To a wonderful
Couple

Happiness Always

D1515312

BARNES&NOBLE

ESSENTIALS
OF COOKING

First published in 1980 as *The Cook Book* by
Mitchell Beazley Publishers
This new edition first published in 1997 by Conran Octopus Limited,
2-4 Heron Quays, London E14 4JP

This edition published by Barnes & Noble, Inc., by arrangement with
Conran Octopus Publishing

2001 Barnes & Noble Books

M 10 9 8 7 6 5 4 3 2 1

ISBN 0-7607-2642-6

COMMISSIONING EDITOR: Suzannah Gough
PROJECT EDITOR: Kate Bell
GENERAL EDITOR: Norma MacMillan
ART DIRECTION: Helen Lewis, assisted by Sue Storey
ART EDITOR: Alistair Plumb
PRODUCTION: Jill Beed, Suzanne Bayliss

Printed and bound by Toppan Printing, China
Origination by Mandarin Offset, Singapore

Page 2: Rhubarb and Raisin Pie   *Page 6:* Salade Niçoise

BARNES&NOBLE

ESSENTIALS OF COOKING

The Back-to-Basics Guide to Selecting, Preparing,
Cooking, and Serving the Very Best of Foods

Caroline Conran

Terence Conran

and

Simon Hopkinson

Recipe Photography by James Murphy
Additional Recipes: Rick Rodgers
Editorial Consultant: Judith Sutton

Contents

HOW THE BOOK WORKS

The three main sections chart the progress of food from the market to the kitchen to the table. All sections are cross-referenced—for example, when reading about scallops in Part One, the reader will find, at the side of the page, cross-references to the preparation of scallops (also in Part One), the recommended specialist equipment for dealing with scallops (Part Two), and recipes including scallops (Part Three). This system allows the book to be used on many different levels. Novices can explore any subject in depth, while experienced cooks can easily find whatever information they require.

Introduction

This book is about food, and is intended as a reference book for cooks. It is significantly different from the many recent cookbooks by restaurant chefs, in that it concentrates solely on the terms and practices of home cooking. This is the book for home cooks who want practical information and a straightforward approach, and who like food cooked beautifully but without pretension.

It is concerned with food in all aspects—it is about raw ingredients and their preparation, and about the cooking and presentation of food. Fortunately, where food is concerned, the material is always fascinating. Food has a marvelous sensuality about it; even the simplest raw vegetable has a vitality and beauty of its own. The colors, texture, and smells of food are all stimulating to the cook, inspiring a desire to cook in the same way that a writer wants to write or a painter to paint. And, like a painter or writer, the cook never knows exactly what will emerge at the end. Good ingredients are so individual—one tomato varying from the next according to the sun, the soil, the season—that there are constant surprises to keep up interest.

Many variations can be made on each theme too. Every time a dish is cooked, there is a feeling that it can be improved upon, that it can be done a little differently from the time before. But to add this dimension to cooking, the cook's response must be both intuitive and well informed; the more one understands the subject, the more one's feeling for ingredients will develop, and the surer one's instincts will become. Therefore the wider the knowledge, the more interesting and successful will be the experiments. This book sets out to provide a knowledge of a vast range of different foods, so that the cook—like someone with an extensive vocabulary—can be fluent and confident. Take, for example, olive oil: you may go to the supermarket and buy an olive oil that has been refined, treated, and blended in order to keep the price to a minimum, and which therefore cannot afford to have much character. But, if you first find out about olive oil and then try different qualities and pressings with their strong individual flavors, you will be in a much better position to judge what the true olive oil taste is like, and which particular oil would be best suited to your purpose. Whether it is oils or cheeses, this book will encourage you to learn to hunt for and try individual products sold in specialty shops or markets, and to recognize the quality of foods not manufactured for mass appeal, but produced individually by people who are passionate about maintaining their high standards, and whose products have a unique character of their own.

As a matter of fact, all good food starts with the shopping—certainly living out of the freezer is convenient, but it does away with a good deal of enjoyment. The seasons and their differences are part of the experience of life. If you eat frozen green peas throughout the winter, where is the pleasure when the first young peas appear in the spring?

Obviously it is foolish not to freeze or preserve food when it is in abundance, and would go to waste otherwise, but does it make sense to ship or fly food many thousands of miles so that we can eat it all the year through? And surely shopping for fresh food in the market is a much more inspiring and entertaining activity than burrowing in the freezer for anonymous-looking frosty packages.

The recipes we have chosen for this book will provide a basis for everyday cooking. With these recipes, which for the most part are very simple, you can cook throughout the year. There are flights of culinary fantasy—stuffed breast of veal for example, and Mussels with Coconut Milk and Chiles—but we have, for the most part, tried to give recipes at a level that the busy cook can live with. Nowadays, with life getting more and more complicated, it is good to be both quick and simple whenever possible—simple surroundings and simple food, with the occasional elaborate dish for days when you want to glory in the whole process.

Simplicity does not mean dullness. There are countless enjoyable tastes, flavors, and experiences available to people who take the trouble to find and try them. This book is intended to help you to do so.

1

The purchase and preparation of food

Fish

Fish is a food of tremendous character and charm. To a cook who has true feeling for raw materials, there is great satisfaction to be found in the beauty of form, the shimmering colors of scale and skin, and the distinctive flavors and textures of fish of all kinds.

It pays to look beyond the inevitable cod, haddock, and sole—although these are no less good for their predictability. But the seas, rivers, and lakes are filled with an extravagant variety of fish, each with its own character. It is comparatively easy to obtain a thick slice of swordfish or a fresh trout, but more of a triumph to find a beautiful sea bass, a colorful red drum, or a fresh halibut steak. Cooking becomes more of a pleasure if one can make an occasional experiment or discovery, and among fish there are endless discoveries to be made.

Choosing fish

There is no excuse for bad fish being offered for sale any more, now that modern transportation practices make it easy to ship fish for long distances in a freshly caught state. What we are more likely to see in fish shops these days are fresh fish that have been in the shop too long, or fish that have been in and out of the freezer several times, thawed out and sold as "fresh." Unfortunately, the telltale signs of a poorly thawed-out fish are less easy to detect than those of a spoiled fish. If you are an expert, and are lucky enough to live near a large fish market, the best fish to buy are those you see in a crate, packed in ice and obviously straight from the docks or wholesale market. These will have been chilled—not flash-frozen—immediately after they were caught.

However, with frequent visits to the fish market, it soon becomes easy to recognize the differences between good fresh fish that have simply been chilled, old fish, and thawed-out frozen fish. Don't be afraid to sniff the fish if you are suspicious, or to ask pertinent questions. Here are the signs to look for.

Fresh fish A really fresh whole fish looks almost alive and ready to swim away. It gleams, its color is bright, its flesh is firm yet elastic to the touch, and the skin shines with a viscous slime that is clear and evenly distributed. Bright, bulging eyes indicate freshness; dull and sunken eyes with red rims mean the fish is old. The gills should be clean and bright red. And fresh fish smells fresh and pleasant; the more offensive the odor, the older the fish.

It's easier to determine the freshness of a whole fish than of fillets and steaks, but there are still some signs to look for when purchasing these. As with whole fish, fillets and steaks should smell only pleasantly of the sea. The flesh should glisten and look almost translucent, and it should look firm, not mushy, without any gaping. Fillets and steaks from white fish should be pure white; those from dark-fleshed fish like tuna should not have shimmery "rainbows," which are a sign of age.

Frozen fish Commercially frozen fish, usually in fillets, are sold from freezers in shops and supermarkets. But there are other fish that have been frozen less efficiently and thawed out, and these are sometimes sold with no sign to indicate the previously frozen state. This is an unfortunate deception. Whole fish that have been flash-frozen at sea as soon as they are caught can be quite good, but these less well treated thawed-out fish are usually imported and/or have traveled some distance. As long as you are aware of this, they need not be shunned—often they are the only chance you will have of tasting unusual fish from far away.

To detect a badly thawed-out fish, look for a sad appearance and flabby, dull skin that has lost its natural slime and shininess. If a fish has suffered badly from freezing and thawing, it will be unpleasantly watery and will have a soft, cottony texture.

Storing fish

There is only one essential piece of advice on storing fresh fish—don't. If you must keep it overnight, put it, well wrapped in several layers of newspaper, in the coldest part of the refrigerator. If you have the chance to buy fresh mackerel or sardines, or other fresh small oily fish, eat them on the day of purchase; if this is not possible, put them in the freezer overnight.

Freezing fish Most home freezers do not act fast enough to prevent large ice crystals from forming in the flesh of a fish. These destroy the delicate tissues, resulting in the loss of texture, juices, and flavor. So if you want a freezerload of fish as a standby, you would be advised to buy commercially frozen fish, which should keep for 2 to 3 months.

There is a way to preserve a degree of texture and flavor using a home freezer, and this procedure is called glazing. Place the cleaned and gutted whole fish, unwrapped, in the freezer set to the lowest temperature. When the fish is reasonably solid, dip it into cold fresh water. A thin film of ice should instantly form. Return the fish to the freezer immediately and, when the ice has frozen solid, repeat the process two or three times, until the fish is completely encased in a good coating of ice. Then store the fish in a freezer bag in the usual way.

Fish that best withstand the freezing process are those with fine-grained flesh, such as the sole and its flatfish relations. Salmon, and other fish with flesh that falls into flakes, can be frozen but are decidedly nicer fresh; the flesh becomes a little soft with the freezing and thawing process. The shorter the time any fish remains frozen, the better it will be.

Frozen fish should be defrosted before cooking. If it is cooked still-frozen, the outside may be overcooked before the inside has had time to thaw out.

A fresh fish will have bright, bulging eyes and skin that shines with a clear, natural slime (RIGHT). A fish that has dull, discolored, sunken eyes and lifeless skin is well past its best (FAR RIGHT).

SALTWATER FISH

Fish from the sea can be roughly divided into those that have white flesh and those that are oily. Within these broad categories exist several natural culinary groups, such as the flatfish, the cod and its relatives, the sea basses and breams, and the oily salmon, mackerel, and herring. The great ocean fish, such as tuna and swordfish, have a category of their own, and there is a section for the multitude of fish, such as red snapper and skate, that do not fall easily into categories.

Flatfish

All flatfish are fine-fleshed, white, delicate, and lean, and two members of this group—turbot and Dover sole— rank in the top echelon of all sea fish.

Dover sole The true Dover, or Channel, sole is perhaps the cook's perfect fish, a fact that is reflected by its prominence on restaurant menus in Europe and in a few select restaurants in America. The flesh is firm, white, and delicate and keeps well (in fact, sole tastes better if it is 24 hours old). It lends itself to almost any cooking method, and is excellent with many sauces, but is at its finest simply cooked on the bone and served with butter, parsley, and lemon. Only poor-quality fish needs dressing up. *Buying guide:* there is no true sole in American waters—although a number of other flatfish, such as Pacific flounder, may be labeled sole—but imported Dover sole is sometimes available in larger cities. Dover sole is available fresh all year in Europe. Buy whole if serving plainly broiled or panfried, or in fillets if serving in a sauce (it is hard to see and deal with bones in a fish covered with sauce). Each fish provides four good fillets. The price of Dover sole has become inordinately high; however, a 7- to 8-ounce sole is enough for one person, although vegetables will be needed if it is served plain. If you order filleted Dover sole from the fish market, take the head and bones with you—they are the basis of an excellent fish stock. *Best cooking methods:* broiled, sautéed in butter, or filleted and poached in sauce.

Flounder In America, the flounder family includes the excellent fluke (also known as summer flounder), the winter and yellowtail flounders, the gray sole, and the fine-textured petrale sole. (Gray sole, also called witch flounder, may be called witch or Torbay sole, or pole

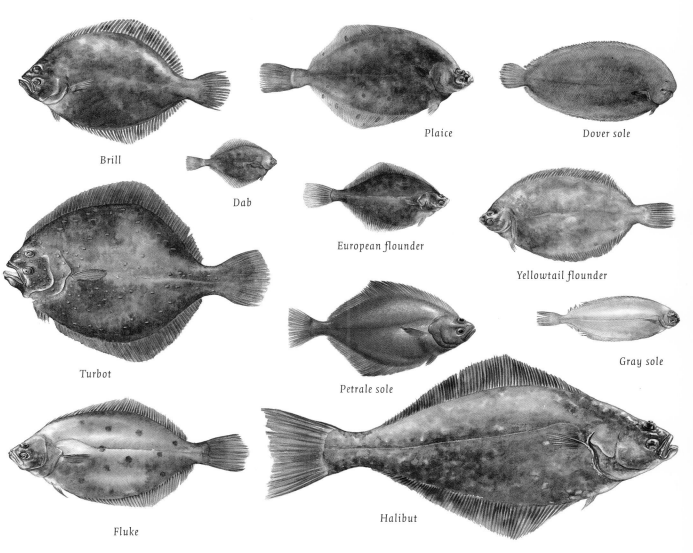

Brill

Dab

Plaice

Dover sole

Turbot

European flounder

Yellowtail flounder

Petrale sole

Gray sole

Fluke

Halibut

flounder in Britain.) These are all quite good eating when freshly caught, and are often used in recipes that call for Dover sole or turbot, since they respond to the same methods of cooking. The European flounder, or fluke, is a fish of poor reputation. It has a dark brown, distinctly rough skin and a pale belly, and little of the other flatfishes' delicacy of flavor. A better choice in England might be the fish labeled lemon sole, which is the American yellowtail flounder. A soft-textured but pleasant fish, it is considered to be slightly superior to plaice.
Buying guide: year-round for American flounder, except fresh summer flounder; winter months for European flounder. Sold whole and in fillets.
Best cooking methods: a good-quality thick flounder can be poached like turbot; a thin one should be sautéed gently in butter, broiled, or filleted and poached in sauce.

Turbot Turbot is one of the finest of sea foods. Its flesh is the firmest and most delicate in flavor of all the white fish, and this has to be paid for dearly these days. Despite this, any opportunity to buy it should not be missed. Unfortunately, "real" (European) turbot is almost never found in American markets at any price. The fish usually sold as turbot is in fact Greenland turbot, which has a much softer flesh; it can be substituted in recipes calling for turbot, but the result will not be the same. Recognize European turbot by its knobbly brown skin and awesome size: a fully grown specimen can weigh up to 28 pounds. In the heyday of the turbot, in the nineteenth century, a huge fish could be poached whole in a special pan, a *turbotière*, designed for the purpose. These days, most of us can only manage to cook chicken turbot (a young turbot weighing 2 to 6 pounds) in this way, substituting a large pan for the turbot kettle. If you can't manage a whole turbot, you can buy fillets or steaks.
Buying guide: imported turbot can on rare occasions be found in large American cities; in Europe, it is available all year, sold whole, in fillets, and in steaks. The flesh should be creamy white; a bluish tinge means that it is old.
Best cooking methods: turbot suits any cooking method, but is best simply poached or broiled and served with a parsley-and-butter sauce, or hollandaise. It is also very good in a salad.

Halibut A giant among flatfish, the halibut can grow up to 6 feet long and is not, in fact, particularly flat. It is a medium to darkish brown on top and pearly white underneath. It has almost as good a flavor as turbot. Atlantic halibut is usually considered finer than Pacific halibut because its flesh is firmer and its flavor somewhat more delicate, but the Pacific is also very good.
Buying guide: available all year. Halibut is almost always sold as steaks, but it is sometimes seen as fillets. Small halibut (weighing less than 3 pounds) may sometimes be sold whole and make a very good-looking lunch or dinner for four to six people. Avoid frozen halibut, which is dull and dry.
Best cooking methods: panfry, poach, or bake, and serve with a good sauce—lobster, parsley, or hollandaise. Halibut is also good when it is eaten very fresh, as in *seviche*.

Plaice Dark brown with russet spots on its upper side and white on its underside, plaice is a mainstay of every British fish-and-chip shop, its mild, soft flesh heavily encased in batter and deep-fried. It is certainly a perfectly palatable fish when served in this way, particularly when it is quite fresh. European plaice, not to be confused with the American dab, and often labeled plaice, turns up in some fish markets in the United States; it can be substituted in most recipes that call for sole or other flatfish fillets.
Buying guide: available all year, sold whole or, more usually, in fillets.
Best cooking methods: deep-fry in a good batter, or coated in beaten egg and bread crumbs, and serve with tartar sauce; or poach and cover with a cheese or parsley-and-butter sauce.

Dab, sand dab The American dab, or sand dab, which is sometimes labeled American or Canadian plaice, has reddish-brown skin and can grow up to 2 feet in length. Its fillets have reddish lines running through them. The European dab is not the most exciting of fish to eat, although its flesh is soft, fragile, and easily digested. It can grow up to 12 inches long, but is usually somewhat smaller than this.
Buying guide: available all year; European dab is best in autumn and winter. Dab is sold whole or in fillets.

Best cooking methods: grilled whole; fillets are very good sautéed in butter or coated in beaten egg and bread crumbs and then panfried.

Brill A very good European fish akin to turbot, the handsome brill has a mixed tweed coloring and is smaller than its cousin. Its flesh is a little softer and not so gelatinous, but it is sweet and delicate to eat. Brill is available in some larger U.S. fish markets.
Buying guide: available all year, sold whole or in fillets.
Best cooking methods: recipes for turbot, halibut, and sole suit brill, and it is one of the fish of choice for the French seafood stew called *matelote*.

Megrim A small, yellowish-gray, rather transparent fish, megrim is common in Britain, where it is also known as whiff, sail-fluke, West Coast sole, white sole, and lantern flounder. Not a particularly tasty fish, it has the advantage of being cheap, and makes a reasonably good contribution to fish soup.
Buying guide: rarely, if ever, seen in U.S. markets; in Europe, available autumn and winter, sold whole or in fillets.
Best cooking methods: as for sole or plaice, but probably best filleted and panfried.

The cod family
The members of this large family of white-fleshed fish—which includes such cornerstones of the fishing industry as cod, haddock, and pollack—keep their succulence best when they are lightly poached or steamed, panfried in batter, or bathed in a good, light homemade sauce. However, cod in particular is quite a versatile fish and will stand up well to most cooking processes, as long as it is treated delicately.

Cod and scrod The cod is a handsome fish and has a dappled skin of brown, greenish-gray, or gray. Once taken for granted as the fisherman's bread and butter, it is becoming more scarce due to overfishing in northern European and American waters. Too often it has been overcooked until dry and gray, and hidden under a blanket of sauce. When treated with care, cod proves to be very fine, but it must be very fresh to be first class. The flesh is succulent and breaks into large flakes—a really fresh fish will produce a cheeselike curd between the flakes, as salmon does. The cod has an excellent roe—used taramasalata—and its liver produces a disagreeable-tasting but effective vitamin supplement. Scrod is not, as many think, the name of a fish but rather a term that is used for young cod and other smaller members of the cod family. An adult cod can weigh as much as 80 pounds; small cod (also known as codling in Britain) are about 1 ½ to 2 ½ pounds.

Buying guide: available all year. Fresh cod is sold mainly as steaks and fillets. If you are able to choose a cut, pick the middle, which combines the tenderness of the tail with the flavor of the shoulder. Never buy fillets or steaks if you can see either yellow or pinkish patches on the flesh. Frozen cod, although reliable, lacks the flavor of really fresh cod, but is certainly a better buy than cod of dubious quality.

Best cooking methods: the flesh of cod falls naturally into large, firm flakes and keeps its texture well. It is splendid poached, and excellent in fish soups or chowders and in fish cakes. Also bake, broil, or panfry or deep-fry and serve with good homemade sauces such as fresh tomato salsa or tartar sauce. In addition to the traditional slices of lemon, *aïoli* (mayonnaise heavily flavored with garlic) is a particularly delicious accompaniment to a whole poached cod (cod is robust enough to take strong Mediterranean flavors). In order to whiten and tenderize the flesh of this fish, it is a good idea to rub it with a cut lemon half an hour or so before cooking.

Haddock Fresh haddock is sometimes preferred to cod by those who declare its texture and flavor finer, but it is really no better a fish. Haddock has a fresh marine flavor and a light, firm texture, and it is blessed with fairly good keeping qualities. It looks similar to cod in appearance, but has a grayer skin, larger eyes, and a marked black lateral line. Haddock is also smoked to make finnan haddie; in Britain it is often used for fish and chips.

Buying guide: available all year, but best in winter and early spring; generally sold in fillets.

Best cooking methods: any of the cooking methods described for cod can also be used for haddock.

Hake An elongated, deep-water member of the cod family, hake appears on some French menus as white salmon (*saumon blanc*), and is familiar all over the United States under a variety of names, including ling and white or red hake. Silver hake, from the East Coast, is a particularly fine fish that also goes under the name of Atlantic or American whiting (not to be confused with the European whiting, a lesser fish). Hake is popular in Spain, fried in a coating of beaten egg or served in an *escabeche*—a cold hors d'oeuvre of fried fish in an herb marinade—but it is sadly becoming an increasingly rare sight in the fish shops of northern Europe. No opportunity should be missed to buy it, though it does tend to be expensive. It has tender, soft, pinkish flesh, somewhat lighter than that of cod, with a delicate flavor, and the advantage of possessing few bones, which are fairly easy to remove.

Buying guide: fresh hake must be very fresh, or it may have an unpleasantly soft texture. It is sold whole, in fillets, and in steaks. It is also available frozen.

Best cooking methods: deep-fried in batter; panfried; baked with pine nuts, bread crumbs, and cheese; or poached and served on a bed of spinach or sorrel mixed with fresh cream.

European whiting This is a common but unexciting European fish not found in American waters (in the United States whiting is another name for the much finer silver hake, above). It is gray and white with a pointed head and backward-slanting teeth. A really fresh whiting is quite good, light, and easily digestible, but a tired and traveled specimen will be dry, dull, and tasteless. In France, whiting is known as *merlan*; in Spain, it is called *merluzzo*.

Buying guide: in Europe, available all year round but best in winter. Sold whole, or in fillets.

Best cooking methods: flaked and used in fish cakes; puréed for mousses and mousselines; poached and served with a julienne of vegetables; or coated with beaten egg and bread crumbs—which will improve the texture—and panfried.

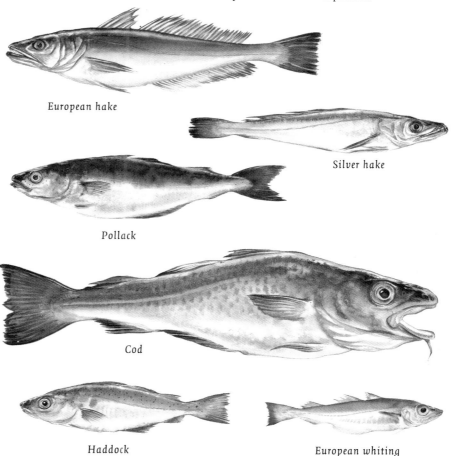

European hake

Silver hake

Pollack

Cod

Haddock

European whiting

Pollack Although pollack does not have quite the firmness and succulence of cod or haddock, it is a well-flavored fish with good texture, and one of its best features is its price. Atlantic pollack has been underappreciated until recently, no doubt in part because of its somewhat off-putting grayish flesh—which, happily, whitens considerably during cooking, even more so if rubbed generously with lemon juice. Pollack is one of the mainstays of the American market; one reason for this is that the heavily fished Alaskan pollack is a major source of Japanese surimi, or imitation seafood, as well as of frozen fish patties and fish sticks. It is also known as coley, saithe, and coalfish, both in the United States and in Britain; in France, it is called *lieu*. *Buying guide:* available all year. Pollack is usually sold in fillets or, less often, as steaks; it is rarely sold whole. *Best cooking methods:* in fish cakes and fish soups, or as for cod.

Some less-sought-after members of the cod family

Ling When this is dried, it is known as *lutefisk* or *lutfisk* and is popular in Sweden boiled and eaten with great quantities of butter, where it is also a traditional Christmas dish. (Do not confuse the European ling with the North American lingcod, which is not a cod at all but is in fact a member of the greenling family.) Ling has firm white flesh and can be used in any cod dish.

Cusk is almost always sold in fillets, usually labeled as scrod.

Pouting is a fish found in Britain. It should be eaten very fresh indeed as its main claim to fame is that it spoils very quickly—for this reason it is sometimes known as "stinkalive."

Bass, porgy, and grouper

Firm and white-fleshed, these fish go well with strong Mediterranean flavors—saffron, fennel, olive oil, tomatoes, white wine, and garlic. They are delicious when grilled whole or baked together with olive oil and fresh herbs.

Sea bass Whether one of the North American varieties—striped bass, black sea bass—or the beautiful silver bass of the Mediterranean and warmer northern European waters, sea bass is the ideal fish for a splendid meal at home. It is just the right size for a small family and has delicately flavored milky flesh. *Buying guide:* available all year. Sold whole or in steaks and fillets. *Best cooking methods:* bass up to 2 pounds can be grilled whole—in France they are cooked over charcoal with herbs and a

handful of fennel twigs is put on the fire. Bake larger fish, and bake or poach steaks and fillets. Bass is also excellent in salads or *seviche*, or steamed on a bed of seaweed. Serve with mayonnaise or a butter sauce; with *salsa verde*, the piquant Italian sauce of parsley, lemon, and anchovy; or with a fresh tomato sauce.

Porgy and other bream American porgies are members of the large bream family that has dozens of species throughout the world. Some species are distinctly better than others: the finest of these is the Mediterranean gilt-head, with its gold spot on each cheek and its compact body. Most of the porgies in the United States, which are generally smaller than the European bream, come from the East Coast or the Caribbean. Red porgy is one of the tastier varieties; sheepshead porgy and scup are common types. Red porgy, called sea bream in Britain, is also found in the Mediterranean. The red bream is the bream found in northern European waters, a large fish usually sold in fillets and recognizable by its rosy-gray skin. All bream have rather coarse but juicy flesh and a pleasant taste that suits fairly strong accompanying flavors. They must be scaled—ask your fishmonger to do this for you, or cook the fish with its scales intact and carefully remove them with the skin just before serving. *Buying guide:* available all year but best in autumn. Sold whole or in fillets. *Best cooking methods:* season well and grill or broil, or bake in foil, or roll in cornmeal or flour and panfry briskly in oil. Make two or three slashes on each side if cooking porgy whole, so that the heat can quickly penetrate the thicker parts, ensuring that the fish cooks evenly.

Grouper A delicacy in Mediterranean countries, grouper is not widely available in northern Europe, which is a pity because its flesh is particularly firm and well flavored. The United States enjoys a number of varieties—red grouper is found from Virginia down to Florida, and the Gulf of Mexico has black grouper and the Nassau. Yellowmouth is also common along the East Coast. *Buying guide:* sold whole, weighing up to 10 pounds, and in steaks and fillets. *Best cooking methods:* panfrying or broiling, or otherwise as for sea bass.

Porgy

European silver bass

Striped bass

Red grouper

Mediterranean gilt-head bream

Mediterranean grouper

Oily fish and small fry

Absolute freshness is essential—all oily fish are inedible when anything less. The traditional accompaniments of mustard for bluefish and for herring and, in England, the tart green gooseberry for mackerel, help to counteract their natural oiliness.

Bluefish Familiar along America's East Coast in summer and in the warm waters around Bermuda, the bluefish can be identified by the blue-green sheen along its back. Although popular in New England, bluefish suffers from a reputation as a strong-tasting, oily fish. Part of its ill repute stems from poor handling; because of its high fat content, bluefish does not keep well. When you see very fresh bluefish, it's well worth buying. The delicate flesh is rather soft in texture and goes best with sharp accompanying flavors—lemon juice, capers, or mustard.
Buying guide: best in spring, summer, and autumn. Sold whole—2 to 3 pounds is a manageable size, but it can be up to 10 pounds—or as fillets.
Best cooking methods: brush the fish with melted butter before broiling or grilling, bake with a little white wine and butter, or poach whole and serve accompanied by melted butter.

Mackerel The mackerel is one of the easiest of all fish to recognize—the taut, steel-blue skin, mottled with blues and greens and a pattern of blackish bands, is so smooth it looks almost enameled. The belly is pearly-white, the inside of the mouth black. If the natural markings have lost their brilliance and the fish does not positively shine up at you, do not buy it. The pink-tinted flesh is firm, richly flavored, oily, and rich in vitamins. In Europe, mackerel roe is considered to be a delicacy, and can be served along with the fish or mixed into a stuffing.
Buying guide: at its best in April, May, and June. Mackerel is sold whole, usually weighing up to about 2 pounds, which will serve two people as a main course or four as a first course, or in fillets.
Best cooking methods: whole mackerel can be broiled, grilled over a charcoal or wood fire, or poached in white wine; broil or panfry fillets. Mackerel is also good stuffed. Sauces for mackerel include mustard and horseradish.

Horse mackerel This somewhat off-putting name, and others such as jack mackerel or, in Britain, scad or round robin, belongs to a group of fish regarded as poor man's mackerel—rather unfairly to the mackerel, since although the horse mackerel has much in common with the true mackerel, it is not related. (In fact, it is a member of the jack family.) The horse mackerel lacks the fine markings of the true mackerel and is not considered a quality fish, being rather coarse and bony.
Buying guide: sold whole—a large fish will feed two people, and a small one, one person; also canned.
Best cooking methods: treat as mackerel, or braise.

Herring Once plentiful, popular, and cheap, herring is rapidly becoming less available because of overfishing. This is a pity because it is a tasty fish and rich in protein, fat, iodine, and vitamins A and D. Fresh herring is popular and common in Europe, but in the United States, it is usually sold pickled or smoked.
Buying guide: in the United States, fresh herring is occasionally available at large fish markets; in Europe, it is available all year but best from spring to autumn. Choose large, firm, slippery herring.
Best cooking methods: panfry or score, brush with fat, and grill or broil. Never discard the roe, which is very good.

Smelt These silvery, semitransparent little fish (about 7 inches long) are anadromous, spawning in fresh water, and so are found not only along both the Atlantic and Pacific coasts, and in

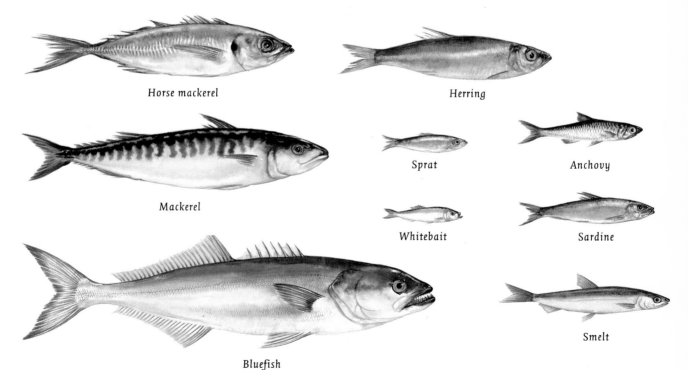

Horse mackerel

Herring

Sprat

Anchovy

Mackerel

Whitebait

Sardine

Bluefish

Smelt

European waters, but also in the Great Lakes, and other freshwater bodies. Smelt have a delicious scent when very fresh—some say of cucumber, others of violets—but this disappears very rapidly, so if they seem scentless when you buy them, it doesn't mean that they are old. They need delicate handling—leave the head and tail on and clean them through the gills.
Buying guide: best in winter and spring, but there are good and bad years, so buy smelt whenever you see them—it may be a long time before you see them again.
Best cooking method: dipped in milk and flour and deep-fried.

Sardine Fresh sardines are a delight, but they must be fresh. They travel badly, and so are usually only found close to where they are caught, such as the Mediterranean coasts of France and North Africa (the true Mediterranean sardine is named after the island of Sardinia); but they are appearing more often in East Coast markets. (The Atlantic sardine is actually a herring.) When you do find them fresh, they are simplicity itself to prepare. Cut the head almost through from the backbone and pull; as the head comes off, the intestines will come with it.
Buying guide: at their best in spring. Fresh sardines are sold whole; sizes vary, so judge by eye how many you need.
Best cooking methods: panfry in olive oil, or coat lightly with salt and olive oil and grill or broil. Eat them with halved lemons, chilled rough wine, and crusty bread.

Anchovy Seeing fresh anchovies for the first time, with their slim bodies and sparkling silvery greenish-blue skin, comes as something of a surprise when one's only previous acquaintance with this useful fish has been as canned fillets. Fresh, they can be distinguished from sardines by their narrower bodies and protruding upper jaws. To enjoy their delicate flavor at its best, they should be straight from the sea, which ideally means the Mediterranean, although varieties appear in northern European and North American waters.
Buying guide: sold whole.
Best cooking methods: panfry or broil as for sardines. Anchovies are also delicious marinated in olive oil and lemon juice with garlic, or boned and panfried with garlic and parsley.

Sprat Although unfamiliar in America, these are worth attention if only for their superabundance in European waters, which means that they are very cheap. Tiny silvery fish, they look rather like small herring but are shorter and stouter.
Buying guide: a winter fish, said to be best when the weather is frosty.
Best cooking methods: sprats are very oily, so are best when broiled; or they can be dusted with flour and panfried in a dry pan sprinkled with salt.

Whitebait The small fry or young of herring and sardines—or in fact almost any tiny, almost translucent specimens, including silversides—whitebait are the most delicious little fish. Bright, silvery, and slender, they are scarcely more than 1½ inches long, and have for a long time been one of the summer treats of the British. In the United States, they can be found on both coasts. Whitebait are eaten whole, so there is no need to clean them—simply rinse them gently.
Buying guide: traditionally available from February to August. Allow about 4 ounces per person.
Best cooking method: the best and only way to cook whitebait is to dip them in milk, shake them in a bag of flour, and then deep-fry them. They should be so crisp that they rustle as they are put on the plates. Serve with lemon wedges and fresh bread and butter.

The great fish

The great ocean fish make firm, meaty eating. Their flesh is inclined to be dry, so it is a good idea to marinate it in olive oil and lemon juice or white wine with herbs before cooking.

Tuna and bonito Found in all the world's warmer waters, the powerful and beautifully shaped tuna family is related to the mackerel, and includes the bluefin, albacore, yellowfin, and skipjack. Bonito is another close relative. When you see fresh tuna, don't be put off by a reddish color—it improves during cooking. Tuna needs plenty of oil and seasoning, and care must be taken not to overcook it, or it will be dry. Bonito can be treated as either tuna or mackerel.
Buying guide: available all year. Sold in steaks; occasionally very small fish are filleted. Avoid tuna steaks with very dark marks, as these indicate bruising.

Best cooking methods: grill, broil, panfry, or bake in steaks, basting often with seasoned oil; or slice very thin into small scallops, dust with flour, and sauté gently in butter and oil for 2 to 3 minutes on each side. Serve with fresh tomato salsa or Italian herb sauce.

Swordfish Familiar in Mediterranean waters and popular in North America as "the steak of the sea," the swordfish is only a very occasional visitor to northern European waters. It makes delicious eating, but the flesh is close-grained and tends to be dry, so it is often marinated in wine, oil, and herbs before cooking.
Buying guide: available all year round. Sold in steaks.
Best cooking methods: grill or broil and serve with plain or herb butter or tomato sauce; or sear in butter and then bake in a sauce. Swordfish is also excellent when used to make kebabs.

Sailfish and marlin Well-known to American sport fishermen, these majestic fish are spectacular fighters and prized trophies. But if you don't want to put them on the wall, they make very good eating.
Buying guide: marlin is commercially fished in Hawaii, but not elsewhere; in other parts of the world, both fish are occasionally sold as steaks in ports near the fishing grounds.
Best cooking methods: as for swordfish.

Opah Whatever you call this splendid fish—moonfish or sunfish (not to be confused with the freshwater sunfish), mariposa, or kingfish—you should never miss a chance to sample it. It lives deep in the Atlantic, Pacific, and Indian oceans; most of the opah seen in the United States comes from Hawaii or California. The skin reflects blue, rose, silver, and gold, and the texture of the flesh may have a markedly different taste—and color—depending on which part of the fish it comes from.
Buying guide: should you ever see opah for sale at a fish market, ask for steaks or scallops.
Best cooking methods: bake, panfry, broil, or poach, but take care not to overcook. Serve with hollandaise sauce.

Shark The shark family includes the mako—or, in Britain, mackerel shark—and its close relative the porbeagle, the dogfish, and the hammerhead and blacktip sharks, as well as angel and thresher sharks. All sharks have very firm flesh, scaleless skin, and a cartilaginous skeleton (like skate). Not attractive fish, they tend to have an ammoniac smell that disappears in cooking. The flavor and texture are good.

Shark is usually presented for sale in steaks. The small dogfish may be euphemistically called grayfish, rock cod, and even—quite shamefully—rock salmon. The flesh is white or slightly pink and firm-textured, and deserves more attention than it gets.
Buying guide: available all year round; sold in steaks.
Best cooking methods: dust with well-seasoned flour and then panfry over gentle heat; or coat with batter and deep-fry; or marinate in an oil-based mixture and grill or broil.

Barracuda A large game fish with vicious teeth, the barracuda can reach 150 pounds. Although found in warmer Atlantic waters, it is also caught mainly on the Pacific coast of North America.

The meaty, firm flesh is rich in oil. Small barracuda (such as the Pacific or California barracuda, or scoot, which normally weighs 4 to 8 pounds) are the best ones to eat.

The Atlantic barracuda, which is fished in the Caribbean as well, can cause a type of poisoning from *ciguatera* toxins, and is best avoided.
Buying guide: sold whole or in steaks and fillets.
Best cooking methods: small fish can be broiled or baked whole; steaks can be marinated and then grilled or broiled.

Assorted fish
Many fish do not fall naturally into a culinary category except that they are good to eat. For many of them, their looks are not their greatest asset, but it is a pity that they should be so often passed by in favor of their better-known and more attractive cousins.

Monkfish Monkfish is also known as angler fish or goosefish; its French name is *lotte*. This unusual-looking fish has a huge head—and mouth—but it is usually sold

headless. Despite its rather endearing ugliness, it is one of the best fish you can buy. The smooth skin is easy to remove, as is the translucent membrane beneath. The flesh is firm, boneless, and white, and has the succulence of lobster—its taste is more associated with shellfish than with fish.
Buying guide: available all year. Ask for a good tail piece—3 pounds for six people. It can then be sliced or cooked whole.
Best cooking methods: can be treated almost as meat—in France it is roasted as *gigot de mer* (lamb of the sea). It can also be poached; or split the tail in half, brush with oil, and grill or broil. Best of all are scallops marinated in lemon and garlic, dusted with flour, and sautéed in butter.

Skate Only the wings of skate, also called ray, are eaten—they contain strips of gelatinous cartilage from which the flesh comes off in long, succulent shreds. Fresh skate is covered with a clear slime, which reappears when wiped dry, and the flesh should be pearly-white, resilient and not flabby. Large skate are generally kept chilled for a day or two before sale as they are inclined to be tough when very fresh.

Bouillabaisse 251–2
Normandy Fish Stew 281, 280
Skate with Brown Butter Sauce 281

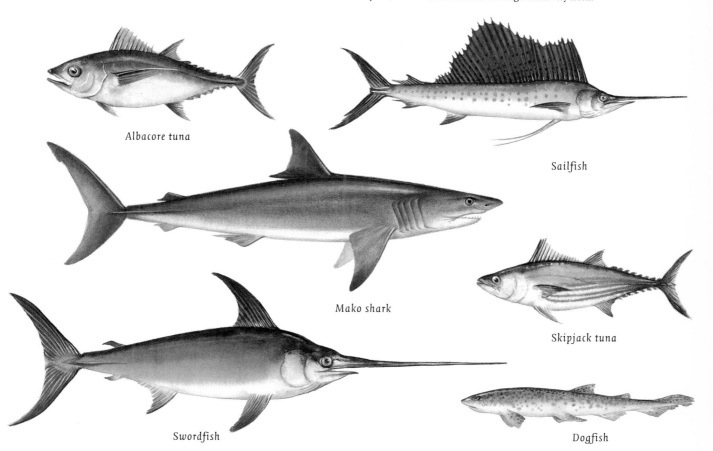

Albacore tuna

Sailfish

Mako shark

Skipjack tuna

Swordfish

Dogfish

salted gray mullet roe 32
scaling round fish 26

Baked Stuffed Pompano 278

Buying guide: best in autumn and winter. Small skate are, rarely, sold whole; usually only the wings are marketed. A very faint smell of ammonia is normal, and will disappear in cooking.

Best cooking methods: The classic French skate dish is *raie au beurre noir*—skate poached in court-bouillon and served with browned butter to which a handful of capers and their vinegar is added. It can also be broiled, deep-fried, or poached. The skin is easy to remove after cooking: simply scrape it carefully, working from the thicker part toward the edge. Because of its gelatinous quality, skate makes a good fish stock.

Red mullet The mullet families can be somewhat confusing. There are two species of fish—not related—called mullet in European waters. One is the gray mullet and the other the red mullet, which is by far the finer of the two species. In America, the term mullet applies to fish of the gray mullet family; fish belonging to the red mullet family that inhabit American waters are known as goatfish.

The Mediterranean red mullet (varying from 2 to 3 inches to 7 to 12 inches) is a superb fish, a shimmering deep silvery-rose with faint golden stripes along each side. The flavor is quite distinctive, something between shrimp and sole. This is the ideal fish to cook together with strong Mediterranean flavors—garlic, saffron, rosemary, and fennel. The liver is often left in the fish during cooking and provides an added richness of flavor, giving red mullet its English nickname of sea woodcock.

Buying guide: sometimes available in ethnic markets or fish markets in larger cities; it may be called by its French name, *rouget*. Look for bright color and transparent, shining eyes. (If the fish seem to be bent sideways, it means that they have been frozen and have just thawed out.) The fish will be sold whole (always ask for the liver to be left in). Large fish are less bony than tiny ones.

Best cooking methods: excellent broiled, baked, or *en papillote*—red mullet is seldom cooked with water—and also ideal for making fish terrines, pâtés, and mousses.

Gray mullet There are several varieties of gray mullet, known variously as striped mullet, black mullet, silver or white mullet, and lisa. In Europe, they are too frequently neglected in favor of the more highly prized red mullet, which is in fact no relation. Gray mullet has large, thick scales and a heavy head with thick, delicate lips. The flesh is coarse and slightly soft, but the flavor is very good, particularly if heightened with fennel or Pernod. The roe is excellent and, used salted, is the proper roe for making the Greek specialty taramasalata.

Buying guide: available all year; sold whole or in fillets. Look for firm fish caught at sea rather than flabby fish caught in estuaries, whose flavor will be muddy.

Best cooking methods: slash the sides and grill, or broil; or if more than 2 pounds, stuff with herbs and garlic, coat with olive oil, and bake. Do not cook gray mullet in water, unless using it as an ingredient for a rich fish soup.

Pompano One of the finest fish in the sea, with firm, white, meaty flesh, pompano is found fresh in Florida and

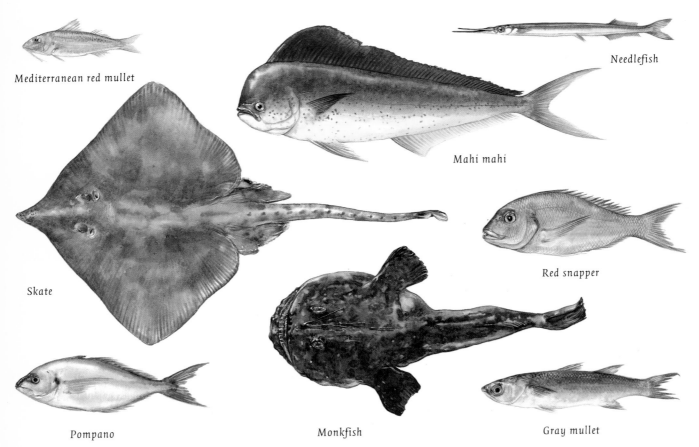

Mediterranean red mullet

Needlefish

Mahi mahi

Skate

Red snapper

Pompano

Monkfish

Gray mullet

appears on the menus of expensive restaurants elsewhere— notably in New Orleans, where Antoine's pompano *en papillote* is a specialty. The California pompano is related not to the Florida pompano but to the butterfish. Pompano are now exported to northern Europe from the Mediterranean.

Buying guide: available all year. Sold whole, or in fillets. Whole fish are usually about 1 ¼ to 2 pounds, but may weigh as much as 3 pounds; avoid larger ones, which may in fact be permit, a similar fish that is not as nice.

Best cooking methods: brush with melted butter and broil, or poach in white wine. Pompano can also be stuffed and baked. Crabmeat or shrimp sauces make an excellent accompaniment.

Mahi mahi Nothing at all to do with the true dolphin, which is a mammal, mahi mahi—also known as dolphinfish or dorado—is a Caribbean native. It is also found in the Mediterranean, where it is often called *lampuga*. Easily recognized by its high ridge of fin, its flesh has a strong, excellent flavor.

Buying guide: sold in steaks or fillets. Steaks are better.

Best cooking methods: bake, grill, broil, or sauté with lemon and garlic. Serve with fresh tomato salsa.

Red snapper You will need to live close to the southern Atlantic or Gulf coasts of America to enjoy this blushing, large-eyed fish fresh from the sea, but red snapper is shipped all over the country—which is fortunate, because it is a fish much in demand, and understandably so. It is weighty, pleasantly textured and well flavored—a 2- to 5-pound specimen, stuffed and baked, makes a delicious meal.

Buying guide: sold whole or in steaks and fillets. Buy carefully, because other snappers, not always as good, may be labeled as red snapper in some markets.

Best cooking methods: bake, broil, or poach.

Needlefish The green and silver needlefish, or garfish—no relation to the freshwater species of fish more correctly called gars—is a pleasant fish to eat although not perhaps of the first order. The flesh is a rather poor grayish-purple in its raw state, but it whitens during cooking. The bones have a rather

startling advantage —they are bright green (this is quite harmless; the color is caused by a phosphate of iron) and easily picked out on the plate. The saury is a similar European fish with colorless bones.

Buying guide: worth trying whenever you see it. Sold whole.

Best cooking methods: cut the fish into segments, then panfry or bake with garlic, or poach and serve with dill or fresh tomato sauce.

Gurnard, sea robin A large family of sweet-tasting fish, despite their armor-plated appearance, the gurnards have several uses and are relatively cheap. In the United States, the best-known member is the sea robin, an often-overlooked fish found along the Atlantic coast. In Europe, the red gurnard—called *grondin* in France—is the best.

Buying guide: usually sold whole; have the fish market do the skinning if possible, as these fish are spiny and tough.

Best cooking methods: excellent in fish soups, sea robins and other gurnards can also be baked with white wine, or coated in beaten egg and bread crumbs, whole or in fillets, sautéed, and served with a Provençal-style or tomato sauce.

John Dory This grandly ugly fish belies its appearance and is, in fact, one of the most delicious of fish—firm, delicate, and excellently flavored. The dark circles on its sides are said to be the marks of St. Peter's fingers, hence its other name, St. Peter's fish. Although there is an American dory, it is not commercially fished and so is rarely seen; John Dory is on occasion available in fish markets in larger cities.

Buying guide: buy whenever you can find it. Remember that almost two-thirds of its weight is taken up by its excessively large, bony head and its intestines.

Best cooking methods: larger fish can be cooked whole or in succulent fillets, as for sole. Small ones are excellent in bouillabaisse.

Butterfish Butterfish, also known as dollarfish, harvest fish, and pomfret, the usual name in Europe, is a small, silvery, coin-shaped fish. The pomfret found in the Mediterranean does not make good eating. However, the pomfret of the Indo-Pacific is excellent, as is the butterfish, found all along the Atlantic

coast. The off-white flesh is rich, tender, and sweet to eat.

Buying guide: available all year round, but best in spring and summer.

Best cooking methods: usually sold whole, butterfish can be baked, broiled or grilled, panfried, poached, or steamed. A piquant sauce will complement the rich, fatty flesh.

Red drum The red drum, also known as redfish and channel bass or red sea bass, is part of a diverse family named for the distinctive drumming sounds the fish make—so loud they can be heard on land. Smaller members of the family are called croakers, for the particular sound they make. The moist, flaky flesh of the red drum is more flavorful than that of its close relative, the black drum. The two fish can easily be distinguished by the fact that only the black drum has barbels, or small whiskers, along its chin; the red drum also has a black spot on either side of its tail.

Found off the Atlantic and Gulf coasts of the United States, red drums can be as heavy as 30 pounds or more, but are usually marketed at about 2 to 5 pounds. Red drum is the fish that is used for blackened redfish, the Cajun dish that became so popular ten years ago or so; the result was overfishing so that red drum became a rarity. Now, however, it is being farmed in Texas, among other places, and so should become more readily available.

Buying guide: available year-round, whole or in fillets.

Best cooking methods: whole fish can be baked, grilled, poached, or braised; fillets can be broiled, poached, and panfried—with "blackening" spices or not. Red drum is also good when used in fish stews and soups.

Weakfish Another member of the drum/croaker family, the weakfish is found along the Atlantic and Gulf coasts. It is sometimes called sea trout or gray trout, but it is not in fact a relative. The weakfish is usually silvery-gray in color but may be multicolored, and some specimens have spots on the flesh, while others look striped. The delicious flesh is delicate in texture and sometimes has a pinkish hue. Whole fish are usually marketed at about 2-5 pounds.

Buying guide: available year-round, whole or in fillets.

sheepshead 25

Cajun Dry Rub 261

Mexican Salsa Cruda 258

freshwater eel and elver 25

Best cooking methods: whole fish are good panfried (weakfish have no pin bones, making it easy to deal with the whole fish) or baked. Fillets can be cooked in various ways: broiled, sautéed or shallow-fried, or baked.

Orange roughy This increasingly popular fish was only discovered about 20 years ago in the deep waters off the coasts of New Zealand. It is normally sold frozen, but some is air-freighted to American and British markets to be sold "fresh" (the fish is always cleaned and frozen at sea, and then partially thawed later on shore for skinning and filleting). The firm white flesh of the orange roughy is moist and tender, and has a sweet, mild, and almost crab-like flavor.
Buying guide: available all year round, most often in fillets weighing about 8 ounces each.
Best cooking methods: a very versatile fish, the orange roughy can be baked, grilled, panfried, coated with batter and then deep-fried, steamed, or poached. It can also be used in a range of fish soups and fish stews.

Tilapia, telapia This small African fish, usually only 1 to 1¼ pounds in weight, can live in both salt and fresh water. New hybrids are being developed and farmed all over the world, with skin color ranging from dark gray-black to bright red. The white flesh of tilapia is moist, fine-textured, and tender with a mild, sweet flavor.
Buying guide: available year-round, whole and in fillets.
Best cooking methods: whole fish can be baked, with or without a stuffing, or grilled. Fillets are best coated with beaten egg and bread crumbs, or a batter, before broiling or panfrying, as this will help to keep them moist; alternatively, fillets can be either poached or steamed, notably with Chinese flavorings.

Sea lamprey A legendary fish that resembles a thick eel in appearance, the sea lamprey is distinguishable by the seven holes that lie behind its eyes and have given rise to its nicknames of flute and *sept-yeux* (French for "seven eyes"). It has a thick body, which is dark gray with mottled markings, and no scales.

The flesh is richly flavored, firm, and fatty. The sea lamprey is not seen in America, but is found on French tables and in Portugal and Spain.
Buying guide: sold whole.
Best cooking methods: prepare and cook as for eel, although you will need to scald the fish before skinning and marinate it before cooking. Sea lamprey can also be pickled in vinegar, or stewed with either port or red wine.

Conger eel The conger eel, or American conger, is one of two edible saltwater eels—the other is the moray, which is really only suitable for bouillabaisse. If you can contemplate eating conger eel, it makes a good meal, in spite of its long, sharp bones.
Buying guide: conger eels are available in some ethnic fish markets. When you buy, ask for a thick cut taken from the head end of the eel.
Best cooking methods: use in fish soups, and also in fish terrines. A good-sized, thick cut of conger eel can be roasted, basted with cider and butter, or simply poached in cider.

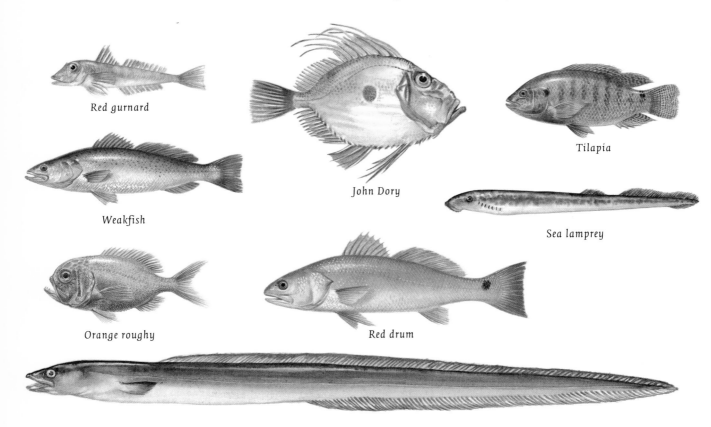

Red gurnard

John Dory

Tilapia

Weakfish

Sea lamprey

Orange roughy

Red drum

Conger eel

FRESHWATER FISH

Lake and river fish are often more frail than sea fish. Their tissues and organs take up a larger proportion of their bodies, and their skin, once scaled, is easily torn. The flesh is much lighter, tends to be dry, and is often riddled with a structure of hairlike forked bones of amazing intricacy. Because of the vulnerable nature of freshwater fish, it is imperative that they should be eaten in the freshest-possible state.

It has been said that freshwater fish should never touch another drop of water once they have left it, so when they are cleaned and scaled, they should be wiped down without washing whenever possible, and baked, grilled or broiled, or panfried in preference to being boiled or poached. If liquids are used, they should be wine, cider, or melted butter or cream rather than water.

The exceptions to the no-water rule are the members of the salmon family—these are exquisite poached in court-bouillon and eaten warm or at room temperature; do not chill.

When cleaning a freshwater fish, be sure to remove the gills, and see that no weed is left in its throat, because this can give a sour and reedy taste. Take particular care to remove the blood that lies along the backbone—this is bitter and must be cleaned away until there is not a trace left.

If you can choose your fish, take those with a silvery or green rather than a brownish hue—brown fish are more likely to have come from slow-moving, muddy haunts. (Various remedies have been suggested—keep the fish alive in a tank of clear water for a day or so, or pour a cup or so of vinegar or a couple of handfuls of salt into its mouth as soon as it is caught and killed, or bake it unscaled in clay, which means that the mud-flavored skin and scales can be removed all at once. But, in fact, there seems little point in trying to rid fish of their inherent taste, so if you dislike the flavor of one, choose some other fish that has a different character.)

Most freshwater fish need quite a lot of salt and other seasoning—in Spain, river fish are gutted, rubbed with salt, and left for several hours, or even buried in salt overnight, to make the flesh firmer and tastier. If you catch your own fish and there are herbs growing near the pool or river, such as watercress or mint, it is a good idea to gather these and take them home for flavoring the fish—it may have been feeding on them and have a hint of their aroma in its flesh.

Small river fish have such a plethora of tiny bones that they are best pickled, so that the bones are softened by the vinegar, or used in a fish soup or a stew. If the fish are very small, they make an excellent "mixed fry" (a dish of deep-fried tiny fish) of the sort often served in the Dordogne region of France as a *friture de la Dordogne*; then the bones can be happily crunched along with the crisp golden-brown skin.

Salmon Known as the king of fish, the salmon is a majestic creature whose life is mysterious and exhausting. Spawned in fresh water, it spends most of its life in the sea, only returning to fresh water—usually to the river where it was born—to spawn. In fresh water, salmon take no sustenance, so on their way back to the sea after spawning, they are miserably thin and worn, and certainly not fit to eat.

A Scotch or Irish wild salmon in good condition, in May, June, or July, is considered by many to be the best in the world. It is a glossy, steely-blue fish shading to bright silver underneath, with black spots on the head and upper part of the body; the flesh is fine and pink.

Of the Pacific salmon, from the Northwest, Canada, and Alaska, the tastiest are the red-fleshed chinook, or king salmon, and the sockeye. Atlantic salmon is widely available; it is a somewhat richer fish than Pacific salmon. Salmon from Norwegian waters is also excellent, and so is that from Greenland.

Today, farmed salmon is readily available and a very good buy. Most of the salmon we see in the marketplace is farmed; almost all Atlantic salmon is farm-raised.

The author of *The Sportsman's Cookery Book*, written in 1926, said: "Salmon, which has a particular virtue of its own, is best plain, so do not attempt to better it." It should be cooked simply and served unadorned, except for an appropriate sauce or herbed mayonnaise and boiled new potatoes. If you are presented with a salmon straight from the river, you will need to clean it, but leave on the head and tail. It is better to cook it a day after it is caught, when it is more succulent, unless you intend to prepare sashimi or sushi and eat it raw. After cooking, skin the salmon very carefully, removing the skin from each side in one piece.

Buying guide: good all year round, but wild salmon is at its best in spring and summer. It is sold whole or in steaks. When salmon is really fresh, there is a creamy substance between the flakes of flesh that sets to a cheeselike curd when cooked. Avoid steaks that look soft, grayish, oily, or watery. You will need to allow 6 to 8 ounces per person.

Best cooking methods: unless you have a truly enormous fish poacher, the best way to cook a salmon whole is to bake it in foil. If you do have a large fish poacher, or can borrow one, poach the salmon in court bouillon at the lowest possible simmer for a really succulent result. Hot, salmon is best with hollandaise or other creamy sauces, or with beurre blanc, a lobster sauce, or plain melted butter, with or without herbs such as chervil, tarragon, or parsley. Salmon steaks can be brushed with butter or oil, grilled or broiled, and served with the same kinds of sauces. Panseared salmon fillets are delicious. Cold, salmon is best eaten with plain or herbed mayonnaise or with a horseradish cream, and served with thinly sliced cucumbers and boiled potatoes.

Salmon trout, sea trout The European salmon trout—closely related to the brown trout found in rivers and lakes in both the United States and Europe—is perhaps the perfect fish. As the name suggests, it combines the best of both the salmon and the trout: it has the superior texture of trout, being less dense and more succulent than salmon, but has salmon's excellent flavor and pale pink-colored flesh. Salmon trout is also a much more useful size than salmon for cooking whole because it usually weighs less than 5 pounds, although it can grow to 10 pounds or even more.

The correct name for salmon trout is sea trout and that, too, is apt since the fish is really a trout that has taken it into its head to wander down to the sea to feed, returning to fresh water to spawn. It is a beautiful silver fish with a small head, not as pointed as that of the salmon, and with dark X-shaped spots on the gill cover.

In America, the steelhead trout, an anadromous rainbow trout, is the most similar to salmon trout, but other brown trout may be called salmon or sea trout. Steelhead may be as small as 1 pound or as large as 10 pounds, or more. *Buying guide:* spring and summer. Sold whole or in fillets. Allow about 8 ounces per person.

Best cooking methods: salmon trout can be dealt with in the same ways as salmon and is particularly good baked in foil. Poached, it makes a delicious summer lunch. Allow the same cooking time as for salmon, or a few minutes less, and use the same sauces as you would for salmon.

Trout Of the many members of the trout family, wild brook trout may be the most delicious of all. Farmed fish cannot match it—it is sometimes so mild as to be almost tasteless—but occasionally does come close. Brook trout, native to the northeastern United States and Canada, may also be found in other parts of North America and in parts of Europe. Although the wild trout can be quite large, farmed brook trout is usually about 1 pound in weight.

The rainbow trout, which is native to California, is a familiar and delicious fish—it appears almost unfailingly on restaurant menus, and a very neat parcel of food it makes, just the right size for one person, pretty to look at, and sweet to eat. The farm-reared rainbow trout is

most familiar: white-fleshed and delicate and deserving better treatment than it often receives in restaurants. A hardy fish, it responds well to freezing, and frozen rainbow trout is quite a good buy. Farmed rainbow trout usually weigh 12 to 16 ounces. Wild rainbow trout, which has pink to deep-red flesh—and more flavor than the farmed fish—may be as large as 10 pounds.

Brown trout, the wild native trout of British rivers and streams, is a beautiful brown with red and dark gray spots. In Britain, it is usually only available to fly fishermen's families—a great pity, for it is quite delicious. In North America, however, the brown trout has thrived since its introduction at the end of last century, and is a hardy and popular fish.

Take care when cleaning trout to wipe rather than wash it. Remove the gills but leave the head on—the eyes will turn quite white as the fish is cooking. The skin can be removed after cooking, if desired, in one whole piece. *Buying guide:* available all year, fresh (farmed) or frozen. Sold whole or in fillets. Allow one trout per person, unless the trout are particularly large. *Best cooking methods:* trout can be poached in court-bouillon, sautéed and served *à la meunière* (in browned butter with parsley and lemon), baked, broiled, or simply panfried, preferably outdoors over a fire, or smoked in a home smoker. It can also be cooked in beer with horseradish and

served with horseradish sauce. Whole trout can be grilled; it's best to use a grilling basket so the skin doesn't stick or tear. If the trout is still alive or is extremely fresh, it can be cooked "au bleu," in water with vinegar in it; served with hollandaise, it is worth the trouble. In Sweden, trout is boiled in salt water and served with butter.

Char The Arctic char of Canada and northern Europe, the Dolly Varden, alpine trout, and lake trout of North America (also chars), and the *omble chevalier* (char) of the deep lakes of the French and Swiss Alps all belong to the enormous and excellent salmon family.

The Arctic char is a silver, salmon-like fish with a pink underside, which flushes deep red during spawning. It has firm, delicate flesh and makes a delicious meal. Most of the Arctic char in the marketplace is farm-raised in Canada or the northern United States, but wild char from Canada can sometimes be found. The Dolly Varden, alpine trout, and lake trout are very good table fish and deservedly popular. In France, the *omble chevalier*, which resembles trout, is eaten throughout the summer, and is definitely worth ordering if you see it on a menu. *Buying guide:* the wild Arctic char is best in early autumn; farm-raised Arctic char and American chars are available all year. The small trout and sometimes small farmed Arctic char are sold whole; larger trout and Arctic char are sold in steaks or fillets.

Grayling

Salmon

Salmon trout

Arctic char

Brook trout

Brown trout

Rainbow trout

Best cooking methods: as for trout or salmon. Steaks can be poached, perhaps with bay leaves, and eaten cold.

Grayling A delicious, thyme-scented fish, called by St. Ambrose the flower fish or flower of fishes, grayling should ideally be eaten as soon as it is caught because the delicate flavor is fleeting. It is a graceful fish, silver with finely marked geometric scales and a long spotted backfin. It cannot survive in even slightly polluted water and thrives only in cold, crystal-clear, turbulent rivers, often living alongside trout and eating the same food. A very fresh grayling has much in common, in both taste and texture, with trout, and bears up well in comparison.

You will probably have to catch your own grayling to try one. Scale it before cooking—scald with boiling water and use a knife or a fish scaler, or pick the scales off with your fingernails. Grayling never weigh more than 4 pounds, and are usually less than 2 pounds.
Best cooking methods: brush with butter, flavor with thyme—especially if you find thyme near where the fish was caught—and broil; or sauté gently in butter.

Carp One of the hardiest of all fish, the carp is known to have existed in Asia thousands of years ago and is reputed to live to a grand old age. A somewhat lumbering fish, in its natural state it lives in slow and muddy rivers or lakes, but it can survive well in domestic ponds and is extensively farmed. In Poland, carp is traditionally eaten on Christmas Eve.

Although variants have been bred with just a few large scales that can be picked off with your fingernails, or with no scales at all, the common carp is covered with large scales that are difficult to remove. To scale a common carp, pour some boiling water over it first—better still, ask the fish seller to scale it for you. A compact and meaty fish, carp needs to be cooked with plenty of interesting flavors.
Buying guide: almost always sold whole, and usually a good size for four people.
Best cooking methods: stuffed and baked, or poached and served with horseradish or sorrel sauce.

Catfish So called because of the long barbels that hang about its mouth like drooping cat's whiskers, the catfish is a particularly hardy creature. It is easily transplanted from one region to another, and is a candidate for intensive farming. It should be skinned before cooking.
Buying guide: almost always sold in fillets. The fillets should be white in color and sweet-smelling.
Best cooking methods: fillets are often deep-fried and served with tartar sauce. They can be panfried or baked; they also make a good basis for a fish soup that should include plenty of tomatoes, garlic, herbs, and white wine.

Pike, pickerel, and muskellunge
The predatory pike is quite handsome in its way, especially the younger fish, which has bold markings on a golden-brown or greenish-silver background. An adult pike can weigh up to 40 pounds or more, although those at the market are usually 5 to 10 pounds, and the flesh is white and firm. The muskellunge of northeastern and north-central North America can grow even larger, but the pickerel, or chain pickerel, of the eastern and southern United States is much smaller, usually around 3 pounds. In France, pike is much admired, and *quenelles de brochet,* the lightest of fish dumplings, served with a white wine sauce, is a classic dish.

The theories about cooking pike are many: it should be bled to remove the sharp, reedy taste; it should have quantities of salt forced down its throat and be left to stand overnight to dissolve the bones; it should not be washed because its natural slime keeps it tender. However, a medium-sized pike is perfectly good cooked without any of these refinements. Simply scale it before cooking—pour a little boiling water over it first. Watch out for the bones when you eat it, for they are vicious and plentiful; and don't ever eat the roe, which in some cases can be poisonous.
Buying guide: best in autumn and early winter. If you do see pike for sale, a small whole one is best. Large pike are usually cut into fillets or steaks. Pickerel and muskellunge are both sport fish, not seen in the market.
Best cooking methods: pike tends to be dry, and a very large one may also be tough, so a whole fish should be stuffed before baking and steaks should be marinated before being panfried or broiled. Small pike can be poached and served with beurre blanc,

melted butter, or a parsley-butter or caper sauce. Pike is also traditionally used for gefilte fish. In Scandinavia, pike is boiled and eaten with horseradish.

Perch and pike perch The perch is a beautiful little fish, pale greenish-gold with a white or yellowish belly and superb coral-colored fins. The back has dangerously sharp spines and the scales are stubborn, but the fish is well worth the trouble of preparing: it is firm-fleshed, delicate, and light, and has a very good flavor. It is a fish that should only be eaten when it is gleamingly fresh.

The pike perch is also known as the walleye, wall-eyed pike, or yellow pike. Looking somewhat like a cross between pike and perch, with a bony head, thick skin, and spiny dorsal fin, it is a most delicious fish, with firm, white, well-flavored flesh, more interesting than trout and well worth purchasing whenever you see it. The European pike perch, or sander (*sandre* in France), is farmed, like trout, in special conditions for fast growth.

The yellow perch, which is abundant in the Great Lakes and throughout the Midwest, is also found in the eastern part of the country and in eastern Canada. A popular sport fish, it is closely related to the common perch and can be cooked in the same ways.

To prepare perch and pike perch for cooking, first carefully cut off the spines and fins with strong scissors, then bend the fish over and scrape off the scales, which will be raised a little from their usual flat position. The procedure is slightly easier if you hold the fish firmly by the tail with a cloth or paper towel; or you can sprinkle your hands with salt. A pair of strong scissors is also useful for opening the fish to gut it.
Buying guide: these fish are generally sold whole, although large pike perch are sometimes filleted. Smaller fish are more delicate in flavor than the large ones.
Best cooking methods: perch and pike perch are probably best panfried very slowly in butter, about 10 minutes on each side for a 1½-pound fish. They can also be baked, boiled, or broiled. Small perch are good when split to butterfly them, seasoned, and grilled, and then served with plenty of melted butter and chopped parsley. Crisply fried sage leaves can be substituted for the parsley.

scaling round fish 26

Beurre Blanc 257
Oven-Fried Catfish with Remoulade Sauce 281–2
Tartar Sauce 259

Shad The shad is a large migratory member of the herring family that spawns in fresh water. White-fleshed and nutritious, it has a good flavor, but also, unfortunately, a multitude of fine, wirelike bones. The roe is particularly good to eat—it is even classed as an aphrodisiac by more hopeful gourmets.

The American shad has been successfully transplanted from the Atlantic to the Pacific, and in the spring can be found in the St. Lawrence River in the East and the Columbia River on the West Coast. In Europe, the allis shad, which can grow up to 2 feet long, and the smaller twaite shad are caught in the Loire and Garonne rivers of France in the springtime, when they are spawning.

Remove as many of the bones as possible before cooking shad, using tweezers if necessary. When the fish is cooked, cut deep lengthwise parallel slits about 4 inches apart in the flesh, and remove any accessible bones before serving, moving your finger over the flesh to detect the hidden ones.

Buying guide: best in spring in spawning season. Sold whole, or in fillets (sometimes boned). A 3-pound shad will feed six. Ask the fish dealer to scale and possibly bone the fish when he cleans it. Shad roe is sold frozen and canned as well as fresh.

Best cooking methods: stuff whole shad with sorrel and then bake, or bake and serve on a bed of sorrel. Shad can also be filleted, with the skin left on, and gently broiled. Serve with fresh tomato sauce, beurre blanc, or a sorrel purée mixed with fresh cream. The delicate roe can be quickly sautéed in butter or gently baked in butter.

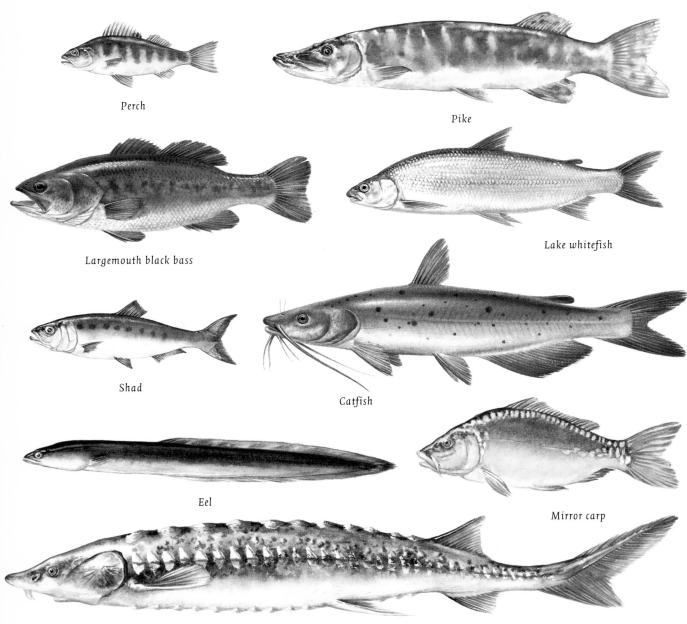

Perch

Pike

Largemouth black bass

Lake whitefish

Shad

Catfish

Eel

Mirror carp

Sturgeon

Sturgeon A huge and somewhat prehistoric-looking creature, the sturgeon spends most of its life in the sea, but is most sought after when it comes into rivers to spawn. It can grow up to 20 feet or more, and the beluga sturgeon—usually a more modest size and the source of the most expensive caviar—can live to the ripe age of 100. Sturgeon are still caught today in some American and European rivers, but they are most plentiful in the Caspian Sea, using its southern rivers for spawning. Recently, sturgeon has begun to be farm-raised in California.

The flesh of sturgeon is white, very firm, rich, and firm-textured, and it is frequently likened to veal. It is inclined to be dry and is improved by being smoked or steeped in a white wine marinade before it is cooked.

Buying guide: best in spring. Sold as steaks or fillets.

Best cooking methods: broil or sauté in butter, like veal; or poach in white wine and serve with a creamy sauce. In France, a luxurious dish is sturgeon poached in Champagne. It is also very good smoked and cut into thick slices, eaten with lemon, horseradish, and brown bread and butter.

Bass This is the collective name for a large family of bony fish equipped with spiny fins, which includes the magnificent sea bass. All make good eating. There are numerous freshwater bass, but the most well-known are the largemouth and smallmouth black bass; other bass include the white, yellow, and spotted bass. Farmed striped bass are actually a cross between wild white bass and sea bass. Cook small ones whole, panfried, baked and stuffed, or grilled over fennel twigs. Larger fish are best filleted and skinned, or the flesh may taste muddy; the fillets can be poached, served *à la meunière*, or fried.

Eel and elver Eels have a life cycle as strange as that of any fish. The American and European eel is spawned in the Sargasso Sea and promptly travels up to 4000 miles to find the fresh waters of its ancestors, where it will spend most of its life, only returning to the Sargasso to spawn and then die. (Australian and Japanese eels have spawning grounds closer to land, but still have a very long

way to travel.) By the time they reach the river mouths, the tiny baby eels have grown into elvers 2 to 3 inches long. These little creatures, looking like transparent spaghetti, are good to eat, deep-fried (they must be soaked for some hours in salt water with a dash of vinegar before cooking). In Spain they are a seasonal delicacy. By their second winter in fresh water the elvers have become small yellow eels, which are not so good to eat. These then mature into the familiar silver eels, velvety-brown on their backs and silver below, and are excellent to eat—meaty, even-textured, succulent, and very rich.

Buying guide: elvers appear in the spring; eels are in season all year but are best in autumn to winter. Try to buy live eels—they become tough and spoil almost instantly once killed. If you flinch at the prospect of having to deal with a live eel yourself, have the fish dealer kill and skin it for you and chop it into pieces. Ask for 3-inch pieces, which look better and are better able to keep their moisture during cooking than smaller lengths; for deep-frying, have it cut into ½-inch slices. Skinned eel is also available frozen.

Best cooking methods: An eel dish is always part of the traditional Italian Christmas Eve dinner; jellied eels are an English seaside treat. You may prefer to stew your eel in red wine, wrap it in bacon and sage leaves and broil it, or sauté it with a few bay leaves and serve it with Italian herb sauce. Elvers should be rinsed and patted dry, then dipped in flour and cooked immediately in hot oil with chile peppers and garlic. In Spain they are served in a fried tangle with a fiery tomato sauce.

Other freshwater fish

Most of the following fish are not commercially fished or farmed, and are unlikely to be in a fish shop. These are mainly fished for sport, and are trophies for the angler rather than the cook.

Bleak A small, slim, silvery fish found in the rivers of northern Europe, which can be cooked just like whitebait.

Bream Freshwater bream needs interesting seasonings and ingredients because the flesh is somewhat dry and tasteless. The European bream can be cooked like carp.

Buffalofish A popular freshwater fish from the Great Lakes and the Mississippi Valley, which makes good eating. It is often

smoked, but can be prepared like carp when fresh. Buffalofish are actually several different species of the fish known as suckers. The three types are the bigmouth, or redmouth; the black buffalo; and the smallmouth, or razorback.

Burbot This handsome golden fish, also called ling fish, is the only member of the cod family to inhabit fresh water, and it is found in North America, the British Isles, and throughout Europe. Burbot has good, firm, fatty flesh and a richly flavored liver that can be sliced to release its oils and then baked or poached with the fish; the roe is poisonous. The fish may be cooked in red wine, or served with a tomato, cheese, and cream sauce.

Chub A fish that precisely fits the description "cotton wool stuffed with needles," chub is watery-fleshed, full of small forked bones, and not really worth eating. If, however, you do catch one and don't want to waste it, try stewing it, panfrying it, or baking it in foil with herbs. It should be cooked as soon as possible after being caught as the flavor deteriorates in a very short time. The chub available in the American marketplace, often smoked, is actually cisco, a member of the whitefish family.

Crappie Known to anglers as white or black crappie, this is an excellent Mississippi Valley and New England freshwater fish. Members of the sunfish family, crappies are also known as calico bass, speckled perch, and strawberry bass. They are usually panfried.

Sheepshead Not to be confused with the saltwater porgy of the same name, this is the only freshwater drum, found in Canada, the Midwest, and the southern states. It can be either poached or panfried when very fresh.

Whitefish This large group of fish, related to salmon and trout, is found in deep-water lakes and rivers throughout the northern United States and Canada. American whitefish, which include the ciscoes and lake whitefish, are fished by anglers and commercially, and are sold fresh and frozen as well as smoked. Lake whitefish, found in plentiful supply in the Great Lakes and Canada, is good to eat and can be used in trout or salmon recipes. Vendace, the European cisco, and powan, or lavaret, are fished in the clear lakes of northern Europe, including the lochs of Scotland and Ireland. The whitefish roe is much prized.

Trimming flatfish

1 Snip off the tough upper pectoral fin.

2 Trim the tail, and cut away the dorsal and anal fins.

1

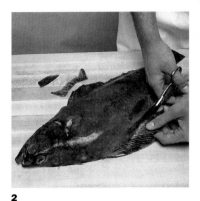

2

3 Cut off the head just behind the gills. If you are planning to serve the fish whole, gently press on it to release the viscera (intestines), and rinse the fish thoroughly under cold running water.

3

1

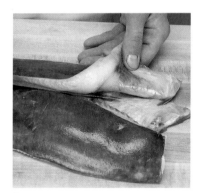

2

3

Filleting and skinning flatfish
(above and above right)
1 With a sharp knife, make a slit down the backbone from head to tail.

2 Slice down one side of the fish from head to tail, sliding the knife between the flesh and the bones. For the second fillet, slice away the flesh from the opposite side of the fish. For the third and fourth fillets, turn the fish over and repeat the process.

3 To skin the fillets, hold each firmly by the tail end and work the knife down the length of the fillet, keeping the blade as close to the skin as possible.

Scaling round fish *(left)*
Holding the fish by the tail, scrape away the scales with the back of a knife, working toward the head.

Cleaning round fish

1 Before cooking a fish whole, it is important to remove the bitter-tasting gills. To do this, lay the fish on its back and ease open the gill flaps. Carefully push the fan of gills (they can be sharp) out from between the gill flaps; sever and discard them.

round fish 12–16, 18–25

filleting knife 224

1

2 Cut off all the fins.

3 Slit open the fish's belly and ease out the viscera (intestines). Rinse the fish thoroughly, inside and out, under cold running water.

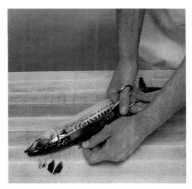

2

3

1

2

Filleting round fish

1 Starting just behind the head, cut into the back of the fish and slide the knife along one side of the backbone to release the fillet, keeping the knife close to the bone.

2 Continue slicing down the length of the fish, severing the fillet just behind the gills and at the tail.

3 Cut the second fillet from the other side of the fish. Skin the fillets in the same way as for flatfish.

3

round fish 12–16, 18–25
salmon 21

knives 222–4
meat pounder 226

Boning round fish

1 Cut off the head behind the gills, without cutting quite through the bottom part of the fish; ease the head away from the body, taking most of the viscera (intestines) with it. Remove the rest with the help of the knife.

2 Carefully slice down the back of the fish between the flesh and backbone, keeping the knife against the backbone; do not puncture the belly. Open the fish out like a book.

3 Turn the fish flesh side down, and cut away the backbone and small adjoining bones.

4 This method of boning is particularly suitable when the fish is to be stuffed, or it is to be opened out flat for grilling, sautéing, or frying.

1

2

3

4

1

2

Cutting salmon scallops

1 Take a tailend section of fresh salmon.

2 Slice off the top fillet, starting at the tail and holding the knife as close to the backbone as possible. Turn the fish over and repeat the process to remove the second fillet. Discard the backbone, and skin each fillet as for flatfish.

3

4

3 Cut each fillet horizontally into two thin slices, using a long, sharp, and flexible knife.

4 Place each slice of salmon between two pieces of dampened parchment paper or between two sheets of plastic wrap. Gently but firmly flatten the fish into scallops, using a rolling pin or a meat pounder.

Preserved Fish

Fresh fish deteriorates fast and has always been a natural subject for traditional preserving methods. Indeed, the smoking, pickling, salting, and drying of fish used to be a matter of simple necessity—when fishing boats relied on the wind, and overland transport on the horse and cart, fresh sea fish was practically unknown inland. Moreover, as fish was the prescribed food for the numerous meatless days in the Christian calendar (as many as twelve a month), to preserve it, and to preserve it palatably, was a matter of great importance.

Smoked fish

Fish must be salted before smoking. This process, which entails either soaking the fish in a brine strong enough to keep a potato afloat, or rubbing into it a generous amount of dry salt, improves both the flavor and the keeping qualities. After salting, the fish is dried and then cold- or hot-smoked. The protein content remains unchanged, but calories are diminished.

To find smoked fish you like, try different varieties, because they vary enormously, and regional specialties still find their way into the marketplace. Some are pale and oak-smoked, while others are oversalted and artificially dyed in fierce hues of red or yellow.

There are several ways of improvising a smoker in your backyard—all you need is a large container/chimney for the smoke with a few airholes for the fire. Although you can convert your barbecue grill to a smoker, if you intend to smoke a great deal it will be worth rigging up a real smoker. For the less ambitious, a small stove-top smoker is much less of a production. It is used indoors, and will quickly hot-smoke a gutted, salted fish. These smokers use sawdust, to which you could add thyme, rosemary, or juniper berries; this will make your fish smell and taste much more interesting.

Store-bought smoked fish will keep for about 3 days, or up to 20 days in the freezer. Home-smoked fish should be eaten at once. Only dried and salted fish keeps indefinitely.

Cold-smoked fish Cold-smoking takes place at temperatures of around 75°F, which smoke the fish but do not cook it. Products of the cold-smoking process are either eaten raw, like smoked salmon, or may require further cooking, like finnan haddie.

Smoked salmon The British think that salmon is best when caught in Scottish waters; Norwegians say that those caught in Norwegian waters are better still; and others argue for the salmon from the Pacific Northwest or Canada. All agree that farmed salmon come fourth, but can still be excellent when smoked. Smoked salmon should be fresh and succulent, melting away under the knife as it is sliced. The best of all is the pale pink-gold, rather undersalted salmon. A darker red or a deep orange color usually means dyed or overcured fish, and is not a good sign.

The traditional Scottish way of kippering salmon, as the process used to be called (kippers—kippered herring—having merely borrowed the word), involves brining boned sides of salmon, wiping them, drying them, oiling them, and then covering them in brown sugar. Another wipe with a cloth, often soaked in whisky, another anointing with oil, and another whisky wipe, and then the sides are smoked over a fire of peat and oak chips.

Fresh cold-smoked salmon is usually sliced for you in the market, but if you can afford it, buying a whole side often works out to be more economical. A side runs the whole length of the fish from shoulder to tail. Buying a whole side has the advantage of giving you both the richer, fattier cuts toward the tail and the fine-grained center. To slice the salmon, go across the grain of the flesh—that is, cut from the shoulder toward the tail. You need an extremely sharp, long, flexible knife—a slicer with a scalloped edge is best. Or you can buy a side of salmon presliced and reassembled.

Smoked salmon is eaten sliced transparently thin, with lemon and thin brown bread and butter. Lox (from the Yiddish word for smoked salmon) tends to be more heavily cured than other smoked salmon; it is most often served with cream cheese and bagels. *Royktlaks*—Norwegian smoked salmon—is used for *smørbrød*, the Scandinavian open-faced sandwiches.

Frozen and canned smoked salmon are available, but both are no more than vividly pink shadows of the fresh variety. However, sliced vacuum-packed and chilled smoked salmon can be perfectly acceptable. And what can be a good buy at the delicatessen are "trimmings"—untidy scraps of fresh smoked salmon with bits of skin attached. Provided they are moist and soft, they are ideal for smoked salmon mousse or for any dish requiring chopped smoked salmon.

Finnan haddie Finnan haddie, or smoked haddock, is so called because it was in the village of Findon, in Scotland, that the method of curing this fish, giving it its distinctive pale appearance, was invented. Originally the beheaded fish were dried and cold-smoked in the smoke of seaweed. By a modernized process, finnan haddie is now produced far beyond Scotland, in New England, among other places. So too are its imitations—fillets of white fish that are artificially dyed a bright, bright yellow and may be chemically treated to taste of smoke. It is easy to tell the true from the false: the color is a complete giveaway.

Finnan haddie is eaten hot. Broil it, or poach it for a few minutes in milk or water, then simply serve it with butter, or with a poached egg on top and a piece of hot buttered toast. Or use it to make dishes such as the creamed finnan haddie that is a favorite in New England; the Anglo-Indian kedgeree, a rice and lentil dish; or the poached smoked haddock of Scandinavia, served with carrots, eggs, and butter. Scotland eats "ham and haddie," frying the fish in fat rendered from slices of smoked ham.

Kipper Kippers, or kippered herring, are split washed herring that are briefly brined, hung on "tenterhooks" to dry, and then smoked for 4 to 6 hours. Kippers are a mainstay of the British table—grilled with a lump of butter for breakfast or high tea, or served cold in salads and pâtés for lunch.

Many kippers are dyed during brining, emerging mahogany-colored after smoking. There are, however, undyed kippers to be had, and these are worth finding. Buy a fat kipper—lean kippers tend to be dry. And buy kippers fresh—frozen kippers, although they keep their texture fairly well, do not taste as good.

Smoked halibut Young halibut is sometimes lightly smoked. Its taste is delicate and its texture firm. It is served in the same way as finnan haddie.

Bloater Bloaters are herring that are lightly salted and then smoked without the intestine being removed. The slight fermentation of the enzymes occurring during this process causes the fish to get bloated and develop a somewhat gamy flavor. Bloaters are silvery in appearance, and the flesh is soft and moist. They do not keep as long as kippers, and must be gutted before they are served. They may be broiled, or simply mashed to make a sandwich filling. The famous *harengs saur* of Boulogne, on France's northern coast, are even more plumped up than the ordinary bloater, and the Swedish *surströmming* is so bloated that it seems on the point of explosion. This last is not much exported, but is deeply loved at home, where it is eaten with thin crispbread or potatoes.

Smoked sturgeon If fresh sturgeon, with its fine-grained white flesh, tastes rather like veal, smoked sturgeon resembles nothing so much as smoked turkey both in color and taste. It is, however, more delicious still, more buttery and melting in the mouth, and of course a great deal more expensive. Eat it like smoked salmon.

Smoked roes Fish eggs from any number of species are smoked and enjoyed. Note that what are called hard roes alone are eggs—soft roes are not roes at all but "milt," or sperm, from the male of the species. Smoked roes should be firm and moist with no signs of skin breakage. Smoked cod roe is deliciously grainy and glutinous. This or smoked carp roe can be used to make taramasalata, the creamy Greek spread, or dip.

Hot-smoked fish Hot-smoking takes place at temperatures of about 180°F, and is the method used for eel, trout, and mackerel, which are smoked and lightly cooked at one and the same time. They are bought ready to eat and can also be served hot.

Smoked trout The best smoked trout has gone into brine as soon as it left the water. It is gutted only after it has been drained, and is then ready for smoking. In England, silver birchwood is said to give it the best and sweetest flavor, and a little peat and a few pine cones make it taste even better. The fish turns golden and then, if left longer, to bronze. Look for springiness in a smoked trout: the flesh should be neither mushy nor dry—the fine, firm texture of a nice plump smoked trout is as much of a pleasure as its delicate flavor. Serve smoked trout for a summer lunch or supper with lemon wedges, thin brown bread and butter, and a dash of horseradish mixed with lightly whipped cream; or serve it in a salad.

Smoked mackerel Silvery-gold smoked mackerel can be very good indeed. As this is not a very subtly flavored fish, it emerges from smoking tasting straightforwardly of itself and is, usually, rich and juicy. Best bought whole, it is also available filleted. Avoid any smoked mackerel in a package that oozes with oil: this indicates that the fish has been stored for too long or at the wrong temperature, and the flesh will be dry.

Eat smoked mackerel cold accompanied by horseradish sauce or lemon.

Bucklings are popular in Europe, and allegedly get their name from a fourteenth-century Dutchman, William Beukels, who invented this method of preserving ungutted herring. A nice fat buckling is tasty eaten with brown bread and butter and lemon wedges, and also good mashed to a paste. In Germany, buckling is sometimes lightly broiled or gently panfried, with the roe, and served with sauerkraut or scrambled eggs.

Sprat, sild, and brisling are all small European herring that, when smoked, are simply served with brown bread, butter, lemon, and a glass of beer. (Sild, or *sill*, is the Scandinavian term for herring.) As well as being candidates for smoking, they also sometimes find themselves canned as sardines.

Arbroath smokie A British delicacy, these are small smoked haddock that have been beheaded and gutted but not split, and hot-smoked. After brining, they are placed over birch and oak smoke until pale golden. A favorite way of serving them is to put butter in the cavity of the fish, season with black pepper, and heat gently under a broiler or in the oven. The dark skin is then peeled off to reveal a golden outer crust and gradually paling flesh.

Smoked eel Some say that the densely textured smoked eel is even more delicious than smoked salmon. Smoked

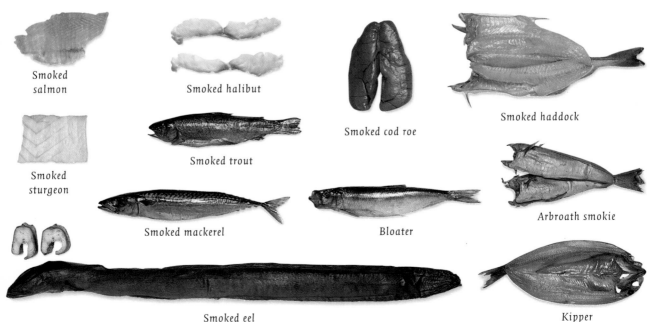

Smoked
salmon

Smoked halibut

Smoked cod roe

Smoked haddock

Smoked
sturgeon

Smoked trout

Smoked mackerel

Bloater

Arbroath smokie

Smoked eel

Kipper

eel is very rich and filling, and is usually served with pepper, lemon juice, and brown bread and butter. Pinky-beige smoked eel fillets laid over a plateful of golden scrambled eggs make a first course that is especially delicious. Or buy it whole, skin on, if you want larger, more succulent fillets. It is easy to skin and then serve with horseradish sauce.

Cured, pickled, and salted fish

The curing process is particularly suited to oily fish, such as herring. They are steeped in a vinegar or brine solution, which halts enzyme action in the same way that cooking does.

Gravlax is a most delicious Swedish specialty—it is raw salmon cured with dill, sugar, salt, and white peppercorns. It is traditionally eaten with a rather sweet mustard and dill sauce. Gravlax is quite popular in the United States, and it and other variations on the theme—such as tequila-and-cilantro-cured salmon—appear on trendy restaurant menus.

Salted herring are sold whole in many European markets. They must be soaked for up to 12 hours, and then filleted and chopped for salads or bathed in sour cream for an hors d'oeuvre.

Matjes herring are considered to be the best salted herring. They are lightly salted fat female fish with translucent, slippery flesh of a beautiful old-rose color. They need no soaking.

Pickled herring, marinated herring These are marinated in spices and vinegar, then bottled in a sour cream or wine sauce.

Schmaltz herring These are larger herring (schmaltz is the German word for fat) that are skinned, filleted, and preserved in brine.

Bismarck herring These herring, blue of skin and white of flesh, are first steeped in white wine vinegar. Then, after they are gutted and boned, their heads and tails removed, and split, they are cured for 24 hours layered in a dish, well seasoned and interspersed with onion rings and sometimes with raw carrot. Eat them with new potatoes, or bathed in sour cream or a mayonnaise dressing.

Rollmop These are Bismarck herring—halved lengthwise—that have been rolled up tightly around peppercorns and slices of onion and fastened with toothpicks before being put into jars with hot spiced white wine vinegar.

Soused herring, potted herring These are a favorite in Britain, where many people like to souse herring at home by steeping them in a vinegary marinade to which herbs and spices are added. Soused herring can be found in specialty shops.

Anchovy Preserved salted anchovy fillets usually come canned in oil, those in olive oil being the best. Plain salted anchovies, sold direct from a barrel or a large can, need a brief soaking in fresh water to make them less harsh.

An anchovy is the most versatile of piquant ingredients, seasoning a great many dishes without imparting the least hint of fishiness. Anchovies are good for *salsa verde*, the Italian herb sauce, or for braised veal, stews, and pizzas, and in potato salad and salade Niçoise. Melted in butter with garlic, they make the Italian *bagna cauda*, a sauce served with raw vegetables as an antipasto.

Dried fish

Fish hung up to dry in the sun and wind provided an almost indestructible food supply for our ancestors. This earliest method of preserving fish is the precursor of modern freeze-drying. Salting is another way to extract moisture from fish, thus discouraging spoilage.

Salt cod, stockfish Dried to a flatness and hardness resembling hide, cod and other members of its family—haddock, pollack, ling—spring back to life when they are soaked. Salt cod has been salted and dried, while what is called stockfish has just been air-dried. In Scandinavia, where stockfish is much eaten, it appears in a fish pudding, light as a soufflé, which is served with hollandaise sauce. In Holland, Belgium, and Germany, stockfish is often soaked in lime water before being cooked.

In Portugal, where *bacalhau*—salt cod—is almost a staple food, they boast that they have more than a thousand different ways of cooking it. Some of the best recipes for dried cod are from the Basque region of Spain, and variously involve the fish—*bacalao*—with garlic, oil, tomatoes, peppers, onions, and potatoes. The French make a rich garlicky purée of salt cod that is called *brandade de morue*.

Bombay duck Made from a cured dried fish found in the Indian Ocean, Bombay duck has a pungent aroma. It can be obtained from Indian and specialty

markets and is used to season rice that is eaten with curry.

Dried shark's fin This is delicately flavored cartilage of the fin, which, when you buy it whole, looks like the tousled beard of Santa Claus. It requires soaking overnight, or even longer, in many changes of water, until it softens. In China, shark's fin is banquet food: it goes into party soups, into rather liquid stews and braises, and, shredded finely, into omelets. Its gelatinous properties have been likened to those of calf's foot. Found in Asian markets, dried shark's fin is also sold in strands. In some shops, frozen shark's fin is available; even more expensive than the dried, it is prepared and ready to use.

Salted roes

Into this category fall the costly caviar and its less exotic alternatives.

Caviar The fish that are used for commercial caviar production are the sevruga, the large osetra, and the giant beluga, which has a huge roe to match. All are members of the *Acipenser* tribe, and are collectively known as sturgeon. The roes are passed through fine-meshed sieves to separate the eggs, which are then salted. The brining of caviar is a delicate business. The condition of the fish and the size of the eggs both have a bearing on it, and the finest grade emerges from the care of the master tasters as *malassol*, a Russian term meaning "slightly salted."

Caviars come in a variety of sizes and colors. Sevruga is small-grained and greenish-black. Osetra, larger-grained, may be golden-brown, deep-green, or slate-gray; it can also be pale—almost bluish-white. Beluga, the largest and the most rare, is gray or, very rarely, golden. The closer to spawning the fish is caught, the paler the roe—and all of these, depending on their quality, make what is called "first-grade" caviar.

First-grade caviar is sometimes pasteurized, which lengthens its shelf life. Nonpasteurized caviar is kept refrigerated at 32°F: warmer, and it loses its texture and becomes oily; colder, and its flavor is ruined. The contents of an open container may be kept, covered, in the refrigerator, but should certainly be eaten within a week.

This also applies to pressed caviar—which is slightly less expensive than the *malassol* but is, in fact, the first choice of some caviar experts. It is caviar that has been drained of some of its liquid. The eggs, of course, are squashed in the process, and what emerges is a fairly solid mass, saltier than *malassol*, but tasting more intensely of sturgeon, since 2 pounds of fresh caviar are reduced to make 1 pound of pressed. Second-grade caviar may be saltier caviar of a single variety, or a mixture of different caviars, some of them highly superior.

To educate the palate, one really needs to eat a lot of caviar, not with tiny special caviar spoons but by the mouthful. In Russia, where large helpings of second-grade caviar are fairly unceremoniously served, it is often eaten with blinis—fat little buckwheat pancakes—and sour cream. But as a rule it is best with a little lemon, some fresh Melba toast and unsalted butter.

Gray mullet roe Known as *tarama* in Greece, the salted, dried, pressed roe of the mullet is considered a great delicacy, ranking only slightly lower than caviar and above salmon roe. As the name suggests, it makes taramasalata—the creamy Greek fish spread served as an appetizer. For this purpose, the roe is pounded with oil, lemon juice, and

crushed garlic, and bound with soft white bread crumbs or mashed potato, and sometimes with an egg yolk. Smoked carp or cod roe makes a good substitute.

Salmon caviar The roe of the salmon, this is bright orange and large-grained, not so much an imitation caviar but a fresh-tasting product in its own right. Sometimes called red caviar, it too can be eaten with sour cream, or just with toast, butter, and a squeeze of lemon.

Lumpfish caviar The pink eggs of the lumpfish are salted, colored black, or sometimes red, and pressed. Lumpfish caviar is used on cocktail party canapés. Alone, it is less interesting than true caviar but is pleasant with sour cream and raw onion, and is fairly inexpensive.

Whitefish caviar Sometimes called American golden caviar, whitefish caviar is composed of small yellowish eggs. It can be served like lumpfish caviar.

Canned fish

Fish is one of the few foods that stand up well to canning. Canned tuna and sardines are foods worth eating in their own right—quite different from their fresh counterparts, but still good.

Salmon Canned salmon comes in many grades, from the not-so-good bright red

to a more acceptable pink (the darker it is, the oilier). It can be good and is useful in fish cakes and sandwich fillings.

Sardines Good brands of sardines have been gently brined, correctly dried, and lightly cooked in olive oil, then stored for about a year, so that the flavors of fish and oil are mingled. Sardine is actually more a general term for a number of soft-boned saltwater fish, including pilchards, sprat, and some herring. The sardines caught off the western coast of France are the best and most expensive. Portuguese and Spanish sardines are less fine but much cheaper. Eat sardines bones and all, with brown bread and butter and a squeeze of lemon.

Tuna The best canned tuna is taken from the albacore, king of the tunas, which alone is permitted to be described as "white meat." Other tuna varieties— skipjack, yellowfin, bluefin—are a little darker, but all make good salads. Use canned tuna for the classic Italian *vitello tonnato* (cold veal with a creamy tuna sauce). Buy good-quality tuna, which comes in solid pieces, packed in olive oil.

Jellied eel A traditional Cockney delicacy, jellied eel is sold in cans, and makes a good appetizer; serve it with little bunches of watercress.

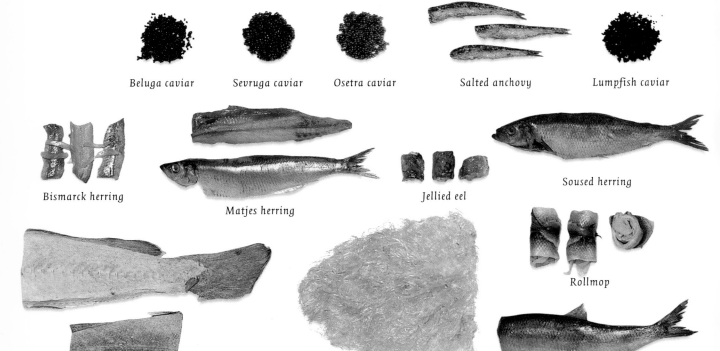

Beluga caviar   Sevruga caviar   Osetra caviar   Salted anchovy   Lumpfish caviar

Bismarck herring   Matjes herring   Jellied eel   Soused herring

Rollmop

Salt cod   Dried shark's fin   Salted herring

Shellfish

Although overfishing and pollution have taken their toll of shellfish, there are signs that things are improving. Waters that were a hazard to the health of both shellfish and consumers have been radically cleaned up, and new farming methods are making it possible to harvest fast-growing shrimp, for example, in large quantities.

True, the shrimp most readily available may not be the high-quality Gulf of Mexico ones, or we may find oysters on the market the size of tennis balls that can only be eaten chopped like large clams and cooked. But we should be able to enjoy more abundant and possibly less costly supplies; and the delicious local varieties of shellfish are still available. Buy them from a dealer who specializes in them and can be trusted to sell them only when they are sweet and fresh.

If you are buying cooked shellfish, a quick sniff should distinguish the freshly cooked from the fading. Shrimp lose the color in their shells and become lighter as they dry up. Lobsters and crabs also lose weight—choose heavy specimens with tension in the tail or claws. If they are floppy and unresisting, they are less than fresh. If you want to cook them live, plunge them into rapidly boiling salted water, seawater, or court-bouillon. Take care not to overcook them—all shellfish toughens and becomes rubbery if it is cooked for too long.

Crab To pick the meat out of a crab is a labor of love but always worth the effort—the flavor and texture are almost equal to that of lobster, and certainly less expensive. The sweet spider crabs beloved of the French, the soft green-backed shore crabs that are a Venetian

specialty, and the large crabs with fearsome claws that are found around the British coast are all delicious. But in America, the crab really comes into its own, with an abundance of blue crabs from the Atlantic and Gulf coasts; the superbly flavored Pacific Coast crab, the Dungeness; the Florida stone crabs; the Alaska king crab and snow crab; and the rock crabs and Jonah crabs found all along the Atlantic coast.

Soft shell crabs are actually blue crabs that have just shed their hard shells and so can be eaten shell and all. They are available from May to September.
Buying guide: whether they are alive or cooked, choose crabs that feel heavy for their size and smell fresh and sweet, with no hint of ammonia. Soft shell crabs should always be purchased alive. About 1 pound of crab in the shell, or 4 ounces of crabmeat, is usually sufficient for each person, depending on how it is prepared. Fresh crabmeat, which may have been pasteurized, is most often from blue crabs; lump or jumbo, then backfin, are the best.
Best cooking methods: the best crab is the one you boil and pick yourself, eaten cold with mayonnaise. Hard-shelled crabs are also good steamed and eaten hot, and can be used to make a very delicious bisque. Soft shell crabs can be eaten sautéed in butter, or broiled, grilled, or deep-fried.

Lobster "There is nothing more delicious in life," said Byron, "than the fireside, a lobster salad, and good conversation." With or without the embellishments, lobster is a treat for both the eye and the palate. The colors—creamy-pink flesh, and a shell speckled cream and coral underneath and deep,

old brick-red on the back; the texture—firm, delicate, and luscious; and the flavor—an appetizing, elusive marine taste—are all highly desirable. And, alas, expensive.

Lobsters from colder waters are generally the finest. The best are the northern lobsters from Maine to Nova Scotia, on the American side of the Atlantic, and the smaller Irish and Scottish lobsters and those from Brittany, on the European side. The male lobster is firmer-fleshed than the female and has larger, meatier claws, but the female has a more delicate flavor, a broader tail, and the delicious coral, or roe, which turns scarlet when it is cooked.
Buying guide: fresh lobsters are available all year, but are at their best and most abundant during the summer. Choose a lobster that is heavy for its size and has both its claws—sometimes a claw is lost in a fight, and some of the best meat is in the claws. Alive, by far the best way to buy lobsters, the shell is dark red to black; if already boiled, the shell should be bright red. If the lobster is precooked, check that its tail springs back into a tight curl when pulled out straight. This shows that it was cooked when alive. If you are brave enough, give it a sniff underneath, too, to make sure it is quite fresh.

If you are intending to cook the lobster yourself, make sure that you get a lively specimen and, again, that it is a heavy one—sometimes lobsters get quite thin in captivity waiting for someone to come along and buy them. To keep a live lobster in the refrigerator—although you should not keep it like this for more than a day or two—roll it loosely in damp newspaper to prevent it crawling about, enclose it in a paper bag pierced with air holes, and put it in the vegetable crisper.

European crab

Blue crab

Dungeness crab

If you are called upon to face cutting a live lobster in half or in pieces before cooking it, lay it on a cutting board, stomach down, and cover the tail with a wet cloth (the claws should be secured with rubber bands). Hold the lobster down firmly and, with a strong, sharp, pointed knife, make a swift incision into the cross mark in the head and push the knife down. This severs the spinal cord and kills the lobster instantly. Leave for a few minutes for the reflexes to cease, then cut the lobster into pieces, or split it in half lengthwise through the stomach shell and open it out flat, or cut it completely in half right through the hard back shell. Clean it, removing the grain sac from the head and reserving any coral and the delicious creamy tomalley, or liver, to use in lobster sauce if you like. Cook the lobster immediately.

Small lobsters are usually the most tender: a 1¼-pound lobster will feed one person. Large lobsters are excellent — and work out to be less expensive—for salads and sauces. Fresh cooked lobster meat is sometimes available; frozen and canned lobster meat is really best forgotten or used as an ingredient in a shellfish salad. Never have anything to do with a dead uncooked lobster—the meat spoils very quickly.

Best cooking methods: the simplest are the best: plain boiled, steamed, or broiled, served hot or cold with melted butter and either a little lemon juice or a good mayonnaise. Keep the shells to put into fish soup, or use them as a basis for lobster bisque or lobster stock.

Spiny lobster Depending on where you find it, this comparatively clawless cousin of the lobster is also known as rock lobster, crawfish, or crayfish— but do not confuse it with the little freshwater crayfish which, in turn, is sometimes known as a crawfish. Depending, too, on where it comes from—it thrives in the warm waters of the Pacific, the Caribbean, and the Mediterranean—it ranges in color from brownish-green to reddish-brown with yellow and white markings. Slightly paler than regular lobster when cooked, it has dense white flesh, which is well flavored but inclined to be coarse. The choicest meat is in the tail, and there is a lively market for frozen tails.

Buying guide: fresh is best, in late spring or early autumn, but fresh spiny lobsters are usually found only locally. The frozen tails are far more widely available. If you see fresh spiny lobsters for sale, choose specimens without eggs, as those that have eggs are not considered to be wholesome. Otherwise, follow the same guidelines as for ordinary lobsters.

Best cooking methods: when fresh, they are best eaten simply boiled with melted butter. Anything leftover makes a fine salad, with mayonnaise, or a very good bisque together with some shrimp in their shells, and plenty of cream and Madeira or brandy. Otherwise, use the same recipes for spiny lobster as for lobster.

Lobster

Cooked spiny lobster

Crayfish A sweet-fleshed miniature of the lobster, the crayfish (alias crawfish, crawdad, and freshwater lobster) is the only edible freshwater shellfish. Almost an institution in Louisiana, crayfish are also relished in France, where they are called *ecrevisses*; in Spain, where they are known as *astaco* or *cangrejo de rio*; and in Scandinavia. They were once a great feature of country-house tables in Britain, but there the native wild crayfish is now scarce. Although fresh crayfish were at one time limited to Louisiana and the West Coast, they are now farmed and fresh crayfish are often available in larger markets throughout the United States. They may also be found frozen, or cooked whole. Keep fresh crayfish in a bowl in the refrigerator, covered with a damp towel, for no longer than 24 hours. Before cooking them, remove the dark intestine by twisting off the middle tail fin, which will bring the intestine with it (or do this after cooking).

Buying guide: If you buy crayfish fresh, make sure they are lively—they spoil very quickly once dead. Allow at least ten to twelve crayfish per person.

Best cooking methods: boiling is best. In New Orleans, where a crayfish boil is an event, they are boiled in large pots of court-bouillon or water flavored with Creole spices. For simple boiled crayfish, put some smooth stones in the bottom of a large pot of water—this will keep the heat up so that the crayfish don't suffer when they are dropped in. Bring the water, into which you have put plenty of salt and fresh dill, to a rapid boil. Drop each crayfish in separately so that the water keeps boiling all the time and cook for about 5 minutes, until they turn bright scarlet. Remove from the heat and let them cool in the cooking liquid; serve cool or chilled. The French cook them *à la nage*—in a well-flavored court-bouillon—and serve them hot in an appetizing scarlet mound with hot melted butter, or cold with mayonnaise. Crayfish are also used to make a beautiful creamy bisque, and for *sauce Nantua*, the most delicate of sauces, frequently served with *quenelles de brochet* (pike dumplings).

Dublin Bay prawn Whether you meet them as *langoustines*, their French name, lobsterettes, Norway lobster (their Latin name is *Nephrops norvegicus*), Italian *scampi*, or Dublin Bay prawns, these pretty pinky-orange-shelled creatures with their pale claws can be treated as exceedingly large shrimp or very small lobsters, depending on which way you like to look at them. The predictability of finding them in their frozen shelled form on the menus of bad, expensive, and pretentious European restaurants has led to their being passed over by many people interested in food, but cooked with care, and not surrounded by soggy batter, they make many delicate dishes.

Buying guide: at present, Dublin Bay prawns are a rarity in U.S. markets, and are most likely to be frozen. If you are lucky enough to find them fresh, they may be preboiled. Sometimes only the tails are sold. To feed four people, buy 2 pounds in their shells, or half that amount if they are already shelled.

Best cooking methods: if raw, cook them in their shells in gently boiling, well-salted water for not more than 10 minutes and then serve them with melted butter.

Overcooking makes them soggy and tasteless. Preboiled, reheat them gently for a hot dish; never recook them, as they easily toughen. Cold, they make a very good salad with oil and vinegar dressing or mayonnaise. In Venice they are dipped into a very light eggless batter, with a few other kinds of small fish and shellfish, then deep-fried and served with lemon wedges. They are also excellent grilled with oil and garlic—even frozen ones are good cooked in this way.

Shrimp and prawn There are so many species in the shrimp family that distinguishing them is often difficult, particularly because in different parts of the world—and in different regions of the United States—the names shrimp and prawn often do not refer to the same variety. In the United States, where more shrimp is consumed than anywhere else, classification is usually by size, from the largest of the luscious Gulf shrimp (ten to twelve make 1 pound) to the tiny cold-

Court-Bouillon 246
Italian Seafood Salad 361, 360
Mayonnaise 259

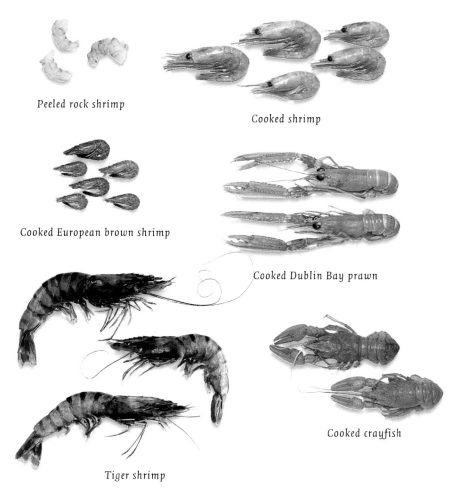

Peeled rock shrimp

Cooked shrimp

Cooked European brown shrimp

Cooked Dublin Bay prawn

Cooked crayfish

Tiger shrimp

water specimens that need 100 or more to tip the scales at that weight. Shrimp is the preferred term in much of the country, but prawn may also be used, usually but not always to refer to the larger varieties. In Europe, any member of the family that is more than about 2 inches long is often called a prawn, and it is the discerning French and Italians who award them the distinction of separate names. The *crevette rouge*, or *gambero rosso*, for example, is the large, expensive shrimp, very strong-flavored, and greatly enjoyed by the Italians, who often eat a whole pyramid of them with a bowl of mayonnaise and a bottle of white wine. A clear, deep-coral color with a violet splotch showing through the transparent shell of the head, it turns a bright pink-red when cooked. The delicious *crevette rose*, or *gamberello*, is the common large pink shrimp seen throughout Europe, best eaten cold with brown bread and butter and lemon juice, or with mayonnaise or in a salad. The *crevette rose du large*, or *gambero rosa*, with pretty red markings on its crested head, is one of the best, very delicate and much appreciated in northern France, where it is simply boiled, laid on a bed of brown seaweed with ice and halved lemons, and served with brown bread and butter.

Also delicious are the cold-water shrimp of Scandinavia, with their firm meat and fresh taste. They are usually boiled in seawater on board the trawler as soon as they are caught, which gives them a mild, sweetish flavor. These are often found frozen or canned throughout Europe.

Freshly caught and freshly boiled, little brown shrimp (in France *grises*) are difficult to shell because they are so small, but perhaps it is this job that makes the reward so worthwhile. Much more delicate than their larger cousins, these are delicious. Brown shrimp will turn browner when cooked; pink shrimp are grayish-brown when caught and turn pink when they are cooked.

Large warm-water shrimp or prawns, farmed by aquaculture methods all over the world, are now widely available raw, in the shell, with or without heads. These include the famed black tiger shrimp from the Indo-Pacific region, the East Asian king prawn, and the Hawaiian blue prawn, or giant river prawn, a freshwater prawn with a brilliant blue tail.
Buying guide: almost all the shrimp sold in the U.S. marketplace is frozen (not necessarily a bad thing, if it was flash-frozen at sea as soon as it was caught)—or was once. Among the more common

types are the delicious Gulf white and Gulf pink, along with the less-exciting Gulf brown shrimp. Others you are likely to see are the black tiger shrimp, usually quite flavorful, and the Chinese white, which varies in quality but may be quite good. Rock shrimp, cold-water shrimp found off the southern Atlantic Coast, are usually sold peeled because they're so difficult to shell, and often cooked. If you do come across fresh raw shrimp or prawns, they should be springy, with bright, crisp shells—avoid any that are soft or limp or have a smell of ammonia about them. Frozen shrimp really should be bought frozen—those thawed-out specimens in packages at the fish market may have been around for some time, and defrosted food spoils much more quickly than fresh food. If you must buy them thawed, make sure they smell fresh, and avoid any with black spots on the shell, which are a sign of deterioration.
Best cooking methods: simply drop them into a large pan of boiling seawater or salted water and simmer them for a minute or two, depending on their size—don't overcook them, as they will lose their delicate texture and turn tough. Recooking shrimp toughens them, so those bought already boiled should be

Blue mussel

Belon oyster

Green-lipped mussel

Pacific oyster

Atlantic oyster

heated gently and for as short a time as possible when being used in a hot dish. Shrimp can be shelled and deveined before or after cooking. The larger the species, the better it lends itself to grilling, panfrying, or broiling.

Oyster Oysters are a luxury you either love or loathe. To some people they are the height of ecstasy, to others a cause of revulsion. Aldous Huxley once said, "I suppose that when the sapid and slippery morsel—which is gone like a flash of gustatory summer lightning—glides along the palate, few people imagine that they are swallowing a piece of machinery (and going machinery too) greatly more complicated than a watch." Perhaps oyster lovers prefer not to think about it. It is certainly hard to believe that oysters were once the food of the poor: they only became fashionable and expensive as they became scarce, and in Europe might have disappeared altogether if a French marine biologist had not discovered the ancient oyster beds at Lake Fusaro, near Naples, and learned how oysters could be artificially reared.

Most American oysters, in contrast to those in Europe, are harvested in the wild. The Atlantic, or Eastern, oyster,

Crassostrea virginica, goes under a variety of names, usually denoting the area where it was caught—Blue Point, Wellfleet, Chincoteague, and Apalachicola are some of the best-known. On the West Coast, the Pacific (*C. gigas*), or Japanese, oyster is the most common type. The Olympia, *Ostrea lurida*, another Pacific oyster, is the only one native to the West Coast.

There are three species of European oyster, all of which are farmed by aquaculture. The best British oysters, *Ostrea edulis*, known as natives or flats, include the Whitstable, the Colchester, and the Helford. These have rounded shells and a subtle flavor. In France, this type is known as *belon*; the American Olympia oyster is a relative. The second type, known as the rock oyster, is *Crassostrea gigas*, the Pacific oyster when it's in America. In France, these are *huîtres creuses*. They have elongated shells and a sharper, more oceanic flavor. The third species, *Crassostrea angulata* or the Portuguese oyster, is being supplanted by *C. gigas*, which is thought to be finer.

Oysters come in many sizes, and not everyone prefers the largest ones. There are stringent regulations to keep oysters safe from pollution, but if you do have one that tastes bad, spit it out.

Oysters are best eaten raw, on the half-shell. Serve them in the deep halves of their shells, on a bed of crushed ice, and take care not to spill the liquid they contain—it has an exquisite salty, marine flavor with a hint of iodine. Accompany them with halved lemons and, if you like, Tabasco sauce or cayenne pepper, or with red wine vinegar with a few chopped shallots afloat in it, and brown bread and butter. Drink a chilled Chablis or an Alsatian wine.
Buying guide: oysters are at their best from about the end of October to the end of February, when the sea is coldest. In summer, as the sea warms up, they may start breeding and can be milky, fat, and soft. Canned smoked oysters make a good hors d'oeuvre.
Best cooking methods: oysters are delicious in a creamy oyster stew or chowder, or with a dry white wine and cheese sauce spooned over them, sprinkled with bread crumbs and placed under the broiler until the crumbs are golden-brown.

Scallop These are a particular favorite among shellfish lovers, partly because they are such a delight to eat and partly because they are beautiful and symbolic. Often represented in painting (notably Botticelli's *Venus*), the scallop shell is a

Queen scallop

Littleneck clam

Cherrystone clam

Chowder clam

Sea scallop

Manila clam

Cockle

symbol of Christianity and a badge of the religious pilgrim.

The most common American scallops are the large sea scallop and the small, tender bay scallop—a third type is the calico, smaller than bays and with less flavor. Europe can boast some of the best of the many species of scallop that abound, including the most common great scallop, the pilgrim scallop, and the queen scallop, or queenie. These latter are much smaller than ordinary scallops, with two slightly hollow shells rather than one convex and one flat. Small and delicate, they have the texture of butter. Unlike American scallops, European scallops are always sold with their scarlet coral, or roe, which is considered by some to be the best part. *Buying guide:* at their best in late fall and winter, scallops are becoming expensive, but fortunately you do not need many—three or four large ones per person is usually sufficient. If using smaller scallops, allow between ten and fifteen per person. Look for "diver scallops"—especially from Maine—which are prime handpicked specimens. In America they are always sold already shelled and cleaned, whereas in Europe you can often buy them still in the shell (and then use the shells as serving dishes). In America, scallop shells are more likely to be found in gourmet shops.
Best cooking methods: be careful not to overcook scallops, or they will be tough—small ones take only a few seconds, large ones a minute or two at the most. They can be pan-seared with garlic and parsley or baked in the oven in butter with parsley, garlic, and lemon juice. Or, sauté and serve perhaps with a little port and cream stirred in to make a sauce. They can be broiled with bacon on skewers, made into a chowder, or lightly poached or steamed and served in a white wine sauce, sprinkled with bread crumbs and browned under the broiler. Served in Mornay sauce, the rich cheese sauce, they have become known simply by their French name, *coquilles St. Jacques.*

Clam America is the place to appreciate clams: aficionados can take delight in steamers, or long-necks, and littlenecks, cherrystones, Manila clams and razors, surf clams, butter clams, and the enormous geoduck. The familiar Atlantic clams called littleneck (which should not be confused with Pacific littleneck), cherrystone, and chowder clams are not in fact separate species, as many people think, but merely different sizes of the hard-shell quahog. Clam chowder is almost a national dish, and a clam bake is a serious and favorite pastime, while expressions like "happy as a clam" are frequently heard along the shorelines—and inland as well. At clam bakes, the shellfish, and usually lobsters too, along with fresh corn, is steamed on a bed of seaweed over heated stones on the beach. Clam bakes are most popular on the East Coast, especially in Massachusetts and Maine, and here too you can find roadside stands where clams, gathered from the shore, are sold, deep-fried in batter and served with tartar sauce.

In France you may be offered *tellines, clovisses, palourdes, olives,* or *praires* (the best, called Warty Venus in England!); in Italy, *vongoli* or *tartufi di mare;* in Spain, *almejas, margaritas,* or *amayuelas.* In England, clams are not as impossible to find as they once were, and the large quahogs are sometimes available.
Buying guide: available all year. Since clams vary so much in size from one variety to another, ask the clam seller how many to allow for each person. Canned clams are also widely available.
Best cooking methods: the soft-shell or long-neck varieties such as razor and Ipswich clams can be eaten raw, just like oysters, and so can small hard-shell clams such as cherrystones. Larger ones like quahogs can be steamed open and chopped for chowder; sautéed in olive oil with lemon juice and parsley; broiled with butter, bread crumbs, and garlic; or chopped and made into the excellent sauce for spaghetti *alla vongole,* which is also delicious made with tiny cherrystone clams.

Mussel Clumped in blue-black masses on rocks and piers or attached singly to shingle stones in estuaries, mussels have in the past quite unfairly been considered the poor man's shellfish. Their status, however, has been improving rapidly. In America, where they are to be found on both coasts and are widely farmed, they have grown steadily in popularity, and in Europe, where they are extremely popular, there are mussel farms around Mediterranean coasts, where the mussels are bred on long stakes in clean seawater. If you are collecting your own mussels, make sure that they are living in unpolluted water and known to be safe. Discard any that are even remotely damaged.

Mussels are usually sold cleaned, but wash them in several changes of water to rid them of grit, then scrape the shells clean with the back of a knife if necessary and rinse thoroughly in cold water. If the stringy "beard" is attached, pull it out (cut it off if necessary) and rinse the mussels again in a bowl of clean water. Discard any that float to the surface or whose shells are damaged or open.

The French are enthusiastic about raw shellfish and will eat whole platefuls of raw mussels with lemon juice as if they were oysters. The smooth, thin-shelled French species are the best to eat in this way, and they should be from a very pure source.

A more recent arrival is the green-lipped mussel from New Zealand. It is larger and meatier than the blue mussel and has a more pronounced flavor.
Buying guide: mussels are inexpensive. Medium-sized or smaller ones are best; large mussels are not so appetizing. Always buy slightly more than you need, to allow for any you must discard. For two people, buy a quart (2 pounds).
Best cooking methods: one of the best-known recipes for mussels is the excellent *moules à la marinière,* mussels steamed in white wine with shallots, herbs, and butter. They can also be, once opened, broiled with bread crumbs, garlic, parsley, and butter, or used in a garlicky tomato sauce, pasta sauce, or seafood salad, or deep-fried.

Cockle Although these can be found along the Atlantic coast, cockles are more favored in Britain than in America, traditionally sold with periwinkles and whelks at the seaside, accompanied by vinegar and brown bread and butter, and outside London pubs. Cockles are a traditional ingredient in *char kway teow,* a Southeast Asian fried noodle dish. Here, cockles are also steamed and served with a piquant chile dipping sauce.
Buying guide: cockles are at their best in the summer.
Best cooking methods: eat them raw, or steam them in court-bouillon until their shells open. They also make a splendid soup, with mussels, garlic, potato, bacon, and milk, and are a good addition to risottos; or they can be stewed in a tomato sauce and served with pasta.

PREPARING SHELLFISH

lobster 33–4

knives 222–4
lobster
crackers, pick,
and pincers 229

Killing a live lobster

In some recipes a lobster is cut up before cooking. First, cover the tail with a cloth and hold it firmly. Insert the point of a sharp, heavy knife into the center of the cross mark in the head, and quickly push it down to the board; this will kill the lobster immediately.

1

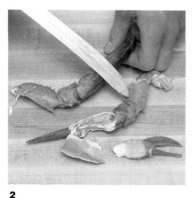

2

Preparing a cooked lobster

1 If you wish to remove the claws and legs, simply twist them off.

2 To extract the meat from the claws and legs, crack them open, using the back of a knife, lobster crackers or nutcrackers, or a small hammer.

3

4

3 Splitting a lobster in half is easiest to do in two stages (you can prepare an uncooked lobster in the same way). First, draw a sharp knife through the head from the tail section toward the eyes.

4 Reinsert the knife and move it in the opposite direction, cutting down to the tip of the tail and splitting the lobster completely in two.

5

6

5 Pull the halves apart to expose the flesh. This fine female lobster has an excellent red coral, and also some darker external roe, which is unusual. Both are edible and should be reserved.

6 Discard the grain sac from the top of the head, and the intestinal tract, which runs down the middle of the tail. As well as the coral, the creamy green tomalley, or liver, of the lobster should be reserved to make a sauce.

Removing the meat from a cooked crab

1 Pull off and discard the narrow triangular "apron" from the underside of the crab (this is a Dungeness crab).

2 Turn the crab over and carefully pull off the top shell.

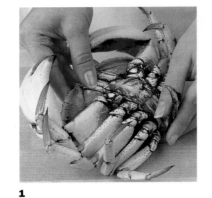

1

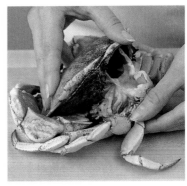

2

3 Pull out and discard the gills (known as "dead man's fingers") and the intestines from each side of the crab.

4 Twist off the claws and legs.

3

4

5

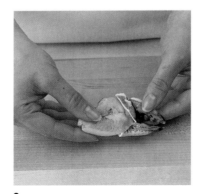

6

5 Crack the claws and legs with lobster crackers, nutcrackers, or small hammer, or with the back of a large, heavy knife.

6 Pull out the meat from the claws, removing it in large pieces; use a lobster pick if necessary to remove the meat from the tips of the claws.

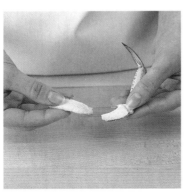

7

8

7 Remove the meat from the legs, using a lobster pick if necessary.

8 Cut the body into several large pieces with a large, heavy knife.

9 Use a lobster pick to remove the meat from the body.

10 The crabmeat from the body, legs, and claws is now ready to be eaten or used in a recipe.

9

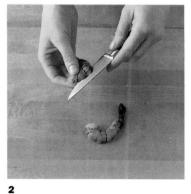

10

clam 38
shrimp and
prawn 35–7

clam knife 225

Peeling, deveining, and butterflying shrimp

1 Pull off the legs with your fingers, and then peel the shell away from the body. If you like, leave the last section of tail on the shrimp.

2 To devein, use a small, sharp knife and carefully cut a shallow slit down the back of each shrimp.

1

2

3 If the intestinal vein is black or brown, pull it out with the tip of the knife or with your fingers and discard it. (The vein is removed only because of its appearance.)

4 To butterfly, slice the shrimp down the back but without cutting quite all the way through, and then open the shrimp out like a book.

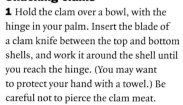

3

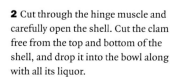

4

Shucking clams

1 Hold the clam over a bowl, with the hinge in your palm. Insert the blade of a clam knife between the top and bottom shells, and work it around the shell until you reach the hinge. (You may want to protect your hand with a towel.) Be careful not to pierce the clam meat.

2 Cut through the hinge muscle and carefully open the shell. Cut the clam free from the top and bottom of the shell, and drop it into the bowl along with all its liquor.

1

2

Shucking oysters

1 Hold the oyster steady, and carefully insert an oyster knife between the top and bottom shells, next to the hinge. (Unless you are very proficient, you may want to hold the oyster in a towel to protect your hand.)

2 Keep a firm grip on the oyster and, pushing against the hinge, carefully work the knife in, twisting it slightly until the hinge breaks.

3 Open the oyster and sever the muscle that adheres to the flatter upper shell.

4 Run the knife underneath the oyster to free it from the rounded lower shell. Remove the oyster, or serve it with its own juices in the rounded bottom shell.

1

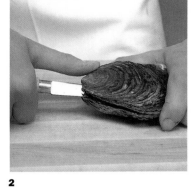

2

3

4

Preparing scallops

1 Using a strong, sharp, wide knife, pry the shells apart and detach the scallop from the rounded shell by carefully sliding the knife underneath the muscle.

2 Rinse the scallop under cold running water. Pull away the film of membrane and discard it.

1

2

3 With the scallop still under cold running water, and holding back the white flesh and coral with your thumb, push away and sever the black intestine.

4 The scallop and the delicious orange coral are now ready to cook.

3

4

Other Seafood, Snails, and Frog's Legs

Many creatures are so strange to look at and are so unlike anything else that they are usually, for want of a better label, called "miscellaneous." But unappetizing though they may look to some people, with their spiny, shell-y, jelly-like, or leathery exteriors, many of us really like to eat them. Indeed, some of these creatures, such as squid, snails, sea urchins, and octopus, rank among the most delicious of foods, and all of them provide a challenge to the adventurous cook.

Some seafood—such as limpets—although it is perfectly edible, is not worth marketing commercially and so you will have to rely on gathering it yourself, always remembering that any living thing gathered from the sea and its shores is potentially dangerous if it comes from a polluted area, and that many varieties are simply inedible. If in any doubt about the safety of your haul, check with the local office of the E.P.A. (Environmental Protection Agency) or the state or local health department.

Squid, octopus, and cuttlefish

The Mediterranean countries understand best how to deal with these extraordinary creatures, having long eaten them in great quantities. They also play an important role in the cuisine of China and Japan. All are at their sweetest and most tender when they are small in size; however, larger specimens can be improved by soaking for several hours in a marinade of wine vinegar, sliced onion, and salt and pepper.

Squid Familiar in Mediterranean dishes as *calamari, calmar* or *encornet, calamaro,* or *calamar,* squid is delicious to eat if you understand the principle that the cooking must be either very brief or very long—anything in between and your squid will be as tough as rubber. Once cleaned, the squid can be rapidly broiled, or stuffed with chopped meat and the chopped tentacles, and then baked in a tomato- and garlic-flavored sauce. Sliced into rings, it can be deep-fried plain or dipped first into a light batter. Larger specimens can be stewed gently with olive oil, wine, and tomatoes.

It is a pleasure, in Spain, to be served two little dishes at the same time, one holding a fragrant stew of the tentacles, with onions and garlic, and the other the sliced, crisply fried rings of the body. Squid can also be cut into rings and boiled very briefly—no more than a minute or two, until the rings lose their pearly, translucent look—and then put into a seafood salad. The squid ink found in a sac inside can be used in risotto, pasta, and sauces. The tiniest squid, with fragile bodies no more than 3 inches long, can be very quickly deep-fried in a coating of beaten egg and flour.

Octopus can be very tough, and the larger it grows, the tougher it gets, so it is a wise precaution, having removed the beak and head (if the fish dealer has not already done so) and turned out the contents of the body, to pound the legs and body with a meat mallet until they are soft. The octopus contains its ink within its liver, and this is sometimes used to make a very strong and heavily scented gravy. The ink can also be used as a pasta sauce. Frozen cleaned octopus

preparing squid
47

meat tenderizer
226

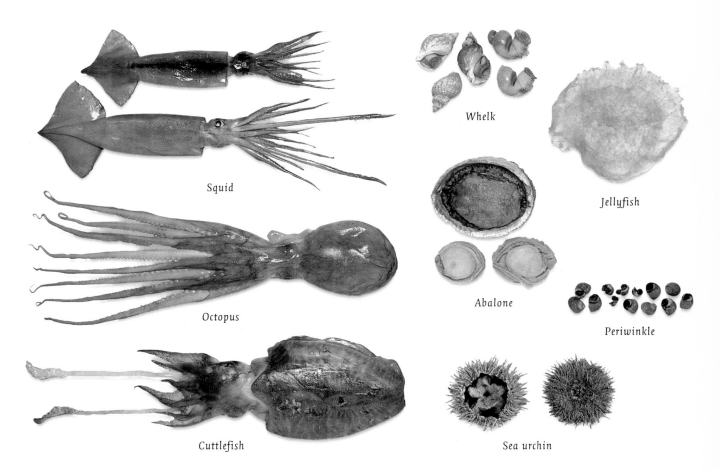

Squid

Whelk

Jellyfish

Octopus

Abalone

Periwinkle

Cuttlefish

Sea urchin

seviche 423

meat tenderizer 226

has recently become available in many supermarkets and good fish shops.

Octopus can be stewed, or stuffed and baked like squid, but a large specimen will need up to 2 hours or more to become tender. Little ones can also be panfried gently in olive oil and make a delicious salad, often eaten warm, with lemon juice, olive oil, garlic, and chopped parsley.

Cuttlefish Often rather gracefully camouflaged by striped markings, the cuttlefish has a larger head than the squid and a much wider, dumpier body. Inside lies the white shell, or cuttlebone, found washed up on Mediterranean beaches and given to pet birds to peck at (ground, it was once used as tooth powder, jewel polish, and as face powder by Roman ladies who wanted to look delicate). More tender than octopus or squid, cuttlefish, only rarely available in the United States—imported and expensive—can be cooked in the same ways, and very small ones are delicious deep-fried. They are prepared in the same way as squid. The ink, or *sepia*, can be used to make a sauce in which the cuttlefish can be stewed, and goes into the Italian dish *risotto nero* (black rice).

Single-shelled creatures

These all belong to the same family that includes the familiar garden snail, and all move around on a muscular "foot." They can go into fish soups, sauces, and stews as well as being tasty snacks on their own, served with plenty of vinegar, pepper, and brown bread and butter.

Abalone "Delicious ambrosia," an enthusiast wrote in the 1600s about these white-fleshed shellfish. With their curiously ear-shaped shells, the inside gleaming with pearly colors, abalone, also called ormer in Britain, can be found fresh in the warm waters off California and around the Channel Islands and the Breton coast at certain times of the year.

Fresh abalone, even little ones, need to be well beaten with a mallet to make them tender. Very small abalones can then be eaten raw with a squeeze of lemon juice; larger ones are usually thinly sliced and marinated in white wine, oil, herbs, and chopped shallots, then sautéed very briefly in butter—overcooking only toughens them. They can also be used like clams in soup or chowder. Canned abalone is a good substitute for fresh. Frozen abalone,

sold in Asian markets, is ready to use and often quite good; should you come across dried abalone, it is hardly worth the effort of making it edible—it needs to be soaked for 4 days before anything can be done with it.

Periwinkle, winkle There is something homely and comfortable about periwinkles, and their little dark shells are small enough to make them completely acceptable in a way that many large snails are not. In France, you are likely to be given a plate of *bigorneaux* with a glass of kir—cassis and white wine— in an Alsatian brasserie while waiting for your *choucroute garnie* or your slice of foie gras. In England, winkles are eaten with bread and butter and a pot of tea, and make a tasty snack on seaside piers, accompanied by vinegar. Whatever the circumstance, a long pin is indispensable for wheedling the little shellfish out of their shells. To cook periwinkles, which may be found fresh in Asian markets along the East Coast, boil them in their shells in salted water for 10 minutes. Eat only the first part of the body—the second part is easily separated.

Whelk These handsome but decidedly unaristocratic shellfish, with their ribbed, deeply whorled shells, are sold already boiled, fresh or frozen. In the United States, they can be found in Italian markets, where they are called *scungilli*, and in other ethnic markets. Whelks look something like periwinkles, but are a much more substantial mouthful and easier to remove from their shells. The large "foot" is the part that is usually eaten. Whelks can also be used in fish soups and stews. On the Scottish island of Iona, where whelks are a traditional part of the islanders' diet, whelk soup is made by thickening seasoned whelk stock with oatmeal and finely chopped onion.

Conch The term conch—pronounced "konk"—is often used to include the periwinkle and whelk, but what is usually thought of as being the best of the family is the large Caribbean conch with the graceful spiral-shaped shell in which one seems to hear the sound of the sea. Fresh conch meat needs to be tenderized by vigorous beating and can then be stewed in a wine sauce with herbs and spices, or thinly sliced and deep-fried. It also goes into chowders and in parts of the Caribbean it is used for *seviche*.

Limpet Limpets are exceptionally tough—you can tell they are going to be tough by the strength of the muscle that clamps them to the rocks as soon as they are touched and makes them almost impossible to pry off, unless you can take them by surprise. With persistence they can be gathered at low tide (they are rarely marketed, except in some fish stores in coastal areas) and eaten raw or used to flavor a soup. They can also be panfried in butter with chopped parsley, pepper, and vinegar, or baked for a few minutes with a little butter in each shell. The smaller ones are better boiled and eaten with vinegar, pepper, and bread and butter. Slipper limpets, native to North America, prey on oysters, which makes them very unpopular with oyster lovers, but they too are good to eat either cooked or raw.

"Fruits" of the sea

Some of the most astonishing candidates for any sort of cuisine are nonetheless considered delicacies by their devotees.

Sea urchin A menace to the bather but a pleasure to the gourmet, the sharp-spined sea urchin is plentiful in many parts of the world, and its pretty lacy-patterned shell—minus the spines— is often brought home as a memento of seaside vacations. Best for eating are the green sea urchin and the black sea urchin. These can be lightly boiled and are sometimes pickled, but are best eaten fresh, raw and straight from the shell. To accomplish this, the sea urchin is cut in half using a sharp knife (in France, sea urchin is called *oursin* and is cut with a *coupe-oursin*, designed for this task). This exposes the rose-colored or orange ovaries, or roe, which are simply given a drop of lemon juice and scooped out with pieces of fresh crusty bread. The crushed roe can also be used in omelets and as a garnish for fish.

Sea anemone These inhabitants of rocky pools, enticingly waving their multitude of soft arms, are sometimes eaten in Japan, Samoa, and France. The snake-locks anemones, known as *orties de mer*, are carefully gathered in France, then marinated, dipped into a light batter, and fried. They also go, together with a few red *tomates de mer* and a lot of shellfish, into a Mediterranean soup.

Figue de mer, violet This very odd, leathery-skinned creature is particularly relished in France's Provence, where it has the proper accompaniment of hot sun and a plentiful supply of white wine. Found anchored to rocks or the sea floor, syphoning water in through one spout and out of the other, it is cut in half and the yellow part inside eaten raw.

Bêche de mer Also known as sea cucumber, because of its shape, and as sea slug, *trepang*, and *balatin*, this warm-water creature is sliced and eaten raw in Japan with soy sauce, vinegar, or mustard. Several species are smoke-dried and used in soup. In China it has a reputation as an aphrodisiac. One recipe using dried sea cucumber involves 4 days of preparation and yields twelve Chinese servings or ninety-five Western servings, which is either a miscalculation or says a great deal about the sea slug's lack of appeal to the Western palate.

Jellyfish The Chinese are great users of dried jellyfish, primarily to add texture to a meal, and slabs of dried jellyfish can usually be found in Chinese markets. If the jellyfish has been salted, it will need to be washed and allowed to soak for some hours in several changes of water. Once soaked, it should be briefly blanched in boiling water, then refreshed in cold water. It can be cut into slivers and stir-fried with chicken, or scalded, which produces crunchy curls that are served with a sauce of sesame oil, soy sauce, vinegar, and sugar. In Japan, jellyfish is cooked into crisp-textured strips and eaten with vinegar as a side dish.

Samphire and seaweeds

Apart from being such a pleasure to gather, in the early months of summer when most of them are at their most luxuriant, seaweeds are a rich source of minerals as well as of intriguing textures and flavors. If you gather your own, cut the plant well above its base so that it can grow again, and always be sure to wash it thoroughly in fresh water before cooking. Most of the better-known seaweeds can be found in dried form in health food stores or Asian markets, and can be restored by soaking. Samphire is occasionally sold in specialty produce markets, when in season.

Samphire, marsh samphire This succulent green plant, also known as glasswort or pickle plant, or, in French, *pousse-pierre* or *saint-pierre* can be found growing in seaside marshes. It is best at midsummer. The flavor of fresh marsh samphire is salty and iodiney—like seawater but green; it is the crisp texture that is interesting.

Samphire can go fresh into salads and is often steeped in vinegar to make a delicate pickle. In many regions, it is greatly appreciated as a vegetable served

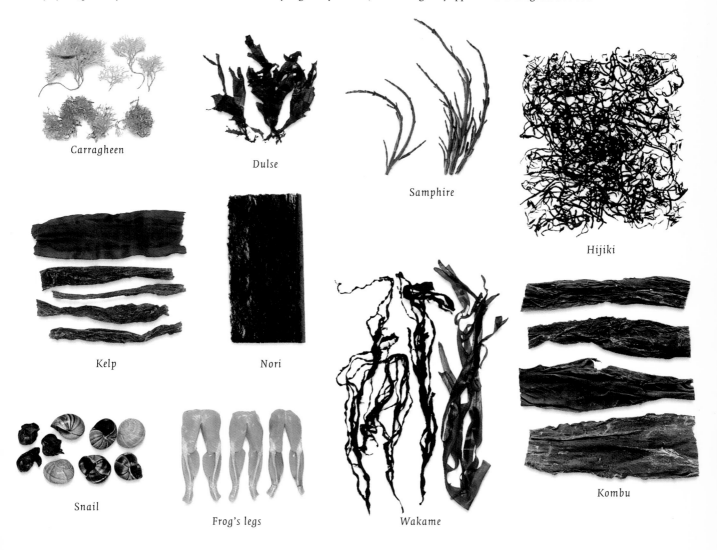

Carragheen

Dulse

Samphire

Hijiki

Kelp

Nori

Snail

Frog's legs

Wakame

Kombu

with fish, or on its own simply boiled and dipped in melted butter, then drawn through the teeth like asparagus to strip the succulent part from the central core.

Nori With its delicate taste of the sea, this reddish-purple seaweed, also known as laver, was very popular in England in the eighteenth century. When fresh, nori is seldom appreciated in the West today, except in Wales, where it is enthusiastically boiled until it turns into the spinach-like pulp called laverbread—although why it should be called bread is a mystery. But dried, it is well-known to aficionados of Chinese and Japanese cuisine, and to any sushi lover. In Japan, where nori is cultivated, it is pressed and dried in thin sheets. Nori is toasted lightly before being wrapped around vinegared rice to make sushi; or it may be crumbled over rice as a salty garnish. In China, nori is dried and then simmered to produce a nutritious jelly.

Carragheen, Irish moss Although Ireland and the village of Carragheen have given it its most commonly used names, this pretty red-tinged, frond-like plant is found along most northerly Atlantic shorelines growing on rocks and stones. It can be used fresh or dried, when it bleaches to a creamy white, and is an important source of agar-agar, a vegetable gelatin much used in the food industry. In Britain a carragheen gelatin dessert is made by simmering the moss in milk or water until most of it dissolves, then straining it and allowing it to set. The result is very nourishing. For those who don't like its faint taste of the sea, it can be flavored with vanilla, honey, or fruit.

Kelp A number of large seaweeds are popularly known as kelp and have long been used as a source of food and of medicine, being particularly rich in iodine. Much liked in Japan, where it is called kombu, kelp, also called sea tangle, finds its way to the table as a delicate salad vegetable, a seasoning for root vegetables, or a garnish for rice, or fashioned into miniature baskets, deep-fried, and stuffed with vegetables. It is also used for making soups and stocks, such as *dashi*, or can simply be cooked as a vegetable to accompany fish.

To make the all-purpose Japanese stock called *dashi*, cut a piece of kombu into quarters using scissors and place it in a pan with 4 cups water. Bring to a boil, then remove the pan from the heat at once and cool the boiling liquid by adding ¼ cup cold water. Add 1 cup dried bonito flakes (*katsuo bushi*), bring the liquid back to a boil, and immediately remove from the heat. Strain the liquid through cheesecloth or a fine sieve. For a vegetarian version of the stock, omit the *katsuo bushi*.

Dulse Another of the familiar purplish-red seaweeds, with fan-shaped fronds up to 10 inches long, dulse is to be found growing plentifully on rocks and on larger weeds throughout the British Isles and the Mediterranean. Known in Ireland as *dillisk*, dulse can be eaten raw as a salad, and around the Mediterranean it sometimes goes into ragouts, but it is a very tough, rubbery plant and needs to be cooked for up to 5 hours. Dried, it can be chewed as a rather unconventional appetizer, without any further preparation, or used as a relish. It has a salty, fish-like flavor, and is said to be "principally eaten by sailors and children."

Wakame A rich source of minerals, this dark green seaweed is much used in Japan. The soft leaves go into salads or are cooked with other vegetables, and both leaves and stems are used in soups. In the United States, wakame is sold dried and must be soaked in lukewarm water before using.

Snail

The French, of course, are the major eaters of snails, and the snails the French prize most are the hefty specimens from the vineyards of Burgundy, where they are fed—like the snails of ancient Rome—on grape leaves until they have grown fat and luscious. The classic method of preparing snails is the Burgundian way, in which case they become *escargots à la bourguignonne*, served sizzling in their shells with great quantities of rich garlic butter and fresh crusty bread for mopping. However, as there are never enough Burgundian snails to meet the demand in France, the alternative is a smaller striped snail, the *petit gris*, which makes up for its lack of size by being sweet, tasty, and tender. (A drawback is that the *petit gris* shells, unlike those of the Burgundian snail, may be too fragile to be used once their occupants have been removed, but this is solved by using special little ceramic pots, easily washed and always ready to be used again. Other essentials for the enjoyment of snails are the dimpled plates called *escargotières*, which hold six or twelve snail shells, tongs for picking up the piping hot shells, and special forks with two prongs for twisting the snails out of their shells.)

The business of preparing live snails means that it is much simpler to buy snails canned, or fresh already cleaned and ready to cook. As a change from garlic butter, snails are very good simmered in olive oil with garlic, tomatoes, and fresh rosemary or mint—the traditional dish to serve on Midsummer's Eve in Rome.

Frog's legs

Like snails, frog's legs as a delicacy have long been associated with the French. Escoffier, the "king of chefs," is credited with making them acceptable to the English: in the 1890s, for a party held by the Prince of Wales at the Savoy Hotel, London, he prepared what he called *nymphes à l'aurore*, frog's legs poached in white wine and served cold in aspic with a little paprika to evoke the rose-gold glow of dawn. Presumably he called his frog's legs "nymphs" out of delicacy of feeling for the English diners. When he wasn't preparing them for the Prince of Wales, Escoffier simply seasoned them with salt and pepper, dusted them with flour, and sautéed them in butter, serving them with a squeeze of lemon juice and a sprinkling of parsley.

Today, in the Dombes region of eastern France, those who know their frogs still go frogging in the ponds and lakes; however, not all frogs are edible and what appears fresh or frozen in the market and on restaurant menus will have come from special frog farms. Frog's legs are light and easily digestible, rather like chicken in flavor—in China, where frogs thrive in the paddy fields and frog's legs are much enjoyed at banquets, they are known as "field chickens." In America, frog's legs are often big enough to be fried like chicken legs, but the smaller legs are usually more tender and have subtler flavors. In any case, Escoffier's way with them is still the best: cooked in oil or butter for 5 minutes until they are golden-brown, and served with lemon and a sprinkling of parsley; or they can be poached in a little white wine and served hot with a creamy sauce. They can also be prepared *à la provençale*, with garlic and tomato.

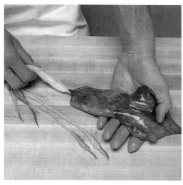

1

Preparing squid

1 Grasp the squid with one hand and, with the other, reach inside the body and pull out the head and tentacles.

squid 43

knives 222–4

2 Pull off and then discard the body's mottled skin.

3 Feel inside the body for the long piece of transparent cartilage, or "quill." Pull this out and discard it.

2

3

4 Wash the body thoroughly, inside and out, under cold running water and then pull off the two flaps from the body. You will find that they separate quite easily, as if held in place only by suction.

5 Cut the tentacles from the head. If the long, narrow ink sac is present and still intact, you will find it attached to the head; remove it carefully and put it aside to use in an accompanying sauce. The head itself, which contains the viscera, can be discarded.

4

5

6 Leave the body whole for stuffing or cut it into thick rings. Slice the flaps into strips, and cut the tentacles to a manageable size. The squid is now ready to cook.

6

Meat

Meat is such an important and delicious part of our diet that it makes sense to buy it as intelligently as possible. If you go to a high-class specialty butcher (possibly one who sells organic meat), who buys meat by the carcass and then hangs it until it has reached the peak of juiciness and flavor, and who butchers it with finesse, you will seldom have a disappointing piece of meat.

You will also be able to buy meat in greater variety, as the butcher will be able to offer you the lesser-known cuts that can go a long way toward making your food more interesting. Because there will be little waste by way of unwanted fat, gristle, and awkward bones, his prices will be high, but cooking will be a joy.

Choosing meat

Failing such a paragon, it pays to develop your own expertise when it comes to shopping. Most butchers will give friendly and sometimes disinterested advice when asked. However, at the supermarket there often is no one to turn to, and the packages of meat can look distressingly similar. Some stores do label their meat as suitable for "roasting," "broiling," and "stewing," for example, but many others will simply give you the name of the cut, and leave it at that.

Although all meat must be inspected by the United States Department of Agriculture before sale, grading meat for quality is only voluntary. Some packing plants follow U.S.D.A. grading, but others use their own systems. The U.S.D.A. system is based on the amount of marbling—the flecks of fat in the meat—and on the age of the animal. Marbling gives meat its tenderness, flavor and juiciness. Beef and lamb are the most commonly graded; veal sometimes is. Beef and lamb may be labeled prime, choice, or standard; veal is usually labeled either prime or choice. Prime meat is the best and most expensive; prime beef is not usually found in the average supermarket. Choice beef is the most common grade found in the supermarket; although choice meat is less marbled than prime, it can still be tender and juicy to eat. Standard beef is the leanest and least expensive; it is also tougher and less flavorful than choice.

Today, with fat definitely off the menu, special attention is paid to the ratio of fat to lean when the herd is still on the hoof, while organic farms, where the animals' diet is carefully supervised, offer the healthiest meat.

The look of meat At a really good store all the cuts, even the cheapest, will look appetizing. They should look silky, not wet. All boned and rolled roasts should be neatly tied. Where there are bones, these should be sawn smoothly, not jaggedly chopped, and smaller cuts of meat, particularly chops and cutlets, should be neatly and thoroughly trimmed, with excess fat removed.

The cut surface of meat exposes the grain, or muscle fibers, which are potentially coarser and tougher in an older animal, or in parts of the anatomy, such as the leg or the neck, that have had more active use. However, the fineness or otherwise of grain is not really a reliable indicator of either the meat's flavor or its tenderness.

Tenderness When all pieces of meat look equally good, it can be hard to distinguish between the tender and the not so tender, and many factors, apart from anatomy, contribute to this: the age and breed of the animal, the way it was handled before slaughter, the way the meat is cut, and so on.

There are many schools of butchery, producing different cuts of meat not only in different countries but in different regions; in fact, there are as many regional variations and names for the different cuts as there are regional recipes. However, no matter where and how a carcass is divided, most of the best meat of each animal comes from the hindquarter and loin, and the tenderest meat of all comes from the parts that have had the least exercise. Exercise means the development of muscle fiber and of the connective tissue that holds the muscles together in bundles, and it is connective tissue that is primarily responsible for toughness.

The tender cuts with little connective tissue respond to dry heat (roasting, panfrying, and broiling/grilling), but the others will need slow cooking in moist heat (braising, stewing, or boiling), which breaks down the connective tissue into gelatin. Although commercial

tenderizers are sometimes used on beef, this is not, fortunately, general practice. Based on papain (from papayas), with its tenderizing enzymes that "digest" proteins, they may be applied to the tougher pieces by the wholesaler. Although the meat will be more tender, it will also become duller to eat. As the enzymes work on all the flesh, the tender parts as well as the tougher ones, the advantage of the breaking down of connective tissues is often balanced by a general loss in character and flavor— a decided disadvantage. Tenderized meat does not become any less fibrous—the fiber merely becomes soft as it is "digested" in this process.

There are ways of preparing tough meat in the kitchen so that it arrives at table full of flavor and juice, fit to be cut with a spoon. Try marinating the meat in a marinade including wine, lemon juice, vinegar, yogurt, or even chopped tomatoes. The acids present in all these ingredients will help to break down connective tissue. Oil, too, is used in many marinades to add succulence, especially in the cooking of Greece and the Middle East. Of course, lengthy cooking in moist heat must follow to complete the process, but this is no disadvantage since the tougher cuts need time, above all, to develop their flavor to the fullest.

Pounding or scoring is another way to break up connective tissue, thus making tough meat more tender, but then quite a lot of flavoring—chopped onions, garlic, herbs both fresh and dried, spices, seasoning, assertive sauces or relishes— is needed to make it taste good. Cube steak is beef top or bottom round that has been commercially tenderized with a cutting machine that chops the meat first one way and then the other. You can perform the tenderizing operation on meats yourself with a sharp, heavy knife or by pounding with a rolling pin.

Aging Aging improves the taste and tenderness of meat; unfortunately, aging meat is no longer a matter of course in this country. Carcasses to be aged are hung in a refrigerated storage space for a certain period of the time so that their moisture evaporates, and enzymes in the meat break down tendons and tough tissues. Beef should be aged for up to 3 weeks, or even longer. Lamb can be aged for a shorter period of time, but the stronger flavor of aged lamb does not appeal to most American tastes; it is more popular in Europe. Pork may be cured, but it is not aged, nor is veal. Kosher meat is never aged.

Since aging leads inevitably to weight loss, properly aged meat costs more to buy than fresh meat. However, it is well worth the difference in price, and a butcher who can supply you with meat that has been correctly aged is certainly worth cultivating.

Storing in the refrigerator Always unwrap and then rewrap meat as soon as you get it home, and put it in the coldest part of the refrigerator. All cuts keep best when they are loosely covered, not so tightly wrapped as to rule out the circulation of air. Waxed paper serves this purpose well. Despite advice to the contrary, never put meat away wrapped in plastic wrap, as this will cause it to deteriorate rapidly, developing a sticky and bad-smelling film over the outside.

Cooking processes
Obviously, it is wisest to use the correct cooking process for each cut: dry heat for the tender ones, moist for those not so tender. Broiling and grilling, panfrying, and roasting come into the first category; braising or pot-roasting, stewing, and boiling into the second. Of course, delicious results can be achieved by using a superior cut for the humbler processes, but the reverse is not the case.

Broiling and grilling Broiling is suitable for small, reasonably thick pieces of good-quality meat from the most tender parts of the animal. The meat, sometimes first brushed with butter or oil to prevent it from drying out, is seared on both sides close to the source of heat to produce color and flavor. Generally speaking, the thinner the piece of meat, the closer it should be to the heat source to sear it. It should then be moved a little way from the heat so that it can finish cooking more slowly. Salt should not be added until halfway through the process, as its moisture-retaining properties would inhibit searing and browning. Always allow broiled meat to rest for a few minutes after cooking so that the juices

---

APPROXIMATE MAXIMUM STORAGE TIMES FOR MEAT

Uncooked meat	In the refrigerator	In the freezer
BEEF		
roasts, steaks	3–5 days	6–12 months
ground, cut up	1–2 days	3 months
VEAL		
roasts	1–2 days	4–8 months
steaks, chops, ground	1–2 days	3–4 months
LAMB		
roasts, chops	3–5 days	6–9 months
ground, cut up	1–2 days	3–4 months
PORK		
roasts, chops	3–5 days	4–6 months
ground	1–2 days	3–4 months
sausage	1–2 days	1–2 months
VARIETY MEATS	1–2 days	3–4 months
Cooked/processed meat		
HAM	3–5 days	1–2 months
BACON		
unopened package	2 weeks	1 month
opened package	1 week	1 month
CORNED BEEF	1 week	2–3 months
ROASTED MEAT		
sliced in sauce	2–3 days	3 months
whole	3–4 days	2 months
CASSEROLES	2 days	3–6 months
PÂTÉ	1 week	3 months

INTERNAL TEMPERATURES FOR MEAT

The following temperatures are a guide to doneness when roasting meat. Cuts of meat will continue to cook after being removed from the oven, so take the meat out when the thermometer registers 5 to 10°F below the final desired internal temperature. During the 10- or 15-minute period of resting before carving and serving, the internal temperature will rise to the correct temperature.

Meat	Rare	Medium-rare	Medium	Well-done
Beef★	125°F	130°F	140–145°F	160°F
Veal			140–145°F	160°F
Lamb★		130°F	140–145°F	160°F
Pork			155–160°F	170°F

★ Because of concern over bacteria in rare meat, the U.S. Department of Agriculture currently recommends cooking beef and lamb to a higher internal temperature. The recommendations for beef are: 145°F for medium-rare, 160°F for medium, and 170°F for well-done. The recommendations for lamb are 145°F for medium-rare, 160°F for medium, and 170°F for well-done.

will be evenly redistributed. Since with this process there is no pan gravy, or cooking juices, broiled meat is often served accompanied by a sauce or a pat of herb butter.

Much of the same applies to grilling meat outdoors: the meat may be lightly brushed with oil, though more often this is merely to keep it from sticking to the grill. It is seared on both sides, as for broiling, and then the grill rack may be raised or the meat moved away from the hottest part of the fire to finish cooking. Allow grilled meat to rest for at least a few minutes, and serve it with a sauce or salsa if desired. Although steaks, chops, and other smaller tender cuts are most often used for grilling, larger cuts can also be grilled, sometimes with the grill covered for part of the cooking time. Or cuts such as leg of lamb may be butterflied for grilling.

Panfrying Thinner, good-quality cuts are needed for this process. They are cooked in a very little hot oil or butter, or a mixture of the two, in a shallow preheated pan so that the meat browns rapidly. The meat is usually turned once as it cooks to sear it on both sides. Do not pierce it while it cooks, and keep a fairly high heat going under the pan, or the juices will escape too fast (if they do, the meat will boil in its own juices and toughen). Do not overheat the fat, as it will burn, and burnt fat imparts an unpleasant, bitter flavor. Panfried meat, like broiled meat, should be allowed to rest for a few minutes after cooking, before it is served.

Choose a frying pan with a good, heavy bottom, and make sure it is the right size. Meat has a tendency to stew in its own juice and steam in an overcrowded pan; in contrast, if the pan is too big, the cooking juices may evaporate too quickly and the meat may all too easily burn. A very good reason for not allowing this to happen is that the pan juices, deglazed with a little wine, water, or stock, make the best possible accompaniment to panfried steaks or chops.

Roasting Top-quality meat goes into a hot oven in an open pan so that it is browned on all sides as the outside is seared. The meat can go straight into a dry pan, fat side down, or into a little hot oil, or it can be cooked on a rack in a dry

pan or in a pan with a little water or wine in it. Some people like to put all meat on a rack in a pan, so that the fat collects beneath it as it roasts, but this is only essential for really fatty cuts. Frequent basting with the pan juices helps to prevent the meat from drying out.

Roasting times and temperatures vary according to the type of meat, the cut, and its quality, but after the initial searing it is a good idea to lower the oven temperature so that the interior of the meat is able to cook more slowly. However, top-quality cuts of meat will always be tender, no matter how briefly or how fast they may have been cooked. A regular meat thermometer or an instant-read thermometer is a foolproof gadget for determining the exact moment when the meat is cooked to the required degree.

There are two golden rules for all cuts of meat: do not season with salt until after roasting, and let the meat sit in a warm place for at least 20 minutes after it comes out of the oven to allow the juices time to settle, making the texture and color more even and the meat easier to carve.

Braising or pot-roasting Large pieces of medium-quality meat respond well to this process, which can be carried out either in the oven or on the stove top.

Braising means slow cooking in a small amount of liquid in a covered pot. The term pot-roasting means essentially the same thing. Braising needs a tightly covered pan so the steam from the cooking meat can condense on the bottom of the lid, falling back onto the meat and basting it as it cooks. The meat is browned first. Then it may be placed on a bed of chopped vegetables, which can be tossed in hot oil or butter first, or sliced onions and other aromatic vegetables may be scattered around the meat. Bacon or salt pork that has also been sautéed beforehand is a possible addition. Usually, stock, tomatoes, water, wine, cider, or beer is added—just enough to cover the vegetables. The meat is then slowly cooked in the casserole at a very moderate temperature (325°F) until meltingly tender. This usually takes about 30 minutes per pound, plus an extra 30 minutes, but the times will vary according to quality. The meat is turned and basted once or twice during cooking, and seasoned halfway through. If the

meat is salted at the outset, there is a danger the salt may draw out too much moisture too quickly.

If you plan to serve the braising vegetables, you may find it better to replace them with a fresh batch towards the end of the cooking time, as the hours they have spent in the pot may well have rendered them lifeless and tasteless.

Stewing A tougher cut of meat does best when cut into smaller pieces and cooked long and slowly in a little liquid—not too much, or the meat will be boiled rather than stewed. The liquid is provided by the meat juices as well as whatever is specified in the recipe. Many recipes call for an initial browning of the meat to give both color and flavor—usually in fat in which a few vegetables have been gently sautéed until they are golden; cooking liquid, flavorings, and seasonings are then added. When the meat is tender (which may take from 1½ to 3½ hours, depending on the type of meat), the gravy may be thickened. Sometimes the thickener, usually flour, is added early in the cooking process; the meat is usually coated with it before or while being browned, and care must be taken not to burn it. Stews cooked on the top of the stove will need stirring occasionally to prevent the meat from sticking to the pan.

Boiling Simmering in liquid, rather than actually boiling, is the best way to render large pieces of meat tender. Such good things as New England boiled beef dinner and all the other dishes served in the rich broth characteristic of the process really need at least a medium-quality meat. If you want to keep most of the flavor in the meat, plunge it into unsalted boiling water or, better still, into boiling stock. If, on the other hand, you want to create a rich, well-flavored broth at the expense of the meat, put the meat into a pan of cold water and then bring it slowly to the boil.

Once the liquid has reached the boiling point, turn it down to the gentlest of simmers. If meat is subjected to the intense heat of rapidly boiling water, the gelatinous connective tissue will dissolve and the meat will become tough and dry, while at a gentle simmer the connective tissues melt gradually, keeping the meat succulently moist and tender.

After the scum has been skimmed off, and foam has ceased to appear on top of the broth, salt, vegetables, and herbs are added for flavoring both the meat and broth, and the meat is simmered to tenderness. The slower the simmer, the less cloudy the broth will be. Allow 20 minutes per pound plus 20 minutes extra for pieces more than 6 pounds in weight; 30 minutes per pound plus 30 minutes extra for smaller pieces. The meat can be served with the cooking liquid as is, or it may be thickened for gravy. Or the liquid can be served separately as a first-course broth, or reserved for another dish. To serve the broth as consommé, it must be clarified to render it crystal-clear.

Meat for the freezer

When freezing meat, it makes the most sense to freeze it in the quantities you will be serving, whether as individual steaks or larger roasts. Smaller cuts or individual portions are best because they will freeze more quickly, preserving more of their texture and juiciness, but larger cuts such as pot roasts can be successfully frozen as well. It's nice to have cut-up stewing meat and ground meat on hand, as well as beef steaks and other cuts. Cooked meat can also be frozen, but usually for no longer than a month or two.

Always place meat that is to be frozen in the coldest part of the freezer (the temperature should be 0°F or lower).

Storing meat in the freezer Limits are placed on the storage times for meat not because the meat will become unsafe to eat, but because the quality deteriorates. Meat storage times are determined largely by the fat content, as fat eventually turns rancid even in the freezer. Pork fat turns rancid more quickly than lamb or beef fat, and salted meats (such as bacon or ham) become tough and can retain water; these are best frozen at the lowest possible temperature setting.

Meat that has been inadequately wrapped for the freezer will develop so-called freezer burn, which manifests itself as grayish-white or brownish patches on the meat. These patches are caused by dehydration at the surface, which results in changes in color, texture, and flavor. The meat will be perfectly safe to eat but will taste dry

and unpleasant, so be sure to wrap all meat securely in heavy-duty freezer bags, and then to expel all the air before sealing the bags.

Cooking frozen meat All meat is infinitely better if thoroughly thawed before cooking. Bone-in roasts and small cuts of beef or lamb may be cooked still-frozen without any risk to health, but inevitably the outside will be overdone before the inside is cooked. For frozen roasts, you will need a meat thermometer to check on the internal temperature. For frozen steaks, chops, cutlets, and so on, it will be necessary to start the cooking at a lower temperature and to cook for almost twice as long as usual. Boneless rolled roasts, however, must never be cooked still-frozen, as the inside and outside surfaces of the meat will have been handled when the roast was boned and tied, and it is therefore important to destroy any bacteria that may be present by thorough cooking. Nor should pork be cooked still-frozen; although today's pork is quite safe and can be cooked to medium rather than well-done, it should be completely thawed out first.

To thaw large cuts, allow 6 to 7 hours per pound in the refrigerator, leaving the meat still wrapped. This is much the best way, as the slower the thaw, the more the juices get reabsorbed. Only about 2 to 3 hours per pound are needed at room temperature. Start to cook the meat as soon as it has thawed—while still cold to the touch. If it is left to thaw longer than necessary, the juices will have further opportunity to escape.

Steaks and chops need about 5 hours in the refrigerator in order to thaw out properly, or 2 to 4 hours in the warmth of the kitchen. If you are in a hurry, thawing the meat in cold water will help, as long as the package is watertight.

Another means of thawing frozen meat is to use the microwave, but this must be done carefully to ensure that some parts do not start to cook before others have finished thawing. Use the Defrost power level, and follow the manufacturer's instructions.

BEEF

The best beef of all is aged, by being hung, usually for around 3 weeks, sometimes longer, to reach its peak

of flavor and tenderness. However, this process results in considerable weight loss, which is reflected in the price, so expect aged beef to be expensive.

Choosing beef

The color of lean beef varies from coral pink to a deep burgundy-red. The color variations of the lean meat indicate the age, sex, and breed of the animal, not the quality. Freshly cut surfaces of any piece of beef will be bright red, deepening to a brownish-red on exposure to air—thus a well-aged piece of beef will have a dark, plum-colored crust. The color of the fat will vary according to the animal's diet. Something positive to look for is the marbling—the meat of good roasting beef should be well endowed with flecks and streaks of fat that melt during cooking, basting the roast from within and guaranteeing tenderness.

The quality of ground beef is fairly simple to judge—it should look red. If it is pink, the proportion of fat will be too high.

As a provider of beef, the steer, or bullock (a young castrated male), is the undoubted king. Different countries consider him to be at his peak at different ages—from ten months to six years old— but all agree that a steer, and perhaps a heifer (a cow that has not calved), produce the most succulent meat. In the British Isles, the Scotch beef is considered the best, with Aberdeen Angus the most highly prized of all. In the United States, the Black Angus are the descendants of the Scotch Angus cattle imported into the country in the late 1800s, and Black Angus beef is much valued.

Cooking with beef

When beef is good and succulent, little is needed in the way of added flavors. Horseradish sauce or mustard makes a good accompaniment to roast beef, while the gravy of roast beef is nicest when the pan juices are simply reduced together with a little water and perhaps some red wine, and plainly seasoned with salt and pepper. Most vegetables go well with beef—from green beans to carrots—but potatoes are the traditional and favorite vegetable, whether mashed, oven-roasted or french-fried. In England, the Sunday roast beef always comes to the table accompanied by a golden Yorkshire pudding.

Tastes in beef eating have changed over the years. There was a time when beef was considered at its best when roasted to a crisp. Today more and more people are enjoying their roasts and steaks rare or on the "blue" side of rare—or even raw. The Italians introduced beef *carpaccio*—raw fillet steak cut very thin and served with olive oil and lemon juice or a mustardy dressing—which appears on fashionable menus.

Broiling, grilling, and panfrying The timing depends so much on the thickness of the steak that you can only be sure whether it is done to your liking by pressing it with your finger as it cooks. If the steak feels soft and wobbly, it is rare; a little give, and it will be medium-rare; firm, and it will be well-done; hard, and it will be quite ruined.

Roasting The finest cuts of prime beef respond best when roasted at a high temperature, which makes them crisp on the outside and leaves them a tender rosy-pink within. Overcooked beef turns leathery, even when it is meat of the very best quality. For larger, choice cuts such as beef tenderloin, allow 12 minutes per pound at 450°F for rare meat; 15 minutes for each pound for medium-rare, and 18 minutes per pound for medium. The coarser cuts, such as the thick ribs, make juicier eating when roasted more slowly—allow 20 minutes per pound at 375°F for thinner pieces or for bone-in cuts; allow 30 minutes per pound for thicker cuts or roasts that are boned and rolled. Roast beef should be allowed to rest for at least 20 minutes after it is removed from the oven before carving.

Braising or pot-roasting In general, you should allow 30 to 40 minutes per pound over medium heat on the stove top, and 40 minutes per pound in the oven at 325°F for pot roasts, but a great deal depends on the quality of the meat chosen for this cooking process.

Boiling The tougher boiling cuts may need up to 1 hour per pound of beef at a gentle simmer.

The cuts
Since butchering techniques vary from country to country, and indeed from region to region, the various cuts used for roasting, braising or pot-roasting, stewing, and boiling differ slightly all over the world. It remains true, of course, that in the case of beef (as well as the other animals raised for the table), the very best and most expensive cuts come from the back half of the animal, and most of the very best of those from the fleshy hindquarters; but the actual names of the cuts and their shapes differ considerably, as do the direction of the grain and the way the bones are dealt with.

Cuts for panfrying, broiling, grilling, and roasting These are the top-quality cuts that respond best to cooking in dry heat.

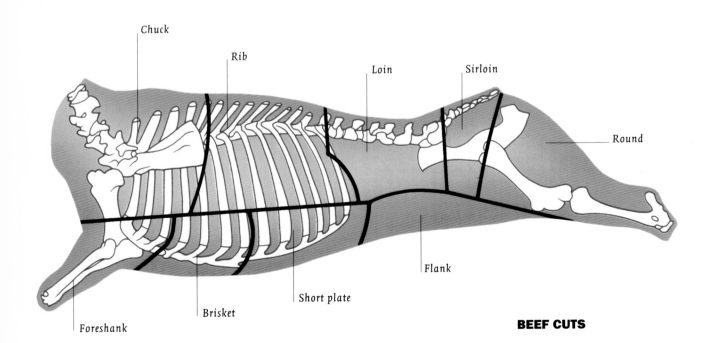

Chuck
Rib
Loin
Sirloin
Round
Flank
Short plate
Brisket
Foreshank

BEEF CUTS

Loin provides the most tender meat that beef or any other animal has to offer. The most luxurious piece of all is the tenderloin or fillet—a tapering strip of practically grainless flesh running inside the rib cage, parallel with the spine. Some butchers offer the tenderloin in its entirety: it can be roasted, sometimes brushed with butter or oil to keep it moist. The tenderloin is also used for the once-classic dinner party dish Beef Wellington, where the meat is enclosed in pastry, with a stuffing between the pastry and the meat to add moisture. The tenderloin is often cut into steaks—the thinnest part makes filets mignons; the wide end can be used for Châteaubriand, a steak so hefty that it is considered a meal for two hungry people.

Finely chopped raw beef tenderloin, spiced to taste with cayenne, Tabasco, Worcestershire sauce, and capers and bound with a raw beaten egg, makes the classic steak tartar. Cut into thin strips, tenderloin is the meat to use for beef Stroganoff, though many unfortunate versions are made with lesser cuts.

There are many people who consider any part of the tenderloin too bland, soft, and almost cottony, much preferring for texture and flavor shell (or New York) steaks, porterhouse steaks, sirloin steaks, and T-bone steaks (which include the end of the sirloin and a piece of tenderloin).

The various national schools cut their steaks differently, some leaving the tenderloin in place to form part of larger steaks, but this does not really affect the cook, since the principle of cooking steak remains constant, and the various forms of serving it differ only in the presentation. As steaks that are grilled are seared so fast that they do not make their own gravy, they may be sent to the table with a separate sauce or an herb or other compound butter. Steaks may also be panfried—filets mignons are usually cooked by this process. Classically they were served on large croutons to absorb the juices; today they are more likely to appear simply, perhaps with a light pan sauce. Panfried, broiled, or grilled, steaks are much enhanced by lighter sauces such as a simple shallot sauce, the classic béarnaise, or even an uncooked sauce of shallots, lemon juice, and oil, similar to a vinaigrette. Crisp french fries and a green salad are the best accompaniments.

The top loin lies above the tenderloin; with the tenderloin, it is called the short loin. The sirloin, which is behind the short loin, may be sold in a single piece for roasting, either on or off the bone, with or without the tenderloin.

In America and in France, the sirloin is often cut into large steaks, which are cooked on the bone and carved into slices at the table. In Britain, steaks are usually cooked in individual portions. Porterhouse, T-bones, and shell or strip steaks come from the top loin.

Rump This is part of the round, and yields rump roasts and beautiful juicy steaks for broiling, grilling, and panfrying. There will be a few tough sinews running through the meat, and these should be lifted out with a sharp knife. Rump roasts are often cooked using moist heat.

Rib When Americans say roast beef, what first come to mind are the great standing roasts from the rib section. Such roasts may be referred to as prime rib roasts, but in fact, with most beef graded prime going to restaurants, these roasts are almost always choice beef. Rolled rib roasts are not quite as flavorful when cooked as rib roasts on the bone, but the boneless rib-eye roast from the middle of the rib section is tender and a luxury. The French rib roast is boned and rolled, and served *au jus* (with its pan juices), accompanied by *pommes frites* and a simple green salad. The traditional English Sunday joint (roast) is the rib or forerib—served with Yorkshire pudding, roast potatoes, and lightly cooked vegetables, not forgetting the horseradish sauce.

Cuts from farther down the rib cage, toward the chuck, fare best braised or pot-roasted, rather than roasted by dry heat. They are juicier when left on the bone but can be tricky to carve. Below lie the short ribs, with a lot of fat and bone, which can be precooked, or marinated, and then barbecued.

For stewing, pot-roasting, and boiling The cuts used for these processes are the tougher pieces that benefit from slow cooking in moist heat. **The round** is the meat from the hind leg, which is divided into top round, eye of round, and bottom round; it is called topside or silverside in Britain. Although part of the round may be cut into steaks,

it is usually used for boneless roasts. From the round comes the very best *boeuf bouilli*, France's classic boiled beef dish, which is eaten in its bouillon with boiled potatoes and the vegetables that were cooked alongside it; little gherkins called cornichons are often served separately. Top round is good pot-roasting meat—being very lean, it often gets a wrapping of fat. Top round can also be roasted, although it may well be rather on the dry and tough side; it remains much juicier when it is kept very rare, in which case it is also excellent cold.

Salted and spiced, top round makes the traditional English boiled salt beef, eaten with carrots and dumplings. As well as nice pot roasts, the round makes good stews, and ground round makes tasty lean hamburgers.

Boneless sirloin tip Called top rump, or thick flank in Britain, this comes from the underside of the hind leg, where leg meets flank. Whole, it can be roasted or pot-roasted, and cut into cubes it makes excellent stews of all sorts, including France's *boeuf bourguignonne*. Ground, it makes good hamburgers.

Shoulder The shoulder area of the carcass is juicy and well flavored. It is known as chuck in the United States and chuck or blade in Britain. Blade steak is cut from the flat of the shoulder blade. When scored across with a heavy knife to cut through all the fine connective tissues, it can be panfried like any steak. Chuck is excellent for pot roast, stews, and other slow-cooked dishes. Ground chuck can be used to make good meat loaves, meatballs, and of course, hamburgers.

Brisket is the flesh of the breast, running from between the forelegs to the front end of the flank. It is fatty meat but is very versatile. It is the favored cut for traditional New England boiled dinner; in Texas, real barbecue always means beef brisket. Corned beef (called salted beef in Britain) is usually brisket, though beef round is sometimes corned; it is boiled and often eaten cold, cut into very thin slices.

Flank meat is coarse, and there can be plenty of fat. The flank may be braised or used for making stews, but the fattier part of the flank is more often ground for patties and the like. Flank steak is a lean boneless muscle that most often appears as London broil. It benefits from marinating before cooking, and, after grilling or broiling, must be sliced thinly across the grain.

Skirt is another muscle from the same region. Like hanger steak, or *onglet*, skirt steak is what is sometimes referred to as a "butcher's cut." Although such cuts are overlooked by the average consumer, butchers know them as some of the most flavorful parts of the animal. Along with flank, this is the cut of choice for fajitas, the Southwestern/Tex-Mex dish.

Foreshank The foreleg is known as the shank or shin. It gives gelatinous stewing meat with a lovely flavor, but takes several hours to cook. The shank—or meat from the flank—is used in the Indonesian dish *rendang*, slowly simmered in spiced coconut milk.

Leg This is the hind leg; it has more gristle and sinew than the foreleg, but it can be slowly cooked to make a well-flavored stew.

Marrow

This is the soft, fatty substance found inside the large bones of beef and veal. Although marrow is not particularly

fancied for eating in the United States, it is regarded as a delicacy throughout much of Europe. It is an integral part of Italy's famous *osso bucco*, made from veal shanks, with their rich supply of marrow, and it is a favorite of restaurant chefs and other gourmands in this country. Beef leg bones are fairly widely available, cut into pieces, although they may have to be special-ordered at the supermarket or butcher.

Marrow makes a wonderful addition to stocks, in which case the split bones are boiled along with the other ingredients to give up their goodness. If you want to use the marrow for sauces or for spreading on toast, the bones should be soaked overnight in cold water, then wrapped in aluminum foil and cooked in a fairly hot oven for 45 minutes. The marrow can then be scooped out from the center of the bones. (In Victorian times, marrow spread on toast was very popular; the bones were served wrapped in starched white napkins and the goodness was scooped from inside with long, narrow marrow spoons.)

VEAL

Veal is a light, delicate, and versatile meat—it is the perfect vehicle for a range of flavors, from subtle and creamy to strong and piquant.

Choosing veal

There are two types of veal: the first and more delicate type comes from milk-fed calves that were slaughtered between 8 and 12 weeks of age, and the second from grass-fed calves, which are usually slaughtered at between 3 and 6 months old.

Milk-fed veal should be the palest pearly-pink in color. It should look firm and moist, but never wet, and have bright, pinky-white, translucent bones. Grass-fed veal is a little darker in color, but never red. Redness is a sure sign that the animal was too old before slaughter. If veal has a brown or gray tinge, it is old and should be avoided. Veal has a little marbling, which should be hard to spot because the fat is practically the same color as the meat. If there is too much marbling and too much covering fat, it means the calf was

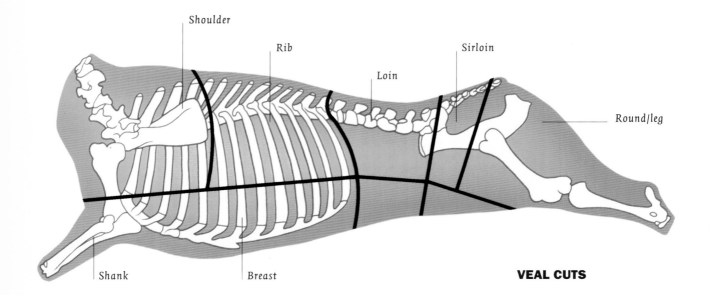

Shoulder • Rib • Loin • Sirloin • Round/leg • Shank • Breast

VEAL CUTS

overfed. What fat there is should look like white satin, and there shouldn't be much of it.

Cooking with veal

Because it hasn't much marbling, there is little interior lubrication while the meat is cooking, and veal can be dry unless other fat is added by way of basting (or, sometimes, larding or barding) for roasting, or by using plenty of butter, good olive oil, or even bacon in sautéed, pot-roasted, and stewed dishes.

The flavor of veal is unassertive, so a strongly flavored garnish is often welcome: the combination of veal and anchovies dates from the earliest times. Lemon and orange often feature in the best sauces, as does white wine and, particularly, Marsala. In Italy, a veal roast may be studded with strips of anchovies; in Parma, they slit a leg of veal and insert strips of paper-thin prosciutto. Scallops and cutlets of veal may also appear under a slice of mildly cured ham on which a generous slice of cheese is gently melting.

Onions have a special affinity with veal, not only because of their taste but also because of their texture—they are often put into the pan with a roast. As for accompaniments: any really fresh-looking vegetable is good, as is salad. Veal is pale in color, so both dark-green spinach or beans will provide a beautiful background. Potatoes, of course, go with veal in almost any form, and so do rice and noodles. Golden saffron rice is the traditional side dish for *osso bucco*, and a ring of snow-white rice often surrounds a pale-golden creamy *fricassée* of veal or a *blanquette*. Tagliatelle is often served with veal in Italy, the texture of the delicate pasta compensating for any possible dryness in the meat.

All veal bones are extremely gelatinous and give an excellent texture and flavor to sauces and stocks: if the butcher has trimmed the meat for you, be sure to carry a few of the bones home with you and add them to the pot when braising a piece of veal, removing them before you serve it.

Broiling and frying Because of the lack of interior fat, the smaller cuts of veal—chops, cutlets, scallopine, or scallops, medallions, and the like—are more often panfried or sautéed than broiled. Thin scallops or cutlets should be sautéed quickly over medium heat;

chops should be first seared over high heat and then allowed to finish cooking slowly, or they will become tough and dry. Because of the high temperature of the initial cooking, chops will need to be panfried in oil or in an oil-and-butter mixture, as butter alone would burn, but scallops can be successfully sautéed in butter. Serve them with wedges of lemon.

Roasting Baste veal frequently if you do decide to try roasting it—braising is often more successful with this dry meat. Roast for 25 minutes per pound plus 20 minutes in a moderate oven (375°F) for cuts that are thinner or on the bone; 30 minutes per pound at 325°F, for those that are thicker, boned and rolled, or stuffed.

A hefty cut, like a leg, will preserve its succulence better if covered with strips of bacon before it goes into the oven. The lean little roasts, such as a boneless loin, are best threaded with strips of fatback (larded) or covered with a layer of pork fat (barded). This extra fat will ensure that the meat remains moist.

Braising This is the best method of cooking a large piece of veal. Add some little onions, shallots, or carrots to the pot to help produce the moisture that will prevent the veal from drying out. In Italy, a carrot is sometimes inserted in the center of the meat for the same purpose. Allow 40 to 50 minutes per pound at 325°F, basting frequently with wine and butter.

Stewing This should be carried out very gently, for well over an hour. Veal is good in the traditional *blanquette*, stewed in a flavorful broth that is thickened and enriched at the end of the cooking time with egg yolks and cream.

Boiling This is, more strictly speaking, poaching, and should only involve a mere simmering.

The cuts

Like beef, cuts of veal vary according to the various butchering techniques. However, since calves are smaller than full-grown beef cattle, there is not quite so much scope for variations and not as much difference among the cuts. In fact, most countries follow the economical French style of butchering for veal—and that involves trimming away all

gristle and sinew most meticulously and dividing the meat neatly along the natural seams in the muscles.

Cuts for panfrying, broiling, and roasting Veal needs plenty of additional fat to stop it drying out completely in the dry heat of these processes.

Leg/Round Only the hind leg of veal is referred to as the leg, as the foreleg is called the shank. The cuts from this large and fleshy joint can be roasted under a layer of sliced bacon; alternatively, and better still, braise them with vegetables in order to keep them moist and juicy.

The roast from the leg is called round roast, the top slices of which go by the name of round steak. Round steak is often boned and tied; it is good stuffed with a mixture of fatback, anchovy fillets, and currants and then braised.

The most delicate leg meat is from the muscle that runs vertically along the thigh bone. In France, this cut may be sold separately as the *rouelle*, but, in general, leg of veal cuts tend to be sliced crosswise, containing some of each of the three muscles, which are very similar in taste. So, whether on or off the bone, a cut from the center part of the leg makes good eating. It is this bit that is used for the famous Italian dish *vitello tonnato*—always eaten cool and coated with a sauce of tuna fish pounded to an emulsion with olive oil, lemon juice, and capers.

Rump Situated at the point where leg meets loin, this is usually boned and rolled for slow roasting and braising.

Scallops It is from the leg that the best veal scallops are cut, across the grain and on the bias. Of course, many shops sell thin pink slices of fatless, trimmed veal under the name of escalopes, *scallopine*, or medallions from other parts of a calf's anatomy, but high-class butchers only recognize those from the leg as the real thing. Ask the butcher to pound them flat for you for extra tenderness. When you dip these diaphanous slices in egg and a Parmesan-bread crumb mixture and quickly panfry them, you get the perfect Veal Parmigiana.

If you have to pound the scallops yourself, do take care not to beat the life out of them—a well-cut scallop will require only a gentle flattening. If you don't possess a meat mallet, then use a rolling pin, or ease the meat into shape with the heel of your hand.

There are many, many ways to serve veal scallops. This rich diversity is in part due to the fact that the scallop is one of the mainstays of Italian cooking, and it features often in the varied cuisines of France, Germany, and Austria. In Italy, for example, a great favorite is *saltimbocca*—which means, literally, to "jump into the mouth." This is a dish consisting of small scallops, each one rolled up around a stuffing of prosciutto and fresh sage. *Piccate* are tiny scallops; traditionally, these are dipped in flour and panfried. They are usually sautéed in butter and served with a good lemony sauce.

In France, veal scallops are often simply browned in butter, with the last-minute addition of a handful of finely chopped shallots or scallions and a slice of lemon. The Germans and Austrians are, of course, famed for their *Weinerschnitzel*—traditionally dipped first into flour, then into beaten egg and in bread crumbs, and briefly deep-fried in hot oil.

Loin A lean cut, the loin contains the tenderloin, which is the equivalent of a beef tenderloin. In Europe, it often contains the kidneys, but these, as well as the tenderloin, are often removed to be sold separately. The tenderloin makes nice little medallions. The loin can be sold as chops or whole for roasting.

When roasting a loin, keep it very well basted with butter or olive oil, or cook it in a covered casserole to keep it moist.
Rib This is sold whole, bone in or boneless, for roasting, or it is divided into delicious chops, which should not be cut too thin. Chops should be cooked very gently after browning, or they may become dry. Veal chops are often served with their garnish sitting on top. Fontina cheese, prosciutto, white mushrooms, and, of course, anchovies may all feature. When rib chops are not quite severed at the base of the veal rack, and are curved around to form a crown roast of veal, an onion and mushroom stuffing may go into the center before roasting.
Shoulder This can be roasted, but is better braised. It provides shoulder chops or steaks, also called blade steaks. They can be prepared in much the same way as loin or rib chops, though they are sometimes seared in butter and then enclosed in foil together with shallots, mushrooms, onion and parsley and baked, to be served

en papillote. Off the bone, the shoulder meat is good for stews and goulash.

For braising or pot-roasting and boiling Veal adapts particularly well to moist heat, absorbing both moisture and any flavorings added to the pot.
Shoulder A fairly lean cut, this is suitable for slow-roasting or pot-roasting. It is almost always sold boned and rolled, sometimes with stuffing, although it is vastly preferable to make your own. For this purpose, good butchers may leave an empty pocket in the center. Boned and cubed shoulder is a prime candidate for stews and ragouts—especially when mixed with the meat from the breast region. Particularly good is a simple braise made with plenty of oil, garlic, tomatoes, and mushrooms.

Ground shoulder meat, flavored with marjoram and rosemary and bound with egg, makes delicious meatballs—made more so with the addition of a sauce of white wine, cream, shallots, and dill.
Breast This is often seen boned, and provides a vehicle for some very good stuffings. Traditionally, something green is included in these: spinach, perhaps, or peas, or pistachio nuts. Served cold, a stuffed breast of veal, simmered, then gently weighted down and allowed to cool in its own cooking broth, makes a beautiful summer lunch. A breast is also very good hot—braised with a chunk of slab bacon and some large, juicy onions.
Shank This is a gelatinous, sinewy, but well-flavored piece of meat consisting mainly of bone. Sawn into thick slices and long-cooked, it makes one of the most delicious veal dishes of all—*osso bucco.*
Neck This is actually a versatile cut; in Britain, it may be used for stewed dishes, as it provides meat that is suitable for long simmering. Ground, it makes meat loaves, meatballs, and stuffings, and can be used in pâtés. Veal neck bones make an excellent stock.

LAMB

The choicest lamb has rosy flesh. Its bones are slender, and the fat is white, silky, and resilient. The very best lamb, meltingly tender but expensive and difficult to find, is baby lamb, with flesh of the palest pink that turns almost white when cooked. It is especially good when cooked in the ancient way, grilled over an herb-strewn glowing wood fire.

Next comes spring lamb, which once referred to "lamb season," when most lambs were born in the fall and sold in the spring. Now spring lamb, which is available all year long, simply means lamb that was butchered at between 3 and 5 months of age. Regular lamb has darker flesh than spring lamb. Lamb only qualifies for the name when it has been slaughtered before its first birthday. After that, it becomes yearling, and then mutton.

Although they do not appeal to most American tastes, mutton and yearling remain popular in Britain. Yearling meat is a little darker and a little stronger-tasting than lamb. The more strongly flavored mutton is dark red, not at all pink. Fans of mutton find it just the right sort of meat for heftier regional dishes. Ironically, however, even in Britain, because good lamb is now so readily available (not least because this meat freezes particularly well), people who actually want to buy good old-fashioned mutton often experience considerable difficulty in finding it.

Choosing lamb

When buying lamb, go for the leanest piece you can see—even the fatty cuts vary greatly in their proportions of fat to lean. Avoid those with fat that looks brittle and crumbly or discolored—the most appetizing-looking pieces will make the best eating and will have the most flavor.

Where sheep are raised can affect the flavor of the meat. Some of the most delicious lamb in the world comes from sheep that have grazed on salt marshes: the *pré-salé* ("pre-salted") lamb of France's Atlantic coast is justifiably famous. Mountain, or hillside lamb, small and slender-boned, is a regional specialty in many countries, from Wales to Greece. Mountain lamb is a touch gamier in flavor than other lamb, and this is the reason that there are many recipes for cooking lamb like venison, using the traditional marinades and the same accompaniments: red-currant jelly or a compote of cranberries.

Cooking with lamb

Lamb is basically a tender, succulent meat, so take care not to overcook it—generally, lamb should be pink and juicy inside.

Broiling and panfrying Chops and cutlets of lamb, nicely trimmed, are equally good broiled or panfried. The timing depends on the thickness of the pieces. Test them by pressing them with your finger during cooking: when they are becoming firmer but are still supple, they are done.

Roasting Much depends on the age of the animal and the quality of the meat. The timing varies according to whether you like your roast rosy-pink or well-done.

A leg of lamb should be pink within, most gourmets would agree, although not everyone shares the taste of the French, who like it rose-red in the center. The rib and loin are best fairly rare—cook these cuts at 375°F, allowing about 20 minutes per pound and maybe 15 minutes more for larger cuts, but test by piercing: when the juice runs red, the meat is rare; rosy, it is fairly rare; when it runs clear, the meat is well-done.

The shoulder and all boned, rolled cuts, including stuffed breast, are better when they are well-done: cook them at 325°F, allowing about 30 minutes per pound.

Pot-roasting or braising This is done at an even lower temperature: 300°F,

allowing approximately 2 hours for a whole leg or shoulder, and 1½ hours for smaller cuts. A lamb stew should be ready for eating after 1½ hours of cooking. Because lamb fat congeals so quickly, it is important to take your stew to the table in a preheated dish and to serve it as soon as possible on very hot plates.

The cuts

Most large cuts of lamb can be roasted successfully; even the fattier ones will taste very good.

Leg This succulent piece, simply roasted on the bone, is one of the greatest cuts of meat there is. It may be subdivided into the shank half and the sirloin half. The sirloin half, in turn, makes sirloin chops. Divested of all membranes, this meat, cut into cubes, makes lovely little kebabs. Leg of lamb is much easier to carve if it is partially boned. The butcher can remove the hip and tail bones.

The leg is also sold completely boned. It is usually rolled, but is sometimes butterflied—cut so that it can be opened out flat. Butterflied leg of lamb is delicious grilled outdoors; marinating it beforehand in olive oil and fresh herbs

will produce delicious results. In whatever form, this cut makes a lovely roast. Roast lamb should be left to rest for at least 15 minutes after it is removed from the oven and before carving.

Serve young spring lamb with freshly made mint sauce if possible, rather than the ubiquitous green jelly, and spring vegetables, and older lamb with root vegetables. Rosemary or thyme and garlic are favorite flavorings for lamb in France; or if half a leg of lamb is braised on a bed of vegetables, with cream and tarragon used in the sauce, it becomes *agneau jardinière*. But what is particularly delicious and all too rarely encountered, even in Britain, is a noble, very English, boiled leg of lamb—the shank end—served with caper or onion sauce.

Sirloin The upper part of the sirloin half of the leg, lying next to the loin, is sometimes sold as a separate cut for roasting, on or off the bone. In some types of butchering, it simply forms part of the leg itself.

Loin The two unseparated loins make a saddle roast, an elegant but extravagant roast for a dinner party. A regular single-loin roast may be bought on the bone, but it also comes boned and rolled.

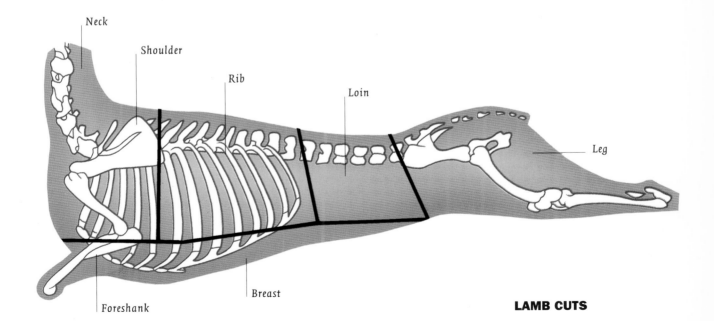

LAMB CUTS

The loin is divided into delicious chops—each with a small T-shaped bone dividing the two pieces of lean meat, double lamb chops are cut from the saddle. There are a hundred ways of garnishing chops; when they are simply panfried or broiled, serve them pink inside with watercress and mashed potatoes. Loin chops may also be boned and trimmed of any excess fat.

Rib Rack of lamb, or the rib roast, lies next to the loin. If you mean to roast or braise it, ask the butcher to remove the chine bone for you, to enable you to carve neat chops after cooking. Two racks of lamb, placed opposite each other, fat side out, bones in the air, and interlinked like swords at a military wedding, make a good dinner-party indulgence, called guard of honor. A good, moist stuffing goes in between the two racks, the same type that you would put into the center of a crown roast of lamb, which is made from the identical two cuts, joined at both ends. The rack can also be boned and sliced into noisettes.

The rack gives chops that are a fraction less juicy than loin chops, but these are still very good. When they are "Frenched" (a reference to the elegance and care the best French butchers bestow on all the meat they handle, in this case meaning that the bones extending from the chops are thoroughly trimmed of fat and meat), they are sometimes eaten with the fingers. The farther back the rib chops lie, the leaner they are; toward the front, they tend to become quite fatty.

Rib chops are probably best of all when sprinkled with olive oil and lemon juice and broiled; boneless chops, or cutlets, from the rib, or the loin or leg, may be coated in egg and bread crumbs before panfrying.

Shoulder Easy to cook, this makes a sweet and juicy roast. It is fattier than the leg, and harder to carve, especially when it is on the bone, but is often a more succulent roast. Boned and tied, it may be stuffed. The shoulder also provides the blade and arm chops, which are good for braising.

Shoulder, trimmed of all fat and membrane, is the cut that is often ground, perhaps together with meat from the foreshank, for use in moussaka, stuffed peppers, *dolmades* (stuffed grape leaves), and the like. In the Middle East, this cut of lamb is sometimes pounded to the consistency of an ointment: this smooth paste, which also includes bulgur, is called *kibbeh* and may be eaten raw or cooked.

Neck The neck is a decidedly bony and fatty cut, but it is useful for broth and lamb stew, including the famous British dish that is known as Lancashire hotpot. This is also the cut used for Moroccan tagines, made with apricots or prunes, almonds, and spices; or use neck to make a good Irish stew—a dish that once used to be made with kid.

Because neck is fatty, add plenty of starchy ingredients to soak up the juices. In Lancashire hotpot, a top layer of thickly cut slices of potato benefits from the rich aromatic fat that rises as the meat cooks. Shepherd's pie, with its covering of mashed potatoes over ground lamb, works on the same principle, as do French *haricots* of lamb or mutton, where dried beans act as the blotting paper. Pilafs, too, use stewing lamb, but this time with rice.

Breast This thin, fatty cut tastes better when it has been slowly cooked. The breast cage makes riblets for barbecuing; the less bony parts can be boned, stuffed, and rolled, or tied flat, like a sandwich, with the stuffing in the middle. In Britain, boneless breast is simmered, cooled, cut into squares, then coated with egg and bread crumbs and panfried; these morsels are called epigrams, a charming name and a good dish.

Shank is from the foreleg. It is full of flavor, but needs long, slow cooking to make it tender.

Kid

Athletic lamb from craggy hillsides with no pasture to speak of produces meat that is notable for flavor, but it can be tough or dry. This is where kid, better adapted to such regions, is much preferred to lamb.

Cooked in oil and wine with garlic, wreathed in rosemary or myrtle, young kid, creamy-white and tender, makes the festive dishes in Corsica and Sardinia, while lamb is for everyday. Saudi Arabia, too, feasts on kid: rubbed with coriander and ginger and onion juices, stuffed with rice, dried fruits, and nuts, and served with clouds of rice and hard-boiled eggs. Lamb can be substituted—as far as recipes go, the two meats are interchangeable. But as kid is mild in taste, it needs plenty of flavoring.

PORK

Prime fresh pork should be a lovely pearly-pink and fine-textured; the fat should be dense and milk-white. The pork that we buy today is very different from that available 20, or even 10, years ago. Pork used to be a very rich, fatty meat; even a suckling pig, slaughtered at about 3 weeks, would make a rich, filling meal, although it had hardly had time to grow stout. Now pigs are much leaner, the meat offering more protein and much less fat.

Choosing pork

The term pork refers to any pig under 1 year old, but most of the pork in the market comes from animals slaughtered at between 6 and 9 months. In older swine, the meat has darkened to rose-pink and the bones, pinkish in young animals, are white. Deep rose-colored meat and white, brittle bones are signs of advanced age. Although pork that is not well trimmed or is fatty-looking is to be avoided, with some cuts—chops particularly—you should choose those that have some marbling (the small flecks of fat that are a sign of good beefsteak as well), or the meat will be dry. If the meat looks wet and slippery rather than moist, it will be of poor quality. If there is any kind of smell, the meat is spoiled or close to it.

Cooking with pork

Today's pork usually benefits from cooking at lower temperatures than those recommended in earlier times. The leg, for example, does not have much in the way of intramuscular fat, so meat from this part of the animal may appear to be on the dry side: to remain as juicy as possible, it should be cooked slowly.

All cuts of pork, without exception, need to be cooked through—this is both because raw pork may contain microscopic parasites that are killed only when the meat reaches an internal temperature of about 140°F and because underdone pork tastes less good, but it is no longer necessary to overcook it. However, to be on the safe side, most pork should be cooked until it reaches an internal temperature of 155 to 160°F—a far cry from the 185°F recommended in cookbooks of just a decade or so ago—which will still leave it juicy and tender.

The humbler cuts of pork tend to be cooked and served with more fat on the meat, and so the best accompaniments are those such as mashed potatoes, beans, dried peas, and lentils, which will absorb some of the fat. Chestnuts have the same effect. In Spain and Portugal, potatoes are added to braised or stewed fatty pork dishes about half an hour before serving to soak up the fat that has risen to the top of the pot.

The more expensive, less fatty cuts of pork—leg and loin—are often served with fruit or vegetables to provide a contrast to the rich, dense meat. Apples are probably the best-known such accompaniment, while in France's Loire Valley, noisettes or medallions of pork are cooked with prunes. In Denmark, prunes are used to stuff a loin roast, and a mixture of soaked dried fruit is used in Poland. In Germany, the starchy and fruity elements are combined in a dish called "heaven and earth"—a mixture of puréed potatoes and apples.

For moistening purposes, beer, wine, and stock are all used, but cider is the liquid that is most traditionally associated with pork.

By way of herbs, pork takes kindly to the warm flavor of fennel and caraway seeds, as well as to the pungent flavor of sage. Sage and onion is a classic stuffing for roast pork or stuffed pork chops. In Italy, pork is often cooked with rosemary or bay leaves; it is good also with juniper berries or whole peppercorns and with thyme. And, of course, a loin of pork is wonderful with truffles.

As for side dishes, all the cruciferous vegetables, led by sweet-and-sour red cabbage, are naturals for pork. The more delicate roasts, such as leg or loin, look most appetizing with something fresh, such as little carrots or turnips, leeks, bright-green cabbage, or spinach. Young peas and artichoke hearts bathed in melted butter make one of the best combinations. A simple lettuce salad, served on the same plate with a broiled or fried chop, and eaten bathed in the meat juices, is extremely delicious.

Broiling and panfrying A medium chop should take about 15 minutes at medium heat. Turn it from time to time as it cooks, and test it by piercing—when the juices run clear, it is ready to serve.

Roasting This must be thorough. For smaller, thinner cuts allow a full 25 minutes per pound, plus 25 minutes extra, at 350°F; and 30 minutes per pound, plus 30 minutes extra, for thicker pieces like leg or shoulder roasts. Fresh pork is not seen with the skin on in our markets, but in some regions, and in many countries, the skin is regarded as a treat. Many Englishmen, at least, think the crisp "crackling" that results from rubbing the skin with oil or salt (but not both) before cooking the pork is the best part of the roast.

Braising or pot-roasting On top of the stove, simmer pork over medium heat. Or place it in a casserole with a little vinegar, whole black peppercorns, and bay leaves and cook slowly in the oven at 325°F.

Boiling It is not usual to boil fresh pork, except for the pig's feet (trotters to the British), but any of the pickled or salted and smoked cuts make perfect candidates for boiling, or, rather, simmering. These may need soaking beforehand: if necessary, ask the butcher how long to soak.

The cuts

There is no cut of pork that cannot be satisfactorily roasted—the pig is too lethargic a beast to develop much by way of tough muscle and connective tissue. The coarser cuts with little in the way of visible fat may be better braised or slowly stewed. A coarse, fatty cut will still make a lovely braise or stew,

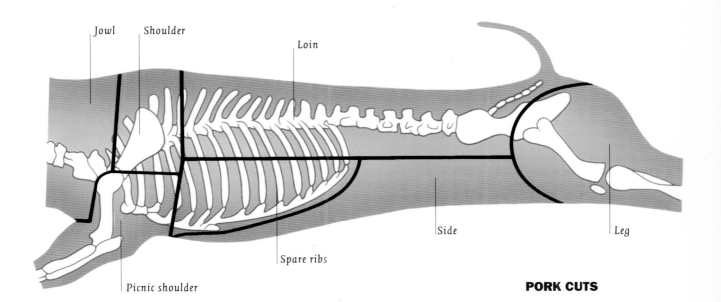

PORK CUTS

Jowl Shoulder Loin

Picnic shoulder Spare ribs Side Leg

provided it is trimmed of most of the fat, which would make the sauce too rich and indigestible.

Leg A whole leg of pork, or fresh ham, makes a really imposing dish. But even a small one—larger ones may weigh up to 15 pounds—can be rather daunting, so it is often divided into the shank or leg end and the butt end or top leg (called, somewhat more elegantly, fillet end in Britain). Leg of pork is more often sold boned than not.

The shank end is easier to cook evenly when it is boned and rolled, but it will then look less handsome on the serving platter. When cooking shank on the bone, it is a good idea to protect the thinner bony part by wrapping it in aluminum foil halfway through the cooking time, leaving the meatier end exposed to the full heat.

The butt end of the leg can be cooked as a roast, boneless or not. It may also be sliced into lean cutlets about ½- to 1-inch thick—and cooked as you would a steak. The butt end of leg may be cut into cubes to be cooked as kebabs.

A fresh leg of pork is sometimes, especially in Italy, first simmered in milk and then finished off in the oven, surrounded by quantities of garlic (the milk ends up as a light, golden gravy). Some countries pickle the leg, which can then be boiled. This is eaten with the coarse purée of green split peas that is known and loved as pease pudding in the north of England.

Loin The sirloin, the fleshy part of the loin, is usually cut into delicious large chops, called sirloin or butterfly chops, or into thick sirloin cutlets, but this is another cut that may be roasted either on or off the bone, seasoned with sage, rosemary, or thyme.

Delicate and very tender, the loin itself makes a wonderful meal if it is boned, stuffed with chopped garlic, a few prunes or herbs, and mushrooms, or even truffles, then rolled, and roasted. On the bone, a loin cut is sometimes served sitting on a bed of unsweetened apples and sweet chestnuts.

It is the loin that provides most pork chops: rib or loin chops to be panfried, broiled, after being lightly brushed with oil; or braised, moistened with beer, white wine, or cider. Pounded thin, dipped in beaten egg and seasoned bread crumbs, and panfried, they become pork

chops *alla milanese*. Chops taken from the hind end of the loin may bring with them a portion of the tenderloin.

Tenderloin Pork tenderloins are now sold in most supermarkets, usually vacuum-packed in plastic. They generally come two to a package, weighing ¾ to 1¼ pounds each. Lean and tender, pork tenderloin is a versatile cut. Tenderloin is good roasted—perhaps slit down the middle and stuffed, or wrapped in bacon and roasted whole like a miniature pork roast. Whole tenderloins can be grilled for a change-of-pace summer meal. The tenderloin may also be cut into medallions or scallops, but their taste, like that of veal, is delicate, so some interesting flavoring is needed to give them character. In France, apples or prunes are used as a garnish for tenderloin cutlets or medallions, which are lovely cooked with crushed allspice berries or fennel seeds. In Germany, they are cooked with caraway seeds or with a rich sauce made with sour cream and the delicious pan juices.

Shoulder Pork shoulder, or butt, is often referred to as Boston butt. Blade roasts and steaks come from the shoulder too, as does the picnic roast (and picnic ham). In addition to being roasted, this rather rich cut can be ground for sausages, meatballs, or patties and for the famous Pennsylvania Dutch scrapple—a cooked mixture of pork and cornmeal, sliced and fried in butter or bacon drippings. Pork shoulder is a favorite for traditional barbecues, and the steaks sliced from the shoulder are particularly good cooked over charcoal.

Ribs Spareribs come from the lower part of the rib cage and the breast, and are either sold in slabs or separated into single or double bones, each with its cartilage. The sheets of ribs are sometimes cooked sandwiched together with a stuffing in between them—the Pennsylvania Dutch like to spread this sandwich with apples, the Germans with cabbage and caraway. But the favorite way to prepare spareribs, and other pork ribs, is to barbecue them—and each region has its own special variations of barbecue sauces, marinades, and rubs.

Spareribs are always eaten with the fingers. Because they are so bony, allow at least 3 pounds for two people.

Back ribs come from the loin, above the spareribs; baby back ribs are from

younger animals and so are smaller than ordinary back ribs. Country-style ribs come from the blade, or shoulder, end of the loin. These are big, thick, meaty ribs.

Side The side, or belly, provides bacon and the rather fatty meat that is cured to become salt pork. It is good for enriching dishes of beans, lentils, and cabbage. It is useful for making pâtés, and, if you don't mind the fat, it can be roasted, sliced, and then broiled, sautéed (allowed to render its fat, it makes delicious cracklings), or braised Chinese-style with star anise.

Suckling pig

These young pigs, which have been slaughtered between the ages of 3 to 8 weeks, contain proportionally little meat; however, what there is, is perhaps the sweetest and richest of all pork.

In northern Spain, suckling pigs are a specialty. These pigs start their short lives on a diet of mother's milk and wild herbs. They are traditionally roasted in a slow-burning wood oven, and served simply with boiled potatoes and apple sauce.

Choosing suckling pig You will need to order a suckling pig specially from your butcher. They range from about 10 to 20 pounds, and a medium-sized one is a good buy because it will have developed enough meaty parts without sacrificing the tender succulence of the smaller pigs. As a rough guide, a 12-pound suckling pig should feed ten people.

Roasting a suckling pig Suckling pig, which should have been prepared for you by the butcher, can be stuffed with any stuffing suitable for pork (a combination of bread crumbs, parsley, onions, sausage, chestnuts, and brandy is good), or simply brushed with oil or rubbed with salt and lemon juice and sprinkled with herbs. Place the suckling pig on a rack and prick the skin before and during roasting to allow the fat to drip out into the roasting pan. It won't need basting, and the skin will turn a shiny, crisp brown. A medium-sized stuffed pig will take 2½ to 3 hours to cook; an unstuffed one will be ready in 2 hours. Allow 20 minutes per pound at 350°F.

Suckling pigs are usually reserved for festive occasions, such as colorful Hawaiian luaus, where the central feature is a spit-roasted suckling pig, liberally basted with barbecue sauce and presented on a tray with a red apple in its mouth.

VARIETY MEATS

Some of the best dishes in the world are made with humble pieces of meat that are collectively known as variety meats, or offal. While, unfortunately, Americans tend to shy away from these, they are treated with special respect in France and the Mediterranean countries, where their distinctive flavors and textures are preserved by careful cooking.

Luckily, many of these meats are among the most economical buys. While some of them, particularly those from veal, may command a high price, only small amounts need to be purchased because of their rich flavor and lack of bones; those from less expensive animals are full of wholesome flavor. Whichever type you buy, make sure it is fresh, and cook it as soon as possible.

Sweetbreads A fine delicacy, sweetbreads are sold in pairs, being two parts of the thymus gland, which sits in the throat and chest of young animals. The rounder, fatter one is the better of the two. (The sweetbreads that come from the pancreas gland, and that are sometimes referred to as belly or stomach sweetbreads, are coarser than true sweetbreads.) Calf's sweetbreads are the best, especially the very large ones from milk-fed veal. They are whiter and larger than beef or lamb sweetbreads and less tedious to prepare, and they have a finer flavor. Pork sweetbreads are small and not particularly good.

No matter how they are to be cooked, all sweetbreads need to be prepared first to make them white and firm. To prepare them, soak them in salted water for 2 hours, changing the water from time to time, until they lose all trace of pinkness and turn white. Put them in a pan of cold salted water, bring to a boil, and simmer for 2 minutes. Drain and rinse them under cold running water. This process firms up the sweetbreads and makes them easier to handle. Peel away the skin, connective tissues, and gristle—some sweetbreads will fall naturally into smaller portions. Finally, flatten the sweetbreads between two plates for an hour before cooking. One of the best ways of cooking them after the initial preparation is to coat them in beaten egg and bread crumbs and to sauté them gently in butter until brown.

Liver Fresh liver is the most nutritious and widely eaten of all organ meats. It is sold either whole or in slices and is often already trimmed, but if it still has a thin covering of membrane, this needs to be removed or the liver will curl up in the pan. Less delicate livers, such as pork or beef liver, will become more tender if soaked in milk before cooking.

Calf's liver Pale and plump, liver from milk-fed veal is the most delicious, but is expensive. Liver from grass-fed veal will be thinner, darker, and not as mild. Panfried liver is delicious if it is cooked very lightly and rapidly and is still rosy inside—overcooking makes liver unappetizingly tough, dry, and leathery. In the famous *fegato alla veneziana*, calf's liver is cut into the thinnest slices, fried for mere seconds, and served on a bed of golden fried onions. Liver is also good when served with fried bacon and watercress.

Beef liver is often the only liver available in the supermarket, and is usually a darker red than calf's liver. Its flavor is stronger and it is not at all as delicate. It should be prepared in the same ways as calf's liver.

Lamb's liver is a deeper color than calf's liver and doesn't have as good a flavor, but it is as tender. It is served in the same ways as calf's liver.

Pork liver is not ideal for frying, as its texture is granular and its taste rather powerful. It is best used in pâtés, or braised in one large piece with wine and vegetables.

Kidneys All kidneys should be firm and smell sweet. Once prepared, they can be broiled or sautéed briefly or simmered slowly and for a long time—anything in between and they will be tough.

Veal kidneys are multilobed and will be very large and pale when they come from milk-fed veal, darker and much smaller from grass-fed veal. They are best when broiled and served with bacon, or briskly browned in butter to seal in their juices. The piquancy of a mustard and cream sauce is the perfect complement. In Europe, kidneys may be sold still in their fresh white surrounding fat, and they can be roasted in this fat; this takes about an hour, and the resulting kidneys will be pink and succulent.

Lamb kidneys have a mild but delicious flavor, and are excellent fried in butter. With the two halves not quite severed, they form an essential part of the dish called a mixed grill.

Pork kidneys are larger than lamb kidneys and are thought by some people to be strong flavored, but they are tender enough to be broiled or panfried, and are a favorite dish on the menu in French brasseries. They are also good cooked slowly in wine and served with boiled potatoes and watercress to offset their richness.

Beef kidneys are dark and quite strongly flavored, and are best suited to braising. They also provide just the right flavor and plenty of rich gravy in Britain's famous steak and kidney pie.

Honeycomb tripe

Veal sweetbreads

Oxtail

Beef tongue

Caul fat

Veal kidneys

Calf's liver

Tongue While tongue can be purchased fresh, it is more usual to find it cured, smoked, or pickled. It is a very smooth meat. Beef tongue is best; calf's tongue, although good, has less flavor; and lamb's tongue is rather dull. Pork tongue is not very often seen.

Whether it is fresh or cured, choose a tongue that feels soft to the touch. Soak cured tongue overnight if necessary to remove the salt, and then simmer it with vegetables and herbs until tender (this can take 3 hours or more, so allow plenty of time). Skin it carefully and serve it hot with Italian herb sauce, or walnut or raisin sauce, and with mashed or boiled new potatoes. Cold, tongue is usually eaten with pickles, horseradish or mustard, and green salad.

Tripe Usually from beef, tripe is the lining of the animal's first and second stomachs. It comes in a variety of textures, some honeycombed, which are considered to be the best, some just slightly rough (called pocket tripe, this is less common), and some smooth. Tripe has to be cleaned and blanched meticulously before cooking, and would take hours to cook if bought truly fresh—an authentic *tripe à la mode de Caen*, the Normandy dish flavored with vegetables and Calvados, needs about 12 hours of simmering before it will reach its gelatinous best.

Thankfully, tripe is usually sold already prepared and partly cooked; always buy tripe that looks white and fresh. In Provence, lamb's tripe is folded into little parcels enclosing garlic, herbs, and salt pork, and simmered with sheep's feet, to make the famous dish called *pieds et pacquets*. Menudo is a much-loved hearty Mexican tripe stew.

Caul fat After the fat has been removed to make fine-quality leaf lard, a very thin membrane of fat that lines the abdominal cavity of the pig is separated to become the delicious and delicate caul fat. This fat, with its lace-like appearance, may need to be special-ordered from the butcher. The sheets usually have to be soaked in warm water until they soften and become pliable for cutting into squares with scissors and wrapping around sausages and chopped meats, as in French *charcuterie*. In Chinese cooking, caul fat is used to envelop poultry before it is deep-fried or baked. The fat provides a basting layer, melting into nothing and leaving behind a delicate, delicious, golden-brown crust.

Heart A heart is a hard-working muscle and, as a result, is never especially tender to eat. Beef heart is particularly tough, and is best prepared by slicing and braising it with plenty of onions to give it a good flavor. Lamb, pork, and calf's hearts, being more tender, can be blanched, stuffed, wrapped in bacon, and roasted.

Brains Calf's brains are decidedly the best, although lamb brains are also quite good. Pork and beef brains are less favored. Like sweetbreads, brains need preparation before they are used, and thorough cooking. They can be gently fried or poached. *Beurre noir* (butter cooked to a rich dark brown), with a few capers added, is the classic sauce. Brains are also good *à la meunière*—sautéed and served with brown butter, lemon, and parsley—or made into a salad with chopped garlic, chiles, and coriander.

Head, tail, and feet

Although not always available, heads, tails, and feet are often well worth the trouble and the long, slow cooking needed to make them tender and to bring out their velvety, gelatinous qualities.

Head Daunting to look at, the head of a calf, pig, or sheep can be a lengthy business to prepare, but an obliging butcher will do this for you and split it into manageable pieces.
Pig's head makes head cheese (called *fromage de tête* in France, and brawn in Britain), the chopped meat suspended in a translucent jelly flavored with herbs, spices, and vinegar (heads are very gelatinous). This is eaten cold with mustard and a green salad.
Calf's head can be cooked, boned and sliced, and covered with a vinaigrette containing capers and onions, to make the *tête de veau vinaigrette* sold in French *charcuteries*. It is sometimes used to make head cheese.
Sheep's head makes a broth much liked in Scotland but thought depressing elsewhere. Sheep's head is, however, a great favorite much on view in Morocco's street food markets.
Calf's and pig's ears are cartilaginous, and considered a delicacy by the Chinese.

Braised pig's ears sometimes appear in the beloved *choucroute garnie* of Alsace, and in some of the pork dishes of Portugal.

Oxtail Oxtail stew, in winter, is one of the very best and most warming dishes. Choose an oxtail with a high proportion of lean, and with fresh, creamy fat. Allow a whole oxtail for two to three people. It will usually be sold cut up and needs only to be trimmed of any large lumps of fat. Generally only the meatier upper joints need trimming.

Oxtail needs long, slow cooking to develop its excellent gelatinous texture. The large amounts of fat that rise to the surface will be easier to remove if the stew is made the day before serving and allowed to get completely cold. Oxtail stew reheats particularly well.

Feet Calf's foot is not much seen today, but pig's feet are quite readily available. **Pig's feet**—trotters in the British Isles—are sold fresh, pickled, or smoked. They are usually split in half, and can be quite plump and meaty. Often they are just simmered and then served either hot with sauerkraut or cold in their own jelly. They are also very good cooked and then coated in bread crumbs and broiled, served with mustard.
Calf's foot can be stewed, and it goes into the making of rich stocks and glazes. Traditionally, calf's foot jelly was given to invalids, being both nutritious and easy to eat and digest.

Gelatin Extracted from calf's feet, pig's knuckles, and the like, gelatin is sold either in powdered form in individual packets, or in shiny sheets. The sheets are the preferred form in Europe; in the United States, sheets may be found in pastry supply shops or through specialty mail-order sources. Gelatin has virtually no taste and dissolves into a clear liquid. Sheet or leaf gelatin is less likely than powdered to turn lumpy. Do not boil gelatin. Powdered gelatin should be softened in cold water before dissolving it; sheet gelatin can simply be dissolved in a little hot liquid in a cup standing in a shallow pan of hot water. Gelatin does not take kindly to freezing.

An alternative to animal gelatin is agar-agar, the jellying agent extracted from seaweed. It can be found in health food stores and Asian markets.

PREPARING MEAT

Preparing a beef tenderloin

1 With the rounded, neater side of the tenderloin uppermost, start cutting and pulling away the fat from the wide end.

2 Cut away all the fat that lies along one side of the tenderloin.

3 Cut off the large lump of fat that is attached to the wide end.

4 Turn the tenderloin over, and pull and cut away the fatty strip, or chain muscle.

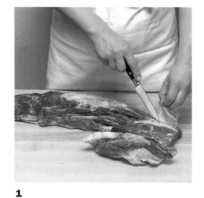

1

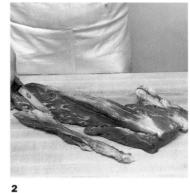

2

beef cuts for panfrying, broiling, grilling, and roasting 52–3

knives 222–4
meat pounder 226

Filets Mignons with Shallot Sauce 292

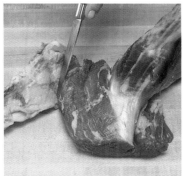

3

4

5

5 Return the tenderloin to its original position. Using a sharp knife, remove the shiny layer of membrane, or silverskin. This should leave the meat completely free of fat and membrane.

6 Prepare the tenderloin for roasting whole by securing any loose pieces neatly with kitchen string. Fold the thin end of the tenderloin under itself and secure it, if you like, for more even cooking.

7 Alternatively, cut small filet mignon steaks from the thin end of the tenderloin, and medium-size tournedos from the center. The wide end can be used as a small roast as is, or prepared for Châteaubriand: wrap it in a clean cloth, turn it on its side, and, using the side of a cleaver or a meat mallet, flatten it to half its original thickness.

8 In this way, the tenderloin has been divided into a Châteaubriand (bottom), three tournedos (top), and three filets mignons. Use the trimmings to make beef Stroganoff or another dish, or for steak tartar.

6

7

8

Preparing veal scallops

1 Using a sharp knife, cut even slices from a boneless cut from leg of veal, such as top or bottom round.

2 Place each slice between two pieces of dampened parchment paper or two sheets of plastic wrap, and flatten it gently but firmly, using a rolling pin or a meat pounder. Here, a prepared scallop is compared with a freshly cut slice.

1

2

1

Preparing a large pork scallop

1 Pork tenderloin is normally cooked whole or cut into slices or chunks, but a large tenderloin can also be flattened and then rolled around a stuffing. Slit the tenderloin open down the middle, being careful not to cut all the way through it.

2

3

2 Open the meat out like a book and then place it on a dampened piece of parchment paper or on a sheet of plastic wrap.

3 Cover the meat with a second piece of parchment paper or plastic wrap, and flatten it gently but firmly with a rolling pin or a meat pounder.

4

4 The scallop can now be stuffed, rolled, and secured with kitchen string. Alternatively, cut it into smaller pieces and use as pork scallopine.

Boning a shoulder of lamb

1 Lay the shoulder fat side down and grasp the exposed end of the shank bone. Cut around the bone with a sharp knife, pushing the meat back as you work toward the joint.

shoulder of
lamb 58

knives 222–4

**Lamb with
Indian Spices**
302, 303

1

2 Cut into the joint between the shank and the center (arm) bone, then bend the shank bone back until the joint breaks. Remove the shank bone.

3 Grasp the exposed end of the center bone and cut back the meat in the same way as with the shank bone, cutting as close to the bone as possible. Avoid cutting through the meat. Pull the center bone away from the blade bone to which it is attached and pull it out.

2

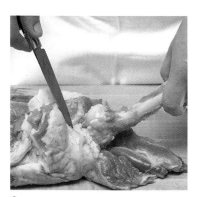

3

4 Turn the meat around so that the triangular blade bone is facing you. Insert the knife into the meat against the bone, and cut the meat away from either side of the flat bone. Pull the bone out, and trim any excess fat from the meat.

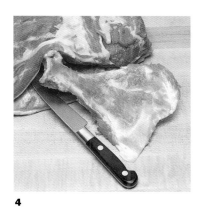

4

5 Roll up the boned meat, with the fat on the outside, and secure it with kitchen string. The three bones that have been removed are, from left to right, the blade bone, the center (arm) bone, and the shank.

5

Boning a leg of lamb

1 Grasp the broad, curved hip bone, which protrudes at the wider end of the leg, and carefully run a sharp knife around it, releasing it from the meat and the tendons that attach it to the leg bone. Pull out the bone.

1

2 Grasp the shank bone at the other end of the leg, cut it away from the meat, severing the tendons that attach it, and then pull it out.

3 Set the leg with the wide end up, and, using the knife, tunnel into the cavity left by the hip bone, cutting as close to the leg bone as possible.

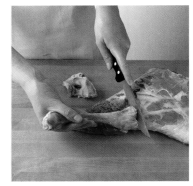

2

3

4 When all the meat has been separated from the bone, pull the bone out of the hip cavity. Trim away the excess fat from the meat.

5 The three bones that have been removed here are, from left to right, the shank bone, the main leg bone, and the hip bone.

4

5

6 Tuck the shank end of the meat into the cavity left by the bones, and roll up the boned meat to make a neat roast. Tie with kitchen string.

6

Butterflying a leg of lamb

1 Lay a boned leg of lamb fat side down. Cut down to the cavity left by the leg bone and slit open the leg, without cutting it all the way through. Trim off all the excess fat and the sinews.

2 Open the leg out flat, then slash it lengthwise in the thickest parts so that it will be reasonably even in thickness; do not cut all the way through the meat.

1

2

leg of lamb 57
rack of lamb 58

Grilled Butterflied Leg of Lamb with Dijon and Herbs 304

Preparing a rack of lamb

1 If the butcher has not already done so, cut away the backbone, or chine, from the meaty end of the rack, using a strong, sharp knife or a cleaver.

1

2

3

2 Trim off most of the fat from the rack, leaving only a thin layer.

3 Cut through the fat across the rib bones, about 2 inches from the meaty part of the rack, and then cut off the layer of fat and meat over the ends of the rib bones.

4 Strip the meat and fat from between the exposed rib bones, and scrape the bones clean.

4

Ham, Bacon, and Salted Pork

Theoretically, and indeed in practice, every kind of meat can be cured, but pork has long been the prime candidate—not only because of pork's doubtful keeping qualities in the days before refrigeration, but also because this fine-grained and well-lubricated meat emerges from the cure in a succulent and delicious state, and remains so juicy and tender when it is boiled, fried, or roasted.

Dry air, salt, and smoke are the age-old curing agents. Nitrates and nitrites, added in minute quantities to reinforce the preservative powers of salt, are comparative newcomers, and it is these additives that cause the pinkness in cured pork products.

Ham

Pigs used for ham tend to be older and heavier than those that yield fresh pork for our tables. Before the cure, their meat is deep pink or clear red, and the fat is firm and white rather than ivory-colored. After the cure, the outside skin may be creamy-gray to mahogany, depending on whether it has been smoked or not.

Most but not all hams are smoked: some of the finest are simply salted, either in a bath of brine or by the dry-cure method, which involves massaging salt into the ham and storing it for a certain period of time to allow the salt

to permeate the meat, then rinsing and drying the ham. Sometimes, but not always, the cure is repeated several times. This is a slow process, but it ensures that the minimum of salt that is necessary for preservation penetrates the meat; the brine treatment is faster but tends to introduce more salt into the flesh. Some brine-cured hams are injected with brine before they go into their salty bath to speed up the process. In both brine-curing and dry-curing, certain flavoring agents—herbs, spices, and sweeteners—may be added. When sugar is added, the ham may be labeled "sugar-cured."

After they are cured, almost all hams are smoked. "Supermarket"-type canned hams may be smoked lightly, for a short time, while "gourmet" hams are smoked for a longer time, ensuring a stronger flavor. (Some excellent American country hams, however, are not smoked.)

Once cured, and perhaps smoked, most hams are matured. The time and methods for this process vary from place to place (some are buried in wood ash, some hung up in an airy place for months on end) and it is to these differences, as well as to the type and diet of the pigs, that we owe our immense variety of hams. There are also differences in the cuts. Strictly speaking, hams are the hind legs of pigs, but there are other parts of the anatomy, such as the loin, hock, and shoulder, that are cured in similar ways.

Whole hams may be bought cooked, partially cooked, or uncooked.

Cooked ham Baked or boiled ham is an extremely versatile meat: it can be served whole as a hot main course with

a parsley sauce and young vegetables, or plain with velvety spinach. It may also be eaten with heartier vegetables, such as root vegetables or cabbage, or dried peas and beans, which may themselves be cooked together with a ham bone or a piece of bacon. Sliced reasonably thick, ham often comes in a mustard, cream, or tomato sauce, although gourmets insist that a spoonful of Champagne is all the moistening a first-class boiled ham really needs. Cold, in thinner slices, ham can make a first course, or, with a salad, a nice lunch. Chopped, it adds flavor and character to a vast number of dishes. Ham with red-eye gravy, a traditional dish from the American South, is made with a slice of regular or country ham.

Specialty hams When buying one of these hams to cook at home, do not be put off by a little bloom on its rind, since this indicates that the ham is cured to perfection. This must, however, be scraped off before the ham is immersed in the cooking liquid for boiling or simmering, or is baked, as country hams occasionally are. Do note that many of these hams must be soaked, often for as long as 2 to 3 days, before cooking. Some of these hams are sold at specialty butchers; others, like Smithfield ham, can be mail-ordered.

Virginia ham is among the more well-known "country-cured" hams. Pigs destined to become Virginia hams were originally fattened on peanuts and acorns, but today they are grain-fed; the meat is usually smoked over scented hickory and applewood.

Smithfield ham is cured and smoked in Smithfield, Virginia. This is probably the

Coppa

Kaiserfleisch

Kasseler

Westphalian ham

Prosciutto

Bayonne ham

Cooked ham

York ham

Black Forest ham

most famous country ham. It is spiced with pepper and heavily smoked.

Kentucky ham is another country ham, and is perhaps a little drier than the Virginia hams. It owes its flavor to a large proportion of clover in the young pigs' food and a diet of grain toward the end of their lives.

York ham is firm and tender and is the best known of the British "boiling hams." It is delicately pink, with fat that is white and translucent. It is cured by the dry-cure method, and smoked over oak sawdust until it develops its fine, mild flavor.

Suffolk ham is traditionally cured in brine with spices and honey. This British ham is then smoked and hung to mature. During this process it develops its characteristic blue mold and a full, delicate flavor.

Bradenham ham has coal-black skin and deep red flesh, and is another famous English ham. It is cured with molasses and so has a sweet but robust flavor.

Gammon or Wiltshire ham is unlike true hams, which are first cut and then cured; it is cured instead as part of the whole pig, which is then divided into various cuts. English gammon is mild and does not keep as well as most other hams. It is sold smoked or unsmoked, and comes in a variety of cuts. It is best boiled and served with root vegetables or dried peas or beans.

Prague ham is perhaps the most admired central European ham. It is traditionally salted and mildly brined before being lightly smoked over beechwood embers, from which it emerges as perhaps the sweetest of all smoked hams.

Jambon de Paris In France, ham ready to be cooked is sold as *jambon de Paris*, and cooked ham as *jambon glacé*.

Other hams Buying a whole hams is a substantial investment usually reserved for festive occasions, and so ham is usually sold in portions as well. Half-hams (called *jambonneau* in France) come from either the meaty, more expensive butt end of the leg or from the bonier, cheaper shank portion. Hams are also sold boned, or partially boned, and cut into either steaks or slices. Hams can be bought with the fat and rind left on, or partly skinned with the fat trimmed. Skinless hams, although popular, tend to lack the flavor of hams with their skin and fat still intact.

Hams may also be bought canned, the better among them being the Dutch, Danish, and Polish. Lean and flavorful,

they are boneless and ready to eat, but taste better baked with cider, brown sugar, mustard, and cloves. Other canned hams may have little flavor.

Kaiserfleisch and Kasseler Other cured pork products include the delicate smoked Austrian *Kaiserfleisch*, and the *Kasseler* so popular in Germany, Denmark, and Poland. Taken from the loin of the pig, these cuts look like a row of pork chops, but they may also be sold by the chop, boned or unboned, or sliced. In Germany, *Kasseler* is so popular that pigs have been bred with an extra set of ribs to yield more of this cut. Austria eats its *Kaiserfleisch* with bread-based dumplings and red cabbage. German *Kasseler* is sold uncooked in its native country, but is usually sold cooked and sliced elsewhere.

Raw ham Local differences in the traditional cures show most clearly in the hams that are not meant to be cooked but are eaten raw.

Prosciutto When you go into a shop in Italy to buy prosciutto, you will be asked if you want it *cotto* (cooked) or *crudo* (raw), because the word simply means "ham." But outside Italy, prosciutto means raw ham, and the best comes from Parma.

Prosciutto is lightly salted and air-cured for many months. A crown stamped upon its golden hide tells you that it is the genuine article produced from local pigs. The thousands of hams sent to Parma for the cure from all over Italy are less delicate and do not bear this hallmark.

Eat prosciutto in paper-thin slices, with melon, fresh figs, or butter.

Culatello Looking like a half-size Parma ham, culatello comes from the choice butt end of the leg. It is less fatty and more spicy than prosciutto.

Coppa When Italian recipes specify raw ham, most Italian housewives tend to use coppa. This is the cured shoulder and neck portion of a pig, pressed into a skin, and is fattier and less expensive than prosciutto. It can also be thinly sliced and served as an antipasto.

Bayonne This most celebrated of French hams comes from the Pyrenees. Wine plays an important part in the curing process and accounts for its special taste. Locally, Bayonne ham is eaten with eggs or added at the last moment to stews; however, it is most delicious eaten raw like prosciutto, but sliced thicker.

Westphalian ham is the best-known of the German hams and the star of a German *schinkenplatte*, a plate of assorted cold hams. Traditionally, it is cured and then smoked over ash or beech with a bit of juniper. It is a deep golden-pink. Eat it thinly sliced on dark bread such as pumpernickel.

Black Forest ham Strongly brined and strongly smoked, this German ham has well-flavored flesh and milk-white fat. Its robust taste goes well with sourdough bread.

Jambons de campagne and other European country hams The Dordogne area of France is well known for its splendid farm-cured hams. These are often rather salty and chewy because the cure is very heavy, but are delicious when thickly sliced and served with unsalted butter and French bread. Spanish and Italian country hams are also excellent.

Jambon de Grisons This Swiss ham comes from a region with a climate that is ideal for the curing of meats. It is first lightly salted and then dried in the cold, clear air of the Alps.

Lachsschinken comes from Germany. It is smoked pork loin, wrapped in snow-white pork fat and bound with string; it should be pink and moist inside. It can be bought sliced or in its entirety, but should be eaten thinly sliced or minutely diced, with crusty buttered rolls.

Jamón serrano This highly esteemed but chewy delicacy is always eaten raw. Cured and air-dried in the Sierra Morena mountains in southwestern Spain, it is delicious on rough peasant bread. It is reputed to be the sweetest ham in the world. The variety from the province of Huelva is thought to be the best.

Bacon, pork belly

Whether you buy *pancetta*, *lard de poitrine*, *poitrine fumé*, *speck*, *paprikaschinken*, or *tocino*, what you carry home is cured belly of pork, which, when sliced, is known as bacon. Cures, and fattiness, vary.

Pancetta is pink and white in even proportions, and may be smoked or unsmoked. *Pancetta stesa* is left flat; it is used mainly in cooking, in such Italian dishes as *spaghetti alla carbonara*, and in other pasta sauces and bean casseroles. *Pancetta arrotolata* is rolled, flavored with cloves and peppercorns, and used for cooking, or, if smoked, eaten as it is.

Lard de poitrine France's version of bacon can be extremely fatty and generally has less lean meat than its pickled *petit salé*. *Lard de poitrine* is given a bacon cure and comes smoked, when it is called *poitrine fumé*, or unsmoked. It is used to enrich stews and stuffings, and is an essential part of *coq au vin* and many beef stews. It is also used to bard roasting birds or dry cuts of meat. Cut into strips, it becomes lardons. *Poitrine fumé* is splendid fried like bacon, or added to omelets.

Speck is basically fat with a thin layer of lean. When it is more meaty, it becomes *schinkenspeck*. In Germany, Holland, Scandinavia, and other European countries, speck, which can be smoked or unsmoked, appears as a garnish on dishes that need the taste of bacon fat. Speck yields such a large quantity of rendered fat that part of it is often poured off and eaten on bread. The drippings are also used for frying potatoes or mushrooms, and for browning beef or veal before roasting.

Paprika speck is translucent white and rindless, and dusted on the outside with bright red paprika. It is not used so much in cooking, but may turn up in various European countries on a platter of cold cuts.

Tocino is the Spanish version of speck; it is strong-flavored and packed in salt. It goes into *fabadas*—bean stews slowly simmered with vegetables and sausages.

Bacon Although most American bacon is smoked, in other countries, bacon can be bought smoked and unsmoked—or "green" in Britain. Smoking makes the rind look golden-orange and turns the flesh a nice deep pink. Unsmoked flesh is pale pink, and the rind looks anything from off-white to dark cream. As far as the taste is concerned, smoking adds depth and interest to the flavor.

Americans tend to like their bacon crisp, and the diet our pigs are fed causes their fat to be on the soft side, so that it melts easily and our bacon curls and crinkles as it cooks, becoming crisp and crumbly. In other parts of the world, crispness is only possible if the bacon is sliced almost paper-thin.

Center-cut bacon is the leanest. Sliced bacon comes thin, regular, and thick cut. Unsliced bacon is called slab bacon; its rind may need to be removed.

In those countries, especially England, where entire carcasses of pigs are cured in brine, a number of ham-like cuts appear on the market. The leaner cuts are good hot or cold, boiled with onions and root vegetables, or first boiled and then liberally basted with fruit juice or cider and roasted. Bacon chops and steaks can be broiled or fried, and served with applesauce.

British sliced bacon comes not only from the belly (streaky bacon), but also from the back of the pig and from the meaty part of the leg.

Canadian bacon comes from the loin. Called back bacon in Canada and top back in Britain, this smoked pork is quite lean and needs to be fried in a little fat. It comes in rough cylindrical cuts.

Salted pork

The salt pork of the United States, the *petit salé* of France, and the pickled pork belly of Great Britain fall into a category all of their own, being not fully cured but lightly salted in brine.

Salt pork Not to be confused with fatback, salt pork comes from the belly, and may be well streaked with lean or virtually all fat. Salt pork from the leaner end of the belly is what goes into Boston baked beans. Salt pork is also known as corned belly and is chiefly used as a flavoring agent. As such, it is an essential part of a New England clam chowder.

Petit salé is lightly brined, and can be either the leg end of pork belly or the fatty parts of the neck. It is eaten in the traditional French *potée*, a rich cabbage soup containing other cured meats and vegetables. It may also sit in pink-and-white slices on top of puréed peas and beans, or on a dish of cabbage, when it is called *petit salé aux choux*, and it is a vital ingredient in the cooking of sauerkraut.

Pickled pork The English contribution tends to be slightly more heavily cured in brine, with sugar added. It usually consists of belly, although shank is sometimes also prepared in the same way. This meat may need soaking before it is simmered with carrots, turnips, and other root vegetables. Pease pudding is a traditional accompaniment.

Sylte is pickled belly of pork, rolled around crushed peppercorns and mustard seed. It is delicious thinly sliced and often appears on Scandinavian cold tables.

Jowls Pork jowls are cured and usually smoked, and are good when not too fatty. They turn up in Southern regional cooking, in boiled dishes or with black-eyed peas. England calls pork jowls bath chaps, and serves them bread-crumbed.

Lard de poitrine

Smoked speck

British unsmoked streaky bacon

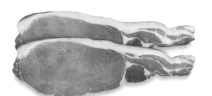

British smoked back bacon

Pancetta

Canadian bacon

Bacon

Cured Meat and Poultry

By far the greatest number of preserved meats, whether brined, air-dried, smoked, or canned, contain pork and pork mixtures. But other meats, game, and poultry also lend themselves to the curing process, producing interesting and luxurious alternatives to ham.

Salted beef There are many ways to treat a corned or salted cut of beef, a number of them a welcome legacy from kosher Jewish cuisine.

Corned beef Corning is an old term for salting, and in the United States corned beef means the salted and well-spiced briskets that go whole into a New England boiled dinner and chopped into corned-beef hash. To most Europeans, however, corned beef means what is called bully beef, canned, pressed, salted beef, pink in color and speckled with fat, that is eaten with salad or in fritters or hash.

Salt beef The British alternative to corned beef, this is simply beef soaked in brine. The addition of saltpeter makes it red—in its natural state it is grayish-brown. Some types of salt beef are so heavily brined that some soaking will be necessary before the meat goes into the pot, while others may be ready for cooking just as they are. Salt beef—beef round is the traditional cut—is often boiled with plenty of carrots and served with potatoes and dumplings.

Pastrami In the Balkans, the word pastrami is used to describe any kind of preserved meat, from beef, pork, and lamb to goose. Elsewhere, it has come to mean salt beef that has been highly seasoned, usually with whole black peppercorns, dry-cured, and then smoked. Since Rumania, above all other Balkan countries, excels in making pastrami, its methods are the model for the rest of the world. Sold fully cooked in slabs or slices, pastrami is delicious with rye bread or hot potato salad.

Dried beef This is beef spiced and salted and then air-dried to the very essence of beefiness.

Bündnerfleisch Grisons in Switzerland is the home of this mountain air-cured beef. As it tends to be rather dry, slivers of it, scraped rather than cut, are eaten with an oil and vinegar dressing.

Bresaola is the Italian counterpart. It is a specialty of Lombardy and is eaten thinly sliced. The usual dressing is made with olive oil, chopped parsley, and lemon; or bresaola may be served with olive oil and slivers of Parmesan or white truffle.

Chipped beef is a rather poor American relation sold in jars. It is sometimes served on toast, or can be mixed with scrambled eggs.

Biltong comes from South Africa, and it is strips of cured, air-dried beef or game, or, more recently, meat such as ostrich. Biltong can be very good indeed, and will keep indefinitely.

Jerky is the American version of biltong, and is strips of beef, traditionally dried in the sun. It is chewy, but full of flavor.

Smoked poultry and game Unlike hams, smoked poultry and game are always hot-smoked, or first cooked and then smoked. The birds can be bought either whole or sliced and resemble ham in flavor, but are as perishable as fresh-roasted birds. Smoked chicken and smoked turkey breast offer plenty of delicate meat; smoked duck is excellent, and smoked quail extravagant. In Europe, smoked guinea fowl is common, but the most prized of all is smoked goose breast obtained from the Baltic coast of Germany, where the geese tend to be the most deep-breasted. Also excellent is smoked reindeer meat from Scandinavia.

Confit d'oie and confit de canard

An everyday food in southwestern France, where vast numbers of geese and ducks are fattened for foie gras, confits are simply salted or salted and spiced pieces of goose (oie) or duck (canard) preserved in fat. Confit can be bought in a jar and will keep for several months, but all that is needed to make it at home is the bird, its rendered fat, coarse salt, and patience. The wings and legs are heavily salted and refrigerated for 12 hours, then wiped dry and gently cooked in their own fat, plus extra pork fat if necessary. After this, they are placed in jars, where they must be completely covered with their own fat. They will keep well in the refrigerator for several months.

A portion of confit is an essential ingredient in a cassoulet, but confit can also be eaten on its own, gently sautéed in a little of its preserving fat, and served crisp on the outside, succulent inside, with a green salad dressed with walnut oil.

Smoked mutton "No sort of meat," say the Scots, "is more improved by smoking with aromatic woods than mutton." The people of Norway are in perfect agreement. Norwegian fenalar is smoked and air-dried until it develops a highly concentrated flavor, to be enjoyed with crisp Norwegian flatbrød and butter. The Scottish mutton ham has a rich, interesting flavor, and is good sliced and eaten raw, or braised with vegetables.

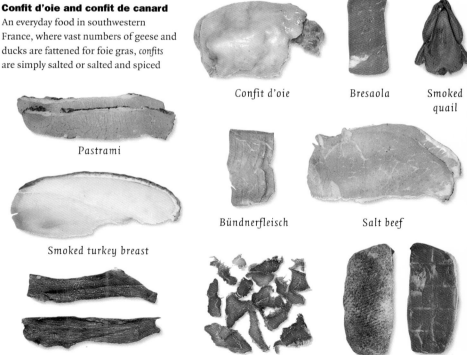

Confit d'oie

Bresaola

Smoked quail

Pastrami

Smoked turkey breast

Bündnerfleisch

Salt beef

Beef jerky

Biltong

Smoked duck breast

Sausages

When country people killed their own animals, particularly pigs, to provide themselves with meat, there was always a tremendous amount of work to be done to make sure that every part of the animal could be either eaten at once or, for the most part, stored for later use.

The liver, heart, kidneys, and so forth were eaten at once, and the legs, bellies, shoulders, feet, and heads salted for the winter, while certain cuts and all the scraps were gathered together and turned into sausages, with the animals' own intestines serving as casings. These sausages were either spiced, to help prolong their life by a few days, and eaten fresh, or dried and preserved by various means, often by salting and smoking, for eating later.

The type of meat, the proportion of fat to lean, and the endless variations of seasonings and cures account for the myriad different sausages we enjoy today. What makes the ideal sausage is largely a matter of regional taste. Some people like sausages so coarse that the meat seems to be chopped, not ground; others prefer the stuffing ground to a paste. But all agree that the meatiest sausages are the best. The seasonings used also vary tremendously from country to country and from region to region.

Most interested sausage eaters prefer their sausages in natural casings, true intestines being marginally more digestible than the artificial kind, less liable to burst during cooking, and producing a more attractive, rustic, natural-looking result. Natural casing can be recognized by the fine, slim knots between the links; artificial casings tend to be less elastic and to untwist, leaving air spaces between the individual sausages.

Fresh sausages

While fresh homemade sausages are fairly simple to make and easily rival the best store-bought ones, farmers' markets, some butchers, and specialty shops now offer some very good fresh sausages. These should be treated like fresh meat and eaten within a few days of purchase. They need really slow cooking—too much heat and they burst their skins, because the contents swell at a faster rate than the casings. Prick them in one or two places before frying in a little oil, and make sure they are thoroughly cooked. In England, fresh sausages and sausage meat go into sausage rolls, pies, and toad-in-the-hole. In Italy and France, sausages are poached and boiled and used in soups, *choucroute garnie*, and *cassoulet*. Also in

France, cervelas sausages are sometimes wrapped in brioche dough and then baked. Algerian merguez, heavily spiced lamb sausages, are the favorite for barbecues in the South of France. In Spain, blood sausages and chorizo are essential components of bean stews.

American and British sausages

Usually bought by weight, these can be made from fresh pork or, usually less good, from fresh beef, veal, or venison. Smoked and unsmoked chicken and turkey sausages are also becoming increasingly popular. Sage is the traditional sausage seasoning, but new types are introduced all the time—one excellent combination is pork and leeks, while pork and fresh chile peppers is another. The best are made of pure, coarsely chopped pork. Broiled and served with fried eggs, fat sausages make a filling and delicious breakfast. Accompanied by mashed potatoes, when they are called bangers and mash in England, they are lovely for lunch or supper. Slender, half-sized sausages, filled with pork or beef, are known as chipolatas in England and France, although the term is in fact Italian.

Unless they are labeled 100 percent meat, sausages are likely to contain a filler: this filler was once fresh bread crumbs, but cereals and other additives are now generally used. Sausages often contain a good deal of moisture, since crushed ice may be introduced into the sausage machine to prevent overheating of the meat as it is ground.

Bratwurst and weisswurst These fine-grained, pale, almost white sausages—the best known are those from Germany and Switzerland—are usually made of veal, though bratwurst sometimes contain pork as well. Literally "frying sausages," bratwurst, and weisswurst, can indeed be fried, or they can be grilled so that they are branded with golden stripes. These sausages are of a fine consistency and have a delicate taste. Bratwurst is particularly popular in the Midwest, where it's sold precooked as well as fresh.

Saucisse Small fresh sausages in France generally go under the name of *saucisses*, while larger ones are *saucissons*. Regional recipes make for difference of

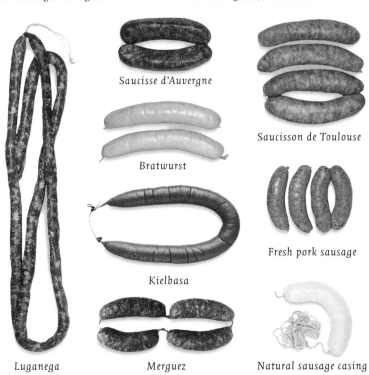

Saucisse d'Auvergne

Bratwurst

Kielbasa

Luganega

Merguez

Saucisson de Toulouse

Fresh pork sausage

Natural sausage casing

texture and taste, but whether coarse or fine, highly seasoned or not, all are made of pure meat, which is so important when making the *saucisses en brioche* (sausages in brioche) encountered throughout France, if the result is to be light and delicate. There are any number of excellent locally made French country sausages—called *saucisses de campagne*—that go into cabbage soups and stuffings as well as being broiled. A wide variety of seasonings is used for these sausages, ranging from pistachio nuts, chard, truffles, or Champagne to sage, sweet and hot peppers, or fresh parsley.

Saucisse d'Auvergne These are *saucisses fumées*, or smoked sausages. They are eaten either broiled or fried, and their rich flavor combines beautifully with a hot potato salad.

Cumberland sausage This meatiest of all British pork sausages is made in a continuous spiral, rather than being twisted into links. The filling is coarsely chopped and spiced with peppercorns. It is sold by length and is usually fried.

Kielbasa In Poland any number of fresh sausages, called kielbasa, are added to hearty *bigos*—cabbage and meat stews—but in the United States and elsewhere kielbasa refers to a particular garlicky and spicy sausage sold either smoked or fresh, sometimes already fully cooked. It is good broiled and served with sauerkraut and a mild mustard.

Luganega This sausage from northern Italy, which consists of pure pork shoulder, often seasoned with Parmesan cheese, is made in enormous lengths; it is narrow, unlinked, and cut to the customer's order. Italian housewives fry it in oil, adding tomatoes or sage, and serve it with polenta; or they may simply scrape all the meat out of the casings and use it as a basis for a thick pasta sauce.

Salsicce Seen hanging in Italian shops, *salsicces* have a rustic flavor and may either be highly spiced with chile peppers or may be very mild, especially if they are made simply with ground pork and pancetta. The common Italian link sausages (and bulk Italian sausage meat) are seasoned with fennel seeds and garlic and may be hot, with red chile peppers, or sweet.

Homemade sausages

While it may be a tedious job to stuff the sausage meat into its casings, nothing can be more rewarding than to see links of fresh homemade sausages emerging in your own kitchen. Using a basic chopped or ground pork mixture, any number of delicious varieties of sausages can be made by simply adding various herbs and spices, and if you have your own smoking equipment in which to smoke the sausages, the possibilities become even greater. Seasonings can range from sage, oregano, marjoram, onions, or garlic to sliced truffles and pistachio nuts. Chopped pancetta or bits of ham or smoked tongue can also be added, and the mixture can be enriched with eggs. If you don't want to bother with sausage casings, form fresh sausage meat into little patties and panfry them.

Sausage meat A basic sausage mixture consists of about half lean meat to half fat, although some may use less fat to meat. For pure pork sausages, use lean meat from the shoulder, or loin, and an equal amount of fatback. For other sausages, veal and game such as venison can be used. Fatback is the best fat to use for any type of sausage. Cut it into cubes along with the meat, and put them both through a grinder. Alternatively, you can chop them briefly in a food processor, which works particularly well, especially for the coarser-textured sausages. Take care to remove gristle and sinew from the chopped meat. The ground ingredients should be mixed together well before the seasonings are added. The best way to determine how the sausages will finally taste is to panfry a little patty of the mixture and, after tasting it, to adjust the seasonings accordingly.

Casings Some sausages, such as *crépinettes*—the flat little sausages made in vast varieties in France—are merely encased in caul fat. Others can be skinless, in which case they are bound with eggs or dipped in beaten egg and bread crumbs or simply floured. Sausage meat can also be poached wrapped in cheesecloth or foil, but natural casings are best for neatly bound sausages.

Casings can be bought in specialty butchers and from butchers' suppliers, or through mail-order sources. These 1¼-inch hog casings usually come in approximately 20-foot lengths and can then be cut and used as required. Store the casings, layered in salt, in a screwtop jar in the refrigerator.

Stuffing sausages It is not difficult to force the freshly ground, seasoned meat into the casings, and although there is a certain amount of domestic machinery available that will help you to turn out professional-looking specimens, you really only need a funnel and a pastry bag, some string, a pusher, such as the handle of a wooden spoon, and a faucet.

After disentangling the casing and soaking it in warm water until it is soft (1 to 2 hours), slip it over the faucet and run cold water through it, cutting out and discarding any sections with holes. Then cut lengths for convenient handling and wrinkle each one up over the funnel, leaving a good bit dangling at the end. Knot the end and start to feed in your mixture; force out any air bubbles, and then tie or twist the casing at intervals. Dry your handiwork for about 24 hours—in an airy, cool place if you are sure the temperature is below 40°F, on a rack in the refrigerator if not—and then cook in the usual way.

Other cooking sausages

Apart from fresh raw sausages, there are those that have been treated in some way to preserve them. Some, such as the frankfurter, have been fully cooked, but are reheated and served hot. Others have been salted and smoked and then left to mature but still require further cooking.

Saucisson de Toulouse These large, delicately seasoned sausages are made from coarsely chopped pork. They are an essential ingredient of *cassoulets*, but are also fried or broiled and served with sautéed apples and mashed potatoes.

Frankfurter It is the light smoking that gives the skins of frankfurters their familiar color. Unless marked kosher, in which case they are made of pure beef, authentic European frankfurters contain a mixture of finely ground beef and pork, and are usually quite highly spiced and salted. Genuine frankfurters are always sold in pairs. The classic accompaniments are potato salad, or sauerkraut and mustard; they are also sometimes added to potato soup.

In the United States, hot dogs—from miniature cocktail franks to "foot-longs"—may be made of pork, beef, chicken, or turkey, and are always precooked. Those labeled "beef" or "all-beef"—or "kosher"—by law contain only beef, without added fillers. Those labeled "meat" may be a combination of beef and pork, but cannot contain fillers; "frankfurters" can contain added fillers and are usually a combination of meats.

In Austria a piece of lean roast beef becomes a *wurstelbraten* when small frankfurter-type sausages called *wurstel* are inserted into it before braising.

When heating frankfurters, it is best to put them into a saucepan filled with water that is just below the boil, not actually boiling; too much heat and their thin skins will split.

Knackwurst, knockwurst This short, stumpy, precooked sausage is made of finely ground pork, beef, and fresh pork fat, flavored with salt, cumin, and garlic. Knackwurst are usually sold in pairs or in long links. They are often served with an accompaniment of sauerkraut.

Bockwurst These fresh sausages are prepared in the same way as frankfurters. In Germany they are traditionally made in the spring, when the winter-made

bock beer is ready to drink. The *Berliner bockwurst* is a smoky red cooked sausage, while a Düsseldorf favorite is bockwurst wrapped in bacon with mustard.

Cervelas The best version of this pure pork sausage, which is a type of *saucisson*, also called saveloy in the United States, comes from Lyons. It is a large, fine-grained sausage and is sometimes delicately flavored with pistachio nuts or with truffles and truffled brandy. It is best poached, or wrapped in foil, together with a few spoonfuls of red wine, and baked. It is served hot, sliced, with warm potato salad or *choucroute garnie*. It may also be wrapped in brioche dough before being baked. The English version of the cervelas, the saveloy, is a very poor substitute.

Cotechino From northern Italy, this fresh sausage is made of pork moistened with white wine and subtly seasoned with spices. It comes in various sizes and is usually salted for a few days. Cotechino is simmered with dried white beans, lentils, or other legumes, or is sometimes served simply alongside helpings of rather soupy mashed potatoes. It is one of the essential ingredients of *bollito misto*—an Italian dish of mixed boiled meats.

Zampone and stuffed goose neck Besides intestines, stomachs, and bladders, which medieval jesters used to flaunt indecently, other parts of a range of animals can be turned into interesting sausages.

Zampone—a specialty from Modena, Italy—is one such example, and is really a cotechino stuffed into a boned pig's foot. Fresh, zampone is sometimes available in Italian markets. It usually needs soaking and then simmering for about an hour, but some of these sausages are precooked and only need heating through.

Stuffed goose neck In Europe, the fat skin of a goose neck is used in a similar way. The filling consists of meat and innards—liver, stomach, heart—perhaps morels or truffles, air-cured bacon, bread crumbs, and an egg for binding it all together. It is sewn up or tied at both ends and may then be fried to a golden-brown; poached, weighted, and then eaten in slices; or simply poached in stock fortified with a little white wine.

Loukanika Sliced and then served as a Greek *mezze*—hors d'oeuvre—a loukanika usually means coarsely ground pork seasoned with coriander, marinated in red wine, stuffed into casings, and, sometimes, left to air-dry. A loukanika in Greek communities in North America, however, is a combination of ground lamb and pork seasoned with orange rind, and is usually grilled and served at barbecues or for breakfast.

Chinese sausage These narrow sausages are dark red in color with white bits of fat. They are cured and air-dried. Chinese sausages flavor a number of chicken and vegetable dishes and are sometimes mixed with rice.

Andouillette and andouille French andouillettes can contain beef, pork, or veal tripe and chitterlings (large intestines), cooked to a gelatinous tenderness. The skins are made from pig's intestines. Veal andouillettes are the most sought after. They often come covered in lard, and are broiled or sautéed and eaten with mashed potatoes or sautéed apples. The larger andouilles, which may be black-skinned, are hung to dry, and are sliced and eaten cold.

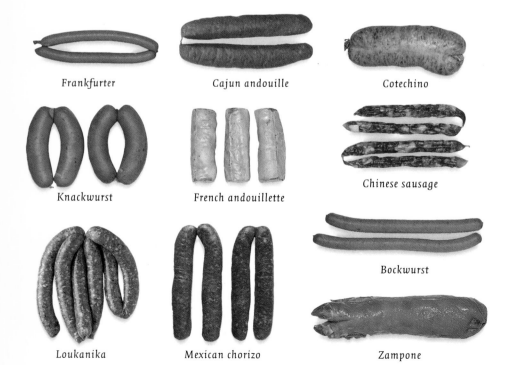

Frankfurter

Cajun andouille

Cotechino

Knackwurst

French andouillette

Chinese sausage

Loukanika

Mexican chorizo

Bockwurst

Zampone

Cajun andouille This large, rich sausage, from Louisiana, is made with lean pork and pork fat, generously spiced with cayenne or chile peppers and flavored with herbs and lots of garlic. Like the French andouille sausage, Cajun-style andouille was traditionally made with chitterlings, but this is not always the case today. It is often heavily smoked, and is the traditional sausage to use in Cajun dishes such as jambalaya and gumbo.

Blood pudding and other cooked sausages

These are the ancestors of all the fresh sausages, and contain cereal additives as well as meat.

Blood pudding These get their color from pig's blood, their richness from cubes of pork fat, and their body from oatmeal—at least it is this cereal that is always used in Scotland and northern England. Elsewhere, other cereals, even bread crumbs, may be used. In Ireland, lamb's blood goes into the local version, which is called drisheen. The French boudins noirs may, variously, also contain onions, apples, chestnuts, eggs, garlic, and the leaves of chard. They are simmered by their makers, but may afterwards be poached, baked, or fried. In France, they are sometimes served with thinly sliced, fried onions, but are at their best when broiled and served with fried apples.

Blood sausage These are also known as black sausages, but differ from blood puddings in that they have fewer cereal additives and less seasoning. They always contain pig's blood, and come in a great variety.

Blutwurst There are many varieties of German blood sausages, but perhaps the blutwurst is the best known. It is made of diced bacon and calf's or pig's lungs, and is seasoned with cloves, mace, and marjoram. It is often served with boiled potatoes and cooked apples. Other German blood sausages include *rotwurst*, which is usually sliced and eaten on bread, and *schwarzwurst*, which is smoked and air-dried, and seasoned with garlic, cloves, and pepper and salt.

Morcilla Made and smoked in Asturias, Spain, this blood sausage is made of pig's blood, fat, spices, and onions,

and is an essential ingredient of *fabada asturiana*, or bean stew. There are two varieties—ordinary morcilla, which is the most popular and has a strong smoky flavor, and *morcilla dulce*, which has a sweet, spicy flavor.

Boudin blanc Made of white meat such as chicken, veal, rabbit, or pale pork, with bread crumbs or ground rice, cream, and perhaps eggs, these sausages are precooked, and may be slowly sautéed, grilled, broiled, or baked. Called white puddings in Britain, they are delicate and should be cooked slowly and at a gentle temperature, or they will burst and brown, losing their succulent softness. As with boudin noirs, these can be served accompanied by succulent fried apples.

Haggis Although called a glorified sausage, a haggis is really in a class of its own. In Scotland it is regarded with reverence and treated with ceremony, and is often the centerpiece of special occasions. Haggis is made of roughly chopped, freshly cooked sheep's innards (liver, lungs, and heart), toasted oatmeal, onions, suet, and herbs, all loosely packed into a sheep's stomach, which is then sewn up. The filling swells as the haggis is boiled, and makes it look like a grayish baseball.

Faggot These British sausages are little round parcels that contain pig's liver and lungs, cereal, and salt pork, or bacon. They are wrapped in caul fat (the lacy, fatty membrane that lines the abdominal cavity of a pig), and are then cooked slowly in the oven. Faggots are also known as poor man's goose or savory duck.

Cayette, caillette These flat sausages from the Ardèche, in France, contain chopped Swiss chard leaves, along with a mixture of ground pork, liver, garlic, herbs, and other seasonings, wrapped in caul fat. The sausages are cooked in the oven, like the aforementioned British faggots, but are usually far more appetizing in appearance.

Slicing sausages

These are usually available either cooked or smoked. The sausages in the following list are eaten cold, often in

sandwiches or as part of a simple lunch, accompanied by bread, olives, and plenty of red wine. They are best bought uncut or freshly sliced, although it is important to remember that once they are sliced they don't last very well. The varieties that are sold presliced in vacuum-packed packets are usually mass-produced and of inferior quality.

Mortadella Made of finely ground pure pork, this is the best and most famous of all Italian sausages, patterned perhaps with green flecks of pistachio nuts and white cubes of fat. The best mortadellas, which are made in enormous sizes, come from Bologna, where only the finest ingredients are used in their production, and where the flavorings include wine and coriander.

There are, however, other varieties— some good, some very pale imitations. Although these have never been anywhere near Bologna, they are still called bologna, or Bologna sausages, or, rather contemptuously, baloney. As well as the ubiquitous bologna sandwich meat, there is an American mortadella sausage, flavored with garlic and studded with pork fat. Canned cooked versions of Italian mortadella are available in the United States, but they are vastly inferior to the real thing, which, unfortunately, cannot be imported.

Eat mortadella with a plate of mixed antipasto or in sandwiches.

Jagdwurst This German sausage owes its character to quite sizeable pieces of pork fat and rosy pork meat embedded

Blood pudding

Blood sausage

Haggis

Boudin blanc

in the pale-pink pâté base, which is slightly porous due to the fact that it is made by a process that involves the use of moist heat.

Bierwurst Although much larger in circumference than jagdwurst, this sausage has a similar taste and texture. Ham bierwurst, or *bierschinken*, shows bits of ham in each of its large slices. It is also known as beerwurst (*bier* being German for beer), and is often flavored with garlic.

Mettwurst The word *mett* is the medieval German description for lean pounded pork. There is *grosse mettwurst*, which is coarse in texture and red, and *feine mettwurst*, which is pink and smooth enough to spread.

Zungenwurst When a blutwurst is interlarded with bits of tongue, it becomes a zungenwurst. Bits of pork fat and a lot of pig's blood are used to make this dried black German sausage, which, unlike blood sausages, does not usually contain cereal additives.

Presswurst Reminiscent of a head cheese, Hungarian presswurst consists of meat from the pig's head, neck, and feet, blood, and seasonings. Cased or uncased, it is cooked, lightly pressed, and cooled until the mixture jells. Sage is the most usual flavoring.

Sulzwurst Similar to presswurst, this sausage is made of large pork pieces. It can be spread on bread, or eaten with sliced onions and accompanied by an oil and vinegar dressing.

Cervelat sausages

Almost always smoked, cervelats (not to be confused with cervelas) are far less firm than salami sausages because their maturing time is half as long. There is, however, a slight resemblance between the two. They are always moist, and, being made of finely pounded meat and fat, they have, when cut, a velvety surface and a color of mottled pink. Fat or thin, cervelats are always pliable and look rather like large frankfurters.

German cervelat Made of finely ground beef and pork, these are very popular in Germany. They are delicate, mild in taste, and easy to slice.

Holsteinerwurst Elastic enough to be sold in rings as well as straight lengths of sausages, the Holsteinerwurst

originated in Holstein on the German-Danish border. Although counted among the cervelat-type sausages, the Holsteinerwurst is so heavily smoked that it could also be categorized among the German country sausages—the sort that used to hang above heather, beech, or peat smoke in northern chimneys.

Plockwurst With its smoke-darkened skin and dark meat, which contains a high proportion of beef, this tasty sausage often comes studded with whole peppercorns.

Katenrauchwurst This cottage-smoked German sausage is produced in some quantity and is eaten throughout much of northern Europe. It is made of coarse pieces of pork, and is dark in color and firm in texture. For serving, it should be cut diagonally into thick, oval slices.

Thuringer Among the American cervelats—also sometimes called summer sausages because they keep well, not requiring refrigeration—is the coriander-spiced variety called Thuringer. It is named after a sausage-producing area in central Germany. In the Midwest, where many German immigrants settled, dozens of different cervelats are still made today.

Danish cervelat Air-dried and hot-smoked, this is rather a bouncy cervelat. Its skin is a glossy red.

Salami sausages

Among the thousands of traditional sausages, it is the salami, or *salame*, that is perhaps the most celebrated. The Italian salamis—and there are almost as many regional variations as there are villages in Italy—may be considered by purists to be the only authentic salamis, but it is worth noting that most of central Europe has made this type of tightly stuffed sausage for a number of centuries, so that German and Hungarian salamis, for example, are not pale imitations of the Italian original but indigenous sausages; only the Italian name is borrowed.

Most salamis, wherever they are made, consist of a mixture of lean pork and pork fat and sometimes beef. Occasionally veal takes the place of beef,

German cervelat

Plockwurst

Ham bierwurst

Presswurst

Zungenwurst

Bierwurst

Mettwurst

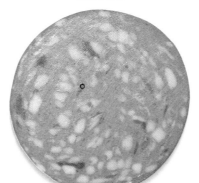

Mortadella

and sometimes donkey or wild boar is used. They can be flavored with red or white wine, with rum, with peppercorns, fennel or other herbs or spices, garlic, paprika, or chiles, and perhaps a few teaspoons of sugar.

Only a few types of salami are smoked, but all are matured for periods that may vary from a few weeks to a few months. During this time they lose a good deal of weight in the form of moisture, while the flavor of the meats and the seasonings added to them—wine, spices, garlic—in turn becomes more concentrated.

Buy salami that is a fine fresh red or pink in color, not brown or greasy, on its outside surface. If you squeeze the salami in your hand and it gives a little, you can be sure that it will be fresh and fragrant. The harder the salami sausage, the more thinly it should be sliced. Cut it at an angle, whether you serve it as an hors d'oeuvre, as they do in Italy (where the Genoese eat their local salami with raw young fava beans), or whether you mean to serve it as a meal in its own right with bread and butter.

Genoa salami This is one of the salamis that traditionally contains a high proportion of veal. To make up for the possible dryness of this meat, a little more pork fat than usual goes into the mixture; as a result, this type of salami is quite fatty.

Cotto salami Almost as well known as Genoa in the United States, this salami is garlicky and comes studded with whole black peppercorns.

Salame di Felino Made near Parma, this pure pork sausage is among the best of all the Italian salamis. Since it is made by hand, it is less perfectly geometrical in shape than most of the other sausages. Containing white wine, garlic, and whole peppercorns, it is subtle in flavor and succulent in texture. It does not keep well, but when sent abroad is encased in wax for a longer life.

Salame napolitano Seasoned with chile peppers, this salami is made with pork and beef. It is usually garlicky and extremely peppery and hot.

Salame finocchiona This pure pork salami has the unusual but very good flavor of fennel seeds. A similar salami, known as *frizzes*, is flavored with aniseed and comes in both spicy and mild or sweet varieties.

German salami Because this is not usually cured for long, it is fairly moist. It is mild with a hint of garlic and usually has a medium-fine texture.

Danish salami This is bright pink or red because it usually contains a coloring agent. Made since the fifteenth century, this is one of the types that is salted and then sometimes hung over smoke that is just cool enough to make the flavor more interesting and to brown the casing, but not warm enough to cook the meat. Danish salami tends to be fine-textured and rather fatty and to have a bland, rather predictable flavor.

Hungarian salami One of the densest of salamis, this is not necessarily made in Hungary, despite its name. Other countries, especially Italy, also produce this type of salami, which contains paprika as well as other peppers. It is surprisingly mild and is often smoked. Since it is matured for about 6 months, it is one of the really hard salamis and is ideal for slicing.

Genoa salami

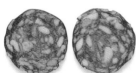

Salame napolitano

Saucisson de Lyon

Hungarian salami

Salame di Felino

Saucisson de l'ail

Rosette

Chorizo de Lomo

Pepperoni

Landjäger

Cacciatore

Kabanos

Saucisson de Lyon In France, salami is known as *saucisson sec*. Perhaps the most famous of the French salami-type sausages is the saucisson de Lyon, which is made of pure pork or of pork and beef flavored with spices and garlic. Cotton twine is used to keep the salami straight while it dries. It has a medium-fine texture with large cubes of fat, a good rose-pink color, and an excellent flavor.

Rosette Perhaps the finest of the Lyonnaise sausages is the rosette, which is ridged, large, and tapering. It is slowly matured and, due to its extra fat and strong casing, made from the lower end of the pig's intestine, is more moist than other salamis.

Saucisson de l'ail Many of the salamis of France, no less than those of Italy, are flavored with garlic. However, the one that is known as garlic sausage ("*de l'ail*") is different insofar as it is only lightly spiced, so that the strong, distinct taste of garlic predominates.

Chorizo Widely used in Spanish and Mexican cooking, chorizos are coarsely textured, strongly flavored with paprika and garlic, and either mild or hot. In Spain they are normally cured or smoked, while the Mexican version is a fresh pork sausage, which may be air-dried. Chorizos imported from Spain are usually air-dried and are suitable for

Leberkäse

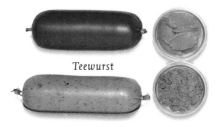

Teewurst

Liver sausage with herbs

slicing or cutting into chunks to be eaten raw or used in a dish; fresh Mexican chorizo is usually removed from the casing and crumbled before cooking. Chorizo de Lomo is one of the finest Spanish chorizos for slicing and eating.

Salsicha This salami-type Spanish sausage is usually served as a snack. It is made of a combination of finely chopped pork, pork fat, and whole white peppercorns.

Small salamis

These are usually bought whole rather than by the slice, and can be short or long.

Pepperoni A Sardinian salami, pepperoni can be mild or spicy. It is usually eaten hot. Sliced, it's a familiar pizza topping.

Kabanos These slim, garlic-flavored sausages of Polish origin are smoked until they show wrinkles. Too thin to slice, they are bought whole and then eaten in chunks.

Landjäger, gendarmes, and cacciatore Landjäger and gendarmes presumably owe their names to the uniformed officials who used to patrol and administrate the German and French Alpine regions, carrying a good supply of these hard, salami-type sausages in the pockets of their tunics. The sausages are usually smoked in little frames, which accounts for their strap-like shape. They are normally eaten in chunks.

The Italian version, called cacciatore, or "hunter's sausage," is somewhat thicker than the others. It is not usually smoked but instead is briefly cured and matured, and is just about large enough to slice. Chunks of these sausages are sometimes added to Italian stews, which they enrich and flavor.

Linguiça A slim and very garlicky Portuguese sausage, this is used in *caldo verde*, the traditional Portuguese kale and potato soup.

Pâté-type sausages

Some pâté-type sausages, such as liver sausages and teewurst, can be soft in consistency and are meant for spreading, while others, such as leberkäse, are firm enough to be sliced.

Liver sausage, liverwurst These may be large or small, curved or straight, or fine- or coarse-textured. They may contain chunks of fat, bits of liver (which is especially good in the case of goose-liver sausage), truffles, garlic, and any number of finely chopped herbs. Some liver sausages are soft and smooth and are intended for spreading, while others, such as France's Strasbourg liver sausage, which also includes pork meat and is smoked, are meant to be thickly sliced.

All liver sausages can be eaten just as they are, but they are occasionally an essential ingredient of cooked dishes: the Swedish black soup, for example, needs the Swedish *gåsleverkorv*. Flavorings, besides herbs and truffles, may include nutmeg, cinnamon, browned onions, or anchovies; where anchovies predominate, liver sausage is known as a *sardellenwurst*.

Most liver sausages are made of pig's liver mixed with pork or veal—some may contain other innards as well as liver—but there are also pure liver sausages. Calf's liver sausages are particularly good, and there are also the sausages made of goose and other poultry livers.

German liver sausage The authentic German liver sausage is almost always smoked. It is prepared by a blanching process, which tends to lead to the formation of a harmless whitish film on the natural casings. Braunschweiger is the most well known German liverwurst.

French liver sausage These have more in common with blood puddings than with the creamy German liver sausages. They are eaten hot, often with lightly sautéed apple rings.

Danish liver sausage These are made of pig's or calf's livers to which anchovy is often added. They are excellent spread on dark Danish rye bread, garnished with slices of cucumber.

Leberkäse A mixture of pork and liver baked in an oblong tin, this German sausage/pâté has no skin. Sliced, it can be eaten as it is, or it can be sautéed.

Teewurst This is the name given to small liver sausages of the spreadable type. They are usually made of a spiced, finely pounded mixture of pork and beef.

Game

In the city, most game is a luxury, and the best restaurants feature it on their menus. It is usually served carefully carved or boned on a dainty bed of exquisite vegetables. The situation is somewhat different in the countryside where, during the open season, you might be given some as a present. Fortunately, however, farm-raised— or ranch-raised—game is increasingly available, and the price should become more reasonable as game becomes more familiar on American tables again. You will find that this meat above any other is worth your time, skill, and attention. Apart from the subtlety of flavor and texture, game is considered to be one of the healthiest of meats.

To tenderize the more athletic and older creatures, particularly wild game, a marinade is useful. This, as a rule, contains vinegar to break down tough fibers, oil to add succulence, and wine, herbs, and spices to permeate the meat with flavor. There are cooked and uncooked marinades, the cooked ones being more powerful. The marinade should completely cover the meat, which should be turned periodically during the time it is steeped.

All wild game is protected by laws, which vary from country to country. These laws are intended to prevent the shooting of creatures that are too young and to allow mating and the rearing of young to take place; they are also important because the game population of any given area will vary from year to year. As a further safeguard, the numbers of any species allowed to be shot by each sportsman are limited in many parts of the world. Some species of game have been hunted almost to extinction—the American buffalo is an example of this, but fortunately it has been reintroduced and is now being successfully raised on game ranches.

Venison

Once bagged, deer becomes venison. It does not matter whether it started life in the wild as red deer, roe deer, fallow deer, white-tailed Virginia deer, axis deer, or the black-tailed variety called mule deer. The term can even be used for antelope, reindeer, caribou, elk, and moose. Nor does it matter if these animals have been bred especially for the table, have lived in the wild, or, as in the case of European roe and fallow deer, have been raised in parks; wild or semi-tame, they all become venison.

With the advent of farm-raised venison, this meat has become relatively easy to obtain. In the United States, venison is farmed in Texas, Wisconsin, and Upstate New York; many of these farms raise the axis deer, which has a fairly mild flavor. New Zealand venison, relatively mild but flavorful, has become rather popular; the collective name for the venison from the many small farms there is Cervena venison. Venison is available from game purveyors and also at many specialty butchers; the meat freezes well, so don't hesitate to try venison if frozen is your only choice.

Buying venison When buying venison, make sure that the flesh is bright red and close-grained and that the fat is clear and bright. Among the cuts game purveyors are likely to offer are the saddle and loin, both on the bone and boneless, the rack, and the leg (sometimes boneless), along with cutlets from the leg, chops or steaks, and meat for stewing. Trim off the fat before cooking venison; however, the farm-raised meat will usually have been well trimmed already.

Cooking with venison Venison is by nature a dry meat, and the fat is often replaced by pork fat or bacon before cooking—the venison having been placed first in a marinade of oil, vinegar, spices, and plenty of red wine, to which juniper berries may have been added. In Italy, venison is sometimes soaked in olive oil with excellent results.

When it is time to cook a venison roast, lift it out of the marinade and wipe it dry. Brown it in butter in a large frying pan. Then, if you like, cover the roast with a jacket of sliced fatback or strips of bacon. (Some cooks find it best to lard the meat with thick strips of fatback, then to cover it with foil.) When cooking venison, it is usual to allow 20 to 25 minutes per pound, in a fairly hot oven (375 to 400°F). The meat will be cooked when, on piercing the skin with a metal skewer or the tip of a sharp knife, the juices run out clear. Any sign of blood in the juices indicates that the meat needs more time, unless you wish to eat it rare or medium-rare.

Prepared with devotion, venison makes a memorable meal. The tenderloin, saddle, loin, and the leg make the best roasting cuts. The loin can also be eaten as chops or steaks, while the rest of the animal is usually used for sausages, stews, ragouts, and pâtés. Spicy venison chili is a favorite in Texas and on the menus of Southwestern restaurants. Smoked reindeer tongue is a delicacy in Scandinavia, as is smoked and salted reindeer meat, and moose.

Serving venison Wild venison has a strong but muted flavor, sometimes described as old lamb that tastes of beef. Farm-raised venison, however, has less of a gamy taste. In either case, it generally needs the encouragement of some sharp, sweet, spicy, or piquant accompaniment to taste its best, so serve it with red-currant jelly, cranberry sauce, a sauce of spiced cherries, or a classic Cumberland sauce. Other flavors that marry particularly well with venison include those of thyme, rosemary, lemon or orange juice (if possible from the bitter Seville orange), and spices such as cloves, cinnamon, mace, allspice, and nutmeg.

Among the many dishes that have an affinity with venison are wild rice, which is traditional—but expensive—with game in America, and the noodles or dumplings, made of pasta dough, eaten in southern Germany, Switzerland, and Austria. There venison is also sometimes served with a sauce made of sour cream blended with the pan juices. This sauce also accompanies venison in northern Germany and in Scandinavia, where it is mopped up with mashed potatoes or potato dumplings. Spiced red cabbage often appears with venison, and chestnut purée is invariably served with it in France, while both celery and celeriac complement its taste and smooth texture beautifully.

Rabbit

The rabbit is both the ancient enemy and old friend of the countryman: ancient enemy because it eats crops, and old friend because it can, in turn, be eaten.

Buying rabbit Wild rabbits are stronger-tasting than domestic ones; they are also less plump and tender. Perhaps the best is a fat, farmed rabbit that is not too young, when it will be tasteless, nor too old, when it becomes dry and tough. Rabbit meat is very lean, almost fat-free, and has a slightly sweet taste. It is also high in protein, as well as low in calories. (In short, rabbit would certainly be a great deal more popular in the United States if Americans could just get over the idea of "bunnies.") Avoid any rabbit meat that does not seem fresh (e.g., that looks discolored and has lost its resilient quality and glossiness).

Frozen rabbit is available in many supermarkets, but fresh rabbit can often be ordered by the market or at the butcher's shop. Try to find rabbit that is not frozen, as freezing tends to make it dry and fibrous. Look for pink meat, and do not be put off by a pearly sheen. Allow half a young rabbit per person.

Tenderloin of venison

Rack of venison

Leg of venison

Cooking with rabbit Although it has a definite flavor of its own, rabbit also makes a good vehicle for other flavors. This works to the lucky cook's advantage in the case of cooking the wild rabbits of Provence, which feed on the tender shoots of wild rosemary and thyme and come with an added herby flavor. Farmed rabbits, however, no longer brought up on lettuce leaves and dandelions, are unlikely to offer unexpected flavors, so it is worth adding a variety of herbs and spices to make them more interesting. Rabbits do not have to be marinated, although a large rabbit, especially a wild one, will develop a good flavor if it is marinated in white wine, olive oil, garlic, and herbs.

Rabbit stew and braised rabbit have long been favorite country dishes. The pioneers used to enjoy rabbit in a delicate *fricassée*. Once eaten as an everyday food throughout the South, rabbit featured in the traditional Cajun and Creole cooking of New Orleans, where, cooked in red wine with tomatoes and hot pepper, it was served as *lapin en matelote*.

Apart from the famous French rabbit dishes, such as *lapin à la moutarde* (rabbit with mustard), there are some splendid traditional British recipes, such as rabbit pie, flavored with salt pork or bacon, grated lemon zest, and nutmeg, or rabbit stew with bay leaves, carrots, and onions. In some parts of England, the stew is moistened with cider, which gives a delicious flavor.

In Spain, rabbit is practically a staple food. When it is not roasted, covered in olive oil and sprinkled with sprigs of rosemary or chopped garlic and parsley, it is stewed in wine or served in a light potato pastry shell. In Italy, it is cooked with tomatoes, eggplant, ham, or bacon; and Sicilians, true to their early Arab heritage, eat it with pine nuts and an *agrodolce* (sweet-and-sour) sauce made with raisins, herbs, stock, and vinegar. Scandinavians roast rabbit like hare and serve it with red cabbage.

Hare

The flesh of the hare is always a dark mahogany-brown regardless of the color of its coat, which varies from species to species. The blue Scotch hare is a first cousin of the Arctic hare of North America, called the snowshoe rabbit; this name is an example of the linguistic

confusion that has overtaken the hare, which is not helped by the fact that the highly palatable, domestically bred Belgian hare is, in fact, a rabbit. American jackrabbits are actually hares too, which becomes clear when it comes to eating them, because there can be no confusion between the strong, gamy flavor of hare and the mild and more delicate taste of rabbit.

Unless you have a sportsman to provide you with hare, it may be almost impossible to find. Specialty purveyors occasionally offer wild blue hare, and brown hare imported from Scotland.

Hare is best eaten when young, under one year of age. The meaty hind legs and the fleshy saddle are particularly esteemed in haute cuisine. The other classic cuts are the saddle or the saddle with the hind legs included, but a tender, less muscular foreleg can be more succulent than either.

Cooking with hare Hare may be marinated and then larded or wrapped in pork fatback to counteract its tendency to be dry. It can then be roasted slowly and served quite rosy if young and tender. The larger the hare, the longer it should be cooked—give it 15 to 20 minutes per pound in a medium oven (350°F).

The flavor of hare, which should never be too pronounced, is improved by the addition of cloves in moderation and red wine in abundance, and also by port, red-currant jelly, bacon, mushrooms, shallots, juniper berries, and cream or sour cream. In France noodles, in Italy polenta, and in Switzerland celeriac purée are served with roast or braised hare. In Italy, hare makes a superb pasta dish, *pappardelle alla lepre*.

Jugged hare is a famous English dish. The original method was to place the hare in a jug with herbs, vegetables, spices, and port and then to put the covered jug in a pot of boiling water; nowadays, however, the hare is often simply stewed or braised.

Wild boar

Any wild pig, whether it is male or female, once killed becomes wild boar. Although wild boar still roam the woods of the world, especially in the wilder districts of southern France, much of the wild boar found in the butcher's shop has been reared on preserves—

environments that are as similar as possible to the wild woods, but where the animals can be fed and are able to raise their young successfully.

Despite the fact that there are wild pigs to be found throughout Texas and the American Southwest, wild boar generally needs to be ordered from a specialty game purveyor.

Wild boar meat should be dark, with little fat. It tastes of pork with strong gamy overtones and, like pork, has a certain natural succulence. Younger animals, under one year, make the best eating. Very young boar may not need it, but meat from larger animals is usually tougher and requires marinating. The top part of the leg and the saddle make noble roasts; the smaller cuts, such as steaks and chops, are often broiled or braised. But no matter how you cook wild boar, it is a lengthy operation, and the meat must be thoroughly cooked, with no trace of pinkness.

In elegant French country restaurants the mounted mask of a ferocious boar with its tusks at a war-like angle may look down on you as you are served, in the autumn, *marcassin* accompanied by chestnut purée and a *poivrade* sauce, which owes its flavor to wine, spices, and Cognac. In America, where boar was introduced from Germany in the early twentieth century, steaks of wild boar may be broiled and eaten with a pepper and mushroom sauce, flavored with plenty of garlic and onion. It is also often marinated in cider and served with applesauce or sautéed apples. In German country inns, wild boar is served with a sour cream sauce, boiled potatoes, and a side dish of golden chanterelles. As with venison, a spicy accompaniment is required, such as cranberry sauce, or sour cherries poached in red wine and cinnamon.

Since boar is eaten wherever it is found, and the method of preparing it follows national traditions, it is no surprise that it is made into curry in India. And in Italy, it is used to make a prosciutto, as well as salami and other sausages (although some of these come from farm-raised animals that are a cross between a wild boar and a pig).

Other game

As Americans' tastes become more adventurous, some types of game, such as buffalo, are now being rediscovered.

Upscale restaurants have also been known to feature such items as antelope chops. But other game, such as squirrel and bear, seem somewhat less likely to become trendy. And alligator and rattlesnake—despite recipes for alligator steaks or grilled rattlesnake—surely will remain in the category of exotic game.

Buffalo is now being raised on ranches throughout the American West and Canada. The meat tastes much like beef, not at all gamy, but it is leaner and higher in protein. It may be found at some specialty butchers, but usually must be mail-ordered. The cuts are similar to those for beef, and buffalo can be cooked following any beef recipe. Buffalo chili, grilled buffalo steaks, and even buffalo rib roast can be delicious.

A decade or so ago, there was much talk about beefalo, a cross between buffalo and beef, as "the new meat"—like buffalo, the meat is lean, but with a somewhat stronger taste. However, little has been heard recently about this "pseudo" buffalo, while interest in ranch-raised buffalo is growing.

Squirrel The squirrel was once highly sought after. A sixteenth-century cook's manual ends its recipe for rabbit pie with the words: "If you cook for a lord, use squirrel instead of coney [rabbit]—it is the fitter meat for the table." The squirrel is no longer regarded as a delicacy in Europe; indeed, it is now not eaten at all and as a result has become a destructive pest.

In the American South, Brunswick stew was traditionally made with squirrel. Today chicken, or perhaps rabbit, is used. Kentucky burgoo was once a squirrel—or rabbit—dish too, but various other meats are used today. A Louisianan Creole recipe from earlier this century suggests stewing squirrel (or opossum) with garlic, herbs, red wine, and the zest of a lemon.

Bear is now so rare that few of us will be faced with the problem of having to prepare it for the pot. Those who are should know that the paw is reckoned to be the best bit, and that every part of the animal needs to be thoroughly cooked, because bear, like pork, can be dangerous if it is eaten underdone.

biltong 71
chanterelle mushroom 159
prosciutto 69

1

2

3

Cutting up a rabbit or hare

1 Cut off the hind legs by inserting a strong, pointed knife into the ball joint just above each thigh.

2 Cut off the forelegs in one piece, slicing cleanly through the rib cage.

3 Split the forelegs down the middle. The forelegs, saddle, and hind legs of this rabbit have been divided into five pieces. If you do not want to keep the saddle whole for roasting, cut it into serving-sized pieces.

Game Birds

For many cooks, one of the traditional pleasures of autumn is the arrival of game on our tables. Today, however, many of the game birds once found only in the wild are being raised on game farms, so the season is, in many cases, no longer limited to the fall. While farm-raised game birds are often milder-tasting than those in the wild, they can still be quite good.

It is the general rule that the natural foods of the bird provide the best and most appropriate company with which to send it to the table. So cranberries, juniper berries, and chestnuts, as well as watercress and celery, play their part in game bird recipes.

Wild goose

This migratory bird flies vast distances and as a result is usually more muscular and has none of the fat of the domestic goose. Like the duck, the wild goose should be eaten within a day or two of being shot. It is best well barded with fatback and roasted with a moist stuffing of apples or prunes. An older bird is best stuffed and braised in red wine or cider. Serve wild goose with red cabbage, a sour cream sauce, and perhaps a tart orange and Belgian endive salad.

Wild duck

The **mallard** is the most common variety of wild duck and also the largest—a fat mallard will feed from two to three people. The **canvasback** obligingly feeds on wild celery and the aquatic plant tape grass, which make its flavor interesting and delicate, lacking any fishy overtones. The **widgeon** is considered superior to the mallard in flavor. One bird will feed one hungry person, or two at a pinch. The **teal** is an ornamental duck, tender of flesh, and looks almost too pretty to eat. It will feed one.

Other varieties include the excellent pintail, the Nantais, the black duck, and the gadwall.

Most species of wild duck enjoy a diet of plants growing below the water and so the flavor is, according to their particular biochemical processes, more or less strong, distinctly aquatic, and, not to put too fine a point on it, fishy. This can be countered by placing a raw onion inside the bird for an hour or two (remove it before cooking) or by rubbing the bird inside and out with half a lemon dipped in salt; or you may find that it is enough just to spike the gravy with lemon juice and cayenne or Tabasco.

No matter what the species, wild duck should be cooked within 24 hours of killing. The two small nodules by the tail, which exude a fluid that helps to waterproof the bird, should be removed, as they can give the flesh a musky taste. Leaner and dryer than domestic ducks, all species of wild duck should be roasted at a high temperature on a rack, alternately basted with butter and whisky, red wine, or port; most benefit from barding before roasting. They must be served juicy and slightly pink—the longer they cook, the tougher they get. The juices that run out when the bird is carved make the best gravy, mixed with orange or lemon juice, red wine, port, and Tabasco. Skim the drippings in the roasting pan and taste—if the juices are not bitter, they too can be added to the gravy. Serve very hot, with homemade potato chips, and a tangy salad of orange, celery, and watercress, or Belgian endive and oranges. Braised wild duck is good with red cabbage.

Pigeon and squab

All varieties of pigeon—including wood pigeon, mourning dove, and other wild doves—and squabs (commercially raised young pigeons) have an agreeable beefy flavor and produce a most appetizing brown gravy. If wild pigeons have fallen from favor, it is because older birds especially can be so tough that preparing and cooking them can be difficult. Today, however, squabs, the farm-raised birds, are increasingly available both fresh and frozen in specialty markets and even in some supermarkets. Although no longer served under glass, as both squab and pheasant once were, squab appears in many upscale restaurants and makes a good special-occasion dish at home.

A Malaysian recipe recommends that pigeons be given a swig of alcohol before their thus-intoxicated and unsuspected demise. This is thought both to be kinder and to improve their taste. They are then rubbed with aniseed inside and honey outside and sautéed in sesame oil. In the Western world, it is usual to serve squab with baby peas, braised onions and mushrooms, cabbage, and bacon, or, for a homier dish, with braised red cabbage.

Partridge

Partridges are a more common sight in Europe than in the United States. In England, these round little birds explode from the stubble in small groups during autumnal country walks. The most common types are the red-legged and the gray partridge. The chuka partridge, which is related to the wild Scottish red-legged bird, is likely to be the partridge found in the marketplace. Confusingly enough, other small birds such as ruffled grouse and quail are referred to as partridge in some parts of the country. Partridges are available frozen, or sometimes fresh, at specialty butchers; a few purveyors offer partridge imported from Scotland. Partridges make the best eating when they are young—about 3 months old, weighing about 1 pound, most of which is supplied by the plump breast. Allow one bird per person.

Roast partridge is a great delicacy. In Europe, *partridge en chartreuse*—a pie of partridge, cabbage, sausage, carrots, onions, and cloves covered with pastry—is a welcome dish on a cold winter's day.

Young wild partridges and farm-raised partridges have a delicate taste that should not be overpowered by strong flavors. Place a lump of butter and two to three sage leaves inside the cavity before roasting. The more tender farmed birds can be grilled or sautéed, as well as braised or roasted. A simple gravy, sautéed potatoes or homemade potato chips, and watercress are really all that is needed with roast partridge. Cold roast partridge with a green salad is a delicious lunch.

Quail

The American quail is the bobwhite, also called blue quail, or partridge in the South. Unlike the American quail, the European quail is a migratory bird, and in Egypt and around the Mediterranean, particularly in southern Italy and Sicily, these birds are easily caught on their journey to or from North Africa. Now, however, since wild quail are scarce and are protected all the year round in many parts of the world, most birds that find their way into kitchens come from quail farms. Quail can be found frozen, and sometimes ordered fresh, at specialty butchers and high-end supermarkets. Some game purveyors offer free-range quail, which has a slightly stronger flavor than the farm-raised birds.

Quail are so small that unless you have run out of appetite, you are likely to eat at least two. They are best roasted in butter, first on one side, then the other, and finally breastside up. This keeps the meat moist—what there is of it. Make a sauce with the pan juices and a little Madeira or vermouth, and, if you like, add a few tablespoons of cream and some raisins soaked in Madeira. The birds can also be rubbed with crushed juniper, allspice, and fennel seeds or wrapped in grape leaves and then roasted. Or cook them in a casserole with shallots and garlic, softened in butter. Quail are a nice indulgence, even though more delicate in flavor than other game birds.

Most farm-raised quail weigh only about 4 ounces, but some producers are now raising "jumbo" quail, which may be as large as ½ pound. These plumper, meatier birds are suitable for broiling and grilling—marinating first is best— and braising, as well as any of the methods used for the tinier quail.

The grouse family

Grouse are neither as popular nor as common in the United States as in the British Isles, where they are deemed one of the greatest treats of late summer and early autumn, and in the rest of Europe. This is no doubt in part because grouse has a gamier taste than other small birds, which is a flavor much prized by gourmands in England and Scotland, but not always by Americans. The question of which makes better eating, partridge or grouse, is a subject of debate among serious game lovers; in England, the northern British red grouse is thought to be the best. Smaller than any of its relations, it has a delicious gamy taste.

To enjoy wild grouse, you will have to rely on a hunter friend—or perhaps on a specialty game purveyor who may import this favorite bird from Scotland in season, at a price to be sure.

Grouse are quite easy to cook to perfection. Young birds, less than 1 year old, need simply a vest of slices of bacon; roast in a hot oven for 20 minutes, until they are just pink and slightly rare. The classic way to serve them is to sit them on a piece of toast with a few straw potatoes and a little watercress. Older birds, while very delicious, take more time to prepare. They are good braised in red wine and stock with plenty of celery, onions, and carrots, and tiny pearl onions added just before the end of their cooking.

The **wood grouse** is also known as the capercaillie, and is the largest of the grouse tribe. It is a northern European bird, and owing to its habit of feeding off the tops of young pine trees, it tastes distinctly of turpentine, which is not agreeable, to say the least. Old English recipes suggest that to remove the pungent tang the bird should be soaked in milk or vinegar; another good method is to stuff the bird with raw potatoes, which are discarded after cooking.

In Scandinavia, cream plays an important part in the cooking process. In Denmark, this might take place in a covered oven dish. Toward the end of the lengthy cooking time, the bird is allowed to brown, and it is served in its sauce with a tart cranberry sauce, little gherkins, and potatoes. In Norway, a creamy, cheesy sauce is poured over the carved roasted bird.

The **ptarmigan** is a northern game bird also called the rock partridge, and is becoming scarcer. Its size is similar to that of the British red grouse, as is its taste, which makes it excellent eating. It is cooked in much the same way as grouse, but in northern Europe slices of bacon may be inserted under the skin as well as tied over the top. Sour cream goes into the sauce, or there might be a cold sauce of apples cooked in wine, blended with mayonnaise.

Pheasant

Pheasant makes delicious eating. The wild cock (male) pheasant is the more handsome, but the hen, although slighter and less gloriously plumaged, is often the plumper, juicier bird. A hen makes a superlative meal for two; a large cock can just feed four.

celeriac 149
Seville orange 165

Pheasant with Chestnuts 311–12

Quail

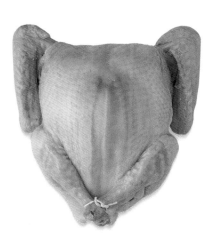

Squab

Partridge

Today pheasants are being farmed throughout the United States. Their flavor is not really the same as that of the wild bird; the free-range birds, however, are more succulent than the ordinary farmed pheasants. Pheasants are available from various game purveyors and, occasionally, at butcher shops.

In Europe, the bird is traditionally hung to improve its succulence and flavor; Americans prefer the less gamy taste of birds that are not aged this way. Since pheasant tends toward dryness—it can sometimes taste rather like a dry version of the chicken (to which it is closely related)—it usually needs a jacket of bacon (very young farm-raised birds may not need this treatment). It also needs basting with butter and/or bacon fat, partly to keep it moist, partly to make the skin crisp. Traditionally a young pheasant is served roasted, with Brussels sprouts and braised celeriac, creamed celery or braised Belgian endive, watercress, and a simple pan gravy.

Pheasant is also good braised and, cut into serving pieces and marinated, grilled over a hot fire. Older birds may need to be stewed or boiled, like older

hens. A plump pheasant boiled and served on a bed of celery, accompanied by a celery sauce with the merest dash of lemon juice, has been described as a dish for the gods. Roast pheasant with bitter orange is also good: the juice of a Seville orange is used to baste the bird toward the end of the cooking. Spiced cabbage, even mild sauerkraut, accompanies pheasant in parts of Europe.

Wild turkey

This is almost a different bird from the plump Thanksgiving turkey, with darker flesh and a stronger, more gamy taste. Wild turkey is not easy to find, although it is being farm-raised today in some parts of the country. It can be ordered from a few specialty purveyors. It is more likely to be available frozen, but fresh wild turkey can sometimes be found in the holiday season.

Woodcock and other small game birds

A few small game birds are farm-raised and may be available from specialty purveyors, but most are only found in the wild. Among these are the woodcock,

the coot, the thrush, and the snipe. Ortolans, one of the tiniest, have long been considered a delicacy in France; in the United States, however, it is illegal to hunt these birds.

The **woodcock** is gently dappled and speckled with a brown-leaf light-and-shade pattern, and has a long and very distinctive beak. It eats greedily of almost anything it comes across, and as a result of its omnivorous diet it should be a fat little bird with a fair amount of meat for its size. One bird will provide just the right amount to feed one person. Traditionally, woodcock is plainly roasted and is then served on toast together with the cooked mashed entrails, which are considered to be a delicacy by connoisseurs.

The **snipe** is a smaller bird than the woodcock, with a similar long beak. It may be cooked in the same way as the woodcock, but in Britain its more diminutive size has given it a cooking method of its own: it is encased in a hollowed-out baking potato that has been cut in half and is then carefully tied together again. When the potato is done, so is the bird.

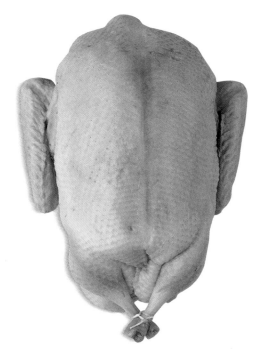

Mallard

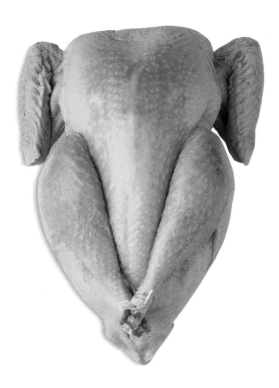

Pheasant

Poultry

When France's King Henry IV summed up his plans for making his people happy, he wished that all his subjects should be prosperous enough to enjoy a succulent chicken in a pot every Sunday. He was not the last ruler, or politician, to offer such a promise (think Herbert Hoover), but in spite of his best intentions, it is only relatively recently that poultry has moved out of the luxury class.

Chicken

In the days before factory-raised poultry became available, when chicken was a rare Sunday treat, young farmyard fowls had to be specially fattened for the table. In France, a young fowl would be roasted; an older bird, nicely stuffed and boiled with plenty of vegetables, would become *poule au pot*; and a large, heavy cockerel would go into a *coq au vin* with its heady smell of wine, onions, mushrooms, and herbs. The *backhähndl* of Austria (a young roasted rooster) was accompanied by a paprika-sprinkled salad of cucumber cut transparently thin. In America, the Sunday roast chicken would be served with fresh garden peas and possibly other vegetables, but always accompanied by mashed potatoes for dousing with flavorful gravy. With its crisp skin and juicy flesh, roast chicken is still always a success. And then, of course, there is the Jewish mother's panacea for any kind of debilitation, from flu to stress—chicken soup made from a fully matured hen, which is by far the best provider of sustaining broth.

Today we eat chicken often and in a thousand and one ways. Unlike its ancestors, the factory-raised chicken is fattened so fast and killed so young that it does not have time to develop its full flavor. Sad though this is, a modern chicken responds to being enhanced and improved and makes a good vehicle for any number of different flavors. Even so, it pays to begin with the best chicken you can find. Free-range birds undoubtedly have the best flavor because of the variety of their diet as they scratch happily for their living, and the fact that they have been able to run about in the sunshine gives them altogether more character. But even among the pale, battery-reared supermarket poultry, there are varying degrees of taste.

The diet on which the chicken has been fed will determine the color of its skin. There are, for example, the yellow corn-fed chickens, that often have richer flesh and an old-fashioned chicken flavor. But be aware that other chickens may be yellow—sometimes unnaturally so—because of additives in their diets. And a bird that has a pale skin is not necessarily lacking in flavor—despite advertising to the contrary. Kosher chickens, which are available in many supermarkets, often have more flavor than the battery-raised birds.

Chicken, whole and cut up, is sold either fresh or frozen. However, some chickens sold as fresh have actually been chilled to below the freezing point during packaging and transport; there are currently efforts by consumer advocates to prohibit producers from marketing these partially frozen chickens as fresh.

In any case, birds bought from a butcher or market will not be free-range unless specifically advertised as such. The majority will be intensively reared birds. These chickens, cut up or whole, and wrapped in plastic, are usually the cheapest variety. Frozen mass-produced chicken may be even cheaper because, provided the bird is stored at the correct temperature, it will not deteriorate. Also, for both fresh and frozen birds, the plastic wrap substantially retards the weight loss through evaporation that the unwrapped birds presented for sale in the display case undergo.

The quality of free-range chickens can vary, and they are more expensive, so if you decide to purchase these birds, you may want to try a selection from several different farms. Some of these will be more tender and flavorful than others. Needless to say, mass-produced chickens, fresh or frozen, can be rather characterless, needing quite a lot of flavoring and enhancement to make them taste of anything.

When buying frozen chicken—or the so-called fresh chicken that has been deeply chilled—avoid any with freezer burn (they will be dry and tasteless) and also those with noticeable chunks of ice between them and the bottom of their wrappings—these have at some time been partially thawed and refrozen, which is not good for the quality of the flesh. All chickens, fresh or frozen, are immersed in a bath of water as soon as they have been plucked and drawn. In the case of the fresh bird, the water has evaporated before it reaches your kitchen. In the case of the frozen bird, however, the water drains off only when the chicken is defrosted at home, and the bird ends up in a pool of pink liquid.

Thaw your frozen bird thoroughly and cook it soon afterwards. Not to do so is dangerous, since bacteria develop as the bird is exposed to the warmer temperature, and these must be killed by thorough cooking. Salmonella is always a concern when dealing with chicken, whether it has been frozen or not.

Thawing is best done slowly in the refrigerator. The second-best method is to plunge the bird into cold water. Change the water every 30 minutes or so as the bird thaws, to keep it cold. Never give a stiffly frozen chicken a bath of warm water: not only does rapid defrosting spoil the texture of the meat beyond redemption, it also promotes bacterial growth and is dangerous.

As soon as you can while it is thawing, remove the wrapped giblets from the chicken so that air can get to the cavity. Never forget to remove the giblet package from any bird before it goes into the oven. This may sound a little basic, but there have been too many surprise stuffings for the advice not to bear repetition.

Poussin, squab (baby) chicken

These are small immature birds and are, generally speaking, rather dull. They do not have a great deal of flavor, but can be good split, butterflied, and grilled over charcoal or broiled under fierce heat. Marinate in olive oil, lemon juice, and herbs before grilling or broiling. Poussin can also be tasty when roasted at high temperatures. Poussin weigh about 1½ pounds; the smaller ones almost have to be eaten with the fingers. Allow one poussin per person.

Do not confuse these small chickens with the true squab, which is a farm-raised young pigeon.

Cornish game hen
Game hens, or Rock Cornish hens, are not game birds at all but a type of small chicken that is a cross between the Cornish and White Rock breeds. They usually weigh about 1½ pounds. The smaller ones make an elegant main course at a dinner party— one for each guest—and the larger ones are just the right size to serve two.

Cornish hens are at their best roasted or butterflied and grilled or broiled. They benefit from marinating, as for poussin.

Broiler-fryer These tender young chickens, found in every supermarket, range from 2½ to 4 pounds in weight. They can be used in most recipes and are often sold cut into serving pieces.

Capon These are young neutered roosters fattened on corn or a similar diet, sometimes to an immense girth. Often considered the best chicken available, they are especially succulent because their flesh is marbled with fat, which melts during the cooking process. Capons are best roasted.

In France, fat, neutered young hens, firm and tender and as prized as capons, are called *poulardes*. The most famous come from Bresse, a district so jealous of its superiority that a true *poularde de Bresse*

proclaims its provenance by a metal disk clipped to its wing and is displayed with great pride at the poultry shop (or touted on a restaurant menu).

Stewing hen, boiling fowl Once abundant, these are now hard to find, but any of the older recipes that specify boiling fowl can be made at a pinch with a young roasting chicken. The stewing hen is an older bird and therefore a good deal tougher as well as stronger in flavor—and cheaper. But treated to long, gentle simmering, it can be made tender. Like that of a turkey, the light and the dark meat has a pronounced flavor of its own. Useful in pot pies and salads, a stewing chicken also provides a very good broth.

Roasting chicken Roasting chickens may be as small as 3 pounds or as large as 7 to 8 pounds, but they are usually

around 4 to 5 pounds. These flavorful chickens can be used in most recipes, as well as simply roasted. You should allow a 3½- to 4-pound roaster to feed four people.

Chicken parts Of course, you can also buy cut-up chicken, chicken quarters, legs, thighs (both boneless and on the bone), and whole or boneless, skinless chicken breast halves. Chicken parts are particularly convenient if you are short of time. Fried with a lovely crisp golden coating—seasoned flour, a delicate batter, or even crumbs, depending on regional allegiances—a cut-up chicken becomes wonderful Southern fried chicken. Boneless chicken breasts wrapped around a piece of chilled herbed butter, dipped in egg and bread crumbs, and then deep-fried, make the aromatic and delicious chicken Kiev that spurts hot butter when the eater's fork is inserted; it is

Cornish game hen

Poussin

Roasting chicken

Capon

Stewing hen

Broiler-fryer

a gastronomic indulgence to be sure these days, but a delicious one.

Chicken breasts and legs are staple grilling items, with barbecued chicken a classic. Chicken wings can be marinated in Asian seasonings and served as an hors d'oeuvre, while "buffalo wings," deep-fried and served with a spicy sauce and a blue cheese dressing, are an ever-popular snack. Boneless chicken thighs, a relative newcomer to the supermarket, cook much more quickly than bone-in thighs, and their dark meat offers more flavor than the ubiquitous boned breasts.

Cooking with chicken Since chicken is such a good vehicle for flavors, there are as many ways of preparing it as there are regional tastes. In Morocco, it is rubbed with honey and stuffed with ground almonds and sweet basil or with dried apricots and raisins. It is served with peanuts in the West Indies and with almonds in China, and in West Africa it is cooked inside a scooped-out melon. It is poached with truffle slivers inserted under its skin *en demi-deuil* (in half-mourning) in the higher reaches of French gastronomy, and, as one might expect, it comes with tomatoes and garlic in Italy, where, simply roasted, it is also eaten with a *salsa de fegatini*—a sauce made of chicken livers, diced ham, mushrooms, chicken stock, and Marsala.

If chicken can be said to have a special affinity with any herb, it is with tarragon. Marjoram or oregano, thyme, and, of course, parsley are good too. The best additions and flavorings for cooking a chicken are bacon, garlic, cream, yogurt, olive oil, white wine, sherry, saffron, and ginger; the best accompaniments are mushrooms, shallots, potatoes, and rice. The best fruits and nuts are raisins, walnuts, lemons, apricots, pine nuts, and almonds.

Turkey

An American Thanksgiving and an English Christmas would be incomplete without a fine, plump, roasted turkey, served with all the ceremonial trappings. You will need to calculate 1 pound per person—thus a 20-pound bird will provide twenty helpings as well as seemingly endless sandwiches, stock, and soup.

Turkeys usually weigh between 12 and 18 pounds; smaller birds, sometimes called fryer-roasters, weighing about 5 to 9 pounds, are becoming more widely available. Turkey is sold both fresh and frozen year-round. If you are buying a fresh bird, choose one with fresh-looking but not moist skin and a pearly-white, rather than purple or blue, tint to the flesh. Although frozen birds can, of course, be quite good, the taste may be rather dull. Free-range turkeys are occasionally seen at specialty markets in the holiday season, but despite their expense they are not always much more flavorful than an ordinary fresh bird.

A frozen turkey usually takes at least 48 hours to thaw. Put it in the refrigerator 2 days before you want it (or 3 days before if it is really large) and leave it there to thaw gradually. If turkey isn't completely thawed, it won't be cooked in the middle, and poultry that is not cooked through is dangerous. Once it has thawed, it should be cooked soon. Resist the temptation to prestuff the turkey in order to save time on the day of the dinner, even though there will be so many other traditional bits and pieces to see to. Get the stuffing ready the night before by all means, but refrigerate it separately and put it inside the bird just before it goes into the oven. If the stuffing sits around inside the bird, it may spoil, even if the stuffed bird is kept in the refrigerator.

Although most Americans expect their Thanksgiving turkey to be stuffed, many people find it preferable to cook the stuffing separately, for reasons of both taste and health. An unstuffed bird cooks more evenly and quickly—and because it takes longer to cook the stuffing through in a stuffed bird, the meat, especially breast meat, dries out long before the stuffing is done. Although some people insist that stuffing cooked in the bird is more flavorful because of the juices it absorbs, often it just gets soggy. Stuffing cooked separately in a casserole, added to the oven during the last hour or so as the turkey roasts, is lighter and turns golden-brown and crisp around the edges as it bakes.

Cooking with turkey Everybody has a favorite stuffing for turkey—some cooks even make a special one for the neck cavity, to make a nicely plumped-out shape under the skin, and a different one to go inside the bird. Bread cubes or crumbs combined with sautéed onions and celery, sage, and melted butter make one of the classic stuffings. Cornbread stuffing is particularly popular in the South; sausage is often featured, and many people like chestnuts in the mixture. You can also add truffles, mushrooms, celery, oysters, or prunes. A plain marjoram and onion stuffing flavored with lemon zest is good but can be rather dry in texture unless it has enough butter in it.

Some people like to cook a turkey simply, basting it only with butter, and starting it off, like a chicken, breastside down. This is an excellent way of keeping what is by nature rather a dry-fleshed bird succulent. Some like to wrap the breast with a few strips of bacon; and others to roast it wrapped in foil, which must, however, be folded back toward the end of the cooking time to give the breast a chance to become brown and crisp. In very slow cooking, which gives good results, a cup or two of white wine can be added to the juices in the roasting pan halfway through the cooking.

One noted wine and food expert compares big birds like the turkey to the cygnets (young swans) and peacocks that once upon a time counted among the greatest delicacies. "One should be content to meet them occasionally at some friend's dinner table," he says, "without troubling to order them when one is the host." It is easy to agree with him, except on traditional occasions.

For the Thanksgiving turkey the traditional accompaniments are both mashed potatoes and sweet potatoes, creamed onions or creamed celery, succotash, particularly in New England, or green peas or string beans, giblet gravy, and cranberry sauce. For an English Christmas dinner, the turkey comes with roasted potatoes, Brussels sprouts and chestnuts, gravy, bread sauce, bacon, and perhaps, if there is no sausage stuffing, a chain of crisp little sausages draped about its breast. On national holidays in Mexico—the home of the ancestral turkey, from which the domestic variety descends—the bird is eaten with *mole*, a velvety, not-at-all-sweet chocolate sauce, spiced with chiles. The Spanish, in a festive mood, stuff their turkey with sweetbreads and truffles.

All these rich meals are best enjoyed once a year and then forgotten until next time. However, we meet turkey with increasing frequency on nonfeast days.

Supermarkets now sell it in all sorts of forms, from boneless roasts to drumsticks and thighs to breasts, bone-in breast halves, and boneless cutlets and tenderloins. Because turkey is a lean meat, ground turkey and turkey sausages, spicy or sweet, are becoming ever more popular. And, more and more, the smaller fryer-roasters may appear on the barbecue grill in the summer (or even throughout the year).

Duck

A duck is an odd-shaped bird: it is a bony, flat-breasted creature covered in fat. When you carve it—and here you may come to blows with the bird before you have finished—you will find that there is not enough breast meat to go around. But hot or cold, duck has such an excellent flavor, richness, and succulence that it is well worth the occasional extravagance.

The most popular American variety of duck is the Long Island duckling. This, like the best French ducks, the small Nantais and the larger Rouen, and the English Aylesbury, is a descendant of the Imperial Peking duck, a Chinese snow-white breed of special excellence, which was once reserved for the Emperor alone.

Long Island duck is also called Pekin duck. The other most common breed in the United States is the Muscovy, or Barbary, duck, which has a stronger flavor than the Pekin. The Barbary duck is also a favorite of the French. The Moulard is the duck raised for foie gras, both in France and, increasingly, in the United States. The exceptionally plump, meaty breasts of these ducks are called magrets, and they are more likely to be available, at specialty butcher shops, than the whole birds are.

"Duckling" was once, strictly, the term for birds under 2 months old, but because our farmed ducks are usually slaughtered at a young age, it is now used more or less interchangeably with the word duck. Very young birds do not have enough meat on their bones to be worth eating; older ones can be tough. However, the best eating age and weight vary with the breed. When buying fresh duck, make sure that the duck's breast, when pinched, feels meaty.

As for how many persons a duck will feed, it is hard to say. A wit once observed that the duck was a difficult bird—too much for one, too little for two. However, two people can dine more than well even on a Long Island duckling, and three or even four, if helpings are modest, on a large Muscovy.

Ducks take quite kindly to freezing—their greater fat content, compared with that of the chicken, assures that when defrosted they retain their succulence, and the stronger flavor is not so easily frozen out. However, fresh is still better than frozen. Like chicken or turkey, frozen duck should be properly thawed in the refrigerator, and the process may take 2 or 3 days. Unlike the intensively reared chickens, which may never have set foot to ground throughout their lives, battery ducklings may have been allowed to waddle about the yard in their youth, before the fattening-up process puts an end to exercise. Frozen duck is available year-round; fresh duck may be found from early summer through the fall.

Cooking with duck Before roasting a duck, it is best to prick its skin in all the fatty places; this will allow some of the subcutaneous fat, which insulates the duck against cold water (even though a farmed duck may never have had a swim in its life), to run out during cooking. This makes a wonderful fat to use for frying potatoes. To help crisp the skin, the bird should be roasted on a rack.

Moulard duck breast (magret)

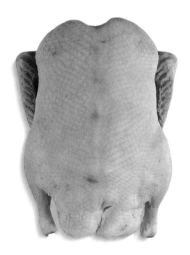

Barbary duck

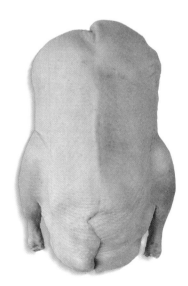

Long Island duck

Like chicken, duck is cooked and eaten in countless ways. The Chinese, especially, who domesticated ducks more than two thousand years ago, have a multitude of delicious dishes composed of crisp duck morsels with steamed pancakes. They also have tea-smoked ducks, and deep-fried ducks that are first steamed to remove the fat; sometimes called lacquered ducks, these are a glistening reddish-mahogany color and so soft that the flesh comes away at a touch. The Chinese even like to chew the brittle bones, saying that the crunchiness is the chief attraction of these vividly glazed ducks, which are often seen hanging in the windows of Chinese markets and restaurants.

The Danes and the Swedes boil their ducks with herbs. The Danes serve theirs with mustard and dark rye bread; the Swedes dish up boiled duck with a creamy horseradish sauce.

The classic flavors for duck include oranges, both bitter and sweet, turnips, and onions—all designed to offset the somewhat richly flavored meat. Other classic accompaniments are crisp sautéed potatoes, young peas, sour Morello cherries, green olives, red wine, and vermouth. Newer "inventions" include duck with eggplant and ginger, and duck with apples, walnuts, and prunes.

Goose

The raucous cry of geese was responsible for saving the ancient Romans from barbarian invasion—but that has not stopped the Italians from eating goose, richly stuffed with sausage meat, olives, and truffles. In northern Europe, St. Martin's Day, November 11, is the traditional day for eating goose. This is, presumably, an extended annual punishment meted out to these birds, whose cackling once gave away the farmyard hiding place of the modest St. Martin as he was attempting to evade admiring followers who wanted him to become Pope.

When you are buying a goose for the table, choose a young bird with a pliable lower beak and breastbone. A well-filled plump breast denotes succulence—and also good value for money. Look too for creamy skin with a warm tinge to it, almost pale apricot, without a trace of blue or brown.

A gosling, or young goose, weighs up to about 5 pounds and can hardly help being tender and delicate. At 8 to 9 months old it becomes a goose (in culinary terms it is never a gander), and, weighing 8 to 12 pounds, is in its prime. With advancing age it becomes fatter and tougher, needing longer and longer periods of braising or stewing—very delicious, but perhaps not quite the rare treat that goose is usually expected to be.

Most geese, available at specialty markets and butchers, are sold frozen. Fresh geese are more likely to be found during the holiday season.

Cooking with goose Roast goose is generally reserved for a special occasion. Goose is eaten on religious and other holidays, especially in northern Europe, where it is the traditional Christmas bird. It comes to the feast magnificently brown, with crackling skin, copious gravy, and a stuffing of tart apples, which may be layered with boiled chestnuts or raisins, or, in Scandinavia, with prunes. (A stuffing of sausage meat, it is rightly agreed, makes this bird far too rich.) In the United States, a wild rice stuffing is the classic one to use for goose, but fruit—particularly dried fruit—stuffings and those with chestnuts are also traditional. In Ireland, geese are stuffed with boiled potatoes, which successfully sop up the fat.

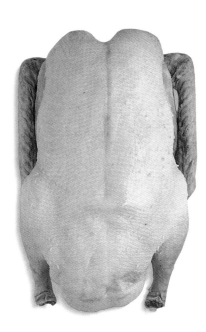

Goose

Turkey

The skin of a roasting goose needs to be well pricked, like that of a duck. Pour a pot of boiling water over the skin before placing the bird on a tall rack in a roasting pan so that it stands clear of the fat that will pour out as it cooks. (Although it is a hot and messy job, it is a good idea to pour off some of the fat halfway through the cooking.) Shortly before the end of the roasting time, some people like to sprinkle the bird with a little flour, which forms dark, crusty speckles. But the best finishing touch is to increase the heat for a few minutes just before the goose comes out of the oven and to splash the bird with drops of cold water. These hiss and evaporate as they would on a hot iron, leaving the skin delicately crisp.

Rendered goose fat makes a wonderful cooking medium, particularly good for frying potatoes. It is more highly flavored than duck fat, and each bird yields so much that in days gone by it was used not only in the kitchen but also on the farm: cows' udders were rubbed with it to prevent chapping, as were the hands of dairymaids; harnesses and leather were kept supple by its liberal application; and cold plasters made with brown paper coated with goose grease were a common household remedy for colds.

Guinea fowl

This elegantly spotted fowl, of West African ancestry, is an endearing but stupid bird. Looking somewhat like a walking sofa cushion, its feathers are a marvel of pattern—white-spotted on black, rather like old ladies' dresses— or sometimes a delicate lavender.

The domesticated breeds are delicious to eat, and are plumper than their wild counterparts, but both have a tendency to be dry and thus require regular basting during cooking with seasoned butter, or barding with strips of bacon. It is nice to put a sprig of marjoram under the bacon if you do not plan to stuff the bird. The meat of the hen is more tender than that of the male. The smaller birds are called guinea squab.

Guinea fowl taste like slightly gamy chicken. Recipes for pheasant, partridge, or smaller roasting chicken will do justice to their delicate flavor, and they make a worthwhile alternative to these. The demand for guinea fowl is not enormous, but they are on the market all year round, fresh and frozen.

Cooking with guinea fowl The prime concern when cooking this bird is to keep the flesh moist, so recipes that call for a stuffing of vegetables or butter under the skin will certainly enhance the texture. In Poland, guinea fowl is rubbed inside and out with ground ginger an hour before roasting, and it is served with chestnut purée. The traditional way to cook guinea fowl is to stuff it, roast it, and serve it with giblet gravy, just like turkey. In the west of England, it is sometimes braised in hard cider.

Older birds are good either stewed or braised in stock and cream. Breasts of guinea fowl can be sautéed in butter and served with a sauce of chestnuts, garlic, and sweet wine such as a Sauternes. A spit-roasted bird, stuffed with a bread crumb, shallot, and marjoram stuffing, sprinkled with Cognac, and served with a well-seasoned "jus," is French bourgeois cooking at its best.

Ostrich

Although still a rarity, the meat of this bird is appearing more and more frequently on restaurant menus and is occasionally available from some specialty purveyors.

Ostrich, which is being farmed in California, is rather like slightly sweet beef, with an agreeable texture similar to tender steak. Because there is very little fat, it is best to cook it like a very lean meat, such as a filet mignon, and to serve it with a sauce—for example, shallot sauce or something a little sharp and fruity, such as a rich red wine sauce enhanced with tomato.

Giblets

The giblets—the neck, heart, gizzard, and liver—of most poultry other than chicken are now removed before packing. However, the giblets of almost any bird make a wonderful stock for gravy and soups. To prepare these for cooking, remove the yellowish gallbladder sac from the liver and trim away all yellowish patches, which will give it a bitter taste. Trim the fat, blood vessels, and membrane from the heart, and discard the outer skin and inner sac containing stones and grit from the gizzard. When making a giblet stock, it seems wasteful to boil the liver too, when it is so good panfried or used in a stuffing or sauce.

Chicken and other poultry livers

Chopped chicken livers are a well-known feature of Jewish cooking, and these and other poultry livers are also an essential part of a wide range of pâtés, terrines, and stuffings. Left whole, chicken livers are delicious when wrapped in slices of bacon, skewered, and grilled, or lightly seasoned and sautéed in butter with a dash of dry vermouth.

Chicken livers, especially, appear in almost every national cuisine: in sauces for spaghetti, in risottos and pilafs, in fancy mousses and simple spreads. Much better fresh than frozen, the fine-grained pale livers are considered to be the best for eating.

Foie gras and goose liver The eighteenth-century English essayist and wit Sydney Smith memorably defined his idea of heaven as "eating foie gras to the sound of trumpets." Indeed, there can be nothing to compare with the exquisite, pale, fattened liver of the goose or duck, for which the birds are expressly bred, particularly in southwestern France.

To make foie gras, geese are force-fed until their livers weigh around 4 pounds. The best type of foie gras comes from a breed that was known even to the ancient Romans. These geese have an extra pleat of skin under the breast, which neatly accommodates the enlarged liver.

Ducks are also increasingly being bred for foie gras. Duck foie gras has been produced in the United States for the last decade or so, with the result that fresh foie gras is now available here for the first time (it is not legal to import fresh foie gras into this country). The breed preferred for foie gras is a cross of the Muscovy and the Pekin duck.

The liver of a goose on a normal diet weighs about 4 ounces. Soaked in milk it will swell a little and become even more tender when cooked. It is good sliced, fried, and added to a risotto or eaten with scrambled eggs. Pounded together with fresh bread crumbs, marjoram, chopped mushrooms, and diced bacon and bound with egg, it is sometimes used to stuff the fatty skin of the neck, to make a sort of sausage, which is then poached in giblet broth and white wine, or panfried in goose fat. In France, no part of a goose is wasted, and in some country areas even the blood is used in little patties flavored with garlic and poached.

PREPARING POULTRY

1

2

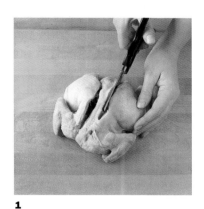

3

Trussing a chicken

1 Place the chicken breast side up with the tail toward you. Take a piece of kitchen string about 3 feet long, and place the center of the string under the tail. Cross the string over the top of the tail, then bring the string up over the ends of the drumsticks and cross it over tightly to tie them together.

2 Bring the ends of the string toward the neck end, passing them under the pointed end of the breastbone and over the thighs.

3 Turn the chicken over. Bring the string over the wings, pressing them close to the body, and tie the string over the neck flap of skin.

chicken 85–7
game birds 82–4

knives 222–4
poultry shears
225
skewers 240
trussing
equipment 230

Butterflying poultry and game birds

1 Place the bird breast side down. With poultry shears or a sharp, heavy knife, cut down along both sides of the backbone, cutting through the skin and bone. Discard the backbone, or reserve it for making stock.

2 Turn the bird over. Press firmly on the breastbone with the heel of your hand to crack the bone and flatten the breast.

3 Make a small slit in the skin on either side of the pointed end of the breast, and then insert the ends of the drumsticks into the slits.

4 Tuck the wing tips under the breast. If you like, insert two metal skewers crosswise through the bird, one at the breast and one at the thigh, to keep the bird flat during cooking.

1

2

3

4

1

2

Cutting up a chicken

1 Using a sharp knife, cut off each of the legs at the point where they join the carcass, forcing the knife blade through the ball joint and slicing down on either side of the tail.

2 Slide a large, heavy knife inside the bird and make two cuts, one on either side of the backbone and as close to the bone as possible.

3 The backbone can now be withdrawn from the body and reserved for making soup or stock.

3

4 Turn the bird over and cut along either side of the breastbone.

5 Discard the breastbone, and cut each breast half crosswise.

4

5

6 The resulting portions are two legs, two wings with a portion of breast, and two breasts. The legs can be cut in half to give two drumsticks and two thighs.

6

Stuffing chicken breasts

1 Take a boneless breast with wing bone attached, and cut off the wing tip at the second joint. Lay the breast skin side down, and push a spoonful of stuffing (a roll of chilled Garlic and Herb Butter is shown here) under the flap of skin.

2 Seal the flap closed by pressing the edges together, then roll the breast up from the pointed tip toward the wing bone. Tie with kitchen string to make a neat parcel.

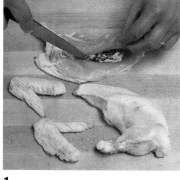

1

2

Stuffing and trussing a turkey

1 Using a small, sharp knife, cut out the wishbone, which is just under the skin at the neck end. (This will make the breast easier to carve.)

2 Spoon some of the stuffing into the neck end, putting in only as much as can be covered by the flap of neck skin. (If you like, loosen the skin over the breast by easing in your fingers, then press a thin layer of stuffing over part of the breast meat.)

1

2

3 Turn the bird over. Pull the neck skin over the stuffing and secure the flap of neck skin to the back by inserting a small skewer.

4 Turn the bird breastside up again. Loosely fill the body cavity with the remaining stuffing (the stuffing will expand as it cooks, so do not pack it).

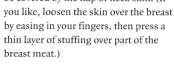

3

4

5 Using kitchen string, tie the ends of the drumsticks to the tail, looping the string under the tail and crossing it as when trussing a chicken. If you like, tuck the wing tips under the turkey, as when butterflying a bird.

5

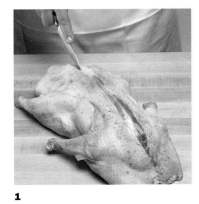

1

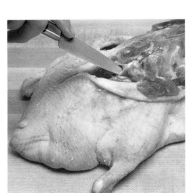

2

Boning and stuffing a duck

1 Lay the duck breastside down. Cut off the wings at the second joint (if you like, reserve the wing tips for making stock). With a strong, sharp, short knife, split the skin down the center of the back from neck to tail.

2 Cut down along each side of the backbone, starting a little behind the neck cavity, and ease back the skin and meat until you encounter the ball joint of the thigh bone.

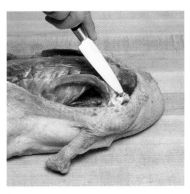

3

3 Place the knife in the thigh joint on one side of the duck, and then twist the knife to sever the thigh bone. Do the same on the other side.

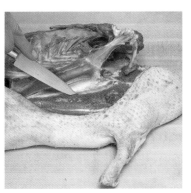

4

4 Slide the knife in the other direction toward the neck until the upper part of the wing bone is well exposed. Free the other wing bone in the same way.

5

5 Cut through the wing joints, and continue to cut, keeping the knife as close to the bones as possible, until you reach the breastbone.

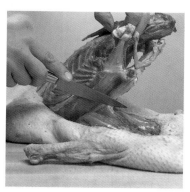

6 Lift up the bones, cutting away the remaining flesh. Take care not to puncture the breast.

6

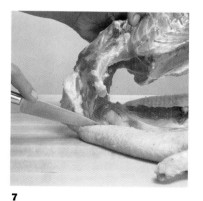

7

8

7 Sever the carcass at the neck, so that you separate it completely from the flesh. Discard the carcass, or reserve it for making stock.

8 Free the leg bones from the body, starting from the inside of the duck and pushing down on the meat, keeping the skin as intact as possible. Once you have reached the "knob" at the end of each drumstick, cut off the leg bone with a cleaver, leaving the "knob" in the duck.

9 Slip out each wing bone in exactly the same way as the leg bones, and leave the "knobs" at the end of the wing joints in the duck.

10 Stuff the bird with a stuffing of your choice; do not to pack the stuffing too tightly, or the duck will split during cooking. Using a trussing needle and kitchen string, sew up the slit.

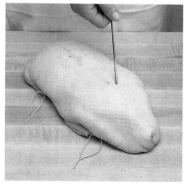

9

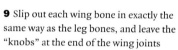

10

11 Press and push the duck into a long oval shape. Prick the bird all over, just piercing the skin, to allow the fat to run out freely as it roasts.

11

Eggs, Milk, Cream, and Butter

EGGS

For primitive man, with a mind far less tortuous than ours, there was no such thing as a chicken-and-egg dilemma: he recognized the egg as the beginning of life and celebrated it as such. It was in this context that people began to decorate eggs, as a symbol of springtime and fertility. In the kitchen, the hen's egg is celebrated still. Indispensable to the cook and rich in vitamins and minerals, it is one of the most versatile and valuable of foods.

There is a popular misconception that brown eggs are somehow better than white (indeed, the Turks simmer their eggs in coffee to give both flavor and a healthy tan). But shell color reflects neither flavor nor nutritional content, merely the breed of the laying bird. The best egg, brown or white, large or small, is one that has been freshly laid by a free-range or organically raised hen. You can determine freshness by checking the pack date on the box, which will run from 1, for January 1, up through 365, for December 31.

From the time when an egg is laid, the membranes weaken and the flavor changes. The white of a fresh egg is thick (making wonderful fried and poached eggs), getting runnier and thinner as time goes by. The yolk of a fresh egg is round and tight when the egg is cracked and dropped into a bowl or pan, while in an older egg the yolk is flatter and more fragile. It is easy enough to tell if an egg is fresh or not once you get it home. At the rounded end of the egg, between the shell and the membrane, there is a small air chamber, all but invisible when the egg is fresh, increasingly large as the egg gets older and loses moisture through its pores. So one way of assessing freshness is to hold the egg upright against a strong light and examine the size of the air space. Another is to weigh it in your hand: the heavier for its size, the better it will be. Yet another method is to lay it down in cold water: a perfectly fresh egg will stay put. An older egg will tilt; if more than 3 weeks old, it will rise to a vertical position. If an egg floats in the water, it is really getting old.

When cookbooks specify eggs they generally mean large ones. Eggs are classified by both size and quality. The best are Grade AA or A; Grade B eggs are more often used for commercial purposes. Sizes, which are determined by weight per dozen eggs, include jumbo, extra-large, large, medium, small, and peewee. Eighteenth- and nineteenth-century recipes instructing the cook to "take three dozen eggs" should cause less amusement than they do, since the average egg used to be a great deal smaller than it is today and was probably laid by a small bantam hen.

"Factory" eggs are no less nutritious than organic ones, and their flavor is standard and good, if rather slight, but they are paler and less rich-tasting than eggs from contented hens scratching about for their food in the farmyard. If you come across genuine farm-fresh eggs, perhaps at a farmers' market, you should eat them as soon as possible, especially if they have been cleaned, because washing removes the natural protective film from the shell.

It has recently been discovered that there is some risk of food poisoning, caused by salmonella bacteria, associated with eating raw or only lightly cooked eggs (the yolks are more likely to carry the bacteria than the whites). For this reason, it is recommended that pregnant women, the elderly, infants, and those whose immune systems are compromised do not eat raw or less-than-completely-cooked eggs. However, the risk is in fact quite minimal, so for most people it makes sense just to be cautious, avoiding any eggs that are cracked or dirty.

Because egg shells are porous, they are highly susceptible to neighboring smells, which is fine if they are intended for truffle omelets and stored in an egg basket together with a truffle, as they are in parts of Périgord. But it is not such a good thing if their near neighbors are strong-smelling foods such as onions or particularly ripe cheese.

Eggs should always be kept in the refrigerator—with the rounded end up to allow the air space to "breathe." For soft-boiling, some cooking, and baking, they should be at room temperature—eggs straight from the refrigerator will crack if plunged into boiling water; a cold yolk will not emulsify reliably in mayonnaise and sauces, for example; and cold whites will not whisk well.

Cooking with eggs A beaten egg will thicken soups, stews, and sauces because heat causes the egg to coagulate, thus holding the liquid in suspension. The raw yolk will emulsify with oil or melted butter, holding it in suspension, and to this happy fact we owe such good things as mayonnaise and hollandaise

Quail egg

White hen egg

Brown hen egg

Duck egg

Goose egg

sauce. An egg is sticky and sets when cooked, and so will bind mixtures for stuffings or meat loaf. As for food that is to be deep-fried, not only will a dip into beaten egg keep the bread crumbs or other coating in place, but the film of egg will protect the food from absorbing the oil and therefore becoming greasy. A light brushing of beaten egg gives a handsome sheen to pastry, and whisked whole eggs, with their millions of tiny trapped air bubbles, give a rise to cakes and other batters.

The volume of beaten egg white—so essential for light soufflés and mousses—depends on the eggs being at room temperature before you start, and on the way you whisk them—electric mixers are very fast and produce a dense texture, whereas "balloon" wire whisks, while taking a little more time and energy, do produce a desirable airy froth.

Apart from omelets and batters, such as those for crêpes or pancakes, which are cooked briefly over high heat, eggs respond best to gentle warmth—too high a heat and too long a cooking time makes them leathery.

Other eggs No other bird has proved anywhere near so obliging as the domestic hen, which lays up to 250 eggs a year, but hens' eggs are by no means the whole story.

Quails' eggs are miniature in size and beautifully speckled, and come both fresh and preserved. When fresh, they make a good first course served hard-boiled with celery salt. Poached, they look charming on salads.

Duck eggs are sold in some parts of the country. These are extremely rich with somewhat gelatinous whites—so, although they taste quite good on their own, they are best in custards, mousses, and other desserts.

Goose eggs are available in some areas. These are also rich and make very good omelets, custards, and mousses.

Ostrich eggs (one ostrich egg is equal to two dozen hens' eggs) are rarely sold these days—but Queen Victoria once tasted one made into a giant omelet and declared it to be very good.

Gull eggs are eaten in England and other parts of Europe, where they are in season briefly in the spring. They are usually eaten hard-boiled, together with celery salt for dipping.

MILK, CREAM, AND BUTTER
The cow is a good friend to mankind, providing us with one of our most complete foods. Milk contains most of the nutrients required by the human body—proteins, vitamins, and minerals, especially calcium—and, since cows are so generous with their supply, milk and other dairy products are still economical.

Milk
Most children and quite a number of adults enjoy drinking milk, and it is also used in a variety of ways, including for cooking. In Italy and Germany, it is even used for roasting pork, the meat bubbling away under a golden skin that eventually caramelizes with the pan juices into a delicious gravy. In Saudi Arabia, lamb cooked with rice in milk is the descendant of an ancient dish. There are also many other sauces and dishes cooked all over the world, as well as cheeses, yogurts, and fermented drinks, that are based on using milk that wouldn't have kept for long in the days before refrigeration.

According to the U.S. Department of Agriculture's Food Pyramid, adults should have two to three servings every day from the milk and milk products food group. Children and teenagers need more than that, and pregnant women and nursing mothers even more.

The vast majority of milk sold today is pasteurized. Pasteurization was one of the successes of Louis Pasteur, whose work in the field of microbiology led to the eradication of many animal-borne diseases. It involves heating the milk to a point where any potentially dangerous bacteria are killed, but without affecting the flavor of the milk. Ultrapasteurized milk is heated to higher temperatures than ordinary pasteurized milk, thus extending its shelf life. However, its flavor is not as good. Unpasteurized milk is now the exception and is sold as raw or untreated milk; it is usually only available at health food stores. It must always be certified—that is, stringently tested at the farm to make sure that no harmful bacteria are present.

Milk should always be heated slowly and cooked at low temperatures. A skin forms on the top when it reaches high temperatures, helping it to boil over the sides of the pan—with the resulting characteristic smell that gives the impression things are getting out of

hand in the kitchen. This skin consists of solidified proteins and milk fat. To avoid it, do not boil, but instead scald the milk: that is, remove it from the heat just as it shows a wreath of tiny bubbles around the edge. Nonstick surfaces have made it much easier to clean pans used for heating milk, but milk tends to scorch on the bottom of the pot if overheated.

If the recipe calls for the addition of flour or sugar, these, too, help prevent a skin from forming. To prevent the skin that appears on the top of a milk-based sauce such as white sauce as it sits rub a small piece of butter over the surface using the point of a knife. This makes a protective film and then can be stirred in at the last minute. Alternatively, place a sheet of plastic wrap directly on the surface of the sauce.

Fresh milk There are two main types of fresh milk, both of which need to be kept cold.
Whole milk This is milk with its natural cream intact, and has one of the best flavors of all milk sold. In days gone by the cream would rise to the top of the milk in a golden layer. Today, however, almost all milk is homogenized, which means that the milk is treated so the cream, or milk fat, is evenly suspended instead of being allowed to float to the top. Milk that has not been homogenized may be found at some small dairy farms.
Low-fat and nonfat, or skim, milk Low-fat and nonfat milk has been divested of some or all of its rich, delicious cream. Our ancestors went to great pains to avoid their milk being skimmed, even to the extent of making the urban dairyman bring his cow to the city streets to be milked on the spot so that the customers could see the cream going into the jug.

Today, the cream is removed by centrifugal force and the result is low-fat milk—called either 2 percent (meaning that it is 98 percent fat-free) or 1 percent (99 percent fat-free) milk—or nonfat, or skim, milk. Skim milk contains less than 0.5 percent milk fat. These milks are sometimes given extra milk solids and vitamins to restore something of the nutrients they have lost.

Long-life milk Heavily sterilized, these milks will keep, unopened, for much longer than ordinary pasteurized milks and are therefore extremely useful for people who are frequently away from home or without refrigeration available. Pasteurized, homogenized, and then held at a high temperature until all the bacteria have been destroyed, they will keep unopened for long periods but have a slightly peculiar taste due to the caramelization of the sugar present in milk, known as lactose. Once opened, however, or reconstituted, they must be refrigerated and will keep only as long as fresh milk.

UHT (Ultra Heat Treated) milk First pasteurized, this milk is then heated to a much higher temperature only briefly, which means that the lactose does not caramelize to such an extent that the flavor is impaired. It will keep unopened for several months and is an invaluable standby in case one runs out of fresh milk.

Evaporated and condensed milk Evaporated milk is the less sweet and sticky of the two, as it is simply regular milk from which 60 percent of the water has been removed. Whole, low-fat, and skimmed evaporated milk are all available, the reduced-fat versions increasingly so. The extra sugar in condensed milk, which is sweetened evaporated milk, helps it to keep better once opened. Condensed milk tends, however, to taste more like caramel than milk. Both can be used in cooking and can even be whipped. Before whipping, chill the milk in the freezer until soft crystals have formed around the edge.

The quality of these milks in cooking is open to controversy; some hold that they enrich foods, while others feel that they impart a strange, oversweet taste.

Dry milk Also called powdered milk, this is milk that has had almost all the water removed; powdered whole milk, nonfat milk, and buttermilk are available. Dry milk has a flat but unobjectionable flavor

that bears little resemblance to real milk. It can be used in cooking either in reconstituted or dried form and can also be used to make yogurt: a few tablespoons of powdered whole milk stirred into the measured quantity of regular milk before heating makes a thicker and slightly richer yogurt.

Soy milk and other milk substitutes Soy milk, made from soybeans, is a nondairy alternative for those allergic to cow's milk. Although high in protein, it is low in calcium; however, many soy milks are enriched with calcium. Nondairy creamers are merely whiteners, used in tea or coffee by those who are allergic to or want to avoid real milk. They are usually made with vegetable, palm, or coconut oil. Other additives such as color, emulsifiers, and sugar are also often present.

Other milk Although Western society drinks mainly cow's milk, there are many other kinds, such as sheep's, goat's, and water buffalo's milk. These latter animals, huge, black, curly-horned beasts, stand up to hot weather better than cows and are found in India and in the hottest parts of southern Italy. Desert dwellers drink camel's milk, and Tibetans drink yak's and donkey's milk, while the Kurds like mare's milk.

Both sheep and goats give milk for cheese such as pecorino, Roquefort, and Spanish Manchego, while buffalo's milk is a fine basis for mozzarella.

Goat's milk has the special quality of being highly digestible and is excellent for babies and people who have poor digestions and for those who are allergic to cow's milk. It should, however, be avoided by those who are unable to cope with a full cream content: since the

cream does not separate as easily from goat's milk as it does from cow's milk, only the whole milk is available.

Soured milk products Milk that has been soured is often looked upon as a food. It also makes a drink that is enjoyed in various parts of the world under different names and soured by various methods. *Kefir* is from the Caucasus and is slightly fermented. The Russian *koumiss* is made from mare's milk that turns sour as it hangs in leather bags on the mare's own warm sides. *Villi* is a Finnish sour milk drink. Yogurt has long been a daily food in the Balkans, parts of India, Russia, Turkey, Greece, and the Middle East, and is now widely available throughout America and Europe.

It is the presence of living lactic acid bacteria in milk that makes it go sour. This used to be a real problem before pasteurization, and it was the need to use milk before it became too sour that led to the making of yogurt and cheese. Pasteurization, however, kills the lactic acid bacteria and now milk, if left, will often not sour but just go bad. Therefore, a souring culture, such as a tablespoon of buttermilk, must be added to make soured milk products.

Acidophilus milk The bacterium *Lactobacillus acidophilus*, killed during pasteurization, is reintroduced in a dormant state to pasteurized milk to produce acidophilus milk. This milk has been found to be easily digestible even by those who cannot manage ordinary milk and is called "the milk of the future" by some nutritionists. It looks and tastes like fresh pasteurized milk. The bacterium is said to be extremely beneficial, as it helps to achieve a better bacterial balance in the digestive tract.

Buttermilk This used to be a favorite drink of farmers' children. It had a fresh, slightly acid flavor, and was made from the liquid left over when butter was made on the farm. It was also used in cooking to activate the bicarbonate of soda that was used as a leavening agent in baking to give a soft, tender quality to cakes and some biscuits. The buttermilk sold today is still delicious, but far less rich; it is made by adding a culture to nonfat or low-fat milk. Powdered buttermilk is also available.

Yogurt Credited with powers of increasing health and prolonging life, yogurt is made daily in those countries where it has a

Buttermilk

Crème fraîche

Heavy cream

Clotted cream

long history. It is eaten as a dessert and is used extensively as a marinade for meat, in soups and salads, and in cooked dishes. For cooking, yogurt can be stabilized to prevent it from separating.

Good yogurt can be easily made at home in a special yogurt maker or simply in an earthenware or ceramic bowl. Commercial yogurts are produced by injecting whole, low-fat, or skim milk with a culture of *Lactobacillus bulgaricus*, *Lactobacillus acidophilus*, or *Streptococcus thermophilus*. A combination of these strains produces the most acidic yogurts, often considered to have the best flavor. Some, especially the varieties with fruit in them, have had milk solids, sugar, cream, edible gums, and/or gelatin added, but none of these contributes to the acid flavor of yogurt, which is particularly desirable in cooking. Although some yogurts are labeled "live," the only ones that are in fact not live are those that have been sterilized.

Heavily sweetened frozen yogurts are now a popular alternative to ice cream.

Cream

Creams vary in thickness and richness according to the amount of butterfat present—the thicker the cream, the more butterfat it contains, and the richer it will be.

The thickest cream—heavy cream, or heavy whipping cream—is for spooning over strawberries, and is whipped for filling cakes and éclairs, and decorating cakes and other desserts. Whipping cream, or light whipping cream, is slightly less rich but can be used for the same purposes. Light cream, also called coffee or table cream, is ideal for soups and sauces, for pouring over puddings, and for putting into coffee.

The richer creams are usually used in soufflés, ice creams, and mousses. Light cream will not whip no matter how long you work at it, because there is not enough butterfat to trap the air bubbles—nor will half-and-half, a combination of milk and cream—so buy heavy cream or whipping cream.

Whipped cream should be light, airy, and about doubled in volume. A balloon or spiral whisk will achieve the best result. An electric mixer can be too fast and even a rotary beater too fierce. To achieve the right texture, the cream, bowl, and whisk should all be cold. A spoonful of cold milk or a crushed ice cube added to each ½ cup of cream as it thickens gives a lighter result. If you add a little sugar to the cream, the whipped result will not separate so easily, although it will not be so "pure" in flavor.

As well as varying in texture, cream can be pasteurized, which is the best for all purposes, or ultrapasteurized, when it has a long life but is not the best choice when flavor is important. Nor does it whip as well as regular pasteurized cream. Pasteurized cream is obviously the first choice and this should keep, refrigerated, for up to a week or even longer. Some farms still offer untreated cream, which may be found at local stores or farmers' markets, and this is the cream with the best flavor of all.

Sour cream Light cream is treated with a souring culture to make sour cream. Light sour cream is made from half-and-half. Nonfat sour cream has none of the taste of the real thing. In Russia, sour cream is called *smetana*, and in that country it is served on borscht and salads and is used in marinades. Germany, Austria, and Scandinavia include sour cream in sauces, which it makes glossy

and slightly acid. A plain grilled pork chop eaten from the same plate as a cucumber salad dressed with sour cream produces the most delicious mixture as the meat juices mingle with the dressing. To make your own version of sour cream, simply add a few drops of lemon juice to heavy cream (don't use ultrapasteurized).

Crème fraîche This thick cream is quite rich and has a lively, nutty taste. Real French crème fraîche is made from unpasteurized cream and so thickens naturally; in the United States, a culture or souring agent must be added to pasteurized cream to thicken it.

Clotted cream This is a specialty of the west of England, where great pans filled with milk are heated, cooled, and then skimmed of their thick, wrinkled, creamy crust. This cream is usually eaten in Devon and Cornwall piled onto scones with strawberry jam. The commercial variety, occasionally available in gourmet markets, is not nearly so good.

Butter

Experts can tell where a particular butter comes from by its color, texture, smell, and taste. There are some superb French butters—ivory-colored and rich—such as *beurre des Charentes* and *Isigny*. Melted, these resemble cream; spread on bread, their taste is sweet and nutty, and their texture firm and smooth. There are no visible beads of water on the surface (if butter has a water content of more than 12 percent, it will not cream well). The aroma of these French butters is delicate and mild. They are all that butter could hope to be and so are really worth buying for a treat, if you see them, expensive though they are.

French butters are available in gourmet markets, and some premium European-style butters are now being produced in the United States. But for normal everyday use we tend to buy butter by brand name or by price. Both for eating and cooking it is always better to buy a good-quality butter, since a low-grade butter can have an off taste that spoils the flavor of fresh vegetables and delicate sauces such as hollandaise. If possible, take your butter out of the refrigerator some time before you intend to use it. Always be sure to keep it well away from strong-smelling foods in the refrigerator, particularly anything flavored with garlic, and soft fruits such as strawberries—butter readily absorbs

Unsalted butter

Salted butter

Ghee

these flavors and, once tainted, no amount of airing will make it recover. Butter does freeze well.

Butter can either be salted or unsalted. Salting used to make all the difference between butter that stayed fresh and butter that quickly turned rancid, and it still improves the keeping qualities of our butter today. Unsalted, or sweet, butter has a sweeter taste. It makes an excellent table butter and is preferred to salted butter (sometimes labeled sweet cream butter) in cooking. Its delicate flavor lends itself particularly well to cakes, and it is better than salted butter for frying or sautéing—salted butter contains deposits that burn at a fairly low temperature. Unsalted butter has fewer of these deposits and is therefore able to withstand higher temperatures. Whipped butter has had air beaten into it to make it softer and more spreadable than regular butter. It may be either salted or unsalted. Do not substitute whipped butter for ordinary butter in recipes because the measurement will not be accurate. Butter-margarine blends, a combination of the two, tend to be cheaper than real butter.

Butter can be blended with a number of ingredients to make delicious garnishes and fillings for sandwiches. Mix it with herbs, especially parsley, to serve with fish or meat. Mixed with garlic, it makes the classic accompaniment for snails. Blended with Roquefort cheese, it is delicious with steak, and with mashed anchovies or mustard (or with lobster coral, should you have any on hand), it makes an excellent garnish for fish.

There are many superb butter sauces, including beurre blanc—velvety-smooth butter flavored with white wine, vinegar, and shallots; *sauce meunière*, a combination

of foaming butter and lemon juice; and beurre noir, which, despite its French name, should on no account be black, but rather golden-brown.

The addition of a little oil will prevent butter from burning when cooking, but perhaps the best butter for frying very delicate foods is clarified butter, from which all the milk solids have been removed. This is the ghee used in India, but only for special occasions—less expensive vegetable ghee is used for everyday cooking. Clarified butter, however, is nowhere near as appetizing on vegetables—particularly on new or baked potatoes—as fresh butter.

Fresh cream butter American butters, and most British butters, are made from fresh cream. The cream is pasteurized, deodorized, cooled, and placed in aging tanks for at least 12 hours before being turned into butter.

Ripened butter This is traditionally made in the Netherlands and Denmark, and like fresh cream butter can be either salted or unsalted. A pure culture of lactic bacteria is added to the cream, which is then allowed to ripen to develop a delicious, slightly acidic flavor before the butter is made. This butter has a slightly more pronounced taste than fresh cream butter and is also softer.

Making your own dairy foods

Many milk-based products can be made quite easily at home. Starter packets for cultured products such as yogurt can be bought from health food stores, or a little of the unflavored ready-made product can be used. All you need then are very clean, well-covered jars or bowls (not metal), an undisturbed environment, and a constant temperature to allow the culture to grow.

Store the culture in the refrigerator and always keep a little aside as a starter for your next batch.

Buttermilk To make buttermilk, add approximately 2 tablespoons of cultured buttermilk to 1 pint skim milk; cover and leave to stand in a warm place for about 12 hours. The buttermilk can be served as a drink or used to make biscuits and soda bread.

Yogurt Any kind of milk (except for evaporated or condensed milk) can be used to make yogurt. The milk should be brought almost to a boil and then kept at a temperature of 170 to 180°F for 15 minutes, before being cooled to about 110°F. The milk then needs to be kept at this temperature throughout the rest of the process so that the bacteria can grow. Stir 1 teaspoon of live yogurt or a packet of culture into each scant quart of milk and leave to stand overnight in a warm place. Alternatively, and much more reliably, buy a yogurt-making kit. When the yogurt has reached the consistency of thick custard, fruit, nuts, and so forth can be added if you like. The yogurt should then go straight into the refrigerator.

When heated, yogurt has a tendency to curdle, so if you intend to cook with it you should stabilize it first to prevent this. Make a little paste with cornstarch and water. Heat the yogurt, stir in the cornstarch paste, and simmer for about 10 minutes, until it thickens. Then proceed with the recipe.

A delicious fresh cheese can be made very easily by putting some yogurt in a cheesecloth bag and then suspending it overnight to drip (attaching it to the taps over the sink is a good method when the weather is not too hot; alternatively, place the bag in a strainer over a bowl and refrigerate it).

Cheeses

There are no rules about serving cheese at home, but if you want to enjoy this most splendid and noble of foods in all its variations, the first thing to do is to find a good cheese shop or cheese department run by someone who really cares, where the cheeses are kept in good condition and allowed to ripen to perfection quite naturally. (If cheeses are stored in an overrefrigerated storeroom, they will not mature properly.)

Having found your source, buy only one or two types of cheese at a time, taking one generous cheese or piece of cheese in perfect condition rather than all sorts of bits and pieces. Keep the cheese, if at all possible, in a cool pantry rather than in a refrigerator, with the cut surfaces covered. If no such cool place is available, keep it loosely wrapped (preferably in plastic-coated paper rather than plastic wrap, and then in aluminum foil, allowing the passage of air) in the lower part of the refrigerator. Take the cheese out a good hour before you intend to serve it, to give it time to recover from the chill, and do not leave it too long before you eat it.

The serving of cheese varies from country to country. In France, it is generally served after the salad, which has then done its job of refreshing the palate. Accompaniments are crusty French bread and good unsalted butter, which sets off the subtlest cheese flavor and will not spoil the most delicate. (Some of the richer Normandy cheeses, obviously, don't need any butter at all.) The burgundy or claret served with the main course is finished off and appreciated with the cheese.

In America, cheese is often served as an hors d'oeuvre with drinks, a practice that horrifies the French because it dulls the appetite for the meal to follow. In Britain, as in America, a cheese or cheese plate may be brought to the table at the end of an elegant dinner, after the dessert. There is usually fresh bread or plain crackers on the table for those who want them, and, again, unsalted butter. A strong cheese may be served with crisp apples or perhaps with walnuts or celery.

When cooking with cheese, it is unwise just to use up any old scraps or ends of on-the-verge-of-moldy cheese. The best results are obtained by using the best cheese. A piece of good, mature farmhouse Cheddar will be worth any amount of cheap mass-produced block cheese in cooking—and, whatever the manufacturers may say, it is possible to tell the difference. Another thing to notice is the difference between cheeses that are made from pasteurized and unpasteurized milk. The unpasteurized cheese, such as some French Bries and Camemberts, for example, will go on developing and maturing because the milk that the cheese was made from was "alive"; cheese made from pasteurized milk does not have the ability to develop the same subtle flavors and textures.

FRESH CHEESES

Also called unripened cheeses, these are the simplest of all . They are made from the curds of soured milk or from milk that has been coagulated with the help of rennet—a curdling substance obtained from the stomachs of unweaned calves or sometimes, in the case of vegetarian rennet, from artichokes. They can also be made from whey, the thin liquid left over from cheese making. The milk used for making fresh cheese has often been skimmed of its fat content, but some fresh "cream" cheeses have a high fat content and are used to make some of the world's most fattening desserts—cheesecake for one.

These cheeses used to be made on country or mountain farms from surplus milk or milk and cream, but are now usually mass-produced in factories from pasteurized milk and, sadly, in the process have become rather bland. Some fresh cheeses, however, are left to ripen and ferment for weeks or months, during which time they develop a characteristic bloom and an agreeable sharpness.

Cottage cheese Made from the curds of low-fat or skim milk and therefore having a low fat content, this cheese is eternally popular with people who are trying to lose weight. The curds are broken into different sizes, resulting in small-curd, medium-curd, and large-curd cottage cheese. Cream is sometimes added, in which case it is known as creamed cottage cheese. Its slightly acid taste makes cottage cheese a refreshing accompaniment to a summer fruit salad. In Germany, where a version known as quark is popular, it is often mixed with fruit purées; in Provence, a similar homemade white cheese, called *fromage frais*, is traditionally eaten with tiny new potatoes cooked in their skins. Pot cheese is cottage cheese allowed to drain longer than usual, so that it is drier; farmer's cheese is cottage cheese that has been drained even longer and is quite firm in texture. Scottish crowdie, a cottage cheese, is made from fresh sweet milk and butter.

Cream cheese Rich and creamy, soft and mild, cream cheese can be made from whole milk or from a combination of whole milk and cream. It is delicious when mixed with scallions, chopped raw vegetables or herbs, or nuts and raisins, and is an essential ingredient of cheesecakes. American neufchâtel is a lower-fat cream cheese. In France, a vast number of fresh cream cheeses are sold, with varying fat contents (*double crème*, *triple crème*), such as Explorateur and Brillat Savarin; when fresh cream cheese is put into heart-shaped molds and drained, it becomes the dessert *coeur à la crème*, eaten with wild strawberries.

Liptauer, Liptoi Originally from Hungary, this ripened fresh cheese is usually made from goat's or sheep's milk. It has a piquant taste and is delicious when blended with butter, seasoned with salt, paprika, and caraway seeds, and spread on rye bread.

Mysost and Gjetost In Norway, any cheese made from thickening the whey after it has been separated from the prepared curd is known as Mysost. There are several varieties, but the most popular is Gjetost. It is cooked until it looks like fudge, and has a sweet flavor.

Gomost This Norwegian fresh cheese is made from soured unsalted milk, and is similar to the French cheese known as Caillebotte. White and creamy, it is sometimes eaten with sugar or mixed with stewed or fresh ripe fruit.

Pultost This is also a Norwegian curd cheese but is stiffer and stronger than Gomost. It is made from buttermilk or whey, and caraway seeds are often added.

Ricotta Traditionally made from the whey left over from making the Italian sheep's-milk pecorino cheese, this can also be made from the whey of other cheeses, or from a combination of whey and milk, or even just milk. Its bland taste makes it ideal for mixing with fruit and raisins, or it can be eaten—as it is in Rome—with salt, or with cinnamon and sugar. It features in numerous Italian dishes—including Italian cheesecake—but it is especially good mixed with Parmesan, spinach, and Swiss chard and used to stuff ravioli.

Fromage blanc A favorite of dieters, this popular creamy French cheese is made from skim milk soured with a culture. It is excellent eaten with fresh raspberries or other berries.

Fontainebleau Rarely available outside its native France, this cream cheese is made from a mixture of curd and whipped cream and is usually eaten with sugar. It can be made at home by blending Petit Suisse with whipped cream, although this method is unlikely to produce the super-aerated result that is achieved by the commercial manufacturers.

Petit Suisse French in origin, but called Swiss because a French-employed Swiss cowman is credited with its invention, this mild, light little cream cheese is delicious with fruit and is excellent in any recipe where cream cheese is required.

Demi-sel Small and square, soft and white, this French cheese is sold under a number of brand names, but it is especially good when it has been made in Normandy, where it originated. It has a high fat content and, as its name implies, is slightly salted.

Neufchâtel This whole cow's-milk cheese (which should not be confused with American neufchâtel) comes from Normandy. It is either eaten fresh, when it is covered with the first growth of a soft white down and has a delicate taste, or is allowed to ripen until it is firm and pungent with a warm-colored, bloomy rind. It comes in a variety of shapes.

Mascarpone Originally made in Lombardy and Tuscany, this rich creamy cheese is now being produced by some American cheese makers. It is used in the popular dessert tiramisù and in other cooking; it is also eaten with fruit or sugar and cinnamon, or spread on slices of sweet bread.

Mozzarella This fresh white cheese was originally made from water buffalo's milk, but now cow's milk is often used; it is sold swimming in water to keep it fresh, and should be soft and springy. Two popular forms are *bocconcini*, or little balls, and a smoked version. Mozzarella is served as an hors d'oeuvre in southern Italy, with olive oil and freshly ground pepper, and is often part of a simple salad with just sliced ripe tomatoes, fresh basil, and a drizzle of olive oil. It is ideal for cooking, being a traditional ingredient of pizza. Once opened, always keep fresh mozzarella in a bowl of water in the lower part of the refrigerator. Commercially produced mozzarella has a less-delicate flavor and texture, but it melts better than the fresh.

Feta Crumbly and salty, this is the best known of the white cheeses ripened in brine or salt and known as "pickled cheeses." It was originally made from sheep's milk by shepherds in the mountain regions near Athens, and is popular in Greek cooking, especially crumbled into the well-known salads of tomatoes, cucumbers, and black olives, with olive oil. It's also made from goat's milk and even from cow's milk. Feta can be made less salty by soaking it in water with a touch of milk.

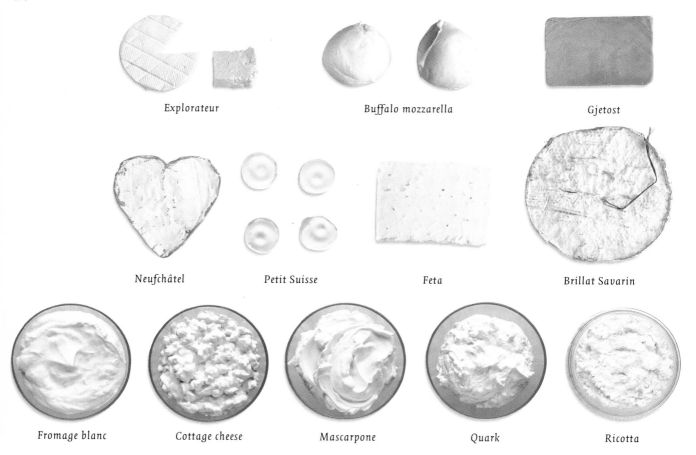

Explorateur

Buffalo mozzarella

Gjetost

Neufchâtel

Petit Suisse

Feta

Brillat Savarin

Fromage blanc

Cottage cheese

Mascarpone

Quark

Ricotta

HARD CHEESES

The word hard, when applied to cheeses, means that they have been subjected to pressure to make them dense. They will be softer or firmer according to their age.

Hard cheeses develop their various characteristics according to the milk used and the methods by which they are made. The speed of coagulation, the way the curd is cut, and whether the curd is then left to ripen or is cut again all affect the taste and texture, as does the treatment the cheese receives during the ripening process.

Some of the cheeses we have today are derivations of more famous originals; while some of them remain only copies, others have developed a character of their own and deserve to be considered as cheeses in their own right.

Grana cheeses

The hard, grainy cheeses that are collectively called *grana* are the well-known Italian grating cheeses, familiar to anyone who has ever eaten a plate of pasta or a bowl of minestrone soup. Their slow aging process and low moisture content give them their long-keeping qualities and their crumbly texture. The younger *grana* cheeses are more delicate, and they are delicious when broken into chunks and eaten accompanied with white wine.

Parmigiano-Reggiano, or simply Parmesan, the most famous and expensive of all the *granas*, is sweet and fragrant. It keeps for years, growing harder and fuller as it ages. When young, it can be served at the end of a meal. It is an essential ingredient of many of the best and most characteristic northern Italian dishes, and it is grated and then scattered on top of soups and pasta.

Of course, there are other Parmesan cheeses made in the United States, of varying quality, but none compares to the real thing. When buying Parmesan, look for the name Parmigiano-Reggiano burned in dots on the rind as proof of authenticity. The cheese should be straw-colored and brittle, with pinprick holes that are scarcely visible but give it a rocky surface. It should never be gray, sweaty, or waxy-looking, and it should always smell fresh. Ground Parmesan cheese is an extremely poor substitute for fresh.

Pecorino is the name given to *grana* cheeses made from sheep's milk, which are used in much the same way as Parmesan. A pecorino is round, hard, and white, with a yellow crust when mature (except for that made in Siena, which is red). The taste is strong, pungent, and salty. There are many varieties, which often go by the names of the districts in which they are made. Pecorino Romano is the original variety and is still considered to be the best.

Grana Padano This is made in the Po valley. Since it is cheaper than true Parmesan, it is often used in cooking.

Asiago is an ancient Italian cheese from the Veneto region, in the northeastern part of the country. Young Asiago can be served as a table cheese, but it is more familiar aged and grated for use in cooking.

Sbrinz This ancient and splendid Swiss cheese is equal in virtue to (although distinct from) Parmesan. Its texture is granular and brittle, and it has an uneven surface with pinprick holes. In central Switzerland, it is often shaved in thin slivers and served with a glass of wine. It is also ideal for cooking.

Sapsago Also known as Schabzieger or simply as green cheese, this cheese from Switzerland is a hard, truncated little green cone. Made from skimmed cow's milk, it ferments naturally, and is mixed with pulverized blue melilot, a sweet clover, which gives it its green color and characteristic pungent flavor. It smells of coriander or cumin, and is grated and used as a condiment for a variety of dishes.

Cheddar-type cheeses

These are the real grass-roots cheeses, made and eaten all over the world and used in all recipes that call for cheese.

Cheddar No hard cheese has been more widely imitated than English Cheddar, which originated in the small town of Cheddar, in Somerset, and was well established by the sixteenth century. It is a splendid all-purpose cheese, good to eat and to cook with. It has a sweet, full flavor when young and mild, and a sharp nutty flavor when mature.

Mature English farmhouse Cheddars, still made on some farms and ripened for months or years, are among the world's greatest cheeses. They compress more than ten times their weight of creamy milk when pressed into a cylindrical form and wrapped in a cloth, which may then be waxed. A traditional Cheddar weighs about 50 to 60 pounds, while small, whole Cheddars, known as truckles, usually weigh about 14 pounds. English Cheddar is also made in large blocks, but these do not develop and mature like the traditional aged cheeses.

Smaller Cheddars of various shapes are made outside England, but may vary widely from the true Cheddar flavor. In New York State, the home of the first Cheddar-cheese factory in America, a number of Cheddars are still made in varying sizes—some even come rindless. Wisconsin is also known for the quality of its Cheddars, but most of these, and most other Cheddars, like the Australian and New Zealand varieties, are made from pasteurized milk and lack the authentic taste of the English farmhouse variety. Tillamook cheese, however, from Oregon, is a delicious raw-milk Cheddar, and other smaller cheese makers are also now using unpasteurized milk for their Cheddars. Canadian Cheddars, which are still sometimes made from unpasteurized milk, have a characteristic tangy, nutty flavor. Look for Black Diamond (with a black waxed surface) or Belleville-Brockville Cheddar (in a plain waxed cloth).

Cantal Sometimes called the French Cheddar, Cantal has a smooth texture and, if the truth be told, a duller flavor than Cheddar. It is large, hard, and yellow and is made in cylindrical forms. Cantal can be good if it is allowed to mature—it takes as long to ripen as farmhouse Cheddars.

Cheshire Known as "Chester" in France and Italy, this is the oldest of the British cheeses. It is crumbly, nutty, and salty, and can be red, white, or blue. The red, which is dyed with annatto and is a marigold-orange, makes excellent eating as well as first-class soufflés. It is fat and rich, with a special piquancy that is also to be found in the white and blue varieties. The white variety, which is in fact a pale cream, is sharper than the red. It ripens faster but does not keep as well. The blue Cheshire is farmhouse-made, and is not often seen outside England.

Gloucester This is a hard and robust English cheese. Single Gloucester is made partly from skim milk and is ready for eating in 6 to 8 weeks; double Gloucester is made from whole milk and is eaten after about 4 to 6 months. In taste, Gloucester lies between Cheddar and Cheshire, although there is none of Cheshire's

Gruyère

English farmhouse Cheddar

New York Cheddar

Cantal

Appenzeller

Leicester

Parmigiano-Reggiano

Cheshire

Gloucester

Pecorino Romano

crumble about it. Farmhouse Gloucester has a natural hard crust. Gloucester is a good cooking cheese and makes delicious cheese crackers.

Caerphilly One of the mildest, softest, crumbliest, and fastest-ripening of the British hard cheeses, this was once known as the Welsh miners' cheese because it was the favorite packed lunch at the mine. The best Caerphilly today, however, is produced on farms in Somerset, England. Made from skim milk, it has a slightly sour taste and is eaten rather immature. It is suitable for dishes calling for a mild cheese flavor.

Wensleydale This English cheese is white, moist, and flaky, with a delicately sour buttermilk flavor.

Leicester The largest English cheese in circumference, Leicester is a rich orange color and shaped like an old millstone, with a hole in the center. It is mild and nutty, moist and flaky, and very different from Cheddar in texture, as the curd is shredded, making it crumbly. It melts easily and is ideal for cheese sauce.

Cotswold is an orange, somewhat crumbly cheese that is often flavored with chives and onions.

Sage Derby Once made for eating at harvest suppers, this English farmhouse cheese is a sage-flavored version of plain Derby, which is similar to Cheddar but with a denser texture and more distinct flavor. It should be aged for at least 9 months and be mottled with natural-looking sage-green streaks; at its worst, however, it is heavily marbled with a vivid green, artificial in taste, and too waxy in texture to even recall the real thing. Sage cheese is a similar cheese, tangy and succulent, made in Vermont.

Gouda-type cheeses

Firm and fat, these familiar round cheeses become drier and sharper with age. Those that are flavored with cumin or caraway seeds are particularly good with rye bread and wine.

Gouda Made in the town of Gouda, outside Amsterdam, this is the archetypal Dutch cheese. It is creamy, golden, and flattish, with a yellow, or sometimes a red, paraffin-waxed protective skin. A mature Gouda will be more pungent than a youthful one and can be very worthwhile. A black coating indicates that the cheese is 7 or more

years old, when it becomes known as an Alt Gouda. Gouda is a simple eating cheese, which in its native Holland appears for breakfast, and in the kitchen it is fried together with potatoes, grated into sauces, and melted to make a type of fondue.

Edam Made from partially skimmed milk, Edam, which is encased in a bright red or yellow coating for the export market, has a lower fat content than Gouda and is less smooth and round-flavored. When young, this cheese tends to have a somewhat boring flavor, but once aged and ripened, it acquires a rather pleasant mellowness.

Mimolette This Dutch cheese, the size and shape of a cannonball, is similar to Edam but bright orange inside, turning a rich red with age. The best Mimolettes are aged for up to 2 years and have a glorious rich flavor; however, most are young and flabby.

Leyden Resembling Gouda, this cheese has a sharp, tangy taste. It is usually flavored with caraway seeds, but varieties with cloves and cumin are also available. It is branded with the crossed keys of the arms of the Dutch city of Leyden.

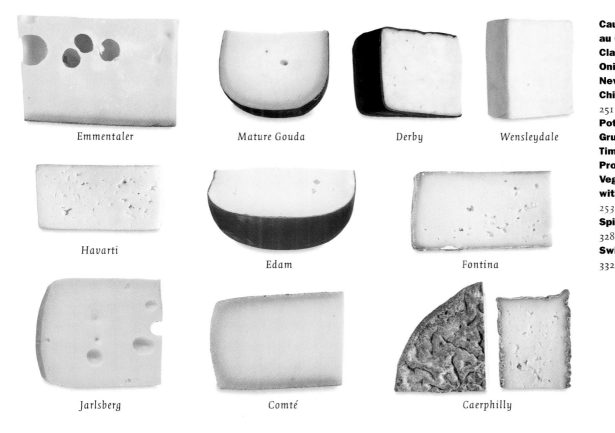

Emmentaler

Mature Gouda

Derby

Wensleydale

Havarti

Edam

Fontina

Jarlsberg

Comté

Caerphilly

Gruyère-type cheeses

Reminiscent of alpine meadows, these cheeses range from mild-flavored to a rich, full nuttiness. Straw-yellow in color, they are characterized by holes caused by gas forming during ripening. These are the cheeses most popular with French cooks, who appreciate their melting qualities, so well suited to the making of gratins and sauces.

Gruyère This Swiss cheese is made of cow's milk and has a fairly smooth rind. Ivory-yellow with tiny pinprick holes spaced far apart, it should have a waxy rather than a velvety surface. It is a main ingredient of the classic cheese fondue because of its fine melting qualities, and is also often served after a meal.

Comté This French cheese is a first cousin to Gruyère. The best, "fruitiest" cheeses are made in one-man village dairies, or *fruitières*, to which the village farmers bring their milk, and they can be identified by a green oval plaque on the outside of the whole cheese. These cheeses often have almost no holes at all.

Emmentaler, Emmental This is the famous Swiss cheese with the large holes. It comes in huge, shiny golden wheels.

Its ivory-colored interior is riddled with bubbles, which form during its fermentation and cooling period. It has a sweet flavor that grows fuller with age, and is excellent for eating and cooking.

Jarlsberg This Norwegian cheese is similar to Emmentaler but milder and more rubbery. Its taste is slightly nutty.

Fontina Made in the Piedmont area of Italy and also in Switzerland, Denmark, and the United States, this is a fat, rich, semi-firm cheese. Experts recommend the Swiss version for the table and the Italian for cooking. It melts beautifully and is used for Piedmontese *fonduta*, a fondue served with sliced white truffles.

Appenzeller, Appenzell A Swiss relation of Emmentaler, washed in a mixture of white wine and brine, this makes a tasty fondue when young. When mature, it is firm but buttery with a rich and sweet flavor.

OTHER SEMI-FIRM CHEESES

These cheeses, some of which resemble Cheddar, are characterized by their firm but elastic feel. They are sometimes soft and tender, but, unlike truly soft cheeses, do not become runny as they mature.

Caciocavallo Made from cow's milk, this Italian cheese is often smoked. An ivory-white cheese with a golden-yellow to gray rind, it is often displayed in pairs joined by a string and is usually eaten at the end of a meal. It is one of the *pasta filata*, or drawn-curd cheeses, so named because they are stretched into strands in hot water during their making.

Provolone There are two main types of provolone, another *pasta filata*, or drawn-curd cow's-milk cheese: *dolce*, which is young and usually dull; and *piccante*, which is strong and often very salty, but a good cheese. The *piccante* is sometimes available from good Italian delicatessens. It may be smoked, and is molded by hand into various shapes. Provolone is also produced in the United States.

Monterey Jack This pale California cheese, with small holes, comes in various shapes and degrees of softness. When it has a high moisture content and is quite soft, it is often simply called Jack. The harder grating varieties are called aged or dry Jack. The softer versions are often flavored with chile peppers.

Colby This cheese of Wisconsin origin is similar to Cheddar but has a more

Provolone

Manchego

Colby

Danbo with caraway

Tilsit

Monterey Jack

open texture. It is a soft, mild cheese, and does not keep as well as Cheddar.

Tilsit German in origin, this yellow cheese is pungent, with a slight smear to its surface. It is sometimes made with caraway seeds.

Havarti A cheese of the Tilsit type, this is named after the farm of one of Denmark's great cheese makers. Havarti is made in round loaf shapes and in blocks, and has a strong individual taste, somewhat sharp when mature.

Danbo and Samsoe These firm, nutty, Swiss-style cheeses are the national standbys of Denmark. (Samsoe is named after the island where it is made.)

Manchego This Spanish cheese has a high fat content, and can be made from cow's or sheep's milk. Young Manchego is called *curado*; aged (*viejo*) Manchego may be left to mature for up to 3 years, sometimes spending a year ripening in olive oil. It may be either white or yellow in color, and with or without holes, and it varies widely in taste.

Brick is an American original that was made in Wisconsin as early as 1875. It has a dry reddish-brown crust and a softish, ivory-colored interior. The flavor should be mellow, stimulating, and somewhat sweet. Depending on its age and its ripeness, it is compared to both Cheddar and limburger.

SOFT CHEESES

The characteristic flavor of the creamy-white soft cheeses comes from bacterial growths, which begin at the outer edges of the cheese and move into the center. A ripe cheese will be soft at the center and can be tested by pressing at the "waist" with the fingers. The bloomy white rinds are also a result of bacterial growth. They are natural in farm or artisan production, where the mold is present in the ripening premises themselves, and are induced in many factory-made cheeses by spraying penicillin or other bacteria onto the crust. (The same applies to cheeses with a russet-brown washed crust.)

These cheeses are considered ready for eating when soft, so they will bulge in the middle of the cut surface, although some people prefer them runny. Any smell of ammonia indicates that the cheese is past its prime. Soft cheeses are delicious on French bread. The most famous varieties come from Normandy, which has some of the best pastures and produces the richest, creamiest milk in the world (although Normandy farmers say that artificial fertilizers are changing the quality of this wonderful milk).

Brie Some decent Bries are now being produced in the United States and in other countries, including England, but French Bries are widely acknowledged to be the best. A whole round, flat Brie usually measures 14 inches across and is most commonly sold in wedges. The unliquefied part in the center of a ripe Brie is called "the soul of the Brie." Farmhouse Brie, known as Brie de Meaux *fermier*, is the creamiest variety and has a bouquet that is full and mild. Nowadays, French Bries are mainly produced in factories and there are many imitations, but do buy unpasteurized farmhouse Brie from Normandy whenever you get the chance. The Brie de Melun *affiné*, a smaller cheese, is one of the finest of all.

Camembert A farmhouse Camembert is made from raw milk, while the more common factory-produced Camembert is always made from pasteurized milk. The best Camemberts are from Normandy, and are made in rounds weighing 8 to 9 ounces. Camembert is also available in half-moons and in wedges, but unfortunately it is only reliable if ripened as a whole cheese: proportion and thickness of the crust and consistency of the interior are all affected by cutting the cheese before it is fully ripe. A well-made and properly ripened Camembert is smooth and buttery, even runny; it should not be eaten if smelling of ammonia.

Pont-l'Evêque This cheese is square, soft, and fat, with a shiny golden or reddish salty rind and a warm, ripe taste. It should always have "Pays d'Auge" and *lait cru* or *nonpasteurisé* stamped on the wrapping paper or box, proving that it comes from unpasteurized milk.

Livarot This strong, pungent cheese, still made at its village of origin and elsewhere in Normandy's Pays d'Auge, is round, weighs about 1 pound, and is about twice as tall as a Pont-l'Evêque. It has a thicker crust and, although it is obviously of the same family, has quite a distinct flavor.

Vacherin Usually banded with spruce bark, which saves it from collapse and gives it a faint aroma of resin, Vacherin is a seasonal cheese, made in winter by the French and Swiss Comté-producing farms when there isn't enough milk, or when transport is too difficult, to produce the Comté that they make in summer. When truly ripe, Vacherin is served with a spoon for digging into the buttery, runny center. It has a sweet, flowery, nutty flavor.

Maroilles Square and strong-smelling, this comes from northwestern France and is ripened for up to 4 months, with much crust-washing as it ages. It is delicious with a full-bodied wine, and is used to make *goyère* and *flamiche*, the cheese pies traditional in the region where it is produced.

Reblochon This fine cheese from the Savoy region in southeast France is smooth and creamy, with a pinkish-gold crust and a strong, ripe flavor.

Port-Salut Also called Port du Salut— "haven of rest"—after the Trappist abbey where it was first made, this is a velvety-smooth whole-milk cheese, semi-soft

or semi-firm, and mildly pungent. One variety, Fermiers-Réunis, is still made by the monks at their Champagne dairy from the unpasteurized milk of their cows. Commercial Port-Salut, made by a farmers' co-operative in the nearby village, is a more rubbery and less tasty affair, as is the Bricquebec—a similar cheese made in the monastic dairy.

Taleggio Made from whole cow's milk, this comes from Lombardy in Italy. It has a smooth pink skin with a straw-colored interior, and is fruity in flavor.

Munster, Muenster Originating in the Vosges, this is the national cheese of France's Alsace. Its interior is firm, and

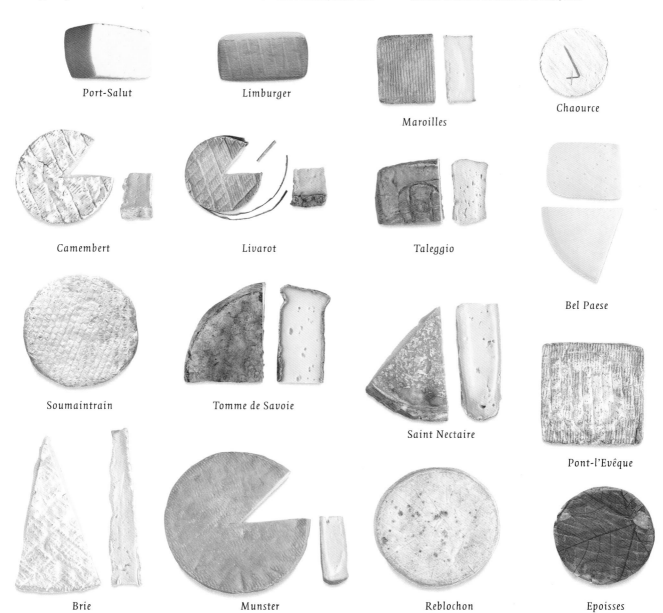

Port-Salut

Limburger

Maroilles

Chaource

Camembert

Livarot

Taleggio

Bel Paese

Soumaintrain

Tomme de Savoie

Saint Nectaire

Pont-l'Evêque

Brie

Munster

Reblochon

Epoisses

Crottin de Chavignol

Chèvre with herbs

Chèvre with herbs and garlic

Selles sur Cher

Pouligny St. Pierre

its rind red and smooth. It has a pungent smell and flavor. American Munster cheese is, unfortunately, only a pale imitation of the original, with an orange rind and a much duller flavor.

Limburger This cheese may take the form of a log, a horizontally corrugated roll, or a little disc or blob, and has a moist, pale rind and an overpowering smell. It is an acquired taste and should be eaten with robust country bread. An American cousin known as Leiderkranz is actually more like a pleasant Pont-l'Evêque than an aged Limburger.

Bel Paese is the trade name for a soft, cream-colored cheese of which there are many local and factory-made variations throughout Italy. Today it is also made in the United States. It is tender and mild.

Tommes This is the family name of a large number of rustic cheeses, made of sheep's, goat's, or cow's milk and in almost any shape. The Tommes were originally from Savoy, the southern mountain ranges of France and the eastern part of Switzerland. Tomme au Marc is coated in fermented grape *marc*—made from the pressed skins and seeds of grapes left over from wine making, which gives it its taste, while Tomme de Savoie has a nutty flavor. At least one artisan cheese maker is now producing a Tomme in the United States.

Saint Nectaire This French mountain cheese is a round, flat cheese with a dark rind and a soft, supple but not creamy, straw-colored inside. It has a nice light flavor.

Epoisses A smelly cow's-milk cheese from Burgundy, this is cylindrical and reddish on the outside, and oozy and rich inside, with a strong earthy taste.

Soumaintrain Like Epoisses, this flat, round cheese comes from Burgundy. It is semi-soft, with a sticky red-brown crust, a strong smell, and an earthy taste.

Chaource is one of those small, white, downy, luxurious-looking cheeses that give a fresh note to an otherwise heavy meal. From the Champagne district, it has a faintly acid, fruity flavor and a velvety rather than a creamy texture.

GOAT CHEESES

In Europe, there are infinite varieties of goat cheeses; most are simply described as *chèvre* (the French for goat) and have no distinguishing names. They are made on farms and dairies all over France and the Mediterranean, and are usually known as *frais* or *mi-frais*, which means fresh; *affiné*, which has been matured and should be velvety, occasionally creamy, and fairly soft; and *vieux*, which is well aged and varies from soft and creamy to rock-hard. They should not be chalky or soapy—often a sign that they have been refrigerated. Over the last decade or so, a number of artisan cheese makers have been producing goat cheese in the United States, most notably in New York and New England and in California.

The flavors of goat cheeses vary according to the ripening period, the locality and altitude (which have a bearing on the taste and quality of the goat's

milk), and on the different mold cultures used. But in general all goat cheeses, whether strong (like Pouligny St. Pierre) or mild (like Selles sur Cher), should taste nutty and sweet with a slight piquancy. Crottin de Chavignol, from the Berry region, has a reddish or gray crust and a white, piquant, and full-flavored interior.

Some goat cheeses are flavored with chives or garlic and other herbs, while others are rolled in wood ashes. Some goat cheeses are sold wrapped in leaves; they may be coated with herbs or pepper, or preserved in oil.

BLUE CHEESES

Blue cheeses first turned blue by a happy accident. Roquefort, the ancestral blue cheese, was once just a humble fresh curd cheese made of sheep's milk. Had it not been for a lovelorn shepherd, who, as legend has it, set off in pursuit of a country girl, leaving his lunchtime cheese in a limestone cave, the blue mold might never have happened. However, returning after a week or so of dalliance, the shepherd found that his lunch had changed in texture, color, and taste and become "blue." Since that time, the penicillin molds that turn cheese blue have been identified, and blue cheeses have multiplied. The cheese may be firm or creamy, buttery or brittle, and any color from chalk-white to golden-yellow.

Roquefort The veining of Roquefort, a sheep's-milk cheese, is due to *Penicillium glaucum*—now better known as *Penicillium roquefortii*—which thrives in the caves high upon the Cambalou plateau in the Aveyron region of southern France. These ancient caves, cool and damp owing to underground springs, are still used for maturing Roquefort. The blue veining is now accelerated by layering the curd with crumbled bread molds, but even so, the ripening process still takes 3 months, and the cheese will not be at its best until at least 6 months old.

A Roquefort in its prime is creamy, with green-blue marbling. *Persillé*—"parsleyed"—is the French term. It is smooth, firm, and buttery, but crumbly owing to the mold. It is strong, with the fine grain and extra pungency that sheep's milk produces. It should not be salty—although cheeses for export tend to be oversalted to prevent spoilage.

Bleu des Causses is a cheese of high quality, somewhat similar to Roquefort.

It is from the same region and has the same mold, but is made from cow's milk.

Gorgonzola Once exclusive to the Italian village of that name, this cheese is now produced all over the lush plain of Lombardy. The squat, cylindrical cheeses, made of cow's milk, are no longer matured in the local caves but rather in the great maturing houses in the district. *Penicillium mycelium* accounts for the streaking. Gorgonzola is often described as an early copy of Roquefort, but it is softer, milder, creamier, and less salty. It should have little rind, being wrapped in foil, and should be rather smooth and cream-colored, marbled with blue-gray or blue-green. The cheese should feel springy. It may smell a little musty, but not overpowering. Other Italian blues include the creamy, mild, factory-made Dolcelatte, also called Gorgonzola latte, and a smaller Mountain Gorgonzola.

Pipo Crème is a round French cheese. It was first produced as a competitor of Gorgonzola, but has its own character.

Danish Blue is similar to Roquefort but is made with cow's milk. It can be round, rectangular, or square, and is white with blue veins. It is high in fat and has the saltiness inevitable in this type of cheese. Danablu is a well-known variety.

Bresse Bleu A French cheese similar to Gorgonzola, this soft blue cheese comes from the Bresse region, which also produces a heavier blue called Bleu de Bresse, another heavy one called France Bresse, and, most recently, Belle Bressane, with a hole in the middle.

Maytag Blue is a tangy and smooth-textured blue-veined white cheese made in Iowa, is one of the best American cheeses. Maytag Dairy Farms is a family operation that has been making its cheese since the early 1940s.

Torta di Gordenza Also marketed as Gorgonzola con mascarpone, this is a cheese made from layers of piquant Gorgonzola and fresh mascarpone—a delicious combination.

Fourme d'Ambert A naturally blued cow's-milk cheese, this is from the Auvergne region of France. It is exceptional in being almost the only non-English blue cheese to have a hard crust, which is gray flecked with yellow and red. The cheese comes in cylinders weighing about 3 pounds, and is sharp and strong in flavor.

Stilton One of the few English foods to be admired by the French, this cheese is made only in Derbyshire, Leicestershire, and parts of Nottinghamshire. Although a noble cheese, Stilton is a comparative latecomer and, in fact, was never made at Stilton. But it was in that small village, in the eighteenth century, that it was first served. Stilton should be a creamy color with greenish-blue veining throughout. It should be open-textured and velvety, never dry, or salty.

Blue Wensleydale Among the other English blue cheeses, Blue Wensleydale is claimed by its admirers to be even better than Stilton. It should be creamier, sweeter, and nuttier, but is nowadays not as soft as it should be.

Dorset Blue Vinny is a hard white cheese with bright-blue veining. It is made using vegetarian rennet and skim milk, which make it agreeably sharp.

Other blues There are a number of lesser-known blue cheeses made in France and elsewhere, including a rather good blue Brie from Germany.

mascarpone 102

Gratinéed Onions in Gorgonzola Sauce 372–3

Danish Blue

Torta di Gordenza

Bresse Bleu

Maytag Blue

Dolcelatte

Roquefort

Bleu des Causses

Fourme d'Ambert

Blue Wensleydale

Dorset Blue Vinny

Stilton

Gorgonzola

Cooking Fats and Oils

Every cook in the world uses fat or oil of some kind as a cooking medium. In the cool northern regions, the fats from grass- and grain-fed animals are traditionally used, while in the hot Mediterranean countries, where the blessed olive tree grows, olive oil is the essential ingredient for a whole range of recipes. Other regions may use goose fat or mustard seed oil, grapeseed oil, or sesame oil, each of which lends its own distinctive flavor to the local dishes.

Today, the limitations of climate count for far less than they used to, and we can obtain and cook with almost any medium we choose. But the flavor of food depends very much on what fat or oil is used, and a good cook will always try to use the right medium for the right dish in order to keep the flavor as authentic as possible.

Unfortunately, the amount of fat, whether animal or vegetable, in our Western diets has come under major criticism from doctors and nutritionists. Not only do we get our chief source of energy from fats that are an "invisible" part of most foods, but we are all too likely to load up on rich fats in the form of butter and other saturated fats. Vegetable fats, unlike the traditionally suspect animal fats, do not contain any cholesterol. Olive oil, canola oil, and sunflower and safflower oil are all recommended as particularly healthy, and suitable in low-cholesterol diets.

Fats

Fats—and oils—are either saturated or unsaturated. Most saturated fats are of animal origin, and they are usually solid at room temperature. Tropical oils, including palm and coconut, are an exception, as they are saturated fats that are liquid at room temperature. Margarine and vegetable shortening are also saturated fats. Animal fats are a source of cholesterol, and all saturated fats are associated with increased cholesterol levels.

Unsaturated fats are mostly plant products and are liquid at room temperature. Monounsaturated fats, such as olive oil and canola oil, are considered somewhat more healthful than polyunsaturated fats, such as corn and soybean oil.

Margarines Margarines are based on vegetable and/or plant oils, such as corn, soybean, or canola. Some contain a small percentage of cream or milk. To make margarine, the oils are "hydrogenated," or converted from their normal liquid form into a solid one. The process of hydrogenation also turns some of the oils' unsaturated fatty acids into what are called trans-fatty acids, which some experts believe have the same—or more—harmful effects on the body as saturated fats.

With the exception of the all-important flavor, the characteristics of margarine in the kitchen are somewhat similar to those of butter. Reduced-fat, or diet, margarine is not particularly suitable for frying since it contains more water and less fat than regular margarine and splutters and burns easily; nor can it be used for baking. Soft margarines are too soft to be rubbed into flour when making pastry; to make a dough with this type of margarine, mix together the margarine, water, and only one third of the flour at the start, then gradually add the rest of the flour until you have a smooth dough that can be rolled out as usual. Whipped margarine, which, like whipped butter, has air beaten into it to make it more easily spreadable, cannot be substituted for regular margarine in baking.

Vegetable oil spreads, which usually appear alongside margarines, cannot be satisfactorily used for cooking and baking purposes.

Lard Lard is rendered pork fat; before technology took a hand, lard had to be used fresh, and it had a strong taste and no creaming properties. The lard we see now is usually light and clean-tasting. Lard is the fat of choice throughout much of South America and is preferred in many European countries as well. In the United States, lard fell out of favor a few decades ago, but recently some cooks have championed it, pointing out that it's no less healthful than many other cooking fats—and more so than some. Lard is used mainly for frying—it was once the traditional medium for English fish and chips—and for baking, where its creaming properties are appreciated. Old-fashioned Southern cooks and many European bakers find lard the essential ingredient in making a good pie crust (when making pastry, a mixture of butter and lard produces a crisp, light, crumbly texture).

The best lard is rendered from the belly fat of the pig; leaf lard, which comes from the fat around the kidneys, is considered the finest and most delicate. Lard made from other parts of the pig has a stronger taste; it is the lard most widely sold.

Suet Suet is the white fat surrounding the kidneys of cows, lambs, and other animals. In England, beef suet is widely used. It goes into sweet dishes such as Christmas pudding and into pastry for savory ones like steak and kidney pie.

Fatback This is the fat that runs along the back of the pig, over the loin. When cut into long, thin sheets, it is used primarily for barding dry meats, such as veal and game birds. The pieces are tied over the birds like a vest, and the fat bastes the flesh during cooking. Cut into strips called lardons, the fat can be inserted with a special needle into the flesh of dry meat to keep it succulent while it cooks.

Fatback is also used for lining terrines for pâtés, and for rendering lard at home. Rendering is done by cutting the fatback into very small cubes and then gently melting the cubes with a little water in a very low oven or over very low heat. When the water has evaporated, the clear liquid fat is poured off into a jar. What is left in the pan are the crisp brown cracklings—used in "cracklin' bread" and other Southern recipes. (In New Orleans, pork cracklings are sometimes called *grattons*, their French name.)

Drippings and poultry fat A good old-fashioned way of acquiring a delicious cooking fat is to strain and reserve the fat that has dripped from poultry or meat as it cooks. Once these drippings have cooled and solidified, the juice or jellied liquid underneath is removed (it is excellent when added to a gravy or stock) and any sediment from the bottom of the cake of drippings is scraped away and disposed of. Drippings from different kinds of meat and poultry should not be mixed.

Chicken fat, when rendered, is fine and delicate and is much used in Jewish cooking. Use the fat from goose or duck for bean dishes, roast vegetables, poultry, and, particularly, fried potatoes. European cooks may use beef drippings to sauté the meat for beef stews, or pork drippings for other savory dishes. (Of course, classic English Yorkshire pudding is made using the drippings from the roast beef it accompanies.) Lamb drippings smell and taste rather unpleasant and are not used very much, except in the Middle East, where lamb's tail fat is much liked.

Shortening Any hard fat, such as butter or lard, is shortening, meaning that it is capable of producing a crumbly "short" pastry crust (the greater the amount of fat in the mixture, the greater the shortening effect). However, it is the solid white vegetable fat that has claimed the name.

Vegetable shortening is made of vegetable oils or plant oils that, like the oils used for margarine, have been hydrogenated to make them solid. Its texture is light and fluffy. Although vegetable shortening makes a flaky pie crust, it is totally flavorless and will not contribute one iota toward the flavor of a pie or tart.

Oils

Oils perform the same function as fats in shallow- and deep-frying, but oils have the advantage of being reusable once or twice, as long as they are not overheated and are carefully strained after each use. (But beware of the taint of overused or overheated oil, which spoils the flavor of so much of the fried food in restaurants.)

When frying, oils should be heated slowly to the correct temperature. If the oil is not hot enough, too much will be absorbed by the food; overheating is dangerous. Overheated oil decomposes and will start to smoke; eventually, if heated further, it develops harmful toxins, and will finally catch fire. Any oil overheated by accident should be thrown away. A simple rule is to wait for a blue haze to rise from the oil but never to allow it to smoke. Test the temperature with a thermometer: the oil should be around 325°F for meat and 375°F for french fries and other vegetables. Poultry and fish come in between. If you do not have a thermometer, add a cube of day-old bread to the heated oil: if the bread turns golden and crisp in 1 minute, the temperature is roughly right.

The object of deep-frying is to seal the surface of the food. The crisp outside crust encloses a food whose inside is cooked in the heat of its own steam. The pieces to be fried should be of uniform size as much as possible so that they cook evenly. If you dip the food in batter, let the excess drain off before you put the food into the oil; if you coat it in bread crumbs, press the crumbs on well so the oil can remain as free as possible of small dark brown—and finally burned—crumbs (these will give the oil a bitter flavor).

You should be able to use good oil up to three times. Strain it well after each use. When reused, it should neither foam nor smoke excessively—the smoking point gradually decreases with age. It should not smell or look dark or thick": these are definite signs that the oil has reached the end of its useful life.

There are a great many oils in the world. Even without going into such exotics as Brazil nut oil, used as hair oil by the inhabitants of the Amazon rain forests, or juniper oil for gin, or even clove oil for toothache, the subject of oils is a complex one. To start with—and this goes a long way to help one make a sensible choice—there is the distinction between oils that are unrefined and refined.

Unrefined oils are those that have simply been cold-pressed and then left to clear and mellow for a few months before being bottled. They tend to be cloudy but come to the customer in full possession of their natural flavor and color. Often called cold-pressed oils, they are—not surprisingly—more expensive than their refined counterparts.

Refined oils have been extracted by pressure under heat. They may then be "degummed," neutralized, heated and blanched, "winterized" to keep them

à la grecque 422
coating with egg and crumbs 423

deep-fryer 239
deep-fry thermometer 233

Margarine

Shortening

Lard

Goose fat

Suet

from turning cloudy, deodorized by an injection of steam, and finally given artificial preservatives to make up for those lost in the processing.

Olive oil Indispensable for pasta dishes, salads, and many Mediterranean recipes, olive oil, the finest of all oils, varies in character from country to country. Choice is often a matter of personal preference. Generally speaking, Spanish olive oil has a strong flavor, Greek a heavy texture, Provençal a fruity taste, and Italian a nutty one.

There are two distinct means of pressing olives: the artisanal olive mill, where the olives are crushed and the oil is extracted by pressure in the traditional manner, and the modern mill where the oil is extracted mechanically. ("Cold-pressed" and "first-pressing" are terms less frequently used today because with hydraulic presses in modern mills the olive pulp is now pressed once only, and requires no heat to facilitate the extraction of the oil.)

The very best and most expensive olive oil, from whatever country it originates, is virgin oil, which is pure enough not to need refining. Virgin olive oils are separated into two grades: "extra virgin" (with 1 percent acidity) and "virgin" (2 percent acidity). Virgin oil is usually a greenish color—often helped by putting a few leaves into the press—but may also be golden-yellow. The best virgin oils come from green Provençal or Tuscan olives (the town of Lucca is reputed to

produce the best Tuscan olive oil). Use virgin olive oil in salads and in cold fish dishes, where its beautiful, fruity flavor can be most appreciated.

Cheaper oils, labeled simply "olive oil" or "pure olive oil," have been refined to remove naturally occurring impurities, and are usually blended with one another; they might then be mixed with a small proportion of virgin olive oil to improve the taste. Olive oil has a blander and less characterful flavor and a paler color than extra virgin and virgin olive oils, but is excellent for cooking. It is unsuitable for deep-frying as it cannot tolerate high frying temperatures.

Peanut oil Known also as groundnut oil in Britain and as *huile d'arachides* in France, this is the favorite cooking oil of those French chefs who do not cling to olive oil. It is also often considered to be a good replacement for olive oil, particularly when used for frying, as it has very little smell and no flavor.

Peanut oil is used for salads and mayonnaise when a delicate flavor is desired, although extra seasoning, lemon juice, or vinegar may be required. Less refined oil can impart a slight peanut flavor to food such as fried chicken. The Chinese, who use this oil a great deal in their cooking, like to flavor it by frying a few slices of fresh ginger, garlic, or scallions in it before use. Chinese oils are generally less processed than Western peanut oils and have more peanut flavor.

Corn oil This is one of the most economical oils for both shallow- and deep-frying, having one of the highest smoking points. Corn oil can also be used for salad dressings, although its detractors find it lifeless, weak, and flabby. Unrefined corn oil, sold in health food stores, has a distinct flavor of corn. Refined corn oil is practically tasteless when cold, but, surprisingly, it produces a strong and not particularly agreeable smell during frying.

Sesame oil There are various types of sesame oil. The thicker and browner the oil, the more aromatic it is. Light sesame oil has only a delicate nutty taste. It can be used for cooking and in salads and other cold dishes. Asian cooks use the dark oil, made from toasted sesame seeds, more for seasoning than for frying, as it burns easily. The Chinese believe that sesame oil added to seafood before cooking will remove fishy odors, but if it is added after cooking, to lamb, vegetables, and sauces, it imparts a pleasant, aromatic flavor.

Ali Baba's efficacious formula "Open sesame" was based on the fact that sesame pods burst open with a sharp sound to release their seeds. The jars in which the thieves hid were no doubt waiting for that year's sesame oil.

Sunflower oil Sunflower oil is light, mild, and thin. Excellent for cooking (although it has a relatively low smoke point), it is also good for using in

Almond oil

Corn oil

Olive oil

Extra virgin olive oil

Grapeseed oil

Walnut oil

combination with more expensive oils when making delicate salad dressings. It is the best oil for recipes where a fairly neutral oil is required.

Safflower oil This oil, so often confused with sunflower oil, is made from the safflower, a pretty thistle-like plant with orange, red, or yellow flowers. Usually a deep golden color, safflower oil is found refined in supermarkets and unrefined in health food stores. It is very light and can be used in the same way as sunflower oil.

Canola oil This bland oil, which is also known as rapeseed oil, is widely used in Mediterranean countries and in Asia for frying and salads. It has become quite popular in the United States in the last few years because it's the lowest in saturated fats of all oils, and only olive oil has more monounsaturated fat. Consequently, it is the oil that is most recommended for use in the diets of heart patients, and has been seized upon by other cholesterol-conscious cooks.

Canola oil is also often blended with other oils to make margarine.

Mustard seed oil Although mustard seed oil has a distinctive smell and taste when cold, most of this dissipates when the oil is heated. This oil is used in parts of India as an alternative to ghee, and in northern Indian curries. It is also used as a preservative in pickles and relishes, including Italy's colorful *mostarda di frutta*.

Soybean oil More oil is produced from the soybean than from any other plant, and most of that oil goes into blended vegetable oils, shortening, and margarines. A good brand, marked 100 percent soybean oil, is quite pleasant in salads, although it tends to have a heavy texture.

Grapeseed oil This light, aromatic oil is a by-product of the wine industry and is popular in France and Italy. The seeds yield a golden oil. Used in salads and for gentle sautéing, this oil comes into its own as the best cooking medium for *fondue bourguignonne* (beef fondue).

Walnut oil Cold-pressed from the new season's walnuts, strong, and with a deliciously nutty flavor, this is an unusual salad oil. Best mixed with a lighter oil, or used a little at a time, as a flavoring, it is especially good on a spinach salad, with a few walnuts added.

Walnut oil does not keep well, so it should be bought in small quantities as needed and kept in the refrigerator. This oil is also very expensive, and is not suitable for frying.

Almond oil When almond kernels are simply pressed, they produce a clear, pale-yellow oil. In European countries, the oil obtained from the bitter almond is used to make a fatty oil that can be used for candy making. When further processed, this oil becomes oil of bitter almonds, a flavoring now often produced synthetically.

Wheat germ oil Extracted by cold-pressing, this strong, nutty-tasting oil is mainly taken by the spoonful as a vitamin E supplement. It is also used in salad dressings, either by itself or, since it is expensive, blended with other oils.

Vegetable oils The most economical oils are the highly refined, pale-golden oils that are a blend of vegetable products—soybean, cottonseed, rapeseed, palm, and coconut oils. They have little taste, but their high smoking point makes them good for frying. Unlike other vegetable oils, palm and coconut oils are high in saturated fat and not suitable for low-cholesterol diets.

Flavored oils Many flavored oils are available in supermarkets and gourmet shops, usually based on olive oil to which flavorings such as herbs, garlic, and sun-dried tomatoes have been added. These are good in dressings, mayonnaise, and other cold preparations—heating can greatly reduce their flavor and aroma. Chile oil—sesame oil tinted red by the hot chiles that have steeped in it—is much used in Chinese cooking.

You can make your own flavored oil by dropping herbs, spices, or aromatics—for example, chiles, sprigs of rosemary or fennel, or lemon zest—into a jar or bottle of good olive oil and leaving it to steep for about a month so that the flavoring can permeate the natural olive oil flavor. A good mixture to use for Provençal cooking would be tiny dried chiles, thyme, and peppercorns.

Peanut oil

Safflower oil

Asian sesame oil

Sunflower oil

Soybean oil

Canola oil

Grains, Thickeners, and Breads

GRAINS

Besides yielding flour for our daily bread, grains are the staple foods of many countries. The polenta of Italy, the couscous of North Africa, the kasha of Russia, the porridge of Scotland, and countless other grain dishes are all basically the same thing: a local grain, in one form or another, cooked in steam or boiling water until swollen and tender, and then eaten either on its own or with whatever else makes up the local diet.

Wheat

One of the first cereals to be cultivated, wheat has become the most valuable of all food grains, widely used in all its stages, from whole and unadulterated to finely milled and sifted. When "flour" is called for in modern recipes, it is wheat flour that is meant. Broadly speaking, the wheat flours can be divided into those made from the high-gluten hard wheats grown in hot, dry areas and used for bread and pasta and the soft wheat varieties grown in temperate places, suitable for cakes, cookies, and general use. The terms spring wheat and winter wheat refer to the time of year the wheat is planted, not to any specific variety.

Wheat berries or whole wheat grains are available in health food stores. To eat them as a grain, soak them overnight before cooking and then boil in plenty of water for about 1 hour. Eat them in the same way as rice with meat, fish, or vegetables, or mixed into a salad.

Cracked wheat is simply the whole wheat berries cracked between rollers. It is eaten in the same way as wheat berries, but takes only about 20 minutes to cook. It is also good cooked like porridge as a hot breakfast cereal.

Bulgur (sometimes called burghul) is wheat that has been parboiled or steamed; it is then dried and some of the bran removed before the wheat is cracked. This process makes the grain easier to cook and gives it a less pronounced flavor and a lighter texture. Eat it in place of rice, or in the Lebanese salad called tabbouleh, for which bulgur is mixed with chopped onions, parsley and mint, olive oil, and lemon juice.

Bran consists of the thin, papery outer covering of the wheat grain. It is a by-product of the refining processes of wheat and can be bought in health food stores and many supermarkets. For extra fiber, sprinkle it on breakfast cereals, eat it plain with milk and sugar, or add it to bread, cake, and cookie doughs and batters.

Wheat germ is the heart of the wheat grain, and is often extracted or destroyed during wheat-refining processes. It can be bought toasted and raw from supermarkets and from health food stores. Wheat germ should be kept in the refrigerator, since the oil in the germ quickly turns rancid (it is often extracted from wheat flour to improve the flour's keeping qualities). Sprinkle it on breakfast cereals or mix it with yogurt. When baking bread, sprinkle wheat germ on the sides of the greased bread pan for a nice finish to the loaf.

Semolina When wheat grain is first milled, it is separated into bran, wheat germ, and endosperm—the floury part of the grain. It is the first millings of the creamy-yellow endosperm that are known as semolina.

Semolina is quite widely used in making desserts, ranging from milk and fruit puddings in England to sweet, round Indian cakes, for which the semolina is first fried and then mixed with raisins, nuts, and honey. The finest ground semolina, called semolina flour, is used to make one kind of Italian gnocchi. Semolina milled from hard durum wheat (*Triticum durum*) is used to make most commercial Italian dried pasta. Flour-coated semolina grains make couscous, part of the excellent North African dish of the same name. Couscous semolina can be purchased precooked; choose the quick-cooking type rather than instant couscous.

Whole wheat flour This is flour from the whole wheat grain. Stoneground flour has a better flavor than the roller-milled supermarket types, since the slow grinding of the stones doesn't overheat and destroy the vitamins in the wheat germ. However, the stoneground flour does not keep as well, so do not buy more than a month's supply and keep it in the refrigerator. Whole wheat flour makes a dense loaf with the warm, earthy taste of the wheat. Using all whole wheat flour would result in a very heavy loaf, so a good compromise is to mix whole wheat flour with bread or all-purpose flour, either in equal amounts or with a higher proportion of the white flour. To make pastry dough with whole wheat flour, sift the flour first and use the fine part in the dough. When the dough is kneaded and ready for shaping, roll it in the remaining coarse particles of bran.

Graham flour was developed by the Reverend Sylvester Graham, inventor of the graham cracker. It is a whole wheat flour that is somewhat coarser and flakier than regular whole wheat flour.

Whole wheat pastry flour is lighter in texture than whole wheat flour and so produces a less dense dough. Baked goods made with whole wheat pastry flour retain some of the sweet, nutty taste of the wheat. Ground from soft wheat, whole wheat pastry flour makes good cookies, pancakes, and waffles and can be used for pastry dough.

All-purpose flour is a blend of soft and hard wheats, and contains virtually none of the grain's bran or germ. However, any flour that doesn't contain the wheat germ is required by law to be fortified, so some of the lost nutrients are restored during processing. Unbleached all-purpose flour, which has been allowed to whiten and mature naturally, has a creamy color and a better flavor than the bleached variety, which, as its name suggests, has been whitened artificially. All-purpose flour is suitable for all types of baking, from bread to light sponge cakes to pie dough, and in cooking, for coating and thickening.

Bread flour is ground from hard flour and is unbleached. It is suitable for all yeast baking, as its high gluten content gives a stronger crumb structure, and it makes excellent loaves and pizza dough.

Cake or pastry flour is the refined and bleached product of soft wheat. Soft wheat flours produce only a small amount of gluten and so give a light, short texture in baking. They are very good for cakes, biscuits, and pastry doughs but are not recommended for yeast baking. All-purpose flour can be substituted for cake or pastry flour, but use 2 tablespoons less all-purpose flour per each cup of cake or pastry flour called for in the recipe.

Self-rising flour is all-purpose flour mixed with baking powder and salt. The baking powder will gradually lose its potency, so use up a box of self-rising flour within 2 or 3 months.

Instant flour is a granular flour that blends well with hot or cold liquids, without lumping. It is used mostly for thickening gravy or sauces.

Corn

Corn (the word was once the generic term for all grains) is second in importance only to wheat. There are countless varieties—some hard, some soft, some golden or white, some red, even some purple. Corn is a New World plant, and Europeans call corn maize, from the Native American word for it.

Cornmeal is ground from white, yellow, or blue corn, is available in coarse and medium grinds. The best cornmeal is ground by the old millstone method, but stoneground cornmeal does not keep as well as cornmeal ground by more modern processes. It should be bought in smaller quantities and kept in a cool place or in the refrigerator.

Throughout the United States there are various traditional cornmeal dishes, such as griddled johnny cakes (or jonny cakes), deep-fried hush puppies, and spoonbreads, lightened with egg whites. Cornbread is often served with chili, and in the South it usually accompanies fried chicken. Fried cornmeal mush is served with syrup for breakfast.

In the south of France, cornmeal is mixed with wheat flour to make rough, flattish loaves. The northern Italian dish of polenta, essentially cornmeal mush, is eaten both soft and, after it has set, sliced and fried. Cornmeal imported from Italy and labeled polenta is sold in gourmet markets; other coarser-ground cornmeals may be used as well.

Hominy is an old Native American name for hulled and dried white or yellow corn. It can be bought either dried or cooked, in cans. The dried grains must be soaked overnight before use. Hominy is also available ground and is then known as hominy grits. The whole grains are cooked and eaten as a side dish, as well as being added to stews. Coarse-ground hominy grits cooked in milk and served with butter and syrup or with gravy is a traditional Southern breakfast dish. Medium- or fine-ground grits are used in cakes and puddings, and to give body to casseroles and stews.

Masa harina is the flour used to make tortillas, and is a hominy relative. It is ground from white corn that is soaked in

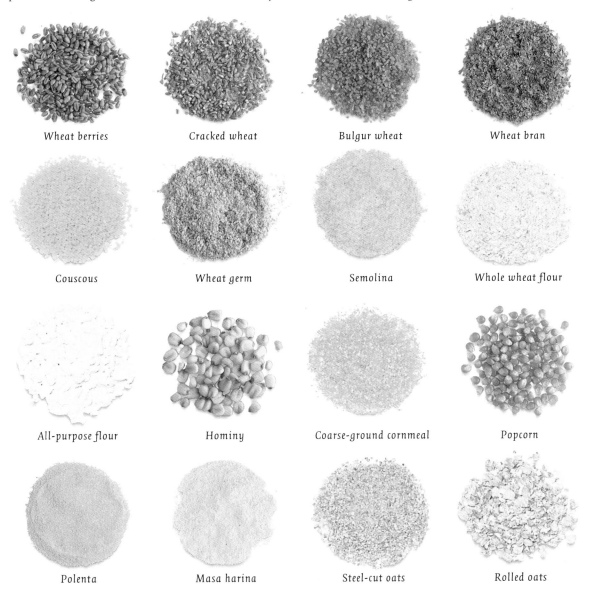

Wheat berries

Cracked wheat

Bulgur wheat

Wheat bran

Couscous

Wheat germ

Semolina

Whole wheat flour

All-purpose flour

Hominy

Coarse-ground cornmeal

Popcorn

Polenta

Masa harina

Steel-cut oats

Rolled oats

limewater. Masa harina can be bought as a wet dough, in Latin American markets, or dried in many supermarkets.

Cornstarch is the white heart of the corn kernel, ground to a silken powder. In England it is known as cornflour. Used primarily as a thickening agent, cornstarch can also be added to cakes, shortbread, and biscuits to give a fine-textured result. A little cornstarch added to an egg custard will stop it from curdling.

Corn flour is finer than cornmeal. It is used for breading foods, as well as for pancakes or waffles and some baked goods. It may be yellow or white.

Oats

These are among the most nutritious of all cereal grains. Being rich in oils, oats soon become rancid, so do not buy more oats or oat products than you can use in about 3 weeks, and keep in a cool place.

Whole oat groats are the whole grain with just the tough outer hull removed.

Steel-cut oats are also called Irish or Scottish oats, and are groats that have been cut into several smaller pieces. Steel-cut oats are good in thick soups and stews. In the British Isles, medium oatmeal, which is cut finer, is also available. It is traditionally used in the north of England and in Scotland to make oatcakes; it is also used for porridge, and to give bulk to sausages.

Rolled oats are oats that have been steamed and flattened between rollers, a process that makes them quicker to cook. Oatmeal takes only 10 minutes to make when using rolled oats. They are a popular ingredient for cookies and muffins, and in Britain they are used to make "flapjacks"—sticky, chewy cookies. Uncooked or toasted rolled oats are the main ingredient of granola and of its cousin, the Swiss breakfast cereal called muesli.

Oatmeal flour is ground from whole oat groats. It can be used in breads and other baked goods; in Britain, it is used for scones and oatcakes.

Rye

This strong-flavored and hardy grain is particularly popular in Scandinavia, Russia, and Germany.

Rye berries are the whole kernels with only the tough outer hulls removed. Boiled until tender, they can be added to stews or mixed with rice.

Rye flour is widely used in bread making in many parts of Europe, and makes a rather heavy and distinctive loaf. Coarse-ground dark rye flour goes into pumpernickel bread; the flour is often called pumpernickel as well. The more finely ground dark rye flour is used for European and Russian black breads. Light rye flour contains less bran than the dark. Light-colored rye breads are made with a combination of rye flour and wheat flour. European rye breads are traditionally made with a sourdough starter. Rye flour is also used to make Scandinavian crispbreads.

Barley

Although more widely used for brewing beer or making whiskey than for eating, barley has a pleasant nutty taste and can be cooked in a variety of ways.

Hulled or whole-grain barley is the whole grain minus the outer hull. Steep it overnight and cook for several hours, then eat it like rice or add it to stews.

Pearl barley is the polished grain. It comes coarse, medium, or fine and will cook to tenderness in 1½ hours or less. It is traditionally used in Scotch broth, to which it adds body and a smooth taste.

Barley flour Ground from pearl barley, barley flour can be added to wheat flour when making bread.

Rice

At least one third of mankind eats rice as its staple food. There is an enormous number of varieties, each with its own special properties, and it is important to choose the right variety for the right dish.

Brown rice is any rice that has been hulled but has not lost its bran. To the regret of dieticians, polished white rice is usually preferred to brown rice, which contains more nutrients, particularly vitamin B (a deficiency of which causes beriberi). It takes rather longer to cook than the white variety. Brown rice is available in short, medium, and long grains. Long and medium grains are best eaten as a vegetable, or as a basis for a pilaf. Short grains are delicious when used to make rice puddings.

Long-grain white rice

Short-grain white rice

Brown rice

Wild rice

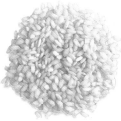

Arborio rice

Basmati rice

White glutinous rice

Long-grain white or polished rice has a long, milk-white grain. It can be simmered in twice its volume of water, cooked in plenty of salted boiling water for about 15 minutes, until just tender, or steamed. The center of each grain, when cooked, should have a slight resistance but no hint of chalkiness. Well-cooked white rice produces a lovely mound of separate grains, good for pilafs, salads, stuffings, and most dishes.

Converted rice This is steam-treated long-grain white rice. It is actually more nutritious than one might think, because it is processed before it is hulled and so has the chance to absorb the bran's nutrients before the bran is discarded.

Basmati rice is available in Asian markets and now in many supermarkets, and is a superior long-grain rice. It is slightly more expensive than regular white rice, but its better flavor and consistency are well worth the extra cost. Before cooking, it sometimes needs to be carefully picked over for any bits of grit and husk, and should then be rinsed thoroughly under cold water. Basmati is ideal for pilafs and as a soothing foil for highly spiced Indian dishes.

Jasmine is an aromatic long-grain Thai rice that is similar to basmati. It is available in many supermarkets as well as Asian and specialty markets.

Short-grain rice is, in fact, a shortish version of long-grain species. When cooked, the grains swell enormously without disintegrating. Popular in Europe, it is very suitable for puddings, whether baked in the oven until caramel-colored within and brown on top, as in England, or cooked on the stovetop and served with sugar and cinnamon as in Germany. This rice is also suitable for making rice rings and for stuffings.

Italian risotto rice These rices have medium-short, roundish grains that are either white or creamy in color. The best varieties include Arborio, which is widely available, and Carnaroli and Vialone Nano. Their grains can absorb a great deal of liquid over a long period without becoming soft or mushy. This, and their distinctive flavor, make them ideal for risottos as well as for any dish such as paella or jambalaya that needs long cooking. Italian rice is often paired with strong-flavored foods such as squid, white truffles, and wild mushrooms, for which it is an excellent vehicle.

White glutinous rice Much used in Asian cooking, this short-grain rice has fat, round, pearly white grains that cook into a sticky mass; it is also called sticky or sweet rice. It must be soaked overnight before steaming or cooking in water. Glutinous rice is also ground into flour, to be used for sweet dumplings, cakes, and pastries, and it is fermented to make low-alcohol wines, such as the Japanese sake and mirin and Chinese Shaoxing, as well as rice vinegar.

Black glutinous rice This rice has a nutty flavor and is used in Southeast-Asian desserts.

Wild rice grows in North America, and is actually the seed of an aquatic grass related to the rice family. Wild rice is expensive, but it has a distinctive, nutty flavor not to be missed. To cook wild rice, add it to a large pot of salted water and bring it to a boil, then reduce the heat, cover, and simmer for 45 to 60 minutes, or until the grains begin to open. Serve plain or in salads, or mix into stuffings for poultry and game birds.

Rice bran is particularly high in dietary fiber. It can be added to cookie or bread doughs for extra texture.

Rice flour is polished white rice finely ground to a silky consistency. Health food stores also sell a coarser, off-white rice flour ground from brown rice. A little rice flour can go into a walnut or hazelnut torte of the type that uses no flour, only grated nuts. It is a useful thickener for dishes to be frozen (wheat flour-thickened sauces are prone to separating when reheated after freezing).

Buckwheat

Buckwheat, a plant related to sorrel and rhubarb, grows in great quantities in northeastern Europe. Buckwheat is available toasted or untoasted. When it is toasted, it is usually called kasha. The toasted grain has a nutty flavor and is a staple in Russian and Eastern European cooking. Kasha comes whole and ground fine, medium, or coarse. Cooked whole-grain kasha is the perfect foil for goose and a comforting dish in cold

Hulled barley

Pearl barley

Buckwheat flour

Kasha

Millet

Quinoa

Sago

Tapioca

Chickpea flour

weather. Buckwheat is the correct flour to use for Russian blini—small, speckled, yeast-risen pancakes that are eaten with caviar. It is also used to make crêpes and can be added to other, lighter flours when making bread.

Millet and sorghum

Millet is invariably sold hulled because the husk is extremely hard. Its greatest characteristic is that the grains swell enormously—at least five parts water are needed to one part millet. Millet has a blandish, slightly nutty taste. It is best cooked and eaten like rice, but bear in mind that a small handful produces a large helping. To reduce the cooking time, toast the grains a little in a dry heavy pan on the stovetop before putting them in the pot to boil. Millet can be toasted, like buckwheat, and cooked like kasha. The cooked toasted whole grain is excellent with sour cream as an accompaniment to chicken. Millet flour produces flattish breads and is best combined with wheat flour.

Sorghum is a close relative of millet and can be eaten in the same way, but in the United States, it is more commonly used as animal feed. A sweet syrup is processed from the sorghum plant.

Quinoa

This tiny South American grain is a healthy addition to the diet, being higher in unsaturated fats and lower in cholesterol than most other grains and very rich in nutrients. Rinse it well, then cook it like rice and use in dishes where its subtle, delicate flavor can provide the background for more assertive flavors, just as rice and couscous do.

Tapioca and sago

Tapioca, prepared from the tuberous roots of the tropical cassava plant, or manioc, is tasteless and starchy. Pearl tapioca is made into the creamy pudding. Tapioca flour is used as a thickener.

The starch obtained from the stem of the Southeast-Asian sago palm, sago is usually exported in pearl form. It comes in varying sizes and consists purely of starch. In Asia and Europe, it is most commonly made into sweet puddings, which are thought to be easily digestible and so are fed to children and the elderly. In Norway, sago is made into a soup with sugar, egg, and sherry. It is sometimes used as a thickener in the United States.

THICKENERS

All starchy meals and flours will, in the presence of heat and moisture, act as thickeners. They cannot simply be used indiscriminately, but the cook can experiment with the two broad categories. Finer flours, before being added to the pan, must first be blended to a lump-free paste with a little of the cooking liquid or with some butter, to make a beurre manié.

As an alternative to all-purpose flour for thickening soups, stews, gravies, and other such dishes, try using something a little more robust, such as fine-ground cornmeal or whole wheat, barley, or chickpea flour. These will add flavor and color as well as body. If you have none of these at hand, a crustless slice of bread or a boiled potato, mashed and blended with a little of the liquid, will work too. Chickpea flour, also known as gram flour or besan, is much used in Indian cookery. It makes a very good batter and is used for *pakoras* (spicy Indian fritters).

Fécule is the general French name for starchy powders used in cooking. It is usually associated with potato flour, which is the thickening agent used by cooks in many European countries when making soups and gravies. The other very fine, quick-thickening flours, such as cornstarch, arrowroot, tapioca flour, and rice flour, are all virtually tasteless. They have double the thickening power of wheat flour, turn translucent when cooked, and are suitable for thickening delicate chicken or game dishes and sauces. Arrowroot and potato flour are particularly suitable for thickening fruit sauces because they turn completely clear when cooked. Arrowroot is also ideal for cooking at low temperatures—an advantage when making such things as sauces that contain eggs. Take care not to overcook these fine flours, as they tend to lose their thickening power.

Yeast and baking powders

When buying flour for baking, you will probably also need a leavening agent, such as yeast for bread, pizza dough, and rolls, and baking powder for biscuits and cakes.

Fresh yeast or compressed yeast is a pale beige, pasty substance that should be solid but crumble easily; it should have a clean, sweet, fruity smell. It will keep for a couple of weeks in the

refrigerator and for several months if stored in the freezer; if frozen, it will need to be thawed thoroughly and brought back to room temperature before use. Look for fresh yeast in health food stores and the refrigerated section of some supermarkets; sometimes a bakery will also sell you fresh yeast.

Active dry yeast has now virtually replaced fresh yeast. It will keep for several months if stored in a cool, dry place, and needs to be dissolved in warm liquid to be reactivated. Never use more of this yeast than the recipe calls for, or you will have a coarse, sour-tasting loaf that quickly becomes stale. Quick-rising dry yeast makes doughs rise in about half the time of regular yeast.

Brewer's yeast Old cookbooks called for brewer's yeast, which was bought at breweries or skimmed off homemade beer and was very temperamental. The brewer's yeast sold these days for home brewing is not suitable for baking.

The brewer's yeast found in health-food stores has no leavening properties but is high in vitamin B. It should be treated as a nutritional additive to mix into drinks and sprinkle over foods.

Baking powder combines acid (such as cream of tartar) and alkaline substances (baking soda) that act together when they come in contact with moisture to create carbon dioxide bubbles; these expand during baking to give a fine and delicate-textured result. Baking powder also contains a small proportion of cornstarch to absorb the moisture in the air. It is sold in airtight containers, and great care should be taken to keep it dry, because any hint of moisture will set the chemicals working. Double-acting baking powder is the most common type today, sold in every supermarket. It reacts in two stages, first when it is combined with a liquid and then later when it is exposed to the heat of the oven. Single-acting baking powder, not often seen, releases all its carbon dioxide when mixed with a liquid; if you use the single-acting type in a recipe, you must work quickly once the liquid and dry ingredients have been combined so that the resulting carbon dioxide cannot escape. You can make your own baking powder: use two parts cream of tartar to one part baking soda.

Baking soda is alkaline, and will work alone as a leavener, without baking powder, in a recipe in which there is an acid ingredient present, such as buttermilk, orange juice, or molasses.

Cream of tartar is a fine white powder crystallized from grape acid. It is an ingredient of some baking powders. A pinch or so helps increase the volume and stability of beaten egg whites.

Ammonium carbonate (sometimes called hartshorn because it was once derived from that deer's horns) is used in Scandinavia as a baking powder to produce light, crisp cookies.

BREADS

The qualities of the plain white loaf are, of course, proper for such things as breakfast toast and croutons, but there is a host of other breads, of completely different tastes and textures. Small artisan bakers are producing a great variety of specialty breads in different parts of the United States today, often inspired by classic European breads.

French bread is most often seen in long sticks, or *baguettes*, and has a hard, crisp crust and a wide-holed crumb. When made in the authentic French manner, it will keep only a few hours, but it is bread at its very best. A thick slice, either plain or toasted, is often floated in soups and consommés.

Light rye bread has a satisfying sour flavor and is popular for sandwiches, particularly those of roast beef, pastrami, or ham and cheese. And of course it's essential in a Reuben sandwich. Light rye bread is also good with smoked fish.

Dark rye bread and pumpernickel A dark rye loaf, with its hard, thick crust, will keep fresh for a week or more, while pumpernickel, which often contains molasses, loses its moisture quickly— it is best wrapped in foil and then stored in a cool place. Both these dark breads should be sliced very thin and are good in open-faced sandwiches, with smoked ham, cheese, or smoked fish.

Bagel These are the ring-shaped rolls that are boiled before baking, and are a well-known Jewish specialty. Cream cheese or cream cheese and lox (smoked salmon) are classic accompaniments. There are endless varieties of these shiny, chewy rolls, including onion, poppy seed, garlic, and egg.

Croissant The soft, doughy crescents that are such an essential part of the French breakfast, these are made from a rich dough of milk and flour layered with butter. Eat hot with butter and jam, or on their own with a cup of good coffee.

Brioche These are rich, feather-light rolls with a crisp golden crust, made from a dough of milk, water, eggs, and butter; they also come as large loaves. Eat warm with butter and jam, sliced and toasted, or hollowed out and stuffed with perhaps sautéed mushrooms or pâté de foie gras.

English muffin These are very popular for breakfast or brunch, when pulled or "forked" in half and toasted. Top with almost anything, sweet or savory.

Crumpet These well-known British breads, about the size of an English muffin, are toasted first on the underside and then on the holey top, then eaten piping hot and dripping with butter.

Bap These are soft, floury rolls from Scotland. They are eaten straight from the oven, split and spread with butter.

Pita bread is originally from the Middle East. It is only slightly leavened and forms flat, hollow rounds. Eaten hot, the breads

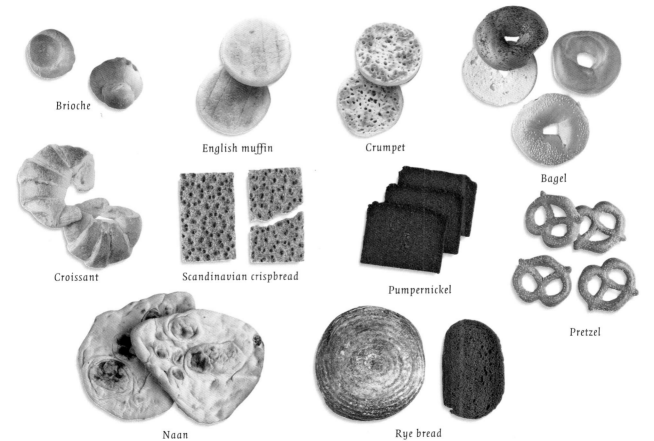

Brioche

English muffin

Crumpet

Bagel

Croissant

Scandinavian crispbread

Pumpernickel

Pretzel

Naan

Rye bread

are sometimes cut in half and filled with grilled lamb and salad. They are always eaten plain with Greek meals, at which it is customary to tear off a bit at a time to use as a scoop for hummus.

Focaccia is thought to be Italy's oldest bread, is usually shaped into a flattened round or slab. It was traditionally baked on a hot stone in a wood-fired oven. The bread can be simply flavored with salt and herbs, or other toppings—such as sautéed vegetables, garlic, olives, chopped tomatoes, and cheese—can be added before baking.

Ciabatta is an Italian slipper-shaped bread with a soft, chewy crust. Freshly baked, it is excellent with salads, soups, and pasta dishes. It can also be used for sandwiches, particularly those with Italian-inspired fillings.

Tortilla This unleavened Mexican bread is made with either masa harina or with white or whole wheat flour. Corn tortillas are fried and filled to make tacos or enchiladas, or are simply fried until they are crisp to make tostadas. Plain wheat tortillas are eaten hot to accompany a main course, or they are filled and rolled or folded to make burritos, fajitas, quesadillas, and so on.

Chapati Unleavened Indian breads made from *atta*—fine-ground whole wheat flour—chapatis are eaten hot with curries and many Indian dishes. They are torn into pieces and used to pick up the food.

Puri This is a deep-fried, puffy, air-filled Indian flat bread.

Paratha is a shallow-fried, butter-enriched, unleavened Indian bread.

Naan, nan Naan is a teardrop-shaped, rich, leavened Indian bread. It is traditionally slapped onto the side of a charcoal tandoori oven to cook. Other versions of naan, made in different sizes and shapes, are eaten throughout Central Asia.

Crackers and crispbreads

There is a huge array of crackers and crispbreads—and their relatives—on the market today. A few varieties, however, deserve special mention.

Scandinavian crispbreads or flatbreads (*flatbrød*) are generally made from rye flour. They are popular with some dieters, as rye is the most filling cereal and so gives one a feeling of satisfaction with relatively fewer calories. These can be eaten spread with almost anything—sweet or savory. Available in light and dark varieties, they are sometimes sprinkled with sesame seeds.

Matzo This crisp unleavened Jewish flatbread, similar to a plain cracker, is traditionally made with only flour and water. Matzos are good when eaten with butter or cheese.

Poppadom, pappadom These wafer-thin, crisp Indian breads are available plain or spiced, and only need to be grilled or deep-fried for a few seconds. Eat them immediately, with curries or drinks.

Pretzel These are often studded with salt crystals, and are available twisted into many shapes and sizes. They are usually crisp but some varieties are soft inside. They are best served with drinks or cheese or simply as a snack; the soft ones are good with spicy mustard.

Breadsticks are also known by the Italian name, *grissini*, and are long, thin sticks of bread with a fine texture, baked until crisp. Eat with drinks, or to accompany an Italian meal instead of bread.

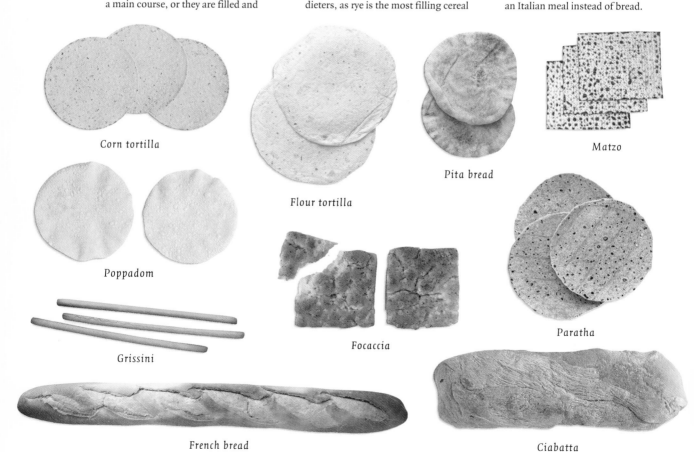

Corn tortilla

Flour tortilla

Pita bread

Matzo

Poppadom

Focaccia

Paratha

Grissini

French bread

Ciabatta

Pasta, Noodles, and Dumplings

Six hundred or so pasta shapes are made in Italy—most Italians rely on a daily supply of pasta in one form or another to keep up their spirits. Many other types of pasta come from China and Japan, where noodles and stuffed dumplings are an important and ancient part of the classic cuisine.

Pasta

Records show that the Chinese were eating pasta as long ago as the Shang dynasty, some 3500 years ago, and it was long believed, rather romantically, that Marco Polo brought pasta to Italy from the court of Kubla Khan. But Etruscan murals in Tuscany show all the kitchen equipment needed for pasta making, from the kind of wooden table still used to roll it out on (so far Formica has not replaced it in Italian households) to the fluted wheel with which to cut pappardelle, lasagne, and ravioli. Even without the murals, the story had been put in doubt by the estate of a military man who died in the thirteenth century, leaving among his effects a precious chest of *maccheroni*.

Whatever its origins, the Neapolitans have always been Italy's most serious pasta eaters, and Naples and the surrounding area have long been regarded as the center of the dried pasta industry. Certainly the best flour for pasta making, milled from the extra-hard wheat *Triticum durum*, comes from the hot, dry south. This flour absorbs a minimum of water as it cooks. The warm, dry, windy climate means, too, that fettuccine, for example, can be dried in the open air, swathed like curtains over long canes that are supported on tall stands—although with industrialization, modern factories have taken the place of the old traditional family enterprises.

Although dried pasta made in the United States can be good, most experts agree that Italian pasta is superior; some assert that the pasta made in southern Italy, especially the Abruzzi, is the best. When buying dried pasta, make sure it is a clear yellow color without any chalky grayish tinge. Thinner pastas should be translucent when held up to the light, with the exception of dried egg pastas, which should be a sunny bright yellow.

Pastas can generally be described as long or short; round, tubular, or flat; smooth or ridged; solid or hollow. An attempt to classify their shapes by name, however, is a problem, since one shape can have several different names and sizes. The north of Italy insists on one appellation, the south another, and even different regions quite close together cannot reach agreement. Miniature pastas, or *pastine*, which come in every shape you can think of, from stars to cars to apple seeds, are in a category of their own. They can be made from egg pasta or plain pasta (without eggs), and are generally cooked and served in *brodo*—in chicken or beef broth and in soups.

The long, round, solid pastas that are coiled around the fork, such as spaghetti, vermicelli, and spaghettini, are generally eaten dry (*asciutta*)—as opposed to in broth—with oil or butter, a tomato-based sauce, or a seafood sauce. Meat sauces, with the exception of Bolognese sauce, are not generally eaten with these, as they do not cling to the pasta well. Short, hollow pastas, such as conchigliette and penne, are the ones to serve with meat sauces as the pieces catch easily in the pasta's hollows and curves.

The larger short, hollow pastas, such as cannelloni and manicotti, are usually boiled and then stuffed with cheese or meat before baking. Macaroni, ziti, and rigatoni are sometimes boiled and then baked in a sauce in the oven—perhaps as part of a molded shape called a timballo, which is among the oldest of all pasta dishes. Lasagne and tagliatelle can also be baked in this way, as can farfalle, conchiglie, ruote, and lumachine.

Serve short, ridged, hollow pastas with cream sauces, since they will catch the cream and do not slip off the fork. Tagliatelle and other flat fresh pastas are generally eaten with rich meat or vegetable sauces, and the same dough is used to make stuffed pastas such as ravioli, anolini, tortelloni, and tortellini.

Spaghetti This is the best-known of all pastas. It is marketed in a number of widths that go under such names as cappellini, spaghettini, vermicelli, and thin or thick spaghetti. Fusilli is a spiral spaghetti, available in long and short lengths. The thicker ones are better with rich sauces, while the thinner ones are better with plainer sauces.

Spaghetti has long been the traditional pasta of Naples, and the traditional way of eating it is still *alla napoletana*—first tossed with oil and then topped with a ladleful of tomato sauce. Naples also eats its spaghetti *all'aglio e olio*—pasta bathed in olive oil with sautéed garlic. Grated *grana* cheese such as Parmesan or pecorino is served with all spaghetti dishes except those with seafood, such as *spaghetti alla vongole*. This is made with tiny clams and is another Neapolitan specialty, although it is, of course, much enjoyed all over Italy.

Macaroni It is not known how the idea of making the tubular pasta called macaroni, or *maccheroni*, started. But the most likely theory is that someone wrapped a piece of rolled-out pasta around a filling, leaving the ends open.

Macaroni comes in an even greater range of sizes than spaghetti. Apart from the long variety, such as bucatini, with center holes that can be measured in fractions of an inch, there are also those that can be measured in inches, or half-inches, such as cannelloni—but these are despised by purists as too modern, invented solely to make filling our pasta easier. However, we ought to be grateful that we are not obliged, as was the composer Rossini, to fill our macaroni with the aid of a silver syringe. He is said to have used this for filling pasta with foie gras, for which he had a passion.

Apart from bucatini and cannelloni, there are ribbed rigatoni, ziti, short or long, penne—cut to resemble quills—and elbow macaroni—the curved, short lengths of macaroni that are used in baked pasta dishes.

Macaroni used to be virtually the only pasta known and loved by English-speaking countries. Called macrow, it was eaten at the court of Richard II of England, in the late fourteenth century. It fell into decline, but was rediscovered by eighteenth-century Englishmen on the Italian part of their "grand tours" and taken back to Britain. Soon macaroni and cheese became an important high-tea dish, and it is now an American classic (in fact, it has even been "rediscovered" by some upscale restaurants).

Egg pasta In northern Italy, until recently, housewives made egg pasta, or *pasta all'uovo*, daily, with eggs and flour. Emilia-Romagna, the area with the richest farming land in Italy, was renowned for its beautiful handmade pasta, and young women from that region were keenly courted by young men—and their mothers—for their pasta-making skills. Egg pastas are richer and lighter than ordinary pastas.

Pasta making is a craft, and to see an expert rolling out a golden circle of dough, as thin as fine suede, to the size of a small tablecloth is a wonderful experience. In Bologna, the gastronomic center of Emilia-Romagna, you can watch it being made in a shop window. It is then turned into tortellini—little stuffed, folded-over pasta triangles—at lightning speed in front of your eyes.

Fresh pasta can be made at home (when, in Italy, it becomes known as *pasta casalinga*), either by hand or with a pasta machine. Perfectionists say the former is better as the machine squeezes the pasta and tends to give it a slippery surface that does not hold sauces as well.

In fact, a great deal of the *pasta all'uovo* now eaten in Italy and elsewhere is made in factories. By law, dried Italian pasta must contain five eggs to each kilo (2.2 pounds) of flour.

The best-known of the egg pastas is fettuccine, or—as it is called in northern Italy—tagliatelle: those golden strands that were supposed to have been inspired by the long blonde hair of Lucretia Borgia. In Bologna and Parma and all the other places of gastronomic pilgrimage with which northern Italy abounds, the tagliarini (thin tagliatelle) is still normally freshly rolled out every day. Malfatte (which means badly made) are irregular shapes of fresh pasta.

Tagliatelle is, of course, even in Bologna, eaten not only *alla bolognese*, but also *in bianco*, mixed with plenty of melted butter, grated Parmesan, and cream; or *al burro*, with just butter and cheese. Bologna also eats its tagliatelle mixed with delicious strips of sautéed pancetta and grated Parmesan.

Lasagne Dried lasagne can be bought in long, wide, flat strips or in curly-edged pieces that will not stick together as readily as flat pieces do when boiling. Fresh lasagne can also be bought as larger sheets or squares, which are easier to fit into a baking dish. In Bologna, strips of green lasagne, or the narrower lasagnette (also called malfadine or trenette), are layered alternately with plain strips, and with Bolognese sauce and rich creamy béchamel sauce. This dish is baked in the oven and emerges, glazed here and there with deep golden flecks, as *lasagne al forno*.

Colored and flavored pasta Lasagne verdi (green) and fettuccine verdi prove that spinach has a special affinity with pasta. Both are widely available, colored by a small amount of spinach purée worked into the dough. Other colorings and flavorings for pasta doughs include tomato paste, saffron, squid ink, herbs, and coarsely ground black pepper.

Tuscany and Umbria serve a pretty mixture of yellow and green tagliatelle or tagliolini, which is called *paglia e fieno*, meaning "straw and hay." It is eaten with melted butter and cream and sprinkled, as usual, with Parmesan.

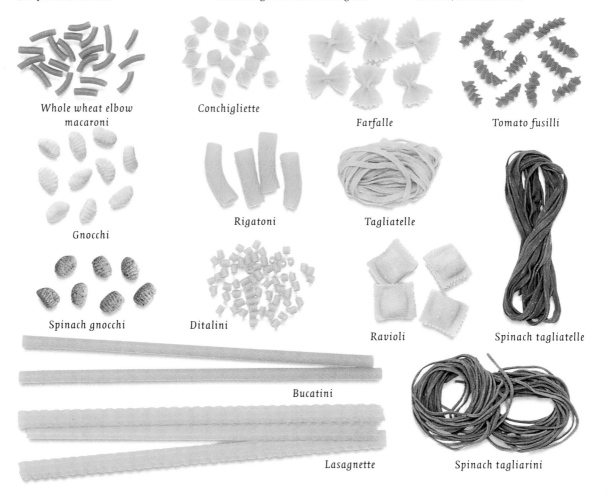

Whole wheat elbow macaroni

Conchigliette

Farfalle

Tomato fusilli

Gnocchi

Rigatoni

Tagliatelle

Spinach gnocchi

Ditalini

Ravioli

Spinach tagliatelle

Bucatini

Lasagnette

Spinach tagliarini

Whole wheat and buckwheat pasta Although Venice has always had its thick whole wheat spaghetti called *bigoli*, it is not common throughout Italy. There are, however, some relative newcomers, such as buckwheat and other whole wheat pastas, which are to be found in health food stores and some supermarkets.

Pastas such as whole wheat lasagne and macaroni and buckwheat spaghetti have a nutty flavor and are richer in vitamins and minerals than the more traditional pale pastas. They take longer to cook, as they contain far more fiber than pale pasta. The Italian whole wheat pastas are, on the whole, lighter than those made elsewhere.

Whole wheat and buckwheat noodles also feature in Japanese cooking. They are often eaten cold as a light snack in the late afternoon.

Stuffed pasta Pasta stuffed with a large variety of finely ground or chopped fillings is eaten throughout Italy. Parmesan cheese and mortadella sausage with pork and veal, diced or pounded and mixed with ground turkey breast, provide the traditional stuffing for tortellini and tortelloni. These are the curved half-moons that are the famous Bolognese version of ravioli; they are by custom eaten on Christmas Eve and for big celebrations. On these same occasions, Perugia, in Tuscany, eats cappelletti, or little hats, whose stuffing includes ground veal and sweetbreads or brains. The shells called conchiglie or the larger conchiglioni and even lumache (the largest shells, whose name means "snails") can also be stuffed.

Throughout Italy, ravioli with delicious spinach, beet greens, or Swiss chard fillings are to be found. The chopped

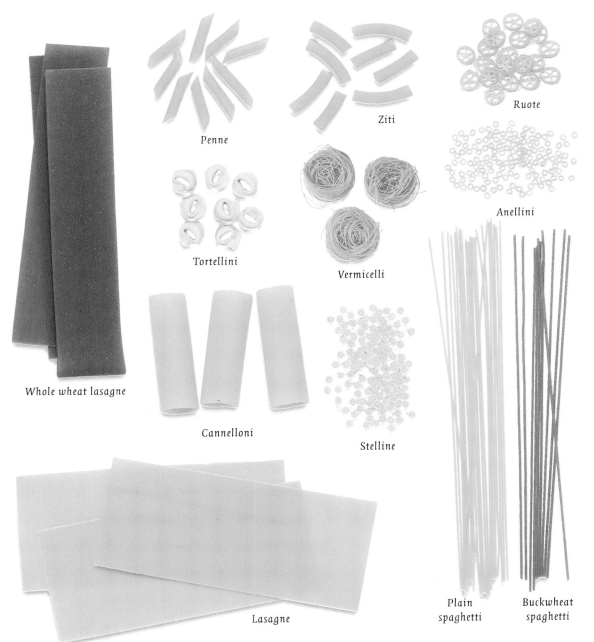

Penne

Ziti

Ruote

Tortellini

Vermicelli

Anellini

Whole wheat lasagne

Cannelloni

Stelline

Plain spaghetti

Buckwheat spaghetti

Lasagne

leaves are mixed with soft white cheese such as ricotta, or with Parmesan or pecorino, bound with egg, and flavored with a touch of nutmeg or garlic, depending on the local preference. They can also be stuffed with pumpkin or squash, wild mushrooms, or even lobster.

Soup pasta If the dough and the basic shape of *pasta asciutta* are fairly consistent—allowing for a thousand and one small regional variations—the same cannot be said of soup pastas. The range of these is vast and includes both anellini and stelline, which are used for serving in clear broth, and larger varieties, such as farfalline, conchigliette, and ditalini, used for making hearty soups such as minestrone or *pasta e fagioli*.

Italy garnishes its soups with tiny car radiators, wheels, flying saucers, hats, boots, and letters and numerals, all made of pasta. The more traditional shapes include grains of rice and melon seeds, twisted bow ties or butterflies, stars, crescent moons, seashells of every description, rings, hoops, elbow macaroni, and noodles that are thinner than matchsticks.

These garnishes are sometimes cooked separately and added to the soup just before serving, as they tend to shed a bit of their starch and so may make a clear broth cloudy.

Pasta sauces Pasta of one kind or another is the main part of most Italians' daily diet, and there are almost as many pasta sauces to be found as there are types of pasta.

All the classic pasta sauces have their origins in regional cookery. They are made from what is readily at hand. Piedmont, with its famous white truffles, makes a delicious sauce of truffled chicken livers. Tuscany makes a richly flavored sauce with hare. Pounded anchovies, truffles, garlic, tomatoes, and onions go into the sauce that, in Spoleto, makes *pasta alla spoletina*. In Sorrento, there is a sauce made of zucchini. Pesto, the mixture of fresh basil, pine nuts, olive oil, garlic, and Parmesan or pecorino cheese, is served with linguine in Genoa. When Tuscany offers a cream sauce to accompany its tagliarini, it saves the sauce from blandness by adding a rich meat glaze (this is made from reduced stock).

Spaghetti alla carbonara, despite the story that it was created during World War II to please the Allied armies, with their vast appetites for eggs and bacon, is a specialty of Rome. The sauce consists of pancetta stirred into spaghetti with some Parmesan and beaten raw egg, which partly sets in the heat of the pasta. The secret is not to drain the spaghetti too enthusiastically, or the result will be dry.

In the Abruzzi and Molise regions of central Italy, one favorite sauce is made with lamb and green peppers, another with smoked pork and tomatoes. The pasta eaten there is *maccheroni alla chitarra*—long strands cut on a frame strung with wires like a guitar. In the Marches, the region between the Abruzzi and Emilia-Romagna, black olives preserved in a special brine are incorporated into the sauces, not only for pasta made with the conventional dough but also for a local variation that is made with a yeast-like bread dough. Chickpeas also appear, in a pasta dish that goes by the name of *tuono e lampo* (thunder and lightning).

Toward the south, sauces include red and green bell peppers and a fiery pinch of ground hot chiles. Since the sea is not far from any spot in Italy, there are often marine accompaniments, such as cockles and clams, and, in the Veneto, the region around Venice, a delicious black sauce is made with squid ink.

Gnocchi

In Italy, the dumplings known as gnocchi are eaten in the same way as pasta and at the same point in the meal, but they are not strictly speaking pasta. There are several local variations, made from ricotta cheese and spinach, or semolina, or mashed potatoes or potato flour. They are usually simmered gently in boiling salted water until cooked, when they rise to the surface. They are then served with a variety of sauces. Gnocchi are generally made fresh, the semolina variety being particularly easy and quick to make.

Nudels, nouilles, and dumplings

In the German-speaking countries, which are supposed to have introduced *nudels* into Italy in the Middle Ages, flat *nudels* have been eaten for centuries. They are often baked with golden raisins and sweetened lemon-flavored fresh cheese and served as a dessert; noodle *kugel*, or pudding, sweet or savory, is a traditional Jewish-American dish. In Alsace, in northeastern France, noodles are known as *nouilles* and are prepared in countless savory and delicious ways. Coq au vin, for example, is often accompanied by *nouilles*—which are always better fresh. In Alsace, we also find the ancestral dumpling known as *noque*, while farther south, in Austria, Germany, and Switzerland, it appears under the name of *nockerln*. By whatever name, it is a pasta dumpling and can be eaten with a number of different sauces.

Chinese noodles

Wheat flour, rice flour, arrowroot, and bean starch are the main ingredients of Chinese noodles. These come in a variety of thicknesses and shapes, some of which can be used interchangeably, and are often tied in bundles or coiled into square packages. The majority, however, are long, as these are thought to symbolize and encourage long life.

Although most Chinese buy their noodles, some do make their own. Fresh noodles are obtainable from Chinese markets and taste best when they are first parboiled and then steamed in a colander over boiling water. Once boiled or steamed, Chinese noodles become part of more elaborate preparations that often involve several cooking methods for one dish.

Soup noodles These are traditionally served in broth with a topping of finely cut meat or seafood and bright, fresh-looking vegetables. The cooked noodles are put into the bottom of the bowl, the hot broth is poured over them, and then the stir-fried meat or seafood and vegetables are added as the garnish.

In northern China, where wheat is the primary grain, wheat noodles, with or without egg, are used. Egg noodles are often sold in little nests, while pure wheat noodles may be packaged in bundles as well as in square-shaped nests. In the southern districts of China, where rice paddies abound, translucent white rice noodles are used. These range from coiled rice sticks in square packets to the thin thread-like rice vermicelli that comes tied in bundles. White arrowroot vermicelli is also available.

Cellophane noodles—also known as transparent or bean thread noodles, bean threads, or vermicelli—are made from ground mung beans. They are never served alone but are used in soups and in stir-fried or braised dishes, to which they add a distinctive slippery texture.

Fried noodles Crispy fried noodles, known as *chow mein*, are a Cantonese specialty. Since many Chinese restaurants in the West are Cantonese, these are among the best-known of all noodle dishes. They can either be flattened in a frying pan with plenty of seasoned oil and then turned like pancakes, or they can be fried gently with leftover vegetables and meat from a noodle and soup dish. Cellophane noodles can also be fried if a crisp garnish is all that is required.

Sauced noodles In the West, where Chinese thickeners such as lotus root flour are not readily available, sauced noodles, or *lo mein*, are usually served in sauces thickened with cornstarch. Since to the Chinese texture is just as important as taste, a crunchy element is often introduced into these sauces with matchstick slivers of bamboo shoots or crisp sticks of scallions and leeks. Protein is provided by meat or chicken, shrimp, or oysters.

Dumplings and spring rolls

Chinese dumplings, or wontons, are similar to the Italian ravioli. The delicate ingredients, finely minced and variously flavored, are wrapped in squares of fine noodle dough. They can be made at home in the same way as fresh pasta. Paper-thin wonton dough, cut into squares or rounds, can also be purchased at Asian markets. Boiled or steamed, wontons are often served floating in a clear broth.

One of the prettiest meals available during the day in a Cantonese Chinese restaurant is dim sum, which is often presented in a towering pagoda of baskets. Each one fits into the other and contains bite-sized morsels, such as steamed buns, savory pastries, and dumplings containing pork, shrimp, or other meat or fish fillings. *Dim sum* are ideal for a brunch or light lunch.

Paper-thin wrappers are also used to make spring and egg rolls, which are filled with a savory mixture of shredded vegetables and sometimes meat or fish and are then deep-fried.

Very thin, semitransparent rice paper wrappers, or *bánh tráng*, are used to make Vietnamese and Thai spring rolls. The wrappers, which are dried on bamboo mats in the sun, need to be soaked briefly in warm water to soften them before rolling them up around the filling mixture.

Japanese noodles

There are four main types of Japanese noodle, all of which play an important part in the national cuisine. *Soba* are thin, brownish noodles made from buckwheat flour. They are used in soups and sometimes served cold with a garnish. *Harusame* are equivalent to Chinese cellophane noodles and can be deep-fried, or soaked and then cooked in various dishes. *Somen* are very fine white noodles—you can substitute Italian *vermicelli* if *somen* are not available. *Udon* are made from white flour and are more substantial.

Chow mein noodles

Somen

Cellophane noodles

Soup vermicelli

Rice paper wrapper

Rice vermicelli

Rice sticks

Fresh rice noodles

Fresh egg noodles

Fresh wheat noodles

Wonton wrapper

Wheat noodles

Arrowroot vermicelli

Udon

Egg noodles

Wheat noodles

Spring roll wrapper

Soba

Dried Beans

The dried seeds of podded plants were first popular many thousands of years ago. In Egypt, the Pyramids have been found to contain little mounds of dried beans—not only to sustain departed pharaohs on their journey to the next world, but also because Egyptians believed beans to be of particular help in conveying the soul to heaven.

Unfortunately, apart from the fact that they are an excellent and sustaining food, and very suitable for those about to embark on long journeys, beans have the annoying property of engendering flatulence. Perhaps this characteristic helped lead to their gradual banishment, after medieval times, from Europe's more elegant tables. Another probable reason for their steady decline in general appeal was the greater availability of fresh vegetables at that time.

It was not until this century, when the Western world found a new taste for simple, sturdy, regional foods, that dried beans and peas were seriously rediscovered. A growing interest in Indian and Middle Eastern cooking brought Eastern species to Western shelves, and with them the Indian word *gram*, which is one of the collective names for dried beans and peas, particularly the chickpea. In the United States, the term dried beans usually includes peas as well; in England, the collective name is pulse, originating from the ancient Roman word *puls*, meaning pottage, a thick stew.

Although thousands of species of beans and peas, botanically known as Leguminosae, now exist, they have many common characteristics. Flavor and mealiness may vary, but all have a straightforward earthy taste and satisfying sturdy quality. All are a rich source of protein and, being a healthy and body-building form of food, make a very sound substitute for meat, especially when combined with cereals.

A popular misconception is that dried beans have an indefinite shelf life. In fact, they should not be stored longer than a year, for they toughen with age and become difficult to cook. There are two methods of preparing them for cooking, both of which help to tenderize them. The most common method is overnight soaking, preferably in soft water, to which all dried peas and beans respond. The dried peas and beans sold in the supermarket are usually quite clean, but it's still best to pick through them for stones or debris. The alternative to overnight soaking, useful when you are short of time, is the quick-soak method: put them into a pan of cold, unsalted water, bring to a boil, and simmer for 5 minutes. Cover the pan, remove it from the heat, and allow the beans or peas to cool. Then drain them and cook them as called for by the recipe.

All these vegetables should be cooked in soft water—a pinch of baking soda will soften hard water—and simmered rather than rapidly boiled. Unless very fresh, they require lengthy cooking. They should be salted toward the end of cooking—if salted at the start, the skins will split and the insides will toughen. A little fat added to the cooking water—salt pork, bacon, or oil—improves the texture of all dried beans and peas. When they are bought canned rather than loose or packaged, they are already cooked, and therefore only need rinsing and draining before heating.

Haricot bean, white bean The word haricot covers the botanical species of beans Phaseolus. It derives from medieval times, when dried beans were used chiefly to go into a pot containing a *haricot*, or *halicot*, of meat—meaning simply that the meat was cut in chunks for stewing. When English and French cookbooks specify dried haricots, what is meant are white beans, smooth and oval rather than kidney-shaped. In the United States, they are known, sensibly enough, as white beans.

Soissons are large and white, and are generally considered to be the finest white beans. They are used in the famous French dish *cassoulet*, from Toulouse, which is cooked with preserved goose, mutton, and sausage.

Flageolets are an important ingredient in another classic French dish, *gigot d'agneau*. They are a delicate pale green in color with a subtle flavor.

Cannellini are also called white kidney beans, and are much used in Italian cooking. They are popular in Tuscany in soups and in dishes such as *tonno e fagioli*—served cold with tuna fish in a garlicky vinaigrette.

Navy beans are also known as Yankee beans. Small and white, they are used in a variety of dishes, particularly for Boston baked beans. At one time, these small round beans were served by the U.S. Navy—hence their name.

Great Northern beans are grown in the Midwest, and are larger than navy beans. They can be used in the same ways as navy or other white beans.

Pea beans are sought out by discerning New Englanders for authentic Boston baked beans, but, although they are smaller, they are used interchangeably with navy beans in canning.

Lima bean Also known as butter beans, these can be large or small. Although they are highly prized when fresh, the large dried bean easily becomes mushy when cooked and so is best used in soups and purées. When a recipe calls for either white or lima beans, it is the smaller lima beans that should be used.

Red kidney bean Probably best known for their part in chili con carne—although Texans, among others, think that beans have no place in real chili—red kidney beans are a staple in Central America. These are the beans that, with black beans, were cooked by the Central American Indians in their earthenware pots (still the best receptacle for baked beans, which should be served from the pot). After the introduction of lard from Spain, beans were often mashed, formed into a stiff paste, and fried to become *frijoles refritos* (refried beans)—still a very popular way of eating beans in Mexico. In this form they may be used to accompany a main dish, or as a filling for tacos or tostadas. Red kidney beans also appear in many dishes in New Orleans, particularly in red beans and rice. A smaller red bean, also called red Mexican bean or red chili bean, is used in many of the same dishes as the red kidney bean, particularly chili.

Black bean As well as being used interchangeably with red kidney and pinto beans to make *frijoles refritos*, black beans, also called turtle beans, with their glistening black skins and creamy flesh, are the staple of many soups and stews in South and Central America. There they are often baked with ham or other cured pork and flavored with garlic, cumin, and liberal amounts of chiles, and they are an essential ingredient in *feijoada*, the Brazilian national dish. In the South and other parts of the United States, black bean soup is a great favorite. The beans are cooked with a ham bone or hock, blended to the consistency of a heavy sauce, and served with chopped hard-boiled eggs and with slices of lemon floating on top.

Pinto bean Often mottled in color, the pink-splotched pinto bean grows all over Latin America and throughout the American Southwest. It is an ingredient in many regional stews and is often mixed with rice. Appaloosa beans are a recent hybrid of the pinto bean.

Cranberry bean The cranberry bean is often mottled like the pinto bean, but it is rounder and a darker red in color. It is popular in Italy, where it is known as the borlotti bean; mixed with pasta, it makes the soup called *pasta e fagioli*.

Black-eyed pea These white beans with their characteristic black splotch came to America and Europe from Africa, brought over in the late seventeenth century by the slave traders. The black-eyed pea thrives in warm climates and is a favorite food crop in the southern United States, where it is eaten fresh

as well as dried. It is often served with pork and corn bread, and is the essential ingredient in the dish called Hoppin' John—a mixture of black-eyed peas, white rice, and salt pork or bacon—which is traditionally eaten on New Year's Day to bring good luck.

Fava bean Also known as broad beans, these are the strongly flavored beans that form the basis of the Egyptian *ta'amia*, or falafel: deep-fried little patties made with soaked and pounded dried beans and flavored with garlic, onions, cumin, coriander, and parsley. Most often used in their fresh green state, as in the rib-sticking *fabada* from northern Spain—a mixture of beans, cured meats, sausage, and plenty of garlic—they become brown in color when dried.

Ful medame, Egyptian brown bean These small, brown, knobbly beans, actually a type of fava bean, are grown in Southeast Asia and in Egypt, where they are a staple food. In Egypt the cooked beans are usually sprinkled with garlic and parsley, with oil and seasonings passed separately. They also make a filling

for an Arabian bread to become a sort of meatless hamburger, eaten with tomato and onion salad, and they are good when served in a tomato sauce. These beans require lengthy soaking and cooking.

Chickpea, garbanzo bean The botanical name for this bean is *Cicer arietinum*—this is because of its alleged resemblance to the skull of a ram, although to those of us with a less-discerning eye it looks more like a small hazelnut. The flavor of chickpeas vaguely recalls that of roasted nuts, and indeed they are eaten with drinks in Greece. Like other dried beans, they should be soaked overnight before cooking. Once cooked, *ceci*, as they are called in Italy, are very good dressed simply with oil and eaten as a salad. The Italians also make chickpea soup, and mix them with pasta—a dish known as *tuono e lampo* (thunder and lightning). In France, where chickpeas are called *pois chiches*, they are stewed in good stock with herbs and also used in soups and as a garnish. In Spain, *garbanzos* form the basis of *olla podrida* ("rotten pot"; traditionally this contains chickpeas, chunks of meat,

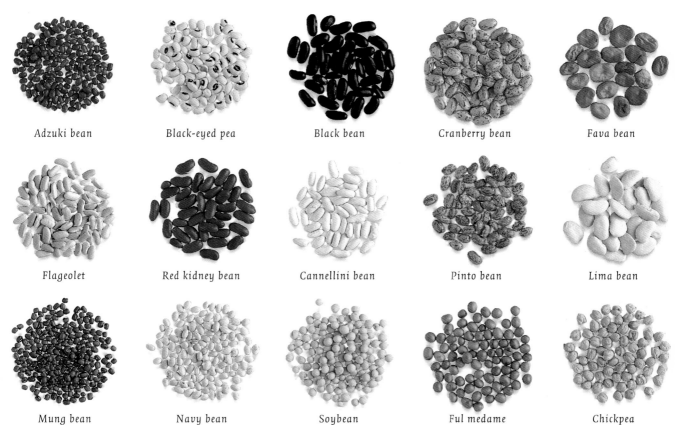

Adzuki bean

Black-eyed pea

Black bean

Cranberry bean

Fava bean

Flageolet

Red kidney bean

Cannellini bean

Pinto bean

Lima bean

Mung bean

Navy bean

Soybean

Ful medame

Chickpea

pig's feet or ears, preserved pork, sausages, and vegetables, all simmered together slowly); in Portugal, they are combined with spinach and eaten with *bacalhau*—salt cod—and other dishes. In the Middle East, chickpeas are mashed with tahini, lemon, and garlic to make the delicious spread hummus, and Israel uses them for its version of falafel, which is so widely eaten that it has almost become the national dish. Chickpeas are a common ingredient of couscous, and they are also mixed with beef and vegetables to make a rich and filling Israeli dish called *deene*, or *daphna*. They are an important crop in India, where they are often cooked with garlic and chiles and tossed with aromatics before being fried with herbs and spices in the clarified butter known as ghee.

Split pea Although there are still some dingy-gray, whole dried peas to be had, most are now sold skinned and split, a bright green or golden yellow. Thick yellow pea soup—*ärter med flask*—is the traditional Thursday evening dish in Sweden, keeping alive the memory of the unpopular King Eric XIV—whose last

supper eaten on earth, on a Thursday, consisted of this very dish. His brother had contrived to slip a dash of arsenic into this humble food, which would hardly have crossed royal lips had Eric not been imprisoned at the time by his eventual successor. Split pea soup made with green peas, or yellow ones, is popular throughout the United States and in many other European countries as well. Green split peas form the basis of a traditional English dish, pease pudding. Although an egg is sometimes beaten into the mushy pea mixture to make it creamier still, it is one of the characteristics of split peas, yellow or green, that they turn into a purée by themselves and do not have to be mashed. Nor do they have to be soaked before cooking.

Lentil Red, brown, and green lentils have all the virtues of dried peas and beans, and the additional one of needing less cooking time (particularly split lentils) and no presoaking. The small red split lentil, originally a native of India, becomes tender with about 20 minutes' cooking, quickly turning into a mush if overcooked. The brown lentil, the ordinary green lentil, and the green lentil of France, *lentille de Puy*, take a little longer to cook.

Lentils make excellent purées and soups. In Germany, they sometimes accompany roast duck, while in France, lentils cooked with garlic and flavored with a squeeze of lemon juice are eaten with a *petit salé*—hot salt pork.

Dal, Dhal This is not a particular type of bean but the Hindi word for dried beans and peas. Most packages labeled dal in the West will contain split varieties, such as chickpeas, lentils, and the pigeon pea, which is known as *tur dal*. They are not soaked but are cooked for 40 to 45 minutes and served spiced as a thick purée, or are mashed to make thick soups. Another of the dals, *urad dal*, is often ground and becomes the basis of the crisp Indian bread poppadom, without which no curry dish is complete.

Mung bean These beans, also called green gram or golden gram, can of course be cooked in the usual way, but they tend to become rather sticky. In India, they are ground into a flour, and the ground beans are the basis

of some Chinese and Japanese noodles. In the West, mung beans are now chiefly used, like alfalfa seeds and soybeans, for sprouting.

Soybean The soybean is the most nutritious of all beans and the most easily digested. Better known for its products than for the bean itself, it is one of the few sources of complete protein. It has been periodically rediscovered by the West, but was first brought to Europe in the eighteenth century, when it confounded scientists with its amazing qualities. It is still the subject of considerable research.

But while the West has only recently started turning soybeans into steaks of tempeh and processing them into cheese, the Chinese have for thousands of years called soybeans "the meat of the earth." They use soybean curd—the bland cakes known as tofu, which readily soak up other flavors—as a substitute for meat, fish, and chicken. The extracted "milk" is used in cooking many vegetable dishes; soy sauce is used for flavoring; and a fermented paste made from the bean, called miso, is used as a basic seasoning in everything from sauces, soups, and salad dressings to casseroles and, when sweetened, in desserts and other sweets in the manner of jam.

Of the thousand or so known varieties, two soybeans are chiefly cultivated—one sort for commercial purposes, the other to be eaten both fresh (when young) and dried, in which case they are prepared and cooked just like other dried beans. Soy milk is a useful substitute for those allergic to dairy products.

Adzuki bean The adzuki, or azuki, bean is one of the most delicious of the dried beans, and also one of the more expensive. A native of Japan, it is small and red with a curiously shaped white-striped ridge. It is a fairly recent arrival in the West and is found mainly in health food stores and Asian markets.

The adzuki bean is cooked in the same ways as other dried beans, both in Japan and abroad, but since it is very much sweeter than most other beans, its flour is also much used for cakes and pastries in Japan, and the crushed bean is made into puddings and ice cream by the Chinese. It is one of the most easily digestible of all the dried beans.

Yellow split pea

Green split pea

De Puy lentil

Split red lentil

Brown lentils

Green lentils

Vegetables

SALAD GREENS

It was a scholarly seventeenth-century English diarist, John Evelyn, who said of a salad that it should be composed like a piece of music, with each ingredient playing its due part without being overpowered by anything of strong taste. Since his time, a salad has come to be widely regarded as an essential part of the everyday diet, so much so that in many countries it is served instead of a vegetable.

Exactly at what point of the meal to serve a green salad is a matter of taste. Ancient Romans, who regarded lettuce as a panacea for all ills, believed that its milky juices "lined the stomach," enabling people to drink more with their food. Accordingly, lettuce was served as a first course—as it is still sometimes eaten today, although hardly for the same reason, in the United States. It is becoming more usual, however, to eat it immediately following the main course, as in France and England, or at the same time, on a side plate or, not so agreeably, on the same plate (although this has something to recommend it in the case of such dishes as chops, steaks, or roast chicken because the meat juices mingle so delectably with the dressing).

Green salads should not meet their dressings until they are on the point of being served, since once dressed, they will rapidly become limp. A good compromise is to prepare the dressing in the bowl, put the crossed salad servers over it, and place the leaves lightly on top, without mixing them. Some people prefer to mix the dressing at the table, while Italians simply pour olive oil and then vinegar onto the salad—they say you need a generous person for the oil, a miser for the vinegar, a judge for the salt, and a madman to mix it.

To make sure that your salad greens are fresh and good, see that the leaves look vigorous and show no sign of brown. Inspect the trimmed parts: they should be sound, neither discolored nor soggy. The heavier the lettuce for its size, the more tightly packed it will be, giving you more leaves for your money.

A lettuce in good condition will stay fresh in the refrigerator if it is wrapped in a plastic bag to retard the evaporation of its moisture. Should it already have wilted, it can be refreshed by being plunged briefly into cold water, shaken dry, and then put into the refrigerator either in a plastic bag or wrapped in a damp dish towel.

Shortly before you use them, salad greens should be washed well and then thoroughly dried—either by absorbing the moisture by shaking the lettuce in a clean dish towel or by getting rid of it in a salad spinner or shaker. The leaves should be torn rather than cut, to avoid bruising.

Apart from being used in salads, lettuces and other leafy plants can be cooked. The less substantial the leaf, the faster it collapses, and while heavier leaves may retain a bit of body, lighter ones do not. For braising, choose small, plump lettuces and cut them in half or braise them whole.

Round and head lettuce

These vary greatly in size and crispness but have in common their general round shape. Although there are many varieties, ranging from soft to very crisp, there are three main types.

Butterhead or butter lettuce These are floppy, loosely packed, and delicate head lettuces. Bibb, a particularly melting variety, is prized in the United States; Boston is another favorite. Continuity, a variety grown in England, sports leaves with a reddish tinge to them. Butterheads tend to be rather floppy, a characteristic that is by no means a defect, as long as the loose leaves are fresh.

Iceberg Whereas there is not much joy in eating a tired and wilting butterhead, these hearty head lettuces, when fading on the outside, may still be full of vitality in the middle. (Despite the fact that all the head lettuces of this type are usually called icebergs, iceberg is actually just one type of crisphead lettuce.) Although not strong in flavor, icebergs are by far the crispest lettuces. They are usually sold without their aureole of outer leaves, looking like tightly wrapped heads of cabbage. Webb's Wonderful is a favorite British iceberg.

Leaf or looseleaf lettuce These lettuces have no heart at all. Instead of the leaves, which are often crinkled, becoming more tightly packed toward the center, they all splay outward from the middle. Some varieties have red-, bronze-, or ruby-tipped leaves. Lollo Rossa is a red-tipped, curly, and somewhat tough example of a looseleaf lettuce. It is a good salad lettuce but is often used indiscriminately as a garnish.

Romaine lettuce, cos lettuce

Far more elongated in shape than the round lettuces is the romaine or cos lettuce. Tall and large, with a nutty flavor to its vigorous leaves, it has a beautifully crisp and tender heart. Its two names—romaine in the United States and France and cos in England—testify to its origins: the Romans found it on the Greek island of Cos and brought it back to Rome, whence it was introduced to the rest of Europe. A lovely small variety, Little Gem, shares the same good qualities as ordinary romaine, and has a vivid young heart.

Celtuce

This tall Far Eastern specimen is among the less well-known salad plants. So called because it tastes just slightly of celery and looks rather like a head of lettuce with long, pale stalks and a head of leaves, it also used to be called asparagus lettuce. However, it tastes neither like asparagus nor much like celery, or even lettuce. The similarity to celery lies mostly in the crunch of the stalks, which, like celery, can be eaten raw, making a good salad when peeled and chopped. The similarity to lettuce is confined to the tender central leaves. The stalks can also be cooked like Swiss chard, and make a similar vegetable dish to be eaten with butter or a creamy sauce, while the tough outer leaves can be cooked like spinach.

Lamb's lettuce, corn salad

This is what you are served when you order a dish of *mâche* in France; the French name is increasingly being used in America as well by gourmet markets and trendy restaurants. The spoon-shaped leaves grow in dark-green rosettes, which are hard to wash as they harbor sand. It is more substantial than other lettuce and has a nutty taste that blends very well with the sweetness of beets for a winter salad.

Chicory, endive, and escarole

Wild chicory has pretty blue flowers, and is the ancestor of varieties now grown primarily for their roots. These are roasted and ground to make a coffee substitute. Its leaves are bitter and can be mixed with other salad greens.

Belgian endive First bred in Belgium, and sometimes called by its Flemish name, *witloof*, this is the best-known of the cultivated chicories. It is "blanched" by being grown in the dark or under sand or peat, and with its tightly furled leaves, it resembles a fat white cigar with a pale yellow (not green) tip. Sliced crosswise or with the leaves separated, it makes an interesting salad on its own, or it can be mixed with sliced orange or watercress and some oil and fresh lemon juice. In England, Belgian endive is called chicory.

What little bitterness there is in Belgian endive tends to come to the fore when it is cooked, so it is usually blanched in a little stock and a few drops of lemon juice before being braised. In this way it is particularly good with ham, veal, chicken, and pheasant.

Radicchio There are several types of this chicory introduced from Italy. Looking like miniature colored lettuces, the plants can be either deep ruby-red,

cream splashed with a fine wine red, or marbled pink. When they have not been carefully shaded, they look green or dark copper-colored and less pretty.

It is its beauty that recommends radicchio: it tastes much like a lettuce but with more bitterness, and has somewhat tougher ribs. It makes a very beautiful salad mixed with bright green lettuce and pale green escarole.

Curly endive and escarole The curly-leaved endive, often called chicory in the United States, and the broad-leaved escarole are more robust than the lettuce tribe. Although by nature they are bitter, they become less so when the jagged rosettes are shielded from the light and blanched to a succulent pale golden-green. Look for these in winter—they have much more character than most hothouse-reared winter lettuces.

Curly endive looks like a frizzy, pale greenish-white mop, and escarole has long, broad, crinkled leaves with a rather leathery texture and a pale yellow center. Prepare curly endive and escarole as you would any lettuce, but with a more highly flavored dressing; use them to give texture to a salad made of more delicate leaves, or on their own. A few walnuts and perhaps some small strips of bacon make good additions, and these are the greens to eat with a Roquefort dressing.

In Britain, escarole is often called by its variety name, Batavia, while the other names used for endive must stem from its Latin name, *Chicorium endiva*—in France it is known as *chicorée frisée*. French frisée, more delicate than regular curly-leaf endive but just as bitter, can be found in some gourmet produce markets, usually at exorbitant cost.

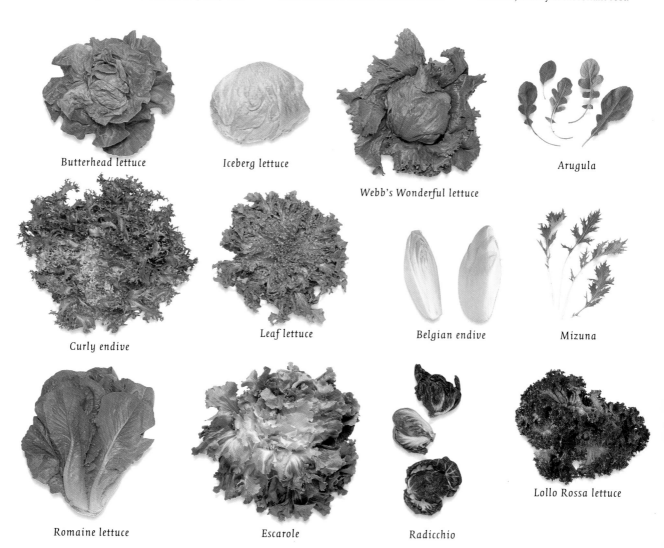

Butterhead lettuce

Iceberg lettuce

Webb's Wonderful lettuce

Arugula

Curly endive

Leaf lettuce

Belgian endive

Mizuna

Romaine lettuce

Escarole

Radicchio

Lollo Rossa lettuce

Cress

Watercress Dark-green, bunched sprigs of watercress make a beautiful garnish for grilled lamb chops or rack of lamb and game, and little sprigs enhance both the taste and look of a green salad or one containing sliced oranges. A watercress sauce is an excellent and pretty complement to fish, while nothing is fresher-tasting than a good watercress soup. When buying watercress, the rule is the darker and the larger the leaves, the better they are. Use watercress soon after purchase, keeping it meanwhile in the refrigerator in a plastic bag or in water, leaves down, like an upside-down bouquet, in a jelly jar—or even completely submerged in a bowl.

Other cress The tiny embryonic leaves of pepper cress, or curly cress, and garden cress are delicious in the thinnest and most delicate sandwiches—especially those containing hard-boiled egg or chicken, to which they bring a warm, sharp flavor—and as a garnish sprinkled over salads. Look for these and other cresses at farmers' and specialty markets; store them in the same way as watercress.

Arugula

This salad green, with its pale yellow flowers, looks something like a cross between mustard greens and radish leaves. The young leaves give a pungent, peppery taste to plain green salads, and in southern Italy wild arugula is used for extra flavor in the mixed salads eaten with pasta or veal. Arugula is also known as rocket, rugola, and rucola.

Mizuna

This feathery, delicate salad green has been cultivated in Japan since antiquity. Its flavor is mildly peppery, and it makes a good addition to *mesclun*, the mixture of young and tender salad leaves.

Radish

As a family, these roots belong to the mustard tribe, which, considering their hot pungency, is not surprising. In shape and color they range from little scarlet or white globes to long red and white types such as the Icicle radish. There is even a black radish, which has snow-white flesh.

Pungency varies not only according to type but also according to the soil in which the plants are grown. The elongated red-and-white type tends to be the mildest and goes by the name of French Breakfast radish, although one has yet to meet a Frenchman who actually eats them first thing in the morning. The most pungent of the pure white radishes is the type offered in Bavarian beer halls to encourage thirst. Except in Asia, where radishes are eaten as a full-fledged vegetable, they mostly provide an appetizer. As "they carry their pepper within," they can simply be dipped in salt and eaten with crusty French bread and butter, or may themselves be buttered and then sprinkled with sea salt. To serve them this way, wash them, trim off the roots and leaves, leaving a tuft about ½ inch long, and crisp them in the refrigerator with a few ice cubes on top. Radishes often appear on *crudités* platters, but they are more likely to be thought of as a garnish. In Italy, thin white slices of radish with their pretty red edges are scattered over green salads, perhaps with some equally thin slices of carrot.

Spring and winter radishes Radishes like the familiar globe, the French Breakfast, and the Icicle are

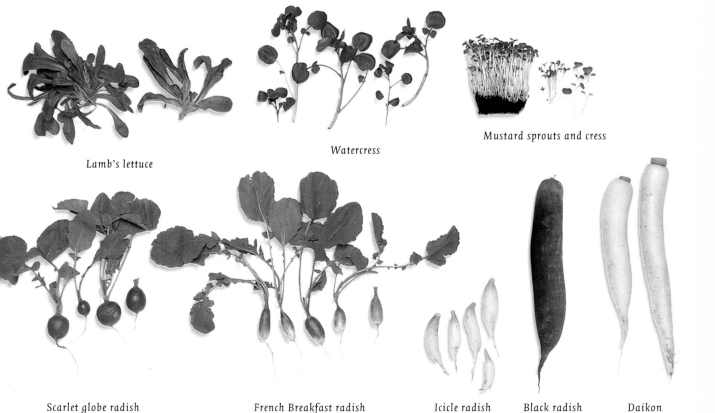

Lamb's lettuce

Watercress

Mustard sprouts and cress

Scarlet globe radish

French Breakfast radish

Icicle radish

Black radish

Daikon

all considered spring radishes. Their growing season may be as short as 4 weeks. Winter radishes, such as some black radishes, take much longer to mature; these large varieties, with flesh that is compact and firm, can be cooked or grated into salads.

Daikon This is the winter radish from Asia, the birthplace of radishes. Long, white, cylindrical, and enormous, with a less peppery flavor than ordinary radishes, it can be pickled, or grated and mixed with grated fresh ginger to make a sauce for stir-fried vegetables. It also features in tempura dishes.

OTHER GREENS

This group of green-leaved vegetables includes several that are now considered to be weeds. Once they were as well known as spinach, which, since its wide cultivation, has displaced them. But while spinach is now the most widely grown and popular of all our leaf vegetables, there should still be a place in the kitchen for its old-fashioned relations. All types of greens should be very fresh and need to be bought in generous quantities; this is because they will reduce significantly in volume when they are cooked.

Spinach

The long cultivation of spinach, since its first appearance in Persia many thousands of years ago, has resulted in succulent leaves of a beautiful green, which may be small and rounded—the best type to use for salads—or larger and more pointed, and either smooth or curly.

Since spinach greatly reduces in volume when cooked, you need to allow ¼ pound for each person. If the stems are coarse, they should be removed, and the center ribs should be torn from larger leaves, by folding the leaf inward and pulling the stem toward the tip. The spinach should then be well washed in several changes of water to remove the grit it often contains. Cook over low heat, the pan uncovered, with only the water that clings to the leaves. As the lower layer softens, stir the spinach, and continue in this way until all the leaves have wilted. Spinach must be very thoroughly drained, because it tends to exude water after it is cooked.

Spinach can be used in a multitude of ways. As a side dish, it can be served simply with plenty of butter, or in a creamy cheese sauce, or as a purée with cream. Sweet spinach purée, although it sounds rather odd, is an ancient dish:

Queen Elizabeth I sat down to a bowl of boiled spinach mixed with rose water, raisins, vinegar, butter, and sugar. And a pastry shell filled with spinach and candied orange and lemon peel, bathed in a rich creamy custard, is a Christmas dish in southern France.

In Italy, there are dozens of lovely spinach recipes: spinach is eaten in soufflés, frittatas, and dumplings; mixed with ricotta, Parmesan, and nutmeg to make a filling for stuffed pasta; and used to make the fresh green pasta that looks so pretty when combined with a cream or tomato sauce. No wonder that on French menus a spinach garnish goes under the Italian name of *alla fiorentina*. Eggs Florentine are eggs arranged on a bed of cooked spinach under a covering of cream or cheese sauce; fish and sweetbreads *à la florentine* have spinach in the sauce.

Spinach can also be eaten raw: delicious salads can be made with small, young spinach leaves garnished with pieces of crisply fried bacon and hard-boiled eggs, tossed in a garlic-laden vinaigrette.

There are also some wild plants that are reminiscent of spinach in flavor, two of them so close to spinach in taste that they are sometimes cultivated.

Nettle

Purslane

Sorrel

Dandelion greens

Spinach

Chinese mustard cabbage

Collards

New Zealand spinach is a fleshy-leaved plant discovered by Sir Joseph Banks, botanist on Captain Cook's *Endeavour*, who brought it back to Europe. It is still grown outside its native land, flourishing where excessive heat and lack of water would make true spinach bolt. Somewhat tougher than true spinach, it may be sold in specialty markets, or at farmers' markets.

Malabar spinach This thrives in tropical Asia and in tropical parts of Latin America. The large, bright, shiny leaves have a distinctive but good taste and are treated in the same way as spinach. In China, it is cultivated for its fleshy berries, which yield a dye that has been used by women as a rouge and also by high-ranking officials for sealing documents.

Cabbage greens

Any member of the cabbage family that does not form a proper head becomes simply one of many "greens," sometimes called spring or winter greens. See that the center ribs are crisp and firm. Any woody stems, coarse center ribs, or damaged leaves must be ruthlessly discarded.

Collards are the Cinderellas of the vegetable world, but, like Cinderella,

Beet greens

Kale

they are good and can be quite splendid when properly dressed. The leaves are particularly tender and delicate when cooked. They are excellent for heartier side dishes such as the Southern "mess o' greens," which usually contains salt pork or bacon; the cooking juices are referred to as "pot likker." These braised greens are always eaten with corn bread to mop up the broth.

Kale or curly kale has crimped leaves, like frisée or chicory. It was known by the early Greeks and Romans, whose climate was too warm to grow cabbage. There are many varieties of kale; some are grown as ornamental plants, and there is even one type whose stems become so hard and woody that when dried they are made into walking sticks. The edible ones taste rather like spring greens but stronger, and can be used for all cabbage recipes.

Cavolo nero is an Italian kale with dark green, strong-flavored leaves. It is much used in vegetable soups or eaten sautéed in oil with chile pepper.

Beet greens

The first-century Roman gourmet Apicius included in his book recipes for beet greens with mustard, oil, and vinegar, and for barley soup with beet greens. Beet greens are still grown extensively in Italy and in eastern districts of France, where, together with Swiss chard, they are known as *blettes* and are used interchangeably with chard. They are often mixed with sorrel to counteract the latter's acidity, being themselves extremely mild but earthy. When cooked, beet greens are used like spinach, and in Italy they are very popular as a stuffing for ravioli or agnolotti, together with ricotta and Parmesan cheese.

Mustard greens

This dark green leafy vegetable is very popular in the South. The leaves have a hot taste and are delicious when lightly braised with garlic and chile flakes. The young leaves, far less pungent than the larger older ones, make a zesty addition to a green salad.

Chinese mustard cabbage or greens (*gai choy*) resemble collards in appearance. They are eaten fresh, as well as stir-fried, used in soups, and pickled in a sweet-sour sauce.

Sorrel, dandelion greens, and purslane

Sorrel Of all the different types of sorrel, it is the cultivated French variety that is best for eating, adding an acid, lemony note to salads, soups, purées, sauces, and omelets. The classic *potage Germiny* consists of sorrel cut into delicate ribbons—called a *chiffonade*—cooked in butter and then moistened with chicken stock and thickened with egg yolk. A purée of sorrel is the traditional accompaniment to grilled shad and is also an exceedingly good foil for salmon. Because sorrel, even more than spinach, is rich in oxalic acid, it should be eaten in moderation.

Dandelion greens In some countries, gardeners wage constant, if ineffectual, war against this golden flower, regarding it as a particularly troublesome weed. In other places, they carefully sow seeds and then take great trouble "blanching" the plants with soil or a cover to keep the leaves tender and white for use in salads. In France, where housewives buy dandelion greens from market stalls, they are called *pissenlits* (literally, "piss-in-bed," illustrating their diuretic properties—so those who are addicted to dandelions should be warned). Their other French name, which is the source of the English word, is *dent de lion*, meaning "lion's tooth," because of their jagged edges.

Weed though they may be, they are certainly useful. The roots can be used as a caffeine-free coffee substitute, and the leaves make excellent salads. Perhaps the best is the French *pissenlits au lard*, a bowl of small, fat, juicy, whole dandelion plants in vinaigrette, over which is thrown a panful of sizzling pieces of salt pork or bacon and bacon fat.

You can remove most of the bitterness from wild dandelion greens by placing a plate over a patch of young plants to blanch them. But the juiciest, least bitter dandelion greens are those grown from a packet of domestic seed. Blanch them before they start to produce flower buds, and pick them young.

Purslane A native of India, where it has grown wild for thousands of years, fleshy-leaved purslane spread to England in the Middle Ages and was popular pickled and as a salad. It was introduced to North America by the early colonists, but today most people discard it as a weed. In England, too, it was once cultivated in gardens, but it is now uncommon. The French are more astute and still consider purslane—which they know as *pourpier*—to be a salad plant worth cultivating. The succulent leaves can also be boiled, and are good when quickly fried in butter and then used to fill an omelet. In the Middle East, where it is also cultivated, purslane is an important ingredient in *fattoush*— a salad mixture including tomatoes and cucumber eaten with pita bread.

Wild greens

There are still many edible green-leaved plants growing wild and free which, if nothing else, can be regarded as survival food. However, much enjoyment can be had gathering these plants on country walks and experimenting with cooking and eating them at home. Make sure, though, that you know exactly what you are gathering. If you are uncertain of what the plants look like, take an illustrated field guide with you so that you can identify the plants you want to find.

Nettle Northern countries used to prize the nettle, but it is now something most people avoid because of its sting (which completely disappears when the nettle is cooked). In Scandinavia, the leaves were boiled like spinach, and the coarse fibers of the stalks used for cloth, in the manner of flax. (This explains, without making it any less sad, the task of the fairy-tale maiden set to stitching nettle garments for her seven brothers, to lift the spell that had transformed them into swans.) Ireland combined nettles and oats in a broth, but her nettle haggis— a purée of nettles, leeks, cabbage, bacon, and oatmeal boiled in a bag—would not, one imagines, pass muster with a Scot. Italians still eat nettle purée or soup in the spring, as it is supposed to be excellent for cleansing the blood.

Nettles should be picked when they are only about a finger-length high; later on, they become bitter and tough. Remember to wear gloves, and use scissors to snip off the leaves.

Goosefoot Goosefoot is better known in Europe than in the United States. In Britain, two of the more delightfully named members of the family are Good King Henry and Fat Hen, both of which were staples in antiquity but have now been superseded by spinach. Fat Hen is a tall, stiff-stemmed plant, which grows prodigiously wherever there are people— or weeds. It tastes much like spinach but is considerably milder. The leaves of Good King Henry are also treated like spinach, and some suggest that the shoots can be prepared and eaten like asparagus.

Amaranth The green leaves of this species, also known as pigweed, have a taste similar to spinach, although more tender and sweet. The celery-like stalks taste somewhat of artichokes.

Chickweed is so called because poultry has a particular yen for it. It grows in all temperate climates of the world. Probably the most common of all edible weeds, it is a tender vegetable that, cooked in butter with chopped onion, goes well with rich meats.

Brooklime This makes a perfectly acceptable, though slightly bitter, substitute for watercress. Brooklime is found by streams and in marshy places in North America and in northern Europe.

CRUCIFEROUS VEGETABLES

Cabbages that form a head are members of the vast Brassica family, which also includes cauliflower, broccoli, and Brussels sprouts (as well as turnips and kohlrabi, which are eaten, respectively, for their roots and their swollen stems). In America, brassicas are referred to as cruciferous vegetables, or crucifers; all the members of the family have gained more respect than they once had, for crucifers are believed to have cancer-fighting properties.

All crucifers are descendants of the wild cabbage, which still grows in coastal regions of Italy and France—a tough, tall plant, almost all trunk. They are rich in vitamin C and minerals, but half of the vitamin content is lost when they are cooked. They all contain sulfur compounds, which give them their characteristic "cabbagey" smell when they are overcooked.

Cabbage

There are three main types of cabbage that form a head, distinguished mainly by color and texture: green, Savoy, and red.

Green cabbage Early-season green cabbages are a deeper green and more loosely packed than the later ones, and often have pointed heads. Buy them in the spring, checking that the leaves— frequently curly at the edges—are fresh and crisp; if you're buying at the farmers' market, where they are likely to be sold with all their outer leaves intact, even the outer leaves should be tender. Do not worry about the lack of heart—they simply have not had time to develop the firmness associated with the later kind. The later-season green cabbages, the type we usually see in the supermarket, are altogether tougher, and have solid hearts.

Green cabbages that are the very palest of green, almost white, are called white cabbages, or sometimes Dutch cabbages, in Britain. They have smooth leaves and are quite hard and firm. These pale-white cabbages are used in the coleslaw mixes available in the supermarket produce department and in some commercial coleslaws.

Savoy cabbage The crimped-leaved Savoy cabbage is particularly tender and mild-flavored and needs less cooking than other cabbages. The Savoy's head

Bok choy

Napa cabbage

is quite firm, for all its crinkliness, and is a beautiful green with a touch of blue. It stands up well to frosty weather and is therefore readily available throughout late winter. This is the best variety for stuffing.

Red cabbage Although this cabbage has magenta or dark purple skin, the color fades during cooking unless a little vinegar is added (the flavor is also improved by this added sharpness). Red cabbage is at its most delicious when braised with oil or another fat, vinegar, sugar, and plenty of spices and flavorings, and it is also good eaten raw or pickled.

Buying and storing cabbage When buying cabbages, no matter what kind, look not only at the leaves, which should be sound and unblemished, but also at the core. This should be neither dry and split nor woody and slimy. Those heads that have wilted outer leaves or a puffy appearance should be avoided.

The firmer the cabbage, the longer it will keep—Savoys can be kept in the refrigerator for several days at least; green and red cabbages will keep for one week or longer.

Cooking with cabbage Red cabbage is cooked very differently from the green variety, with such ingredients as wine vinegar, red wine, apples, raisins, onions, brown sugar, and spices going into the pot after the cabbage has been sautéed in oil or butter (or goose fat).

A sweet-and-sour red cabbage dish is also much improved by the addition of some dried prunes during the cooking. Red cabbage is traditionally served with the Christmas goose in many northern European countries and is also excellent with pork or game.

The simplest way to cook green cabbage is to boil it, after removing the core and tough outer leaves, and

washing it well in a bowl of cold water with 1 tablespoon salt to deal with any creatures that might lurk between the leaves. Cut into quarters or shreds, it needs no more than a few minutes to cook—the moment it starts to sink to the bottom of the pot, it is ready—and it should be cooked uncovered.

The smell of overcooked cabbage is a dreary one, and the sodden leaves that mark overcooked cabbage have to take much of the blame for the ruin of Britain's culinary reputation. Yet cabbage that has been carefully cooked and gently but thoroughly drained, and then heated with a generous quantity of butter, makes a delicate, light vegetable dish. Long, slow cooking gives it a succulent texture quite different from cabbage cooked quickly and served quite green.

There are several good slow-cooked dishes in which the cabbage is started off with fat and onions and then cooked

rendered goose fat 110

Braised Red Cabbage 368

Cauliflower

Purple sprouting broccoli

Broccoli

Savoy cabbage

Red cabbage

Purple cauliflower

White cabbage

Brussels sprout

Green cabbage

with meat added to the pot, including the Irish-American dish of corned beef and cabbage. Then there are the filling, stock-based cabbage soups, poured over slices of bread for extra body, which make complete meals by themselves.

In northern Germany, there is the famous hunter's cabbage, with golden cubes of bacon bathed in a piquant sauce, which accompanies the equally famous bratwurst. In Bavaria, in the southeast, cabbage is braised with chopped bacon, caraway seeds, and white wine. The nineteenth-century Bavarian king of the dream castles, the eccentric Ludwig, liked to eat his cabbage braised with pike and served with a crayfish sauce.

Stuffed cabbages are a category of their own: stuffings of all descriptions are layered between the blanched and semi-unfurled leaves. Ingredients may include different kinds of meat, bacon, chicken livers, herbs, rice, onions, and chestnuts, all bound with eggs and possibly rice or bread crumbs. Cabbages can also be stuffed after being hollowed out, with their tops cut off but replaced before going into the oven; or the individual leaves can be stuffed and tied into little parcels.

Sweet-and-sour cabbage dishes are popular in Jewish cooking, and in Russia, cabbage baked with apples is eaten with smoked meats. From sweet-and-sour it is only a small step to sour; cabbage ferments and becomes sauerkraut when packed in a barrel with salt. Fresh sauerkraut, or that sold in plastic bags, is preferable to the canned or jarred versions. Raw green cabbage makes a good salad either as coleslaw, with its thick creamy dressing, or simply shredded into a bowl and dressed with oil and vinegar.

Chinese cabbage

A wide variety of cabbages is grown in China, and they frequently end up in large wooden barrels, coarsely chopped and pickled in brine. Pickled cabbage is often used for dishes that need a piquancy or bite to them.

The Chinese cabbage that we know best is a variety called, in Chinese, *pe-tsai*; we know it simply as Chinese cabbage, or Chinese celery cabbage, or as Napa cabbage. It somewhat resembles a large, pale head of romaine lettuce, and is crisp and delicate with a faint cabbage flavor. Its crinkly inner leaves are best used in salads, while the outer leaves, once divested of their tough ribs, can be braised, stir-fried, simmered, or treated like ordinary cabbages.

Another Chinese cabbage is *bok choy*, or *pak choi*. It has large dark-green leaves at the top of long white stalks. Bok choy is used in soups and stir-fried meat dishes as well as being prepared in the same ways as spinach or cabbage.

Broccoli

Like the cauliflower, broccoli started life in the Mediterranean region, where the warm, dry climate encouraged wild cabbages to shoot into buds rather than concentrate on making leaves. The earliest broccoli was the purple sprouting type, which has green stalks and loose green rudimentary flowers. Broccoli is a delicate vegetable, and the best broccoli can be said to combine the subtle, fresh texture of cauliflower with the succulence of asparagus.

Look for broccoli that is deeply colored a brilliant emerald green. Broccoli that is tinged with purple or bluish green is considered the best. The spears should look firm and fresh, and the florets should be tightly closed; avoid any that show the least sign of turning yellow.

Broccoli is best steamed or boiled briefly so that it still preserves some crispness. It is often eaten with hollandaise or a cheese sauce, or simply with butter and a squeeze of lemon juice. Bright green broccoli florets and pure white cauliflower make a lovely combination.

Sprouting broccoli The Romans ate purple sprouting broccoli either cooked in wine or dressed in oil and sharp *garum*—a sauce of fermented fish—and also added it as a garnish to a soup of chickpeas and lentils, peas, and barley. In Sicily, broccoli is still cooked in the oven with anchovies and onions. In the rest of Italy, it is often parboiled and finished off with oil, garlic, and chile flakes in the frying pan, perhaps eaten with pasta.

Although less succulent than regular broccoli, sprouting broccoli is a very fine vegetable. In addition to the purple sprouting broccoli, there are white and green varieties; the stalks of all types are usually cooked whole, with the small loose buds still attached, and served drenched in butter. Purple sprouting broccoli turns green when cooked; the others keep their original color. The flavor of all kinds is excellent, but sprouting broccoli must be picked young, or it becomes stringy and tough.

Cauliflower

Since early cauliflowers used to be no larger than tennis balls, one can justify the complaint made by six seventeenth-century travelers to Italy who rose from the table in a marble palazzo as hungry as they arrived, having shared among them one cauliflower, a dish of anchovies, and three hard-boiled eggs. Modern cauliflowers can be enormous, although ironically a strain no larger than golf balls is being grown once more. One type of cauliflower, originally from Sardinia and southern Italy, is purple but turns green when cooked and another is green with a pointed head. Another beautiful cauliflower, rather confusingly called broccoli Romanesco in the United States (but Romanesca or Roman cauliflower in the British Isles), is bright green all the way through— a more grassy green than broccoli. Its curds (these are so called because they resemble soured-milk curds) grow in whorls like a snail shell. And despite its name, the pale-green broccoflower is not a cross between broccoli and cauliflower, but simply a variety of cauliflower.

A fresh head of cauliflower will have a compact cluster of creamy white florets, or curds, and will feel heavy for its size. Loose or spreading florets mean the cauliflower is overmature.

When cooking cauliflower whole, test for tenderness after 8 to 10 minutes by carefully sticking a skewer into a side stalk; continue testing until there is little, but still some, resistance. Florets take 6 to 8 minutes and will cook more evenly.

Cauliflower needs sauce—a light creamy sauce flavored with cheese or mustard; or perhaps an Italian sauce incorporating chopped onion, capers, olives, and anchovies—or fried bread crumbs and chopped hard-boiled eggs. Cauliflower and cheese have a special affinity: cauliflower *au gratin* is a classic. Florets of raw cauliflower, as part of a plate of *crudités*, arranged around a bowl of mustardy mayonnaise, make a good cocktail party offering, and cold cooked florets in a mustard vinaigrette make a delicious salad.

Brussels sprout

At their best, Brussels sprouts look like tiny green buds, and at their worst, like miniature full-blown cabbages. Developed in Flanders, the vegetable garden of Europe, some time in the Middle Ages, Brussels sprouts grow at the intersection of leaf and stalk on a tall plant that much resembles the old wild cabbage. They have a delicate nutty taste, especially when they are small. Cooked until just tender but not too soft, they are an excellent vegetable.

The ideal size for Brussels sprouts is no bigger than about an inch in diameter; the smaller the sprout, the more tender. Do not waste much time before using them—they soon turn yellow. Look for compact green heads and uniform size so that they will cook evenly. Some people cut a cross in the stem, but this is really only necessary in large specimens cut from coarse, wide stalks; fresh small ones do not need such incisions. Prepare by washing and trimming off any yellowing leaves, then cook in rapidly boiling well-salted water without a lid so that they preserve their good green color.

Brussels sprouts are a traditional accompaniment to turkey, together with separately braised chestnuts, at many Christmas dinners. On less festive occasions, they appear simply tossed in butter, or with browned butter and toasted bread crumbs. If they are used to garnish a meat dish or game birds in France, the dish is called *à la bruxelloise*. Some people like Brussels sprouts with a white or cheese sauce, or with crisply fried and crumbled bacon.

SHOOTS AND STALKS

Although shoots and buds often look appetizing, there are in fact only a handful that make serious eating: the buds of the palm tree are familiar to us as hearts of palm, and asparagus and bamboo shoots are two of the best vegetables there are—particularly asparagus, one of nature's kindest gifts to man. Stalks are mainly enjoyed in the form of celery and sweet fennel, chard and cardoons, while the globe artichoke, a companion delicacy, is a flower bud.

Fennel

Looking like a short, bulbous celery plant, fennel is also called Florence or sweet fennel or finocchio, and it is sometimes incorrectly referred to as anise. Florence fennel is a close relation of common fennel, the herb, and the same feathery leaves can be seen emerging from its fat, overlapping stalks. Like the herb, it tastes of anise, and its leaves can be used to flavor a court-bouillon for a fish dish. Southern Italians eat it raw, very thinly sliced and simply dressed with a fruity olive oil or with garlicky *aïoli*; northern Italians slice and parboil it, then bake it with butter and grated Parmesan. It makes a very good addition to a green salad.

When braising fennel, allow one bulb per person. Trim away the base and, if the outer leaves are tough, string it as you would celery, then halve or quarter the bulbs. Choose rounded, fat bulbs in preference to long, thin ones, which tend to be less succulent. Buy fennel as fresh as possible; the bulb should be white in color and firm in texture—any yellowness is a sign of age. It will keep crisp in a plastic bag in the refrigerator.

Asparagus

Although there are many species of asparagus, ranging from the thorny ones of Spain to the shiny ones of the Far East, it is always something of a luxury because its season is so short. There are also many differences in the way it is raised: white French asparagus is cut below the sand that covers the crown once the tip has emerged above the soil; American and English asparagus is allowed to grow above the ground, which gives it its green color all the way down the stalk; Dutch and German ivory-tipped asparagus is always grown under mounds of soil, which help to blanch it, and it is cut as soon as the tips begin to show.

Whatever the color, the thick varieties of asparagus are usually the most

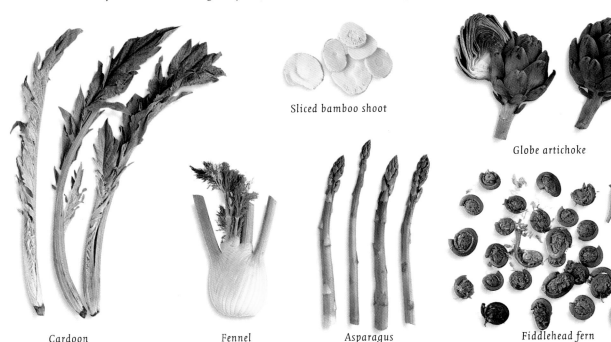

Cardoon

Fennel

Sliced bamboo shoot

Asparagus

Globe artichoke

Fiddlehead fern

expensive. The famed asparagus of Argenteuil, with their white stalks showing a purple tinge toward the top, and their pointed green and purple heads, are considered to be the very best, certainly in France, but this does not stop America from considering its more modest green asparagus to have a superior flavor. In fact, each of the great asparagus-growing areas, no matter the country, tends to prefer its own asparagus above all others, because although asparagus travels well, it starts to lose flavor from the moment it is cut. It is a revelation to eat asparagus fresh from the garden, cut and cooked within the hour or even sooner.

Thick or thin, the tips are the best part, and this is the part to inspect when buying asparagus. The tips should be tightly furled, with the scales close together, and none of them discolored or moist.

The difficulty encountered in cooking asparagus arises from the fact that the tips, being much more tender than the stalks, cook more quickly and may break off when you transfer the asparagus to the serving dish. The answer is to cook asparagus in an asparagus cooker or steamer, a special pot with a perforated insert. Failing this, cook them tied together in bundles in a wide shallow pan. With the second method, it is extremely important not to overcook the asparagus, or to boil it too fast, or the tips will become damaged.

To prepare the asparagus, wash it well, cut off the hard ends, and peel the lower part of the stalks with a knife or potato peeler. Then tie the asparagus into small bundles, if you are not using an asparagus cooker. Bring well-salted water to a boil in the cooker (or a wide pan). Lower the asparagus into the water (in the cooker just the stalks are in water; the tips will cook in the steam) and return to the boil as rapidly as possible. Cover and cook for 8 to 10 minutes, until the lower parts of the stalks are easily pierced with the tip of a knife. Don't overcook them—they should be just tender when pierced, and the tips will break up if boiled for too long. If you like, save the asparagus water as well as a few token stalks of asparagus for making soup. Serve the rest, carefully drained.

Asparagus can be served as a course on its own, at the beginning of the meal.

Swiss chard

Celery

It is best eaten with the fingers. Served warm, asparagus is best with melted butter, or with hollandaise or mousseline sauce (hollandaise with whipped cream added to it). In France, asparagus *à la flamande* has halved hard-boiled eggs and browned butter served separately. When it is served *à la polonaise*, the browned butter—butter that is heated in a pan until it is a pale hazelnut color—is poured over the tips, which have been sprinkled with finely chopped hard-boiled eggs. In Italy, asparagus is eaten with freshly grated Parmesan cheese and butter over the tips, melted just for a moment under a broiler.

If asparagus is to be served cold, either mayonnaise or a vinaigrette dressing is the usual accompaniment. As asparagus contains a certain amount of sulfur, it spoils the taste of wine, so save the wine for other courses when you are serving the asparagus separately.

Asparagus also makes a good vegetable dish, of course, and goes well with delicate, light meats: veal, sweetbreads, chicken breasts, slices of turkey, or rosy boiled ham, thinly sliced. And asparagus can also go into risottos or omelets.

Celery

Although this can be white or golden in color, which means that it has been blanched during cultivation or is the self-blanching kind, most of the celery in the market is the green Pascal variety. The ribs, or stalks, should be thick and crisp, the leaves green and full of vitality, and the base sound. Revive limp celery by wrapping it in moist paper towels and standing it in a jar of water. Celery should be thoroughly washed before use.

Raw celery is excellent served with cheese, standing in a tall jar with the decorative leaves intact; however, the coarse outer strings should be removed first. Do this by cutting partway through the rib bases and pulling off the attached strings down the length of the ribs.

Chopped, raw celery is often mixed with tuna or egg salad as a sandwich filling. Celery also goes into poultry stuffings and sauces, and can be stewed with bacon to accompany game and other meats. It is delicious parboiled and served *au gratin*, and it is equally good when braised in broth or water, or *à la grecque*—with olive oil and lemon juice—and eaten cold.

Swiss chard

Swiss chard is grown both for its pale, wide center ribs and for its leaves. Green chard, with its white ribs, is more familiar, but there is also red chard, with green leaves and red ribs, and ruby chard, which has reddish leaves and ribs. Although baby chard can be cooked whole, usually the stalks and leaves are cooked separately. The leaves can be prepared like spinach or beet greens, while the stalks have a delicate flavor and are extremely succulent when boiled or steamed. They can be served *au gratin* or simply with melted butter. In France, chard, or *blettes*, is served with béchamel sauce and sausages, while in Italy, it makes stuffings for tarts and ravioli or is chopped and cooked in risotto.

Globe artichoke

Although not strictly a shoot or stalk, but rather a bud, the globe artichoke is usually considered in the same group as delicacies such as asparagus. While some of its flavor lies in the fat base of each of its leaves, the best part—the *fond* (bottom)—lies deep within its center.

When you buy artichokes—they can be green or purplish—make sure they still have a good bloom on their leaves and that the centers are well closed, not looking almost ready to burst into great purple thistle-like flower heads. They don't keep well and should be used at once, but if you must keep them, place them in a plastic bag in the refrigerator.

To prepare artichokes for cooking, if the stalks are long enough, twist them off, which will also remove some of the tougher fibers from the base. Then, with a stainless steel knife, cut the base of each globe flush so that it won't wobble on the plate when it is served and rub the cut surface with lemon to prevent it from turning black. If the leaves are very spiky, cut them into a pretty V shape or simply trim off the tops. Wash the artichokes and then boil with a little lemon juice in a stainless steel or other nonreactive pan— perhaps with a slice of lemon tied to each base. Test for readiness by tugging at a leaf: when it comes away and is tender, the artichoke is done and ready to be drained upside down on a rack.

One of the best ways to eat globe artichokes is simply to pull off the leaves with your fingers, one at a time; dip the fleshy part in turn into melted butter, vinaigrette, or hollandaise, then draw it through your teeth, eating the fleshy part, and put the remains of the leaf on your plate. When you reach the tiny pale leaves in the center, which seem to be arranged in the form of a little pointed hat, grasp them tightly at the top and pull off the whole rosette. Then pull away and discard the prickly, straw-like choke, which may come away with one tug or

1

2

3

5

Preparing globe artichoke bottoms

As you work, rub all the cut surfaces with lemon halves to prevent discoloration.

1 Snap the stalk off at the base of the artichoke, pulling out the coarse fibers with it.

2 Bend a large lower leaf out and over toward the base until the leaf snaps, then pull it off. Continue snapping off all the large outer leaves in this way.

3 Cut off the cone of paler green, soft inner leaves, cutting straight across just above the hairy choke.

4

4 Using a small knife, trim off all the dark green parts from around the sides and base of the artichoke bottom, trimming it into a neat round shape.

5 Scoop out the hairy choke in the center using a teaspoon (or do this after cooking the artichoke bottom according to the recipe instructions). Cook the artichoke bottom immediately, or immerse it in water acidulated with lemon juice, to prevent discoloration.

need a bit of scraping. Finally, eat the bottom, which is slightly pitted, with a knife and fork.

It is possible to remove the chokes before cooking, to form little cups. The artichokes can also be trimmed and the artichoke bottoms then filled or stuffed, perhaps with a béchamel sauce and Parmesan, or with a purée of mushrooms. They are usually parboiled before they are stuffed, and then go into the oven, anointed with butter or oil, until the stuffing is cooked. For delicate dishes, or when artichoke bottoms are required as a garnish, all the leaves are removed and the bottom trimmed; this is often done in sophisticated restaurants, where artichoke bottoms, whole or trimmed, appear in various dishes.

Among the many ways of preparing artichokes, the Italians have produced the most inventive. They simmer artichoke bottoms in broth or wine, or in wine with oil, tomatoes, and garlic, and fry small, tender artichokes in oil. Sometimes they blanch the smaller ones and then dip them in batter before deep-frying them. As elsewhere, artichokes are also eaten cold in Italy.

Sliced sautéed artichoke bottoms may be mixed with peas and ham or scrambled eggs, and if in France you are given a soup called *Chatelaine*, you will find that it is made of puréed artichoke bottoms. In the south of France and some parts of Italy, tiny young artichokes are eaten raw, either whole with *aïoli* or *bagna cauda*—a hot anchovy-and-garlic-flavored dip—or thinly sliced and tossed with Parmesan in olive oil.

Seakale

Highly popular in earlier times, although less often seen now, this European plant is a member of the mustard family. A frail, pale vegetable, it grows wild in English coastal districts, forcing its stalks up through mounds of sand so that they emerge perfectly white. The juicy but delicate stems of cultivated seakale are sometimes found in the market.

Cardoon

A relative of the globe artichoke, the cardoon is cultivated for its young leaf stalks and has a flavor that faintly resembles that of the artichoke. Left to itself, it produces smaller, spikier heads than the artichoke, which in Greece are

picked and eaten stewed, but what you may find in markets in winter and early spring is the bottom part of the plant, looking like overgrown gray-green celery. Cardoons are grown covered with soil to blanch the stalks, which gives them their delicate texture and delicious flavor.

The finest cardoons are those from the region of Tours in the center of France, but since Italians enjoy their *cardoni* even more than do the French, you are likely to come across cardoons in Italian markets.

To prepare them, trim off the skin, which is fibrous and prickly at the ridges, blanch the cardoons in boiling water, and then cook them for about 30 minutes in a *blanc* (boiling water to which 1 tablespoon of flour has been added); this helps to keep the color, because, like artichokes, cardoons will discolor easily when cooked. Serve them with a béchamel or cheese sauce, or *alla piedmontese*—dipped into a sauce of anchovies, oil, and garlic—or simply eat them with melted butter. In North Africa, they are used to flavor meat stews.

Bamboo shoot and heart of palm

Edible young bamboo shoots—not all bamboos are edible—are bought fresh in the Far East and stripped of their tough brown outer skins before being eaten. Their texture is similar to celery and their taste to a globe artichoke.

The canned variety is the most readily available outside Asia. It needs no peeling, but it should be rinsed before use, whether packed in brine or water, because it otherwise has a pronounced tinny taste. Chopped bamboo shoots can be used in a number of stir-fried vegetable and meat dishes, and as a garnish for clear chicken broth. They can also be served with any of the sauces that are suitable for asparagus.

Hearts of palm are the buds of cabbage palm trees. Fresh hearts of palm are sometimes available in Florida, where they are grown, but in the rest of the country, only canned are available. The fresh ones need to be blanched before being cooked to get rid of their bitter flavor. Served hot, they are eaten with any of the sauces suitable for asparagus; cold, they need a vinaigrette dressing. They are also good in mixed salads. Hot or cold, they are usually served cut in half lengthwise.

Hop shoot

While the dried flowers of hops are used for brewing, the young blanched shoots, popular throughout Europe, can be cooked and eaten with melted butter, like asparagus. In France, where they are known as *jets de houblon*, they are considered to be a delicacy. Their delicate flavor goes especially well with creamy sauces. In Belgium, young hop shoots are served with eggs.

Fiddlehead fern

Found in the eastern part of the United States and Canada, fiddlehead ferns are not, in fact, a particular type of fern, but simply young ferns of any type, with their shoots still tightly coiled. The small, rich green shoots have a satisfying chewy texture and a flavor that has been described as a mixture of asparagus, green beans, and mushrooms. Eat them raw, in a salad, or sauté in butter with lemon juice and black pepper.

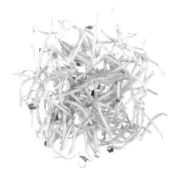

Bean sprout

Corn

PEA, BEAN, AND CORN

From the moment they are picked, peas, beans, and corn start converting their sugar into starch. Because this process subtly alters both their taste and texture, it is freshness just as much as youth that matters, and they should be chosen carefully and eaten the very day they are bought. Freezing, however, arrests these changes, which is why frozen peas, beans, and corn retain their sweetness and texture so well.

Pea

Once inordinately expensive and considered a great luxury, peas have become one of the best loved of all vegetables. Endless varieties have been developed, especially in England, where the climate suits them to perfection.

Garden pea The green garden pea is also known as the English pea. Although there are dozens of varieties of English pea, most have disappeared from the marketplace. The reason is, of course, the ubiquitous frozen pea—a great timesaver.

Green peas respond to all sorts of treatment: in the United States and England they are liked best of all plain, boiled and bathed in butter, although some cooks add a sprig of fresh mint. In Italy, peas are often mixed with fine shreds of raw ham, or with rice, in which case the dish becomes *risi e bisi*. In the countries, such as France, where vegetables are habitually served in a light coating of white sauce, peas, too, are given this treatment.

Contrary to popular belief, the small garden peas called petits pois are small not because they are immature but because they are a dwarf variety. These are the peas that are canned in vast quantities by the French and Belgians, and they are excellent: tiny, dull green, and very sweet, they are quite unlike most other types of canned peas, which are best avoided altogether.

Snow pea These are also called Chinese pea pods; as their French name, *mangetout* (literally, "eat-all") suggests, they are eaten pods and all. There are many varieties, all bred with the minimum of thin, tough membrane that lines the pod of the common green pea. Look for young snow peas, bright green and with scarcely visible seeds. If they have strings at the sides, these should be removed during topping and tailing.

Snow peas taste best when they are briefly boiled or steamed. When cooked, they should still have a little bite to them, and they are best served perfectly simply, with just enough butter to coat each pod. Very young snow peas are good in salads, and all snow peas are also excellent when stir-fried.

Sugar snap pea These are like snow peas in that they have an edible pod, but they are eaten after the peas inside have matured and swollen. As a result, the pod is lumpy rather than flat.

Béchamel Sauce 256
Fresh Peas with Lettuce Française 373
Peas in the Indian Fashion 373

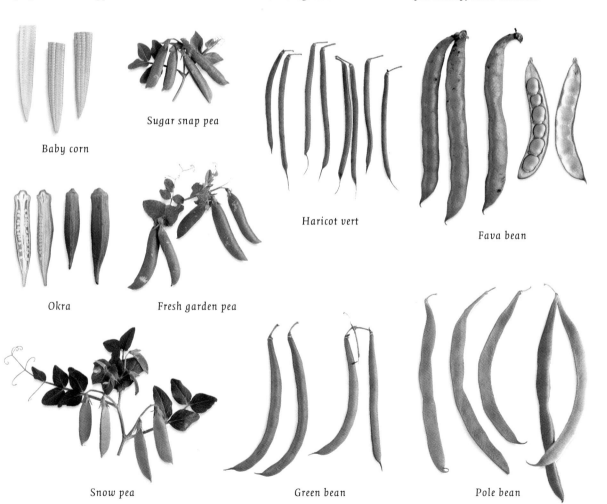

Baby corn

Sugar snap pea

Haricot vert

Fava bean

Okra

Fresh garden pea

Snow pea

Green bean

Pole bean

Green bean

This is a general term that is used to describe beans with edible pods, but in fact they come in colors ranging from deep green and purple to pale yellow. The two main types, however, are the round green bean and the flatter pole, or runner, bean. Beans of either type may also be known as snap beans, because they should snap in half juicily if they are fresh.

Of the round green beans, there are dozens of varieties available. The highly prized haricot vert is slim and delicate and should be eaten very young, when it is no larger in size than the prong of a carving fork. The yellow wax bean is also a round bean and is somewhat mild in taste.

Pole beans have long, rough, and usually stringy pods, although stringless varieties are available. As their name suggests, they are a type of climbing bean, rather than a bush bean, like most other green beans. There is a delicious purple-podded pole bean that has stringless purple pods, but these turn the normal green when they are cooked.

Whatever the type, podded beans should always look both crisp and bright—avoid buying wilted ones or overly mature beans with tough-looking pods. They all need their ends trimmed, and some types still need de-stringing. Test for stringiness by keeping the top or tail end just attached to the pod and drawing it downward: if a portion of tough string comes away, careful de-stringing is indicated.

All podded beans are cooked in the same way. They should be briefly steamed or plunged into well-salted, rapidly boiling water and cooked until just *al dente*—too often they suffer from overcooking. Once drained, they can be tossed in butter until they glisten. Green beans especially can be served in a sauce containing shallots, or cream and butter with chives, or bathed in a tomato purée with a touch of onion.

Lima bean and fava bean

In their first youth, neither lima beans nor fava beans strictly require shelling, but the pods are nearly always discarded to reveal large, flattish seeds.

Lima bean These are named after the capital of Peru. They are most familiar in America in their shelled and frozen state, but are at their best when they can be bought fresh and in their pods. They appear in the American Indian dish succotash, which also includes corn. Lima beans are sometimes called butter beans in the South. There are two types of lima bean—the baby Sieva, pale in color, and the larger Fordhook.

Fava bean Also called broad beans, these are the original Old World bean, much appreciated in Italy and Spain. (*Fava* is the Italian name.) These large, lumpy beans with their furry lined pods should be shelled immediately before going into the pot, unless they are very young, in which case they need only to be trimmed and can then be cut up, cooked, and eaten pods and all. Older fava beans will need skinning after they are cooked.

For a plain dish of lima beans or fava beans, plunge the shelled beans into a large pan of rapidly boiling water and cook until they are just tender, but not a moment longer. These beans are also delicious with cooked ham or bacon.

Okra

These curved and pointed seed pods originally came from Africa. They traveled to America with the slaves and feature a great deal in Creole cooking. The flavor of this vegetable resembles that of eggplant, but the texture is mucilaginous, and this is what gives the body to the Creole stews and gumbos to which okra is added.

Crossbreeding has produced a range of colors and surfaces, but the slim, green, octagonal okra is the one that is usually sold in our markets. Look for small, crisp pods and avoid any that are shriveled or bruised.

To cook okra whole, trim off the tip and the cap, but be sure not to expose the seeds and sticky juices inside, or the okra will split and lose shape during cooking. Steamed or cooked in boiling salted water until tender, okra can be served with a tomato sauce or simply tossed in butter, or it can be used in vegetable ragouts and stews.

Corn

One of the delights of late summer is the appearance on the market of fresh, tender young corn. The husks should be clean and green; the silk tassels bright and golden-brown with no sign of dampness or matting; and the kernels plump, well filled, and milky, with no space between the rows. Avoid ears with dark yellow kernels or older large ones that look tough and dry.

When dealing with fresh corn, time is of the essence—the briefer the span between picking and eating, the sweeter and more tender the corn will be. There are now supersweet varieties being bred that will stay sweeter much longer than other types, but even with these, the fresher, the better. If you are not able to use corn immediately, then keep it stored in plastic bags in the refrigerator for no more than 2 or 3 days. Be sure to allow the corn plenty of space—if the ears are piled on top of one other, this will tend to generate warmth and "cook" the corn.

To cook corn on the cob, strip away the green packaging and silk tassel, then steam or plunge into briskly boiling water. A little sugar can be added for extra sweetness—especially for the corn sold in Europe, which is never quite as sweet and tender as American corn. Never salt the water used for boiling corn—salt will toughen it. Serve with plenty of butter, salt, and freshly ground pepper, and with large napkins. Fresh corn on the cob can also be grilled, either in the husk (don't soak the husks first, as many books advise—you'll just be steaming the corn) or out, and it can be roasted, husked, in a hot oven.

Baby corn, which is imported from Thailand, is a popular addition to stir-fry dishes. It has a crisp yet tender texture but not much flavor.

Bean sprout

The sprouts that can be bought in plastic bags, or sometimes in plastic boxes, and are an ingredient in many Asian dishes have usually been sprouted from mung beans or soybeans. Look for crisp, pale sprouts; even a hint of exuding brown juice means that they are past their prime.

Mild-flavored bean sprouts will add a crunchy texture to a range of salads, or they can be stir-fried briefly over high heat and seasoned with soy sauce, fresh ginger, garlic, and scallions. Always serve the sprouts immediately, or they will lose their crunch.

Keep bean sprouts in their plastic bag or box in the refrigerator while they are waiting to be used.

THE ONION FAMILY

The onion, or Allium, family, including garlic and leeks, has a great many members, both cultivated and wild. It is because the onion is such an ancient vegetable that it has been bred in so many forms. While many of these can be used interchangeably, each type has a particular use.

Onion

Being both flavoring agent and vegetable in its own right, the onion is something that no kitchen can ever be without. There are few savory dishes that don't start with a sliced or chopped onion, and few that would be good without it. Then there are onions in onion soup, creamy or clear, quiches like *zwiebelkuchen* from Austria or the French *tarte à l'oignon*, as well as all the garnishes that this versatile vegetable provides. Among these are the glazed, bronzed pearl onions, good with any plainly roasted meat, particularly veal; fried onions that go with steak and liver; little pickled onions; and the smaller, fresh green-tailed scallions that are sometimes part of a *crudités* platter and can be eaten with cheese.

Green or fresh onions

These are generally eaten raw in salads, but can also be cooked. There are two types of fresh green onions, which are so called because of the green leaves that form above the white part. These are scallions and Welsh onions, or Japanese bunching onions.

Scallion These may be tiny and thin, like miniature leeks, except that their leaves are tubular, or they may have been lifted from the soil after small silvery bulbs have formed just above the roots. On the West Coast and in some other parts of the United States, these are usually called green onions. They taste mild and quite delicate, and both the white bottoms and the green tops are used as lively additions to salads and salad dressings. When cooked, scallions are added to some savory dishes where other onions would add too strong a flavor. They are also good when finely chopped and mixed with mashed potatoes, in omelets, and as a fresh-looking garnish on pork dishes.

Welsh onion, Japanese bunching onion If you find scallions mentioned in Chinese or Japanese recipes, these are the onions you should use, if you can get hold of them—they are not widely known in the West and certainly not in Wales, despite their name. The names Japanese bunching onion and Chinese onion are more precise, since they are very popular in Asia. Welsh onions grow in clusters, and, if the young leaves are harvested early in the year, the bulbs will grow more leaves. Eat the small, young green leaves raw in salads, and the mature stems in any recipe that is suitable for leeks, or in onion soup.

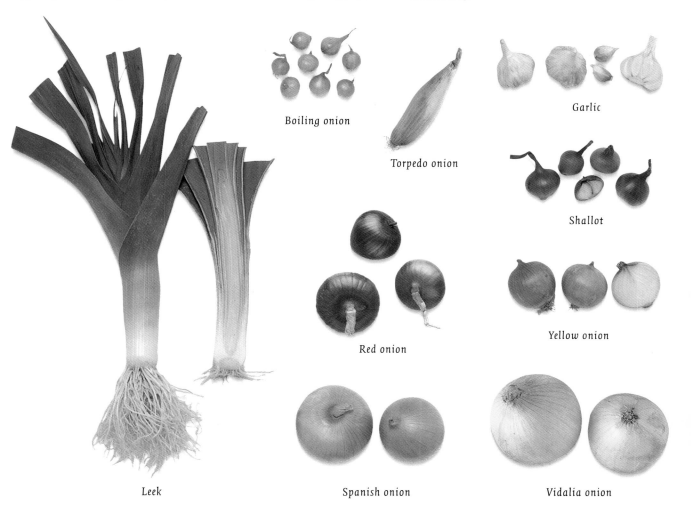

Leek

Boiling onion

Torpedo onion

Garlic

Shallot

Red onion

Yellow onion

Spanish onion

Vidalia onion

Dry or storage onions It is a good idea to try to buy ordinary dry onions in assorted sizes, or to choose smaller rather than larger specimens, because once cut, they do not keep well. To keep back the tears when peeling an onion, try peeling it under running water.

Chopping an onion into dice can be quite a fast business if efficiently tackled. Peel the onion but do not cut off the root end. Halve the onion through the root and lay the half-onion cut side down. Slice down into narrow strips, cutting from tip end to root end, but do not let the strips fall apart. Now, holding the half-onion together, cut across the strips, at right angles to the first cuts. Remove the root end and the onion will fall into dice.

Once chopped, the onion is often "sweated" in hot fat—meaning that it is allowed to become soft and translucent without coloring—or is sautéed to a more or less deep gold in order to develop its characteristic flavor. It is then incorporated with the other ingredients for the dish in the making.

Storage onions come in all sizes, from small white pearl onions to coppery spheres as large as grapefruit, and in a variety of shapes: oval, round, slender, and flat. All come to a peak at the top, like the domes of the Kremlin, which owe their shape to the fact that the many-layered onion—"a sky within a sky"—was regarded as a symbol of eternity in its native Asia and beyond.

Yellow onion Known by this name although its outer skin is golden-brown rather than yellow, this is considered to be the most pungent of all onions. Look for sound, dry specimens, with no trace of moisture at the base or the neck, and no growth of light greenery at the top—a sign that they have begun to sprout again at the expense of the soundness of their core. The yellow globe onion is the basic all-purpose onion.

White onion This globe onion, which can be quite large in size, is not quite as pungent as the yellow. White globe onions are favored in Mexican cooking.

Spanish onion This large, flattened, pale copper-colored onion is generally inclined to be milder and sweeter in flavor than either the yellow or the white variety. Its size makes it particularly suitable for stuffing and baking, and its comparative gentleness makes it ideal as fried onions, in salads, and for use in dishes that need its additional substance, such as creamy soups and sauces.

Bermuda onion Large but rather more squat, this can be used in the same ways as Spanish onions and is ideal with hamburgers.

Red onion This is relatively mild and distinguished by its deep red skin and the red-tinged layers below the skin. Sweet in flavor, it can be used for the same purposes as Spanish onions, and is good raw in antipasto and in salads.

Boiling onion This is a small yellow or white globe onion, about 1¼ inches in diameter. Despite the name, boiling onions are often added whole to braised dishes and stews.

Pearl onion This relatively mild little onion has a shimmery silver skin. It is about the size of a walnut, and is best either added to stews or served in a cream sauce. Small pearl onions are used for pickling, and in many French dishes such as coq au vin. They are delicious, too, made into a *confit*, by slow cooking in a caramelized, tart-flavored syrup. Very tiny white onions are called cocktail onions. Sold in jars, these are used as a garnish in various cocktails such as the Gibson—which is what a Martini becomes when an onion replaces the usual olive.

Vidalia onion This very juicy onion from Georgia is much sweeter than the Spanish or Bermuda onion, and is excellent both raw and cooked. Walla Walla onions, from Washington State, and Maui onions, from Hawaii, are similar large, sweet onions. New varieties are being developed all the time.

Rocambole Also known as Italian or serpent garlic, or in England as tree onion or garlic-onion, this is a curiosity for the gardener. It produces a cluster of little copper-colored bulbs at the top of the plant, where one normally expects to see only flowers. If these are planted in winter or spring, they will produce larger bulbs with a good flavor, somewhere between garlic and shallots.

Torpedo onion This is spindle-shaped and up to 6 inches long, with a sweet, mild flavor.

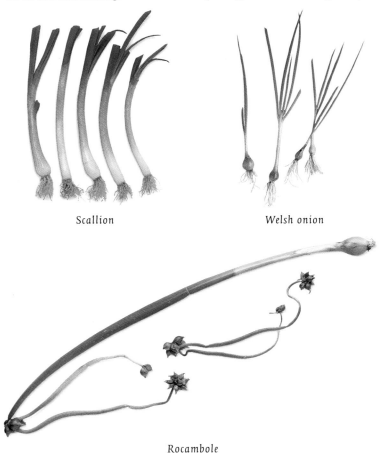

Scallion

Welsh onion

Rocambole

Shallot

This pear-shaped bulb with a long neck and skin that ranges from copper to pinkish to the gray of French shallots, is intense in taste without being unduly pungent. Shallots grow singly or in clusters. The crisp layers of their flesh are finely textured. Because shallots taste sweet and delicate, they are mostly used for flavoring. No other member of the onion family produces such an exquisite flavor in a sauce such as beurre blanc, the butter sauce that features them cooked in wine or in wine vinegar.

When recipes specify shallots, they should be used. And, although it would be extravagant, you can use shallots instead of onions if you want a lighter, more delicate taste. The exception comes when browning is involved, as this makes shallots taste a little bitter; shallots cook much faster than onions.

Shallots are an important ingredient in the cooking of northern France, featuring in *marchand de vin* sauces, made by reducing shallots to a purée with wine (red wine to go with steak and white wine for fish dishes).

Garlic

By far the most pungent member of the onion family, garlic grows in a cluster of pointed cloves from a single base. Many people are prejudiced against garlic because it lingers on the breath, but by way of compensation, when garlic is eaten in company, the nose develops a tolerance toward the garlic-laden breath of others. A slowly cooked dish using a great deal of garlic—say a chicken cooked on a bed of whole cloves of garlic—or even whole heads of garlic, which can be roasted unpeeled and eaten by picking up the cloves at the end and squeezing out the pulp within, taste much sweeter and far less garlicky than something like a salad with peeled and bruised raw garlic included in the dressing.

Garlic grown in a hot climate is considered to be the most pungent. But wherever it comes from, whether it is sold in little nets or loose, and whether it is snow-white, gray, purple, or pinkish, look for fat, round, hard bulbs.

Very fresh garlic, available in the spring, when garlic is harvested, has an especially subtle flavor and is favored by connoisseurs for their salads. However,

most garlic is allowed to dry: it keeps well in cool, dry, airy storage conditions. Too much moisture in the air, and it will start sprouting in due course; too much warmth, and the interior cloves will eventually turn to black dust. In Provence, garlic is sometimes smoked to help it keep a little longer.

To prepare garlic, carefully peel as many cloves as you plan to use. Whether you chop them in the ordinary way, mash them with salt under the flat of a knife, or crush them in a garlic press is a matter of taste: the finer the result, the more of the pungent oil is released, and it is probably true that the garlic press produces the least subtle taste. If the garlic clove has a green shoot inside, remove it before chopping, as it has a bitter taste.

There are many dishes to which garlic gives its essential flavor. It bonds well with meat, particularly lamb, with chicken and fish and many vegetables, especially the Mediterranean ones such as tomatoes and eggplant, and with mushrooms, whose flavor it enhances. Without it there would be no aïoli, the garlic-laden mayonnaise served in France with fish soups, boiled chicken, and every sort of fresh vegetable. And garlic is an essential ingredient in the cooking of southern Europe, of India and Southeast Asia, and of China.

Leek

The leek that the Welsh adopted as their national symbol was, in fact, their native non-bulb-forming onion. Leeks were once used interchangeably with onions, but they are, with their flat leaves arranged in chevron formation, more delicate in taste than onions. A leek is certainly a more subtle flavoring for broth, earning it the title of "king of the soup onions." Scotland's cock-a-leekie is a justifiably renowned soup composed of chicken and leeks, and the leek's talents were taken to their logical end when the *chef des chefs* of New York's Ritz-Carlton Hotel invented his *crème vichyssoise*.

Sadly, many cooks quite ignore the leek's virtues as a vegetable on its own. It is excellent simmered in butter or stewed in red wine, lightly browned and then cooked in a tomato sauce, or eaten cold with a vinaigrette.

If leeks have a drawback, it is that they can be rather a bore to clean. There is no problem when recipes call for chopped

leeks, when it is a case of chopping them first—after pulling off any outer membrane and trimming the wilted part of the greenery—and cleaning later. This is best done by placing the chopped leeks in a colander set in a bowl in the sink and running cold water over them until all the grit has settled at the bottom of the bowl. But when recipes call for whole or split leeks, it is necessary to loosen the leaves gently so that the water can run right into the furled vegetable. Most leeks on sale appear to be quite clean, but in fact it is only the outside dirt that has been removed by the growers; when you get it home and into the kitchen, it is usually a question of making little slits with the point of a knife in appropriate places and of rinsing until all the grit has gone, or cutting them almost in half down the middle if they are very gritty.

When you buy leeks, examine them at both ends. The white part should be firm and unblemished and the green part fresh and lively—the green is useful for soups or stock even if your dish only calls for the white part. When leeks are sold trimmed, without much greenery, you may suspect that they are not only elderly, but so mature as already to have formed a solid tubular flower stalk in the middle. This you will have to discard, being left with a disappointingly hollow stem as a result.

ROOTS AND TUBERS

The root vegetables and the tubers—turnips, parsnips, and rutabagas, carrots, beets, and potatoes—certainly make rather a humble-sounding list when they are all lumped together. It is true they are of the earth, rustic, robust, and ordinary, but it is because of this that they have always been so useful.

In hard times, when people couldn't afford to buy bread, or were forced to make it out of whatever roots they could find, including fern roots, it was root vegetables, particularly turnips, and herbs that kept them alive: herbs can be gathered wild, and roots, surviving the worst rains or droughts, can be stored through the winter. And in better times, roots were the vegetables liked best in most households, alongside a piece of boiled or roasted meat—hence boiled beef and carrots, roast duck with turnips, and everything with potatoes.

Potato

Potatoes, whose mysterious underground swellings make better use of their patch of ground than any cereal, are one of the world's most important food crops. They are a most obliging and good-natured vegetable. Easy to grow, cheap to buy, simple to cook, and tremendously filling, they also seem to be the one vegetable, apart perhaps from tomatoes, that nobody ever gets tired of.

There are endless varieties of potatoes. Popular varieties change rapidly, coming into favor with the growers because they keep well or are resistant to disease, and then being ousted by newer, even hardier kinds with higher yields or fewer eyes. This makes it extremely difficult to prepare a catalogue of varieties.

However, different types of potatoes, round, oval, or kidney-shaped, pink, red, white, or, more rarely, blue or purple, do have very different qualities. In Europe, potatoes can be differentiated by variety—at least if you have a well-informed supplier. In the United States, the wholesale marketers do not identify them this way, but, often, instead, by where they were grown. However, all potatoes can be classified by their starch content. There are floury or mealy high-starch potatoes, which are ideal for mashing and baking, but annoying if you want to boil them whole, as they tend to

fall apart in the water. Waxy low-starch potatoes, such as red-skin potatoes and fingerlings, are very firm-fleshed and not at all good for mashing because they become glutinous, but they make excellent potato salads, lovely boiled potatoes, and excellent potato gratins, when the potatoes are cooked in slices that are supposed to remain whole.

There are also medium-starch all-purpose potatoes, whose texture is quite firm. These can be used for almost anything, except perhaps potato salads. They don't disintegrate, can be made into good french fries, and are excellent for baking. Most of the all-purpose potatoes grown in America have white flesh, while many European varieties, including some of the best, are yellow-fleshed. However, the Yukon Gold is a delicious new medium-starch yellow-fleshed potato from Canada that is increasingly available throughout the United States.

As well as different types and varieties, there are also new—and not-so-new—potatoes. New potatoes are not a specific variety of potato, but any potato harvested when small and young. True new potatoes are dug in the spring and early summer. The small red- or white-skinned waxy potatoes available year-round can be treated like new potatoes, but they are not the real thing.

Buying and storing potatoes New potatoes should be small and faintly translucent; the skin should be taut, but if it is a little ragged and so tender that you can pull it off in strips, so much the better—this shows that the potatoes are fresh and will be easy to peel if so desired. New potatoes do not keep particularly well, as they lose flavor after a few days, so buy them in small quantities and keep them in a cool, dark place. New potatoes can be difficult to peel if not perfectly fresh, but the skins are thin and delicate, so many cooks just scrub them and cook them in their skins.

Older potatoes are more amenable and some can be stored in a cool, dark, dry place for months on end. Choose dry potatoes free of sprouts and without the green patches that appear when potatoes are exposed to light—these contain poisonous alkaloids. If your potatoes do have green parts, cut them off. Avoid potatoes that have scaly or soft patches. If buying potatoes in plastic bags, avoid those that look damp or show signs of condensation, as you may find that they have an unpleasant, moldy flavor.

Potatoes for boiling The very best dish in the world is probably new potatoes boiled and served with lots of melted butter and a sprinkling of coarse salt. For perfection, choose walnut-sized

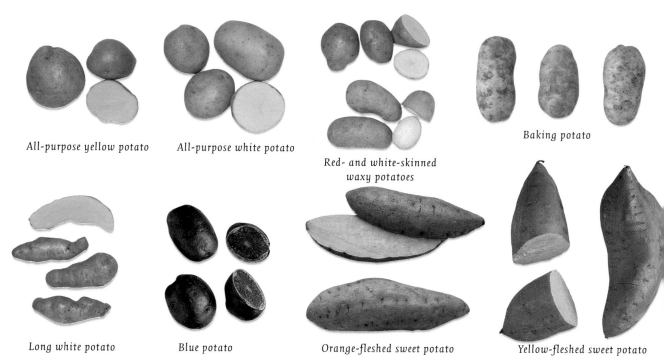

All-purpose yellow potato

All-purpose white potato

Red- and white-skinned waxy potatoes

Baking potato

Long white potato

Blue potato

Orange-fleshed sweet potato

Yellow-fleshed sweet potato

potatoes, peel or scrub them, and drop them into already boiling salted water. Bring them back to a boil, and after 8 to 10 minutes of gentle boiling, test frequently with a thin-bladed knife or skewer. Drain as soon as they are tender. A small sprig of fresh mint added to the water heightens the flavor.

When peeling potatoes, remove as thin a layer of flesh as possible, because many of the vitamins are concentrated just under the skin. If they are not to be cooked immediately, the peeled potatoes must be put straight into a bowl of water, or they will discolor on contact with the air. But don't soak them too long, as this can also lead to a loss of vitamins.

For a delicate but somewhat earthy flavor, older waxy and all-purpose potatoes can be scrubbed and boiled in their skins (this conserves the vitamins too), then peeled while still hot—unless you want to be rustic and serve them with skins on. But peeling the skin from hot potatoes can be tedious, so don't attempt it when you are preparing potatoes for more than two or three people.

To cook potatoes other than the little new ones, put them in a pan of salted cold water, bring it to a boil, and then cook them fairly gently—fast boiling causes them to bump against each other, which breaks them up. When they are just tender, drain them thoroughly and return them to the pan. Let them steam for a minute, then drop in a few chunks of butter and turn the potatoes over gently until they are well coated.

Boiled potatoes are very absorbent and good for all dishes with a lot of gravy to mop up. In some countries, raw potatoes are placed on the top of stews about 30 minutes before the end of cooking—the potatoes absorb any fat that has risen to the top of the stew and also help to stretch the dish a bit further.

Potatoes for sautéing The dry, firm texture of all-purpose potatoes makes them ideal for sautéing. Cut them up and drop them into a large pan of boiling, well-salted water to blanch for about 5 minutes before sautéing them, or fry them from their raw state, drying them with a kitchen towel before putting them into the hot fat.

Potatoes can also be grated before they are sautéed. *Rösti*, the Swiss national dish, is usually made with potatoes that have been boiled the previous day and kept overnight—traditionally in the snow but the refrigerator will do—to dry them out a little. They are then grated, formed into a pancake, and fried gently in butter; for serving, they are inverted onto a plate with the golden crust upward. *Pommes lyonnaise* are potatoes sautéed with fried onions.

Potatoes for deep-frying For french fries, choose firm, dry potatoes. Baking potatoes or a variety such as Yukon Gold are best, although all-purpose white potatoes can be used; in Europe, the yellow-fleshed varieties are preferred. These are also the potatoes to use for homemade potato chips, *gaufrettes* (waffle-cut potato chips), matchsticks, croquettes, potato puffs, and all the many other varieties of fried potatoes.

Sliced or cut-up raw potatoes for fries or chips should be soaked in cold water for at least half an hour to rid them of their surface starch, or the slices will stick together when deep-fried. Dry them well, since hot fat foams up over wet potatoes and could bubble over. Fried potatoes should be salted after cooking, and like other fried foods they will turn soft if covered to keep them warm.

Potatoes for roasting Most all-purpose potatoes are fine for roasting, but small potatoes should be avoided because roasting tends to dry them out. New potatoes do not roast well (sauté them instead). Potatoes roast better if they are first boiled in well-salted water for about 5 minutes, then drained well and returned to the pan to dry off over low heat, uncovered, for a minute or two, before they go into the oven.

Potatoes for mashing Baking potatoes are ideal for mashing. Peel and boil them until they are very tender, drain them well, and mash them thoroughly or purée with a potato ricer or a food mill—but not a food processor, as it will ruin the texture. Then add any liquid, which should be hot for best results. Add butter at the end, beat thoroughly, and taste for seasoning—potatoes always need extra salt. In France, meat juices are sometimes added to mashed potatoes instead of milk.

In the United States, mashed potatoes flavored with everything from roasted garlic to truffle oil have turned up on the menus of trendy restaurants, but these variations will never replace the simple and delicious original.

Potatoes for baking The large russet potatoes, such as Idahos, are the ideal ones for baking. Baked potatoes are extremely healthful, since there is no loss of goodness or flavor into water that is then thrown away. They are also a wonderful vehicle for fillings such as cheese, sour cream, bacon bits, and chopped fresh chives.

Prick the potatoes in a few places with a fork before baking—this allows the steam to escape, and the flesh will be light and fluffy. Never wrap potatoes in aluminum foil for baking—they will steam inside the foil and the skin will be soft rather than nice and crisp.

Potatoes for salads The classic potato salad is plainly boiled and sliced waxy potatoes mixed with a simple, sharpish vinaigrette while they are still hot. A little more dressing is added just before serving. Another version mixes the potatoes first with a little dressing while still warm, and then with some good, creamy homemade mayonnaise when cool. Celery, freshly cooked thin green beans, and dill are all good additions to fresh potato salad.

No summer picnic would be complete without potato salad to go along with the hamburgers and hot dogs. Serve potato salad, too, with sausages or salted fish—its mild flavor is an excellent foil to their assertiveness. For the same reason, potato salad is good with smoked fish, such as trout.

Sweet potato

The tuberous roots of a tropical vine, sweet potatoes have a taste of faintly scented artichoke. The small or medium-sized ones are best: they should be firm and well shaped. Avoid any with cracks and damp patches.

Sweet potatoes are one of the key ingredients used in Creole cookery. Throughout the American South, these potatoes are eaten fried, whipped up into soufflés, and with sugar-cured Virginia ham. (They were the traditional accompaniment to possum.) They are often boiled and mashed with nutmeg, as well, or made into a sweet potato pie.

Taro

Yam

Cassava

Candied, sweet potatoes are a traditional accompaniment for the Thanksgiving turkey. In Australia, they are parboiled and roasted with pork.

Yam, taro, and cassava

The yam belongs to a family of climbing plants that flourish in tropical climates. It comes in a large number of shapes and sizes, and the flesh is white or yellow, with a texture similar to potatoes. In the United States, where true yams are not cultivated, orange-fleshed sweet potatoes with brownish skins are often erroneously called yams. The true yam, however, is much sweeter and moister than the sweet potato, although both are usually prepared in much the same ways: boiled and served with butter, nutmeg, and other spices, as well as with apples, oranges, and nuts. Like sweet potatoes, they are delicious when fried.

Looking something like yams (and found in the same markets) are taro root, or dasheen, and cassava, also called yuca—the source of tapioca. They taste much like potatoes and can be prepared in the same ways, but the taro root will turn a grayish-green color when boiled. Try them sautéed, or mashed together with milk and butter, chopped scallions, and salt and pepper.

Carrot

These range from slim little slips, pale apricot in color and no longer than a little finger, to long, stout cylinders, light orange to the deep color of nectarines.

Young carrots, tender and melting, have a most delicate flavor. Washed and cooked in boiling water for no more than about 7 minutes, then simply tossed in butter and sprinkled with parsley, they are one of the celebratory dishes of early summer. Parboiled and then glazed with butter and possibly a little sugar to emphasize their natural sweetness, they become one of the essentials of *haute cuisine*. Young carrots are best if they are boiled unpeeled. They can then be drained and eaten with their skins on, or rubbed in a towel to slip off the skin.

Sturdier carrots are the great standby for winter, and accompany such hearty dishes as boiled beef and dumplings. And it is to carrots, together with onions, celery, and leeks, that good warming broths owe their flavor—but don't put in too many, or the broth will become so sweet that people will think there is sugar in it. Carrots are also used to make the excellent classic French carrot soup, *potage de Crécy*.

The bright orange, almost translucent carrots of uniform size usually found in supermarkets are bred more for the convenience of the seller than the buyer, because they travel well. Although their flavor is a little elusive, they are delicious raw, and they make a good dish on their own, either sliced and simmered in water and butter, then sprinkled with parsley, or simply served with butter and parsley.

Buying and storing carrots Avoid specimens that have a rubbery texture, are blemished or cracked with age, or are sprouting little roots. Store carrots in the vegetable compartment of the refrigerator after taking them out of their plastic wrapping.

Parsnip

Related to the carrot, the parsnip is almost as sweet but blander. It is delicious in soups and stews. Parsnips are more popular in Europe than in the United States, and there particularly many old-fashioned recipes exist for parsnip custards or flans and other desserts that make good use of the vegetable's sweetness. This is often emphasized by the addition of ginger, spices, and honey. Sweet parsnip dishes are part of the English country tradition, as is parsnip wine, a clear, pale gold, and delicious drink. In England as well, boiled parsnips mixed with mayonnaise were once served as mock lobster, but they are actually nicer without the pretentious title.

Parsnips are available year-round, but the peak season is from early fall until spring. They are at their best in midwinter, especially when their ivory skin has been touched by frost. They are usually sold already washed, but those with traces of soil still clinging to them will keep better. Those with brown patches or that look wizened or dry should be avoided.

Store parsnips in a cool place—the Dutch seventeenth-century paintings that show root vegetables spread around the housewife's feet do not signify untidiness but the fact that the tiled floor of the kitchen was the coolest place. The crisper compartment of the refrigerator is more convenient nowadays.

Salsify

Black-skinned salsify, which has snowy white flesh, is also known as scorzonera; white salsify is sometimes known as the oyster plant because its taste is supposedly reminiscent of oysters. In fact, the flavor of both black and white salsify has a nodding acquaintance with that of asparagus. It is just as delicate and therefore at its best when simply boiled or poached and served with a good chunk of butter, or perhaps with a creamy white sauce made from a roux

Carrot

Parsnip

and be no more than pale shadows of themselves when they are cooked. For the same reason, beets are never peeled before cooking.

When making borscht, the ruby-colored Russian soup, however, it is desirable to make use of the beet's tendency to bleed. For this reason, the beets are chopped before being cooked into a soup. The purple color can become almost brownish with long cooking, though, so it is generally a good idea to cook one or two beets whole and cut them into julienne strips to add shortly before serving, or to add some fresh beet stock, to bring the fine dark red color to the soup.

To serve sliced beets as a vegetable dish, sauté them gently, moistening them with red wine vinegar to set the brilliant color and give them a perfect flavor. The greenery attached to beets can be cooked separately and tastes like spinach.

You can also find golden and white beets, which taste the same as the red, but are rather disappointing to look at. Chioggia beets, however, are striped with red and white—thus their other name, candy cane beet.

Roasted beets are delicious, with a more intense flavor than when boiled. In France, beets are sometimes roasted in the ashes of a wood fire, which gives a charred skin and an earthy, smoky flavor.

Rutabaga and turnip

Both these roots are, in fact, members of the cabbage family, and are so closely related that it is not surprising to find their names sometimes used interchangeably, or the rutabaga referred to as yellow turnip. To add to the confusion, rutabagas are also called swedes or Swedish turnips. However, rutabagas, with their pale, dense flesh, grow to immense sizes without impairment to taste or texture, while white-fleshed turnips will coarsen if they become any larger than tennis balls.

Rutabagas and turnips should be heavy for their size, with no signs of spongy patches, worm holes, or large blemishes. Those with side roots should be avoided.

Rutabagas have a warm, strong flavor and make a delicious winter dish when mashed on their own or cooked in stews. They are the essential ingredient for "mashed neeps," a Scottish dish served with haggis, in which the rutabagas are mashed with potatoes and butter.

moistened with the cooking liquid and a dash of cream.

Salsify is not easy to peel or to clean, so it is best boiled in its skin and peeled afterward, or thinly peeled with a swivel-bladed potato peeler and plunged immediately into a saucepan containing a "*blanc*"—boiling water to which 1 tablespoon of flour has been added (vegetables cooked in a *blanc* will keep their color). It should then be cooked, drained, and finished with a little butter. As it is water-retaining, salsify will not easily burn, provided the pan is heavy and has a well-fitting lid.

Salsify is generally available from fall through late winter. When buying it, choose white salsify with a topknot of fresh-looking leaves; black salsify is usually already trimmed of its leaves. Avoid any, of either type, that look sad or shriveled.

Celeriac, celery root

The edible bulbous root of a member of the celery family, celeriac is not a neat-looking vegetable and needs to be peeled with a sharp knife. Under its brown exterior, the flesh is pale, but it discolors when exposed to the air so should be

plunged immediately into a bowl of acidulated (lemon) water. Cooked, its texture is similar to that of a potato, but less smooth and with more bite to it. Celeriac is a great standby, not only because soups and broth are often improved by a slight celery flavor, and it is milder and less overpowering than regular celery, but also because *céleri rémoulade*—grated raw celeriac coated in mustard mayonnaise, one of the delights of French cuisine—cannot, of course, be made without it. Boiled and diced, celeriac is delicious in potato salads, and in Germany it is served with diced apples, potatoes, and beets in a herring salad. Puréed with potatoes, it is also excellent with duck and game.

Beet

Globe-shaped or somewhat elongated, beets come in bunches with edible greenery at the top when young; older ones may be trimmed of their leaves and sold loose. When buying beets, make sure that their "whiskers" are intact and that they have at least 1 to 2 inches of stem at the top—if too closely trimmed, they will bleed, meaning that they will give up their color to the cooking water

acidulated water 422

Baby turnips, globe-shaped, conical, or flattened, with a sweet, mild radishy flavor but not the hot sting, are as different from older turnips as new potatoes are from more mature ones. They should not be peeled before cooking, but rubbed afterward: the skin comes off easily and beneath it lies their flavor and goodness. Although it seems a pity to do more to any young vegetable than to boil it for a few minutes, glazed baby turnips are delicious and a classic accompaniment to roast duck. Their fresh greenery can be cooked in the same way as other greens. Older, larger turnips may have a purplish tinge to their tops, and are peeled before roasting or boiling.

Kohlrabi

White, pale green, or purple, kohlrabi is a member of the cruciferous family that is bred for its bulbous stem. It looks like a horizontally ridged turnip, and is at its best when young and small, since it becomes coarse and fibrous as it grows larger. The leaves, which grow in stalks from the spaced-out ridges, can be used in the same way as young turnip tops, but are usually removed before the vegetable reaches the market. The skin can be peeled easily with a kitchen knife to expose the pale green flesh below. Tiny kohlrabi can be cooked whole, but the larger ones need to be sliced. They can then be boiled, eaten with fresh butter or a creamy sauce, served with any meat that responds to a delicate cabbagey taste.

Jerusalem artichoke

These knobbly tubers are not artichokes, and nor do they come from the Holy City—in fact, they are from the New World. Like the sunflower, to which they are related, they were christened *girasole* by the Italians—from whence "Jerusalem"—because their yellow flowers tend to turn toward the sun. They may also be called sunchokes.

Jerusalem artichokes are at their best from winter to spring. When buying them, look for neat specimens with the minimum of knobs. Their skin is brownish, like that of potatoes, but more delicate. The white flesh must not be exposed to the air, as it quickly turns a gray-purple color. When boiling Jerusalem artichokes, add a squeeze of lemon juice to the water. This will prevent them from discoloring, especially if you plan to make the delicious white soup, sometimes called Palestine soup, that owes its pearly color as much to the artichokes as it does to the milk or cream that goes into its making. Jerusalem artichokes are delicious roasted like potatoes.

Crosne Also known as Chinese or Japanese artichokes, these taste similar to Jerusalem artichokes but are nuttier and more delicate. These tiny, spindle-shaped vegetables dry out too quickly after being pulled to be widely available. The yellowish patches that tend to develop on fresh white crosnes in no way impair the flavor. Crosnes were once quite popular in France but are no longer common in Europe; you may come across them at a farmers' market here. They should be scrubbed—a tedious job as they are so tiny—and cooked very briefly in boiling salted water, then tossed in plenty of butter.

Jícama

A tropical tuber that looks somewhat like a turnip-shaped yam—and is sometimes called yam bean—jícama has crisp, sweet, juicy flesh. Popular in Mexican and Southwest dishes, it can be peeled and eaten raw or sliced and stir-fried with other vegetables; it can also be roasted like a potato.

Jerusalem artichoke

Jícama

Black salsify

Turnip

Beet

Kohlrabi

Celeriac

Rutabaga

VEGETABLE FRUIT

Glossy black olives, rich purple eggplants, bright scarlet tomatoes, red, green, yellow, and purple peppers, and green cucumbers need hot sun to ripen, and these vegetables bring Mediterranean color and warmth into the kitchen. Others in this group—avocados, tender squash, and huge pumpkins—provide exotic shapes, textures, and tastes.

Tomato

Ripened to a marvelous blazing red in the sun, tomatoes are one of the cook's most essential provisions. Ideally, one should have tomatoes in the kitchen at all times, both fresh and in cans (fortunately, tomatoes are one of the very few vegetables that take happily to being canned).

Belonging to the Solanum family (as does nightshade), the tomato used to be considered unhealthy and was not eaten raw for many centuries after it arrived in Europe from its native South America, via Central America. Spain was the first country to use tomatoes in cooked dishes, and the rest of Europe followed suit, but it was not until the middle of the nineteenth century that tomatoes were eaten raw. Even then they do not seem to have been highly regarded. And the tomato did not have much of a following in the United States before the turn of the century.

Today, however, there is no better salad than a tomato salad, preferably scattered with fresh basil leaves, which have a great affinity with tomatoes. The Italians often add slices of mozzarella, the fresh cheese that goes so well with tomatoes. As dressing, a good sun-ripened tomato needs only olive oil, since it provides its own astringency, but a duller one needs vinaigrette. Tomatoes should never be allowed to sit in their dressing, because this will turn them soggy.

The large beefsteak tomatoes, deep red and often quite misshapen, tend to be the best. The more ordinary globe tomatoes, grown to uniform medium size, often have very little flavor. Cherry tomatoes can be used whole in salads, while the richly flavored Italian plum tomatoes, with relatively small seed clusters and pulp that is inclined to be dry, are perfect for sauces and purées. Fleshy tomatoes are best for sandwiches as there is less liquid; slice them across rather than downward.

Golden-yellow tomatoes are like red tomatoes in every aspect except color, and make a pretty salad when mixed with the reds or on their own. Yellow pear tomatoes are the size of cherry tomatoes, but are, not surprisingly, the shape of a pear. Tiny currant tomatoes sometimes appear at specialty markets, and unusual heirloom varieties of many hues and shapes may be found at the farmers' market.

Buying and storing tomatoes The best tomatoes are those that have been allowed to ripen slowly on the vine, developing their flavor in the warm sun.

Buy bright red, ripe tomatoes for immediate use; for use in the near future, choose those of a paler red color—after a day or two in a cool spot, they will be a vivid red. If tomatoes have been picked when green but after reaching maturity, they will redden well if they are kept in a brown paper bag (they will ripen faster with a red tomato keeping them company, exuding its ethylene gas, which is responsible for the color change). Tomatoes picked when green and unripe will never turn red naturally and are best used for making pickles and chutneys, and, of course, fried green tomatoes. The cottony flavorless tomatoes found in the supermarket are picked green and "force-ripened"— to no more than a pale imitation of a true vine-ripened red tomato.

Cooking with tomatoes Traditional tomato dishes include tomato soup, which may be delicate and translucent or creamy and strong, perhaps flavored with basil or chives; tomatoes with stuffings of cooked seasoned rice mixed with lamb, currants, onion, and garlic, or with bread crumb-bound fillings of olives, herbs, or mushrooms; and fragrant tomatoes *provençale*, which are broiled with a sprinkling of herbs, garlic, and olive oil. A la *provençale* invariably means the presence of tomatoes in a dish, and just as Provençal cooking relies

Cherry tomato

Sun-dried tomato

Tomatillo

Beefsteak tomato

Plum tomato

on tomatoes, so does Italian cooking, using them liberally for pastas and pizzas, in soups and vegetable stews.

Many recipes require tomatoes to be peeled, seeded, and roughly chopped (the French culinary term is *concasséed*). The skin of Italian plum tomatoes may come off easily, but most tomatoes need a quick dip in boiling water first.

Sun-dried tomato These are tomatoes that have been halved and dried—not always in the sun. The drying intensifies and sweetens the flavor and makes the texture leathery. It's much cheaper to buy the tomatoes loose, in bags, rather than packed in oil in jars. Then soak them for an hour before storing in good olive oil with herbs and chiles if you like. Sun-dried tomatoes are eaten as an antipasto or with prosciutto in sandwiches. They are also used in cooked dishes, such as stews and braised vegetables, in pasta sauces and on pizzas, and in salads.

Tomatillo

Related to the Cape gooseberry and belonging to the same family as the tomato, the tomatillo does in fact look very like a walnut-sized green tomato, except that it comes wrapped in a thin,

papery husk. It is firm in texture, with a flavor like that of a tart apple. Tomatillos are much used in Mexican cooking, in meat stews and green *mole* sauces, and with onions and chiles to make *salsa verde*, served with tacos and enchiladas.

Pepper

Peppers may be mild and sweet, or hot and unbearably fiery, but they are all members of the Capsicum family. The large sweet peppers include the bell, the cubanelle, the frying or Italian frying pepper, and the sweet banana. Sweet peppers may be red, yellow, orange, purple, white, or green, and squarish or long in shape.

Chile peppers add heat as well as flavor to a dish, although some of them are quite mild. They can be green, red, yellow, or purple-black; in general, the smaller the chile, the hotter it is. When testing them for heat, simply touch a piece of the broken flesh to your tongue.

Most peppers are green to begin with, ripening to red and finally becoming red-brown when dried, although some peppers turn a pale yellow or bright orange, or a deep mahogany color, when ripe. Peppers that are sold half-ripe—part red and part green—may never ripen to a full red.

Paprika, cayenne pepper, and Tabasco sauce are all made from peppers.

Sweet pepper Bought fresh, large sweet peppers (which are a good source of vitamin C) are quite light in weight. Red peppers are sweeter than green, and the yellow and orange ones are closer in flavor to red peppers than to green.

Capsicum means box, and the fleshy walls of sweet peppers contain no more than a few ribs and a cluster of seeds. These should all be discarded to the last flat seed, which even in the mildest pepper can occasionally be bitingly hot. The empty "boxes" can then be filled with any number of stuffings—cooked rice mixed with ground meat and perhaps yogurt, or with a mixture of tomatoes, anchovies, and garlic, or olives and capers. They are then put in an oiled pan and baked slowly. Some people like to blanch the peppers in boiling water for a minute or two before stuffing them.

As well as being stuffed, sweet peppers can be cut into strips and used in a variety of dishes. Sicilians make lovely salads with grilled red or yellow peppers, mixing them with anchovy fillets, capers, garlic, and olive oil. Yugoslavians have a similar salad, which is made using peppers roasted until they

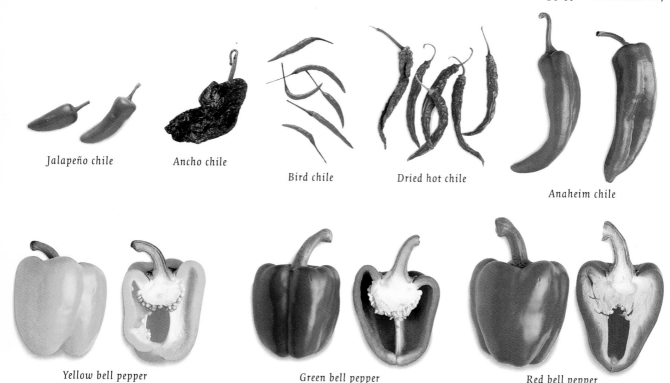

Jalapeño chile

Ancho chile

Bird chile

Dried hot chile

Anaheim chile

Yellow bell pepper

Green bell pepper

Red bell pepper

have blistered and then skinning them. In the South of France, there is the beautiful *pipérade*, a mixture of sweet peppers, tomatoes, onions, garlic, and, sometimes, bacon, to which beaten eggs are added at the last moment. Sweet peppers are also sometimes combined with chile peppers, as in rouille—the bright orange, fiery sauce that floats in a bowl of bouillabaisse, and is served with a number of other fish dishes that have their origins in the South of France.

Pimiento, the Spanish word for peppers, has come to mean the peeled and seeded cooked red peppers that are sold in jars. But you can roast or grill any bell peppers at home, and peel and seed them. Once prepared, they will keep in the refrigerator, covered, for up to a week.

Chile pepper When fresh, a chile pepper should look bright—dullness is a sure sign of overmaturity—with no brown patches or black spots. Chiles can vary in size from 12 inches in length down to just ¼ inch, and in taste they may be anywhere from mildly warm to blisteringly hot. As well as fresh, they are sold dried (whole, crushed into small flakes, or ground to a powder), canned, and bottled, often pickled.

In Central America, notably Mexico, chiles are second only to corn in their importance in cooking. They are widely used in the cuisines of other countries, including Africa, India, China (Hunan and Sichuan cooking), and Thailand. In North America and most of Europe, hot chiles are generally used sparingly.

Chile experts, of course, are able to distinguish between the dozens of varieties, but nonexperts tend to differentiate only between the mild, the hot, and the unbearable. Large chiles include the mild Anaheim or California (when fresh and green this is used for *chiles rellenos*—stuffed with cheese and deep-fried; the fresh red pepper is also called Colorado chile); the similar but slightly longer and hotter New Mexico; the poblano, which can range from slightly hot to hot (when ripened to red and dried this is called an ancho, which is sweet but can be quite pungent); and the pungent yellow Santa Fe Grande. Among the smaller chiles are the hot to very hot jalapeño (when smoked, this becomes a chipotle) and the cayenne, Thai, and bird—all three similar in size

and shape and all quite hot. Other small chiles include the extremely hot, slender green serrano, the fiery, lantern-shaped habanero and its cousin the Scotch bonnet, and the blistering, tiny tabasco, which is used to make Tabasco sauce.

With chiles, not only are the seeds hot, but the box itself is pungent. It is a volatile oil called capsaicin, found mainly in the seeds and ribs, that accounts for the heat. Capsaicin irritates the skin and especially the eyes, so keep your hands—even after washing—away from your eyes, lips, and other sensitive areas for a while after you have prepared chiles. Also, rinse the chiles in cold, not hot, water, or the irritating fumes may rise into your face. To prepare chiles, pull off their stems and cut each in half, all under cold running water. Chiles soaked in cold salted water will be less hot. They can also be blistered on the grill or under a broiler for a lovely smoky flavor.

Canned chiles should be washed to remove the brine in which they have been preserved. They may be already sliced or diced, or they may need to be seeded like fresh ones. Dried whole chiles, torn into small pieces, can be used as they are to season dishes, or they can be rehydrated in water first. For a much milder flavor, put dried hot chiles into a pan of cold water, bring slowly to a boil, and then drain. They can then be used, more or less discreetly, to heat up dishes such as chili con carne and other Tex-Mex favorites; for curries, especially Thai curries; for any number of Creole and Cajun dishes, especially those that include shrimp or pork; and in many of the dishes of the American Southwest.

Eggplant

This can be long and slim or as fat as a blimp, with a glossy purple or almost black skin, or it can be a plump ivory-white oval (to which version it owes its American name; in France and Britain, it is known as *aubergine*). All varieties have the same slightly acrid taste. The difference lies in consistency: the plump ones, marginally juicier, are the ones to use for such dishes as moussaka, with its golden layers; or the Balkan *okrochka*, also layered but without the white sauce or eggs; or in eggplant Parmesan. The long, slim ones, being drier, are best for frying.

When buying eggplants, chose those that feel heavy for their size—they are

likely to have the smallest seed channels because their flesh will have filled out. They should have smooth, unblemished skins with no rough, spongy patches or brown spots.

It is a good idea to salt eggplant before cooking to sweat out some of the moisture and possible bitterness, although some modern varieties do not really need this treatment. To salt them, cut them into thin slices, sprinkle with salt, and allow them to drain in a colander for half an hour, then rinse them and pat dry with paper towels.

It is not usually necessary to peel eggplant, because the skin contributes to their flavor and color, and in dishes such as stuffed eggplant, it prevents them from disintegrating. But in dishes that involve puréed eggplant, such as the dish sometimes known as "poor man's caviar," the traditional way of peeling them is to roast them in their skins over a charcoal fire or under a broiler until they are soft, and then to scoop out the flesh, which will have acquired a delicious smoky taste.

Although ratatouille—the delicious Provençal stew of eggplant, tomatoes, zucchini, onions, and sweet peppers—is one of the great Mediterranean dishes, the best eggplant recipes come from southern Italy and the Middle East. In the Middle East, eggplant purées are flavored with tahini and garlic and served as a salad.

The most famous eggplant dish is the Turkish *Imam Bayildi*, or "the Imam has fainted"; this is apparently what an *imam* (Turkish priest) did when presented with an incredibly rich dish of fried eggplant mixed with onions, tomatoes, spices, and golden raisins, all swimming in oil.

Eggplants may be halved and stuffed, or filled from the stem end after the seeds and a portion of the flesh have been removed to make room for the stuffing. They look very beautiful if they are first peeled in strips so that white flesh and purple skin make handsome stripes around the outside. Fill them with cooked ground lamb or beef, rice, tomatoes, garlic, onions and spices, and their own chopped pulp. Then sprinkle them with oil and bake until tender.

Whether eaten hot or cold, in batter, or in a garlicky marinade, eggplant is almost always first fried in hot olive oil. It absorbs vast quantities of oil, so should be fried quickly and drained well.

Avocado

The avocado was once called the alligator pear because its original Spanish name, *aguacate*, based on the Aztec word, was too difficult to pronounce; in Britain, it was also called the butter pear, because of its consistency. It is, strictly speaking, a fruit, but is used mainly as a salad vegetable because its flavor is bland, mild, and nutty.

Particularly rich in oils, proteins, and vitamins, the avocado was used by the ancient Mayans, Incas, and Aztecs both as a food and for skin care. Avocados were a luxury in northern countries until Floridians and then Californians began to cultivate them in the nineteenth century. Some people consider these comparatively northerly avocados to be only pale replicas of those grown in the tropics, but they are still very good, as are the Israeli avocados that supply many European markets in their season.

There are two main types of avocado: those varieties grown in California and those grown in Florida. The California avocados, of which the Hass is the most common variety, have rough, pebbly skin that is green when unripe and purple-black when ripe, and golden-yellow flesh. The Fuerte and other Florida varieties are usually larger, with smooth green skin and pale green to yellow flesh. In the case of Florida avocados, the skin color is no indication of ripeness; the test for this is to apply gentle pressure at the stem end—if there is some give, the avocado is ready.

In Mexico, where avocados are abundant, they are eaten in soups, salads, and stews. They are also the essential ingredient in guacamole—the coarse avocado purée with green chiles, chopped onions, and lime or lemon juice which may be eaten on its own or, as in Mexico, with tortillas. It is best to purée avocado shortly before it is to be eaten, because it turns brown when exposed to the air. So does the flesh of a cut avocado, so either halve or slice it just before serving, or rub or sprinkle the cut surfaces with lemon.

In the Caribbean, avocados baked in their skins are sometimes served with turkey and chicken. But there is no better way to serve them than halved, or sliced, with a good vinaigrette, or, even more simply, with a sprinkling of fresh lime juice and salt.

Olive

Groves of gnarled olive trees flourish in the Mediterranean countries and in California, producing a great variety of olives, large and small. Greek and Italian olives are reckoned to be the finest—in ancient Rome, olives were eaten both at the beginning and at the end of meals from sheer love of them.

Whether olives are green or black (they may actually be brown or purple) is not a matter of type but of timing: olives picked young are still hard and pale green; black olives have had time to ripen and darken on the tree and have developed more of their oil. In order to make them edible, black olives are soaked in an alkaline solution—traditionally rainwater and wood ash (lye), now more likely to be caustic soda—and exposed to the air to remove their excessive bitterness.

Green olives are treated rather differently, first soaked under running water or steeped in an alkaline solution, then put into tightly sealed barrels of brine and left for up to a year to develop their olive-green, smooth succulence. Olives destined for the

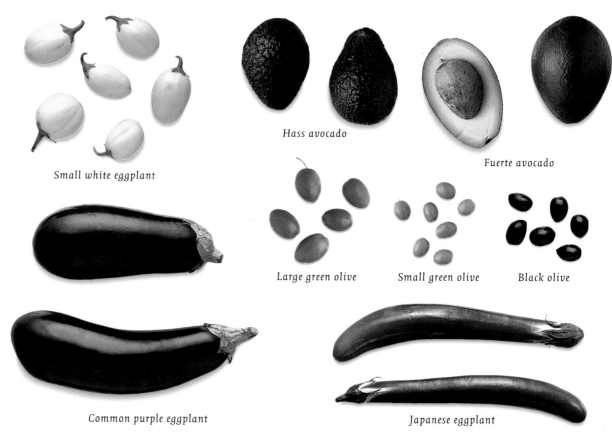

Small white eggplant

Hass avocado

Fuerte avocado

Large green olive   *Small green olive*   *Black olive*

Common purple eggplant

Japanese eggplant

oil presses are allowed to ripen fully; some of these, looking a little shriveled and quite small, are also cured in salt to be eaten, and can be the best of all.

Olives are preserved in a number of different ways. The black ones range from those that are marinated in oil with herbs to those in brine. There are also cracked green olives—which may be plain or flavored with garlic, spices, or herbs— and whole pitted black or green olives spiced with chiles.

Of the many olives on the market, among the most commercial and widely available are the big, green, solid Spanish olives, which are slightly acid— and which connoisseurs like to dip in olive oil before eating—and the small, succulent Spanish Manzanillas. These are often stuffed with strips of *pimiento* or, less frequently, with almonds, anchovies, lemon or orange peel, or pieces of black olive. Italian olives, such as the large green Cerignola, the black olives from Castellamare, and the tiny black wrinkled ones from around Rome, go on top of pizzas and focaccia. Plump Kalamatas and other olives from Greece go into a salad with tomatoes and sliced onions. And the black olives of Provence are used in rich *estouffades* and *daubes*, and in other braised dishes, as well as in an olive pâté or purée and stuffings with mushrooms, anchovies, herbs, and bread crumbs.

Besides the best-known green and black olives, there are also the pale or dark brown ones found in Italy and Cyprus, the tiny, delicate black Niçoise ones, and the straw-colored California olives, which some people prefer above all others.

If you buy olives and do not use them all at once, store them in the refrigerator, perhaps in some olive oil or in a mixture of water, oil, and vinegar. You can roll olives in fresh olive oil, perhaps with a few herbs, chiles, or crushed coriander seeds, to liven them up before eating. If you want black olives without pits for cooking, use an olive pitter, or simply split the flesh and remove the pits.

CUCUMBER, SQUASHES, AND PUMPKIN

These belong to the climbing or rambling family known as Cucurbitas, together with melons and the decorative autumn gourds.

Cucumber

English cucumber

Cucumber

Before cucumbers had the bitterness bred out of them, they were invariably peeled, salted, and drained. This is no longer necessary, unless you want to make a delicate Austrian or French cucumber salad, for which salting and draining are essential—this alters the texture to a soft crispness by extracting some of the water, and heightens the flavor. Otherwise, cucumber salads are likely to consist of slices cut paper-thin and dressed with sour cream or vinaigrette, or, in the Hungarian version, of little dice dressed with yogurt and chives and sprinkled with paprika. Cucumbers are also good peeled, cut into strips or cubes, and cooked briefly in butter, to be served hot.

Small kirby cucumbers have plentiful seeds and smooth, dark green skins. They are also called pickling cucumbers because they are the ones that are brined, or used to make sweet or dill pickles.

The long, clear green cucumber (known as the English or hothouse cucumber) has fewer seeds than regular cucumbers and an exceedingly thin skin. It is often sold in a tight plastic jacket to keep it fresh. Europe has the enormous Zeppelin cucumber, firm and juicy, that turns a pale yellow when fully ripe. Another unusual variety is the lemon cucumber, almost round and with crisp, juicy flesh and tough yellowish skin; this should always be peeled.

Cucumbers are best when they are young and tender and look as if they are bursting with juice. They can be stored in the refrigerator for about a week at most. Avoid waxed cucumbers if you can; peel them if you can't.

Tiny gherkin cucumbers are usually found pickled in vinegar (then often called cornichons), and are eaten with cold meats or with *pâté de campagne*, or chopped and used in sauces such as tartar sauce.

Squashes and pumpkin

Some squashes are soft-skinned and for eating when young and tender, which is why they are known as summer squashes; these should be cooked as soon as possible after being picked. Others are best when they have been allowed to mature slowly to develop firm, sweet flesh and tough, inedible skins; these are known as winter squashes.

Zucchini Smaller zucchini are infinitely superior to the larger overgrown ones, with a much more interesting and delicate taste. They may have green or yellow skins. There is hardly any work involved in their preparation: just give them a little wash, then leave tiny ones whole and cut larger ones into circles, or slice them lengthwise into halves or quarters. Give them a very few minutes' boiling, steaming, or sautéing, add some herbs such as basil or parsley and, perhaps, a dash of cream or some butter or olive oil, and an extremely good dish is ready to eat. But don't keep it waiting, because the vegetable continues to soften even after it has been taken off the heat.

Zucchini are excellent fried in oil, either plain or in batter, and their big golden flowers are also sometimes stuffed and deep-fried in a crisp batter or chopped and used in risotto. They form part of an Italian *fritto misto*, in which there may also be apples, artichoke hearts, eggplant, brains, tiny veal chops, croquettes, pumpkin, and peeled figs.

A parboiled or a blanched large zucchini, halved and hollowed out, makes a good vehicle for a ground beef and onion stuffing bound with an egg, or a rice and meat stuffing, but both will need lively flavoring because the squash itself is bland in taste.

Straightneck and crookneck yellow squash Much like zucchini in flavor and texture, these can be used in the same ways. The crookneck has somewhat bumpy yellow skin and curves at the neck; the straightnecks often have smooth skin.

Vegetable marrow The large vegetable marrow is the pride of many English gardens. The enormous prize-winning specimens, however, are not very delicate as a vegetable. Boiled into a watery mush, medium-sized marrows can be equally disappointing, but started off with a little butter and chopped onion and steamed in their own juice, and then sprinkled with a generous handful of chopped parsley, they can be fresh-looking and delicious, especially when tomatoes are added.

Spaghetti squash Sometimes known as vegetable spaghetti, this stubby yellow watermelon-shaped squash is grown with particular attention to its tendency to produce stringy flesh, and is eaten, with sauce, just like spaghetti. It is baked or boiled, the end pierced so that the heat reaches the interior. Then it is served cut in half lengthwise, or the flesh is scooped out; pass a tomato sauce separately. It is also quite good eaten simply with butter and grated cheese.

Pattypan squash Usually creamy in color, although it also comes in shades of yellow and pale green, this tastes rather like zucchini. It is best no bigger than 4 inches across, when the skin is soft and the interior tender, and the scalloped shape need not be spoiled by slicing. Boil it or bake it whole, then cut off the top, scoop out the seeds, and fill the hollow with melted butter; eat with a spoon. It also makes good fritters.

Chayote, mirliton, christophene This small, pear-shaped squash has a large seed, which in very young chayotes

Pattypan squash

Chayote

Straightneck yellow squash

Chinese hairy melon

Spaghetti squash

Zucchini

Vegetable marrow

is edible. It features in Central and South American cooking, where besides being used like other soft-skinned squashes, it is candied, filled with nuts and raisins, and eaten as a dessert.

Chinese hairy melon, fuzzy melon Looking like a large green or bluish-green torpedo, this can be bought in Chinese markets. When young, the melon is covered with a silky fuzz, which is easily washed off by running your hand over its skin under cold running water. In maturity, it is usually coated with a white wax-like layer, and needs to be peeled.

This melon has a slight bitterness but is excellent stir-fried, braised, and used in soups. A half-ripe specimen makes the best eating. In Indonesia, it is candied to be eaten with tea, and is used in cakes and cookies.

Winter squashes A favorite winter vegetable in North America, winter squashes, or many of them at least, can now be found year-round. The most common varieties of winter squash include the acorn, which can be green

or orange or a combination of the two; the smooth-skinned, long, pale butternut squash, which swells toward the blossom end; the colorful, bumpy-skinned turban squash, of which the dark green buttercup, with its lighter-colored turban, is one variety; and the large, warty Hubbard squash, often sold in chunks or wedges. Look for firm, unbruised specimens, or chunks that show no signs of softening around the edges.

Peeled, cut into pieces, and boiled or steamed for about 20 minutes, winter squash can be served mashed with butter and salt and pepper, or a little orange juice. The smaller squashes can be left unpeeled, halved, seeded, and baked in the oven for about 30 minutes with butter and brown sugar or maple syrup in their hollows.

Calabaza Often sold in wedges to display its golden-orange flesh, this squash, also called West Indian pumpkin, features in Caribbean soups. Otherwise, it can be used in any hard-skinned squash or pumpkin recipe.

Pumpkin Best-known of all are the handsome, golden field pumpkins that are carved into smiling, gap-toothed faces for Halloween. However, these are not really the ones for pumpkin pie, pumpkin soup, or pumpkin bread; instead, for cooking, choose smaller varieties like sugar pumpkins, also called pie pumpkins. Nowadays, of course, because of the business of baking, straining, seeding, scraping, and puréeing pumpkin, many people use canned purée—one of the few foods that can be better canned than fresh. For pies and for pumpkin soup, canned purée can also be used, but for baked and sautéed pumpkin, you need fresh ones.

Italians use pumpkins in soups and risotto, and also as a stuffing for ravioli. The English pumpkins are much softer fleshed, and because they cook so readily into a mush, they are best used for pumpkin soup. Alternatively, they may be combined with potatoes or root vegetables to give them a little extra body when used in vegetable soups.

Acorn squash

Butternut squash

Turban squash

Pumpkin

Hubbard squash

Mushrooms and Other Fungi

In many countries, mushroom foraging is an autumn treat, with whole families combing the ground for the eighty or so edible species of fungi that are sold in the local markets, dried, or enjoyed fresh as a luxurious addition to the normal diet. It is important to remember, however, that for the amateur picker going out in the morning dew, the business of mushrooming is fraught with risk. Some mushrooms are indigestible; a few are lethal. In France and Germany, where mushroom gathering is particularly popular, pharmacists will check the morning's pick.

Plenty of wild mushrooms do find their way to the world's vegetable markets, harvested by people with a long tradition of mushroom gathering. As a change from the ubiquitous cultivated white mushroom, it is one of the greatest pleasures of autumn to see a selection of wild forms, including the fat brown cèpe and the golden-pleated chanterelle, both worldwide in distribution and probably far and away the best of the woodland mushrooms. These, along with the morel, a springtime delicacy, are the truly great mushrooms of fine cooking. For those who can find an expert to tell them which varieties to choose, there are also many other pleasant treats to be had.

Gathering your own wild mushrooms

Fungi are plants that lack chlorophyll, and so cannot use direct sunlight to provide themselves with energy. Instead they get their energy by decomposing the life around them that contains energy in the forms of sugars and starches. The word fungi covers everything, including the mold that grows on your ceiling or on old jam, so the term mushroom has been used for those covered here.

Each species of mushroom inhabits a specific environment. There are three main types: the parasitic, which live on a living organism without benefiting the host; the saprophytic, which live on dead material such as tree stumps; and the mycorrhizal, which associate with the root hairs of a tree—the mushrooms get nutrients from the tree and the tree gets nutrients from association with the mushroom (usually a very precise association—some types will only grow on pine trees or even on a particular pine, others only on an oak or birch).

What you see above ground is the fruit of an underground plant. The hidden *mycelium* is actually the plant; it grows well in a warm summer. When its season comes, and after a period of high humidity, the fruiting bodies emerge above the ground, fed by the rapid intake of water. The mushroom comes up in a matter of hours; it emerges to release spores when the *mycelium* stops growing, as the days shorten and it gets colder. Most mushrooms grow from autumn to the first frosts, September and October being the best months, but as it gets

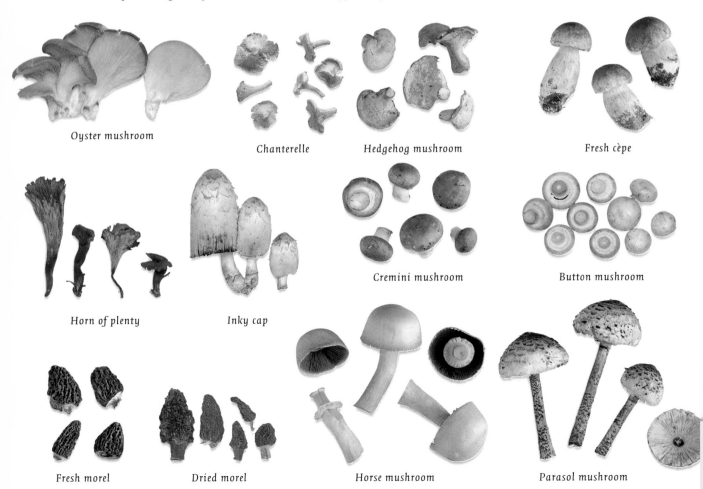

Oyster mushroom

Chanterelle

Hedgehog mushroom

Fresh cèpe

Horn of plenty

Inky cap

Cremini mushroom

Button mushroom

Fresh morel

Dried morel

Horse mushroom

Parasol mushroom

farther into autumn, the leaves cover the mushrooms, so they are harder to find. September rain is crucial to many species—it is more important than heat at this time of year. Because they lack chlorophyll, most mushrooms will grow regardless of whether it is light or dark, or the days long or short. Only the first frosts will end their growth.

(Essential advice for anyone who is considering taking up the hunt for the first time: LEARN YOUR SUBJECT. The means of identifying edible mushrooms and avoiding all poisonous or dubious species is of crucial importance. It is vital to use a guide that gives clear identification information.)

Some edible wild mushrooms

Cèpe or porcini (*Boletus edulis*) This is considered by the French and Italians to be the king of mushrooms, and in Austria it is called *Herrenpilz* (gentleman's fungus). While fresh cèpes are relatively abundant in much of Europe in autumn, they are

Dried cèpe (porcini)

Portobello mushroom

Giant puffball

unfortunately a rarity in the United States. The fresh mushrooms are sometimes offered, at a price, in specialty markets; otherwise, only the dried are available. The flesh of the fresh mushroom is almost white, firm and fleshy, tasting sweet and nutty with a pleasant smell. Firm, fresh cèpes will keep in the refrigerator for up to a week. The dried ones are usually labeled porcini, the Italian name; choose creamy-fawn ones (they blacken with age).

Do not wash fresh cèpes; just wipe with a damp cloth. Then, if young, they can be sliced to eat raw in a green salad, possibly dressed with walnut oil. They make the best risotto, and in France's Dordogne are eaten in omelets with garlic and parsley, or sautéed with potatoes and garlic. Dried porcini must be soaked in warm water for 20 to 30 minutes before use (use the soaking liquid in the recipe as stock).

Horn of plenty (*Craterellus cornucopioides*) Also known as *trompette des morts*, black trumpet, or black chanterelle, this mushroom is trumpet- or funnel-shaped and looks like old, dusty black leather. The cap is 1 to 3 inches long, and deep brown to black when the weather is damp, but paler grayish-brown in dry weather. It is hollow all the way down the center and paler inside. The gills are more like radiating folds or wrinkles. Horn of plenty grows in autumn in deciduous woods, sometimes in large colonies beneath beeches, but can be hard to see.

The taste is strong and earthy and the flesh remains black in cooking. Cut open down one side to clean them. They should be sautéed gently in butter with garlic and parsley and used in an omelet, or perhaps in a cream sauce with chicken instead of the more expensive morels, which have a short spring season.

Chanterelle (*Cantharellus cibarius*) In Germany, golden chanterelles are known as *pfefferling* or *eierschwamm*, on account of their egg-yellow color. The small ones in France are known as *girolles*. They are both beautiful and delicious, bright golden-yellow all over, 1 to 4 inches across, smooth, and funnel-shaped, with edges that are rolled at first and then wavy and irregular. The underside has blunt, gill-like waves and folds. The stem is short and thick, and the flesh smells of apricots and pepper. They are found in

autumn in little clumps in mixed woods, often under moss, and also on banks of ditches or paths or among leaves.

Chanterelles are hard to clean, but very good to cook with—any mushroom recipe will be even better made with chanterelles. They are particularly good with scrambled eggs or in an omelet, flavored with garlic and parsley, and they are wonderful with chicken or squab.

There are other good edible chanterelles in addition to the golden one, such as yellow leg (*Cantharellus infundibuliformis*), which has a small, funnel-shaped, dark brown cap and hollow, bright golden stem. The flesh is yellowish and thin, slightly bitter when raw, and it smells aromatic. It grows in autumn in acid soils, in woods, usually in clumps. The golden chanterelle grows particularly well in California; other varieties are more common in the East and other parts of the United States.

Morel (*Morchella esculenta, M. augusticeps, M. elata,* and *M. deliciosa*) These are spring mushrooms, very highly prized by serious mushroom hunters. Wild morels grow in parts of New England, in Michigan, and in the Northwest; morels are now being cultivated as well but are usually less flavorful. Fresh morels are quite expensive and limited in availability; dried morels are easier to come by. Characteristically sponge-like, with domed caps 2 to 5 inches tall and hollow stems, morels come in a range of colors—from white or pale buff to cream-colored to black. Fresh morels should be trimmed of their tough stems, then thoroughly washed before cooking. Dried morels are very good indeed, retaining the rich nutty flavor well; cook them, after soaking, in cream and serve with free-range chicken or with veal.

Horse mushroom (*Agaricus arvensis*) Called *boule de neige* in French, this does look somewhat like a snowball when young, but when fully opened, a horse mushroom found in a grassy field looks more like a dish on a green tablecloth. It is large and thick, 4 to 8 inches across, with a bright creamy-white cap that slowly turns yellowish with age. The cap is smooth and silky and can stain brownish-yellow when handled; the flesh is firm and white and smells of anise seeds. The closely packed gills are grayish-white, quickly turning to chocolate-brown and finally black. The stem is white shaded

Chicken with Potatoes and Mushrooms 315–16
Tagliatelle with Tuscan Meat Sauce 339
Trattoria Beef Stew with Polenta Dumplings 294–5

with rose and up to 1 inch thick; it has a double ring around it. Horse mushrooms can be found in unplowed fields and old grassy meadows from July onward. They can be seen from a long way off.

This mushroom is very fine. It has a much stronger flavor than its close relative the field mushroom and is less watery. Eat it young, as it gets tough and and dry with age.

Horse mushrooms can be cooked in all the best ways you might prepare ordinary mushrooms. A rather nice Swiss recipe suggests cooking them in butter and then setting them on a mound of spinach flavored with finely chopped onion cooked in butter, to look as if they were growing on a grassy bank.

Cauliflower fungus (*Sparassis crispa*) This wonderful cream-colored mushroom looks like a large sponge, up to 12 inches across. In Switzerland, it is called a broody hen; in Britain it is sometimes known as brain fungus. It has brittle, wax-like flesh and a pleasant smell; with age it becomes darker and tougher. It is not uncommon and can be found growing at the foot of old fir trees and around pine stumps. It is good to eat when young, but needs careful cleaning. Slice it and fry in butter with garlic and parsley. You can also pull it into pieces and, having washed and dried it, dredge it with flour and then sauté in butter with finely chopped onions or shallots.

Giant puffball (*Lycoperdon giganteum/Langermannia gigantea*) This lovely mushroom ranges in size from that of a large turnip to almost a full yard across, when it can be seen for miles. White at first, it has a kid-glove-like, smooth exterior, taut to the touch when it is young, becoming softer and somewhat dingier-looking with age. It is found between May and November in fields, pastures, and gardens; it often reappears in the same place year after year. Picked young, sliced, and sautéed, puffballs have a flavor like a mixture of bacon, mushrooms, eggplant, and fried pototoes all at once, especially if cooked in bacon fat. Some books say that the mushroom is exactly like sweetbreads in taste and flavor. You can sprinkle it with lemon juice before or after sautéing, but don't overcook it. Puffball with bacon is a good start to a day in the country.

Inky cap (*Coprinus comatus*) Known as lawyer's wig or shaggy inky cap in Britain, these tall, white, bell-shaped mushrooms liquefy as they age, and the resulting black fluid has been used as a substitute for ink.

Inky caps are a familiar sight on grassy roadsides and recently disturbed soil. The caps are shaggy, and gills are white at first, then pink and finally black. The best specimens are very young and firm: peel them, discard the stems, and sauté them in butter with salt, pepper, and a last-minute sprinkle of lemon juice, or bake them in cream for at least an hour, or possibly longer. They will taste like Dover sole.

Blewit (*Lepista nuda*) The blewit, or wood blewit, is a beauty—bluish-lilac or violet when young, with lilac gills. Usually found late in the season in woods, or in heaps of garden compost and leaves, it is good to eat if gathered when it is dry and sound; it's a useful mushroom at the end of the season. The larger caps have a particularly nice texture; slice them and sauté in butter, or grill them whole. Another blewit (*L. saeva*), called blue legs, is one of the few species that the English feel is safe to eat. Its flesh is fragile and tends to be watery, so it is best stewed in butter with softened onions, then coated with sour cream and chives, and a little flour, until bathed in a creamy sauce. In Switzerland, blewits are eaten in a sauce flavored with paprika, onion, and parsley.

Parasol mushroom (*Lepiota procera*) This handsome mushroom starts off as a tight brown dome that is quite hard to spot in the shortish grass it favors. It emerges as a glorious tall, shaggy-topped umbrella up to 12 inches across, which can be seen for miles.

With its characteristic shape, and creamy flesh and gills, goes a pungent, meaty smell, which makes it easy to identify. A larger version (*L. rachodes*) is called the shaggy parasol. However, not everybody is attracted by the strong flavor. The parasol mushroom should be eaten young. Discard the stems, and fry with eggs and bacon.

Hedgehog mushroom (*Hydnum repandum*) This is easily identified by the clustered spines beneath the cap, which gave it its name. It is golden-yellow, with an undulating top 1 to 4 inches across that sometimes becomes slightly funnel-shaped, and it has a slightly acrid smell. Found in deciduous woods from autumn to late winter, the hedgehog mushroom is not particularly special to eat. To cook it, scrape away the gills (some people leave them, but the texture is not good), wipe the caps clean, and sauté in butter; or use in soups and stews, risottos, and pasta sauces where a mixture of different mushrooms is called for.

Oyster mushroom (*Pleurotus ostreatus*) This mushroom is now cultivated widely, but is also found growing in the wild. It looks like an ear or a bracket, and grows in tiers on the stumps, logs, and branches of hardwood trees, especially beech trees. Colors vary from oyster-gray, pale buff, or white to yellowish-brown to almost black. The flesh is thick and soft with an almost waxy surface. The stems are short and tough, and the gills are white to pallid, often fused near the stalk.

There are dozens of varieties of oyster mushrooms and, as they tend to be in season at different times, oyster mushrooms now appear almost all year round. They are good to eat when young, but toughen as they age, becoming bitter. The wild ones need long, slow cooking as they can be hard to digest. Snip off the woody stems and either slice and fry until crisp or sauté in butter. They can also be used in stews or stir-fries, or pickled. The texture is good, slightly gelatinous and crunchy.

Shiitake mushroom (*Lentinus edodes*) These mushrooms also grow on trees. First cultivated by the Chinese, and then commercially developed by the Japanese, they were originally grown on teak, mahogany, or oak logs. Now they are often grown indoors on sterile wood sawdust.

Shiitake mushrooms, which have dark brown caps with inwardly rolling edges and a small, tough stem, do not grow in the wild in North America. They are, however, extensively cultivated for today's market, in Pennsylvania, California, and other states.

Fresh shiitakes have a firm and meaty texture; the stems are tough and should be removed. They are good in tempura, with shrimp and vegetables, and in stir-fries. They can be used together with dried shiitakes to make a good sauce for pasta, or in rice pilafs and risotto.

Dried shiitakes are also called Chinese black mushrooms. They can be used, soaked for at least 30 minutes, in any recipe where a small quantity of mushrooms is needed for flavoring.

Cultivated mushrooms

Although lacking the pleasing diversity of wild mushrooms gathered by season, cultivated forms have the merit of year-round availability. Moreover, they are consistent and utterly safe. Most common, of course, is the common white mushroom (*Agaricus bisporus*), cultivated relative of the field and horse mushrooms, and sold in several sizes.

Now that a wider range of mushrooms is becoming available, large mushroom farms, which formerly stuck to rearing our good old agaric species, are experimenting with other types: straw mushrooms, which have been grown in China for something like 2000 years, and enoki, as well as morels. Growers are also doing research on the requirements of mycorrhizal fungi, those species such as chanterelles and cèpes that can only grow in partnership with another plant.

Button mushrooms are small and succulent, and slightly weaker in flavor than the more mature grades. Remaining pale (although an aluminum saucepan may darken them slightly), they are useful for white, creamy sauces and also for salads. The larger white mushrooms, the kind where the membrane is just breaking to expose the gills, can be kept pale if rubbed with a cut lemon, or if a few drops of lemon juice or white wine are added to the cooking liquid. These mushrooms are ideal for stews and casseroles. The largest ones can be stuffed or, with the stems trimmed off level with the cap, can be filled with cream and cooked in the oven.

Cremini Also called common brown mushrooms or Italian mushrooms, these are actually a variety of the ordinary white mushroom. They are pale brown in color with a deeper flavor than the white mushroom. They can be used in any mushroom recipe.

Portobello These large mushrooms—from about 3 inches up to 8 inches across—are the mature version of the cultivated white mushroom, the grown-up cremini. They resemble wild field mushrooms and have a rich flavor and meaty texture. They can be grilled whole and served on a salad of arugula with olive oil. Or slice the caps and sauté with garlic and plenty of black pepper and chopped parsley.

It is best to buy mushrooms a few at a time and often. Mushrooms can lose moisture and dry out even in the refrigerator, and their flesh soon starts to shrivel. To limit evaporation, they can be kept in brown paper bags. All but the densely fleshed button mushrooms act like sponges when they are cooking, absorbing more than their own weight in liquid, so add them to stews or casseroles toward the end of the cooking time.

Japanese and Chinese mushrooms

Long before mushrooms were first cultivated in Europe, the Japanese were harvesting *take* specially grown in the water-softened bark of various tree trunks. In addition to shiitakes there are enoki, also called golden mushrooms or golden needles (*Flammulina velutipes*), and the meaty-tasting matsutake, grown on pine logs. Unlike the shiitake and the enoki, the matsutake has not been successfully cultivated.

As well as dried shiitakes, which are the black mushrooms served in Chinese restaurants, Chinese markets carry a stemless mushroom known as cloud ear, tree ear, or wood ear, used for texture rather than flavor. These dried mushrooms must be soaked for half an hour to revive their unusual texture.

Another Chinese mushroom is the tiny straw mushroom (*Volvariella volvaceae*), so called because it is grown on straw from paddy fields. It is normally sold canned.

Truffles

One of the rarest and certainly the most expensive of all fungi, the black Périgord truffle (*Tuber melanosporum*) grows on the roots of young oak trees. This is the most sought after of the truffle species, and is detected beneath the soil by pigs or specially trained truffle hounds.

With its rich, mold-like flavor, a little of the black truffle goes a long way—one of the good reasons it is used sparingly in such things as omelets, scrambled eggs, or stuffing for roast chicken. The classic dish *truffe sous cendre*—truffle wrapped in bacon fat or pastry and baked (traditionally under cinders)—is highly rated by gourmets. Sadly, truffles found in pâtés often have no flavor at all and were probably canned.

The white truffle of Italy's Piedmont is larger, stronger in flavor, and almost as expensive as its Périgord cousin. While the latter is invariably eaten cooked, the Italians use their white truffle raw, grating or slicing it over risottos and salads.

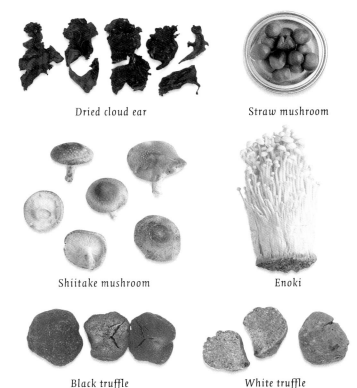

Dried cloud ear

Straw mushroom

Shiitake mushroom

Enoki

Black truffle

White truffle

Fruit

APPLE AND PEAR

Apples and pears, although frequently bracketed as if they were almost one and the same fruit, could scarcely be more different.

Apples are the most common, the most easy-going, and the most useful of all fruits, both to eat casually at any time of the day and to cook with—there are more apple desserts than any other sort. Pears, on the other hand, are a fragile luxury—large and aesthetically pleasing, they make a grand ending to a grand meal, and speak to the diner of sunny orchards and of careful harvesting and marketing.

Apple

Today, the choice of apples is getting smaller and smaller—although there are several thousand different apples cultivated in gardens and nurseries, very few find their way into commercial orchards, where the fruit must keep well and be tough, disease-resistant, and good at traveling. Of the seven thousand varieties known in the United States, only twenty or so are seriously marketed.

This is sad, since there are so many aromatic old-fashioned apples that are worth growing. But there has been a marked interest in some of the antique or heirloom varieties, and more of these are being cultivated now. So hunt through country markets and the more enlightened supermarkets, and you may come across some interesting varieties.

Apples sold as windfalls are also good buys and are perfect for cooking, since these unripe apples have plenty of acid, essential to the flavor of apple pies, tarts, and crisps. The best eating apples are those that retain some acidity even in their final sweetness, and have a mellow flavor and firm, juicy texture. The bright red apples known as Empires and the tart, green Granny Smith are especially good. The most popular American varieties are listed in the chart; others to look for are Baldwin, Northern Spy, Jonathan, Gravenstein, and Winesap.

Buying and storing apples While obviously one should avoid apples with bruises and soft spots, do not be put off by a few dull, rough, brown patches on sound apples. This is called russeting, and does not indicate spoilage. The term russet, in fact, refers to a whole category of winter apples with rough brownish

NAME	APPEARANCE	FLESH	TYPE
Red Delicious	large, elongated, thick-skinned, shiny red	juicy, very tender, no acidity	eating
Golden Delicious	large, conical, green ripening to yellow	tender, very sweet, no acidity when ripe	all-purpose
Granny Smith	medium to large, conical, green with whitish flecks	crisp, juicy, sweet-tart	all-purpose
McIntosh	medium, round, two-tone red and green to red	crisp, juicy, firm, slightly tart	all-purpose
Rome Beauty	large, round, thick-skinned, shiny red	crisp, juicy, firm, slightly tart	baking whole
Empire	medium, round, strong dark red	crisp, juicy, firm	all-purpose
Newtown Pippin	medium, round, greenish-yellow	crisp, juicy, firm, mildly tart	all-purpose
Cortland	medium, round, red tinged with green	crisp, firm, slightly tart	all-purpose
Gala	medium, round, yellow flushed and striped with orange and red	crisp, juicy, sweet-tart, aromatic	eating
Crispin (Mutsu)	medium to large, yellow-green	crisp, juicy, mild but slightly acid	eating
Cox's Orange Pippin	small, round, greenish-yellow tinged with red	crisp, juicy, firm, sweet, some acidity	all-purpose, best for eating
Orleans Reinette	small, flat, golden tinged with crimson	crisp, juicy, firm, some acidity	all-purpose
Egremont Russet	medium, round, with brown-orange russeting	soft, very sweet, some acidity	all-purpose
Laxton's Superb	medium, round, greenish-yellow, flushed with red	juicy, firm, sweet, some acidity	all-purpose
Bramley's Seedling	extra-large, irregular, green sometimes flushed with red	crisp, juicy, acid	cooking
Worcester Pearmain	medium, round, red, sometimes two-tone red and green	crisp, juicy, firm, sweet, slightly tart	all-purpose

skins; since Americans tend to like bright, shiny apples, russets are more popular in Europe. They are splendid with cheese, and cook well.

Those buying for the trade test for ripeness by grasping apples around the waist and applying gentle pressure: if the flesh is firm or the skin wrinkles only slightly, the apples are at the peak of perfection. Fragrance is also important, and the fruit should be firm.

Apples continue to ripen after they have been picked. If they are to be stored, they should be spread out so that they are not touching one other. If you want to buy apples in quantity, at one of the pick-your-own farms, for example, keep them on racks in a cool, dry, dark place.

Cooking with apples Selecting the right apples for cooking is important if you do not want your pies to end up watery or your baked apples to collapse in a frothy mess all over the oven. Some apples, such as America's favorite eating apple, the Red Delicious, are too tender for cooking and lack the acidity that gives apple dishes their delicious flavor.

The hard, crisp apples such as the popular Granny Smith or baking apples like the Rome Beauty will require longer cooking than the softer-fleshed ones.

Applesauce When making applesauce, choose crisp, juicy apples with plenty of acid—adding sugar toward the end of the cooking time—as these will quickly turn to a froth. Tart apples give a sweet-acid taste that is delicious with pork, pheasant, or goose.

Cooking sliced apples Many of the dishes involving apples, such as pies and tarts, turnovers, crisps, and fritters, depend on apples keeping their shape. Sugar and/or butter added at the start of cooking helps to prevent them from disintegrating. Among the best "pie apples" are Empires and Newtown Pippins. The Golden Delicious retains its shape well, but lacks flavor, so cook it with cinnamon and plenty of butter and sugar. Europe's favorite reinettes and russets, noted for their unique subtle flavor, are excellent for cooking: these are the apples that French cooks use when making *tartes aux pommes*.

Baking apples These are cored with an apple corer and the cavity filled with sugar, butter, and perhaps raisins, almonds, or blackberries. They are then baked, possibly basted or flamed with Calvados or brandy, and served with heavy cream. The best apples for baking are the large ones. Run your knife around the circumference of the apple (to prevent the skin from splitting) before you stuff them and put them in the baking dish. Thick-skinned varieties such as Rome Beauty are ideal, since their skins are less likely to burst. The harder the apple, the longer it will take to bake: it is done when the top is frothy and seeping with juice.

Fried apples A classic accompaniment to pork chops is peeled, sliced apples fried until golden in butter. Fried apples are good with sausages at breakfast, and they are also very good with pheasant.

Stewing apples When stewing apples, as for a compote, use the same varieties as you would use for pies and tarts. To vary the flavor, you can add cloves, cinnamon, or perhaps coriander seeds and grated lemon zest. Rum or Calvados and butter are also good with stewed apples. Some savory dishes, such as Iran's *khoresh*, involve apples with cinnamon and onions. In West Germany, apples are stewed, sprinkled with bread crumbs, and then fried, to be served with ham.

Raw apples Sliced or chopped apples give a crisp, crunchy texture to salad. The famous Waldorf salad of celery, apples, and walnuts tossed in mayonnaise is especially good if made right. A squeeze of lemon juice will prevent cut-up apples from turning brown. Any crisp, sharp eating apple will make a good salad.

Lady apple

Lady apples, usually found in specialty markets or farmers' markets, are miniature apples about the size of a crabapple. They may be red or yellow flushed with red. They can be eaten raw or cooked—there's no need to peel them—and are often used as a garnish.

apple corer 225

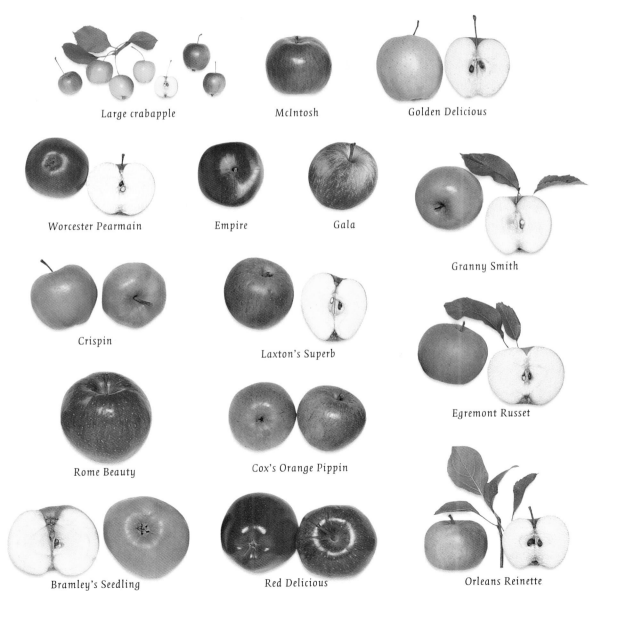

Large crabapple

McIntosh

Golden Delicious

Worcester Pearmain

Empire

Gala

Granny Smith

Crispin

Laxton's Superb

Egremont Russet

Rome Beauty

Cox's Orange Pippin

Bramley's Seedling

Red Delicious

Orleans Reinette

Crabapple, quince, and medlar

These three fruits, like the apple, are related to the rose family.

Crabapple Roasted and still hot, the crabapples that "hissed in the bowl" in the hot spiced ale punches of Shakespeare's day were most likely the small, sour apples that grow wild or in gardens and that are the ancestors of all our modern apples. These beautiful tiny fruits, which can be yellow, red, or green, are no longer eaten (except by birds), because they are generally not worth the bother, being mostly core and often very sour. They do, however, make a lovely clear, golden-pink jelly, which is excellent on buttered bread and with good cream cheese. Larger crabapples, which are slightly sweeter, grow from the seeds of cultivated apples that have become wild. They have a crisp, tart flavor.

Quinces came originally from Central Asia. Yellow-gold and aromatic, they are a pleasing sight in autumn and are usually used to make jellies or jams. The astringent fruit, always eaten cooked, is not as popular in America as in Europe, which is unfortunate. A slice or two added to an apple pie or tart gives these dishes a delicious scent and flavor. Quinces can also be boiled down with sugar to a thick paste—called *membrillo* in Spain, *cotignac* in southwestern France, and quince cheese in Britain—which is then dried and eaten as a sweet.

Medlar This unusual European fruit rarely comes to market, but is sometimes cultivated in gardens or seen growing wild in hedges. Medlars look like open cups of a warm golden-brown and resemble a large rose hip. Since they do not ripen on the tree, they need to be picked and kept until they turn soft before they are edible. The ripe state is easily recognizable, because the unripe fruit is rock-hard. Medlars are usually baked or made into jam or jelly, or the flesh is scraped out and eaten with sugar and cream. The taste and texture are slightly reminiscent of marzipan.

Pear

This fruit, which can be so delicious, is more temperamental than the apple. It has an unpleasant habit of becoming mealy from the core outward, a state that is described by English growers as "sleepiness," and it does not keep as well as the apple.

Pears come in almost as great a variety as apples. Europe has about five thousand named varieties and America about one thousand, but, as with apples, only a small proportion reach the market. Three shapes predominate: the ordinary pear shape, the long-necked shape, and the oval, almost round shape. Colors, too, vary a great deal, from a soft blurred brown to bright green with dark brown, gray-black, or green flecks, to golden with a handsome red-gold flush.

Comice pear This French variety, properly known as *Doyenné de Comice*, is considered to be one of the best pears. It has a perfect balance of sweetness and acidity and a certain spiciness. Its juicy, sweet flesh is buttery—meaning that it is melting and not grainy. Medium to large and greenish-yellow, it has a red blush where it has been exposed to the sun. Its thick, shiny skin is stippled with tiny gray spots and fawn patches.

Bartlett This popular pear is usually known as the Williams' pear in Europe, as it was propagated by an English grower named Williams. It was first introduced to North America by an American called Bartlett. It has a sweet, musky flavor and a smooth skin that turns from dark green to yellow as it ripens; eat it when its speckles are still surrounded by a tiny halo of green on an otherwise golden skin. These superb pears are unfortunately bad travelers and extremely perishable.

Anjou One of the most widely grown varieties of pear in the United States, the Anjou remains green even when fully ripe. It has sweet, spicy, juicy flesh speckled with tiny brown spots.

Packham's Triumph This descendant of the Bartlett or Williams' pear looks somewhat like its distinguished ancestor but is not nearly so delicate. It keeps well and is therefore exported in great numbers from Australia, where it is grown in profusion.

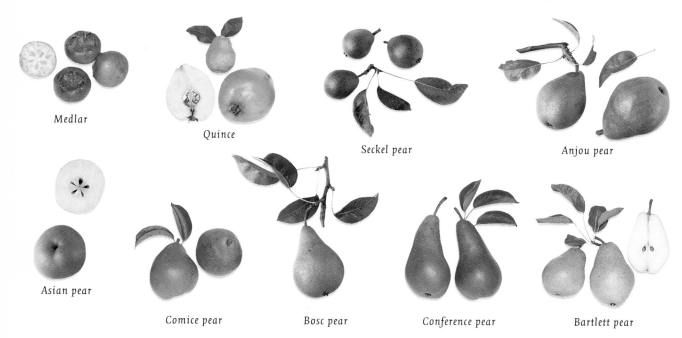

Medlar

Quince

Seckel pear

Anjou pear

Asian pear

Comice pear

Bosc pear

Conference pear

Bartlett pear

Conference pear A favorite English pear, this was so named when it won the top prize at a fruit growers' conference because of its fine, tender, melting flesh and delicious flavor. This pear is slim and long-necked, stippled with fawn and gray russeting, and turns pale yellow when it is ripe.

Bosc More properly known as the Beurré Bosc, this is one of a number of pear varieties that have the French word for butter in their names and are characterized by their creamy, melting quality. The Beurré Bosc is so named in honor of a former director of the Jardin des Plantes in Paris, who propagated it. It has a long neck and a fine brown russeting. Juicier and plumper than the Beurré Bosc, the Beurré Hardy, a popular European variety, takes its name from a nineteenth-century Belgian and is a plumper pear. Both pears in their youth have enough juice for delicious eating and are also excellent when poached.

Bonne Louise This French pear is now also known as Louise Bonne de Jersey, and in German-speaking countries as *gute Louise von Avranches*. Good it certainly is, and well known not only in its native country but wherever French pears are exported. Smooth-skinned, with the merest speckle of russeting, the Louise tends to be greenish on the shaded side and yellow washed with pink on the side ripened in the sun. It makes an excellent dessert pear.

Seckel, Seckle This was discovered growing wild in Pennsylvania by an eighteenth-century trapper. It is small and rather round, with a green to russet skin sometimes tinged with rose. It is sweet, juicy, and spicy.

Clapp's Favorite This medium pear has green skin that turns golden-yellow when fully ripe, with some russeting and, occasionally, faintly red cheeks. It is a popular variety for cooking.

Passe crassane This fat, juicy, rounded Italian pear has a lovely flavor and makes an excellent dessert pear. It keeps well.

Asian pear The many varieties of Asian pear range in size from tiny to huge, and may be round like an apple or elongated like a pear. Skin color is golden-brown or greenish-yellow. The flesh is firm and crunchy when ripe and extremely juicy.

Buying pears Pears for eating or cooking should always be sound. Test for ripeness near the stem end, where there should be more than a little give, and at the blossom end, where there should be no oozing softness, since this usually indicates trouble within. Pears are at their best for a very short time, and although they can be left to mature for a little while, they must be inspected frequently.

Cooking with pears Most large pears are eating pears, although some are juicier than others. All pears, however, can also be poached in wine or light syrup, and well-flavored eating pears such as Bartletts are, in fact, best for such dishes as pear sorbet.

The best pears for cooking are the harder, firmer varieties. Poached in vanilla-flavored syrup, they make good compotes and can also be cooked in spiced red wine, in the process of which they become dyed to "a fine Oriental red." In Italy, they are halved and baked in Marsala, the cavity of each half stuffed with a mixture of ground almonds and crystallized fruit. They can also be made into a relish or chutney with lemon juice and ginger or with horseradish, mustard seeds, and black pepper; or they can be preserved or pickled with sugar, cinnamon, and white wine vinegar. Cooked with butter and sugar, they used to be served hot with game in Germany. They are still served cold there, poached in lemon juice with cranberries.

Around the North Sea, pears also go into main dishes: in the Netherlands, they are boiled along with green beans, potatoes, and beef, while in Hamburg they are cooked with beans and bacon or with cured meats. Boiled potatoes mixed with pears and a dash of vinegar are also sometimes served in northern Europe; try pear and spinach purée with roast duck.

CITRUS FRUIT

The beautiful citrus fruits, probably East Asian in origin, all have one thing in common: they ripen while they are still on the tree. Once they have been picked, they stop developing and will not get sweeter or improve in flavor. But most of them travel well and remain in good condition for many weeks in the right environment, only gradually losing weight and pliancy as their juices and oils lose freshness.

Natural untreated citrus fruits are subject to what is called regreening. This does not necessarily mean that the fruits are unripe, but is simply a matter of temperature: the chlorophyll in ripe fruit fades as the thermometer drops and revives as it rises again; inside the skin, the fruit remains unaffected. However, since green patches are unattractive on citrus fruit that should by rights be orange or lemon-yellow, they are often treated with ethylene gas, which fades the chlorophyll, making the fruit more acceptable to the consumer.

When buying citrus fruits, choose those that feel heavy for their size, as this means plenty of juice. The fruit should be sound, with no signs of bruising, damp patches, or soft spots. If you want to use the peel in cooking or for making marmalade, try to find fruit that is unwaxed, and wash or scrub it well to remove any residues of pesticides or other treatments it may have had.

Citron

This fruit is the elder of the citrus tribe. It has a thick corrugated skin, and looks similar to a large, rough lemon. Since its pulp is too bitter to eat, the citron is now mostly grown to make the most beautiful translucently green candied peel, which is used in fruitcakes.

Orange

Oranges may be orange, but they can also be green, greenish-yellow, and even red. There are three main varieties of orange: the smooth, thin-skinned sweet oranges, such as the Valencias and blood oranges, which range from bright gold to blood red and are full of juice; the larger, rougher, thick-skinned seedless navel oranges, which have the best flavor and are easy to peel; and the bitter oranges, also known as Seville or Bigarade oranges, which are used for making the best marmalade. The bergamot, a small, acidic citrus fruit similar to an orange, yields an essential oil from its rind that is used in perfumes, confectionery, and Earl Grey tea.

Orange marmalade, which was invented in Scotland, owes its origins to a boatload of Portuguese oranges that arrived in Dundee in the eighteenth century and unexpectedly turned out to be extremely bitter. Bitter oranges occasionally come onto the market in their short New Year season, and marmalade making is about the only occasion on which we boil oranges to good purpose.

For the most part, however, we like our oranges fresh. In Trinidad, they are sold in the street, halved and sprinkled with salt. Orange juice, freshly squeezed and served with ice, used to be standard refreshment in all countries. In Sicily, a paradise for oranges, the juice is drunk not so much as an appetizer but as a final refreshment after a meal—especially the glorious tomato-red juice of blood oranges, which is particularly sweet and full of flavor.

When making orange juice, thin-skinned oranges such as the virtually seedless Valencias are the best choice. This is not so much because navel oranges lack juice, but because their imposing size makes them more expensive, and since their skins have a thick padding of pith, a lot of what we pay for is thrown away. The thin-skinned oranges are, of course, in fact sometimes simply called juice oranges. The navel orange, which can be peeled neatly and is virtually seedless, is the best one to eat as a dessert or snack.

Mandarin and tangerine

These and their many cultivars such as clementines and satsumas are the smaller members of the citrus family and their names are sometimes used interchangeably. All are distinguished by having skin that does not cling to the fruit, and flesh that separates easily into segments.

These fruits are known as various mandarin cultivars to the botanist, but simply as different types of tangerines to the shopper. Those of North African descent, which are grown in and exported from Tangiers, with loose skins and perfumed juice, are responsible for the name tangerine. Canned segments are sold under this name, although most are actually satsumas.

Clementine These are considered by some people to be mandarins crossed with the Algerian wild orange, but clementines are generally recognized as a variety of tangerine. They are usually tiny, with a very good flavor—children are particularly fond of them.

Satsuma These are the tangerines that are grown and exported from Japan and Cyprus. They can have quite a sour taste and are very refreshing.

Temple orange A cross between a tangerine and a sweet orange, temple oranges have loose, deep-orange skins and a sweet-tart flavor.

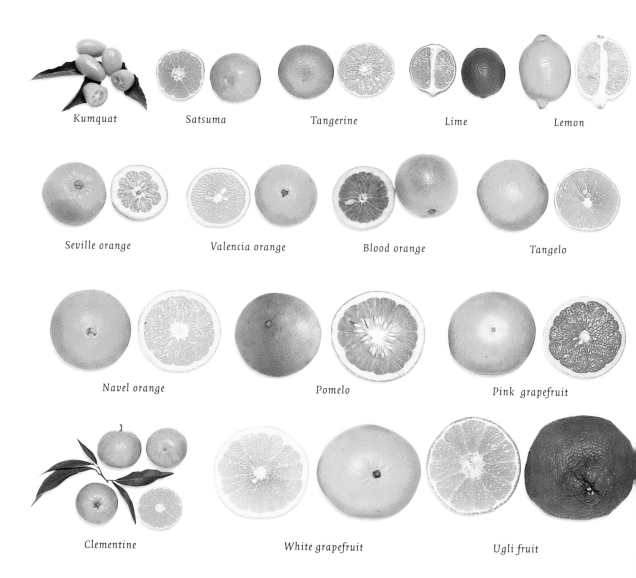

Kumquat   Satsuma   Tangerine   Lime   Lemon

Seville orange   Valencia orange   Blood orange   Tangelo

Navel orange   Pomelo   Pink grapefruit

Clementine   White grapefruit   Ugli fruit

Murcott (honey tangerine), ortanique, king, and tangor Along with many other small hybrids, these are related to both tangerines and oranges. They are often found growing together on the same tree, which shows how easily they cross with each other. All are sweet, spicy dessert fruits, and all are easy to peel.

Tangelo and ugli fruit

The tangelo is a cross between a tangerine and a grapefruit. It is loose-skinned and ranges from deep-red orange to orange-yellow. The Minneola, or Mineola, variety is particularly sweet and juicy and easy to peel.

The ugli fruit, larger than most tangelos, is another tangerine-grapefruit cross (or, possibly, a tangerine-pomelo hybrid). Its extraordinary bumpy, mottled skin is greenish-yellow, but the light orange flesh is sweet, juicy, and delicately flavored, with a flower-like perfume.

Grapefruit and pomelo

The large familiar globe of the grapefruit—either yellow, when it is called white; rosy, when it is called pink; or ruby-red fleshed inside a yellow or pinkish-yellow skin, when it is called ruby—is a descendant of the pomelo, a citrus plant brought from Polynesia to the West Indies in the seventeenth century by an English sea captain. The grapefruit is perhaps more popular in America than anywhere else. It is primarily a breakfast fruit, but it also ends meals in mousses and sorbets, and in between turns up in salads mixed with avocado, or with oranges and mint, and served on a bed of lettuce.

The pomelo, or pumelo, is also called shaddock, after that English sea captain. It may be found in Asian or specialty produce markets in winter, at least as large as a grapefruit and often larger, and ranging in color from greenish to yellow. The pink or pale-yellow flesh can be very juicy but is sometimes dry, and the taste may be either sweet or pleasantly tangy.

Kumquat

This originated in Japan and has recently been cast from the citrus family by botanists, although it continues to look and taste like a tiny orange. Tart in flavor, kumquats are usually eaten with their skin, and are often bottled in syrup.

Lemon

This most indispensable of fruits, which is rich in vitamin C, can be either large or small, with a smooth, thin skin or a thick and knobbly one. For culinary purposes, such as mousses and sorbets, lemon curd, lemon soups, and frothy sauces, and for the wedges served with fish for squeezing over, it is always better to use smooth-skinned lemons if possible, as they have more juice.

Choose specimens that are truly lemon-yellow in color. Butter-yellow lemons may have lost some of their acidity during the ripening process, and lemons that look dull and do not have a moist-looking sheen may be dry and "ricy," meaning that the almost invisible little sacs containing the juice have turned grainy through evaporation.

Lemons owe much of their flavor and aroma to the oil contained in the outer part of their skin, which is known as the zest. When serving lemon quarters, cut them lengthwise so that, when they are squeezed, the juice will be directed downward onto the food. Whenever possible, lemon juice should be added to dishes after they have been cooked, to avoid any loss of its valuable vitamin C, which disappears when heated.

In addition to its use as a flavoring, lemon juice has certain other qualities that are of value to the cook. When poaching or stewing fruit, 1 teaspoon lemon juice added to each ¼ cup water will help prevent the fruit from breaking up or losing its shape. A few squeezes of juice will help poached eggs set, and a few drops will acidulate water sufficiently to prevent the discoloration of vegetables such as Jerusalem artichokes or salsify. Lemon juice can be used instead of vinegar in salad dressings, and, since it helps to counteract the richness of foods, it can aid digestion when used with fried foods.

Lime

This can be pale or dark green and has a tart greenish pulp; if the skin is yellowish, it usually means that the tang has gone. The Mexican or West Indian lime, which features so much in Southwest and Creole cooking, is sharp and aromatic in flavor, as are the larger Tahitian limes, of which the Persian and the Bearss are two types. The Key limes of Florida have a delicious sharpness to them and are used to make Key lime pie.

Limes are the most perishable of all citrus fruits: unfortunately, they dry up and shrivel all too fast, and develop soft brown patches on their skins. They can be used for many of the same purposes as lemons, and their juice, which is pale when fresh but often has added green color when it's been commercially extracted, goes into daiquiris, margaritas, and other tequila drinks.

1

2

Peeling and sectioning citrus fruits

1 Using a serrated knife, cut a slice from the top and bottom of the fruit to expose the flesh. Peel the fruit in the same way as you would an apple, cutting just beneath the pith.

2 Hold the fruit in one hand and cut out each segment, freeing it from its membrane as you cut. The resulting sections should be completely free of membrane and pith.

STONE FRUIT

Although imported peaches can be found for much of the year, there is still something wonderfully seasonal about stone fruits. Their year begins with the first cherries and ends with the last of the plums, with local peaches, nectarines, and apricots in between. All are closely related members of the Prunus family and when talked about collectively are known as drupes.

Cherry

Firm-fleshed or melting, deepest lip-staining black, or the palest cream tinged with a rosy blush, the cherry comes in hundreds of varieties. They are generally classified by their growers as sweet or sour. There is also a third type, which is a mixture of sweet and sour; two of these hybrids are Dukes and Royales. Usually black or translucent red, these are all-purpose cherries and can be eaten and cooked in a variety of ways.

Sweet cherry Sweet cherries (*Prunus avium*) used to be neatly divided into the hard, crisp bigarreaus and the soft, sweet cherries known as hearts or heart

cherries in America (or, sometimes, jeans), *guignes* in France, and geans in England. Now, however, with the appearance of many hybrids, the distinction has become blurred.

Among the most delicious of the bigarreaus is the Bing—large, heart-shaped, and deep red to almost black, with firm, sweet flesh. The Royal Anne is also a bigarreau—big, crisp, and golden with a red cheek.

Another red-black cherry that is tender and has an excellent flavor is the black Tartarian, a type of *guigne*. The Lambert is a large deep-red sweet cherry that is similar to the Bing but slightly smaller and not quite as good. The Ranier is a sweet golden cherry with a pink blush.

Bings are the first choice for a fresh sweet cherry pie. Sweet, juicy, black *guignes* are used to make the delicious dessert clafoutis, which comes from France's Dordogne; in Kent, England's cherry-orchard county, a similar dish goes by the name of battered cherries. The same juicy cherries also go into the exquisite Swiss black cherry jam, shiny, slippery, and full of whole cherries.

Sour cherry If the word sweet is sometimes used too optimistically as far as cherries are concerned, sour is almost an understatement. The dark, short-stemmed, juicy Morellos, or *griottes* as they are known in France, are so acidic that they are almost impossible to eat. They are small, round, and deep red to almost black. The famous Black Forest cherry cake called *schwarzwälder kirschtorte* is authentically made with Morellos grown in the Black Forest region, and with *kirschwasser*, the Black Forest version of cherry brandy. Cherries such as the Montmorency, brighter in color and with pale, clear juice, are so sour that they are not normally eaten uncooked. Early Richmond is another sour cherry.

Sour cherries (*Prunus cerasus*) go into translucent jams; into pickles to eat with game, pork, poultry, rich meat dishes, and pâtés; and into liqueurs and cherry brandies. Fresh sour cherries make the most delicious pie. Duck Montmorency, now something of a cliché, requires cherries for its fruity wine sauce, although they do not have to be the sour Montmorency cherries of France; any

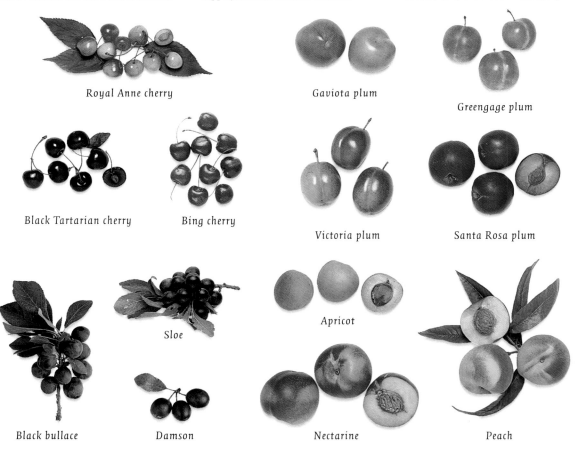

Royal Anne cherry

Gaviota plum

Greengage plum

Black Tartarian cherry

Bing cherry

Victoria plum

Santa Rosa plum

Sloe

Apricot

Black bullace

Damson

Nectarine

Peach

acidic red cherries will do. And cherries set alight in a brandy sauce and poured over vanilla ice cream make Cherries Jubilee. Morello cherries are often preserved and make good tarts and pies.

Maraschino cherry The sweet, sticky liqueur maraschino is made from a small, wild cherry from the Dalmatian region of Yugoslavia, the *damasca*, or *marasca*. Maraschino cherries, however, which were originally preserved by being steeped in the liqueur, are now more likely to be ordinary cherries that have been bleached and then steeped in syrup flavored with almond or mint.

Buying and storing cherries Look for brightly colored fruit; whether heart-shaped or spherical, the plump ones are always best. The fruit should be clean and glossy, with unbroken skins and stems that are fresh and green. Make sure the stems are attached on most of the fruit, or the fruit may have been spoiled by mold or rot in transit. Ripe cherries are perishable, but will keep for a few days in the refrigerator; wash them just before they are to be eaten.

Cooking with cherries Prepare cherries for cooking by pushing out the pits with a cherry pitter or hooking them out with the U-bend of a paper clip or hairpin. If you try to squeeze the pits out, too much juice will be lost.

Canned cherries lack firmness and flavor and are best used in sweet, rather than savory, dishes, although they still won't be very good.

Plum

"No other fruit," said Pliny, "has been so cleverly crossed"—and since he wrote this some 2000 years ago, the growers have not been idle. Some plums are grown primarily to be eaten fresh, although many, like the greengage, are equally delicious cooked.

Eating plums These are usually larger and juicier than cooking plums, with a higher sugar content.

Santa Rosa These pleasantly tart, bright red plums are grown largely in California, where the climate suits their warm temperament. Derivatives of the wild Asiatic plum, they are often referred to as Japanese plums, although they were grown originally in China. Others of this type are the Laroda, with reddish-yellow skin, Friar, Queen Anne, and the Kelsey, a dark-green to yellow plum.

Greengage Of all the European plums, none is more sweetly perfumed than the greengage, known in France as the Reine-Claude. In the United States, the Kelsey is sometimes marketed as a greengage plum, but it is not the real thing. In Europe, there are several other varieties in addition to the old greengage, round and firm-fleshed, with its rose-flushed cheek. There are also many golden descendants of the old French "transparent gage," large and translucent, with the delicious honeyed flesh characteristic of all the gages.

Italian or prune plum These small purple plums are quite good eaten out of the hand, but are usually at their best in the kitchen, stewed or used in baking.

Gaviota and Victoria The Gaviota is one of the newer European varieties, grown to giant proportions; it is sweet and juicy, and ruby-colored right down to the pit. Golden-red and pink-bloomed, the Victoria is one of the most prolific of plums. Oval-shaped with golden flesh, it is a favorite in the kitchen and is also excellent eaten out of hand.

Cooking plums These are usually the smaller, drier, sharp-flavored plums that retain enough acidity to make them delicious when cooked.

Damson These have a lovely acidity even when ripe, and are used for jams, pies, and other desserts. Damsons are not as common as they once were, but are well worth seeking out. In England, they may be turned into damson cheese, an old country confection made of puréed fruit and plenty of sugar, which is aged before it is ready to eat. Damson cheese is a close relation to the more pliable *mus*—made from the quetsch plum—which used to be very popular.

Beach plum These grow wild along the Atlantic Coast, especially on Cape Cod. The small, tart, dark purple fruits grow in large clusters and are avidly gathered to be made into beach plum jelly or jam.

Sloe and bullace Dark and mouth-drying, the sloe is a wild European plum that grows on spiky hedges and is used for making sloe gin. The wild bullace, larger than the sloe, is less acidic and can be stewed or made into jelly or preserves. These are rarely seen in U.S. markets.

Zwetschen, Quetsch plum Also known as *switzen*, or, in the Slavonic languages, *slivy*, these are small, dark blue plums with a heavy bloom. They thrive in central Europe, where they are made into the plum brandy *slivovitz*, and in Germany and in Alsace, where they are used to make a potent fruit brandy.

Mirabelles are also called myrobalans or, in Britain, cherry plums. They are very small, with red or yellow skins and golden flesh. These European plums are soft and juicy and are excellent stewed or made into jams. They are also used to make an *eau-de-vie* called mirabelle.

Buying and storing plums When buying plums, make sure that they are firm and free from damage. They should be stored in a cool place, but not for too long; ripened plums do not keep for more than 2 or 3 days.

Cooking with plums All dark plums, like the purple Empress and the almost black El Dorado, and some of the lighter varieties, such as the small golden-yellow Mirabelle, have bitter skins. This makes a delicious contrast to the sweetness of their flesh when cooked. They can be used to make jams and jellies that are transparently luminous when freshly cooked, but darken with aging. They also make a delicious sweet-sour sauce to serve with meat and with the pancakes that accompany Peking duck.

In Austria, plums, fresh or dried, go into the middle of lovely deep-fried little dumplings that are rolled in fine sugar mixed with grated chocolate, and go into strudels. Throughout Germany, the plum season means *Pflaumenkuchen*—plums riding on a yeast-based dough that absorbs the juice of the fruit. In Britain, many recipes such as plum pudding do not require plums at all, the word being used to mean raisins.

Peach

The flesh of peaches ranges from almost silvery-white to deep gold or deep red. White-fleshed peaches are tender and juicy, yellow ones slightly coarser but often very good; the little-known red-fleshed *pêches-de-vignes* of France can be the richest in flavor. With some peaches, the flesh clings to the stone, hence clingstone peaches, while with freestone varieties, the flesh comes away cleanly.

Known as *Prunus persica*, the peach reached Greece from its native China via Persia, and then Rome and the rest of Europe via Greece. It arrived in America by way of peach pits carried by Columbus, and the American soil and

cooking with wine and spirits 208–9
dried peach 184
prune 184
cherry pitter 225

Peach Melba Cobbler 398

climate suited the peach tree so well that it spread faster than the settlers. But it is Georgia, especially, that is known as the peach state. The freestone Belle of Georgia, crimson cheeked, its creamy flesh delicately marbled and its stone sitting in a carmine-tinted pit, comes from seed that was sent directly from China at the end of the nineteenth century. Elberta, another favorite Georgian, has juicy yellow flesh, firm but tender. It is equally popular fresh or canned, but while canned peaches in heavy syrup are nice enough, they differ almost more than any other fruit from their fresh counterparts.

Buying and storing peaches Large peaches command the highest price but are not always the most delicately flavored. In China, where peaches symbolize longevity, the highly venerated ancestor of all the peach trees in the world bears fruit that is relatively small, with large pits, and yet its flavor is said to be unsurpassed by any of our hybrids.

Peaches are a fragile fruit and should be handled very gently. They should feel firm with a little give; greenish fruit should be avoided, as it will never ripen at home. Store ripe peaches in the refrigerator, but keep those that are still a little too firm at room temperature.

Cooking with peaches Some people eat peaches in salads, and spiced or pickled peaches are excellent with ham, but it is in desserts that peaches come into real use. Peach sorbets and ice creams are both delicate and subtle, and there are scores of sundaes and *coûpes* made with peaches, the most famous of which must undoubtedly be Peach Melba. Invented by Escoffier for a late dinner for Dame Nellie Melba, the opera singer, this involves a ripe fresh peach gently poached in syrup, with vanilla ice cream, whipped fresh cream, and crushed fresh raspberries for the sauce. In France, peaches and raspberries are combined in an exquisite fruit salad.

Nectarine

One of the most beautiful of all fruits, with rosy cheeks like those of a blushing girl, the nectarine is smooth-skinned like a plum. It is like a ripe plum in texture, but tastes of peach, although it is a little sharper and more scented. Nectarines can be used in all the same ways as peaches, but are usually devoured, messily, as a

dessert fruit or snack—much juicier than peaches, they are rarely peeled, because their skin is much thinner. Called *brugnons* in France, they are eaten there in vast quantities in July and August, the white-fleshed varieties fetching higher prices than the yellow ones. Nectarines can be purchased underripe, as they will ripen at room temperature.

Apricot

Even in the days when fresh fruit was regarded with suspicion, apricots were generally accepted as wholesome food. Known as *Prunus armeniaca* because the Romans obtained them from the Far East via Armenia, they span the spectrum of gentle orangey tones, from the very pale to the very rich. Depth of color, however, is not necessarily an indication of flavor; it merely means that some varieties have more carotene than others and are richer in vitamin A. The deep-orange apricot called Moorpark is always sweet and delicious to eat.

The flesh of apricots is much firmer and drier than that of peaches and nectarines, which makes them ideal for eating fresh as well as for cooking—they will not turn into a mush, thereby ruining your tart or whatever else.

Buying and storing apricots An apricot picked before its time does not sweeten, it only matures a little, so test for ripeness by pressing the fruit gently between two fingers; it should feel soft. Ripe fruits will keep in the refrigerator for a few days. Unripe, they will keep for longer, and if they are too hard and sour to be eaten fresh, they can be cooked in tarts, and a compote, or pickled in vinegar with cloves; this treatment makes an excellent relish that is delicious when eaten with cold pork or ham.

Cooking with apricots In France, large, fresh apricots, arranged on light flaky pastry, make mouthwatering tarts, and a compote of apricots, sometimes flavored with Madeira, is served hot on crisp, golden croutons. Austria's *knoedels*, or apricot dumplings, are made from fresh peeled apricots individually wrapped in thin pastry, and then poached and eaten with hot melted butter, sugar, and cinnamon. And brandied apricots are delicious, the fruit poached with sugar and put up with brandy in equal quantity to the syrup.

BERRIES AND RHUBARB

The arrival of berries heralds the coming of summer, but they will not be so fully flavored and sweet as later on in the season, and they are also likely to be expensive. In the case of most berries, however, it is a pleasure to buy at least a few early ones for decorating creamy mousses or other desserts, to which they give an allure that is quite disproportionate to their numbers.

The real feasting begins in the high season, and it is then that most berries taste best, simply sprinkled with sugar and eaten with milk or cream or possibly sprinkled with wine. When the first flush of excitement has worn off somewhat, they can be combined with other fruit or made into ice creams and sorbets.

There are usually at least 2 weeks each summer when a great number of berries are available simultaneously. This is the time to make fresh berry desserts or to offer great bowls of mixed berries, sugared well beforehand so that they yield some of their juice. Later in the season, when berries are more abundant, and cheaper, it is time to think about making jams, jellies, and syrups.

When buying berries, it is important to look not only at the top of the box in which they are likely to be packed, but also at the underside. Bad staining or wetness suggests squashed fruit, which will soon turn moldy. Some packers still call to mind the Elizabethan "strawberry wives," who, according to their monarch, were given to "laying two or three great ones at the mouth of their pot, and all the rest were little ones."

If you buy berries loose, ask for them to be weighed and packed ½ pound at a time, since this prevents them from being crushed by their own weight on the way home. If you go fruit picking at a farm—every year more of them open their gates to the public—use plenty of small baskets or other containers so that your harvest remains in good condition.

Berries, whether bought or picked, are fragile and perishable, so the sooner you eat them, the better. If they must be stored, spread them out well so that furry casualties do not infect their neighbors. A cool, dark, airy spot other than the refrigerator is in fact the best place to store them because no berries, except perhaps the firmer ones that come in the autumn, will thrive for very long in the refrigerator—it is too humid for them. Also, the more highly scented berries such as strawberries tend to permeate other foods, particularly butter, with their smell. Nevertheless, the refrigerator will be the storage place of necessity for most.

Strawberry

"Doubtless God could have made a better fruit than the strawberry, but doubtless God never did." Best loved among the soft fruits, strawberries conjure up all the well-being of summer. Strawberry shortcake is one of the all-time favorite American desserts. In England, the fruit is built into the summer way of life— garden parties at Buckingham Palace traditionally include what a sixteenth-century writer described as "strawberries swimming in the cream."

The ancestor of the cultivated strawberries we delight in these days was the native wild Virginia berry, introduced to Europe by the early colonists. It was smaller than today's prize specimens, but a positive giant compared with the indigenous European fragrant wood strawberries (*fraises des bois*) that had long been transplanted into gardens and regarded as a cure for all ills. Alpine strawberries (*fraises des Alpes*) are slightly larger, and some are white. Both these wild varieties have not changed in their intense fragrance and size, and still remain the best of all strawberries.

The advent of the Virginian strawberry led to unceasing attempts to grow even larger strawberries. Sadly, it was found that what the fruit gained in size it lost in flavor. It was not until a particularly fragrant strawberry arrived from Chile and was crossbred with the Virginian that the balance between size and taste was finally adjusted. This hybrid is the ancestral strawberry of all modern varieties cultivated on both sides of the Atlantic.

Today new varieties of strawberries are regularly introduced and old ones discarded as being too fragile or not sufficiently resistant to disease, or too small: size rather than flavor has been the important factor in marketing, and the big strawberries command the highest prices. They may look luscious, but from the eater's point of view, bigger is not necessarily better; nor do the deep scarlet varieties necessarily taste best.

Do not be put off by the lighter berries or those that have paler tips, but make sure that the strawberries are plump and glossy. They should be bought with their green frills intact, and if washing them, do so immediately before hulling. Hulled strawberries yield their juice when they are sugared. Only in jam making should strawberries be cooked at all. Even when making strawberry sauce to go with ice creams or sorbets, simply purée the fresh fruit with sugar and perhaps with a little lemon juice.

The way in which strawberries are served is really a matter of personal preference. Some people like their strawberries simply hulled and sugared, or—using a serving method that is especially pretty—hulled and arranged in a pyramid with strawberry leaves tucked in here and there. Others prefer to eat them with a dusting of black pepper or a sprinkling of orange or lemon juice or balsamic vinegar to bring out the flavor. There is also a school of thought that considers a sprinkling or even a dousing of Beaujolais, claret, or Champagne perfection on strawberries.

Raspberry

This beautiful, velvety berry, from which the liqueur *crème de framboises* is made, is at its best when a deep garnet red. Black raspberries taste much like the red ones, as do the golden ones, which do not often find their way onto the market. Raspberries are always sold hulled, which makes them fragile and particularly vulnerable to crushing. When picking them, gently slide the beaded lantern shape off its conical center, as this will turn brown and mushy, quickly spoiling the flavor of the fruit.

The flavor of raspberries is intense, and their presence will be apparent even if only a handful is mixed with other fruit, or if the juice of a few is mixed with the juice of, say, red currants, for the Scandinavian dessert called *rødgrød*.

Raspberry juice is much loved in Germany and Scandinavia as a refreshing drink. And in Berlin, when you order a *weisse mit Schuss* in a beerhall, you will be served a goblet containing a drink made from pale ale, raspberry syrup, and soda. Finally, among the raspberry-flavored liquids is raspberry vinegar, which is

balsamic vinegar 205
raspberry leaf tea 219
raspberry vinegar 205

Cranberry and Raspberry Mold 268
Hot Raspberry Soufflé 385
Peach Melba Cobbler 398
Pink Raspberry Lemonade 268
Raspberry and Lime Sherbet 388
Raspberry Ice Cream 387
Strawberry Ice Cream 387
Strawberry Jam 270, 271
Strawberry-Chocolate Truffles 386

Fraise des bois

Tayberry

Boysenberry

Raspberry

Loganberry

Strawberry

Blackberry

Gooseberry

made by steeping crushed berries in wine vinegar. It is a delicious addition to fruit salads, and when mixed with sugar and water and poured over ice, it makes a cool, thirst-quenching drink.

A few savory dishes are improved by the addition of raspberries—the Scots stuff grouse with the wild raspberries that grow in abundance in the hedges. It is in desserts, however, that raspberries come into their own, either served quite plain with a dollop of whipped cream, or crushed into fresh sorbets, or puréed with a little sugar and served as a sauce.

Blackberry and dewberry

From the shopper's point of view, the distinction between these two berries is purely academic. From the picker's point of view, these relations of the raspberry are distinguished by their growing habits: upright plants are thought of as blackberry bushes, trailing ones as dewberries.

Although blackberries are generally larger than dewberries, and shiny while dewberries are dull, sometimes with a white bloom, their names are used interchangeably in many places. In the United States, the word blackberry is almost always used for any variety. Neither their taste nor their properties differ, and both are exceptionally rich in vitamin C. Both remain sour for a long time after turning black and are only fully ripe when they are soft to the touch.

The plant, which is a bramble, grows freely and can often be found growing along the roadside. In peak season, pickers who know where to look are out in full force, and kitchens are filled with the aroma of the berries, which, besides preserves, are also made into syrup, wine, and any number of desserts. Like raspberries, blackberries can also be eaten with sugar and cream, but this is a success only when the berries are ripe and fresh—once off the brambles, wild blackberries lose their flavor fast.

Cultivated blackberries are more stable and keep their taste longer. They are always sold with their core but without their green stem. They, too, make lovely pies, tarts, crisps, and fools. Blackberries are particularly good cooked with apples, not only because apples give an agreeable texture to the dish, but also because their mellowness accentuates the blackberry's delicious acidic flavor.

Hybrid berries

Whether in an attempt to improve the humble blackberry or to make the raspberry more robust, Messieurs Logan, Young, and Boysen in turn did us a great service in crossbreeding. All three of these hybrid berries can be made into cooked and uncooked desserts and preserves using any recipe in which raspberries are called for.

Loganberry The loganberry is essentially a cross between a blackberry and a raspberry; it is more acidic than the blackberry but less intensely flavored than the raspberry. It is purple with a delicate bloom, is almost conical in shape, and has no seeds. It needs plenty of sugar if eaten uncooked.

Youngberry This is the result of crossing a dewberry with a raspberry. It looks like an elongated blackberry and tastes rather like a loganberry.

Boysenberry This is a cross between a youngberry and a raspberry. Dark red to black and very juicy, it is similar in taste and shape to the raspberry. The size of this fruit causes amazement to those unfamiliar with it, as it is twice or even three times the size of its ancestors.

Marionberry A cross between wild and cultivated blackberries, the marionberry is dark black or scarlet, with a sweet-tart flavor. It is eaten sprinkled with sugar or cooked in pies or preserves.

Tayberry Another blackberry/raspberry cross, the tayberry was bred in Scotland. Large and scarlet-red, it is quite tart.

Cloudberry and mulberry

Cloudberry This is the raspberry's slow-ripening, cold-weather cousin. It has been found as far north as the Arctic Circle, and grows in Siberia, Canada, cold districts of the northern United States, and in Scandinavia, where it forms the basis of many fruit desserts and soups. Fully ripe, it is orange, tinged with red where it catches the sun, and resembles a golden mulberry. Its taste is reminiscent of apples with honey—in Canada it is called the baked-apple berry.

Mulberry Although this berry is not botanically related to the raspberry members of the Rubus tribe, it is used in much the same way. The leaves of the mulberry tree form the silkworm's diet, and many trees of great antiquity are to be found in old gardens, dropping their deep-purple fruit to the ground below.

Mulberries may also be red, and there are even white ones. Ripe and sweet-scented, mulberries are good to eat fresh, although sometimes a little musty and watery. They also make delicious ice creams and sorbets, and a superb jam. They are often used in summer pudding, the traditional English dessert. Take care not to get mulberry juice on your clothes: the stains are hard to remove. One method of removing them, which does work, is to rub the ripe berry juice marks with an unripe mulberry.

Gooseberry

This can be a golden, green, or red globe, translucent or opaque, covered in whiskers or smooth; one variety is also milky-white. The gooseberry is the only berry among the soft fruits that makes the most delicious dishes when it is unripe. No matter what the final color, immature gooseberries are pea-green.

If you find fresh gooseberries, cook them, their spiky stems and tails removed, into a purée with a little water over the lowest heat, adding sugar to taste. They are always sour and require some sweetening even when making the classic sauce for the famous French mackerel dish, to which a little fennel is sometimes added. For pies and crisps or cobblers, gooseberries are also best when they are slightly immature.

When fully ripe, the bigger varieties— full globes of yellow or red— make glorious eating. The common green gooseberries are also good to eat, but are really better for jam making.

Currant

Red currants, white currants, and black currants belong, like gooseberries, to the Rubus tribe, but here the similarity ends. They hang like tiny translucent grapes in little bunches on the bush, and the longer they hang, the sweeter they become. They are, however, never really sweet and even the ripest retain a good percentage of pectin.

Red currant There are those who love eating fresh red currants, raked off their stalks with a fork and covered with sugar and milk. Others prefer them in a berry mixture, or bathed in a real vanilla custard sauce to mitigate their acidity. Red currants are also delicious with melon and are an essential ingredient of summer pudding.

Perhaps best loved of all red-currant preparations, however, is red-currant jelly. Eat this with roast lamb, or with croissants and butter. Add a spoonful when cooking red cabbage or transform it, with the addition of port and orange juice and zest, into a sweet-sharp Cumberland sauce that is ideal for serving with ham and game.

White currant These are less acidic than their red counterparts and can be eaten just as they are, with their thin, almost transparent, silver-gold skins liberally dusted with sugar.

Black currant These, too, make lovely jams and jellies, as well as the liqueur *crème de cassis*, but are rarely eaten fresh, except by those who like sharp-tasting berries.

Black currants are more commonly found in Europe and Central Asia than in America. The Russians, who often add spoonfuls of jam to lemon tea, add black-currant jam to the real brew in cases of colds and coughs. Black currants are rich in vitamin C, and an herbal tea made of their leaves is often taken as a health-giving drink. A few black currant leaves are also sometimes included in a sauce for desserts, and a fragrant spring sorbet can be made with lemons and black currant leaves.

Blueberry

Blueberries, borne by low bushes in Canada and the northern United States and in northern Europe, are one of our oldest berries; they once were an important part of the diet of Native Americans and the Eskimos. The berries have a silvery bloom that intensifies their blueness. They can be small or large, although cultivated blueberries are usually larger than the wild ones.

The bilberry is a European cousin of the blueberry that grows throughout the British Isles. Also called whortleberries, bilberries are usually somewhat tarter and smaller than blueberries.

Wild blueberries were at one time so widespread in both America and northern Europe that there was little to be commercially gained by putting them under cultivation. But their numbers declined as our appetite increased for blueberry pancakes, cheesecake, pie, and cobblers and grunts—those delicious concoctions of cooked fruit and dumplings—and now it is possible to buy cultivated berries that are the size of marbles and twice the size of the wild ones. Flavor has suffered considerably with cultivation, but becomes stronger when the berries are cooked and turn to a deep, teeth-staining purple.

The huckleberry is another wild berry that is sometimes confused with the blueberry. Huckleberries, however, are a darker blue-black, and each berry has ten tiny seeds at its center.

Cranberry

Although their association with Thanksgiving makes cranberries one of the quintessential American berries, they are also plentiful in northern Europe, where they go into a sharp fruit relish that traditionally accompanies venison and roast game birds. Cranberries used to be as popular in Britain as elsewhere, but with the advent of red currants fell out of favor. However, they are still traditional there at Christmas.

A native fruit of North America, cranberries are extensively cultivated in Massachusetts, particularly on Cape Cod, and in Wisconsin and in New Jersey. When buying cranberries, make sure that they are bright, dry, plump, and unshriveled. They will keep, unwashed, in the refrigerator for up to 2 weeks and also freeze well. When preparing them for sauce, chutneys, fritters, jellies, compotes, relishes, or pies, cook them slowly with plenty of sugar and a little water until they pop their skins and turn into a ruby-colored purée.

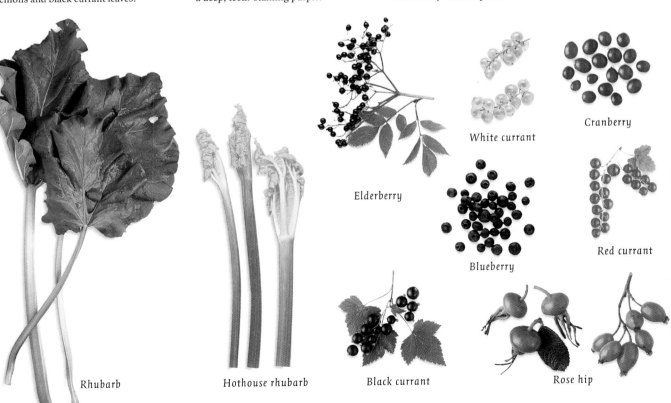

Rhubarb

Hothouse rhubarb

Elderberry

White currant

Cranberry

Blueberry

Red currant

Black currant

Rose hip

Elderberry and rose hip

These two berries are not usually found in the market, but each is well worth picking and using for various purposes.

Elderberry Growing black and shiny in flat clusters, elderberries are a good addition to blackberry desserts and ripen at about the same time. On their own they may be a little sour, but a syrup made of the berries can add a delicious flavors to apple pies all winter long.

Sprigs of the cream-colored flowers can be dipped in batter and eaten as fritters; they are surprisingly good, light and delicate.

Rose hip Either the scarlet oval fruits that appear when wild roses have gone to seed, or the flat, squat fruits of the Rugosa roses, these are the essential ingredients of delicate rose-hip jelly. They also make a health-giving syrup, which is full of vitamin C.

Care must always be taken to strain out the sharp, prickly hairs that surround the abundant seeds found in each rose hip, so after steeping the finely chopped hips in boiling water, you must pass the liquid at least twice through a double layer of cheesecloth.

Rhubarb

Odd man out in the world of fruit, rhubarb is used for the same types of dishes that call for apples and plums. It is probably best known stewed and in pies—in fact, it used to be known as the pie plant—and its tart taste combines well with blander, sweeter fruits and particularly with strawberries. When you are buying rhubarb, look out for stalks that are crisp and firm. Use the rhubarb as soon as possible, because the stalks are very perishable; keep them in the refrigerator until you are ready to cook them.

Hothouse rhubarb, with its brilliant pink stalks of a delicate texture, needs only the briefest of cooking, as it softens so quickly. Tougher, greenish field-grown rhubarb takes longer, and both need lots of sugar. If the rhubarb is particularly tart, a teaspoon of red-currant jelly added to the cooking water will often help.

Rhubarb is sometimes sold with its leaves because these prevent it from wilting, but the leaves must be discarded before cooking, as they contain toxic amounts of oxalic acid.

GRAPE

Grapes can be pale, straw-colored or amber, shades of green, rose or scarlet, or deepest blue-black with a rich silvery bloom. They can be tear-shaped, oval or round, large or small, and in tight or straggly bunches. All of today's grapes are descended from the wild grape.

The main role of grapes, of course, is to provide us with "God's choicest gift to man"—wine. The grape contains all that is necessary for making wine: it has yeast in its bloom, natural sugar to feed the yeast, tannin in the skin and seeds, and natural acids to help provide the right environment for the yeast to make alcohol.

But grapes have long been celebrated for more than the wine they yield. Fresh grape juice was much used in medieval kitchens. The acid juice that characterizes grapes when they are unripe and sour was pressed out for verjuice—a piquant green liquid used in place of vinegar for flavoring tart sauces. The sweet juice of mature grapes, when not concentrated by sun-drying, which transforms the grapes into raisins, or currants, was boiled down into a syrup that was used as an alternative to honey.

Grape "cures," too, were once very popular. In the early days of this century, British society, after a season's overeating, would spend a week or so eating nothing but grapes, in an attempt to restore the figure and cleanse the system. These grapes would probably have been huge, perfectly flavored hothouse Muscats—still the most elegant of all the dessert grapes—which became the pride of landowners all over northern Europe as soon as greenhouses appeared in the seventeenth century.

Grapes are to be seen in the market almost all the year round, the hothouse varieties swaddled in tissue paper to protect their yeasty bloom. They may be translucent green with a golden tinge, a deep blue, or anywhere from scarlet to purple. Grapes can be classified by their color—white (or green) and black (or red)—or as table or wine grapes, although some varieties can both be eaten out of hand and made into wine.

Most of the grapes in the United States come from California. All California grapes are of the European type, descended from the *Vinifera* grape. They include the Muscat grapes and others. Muscats in their turn actually encompass a number of different varieties, but all of them are large, with the richly perfumed flesh that makes muscatel wines so distinctive. Muscat grapes are more common on European tables than in America.

Grapes with seeds

White/green grape These grapes include the Italia Muscat, large, golden-amber, and very sweet and flavorful; the Calmeria, long and oval-shaped, with a sweet flavor and few seeds; and the fleshy green Almeria, of Spanish stock. Popular in Europe are the green (or amber when fully ripe (oval-shaped Muscat of Alexandria, with a bloom that rubs off easily unless carefully handled; and the prized Golden Chasselas, green with an amber tinge.

Black and red grapes Among the blue-black grapes are the Ribier, oval-shaped and sweetly perfumed, with a vine-like flavor; and the beautiful Exotic, large black grapes with a milder flavor. Among the best of these grapes in Europe are the delicately flavored Gros Colmar and the large round Royal, with a heavy bloom, and very juicy and sweet.

Red grape These range from the Cardinal, scarlet, crisp, and aromatic; to the Flame Tokay, a deep red; and the Emperor, red or purple, firm, and bland.

Labrusca and Muscadine The *Vitis labrusca*—not to be confused with Lambrusco, the sparkling red wine of Lombardy—is the native American vine that thrives in the colder climate of the eastern United States, where more tender varieties of grape refuse to grow. (Some of these are now grown in the Pacific Northwest as well.) Labruscas, such as the round, blue-black Concord, are rich in pectin and ideal for making grape juice and grape jam. Delaware, small and a pale rose-red, has a juicy, sweet flesh, and Catawba is red-purple and sweet.

Muscadines, such as the large, bronze, sweet-fleshed Scuppernong, are grown mainly in the southern states. They have a rich, spicy flavor.

Seedless grapes

These grapes, which have much less tannin than the varieties with seeds, dominate the market in the United States. Sweet, juicy, and green, with smallish fruit, varieties such as Thompson eedless and the smaller Perlette Seedless, oth descendents of the European ultana, are among the most abundant rape varieties in the world. Flame eedless is a red-skinned variety with weet flesh. Ruby Seedless have purplish- ed skin and are also sweet.

uying grapes Although some grapes ave ceased to be seasonal, and are either sued from greenhouses all the year ound, or imported from the Southern lemisphere, the end of summer is the raditional grape season.

When buying grapes, make sure that he red or black kinds have lost any tinge f green, and that green or white ones ave a tone of amber about them. The tems of both kinds should be fresh- ooking but show a few brown patches, xcepting Emperor grapes, whose stems hould be woody-brown all over.

From the trade's point of view, the erfect bunch consists of grapes that re uniform in size, with no lurking tiny nes, and all of them firmly attached o their stems. From the consumer's iewpoint, bunches with a tendency to hedding are often the sweetest, as nyone who has bought local grapes rom a huge mound in an open market,

through a haze of wasps, can testify, for these straggly bunches and loose grapes can be delicious and more aromatic than the cosseted sort. But if perfect fruit is desired, it should be plump with no wrinkling and no brown patches at the stems. Avoid bunches with little or no bloom, which shows they have been handled too much, or with any small, shriveled grapes; these will be sour.

Storing grapes Grapes will keep in good condition for about 2 weeks if stored in the refrigerator, wrapped in their perforated plastic bags—a long way from the barrels in which the ancient Romans sealed their oil-dipped grapes, hoping to keep them fresh and luscious. But since part of the pleasure of grapes is their appearance, it seems a pity to banish them from sight. A fine bunch placed in a glass bowl or a basket makes a perfect centerpiece on the dining table for a special meal.

Serving grapes Grapes are usually eaten as a snack or served at the end of a meal, either on their own or with one of the soft French cheeses from Normandy—or perhaps a hard cheese from Switzerland, where grapes are a frequent accompaniment to cheese. In Italy, you may be offered your grapes

in a huge bowl of ice water, with a few floating ice cubes.

In the kitchen, grapes are used to make pies and tarts, jam, jelly, and juice, and sorbets. They can also be frosted with egg white and sugar. In France, grape juice is sometimes boiled down until syrupy, then boiled again with sliced apples, quinces, pears, or lemons until sticky: such fruit is called *raisiné*.

Sole becomes *sole Véronique* when the rolled, poached fillets in a light white wine sauce are garnished with scented Muscat grapes. Richly flavored grapes are good, too, with duck foie gras, and pheasant is sometimes stuffed with peeled, seeded grapes.

If you wish to peel grapes, you will find that some types slip easily from their skins, while others may need to be dipped in scalding water for a minute. Seeding grapes is easy if you halve them first.

If you like salads with fresh fruit, try grapes in a mixture of apples and watercress, dressed with oil and lemon juice. Grapes and cottage cheese also combine well. Make fruit salads prettier with the addition of black grapes, seeded but not peeled, even though the skins of black grapes may be tougher than those of the white varieties.

Concord

Muscat of
Alexandria

Sultana

Thompson Seedless

Emperor

Flame Seedless

MELON

A melon is a luxurious thing. Beautiful and intricately patterned on the outside, a ripe melon no larger than an orange can entirely fill a good-sized room with its fragrance. Inside, cool and full of juice, it offers to quench your thirst and provide you with a delicate sensation rather like eating snow. "There is," say the Arabs, "a blessing in melons. He who fills his belly with melons fills it with light."

Sweet melons, ribbed and encrusted with lacy patterns, were brought to Spain by the Moors, who had in turn received them from Persia or from the depths of Africa—both the Middle East and Africa claim to be the home of this honey-sweet fruit, described as "the masterpiece of Apollo" and celebrated for being as beneficial as the sun itself.

Melons appeared in France toward the end of the fifteenth century, to extravagant praise, and were eaten in astonishing quantities by the royal court. Served piled in pyramids and mountains, "as if it were necessary to eat to the point of suffocation, and as if everyone in the company ought to eat a dozen," they were washed down with glasses of Muscat wine.

Melons were brought to the New World by Christopher Columbus. At that time, of course, sweet melons were no larger than oranges, but over the centuries, they have been cultivated and expanded in both their size and their variety.

Muskmelon and cantaloupe

It is most likely that the muskmelon, or "nutmeg" melon as it is sometimes known, was the kind eaten by the ancient Romans, who served it with a sprinkling of powdered musk in order to accentuate the delicate flavor.

Muskmelons, which include the cantaloupe, are easily recognized by the distinctive raised netting on their skin, which may be coarse like crochetwork or fine like lace. It is for this reason that cantaloupes are also called "embroidered" melons in France and "netted" melons in North America and Britain. They may be sharply segmented or grooved, with a green or yellow-orange skin, and the flesh ranges from green to salmon-pink.

The cantaloupe is among the most aromatic types of muskmelon. Despite the mounds of netted fruit seen in every produce market, however, the true cantaloupe is not grown commercially in the United States. Named for the Italian town of Cantalupo, it is seen all through Europe. Its rind is ribbed and warty, and the flesh is usually a pale orange, rich and juicy.

The French prefer to grow this type, especially the Charentais, with its deep-orange, faintly scented flesh, although new similar hybrids are always being introduced. The delicate, pale yellow-fleshed Ogen melon from Israel is a small, smooth-skinned cantaloupe hybrid. The Persian melon is another of the netted melons, large with flavorful salmon-colored flesh.

Winter melon

The skin of this melon is either smooth or shallowly ribbed. It is less aromatic than the cantaloupe and other netted melons. Principal varieties are the onion-shaped Casaba, with its thick golden-yellow skin and creamy-white to golden flesh; the Crenshaw, with green-gold skin and aromatic golden-salmon flesh; and the ubiquitous pale green or yellow honeydew melon, which has delicate pale green flesh.

Buying sweet melons Whatever type of melon you buy, there are a few sound rules to follow. Choose firm, plump melons with clean scars at the stem ends (a roughness here indicates they were picked before they were fully ripe). Netted melons should have no bald patches on their skins, as these are a sure indication that the melon has suffered a setback of some kind during its development.

You should reject any fruits that are soft or scarred or that show moist bruises on the skin. It is a bad sign, too, if the stem end has started to rot; however, light cracking at this end is a sign of ripeness. If you press them gently at the blossom end with your fingers, both the cantaloupe and the honeydew melon should feel slightly springy to the touch.

If you are able to shake the melon before buying it and you hear a sloshing sound as you do so, this indicates that the fruit is too ripe and

may have started to deteriorate. All melons should feel heavy for their size and—most importantly—ripe melons should have a pleasant, sweet melon scent about them.

Storing melons A cool, airy place is best for storing all types of melons—although this should be warmer if you suspect that your melon is not quite ripe. When you think that it is ready to eat, and if you do not want it to scent everything in your refrigerator, put your melon to chill in a tightly closed plastic bag before cutting it up, ready for serving.

Serving melons Although the most-scented varieties are nicest when served all on their own for desserts, melon can also be served in salads with leaves of fresh mint and an oil and lemon dressing; with oranges and watercress; or with finely chopped celery, onions, olives, and mayonnaise. This last mixture may sound rather strange, but it rests on an old tradition: a seventeenth-century list of "sallet" herbs includes the melon, and ideas for eating it with salt and pepper.

Sugar or a squeeze of fresh lime juice has today taken the place of pepper—which had ousted powdered musk—as the melon's usual condiment. Even the sweetest melon will be enhanced by a fine dusting of sugar, but to pour port or another type of fortified wine into the cavity of a small scented melon, as some people like to do, is a mistake, since it actually ruins both.

Fragrant melon slices, resting on the rind from which they have been separated with a sharp knife, beside thin, translucent slices of prosciutto, is as delicious a start to a meal as one could hope for.

The French traditionally used to offer melons only as an hors d'oeuvre—these were usually chilled, halved cantaloupes sitting in a bowl of crushed ice, but sometimes, in the case of larger light-fleshed varieties, the melon was served in wedges, the flesh already cut and resting on the rind in an attractive sawtooth arrangement.

These days, melons have rightly taken a place in the dessert course and are to be met in fruit salads, filled with an assortment of fresh fruit, or diced and mixed with grapes or red currants. Or they may appear as melon sorbet or even melon ice cream, made with orange and lemon juices and served, if possible, together with wild strawberries. The best melons, of course, really need no dressing up at all, but a very cool and refreshing sweet melon salad can be made with an assortment of melon balls or cubes—orange, white, green, and scarlet—sugared and chilled: this will provide a feast for the eye as well as an opportunity for the palate to distinguish between all the slightly different flavors of the fruits.

Watermelon

The watermelon—which Mark Twain once memorably described as "the food that angels eat"—is a different proposition altogether. Considerably larger in size than the sweet melons, and either oblong or round in shape, this is an entirely separate species of fruit that originated in tropical Africa and in India.

Small round watermelons, weighing anywhere from 6 to 10 pounds, with sweet red flesh and pitch-black seeds, may have deep green rinds with a bloom, as found on the Sugar Baby, or they may be striped on a light green background, such as on the appropriately named Tiger watermelon.

However, the favorites at family picnics are the large spherical or oblong watermelons, which are often sold in wedges. These usually have a much paler flesh than the smaller varieties because of their higher water content. There are also yellow-fleshed varieties, as well as seedless watermelons—which, in spite of their name, usually do have a few small edible seeds in their flesh.

When you buy a watermelon, there are various things to look out for. The spot where the melon rested on the ground should be amber-colored, not white or green. The fruit should sound hollow when tapped. If you buy your melon by the piece, avoid pieces with visible fibers: the flesh should not have any hard white streaks in it.

Watermelon is often eaten chilled in slices. When cut into smaller pieces, it makes a decorative and delicious addition to a fruit salad.

wild strawberries 171

Sugar Baby watermelon

Cantaloupe

Casaba

Ogen

Charentais

Honeydew

Tiger watermelon

Crenshaw

Watermelon

TROPICAL AND EXOTIC FRUIT

Before steamships began to cross the seas regularly in the nineteenth century, trading in perishable tropical fruits such as bananas and pineapples was an impossibility. Now, unfamiliar fruits appear by boat or plane and make strange, exotic-looking piles among the more familiar fruits, appearing, conveniently, just at the time of year when most fresh fruit, apart from apples and oranges, is usually scarce.

Banana and plantain

There are many varieties of this perfectly packaged fruit. One is grown only for making beer, and there are red bananas, purple bananas, and pink bananas, slim bananas, and fat ones like little pigs. Plantains, also called cooking bananas, tend to be starchier and less sweet than the eating variety and are often used before they ripen. Bananas for the table are picked while they are still hard and green, and may not be perfectly ripe when they reach the market. They will, however, ripen quickly at room temperature, turning first yellow, when they are ready for eating, then spotted, when they become softer and more scented, and finally black, when they can still be used to make banana bread. Buy them in the bunch rather than loose, since the skin of loose bananas may well be ripped at the top, thus exposing the flesh.

The first bananas to reach us came from the Caribbean, and many early desserts using bananas have a distinctly Latin flavor: raw brown sugar and rum, coffee flavoring and rice, and coffee ice cream feature widely. Bananas Foster, a more recent invention from Brennan's Restaurant in New Orleans, consists of bananas sautéed in butter with brown sugar, then flambéed with rum and orange juice. Bananas are also eaten baked with slices of lemon, or plain in their skins. Chicken Maryland is often accompanied by fried bananas, and in Central America and the Caribbean plantains are found in many dishes.

Bananas, however, are most enjoyed fresh. Sliced, they form part of many savory dishes, including curries. In fruit mixtures, their slightly scented taste and smooth texture complement juicy or crisp fruits such as oranges and apples. They also make a delicious cream pie.

Pineapple

A whole pineapple on the table is a truly luxurious sight. Fresh pineapples form part of many main courses in their native tropical habitat, and it was there that the idea of serving them hot with poultry, pork chops, and ham originated.

It is when fresh and simply served with sugar and perhaps kirsch that the pineapple is really at its best. However, now that bananas from Hawaii and Central America are shipped in quantity, they are sometimes grilled or broiled, baked in the shell, flambéed with cinnamon and rum, sprinkled with lime juice, or used to make relishes or salsas.

When buying a pineapple, look for one that is fully ripe and fragrant. If the stem end is very soft or discolored, the fruit bruised, or the leaves wilting, the pineapple is not at its best. A pineapple will continue to ripen after it is picked, and one that is almost ripe will ripen completely at home—but an unripe pineapple that has no scent and is not uniformly colored will probably never develop its full flavor. Small pineapples often have a more delicate flavor.

Mango

This beautiful fruit may be as large as a melon or as small as an apple. It may be green, gold, rosy, or a mixture of all three. The vivid pinky-golden, yellow, or orange flesh of the best ripe mangoes is smooth, juicy, and fiberless, with a slightly resinous taste that has been compared to that of peaches, apricots, and pineapples.

When buying mangoes, choose fruits that are just soft, with a good perfume. If they are completely green, they will not ripen properly; those with large soft areas or black spots tend to be overripe.

Mangoes can be scored from top to bottom in several places and peeled, or cut in half by slicing down either side of the large, flat pit, and then eaten with a spoon. A better way is to prepare them "hedgehog" fashion: slice them lengthwise into two pieces, discarding the pit, and then score the flesh diagonally at $\frac{1}{2}$-inch intervals in both directions, cutting almost to the skin but without piercing it. Turn each half inside out, and the little squares of mango will be easy to eat with a spoon.

Chilled mangoes are sometimes served halved in their skin, sprinkled with lemon juice, sugar, rum, or ginger. Peeled and cut up, they are delicious in fruit salads, and they make excellent sorbets.

It was in India that the British found their taste for mango chutney, and Major Grey's mango chutney can be found in almost any American supermarket today.

Papaya

Columbus anticipated Mark Twain—in a different context—by declaring that the papaya, which he called a tree melon, tasted, when ripe, like the "food of the angels." The papaya's skin is green to golden, its flesh orangey, and its seeds black. It is sweet and subtly flavored.

When buying papaya, make sure that it is firm, unblemished except for its speckles, and just turning yellow, then

Passion fruit

Kiwifruit

Pomegranate

Papaya

allow it to ripen at home. Ripe papaya is distinctive in fruit salads, pies, and sorbets, and can also be served simply sprinkled with lemon or lime juice and sugar or ginger.

The unripe papaya is used like a vegetable in Latin America. It tastes like a squash and may be served stuffed or baked with butter, added to salads, or pickled. It is good in hot chile salsas.

South American Indians have traditionally wrapped papaya leaves, freshly plucked, around tough meat to act as a tenderizer—the plant contains a powerful enzyme that breaks down protein. A derivative of the leaves, the enzyme papain, is used in commercial tenderizing powders for meat.

The papaya is sometimes called pawpaw, as is another fruit, the papaw, that is similar to look at but is, in fact, related to the cherimoya. The papaw is a wild North American fruit that can be good to eat or unpleasantly scented and flavored, depending on the type.

Guava

Pink- or pale-yellow-fleshed, strongly aromatic, and sweet, this fruit can be as small as a walnut or as large as an apple. It can be puréed or baked, or eaten fresh with sugar and cream, and it goes well with fruit such as pineapple or banana. Guavas make a delicious jelly, and a sauce made from puréed guavas can be served with meat or duck.

Pomegranate

The lark, which Shakespeare's Juliet insisted was a nightingale, "sang on yon pomegranate tree"—a shrub-like plant introduced to the Western world from Persia via Africa. Its beautifully shaped fruit, scarlet or golden flushed with crimson outside and filled with crimson beads, each with its central seed, is an intricate construction.

To admire its crimson glory at its best, cut the fruit in half or into segments, slicing through the leather-like skin. Although the juicy pulp surrounding each of the seeds is beautifully refreshing and aromatic, it can be rather tiresome to eat. You can take a few grains, suck the flesh off the seeds, discard the seeds—

Fuyu persimmon

Hachiya persimmon

Guava

Banana

Pineapple

Mango

and continue to eat and discard until the shell is empty. A much easier way, however, is to crunch and swallow the seeds, which have a nice texture. Avoid the pale yellow pith, which is bitter.

Persimmon

Looking like a golden-red tomato, the persimmon, when it is completely ripe and plumply soft, is often compared in taste to guavas, apricots, tomatoes, and mangoes; however, when less than perfect, its astringency "draws the mouth awry with much torment." Wrinkled fruit of the common acorn-shaped Hachiya type should therefore never be shunned, since by the time it has reached this stage, the acidity and tannin are sure to have disappeared. There is also a

smaller, rounder variety, called the Fuyu, which is not at all astringent and which remains firm when ripe.

The handsome persimmon stays glossy and plump when plucked early and artificially matured. Provided it is ripe, with cap and stem intact, its tough skin can be slit and peeled back, and the soft flesh eaten as is or sliced. A seedless variety of persimmon, the Sharon fruit, has tender, edible skin and less tannic flavor than the Hachiya.

Kiwifruit

The brown furry skin covering this egg-shaped fruit hides glistening, translucent green flesh with decorative edible black seeds. Once known as the Chinese gooseberry, it is now best known by the

name of New Zealand's national bird, the kiwi. The fruit is used to best effect when it is peeled and thinly sliced, since the pattern of the black seeds in the bland but fresh-tasting green flesh is so pleasing.

One kiwi contains huge quantities of vitamin C—as much as ten lemons. Unripe fruit can be ripened in a plastic bag with a ripe banana, apple, or pear; the ethylene gas given off by the ripe fruit accelerates the ripening process.

Passion fruit

This fruit is so called because the flower of the plant is said to symbolize the Passion of Christ. The fruit of some species of the passion flower is also called granadilla (which has yellow skin) or, in the West Indies, calabesh. The size and shape of

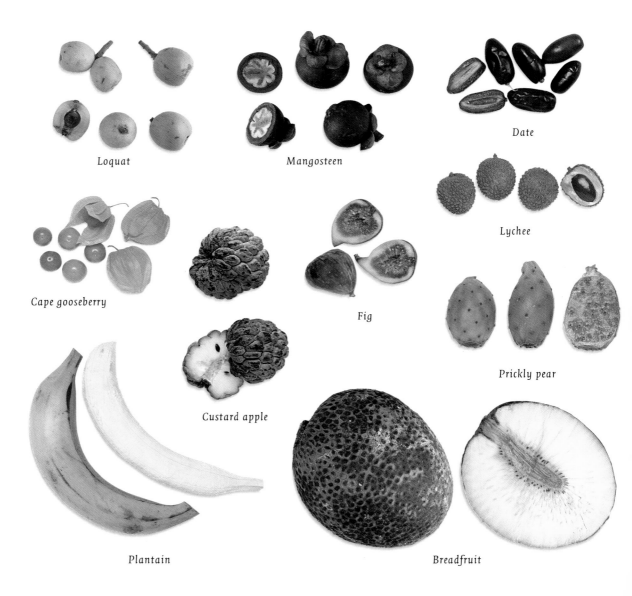

Loquat

Mangosteen

Date

Cape gooseberry

Custard apple

Fig

Lychee

Prickly pear

Plantain

Breadfruit

an egg, the passion fruit normally has a purple-brown, hard skin that becomes crinkly as the fruit gradually ripens.

The richly perfumed, sweet-sour flesh is inseparable from the many small black seeds, which are edible. The fruit is usually halved and perhaps sprinkled with sherry or cream, or the flesh may be scooped out and mixed into fruit salads. It is delicious made into mousses, sorbets or ice cream, or sauces.

Custard apple

This can be any of the fleshy, round or elongated, thick-skinned fruits of the large family of Annona trees in the American tropics. There is the apple-shaped cherimoya, the one most likely to be found in our markets, and the llama, whose taste has been compared

Feijoa

Star fruit

Tamarillo

to that of a banana and pineapple. The soncoya is similar but larger, and the sweetsop, or sugar apple, is green, heart-shaped, and more acidic, with a taste similar to that of a black currant. The atemoya is a cross between a cherimoya and the sweetsop; its delicate flesh tastes of mango and vanilla. All are eaten fresh, the flesh being spooned from the shell. The fruit can also be used for jam and jelly, in milk shakes, and for sorbets.

Loquat

Also known as Japanese medlar, the orangey-yellow loquat is the size of a crabapple but more pear-shaped; it contains a few shiny seeds. Although thirst-quenching, it does not have much flavor when raw and is principally used to make jams, jellies, and sauces. A few of the seeds are usually included, as they add a delicious bitter-almond flavor.

Cape gooseberry

Native to South America, this tart-sweet, pleasant, small fruit of the shrub *Physalis peruviana* is encased in a papery balloon shaped like a Chinese lantern. In South Africa, the plants are grown on such a large scale that they have come to be known as Cape gooseberries. Golden when ripe, the berries—also called ground cherries—can be eaten out of hand or used decoratively (peel back the papery skin to form "petals" around the golden globe of the fruit), and in Europe they may be coated with fondant and served with *petits fours*, but they are chiefly used to make jellies and jams.

Lychee and rambutan

These fruits, encased in brown, papery shells with a delicate pink lining, both have translucent, colorless flesh enclosing a single brown, glossy seed. Fresh lychees have a delicious perfumed flavor and a refreshing tang that all but disappears when the fruit is canned. In China, the lychee, or *litchi*, has been cultivated for thousands of years. With its sweet-tart flavor, it is used in pork and duck dishes, much as apples and oranges are used in the West.

A rambutan has a hairier shell than a lychee; in Southeast Asia it is peeled and eaten fresh, and is enjoyed for its refreshing, sweet juiciness. Canned rambutans are also available, but these are overly sweet.

Both fruits can be bought in Asian markets in the West—although you are more likely to find lychees—but should be avoided if they look shriveled, since this means their pulp is turning black and their delicate flavor will be lost.

Prickly pear

This is the fruit of a cactus (*Opuntia ficus indica*), and is sometimes known as cactus pear or Indian fig. It is pear-shaped, varies in color from green to rosy, and is covered with small clumps of sharp prickles.

When buying a prickly pear, make sure that it is orange to red and reasonably bright in color, and firm but not too hard. It is mild-flavored and sweet, somewhat pear-like in flavor but more melon-like in texture, and is usually eaten raw. The fruit should be slit lengthwise; the prickly skin will come off easily. The flesh can then be eaten with sugar and cream or sprinkled with lemon juice. Take care when handling prickly pears, as the prickles will irritate the skin. Wear gloves or encase your hand in a paper bag before you pick them up.

Mangosteen

This thick-skinned, glossy, dark-mahogany-colored fruit is very popular in Southeast Asia. The white, soft flesh is segmented like that of an orange; some segments contain a large, inedible seed. The taste of the mangosteen is sweet-sharp, delicate, perfumed, and refreshing.

Fig

This is perhaps the most sensual of all fruits, with its bloomy, bursting skin and luscious flesh. Ancient Greeks thought figs so health-giving that they formed part of the athletes' diet for the original Olympic games, and so delicious that poets and philosophers sang their praises. White, green, brown, or purple, figs are always beautiful. When cut open, they reveal their pulpy flesh, deep purple, red, or pink, embedded with a mass of seeds, which are in fact tiny fruits. Calimyrna, or the Turkish Smyrna, Mission, and Kadota are some of the more familiar varieties.

The entire fruit is edible. In Italy, where the Sicilian figs are most prized, they are served with prosciutto or as a dessert. In France, the purple, white-fleshed Barbillone and many other

dried fig 183
prosciutto 69
tomatillo 152

varieties are also served as a dessert. All are good, especially when eaten fresh and ripe. Being perishable, figs will only keep for up to 3 days in the refrigerator.

Date

In its fresh state, the sumptuous, rich date—called "bread of the desert"—has a glowing brown skin that promises more juice than the flesh actually delivers, and the plumpest date has a warm, fudge-like consistency. When buying fresh dates, pick fat, wrinkly skinned, nonsticky specimens.

Star fruit, carambola

Somewhat cucumber-like in texture, the star fruit, uncut, resembles an elongated yellow Chinese lantern with deep ridges running from top to bottom. When sliced, it reveals that the cross-section is a perfect-star—very beautiful, but when it comes to flavor, it hasn't much to offer. Star fruit can be either sweet or sour and tangy; both are refreshing. They are best sliced and used in a fruit salad, or poached in a sugar syrup.

Tamarillo, tree tomato

Orangey-red, smooth, and glossy, this fruit resembles the small oval eggplant in shape, and, like it, is a member of the family of solanums, together with Cape gooseberries, potatoes and tomatoes. The orange flesh with its black seeds is sweet-tart, but the skin is intensely bitter and should be removed either by plunging the fruit into boiling water for a minute, like a tomato, or, if the fruit is very ripe, by peeling. Eat tamarillos raw with sugar or in fruit salads, or use to make chutney.

Feijoa

A round or oval shiny green fruit related to the guava, the feijoa has a flavor said to resemble pineapple, and it is also known as the pineapple guava. The flesh contains tiny seeds. Eat raw by cutting in half and scooping out the flesh.

Breadfruit

This large and imposing green fruit, covered in short, knobbly spines, can weigh up to 9 pounds. An unripe specimen can be cut up and baked or roasted, while an entirely ripe one may be sliced and eaten raw. Breadfruit is often used in savory dishes.

DRIED AND CANDIED FRUIT

Dried fruit does not so much prolong the taste of summer as provide us with sweetness of a different kind. Drying concentrates the sugar content of the fresh fruit, and although vitamin C is usually lost, vitamin A and the minerals remain. Some dried fruits are completely dried; the larger ones like apricots may need soaking before cooking. Others still contain a percentage of their original moisture. These are succulent and can be eaten as they are or cooked, but tend to be heavy on preservatives.

Dried fruits such as "datyes, figges, and great raysings" have been valued in Europe since they were imported in the thirteenth century from the Levant, to sit in the larder alongside dried domestic "prunellas, apricocks, and pippins [apples]." There were also dried pears (a special delicacy) and the dried cherries and berries that the medieval housewife would prepare in due season. These dried fruits went into a number of what now seem curious dishes. The taste was for the sweet-savory—the sort of dish still found in countries that were once part of the great Ottoman Empire. In Turkey, Iran, Saudi Arabia, Yemen, and North Africa, traditional cookery still allies lamb with prunes, apricots, almonds, honey, and spices. Chicken is simmered with prunes, or with quinces, dates, or raisins.

Medieval Europe ate veal tartlets with prunes and dates, pickled fish was enhanced with raisins and figs, and ducks were smothered with fruit. The "Great Pyes," without which no great dinner was complete, contained a mixture of beef, chicken, bone marrow, eggs, dates, prunes, and raisins, all highly spiced and saffroned before being entombed in the "coffyn," as the crust was called.

The taste for such things lives on. The seventeenth-century recipe for raisin sauce to eat with ham differs very little from that found in modern American cookbooks, or the raisin sauce eaten with boiled tongue in northern Europe. And the eighteenth-century ham stuffed with "apricocks" is not far from Virginia ham with peaches. Indeed, that most British of institutions, the plum pudding, is a descendant of the sweet-savory puddings of the Middle Ages—until the eighteenth century, one of its main ingredients was

a leg or shin of beef. Look farther back and you find that the Christmas pudding is not English at all, but of ancient Greek origin—a less astonishing fact when you think that the very word currant (with which plum pudding is actually made, not plums) is derived from Corinth, its place of origin.

The too-liberal use of sulfur dioxide to keep dried fruit from becoming too dry is a deplorable innovation. The flavor can and occasionally does permeate the fruit and cannot be removed by soaking. So buy unsulfured or organic fruit where possible.

Raisin

The large, sweet raisins made from Spanish Muscat grapes and called muscatels used to be the kings of the tribe. Now, similar giants are produced in other places in the world, especially California. These can be eaten on their own and are also useful in cooking. Sometimes available in specialty markets, Muscat raisins may be sold dried in whole bunches, seedless or complete with seeds. The more familiar smaller dark and golden raisins sold loose and in boxes come from Thompson Seedless grapes; the dark ones are naturally sun-dried, while the golden ones are treated with sulfur dioxide to preserve their color. Raisins are used in cakes, cookies, breads, granola, and mincemeat. They are also good in couscous, and for stuffed vegetables and onions *à la grecque*. Raisins also come packed together with nuts and other dried fruits, as a snack sometimes called trail mix. Combined with peanuts, hazelnuts, and almonds, they make a mixture known as *Studenten Futter* in Germany, because the sugar content of the raisins and the protein content of the nuts quickly revives the energy of poor scholars while they pore over their books.

Currant and sultana

The dried currant comes from the small, black seedless grape that is a native of the slopes around Corinth in Greece, while sultanas are made from the seedless white grapes once grown only in the neighborhood of biblical Smyrna in Turkey. Although both varieties have long been produced elsewhere, the old names have stuck. In some parts of the world, currants and sultanas are still sun-dried, without the help of chemical treatments. In others, science gives nature a helping hand and the fruit is artificially dried.

Sultanas are rarely seen in U.S. markets; seedless golden raisins can be substituted in any recipe that calls for them. If you mean to use currants or sultanas with yeast for baking, it is a good idea to place them in a strainer over a pot of boiling water for a few minutes. This warms and moistens the fruit just enough to prevent it from retarding fermentation of the temperamental yeast.

Dried fig

The yellow fig of Smyrna was originally the most highly prized, and this is now extensively grown elsewhere, together with many other varieties, including the dark, juicy Mission fig. Calimyrna figs from California are actually Smyrna figs, their name a combination of their place of origin and where they are now grown. Although dried figs pack and travel well, blocks of squashed figs can have

a depressing look; so if you mean to enjoy figs with a dessert wine after a winter dinner, look for those whose plump, cushiony shapes are still discernible. In France, in Provence, a dessert offered at New Year's and known as les quatres mendiants (the four mendicants) is a mixture of figs, raisins, hazelnuts, and almonds, their colors recalling the habits worn by the four Roman Catholic mendicant orders.

For compotes or other desserts, dried figs need soaking for a few hours before they are used: try wine instead of water for a good flavor.

Dried banana

Slices of dried banana are eaten as a snack on their own or as part of prepackaged mixes with other dried fruits. Look for banana chips in health food stores and some markets, together with strips of dried banana which can be used in the same way as dried figs.

Date

The date palm has flourished well in favorable places since 5000 BC, and has always been a good and useful friend to mankind. Only the stickiest, juiciest dates—"candy that grows on trees"— are sent into the world from their native Middle East and North Africa. Of them all, the Tunisian date, the Deglet Noor, "date of the light," is considered the finest, although some people prefer Medjool dates, with their wrinkled skins and rich fudge-like texture. Dried dates, black, dark red, or golden yellow, imported from the Middle East, are available year-round, as are those from California; Arizona grows some dates too, but California is the major producer.

Most easily obtained are the shiny or wrinkled dates that have been left on their palm trees to sweeten and mature in the sun, and are then packed in boxes, sometimes with desert scenes on the lid. Most are pitted; dates sold in bulk may

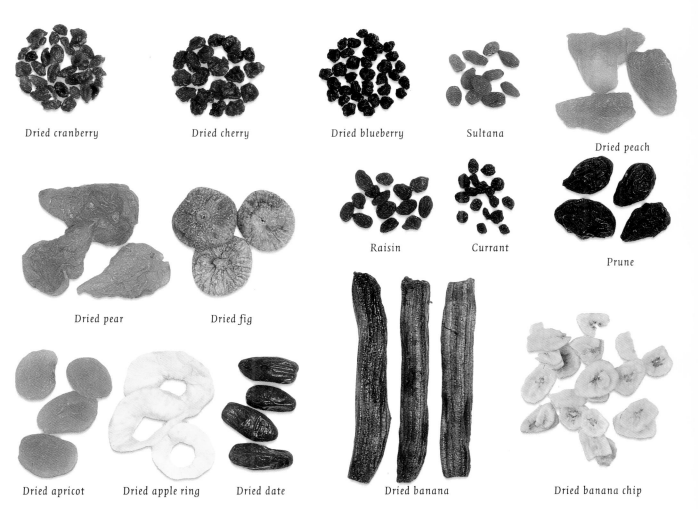

Dried cranberry

Dried cherry

Dried blueberry

Sultana

Dried peach

Dried pear

Dried fig

Raisin

Currant

Prune

Dried apricot

Dried apple ring

Dried date

Dried banana

Dried banana chip

sometimes still have their pits. If you plan to stuff dates with nuts or marzipan, making *petits fours* to be offered after dinner, you would, of course, use the handsomest dates you could find. Inexpensive pressed blocks of dates are perfectly adequate to use in breads, cakes, and other desserts.

Prune

Until the nineteenth century, prunes were far more popular than plums. Traditionally eaten with game, goose, and pork, prunes can be cooked with red cabbage. They are also used to make ice creams, soufflés, and delicate whips. Prunes are essential for *tsimmes*, the Jewish-American Passover dish, and they may be used in a stuffing for chicken or turkey. The drying process makes prunes good keepers, and nothing is easier than to reconstitute their plumpness by soaking them overnight. (Better still, keep them in a jar of brandy, ready to eat.)

The finest prunes are from the red and purple plums of Agen and from those of Tours, the orchard of France. It is these varieties that are grown in California and have made the Santa Clara Valley the center of the excellent American prune industry. Some of the French maintain that the flesh of a California plum is less delicate than that of their native produce, but then, in France, plum drying has developed into a fine art. There the Perdrigon plum, for example, is not simply dried. It may be either peeled, pitted, exposed to the sun, and flattened to become a *pistole*, or scalded in its entirety and slowly dried in the shade to become a *brignole* or *pruneau fleuri*. This is plumper and less wrinkled than the humble grocery store prune. It somewhat resembles the Karlsbad plum, a glamorous prune with a blue sheen, tasting strongly of fruit, that is on sale in gourmet shops around Christmastime, packed in handsome wooden boxes. Famous, too, are Elvas plums, semidried and candied greengage plums from Portugal, a very sweet Christmas treat.

Dried peach, pear, and apricot

Dried peaches and pears are most delicious eaten simply as a snack or sweet: their taste is delicate and does not always survive cooking.

On the tart side even when they're ripe, when dried, apricots keep a good deal of their original flavor. Of all the dried fruits, they are the least sickly-sweet. Soaked and cooked, they can be used to make a sharp, fragrant purée, good for desserts, sauces, and jam making. Roughly chopped, they can go into rice pilaf; soaked, they make a good stuffing for poultry and lamb.

Apricots from health food stores are most likely to be sun-dried. Supermarket apricots may have been assisted in drying by sulfur dioxide—the label should reveal the process. If the fruits are sold in bulk, ask if they have been treated. The best dried apricots are tender and chewy, fruit that tastes strongly of itself and doesn't need soaking. Apricot paste, a sweet much appreciated in Arabian countries, where it is called *kem-reddine*, "moon of religion," can be found in the more exotic stores, and apricot leather is available in many markets.

Dried apple

This can be reminiscent of faintly scented rings of soft chamois leather; only by shopping around, particularly at health food stores, can you find dried apples actually tasting of fruit.

Apple rings have only come into fashion during the last century or so. Before that, and before apple drying became a commercial operation, there were several methods for drying apples whole—all of them considerably more trouble than to simply core, peel, and slice apples, soak them for a few minutes in salted water to prevent discoloration (the salt draws out the moisture quickly), and thread them onto string looped around the ceiling, where air can circulate around them until the rings are thoroughly dried.

In whatever way apples have been dried, they have many uses. Chopped and mixed with currants and raisins, they usefully stretch and flavor a cake batter. If you use dried apples for a compote, stew them slowly with cinnamon or cloves and add a dash of lemon juice for tartness. If you make your own granola or mincemeat, you can add chopped dried apple together with the raisins. Indeed, dried apples combined with any other dried fruit and every type of nut, particularly prunes, blanched almonds, and apricots, make nourishing winter fruit salads, steeped either in water or in a syrup.

Dried cherries and berries

Dried cherries can be made from sweet or sour cherries. The sour ones are bright mahogany-red and have a sweet-sour tang and an intense flavor. They can be used in desserts and sweet sauces, and they make a delicious sauce for duck or lamb. Dried sweet cherries are less tangy and lighter in color than the sour ones. Use them in the same way for cooking, or to make a dessert with sugar, lemon juice, and cream. Dried sweet and sour cherries can also be eaten like candy, and are sometimes sold enrobed in chocolate.

Dried blueberries These look like dark raisins and almost lose their blueberry taste in the drying. You may need to soak them for an hour or so before using them, raw or lightly poached and sweetened, in blueberry muffins or with apples in apple and blueberry pies and crisps.

Dried cranberries These dark-rose-colored berries are a great deal sweeter than their fresh counterparts; some have added sugar. They can be eaten raw or soaked and cooked in sauces and stuffings. Or, use them in fruit salads.

Dried mango and papaya

Golden, leathery dried mangoes can be found in health food stores and gourmet shops as small pieces, long strips, or, best of all, whole mango-sized slices. They need to be soaked for several hours before cooking. Like dried apricots, they can eaten in their dried state, making delicious chewy snacks with a full, deep, almost parsnippy mango flavor.

Small cubes of dried papaya, pink and glowing, are usually sugared and eaten like candy. They can also be cut up and used like candied citrus peel in cakes.

Candied citrus peel

The delicate green variety is the candied, aromatic skin of the citron—the large, scented, extremely thick-skinned cousin of the lemon. Orange peel—sometimes sold mixed with citron—and lemon peel may be found in large pieces at gourmet or specialty markets. If you can buy the peel in a large slice, you will find that it has more flavor than the "cut" peel, not only because there has been less chance for its essential oils to evaporate, but also because only the fattest, juiciest peels are sent to market in their entirety. When chopping candied citrus peel, if the pieces are very sticky, separate them with a dusting of flour and then use that much less flour in your recipe. Store candied citrus peel in airtight jars to prevent it from becoming tough and difficult to cut. If it becomes hard, steam it to soften it.

Mixed citrus peel is sold for use in cakes, other desserts, and tea breads, but it is always better to chop your own whenever possible.

Glacé and crystallized fruit

Strictly speaking, crystallized fruit is candied fruit with a coating of granulated sugar, such as that on strips of crystallized orange. *Glacé* refers to the glossy coating of sugar syrup found, for example, on pineapple rings and whole candied fruit such as oranges. The terms, however, have become almost interchangeable.

Cherries for fruitcakes are candied and glazed with a heavy syrup to aid their preservation. This accounts for their extreme stickiness, and makes it advisable to rinse and dry them before adding them to a cake batter; or steam them for 5 to 10 minutes in a strainer placed over a pan of boiling water and then dry them. Without this precaution, they may sink to the bottom of the cake. A dusting of flour helps to keep them suspended in the batter. No need, of course, to wash the cherries you use for decoration—their charm depends on their glistening lusciousness. Candied cherries are often artificially dyed, not just bright red but also yellow or even green; the package label should indicate whether artificial dyes, and other additives best avoided, have been used.

Ginger Made with fiery mature ginger in Asia, and milder, immature ginger in Australia and other parts of the world, crystallized ginger is a delicious alternative to chocolates at Christmas, and far less rich. The Chinese believe that ginger warms and sends energy to the solar plexus, and it certainly cuts the richness after a fatty meal.

Angelica This is an herb related to parsley, and is used primarily for decorating. If you are a gardener, it is quite easy to candy angelica yourself.

Blanch the stalks and peel off the outer skin, then boil the inner stems in a syrup made of ½ cup water and a generous 1 cup sugar. When the stems are soft and translucent, let them cool and then soak in the syrup for two weeks. Finally, dry the sticks in a low oven. The same technique works for all sorts of small fruit, or for chunks or segments of larger fruits.

Crystallized flowers

To crystallize violets or rose petals, or other edible (and nonsprayed) flowers, you will need a light touch.

First prepare a sugar syrup (2¼ cups sugar to each 1 cup water), and boil to just under the hard crack stage (295°F); it will form brittle threads when dropped into cold water. Remove from the heat and dip in the petals or blossoms.

Dry them in a strainer, sprinkling them with a little confectioners' sugar. Shake off the excess sugar and then scatter the flowers over cakes frosted with white buttercream, or use them to decorate chocolate mousse and trifle.

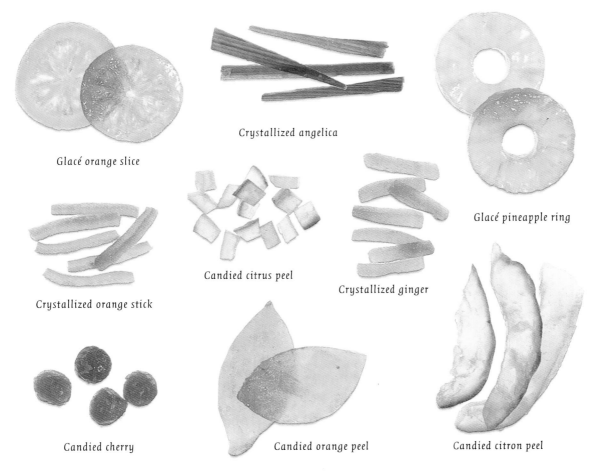

Glacé orange slice

Crystallized angelica

Glacé pineapple ring

Crystallized orange stick

Candied citrus peel

Crystallized ginger

Candied cherry

Candied orange peel

Candied citron peel

Nuts

The sound of cracking nuts has always been a pleasant accompaniment to conversation: "after-dinner talk across the walnuts and the wine" is Tennyson's description of the ritual, while in the Middle East pistachio nuts and cashews are eaten before a meal as part of the varied *mezze*, the morsels that precede a meal, and are "savored accompanied by feelings of peace and serenity."

As well as spreading serenity and tranquil enjoyment, nuts have been used since the earliest times in a huge variety of cooked dishes. Egyptians and Iranians, many of whose favorite recipes have changed very little for almost twelve centuries, may use almonds and pine nuts to thicken their sauces; in stuffings for lamb, chicken and vegetables, and in every kind of pastry and sweet—dates stuffed with walnuts and almonds were one of the earliest sweets invented. In India, pilafs and rich rice dishes are decorated with almonds or cashew nuts, and coconut is a vital ingredient of soups and curries in many areas, particularly in Kerala in the southwest of India. And peanuts are used throughout Africa in all sorts of stews.

Pecan pie is one of the traditional great American dishes, and of course nut-flavored ice creams abound. In Europe, chestnuts are much enjoyed with turkey and with game of all sorts. The French serve wonderful green salads sprinkled with fresh walnuts, while Eastern Europe specializes in rich nut cakes with ground almonds or hazelnuts taking the place of flour.

Since nuts are so rich in protein, vitamins, calcium, iron, and oils (nut cooking oils are used everywhere) and are so extremely versatile, no good cook should be without them. Buy them frequently in small quantities rather than large, preferably in their shells, and store them in a cool environment such as the refrigerator, as their high oil content makes them subject to dire alterations of flavor if they get hot or are kept too long. Make a particular point of enjoying fresh nuts in the autumn and early winter when they are sweet and milky.

Cashew nut (*Anacardium occidentale*) Kidney-shaped cashew nuts come from a tropical tree, which found its way from South America to the rest of the world by way of the early Portuguese explorers. The nuts grow suspended from a large fruit that is liked by monkeys, who ruin the crops in India and Asia. Cashews are widely eaten throughout South America, India, and Asia. They often appear—blanched and plain, roasted, and/or salted—with drinks or as a dessert nut in the colder continents (they are easy to toast and salt yourself at home). Cashews are always sold shelled, as the shells are toxic. In Brazil, they are also used for making wine and producing the famous *anacard*, or cashew nut vinegar. In Chinese cooking, of course, they often appear as an ingredient, especially in chicken dishes. Use raw unsalted cashews for cooking—they are usually sautéed in oil until golden-brown and added to the dish at the last moment.

Pine nut or pignolia (*Pinus pinea*) This nut actually does come from the beautiful glossy cones of pine trees. It is contained inside a hard little torpedo-shaped shell that is covered with a sooty dust. In the southwestern United States, the nuts come from the piñon pine. In the Mediterranean, the shells can be found lying all over the sand or rocks in September, wherever the handsome umbrella-shaped stone pines grow. Chinese and Koreans use the nut of *Pinus kovaiensis* in sweets and desserts.

Pignoli are the classic resinous pine kernels used in Mediterranean cooking. They are delicious in stuffed vegetables—eggplant or zucchini—or wrapped in grape leaves, and are essential for pesto, the smooth green paste of basil that is so irresistible with tagliatelle or linguine. They combine with rice and raisins in a rich stuffing for chicken, duck, or turkey, and are mixed with prunes, dried apricots, pomegranate seeds, and almonds in *khoshaf*—an exotic dried-fruit salad.

Pine nuts can be found in health food stores and other shops. Keep them refrigerated, but don't store them for too long, as their resinous oil spoils easily.

Macadamia nut (*Macadamia ternifolia*) Sweet and buttery, with a waxy texture, this is of the predinner drinks and dessert-nut variety. Native to Australia, where it is sometimes known as the "Queensland" nut, it is also grown extensively in Hawaii and in California and Florida. The hard, shiny shell is cracked open and the kernel roasted in coconut oil before being marketed.

Almond (*Prunus dulcis*) No other nut features as widely in old recipe books as the almond. Milk of almonds—the juice extracted from ground almonds steeped in water—used to take the place of milk on fast days or in hot weather (it is almost as rich in calcium as cow's milk). This technique of dealing with ground almonds is still used in such dishes as almond soup. Slivered almonds, fried golden, were much used for seasoning; they are still sometimes scattered on panfried river fish, particularly trout.

Ground almonds do more than provide their liquor. They can be used in the place of flour for rich, moist cakes and for crisp cookies. Sweet almonds are the chief ingredient of marzipan for coating or decorating cakes, and smooth sugared almonds, ovoids in silver, white, pink, and pale blue, in silver baskets, traditionally grace French wedding feasts (and candy shops). "Burnt almonds," cooked in sugar until caramelized and the color of burnt siena—the classic praline—are superb in ice cream. In India's delicate Mogul dishes, almonds are combined with chicken in a variety of ways, while fresh almonds in their delicate green velvet coats form part of the early autumn fruit baskets in France and Italy—although these must be soaked in cold water before eating.

Almonds can be bought in their shells or out of them, and also come blanched, sliced, slivered, and ground. There are also bitter almonds (*Prunus amara*), which some European recipes for cookies and sweets may specify. The pungent taste of bitter almonds—like that of the crushed peach kernels you would add to jam—is related to the same enzyme reaction by which prussic acid is produced. Although they are inedible raw, bitter almonds, like peach kernels, are quite safe to use in cooking, as the poison is highly volatile and evaporates when heated. However, it is illegal to sell bitter almonds in the United States, although almond extract, made from bitter almonds, is a supermarket staple. Bitter almonds are much used in Italian confectionery and in cookies.

Peanut (*Arachis hypogaea*) Whether one knows them as peanuts, ground nuts, or goobers or goober peas, these are the success story of our age. Dry-roasted, salted, shelled, or unshelled, they come to more cocktail parties than any other nut. In North African countries, you will find whole peanuts scattered over couscous; in Indonesia, ground peanuts go into salads and sauces; and all over the world pressed peanuts give their oil—for use in cooking and as a salad oil.

Raw peanuts have a faint taste of green beans—which is not surprising, as the peanut is a member of the legume family. These are the peanuts that can be so useful in cooking. You can deep-fry, fry, or roast raw peanuts. Try tossing them in a little heated oil and some salt, then toasting them to a light golden color in a moderate oven. To make spiced nuts, first coat them in oil with a little chili powder instead of salt, or season the oil with ground coriander, cumin, and cayenne pepper.

When you buy peanut butter, you may find the highly nutritious oil sitting on top—stir it in before you start spreading. You can make your own peanut butter by grinding shelled whole peanuts, with their skins removed, together with a little peanut oil in a blender. Add a little salt, and do not make too much at a time, because fresh peanut butter is inclined to turn rancid quickly. However, it will soon be used up if you make peanut butter cookies or use it as a foundation for peanut butter fudge, in which to encase chopped blanched nuts.

Pistachio nut (*Pistacia vera*) These exquisite pale-green nuts—marketed with usefully half-open shells and, often, with their papery skins marked by a rosy fingerprint—are the greatest luxury. They are grown in California, Italy, Iran, and Turkey, and are usually roasted and salted, to eat between meals or with drinks. Those from the Middle East are sometimes flavored with rose water or lemon juice. They are also found, blanched and skinned, in mortadella in Italy, and studding the galantines and terrines and even the sausages in provincial French restaurants (you can

use hazelnuts instead in duck pâté). The best halvah, Turkish delight, and nougat contains pistachio nuts. They also make a delicious ice cream.

Betel nut (*Areca catechu*) This is the tough little nut much beloved in India. Chopped and mixed with spices, pink-dyed coconut shreds, other nuts, or tiny candy balls, they are wrapped in betel leaves to make the small triangular packages called *paans* that Indian hostesses (and restaurants) may offer to guests after a meal. Chewing these aromatic little parcels is said to aid the

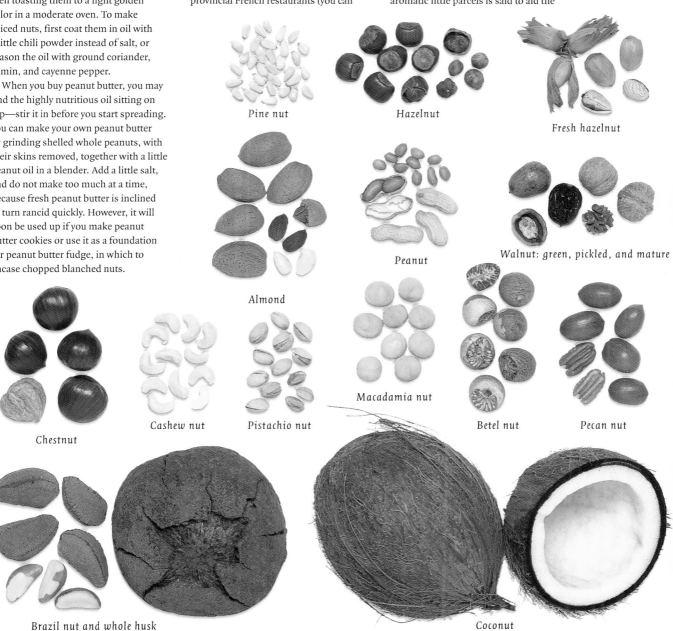

Pine nut

Hazelnut

Fresh hazelnut

Almond

Peanut

Walnut: green, pickled, and mature

Chestnut

Cashew nut

Pistachio nut

Macadamia nut

Betel nut

Pecan nut

Brazil nut and whole husk

Coconut

digestion and sweeten the breath. It can also turn the mouth an alarming red. Betel nuts may be found in some Indian or Asian markets.

Pecan nut (*Carya illinoensis*) Pecans, thin-shelled and richly flavored, are grown mainly in the United States, their natural home. Their very name is Native American, and the nut was widely used in tribal Indian cookery. Heavier in fats than walnuts, which belong to the same family and which pecans somewhat resemble in taste and in the appearance of their kernels, pecans were particularly cherished for their oil. Their flesh, having been ground to a fine meal, was used to thicken soups and stews.

Nowadays, pecans are used to enrich cakes, candies, and ice cream, but their proudest moment comes in pecan pie—that rich, sweet mixture of corn syrup, brown sugar, eggs, vanilla, and nuts in a buttery pastry crust. Pecans can be found in most supermarkets.

Hazelnut, filbert (*Corylus*) In Europe, these are the joy of the autumn countryside, but in the United States, fresh hazelnuts are a rarity. Most of our hazelnuts are imported, from Italy or Turkey, although Oregon does produce a small crop. The best hazelnuts grow on trees, but some are the fruit of a shrub; some varieties are more elongated than the familiar round brown nut.

In America, the terms hazelnut and filbert are used interchangeably. In England, these common nuts are known as hazelnuts or cob nuts, and filbert refers to a larger variety that may be called giant filbert in the United States. Europeans buy the fresh nuts, moist and juicy, in good stores throughout the fall. By Christmas, the pretty leafy husks have shriveled, and the shells hardened and darkened to the familiar hazel color. The nut kernels themselves will be less milky, but, in their own way, still as good to eat as the fresh nuts and to use in cooking.

Hazelnuts are perfect with goat cheese and in green salads, but where they come into their own is in the preparation of candies, tortes, cakes, and other desserts. To make cakes and many other sweets, you need neither fat nor flour: hazelnuts have enough oil, balanced with mealiness, to provide it all. Just combine them, ground, with

eggs and sugar and/or cream, as the case may be, and you have a whole repertoire of rich desserts. In supermarkets, you can buy shelled hazelnuts whole or chopped. In produce markets they'll be sold complete with their shells.

Chestnut (*Castanea sativa*) Edible chestnuts are first cousins to horse chestnuts or buckeyes. They are a prettier shape, but have none of their cousin's flamboyant mahogany sheen. Their pointed shell encloses a truly delicious nut—good to eat with Brussels sprouts, wonderful for stuffings, and warming when roasted over the fire on a winter's day. Unfortunately, most of America's once-common chestnut trees were wiped out by a blight in the early 1900s, and all of the chestnuts in our markets today—or roasted by vendors on the streets of New York—are imported.

Marrons glacés, chestnuts preserved in syrup, are easy to make and are a great treat, although they do not often look as stunning as the French ones bought sitting in individual frilled paper cups. Puréed sweet chestnuts make the basis for the creamy and delicious dessert known as *mont blanc* and for frozen Nesselrode pudding (invented for the nobleman of that name by his gifted cook). In Italy, chestnuts are stewed in wine, and in France, these useful nuts, braised or puréed, provide garnishes for chicken, squab, and turkey.

When shopping for fresh chestnuts, look for smooth, shiny shells and buy nuts that feel heavy for their size. Preserved chestnuts come vacuum-packed, which saves the laborious business of shelling and skinning them—the inner skin is bitter even when cooked, so it must be removed. Less good are chestnuts canned in water. They are also preserved in syrup or, of course, in the form of purée, sweetened or unsweetened. Chestnuts are also sold dried, ready for soaking and making into chestnut purée, a traditional accompaniment for game.

Brazil nut (*Bertholletia excelsa*) This is the seed of a mighty tree that towers above the Brazilian jungle. The trees have never been cultivated: their seeds are gathered and buried by the cotia, the Amazonian hare, and those that the hare forgets to retrieve take root. The fruit that the tree produces is as large as a coconut and

a considerable weight; it falls to the ground when ripe. Inside the hard, woody shell are the twelve to twenty triangular seeds, packed tightly together like segments of an orange. These are the Brazil nuts that we buy, either in their shells (don't buy those that rattle when shaken or that feel light) or shelled, often in containers of mixed nuts.

Rich and creamy-fleshed, Brazil nuts are available all year, but are best in winter. However, they do not keep well—a high oil content gives them a rich flavor but soon turns them rancid.

Walnut (*Juglans regia*) Fresh walnuts have flesh that is pearly-white and soft, easily peeled inner skins, and shells that still have a trace of moisture about them. In Britain and other parts of Europe, these "wet" walnuts are a great delicacy, eaten raw with cheese—particularly goat cheese—and as soon as possible, so that their moisture has had no chance to evaporate. The British like to pickle very young green walnuts, before the shells have hardened, in vinegar, which turns them black.

After the first flush of youth, walnuts become both drier and more oily in consistency. It is in this state that their kernels, halved or chopped, are used raw in salads or in cooking. Walnuts are good in stuffings, pressed into cream cheese, and baked in breads and cakes. They are excellent in a winter fruit compote of prunes, pears, and dried apricots, cooked in spiced red wine. Walnut toffee and walnut fudge are delicious, and so are halved nuts, coated in caramel, to make walnut brittle. In addition, nothing goes better with after-dinner port than a dish of fat walnuts.

The common walnut is also known as the English walnut, although it is a native of the Middle East. The United States is the largest producer of these nuts, grown throughout California. Black walnuts (*Juglans nigra*) and butternuts, or white walnuts (*Juglans cinerea*), are the native North American branch of the family. Black walnut shells are so hard that special nutcrackers are needed. These nuts have a stronger taste than common walnuts, which some find bitter, but are prized in candies, ice creams, and cake. Butternuts are less difficult to crack, and have a rich flavor. Both nuts have a high oil content and turn rancid quickly.

Coconut (*Cocos nucifera*) The coconut is harvested when its outer husk is green, its shell pliable, and its flesh soft and moist. It grows in great clusters on giant palm trees, native to and once found only in Malaysia. It is now cultivated on tropical coasts all over the world. This is because, apart from providing an invaluable source of food, the coconut palm supplies a vast range of products, from coir for rugs and matting to palm wine. And in world kitchens, the coconut proves its worth in any number of ways.

By the time it arrives in our markets, its shell is dark and its flesh thick, and a great deal of the coconut juice—the thin white liquid present in the center of the unripe nut—will have been absorbed. When you buy a fresh coconut, weight is the factor to watch—the heavier the nut, the juicier it will be. When you have opened it and extracted the juice, which makes a sweet, refreshing drink, you only have to peel away the brown skin with a sharp knife and grate your coconut meat to use in pies, cakes, and other desserts, candies, and savory dishes such as curries. You can also mix fresh grated coconut with an equal amount of boiling water and then squeeze the liquid from the shreds to get coconut milk. To make coconut cream, simply use less water—approximately four parts coconut to one part water. Alternatively, buy canned coconut milk, or slabs of creamed coconut. The canned or fresh milk can be used in soups, curries, stews, roasts, drinks, candies, cakes, and other desserts, and even for cooking rice.

Shredded or flaked coconut, usually sweetened, is sold in cans and packages. Unsweetened dried, or desiccated, coconut is also available. It is made from dried coconut meat from which most of the oil has been extracted, and has less flavor than freshly grated flesh, but can be used in desserts and other dishes.

1

2

3

Splitting a coconut

1 Pierce two of the coconut "eyes" with a strong, sharp instrument such as a screwdriver, or, as shown here, an awl.

2 Shake out the juice; bake the empty coconut in a hot oven (400°F) for 15 minutes.

3 Lay the coconut on a board and give the center of the shell a sharp blow with a hammer; it should break cleanly in two.

Blanching almonds

Plunge shelled almonds into boiling water and leave for a few seconds, until the skins expand and loosen. Drain the nuts, and then pinch the almonds out of their skins. (Pistachios are skinned in the same way.)

Skinning hazelnuts

Toast shelled nuts under the broiler or in a moderate oven (350°F) until the skins begin to color and loosen. Put the nuts in a paper bag and then rub them against one another to free most of the skins from the nuts.

Peeling chestnuts

With a sharp pointed knife, score a cross on the flat side of each nut. Blanch the scored chestnuts in boiling water for a few minutes, then drain. While they are still warm, peel away the hard outer shell and the furry inner skin.

Herbs

Each herb used in the kitchen has a special and well-known affinity with certain kinds of food—fresh basil with tomatoes, rosemary with lamb, sage with pork—but there are no rules laid down about these harmonies. One of the great pleasures of cooking is improvising with the fresh green flavors that herbs bring to food, playing around to produce sometimes fierce, sometimes delicate tones. This is especially enjoyable for those who can stroll out into the herb garden for inspiration and cast their eye over the fresh greenery growing there.

The judicious use of dried herbs, too, can lead to some very memorable discoveries, so always keep a wide variety at hand—not simply a jar or two of mixed herbs to fling into everything.

Herbs from the garden can be dried at home, but they must be picked at the right moment, just before they flower, or they will have lost their flavor. Gather them on a dry but gray day, and wash them quickly. Divide the small-leafed herbs such as thyme, tarragon, and summer savory into bunches and tie them loosely with string. Either hang them up in cheesecloth bags or spread them on a cloth or on newspaper laid over a rack, and then leave them to dry in a warm place (this should not be out in the sunshine).

Large-leafed herbs such as bay, sage, and mint can be tied loosely and dried in the same way, or dipped into boiling water for a minute, shaken dry, and dried to a crisp in a very low oven. Parsley is more difficult, as it is a very juicy herb. Dry it on a rack in a hot oven (400°F) for 1 minute, then turn the heat off and leave the parsley in the oven until it is quite crisp.

If you want to crush dried herbs for storage in glass jars, use a rolling pin or whiz them in a little spice grinder, which will turn them a nice green color again. Fill the jars loosely to the top and make sure the tops fit properly, to preserve the herb's aroma.

Most of the more tender herbs—dill, mint, tarragon, parsley, chives, basil, chervil, and so forth—can be frozen. They will darken in color when they are thawed, but the flavor will be well preserved. Since most herbs are very strongly scented, be sure to store them in airtight freezer containers or bags, otherwise they will flavor everything in the freezer.

Bouquet garni Traditionally this is a few sprigs of parsley, some thyme, and a bay leaf. Tied with kitchen twine, it goes into the soup, stew, or whatever dish calls for it and is discarded when the dish is cooked. When used to flavor a stock, the herbs can be tied inside a rib of celery or leek greens. A bouquet garni can also be a mixture of dried herbs tied up in a little square of cheesecloth or muslin. To the basic bouquet can be added a piece of orange peel, a clove of garlic, a few celery leaves, a couple of twigs of fennel, or whatever herbs you choose to go with the particular dish you are making.

Fines herbes This is a delicate mixture of the more tender herbs— parsley, chervil, chives, and sometimes tarragon—all chopped very fine. The alchemy of this mixture has a hundred and one uses, flavoring everything from subtly cooked egg dishes and omelets to poached sole or any delicate fish with a cream and white wine sauce.

Angelica (*Angelica archangelica*) Nobody knows why angelica is associated with angels, although it has been helpful in its time for curing coughs, colds, and colic. It is best known today as a candied stem used for decorating cakes and other desserts. Freshly shredded angelica leaves are a good flavoring for rhubarb, and can also be used in jam making, particularly in rhubarb jam.

Basil (*Ocimum basilicum*) Sweet basil, so necessary to the well-being of anyone who loves the Mediterranean, has large, tender leaves that bruise easily and smell sweetly of cloves. It should be picked young and eaten raw, or almost so, since the aroma and flavor are fleeting. Use it lavishly on tomato salad—it has a great affinity with tomatoes—and with eggplant and zucchini. In the South of France, a few chopped leaves are sometimes thrust into a ratatouille at the last moment. The famous *pesto alla genovese*—basil and pine nut paste—is one of the greatest pasta sauces. And Provençal vegetable soup would be no more than an ordinary vegetable soup were it not for the similar *pommade* made with oil, garlic, and basil pounded together and added to the bowl at the last moment. Fresh basil is also delicious

with mozzarella cheese, in a potato salad or a salad of white beans, as well as with steak and chicken.

There are many varieties of basil in addition to common sweet basil. Small-leaved pot basil is particularly sweet, while Thai or Asian basil has a pungent anise aroma, purple stems, and sharply pointed leaves—delicious in salads, stir-fried dishes, and soups. Lemon basil has a citrus fragrance, and purple or opal basil has beautiful dark red-purple leaves with a slightly muted flavor.

To preserve basil, push the leaves into a jar, sprinkling a little salt between the layers, and fill the jar with olive oil. Both leaves (which become black) and oil are good, and impart their flavor to whatever ingredient or dish they are added to. Basil can also be preserved by freezing, after a brief blanching, but the flavor of frozen or dried basil can never compare with that of the freshly picked herb.

Bay (*Laurus nobilis*) Anyone who is familiar with cooking is familiar with the sweet, resinous smell of bay. The leaves or sprigs go into stocks, broths, and marinades, court-bouillons for fish, pickles, stews, and spaghetti sauces— into anything, in fact, that demands a bouquet garni. In the past, fresh bay leaves were used to flavor custards— bay infused in boiled milk adds a very agreeable, subtle flavor.

Fresh bay leaves are not often seen in the United States even in produce markets, but they can sometimes be found at herb growers' stands in farmers' markets. Buy Turkish bay leaves if you can; California bay leaves have a harsher flavor. Avoid buying old bay leaves; if they are more than a year old, they will have lost their flavor as well as their color. In France, bay leaves are called *laurier*, which is sometimes dangerously translated as "laurel leaves" in cookbooks (including Alice B. Toklas's famous cookbook, where there is a laurel soup recipe that would fell a horse), as leaves of laurels other than the sweet bay can be poisonous.

Borage (*Borago officinalis*) A hairy, bristly plant that stings the fingers, borage makes up for the discomfort it inflicts by its flowers, which are a heart-breakingly intense blue. Together with the cucumber-flavored furry leaves, they complete that fruit salad of an English summer drink called Pimms cup. Borage leaves also go into teas and other refreshing summer drinks. The flowers make a pretty garnish for crab salad.

Burnet (*Poterium sanguisorba*) Salad burnet, with its gray-green leaves and cool cucumber flavor, was eaten a great deal by our ancestors. The young leaves of this European plant are very tender and can be sprinkled into the salad bowl with the lettuce. Used a great deal in France and Italy, burnet can also be used, like borage, in cooling drinks, and is an excellent flavoring for vinegar.

Chervil (*Anthriscus cerefolium*) One of the classic fines herbes, chervil has a delicate, anise flavor, so subtle that it needs to be

used lavishly. It is good in green salads, with eggs, and in an herb butter for steak or sole. In Korea, it is used as a salad green instead of lettuce, served by itself or with a dish of grilled or curried shrimp. It makes a very good light soup, and chervil and sorrel, both shredded fairly finely, are a traditional garnish for chicken soup. Fresh chervil can be frozen, but it doesn't dry very well.

Chinese chive, garlic chive (*Allium tuberosum*) These garlic-scented and -flavored chives, also known as ku chai, have narrow, flat green leaves and edible white flowers. They are much used in Chinese and Indian cooking, and in South Africa they are used for flavoring salads. Usually eaten while still in bud, they can also be picked in full flower and

scattered lightly on top of salad greens to add beauty and a delicate garlic flavor. The buds may also be fried.

Chive (*Allium schoenoprasum*) With a flavor faintly redolent of onions but far finer and more delicate, grassy-looking chives are best with eggs, especially in omelets. They are also delicious with potatoes —particularly baked potatoes split open and piled with sour cream mixed with chopped chives—and with raw or cooked tomatoes. As they are such a clean, fresh green, they look pretty snipped and sprinkled over puréed soups—tomato, vichyssoise, avocado, potato, or artichoke—as well as in a mixed green salad and as a garnish for potato salad and glazed carrots. Chives freeze well but lose their flavor if dried.

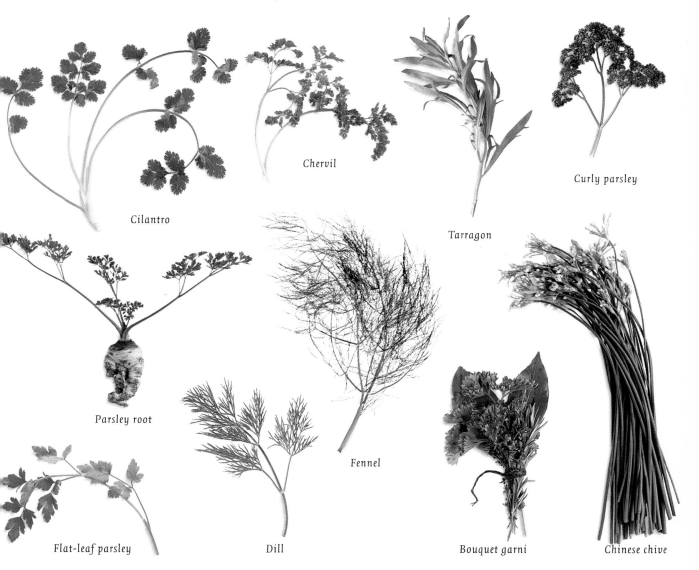

Chervil

Curly parsley

Cilantro

Tarragon

Parsley root

Fennel

Flat-leaf parsley

Dill

Bouquet garni

Chinese chive

Cilantro, fresh coriander
(*Coriandrum sativum*) The soft, floppy green leaves of this now well-known herb look like rather lacy, flat parsley. They don't smell particularly strong unless you bruise them, and their taste, on its own, is harsh with a green note (said by some to be reminiscent of soap)—quite unlike the warm flavor of the seeds. But chopped and used in fresh salsas and in many other Mexican and Southwestern dishes, cilantro has a superb flavor. It is also an essential flavor in many types of Indian curry, particularly shrimp, and a very good addition to a Southeast-Asian meat or chicken curry is a paste made from fresh ginger, garlic, hot green chiles, and fresh cilantro, all pounded together. Cilantro can be delicious in meatballs and lamb stews, or with lamb or pork kebabs, and in Mediterranean vegetable dishes. It is widely used in Thai and other Asian cuisines. It does not dry well, but can be frozen or preserved with salt in oil.

The roots of the cilantro plant are also delicious in cooking. In Thailand, the roots are added to dishes that are to be long-simmered, and then the leaves are stirred in at the last moment.

Dill (*Anethum graveolens*) Scandinavians are as fond of dill as they are of summer, the height of which is the first day of the *krefta* season, when thousands of crayfish are cooked with generous amounts of dill and served in their scarlet shells on a bed of the green herb, accompanied by numerous glasses of aquavit interspersed with beer. Dill is the flavor that makes gravlax, the Scandinavian cured salmon, so delicious, and it is also used there with boiled and mashed potatoes. In Greece, it is the herb used to flavor fava beans and artichokes. With white fish, serve dill in melted butter or made into an herb sauce.

To preserve dill, freeze it in plastic bags. (Or use dill seeds when fresh dill is out of season.)

Fennel (*Foeniculum vulgare*) The sweet herb fennel—not to be confused with the bulb vegetable fennel—is used both as an herb and for its seeds. A few of the small twigs are invaluable for bouillabaisse and fish soup and with fresh fish; if you find fresh crayfish and cook them in boiling water with a jungle of fennel, it gives them a most delicate flavor and is a good alternative to the dill the Scandinavians prefer. Burn a few dried twigs when you are grilling fish or lamb outdoors, and put sprigs inside and under a fish when you roast it in the oven. The anise-flavored oils will permeate the food with a wonderful flavor. In Sardinia, wild fennel is often used to flavor a bean and pork stew, and occasionally with lamb.

Horseradish (*Armoracia rusticana*) A fresh, sharp horseradish sauce with roast beef is one of life's pleasures and is very good, too, with hot boiled tongue. In Germany, horseradish is grated and mixed with vinegar as a sauce for fish, and creamed horseradish sauce is particularly good with smoked trout or eel. Bottled horseradish is an adequate substitute for the fresh root but is often quite vinegary; a better substitute, if available, is dried horseradish.

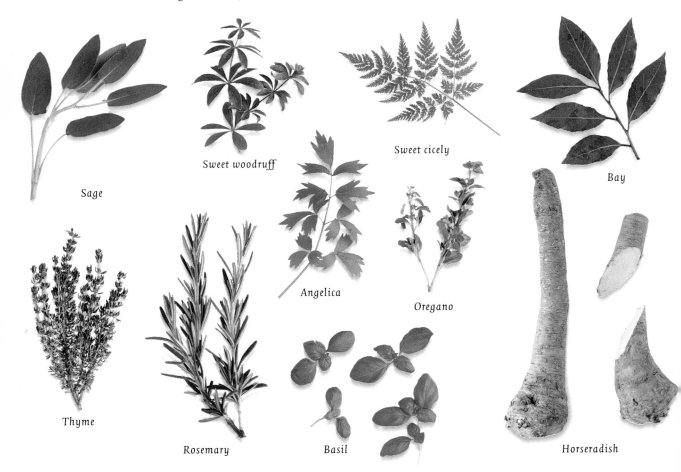

Sage

Sweet woodruff

Sweet cicely

Bay

Thyme

Angelica

Oregano

Horseradish

Rosemary

Basil

Kaffir lime leaf (*Cistus hystrix*) Only the leaves of the Southeast-Asian kaffir lime, or *makrut*, tree and sometimes the peel of its fruit are used in cooking. The glossy, waisted leaves have an aromatic, floral-citrus smell and are used in the same way as bay leaves to flavor Thai and other Southeast-Asian soups and curries. They are usually sold dried in Asian markets, but the fresh leaves are becoming more available. The peel can sometimes be found, dried, and needs soaking before it is used, like the leaves, to flavor soups, marinades, and curries— even marmalade.

Lemon balm, balm (*Melissa officinalis*) Beloved of bees, balm was the vital ingredient of the *elixir vital* created by the Swiss alchemist Paracelsus, which was designed to make man immortal. It now gives its essence to Chartreuse, that green and potent liqueur made by monks, who keep most of the other ingredients a secret. The fresh, lemon-scented leaves and small white flowers of this plant are delicious in a white wine punch, and

a few freshly picked leaves can also go into a green salad, but the taste is rather overpowering and more bitter than you might expect.

Lemon grass (*Ambopogon citratus/ Cymbopogon citratus*) Perfumed, spicy, and balm-like, lemon grass adds a light, rather elusive flavor to many Thai and Indonesian dishes. Tough on the outside, the stalks contain tender inner leaves that are cut into rounds or shredded and used to flavor soups, curries, pork, seafood—particularly crab—and chicken. Lemon grass can be grown in a frost-free place like any other herb. Best fresh, it can also be bought dried: soak for half an hour before use.

Lovage (*Ligusticum officinalis*) This old-fashioned herb looks rather like immensely tall, dark green celery that has gotten out of hand. It has a strange, pleasant but heavy smell (it is called the Maggi plant in Holland because the flavor is reminiscent of the stock cubes, with monosodium glutamate lurking

somewhere in its nuances). It is a strong-flavored herb and should be used sparingly to season stocks or soups when a meaty flavor is wanted; its seeds can be used like celery seed.

Marjoram (*Origanum majorana*) **Sweet, or knotted, marjoram** smells very sweet, both when it is fresh and the bees are enjoying it and when it is cut, just after flowering, and dried in bunches like thyme and sage. Use fresh leaves in a salad, on grilled or roast lamb, or in stuffings for chicken or squab. Dried marjoram can be added to spaghetti and tomato sauces, and to any tomato-based soup or stew.
Pot marjoram (*Origanum onites*) This is less warm-flavored than sweet marjoram, but can be used in all the same ways.
Rigani is the wild marjoram of Greece; the dried herb is sometimes available in specialty markets. Use the dried flowers rather than the leaves to give the authentic Greek flavor to grilled lamb kebabs and to the Greek salad of feta cheese, tomatoes, olives, and onion.

Burnet

Lemon balm

Marjoram

Mint

Borage

Chive

Lovage

Summer savory

Winter savory

Mint (*Mentha*) One of the oldest and most familiar of all the herbs, mint has almost as many varieties as it has uses. Spearmint (*Mentha spicata*), with its pointed leaves and fresh taste, is the most commonly used. Peppermint (*Mentha piperita*) has longer, darker green leaves and a more pungent taste. Pretty apple mint (*Mentha rotundifolia*), which has woolly, rounded leaves, has a superior, fruitier flavor (its woolly texture disappears when it is finely chopped or cooked).

Americans like mint in candies and desserts. For some, an all-too-vividly-green mint jelly is essential with lamb chops or roast lamb. And in Kentucky, mint juleps are always served on Derby Day (and on other days as well). In England, mint is best known in a sauce to accompany roast lamb. A few sprigs of fresh mint are often boiled with new potatoes, when it is delicious, and with garden peas, when it is a mistake. Mint features a good deal in Middle Eastern cookery—for example, finely chopped and stirred into yogurt as a dressing for the cucumber salad called *raita*. In northern India, chopped mint is mixed with hot green chiles and yogurt to make a fresh chutney that is very good with tandoori chicken. In Italy, wild mint is used instead of parsley with grilled or sautéed porcini mushrooms.

Mint is also used with shellfish, particularly grilled shrimp, and in the making of desserts that contain fresh oranges (with which the herb has an affinity). Sprigs of mint go into fruit drinks and iced tea. Sun-brewed mint tea is made by putting mint sprigs and tea bags in a pitcher of cold water and leaving it to brew in the sun—the resulting tea has no hint of bitterness.

Oregano (*Origanum vulgare*) This Mediterranean herb, sometimes known as wild marjoram, has a wonderfully warm, heady scent and flavor. In Italy, it is used for the same dishes as marjoram. The dried leaves give a strong, spicy flavor to an oil and lemon sauce for fish and roast meats, and to pizza and spaghetti sauces, chicken broths, beef stews, and grilled fish, especially the prized red mullet. Oregano is delicious with mozzarella and tomatoes, and is one of the flavors in the best chilis. The oregano of Mexico is stronger than the common Mediterranean variety.

Parsley (*Petroselinum crispum*) The most serviceable of herbs and one that you can always buy fresh, parsley seems to have just as much affinity with garlic and strongly flavor Mediterranean dishes—salty with olives, anchovies, goat cheese, garlic, and capers—as it does with the heartier cooking of cooler northern regions, and many a pallid dish has been saved with a sprinkling of this chopped green. Flat-leaf parsley is tastier and has a better texture than the curled, and parsley root—also called Hamburg parsley—is good for flavoring stews. Use parsley in stock and court-bouillon, soups, and, stews. *Persillade* is the term for garlic and parsley chopped together, and it flavors many dishes; rack of lamb *en persillade*, coated with bread crumbs tossed with this mixture before roasting, is delicious. Parsley can be cooked with cream and served as a vegetable in its own right. Put plenty of coarsely chopped flat-leaf parsley, which is also called Italian parsley, in any green salad.

Rosemary (*Rosmarinus officinalis*) One of the prettiest of shrubs, rosemary loves the baking heat and dryness of the Mediterranean, but will grow to quite a good size in cooler climates if given a warm, dry, sheltered place. It particularly likes the seaside—its name comes from the Latin for "dew of the sea." It has a great affinity with veal, lamb, chicken, and also with rabbit—put a sprig under a rack or leg of veal or lamb before roasting, or into the butter in which you are softening onions for a veal stew, and drop a sprig into the oil in which you are frying potatoes. Rosemary is better fresh than dried, and a fresh rosemary sprig has the added advantage of staying in one piece in the cooking—which is lucky, as it is very disagreeable to get a mouthful of the needle-like leaves. But be miserly, because it is all too easy to overdo the gingery, pungent flavor of this herb.

Sage (*Salvia officinalis*) Sage was once believed to give wisdom and prolong life. It is certainly a powerful herb, musky and fragrant. The leaves go into stuffings for roast pork and turkey, and sage is an important ingredient—usefully cutting the richness of the fat—in pork sausages. Quail and other small game birds are sometimes cooked with sage. In Italy, fresh sage is fried in the oil in which veal or calf's liver is to be cooked, to give it an interesting flavor, and, sprinkled on ravioli, sage leaves fried in butter add a warm, satisfying note.

Savory (*Satureia hortensis*)
Summer savory Aromatic and pleasantly bitter, with a scent a little like thyme, summer savory was used by the Romans to flavor vinegar in much the same way as we use tarragon and other herb vinegars today. In France, where it is called *sarriette*, it is used with thyme to flavor rabbit, and fresh sprigs are cooked with fava beans and peas. It is also good in long-simmered stews and *daubes*. Summer savory dries well, and can be used with other herbs in stuffings for turkey and veal. It is said to be a good antidote to beestings.
Winter savory (*Satureia montana*), with its blue flowers, is a tougher herb than summer savory. Its rough, pointed evergreen leaves cannot be eaten raw, as they tickle the throat. It has a similar, strong earthy flavor, perfect with beef and rabbit stews, and in stuffings.

Sweet woodruff (*Asperula odorata*) A small woodland herb, sweet woodruff is a native European flowering plant that has a ravishing hay-like perfume. In Germany, it is used in May, before it flowers, to flavor the delicate wine punch known as May wine: steep the well-washed plants in a pitcher of white wine overnight in the refrigerator, then add brandy and sugar or Bénédictine and serve with a garnish of the green leaves.

Tarragon (*Artemisia dracunculus*) Like basil and dill, tarragon has an addictive flavor—that is to say, those who have eaten it fresh can't very well get through the summer without it, since it is so delicious. French tarragon tastes sweetly of vanilla and anise, and harmonizes with all kinds of egg dishes, with cream sauces, and with roast chicken or steak. It is good in green salads and potato salad, and with cold salmon or trout. Tarragon is excellent in homemade mayonnaise for potato salad or chicken, and is essential for béarnaise sauce. Dried tarragon takes on a hay-like flavor, but frozen tarragon is very good.
Russian tarragon (*Artemisia dracunculoides*) Unlike the true French herb, this has a disappointing flavor.

Thyme (*Thymus vulgaris*) Sun-loving, tiny-leafed, but tough, thyme tastes and smells warm, earthy, and flowery. Use it in every kind of long-simmered red-wine dish; with veal and chicken in all their tomatoey incarnations; in a bouquet garni; in marinades; and—instead of rosemary—with lamb. In Marseilles, thyme is sprinkled into everything including vinaigrettes, on fried potatoes, and onto fish to be grilled over a wood fire. It gives pungency to pâtés, terrines, and meatballs and has an affinity with Mediterranean vegetables such as eggplant, zucchini, and sweet peppers.

Lemon thyme (*Thymus citriodorus*) is superb in stuffings for both pork and veal. Home-dried or frozen thyme is incomparably better than commercially dried or ground thyme.

Garden leaves and flowers

Always use only unsprayed (pesticide-free) leaves and flowers.

Geranium (*Pelargonium graveolens*) The curling, slightly furry leaves of the rose-scented geranium add a delicate rose fragrance to a clear amber-pink crabapple jelly or to lemon granita or sorbet. Pick the larger leaves.

Grape (*Vitis*) Every vine that produces edible grapes produces leaves that are edible when young. As rice-filled Greek *dolmades*, and as a wrapping, with bacon, for little birds such as quail, grape leaves impart a delicious, faint lemon flavor. Choose large, tender young leaves; or if they are older, blanch them briefly in boiling salted water to soften them before they are used. Of course, canned grape leaves are also available; rinse them well before using.

Marigold (*Calendula officinalis*) This pretty golden flower was once used a great deal to color and flavor fish soups and meat broths and to decorate salads—especially shrimp, crab, or lobster. Since the petals are surprisingly tough, they are best chopped. Mixed with other chopped petals, such as borage, rose, and hyssop, the effect is colorful and quite charming. Marigolds are still sometimes used as a coloring agent, and can be employed as a substitute for saffron if you don't like the strong flavor of that spice. The petals can be fresh or dried, but don't use the flower centers. The small Signet marigold is one of the nicest.

Nasturtium (*Trapaeolum majus*) Almost every part of this tender plant has a place in the kitchen. The flowers and young leaves can be used in salads—the leaves taste like watercress, but don't use too many, because they are very spicy. The buds and seeds can also be pickled, to make "false capers." Gather the seeds as soon as the blossoms have fallen, before they get hard, rinse them in cold water, and soak overnight in cold salted water. Then drain, cover with cold spiced vinegar, and seal; keep for a year or so before using.

Peach (*Prunus persica*) Fresh peach leaves make a delicate flavoring for custard, more interesting than the usual vanilla and tasting faintly of almonds. Pick five or six fresh leaves and infuse them in the milk for 5 to 10 minutes, then proceed with the custard in the usual way.

Rose (*Rosa*) Although much of life was probably far from rosy in medieval days, it must have been a great pleasure, on a fine day, to gather dark red rose petals to make into rose syrup, rose candy, and rose vinegar. In the Middle East, roses are still definitely the domain of the cook, who will sprinkle rose water into fruit salads made with pomegranates and make clear rose petal jelly with nuts suspended in it, or chewy, scented rose petal jam. In the last century, the American Shakers used their own rose water to flavor apple pie—an unexpectedly exotic touch for such a "plain" people; in England, the Victorians made rose petal sandwiches. Rose petals are also good in cherry pie.

Scented geranium leaf

Nasturtium

Kaffir lime leaf

Marigold

Rose

Grape leaf

Lemon grass

Spices

Although spices have been in wide use since the Middle Ages—and Christopher Columbus would never have landed in America had he not been seeking an easier route to the spices of India—they rather fell into disrepute here as "good plain cooking" took hold. Now the heady, aromatic smells of the spice bazaars are back, with the wave of new ethnic food shops, and with them a revived interest in the cooking of India, the Middle East, and Asia.

Kitchen cupboards are loaded with little pots and jars of cumin, coriander seeds, and cardamom, which are becoming as familiar as the ginger, cloves, and cinnamon many cooks have relied on in the past. Buy in small quantities and use whole spices whenever possible, pounding or grinding them fresh for each dish that calls for ground spice. A small, specially designated coffee grinder can be used for this purpose, as can a spice grinder—but grinding the spices with ingredients such as garlic, fresh cilantro leaves, fresh ginger, and chile pepper in a large mortar and pestle is a pleasure not to be missed.

Mixtures

Five-spice powder This is a Chinese mixture of ground star anise, fennel seeds, cloves, cinnamon, and Sichuan pepper. Its subtle anise flavor is particularly good with roast pork.

Garam masala This Indian mixture of spices is added to a dish toward the end of cooking to enhance the aromas and flavors. It can be bought at Indian markets and well-stocked supermarkets or ground at home from a mixture of whole spices. The powder can be mixed to a paste with water, to be used in curry, stirred into yogurt, or eaten with other foods like a condiment.

Pickling spice Although these mixtures vary according to their manufacturer, most will probably contain a great deal of mustard seed, some small dried chiles, white peppercorns, allspice, cloves, mace, a few coriander seeds, and perhaps some ginger. But it is better to use measured amounts of the individual spices in pickling, because appropriate quantities and ingredients vary from vegetable to vegetable, as well as recipe to recipe.

Quatre épices Although called "four spices" in French, the actual number of spices used in this mixture may vary. The base spices are star anise, cassia or cinnamon, cloves, and fennel seeds; the "extra" spices often added are Sichuan peppercorns, ginger, or cardamom. Quatre épices is used in the making of pâtés, savory pies, and sausages. Buy it from a specialty market or spice purveyor, or make only a small quantity at a time.

Other spice blends commonly available include curry powder and chili powder, and the sweeter mixtures for seasoning pumpkin and apple pies.

Allspice (*Pimenta officinalis*) Allspice, or Jamaica pepper, is a hard brown berry, larger and smoother than a peppercorn. It tastes faintly of cinnamon and strongly of cloves, with a touch of nutmeg, which is why it is sometimes mistakenly thought to be a mixture of spices when it is bought ground. It is called *pimienta* in Jamaica, where it is an essential ingredient in jerk seasoning, the spicy paste rubbed on chicken, pork, and other meats before grilling them. Ground allspice can also go into pâtés and sausages. It is used in gingerbread and spice cake, in marinades, with cured beef, and in chutneys. It seems to impart something of a peppery as well as a spicy flavor.

Anise seeds (*Pimpinella anisum*) Anise seeds, or aniseed, flavor Pernod, ouzo, and other addictive licorice-flavored drinks of the same genre. From a delicate bush of the hemlock family, the seeds give a sweet flavor to fish and particularly to mussels, to some sweets, and, in parts of Europe, to cakes and bread. In the Middle East, anise flavors preserved green figs (it is added to the syrup in which the figs are cooked), and it is a seasoning in some Indian vegetable and fish curries. Buy aniseed in small quantities, as it quickly loses its strength.

Asafoetida (*Ferula asafoetida*) An ingredient in Indian vegetable dishes, curries, and pickles, asafoetida is an evil-smelling resin that is obtained from equally pungent plants of the giant fennel family. It should be used in exceedingly small quantities—or it can be omitted entirely from recipes that call for it.

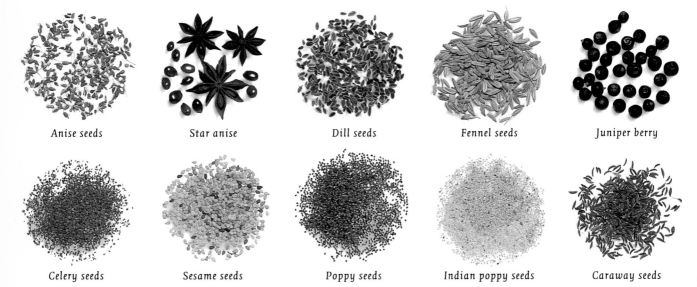

Anise seeds   Star anise   Dill seeds   Fennel seeds   Juniper berry

Celery seeds   Sesame seeds   Poppy seeds   Indian poppy seeds   Caraway seeds

Caraway seeds (*Carum carvi*) It could be the fact that they aid digestion that makes these an ingredient of so many hearty, delicious rye breads. In Germany, caraway is called *kümmel* and gives the typical flavor to the liquor of the same name—a warm and comforting drink. With anise, star anise, fennel, and coriander, it also flavors aquavit, the superb but lethal white liquor tossed down by the Scandinavians with herring, crayfish, and smoked eel. And there are at least a dozen good cheeses flecked with caraway seeds. Caraway seeds are good in coleslaw, and with cooked cabbage too.

Cardamom (*Elettaria cardamomum*) Genuine cardamom is costly and has a great many inferior relatives, so it pays to look carefully at what you are buying. The best cardamom pods are the size of peas, pale brown or greenish, and the tiny seeds, when you split open a pod, should be dark, shiny, and richly aromatic. The flavor of cardamom is essential in some curries—it has a warm, aromatic, but sharp taste, and an anesthetic effect on the tongue. Sometimes the whole pod is used, but usually the seeds are taken out and ground with other spices. Ready-ground cardamom is sold, but has a much more floury flavor than the freshly ground seeds. In Arab countries, cardamom is put into the sweet coffee, and in Scandinavian countries, it flavors cakes and pastries. White cardamom is dried in the sun—or, more commonly, is bleached with sulfur dioxide—and is the one to use to flavor hot drinks.

Celery seeds (*Apium graveolens*) Although inclined to be bitter, celery seeds give a lift to soups and stews. They can also go into dishes that combine rice with tomatoes, into bread, and into pickling mixtures.

Cinnamon (*Cinnamomum zeylanicum*) Cinnamon sticks are curled, thin pieces of the bark of a tropical evergreen tree. Use them for flavoring the milk for rice pudding and baked custard, or put a few pieces in a rice pilaf. The sticks are also used in hot punches and sweet pickles.

Ground cinnamon is used in baking—in cinnamon rolls and raisin bread, hot-cross buns, apple pie, and cookies, on cinnamon toast, and in sweet and savory spiced dishes all over the Middle East and India. It has a marvelous affinity with chocolate, a combination that is particularly liked in Spain and Mexico. **Cassia** (*Cinnamomum cassia*) is the inner bark of a relative tree. Mainly produced in China and Southeast Asia, it comes in thicker, harder pieces than true cinnamon and is less delicate, more pungent, and less expensive. The cinnamon, ground or in stick form, found on most supermarket shelves is actually cassia. True cinnamon is much more common in Europe and Asia.

Clove (*Eugenia caryophyllus*) Cloves have the scent of the Spice Islands, sweet and warm, with a rather numbing quality that has also made them since the earliest days of medicine an excellent remedy for toothache. They are not, however, particularly pleasant to bite on, so are usually fixed firmly in an onion—for lamb or oxtail stew, and other long-cooked meat dishes—or used ground. Cloves flavor pumpkin pie, gingerbread, and other baked goods, and they are traditional with cooked apples and pears, in sweet spiced pickles, and in mulled wine. The best cloves are large, dark, and plump, and not easily broken.

Coriander seeds (*Coriandrum sativum*) These round, brittle, easily crushed seeds are the basis of all that is delicious in many curry dishes and in vegetables *à la grecque*, marinated in olive oil and lemon juice. They have a warm, faintly orangey fragrance that is much enhanced if they are toasted by gentle heating in a heavy frying pan just before use. Coriander seeds, together with lemon zest, make a delicate and unusual substitute for vanilla in custards and ice creams, and an excellent flavoring for cooked apples—puréed or in an apple tart or pie. Ground coriander seeds are often used in Scandinavian baked goods.

Cumin (*Cuminum cyminum*) Cumin is an essential spice. Its scent is hard to define: powerful, warm, sweet, and slightly oily, but quite unmistakable—which is fortunate, because it looks rather like caraway and the two are often confused. In Spain, cumin is the traditional seasoning for chickpeas; in Mexico, it is part of the background in chili; and in the Canary Islands, it flavors fish soup. In North Africa and countries

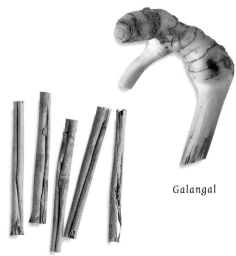

Clove

Ground cinnamon

Allspice

Galangal

Dried ginger

Fresh ginger

Japanese pickled ginger

Cinnamon stick

of the eastern Mediterranean, it is used in couscous, on kebabs, with stewed lamb, and to spice rice and vegetable dishes and yogurt. In India, it is an element of every sort of dish. Toasting the seeds before grinding releases their aroma and makes them easier to grind.

Dill seeds (*Anethum graveolens*) Sprigs of dill complete with half-ripe seeds are a familiar sight in jars of pickles and may be used to make dill vinegar. Dill seeds are also excellent as a flavoring for fish soups and stews and in a court-bouillon. In Scandinavia and other parts of Europe, they are used to flavor cakes and breads.

Fennel seeds (*Foeniculum vulgare*) These have a sweet anise flavor, and a few seeds chewed after meals will help the digestion and sweeten the breath. In Italy, they are used in the manufacture of a marvelous salami called *finocchiona*, and are also found in a kind of nougat called *mandorlotto*. Use them to flavor the liquid in which fish is poached or in fish soups.

Fenugreek seeds (*Trigonella foenum-graecum*) Floury, somewhat bitter, and smelling of maple or fresh hay, the

ground seeds of fenugreek are used in many Indian dishes and are a common ingredient of commercial curry powders and garam masala. The seeds need to be lightly toasted before they are ground—don't overdo it, or they become bitter.

Galangal (*Alpinia galanga*) Galangal, popular in European cooking during the Middle Ages and then forgotten, has made a reappearance in Thai and Indonesian markets. An underground rhizome, it takes the place of ginger in Thai cooking. Fresh galangal may occasionally be found in Asian markets, but dried is the more usual form.

Ginger (*Zingiber officinale*) This romantic spice is associated with Asia. The fresh root (actually a rhizome) is used a great deal in Chinese cooking, with pork, beef, chicken, and duck, and with fish, shrimp, and crab. It has a delicious scent and a crisp texture. In India, fresh ginger is a favorite curry ingredient. Ginger has long been used to make ginger beer and ginger ale. Ground ginger—Jamaican is best—goes into ginger snaps, brandy snaps, and gingerbread. It's good in fruit compotes; or mix it with sugar to

sprinkle on chilled melon—the pleasant contrast of hot and fiery with icy and juicy being interesting, if slightly detrimental to the flavor of the melon.

Stem ginger preserved in syrup and packed into Chinese jars goes, with its syrup, into many desserts and over—or sometimes into—ice cream. Pickled ginger, called *gari* in Japan, is made from baby ginger, thinly sliced and cured in vinegar, salt, and sugar. It is usually a pale pinky-beige, but it may be dyed red. Serve it with *sushi* or *sashimi*.

Juniper berry (*Juniperus communis*) The flavor of the juniper berry, familiar to gin drinkers and especially to those who drink Dutch gin, is strangely harsh and turpentiney on its own. The hard blue-purple berries, the fruit of a pretty but prickly evergreen bush, take 2 years to ripen, so that green and ripe berries appear together. When combined with game, red cabbage, sautéed pork, chops or tenderloin, or beef stews, they add a delicious, rather somber, spicy background flavor. They are good in pork-based pâtés, in marinades for game, especially venison, and in stuffings for small game birds.

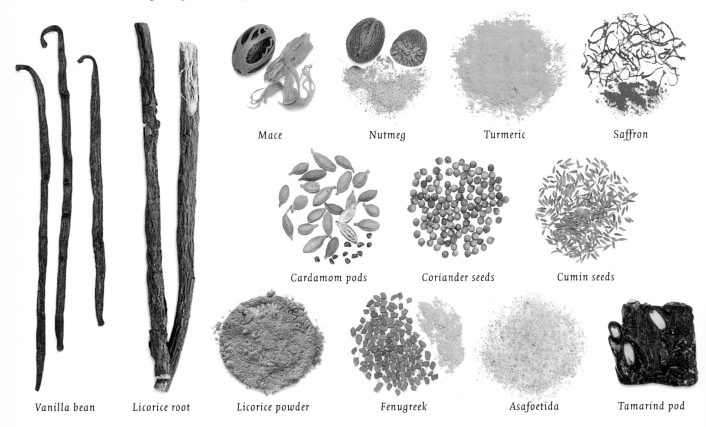

Mace Nutmeg Turmeric Saffron

Cardamom pods Coriander seeds Cumin seeds

Vanilla bean Licorice root Licorice powder Fenugreek Asafoetida Tamarind pod

Licorice (*Glycrriza glabra*) Licorice root is a natural sweetener and can be made into a strong-flavored herbal tea. Once given to children to chew instead of sweets, it is supposedly an aphrodisiac, especially for women. Licorice extract is used commercially in candies and other sweets, but you may find the dried or ground root in an ethnic market.

Mace (*Myristica fragrans*) This is the frond-like outer coat, or aril, of the nutmeg, dried to an orange-brown. More delicate than nutmeg, it is almost always sold ground. It has an affinity with chicken and shrimp and is invaluable in sausages, pâtés, and terrines, as well as in marinades and chutneys. Its warm, sweet, spicy flavor is delicious in cakes and other desserts, and in Italy it flavors the milk for white and cheese sauces.

Nutmeg (*Myristica fragrans*) Beautifully aromatic, with a warm, slightly bitter flavor, nutmeg is equally at home in sweet and nonsweet dishes. While its pretty outer coating is dried to make mace, the nutmeg or seed is dried and will keep, whole, for months or even years. Buy good-quality, large whole nutmeg rather than ground nutmeg, and grate it as you need it.

Northern Italians use nutmeg in many of their stuffed pastas, and in India it is a frequent ingredient of garam masala. Nutmeg is also essential in eggnog and in mulled wine (an excellent sleeping potion, since nutmeg is mildly narcotic).

Poppy seeds (*Papaver rhoeas*) Although they come from a variety of the opium poppy, there is nothing narcotic about poppy seeds. The blue-gray seeds, scattered over loaves, rolls, and bagels, add a pretty decoration and a warm and dusty flavor. Poppy seed cake or coffee cake is a favorite. The creamy-yellow poppy seeds used in India are ground to make a floury curry spice that adds texture rather than flavor. Because poppy seeds have a high oil content, they turn rancid quickly; they're best stored in a cool spot or in the refrigerator.

Saffron (*Crocus sativus*) Saffron is fabulously expensive—each red-gold shred is a crocus stigma, and each saffron crocus has only three stigmas to be hand-gathered and dried.

It is in Spain that one becomes truly addicted to the flavor of saffron, although it is used a great deal in the South of France for soups, particularly fish soups, and is essential in Milanese risotto. But the Spanish must have it. They like their rice bright yellow, and they have saffron in their fish stews, in vegetable soups, and with mussels and shrimp or prawns. Very little is needed: a pinch soaked in a little warm water or white wine will infuse the liquid with its powerful flavor and characteristic color. Saffron is almost always steeped in the liquid with which the dish is cooked, but sometimes, as in certain types of rice pilaf, it is kept until the end of the cooking and then stirred in for a dish of many shades of yellow and orange.

Saffron powder, also expensive and liable to be adulterated, is a poor substitute for saffron strands. Saffron and turmeric are sometimes substituted for each other, but this is a mistake. Saffron is perfect with garlic, fennel, white wine, mussels, and fish, while turmeric belongs with vegetables and meat; but both can be used to color rice.

Sesame seeds (*Sesamum indicum*) The nutty taste of toasted sesame seeds is probably most familiar topping on bread and crackers, but sesame comes in many guises. Tahini, the oily paste made from the finely ground seeds, is used with chickpeas to make hummus, a delicious smooth, creamy sauce into which pita bread is dipped—an hors d'oeuvre well known to everyone who has eaten a Middle Eastern meal. Halvah, a sweet, compressed, oily bar of crushed sesame seeds, has a delicate scrunch and is good as an unusual dessert. Gomasio— a seasoning popular in macrobiotic cooking—is a Japanese mixture of lightly toasted sesame seeds and sea salt. In the American South, sesame seeds are also called benne seeds (*benne* is the African name for these seeds brought over by the slaves), used to make cookies and benne wafers, and in many other recipes.

Star anise (*Illicium verum*) The fruit of a small evergreen tree that belongs to the magnolia family, star anise has the same essential oil that gives aniseed its flavor but is much stronger and more licoricey. It is used in Chinese cooking, particularly with pork and duck.

Tamarind (*Tamarindus indica*) Sharply sour, the sticky, dried pods of the tamarind tree—which are also known as Indian dates—are used instead of limes or lemons to add a sweet-sour tang and a bit of body to many Middle Eastern, Indian, and Southeast-Asian dishes. Tamarind also makes delicious fresh chutneys to eat with curry. The dried pods, shaped into bricks, can be found in ethnic markets; to obtain tamarind juice, steep the pulp in a bowl of hot water until the sour brown juice can easily be squeezed out or strained. Either vinegar or lemon juice makes a reasonable substitute.

Turmeric (*Curcuma longa*) Turmeric, which is a spice much used in Indian cooking, has a harsh taste, somehow reminiscent of freshly scrubbed wood, but its color is indisputably useful. A deep yellow ocher, turmeric is delightful with potatoes and other pale vegetables, such as cauliflower, and in many curries. Use it in moderation, and do not try to use it in place of saffron—the flavor is quite different.

Vanilla (*Vanilla planifolia*) Vanilla is associated with the exotic because of the drowsy, lotus-eating quality of its perfume. In fact, it does have an exotic quality, for it comes from a climbing orchid found in tropical rain forests. It was used to flavor chocolate by the Aztecs, the original chocolate addicts.

The vanilla beans are picked unripe, when they are yellow, and are then allowed to cure to a dark brown. When you buy them, the beans should be somewhat soft, ribbed, and pointed at one end, and they should have a frosting of crystals—the vanillin essence. A favorite way of using vanilla beans is to keep them in a jar of sugar, refilling the jar as you use the sugar in whipped cream, rice pudding, baked custard, and so forth. Another method, useful when making ice cream and crème brûlée, is to infuse the bruised or split bean in the milk or cream. The bean imparts a flowery and spicy aroma, and it can then be gently washed and dried, and stored for another time.

The only vanilla substitute that has genuine flavor is pure vanilla extract; imitation vanilla extract is synthetic and comes nowhere near the real thing.

Salt and Pepper

It has long been considered a measure of a cook's talent as to whether his or her food can be sent perfectly seasoned to the table, and of all the condiments, salt and pepper are the cook's greatest allies. But there are two aspects to the proper seasoning of food. One is what goes into the food in the kitchen, the other is what goes onto it at the table.

SALT

One of the properties of salt—which is an invaluable preservative as well as a seasoning—is to draw the moisture out of foods. This is an advantage with vegetables such as eggplant that may have bitter juices; they can be sliced and salted before cooking so that the bitterness is drawn out. Meat, however, should not be salted before panfrying, grilling, broiling, or roasting, as the moisture raised on its surface will prevent it from searing and browning; salt it only halfway through cooking, after the surface is seared.

Salt also toughens food, which can be helpful, for example, when pickling with vinegar—food salted before being pickled will not turn soggy in the jar. But this is a disadvantage when braising or stewing meat, and with legumes such as dried beans—start these in unsalted water or other cooking liquid and do not add salt until at least 15 minutes after they have reached a simmer.

Sea salt This is the best of all salts for both kitchen and table. It is made by evaporating sea water, either naturally by sun and wind or by artificial heat. The result is large crystals of pure salt that retain their natural iodine and have no bitter aftertaste. They can be sprinkled directly onto foods such as salmon and tuna before cooking, or ground in a salt mill or wooden mortar. This is also the salt to sprinkle over certain breads, rolls, and pretzels before they go into the oven—the crystals dissolve so slowly that they will still be a sparkling presence after baking. Fine sea salt is in most cases the best to use in cooking. Most of our sea salt comes from France, but Britain's Maldon sea salt is considered one of the finest of all.

Sel gris is a coarse, grayish, unrefined French sea salt that contains traces of other minerals. Preferred by some discerning cooks, it is for kitchen use rather than at table.

Kosher salt is widely used in the United States by cooks who prefer its flavor (it is half as salty per volume as table salt) and its coarse-grained, flaky texture; and it contains no additives.

Table salt Ordinary table salt is made by dissolving the salt found in underground deposits and then drying it in a vacuum. It is refined and coated with magnesium carbonate or some other additive to prevent it from absorbing moisture from the air and to keep it free-flowing. Table salt has a decidedly bitter aftertaste, but it is better than any other salt for baking.

Iodized salt is table salt to which iodine has been added. It is useful in areas where the water and soils are lacking in this essential trace element.

Rock salt More widely available in Europe than in the United States (in France it is known as *sel-gemme*), this is a hard, coarse, crystalline salt that needs a salt mill or mortar to make it manageable. At its best, it can be the finest of all the salts. Don't confuse it with the nonedible rock salt, used when making homemade ice cream in an old-fashioned ice cream freezer.

Pickling salt is pure, refined rock salt. It is good for all cooking and is the salt to use for pickling, because it has no additives that might spoil the clarity of the pickling liquid. Other names for it are block salt, cut lump salt, and dairy salt.

Seasoned salts Salts such as garlic salt and celery salt contain extracts of the vegetable—or, in the case of celery salt, the seeds—that give the salt its name, but they add an instantly recognizable "packaged" flavor so often found in convenience foods. Many seasoned salts contain monosodium glutamate plus flavoring agents.

Saltpeter Saltpeter is potassium nitrate, a preservative that has been used in the making of brines and dry salt curing mixtures for hundreds of years. It has the culinary quality of turning meat a beautiful pink—in France, many restaurateurs put a pinch of saltpeter in their pâté to keep it a wholesome rosy color. But saltpeter has been found to be harmful when eaten in large quantities, and, in fact, the U.S. Department of Agriculture no longer recommends it as a curing agent.

PEPPER

The vine that gives us peppercorns and the pepper, or capsicum, plants that give us chili powders, cayenne, and paprika are not related, although all these seasonings add a pungent heat to food.

Preground pepper soon tastes dull and dusty, so buy whole peppercorns—they should be evenly colored, aromatic, free from dust, and too hard to be crushed between the fingers. Nothing could be easier than keeping a peppermill in the kitchen and on the table, and the aroma and flavor of freshly ground pepper, black or white, is quite different from the dry smell and taste of the preground product.

Coarse sea salt

Fine sea salt

Sel gris

Table salt

Rock salt

Kosher salt

Different peppers vary in pungency and size of the peppercorn. Usually they are called after their place of origin—Malabar black, for instance, is one of the best of the black peppercorns; Tellicherry and Lampung are also excellent.

Black peppercorns are the dried, shriveled berries of the pepper vine, *Piper nigrum*. They are picked before they are quite ripe and dried in the sun, where they blacken within a day or two. Coarse "butcher-grind," coarse-ground black pepper, and cracked black pepper are all available in larger supermarkets. These can be used in pâtés to give an aromatic flavor without bringing tears to the eyes, as happens when peppercorns are thrown in whole, and they can also be used for steak au poivre, although freshly crushed whole peppercorns are preferable.

White peppercorns are the ripened berries, soaked, rubbed to remove their husks, and then dried. White pepper is slightly less warm and spicy than black pepper, and has a drier smell. It is useful in pale soups or sauces when black specks would spoil the appearance.

Green peppercorns are unripe pepper berries, milder than the dried black peppercorns and with a crisp texture. Picked when green, they turn black in a day or two and so are rarely seen fresh, but freeze-dried or canned green peppercorns, preserved in brine, are quite good. Use them in a sauce for lamb, steak, or duck, in pâtés and fish terrines, and with shellfish.

Pink peppercorns (*Schinus terepinthifolius*) Not true pepper but the berries of another tree, these are more subtle than green peppercorns and with little of the hotness associated with pepper. They are much used in the South of France in fish dishes. Preserved in vinegar or water and sold in jars, or freeze-dried, they are quite soft.

Sichuan or Szechwan pepper (*Xanthoxylum piperitum*) The dried red berries of a small shrub, this spice comes from the Sichuan region in China. It has a peculiar delayed reaction: nothing happens when you first bite it, but then it floods your mouth with a hot flavor.

Chili or chile powders and chile (red pepper) flakes are dried and ground or crushed chiles. They are usually red but also black, and vary enormously. The powders can be pungent, mild, tasty, or absolutely red-hot, and only by experience can you know what you are getting. Use chili powder in curry and of course in chili con carne, with beans and chickpeas, and in couscous (although authentically for couscous you should use harissa, a hot Tunisian mixture of crushed dried chiles, ground cumin, and salt). The chili powders that contain spices such as cumin and oregano are made specifically for chili con carne, but pure ground chile pepper is usually preferable. Chile flakes, commonly called crushed red pepper or red pepper flakes, can be used to heat tomato sauces, and will give a lift to many stir-fried and sautéed dishes. They are excellent combined with garlic and anchovies and used to sauce pasta; quickly sautéed slices of pork tenderloin are also splendid with this mixture.

Cayenne pepper is made from ground dried chiles (both pods and seeds), and came originally from Cayenne in French Guiana. The red-orange powder is very hot and rather delicious. Cayenne pepper, or red pepper, is often used in Cajun cooking. It is also used in dishes with "deviled" in their name, such as deviled chicken, in spiced almonds, and in the gravy served with roasted game birds, particularly duck. Cayenne also makes a pretty finish for deviled eggs.

Paprika Although it may be either sweet or hot, paprika by nature has a sweet flavor and is made from sweet red peppers. In Spain and Portugal, it is used in fish stews and potato and vegetable soups and with salt cod, as well as in most of the chorizos and *salsichas* (sausages). But it is in Hungary that paprika really comes into its own, so the best to buy is the original mild Hungarian paprika, described as "noble and sweet," or, for some dishes, the hot version. The combination of sweet paprika and sour cream has the most appetizing delicacy to it, and, although chicken paprikash and goulash may be somewhat overworked dishes, both are wonderful food. Hungarians sometimes use paprika and cayenne in the same dish—in cabbage soup, for example.

White peppercorns

Black peppercorns

Pink peppercorns

Green peppercorns

Sichuan pepper

Chili powder

Chile flakes

Cayenne pepper

Paprika

Mustard

Mustard has been adding its hot spiciness to food for thousands of years—the ancient Egyptians, and the Greeks and Romans used to crunch the seeds between their teeth during meals, and the Romans used mustard to preserve vegetables—their pickled turnips in mustard were the forerunners of our highly seasoned piccalilli.

In the course of time, it was discovered that mustard helps the digestion, and it came to be eaten particularly with pork dishes and with cheese, which was thought to "sit heavy on the stomach." It had a place in home medicine too: hot mustard poultices were frequently applied to relieve aching joints, and sportsmen, when they came home cold and wet from the hunt, used to thrust their feet into a comforting mustard bath to ward off chills.

Mustard as we know it is basically a paste made from the ground seeds of black (*Brassica nigra*), or brown (*B. juncea*), and white mustard (*B. alba*), which is also called yellow mustard. *Nigra* is hot; *alba* is cooler. It is *alba* that, when young, gives us the tender mustard greens to be added to salads, and when mature, yields the seeds that are used whole in pickling.

B. juncea, the brown variety, is less pungent than *nigra*. It is the seed that is usually called for in Indian recipes. And although black mustard seeds were traditionally used in European mustards, they have mostly been replaced today by the brown seeds.

French mustards

The most famous French mustards are those of Dijon, Bordeaux, and Meaux.

In Dijon, mustard center of the world, the mustard is blended with salt, spices, and white wine or verjuice—an acidic juice made from unripe green grapes. Some Dijon mustards rival powerful English mustard in strength, but are a creamy grayish-lemon color rather than yellow and have a more subtle flavor. Other Dijon mustards are milky-pale and delicate rather than sharp. The famous house of Poupon—one of the sights of Dijon—sells dozens of different blends and exports them all over the world.

Most good cooks use Dijon mustard in preference to any other: for vinaigrettes, for mayonnaise (which mustard helps to emulsify), and for the more delicate creamy sauces to go with egg dishes and chicken or fish. Generally, when mustard is called for in a recipe it is safe to use a strong Dijon, such as Grey Poupon.

Blended with unfermented red wine, Bordeaux mustard is strong, dark brown, and both more acid and more aromatic than that of Dijon. It is unsurpassed for eating with steak, complementing rather than overpowering the flavor of the meat.

Moutarde de Meaux is an interesting mixture of ground and half-ground seeds, with a grainy texture and an attractive musty taste. It is pleasantly hot, and was once described by Brillat-Savarin—the eighteenth-century French gastronome—as "the gourmet's mustard." It comes in widemouthed stoneware jars, their corks secured by sealing wax. It is made to a formula that has been a closely guarded secret since 1760, when it was handed by the abbots of Meaux to the Pommery family, of Champagne fame. The most superior of the coarse-grained mustards, with a taste all its own, it is best appreciated when eaten with humble food—bacon, sausages, and cold meats.

There are, of course, a thousand other French mustards: sometimes tarragon is added, or a mixture of fresh herbs (which produce a pleasant-tasting but rather alarming-looking result). There is a mustard containing tomato purée, making a red-brown mustard that is designed to go with hamburgers; and a mustard that is basically mild, but with the bite of crushed green peppercorns, called *moutarde au poivre vert*.

American mustards

Owing to the wide range of national tastes, every kind of mustard, plain and spiced, can be found in American supermarkets. What is thought of as the true American mustard, however, is yellow (it's colored with turmeric), mild, and sweet, and has a consistency rather more like a thick sauce than a French mustard. It is made from yellow mustard seeds and is flavored with sugar, vinegar, or white wine—which accounts for its cool character and for the fact that it can be applied in such quantities to hot dogs and be lavished on that other all-American specialty, the hamburger. (It's sometimes referred to as "ballpark mustard.")

This mustard can be used when making homemade mayonnaise, not only to speed up the emulsion of the egg yolks and the oil but also to give the mayonnaise a sweetish mustard flavor. Such mayonnaises are good in egg, potato, and tunafish salads.

A German-style mustard, which is brown, sweet-sour, and spicy, is also very popular, particularly on ham sandwiches. Among the many other flavored mustards on the grocery store shelves are hot, spicy Creole mustard, and sweet, mild honey mustard.

English mustard

This dry mustard is a hot yellow in color and its taste is biting and hot; it is good with plain home-cooked food. For its texture, we owe a debt to an eighteenth-century housewife from Durham, who

Mustard seeds: Brassica alba

Mustard seeds: Brassica nigra

Dijon mustard

Dijon mustard with tarragon

Moutarde de Meaux

Bordeaux mustard

French mustard with tomato

German mustard with herbs

decided to grind and sift her mustard seeds rather than pound them. She took her new "mustard flour" to London, where it was championed by King George I, and commercial production followed. Mr. Colman began milling his mustard powder in 1814.

Today you can buy Colman's mustard, the best-known powdered mustard, in its powdered form or—more convenient but perhaps not as good—prepared. A straightforward blend of ground and sifted seeds, wheat flour, and spices, it contains no wine or vinegar to lessen the natural impact of the seeds.

To mix "common" hot English mustard, simply add cold water to the powder, in equal quantities—the water must never be hot, or it will release bitter oils that spoil the taste. To be at its best, the mustard should be freshly prepared in a small quantity. Allow it to stand, well covered, for half an hour before use, to develop its full flavor and heat. For milder mustard, mix 1 teaspoon each of milk and cream and a pinch of sugar, with 2 teaspoons of mustard powder and water. To make a thick mustard, with a more delicate flavor and a biting aftertaste, moisten the powder with wine vinegar, grape or apple juice, or ale or claret.

Common English mustard is perfect with roast beef, its classic partner, as well as with other plain roast meats, ham, English pork pie, and beef or pork sausages. It goes well with Cheddar cheese (especially in Welsh rarebit), and it is the best mustard to use when making strong mustard sauce to go with richly flavored oily fish such as herring or mackerel. But simmered for any length of time in dishes that call for mustard, even English mustard loses some of its taste and piquancy, and in fact mustard sauces of all types benefit from being given a boost of a little more mustard shortly before the end of cooking.

German mustards

Made from a blend of strong mustard flour and vinegar, German mustard—*senf*—generally combines pungency with aroma, and comes halfway between the earthy, aromatic flavor of Bordeaux mustard and that of hot, sharp English mustard. Stronger palates go for mustard that is *scharf* or *extra scharf*—hot or extra-hot.

A lot of mustard is consumed in Germany: it is specifically designed to be eaten with the profusion of sausages of the frankfurter type—knackwurst, bockwurst, and of course with frankfurters themselves. So it is not surprising that the Bavarians and other southern Germans, whose pale local sausage is made of veal and called weisswurst, have a mild, pale mustard to go with it: coarse-grained and sweet, it is just right for this bland sausage, which is eaten fried to a golden color. The Rhineland favors a herb mustard, thought to be excellent with lamb.

Mustard preserves

Mostarda di frutta, mostarda di cremona This is an Italian confection of fruits—figs and cherries, and chunks of pears, lemons, and peaches—candied in a syrup containing mustard oil. Enjoyed from about the sixteenth century on, it is still eaten, like jam, by the spoonful on bread. Its delicate, strange, sweet-sharp flavor makes it an interesting relish for cold meats, particularly ham, boiled beef, and zampone (stuffed pig's foot that is a New Year's Eve specialty). Look for *mostarda di frutta* in gourmet shops and Italian markets. *Bollito misto*—mixed boiled chicken, ham, sausage, and beef—can be served with *mostarda* on the side.
Mostarda di Voghera Even more special is a *mostarda* of whole, translucent pale pears, complete with their stems, in a jar that looks as if it might float off the table; the taste is ethereal too. Eat them with game, particularly roasted venison,

and with the same meats as *mostarda di frutta*. This also comes as a yellow-brown mush—a less extravagant version. It may sometimes be found in gourmet shops.
Piccalilli is a strong, mustardy pickled relish with a crunch to it. It contains cauliflower among other things, including onions, chiles, ginger, and plenty of turmeric to color it a gorgeous bright yellow. Eaten with ham and cold meats, it is very refreshing, cutting the fattiness of the meat.

Making your own mustard

Experimenting with your own blends can produce interesting results. To grind the seeds, use a small coffee grinder (clean it very well after use) or a spice grinder—or, for a coarser mixture, simply pound the seeds in a mortar.

The first time you make your own mustard, use equal amounts of black and yellow seeds and, if necessary, gradually alter the balance according to taste. (Black mustard seeds are available in Indian and Asian markets; if you can't find them, substitute the brown seeds, available in specialty markets.) Moisten the ground mustard with water until just saturated, then add white wine vinegar, salt, and the flavorings of your choice—tarragon, green peppercorns, horseradish, honey, etc.—and leave to ferment for several days. A little olive oil takes the edge off a hot mixture. Store in a tightly sealed jar, in the refrigerator.

To enjoy all mustards at their best, store them in the refrigerator, and keep them for no longer than 6 months.

Hot German mustard

Bavarian mustard

American mild mustard

American spicy brown mustard

Green peppercorn mustard

Mostarda di frutta

Prepared English mustard

English mustard powder

Vinegar

Vinaigre, the French word for vinegar, means sour wine, and this is what wine vinegar is, being produced by an acid fermentation of fresh wine. By the same process, cider vinegar is made from cider, malt vinegar from malted barley, and Chinese and Japanese vinegars from fermented rice.

"The grateful acid," as vinegar was called in the seventeenth century, has had its abuses. In England, in Elizabethan days, salads were served dressed in malt vinegar—a condiment much loved by the British—without benefit of either salt or oil. And in America, until quite recently, the only vinegar found in the kitchen might well have been harsh distilled white vinegar. But things have improved. Although vinegary pickles and relishes still go well with rich foods such as cold roast pork, the biting character of vinegar has been tempered—by the increased use of wine vinegar, which is an altogether milder, subtler, and more flavorful affair than distilled vinegar, by reducing the quantity of vinegar classically used in such things as salad dressings and increasing the proportion of oil, and sometimes— which is rather a pity—by the increased use of sugar in these recipes.

Apart from its role in salad dressings, vinegar can be used instead of lemon juice in mayonnaise, hollandaise, and béarnaise, and is essential in horseradish and fresh mint sauces. It is used in countless marinades for meat, poultry, and game, and a little vinegar can improve the flavor of stews and other dishes—a dash of vinegar sometimes works wonders with a dull sauce or gravy. A little vinegar in the water when steaming food stops the pan from discoloring—but vinegar is corrosive, so when cooking food that includes vinegar, use pans of stainless steel, glass, or earthenware, or enameled ones.

Good vinegars are always worth their price. Cheap vinegars are usually inferior and frequently synthetic.

Wine vinegar The best wine vinegar is produced by a slow, gentle process that allows it to mature naturally. The French wine vinegars from Orléans are expensive but still probably the best and the purest. It is encouraging that a few specialized producers in the United States are making vinegar using the Orléans method (also called the slow method). Wine vinegar can be red or white and is sometimes very powerful, but it has a delicious flavor.

If you are offered a "vinegar mother," accept it with alacrity. It is a fungus that lives in wine and will turn your left-over wine into excellent vinegar. Keep this "mother" in a warm place in an earthenware jar with a loose-fitting lid, so that air can get in, and add wine as often as you have it to spare. If it is not very active, feed it a large dose of cheap wine (avoid the cheapest jug wines) and a pinch of sugar.

When the wine vinegar smells sharp and strongly acetic, decant it carefully into a bottle and let it stand for a month to mature and mellow before using it. Red wine seems to produce the best-flavored vinegar, but white is more useful in mayonnaise.

Cider vinegar Apple cider vinegar has been touted as a cure for all ills, from indigestion to hair loss. As a seasoning, it has a strong, distinctive taste of cider and in sharpness is midway between wine vinegar and malt vinegar. Use it

White wine vinegar

Red wine vinegar

Balsamic vinegar

Sherry vinegar

Raspberry vinegar

when making pickles and fruit chutneys, especially those with apples in them, and for a refreshing vinaigrette to use with fresh tomatoes.

Malt vinegar Brewed from malted barley, malt vinegar is colored with caramel to varying shades of brown. The color is no longer an indication of the strength of the vinegar—although originally a deeper color probably did mean a well-matured vinegar, since it was kept in oak barrels that colored the clear vinegar as it aged.

The best malt vinegar, with an acetic acid content of at least 5 percent, is excellent for pickling, which needs a strong vinegar. This is also the vinegar always served with fish and chips.

Distilled vinegar Being colorless, this is often simply labeled white vinegar. It is the vinegar to use for pickling onions and for any pickling when color is important.

Sherry vinegar A delicious vinegar made from sweet sherry, this varies in strength of flavor—a good-quality one is worth its place in the kitchen and can be used instead of balsamic vinegar for a slightly drier result. Sherry vinegar used with an equal amount of lemon juice in a vinaigrette gives it a very nutty taste, almost like walnut oil. French chefs sometimes use sherry vinegar in the classic chicken dish *poulet au vinaigre*. The best sherry vinegars come from Spain.

Balsamic vinegar—*aceto balsamico*—is a traditional farm-made vinegar from the Modena region of Italy. It is made from white wine must (the unfermented juice from pressed grapes), which is boiled until it is thick and then matured in barrels. Each year for 5 years, as it reduces in volume by evaporation, it is moved to a smaller barrel made from a different wood: oak, chestnut, mulberry, ash, and cherry are favorites. Then it may be left to age for a further 5 years, or for as many as 50 years. Sweet, dark brown, highly concentrated, and mellow, it was traditionally used sparingly, and often for medicinal purposes. It is exquisite on cold vegetables, both cooked and raw, on fish and shellfish, and on raw steak *carpaccio*. Look out for *Aceto Balsamico di Modena Tradizionale*, as there are many imitations.

Rice vinegar features in Japanese and Southeast-Asian cooking, where its sweet, delicate flavor is used in *sushi* rice. In China, rice vinegar may be "black," with a rich, smoky, complex flavor; clear pale red, when it is slightly tart; or white and mild—the vinegar for sweet-and-sour dishes. Black vinegar may also be made from grains, such as wheat, millet, or sorghum. There is also a sweet rice vinegar that is dark, thick, and aromatic.

Flavored vinegars Wine vinegar can be flavored by putting fresh herbs—tarragon, basil, mint, or thyme, for example—into a jar, filling it with vinegar, and then keeping it in a fairly warm place for a week, giving the jar an occasional shake. Then decant the vinegar, keeping a token sprig of herb to show what's what. Three herb sprigs to a scant quart of wine vinegar will be ample. Fruits such as raspberries can be used to flavor vinegar in the same way.

To make garlic vinegar, crush the garlic and then leave it in the vinegar for 24 hours. For a really good chile vinegar, steep the dried chiles for 10 days, and give the jar a daily shake.

Tarragon vinegar is excellent for hollandaise. Use chile vinegar with shellfish, and garlic vinegar for salad dressings when sharp flavors such as anchovies and capers are used.

Tarragon vinegar   Rice vinegar   Cider vinegar   Distilled vinegar   Malt vinegar

Sauces, Flavorings, and Colorings

There is no dispute that sauces, relishes, and other condiments are best made at home, although in a busy world it is often not possible to brew great batches of ketchup, to crack the secret formula of Worcestershire sauce, or to find the time to make a zesty tomatillo salsa.

Sauces, ketchups, and pastes

Some store-bought sauces have been able to withstand the test of time and changing tastes, and are to be found in almost every kitchen.

Tomato ketchup must head the list. Properly made, it is thick and almost chunky in appearance. It should be bright red and contain no artificial coloring. Homemade ketchup is delicious, but only viable if you grow your own tomatoes. We tend to think of ketchup as solely a tomato condiment, but walnut and mushroom ketchups were once very popular. Even fruits such as peaches can be made into ketchup.

Salsa A wide range of bottled salsas can be found in any grocery store. Larger supermarkets often carry fresh salsas as well, and specialty shops may offer a mind-boggling array of salsas.

Tomato paste is used in cooking rather than at the table and is highly concentrated—a tablespoonful will improve the taste and texture of Mediterranean casseroles and provide melting juices for Greek braised lamb.

Worcestershire sauce There is only one true variety, which is of Indian origin, although there are many similar concoctions, including bottled steak sauces. The real thing is hot, spicy, and vinegary and contains tamarind, molasses, sugar, anchovies, garlic, salt, and other natural flavors. This sauce, besides adding its own ineffable taste, heightens the flavor of whatever is being cooked. It is essential for Bloody Mary.

Chile or chili sauce is thick and bright red and can vary considerably in hotness. This Asian condiment also goes under the names Sichuan chile sauce and, in Malaysia, sambal oelek. Use it sparingly in stews and discreetly as a dip for Chinese and Southeast-Asian food or spareribs.

Chile or chili paste is used in Chinese cooking. Most of these red pastes are quite hot; some include soybeans or black beans.

Tabasco sauce is an exceedingly hot, peppery liquid made from vinegar, red chiles, and salt. The label suggests a multitude of uses: soup, gravy, breakfast eggs, even milk, and insists "no seafood to be eaten without it." It also adds its heat to Creole and Cajun cookery. There is also now a jalapeño Tabasco sauce, but the original is still the favorite. There are dozens of other hot sauces on the market—some good, some less so.

Hoisin sauce This anise-flavored sweet and spicy red-brown sauce is, like soy sauce, soybean-based. The texture varies from a thick, creamy sludge to a sauce that can be poured, and the flavor is inclined to be overpowering, containing as it does garlic, chiles, and several spices. However, it is served to advantage, mixed with sugar and sesame oil, with Peking duck, when it is spread over the pancakes before the cucumber, scallions, and shredded duck are placed on top.

Plum sauce Thick and sweet-tart, this is made from plums preserved with chiles, ginger, vinegar, sugar, and spices. Also called duck sauce, it is a popular ingredient in Chinese cookery.

Fish sauce This is made by fermenting barrels of small fish (often anchovies) in brine for several months under the tropical sun. The end result is a strange-smelling, salty brown liquid, highly nutritious, which is a major element of the cooking of Southeast Asia. It is called *nam pla* in Thailand and *nuoc nam* or *nuoc cham* in Vietnam and Laos. Fish sauce is mixed with garlic, lime juice, sugar, and chile oil to make a wonderful dipping sauce for fried foods or dumplings. It can be added to chopped tomatoes together with red onion, vinegar, and plenty of fresh cilantro, to make a salsa to serve with braised chicken and pork.

Anchovy paste comes in tubes and is good in a green herb sauce for fish. It is also nice in canapés or on buttered toast.

Shrimp paste (*terasi*, *kapee*, or *blachan*) is a common general flavoring in Asian cookery. It is pungent and salty, so use it sparingly. Chinese shrimp paste is the consistency of a thick sauce; the Southeast-Asian version comes either fresh, in jars and bottles, or dried in cakes. Before using the dried paste, bake it, wrapped in foil, then crumble it. Shrimp paste keeps well, but store it well wrapped because of its pungent odor.

Oyster sauce is a flavoring used a great deal by the Chinese. It is a thick brown sauce made with oysters cooked in soy sauce and brine.

Tahini This is a Middle Eastern, Turkish, and Greek staple. A thick, oily beige paste made from ground toasted sesame seeds, tahini resembles peanut butter in texture, being rich and dense. It forms the basis of several delicious *mezze*, such as hummus, a mixture of cooked chickpeas, tahini, lemon juice, and olive oil, puréed and eaten with pita bread.

Wasabi or Japanese horseradish Unrelated to our horseradish, despite its popular name, wasabi root, grated or powdered, makes the eye-watering accompaniment that gives *sushi* and *sashimi* such a fresh lift. Wasabi powder, available in Japanese and specialty markets, is mixed with water to make the familiar stiff paste. Wasabi paste is also sold, in tubes, but the fresh root is only found in Japan.

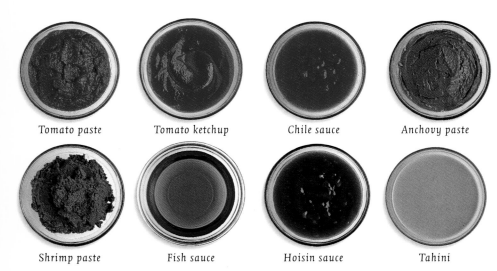

Tomato paste   Tomato ketchup   Chile sauce   Anchovy paste

Shrimp paste   Fish sauce   Hoisin sauce   Tahini

Soy sauce

True soy sauce is a thin liquid distilled from a naturally fermented mixture of soybeans, wheat or barley flour, and water. Most commercially prepared brands are chemically fermented from defatted soybean pulp. When selecting soy sauce, shake the bottle vigorously until bubbles form at the top. Naturally fermented soy will form a thick, foamy head that takes quite a while to disperse.

Good soy sauce has a rich aroma and a flavor both salty and pungent. It heightens the flavor of whatever is being eaten with it. In China and Japan, it is a staple condiment, used extensively in cooking and at the table in place of salt. In Western cooking, it has become a common ingredient in marinades and barbecue sauces.

Tamari is pure, naturally fermented soy sauce complete with nutritious oils and free from coloring and flavorings.

Light soy sauce is sometimes labeled "superior soy," and is salty, while **dark soy sauce** is thick and sweet. Use light soy for cooking, and dark for dipping.

Miso is a thickened paste made from soybeans, and tastes much like soy sauce. It is used in Asian cooking to make soups and to enrich sauces.

Teriyaki marinade or sauce can be bought prepared in bottles, and is a mix of soy sauce, sugar, ginger, and spices.

Angostura bitters

Originally created as a remedy for fever, as they contain quinine, Angostura bitters are clove-scented, spiced, and pink in color. Found more often at the bar than in the kitchen, this bitter liquid can do a great deal more than flavor Champagne cocktails. In cooking, it makes a good contribution to several sauces, particularly mustard sauce and tarragon sauce.

Capers

These little green flower buds, tasting of goats and the sea, are both a seasoning and a condiment. They are an essential part of Italian and Provençal cooking. Use capers in any sharp sauce to be eaten with fish, such as the Italian herb sauce, or with "black" butter and lemon juice in the classic sauce for skate. Steak tartare would be unthinkable without its caper seasoning. The buds imported from Spain are usually called caperberries.

Chutneys, pickles, and relishes

Chutneys (the Indian word *chatni* means literally "to lick something in small amounts") form an important part of every meal in India and accompany most basic curries. We are used to seeing them in jars, but they are often freshly made, from a wide range of ingredients. One of the most popular is mango chutney, which comes in several different guises, some hot, some sweet, but all made from green, unripe mangoes. A chutney that takes just 10 minutes to make consists of green mangoes, onion, hot green chiles, fresh cilantro, and salt, all blended together with a little water to make a smooth paste.

Pickles are made from vegetables and fruits—just one kind or a mixture—preserved in a seasoned and often highly spiced vinegar. Like chutneys, they are mainly eaten as a condiment. Vegetables commonly pickled include cucumbers, peppers, beets, onions, and red cabbage. Other foods that are pickled are ginger and radishes (both popular in Japan), walnuts (in Britain), and herring (especially in Scandinavia and the United States); watermelon rind is a popular pickle in the American South.

Relish is the term often used for pickles made from chopped vegetables and/or fruit. Because of their texture, relishes are ideal in sandwiches.

Flavoring extracts

These volatile substances are the essential oils extracted from flowers, nuts, fruits, and herbs, mixed with alcohol—vanilla, orange extract, almond extract, peppermint extract, and so on. There are, of course, endless artificial flavorings that are cheaper than the true extracts, but these imitation extracts have little of the flavor of the real thing and are best avoided. Even more intense are citrus and herb oils, such as lemon oil and oil of peppermint, which can be used in candy making and some baking; these are usually available only at specialty shops or through mail-order sources.

Colorings

In countries where the sun shines at its brightest—in Sicily, for example, and southern Italy, India, and also South America—food tends to be extravagantly brightly colored.

Shocking pink and silver, bright orange and magenta, and glaring yellow and green make the dinner table look like a carnival and the food rather exotic to most of us. Ideally these hues are achieved with vegetable colorings, but even in these locales food may be artificially colored with chemicals that are potentially harmful.

Cooks at home can avoid artificial colorings: forget about the garish chemical food colorings and gravy brownings and use the gentler natural colorings. Use saffron or annatto for a beautiful golden yellow and turmeric for a brighter, harsher yellow; onion skins for golden broths; spinach juice or chopped herbs for green sauces and mayonnaise; beet juice for a ruby-colored soup; and tomato paste for healthy reddish-brown stews or delicately pink sauces for shellfish.

Capers Fruit relish Mango chutney

Pickled walnuts Pickled radish Wasabi powder

Cooking with Wine and Spirits

In a good restaurant kitchen there will be, within easy reach of the bubbling and simmering pots and pans, a lineup of interesting bottles of wines, fortified wines, and *eaux-de-vie*. This alcohol supply is not for fortifying the cooks but to be used judiciously as an ingredient in cooking—an ingredient as vital as butter, flour, salt, pepper, or eggs.

There is no reason why the home cook should not emulate the professional here. Use leftover wine for cooking, and raid the liquor cabinet or buy small bottles of sherry, port, rum, vermouth, brandy, and the more exotic spirits. Do not make false economies—"cooking" sherry, cheap brandy, and wine-flavored extracts will defeat the purpose, which is not to swamp food in alcohol (which evaporates in cooking anyway) but to add flavor. If a wine or spirit is too awful to drink, then it is too awful to cook with.

Wine is an important ingredient in marinades. It impregnates food with its flavor, and it will soften the fibers of meat and draw out the juices from fruit. Wines for cooking should, in general, be young and dry. It is easy enough to find a reasonably priced red, but cheap white wines do tend to sourness—a light French vermouth such as Noilly Prat is an excellent substitute. Cooking with Champagne may seem extravagant, but

often a glass or two is all that is required to make a superlative sauce for sole or scallops, or an unforgettable sorbet.

Liqueurs and *eaux-de-vie* (clear fruit brandies or spirits) will turn a simple dish of fruit into a deliciously alcoholic dessert worthy of any occasion. Apart from the fact that it is fun, flaming or *flambéing* crêpes Suzette or an elegant dessert can add to the dish. The purpose of pouring spirits over food and igniting it is, of course, to flavor the food—but also to lose the raw taste of the straight alcohol.

Liqueurs and *eaux-de-vie* distilled from fruit or flavored with it have an obvious affinity with the fruit from which they were made—hence oranges in Grand Marnier—and they share with the parent fruit affinities with certain foods—hence pork cooked with Calvados, the dry French apple brandy. The same logic applies to liqueurs flavored with herbs and essences.

Rice wines are enjoyed in Japan and China. Crystal-clear colorless sake is used in Japanese cooking to remove strong flavors and enhance delicate ones. The Japanese like the lightness of vegetables that are cooked with sake, and also use it in marinades for chicken and other meats. In one recipe, the chicken is pricked all over and marinated in sake, soy sauce, and salt for 20 minutes before being steamed with ginger and scallions. (Although sake

is thought of as a wine, this is not really accurate, because the rice is boiled and yeast is then added, in a method more akin to brewing than wine making.)

Mirin, a sweet, lustrous, amber-colored Japanese rice wine, contains 10 percent alcohol and a huge 40 percent sugar. It is used as a seasoning for *sushi* and, together with dark soy sauce, as an ingredient in marinades and for basting grilled foods such as *teriyaki*, when it forms a sticky golden glaze.

Shaoxing, a very clear yellow wine, is more like a sherry in color and flavor than sake. This Chinese wine has been made for thousands of years and is always aged before drinking. It is traditional to buy it when a daughter is born, and to keep it to celebrate her coming-of-age at 15 and her wedding. It is used in stir-fried dishes to moisten the ingredients and in the marinades for cuttlefish and for *char-siu* pork. When drunk, it is served warm, as sake often is.

Beers and ales have their place in the kitchen too. The dry taste of beer makes an interesting addition to a soup or a stew, fruity hard cider complements pork and rabbit, and bittersweet English stout is a good addition to beef stews.

These charts are not intended to be exhaustive lists—merely a guide to inspire you to tip the right bottle into the dish that will benefit from the added flavor.

Liqueurs/*Eaux-de-vie*	Made from	Uses
Advocaat	Eggs and brandy	Whip into cream for trifles and rich custards
Apricot brandy	Apricots	Flame over roast chicken; use to soak dried apricots
Cointreau, Curaçao, Grand Marnier	The rind of bitter oranges, oranges	Chicken, duck; lemon soufflé, chocolate mousse, sweet omelets, crêpes, fruit salads; apples, pears, figs, strawberries, oranges
Crème de cassis	Black currants	Pour over ice cream; use in sorbets
Amaretto, crème d'amandes	Almonds and apricot kernels	Cookies, icings, cakes, tiramisù
Crème de cacao	Chocolate flavored with vanilla	Ice cream, mousses, cakes
Calvados	Apples	Pheasant and other game birds; pork and veal dishes; cooked apple desserts
Maraschino (sweet), Kirsch (dry)	Cherries	Black Forest cake, fruit compotes, clafoutis; cheese fondue; fruit salad; strawberries, pineapple, cherries, figs, peaches, apples
Izarra	Herbs and mimosa honey	Sweet fruity desserts
Kahlúa; Tía Maria; Bailey's	Coffee; coffee and cream	Cakes, ice creams, other desserts
Kümmel	Caraway, cumin, and fennel	Cabbage, sauerkraut
Crème de menthe	Peppermint	Pour over chocolate ice cream; use in chocolate milk shakes and puddings
Pernod, Anis, Pastis	Anise	Trout, sea bass, striped mullet; fennel; pork
Mirabelle, Slivovitz, plum brandy	Yellow plums, plums	Plum desserts, compotes
Southern Comfort	Bourbon flavored with peaches	Peach desserts
Poire Williams', eau-de-vie de poire	Pears	Pear desserts
Eau-de-vie de fraise, de framboise, de pêche	Strawberries, raspberries, peaches	Strawberries, raspberries, melon; sorbets

Wines and Spirits	Soup	Fish and shellfish		Poultry	Game	Meat	Vegetables	Sauces	Fruit and desserts	Cheese and eggs
Red wine	Cherry	Salmon, mackerel, sole		Chicken, duck, goose, squab	Duck, pheasant, squab, venison; marinades for all game	Beef stews, steaks and braises; lamb, liver, oxtail, pork, veal; marinades for all cuts of beef	Broccoli, leeks, red cabbage	Gravy (meat); anything à la bordelaise (in red wine sauce), such as steak, etc.	Cherries, peaches, pears, prunes, raspberries, strawberries	Poached eggs
White wine (or substitute dry vermouth or hard cider)	Crab and lobster bisque, strawberry	Haddock, salmon, sole, trout, turbot, herring, mackerel	Clams, lobster, mussels, scallops, shrimp	Pâtés; chicken, duck, squab	Pâtés; duck, squab, rabbit	Pâtés; beef stews; ham, lamb, liver, pork, veal, sweetbreads, sausages	Artichoke bottoms, carrots, cauliflower, green beans, leeks, sauerkraut	Court-bouillon; sauces for fish, poultry, vegetables	Peaches, raspberries; sorbet	Fondue, sabayon
Rosé wine	Shrimp	Salmon		Chicken						
Champagne		Salmon, sole, turbot	Oysters	Chicken		Ham, sweetbreads		Sauces for fish, poultry, oysters	Peaches, raspberries, strawberries; sorbet	
Sherry	Asparagus, tomato, chicken consommé, game consommé	Salmon, any firm-fleshed white fish; lobster		Pâtés; chicken, chicken livers, duck, turkey; foie gras	Pâtés; pheasant	Pâtés; beef, veal	Stir-fried vegetables; avocado	Applesauce; gravy (meat), sauce for poultry, seafood sauces	Apricots, oranges, fruitcake, trifle	Cheese spread, Welsh rarebit; sabayon, zabaglione
Port	Duck	Scallops		Duck	Duck, rabbit		Mushrooms	Applesauce	Cherries, melon, peaches, plums, prunes, strawberries	
Madeira	Consommé	Crab, lobster		Pâtés; chicken, duck	Pâtés; quail	Pâtés; veal		Sauce for veal	Cakes, tea breads	
Marsala (dry)				Chicken livers		Veal scallops		Sauce for sweetbreads	Pears	Zabaglione
Vermouth (dry)		Sole				Pork		Sauce for fish		
Brandy	All bisques	Sole; all shellfish, especially lobster		Pâtés; chicken, chicken livers, duck, squab	Pâtés; quail, rabbit, venison, partridge	Pâtés; beef stews and steaks, lamb	Mushrooms	Brandy butter, brandy cream, lobster sauce	Apricots, cherries, oranges, peaches; fruitcake, mince pies	Custard
Rum		Oysters						Rum butter	Apple desserts, baked apples, baked bananas, fruit compotes, ice cream, mixed berries, babas au rhum, anything flambéed; oranges	Omelets, soufflés
Whisky (scotch) and whiskey (bourbon, rye)		Lobster						Sauce for lobster	Mincemeat pie, trifle, bourbon balls	
Gin					Quail	Venison, pork				

Honey, Syrups, Sugars, and Chocolate

Man was probably born with a sweet tooth. Wild fruits and honey taken from wild bees provided the first sweet foods, and since then the craving for sweet things has continued unabated.

Obviously, any sensible household is now aware that it is unwise to eat too many sweet things, but sweeteners do have an important part to play in the kitchen. As seasonings and preservatives, they have always been as important as salt to the cook. There are many foods too bitter, like cocoa; too sour, like lemons and sour cherries; too acid, like some plums and rhubarb; or too bland, like applesauce, to be enjoyable without added sweeteners.

Without sugar it would not be possible to preserve strawberries and raspberries as jam, and there would be no breakfast marmalade. By using honey, syrups, and sugars in their original roles, and cutting down on highly sweetened convenience and other manufactured foods and drinks, it is possible to enjoy sweet things without undue concern.

HONEY

Like all natural things, honey can vary enormously. It can be runny, or gritty, or so stiff that you can hardly dig it out of the jar. It can vary in color from darkest amber to almost white. Connoisseurs look out for a honey with a clean flavor, with no undertones of bitterness.

For a single pot of honey, bees have to visit myriad flowers, and the honey's taste, color, and runniness depend on the sort of flowers they choose. Normally, the bees' main diet will be written on the label—clover, lavender, heather, and so on.

Generally, the paler honeys, gathered from meadow flowers such as clover, have a mild, clean, delicate flavor. Orange blossom honey from California has its own distinctive flavor, and heather honey is light golden with an aromatic tang to it. Other honeys, such as lavender from Provence or the dark Greek Hymettus honeys, have heavily scented flavors. Although not the finest, blended honeys are reliable.

Clover honey is best for all-round cooking and eating. If you bake yeast breads or rolls sweetened with honey, note that the presence of honey will slightly lengthens the rising time. If you substitute honey for sugar in any recipe, remember that honey is much sweeter than sugar, so you need less of it. Frozen yogurt and ice creams that are made with honey will usually have a softer consistency than those sweetened with sugar, because the freezing point of honey is lower.

Honeycombs, or comb honey, give us the honey sealed in the cells with a capping of wax (scoop horizontally, so that the honey does not run out); chunk-style honey includes pieces of the comb bottled in liquid honey. Clear, runny honeys have usually been heat-treated to prevent them from crystallizing—which most honeys will do naturally within a few weeks of being taken out of the comb. If your honey does begin to crystallize, loosen or remove the top and set the jar in hot water (no hotter than 160°F) until it reliquifies. Creamed or whipped honeys should be smooth and fine-grained, with no coarse crystals.

SYRUPS

Some syrups are made by God, others are made by man.

Maple syrup is among the former, and is the best known and most delicious: the grades generally considered to be among the best are light in color and crystal-clear and come from the maples of Vermont. The clear, thin sap tapped from the trunks of the maple trees is boiled for hours to reduce it to the syrup that goes onto hot buttered waffles and pancakes, and over ice cream. There are also various maple-flavored syrups on the market, less pure, less fragrant, and less expensive. Maple sugar is produced by boiling the syrup until most of the liquid has evaporated. Much sweeter than ordinary granulated sugar, it is used to make the candies sold all over New England.

Palm syrup Another natural syrup, this is the sap of date palms (which also gives us the sugar known as jaggery). Very dark and extremely sticky, it can be bought in Asian grocery stores, and often features in Indian recipes.

Corn syrup is produced from corn. It can be light or dark (the dark syrup tastes stronger), and is used in baking and candy making.

Golden syrup is a byproduct of sugar refining that has been through its own refining process. It can be used in cakes and other desserts, and as a substitute for corn syrup in most recipes. It is less sweet than sugar, so when it is used in baking, sugar is usually added. It can be useful when making such things as brandy snaps, since it is not as granular as sugar when heated.

Sorghum syrup, molasses This comes from the sorghum plant, which grows throughout the American South. Sweet and thick, it is used like molasses and as a pancake syrup. A rich source of vitamins and minerals, it can be found in health food stores.

Honeycomb

Clear clover honey

Creamed clover honey

Orange blossom honey

Hymettus honey

Scottish heather honey

Molasses This dark, heavy syrup is a good friend to the cook. Far less sweet than honey, it goes into gingerbreads and hefty fruitcakes and into such traditional dishes as Boston baked beans and Indian pudding. A byproduct of sugar refining, molasses comes light and dark—the darker the molasses, the less sugar it contains. Molasses can be sulfured or unsulfured; unsulfured has a somewhat richer flavor and a lighter color.

Being slightly bitter, molasses should be used in smallish amounts for the best flavor. It is much more nutritious than sugar. Britain's black treacle is a molasses-like syrup, but it contains more sugar and is sweeter than molasses.

SUGAR

Sugar first started to replace honey as a sweetener in European kitchens in medieval times, although it was being used in China and India over two thousand years ago. It was introduced into the Americas by Columbus, and it was the first sugar plantations that formed the basis for the slave trade.

While the natural brown sugars still bring us some of the flavor and goodness of the sugarcane from which they come, the white sugars contain no proteins, no minerals, and no vitamins—simply instant energy. For the cook, sugar, used discriminatingly, is an indispensable ally.

Brown sugar

The natural brown sugars come from raw sugarcane, and if you like the warm taste of molasses that still clings to them, you can use them all the time. Any "raw" brown sugar sold in the United States has been purified and cleaned, a process that also removes some of the flavor and nutrients. Being moist, brown sugar has a tendency to harden in the bag or box, but if covered with a damp cloth for a few hours, it softens up again.

Light and dark brown sugar The ordinary brown sugars used so much in baking are simply fully refined white sugar combined with molasses. Dark brown sugar, which has a greater proportion of molasses added, has a somewhat deeper flavor than the light.

Muscovado sugar is sometimes also called Barbados sugar. It is soft, fine-grained, and very moist. It is good in dark, rich fruitcakes and in desserts made with dried fruit, gingerbread,

and homemade toffee. Molasses sugar, popular in Britain, is similar to dark muscovado and can be used in the same ways. Pale muscovado sugar is excellent for making crunchy toppings, and in pickles and chutneys.

Demerara is gritty, with golden crystals; it is crystallized from partly refined sugar syrup and contains 2 percent molasses. It can be used in the same ways as pale muscovado sugar. Although, like honey, demerara slightly retards the action of yeast in the early stages of rising, it is particularly useful in spiced breads and other yeasted baked goods, giving them a creamy color and a nice flavor.

Turbinado is refined one stage beyond demerara and lighter in color. It can be used in recipes that call for demerara.

White sugar

All white sugars are equally sweet, but the finer the sugar, the faster it dissolves and the sweeter it seems. There is one thing that white sugars have in common: they taste sweeter when hot than when cool. This is why ice cream mixtures, before freezing, need to taste almost too sweet, and why recipes for warm desserts specify, as a rule, less sugar than for cold ones.

Granulated or white sugar is a highly refined white crystal sugar, primarily made from sugarcane but sometimes from sugar beets (both are pure sucrose). If there is such a thing as an all-purpose

sugar, this is it, used in all sorts of desserts and candies, cooking, and in coffee and tea. Use it, too, to make your own vanilla sugar by sticking a vanilla bean or two into a large jar of sugar and leaving it for at least two weeks. Make cinnamon-scented sugar—good on pancakes, French toast, and even creamy fresh dessert cheese—in the same way, substituting two cinnamon sticks for the vanilla beans. Or try rosemary sugar: clean and dry sprigs of rosemary, put them in the sugar, and shake well; after 24 hours, shake again, and then leave for a week. This unusual sugar is good in puddings and other creamy desserts.

Lump sugar Once hacked from cones of sugar, this is now granulated sugar pressed into cubes to use in coffee or tea.

Superfine sugar is a smaller-grained crystal. It is very fine and dissolves easily: use it when cooking soft fruit and in meringues, in custards or mousses, and, in fact, whenever it is desirable for the sugar to dissolve before the mixture starts cooking. Because it dissolves so quickly, it is often used to sweeten iced tea and other cold drinks, and it is the best sugar to use in sorbets made with uncooked fruit purées.

Confectioners' or powdered sugar tastes the sweetest of all and dissolves the fastest. It is known as icing sugar in Britain, and, of course, there are countless icings made with confectioners' sugar.

Light corn syrup

Dark corn syrup

Golden syrup

Maple syrup

Molasses

In the new wave of restaurant cooking, it is sifted over many desserts—especially those made with dark red berries and pastry—and over the edges of dessert plates as decoration.

Decorating, coarse, or pearl sugar has large, round granules. Because it dissolves less quickly than granulated, it is often sprinkled on cookies before baking and on other baked goods. It's found in gourmet markets and cake-decorating supply stores.

Preserving sugar is a coarse sugar used for jam making: the large crystals retain enough air between them to prevent the sugar from sinking in a solid mass to the bottom of the pan, so they dissolve evenly and quickly without burning or forming too much scum. Jams, jellies, and marmalades will then need less skimming, and will be crystal clear. Unfortunately, preserving sugar has become difficult to find in the United States, although some ethnic or specialty shops may have it.

Jaggery

In India and Southeast Asia, sugar is regarded as quite good for you, and many of the little sweet snacks eaten during the day, rather than at meals, are intensely sweet. The dark, coarse unrefined sugar used is called jaggery, and it may be processed from the sap of palm trees or from sugarcane.

COCOA, CHOCOLATE, AND CAROB

A century before coffee arrived in the West, the Spanish conquistadores had brought chocolate home with them from the New World. They had seen the Aztecs whisk up a hot, frothy drink called *cacahuatl* ("bitter water,") and at the court of Montezuma, the Mexican emperor, they had savored a richer brew that the Mexicans called *chocolatl*.

Cocoa beans, each the size of an almond, grow thirty or forty at a time in large pods. Their characteristics vary widely depending on the region in which they are grown, and a closely guarded secret of the chocolate industry is the formula for handling and blending different varieties.

When cocoa beans are fermented, roasted, hulled, and ground, a rich reddish-brown liquid, the chocolate liquor, is extracted, which contains a fat called cocoa butter. It is at this stage that cocoa and chocolate undergo their separate processes.

Cocoa

To make cocoa, a proportion of the cocoa butter—it varies from one maker to the next—is removed from the chocolate liquor. The remaining liquid sets hard and is then pulverized. The result, pure, naturally acid cocoa, needs sweetening before it becomes palatable. Dutch, or alkalized, cocoa undergoes a further process known as Dutching to neutralize the acids, making it mellower and darker.

Cocoa powder contains starch, so when it is being made into a hot drink it should, like flour, be mixed to a paste with a little milk or water before being added to the heated milk, or it will turn lumpy. Instant cocoa, or cocoa mix, is precooked cocoa to which sugar and flavorings have been added. When buying cocoa powder, avoid any that is labeled "chocolate-flavored."

Hot cocoa is very popular in Europe, as well as in America, particularly during the long winters. In the United States, steaming cups of cocoa are traditionally topped with whipped cream, or have a melting marshmallow floating on the top. In France, cream is often added, and in Spain, they make a rich chocolate drink thick enough to eat with a spoon. In Russia and Brazil, coffee is added (when coffee is added to cocoa or chocolate, the flavor is called mocha).

Cocoa powder can also be used as a flavoring for cookies, cakes, and other desserts. When unsweetened baking chocolate is called for in a recipe, you can substitute 3 tablespoons cocoa plus 1 tablespoon vegetable shortening or unsalted butter for each 1 ounce chocolate. If bittersweet or semisweet chocolate is required, do the same, but add an extra 3 tablespoons sugar.

Light brown sugar

Dark muscovado sugar

Dark brown sugar

Demerara sugar

Molasses sugar

Granulated sugar

Lump sugar

Superfine sugar

Confectioners' sugar

Preserving sugar

Chocolate

The quality of chocolate is a subject of great interest to chocolate lovers and serious connoisseurs alike. Whole books have been written about chocolate, discussing the merits and drawbacks of the many types and the individual characteristics of the beans from which chocolate is made. This should not be surprising, though, considering that good chocolate makers use a blend of as many as twelve different varieties of beans to achieve just the right balance of richness, aroma, and depth of flavor.

Unlike cocoa, chocolate may retain all the natural cocoa butter found in the liquor extracted from the beans. However, the proportion of cocoa butter varies considerably; in some instances extra cocoa butter is added to the liquor to make the chocolate even richer. The higher the cocoa butter content, the more delectable the chocolate—and also the more expensive. Sugar may be added too, and the sweetness or otherwise is another quality to consider. Connoisseurs like bittersweet chocolate, but more popular by far is chocolate with lots of added sugar and, often, milk solids. Chocolate to which sugar and extra cocoa butter have been added ranges from the darkest bitter chocolate to mild milk chocolate.

When cooking with chocolate, it is generally best to use the least-sweet variety that you can find (the less sugar that is added to chocolate, the stronger and more chocolaty will be the flavor— you can always add more sugar). To ensure the best flavor, unsweetened or bittersweet chocolate with at least 50 percent cocoa butter content is ideal, though 60 to 70 percent is even better, whether it is for cooking or eating. However, although a few imported European chocolates may include these percentages on their labels, most brands of chocolate do not. Experiment to find the ones you like best; higher price often indicates better quality and fuller flavor, but this is not always the case. For icings and frostings, semisweet chocolate is better: it has a higher fat content than unsweetened or bittersweet chocolate so is easier to melt, and the sugar in it produces a good sheen when dry. Beware of cheap baking chocolates, which have often been blended from rather inferior beans, or may not even be real chocolate: as with cocoa mixes, products that are labeled "chocolate-flavored" or "artificial chocolate" are to be avoided. Liquid chocolate, although it may seem convenient for baking, is made with vegetable oil rather than cocoa butter.

Great care is needed when melting any sort of chocolate: it should be done in a bowl set over a pan of boiling water or a double boiler—if it is overheated, it scorches. It is also important to prevent any steam or the smallest drop of water from coming into contact with the melting chocolate, as this will cause it to "seize," or become a thick, lumpy mass.

Chocolate is, of course, essential to the making of some of the world's most delicious cakes and tortes, truffles, pastries, and other desserts and candies. It has a special affinity with rum and brandy, particularly in mousses and ice creams. To make a particularly rich and glorious-tasting drink, melt grated chocolate slowly with sugar and then whisk in hot milk.

Unsweetened chocolate is also used as a flavoring in extraordinary dishes, such as the Mexican holiday dish, *mole poblano de guajolote* (turkey in Pueblan sauce); while in Spain, two casseroles, one of veal tongue *a la aragonesa* and one of braised pigeon, *pichones estofados*, are served in sauces containing chocolate. It can be used very sparingly to improve the color and texture of other sauces—with rabbit and other game, for example.

White chocolate is made with cocoa butter, milk solids, and sugar, and contains no chocolate liquor. Some types, in fact, do not even contain cocoa butter; these, however, cannot be labeled white chocolate. It is not suitable for much in cooking except decoration, and is more cloying than real chocolate.

Carob

Naturally sweet and nutritious, carob provides a satisfying alternative to chocolate. In their natural state, carob beans are the long, elegant pods of a Mediterranean tree belonging to the legume family (it is the carob, or locust bean, on which St. John reputedly lived in the wilderness—hence another of its names, St. John's bread).

Carob contains fewer calories than chocolate and none of the substance theobromine, found in chocolate, that can be a cause of migraine. Carob powder is ground from the whole pod, which is also very palatable in its natural state. As a powder, carob can be used in the same way as cocoa in cakes, cookies, and homemade candies, but carob is sweeter than cocoa, so use less sugar or other sweetener with it. Its mild, milk-chocolate taste is good in cake icings, ice creams, and some baked goods, but it is not recommended for use in recipes that require a really strong chocolate flavor, such as mousses and rich chocolate cakes.

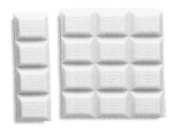

White chocolate

Milk chocolate

Bittersweet chocolate

Cocoa powder

Carob powder

Carob pod

Coffee, Tea, and Herbal Tea

COFFEE

In the Arab world, where coffee is drunk throughout the day in countless ceremonial cups, the old rule for a good brew is that it should be "as black as hell and as sweet as sin."

Good coffee, to suit the Western palate, is made from freshly roasted beans of the particular kind you like best, preferably ground just before brewing. Freshness is vital: coffee rapidly loses quality if exposed to air. There must be a generous amount of beans to the cup, the grind must be suitable for your method of making coffee, and the water sparkling fresh. Our breakfast coffee loses nothing by the addition of milk, however, or our after-dinner coffee by a layer of cream.

Sadly, however, the promise in the delicious smell of real coffee is not always fulfilled. This is one of the reasons why coffee making has become surrounded by mystique—quite unnecessarily, for it is really only a matter of knowing a little bit about the properties of coffee, the way it has been roasted, the grind, and the method of infusion. But the beginning of a good cup of coffee lies in the beans.

The beans

These are, in fact, not beans at all but the twin seeds of the cherry-red fruit produced by the tropical coffee plant. The seeds lie, flat sides facing, in a parchment-like covering. If, as occasionally happens, only one seed develops, it is called a peaberry, because of its rounded shape. (This is noted for its even roasting qualities and so is especially good for home-roasting.)

Once picked and with some of its pulp removed, the fruit is usually fermented in water for varying periods. The seeds are then extracted from their natural wrapping, dried, washed, dried again, and graded according to size.

Before roasting, coffee beans are quite pale. The type called Mochas are yellowish, small, uneven beans; the Bourbon Santos are the same color but oblong and a little larger; and the Martiniques are greenish, rounder, and larger still.

The true Mocha that comes from the Yemen is now a rarity. There had been hardly enough to go around when only the Arab and Levantine world drank what was described by an astonished British traveler as "that black liquid called *kahveh*." But when Europe took to coffee in the seventeenth century, enterprising colonists were quick to spread the tree now known as *Coffea arabica* to new parts of the world. The Dutch were soon providing coffee from plantations in their East Indian possessions, while in France the ever-growing demand for coffee led to its cultivation in Martinique. France was also to grow coffee on its Indian Ocean island of Bourbon (now called Réunion); it was from here that the Brazilians imported the seed for the famous Bourbon Santos coffee.

These *arabica* coffees all do best at high altitudes; they are often labeled "mountain grown" and are a good deal more temperamental than the group of coffees called *robusta*. The *robustas* can be grown in lower regions and are, as the name implies, hardier, easier to grow, and therefore cheaper. Mostly grown in Africa, the *robustas* are less delicately flavored, but are steadily improving.

However, the *arabicas*, which the trade now also divides into the Brazilians and the Milds, make up most of the coffees you are likely to find at a specialty store. If you buy preground, vacuum-packed coffee, always look for "100 percent arabica" or "Pure arabica" on the package.

Brazil is the world's largest coffee grower, and produces all grades from exquisite to indifferent. Santos is the word to look out for: the Brazilian Santos, especially Bourbon Santos, give a good, full-bodied cup of coffee. "Prime Brazilian" on a coffee label is actually meaningless as far as flavor goes.

Colombia Second only to Brazil as a coffee exporter, Colombia produces some excellent coffees that brew so well that you need fewer beans than of other coffee to the amount of water. Among the best Colombians are Medellin, mildly acid, which means that it has a much-valued sharpness, just short of being sour; Manizales, a little sharper; and Excelsio, which is slightly bitter.

Jamaica If you find Jamaican Blue Ridge Mountain coffee, which is all too rarely available, you can be sure that it will be mellow and "sweet"—it is rich in natural sugars, which caramelize in the roasting. It is hailed by many as the best coffee in the world. The Jamaican High Mountain Supremes are less full-bodied.

Venezuela Coffee from Venezuela, if it has grown in the mountain districts, can be rich, winy, and light in body.

Guatemala Mountain-grown coffees from Guatemala are noted for their acidity and fullness. Antiquas and Cobans are the best varieties.

Costa Rica Coffee grown in the high areas of Costa Rica is renowned for its acidity—it has the reputation of being able to curdle milk in the cup—but other Costa Rican *arabicas* are famed for their fragrance, mild flavor, and full body.

Mexico Coffee grown in Mexico is light, mellow, and on the bitter side.

Hawaii This is where Kona coffee comes from. It is rich, mellow, full-bodied, and full of flavor.

Sumatra and Java Sumatra *arabica* coffee is wonderful: sweet, mellow, and full-bodied. It is Sumatra coffee that is still most sought after by the Dutch, who take great pride in perfect coffee making. However, both Sumatra and Java now also grow *robustas*, so ask specifically for a Sumatran *arabica*. Take the same precaution when you buy Java coffee. Old Java ("old" means that it has been stored in tropical conditions for a decade or so) is always of the *arabica* variety; *robustas* are not worth storing for so long and would not in a hundred years develop the fine flavor associated with Old Java.

Mysore This Indian coffee is velvety, acidy, and aromatic. It is delicious, especially when blended with Mocha.

Malabar Monsooned Malabar, from India, is coffee grown throughout the monsoon period, which is supposed to give a very aromatic and mellow flavor. It is indeed wonderful coffee.

Ethiopia This coffee is acid and has a slightly spicy aroma. A type known as Longberry Harrar is now replacing the traditional descendants of Yemen Mocha, and in this there is a poetic justice: the Yemen's first coffee came from Ethiopia, after a legendary Abyssinian goatherd observed his goats skipping and dancing after feeding off the hitherto-ignored coffee plant growing in the wild.

Kenya The *arabicas* of Kenya are among the best-quality coffees: one, the Kenya Peaberry, a variant producing a single round bean, is much admired for its flavor and is one of the coffees always drunk straight, unmixed with any other.

Although there are these, and many more, distinctive varieties of coffee beans, most coffees are blended, producing a pleasant balance of body, flavor, sweetness, and acidity. This is where the skill and knowledge of a discerning coffee merchant, or of a knowledgeable department manager in a large gourmet market, is an invaluable help. The names of house blends—Connoisseur and such like—signify nothing, so it will pay to cultivate a discerning coffee merchant who can be relied upon to offer freshly roasted beans and will explain which combinations of beans constitute his particular blends.

The roast

Roasting brings out the flavor of the bean and determines the mellowness, richness, nuttiness, smoothness, or otherwise of the final brew. The roast does not determine the strength of the coffee—this depends on the ratio of coffee to water when brewing.

Light roast is also called light city roast. It results in a cinnamon-colored bean and a brew called delicate by those who like it and thin by those who don't.

Medium or American roast, regular roast, or city roast will give beans a stronger character and flavor, but the flavor is still on the acid side.

French roast produces shiny beans, burnt umber in color, for coffee that is still smooth, but only just.

Heavy roast or continental roast produces dark brown beans and a flavor that is deeper still.

High roast, dark continental roast, or dark French roast burns the beans almost black, for after-dinner coffee with a strong kick. Dark continental roast is a favorite of gourmets.

Viennese roast is two thirds regular-roasted beans and one third heavy roast.

European roast is stronger, with the proportions reversed: two thirds heavy-roasted beans and one third regular roast.

Espresso or Italian roast is dark to the point of carbonization, but can be mellow in flavor.

The higher the roast, the lower the acidity of the bean and the less varied the aroma, so the most precious beans are not used for very high roasts. However, the high-roasted coffees are preferred by many coffee connoisseurs who dislike the acid flavors of lightly roasted beans.

Only countries that take their coffee drinking very seriously go in for large-scale home-roasting, with appropriate machinery. If you want to try roasting your own "green" beans (which you can buy from specialty coffee merchants and which will keep, before roasting, for long periods) but lack an electric roaster, use a frying pan, shaking it continuously over the heat until the beans are the right color all over. However, for the very best coffee, it is easier to buy your beans freshly roasted and in small quantities. Store them in an airtight container to preserve their aroma. In this state they will keep in good condition for up to 3 weeks. You can also freeze them.

If you buy your coffee preground in vacuum packs, you may not be told on the package the exact types of beans used to make the blend, but you should be informed of the degree of roast and the grind. Many of these coffees are excellent, and blended for consistency of flavor, although coffees, like wines, do vary according to conditions during the growing season. Once the package has been opened, store the ground coffee in an airtight container and use it up within a week if possible, or freeze it.

The grind

Choosing the right grind is essential. The finer the grind, the greater the surface area of coffee that is exposed to the water, and the longer the water takes to run through it as it is brewed. A coarser grind has less surface area and the water passes through more rapidly. The various machines for making coffee are designed so that with the right grind the coffee is exposed to the water for just the right length of time. If the grind is not right, it will result in underextraction, which is wasteful and gives a weak-bodied brew, or overextraction, which makes coffee bitter and can leave a lot of sediment in the cup. If you don't grind your coffee yourself, tell the store where you buy the beans by what method you make your coffee and have it ground accordingly.

Turkish grind Powder-fine, this is the grind that is used to make intensely strong, sweet Greek and Turkish coffee.

Very fine grind (sometimes referred to as Melitta grind) is the grind to use for the paper-filter method. It is too fine to use in an infusion—the fine grounds would turn into an unstrainable mud.

Fine or drip grind is the coffee to use in an espresso machine and in the Italian-style drip pot, or Neapolitan. Brillat-Savarin, the French gastronome,

Unroasted peaberry	*Light roast*	*Medium roast*	*Turkish grind*	*Very fine grind*
Heavy roast	*High roast*	*Espresso roast*	*Fine grind*	*Regular grind*

writing on coffee in the early eighteenth century, preferred this type to others; it is what the French still call for when they order *un filtre*.

Medium-fine grind This is the grind for the cafetière method, using the glass pots that have a pump filter. The coffee comes up through the mesh filter and the grounds stay at the bottom.

Regular grind is the one to use in an electric coffee maker or percolator, since it requires an extraction time of 6 to 8 minutes.

The brew

When making coffee, it is important to use coffee and water in the right proportions. Nineteenth-century visitors to England—notorious for its awful coffee—once were urged by experienced travelers to specify the precise number of beans to the cup, or they would be served with a prodigious quantity of pale brown liquid. "Waiter, is this tea? Bring me a cup of coffee. Or is this coffee? In that case bring me a cup of tea"—ran a famous joke in *Punch*. Sixty-five beans to the cup was Brillat-Savarin's recipe, but he and his peers liked their coffee extra-strong. ("I know it is a poison," said Voltaire, whose clarity of thought Brillat-Savarin ascribed to copious coffee consumption, "but it is a slow one." He was over eighty at the time.) Today, the recommended amount of ground coffee is 2 tablespoons per regular coffee cup, or per each cup of water used.

There is much controversy among experts over which proportions produce the best brew. Internationally recognized styles of serving coffee include:

Café au lait or café con leche, the breakfast drink served in France and in Spain, is made with equal amounts of strong dark-roasted coffee and hot milk.

Demitasse, an after-dinner coffee that is a regular medium-roasted coffee served double-strength.

Espresso, the Italian favorite. The small, strong, foaming cup is the product of a machine that forces steam and boiling water through finely ground Italian-roast coffee. Use a high-roast coffee at double strength to make espresso, if you haven't bought espresso roast. It should be drunk immediately.

Cappuccino, espresso served with steaming, frothy milk from the espresso machine. It can be dusted with cocoa

powder or cinnamon. In France, *café crème* is espresso with milk but without the froth, while in Italy, *caffè latte* is espresso combined with a much larger quantity of steamed milk.

Viennese coffee, made with dark-roasted beans and topped with sweetened, whipped cream, often spiced with cinnamon and nutmeg.

Turkish or Greek coffee, usually drunk very sweet and after dinner. It is traditionally made in an *ibrik*, a long-handled copper pot. The powdered coffee beans, sugar—plenty of it—and water are slowly brought to a boil and simmered to a froth, then left to stand for a few seconds to allow the grounds to settle. This rich, thick coffee is served in a tiny cup and should not be drunk until the grounds have settled at the bottom.

By long tradition, the enjoyment of really good coffee is something of an event. There are still individual flourishes to be seen in Africa and the Middle East. The Moroccans, for instance, add whole peppercorns to the brew for extra kick. The Ethiopians take it with a pinch of salt, and in some Arab countries pounded saffron or cardamom pods are added to a foam called the "face of the coffee." Most evocative of all, perhaps, when the Turks gather around the polished *ibrik*, is the practice of taking coffee with extra sugar for happy occasions such as a wedding, but with no sugar at all at somber gatherings such as funerals.

Additives and extractions

Unless you are positively fond of the taste, avoid coffees that are "stretched" with additives, or coffee substitutes. The reason for using them is, of course, economy, but chicory "coffee" and other mixtures that appear in abundance whenever the Brazilian crops are decimated by frost are, even so, quite popular in their own right. In New Orleans, a chicory-coffee blend that is sometimes called Creole coffee is often served. In various parts of the world, such things as dandelion roots, toasted and ground, sometimes feature in mass-produced coffee; so do toasted figs and barley, which make what is called malt coffee. If you buy packaged coffee, the label will tell you what it contains.

Decaffeinated coffee is pure coffee from which the stimulating properties have been extracted. With them, alas, goes a proportion of the aromatics,

too: using the traditional extraction method, to produce a product that is 97 percent caffeine-free, the beans have to swirl in a solvent and then be dried off twenty-four times. Some coffee is decaffeinated using the Swiss water method. With this process, rather than using a solvent the beans are steamed and then their outer layers, where the caffeine is concentrated, are removed. Decaffeinated coffee beans need a higher, darker roast than the unprocessed ones to develop their flavor.

"Gourmet" coffee If tea can be flavored with anything God can create in the way of fruits, flowers, and spices, it seems to follow that coffee can be too. So we now have designer coffees, with flavors such as vanilla nut crème, Irish crème, chocolate hazelnut, and so on. Many coffee lovers don't seem interested, but if you like the idea, the time to serve these coffees is after dinner. Look for those without artifical flavorings.

Instant coffee

Purists may despise them, but these are nevertheless pure coffee, if not of the most delicately flavored sort; few (but discriminating) are the people who insist on making the real thing for every cup they drink. Instant coffee is also an asset in the kitchen when you want just a coffee flavor, not a pot of liquid.

What is true is that instant coffees vary. Their taste is affected not only by the blends of coffee going into their making (they are made entirely from *robustas*) but also by the way they are produced. The freeze-dried varieties are most like the real thing. For these, brewed coffee is frozen and the resulting ice is ground and vacuum-dried. The strongest and most flavorful of all are the individual sachets of Italian espresso coffee, recently introduced in the United States. Other, cheaper varieties are spray-dried at high temperatures, a process that drives away the aromatics. These are sometimes reintroduced by means of a spray of coffee oil, which evaporates as soon as the jar is opened—the result is a poor apology for the real thing. Some instant coffees are composed of partly freeze-dried and partly heat-dried types.

Of course, with instant coffee one gains in convenience but loses in flavor and the delicious aroma that heralds a pot of fresh coffee in the making.

TEA AND HERBAL TEA

When, in the early seventeenth century, the Dutch first brought tea to the West— it had been cultivated in China for centuries—it was the rich who savored its various aromas, not the poor. For another century or more, ordinary people continued drinking their habitual cheap ale and wine, while the gentry sipped the costly new brew from the East.

It was not until the middle of the eighteenth century that tea became a popular drink as a result of the British East India Company cutting prices and opening up the trade. Today, still single-minded about their tea, the British lead the field in consumption, drinking three times as much as the Japanese (to whom tea is as much a ceremony as a refreshment) and ten times as much as the Americans, who much prefer coffee. In Russia, tea is served very strong, sometimes with lemon but never with milk, while Moroccans like their milkless tea very sweet, adding great quantities of sugar and honey and, frequently, mint leaves. Indian masala tea is brewed with spices—cinnamon, cardamom, and so on—and, usually, made with milk and plenty of sugar. It is deliciously reviving for the traveler.

What is a curious anomaly, now that tea is such a universal beverage, is that the terminology under which it is graded and sold remains utterly cryptic to the bulk of the tea-buying public. True, most people readily distinguish black tea, the kind most commonly drunk in the West, from green, which is the favorite in the East. But other terms are for the most part incomprehensible outside the trade. The term Orange Pekoe, for example, on the label of many black teas, simply indicates the size of the leaf and has nothing to do with the taste of the tea.

Although all tea comes from variants of the same evergreen plant, *Camellia sinensis*, it varies noticeably according to the region in which it is grown and after which it tends to be named. The factors mainly associated with superior teas are good soil and water conditions, high elevation, attentive picking, or plucking, and a favorable harvest season.

Generally, the finest flavors are to be found among what are known as high-grown teas—varieties cultivated on terraced hillsides at high altitude. Scarcer and more difficult to harvest, these hill varieties invariably cost more than the lowland teas.

Following the harvest, what happens to the leaf during its processing has a considerable bearing on the quality of tea in the cup. Tea processing not only changes the leaf to bring out its inherent qualities, but also ensures that the finished leaf will not spoil. In addition, it confirms it in one of the three classifications into which all teas are grouped: black tea, fermented and with the highest concentration of essential oil; green tea, which is unfermented and retains the closest resemblance to the natural leaf; and oolong, semi-fermented tea.

Black tea

Rich, aromatic, and full flavored, black teas make up by far the largest proportion of international tea sales. The oxidization that takes place during fermentation largely accounts for their flavor, strength, body, and color—all characteristics that hinge on chemical changes in the tea tannin and the development of the essential oil. The longer the tannin ferments, the more color it has and the less pungent it is to the taste, so that a very black tea might, in fact, have little pungency—in tea terms, astringency without bitterness.

Black teas are graded by the size of the leaf into leaf teas—those with large leaves, which develop flavor and color more slowly to make a lighter, more fragrant brew—and broken-leaf teas, covering the smaller, broken leaves, which yield a stronger, darker, quicker brew.

Among the leaf teas, the term Orange Pekoe means that the leaves are long and well defined, perhaps with a few yellow tips or mixed with a few leaf buds. (1000 years ago, the term pekoe—"white haired"— was applied by the Chinese to teas that showed a touch of white on the leaves and to which they sometimes added orange blossoms for extra fragrance, but the name no longer denotes this agreeable custom.) Pekoe, with smaller and more tightly rolled leaves, produces a brew that is darker in color but not necessarily stronger in taste than Orange Pekoe. Souchong, the largest, coarsest leaf picked, makes a tea that is pale and quite pungent.

Crystal-Clear Iced Tea 268

Black: Darjeeling

Black: Ceylon spiced with lemon

Black: Keemun

Black: Ceylon

Black: Assam

Japanese Three-year tea

Green: Taiwan Special Chun Mee

Green: China Young Hyson

Green: Japanese Sencha (pan-fired)

Green: China Gunpowder

bergamot 165

Of the broken-leaf teas, Broken Orange Pekoe, which yields good strength and color in the cup, is the one most often used as the mainstay of a blend. Fannings, much smaller, make a strong, quick brew, as does Dust, the smallest grade produced.

Outstanding among the black teas are Keemun, a full-bodied, aromatic tea from North China, and the rich, tarry-flavored, smoke-cured Lapsang Souchong from South China and Taiwan, which is best without milk. With its penetrating bouquet, Keemun makes a good alternative to after-dinner coffee.

The classic Indian teas include high-grown Darjeeling, the Champagne of teas and one of the world's most prized, with a rich, pale liquor and exquisite, penetrating aroma; and the full, strong, malty-tasting Assam. Ceylon teas (from what is now known as Sri Lanka) are generally softer in character than other blacks, and the high-grown varieties are known for their strength, delicacy of flavor, and scented aroma. Dimbula, a rich, mellow Ceylon, makes a good bedtime drink. Indonesian black teas are favored mainly by Dutch blenders and packers.

Green tea

Primarily from China, Japan, and Taiwan, green tea is cool, clean, and refreshing. Said to aid digestion, it is often served with highly flavored or fried foods. It has a mellow, subtle flavor and brews to a pale golden-green. But where green tea is concerned, pallor does not signify lack of strength: the lighter the liquor, the younger the leaf and the better the brew.

Green tea is steamed and heat-dried but not fermented. It is graded by the age as well as by the size of the leaf. The top grades are Gunpowder (young leaves rolled into tiny balls), and Young Hyson (long, thinly rolled leaves). Other grades are Imperial (loosely balled leaves), and Hyson, which is a mixture of Young Hyson and Imperial.

Among the Chinese green teas, look for the type known as Moyunes, celebrated for its richness and clarity, and Dragon Well, a variety that takes its name from a spring outside Hanzhou and is considered the best in China.

Japan, which meets a good deal of the U.S. demand for green tea, grows its finest varieties in the district of Yamashiro, near Kyoto. Sadly, the most prized, Gyokuro or "Pearl Dew," is not normally exported, nor is the leaf from which Mattcha, the ceremonial tea of Japan, is made. Most of Japan's tea is Sencha, or "ordinary" tea, which finds its way abroad as pan-fired teas—delicate, light-colored, and similar to the Young Hyson of China—and the long-leafed, basket-fired teas, which have been cured to a dark olive-green.

The green teas of Taiwan are graded as Special Chun Mee, Chun Mee, Sow Mee, and Gunpowder.

Oolong tea

Named after the Chinese words *wu* (black) and *lung* (dragon), the oolongs combine the characteristics of black and green teas. Best known—and the best of all teas, some experts believe—are those from Taiwan, known as Formosa oolongs, with their deep amber color and magnificent fruity taste. Also very distinctive is Pouchong—oolong mixed with highly scented flowers such as jasmine and gardenia.

Much better than other countries (China included) at cultivating oolongs, Taiwan is the one exception to the high-altitude rule: here on this subtropical island, the best teas are grown on the yellow clay soils of the *teela*, or broken lands, many of which are at sea level. It is the summer pluckings that yield the highest-grade, rich golden oolongs.

Blended teas

Perhaps not surprisingly, the hub of the tea trade is London. Here firms base their bidding on the verdicts of tea tasters, who are much preoccupied with appearance, aroma, and taste. For although there are only three basic types of tea, there are something like three thousand commercial blends.

Given the fluctuations in price and availability from year to year, the major tea packers mostly market products that are blends using perhaps fifteen or twenty varieties. The most distinguished of these tea blends include English Breakfast, traditionally a straight Keemun but now more likely to be a strong blend of India and Ceylon teas; Irish Breakfast, high-grown Ceylon with hearty Assam; Russian Style (also known as Russian Caravan or Russian Blossom), a blend of Keemun, Assam, and China green well suited to the samovar; and Uva, a blended Ceylon, golden when brewed and with a distinctive flowery bouquet.

Another well-known blend is Earl Grey—so called because its secret was said to have been passed by a Chinese mandarin in 1830 to the Earl Grey, who had it made up for himself by a London tea merchant. Earl Grey is made from Indian and Chinese teas, and is scented with oil of bergamot. Ideal for afternoon tea, it yields a pale, clear liquor with a slight citrus flavor—a reminder of how well a hint of citrus combines with tea.

Spiced blends on the market, such as the orange-flavored teas particularly popular in the United States, usually feature a smooth-drinking Ceylon tea

Oolong: Formosa   *Blend: Earl Grey*   *Blend: Uva*

Oolong: Pouchong with jasmine   *Blend: English Breakfast*   *Blend: Irish Breakfast*

with added cloves, dried orange peel, or lemon. Various teas can also be deliciously spiced with cinnamon, anise, or cardamom.

Japanese three-year tea, also known as twig tea or *kukicha*, is a natural tea with no caffeine, made from the roasted 3-year-old twigs and leaves of the tea bush. It is best sipped slowly after meals.

Herbal teas

Long eclipsed by ordinary tea, herbal teas, also known as tisanes, are making a comeback as more and more people realize that, as well as being refreshing in summer and a fragrant reminder in winter of sunny gardens, herbal teas can be soothing and beneficial. And, of course, they are caffeine-free.

Modern-day herbal teas and blends are sold either in packages, complete with instructions, in the ubiquitous tea bag, or loose, by retailers who should be able to advise on their use. The ingredients can also be gathered from the garden, as long as one keeps to the absolutely safe, well-known plants (be sure that they have not been sprayed with pesticides). The flowers, leaves, seeds, and/or roots can then be used fresh or dried gently, out of the sun, to use later.

Most of the teas made from dried herbs, flowers, and leaves are infused—made like regular tea—in a stainless steel or ceramic container (never aluminum). Measure about 1 teaspoonful of the dried herb or 2 teaspoonfuls of the fresh (or a few sprigs) per cup of water, add boiling water as if making ordinary tea, cover,

and allow to stand for no more than 5 minutes—long enough to bring out the fragrance, but not too long, or the tea will become bitter. Strain and, if you like, flavor with lemon or honey. Teas made from seeds, roots, or bark are prepared by boiling them to extract the flavors: allow 2 tablespoons of seeds, or a small handful of roots or bark, per 2 cups water. Bring to a boil, cover, and allow to simmer gently for about 15 minutes. Strain into a teapot, cover, and leave the tea to steep for a few minutes.

Ginseng (*Panax quinquefolium*) An ancient Chinese cure-all and aphrodisiac, said to be good for the mind, ginseng makes a tea with a licorice-like taste. Ginseng root, with fifteen other herbs, features in the powerful, spicy Japanese mu tea.

Linden (*Tilia americana, T. vulgaris*) Beautifully scented flowers from the linden tree, which may be called lime flowers in Europe, are dried to yield relaxing linden-blossom tea, which can be drunk hot or cold (disconcertingly, some recent studies say that frequent consumption of linden tea may affect the heart). A pale amber liquid, this is sometimes known as basswood tea.

Bergamot (*Monarda didyma, M. citriodora, M. fistulosa*) Tea made from the leaves and flowers has a slightly bitter taste.

Mint (*Mentha*) A great Arabian beverage, mint tea, which contains both mint and tea leaves, is served hot and heavily sweetened, in glasses, with sprigs of fresh mint. This refreshing tea is stimulating to drink and is also a good aid to digestion. The many mint teas

include peppermint, with menthol coolness, giving a pungent tea, and sharp, aromatic spearmint.

Chamomile (*Anthemis nobilis*) The dried flowers of chamomile make a rather bitter but soothing tea, excellent for settling the stomach and supposed to induce tranquil sleep. (It should be drunk in moderation.)

Maté (*Ilex paraguensis*) This stimulating tea, made from the dried leaves of a small tropical tree, is a favorite South American drink. Also known as yerba maté, it can be drunk hot or cold.

Lemon verbena (*Lippia citriodora*) The lemon-scented leaves make a delicious tea, strongly reminiscent of lemon and excellent for the digestion.

Marigold (*Calendula officinalis*) The warm orange flowers of pot marigold make a very pretty but somewhat bitter tea, supposed to be healing and to have antiseptic properties. Make it weak and sweeten it, or mix a few marigold flowers with lemon verbena tea.

Raspberry, black currant The leaves from both bushes make lightly flavored teas faintly evocative of the fruits.

Rose hip (*Rosa*) Wild rose hips yield a sweet, astringent tea popular for its high vitamin C content.

Fruit teas Refreshing and astringent, these are often spiced with cinnamon or cloves. Some common ones include a fragrant apple-based tea, a refreshing orange-based tea, a spicy ginger and red fruit blend, and lemon and ginger, a good morning tea. To sweeten a fruit tea, use honey rather than sugar.

Mint   Bergamot   Rose hip   Ginseng   Japanese mu

Maté   Linden   Raspberry leaf   Chamomile   Lemon verbena

2

Equipment:
How to choose it
and use it

Equipment

KNIVES

A good sharp knife that is comfortable to hold is the most essential tool to have in the kitchen—and one that makes the preparation of food a pleasure rather than a troublesome chore.

Quality and materials

Before selecting the right knife for the particular task you have in mind, it is important to know what qualities raise a kitchen knife into the top-quality class.

Balance It is critical that the weight of a knife be evenly distributed along the blade and handle, as an unbalanced knife is tiring to use. Knives are balanced by a tang (the metal that extends from the base of the blade through the handle), and in the case of heavy-bladed knives, the tang should run the full length of the handle. A full tang will also lend extra strength to a knife designed for tough tasks. Whether the knife is light- or heavy-bladed, the tang should be securely fixed inside the handle, preferably with rivets.

Machine-ground edge Grinding gives a blade both sharpness and strength. The best knives are taper-ground, with grinding marks at right angles to the cutting edge.

Hollow-ground blades are recognizable by their profile—a thick blade abruptly punched in at the cutting edge. The blade is machined so it cannot be sharpened, and it does not make a good edge for a chopping knife, but hollow grinding does make the hardest, most durable serrated edge.

Handles on the best-quality kitchen knives will be either of close-grained hardwood, which will not split or warp—and the slight texture of which gives a secure grip—or of plastic, or plastic-impregnated wood, which combines extreme toughness with the natural properties of wood. High-quality plastic handles are practical.

Stainless steel is a rust-resisting alloy of iron and chromium. Many people are disparaging of stainless steel, claiming that it is impossible to give it a really sharp edge. This is certainly true of inferior-quality knives stamped out of a flat piece of metal, but those forged from tempered stainless steel with a high carbon content (sometimes described as carbon stainless) are among the best knives you can buy, and they hold a very fine edge indeed.

Carbon steel has the advantage of being cheaper to buy than stainless steel, and it will sharpen to a razor-sharp edge. The disadvantage is that it is particularly susceptible to corrosion and staining, especially when used for foods with a high acid content, such as lemons and tomatoes, so it needs careful looking after and cleaning.

Shape and size

There are dozens of knives available today, designed for all the specialized tasks a professional chef may have to perform, but a carefully chosen collection of six or seven will equip most kitchens admirably.

Chopping To finely chop vegetables, herbs, garlic, nuts, and so on, you will need a tough, well-balanced, general-purpose cook's, or chef's, knife with a deep, smoothly curved blade that tapers toward a pointed tip. The handle should be shaped to the grip, with a downturned curve at the end to prevent the hand from slipping backward. It should have a full tang in order to balance the weight of the blade and to absorb the chopping vibrations as the knife is used.

The bolster (the thicker back end of the blade, also called the shoulder or guard) must be thick and deep to shield the hand and to allow the full length of the cutting edge to be used without hitting the knuckles on the chopping surface. The correct way to use this type of knife for fine chopping is to rest one hand lightly on the back of the blade at the tip to keep the blade in contact with the cutting board, while the other hand simply rocks the handle up and down, gradually moving the knife across the food. For coarser chopping, raise and lower the whole blade.

For tough chopping jobs, a cleaver should be used. This tool relies for its strength on a wide, really hefty, full-tanged blade, and it is one of the few instances where an imbalance between handle and blade is desirable. Butchers may be seen wielding this implement with considerable force and accuracy, but ferocious hacking can chip and blunt the cutting edge very quickly. To chop through bones, rest the cleaver in the proper position and hit the back of the blade with a mallet.

Cleavers are traditionally used for all the chopping and shredding that goes into the preparation of Asian dishes. Chinese and Japanese chefs are able to cut a thin scallop of meat or fish by placing the ingredient under one palm and passing the cleaver through the meat or fish, their palm acting as a sort of radar device. This skill takes years of practice, however, and nonprofessionals should always treat cleavers with respect—and a fair amount of caution.

Slicing The type of knife you use will depend entirely on what you are slicing.

Bread A long serrated edge is good for cleanly penetrating the rough outer crust. Choose a straight, firm knife with hollow-ground serrations.

Cold meats The compact, tender fibers of cooked cold meats offer little resistance to a sharp knife and thus can be sliced very thin. Choose a knife with a long, narrow blade, which should be flexible and strong. Special ham slicers have a rounded tip to prevent accidental slashes to the meat and a fluted edge that gives a little purchase to the first stroke and reduces friction. Fluted or scalloped smoked salmon knives are also available; they make light work of slicing smoked salmon wafer-thin, and are also useful for cutting raw meat and fish for carpaccio.

Fruit and vegetables A small serrated stainless steel blade is wonderfully efficient for slicing lemons, tomatoes, cucumbers, peppers, and all those other fruits and vegetables with tough or slippery outer skins. The serration pierces the skin so easily that the flesh beneath is not bruised or squashed, and each slice keeps all its juice.

Paring, peeling, and scraping

Everyone has a favorite little knife that tucks under the index finger and can be used almost as an extension of the hand. As the hand should be in close contact with the food, choose a light knife with a comfortable, well-shaped handle. The blade should be short and made of good-quality stainless steel capable of holding a really sharp edge.

Boning This operation is carried out in a series of small cutting movements, using the tip of the knife to follow the contours of the bone, so good control of the blade is important. For lightweight cuts of meat or poultry, a short, rigid knife is best, with a slim, pointed blade and a broad handle. The larger the piece of meat to be boned, the larger and more rigid the blade should be.

Filleting Choose a pointed straight-edged knife with a flexible blade that will feel its way around soft cartilaginous fish bones—this is a task requiring precision and dexterity. The blade should be protected by a bolster and the knife should have a full-tanged handle. This kind of knife is useful for almost every sort of cutting, slicing, carving, etc., except chopping.

Mincing The Italians have a very practical instrument called a *mezzaluna* ("half-moon"). It is a double-handled knife with a crescent-shaped single or double blade that is rocked over herbs, peppers, strips of meat, garlic, and already sliced vegetables, mincing them to fine bits. Small *mezzalunas* are sometimes sold together with a wooden herb-chopping bowl.

Carving Happily the days are past when carving was a competitive performance, but a good sharp knife is still a reassuring ally on these occasions. So too is a strong carving fork, traditionally used to hold the roast steady while slicing. A chicken can be carved with a small, handy knife, while a bulky hot roast with a bone requires a straight, sharply pointed knife. It helps when carving meat around a bone if the blade curves slightly upward toward the tip. The handle should be shaped to the hand, preferably with a full tang and a bolster to prevent the hand from slipping onto the blade. A slim blade that is slightly flexible will enable the carver to slice the meat quite thin.

Care and cleaning

Dishwashers can be very unkind to knives. The high temperature and harsh detergents loosen, warp, and split the handles, so it is better to wash them by hand unless they are guaranteed dishwasherproof. Wash them in hot, soapy water and dry immediately. Knives made of carbon steel are inclined to become rusty very quickly, so they must be cleaned and dried immediately after use. If the blades do become stained, polish them with a cork sprinkled with an abrasive cleaning powder, or scrub with a plastic scouring pad and a scouring cream or powder.

If by any chance a knife gets put in the dishwasher, you may find that its handle turns out of alignment with the blade. This will be because the tang is fixed to the handle not with rivets, but with resin

that softens with heat. To realign the knife, put the handle in boiling water for a few minutes, then twist it straight.

Sharpening Knives should always be kept in razor-sharp condition. A blunt knife is frustrating and dangerous to use—it performs badly, needing a great deal of force, and it can all too easily slip out of control. To help preserve their cutting edges, always chop on a wooden or polyethylene or acrylic board.

The best way to keep a sharp edge on a knife is to use a hand-held steel: draw the blade lightly down the steel at a shallow angle. Repeat, drawing the knife first down one side of the steel, then the other. To resharpen a dull blade you will have to resort to a whetstone—a block made of very hard Carborundum or very hard stone. There are many other devices for sharpening knives, but these usually grind down blades quickly and are not recommended.

Storage Kitchen knives should not be stored in drawers where the blades will clash together, bending the tips and dulling the fine edges. Each knife should be separated from its neighbors and clearly visible to the cook, who can then easily select the right knife for the job.

The best solution is to slot the knives into a wooden knife block or into a wall-fixed rack within easy reach of the work surface (but inaccessible to children.) Magnetic racks are good, but they may not be strong enough to hold very heavy knives or cleavers.

OTHER CUTTING UTENSILS

There are some cutting tasks that are really quite difficult to carry out with a straight-bladed knife, however sharp it may be. Fortunately, over the centuries a wide variety of special tools has been invented to do these jobs more quickly, safely, and efficiently. Some tools, like scissors, are strokes of genius, invaluable in the kitchen and elsewhere. Other tools are so specialized that it is advisable to examine your needs quite dispassionately before you go ahead and acquire them, as they might well spend more time collecting dust than attracting compliments for your prowess.

The following tools, used in conjunction with a basic collection of knives, should equip the cook to deal with most cutting tasks in the kitchen.

Graters

Choose a sturdy stainless steel box (or octagonal) grater that will sit firmly in a bowl or on a work surface without slipping or sliding. Each face should offer a different grating surface, and the grater should be large enough for the food to collect neatly inside without being squashed.

The face with fine holes is useful for Parmesan and other hard cheeses, while the abrading face consists of a series of jagged puncture holes for rasping tough or brittle foods, such as lemon zest and nutmeg. (Some graters have two abrading faces, one with large puncture holes, the other with small ones, rather than a side with fine slightly oval holes.) The smoother directional face cuts smooth slices or slivers from softer cheeses and vegetables.

A small flat or conical abrading grater is useful for holding over dishes to add a dash of nutmeg or lemon zest at a stroke.

Hand-operated rotary graters are speedy and pleasant to use, keeping the fingers at a safe handle's length from the grating surface. A curved plate holds the food tightly against the grating drum, which is turned by hand. Choose a model with a selection of drums of fine and coarse gauges.

Small nutmeg graters are nice to have, but are not essential.

Peelers and corers

Potato peeler It is perfectly possible to peel a potato quickly and easily with a small sharp knife, but the chances are that the discarded peel will contain more nourishment and flavor than the potato on the table. The *raison d'être* of a good potato peeler is to shave off the skin so finely that nothing of value is lost.

Fixed-blade peelers are used in the same way as knives, but left-handed people should make sure they buy a left-handed version. The slotted blade of the swivel-action peeler adapts to the shape of the fruit or vegetable as it is moved quickly over it; the sharp steel blade will cut equally well in either direction, meaning it is adaptable to either right-handed or left-handed use.

Citrus zester and canelle knife There are several types of peeler available that will remove only the zest, the thin colored top layer of citrus peel. A zester has a row of small holes that remove the zest in tiny strips, while a canelle knife, also called a citrus stripper, has a V-shaped tooth that removes the zest in ribbons or fatter strips—it's especially good for making martini-sized twists. The object of these specialized peelers is to leave behind the bitter pith, which is harder to do when using a knife.

Apple corer The end of this tool should be placed over the target area and pushed firmly through the apple; when it is withdrawn, the core will be retained in the center of the corer. It is a most useful gadget for preparing baked apples, the only drawback being that not every apple has an obligingly straight core of a standard size. Choose a corer with a sharp bottom edge.

Olive or cherry pitter This little gadget ejects pits from cherries and olives, and a sturdy stainless steel pitter will do the job very efficiently—a boon if you make a great deal of cherry pies or want pitted olives for cooking.

Slicers

Mandoline This instrument is used for high-speed slicing of firm, crisp foods—such as potatoes, onions, zucchini, carrots, cucumbers, or celeriac. While the cutting disks of a food processor can be used for slicing and shredding, they are never as fine and precise as the blades of a mandoline. Professional mandolines made of stainless steel have several blades and attachments for a variety of thicknesses and shapes; wooden mandolines usually have just two adjustable blades (preferably of high-carbon stainless steel), for slicing thick or thin. Plastic mandolines may have several interchangeable blades. In any case, the mandoline is held firmly in place with one hand while the other hand moves the food over the chosen blade with a regular strumming movement.

Cheese plane, cheese slicer These slicers are intended for semi-hard cheeses, such as Edam, that are traditionally cut very thin, and they are extremely good once you are accustomed to using them.

Cheese wire This is only useful if you buy cheese in large pieces. However hard or crumbly the cheese, a stainless steel cutting wire, when drawn taut, will melt through it and leave a clean, straight cut.

Egg slicer Wire slicers are a very good way of cutting hard-boiled eggs without displacing or crumbling the yolk. Some kinds cut wedges, some slices. Make sure that the wires are of stainless steel.

French fry cutter If you make a lot of french fries, then this gadget is quite useful. The whole peeled potato is placed under it, the stainless steel cutter pushed down, and within a few minutes you have a bowl of neatly cut potatoes ready for frying. Instruments for cutting raw potatoes must be sturdy, so be prepared to pay for a heavy-duty steel model. A flimsy cutter is worse than useless.

Scissors and shears

Kitchen scissors should be very sharp, strong, and chrome-plated or made of stainless steel with plastic handles because they must be impervious to rust. For tough jobs, their power will be strengthened if the lower handle is large enough to take the first three fingers of the cutting hand, and a serrated edge is sometimes useful for giving an extra bite to the first cut.

The blades should cut evenly right down to their tips—in fact, especially at the tips, because snipping is an important function of this tool. Scissors should be professionally sharpened when they become blunt.

Poultry shears Like garden clippers, this tool gains its strength from the tension in the coiled spring just below the pivot point of the blades. Usually one blade is serrated to give a firm grip when tackling tough assignments such as small bones, and the pointed tips enable the shears to reach and operate effectively in small awkward places.

Some versions are quite attractive, and as well as being invaluable in the kitchen, they can be used at the table for dividing a roast duck (or a small game bird) into neat and manageable portions. This is an especially good way to serve duck, as its bony carcass makes carving awkward.

Cutters

Graded sets Tin-plated steel plain- and crinkly-edged cutters are basic equipment for small pastries and can be used for cookies; the top edge should be rolled for strength, the cutting edge sharp. For convenient storage, buy graded sets that fit inside each other in their own tin.

Fancy cutters These are usually tin-plated steel, although occasionally stainless steel or plastic, in every imaginable shape and for every possible occasion. In addition to making cookies, these are fun to use for pastries, cakes, icings, marzipan, canapés, etc.

Pastry wheel This can cut straight or crimped lines through pastry or through sheets of pasta for pappardelle and ravioli with professional panache, dividing dough with a smooth, even pressure.

Ravioli cutter This is a fluted-edged metal cutter with a wooden handle, for stamping out individual rounds of ravioli. Different sizes are available. Ravioli trays are used for sheets of pasta—a rolling pin is rolled over the stuffed sheets and up to forty small squares of ravioli are cut at one time.

Pizza cutter This is a wheel with a sharp cutting edge to cut through cooked pizza dough and its toppings to make neat portions.

Specialty knives

Oyster and clam knives These tough knives are designed to open the shells of oysters and clams while they are raw and still alive. The blades of oyster knives and some supposedly dual-purpose knives have cutting edges on both sides to pry open the shells, and there is usually a guard to protect your hands. Clam knives usually have just one sharp side. Shucking raw shellfish is a tricky task. For safety's sake, choose one of the short, stubby knives, and hold the shellfish in a cloth—this will improve your grip and also protect your hand.

Grapefruit knife This double-edged, serrated knife is curved to fit the shape of a grapefruit half. It's easier than using a straight-edged knife for separating and removing individual grapefruit segments from tough membranes.

Sandwich spatula, sandwich spreader This is similar to a metal icing spatula, but has a shorter, broader, and more flexible blade. It is useful for spreading butter and sandwich fillings, whipped cream, icings, and frostings.

Cleaning

It is an unpleasant fact that behind every meal there looms the inevitable pile of dirty dishes. Even if there is a dishwasher in the kitchen, there will still be a hard core of gadgets, knives, and pots that has to be hand-washed. Some of the items listed in this section come into this rather unfortunate category.

Mandolines should be cleaned with a brush, rinsed, and dried quickly to preserve the cutting edge of their blades; wooden ones should never be left to soak, or they will warp. Brushing is also the best way to clean graters, although the larger box-shaped ones usually come clean perfectly well in the dishwasher.

Storage

Most of these implements have sharp cutting edges, so do not jumble them all into a drawer. This will ruin the blades and you will most probably cut your fingers as you root about searching for the appropriate gadget. Some can be hung from a rack or a rail on hooks, while larger items can be kept on a shelf. In all cases, the cook must be able to see and reach them easily.

GRINDERS, MASHERS, AND SIEVES

When you look at a collection of modern kitchen tools—efficient, easy to use, light, and simple to clean—it is easy to believe that they are all twentieth-century inventions. But most of them have a long and interesting lineage, and this is certainly true of the diverse group of tools in this section, designed to refine or change the texture of food.

Even before the advent of bread, our ancestors had realized that seeds and grains could be made more digestible or aromatic by pounding and grinding; pieces of cloth filled with berries and then wrung tightly were the first juice extractors. And loosely woven cloths suspended on wooden frames were the predecessors of modern sieves and strainers.

Grinders

Mortar and pestle This elegant descendant of the primitive pounding pole is still the most effective tool for pulverizing nuts, garlic, berries, grains, seeds, herbs, and spices.

The mortar should have a smooth, regularly curved bowl and a compatibly shaped pestle. The grinding surfaces should be slightly rough to provide the necessary friction and prevent the food sliding away from the pestle.

Mortars and pestles are available in wood, glass, tough unglazed porcelain, stone, metal, and marble. The small wooden ones are excellent for crushing most things, but because they are fairly lightweight, they require a fair amount of force to crush seeds, grains, and spices. The off-white vitrified porcelain versions are probably the most handsome and best all-round performers at a reasonable price.

Peppermill Peppercorns should be ground when and where they are needed so that their fugitive pungency can be enjoyed before it fades. The mealtime musings of many designers have resulted in an enormous variety of pepper mills to choose from, but perhaps the favorite is still the classic wooden mill with a removable top for easy filling and a highly efficient steel grinding mechanism.

Salt mill Where the pepper goes, salt goes too, so many manufacturers make a salt mill to match their peppermill. They will reduce coarse sea salt to usable size.

Coffee grinder Freshness is the essence of good coffee, and one way to ensure it is to grind your own. Hand-operated mills are preferred to electric grinders by some purists, as the beans are truly ground rather than cut, and the grind is cooler.

Grinder, meat grinder A hand-operated grinder should be very strong and have clamps or suction cups for fixing it rigidly to the work surface. The handle turns a small Archimedean screw, which inexorably pushes the food from the hopper onto the rotating stainless steel grinding plates, or disks, which will process almost anything except bones. Make sure that the machine has been designed to come apart completely so that every part can be easily cleaned.

Pounders and tenderizers

Meat pounder, meat mallet Thin slices of raw meat, such as veal scallops that are to be cooked quickly, should be flattened to half their original thickness. This is best done by gently pounding the meat, using a stroking motion, with a smooth, heavy meat pounder. Doing this homogenizes the texture of the flesh and breaks down the fibers, which will otherwise contract when the meat is cooked, causing shrinkage and toughness.

Meat tenderizer A mallet with a flat grid-shaped face is less brutal than the type with steel protuberances—which cut through fibrous tissues. Use a tenderizer only on very thick, tough cuts of meat.

Mashers

Potato masher Choose a strong masher that deals severely with the food and will not collapse under pressure. Traditional-style mashers are extremely efficient at mashing and puréeing cooked potatoes and other root vegetables, and can be used in the pan in which the vegetables were cooked. Stylish, modern mashers, which are made of zigzagging stainless steel are quite efficient, but they do seem to require more hard work than the traditional kind.

Ricer Chrome-plated steel ricers are excellent for making ultrasmooth mashed potatoes and other vegetable and fruit purées. The food is put into a mesh basket or hopper, then pressed through by means of a metal pusher attached to a handle. The end result is light, dry, and fluffy. Buy a ricer of a decent size, and preferably one that is dishwasherproof, as the basket can be a bore to clean by hand.

Garlic press For all those who are wary about impregnating a wooden cutting board or a mortar and pestle with the all-pervading odor and flavor of garlic, the garlic press is the answer. Select a sturdy cast aluminum or stainless steel press with a fairly coarse mesh—then there is no need to peel the clove of garlic before you squeeze. (Beware—crushed garlic is more overpowering than chopped.)

Sieves and strainers

There are sieves for sifting, sieves for straining, and sieves for puréeing: versatility breeds variation, and the sieve family is no exception.

Round stainless steel sieves are suitable for all sifting and puréeing tasks. They are preferable to the wire- or nylon-mesh type because they do not stain or corrode in contact with acid, and they do not wear out as quickly or come apart with constant pushing. To help with puréeing, you can use a wooden mushroom-shaped pestle called a *champignon* (French for mushroom) or the back of a spoon.

Sieves should not be filled too full for sifting—simply knock the side of the frame gently against the palm of the free hand to help the contents pass through.

Sieves can be very difficult to clean, and for this reason the wood-framed drum sieves, or tamis, are best avoided for puréeing—metal-framed drum sieves are better, as they are stronger and can be immersed in really hot, soapy water, or, better still, left for the dishwasher.

Conical strainer For fine puréeing jobs, a stainless steel *chinois*, or cone-shaped strainer, is preferable. Look for one with the frame and perforations formed from one piece of metal, with no seams or welds. The food is forced through the perforations by a pumping action using a small ladle or a wooden spoon, or by a long narrow pestle that fits right into the tip. A conical strainer is also excellent for straining, the tapering point channeling the liquid neatly down in a trickle into a deep bowl or saucepan.

Food mill This rotary sieve produces a range of purées, from the most delicate tomato sauces to a robust vegetable soup. A food processor, of course, would do the same, but a hand-cranked food mill often gives better results as it does not rob the food entirely of its intrinsic texture—it takes out, rather than chops up, lumps, fibers, or fine bones. Most food mills have a set of interchangeable plates or disks for a coarse, medium, or fine finish, and are easily dismantled for cleaning. The best food mills have bodies of stainless steel.

Juicers

A citrus fruit juicer must be able to extract the maximum amount of juice free of seeds, pith, and other solids. There are good models available with the reamer and strainer molded in one piece, which fits onto a container with a lip for pouring. Stainless steel versions are the most stylish, although plastic ones do the job just as well.

More traditional but not so efficient is the familiar glass version. It has teeth, which only halfheartedly trap the seeds and pieces, and a moat that barely holds the juice of one lemon.

For extracting just a few drops of juice without sacrificing a whole lemon or lime, there is a very clever little gadget called a citrus spigot. When plugged into the fruit, it will produce the required number of drops.

Ultramodern citrus presses are made of stainless steel. They look beautiful on the kitchen countertop, and most do the job exceedingly well. The most efficient types have a geared mechanism with sufficient power to squeeze every last drop of juice out of the fruit. Electric juicers are also widely available.

ESSENTIAL KITCHEN TOOLS

Some tools are never far from the cook's hand—usually tucked into a jar by the stove ready in an instant to tend those dishes that need stirring, whisking, or skimming while they cook.

Cutting boards

Wooden cutting boards are tough, but they are porous and so not only stain easily but also take on the flavors of foods that are chopped on them. If you choose wooden boards, you need to have several, each one for a specific task—chopping onions and garlic, rolling out pastry, slicing bread, etc. When you clean wooden boards, they should never be saturated or left to soak in water, as this will warp and crack the wood, and they should be kept away from heat. Polyethylene or acrylic boards are easier to keep clean than wood, but wooden boards are often preferred for their natural look and feel.

Whisks and beaters

Substances are whisked to lighten their texture by the introduction of air, to emulsify and blend ingredients, or to thicken those substances that contain fat. Egg whites, for example, have an almost infinite capacity for trapping air as they are whipped—when gently folded into sponge cakes, soufflés, or meringues, the air bubbles expand on heating to give the food a texture of honeycombed lightness.

A brisk whisking will rescue a lumpy sauce, and transform egg yolks and oil into a pale-golden mayonnaise.

There are many varieties of whisks. These are the most effective types:

Balloon whisk Made of several loops of stainless steel or tin-plated steel wire bound together around a central handle, these are simple and very effective instruments with no moving parts to break. However, they do need a strong arm to keep up the whisking motion for some minutes without tiring. Sizes range from large heavy-duty models for egg whites to small, dainty ones for light sauces and delicate dressings.

Rotary beater This can be heaven or hell depending on the quality. A cheap version is really a waste of money; unless the gear mechanism is carefully made of high-quality materials, the beater will not operate smoothly at high speed. The best types work very well indeed and are

less tiring to use than balloon whisks, but they do not achieve the same volume, particularly in the case of egg whites. They also require both hands, which is sometimes a disadvantage.

Flat coiled whisk, whip This is a neat spoon-shaped tool that can get right into the corners of a pan, or control one or two egg whites so well that they can be whisked on a plate. It is most effective at beating lumps out of sauces.

Spoons

Wooden spoons The wooden spoon is regarded by most people with affection, not only because it is associated with childhood treats like scraping the mixing bowl, but also because it is one of the most useful tools in the kitchen. A wooden spoon is invaluable for beating, mixing, and stirring; it will never burn your hand, because wood is a very bad conductor of heat; it will not scratch saucepans; and it is quiet and strong in use.

Choose a spoon of a close-grained wood that is not likely to split. The bowl of the spoon should have a fairly thin edge that can get right into the bottom corner of deep saucepans—some spoons are specially shaped to help you do this.

Metal spoons Although wooden and metal spoons share the same shape, their functions do not often overlap. While wooden spoons are good for stirring and beating, metal ones excel at transferring food quickly from pan to dish, and at gently folding together delicate mixtures. A metal spoon should always be used for last-minute taste checks on soups and sauces, as wood can hold a tiny bit of the flavor from its last use.

Perforated and slotted metal spoons are excellent for removing and serving pieces of food that have been cooked in liquid; the excess liquid drains through the holes or slots, keeping the food whole and fairly dry.

Ladle The familiar shape of the ladle has remained unchanged since very ancient times. Like most classics, ladles are satisfying to use because of their geometric balance, and they are also pleasing to the eye. Soups and stews can be dexterously served without fear of spilling a drop; just the right quantity of batter can be poured into a crêpe pan for feather-light crêpes; and lipped ladles will transfer punches from serving bowl to glasses with ease.

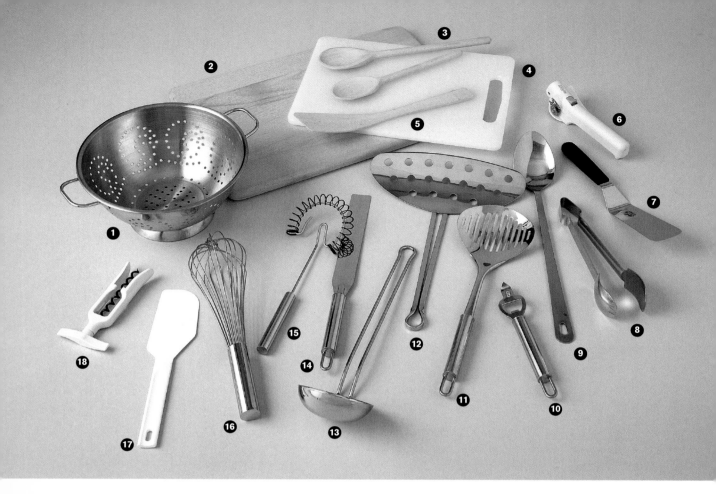

Essential kitchen tools

1 colander
2 wooden cutting board
3 wooden spoons
4 polyethylene cutting board
5 wooden spatula
6 can opener
7 angled spatula
8 tongs
9 large metal spoon
10 bottle opener
11 slotted turner
12 fish lifter
13 ladle
14 metal icing spatula
15 flat coiled whisk
16 balloon whisk
17 plastic spatula
18 corkscrew

Skimmers

Wire mesh skimmer Sometimes called a spider, a mesh skimmer is a shallow lightweight wire basket on a long handle that will scour bubbling oil, soup, or stock, gathering up impurities or removing food as it cooks. It is also good for scooping up fritters from hot oil at just the right moment to be rolled crisp and hot in sugar.

Solid perforated disk skimmer This can both skim liquids and remove pieces of food from their cooking liquid. They are not as good as mesh skimmers for deep-frying, because their bulk lowers the oil temperature and the perforations are not large enough to allow the oil to drain freely from the food.

Turners, spatulas, and tongs

Metal turner The flexibility of a good turner must be finely judged: slim and flexible enough to slide under the food without causing damage, but broad and firm enough to support it as it is turned or lifted from the pan. Perforations in the blade will allow excess fat or oil to escape, and a sturdy handle will help insulate the hand from the transferred heat of the pan. A fish lifter is a specialized metal turner

designed for removing a nicely cooked whole fish from its poaching liquid. (Turners are sometimes called spatulas, although this is incorrect.)

Wooden spatula It is strange that this archaic tool should be the perfect companion to the nonstick pan—that culinary spin-off from our space-age technology—and although as a turner it is somewhat lacking in flexibility, nothing harsher than wood should be used on this vulnerable finish.

Wooden spatulas are available in rounded spoon shapes, or with a flat blade and a slanted straight end, which fits snugly against the sides of pans and bowls, and gathers up everything in its path. Pierced or slotted wooden spatulas are useful for lifting and draining off fried food.

Rubber or plastic spatula These tools are the delight of a frugal cook's heart. Nothing else can scrape a bowl or jar as clean. Their rubber or plastic heads have a rounded side and an angular edge so they will fit a wide variety of pots, pans, and surfaces. Unless it's of the more expensive heat-resistant type, never put a rubber spatula into the dishwasher or very hot liquid—it will perish.

Metal spatula The long, thin, flexible blade of a metal icing spatula, also called a palette knife, is ideally suited to large-scale spreading jobs—like professionally smoothing a layer of buttercream on a cake or deftly distributing its filling. It is also a handy tool for lifting and turning pancakes or crêpes.

Angled or offset spatula This is useful for removing slices of tart or pie from rimmed pans without breaking them, and for lifting very delicate items like meringues.

Tongs These reach like heatproof fingers into sizzling pots and pans to grip small or awkwardly shaped items. They are invaluable for removing individual strands or pieces of pasta from the water to test for doneness, or for serving pasta.

Forks

Metal fork The long two-pronged kitchen forks, which are also known as pot forks or cook's forks, are mostly for various tasks such as removing a whole chicken from a deep pot or turning a roast. Smaller three-tined forks are called granny forks.

A strong fork with two long tines is necessary for holding meat firmly while it is carved. The best forks have a full tang riveted to a wooden or plastic handle. A carving fork may have a guard to protect the hand.

Wooden fork This friendly giant is ideal for gently swirling spaghetti while it cooks in the pot. Some cooks also find its light touch useful when adding liquid to pastry or dough mixtures.

Colander For the speedy separation of food from liquid, a round, double-handled metal bowl standing on a firm base and laced with a pattern of perforations is the most effective instrument to use. Choose the most roomy colander you can find so that when you are washing fruit, vegetables, or greens, there is plenty of space to swish them around.

Corkscrew There are so many different corkscrews that it's difficult to decide which is best for you. Corkscrews are very personal things—some people swear by one type of mechanism, others by another. The coil (or worm) should be a very sharp, thin spiral, preferably of a triangular section so that it really cuts into the cork. It should have a solid, comfortable handle, and should be long enough so that it can penetrate the whole cork.

The corkscrew that is known as the Screwpull is very simple and effective because it involves no pulling, and the screw itself is wider than most, making it extremely effective at holding the cork firmly. As you turn the handle, the screw goes into the cork and lifts it out in one action. Some models incorporate a blade for cutting the foil.

The winged or double-lever corkscrew is also easy to use. No pulling is required: the coil is screwed in and the two arms slowly depressed to raise the cork.

The simple waiter's corkscrew needs only a little strength to use and is quite efficient and reliable, if it is inserted and pulled out straight—otherwise, it breaks the cork. The classic corkscrew with a simple wooden crossbar can require a lot of effort, especially if the cork is stubborn.

Bottle opener Choose the simplest and sturdiest bottle opener you can find. Wooden handles have a nice feel to them. Make sure that the shape fits your hand comfortably.

Can opener Easy to use is the type that clamps onto the rim of the can and then cuts through the metal by means of two gear-driven cutting wheels, which are turned by means of a butterfly handle. It grips the can very firmly and leaves a very clean cut edge. Dishwasherproof, this type of can opener is a sophisticated and much improved version of the original all-metal butterfly-action opener.

A wall-mounted opener is also very convenient to use, in that the can is slotted into the jaws and held there by a lever as the lid is removed.

The old-fashioned scythe-cutting-action manual can opener has no moving parts to wear out, but it requires a firm pushing action to cut through the lid, and makes a rather messy job of it.

OTHER USEFUL ITEMS

Depending on the kind of cooking you do, you may consider some, or all, of the following to be essential.

Pasta machine This operates in a similar way to an old-fashioned clothes mangle with adjustable rollers. It has attachments to produce different shapes and sizes of pasta. The best machines are made of chrome-plated steel with stainless steel rollers.

Salad basket and spinner A salad basket, that airy balloon of wire, will contain a leafy salad with the minimum of restriction while it is whirled around out in the garden by energetic arms to extract the water by centrifugal force. If you don't have revolving arm sockets, try instead one of the ingenious plastic salad spinners operated by a handle.

Bulb baster A useful tool, this looks rather like a large syringe and acts on the same principle. Inserting the plastic tube of the baster into a liquid and squeezing the rubber bulb at the top draws the liquid up into the tube. It can then be squirted back out again, for basting meat during roasting. The added advantage of a bulb baster is that it can also be used as a fat separator—any fat in the liquid settles at the top of the tube, and can be left behind. Some basters come with a needle that can be screwed onto the tip and used to inject the basting liquid into the meat, or under the skin of a roasting chicken or turkey.

Gravy separator As a fat separator, this is an alternative to the bulb baster. The original version of the gravy separator, which was invented by the French, is an ingenious gravy boat with two spouts, one at either side. One spout has a deep funnel that pours the nonfatty gravy (*maigre*) from the bottom of the pitcher, while the other is shallow and pours the fat (*gras*) on the surface; its French name is *maigre et gras*, or *gras-maigre*. The newer plastic types have just one spout for pouring out the nonfatty gravy or pan juices.

Funnel This can be made of stainless steel, aluminum, or plastic, and is an invaluable tool for decanting liquids into bottles or other narrow-necked containers.

Lobster crackers These look like nutcrackers in the shape of lobster claws. They are hinged, with ridges inside near the hinge, and are indispensable for cracking open the very hard shells of both lobster and crab claws.

Lobster pick These are for extracting every last bit of meat from the awkward parts of lobsters and crabs. The most efficient picks have a two-pronged fork at the end, which helps pull the meat from hidden crevices.

Lobster pincer This is a two-in-one tool that in essence combines both lobster crackers and pick.

Nutcrackers Heavy chrome- or silver-plated crackers with a squeezing action are probably the most popular shape, but people with weak wrists may find them difficult; a wooden version of the screw-type nutcracker is a good alternative.

Cake tester Resembling a long needle with a handle, a cake tester is inserted into a cake to check for doneness. A toothpick will often do this job, but cake testers are especially useful for tall cakes baked in deep Bundt or other such pans.

Wire cake rack Raised wire racks are essential for cooling just-baked pastries, cookies, and cakes. If the steamy moisture is not allowed to escape after baking, it will condense inside the dough, making it leaden. Choose large racks made of strong stainless steel.

Useful utensils, bowls, and measuring equipment

1 gravy separator
2 meat thermometer
3 deep-fry/candy thermometer
4 bulb baster
5 glass mixing bowls
6 English pudding basins
7 ceramic mixing bowl
8 wooden salad bowl with salad servers
9 salad spinner
10 stainless steel bowls
11 blowtorch
12 pasta machine
13 lobster cracker
14 nutcracker
15 lobster pick
16 cake tester
17 wire cooling rack
18 dry measuring cups
19 glass measuring cups
20 funnel
21 electronic scale
22 ice cream scoop
23 measuring spoons

Blowtorch This is used by chefs to rapidly caramelize the sugared tops of desserts such as crème brûlée. Buy a small blowtorch for your kitchen from a hardware store—it will be invaluable for that professional touch with desserts that would otherwise melt or overcook if caramelized using the conventional broiler method.

Ice cream scoop There are two main types. One has a blade that sweeps between the bowl of the scoop and the ice cream, shaping the ice cream into a perfect ball as if by magic. This is the traditional kind used in ice cream parlors; it is easy to use, but needs to be dunked in water in between each scooping or the ice cream will stick. It is also useful for serving mashed potatoes and other vegetable purées, and for making cookies (especially the smaller sizes).

A second, rather more sophisticated type of ice cream scoop has no blade mechanism, but inside the handle there is a type of (nontoxic) antifreeze fluid. This enables you to scoop out very hard ice cream, sorbets, and granitas (be sure not to put this type of scoop in the dishwasher, or the antifreeze fluid will solidify). A similar version is made without the antifreeze.

Trussing equipment For the simple trussing of whole birds, especially small ones, kitchen string is usually sufficient. Short metal skewers or poultry lacers are useful for larger birds and those that are stuffed. Trussing with a needle and butcher's twine keeps a large stuffed bird in good shape. Trussing needles have very sharp points and eyes that are large enough for threading the quite thick twine. The length of a trussing needle is important—it should be at least 10 inches long so that it can be used to pierce a bird from one side to the other, through wings or legs and the body in between. The butcher's twine or kitchen string should be strong, undyed, and not waxed.

Larding needle This is the type of needle used for larding roasts of meat with bacon or other fat. It is long and hollow, and often has one pointed end and a clasp at the other end to hold the fat.

BOWLS

Bowls are used for food preparation, cooking, storing, and serving. They are available in a huge variety of materials and sizes, each having qualities suited more to one purpose than another. Bowls must be suited to the job in hand—too large, and the ingredients spread themselves in a thin film around the sides; too small, and the contents will overflow.

Every serious kitchen needs at least one huge bowl, suitable for soaking dried beans, or perhaps a country ham, and for mixing layer cake batters and bread doughs. It will also be useful for salads.

Glass bowls Tempered glass bowls are good for all mixing tasks, and the sets of different sizes that fit neatly inside one another are most convenient for easy storage. All are heatproof, and some are also ovenproof. Many of us grew up mixing cookie dough in—or licking icing from—the nested set of colored Pyrex bowls, and Pyrex bowls are still the cornerstone of many a cook's collection.

Ceramic bowls The classic yellow mixing bowl with a white interior, made of stoneware, is a favorite of many cooks, especially those who bake their own bread, as it is the ideal bowl for dough making. At the bottom of one side, there is a small flat area that acts as a base for holding the bowl steady when tilting the bowl for beating or creaming.

China pudding basins These useful bowls are a standard of the English kitchen. The sides of a pudding basin are steeper and more tapered than those of a regular mixing bowl because this shape gives support to the center of the cooked dessert or pudding, and prevents it from collapsing when turned out. The tough glazed finish will withstand even the high temperatures of a pressure cooker when steaming a pudding, and its raised rim holds a cover and string in place.

Plastic bowls Good-quality plastic bowls are quiet, nonporous, virtually unbreakable, and good insulators, but they have to be treated carefully, as they are vulnerable to scratching and to distortion through heat. And of course they cannot be used in the oven. A rubber-ringed base will keep the bowl anchored safely in place. Melamine is one of the toughest plastics used to manufacture mixing bowls, and it can be put in the dishwasher.

Stainless steel bowls It is not surprising that most restaurant kitchens choose to use stainless steel bowls almost to the exclusion of all others. The conductivity of metal makes these bowls ideal for ingredients that need to be cooled or heated over water; stainless steel is also an excellent alternative to the once-popular copper for beating egg whites.

Wooden bowls A handsome wooden bowl is the perfect setting for fresh green lettuce leaves. It should be wide and deep enough to contain an exuberant curly salad while it is being tossed.

Wooden bowls need to be washed briefly soon after they have been used, as they absorb the flavor of food. When washing, use the minimum amount of detergent, and never soak these bowls, or dry them next to direct heat.

Other bowls There are all sorts of small porcelain, earthenware, terracotta, and stoneware bowls of ancient and modern design that are endlessly useful. Handmade bowls with slightly rough interiors are good for making mayonnaise and vinaigrette—the surface helps the mixture to emulsify.

MEASURING EQUIPMENT

It is obvious from just a cursory glance at any cookbook that artistry needs to be underpinned by a solid foundation of knowledge. Ingredients must often be measured in exact amounts, assembled and prepared in an ordered sequence, and then cooked at precise temperatures for a predetermined length of time. Measuring equipment is therefore an important component of the *batterie de cuisine*, enabling recipes to be perfectly balanced every time.

In these days of international recipe exchanges, measuring is complicated by the different systems used in America and Europe. Americans mete out their ingredients, liquid and dry, in cups (which sounds like a vague term for what is in fact a precise volume), and only rarely weigh ingredients in ounces and pounds, whereas Europeans measure their dry ingredients by metric weights. (To further complicate the issue, the American pints, quarts, and gallons are quite different from English imperial measures, their counterparts that share the same names.) So it makes sense, whenever possible, to buy measuring

devices that are marked with metric calibrations, as well as with our regular American measures.

Scales

Balancing quantities of goods against weights of constant or standard size is a very ancient practice that began in the marketplace as a fair method of trading. In these days of high technology, scales are more important than ever, not least in the kitchen, where serious cooks know they are one of the keys to successful baking and useful for some other recipes as well.

Balance scale A strong balance scale will last a lifetime because it operates on a simple seesaw principle and there is no complicated mechanism to wear out. The weight is not indicated on a register, but when the weights on the two sides exactly match, a pointer lines up with a central marker on the fulcrum. These scales are usually so sensitive that two or three crumbs added to either side are enough to tip the balance.

American or metric weights may be used according to the manufacturer, and these are available in brass or, less expensively, in cast iron, especially for the heavier weights. The pan for containing the food should ideally be a pear-shaped brass, stainless steel, or enamel bowl that, when tipped, will funnel its contents neatly into a mixing bowl or saucepan.

Electronic battery-operated scales have a digital display that shows either just American weights or both American and metric weights. Many models incorporate an ingenious device by which the display can be returned to zero when weighing more than one ingredient in the bowl at the same time. The disadvantage of these scales is that they are not very accurate with small amounts (under 1 ounce).

Spring-balance scale In this type of scale, the weights have been replaced by a metal coil or spring. The ingredients are balanced against the tension stored in the spring and the weight is registered on a calibrated scale, usually marked with both American and metric measures. The capacity is limited by the power of the spring, so check before purchase that the scale is not just suited to light loads— the best balance scales will weigh up to 26 pounds. There is a tendency for spring balance scales to wander out of true, so choose one where accuracy can be restored by means of an adjustment screw when the scale is at rest.

Measuring cups

For cooking purposes, ingredients are usually measured in cups, or fractions thereof (and smaller amounts in teaspoons and tablespoons). Many cooks who do a lot of baking, especially bread making, however, prefer to weigh dry ingredients such as flour and sugar for more accurate measurement.

For liquids, a measuring cup made of tempered glass is the most useful; the glass, which can withstand the impact of boiling liquids, enables the cook to see exactly how much is in the cup, and, because glass is such a poor conductor of heat, the handle always remains cool.

Clear plastic measuring cups are cheaper than glass, but they must be treated more carefully; heat can craze or distort the plastic, and if the shape of the

cup changes, it may no longer provide an accurate measure. Liquid measuring cups come in 1-cup, 2-cup, 1-quart, and even larger sizes. Most also have metric markings.

The best dry measuring cups are sturdy metal ones; cheaper plastic ones are often inaccurate. Dry measuring cups come in sets that nest neatly inside each other. Most sets include ¼-cup, ⅓-cup, ½-cup, and 1-cup measures; some have an ⅛-cup measure too, and 2-cup dry measuring cups are also available. Dry ingredients should be spooned or scooped into the cup, without packing (except for brown sugar, which is measured by the packed cup), and the top leveled off with a knife or other straight edge.

Measuring spoons

Smaller amounts of ingredients, both liquid and dry, are measured using measuring spoons. The best are metal, but plastic ones are also common; avoid cheaper sets, which are likely to be inaccurate. Measuring spoons always come in sets, which usually include ⅛-teaspoon, ¼-teaspoon, ½-teaspoon, and 1-tablespoon measures; some also have a handy ½-tablespoon measure (which is, of course, the same as 1½ teaspoons). The ingredients in the spoon should be leveled off with a knife unless the recipe specifies a heaped measure.

Thermometers

A well-equipped kitchen will ideally have a variety of thermometers to cope with the whole gamut of culinary needs, from monitoring the coldest depths of the freezer to recognizing the different stages of cooking sugar. Precise temperature control is also essential for the safety and the success of many dishes and methods, such as making custard or yogurt, yeast baking, deep-fat frying, and jam making.

Freezer thermometer There are two enemies to be faced when preserving food by freezing: first, the bacteria that cause the food to decay, and second, the enzymes that break down its structure and impair the flavor. Food frozen to 0°F will be safe from bacteriological activity. You should check that this temperature is constantly maintained, as the enzymes will begin to function at 14°F.

Deep-fry and sugar/candy thermometers These register the highest temperatures that are encountered in cooking. The secret of successful deep-frying lies in preheating the oil until it registers about 375°F on a deep-fry thermometer before adding the food. At this temperature, the oil will sear the food instantly, preventing the escape of any juices or flavor; conversely, the food will not absorb the oil.

When sugar is heated, it passes through various stages of crystallization at certain critical temperatures, until at 356°F it becomes dark caramel. A candy thermometer is required to catch the sugar at just the right moment before it passes to the next stage. Combination deep-fry/candy thermometers are also widely available. Some of these high-temperature thermometers are made of glass, so warm them in hot water before use to avoid any danger of cracking.

Oven thermometer In a perfect world this would be superfluous, but ovens are notorious for their idiosyncrasies and their temperature variations between the top and bottom racks and the front and back. You can establish the temperature pattern inside your oven by standing or hanging a mercury-filled or spring-type thermometer in various positions and noting the differences.

Meat thermometer This will take all the guesswork out of roasting meat by enabling you to gauge the exact degree of doneness. A meat thermometer is also vital for checking the internal temperature of whole roast chickens and turkeys—this should be at least 180° to 185°F to kill any dangerous bacteria such as salmonella. "Instant-read" meat thermometers are used for spot checks, but the more common type is inserted into the meat or poultry before cooking begins and left until the hand points to the appropriate place on the dial.

Timers

Automatic timer Very often it is the sense of smell that alerts a busy or forgetful person that something is not only cooked but overcooked. An automatic timer preset to ring at a certain time will help avoid disaster.

Sand timer Egg timers and hourglasses have now been largely superseded by automatic timers, but they are quiet and accurate, and cost a fraction of the price.

STOVETOP POTS AND PANS

Before purchasing, take care to find out what the qualities of good saucepans are and the various properties of the metals they are made from. Equipped with this information, it is possible to make a selection that will suit all needs and give a lifetime's reliable service.

The materials

Stainless steel The most durable metal found in the kitchen, stainless steel will retain a polished finish throughout its long life and is completely impervious to acid or alkaline ingredients. Alas, this promising metal is not the best conductor of heat—which is of course an enormous drawback in a pan—but thankfully, modern technology has found a solution. Good-quality stainless steel pans now have heavy-gauge bases made of a "sandwich" of stainless steel with a metal filling that is a good conductor of heat. This may be copper, copper and silver alloy, or aluminum or aluminum alloy. These types of pans are expensive, but they should last a lifetime. *Care* Soak pans to loosen food deposits, then clean with a brush and hot soapy water. Scouring pads and powders can be used without risk of damage.

Iron and steel In spite of its propensity to rust, cast iron is popular for some pans, such as stovetop griddles, frying pans, paella pans, blini pans, and Belgian waffle pans, when cooking the food evenly at high temperatures is important.

Untreated black steel pans are very susceptible to corrosion and distortion by heat, and although a well-seasoned heavy steel frying pan, crêpe pan, or omelet pan is a very satisfying thing to use, saucepans made of steel are always covered with a layer of vitrified enamel. *Care* Maintenance is a continuous battle against rust. Pans should be thoroughly dried before being stored, and if they are not used very often, coated with a light layer of vegetable oil before being put away. New cast-iron and black steel pans should be prepared for use by seasoning them: first heat the pan slightly and then wash thoroughly in hot soapy water to remove any protective coating. Dry the pan and heat again, with some vegetable oil in the pan, over fairly high heat until it smokes. Keep the pan at this high temperature for several minutes, tilting the pan so that the oil runs over the

Stovetop pots and pans, ovenware, and bakeware

1 pasta pot
2 enameled cast-iron casseroles
3 baking and gratin dishes
4 ramekins
5 soufflé dish
6 glass custard cups
7 stainless steel roasting pan with rack
8 nonstick frying pan
9 baking sheet
10 cast-iron griddle
11 long chopsticks
12 wooden spatula
13 wok
14 ridged cast-iron grill pan
15 cast-iron frying pan
16 stainless steel saucepans

bottom and up the sides until the whole surface of the pan has been covered. Cool, then vigorously rub and wipe out excess oil using a pad of paper towels and some coarse salt. Cast-iron pans may also be seasoned in the oven: brush with oil and add about ¼ inch oil to the pan. Heat in a 300°F oven for 1 hour, then cool and wipe out the excess oil.

Enameled cast iron and steel Enameled cast iron is a good, even conductor of heat, and it does not rust. It makes very strong, sturdy vessels, which are excellent for both stovetop and oven cooking—ideal for casseroles and stews or braises that are started off on top of the stove and then left to simmer slowly in the oven. Allow time for the metal to heat up at the start of cooking, and remember that it will retain the heat exceptionally well, so it is rare that a very high heat need be used.

Care Wash these types of pans in hot soapy water, scrubbing off any food that has adhered during cooking with a brush. Soaking helps loosen stubborn food stuck on the inside of pans. Plastic scouring pads can be used, and if all else fails, diluted bleach.

Enameled steel pans need to be treated with care—don't allow empty pans to sit over the heat, or they will distort and shed their protective enamel coating, and never clean them with an abrasive substance, or you will eventually expose the metal. Harsh scouring powders or pads will destroy the glassy surface and eventually wear through the enamel; any stains can be easily removed by soaking the pan in a solution of diluted bleach. Be careful not to bang or knock these pans, particularly when they are hot, as the enamel may chip. They scorch easily, are not very flat, and are not good conductors of heat, so are only really appropriate when cooking with gas, not on an electric stove.

Copper The great advantage of copper is that it is an excellent conductor of heat, and its rich golden-red color adds a warm glow to the kitchen. But it is expensive and, regrettably, readily combines chemically with food, liquids, and the air to form a poisonous layer of green verdigris. For this reason, copper cooking vessels must always be lined. Tin or silver were the traditional lining materials, but nowadays the more durable stainless steel is preferred.

Care Copper needs constant polishing to keep it bright, and for some this is just one chore too many. Salt and lemon halves will keep copper pans shining— commercial cleaners give the copper a light finish that is difficult to maintain. Avoid using harsh scouring pads, cream, or powder when cleaning the copper outside of the pans.

Nonstick Nonstick surfaces are a gift from modern technology and daily appear in more durable and long-lived forms. They are particularly useful for lining frying pans, where, for example, eggs and fillets of fish will cook happily with little or no fat and be released completely intact at the end, leaving scarcely a trace in the pan.

Care Clean with a plastic scouring pad or cloth in hot soapy water, rinse, and dry. Avoid using metal spoons: these will scratch, exposing the metal beneath.

The perfect metal Unfortunately, no one particular metal is capable of providing the perfect pan, but until a single hybrid alloy can be produced combining the beauty and conductivity of copper and the stability of stainless steel, the next best thing is to laminate the various metals in such a way as to combine all their best qualities and minimize their negative points. Combinations that give excellent results are: aluminum sandwiched between an outer layer of copper and an inner lining of stainless steel; copper lined with stainless steel; aluminum lined with a nonstick finish; cast iron coated with enamel; and stainless steel with a thick copper or aluminum base.

Choosing pans

Once you have decided on the best metal or combination of metals, you should consider the design and quality of the pan. Look for the following points:

- Thick, heavy-gauge metal, particularly at the bottom, which will not distort or dent and will spread the heat evenly from the source to all parts of the pan.
- Sides that curve gently into the base so that no part of the pan will be inaccessible to the spoon. This is a good feature to look for in a frying pan—curved sides enable delicate omelets, for example, to be rolled gently onto a plate without damage.
- Handles should be strong, securely riveted to the pan, and preferably

insulated so they always remain cool enough to hold. They should have well-rounded contours—thin angular shapes cut into the hand when you are pouring or lifting heavy pans. Plastic or wooden handles are the best insulators, but may loosen and split if cleaned in a dishwasher, and of course they can't go in the oven. A sturdy ring or a hole at the end of the handle is useful for hanging the pan on a rack.

- Lids must give a tight seal and be shaped so that condensed water vapor is returned to the pan and does not escape in trickles down the outside of it. Lid knobs, like handles, should remain cool enough to touch—again, plastic or wood is best.

Storage

If possible, pans should be kept at eye level, or at least above the waist, either hanging from a rack or lined up on a shelf. Crowded, low cupboards infuriate the busy cook, while pans piled together indiscriminately are very likely to become scratched, or will be pushed to inaccessible corners.

Useful pots and pans

The following pans will make a good "starter pack" if you are equipping a kitchen from scratch. There are many more pans you can have, but most are suited to specific tasks, so it is best to buy them only if and when you need them. Good-quality pans are expensive, but they will last a very long time.

Set of stainless steel pans

A stacking set of three or four saucepans is adequate for most tasks. Sizes vary enormously, so choose the ones that suit your needs and size of household. A large pot with two handles is an essential purchase even if you normally cook small quantities—you can use it for cooking pasta and making stocks and soups, and it can also double as a casserole to be used in the oven.

Frying pan Cast-iron frying pans are traditional, especially for sautéing and making pancakes. They improve with age and can last a lifetime. However, they are heavy and not always easy to clean, so a couple of good-quality nonstick frying pans will also come in handy. These will not last as long as cast iron, so expect to replace them from time to time.

OVENWARE AND BAKEWARE

From everyday roasting pans and baking sheets to "country kitchen" casseroles, porcelain ramekins, and fancifully shaped metal molds, this section covers items that you will use time and again, and more specialized equipment that may be used only once a year.

The materials

Stainless steel This conducts heat slowly, so its use in the oven is generally limited to roasting pans, although some other baking equipment is made in stainless.

Enamel High-quality enamel on steel or cast iron is a most durable, hard-wearing combination—the glassy finish will not be affected by even the most corrosive ingredients. Its weakness lies in the different expansion rates of the enamel and base metal, so it is particularly vulnerable to chipping when it is heated or cooled.

Glass Ovenproof glass behaves in the same way as dark metal surfaces when it is heated, and oven temperatures should be reduced slightly (by about 25°F) when using glass baking dishes. The brittleness, however, and sensitivity of glass to temperature changes means that careful handling is essential. It is not as good a conductor of heat as metal, so if used for pies and other pastry-based dishes, the pastry bottom will never achieve such a crisp result.

Porcelain This is especially suitable for dishes such as soufflés that must be served straight from the oven. Although porcelain is prone to chipping, the highly vitrified surface is very tough.

Stoneware is another tough ceramic, with a homey quality and the ability to withstand high temperatures in the oven.

Glazed earthenware is not as highly fired as stoneware, so will chip more easily.

Unglazed terracotta pots for cooking meats or vegetables without fat will be essential for the diet-conscious, or for those who enjoy the flavor of meat and vegetables stewed in their own juices.

The equipment

Casserole Casseroles require slow, lengthy cooking, so conservation of moisture is of paramount importance. Whatever the material the dish is made from, it should be heavy so that it absorbs heat slowly and then retains heat and moisture for the longest possible time. The lid must fit very tightly to prevent the

---

Sauté pan Deeper than ordinary frying pans, sauté pans have straight or slightly rounded sides. A good sauté pan is very versatile; it can be used both as a regular frying pan and for risottos, sautés, stir-fries, sauces, etc., and for poaching.

Pasta pot This is stainless steel, with a perforated inner basket. It is expensive, but ideal for cooking pasta in a large quantity of water, and the basket makes for easy draining. Some pasta pots also come with a second insert for steaming.

Steamer set The best is stainless steel, with one or two stackable steamer compartments. The bottom pot can also serve as a stovetop pot. The Chinese bamboo steamer that fits in a wok is cheaper, but its use is more limited.

Wok and accessories An inexpensive carbon-steel wok is more than adequate, but the more expensive preseasoned carbon steel woks are easier to keep clean. Carbon steel is the best metal because it is such an excellent conductor of heat. The most useful accessories are wooden spatulas and long chopsticks, plus a long-handled spatula or scoop.

Clean your wok with hot soapy water, and dry it well. To prevent rusting, wipe it with vegetable oil before putting away.

Cake and pastry making equipment

1 loaf pan
2 rolling pin
3 tube pan
4 flour sifter
5 Bundt pan
6 deep pie dish
7 ceramic tart pan
8 dough scraper
9 jellyroll pan
10 pastry brush
11 marble slab
12 pastry blender
13 madeleine pan
14 muffin pan
15 round cake pan
16 brioche mold
17 springform pan
18 ring mold
19 removable-bottomed tart pan
20 pastry bag with tips

escape of steam, and the seal must be designed so that condensed water vapor is channeled back into the dish. Handles should be easy to grip, yet small enough for the dish to fit easily into the oven.

Casseroles made of enameled cast iron, or other suitable heavy-gauge metals, can be used on top of the stove, for searing the meat over high heat (if required) and for lengthy simmering. Earthenware or heat-resistant glass dishes should only be used in the oven.

It is useful to have casseroles of various sizes because the contents should fill the pots in the correct proportion—a small stew in a large casserole, for instance, will dry out long before it is cooked.

Baking dish and gratin dish It is impossible to have too many of these, in different shapes and sizes, full-size and individual. They are used for lasagne and other baked pastas, moussaka, chicken pot pie, vegetable gratins and roasts—in fact any dish with a topping that needs to be crisped and browned at a high temperature. Baking dishes may be rectangular or oval and made of porcelain, enameled cast iron or steel, glass, or earthenware or stoneware. French gratin dishes were traditionally made of copper, but nowadays enameled cast iron, porcelain, and stoneware are more common. They can be put safely under the broiler or into a very hot oven and yet still look presentable enough for the table.

Roasting pan Roasting pans in one or two sizes are useful, in stainless steel or anodized aluminum, which are both easy to clean—an important consideration with a roasting pan. Buy them with racks that fit inside for keeping meat and poultry above the fat as it runs out during roasting. Racks are especially good for fatty birds like duck and geese, and long-cooking poultry such as turkey.

Ovenproof skillet A useful pan for dishes that need to start off on top of the stove, finish cooking in the oven, and then be turned out for serving. French *tarte tatin* and potato galette are such dishes, as are some Italian frittatas. Most frying pans do not have ovenproof handles, so would not be suitable, whereas cast iron is.

Soufflé dish These are traditionally straight-sided so the soufflé mixture can rise unimpeded above the edge. Made of porcelain, glass, or stoneware, they can be

taken straight from oven to table. Available in different sizes and as individal ramekins, they are also useful for general baking, and for such things as baked custard and gelatin-based cold mousses and soufflés.

Terrine Deep enameled cast-iron or earthenware terrines are traditional for baking pâtés and terrines. They are often long and narrow, which makes for elegant presentation.

Baking sheet Heavy-duty steel sheets are best. Flat and rigid, they are good conductors of heat, and will not buckle or warp in the hottest of ovens. Baking sheets usually have four slightly flared upturned edges. Cookie sheets have only one, or sometimes two, rims; the flat sheet allows hot air to circulate around the cookies for more even baking.

CAKE AND PASTRY MAKING EQUIPMENT

When food is placed in the dry, hot atmosphere of the oven, it is cooked equally from all directions, and the containers do not have to withstand and conduct heat from a single intense source as saucepans do. The function of a baking pan is to mold and contain, and to respond as quickly as possible to the ambient heat of the oven.

The materials

Some baking pans have bright shining surfaces, which deflect the heat away from the contents so that they will not scorch. Others have dark finishes, which absorb and hold the heat and need an oven temperature reduction of 25°F to achieve the same results.

Tinned steel, black steel This is the most widely used material for baking containers. It is really worth spending money on good-quality baking pans that have the minimum number of seams, as nooks and crannies are difficult to clean and dry. Corrosion is the chief enemy of tinned steel, for underneath the shining exterior lurks a metal that is addicted to oxidation through even the smallest pinhole in the tin coating. Never use steel wool or other abrasive cleaning materials; wash and dry baking pans as soon as possible after use. A good-quality, well-treated tinned steel baking pan will last a lifetime.

Some baking equipment, such as tart pans and loaf pans, is made of plain black or blue steel. Black steel conducts heat well and evenly, but it rusts easily

and so must be well dried after washing.

Aluminum Impervious to atmospheric oxidation, aluminum is a metal that is often used for cake pans, but it is thinner and lighter than tinned steel, making it unsuitable for dense rich fruit mixtures or other cakes that need a long baking time. They are likely to dry out and even burn if baked in aluminum pans. In any case, choose heavier-weight aluminum pans.

Stainless steel Stainless steel baking pans are sturdy, nonreactive, and easy to clean. However, stainless steel does not conduct heat well, and can be expensive.

Nonstick silicone surfaces These can be applied to tinned steel or aluminum, but the surface will not last if metal utensils are used to cut or scoop out the contents of the pan. To clean nonstick surfaces, soak for a few minutes, then wipe with a soapy cloth and rinse.

Aluminum foil If you are baking for the freezer, it is a nuisance to lose the use of baking containers for weeks on end. Aluminum foil dishes can be used in the oven, then put in the freezer once cool.

Cake pans

Even if you are not a prolific baker or cake maker, a few basic pans are very versatile and well worth buying.

Round cake pan The standard size of these is 8 or 9 inches in diameter and about 1 inch deep; some, which are usually of better quality, are 2 inches deep. Shiny metal pans are best for these because they deflect the heat and the cake cooks quickly and evenly. Loose-bottomed pans facilitate unmolding.

Square cake pan Used for brownies and gingerbread as well as for cakes, the standard sizes are 8 and 9 inches square. Square cake pans are available in the same materials as round cake pans, and also in glass.

Springform pan This is one of the most useful pans in that it can be used for most cake batters. It can also be used for cheesecakes and for layered mousse cakes. The combination of the spring-clip mechanism and loose bottom makes it an excellent pan for easy unmolding of delicate or crumbly textures.

Jelly-roll pan Indispensable for making jelly rolls and other rolled cakes, this pan is also useful as a baking sheet.

Loaf pan These are sold in different sizes, but 5 by 9 inches and 4½ by 8½ inches are the most common. Also called bread pans, these are useful for pound cakes and tea breads as well as the daily loaves, and are the standard pan for meat loaf. Nonstick pans are useful for both bread and cakes.

Muffin pan Muffin pans have 6 or 12 cups and come in three sizes, for regular, miniature, and giant muffins. Related pans, with cups of varying sizes, include those for making mini Bundt cakes, miniature tea cake pans, and fancy bun or muffin pans. These latter, often in cast iron, have decorative cups. Nonstick pans make for easy unmolding.

Specialty cake pans and molds

Some traditional and classic cakes require specially shaped pans; among these is the tube pan used for angel food cake. Pans with loose bottoms are best. Some have three little feet along the top edge for raising the cake up during its upside-down cooling. Bundt pans, used for dense cakes like pound cakes, are fluted tube pans that come in various sizes; a 10-inch pan with a 12-cup capacity is the most useful. The Austrian *kugelhopf* pan is a fluted tube pan used for the enriched sweet bread of the same name.

Other special pans include those for savarins, brioches, and charlottes, all of which can double as molds for mousses and other gelatin-based desserts, so are worth buying to add interest to your culinary repertoire. Pans or molds with depressions for individual madeleines, éclairs, and petits fours are more specialized and therefore less generally useful. Molds for cannoli and cream horns, *coeurs à la crème*, and darioles, etc., also fall into this latter category.

Decorating equipment

Desserts, pastries, and cakes are often decorated using a pastry bag for piping, whether it is writing messages on frosting or making a ring of whipped cream rosettes. Pastry bags are also used for shaping meringues and choux pastry.

Pastry bag These cone-shaped bags are usually made of flexible nylon fabric or plastic-lined cotton that can be easily washed and dried after use. A decorating tube or tip is fitted into the opening in the tip of the bag and the contents are forced through by twisting the top of the bag and then applying gentle hand pressure.

Pastry tube or tip A good set of these will contain large, plain round tips for shaping meringues, cream puffs, or

éclairs, large star tips for piping whipped cream, and a galaxy of smaller tips for delicate and intricate cake icing.

Revolving turntable When decorating a cake, you must have the part you are working on facing you; turntables can be rotated with just a flick of a finger.

Pastry making

Anyone who makes pastry needs good tools because pastry is not improved by handling, and because pastry making turns from a chore to a pleasure if your equipment is well designed and efficient.

Rolling pin Some cooks are perfectly happy to be up to their elbows in flour; those who have this tactile approach to baking will probably opt for a rolling pin made from a single length of wood, which keeps the palms near the dough.

The handled pin is more likely to suit people who prefer to keep food at a distance. The two handles, which are set on an axle and remain stationary in the hands, guide the pin.

The best rolling pins of either type are heavy and of a good size, made of hard, close-grained wood smoothed to a fine, silky finish. Ceramic and marble rolling pins are available, but these break easily and do not roll as well—the smooth surface will not hold a dusting of flour.

Boards and slabs Pastry can be rolled perfectly well on smooth kitchen countertops. A large wooden board can also be used, but to preserve its smooth surface, it should only be used for pastry and not as a bread or cutting board. Polyethylene or acrylic boards are very good for pastry because they are smooth, stay cool, and are easy to clean after use.

Marble slabs These are satin-smooth, impervious to flavors, and keep the pastry cold while it is being worked.

Pie and tart pans

Pie pan Aluminum or black or tinned steel are best. The bottom crust of a pie really needs metal beneath it to crisp—glass and ceramic do not conduct heat well enough and so result in a soggy crust under the filling. This is especially true with wet or juicy fruit fillings.

Deep-dish pie pan For deep-dish pies, choose from earthenware, tempered glass, or porcelain. Pans for deep-dish apple pie and the like are $\frac{1}{2}$ to 1 inch deeper than regular pie pans; there is also a deeper oval pie dish, used for fruit pies and, traditionally, for British savory pies.

Tart pan These are for open-faced tarts, quiches, and flans. Usually fluted for attractive presentation, they come in different shapes and sizes, and may be made of metal or porcelain (when they are sometimes called quiche pans). Removable-bottomed pans are especially good for sweet, rich pastries that are likely to break. To unmold, the bottom is pushed up from the side of the pan so that the tart comes out in one piece. For serving, the tart can be slid off the bottom or left on.

Flan ring and frame An alternative to removable-bottomed tart pans, these come in many more shapes and sizes. Some rings are also called cake or tart rings. All of these are used on a baking sheet and lift off so that the quiche, tart, or other pastry can be easily transferred to a plate or dish.

Other useful equipment

Flour sifter This both aerates flour and blends it with other dry ingredients as called for in a recipe. Sifters come in various sizes and in stainless steel, tinned steel, or plastic. Some have a triple screen rather than just a single one, for finer sifting.

Pastry blender This ingenious tool is most adept at cutting fat into flour and aerating it at the same time. It is made of a series of stainless steel wires curved into a half-oval shape and attached to a handle. The best have deep wires to cope with a large volume of ingredients.

Dough scraper This piece of flexible plastic is used by bakers for scraping up rich pastry doughs from marble slabs and other work surfaces, and for marking and dividing dough into portions. Some dough scrapers are rigid and have handles; these are also called bench scrapers, and look more like tools for smoothing plaster.

Pastry brush Soft natural or nylon bristles will spread egg washes, glazes, jam, or melted butter without damaging the surface of delicate or uncooked pastry. They are also useful for buttering or oiling the awkward grooves and ridges in patterned baking pans and molds.

Sugar and flour dredgers are useful items, usually made of aluminum or stainless steel. They can be used for sprinkling cakes and other desserts with confectioners' sugar or cocoa, and for dusting a work surface with flour.

ELECTRICAL APPLIANCES

There is an ever-increasing choice of electrical appliances for the kitchen. Think hard before you purchase, and don't clutter up valuable counter and cupboard space with bulky machines you hardly ever use.

Blender For blending soups and making vegetable purées, pâtés, and baby food, a blender gives excellent results. Many blenders claim to be able to pulverize nuts, chop vegetables, and grate cheese, but few have the power and the capacity to do so, and it is often just as quick to use a sharp knife. Some blenders offer over a dozen speeds, but these are really unnecessary; in fact, the machines called professional or bar blenders have only two speeds, but they are powerful and efficient.

Choose the largest blender you can, because they rarely work well when the container is more than half-full, and it is time-consuming trying to purée a huge pan of soup in a blender that takes a cup or two at a time. The container should be clear, tempered glass or heavyweight plastic to enable you to see how things are going on; avoid lightweight plastic, which may chip or crack. A small "trap door" in the lid allows you to dribble in your oil for mayonnaise without spattering the kitchen.

Hand-held immersion blender This is excellent for puréeing soup in the pan, thus saving on dish washing. It is also very good for whipping cream, making mayonnaise, and blending small quantities of ingredients.

Food processor The ultimate in kitchen machines, this chops, slices, shreds, pulverizes, and grinds, makes pastry and bread dough, and purées soups and pâté mixtures. Some models go even further and, with attachments and different blades, squeeze citrus fruit, grind coffee beans, and peel potatoes. They will not beat egg whites effectively, however, so a separate mixer or a rotary beater, or whisk, is still essential.

The more compact the design, the better for countertop storage, but you will still have to find room for the extra blades, disks, and attachments.

Choose a model that has a heavy-duty motor and a large bowl, as, like blenders, they work better if they are no more than half-full. Rubber foot pads will make the machine stay put during any operation.

Hand-held mixer The main advantage of a hand-held electric mixer is that it is faster than a whisk or old-fashioned rotary beater. It also frees one hand to hold the bowl or add ingredients as you beat, and you can move the mixer to beat in every part of the bowl. Choose a mixer with three speeds (high, medium, low) and a switch that is easy to change using your thumb. The beaters should be easy to remove for cleaning. Unless you want a stand mixer, buy a hand mixer with a heavy-duty motor and beaters for tough jobs such as mixing dough.

Stand mixer A heavy-duty stand mixer is useful for many jobs besides cake making. Most have a dough hook attachment and some a separate blender and/or coffee grinder, which can be used with the same motor and base. When a mixer also has such varied attachments as a food grinder, a juice extractor, a pasta maker, a potato peeler, and a shredder and slicer, it has really moved into the next function and price bracket of the all-in-one food processor. Before buying a multifunction apparatus, check that the motor can cope with heavy-duty jobs and is not just a glorified blender/mixer.

The mixer bowl may be made of plastic, stainless steel, or tempered glass; stainless steel or tempered glass is best for durability. In some mixers, the beaters are simply inserted into the motor housing and rotate only in one spot; these often leave a ring of unbeaten ingredients around the bowl. The best machines are those with beaters that travel in a circle as they rotate and thus beat every part of the mixture efficiently. Make sure, too, if you can, that the beaters can handle a small quantity, such as one egg. Mixers with light plastic bases and bowls may be lighter to move around, but a solid base with a rubber pad or feet will prevent the machine from "creeping" during prolonged activity.

Toaster Toasters are very simple electrical gadgets and the vast majority of them do their job efficiently. Some take four slices—a must for the large family—but standard models take two. Some have adjustable slots that are wide enough to take items like thick slices of bread, English muffins, bagels, and croissants without burning; others have one wider and one narrower slot. When selecting a toaster, look for a removable crumb tray—and a long guarantee.

Waffle iron Most waffle iron griddles have the traditional honeycombed surface, but others are embossed with figures or decorative scenes. A nonstick surface prevents waffles from sticking, and thermostat controls ensure the ideal crisp finish.

Juice extractor This offers effortless juice extraction from all kinds of fresh fruits and vegetables. A juice extractor is a worthwhile purchase if you drink a lot of fresh juice, as it will be less expensive than store-bought juices in the long run. Models range from simple and small citrus juicers to large machines with two juicing functions—one for extracting juice from vegetables and fruits such as apples and peaches, the other for juicing citrus fruits. Some models have filters and strainer baskets to separate the juice from the seeds, pulp, and pith.

Deep-fryer A thermostatically controlled, electric deep-fryer with a lid not only takes the guesswork and odor out of deep-frying, it is also the safest way to deep-fry at home. It brings the fat up to the chosen temperature and holds it there; the best models have a light that indicates the desired temperature is reached. Deep-fryers come in various capacities and designs, some with nonstick linings that are easy to keep clean. A good design feature in some models is a basket with handles that clip on the pan so that the fat from the fried food can drain before serving.

Ice cream machine Old methods of ice cream making involved a great deal of cranking and stirring over buckets of crushed ice and rock salt. The latest state-of-the-art ice cream machines have their own compressors and freezers so they sit on the countertop to make ice cream. This kind works very fast and doesn't take up freezer space—it also makes the most velvety smooth ice creams and sorbets. Professional-style models make a large quantity in a very short time. Less expensive electric ice cream machines with rotation motors are not quite as convenient, because they must be put into the freezer, but they also achieve very good results in a very short time. Choose a compact shape, and check that it makes a generous quantity.

Pasta machine A machine that makes the dough from start to finish, cutting out all the hard work of kneading and rolling by hand. The dough can be extruded in a variety of shapes according to the cutting disk used—from long and thin spaghetti and tagliatelle to ridged ziti, flat sheets of lasagne, and noodles.

Bread machine This popular machine mixes all the ingredients, then kneads the dough and bakes it. Most machines are quite compact and sit neatly on the countertop. A programmer allows you to set the time the machine operates, so you can wake up to freshly baked bread in the morning. The machine itself bakes different types of dough in a set loaf shape, but if you want rolls, different-shaped loaves, pizza, or pita bread, etc., you can use the machine just to ready the dough for shaping by hand and then bake it conventionally.

Coffee grinder The advantage of electric coffee grinders over the manual type is that they are quicker, but they are often noisy. The ideal grinder is quiet, efficient, and neat. It is also useful if you can preselect the grind required, from powder to coarse ground. The safest electric coffee grinders are those that will not work unless the lid is on.

Drip coffee machine The electric drip or filter coffee machine is an elaborate version of the drip coffeepot. It heats the water to the right temperature and pulses it through the ground coffee into the pot below; a hotplate under the pot keeps the coffee warm. As long as you put the correct type and amount of coffee in the filter, it's a foolproof way to make decent coffee. You should avoid leaving the pot on the hotplate for too long, however, or the coffee will taste stewed.

Combination coffee machine The most versatile coffee machine is the type that makes filter coffee in a pot on one side and espresso or cappuccino on the other, thus eliminating the need for two separate machines. Before you buy, check that the instructions are easy to follow, and ask for a demonstration if possible. Some espresso and cappuccino machines may look very glamorous and stylish, but they can be fiendishly difficult to use. Other considerations are whether the pump mechanism for frothing the milk for cappuccino is fast and efficient, and whether the water reservoir can be refilled during brewing for uninterrupted use. Pump espresso machines make the best coffee; also available are steam-type machines, which are less expensive but often produce disappointing results.

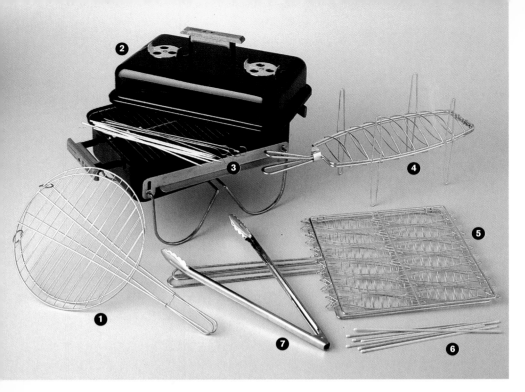

Cooking outdoors is one of the greatest pleasures of summertime and, to many, grilling is one of the easiest and the most enjoyable ways of preparing food.

Devotees of grilling will not need to be convinced of its benefits, but those who have not tried it should not be put off by the apparently vast selection of tools and equipment available: the rule is, the simpler the better. Food that has been cooked on a piece of chicken wire over a driftwood fire on a beach tastes just as good as—if not better than—food prepared on a elaborate gas-fired grill with a motorized spit.

Types of grills

For those with large backyards, a built-in brick barbecue is worth considering; it allows you to design extra warming racks, cupboards, and preparation surfaces. Sturdy grills made of heavy-gauge metals may be more expensive, but cheaper, flimsier ones are best avoided. Heavy metal and cast-iron grates—also called grids and, of course, just grills—are less likely to bend or become misshapen with repeated use than lightweight nickel-plated and chrome-plated grates, which do have the advantage of being rustproof. The grill wires should be positioned fairly close together for grilling chicken wings, sausages, and the like.

Most people find it is convenient to cook at table height and this is certainly safer for the usual grilling conditions of outdoor light and uneven ground; if you buy a small portable grill or hibachi, you will need to set it on a table or on a board on two stools. Some portable braziers have very short legs—check that they are high enough to cook on in comfort.

Kettle grill As the name suggests, kettle grills are totally enclosed by means of a hinged lid. This may be left open during grilling—it also provides a windbreak—but often the food is cooked with the lid down, which reflects the heat like an oven so that even whole chickens and roasts can be grilled. Made from cast-aluminum or vitreous-enameled steel, kettle grills are popular and versatile—they can also be used for smoke-cooking food.

Wagon-type grill Probably the most elaborate of grills, these carts are usually on wheels and sometimes covered. The

Grilling equipment

1 large grill basket
2 portable grill
3 bamboo and metal skewers
4 fish grill basket
5 sardine grill basket
6 long matches
7 long-handled tongs
8 kettle grill

larger kinds are gas-fired and have all manner of modern cooking aids, such as warming racks, electric rotisseries, thermometers, cutting surfaces, equipment racks, and even gas side burners for stovetop-style cooking. They are bulky and need storage room in winter, but they come into their own if you are cooking for a lot of people.

Hibachi These are small Japanese-style black cast-iron troughs, rectangular or round, with strong wooden-handled grids. The height of the grids is adjustable. Especially useful for taking on picnics and other outings, hibachis come with single, double, or even triple grids, which can be raised to different heights, but they are not adaptable for spit-roasting.

Brazier Often made in unsuitably lightweight materials, braziers are basically round or square trays on legs, and sometimes on wheels. Some have hoods, and spits can be fitted, but the main drawback of braziers is that they are often too low to cook on comfortably. Some models have legs that screw in or fold up, making them as portable as picnic grills.

Portable or picnic grill This is a term that may be applied to the small compact types of brazier that can be easily packed for travel. They may be rectangular or round in shape and are usually made of lightweight metal.

The accessories

There is no real need to assemble a battery of gadgets for grilling, but some specialized items will aid the cook considerably and some are essential for safety reasons.

Heatproof gloves and apron Protective gloves and an apron are a must when cooking over an open fire to save you from grease splashes and prevent burns from unexpectedly hot grill rack handles. Choose really thick gloves and heavy aprons—and avoid plastic aprons.

Long-handled fork Useful for lifting and turning food over the heat; those with wooden handles are best.

Tongs Long-handled tongs are useful, both for moving glowing coals and for lifting and turning pieces of food without piercing them. Wooden handles are best.

Basting brush and bulb baster Succulent grilled food needs frequent basting. For steaks and chops, a long-handled basting brush is easiest to use, but for large roasts cooked on a rotisserie, a bulb baster allows you to baste over the heat without burning your arms. (Alternatively, use a bunch of rosemary twigs or bay leaves dipped in the marinade or juices as a brush.)

Stiff wire brush This is ideal for removing burned-on fragments of food from the grill.

Skewers Long ones are preferable because they enable you to leave the handles outside the fire. Stainless steel skewers will not rust, and those with wooden handles will be easier to use.

Grill baskets and hamburger grill For tender fish and crumbly hamburgers, you need a wire grill basket to cradle them gently while cooking and to keep them in one piece. Usually made of stainless steel or chrome- or tin-plated steel, grill baskets consist of two sides made of close-set wires hinged together, with two long, flat wire handles. Steaks and hamburgers are cooked in a flat round, square, or rectangular grill; if heated before use, it sears the food with a lovely pattern. Fish grills are curved so that the delicate flesh is not crushed. They are usually shaped in the form of a single large fish, and some have legs on each side to allow them to stand in the coals. Sardine grills are round, with twelve small fish shapes nose-to-nose. All wire baskets and grills need to be greased with oil or butter and heated before use, or the food will stick to them.

Rotisserie The simplest rotisserie has a long stainless steel spit with a plastic or wooden handle, and two or four sharp angled tines that can be adjusted to hold the bird or roast in place. This sort of rotisserie is usually made to slot into the hood of a barbecue grill. A motor-driven spit with either battery or electrical power is essential for roasting evenly.

Make sure the spit is strong enough to take the heaviest roast without bending, and when loading, always test it for balance before cooking, or you will wear out the motor and the meat will cook most on the heaviest side.

SMOKING

Home smoking—to cook food or to cure it—offers great scope to the adventurous cook. Simply adding aromatic herbs, to enhance the fragrant wood smoke, will produce wonderful flavors.

Hot smoking

Hot smoking is a refinement of grilling: the food is cooked and smoked at the same time. Those people who plan to do a great deal of hot smoking will want to purchase a smoker, but food can also be smoked using an ordinary covered barbecue grill. Sawdust or wood chips are added to the fire to cause a fragrant smoke to flavor and preserve the food. Resinous woods such as pine must never be used, because they will make the food taste more like disinfectant. Favorite woods are apple, hickory, and oak, but any hardwood will do.

The temperature in the smoker depends on the food you are smoking and how strong a smoke flavor you want. Fish and shellfish take well to smoking; most is hot-smoked at temperatures ranging from 120 to 200°F.

Many hot smokers are available, all of which come with full instructions— some use sawdust, or smoke dust, and others use wood chips. No matter what type you have, these are always used outdoors, because there will be a fair amount of smoke and fumes escaping.

Electric smoker This type of smoker is expensive but convenient. With the combination of a heating element and lava rocks, it keeps an even, constant heat and can be used for fish, meat, and poultry. Wood chips are an optional extra, if you like the additional flavor.

Small stovetop hot smoker This type of smoker is convenient for smoking small quantities of food indoors. A stovetop smoker looks like a large covered rectangular baking pan; it is fitted with a wire rack and a drip tray. Sawdust is used for the smoke, most of which is contained by the sliding cover (look for a sturdy smoker with a tight-fitting lid), but good ventilation is still important.

Cold smoking

Hot smoking is essentially a method of cooking, but cold smoking, with which it is often confused, is a long process that does not cook the food—with the exception of very small fish—but instead cures it. Before being cold-smoked, all foods must be brined and air-dried.

You can make your own cold smoker from a barrel, or you can convert a hot smoker to a cold smoker. Cold smoking must always be done outdoors.

3

Recipes

Stocks

Making homemade stock is not a costly proposition—inexpensive meat bones, fish frames, chicken giblets, or even a leftover roast chicken carcass can all be made into stock with very little effort. Add whatever vegetables you have to the stock pot, or do without. Or, if you only have vegetables, you can make a good meatless stock. Homemade stock is always the first choice when preparing a recipe, although you could use canned broth (the low-sodium variety has the best flavor) or the good but pricey fresh or frozen stocks now carried by many specialty butchers. But it is well worth trying to get in the habit of making your own stock when convenient, and freezing it for future use in a range of recipes.

Most stocks consist of a straightforward broth of bones and vegetables, and they may be either **white** (a pale stock, made from unbrowned bones, that won't add significant color to the dish in which it is used) or **brown** (a dark stock, achieved with deeply browned bones, that gives a rich color to the end result). There are also two variations to these basic types. **Jellied stock** is a chicken or meat stock that sets lightly when chilled; this is due to the inclusion of a high proportion of gelatinous veal bones or calf's or pig's feet. This stock gives an especially velvety texture to sauces, gravies, and soups, and is an essential component of some cold dishes. If you reduce jellied stock to about one fourth of its original quantity, you will have **meat glaze**, a syrupy jelly used to enrich many classic sauces. Meat glaze is an important ingredient in French restaurant cooking, where it is called *glace de viande*.

Do not salt long-simmered stocks until the very end of the cooking time (or don't salt at all, as you will be salting the dish the stock is used in), because as the stock reduces during simmering, the saltiness will increase. With long-simmered stocks, add the seasoning vegetables after the bones have already simmered for a couple of hours. If the vegetables are cooked from the beginning, together with the bones, they will certainly be overcooked at the end, and can then give a bitter flavor to the stock.

ROAST CHICKEN STOCK
Don't ever throw away the leftover carcass from a roast chicken dinner—it is the beginning of an excellent light-colored, but full-flavored chicken stock that is perfect for soups, stews, and braising. For a jellied stock, add some veal bones—even if you don't need to have the stock jell, the gelatin extracted from the bones will add body to the stock. Be flexible in your choice of seasoning vegetables; leeks and celery are especially good. Cruciferous vegetables such as cabbage or broccoli should be avoided because they are just too strong in flavor, and too many carrots will give an oversweet note. To give a golden tint to the stock, chop the onions with their skins and add the skins to the pot, too.

MAKES ABOUT 1½ QUARTS
  1 roast chicken carcass, the larger the better, plus the giblets (no liver) if you have them
  1 pound veal bones, sawed into 1-inch-thick pieces by the butcher, or 1 calf's or pig's foot, halved lengthwise (optional)
  ½ cup dry white wine (optional)
  2 medium onions, coarsely chopped
  2 medium carrots, coarsely chopped
  2 medium leeks, white part only, coarsely chopped
  2 medium celery ribs, coarsely chopped
  1 bouquet garni of 1 sprig fresh thyme, 1 sprig fresh parsley, and 1 bay leaf
  6 whole black peppercorns
  Salt, to taste

Break up the chicken carcass and place in a large soup pot with the optional giblets and veal bones. Add enough cold water to cover by 2 inches. Slowly bring to a simmer over medium heat, skimming off any foam that rises to the surface. Add the wine, if using, along with the onions, carrots, leeks, celery, bouquet garni, and peppercorns. Reduce the heat to low. Simmer until the flavor is well concentrated, at least 2 and up to 3 hours. Do not allow the stock to boil, or it will become cloudy. Season with salt.

Strain the stock into a large bowl, pressing lightly on the vegetables to extract all the flavor. (If you want a clear stock, do not press the vegetables.) Let the stock cool to room temperature, then cover and refrigerate until chilled. Scrape off the solidified fat on the surface (save it, if desired, to use in other recipes as an excellent cooking fat). The stock can be kept in the refrigerator for up to 3 days, or frozen for up to 3 months.

Roast Duck Stock: Substitute a roast duck carcass for the chicken carcass.

WHITE VEAL STOCK
Veal stock is very versatile, and can be used for veal, beef, or even chicken dishes, especially stews and roasts. Although marrow bones give lots of flavor to the stock, always include some additional meat, or choose meaty bones like shanks. Not only does the meat enrich the stock, it also helps to keep it relatively clear. Long, slow cooking is very important to draw out the gelatin, salts, and flavor deep in the bones.

MAKES ABOUT 2 QUARTS

3 pounds veal bones, sawed into 1-inch pieces by
   the butcher
12 ounces boneless veal shoulder, cut into 1-inch pieces
½ cup dry white wine (optional)
2 medium onions, coarsely chopped
2 medium carrots, coarsely chopped
3 small leeks, white part only, coarsely chopped
2 medium celery ribs, coarsely chopped
1 bouquet garni of 1 sprig fresh thyme, 1 sprig fresh
   parsley, and 1 bay leaf
6 whole black peppercorns
Salt, to taste

Place the veal bones and shoulder in a large soup pot, and add enough cold water to cover by 2 inches. Slowly bring to a simmer over medium heat, skimming off any foam that rises to the surface. Reduce the heat to low. Simmer for 2 hours. Add the wine, if using, along with the onions, carrots, leeks, celery, bouquet garni, and peppercorns. Continue simmering until the flavor is well concentrated, 2 to 3 more hours. Do not allow the stock to boil at any time. Season with salt.

Strain the stock into a large bowl. Let cool to room temperature, then cover and refrigerate until chilled. Scrape off the solidified fat on the surface. The stock can be kept in the refrigerator for up to 3 days, or frozen for up to 3 months.

White Beef Stock: Use 3 pounds beef bones and 1 pound veal bones, sawed into 1-inch pieces by the butcher, instead of the 3 pounds veal bones. Substitute beef chuck for the veal shoulder.
White Chicken Stock: Substitute 3 pounds chopped chicken bones (such as backs, necks, or wings) and giblets (no liver) for the veal bones and veal shoulder.

BROWN BEEF STOCK

When a hearty, meaty flavor is required in robust soups, stews, and sauces, use this stock. The bones from a roast prime rib of beef would be an excellent addition to the stock pot. Veal stock can be made using veal bones and veal shoulder, and lamb stock using meaty lamb neck bones.

MAKES ABOUT 2 QUARTS, OR ABOUT 3 QUARTS
IF USING PRIME RIB BONES

4 tablespoons lard or vegetable oil
3 pounds beef bones, sawed into 1-inch pieces by
   the butcher
12 ounces boneless beef chuck, cut into 1-inch pieces
Leftover roast prime rib bones (optional)
2 medium onions, unpeeled, coarsely chopped

2 medium leeks, coarsely chopped
2 medium carrots, coarsely chopped
2 medium celery ribs, coarsely chopped
½ cup hearty red wine (optional)
2 medium tomatoes, seeded and coarsely chopped
2 whole cloves
4 sprigs fresh parsley
3 sprigs fresh thyme
1 bay leaf
¼ teaspoon whole black peppercorns
Salt, to taste

In a large stock pot, heat 2 tablespoons of the lard over medium-high heat. In batches, and without crowding, brown the bones and beef chuck on all sides, about 8 minutes. Transfer to a plate. Pour off the fat from the pot. (Alternatively, the bones and chuck can be roasted in a preheated 425°F oven. Put them in a roasting pan, without the fat, and roast, turning occasionally, until well browned, about 45 minutes; remove the bones and set aside. Deglaze the browned bits in the pan on top of the stove with 2 cups water; add this liquid to the stock pot.)

Return the bones and beef chuck to the stock pot, along with the optional roast prime rib bones. Add enough water to cover by 2 inches. Slowly bring to a simmer over medium heat, skimming off any foam that rises to the surface. Simmer for 2 to 3 hours, skimming occasionally.

In a saucepan, heat the remaining 2 tablespoons lard over medium heat. Add the onions, leeks, carrots, and celery and then cook the vegetables, stirring occasionally, until browned, 10 to 15 minutes. Drain off the fat, then add the vegetables to the stock, along with the optional wine, the tomatoes, cloves, parsley, thyme, bay leaf, and peppercorns. Continue simmering until the stock is well flavored, about 2 more hours. Season with salt.

Strain the stock into a large bowl. Let cool to room temperature, then cover and refrigerate the stock until chilled. Scrape off the solidified fat on the surface. The stock can be kept in the refrigerator for up to 3 days, or frozen for up to 3 months.

Meat Glaze: In a large pot, bring the degreased and unsalted stock to a boil over high heat. Reduce the heat to medium and cook at a steady simmer until the stock has reduced to about 1½ quarts, about 1 hour. Transfer to a medium saucepan and continue simmering until reduced to a thick, dark syrup, about 30 minutes. The yield will be about 3 cups. Transfer to small containers (meat glaze is usually used in small quantities). The glaze can be kept in the refrigerator for up to 2 weeks, or frozen for up to 6 months.

Brown Chicken Stock: Substitute 3 pounds chopped chicken bones (such as backs, necks, or wings) and giblets (no liver) for the beef bones and chuck. Roast the chicken bones in a roasting pan in a preheated 400°F oven until browned, about 45 minutes. Discard any fat in the roasting pan, and deglaze the browned bits in the bottom of the pan with 2 cups water. Continue as for Brown Beef Stock above, using white wine instead of red.

Brown Duck Stock: Substitute the chopped carcass, wing tips, neck, giblets (no liver), and excess skin of a 5-pound duck (or 3 pounds chopped duck wings and giblets, available at many Asian butchers) for the beef bones and chuck. Roast the duck bones, following the instructions above for Brown Chicken Stock. Continue as for Brown Beef Stock above.

COURT-BOUILLON

Court-bouillon is used as a poaching medium for fish, and also forms the basis for many fish soups. Before adding fish to court-bouillon for poaching, cool the liquid to room temperature.

MAKES ABOUT 1½ QUARTS
  2½ cups dry white wine or 1¼ cups white wine vinegar
  1 medium onion, sliced
  3 medium carrots, sliced
  1 tablespoon unsalted butter
  6 sprigs fresh parsley
  2 slices of lemon
  6 whole black peppercorns
  2 bay leaves
  Salt, to taste

Combine all of the ingredients in a pot. Season well with salt if using as a poaching liquid for fish; do not salt if using in a soup. Add 5 cups cold water. Bring to a simmer over medium heat. Cook for 20 minutes. If using in a soup, strain the court-bouillon. The court-bouillon can be prepared up to 3 days ahead and kept in the refrigerator.

FISH STOCK

Fish stock is an important ingredient in seafood soups and stews, and, when reduced, is excellent in sauces for fish. Use the bones of white-fleshed fish, such as flounder or cod, and avoid oily, strong-flavored varieties, such as salmon, mackerel, and bluefish. Fish stock is simmered just long enough to release the flavors and gelatin from the bones—long cooking will make the stock bitter. If desired, substitute 1 to 1½ cups dry white wine for some of the water.

MAKES ABOUT 1½ QUARTS
  2 pounds fish bones and heads without gills, well rinsed in cold water
  3 medium celery ribs, sliced
  2 medium onions, sliced
  1 medium carrot, sliced
  1 bay leaf
  Salt, to taste

Place all the ingredients in a large pot (do not add salt if you intend to use the reduced stock in a sauce). Add 10 cups cold water. Bring to a boil over medium heat. Reduce the heat to low and simmer, occasionally skimming off the foam that rises to the surface, until the stock is well flavored, 30 to 45 minutes. Strain into a bowl. The stock can be kept in the refrigerator for up to 3 days, or frozen for up to 3 months.

VEGETABLE STOCK

This vegetable stock may appear to include some unusual ingredients, but these have in fact been carefully chosen to give a very satisfying, savory flavor. You can use this vegetable stock in recipes as a substitute for chicken stock, or in any recipe that is based on legumes, onions, root vegetables, or mushrooms (it is especially good when used as a base for yellow pea, onion, beet, or mushroom soups).

MAKES ABOUT 1½ QUARTS
  ¾ cup dry white wine
  2 tablespoons light soy sauce
  2 medium leeks, chopped
  1 medium red onion, chopped
  4 large mushrooms, sliced
  ½ cup yellow split peas
  ½ cup pearl barley
  1 teaspoon brown mustard seeds
  ½ teaspoon fenugreek seeds
  Sprigs of fresh parsley
  1 bay leaf
  A pinch of sugar
  Salt and freshly ground pepper, to taste

Place all of the ingredients in a large pot and then add 10 cups water. Bring to a boil over high heat, skimming off all the foam that rises to the surface. Reduce the heat to low and simmer for 1 hour. Strain into a bowl, discarding the last bit of stock, which will be dark and cloudy with sediment. Taste the stock to check the seasoning and adjust if necessary. The stock can be kept in the refrigerator for up to 3 days, or frozen for up to 1 month.

Soups

DELICATE CARROT SOUP

Carrots and potatoes, simmered until tender, are blended to make a light-bodied, pale orange soup.

MAKES 6 SERVINGS

    6 medium carrots, coarsely grated
    2 medium boiling potatoes, coarsely grated
    2 medium onions, coarsely grated
    2 tablespoons unsalted butter
    3¾ cups chicken stock
    3 tablespoons heavy cream
    Salt and freshly ground pepper, to taste
    2 teaspoons chopped fresh chervil or parsley

In a large, heavy-bottomed saucepan, combine the carrots, potatoes, onions, and butter. Stir over medium heat until the butter melts, then cover the pan and reduce the heat to low. Cook, stirring occasionally, until the vegetables are softened, about 10 minutes. Stir in the stock and bring to a simmer. Cook, uncovered, until the vegetables are very tender, about 20 minutes.

   In batches, purée the soup in a blender. Stir in the cream, and season with salt and pepper. At the last minute, stir in the chervil. Serve hot.

CREAMY WILD MUSHROOM SOUP

Mushrooms of all sizes and shapes now fill the produce shelves—make this soup with your favorite, or use a combination. For a richer soup, you can thicken with an egg yolk and cream mixture (called a *liaison* in classic French cooking) rather than flour: in a small bowl, lightly whisk the cream with 3 egg yolks, add a few ladles of the soup, and stir this mixture into the rest of the soup in the pan, along with the parsley and seasoning. Cook over very low heat, stirring, until the soup thickens; do not let it boil or it will curdle.

MAKES 6 SERVINGS

    4 tablespoons unsalted butter
    ½ cup minced shallots
    1 garlic clove, minced
    8 ounces cultivated wild mushrooms (such as oyster
       or cremini mushrooms), finely chopped
    2 tablespoons all-purpose flour
    3 tablespoons dry vermouth
    5 cups chicken or vegetable stock
    1 cup heavy cream
    2 teaspoons chopped fresh parsley
    Salt and freshly ground pepper, to taste

In a large saucepan, melt the butter over medium heat. Add the shallots and garlic and cook until softened,

about 3 minutes. Add the mushrooms and stir to mix with the shallots and garlic. Sprinkle with the flour and cook, stirring often, for 2 minutes. Stir in the vermouth. Add the stock and bring to a simmer. Cook over medium-low heat until the mushrooms are very tender, about 15 minutes. Reduce the heat to low. Stir in the heavy cream and parsley, and season with salt and pepper. Heat thoroughly, stirring all the time. Serve hot.

TOMATO AND LEEK SOUP

This is a simple, yet sophisticated, soup, without any need for herbs or spices—as long as you use ripe tomatoes that are full of flavor.

MAKES 6 SERVINGS

    1 pound ripe plum tomatoes, cut into quarters
    2 medium leeks, white part only, chopped
    2 small boiling potatoes, peeled and cut into
       ½-inch cubes
    5 cups chicken stock
    Salt and freshly ground white pepper, to taste
    3 to 4 tablespoons crème fraîche or sour cream

Place the tomatoes, leeks, and potatoes in a large saucepan. Cover with the stock and bring to a boil over medium heat. Simmer over low heat just until the vegetables are tender, 25 to 30 minutes. In batches, purée the soup in a blender, then strain through a sieve to remove the tomato seeds and skin. Season to taste, and stir in half the crème fraîche. Serve in soup bowls, topping each serving with a swirl of the remaining crème fraîche.

SPRING GREENS SOUP

Sorrel gives this soup a beautiful velvety consistency and a refreshing, slightly acidic edge that will lift jaded appetites. If desired, top with freshly made small croutons.

MAKES 4 TO 6 SERVINGS

    3 tablespoons unsalted butter
    1 medium onion, chopped
    12 ounces fresh sorrel, tough stems discarded
       and leaves chopped
    1 small head Boston lettuce, cored and
       coarsely chopped
    1 tablespoon chopped fresh chervil or parsley
    3¾ cups chicken stock, heated to boiling
    3 large egg yolks
    Salt and freshly ground pepper, to taste
    4 to 6 tablespoons heavy cream, for garnish

RUSSIAN BORSCHT

In a large saucepan, melt the butter over medium-low heat. Add the chopped onion and cook until soft and translucent, about 5 minutes. Add the sorrel, lettuce, and chervil. Continue cooking until the greens have all wilted, about 5 minutes, turning them over occasionally. Add the boiling stock. Simmer over low heat until the greens are very tender, 10 to 15 minutes.

In batches, purée in a blender. Strain the soup through a fine wire sieve to remove the sorrel fibers. Return the soup to the saucepan and heat to just below a simmer. Reduce the heat to low. In a small bowl, whisk the egg yolks. Gradually whisk in about 3 to 4 tablespoons of the hot soup. Stir this mixture into the remaining soup in the saucepan and continue stirring just until the soup is slightly thickened. Do not boil, or the soup will curdle. Season with salt and pepper. Serve the soup in individual bowls, adding a tablespoon of cream to each serving.

Cream of Spinach Soup: Substitute 1 pound fresh spinach leaves, tough stems discarded and leaves coarsely chopped, for the sorrel and lettuce.

PUMPKIN SOUP
Cheese or sugar pumpkins make better soup than the jack o'lantern variety. Rather than using a whole pumpkin, you can also use a wedge of pumpkin or another large winter squash such as calabasa or hubbard. For a dramatic presentation, hollow out a pumpkin and use it as a soup tureen (double the quantities for a large pumpkin).

MAKES 8 OR MORE SERVINGS
 1 small (1-pound) pumpkin or 1-pound winter squash
 2 large leeks
 5 cups chicken stock
 2 cups milk
 2 sprigs fresh basil, leaves chopped, or ½ teaspoon
   dried basil

A pinch of grated nutmeg
Salt and freshly ground pepper, to taste
2 tablespoons unsalted butter
3 tablespoons heavy cream

Cut the pumpkin into 1-inch cubes, discarding the seeds and fibers, and pare away the skin. Thinly slice the white part of the leeks into rounds. Thinly slice enough of the tender pale green part of the leeks to make ½ cup; set aside. Place the pumpkin cubes and white leek rounds in a medium saucepan. Add ⅓ cup water. Cover and cook over medium-low heat, stirring often to be sure the vegetables aren't sticking to the pan, until they are very soft and can be mashed, about 20 minutes. Transfer to a blender in batches and purée.

Return the purée to the cleaned saucepan and stir in the stock, milk, basil, and nutmeg. Season with salt and pepper. Let cook over low heat, stirring often, until heated through. Meanwhile, in a medium saucepan, melt the butter over medium-low heat. Add the pale green leek rounds and cook just until tender, about 5 minutes. Stir the green leek rounds and cream into the soup and heat through. Serve immediately.

RUSSIAN BORSCHT
Borscht can be made with either beef stock, which gives it more depth of flavor, or vegetable stock, which lightens its character considerably.

MAKES 8 OR MORE SERVINGS
2 tablespoons unsalted butter
2 medium beets, peeled and finely chopped
½ small head white cabbage, cored and finely chopped
2 medium onions, finely chopped
2 medium leeks, white part only, finely chopped
2 medium celery ribs, finely chopped
2½ quarts beef stock, well skimmed of fat, or vegetable stock
1 teaspoon caraway seeds
1 bouquet garni of 1 sprig fresh thyme, 1 sprig fresh parsley, and 1 bay leaf
A pinch of grated nutmeg
Salt and freshly ground pepper, to taste
½ cup hearty red wine
2 tablespoons red wine vinegar
2 teaspoons granulated sugar
1 large cooked beet, grated or cut into thin strips
⅔ cup sour cream, for garnish

In a large soup pot, melt the butter over medium-low heat. Add the beets, cabbage, onions, leeks, and celery, and cook until the vegetables are softened, about 5 minutes. Add the stock, caraway seeds, bouquet garni, and nutmeg, and season lightly with salt and pepper. Bring to a simmer over medium heat, then reduce the heat to low. Simmer for 1 hour. Add the wine, vinegar, and sugar, and simmer until the vegetables are very tender, about 20 minutes longer. Add the grated cooked beet and heat through. Remove the bouquet garni and taste the soup to check the seasoning. Serve in soup bowls, garnishing each serving with a dollop of sour cream.

CLASSIC FRENCH ONION SOUP
In France, this famous and filling soup is often enjoyed in trencherman proportions as a late-night meal in itself, but here it is usually presented in more manageable servings as a first course. While a French cook would traditionally use beef stock, vegetable stock makes this an excellent meatless soup. One important note of authenticity is the spoonful of caramelized sugar; this is added to give a mellow brown color to the soup.

MAKES 6 SERVINGS
4 tablespoons unsalted butter
2 to 3 Spanish onions (1 pound), thinly sliced
5 cups beef stock, heated to boiling
2 sprigs fresh fennel leaves or ¼ teaspoon fennel seeds
1 whole clove
Salt and freshly ground pepper, to taste
1 teaspoon granulated sugar
12 (½-inch-thick) slices crusty French bread, cut on the diagonal
1 tablespoon brandy
1½ cups shredded Gruyère or other Swiss cheese

In a large saucepan, melt the butter over medium-low heat. Add the onions and cook, stirring occasionally, until they are very soft, translucent, and golden, about 10 minutes. Add the boiling stock, fennel, and clove, and season with salt and pepper.

Place the granulated sugar in a long-handled, large metal spoon. Hold it under a broiler or, alternatively, over a gas flame and heat until the sugar melts and caramelizes to a deep brown color. Stir this into the soup. Bring the soup to a boil, then simmer over low heat for 30 minutes.

Preheat the broiler. Toast the slices of bread under the broiler, turning once, until golden-brown on both sides. Discard the fennel sprigs from the soup, and stir in the brandy. Ladle the soup into heatproof bowls. Thickly cover each piece of toast with shredded Gruyère. Float 2 pieces of toast on top of each serving. Broil until the cheese is melted and bubbling, 1 to 2 minutes. Serve immediately.

OLD-FASHIONED CHICKEN SOUP

The best chicken soup has a golden broth so delicious you can enjoy it all by itself—the extras, like rice and noodles, are really superfluous. Chicken soup is best understood by the Italians, who use it in delicate ways such as *stracciatella* (with just a couple of eggs stirred into it to form tender flakes). Start with a good chicken, preferably free-range. If you can find one, a stewing hen will give superior flavor. For a really terrific, doubly delicious soup, simmer the chicken in previously made chicken stock.

MAKES 6 TO 8 SERVINGS

   1 (4-pound) roasting chicken or 1 (5-pound) stewing hen, with the giblets (no liver), rinsed and patted dry

   2 medium onions, unpeeled, coarsely chopped

   1 medium leek, coarsely chopped

   1 medium carrot, coarsely chopped

   1 medium celery rib, coarsely chopped

   2 medium shallots, coarsely chopped

   1/2 cup dry white wine

   6 whole black peppercorns

   8 sprigs fresh parsley

   2 1/2 quarts chicken stock or water

   Salt, to taste

Place the chicken, breastside down, in a large pot. Add the remaining ingredients. Bring to a simmer over medium heat, skimming off any foam that rises to the surface. Reduce the heat to medium-low and simmer, skimming occasionally, until the chicken is tender, about 1 hour for the roasting chicken and 2 to 2 1/2 hours for the stewing hen.

   Remove the chicken from the broth. Strain the broth, but do not press on the vegetables. Let the broth stand for about 5 minutes, then skim off the clear yellow fat from the surface. Season with salt. Serve the soup in bowls, with the carved chicken served as a separate main course. Or, discard the chicken bones and skin, cut the meat into bite-sized pieces, and stir into the soup. If desired, save any leftover soup for use as a chicken stock.

Stracciatella: In a large saucepan, bring the strained broth to a boil over medium heat. In a small bowl, lightly beat 2 large eggs with an optional 2 tablespoons freshly grated Parmesan cheese and a seasoning of salt and pepper. Whisking constantly, pour the eggs into the boiling broth, and continue whisking until the eggs form tiny flakes, about 2 minutes.

Chicken and Rice Soup: In a large saucepan, bring the strained broth to a boil over medium heat. Add 1/2 cup long-grain rice and cook until the rice is tender, about 15 minutes.

Chicken and Noodle Soup: In a large saucepan, bring the strained broth to a boil over medium heat. Add 6 ounces dried egg noodles and cook until the noodles are tender, about 15 minutes.

RIBOLLITA

This hearty Tuscan soup is called *ribollita* (reboiled) because it was originally made with leftover vegetables, cooked with the addition of beans and their liquid. The version here reheats very well. It is traditional to douse chunks of day-old country bread in the soup. Try using rosemary bread for a particularly delicious winter lunch.

MAKES AT LEAST 8 SERVINGS

   4 tablespoons olive oil, plus extra for serving

   1 medium red onion, chopped

   2 garlic cloves, chopped

   1/2 cup chopped fresh parsley

   1 small head green cabbage, preferably Savoy, coarsely chopped

   8 ounces Swiss chard, including stems, coarsely chopped

   4 large ripe tomatoes, peeled, seeded, and chopped

   3 medium boiling potatoes, peeled and cut into 1/2-inch cubes

   2 quarts chicken or vegetable stock

   2 medium yellow squash or zucchini, cut into 1/2-inch pieces

   1 cup dried white beans, cooked and drained

   Salt and freshly ground pepper, to taste

   Chunks of day-old country-style bread

   Freshly grated Parmesan cheese, for serving.

In a large soup pot, heat the oil over medium heat. Add the onion, garlic, and parsley and cook until the onion is softened, about 5 minutes. Add half of the cabbage (with the thick ribs) and the chard stems, reserving the more tender leaves. Stir in the tomatoes and potatoes. Cook, stirring all the time, for about 2 minutes. Add the stock and bring to a boil over high heat. Reduce the heat to low and simmer for 1 hour. Add the squash or zucchini and cooked white beans and simmer about 20 minutes longer. Season with salt and pepper.

   In another large pot, plunge the reserved cabbage and chard leaves into lightly salted boiling water and cook until just tender, about 2 minutes. Drain well and add to the soup. Bring it back to a boil.

   Put chunks of bread into warmed soup bowls and ladle the hot soup over the top. Pass a bowl of Parmesan cheese and a cruet of olive oil on the side, so each guest can add them to taste.

VARIATION: After adding the cabbage and chard to the soup, put it into a casserole. Cover the surface of the soup with slices of toasted Italian bread and sprinkle with freshly grated Parmesan cheese. Bake in a preheated 350°F oven for 30 minutes.

NEW MEXICAN CHICKEN POZOLE

Pozole (which is also the Mexican word for hominy) is usually made with pork. This is a lighter, but equally satisfying, version. Each guest can sprinkle their serving with an assortment of garnishes to taste.

MAKES 6 TO 8 SERVINGS

2 tablespoons olive oil
6 chicken thighs
1 large zucchini, cut into ½-inch-thick rounds
1 medium onion, chopped
1 medium bell pepper, seeded and chopped
1 fresh hot green chile pepper (such as jalapeño), seeded and minced
2 garlic cloves, minced
4 cups chicken stock
1 teaspoon dried oregano
1 bay leaf
2 cups canned hominy, drained and rinsed
Salt and freshly ground pepper, to taste
Grated radishes, cubed avocado, shredded Monterey Jack cheese, lime wedges, and chopped black olives, for garnish

In a soup pot, heat the oil over medium heat. Add the chicken thighs and brown on both sides, about 8 minutes. Transfer to a plate and set aside. Add the zucchini, onion, bell pepper, chile pepper, and garlic to the pot. Cover and cook, stirring occasionally, until the vegetables are softened, about 10 minutes. Return the chicken to the pot. Stir in the chicken stock, oregano, and bay leaf. Bring to a simmer, then reduce the heat to low and simmer until the chicken is tender, about 40 minutes. Remove the chicken, discard the skin and bones, and chop the meat into bite-sized pieces. Stir the chicken back into the soup, along with the hominy, and season with salt and pepper. Cook until the hominy is heated through, about 5 minutes. Serve the soup in deep soup bowls, accompanied by small bowls of the garnishes.

SAUSAGE AND BEER GUMBO

Gumbo is a spicy, rib-sticking meal-in-a-pot that has dozens of variations. The name probably comes from the Bantu word for okra, the vegetable whose juices act as a natural thickening.

MAKES 8 SERVINGS

2 tablespoons vegetable oil
1 pound Cajun andouille or kielbasa sausage, cut into ½-inch-thick rounds
1 large onion, chopped
1 medium green bell pepper, seeded and chopped
2 medium celery ribs with leaves, chopped
2 garlic cloves, minced
¼ cup all-purpose flour
1 teaspoon sweet or hot Hungarian paprika
1 teaspoon dried basil
1 teaspoon dried thyme
½ teaspoon freshly ground pepper
¼ teaspoon cayenne pepper
4 cups chicken stock
1½ pounds ripe plum tomatoes, peeled, seeded, and chopped; or use drained canned tomatoes
1 (12-ounce) bottle or can lager beer
10 ounces fresh or frozen okra, cut into ¼-inch-thick rounds
Salt, to taste
Hot cooked rice, for serving

In a large soup pot, heat the oil over medium heat. Add the sausage and cook, turning once, until browned on both sides, about 5 minutes. Transfer to paper towels to drain, leaving the oil in the pot. Add the onion, bell pepper, and celery to the pot. Cover and cook, stirring often, until the vegetables are well softened, about 10 minutes. Add the garlic and cook for 1 minute. Stir in the flour and cook, stirring almost constantly, until well browned but not scorched, about 4 minutes. Stir in the paprika, basil, thyme, pepper, and cayenne and stir for 1 minute. Add the chicken stock, tomatoes, and beer and bring to a boil. Reduce the heat to low and simmer for 30 minutes. Stir in the okra and the reserved sausage, and cook until the okra is tender, about 10 minutes. Season with salt. To serve, spoon rice into individual soup bowls, and ladle in the gumbo.

BOUILLABAISSE

It is often argued that bouillabaisse is very much a fish stew of its birthplace, and cannot be made authentically outside of Provence. Authenticity is hardly to the point when something is as delicious as this, made with the best local fish at hand. If possible, buy fish with bones and have it filleted, so that you will have the bones to make the stock. Bouillabaisse is traditionally served in two courses, with the broth served first, then the fish presented as the entrée, both accompanied by the spicy garlic mayonnaise, rouille. Here, bouillabaisse is served as a hearty main course soup.

MAKES 6 TO 8 SERVINGS

3 pounds assorted boneless fresh fish (fillets or steaks),
   such as monkfish, cod, haddock, snapper, and bass
3 large ripe tomatoes, peeled, seeded, and chopped
2 medium onions, chopped
3 garlic cloves, minced
½ cup olive oil
1 bouquet garni of 4 sprigs fresh fennel or ½ teaspoon
   fennel seeds, 3 sprigs fresh thyme, a 3-inch strip of
   orange zest, and 1 bay leaf
A large pinch of saffron threads, soaked in ½ cup
   white wine
Salt and freshly ground pepper, to taste
6 cups fish stock
6 slices crusty French bread, dried in the oven or toasted
Rouille, for serving
1 cup shredded Gruyère or Swiss cheese
2 tablespoons chopped fresh parsley

Cut all the fish into thick slices or chunks. Cover and
refrigerate until ready to add to the soup.

   In a large saucepan, combine the tomatoes,
onions, garlic, olive oil, bouquet garni, and saffron
and wine mixture. Season with salt and pepper. Bring
to a boil over medium-high heat and boil rapidly,
stirring often, until the onion is softened, about
5 minutes. Add the fish stock. Return to a rapid boil
and boil furiously for 10 minutes. (It is important that
the broth is boiled, to amalgamate the oil and stock.)
Reduce the heat to low and add the fish. Cook at a
gentle simmer until the fish is just firm and opaque,
4 to 5 minutes.

   Remove the bouquet garni. Ladle the soup into
individual bowls. Spread each slice of bread with rouille
and sprinkle with a little Gruyère cheese. Float a slice
on each serving and sprinkle with chopped parsley.
Serve immediately.

PROVENÇAL VEGETABLE SOUP WITH BASIL

Another vegetable and bean soup from the
Mediterranean canon, this one is made especially
aromatic with the addition of *pistou*, a basil purée that
is very closely related to Italian pesto. The soup can
be made ahead and reheated, but don't add the *pistou*
until just before serving, as the heat will eventually
darken the basil.

MAKES 6 SERVINGS

3 tablespoons olive oil
1 large onion, finely chopped
1 pound ripe plum tomatoes, peeled, seeded, and
   chopped, or use canned

Salt and freshly ground pepper, to taste
8 ounces green beans, cut into ½-inch lengths
1 large zucchini, cut into ½-inch cubes
2 medium boiling potatoes, peeled and cut into
   ½-inch cubes
¾ cup dried white beans, cooked (reserve the cooking
   water), or 1 (16-ounce) can cannellini beans, drained
¼ cup broken (½-inch pieces) thin pasta, such
   as vermicelli
1 cup coarsely shredded Emmentaler or Swiss cheese
Pistou
   1 cup packed fresh basil leaves
   3 garlic cloves, chopped
   3 tablespoons olive oil
   Salt and freshly ground pepper, to taste

In a large soup pot, heat the oil over medium heat.
Add the onion and cook, stirring often, until soft and
translucent, about 5 minutes. Add the tomatoes and
cook, stirring often, until they form a sauce, 10 to
15 minutes. Add 6 cups water, and season with salt
and pepper. Increase the heat to medium-high and
bring to a boil. Add the green beans, zucchini, and
potatoes, and simmer for 10 minutes. Add the cooked
white beans, along with their cooking water (if using
canned beans, add them with 2 cups water). Add the
vermicelli. Cook until all the vegetables and the pasta
are tender, about 5 minutes longer.

   Meanwhile, to make the *pistou*, place the basil and
garlic in a blender or a food processor fitted with the
metal blade and blend to a coarse paste. With the
machine running, add the oil to make a thick, green
paste. Season with salt and pepper.

   Stir the *pistou* into the soup. Serve the soup in
individual bowls, passing a bowl of Emmentaler
cheese so each guest can add it to taste.

SALMON CIOPPINO

From Monterey to Seattle, Italian and Portuguese
fishermen argue about whose cuisine introduced the fish
soup, cioppino, into West Coast cookery. It can be made
with just about any Pacific fish, but its sturdy tomato,
wine, and herb basis is especially good with salmon.

MAKES 6 SERVINGS

3 tablespoons olive oil
1 medium onion, chopped
2 medium celery ribs, chopped
½ cup chopped fennel bulb, or 1 additional celery rib
2 garlic cloves, minced
1 cup hearty red wine
2 pounds ripe plum tomatoes, peeled, seeded, and
   chopped; or use drained canned tomatoes

PROVENÇAL VEGETABLE SOUP WITH BASIL

¼ cup chopped fresh parsley
1 teaspoon dried basil
1 teaspoon dried oregano
1 bay leaf
¼ teaspoon chile flakes
3 cups fish stock
1½ pounds skinless salmon fillets, cut into 1-inch cubes
Salt and freshly ground pepper, to taste

In a very large soup pot, heat the oil over medium heat. Add the onion, celery, fennel, and garlic. Cover and cook until the vegetables are softened, about 10 minutes. Add the wine and cook, uncovered, until reduced by half, about 5 minutes. Add the tomatoes, parsley, basil, oregano, bay leaf, and chile flakes and cook for 5 minutes. Stir in the fish stock and bring to a boil. Reduce the heat to low and simmer, with the pot partially covered, for 30 minutes. Add the cubes of salmon and cook, covered, until the fish is firm, about 5 minutes. Season with salt and pepper to taste, and serve hot.

NEW ENGLAND FISH CHOWDER

This ivory-colored stew, slightly thickened with potatoes and cream, is appetizing in both appearance and taste.

MAKES 6 TO 8 SERVINGS
   1½ pounds cod or haddock steaks
   4 ounces salt pork or slab bacon, rind removed, cut into small dice
   1 large onion, thinly sliced
   3 large boiling potatoes, peeled and sliced into rounds
   Salt and freshly ground pepper, to taste
   2 cups milk
   ⅔ cup heavy cream, heated
   2 to 4 tablespoons unsalted butter

Remove the skin and bones from the fish and place in a medium saucepan. Cut the fish into 1-inch pieces and set aside. Add 2 cups water to the skin and bones in the saucepan and bring to a boil. Reduce the heat to low and simmer for 15 minutes. Strain the fish stock into a bowl and set aside.

In a medium saucepan, cook the salt pork over medium-low heat until the fat begins to render, about 5 minutes. Stir in the onion, cover the pan, and cook until the onion is translucent and very soft, about 10 minutes. Set aside.

In a large saucepan, combine the potatoes, 2 cups water, and a pinch of salt. Bring to a boil over medium heat, then reduce the heat to low. Cover and simmer for 15 minutes. Add the reserved fish stock, the milk, and the onion and salt pork mixture. Bring to a simmer. Add the pieces of fish and cook, uncovered, until firm and opaque, about 10 minutes. Add the hot cream and butter, and heat through without boiling. Season with pepper and serve hot.

Clam Chowder: Omit the cod or haddock steaks. Place 2 dozen littleneck clams, well scrubbed, in a large pot with ½ cup water. Cover tightly and cook over high heat, shaking the pot often, until the clams are opened, about 5 minutes. Discard any unopened clams. Remove the meat from the shells and reserve. Strain the clam broth through cheesecloth; if necessary add enough water to make 2 cups. Use the clam broth instead of the fish stock. After adding the broth (with the milk and onion/salt pork mixture) simmer for about 10 minutes. Stir in the reserved clams with the cream and butter.

Oyster Chowder: Omit the cod or haddock. Shuck 16 oysters, reserving and straining the oyster liquor. Set the oyster meat aside. Add enough fish stock or water to the oyster liquor to make 2 cups and use instead of the fish stock. Stir in the oysters with the cream and butter.

SHRIMP AND CORN CHOWDER

A fine representative of New American cooking that blends regional specialties to make a delicious hybrid.

MAKES 6 TO 8 SERVINGS
  1 pound medium shrimp, peeled (shells reserved)
    and deveined
  3 cups fish or chicken stock
  4 strips bacon
  2 medium celery ribs, chopped
  1 medium red bell pepper, seeded and chopped
  2 cups fresh or defrosted corn kernels
  4 scallions, white and green parts, chopped
  2 cups half-and-half
  Salt and Tabasco sauce, to taste
  Chopped fresh parsley, for garnish

In a small pot, simmer the shrimp shells with the stock over medium-low heat for 10 minutes. Strain the broth and reserve. In a large soup pot, cook the bacon over medium heat until crisp, about 5 minutes. Transfer to paper towels to drain, leaving the bacon fat in the pot. Add the celery, red bell pepper, and corn to the pot. Cook until the peppers are softened, about 5 minutes. Add the scallions and cook until wilted, about 3 minutes. Stir in the reserved broth and the half-and-half. Bring to a simmer and then cook for 5 minutes over low heat. Stir in the shrimp and cook just until firm and pink, about 5 minutes. Season with salt and Tabasco sauce. Serve hot, sprinkled with the parsley and crumbled bacon.

Crab and Corn Chowder: Use fish stock and do not simmer the shrimp shells. Substitute ½ pound crabmeat, picked over for cartilage, for the shrimp.

SHRIMP AND FENNEL BISQUE

Bisques, the richest and creamiest of soups, are usually made from shellfish. This version is enhanced with the licorice-like taste of fennel. If you like, set aside some of the fennel greens to sprinkle on the soup as a garnish.

MAKES 6 SERVINGS
  1 pound medium shrimp, peeled (shells reserved),
    deveined, and coarsely chopped
  5 cups fish stock
  ⅔ cup dry white wine
  1 small head fennel, white bulb sliced and leafy green
    tops reserved
  2 medium onions, thinly sliced
  1 sprig fresh parsley
  2 bay leaves
  4 tablespoons unsalted butter
  1 sprig fresh thyme
  4 tablespoons all-purpose flour
  1¼ cups milk
  ¼ cup heavy cream
  1 tablespoon brandy
  Salt and freshly ground white pepper, to taste

Combine the shrimp shells, fish stock, wine, fennel greens, 1 sliced onion, parsley, and 1 bay leaf in a medium saucepan. Bring to a boil over high heat. Reduce the heat to low and simmer for 25 minutes. Strain the stock and set aside.

In a large saucepan, heat 3 tablespoons of the butter over medium heat. Add the remaining sliced onion and bay leaf with the thyme. Cook, stirring often, until the onion has softened, about 5 minutes. Add the shrimp and cook for 2 minutes. Sprinkle with the flour and stir well. Gradually add the reserved stock, stirring. Bring to a simmer, then cook over medium-low heat for 20 minutes. Discard the bay leaf and thyme sprig. In batches, purée the soup in a blender, and return to the saucepan. Add the milk and set aside.

In a saucepan, heat the remaining 1 tablespoon butter over medium-low heat. Add the sliced fennel bulb. Cover and cook until tender, 15 to 20 minutes. Stir the fennel into the soup, with the cream and brandy, and heat gently. Season and serve hot.

HOT-AND-SOUR SHELLFISH SOUP

This soup is loosely based on a Thai soup, with a bit of hot-and-sour Chinese influence thrown in. You can use any kind of shellfish, but mussels will contribute a good amount of juices to the broth.

MAKES 4 SERVINGS
2 tablespoons vegetable oil
2 medium onions, finely chopped
4 garlic cloves, sliced
2 pounds mussels, scrubbed and debearded, if necessary
2½ cups chicken stock
2 stems lemon grass, tender inner leaves only, chopped
1 (2-inch) piece fresh ginger, sliced
6 kaffir lime leaves, or grated zest of 1 lime
12 fresh cilantro sprigs with stems and leaves chopped separately
3 tablespoons rice vinegar
1 teaspoon granulated sugar
¼ cup fish sauce
2 tablespoons lime juice
1 pound medium shrimp, cooked, peeled, and deveined
1 teaspoon arrowroot or cornstarch, mixed with 1 tablespoon water
3 hot fresh chile peppers (such as bird or serrano), seeded and finely chopped

In a large saucepan, heat the oil over medium heat. Add the onions and garlic and cook until lightly browned, about 8 minutes. Add the mussels. Cover the pan and cook until the mussels have opened, about 5 minutes. Using a slotted spoon, lift out the mussels and set aside on a plate. When cool enough to handle, shell the mussels and reserve the meat.

Add the chicken stock to the mussel juices in the saucepan, along with the lemon grass, ginger, lime leaves, and cilantro stems. Bring to a boil. Reduce the heat, and simmer for 30 minutes. Add the vinegar and sugar and simmer for 3 or 4 minutes. Strain the broth.

Return the broth to the pan, add the fish sauce and lime juice, and bring to a simmer. Add the shrimp and mussels. Stir in the arrowroot mixture and cook until the broth is slightly thickened, 1 minute. Stir in the chiles and cilantro leaves. Remove from the heat, cover, and leave to stand for 5 minutes before serving.

COLD CUCUMBER AND MINT SOUP

This refreshing soup is for occasions calling for an elegant first course that can be prepared quickly.

MAKES 4 TO 6 SERVINGS
1½ large English cucumbers, coarsely chopped
1¼ cups sour cream
1¼ cups plain low-fat yogurt
2 cups cold chicken stock, well skimmed of fat
¼ cup chopped fresh mint leaves
Salt, to taste
½ cup heavy cream, chilled
Sweet Hungarian paprika, for garnish

In batches, purée the cucumbers, sour cream, and yogurt in a blender. Transfer to a bowl and stir in the stock and mint. Cover and chill, about 2 hours. Season with salt. Whip the cream. Serve topped with a dollop of cream and a sprinkling of paprika.

CAULIFLOWER VICHYSSOISE

A particularly fresh and delicate version of the classic summertime soup. Serve with croutons.

MAKES 8 SERVINGS
4 tablespoons unsalted butter
1 (1-pound) head cauliflower, trimmed and cut into small florets
2 small boiling potatoes (8 ounces), peeled and cut into ½-inch cubes
2 shallots or 1 small onion, chopped
2 cups chicken stock, well skimmed of fat
⅔ cup dry white wine
A pinch of grated nutmeg
Salt and freshly ground white pepper, to taste
4 cups milk
⅔ cup heavy cream

In a heavy-bottomed saucepan, melt the butter. Add the cauliflower, potatoes, and shallots and cook, stirring, until softened but not browned, 5 minutes. Add the stock and wine and bring to a boil. Add the nutmeg, and season. Simmer over medium-low heat until the vegetables are very tender, about 25 minutes.

In batches, purée the soup in a blender. Transfer to a large bowl and stir in the milk. Cover and refrigerate until well chilled, at least 2 hours. Check the seasoning and serve, drizzling each serving with heavy cream.

Sauces and Marinades

WHITE SAUCE

White sauce is one of the most versatile of all sauces. To name just three variations, it can be turned into a classic *sauce béchamel*, or flavored with cheese, or made with stock to achieve a totally different result. To make a thin white sauce, suitable for serving as an accompaniment to poached fish or chicken, use 1 tablespoon each butter and flour. The secret of a fine white sauce is to let the roux bubble gently at the beginning without browning.

MAKES ABOUT 2 CUPS
    3 tablespoons unsalted butter
    2 tablespoons all-purpose flour
    2 cups milk
    Salt and freshly ground white pepper, to taste

In a medium saucepan, heat 2 tablespoons of the butter over medium-low heat. Stir in the flour. Let cook and bubble gently without browning for 1 to 2 minutes. Gradually stir in the milk, using a wooden spoon. Season with salt and pepper. Cover the pan and simmer the sauce over very low heat, stirring occasionally, for about 15 minutes. Off the heat, whisk in the remaining 1 tablespoon butter in small pieces to give the sauce a velvety texture.

Béchamel Sauce: Pour the milk into a medium saucepan and add 1 sliced onion, 1 bay leaf, and 4 or 5 whole cloves. Scald the milk over medium heat, then remove from the heat, cover the pan, and let infuse for 10 minutes. Strain the flavored milk. Make the roux as for White Sauce, then let it cool a little before stirring in the hot milk. Continue making the sauce as above.
Cheese Sauce (*Sauce Mornay*): Remove the White Sauce or Béchamel Sauce from the heat, and stir in ¼ cup freshly grated Parmesan cheese and ¼ cup shredded Emmentaler cheese. Do not season the sauce until after the cheese has been added, as the cheese is salty. Add a little cayenne pepper and a pinch of grated nutmeg, too.
Velvety White Sauce (*Sauce Velouté*): Substitute 3 cups white chicken stock (or 2¾ cups stock and ¼ cup dry white wine) for the milk. Season with salt, pepper, and a pinch of grated nutmeg. If desired, add a bouquet garni. Cover and cook for about 25 minutes. Remove the bouquet garni before serving.

BROWN SAUCE

Brown sauce is an important component of classic French cooking, used as an ingredient and to create other sauces. Originally thickened with a flour and butter roux, most contemporary chefs prefer the lighter (and quicker) results achieved with arrowroot or potato starch. The sauce is only as good as the stock it is made with, so always use homemade.

MAKES ABOUT 2 CUPS
    2 cups brown beef or veal stock
    4 teaspoons arrowroot, potato starch, or cornstarch
    2 tablespoons Madeira or dry sherry

In a medium saucepan, bring the stock to a simmer over medium heat. Mix the arrowroot with the Madeira, and whisk into the stock. Simmer, whisking constantly, just until the sauce is thickened. The sauce can be kept, covered, in the refrigerator for up to 3 days; reheat gently for serving.

Red Wine Sauce (*Sauce Bordelaise*): This is a classic sauce for grilled beef steaks. In a medium saucepan, melt 1 tablespoon butter over medium heat. Add 2 tablespoons minced shallot and cook until softened, about 3 minutes. Add 1 cup red wine. Bring to a boil and boil until reduced to 2 tablespoons. Stir in the Brown Sauce and bring just to a simmer.

HOLLANDAISE SAUCE

Serve warm with poached fish (especially salmon) or shellfish, and with asparagus or broccoli.

MAKES ABOUT 1 CUP
    2 extra large egg yolks
    1 tablespoon white wine vinegar or lemon juice
    10 tablespoons (1¼ sticks) unsalted butter,
        at room temperature
    Salt and freshly ground white pepper, to taste

Whisk the egg yolks and vinegar in a double boiler insert. Place the insert over a saucepan of hot, not simmering, water, over low heat (do not let the base of the insert touch the water). Stirring constantly with a wooden spoon, add the butter, 1 tablespoon at a time. Stir until each addition of butter is thoroughly incorporated before adding the next. Occasionally scrape down any sauce that splashes onto the side of the insert. If the sauce seems to be thickening too fast, immediately remove the insert to a bowl of cold water and stir the sauce to cool it quickly. If the sauce isn't thickening at all, increase the heat slightly. The finished sauce should be smooth and creamy. If desired, thin the sauce slightly with a small amount of cold water or milk. Season with salt and pepper.

Hollandaise can be prepared up to 1 hour ahead, and kept warm over hot water, off the heat; cover with plastic wrap pressed directly onto the surface of the sauce.

BÉARNAISE SAUCE

A tarragon-scented derivative of hollandaise, this is one of the best sauces for lamb or beef.

MAKES ABOUT 1 CUP

⅓ cup minced shallots
3 tablespoons white wine vinegar
12 whole black peppercorns, coarsely crushed
3 sprigs fresh tarragon
3 large egg yolks
10 tablespoons (1¼ sticks) unsalted butter, at room temperature
Salt, to taste

Place the shallots, vinegar, peppercorns, and tarragon in a small saucepan and bring to a boil over medium-high heat. Cook until the liquid is reduced to about 1 tablespoon. Let cool and then strain into a double boiler insert. Beat the egg yolks into the strained liquid. Place the insert over a saucepan of hot, not simmering, water, over low heat (do not let the base of the insert touch the water). Whisk until the egg mixture is slightly thickened and creamy. Still whisking constantly, add the butter, 1 tablespoon at a time. Whisk until each addition of butter is thoroughly incorporated before adding the next. Occasionally scrape down any sauce that splashes onto the side of the insert. If the sauce seems to be thickening too fast, immediately remove the insert to a bowl of cold water and stir the sauce to cool it quickly. If the sauce isn't thickening at all, increase the heat slightly. When all the butter has been added, season with salt.

Béarnaise can be prepared up to 1 hour ahead, and kept warm over hot water, off the heat; cover with plastic wrap pressed onto the sauce. If it is too thick, add a few drops of cold water just before serving.

BEURRE BLANC

Beurre blanc, a smooth sauce perfect for grilled fish, depends on the gentle melting and emulsion of butter to create a creamy consistency. It can be seasoned with your choice of fresh herbs—tarragon or dill are very good.

MAKES ABOUT ¾ CUP

3 shallots, finely chopped
3 tablespoons white wine vinegar
3 tablespoons dry white wine
8 tablespoons (1 stick) unsalted butter, chilled
A few drops of lemon juice
Salt and freshly ground white pepper, to taste

Place the shallots, vinegar, and wine in a small saucepan and bring to a boil over medium-high heat.

Boil until reduced to about 2 tablespoons. Remove from the heat and let cool slightly. Whisking constantly, add the butter, 1 tablespoon at a time. Whisk until each addition of butter is thoroughly incorporated before adding the next. After 2 or 3 tablespoons have been added, return the saucepan to very low heat. Continue gradually whisking in the butter. When it has all been incorporated, season the sauce with lemon juice, salt, and pepper. If desired, strain the sauce before serving.

DELICATE TOMATO SAUCE

Not all tomato sauces need to be long-simmered with olive oil and garlic. This one is best served right after preparation, and is excellent with pasta or gnocchi, and with grilled meat or fish.

MAKES ABOUT 2½ CUPS

4 tablespoons unsalted butter
2 pounds ripe plum tomatoes, peeled, seeded, and coarsely chopped
2 teaspoons chopped fresh basil or 1 teaspoon dried basil
1 teaspoon chopped fresh tarragon or ½ teaspoon dried tarragon
Salt, to taste

In a medium saucepan, melt the butter over low heat. Add the tomatoes and cook gently for about 10 minutes. Purée in a blender or food processor fitted with the metal blade. Stir in the basil and tarragon, and season with salt. Let stand for at least 10 minutes to allow the flavors to blend. If necessary, reheat the sauce before serving.

ROASTED TOMATO SAUCE

Roasting is an easy way to add flavor to less-than-perfect tomatoes. When made with the best summer tomatoes, the results are spectacular.

MAKES ABOUT 2 CUPS

2 pounds ripe plum tomatoes
4 tablespoons unsalted butter
2 teaspoons chopped fresh parsley
Salt and freshly ground pepper, to taste

Preheat the oven to 400°F. Place the whole tomatoes on a baking sheet. Roast until the skins are split and blackening, about 30 minutes. Let stand until cool enough to handle, then remove the peels and gently squeeze out the seeds. Purée the tomato flesh in a blender or a food processor fitted with the metal blade.

In a medium saucepan, heat the puréed tomatoes with the butter over medium heat, stirring all the time until the butter melts. Stir in the chopped parsley, and season with salt and freshly ground pepper. The sauce can be prepared up to 2 hours ahead, and reheated gently for serving.

HERB BUTTER

Place a small spoonful of this butter (called *beurre maître d'hôtel* in classic French cuisine) on top of piping hot grilled fish, steaks, or chops. You can form the butter into a log and keep it in the freezer to slice and use as needed.

MAKES ABOUT ½ CUP
8 tablespoons (1 stick) unsalted butter,
at room temperature
2 tablespoons finely chopped fresh parsley
1 tablespoon lemon juice

In a small bowl, combine all of the ingredients and work them together with a fork until well mixed. Cover and refrigerate until slightly firmed. The butter can be kept in the refrigerator for up to 2 days, or frozen for up to 3 months.

Garlic and Herb Butter: Add 1 shallot and 2 garlic cloves, both finely minced. Substitute 1 tablespoon finely chopped fresh tarragon for the parsley, if desired. **Horseradish Butter:** Add 2 tablespoons grated fresh horseradish, 1 teaspoon Dijon mustard, and 1 teaspoon red wine vinegar (or more of any of these ingredients according to taste). If you are unable to find fresh horseradish, use drained, prepared horseradish and omit the vinegar.

ASIAN PEANUT SAUCE

Use this sauce to dress Sichuan Chicken Salad, or serve as an accompaniment to crab cakes or grilled chicken or pork. If you are unable to find stem ginger preserved in syrup, you can substitute 2 tablespoons minced fresh ginger plus 2 tablespoons honey.

MAKES ABOUT 2½ CUPS
1½ cups smooth peanut butter
7 tablespoons soy sauce
⅓ cup lemon juice
⅓ cup Asian dark sesame oil
3 pieces candied stem ginger in syrup plus
3 tablespoons syrup from the jar
1 teaspoon chile flakes
2 garlic cloves, minced

Place all the ingredients in a blender with a scant ½ cup water, and purée until smooth. Strain through a fine sieve, pressing hard on the solids. The sauce should be thick and creamy, but if it is too thick, thin with a little water. The sauce can be kept, covered, in the refrigerator for up to 1 week.

MEXICAN SALSA CRUDA

Salsa has many uses beyond being a dip for tortilla chips. Serve it as a condiment for broiled meat, fish, or chicken, or with steamed vegetables.

MAKES ABOUT 2½ CUPS
3 large ripe tomatoes, peeled, seeded, and chopped
3 hot fresh chile peppers (such as serrano or jalapeño),
seeded and minced, or less to taste
½ small red onion, finely chopped
2 tablespoons chopped fresh cilantro
2 garlic cloves, minced
Salt, to taste
A splash of red wine vinegar (optional)

Combine all the ingredients in a bowl and stir to mix. Season with salt. If you feel the salsa needs a bit of acidity, add the vinegar. Cover and chill, about 1 hour. The salsa can be made up to 1 day ahead and kept, covered, in the refrigerator, but the fresher, the better.

CIDER BBQ SAUCE

Apple juice gives a fruity edge to this thin grilling sauce. It works best brushed onto meats and chicken during the last 10 or 15 minutes of grilling, because the sugars in the tomatoes and cider will scorch if it is applied sooner.

MAKES ABOUT 1½ CUPS
1¼ cups dry apple cider, or 1 cup apple juice and
¼ cup dry white wine
½ cup tomato paste
2 tablespoons cider vinegar
2 tablespoons packed light brown sugar
1 teaspoon soy sauce
1 garlic clove, crushed
¾ teaspoon salt
3 good dashes Tabasco sauce

Combine all the ingredients in a medium, heavy-bottomed saucepan. Bring to a simmer over medium heat. Reduce the heat to low and then simmer, stirring occasionally, until slightly thickened, about 20 minutes. Let cool completely. The sauce can be kept, covered, in the refrigerator for up to 3 days.

SOUTHERN-STYLE BBQ SAUCE

Once you've made BBQ sauce at home, you may never buy another bottle.

MAKES ABOUT 2 CUPS
2 tablespoons unsalted butter
1 medium onion, chopped
2 garlic cloves, minced
1 cup tomato ketchup
1 cup prepared American-style chile sauce
⅓ cup lemon juice
⅓ cup honey
2 tablespoons spicy brown mustard
2 tablespoons Worcestershire sauce
¼ teaspoon cayenne pepper (optional)

In a medium, heavy-bottomed saucepan, melt the butter over medium heat. Add the onion and garlic. Cover and cook until the onion is golden-brown, about 8 minutes. Stir in the remaining ingredients and bring to a simmer. Reduce the heat to low. Simmer, uncovered, stirring often, until the sauce has thickened, about 30 minutes. The sauce can be kept, covered, in the refrigerator for up to 1 month.

HORSERADISH SAUCE

One of the most popular sauces for hot or cold roast beef, this is also excellent with smoked trout. For a milder sauce (or if using prepared horseradish instead of fresh), omit the vinegar.

MAKES ABOUT ¾ CUP
⅔ cup heavy cream
3 tablespoons grated fresh horseradish, or use drained prepared horseradish
1 tablespoon white wine vinegar
1 teaspoon Dijon mustard
A pinch of granulated sugar

In a small bowl, whisk together all of the ingredients until smooth. Taste the sauce and add more vinegar or sugar, if desired. Serve immediately.

MAYONNAISE

Homemade mayonnaise is a real treat. Remember to have all of the ingredients at room temperature. If you use extra virgin olive oil, mix it with another oil, in equal parts, because mayonnaise made with all extra virgin oil tends to "break" after a day or two in the refrigerator. If you prefer to avoid raw egg yolks, use ¼ cup liquid egg substitute; this is pasteurized and makes a surprisingly good mayonnaise.

MAKES ABOUT 1¼ CUPS
2 large egg yolks, at room temperature
1 teaspoon Dijon mustard
Salt and freshly ground white pepper, to taste
1¼ cups olive oil, or sunflower oil, peanut oil, or a mixture of olive and peanut oils
2 tablespoons lemon juice or white wine vinegar

In a medium bowl, combine the egg yolks, mustard, and salt. Beat together with a wire whisk or wooden spoon. Gradually add the oil, ½ teaspoon or so at a time, thoroughly mixing in each addition of oil before adding the next. As the mixture thickens, you can increase the flow of oil, to about 2 teaspoons at a time. After about half of the oil has been added and the mayonnaise is thick, beat in the lemon juice. By this stage it is almost impossible to curdle the mayonnaise, so you can whisk in the rest of the oil quite fast. Taste the mayonnaise, and add more salt and lemon juice if desired. Serve immediately. Or, cover and refrigerate until ready to serve (the mayonnaise can be prepared up to 1 day ahead); before serving, whisk the mayonnaise briefly.

Tartar Sauce: Stir 2 chopped hard-boiled eggs, ⅓ cup finely chopped fresh parsley, 2 tablespoons finely chopped sweet dill pickle, 2 tablespoons capers, chopped, and 2 tablespoons minced shallot into the mayonnaise.

Remoulade Sauce: Stir ½ cup finely chopped scallions, 2 tablespoons chopped fresh parsley, 1 tablespoon Creole or spicy brown mustard, 1 tablespoon prepared horseradish, and 1 teaspoon Worcestershire sauce into the mayonnaise.

Garlic Mayonnaise (Aïoli): Add 3 garlic cloves, crushed, to the egg yolks before adding the oil. Use a mixture of half peanut oil and half olive oil.

ROUILLE

Rouille is the traditional Provençal accompaniment to fish soups, in particular Bouillabaisse. It looks like mayonnaise with a warm red tint, but its gentle color belies its heat.

MAKES ABOUT 1 CUP
1 small red bell pepper
1 fresh hot red chile pepper (such as serrano), or ½ teaspoon chile flakes
1 slice white bread, crusts removed
3 garlic cloves, chopped
1 large egg yolk, at room temperature
Salt, to taste
⅔ cup olive oil

Roast, peel, and seed the red bell pepper and fresh chile pepper, then chop them. Moisten the bread with a little water to soften it, then squeeze out the excess water. In a blender or food processor, combine the bread, bell pepper, chile pepper or chile flakes, garlic, egg yolk, and salt. Blend to a paste. With the machine running, gradually drizzle in oil. The finished rouille should have a thick, smooth, mayonnaise-like texture. Rouille can be kept, covered, in the refrigerator for up to 1 day.

ITALIAN HERB SAUCE

This emerald-green sauce, called *salsa verde* in Italy, is extremely good with poached chicken and fish.

MAKES ABOUT 1½ CUPS
4 scallions, finely chopped
3 tablespoons finely chopped mixed fresh herbs
  (flat-leaf parsley and chives)
2 tablespoons capers, finely chopped
8 anchovy fillets in oil, drained and finely chopped
1 hard-boiled egg, chopped
Grated zest of 1 lemon
1 garlic clove, minced
½ tablespoon wine vinegar or 1 tablespoon lemon juice
6 tablespoons olive oil
Salt, to taste

In a medium bowl, combine the scallions, herbs, capers, anchovies, egg, lemon zest, and garlic. Add the vinegar, then gradually whisk in the oil. Season with salt. Cover and let stand for 1 hour to blend the flavors. Serve at room temperature. The sauce can be kept, covered, in the refrigerator for up to 1 day.

CRANBERRY-ORANGE SAUCE

Cranberry sauce's affinity with turkey is well known, but try this with pork and venison as well.

MAKES ABOUT 3 CUPS
2 large oranges
2 cups cranberries (12 ounces)
1½ cups granulated sugar
2 tablespoons orange-flavored liqueur (optional)

Grate 2 teaspoons of zest from the oranges and set aside. Cut off and discard the thick white pith, then carefully cut between the membranes to release the orange sections.

In a medium, heavy-bottomed saucepan, combine the cranberries, sugar, 1 cup water, the oranges, and zest. Bring to a boil over medium heat, stirring often to help dissolve the sugar. Reduce the heat to low and simmer until the sauce is thick and the cranberries have burst, 10 to 15 minutes. Stir in the liqueur, if using. Let cool completely before serving.

MANGO COULIS

A coulis is nothing more than the French culinary term for a simply prepared sauce made from puréed fruit or vegetables. This vibrant gold mango coulis is excellent in a tropical fruit salad, spooned over exotic-flavored ice creams and sorbets, or stirred into plain yogurt.

MAKES ABOUT 1½ CUPS
2 large ripe mangoes
¼ cup lime juice
¼ cup granulated sugar

The mango pit lies lengthwise in the center of the fruit. Lay one mango on your work surface, plump side down. Holding the mango firmly, use a sharp, thin-bladed knife to slice off the top third of the fruit, cutting around the pit. Turn the mango over and slice off the other side. Repeat with the other mango. Using a large spoon, scoop the flesh from each piece.

In a blender, purée the mango flesh with the lime juice and sugar. Taste, and add more lime juice or sugar to get the proper balance of acid and sweetness. The coulis can be kept, covered with plastic wrap pressed directly onto the surface, in the refrigerator for up to 4 hours.

WARM CHOCOLATE SAUCE

Poured over ice cream, this sauce will harden slightly and be deliciously chewy. Or, serve it as a sauce with pastries such as cream puffs.

MAKES ABOUT ⅔ CUP
6 tablespoons unsalted butter
⅓ cup heavy cream
8 ounces bittersweet or semisweet chocolate,
  finely chopped
2 tablespoons honey
2 tablespoons dark rum or additional heavy cream

In a saucepan, bring the butter and heavy cream to a simmer over medium heat. Remove from the heat and add the chocolate. Let stand for 3 minutes, then whisk until the chocolate has melted and the mixture is smooth. (If necessary, return to very low heat, stirring constantly, until the chocolate has melted.) Stir in the honey and rum. Serve warm. The sauce can be kept, covered, in the refrigerator for up to 5 days; reheat in a double boiler insert over simmering water.

ORANGE CARAMEL SAUCE

The rich flavor of caramelized sugar adds another dimension to many desserts. For a simple dessert, pour this sauce over ripe fresh peach slices garnished with a few raspberries. There are a couple of tips for making this sauce. First, be sure the cream is hot before adding it to the caramel—if cold, it will stiffen the sauce. Also, be careful when adding the liquids, because they will boil up dramatically.

MAKES 1¼ CUPS

1 cup granulated sugar
¼ cup heavy cream, heated until very hot
½ cup orange juice, at room temperature

Put ¼ cup water in a deep, medium saucepan. Add the sugar. Bring to a boil over high heat, stirring to help dissolve the sugar. Then let boil, without stirring, but occasionally swirling the syrup around in the pan, until the syrup is a medium amber color, 3 to 5 minutes. Remove from the heat. Gradually stir in the hot cream, being careful of the sauce bubbling up, then stir in the orange juice. Cool slightly before serving; the sauce will thicken upon cooling. The sauce can be kept, covered, in the refrigerator for up to 3 days; reheat in a double boiler insert over simmering water before serving, adding additional heavy cream or orange juice as needed to thin the sauce to the desired consistency.

PROVENÇAL LEMON MARINADE

Grilling marinades should include enough oil to keep the food from sticking to the grill, but don't use too much oil, or it will drip onto the coals and cause flareups. This marinade uses full-flavored extra virgin olive oil, which adds its own character to the fragrant blend of herbs and garlic.

MAKES ABOUT 1¼ CUPS, ENOUGH FOR 3 POUNDS MEAT, POULTRY, OR FISH

½ cup extra virgin olive oil
½ cup lemon juice
2 garlic cloves, crushed
1 tablespoon chopped fresh rosemary or 1½ teaspoons dried rosemary
1 tablespoon chopped fresh thyme or 1½ teaspoons dried thyme
1 tablespoon chopped fresh oregano or 1½ teaspoons dried oregano
1 teaspoon fennel seed, crushed
Grated zest of 1 orange
¼ teaspoon chile flakes
Salt, to taste

In a medium bowl, combine all of the ingredients. Use the mixture to marinate meat and poultry for up to 8 hours, covered, in the refrigerator. Marinate fish and shellfish for no longer than 2 hours, covered, in the refrigerator.

ITALIAN RED WINE MARINADE

Choose a robust dry red wine, such as Chianti or Zinfandel, to make this Tuscan-inspired marinade. It makes an especially delicious marinade for either lamb or beef.

MAKES ABOUT 1¼ CUPS, ENOUGH FOR 3 POUNDS MEAT, POULTRY, OR VEGETABLES

1 cup hearty red wine
⅓ cup extra virgin olive oil
2 garlic cloves, minced
1 tablespoon chopped fresh rosemary or 1½ teaspoons dried rosemary
1 tablespoon chopped fresh thyme or 1½ teaspoons dried thyme
¼ teaspoon freshly ground pepper
Salt, to taste

In a medium bowl, combine all of the ingredients. Use the mixture to marinate meat and poultry for up to 8 hours, covered, in the refrigerator. Marinate vegetables for no longer than 2 hours, covered, in the refrigerator.

CAJUN DRY RUB

Blackened fish took America by storm, and along with it the concept of rubbing foods with spicy seasoning blends before cooking them became very popular. This Cajun dry rub is a particularly good mixture. New Orleans cooks almost always include both onion and garlic powders, as used in this recipe, in their dry rubs.

MAKES ABOUT ¼ CUP, ENOUGH FOR ABOUT 3 POUNDS MEAT, POULTRY, OR FISH

1 tablespoon sweet Hungarian paprika
1 teaspoon dried oregano
1 teaspoon dried thyme
½ teaspoon garlic powder
½ teaspoon onion powder
½ teaspoon freshly ground pepper
¼ teaspoon cayenne pepper

In a small bowl, combine all of the ingredients. The dry rub, stored in a covered container, will keep indefinitely in a cool, dry spot.

Appetizers, Snacks, and Beverages

CRUDITÉS WITH GARLIC MAYONNAISE

The more vegetables you have on a crudité platter, the better, as you want to create a colorful, eye-catching combination. Other possibilities to use include boiled small new potatoes, slices of fresh fennel bulb, steamed baby beets, sticks of celeriac, and tiny globe artichokes the size of a walnut.

MAKES 6 TO 8 SERVINGS

1 English cucumber

8 ounces small zucchini

8 ounces green beans

1 large red bell pepper, seeded and cut into 2- by ¼-inch sticks

3 medium carrots, cut into 2- by ¼-inch sticks

2 celery ribs, cut into 2- by ¼-inch sticks

4 ripe plum tomatoes, cut into ¼-inch-thick rounds

1 bunch radishes

2 heads Belgian endive, separated into leaves

1½ cups Garlic Mayonnaise

¾ cup black Mediterranean olives

Peel the cucumber, cut crosswise into 2-inch pieces, and cut these into ¼-inch-thick sticks, removing the seeds. Bring a small saucepan of lightly salted water to a boil over high heat. Add the zucchini and cook until they are crisp-tender, about 3 minutes. Remove them with a slotted spoon and let cool. Bring the water back to a boil. Add the green beans and cook until crisp-tender, 1 to 2 minutes. Drain, refresh, and dry on paper towels. When the zucchini are cool, cut them across in half and then into ¼-inch-thick sticks.

Bring another small saucepan of lightly salted water to a boil over high heat. Add the red pepper strips and cook just to soften slightly, about 1 minute. Drain, refresh, and pat dry with paper towels.

Arrange all the vegetables on a large platter, cover with plastic wrap, and chill, about 1 hour. Place the garlic mayonnaise and olives in bowls. Serve the vegetables and olives with the mayonnaise as a dip.

FARMHOUSE CHEESE SPREAD WITH PITA CRISPS

Yogurt, when drained of its whey, has a cheese-like consistency that makes it an admirable low-fat ingredient. Mixed with vegetables, it becomes a versatile spread that can be served with pita crisps or crackers, or even used as a sandwich filling.

MAKES ABOUT 3 CUPS

2 medium kirby cucumbers or 1 large cucumber

¼ teaspoon salt

1 quart plain low-fat yogurt, drained

1 cup shredded radishes (about 6 medium radishes)

2 scallions, finely chopped

2 tablespoons chopped fresh dill

Freshly ground pepper, to taste

6 pita breads

Olive oil, for brushing

Scrub the cucumbers well and cut them in half lengthwise. (Leave kirby cucumbers unpeeled, but peel regular cucumber, if using.) With the tip of a spoon, scoop out and discard the seeds. Chop the cucumbers into ¼-inch dice and place in a small bowl. Toss with the salt, and let stand until they release their juices, about 30 minutes. Rinse well, drain, and squeeze out the excess moisture. Transfer to a medium bowl.

Stir in the drained yogurt, radishes, scallions, and dill. Season with salt and pepper. Cover and refrigerate for at least 2 hours. The spread can be prepared up to 1 day ahead and kept, covered, in the refrigerator.

To make the pita crisps: Preheat the oven to 350°F. Pull apart the two layers of the pita breads. Cut into wedges and arrange in single layers on baking sheets. Lightly brush with olive oil. Bake until crisp and golden-brown, about 10 minutes.

GUACAMOLE

This mixes hot and cool sensations, which stimulates the appetite—no wonder it's so hard to stop eating it.

MAKES 6 TO 8 SERVINGS

3 ripe Hass avocados

2 tablespoons lime juice

1 scallion, chopped

2 small hot chile peppers (such as jalapeño), seeded and chopped, or to taste

1 garlic clove, minced

1 large ripe tomato, peeled, seeded, and chopped

Salt and freshly ground pepper, to taste

2 tablespoons chopped fresh cilantro (optional)

Cut the avocados in half and scoop out the flesh. In a medium bowl, use a fork to mash the avocado flesh with the lime juice. Using a mortar and pestle, or a mini food processor, work the scallion, chiles, and garlic to a paste. Add to the avocado mixture. Fold in the chopped tomato. Season with salt and pepper. Garnish with the cilantro, if using. Press plastic wrap

FARMHOUSE CHEESE SPREAD WITH PITA CRISPS

directly onto the surface of the guacamole, and then refrigerate until well chilled, at least 1 hour. The guacamole can be prepared up to 8 hours ahead; keep it covered with plastic wrap to prevent discoloration.

OLIVADA

Olivada, and its French twin, tapenade, are olive pastes that have many uses in the Mediterranean kitchen. Spread onto toasted baguette slices, they make an admirable antipasto, but they can also be incorporated into recipes as a seasoning.

MAKES ABOUT 1 CUP
2 cups black Mediterranean olives, pitted
3 tablespoons extra virgin olive oil
2 tablespoons coarsely chopped capers
1 tablespoon Dijon mustard
1 tablespoon brandy
2 teaspoons anchovy paste
1 teaspoon chopped fresh rosemary or ½ teaspoon dried rosemary
2 teaspoons chopped fresh thyme or 1 teaspoon dried thyme
¼ teaspoon chile flakes

In a food processor fitted with the metal blade, process all the ingredients together just long enough so that they form a coarse purée. Transfer the paste to a suitable container, cover tightly, and keep refrigerated until you are ready to use it. The olivada can be kept, covered, in the refrigerator for up to 1 week.

Sun-Dried Tomato Olivada: Substitute ½ cup coarsely chopped sun-dried tomatoes packed in oil, well-drained, for 1 cup of the black olives.

BLACK BEAN AND BACON DIP

This is a zesty Southwestern-style bean dip.

MAKES ABOUT 2½ CUPS
4 strips bacon
1 medium onion, chopped
1 hot fresh chile pepper (such as jalapeño), seeded and minced
2 garlic cloves, minced
3 ripe plum tomatoes, seeded and chopped
1 teaspoon dried oregano
½ teaspoon ground cumin
3 cups cooked black beans
¾ cup beef stock, approximately
Tortilla chips, for dipping

In a large frying pan, cook the bacon over medium heat until crisp, about 5 minutes. Transfer to paper towels to drain, leaving the fat in the frying pan. Add the onion, chile pepper, and garlic to the pan and cook, stirring often, until the onion is softened but not browned, about 5 minutes. Stir in the tomatoes, oregano, and cumin, and cook for 5 minutes. Add the cooked black beans. Continue cooking over low heat, mashing the beans with a large spoon and gradually adding the stock, to make a chunky, but soupy, purée. Remove from the heat and stir in the crumbled bacon. Let the dip cool completely—it will thicken as it cools.

The dip can be kept, covered, in the refrigerator for up to 3 days. Before serving, thin down the dip, if necessary, with additional beef stock. Serve with tortilla chips for dipping.

CHICKPEA HUMMUS

Hummus is most delicious when made with freshly cooked chickpeas, but it can also be made with high-quality canned chickpeas—the ones sold at health food stores are the best.

MAKES 4 TO 6 SERVINGS
1 cup dried chickpeas, cooked and drained, or 2½ cups drained canned chickpeas
2 garlic cloves, crushed
⅓ cup tahini
¼ cup lemon juice
2 teaspoons ground cumin
2 teaspoons chili powder
Salt, to taste
2 tablespoons olive oil
Cayenne pepper, for garnish
1 tablespoon chopped fresh parsley
Pita bread, for serving

In a food processor fitted with the metal blade, process the chickpeas until they are smooth. If desired, press the purée through a sieve to remove any bits of skin. Add the garlic, tahini, and lemon juice. Beat in just enough cold water to make a smooth paste with the consistency of mayonnaise, about 5 tablespoons. Add the cumin and chili powder, and season with salt.

Pour the hummus into a serving bowl and smooth over the surface with the back of a spoon or a spatula. Pour the olive oil on top, and sprinkle generously with cayenne pepper in the center and parsley all over the surface. The hummus can be kept, covered, in the refrigerator for up to 3 days; garnish with oil, cayenne, and parsley just before serving. Serve the hummus as a dip, with pita bread.

EGGPLANT CAVIAR

Sometimes called "poor man's caviar," this has an intriguing smoky flavor. Serve it as a delicious snack accompanied by warm pita bread and olives, or as part of a combination of salads, perhaps with hummus and tomatoes.

MAKES 4 TO 6 SERVINGS

2 medium eggplants
1 teaspoon cumin seeds
2 ripe plum tomatoes, peeled, seeded, and
   finely chopped
2 scallions, finely chopped (optional)
2 garlic cloves, minced
6 tablespoons olive oil
1 teaspoon lemon juice, or more to taste
Salt and freshly ground pepper, to taste

Preheat the broiler. Broil the eggplants until the skins have blackened and the eggplants are becoming soft, about 20 minutes. Turn the eggplants and continue broiling until completely soft, about 15 minutes longer. Cool until easy to handle, then split the eggplants open and remove the flesh from the skin with a large spoon. Coarsely chop the flesh and transfer to a medium bowl.

In a small frying pan, toast the cumin seeds over medium heat, stirring often, until fragrant, about 2 minutes. Transfer to a mortar and pestle, and crush. (Or, place the seeds on a work surface and crush under a heavy pot.) Add to the eggplant, along with the tomatoes, optional scallions, and most of the garlic. Stirring constantly, gradually add the oil. Add the lemon juice, and season with salt and pepper. Taste the caviar and add more lemon juice, garlic, and/or seasoning if desired. Serve at cool room temperature. The eggplant caviar can kept, covered, in the refrigerator for up to 2 days.

CRAB CHILE CON QUESO

Hot dips are always a hit at parties, especially when made with sweet crabmeat. This one can be prepared well ahead of serving.

MAKES 12 APPETIZER SERVINGS

1 pound, 3 ounces cream cheese, at room temperature
1 cup Mexican Salsa Cruda, finely chopped, or use
   bottled salsa, drained slightly to remove excess liquid
2/3 cup mayonnaise
1 teaspoon chili powder
1/2 teaspoon Worcestershire sauce
1 pound fresh lump crabmeat, picked over to remove
   any cartilage

Tabasco sauce, to taste
1/2 cup finely crushed unsalted tortilla chips
Assorted raw vegetables, tortilla chips, or crackers,
   for serving

Preheat the oven to 350°F. In a medium bowl, mix together the cream cheese, salsa, mayonnaise, chili powder, and Worcestershire sauce. Fold in the crab, and season with Tabasco sauce. Transfer to a shallow 1-quart baking dish. (The dip can be kept, covered, in the refrigerator for up to 8 hours before baking.)

Sprinkle the top with the crushed tortilla chips. Bake until bubbling, about 30 minutes. Serve warm with vegetables or chips, for dipping.

SQUASH FRITTERS WITH GARLICKY YOGURT DIP

Serve these crispy fritters as a snack with drinks, or as a Mediterranean-style first course.

MAKES 4 TO 6 SERVINGS

1 cup all-purpose flour
2 tablespoons vegetable oil
3 small pattypan squash (1 pound)
Vegetable oil, for deep-frying
1 large egg white
Salt, to taste
Garlicky Yogurt Dip
4 ounces cream cheese, at room temperature
1/2 cup thick, drained plain yogurt
2 garlic cloves, chopped and mashed to a paste with
   a sprinkle of salt

Put the flour in a medium bowl. Make a well in the center, and pour in the oil and 3/4 cup water. Stir just until smooth. Let the batter stand for at least 30 minutes and up to 1 hour.

Meanwhile, for the dip, mash all the ingredients until smooth. Let stand so the flavors can blend.

Slice the pattypan squash vertically into 1/4-inch-thick slices. (If there are seeds in the squash, remove them, and peel the squash rounds.) Pour enough oil into a deep saucepan to come 2 inches up the sides of the pan. Heat to 360°F. Preheat the oven to 200°F. In a small bowl, beat the egg white until it forms stiff peaks, then fold into the batter. Working in small batches, dip the squash slices one at a time in the batter, shake off the excess, and place in the hot oil. Fry until pale golden on both sides, 2 to 3 minutes. Using a slotted spoon, transfer to paper towels to drain, and keep warm in the oven while making the rest of the fritters. Sprinkle the fritters with salt, and serve hot with the dip.

APPETIZERS, SNACKS, AND BEVERAGES

SALMON AND WATERCRESS PÂTÉ

This is an elegant first course for a supper party.

MAKES 6 TO 8 SERVINGS

Pâté

1 pound skinless salmon fillets, cut into long strips
about ½ inch thick

¾ cup dry white wine

Salt and freshly ground white pepper, to taste

2 cups packed watercress leaves

1 cup (2 sticks) unsalted butter, at room temperature

2 tablespoons finely chopped shallot

1 pound skinless white fish fillets, such as snapper
or sea bass, cut into 1-inch cubes, chilled

2 large eggs

Sprigs of watercress, for garnish

Sauce

8 ripe plum tomatoes, peeled, seeded, and cut into
small cubes

¼ cup fromage blanc or sour cream, chilled

¼ cup heavy cream, chilled

2 teaspoons Dijon mustard

2 tablespoons lemon juice

¼ cup chopped fresh parsley

1 teaspoon chopped fresh tarragon

Salt, freshly ground pepper, and Tabasco sauce,
to taste

To make the pâté, place the salmon strips and wine in a glass dish and season lightly with salt and pepper. Cover and let marinate in the refrigerator for 1 hour.

Bring a medium saucepan of lightly salted water to a boil over high heat. Add the watercress and blanch for about 1 minute. Drain, refresh, and pat dry with paper towels. Set aside.

In a small frying pan, melt 1 tablespoon of the butter over medium-low heat. Add the shallot and soften without browning, about 2 minutes. Place in a food processor fitted with the metal blade. Add the cubes of white fish and process until very smooth—this could take 3 minutes or so. With the machine running, add the eggs, one at a time. With the machine still running, add the remaining butter, about 2 tablespoons at a time. Season with salt and pepper.

Remove about two thirds of the white fish purée and set aside in a bowl. Add the watercress to the remaining fish purée in the food processor, and process until the mixture is evenly green. Transfer the green purée to another bowl. Cover both bowls and refrigerate for 30 minutes.

Preheat the oven to 275°F. Lightly oil a 10- by 3½-inch enameled cast-iron terrine mold.

Spread half of the white purée evenly over the bottom of the mold. Layer half of the drained salmon strips on the white purée, then cover with all of the green purée. Top with the remaining salmon strips, then add the rest of the white purée. Cover with buttered aluminum foil, buttered side down. Bake until an instant-read thermometer inserted in the center reads 160°F, about 2 hours. Transfer the mold to a wire cake rack and let cool completely. Refrigerate for at least 4 hours or overnight.

To make the sauce, place the tomato cubes in a strainer and let drain. In a medium bowl, whisk together the fromage blanc, heavy cream, and mustard. Gradually add the lemon juice, whisking it in. Fold in the tomato cubes and herbs. Season with salt, pepper, and Tabasco sauce.

Unmold the pâté onto a platter, discarding any liquid in the mold. Using a thin, sharp knife, cut into slices. Place each slice on a plate, spoon some of the sauce alongside, and garnish with a watercress sprig. Serve chilled, with the sauce.

BISTRO PÂTÉ DE CAMPAGNE

Here's a good, hearty pâté, straight from a bistro menu. Serve it with cornichons, coarse mustard, and plenty of crusty bread.

MAKES 8 SERVINGS

8 ounces slab bacon, rind removed

8 ounces boneless pork shoulder, cut into 1-inch cubes

12 ounces chicken livers, trimmed and cut into
¼-inch cubes

½ cup dry white wine

1 cup fresh bread crumbs

1 extra large egg

2 garlic cloves, minced

1 tablespoon brandy

1 teaspoon dried sage

1 teaspoon dried thyme

½ teaspoon quatre épices or ground allspice

15 black peppercorns, coarsely crushed

4 tablespoons unsalted butter

½ onion or 2 shallots, minced

1½ teaspoons salt

4 ounces fresh pork fatback, thinly sliced and cut into
¼-inch-thick strips

Bring a large saucepan of water to a boil over high heat. Add the bacon and blanch for 5 minutes to remove the smokiness. Drain, refresh, and drain again. Cut into 1-inch cubes. Place the bacon in a food processor fitted with the metal blade, add the pork, and process until coarsely chopped. Or, coarsely grind the bacon and pork in a meat grinder. Transfer to a medium bowl. Add the chicken livers, wine, bread crumbs, egg, garlic,

BISTRO PÂTÉ DE CAMPAGNE

brandy, sage, thyme, quatre épices, and peppercorns. Mix well. Cover with plastic wrap and refrigerate to blend the flavors, about 3 hours.

Preheat the oven to 350°F. In a small frying pan, melt the butter over medium heat. Add the onion and cook until soft and translucent, about 5 minutes. Add to the meat mixture with the salt and mix well. Place in a 1½-quart enameled cast-iron or earthenware terrine mold. Arrange the fatback strips over the top of the pâté in a lattice pattern, then cover with aluminum foil.

Bake for 1 hour. Remove the foil and continue baking until an instant-read thermometer inserted in the center of the pâté reads 160°F, about 30 more minutes. Place on a cooling rack and let cool completely. Cover with plastic wrap and refrigerate for 8 hours or overnight (the pâté can be kept in the refrigerator for up to 3 days).

When ready to use, if desired, unmold the pâté and wipe away any congealed juices. Slice the pâté and serve at cool room temperature.

HERBED CARROT PÂTÉ

Today's pâtés and terrines will just as often be made from vegetables as meat. Like most charcuterie, this carrot and white bean pâté makes enough for a crowd, so it is ideal when you need a light party appetizer.

MAKES ABOUT 20 APPETIZER SERVINGS

 12 ounces carrots, peeled and cut into 1-inch chunks
 2 tablespoons unsalted butter
 ½ cup minced shallots or scallions
 ¾ cup fresh bread crumbs
 ½ cup heavy cream
 3 cups cooked white beans
 2 large eggs plus 1 yolk
 2 tablespoons lemon juice
 2 tablespoons chopped fresh dill
 2 tablespoons chopped fresh parsley
 1 tablespoon chopped fresh tarragon or 1½ teaspoons dried tarragon
 Salt and freshly ground pepper, to taste
 French bread slices or crackers, for serving

Preheat the oven to 325°F. Lightly butter an 8½- by 4½-inch glass loaf pan. Fit a piece of waxed paper on the bottom of the pan. In a medium saucepan of lightly salted water, cook the carrots until very tender, about 20 minutes. Drain well. In a medium frying pan, heat the butter over medium heat. Add the shallots and cook until softened, about 3 minutes. In a small bowl, soak the bread crumbs in the cream until soft.

In a food processor fitted with the metal blade, purée the carrots with the shallots and crumb mixture. Add the beans, eggs, egg yolk, and lemon juice, and purée until smooth. Transfer to a bowl and stir in 1 tablespoon each of the dill and parsley, along with all the tarragon. Season well with salt and pepper. Spoon into the prepared pan and spread evenly. Top with a buttered piece of waxed paper, buttered side down. Put the loaf pan in a larger roasting pan and place in the oven. Pour enough water into the roasting pan to come ½ inch up the sides. Bake until the center of the pâté is firm and an instant-read thermometer inserted in the center reads 160°F, about 1¼ hours.

Remove the loaf pan from the bain marie. Remove the top piece of waxed paper, and cool the pâté in the pan on a wire cake rack. Then run a knife around the edges of the pâté, unmold onto a serving platter, and remove the waxed paper. Cover with plastic wrap and refrigerate until chilled, at least 4 hours or overnight (the pâté can be kept, covered, in the refrigerator for up to 3 days). Before serving, sprinkle the pâté with the remaining dill and parsley. Serve with slices of French bread.

PAN CATALAN

The simplest of ingredients——toasted bread, fine olive oil, robust garlic, and ripe tomatoes—combine in a form of alchemy to make the perfect appetizer. Similar to its better-known Italian cousin, bruschetta, this Spanish specialty has a charm all of its own. You could also toast the bread under the broiler or on a ridged cast-iron grill pan.

MAKES 4 SERVINGS
    4 large, thick slices country-style bread
    2 or 3 garlic cloves, peeled
    1 or 2 large ripe tomatoes, cut in half horizontally
    Extra virgin olive oil, for drizzling
    Salt, to taste
    4 large basil leaves, cut into thin strips (optional)

Light a charcoal (or wood) fire in an outdoor grill and let burn until the coals are covered with ashes. Grill the bread on both sides until toasted and very lightly charred. Fiercely rub one side of each toast with a garlic clove, using as much garlic as you like. (The rough surface of the toast will grate the garlic and the toast will absorb all the garlic juices.) Now rub the same surfaces with the cut side of the tomato halves. Drizzle oil over the tomato-soaked toasts and sprinkle with salt, both to taste. Serve at once, topped with the basil leaves, if desired.

CRYSTAL-CLEAR ICED TEA

The best iced tea takes time—if tea brewed from hot water is chilled, it will become cloudy.

MAKES 5 CUPS, ABOUT 5 SERVINGS
    4 tea bags of your favorite tea
    Sprigs of fresh mint or lemon slices, or both
    Sugar, to taste

Place the tea bags in a large pitcher. Add 5 cups of cold water. Cover and refrigerate until the tea is brewed, at least 4 hours or overnight. Serve over ice cubes, garnishing each serving with mint or lemon, or both. Let each guest sweeten with sugar to taste.

PINK RASPBERRY LEMONADE

Lemonade is the ultimate summer thirst-quencher. It only takes a second to muddle some berries in the bottom of a glass before pouring in the lemonade, producing a lovely pink-colored drink.

MAKES 3 QUARTS, ABOUT 12 SERVINGS
    2 cups fresh lemon juice
    1½ cups granulated sugar
    1 pint fresh raspberries

In a blender, process 1 cup of the lemon juice with the sugar until the sugar dissolves. Pour into a pitcher and stir in the remaining juice and 2 quarts of ice-cold water. Chill until ready to serve.

Just before serving, place a few raspberries in the bottom of each serving glass. Then, using a long spoon, crush the raspberries to release their juices. Pour the lemonade over the top. Add ice cubes, if desired, and serve.

GLÖGG

Mulled wine can be tame, but when it is made the Scandinavian way, it becomes a delicious, heady drink. Glögg is traditionally presented spectacularly flaming.

MAKES ABOUT 8 SERVINGS
    5 cups hearty red wine
    2½ cups Muscat wine
    ⅔ cup raisins

SANGRÍA

²⁄₃ cup packed light brown sugar
3 (3-inch) strips orange zest
5 whole cloves, lightly crushed
5 whole cardamom pods, lightly crushed
1 cinnamon stick, lightly crushed
²⁄₃ cup aquavit
¹⁄₃ cup slivered blanched almonds

Combine the red wine, Muscat wine, raisins, light brown sugar, strips of orange zest, cloves, cardamom pods, and cinnamon in a large nonreactive bowl. Let the mixture stand at room temperature overnight to infuse the flavors.

The next day, pour the mixture into a large nonreactive pot and bring just to a boil over medium heat. Pour 1 tablespoon of the aquavit into a small saucepan and set aside. Stir the remaining aquavit and the almonds into the pot. Heat the aquavit in the saucepan just until warm. Pour it over the top of the

glögg, and, averting your face, set it alight with a match. Serve immediately in tumblers with teaspoons, so the guests can eat the raisins and almonds.

SANGRÍA
Rioja is the best wine to use to give sangría an authentic Spanish flavor.

MAKES ABOUT 8 SERVINGS
1 medium orange, cut into ¼-inch-thick rounds
1 medium lemon, cut into ¼-inch-thick rounds
1 (750-ml) bottle red wine, preferably Rioja
¼ cup brandy, preferably Spanish
²⁄₃ cup sparkling mineral water
Superfine sugar, to taste
Sprigs of fresh mint

Half-fill a pitcher with ice cubes. Add the orange and lemon slices. Stir in the wine and brandy, then pour in the sparkling water. If needed, sweeten with sugar. Serve immediately, garnishing each glass with mint.

Preserves

MAKING PRESERVES AND PICKLES

Making good jams, jellies, preserves, and pickles does not necessarily mean an afternoon's devotion to the kitchen. Preparing small quantities is perfectly practical and doesn't take long. Many recipes don't even need to be processed in a water bath—just be sure to store them in the refrigerator instead of on the pantry shelf. Before you start, here are a few guides to success.

Pectin This substance is naturally present in many fruits, and when combined with sugar and the fruit's acids, ensures that your jam or jelly will set properly. Slightly underripe fruit contains more pectin than ripe. Tart fruits, such as apples, quinces, currants, oranges, and lemons, are particularly rich in pectin. When making preserves low in pectin, the setting is helped by the addition of some lemon juice. Some recipes (not in this book) call for liquid pectin, extracted from apple pulp, which is available at supermarkets during canning season.

Preparation Check jars to be sure they are free of nicks and cracks, and only use brand-new rings and lids. Do not use leftover jars from, say, mayonnaise, as they are not made to withstand the high heat of water-processing. Jars should be washed with soap, and rinsed thoroughly with very hot water. Both jars and rings must be sterilized in boiling water for 10 minutes before using. Have everything else ready and scrupulously clean. If you wish, warm the sugar in a 200°F oven while preparing the fruit—warm sugar will dissolve more quickly.

Setting Point After the jam, jelly, or preserve has boiled for 10 minutes, test it by dropping a spoonful onto a cold plate, and cooling until it looks set (you can speed the cooling in the refrigerator). Nudge with your finger; if the jam, jelly, or preserve wrinkles and clings to where it was dropped, it is ready. Skim the batch at this point to remove any scum or froth on the surface.

Packing into Jars Always pack your preserves in hot jars. After sterilizing, leave the jars standing in the hot water until ready to use, then remove with long tongs. Dry them with a very clean kitchen towel. The lids only need to be placed in a bowl of hot water to soften the rubber seal slightly; drain the lids right before using. To fill the jars most easily, use a widemouthed funnel. Don't fill the jars completely: leave about ½ inch of headspace. Use a clean towel to wipe the rims clean of any drips. Screw on the lids and rings.

Processing in a Water Bath Have a large pot of boiling water ready, filled with enough water to cover the jars by 1 inch. A processing pot with a removable basket works best, but any large pot with a rack on the bottom is fine. Submerge the jars in the water and process for the time indicated in the recipe. Lift the jars out of the hot water with tongs and place on a folded kitchen towel (this helps insulate the bottom of the jars to prevent them from cracking.) Let cool at room temperature.

Checking the Seal The jars must be checked for a proper seal. Unscrew the band and pick up the jar, holding by the seal. If the seal holds, all is well. If it is loose, return the screw band, and use the preserve promptly (or refrigerate and plan to use within the average refrigerated life of the food). If a stored jar shows an unsightly bulge on top, throw the preserve away—do not taste it to see if it is edible.

Storage Store preserves in a cool, dark, dry place.

STRAWBERRY JAM

There is no use making strawberry jam with inspid berries—wait until they are at their peak.

MAKES ABOUT 8 CUPS
4 pounds fresh strawberries, hulled
¼ cup lemon juice
4 pounds granulated sugar, warmed

Put the strawberries and lemon juice in a large, heavy-bottomed pot. Cook over very low heat, stirring from time to time, until the strawberries have softened and released their juices, 20 to 30 minutes.

Gently stir in the warmed sugar until it dissolves. Increase the heat to high and bring to a rapid boil, stirring frequently. Boil until the jam reaches the setting point (the syrup will look thick and the fruit will mound slightly in a metal spoon). Remove the pot from the heat. Draw the scum to the sides and carefully skim it off. Let the jam cool slightly, then ladle into hot, sterilized jars and seal.

PEACH PRESERVES

When peaches are in season and plentiful, but maybe just a little too ripe for eating out of hand, make peach preserves so that you can continue to enjoy the fruit's sweetness until next year's crop comes around.

MAKES ABOUT 5 CUPS
3 pounds ripe peaches, peeled, halved, and pitted
2¼ cups granulated sugar
2 tablespoons lemon juice
⅓ cup brandy

Place the peaches in a pan with 1 tablespoon water. Simmer gently until very soft, about 45 minutes.

STRAWBERRY JAM

Measure the cooked peaches; you should have about 4 cups. Return to the saucepan. Stir in the sugar and lemon juice. Stir over low heat until the sugar dissolves. Increase the heat to medium-high and boil for 6 minutes. Remove from the heat, cover, and let stand in a cool place overnight.

The next day, return the saucepan to medium-high heat and bring to a boil. Remove from the heat and stir in the brandy. Ladle into hot, sterilized jars and seal.

LEMON CURD

Lemon curd is not only an admirable tart filling, but is excellent spread onto English muffins or toast.

MAKES 2 CUPS

    8 tablespoons (1 stick) unsalted butter
    1 cup granulated sugar
    ½ cup fresh lemon juice, strained
    Zest of 2 lemons, removed with a vegetable peeler
    3 large eggs, at room temperature

In a double boiler insert set over a saucepan of hot, not simmering, water, combine the butter, sugar, lemon juice, and zest. When the mixture is smooth, stir in the eggs. Cook, stirring occasionally with a wooden spoon, until the curd is thick enough to coat the spoon (an instant-read thermometer will read about 185°F), about 6 minutes. Strain into a medium bowl. If using within 24 hours, press a sheet of plastic wrap directly onto the surface of the curd, and pierce with a few holes to allow the steam to escape. Let cool to room temperature, then transfer to a covered container and refrigerate for up to 1 week. Otherwise, ladle into hot, sterilized jars and seal, and store, refrigerated, for up to 3 months.

SWEET PEPPER CHUTNEY

This excellent chutney is a good accompaniment to all cold meats and game, and could even replace the cranberry sauce at the Thanksgiving meal.

MAKES ABOUT 2 PINTS

    ¼ cup olive oil
    3 medium onions, chopped
    2 medium red bell peppers, seeded and cut into 1-inch pieces
    2 medium green bell peppers, seeded and cut into 1-inch pieces
    1 garlic clove, minced
    12 allspice berries, coarsely crushed
    ¾ teaspoon ground cinnamon
    ½ teaspoon ground ginger
    ⅛ teaspoon ground cloves
    Salt, to taste
    1 pound ripe plum tomatoes, peeled, seeded, and chopped
    ⅔ cup raisins
    ¾ cup granulated sugar
    ⅔ cup white wine vinegar

In a heavy-bottomed saucepan, heat the oil. Add the onions and cook until soft, about 5 minutes. Add the peppers, garlic, allspice, cinnamon, ginger, cloves, and a seasoning of salt. Reduce the heat and cook for 10 minutes. Stir in the tomatoes and raisins, and cook for another 10 minutes. Add the sugar and vinegar. Increase the heat to medium and, stirring, bring to a simmer. Return the heat to medium-low and simmer until the chutney is thick and a beautiful bronze color, about 2 hours. Ladle into hot, sterilized jars and seal. Let stand in a cool, dark place for at least 2 weeks.

PICKLED BABY CARROTS

This blue-ribbon recipe turns a bag of peeled baby carrots into crisp and crunchy pickles. For crisp-tender pickles, cook the carrots in boiling lightly salted water for 2 minutes and drain before placing in the jar.

MAKES 1 QUART

    1 pound peeled baby carrots
    2 large sprigs fresh dill
    1 garlic clove, cut in half
    1½ cups distilled white vinegar
    1¼ teaspoons pickling salt
    1¼ teaspoons granulated sugar
    1½ teaspoons dill seeds
    ¼ teaspoon whole black peppercorns

In a hot, sterilized quart jar, arrange the carrots (quite a few will stand upright; lay the others across the top). Add the dill sprigs and garlic. In a saucepan, combine the vinegar, ½ cup water, the salt, sugar, dill seeds, and peppercorns. Bring to a boil. Pour the liquid into the jar, adding boiling water, if needed, to bring the liquid up to ½ inch from the top. Screw on the lid and ring, and let stand at room temperature overnight. Store in the refrigerator for 3 days before eating. The pickles will keep in the refrigerator for 1 month.

To store longer, or at room temperature, you must process the pickles in a water bath: Submerge the sealed jar in a saucepan of boiling water and boil for 5 minutes. Remove and let cool to room temperature.

New-Fashioned Dill Pickles: Substitute 6 medium kirby cucumbers for the carrots.

SPICY BREAD AND BUTTER PICKLES

The taste of homemade pickles is incomparable, and this recipe lets you enjoy it.

MAKES 1 QUART

- 4 medium kirby cucumbers, unpeeled, cut into ¼ inch-thick rounds (about 3 cups)
- 1 large onion, cut into ¼-inch-thick half-moons
- 1 medium red bell pepper, seeded and cut into ¼-inch-thick strips
- 2 tablespoons pickling salt
- 1 cup cider vinegar
- 1 cup granulated sugar
- ¼ teaspoon yellow mustard seeds
- ¼ teaspoon celery seed
- ¼ teaspoon coriander seeds
- ¼ teaspoon whole cloves
- ¼ teaspoon ground turmeric
- ¼ teaspoon chile flakes

In a large bowl, toss the cucumbers, onion, and red pepper with the salt. Add enough cold water barely to

SWEET PEPPER CHUTNEY

cover the vegetables, then stir in 2 trays of ice cubes. Let stand for 3 hours. Drain the vegetables, and rinse well under cold water. In a medium pot, combine the vinegar, sugar, and spices, and bring to a boil over high heat. Reduce the heat to low and simmer for 5 minutes. Add the drained vegetables and return just to boiling point. Spoon the hot vegetables into a hot, sterilized quart jar. Pour enough of the syrup into the jar to come up to ¼ inch from the top. Wipe the rim of the jar clean with a dish towel, and then close it with the lid and ring. Let stand at room temperature overnight, then refrigerate for at least 3 days before eating. The pickles can be kept in the refrigerator for up to 1 month.

For longer storage, the pickles must be processed in a water bath: Submerge the sealed jar in a deep saucepan of boiling water and boil for 5 minutes (counting from when the jar is put in the pot). Remove from the water, and let cool to room temperature.

Fish

Where most meat is cooked to make it tender, fish is naturally tender, so heat is only applied to develop the fish's flavor. Cooking fish beyond the moment when the flesh has turned from translucent to opaque will make it tough and dry. Fish is done if the fleshiest part flakes when it is prodded with the tip of a knife. You should start this testing about halfway through the recommended cooking time, in order to ensure succulent results.

There are a number of different ways to cook fish:
Poaching When cooking fish in a court-bouillon or other liquid, take care that the liquid never passes a bare simmer. Boiling extracts flavor from fish, which is fine for soups and stews, but disastrous when you want to serve simply prepared fish fillets or steaks. The poaching liquid should be well salted.
Steaming As the fish will not be cooked in a medium that lends much flavor, the fish itself must be impeccably fresh. Season the fish well with herbs, salt, and pepper, or it could end up as bland as hospital food. Place the fish on a buttered or oiled plate, and steam on a rack in a large covered pan of simmering water until just done.
Baking There is only one firm rule about baking fish—don't let it dry out. Be sure the oven is preheated well. The fish is often protected with a foil or paper wrapping, or insulated with a sauce or stuffing. If you are baking a whole fish, try to leave the head and tail on, as it will then retain more moisture.
Frying Fish should be fried as quickly as possible to seal the exterior and hold in the juices. Clarified butter is a good fat for sautéing, but only use enough to stop the fish from sticking to the pan. When deep-frying fish, preheat the oil to 375°F. Large pieces of fish should be sealed in a batter or with egg and crumbs; small fish, like whitebait, only need a quick dip in milk and seasoned flour.
Broiling The broiler should be preheated so the fish can start to cook immediately, to seal in the juices. If you are cooking a whole fish, leave the head and tail on, and make two diagonal slashes in the thickest parts of the body to help the heat to penetrate. Brush fish steaks or fillets with oil or clarified butter to add moisture. Fish fillets do not need turning over halfway during broiling, but do turn whole fish and steaks.
Grilling Brush the grill well with oil so the fish won't stick. Let the coals burn down for a few minutes after they are covered with white ash—they should be medium-hot, not blazing. For whole fish, use a fish-shaped grilling basket, which makes turning the fish very easy.
Marinating For dishes such as *seviche*, very fresh fish is "cooked" in an acidic marinade (the acids turn the fish opaque, which makes it look as if it has been cooked by heat, when it is actually raw). Fish to be cooked by heat is often marinated in a well-seasoned liquid, to add flavor and, sometimes, moisture (it is important not to marinate fish for longer than 2 hours or the acids will do their "cooking" trick and make the cooked flesh mushy). Always marinate fish in a glass or ceramic dish, as the acids will react with metal and give the marinade a metallic taste.

FILLET OF SOLE MEUNIÈRE
This is a delicious, useful recipe for a quick supper. For the best results, use Dover sole fillets, or another firm fish fillet like snapper, since sole's ubiquitous cousin, flounder, has a tendency to fall apart when panfried. Be sure the butter is good and hot before adding the fish in order to create a nice crust.

MAKES 4 SERVINGS
  4 (7-ounce) sole fillets
  Salt and freshly ground pepper, to taste
  ½ cup all-purpose flour
  7 tablespoons unsalted butter
  3 tablespoons lemon juice
  2 tablespoons finely chopped fresh parsley

Season the fillets with salt and pepper, then coat lightly with flour, shaking off the excess flour. In a large frying pan, heat 2 tablespoons of the butter over medium-high heat until very hot and starting to brown. Add the fillets and cook, turning once, until golden-brown on both sides, about 4 minutes. Transfer the fish to warm dinner plates. Wipe out the pan and then return it to medium-high heat. Add the lemon juice and parsley to the pan, then the remaining 5 tablespoons butter. Swirl the butter in the pan until melted, then pour equal portions of the lemon butter over each fillet. Serve immediately.

Trout Meunière: Substitute 4 whole trout (about 12 ounces each) for the sole. Cook until golden-brown on both sides, turning once, about 8 minutes. If necessary, cook the fish in batches and keep warm.

BAKED HALIBUT STEAKS WITH MUSHROOMS
A delicate dish for a special meal. Serve with boiled new potatoes and brightly colored vegetables such as baby carrots or young peas.

MAKES 4 SERVINGS
  4 tablespoons unsalted butter
  1 cup sliced button mushrooms
  4 shallots, sliced

4 (6- to 8-ounce) halibut steaks
¾ cup dry white wine
Salt and freshly ground pepper, to taste
2 tablespoons heavy cream

Preheat the oven to 350°F. In a flameproof baking dish or an ovenproof frying pan, heat 2 tablespoons of the butter over medium heat. Add one fourth of the mushroom and shallot slices and cook until they absorb the butter, about 1 minute. Place the halibut steaks on top and pour the wine over the fish. Lay the remaining mushrooms and shallots on the fish. Season with salt and pepper, and dot with small pieces of the remaining 2 tablespoons butter. Cover with foil and bake until the fish is barely opaque when flaked with the tip of a sharp knife, 10 to 15 minutes.

Using a perforated metal turner, transfer the halibut steaks, mushrooms, and shallots to a warm platter, and cover with foil to keep warm. Strain the cooking liquid into a small saucepan. Add the cream, bring to a boil over high heat, and cook until slightly thickened, about 3 minutes. Season the sauce with salt and pepper. Transfer the halibut steaks and mushrooms to four warm dinner plates, and spoon the sauce over each serving.

STEAMED COD WITH GINGER AND SCALLIONS

Cantonese restaurants all over the world serve steamed seafood—just about anything that swims, from sea bass or sole to lobster or crab. However, cod is especially good prepared like this. Chinese woks often come with a large steaming rack that will fit a standard dinner plate. Lacking a wok, use a large covered roasting pan with a rack, and place the fish on an oval platter that will fit the pan.

MAKES 4 SERVINGS
    4 (6-ounce) cod fillets, with skin
    2 tablespoons vegetable oil
    2 tablespoons light soy sauce
    1½ teaspoons dry sherry
    2 teaspoons rice vinegar
    1 teaspoon Asian dark sesame oil
    1 (2-inch) piece fresh ginger, peeled and cut into
        matchstick-sized strips
    6 scallions, thinly sliced on the bias
    4 sprigs fresh cilantro

Place the fish on a plate or platter that will fit your steaming utensil. Pour the vegetable oil over the fish. Pour enough water into the steamer to come about 1 inch up the sides. Place the plate of fish in the steamer, cover, and then bring the water to a full boil over high heat.

While the water is coming to a boil, in a small saucepan, combine the soy sauce, sherry, rice vinegar, sesame oil, and ginger. Bring to a simmer over medium heat and cook for 2 minutes. Pour the soy sauce mixture over the fish. Cover again and steam until the fish is barely opaque when flaked in the thickest part with the tip of a knife, 6 to 8 minutes. Sprinkle with the scallions and steam for 2 more minutes.

Using a perforated metal turner, transfer the fish to individual plates. Spoon over the cooking juices, and garnish with the cilantro. Serve immediately.

WHOLE BAKED SEA BASS WITH TOMATOES

A whole baked fish always makes an impressive main dish. This method of preparation is appropriate for any large fish, such as snapper, sea trout, or grouper. To estimate baking times for whole fish, measure the height of the fish in its thickest part, and allow 15 minutes for each inch. For example, a 2-inch-thick fish will take about 30 minutes.

MAKES 4 SERVINGS
    1 (3- to 4-pound) whole sea bass, cleaned and scaled
    3 garlic cloves, halved lengthwise
    2 lemon slices, halved
    Salt and freshly ground pepper, to taste
    A few sprigs fresh fennel leaves, or ½ teaspoon
        fennel seed
    3 large ripe tomatoes, peeled, seeded, and quartered
    2 small onions, sliced
    ¼ cup olive oil

Preheat the oven to 375°F. Butter a large baking dish or roasting pan. Rinse the fish and pat dry with paper towels. Make two deep diagonal slashes in the thickest part on both sides of the fish. In each slash, place a piece of garlic and a half lemon slice, peel side outward. Place a piece of garlic in the head. Put the remaining garlic in the body, and season with salt and pepper. If using fennel seed, sprinkle it inside the fish. Put the fish in the prepared dish and surround with the tomatoes and onions. Pour the olive oil over all, and season with salt and pepper.

Bake in the bottom third of the oven until the fish is opaque in the thickest part when flaked with the tip of a knife, about 35 minutes. If using fennel sprigs, scatter them over the fish 15 minutes before the end of cooking. Lift the fish off the bone, in serving-sized pieces, and serve hot with the vegetables. The fish can also be served cold, with a garlicky tomato sauce.

FISH FILLETS IN BASQUE PEPPER SAUCE

Pipérade, a zesty vegetable mixture featuring different-colored bell peppers, tomatoes, and onions, can be found in various dishes throughout the Pyrenees mountains. Here it acts as a flavorful sauce for baked fish fillets, where the colors of the ingredients add to the appeal of the finished dish.

MAKES 4 SERVINGS

4 tablespoons olive oil

2 medium onions, sliced

2 medium red or yellow bell peppers, seeded and cut
   into ¼-inch-wide strips

2 garlic cloves, minced

3 large ripe tomatoes, peeled, seeded, and
   coarsely chopped

Salt and freshly ground pepper, to taste

4 (6-ounce) skinless fish fillets, such as porgy,
   sea bass, or snapper

12 black Mediterranean olives, pitted

In a large frying pan, heat 2 tablespoons of the olive oil over medium heat. Add the onions and cook until they are soft and translucent, about 5 minutes. Add the peppers and garlic, and cook until the peppers have softened, about 10 minutes. Stir in the tomatoes and cook until the mixture forms a thick sauce, about 15 minutes. Season with salt and pepper. Transfer to a bowl and set aside.

Preheat the oven to 350°F. Lightly oil a shallow baking dish. Season the fish with salt and pepper. Heat 1 tablespoon of the remaining oil in the cleaned frying pan over medium-high heat until very hot but not smoking. Add the fish and cook, turning once, until lightly browned on both sides, about 2 minutes. Place in the baking dish and cover with the tomato-pepper sauce. Bake until the fish is cooked through, about 15 minutes. About 3 minutes before the fish is done, scatter the olives on top and drizzle with the remaining 1 tablespoon oil. Serve hot.

BAKED BLUEFISH WITH SWEET MUSTARD GLAZE

East Coast bluefish has a rich, oily flesh that needs a sharp accent to bring out its flavor. This mustard glaze does the job perfectly.

MAKES 4 SERVINGS

4 (8-ounce) bluefish fillets
⅓ cup Dijon mustard
1 tablespoon packed light brown sugar
2 teaspoons chopped fresh tarragon or 1 teaspoon dried tarragon
1 teaspoon soy sauce

Preheat the oven to 375°F. Place the bluefish, skin side down, in a lightly oiled baking dish. In a small bowl, mix together the Dijon mustard, light brown sugar, fresh or dried tarragon, and soy sauce. Spread evenly over the bluefish. Bake until the fish appears opaque when flaked in the center with the tip of a knife, 15 to 20 minutes. Serve hot.

FRIED SARDINES WITH LEMON

Whenever you see plump fresh sardines in the fish market, think about preparing them this way—simply sautéed in olive oil and served with a good squeeze of lemon juice to offset their oily flesh. This quick preparation is also applicable to other small fresh fish, such as anchovies.

MAKES 4 SERVINGS AS A FIRST COURSE, OR 2 SERVINGS AS A MAIN COURSE

1½ pounds fresh sardines
2 lemons
Salt, to taste
4 tablespoons olive oil

Rinse the sardines well under cold running water, rubbing them to remove their tiny scales. To clean the fish, pinch off their heads and gills, and pull out the innards at the same time. Otherwise, run your finger down the belly to open, and remove the innards. Rinse again and pat dry with paper towels. Place the sardines in a glass baking dish. Squeeze the juice of 1 lemon over the fish and let stand for 30 minutes. Season with salt.

In a large frying pan, heat the oil over medium-high heat until very hot but not smoking. Carefully add the sardines to the pan, standing well back to avoid any spitting fat. Cook, turning once, until golden-brown, about 5 minutes. Transfer to paper towels to drain. Serve hot, with the second lemon cut into wedges.

MEDITERRANEAN SWORDFISH IN TOMATO-ONION SAUCE

The meaty quality of swordfish makes it a good candidate for baking. For an interesting variation of this sauce, substitute ½ teaspoon fennel seed for the oregano, and add ¼ teaspoon crushed saffron threads.

MAKES 4 SERVINGS

½ cup olive oil
1 tablespoon dry white wine
3 sprigs fresh thyme
4 (6-ounce) swordfish steaks
3 medium onions, sliced
2 garlic cloves, minced
1 pound ripe plum tomatoes, peeled, seeded, and coarsely chopped
1 teaspoon finely chopped fresh oregano or ½ teaspoon dried oregano
Salt and freshly ground pepper, to taste
4 slices white bread, cut into triangles

Mix 2 tablespoons of the oil, the wine, and the thyme in a shallow glass baking dish. Add the swordfish. Cover and let marinate in the refrigerator, turning the fish occasionally, for 1 to 2 hours, no longer.

Preheat the oven to 375°F. In a large frying pan, heat 2 tablespoons of the oil over medium heat. Add the onions and garlic and cook, stirring occasionally, until softened, about 5 minutes. Stir in the tomatoes and oregano, and season with the salt and pepper. Pour the tomato-onion sauce over the swordfish steaks and stir to mix with the marinade. Bake until the swordfish is medium-rare (pink) when pierced in the center with a sharp knife, about 20 minutes.

Meanwhile, in a frying pan, heat the remaining oil over medium-high heat. Fry the triangles of bread until golden-brown on both sides, 3 to 4 minutes. Drain on paper towels. Arrange the bread triangles around the fish and serve immediately.

SICILIAN BROILED TUNA

Tuna plays a large part in Sicilian cuisine, and is often cooked in large portions like a meat roast.

MAKES 4 SERVINGS

1 (2-pound) tuna steak, in one piece, skin removed
4 anchovy fillets, cut in half
6 tablespoons lemon juice
6 tablespoons olive oil
1 teaspoon chopped fresh marjoram or oregano, or ½ teaspoon dried oregano
Salt and freshly ground pepper, to taste
Delicate Tomato Sauce, for serving

Using the tip of a sharp knife, make eight incisions all over the tuna, and stuff the incisions with the anchovies. In a medium bowl, whisk the lemon juice with the oil. Add the tuna and cover. Let marinate in the refrigerator, turning often, for at least 1 and up to 2 hours.

Preheat the broiler, and line the broiler pan with aluminum foil. Remove the tuna from the bowl and shake off excess marinade. Place the tuna on the foil-lined pan. Season the tuna with the marjoram, salt, and pepper. Broil, turning once, and occasionally basting with the marinade, until the fish looks medium-rare in the center when flaked with the tip of a knife, 15 to 20 minutes. Serve immediately, with the tomato sauce passed on the side.

BAKED STUFFED POMPANO

A tarragon and chive stuffing adds flavor and keeps the fish succulent during baking. Removing the backbone and ribs makes for easy serving.

MAKES 4 SERVINGS
> 1 (2½-pound) whole pompano, cleaned and scaled
> 1 cup fresh bread crumbs
> ¼ cup milk
> 6 tablespoons butter, at room temperature
> 2 large egg yolks
> 1½ teaspoons finely chopped fresh tarragon
> 1½ teaspoons finely chopped fresh chives
> Salt and freshly ground pepper, to taste
> ⅔ cup dry white wine
> 3 tablespoons heavy cream
> 2 teaspoons finely chopped fresh parsley

Preheat the oven to 325°F. Lightly oil a baking dish large enough to hold the fish. Using a long, flexible, sharp knife, make a long slit down the back of the fish. Running the knife along the rib bones, cut out and remove the backbone and ribs.

In a medium bowl, moisten the bread crumbs with the milk, and then squeeze out the excess milk. Add 4 tablespoons of the butter, the egg yolks, tarragon, chives, and some salt and pepper. Mix well. Stuff the fish with the herb mixture, and use kitchen string to sew up the back and belly incisions.

Place the fish in the prepared baking dish. Pour the wine over the fish, season with salt and pepper, and dot with the remaining butter. Bake until the thickest part of the fish feels tender when pressed with a fingertip, about 30 minutes. Using a fish lifter, carefully transfer the fish to a warmed serving platter. Cover with foil to keep warm.

Pour the cooking juices into a medium saucepan. Bring to a boil and cook until reduced by half, about

5 minutes. Add the cream and parsley and continue cooking until the sauce has thickened slightly, about 3 more minutes. Season with salt. Pour the sauce around the fish and serve immediately.

TUNA WITH HOT RED CHILE SAUCE

Adapted from a North African recipe, this is an aromatic, boldly colored dish. Serve it with fried potatoes or couscous.

MAKES 4 SERVINGS
> 4 (6-ounce) tuna or swordfish steaks
> 4 garlic cloves: 2 crushed to a paste with ½ teaspoon salt, and 2 minced
> 1 teaspoon ground cumin
> 3 medium red bell peppers, roasted, peeled, and seeded
> 3 medium yellow or orange bell peppers, roasted, peeled, and seeded
> ¼ cup olive oil, plus more as needed
> 1¼ pounds ripe plum tomatoes, peeled, seeded, and quartered, or use canned
> 2 hot fresh green chile peppers, seeded and chopped
> Salt and freshly ground pepper, to taste
> Shredded fresh mint and lemon wedges, for garnish

Rub the tuna steaks with the garlic paste and ground cumin. Cover and refrigerate while making the sauce.

Cut the roasted peppers into thin strips. Set aside about ½ cup of the pepper strips to use as a garnish. Stack the remaining strips and cut them crosswise into ¼-inch pieces. In a large frying pan, heat the oil over medium-high heat. Add the tomatoes, chiles, and minced garlic. Cook rapidly, stirring often, until the tomato juices have evaporated and the mixture is caramelizing and beginning to stick to the pan, about 10 minutes. Add a little more oil, if needed. Remove from the heat. Crush the tomatoes with a large spoon, then stir in the chopped peppers. Season this sauce with salt and pepper.

Preheat the oven to 400°F. In the center of four 12-inch squares of aluminum foil, place a heaping tablespoon of the sauce. Top with a tuna steak and cover with the remaining sauce, dividing it equally. Bring up the edges of the foil squares over the fish and tightly crimp together to seal closed. Place the foil packets on a baking sheet. Bake for about 15 minutes.

Open the packets and turn the tuna and sauce onto four dinner plates. Sprinkle each serving with mint, and serve with lemon wedges.

TUNA WITH HOT RED CHILE SAUCE

SKATE WITH BROWN BUTTER SAUCE

Skate, with its deliciously sweet flesh, is finally finding the recognition in America that it has long enjoyed in Europe. This is a classic preparation.

MAKES 4 SERVINGS

1 quart Court-Bouillon
2 (1- to 2-pound) skate wings, skin removed
4 tablespoons unsalted butter
1 teaspoon red wine vinegar
2 teaspoons drained capers (optional)
Salt and freshly ground pepper, to taste
1 teaspoon finely chopped fresh parsley

In a large frying pan, bring the court-bouillon to a simmer over medium heat. Add the skate wings and return to the simmer. Cover and remove from the heat. Let the retained heat cook the fish until it looks opaque when flaked in the center with the tip of a sharp knife, about 15 minutes. Using a perforated metal turner, transfer the skate to a platter and cover to keep warm.

In a small frying pan, heat the butter over medium heat until it is hazelnut brown in color, 1 to 2 minutes. Off the heat, swirl in the red wine vinegar and the optional capers. Season with salt and pepper, and stir in the chopped parsley. To serve, lift off the top fillets from the skate wings and place on dinner plates. Remove the cartilage, and serve the bottom fillets. Pour the sauce over the skate and serve.

NORMANDY FISH STEW

The French province of Normandy is famous for an abundance of apples from its orchards and fish from its coast. Monkfish is used in this rich fish stew, called *matelote normande* in France, but sea bass or snapper is also very good, and if you like eel, this recipe is a traditional way to serve it. Hard, alcoholic apple cider, which is quite dry, almost like a fruity white wine, acts as the cooking liquid. A few American companies are beginning to make hard cider, but if you can't find it and you want to keep an apple flavor in the stew, use a combination of ¾ cup dry white wine and ½ cup regular apple cider.

MAKES 4 SERVINGS

2 pounds mussels, scrubbed and debearded if necessary
6 tablespoons unsalted butter
2 medium onions, finely chopped
1¼ cups dry hard cider or dry white wine

NORMANDY FISH STEW

2 pounds monkfish, boned and cut into 2-inch pieces
3 tablespoons all-purpose flour
8 medium shrimp, cooked, peeled, and deveined
2 tablespoons chopped fresh parsley
Salt and freshly ground pepper, to taste
Juice of ½ lemon (optional)

Place the prepared mussels and 3 tablespoons cold water in a large saucepan. Cover and bring to a boil over high heat. Cook, shaking the saucepan often, until all the mussels have opened, about 5 minutes. Remove the mussels to a platter and leave them to cool. Strain the cooking liquid. When the mussels are cool enough to handle, shell them, discarding the shells, and set them aside.

In a large saucepan, heat 2 tablespoons of the butter over medium heat. Add the onions and cook until they are soft and translucent, about 5 minutes. Add the strained mussel liquid and the cider. Bring to a simmer. Add the monkfish. The liquid should just cover the fish, so add hot water, if necessary. Simmer gently over medium-low heat until the fish is almost cooked through, about 5 minutes.

In a small bowl, work the remaining 4 tablespoons butter and the flour together to make a paste. Add this to the simmering liquid in small pieces, stirring constantly. Continue to simmer until the sauce is lightly thickened and the fish is opaque when pierced in the center with the tip of a knife, 3 to 5 minutes longer. Add the reserved mussels, the shrimp, and the chopped parsley. Season with salt and pepper, and add the optional lemon juice. Cook just until the mussels and shrimp are heated through, about 1 minute. Transfer to a warm soup tureen and serve immediately, accompanied by plenty of fresh, crusty French bread.

OVEN-FRIED CATFISH WITH REMOULADE SAUCE

Crispy catfish fillets in a cornmeal crust, served with a spoonful of spicy remoulade sauce alongside, are a specialty of Southern cuisine. These fillets are oven-fried—a quick and healthy way to prepare this old-fashioned dish.

MAKES 4 SERVINGS

¾ cup buttermilk
1 tablespoon Cajun Dry Rub
1 cup yellow cornmeal, preferably stoneground
Salt, to taste
4 (7-ounce) catfish fillets
3 tablespoons vegetable oil
½ cup Remoulade Sauce

Preheat the oven to 400°F. Lightly oil a large baking sheet and then place this in the oven to heat up for about 3 minutes.

In a shallow dish, mix together the buttermilk and the Cajun dry rub. Place the cornmeal in another shallow dish and season with a little salt. Dip each catfish fillet first in the buttermilk and Cajun dry rub mixture, shaking off the excess, and then coat with the cornmeal.

Place the prepared catfish fillets on the hot baking sheet, and drizzle them with the vegetable oil. Bake until the coating is a lovely golden-brown color, about 20 minutes. Serve hot, accompanied by the remoulade sauce.

SALMON WITH HERBED YOGURT SAUCE

This fish dish is based on an Indian recipe, and is very easy to make. Boiled new potatoes would go well with the salmon.

MAKES 4 SERVINGS
    4 (5- to 6-ounce) skinless salmon fillets
    2 tablespoons lemon juice
    Salt, to taste
    ½ cup packed fresh cilantro leaves
    ½ cup packed fresh flat-leaf parsley leaves
    ¼ cup coarsely chopped fresh chives
    3 hot fresh green chile peppers (such as serrano),
        seeded and chopped
    3 garlic cloves, peeled
    1 cup plain yogurt, drained
    ½ cup vegetable oil

Place the salmon fillets in a shallow glass baking dish and sprinkle them with lemon juice and salt. Cover the dish and leave the salmon to marinate in the refrigerator, turning the fillets from time to time, for 1 to 2 hours, no longer.

In a food processor fitted with the metal blade, purée the cilantro, parsley, chives, chiles, and garlic to a mush, adding a little water if needed to help smooth out the mixture. Pour the processed herb mixture into a shallow dish, and put the thick drained yogurt in another shallow dish.

Heat the vegetable oil in a large frying pan over medium-high heat. Dip each salmon fillet in the yogurt to coat well, and then dip into the herb mixture. Quickly place the fillets in the frying pan, being careful of hot spitting oil. Cook, turning the fish over once, until it looks barely opaque when pierced in the thickest part with the tip of a sharp knife, 6 to 8 minutes. Transfer the fish to paper towels to drain. Serve immediately.

SOY-MARINATED SALMON BROCHETTES

Salmon's inherent oiliness makes it a perfect fish for grilling. Charcoal grilling really brings out the fish's flavor, but these brochettes can also be broiled indoors or cooked on a ridged cast-iron grill pan. Serve the brochettes on a bed of Sesame Spinach.

MAKES 4 SERVINGS
    1½ pounds skinless salmon fillet, cut into 1-inch pieces
    Chopped garlic chives or scallions, and lime wedges,
        for garnish
Marinade
    ¼ cup light soy sauce
    ¼ cup rice wine or dry sherry
    1 (2-inch) piece fresh ginger, unpeeled, thinly sliced
    Thinly pared zest and juice of 1 lime
    2 teaspoons Chinese chile oil
    1 tablespoon syrup from a jar of candied stem ginger,
        or 1 tablespoon honey
    ½ teaspoon five-spice powder
    ½ teaspoon chile flakes

To make the marinade, mix all of the ingredients in a medium nonreactive bowl. Add the salmon. Cover and let marinate in the refrigerator, stirring occasionally, for 1 to 2 hours, no longer.

Build a hot charcoal fire in an outdoor grill. Lightly oil the grill. Drain the salmon, reserving the marinade, and thread onto metal skewers. (If using bamboo skewers, soak them for 30 minutes, then drain.) Grill for 5 minutes, then turn the brochettes over and grill until the salmon is just cooked, about 3 more minutes. The outside should be lightly charred and blistered.

Place the brochettes on dinner plates. If desired, gently heat the marinade in a small saucepan and brush it onto the brochettes to give a glossy finish. Sprinkle with garlic chives or scallions and serve with lime wedges.

GRILLED SALMON WITH COOL AND HOT CUCUMBERS

This combination of hot grilled salmon with cool, spiced cucumber is very pleasing, particularly eaten outdoors on a hot summer day.

MAKES 4 SERVINGS
    4 (9-ounce) salmon steaks
    1 tablespoon vegetable oil
    Salt and freshly ground pepper, to taste
Cucumber Salad
    1 large cucumber, peeled, halved lengthwise, seeded,
        and sliced into ⅛-inch-thick half-moons
    ½ teaspoon salt

2 tablespoons plain yogurt

2 tablespoons chopped fresh cilantro

1 tablespoon chopped fresh mint

1 or 2 hot fresh chile peppers (such as jalapeño or
   serrano), seeded and minced

1 garlic clove, minced

2 teaspoons lime juice

1 teaspoon granulated sugar

½ teaspoon ground cumin

Cayenne pepper, to taste

To make the cucumber salad, toss the cucumbers with
the salt and then refrigerate for 1 hour to draw out some
of the cucumber juices. Drain, rinse under cold water,
drain again, and pat dry with paper towels. Add the
remaining salad ingredients and toss to combine. Cover
and refrigerate until ready to serve. (The salad can be
prepared up to 8 hours ahead.)

Build a hot charcoal fire in an outdoor grill. Lightly
oil the grill. Brush the salmon on both sides with oil,
and season with salt and pepper. Grill, turning once,
until the fish looks barely opaque when pierced in the
thickest part, 8 to 10 minutes. Serve the salmon steaks
with the cucumber salad.

Soy-Marinated Salmon Brochettes
with Sesame Spinach

BAKED WHOLE SALMON FILLET WITH LEMON AND HERBS

A lovely main course for a spring buffet, this recipe
proves that some of the simplest foods are the best.

MAKES 8 TO 12 SERVINGS

1 (3-pound) salmon fillet, fine bones removed
   with tweezers

Salt and freshly ground pepper, to taste

¼ cup chopped mixed fresh herbs, such as tarragon,
   dill, and parsley

2 tablespoons minced shallots

2 lemons, very thinly sliced and seeds removed

Italian Herb Sauce or Remoulade Sauce, for serving

Preheat the oven to 375°F. Lightly oil a large piece of
heavy-duty aluminum foil. Place the fillet on the foil,
skin side down. Season with salt and pepper, sprinkle
with the herbs and shallots, and top with the lemon
slices. Wrap well in the foil. Place on a baking sheet.

Fish/Shellfish

Bake until the salmon looks barely opaque when pierced in the thickest part (unwrap the salmon to check this), 35 to 40 minutes. Open the foil and cool the salmon to room temperature, then rewrap it and refrigerate until chilled. To serve, transfer the salmon onto an oval serving platter. Cut the fish into individual servings, and serve with a bowl of the sauce on the side.

TROUT WITH MUSHROOMS EN PAPILLOTE

Other small fish under 1 pound can also be prepared in this manner, baked in an envelope of parchment paper or foil with a finely chopped mushroom mixture, called a *duxelles* in French.

MAKES 4 SERVINGS

    2 cups finely chopped button mushrooms
    1 tablespoon lemon juice
    2 tablespoons unsalted butter, plus softened butter for
        the parchment paper or foil
    ¼ cup chopped shallots
    1 tablespoon chopped fresh parsley
    Salt and freshly ground pepper, to taste
    4 (12-ounce) whole trout, cleaned and scaled
    Velvety White Sauce, made with fish stock, for serving

Toss the mushrooms with the lemon juice, which will help keep the mushrooms white. In a large frying pan, melt the butter over medium heat. Add the mushrooms and shallots, and cook, stirring often, until the mushrooms give off their liquid. Continue cooking until the liquid has evaporated and the mixture is quite dry, 4 to 5 minutes. Stir in the parsley, and season with salt and pepper.

Preheat the oven to 400°F. Cut four 12-inch rounds of parchment paper or foil. Butter one side of each round, leaving the borders unbuttered. Using a sharp knife, cut two deep slashes on both sides of each trout, in the thickest part. Season the fish, inside and out, with salt and pepper.

Reserve about ⅓ cup of the mushrooms for the sauce. Place a spoonful of the remaining mushrooms on one half of each paper round, buttered side up. Top with a trout, and spoon the remaining mushrooms over the fish. Fold over the paper round to enclose the fish, and pleat the edges together twice to seal them. Place the packets on a baking sheet and bake for 15 minutes. Meanwhile, if necessary, reheat the white sauce; stir in the reserved ⅓ cup mushrooms, and keep warm. Serve the fish in their paper packets, letting each guest open his or her own, and passing the sauce on the side.

VERMOUTH-MARINATED TROUT PIEDMONTESE

Italians love cold marinated fish, served either as a piquant first course or as a cool entrée. This recipe, from the Val d'Aosta, should be made at least a day ahead.

MAKES 6 SERVINGS

    6 (12-ounce) trout, cleaned and scaled
    ½ cup all-purpose flour
    ¼ cup vegetable oil
Marinade
    6 tablespoons vegetable oil
    2 tablespoons olive oil
    2 medium onions, sliced
    2 garlic cloves, sliced
    6 tablespoons dry vermouth
    3 tablespoons white wine vinegar
    4 strips lemon zest
    4 fresh sage leaves
    1 sprig fresh rosemary
    1 teaspoon whole black peppercorns, coarsely crushed
    Salt, to taste

Coat the fish lightly with the flour, shaking off excess flour. Heat the oil in a frying pan over medium heat. Add the fish and cook, turning once, until golden on the outside and opaque when flaked in the thickest part, about 12 minutes. Drain on paper towels. Place the fish, side by side, in an earthenware or glass dish.

To make the marinade, heat both oils in a medium saucepan over medium heat. Add the onions and garlic and cook until softened, about 5 minutes. Add the remaining marinade ingredients and bring to a boil. Pour the hot marinade over the trout. Let cool to room temperature, then cover. Let marinate in the refrigerator, turning the fish occasionally, for at least 1 and up to 3 days. Serve lightly chilled.

VARIATION: Substitute orange zest for the lemon zest, and add 2 tablespoons dark raisins to the marinade.

BACALAO WITH POTATOES

Salt cod is a beloved ingredient of Hispanic cooks, and this way of preparing it with potatoes in a garlicky tomato sauce is known from Spain to Puerto Rico. Salt cod needs at least 24 hours' soaking, to desalt it.

MAKES 4 SERVINGS

    1 pound salt cod fillet
    3 tablespoons olive oil
    ½ cup all-purpose flour
    2 pounds boiling potatoes, peeled and cut into
        ¼-inch-thick rounds

3 medium onions, thinly sliced
4 large ripe tomatoes, peeled, seeded, and sliced
1 garlic clove, chopped
1 tablespoon chopped fresh parsley
⅛ teaspoon crushed saffron threads
Salt and freshly ground white pepper, to taste

Place the salt cod in a bowl. Add enough cold water to cover the fish by at least 2 inches. Refrigerate for 24 hours, changing the water twice. Drain.

Place the cod in a large frying pan and add enough cold water to cover. Bring to a boil over medium-low heat. Remove from the heat and let the cod cool in the liquid. Drain, and cut into 1-inch squares.

Heat the oil in a large frying pan over medium-high heat until hot but not smoking. Coat the squares of cod in the flour, shaking off the excess flour. Cook until golden-brown on all sides, about 4 minutes. Using a perforated metal turner, transfer the cod to paper towels to drain, leaving the oil in the pan.

Reduce the heat to medium-low. Add the potatoes, onions, tomatoes, and garlic to the pan and cook, stirring occasionally, for about 2 minutes. Add the parsley and enough boiling water to cover the vegetables. Cover and simmer until the potatoes are almost tender, about 15 minutes.

Stir in the saffron, and return the cod to the pan. Season with pepper; taste and add a little salt, if desired. Cover and continue cooking until the cod is heated through and the potatoes are tender, about 10 more minutes. Serve hot from the pan.

———————— • ————————

CRAB CAKES WITH ROASTED TOMATO SAUCE

These crab cakes are quick and easy to make, and the roasted tomato sauce provides a tasty alternative to tartar sauce.

MAKES 4 SERVINGS
1 pound crabmeat, preferably lump
¾ cup fresh bread crumbs
4 tablespoons unsalted butter
1 medium onion, grated
2 garlic cloves, minced
¼ teaspoon dried thyme
⅛ teaspoon hot Hungarian paprika, or a large pinch of cayenne pepper
1 tablespoon chopped fresh parsley
Salt and freshly ground pepper, to taste
Lemon wedges, for serving
Roasted Tomato Sauce, for serving

Pick over the crab and discard any cartilage. In a medium bowl, toss the bread crumbs together with 2 to 3 tablespoons water, just to moisten. Add the crabmeat and set aside. In a medium frying pan, melt 2 tablespoons butter over medium heat. Add the onion, garlic, thyme, and paprika. Cook until the onions soften, about 5 minutes. Add to the crab mixture, along with the parsley. Season with salt and pepper. Using floured hands, form into eight cakes. In a large frying pan, heat the remaining butter over medium heat. Add the crab cakes and cook, turning once, until browned on both sides, about 5 minutes. Serve with lemon wedges and the warm tomato sauce.

SOFT SHELL CRABS WITH MACADAMIA-LIME BUTTER

Soft shell crabs are a summertime delicacy on the Atlantic seaboard. Here they are served perfectly crisp, topped with sizzling macadamia nuts. Cook soft shell crabs with caution, as they tend to sputter and spit hot oil when you least expect it.

MAKES 4 SERVINGS
8 large soft shell crabs, cleaned
2 cups all-purpose flour
Salt and freshly ground pepper, to taste
1 cup milk
2 large eggs
Vegetable oil, for frying
4 tablespoons unsalted butter
1 cup coarsely chopped unsalted macadamia nuts
2 tablespoons lime juice

Pat the crabs dry with paper towels. In a shallow dish, combine the flour with a seasoning of salt and pepper. In another dish, beat the milk and eggs together. Dip each crab in the flour to coat lightly, then into the milk mixture, and finally back into the flour again, shaking off excess flour. Place the crabs on a wire cooling rack and refrigerate for 30 minutes to set the coating.

Preheat the oven to 200°F. Pour oil into a frying pan to come ¼ inch up the sides. Heat over medium-high heat until very hot, but not smoking. Carefully add four crabs to the pan. Cook, turning once with kitchen tongs, until golden-brown, 3 to 4 minutes. Transfer to a paper-towel-lined baking sheet, and keep warm in the oven while you cook the remaining crabs.

Discard the oil from the frying pan. Put the butter in the pan and melt over medium heat. Add the macadamia nuts and cook just until lightly browned, about 2 minutes. Remove from the heat and stir in the lime juice. Serve the crabs on dinner plates, spooning the macadamia-lime mixture over the top.

GRILLED LOBSTER

Lobster cooked in this way has a wonderful flavor, and has to be one of summer's greatest pleasures. If you want to broil the lobsters indoors, be sure you can fit the amount of lobsters you want to serve in your broiler at the same time—it may only be large enough to hold two or three.

MAKES 4 SERVINGS

4 (1½-pound) lobsters, freshly killed
¼ cup olive oil
Salt and cayenne pepper, to taste
8 tablespoons (1 stick) unsalted butter, melted

Build a hot charcoal fire in an outdoor grill and let the coals burn down until they are just medium-hot, rather than blazing. Lightly oil the grill. Using a heavy, sharp knife, carefully cut each of the lobsters in half lengthwise, and remove the sacs found in both sides of the head. Using the back of the knife, crack the claw shells, but do not remove them. Brush the lobsters all over with the olive oil and season with salt and cayenne pepper.

Grill the lobsters, shell sides up and covered with the grill lid, for 5 minutes. Turn the lobsters and spoon some of the melted butter over the top. Grill until the flesh is just firm when pressed with a finger, 5 to 7 more minutes. Place the cooked lobsters, with their cut sides up, on four dinner plates. Pour the remaining melted butter over the lobsters and then serve immediately.

GRILLED BUTTERFLIED SHRIMP WITH LEMON

This is an easy and extremely tasty way to serve large shrimp. They will be eaten with your fingers, so serve them at a casual dinner with good friends. If desired, you can thread the shrimp onto skewers, piercing them crosswise to keep them open and butterflied, before grilling them.

MAKES 4 SERVINGS

2 pounds jumbo or extra-large shrimp, unpeeled
2 tablespoons lemon juice
Salt and freshly ground pepper, to taste
¼ cup extra virgin olive oil

Devein and butterfly the shrimp, then flatten them lightly. In a large bowl, whisk together the lemon juice and a seasoning of salt and pepper. Gradually whisk in the olive oil. Add the shrimp and toss to coat them all thoroughly with the marinade. Leave to stand for about 30 minutes.

Build a hot charcoal fire in an outdoor grill, and lightly oil the grill. Put the shrimp on the grill cut sides down, and grill for 2 minutes. Turn them over, baste well with the marinade, and grill until they are pink in color and firm in texture, about 2 more minutes. Serve immediately.

SHRIMP BROCHETTES WITH MINT BUTTER

Mint may seem to be an unusual seasoning for shrimp, but it is both delicious and refreshing. Use a large-leafed variety, such as spearmint.

MAKES 4 SERVINGS

1 large bunch fresh mint
1½ pounds medium or large shrimp, peeled and deveined
8 tablespoons (1 stick) unsalted butter
2 tablespoons lemon juice
Salt and cayenne pepper, to taste

Soak four or eight bamboo skewers in a bowl of cold water for about 30 minutes.

Discard the mint stems, and reserve about 40 of the largest leaves; chop enough of the remaining mint leaves to measure 1 tablespoon and set aside. Thread the shrimp, alternating with the whole mint leaves, onto the skewers (if you use two parallel skewers for each brochette, instead of one skewer, the brochettes will be easier to turn, and this will also prevent the shrimp from twirling around on the skewer). When threading the shrimp onto the skewers, pierce each shrimp through the top and bottom, and keep the natural curve of the shrimp.

Preheat the broiler. In a small saucepan, melt the butter with the lemon juice and a seasoning of salt and cayenne pepper. Baste the brochettes well with the lemon butter.

Broil the brochettes, basting them occasionally and turning once, until the shrimp are firm and pink, 3 to 4 minutes. Stir the chopped mint into the remaining melted butter. Serve the shrimp brochettes immediately, with a little of the mint butter poured over each serving.

GRILLED THAI-MARINATED SHRIMP

During grilling, the shells of the shrimp scorch and blacken, leaving the flesh inside deliciously moist and juicy. A simple salad of thinly sliced English cucumber, seasoned with salt and sugar and moistened with a little white wine vinegar, would be an ideal accompaniment to this dish.

SHRIMP BROCHETTES WITH MINT BUTTER

MAKES 4 SERVINGS
2 pounds large shrimp, unpeeled

Marinade
3 tablespoons vegetable oil
2 tablespoons syrup from a jar of candied stem ginger, or 2 tablespoons honey
¼ cup fish sauce
¼ cup lime juice
4 kaffir lime leaves, torn into pieces, or grated zest of 1 lime
½ cup coarsely chopped cilantro stems
3 tablespoons chopped shallot
1 (2-inch) piece fresh ginger, unpeeled, thinly sliced
4 small hot green chile peppers (such as Thai or serrano), seeded and chopped, or to taste
2 garlic cloves, sliced

Dipping Sauce
½ cup chopped fresh cilantro leaves
6 tablespoons lime juice
¼ cup chopped fresh mint leaves
3 small hot chile peppers (such as Thai or serrano), seeded and chopped, or to taste
5 tablespoons fish sauce
2 teaspoons granulated sugar
2 garlic cloves, chopped

To make the marinade, mix all of the ingredients together in a large bowl. Add the shrimp and turn to coat them thoroughly. Cover and let marinate in the refrigerator, occasionally tossing the shrimp, for at least 6 hours or overnight.

To make the dipping sauce, combine all of the ingredients in a blender or food processor fitted with the metal blade. Add 5 tablespoons water, and blend until well mixed but not completely smooth. Pour into four small serving dishes.

Build a hot charcoal fire in an outdoor grill (or you can use a ridged cast-iron grill pan or the oven broiler if you prefer). Lightly oil the grill. Remove the shrimp from the marinade and heap them onto the grill. Cook, turning once, until the shrimp are pink and firm to the touch, 4 to 5 minutes. Serve together with the dipping sauce.

SHRIMP AND CUCUMBER CURRY

Cucumber is an unusual addition to this curry, but their mild taste and slight crunch are the perfect foil to the spicy sauce. If you wish, you can substitute 2 medium zucchini.

MAKES 4 SERVINGS

1½ pounds medium shrimp, peeled and deveined (shells reserved)
3 or 4 scallions, coarsely chopped
5 garlic cloves, 2 whole and 3 minced
1 large English cucumber, quartered lengthwise and cut into 2-inch pieces
5 tablespoons unsalted butter
1 large onion, thinly sliced
2 tablespoons finely chopped fresh ginger
2 teaspoons garam masala
1 teaspoon turmeric
½ teaspoon ground cinnamon
½ teaspoon ground cloves
1 teaspoon granulated sugar
½ teaspoon salt
1 tablespoon all-purpose flour
1¼ cups thick coconut milk
3 small hot fresh green chile peppers (such as serrano), seeded and cut into thin strips
1 tablespoon lemon juice
Hot cooked rice, preferably basmati rice

Combine the shrimp shells, scallions, whole garlic cloves, and 3 cups water in a large saucepan. Bring to a simmer over medium heat, then cook for 20 to 30 minutes. Strain the broth and reserve 1¼ cups. Cut each shrimp in half lengthwise.

Bring a medium saucepan of lightly salted water to a boil over high heat. Add the cucumber and 1 tablespoon of the butter. Simmer until the cucumber is barely crisp-tender, 4 to 5 minutes. Drain and set aside.

In a saucepan, heat the remaining 4 tablespoons butter over medium heat. Add the onion, ginger, and minced garlic and cook, stirring often, until softened but not browned, about 5 minutes. Sprinkle in the garam masala, turmeric, cinnamon, cloves, sugar, and salt and stir well. Cook for 2 minutes, stirring constantly. Add the flour and stir for 1 minute. Gradually stir in half of the reserved shrimp-shell broth and half of the coconut milk. Bring to a simmer and cook until lightly thickened, about 10 minutes. Remove from the heat, and stir in the shrimp, cucumber, and chiles. Let stand for 30 minutes.

Stir in the remaining broth and coconut milk, along with the lemon juice. Return to a simmer and cook over medium-low heat until heated through, about 2 minutes. Serve hot, with rice.

JAMBALAYA CLASSIQUE

Jambalaya, one of the masterpieces of Louisiana cookery, is a deliciously spicy meal-in-a-pot. It can be prepared in various ways according to the cook's whim on different occasions——for instance, you could try adding spicy smoked sausage (such as Cajun andouille) instead of the ham, or substituting shucked oysters for the shrimp.

MAKES 4 TO 6 SERVINGS

4 tablespoons vegetable oil
1 pound medium shrimp, peeled and deveined
6 ounces smoked ham, coarsely chopped
1 medium onion, chopped
1 medium green bell pepper, seeded and chopped
2 medium celery ribs with leaves, chopped
1 garlic clove, minced
½ teaspoon sweet Hungarian paprika
½ teaspoon dried basil
½ teaspoon dried thyme
½ teaspoon salt
½ teaspoon cayenne pepper
1 (28-ounce) can peeled plum tomatoes, drained (juices reserved) and chopped
1½ cups long-grain rice
1½ cups chicken stock
Chopped scallions, for garnish (optional)

In a large Dutch oven, heat 2 tablespoons vegetable oil over medium heat. Add the shrimp and smoked ham and cook until the shrimp is firm to the touch and pink in color, about 3 minutes. Transfer to a plate and set aside.

Heat the remaining 2 tablespoons vegetable oil in the Dutch oven. Add the onion, bell pepper, celery, and garlic. Cover and cook until the vegetables soften, about 10 minutes. Uncover the pan. Add the paprika, basil, thyme, salt, and cayenne pepper and stir for 1 minute. Add the tomatoes with their juices and bring to a simmer. Cook, uncovered, over medium heat, stirring often, until a thick sauce is formed, 15 to 20 minutes.

Meanwhile, combine the rice, chicken stock, and 1¼ cups cold water in a medium saucepan. Bring to a boil over high heat, then cover and reduce the heat to low. Simmer gently until the rice is tender, about 15 minutes, then remove from the heat and leave to stand for 5 minutes.

Stir the shrimp and ham into the sauce and heat through gently, about 2 minutes. Remove from the heat and then stir in the rice until thoroughly mixed. Serve hot, sprinkling each serving with chopped scallions, if desired.

STUFFED SQUID

Baked, stuffed squid is a wonderful way to make a sumptuous main course from a range of inexpensive ingredients.

MAKES 4 SERVINGS

12 squid, cleaned

Stuffing

1 cup fresh bread crumbs

½ cup milk

2 tablespoons olive oil

1 large onion, finely chopped

5 ripe plum tomatoes, peeled, seeded, and chopped

2 garlic cloves, minced

1 tablespoon chopped fresh parsley

2 large egg yolks

Salt and freshly ground pepper, to taste

Sauce

3 tablespoons olive oil

1 medium onion, chopped

1 garlic clove, crushed

1 bay leaf

2 teaspoons all-purpose flour

¾ cup dry white wine

Salt and freshly ground pepper, to taste

Preheat the oven to 350°F. Lightly oil a shallow baking dish. Cut the tentacles from the squid, leaving the body sacs intact, and coarsely chop the tentacles. Set aside.

To make the stuffing, soak the bread crumbs in the milk in a small bowl for 5 minutes. Squeeze out excess milk and set the softened crumbs aside. Heat the oil in a large frying pan over medium heat. Add the onion and cook until translucent, about 5 minutes. Add the chopped squid tentacles, tomatoes, and garlic and mix until well combined. Add the bread crumbs and chopped parsley. Remove from the heat, and stir in the egg yolks to make a thick stuffing. Season with salt and pepper. Spoon into the squid (the stuffing will expand during cooking, so don't pack it in tightly) and close the ends with wooden toothpicks. Place in the prepared dish.

To make the sauce, in a medium saucepan, heat the olive oil over medium heat. Add the onion, garlic, and bay leaf and cook until the onion is softened and translucent, about 4 minutes. Add the flour and stir for 1 minute. Gradually stir in the wine and ¾ cup hot water, and season well with salt and pepper. Bring to a simmer and cook over low heat until lightly thickened, about 15 minutes. Pour the sauce over the stuffed squid.

Bake, basting occasionally, until the squid is very tender, about 1 hour. Serve hot.

FRIED SQUID WITH AÏOLI

Golden, tender morsels of fried squid can be problem-free if you observe a simple rule: be sure your oil is hot enough, and allow it to return to the proper temperature before frying each batch. Don't fry the squid until deep golden-brown, or it will be overcooked. The garlic mayonnaise called *aïoli* is a perfect accompaniment.

MAKES 4 SERVINGS

Vegetable oil, for deep-frying

½ cup all-purpose flour

Salt and cayenne pepper, to taste

1 pound squid, cleaned, sacs cut crosswise into ⅓-inch-thick rings, and tentacles intact

Garlic Mayonnaise (*Aïoli*), for serving

Preheat the oven to 200°F. Pour enough oil into a large, heavy saucepan to come to a depth of about 2 to 3 inches. Heat the oil to 350°F. In a shallow dish, combine the flour and a seasoning of salt and cayenne pepper. Working in batches, toss the squid in the flour, shaking off excess flour, and fry until golden-brown, 1 to 2 minutes. Drain on a paper-towel-lined baking sheet, and keep warm while preparing the remaining squid. Serve hot, with garlic mayonnaise.

FRIED SCALLOPS WITH LEMON AND GARLIC

Scallops should be sautéed in small amounts—if they are crowded into a pan they will steam and not brown. Do not overcook them, so they remain tender.

MAKES 2 TO 3 SERVINGS

4 tablespoons unsalted butter

1 pound sea or bay scallops

3 tablespoons all-purpose flour

2 garlic cloves, chopped

1 tablespoon chopped fresh parsley

2 tablespoons lemon juice

Salt and freshly ground pepper, to taste

Preheat the oven to 200°F. In a large frying pan, heat 2 tablespoons of the butter over medium-high heat until lightly browned. Toss half of the scallops with about 1½ tablespoons of the flour to coat them lightly, then add to the pan with half of the garlic and parsley. Cook briskly, turning occasionally, until the scallops are golden-brown in color and barely cooked through, 2 to 3 minutes. Transfer to a baking sheet, and keep warm while sautéing the remaining scallops, lightly floured, with the rest of the butter, garlic, and parsley. Add the lemon juice to the pan, swirl it around, and pour over the scallops. Season, and serve immediately.

SCALLOPS WITH TOMATO, BASIL, AND SAFFRON VINAIGRETTE

Serve this on its own as a first course, or add some tender mixed greens to present it as an entrée salad. Use the very best extra virgin olive oil and red wine vinegar available for the vinaigrette.

MAKES 4 SERVINGS

3 tablespoons olive oil (not extra virgin)
12 large sea scallops
Salt and freshly ground pepper, to taste
Vinaigrette
2 tablespoons red wine vinegar
½ garlic clove, minced and crushed to a paste with a sprinkle of salt
Freshly ground pepper, to taste
6 tablespoons extra virgin olive oil
1 teaspoon saffron threads, infused in 2 tablespoons hot water for 2 minutes
2 large ripe tomatoes, peeled, seeded, and chopped into ¼-inch dice
2 tablespoons coarsely chopped fresh basil

To make the vinaigrette, whisk together the vinegar, garlic, and pepper in a medium bowl. Gradually whisk in the oil until emulsified. Stir in the saffron (do not whisk it, as the saffron will become entangled in the whisk). Stir in the tomatoes and basil.

Divide the oil between two large, heavy frying pans and heat over medium-high heat. Add the scallops and cook, turning once, until browned on both sides, 2 to 3 minutes. Do not overcook the scallops.

Place 3 scallops in the center of each warmed plate. Spoon the vinaigrette over, and serve immediately.

MOULES À LA MARINIÈRE

Probably the most classic way to prepare mussels, this is the method preferred by French fishing communities.

MAKES 5 SERVINGS

⅔ cup dry white wine
1 medium onion, chopped
½ cup chopped shallots
4 pounds mussels, scrubbed and debearded if necessary
Salt and freshly ground pepper, to taste
2 tablespoons chopped fresh parsley

Place the wine, onion, and shallots in a large pot and add ⅔ cup water. Bring to a boil over medium-high heat. Cook briskly until reduced by about half, 6 to

MUSSELS WITH COCONUT MILK AND CHILES

8 minutes. Add the mussels. Cover and cook, shaking the pan occasionally, until the mussels open, 4 to 5 minutes. Spoon the mussels into individual bowls. (Leave any unopened mussels in the pot and cook for another couple of minutes. If they remain firmly shut, discard them.) Season the cooking liquid, then strain it through a fine sieve (or a regular sieve lined with moistened paper towels). Divide among the bowls of mussels, sprinkle with parsley, and serve immediately.

Moules à la Crème: Add ⅔ cup heavy cream to the strained cooking liquid and heat through before spooning over the mussels.

MUSSELS WITH COCONUT MILK AND CHILES

The wonderfully aromatic Thai flavorings used here—coconut milk, fish sauce, lemon grass, and kaffir lime leaves—enhance the delicate flavor of mussels.

MAKES 4 SERVINGS

5 pounds mussels, scrubbed and debearded, if necessary
1¾ cups coconut milk
6 scallions, chopped
⅓ cup chopped fresh cilantro stems
4 hot fresh green chiles (such as jalapeño), seeded and chopped
2 stalks lemon grass, tender inner leaves only, chopped
1 (2-inch) piece galangal or fresh ginger, peeled and thinly sliced
¼ cup lime juice
6 kaffir lime leaves or grated zest of 1 lime
1 garlic clove, crushed
⅔ cup heavy cream
3 tablespoons fish sauce
¾ cup chopped fresh cilantro leaves

Place the mussels in a pot with 1¼ cups water. Bring to a boil over high heat. Cover and cook, shaking the pan occasionally, until the mussels open, 3 to 5 minutes. Drain in a colander over a clean saucepan, and reserve the broth. Let the mussels cool, then remove the empty shell halves. Set the mussels aside.

Add the coconut milk, scallions, cilantro stems, chiles, lemon grass, galangal, lime juice, lime leaves, and garlic to the broth. Bring to a simmer and cook over low heat until well flavored, about 30 minutes. Strain into the pot in which you cooked the mussels.

Add the heavy cream, fish sauce, and cilantro leaves and stir well. Return to a simmer. Add the reserved mussels. Cook gently until the mussels are reheated, about 3 minutes. Serve immediately in shallow soup bowls.

Meat

FILETS MIGNONS WITH SHALLOT SAUCE

Filets mignons are a good size for sautéing, making this a quick bistro-style meal. They should be served in the classic way, with french-fried potatoes.

MAKES 4 SERVINGS

8 tablespoons (1 stick) unsalted butter
2 tablespoons olive oil
1 cup chopped shallots
⅔ cup dry white wine
Salt and freshly ground pepper
4 (6-ounce) filet mignon steaks, each about 1 inch thick
1 tablespoon chopped parsley

In a medium saucepan, heat 2 tablespoons of the butter and 1 tablespoon of the oil over medium-low heat. Add the shallots and cook gently until softened, about 3 minutes. Add the wine and increase the heat to high. Boil rapidly until the liquid is syrupy and reduced to about 2 tablespoons, 5 to 10 minutes. Season with salt and pepper. Remove from the heat and keep warm.

In a large frying pan, heat 2 tablespoons butter and the remaining 1 tablespoon oil over medium-high heat until very hot. Add the steaks and cook, turning them once, until well browned, about 6 minutes for medium-rare meat. Season. Transfer the steaks to four warmed dinner plates. Pour off any fat from the pan, leaving the browned bits. Return the pan to low heat. Add the shallot mixture and stir with a wooden spoon to mix in the browned bits on the bottom of the pan. Stir in the remaining 4 tablespoons butter and the parsley, and season. Spoon equal amounts of the shallot sauce over each steak. Serve hot.

STEAK AU POIVRE

Pick a frying pan that is large enough to hold all of the steaks at once, or choose smaller steaks, like filets mignons or rib eye steaks. Another alternative is to cook the steaks in two pans. However, do not, under any circumstances, crowd the steaks, or they will not get a nicely browned exterior. Use freshly crushed peppercorns for the best flavor.

MAKES 4 SERVINGS

4 (6- to 8-ounce) beef steaks (such as club, rib eye, or filet mignon)
1 teaspoon olive oil
2 teaspoons black peppercorns, coarsely crushed
2 tablespoons unsalted butter
Salt, to taste
¾ cup chicken stock
1 tablespoon dry sherry
2 teaspoons Cognac

Rub the steaks lightly with the oil, and press the peppercorns into them on both sides. In a large frying pan, heat 1 tablespoon of the butter over medium-high heat until very hot. Add the steaks and cook, turning once, until browned on both sides, about 6 minutes for medium-rare meat. Season the steaks with salt. Transfer the steaks to four warmed plates and tent with aluminum foil to keep warm.

Add the remaining 1 tablespoon butter to the pan and melt. Add the stock and bring to a boil over high heat, scraping up the browned bits in the pan with a wooden spoon. Add the sherry and boil rapidly until reduced by half. Add the Cognac and cook for another 30 seconds. Season with salt and pepper, and drizzle the sauce evenly over the steaks.

RIB EYE STEAKS WITH CHIMICHURRI SAUCE

In Argentina, countless restaurants specialize in grilled beef, and this is the sauce found on every table.

MAKES 4 SERVINGS

4 (10-ounce) rib eye steaks
Salt and freshly ground pepper, to taste
Chimichurri Sauce
⅓ cup chopped fresh parsley
¼ cup minced onion
¼ cup red wine vinegar
4 garlic cloves, minced
1 teaspoon dried oregano
½ teaspoon salt
½ teaspoon freshly ground pepper
½ cup olive oil

To make the sauce, whisk together all of the ingredients, except the oil, in a medium bowl. Gradually whisk in the oil. Cover and refrigerate for at least 1 hour before serving. (The sauce can be prepared up to 1 day ahead.)

Build a charcoal fire in an outdoor grill or preheat a broiler. Lightly oil the grill. Grill or broil the steaks, turning once, for 8 to 10 minutes for medium-rare meat (or cook longer, if desired). Season the steaks with salt and pepper. Serve the steaks with a bowl of the sauce passed on the side.

ROAST BEEF TENDERLOIN

Roast beef tenderloin is a perfect party entrée. It is quick to prepare, has very little waste, and is equally good served hot or cold. The interior temperature of the meat will continue to rise by about 5 degrees as it rests before serving, so be careful not to overcook.

MAKES 8 TO 12 SERVINGS
- 1 (4-pound) trimmed whole beef tenderloin, all fat and silver membrane removed
- Asian Marinade or Italian Red Wine Marinade
- 2 tablespoons vegetable oil
- Freshly ground pepper, to taste

Fold the thin ends of the tenderloin underneath so the tenderloin is the same thickness throughout its length, and tie with kitchen string. Immerse the tenderloin in the marinade. Cover and leave to marinate in the refrigerator for at least 8 hours and up to 24 hours.

Drain the tenderloin and let stand at room temperature for 1 hour before roasting.

Preheat the oven to 450°F. Pat the tenderloin dry with paper towels. Rub it all over with the oil, and season with pepper. Place on a rack in a large roasting pan. Roast until a meat thermometer inserted in the center of the roast reads 130°F for medium-rare meat, about 45 minutes. Let the tenderloin stand for 10 minutes before carving.

T-BONE STEAKS WITH SMOTHERED VIDALIA ONIONS

Here is another good way to add interest to familiar grilled steak. This sweet-and-sour condiment is an opportunity to use sweet Vidalia, Maui, or Walla Walla onions, but if these are not available, regular Spanish onions will work, too.

MAKES 4 SERVINGS
- 4 (12-ounce) shell (sirloin) steaks

Smothered Vidalia Onions
- 2 tablespoons unsalted butter
- 2 pounds sweet onions (such as Vidalia), cut into ¼-inch half-moons
- ⅓ cup balsamic vinegar
- 2 tablespoons light brown sugar
- 2 teaspoons chopped fresh thyme or 1 teaspoon dried thyme
- Salt and freshly ground pepper, to taste

To make the smothered onions, heat the butter in a large saucepan over medium heat. Add the onions. Cover and cook, stirring often, until the onions are softened, about 8 minutes. Stir in the balsamic vinegar, light brown sugar, and fresh or dried thyme, then reduce the heat to medium-low. Cover the pan once again and continue to cook until the onions are very tender, about 30 minutes. Uncover the pan and cook over medium-high heat until the liquid has reduced to a glaze, about 3 minutes. Season with salt and pepper. Set aside.

Build a charcoal fire in an outdoor grill or preheat the broiler. Lightly oil the grill. Grill or broil the steaks, turning once, for 8 to 10 minutes for medium-rare meat. Top each steak with a mound of onions.

SHORT RIBS BERBERE

There's more to African cuisine than couscous, as these short ribs in a well-spiced sauce will prove. It is based on the Ethiopian spice paste, *berbere*, which oddly resembles the moist red curry pastes of Southeast Asia, thousands of miles away.

MAKES 4 TO 6 SERVINGS
- 6 (1-pound) meaty beef short ribs
- 4 tablespoons vegetable oil
- 2 medium onions, cut into ½-inch-thick half-moons
- 6 garlic cloves, minced
- ½ teaspoon fenugreek seeds
- ½ teaspoon coriander seeds
- ½ teaspoon whole black peppercorns
- 2 tablespoons sweet Hungarian paprika
- 1 teaspoon chile flakes
- ½ teaspoon ground ginger
- ¼ teaspoon ground cardamom
- ¼ teaspoon grated nutmeg
- ¼ teaspoon ground cinnamon
- Salt, to taste
- 1 cup hearty red wine
- 2 tablespoons tomato paste

Preheat the oven to 325°F. In a large Dutch oven or flameproof casserole, heat 2 tablespoons oil over medium-high heat. In batches, add the ribs and brown on all sides, about 10 minutes. Transfer to a plate. Heat the remaining oil in the Dutch oven, and add the onions and garlic. Cook, stirring, until the onions are translucent, about 5 minutes.

Meanwhile, heat a dry medium frying pan over medium heat. Add the fenugreek seeds, coriander seeds, and peppercorns. Cook, stirring often, until very fragrant and lightly toasted, about 1 minute. Transfer to a spice grinder. Let cool completely, then grind to a powder. Add the paprika, chile flakes, ginger, cardamom, nutmeg, and cinnamon, and pulse to combine. Season the browned short ribs with the salt and spice mixture.

Pour the wine and tomato paste into the Dutch oven and bring to a boil, stirring to dissolve the paste. Return the short ribs to the Dutch oven and cover. Transfer to the oven and bake until the meat is fork tender, about 1½ hours. Transfer the short ribs to a deep serving platter and tent with foil to keep hot. Skim off the fat from the cooking liquid, and boil to reduce by half. Pour the sauce over the ribs and serve.

FRENCH BEEF DAUBE WITH OLIVES

A rich *boeuf en daube*, with its aromas of red wine, orange zest, herbs, and garlic, is the pride of many a Provençale cook. If at all possible, let the stew stand for a few hours (preferably overnight), to allow the flavors to mellow, then reheat for serving.

MAKES 6 SERVINGS

   3 tablespoons olive oil, approximately
   4 ounces thick-sliced pancetta or slab bacon
      rind removed, diced
   1 large onion, chopped
   4 garlic cloves, minced
   2½ pounds beef chuck or round, cut into
      1½-inch pieces
   ⅓ cup dry vermouth
   1 cup hearty red wine, heated to boiling
   ⅔ cup beef stock, heated to boiling
   1 tablespoon tomato paste
   1 bouquet garni of 3 sprigs fresh thyme, 1 bay leaf,
      and 1 (3-inch) strip orange zest
   Salt and freshly ground pepper, to taste
   5 ounces black Mediterranean olives, pitted

Preheat the oven to 300°F. In a large Dutch oven or flameproof casserole, heat 1 tablespoon of the oil over medium heat. Add the pancetta and cook until browned, about 5 minutes. Using a slotted spoon, transfer to paper towels to drain, leaving the fat in the Dutch oven. Add the onion and garlic and cook until the onion is golden-brown, 8 to 10 minutes. Transfer to a plate. Add the remaining 2 tablespoons oil to the Dutch oven and heat over medium-high heat. In batches, without crowding, add the beef and brown on all sides, about 8 minutes; add more oil as needed. As the batches of beef are browned, transfer to a plate.

   Return all the beef and its juices, the pancetta, onions, and garlic to the Dutch oven. Pour in the vermouth, boiling wine, and stock. Stir in the tomato paste, then add the bouquet garni. Season with pepper. Cover and transfer to the oven. Cook until the beef is almost tender, about 1½ hours. Add the olives and continue cooking until the beef is very tender, about 30 more minutes. Season with salt. Skim off any fat from the surface of the sauce, and remove the bouquet garni. Serve hot.

BELGIAN BEEF AND BEER STEW

Lots of onions add a delicious touch of sweetness to this stew, which is known as *carbonnade de boeuf* in its country of origin, Belgium. Use a mellow lager beer for this dish, not anything too dark or strong like ale or stout.

MAKES 6 TO 8 SERVINGS

   3 tablespoons vegetable oil, approximately
   4 ounces slab bacon, rind removed, cut into
      ½-inch-wide sticks
   3 pounds beef chuck or round, cut into 1-inch pieces
   3 large onions, sliced
   2 tablespoons all-purpose flour
   2½ cups lager beer
   1 tablespoon red wine vinegar
   1 teaspoon granulated sugar
   2 garlic cloves, minced
   2 bay leaves
   Salt and freshly ground pepper, to taste

Preheat the oven to 300°F. In a large Dutch oven or flameproof casserole, heat 1 tablespoon of the oil over medium heat. Add the bacon and cook until browned, about 5 minutes. Using a slotted spoon, transfer to paper towels to drain, leaving the fat in the Dutch oven. Increase the heat to medium-high.

   In batches, without crowding, add the beef and brown on all sides, about 8 minutes; add more oil as needed. As the beef is browned, transfer to a plate, then set aside. Add the remaining 2 tablespoons oil to the Dutch oven and heat. Add the onions and cook, stirring often, until golden brown, about 10 minutes. Sprinkle the vegetables with the flour and cook, stirring, for 2 minutes. Gradually stir in the beer, then add the vinegar, sugar, garlic, and bay leaves. Season with salt and pepper. Return the beef and its juices to the Dutch oven, along with the bacon. Bring the liquid to a simmer, then cover the pot and transfer to the oven. Cook until the meat is very tender, about 2 hours. Skim off any fat from the surface of the stew. Serve hot.

TRATTORIA BEEF STEW WITH POLENTA DUMPLINGS

When the weather is cool, practically every Italian trattoria serves its own version of a hearty, aromatic beef stew. Topped with plump polenta dumplings, this will become a favorite at home, too.

MAKES 6 TO 8 SERVINGS

   1 cup dried porcini (1 ounce)
   4 tablespoons olive oil, approximately
   3½ pounds beef chuck, cut into 1½-inch pieces
   2 medium red onions, chopped
   4 medium celery ribs with leaves, cut into 1-inch
      lengths and leaves chopped
   6 garlic cloves, minced
   1 cup hearty red wine
   2 cups ripe plum tomatoes, peeled, seeded, and
      chopped; or use canned

1 cup beef stock

2 teaspoons chopped fresh rosemary, or 1 teaspoon dried rosemary

1 bay leaf

Salt and freshly ground pepper, to taste

Beurre Manié made with 2 tablespoons each unsalted butter and all-purpose flour

Polenta Dumplings

½ teaspoon salt

1 cup polenta (not quick-cooking) or yellow cornmeal

In a small bowl, soak the porcini in 1 cup boiling water until softened, 20 to 30 minutes. Lift from the water and chop coarsely. Strain the liquid through a paper-towel-lined sieve over a bowl. Set aside.

In a large Dutch oven or flameproof casserole, heat 2 tablespoons oil over medium-high heat. In batches, without crowding, add the beef and brown on all sides, about 8 minutes; add more oil as needed. As the beef is browned, transfer to a plate, then set aside. Heat the remaining 2 tablespoons oil in the Dutch oven, and add the onions, celery, and garlic. Cover and cook over medium heat until the onions are very soft and translucent, about 10 minutes. Add the wine and strained mushroom liquid. Bring to a boil, scraping up the browned bits on the bottom of the pot. Cook, uncovered, until the liquid has reduced by half, about 8 minutes. Add the tomatoes, beef stock, rosemary, and bay leaf. Return the beef to the Dutch oven, along with the soaked mushrooms, and season. Bring to a boil, then reduce the heat to low. Simmer, covered, until the meat is tender, about 2 hours.

Skim the fat off the top of the cooking liquid. Whisk about 1 cup of the cooking liquid into the beurre manié in a small bowl until smooth. Stir the mixture into the stew, and let simmer over medium-low heat while you make the polenta mixture.

In a saucepan, bring 2 cups water to a boil. Add the salt, then gradually whisk in the polenta. Whisk over medium-low heat until very thick, about 2 minutes. Drop the polenta in six large spoonfuls onto the surface of the stew. Cover the pot and cook until the dumplings are set, 10 to 15 minutes. Serve hot.

BEEF POT ROAST WITH ROOT VEGETABLES

Tender, juicy pot roast is even more delectable when paired with naturally sweet root vegetables.

MAKES 4 TO 6 SERVINGS

2 tablespoons vegetable oil

1 (3½-pound) beef bottom round roast

1 large onion, chopped

3 medium carrots, cut into 1-inch lengths

3 medium parsnips, cut into 1-inch lengths

6 small turnips, scrubbed and quartered

3 medium boiling potatoes, scrubbed and quartered

1 teaspoon dried thyme

Salt and freshly ground pepper, to taste

½ cup beef stock

Preheat the oven to 325°F. Heat the oil in a large Dutch oven or flameproof casserole over medium-high heat. Add the roast and brown on all sides, about 10 minutes. Transfer to a plate and set aside. Add the onion, carrots, parsnips, turnips, potatoes, and thyme to the pot. Cover and cook over medium heat until the onions are soft and golden, about 10 minutes. Season with salt and pepper. Return the roast to the Dutch oven and add the beef stock. Bring to a boil. Cover and transfer to the oven. Cook until the roast is fork-tender, 2½ to 3 hours. To serve, slice the roast across the grain, and serve with the vegetables and juices.

CHINESE BEEF BRISKET

A blend of Chinese spices makes an interesting brew for simmering beef brisket. Serve with plain boiled potatoes—unexpected but very good.

MAKES 4 TO 6 SERVINGS

1 (3-pound) beef brisket, well trimmed

½ cup soy sauce

½ cup sake or dry sherry

2 tablespoons sherry vinegar

1 teaspoon granulated sugar

⅓ cup sliced peeled fresh ginger

10 garlic cloves, peeled

3 whole star anise

4 (3-inch) strips orange zest

2 small dried hot red chile peppers

½ cinnamon stick

12 large Pacific oysters (optional)

Sliced scallions, ¼ teaspoon chile flakes (optional), and cilantro sprigs, for garnish

Preheat the oven to 275°F. Place the brisket in a large flameproof casserole that is just large enough to hold it. Add enough cold water to cover the brisket, and bring to a boil over medium heat. Cook for 2 minutes, then drain. Rinse the beef, drain again, and pat dry with paper towels.

Return the brisket to the casserole and add all of the remaining ingredients, except the oysters (if using) and those for the garnish. Stir well to mix the liquid and flavorings. Bring to a simmer over medium-low heat, and then cook for 5 minutes. Cover the casserole and transfer to the oven. Cook until the brisket is very tender, about 3 hours. Check occasionally to be sure that the braising liquid isn't boiling away; if necessary, add a little more water to the casserole.

Shuck the oysters, if using, and reserve them along with their juice.

Transfer the brisket to a warmed serving platter and cover it loosely with a sheet of foil to keep warm. Strain the braising liquid into a saucepan, and carefully skim off any fat that rises to the surface. Bring the liquid to a boil and cook until it is rich and syrupy, 1 to 2 minutes. Add the oysters with their juices and warm through until they are just firm to the touch. Slice the meat, and pour the sauce over. Sprinkle with the scallions and optional chile flakes, and garnish with cilantro sprigs. Serve immediately.

GRILLED FAJITAS WITH CHILE-LIME MARINADE

For first-class fajitas, you need a zesty marinade to flavor and tenderize the meat. This one is so good, you may want to try it on chicken breasts, too.

MAKES 4 TO 6 SERVINGS
1½ pounds flank steak
2 tablespoons olive oil
1 large onion, cut into half-moons
1 large red bell pepper, seeded and cut into strips
1 teaspoon dried oregano
12 (6-inch) flour tortillas, warmed
Mexican Salsa Cruda, for serving
Guacamole, for serving
Marinade
¼ cup lime juice
¼ cup olive oil
1 tablespoon Worcestershire sauce
2 scallions, trimmed
1 hot fresh chile pepper (such as jalapeño), seeded and chopped
2 garlic cloves, chopped
⅛ teaspoon cayenne pepper
Salt, to taste

In a blender, blend all the marinade ingredients until smooth. Pour into a glass baking dish. Add the steak. Cover and let marinate in the refrigerator for at least 4 and up to 8 hours, turning the steak occasionally. Remove from the refrigerator 1 hour before cooking.

In a large frying pan, heat the oil over medium heat. Add the onion, bell pepper, and oregano. Cook, stirring often, until the onions are soft and golden, about 10 minutes. Remove from the heat, cover, and keep warm.

Build a charcoal fire in an outdoor grill and let burn until the coals are covered with white ash. Lightly oil

the grill. Remove the steak from the marinade. Grill, turning once, for 6 to 8 minutes for medium-rare meat. Leave to stand for about 5 minutes, then cut the meat across the grain into thin slices. Serve the sliced steak accompanied by the warm tortillas and bowls of the vegetables, salsa, and guacamole. Let each guest roll up the steak in a tortilla, adding the condiments to taste.

VEAL SCALLOPINE MARSALA

Veal scallopine make a quick, elegant, and delicious meal. Be sure to use only dry Marsala in the sauce for this dish—sweet Marsala should always be reserved for desserts.

MAKES 4 SERVINGS
2 tablespoons olive oil
4 tablespoons unsalted butter
4 veal scallops (1 pound), pounded until less than ⅛ inch thick
⅓ cup all-purpose flour
Salt and freshly ground pepper, to taste
⅔ cup dry Marsala

In a large frying pan, heat the olive oil together with 2 tablespoons of the butter over medium-high heat until very hot, but not smoking. Dip each piece of veal in the flour to coat, shaking off any excess flour. Working in batches, if necessary, place the veal in the pan and cook, turning once, until browned on both sides, about 2 minutes. Season with salt and pepper. Transfer to a large heated platter and tent with a sheet of foil to keep warm.

Pour the Marsala into the pan. Bring to a boil over a medium heat and cook until the liquid is slightly reduced, about 1 minute. Add the remaining butter and let it melt, swirling it into the Marsala. Return the veal to the pan, along with any juices from the platter, and turn to coat the veal all over with the sauce. Serve immediately.

VEAL STUFFED WITH PROSCIUTTO AND MOZZARELLA

These stuffed veal rolls are excellent dinner party fare, as they can be prepared well ahead of time, and then only need a brief browning and baking to serve. A simple fresh green salad is the only accompaniment that you will need.

GRILLED FAJITAS WITH CHILE-LIME MARINADE

MAKES 4 SERVINGS

1 pound veal scallops, pounded until less than ⅛ inch
    thick and cut into 8 pieces

Salt and freshly ground pepper, to taste

4 ounces thinly sliced prosciutto, cut into 8 pieces
    to fit veal

6 ounces mozzarella cheese, thinly sliced and trimmed
    to fit veal

8 fresh sage leaves or 1 teaspoon crumbled dried sage

½ cup all-purpose flour

4 tablespoons clarified or unsalted butter

⅓ cup freshly grated Parmesan cheese

Preheat the oven to 375°F. Place a piece of veal on
a work surface, and season. Cover with a slice of
prosciutto, a couple of slices of mozzarella, and a sage
leaf. Roll up into a cylinder and secure with a wooden
toothpick. Repeat with the remaining veal, prosciutto,
mozzarella, and sage. Coat the veal rolls with the
flour, shaking off the excess flour.

In a large flameproof casserole or ovenproof
skillet, heat the butter over medium-high heat until
very hot. Add the veal and cook, turning occasionally,
until browned on all sides. Remove the casserole
from the heat and sprinkle the veal with Parmesan
cheese. Baste with the melted butter from the
casserole, and bake until the cheese melts, about
10 minutes. Remove the toothpicks and serve hot.

OSSO BUCCO

Osso bucco, the Italian way of preparing veal shank,
has an especially luscious sauce due to the gelatinous
quality of the meat. The sauce is accented by *gremolata*,
a zesty lemon, parsley, garlic, and anchovy garnish.

MAKES 4 SERVINGS

½ teaspoon saffron threads

⅔ cup dry white wine

6 tablespoons unsalted butter, approximately

3 pounds veal shank, cut in 1½-inch-thick pieces

¼ cup all-purpose flour

1 medium onion, finely chopped

1 medium carrot, finely chopped

1 medium celery rib, finely chopped

1 pound ripe plum tomatoes, peeled, seeded, and
    chopped; or use drained canned tomatoes

1 tablespoon tomato paste

Zest of 1 small lemon, removed in strips with
    a vegetable peeler

2 teaspoons minced fresh parsley

OSSO BUCCO

1 large garlic clove, minced

2 anchovy fillets packed in oil, drained and minced
    (optional)

Salt and freshly ground pepper, to taste

Combine the saffron and wine in a small bowl. Let
infuse while you prepare the veal.

In a large Dutch oven, heat 2 tablespoons of the
butter over medium-high heat. Dust the veal lightly
with the flour. In batches, without crowding, add the
veal to the pot and cook, turning occasionally, until
browned on all sides, about 8 minutes; add more
butter as needed. As the veal is browned, transfer to
a plate, then set aside.

Melt 2 tablespoons of the remaining butter in the
Dutch oven over medium heat. Add the onion, carrot,
and celery and cook until the onion is softened, about
5 minutes. Return the veal to the pot. Add the wine
and saffron mixture and cook until the wine has
almost completely evaporated, about 3 minutes. Stir
in the tomatoes, tomato paste, and 2 strips of lemon
zest. Bring to a simmer. Cover and cook until the veal
is very tender, 1½ to 2 hours; check occasionally to be
sure the liquid isn't evaporating too quickly, and add
a little water if needed.

Meanwhile, finely chop the remaining lemon zest
and place in a small bowl. Add the parsley, garlic, and
optional anchovies. Set this *gremolata* aside. When the
veal is tender, sprinkle with half of the *gremolata*, turn
the veal over, and cook for about 2 more minutes.

Transfer the veal to a heated serving platter. Swirl
the remaining 2 tablespoons butter into the sauce.
Season with salt and pepper. Spoon the sauce over
the veal, sprinkle with the remaining *gremolata*, and
serve immediately.

VEAL POT ROAST WITH MUSHROOMS AND ONIONS

Veal shoulder, which can be dry, benefits from being
cooked slowly in this way. If you wish, the sauce can
be thickened with a teaspoon or so of beurre manié.

MAKES 6 SERVINGS

1 (3-pound) boneless veal shoulder roast, tied

½ teaspoon fresh thyme leaves or ¼ teaspoon
    dried thyme

Salt and freshly ground pepper, to taste

4 tablespoons unsalted butter

3 ounces slab bacon, rind removed, cut into
    ¼-inch-thick sticks

12 ounces small button mushrooms

20 small white boiling onions, peeled

3 tablespoons white veal stock, white wine, or water

Preheat the oven to 325°F. Rub the veal with the thyme and some pepper. In a large Dutch oven just big enough to hold the veal comfortably, heat 2 tablespoons of the butter over medium-high heat. Add the bacon and cook until browned, about 5 minutes. Remove the bacon with a slotted spoon and set aside. Add the veal to the Dutch oven and cook, turning occasionally, until browned on all sides, about 10 minutes. (Reduce the heat as needed so the butter doesn't get too brown.) Pour out the excess fat, and return the bacon to the pot. Cover and transfer to the oven. Cook for 1½ hours, turning the veal over occasionally.

Meanwhile, in a large frying pan, heat the remaining 2 tablespoons butter over medium heat. Add the button mushrooms and cook, stirring occasionally, until lightly browned, about 10 minutes. Set the mushrooms aside. Bring a medium saucepan of lightly salted water to a boil over high heat. Add the onions and blanch for 5 minutes. Drain well. After the veal has cooked for 1½ hours, add the onions to the pot. Continue cooking until the veal is tender, 30 more minutes. Add the mushrooms to the pot for the last 15 minutes of cooking.

Transfer the veal to a warmed serving platter, and use a slotted spoon to place the mushrooms, onions, and bacon around the veal. Skim off the fat from the cooking liquid. Add the stock and bring to a boil over high heat. Cook until slightly reduced, 1 to 2 minutes. Pour into a sauceboat. Slice the veal and serve.

BREADED VEAL CHOPS MILANESE

At the end of cooking the butter will be very dark, but don't worry about it because the chops will be golden and crusty outside, juicy and tender within.

MAKES 4 SERVINGS
    4 veal loin chops, cut about ½ inch thick
    Salt and freshly ground pepper, to taste
    2 large eggs
    1 cup fine fresh bread crumbs
    4 tablespoons unsalted butter
    Lemon wedges, for serving

One at a time, place the chops between two sheets of moistened waxed paper, and pound out the meat, still attached to the bone, until it is about ¼ inch thick. Season with salt and pepper. In a shallow dish, beat the eggs lightly to mix. In another shallow dish, spread out the bread crumbs. Dip each chop in beaten egg and shake off the excess, then coat on both sides with the crumbs, patting them on gently. Let the chops stand on a wire rack for about 15 minute to set the coating.

In a very large frying pan (or use two pans, if necessary), heat the butter over medium-high heat until it is very hot and starting to brown. Add the veal loin chops and cook for 1 minute on each side to brown the crumb coating. Reduce the heat to medium-low and continue cooking, turning once, until the chops are thoroughly cooked, 15 to 20 minutes. Transfer to paper towels to drain. Serve immediately, with lemon wedges.

BREAST OF VEAL WITH RICOTTA AND SPINACH STUFFING

This recipe uses boneless breast of veal, which can be rolled around a stuffing and sliced into neater servings; the bones add richness to the simple sauce.

MAKES 6 TO 8 SERVINGS
    1 (7- to 8-pound) whole veal breast, bones removed
        and reserved, well-trimmed of excess fat (about
        3 pounds after boning)
    4 tablespoons vegetable oil
    1 medium onion, chopped
    1 medium carrot, chopped
    1 medium celery rib, chopped
    1 cup dry white wine
    Salt and freshly ground pepper, to taste
Stuffing
    2 tablespoons unsalted butter
    1 medium onion, chopped
    2 garlic cloves, minced
    1 pound fresh spinach, stems removed, coarsely
        chopped
    ½ cup dry bread crumbs
    ½ cup freshly grated Parmesan cheese
    ½ cup ricotta cheese
    2 tablespoons finely chopped fresh basil
    2 tablespoons finely chopped fresh parsley
    1 large egg
    A pinch of grated nutmeg
    Salt and freshly ground pepper, to taste

To make the stuffing, heat the butter in a large frying pan over medium heat. Add the onion and garlic and cook, stirring often, until the onion is translucent, about 5 minutes. Add the spinach. Cover and cook until the spinach is wilted and tender, about 8 minutes. Transfer to a sieve and drain. Let cool until easy to handle, then squeeze out the excess liquid from the spinach by handfuls, and place the spinach in a medium bowl. Add the remaining stuffing ingredients and mix well, seasoning with salt and pepper.

Place the veal flat, smooth side down, on a work surface. Spread with the cheese mixture, leaving a

1-inch border around all sides. Starting at a long side, roll up the veal into a cylinder. Tucking in the ends of the veal cylinder to enclose the filling, tie up the veal horizontally and vertically using kitchen string.

Preheat the oven to 300°F. In a heavy roasting pan, heat 2 tablespoons of the oil over medium-high heat. Add the veal and cook, turning often, until browned on all sides, about 10 minutes. Transfer to a platter and set aside.

Add the remaining 2 tablespoons oil to the pan and heat. Add the veal bones and cook, turning occasionally, until browned, about 10 minutes. Add the onion, carrot, and celery and cook for 1 minute. Pour in the wine and bring to a simmer. Place the veal breast on top of the bones and vegetables. Cover the pan and transfer to the oven. Cook until the veal is tender and a meat thermometer inserted in the center reads 160°F, about 1½ hours. Transfer the veal to a platter, tent with foil, and let stand for 10 minutes before slicing.

Strain the cooking liquid, and skim off the fat that rises to the surface. Return the liquid to the roasting pan and cook over high heat until reduced and slightly thickened. Season with salt and pepper. Remove the strings from the veal, then cut crosswise into thick slices. Serve with the sauce.

POMEGRANATE-MARINATED LEG OF LAMB

That harbinger of autumn, the pomegranate, has a vibrant red juice that can be the beginnings of a sensational marinade for lamb. Pomegranates are only available for a short time, so you may want to freeze some juice for making this dish throughout the year.

MAKES 8 TO 10 SERVINGS
1 (4-pound) leg of lamb
1 cup brown beef or lamb stock
Salt and freshly ground pepper, to taste
Marinade
3 medium pomegranates
2 tablespoons balsamic vinegar
1 small onion, thinly sliced
1 teaspoon ground cumin
1 teaspoon dried oregano
2 garlic cloves, minced
¼ teaspoon salt
¼ teaspoon freshly ground pepper
⅓ cup extra virgin olive oil

To make the marinade, remove the seeds from the pomegranates. Place the seeds in a strainer set over a medium bowl. Using a large spoon, crush the seeds to

extract the juice. You should have 2 cups pomegranate juice. In the bowl, combine the juice with the balsamic vinegar, onion, cumin, oregano, garlic, salt, and pepper. Whisk in the oil. Pour into a large nonreactive baking dish and add the lamb. Cover and let marinate in the refrigerator, turning the lamb often, for at least 8 and up to 24 hours. Remove from the refrigerator 1 hour before cooking.

Preheat the oven to 450°F. Remove the lamb from the marinade, reserving the marinade, and pat the lamb dry with paper towels. Place the lamb on a roasting rack set in a large roasting pan. Roast for 10 minutes. Reduce the heat to 350°F. Continue roasting, basting often with the marinade, until a meat thermometer inserted in the thickest part of the lamb reads 130°F for medium-rare lamb, about 50 minutes. Transfer the lamb to a serving platter. Let the lamb stand for 10 minutes before carving.

Meanwhile, skim off any fat from the roasting juices in the pan. Place the pan over two stove burners on medium heat. Add the stock and bring to a boil, scraping up the browned bits in the pan with a wooden spoon. Boil until slightly reduced, about 2 minutes. Season with salt and pepper. Carve the lamb and serve with the sauce.

ROAST LEG OF LAMB WITH WHITE BEANS

Roasting a boned leg of lamb makes slicing much easier. While white beans are delicious in the tomato-wine sauce, other legumes work well too. Try tiny dried green flageolets, reducing the cooking time.

MAKES 6 TO 8 SERVINGS
6 tablespoons unsalted butter
¼ cup chopped fresh parsley
3 garlic cloves, minced
1 (4-pound) boneless leg of lamb
Salt and freshly ground pepper, to taste
White Beans
1 pound dried white beans, soaked overnight
  and drained
1 (1-pound) smoked ham hock, sawed in half
1 tablespoon olive oil
1 large onion, finely chopped
2 tablespoons tomato paste
1 cup dry white wine
Salt and freshly ground pepper, to taste

To prepare the beans, place them in a large saucepan with the ham hock and add enough cold water to cover. Bring to a boil over high heat. Reduce the heat to low and simmer until the beans are tender, 1 to

1½ hours. Remove and reserve 1 cup of the liquid. Drain the beans, discard the ham hock, and set aside.

Preheat the oven to 425°F. In a small frying pan, heat 4 tablespoons of the butter over medium-low heat. Add the parsley and garlic and cook, stirring often, until the garlic is softened, but not browned, 1 to 2 minutes. Let cool, then push into the cavity left by the bones in the leg of lamb. Season with salt and pepper. Roll up the lamb and tie crosswise in places with kitchen string. Spread the remaining butter over the lamb. Place on a roasting rack set in a roasting pan. Roast for 30 minutes, basting occasionally with the fat in the pan. Reduce the heat to 350°F, and continue roasting until a meat thermometer inserted in the center of the roast reads 130°F (medium-rare), about 40 minutes. Transfer the lamb to a platter and let stand for 10 minutes before carving.

While the lamb is roasting, finish the beans. In a medium saucepan, heat the oil over medium heat. Add the onion and cook until soft and translucent, about 5 minutes. Stir in the tomato paste and bubble for 1 to 2 minutes. Add the wine and the reserved bean cooking liquid. Bring to a simmer, stirring, and simmer for 1 to 2 minutes. Add the beans and let simmer over low heat until the lamb is cooked.

Skim off any fat from the roasting juices in the pan, and stir the juices into the beans. Season. Transfer the beans to a large platter. Slice the lamb crosswise, and overlap the slices on the beans. Serve hot.

LAMB WITH INDIAN SPICES

This is a fine dish for a dinner party, and looks as beautiful as it tastes. Plan ahead, as it should marinate overnight in the refrigerator. Serve with spiced rice—steamed with 4 cardamom pods and 2 cinnamon sticks—to complement the rich cooking juices.

MAKES 6 SERVINGS

1½ cups plain yogurt

3 tablespoons lemon juice

1 medium onion, minced

2 garlic cloves, minced and mashed to a paste
    with a sprinkle of salt

1 teaspoon ground ginger

1 tablespoon chili powder

Salt, to taste

1 (3-pound) boneless leg of lamb or lamb shoulder,
    well trimmed

¾ cup raisins

½ cup chopped blanched almonds

¼ cup chopped pistachio nuts

4 tablespoons unsalted butter

1 tablespoon honey

Reserve 2 tablespoons of the yogurt. In a medium bowl, mix together the remaining yogurt, the lemon juice, onion, garlic, ginger, chili powder, and salt. Prick the lamb all over with a metal skewer, and place in a shallow nonreactive dish. Spread on both sides with the yogurt mixture. Cover and let marinate in the refrigerator overnight.

Preheat the oven to 325°F. Remove the lamb from the dish, reserving the marinade, and place on the work surface. In a medium bowl, combine the raisins, almonds, pistachios, and reserved 2 tablespoons yogurt. If using a leg of lamb, push the nut mixture into the cavity left by the bones; if using a shoulder of lamb, place it boned side up and spread the nut mixture over the surface. Roll up the lamb and tie it crosswise in several places with kitchen string.

Place the lamb in a deep medium casserole, and add the reserved yogurt marinade and the butter. Cover and cook in the oven for 1 hour. Turn the lamb over and drizzle with the honey. Cook, covered, for another 1 hour, basting about every 30 minutes with the juices in the casserole. Uncover and continue cooking until a meat thermometer inserted in the center of the roast reads 140°F (medium), about 30 more minutes.

Transfer the lamb to a large heated platter and let stand for 5 minutes before removing the string and carving crosswise into fairly thick slices. Skim off the fat from the surface of the cooking liquid, and serve the liquid with the lamb.

FRENCH LAMB RAGOUT WITH PEAS AND POTATOES

The French would call this lamb stew a *navarin*. The best ones are made in the spring with baby new potatoes and fresh peas.

MAKES 6 TO 8 SERVINGS

3 tablespoons vegetable oil

4 pounds boneless lamb shoulder, well trimmed and
    cut into 1-inch chunks

1 large onion, chopped

3 garlic cloves, crushed

2 tablespoons all-purpose flour

2 tablespoons tomato paste

2 cups chicken stock

2 cups dry white wine

1 bouquet garni of 2 sprigs fresh thyme, 2 sprigs
    fresh parsley, and 1 bay leaf

Salt and freshly ground pepper, to taste

1½ pounds boiling potatoes, cut into
    ¼-inch-thick rounds

1 cup shelled fresh peas (from 1 pound unshelled),
    or use frozen

Preheat the oven to 325°F. In a large Dutch oven, heat 2 tablespoons of the oil over medium heat. In batches, without crowding, add the lamb and brown on all sides, about 8 minutes. As the lamb is browned, transfer to a plate.

Add the remaining 1 tablespoon oil to the Dutch oven. Add the onion and garlic, and cook until the onion is golden-brown, about 8 minutes. Sprinkle with the flour and stir for 1 minute. Stir in the tomato paste. Pour in the stock and the wine, and stir to mix. Return the lamb to the pot, and add the bouquet garni. Season with salt and pepper. Bring to a boil, then cover and transfer to the oven. Cook for 1 hour.

Skim off any fat on the surface of the cooking liquid. Layer the potatoes over the lamb, seasoning the slices with salt and pepper as they are layered and pushing them down into the cooking liquid to moisten them. Cover again and cook for 30 minutes. Increase the heat to 375°F. Uncover the pot, and cook until the potatoes are browned and tender, about 30 more minutes.

Meanwhile, in a medium saucepan of lightly salted boiling water, cook the peas over medium heat until barely tender, about 4 minutes. Drain well and keep warm. Scatter the peas over the surface of the stew just before serving.

Lamb with Indian Spices

GARLIC-BRAISED LAMB SHANKS WITH SWEET PEPPERS

Cooking lamb shanks on the bone gives a wonderful sauce that is made more delicious by the addition of sweet peppers. Yellow peppers add a pleasing color, but red peppers, or even a combination of red and yellow, could also be used.

MAKES 6 SERVINGS

6 tablespoons olive oil, or more as needed
6 (1-pound) lamb shanks
2 medium red onions, cut into ¼-inch-thick half-moons
20 garlic cloves, peeled
1 teaspoon dried oregano
12 ounces ripe plum tomatoes, peeled, seeded, chopped, and well drained, or use drained canned tomatoes
6 tablespoons hearty red wine
Salt and freshly ground pepper, to taste
4 medium yellow bell peppers, seeded and cut into 1½-inch pieces

Preheat the oven to 325°F. In a large Dutch oven, heat 3 tablespoons of the oil over medium-high heat. In batches, without crowding, add the lamb shanks and brown on all sides, about 8 minutes. As the shanks are browned, transfer to a plate. Add more oil to the Dutch oven if needed, then add the onions, garlic, and oregano. Cook until the onions are lightly browned, about 8 minutes. Stir in the tomatoes and cook for 3 minutes. Pour in the wine and bring to a simmer. Return the lamb shanks to the pot, and season with salt and pepper. Cover and transfer to the oven. Cook, turning the lamb occasionally, for 1 hour.

Meanwhile, in a large frying pan, heat the remaining 3 tablespoons oil over medium heat. Add the peppers and cook, turning often, until lightly browned, about 5 minutes. When the lamb has cooked for 1 hour, add the peppers to the Dutch oven. Continue cooking, covered, until the lamb is tender, 30 to 45 more minutes, depending on the size of the shanks.

Transfer the shanks to a serving dish. Skim off any fat that has risen to the surface of the sauce. If the sauce is too thin, bring to a boil and reduce until thickened and velvety. Pour the sauce over the shanks and serve hot.

LAMB, ZUCCHINI, AND RED PEPPER KEBABS

You can create a new kebab recipe simply by using a different marinade. Provençal Lemon Marinade is just one alternative to the one suggested here.

MAKES 4 SERVINGS
2½ pounds boneless leg of lamb, cut into 1½ inch cubes
Italian Red Wine Marinade
1 medium zucchini, cut into 8 rounds
1 small red bell pepper, seeded and cut into 8 pieces
Salt and freshly ground pepper, to taste

In a medium bowl, combine the lamb with half of the marinade. Cover and leave to marinate in the refrigerator for at least 4 and up to 12 hours. In another bowl, combine the rounds of zucchini and the pieces of bell pepper with the remaining marinade, and let stand at room temperature for at least 1 and up to 2 hours.

Build a hot charcoal fire in an outdoor grill or preheat the broiler. Lightly oil the grill. Drain the lamb and vegetables, patting the lamb dry with paper towels. Thread the lamb cubes onto metal skewers, alternating them with the pieces of zucchini and red pepper. Grill or broil the kebabs, turning occasionally, until the lamb is browned on all sides and medium-rare, about 10 minutes. Season with salt and pepper.

LAMB RIB CHOPS WITH ROASTED GARLIC BUTTER

This recipe calls for tender rib chops, but of course you could use less expensive lamb shoulder chops instead. The flavor of roasted garlic with a hint of thyme goes perfectly with grilled lamb.

MAKES 6 SERVINGS
8 lamb rib chops, cut about ¾ inch thick
Roasted Garlic Butter
1 large head garlic, with firm, plump cloves
1 tablespoon extra virgin olive oil
6 tablespoons unsalted butter, at room temperature
1 teaspoon chopped fresh thyme or ½ teaspoon dried thyme
Salt and freshly ground pepper, to taste

Preheat the oven to 350°F. To make the butter, cut the head of garlic in half horizontally, then put the two halves back together to form the original shape. Place on a piece of aluminum foil, drizzle with the oil, and wrap tightly. Bake until the garlic feels tender when squeezed, 20 to 30 minutes. Unwrap and let cool. Squeeze the tender garlic pulp out of the hulls into a small bowl. Add the butter and thyme, and mash. Season. Scrape out onto a square of waxed paper. Use the waxed paper to form the butter into a 4-inch-long log. Refrigerate until the butter is firm, at least 2 hours. (The butter can be kept, wrapped in foil, in the freezer for up to 2 months.)

Build a hot charcoal fire in an outdoor grill or preheat the broiler. Lightly oil the grill. Grill or broil the chops, turning once, until medium-rare, 8 to 10 minutes. Cut the butter into eight rounds. Serve the chops hot, topping each with a butter round.

GRILLED BUTTERFLIED LEG OF LAMB WITH DIJON AND HERBS

Here the lamb is grilled by the indirect cooking method (covered, and not directly over the coals), so it cooks through without scorching the outside.

MAKES 4 TO 6 SERVINGS
½ cup Dijon mustard
2 scallions, minced
2 garlic cloves, minced
1 tablespoon chopped fresh rosemary or 1½ teaspoons dried rosemary
1 tablespoon chopped fresh mint or 1½ teaspoons dried mint
Salt and freshly ground pepper, to taste
1 (4-pound) butt portion leg of lamb, boned and butterflied (about 2½ pounds after boning)

In a small bowl, combine the mustard, scallions, garlic, rosemary, and mint with a seasoning of salt and pepper. Place the lamb in a glass baking dish and slather the mustard mixture on both sides. Cover and let marinate in the refrigerator for at least 2 and up to 8 hours. Remove from the refrigerator 1 hour before grilling.

Build a hot charcoal fire in an outdoor grill, banking the coals to one side and leaving the other side empty. Lightly oil the grill. Grill the lamb over the coals, turning once, until seared on both sides, about 5 minutes. Place the lamb over the empty side of the grill and cover. Grill, basting occasionally with the remaining marinade, until a meat thermometer inserted in the thickest part of the lamb reads 130°F, about 20 minutes for medium-rare lamb. (To use a gas grill, heat one side of the grill on High, leaving the other side off. Sear the lamb on the hot side for 5 minutes. Move to the unheated side of the grill and close the lid. Continue cooking as directed.) Transfer to a carving board and leave to stand for about 10 minutes before carving.

ROAST LOIN OF PORK

A fine pork roast needs little attention to make it into a delicious meal. Applesauce and roast potatoes are ideal accompaniments.

MAKES 6 SERVINGS

- 1 (3½-pound) pork loin roast with bone, chine bone cracked by butcher
- 2 sprigs fresh rosemary
- 2 garlic cloves, unpeeled
- 2 tablespoons lemon juice
- ⅔ cup dry white wine or hard cider
- 1 cup chicken stock
- 2 teaspoons all-purpose flour
- Salt and freshly ground pepper, to taste

Preheat the oven to 350°F. Place the pork roast in a roasting pan, bones down (the bones will act as a natural rack). Tuck the rosemary under the pork, and push the garlic cloves into the roast next to the bones. Rub the meat with the lemon juice. Roast, basting occasionally, until a meat thermometer inserted in the center of the roast reads 155°F, about 2 hours. Transfer the pork to a platter and let stand for at least 10 minutes before carving.

Meanwhile, make the gravy. Spoon off the fat from the roasting pan, and discard the rosemary. Squeeze the garlic cloves from their skins into the pan. Place the roasting pan over medium heat. Add the wine and bring to a boil, mixing in the garlic and scraping up all the browned bits and pieces in the pan with a wooden spoon. Cook until the wine is reduced to about 2 tablespoons. In a small bowl, gradually whisk the broth into the flour until completely dissolved. Pour into the roasting pan and bring to a simmer, stirring. Reduce the heat to low and simmer until the gravy has thickened, with no trace of raw flour taste, about 5 minutes. Season with salt and pepper. Strain, if desired. Pour into a warmed sauceboat. Carve the roast and serve with the gravy.

PORK TENDERLOIN WITH CHERRY AND PORT SAUCE

Pork tenderloin is an excellent choice for a special but speedy entrée. Here a dry rub adds extra flavor to the mild meat, and the sauce is an intriguing, sweet-and-sour blend of dried cherries, port, and chile pepper.

MAKES 4 TO 6 SERVINGS

- 2 (12-ounce) pork tenderloins
- 1 teaspoon granulated sugar
- 1 teaspoon dried marjoram
- ½ teaspoon salt
- ¼ teaspoon freshly ground pepper

Cherry and Port Sauce
- 1½ cups dried cherries or cranberries (6 ounces)
- ¾ cup ruby or tawny port
- 3 tablespoons unsalted butter
- ¼ cup minced shallots or scallions (white part only)
- 1 small hot fresh chile pepper (such as jalapeño), seeded and minced
- 1 cup chicken stock
- Salt, to taste

Rinse the pork and pat dry with paper towels. Mix together the sugar, marjoram, salt, and pepper, and rub all over the pork. Place in a plastic bag and refrigerate for at least 4 hours or up to 24 hours. When ready to cook, drain the pork of its released juices, and gently pat dry with paper towels. Fold the thin, elongated end of each tenderloin underneath and tie with kitchen string so each tenderloin is the same thickness along its length, thus ensuring that it will cook evenly.

To start the sauce, soak the cherries in the port in a small bowl until plumped, about 30 minutes.

Build a hot charcoal fire in an outdoor grill or preheat the broiler. Lightly oil the grill. Grill or broil the pork, turning occasionally, until browned on all sides and a meat thermometer inserted in the thickest part reads 155°F, about 20 minutes.

Meanwhile, finish the sauce. In a small saucepan, melt 1 tablespoon butter over medium-low heat. Add the shallots and chile pepper and cook, stirring often, until the shallots are lightly browned, about 3 minutes. Add the cherries and their soaking liquid, along with the chicken stock, and bring to a simmer. Reduce the heat to low and cook until the liquid is reduced by half, about 10 minutes. Remove from the heat, and swirl in the remaining 2 tablespoons butter. Season with salt, and keep warm.

Let the grilled pork stand for 5 minutes before slicing crosswise, and serve with the warm sauce.

NEW MEXICAN PORK AND VEGETABLE CHILI

In the Southwest, whole dried chile peppers are turned into a brick-red cooking sauce that is preferred to one seasoned with chili powder.

MAKES 4 TO 6 SERVINGS
10 mild whole dried chile peppers (preferably New Mexico)
1½ cups beef stock
2 garlic cloves, minced
4 tablespoons olive oil
3 pounds boneless pork shoulder, cut into 1½ inch cubes
1 tablespoon ground cumin
1 tablespoon dried oregano
Salt and freshly ground pepper, to taste
¼ cup yellow cornmeal
3 medium zucchini, cut into ½-inch cubes
1½ cups corn kernels, fresh or defrosted frozen
Chopped fresh cilantro, for garnish

Discard the stems and seeds from the peppers, and tear into pieces. Place in a bowl and add boiling water to cover. Let stand until soft, about 30 minutes. Drain the peppers and place in a blender. Add the beef stock and garlic, and purée. Set the sauce aside.

In a large Dutch oven or flameproof casserole, heat 2 tablespoons oil over medium-high heat. In batches, without crowding, add the pork and brown on all sides, about 8 minutes. Return all the pork to the Dutch oven, and stir in the pepper sauce, the cumin, and oregano. Season with salt and pepper. Bring to a simmer, then reduce the heat to low. Cover and simmer until the pork is tender, about 1½ hours. Carefully skim off any fat that has risen to the surface of the cooking liquid, and then stir in the cornmeal and simmer until it has thickened, about 5 minutes.

Meanwhile, in a large frying pan, heat the remaining 2 tablespoons oil over medium heat. Add the zucchini and cook until lightly browned, about 5 minutes. Stir in the corn and cook until heated through, about 5 minutes. Stir the zucchini and corn into the stew. Serve hot, sprinkling each serving with cilantro.

DOUBLE-COOKED PORK CHOPS

The trouble with panfried pork chops is that by the time they have cooked through, they are very likely to have dried out. But by browning the chops in a frying pan first, and then stacking them in a warm oven where they continue to cook gently, they will turn out perfectly tender and juicy.

MAKES 4 SERVINGS
4 (7-ounce) center-cut loin pork chops
2 tablespoons vegetable oil
1 teaspoon chopped fresh thyme or ½ teaspoon dried thyme
2 garlic cloves, minced
Salt and freshly ground pepper, to taste

Preheat the oven to 350°F. Rub the pork chops with 1 tablespoon of the oil and then the thyme, garlic, and pepper (do not add salt yet). In a large frying pan, heat the remaining 1 tablespoon oil over medium-high heat until very hot, but not smoking. Add the chops and cook, turning once, until seared on both sides, about 2 minutes. Reduce the heat to medium and cook, turning occasionally, until both sides are browned and the meat feels a little resistant when pressed in the center, about 8 minutes. Transfer the pork chops to a baking dish, stacking them on top of each other into a tower. Cover lightly with foil. Place in the oven, and leave the oven door slightly ajar. Cook for about 10 minutes. Season with salt and serve hot.

SHERRY-GLAZED HAM

Here's a nice way to dress up ham.

MAKES 8 TO 12 SERVINGS
1 (4- to 5- pound) boneless smoked ham
¾ cup packed light brown sugar
3 tablespoons sherry vinegar
1 tablespoon dry sherry
1 teaspoon dry mustard
¼ teaspoon ground cloves

Place the ham in a large pot or deep roasting pan and add enough cold water to cover as much as possible. Bring to a simmer over high heat. Reduce the heat to low and simmer for 45 minutes, turning the ham occasionally in the water. Drain and let cool slightly.

Preheat the oven to 325°F. Cut off the rind from the ham, leaving a thin layer of fat. Using the tip of a sharp knife, score the fat in a diamond pattern. Place the ham on a roasting rack set in a foil-lined roasting pan. Mix together all of the remaining ingredients in a medium bowl and set aside.

Bake the ham until a meat thermometer inserted in the thickest part reads 160°F, about 2 hours. During the last 30 minutes of baking, spread the ham with the glaze, and baste occasionally with the melted glaze in the pan.

Increase the oven temperature to 450°F, and continue baking until the glaze is tinged with brown spots, about 10 minutes. Transfer to a platter and let stand for at least 15 minutes before carving, or let cool completely and serve cold.

OVEN-BARBECUED SPARERIBS

Spareribs are almost as delicious when cooked indoors as out.

MAKES 6 SERVINGS

6 pounds spareribs, cut between the ribs into
    2-rib pieces
¼ cup Cajun Dry Rub
Salt, to taste
2 cups Southern-Style BBQ Sauce

Preheat the oven to 350°F. Season the spareribs with the Cajun dry rub and salt. Place in a large roasting pan and cover with aluminum foil. Bake for 1 hour. Pour off the fat from the pan, and increase the heat to 400°F.

SHERRY-GLAZED HAM

Bake until the ribs are beginning to brown and are almost tender, about 20 minutes. Baste with some of the sauce, and continue baking, turning and basting often, until the ribs are tender, about 15 more minutes. Serve immediately, with any remaining sauce passed on the side.

Outdoor BBQ Spareribs: Leave the ribs in 6- to 8-rib slabs, and season with the Cajun dry rub and salt. Wrap each slab in a piece of heavy-duty aluminum foil. Build a hot charcoal fire in an outdoor grill. Place the ribs on the grill and cover with the grill lid. Cook, turning occasionally, until the ribs are almost tender, about 1 hour. Unwrap the ribs, and discard any fat and juices remaining in the foil.

Add more coals to the grill and allow them to continue burning until they are covered with white ash. Lightly oil the grill grate. Grill the parcooked ribs (this time without the aluminum-foil covering), turning them occasionally and basting with the sauce, until they are tender and well glazed, 10 to 15 minutes.

If you are using a gas grill, cook the foil-wrapped ribs at low heat, and then glaze them, turning and basting with the sauce, over medium heat.

pork spareribs
60

grilling
equipment
240–1

meat
thermometer
233

roasting pan
236

Cajun Dry Rub
261

Southern-Style
BBQ Sauce 259

Game

GRILLED VENISON WITH RED WINE AND ROSEMARY

Smoldering fresh rosemary branches add a distinctive smokiness to these grilled venison filets mignons. Try serving them with Sweet Pepper Chutney.

MAKES 6 SERVINGS

1 cup hearty red wine
¼ cup olive oil
1 teaspoon chopped fresh rosemary
6 (6- to 8-ounce) boneless venison tenderloin steaks
20 to 40 (5-inch) sprigs fresh rosemary
Salt and freshly ground pepper, to taste

In a shallow glass dish, whisk together the wine, oil, and chopped rosemary. Add the venison steaks. Cover and let marinate in the refrigerator until ready to grill, at least 2 and up to 8 hours.

Build a hot charcoal fire in an outdoor grill. Lightly oil the grill. Remove the venison from the marinade and pat the steaks dry with paper towels. Toss the rosemary sprigs on the coals, and cover to build up a good head of smoke. Place the venison on the grill and cover again. Grill until seared, about 3 minutes. Turn and continue grilling until the steak is medium-rare, about 3 more minutes. Season and serve.

SPICED VENISON AND BEER RAGOUT

A heady blend of aromatic spices sets this ragout apart. Suitable accompaniments are new potatoes, creamed celeriac, and red-currant jelly.

MAKES 6 TO 8 SERVINGS

2 tablespoons unsalted butter
1 tablespoon olive oil, approximately
3 pounds venison stew meat, such as shoulder, cut into 1½-inch cubes
2 medium onions, chopped
Salt, to taste
1 teaspoon whole black peppercorns, coarsely crushed
1¼ cups stout (such as Guinness)
⅔ cup beef or chicken stock
3 tablespoons malt or cider vinegar
1 teaspoon brown sugar or 1 tablespoon red-currant jelly
8 whole allspice berries
4 whole cloves
3 bay leaves
2 tablespoons heavy cream
About 2 tablespoons Beurre Manié (optional)

In a large Dutch oven, heat the butter and oil over medium-high heat. In batches, without crowding, add the venison and cook until browned on all sides, about 8 minutes. As the venison is browned, transfer to a plate. Add more oil to the Dutch oven, if needed, then add the onions and cook until golden-brown, about 6 minutes. Return the venison to the Dutch oven, and season with salt. Add the peppercorns.

Add the stout, stock, vinegar, sugar, allspice, cloves, and bay leaves. Bring to a simmer, then reduce the heat to low and simmer, partially covered, until the meat is tender, about 1½ hours. Discard the bay leaves. Stir in the cream and heat through. The sauce should be nicely thickened. If not, remove the venison to a heated serving tureen using a slotted spoon, and cover to keep warm. Boil the sauce over high heat until reduced to the consistency of heavy cream. Or, bring the sauce to a boil, whisk in enough beurre manié to thicken the sauce, and simmer over medium heat for 5 minutes.

BRAISED RABBIT WITH PRUNES

At one time, vinegar was used in recipes like this to help mellow the flesh of wild game. Even today's farmed game benefits from a spell in a vinegar- and wine-based marinade.

MAKES 4 SERVINGS

1 (2½- to 3-pound) rabbit, cut into serving pieces
4 tablespoons unsalted butter
2 tablespoons all-purpose flour
1 medium onion, chopped
Salt and freshly ground pepper, to taste
1 cup hearty red wine
½ cup chicken stock
1½ cups packed dried pitted prunes
Marinade
2 cups hearty red wine
½ cup wine vinegar
2 garlic cloves, crushed
1 sprig fresh thyme or ¼ teaspoon dried thyme
3 to 4 sprigs fresh fennel or ¼ teaspoon fennel seed
1 bay leaf
Salt, to taste
6 whole black peppercorns, crushed

Combine all of the marinade ingredients in a large nonreactive bowl. Add the rabbit and cover with plastic wrap. Let marinate in the refrigerator, turning the rabbit pieces occasionally, for at least 4 hours but not longer than 12 hours. Remove the rabbit from the marinade and pat dry with paper towels. Discard the marinade.

In a large Dutch oven, heat 2 tablespoons of the butter over medium-high heat. Dust the rabbit pieces

BRAISED RABBIT WITH PRUNES

lightly with the flour. In batches, without crowding, add the rabbit to the Dutch oven and cook, turning occasionally, until browned on all sides, about 8 minutes. As the pieces are browned, transfer to a plate.

Add the remaining 2 tablespoons butter to the Dutch oven and reduce the heat to medium. Add the onion and cook until soft and translucent, about 5 minutes. Return the rabbit to the Dutch oven, and season with salt and pepper. Add the wine, stock, and prunes and bring to a simmer. Reduce the heat to low, cover, and simmer, turning the rabbit occasionally, for 30 minutes. Uncover and continue simmering until the rabbit is tender, about 15 more minutes. Serve hot.

RABBIT WITH MUSTARD AND THYME

Smothered with a zesty mustard sauce, this rabbit would go well with steamed new potatoes.

MAKES 4 SERVINGS
  ½ cup all-purpose flour
  Salt and freshly ground pepper, to taste
  2 tablespoons unsalted butter
  1 tablespoon olive oil, approximately
  1 (2½- to 3-pound) rabbit, cut into serving pieces
  1 medium onion, thinly sliced
  1 cup dry white wine
  ½ cup chicken stock
  3 teaspoons Dijon mustard
  3 teaspoons prepared "common" English mustard
  3 sprigs fresh thyme or ½ teaspoon dried thyme
  3 tablespoons heavy cream

Put the flour and a seasoning of salt and pepper in a shallow dish. In a large Dutch oven, heat the butter and olive oil together over medium-high heat. Coat the rabbit pieces in the flour, shaking off the excess, then in batches, without crowding, add to the Dutch oven. Cook, turning occasionally, until browned on all sides, about 8 minutes. As the pieces are browned, transfer them to a plate.

Add more oil to the Dutch oven, if needed, and reduce the heat to medium. Add the onion and cook until lightly browned, about 8 minutes. Return the rabbit to the Dutch oven, and pour in the wine and stock. Stir in 1 teaspoon each of the Dijon mustard and English mustard, along with the thyme. Bring to a simmer, then cover and reduce the heat to low. Simmer, turning the rabbit occasionally, for 20 minutes. Stir in the remaining 2 teaspoons of Dijon mustard, and continue simmering until the rabbit is tender, about 25 more minutes. Stir in the heavy cream and the remaining 2 teaspoons of English mustard. Serve hot.

MARINATED ROAST QUAIL

The marinade gives a delicious glossy finish to the birds. Eat them with your fingers so you can really savor every morsel.

MAKES 4 SERVINGS
  8 quail
  Sprigs of fresh cilantro, for garnish
  Lime wedges, for serving
Marinade
  ⅔ cup rice wine or dry sherry
  ½ cup light soy sauce
  ⅓ cup fresh orange juice
  ¼ cup hoisin sauce
  2 tablespoons honey
  1 (2-inch) piece fresh ginger, unpeeled, thinly sliced
  1 tablespoon Asian dark sesame oil
  1 teaspoon five-spice powder
  1 teaspoon chile flakes
  1 teaspoon freshly ground white pepper
  Zest of 1 orange, removed in strips with a vegetable peeler
  1 garlic clove, crushed

To make the marinade, combine all of the ingredients in a food processor fitted with the metal blade, and process for 30 seconds. Pour the marinade into a large nonreactive bowl. Add the quail. Cover and let marinate in the refrigerator, turning the quail occasionally, at least overnight or preferably for 24 hours.

Preheat the oven to 425°F. Remove the quail from the marinade, shaking off any clinging marinade solids. Place the birds, well apart, on a rack in a heavy roasting pan. Pour about 1¼ cups water into the pan (to prevent the drippings from burning).

Strain the marinade into a medium saucepan. Bring to a boil over high heat and boil until reduced to a syrup, about 10 minutes. Spoon a little of the reduced marinade over each bird, reserving the remaining marinade. Roast the quail for 5 minutes. Remove from the oven, and spoon a bit more of the marinade over. Roast for 10 more minutes, then spoon all the remaining marinade over the birds. Continue roasting until the quail are tender and a rich, glossy golden-brown, 5 to 10 minutes. There may be a few scorched patches, which will add to the flavor.

Transfer the quail to a serving platter and place in the turned-off oven to keep warm. Strain the roasting liquid into a medium saucepan and bring to a boil over high heat. Boil until syrupy, about 5 minutes; taste the liquid occasionally and stop boiling if it is becoming very salty. Garnish the quail with the cilantro and lime wedges, spoon the sauce over the birds, and serve.

MARINATED ROAST QUAIL

PHEASANT WITH CHESTNUTS

Pheasant braised in red wine and stock, with fresh chestnuts, is a succulent dish for a winter's night.

MAKES 2 OR 3 SERVINGS

6 ounces slab bacon, rind removed, cut into
 ¼- by 1-inch strips
1 (2- to 3-pound) pheasant
2 tablespoons all-purpose flour
2 tablespoons unsalted butter
4 medium carrots, thinly sliced
2 medium onions, thinly sliced
2 shallots, thinly sliced
½ cup hearty red wine
1 bouquet garni of 1 sprig fresh thyme, 1 sprig fresh
 parsley, and 1 bay leaf
Salt and freshly ground pepper, to taste
8 ounces fresh chestnuts, cooked and peeled
 (about 1½ cups)
1 teaspoon cornstarch, mixed with 2 teaspoons water
Stock
2 teaspoons vegetable oil
Neck, heart, and gizzard from the pheasant
1 small onion, chopped
1 small carrot, chopped
1 bay leaf

To make the stock, in a medium saucepan, heat the oil over medium-high heat. Add the pheasant neck, heart, and gizzard and cook until browned, about 5 minutes. Add the onion and carrot, and cook until softened, about 5 minutes. Pour in 3 cups cold water and bring to a simmer. Skim off any foam that rises to the surface. Add the bay leaf. Reduce the heat to low, and simmer until well flavored, 2 to 3 hours. Strain the stock. If necessary, return to the saucepan and boil over high heat until reduced to 1½ cups. Set aside.

Preheat the oven to 325°F. In a medium Dutch oven or flameproof casserole, just large enough to hold the pheasant, cook the bacon over medium-high heat until crisp and brown, about 5 minutes. Using a slotted spoon, transfer the bacon to paper towels to drain, leaving the fat in the Dutch oven. Dust the pheasant with the flour, shaking off any excess flour. Place in the Dutch oven and cook, turning often, until browned on all sides, about 10 minutes. Set aside on a plate. Pour excess fat from the Dutch oven, then add the butter and heat it. Add the carrots, onions, and shallots to the pot, and reduce the heat to medium.

bouquet garni
190
chestnut 188
peeling
chestnuts 189
pheasant 83
slab bacon 70

casserole 235–6

Game/Poultry

Cook until softened, but not browned, about 5 minutes. Add the red wine, bring to a simmer, and cook for 3 minutes. Return the bacon to the Dutch oven, then the pheasant, placed on one side. Add the stock and bouquet garni, and season with salt and pepper. Cover and cook in the oven for 20 minutes.

Add the chestnuts to the Dutch oven, and turn the pheasant onto its other side. Cover again and continue cooking until the legs of the pheasant show the barest hint of pink when pierced at the bone with the tip of a sharp knife, 20 to 30 more minutes. Transfer the pheasant, chestnuts, and vegetables to a deep serving platter, and cover with aluminum foil to keep warm.

Skim the fat from the sauce. Bring it to a simmer, stir in the cornstarch, and simmer for 2 minutes to thicken. Carve the pheasant and serve with the vegetables and chestnuts, with the sauce on the side.

BRAISED SQUAB WITH CABBAGE

Squabs, those little farm-raised pigeons, turn out beautifully tender after being braised on a bed of cabbage and bacon cooked in white wine.

MAKES 4 SERVINGS

    4 (12-ounce to 1-pound) squabs
    2 tablespoons all-purpose flour
    Salt and freshly ground pepper, to taste
    3 tablespoons unsalted butter
    1 tablespoon vegetable oil
    2 medium onions, thinly sliced
    1 (1-pound) head green cabbage, cored and finely sliced
    3 ounces thick-sliced bacon, coarsely chopped
    ⅔ cup chicken stock
    ½ cup dry white wine
    2 tablespoons cider vinegar
    2 teaspoons granulated sugar
    6 juniper berries, crushed
    4 allspice berries
    1 bay leaf

Preheat the oven to 325°F. Dust the squabs with the flour, shaking off the excess, and season inside and out with salt and pepper. In a large Dutch oven, heat 2 tablespoons of the butter and the oil over medium-high heat. In batches, so they aren't crowded while browning, add the squabs to the Dutch oven and cook, turning occasionally, until browned on all sides, about 8 minutes. Transfer to a plate.

Pour excess fat from the Dutch oven, then add the remaining butter to the pot and heat. Add the onions

and cook, stirring occasionally, until they are lightly browned, about 8 minutes. Add the cabbage and bacon. Cover and cook until the cabbage is softened, about 5 minutes. Add the stock, wine, vinegar, sugar, juniper berries, allspice, and bay leaf. Season with salt and pepper. Bring to a simmer, then reduce the heat to low. Cook, covered, until the cabbage is tender, about 30 minutes.

Return the squabs to the pot, placing them on the bed of cabbage. Cover and place in the oven. Cook until the squabs are tender and the juices run a pale pink when pierced at the bone, 20 to 30 minutes; if you prefer well-done squab, cook for longer. Serve them on a bed of the braised cabbage.

———————— • ————————

ROAST CHICKEN WITH MARJORAM BREAD STUFFING

Everyone loves a simply roasted chicken with an herby bread stuffing. Marjoram is a great flavoring for poultry, but if not available you can substitute fresh parsley or thyme.

MAKES 4 SERVINGS

    1 (3½-pound) chicken, rinsed and patted dry
    Salt and freshly ground pepper, to taste
    5 tablespoons unsalted butter, at room temperature
    1 small onion, finely chopped
    1 cup fresh bread crumbs
    1 tablespoon chopped fresh marjoram or 1½ teaspoons dried marjoram

Preheat the oven to 375°F. Season the chicken inside and out with salt and pepper. In a small frying pan, heat 1 tablespoon of the butter over medium heat. Add the onion and cooked until soft and translucent, about 5 minutes. Transfer to a bowl. Add the bread crumbs, marjoram, and 2 tablespoons of the butter to the bowl. Season with salt and pepper, and mix well. Use to stuff the body cavity, then truss the bird.

Place the chicken on a rack in a roasting pan, and rub the bird with the remaining 2 tablespoons butter. Roast, basting occasionally with the juices in the pan, until golden-brown and the juices show no sign of pink when the chicken's thigh is pierced, about 1 hour.

CHICKEN ON A BED OF GARLIC

Once a regional Provençal favorite, this dish's popularity has traveled far from its place of origin. The quantity of garlic may seem too much, but baking makes the cloves soft and mellow in flavor. Serve this with mashed potatoes to sop up the delicious butter.

BRAISED SQUAB WITH CABBAGE

MAKES 4 SERVINGS

1 (3½-pound) chicken, rinsed and patted dry
2 heads garlic (about 30 cloves), each clove peeled
5 tablespoons unsalted butter
Salt and freshly ground pepper, to taste

Preheat the oven to 375°F. Place 2 garlic cloves and 1 tablespoon butter in the chicken cavity. Season the bird inside and out with salt and pepper. Place the chicken on a rack in a roasting pan. Rub the bird with 2 tablespoons of butter, and put the remaining 2 tablespoons butter into the roasting pan. Roast for 30 minutes.

Add the remaining garlic cloves to the roasting pan. Continue roasting, basting often with the garlic-flavored butter in the pan, until the chicken is golden-brown and the juices show no sign of pink when the thigh is pierced, about 30 more minutes. (If the garlic is tender before the chicken is done, transfer the cloves to a bowl with a slotted spoon and keep warm.) Transfer the chicken to a platter and let stand for 5 minutes before carving. Serve the chicken, spooning a portion of the garlic and butter over each serving.

GRILLED CHICKEN DRUMSTICKS WITH DEVILED SAUCE

Deviled dishes always contain hot and/or spicy seasonings—here mustard, cayenne pepper, and Worcestershire sauce are used. Serve the drumsticks with rice and a green salad for a simple meal.

MAKES 4 SERVINGS

¼ cup dry sherry
1 tablespoon tarragon vinegar, or 1 tablespoon white wine vinegar with ½ teaspoon dried tarragon
2 teaspoons Worcestershire sauce
2 teaspoons Dijon mustard or prepared English mustard
A pinch of cayenne pepper
¼ teaspoon freshly ground black pepper
Salt, to taste
8 chicken drumsticks
3 tablespoons olive oil

In a shallow glass baking dish, mix the sherry, vinegar, Worcestershire sauce, mustard, cayenne, black pepper, and a seasoning of salt. Cut deep slashes in the thickest parts of the drumsticks, parallel to the bone. Place in the marinade, and rub it over the drumsticks and into the slashes. Cover and marinate at room temperature for 1 hour, or in the refrigerator for up to 8 hours.

Build a hot charcoal fire in an outdoor grill. Lightly oil the grill. Remove the drumsticks from the marinade, reserving the marinade. Brush the drumsticks with half of the oil. Grill the drumsticks directly over the coals, turning occasionally, until seared on all sides, about 8 minutes. Move the chicken to the cooler outside edges of the grill. Cover with the grill lid and continue cooking, basting alternately with the marinade and the remaining oil, until the meat of the drumsticks shows no sign of pink at the bone, about 30 minutes. Serve hot.

CHICKEN POT PIE

This is one of the best examples of delicious farmhouse cooking. If you don't have the time to make your own crust, you could use store-bought puff pastry.

MAKES 4 TO 6 SERVINGS

6 chicken thighs
4 small boiling potatoes, cut into cubes
8 small white boiling onions, peeled and an "X" cut into each end
3 medium carrots, cut into ½-inch lengths
3 medium celery ribs, cut into ½-inch lengths
2 tablespoons chopped fresh parsley
¼ teaspoon dried thyme
Salt and freshly ground pepper, to taste
3 tablespoons unsalted butter
3 tablespoons all-purpose flour
½ cup heavy cream
Basic Pie Dough
1 egg yolk, beaten with 1 tablespoon milk

Place the chicken in a large saucepan with the potatoes, onions, carrots, and celery. Add enough cold water to cover by 2 inches. Bring to a simmer over high heat, skimming off the foam that rises to the surface. Add the parsley and thyme, and season with salt and pepper. Reduce the heat to low and simmer until the chicken meat shows no sign of pink near the bone, about 25 minutes. Drain the chicken and vegetables, reserving the cooking liquid. Discard the skin and bones from the chicken, and cut into bite-sized pieces. Set the chicken and vegetables aside. Strain the chicken broth, skim off any fat from the surface, and reserve 2 cups of the broth.

In a medium saucepan, melt the butter over medium-low heat. Whisk in the flour and let bubble without browning for 2 minutes. Gradually whisk in the reserved broth. Bring to a simmer, and simmer for 5 minutes. Stir in the cream and simmer for 5 more minutes. Season. Add the chicken and vegetables to the sauce and stir to mix. Let cool completely.

Meanwhile, on a lightly floured work surface, roll out the pastry dough into a ⅛-inch-thick circle. Trim into a circle about 2 inches larger than the top diameter of a 2½-quart round casserole. Place the circle of dough on a large baking sheet, cover with plastic wrap, and refrigerate for 20 minutes.

Preheat the oven to 375°F. Transfer the cooled chicken mixture to the casserole. Place the circle of dough over the top of the casserole, and press the dough to the sides. Brush the crust lightly with some of the egg mixture, and cut an "X" in the center. Place the casserole on a baking sheet, and bake until the crust is golden-brown, 35 to 45 minutes.

CHICKEN WITH RICE, ALMONDS, AND RAISINS

Dried fruits and nuts are often combined with meat or poultry in Middle Eastern cooking. If you like, make the chicken stock from the chicken giblets, simmering them with a small chopped onion and a few parsley sprigs in 4 cups water and ½ cup dry vermouth or white wine for about 45 minutes.

MAKES 4 SERVINGS

1 (3½-pound) chicken, rinsed and patted dry
3 tablespoons unsalted butter
2 tablespoons lemon juice
Salt and freshly ground pepper, to taste
⅛ teaspoon saffron threads
½ cup dry vermouth or white wine
¾ cup blanched almonds, each separated in half
½ cup raisins
1 cinnamon stick
2 to 3 whole cloves
3 tablespoons olive oil
½ cup chopped shallots
2 cups long-grain rice
3½ cups light chicken stock
2 tablespoons chopped fresh parsley

Preheat the oven to 375°F. Place 1 tablespoon of the butter inside the chicken's body cavity. Rub the outside of the chicken with the lemon juice, then rub with the remaining 2 tablespoons butter. Season inside and out with salt and pepper. Place the bird on a rack in a roasting pan. Roast, basting occasionally with the juices in the pan, until the chicken is golden-brown and the juices show no sign of pink when the thigh is pierced, about 1 hour.

Meanwhile, put the saffron and vermouth in a small bowl and set aside to soak. In a dry medium frying pan, cook the halved almonds and the raisins with the cinnamon and cloves over medium heat, stirring often, until the almonds are lightly toasted, about 3 minutes. Transfer to a plate. In the same frying pan, heat the oil over medium heat. Add the shallots and cook until softened, about 3 minutes. Add the rice and cook, stirring often, until opaque, about 3 minutes. Add the stock, saffron mixture, and reserved spiced almonds and raisins, and season with salt and pepper. Bring to a simmer, then reduce the heat to low. Cover and simmer, without stirring, until the rice has absorbed the liquid and is tender, about 20 minutes.

Pour out all of the juices in the chicken cavity into the roasting pan, and transfer the roasted chicken to a warmed platter. Stir the contents of the roasting pan into the rice, along with the parsley. Carve the chicken and serve with the rice.

CHICKEN WITH POTATOES AND MUSHROOMS

The potatoes and mushrooms play important roles in this dish, so try to get the best ones available at your farmers' market.

MAKES 4 SERVINGS

4 tablespoons unsalted butter
2 tablespoons vegetable oil
1 (3½-pound) chicken, rinsed, patted dry, and cut into 6 pieces
18 small new or fingerling potatoes (preferably no bigger than walnuts), scrubbed, or 1 pound red-skinned potatoes, scrubbed and cut into 1-inch pieces
4 ounces fresh wild mushrooms such as chanterelles, or cultivated mushrooms such as cremini or oyster, sliced
Salt and freshly ground pepper, to taste
1 tablespoon chopped fresh parsley
2 garlic cloves, minced
⅔ cup light chicken stock

In a large frying pan, heat 2 tablespoons of the butter and 1 tablespoon of the oil over medium heat. Add the chicken and cook, turning the pieces occasionally, until golden-brown all over, about 10 minutes.

Meanwhile, in another frying pan, heat the remaining butter and oil over medium heat. Add the potatoes and cook until lightly browned, about 7 minutes. Add the sliced mushrooms, stir to mix with the potatoes, and cook for 2 minutes. Add the potatoes and mushrooms, along with their butter, to the chicken. Season with salt and pepper. Cover and reduce the heat to low. Cook gently until the potatoes are tender and the chicken meat shows no sign of pink at the bone, about 30 minutes. Stir the parsley and garlic into the chicken and vegetables. Cook, uncovered, until the garlic is softened, 3 to 4 minutes.

Transfer the chicken, potatoes, and mushrooms to a serving platter and keep warm. Skim off the fat from the cooking juices in the pan. Add the stock to the pan and bring to a boil, scraping up the browned bits with a wooden spoon. Boil until the liquid has reduced by half, 2 to 3 minutes. Pour over the chicken and serve immediately.

COQ AU VIN

Chicken simmered in red wine is one of the best dishes to make for an autumn supper. All it needs is plain boiled potatoes or turnips, and a green salad.

MAKES 4 SERVINGS

4 tablespoons unsalted butter, at room temperature
1 tablespoon vegetable oil
4 ounces slab bacon, rind removed, cut into
  ¼- by 1½-inch sticks
1 (3½-pound) chicken, rinsed, patted dry, and cut into
  8 pieces
½ cup all-purpose flour
2 garlic cloves, crushed
2 cups hearty red wine
1 bouquet garni of 2 sprigs fresh thyme and 2 sprigs
  fresh parsley
Salt and freshly ground pepper, to taste
12 white boiling onions, peeled
12 button mushrooms
Beurre Manié, made with ½ tablespoon each unsalted
  butter and all-purpose flour (optional)

Preheat the oven to 350°F. In a large flameproof casserole, heat 2 tablespoons of the butter and the oil over medium heat. Add the bacon strips and cook until lightly browned, about 4 minutes. Using a slotted spoon, transfer the bacon to paper towels to drain, leaving the fat in the casserole. Dip the chicken pieces in the flour, and shake off the excess. In batches if necessary, add the chicken pieces to the casserole and cook, turning once, until nicely browned on all sides, about 10 minutes. Return the bacon to the casserole, and add the garlic. Cook until the garlic is fragrant, about 1 minute. Add the wine and bouquet garni, and season with salt and pepper. Bring to a simmer, then cover and transfer to the oven. Cook until the chicken is tender and the meat shows no sign of pink near the bone, about 1 hour.

Meanwhile, bring a medium saucepan of lightly salted water to a boil over high heat. Add the boiling onions and cook until barely tender, about 10 minutes. Drain and pat dry. Heat the remaining 2 tablespoons of butter in a medium frying pan over medium heat. Add the onions and cook, turning occasionally, until

lightly browned, about 5 minutes. Remove with a slotted spoon, and set aside on a plate. Add the mushrooms to the pan, with a little more butter, if needed, and cook until lightly browned, about 8 minutes. Add to the onions.

When the chicken is tender, add the onions and mushrooms to the casserole. Cook, covered, for 5 more minutes, just to heat the vegetables through. Using a slotted spoon, transfer the chicken, bacon, and vegetables to a deep serving bowl. Cover with foil to keep warm. Skim the fat from the surface of the cooking liquid. Bring to a simmer over medium heat, and cook until reduced, 5 to 10 minutes. Taste to check the seasoning, and discard the bouquet garni. If you prefer a thicker sauce, reduce the heat to low, whisk in the beurre manié, and simmer until no trace of raw flour flavor remains, about 5 minutes. Pour the sauce over the chicken and serve immediately.

CHICKEN PAPRIKA

This recipe represents simple home cooking at its best—just a few ingredients cleverly combined to make a satisfying meal. Serve with hot buttered noodles, perhaps sprinkled with poppy seeds.

MAKES 4 SERVINGS

2 tablespoons unsalted butter
1 tablespoon vegetable oil
1 (3½-pound) chicken, rinsed, patted dry, and cut into
  6 pieces
2 large onions, chopped
2 tablespoons sweet Hungarian paprika
Salt, to taste
⅔ cup canned tomato purée
⅔ cup sour cream

Preheat the oven to 300°F. In a flameproof casserole, heat the butter and vegetable oil together over medium-high heat. In batches, if necessary, add the chicken pieces and cook, turning once, until nicely browned all over, about 8 minutes. Transfer to a plate, leaving the fat in the casserole.

Add the onions to the casserole and reduce the heat to medium. Cook, stirring often, until golden-brown, about 8 minutes. Stir in the paprika and cook for 1 minute. Return the chicken to the pot, and season with salt. Cover the casserole with foil, then with the lid to make a tight seal. Transfer to the oven and cook until the chicken shows no sign of pink at the bone, about 1 hour. Stir in the tomato purée. Continue cooking until the purée is heated through, about 5 minutes. Serve on warmed dinner plates, topping each serving with a dollop of sour cream.

TEXAS FRIED CHICKEN BREAST WITH SALSA

This buttermilk-dipped version of popular fried chicken gives a crisp crust with a juicy interior.

MAKES 4 SERVINGS

  1 cup buttermilk
  1 teaspoon Tabasco sauce
  4 (7-ounce) boneless, skinless chicken breast halves, lightly pounded to an even thickness
  1 cup all-purpose flour
  Salt and freshly ground pepper, to taste
  Vegetable oil, for frying
  Mexican Salsa Cruda, for serving

In a shallow dish, mix together the buttermilk and Tabasco sauce. Add the chicken breasts and turn to coat. Cover and refrigerate for at least 1 and up to 8 hours.

In another shallow bowl, mix the flour with a seasoning of salt and pepper. Wipe off the excess buttermilk from the breasts. Dip each chicken breast in the flour, then back into the buttermilk, and then into the flour again. Shake off the excess flour. Place the coated breasts on a wire cake rack and refrigerate for 1 hour to set the coating.

Coq au Vin

Pour enough oil into a large frying pan to come approximately ¼ inch up the sides. Heat the oil over medium heat until it is very hot, but not smoking. Add the chicken breasts and cook them, turning once, until they are golden-brown on both sides, 12 to 15 minutes. (The oil should be bubbling steadily, but not furiously. Adjust the heat as necessary.) Drain the chicken breasts thoroughly on paper towels, and serve with the salsa.

BAKED CHICKEN WITH LEMON AND OLIVES

Mediterranean olives are the key to the success of this dish. Use either brine-cured black olives, such as Kalamata or Gaeta, or cracked Sicilian green olives. The best way to pit the olives is to smash them underneath a large frying pan, one at a time, and then to discard the pits (it doesn't matter that the olives themselves are slightly crushed). Serve the tangy roasting juices from the chicken and the olives over hot cooked rice.

ROAST CHICKEN BREASTS WITH
ASIAN MARINADE

MAKES 4 SERVINGS
  1 (4-pound) chicken, rinsed, patted dry, and cut into
    8 pieces
  2 large lemons
  2 tablespoons extra virgin olive oil
  8 garlic cloves, unpeeled
  1 tablespoon chopped fresh rosemary or 1½ teaspoons
    dried rosemary
  1½ teaspoons dried oregano
  Salt, to taste
  ½ teaspoon chile flakes
  1 cup pitted black or green Mediterranean olives

Place the chicken, skin side up, in a large baking dish.
Squeeze the juice of 1 lemon over the chicken. Add the
oil, garlic, rosemary, oregano, salt, and chile flakes,
and toss well. Cover and let marinate for 30 minutes
at room temperature, or put in the refrigerator and let
marinate for up to 4 hours.

Preheat the oven to 400°F. Slice the other lemon
into thin rounds and place over the chicken. Bake,
basting occasionally, for 35 minutes. Scatter the olives
around the chicken, and continue baking until the
chicken meat shows no sign of pink at the bone,
about 10 more minutes. With a large spoon, crush the
garlic cloves in the pan and discard the skins. Serve
the chicken hot, with the roasting juices and olives.

QUICK-FRIED CHICKEN WITH GARLIC AND CHILE PEPPERS

Cooked like this, chicken legs are very succulent. Ask
your butcher to chop the thighs and drumsticks.

MAKES 4 SERVINGS
  6 tablespoons soy sauce
  3 tablespoons dry sherry
  1 tablespoon honey
  ½ teaspoon freshly ground white pepper
  4 chicken thighs, chopped into 3 pieces
  4 chicken drumsticks, chopped in half
  ¾ cup cornstarch

Peanut or vegetable oil, for frying
10 garlic cloves, sliced
5 hot red chile peppers, seeded and sliced
Salt, to taste
Crisp lettuce leaves, for serving

In a shallow dish, combine the soy sauce, sherry, honey, and white pepper. Add the chicken thighs and drumsticks and toss to combine. Cover and let marinate in the refrigerator, turning the chicken pieces occasionally, for about 2 hours. Drain the chicken and pat dry with paper towels.

Preheat the oven to 200°F. Toss the chicken in the cornstarch, shaking off the excess. Pour enough oil into a large frying pan to come about ¼ inch up the sides. Heat the oil over medium-high heat until very hot and almost smoking. In batches, and without crowding, add the chicken pieces to the pan and cook, turning once, until the chicken is crusty and deep golden-brown all over, 8 to 10 minutes. Transfer to a plate and keep warm in the oven while cooking the rest of the chicken.

Pour off all but 2 tablespoons of the oil from the pan. Add the garlic and chile peppers and cook until crisp and slightly browned, about 2 minutes. Return the chicken to the pan, and mix with the garlic and chiles. Using a slotted spoon, transfer to a warmed serving platter. Season with salt and serve immediately, with a bowl of lettuce leaves passed on the side.

ROAST CHICKEN BREASTS WITH ASIAN MARINADE

Boneless chicken breasts are quick to prepare. You will get more succulent results if you cook them with the skin and bones still attached.

MAKES 6 SERVINGS
6 chicken breast halves
3 tablespoons vegetable oil
Roasted Tomato Sauce, made without butter
Asian Marinade
¼ cup light soy sauce
¼ cup dark soy sauce, or 3 tablespoons light soy sauce and 1 tablespoon molasses
2 tablespoons light brown sugar
1 tablespoon rice vinegar or sherry vinegar
2 teaspoons Asian dark sesame oil
1 (2-inch) piece fresh ginger, thinly sliced
3 garlic cloves, sliced

To make the marinade, mix all the ingredients together in a medium bowl. Place the chicken breasts side by side in a shallow earthenware or glass baking dish. Pour the marinade over the breasts, and cover. Let marinate in the refrigerator, turning the chicken occasionally, for at least 2 and up to 8 hours.

Preheat the oven to 350°F. Drain the chicken breasts, reserving the marinade. In a large frying pan, heat the oil over medium heat. Add the chicken breasts and cook, turning once, until a golden mahogany color on both sides, about 6 minutes.

Transfer the chicken breasts to a large roasting pan. Roast, basting often with the reserved marinade, just until the juices run clear yellow when the breasts are pierced with a knife, about 20 minutes. Remove from the oven, place on a heated serving platter, and cover with foil. Return to the turned-off oven to keep warm while making the sauce.

Tilt the pan and skim off any fat on the surface of the cooking juices. (If there are burned bits on the bottom of the roasting pan, pour the juices into a saucepan.) Add the tomato sauce to the juices. Place the pan over medium heat and bring to a boil, scraping up any browned bits on the bottom of the roasting pan with a wooden spoon. Bubble the sauce for a minute or two, stirring. Serve the chicken with the sauce.

Grilled Chicken Breasts: Build a charcoal fire in an outdoor grill, and let the coals burn until they are covered with white ash. Grill the marinated, drained breasts, basting often with the reserved marinade, until the juices run clear when a breast is pierced with a knife, 20 to 25 minutes. If the coals flare up, move the chicken to the outside edges of the grill, not over the coals. Cover the grill with the lid, leaving all the vents open, and continue grilling. Serve with Asian Peanut Sauce, instead of the roasted tomato sauce.

CHICKEN BREAST WITH SUN-DRIED TOMATOES AND BASIL

Here's a low-fat recipe that is easy to make after a day's work, yet elegant enough for a dinner party.

MAKES 4 SERVINGS
1 tablespoon extra virgin olive oil
4 (6-ounce) boneless, skinless chicken breast halves, lightly pounded to an even thickness
Salt and freshly ground pepper, to taste
⅔ cup dry vermouth
⅓ cup chopped sun-dried tomatoes (packed without oil), soaked in water until plumped and drained
1 garlic clove, minced and mashed to a paste with a sprinkle of salt
2 tablespoons chopped fresh basil
2 tablespoons unsalted butter (optional)
2 tablespoons fresh basil, cut into thin strips

Heat the oil in a large nonstick frying pan over medium heat. Add the chicken breasts and cook, turning once, until browned on both sides and cooked through, about 8 minutes. Season with salt and pepper. Transfer to a plate, and cover to keep warm. Add the vermouth, tomatoes, and garlic to the pan and bring to a boil, scraping up any browned bits from the bottom with a wooden spoon. Cook until reduced by half, about 2 minutes. Stir in the chopped basil. Off the heat, swirl in the optional butter. Place the chicken breasts on dinner plates, spoon the sauce over the breasts, and garnish with the strips of basil.

INDIAN CHICKEN KEBABS

This exotic marinade is a great way to add excitement to chicken, which sometimes can seem just a little too familiar.

MAKES 4 SERVINGS

8 boneless, skinless chicken thighs, cut into 1-inch pieces
1/3 cup lime juice
1/2 teaspoon salt
2/3 cup plain yogurt
1 small onion, coarsely chopped
1 (2-inch) piece fresh ginger, coarsely chopped
3 garlic cloves, halved
2 teaspoons ground cumin
1 teaspoon turmeric
1 teaspoon ground coriander
1 teaspoon paprika
1 teaspoon garam masala
1/2 teaspoon freshly ground black pepper
1/4 teaspoon ground cloves
1/8 teaspoon cayenne pepper
8 sprigs fresh cilantro, for garnish
1 lime, quartered, for garnish

In a shallow glass dish, combine the chicken thighs, lime juice, and salt. Cover and let stand at room temperature for 30 minutes.

In a food processor fitted with the metal blade or a blender, process all of the remaining ingredients, except the cilantro and lime wedges, to make a smooth paste. (If the mixture seems too thick to process smoothly, add a little water.) Rub the paste through a sieve. Add to the chicken and mix well with your fingers. Cover and let marinate in the refrigerator for at least 3 and up to 8 hours.

Build a charcoal fire in an outdoor grill and let burn until the coals are covered with white ash. Lightly oil the grill. Thread the chicken onto eight small skewers. (If you will be using wooden skewers, soak them in water for at least 30 minutes, then drain.) Grill the chicken kebabs until a crust forms on the side nearest the coals, about 5 minutes. Turn the kebabs and continue grilling until they are cooked through, about 5 more minutes. Serve the kebabs garnished with cilantro and lime wedges.

GLAZED CORNISH GAME HENS WITH RICE AND PINE NUT STUFFING

Cornish game hens always add a festive touch, whether they are simply for a family meal or for a company dinner party. These have an Asian accent, with a delicious gingered rice stuffing and glazing of plum sauce. Serve accompanied by a colorful stir-fry of vegetables.

MAKES 4 SERVINGS

4 (1½-pound) Cornish game hens, rinsed and patted dry
1/2 cup plum sauce
Rice Stuffing
1/2 cup long-grain rice
1/4 cup pine nuts
2 teaspoons vegetable oil
2 scallions, chopped
2 teaspoons minced fresh ginger
1 garlic clove, minced
1 tablespoon dry sherry
Salt and freshly ground pepper, to taste

To make the rice stuffing, bring a medium saucepan of lightly salted water to a boil over high heat. Add the long-grain rice and boil, uncovered, until tender, about 15 minutes. Drain and rinse under cold water, then transfer to a bowl.

In a dry medium frying pan placed over medium heat, cook the pine nuts, stirring often, until they are lightly toasted, about 2 minutes. Add these to the rice. In the same pan, heat the vegetable oil. Add the scallions, ginger, and garlic and cook until fragrant, about 30 seconds. Stir in the sherry and cook until evaporated, about 30 more seconds. Stir into the rice. Season with salt and pepper.

Preheat the oven to 450°F. Fill the hens with the stuffing, and close with toothpicks. Place the hens on a rack in a large roasting pan. Roast for 15 minutes. Reduce the oven to 350°F. Roast for 45 minutes longer. Brush the hens lightly with the plum sauce. Continue roasting, brushing occasionally with the remaining plum sauce, until the hens are well glazed and a meat thermometer inserted in the thickest part of the thigh, not touching a bone, reads 180°F, 20 to 30 minutes. (The total baking time for this dish is about 1½ hours.)

ROAST DUCK WITH BACON AND LIVER STUFFING

The stuffing in this duck is quite rich: just a spoonful each will suffice. As to how many people a duck will serve, consider your side dishes—with several, you could serve a quarter of a duck per person.

MAKES 2 TO 4 SERVINGS
1 (5-pound) duck, neck and giblets reserved
1 small onion, chopped
1 medium carrot, chopped
1 medium orange, halved
1 small bunch fresh thyme, or 1 teaspoon dried thyme
1/3 cup chopped shallots
2 strips bacon, chopped
Salt and freshly ground pepper, to taste
1 tablespoon olive oil
1/2 cup dry white wine, heated
2 teaspoons all-purpose flour

Rinse the duck and pat dry. Pull out the fat from both sides at the end of the body cavity. Cut off the excess neck skin and coarsely chop. Chop the neck into 1-inch pieces. Return the duck and its liver to the refrigerator.

In a medium saucepan over medium heat, cook the chopped neck skin until it begins to render its fat, about 5 minutes. Add the chopped neck and giblets and cook, turning occasionally, until browned, about 10 minutes. Add the onion and carrots, and cook until softened, about 5 minutes. Add 5 cups water, half of the orange, and the thyme. Bring to a simmer over medium heat, and skim off the foam that rises to the surface. Reduce the heat to low and simmer for at least 2 and up to 4 hours. Strain the stock and skim off any fat that rises to the surface. Measure out 2 cups of stock, saving the remainder for another use.

Preheat the oven to 425°F. Using a pot fork, prick the duck skin all over, being sure not to pierce the duck meat. Chop the duck liver into 1/4-inch pieces. In a small bowl, combine the liver, shallots, and bacon, and season with salt and pepper. Spoon the liver mixture into the duck body cavity. Squeeze the juice from the remaining orange half all over the duck. Score the skin of the orange half with the tines of a fork, and rub all over with salt. Place the orange half inside the duck with the stuffing. Place the duck on a rack in a roasting pan, and drizzle with the oil.

Roast for 15 minutes, then reduce the oven to 350°F. Continue roasting, basting alternately with hot wine and the pan drippings, until the juices are mostly yellow with a hint of pink when the duck is pierced in the thigh, about 1 1/4 hours. Transfer to a serving dish.

Spoon off all but 1 tablespoon of the fat from the roasting pan. Place the pan over medium-low heat.

Whisk in the flour and cook until lightly browned, 1 to 2 minutes. Whisk in the reserved stock, scraping up the browned bits in the bottom of the pan, and bring to a simmer. Simmer until the sauce has thickened, about 5 minutes. Season, and pour into a warmed sauceboat. Carve the duck, discarding the orange half, and serve with the sauce.

BALLOTINE OF DUCK WITH PRUNE AND MADEIRA STUFFING

A boned roast duck, filled with a luxurious stuffing of veal, pork, and wine-soaked prunes, is a spectacular centerpiece for a special meal. Reserve the bones and giblets for making the stock, which will become a sauce for the sliced duck. Wild rice, baby carrots, and tiny green beans are perfect accompaniments.

MAKES 6 TO 8 SERVINGS
1 (5-pound) duck, boned
Salt and freshly ground pepper, to taste
6 cups brown duck or chicken stock
2 teaspoons cornstarch mixed with 1 tablespoon Madeira
Stuffing
1/3 cup coarsely chopped prunes
1/3 cup Madeira or tawny port
1 tablespoon unsalted butter
1/3 cup chopped shallots
1/2 cup fresh bread crumbs
1 large egg
2 tablespoons coarsely chopped pistachios
1 tablespoon chopped fresh parsley
1 1/4 teaspoons salt
1/4 teaspoon freshly ground pepper
12 ounces ground pork
12 ounces ground veal or turkey

To make the stuffing, put the prunes and Madeira in a small bowl and let soak for at least 15 minutes or up to 1 hour. In a medium frying pan, heat the butter over medium heat. Add the shallots and cook until they are lightly browned, about 4 minutes. Transfer to a bowl and let cool completely. Add the prunes and the Madeira to the shallots, along with the bread crumbs, egg, pistachios, parsley, salt, and pepper. Mix together, then add the ground pork and veal, and mix well.

Place the duck, skin side down, on the work surface. Spread the stuffing inside the duck. Use a sturdy needle and kitchen string to sew it up, pressing the stuffing inside the duck to help form it back into its original shape. Season the duck, and prick the skin all over with a skewer (do not pierce into the meat). (The duck can be prepared up to 2 hours ahead of cooking and kept, covered, in the refrigerator.)

Preheat the oven to 400°F. Place the duck on a rack in a roasting pan. Slowly pour 1 cup boiling water over the duck. Roast, basting occasionally with the pan juices, until a meat thermometer inserted in the center of the duck reads 165°F, about 1½ hours. Transfer to a serving platter and let stand for 10 minutes.

While the duck is roasting, bring the duck stock to a boil in a large saucepan, and boil until reduced to 2 cups, 30 to 40 minutes. Stir in the cornstarch mixture, and cook until slightly thickened. Set the sauce aside; reheat when ready to serve.

Remove the kitchen twine from the duck. Using a sharp, thin knife, slice the duck into ½-inch-thick slices. Serve the duck, spooning a little of the sauce over each portion.

SAUTÉED DUCK BREASTS WITH GINGERED PEARS

In this recipe the duck breasts are sautéed until medium-rare, then ripe pears are tossed in the pan to make a quick side dish that complements the rich duck meat beautifully. In season, you can substitute peaches or nectarines for the pears.

MAKES 4 SERVINGS
4 (10-ounce) boneless duck breasts (magrets)
½ teaspoon ground allspice
Salt and freshly ground pepper, to taste
2 tablespoons minced shallots
1 tablespoon minced fresh ginger
2 large ripe pears (such as Bartletts), cored and cut into ¼-inch-thick wedges
1 teaspoon granulated sugar
1 tablespoon lemon juice
1 teaspoon chopped fresh mint or cilantro

Season the duck breasts with the allspice, salt, and pepper. Place skin side down in a large cold frying pan, preferably nonstick. Cook over medium heat until the skin is deep golden-brown, about 10 minutes, pouring off the fat as it accumulates. Turn the breasts over and continue cooking until they are medium-rare, about 2 more minutes. Transfer to a plate and cover loosely with foil to keep warm.

Pour out all but 1 tablespoon of the fat from the pan. Return the pan to medium heat. Add the shallots and ginger and cook until softened, about 2 minutes. Add the pears, and sprinkle with the sugar. Cook until the pears are lightly browned, about 2 minutes. Gently stir in the lemon juice and mint. Season with salt and pepper. Slice the duck breasts on the bias into thick slices. Place a duck breast on each dinner plate, fanning out the slices, and serve with the gingered pears.

ROAST GOOSE WITH APPLE STUFFING

Geese are not very meaty, but the meat is rich. Good side dishes are sweet and sour cabbage, braised celery, and potato dumplings. A lot of fat will run out of the bird during cooking—you could skim it off the top of the liquid in the roasting pan and save it in a jar in the refrigerator. It makes excellent fried potatoes.

MAKES 6 TO 8 SERVINGS
1 (10- to 12-pound) goose, including the neck and giblets
3 cups chicken stock
Salt and freshly ground pepper
4 or 5 medium Golden Delicious apples, unpeeled, cored and left whole
½ cup semi-dry white wine, such as Riesling
1 medium onion, thinly sliced
1 tablespoon chopped fresh sage or 1½ teaspoons dried crumbled sage
1½ tablespoons all-purpose flour mixed with 3 tablespoons water

Use a cleaver or heavy knife to chop the neck into 2-inch pieces. Place the neck, giblets, and stock in a medium saucepan. Bring to a simmer over medium heat, and simmer for 30 minutes. Strain the stock.

Preheat the oven to 425°F. Place the goose in the sink and slowly pour about 1 quart boiling water all over the top of the bird. (This helps to release the fat.) Season the inside of the bird with salt and pepper. Stuff the goose with the apples. Using wooden skewers or a sturdy needle and kitchen string, close the body cavity and secure the neck skin to the back.

Pour the goose stock and wine into a roasting pan, and add the onion and sage. Place the goose, breast side down, on a rack in the pan. Roast for 1 hour, occasionally basting with the liquid in the pan and pricking the skin all over with a meat fork to help the fat run out (do not pierce the meat). Turn the goose breast side up, and reduce the oven to 350°F. Continue roasting, occasionally basting and pricking with the fork, until a meat thermometer inserted in the thickest part of the thigh reads 180°F, about 1½ hours longer (allow about 15 minutes per pound total roasting time). Transfer to a warmed platter, and keep warm by tenting with foil or returning to the turned-off oven.

Strain all the liquid in the pan into a glass bowl or measuring cup. Let stand for 5 minutes, then skim off all the clear fat. Return the degreased liquid to the pan, and bring to a simmer on the stove over medium heat. Whisk in the flour mixture, and simmer until thickened and no taste of raw flour remains. Season, and pour into a sauceboat. Carve the goose and serve with the sauce and the apples from inside the bird, which will have softened into a delicious stuffing.

ROAST TURKEY WITH HERB AND APPLE BREAD STUFFING

A gorgeous roast turkey is an icon of the holiday table, but a turkey's size alone (what other food does one cook that averages 20 pounds?) can make this a tricky proposition. Here are some basic tips for roasting a perfect bird:

Always choose a fresh bird over one that has been frozen or that has been injected with flavorings and fats. If you must use a frozen bird, defrost it in the refrigerator according to the instructions on the package.

Estimate at least 1 pound turkey for each guest, more if you want plenty of leftovers. Large tom turkeys have a higher proportion of meat to bone than smaller hens.

Roast the turkey in a preheated 325°F oven. This temperature promotes even browning and discourages shrinkage. For large tom turkeys (16 pounds and above), estimate 15 minutes per pound. For smaller hen turkeys (below 16 pounds), estimate 20 minutes per pound. If the birds are not stuffed, decrease the estimated cooking times by 2 minutes per pound.

Turkey roasting times are always an estimate, as there are many variables (from exact oven temperature to the density of the stuffing) that affect the final timing, so always test with a meat thermometer or an instant-read thermometer.

Covering the breast with foil will help keep the breast meat (which is much leaner than dark meat) from drying out. Remove the foil for the last hour of roasting so that the breast will be as browned as the rest of the bird.

Baste every 30 minutes to promote a brown skin.

Let the turkey stand for at least 20 minutes and up to 1 hour before carving. (It will stay perfectly warm—it takes quite a long time for a large bird to get cold.) Not only will this allow the juices to settle in the turkey meat and make for easier carving, but it also gives the cook extra time to gather all of the side dishes and finish the gravy.

MAKES 12 TO 16 SERVINGS

1 (18-pound) fresh turkey, neck and giblets (not liver) reserved, rinsed, patted dry, and excess fat removed

A double recipe of Herbed Bread Stuffing with Onions and Apples

4 tablespoons unsalted butter, softened

Salt and freshly ground pepper, to taste

1 medium onion, chopped

1 medium carrot, chopped

1 medium celery rib, chopped

4 cups chicken stock

2 sprigs parsley

6 tablespoons all-purpose flour

Preheat the oven to 325°F. Fill the neck and body cavities loosely with the stuffing. (Place the excess stuffing in a buttered baking dish, cover, and refrigerate to bake later: put in the oven just before the turkey has finished cooking and bake for 30 to 40 minutes.) Truss the turkey. Rub the bird with 3 tablespoons butter, and season with salt and pepper. Cover the breast tightly with a piece of aluminum foil.

Place on a roasting rack in a large, shallow roasting pan. Pour 1 cup of water into the pan. Roast, basting every 30 minutes with the pan drippings, for 3¼ hours. Remove the foil and continue roasting until a meat thermometer inserted in the thickest part of the thigh reads 180°F, about 1 more hour. If the drippings start to burn during roasting, add additional water to the pan. Transfer the turkey to a serving platter and let stand for at least 20 minutes before carving.

While the turkey is roasting, prepare a turkey stock. In a large saucepan, heat the remaining 1 tablespoon butter over medium heat. Chop the turkey neck into 2-inch pieces. Add the turkey neck and giblets to the pot and brown them all over, about 10 minutes. Add the onion, carrot, and celery. Cover and cook until the vegetables are soft, about 10 minutes. Add the chicken stock and 2 cups water and bring to a simmer, skimming off any foam. Add the parsley. Reduce the heat to low and simmer, uncovered, for 3 hours. Strain. (If desired, chop the giblets and boned turkey neck meat, and reserve to stir into the gravy.) Skim off any fat that rises to the surface of the turkey stock.

To make the gravy, pour off all the drippings from the roasting pan into a glass bowl and let stand for 5 minutes. Skim off and reserve any clear yellow fat that rises to the surface. Measure out 6 tablespoons fat, and discard the remainder. Add enough of the turkey stock to the degreased pan drippings to measure 4 cups. Place the roasting pan over two stove burners at medium-low heat. Pour the reserved fat into the pan, then whisk in the flour. Let cook until lightly browned, 1 to 2 minutes. Whisk in the turkey stock/cooking liquid and bring to a simmer. Cook until thickened and no taste of raw flour remains, about 5 minutes. Season with salt and pepper.

Pour the gravy into a warmed sauceboat and serve with the carved turkey.

VARIATIONS: Use Herbed Bread Stuffing with Sausage; Cornbread Stuffing with Ham and Pecans; or Oyster, Ham, and Cornbread Stuffing instead of the stuffing suggested above.

OVERLEAF: ROAST TURKEY WITH HERB AND APPLE BREAD STUFFING

Eggs and Cheese

Eggs are not always as wholesome as they should be, so care must be taken to be sure they are very fresh, clean, and uncracked. Unfortunately, some raw eggs have been found to be contaminated by the bacteria salmonella. While cooks are warned against serving undercooked eggs, this bacteria will be killed at temperatures about 170°F—a temperature that is easily reached with a hard-boiled egg, for example, but is impossible to achieve for a soft-boiled one. If you want to serve soft-boiled, poached, or sunnyside-up eggs, which will not reach the safe temperature of 170°F, realize that there is a small amount of risk involved. People with impaired immune systems, and the elderly or very young, may want to avoid undercooked eggs completely. The key is not to be alarmed, just sensible.

Soft-Boiled Eggs The old remark about not even being able to boil an egg is no joke. Often, the egg cracks from being bounced around in the boiling water, and the white pours out, and other times the egg yolk gets too hard. The term "boiled" is a misnomer—the eggs should be gently simmered. To cook soft-boiled eggs, bring a medium saucepan of unsalted water to a boil over medium heat (salt toughens the whites). Reduce the heat to low so the water is simmering. Gently lower the eggs into the water, and simmer for 3 to 5 minutes, depending on how soft you like your eggs.

Coddled Eggs These are a foolproof variation of soft-boiled eggs. Place the eggs in a saucepan and add enough unsalted cold water to cover. Bring the water to a boil over high heat. Immediately remove from the heat, cover, and let stand for 5 minutes.

Hard-Boiled Eggs The timing for hard-boiled eggs is crucial—don't overcook them, or the sulfur compounds in the white will be transformed into ferrous sulfide and create a dark gray ring around the yolk. Simmer the eggs in unsalted water for 10 to 12 minutes. Immediately drain the water out of the saucepan, and fill the pan with cold water to stop the eggs from cooking further. Run a gentle stream of cold water into the pan for a couple of minutes until the eggs are cool enough to handle. Shell the eggs as needed. Store hard-boiled eggs in the refrigerator.

Poached Eggs Use the freshest eggs available. Pour enough cold water into a large frying pan to come about halfway up the sides. Add 1 tablespoon vinegar (any type) to help set the whites, but no salt. Bring to a boil over high heat, then reduce the heat so the water is boiling steadily, but not rapidly. One at a time, holding the eggs just over the surface of the water, break them into the pan. For a nice, oval poached egg, use a large spoon to coax the white into shape, spooning the spreading white back over the egg. If the yolks aren't covered by the simmering water, spoon the water over them to help cook the tops. Simmer the eggs just until the whites are set and are no longer translucent. Use a slotted spoon to transfer them to a bowl of very hot water. They can now wait for a few minutes. If desired, trim off any untidy edges from the whites.

Scrambled Eggs These should be rich and creamy, not tough and overcooked. To make them, you need patience and a nonstick pan. Crack the eggs into a medium nonstick frying pan, and season with salt and pepper. Add about 2 tablespoons unsalted butter for every 3 eggs. Now place the pan over low heat. (If you don't have a nonstick frying pan, beat the eggs in a bowl with salt and pepper, and then melt the butter in the pan before adding the eggs.) Using a wooden spoon, constantly stir the eggs with intelligence—that is, moving all of the eggs around, not just stirring them clockwise in the center of the pan. Gradually, the eggs will begin to thicken. When they start to hold shape, but are still runny, remove the pan from the heat, and continue to stir until they become a soft, creamy mass.

Serve the scrambled eggs immediately, preferably with hot buttered toast. If you like, add any of the following to the eggs before they are scrambled: chopped fresh parsley or chives, chopped ham or prosciutto, or shredded fresh truffle. Scrambled eggs are also delicious topped with smoked salmon.

OLIVADA-STUFFED EGGS

These are extraordinary stuffed eggs, a far cry from the usual picnic fare.

MAKES 2 DOZEN
  1 dozen large eggs, hard-boiled
  3 tablespoons Olivada
  3 tablespoons mayonnaise
  Salt and freshly ground pepper, to taste
  Chopped fresh parsley, for garnish

Cut the eggs in half lengthwise; place the yolks in a medium bowl, and reserve the whites. Add the olivada and mayonnaise to the yolks, and mash with a fork until smooth. Season with salt and pepper. Put the mixture in a pastry bag fitted with a large open star pastry tube (Number 5). Pipe the olivada filling into the whites, and sprinkle with the parsley. The eggs can be kept, covered, in the refrigerator for up to 8 hours.

TUNISIAN EGGS IN VEGETABLE SAUCE

This dish originated in Tunisia, where it is called *chakchouka*, but is now enjoyed throughout the Middle East. Here, the eggs are poached directly in a sweet pepper and tomato sauce, rather than in water.

MAKES 4 SERVINGS

2 tablespoons olive oil
1 garlic clove, crushed under a knife and peeled
2 red or green bell peppers, seeded and cut into
  ½-inch-wide strips
1½ cups peeled, seeded, and chopped ripe plum
  tomatoes, or use drained canned tomatoes
Salt and freshly ground pepper, to taste
4 large eggs

In a medium frying pan, heat the oil over medium heat. Add the garlic and cook until golden-brown, about 2 minutes. Remove and discard the garlic clove. Add the peppers to the pan and reduce the heat to medium-low. Gently cook the peppers until soft, about 15 minutes. Stir in the tomatoes, and season with salt and pepper. Bring to a simmer, then partially cover the pan and cook until the sauce has thickened, about 15 minutes. Taste to check the seasoning, and adjust if necessary.

One at a time, carefully break the eggs onto the vegetable sauce. Cover and cook just until the eggs are set, about 5 minutes. Serve immediately, directly from the pan.

SCRAMBLED EGGS WITH PEPPERS

Here's the Basque way to cook eggs with peppers and tomatoes, in a dish called *pipérade*. It's traditionally eaten with Bayonne ham.

MAKES 4 SERVINGS

2 tablespoons olive oil
2 medium onions, thinly sliced
2 bell peppers, 1 red and 1 green, seeded and cut into
  ½-inch-wide strips
2 garlic cloves, crushed and minced to a paste with a
  sprinkle of salt
1½ cups peeled, seeded, and coarsely chopped ripe
  plum tomatoes, or use drained canned tomatoes
Salt and freshly ground pepper, to taste
4 large eggs

In a large frying pan, heat the oil over medium heat. Add the onions and cook until soft and translucent, about 5 minutes. Add the peppers and garlic and cook until the peppers are softened, about 5 minutes. Stir in the tomatoes, and season with salt and pepper. Bring to a simmer, then reduce the heat to medium-low. Cook until the sauce has thickened, about 15 minutes.

In a medium bowl, beat the eggs. Stir them into the pepper stew. Cook, stirring, until the eggs are just beginning to set, 1 to 2 minutes. Serve immediately, directly from the pan.

OMELETS

For a quick meal, an omelet is hard to beat, and the possibilities for flavorings and fillings are practically endless. For each omelet, break 2 or 3 large eggs into a bowl, and season with salt and pepper to taste. Beat just enough to break the eggs down, but not so much that they get foamy and filled with air. Heat 1 tablespoon unsalted butter in a medium nonstick frying pan until it is very hot and the butter foam subsides. Pour in the egg mixture. Using a rubber spatula, lift up the cooked, set edges of the omelet, and tilt the pan to let the uncooked portion run underneath. When the top of the omelet is barely set, but still shiny, use the spatula to fold one third of the omelet toward the center. Then roll the omelet onto a heated plate so that it is folded in three. It should look like a plump golden cushion. Eat at once: speed is essential when serving an omelet, too.

Omelet with Herbs: Add 1 teaspoon each finely chopped fresh tarragon, chives, and parsley and 1½ teaspoons freshly grated Parmesan cheese to the beaten eggs. If you have it, add 1 teaspoon chopped fresh chervil, too.

Cheese Omelet: Just before folding the omelet, sprinkle with ⅓ cup shredded Emmentaler or Gruyère cheese. Or, use half Emmentaler or Gruyère with half freshly grated Parmesan cheese.

Mushroom Omelet: In a medium frying pan, heat 1 tablespoon unsalted butter over medium heat. Add ½ cup sliced mushrooms, 1 tablespoon chopped fresh parsley, and ½ clove garlic, minced. Cook until the mushrooms have given off their liquid and are lightly browned, about 8 minutes. Season with salt and pepper. Scatter the mushrooms over the omelet before folding.

Shrimp Omelet: In a medium frying pan, combine 6 medium shrimp, peeled and deveined, and ⅓ cup heavy cream. Bring to a simmer over medium heat, and cook until the shrimp are firm and pink and the cream has thickened, about 3 minutes. Stir in 2 teaspoons chopped fresh chives, and season with salt and pepper. Spoon over the omelet before folding.

Spinach and Cheese Omelet: In a medium frying pan, heat 1 tablespoon unsalted butter over medium heat. Add 2 cups shredded fresh spinach leaves, and cook until the spinach is wilted and tender, about 5 minutes. Place the spinach in a colander and press to remove any excess moisture. Let cool completely. Add to the beaten eggs, along with 2 tablespoons freshly grated Parmesan cheese.

Ham Omelet: In a frying pan, heat 1 tablespoon unsalted butter over medium heat. Add ¼ cup finely chopped smoked ham and cook until heated through, about 5 minutes. Let cool completely. Add to the beaten eggs (season with less salt than usual, as the ham may be salty).

OMELET WITH ARTICHOKES AND PARSLEY

If you have a 12-inch nonstick frying pan, you can make a single large omelet: in this case, beat all the eggs together, and then use just 2 tablespoons butter for cooking the omelet.

MAKES 4 SERVINGS

Juice of 1 lemon
8 large artichokes
8 tablespoons (1 stick) unsalted butter
1 garlic clove, crushed under a knife and peeled
Salt and freshly ground pepper, to taste
1 tablespoon chopped fresh parsley
8 large eggs

Stir the lemon juice into a large bowl of cold water. Working with 1 artichoke at a time, trim off all the leaves and remove the hairy choke, leaving just the artichoke bottom. Cut the bottom into ¼-inch-thick slices, and drop into the bowl of water.

Drain the artichoke slices thoroughly and then pat them dry with paper towels. In a large frying pan, heat 4 tablespoons of the butter over medium-low heat. Add the artichokes and the crushed garlic, and season with salt and pepper. Cover and cook until the artichokes are beginning to soften, about 10 minutes. Uncover and cook until golden-brown and tender, about 10 more minutes. Stir in the chopped parsley. Transfer to a large plate and cover with aluminum foil to keep warm.

In a bowl, lightly beat 2 of the eggs with a seasoning of salt and pepper. Heat 1 tablespoon of butter in a 7-inch nonstick frying pan over medium-high heat. Pour in the beaten eggs. Using a rubber spatula, lift up the cooked, set edges of the omelet, and tilt the pan to let the uncooked portion run underneath. Cook until the top of the omelet is barely set, but still shiny, about 2 minutes. Spoon about one fourth of the artichokes into the center of the omelet, arranged neatly in a vertical strip. Use the spatula to fold one third of the omelet toward the center, and then roll the omelet onto a heated platter so that it is folded in thirds. Serve the omelet immediately, or keep it warm in a 200°F oven while making the remaining three omelets in the same way.

Artichoke Frittata: Prepare the omelet in a 9-inch nonstick frying pan. When the eggs are barely set, spread the artichokes evenly over the surface of the omelet. Place in a preheated broiler and cook until the eggs are set and the artichokes are golden-brown in color, 1 to 2 minutes. Do not fold the omelet. Instead, cut it into wedges for serving.

FRITTATAS AND TORTILLAS

A frittata is a thick, flat, fairly solid omelet made with eggs and lightly cooked vegetables. It is cut into wedges like a cake, and served hot, warm, or at cool room temperature—the Italians prefer the latter.

A tortilla is the Spanish version of the frittata (not to be confused with the Mexican corn or flour flatbread, also called tortilla). Fried potatoes and onions are the usual ingredients, although spicy chorizo sausage, sweet peppers, and garlic may also be added. Wedges of cold tortilla are an essential part of the appetizers called *tapas*, available at almost every Spanish bar. Frittatas and tortillas are perfect picnic fare.

SPINACH FRITTATA

Serve this frittata accompanied by a bowl of juicy black olives.

MAKES 4 SERVINGS

2 tablespoons olive oil
2 garlic cloves, crushed
8 ounces spinach leaves, tough stems discarded
Salt and freshly ground pepper, to taste
6 large eggs
A pinch of grated nutmeg
¾ cup shredded Gruyère cheese
2 tablespoons heavy cream

In a medium frying pan, heat 1 tablespoon of the oil over medium heat. Add the garlic and crush it into the oil with a large spoon to release the flavor. Cook until the garlic is lightly browned, about 1 minute. Add the spinach, and season with salt. Stir until the spinach has wilted, about 1 minute. Then continue cooking until the most of the liquid has evaporated, about 10 minutes. Let cool completely. Transfer to a sieve and press the spinach to release any excess moisture. Chop coarsely and set aside.

Preheat the oven to 350°F. In a large bowl, lightly beat the eggs with the nutmeg and a seasoning of salt and pepper. Stir in the spinach, cheese, and cream. In a 10-inch flameproof round earthenware dish, or a metal cake pan, heat the remaining 1 tablespoon oil over medium heat. Pour in the egg mixture. Place in the oven and bake until firm and set, 20 to 25 minutes. Cut into wedges and serve hot, directly from the dish, or allow to cool to room temperature.

POTATO AND ONION TORTILLA

If you wish, add ½ cup chopped Serrano ham or prosciutto to the potatoes about 5 minutes before they have finished cooking.

MAKES 6 SERVINGS

5 tablespoons olive oil

3 medium boiling potatoes, peeled, quartered, and
thinly sliced

2 medium onions, thinly sliced parallel to the layers

Salt and freshly ground pepper, to taste

8 large eggs

In a large nonstick frying pan, heat 3 tablespoons of the oil over medium heat. Add the potatoes and onions, and season with salt and pepper. Cover and cook, stirring occasionally, until the potatoes are tender, about 20 minutes.

In a large bowl, lightly beat the eggs with a little salt and pepper. Pour the eggs into the frying pan. Cook uncovered, lifting up the set edges of the tortilla and tilting the pan to let the uncooked portion run underneath, until the eggs are set but the top is still shiny, 4 to 5 minutes. Place a plate on top of the tortilla, and invert the pan and plate together so the tortilla falls out onto the plate. Return the pan to the heat and add the remaining 2 tablespoons oil. When the oil is hot, slide the tortilla, cooked side up, off the plate back into the pan. Continue cooking until the underside is golden-brown, 2 to 3 minutes. Serve hot, warm, or at room temperature.

ZUCCHINI AND GOAT CHEESE FILO TART

A flaky, golden-brown crust of filo pastry encloses a rich zucchini, cheese, and nut filling. Serve the tart cut into wedges with a crisp green salad dressed with a simple vinaigrette.

MAKES 8 SERVINGS

1 pound zucchini (about 3 medium), shredded

Salt and freshly ground pepper, to taste

5 ounces soft goat cheese

¾ cup ricotta cheese

1 large egg

1 teaspoon lemon juice

2 tablespoons olive oil

1 medium onion, chopped

1 garlic clove, sliced

1 cup chopped pecans or walnuts

1 tablespoon chopped fresh basil or 1 teaspoon
dried basil

1 teaspoon chopped fresh thyme or ¼ teaspoon
dried thyme

5 (12- by 17-inch) sheets filo pastry, thawed if frozen

4 tablespoons butter, melted

Toss the shredded zucchini with ½ teaspoon salt in a medium bowl. Let stand for 20 minutes. Meanwhile,

in a large bowl, mash together the goat cheese, ricotta, egg, and lemon juice with a fork until combined. Set aside. In a medium frying pan, heat the oil over medium heat. Add the onion and garlic, and cook until the onion softens, about 5 minutes. Add to the cheese mixture. In the same pan, cook the pecans over medium heat, stirring often, until they are toasted and fragrant, about 3 minutes. Stir half of the pecans into the cheese mixture, setting the remainder aside. A handful at a time, squeeze the zucchini to remove excess juice, and add the zucchini to the bowl. Add the basil and thyme, and season with salt and pepper. Mix well.

Preheat the oven to 325°F. Lightly butter a 10-inch pie pan. Place the filo sheets on the work surface and cover with a damp towel. Lay one filo sheet on the work surface (keep the remaining filo sheets covered to prevent them from drying out), and brush lightly but completely with melted butter. Center the sheet in the pie pan, letting the corners hang over the sides. Repeat with a second filo sheet, placing the corners at different points of the compass from the first. Sprinkle with some of the reserved pecans. Continue with 3 more filo sheets, placing the corners of the progressive sheets at different points and sprinkling with the remaining pecans. Fill the tart with the cheese mixture. Loosely bring up the overhanging filo to enclose the filling completely and form a crown. Brush the top of the tart with the remaining butter. Place on a baking sheet and bake until crisp and golden, 35 to 45 minutes. Remove from the oven, cover with a damp cloth, and let cool for 10 minutes. Remove the cloth and cool until warm on a wire cake rack. To serve, slice into wedges with a serrated knife.

QUICHE

Quiche went through a raging fad in the 1960s, but then fell out of fashion. However, it makes such a pleasant brunch, lunch, or supper entrée, and can so easily be varied, that it is well worth keeping in the cook's repertoire. Like frittatas and tortillas, quiches are excellent served at just about any temperature, from piping hot to tepid.

The basic custard for a 9-inch quiche is 3 large eggs, 1 cup milk, and ⅓ cup heavy cream, seasoned with salt and pepper. Solid ingredients, such as cheese or cooked vegetables, are placed in a partially baked pastry shell, then the custard is poured into the shell. (To avoid spills, it is a good idea to set the quiche pan, filled with the solid ingredients only, on a baking sheet and place it in the oven before pouring in the custard.) You may need slightly more or less custard, depending on the quantity of solid ingredients. If you need more, whisk together 1 large egg, ⅓ cup milk,

BACON AND PARMESAN QUICHE

and 1½ tablespoons heavy cream with a pinch each of salt and pepper. To bake the quiche, follow the recipe for Bacon and Parmesan Quiche below.

Red and Yellow Pepper Quiche: Roast and peel 1 red and 1 yellow bell pepper, then seed and cut into thin strips. Sprinkle ½ cup freshly grated Parmesan cheese over the bottom of the warm, partially baked pastry shell, then arrange the strips of pepper on top and sprinkle with 2 tablespoons chopped fresh basil. Pour in the custard and bake.

Provençal Quiche: Heat ¼ cup olive oil in a large frying pan over medium heat. Add 2 cups diced (¼-inch) eggplant and cook until the eggplant is lightly browned, about 5 minutes. Add 2 peeled, seeded, and coarsely chopped ripe plum tomatoes, and cook until the tomatoes are softened, about 3 more minutes. Season with salt and pepper. Let cool completely. Sprinkle ½ cup shredded Gruyère cheese over the bottom of the warm, partially baked pastry shell. Add the eggplant mixture and sprinkle with 1 teaspoon chopped fresh thyme. Pour in the custard and then bake.

Leek Quiche: In a medium frying pan, heat 2 tablespoons unsalted butter over medium heat. Add 3 medium leeks, white part only, cut into thin rounds. Cook, stirring often, until the leeks are golden, about 8 minutes. Add ⅛ teaspoon crumbled saffron threads. Let cool completely. Sprinkle ½ cup shredded Gruyère cheese over the bottom of the warm, partially baked pastry shell. Add the leek mixture and sprinkle with 1 tablespoon chopped fresh parsley. Pour in the custard and bake.

BACON AND PARMESAN QUICHE

This version of the classic quiche Lorraine uses Parmesan instead of Gruyère cheese.

MAKES 4 TO 6 SERVINGS

  Basic Pie Dough
  4 slices thick-cut bacon, cut into ½-inch-wide strips
  3 large eggs
  1 cup milk
  ⅓ cup heavy cream
  ½ cup freshly grated Parmesan cheese
  Salt and freshly ground pepper, to taste
  A pinch of grated nutmeg

Preheat the oven to 400°F. On a lightly floured work surface, roll out the pastry dough to a ⅛-inch-thick circle. Use to line a 9-inch round tart pan with a removable bottom. Line the pastry shell with foil and fill with dried beans or rice. Bake until the pastry is set (peek under the foil), about 10 minutes. Remove from the oven, keeping the oven on. Lift out the foil with the beans.

In a medium frying pan, cook the bacon over medium heat until crisp, about 5 minutes. Drain on paper towels; reserve 1 tablespoon fat in the pan.

In a medium bowl, whisk the eggs with the milk and cream. Stir in the Parmesan cheese, and season with salt (very lightly as the bacon and cheese may be salty), pepper, and nutmeg. Place the tart pan on a baking sheet. Sprinkle the bacon into the pastry shell, then drizzle with the bacon fat. Pour in the egg mixture. Bake for 10 minutes. Reduce the heat to 375°F, and continue baking until the filling is puffed and browned, and a knife inserted near the center comes out clean, 30 to 40 minutes. Serve hot, warm, or at room temperature.

Spinach and Chèvre Quiche: In a medium frying pan, heat 1 tablespoon unsalted butter over medium heat. Add 2 cups shredded fresh spinach leaves and cook until the spinach is wilted and tender, about 5 minutes. Place the spinach in a colander and press to remove any excess moisture. Let cool completely. Add to the filling, along with ½ cup crumbled soft goat cheese and ⅓ cup chopped scallions.

SOUFFLÉS

The classic French soufflé has an unfair reputation for being difficult. In fact, it is quite simple, and lends itself to advance preparation. The trick is to make the base (actually a thick sauce) a couple of hours ahead. Use a fairly large saucepan, and cover the sauce with plastic wrap pressed onto the surface so a crust won't form. When ready to bake, reheat the sauce until just warm, beat the egg whites, and fold them in.

ASPARAGUS SOUFFLÉ
A delicious way to celebrate spring.

MAKES 4 SERVINGS
8 ounces fresh asparagus, woody ends trimmed
4 large eggs, separated
4 tablespoons unsalted butter
¼ cup all-purpose flour
1¼ cups milk, heated
6 tablespoons freshly grated Parmesan cheese
Salt and freshly ground pepper, to taste

Preheat the oven to 400°F. Lightly butter a 1½-quart soufflé dish and set aside.

In an asparagus cooker or a wide pan of lightly salted water, cook the asparagus until tender, about 8 minutes. Drain and rinse well under cold running water. Cut off the top 2 inches or so from each asparagus spear and set aside. Place the asparagus stalks in a blender with the egg yolks and process into a purée. Set the purée aside.

In a large saucepan, melt the butter over medium heat. Stir in the flour and reduce the heat to low. Let bubble without browning for 1 to 2 minutes. Gradually stir in the milk to make a thick, smooth sauce. Bring to a simmer and cook, stirring frequently to prevent sticking, for 5 minutes. Remove from the heat, and stir in the Parmesan cheese. Let cool slightly, then stir in the asparagus purée. Season with salt and pepper.

In a large, greasefree bowl, beat the egg whites until soft peaks form. Stir about one fourth into the asparagus mixture to lighten it, then fold in the remaining whites. Pour half of the soufflé mixture into the prepared dish, then sprinkle with the asparagus tips, and pour in the remaining mixture. Bake until the soufflé is puffed and golden-brown, about 20 minutes. Serve immediately.

APPLE, CHEDDAR, AND PECAN QUESADILLAS
The concept of the quesadilla, that Tex-Mex favorite, is applied here to the Yankee grilled cheese sandwich. It makes a terrific quick lunch or snack, or can be served as an appetizer.

MAKES 4 SERVINGS
8 (6-inch) flour tortillas
2 cups shredded sharp Cheddar cheese
1 tart green apple, such as Granny Smith, quartered, cored, and cut into very thin wedges
4 tablespoons finely chopped pecans

Preheat the oven to 200°F. For each quesadilla, sprinkle one tortilla with about ¼ cup of the cheese. Arrange one fourth of the apple slices in a spoke pattern on the cheese, then sprinkle with 1 tablespoon pecans and another ¼ cup of the cheese. Top with a second tortilla. Heat an empty large frying pan over medium heat. One at a time, cook the quesadillas in the pan, turning them once, until both sides are lightly browned and the cheese has melted, about 3 minutes. Keep the quesadillas warm in the oven until they are all prepared. Cut them into wedges and serve hot.

MOZZARELLA IN CARROZZA

Mozzarella in carrozza, or "in a carriage," consists of cheese sandwiches dipped in egg and fried to an appetizing golden-brown.

MAKES 4 SERVINGS

6 ounces mozzarella cheese, cut into 4 thick slices
8 slices firm white sandwich bread, crusts removed
8 anchovy fillets (optional)
3 large eggs
Salt, to taste
Olive oil, for frying

Make four sandwiches out of the cheese and bread, including the anchovies, if desired. Cut each sandwich in half. In a small bowl, beat the eggs with a pinch of salt.

Put enough oil in a large frying pan to come ½ inch up the sides. Heat over medium heat until very hot but not smoking. Dip each sandwich into the beaten egg to coat both sides, shaking off the excess egg, and place in the oil. Fry the sandwiches, turning once, until golden, about 3 minutes. Drain briefly on paper towels. Sprinkle lightly with salt and serve hot.

HAM AND MUSHROOM BREAKFAST CASSEROLE

This must be refrigerated overnight before serving, so it is perfect for holiday brunches. It is actually a savory bread pudding with sautéed mushrooms and ham.

MAKES 8 SERVINGS

2 tablespoons unsalted butter
1 pound button mushrooms, thinly sliced
12 ounces smoked ham, cut into ¼-inch cubes
6 scallions, chopped
20 (¼-inch-thick) slices French or Italian bread, approximately
2 cups shredded Cheddar cheese
4 cups milk
6 large eggs
2 tablespoons Dijon mustard
2 tablespoons chopped parsley
1 teaspoon dried thyme
½ teaspoon salt
¼ teaspoon freshly ground pepper

In a large frying pan, heat the butter over medium heat. Add the mushrooms and cook, stirring often, until lightly browned, about 10 minutes. Stir in the ham and scallions, and cook until the scallions are softened, about 2 minutes. Set aside.

Lightly butter a 9- by 13-inch baking dish. Arrange enough bread slices, slightly overlapping or trimmed to fit, in the dish to cover the bottom. Spread the mushroom-ham mixture over the bread, then sprinkle with the cheese. Top with another layer of bread. In a large bowl, whisk together the milk, eggs, mustard, parsley, thyme, salt, and pepper. Slowly pour all over the bread. Cover and refrigerate overnight.

Preheat the oven to 325°F. Set the dish in a larger roasting pan, and place in the oven. Add hot water to the pan to come ½ inch up the sides. Bake until a knife inserted in the center of the casserole comes out clean, about 1½ hours. Remove from the water bath and let stand for 10 minutes before serving.

SWISS FONDUE

Like the quiche, fondue went through a period of decline. But as busy cooks realized that this fun way to enjoy supper with friends was also easy, it returned to the culinary scene. If you don't have a fondue set, improvise with a plate warmer and a saucepan.

MAKES 6 SERVINGS

2 garlic cloves, peeled
1 cup dry white wine
1¼ pounds shredded Emmentaler cheese (about 5 cups), or a mixture of Emmentaler and Gruyère
1 teaspoon potato flour or cornstarch
2 tablespoons kirsch
A drop of corn or vegetable oil
A pinch of grated nutmeg
Freshly ground pepper, to taste
Crusty French or Italian bread, cut into 1-inch cubes

Rub a cheese-fondue pot, a medium earthenware dish, or a medium saucepan with 1 crushed garlic clove; discard the garlic. Add the wine and the remaining whole clove of garlic. Bring to a simmer over medium-low heat on top of the stove. Toss the cheese with the potato flour. Gradually add the cheese to the pot, stirring constantly, until it has melted into a thick sauce. If the fondue seems too thick, add a little more wine. Stir in the kirsch mixed with the corn oil, and season with the nutmeg and freshly ground pepper.

Transfer the fondue in the cooking utensil to the fondue burner and place over a medium flame. Allow each guest to serve themselves, piercing a bread cube onto a fork and dipping into the cheese sauce. Maintain the heat so the fondue is very hot and gently bubbling. A delicious crust will form on the bottom of the pot; this can be scraped up and eaten.

Mozzarella in Carrozza

Pasta

FRESH PASTA DOUGH

Whether you make this dough by hand or in a food processor, the results will be equally fine. You will have to be flexible with the amount of flour and liquid, as the flour will absorb differently according to the humidity of the day and exact size of the eggs.

MAKES ABOUT 1 POUND

2 cups unbleached all-purpose flour

3 large eggs

To make the dough by hand, place the flour in a large bowl and make a well in the center. Put the eggs in the well. Using the fingers of one hand like a fork, break up the eggs. Then, stirring the eggs in a circle, gradually draw the flour into the eggs to make a moist, pliable ball of dough. If the dough is too dry, sprinkle with 1 tablespoon water. If the dough seems too sticky, sprinkle with a tablespoon of flour. Turn the dough onto a lightly floured work surface and knead until the dough is supple, about 5 minutes. If the dough feels at all sticky while you are kneading, sprinkle it with a little flour.

To make the dough in a food processor, fit the bowl with the metal blade and put in the flour. With the food processor running, gradually pour in the beaten eggs through the feed tube. Process until the dough forms a ball that rides on top of the blade. Feel the dough to test its consistency. If it is too dry, sprinkle with 1 tablespoon water. If it is too sticky, sprinkle with 1 tablespoon flour. Process for about 30 seconds and check again. To knead the dough, process for 1 more minute.

Wrap the dough in plastic wrap and allow to relax at room temperature for 30 minutes before rolling out.

Tuscan Pasta Dough: Substitute 1 tablespoon each olive oil and milk for 1 of the eggs.

Rolling Pasta Dough in a Machine

Be sure the pasta machine is very clean and dry. Attach the machine to your work surface. Set the rollers at the widest setting. Cut the dough into thirds. Work with one piece at a time, keeping the remaining dough covered with plastic wrap. Dust the piece of dough lightly with flour and press it into an oblong shape. Cranking the handle of the machine, feed the dough through the rollers. Fold the dough into thirds, dust with flour, and feed it through the rollers again. Do this several times to smooth out and finish kneading the dough.

Now set the rollers one notch closer together. Fold the dough, dust with flour, and feed through the rollers again. Move the machine up another notch, and repeat the procedure, without folding the dough into three. The dough will now be getting fairly long, and you will have to hold it up over the machine. Set the rollers to the next setting, dust the dough with flour, and feed through the machine. Set the rollers to the next-to-last setting, and pass the dough through a final time. (The finest setting is reserved for very thinly rolled pasta, like ravioli, where the edges of each raviolo will have a double thickness.)

Spread out the dough strip on a lightly floured work surface. Repeat the procedure with the remaining dough. If you will be cutting the dough into noodles or other shapes, let the dough strips dry, uncovered, for 15 to 30 minutes (depending on the weather and humidity), turning them over once so that they dry evenly. The dough should be supple and leathery, but not so dry that it will crack when cut. For stuffed pasta, do not let the dough dry at all, and keep the strips covered with a slightly damp dish towel.

Making Pasta Shapes

Tagliatelle (sometimes called fettuccine) are narrow ribbons of pasta. They are eaten with all sorts of sauces—cream, tomato, or meat. To make tagliatelle by hand, roll up each strip of pasta like a jelly roll, and slice across at ¼-inch intervals all the way along the roll. Unroll each spiral of dough. If you wish, hang the tagliatelle on a cloth placed over the back of a chair to dry, but the pasta can be cooked immediately. You can also cut tagliatelle by running the strip of dough through the wide cutters on the pasta machine.

Linguine are ⅛-inch-wide ribbons of pasta. They are normally cut by hand, as most pasta machines do not have cutters of the required width.

Tagliarini are very narrow strands of pasta, about ¹⁄₁₆ inch wide. They can be cut by hand like tagliatelle, but it is easier to run the strips of dough through the thinnest cutters on the pasta machine.

Pappardelle are ¾-inch-wide ribbons of pasta that are about 12 inches long. Use a fluted pastry wheel, or even a plain pizza cutter, to cut the flat strips of dough into pappardelle.

Farfalle are eaten with the same sauces as tagliatelle. To make them, use a fluted pastry wheel to cut the dough into 2-inch squares. With the forefinger and thumb of one hand, pinch each square across the middle to make an even fold, thus creating a butterfly or bow-tie effect.

Lasagne are large strips of pasta that are cooked and then layered with meat or vegetable sauces, cheese, and, sometimes, béchamel sauce. The assembled lasagne is then baked until it is bubbling and browned. To fit a typical 9- by 13-inch lasagne pan,

1

2

Making pasta dough

1 Put the flour in a bowl and make a well in the center. Add the eggs to the well.

2 Using your fingertips, break up the eggs to mix them. Gradually mix the flour into the eggs to make a moist, pliable dough. The dough can now be kneaded and rolled by hand, or using a pasta machine.

flour dredger
237
pasta machine
229, 239

**Fresh Pasta
Dough** 334
**Tuscan Pasta
Dough** 334

3

3 If using a pasta machine, turn the dough out onto a lightly floured work surface. Cut the dough into three portions (or into as many pieces as there are eggs in the dough). Work with one piece at a time and keep the others covered to prevent them from drying out.

Rolling and cutting pasta dough

1 To knead the dough, set the rollers on the pasta machine to the widest setting. Flatten the piece of dough and feed it through the rollers, then fold the dough into thirds.

2 Feed the dough through the rollers again. Repeat several times, folding it into thirds each time.

3 To roll out the dough, set the rollers one notch closer together. Feed the dough through again, but do not fold it into thirds. Continue moving the rollers closer together, one notch at a time, and feeding the dough through, rolling it gradually into a long, thin strip. Repeat with the remaining dough.

4 To cut noodles, let the dough strips dry until they look leathery. Then fit the appropriate cutting rollers onto the machine. Feed through the strips, and catch the emerging nooodles on your hand.

1

2

3

4

Cutting tagliatelle by hand (*right*)
Roll up the sheet of pasta loosely, like a jelly roll. Using a small, sharp knife, cut across the roll at ¼-inch intervals and then unroll the little spirals of dough.

Making farfalle (*far right*)
With a fluted pastry wheel, cut the sheet of dough into strips 2 inches wide, then cut across the strips to make 2-inch squares. Pinch the middle of each square between your thumb and forefinger, to make a butterfly shape.

1

Making ravioli

1 Roll the pasta dough as thinly as possible. With a fluted pastry wheel, cut the pasta sheet into strips about 3 inches wide.

2

3

2 Put heaped teaspoonfuls of the filling down each strip, spacing the mounds of filling about 1½ inches apart and about ¾ inch from one long edge. Lightly moisten the dough around the mounds of filling, then fold the dough over the filling.

3 Press the edges of the dough together, and press all around the mounds of filling to seal the dough.

4 With the pastry wheel, carefully cut between the mounds of filling to form the ravioli.

4

cut the dough with a fluted pastry wheel into 3 ½- by 13-inch strips (this allows a little extra so the strips can overlap slightly in the pan).

Cooking and Serving Pasta

Pasta in Italy is most often served as a first course, but in other parts of the world it is also served as an entrée. If you are serving pasta as an appetizer, 1 pound of pasta will feed six to eight people; as a main course, each pound of pasta will give four to six servings (according to the sauce used to dress the pasta, and individual appetites).

Bring a large pot of water—this should be at least 4 quarts—to a boil over high heat. Salt the water, allowing 2 tablespoons salt for every 4 quarts of water. When cooking fresh pasta, add it to the boiling water all at once and then stir gently for 1 minute to be sure the strands or shapes don't stick together. Continue to cook until the pasta is just tender but still a little resilient (*al dente*): test a strand or piece by biting into it. This will take between 2 and 4 minutes, depending on how dry the pasta is.

To cook dried pasta, add it to the water all at once (spaghetti should be gradually pushed down into the pot as it softens), then stir well for 1 to 2 minutes to be sure the strands or shapes don't stick together. Boil until *al dente*, 10 to 12 minutes or according to the package instructions; test often to be sure the pasta is not overcooked.

Drain spaghetti and other noodles and pasta shapes in a colander, shaking it around gently. Leave a tiny bit of water on the pasta—if it is too well drained it will stick together. Transfer the pasta to a warmed bowl or return it to the empty pot. Add the sauce and toss briefly. Serve immediately, into warmed bowls or onto warmed plates, and provide a bowl of freshly grated Parmesan cheese so each diner can add this to taste (unless you have dressed the pasta with a fish sauce, which in Italy is never accompanied by Parmesan).

To drain lasagne properly, lift the strips out of the water using either a perforated metal turner or a fish lifter. Dip each strip briefly into a bowl of cold water, and then spread it flat on a clean damp cloth to drain and dry completely.

SPAGHETTI WITH TOMATO AND VEGETABLE SAUCE

Tomato sauce is the everyday sauce of northern Italy, where everyday means at least once or even twice a day. Italians make a batch large enough to last a week, and may eat it with pasta, semolina gnocchi, and polenta, with plenty of Parmesan cheese.

MAKES 4 TO 6 SERVINGS

1 pound spaghetti
Freshly grated Parmesan cheese, for serving

Tomato and Vegetable Sauce

¼ cup olive oil
2 medium onions, finely chopped
2 small carrots, finely chopped
2 small celery ribs, finely chopped
3 garlic cloves, minced
1½ pounds ripe plum tomatoes, peeled, seeded, and chopped, or 2 cups canned tomato purée
¾ cup chicken stock or water
Salt and freshly ground pepper, to taste
3 tablespoons unsalted butter

In a large saucepan, heat the oil over medium heat. Add the onions, carrots, celery, and garlic. Cook, stirring often, until softened and starting to brown, about 8 minutes. Add the tomatoes and stock and bring to a simmer. Season with salt and pepper. Reduce the heat to low and simmer until the sauce has thickened, about 1 hour. If desired, purée the sauce in a food processor fitted with the metal blade or in a blender. Stir in the butter, and taste the sauce to check the seasoning. Keep the sauce warm. (The sauce can be cooled and then kept, covered, in the refrigerator for up to 2 days; reheat before serving.)

In a large pot of boiling salted water, cook the spaghetti until *al dente*, about 10 minutes. Drain the pasta and add to the sauce. Cook, stirring to mix the pasta with the sauce, for 1 to 2 minutes. Transfer to a heated bowl and serve, with the cheese on the side.

SPAGHETTI ALLA CARBONARA

This rich and creamy sauce, whose name means "in the charcoal-burner's style," is justifiably popular. The trick is to work very quickly once the pasta has been drained so everything is served piping hot.

MAKES 4 TO 6 SERVINGS

2 tablespoons unsalted butter
5 ounces thick-sliced pancetta or slab bacon, rind removed, cut into ¼-inch-wide sticks
3 large eggs
4 large egg yolks
⅔ cup heavy cream
Freshly ground pepper, to taste
1 pound spaghetti
⅔ cup freshly grated Parmesan cheese

In a frying pan, heat the butter over medium heat. Add the pancetta and cook until lightly browned, about 5 minutes. Remove from the heat and keep warm.

In a medium bowl, whisk together the eggs and yolks, then whisk in the cream. Season with plenty of pepper, and set aside.

In a large pot of boiling salted water over high heat, cook the pasta until *al dente*, about 10 minutes. Drain and return to the empty pot in which the pasta was cooked. Stir in the pancetta and its cooking fat, then add the egg mixture and Parmesan cheese. Toss well, transfer to a warmed bowl, and serve immediately.

SPAGHETTI WITH QUICK TOMATO AND BALSAMIC VINEGAR SAUCE

Make this when tomatoes and basil are at their best. A splash of balsamic vinegar works magic with this simple sauce.

MAKES 4 TO 6 SERVINGS

1 pound spaghetti

¼ cup olive oil

2 garlic cloves, minced

2½ pounds ripe plum tomatoes, seeded and coarsely chopped

3 tablespoons chopped fresh basil

2 tablespoons balsamic vinegar

Salt and freshly ground pepper, to taste

Freshly grated Parmesan cheese, for serving

In a large pot of boiling salted water over high heat, cook the spaghetti until *al dente*, about 10 minutes.

Meanwhile, heat the oil in a large nonreactive frying pan over medium heat. Add the garlic and cook until softened, about 1 minute. Add the tomatoes and cook, stirring often, until just heated through, about 3 minutes. Stir in the basil and balsamic vinegar, and season with salt and pepper.

Drain the pasta and transfer to a warmed serving bowl. Add the sauce and toss well. Serve, with a bowl of Parmesan cheese on the side for sprinkling.

PAPPARDELLE WITH RAGÙ BOLOGNESE

Here is the classic meat sauce of northern Italy. Wide strips of pappardelle match the heartiness of the sauce, but tagliatelle is a good choice, too, either fresh or dry.

MAKES 4 TO 6 SERVINGS

1 pound fresh pappardelle

Ragù

3 tablespoons olive oil, or 1½ tablespoons each olive oil and unsalted butter

1 medium onion, finely chopped

1 large carrot, finely chopped

1 large celery rib with leaves, finely chopped

2 garlic cloves, minced

8 ounces ground veal or beef

8 ounces ground pork

3 large ripe tomatoes, peeled, seeded, and chopped, or 1 cup drained, chopped canned tomatoes

3 chicken livers, cut into ¼-inch dice

½ teaspoon chopped fresh thyme or ¼ teaspoon dried thyme

Salt and freshly ground pepper, to taste

⅔ cup chicken stock

⅔ cup hearty red wine

2 tablespoons heavy cream

To make the *ragù*, heat the oil in a large saucepan over medium heat. Add the onion, carrot, celery, and garlic. Cook until the vegetables are softened, about 5 minutes. Add the ground veal and ground pork and increase the heat to medium-high. Cook, uncovered, breaking up the meat with a spoon, until the meat is browned, about 10 minutes. Stir in the tomatoes, chicken livers, and thyme, and season with salt and pepper. Bring to a simmer, and cook until most of the liquid from the tomatoes has evaporated. Add half of the stock and red wine. Reduce the heat to medium-low, and simmer for 30 minutes. Add the rest of the stock and red wine, and simmer until the sauce is thick, about 1 more hour. Remove from the heat and stir in the cream. Taste the sauce to check the seasoning. (The sauce can be prepared, without the cream, then cooled and kept, covered, in the refrigerator for 1 day; reheat, then remove from the heat and add the cream. The cream may curdle if allowed to boil.)

In a large pot of boiling salted water over high heat, cook the pasta until *al dente*, 3 to 5 minutes. Drain and transfer to a warmed serving bowl. Add the hot sauce and toss. Serve immediately.

TAGLIATELLE WITH PESTO SAUCE

This is a memorable dish, especially when prepared with homemade pasta. The pesto is delicious—an aromatic partner for many kinds of pasta.

MAKES 4 TO 6 SERVINGS

1 pound fresh tagliatelle or fettuccine

Pesto Sauce

3 tablespoons pine nuts

2 cups packed fresh basil leaves

2 large garlic cloves, coarsely chopped

2 tablespoons freshly grated Parmesan cheese, plus more for serving

6 tablespoons olive oil

Salt, to taste

In a small dry frying pan over medium heat, cook the pine nuts, stirring often, until lightly toasted. Transfer to a plate to cool.

In a food processor fitted with the metal blade or a blender, process the basil leaves and garlic until finely chopped. Add the pine nuts and pulse briefly. Add the cheese and pulse again. With the machine running, gradually add the oil to make a smooth, thick sauce. Season with salt. (The pesto can be kept, in a covered container, with a film of olive oil poured over the top of the sauce, for up to 3 days.)

In a large pot of boiling salted water over high heat, cook the pasta until *al dente*, 3 to 5 minutes. Drain well, but reserve ½ cup of the pasta cooking liquid. Transfer the pasta to a heated serving bowl. Add the pesto and toss, adding enough of the reserved pasta liquid to make a smooth sauce. Serve the pasta immediately, with additional grated Parmesan cheese passed on the side.

TAGLIARINI WITH FRESH ARTICHOKES AND GREMOLATA

This is a very light and refreshing pasta dish that is also easy to make.

MAKES 4 TO 6 SERVINGS
    1 large lemon
    2 tablespoons chopped fresh parsley
    4 garlic cloves, thinly sliced
    ½ cup extra virgin olive oil
    8 large artichoke bottoms, cut into ⅛-inch-wide slices
    Salt and freshly ground pepper, to taste
    1 pound fresh tagliarini or linguine
    Freshly grated Parmesan cheese, for serving

Grate the zest from the lemon and put it into a small bowl. Mix in the parsley and garlic, and set this *gremolata* aside. Squeeze the juice from the lemon and set aside.

In a large frying pan, heat ¼ cup of the oil over medium heat. Add the artichoke slices, and season with salt and pepper. Cook until the artichokes are golden-brown and tender, 10 to 15 minutes. Stir in the lemon juice. Remove the frying pan from the heat and keep warm.

In a large pot of boiling salted water over high heat, cook the pasta until *al dente*, 3 to 5 minutes. Drain, and return to the empty pot. Add the remaining ¼ cup of oil, season generously with pepper, and toss well. Divide among warmed pasta bowls. Top with the artichokes, and sprinkle with the *gremolata*. Serve immediately, with the Parmesan cheese passed on the side.

TAGLIATELLE WITH TUSCAN MEAT SAUCE

This exquisite meat sauce, fundamental to the Tuscan kitchen, is a delicious change from its more familiar Bolognese cousin. While beef or veal are excellent in the sauce, a Tuscan cook would use whatever meat were handy or abundant—rabbit, chicken, or squab.

MAKES 4 TO 6 SERVINGS
    1 pound fresh tagliatelle
Sauce
    10 ounces boneless beef round or veal shoulder, cut
        into 2-inch pieces
    2 chicken livers, coarsely chopped
    1 medium onion, chopped
    2 medium carrots, chopped
    1 medium celery rib, chopped
    6 large fresh basil leaves, chopped
    ¼ cup olive oil
    Salt and freshly ground pepper, to taste
    1 cup hearty red wine
    1¼ cups chicken stock
    ½ cup dried porcini mushrooms (½ ounce)
    ¾ cup peeled, seeded, and chopped plum tomatoes,
        or use drained canned tomatoes

In a large saucepan, combine the beef, chicken livers, onion, carrots, celery, and basil. Drizzle with the oil and stir to coat the ingredients. Season with salt and pepper. Place over medium-high heat and then cook, stirring often with a wooden spoon, until the ingredients are well browned, 10 to 15 minutes. Don't worry if the vegetables stick to the bottom of the pan, but take care not to let them burn. Add the red wine. Scrape up the browned bits and pieces on the bottom of the pan, and blend them with the wine. Bring to a boil over medium heat and then cook until the wine has reduced to ¼ cup, about 10 minutes. Add the stock and bring to a simmer. Reduce the heat to low, cover, and simmer until the beef is tender, about 1½ hours.

Meanwhile, in a small bowl, soak the porcini in 1 cup hot water until softened, about 30 minutes. Lift the mushrooms out of the liquid and chop coarsely. Strain the soaking liquid through a sieve lined with a wet paper towel, and reserve the liquid.

Remove the beef and chop coarsely. Return the beef to the sauce, along with the mushrooms and their liquid and the tomatoes. Cook over medium heat, stirring often, until the sauce is thick, about 15 minutes. If the sauce seems too dry, add a little stock or water. (The sauce can be cooled and kept, covered, in the refrigerator for 1 day; reheat before serving.)

In a large pot of boiling salted water over high heat, cook the pasta until *al dente*, 3 to 5 minutes. Drain and put in a warmed bowl. Add the sauce, toss, and serve.

Tuscan Game Sauce: Substitute 2 (1½-pound) squabs, including their giblets, chopped through the bones into 2-inch pieces, for the beef. When the sauce has simmered for 1½ hours, remove the squab pieces and giblets. Discard the skin and bones, and chop coarsely. Return the chopped squab and giblets to the sauce and continue cooking.

RIGATONI WITH SPICY TOMATO AND PANCETTA SAUCE

This dish, known in Italy as *rigatoni all' amatriciana*, should be good and spicy. If you can't find pancetta, just use rindless slab bacon. As pancetta is unsmoked, you may want to remove some of the bacon's smokiness by simmering it in water for 3 minutes, then draining and patting dry before browning it.

MAKES 4 TO 6 SERVINGS

  1½ tablespoons olive oil
  4 ounces thick-sliced pancetta, cut into ¼-inch dice
  1 small onion, chopped
  ¼ teaspoon chile flakes, or to taste
  2 cups peeled, seeded, and chopped ripe plum tomatoes; or use drained canned tomatoes
  Salt, to taste
  1 pound rigatoni or ziti
  ½ cup freshly grated Parmesan cheese, plus more for serving

In a medium saucepan, heat the oil over medium heat. Add the pancetta and cook until lightly browned, about 5 minutes. Using a slotted spoon, remove the pancetta to a plate.

Add the onion and chile flakes to the fat in the pan and cook until the onion is softened, about 5 minutes. Add the plum tomatoes and bring the mixture to a simmer. Cook, stirring often, until the sauce is thick, about 10 minutes. Return the pancetta to the sauce, and season with salt.

In a large pot of boiling salted water over high heat, cook the pasta until *al dente*, about 10 minutes. Drain and place in a warmed serving bowl. Add the sauce and toss well to combine, then add the cheese and toss again. Serve immediately, with more cheese passed on the side.

SEA SHELLS WITH SHRIMP, FETA, AND OLIVES

The flavors in this dish are as lively as a busy Greek taverna. The sauce is made with uncooked tomatoes, so they must be very flavorful. Make it when they are at their summertime peak.

MAKES 4 TO 6 SERVINGS

  3 large ripe tomatoes, chopped
  1 cup Mediterranean black olives, pitted and coarsely chopped
  4 tablespoons extra virgin olive oil
  2 tablespoons minced fresh dill or oregano
  1 garlic clove, minced
  Salt and freshly ground pepper, to taste
  1 pound medium shrimp, peeled and deveined
  1 pound conchiglie (sea shells)
  6 ounces feta cheese, crumbled

In a large bowl, combine the tomatoes, olives, 2 tablespoons oil, the dill, garlic, and a seasoning of salt and pepper. Let stand for 1 hour.

Heat the remaining 2 tablespoons oil in a large frying pan over medium-high heat. Add the shrimp and cook, stirring occasionally, until firm and pink, about 3 minutes. Remove from the heat, and cover the pan to keep the shrimp warm.

In a large pot of boiling salted water over high heat, cook the pasta until *al dente*, 10 to 12 minutes. Drain well. Return the pasta to the empty pot, and add the tomato mixture, shrimp, and feta. Toss until the feta begins to melt, then season with salt and pepper, and serve.

BUCATINI WITH TOMATOES, VEGETABLES, AND HAM

If you were to order pasta with tomato sauce in the Marches, in the central part of Italy, this is what you would be given. The cooking of this region features pork, so try to cook the sauce with lard to create an authentic flavor. Bucatini is a long, hollow macaroni, but if you prefer you can use other hollow pasta such as penne.

MAKES 4 TO 6 SERVINGS

  2 tablespoons lard or olive oil
  1 medium onion, finely chopped
  1 medium carrot, finely chopped
  1 medium celery rib, finely chopped
  4 ounces (¼-inch-thick) sliced boiled ham, cut into ¼-inch-wide strips
  ½ cup hearty red wine
  3 cups peeled, seeded, and chopped ripe plum tomatoes, or use drained canned tomatoes
  2 tablespoons tomato paste
  A pinch of dried marjoram
  A pinch of dried thyme
  Salt and freshly ground pepper, to taste
  1 pound bucatini
  1 cup freshly grated Parmesan cheese

In a medium saucepan, heat the lard over medium heat. Add the onion, carrot, and celery. Cook, stirring often, until lightly browned, about 10 minutes. Add the ham and stir for 2 minutes. Add the wine, increase the heat to high, and bring to a boil. Boil until the wine has almost all evaporated, about 5 minutes. Stir in the tomatoes, tomato paste, marjoram, and thyme. Season with salt and pepper. Bring to a simmer, then reduce the heat to low and let simmer until rich and thick, about 30 minutes.

In a large pot of boiling salted water, cook the pasta until *al dente*, about 10 minutes. Drain and place in a heated bowl. Mix in half of the sauce and a few heaping tablespoons of cheese. Serve immediately, with the remaining sauce and cheese on the side.

PASTA WITH GRILLED VEGETABLES AND MOZZARELLA

Grilled vegetables add a smoky dimension to this pasta sauce that works in harmony with the mozzarella's creaminess. It is easiest to grill the onion rounds on a perforated vegetable grilling grid,

SEA SHELLS WITH SHRIMP, FETA, AND OLIVES

available at kitchenware stores, so they don't fall onto the coals. An alternative is to chop the onion and sauté in a little olive oil.

MAKES 4 TO 6 SERVINGS
¼ cup extra virgin olive oil
2 garlic cloves, coarsely chopped
8 ripe plum tomatoes, cut in half lengthwise
1 medium eggplant, cut into ½-inch-thick rounds
2 medium zucchini, cut in half lengthwise
1 medium red onion, cut into ½-inch-thick rounds
1 large red bell pepper, seeded and cut
   in half lengthwise
3 tablespoons chopped fresh basil
Salt and freshly ground pepper, to taste
1 pound penne or ziti
2 cups shredded mozzarella

In a small saucepan, heat the olive oil with the garlic over medium heat until the garlic is golden, about

3 minutes. Discard the garlic, and then set the garlic-flavored oil aside.

Build a hot charcoal fire in an outdoor grill or preheat a gas grill. Lightly oil the grill. Brush the vegetables lightly with the garlic-flavored oil. Grill the vegetables, turning and basting with the oil occasionally. Cook the tomatoes until tender but still holding their shape, about 8 minutes. Cook the eggplant and zucchini until browned on both sides, about 10 minutes. Cook the onion until crisp-tender and the edges are charred, 10 to 12 minutes. Cook the red pepper until the skin is charred, about 12 minutes. As the vegetables cook, transfer them to a large bowl and cover with a sheet of foil to keep warm. When the pepper is cool enough to handle, remove and discard the charred skin.

Transfer the vegetables to a food processor fitted with a metal blade and coarsely chop. (The sauce can be prepared up to 1 hour ahead, and kept at room temperature; reheat until hot in a medium saucepan over medium heat.) Stir in the basil, and season with salt and pepper. Keep warm.

LASAGNE WITH PORTOBELLO MUSHROOMS, ARTICHOKES, AND PANCETTA

In a large pot of boiling salted water, cook the pasta until *al dente*, about 10 minutes. Drain well, but reserve ½ cup of the pasta cooking water. Place the hot pasta in a warmed serving bowl. Add the sauce and mozzarella and toss thoroughly to combine, adding enough of the reserved water to make a creamy sauce. Serve immediately.

PENNE WITH EGGPLANT AND RICOTTA

A satisfying vegetarian pasta dish, this is both easy and quick to make.

MAKES 4 TO 6 SERVINGS
4 tablespoons olive oil
1 medium onion, chopped
1 medium red bell pepper, seeded and chopped
1 medium eggplant, unpeeled, cut into ½-inch cubes

2 garlic cloves, minced

1 teaspoon dried oregano

¼ teaspoon chile flakes

2 cups peeled, seeded, and chopped ripe plum
  tomatoes, or use canned tomatoes

Salt, to taste

1 pound penne or ziti

1 cup ricotta cheese

⅓ cup grated pecorino romano cheese, plus more
  for serving

2 tablespoons chopped fresh basil (optional)

In a large frying pan, heat 2 tablespoons oil over medium heat. Add the onion and bell pepper and cook until the onion is golden, about 8 minutes. Add the remaining 2 tablespoons oil, then the eggplant, garlic, oregano, and chile flakes. Cover and cook until the eggplant softens, about 5 minutes. Add the tomatoes and bring to a boil. Reduce the heat to low and simmer, uncovered, until the eggplant is tender and the sauce is thick, about 20 minutes.

In a large pot of boiling salted water over high heat, cook the penne until *al dente*, about 10 minutes. Drain well and return to the empty pot. Add the sauce, ricotta and romano cheeses, and the optional basil, and toss well. Season with salt. Serve immediately, with a bowl of romano cheese passed on the side.

LASAGNE WITH PORTOBELLO MUSHROOMS, ARTICHOKES, AND PANCETTA

Made without the pancetta, this is an excellent vegetarian main course.

MAKES 6 SERVINGS

Béchamel Sauce, made with 2½ cups milk flavored
  with onion, bay leaf, and cloves, 4 tablespoons
  unsalted butter, and ⅓ cup all-purpose flour

⅔ cup half-and-half

A pinch of grated nutmeg

Salt and freshly ground pepper, to taste

1 pound large portobello mushrooms

3 tablespoons olive oil

2 tablespoons lemon juice

2 garlic cloves, sliced

6 ounces thick-sliced pancetta or thinly
  sliced bacon

6 large artichoke bottoms

12 dried lasagne strips (9 ounces)

1 tablespoon chopped fresh oregano

3 tablespoons freshly grated Parmesan cheese

6 tablespoons unsalted butter

12 large fresh sage leaves

Preheat the oven to 400°F.

Add the half-and-half to the béchamel sauce, and simmer until it returns to its original thickness, about 5 minutes. Season with the nutmeg, salt, and pepper. Remove from the heat. Press a piece of buttered waxed paper directly onto the surface of the sauce, and set aside.

Cut off the stems from the mushrooms. Put the mushroom caps and stems in a baking dish just large enough to hold them. Drizzle with the oil and lemon juice. Tuck the garlic slices under the mushrooms, and season. Bake until the mushrooms are tender, 30 to 40 minutes. Let cool. Discard the garlic. Cut the mushroom caps into ¼-inch-thick slices, and the stems into ¼-inch-thick rounds. Set aside.

Cook the pancetta in a preheated broiler until crisp and golden-brown. Set aside.

In a large pot of lightly salted water over high heat, cook the artichoke bottoms until tender, about 20 minutes. Drain and rinse under cold running water to cool. Cut into ¼-inch-thick slices. Set aside.

In a large pot of boiling salted water over high heat, cook the lasagne until it is barely tender, about 10 minutes. Do not overcook. Drain.

Oil a 9- by 13-inch baking dish well. Spread with a thin layer of the béchamel sauce. Place an overlapping layer of four lasagne strips in the dish (three placed horizontally, and one vertically). Spread with another thin layer of béchamel, then sprinkle with half of the oregano. Arrange half of the mushrooms on top. Spread with another thin layer of béchamel, then add half of the pancetta and half of the artichokes. Top with another layer of four lasagne strips. Repeat the layering process, using thin layers of béchamel and the remaining oregano, mushrooms, pancetta, and artichokes. Finish with the final four lasagne strips and a thick coating of béchamel. Cover with plastic wrap and then refrigerate until firm, at least 6 hours or overnight.

Preheat the oven to 400°F. Lightly oil two baking sheets. Using a sharp knife, cut the lasagne into six portions. Carefully lift out each of the portions with a metal spatula, and place on the baking sheets, being sure to space the portions well apart. Sprinkle each portion with some grated Parmesan cheese. Bake until the tops are bubbling and golden-brown in color, about 30 minutes.

Just before serving, heat the butter in a medium frying pan over medium heat. Add the sage leaves and cook until they are crisp, 1 to 2 minutes. Season the leaves with salt.

Transfer each lasagne portion to a warmed dinner plate. Spoon equal amounts of the sage leaves and butter over each, and serve immediately.

LASAGNE WITH TWO SAUCES

Authentic *lasagne alla bolognese* is prepared with two sauces—a rich, meaty tomato sauce and a creamy béchamel (or, as the Italian would say, *besciamella*).

MAKES 8 SERVINGS

6 (3½- by 13-inch) strips fresh lasagne
Béchamel Sauce, made with 4 cups milk flavored with onion, bay leaf, and cloves, 6 tablespoons unsalted butter, and ½ cup all-purpose flour
1 pound mozzarella cheese, shredded
¾ cup freshly grated Parmesan cheese
Meaty Tomato Sauce
¼ cup olive oil
2 medium onions, chopped
1 pound ground round
8 ounces ground pork
1½ cups peeled, seeded, and chopped ripe plum tomatoes; or use drained canned tomatoes
¾ cup chicken or beef stock
1 heaping teaspoon dried oregano
1 heaping teaspoon dried basil
3 garlic cloves, minced
Salt and freshly ground pepper, to taste

To make the meaty tomato sauce, heat the oil in a large saucepan over medium heat. Add the onions and cook until soft and translucent, about 5 minutes. Add the ground round and pork, and cook, stirring with a spoon to break up the meat, until browned, about 10 minutes. Add the tomatoes, stock, oregano, basil, and garlic, and season with salt and pepper. Bring to a simmer, then reduce the heat to low. Let simmer, adding more stock if the sauce seems too dry, until thickened, about 1 hour. Set aside.

In a large pot of boiling salted water over high heat, cook the lasagne until barely tender, 3 to 4 minutes. Do not overcook. Drain.

Preheat the oven to 350°F. Lightly butter a 9- by 13-inch baking dish. Spread one third of the meat sauce in the bottom of the dish, then spoon on one third of the béchamel. Top with half of the mozzarella and Parmesan cheeses, then add a neat layer of half of the lasagne. Repeat the layers of meat and béchamel sauces and pasta, then top with the remaining meat and béchamel sauces. Sprinkle with the remaining mozzarella, then with the rest of the Parmesan cheese. Bake until the cheese topping is golden-brown, about 45 minutes.

BAKED RIGATONI WITH CREAMY PROSCIUTTO SAUCE

This is incredibly rich and satisfying. Don't overcook the pasta, as it will be baked with the sauce.

MAKES 4 SERVINGS

2½ cups heavy cream, or 1½ cups heavy cream and 1 cup half-and-half
A pinch of grated nutmeg
Salt and freshly ground pepper, to taste
5 ounces (⅛-inch-thick) sliced prosciutto or boiled ham, cut into thin strips
1 pound rigatoni or ziti
1 cup freshly grated Parmesan cheese
5 tablespoons unsalted butter, cut into small pieces

Preheat the oven to 400°F. In a medium saucepan, bring the cream to a simmer. Season with the nutmeg, salt, and pepper. Stir in the prosciutto and set aside.

In a large pot of boiling salted water over high heat, cook the pasta until barely tender, about 9 minutes. Do not overcook. Drain and return to the empty pot. Add the cream mixture and ½ cup of the Parmesan cheese and toss well.

Transfer to a well-buttered 9- by 13-inch baking dish. Sprinkle with the remaining ½ cup of Parmesan cheese and dot with the butter. Bake until the top is golden-brown and the sauce is bubbling nicely, about 15 to 20 minutes.

MACARONI AND THREE CHEESES

In this delicious trio of cheeses, each adds its own characteristics to create a special version of this well-loved dish.

MAKES 4 TO 6 SERVINGS

1 pound elbow macaroni
8 ounces cream cheese, at room temperature
2 cups shredded sharp Cheddar cheese
1 cup heavy cream or milk
½ cup fresh bread crumbs
½ cup freshly grated Parmesan cheese
⅛ teaspoon cayenne pepper
1 tablespoon unsalted butter, cut into bits

Preheat the oven to 350°F. Lightly butter a 2½-quart round baking dish. In a large pot of boiling salted water over high heat, cook the macaroni until just tender, about 8 minutes. Do not overcook, as it will cook further in the sauce. Drain and return to the empty pot. Add the cream cheese and stir until it melts. Stir in the Cheddar cheese and cream. Transfer to the prepared baking dish.

In a small bowl, combine the bread crumbs, Parmesan cheese, and cayenne pepper. Sprinkle this mixture over the macaroni, and dot with the butter. Bake until the top is golden-brown and the macaroni is bubbling, about 35 minutes.

SPINACH AND RICOTTA RAVIOLI

Homemade ravioli are a real treat. They require a bit of effort, however, so are not everyday fare. Save them for very special holiday meals, which is exactly what the Italians would do.

MAKES 4 SERVINGS

   1 pound Fresh Pasta Dough
   ⅔ cup light cream
   2 tablespoons unsalted butter
   Freshly grated Parmesan cheese, for serving
Filling
   1 pound fresh spinach, tough stems
      discarded
   ⅔ cup ricotta cheese
   ¼ cup freshly grated Parmesan cheese
   3 tablespoons chopped fresh basil leaves
   ¼ teaspoon freshly grated nutmeg
   Salt and freshly ground pepper, to taste

To make the filling for the ravioli, place the spinach (with the rinsing water still clinging to its leaves) in a large saucepan. Cover and cook over medium-low heat until wilted and just tender, 4 to 5 minutes. Drain thoroughly and let cool. Chop finely and place in a medium bowl. Add the remaining filling ingredients and mix well.

Roll out the pasta dough to the thinnest setting on the pasta machine. It is important for the pasta to be very thin, as each raviolo will have a double thickness around the edges. Using a fluted pastry wheel, cut the pasta into strips about 3 inches wide (they can be as long as you like). Place heaped teaspoons of the filling about 1½ inches apart along the length of one strip, about ¾ inch from one long edge. Dampen the pasta dough around the filling. Fold the dough over so the long edges meet. Press all around the mounds of filling, sealing carefully. Using the fluted pastry wheel, cut between the mounds of filling to form ravioli. Place the ravioli on baking sheets lined with flour-dusted dish towels. Repeat with the remaining filling and dough. Cover with plastic wrap and refrigerate until ready to cook.

Preheat the oven to 350°F. Bring a large pot of salted water to a boil over high heat. In a small saucepan, heat the cream and butter together gently over low heat, stirring. Season with salt and pepper, and keep warm.

In batches, without crowding, cook the ravioli in the boiling water until al dente, 3 to 4 minutes. Using a slotted spoon or a skimmer, remove the ravioli from the water and transfer to a warmed heatproof serving dish. Sprinkle each layer of ravioli with a little of the cream sauce. When all the ravioli are in the dish, bake until heated through, 5 to 10 minutes. Sprinkle with grated Parmesan cheese and serve immediately, with more Parmesan passed on the side so that guests can help themselves.

SEMOLINA GNOCCHI

Semolina flour is a golden and gritty-textured flour that is ground from durum wheat. It is used to make very light Italian dumplings, which are known as *gnocchi alla romana*. If you would like to serve the gnocchi with a sauce, Delicate Tomato Sauce would be a very good choice.

MAKES 4 TO 6 SERVINGS

   2½ cups milk
   1 small onion, thickly sliced
   1 bay leaf
   1 mace blade or a pinch of grated nutmeg
   ¾ cup semolina flour
   1 large egg yolk
   4 tablespoons unsalted butter
   ½ cup freshly grated Parmesan cheese
   Salt and freshly ground pepper, to taste

In a large saucepan, heat the milk with the thickly sliced onion, the bay leaf, and mace over low heat until bubbles start forming around the edge of the milk. Spoon the onion, bay leaf, and mace out of the milk and discard them. Stirring constantly, gradually add the semolina, and continue stirring until the mixture is very thick, 2 to 3 minutes. Cover the pan, reduce the heat to very low, and cook very gently, stirring often, for 15 minutes. Remove from the heat. Stirring briskly, add the egg yolk, 2 tablespoons of the butter, and ¼ cup of the Parmesan. Season with salt and pepper. Wet a baking sheet with water. Pour the semolina onto the baking sheet and, using the palm of your hand, spread into a ½-inch-thick slab. Leave to cool until firm.

Preheat the oven to 325°F. Lightly butter a 9- by 13-inch baking dish. Using a 1½-inch round biscuit cutter (or, alternatively, the top of a wine glass if you do not have a biscuit cutter), cut out rounds from the semolina. Or, if you prefer, use a sharp knife to cut it into squares or triangles. When you have cut out as many shapes as you can, press the leftover scraps together until smooth, and cut out more rounds until the semolina is all used.

Arrange the semolina rounds in rows, slightly overlapping, in the dish. Sprinkle with the remaining Parmesan cheese and dot all over with the remaining 2 tablespoons butter. Bake until nicely browned, about 30 minutes.

SPINACH GNOCCHI WITH BUTTER AND SAGE

These gnocchi are actually quite easy to make, and have a sublime texture. To guarantee success with this recipe, be sure not to overhandle the gnocchi when you are shaping them.

MAKES 4 SERVINGS

    1½ pounds fresh spinach leaves, thick stems discarded
    1 cup freshly grated Parmesan cheese
    ½ cup ricotta cheese
    3 large egg yolks
    ¼ teaspoon freshly grated nutmeg
    Salt and freshly ground pepper, to taste
    All-purpose flour, for coating
    8 tablespoons (1 stick) unsalted butter
    16 large fresh sage leaves
    1 lemon, cut into quarters

In a large pot of boiling salted water, cook the spinach until wilted and tender, about 3 minutes. Drain and refresh the spinach in cold water, then squeeze by handfuls in a clean dish towel to remove all the excess moisture.

In a food processor fitted with the metal blade, process the spinach with ¾ cup Parmesan cheese, the ricotta, egg yolks, nutmeg, and a seasoning of salt and pepper until the spinach is evenly chopped and the mixture is well combined. Spread in a shallow baking dish, cover with plastic wrap, and refrigerate until firm, at least 2 hours.

Using a pair of tablespoons, form the spinach mixture into small egg shapes, and roll each one in flour. As they are shaped, place the gnocchi on a lightly floured baking sheet.

Preheat the oven to 200°F. In a large saucepan, bring 2 quarts salted water to a boil over high heat, then reduce the heat so that the water remains just at a steady simmer. In batches, and taking care not to crowd them, cook the gnocchi until they are swollen and floating buoyantly on the surface, about 5 minutes. Remove the gnocchi from the water with a slotted spoon or skimmer and transfer them to a heatproof serving bowl. Cover loosely with aluminum foil and keep warm in the oven while cooking the remaining gnocchi.

In a medium frying pan, melt the butter over medium heat and continue to cook until it is a nut-brown color. Add the sage leaves and cook until slightly crisp, about 1 minute. Pour the sage and butter over the gnocchi, sprinkle with the remaining grated Parmesan cheese, and serve immediately, with lemon wedges.

CHINESE EGG NOODLES WITH BROWNED GARLIC, CHILES, AND CILANTRO

Garlic fans will love this easy lunch or supper dish. Whenever you find them, purchase fresh Chinese egg noodles—they freeze very well. You can make this dish with fresh or dried tagliatelle or linguine, too.

MAKES 4 SERVINGS

    1 pound fresh Chinese egg noodles
    6 tablespoons peanut oil
    2 tablespoons Asian dark sesame oil
    8 garlic cloves, thinly sliced
    2 hot green chile peppers (such as jalapeño), seeded and thinly sliced
    ⅓ cup chopped fresh cilantro leaves

In a pot of boiling salted water, cook the egg noodles until just tender, about 3 minutes. Drain well.

Meanwhile, in a wok or large nonstick frying pan, heat the peanut and sesame oils over medium heat until hot. Add the garlic and stir-fry until golden-brown, about 1 minute. Ad the chiles and stir briefly. Add the drained noodles and toss to coat with the flavored oil. Stir in the cilantro, and serve.

VEGETABLE STIR-FRY ON A NOODLE PILLOW

You'll need a 12-inch nonstick frying pan to prepare this colorful dish. The vegetables can be stir-fried in a wok, or a frying pan works just as well.

MAKES 6 SERVINGS

    2 cups broccoli florets
    2 tablespoons vegetable oil
    2 scallions, chopped
    2 tablespoons minced fresh ginger
    2 garlic cloves, minced
    3 medium celery ribs, thinly sliced on the diagonal
    2 medium carrots, thinly sliced on the diagonal
    1 medium red bell pepper, seeded and cut into ½-inch-wide strips
    2 medium zucchini (or 1 zucchini and 1 yellow squash), cut in half lengthwise and then into ¼-inch-thick slices
    1 (10-ounce) can baby corn, drained and rinsed
    1 cup bean sprouts
Noodle Pillow
    1 pound fresh Chinese noodles or linguine
    3 tablespoons vegetable oil
Stir-Fry Sauce
    ¾ cup chicken stock
    ¼ cup soy sauce

1 tablespoon rice vinegar

1 tablespoon dry sherry

1 tablespoon light brown sugar

½ teaspoon chile sauce with garlic, or ¼ teaspoon
chile flakes

4 teaspoons cornstarch

Preheat the oven to 200°F.

To make the noodle pillow, cook the noodles in
a large pot of boiling salted water until just tender,
about 3 minutes. Drain, rinse well under cold water,
and drain again. Toss with 1 tablespoon of the oil.
Heat the remaining 2 tablespoons oil in a 12-inch
nonstick frying pan over medium heat. Add the
noodles and spread into a thick cake. Cook until the
underside is golden-brown, about 5 minutes. Slide the
noodle cake out of the pan onto a large rimless baking
sheet. Return to the pan, crisp-side up, and cook until
the other side is golden, about 4 minutes. Transfer
the noodle cake to a paper-towel-lined baking sheet,
and keep it warm in the oven while you are stir-frying
the vegetables.

VEGETABLE STIR-FRY ON A NOODLE PILLOW

To make the stir-fry sauce, mix together all of the
ingredients except the cornstarch in a medium bowl.
Add the cornstarch and whisk to mix thoroughly, then
set the bowl aside.

In a medium saucepan of boiling salted water,
cook the broccoli until crisp-tender, about 2 minutes.
Drain, refresh, and set aside.

Heat the oil in the frying pan over high heat. Add
the scallions, ginger, and garlic and stir until very
fragrant, about 30 seconds. Add the celery, carrots,
and red pepper and stir-fry for 1 minute. Add the
zucchini and stir-fry for 1 more minute. Add the
broccoli florets and corn, and stir-fry until all the
vegetables are heated through, about 1 minute longer.
Add the bean sprouts and the sauce mixture and cook,
stirring, until the sauce thickens, about 1 minute.
Place the noodle pillow on a large serving platter,
and pour the vegetables on top. Serve immediately.

Rice, Grains, and Legumes

PLAIN STEAMED RICE

This method works well with any kind of long-grain rice, from basmati and jasmine to supermarket extra-fancy. There is no need to rinse domestic rice. If you are feeling lazy, and don't want to measure the rice, it can be cooked in boiling water, just like pasta.

MAKES 4 SERVINGS

½ teaspoon salt
1½ cups long-grain rice

In a medium saucepan, bring 3 cups water and the salt to a boil over high heat. Add the rice and return to the boil. Reduce the heat to low, cover, and simmer until the rice is tender, about 15 minutes. Remove from the heat and let stand, covered, for 5 minutes before serving.

BROWN RICE PILAF

Brown rice is much denser than white rice, and takes longer to cook. When plainly steamed, it can be a bit stodgy, but cooking it in a flavorful stock makes it much more interesting.

MAKES 4 SERVINGS

4 tablespoons unsalted butter
2 tablespoons olive oil
1 medium onion, chopped
1 cup brown rice
3½ cups chicken stock
¼ teaspoon salt

In a medium saucepan, heat the butter and oil over medium heat. Add the onion and cook until softened, about 5 minutes. Add the rice and stir until completely coated with butter and oil, about 1 minute. Add the stock and salt, and bring to a boil. Reduce the heat to low, cover, and simmer until all of the liquid has been absorbed and the rice is tender, about 1 hour.

RISOTTO MILANESE

Risotto must be made with Italian rice, such as Arborio or Carnaroli, as only they have the proper amount of starch to give a creamy quality to the sauce. The stock is added gradually so the rice swells and cooks slowly. Serve this as a first course, or as the classic accompaniment to osso bucco.

MAKES 4 SERVINGS

5 cups chicken or beef stock
¼ teaspoon crushed saffron threads
4 tablespoons unsalted butter
2 tablespoons olive oil
1 small onion, finely chopped
1⅓ cups Italian rice for risotto
½ cup freshly grated Parmesan cheese
Salt and freshly ground pepper, to taste

In a medium saucepan, heat the stock with the saffron until simmering. Reduce the heat to very low, and keep the stock at the barest simmer while making the risotto.

In a large, heavy-bottomed frying pan or sauté pan, heat 2 tablespoons of the butter and the oil over medium heat. Add the onion and cook until softened, about 5 minutes. Add the rice and cook, stirring often, until it becomes a little translucent, about 2 minutes. Reduce the heat to medium-low. Add about ½ cup of the simmering stock: it will hiss and bubble violently, but will then subside to a fairly quiet simmer. Stir constantly until the rice absorbs almost all the stock, then add another ½ cup of the stock, and stir until this has been absorbed. Continue adding stock and stirring until the rice is barely tender (*al dente*, like pasta, with a slightly resistant bite), about 25 minutes. The finished risotto should have a creamy, but not soupy, consistency. If you run out of stock, you can use hot water. (Conversely, you may not use all of the stock.) Stir in the Parmesan cheese and the remaining butter, and season with salt and pepper. Serve hot.

Chicken Liver Risotto: Omit the saffron, and add 6 large sage leaves to the stock. Cook 3 chopped chicken livers with the onion. Before adding the stock to the rice, stir in ½ cup dry Marsala or vermouth.

ASPARAGUS RISOTTO

If you use vegetable stock, this can be a vegetarian main course.

MAKES 4 SERVINGS

1 pound asparagus spears, woody stems discarded
5 cups chicken stock
½ cup dry white wine
4 tablespoons unsalted butter
1 medium onion, finely chopped
1⅓ cups Italian rice for risotto
1 heaped tablespoon chopped fresh mint or tarragon
3 tablespoons freshly grated Parmesan cheese
Salt and freshly ground pepper, to taste

Cut off the top 3 or 4 inches from each asparagus spear; cut each asparagus tip into 3 pieces, and set aside. Coarsely chop the asparagus stalks. In a medium saucepan, bring the stock and wine to a boil over high heat. Add the chopped asparagus stalks and reduce the heat to low. Cover and simmer until the stock is flavored with asparagus, about 20 minutes. Strain the stock and discard the stalks. Return the strained stock to the saucepan and bring back to a boil. Add the reserved asparagus tips and cook until just tender, about 3 minutes. Remove the tips with a slotted spoon and set aside. Keep the stock at a bare simmer while making the risotto.

In a large, heavy-bottomed frying pan or sauté pan, heat the butter over medium heat. Add the onion and cook until softened, about 5 minutes. Add the rice and stir until slightly translucent and coated with butter, about 2 minutes. Reduce the heat to medium-low. Add about ½ cup of the simmering stock; it will hiss and bubble violently, but will then subside to a fairly quiet simmer. Stir constantly until the rice absorbs almost all the stock, then add another ½ cup of the stock, and stir until this has been absorbed.

Continue adding stock and stirring until the rice is barely tender (al dente, like pasta, with a slightly resistant bite), about 25 minutes. The finished risotto should have a creamy, but not soupy, consistency. If you run out of stock, you can use hot water instead. (Conversely, you may not use all of the stock.) When the rice is almost tender, add the reserved asparagus tips and mint. Just before serving, stir in the Parmesan cheese, and season with salt and pepper. Serve immediately in warmed soup bowls.

WILD RICE PILAF WITH WILD MUSHROOMS

An interesting mix of European and American ingredients makes an enticing side dish for poultry, game, or pork. When cleaning the fresh mushrooms, wipe them with a damp cloth, and only rinse them quickly under cold water if absolutely necessary.

MAKES 6 SERVINGS
  1 cup dried wild mushrooms, such as porcini (1 ounce)
  1½ cups wild rice, soaked in water overnight and drained well
  2 cups chicken stock
  6 tablespoons olive oil
  1 pound assorted fresh mushrooms, preferably a mixture of cremini, oyster mushrooms, and stemmed shiitakes, trimmed and sliced
  1 medium red onion, chopped
  2 garlic cloves, minced
  1 tablespoon chopped parsley
  2 tablespoons unsalted butter
  3 tablespoons freshly grated Parmesan cheese, plus more for serving

In a small bowl, soak the dried mushrooms in 1 cup warm water until they are softened, about 30 minutes. Lift the mushrooms out of the liquid and squeeze them dry over the bowl of soaking liquid. Drain the liquid through a cheesecloth- or paper-towel-lined sieve to remove the grit. Set the mushrooms and liquid to one side.

In a medium saucepan, combine the drained wild rice and chicken stock, and bring to a simmer. Cover and cook over medium-low heat until the rice is just tender, about 30 minutes.

Meanwhile, in a frying pan, heat 4 tablespoons of the oil over medium heat. Add the fresh mushrooms and cook, stirring often, until golden-brown, about 10 minutes. Transfer to a bowl and set aside. In the same pan, heat the remaining 2 tablespoons oil and cook the onion and garlic until softened, about 5 minutes. Add the soaked mushrooms and parsley, and cook for 2 more minutes. Stir into the wild rice, along with the strained soaking liquid. Cook, uncovered, over low heat, stirring often, until rice absorbs almost all of the liquid, about 10 minutes. Stir in the cooked mushrooms and continue cooking until the liquid is totally absorbed, about 5 minutes. Add the butter and cheese, and stir until melted.

Serve immediately, passing a bowl of Parmesan cheese on the side.

SPICED BASMATI RICE

Spiced rice makes a wonderful accompaniment to curries as well as roast chicken. However, you should warn your guests in advance to look out for the spice pieces!

MAKES 4 SERVINGS
  1 (2-inch) cinnamon stick
  8 cardamom pods
  4 whole cloves
  4 tablespoons clarified butter
  1 large onion, cut into very thin rings
  2 bay leaves
  1⅓ cups basmati rice
  ⅓ cup raisins
  ¼ cup blanched slivered almonds
  ¼ teaspoon salt

Coarsely crush the cinnamon, cardamom, and cloves with a rolling pin or under a heavy pan. In a medium frying pan, heat 1 tablespoon of the butter over medium heat. Add the onions and cook, stirring occasionally, until the onions are a deep cinnamon-brown, about 12 minutes or so. Transfer them to a plate and then set aside.

In the same pan, melt the remaining 3 tablespoons of butter over low heat. Stir in the crushed spices and bay leaves. Add the rice and cook, stirring often, until translucent, about 7 minutes. Add 2⅔ cups water, and stir in the raisins, almonds, and salt. Bring to a boil, then cover and reduce the heat to low. Simmer until the rice is tender and has absorbed the liquid, about 15 minutes. Remove from the heat and let stand, covered, for 5 minutes. Scatter the onion rings over the rice and serve.

PAELLA

What a great dish for a party! It can be prepared with clams instead of mussels if you prefer, or with 6 ounces chopped smoked chorizo sausage, sautéed with the onions. Use Italian rice for risotto, as this most closely resembles the Spanish rice that gives the dish its character.

MAKES 4 TO 6 SERVINGS
    1 (2½-pound) chicken, rinsed, patted dry, and cut into
        4 pieces; or 2 pounds chicken thighs
    ¼ teaspoon crumbled saffron threads
    5 cups chicken stock
    1 pound mussels, scrubbed and debearded if necessary
    4 tablespoons olive oil
    1 medium onion, finely chopped
    1 medium red bell pepper, peeled, seeded, and finely
        chopped
    2 garlic cloves, minced
    1½ cups drained and chopped canned plum tomatoes
    1 bay leaf
    2 cups Italian rice for risotto
    8 ounces squid, cleaned, bodies cut into ¼-inch rings,
        and tentacles coarsely chopped
    Salt and freshly ground pepper, to taste
    ¾ cup shelled fresh or frozen peas
    12 medium shrimp, unpeeled
    ½ cup black Mediterranean olives
    1 lemon, thinly sliced into rounds

Chop the chicken pieces, except the drumsticks, through the bone into 1½-inch pieces; leave the drumsticks whole. Add the saffron to the stock and let soak. In a large saucepan, combine the mussels and ½ cup water, and bring to a boil over high heat. Cover and cook until all the mussels have opened, 4 to 5 minutes. Remove the mussels and set aside. Strain the mussel liquid through a sieve lined with a damp paper towel, and reserve the liquid.

PAELLA

In a very large, heavy-bottomed paella pan or frying pan, heat the oil over medium-high heat. Add the pieces of chicken and cook until browned on all sides, about 8 minutes. Add the onion, red pepper, and garlic and cook, stirring often, until the vegetables soften, about 5 minutes. Add the chicken stock mixture, tomatoes, and bay leaf and bring to a simmer. Stir in the rice and squid, and season with salt and pepper. Spread out the ingredients in the pan.

Reduce the heat to low, put a heat diffuser under the pan, cover, and simmer gently until the rice is almost tender, about 20 minutes. Stir in the peas, and arrange the shrimp and mussels over the rice. Place the olives around the edge. Add the reserved mussel liquid, then cover and continue cooking until the rice has absorbed all of the liquid and is tender, about 5 more minutes.

Serve from the frying pan, garnishing each serving with a slice of lemon.

CURRIED FRIED RICE WITH SHRIMP AND ASPARAGUS

There is a trick to cooking good fried rice—the rice must be well chilled, or it will clump up in the pan. This version uses basmati rice and curry to make fragrant fried rice, Indian style.

MAKES 4 SERVINGS
    2 tablespoons vegetable oil
    8 ounces medium shrimp, peeled and deveined
    1 medium onion, chopped
    1 medium red bell pepper, seeded and chopped
    1 tablespoon minced fresh ginger
    2 garlic cloves, minced
    1 tablespoon Madras-style curry powder
    3 cups cold cooked basmati rice
    3 tablespoons chicken stock
    1 tablespoon soy sauce
    Chopped scallions, for garnish

In a large wok or frying pan, heat 1 tablespoon of the oil over medium heat. Add the shrimp and cook until firm and pink, about 3 minutes. Transfer the shrimp to a plate and set aside.

In the same pan, heat the remaining 1 tablespoon oil over medium heat. Add the onion, red pepper, ginger, and garlic, and cook until the onion is translucent, about 5 minutes. Add the curry powder and stir for 30 seconds. Add the rice, chicken stock, and soy sauce and stir-fry until the rice is heated through, about 3 minutes, returning the shrimp to the pan during the last minute. Serve, garnishing each serving with chopped scallions.

BULGUR PILAF

Bulgur pilaf is a wonderful alternative to rice as a side dish, but can also serve as a light entrée.

MAKES 4 SERVINGS

2 tablespoons olive oil
1 small onion, chopped
2 garlic cloves, minced
1⅓ cups medium or coarse bulgur
3 cups chicken stock
Salt, to taste
A pinch of cayenne pepper
¼ cup chopped fresh parsley
3 tablespoons lemon juice
⅔ cup plain yogurt, for serving

In a large frying pan, heat the oil over medium heat. Add the onion and cook, stirring occasionally, until golden-brown, 6 to 8 minutes. Add the garlic and cook for 1 more minute. Add the bulgur and stir until well coated with the oil. Add 1½ cups of the stock, and season with salt and cayenne. Bring just to a boil, then reduce the heat to low. Cover and cook gently for 10 minutes. Add the remaining 1½ cups of the stock, cover again, and continue cooking for 10 minutes.

Remove from the heat. Stir the bulgur, then cover the pan with a dish towel and the lid. Let steam until the grains are light and separate, about 10 minutes. Stir in the parsley and lemon juice, and taste to check the seasoning. Serve hot or cold, with the yogurt on the side.

TABBOULEH

Tabbouleh is the perfect hot weather salad, since it doesn't need to be cooked. The bulgur is merely soaked until it is nice and tender, and then mixed with lots of good things.

MAKES 4 SERVINGS

1 cup fine bulgur
1 cup chopped scallions
2 large tomatoes, peeled, seeded, and chopped
¼ cup chopped fresh parsley
¼ cup chopped fresh mint
¼ cup lemon juice, or more as needed
3 tablespoons olive oil, or more as needed
Salt and freshly ground pepper, to taste
Crisp romaine lettuce leaves, for garnish

In a bowl, combine the bulgur with enough cold water to cover by 2 inches. Let soak for 15 minutes. Drain in a fine sieve. By handfuls, squeeze the excess water from the bulgur, then place in a large bowl.

Add the scallions, tomatoes, parsley, and mint. Mix in the lemon juice and oil. Taste and balance the flavors with more lemon juice and oil, if needed, and season with salt and pepper. Place the tabbouleh on a deep platter, and surround with lettuce leaves. To eat, scoop up the tabbouleh in a lettuce leaf.

SOFT POLENTA VENETO-STYLE

There are two ways to enjoy polenta, soft and firm. Cooked soft, as in this method, the polenta can be served as an accompaniment to stews, or even served as a main course, topped with a spoonful of *ragù*. To vary, you could stir in chopped ham or minced fresh herbs, instead of or in addition to the Parmesan.

MAKES 6 TO 8 SERVINGS

1½ teaspoons salt
4 cups polenta (not quick-cooking) or stoneground yellow cornmeal
½ cup freshly grated Parmesan cheese
4 to 6 tablespoons unsalted butter, cut into pieces

Bring 2 quarts water to a boil in a large, heavy-bottomed saucepan over high heat. Add the salt. Reduce the heat to low so the water is simmering steadily. Gradually whisk in the polenta. Whisk the polenta vigorously to dissolve any lumps. Reduce the heat to very low and cook, whisking often (if you have a heavy-bottomed pan, you don't have to whisk constantly as old recipes state), until the polenta is tender and pulls away from the sides, about 20 minutes. Remove from the heat, and whisk in the Parmesan and butter. Serve immediately.

Grilled Polenta: Pour the hot polenta mixture into an oiled straight-sided rectangular pan, to make a layer ¾ inch thick. Cover with plastic wrap and let cool until firm. Then cut into squares. Heat a ridged cast-iron grill pan over medium heat. Brush the polenta squares with olive oil, then cook until crisp and lightly charred on both sides, 4 to 5 minutes. Serve hot.

POLENTA FRITTI

Firm, golden, fried polenta is perfect with lightly sauced meat and poultry. It can also be a luscious first course, topped with crumbled Gorgonzola cheese.

MAKES 4 TO 6 SERVINGS

1 cup milk
¼ teaspoon salt
1 cup yellow cornmeal, preferably stoneground
½ cup freshly grated Parmesan cheese
Olive oil, for frying

Lightly oil a 6- by 11-inch baking dish. In a heavy-bottomed saucepan, bring the milk, 1 cup water, and salt to a boil. Gradually whisk in the cornmeal. Reduce the heat to low and cook until very thick, about 2 minutes. Remove from the heat, and whisk in the cheese. Immediately pour into the pan and spread evenly. Let cool until firm, about 1 hour.

Cut the polenta into eight rectangles. Lightly oil a griddle or a large frying pan and heat over medium heat. Cook the polenta squares, turning once, until golden-brown on both sides, about 4 minutes. Serve hot.

TAMALE SPOONBREAD

This cornmeal-based side dish is almost a cornbread, but its spoonable quality resembles a zesty polenta. It has a firm topping and a creamy layer underneath.

MAKES 6 SERVINGS

1 cup yellow cornmeal, preferably stoneground
½ cup all-purpose flour
2 teaspoons chili powder
1 teaspoon baking soda
1 teaspoon salt
1 cup buttermilk
2 large eggs, beaten
1½ cups milk
1 cup shredded sharp Cheddar cheese
1 hot fresh green chile pepper (such as jalepeño), seeded and minced
1 cup fresh or defrosted frozen corn kernels
2 tablespoons unsalted butter, cut into pieces

Preheat the oven to 400°F. Whisk the cornmeal, flour, chili powder, baking soda, and salt. Stir in the buttermilk and eggs. Add 1 cup of the milk, the cheese, chile pepper, and corn, and mix just until they are all combined.

Put the butter in a 10-inch round cake pan and heat in the oven until the butter has melted. Pour in the cornmeal mixture, and top with the remaining ½ cup milk. Bake until a toothpick inserted 2 inches from the center comes out clean and the center is barely set, about 25 minutes. Let stand for 5 minutes, then serve.

KASHA WITH APPLES

Kasha has an elusive nutty flavor that blends well with apples. Serve this with roast pork, duck, or chicken.

MAKES 4 SERVINGS

2 tablespoons unsalted butter
1 tart green apple (such as Granny Smith), peeled, cored, and cut into ¼-inch pieces
1 large egg
1 cup kasha
2 cups chicken stock
Salt and freshly ground pepper, to taste

In a medium nonstick frying pan, heat 1 tablespoon butter over medium heat. Add the apple and cook until tender and lightly browned, about 4 minutes. Transfer the apple to a plate and set aside.

Add the remaining 1 tablespoon butter to the pan and heat over medium-low heat. In a medium bowl, beat the egg. Add the kasha and mix well to coat with egg. Pour into the pan and cook, stirring often, until the egg is set, about 3 minutes. Add the chicken stock, and season with salt and pepper. Bring to a simmer. Cover tightly and cook until the kasha is tender and the liquid is absorbed, about 15 minutes. Stir in the apple and cook for 1 more minute. Transfer to a warmed serving bowl and serve.

INDIAN MILLET

Here, cauliflower and zucchini add their color to a simple pot of spiced millet, to make a delicious lunch, supper, or side dish.

MAKES 6 SERVINGS

4 tablespoons unsalted butter
2 medium onions, 1 thinly sliced and 1 chopped
½ small head cauliflower, cut into small florets (about 3 cups)
2 medium zucchini, cut into ¼-inch dice
1 cup millet
2 garlic cloves, minced
1 teaspoon cumin seeds
4 whole cardamom pods
4 whole cloves
Salt and freshly ground pepper, to taste

In a medium frying pan, heat 2 tablespoons of the butter over medium heat. Add the sliced onion and cook, stirring occasionally, until a deep cinnamon-brown, about 12 minutes. Transfer to a plate, and cover to keep warm.

In the same pan, heat the remaining 2 tablespoons of butter over medium heat. Add the chopped onion, cauliflower, and zucchini, and cook, stirring often, until lightly browned, about 6 minutes. Add the millet, garlic, cumin, cardamom, and cloves, and cook, stirring often, until well combined and the spices are fragrant, about 4 minutes. Pour in enough water just to cover the millet. Season. Bring to a boil, then reduce the heat to low. Cover and cook, fluffing the millet occasionally with a fork, until just tender,

20 to 25 minutes. Remove from the heat. Cover the pan with a dish towel and then the lid, and let steam for 5 minutes. Fluff the millet a final time with a fork. Scatter the onions on top, then serve hot.

BOSTON BAKED BEANS

Long, slow cooking and a good heavy cooking utensil (preferably an old-fashioned earthenware bean pot) are the keys to this traditional dish's success.

MAKES 4 TO 6 SERVINGS

1 pound dried Great Northern or navy beans, soaked overnight and drained

2 tablespoons unsalted butter

¼ pound rindless salt pork or bacon, thickly sliced

1 medium onion, peeled

2 tablespoons unsulfured molasses

2 tablespoons tomato paste

1 tablespoon spicy brown mustard

1 teaspoon cider vinegar

1 teaspoon salt

Place the drained beans in a large pot and add enough cold water to cover by 2 inches. Bring to a boil over high heat. Reduce the heat to medium-low and simmer until the beans are tender, about 1 hour, depending on their dryness. Drain, reserving the cooking liquid. Place the beans in a 4- to 5-quart bean pot or Dutch oven.

Preheat the oven to 300°F. In a medium frying pan, heat the butter over medium heat. Add the salt pork and cook until browned on both sides, about 5 minutes. Bury the salt pork and onion in the beans, and stir in the fat from the frying pan. Stir the molasses, tomato paste, mustard, vinegar, and salt into the reserved cooking liquid, and pour over the beans. Cover tightly and bake for 2 hours. Remove the lid and continue baking until the liquid has thickened, about 30 minutes. Let stand for 10 minutes; serve hot.

WHITE BEAN, VEGETABLE, AND ROSEMARY STEW

This makes a large batch of hearty vegetarian stew, and it reheats well. You can substitute 6 cups canned cannellini beans, well rinsed, for the freshly cooked beans.

MAKES 8 TO 12 SERVINGS

¼ cup olive oil

1 large onion, chopped

1 large red bell pepper, seeded and chopped

2 medium zucchini, cut into ½-inch pieces

2 medium carrots, cut into ½-inch pieces

2 medium celery ribs, chopped

2 garlic cloves, chopped

1 cup hearty red wine

1 pound dried white beans, cooked and drained

1½ cups peeled, seeded, and chopped ripe plum tomatoes; or use drained canned tomatoes

1½ tablespoons chopped fresh rosemary or 2 teaspoons dried rosemary

1 bay leaf

½ teaspoon chile flakes

Extra virgin olive oil, for serving

Freshly grated Parmesan cheese, for serving

In a large Dutch oven or flameproof casserole, heat the oil over medium heat. Add the onion, bell pepper, zucchini, carrots, celery, and garlic. Cover and cook, stirring often, until the onion is soft and golden, about 10 minutes. Add the red wine and bring to a boil over high heat. Stir in the cooked white beans, tomatoes, rosemary, bay leaf, and chile flakes, and bring to a simmer. Reduce the heat to low and simmer, uncovered, until the vegetables are tender, about 30 minutes. Serve hot, drizzling each serving with extra virgin olive oil, and passing a bowl of Parmesan cheese on the side.

CUBAN BLACK BEANS AND RICE

Bean and rice dishes are daily fare in many Central and South American countries. This Cuban recipe is one of the most tasty examples.

MAKES 6 SERVINGS

1 cup dried black beans, soaked overnight and drained

2 tablespoons olive oil

1 large onion, chopped

1 small green bell pepper, seeded and chopped

1 hot fresh green chile pepper (such as jalapeño), seeded and minced

1 garlic clove, minced

½ cup coarsely chopped smoked or boiled ham (optional)

⅔ cup long-grain rice

2 ripe plum tomatoes, peeled, seeded, and chopped

Salt, to taste

Put the beans in a medium saucepan, and add enough cold water to cover by 1 inch. Bring to a boil over medium heat. Reduce the heat to medium-low and simmer until just tender, about 1 hour.

Meanwhile, in a medium frying pan, heat the oil over medium heat. Add the onion and cook until soft and lightly browned, about 7 minutes. Stir in the green pepper, chile pepper, and garlic, along with the

ham, if using. Continue cooking for about 5 minutes. Add the rice and stir until well coated with the oil, about 2 minutes. Stir in the tomatoes.

Add the rice mixture to the pot of beans and stir to mix. Pour in enough cold water so that all the ingredients are covered by liquid. Bring to a boil over high heat, then return the heat to medium-low. Season with salt to taste. Simmer until the rice is tender, about 20 minutes. If necessary, add a little more water during cooking: the beans and rice should be bathed in a light sauce.

LENTILS AND RICE WITH FRIED ONIONS

This dish from Baghdad, called *magedra*, is known as "the food of the poor." Serve it with a spoonful of plain yogurt or chopped tomatoes and scallions.

MAKES 4 SERVINGS
⅔ cup brown lentils
3 tablespoons olive oil
2 large onions, thinly sliced

CUBAN BLACK BEANS AND RICE

1⅓ cups long-grain rice
Salt, to taste

Put the lentils in a saucepan with 5 cups cold water. Bring to a boil, then simmer until tender, about 30 minutes. In a frying pan, heat 1½ tablespoons of oil. Add the onions and cook, stirring occasionally, until cinnamon-brown, about 12 minutes. Transfer to a plate, and cover to keep warm.

Drain the lentils, reserving the liquid. Return this to the saucepan and bring to a boil. Add the remaining 1½ tablespoons oil, then the rice and salt. Reduce the heat to medium-low. Partially cover the pan and cook until the rice has absorbed most of the liquid and is tender, about 15 minutes. Let stand, uncovered, until all of the liquid has been absorbed, about 5 minutes. Stir in the lentils and cook over low heat, stirring constantly, just until heated through, 1 or 2 minutes. Transfer to a dish and scatter with onions. Serve hot.

Salads

ARUGULA AND BACON SALAD

The slightly bitter edge of arugula is tempered by the crisp saltiness of bacon in this great salad. Another time, substitute dandelion or curly endive for the arugula, or use tender young spinach leaves plus a diced avocado.

MAKES 4 TO 6 SERVINGS

1 tablespoon white wine vinegar or sherry vinegar
A pinch of granulated sugar
Salt and freshly ground pepper, to taste
2 tablespoons olive oil
6 strips thick-sliced bacon, cut into ¼-inch-wide pieces
1 pound arugula (about 2 large bunches), tough stems discarded

In a small bowl, whisk the vinegar with the sugar and a seasoning of salt and pepper. Gradually whisk in the oil, and set the dressing aside.

Just before you are ready to serve, cook the bacon in a medium frying pan over medium heat until crisp, about 5 minutes.

Toss the arugula with the dressing. Pour the bacon with its fat over the arugula and toss again. Taste a leaf and balance the flavor of the dressing with more vinegar or oil if needed. Serve immediately.

SPINACH AND WALNUT SALAD

This simple but delicious salad can easily be varied, for example by sprinkling over about 2 ounces crumbled Gorgonzola cheese or 1 or 2 chopped hard-boiled eggs.

MAKES 4 SERVINGS

12 ounces fresh young spinach leaves, tough stems removed
1 cup walnut halves or pieces, preferably freshly shelled
Dressing
½ tablespoon white wine vinegar
½ tablespoon white wine
¾ teaspoon Dijon mustard
1 garlic clove, minced with a sprinkle of salt
Salt and freshly ground pepper, to taste
¼ cup walnut oil
1 tablespoon extra-virgin olive oil

To make the dressing, whisk together the white wine vinegar, wine, Dijon mustard, minced garlic, and a seasoning of salt and pepper. Gradually whisk in the walnut and olive oils.

Put the spinach in a large salad bowl, and sprinkle with the walnut halves or pieces. Add the dressing, toss, and serve immediately.

ROMAINE SALAD WITH BALSAMIC CAESAR DRESSING

The original Caesar salad used a coddled egg in the dressing, but this updated version leaves it out as a concession to modern tastes.

MAKES 4 SERVINGS

1 large head romaine lettuce, torn into bite-sized pieces
1 cup croutons, fried or baked
½ cup freshly grated Parmesan cheese
Dressing
2 tablespoons balsamic vinegar
1 teaspoon anchovy paste
1 garlic clove, crushed through a press
½ cup olive oil
Salt and freshly ground pepper, to taste

To make the dressing, in a bowl, whisk together the vinegar, anchovy paste, and garlic. Gradually whisk in the oil. Season with salt and pepper.

In a large bowl, toss the lettuce thoroughly with the dressing until well combined. Add the fried or baked croutons and the Parmesan cheese, and toss again. Serve immediately.

Romaine Salad with Balsamic Herb Vinaigrette: In a medium bowl, whisk together 2 teaspoons each balsamic vinegar and lemon juice with a seasoning of salt and pepper. Gradually whisk in ¼ cup each olive oil and vegetable oil, then add 2 shallots, finely chopped, and 2 teaspoons each chopped fresh tarragon, chopped fresh chives or scallions, and chopped fresh parsley or chervil. Toss the lettuce thoroughly with the dressing and serve immediately.

BIBB LETTUCE WITH LEMON-POPPY SEED DRESSING

A sweet-and-sour dressing with roots in Pennsylvania Dutch cooking, this is excellent on Bibb lettuce.

MAKES 4 SERVINGS

2 large heads Bibb lettuce, torn into bite-sized pieces
1 medium cucumber, peeled and thinly sliced
Dressing
3 tablespoons lemon juice
Grated zest of 1 lemon
1 tablespoon red wine vinegar
1 tablespoon brown sugar
1 tablespoon Dijon mustard
2 tablespoons poppy seeds
¾ cup vegetable oil
Salt and freshly ground pepper, to taste

To make the dressing, combine all of the ingredients except the vegetable oil in a blender. With the machine running, gradually pour in the oil until the dressing is thick and smooth. Season with salt and pepper. (The dressing can be kept, covered, in the refrigerator for up to 3 days.)

Place the lettuce and cucumber in a large bowl and add the dressing. Toss well, and serve immediately.

CELERY AND PARMESAN SALAD

Serve this simple salad as an unusual first course, or as a separate salad course after roast veal or pork. Use a piece of fresh Parmesan that is young and moist, not aged and dry.

MAKES 6 SERVINGS

 1 (2-ounce) piece Parmesan cheese
 8 medium celery ribs, thinly sliced
 ¼ cup olive oil
 1 tablespoon lemon juice (optional)
 Salt and freshly ground pepper, to taste

Using a Parmesan knife or a small, sharp knife, cut the Parmesan into the thinnest possible flakes. (This can also be done by using a swivel-bladed vegetable

SPINACH AND WALNUT SALAD

peeler, shaving off the cheese in curls.) Place the flakes of Parmesan in a medium bowl and add the sliced celery ribs. Sprinkle with the olive oil and optional lemon juice, and season to taste with salt and pepper. Toss the salad gently to mix, and then serve it immediately.

CELERIAC REMOULADE

Celeriac, also called celery root, is a very popular vegetable in France, but it really deserves to be better known with American cooks. The brief blanching will keep the celeriac white, although many people prefer it raw and crunchy.

MAKES 4 SERVINGS

 2 tablespoons lemon juice
 1 pound celeriac (2 medium heads)
 1 large egg yolk, at room temperature
 1½ teaspoons Dijon mustard, or more as needed
 2/3 cup peanut or vegetable oil
 3 tablespoons light cream or half-and-half
 Salt and freshly ground pepper, to taste

Fill a medium bowl with cold water and add the lemon juice. Using a sharp paring knife, remove the thick brown skin from the celeriac. Cut the celeriac into quarters and remove any soft core. Using a mandoline, cut the celeriac into thin shreds. (The celeriac can also be shredded on a box grater or with a food processor fitted with the shredding blade.) Drop the celeriac immediately into the acidulated water to prevent discoloration.

Bring a large saucepan of salted water to a boil over high heat. Add the celeriac and stir briefly, then immediately drain. Rinse the celeriac under cold water until cooled. Drain thoroughly and pat dry with paper towels. Cover and refrigerate until well chilled, at least 2 hours.

Whisk the egg yolk and mustard. Gradually whisk in the oil as if making mayonnaise, then add the cream. Season. Taste and add more mustard if the dressing is too bland. Add the celeriac and toss with the dressing. Serve within 8 hours.

TOMATO AND CHÈVRE SALAD WITH PESTO VINAIGRETTE

This is a twist on the classic tomato and basil salad. Make it with the best summer tomatoes you can find for the tastiest results.

MAKES 6 TO 8 SERVINGS
 ¾ pound arugula, tough stems removed
 6 large ripe tomatoes, sliced into ½-inch-thick rounds
 3 ounces chèvre (goat cheese) or feta, crumbled
 ½ cup black Mediterranean olives, pitted
Pesto Vinaigrette
 ⅓ cup packed chopped fresh basil leaves
 2 tablespoons red wine vinegar
 1 garlic clove, crushed
 Salt and freshly ground pepper, to taste
 ⅔ cup extra virgin olive oil

To make the dressing, combine the basil, vinegar, garlic, and a seasoning of salt and pepper in a blender. With the machine running, gradually pour in the olive oil.

Arrange the arugula on a round platter. Top with the tomatoes, overlapping the slices in a circle. Sprinkle with cheese and olives. Serve immediately, with the pesto vinaigrette on the side.

ROASTED SWEET PEPPER SALAD

This is frequently served as part of an antipasto plate, along with fresh cheese, olives, and bread. The salad can also accompany main courses, from grilled chicken to roast beef tenderloin.

MAKES 4 SERVINGS
 2 medium red bell peppers, roasted, peeled, seeded, and cut into 1-inch-wide strips
 2 medium yellow bell peppers, roasted, peeled, seeded, and cut into 1-inch-wide strips
 1 tablespoon lemon juice
 ¼ cup olive oil
 1 garlic clove, minced
 Salt, to taste
 A handful of small basil leaves

On a serving platter, arrange the peppers, alternating the two colors. Sprinkle with the lemon juice, olive oil, and garlic, and season with the salt. Turn the pepper strips over in this dressing to coat both sides. (The peppers can be prepared up to 4 hours ahead of serving, and kept at room temperature.) Just before serving, scatter the basil leaves over the top.

APPLE AND CABBAGE SLAW

This is a delicious year-round salad.

MAKES 6 SERVINGS
 12 ounces green cabbage (about ½ medium head), cored and shredded
 1 medium carrot, shredded
 1 medium celery rib, cut into ⅛- by 1½-inch strips
 1 tart green apple (such as Granny Smith), peeled, cored, and cut into ⅛- by 1½-inch strips
 ⅓ cup chopped walnuts
 1 tablespoon red wine vinegar
 1 teaspoon Dijon mustard
 1¼ cups mayonnaise
 3 tablespoons light cream or half-and-half
 Salt and freshly ground pepper, to taste

In a bowl, combine the cabbage, carrot, celery, apple, and walnuts, and toss. In a small bowl, mix the vinegar with the mustard. Add the mayonnaise and cream, and blend. Season. Add to the vegetables and toss to coat.

GREEN BEAN SALAD WITH ANCHOVY-CREAM DRESSING

In Italy, green-vegetable salads with a creamy anchovy dressing are often enjoyed during the summer. If you don't want to use all the dressing for the beans, keep the remains in a covered jar in the refrigerator.

MAKES 4 SERVINGS
 1 pound haricots verts or thin green beans
 2 tablespoons minced shallot
 Lemon wedges, for garnish

Dressing
- 1 tablespoon red wine vinegar
- 1 tablespoon Dijon mustard
- 1 small garlic clove, chopped
- ⅔ cup peanut or vegetable oil
- ⅔ cup extra virgin olive oil
- 1 (2-ounce) can anchovy fillets packed in oil, undrained
- Freshly ground pepper, to taste

To make the dressing, place the vinegar, mustard, garlic, and ¼ cup water in a blender. Blend until smooth. With the machine running, gradually add the peanut and olive oils to make a thick dressing. Add the anchovies and their oil, and blend until smooth. Season with pepper. Taste the dressing, and add salt and more vinegar if needed.

Bring a large saucepan of lightly salted water to a boil over high heat. Add the haricots verts and cook until crisp-tender, 2 to 4 minutes. Drain and refresh, then pat dry with paper towels.

Arrange the haricots verts in bundles on four chilled salad plates. Spoon the dressing over the green beans. Sprinkle with the shallots. Serve with the lemon wedges for squeezing over the salad.

MEXICALI BEAN SALAD

Great as an extra for a picnic or barbecue, this salad is also filling enough to make a good lunch on its own.

MAKES 6 SERVINGS
- ¼ cup red wine vinegar
- 1 tablespoon chili powder
- 1 hot fresh chile pepper (such as jalapeño), seeded and minced
- 2 garlic cloves, minced
- ¾ cup olive oil
- 3 cups cooked pinto beans
- 3 cups cooked black beans
- 2 medium celery ribs, finely chopped
- 1 medium red onion, finely chopped
- 1 medium red bell pepper, seeded and chopped
- 1 pint cherry tomatoes, cut in half horizontally
- 2 tablespoons chopped fresh cilantro
- Salt and freshly ground pepper, to taste
- 1 cup shredded sharp Cheddar cheese

In a medium bowl, whisk together the vinegar, chili powder, chile pepper, and garlic. Gradually whisk in the oil. Set the dressing aside.

In a large bowl, combine the pinto and black beans, celery, red onion, red pepper, cherry tomatoes, and cilantro. Add the dressing, season with salt and pepper, and toss well. Cover and refrigerate until chilled, about 1 hour. (The salad can be prepared up to 2 days ahead and kept, covered, in the refrigerator.) Just before serving, sprinkle with the cheese.

RICE SALAD WITH ORANGES AND OLIVES

Rice hardens when chilled, so serve this Moroccan-inspired salad at room temperature.

MAKES 6 TO 8 SERVINGS
- 1½ cups long-grain rice
- Salt and freshly ground pepper
- 3 tablespoons balsamic vinegar
- Grated zest of 1 orange
- ⅔ cup olive oil
- 2 oranges, peeled and sectioned
- 1 cup black Mediterranean olives, pitted and chopped
- 4 scallions, chopped

Bring 4 cups of water to a boil over high heat. Add the rice and ½ teaspoon salt. Reduce the heat to low, cover, and simmer until the rice is tender, about 15 minutes. If necessary, drain the cooked rice of excess water. Transfer to a large bowl and let cool to lukewarm.

In a medium bowl, whisk together the balsamic vinegar and orange zest with a seasoning of salt and pepper. Gradually whisk in the oil. Pour half of the dressing over the rice, and reserve the remainder. Toss the rice with the orange sections, olives, and scallions. Cover and let stand at room temperature for 1 hour to blend the flavors. (The salad can be kept, covered, in the refrigerator for up to 1 day, but bring to room temperature before serving.) Just before serving, toss with the remaining dressing, and taste to check the seasoning.

CREAMY SCANDINAVIAN POTATO SALAD WITH DILL

Everyone loves potato salad. Here's an unusual version with dill and capers.

MAKES 6 TO 8 SERVINGS
- 3 pounds boiling potatoes, scrubbed
- 2 tablespoons white wine vinegar or cider vinegar
- ¾ cup mayonnaise
- ½ cup sour cream
- 4 hard-boiled eggs, chopped
- 3 scallions, chopped
- 3 tablespoons chopped fresh dill
- 3 tablespoons capers, rinsed
- Salt and freshly ground pepper, to taste

ITALIAN SEAFOOD SALAD

Bring a large pot of lightly salted water to a boil over high heat. Add the potatoes and cook until they are just tender, about 20 minutes. Drain well and leave until cool enough to handle. Peel the potatoes, if desired (this is not essential), and use a sharp knife to cut them into thick rounds.

Put the potatoes in a large bowl and sprinkle them with the vinegar, tossing the potatoes around in the bowl so that they are all moistened. Add the mayonnaise, sour cream, hard-boiled eggs, chopped scallions, dill, and capers, and season with salt and pepper. Fold all the ingredients together gently but thoroughly. Cover the bowl and put in the refrigerator to chill for at least 2 hours.

Just before you wish to serve the salad, taste the potatoes to check the seasoning, and adjust if necessary. The salad can be kept, covered, in the refrigerator for up to 1 day.

INDIAN POTATO SALAD WITH YOGURT AND SCALLION DRESSING

This is just the dressing to complement a potato salad, with its smooth, creamy texture; it is also good over greens.

MAKES 6 SERVINGS
  2 pounds new potatoes, unpeeled
Dressing
  6 scallions, cut into thin rounds
  Salt, to taste
  ⅔ cup plain yogurt, preferably goat-milk yogurt
  4 ounces cream cheese, at room temperature
  1 teaspoon chopped fresh dill

In a small bowl, sprinkle the scallion rounds lightly with salt. Let stand until limp, 20 to 30 minutes. Drain, rinse, and pat dry with paper towels. In a bowl, mash the yogurt with the cream cheese until well blended and smooth. Stir in the scallions and dill, and season with salt.

Bring a large pot of lightly salted water to a boil. Add the potatoes and cook until they are just tender, about 20 minutes. Drain the potatoes thoroughly and leave on one side to cool. Peel the potatoes, if desired, and then cut them into thick rounds. Add to the dressing and toss well to combine. Cover the potatoes and then place in the refrigerator to chill until you are ready to serve them.

CRANBERRY AND RASPBERRY MOLD

For many families, the American Thanksgiving menu would be incomplete without a deliciously chilled gelatin fruit-salad mold. The version that is given here eschews artificially-flavored gelatin in favour of a combination of cranberries and raspberries that is truly mouthwatering. If fresh raspberries are not available, frozen ones, thawed before use, will be just as good.

MAKES 12 SERVINGS

- 2 envelopes unflavored gelatin
- 4 cups apple juice
- 1 (12-ounce) bag fresh cranberries
- 2 cups sugar
- 1 cup heavy cream
- 2 cups fresh or defrosted frozen raspberries

In a medium bowl, sprinkle the gelatin over ½ cup of the apple juice. Let stand while preparing the cranberry mixture.

In a medium saucepan over medium-high heat, bring the cranberries, sugar, and remaining 3½ cups apple juice to a boil, stirring to dissolve the sugar. Cook until all of the cranberries have burst, about 3 minutes. Reduce the heat to very low. Add the softened gelatin mixture and stir until the gelatin has completely dissolved, about 2 minutes. Transfer to a large bowl set in a larger bowl of ice water. Let stand, stirring occasionally, until cool, but not set, about 20 minutes.

In a chilled medium bowl, whip the cream until it forms stiff peaks, and then fold it into the cooled gelatin mixture. Fold in the raspberries. Spoon the mixture into a lightly oiled 12-cup fluted mold. Cover the mold and refrigerate until it is set, at least 4 hours or overnight.

When you are ready to serve the mold, dip the outside of the mold into a large bowl filled with hot water and let stand in the water for about 10 seconds or so. Wipe the outside of the mold dry with a dish towel, then invert the mold onto a chilled serving platter. Serve cold.

ITALIAN SEAFOOD SALAD

This makes a perfect luncheon salad, or a special first course. If you prefer, use 8 ounces of thinly sliced white mushrooms instead of the squid (there is no need to cook the mushrooms), and let the salad marinate for an hour or two before serving so that the flavors can mingle together.

MAKES 6 SERVINGS

- 20 mussels, scrubbed well and debearded, if necessary
- 12 littleneck clams
- 8 small squid, cleaned, bodies cut into ¼-inch-thick rings and tentacles left whole
- 12 ounces medium shrimp
- 24 Dublin Bay prawns or jumbo shrimp
- 1 tablespoon lemon juice
- 6 tablespoons olive oil
- ⅛ teaspoon chile flakes
- 2 tablespoons chopped fresh parsley, oregano, or dill (optional)
- Salt and freshly ground pepper, to taste

In a large saucepan, combine the mussels, clams, and 1¼ cups water. Bring to a boil over high heat, then cover and cook, shaking the pan often, until all the shells have opened, about 5 minutes. Using a slotted spoon, transfer the mussels and clams to a bowl and set to one side.

Return the cooking liquid to a simmer over medium-low heat. Add the prepared squid and cook, uncovered, until barely tender, 1 to 2 minutes. Do not overcook. Using a slotted spoon, quickly transfer the squid to another bowl. Add the shrimp and Dublin Bay prawns to the saucepan, cover, and cook until they turn pink and firm, about 3 minutes. Drain the shrimp and prawns. When the seafood is cool enough to handle, discard the mussel shells, and peel and devein the shrimp and prawns.

Add the mussels, shrimp, and prawns to the squid, along with the clams still in their shell (or shelled if you prefer). Toss the seafood, adding the lemon juice, then the oil, chile flakes, and optional herbs. Season with salt and pepper. Refrigerate the seafood salad until ready to serve, up to 2 hours.

SALADE NIÇOISE

While salade niçoise conjures up an image of a glorified tuna salad to many cooks, it can be simply a wonderful combination of colorful vegetables dressed with vinaigrette. If you wish, add canned tuna, preferably an excellent imported brand packed in olive oil, to the center of the platter.

MAKES 4 TO 6 SERVINGS

4 small boiling potatoes, unpeeled

8 ounces haricots verts or thin green beans

1 small head romaine lettuce, separated into
    individual leaves

1 small head curly-leaved red lettuce, separated
    into individual leaves

3 large ripe tomatoes, sliced

2 medium red bell peppers (or 1 red and 1 yellow),
    peeled, seeded, and cut into thin strips

3 hard-boiled eggs, cut in half lengthwise

12 anchovy fillets packed in oil, drained

¼ cup drained capers, rinsed

½ cup black Mediterranean olives

Balsamic Herb Vinaigrette, made with 1 garlic clove,
    crushed through a press

1 small red onion, thinly sliced

A handful of small fresh basil leaves

In a medium saucepan of boiling salted water,
cook the potatoes until they are just tender, 15 to
20 minutes. Drain the potatoes and rinse under cold
running water until cool enough to handle, then slice
into thick rounds. In another medium saucepan of
boiling salted water, cook the haricots verts until they
are crisp-tender, about 2 minutes (if using green
beans, cook for 4 minutes). Drain and refresh, then
pat dry with paper towels.

Arrange the lettuce leaves around the edge of
a large serving platter. Place the sliced tomatoes and
potatoes in rings in the center. Arrange the pepper
strips, radiating outward, on top of the lettuce leaves.
Add small bundles of haricots verts here and there,
and place the egg halves on the peppers. Lay 1 anchovy
over each yolk. Add little mounds of capers, and place
the olives on the tomato slices. Drizzle ½ cup of the
dressing over the salad, and pour the remainder into
a sauceboat. Scatter the red onion and basil leaves
over all. Serve immediately, with the remaining
dressing passed on the side.

GRILLED SHRIMP LOUIS

This classic seafood salad (named after its forgotten
originator) gets an update with grilled shrimp.

MAKES 4 SERVINGS

2 tablespoons olive oil

2 tablespoons lemon juice

16 jumbo shrimp, peeled, with last tail section left
    attached, deveined, and butterflied

Salt and freshly ground pepper, to taste

6 cups *mesclun* salad leaves

1 cup halved cherry tomatoes

1 medium cucumber, peeled, seeded, and cut into
    thin half-moons

2 hard-boiled eggs, chopped

Dressing

⅓ cup finely chopped sun-dried tomatoes packed in
    oil, well drained

1 cup mayonnaise

2 tablespoons lemon juice

2 tablespoons chopped capers, rinsed

1 scallion, finely chopped

1 teaspoon chili powder

2 tablespoons lemon juice

Salt and freshly ground pepper, to taste

2 tablespoons milk, approximately

To make the dressing, mix all of the ingredients in
a small bowl, thinning with milk as needed. Cover
and refrigerate for 1 hour to blend the flavors.

In a medium bowl, whisk together the olive oil and
lemon juice. Add the shrimp, and season with salt and
pepper. Cover and let marinate in the refrigerator for
1 to 2 hours, no longer.

Build a hot charcoal fire in an outdoor grill. Lightly
oil the grill. Place the shrimp on the grill, opened up,
cut side down. Grill, turning once, until firm, about
3 minutes. Set aside.

Divide the *mesclun*, cherry tomatoes, and cucumber
among four large plates. Top each with four grilled
shrimp, and sprinkle with the hard-boiled egg. Serve
immediately, with the dressing passed on the side.

CHICKEN, FENNEL, AND PEAR SALAD

The crisp texture and herbaceous flavor of fennel
make it a fine addition to this luncheon salad.

MAKES 4 TO 6 SERVINGS

4 (10-ounce) chicken breast halves

2 cups chicken stock

2 cups chopped fennel bulb

2 ripe medium pears (such as Bartlett), peeled, cored,
    and chopped

1 cup mayonnaise

2 scallions, chopped

1 tablespoon chopped leafy fennel tops or herb fennel

1 cup chopped pecans

Salt and freshly ground pepper, to taste

3 cups watercress leaves, tough stems removed

Fresh fennel or tarragon sprigs, for garnish

Place the chicken breasts and stock in a large frying
pan, and add enough cold water so that the breasts are
just covered with liquid. Bring to a simmer over high
heat, then reduce the heat to low. Cover and simmer

for 20 minutes. Remove from the heat and let stand, covered, until cool and the chicken meat shows no sign of pinkness at the bone, about 1 hour. Discard the skin and bones, and use a sharp knife to cut the chicken into bite-sized pieces. (You can save the broth for another use.)

In a large bowl, combine the chicken with the fennel, pears, mayonnaise, scallions, and fennel leaves. Stir in the pecans, and season with salt and pepper. Cover and refrigerate until chilled, about 1 hour. (The salad can be prepared up to 8 hours ahead.)

Place the watercress leaves on large plates, and top each with a large spoonful of the chicken salad. Garnish with fennel sprigs and serve immediately.

SICHUAN CHICKEN SALAD

In Chinese restaurants, this tasty chicken salad often goes by the name bang-bang chicken. It's a good way of using up leftover roast chicken—substitute 3 cups shredded cooked chicken for the chicken thighs.

MAKES 4 SERVINGS

4 (6-ounce) chicken thighs
2 teaspoons sesame seeds

Sɪcʜᴜᴀɴ Cʜɪᴄᴋᴇɴ Sᴀʟᴀᴅ

1 large English cucumber, cut into ⅛- by 3-inch strips
1 large carrot, cut into ⅛- by 3-inch strips
8 scallions, shredded lengthwise
2 tablespoons lime juice
½ teaspoon granulated sugar
Salt, to taste
1 cup Asian Peanut Sauce
½ teaspoon chile flakes
2 teaspoons Asian dark sesame oil
Sprigs of fresh cilantro, for garnish
Poaching Liquid
3 tablespoons soy sauce
2 tablespoons rice vinegar
2 teaspoons Asian dark sesame oil
4 scallions, sliced
2 garlic cloves, crushed
4 slices fresh ginger, unpeeled
2 small hot fresh chile peppers (such as serrano), thinly sliced
2 star anise

Put the chicken thighs in a saucepan just big enough to hold them snugly. Add all the ingredients for the poaching liquid, and pour in enough cold water to cover the chicken. Shake the pan to mix everything together. Bring to a simmer, then cover and simmer gently for 30 minutes. Remove from the heat and let stand, still covered, until cool, about 1 hour. Remove the chicken from the poaching liquid. Discard the skin and bones, and shred the meat. Cover and refrigerate the chicken until chilled, about 2 hours. (You can strain the poaching liquid and keep it in the freezer for the next time you want to make this salad.)

In a small dry frying pan over medium heat, cook the sesame seeds until nicely toasted. Tip them onto a plate to cool.

Toss the cucumber, carrot, and scallions with the lime juice, sugar, and salt. Place on a serving platter. Top with the shredded chicken, and spoon the peanut sauce over the chicken. Sprinkle with the toasted sesame seeds, chile flakes, and sesame oil, and garnish with cilantro.

SIX VEGETABLE COUSCOUS SALAD

LIDO PASTA SALAD

Summer is the time to make this simple, delicious salad. Salted capers, available at many Italian grocers, are the best, although you could use bottled ones.

MAKES 6 TO 8 SERVINGS

3 tablespoons salted capers
5 ounces black olives (preferably herb-marinated Kalamata olives), pitted
1 large red onion or 6 scallions, chopped
20 anchovy fillets packed in oil, drained and chopped (optional)
5 garlic cloves, minced
2 tablespoons lemon juice
½ cup olive oil
1 pound penne, ziti, or rigatoni
1 pound cherry tomatoes, halved crosswise
3 tablespoons chopped fresh basil

Salads/Vegetables

3 tablespoons chopped fresh parsley
2 tablespoons chopped fresh mint
Salt and freshly ground pepper, to taste

Soak the capers in cold water for 5 minutes, then drain and pat dry with paper towels. In a large bowl, combine the capers, olives, onion, optional anchovies, and garlic. Mix in the lemon juice, then the oil.

In a large pot of boiling salted water over high heat, cook the pasta until *al dente*, 10 to 12 minutes. Drain thoroughly, and add to the bowl. Toss well with the olive mixture. Reserve about one fourth of the tomatoes and herbs, and mix the remainder into the salad. Check the seasoning. Scatter the reserved tomatoes and herbs on top, and serve warm.

SIX VEGETABLE COUSCOUS SALAD

The combination of vegetables here is typically Moroccan, but other mixes are possible, according to the cook's inspiration. Serve with a green salad.

MAKES 6 TO 8 SERVINGS
    1 (1-pound) acorn squash, halved crosswise and
        seeds discarded
    8 ounces green beans, cut in half crosswise
    3 medium zucchini, sliced into ½-inch-thick
        rounds
    3 tablespoons butter
    Salt and freshly ground black pepper
    1¾ cups instant couscous
    2 tablespoons vegetable oil
    ½ cup dark raisins
    1 teaspoon cumin seeds
    ½ teaspoon chile flakes
    2 medium red bell peppers, peeled, seeded,
        and chopped
    1½ cups cooked chickpeas, either fresh
        or canned
    10 scallions, thinly sliced
    1 tablespoon chopped fresh cilantro
    1 tablespoon chopped fresh parsley
Harissa Dressing
    2 tablespoons lemon juice
    2 teaspoons harissa
    6 tablespoons vegetable oil
    2 tablespoons olive oil

Preheat the oven to 350°F. Place the acorn squash, cut side down, on a lightly oiled baking sheet. Bake until tender, 30 to 40 minutes. Let cool, then peel and cut into 1-inch chunks. In a medium saucepan of boiling salted water, cook the green beans until crisp-tender, 3 to 5 minutes. Drain and refresh, then pat dry with

paper towels. In another medium saucepan, steam the zucchini, covered, over simmering water until crisp-tender, about 4 minutes. Drain well and pat dry with paper towels. Set the acorn squash, green beans, and zucchini aside.

In a medium saucepan, combine 1¾ cups water, the butter, and 1 teaspoon salt. Bring to a boil over high heat. Stir in the couscous, then immediately remove from the heat. Cover tightly and let stand until the couscous absorbs the water, about 5 minutes. Uncover, and stir over low heat to separate the couscous grains and evaporate any excess moisture, 1 to 2 minutes. Transfer to a large bowl.

In a medium frying pan, heat the oil over medium heat. Add the raisins, cumin seeds, and chile flakes, and stir until the cumin seeds are lightly toasted, about 1 minute. Stir into the couscous, and season with salt and pepper.

To make the dressing, whisk the ingredients in a small bowl. Stir about one third of the dressing into the couscous. In another bowl, combine the green beans, zucchini, acorn squash, red peppers, chickpeas, and scallions. Add the remaining dressing to the bowl, and season with salt and pepper. Toss gently to mix, then arrange the vegetables on top of the couscous.

The salad can be made up to 4 hours ahead, and kept in a cool place. Just before serving, sprinkle with the cilantro and parsley.

———————— • ————————

ORANGE-GLAZED ACORN SQUASH

Here baked acorn squashes are finished with a simple marmalade and butter glaze. These go well with grilled pork chops.

MAKES 6 SERVINGS
    2 (1-pound) acorn squashes, halved horizontally and
        ends trimmed
    ¼ cup orange marmalade, preferably bitter orange
    2 tablespoons unsalted butter
    ¼ teaspoon ground cinnamon

Preheat the oven to 350°F. Line a baking sheet with foil, then butter it lightly. Place the squash halves, cut side down, on the baking sheet. Bake until the squash is tender when pierced with the tip of a sharp knife, 30 to 40 minutes.

Meanwhile, in a small saucepan over low heat, heat the marmalade, butter, and cinnamon until melted; set aside. Preheat the broiler. Turn the squash cut sides up, and brush with the marmalade mixture. Broil until glazed, about 2 minutes.

STIR-FRIED ASPARAGUS WITH GINGER

Asparagus lends itself beautifully to stir-frying.

MAKES 4 SERVINGS

1½ pounds asparagus

2 tablespoons vegetable oil

1 tablespoon shredded fresh ginger

1 garlic clove, minced

¼ cup chicken stock or water

Salt and freshly ground pepper, to taste

Snap off and discard the woody ends from the asparagus. Cut the spears into 1-inch lengths. In a large wok or frying pan, heat the oil over medium-high heat until very hot. Add the asparagus and stir-fry for 2 minutes. Add the ginger and garlic and stir until fragrant, about 30 seconds. Add the stock, then cover tightly and reduce the heat to medium-low. Cook until the asparagus is crisp-tender, 2 to 3 minutes. Season with salt and pepper, and serve hot.

GREEN BEANS WITH PORTOBELLO MUSHROOMS AND PROSCIUTTO

This is a super blend of flavors that could well become a favorite, especially at holiday meals.

MAKES 6 SERVINGS

½ cup dried porcini (½ ounce)

2 tablespoons unsalted butter

2 large portobello mushrooms, stems discarded, caps cut into ½- by 3-inch strips

4 ounces prosciutto, chopped into ¼-inch pieces

12 ounces green beans

Salt and freshly ground pepper, to taste

In a small bowl, soak the porcini in 1 cup boiling water until softened, about 20 to 30 minutes. Lift the mushrooms out of the water and coarsely chop. Strain the soaking liquid through a paper-towel-lined sieve set over a bowl. Set aside.

In a large frying pan, heat the butter over medium heat. Add the portobello strips and cook, stirring occasionally, until the mushrooms give off their liquid, about 5 minutes. Add the chopped porcini and their soaking liquid, and cook until the mushrooms are tender and the liquid has reduced to about 2 tablespoons, about 5 more minutes. Add the prosciutto and stir for 1 minute.

Meanwhile, in a large saucepan of lightly salted boiling water, cook the green beans over high heat until crisp-tender, about 4 minutes. Drain and refresh. (The mushrooms and beans can be prepared up to 2 hours ahead, and kept at room temperature.)

Stir the green beans into the mushroom mixture, and cook over medium heat, stirring often, until heated through, 3 to 5 minutes. Season with salt and pepper, and serve hot.

GREEN BEANS ATHENA

The Greeks appreciate long-cooked vegetables where the flavors have time to mingle. Here, green beans and tomatoes are combined.

MAKES 6 SERVINGS

2 tablespoons olive oil

1 large onion, cut into thin half-moons

2 garlic cloves, minced

1 pound green beans

6 ripe plum tomatoes, peeled, seeded, and chopped

Salt and freshly ground pepper, to taste

2 ounces feta cheese, crumbled

In a large frying pan, heat the oil over medium heat. Add the onion and garlic and cook, stirring often, until the onion is soft and translucent, about 5 minutes. Add the green beans, tomatoes, and 2 tablespoons water, and season with salt and pepper. Cover and cook over medium-low heat until the green beans are very tender and the tomatoes have softened into a sauce, about 40 minutes. Sprinkle with the cheese, and serve hot or warm.

ROASTED BEETS WITH GREENS

Roasting beets emphasizes their natural sugars, and helps them keep their vibrant color. Try to purchase beets with the tops attached. Not only are the greens a good sign of freshness, they are also delicious. Balsamic vinegar, with its sweet note, is a perfect condiment.

MAKES 4 TO 6 SERVINGS

6 medium beets, with green tops attached

3 tablespoons balsamic vinegar

Grated zest of 1 orange

3 tablespoons extra virgin olive oil

Salt and freshly ground pepper, to taste

Preheat the oven to 350°F. Cut off the beet greens about 1 inch from the top of the beets, and set the greens aside. Wrap each beet in aluminum foil. Bake until tender, about 1 hour, depending on the size of the beet. Unwrap the beets and let cool until easy to handle. Slip off the skins and slice into rounds.

STIR-FRIED ASPARAGUS WITH GINGER

While the beets are cooling, rinse the beet greens well. Coarsely chop the tough stems. Bring a medium saucepan of lightly salted water to a boil over high heat. Add the stems and cook for 5 minutes. Add the beet greens and continue cooking until the greens and stems are tender, about 10 minutes. Drain well.

Place the beet greens and stems on a platter and top with the sliced beets. In a bowl, whisk together the balsamic vinegar, orange zest, and olive oil, and season with salt and pepper. Pour over the beets and greens, and serve warm or at room temperature. (If the latter, add the dressing just before serving.)

CREAMED BELGIAN ENDIVE

Belgian endive is usually thought of as a salad vegetable. Here it is eaten hot, cloaked in a suave cream sauce.

MAKES 4 SERVINGS
4 plump heads Belgian endive, tough cores removed
1 cup chicken stock
2 tablespoons unsalted butter
1 tablespoon lemon juice
6 tablespoons heavy cream
Salt, to taste

Cut the endive lengthwise into ½-inch-wide strips. Cut the strips crosswise into pieces about 2 inches long. Place in a medium frying pan with the stock, butter, and lemon juice. Bring to a simmer over medium heat. Cook, stirring occasionally, until the stock has reduced to 2 tablespoons, about 8 minutes.

Add the cream and cook until the liquid has reduced by half and the endive is coated with a light sauce. Season with salt. Serve hot. (The endive can be prepared up to 2 hours ahead; reheat gently to serve.)

IRISH CABBAGE AND POTATOES

Called colcannon in Ireland, this hearty side dish is just the thing for a St. Patrick's Day dinner. Leftovers can be shaped into patties and fried in butter until crisp.

MAKES 4 TO 6 SERVINGS
1 (1½-pound) head green cabbage (about 1 medium head), quartered and cored
1 pound boiling potatoes, peeled and cut into 2-inch chunks
2 small leeks, chopped
1 cup half-and-half
A pinch of ground mace or nutmeg
Salt and freshly ground pepper, to taste
4 tablespoons unsalted butter, melted

Bring a large pot of salted water to a boil over high heat. Add the cabbage and cook until just tender, about 15 minutes. Drain and rinse under cold running water until cool enough to handle. Cut the cabbage into shreds.

In a medium saucepan of boiling salted water, cook the potatoes until tender, about 15 minutes. Meanwhile, in a small saucepan, bring the leeks and half-and-half to a simmer over medium-low heat. Cook until the leeks are tender, about 10 minutes. Drain the potatoes well and return to the pan. Mash the potatoes, then add the leeks and cream. Beat in the shredded cabbage. Cook over low heat, beating continuously, until hot and fluffy, 2 to 3 minutes. Season with the mace, salt, and pepper.

Transfer to a heated serving dish. Make a little hollow in the potato mixture and fill with the melted butter. Serve hot.

BRAISED RED CABBAGE

Is there anything that goes better with roast pork or game than tangy red cabbage?

MAKES 4 SERVINGS
1 tablespoon unsalted butter
1 medium onion, finely chopped
1 (1-pound) head red cabbage, halved lengthwise, cored, and cut into ¼-inch-thick slices
2 tart green apples (such as Granny Smith), peeled, quartered, and cored
⅔ cup red wine
⅓ cup red wine vinegar, or more to taste
3 tablespoons light brown sugar, or more to taste
1 (3-inch) strip orange zest
3 juniper berries, crushed (optional)
2 bay leaves
Salt and freshly ground pepper, to taste

Preheat the oven to 325°F. In a Dutch oven or flameproof casserole, heat the butter over medium heat. Add the onion and cook until softened, about 5 minutes. Add the cabbage and stir until well coated with butter. Stir in the remaining ingredients, and season with salt and pepper. Bring to a simmer.

Cover with aluminum foil and then a lid. Transfer to the oven and cook, stirring occasionally, until the cabbage is very tender, about 1½ hours. If the casserole is well sealed, there will be enough liquid; however, if the cabbage seems to be getting too dry, add a little more red wine or water. During the last 30 minutes of cooking, taste the cabbage and add more vinegar or sugar, if needed—some cabbages are full-flavored, but others are bland and need the extra seasoning. Serve hot.

GLAZED BABY CARROTS

Peeled baby carrots make a lovely side dish for many different entrées, especially roasts.

MAKES 4 SERVINGS

1 pound peeled baby carrots
2 teaspoons granulated sugar
4 tablespoons unsalted butter
2 teaspoons chopped fresh chives or parsley

Bring a pan of lightly salted water to a boil. Add the carrots and cook until barely tender, 6 to 8 minutes. Drain off all but 2 tablespoons of the cooking water. Reduce the heat to medium-low. Add the sugar and let it dissolve in the cooking water. Add the butter and melt. Increase the heat to medium-high and cook until the liquid reduces to a thick, golden-brown syrup, rolling the carrots in this to glaze, about 5 minutes. Sprinkle with the herbs, and serve hot.

CAULIFLOWER AU GRATIN

This is an excellent way to prepare broccoli, too.

MAKES 4 TO 6 SERVINGS

4 tablespoons unsalted butter
3 tablespoons all-purpose flour
2 cups milk
1 large head cauliflower, broken into florets
1/2 cup light cream or half-and-half
3/4 cup shredded Emmentaler or Gruyère cheese,
   or freshly grated Parmesan cheese
Salt and freshly ground pepper, to taste
1 cup fresh bread crumbs

In a saucepan, melt 2 tablespoons of the butter over medium-low heat. Stir in the flour and let bubble gently without browning for 1 to 2 minutes. Gradually stir in the milk, then bring to a simmer. Cover and simmer over low heat, stirring occasionally, for about 15 minutes.

Meanwhile, bring a large saucepan of lightly salted water to a boil. Add the cauliflower and cook until just tender, about 8 minutes. Drain and keep warm.

Preheat the broiler. Stir the cream into the sauce, then remove from the heat. (The sauce should be thin but creamy.) Reserve 3 tablespoons of the cheese for the topping, then stir the remaining cheese into the sauce. Season with salt and pepper. Keep warm.

In a medium frying pan, heat the remaining 2 tablespoons of butter over medium-high heat. Add the bread crumbs and cook, stirring often, until golden-brown, about 3 minutes. Add the cauliflower, and stir and mix until each floret is coated with bread crumbs. Transfer to a buttered baking dish. Pour the sauce around the cauliflower, and sprinkle the reserved cheese over the top. Broil until the top is lightly browned, 1 to 2 minutes. Serve hot.

CAJUN SMOTHERED CORN

Cajun cooks know how to season humble ingredients and get delicious results. If desired, substitute 1/4 cup olive oil for the bacon and its rendered fat.

MAKES 6 TO 8 SERVINGS

6 strips thick-sliced bacon
1 medium onion, chopped
1 medium red bell pepper, seeded and chopped
2 medium celery ribs, chopped
4 cups fresh or defrosted frozen corn kernels
2 garlic cloves, minced
1/2 teaspoon Hungarian paprika
1/2 teaspoon dried thyme
1/2 teaspoon dried basil
1/4 teaspoon freshly ground pepper
2 large ripe tomatoes, seeded and chopped
Salt, to taste

In a large frying pan over medium heat, cook the bacon until crisp, about 5 minutes. Transfer to paper towels to drain. Pour out all but 2 tablespoons of the bacon fat from the pan. Add the onion, bell pepper, and celery to the pan, and cook until the onion is golden-brown, about 10 minutes. Add the corn, garlic, paprika, thyme, basil, and pepper, and cook, stirring frequently, until the corn is beginning to brown around the edges, about 5 minutes. Stir in the tomatoes and cook until they are heated through, about 5 minutes. Crumble the bacon, stir it in, and season with salt. Serve hot.

STIR-FRIED EGGPLANT WITH CHILES AND CILANTRO

This vegetable dish is just as good hot or warm as it is cool. If you can find them, use Asian eggplants.

MAKES 4 SERVINGS

1/4 cup vegetable oil
1 pound eggplant, cut into 1-inch cubes
1/4 cup balsamic vinegar
2 tablespoons soy sauce
2 tablespoons finely sliced scallions
1 tablespoon shredded fresh ginger
1/2 teaspoon chile flakes, or more to taste
Salt and freshly ground pepper, to taste
Fresh cilantro sprigs, for garnish

In a wok or large nonstick frying pan, heat the oil over medium-high heat until very hot. Add the eggplant and cook, turning often, until browned on all sides, about 3 minutes. Transfer to paper towels to drain.

Add the vinegar and soy sauce to the pan and heat to boiling. Return the eggplant to the pan. Reduce the heat to medium-low and simmer for 5 minutes. Stir in the scallions, ginger, and chile flakes, and season with salt and pepper. Cook until the liquid is reduced and the eggplant is very tender, about 2 more minutes. Transfer to a serving dish and garnish with cilantro sprigs. Serve hot, warm, or at room temperature.

BAKED EGGPLANT PARMESAN

Melanzane alla parmigiana, a dish that is found on menus in Italian restaurants all around the world, is a good example of how peasant food has been popularized, if not glamorized, in recent years. Until recently, only the wealthiest Italian families could afford meat, and recipes like this were served in its stead, so deliciously that one wonders how much the meat was missed.

MAKES 6 SERVINGS
  2 (1-pound) eggplants, cut lengthwise into
    ¼-inch-thick slices
  Salt and freshly ground pepper, to taste
  ¾ cup vegetable oil, plus more as needed
  All-purpose flour, for dusting the eggplant
  ⅓ cup olive oil
  1 medium onion, chopped
  2 garlic cloves, minced
  2 pounds ripe plum tomatoes, peeled, seeded, and
    chopped, or use drained canned tomatoes
  3 tablespoons chopped fresh basil
  2 tablespoons chopped fresh parsley
  12 ounces mozzarella cheese, cut into cubes
  1 teaspoon dried oregano
  ¼ cup freshly grated Parmesan cheese

Sprinkle the eggplant slices lightly with salt. Let stand for 30 minutes to draw out the juices. Pat dry with paper towels.

In a large frying pan over medium-high heat, heat the vegetable oil until very hot, but not smoking. In batches, dust the eggplant slices with flour and add to the oil. Cook, turning once, until golden-brown on both sides, about 5 minutes. Add more oil to the pan, if needed. As the eggplant is browned, place on paper towels to drain.

GLOBE ARTICHOKES ROMAN-STYLE

In a medium saucepan, heat the olive oil over medium heat. Add the onions and garlic and cook, stirring often, until softened and translucent, about 5 minutes. Stir in the tomatoes and 1 tablespoon each of the basil and parsley. Season with salt and pepper. Bring to a simmer, then reduce the heat to low and simmer until the tomatoes have formed a thick sauce, about 30 minutes.

Preheat the oven to 350°F. Lightly oil a 9- by 13-inch baking dish. Layer half of the eggplant slices in the dish, then spread with half of the tomato sauce and half of the mozzarella cheese. Sprinkle with half of the remaining basil and parsley, and half of the oregano. Top with the remaining eggplant, tomato sauce, and mozzarella. Sprinkle with the Parmesan and the remaining herbs. Bake until the cheese has melted and the juices are bubbling, about 30 minutes. Let stand for 5 minutes before serving hot.

FENNEL PARMIGIANO

This superior side dish makes an excellent accompaniment for grilled pork chops or roast pork tenderloin.

MAKES 6 SERVINGS
  3 heads fennel
  Salt and freshly ground pepper, to taste
  ¾ cup freshly grated Parmesan cheese
  5 tablespoons unsalted butter, cut into small pieces

Preheat the oven to 375°F. Cut the fennel bulbs crosswise into ⅓-inch-thick slices, or cut them lengthwise into quarters. Bring a large pot of lightly salted water to a boil over high heat. Add the fennel and cook until barely tender, about 5 minutes for slices and 8 minutes for quarters. Drain thoroughly and pat dry with paper towels.

Lightly butter a medium-sized baking dish. If you have cut the fennel into slices, layer them in the dish, seasoning each layer lightly with salt and pepper, sprinkling with cheese, and dotting with butter; finish with a layer of cheese dotted with butter. If you have cut the fennel into quarters, arrange them in the dish and sprinkle with seasoning and cheese, then dot with butter. Bake until the top is golden, 20 to 25 minutes. Serve hot.

GLOBE ARTICHOKES ROMAN-STYLE

Romans treat their artichokes with loving care. Instead of simply serving them boiled, they braise them in a fragrant broth of olive oil, mint, and garlic. Serve with plenty of bread for mopping up the cooking juices.

MAKES 4 APPETIZER SERVINGS

   2 tablespoons lemon juice

   8 or 12 small artichokes (preferably less than 2 inches
      across)

   2/3 cup extra virgin olive oil

   3 tablespoons chopped fresh mint

   4 garlic cloves, chopped

   Salt and freshly ground pepper, to taste

Fill a large bowl with cold water and add the lemon juice. If using very small artichokes, peel the stems and lower parts, cutting away the outer layer of leaves. If using larger artichokes (but still no more than 3 inches across), you will need to remove the hairy choke in the center. As each artichoke is prepared, place it in the bowl of acidulated water.

    In a medium frying pan, heat 1 tablespoon of the oil over medium-low heat. Add the mint and garlic and cook gently until the garlic is fragrant, about 2 minutes. Drain the artichokes and shake each one upside-down to remove excess water. Divide the mint mixture evenly among the artichokes, randomly stuffing teaspoonfuls of it between the leaves (and in the center if you have removed the chokes).

    Pack the artichokes in a saucepan just large enough to hold them snugly. Pour in 1 1/4 cups water and the remaining olive oil. Season lightly with salt and pepper. Bring to a boil over high heat, then cover and reduce the heat to low. Simmer until the artichokes are tender, 30 to 45 minutes. Uncover, increase the heat to high, and cook until the liquid has reduced by about half, 10 to 15 minutes. Transfer the artichokes to a platter and spoon the cooking juices over them. Serve hot, warm, or at room temperature.

STEWED ARTICHOKE BOTTOMS WITH SPINACH

You can also make this springtime dish with sorrel instead of spinach. Serve with plainly grilled or broiled meat or fish.

MAKES 4 SERVINGS

   2 tablespoons unsalted butter, cut into small pieces

   1 pound fresh spinach leaves, tough stems discarded

   10 fresh artichoke bottoms, or 1 (10-ounce) package
      frozen artichoke hearts, defrosted, cut into quarters

   2 tablespoons olive oil

   1 garlic clove, peeled

   A pinch of granulated sugar

   Salt and freshly ground pepper, to taste

Scatter the butter on the bottom of a large, heavy-bottomed saucepan. Add one fourth of the spinach

(still wet from its rinsing), then one fourth of the artichoke pieces. Repeat the layers until all the spinach and artichokes are in the pan. Drizzle with the oil, add the garlic clove and sugar, and season with salt and pepper. Cover the pan tightly. Cook over very low heat for 1 hour, checking occasionally to be sure the bottom layer of spinach isn't sticking and burning, and adding a few tablespoons of water, if needed. (If using frozen artichokes, cook for about 30 minutes.) If too much liquid remains, remove the lid for the last few minutes of cooking so the excess moisture can evaporate. Serve hot.

MUSHROOMS WITH SWEET PEPPERS

Serve this as an unusual first course for a summer lunch.

MAKES 4 APPETIZER SERVINGS

   3 tablespoons olive oil

   2 medium red or yellow bell peppers, seeded and cut
      into 1/4-inch-wide strips

   8 ounces button mushrooms, thinly sliced

   3 tablespoons hearty red wine

   1 tablespoon lemon juice

   2 tablespoons chopped fresh parsley

   1/2 tablespoon chopped fresh thyme or 1 teaspoon
      dried thyme

   12 coriander seeds, crushed, or 1/3 cup chopped
      fresh cilantro

   1 garlic clove, thinly sliced

   Salt and freshly ground pepper, to taste

In a medium frying pan, heat the oil over medium heat. Add the peppers and cook until softened, about 5 minutes. Add the mushrooms, 3 tablespoons water, the wine, lemon juice, parsley, thyme, coriander, and garlic. Season. Simmer, uncovered, stirring occasionally, until the mushrooms are tender, about 15 minutes. Cool to room temperature before serving.

GRATINÉED ONIONS IN GORGONZOLA SAUCE

Creamed onions are given a very sophisticated finish in this recipe.

MAKES 8 SERVINGS

   2 pounds small white boiling onions

   5 tablespoons unsalted butter

   3 tablespoons all-purpose flour

   1 1/2 cups milk

   3 ounces Gorgonzola cheese, crumbled

   Salt and freshly ground pepper, to taste

   1/2 cup fresh bread crumbs

In a large saucepan of boiling water, blanch the onions for 1 minute. Drain well and refresh under cold running water. Using a small sharp knife, peel and trim the onions. Cut a small "X" in the end of each onion. In a large saucepan of lightly salted boiling water, cook the onions over medium heat until they are just tender, 10 to 15 minutes, then drain well.

Preheat the oven to 350°F. Lightly butter a 2-quart round baking dish. Transfer the cooked onions to the dish. In a medium, heavy-bottomed saucepan, heat 4 tablespoons of the butter over medium-low heat until melted. Stir in the flour and let bubble gently without browning for 2 minutes. Gradually stir in the milk and bring the sauce to a simmer. Reduce the heat to low and simmer for 2 minutes. Remove from the heat, and stir in the Gorgonzola cheese until melted. Season with salt and pepper.

Pour the sauce over the onions. Sprinkle with the crumbs and dot with the remaining 1 tablespoon butter. Bake until bubbling and the top is golden-brown, about 30 minutes.

GLAZED PEARL ONIONS

Pearl onions are now available in many supermarkets in a variety of colors—yellow and red, as well as white. If you can, use an assortment. To peel the onions, drop them in a large saucepan of boiling water and boil for 1 minute, then drain and rinse under cold water—this blanching loosens the skins and makes them easier to peel.

MAKES 4 TO 6 SERVINGS

1½ pounds pearl or small white boiling
   onions, peeled
⅔ cup chicken or beef stock
2 teaspoons granulated sugar
Salt, to taste

Choose a frying pan just large enough to hold the onions snugly in one layer. Half fill the pan with salted water and bring to a boil over high heat. Add the onions and cook for 5 minutes, then pour off all but 3 tablespoons of the water. Add the stock, sugar, and just a pinch of salt (the saltiness will intensify as the liquid cooks and reduces).

Bring to a simmer, then reduce the heat to low. Cook gently until the onions are very tender and the liquid has reduced to a glaze, 15 to 20 minutes. Shake the pan occasionally during cooking to turn the onions, so they become evenly coated with the glaze. The onions can be prepared up to 30 minutes before serving, and kept covered; reheat gently before serving, if necessary.

FRESH PEAS WITH LETTUCE FRANÇAISE

The French like to cook fresh peas with lettuce hearts—both are sweet vegetables and complement each other very well.

MAKES 4 SERVINGS

4 sprigs fresh savory or thyme, or ¼ teaspoon dried
   savory or thyme
2 heads Bibb lettuce, outer leaves removed (reserve for
   another use)
2½ cups shelled fresh peas (about 2 pounds unshelled)
4 tablespoons unsalted butter
A pinch of granulated sugar
Salt, to taste

Tuck the herb sprigs into the lettuce hearts and then place them in a medium saucepan. Add the peas, butter, and sugar, and season with salt. Pour in ½ cup water. Bring to a simmer over medium heat, then cover and reduce the heat to low. Simmer gently until the peas are tender, 10 to 15 minutes (this will depend on the age of the peas; older ones will take slightly longer). Drain well. Serve hot.

PEAS IN THE INDIAN FASHION

Here fresh peas are cooked together with Indian seasonings. This method can also be adapted to add interest to frozen peas—just adjust the cooking time accordingly.

MAKES 4 SERVINGS

3 tablespoons clarified butter, or 2 tablespoons
   vegetable oil and 1 tablespoon unsalted butter
1 large onion, finely chopped
½ teaspoon ground cumin
2½ cups shelled fresh peas (about 2 pounds
   unshelled)
1 small hot fresh chile pepper (such as serrano),
   seeded and minced
3 tablespoons chopped fresh cilantro
Salt, to taste

In a medium frying pan, heat the clarified butter over medium heat. Add the onion and ground cumin and cook until the onion is soft and golden, but not browned, about 6 minutes. Add the peas, minced chile pepper, and chopped cilantro, and stir for 1 to 2 minutes. Add ¼ cup water and season with salt. Cover and cook over medium-low heat until the peas are tender, 10 to 15 minutes, depending on the age of the peas.

Serve the peas hot, with the fragrant cooking juices poured over them.

STUFFED RED PEPPERS WITH TOMATOES AND ANCHOVIES

Elizabeth David included this simple recipe in her book *Italian Food*, published in the 1950s.

MAKES 4 SERVINGS
4 medium red bell peppers, halved lengthwise and seeded
4 garlic cloves, sliced
Salt and freshly ground pepper, to taste
4 large ripe tomatoes, peeled and halved crosswise
½ cup olive oil
16 anchovy fillets packed in oil, drained

Preheat the oven to 375°F. Lightly oil a baking dish. Arrange the pepper halves, cut side up, in the dish, and distribute the garlic evenly in the cavities. Season with salt and pepper. Push a halved tomato, cut side down, into each pepper half. Season lightly with pepper, then drizzle with the oil.

Bake until the peppers are very tender, with scorched edges, about 1 hour. Remove from the oven, and criss-cross 2 anchovy fillets over each stuffed pepper. Let cool to room temperature before serving.

ROASTED POTATOES

If you are cooking a roast, you can add the potatoes to the roasting pan, using the meat drippings in the pan instead of the butter and oil.

MAKES 8 SERVINGS
4 large russet potatoes, peeled and halved
6 tablespoons unsalted butter, or goose or duck fat
¼ cup vegetable oil
Salt and freshly ground pepper, to taste

Preheat the oven to 400°F. Place the potatoes in a large saucepan of lightly salted water and bring to a boil over high heat. Cover and cook for 5 minutes. Drain. Return the potatoes to the pan and cook uncovered over low heat, shaking the pan occasionally, to dry out them out and give them a rough surface, 1 to 2 minutes.

Put the butter and oil in a roasting pan, and heat in the oven. Arrange the potatoes in the pan and baste with the hot fat. Roast, turning occasionally, until golden-brown and tender, about 1 hour. Using a slotted spoon, transfer to a warmed serving bowl. Season with salt and pepper, and serve hot.

POTATO AND GRUYÈRE TIMBALE

This satisfying potato dish can be prepared with whatever favorite cheese you have in the house.

MAKES 6 SERVINGS
6 tablespoons unsalted butter, at room temperature
2 tablespoons dry bread crumbs
2 pounds boiling potatoes, peeled and quartered
½ cup milk
2 large eggs, beaten
1½ cups shredded Gruyère cheese
Salt and freshly ground pepper, to taste

Preheat the oven to 350°F. Grease a 9-inch round cake pan with 1 tablespoon of the unsalted butter, and then coat it with about 1 tablespoon of the dry bread crumbs.

In a large pot of lightly salted boiling water, cook the potatoes until tender, about 20 minutes. Drain well. Return to the pot and cook over low heat, stirring constantly, to evaporate any excess moisture, about 3 minutes. Using a potato masher or a hand-held electric mixer on low speed, mash the potatoes with the milk. Stir in the eggs and cheese. Season with salt and pepper.

Spread the potatoes in the prepared pan. Sprinkle the top with the remaining 1 tablespoon bread crumbs, and dot with the remaining 1 tablespoon butter. Bake until the top is golden-brown, 30 to 35 minutes. Let stand for 5 minutes, then invert and unmold onto a serving plate. Serve hot.

BAKED STUFFED POTATOES

Serve these with grilled steak or a vegetable stew.

MAKES 8 SIDE DISH SERVINGS
4 large russet potatoes, unpeeled, pricked all over with a skewer
⅔ cup half-and-half or milk, heated
1½ cups shredded sharp Cheddar cheese
4 tablespoons unsalted butter
1 large egg, beaten
Salt and cayenne pepper, to taste

Preheat the oven to 400°F. Place the potatoes directly on the oven rack and bake until tender, about 1 hour. Let cool until easy to handle. Cut each potato in half lengthwise, then use a fork to scrape out the flesh into a bowl, leaving a ¼-inch-thick layer of flesh in the skins to form shells. Set the skins aside.

Add the half-and-half to the potato flesh, mashing with a fork until smooth. Add the cheese, butter, and egg, and mix well. Season with salt and cayenne pepper. Heap into the potato skins and place on a lightly greased baking sheet. Bake until the tops are golden-brown, about 15 minutes. Serve hot.

PARSLEY MASHED POTATOES

Plain mashed potatoes are just fine, but they can also be embellished with herbs and other flavorings. This version is one of the most versatile.

MAKES 4 SERVINGS

2 pounds boiling potatoes, peeled
½ cup packed fresh flat-leaf parsley leaves
1¼ cups heavy cream
8 tablespoons (1 stick) unsalted butter, cut up
Salt and freshly ground pepper, to taste

Bring a large saucepan of lightly salted water to a boil over high heat. Add the potatoes and cook until tender, about 20 minutes, depending on the size of the potatoes.

Meanwhile, bring a small saucepan of water to a boil over high heat. Add the parsley and blanch for 1 minute. Drain and refresh. Squeeze dry in a dish towel. Place the blanched parsley in a blender. In another small saucepan, bring the cream and butter to a simmer over low heat, stirring to melt the butter. Pour into the blender and process until smooth. Season with salt and pepper.

Drain the potatoes and return to the warm saucepan. Mash the potatoes, adding the parsley cream. Taste to check the seasoning. Serve hot.

Pesto Mashed Potatoes: Subsitute ½ cup packed fresh basil leaves for the parsley. Stir ½ cup freshly grated Parmesan cheese into the mashed potatoes.

PAN-ROASTED NEW POTATOES

Sometimes you want roasted potatoes, but the oven is packed with other foods. This method gives delicious results on top of the stove. If you can find very small new potatoes about the size of a large walnut, leave them whole.

MAKES 4 SERVINGS

6 tablespoons unsalted butter
1½ pounds small new potatoes, unpeeled, cut into 1-inch pieces
Salt and freshly ground pepper, to taste

In a large frying pan that will hold the potatoes in a single layer, heat the butter over medium heat. Add the potatoes and cook, turning occasionally, until browned on all sides, 8 to 10 minutes. Season with salt and pepper. Cover and reduce the heat to medium-low. Cook until the potatoes are tender when pierced with the tip of a sharp knife, about 30 minutes. Remove the lid, increase the heat to medium-high, and cook, shaking the pan often, until the potatoes become a bit crispier, 2 to 3 minutes. Using a slotted spoon, transfer to a warmed serving bowl and serve hot.

FRIED NEW POTATOES WITH MINTED YOGURT DRESSING

Many Indian vegetable dishes include potatoes, which are an ideal bland background for the aromatic blends of onions, garlic, chiles, and spices.

MAKES 4 SERVINGS

8 medium boiling potatoes (2 pounds), peeled and cut into 1½-inch pieces
½ cup clarified butter or vegetable oil
1 large onion, thinly sliced
4 garlic cloves, thinly sliced
1 tablespoon shredded fresh ginger
2 teaspoons ground coriander
1 teaspoon ground cumin
2 small hot fresh chile peppers (such as serrano), seeded and chopped
Salt and freshly ground pepper, to taste
2 tablespoons chopped fresh cilantro
1 tablespoon lime juice
Dressing
⅔ cup plain yogurt
2 tablespoons chopped fresh mint
¼ teaspoon cayenne pepper, or more to taste
Salt, to taste

To make the dressing, combine all of the ingredients in a small bowl. Let stand at room temperature while preparing the potatoes.

Bring a large pot of lightly salted water to a boil over high heat. Add the potatoes and cook until half done, about 10 minutes. Drain well.

In a large frying pan, heat the clarified butter over medium heat. Add the onion and garlic and cook until the onion is golden-brown, about 7 minutes. Add the ginger, coriander, and cumin, and reduce the heat to very low. Cook, stirring often, until very fragrant, 3 to 5 minutes. Stir in the chiles, and season with salt and pepper. Add the potatoes and mix well to coat with the spices. Add ½ cup water, and increase the heat to medium-low. Simmer the potatoes until they are tender and the water has almost completely evaporated, about 15 minutes. Sprinkle with the cilantro and lime juice. Increase the heat to high and continue cooking, stirring often, until the potatoes are crisped, about 3 more minutes. If desired, drain the potatoes to remove excess fat. Allow to cool to warm, then spoon the dressing over the potatoes and serve.

BAKED NEW POTATOES WITH SAFFRON, CREAM, AND GARLIC

Prepared this way, the potatoes become wonderfully soft and creamy in texture, and the saffron adds a new flavor dimension.

MAKES 8 SERVINGS
8 medium boiling potatoes (2 pounds), peeled and cut into 1½-inch pieces
⅔ cup heavy cream
⅔ cup milk
2 garlic cloves, minced
½ to 1 teaspoon crushed saffron threads
Salt and freshly ground pepper, to taste
Chopped fresh chives, for garnish

Preheat the oven to 350°F. Lightly butter a baking dish large enough to hold the potatoes in a single layer. Bring a large saucepan of lightly salted water to a boil over high heat. Add the potatoes and cook until half done, about 10 minutes. Drain and refresh. Place in the prepared baking dish.

In a medium saucepan, combine the heavy cream, milk, garlic, and saffron, and season with salt. Bring to a simmer over medium heat. Remove from the heat and let stand for 5 minutes or so. Pour evenly over the potatoes. Bake until the potatoes are tender when pierced with the tip of a sharp knife and the cream has thickened, about 30 minutes. Sprinkle generously with pepper and with chives, and serve hot.

CARAMELIZED SWEET POTATOES

These are perfect with baked ham, roast pork, and, of course, the holiday turkey.

MAKES 6 SERVINGS
4 medium sweet potatoes (about 2 pounds), unpeeled
3 tablespoons sugar
4 tablespoons butter, cut into pieces

In a saucepan of boiling salted water, cook the sweet potatoes until barely tender when pierced with a knife, 20 to 25 minutes. Cool until easy to handle, then peel. Cut into 1½-inch rounds, and cover to keep warm.

In a large frying pan, heat the sugar over medium heat, shaking the pan often, until the sugar melts and caramelizes to a golden amber color. Add the butter, and swirl the pan to incorporate the butter into the caramel. Quickly rinse the sweet potatoes under cold running water, shake off excess water, and carefully place the sweet potatoes in the pan. Turn them in the caramel until well coated, then heat through for about 2 minutes. Serve hot.

BAKED SWEET POTATOES WITH PINEAPPLE

Use either yellow-fleshed sweet potatoes or orange-fleshed sweet potatoes (often called yams) for this holiday specialty.

MAKES 8 TO 12 SERVINGS
1 small ripe pineapple
3 pounds sweet potatoes, peeled and cut into ¼-inch-thick slices
8 tablespoons (1 stick) unsalted butter
1½ cups unsweetened pineapple juice, fresh or canned
¾ cup packed light brown sugar
3 tablespoons dark rum, bourbon, or additional pineapple juice
1 tablespoon minced fresh ginger
2 tablespoons cornstarch mixed with 2 tablespoons water

Using a large, sharp knife, cut away the crown and the thick skin from the pineapple, and then remove the small "eyes" with the tip of the knife. Quarter the pineapple lengthwise. Cut away and discard the thick core from each quarter, then cut crosswise into ¼-inch-thick slices.

Bring a large pot of lightly salted water to a boil over high heat. Add the sweet potatoes and cook until crisp-tender, about 5 minutes; do not overcook. Drain and rinse under cold running water.

Lightly butter a 9- by 13-inch baking dish. Layer the sweet potatoes in the dish in overlapping rows, slipping in a pineapple quarter every few potatoes, letting the curved edge of the pineapple peek out. (The dish can be prepared up to 8 hours ahead and kept, covered, in the refrigerator.)

Preheat the oven to 350°F. In a medium saucepan, melt the butter over medium heat. Add the pineapple juice, brown sugar, rum, and ginger and bring to a boil. Stir in the cornstarch and cook until thickened. Drizzle over the sweet potatoes and pineapple. Bake, basting the top often with the juices in the dish, until the sweet potatoes are tender and the cooking liquid is syrupy, about 35 minutes. Serve hot.

MASHED RUTABAGA WITH POTATOES

Rutabaga is a humble root vegetable in itself, but it can be very good when treated properly. Here, it is mashed together with potatoes, and enriched with the addition of a little cream.

BAKED NEW POTATOES WITH SAFFRON, CREAM, AND GARLIC

STUFFED TOMATOES

MAKES 4 SERVINGS
  1 pound rutabagas, peeled and cut into 1-inch chunks
  1 pound boiling potatoes, peeled and cut into
    1-inch chunks
  ¼ cup heavy cream
  2 tablespoons unsalted butter
  Salt and freshly ground pepper, to taste

Put the rutabaga and potatoes in a saucepan and add water to cover. Bring to a boil and cook until tender, 15 to 20 minutes. Drain, then return to the pan. Mash, adding the cream and butter and a seasoning of salt and pepper. If desired, beat until fluffy. Serve hot.

SPINACH AND CHICKPEA STEW

This is a fragrant vegetable stew with a sumptuous, deep flavor, substantial enough to make a whole meal. It is especially welcome on a cold day. Dried black-eyed peas could be substituted for the chickpeas.

MAKES 4 TO 6 SERVINGS
  4 tablespoons olive oil
  1 slice country-style bread

  1 medium onion, chopped
  4 ripe plum tomatoes, peeled, seeded, and chopped
  1 garlic clove, chopped
  1 tablespoon sweet Hungarian paprika
  1 pound fresh spinach leaves, tough stems discarded
  Salt, to taste
  1 generous cup dried chickpeas, cooked and drained

In a medium frying pan, heat 2 tablespoons of the oil over medium heat. Add the bread and fry, turning once, until golden-brown, about 3 minutes. Transfer the bread to paper towels to drain, leaving the oil in the pan, and let the bread cool. In the same pan, cook the onion until golden-brown, about 6 minutes. Stir in the tomatoes. Set aside.

Using a mortar and pestle or a blender, crush the garlic. Crumble in the fried bread and crush to a paste. Set aside.

In a large saucepan, heat the remaining 2 tablespoons of oil. Stir in the paprika. Immediately, in batches, add the spinach, waiting for the first batch to wilt before adding the next. Season with salt. Add the chickpeas, garlic and bread paste, and onion-tomato mixture. Add 1 cup of water. Cover and simmer very gently until the flavors are well blended, about 30 minutes, adding more water, if needed, to keep the mixture moist. Serve hot.

SESAME SPINACH

Grit has a tendency to hide in the crevices of spinach leaves, so be sure to rinse them thoroughly.

MAKES 4 SERVINGS

1 tablespoon Asian dark sesame oil
1 garlic clove, crushed under a knife and peeled
1 tablespoon sesame seeds
1½ pounds fresh spinach, tough stems discarded
Salt, to tase

Heat a large frying pan or wok, then add the oil and garlic and cook until the garlic begins to brown. Discard the garlic. Add the sesame seeds and fry until golden, about 30 seconds. Add the spinach. Increase the heat and cook, stirring and tossing, until the spinach is wilted, about 3 minutes. Season with salt.

Drain well in a sieve, pressing the spinach with the back of a spoon to remove excess moisture. Serve hot.

STUFFED TOMATOES

Serve these as a light lunch dish with salad.

MAKES 6 SERVINGS

6 large ripe but firm tomatoes
⅔ cup fresh bread crumbs
6 green Mediterranean olives, pitted and chopped
6 anchovy fillets packed in oil, drained and chopped
1 teaspoon chopped fresh basil or marjoram
1 large garlic clove, minced
4 tablespoons unsalted butter, melted
Salt and freshly ground pepper, to taste

Preheat the oven to 325°F. Lightly oil a baking dish. Cut the tomatoes in half horizontally. Over a bowl, scoop out the inside of each tomato half, leaving a ¼-inch-thick shell. Set the shells aside. If desired, remove the tomato seeds from the flesh. Add the bread crumbs, olives, anchovies, basil, and garlic to the tomato flesh. Moisten with the butter, and season. Stuff the mixture into the tomato shells. Bake until tender and browned on top, 30 to 40 minutes.

ZUCCHINI AND TOMATO GRATIN

This crusty gratin is a substantial side dish, or it could be served as a vegetarian main course.

MAKES 4 TO 6 SERVINGS

4 tablespoons olive oil
5 medium zucchini, cut into ½-inch-thick rounds
2 garlic cloves, minced
Salt and freshly ground pepper, to taste
¾ cup fresh bread crumbs
⅓ cup freshly grated Parmesan cheese
1 tablespoon chopped fresh basil
1 teaspoon chopped fresh rosemary
2 large ripe tomatoes, cut into ½-inch-thick rounds and lightly squeezed to remove seeds
1 cup shredded mozzarella cheese

Preheat the oven to 350°F. Lightly oil a 2½-quart baking dish. In a frying pan, heat 3 tablespoons of the oil. Add the zucchini and cook, stirring often, until lightly browned, about 10 minutes. Add the garlic and cook for 1 minute. Season, and set aside.

Mix the bread crumbs, Parmesan, basil, and rosemary. Sprinkle 2 tablespoons into the baking dish. Arrange half of the zucchini in the dish, then cover with half of the tomato slices. Sprinkle with half of the remaining crumbs, and all the mozzarella. Top with the remaining zucchini, tomatoes, and crumb mixture. Drizzle with the remaining 1 tablespoon oil. Bake until browned and bubbling, 30 minutes. Let stand for 5 minutes before serving.

RATATOUILLE

Here a rich and moist mélange of vegetables is just distinguishable in a smooth, aromatic tomato sauce.

MAKES 6 SERVINGS

⅔ cup olive oil
2 pounds ripe plum tomatoes, peeled, seeded, and chopped, or use drained canned tomatoes
Salt and freshly ground pepper, to taste
2 medium onions, sliced
3 garlic cloves, sliced
2 medium red or green bell peppers, seeded and cut into ¼-inch-wide strips
3 medium zucchini, cut into ¼-inch-thick rounds
1 eggplant, cut into ¼-inch slices, then quartered
½ cup black Mediterranean olives, pitted
2 tablespoon shredded fresh basil

In a saucepan, heat ⅓ cup of the oil. Add the tomatoes, and season with salt and pepper. Bring to a simmer, then cook, stirring, until the tomatoes form a thick sauce, 10 to 15 minutes.

Meanwhile, heat the remaining ⅓ cup olive oil over medium heat. Add the onions and garlic, and cook until translucent, about 5 minutes. Add the red peppers, zucchini, and eggplant. Season. Reduce the heat and cook, stirring, until the vegetables are almost tender, about 20 minutes. Stir in the tomato sauce and olives. Cook until the vegetables are tender, 5 to 10 minutes. Stir in the basil. Serve hot, warm, or cool.

Desserts and Candies

APPLE FRITTERS

Golden Delicious apples are the best choice of apples for making these fritters, as, unlike some others, they hold their shape well when cooked. The fritters are a nice dessert, but would also make a pleasant surprise to finish off brunch.

MAKES 4 TO 6 SERVINGS

¾ cup all-purpose flour
3 tablespoons unsalted butter, melted
⅓ cup granulated sugar
⅛ teaspoon ground cinnamon
A large pinch of ground cloves
A pinch of salt
8 Golden Delicious apples
Vegetable oil, for deep-frying
1 large egg white

About 1 hour before making the fritters, mix the flour and melted butter in a medium bowl. Gradually stir in 1 cup lukewarm water. Cover and let stand in a cool place, but not the refrigerator.

Just before serving, mix together the sugar, cinnamon, cloves, and salt in a small bowl. Peel and core the apples, and slice into ⅓-inch-thick rings. Toss the apple rings with about 2 tablespoons of the spiced sugar mixture.

Pour enough oil into a deep saucepan to come 2 or 3 inches up the sides, and heat to 350°F. Preheat the oven to 200°F.

In a small bowl, beat the egg white until it is stiff. Fold into the flour batter. In batches, dip the apple slices in the batter, gently shake off the excess batter, and add to the oil. Fry until golden-brown, turning once, about 3 minutes. Drain on paper towels and keep warm in the oven while making the remaining fritters. Serve hot, sprinkled with the remaining spiced sugar.

PEARS IN RED WINE

There are few desserts that are more appropriate as the finale to an autumn dinner than these beautiful pears in a deep ruby-colored syrup.

MAKES 4 SERVINGS

2½ cups hearty red wine
⅓ cup granulated sugar
½ vanilla bean (optional)
2 (3-inch) strips orange zest
1 cinnamon stick
6 whole cloves
4 large Bosc pears
1 lemon, halved

In a large saucepan, combine the wine, sugar, optional vanilla bean, orange zest, cinnamon stick, and cloves. Bring to a simmer over medium heat. Cook for 5 minutes.

Peel the pears, rubbing with the lemon halves to keep them from discoloring; leave the stems attached. Place the pears on their sides in the wine syrup. Cover and reduce the heat to low. Simmer gently, turning the pears occasionally in the syrup to ensure even coloring, until tender, about 1 hour. Using a slotted spoon, lift the pears onto a platter, standing them upright. Increase the heat to high and boil the wine syrup until it has reduced to about ⅔ cup, about 15 minutes. Pour over the pears. Serve warm or chilled, with cream.

FRENCH CHERRY CLAFOUTIS

This is a specialty of French country cooking, simple to make and delicious hot or cold.

MAKES 6 TO 8 SERVINGS

⅓ cup all-purpose flour
A pinch of salt
3 large eggs, beaten
2 cups milk
3 tablespoons granulated sugar, plus more
   for serving
3 tablespoons kirsch
1½ pounds fresh sweet cherries, pitted
Sweetened whipped cream, for serving

Preheat the oven to 375°F. Lightly butter a 10-inch round pie plate or baking dish.

Place the flour and salt in a medium bowl. Make a well in the center and pour in the eggs. Gradually beat in the milk until smooth, then add the sugar and kirsch. Beat with a wooden spoon for about 3 minutes. (The batter can also be prepared in a blender, and blended until smooth, about 20 seconds.)

Spread the cherries in the prepared pie plate. Pour in the batter, straining it through a sieve to remove any lumps, if necessary. Bake until a toothpick inserted in the center comes out clean, about 1 hour.

Sprinkle with additional sugar and serve warm, with whipped cream.

SUMMER BERRY FOOL

Fools, those extremely simple desserts, are hard to beat when you want something sweet that requires little effort to make.

FRENCH CHERRY CLAFOUTIS

MAKES 4 SERVINGS
1½ pints strawberries or raspberries
¾ cup granulated sugar
1¼ cups heavy cream, chilled

Reserve a few whole berries, and chop the rest. In a medium bowl, mix the chopped strawberries with 6 tablespoons of the sugar. Cover and chill until the strawberries give off some juices, at least 1 hour. Crush the berries with a fork.

In a chilled large bowl, whip the cream with the remaining sugar just until it forms soft peaks—do not overwhip. Fold the berries into the cream. Spoon into individual glasses and garnish with the reserved berries, either whole or sliced. Serve cold.

JAMAICAN BAKED BANANAS

This dessert will appeal to everyone with a sweet tooth—the bananas are gorgeously sticky.

MAKES 4 SERVINGS
8 tablespoons (1 stick) unsalted butter
8 small ripe bananas, peeled
½ cup packed light brown sugar
2 tablespoons lime juice
3 tablespoons dark rum
Coconut Ice Cream, for serving

Preheat the oven to 425°F. Place the butter in a flameproof baking dish (preferably enameled cast iron) large enough to hold the bananas in one layer. Melt the butter over medium heat. Add the bananas and turn to coat with butter. Sprinkle with the brown sugar, and turn the bananas until coated with the resulting sticky syrup. Sprinkle with the lime juice. Transfer to the oven and bake for 10 minutes.

Remove from the oven and place over medium heat again. Add the rum—be careful, as it may splatter. Bring to a simmer, holding the dish with a pot holder and swirling the liquids in the dish to mix them. Return to the oven and bake until nicely browned, about 5 minutes. (The bananas can also be browned in a preheated broiler.) Serve hot, with coconut ice cream.

RASPBERRY AND SHERRY TRIFLE

This delicious trifle is a holiday classic, and is simple to put together. The ingredients given here can easily be doubled to make a larger trifle when you have a bigger crowd to serve.

RASPBERRY AND SHERRY TRIFLE

MAKES 6 SERVINGS
½ (12-ounce) store-bought pound cake, cut into ⅓-inch-thick slices
½ cup sherry, preferably oloroso
⅓ cup seedless raspberry jam
1 cup fresh raspberries, plus more for garnish
1 cup slivered blanched almonds, plus more for garnish
⅔ cup heavy cream, chilled
2 tablespoons granulated sugar
1 teaspoon vanilla extract
Custard
2 cups milk
⅓ cup granulated sugar
2 large strips lemon zest
5 large egg yolks, at room temperature

For the custard, in a double boiler insert, heat the milk with the sugar and lemon zest over medium heat until bubbles form around the edge, stirring occasionally to dissolve the sugar. Remove from the heat and let stand for 10 minutes. Remove the lemon zest. In a large bowl, whisk the egg yolks until light and frothy. Gradually stir the hot milk into the eggs. Return to the double boiler insert and place over a saucepan of hot, not simmering, water over low heat. Cook, stirring constantly with a wooden spoon, until the custard is thick enough to coat the spoon (an instant-read thermometer will read 185°F), 5 to 10 minutes. Strain the custard through a sieve into a large bowl. Let cool to room temperature.

Place the cake slices in a 1½- to 2-quart glass bowl or trifle dish. Sprinkle with the sherry, then spread with the jam. Sprinkle with the raspberries and almonds. Pour in the cooled custard. (The trifle can be prepared up to 4 hours ahead, and kept, covered with plastic wrap, in the refrigerator.)

In a chilled medium bowl, whip the cream with the sugar and vanilla until soft peaks form. Spread over the trifle, and garnish with more raspberries and slivered almonds. Serve chilled.

CRÈME BRÛLÉE

For this version of the international favorite, the custard is cooked entirely on top of the stove, and not baked at all. Also, most of the sweetness comes from the caramelized sugar topping.

MAKES 4 SERVINGS
2 cups heavy cream
1 vanilla bean, split lengthwise
4 large egg yolks
¼ cup granulated sugar
3 tablespoons light brown sugar

In a medium heavy-bottomed saucepan, heat the cream with the vanilla bean over low heat until bubbles appear around the edge. Remove from the heat, and let stand for 10 minutes to infuse the cream with the vanilla flavor.

Whisk the egg yolks and sugar in a double boiler insert until the mixture is light and a little thickened. Gradually stir in the hot cream, adding the vanilla bean too. Place the insert over a saucepan of hot, not simmering, water over low heat. Do not let the base of the insert touch the water. Stir constantly until the custard is thick enough to coat a wooden spoon (about 185°F on an instant-read thermometer), 5 to 10 minutes. Discard the vanilla bean. Pour the custard into four ¾-cup ramekin cups. Let cool, then cover each and refrigerate until well chilled and set, at least 4 hours or overnight.

When ready to serve, preheat the boiler. Unwrap the custards. Place the brown sugar in a sieve, and rub it through the sieve to make an even layer about ¼ inch thick on the top of each custard. Place the ramekins on a baking sheet, and broil until the sugar melts and caramelizes, 1 to 2 minutes. Watch the sugar closely so it doesn't burn; don't worry if it colors unevenly. Let the caramel cool and harden before serving.

CHOCOLATE MOUSSE

Some things never go out of fashion. It's easy to see why chocolate mousse is a perennial favorite.

MAKES 4 TO 6 SERVINGS
2 cups heavy cream
3 egg yolks
3½ ounces high-quality bittersweet chocolate, grated
¼ cup granulated sugar
A tiny pinch of salt

In a double boiler insert, combine ⅔ cup of the cream, the egg yolks, chocolate, and sugar. Whisk until the mixture is light and foamy. Place the insert over a saucepan of hot, not simmering, water over low heat. Do not let the base of the insert touch the water. Cook, stirring occasionally, until the chocolate melts and the mixture is thick and creamy, 5 to 10 minutes. Remove from the heat and leave to cool to room temperature. Stir in the salt.

In a chilled medium bowl, whip the remaining 1⅓ cups cream until it forms soft peaks. Stir a spoonful of the whipped cream into the chocolate mixture to lighten it, then fold in the remaining cream. Spoon into individual ramekins, cover each, and refrigerate until well chilled and set, at least 4 hours or overnight. Serve chilled.

Orange Chocolate Mousse: Add the grated zest of ½ orange to the chocolate mixture just before folding in the whipped cream.

TIRAMISÙ

This little Italian sweet is popular the world over. Dry ladyfingers (*savoiardi*) are the ones to use if you can buy them, but if you can't find those you can use stale sponge-like ladyfingers.

MAKES 8 SERVINGS
2 cups mascarpone, at room temperature
½ cup confectioners' sugar
1 cup heavy cream, chilled
1 teaspoon vanilla extract
1½ cups cool, brewed espresso coffee, or 1 tablespoon instant espresso dissolved in 1½ cups boiling water
⅓ cup sweet marsala
1 (7-ounce) package Italian dry ladyfingers (*savoiardi*)
1 ounce bittersweet chocolate

In a medium bowl, gently work the mascarpone and confectioners' sugar together until smooth. In a chilled medium bowl, whip the cream together with the vanilla extract until soft peaks form. Fold the whipped cream into the mascarpone.

In a shallow dish, mix together the espresso and the marsala. One at a time, dip about half of the ladyfingers very briefly in the espresso mixture on both sides, just to moisten (do not soak them), then arrange in a single layer in an 7- by 11-inch serving dish. Spread with half of the mascarpone mixture. Moisten the remaining ladyfingers, and make a second layer, then spread with the remaining mascarpone mixture. Cover tightly with plastic wrap and refrigerate for at least 4 hours or overnight. When ready to serve, using the coarse holes of a cheese grater, grate the chocolate over the top.

MERINGUE CUPS WITH FRESH FRUIT

This is a sumptuous dessert, to be sure, but one that also enjoys the virtue of being low-fat. With the substitution of 1 cup sweetened whipped cream for the orange liqueur, it can be transformed into Pavlova, the beloved Australian sweet.

MAKES 6 SERVINGS
3 cups mixed fresh fruit, such as sliced strawberries and chunks of mango
2 tablespoons orange-flavored liqueur, such as Grand Marnier
1 tablespoon granulated sugar

Meringue Cups
  3 large egg whites, at room temperature
  ⅛ teaspoon cream of tartar
  ¾ cup granulated sugar
  ½ teaspoon vanilla extract

Preheat the oven to 250°F. Line a baking sheet with parchment paper or aluminum foil. Draw six 3-inch circles on the paper.

To make the meringue cups, in a large bowl, beat the egg whites at low speed until foamy. Add the cream of tartar and increase the speed to high. Beat until soft peaks form. Gradually beat in the sugar, and beat until very stiff, shiny peaks form. Beat in the vanilla. Transfer the meringue to a pastry bag fitted with a large plain tube (Number 5). Pipe a flat spiral of meringue inside each of the circles on the baking sheet, to form the bases. Pipe one or two rings, on top of each other, on the edge of each base, to make the wall of the cups. Or, simply drop six mounds of meringue onto the parchment paper, and form into cups with the back of a tablespoon dipped into water. Bake until the meringues are set but not browned, about 45 minutes. Let the meringues stand in the turned-off oven until crisp, at least 1 hour. (The meringue cups can be baked up to 1 day ahead, and kept, uncovered, at room temperature.)

In a bowl, toss the fruit with the liqueur and sugar. Fill the meringue cups with the fruit, and serve.

HOT RASPBERRY SOUFFLÉ

Here's a low-fat dessert that is no less delicious for its healthy profile. Soufflés are one of the most dramatic of all dishes, and always win praise for the cook.

MAKES 4 SERVINGS
  Butter and granulated sugar, for the soufflé dish
  3 cups fresh raspberries
  ½ cup granulated sugar
  1 tablespoon lemon juice
  5 large egg whites, at room temperature

Preheat the oven to 375°F. Lightly butter a 2-quart soufflé dish, then dust with sugar, tapping out the excess sugar. In a blender, purée the raspberries with the sugar and lemon juice. Strain through a fine sieve to remove the seeds. Pour the raspberry sauce into a medium saucepan and bring to a simmer over medium heat. Transfer ¾ cup of the sauce to a small saucepan and set aside.

In a large bowl, beat the egg whites at low speed until foamy. Increase the heat to high and beat until soft peaks form. Fold the beaten egg whites into the purée in the larger saucepan. Pour into the prepared

dish. Bake until the top of the soufflé is browned and a long wooden skewer inserted in the center comes out clean, 20 to 25 minutes.

Reheat the raspberry sauce in the small saucepan. Present the soufflé at the table and serve, spooning some of the warm sauce over each portion.

BREAD AND BUTTER PUDDING

This is one of the best ways to use day-old bread.

MAKES 8 SERVINGS
  6 slices day-old, firm white sandwich bread,
    crusts removed
  3 tablespoons unsalted butter, at room temperature
  ⅓ cup raisins
  3 large eggs
  ⅓ cup granulated sugar
  ⅛ teaspoon ground cinnamon
  1 cup milk
  1 cup light cream or half-and-half

Lightly butter a 1-quart baking dish. Butter the bread slices on one side. Buttered side up, layer the bread in the dish, sprinkling each layer with the raisins. In a medium bowl, whisk the eggs with 3 tablespoons of the sugar and the cinnamon. Gradually whisk in the milk and cream. Pour over the bread and let stand for 1 hour.

Preheat the oven to 275°F. Sprinkle the pudding with the remaining sugar. Bake until a knife inserted in the center comes out clean and the top is puffed and golden, 1 to 1¼ hours. Serve warm or chilled.

RICE PUDDING

The bay leaf adds an unusual, elusive flavor to this simple baked rice pudding.

MAKES 4 TO 6 SERVINGS
  7 tablespoons short-grain rice, or use Arborio rice
  2½ cups milk
  2 tablespoons heavy cream
  1 bay leaf
  ¼ cup vanilla sugar, or ¼ cup granulated sugar and
    1 teaspoon vanilla extract

Preheat the oven to 300°F. Lightly butter a 1-quart baking dish. Put the rice in the dish. In a medium saucepan, heat the milk and cream with the bay leaf over medium heat until bubbles appear around the edge. Remove from the heat and let stand for 5 minutes. Pour the mixture over the rice, and stir in the sugar.

Bake until the pudding is thick and creamy and the rice is very tender, about 2 hours.

STRAWBERRY-CHOCOLATE TRUFFLES

Use mellow-flavored Dutch-processed cocoa for coating these melt-in-the-mouth truffles.

MAKES ABOUT 30 TRUFFLES
    6 tablespoons unsalted butter, cut up
    8 ounces good bittersweet chocolate, finely chopped
    ¼ cup strawberry preserves
    2 tablespoons strawberry liqueur or Cognac
    ⅓ cup Dutch-processed cocoa powder

In a double boiler insert set over a saucepan of hot water, melt the butter. Add the chocolate and melt, stirring. Remove from the heat, and whisk in the strawberry preserves and liqueur. Cool, cover with plastic wrap, and chill until firm, at least 2 hours.

Using a melon baller, scoop out 1 tablespoon of the chocolate mixture for each truffle. (If the mixture is too firm, leave at room temperature to soften.) Roll between your palms into balls, and roll in the cocoa to coat. Keep refrigerated, in a covered container, until ready to serve. The truffles can be kept like this for up to 5 days or frozen for up to 1 month.

PINE NUT PRALINES

In New Orleans, pralines are made with pecans. This delicious Southwest version uses pine nuts instead.

MAKES ABOUT 2 DOZEN
    3 cups packed light brown sugar
    1 tablespoon unsalted butter
    1 cup pine nuts
    1 teaspoon vanilla extract

Line a work area with waxed paper. In a medium, heavy-bottomed saucepan, with a candy thermometer attached, combine the sugar, butter, and ¼ cup water. Bring to a boil and cook until the thermometer reads 238°F (soft-ball stage). Stir in the pine nuts and vanilla. Remove from the heat, and stir until the mixture is opaque and thickened, but still pourable. Drop from a heaping tablespoon onto the waxed paper to form small patties about 2½ inches wide. Let cool completely. Keep in an airtight container at room temperature for up to 5 days.

MACADAMIA-COCONUT CRUNCH

The texture of this golden candy is similar to toffee or brittle, but the flavor goes Hawaiian with macadamia nuts and coconut. If you can find it, substitute unsweetened coconut ribbons for the sweetened flaked coconut—it gives a better look and texture.

MAKES ABOUT 2 POUNDS
    1 cup sweetened flaked coconut
    2 cups granulated sugar
    1 cup light corn syrup
    1 cup (2 sticks) unsalted butter
    2 teaspoons baking soda
    1 teaspoon vanilla extract
    2 cups salted macadamia nuts, coarsely chopped

Preheat the oven to 400°F. Spread the coconut on a baking sheet and bake, stirring often, until lightly toasted, about 5 minutes. Let cool completely.

Lightly butter two baking sheets. Butter a 3-quart saucepan and attach a candy thermometer. Put the sugar, corn syrup, butter, and ½ cup water in the saucepan, and bring to a boil over high heat, stirring constantly to dissolve the sugar. Stop stirring, and continue cooking until the thermometer reads 295°F (hard-crack stage). Remove from the heat and immediately sift the baking soda over the mixture. Add the vanilla and stir gently. (Be careful, because the mixture will froth up.) Stir in the toasted coconut and macadamia nuts. Quickly pour onto the prepared baking sheets and tilt them to spread the crunch into a layer about ½ inch thick. Let cool completely. Break into pieces of random size and shape. The crunch can be kept, in an airtight container at room temperature, for up to 1 week.

CASHEW ROCKY ROAD

This is one of the most popular of all American candies, and certainly one of the easiest to make. Other nuts, such as walnuts, peanuts, or pecans, can be used instead of the cashews.

MAKES ABOUT 2 POUNDS
    1 pound milk chocolate, coarsely chopped
    8 ounces large marshmallows, snipped with scissors into quarters
    1 cup unsalted cashews, coarsely chopped

Lightly butter a baking sheet. In a double boiler insert set over a saucepan of hot, not simmering, water, heat the chocolate until almost completely melted. Remove from the heat, and stir until the chocolate is melted and smooth. Let cool until barely tepid (if the chocolate is too hot, the marshmallows will melt when added). Fold in the marshmallows and cashews. Spread out on the prepared baking sheet in a thick layer about 12 inches square. Refrigerate until completely chilled and firm. To serve, cut into squares with a sharp knife. The candy can be kept, in an airtight container stored at room temperature, for up to 1 week.

Frozen Desserts

SCENTED VANILLA ICE CREAM

This ice cream is a beautiful golden-yellow, and is scented deliciously with coriander and lemon zest along with the vanilla.

MAKES ABOUT 1½ QUARTS
  6 large egg yolks
  ¾ cup plus 2 tablespoons granulated sugar
  1¼ cups milk
  1¼ cups light cream or half-and-half
  1 vanilla bean, split lengthwise, or 1 teaspoon vanilla extract
  1 (3-inch) strip lemon zest
  1 teaspoon coriander seeds
  ⅔ cup heavy cream, chilled

In a double boiler insert, whisk the egg yolks with the sugar until the mixture is light in color and frothy. In a medium saucepan, heat the milk and light cream with the vanilla bean until bubbles form around the edge. Remove the vanilla bean and set aside. Gradually stir the hot liquid into the egg mixture. Return the vanilla bean, and add the lemon zest and coriander seeds. Set the insert over a saucepan of hot, not simmering, water. Stirring constantly with a wooden spoon, cook until the custard is thick enough to coat the spoon (an instant-read thermometer will read about 185°F), 5 to 10 minutes. If using vanilla extract, stir it in now. Strain into a medium bowl set in a larger bowl of ice water. Let stand until chilled, stirring often.

  In a chilled medium bowl, whip the heavy cream until it is stiff, then whisk the cream into the custard. Transfer to the container of an ice cream machine and freeze according to the manufacturer's instructions. Pack the ice cream into a container, cover, and let harden in the freezer for at least 4 hours before serving. Transfer the ice cream to the refrigerator about 20 minutes before serving, in order to allow it to soften slightly.

Scented Vanilla Gelato: An Italian-style ice cream, with a slightly less smooth texture but excellent flavor, this can be made without an ice cream machine. (This technique can be applied to any ice cream recipe.) Chill a 9- by 13-inch metal baking pan in the freezer until very cold. Pour the mixture into the chilled pan, and freeze until partially frozen, about 1½ hours. Whisk the mixture well to break up any ice crystals, or transfer to a food processor fitted with the metal blade and process. Repeat the freezing and whisking procedures two more times. After the third whisking, let the ice cream freeze until it can be scooped. The procedure will take about 6 hours.

STRAWBERRY ICE CREAM

Try to use the sweetest berries to make this summer treat. Taste the mixture before it goes into the ice cream machine—it should be sweeter than you want the finished ice cream to be.

MAKES ABOUT 1 QUART
  3 large egg yolks
  ¾ cup granulated sugar, plus more as needed
  ⅔ cup milk
  ⅔ cup heavy or light cream
  1½ pints fresh strawberries, hulled

In a double boiler insert, whisk the yolks with the sugar until light in color and frothy. In a medium saucepan, bring the milk and cream to a simmer. Gradually stir into the egg mixture. Set the insert over a saucepan of hot water. Stirring with a wooden spoon, cook until the custard is thick enough to coat it (an instant-read thermometer will read about 185°F), 5 to 10 minutes. Strain into a medium bowl set in a bowl of ice water. Leave until chilled, stirring often.

  In a food processor fitted with the metal blade or in a blender, purée the berries. Whisk into the chilled custard. Taste and whisk in more sugar, if needed. Transfer to the container of an ice cream machine and freeze according to the manufacturer's instructions. Pack the ice cream into a container, cover, and harden in the freezer for at least 4 hours. Or, make a strawberry gelato, freezing according to the directions for Scented Vanilla Gelato. Transfer the ice cream or gelato to the refrigerator about 20 minutes before serving.

Raspberry Ice Cream: Substitute raspberries for the strawberries, and, if you wish, add 2 teaspoons framboise *eau-de-vie* or other raspberry-flavored liqueur.

COCONUT ICE CREAM

This makes an exotic finale to a Caribbean or Indian meal. Desiccated coconut is available at health food stores. If necessary, use flaked coconut, rinsed under hot water to remove the sugar coating, and drained.

MAKES ABOUT 1 QUART
  1¼ cups milk
  ½ vanilla bean, split lengthwise, or ½ teaspoon vanilla extract
  Pared zest of ½ lime
  ½ cup unsweetened desiccated coconut
  5 large egg yolks
  ½ cup granulated sugar
  ⅔ cup heavy cream
  A pinch of salt

In a medium heavy-bottomed saucepan, heat the milk with the vanilla bean and lime zest over medium heat until bubbles form around the edge. Remove from the heat. Stir in the coconut, cover the pan, and let stand for 30 minutes. Strain through a fine sieve into a bowl. Discard the vanilla bean and lime zest, then press the coconut in the sieve to extract all the remaining milk; discard the coconut.

In a double boiler insert, whisk the yolks with the sugar until light in color and frothy. Gradually whisk in the flavored milk. Set the insert over a saucepan of hot water. Stirring with a wooden spoon, cook until the custard is thick enough to coat the spoon (an instant-read thermometer will read about 185°F), 5 to 10 minutes. Strain into a medium bowl, and stir in the cream, and salt. (If using vanilla extract, add it now.) Place the bowl in a larger bowl of ice water and let stand until chilled, stirring often.

Transfer to the container of an ice cream machine and freeze according to the manufacturer's instructions. Pack the ice cream into a container, cover, and let harden in the freezer for at least 4 hours before serving. Or, make a coconut gelato, freezing according to the directions for Scented Vanilla Gelato. Transfer the ice cream or gelato to the refrigerator about 20 minutes before serving, to allow it to soften slightly.

CASSATA

Many Sicilian desserts have their origins in Arabic cooking. For example, their ice cream specialty, cassata, is actually named for a certain type of Arabic bowl.

MAKES 6 TO 8 SERVINGS
   1 pint high-quality vanilla ice cream, slightly softened
   1 pint high-quality chocolate ice cream,
     slightly softened
   2/3 cup heavy cream, chilled
   1/2 cup confectioners' sugar
   3/4 cup chopped mixed candied fruit
   1 large egg white, at room temperature

Using a metal spoon dipped in hot water, spread the vanilla ice cream in a thick, even layer in a 1½-quart melon-shaped metal mold or bowl. Press a piece of plastic wrap onto the surface of the ice cream, and freeze until it is firm. Cover the vanilla ice cream with the chocolate ice cream in an even layer, leaving a well in the center for the filling. Cover and freeze again until firm.

In a chilled medium bowl, whip the cream with the confectioners' sugar until just before it reaches soft peak stage. Stir in the candied fruit. In a small bowl, beat the egg white until it forms soft peaks, and fold into the cream. Spoon into the well in the ice-cream-lined mold. Cover tightly and freeze until firm. To serve, dip the mold briefly in hot water, and invert the cassata onto a well-chilled serving plate. Refrigerate the cassata for about 20 minutes, to allow it to soften slightly, then cut into wedges.

RASPBERRY AND LIME SHERBET

Sherbets generally feature fruit juices frozen with milk. This combination of raspberry and lime is deliciously tangy.

MAKES ABOUT 1 QUART
   1½ cups fresh or frozen raspberries
   2 cups milk
   ½ cup granulated sugar
   Grated zest of 1 lime
   2 tablespoons lime juice

In a food processor fitted with the metal blade, or a blender, purée the raspberries. Strain through a fine sieve to remove the seeds. You should have 1 cup purée. In a large bowl, combine the raspberry purée with the milk, sugar, and lime zest and juice. Pour into the container of an ice cream machine and freeze according to the manufacturer's instructions. Pack into a container, cover, and let harden in the freezer for at least 4 hours before serving. Transfer the sherbet to the refrigerator about 30 minutes before serving, to allow it to soften slightly.

ORANGE SORBET

Be sure to make this with freshly squeezed juices. If you can find them during their short winter season, use garnet-hued blood oranges.

MAKES ABOUT 1 QUART
   2⅓ cups fresh orange juice
   3 tablespoons fresh lemon juice
   1 cup confectioners' sugar

Combine all of the ingredients, and whisk to dissolve the sugar. Strain into the container of an ice cream machine and freeze according to the manufacturer's instructions. Pack the sorbet into a container, cover, and let harden in the freezer for at least 4 hours before serving. Transfer the sorbet to the refrigerator about 30 minutes before serving, to allow it to soften slightly.

Or, make an orange granita, freezing according to the directions for Coffee Granita.

SORBETS

Frozen Desserts/Pastries

GRAPEFRUIT SORBET

One of the most refreshing, sophisticated ways to serve this sorbet for a dinner party is to put a scoop of the sorbet in a chilled martini glass, and then to drizzle Campari over it.

MAKES ABOUT 1 QUART
   ½ cup plus 1 tablespoon granulated sugar
   2 cups fresh grapefruit juice

In a saucepan, dissolve the sugar in 3 tablespoons water over high heat, and bring to a boil. Boil for 5 minutes. Transfer to a medium bowl and leave to cool completely. Whisk in the fresh grapefruit juice. Strain into the container of an ice cream machine and freeze according to the manufacturer's instructions. Pack the sorbet into a container, cover, and let harden in the freezer for at least 4 hours before serving. Transfer the sorbet to the refrigerator about 30 minutes before you wish to serve it, to allow it to soften slightly.

   Alternatively, make a grapefruit granita, freezing according to the directions for Coffee Granita.

MELON SORBET

Be sure the melons are sweet and full of juice—underripe melons won't do.

MAKES ABOUT 1 QUART
   2 (1-pound) ripe cantaloupe or
      honeydew melons
   2 cups confectioners' sugar
   ¼ cup lemon juice

Cut the melons in half and then discard the seeds. Using a large spoon, scoop out the flesh from both melons. In a food processor fitted with the metal blade, purée the melon flesh with the sugar and lemon juice. Transfer to the container of an ice cream machine and freeze according to the manufacturer's instructions. Pack the sorbet into a container, cover, and let harden in the freezer for at least 4 hours before serving. Transfer the sorbet to the refrigerator about 30 minutes before you wish to serve it, to allow it to soften slightly.

COFFEE GRANITA

This is the cooling late-morning favorite which many tourists (and of course the Italians) enjoy at the myriad pavement cafés in Rome and other big cities. The coffee must be really strong, preferably brewed from espresso or Viennese Roast.

MAKES ABOUT 1 QUART
   ½ cup plus 1 tablespoon granulated sugar
   2¼ cups hot, very strong brewed coffee
   1¼ cups heavy cream
   2 tablespoons Tia Maria (optional)

Place a 9- by 13-inch metal baking dish in the freezer and chill while making the coffee mixture. In a bowl, dissolve the sugar in the coffee, stirring. Place the bowl in a larger bowl of ice water and leave to chill. Pour into the chilled pan. Freeze until the edges of the coffee mixture are icy and semi-solid, about 1 hour.

   Using a fork, mix the icy crystals at the edge into the still-liquid center. Do not use a whisk: you want to coax ice crystals into forming. Return to the freezer and freeze until the edges are icy again, about 30 minutes. Mix with a fork again. Continue freezing, mixing with a fork about every 30 minutes, until the mixture has frozen into a slush of separate, soft crystals of pale-brown coffee ice, about 2 hours.

   In a chilled medium bowl, whip the cream until it forms soft peaks. To serve, layer the granita and whipped cream in well-chilled goblets, drizzling the layers with the optional Tia Maria.

———————— • ————————

BASIC PIE DOUGH

This is a superlative pie dough, with a crispness and flavor provided by the butter and flakiness from the vegetable shortening.

MAKES ENOUGH FOR ONE 9-INCH PIE SHELL
   1½ cups all-purpose flour
   ¼ teaspoon salt
   6 tablespoons unsalted butter, cut into small
      pieces, chilled
   2 tablespoons vegetable shortening, cut into small
      pieces, chilled

Place the flour and salt in a medium bowl. Add the butter and shortening. Using a pastry blender or two knives, cut the fats into the flour until the mixture is crumbly with some pieces about the size of small peas. Stirring with a fork, gradually add about ⅓ cup ice water to moisten the dough—it should be just moist enough to hold together when pressed between your fingertips. Gather up the dough into a flat disk and wrap in plastic wrap. Chill for at least 20 minutes before rolling out.

Double Crust Pie Dough: Use 2 cups all-purpose flour, ¼ teaspoon salt, 7 tablespoons unsalted butter, and 3 tablespoons vegetable shortening. Moisten with a scant ½ cup ice water.

SWEET TART DOUGH

Use this for French-style dessert tarts.

MAKES ENOUGH FOR ONE 9-INCH TART SHELL
  1¼ cups all-purpose flour
  2 tablespoons granulated sugar
  ⅛ teaspoon salt
  6 tablespoons unsalted butter, cut into small
      pieces, chilled
  1 large egg yolk

Mix the flour, sugar, and salt in a medium bowl. Add the butter. Using a pastry blender or two knives, cut the fats into the flour until the mixture is crumbly with some pieces about the size of small peas. In a small bowl, mix the egg yolk and 3 tablespoons ice water. Stirring with a fork, gradually add enough of the yolk mixture to moisten the dough—it should be just moist enough to hold together when pressed between your fingertips. Gather up the dough into a flat disk and wrap in plastic wrap. Chill for at least 20 minutes before rolling out.

ROUGH PUFF PASTRY DOUGH

This is a variation of classic French puff pastry. It takes much less time to make than the French version, but you'll still end up with a light, flaky pastry that has 81 paper-thin layers!

MAKES ENOUGH FOR 2 DOUBLE-CRUST 9-INCH PIES
  2 cups all-purpose flour
  ¼ teaspoon salt
  6 tablespoons unsalted butter, cut into
      ½-inch cubes, chilled
  6 tablespoons vegetable shortening, cut into
      ½-inch cubes, chilled

Mix the flour and salt in a large bowl. Add the butter and shortening. Using a pastry blender or two knives, cut in the fats until they are in pieces about ¼-inch square. Stirring with a fork, gradually add about ½ cup ice water, to make a lumpy dough. Cover with plastic wrap and refrigerate for 30 minutes.

Turn out the dough onto a well-floured work surface, and dust the top of the dough with flour. Roll out the dough into a ¼-inch-thick rectangle. Fold the dough into thirds, like a business letter, brushing off the excess flour as you do so. With the rolling pin, gently press the edges of the dough rectangle together to seal in the air. Wrap in plastic wrap and chill for 15 minutes.

Repeat the rolling, folding and chilling procedure three more times. Wrap and chill the dough for at least 15 minutes before using.

CREAM PUFF DOUGH

Cream puff dough is called *pâte au choux* ("cabbage dough") in French because baked cream puffs look like little cabbages. Use it for éclairs, profiteroles, and cream puffs, as well as puffs to be filled with savory mixtures such as herbed cream cheese.

MAKES ENOUGH FOR 10 TO 12 3-INCH CREAM PUFFS
  8 tablespoons (1 stick) unsalted butter, cut into pieces
  ¼ teaspoon granulated sugar
  ¼ teaspoon salt, plus a pinch for the glazing mixture
  1 cup plus all-purpose flour
  4 large eggs, at room temperature

In a medium heavy-bottomed saucepan, combine 1 cup water, the butter, sugar, and ¼ teaspoon salt. Bring to a boil over medium heat, stirring occasionally to help the butter melt. Remove from the heat and let cool slightly, then sift the flour into the saucepan. Beat with a wooden spoon until smooth. Return to medium-low heat and continue beating until the mixture pulls away from the pan sides and forms a ball on the spoon, 1 to 2 minutes.

Remove from the heat and cool slightly. Break an egg into the saucepan and beat vigorously until the egg is absorbed. Beat in a second and third egg the same way. Beat the fourth egg in a small bowl. Beat in just enough of the fourth egg to make a soft dough that holds its shape—you may not need the whole egg. Mix the remaining beaten egg with a pinch of salt; cover and set aside for glazing the shaped dough before baking. Use the dough while still warm.

PRE-BAKING PASTRY SHELLS

To prevent the bottom of a pastry shell from becoming soggy, it is often suggested that the pastry is baked (either partially or fully) before the filling is added.

Roll out the pastry dough and use to line the pie or tart pan. Prick the bottom of the pastry shell a few times with a fork. Line the pastry shell with lightly buttered aluminum foil, buttered side down, or with parchment paper. (To discourage shrinkage, freeze the lined pan for about 30 minutes before baking.) Fill to the brim with about 2 cups of dried beans, rice, or ceramic pie weights, to weight down the dough and keep it from bubbling up or collapsing when heated in the oven. It is especially important to bank the beans against the sides of the pastry shell.

Bake in a preheated 400°F oven until the pastry looks set, 8 to 10 minutes. Lift off the foil or paper and beans. For a partially baked shell, continue baking until the pastry has lost its raw look but is not dry, 3 to 5 more minutes. For a completely baked shell, bake until lightly browned, about 10 more minutes.

1

2

3

4

5

6

7

Making pie dough and lining a pie pan

1 Combine the flour and salt in a bowl. Using a pastry blender, cut in the butter and/or shortening.

2 Gradually add just enough ice water to moisten the mixture.

3 Gather the dough into a flat disk, wrap, and chill for 20 minutes.

4 On a floured surface, roll out the dough to a round about ⅛ inch thick.

5 Roll the dough around the rolling pin, then unroll it over the pan.

6 Lift the edges of the dough and gently press it over the bottom and up the sides of the pan.

7 For a single-crust pie, cut off the excess dough. For a double-crust pie, trim the dough after adding the top crust.

Pre-baking a pastry shell

1 Prick the bottom of the pastry shell all over with a fork.

2 Line the pastry shell with foil or parchment paper. Fill with dried beans, rice, or pie weights. Bake until the dough is set, then remove the foil or paper and weights and continue baking until the pastry is partially or completely baked, according to the recipe instructions.

1

2

Making a decorative edge
For a **forked edge**, trim the dough even with the edge of the pan. With the back of a fork, press firmly and evenly all around the edge. If the fork sticks, dip it in flour.

For a **crimped edge**, trim the dough to a ½-inch overhang. Put the tip of one index finger inside the dough edge. With the thumb and finger of your other hand, pinch the dough in a "V". Continue all around the edge.

For a **forked-fluted edge**, trim the dough to a ½-inch overhang. Put one thumb inside the dough edge, and use your other thumb and index finger to press the dough into a flute. Press a fork into each flute.

RHUBARB AND RAISIN PIE

This pie is at its best when served piping hot from the oven, accompanied by a bowl of whipped cream for guests to help themselves.

MAKES 6 SERVINGS
⅓ cup raisins
2 tablespoons tawny or ruby port or red wine
Double-Crust Pie Dough
2 pounds rhubarb, cut into 1-inch lengths
8 tablespoons granulated sugar
2 teaspoons all-purpose flour
1 tablespoon heavy cream or milk

In a small bowl, soak the raisins in the port or the red wine for 30 minutes.

Preheat the oven to 425°F. Divide the dough into two portions, one twice as large as the other. On a lightly floured surface, roll out the larger portion of dough into a ⅛-inch-thick round. Use to line a 9-inch pie pan, letting the excess dough hang over the edges. Fill with the rhubarb. Sprinkle with 7 tablespoons of the sugar and the flour, then add the raisins and their port. Roll out the smaller portion of dough into a ⅛-inch-thick round, and center over the pie. Seal and flute the edges. Make several cuts in the top crust. Lightly brush the top of the pie with the cream, then sprinkle with the remaining 1 tablespoon of sugar.

Bake for 15 minutes, then reduce the oven to 350°F. Continue baking until the filling is bubbling and the crust is nicely golden-brown in color, 20 to 25 more minutes. If the pastry browns too quickly, cover loosely with foil.

PUMPKIN "SOUFFLÉ" PIE

This light-textured version of pumpkin pie is a nice change from the usual, and seems less filling after a holiday meal. The recipe makes a good amount of filling, so try to get the pastry to stand a bit above the edge of the pie pan, to contain it all. If you still have a little too much filling for the pie, use what you need and pour the rest into a buttered ramekin, bake at 350°F until set, about 30 minutes, and enjoy it as the cook's treat.

MAKES 8 SERVINGS
Basic Pie Dough
1¾ cups canned pumpkin (15-ounce can)
¾ cup granulated sugar
½ cup packed light brown sugar
2 tablespoons all-purpose flour
2 teaspoons ground cinnamon
1 teaspoon ground ginger
1 teaspoon grated nutmeg
¼ teaspoon ground cloves
¼ teaspoon salt
1⅓ cups evaporated milk
3 large eggs, at room temperature
Sweetened whipped cream, for serving

Preheat the oven to 400°F. Roll out the dough to a ⅛-inch-thick round, and use to line a 10-inch deep-dish glass pie pan. Fold the excess dough over into the pan. Press the dough against the sides of the pan, pushing gently so that the dough rises to stand about ½ inch above the edge of the pan. Partially bake the pastry shell. Set aside; leave the oven on at 400°F.

In a medium bowl, whisk together all of the remaining ingredients, except the eggs and whipped cream, until smooth. In another medium bowl, beat the eggs at high speed until very light and tripled in volume, about 3 minutes. Fold the eggs into the pumpkin mixture. Pour into the pastry shell. Bake for 15 minutes, then reduce the heat to 350°F. Continue baking until a knife inserted into the filling 2 inches from the center comes out clean, 40 to 50 minutes. The center will seem slightly unset when shaken, but will firm upon standing. Let cool completely on a wire cake rack. Then cover with plastic wrap and refrigerate until chilled, at least 2 hours or overnight. Serve the pie chilled or at room temperature, with whipped cream.

SWEET POTATO AND ORANGE PIE

Sweet potato pie is to Southerners what pumpkin pie is to Yankees—an absolutely essential part of a holiday meal. This version gets a fillip from orange marmalade. Note that the recipe uses orange-fleshed sweet potatoes, which may be called yams, depending on where you live.

MAKES 6 TO 8 SERVINGS

Basic Pie Dough

2 medium orange-fleshed sweet potatoes
    (1 pound), unpeeled

2 tablespoons unsalted butter

½ cup orange marmalade

⅓ cup packed dark brown sugar

¼ teaspoon ground cinnamon

¼ teaspoon salt

2 large eggs plus 1 large yolk, beaten together

1 cup half-and-half

About 20 pecan halves

1 cup heavy cream, chilled

2 tablespoons granulated sugar

1 tablespoon orange-flavored liqueur (optional)

Preheat the oven to 400°F. Roll out the dough to a ⅛-inch-thick round, and use to line a 10-inch deep-dish glass pie dish. Partially bake the pastry shell. Leave the oven on at 400°F.

In a large saucepan of boiling salted water, cook the whole sweet potatoes until they are tender, about 30 minutes. Drain and rinse under cold water until easy to handle, then peel and place in a medium bowl. Add the butter and mash until smooth. Stir in the orange marmalade, brown sugar, cinnamon, and salt. Beat in the eggs and half-and-half. Pour into the pie shell and smooth the top. Arrange pecan halves around the edge of the pie.

Bake for 10 minutes, then reduce the oven temperature to 350°F. Continue baking until a knife inserted into the center of the filling comes out clean, about 45 more minutes. Leave to cool completely on a wire cake rack.

In a chilled medium bowl, whip the cream with the sugar and optional liqueur until soft peaks form. Serve the pie at room temperature or chilled, along with the whipped cream.

HONEY PECAN TART

Honey makes a nice change from corn syrup in this pecan pie. Serve it warm with vanilla ice cream. A delicious variation can be made by substituting walnuts for the pecans.

MAKES 6 SERVINGS

Sweet Tart Dough

6 tablespoons unsalted butter, at room temperature

⅓ cup packed light brown sugar

1 tablespoon granulated sugar

3 large eggs

¼ cup honey

1 teaspoon vanilla extract

A pinch of salt

2 cups pecan halves

Preheat the oven to 400°F. Roll out the dough and use to line a 9-inch pie pan. Partially bake the pastry shell. Increase the oven temperature to 425°F.

In a medium bowl, beat the butter, brown sugar, and granulated sugar together until smooth and fluffy, about 5 minutes. One at a time, beat in the eggs. Beat in the honey, vanilla, and salt.

Fill the pastry shell with the pecan halves. Pour in the honey mixture. Bake until a knife inserted in the center of the filling comes out clean, about 30 minutes. Let cool slightly, and serve warm.

TROPICAL CREAM PIE

Here's an irresistible combination—a banana and coconut pie with a crystallized ginger and whipped cream topping.

MAKES 8 SERVINGS

¾ cup plus 2 tablespoons granulated sugar

¼ cup cornstarch

3 cups milk

4 large egg yolks

1 cup unsweetened desiccated coconut

1 tablespoon unsalted butter

1 teaspoon vanilla extract

1 (9-inch) baked pie shell, made with Basic Pie Dough
2 ripe medium bananas, sliced
1 cup heavy cream
¼ cup finely chopped crystallized ginger

In a medium, heavy-bottomed saucepan, whisk ¾ cup of the sugar and the cornstarch to combine. Gradually whisk in the milk until the mixture is smooth. Bring to a boil over medium heat, stirring constantly, then reduce the heat to low and cook for 2 minutes. In a small bowl, beat the egg yolks. Gradually stir in about 1 cup of the hot milk mixture. Pour into the saucepan and cook, stirring, for 2 minutes. Stir in the coconut, butter, and vanilla. Transfer to a medium bowl and cover with plastic wrap, pressing the wrap directly on the surface of the filling. Pierce several holes in the wrap with a sharp knife. Cool to room temperature.

Cover the bottom of the baked pie shell with the banana slices. Spoon in the coconut filling and spread evenly (do not stir the filling, or it will thin out). Cover with plastic wrap and refrigerate until chilled, at least 2 hours. (The pie can be prepared up to 1 day ahead, and kept, covered, in the refrigerator.)

In a chilled medium bowl, whip the heavy cream with the remaining 2 tablespoons of sugar until soft peaks form. Spread over the top of the pie. Sprinkle with the chopped ginger. Serve the pie chilled.

DOUBLE-COOKED, TWO-APPLE PIE

Precooking the filling before baking gives you a plump pie full of apples. With two varieties of apples, you can have a blend of different textures and flavors.

MAKES 8 SERVINGS
    4 tablespoons unsalted butter
    5 Granny Smith apples, peeled, cored, and cut into
        ½-inch-thick wedges
    5 Golden Delicious apples, peeled, cored, and cut into
        ½-inch-thick wedges
    ¼ cup granulated sugar
    ½ teaspoon ground cinnamon
    2 tablespoons all-purpose flour
    Double-Crust Pie Dough

In a large frying pan, heat the butter over medium heat. Add the apples, sugar, and cinnamon. Cook, stirring often, until the apples have reduced in volume by about half, 5 to 7 minutes. (If necessary, do this in batches.) Transfer to a large bowl and let cool completely. Stir in the flour.

Preheat the oven to 375°F. Divide the dough into two portions, one twice as large as the other. Roll out the larger portion of the dough into a round about ⅛ inch thick, and use to line a 10-inch pie pan. Fill the pastry shell with the cooled apples. Roll out the smaller portion of dough into a round about ⅛ inch thick, and center over the pie. Seal and flute the edges. Cut an "X" in the center of the top crust. Bake until the filling is bubbling and the crust is golden-brown, 35 to 45 minutes. If the pastry browns too quickly, cover loosely with foil.

STRAWBERRY GALETTE

A galette is a kind of free-form tart. The pastry base here can also be topped with raspberries.

MAKES 8 SERVINGS
    Sweet Tart Dough
    1 egg yolk beaten with 1 teaspoon milk
    3 tablespoons raspberry or red-currant jelly
    Grated zest of ½ orange
    2 pints fresh strawberries, hulled

Preheat the oven to 400°F. Lightly butter a large baking sheet or metal pizza pan. On a lightly floured work surface, roll out the dough to a ⅛-inch-thick round. If you wish, trim the dough into a perfect circle, although part of a galette's charm is in its rustic look. Transfer to the prepared sheet. Prick the dough all over with a fork, and lightly brush with some of the egg mixture. Bake until crisp and golden-brown, about 20 minutes. If the dough bubbles up while baking, deflate it by piercing with a fork. Let cool slightly on the sheet. If you wish, slide the pastry base onto a flat serving dish.

In a small saucepan, warm the jelly with the orange zest over medium heat until melted, then bring just to a boil. Brush the pastry with the melted jelly. Arrange the strawberries, pointed ends up, on the pastry base in concentric circles. Serve warm or cool.

Lemon Galette: Spread the pastry base with about 1½ cups of warm, freshly made Lemon Curd.

LEMON MERINGUE TART

Here's a wonderful European-style reworking of an American specialty.

MAKES 6 TO 8 SERVINGS
    1 (9-inch) baked tart shell, made with Sweet
        Tart Dough
    Lemon Curd
    3 large egg whites, at room temperature
    ½ teaspoon vanilla extract
    ¼ teaspoon cream of tartar
    6 tablespoons granulated sugar

Preheat the oven to 350°F. Fill the tart shell with the lemon curd, spreading evenly. In a medium bowl, beat the egg whites on low speed until foamy. Add the vanilla and cream of tartar, increase the speed to high, and beat until soft peaks form. Gradually beat in the sugar until stiff, shiny peaks form. Transfer the meringue to a pastry bag fitted with a large open star tube. Randomly pipe large swirls of meringue over the lemon curd. (The lemon curd does not have to be completely covered.) Bake until the meringue is lightly browned, about 10 minutes. The lemon curd will melt slightly, but will firm again when chilled. Let cool, then refrigerate the tart until chilled, about 1 hour. Dip a sharp knife in hot water before each cutting each slice.

APRICOT TART

Make this with sweet, aromatic apricots in the summer, or with drained canned apricots at other times of the year. Thinly sliced apples can also be used.

MAKES 4 SERVINGS
Rough Puff Pastry Dough
1 pound apricots, halved and pitted
¼ cup granulated sugar
4 tablespoons unsalted butter, cut into small pieces

Preheat the oven to 425°F. Cut the pastry dough in half, and save one half for another use. On a lightly floured work surface, roll out the dough into an 8- by 12-inch rectangle about ⅛ inch thick. Using a very sharp knife, trim the edges neatly—they must be cut cleanly, or the pastry won't rise. Transfer the rectangle to a lightly dampened baking sheet. Top with the apricots, cut sides up, arranging them in neat rows and leaving a ½-inch margin around the edges. Press the apricots gently into the pastry. Sprinkle with the sugar, then dot with the butter.

Bake for 10 minutes. Reduce the heat to 400°F, and continue baking until the pastry is browned and the apricots are glazed and beginning to blacken around the edges, about 25 more minutes. Serve warm.

FRENCH ALMOND PIE

This shiny brown puff, called a Pithiviers, is often seen in French *pâtisseries*, decorated with geometric designs, and with the almond filling varying from a smooth honey-colored paste to a chocolate marzipan.

MAKES 8 SERVINGS
Rough Puff Pastry Dough
8 tablespoons (1 stick) unsalted butter, at
room temperature
½ cup granulated sugar, plus extra for sprinkling
3 large egg yolks
2 cups ground almonds
⅓ cup heavy cream, chilled
2 teaspoons dark rum or ½ teaspoon grated lemon zest
1 large egg yolk beaten with 2 teaspoons milk,
for glazing

Cut the pastry dough in half, and save one half for another use. In a medium bowl, beat the butter with the sugar at medium speed until light in color and texture, about 2 minutes. Add the yolks and beat for 2 more minutes. Stir in the almonds, heavy cream, and rum.

Preheat the oven to 400°F. Dampen a baking sheet or metal pizza pan. Cut the dough into two pieces, one slightly larger than the other. On a lightly floured work surface, roll out the smaller piece into an 8½-inch round about ⅛ inch thick. Transfer to the prepared baking sheet. Spread the almond mixture on the pastry base, leaving a 1-inch border around the edges.

Roll out the other piece of dough into a ⅛-inch-thick round, slightly larger than the first round. Moisten the edges of the first round, then center the second round on top and press the edges together lightly to seal. Trim the edges cleanly with a sharp knife to make a neat circle. With the back of the knife, notch the edge of the dough at 2-inch intervals. Brush the top of the pastry lightly with the egg glaze. Using the tip of a sharp knife, make a crisscross pattern of very shallow lines across the top of the pie. Bake until the pastry is puffed and golden-brown, 35 to 40 minutes. Sprinkle the the pastry with sugar. Let cool completely on the baking sheet before serving.

CHOCOLATE CREAM PUFFS

Light, golden puffs of *pâte au choux* are filled with sweetened cream and topped with a chocolate icing.

MAKES 10 TO 12 CREAM PUFFS
Cream Puff Dough
1 large egg beaten with a pinch of salt, for glazing
2 cups heavy cream
1 tablespoon vanilla sugar, or 1 tablespoon granulated
sugar and ½ teaspoon vanilla extract
4 ounces high-quality bittersweet chocolate,
finely chopped
2 teaspoons light rum
8 tablespoons (1 stick) unsalted butter, at
room temperature

Preheat the oven to 400°F. Lightly dampen two baking sheets. Place heaping tablespoons of the warm dough on the sheets, spacing them well apart. (Or, pipe out

APRICOT TART

mounds of the dough about 1½ inches across and 1 inch high, using a pastry bag fitted with a ½-inch-wide plain tube.) Brush the tops with the leftover beaten egg from making the pastry (or, use freshly made egg glaze), flattening any peaks of dough with the pastry brush.

Bake until the puffs are firm and golden, about 20 minutes. Make a small hole in the bottom of each puff with the tip of a knife, to allow the steam to escape. Transfer to a wire cake rack to cool completely.

In a chilled medium bowl, whip the cream with the vanilla sugar until soft peaks form. Using a serrated knife, slice open the puffs a little, and fill with the whipped cream. (Or, put the cream into the pastry bag fitted with the tube, and pipe into the puffs through the holes in the bottoms.)

To make the icing, melt the chocolate with the rum in a double boiler insert set over a saucepan of hot, not simmering, water. Remove from the heat, and add the butter, 1 tablespoon at a time, stirring to incorporate each addition before adding another. Place the double boiler insert in a bowl of cold water,

and beat the icing with a wooden spoon until thick enough to spread. Spoon the icing over the tops of the puffs, and let cool and set before serving.

AUTUMN FRUIT CRISP

Here fruits are baked with a crumbled pastrylike topping to make an easy, warming dessert. All varieties of apples and pears are suitable, and you can combine them for different results.

MAKES 6 SERVINGS

2 medium apples, peeled, cored, and cut into
½-inch-thick wedges
2 medium pears, peeled, cored, and cut into
½-inch-thick wedges
½ cup granulated sugar
¼ teaspoon ground cinnamon
Grated zest of 1 lemon
8 tablespoons (1 stick) unsalted butter, in small pieces
⅔ cup all-purpose flour
A pinch of salt
Sweetened whipped cream or vanilla ice cream,
for serving

Preheat the oven to 350°F. Lightly butter a 2-quart baking dish. Put the apples and pears in the baking dish. Add 2 tablespoons of the sugar, the ground cinnamon, and the grated lemon zest, and toss to mix with the fruit. Dot with 1 tablespoon of the butter.

Put the remaining sugar in a medium bowl with the flour and salt. Add the remaining butter. Using your fingertips, quickly and lightly rub together until the mixture resembles fine bread crumbs. Sprinkle the crumb topping evenly over the fruit.

Bake until the topping is nicely browned and the fruit is tender, about 40 minutes. Serve warm, with whipped cream.

PEACH MELBA COBBLER

Pastry chefs often name desserts made with peaches and raspberries "Melba," after the famous Australian soprano of the Victorian era.

MAKES 8 SERVINGS

3 pounds ripe peaches, peeled, pitted, and sliced into
½-inch-thick wedges
2 cups fresh raspberries
1 cup granulated sugar
4 tablespoons butter, cut into pieces
2 tablespoons cornstarch
Grated zest and juice of 1 lemon
Vanilla ice cream or sweetened whipped cream,
for serving

Cobbler Dough
1¾ cups all-purpose flour
⅓ cup granulated sugar
1 tablespoon baking powder
½ teaspoon salt
8 tablespoons (1 stick) unsalted butter, chilled,
cut into ¼-inch pieces
½ cup milk
1 large egg

Preheat the oven to 400°F. In a 9- by 13-inch baking dish, combine the peaches, raspberries, sugar, butter, cornstarch, and the grated lemon zest and juice. Toss gently together.

To make the dough, in a medium bowl, whisk the flour, sugar, baking powder, and salt to combine. Add the butter, and cut it into the flour with a pastry blender or two knives until the mixture resembles coarse crumbs with some pea-sized pieces of butter. In a small bowl, beat the milk with the egg. Stir enough of the milk and egg mixture into the dry ingredients to make a soft, sticky dough (you may not need all of the liquid, so add it gradually). Drop the dough by large tablespoons randomly over the top of the fruit. Bake until the cobbler topping is browned and the fruit juices are bubbling, about 45 minutes. (If the topping seems to be browning too quickly, cover the cobbler loosely with a sheet of aluminum foil.) Serve the cobbler warm, topped with ice cream.

MANGO SHORTCAKES WITH ORANGE CARAMEL SAUCE

Fresh mangoes make a lovely, refreshing filling for America's favorite shortcake.

MAKES 8 SERVINGS

4 ripe mangoes, peeled and sliced
2 tablespoons lime juice
2 cups heavy cream
3 tablespoons confectioners' sugar
1 teaspoon vanilla extract
2 cups Orange Caramel Sauce

Shortcakes
1 cup cake flour (not self-rising)
1 cup all-purpose flour
2 tablespoons granulated sugar
1 tablespoon baking powder
½ teaspoon salt
8 tablespoons (1 stick) unsalted butter, chilled,
cut into small pieces
¾ cup milk

Preheat the oven to 400°F. To make the shortcakes, in a medium bowl, whisk the cake flour, all-purpose flour, sugar, baking powder, and salt to combine. Add the butter, and cut into the flour mixture with a pastry blender or two knives until the mixture resembles coarse crumbs. Add the milk and stir until just combined. Knead lightly in the bowl just to form a soft, sticky dough. Turn out onto a lightly floured work surface and pat out until ½ inch thick. Using a 3½-inch cookie cutter, cut out rounds and transfer them to an ungreased baking sheet. When you have used up the dough, gather up the scraps, knead lightly, and cut out more rounds. Bake the shortcakes until golden-brown, about 15 minutes. Let cool slightly.

Meanwhile, in a medium bowl, combine the mangoes and the lime juice. In a chilled medium bowl, whip the cream with the confectioners' sugar and vanilla extract until soft peaks form.

Using a serrated knife, split the shortcakes horizontally. On each plate, pour ¼ cup of the caramel sauce. Place a shortcake bottom on each plate, top with mangoes and whipped cream, and then replace the shortcake top. Serve immediately.

Cakes and Cookies

YELLOW LAYER CAKE WITH LEMON BUTTER FROSTING

Here is the classic American layer cake that even beginning bakers can master. Instead of trying to decorate with fancy frosting flowers and swirls, just garnish simply with fresh flowers. However, be sure they are nontoxic and unsprayed—violets, nasturtiums, and roses are good choices.

MAKES 8 TO 12 SERVINGS

Cake
- 10 tablespoons (1 stick plus 2 tablespoons) unsalted butter, at room temperature
- 1¾ cups granulated sugar
- 2 large eggs, at room temperature
- 1 teaspoon vanilla extract
- 3 cups cake flour
- 2½ teaspoons baking powder
- ¼ teaspoon salt
- 1¼ cups milk

Lemon Butter Frosting
- 6 tablespoons unsalted butter, at room temperature
- 4 cups confectioners' sugar (1 pound), sifted
- Grated zest of 1 lemon
- 1 tablespoon lemon juice
- ¼ cup milk, approximately

To make the cake, preheat the oven to 350°F. Lightly butter two 9-inch round cake pans and line the bottoms with waxed paper. Dust with flour and tap out the excess. In a large bowl, cream the butter with the sugar at medium speed until light in color and texture, about 2 minutes. One at a time, beat in the eggs, then the vanilla. Sift the flour, baking powder, and salt together. Alternately, one third at a time, beat the flour mixture and milk into the creamed mixture, beating on low speed just until smooth. Transfer the batter to the pans and smooth the tops. Bake until the tops spring back when pressed in the center, 25 to 30 minutes. Cool on a wire cake rack for 5 minutes. Invert and unmold the cakes, removing the waxed paper. Let cool completely, right sides up, on the rack.

To make the frosting, in a medium bowl, beat the butter at low speed until creamy. Gradually beat in the confectioners' sugar. Beat in the lemon zest and juice, then enough of the milk to make a spreadable frosting.

Put a small dab of frosting in the center of a serving platter. Place one cake layer, rounded side down, on the platter. Spread with about ½ cup of the frosting. Top with the remaining cake layer, rounded side up. Cover the top and then the sides of the cake with the remaining frosting. The cake can be kept, covered, in the refrigerator for up to 1 day. Remove it prior to serving, and serve at room temperature.

Orange Butter Frosting: Substitute the grated zest of 1 orange and 1 tablespoon orange juice for the lemon zest and juice.

Chocolate Butter Frosting: Omit the lemon zest and juice. When the frosting is thick, beat in 2 ounces melted, tepid unsweetened chocolate.

DEVIL'S FOOD CAKE WITH CHOCOLATE-CREAM FROSTING

This deep, dark chocolate layer cake gets its name from the tinge of red in the crumb, a phenomenon that results from the effect of baking soda on the chocolate. While the cake is all-American, the chocolate-cream frosting is a staple of European bakers, who call it ganache. A simple garnish would be chocolate shavings sprinkled over the top (make them from a block of bittersweet chocolate grated on the large holes of a box grater).

MAKES 8 SERVINGS

Cake
- 3 ounces unsweetened chocolate, finely chopped
- 8 tablespoons (1 stick) unsalted butter, at room temperature
- 1½ cups granulated sugar
- 2 large eggs, at room temperature
- 1 teaspoon vanilla extract
- 2 cups cake flour
- 1¼ teaspoons baking soda
- ½ teaspoon salt
- 1¼ cups buttermilk

Frosting
- 1½ cups heavy cream
- 12 ounces high-quality bittersweet or semisweet chocolate, finely chopped

To make the cake, preheat the oven to 350°F. Lightly butter two 9-inch round cake pans and line the bottoms with waxed paper. Dust with flour and tap out the excess. In a double boiler insert set over a saucepan of hot, not simmering, water, melt the chocolate. Remove from the heat and let stand until tepid. In a medium bowl, beat the butter with the sugar at medium speed until light in color and texture, about 2 minutes. One at a time, beat in the eggs, then the vanilla. Beat in the cooled chocolate. Sift together the flour, baking soda, and salt. Alternately, one third at a time, beat in the flour and buttermilk, beating well after each addition until smooth. Transfer the batter to the prepared pans and smooth the tops. Bake until the tops spring back when pressed in the center, about 25 minutes. Cool in the pans on a wire cake rack for 5 minutes. Invert and unmold onto the rack,

Coffee-Walnut Cake with White Frosting

then remove the waxed paper. Let cool completely, right sides up, on the rack.

To make the frosting, in a medium saucepan, bring the cream to a simmer over medium heat. Remove from the heat and add the chocolate. Let stand for 3 minutes to soften the chocolate, then whisk until smooth. Transfer to a medium bowl and let stand at room temperature until the mixture is as thick as pudding, about 3 hours. (To speed the cooling, place the bowl in a larger bowl of ice water, and let stand, folding often with a rubber spatula, until cooled but not set.) Whisk until soft peaks form and the frosting is spreadable. Do not overbeat, or the frosting will be grainy.

Put a small dab of frosting on a serving platter. Place one cake layer, upside down, on the platter. Spread with about ½ cup of the frosting. Top with the second cake layer, right side up. Cover the top and sides of the cake with the remaining frosting. Refrigerate until the frosting is firm, about 1 hour. The cake can be kept, covered loosely with plastic wrap, in the refrigerator for up to 1 day. Serve at room temperature.

COFFEE-WALNUT CAKE WITH WHITE FROSTING

Cakes like this are popular in the coffeehouses of Eastern Europe.

MAKES 6 TO 8 SERVINGS

Cake
- 12 tablespoons (1½ sticks) unsalted butter, at room temperature
- 1 cup granulated sugar
- 3 large eggs, at room temperature
- 1 teaspoon vanilla extract
- 1¼ cups all-purpose flour
- 1 teaspoon baking powder
- A pinch of salt
- ¾ cup coarsely chopped walnuts

Coffee Filling
- 5 tablespoons unsalted butter, at room temperature
- 1½ cups confectioners' sugar
- 3 tablespoons strong brewed coffee, preferably espresso, cooled

White Frosting
- 1 cup granulated sugar
- 2 tablespoons vanilla sugar, or 2 tablespoons granulated sugar and 1 teaspoon vanilla extract

1 large egg white, at room temperature

8 walnut halves, for garnish

To make the cake, preheat the oven to 325°F. Lightly butter and 8-inch springform cake pan and line the bottom with waxed paper. In a large bowl, cream the butter with the sugar at medium speed until light in color and texture, about 2 minutes. One at a time, beat in the eggs, then the vanilla. Sift the flour, baking powder, and salt together. One third at a time, stir the flour mixture into the egg mixture using a rubber spatula. Fold in the walnuts. Transfer the batter to the prepared pan and smooth the top. Bake until a tester inserted into the center of the cake comes out clean, about 1 hour. Cool on a wire cake rack for 5 minutes. Invert and unmold the cake, and remove the waxed paper. Let cool completely, right sides up, on the rack.

To make the filling, in a small bowl, beat the butter with the confectioners' sugar at low speed until combined. Gradually beat in enough of the coffee to make a spreadable mixture. Slice the cake into two layers. Place one cake layer, upside down, on a serving platter. Spread with the filling. Place the second cake layer, right side up, on the filling.

To make the frosting, in a medium saucepan with a candy thermometer attached, dissolve the granulated sugar and vanilla sugar in ⅓ cup water over low heat. Increase the heat to high and bring to a boil. Boil, without stirring, until the thermometer reads 240°F (soft-ball stage). Remove from the heat. Immediately, using an electric mixer (a heavy-duty standing mixer works best), beat the egg white at medium speed until stiff. Reduce the mixer speed to low, and beat in the sugar syrup, pouring it in a thin stream and avoiding the beaters. Continue beating until the frosting is very thick. Beat in the vanilla extract, if using.

Pour the warm frosting over the top of the cake, and smooth out with a metal spatula; frost the sides of the cake too, if desired. Decorate with the walnut halves. Let cool until the frosting is completely set, about 2 hours.

ORANGE SPONGE CAKE WITH BUTTERCREAM FROSTING

Sponge cakes are butter-free, so a rich, luxurious buttercream frosting is the perfect finish. This elegant cake is an excellent choice for a celebration.

MAKES 8 SERVINGS

Cake

4 large eggs, at room temperature

1½ cups granulated sugar

½ cup boiling water

2 cups cake flour

2 teaspoons baking powder

¼ teaspoon salt

Frosting

1½ cups granulated sugar

3 large egg yolks

1½ cups (3 sticks) unsalted butter, at cool room temperature so it is soft and malleable

Grated zest of 1 large orange

To finish

4 tablespoons orange-flavored liqueur or orange juice

½ cup orange marmalade

½ cup sliced blanched almonds, toasted (optional)

To make the cake, preheat the oven to 350°F. Lightly butter two 9-inch round cake pans and line the bottoms with waxed paper. Dust with flour and tap out the excess. In a medium bowl, beat the eggs with the sugar at high speed until very thick and fluffy, about 2 minutes. Beat in the boiling water. Sift the flour, baking powder, and salt together, and beat into the egg mixture at low speed. Transfer the batter to the prepared pans and smooth the tops. Bake until the tops of the cakes spring back when pressed in the center, 20 to 25 minutes. Cool in the pans on a wire cake rack for 5 minutes. Invert and unmold onto the rack, and remove the waxed paper. Let cool completely, right sides up, on the rack.

To make the frosting, combine the sugar and ¾ cup water in a medium saucepan. Fit a candy thermometer on the side. Bring to a boil over high heat. Boil, using a wet brush to wash down any sugar crystals that form on the sides, until the thermometer reads 240°F (hard-ball stage). Using an electric mixer (a heavy-duty standing mixer works best) set on high speed, gradually beat the hot syrup into the egg yolks, drizzling the syrup down the sides of the bowl and avoiding the beaters. Beat until the mixture is thick and completely cooled, about 10 minutes. (To speed up the cooling process, place the bowl on a wire cake rack so the bottom of the bowl is exposed to cool air.) Adding 1 tablespoon at a time, beat in the butter to make a thick frosting. Beat in the orange zest.

Put a dab of frosting in the center of a serving platter. Place one cake layer upside down on the platter. Sprinkle with 2 tablespoons of the liqueur. Spread with the orange marmalade. Top with the second cake layer, right side up, and sprinkle with the remaining liqueur. Transfer about ½ cup of the frosting to a pastry bag fitted with a large open star pastry tube (Number 5). Cover the top and sides of the cake with the remaining frosting. Pipe eight large rosettes of frosting around the edge of the cake. If desired, press the almonds onto the side of the cake. Refrigerate until the frosting is set, about 1 hour. The cake can be kept, loosely covered with plastic wrap (protect the frosting by first inserting toothpicks in the top of the cake), in the refrigerator for up to 1 day. The cake can be served either chilled or at room temperature.

ANGEL FOOD CAKE WITH BERRY FOOL

For the times when a light dessert is in order, look no further than angel food cake. One of the nicest ways to serve it is with an accompaniment of fresh berries, with (or without) whipped cream.

MAKES 10 SERVINGS
12 large egg whites, at room temperature
1½ teaspoons cream of tartar
¼ teaspoon salt
1 cup granulated sugar
1 teaspoon vanilla extract
1 cup cake flour
Summer Berry Fool, for serving

To make the cake, preheat the oven to 325°F. Using an electric mixer (a heavy-duty standing mixer will work best), beat the egg whites at low speed until they are foamy. Add the cream of tartar and salt, and continue to beat on high speed until soft peaks begin to form. Gradually beat in the sugar, and continue beating until stiff, shiny peaks form. Beat in the vanilla. One third at a time, sift the flour over the beaten egg whites and gently fold it in.

Transfer the batter to an ungreased 10-inch tube pan and smooth the top. Bake until the top springs back when pressed lightly with a finger, 50 to 60 minutes. Cool the cake in the pan upside-down, placing the edges of the pan on inverted coffee cups to hold it, if necessary. Using a long, thin serrated knife, cut the cake away from the pan, and gently pull it out. Cut the cake wedges with a serrated knife, and serve with spoonfuls of berry fool.

RICH CHOCOLATE CAKE

The recipe for this flourless cake may well have come about when someone decided to bake chocolate mousse just to see what would happen. The result is a rich though light-textured cake.

MAKES 8 TO 10 SERVINGS
12 tablespoons (1½ sticks) unsalted butter
12 ounces high-quality bittersweet chocolate, chopped
1 cup granulated sugar
6 large eggs, at room temperature
Whipped cream, for serving

Preheat the oven to 300°F. Lightly butter and flour a 9-inch round cake pan. Line the bottom with a round of parchment paper.

In a double boiler insert set over a saucepan of hot, not simmering, water, melt the butter and chocolate. Whisk until smooth. Remove from the heat, but keep warm over the hot water.

In a small saucepan, dissolve the sugar in ½ cup water. Bring to a boil over high heat, and boil without stirring for 3 minutes. While the syrup is boiling, using an electric mixer (a heavy-duty standing mixer works best), beat the eggs on medium-high speed until they are light in color and texture, about 2 minutes. With the mixer still running, pour in the hot sugar syrup in a thin stream, taking care to avoid the beaters. Beat until the egg mixture is very thick and cooled, 8 to 10 minutes. (You can also use a hand-held mixer for this, but it will take longer. Place the bowl on a wire cake rack to increase air circulation around the bowl and encourage cooling.) Using a large rubber spatula, fold the warm chocolate mixture into the beaten eggs until completely combined, trying not to deflate the batter too much.

Pour into the prepared pan, and set in a larger roasting pan. Place in the oven, and add enough hot water to the roasting pan to come three fourths up the sides of the cake pan. Bake until the top of the cake springs back when pressed lightly in the center with a finger, 40 to 45 minutes.

Remove from the oven and let the cake cool completely, still standing in the water. (If you prefer a firmer texture, lift out of the water, cover with plastic wrap, and refrigerate for 4 to 5 hours.)

Run a sharp knife around the inside of the pan, being careful not to tear the parchment paper on the bottom. Invert onto a serving plate to unmold, and peel off the parchment paper. Cut into wedges and serve chilled, with cream.

HAZELNUT MACAROONS

These are a rustic kind of macaroon, cut into squares, not shaped into mounds. They are have soft, chewy centers with crunchy edges. If you don't have superfine sugar, you can whirl granulated sugar in a blender until it has a finer texture.

MAKES ABOUT 16 COOKIES
3 large egg whites, at room temperature
2 cups ground hazelnuts
¾ cup plus 2 tablespoons superfine sugar

Preheat the oven to 350°F. Line a jellyroll pan with aluminum foil and dust with flour.

RICH CHOCOLATE CAKE

In a medium bowl, beat the egg whites at high speed until they form stiff, but not dry, peaks. With a rubber spatula, gently fold in the ground hazelnuts and sugar until they are evenly mixed. Pour the mixture onto the prepared pan, and spread into a rectangle about ½ inch thick.

Bake until lightly browned and crisp on top, about 20 minutes. Remove from the oven and cut into sixteen squares. Carefully slide a metal spatula under the macaroons to release them from the foil, then gently turn the macaroons over.

Reduce the oven temperature to 275°F. Return the macaroons to the oven and bake until the edges are beginning to crisp, about 10 minutes. Transfer to a wire cake rack and cool completely.

BLACK FOREST CHOCOLATE CHIP COOKIES

Butter drop cookies have long been very popular, appearing as far back as 1796 in Amelia Simmon's *American Cookery*, one of the first American cookbooks. However, they reached new heights when Mrs. Ruth Wakefield added chopped chocolate bars to the dough at her Toll House Inn in Massachusetts. This version includes dried cherries, too.

MAKES ABOUT 30 COOKIES

1 cup (2 sticks) unsalted butter,
   at room temperature
¾ cup granulated sugar
¾ cup packed light brown sugar
2 large eggs
1 teaspoon vanilla extract
2¼ cups all-purpose flour
1 teaspoon baking soda
1 teaspoon salt
2 (3-ounce) bars high-quality bittersweet chocolate,
   cut into ¼-inch pieces
1 cup dried cherries

Preheat the oven to 375°F. Lightly butter two baking sheets. In a medium bowl, beat the butter with the granulated sugar and brown sugar at medium speed until light in color and texture, about 2 minutes. One at a time, beat in the eggs, then the vanilla. Sift the flour, baking soda, and salt together. Using a wooden spoon, stir into the butter mixture. Stir in the chocolate and cherries.

Drop by tablespoons onto the prepared baking sheets, spacing the cookies 2 inches apart. Bake until golden-brown, 10 to 12 minutes. Cool on the baking sheets for 5 minutes, then transfer to wire cake racks to cool completely. The cookies can be kept in an airtight container for up to 5 days.

PEANUT BISCOTTI

Peanuts are hardly a traditional biscotti ingredient, but they work extremely well. Dunk these cookies into a cup of coffee or tea, or nibble them with a glass of sweet wine.

MAKES ABOUT 30 COOKIES

    8 tablespoons (1 stick) unsalted butter,
      at room temperature
    1 cup granulated sugar
    2 large eggs
    ½ teaspoon almond extract
    2 cups plus 2 tablespoons all-purpose flour
    1 teaspoon baking powder
    ¼ teaspoon salt
    1 cup coarsely chopped unsalted peanuts

Preheat the oven to 350°F. Lightly butter two baking sheets. In a medium bowl, beat the butter with the sugar at medium speed until light in color and texture, about 2 minutes. One at a time, beat in the eggs, then the almond extract. Sift together the flour, baking powder, and salt. Using a wooden spoon, stir the dry ingredients into the butter mixture. Stir in the peanuts. Turn the dough onto one of the baking sheets, and form the dough into two 10- by 2-inch logs, spacing them 2 inches apart. Bake until set and golden-brown,

ALMOND SHORTBREAD

about 30 minutes. Cool on the baking sheet for 20 minutes. Using a serrated knife, cut the logs on a slight diagonal into ½-inch-thick slices. Arrange the slices on the two baking sheets. Return to the oven and bake, turning once, until crisp, about 16 minutes. Let cool completely on wire cake racks. The cookies can be kept in an airtight container for up to 5 days.

MELT-IN-THE-MOUTH LEMON COOKIES

These are the tenderest, crumbliest cookies around.

MAKES ABOUT 2½ DOZEN LARGE COOKIES

    8 tablespoons (1 stick) unsalted butter, at room
      temperature
    ½ cup vegetable oil
    Grated zest of 2 lemons
    ½ cup granulated sugar, plus more for baking
    ½ cup confectioners' sugar
    1 large egg
    ½ teaspoon vanilla extract
    2¼ cups all-purpose flour
    1 teaspoon baking powder
    ¼ teaspoon salt

In a medium bowl, beat the butter, oil, and lemon zest at low speed until combined. Add ½ cup of the granulated sugar and the confectioners' sugar, and beat at medium speed until light in color, about 2 minutes. Beat in the egg and vanilla. Sift together the flour, baking powder, and salt. Add to the butter mixture, and mix to form a soft dough. Cover tightly with plastic wrap and refrigerate until chilled, about 2 hours.

Preheat the oven to 375°F. Using a tablespoon of dough for each cookie, roll into balls. Place on ungreased baking sheets about 2 inches apart. Dip the flat bottom of a large glass in water, then in a shallow bowl of granulated sugar, and use to flatten the balls of dough. Bake until the edges of the cookies are golden, 10 to 12 minutes. Let cool on the sheets for 2 minutes, then transfer to a wire cake rack to cool completely. The cookies can be kept in an airtight container for up to 5 days.

COCOA BROWNIES

This is a nice and easy recipe for everyone's favorite, brownies. Optional additions are 1 cup chocolate or peanut butter chips, or chopped walnuts or pecans.

MAKES 9 BROWNIES
- 6 tablespoons unsalted butter
- 1 cup plus 2 tablespoons granulated sugar
- ½ cup unsweetened cocoa powder
- 2 large eggs plus 1 egg yolk
- ⅓ cup plus 1 tablespoon all-purpose flour
- ½ teaspoon baking powder
- ¼ teaspoon salt
- 1 teaspoon vanilla extract

Preheat the oven to 350°F. Lightly butter an 8-inch square pan. In a medium saucepan, melt the butter over low heat. Remove from the heat and stir in the sugar and cocoa. One at a time, add the eggs, beating in well with a spoon. Sift the flour, baking powder, and salt together, and stir into the chocolate mixture with the vanilla. Spread evenly in the prepared pan.

Bake until a toothpick inserted in the center comes out with a moist crumb, 25 to 30 minutes. Let cool in the pan on a wire cake rack, and cut into squares for serving.

ALMOND SHORTBREAD

Almonds and a quick dip of milk chocolate add distinction to buttery shortbread cookies.

MAKES 20 COOKIES
- 1 cup (2 sticks) unsalted butter, at room temperature
- ½ cup granulated sugar
- 2 cups all-purpose flour
- ½ cup ground almonds
- ¼ teaspoon salt
- 5 ounces milk chocolate, finely chopped

Preheat the oven to 350°F. In a medium bowl, beat the butter with the sugar at medium speed until light in color and texture, about 2 minutes. Stir in the flour, ground almonds, and salt.

On a lightly floured surface, roll out the dough into a 6- by 12-inch rectangle. Cut the rectangle in half horizontally, then cut vertically into 20 rectangles. Use a spatula to transfer the cookies to an ungreased baking sheet, placing them about 1 inch apart. With a fork, prick each cookie once in the center. Bake until lightly browned around the edges, about 20 minutes. Let cool completely on a wire cake rack.

In a double boiler insert, or a medium heatproof bowl, set over a saucepan of hot, not simmering, water, heat the chocolate until almost melted. Remove from the heat and let stand until completely melted. Cool until slightly thickened, about 5 minutes. Tilt the boiler insert so the chocolate gathers in a pool (use a rubber spatula to clean off all the chocolate on the sides of the insert). One at a time, dip each cookie about 1 inch into the melted chocolate. Lift out and drag the underside of the cookie on the lip of the insert to remove excess chocolate. Place on a waxed-paper-lined baking sheet. Refrigerate until the chocolate is firm. The cookies can be kept in an airtight container for up to 5 days.

MAPLE-OAT BARS

Be sure to use pure maple syrup for these delicious, chewy bar cookies.

MAKES 16 TO 20 BARS
- 9 tablespoons (1 stick plus 1 tablespoon) unsalted butter
- ½ cup plus 1 tablespoon granulated sugar
- ¼ cup maple syrup
- 3 cups rolled oats
- 1 cup raisins

Preheat the oven to 350°F. In a saucepan, warm the butter, sugar, and syrup until melted, 2 to 3 minutes. Remove from the heat, and add the oats and raisins. Stir to mix. Pour into a lightly buttered 9- by 13-inch shallow pan, and spread evenly into a layer about ½ inch thick. Bake until golden, 15 to 20 minutes. Let cool in the pan for 5 minutes, then mark into bars with a knife. Leave to cool completely in the pan, and break into bars for serving. The bars can be kept, in an airtight container, for up to 5 days.

Yeast and Quick Breads

Baking bread is one of the most enjoyable tasks the kitchen has to offer. While making bread at home requires tools no more complicated than a bowl, a spoon, and a strong pair of hands for kneading, you can make use of machines to help. For example, a food processor or a heavy-duty standing mixer both do an admirable job of mixing and kneading dough. Electric bread machines, which can do everything, make bread that is acceptable to many people. However, they rob the cook of the pleasure and feeling of accomplishment provided by handmade bread.

Using Yeast There are four kinds of yeast available: active dry yeast, fresh compressed yeast, rapid-rise yeast, and instant yeast. You can use all of them interchangeably, following certain rules of substitution. No matter what kind you use, pay attention to the "use-by" dates printed on the package, as yeast will diminish in strength with age. Store yeast in a cool place, preferably the refrigerator. It can be frozen for convenience, but freezing won't extend its shelf life.

If you dissolve yeast in water before adding it to the dry ingredients, realize that not all yeasts will become foamy—some will just look creamy. The optimum water temperature for dissolving active dry yeast and fresh yeast is 100 to 110°F. Don't use liquid that is warmer than 110°F, as the heat will kill the yeast (it is a living organism). To test for water temperature, dip in your finger—the water should be comfortably warm, but not hot. Once mixed with the other ingredients, yeast will not make dough rise unless it has been "fed" with sugar in some form: as the yeast "eats" the sugar, carbon dioxide bubbles form.

Active dry yeast is the most common variety. A ¼-ounce package holds about 2¼ teaspoons. Fresh compressed yeast can be found in 0.6-ounce cakes in the refrigerated section of well-stocked supermarkets. Some bakers feel that fresh yeast gives bread better flavor than active dry. To substitute fresh yeast for dry, use twice as much—for example, 2 teaspoons (crumbled and packed) fresh yeast for 1 teaspoon active dry yeast.

Rapid-rise yeast is becoming popular with busy cooks, as it dramatically reduces the rising times. Many bread bakers report that they cannot taste the difference when breads are leavened with rapid-rise yeast. It is best to follow the instructions on the package if you are adjusting a recipe for rapid-rise yeast, but, in general, the yeast is mixed directly with the dry ingredients and then liquid (heated until quite hot, around 130°F) is added. Some specialty stores now carry instant yeast, which has a rising power

1

2

3

Making a yeast dough

1 Mix the yeast with the warm liquid, and then let it sit in a warm place until it is creamy or foamy.

2 Combine the flour and other dry ingredients in a large bowl, make a well in the center, and pour in the yeast mixture and the other liquids.

3 With your fingers, start mixing the flour into the liquid. Continue mixing in the flour in this way to make a rough dough.

1

2

3

Kneading and rising

1 Turn the dough out onto a lightly floured surface. Start kneading by pressing and pushing the dough firmly with the heel of your hand, stretching the dough away from you.

2 Turn the dough over on itself, rotate it slightly, and press and push it away again. Continue kneading, working with a rhythmic action.

3 After 8 to 10 minutes of kneading, the dough will be smooth and elastic. Shape it into a ball.

4 Put the dough in a greased bowl and turn the dough to coat on all sides. Cover the bowl with plastic wrap and let rise in a warm place.

5 During rising, the dough will double in size. When it has risen properly, a finger pressed down into the center of the dough will leave an indentation.

4

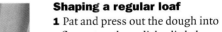

5

6

6 Punch down the ball of dough with your fist to knock out the air, then turn the dough out onto a work surface. Knead the dough briefly to return it to its original size and texture. The dough is now ready to be shaped.

1

2

Shaping a regular loaf

1 Pat and press out the dough into a flat rectangle or disk a little longer than the loaf pan. Roll up the dough like a jelly roll.

2 Turn the loaf seam-side down, tuck the ends under, and place in the pan. Cover and let rise again in a warm place before baking.

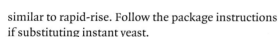

Shaping rolls

For **round rolls** (*top left*), on a lightly floured surface, roll each piece of dough under your cupped hand to make a neat, smooth ball.

For **knot rolls** (*top right*), roll each piece of dough under the palms of your hands into a 9-inch rope. Tie this loosely into a knot, with the knot in the center of the rope.

For **cloverleaf rolls** (*bottom left*), divide each piece of dough into three equal pieces and shape each one into a small ball. Put the three balls, side by side, in a buttered muffin pan.

Shaping pizza dough

(*bottom right*) Roll out the dough to a thin round to fit your baking sheet or pizza pan, stretching the dough with the rolling pin. Transfer to the floured baking sheet or pan. Push up the edge all around with your fingertips to make a rim.

similar to rapid-rise. Follow the package instructions if substituting instant yeast.

Kneading Kneading is important for distributing the yeast evenly and for developing the gluten contained in the flour. Put the dough on a lightly floured work surface, and fold the dough over toward you. Press with the heel of your hand, and push the dough away. Turn the dough slightly, and repeat the folding and pushing process. Keep turning and kneading the dough, with a rhythmic, regular action, until it is firm, supple, and elastic (that is, it retracts when pulled apart), 8 to 10 minutes. Resist the temptation to add too much flour during kneading—as long as the dough is not sticking to the board, there is enough flour. Some whole grain doughs will retain a slightly sticky texture, so it is especially important to hold back on adding too much flour to them, lest your bread bake up dry and crumbly.

Rising and Punching Down After kneading, form the dough into a smooth ball. Place it in a lightly buttered or oiled bowl, and turn the dough so that it is lightly coated with butter or oil all over (this will allow it to stretch and expand more easily as it rises). Cover the bowl tightly with plastic wrap. Let rise in a warm, draft-free place, such as a warm closet or an oven

with a pilot light. When the dough has roughly doubled in volume, punch it in the center with your fist to expel the air. Turn the dough onto the work surface (it is not necessary to dust the surface with flour), and knead briefly until the dough is even in texture and has returned to its original volume. If the recipe requires a second kneading, shape the dough into a ball again, return to the bowl, cover, and let rise once more.

After shaping, most breads are given a final rising before baking. For loaf breads, cover loosely with plastic wrap, and let rise in a warm place until the dough almost reaches the top of the pan. For country-style bread, where the shaped dough is placed directly on a baker's peel or baking sheet, cover loosely with plastic wrap and let rise in a warm place until the dough has almost doubled in volume.

Baking To test whether a loaf is done, remove the bread from the pan (or turn a country-style loaf upside down), and rap on the underside with your knuckles—the bread should sound hollow, like a drum. If it doesn't sound hollow, return the bread to the oven (loaf breads can be placed on their sides directly on the oven rack) and bake for 5 to 10 more minutes or until they test done.

OLD-FASHIONED WHITE LOAF BREAD

There's nothing like good, old-fashioned homemade bread—slightly sweet, with a firm crumb and a thin, tender crust. This recipe makes two loaves, so you'll have one to freeze for another day, if you wish.

MAKES TWO 9-INCH LOAVES

   1 (¼-ounce) package active dry yeast
   4 tablespoons unsalted butter
   2 cups milk
   2 tablespoons granulated sugar
   2½ teaspoons salt
   6 cups bread flour or unbleached all-purpose flour, approximately

In a small bowl, dissolve the yeast in ¼ cup warm water, and let stand until creamy, about 5 minutes. In a small saucepan, heat the butter with ½ cup of the milk until the butter melts. Remove from the heat, and stir in the remaining 1½ cups milk to make a lukewarm mixture. Add the sugar and salt. Put the flour into a large bowl and make a well in the center. Pour the yeast mixture and milk mixture into the well. Gradually mix the flour into the liquid to make a stiff dough. Turn onto a lightly floured work surface. Knead, adding more flour as needed, until the dough is smooth and elastic, 8 to 10 minutes. Form into a ball and place in a buttered bowl. Cover with plastic wrap and let rise in a warm place until doubled in volume, about 1½ hours.

   Lightly butter two 5- by 9-inch loaf pans. Punch down the dough, then divide it in half. Form each piece into a flat disk about 11 inches in diameter, then roll up loosely into a log shape. Tuck the ends under and place, seam sides down, in the prepared pans. Cover loosely with plastic wrap and let rise in a warm place until the dough has almost reached the top of the pans, about 45 minutes.

   Preheat the oven to 400°F. Bake until the tops are golden-brown and the loaves sound hollow when tapped on the base, 25 to 30 minutes. Cool in the pans on a wire cake rack for 10 minutes, then unmold onto the rack and let cool completely.

Raisin-Cinnamon Loaf: Combine 1 cup dark raisins, 2 tablespoons granulated sugar, and 1 teaspoon ground cinnamon. After dividing the dough in half, roll out one portion into a 9-inch square. Brush with 1 tablespoon melted butter. Sprinkle with half of the raisin mixture, leaving a 1-inch border around the edges, and press the raisins lightly into the dough. Tightly roll up the dough, like a jelly roll. Pinch the seams closed. Place in a buttered loaf pan and cover loosely with plastic wrap. Repeat with the remaining ingredients. Let rise and bake as directed above.

WHOLE WHEAT BREAD

Breads made entirely with whole wheat flour are too firm in texture for most people, so this recipe combines whole wheat with white flour for a lighter texture. If possible, use stoneground flours (these are obtainable from health food stores) for the best flavor in this bread.

MAKES TWO 9-INCH LOAVES

   2 (¼-ounce) packages active dry yeast
   2 tablespoons unsulfured molasses
   2½ teaspoons salt
   2 cups whole wheat flour
   4 cups bread flour or unbleached all-purpose flour, approximately

In a medium bowl, dissolve the active dry yeast in ½ cup warm water, and let stand until creamy, about 5 minutes. Add another 2 cups warm water, and stir in the molasses and salt. Put the whole wheat flour and 3 cups of the bread flour in a large bowl and make a well in the center. Pour the yeast mixture into the well. Gradually mix the flour into the liquid to make a stiff dough, adding more of the bread flour if necessary. Turn onto a lightly floured work surface. Knead, adding more bread flour as needed, until the dough is smooth and elastic, 8 to 10 minutes. Form into a ball and place in a buttered bowl. Cover with plastic wrap and let rise in a warm place until doubled in volume, about 1½ hours.

   Lightly butter two 5- by 9-inch loaf pans. Punch down the dough, then divide it in half. Form each piece into a flat disk about 11 inches in diameter, then roll up loosely into a log shape. Tuck the ends under and place, seam sides down, in the prepared pans. Cover loosely with plastic wrap and let rise in a warm place until the dough has almost reached the top of the pans, about 45 minutes.

   Preheat the oven to 400°F. Bake until the tops are golden-brown and the loaves sound hollow when tapped on the base, 25 to 30 minutes. Cool in the pans on a wire cake rack for 10 minutes, then unmold onto the rack and let cool completely.

Walnut Bread: For this variation on the bread, add ½ cup finely chopped walnuts to the well in the flour along with the liquid.

COUNTRY RYE BREAD

Rye bread—which is firm in texture, dark in color, and pleasantly sour to the taste—is especially delicious when served with sliced ham and assorted sharp cheeses.

MAKES 2 LARGE LOAVES

4½ cups rye flour

3 cups unbleached all-purpose flour

¼ cup whole wheat flour

2 (¼-ounce) packages active dry yeast

1 teaspoon granulated sugar

1 tablespoon plain yogurt

1 tablespoon salt

2 tablespoons caraway seeds (optional)

Cornmeal, for dusting baker's peel

In a large bowl, combine the rye, all-purpose, and whole wheat flours. In a small bowl, dissolve the yeast in ⅔ cup warm water, and let stand until creamy, about 5 minutes. Stir in ⅓ cup of the combined flours and a pinch of the sugar. Stir for one hundred strokes. Cover with plastic wrap and let the sponge stand in a warm place until risen and very bubbly, about 1 hour.

In another small bowl, mix 2 cups warm water with the remaining sugar, the yogurt, and salt. Stir in the caraway seeds, if using. Make a well in the flour in the large bowl and pour in the sponge and the yogurt mixture. Using a wooden spoon, mix to make a rough dough. Turn onto a lightly floured surface and knead, adding more flour as needed, until the dough is smooth and elastic, 8 to 10 minutes. (Rye doughs always retain a slight stickiness, so don't add too much flour.)

Form into a ball and place in a buttered bowl. Cover with plastic wrap, and let rise in a warm place until doubled in volume, about 2 to 3 hours. Or, even better, let rise in the refrigerator overnight. (If refrigerated, let the dough stand at room temperature for about 2 hours to warm up before proceeding.)

Punch down the dough, then cut in half. Form each portion into a ball and place on baking sheets or baker's peels sprinkled with cornmeal. Sprinkle the the balls with flour. Cover with plastic wrap and let rise until almost doubled in volume, about 1 hour.

Place a baker's stone or a large heavy baking sheet on the center rack and preheat the oven to 425°F. Using a sharp knife, cut a shallow cross in the tops of the loaves, then slide onto the heated baking stone. Bake for 15 minutes. Reduce the heat to 350°F, and continue baking until the loaves sound hollow when tapped on the base, about 40 minutes. Place on a wire cake rack to cool.

BRIOCHE LOAF

This buttery, rich loaf is exquisite when toasted and served with the best jam or preserves. If you have a large fluted brioche tin, you can form the dough into the traditional brioche shape: divide the dough into a large ball and a much smaller ball. Put the large ball in the buttered brioche tin, brush with beaten egg, and set the small ball on top in the center; glaze this with egg too. Bake as for the loaf.

MAKES 2 LOAVES

2 (¼-ounce) packages active dry yeast

2 tablespoons granulated sugar

4 large eggs

⅓ cup milk, heated (100° to 110°F)

2 teaspoons salt

5 cups unbleached all-purpose flour

8 tablespoons (1 stick) unsalted butter,
    at room temperature

Beaten egg, for glazing

In a small bowl, dissolve the yeast and ½ teaspoon of the sugar in ⅓ cup warm water. Let stand until creamy, about 5 minutes. In a medium bowl, mix the remaining sugar with the eggs, milk, and salt.

Put the flour in a large bowl and make a well in the center. Pour the dissolved yeast and the egg mixture into the well. Gradually mix the flour into the liquid to make a rough dough. Turn onto a lightly floured work surface. Knead, adding more flour as needed, until the dough is smooth and elastic, 8 to 10 minutes. Cover the dough loosely with plastic wrap and let rest for 5 minutes.

Flatten the dough into a thick disk and dot with about 1 tablespoon of the butter. Fold the dough in half, then knead to work in the butter. Repeat the procedure, 1 tablespoon of butter at a time. It will be a little messy to do, but eventually all the butter will be incorporated and the dough will be satiny smooth. Cover and let rest for a couple of minutes, then form into a smooth ball. Place the ball in a buttered bowl. Cover with plastic wrap and let rise in a warm place until the dough has almost doubled in volume, about 1½ hours.

Punch down the dough, then knead briefly. Reform into a ball, return to the bowl, and cover again with plastic wrap. Let rise again until almost doubled in volume, about 1½ hours.

Lightly butter two 5- by 9-inch loaf pans. Punch down the dough again, then divide in half. Form each portion into a flat disk about 11 inches in diameter, then roll up loosely into a log shape. Tuck the ends under and place, seam sides down, in the loaf pans. Cover loosely with plastic wrap and let rise in a warm place until the dough almost reaches the top of the pan, about 45 minutes.

Preheat the oven to 400°F. Brush the top of the loaves lightly with beaten egg. Bake until the tops are glazed and golden-brown, and the loaves sound hollow when tapped on the base, 20 to 25 minutes. Cool in the pans on a wire cake rack for 10 minutes, then unmold onto the rack and let cool completely.

CRUSTY SOURDOUGH BREAD

Once you have a sourdough starter in the refrigerator, making a crusty, sourdough loaf is no more difficult than any other bread. However, you will need some special utensils that are essential to creating excellent rustic breads: a baking stone or heavy baking sheet, a baker's peel or a thin, rimless baking sheet, and a water-filled spray bottle. For superior results, use stoneground flours, preferably an organic variety.

MAKES 2 LARGE LOAVES

6 cups unbleached all-purpose flour
½ cup rye flour
½ cup whole wheat flour
1 tablespoon salt
Yellow cornmeal or semolina, for dusting baker's peel

Sourdough Starter
2½ cups unbleached all-purpose flour, preferably stoneground
A scant ¹⁄₁₆ teaspoon active dry yeast

To make the starter, mix the flour and yeast with 1 cup water (at room temperature) to make a thick batter. Stir for 100 strokes. Transfer to a 1-quart jar and cover tightly. Let stand for 24 hours at warm room temperature; the starter will be bubbling and have a pleasantly sour aroma. The starter is now fermented and ready to use, but will be stronger in flavor and rising power if allowed to stand for up to 72 hours.

The starter will keep for up to a week, refrigerated, (the initial batch makes 1½ cups, enough for two loaves, with ½ cup starter left over), or indefinitely if fed at least once a week. To feed the starter: after using 1 cup of starter to make two sourdough loaves, stir ½ cup water and ½ cup flour into the remaining starter in the jar. Let stand overnight at room temperature to ferment again, then refrigerate until the next use or feeding, within 1 week. If any clear liquid forms on the top of the starter, just stir it in. The sour flavor will develop as the starter ages.

To make the bread, measure 1 cup sourdough starter using a rinsed metal cup measure. Put into a large bowl. Add 2 cups water (at room temperature) and stir to dissolve the starter. Stir in about 2½ cups unbleached flour to make a thick batter, and stir for 100 strokes. Cover tightly with plastic wrap and let the sponge stand in a warm spot until bubbling and approximately double in volume, about 2 hours.

Stir in the rye flour, whole wheat flour, and salt. Gradually stir in enough of the remaining unbleached flour to make a stiff dough. Turn onto a lightly floured surface. Knead until the dough is smooth and elastic, 8 to 10 minutes. Form into a ball and place in a lightly oiled bowl. Tightly cover the bowl with plastic wrap,

and let rise in a warm place until doubled in volume, about 2 hours. Punch down the dough and knead briefly. Re-form into a ball, return to the bowl, and cover again. Let rise until almost doubled in volume, about 1 hour. Punch down the dough again, then cut in half. Form each portion into a taut ball. Place each ball on a large rimless baking sheet or baker's peel that has been sprinkled with cornmeal. Cover and let rise until doubled in size, about 1 hour.

Place a baker's stone or a heavy baking sheet on the center rack and preheat the oven to 450°F. Using a sharp knife, cut a 3-inch crescent in the top of one loaf. Slide the loaf onto the heated baking stone. (Refrigerate the other loaf while the first is baking.) Spray the loaf with water. Start baking, spraying the loaf two more times at 3-minute intervals, then continue to bake until golden-brown and the loaf sounds hollow when tapped on the base, about 30 minutes in all. Let cool on a wire cake rack for at least 20 minutes before serving. Bake the other loaf in the same way.

BUTTERMILK DINNER ROLLS

These chewy rolls, with a thin, golden crust and wholesome, old-fashioned flavor, can be formed into a variety of shapes, so let your imagination go to work.

MAKES 18 ROLLS

1 (¼-ounce) package active dry yeast
5 cups bread flour or unbleached all-purpose flour, approximately
1½ cups buttermilk, heated (100° to 110°F)
6 tablespoons unsalted butter, melted
2 large eggs
3 tablespoons granulated sugar
1½ teaspoons salt
¾ teaspoon baking soda
Milk, for brushing

In a small bowl, dissolve the yeast in ¼ cup warm water, and let stand until creamy, about 5 minutes. Put the flour in a large bowl and make a well in the center. Pour the yeast mixture, buttermilk, melted butter, and eggs into the well, and add the sugar, salt, and baking soda. Gradually mix the flour into the liquid to make a stiff dough. Turn onto a lightly floured work surface. Knead, adding more flour as needed, until the dough is smooth and elastic, 8 to 10 minutes. Form into a ball and place in a buttered bowl. Cover with plastic wrap and let rise in a warm place until doubled in volume, about 1½ hours.

Lightly butter two 9-inch round cake pans. Punch down the dough, then cut into 18 pieces. Form each into a taut ball and place in the pans. Cover with

plastic wrap and let rise in a warm place until almost doubled in volume, about 40 minutes.

Preheat the oven to 400°F. Brush the tops of the rolls lightly with a little milk. Bake until golden-brown, about 20 minutes. Remove from the pans and serve warm.

Buttermilk Knots: Form each piece of dough into a 9-inch-long rope. Tie each into an overhand knot, with the knot positioned in the center of the rope. Place on ungreased baking sheets. Cover loosely with plastic wrap and let rise until almost doubled in size. Bake as directed above.

Cloverleaf Rolls: Cut each piece of dough into thirds and form into small balls. Lightly butter 18 muffin tins. Place three balls side by side in each tin. Cover loosely with plastic wrap and let rise until almost doubled. Bake as directed.

SAFFRON BREAD

Golden saffron bread is especially good with fish soups and chowders, or with steamed shellfish such as moules à la marinière.

MAKES 1 LARGE ROUND LOAF

1 (¼-ounce) package active dry yeast
½ teaspoon granulated sugar
7 cups unbleached all-purpose flour, approximately
½ teaspoon crushed saffron threads
1 large egg, beaten
3 tablespoons olive oil
2½ teaspoons salt

In a medium bowl, dissolve the yeast and sugar in ⅔ cup warm water. Stir in ½ cup of the flour to make a batter. Cover tightly with plastic wrap and let the sponge stand in a warm place until bubbly and well risen, about 30 minutes. Meanwhile, soak the saffron in 1¼ cups warm water.

Put the remaining flour in a large bowl and make a well in the center. Pour the sponge mixture, saffron water, egg, and oil into the well, and add the salt. Gradually mix the flour into the liquid to make a rough dough. Turn onto a lightly floured work surface. Knead, adding more flour if needed, until the dough is smooth and elastic, 8 to 10 minutes. Form into a ball and place in a buttered bowl. Cover with plastic wrap and let rise in a warm place until doubled, about 1½ hours.

SAFFRON BREAD

Lightly butter a large baking sheet and dust with flour. Punch down the dough, then knead briefly. Form into a large ball and place on the baking sheet. Cover loosely with a lightly oiled sheet of plastic wrap, then with a clean dish towel. Let rise until the dough has doubled in volume, about 1 hour.

Preheat the oven to 425°F. Using a sharp knife, cut a shallow "X" in the top of the ball of dough. Bake for 15 minutes. Reduce the oven temperature to 350°F, and continue baking until the bread sounds hollow when tapped on the base, 30 to 40 minutes more. Let cool on a wire cake rack.

FLUFFY YEAST BISCUITS

These biscuits bake up incredibly light and fluffy, thanks to the addition of a bit of yeast. The dough can be refrigerated for up to 2 days, combining convenience with good flavor.

MAKES ABOUT 2 DOZEN

1 teaspoon active dry yeast
5 cups all-purpose flour
3 tablespoons granulated sugar
1 tablespoon baking powder
1 teaspoon baking soda
1 teaspoon salt
1 cup vegetable shortening, chilled, cut into small pieces
2 cups buttermilk, or 1½ cups plain low-fat yogurt mixed with ½ cup milk, approximately

In a small bowl, dissolve the yeast in 2 tablespoons warm water, and let stand until creamy, about 5 minutes. In a large bowl, combine the flour, sugar, baking powder, baking soda, and salt. Add the shortening, and cut into the flour with a pastry blender or two knives until the mixture resembles coarse crumbs. Mix in the dissolved yeast and the buttermilk. Knead in the bowl to make a soft, sticky dough. Cover tightly with plastic wrap, and refrigerate for at least 2 hours and up to 2 days.

Preheat the oven to 450°F. On a lightly floured work surface, knead the dough briefly. Roll out the dough into a ½-inch-thick rectangle. Using a 2½-inch biscuit cutter, cut out rounds and place on ungreased baking sheets. Knead the dough scraps together, reroll, and cut rounds until all the dough is used. Bake until the biscuits are lightly browned, 12 to 15 minutes. Serve warm.

EGGPLANT, TOMATO, AND PEPPER PIZZA

Pizza is fun to make at home. The dough can be shaped into six mini-pizzas if you prefer, and you can vary the toppings as you wish.

MAKES 6 SERVINGS

Pizza Dough

1 (¼-ounce) package active dry yeast

1½ tablespoons olive oil

1 teaspoon salt

3½ cups unbleached all-purpose flour

2 tablespoons semolina or cornmeal, approximately

Topping

1 large eggplant, sliced into ½-inch-thick rounds

3 medium ripe tomatoes, sliced into ½-inch-thick rounds

2 tablespoons chopped fresh thyme or ½ tablespoon
   dried thyme

5 tablespoons olive oil, plus more as needed

1 garlic clove, crushed with the side of a knife

2 medium bell peppers (1 red and 1 yellow), seeded and
   cut into ½-inch-thick strips

6 ounces mozzarella cheese, cut into thin strips

24 black Mediterranean olives, pitted

2 tablespoons drained capers

24 anchovy fillets packed in oil, drained (optional)

Salt, to taste

To make the pizza dough, in a small bowl, dissolve the yeast in 1½ cups warm water, and let stand until creamy, about 5 minutes. Stir in the olive oil and salt. Put the flour in a large bowl and make a well in the center. Pour the yeast mixture into the well. Gradually mix the flour into the liquid to make a soft dough. Turn onto a floured work surface. Knead, adding more flour as needed, until the dough is smooth and elastic, 8 to 10 minutes. Form into a ball and place in a lightly oiled bowl. Cover with plastic wrap and let rise in a warm place until tripled in volume, about 1½ hours.

To make the topping, sprinkle the eggplant and tomato slices with some of the thyme, and set aside. Heat 3 tablespoons of the oil in a large frying pan over medium heat. Add the garlic and cook until golden-brown; discard the garlic. In batches, cook the eggplant, turning once, until lightly browned and tender, about 5 minutes. Transfer to paper towels to drain. Heat the remaining 2 tablespoons oil in the pan. Cook the tomato slices, in batches, just until lightly browned, about 3 minutes; drain on paper towels. Add the pepper strips to the pan, and cook just until crisp-tender, about 5 minutes; drain on paper towels.

Preheat the oven to 400°F. Dust three baking sheets lightly with semolina. Punch down the dough and cut into thirds. Keep two pieces covered with plastic wrap, and put the third piece on a lightly floured work surface. Shape the dough into a ball, then flatten and roll out into a 10-inch round. Place the round on the baking sheet, and press all around the edge to make a rim. Top with one third each of the mozzarella, the cooked vegetables, olives, capers, and optional

anchovies. Sprinkle with a little of the remaining thyme and a seasoning of salt. Repeat with the remaining dough and topping ingredients to make two more pizzas. Bake until the pizza crust is golden-brown and the cheese has melted, about 20 minutes. (If you can only fit two pizzas in your oven, cover the third pizza with plastic wrap, and refrigerate for up to 30 minutes, until ready to bake.) Serve hot.

FOCACCIA WITH CARAMELIZED ONIONS AND GARLIC

Focaccia can be served in any number of ways: as a snack, as a bread with meals, or even used to make sandwiches. This version uses the "sponge" method, where the dough is built upon a fermented batter to give extra flavor and moisture.

MAKES 8 TO 12 SERVINGS

1 (¼-ounce) package active dry yeast

3½ cups bread flour

7 tablespoons olive oil

¼ teaspoons salt

2 medium onions, sliced into ¼-inch-thick half-moons

2 garlic cloves, sliced

Coarse kosher salt, for sprinkling

In a medium bowl, dissolve ½ teaspoon of the yeast in ½ cup warm water. Stir in ¾ cup of the flour to make a thick batter. Beat for 100 strokes. Cover with plastic wrap and let the sponge stand until doubled in volume and bubbly, about 2 hours.

Scrape the sponge into a bowl. Add 4 tablespoons of the oil, the salt, the remaining 1½ teaspoons yeast, and ¾ cup warm water. Mix vigorously to break up and dissolve the sponge. Gradually stir in enough of the remaining 2¾ cups flour to make a stiff, sticky dough. Turn onto a lightly floured work surface. Knead, adding more flour as needed, until the dough is smooth and elastic, 8 to 10 minutes. Form into a ball and place in an oiled bowl. Cover with plastic wrap and let rise in a warm place until doubled in volume, about 1½ hours. Punch down the dough, and then cover again and let rise until doubled in volume, about 45 minutes.

Meanwhile, in a frying pan, heat 2 tablespoons of the remaining oil over medium heat. Add the onions and cook, stirring often, until golden-brown, about 10 minutes. Stir in the garlic and cook for 1 more minute. Set aside.

Preheat the oven to 400°F. Lightly oil a 10- by 15-inch jelly-roll pan. Punch down the dough, then turn it onto a lightly floured work surface. Roll out the dough into a 10- by 15-inch rectangle (if the dough seems too elastic,

FOCACCIA WITH CARAMELIZED ONIONS
AND GARLIC

cover and let stand for 10 minutes to relax, and roll
out again). Fit the dough into the pan, stretching it, if
necessary, to fit the corners. Spread the onion mixture
over the top, drizzle with the remaining 1 tablespoon
oil, and sprinkle with coarse salt. Bake until the
focaccia is puffed and golden, 18 to 22 minutes. Let
cool in the pan for at least 20 minutes. Cut into serving
portions and serve warm or at room temperature.

STICKY CARAMEL-NUT BUNS
These rolls have wonderful buttery caramel flavor
packed into every bite.

MAKES 15 BUNS
  ½ cup chopped pecans
  ¼ cup granulated sugar
  1 teaspoon ground cinnamon
  10 tablespoons (1 stick plus 2 tablespoons)
    unsalted butter
  ½ cup packed light brown sugar
  2 tablespoons corn syrup

Sweet Dough
  2 cups bread flour, approximately
  ¼ cup granulated sugar
  1 teaspoon active dry yeast
  ¼ teaspoon salt
  ½ cup milk
  4 tablespoons unsalted butter
  1 large egg

To make the sweet dough, in a medium bowl, mix
½ cup of the flour with the sugar, yeast, and salt. In a
small saucepan, heat the milk with the butter just until
the milk is warm (the butter doesn't have to melt
completely). Pour into the flour mixture, and add the
egg. Using an electric mixer at high speed, beat until
thick and elastic, about 3 minutes. Using a spoon,
work in enough of the remaining flour to make a soft
dough. Turn onto a lightly floured work surface.
Knead, adding more flour as needed, until the dough
is smooth and elastic, about 8 minutes. (The dough
should be soft and supple—do not add too much
flour.) Shape into a ball and place in a buttered bowl.
Cover with plastic wrap and let rise in a warm place
until doubled in volume, about 1½ hours.

  Meanwhile, mix together the pecans, sugar,
and cinnamon in a small bowl. Set aside. Melt

2 tablespoons of the butter and set aside. In a medium saucepan, combine the remaining 8 tablespoons butter with the light brown sugar and corn syrup, and bring to a simmer. Pour the syrup mixture into a buttered 9- by 13-inch baking pan, tilting the pan to coat the bottom evenly with syrup.

Punch down the dough. On a lightly floured work surface, roll out the dough into a 9- by 15-inch rectangle. Brush the dough with the melted butter. Sprinkle with the pecan mixture, leaving a 1-inch border on the long sides. Starting at a long side, tightly roll up the dough. Cut the dough crosswise into 1-inch-thick rounds, and place, cut sides up, on the syrup in the pan. Cover loosely with plastic wrap and let rise until the buns have almost doubled in volume, about 45 minutes. (They will not fill the pan completely.)

Preheat the oven to 350°F. Bake until the buns are golden-brown, about 25 minutes. Cool for 5 minutes. Place a baking sheet over the pan, and invert with the pan to unmold the buns. Serve warm.

BLUEBERRY AND CORN MUFFINS

These muffins are chunky with corn and blueberries. For an optional crunchy topping, sprinkle them with amber, coarse-crystal raw sugar, which is available at health food stores.

MAKES 12 MUFFINS
1½ cups all-purpose flour
¾ cup yellow cornmeal
½ cup granulated sugar
1 tablespoon baking powder
1 teaspoon salt
1 cup milk
½ cup vegetable oil
2 large eggs
1½ cups fresh blueberries
½ cup fresh or defrosted frozen corn kernels
1 tablespoon raw sugar crystals, for sprinkling (optional)

Preheat the oven to 350°F. Lightly oil 12 (2½-inch) muffin cups. In a medium bowl, combine the flour, cornmeal, sugar, baking powder, and salt. In another bowl, whisk together the milk, oil, and eggs. Stir into the dry ingredients, just until blended. Fold in the blueberries and corn. Spoon into the prepared muffin cups. Sprinkle the tops with the raw sugar, if desired. Bake until golden-brown, 25 to 30 minutes. Cool for 5 minutes on a wire cake rack, then unmold and serve warm.

BLUEBERRY AND CORN MUFFINS

SOUTHERN CORNBREAD

It's no trouble to serve warm bread with dinner (or breakfast or lunch) when it is as easy to make as this.

MAKES 6 TO 8 SERVINGS
1¼ cups all-purpose flour
1 cup yellow cornmeal, preferably stoneground
2 teaspoons granulated sugar (optional)
1 teaspoon baking powder
1 teaspoon salt
1½ cups milk
¼ cup unsalted butter, melted
1 large egg

Preheat the oven to 425°F. Lightly butter an 8-inch square baking dish. In a medium bowl, whisk the flour, cornmeal, optional sugar, baking powder, and salt to mix. Make a well in the center, and pour in the milk, melted butter, and egg. Mix just until smoothly blended, and spread in the prepared dish.

Bake until golden-brown and a tester inserted in the center comes out clean, about 35 minutes. Leave to cool on a wire cake rack. Serve either warm or at room temperature, with plenty of butter.

BUTTERMILK SCONES

Britain used to be the only place where you could get a good scone, but as muffins increased in popularity in America, scones became better known. Buttermilk makes the lightest scones. If you like sweet scones, add 3 tablespoons granulated sugar to the flour.

MAKES 15 (2-INCH) SCONES
1¾ cups all-purpose flour
2 teaspoons baking powder
¼ teaspoon baking soda
⅛ teaspoon salt
3 tablespoons unsalted butter, chilled
⅔ cup buttermilk

Preheat the oven to 375°F. Sift the flour, baking powder, baking soda, and salt into a bowl. Using a pastry blender or two knives, cut the butter into the flour until the mixture is in coarse crumbs. Add the buttermilk and mix to a soft dough.

Turn the dough onto a lightly floured work surface. Lightly roll out the dough to ½ inch thick. Using a 2-inch round biscuit cutter, cut out the scones. Gather up the scraps and knead briefly, then roll and cut more scones until the dough is used. Dust each scone with flour, and put on an ungreased baking sheet. Bake until puffed and golden, 10 to 15 minutes. Cool on a wire cake rack. Serve warm or at room temperature.

CINNAMON CRUMB COFFEE CAKE

Every cook needs a fast coffee cake recipe. Make this on a Saturday morning, and there will certainly be nothing but crumbs left by Sunday evening.

MAKES 12 SERVINGS

2½ cups all-purpose flour
1 cup granulated sugar
1 cup packed light brown sugar
10 tablespoons (1 stick plus 2 tablespoons) unsalted
    butter, chilled, cut into small pieces
½ cup chopped pecans
¾ teaspoon ground cinnamon
2 teaspoons baking powder
½ teaspoon baking soda
½ teaspoon grated nutmeg
¼ teaspoon salt
¾ cup plain low-fat yogurt
¼ cup milk
2 large eggs, beaten

Preheat the oven to 375°F. Lightly butter a 9- by 13-inch baking dish. In a bowl, combine the flour, sugar, brown sugar, and butter, and use your fingertips to blend until crumbly. In a small bowl, stir ½ cup of the crumb mixture with the pecans and ¼ teaspoon of the cinnamon; set aside. To the remaining crumb mixture, add the remaining ½ teaspoon cinnamon, the baking powder, baking soda, nutmeg, and salt. Add the yogurt, milk, and eggs, and mix.

Pour into the dish and smooth the top. Sprinkle with the crumb mixture. Bake until a tester inserted in the center of the cake comes out clean, about 25 minutes. Leave to cool on a wire cake rack, and serve warm or at room temperature.

HERBED BREAD STUFFING WITH ONIONS AND APPLES

Fresh herbs and a good, firm bread from your favorite bakery will make all the difference in this stuffing for the holiday bird. Allow about ¾ cup stuffing for each pound of turkey. The recipe is easy to double, or even triple, when serving a crowd.

MAKES ABOUT 8 CUPS STUFFING (ENOUGH FOR A 12-POUND TURKEY)

8 tablespoons (1 stick) unsalted butter
1 large onion, chopped
1 medium tart apple (such as Granny Smith), peeled,
    cored, and chopped
2 medium celery ribs, chopped
8 cups (½-inch cubes) day-old, firm white bread
¼ cup chopped fresh parsley
2 teaspoons chopped fresh rosemary or 1 teaspoon
    dried rosemary
2 teaspoons chopped fresh sage or 1 teaspoon dried sage
1 teaspoon chopped fresh marjoram or ½ teaspoon
    dried marjoram or oregano
1 teaspoon salt
½ teaspoon freshly ground pepper
1 cup chicken stock, approximately

In a frying pan, melt the butter over medium-high heat. Add the onion, apple, and celery, and cook until the onion is golden, about 10 minutes. Transfer to a large bowl. Add the remaining ingredients, and stir in enough stock to moisten. Use as a poultry stuffing, stuffing the neck and body cavities loosely. Or, place the stuffing in a buttered baking dish, cover with foil, and bake in a 325°F oven for 30 to 40 minutes.

Herb Bread Stuffing with Sausage: In a large frying pan, heat 2 tablespoons vegetable oil over medium heat. Add 1 pound bulk pork sausage and cook, breaking up the meat with spoon, until browned, about 10 minutes. Drain well. Stir into the stuffing mixture.

CORNBREAD STUFFING WITH HAM AND PECANS

Bake the cornbread the day before, crumble, and let stand, uncovered, overnight, to dry out.

MAKES ABOUT 12 CUPS STUFFING (ENOUGH FOR A 16-POUND TURKEY)

4 tablespoons unsalted butter
8 ounces smoked ham, cut into ¼-inch dice
2 celery ribs, chopped
1 cup chopped scallions
1 recipe Southern Cornbread, crumbled
3 cups (½-inch cubes) day-old, firm white bread
½ cup coarsely chopped pecans
2 teaspoons chopped fresh rosemary or 1 teaspoon
    dried rosemary
1 teaspoon chopped fresh thyme or ½ teaspoon
    dried thyme
½ cup half-and-half
1 cup chicken stock, approximately
Salt and freshly ground pepper, to taste

In a medium frying pan, melt the butter over medium heat. Add the ham and celery, and cook until the celery is soft, about 5 minutes. Stir in the scallions and cook until wilted, about 3 minutes. Transfer to a bowl. Add the cornbread, bread, pecans, rosemary, thyme, and half-and-half. Mix in enough stock to moisten, and season to taste. Use as a poultry stuffing, filling the neck and body cavities loosely. Or, place the stuffing in a buttered baking dish, cover with foil, and bake in a 350°F oven until heated through, 30 to 40 minutes.

Oyster, Ham, and Cornbread Stuffing: Omit the pecans. Shuck 1 dozen oysters, reserving their juices, and coarsely chop into bite-sized pieces. Add the oysters with the cornbread. Use the oyster juices to moisten the stuffing, adding chicken stock, if needed.

SPICED APPLE PANCAKES

Adding grated apples and spices to the batter puts these pancakes in their own special class.

MAKES ABOUT 12 PANCAKES

2 cups all-purpose flour
1/4 cup granulated sugar
1 teaspoon baking powder
1 teaspoon baking soda
1 teaspoon ground cinnamon
1/4 teaspoon ground allspice
1/4 teaspoon salt
1 cup plain yogurt
3/4 cup milk
3/4 cup vegetable oil
3 large eggs
1 cup grated tart apple, peeled, cored, and grated
Butter and maple syrup, for serving

In a large bowl, combine the flour, sugar, baking powder, baking soda, cinnamon, allspice, and salt. In a small bowl, whisk together the yogurt, milk, oil, and eggs. Pour into the dry ingredients and mix just until moistened. Fold in the apple. Do not overbeat.

Preheat a greased griddle until a splash of water flicked on it sizzles and forms tiny balls. In batches, using about 1/3 cup batter for each pancake, pour the batter onto the griddle, and cook until tiny bubbles appear on the surface and the edges look dry, about 2 minutes. Turn and cook until the other sides are golden. Serve hot, with butter and maple syrup.

PECAN WAFFLES

Finely ground pecans provide a nutty flavor.

MAKES 6 (8-INCH-SQUARE) WAFFLES

Vegetable oil or nonstick vegetable oil spray, for waffle iron
2 cups pecans
2 cups all-purpose flour
1/2 cup granulated sugar
1 tablespoon baking powder

1/2 teaspoon baking soda
1/2 teaspoon salt
1 1/2 cups plain low-fat yogurt
1 cup milk
4 large eggs
2/3 cup vegetable oil
Maple syrup and butter, for serving

Preheat a waffle iron. Lightly oil the waffle grids. Preheat the oven to 200°F. In a food processor fitted with the metal blade, pulse the pecans with 1 cup of the flour until the nuts are very finely chopped—the consistency should be just short of a flour. Transfer to a large bowl, and stir in the remaining 1 cup flour, the sugar, baking powder, baking soda, and salt. In a medium bowl, whisk the yogurt, milk, eggs, and oil. Add to the flour mixture and mix just until blended. Do not overbeat. Pour 1/4 cup of the batter into the center of the waffle iron and close it. Bake for about 2 minutes—the waffle is done when no steam comes from the sides of the waffle iron. Transfer to a baking sheet and keep warm while making the remaining waffles. If the batter thickens on standing, thin with a little milk. Serve warm, with maple syrup and butter.

CRUMBS, CROUTONS, AND TOASTS

Fresh Bread Crumbs: Remove crusts from thick slices of day-old white bread, and cut the slices into large cubes. In a food processor fitted with the metal blade, or a blender, reduce the bread to crumbs.

Dry Bread Crumbs: Preheat the oven to 300°F. Spread out slices of bread on baking sheets and bake until golden-brown, 15 to 20 minutes. Cool. Wrap in a dish towel, and pound and roll with a rolling pin to crush into crumbs. Sift the crumbs through a sieve so they are uniform in size (pound any remaining large bits). Or, reduce the dried bread to crumbs in a food processor fitted with the metal blade, or a blender.

Croutons: Remove crusts from 1/2-inch-thick slices of bread, then cut the bread into 1/4- or 1/2-inch dice. In a frying pan, heat equal quantities of unsalted butter and vegetable oil (about 1/4 inch deep) over medium heat. Add the bread dice and cook, stirring and tossing, until golden-brown all over. Remove with a slotted spoon and drain on paper towels. Or, spread out the bread dice on a baking sheet and bake in a preheated 350°F oven until crisp and lightly browned, 10 to 15 minutes.

Melba Toast: Preheat the oven to 350°F. Toast medium slices of white bread. With a serrated knife, cut each slice horizontally in half. Scrape away the untoasted side, and cut off the crusts. Spread out the wafer-thin slices, untoasted side up, on baking sheets and bake until crisp and lightly browned, about 5 minutes.

Planning menus

Memorable meals come in all shapes and sizes. From a casual picnic on a perfect summer's day to a celebratory dinner party, from a quiet night at home without the children to a classic Sunday lunch with all the family. Good company, a comfortable and attractive environment, and a relaxed and happy atmosphere will all shape our experience of a meal, but generally the cornerstone will be the food itself.

The emphasis of this book, quite deliberately, is on the quality and availability of ingredients. If you know what to look for when you are shopping; if you select from produce in season that is at its best and full of flavor; and if you know how to identify the good from the average—and from the bad— then you have already won half the battle. If you are like me, you will take great pleasure in going shopping and planning a meal around just what happens to be available: you might see some wonderful cod at the fish market, and this might inspire you to buy some ginger and scallions so that you can cook it in a slightly different and more interesting way than usual.

Of course, some people prefer to go shopping armed with a list of ingredients for the dishes they have decided to cook, and here the season should give you a good idea of what to expect: asparagus and lamb in spring, for example. But whichever method you adopt, you have to consider how the various ingredients will combine in a dish, and how the various dishes will complement each other. Garlic, for example, has a capacity to overwhelm other flavors, and, indeed, it's the garlic we taste first and foremost when it is served with mushrooms or shrimp or perhaps escargots; but when you think about it, the subtlety of the mushrooms or shrimp or escargots remains and produces something quite different in each case.

Still other foods act as a vehicle for the ingredients with which they are combined. Chicken is a fine example: depending on how it's cooked, you get amazingly diverse results—Coq au Vin is vastly different from roast chicken, and neither is remotely similar to chicken that has been used as the base for a curry or one that has been cooked with soy sauce and sesame for a Sichuan Chicken Salad.

This confidence in handling and balancing ingredients is something that comes with experience, not just in cooking but in eating out at restaurants or at other people's houses. The true cook develops an instinct for combining ingredients in the right quantities to produce

something exceptional: I don't know who it was who first thought of combining poultry and chocolate in a *mole* sauce—it sounds so unpromising, and yet it works wonderfully well. As culinary influences circle the world in search of new and exciting ingredients and recipes, the repertoire of combinations at our disposal becomes ever more eclectic.

The care we apply to the combination of ingredients in a single dish applies equally to the balance of dishes that makes up a meal. Only a greedy child, I suspect, would want to follow up a rich first course with an equally rich entrée, finishing the meal with a rich chocolate pudding and whipped cream. Most of us prefer to balance flavors and courses according to the time of year and the type of occasion—even, perhaps, the day of the week.

When it comes to presentation of the food on the plate, balance is equally important. Most of us, from time to time, succumb to the temptations of "comfort food," filling the plate with a favorite dish. Yet I sigh when confronted by the classic Sunday roast with its many elements on one cluttered plate. Each item on its own is often quite delicious, but they lose their individual flavors and qualities when indiscriminately heaped together. Although the faddish precision of nouvelle cuisine (the opposite extreme) is now, largely, a thing of the past, we have undoubtedly taken from it some important lessons about presentation. A good-looking dish excites the eyes and gets the tastebuds going just as surely as tempting smells from the kitchen do.

The recipes in this book cover food for every occasion, from hearty winter soups to light summer salads, from pasta dishes that can be brought to the table within minutes, to stews and roasts that repay the preparation time in their wonderful combination of textures and flavors.

Above all, food is for pleasure. In the last twenty years, we have thankfully become less concerned with pretentious social niceties: pressures of space at home and pressures on time at work mean that a dinner party is just as likely to take place around the kitchen table as it is in a separate diningroom. A sense of pleasure in the rituals of serving dinner is simply and easily suggested: homemade food, large white cloth napkins, plain knives and forks, a couple of well-shaped wine glasses each, good wine, and perhaps a bunch of fresh flowers are, for me, all the accompaniments you need.

SPRING

Squash Fritters with
Garlicky Yogurt Dip

Bouillabaisse

Strawberry Galette

Spring Greens Soup

Shrimp Brochettes with
Mint Butter
Spiced Basmati Rice
Peas in the Indian Fashion

Orange Sorbet

Apple, Cheddar, and
Pecan Quesadillas

New Mexican Pork and
Vegetable Chili
Southern Cornbread

Tropical Cream Pie

Artichokes Roman-Style

Garlic-Braised Lamb
Shanks with Sweet
Peppers
Soft Polenta Veneto-Style

Meringue Cups with
Fresh Fruit

Hot and Sour Shellfish
Soup

Glazed Cornish Game
Hens with Rice and Pine
Nut Stuffing
Stir-Fried Asparagus with
Ginger

Melon Sorbet

SUMMER

Cauliflower Vichysoisse

Baked Bluefish with
Sweet Mustard Glaze
Roasted Sweet Pepper
Salad

Apricot Tart

Pan Catalan

Grilled Butterflied Leg
of Lamb with Dijon
and Herbs
Green Bean Salad with
Anchovy-Cream Dressing
Rice Salad with Oranges
and Olives

Angel Food Cake
Summer Berry Fool

Pink Raspberry Lemonade

Olivada with grilled
baguette slices

Salade Niçoise

Raspberry and Lime Sherbert

Cool Cucumber and Mint
Soup

Indian Chicken Kebabs
Lentils with Rice and
Fried Onions
Indian Potato Salad with
Yogurt and Scallion
Dressing

Coconut Ice Cream

Ratatouille

Moules à la Marinière
Saffron Bread

French Cherry Clafoutis

AUTUMN

Bibb Lettuce with Lemon-
Poppy Seed Dressing

Sausage and Beer Gumbo
Fluffy Yeast Biscuits

Pine Nut Pralines

Creamy Wild Mushroom
Soup

Roast Loin of Pork
Orange-Glazed Acorn
Squash
Cajun Smothered Corn

Double-Cooked, Two-
Apple Pie

Arugula and Bacon Salad

Eggplant, Tomato, and
Pepper Pizza

Coffee Granita

Spinach and Walnut Salad

Braised Rabbit with
Prunes
Pan-Roasted New
Potatoes
Glazed Baby Carrots

Autumn Fruit Crisp

A Thanksgiving Menu

Shrimp and Corn
Chowder

Roast Turkey with Herb
and Apple Bread Stuffing
or Cornbread Stuffing
with Ham and Pecans
Green Beans with
Portobello Mushrooms
and Prosciutto
Gratinéed Onions in
Gorgonzola Sauce
Parsley Mashed Potatoes
Baked Sweet Potatoes
with Pineapple
Cranberry-Orange Sauce
Cranberry and Raspberry
Mold
Buttermilk Dinner Rolls

Pumpkin "Soufflé" Pie
Sweet Potato and Orange Pie

WINTER

Romaine Salad with
Balsamic Herb
Vinaigrette

Lasagne with Portobello
Mushrooms, Artichokes,
and Pancetta

Grapefruit Sorbet

Zucchini and Goat Cheese
Filo Tart

Pomegranate-Marinated
Leg of Lamb
Pan-Roasted New
Potatoes
Fennel Parmigiano

Pears in Red Wine

Crab Chile con Queso

Jambalaya Classique

Bread and Butter Pudding

A Holiday Buffet

Crudités with Garlic
Mayonnaise
Bistro Pâté de Campagne
with baguette slices
Herbed Carrot Pâté with
crackers
Eggplant Caviar with
pita bread

Baked Chicken with
Lemon and Olives
Sherry-Glazed Ham with
Sweet Pepper Chutney
Italian Seafood Salad
Lido Pasta Salad

Cocoa Brownies
Chocolate-Hazelnut
Shortbread
Macadamia-Coconut
Crunch

Glögg

A Holiday Dinner

Oyster Chowder

Celery and Parmesan
Salad

Roast Beef Tenderloin
Baked Stuffed Potatoes
Glazed Baby Carrots
Buttermilk Dinner Rolls

Crème Brûlée

Glossary

Cooking terms

acidulated water: water to which lemon juice or vinegar, preferably white wine vinegar, is added, and in which certain vegetables, such as celeriac, salsify, and globe artichokes, are immersed to prevent discoloration.

à la grecque: refers to a preparation of vegetables, particularly mushrooms, onions, and artichoke bottoms, cooked in olive oil with coriander seeds and other seasonings and served cold.

à la meunière: refers to a mixture of browned butter, lemon juice, and parsley served with food such as fish.

al dente: Italian term (literally "to the tooth") used to describe the texture of food, mainly pasta, when it is properly cooked and just firm to the bite.

antipasto: literally meaning "before the pasta," this is the Italian equivalent of hors d'oeuvres and may consist of slices of salami and other cured meats, vegetables grilled or marinated in oil, seafood salads, and other hot and cold dishes.

au gratin: refers to dishes that are sprinkled with cheese and/or bread crumbs, then broiled or cooked in the oven just long enough to brown the top.

baker's peel and stone: the pizza or bread dough is shaped on the large, flat, wooden peel, then slid directly onto the hot baking stone in the oven; the baking stone duplicates the baking properties of commercial brick-floored pizza ovens.

bard: originating from the old French word *barde*, which was a horse's iron armor, this means to wrap thin sheets of fat, usually pork fat, around meat, poultry, or game to prevent the flesh from drying out while roasting.

baste: to spoon cooking juices or another liquid over food while it cooks to keep it moist.

battuto: Italian term for a mixture of very finely chopped vegetables and pancetta or pork fat, which is cooked and then used for flavoring sauces, stews, and soups.

beurre manié: flour and softened butter worked together to a paste, used to thicken soups, sauces, and stews.

beurre noir: literally, in French, black butter, this usually refers to a sauce for skate and other fish, made by cooking butter until nut brown (not black, despite the name) and mixing in vinegar, parsley, and capers.

beurre noisette: butter cooked until just brown; lemon juice and seasoning may be added when used as a sauce.

bind: to add egg, liquid, or a thickening agent to a mixture to hold it together. Foods such as pâtés and stuffings sometimes require binding.

bisque: thick creamy soup based usually on seafood—especially lobster, crayfish, or shrimp—but sometimes game or poultry.

blanch: to immerse food briefly in boiling water to soften it, to keep it white, to make it easy to remove its skin (as for almonds and some fruits and vegetables), or to remove excess salt or bitterness.

braise: to cook food slowly, after it has been browned, in a minimum of liquid in a tightly covered pan or casserole.

brine: saltwater solution used to preserve or flavor meat, fish, or vegetables.

canapés: small appetizers made of bread— fresh or toasted—topped with various savory mixtures, or other small foods that can be eaten with the fingers, to be served with cocktails.

charcuterie: French term that refers to the wide assortment of pork products—sausages, pâtés, hams, etc.—sold in the specialty shops called *charcuteries*. The Italian equivalent is *salumi*, sold at *salumerie*.

chine: the backbone of an animal; this is often loosened or severed from the ribs in a roast, to allow easier carving.

choucroute garnie: classic dish from the Alsace region in France of sauerkraut garnished with sausages, pig's ears or feet, ham, pickled pork knuckles, and similar meats.

chowder: thick soup, most often of seafood, notably clams, that takes its name from the French word for pot or cauldron, *chaudière*.

chutney: From the Indian word *chatni*, a relish, cooked or uncooked, of fruits or vegetables and spices, served with curries, cold meats, and other dishes.

clarify: to remove impurities from fats— particularly from butter, for cooking—and from stocks, and consommés.

compote: fruit cooked in a sugar syrup.

confits: meat or poultry preserved in its own fat, such as *confit d'oie* (goose) and *confit de canard* (duck); or fruits candied in sugar, often with brandy added.

cream: to beat butter or butter and sugar to a light consistency.

croquette: cylindrical- or oval-shaped mixtures of chopped meat, fish, eggs, or vegetables, coated in beaten eggs and bread crumbs and deepfried.

curd: coagulated substance that is produced in milk when it is soured; cheese is made from curds.

cut in: to mix fat, usually butter or lard, with flour or other dry ingredients using a pastry cutter to give a crumbly rather than a smooth result. This technique is especially important in the making of pie crusts and biscuits.

daube: French stew of braised meat and vegetables.

deglaze: to scrape browned solidified cooking juices from the bottom of a roasting pan, frying pan, or saucepan, loosening them with the help of a liquid such as wine, brandy, or stock.

devil: to season foods with spicy ingredients, usually mustard, cayenne, and Tabasco sauce.

disgorge: to salt vegetables such as egg plant and cucumber to draw out their bitter juices; also to soak certain foods, such as sweetbreads, in water to remove a strong flavor and blood or to improve color.

dredge: to coat foods lightly with flour, confectioners' sugar, or other fine powder.

duxelles: finely chopped mushrooms, often mixed with chopped shallots or onions, sautéed in butter, and used for stuffings and garnishes.

emulsion: mixture, such as mayonnaise or vinaigrette, in which fat or oil is held in suspension in another liquid.

en croûte: refers to cooking food, particularly pâté and meat, entirely encased in pastry.

en papillote: refers to cooking food, and often serving it, wrapped in parchment paper; today, foil is often used instead.

escabèche: Portuguese, Spanish, and Latin American way of preparing fish, poultry, and game by cooking it, often by frying it, and then marinating it and serving cold.

filo, phyllo pastry: paper-thin pastry dough sheets, very similar to strudel dough. Filo is usually brushed with butter and then layered; sweet or savory fillings may be layered with the pastry or wrapped in it, before baking.

flan: open-faced pie or tart, normally cooked in a metal flan ring. In Spain and Mexico, flan is a baked caramel custard.

fumet: reduced stock, usually made with fish, used to give flavor to other stocks and sauces.

galantine: boned and stuffed poultry, game, or meat, often glazed with aspic, decorated and served cold.

glaze: to make food shiny by coating it with a sugar syrup, aspic, beaten egg, milk, melted chocolate, etc.

gluten: elastic protein found in some grains, such as hard or strong wheat; it develops with kneading and in the presence of water, and helps to trap the air bubbles produced by fermenting yeast, resulting in a light, well-risen bread.

granita: sweet Italian ice with a granular texture, flavored with fruit, coffee, etc.

infuse: to extract flavor from food by steeping in a hot liquid—the resulting liquid is an infusion. This technique is usually applied when making coffee and tea, including herbal tea. Milk is infused with onion and other flavorings for béchamel sauce or with vanilla for custard.

julienne: thin matchstick-like strips of vegetables, ham, etc., often used as a garnish.

lard: to insert strips of fat (lardons), usually pork fat, or bacon, into meat to be roasted, using a special needle, to make the meat more succulent.

lardons, lardoons: strips of pork fat or bacon.

liaison: thickening for a sauce or soup, which may be a starch such as flour or cornstarch, a mixture of egg yolk and cream, or a combination of flour and butter; in mayonnaise, the liaison is oil and egg yolk.

macedoine: mixture, cooked or uncooked, of fruits, usually, or vegetables cut into small cubes.

macerate: to steep in liquid, often liquor or liqueurs, so that the food (usually fruit) becomes infused with the liquid's flavor.

marinate: to soak raw meat, fish, or vegetables in a seasoned liquid (a marinade) to make it more tender and/or flavorful.

mezze: Middle Eastern hors d'oeuvres, often including olives, baked or broiled cheese, small spiced meatballs, cooked vegetable salads and purées, and nuts such as pistachios and almonds.

mirepoix: diced vegetables such as carrots, onions, and leeks used as a base for a sauce, soup, or stew, or, cooked in butter, as a garnish for some meat or fish dishes.

navarin: French lamb or mutton stew made with turnips, carrots, onions, and potatoes, and, in spring, with peas and young vegetables— when it becomes *navarin printemps*.

pâté: savory mixture of chopped meat or game, usually containing some pork and pork fat, which is baked, either with or without a casing of pastry, and served cold. The word is also used to cover similar mixtures that are not baked, such as smoked fish pâtés.

poach: to cook food immersed in gently simmering liquid.

purée: raw or cooked food, usually vegetables or fruit, that is finely mashed and then strained, or processed in a food processor or blender (or put through a food mill) until smooth.

quenelles: lightly cooked dumplings made of finely chopped fish or meat; a French delicacy.

quiche: a savory custard tart, originally from France's Lorraine.

ragout: French stew of meat and vegetables.

ragù: Italian term for a meat stew or sauce.

ramekin: small round baking dish for individual servings.

reduce: to concentrate or thicken a liquid by evaporation through rapid boiling.

refresh: to rinse or immerse hot food (usually green vegetables) in very cold or ice water to stop further cooking and to set the color of the food.

render: to melt animal fat, such as duck, slowly so that it separates into, mostly, liquid and particles usually called cracklings.

risotto: Italian rice dish, usually with a creamy consistency; it should be made with round Italian long-grain rice.

roux: cooked mixture of flour and fat, usually butter, used as the basis for savory sauces and soups.

sauté: to cook briskly in a small amount of fat in a shallow pan, shaking the pan to make sure that the pieces being cooked are evenly browned.

scald: to heat liquid, usually milk, to just below boiling point, until bubbles form around the edge of the pan.

score: to make shallow cuts in the surface of food. Steaks may be scored before they are grilled, broiled, or panfried to tenderize them (by cutting through the fine connective tissues), and some whole fish or skin-on fillets are scored before broiling or grilling so that they will cook through quickly and evenly.

seviche: a dish of raw fish marinated in lemon or lime juice, the acidity of which "cooks" the fish.

simmer: to keep a liquid at just below boiling point so that it remains gently "shivering."

steam: to cook food in steam, usually in a perforated container set above boiling water.

stir-fry: to cook food quickly in a little oil over high heat, stirring and tossing it constantly. A wok is the best pan for this as the rounded shape distributes the heat evenly and a lot of food can be cooked in a very little fat.

stock: well-flavored broth in which meat, poultry, or vegetables or a combination of these have been cooked. It is used instead of water in many dishes, particularly soups and sauces, to enhance their flavor.

sweat: to soften vegetables, particularly onions, by cooking them gently so that they release their juices but do not brown.

tapas: snacks or appetizers traditionally served in Spanish bars, consisting of marinated vegetables, olives, meats, slices of cold Spanish omelet, and the like.

tart: basically an open-faced pie, usually no more than an inch high, made with fruit or other sweet fillings or with savory custard mixtures.

terrine: both a deep rectangular or oval mold used for cooking a pâté, and the pâté itself. Terrines are traditionally made of earthenware, but may also be enameled cast iron.

timbale: both a cup-shaped earthenware or metal mold and the food cooked in such a mold, often rice or pasta.

water bath: also known as a bain marie, this consists of a large saucepan or a roasting pan filled with water in which baking dishes or ramekins, or saucepans or bowls, containing food are set (ideally on a special trivet). The water bath may be used to keep prepared foods hot and moist, but its most useful purpose is to ensure that certain delicate foods, such as custards and sauces, cook at a constant low temperature without drying out, curdling, or scorching. The advantage of a water bath over a double boiler is that the former ensures that the food remains moist while cooking and cooks evenly, due to the surrounding steam caused by evaporation.

whey: watery liquid that separates out when milk or cream curdles; unlike most cheeses, which are made from the curds left behind, ricotta is usually made from whey.

zest: oily, colored part of citrus peel, used as a flavoring agent or garnish.

Basic cooking techniques

making beurre manié: mash together equal parts of softened butter and flour to make a paste. Add it in small pieces to a hot sauce, soup, etc., at the end of cooking, whisking in enough of the beurre manié to thicken the liquid to the desired consistency.

clarifying butter: melt butter over low heat, then continue to heat gently, without allowing the butter to color, until the milk solids separate and sink to the bottom of the pan. Remove from the heat and allow to settle for 10 minutes, then strain through a strainer lined with moist paper towels. Clarified butter can be refrigerated, tightly covered, for weeks or frozen for months.

whipping cream: pour chilled cream into a chilled bowl. Use a whisk, a rotary beater, or electric mixer to whip the cream until it is thickened or stiff enough to pipe, according to the recipe instructions. A tablespoon or two of ice water can be added to lighten the cream. For sweetened whipped cream, add 2 tablespoons granulated sugar to each cup of cream before whipping.

making crème fraîche: stir 2 tablespoons buttermilk into 1 cup whipping or heavy cream and keep in a warm place (75 to 85°F) for about 8 hours or until thickened and slightly soured in flavor. Store in the refrigerator.

draining yogurt: put plain yogurt into a sieve lined with a paper towel (or a coffee filter) set over a bowl, or put it in a cheesecloth bag hung over the sink. Let drain at room temperature for about 2 hours, and use the thick yogurt for dishes such as the Indian *raita*; or let drain overnight to make a yogurt cheese.

beating egg whites: if using an electric mixer, start at low speed; or beat slowly with a whisk. When the egg whites are foamy, increase the speed (to high for an electric mixer) and beat until stiff peaks form. If adding sugar, beat the whites just until soft peaks form, then beat in the sugar gradually and continue beating until the mixture holds stiff, shiny peaks.

coating with egg and crumbs: first dip the food to be coated into seasoned flour, turning to coat both sides, and shake off excess flour; then dip into beaten egg, moistening both sides; and finally, dip into fine bread crumbs, coating both sides and pressing lightly so the crumbs adhere.

dissolving gelatin: sprinkle the gelatin over liquid as specified in the recipe and let soften for about 5 minutes, then heat gently, without stirring, until the gelatin has completely dissolved.

peeling and seeding tomatoes: cut a small cross in the bottom of each tomato, then plunge into boiling water. Leave for about 10 seconds, or until the skin begins to peel away from the cuts, then lift out the tomatoes and immerse in cold water. As soon as the tomatoes are cool enough to handle, drain them and slip off the skin. To remove the seeds, cut each tomato in half crosswise. Gently squeeze each half and shake out the seeds; remove any remaining seeds with the tip of a teaspoon or your fingers.

roasting and peeling peppers: roast, grill, or broil the peppers until the skin is blistered and blackened all over, turning the peppers as necessary. Put the peppers in a plastic bag and let cool. Peel off the skins with the help of a small knife, then core and seed.

seeding chile peppers: cut each chile lengthwise in half, then scrape out the seeds and cut away the white ribs with a small knife. Take care not to touch your eyes or any other sensitive area when handling chiles, and be sure to wash your hands thoroughly in hot soapy water when you have finished.

crushing and chopping garlic: put a cook's knife flat on top of the garlic clove and bang the knife with the side of your fist to crush the garlic slightly. This will loosen the skin, which can then easily be peeled off. Crush the garlic further under the side of the knife, to flatten it completely. Then, according to the recipe instructions, coarsely or finely chop the garlic with the knife blade.

cooking dried beans: most dried beans need to be soaked for at least 8 hours, or overnight, in cold water before cooking (lentils and split peas are exceptions). Drain off the soaking water and replace with fresh water. To cook all dried beans, simmer in plenty of unsalted water until they are tender. The cooking time will vary according to the age and dryness of the bean, but in general most need 1¼ to 2 hours; split peas and lentils require less time. Add salt just before they're tender.

peeling peaches: as for tomatoes.

zesting citrus fruits: for large strips of zest, use a vegetable peeler to shave off just the colored part (the strips can then be cut into very thin shreds with a knife); for small, curled strips, use a canelle knife; for very fine filaments use a citrus zester. Zest can be grated using the fine holes of a box or other grater.

toasting and grinding nuts: spread the nuts on a baking sheet and toast in a preheated 350°F oven, stirring occasionally, until golden brown; or toast in a dry frying pan over moderate heat, stirring frequently. Grind nuts in a nut mill, clean coffee grinder or a food processor, taking care not to overgrind the nuts to an oily paste (adding a little sugar or flour will help prevent this).

making coconut milk: mix equal parts grated fresh or dried (desiccated) coconut and boiling water, then let cool; strain through cheesecloth, squeezing to extract all the liquid. Canned coconut milk will normally separate into thin milk with a thick layer at the top (which can be spooned off to use as coconut cream). For a thicker coconut milk, shake the can well before opening.

Index

ACKNOWLEDGMENTS

The Authors would like to thank the following:
Sophie Grigson, Dee MacQuillan and Robert Neild

The Publisher would like to thank the following for their invaluable assistance
in preparing this book:

Lewis Esson, for first suggesting a new edition of *The Cook Book*

Editorial
Tessa Clayton, Indexing Specialists, Jenny Linford, Kate Quarry, Jane Royston, Susanna Tee,
Kate Whiteman, Sarah Widdecombe, Simon Willis, Jeni Wright.

Photography and illustration
Meg Jansz (recipe home economist), Róisín Neild (recipe stylist), Amanda Hills (ingredients buyer and stylist),
Dave King and Allison Tyler (additional ingredients photography), Nato Welton (equipment stylist),
Denys Ovenden (new fish artworks), Susan Campbell/King and King (meat cut artworks).

Ingredients
City Herbs, New Spitalfields Market; C. Lidgates, London W11; Jarvis & Co., Kingston; R.A. Bevan & Son, Kingston;
Harrods Food Halls; Brogdale Horticultural Trust; Wild Harvest Mushrooms, London; Henry Doubleday Research Association;
Harvey Nichols Food Halls; Selfridges Food Halls; Idencroft Herb Nursery, Staplehurst; Yaohan Oriental Supermarket,
Colindale; G.M. & E.A. Innes, Newmachar, Aberdeen; Winterwood Soft Fruit Farm, Nr Maidstone; Remfresh, Colchester;
E.W. King's, Chertsey; Garson Farm, Esher; Potato Marketing Board; Vivians, Richmond; Mrs Tee's Wild Mushrooms,
Haslemere; C.R. Upton Pumpkins & Squashes, Arundel; Tawana Supermarket, London; Syon Park Garden Centre.

Equipment and props
Braun, The Conran Shop, Le Creuset, Divertimenti, Kenwood, Krups, Petra (Beam Group Ltd), Sabatier, Salter.

Contributors to the original edition of the book
Maria Kroll, Ann Sayer (contributors), Clive Corless (photography), Ingrid Jacob, Andrew Davidson, Paul Brooks (illustrators).

The
MEDICAL and HEALTH
ENCYCLOPEDIA

The
MEDICAL and HEALTH
ENCYCLOPEDIA

EDITED BY
RICHARD J. WAGMAN, M.D., F.A.C.P.
Associate Clinical Professor of Medicine
Downstate Medical Center
New York, New York

J. G. FERGUSON PUBLISHING COMPANY • CHICAGO, ILLINOIS

Portions of *The New Complete Medical and Health Encyclopedia* have
been previously published under the title of *The Complete Illustrated
Book of Better Health,* and *The Illustrated Encyclopedia of Better
Health,* edited by Richard J. Wagman, M.D.

Printed in the United States of America
S-8

Editor

Richard J. Wagman, M.D.,
F.A.C.P.
Associate Clinical Professor of
    Medicine
Downstate Medical Center
New York, New York

Consultant in Gynecology

Douglas S. Thompson, M.D.
Clinical Professor of Obstetrics and
    Gynecology and Clinical Associate
    Professor of Community Medicine
University of Pittsburgh School of
    Medicine
Pittsburgh, Pennsylvania

Consultant in Pediatrics

Charles H. Bauer, M.D.
Clinical Associate Professor of
    Pediatrics and Chief of Pediatric
    Gastroenterology
The New York Hospital-Cornell
    Medical Center
New York, New York

Consultants in Psychiatry

Julian J. Clark, M.D.
Assistant Professor of Psychiatry
                and
Rita W. Clark, M.D.
Clinical Assistant Professor of
    Psychiatry
Downstate Medical Center
New York, New York

Contents

INTRODUCTION

THE MEDICAL AND HEALTH ENCYCLOPEDIA provides for you answers to your health questions. This encyclopedia can serve as a guide for you in learning about and understanding the medical terms and conditions that you or your family may experience during your life. The books cover a wide range of topics, from skin care to how to choose a daycare center for your toddler.

We have compiled the most up-to-date information on health care, medicine, and treatment of diseases and illnesses. We give you thorough coverage on major diseases such as cancer and heart problems. We also cover the day-to-day changes that you experience from growing older. THE MEDICAL AND HEALTH ENCYCLOPEDIA takes you from health care for newborns through early childhood, to adolescence, adulthood, and the concerns of the middle and later years in life. Each stage provides fundamental information about what to expect, what happens, and how to find out if something is wrong.

To understand your health needs and problems, you need to have some knowledge of how your body works. We start the encyclopedia with a basic guide to your body and all its functioning parts. If you come across something in the chapters following, you can turn back to the first chapter to learn about that particular part of your body.

From there you can look up whatever concerns you about your health or your family's health. Simple problems like treating poison ivy rashes are explained. Problems that are serious or difficult to understand are also explained, like mastectomies and breast cancer. After you discuss a problem with your doctor, you can turn to THE MEDICAL AND HEALTH ENCYCLOPEDIA to see diagrams and illustrations of the body part affected and the types of surgery involved. This helps you to understand what is being discussed, and may also provide for you guidance for some questions you may have for the doctor.

The key to better health is preventing injuries and illness whenever possible. By following a healthy diet, combined with some exercise, you set yourself on a good start. THE MEDICAL AND HEALTH ENCYCLOPEDIA can give you some guidance about your diet and exercise needs. It also provides guidance for making you home a safe environment. The Medical Emergency section, edged in color for easy finding, includes how to provide first aid for injuries. It also guides you through making your home emergency-free. The chapter shows you how to eliminate some of the dangers you may have in your home without realizing it.

The best thing you can do for your family's and your own health is to learn about it. This set of books can give you the information you need about what to ask and what to expect of your doctor and your medical care. It can give you a good start on providing a safe, healthy, and happy life for you and those you love.

1

Your Body

The Skeleton

Say "skeleton" to children and you probably conjure up in their minds a rickety structure of rigid sticks, or, to the more fanciful child, a clickety-clacketing collection of rattling bones cavorting under a Halloween moon. A look at almost any anatomical drawing of the human skeletal system bears out the child's image: dry sticks of bones, stripped of skin and flesh, muscle and tendon—a grotesque caricature of a living human being.

Our living bones are something quite different. They are rigid, yes, but not entirely so: they also may bend a little and grow and repair themselves; and they are shaped and fitted so that—rather than the herky-jerky motions of a wooden puppet—they permit the smooth grace and co-ordination power displayed by an accomplished athlete or a prima ballerina.

Our bones do not do just one thing but many things. Some bones, like the collarbone or *clavicle*, mainly give support to other body structures. Others, like the skull and ribs, encase and protect vulnerable organs. Still others, like the *metacarpus* and *phalanges* that make up our hands and fingers, give us mechanical advan-

tages—leverage and movement. There are even bones, the tiny *ossicles* in the middle ear, whose vibrations enable us to hear.

Finally, to think of bone simply as a structural member, like a solid steel girder in a skyscraper, ignores the fact that bone is living tissue. It is one of the busiest tissues in our bodies, a chemical factory that is continually receiving, processing and shipping a wide variety of mineral salts, blood components, and a host of other vital materials.

How the Bones of the Skeletal System Fit and Work Together

Medical textbooks name a total of 206 bones making up the skeletal system of the normal, adult human being. The words "normal" and "adult" are significant. A newborn baby normally has 33 vertebrae making up its backbone (also called *spinal column* or simply *spine*); but by the time a person reaches adulthood, the number of individual vertebrae has shrunk to 26. The explanation: during the growth process, the nine bottom vertebrae

fuse naturally into just two. In like fashion, we "lose" some 60 bones as we grow up. Some otherwise perfectly normal adults have "extra" bones or "missing" bones. For example, although the normal number of ribs is 12 pairs, some adults may have 11; others may have 13 pairs.

Even a practicing physician might be hard-pressed to identify each of our 200-plus bones and describe its function. An easier way to gain a general understanding of the various functions, capabilities—and weaknesses, too—of our bones is to visualize the skeletal system as a standing coatrack, say, about six feet high.

Call the central pole the backbone. About ten inches down from its top (the top of your skull) is a horizontal crossbar (your shoulders—collarbones and shoulder blades), approximately a foot-and-a-half across. Sixteen or so inches below the bottom of the top crossbar is another, shorter crossbar, broader and thicker—the *pelvic girdle*. The coatrack with its two crossbars is now a crude model of the bones of the head and trunk, collectively called the *axial skeleton*. Its basic unit is the backbone, to which are attached the skull at the top, then the bones of the shoulder girdle, the ribs, and at the bottom, the bones of the pelvic girdle.

By hanging down (or appending) members from the two ends of the top crossbar, and doing the same at the lower crossbar, we would simulate what is called the *appendicular skeleton*—arms and hands, legs and feet.

Now, make the coatrack stand on its new legs, cut off the central pole just below the lower bar (if you wish, calling it man's lost tail), and you have the two main components of the skeletal system, joined together before you. Let us look at each more closely.

The Axial Skeleton

Within the framework of the axial skeleton lie all the most vital organs of the body. People have gone on living with the loss of a hand or a leg—indeed, with the loss of any or all of their limbs. But nobody can live without a brain, a heart, a liver, lungs, or kidneys—all of which are carried within the framework of the axial skeleton.

The Skull

The bones of the skull have as their most important function the protection of the brain and sense organs.

There are also, of course, the jawbones that support the teeth and gums and which enable us to bite and chew our food.

Most of the skull appears to consist of a single bone—a hard, unbroken dome. Actually, the brain cage or *cranium* consists of eight individual platelike bones which have fused together in the process of growth. At birth, these bones are separated, causing the soft spots or *fontanelles* we can readily feel on a baby's head. As the baby's brain enlarges, the bones grow along their edges to fill in the fontanelles, finally knitting together in what are called *suture lines*, somewhat resembling inexpertly mended clothes seams. Along the suture lines, the skull bones continue to grow until the individual's mature skull size is reached.

Teeth

The hardest substance in the human body is the *enamel* that covers the exposed surface of a tooth. Below the gum, the tooth's outside surface is composed of somewhat softer *cementum*. Beneath enamel and cementum is a bonelike substance, called *dentin*, which covers the soft interior of the tooth, called *pulp*. Pulp is serviced by blood vessels and nerves through the root or roots of the tooth. The passageway of nerves and blood vessels that lead up through the tooth from the gum sockets is called a *root canal*. Tooth and gum are stuck to each other by a tough, adhesive tissue called *periodontal* (or peridental—"surrounding the tooth") *membrane*. See Ch. 22, *The Teeth and Gums*, for further information on teeth.

The Backbone

At the base of the skull, the backbone begins. The skull is supported by the

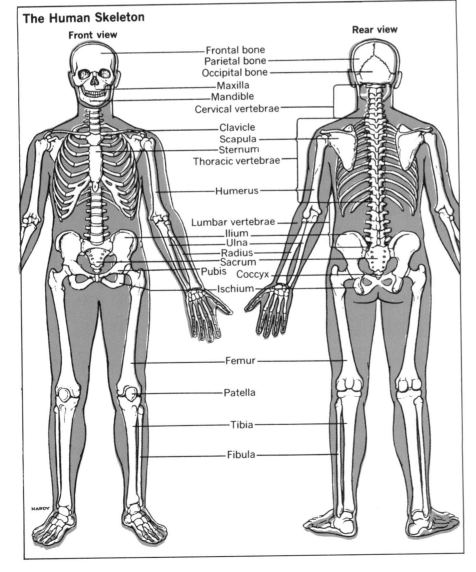

The Human Skeleton

Front view

Frontal bone
Parietal bone
Occipital bone
Maxilla
Mandible
Cervical vertebrae
Clavicle
Scapula
Sternum
Thoracic vertebrae
Humerus
Lumbar vertebrae
Ilium
Ulna
Radius
Sacrum
Pubis
Coccyx
Ischium
Femur
Patella
Tibia
Fibula

Rear view

HARDY

topmost *cervical* (neck) vertebra. The curious thing about a backbone is that the word has come to suggest something solid, straight, and unbending. The backbone, however, just isn't like that: it consists of 26 knobby, hollowed-out bones—*vertebrae,* rather improbably held together by muscles, ligaments, and tendons. It is not straight when we stand, but has definite backward and forward curvatures; and even some of its most important structures (the disks between the vertebrae) aren't made of bone, but of cartilage.

All in all, however, the backbone is a fairly well designed structure in terms of the several different functions it serves—but with some built-in weaknesses. For a discussion of backache, see Ch. 23, *Aches, Pains, Nuisances, Worries.*

The Vertebrae

Although they will have features in common, no two of our 26 vertebrae are exactly alike in shape, size, or function. This is hardly surprising if we consider, for example, that the cervical vertebrae do not support ribs, while the *thoracic* vertebrae (upper trunk, or chest) do support them.

But for a sample vertebra, let us pick a rib-carrying vertebra, if for no other reason than that it lies about midway along the backbone. If viewed from above or below, a thoracic vertebra, like most of the others, would look like a roundish piece of bone with roughly scalloped edges on the side facing inward toward the chest and on the side facing outward toward the surface of the back, and would reveal several bony projections. These knobby portions of a vertebra—some of which you can feel as bumps along your backbone—are called *processes.* They serve as the vertebra's points of connection to muscles and tendons,

to ribs, and to the other vertebrae above and below.

A further conspicuous feature is a hole, more or less in the middle of the typical vertebra, through which passes the master nerve bundle of our bodies, the spinal cord, running from the base of the skull to the top of the pelvis. Thus, one of the important functions of the backbone is to provide flexible, protective tubing for the spinal cord.

Between the bones of one vertebra and the next is a piece of more resilient cartilage that acts as a cushion or shock absorber to prevent two vertebrae from scraping or bumping each other if the backbone gets a sudden jolt, or as the backbone twists and turns and bends. These pieces of cartilage are the intervertebral disks—infamous for pain and misery if they become ruptured or slipped disks.

Regions of the Backbone

The backbone can be divided into five regions, starting with the uppermost, or *cervical* region, which normally has seven vertebrae. Next down is the *thoracic* (chest) section, normally with 12 vertebrae. From each vertebra a rib extends to curl protectively around the chest area. Usually, the top ten ribs come all the way around the trunk and attach to the breastbone (or *sternum*); but the bottom two ribs do not reach the breastbone and are thus called floating ribs. The thoracic section also must support the shoulder girdle, consisting of the collarbones (*clavicles*) and shoulder blades (*scapulas*). At the end of each shoulder blade is a shoulder joint—actually three distinct joints working together—where the arm connects to the axial skeleton.

Below the thoracic vertebrae come the five vertebrae of the *lumbar* sec-

tion. This area gets a good deal of blame for back miseries: lower back pain often occurs around the area where the bottom thoracic vertebra joins the top lumbar vertebra. Furthermore, the lumbar region or small of the back is also a well-known site of back pain; indeed, from the word "lumbar" comes *lumbago,* medically an imprecise term, but popularly used to describe very real back pain.

Below the lumbar region are two vertebrae so completely different from the 24 above them—and even from each other—that it seems strange they are called vertebrae at all: the *sacrum* and the *coccyx.* These two vertebrae are both made up of several distinct vertebrae that are present at birth. The sacrum is a large bone that was once five vertebrae. The coccyx was originally four vertebrae—and, incidentally, is all that remains of man's tail in his evolution from the primates.

The Pelvic Girdle

The sacrum is the more important of these two strange-looking vertebrae. It is the backbone's connection to the *pelvic girdle,* or pelvis. On each side of the sacrum, connected by the sacroiliac joint, is a very large, curving bone called the *ilium,* tilting (when we stand) slightly forward and downward from the sacrum toward the front of the groin. We feel the top of the ilium as the top of the hip—a place mothers and fathers often find convenient for toting a toddler.

Fused at each side of the ilium and slanting toward the back is the *ischium,* the bone we sit on. The two *pubis* bones, also fused to the ilium, meet in front to complete the pelvic girdle. All the bones of the pelvis—ilium, ischium, and pubis—fuse together so as to form the hip joint (*acetabulum*), a deep socket into which the "ball" or upper end of the thigh-bone fits.

The Appendicular Skeleton

The bones of the appendages—arms, hands, and fingers; legs, feet, and toes—allow human beings to perform an astonishing array of complex movements, from pushing themselves through the physical rigors of the Olympic decathlon to creating an elaborate piece of needlework. The key points in the appendicular skeleton, as indeed, in the axial skeleton, are where the ends or edges of bones lie close together and must work with or against one another in order to achieve coordinated movement. These key points are the *joints*—not really bones at all but the non-bony spaces between bones.

The Joints

A typical joint consists of several different structures. First, there are the bones themselves—two, three, four, or more almost touching in the area of the joint—with their ends or edges shaped to fit in their respective niches. Between the bones of an appendage joint (as between the verte-

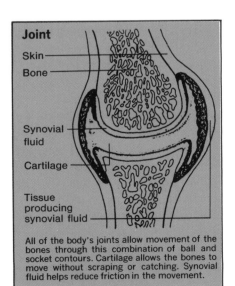

Joint

Skin
Bone

Synovial fluid

Cartilage

Tissue producing synovial fluid

All of the body's joints allow movement of the bones through this combination of ball and socket contours. Cartilage allows the bones to move without scraping or catching. Synovial fluid helps reduce friction in the movement.

brae of the back) is the smooth, resilient material called *cartilage* that allows the bones to move over one another without scraping or catching. At the joint, the bones, with their layer of cartilage between them, are held together by tough bonds of muscle. *Bursas,* tiny sacs containing a lubricating fluid, are also found at joints; they help to reduce the friction between a joint's moving parts.

The Hip and Knee

The hip joint must not only support the weight of the head and trunk, but must allow for movement of the leg and also play a part in the constant balancing required to maintain upright posture. Similar stresses and strains, often literally tending to tear the joint apart, are placed on every joint in the body.

The notoriety of athletes' bad knees attests to the forces battering at the knee joint, the largest in the human body. Sports involving leaping or sudden changes in direction, such as basketball, are especially hard on the knee. However, the fact that there are not more disabled sports heroes speaks well for the design of the knee joint. The same can be said of the ankle joint and the joints of the foot and toes.

The Shoulder, Elbow, and Wrist

The counterpart of the hip joint in the upper trunk is the shoulder joint. Free of weight-bearing responsibilities, the shoulder has a system of three interconnected joints that allow it and the arm far more versatile movements than the hip and leg.

The elbow connects the upper arm bone (*humerus*) with the two bones of the lower arm (*radius* and *ulna*). Like the knee, it is basically a hinge joint, which allows the lower arm to be

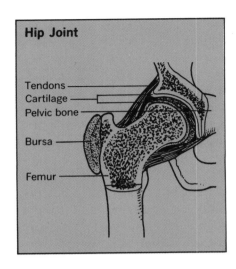

Hip Joint

Tendons
Cartilage
Pelvic bone

Bursa

Femur

raised and lowered. The elbow is also constructed to allow some rotation by the hand; likewise, the knee joint allows us to waggle the foot.

Of all our body parts, the wrist, hand, and fingers are perhaps the most elegantly and finely jointed—witness the performance of a concert pianist—and our ankles, feet, and toes probably the most subject to everyday misery.

Bone as Living Tissue

Our bones, like all our tissues, change as we grow up, mature, and finally grow old. There are changes in the chemical activity and composition of bone representative of each stage of life.

In young children, the ends and edges of bones are mainly cartilage, forming a growing surface on the bone that is gradually replaced by hard bone as full size is attained. The bones of a child are more pliable and less likely to break than those of a full-grown adult.

Similarly, as an adult ages, the bones turn from a resilient hardness to a more brittle hardness. This accounts for the much greater danger of broken bones in older people.

These changes with age are an indication of the great amount of chemical activity going on within bone. We sometimes forget that our bones are amply supplied and penetrated by blood vessels. There is a constant building up and breaking down, an interchange of materials between blood and bone.

The Composition of Bone

A living bone does not have a single uniform composition, but instead is composed of several different kinds of tissue. To begin with, there are actually two types of bone tissue in the same bone: compact and spongy. In addition, bone is sheathed in a tough membranous tissue called the *periosteum,* interlaced with blood vessels. Finally, within most of the larger and longer bones of the body, as well as in the interior of the skull bones and vertebrae, are two more kinds of tissue: red marrow and yellow marrow.

Marrow

Within the spongy bone areas, *red marrow* produces enormous numbers of red blood cells, at a rate of millions per minute. These are needed for growth as well as for replacement of red cells, which also die in enormous numbers. Children's bones contain greater proportions of red marrow than adults'. With age, *yellow marrow,* composed mainly of fat cells, begins to fill the interior bone cavities formerly occupied by red marrow.

Calcium

Bone also serves as a storage and distribution center for one of the most important elements in our body. Calcium, in the form of calcium phosphate, is the basic chemical of bone tissue, but this element also must always be present in the bloodstream at a certain level to ensure normal heartbeat, blood clotting, and muscle contraction. When the calcium level in the blood is deficient, the bones release some calcium into the bloodstream; when the blood has a surplus of calcium, the bones reabsorb it.

Fractures

Like most other tissues, broken bone can repair itself, and it is a remarkable process to observe. It is a process, however, that will proceed even if the ends are not aligned or set—an important reason why any suspected fracture should be checked by a physician.

A break in a bone causes a sticky material to be deposited by the blood around the broken ends. This material begins the formation of a kind of protective, lumpy sleeve, called a *callus,* around the broken ends. Mainly cartilage, the callus hardens into spongy bone, normally within a month or two. Then, the spongy bone begins to be reduced in size by bone-dissolving cells produced in the marrow, while at the same time the spongy bone in the area of the break is beginning to be replaced by hard bone.

Depending on the particular bone involved and the severity of the fracture, the broken bone can be completely healed within four to ten months.

Potential Trouble Spots

Essentially there are two kinds of things that can go wrong with the skeletal system and cause trouble.

Mechanical Difficulties

A healthy bone's main mechanical functions—support, movement, protection—can be impaired. This can happen as a result of a physical injury resulting in a fracture or dislocation.

The stack of vertebrae called the backbone is vulnerable to a number of painful conditions from top to bottom, especially in the region of the lower back. Unfortunately, man seems to have evolved relatively quickly from a four-footed creature, and his backbone is not ideally suited for standing and walking on two feet. Back troubles become increasingly common with age.

Areas where bones interact are also very susceptible to injury because of the stresses and strains they undergo even in people who are not

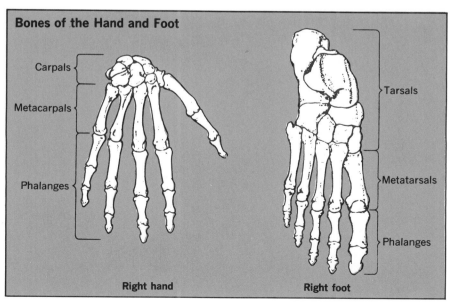

Bones of the Hand and Foot

Carpals

Metacarpals

Phalanges

Right hand

Tarsals

Metatarsals

Phalanges

Right foot

especially active. Normal wear and tear also takes its toll on our bones and joints; for example, the bones' structure or their alignment at a joint may be altered slightly with age, making one bone or another prone to slipping out of the joint causing a dislocation. In any case, it is not advisable to make the same demands on our skeletal system at 40 as we did at 20. Joints are also the site of arthritis.

Disease

Second, and generally more serious if untreated, the interior bone tissues themselves may become infected and diseased. This can lead as a secondary effect to impairment of the bones' mechanical functions. *Osteomyelitis,* for example, a bacterial infection of bony tissues, can destroy large portions of bone unless antibiotics are started at once.

Fortunately, disorders of the skeletal system generally reveal themselves early and clearly by pain. Any severe or lingering pain of the joints or bones should be reported to a physician. For example, some people may feel that aching feet are unavoidable—and a little undignified. But a foot is not meant to hurt, nor is any part of the skeletal system. Consulting a physician could prevent much present and future misery. See also Ch. 7, *Diseases of the Skeletal System.*

The Muscles

Some 600 muscles of all sizes and shapes are attached to the framework of the skeletal system. Altogether these muscles make up nearly half of a normal adult's weight. They hold the skeleton together and, on signals originating in the brain, empower its various parts to move. Everywhere throughout the skeletal system, muscles work together with bones to protect the body's vital organs and to support and move its parts.

Skeletal Muscle

Such muscles are called, collectively, *skeletal muscle.* They are also called *voluntary muscles* because, for the most part, we can choose when we want them to act and what we want them to do—drive a car, kick a football, turn a page, jump a brook, ride a bicycle. Skeletal muscle also goes by two other names, based on its appearance under a microscope—striped and striated.

Skeletal, voluntary, striped, striated—all refer to the same general type of muscle. To avoid confusion, the term used throughout this section is skeletal muscle.

Smooth Muscle

There are two other general types of muscle. One is called *smooth muscle* because, under the microscope, it lacks the clearly defined stripes of skeletal muscle. Smooth muscle has another name, *involuntary muscle,* so called because the brain does not voluntarily control its actions. Smooth muscle is responsible for movements such as the muscular action that moves food and waste along the

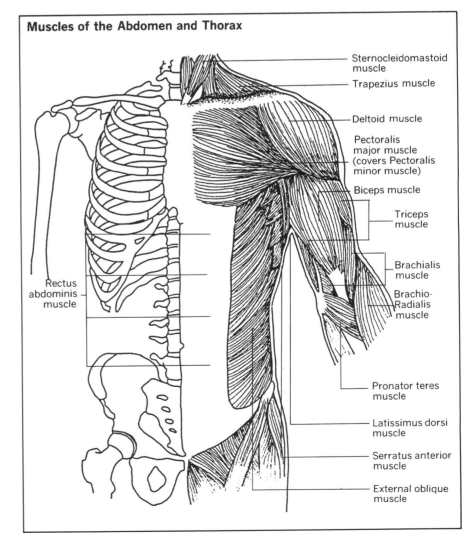

Muscles of the Abdomen and Thorax

Sternocleidomastoid muscle
Trapezius muscle
Deltoid muscle
Pectoralis major muscle (covers Pectoralis minor muscle)
Biceps muscle
Triceps muscle
Brachialis muscle
Brachio-Radialis muscle
Pronator teres muscle
Latissimus dorsi muscle
Serratus anterior muscle
External oblique muscle
Rectus abdominis muscle

digestive tract, or the contraction and dilation of the pupil of the eye, as well as countless other involuntary movements of the sense and internal organs—with the exception of the heart.

Cardiac Muscle

The third and last general type of muscle is confined to the heart area, and is called *cardiac muscle.* (Cardiac means having to do with the heart.) It is involved in the rhythmic beating and contractions of the heart, which are not under conscious control, and cardiac muscle is therefore termed involuntary.

Structure of the Muscles

Each of the three kinds of muscle shares certain structural similarities with one or both of the others. All are made up of bundles of varying numbers of hair-thin fibers. In skeletal and smooth muscles, these fibers are lined up side by side in the bundle, while in cardiac muscle the fibers tend more to crisscross over one another. Skeletal muscle and cardiac muscle are both striped, that is, they show darker and lighter bands crossing over a group of adjacent fibers, while smooth muscle lacks these distinct cross-bands.

Both involuntary muscle types, smooth and cardiac, are controlled by signals carried by the autonomic nervous system. Signals that result in movements of the skeletal muscles are carried by a different nerve network, the central nervous system. The individual fibers in a muscle bundle with a particular function all react simultaneously to a signal from the nervous system; there is no apparent time lag from fiber to fiber.

How the Skeletal Muscles Work

The great range and variety of functions served by skeletal muscles can be suggested by naming just four: the diaphragm, used in breathing; the muscles that make the eye wink; the deltoid muscle that gives the shoulder its shape; and the tongue.

As with the bones, the body tends to make its greatest demands on muscle tissue in the area of the joints and the backbone. A smoothly functioning joint requires that bone, cartilage, and muscle all be sound and able to work together effectively.

Tendons and Ligaments

We often hear the words tendon and ligament used in the description of the knee or another joint. These are actually two types of skeletal muscles, distinguished as to their function.

A *tendon* can be described as a tight cord of muscle tissue that attaches other skeletal muscle to bone. For example, the Achilles tendon running down the back of the calf, the strongest tendon in the body, connects the muscles of the calf with the bone of the heel. A *ligament* is a somewhat more elastic band of muscle fibers that attaches bone to bone.

A tendon is not always evident in the connection of muscle to bone. Various groups and shapes of muscle fibers may be similarly employed,

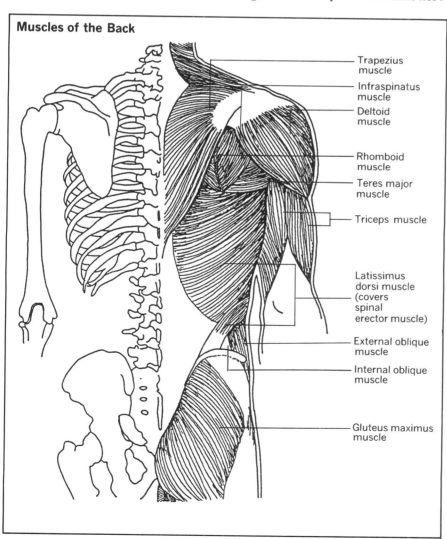

Muscles of the Back

- Trapezius muscle
- Infraspinatus muscle
- Deltoid muscle
- Rhomboid muscle
- Teres major muscle
- Triceps muscle
- Latissimus dorsi muscle (covers spinal erector muscle)
- External oblique muscle
- Internal oblique muscle
- Gluteus maximus muscle

Tendon

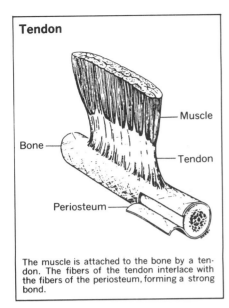

The muscle is attached to the bone by a tendon. The fibers of the tendon interlace with the fibers of the periosteum, forming a strong bond.

Muscles, Their Locations, and Exercises that Strengthen Them

Muscle	Location	Movement
Trapezius	Upper back and each side of neck	Shoulder-shrugging and upward-pulling movements
Deltoids	Shoulders	Arm raising and overhead pressing
Pectorals	Chest	Horizontal pressing and drawing arms across body
Latissimus dorsi	Wide back muscle stretching over back up to rear Deltoids	Pulling and rowing movements
Serratus	Jagged sawtooth muscles between Pectorals and lattissimus Dorsi	Pullover and Serratus leverage movements
Spinal erectors	Lower length of spinal column	Raising upper body from a bent-over position
Biceps	Front portion of upper arm	Arm bending and twisting
Forearms	Between wrist and elbow	Reverse-grip arm bending
Triceps	Back of upper arm	Pushing and straightening movements of upper arms
Rectus abdominals	Muscular area between sternum and pelvis	Sit-up, leg-raising, knee-in movements
Intercostals	Sides of waist, running diagonally to Serratus	Waist twisting
External oblique abdominals	Lower sides of waist	Waist twisting and bending
Buttocks	Muscular area covering seat	Lunging, stooping, leg raising
Leg biceps	Back of thighs	Raising lower leg to buttocks, bending forward and stretching
Frontal thighs	Front of thighs	Extending lower leg and knee bending
Calves	Lower leg between ankle and knee	Raising and lowering on toes

forming connective tissue without the formation of tendon.

Various associated tissues between or around skeletal muscles serve to reduce the wear and tear of friction in areas such as a joint, where muscle, bone, and cartilage may rub against one another. For example, the tendons that pass along the back of the hand from the wrist to the fingertips, as well as many other muscle groups throughout the body, are enclosed in lubricated sheaths. The muscle-sheathed *bursas,* lined inside with lubricating fluid, are also found in areas subject to friction, such as where a tendon passes closely over a bone.

Man's upright posture and two-legged locomotion subject the backbone to heavy stresses. It is buttressed, however, with scores of tightly packed bundles of muscle attached to either side of the spinal column.

Flexors and Extensors

Most of us probably first used the word "muscle" when, as children, we watched an older child or adult flex an arm and proudly display the bump of muscle between the crook of elbow and shoulder. This biceps muscle works together with the triceps muscle on the underside of the arm. The arm is bent at the elbow by contraction of the biceps, which makes this muscle get shorter and thicker; in this position, called *flexion,* the triceps muscle is relaxed. To return the arm to its normal straight position, called *extension,* the biceps relaxes and the triceps contracts. In this bit of muscle teamwork, the biceps, which bends the arm at the elbow joint, is called the *flexor,* while the triceps straightens the arm and is called the *extensor.* Similar flexor–extensor action can be observed at many body joints, including the fingers.

Smooth Muscle

Beginning about midway down the esophagus, layers of smooth muscle line the walls of the 25 feet of digestive tract, extending into the stomach and through the intestines. These muscles keep the stomach and intes-

Muscle Action in Forearm Movement

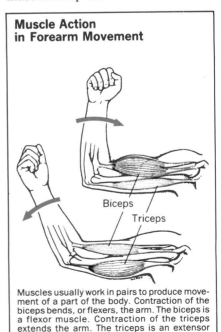

Muscles usually work in pairs to produce movement of a part of the body. Contraction of the biceps bends, or flexers, the arm. The biceps is a flexor muscle. Contraction of the triceps extends the arm. The triceps is an extensor muscle.

tinal walls continually in motion, constricting and relaxing to push food along. Smooth muscle also effects the opening and closing of important valves, called *sphincters,* along the digestive tract.

Trouble Spots

The functions and failures of the skeletal muscles are closely allied to those of the skeletal system. The same areas are vulnerable—joints and back—and the same rule holds: severe or persistent muscle pain is a cause to consult your physician.

Hernia

One type of disorder associated exclusively with a weakness or abnormality of muscle is a rupture or *hernia.* This is the protrusion of part of another organ through a gap in the protective muscle. A likely area for a hernia to appear is in the muscles lining the abdomen, although hernias may occur in any other part of the body where there is pressure against a muscle wall that is not as strong as it should be. Weight control and a sensible program of exercise—abdominal muscles being particularly liable to slackness—are good preventive measures against hernia.

All our muscles, in fact, benefit from regular exercise; but you don't have to exhaust yourself physically every day to reach and maintain the desirable plateau physicians describe as good muscle tone.

Atrophy of Muscle Tissue

Muscle tissues are likely to *atrophy* (shrink and weaken) if they are not used for too long a time. Thus, illness or injuries that cause paralysis or an extended period of immobility for the body or a part of it must be followed by a supervised program of physical therapy.   See also Ch. 8, *Diseases of the Muscles and Nervous System.*

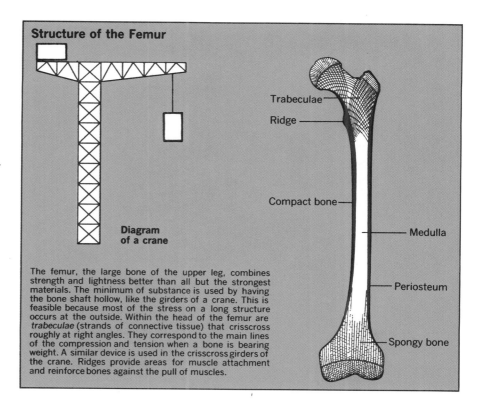

Structure of the Femur

Trabeculae
Ridge
Compact bone
Medulla
Periosteum
Spongy bone

Diagram of a crane

The femur, the large bone of the upper leg, combines strength and lightness better than all but the strongest materials. The minimum of substance is used by having the bone shaft hollow, like the girders of a crane. This is feasible because most of the stress on a long structure occurs at the outside. Within the head of the femur are *trabeculae* (strands of connective tissue) that crisscross roughly at right angles. They correspond to the main lines of the compression and tension when a bone is bearing weight. A similar device is used in the crisscross girders of the crane. Ridges provide areas for muscle attachment and reinforce bones against the pull of muscles.

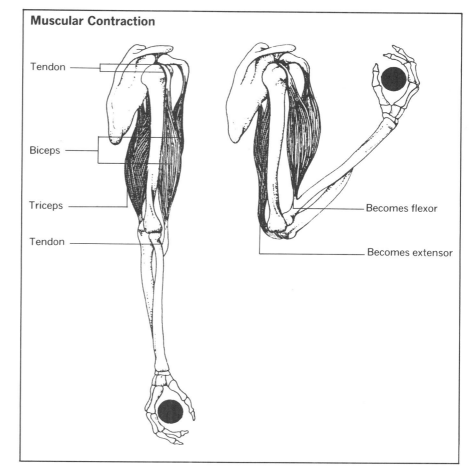

Muscular Contraction

Tendon
Biceps
Triceps
Tendon
Becomes flexor
Becomes extensor

Skin, Hair, and Nails

Perhaps no other organ of the human body receives so much attention both from its owner and the eyes of others as the skin and its associated structures—hair and nails.

Vanity is hardly the issue. The simple facts are that skin is the last frontier of our internal selves, the final boundary between our inside and outside, and our principal first line of defense against the dangers of the outside world. It shows, not always clearly, evidence of some internal disorders; and it shows, often quite clearly, the evidence of external affronts—a bump, a cut, a chafe, an insect bite, or an angry reaction to the attack of germs.

In personal encounters, the unclothed portion of our skin is one of the first things other people observe, and—if we happen to have some unsightly scratch, rash, or blemish—the last thing by which we wish to be remembered. Of all our organs, the skin is the most likely candidate for a program of self-improvement.

The Organ Called Skin

It is always a little surprising to hear, for the first time, the skin referred to as a single organ. This is not to say it is a simple organ; on the contrary, it is an exceedingly complex and varied one. However, despite variations in appearance from part to part of the body, our entire outer wrapper (the more technical word is *integument*) is similarly constructed.

One might object: "But my nails and hair certainly look different from the skin on my nose!" This is perfectly true, but nails and hair are extensions of the skin, and wherever they occur are composed of similar tissues: the nail on a little toe is made of the same material as the hair.

Functions of the Skin

The skin has three main functions, and its different outward appearance on different parts of the body reflects to some extent which of these functions a certain area of skin primarily serves. The three main functions are protection (from germs or blows), temperature control (e.g., through perspiration, to aid in keeping the body's internal organs near our normal internal temperature of 98.6° F.), and perception. Nerve endings in the skin give us our sensations of touch, pain, heat, and cold. Associated with the skin's important role in temperature regulation is its function as an organ of excretion—the elimination, via perspiration, and subsequent evaporation of water and other substances. Skin is also the site of the body's natural production of vitamin D, stimulated by exposure to sunlight.

Anatomy of the Skin

Skin has three more or less distinct layers. The outermost is called the *epidermis;* the middle, the *dermis;* and the innermost, *subcutaneous* (underskin) tissue. The epidermis may also be called *cuticle;* and the dermis either *corium* or *true skin.*

The Subcutaneous Layer

The subcutaneous layer is really a rather vague border zone between muscle and bone tissues on one side, and the dermis on the other, a kind of springy, fatty padding that gives bounce and a look of firmness to the skin above it. With age, the fatty cells of the subcutaneous layer are not continually replaced as they die, and this layer tends to thin out. The result is wrinkles, which form where the outer layers of skin lose their subcutaneous support, much like the slipcover of a cushion that has lost some of its stuffing.

Anatomy of the Skin

Approximate depth of section shown

Sebaceous glands

The epidermis has been lifted to show the papillae on the dermal layer. The pattern of these papillae creates the fingerprints.

Epidermis

Dermis

Subcutaneous tissue

Touch receptor

Sweat gland

Pressure receptor nerve ending

Capillary tufts bring blood close to surface for cooling.

Erector pili muscle causes gooseflesh.

Hair follicle

Nutrient blood vessel to hair follicle

The Dermis

The dermis is serviced by the multitude of tiny blood vessels and nerve fibers that reach it through the subcutaneous tissue. In addition, many special structures and tissues that enable the skin to perform its various functions are found in the dermis: *sebaceous* (skin oil) glands and sweat glands; minuscule muscles; and the roots of hairs encased in narrow pits called *follicles*.

The topmost layer of the dermis, interconnecting with the epidermis above it, resembles, under a microscope, nothing so much as a rugged, ridge-crossed landscape carved with valleys, caves, and tunnels. The basic forms of this microscopic terrain are cone-shaped hills called *papillae;* between 100 and 200 million of them are found in the dermis of an adult human being.

Because the dermal papillae serve as the bedrock for the surface layer of skin, the epidermis, we can understand why there is really no such thing as smooth skin; even the smoothest patch of a baby's skin appears ridged and cratered under a magnifying glass.

The distribution of papillae in the skin falls into certain distinctive patterns that are particularly conspicuous on the soles of babies' feet and on the fingertips, and give each of us our unique finger, toe, and footprints. The mathematical possibility of one person having the same fingerprints as another is thought to be about one in 25 billion. The papillae ridges on the fingertips also make it easier for us to pick up and handle such things as needles or pencils or buttons.

Finally, because there are relatively more papillae concentrated at the fingertips than on most other areas of the body, and because papillae are often associated with dense concentrations of nerve endings, the fingertips tend to be more responsive to touch sensations than other parts of the body.

The Epidermis

The bottom layer of the epidermis, its papillae fitted into the pockets of the layers of the dermis beneath it, is occupied by new young cells. These cells gradually mature and move upward. As they near the surface of the skin, they die, becoming tough, horny, lifeless tissue. This is the outmost layer of the epidermis, called the *stratum corneum* (horny layer), which we are continually shedding, usually unnoticed, as when we towel off after a bath, but sometimes very noticeably, as when we peel after a sunburn.

A suntan, incidentally, is caused by the presence of tiny grains of pigment, called *melanin,* in the bottom layers of epidermis. Sunlight stimulates the production of melanin, giving the skin a darker color. A suntan fades as the melanin granules move to the surface and are shed with dead skin cells.

Hair and Nails

Certainly the most noticeable of the specialized forms of skin are our hair and nails. What we see of them is really a dead tissue, called *keratin,* similar to the dead skin cells that are continually being shed by our bodies, but much more firmly packed together. However, hair and nails both originate in cells that are very much alive—as anyone who has plucked a group of hairs or suffered the pain of a torn-out nail knows very well. Growth occurs in this living region, with new cells pushing the dead, hard hair and nail stalks upward, then dying themselves and being replaced from below.

The bottom end or root of a hair is

Fingerprint

The pattern of ridges in a fingerprint reflects the contours of the papillae (conelike bumps) of the upper layer of the dermis, just below the epidermis.

lodged, as noted above, in a *follicle,* a hollow resembling a rounded bottle with a long, narrow neck slanting toward the skin's surface. Each follicle is supported by the little hummock of a papilla, and is serviced by tiny oil glands that lubricate the shaft (or neck) through which the hair pushes toward the surface.

The follicles of the long hairs of the scalp, groin, and armpits may be found deep in the subcutaneous layers of the skin; others are no deeper than the top layers of dermis. Attached to a follicle are microscopic muscle fibers that, if stimulated by cold or emotional factors, can contract around the follicle; the result is gooseflesh or sometimes even the sensation that our hair is standing on end.

A nail's living, growing part is found beneath the whitish half moon, or *lunula,* at its base. The lunula is sometimes obscured because a layer of epidermis (cuticle) has grown over it. Except at its very top (the part we can trim without pain), the nail is firmly attached to the ridged upper layer of the dermis, a region richly laced with tiny blood vessels.

Oil Glands

The skin's oil-producing (or *seba-*

ceous) glands are almost always associated with hair follicles, into which they seep their oils (or *sebum*). The oily substance works its way up toward the surface, lubricating both the hair and outer layers of epidermis, which need continual lubrication in order to stay soft and flexible. Also, skin oils serve as a kind of protective coat against painful drying and chapping.

Sweat Glands and Blood Vessels

While everybody is aware that the amount we perspire is related to the temperature around us, not everybody is aware that the countless tiny blood vessels in our skin—some 15 feet of them coursing beneath every square inch of skin—also react to changes in outside temperatures. Working together, and both controlled by an automatic "thermostat" in our brain, sweat glands and blood vessels have the all-important role of keeping our internal organs near their normal 98.6° Fahrenheit temperature.

The trick in maintaining an internal body temperature near normal is to conserve body heat when it is colder outside and to lose heat when it is warmer. Blood circulating near the surface of the skin is warmed (gains heat) or cooled (loses heat) according to the outside temperature.

The skin's myriad blood vessels constrict when the outside temperature is colder. This means that less blood can come into contact with the colder outside air, and therefore the overall temperature level of the blood remains warmer than if the blood vessels had not become constricted. On the other hand, when the body needs to lose heat—for example, during and after a vigorous tennis match—the skin's blood vessels dilate. This accounts for the "heat flush" or reddening of skin that light-skinned people exhibit when very heated.

Sweat glands aid in temperature regulation by secreting moisture, which, evaporating on the skin's surface, cools the skin and therefore the blood flowing beneath it. Moisture that does not evaporate but remains as liquid on the skin or runs off in rivulets is not efficient in cooling. Humid air tends to prevent evaporation, while moving air or wind aids it. Sweat that evaporates as soon as it reaches the skin's surface usually goes unnoticed. Fresh sweat has no odor; but if it remains without evaporating, bacteria begin to give it the odor known medically as *bromhidrosis*.

There are some two million sweat glands in the skin. Each consists of a coiled, corkscrewlike tube that tunnels its way up to the surface of the skin from the dermis or from the deeper subcutaneous layer.

Potential Trouble Spots

All of us are very conscious of the condition of our skin and worry when something seems to be wrong with it. The temptations to worry too much, to overtreat, to take the advice of a well-meaning friend, to use the wrong (but heavily advertised) product are very great. Knowing about the properties of the skin and what medical knowledge has to say about skin problems can help to avoid mistakes in caring for it. See Ch. 21, *Skin and Hair.* For a discussion of adolescent skin problems, see also Ch. 3, *The Teens.*

The Nervous System and the Brain

Most of us have heard often enough that the brain, acting as control center for a communication network we call our nervous system, is an incredible computer, weighing a mere three pounds. Its form and functions, however, are often described as being so much more intricate and complex than any existing or imagined computer that thorough knowledge of the brain seems very remote. This is certainly true. But it doesn't prevent us from knowing some general things about the brain and nervous system, or what its most significant parts are and how they work.

Basically, the nervous system has just two functions: first, getting information (impulses, signals, messages) from outside or inside the body to where it can be acted upon, usually in the brain; and secondly, feeding back information (for example, to the muscles) so that the indicated action can be taken. Thus, nerves can be divided by their function into two general types, each following a separate pathway. Those that receive information—for example, from our senses—and pass it along are called *sensory,* or *afferent* (inward-traveling). Those that relay information back, with a directive for action, are called *motor,* or *efferent* (outward-traveling).

The brain and the spinal cord can be considered as the basic unit of the *central nervous system.* All sensory and motor information comes or goes from this central core. The spinal cord is the master nerve tract (or nerve trunk) in our body and consists of millions of nerve fibers bundled together, somewhat like many small threads making up a large rope.

Like the spinal cord, all the lesser nerves, shown as single cords in a typical anatomical drawing, are made up of hundreds of thousands of individual fibers. Each fiber is part of a single nerve cell, or *neuron.* Neurons—there are 12 to 15 billion of them in our brain alone—are the basic structural units of the brain and nervous system, the tubes and transistors and circuits of which our personal computer is built.

The Brain

The appearance of the brain within the skull has been described as a huge gray walnut and a cauliflower. The inelegance of such descriptions is the least of many good reasons why we should be happy our brains are not exposed to public view.

Brain tissue—pinkish gray and white—is among the most delicate in our body, and the destruction of even a small part may mean lasting impairment or death. Its protection is vital and begins (if we are so fortunate) with a mat of hair on the top, back, and sides of our skull. Next comes the resilient layer of padding we call the scalp, and then the main line of defense—the rounded, bony helmet of skull.

The brain's armor does not stop with bone. Beneath are three strong, fibrous membranes called *meninges* that encase the brain in protective envelopes. Meninges also overlie the tissue of the spinal cord; infection or inflammation of these membranes by bacteria or viruses is called *cerebrospinal meningitis*.

Between two of the meninges is a region laced with veins and arteries and filled with *cerebrospinal fluid*. This fluid-filled space cushions the brain against sudden blows and collisions. The cerebrospinal fluid circulates not only about the brain but through the entire central nervous system. Incidentally, chemical analysis of this fluid, withdrawn by inserting a hypodermic needle between vertebrae of the spinal column (a spinal tap), can provide clues to the nature of brain and nervous system disorders.

The Cerebrum

What we usually mean by "brain" is that part of the brain called the *cerebrum*. It is the cerebrum that permits us all our distinctly human activities—thinking, speaking, reading, writing.

Only in man does the cerebrum reach such size, occupying the interior of our entire dome above the level of the eyes.

The surface of the cerebrum is wrinkled, furrowed, folded and infolded, convoluted, fissured—anything but smooth. This lavishly wrinkled outer layer of the cerebrum, about an eighth of an inch thick, is called the *cerebral cortex*. From its grayish color comes the term "gray matter" for brain tissue. There is a pattern among its wrinkles, marked out by wider, or deeper fissures, or furrows, running through the brain tissue. The most conspicuous fissure runs down the middle, front to back, dividing the cerebrum into two halves, the left hemisphere and the right hemisphere. The nerves from the left half of the body are served by the right hemisphere, and the right half of the body by the left hemisphere, so that damage to one side of the brain affects the other side of the body.

The Lobes of the Cerebrum

Smaller fissures crisscross the cerebrum and mark out various specific areas of function called *lobes*. The frontal lobes, one on the left hemisphere and one on the right in back of our eyes and extending upward behind the forehead, are perhaps the most talked about and the least understood by medical researchers. The specific functions of most other lobes in the cerebrum, such as the two occipital lobes (centers for seeing), the olfactory lobes (centers for smelling), and the temporal lobes (centers for hearing) are much better known.

The Brain Stem

The cerebrum, like a large flower obscuring part of its stalk, droops down

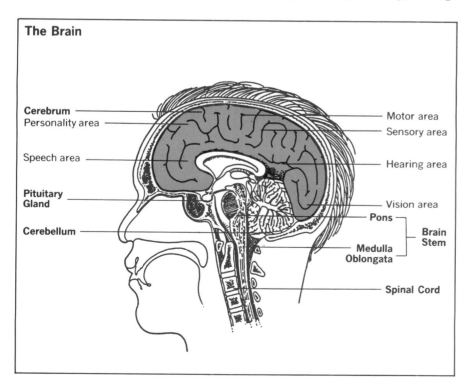

The Brain

- Cerebrum
- Personality area
- Speech area
- Pituitary Gland
- Cerebellum
- Motor area
- Sensory area
- Hearing area
- Vision area
- Pons
- Brain Stem
- Medulla Oblongata
- Spinal Cord

The Brain and the Cranial Nerves

Cranial nerves

1. Olfactory: smell
2. Optic: vision
3. Oculomotor: muscle of eyes
4. Trochlear: muscle of eyes
5. Trigeminal: sense of touch in face
6. Abducens: muscle of eyes
7. Facial: muscles of face
8. Acoustic: hearing and balance
9. Glossopharyngeal: taste
10. Vagus: heart, lungs, abdomen
11. Hypoglossal: tongue muscles
12. Accessory: neck muscles, eyeball

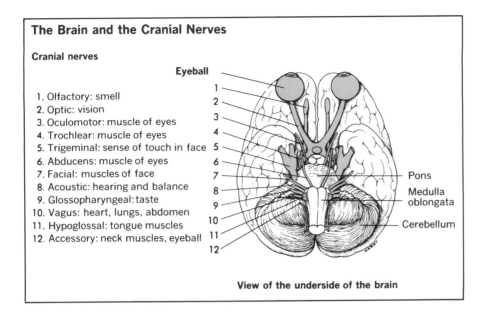

View of the underside of the brain

around the *brain stem.* Thus, while the brain stem originates just about in the middle of our skull, it does not emerge completely from the folds of the cerebral hemispheres until it reaches the back of the neck. Then it soon merges into the spinal cord.

Associated with this portion of the brain—roughly speaking, between the cerebrum and the spinal cord— are centers that take care of the countless necessary details involved in just plain existing, and structures (such as the *medulla oblongata* and the *pons*) that serve also as traffic control points for the billions of nerve impulses traveling to and from the cerebrum. The largest of these "lesser brains" is the *cerebellum,* whose two hemispheres straddle the brain stem at the back of the head.

The Cerebellum

The cerebellum is the site of balance and body and muscle coordination, allowing us, for example, to "rub the tummy and pat the head" simultaneously, or tap the foot and strum a guitar, or steer a car and operate the foot pedals. Such muscle-coordinated movements, though sometimes learned only by long repetition and

practice, can become almost automatic—such as reaching for and flicking on the light switch as we move into a darkened room.

But many other activities and kinds of behavior regulated by the part of the brain below the cerebrum are more fully automatic: the control of eye movement and focusing, for example, as well as the timing of heartbeat, sleep, appetite, and metabolism; the arousal and decline of sexual drives; body temperature; the dilation and constriction of blood vessels; swallowing; and breathing. All these are mainly functions of the *autonomic nervous system,* as opposed to the more voluntary actions controlled by the *central nervous system.*

The Body's Nervous Systems

Simply speaking, the human body has only one nervous system, and that is all the nerve cells, nerve cords, nerve centers (both voluntary and involuntary) in the body. It is helpful, however, though quite arbitrary, to divide our nerves into the central and autonomic nervous systems. This division tends to obscure the countless interconnections and interplay between

the two systems. For example, where do you place the control of breathing or blinking? Such actions are automatic except when we choose to regulate them.

The Central Nervous System

The central nervous system, as noted above, includes the brain and the spinal cord. It also includes all the nerves of conscious response and voluntary action that link up with the brain and spinal cord.

Twelve pairs of *cranial nerves* originate within the brain and emerge at its base. These include the very important nerves that connect with our sense organs, nerve bundles that control the facial and neck muscles, and the *vagus* (or tenth cranial nerve) that serves the heart, lungs, stomach, intestines, esophagus, larynx, liver, kidneys, spleen, and pancreas. The vagus nerve, although anatomically part of the central nervous system, controls bodily functions that are mainly automatic.

Spinal nerves branch out from the spinal cord as it snakes its way through the vertebrae of the spinal column. All the major nerve cords that wrap around the trunk and reach the arms and hands, legs and feet, originate from spinal nerves.

The cranial nerves and the spinal nerves, together with all those nerves lying outside the confines of the brain and spinal cord, are sometimes referred to as the *peripheral nervous system.* This term can be confusing, however, because it is also used to include all the nerves of the autonomic nervous system, next discussed.

The Autonomic Nervous System

The muscles served by the central nervous system are all of one general type (striated), while the muscles served by the autonomic system are called involuntary or smooth. The autonomic nerves regulate body activity without our conscious control—for example, as we sleep. They are rather elegantly divided into two categories: *sympathetic* and *parasympathetic* nervous systems. These are distinguishable primarily by their opposite effects on the body organs. For example, impulses along parasympathetic nerve trunks dilate blood vessels, slow the heartbeat rate, and increase stomach secretions, while the sympathetic system constricts blood vessels, increases rate of heartbeat, and inhibits stomach secretions.

The Neuron—What Nerves Are Made Of

A nerve cell is a grayish blob of tissue from which protrude several short gray fibers, *dendrites,* and one longer whitish fiber, an *axon.* Both the dendrites and the axon resemble ropes with their ends splayed and frayed. Dendrites register impulses coming into the central blob of the neuron (perhaps from a neighboring neuron's axon); an axon picks up the incoming impulses and carries them away.

Both units are equally important for normal nerve functioning, but the axon is far more showy as an anatomical structure. All nerve cords are made up of the single strands of many axons, which may reach lengths of several feet. In other words, if we could stretch out certain neurons in our body—for example, those making up the sciatic nerve that runs from the small of the back to the toes—their axon "tails" would make them three or four feet long.

Myelin

A normal axon usually has a fatty coating of insulation called *myelin.* An axon severed into two pieces cannot grow together again; but if the myelin sheath is pretty much intact, a surgeon can sometimes restore nerve function by sewing the two ends together, or replace the nerve with one from another part of the body. The part of the severed axon connecting to the central portion usually remains alive in any case—which is why a person can often retain the sensation of feeling in an amputated part.

Certain serious and progressively disabling diseases involve the gradual loss (*demyelination*) of this coating, causing paralysis, numbness, or other loss of function in an organ; a demyelinated nerve fiber is not able to carry impulses to and from the brain. Two such diseases are multiple sclerosis and "Lou Gehrig's disease" (amyotrophic lateral sclerosis).

Effects of Aging

Once we reach maturity, the number of our nerve cells begins to decrease, because our bodies cannot manufacture new neurons to replace the ones that die in the normal process of living. (Other kinds of tissue are continually replenished with new cells.) This has some relation to senility, but the loss of a few million out of many billions of brain and nerve cells has

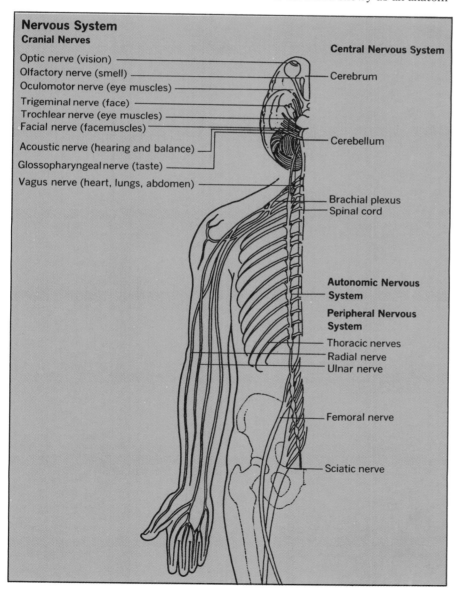

Nervous System
Cranial Nerves

Optic nerve (vision)
Olfactory nerve (smell)
Oculomotor nerve (eye muscles)
Trigeminal nerve (face)
Trochlear nerve (eye muscles)
Facial nerve (facemuscles)
Acoustic nerve (hearing and balance)
Glossopharyngeal nerve (taste)
Vagus nerve (heart, lungs, abdomen)

Central Nervous System

Cerebrum

Cerebellum

Brachial plexus
Spinal cord

Autonomic Nervous System

Peripheral Nervous System

Thoracic nerves
Radial nerve
Ulnar nerve

Femoral nerve

Sciatic nerve

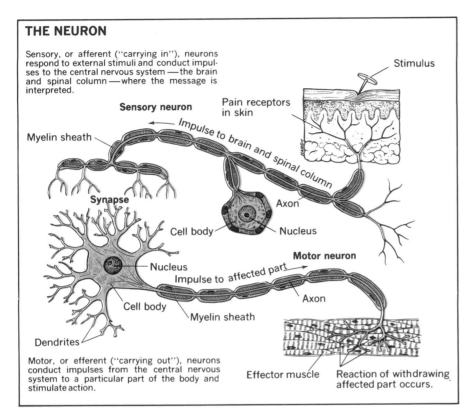

THE NEURON

Sensory, or afferent ("carrying in"), neurons respond to external stimuli and conduct impulses to the central nervous system — the brain and spinal column — where the message is interpreted.

Sensory neuron

Myelin sheath

Impulse to brain and spinal column

Synapse

Cell body

Nucleus

Motor neuron

Nucleus

Impulse to affected part

Cell body

Myelin sheath

Axon

Dendrites

Stimulus

Pain receptors in skin

Axon

Nucleus

Effector muscle

Reaction of withdrawing affected part occurs.

Motor, or efferent ("carrying out"), neurons conduct impulses from the central nervous system to a particular part of the body and stimulate action.

little effect on mental powers unless the losses are concentrated in one area.

Synapse, Ganglion, and Plexus

When a nerve impulse, traveling away from the neuron's central part, reaches the ends of an axon, it meets a gap that it must jump to get to the tentaclelike dendrites of the next neuron. This gap is called a *synapse*.

At certain points in the body a great many nerve cell bodies and branches are packed closely together, with a resulting profusion of interwoven axons, dendrites, and synapses. Such a concentration of nervous tissue is called a *ganglion,* or *plexus*. A blow or jolt to such an area can be extremely painful and even stupefying—affecting as it does a whole network of nerves—as anyone who has been hit in the solar plexus or learned the pressure points of karate knows.

The Movement of Impulses along Nerve Fibers

There is really no exact counterpart in the mechanical world for how an impulse moves along a nerve fiber and then jumps across a synapse to the next nerve. Nor is this movement completely understood by scientists. Suffice it to say that it is somewhat like an electrical current moving along in a chemical environment that allows the impulse to travel, in discreet little jumps, at a speed of about 200 miles per hour—quite slowly when we compare it to the speed of light or electricity: 186,000 miles per second. This speed serves us quite well in most situations, but there are times when we wish human beings' nerves could act more quickly—on the highway, for example, or when a cherished vase starts to topple off the mantelpiece.

One of the simplest and quickest kinds of reactions to an outside stimulus is one that bypasses the brain. We don't really think to pull our hand

away from a piping hot radiator. This is called a *spinal reflex*. What happens is that the sensory nerve endings in the finger pick up the "too hot" impulse from the radiator; the impulse then travels to the spinal cord where it activates the motor nerve pathway back to the burned finger, carrying the message, "Jerk your finger away!"

When to Suspect Trouble

Our entire existence as human beings depends so much on the normal functioning of our brain and nervous system that any real brain or nervous disorder or disease is a very serious matter. A sprained joint or cut foot can spell doom for an animal that depends on speed and mobility for survival; but the same injury is often not much more than a painful inconvenience to us. Impairment of our brain or nervous system is far more of a threat to our survival.

Multiple sclerosis and meningitis have been mentioned as serious disorders affecting the nerves, others are Parkinsonism, shingles, encephalitis, and brain tumors. The possible presence of one of these disorders is reason enough not to shrug off any of the following signs and symptoms: recurrent headaches, intense pain of unknown cause, tremors, numbness, loss of coordination, dizziness, blackouts, tics, cramps, visual difficulties, and loss of bowel and bladder control. Also, any person who has remained unconscious for more than a few minutes should be taken to a physician as soon as possible. This applies even when the person has regained consciousness and says he feels fine.

Our complex emotions, of course, are linked to the functioning of our brain and nervous system. A mind free of undue anxiety, guilt, and frustration functions better than a mind racked with worries and conflicts, and is a much more efficient and reliable leader of the body. See also Ch. 8, *Diseases of the Muscles and Nervous System.* For a discussion of mental and emotional health, see Ch. 36.

The Circulatory System, the Heart, and Blood

When the heart stops beating— that is to say, stops pumping blood— for longer than a couple of minutes, we stop living. But the heart, fortunately, is extremely sturdy. It is also simple in construction, capable of operating at a great many different speeds, in many cases self-repairing if damaged, and probably the one continuously operating automatic pump that we could, with any confidence, expect to last 70 years or longer.

These simple facts tend to be forgotten today, in what is probably the most heart-conscious era in history. True, heart disease, along with cancer, is statistically one of today's major killers. But we should remember two circumstances: not until about 50 years ago did deaths from heart disease begin to be accurately recognized and reported; second, with longer and longer life spans, it becomes more likely that a nonstop vital organ like the heart will simply wear out. Heart transplants, open heart surgery, and artificial heart parts— often reported sensationally in the public media—have also conditioned us to think of our hearts as terribly vulnerable, rather delicate, a bit inadequate to their tasks, and quite open to improvement.

Advances in heart surgery do, indeed, hold greater promise for persons whose hearts had been considered, until now, irreversibly damaged or diseased. But the great attention accorded such miracles of medicine tends to obscure the humdrum, day-in-day-out, low-key drama performed for a lifetime by a healthy, uncomplaining heart.

The Heart and Circulatory Network

Perhaps the best way to put the heart in perspective is to place it where it belongs, at the hub of the body's circulatory system. This hollow, fist-sized lump of sinewy tissue is located behind the breastbone, centered just about at the vertical midline of our chest. It is connected into a closed system of flexible tubes, called blood vessels, ranging down from finger-thick to microscopically slender, that reach into every cavern, crevice, and outpost of our body—a network of some 70,000 miles.

The heart has essentially one function—to push blood, by pumping action, through this enormous network of blood vessels. We have about six quarts of blood in our body, pumped at the rate of about five ounces every time the heart beats (normally about 72 times a minute for an adult), which we feel as our pulse. The blood circulates and recirculates through the blood vessels, pushed along by the pumping of the heart.

Arteries and Veins

The blood vessels are generally described as *arterial,* referring to the *arteries* that carry blood away from the heart; or *venous,* referring to the *veins* through which blood seeps and flows back toward the heart to be re-pumped. A large artery such as the *aorta* branches into smaller arteries, and these eventually into still smaller vessels called *arterioles,* and the arterioles, finally, into the smallest

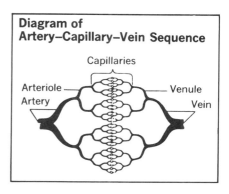

Diagram of Artery–Capillary–Vein Sequence

Capillaries

Arteriole — Venule
Artery — Vein

blood vessels, the *capillaries.* These in turn open onto other capillaries, which are the starting point for the return of blood to the heart.

The microscopic capillaries typically form a kind of cat's cradle connection, sometimes called a capillary bed, at the transition zone where arterial blood becomes venous blood. The returning blood moves from the capillaries to small veins called *venules* (the counterparts of arterioles) and through successively larger veins back to the heart.

Blood and Our Internal Fluid Environment

What makes this fairly rudimentary collection of plumbing so absolutely indispensable to life is the fluid it pumps—blood. If any part of the body—cell, tissue, or major organ— is denied circulating blood and the substances it carries with it for longer than a few minutes, that part will fail. It is the job of the heart and the blood vessels to get blood to all the body's far-flung tissues, where it both picks up and deposits substances.

Blood is really a kind of fluid tissue. About 80 percent of its volume is water, and blood's indispensable, life-sustaining power is owed in great part to its watery base, which permits it both to flow and to take up and carry materials in solution. All our tissues and organs have a kind of give-and-take arrangement with the circulating blood.

The Circulatory System

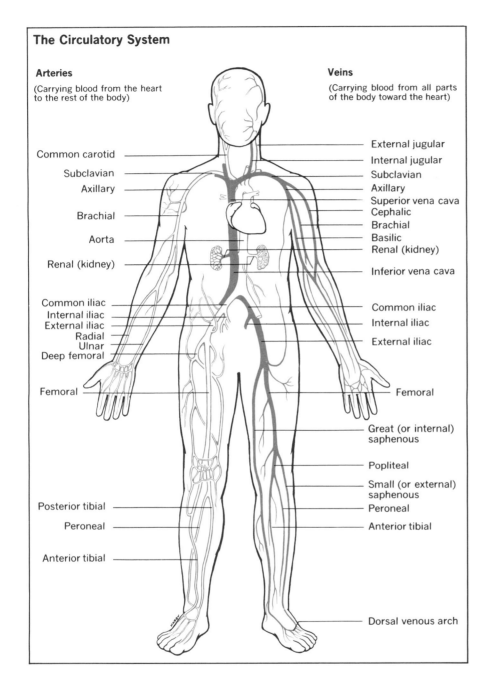

Arteries

(Carrying blood from the heart to the rest of the body)

Veins

(Carrying blood from all parts of the body toward the heart)

Common carotid
Subclavian
Axillary
Brachial
Aorta
Renal (kidney)
Common iliac
Internal iliac
External iliac
Radial
Ulnar
Deep femoral
Femoral
Posterior tibial
Peroneal
Anterior tibial

External jugular
Internal jugular
Subclavian
Axillary
Superior vena cava
Cephalic
Brachial
Basilic
Renal (kidney)
Inferior vena cava
Common iliac
Internal iliac
External iliac
Femoral
Great (or internal) saphenous
Popliteal
Small (or external) saphenous
Peroneal
Anterior tibial
Dorsal venous arch

Distributor of Nutrients

Food, or more accurately the nutrient molecules needed by cells, are also transported throughout the body by the blood. In the digestive tract, food is broken down into tiny submicroscopic pieces that can pass through the tract's walls (mainly along the small intestine) and be picked up by the blood for distribution around the body.

One of the specialized, small-volume transportation jobs handled by the blood is to pick up hormones from the endocrine glands and present these chemical messengers to the organs they affect.

Composition of Blood

Blood is a distinctive and recognizable type of tissue, but this does not mean it is a stable, uniform substance with a fixed proportion of ingredients. Quite the opposite is true; its composition is ever changing in response to the demands of other body systems. Other organs are constantly pouring substances into the blood, or removing things from it. Blood in one part of the body at a given moment may be vastly different in chemical makeup from blood in another part of the body.

Despite its changing makeup, blood does have certain basic components. A sample of blood left to stand for an hour or so separates into a clear, watery fluid with a yellowish tinge and a darker, more solid clump. The clear yellow liquid is called *plasma*, and accounts for about 55 percent of the volume of normal blood. The darker clump is made up mainly of the blood's most conspicuous and populous inhabitants, the red cells that give blood its color.

Plasma

It is the plasma that enables our blood

Carrier of Oxygen

Perhaps the most critical of these give-and-take transactions occurs in the lungs; it is this transaction that if interrupted by heartbeat stoppage for more than a few minutes causes death by oxygen starvation of vital tissues. Before a unit of blood is pumped out by the heart to the body, it picks up in the lungs the oxygen that we have inhaled and which every cell in the body needs to function. The blood then transports the oxygen, delivering it to other parts of the body. By the time a given unit of blood has made a tour of the blood vessels and returned to the lungs, it has given up most of its oxygen and is laden instead with carbon dioxide, the principal waste product of living processes. The venous blood releases its carbon dioxide, to be exhaled by the lungs.

to carry out most of the transportation tasks assigned it. Being over 90 percent water, the plasma has water's property of being able to carry substances both in solution and in suspension. (A substance in solution is one, like salt, that must be removed from water by chemical or physical action, such as boiling; while a substance in suspension—such as red blood cells within whole blood in a standing test tube—separates out more readily, particularly when its watery carrier has been contained and its flow stilled.)

Red Blood Cells

Red blood cells (or *erythrocytes*) numbering in the trillions are carried in suspension by the plasma. In turn, the red blood cells carry the single most important substance needed by the body's cells—oxygen. For such an important task, the red blood cell looks hardly adequate. As it matures, this cell loses its nucleus. Lacking a nucleus, it is sometimes not even called a cell but a red blood *corpuscle*. What gives red blood cells their special oxygen-carrying ability, and also their color, is their possession of a complex iron-protein substance called *hemoglobin*.

Hemoglobin

Molecules of hemoglobin have the property of loosely combining with oxygen where it is plentiful, as in the lungs. They can then hold on to oxygen until they reach an area where oxygen has been depleted by the demands of living processes. There— usually in the fine tubes of the capillaries—hemoglobin's hold on oxygen is challenged by the demands of other cells, and the red cells give up their oxygen. The hemoglobin of red cells develops an immediate affinity for car-

bon dioxide, the waste product of cell metabolism, and the red blood cells then carry this carbon dioxide back to the lungs for exhalation.

Hemoglobin's ability to carry oxygen is not unique. Water, and therefore plasma, also have this ability. Hemoglobin's specialness lies in how much oxygen it can carry. Hemoglobin increases by more than 50 times the oxygen-carrying capacity of our blood.

White Blood Cells

White blood cells have many different shapes and sizes, all going under the general scientific name of *leukocytes*. They are typically larger than red blood cells, but far less numerous. If we accept an estimate of 25 trillion as the number of living red blood cells in our body, then the number of white blood cells might be generously estimated at around 40 billion, a ratio of one white cell to about 600–700 reds.

According to their shape, size, and other characteristics, white blood cells have been divided into various categories such as lymphocytes, monocytes, and granulocytes. But as a group these blood cells are distinguished by their common propensity for attacking foreign bodies that invade our tissues, whether these invaders be sizable splinters or microscopic bacteria. White blood cells move in force to the site of an infection, do battle with the intruding agents, and frequently strew the area with the wreckage of the encounter— a collection of dismantled alien bacteria and dead white cells, which we know as pus.

Platelets

Platelets, also called *thrombocytes,* initiate some of the first steps in the complex biochemical process that leads to the clotting of blood. They

thus help to spare us from bleeding to death from a slight injury. Platelets are the most rudimentary and diminutive of the major blood components. Like mature red blood cells, they lack nuclei, but are only one-quarter as big. By no stretch of the imagination can they be called blood cells. Rather, they are blood elements—bits of cell substance with a recognizable size and shape, circulating with the blood.

The Proportions of Blood Cells

All the several types of blood cells and subcells in a healthy body occur in proportions that, though never precisely fixed and unchanging, are recognized as having normal upper and lower limits. If a particular type of cell shows a sudden increase or decrease in population, so that its proportion relative to other blood cells shows a variation markedly outside its normal range, some infection, disease, or disorder must be suspected.

In addition to occurring in certain normal-range proportions, each type of cellular blood component has a typical shape, appearance, and set of chemical and physical properties. Variations from these norms occur in many diseases.

The analysis of blood samples (usually taken from the finger or arm) and their inspection under a microscope have proved invaluable in diagnosing illness and disease, often before a person feels any symptoms whatsoever. This is why a thorough medical checkup should always include taking a sample of your blood. It is then up to the physician to decide which of the dozens of tests should be made on your blood in the medical laboratory. One common test is a *blood count,* in which the number of a certain type of cell in a given unit of your blood can be estimated, and then compared to the normal number in the same amount of blood.

Blood Groups and Rh Factors

The identification of *blood groups* and *Rh factors* is another aspect of blood analysis. The four most common blood groups are called A, B, AB, and O, classifications based on chemical differences that may be incompatible if one group is mixed with another. Thus, it is absolutely essential before a person receives a blood transfusion to know both his own blood type and the type of the blood he is to be given. Blood group O is considered the safety for transfusion, and people with type O blood are sometimes called "universal donors." It is a wise practice to carry, along with your other important cards, a card giving your own blood type. The blood of a donor, however, is always *cross-matched* (checked for compatibility) with the blood of the person who is to receive it in order to avoid transfusion reactions.

Blood Cell Manufacture and Turnover

Most types of blood cells, both red and white, are manufactured in the red marrow of bones. The rate and quantity of total production is staggering; estimates range from one to five million red blood cells per second. This prodigious output is necessary because blood cells are disintegrating, having served their useful lives, in the same enormous numbers every second. The normal life span of a red blood cell is about four months, which means that four months from now every blood cell in your body will have died and been replaced with new cells.

The Liver As a Producer of Red Blood Cells

The red bone marrow is backed up by several other tissues that can, if called upon, turn out blood cells in quantity or serve as specialized producers of certain blood cells and blood elements. One such organ is the liver, which, before and after birth and into childhood, is a site of red blood cell production. In an emergency, such as severe internal hemorrhage, the liver sometimes reverts to its earlier function of manufacturing red cells. The liver also serves as a kind of salvage yard for the iron from dead red cells. It stores the iron for later combination into hemoglobin and passes off the rest of the red blood cell fragments as part of the bile pigments that empty into the duodenum of the small intestine.

The Spleen As a Producer of Blood Cells

Certain white blood cells, in particular the lymphocytes, are produced at a variety of locations in the body—for example, by the lymph nodes, by little clumps of tissue called *Peyer's patches* in the intestinal tract, and by the spleen.

The spleen plays a number of interesting secondary roles in blood cell production. Like the liver, it can be pressed into service as a manufacturer of red blood cells and serve as a salvage yard for iron reclaimed from worn-out red blood cells. A newborn baby is almost totally dependent on its spleen for the production of red blood cells, with a little help from the liver. In an adult, however, a damaged or diseased spleen can be surgically removed, with little or no apparent effect on the health or life span of the person, provided the patient's bone marrow is in good functioning order.

Movement of Blood Cells through the Capillaries

A blood cell must be able to slip through the microscopic, twisting and turning tunnels of the capillaries that mark the turn-about point in the blood cell's round-trip voyage from the heart. Blood cells, therefore, must be small (the point of a pin could hold dozens of red blood cells), and they must be jellylike in order to navigate the tight tortuous, capillary channels without either blocking the channel or breaking apart themselves. A red blood cell is further adapted to sneaking through the capillaries by its concave-disk shape, which allows it to bend and fold around itself. Nevertheless, so narrow are the passageways within some of the capillaries that blood cells must move through them in single file. If a substantial number of the cells are misshapen, as in sickle-cell anemia, they tend to move sluggishly or clog up the passageway—a condition that can have serious consequences. See also Ch. 9, *Diseases of the Circulatory System.*

Lymph and the Lymphatic System

Of all our body systems, perhaps the most ignored is the lymphatic system, although it forms a network throughout our body comparable to the blood vessels of our circulatory system.

Lymph is a whitish fluid that is derived from blood plasma. As plasma circulates through the body, some of it seeps through the walls of capillaries and other blood vessels. This leakage is of the utmost importance, because the leaked fluid, lymph, supplies the liquid environment around and between individual cells and tissues that is essential for their survival.

The presence of lymph requires a drainage system to keep the fluid moving. If there were no drainage system, two things could happen: the dammed-up lymph could create areas swollen with water in which cells would literally drown, or stagnant pools of lymph could become breeding

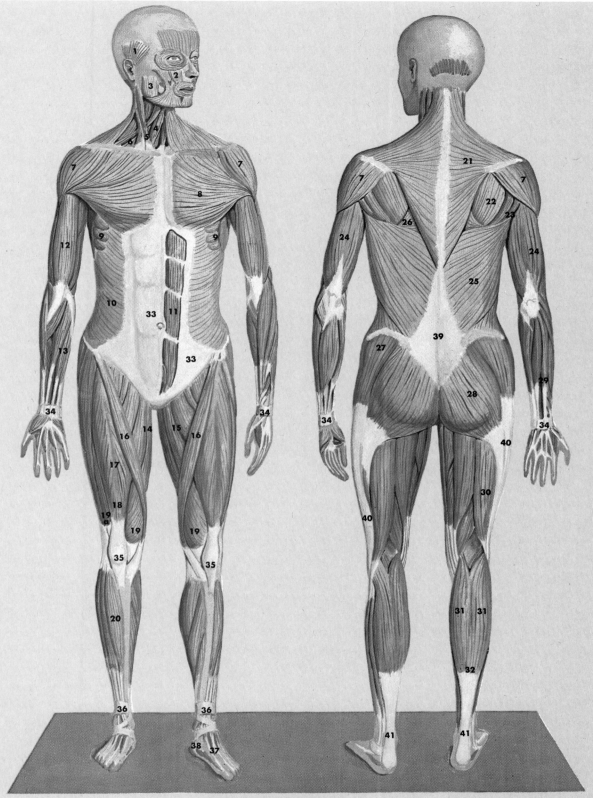

MUSCLES AND TENDONS

MUSCLES

1. Temporal
2. Mimetic muscles
3. Masseter (a muscle of mastication)
4. Infrahyoid muscles
5. Sternomastoid
6. Omohyoid
7. Deltoid
8. Pectoral muscles
9. Serratus anterior
10. External oblique
11. Rectus abdominus
12. Biceps brachii
13. Flexor digitorum superficialis (sublimis)
14. Gracilis

15. Adductor group
16. Sartorius
17. Rectus femoris
18. Quadriceps femoris
19. Vastus medialis
19a. Vastus lateralis
20. Dorsiflexors
21. Trapezius
22. Infraspinatus
23. Teres major
24. Triceps brachii
25. Latissimus dorsi
26. Rhomboideus major
27. Gluteus medius
28. Gluteus maximus

29. Digital extensors
30. Hamstring muscles
31. Gastrocnemius
32. Plantar flexors

TENDONS

33. Rectus sheath
34. Flexor retinaculum of carpal tunnel
35. Patellar tendon
36. Retinaculum of tarsal tunnel
37. Tendons of long digital extensors
38. Tendon of tibialis anterior
39. Lumbodorsal fascia
40. Fascia lata
41. Achilles

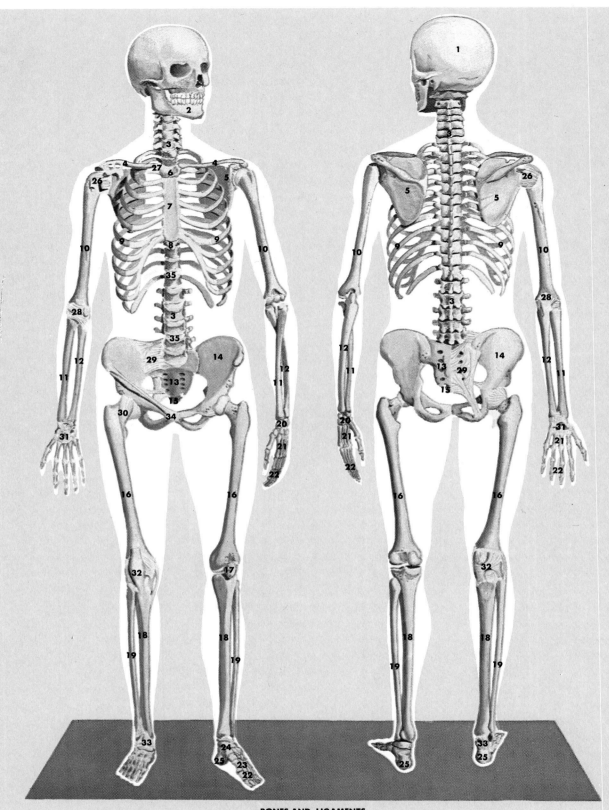

BONES AND LIGAMENTS

BONES
1. Skull
2. Mandible
3. Vertebrae
4. Clavicle
5. Scapula
6. Manubrium
7. Body of sternum
8. Xiphoid process
9. Ribs
10. Humerus
11. Radius
12. Ulna
13. Sacrum
14. Ilium
15. Coccyx
16. Femur
17. Patella
18. Tibia
19. Fibula
20. Carpals
21. Metacarpals
22. Phalanges
23. Metatarsals
24. Tarsals
25. Heel

LIGAMENTS AND JOINTS
26. Capsule of shoulder
27. Sternoclavicular
28. Capsule of elbow
29. Sacroiliac
30. Iliofemoral
31. Wrist
32. Capsule of knee
33. Ankle
34. Pubic symphysis
35. Intervertebral discs

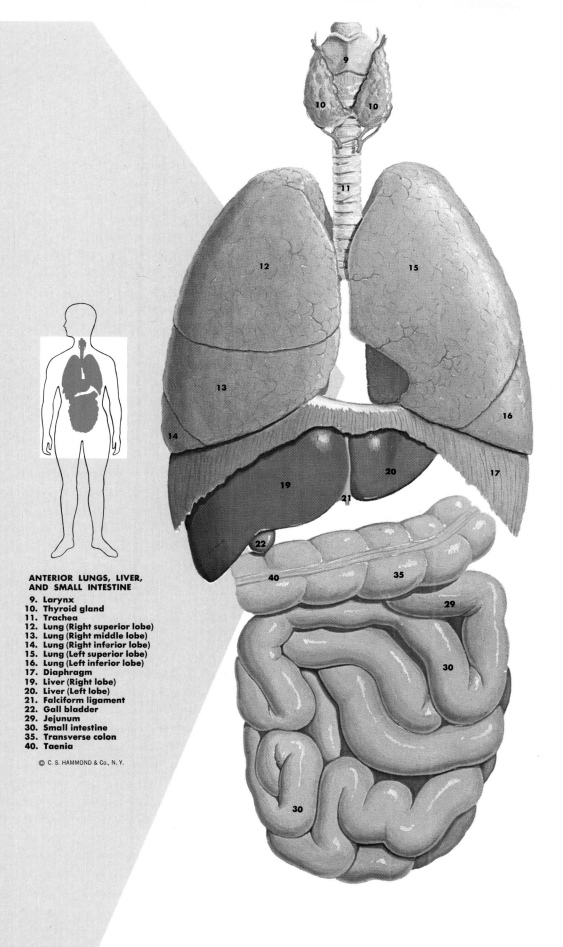

ANTERIOR LUNGS, LIVER, AND SMALL INTESTINE

9. Larynx
10. Thyroid gland
11. Trachea
12. Lung (Right superior lobe)
13. Lung (Right middle lobe)
14. Lung (Right inferior lobe)
15. Lung (Left superior lobe)
16. Lung (Left inferior lobe)
17. Diaphragm
19. Liver (Right lobe)
20. Liver (Left lobe)
21. Falciform ligament
22. Gall bladder
29. Jejunum
30. Small intestine
35. Transverse colon
40. Taenia

© C. S. HAMMOND & Co., N. Y.

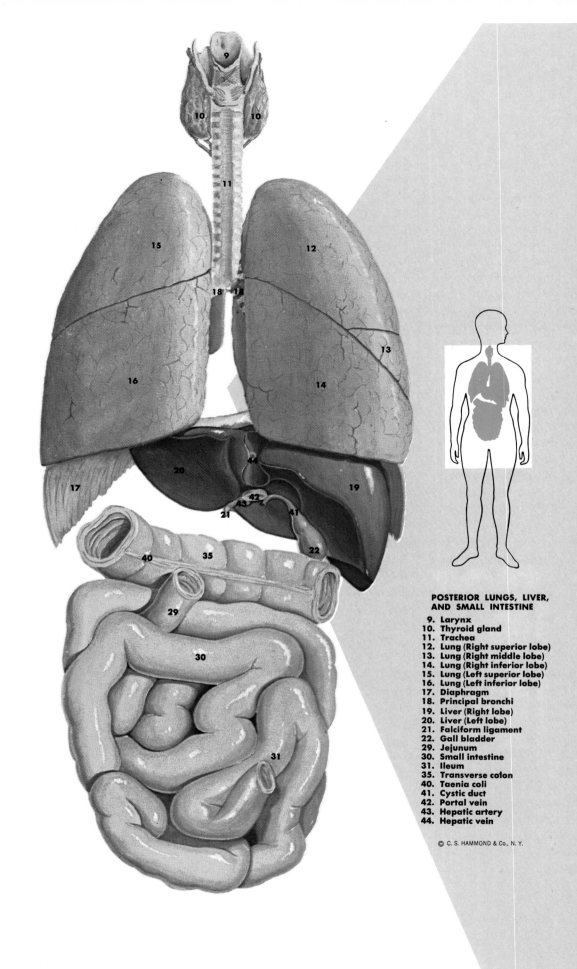

POSTERIOR LUNGS, LIVER, AND SMALL INTESTINE

9. Larynx
10. Thyroid gland
11. Trachea
12. Lung (Right superior lobe)
13. Lung (Right middle lobe)
14. Lung (Right inferior lobe)
15. Lung (Left superior lobe)
16. Lung (Left inferior lobe)
17. Diaphragm
18. Principal bronchi
19. Liver (Right lobe)
20. Liver (Left lobe)
21. Falciform ligament
22. Gall bladder
29. Jejunum
30. Small intestine
31. Ileum
35. Transverse colon
40. Taenia coli
41. Cystic duct
42. Portal vein
43. Hepatic artery
44. Hepatic vein

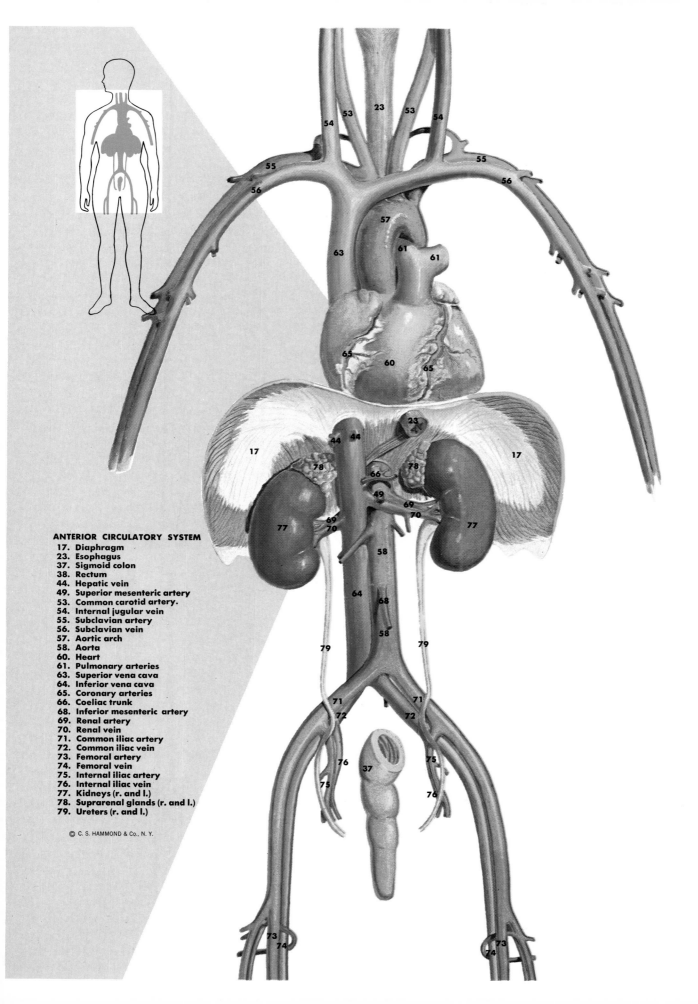

ANTERIOR CIRCULATORY SYSTEM

17. Diaphragm
23. Esophagus
37. Sigmoid colon
38. Rectum
44. Hepatic vein
49. Superior mesenteric artery
53. Common carotid artery.
54. Internal jugular vein
55. Subclavian artery
56. Subclavian vein
57. Aortic arch
58. Aorta
60. Heart
61. Pulmonary arteries
63. Superior vena cava
64. Inferior vena cava
65. Coronary arteries
66. Coeliac trunk
68. Inferior mesenteric artery
69. Renal artery
70. Renal vein
71. Common iliac artery
72. Common iliac vein
73. Femoral artery
74. Femoral vein
75. Internal iliac artery
76. Internal iliac vein
77. Kidneys (r. and l.)
78. Suprarenal glands (r. and l.)
79. Ureters (r. and l.)

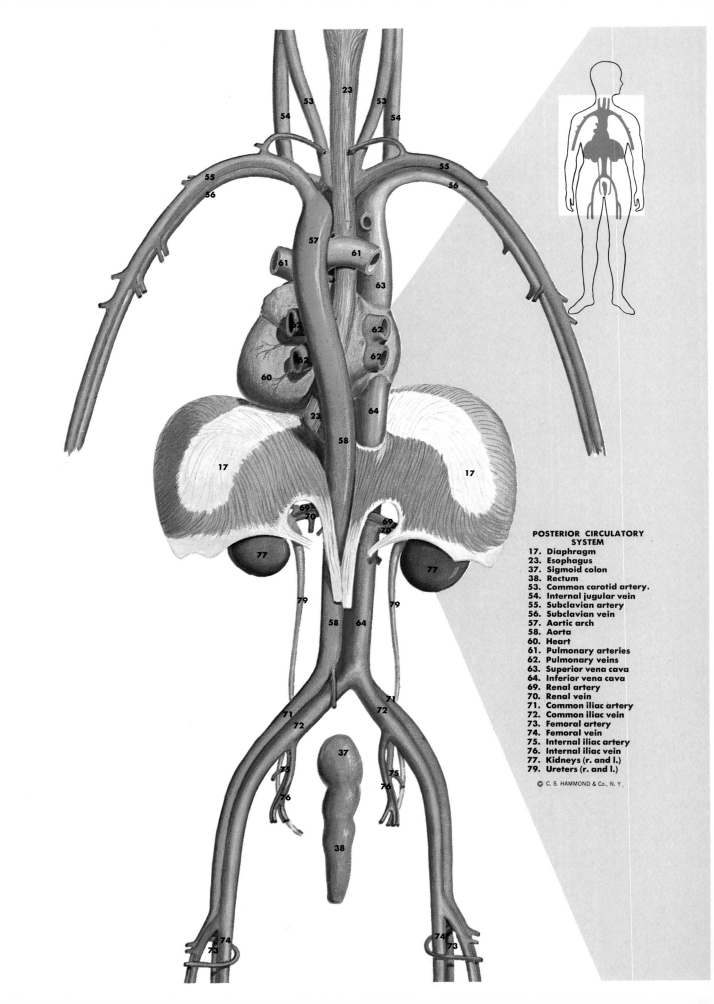

POSTERIOR CIRCULATORY SYSTEM

17. Diaphragm
23. Esophagus
37. Sigmoid colon
38. Rectum
53. Common carotid artery.
54. Internal jugular vein
55. Subclavian artery
56. Subclavian vein
57. Aortic arch
58. Aorta
60. Heart
61. Pulmonary arteries
62. Pulmonary veins
63. Superior vena cava
64. Inferior vena cava
69. Renal artery
70. Renal vein
71. Common iliac artery
72. Common iliac vein
73. Femoral artery
74. Femoral vein
75. Internal iliac artery
76. Internal iliac vein
77. Kidneys (r. and l.)
79. Ureters (r. and l.)

© C. S. HAMMOND & Co., N. Y.

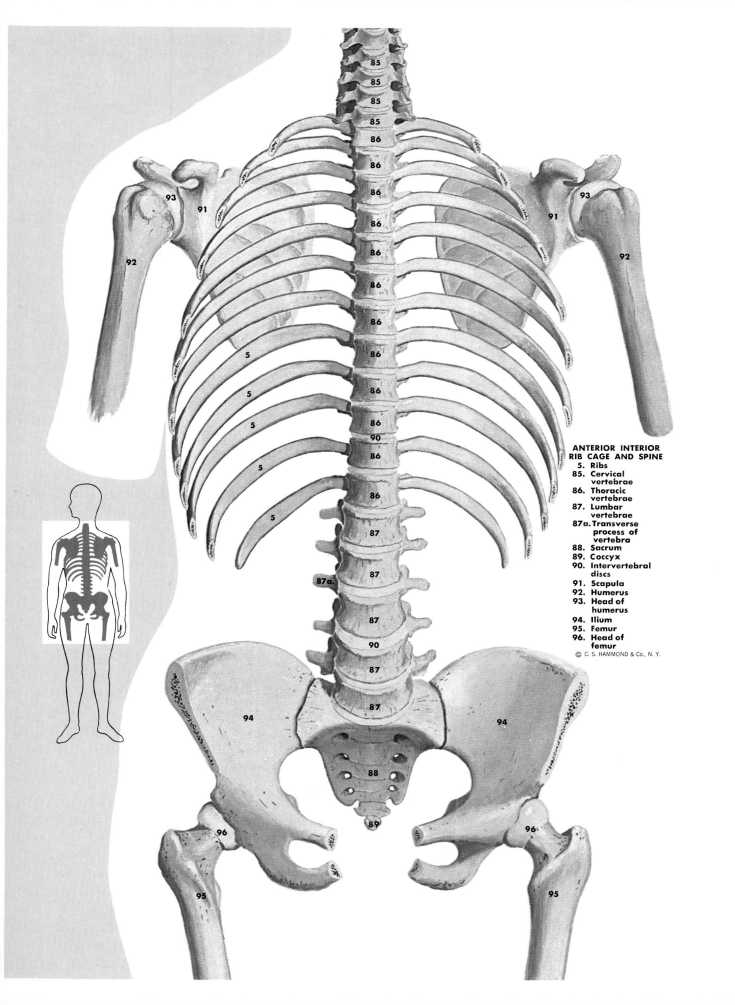

**ANTERIOR INTERIOR
RIB CAGE AND SPINE**
  5. Ribs
 85. Cervical
     vertebrae
 86. Thoracic
     vertebrae
 87. Lumbar
     vertebrae
87a. Transverse
     process of
     vertebra
 88. Sacrum
 89. Coccyx
 90. Intervertebral
     discs
 91. Scapula
 92. Humerus
 93. Head of
     humerus
 94. Ilium
 95. Femur
 96. Head of
     femur

© C. S. HAMMOND & Co., N. Y.

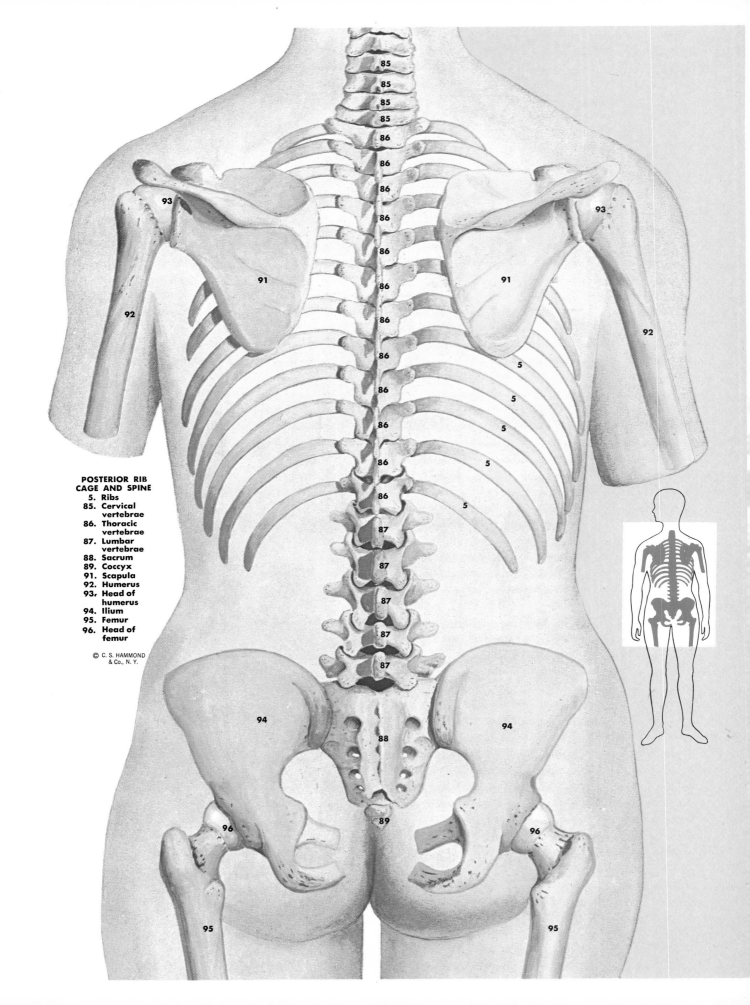

**POSTERIOR RIB
CAGE AND SPINE**
5. Ribs
85. Cervical
    vertebrae
86. Thoracic
    vertebrae
87. Lumbar
    vertebrae
88. Sacrum
89. Coccyx
91. Scapula
92. Humerus
93. Head of
    humerus
94. Ilium
95. Femur
96. Head of
    femur

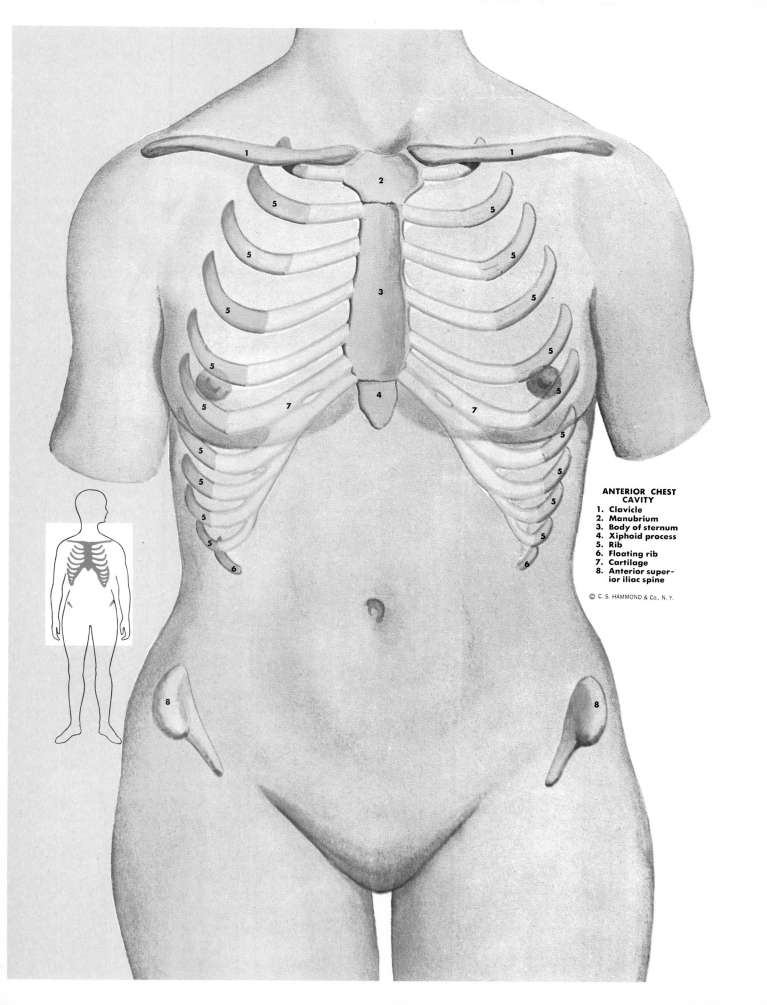

ANTERIOR CHEST CAVITY

1. Clavicle
2. Manubrium
3. Body of sternum
4. Xiphoid process
5. Rib
6. Floating rib
7. Cartilage
8. Anterior super-ior iliac spine

© C. S. HAMMOND & Co., N. Y.

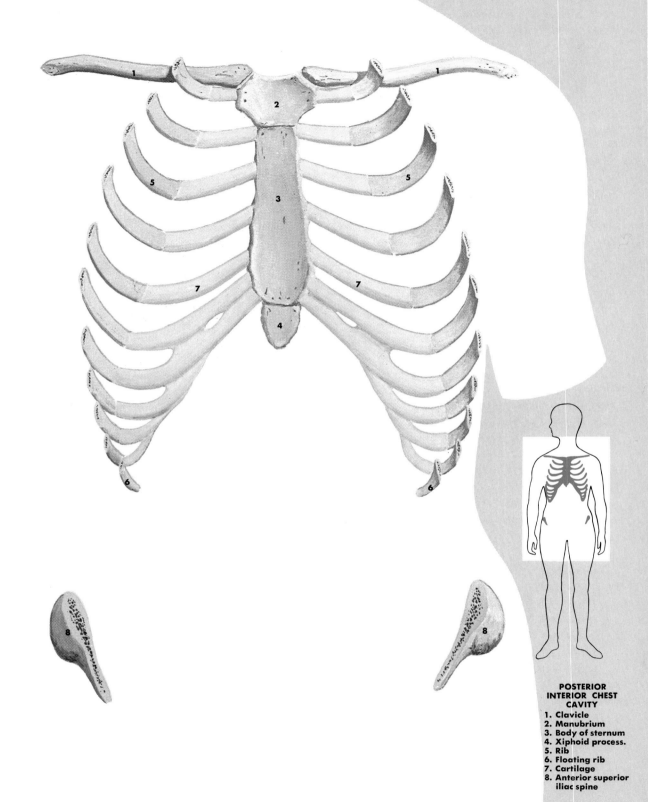

POSTERIOR INTERIOR CHEST CAVITY

1. Clavicle
2. Manubrium
3. Body of sternum
4. Xiphoid process.
5. Rib
6. Floating rib
7. Cartilage
8. Anterior superior iliac spine

© C. S. HAMMOND & Co., N. Y.

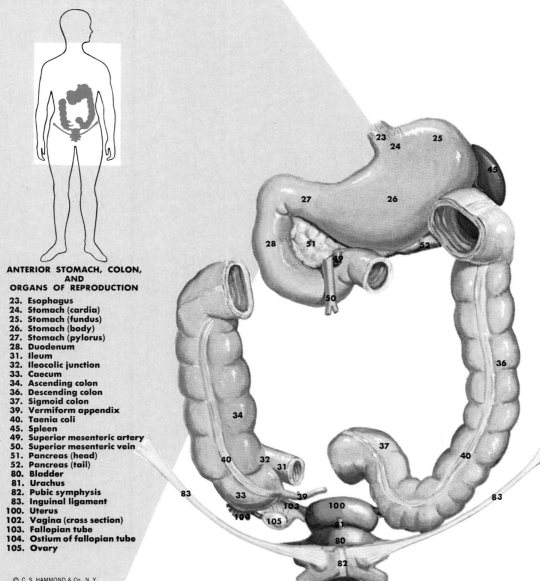

ANTERIOR STOMACH, COLON,
AND
ORGANS OF REPRODUCTION

23. Esophagus
24. Stomach (cardia)
25. Stomach (fundus)
26. Stomach (body)
27. Stomach (pylorus)
28. Duodenum
31. Ileum
32. Ileocolic junction
33. Caecum
34. Ascending colon
36. Descending colon
37. Sigmoid colon
39. Vermiform appendix
40. Taenia coli
45. Spleen
49. Superior mesenteric artery
50. Superior mesenteric vein
51. Pancreas (head)
52. Pancreas (tail)
80. Bladder
81. Urachus
82. Pubic symphysis
83. Inguinal ligament
100. Uterus
102. Vagina (cross section)
103. Fallopian tube
104. Ostium of fallopian tube
105. Ovary

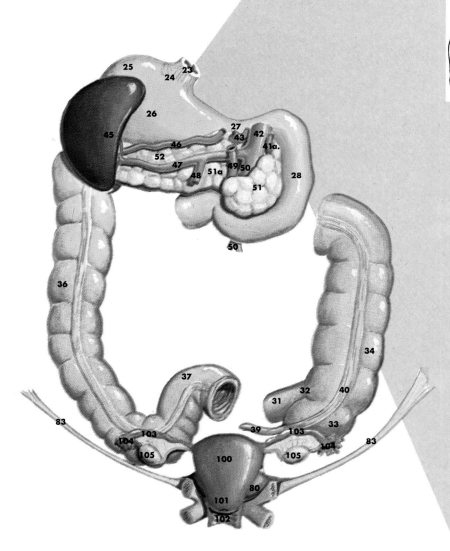

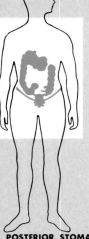

**POSTERIOR STOMACH, COLON,
AND
ORGANS OF REPRODUCTION**

23. Esophagus
24. Stomach (cardia)
25. Stomach (fundus)
26. Stomach (body)
27. Stomach (pylorus)
28. Duodenum
31. Ileum
32. Ileocolic junction
33. Caecum
34. Ascending colon
36. Descending colon
37. Sigmoid colon
39. Vermiform appendix
40. Taenia coli
41. Cystic duct
41a. Common bile duct
42. Portal vein
43. Hepatic artery
45. Spleen
46. Splenic artery
47. Splenic vein
48. Inferior mesenteric vein
49. Superior mesenteric artery
50. Superior mesenteric vein
51. Pancreas (head)
51a. Pancreas (body)
52. Pancreas (tail)
80. Bladder
83. Inguinal ligament
100. Uterus
101. Cervix
102. Vagina (cross section)
103. Fallopian tube
104. Ostium of fallopian tube
105. Ovary

grounds for infection.

As it moves through the vessels of the lymphatic system, lymph carries away from the tissues the bits and pieces of cells that have died and disintegrated, and also potentially harmful bacteria and viruses.

Lymph and Lymphocytes

Confusion often arises about the connection between the white blood cells called *lymphocytes* and the lymph itself. Lymph is not made up of lymphocytes, although it often carries

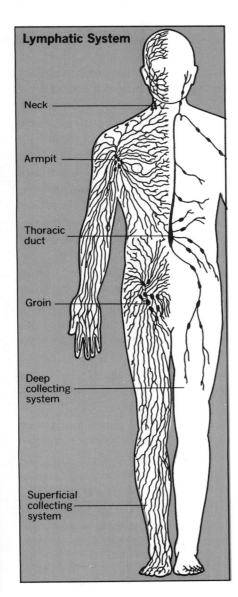

Lymphatic System

Neck

Armpit

Thoracic duct

Groin

Deep collecting system

Superficial collecting system

them; lymph is simply a watery vehicle moving through the lymphatic network. At certain points along this network, the vessels enlarge into clumpy structures called *lymph nodes* (or, misleadingly, lymph glands). Lymph nodes are major manufacturing sites for lymphocytes.

Lymph Nodes

Swollen glands are actually swollen lymph nodes, where a small army of lymphocytes is doing battle against invading bacteria or other harmful microscopic organisms. The lymph nodes, more than a hundred of them distributed around the body, serve as defense outposts against germs approaching the interior of the body. Those in the neck, groin, and armpits most frequently exhibit the pain and swelling that may accompany germ-fighting.

Circulation of Lymph

Lymph circulates without any help from the heart. From the spaces between cells, it diffuses into lymph capillaries which, like the venous capillaries, merge into larger and larger vessels moving inward toward the heart. The lymph moves—even upward from the legs and lower part of the body—because the muscles and movements of the body are constantly kneading and squeezing the lymph vessels. These vessels are equipped with valves that prevent back-flow. This is not so very different from the way venous blood makes its way back to the heart.

Eventually, master lymph vessels from the head, abdomen, and torso join in the thoracic lymph duct, which then empties into large neck veins that carry lymph and venous blood, mixed together, back to the heart.

The Heart at Work

The structure and performance of the heart, at first glance rather complicated, assume a magnificent simplicity once we observe that this pulsating knot of hollow, intertwining muscle uses only one beat to perform two distinct pumping jobs.

The heart has a right side (your right) and a left side (your left), divided by a tough wall of muscle called a *septum*. Each side has two chambers, an upper one called an *atrium* (or *auricle*), and a lower one called a *ventricle*.

How the Heart Pumps the Blood

Venous blood from the body flows into the right atrium via two large veins called the *superior vena cava* (bringing blood from the upper body) and the *inferior vena cava* (bringing blood from the lower part of the body). Where the blood enters the right atrium are valves that close when the atrium chamber is full.

Then, through a kind of trapdoor valve, blood is released from the right atrium into the right ventricle. When the right ventricle is full, and its outlet valve opens, the heart as a whole contracts—that is, pumps.

To the Lungs

The blood from the right ventricle is pumped to the lungs through the pulmonary artery to pick up oxygen. The trapdoor valve between the right atrium and ventricle has meanwhile closed, and venous blood again fills the right atrium.

Having picked up oxygen in the lungs, blood enters the left atrium through two pulmonary veins. (They are called veins despite the fact that they carry the most oxygen-rich blood, because they lead *to* the heart; just as the pulmonary artery carries the oxygen-poorest blood away from

How Blood Circulates through the Heart

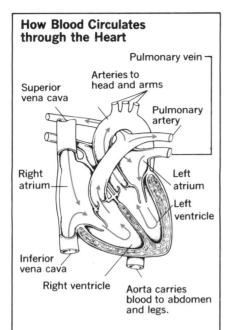

Blood from the head and arms enters the right atrium from the superior (i.e., upper) vena cava. Blood from the torso and legs enters from the inferior (i.e., lower) vena cava. The blood, controlled by a valve, passes to the right ventricle. It is then pumped into the pulmonary artery, which divides into two vessels, one leading to each lung. After being enriched with oxygen, the blood is brought back to the left atrium via the pulmonary veins, is admitted by a valve into the left ventricle, and is pumped through the aorta to be distributed to all parts of the body.

Both atria contract at the same time, forcing blood into the ventricles. Then both ventricles contract (while the atria relax), forcing blood into the great arteries. This period of contraction is called systole, and is followed by a period of relaxation called diastole.

the heart, to the lungs.) Like the right atrium, the left atrium serves as a holding reservoir and, when full, releases its contents into the left ventricle. A valve between left atrium and ventricle closes, and the heart pumps.

To the Body

Blood surges through an opening valve of the left ventricle into the aorta, the major artery that marks the beginning of blood's circulation throughout the body. The left ventricle, because it has the job of pumping blood to the entire body rather than just to the lungs, is slightly larger and more muscular than the right ventri-

cle. It is for this reason, incidentally, that the heart is commonly considered to be on our left. The organ as a whole, as noted earlier, is located at the center of the chest.

The Heart's Own Circulatory System

Heart tissue, like that of every other organ in the body, must be continually supplied with fresh, oxygen-rich blood, and used blood must be returned to the lungs for reoxygenation. The blood inside the heart cannot serve these needs. Thus the heart has its own circulation network, called *coronary arteries* and *veins,* to nourish its muscular tissues. There are two major arteries on the surface of the heart, branching and rebranching eventually into capillaries. Coronary veins then take blood back to the right atrium.

Structure of the Heart

The musculature of the heart is called cardiac muscle because it is different in appearance from the two other major types of muscle. The heart muscle is sometimes considered as one anatomical unit, called the *myocardium.* A tough outer layer of membranous tissue, called the *pericardium,* surrounds the myocardium. Lining the internal chambers and valves of the heart, on the walls of the atria and ventricles, is a tissue called the *endocardium.*

These tissues, like any others, are subject to infections and other disorders. An infection of the endocardium by bacteria is called *bacterial endocarditis.* (Disease of the valves is also called *endocarditis,* although it is a misnomer.) An interruption of the blood supply to the heart muscle is called a *myocardial infarction,* which results in the weakening or death of the portion of the myocardium whose blood supply is blocked. Fortunately,

in many cases, other blood vessels may eventually take over the job of supplying the blood-starved area of heart muscle.

Heartbeat

The rate at which the heart beats is controlled by both the autonomic nervous system and by hormones of the endocrine system. The precise means by which the chambers and valves of the heart are made to work in perfect coordination are not fully understood. It is known, however, that the heart has one or more natural cardiac pacemakers that send electrical waves through the heart, causing the opening and closing of valves and muscular contraction, or pumping, of the ventricles near the normal adult rate of about 72 times per minute.

One particular electrical impulse (there may be others) originates in a small area in the upper part of the right atrium called the *sinus node.* Because it is definitely known that the contraction of the heart is electrically activated, tiny battery-powered devices called *artificial pacemakers* have been developed that can take the place of a natural pacemaker whose function has been impaired by heart injury or disease. Through electrodes implanted in heart tissue, such devices supply the correct beat for a defective heart. The bulk of the device is usually worn outside the body or is implanted just under the skin.

The fact that both ventricles give their push at the same time is very significant. It allows the entire heart muscle to rest between contractions—a rest period that adds up to a little more than half of a person's lifetime. Without this rest period, it is more than likely that our hearts would wear out considerably sooner than they do.

Blood Pressure

A physician's taking of blood pressure is based upon the difference between the heart's action at its period of momentary rest and at the moment of maximum work (the contraction or push). The split-second of maximum work, at the peak of the ventricles' contraction, is called the *systole*. The split-second of peak relaxation, when blood from the atria is draining into and filling up the ventricles, is called the *diastole*.

Blood pressure measures the force with which blood is passing through a major artery, such as one in the arm, and this pressure varies between a higher *systolic* pressure, corresponding to the heart's systole, and a lower *diastolic* pressure, reflecting the heart's diastole, or resting phase. The device with which a physician takes your blood pressure, called a *sphygmomanometer,* registers these

higher and lower figures in numbers equivalent to the number of millimeters the force of your arterial blood would raise a column of mercury. The higher systolic force (pressure) is given first, then the diastolic figure. For example, 125/80 is within the normal range of blood pressure. Readings that are above the normal range—and stay elevated over a period of time—indicate a person has high blood pressure, or hypertension.

Hypertension has no direct connection with nervous tension, although the two may be associated in the same person. What it does indicate is that a heart is working harder than the average heart to push blood through the system. In turn, this may indicate the presence of a circulatory problem that might eventually endanger health. See also Ch. 9, *Diseases of the Circulatory System* and Ch. 10, *Heart Disease.*

The Digestive System and the Liver

A physician once remarked that a great many people seem to spend about half their time getting food into their digestive tracts and the other half worrying about how that food is doing on its travels. The physician was exaggerating, but he made his point.

The digestive tract has essentially one purpose: to break down food, both solid and fluid, into a form that can be used by the body. The food is used as energy to fuel daily activities or to nourish the various tissues that are always in the process of wearing out and needing replacement.

A normally functioning digestive tract, dealing with a reasonable variety and quantity of food, is designed to extract the maximum benefit from what we eat. Urine and feces are the waste products—things from which our body has selected everything that is of use.

Our digestive system's efficiency and economy in getting food into our bodies, to be utilized in all our living processes, can be attributed basically to three facts.

First, although the straight-line distance from the mouth to the bottom of the trunk is only two or three feet, the distance along the intestinal tract is about 10 times as great—30 feet—a winding, twisting, looping passageway that has more than enough footage to accommodate a number of ingeniously constructed way stations, checkpoints, and traffic-control devices.

Second, from the moment food enters the mouth, it is subjected to both chemical and mechanical actions that begin to break it apart, leading eventually to its reduction to submicro-

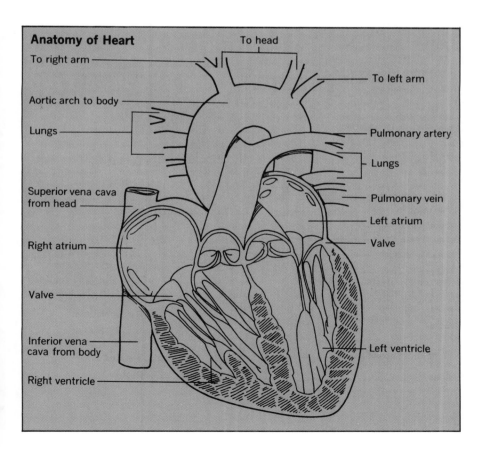

Anatomy of Heart

To right arm

To head

To left arm

Aortic arch to body

Lungs

Pulmonary artery

Lungs

Superior vena cava from head

Pulmonary vein

Left atrium

Right atrium

Valve

Valve

Inferior vena cava from body

Left ventricle

Right ventricle

scopic molecules that can be absorbed through the intestinal walls into the circulatory system.

Finally, each of the three main types of food—carbohydrates, fats, and proteins—receives special treatment that results in the body deriving maximum benefit from each.

Sensing the Right Kind of Food

Lips, eyes, and nose are generally given scant notice in discussions of the digestive process. But if we consider digestion to include selection of food and rejection of substances that might do us harm, then all three play very important roles.

The sensitive skin of our lips represents one of our first warning station that food may be harmful if taken into the mouth. It may tell us if a forkful of food is too hot or warn us of a concealed fishbone.

Our eyes, too, are important selection-rejection monitors for food. What else keeps us from sitting down to a crisp salad of poison ivy, or, less facetiously, popping a moldy piece of cake into our mouth?

As mammals' noses go, man's is a very inferior and insensitive organ. Nevertheless, we make good use of our sense of smell in the selection and enjoyment of foods. The nose adds to our enjoyment of favorite food and drink not only before they enter the mouth, but also after, because stimulation of the olfactory cells in the nasal passages combines with the stimulation of the taste cells on the tongue to produce the sensation-and-discrimination gradations of taste.

The Mouth: Saliva, Teeth, and Tongue

By the time food leaves the mouth and is pushed down into the gullet (or esophagus), it has already received a sampling of all the kinds of punishment and prodding that will be provided by the 30-foot tube that lies ahead of it. The chances are slim that any piece of food will end that journey in the same condition it started, but if it did it would have traveled those 30 tortuous feet at the rate of something less than two feet per hour. Normally, the elapsed time is between 17 and 25 hours.

As in the rest of the digestive tract, the mouth puts both chemical and mechanical apparatus to work on a bite of food. Saliva supplies the chemical action. Teeth and tongue, backed up by powerful sets of muscles, are the mashers, crushers, and prodders.

Saliva

The mere presence of food in our mouth—or even the smell, memory, or anticipation of it—sends signals to our brain, and our brain in turn sends messages back to a system of six salivary glands: one pair, called the *sublingual glands,* located under the tongue toward the front of the mouth; another pair, the *submaxillary* (or *submandibular*) glands, a bit behind and below them; and the largest, the *parotid glands,* tucked in the region where jaw meets neck behind the ear lobes.

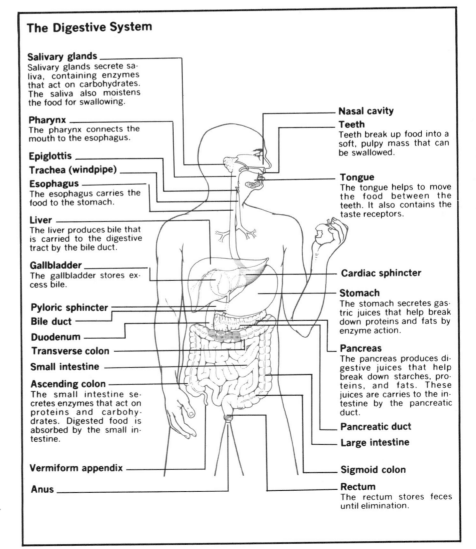

The Digestive System

Salivary glands _____
Salivary glands secrete saliva, containing enzymes that act on carbohydrates. The saliva also moistens the food for swallowing.

Pharynx _____
The pharynx connects the mouth to the esophagus.

Epiglottis _____

Trachea (windpipe) _____

Esophagus _____
The esophagus carries the food to the stomach.

Liver _____
The liver produces bile that is carried to the digestive tract by the bile duct.

Gallbladder _____
The gallbladder stores excess bile.

Pyloric sphincter _____

Bile duct _____

Duodenum _____

Transverse colon _____

Small intestine _____

Ascending colon _____
The small intestine secretes enzymes that act on proteins and carbohydrates. Digested food is absorbed by the small intestine.

Vermiform appendix _____

Anus _____

Nasal cavity

Teeth
Teeth break up food into a soft, pulpy mass that can be swallowed.

Tongue
The tongue helps to move the food between the teeth. It also contains the taste receptors.

Cardiac sphincter

Stomach
The stomach secretes gastric juices that help break down proteins and fats by enzyme action.

Pancreas
The pancreas produces digestive juices that help break down starches, proteins, and fats. These juices are carries to the intestine by the pancreatic duct.

Pancreatic duct

Large intestine

Sigmoid colon

Rectum
The rectum stores feces until elimination.

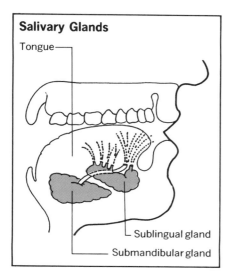

Salivary Glands

Tongue

Sublingual gland

Submandibular gland

Saliva is mainly composed of water, and water alone begins to soften up food so that it can pass more smoothly down the esophagus toward encounters with more powerful chemical agents.

There is also a very special substance in saliva, an enzyme called *ptyalin,* whose specific job is to begin the breakdown of one of the toughest kinds of food our digestive system has to handle—starches. Starch is a kind of carbohydrate, the group of foods from which we principally derive energy; but in order for the body to utilize carbohydrate, it must be broken down into simpler forms, which are called simply sugars. Ptyalin, then, begins the simplification of carbohydrate starch into carbohydrate sugar.

Saliva also does a favor or two for the dominating structures of the mouth—the tongue and teeth. Without its bathing action, the tongue's taste cells could not function up to par; and because it has a mild germicidal effect in addition to a simple rinsing action, saliva helps protect our mouth and teeth from bacterial infection.

Teeth

The role of the teeth in digestion can be summed up in one word: destruc-

tion. What the wrecker's ball is to a standing building, our teeth are to a lump of solid food. They do the first, dramatic demolishing, leaving smaller fragments to be dealt with and disposed of in other ways.

Starting from the center of the mouth, we have two incisors on either side, top and bottom, followed by a canine, a couple of premolars, and three molars, the most backward of which (it never appears in some people) is the curiously named "wisdom" tooth, so called because it commonly appears as physical maturity is reached, at about 20 years of age.

Our teeth equip us for destroying chunks of food by a gamut of mechanical actions ranging from gripping and puncturing to grinding and pulverizing. The teeth in front—canines and incisors—do most of the gripping, ripping, and tearing, while the premolars and molars at the back of the jaws do the grinding.

The Tongue

The surface of the tongue is not smooth, but has a finely corrugated look and feel. This slightly sandpapery surface results from the presence of thousands of tiny papillae, little pyramid-shaped bumps. When we are young, the walls of a single papilla may contain up to 300 taste cells, or buds. As we get older, the maximum number of taste buds per papilla may decline to under 100.

There are four kinds of taste cells, distinguished by the type of taste message each sends to the brain: salty, sweet, sour, and bitter. Each of the four types is a narrow specialist in one type of taste. However, simultaneous or successive stimulation of all four types (combined almost always with information picked up by our sense of smell) can produce a tremendous variety of recognizable tastes—although perhaps not so many as some gourmets or wine-tasters might have us believe.

All four types of taste buds—salty, sweet, sour, and bitter—are found associated with papillae in all areas on the surface of the tongue; but there tend to be denser populations of one

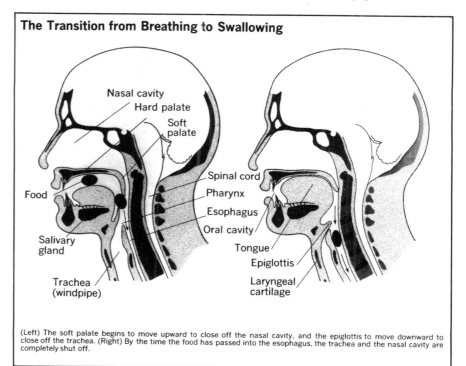

The Transition from Breathing to Swallowing

Nasal cavity
Hard palate
Soft palate
Spinal cord
Pharynx
Esophagus
Oral cavity
Food
Tongue
Salivary gland
Epiglottis
Laryngeal cartilage
Trachea (windpipe)

(Left) The soft palate begins to move upward to close off the nasal cavity, and the epiglottis to move downward to close off the trachea. (Right) By the time the food has passed into the esophagus, the trachea and the nasal cavity are completely shut off.

or the other kinds of taste cells in certain places. For example, salty and sweet cells predominate at the tip of the tongue and about halfway back along its sides; sour cells are more numerous all the way back along the sides; bitter buds are densest at the back of the tongue.

In addition to its tasting abilities, the tongue is a very versatile, flexible, and admirably shaped bundle of muscle. Not only can it flick out to moisten dry lips and ferret out and dislodge food particles in the oral cavity, but it also performs the first mechanical step in the all-important act of swallowing.

Swallowing

Swallow. You'll find that you feel the top of your tongue pressing up against the roof of your mouth (hard palate). You may never have thought about it consciously, but the pressing of the tongue against the hard palate prevents food from slipping to the front of your mouth—and also gives the food a good shove up and to the back of your mouth. At this point, the *soft palate* (from which the teardrop-shaped piece of tissue called the *uvula* hangs down) slips up to cover the passageway between mouth (oral cavity) and nasal cavity, nicely preventing the food from being misdirected toward your nose.

Once past the soft palate, the food is in the *pharynx,* a kind of anatomical traffic circle with two roads entering at the top, those from the mouth and nasal cavity, and two roads leading away from the bottom, the *trachea* (windpipe) and the *esophagus* or food tube.

The Epiglottis

A wedge of cartilage called the *epiglottis* protrudes from the trachea side, the side toward the front of the neck.

When we are breathing, the epiglottis is flattened up against the front wall of the pharynx, allowing free movement of air up and down the trachea. Simultaneously, the epiglottis helps to close off the entrance to the esophagus; a good part of the esophagus-closing work is done by a bundle of sinewy, elastic tissue we associate primarily with speech—the tissue of the vocal cords, otherwise known as the voice box or *larynx.* The laryngeal tissue is connected to the epiglottis above it, and supplies the epiglottis with most of its muscle for movement.

During the movement of a swallow, the larynx exerts an upward force against the epiglottis that serves to block off the trachea. At the same time, the larynx relaxes some of its pressure on the esophagus. Result: food enters the esophagus, where it is meant to go, and not the windpipe, which as we all know from having had something "go down the wrong way," produces an immediate fit of coughing.

Once we have swallowed, we lose almost completely the conscious ability to control the passage of food along the intestinal tract. Only when wastes reach the point of elimination do we begin to reassert some conscious control.

Peristalsis

The mechanical action called *peristalsis,* affected by muscles in the walls of all the organs of the gastrointestinal tract, first comes into play in the esophagus. Two layers of muscles intermesh in the intestinal walls: the inner layer encircles the esophagus in a series of rings; the outer layer stretches lengthwise along the tube. These two sets of muscles work in tandem to produce the basic action of persistalsis, called a *peristaltic wave.*

The alternative contraction and relaxation of the muscles—closing behind swallowed food and opening in front of it—combine to move both liquid and solid food (medical term, *bolus*) along the digestive tract. Gravity, in a sense, is left behind once food enters the esophagus. Because of peristalsis, we can swallow lying down or even standing on our heads; and astronauts are able to eat in near zero-gravity or under weightless conditions.

Peristalsis has another important function besides moving food through the body. The constricting and relaxing muscles serve also to knead, churn, and pummel the solid remains of the food left after our teeth have done their best.

Digestive Sphincters

If you think about it, the gastrointestinal tract has to be equipped with a number of gates that can open or shut, depending on the amount of food that is passing through. Otherwise, the food might push through so fast that little nourishment could be extracted from it: we would feel hungry one minute and glutted the next. The gastrointestinal tract is thus equipped at critical junctures with a number of muscular valves, or *sphincters,* which, usually under the direction of the autonomic nervous system, can regulate the movement of food through the digestive tube. Another function of a sphincter is to prevent backflow of partially digested food.

The muscles of a sphincter are often described as "pursestring muscles" because the way they draw together the sides of the digestive tube is roughly similar to drawing up the strings of a purse. The first of these pursestring valves occurs at the *cardia,* the opening where the esophagus meets the stomach, and is called the *cardiac sphincter,* from its location almost directly in front of the heart. (But there is no physical connection.)

Another important muscle ring is the *pyloric sphincter,* at the opening called the *pylorus,* located at the other end of the stomach, at the connection between stomach and small intestine. The release of waste from the rectum is controlled, partly voluntarily, by an *anal sphincter,* located at the *anus,* which marks the end of the tract.

The Stomach

About ten inches down the esophagus, the food we swallow must pass the cardiac sphincter. Then the food, by now fairly well diced and mashed, passes into the stomach.

Inelegant as it sounds, the stomach is best described as a rough, leather-skinned balloon. When empty, its skin shrivels around itself like a deflated balloon; but when "pumped up" by a hearty meal, the stomach becomes a plump, J-shaped bag about a foot long and six inches wide, holding about two quarts of food and drink.

The Passage of Food through the Stomach

Although its food-processing function tends to get more attention, the stomach's role as a storage reservoir is equally important. A moderate, well-rounded meal with a good blend of carbohydrates, proteins, and fats takes usually a minimum of three hours to pass out of the pyloric sphincter into the small intestine—more if the meal is heavy in fats and rich foods. Thus, a meal that might take us 15 minutes to eat, may take up to 20 times as long to pass from the stomach into the small intestine. This decelerating of food's rate of passage has two very significant re-

sults: first, it allows time for the food-processing activities within the stomach; and second, it releases food (in a mushy form called *chyme*) in small, well-spaced amounts that can be efficiently handled by the small intestine.

Although the stomach is not an absolutely essential organ—a person can live a full life with part or even all of it removed—it is a tremendous convenience. Without a stomach, frequent, carefully selected, well-chewed small feedings rather than "three square meals a day" are necessary so as not to overburden the small intestine, which can handle only a small quantity of food, well-mashed, at one time. If too much food goes directly to the small intestine, only so much nourishment (carbohydrates, proteins, fats) per meal can be supplied to the body, with the result that we would be weak from hunger after going a few hours without eating.

It will come as no surprise to know that the food processing done in the stomach is both mechanical and chemical. The three layers of crisscrossing muscles in the stomach walls are rarely still. They contract and relax continually, squeezing, pummeling, and mixing the stomach's contents into chyme. So active and relentless is the stomach's muscular activity that it actually "chews up" pieces of food that have been swallowed too hastily.

Stomach Chemicals

The various chemicals found in the stomach are produced and secreted into the stomach cavity by some 40 million gland cells that line the interior stomach walls. The constant wiggling and jouncing of the stomach helps to mix these chemicals thoroughly into the food. Each of the chemicals is secreted by a special type of cell and has a specific function. They include the digestive enzymes pepsin, rennin, and lipase; hydrochloric acid; and wa-

tery mucus.

A look at the special assignments of rennin, pepsin, hydrochloric acid, and mucus—and how they interact with and depend upon one another—provides a good glimpse into the elegant and complex chemical events that occur when the stomach encounters a swallow of food.

Rennin and Pepsin

Rennin, well known to cheesemakers, has essentially one task: to turn milk

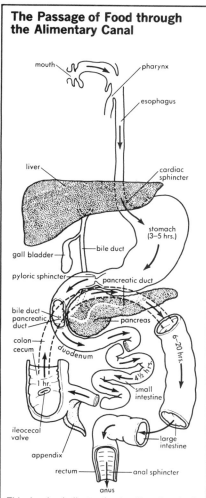

The Passage of Food through the Alimentary Canal

This drawing indicates the duration of each digestive process. Food enters the mouth and is passed through the pharynx and esophagus into the stomach, where it is partly digested. The small intestine completes digestion and absorbs digested food. The large intestine absorbs excess water. Indigestible residue collects in the rectum for later disposal.

into milk curds. But the curds are not ready to pass on to the small intestine until they are further dismantled by *pepsin*. Pepsin has other duties as well: one of them is to begin the breakdown of proteins. But pepsin can only begin to split up protein foods after they have been worked on by *hydrochloric acid*.

Hydrochloric Acid

Hydrochloric acid is a corrosive substance and, except in very dilute strengths, could quite literally eat away the lining of the stomach. (This is apparently what happens in cases of gastric ulcers.) Mucus secretions, with the help of fluids in the food itself, dilute the hydrochloric acid to a point where (in a normal stomach) it is rendered harmless. Even so, the normal, healthy condition inside our stomach is slightly acid. The slight acidity of the stomach serves to inhibit the growth of organisms such as bacteria.

The Small Intestine

By the time food-turned-chyme gets through the pyloric sphincter, it has already traveled about two-and-a-half feet: about 6 inches from lips to epiglottis; 10 or 12 inches down the esophagus; and about a foot through the stomach. But at this point it has actually traveled less than one-tenth of the gastrointestinal (GI) tract, and the longest stretch lies just ahead: the 20-plus feet of the small intestine, so named because of its relatively small one-to-two inch diameter. The preparation of food particles to pass through the walls of the GI tract is completed in the small intestine—almost completed, in fact, before the chyme has traveled the first foot of the small intestine. By the time it leaves the small intestine, chyme has

given up virtually all its nutrients. In other words, the process called *absorption* or *assimilation* has taken place: the nutrients have left the GI tract for other parts of the body via the circulating blood and lymph. What passes on to the large intestine is principally waste and water.

The small intestine is somewhat arbitrarily divided into three sections: the *duodenum*, the *jejunum*, and the *ileum*.

The Duodenum

Within this horseshoe loop, eight to ten inches long and about two inches in diameter, more chemical interactions are concentrated than in any other section of the GI tract. One of the first jobs in the duodenum is to neutralize the acidity of the chyme. The final steps of digestion, and the absorption of food through the intestinal lining, proceed best in a slightly alkaline environment.

The alkaline juices needed to neutralize the acidity of the chyme come mainly from the liver in the form of bile. Bile produced by the liver but not needed immediately in the duodenum is stored in concentrated form in the gallbladder, a pouchlike, three-inch-long organ. On signal from the autonomic nervous system, the membranous muscular walls of the gallbladder contract, squeezing concentrated, highly alkaline bile into a short duct that leads to the duodenum. Bile components are indispensable for the digestion and absorption of stubborn fatty materials.

Through a duct from the pancreas, a host of pancreatic enzymes, capable of splitting apart large, tough molecules of carbohydrate, protein, and fat, enters the duodenum. These digestive enzymes manufactured by the pancreas are the most powerful in the GI tract.

What triggers the production of

bile and pancreatic juice for the duodenum? Apparently, it is a two-step process involving hormones. When the stomach walls secrete hydrochloric acid on the arrival of food, hormones are released; they travel to the liver and pancreas with instructions to step up their production of digestive juices.

Still other strong enzymes are secreted by the walls of the duodenum and join the bile and pancreatic enzymes in the duodenum.

Thus, in the not quite foot-long tube of the duodenum, the final breakdown of food—digestion—reaches a dramatic climax. The nutrients in the food eaten some hours ago have almost all been reduced to molecules small enough to be absorbed through the intestinal walls into the bloodstream. Carbohydrates are reduced to simpler sugars; proteins to amino acids; and fats to fatty acids and glycerol.

Some absorption of these nutrients occurs in the duodenum, but the far greater proportion takes place in the next two, longer sections of the small intestine: the eight- to ten-foot jejunum and the twelve-foot ileum. Likewise, some oversize food molecules that get past the duodenum may be digested further along in their passage through the small intestine.

The Jejunum

As peristalsis pushes the nutrient broth out of the duodenum and into the first reaches of the jejunum, a gradual change in the appearance of the intestinal lining is evident. Greater and greater number of *villi*—microscopic, hairlike structures—sprout from the already bumpy walls of the intestinal lining into the GI tube.

The Villi

The villi (singular, *villus*) have the primary responsibility for absorbing amino acids (from protein), sugars (from carbohydrates), and fatty acids and glycerol (from fats) from the digested contents of the small intestine, and starting them on their way to other parts of the body. What the villi do not remove from the chyme—such as the cellulose fragments of fruits and vegetables—passes on to the large intestine in a thin, watery soup almost completely lacking in nutritional value.

Gland cells near the bottom of a villus secrete various enzymes, mucus, and other substances that perform digestive "mop-up operations" along the whole length of the small intestine.

The Ileum

In this third and final 12-foot section of the small intestine, villi line the walls in such profusion that the intestinal lining resembles, under moderate magnification, nothing so much as a plush, velvety carpet. The greatest numbers of the estimated five or six million villi in the small intestine are found along the lining of the ileum, making it the primary absorption site of the GI tract.

Also adding to the ileum's absorption efficiency is its gradually narrowing diameter (just one inch at its junction with the large intestine), which helps to keep the chyme always in close contact with the swishing villi. The end of the ileum is marked by the *ileocecal valve,* beyond which lies the first bulge of the large intestine, the *cecum.*

Principally because of vigorous peristaltic contractions and relaxations, the walls of the small intestine are always moving like the walls within some spasmodically flexing, nightmarish tunnel. Attached to the intestinal walls, the villi, too, are always in restless motion: waving and

thrashing, protracting and retracting, even growing thinner or fatter.

Although the entire distance through the small intestine, from the pyloric sphincter to the ileocecal valve at the junction with the large intestine, is only a bit over 20 feet, the villi give the small intestine's internal lining a relatively gigantic surface area—over 100 square feet. This is about five times the surface area of our body's skin. Of course, the greatly enlarged surface area gives the small intestine lining that much more space in which to absorb nutrients.

The small intestine is supported in the abdomen by a fan-shaped web of tissues called the *mesentery.* Attached at the back of the abdomen, the mesentery connects to the small intestine at various points, and yet allows it some freedom to squirm and sway—much like the V network of ropes that attaches either end of a hammock to a tree. Nerve fibers and blood vessels also reach the small intestine via the mesentery.

The Liver, Gallbladder, and Pancreas

These three organs all share a common function—sending digestive substances to the duodenum—although, except in the case of the gallbladder, it is not their only function. Lying outside the GI tract proper, they nevertheless are indispensable in the processes of digestion and absorption. Digestive fluids from all three converge like tributaries of a river at the common bile duct, and their flow from there into the duodenum is controlled by a sphincter muscle-ring separating the duodenum and common bile duct.

From the liver, bile drips into the *hepatic duct,* which soon meets the *cystic duct* arriving from the gallbladder. Converging, they form one duct,

the *common bile duct,* which meets the *pancreatic duct,* carrying enzymatic fluid from the pancreas. Like a smaller river meeting a larger one, the pancreatic duct loses its own name at this confluence and becomes part of the common bile duct, which empties on demand into the duodenum. When the sphincter of the bile duct is closed, bile from the liver is forced to back up into the cystic duct, and eventually into the gallbladder. There it is stored and concentrated until needed, when it flows back down the cystic duct.

The Liver

Four pounds of highly efficient chemical-processing tissues, the liver is the largest solid organ in the body. You can locate it by placing your left hand over your right, lowermost ribs; your hand then just about covers the area of the liver. More than any other organ, the liver enables our bodies to benefit from the food we eat. Without it, digestion would be impossible, and the conversion of food into living cells and energy practically nonexistent. Insofar as they affect our body's handling of food—all the many processes that go by the collective name of nutrition—the liver's functions can be roughly divided into those that break down food molecules and those that build up or reconstitute these nutrients into a form that the body can use or store efficiently.

Breaking Down Food Molecules

Bile, as we have seen, assists in the destruction of large food molecules in the small intestine, enabling absorption of nutrients by the villi. Bile acts to increase alkalinity, breaking down big fat molecules; stimulates peristalsis; and prevents food from putrefying within the digestive tract. Unusable portions of the bile, destined to be eliminated as waste, include excess cholesterol, fats, and various components of dead disintegrated cells. Pigments from dead cells in bile give feces its normal, dark, yellow-brown color. Other cell fragments in bile, especially iron from disintegrated red blood cells, are reclaimed from the intestines and eventually make their way via the bloodstream to other parts of the body, where they are built into new cells.

Reconstituting Nutrients

Oddly enough, the liver rebuilds some of the proteins and carbohydrates that the bile has just so effectively helped to break down in the digestive tract. But this is really not so strange as it sounds. The types of proteins and carbohydrates that can be used by man for cell-rebuilding and energy are usually somewhat different in fine structure from those in food. Thus, the liver receives the basic building blocks of proteins and carbohydrates—amino acids and sugars—and with them builds up molecules and cells that can be utilized by the human body. The amino acids and sugars reach the liver through the *portal vein,* which is the great collection tube for nutrient-carrying blood returning from capillaries along the stomach and small intestine.

Glycogen and Glucose

In the liver, sugars from the small intestine are converted into a special substance called *glycogen;* amino acids are made available as needed for building new cells to replace the cells that are always naturally dying in a healthy normal body. Glycogen, simply speaking, is the liver's solution to a difficult space and storage problem. The form of carbohydrate the body can use best is a sugar called *glucose,*

but the liver isn't large enough to store the necessary amount of glucose. The answer is glycogen, a tidy, compact sugar molecule that the liver can store in great quantities. When a call comes from any part of the body for glucose, the liver quickly converts some glycogen to glucose and releases it into the bloodstream. By this mechanism, healthy blood sugar levels are maintained.

The liver also builds up human fats from fatty acids and glycerol, packs them off to storage, then reverses the process when necessary by breaking down body fats into forms that can serve as fuel to be burned by the body for energy.

Other Functions

In addition to its functions closely related to digestion and nutrition, the liver also serves as a storehouse and processor of vitamins and minerals—it is, in fact, the manufacturer of vitamin A. It can remove many toxic substances from the blood and render their poisons harmless. It picks up spent red blood cells from the circulation and dismantles them; and it continually manufactures new blood elements.

The liver is also a manufacturing site for *cholesterol,* a substance belonging to the class of body chemicals called steroids. Above-normal levels of cholesterol in the blood have been linked to hardening of the arteries and heart disease; but cholesterol in the proper amounts is needed by almost every tissue in the body. Some brain and spinal tissues, for example, have cholesterol as one of their main structural components.

With all these vital chemical activities and more, the liver might be expected to be a most delicate and fragile organ. In a sense it is: minor liver damage from one cause or another is thought to be fairly common. But

what saves our lives (and us) is that we have a great deal more of it than we need for a normal healthy life. Before symptoms of a liver deficiency appear, more than 50 percent of the liver cells may be destroyed. Furthermore, the liver has a great capacity for regeneration, rebuilding diseased tissues with new liver cells.

The Gallbladder

Bile stored in the gallbladder is much more concentrated and thicker than bile that is fresh from the liver. This allows the three-inch gallbladder to store a great deal of bile components. But the thickening process can also create problems in the form of extremely painful gallstones, which are dried, crystallized bile. Fortunately, the entire gallbladder can be removed with little or no lasting ill effect. All that is missing is a small storage sac for bile.

The Pancreas

This manufacturer of powerful digestive enzymes, only six inches long, resembles a branchlet heavily laden with ripe berries. Its important role in digestion is often overshadowed by the fact that it also manufactures the hormone *insulin.* The pancreas cells that manufacture digestive enzymes are completely different from those that manufacture insulin. The latter are grouped into little clusters called the *islets of Langerhans,* which are discussed under *The Endocrine Glands* in this chapter.

The Large Intestine

The large intestine, also called the large bowel, is shaped like a great, lumpy, drooping question mark—arching, from its beginning at the ileocecal valve, over the folds of the small intestine, then curving down and descending past more coiled small intestine to the anus, which marks the end of the GI tract. From ileocecal valve to anus, the large intestine is five to six feet in length.

The junction between the ileum and the *cecum,* the first section of the large intestine, occurs very low in the abdomen, normally on the right-hand side. The cecum is a bowl-like receptacle at the bottom of the colon, the longest section of the large intestine.

Just below the entrance of the ileum, a dead-end tube dangles down from the cecum. This is the *appendix vermiformis* (Latin, "worm-shaped appendage") commonly known as the appendix. Three to six inches long and one-third inch in diameter, the appendix may get jammed with stray pieces of solid food, become infected, swell, and rupture, spewing infection into the abdominal cavity. This is why early diagnosis of *appendicitis* and removal (*appendectomy*) are critically important.

Sections of the Colon

The colon is divided into three sections by pronounced *flexures,* or bends, where the colon makes almost right-angle changes of direction. Above the bowl of the cecum, the *ascending colon* rises almost vertically for about a foot and a half.

Then there is a flexure in the colon, after which the *transverse colon* travels horizontally for a couple of feet along a line at navel height. At another flexure, the colon turns vertically down again, giving the name of *descending colon* to this approximately two feet of large intestine. At the end of the descending colon, the large intestine executes an S-shaped curve, the *sigmoid flexure,* after which the remaining several inches of large intestine are known as the *rectum.*

Some people confuse the terms rectum and anus: the rectum refers specifically to the last section of the large intestinal tube, between sigmoid flexure and the anal sphincters, while the anus refers only to the opening controlled by the outlet valves of the large intestine. These valves consist of two ringlike voluntary muscles called anal sphincters.

Any solid materials that pass into the large intestine through the ileocecal valve (which prevents backflow into the small intestine) are usually indigestible, such as cellulose, or substances that have been broken down in the body and blood in the normal process of cell death and renewal, such as some bile components. But what the cecum mainly receives is water.

Functions of the Large Intestine

The principal activity of the large intestine—other than as a channel for elimination of body wastes—is as a temporary storage area for water, which is then reabsorbed into the circulation through the walls of the colon. Villi are absent in the large intestine, and peristalsis is much less vigorous than in the small intestine.

As water is absorbed, the contents of the large intestine turn from a watery soup into the semisolid feces. Meanwhile, bacteria—which colonize the normal colon in countless millions—have begun to work on and decompose the remaining solid materials. These bacteria do no harm as long as they remain inside the large intestine, and the eliminated feces is heavily populated with them. Nerve endings in the large intestine signal the brain that it is time for a bowel movement.

The Peritoneum

Lining the entire abdominal cavity, as well as the digestive and other abdominal organs, is a thin, tough, lubricated membrane called the *peritoneum.* In addition to protecting and supporting the abdominal organs, the peritoneum permits these organs to slip and slide against each other without any harm from friction. The peritoneum also contains blood and lymph vessels that serve the digestive organs. See Ch. 11, *Diseases of the Digestive System.*

The Respiratory System and the Lungs

The heart, by its construction and shape, tells us a great deal about the lungs and respiration.

Interaction between Heart and Lungs

The heart is divided vertically by a wall called a septum into right (your right) and left parts. The right part is smaller than the left: its muscles only have to pump blood a few inches to the lungs, while the muscles of the left half have to pump blood to the whole body.

The function of the right half of our heart is to receive oxygen-poor blood from the veins of the body. Venous blood empties into the top-right chamber, or right atrium, of the heart, and the right ventricle pumps that oxygen-poor blood (via the pulmonary artery) to the lungs, where the blood, passing through minute capillaries, picks up oxygen.

From the lungs, the oxygen-rich blood flows back into the heart's left atrium via the pulmonary veins; and from the left atrium, the oxygen-rich blood drains into the left ventricle,

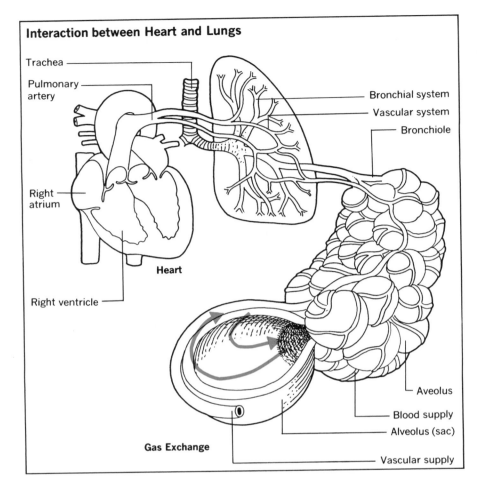

Interaction between Heart and Lungs

Trachea
Pulmonary artery
Right atrium
Right ventricle
Heart

Bronchial system
Vascular system
Bronchiole

Gas Exchange

Aveolus
Blood supply
Alveolus (sac)
Vascular supply

from whence it is pumped via the aorta to the body.

The blood pumped to the lungs by the right ventricle is oxygen-poor blood; it has given up its oxygen to the cells that need it around the body. But this "used blood" is rich in something else—carbon dioxide. As the body's cells have taken oxygen, they have given up carbon dioxide to the circulating blood. For both oxygen and carbon dioxide, the "carrier" has been *hemoglobin,* a complex iron-protein substance that is part of our red blood cells.

Capillaries and Alveoli

The pulmonary artery carrying this lung-bound blood soon branches into smaller and smaller vessels, and eventually into microscopic capillaries that reach into every crook and crev-

ice of the lungs.

In the lungs, the walls of the capillaries touch the walls of equally microscopic structures called *alveoli* (singular, *alveolus*). The alveoli are the smallest air sacs of the lungs. These tiny, expandable air cells are the destination of every breath of air we take. Estimates of the total number of alveoli in both our lungs vary between 300 million and a billion—in any case, we normally have several hundred million of them.

Carbon Dioxide and Oxygen Exchange

Where they meet, the membranous walls of both a capillary and an alveolus are both about as thin as any living tissue can be—a thickness that is only the width of one cell. Under such

conditions, the carbon dioxide carried by the hemoglobin in our blood to the lungs diffuses (as tiny gaseous "bubbles") across both the wall of a capillary and the wall of an alveolus.

Once inside the sac of the alveolus, carbon dioxide is ready to be exhaled from the body by "breathing out." One indication of just how well this system works is the fact that the air we exhale has roughly 100 times more carbon dioxide than the air we breathe in.

At the same time that hemoglobin dumps carbon dioxide at the interface of the capillary and alveolus walls, it picks up the oxygen made available from inhaled fresh air that has reached the alveoli. The molecular oxygen bubbles cross the membranes in the same way—but in the opposite direction—as the carbon dioxide.

Hemoglobin in the capillaries picks up the oxygen and carries it via veins leading away from the lungs, to the left atrium of the heart.

Essential Role of Moisture

The alveolar membranes are supplied with a thin film of moisture that is absolutely indispensable to the exchange of gases in the lungs. As in so many of our body's reactions, our evolutionary descent from water-dwelling ancestors is revealed by the wet environment demanded if our lungs are to supply our body with oxygen.

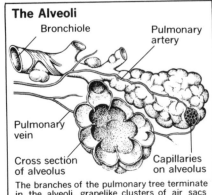

The Alveoli

Bronchiole
Pulmonary artery
Pulmonary vein
Cross section of alveolus
Capillaries on alveolus

The branches of the pulmonary tree terminate in the alveoli, grapelike clusters of air sacs covered by capillaries, where the gaseous exchange occurs.

Respiration at the One-Cell Level

Oxygen molecules, then, are carried to the body's cells by the hemoglobin of the arterial blood pumped by the heart's left ventricle. But how does a cell take oxygen from the blood and use it?

Exchange of Gases

The transfer of oxygen from blood to cell is accomplished in much the same way as the exhanges that take place in the lungs. The circulating arterial blood has a surplus of oxygen; the cells have a surplus of carbon dioxide. When the oxygen-rich blood reaches the finest capillaries, only the very thinnest membranous walls (of cell and capillary) separate it from the carbon-dioxide-rich cells. As in the lungs, both these gases (dissolved in water) diffuse through these thinnest of membranes: the oxygen into the cell, the carbon dioxide into the blood for eventual deposit in the alveoli, and exhalation.

Within the cell, the oxygen is needed so that food, the body's fuel, can be burned to produce energy. At the cellular level, the most convenient and common food is a fairly simple carbohydrate molecule called glucose.

Conversion of Carbohydrates into Energy

Energy is locked into a carbohydrate molecule such as glucose in the form of chemical bonds between its atoms. If one of these bonds is broken—say, a bond holding together a carbon and a hydrogen atom—a bit of pent-up energy is released as if, in a stalemated tug of war, the rope suddenly broke and both teams went hurtling off a few feet in opposite directions. This is precisely the effect of respiration within a cell: the cell "breaks the ropes" holding together a carbo-

hydrate molecule. The result is the release of energy—either as body heat or to power other activities within the cell.

It is useful—but a somewhat misleading oversimplification—to consider cellular respiration as a type of burning, or combustion. When a typical cell burns food, a carbohydrate molecule (glucose) together with molecules of oxygen are changed into carbon dioxide and water. During this change, chemical energy is released—energy that has been trapped, as we have seen, in the carbohydrate molecule. That complex, energy-rich molecule has been dismantled into the simpler molecules of carbon dioxide (CO_2) and water (H_2O). Oxygen is necessary here just as it is in fiery combustion. But the energy released here, instead of rushing out as heat and flame, is used to power the living activities of the cell.

This description of cellular respiration is all right in principle, but the trouble is this: if it all happened at once—if carbohydrate was so abruptly dismantled, split up at one stroke to water and carbon dioxide—such a great amount of energy would be released that the cell would simply burn itself up. As one biologist has said, the cell would be in exactly the same position as a wood furnace built of wood.

What protects the cell is its army of enzymes. These remarkable protein molecules combine briefly with energy-containing food molecules, causing them to break down bit by bit, so that energy is released gradually rather than all at once.

Carbon Dioxide— Precious Waste

In most of our minds, oxygen tends to be the hero of respiration and car-

bon dioxide the villain or at least the undesirable waste gas. This isn't really a fair picture. While it is true that too much carbon dioxide would act as a poison in our body, it is also true that we must always have a certain amount of the gas dissolved in our tissues. If we did not, two potentially fatal events could occur. First, our blood chemistry, especially its delicate acid-alkali balance, would get completely out of control. Second—and something of a paradox—the body's whole automatic system of regulating breathing would be knocked out.

It is the level of carbon dioxide in the bloodstream that controls our breathing. This level is continuously being monitored by the autonomic nervous system, specifically by the lower brain's "breathing center" in the medulla at the top of the spinal cord. When the level of carbon dioxide in our body goes above a certain level, signals from the medulla force us to breathe. Almost everybody has played, "How long can you hold your breath?" and knows that, past a certain point, it becomes impossible *not* to breathe. When you are holding your breath, the unexhaled carbon dioxide rapidly builds up in your system until the breathing center is besieged with signals that say "Breathe!" And you do.

Our Big Breathing Muscle: The Diaphragm

What gets air into and out of our lungs? The answer may seem as obvious as breathing in and out. But except for those rare instances when we consciously regulate our breathing pattern—which physicians call "force breathing"—we do not decide when to inhale and when to exhale. And even when we do force-breathe, it is not primarily the action of opening the

Diaphragm

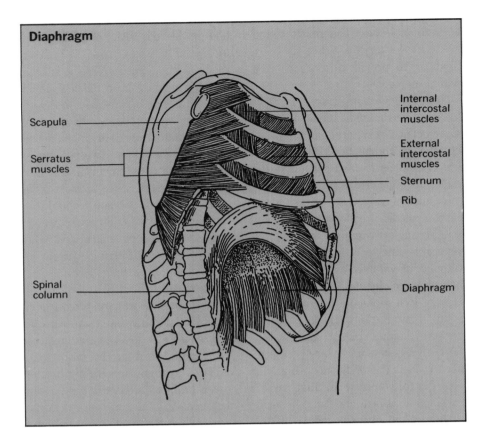

Scapula

Serratus muscles

Spinal column

Internal intercostal muscles

External intercostal muscles

Sternum

Rib

Diaphragm

mouth and gulping in air, then blowing it out, that gets air down the windpipe and into the alveoli of the lungs. The main work of inhaling and exhaling is done by the contraction and relaxation of the big helmet-shaped muscle on which the lungs rest and which marks the "floor" of the chest or thoracic cavity and the "ceiling" of the abdominal cavity. This muscle is the *diaphragm.*

It is the diaphragm that causes the lungs to swell and fill with fresh air, then partially collapse to expel used gases. The muscles and tendons of the sinewy diaphragm are attached at the back to the spinal column, at the front to the breastbone (*sternum*), and at the lower sides to the lower ribs.

The diaphragm contracts and relaxes on orders from the brain's breathing center, orders that are carried along the pathways of the autonomic nervous system. When the medulla sends messages to the

breathing muscles to contract, the diaphragm is pulled downward, enlarging the space filled by the lungs. This creates a temporary partial vacuum, into which air rushes, inflating and expanding the lungs. When the diaphragm relaxes, the lung space is reduced, pushing air out.

Other Breathing Muscles

The diaphragm muscle's leading role in breathing is supported by several other muscles that play minor parts. Among these are the *intercostal muscles* between the ribs that give the rib cage a slight push upward and outward, enlarging the thoracic cavity, and the *serratus muscles,* which are mainly muscular sheaths along the ribs, to which other muscles are attached.

The Trachea and the Lungs

The right lung (your right) is somewhat bigger than the left. The lungs

hang in the chest attached to the windpipe or *trachea.*

The Trachea

The trachea itself branches off at the back of the throat, or *pharynx,* where the epiglottis prevents food from entering the trachea and channels swallowed food along its proper route, the esophagus. The top part of the trachea forms the voice box or *larynx,* made up of vocal cords—actually two flaps of cartilage, muscle, and membranous tissue that protrude into the windpipe—whose vibrations in response to air exhaled from the lungs give us our voice.

Below the larynx, the trachea descends five or six inches to a spot just about directly behind your breastbone, where the first of many thousands of branchings into *bronchi, bronchioles,* and alveoli occurs. C-shaped rings of cartilage give the trachea both support and flexibility. Running your finger down the front of your neck, you can feel the bumps made by the cartilage rings.

Above the base of the trachea in midchest the lungs arch on either side like giant butterfly wings, then fall to fill out the bottom of each side of the thoracic cavity.

The Pleural Membranes

Both lungs are encased in moist, clinging, tissue-thin membrane called the *pleura,* which also lines the inside of the thoracic cavity where it comes into contact with the pleural coating of the lungs. The slippery pleural membranes hold tightly to each other, because there is an air lock or vacuum between them, but at the same time are free to slide over each other. The principle is the same as that illustrated by moistening the surfaces of two pieces of plate glass and placing the moistened surfaces together: the two pieces of glass will slide over each other but will resist being pried apart, because a partial vacuum exists between them.

The Pleural Cavity

The vacuum space between the pleura of the lung and the pleura of the thoracic cavity—although it is normally not a space at all—is called the *pleural cavity*. Each lung has its own pleural membrane: that of one lung does not interconnect with the other, so that one pleura may be injured without affecting the other.

It is extremely fortunate for us that the pleural linings both stick fast and can slide along each other's surfaces. Although the lungs are virtually without muscle, they are extremely elastic and in their natural condition are stretched fairly taut, held to the sides of the thoracic cavity by the suction of the pleura.

Collapsed Lung

Should this suction be broken and the pleural linings pull apart, the lung would shrink up like a deflated balloon. Such a condition, caused by the rush of outside air into the pleural cavity, is known medically as *pneumothorax* and causes a lung collapse. Violent injuries such as gun and stab wounds, various lung diseases, and obstructions of the breathing tubes can cause a lung or portion of a lung to collapse.

In the surgical procedure called *artificial pneumothorax*, a physician deliberately injects air between the pleural linings to collapse a portion of a lung. This is done to rest a lung in severe diseases such as tuberculosis, or to control heavy bleeding within the thoracic cavity.

Pleurisy

The intense chest pains called *pleurisy*

are caused by inflammation of the pleura. The pleural linings lose their slipperiness and the increased friction stimulates pain receptors in the pleural lining of the chest. There are, however, no pain receptors in the lungs' pleural linings nor in the lungs themselves: this is why pain is not an early warning signal of lung cancer.

The Bronchi

Just behind the breastbone and just in front of the heart, the trachea divides into the right bronchus and the left bronchus, leading respectively to the right and left lungs. These are the primary two *bronchi* or *bronchial tubes*. Each is the main trunk of a bronchial tree that serves its respective lung.

Soon after leaving the trachea, each bronchus branches repeatedly into smaller tubes called *bronchioles,* which in turn branch into alveolar ducts, which terminate finally with the hundreds of millions of microscopic air sacs called alveoli, discussed at the beginning of this section. The alveoli are the site of the all-important exchange of carbon dioxide and oxygen.

Lobes and Segments

The larger right lung has three distinctive sections, or *lobes*—upper, middle, and lower. The left lung has only an upper and lower lobe. The lobes themselves are divided into smaller segments. Medically, these lobes and segments are important because they are somewhat independent of each other and can be damaged or removed surgically, as in operations for lung cancer, usually without damaging the function of adjacent, healthy segments or lobes.

The fact that a lung segment, lobe, or even an entire lung can be removed implies that we have plenty of reserve lung tissue, and this is indeed the case. When we are at rest, we use

only about one-tenth of our total lung capacity. The total surface area exposed within our lungs to outside air is, amazingly, 600 square feet. This compares to a mere 20 square feet of skin surface. To appreciate the incredibly intricate, lacelike finery of the lungs' structure, we need only know that those 600 square feet of surface area are contained within two organs that together weigh only two-and-a-half pounds.

Oxygen Requirements

How much air do we breathe, and how much oxygen do we absorb into our body from the air? A normal, moderately active person breathes in and out (a complete respiration or breath cycle) about 18 times a minute; that is, the diaphragm contracts and relaxes 18 times a minute, or something over 25,000 times every day. At about four-fifths of a pint of air per breath cycle, this means that we inhale and exhale about 20,000 pints, or 10,000 quarts, or 2,500 gallons of air every day.

Only a very small proportion of this volume is oxygen that finds its way into our bloodstream: about a pint every minute in normal, quiet breathing, a little over 1,400 pints, or 700 quarts, or 175 gallons of oxygen every day. The amount of oxygen our lungs are capable of delivering to our body, however, varies tremendously: during sleep a person may need only a half-pint of oxygen per minute, half the average, while the lungs of a hard-driving athlete striving to break the mile record can deliver up to five quarts to the bloodstream—ten times the average.

At any given time, there are about two quarts of oxygen circulating in our blood. This is why a stoppage of breathing has an upper time limit of about four minutes before it causes irreversible damage or death. With our body needing about a pint of oxygen every minute for normal functioning, we have about four minutes before we use up the oxygen dissolved in our blood and other tissues.

Pollution Control—Filters, Cleaners, and Traps

Air pollution being what it is these days, it is fortunate that we have several natural devices that serve to filter out and wash away most of the impurities in the air we inhale.

Air gets into the lungs from outside about equally well via the nose or mouth. The mouth offers the advantage of getting more air in at a faster rate—absolutely a must if we have to push our body physically. But the nose has more and better equipment for cleaning air before it reaches the trachea. Via the mouth, air must only pass over a few mucous membranes and the tonsils, which can collect only so many germs and impurities.

Nose Filter System

Air taken in through the nose, however, first meets the "guard hairs" (*vibrissae*) of the nostrils, and then must circulate through the nasal cavity, a kind of cavern framed by elaborate scroll-shaped bones called *turbinates,* and lined with mucus-secreting membranes and waving, hairlike fibers called *cilia.* Foreign particles are caught by the cilia and carried away by the mucus, which drains slowly down the back of the throat.

It would be nice to be able to ascribe an important function to the eight *paranasal sinuses,* four on either side of the nose: the headache and discomfort of sinusitis might then be more bearable. But these "holes in the head" seem to exist simply to cause us trouble; for example—swelling to close the nasal air passages, making it impossible to breathe, as recommended, through the nose.

Filter System beyond the Nose

The cleansing and filtering action started in the nose and mouth does not stop there, but is repeated wherever air travels along the air passages of the lungs. Cilia project inward from the walls of even the tiniest bronchioles of the lungs, and impurities are carried from the alveoli on films of mucus that move ever back toward the trachea for expulsion—as when we cough. See also Ch. 12, *Diseases of the Respiratory System* and Ch. 13, *Lung Disease.*

The Endocrine Glands

Technically speaking, a gland is any cell or organ in our bodies that secretes some substance. In this broad sense, our liver is a gland, because one of its many functions is to secrete bile. So too, is the placenta that encloses a developing baby and supplies it with chemicals that assure normal growth. Even the brain has been shown by modern research to secrete special substances. But lymph glands are not considered true glands and are more correctly called lymph nodes.

Physicians divide the glands into two categories. *Endocrine glands* are also known as *ductless glands,* because they release their secretions directly into the bloodstream. *Exocrine glands,* by contrast, usually release their substances through a duct or tube. Exocrine glands include the sebaceous and sweat glands of the skin; the mammary or milk glands; the mucous glands, some of which moisten the digestive and respiratory tract; and the salivary glands, whose secretions soften food after it enters the mouth. The pancreas has both an endocrine and an exocrine function and structure.

Role of the Endocrine Glands

The *endocrine glands* have the all-important role of regulating our body's internal chemistry. The substances they secrete are complex compounds called *hormones,* or chemical messengers.

Together with the brain and nerves, the system of endocrine glands controls the body's activities. The nervous system, however, is tuned for rapid responses, enabling the body to make speedy adjustments to changing circumstances, internal and external. The endocrine glands, with some exceptions, like the adrenal, are more concerned with the body's reactions over a longer period of time—from season to season, as it were. They regulate such processes as growth, levels of metabolism, fertility, and pregnancy.

For a group of tissues that exercise awesome power over our body's well-being, the endocrine glands are surprisingly small and inconspicuous—all of them together would weigh less than half a pound. Nor are they placed with any particular prominence in our body. They tend to be little lumps of tissue attached to or tucked behind grander bodily structures. Their power comes from the hormones they release into the bloodstream.

Scientists have discovered the exact chemical makeup of a number of these complex substances, have extracted several in pure form from living tissue, and have succeeded in making a few synthetically in the lab-

Endocrine Glands

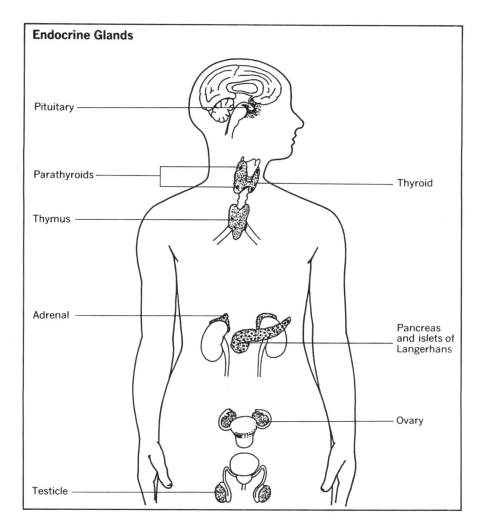

Pituitary

Parathyroids

Thymus

Adrenal

Testicle

Thyroid

Pancreas and islets of Langerhans

Ovary

The Posterior Lobe and the Hypothalamus

The posterior lobe, so far as is known, does not make any of its own hormones, but serves as a store-house for two hormones manufactured by the *hypothalamus,* located in the brain's cerebellum. The hypothalamus, apart from having a role in controlling the body's autonomic nervous system, also functions as an endocrine gland, secreting its own hormones, and as a connecting link between the brain's cerebral cortex and the pituitary gland.

The posterior lobe of the pituitary releases the two hormones it receives from the hypothalamus, called *vasopressin* and *oxytocin,* into the bloodstream. Vasopressin plays a role in the fluid balance of the body; oxytocin is thought to pace the onset and progress of labor during childbirth.

The Anterior Lobe

The anterior lobe secretes no less than six known hormones, five of which act as stimulators of hormone production by other endocrine glands. The sixth, identified as *somatotrophin*

oratory. This avenue of research, called *endocrinology,* has enabled physicians to treat persons suffering from certain endocrine gland disorders.

Hormones have been aptly described as chemical messengers. Their action, while still not completely understood, is that of catalysts. This means that the presence of a hormone (the name comes from a Greek word meaning "arouse to activity"), even in very small quantities, can affect the rate at which a chemical change occurs or otherwise stimulate a reaction, and without itself being affected. The hormone is a promoter, either of a positive or negative sort; it speeds up a process or slows it down.

The endocrine glands form an interdependent family. The functioning

or malfunctioning of one can affect all the others.

The Pituitary—Master Gland

The *pituitary* is often called the master gland because the hormones it secretes play an active part in controlling the activities of all the other endocrine glands. This impressive power is wielded from two little bumps at the base of the brain, about midway between the ears at eye level. The two parts, or lobes, are connected by a tiny bridge of tissue, the three structures together being about the size of a small acorn. The lobe lying toward the front of the head is the *anterior lobe;* the one at the back, the *posterior lobe.* Each lobe is really an independent gland in itself, with its own quite distinct activities.

The Pituitary Gland

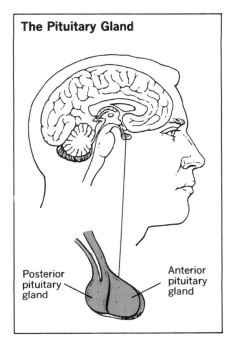

Posterior pituitary gland

Anterior pituitary gland

in medical textbooks, is more popularly known as the *growth-stimulating hormone* or simply as the growth hormone. It controls the rate of growth and multiplication of all the cells and tissues in our bodies—muscle, bone, and all our specialized organs.

Gigantism

In rare instances, during childhood, the pituitary releases too much or too little somatotrophin. If too much is secreted, the result is an overstimulation of growth processes, causing a disorder known as *gigantism*. Victims of this disorder have been known to grow nine feet tall and weigh 500 pounds.

Dwarfism

If too little somatotrophin is secreted, *dwarfism* results. This pituitary-type dwarf, of which Tom Thumb was one, is different from a dwarf suffering from a disorder of the thyroid (another endocrine gland, discussed below). The pituitary dwarf is usually well proportioned despite a miniature size, while the thyroid dwarf typically has short, deformed limbs.

Neither pituitary gigantism nor dwarfism affects basic intelligence. If oversecretion of somatotrophin occurs after full size has been reached—as, for example, because of a tumor affecting the pituitary, the condition known as *acromegaly* occurs. The bones enlarge abnormally, especially those of the hands, feet, and face.

Anterior Pituitary Hormones

Of the five anterior pituitary hormones that regulate other endocrine glands, one affects the adrenal glands, one the thyroid, and the remaining three the sex glands or gonads (the

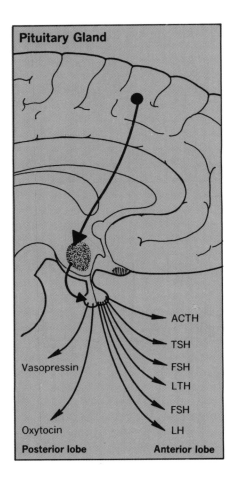

Pituitary Gland

Vasopressin

Oxytocin

Posterior lobe

ACTH
TSH
FSH
LTH
FSH
LH

Anterior lobe

testicles in men and the ovaries in women). Each is identified by a set of initials derived from its full name, as follows:

- *ACTH,* the *a*dreno*c*orti*cotrophic h*ormone, affects the production of hormones by the outer "bark" of the adrenal glands, called the *adrenal cortex.*

- *TSH,* the *th*yroid-*s*timulating *h*ormone, also known as *thyrotrophin,* causes the thyroid gland to step up production of its hormone, *thyroxin.*

- *FSH,* the *f*ollicle-*s*timulating *h*ormone, spurs production in women of estrogen, a sex hormone produced by the ovaries; and in men, of sperm by the testicles. Follicle here refers to the *Graafian follicles* in the ovary, which contain developing female egg cells whose

growth is also stimulated by FSH. Graafian follicles have approximate counterparts in the male—tiny pouches (seminal vesicles) on either side of the prostate gland that store mature sperm cells.

- *LH,* the *l*uteinizing *h*ormone, transforms a Graafian follicle, after the follicle has released a ripened egg cell, into a kind of tissue called *corpus luteum.* The corpus luteum, in turn, produces *progesterone,* a hormone that prepares the mucous membrane lining the uterus (the endometrium) to receive a fertilized egg.

- *LTH,* the *l*actogenic *h*ormone, or *luteotrophin,* stimulates the mother's mammary glands to produce milk; LTH also joins with LH in promoting the production of progesterone by the sex glands.

The last three hormones mentioned—follicle-stimulating, luteinizing, and lactogenic—are sometimes called the *gonadotrophic* hormones because they all stimulate activity of the gonads.

The Adrenal Glands

Resting like skull caps on the top of both kidneys are the two identical *adrenal glands.* Each has two distinct parts, secreting different hormones.

Adrenaline

The central internal portion of an adrenal gland is called the *medulla.* Its most potent contribution to our body is the hormone *adrenaline* (also called *epinephrine*). This is the hormone that, almost instantaneously, pours into our bloodstream when we face a situation that calls for extraordinary physical reaction—or keeps us going past what we think to be our normal

Adrenal Glands

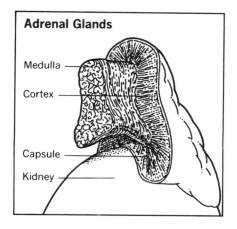

limit of endurance.

A surge of adrenaline into the bloodstream stimulates our body to a whole array of alarm reactions—accelerating the conversion of stored foods into quick energy; raising the blood pressure; speeding up breathing; dilating the pupils of the eyes for more sensitive vision; and constricting the blood vessels, making them less vulnerable to bleeding.

Adrenaline provides a good example of the interdependence of the endocrine system. Its production stimulates the secretion of ACTH by the pituitary gland. And ACTH, as noted above, causes the adrenal cortex to accelerate production of its hormones. Some of these adrenal cortex hormones enable the body to call up the reserves of energy it does not normally need. For example, body proteins are not usually a source of quick energy, but in an emergency situation, the adrenal cortex hormones can convert them to energy-rich sugar compounds.

The Corticoids

There are some 30 different hormones, called the *corticoids,* manufactured in the adrenal cortex—the outer layer of the adrenal. A few of these influence male and female sexual characteristics, supplementing the hormones produced in the gonads. The others fall into two general cat-

egories: those that affect the body's metabolism (rate of energy use), and those that regulate the composition of blood and internal fluids. Without the latter hormones, for example, the kidneys could not maintain the water–salt balance that provides the most suitable environment for our cells and tissues at any given time.

Corticoids also influence the formation of antibodies against viruses, bacteria, and other disease-causing agents.

Extracts or laboratory preparations of corticoids, such as the well-known cortisone compounds, were found in the 1950s to be almost "miracle" medicines. They work dramatically to reduce pain, especially around joints, and hasten the healing of skin inflammations. Prolonged use, however, can cause serious side effects.

The Islets of Langerhans

Strewn at random throughout the pancreas are hundreds of thousands of tiny clusters of cells. Each of them, when seen under a powerful microscope, forms an "islet" of its own, similar to the other distinct islets, but markedly different from the pan-

The Pancreas and the Islets of Langerhans

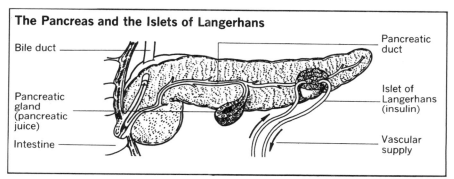

The Pancreas and the Islets of Langerhans

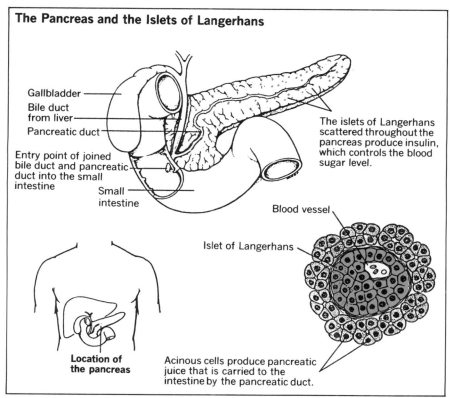

The islets of Langerhans scattered throughout the pancreas produce insulin, which controls the blood sugar level.

Location of the pancreas

Acinous cells produce pancreatic juice that is carried to the intestine by the pancreatic duct.

creatic tissue surrounding it. These are the *islets of Langerhans,* named after the German scientist who first reported their existence in 1869. Each of these little cell clumps—up to two million or more of them—is a microscopic endocrine gland.

They secrete the hormone *insulin,* and the disease that occurs if they are not functioning properly is *diabetes mellitus.*

Actually, the islets of Langerhans produce not only insulin, but also a related hormone called *glucagon.* Both regulate the amount of sugar (glucose) that is present in the bloodstream and the rate at which it is used by the body's cells and tissues. Glucose supplies the energy for life and living processes.

When insulin and glucagon are not in sufficient supply, the cells' ability to absorb and use blood sugar is restricted, and much of the sugar passes unutilized out of the body in urine. Because the body's ability to obtain energy from food is one of the very foundations of life, diabetes calls for the most careful treatment.

One of the great advances of twentieth century medicine has been the pharmaceutical manufacture of insulin and its wide availability to diabetics. With regulated doses of insulin, a diabetic can now lead a normal life. See Ch. 15, *Diabetes Mellitus* for a full discussion of this disease.

The Thyroid Gland

The *thyroid gland* folds around the front and either side of the trachea (windpipe), at the base of the neck, just below the larynx. It resembles a somewhat large, stocky butterfly facing downward toward the chest.

Thyroxin

The thyroid hormone, *thyroxin,* is a complex protein-type chemical con-

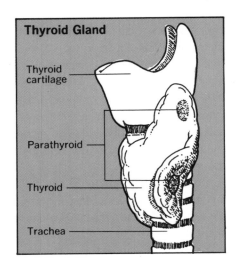

Thyroid Gland

Thyroid cartilage

Parathyroid

Thyroid

Trachea

taining, along with various other elements, a large percentage of iodine. Like a number of other hormones manufactured by the endocrine glands, thyroxin affects various steps in the body's metabolism—in particular, the rate at which our cells and tissues use inhaled oxygen to burn the food we eat.

Hypothyroidism

A thyroid that is not producing enough thyroxin tends to make a person feel drowsy and sluggish, put on weight (even though his appetite is poor), and in general make his everyday activities tiresome and wearying. This condition is called *hypothyroidism.*

Hyperthyroidism

Its opposite—caused by too much secretion of thyroxin—is *hyyperthyroidism.* A hyperthyroid person is jumpy, restless, and may eat hugely without gaining weight. The difference between the two extremes can be compared to environments regulated by two different thermostats, one set too high and the other set too low.

Although a normally functioning thyroid plays a significant part in making a person feel well, physicians to-

day are less willing than in former years to blame a defective thyroid alone for listlessness or jittery nerves. Thirty or forty years ago it was quite fashionable to prescribe thyroid pills (containing thyroid extract) almost as readily as vitamins or aspirin; but subsequent medical research, revealing the interdependence of many glands and other body systems, made thyroxin's reign as a cure-all a short one.

Of course, where physical discomfort or lethargy can be traced to an underfunctioning thyroid, thyroxin remains an invaluable medicine.

Goiter

One disorder of the thyroid gland—the sometimes massive swelling called *goiter*—is the direct result of a lack of iodine in the diet. The normal thyroid gland, in effect, collects iodine from the bloodstream, which is then synthesized into the chemical makeup of thyroxin. Lacking iodine, the thyroid gland enlarges, creating a goiter. The abnormal growth will stop if iodine is reintroduced into the person's diet. This is the reason why most commercial table salt is iodized—that is, a harmless bit of iodine compound has been added to it.

The Parathyroid Glands

Four small glands, each about the size of a small pea, cling to the base of the thyroid gland, two on each of the thyroid's lobes curving back of the trachea. These are the *parathyroids,* whose main role is to control the level of calcium—as well as other elements needed in carefully regulated amounts by the body—in the bloodstream and tissues. The parathyroids secrete two hormones: *parathormone* when blood calcium is too low; *calcitonin* when the calcium level is too high. These hormones work by controlling the interchange of calcium between bones and blood.

The most common symptom of defective parathyroids is *tetany*—a chronic or acute case of muscle spasms, which can be controlled by administration of synthetic parathyroidlike chemicals or concentrated vitamin D preparations.

The Gonads

The *gonads* refer to both the two male testicles and the two female ovaries.

There are four hormones secreted by the gonads: the female sex hormones, *estrogen* and *progesterone;* and the male hormones, *testosterone* and *androsterone.* Each sex merely has a predominance of one or the other pair of hormones. Men have some of the female hormones, and women some of the male hormones.

In both sexes, puberty is signaled by the release of the gonadotrophic hormones (or *gonadotrophins*) of the pituitary gland. These stimulate the production of sex hormones by the sex glands and the subsequent appearance of secondary sexual characteristics. In men, these include the enlargement of testicles and penis, growth of facial, axillary (armpit) and pubic hair, and enlargement of the larynx, resulting in deepening of the voice. Pubescent women also experi-

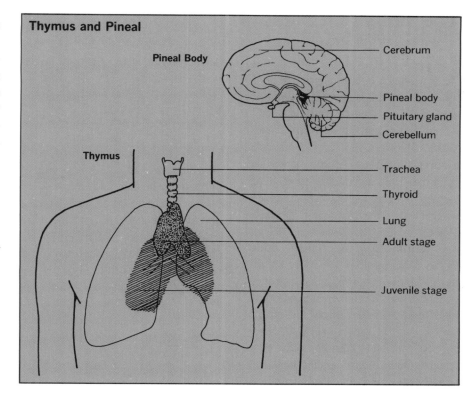

Thymus and Pineal

Pineal Body

Cerebrum

Pineal body

Pituitary gland

Cerebellum

Thymus

Trachea

Thyroid

Lung

Adult stage

Juvenile stage

ence pubic and axillary hair growth, in addition to breast growth and changes in the genital tract that give it childbearing capability.

Estrogen and progesterone control the cyclic changes within the uterus that involve the development, ripening, and discharge of the egg (ovulation) to be fertilized; the preparation of the lining of the uterus to receive a fertilized egg; and this lining's subsequent dismantling—all the complex biochemical events that occur as part of every woman's menstrual cycle.

The Thymus and Pineal Glands

These are the least known of the endocrine family; in fact, physicians do not know the function of one of them—the *pineal*—and are not even agreed that it is an endocrine gland. Situated near the hypothalamus, at the base of the brain, this tiny, pinecone-shaped body has follicles that suggest a glandular function and some calcium-containing bits that medical researchers have descriptively dubbed "brain sand."

The *thymus,* only slightly better understood, has the intriguing characteristic of shrinking in size as a person grows up. It is located in the middle of the chest, about midway between the base of the neck and the breast line. There is some evidence that the secretions of the thymus play a role in the body's natural immunity defenses. See also Ch. 14, *Diseases of the Endocrine Glands.*

The Gonads

Sperm

Egg

Corpus luteum

Primary follicle

Mature follicle

Stroma

Ovary

Ductus deferens

Epididymis

Seminiferous tubules

Testis

The Sense Organs

Once upon a time, a grade-school teacher would ask, "How many senses do we have?" And his pupils would confidently chorus back, "Five!" People who displayed a knack for predicting future events, or whose quick reactions seemed to give them a jump over most everybody else, were credited with having a "sixth sense."

Scientists now recognize about twice that number—12 or 13 or more. Man, of course, has not grown a number of new senses in addition to the traditional five: sight, hearing, touch, smell, and taste. What has happened is that scientists have discovered many more specific kinds of sense receptor cells. For example, whereas touch was formerly thought of as just one sense, it has now been divided into no less than five different senses, each having its own special kind of receptor cell in the skin.

We can talk with a little more justification of the five sense organs, the five anatomical structures we associate with our senses—the eyes, ears, nose, tongue, and skin. But here, too, it does seem to be oversimplifying things to thus equate the nose—having only a tiny patch of olfactory (sense of smell) receptor cells—with the marvelously complex arrangement of sensing structures that make up the eye. Moreover, the other sense organs are not nearly so specialized as the eye. For example, a good case could be made for the nose being more valuable as an air purifier than as an organ of smell, or for the tongue being more valuable as an aid in digestion than as a source of the taste sensation.

Suppose we accept the proposition that pain is one of the senses of the skin; how then do we explain a pain from inside our bodies—say, a stomachache or a deep muscle pain? The answer, of course, is that there are pain receptors in many other places besides the skin.

What Is a Sense?

A sense is a nerve pathway, one end of which (the receptor end) responds in a certain way to a certain condition affecting our bodies, and whose other end reaches to a part of our brain that informs our conscious mind of what has happened or is happening. A sense is thus distinguished from the body's countless other nerve pathways by the fact that our brain *consciously* registers its impulses, although the impulses themselves are no different from those of the autonomic nervous system.

While remaining aware of the limitations of the traditional list of five sense organs, let us now analyze what they can do and how they operate:

- The eye (vision): Nerve impulses to the brain are stimulated by light waves, from which the brain forms visual images.

- The ears (hearing): Nerve impulses to the brain are stimulated by sound waves, out of which the brain forms meaningful noise, such as speech. Deep within the ear, also, are structures that give us balance.

- The nose (olfaction): Nerve impulses to the brain are stimulated by airborne chemical substances, moistened within the nasal cavity, from which the brain elicits distinctive smells.

- The tongue (taste): Nerve impulses to the brain are stimulated (in presence of water) by chemical substances in food, from which the brain forms sensations of sweet, salty, sour, bitter, or combinations of these tastes.

- Skin (touch): Nerve impulses to the brain are stimulated by the presence of outside physical forces and changes in the physical environment, including varying temperatures, which the brain registers as feelings of contact, pressure, cold, heat, and pain. (Some medical texts add traction, as when the skin is pulled or pinched, as well as the sensation of tickle.)

The Eye

Rather than take a name-by-name anatomical tour of the eye, let's instead take just three programmed tours of the eye to explore:

- the transformation of light energy into vision;

- focusing, or how the structure of the eye prepares light for transformation into vision; and

- the supporting structures and service units of the eye.

Transforming Light Energy into Vision

If you could look through the opening in the front of your eye (the *pupil*), and see to the very back surface of your eye (as if you could see through the needle valve opening to the inside skin of a basketball), you would see your own *retina*. On your retina are located all the sense receptor cells that enable us to see. There are none anywhere else in the body.

Rods and Cones

A good argument can be made that man's vision is really *two* senses. For on the paper-thin retina are two quite anatomically distinct sense receptors (nerve endings) named, for their appearance under high magnification, *cones* and *rods*. The cones are concentrated at a tiny spot on the retina called the *fovea*.

If the focusing machinery of the eye (cornea, lens, etc.) is working just right, light rays from the outside have their sharpest focus on the fovea. Surrounding the fovea is a yellowish area called the *macula lutea* (Latin, "yellow spot"). Together, the fovea and macula lutea make a circle not much bigger than the head of a pin.

All our seeing of colors and fine details is accomplished by the cones of the fovea and the macula lutea. Beyond the yellowish circumference of the macula lutea, there are fewer and fewer cones: rods become the dominant structures on the retina. It has been estimated that there are something less than 10 million cones on the retina of each eye, but more than 10 times as many rods—100 million of them or more.

Although the tight circle of cones in each eye gives man his ability to do close, detailed work (including reading) and to discriminate colors, the cones are virtually useless in detecting objects that are a bit off center from our direct focus, and furthermore operate only in good lighting conditions or in response to bright light sources.

The rods compensate for the specialized limits of the cones. They take over completely in dim light, and also give us the ability to detect peripheral objects and movements—"out of the corner of the eye." Because the rods are not sensitive to colors, our seeing at night is almost completely in black-and-white.

You can give yourself an interesting demonstration of the interacting functions of your own cones and rods if you walk from bright, sunny daylight into a dimly lit theater. In the bright light, your cones have been picking out sharp images and colors. But once

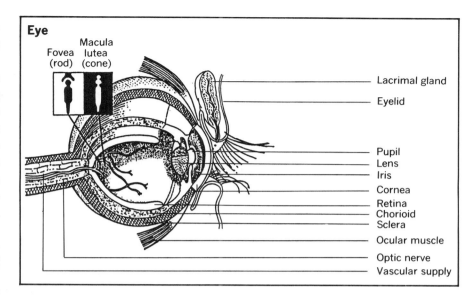

Eye

Fovea (rod)   Macula lutea (cone)

Lacrimal gland
Eyelid
Pupil
Lens
Iris
Cornea
Retina
Chorioid
Sclera
Ocular muscle
Optic nerve
Vascular supply

in dimness, the cones become inoperative. For a few moments, in fact, you may see almost nothing at all.

Visual Purple

The momentary interval after the cones stop working but before the rods begin to function is explained by a curious pigment present in the eye called *visual purple*. This substance is manufactured constantly by the rods, and must be present for the rods to respond to dim light—but it is destroyed when exposed to bright light. Thus, after entering a darkened room, it takes a few moments for visual purple to build up in the retina.

One of the principal constituents of visual purple is vitamin A, which is why this vitamin (present in carrots and other yellow produce) is said to increase our capacity to see in the dark.

The Optic Nerve

Every nerve ending is part of a larger unit, a neuron or nerve cell, and the sense receptors called rods and cones are no exception. Like all nerve cells, each rod and cone sports a long nerve fiber or *axon* leading away from the site of reception. In each eye, fibers serving the hundred-million-plus rods and cones all converge at a certain

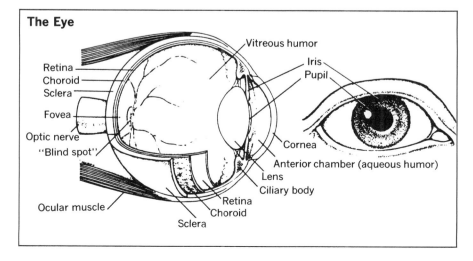

The Eye

Retina
Choroid
Sclera
Fovea
Optic nerve
"Blind spot"
Ocular muscle
Vitreous humor
Iris
Pupil
Cornea
Anterior chamber (aqueous humor)
Lens
Ciliary body
Retina
Choroid
Sclera

spot just behind the retina, forming the *optic nerve.* There are no rods and cones at the point where the optic nerve exits from behind the retina at the back of the eyeball: that is why everybody has a "blind spot" at that point. An image passing through that spot completely disappears.

From the retina, both optic nerves set a course almost directly through the middle of the brain. Right and left optic nerves converge, their individual fibers partially intertwining a short distance behind the eyes. Then this joint optic nerve trunk proceeds toward the rear of the head, where the *occipital lobes,* the brain's "centers for seeing," are located. Just before reaching the occipital lobes, the optic nerve splits again into thousands of smaller nerve bundles (called *visual radiations*) that disappear into the visual cortex or "outer bark" of the occipital lobes. Only at this point are the bits of light energy that have stimulated our rods and cones transformed into images that our brain can "see."

Focusing and Light Control

Lacking the structures of the retina and their connection to the brain via the optic nerve, we could not see. Lacking reasonably normal functioning of the cornea, lens, and iris, we do not see well.

Good vision depends upon the eye being able to bend incoming light rays in such a way that the image being observed falls directly on the retina—in other words, upon proper focusing. The bending or *refraction* of light rays is the joint work of two curves, transparent slivers of specialized tissue through which light passes on its way to the retina. These are the *cornea* and the *lens.* Broadly speaking, the degree of curvature and thickness of these two structures determines whether we see well or poorly, are nearsighted or farsighted.

The Cornea and Lens

The cornea, which does the major light-bending, has a virtually fixed curvature and thickness. The lens puts the finishing touches on the focusing. Its thickness and curvature are adjustable—more or less without our conscious awareness—depending on whether we wish to focus on something nearer or farther away. The lens is made thicker or thinner, a process called *accommodation,* by the relaxing and contracting of tiny, attached *ciliary muscles.* Normally, these muscles do not have to work at all if we are looking at objects more than 20 feet away: but they often are overworked by a great deal of close work.

The Pupil and Iris

Effective focusing in various light conditions also depends upon the diameter of the hole through which light enters the eye. This hole is the *pupil.* Its diameter is controlled automatically—wider in dim light, narrower in bright light—by the muscles of the surrounding *iris.* The iris muscle contains pigment that gives our eyes color (brown, blue, green, etc.). The pupil, opening into the dark interior chamber of the eye, is black. A fully dilated (widened) pupil, as would occur in the dimmest light, illuminates over 15 times more retinal surface than the tiny "pinhole" pupil of an eye exposed to very bright light.

Structural Support and Protection of Eye

Two outer layers protect the eye. The tough outermost layer is the *sclera,* the white of the eye. Underlying the sclera is another layer, the *choroid,* which contains numerous tiny blood vessels that service the sclera and other structures on the eyeball. Both sclera and choroid have concentric openings that allow for the hole of the pupil. The cornea is really a specialized extension of the sclera,

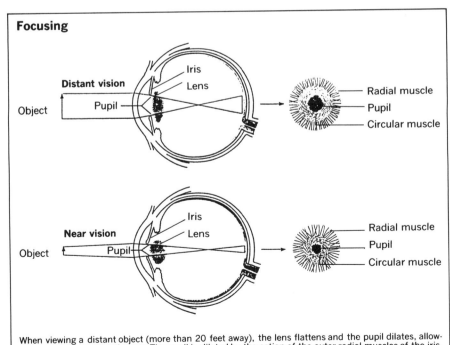

Focusing

Distant vision / Object / Pupil / Iris / Lens / Radial muscle / Pupil / Circular muscle

Near vision / Object / Pupil / Iris / Lens / Radial muscle / Pupil / Circular muscle

When viewing a distant object (more than 20 feet away), the lens flattens and the pupil dilates, allowing more light to enter the eye. The pupil is dilated by the action of the outer radial muscles of the iris, which contract and thus stretch the previously contracted circular muscles. When viewing a near object, the lens becomes more oval and the pupil contracts as more light enters the eye. This prevents overstimulation of the retina. The pupil is reduced in size by the contraction of the inner circular muscles, which serve to stretch the previously contracted radial muscles.

Muscles of the Eye

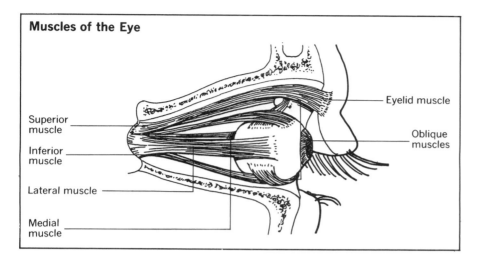

- Superior muscle
- Inferior muscle
- Lateral muscle
- Medial muscle
- Eyelid muscle
- Oblique muscles

and the iris of the choroid.

Two trapped reservoirs of fluid within the eye are important in maintaining the eye's shape as well as the frictionless operation of its moving parts. These two reservoirs contain fluids called the *aqueous humor* and *vitreous humor.* The tiny space between the cornea and lens, corresponding to the pupil, is called the anterior chamber and is filled with the clear, watery, aqueous humor. The larger interior space behind the lens is called the posterior chamber, and is filled with the vitreous humor.

Muscles for Movement of Eye

In addition to the tiny muscles within the eye that control the opening of the pupil and the shape of the lens, we also have a number of elegant muscles that control the movements of each eyeball, and make both eyeballs move together in unison.

The movements of each eyeball are affected by six muscles attached to its top, bottom, and sides. The teamwork between these muscles—some contracting while others relax—allows the eye to move from side to side, up and down, and at all intermediate angles (obliquely). One of our eyes is always a dominant or leading eye; that is, its movements are always followed by the other eye.

Our protective eyelids, of course, are controlled by opening and closing muscles that lie outside the eye proper. These muscles can function both voluntarily and involuntarily.

Lubrication and Hygiene of Eye

Without the moisture provided by tears, our eyeball would scrape excruciatingly on the inside lining (*conjunctiva*) of the eyelid. In addition to lubrication, tears also have a cleansing action, not only because they supply water for washing and rinsing but also because they contain a mild germicide called *lysozyme* that kills bacteria and other potentially harmful microbes.

Ciliary Muscle Contraction

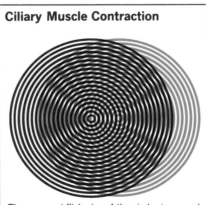

The apparent flickering of the circles is caused by contractions of the ciliary muscles, which control the accommodation (or change in thickness) of the lens for accurate focusing of objects at a variety of distances.

Tears are produced by the *lacrimal glands* above the eyeball, just under the eyebrow, a bit further toward the temple side than the nose side. They are discharged from several short ducts and spread over the surface of the eyeball by blinking. The *conjunctival sac* at the bottom inner (nose) side of the eye—visible in the mirror as a pinkish flap of tissue—serves as a collecting pool for tears; from there, they drain down a duct into the nasal cavity. This is why somebody who is crying also snuffles and must blow his nose.

There is another tiny drainage network in the eye, located at the interconnection of the cornea and iris, which serves to keep the fluid pressure of the space filled by the aqueous humor within normal limits. Drainage of this area is through microscopic conduits called the *canals of Schlemm.* Improper drainage can cause build-up of pressure, such as occurs in glaucoma, and impairment or loss of vision.

The Ear

Within the tunnels and chambers of the ear lie the two special types of sense receptors that give us, respectively, the sense of hearing and the sense of balance.

The Outer Ear

The *outer ear* includes that rather oddly shaped and folded piece of flesh and cartilage from which earrings are hung, and more important, the external *auditory canal,* a tunnel leading from the ear's opening to the *tympanic membrane,* or *eardrum.*

The Middle Ear

The *middle ear* includes the inner surface of the eardrum and the three

Ear

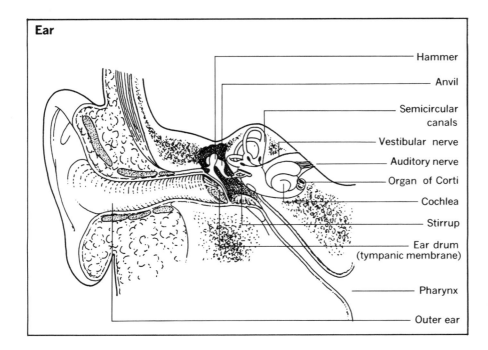

- Hammer
- Anvil
- Semicircular canals
- Vestibular nerve
- Auditory nerve
- Organ of Corti
- Cochlea
- Stirrup
- Ear drum (tympanic membrane)
- Pharynx
- Outer ear

tiny, bony *ossicles,* named long ago for their shape (apparently by some blacksmithing anatomist), *the hammer, the anvil,* and *the stirrup;* or in Latin: *the malleus, the incus,* and *the stapes.* These bones respond to the vibrations in the air that are the basis of sound, vibrate themselves, and transmit their vibrations to the inner ear, where the sense receptors for hearing are located, and the *auditory* (or *acoustic*) *nerve* to the brain begins.

The middle ear is connected to the back of the throat (pharynx) by the Eustachian tube. This tunnel between throat and middle ear makes the pressure on the inside of the eardrum, via the mouth, the same as the pressure of the atmosphere on the outside of the eardrum. (Thus yawning helps to equalize pressure.) Without it, or if the Eustachian tube becomes clogged, the taut membrane of the eardrum would always be in imminent danger of bursting.

The Inner Ear

The chambers of the *inner ear* are completely filled with fluid, which is jostled by the ossicles "knocking" on

a thin membrane called the oval window, separating the middle from the inner ear. Another flexible membrane, the round window, serves to restrict the motion of the inner ear fluid when the movement is too stormy.

Organ of Hearing

Within the inner ear is a bony structure coiled like a snail shell about the size of a pea. This is the *cochlea,* the actual Latin word for snail or snail shell. Following the internal spiral of the cochlea is the *organ of Corti,* the true sense receptors for hearing.

The organ of Corti is made up of thousands of specialized nerve endings that are the individual sense receptors for sound. These are in the form of tiny hairs projecting up from the internal membrane lining the cochlea; they wave like stalks of underwater plants in response to the oscillating currents of the inner ear fluid. There are some 20,000 of these hairs within the cochlea, responsive to almost as many degrees of movement of the fluid. These thousands of nerve endings merge at the core of the

cochlea and exit from its floor as the nerve bundle of the *auditory nerve.*

Organ of Balance

The organ of balance, or equilibrium, is also behind the oval window that marks the beginning of the inner ear. The principal structure consists of three fluid-filled *semicircular canals* arranged, like the wheels of a gyroscope spinning on a perfectly flat plane or surface, at right angles to each other. When we are in a normal, upright position, the fluid in the canals is also in its normal resting state. But when we begin to tilt or turn or wobble, the fluid runs one way or another in one or more of the canals. This fluid movement is picked up by crested, hairlike nerve endings lining the inside of the canals and relayed as nerve impulses along the *vestibular nerve* to the brain. Then, the brain sends messages to the muscles that can restore our equilibrium.

The Semicircular Canals

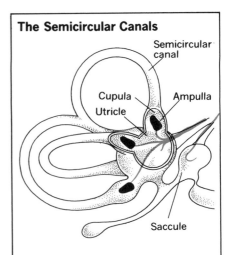

- Semicircular canal
- Cupula
- Utricle
- Ampulla
- Saccule

The semicircular canals are swollen at their bases into three ampullae in which receptors are located. When the head moves or accelerates, the fluid within the canals (endolymph), tends to move slower than the head, and the cupula is displaced. This is communicated to the hairlike nerve receptors. Soon the endolymph catches up to the head movement and the cupula returns to its normal position. When movement stops, the endolymph continues to move, the cupula is again displaced, and the nerve receptors are activated until the endolymph ceases to move.

The Ear and the Perception of Sound

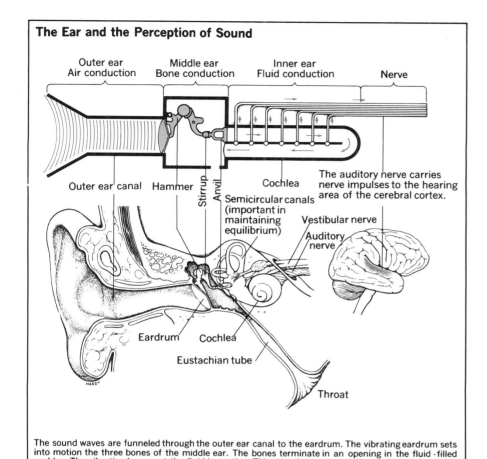

The sound waves are funneled through the outer ear canal to the eardrum. The vibrating eardrum sets into motion the three bones of the middle ear. The bones terminate in an opening in the fluid-filled cochlea. The vibrating bones set the fluid in motion. This stimulates nerve endings, which unite to become the auditory nerve. The nerve impulses are carried to the hearing area in the cerebral cortex.

drop."

Tiny muscles in the middle ear relax or tighten the eardrum and adjust to changing volumes of sound. For example, a muscle connecting the stirrup and the eardrum relaxes when the stirrup is vibrating violently in the presence of very loud noises. A lax eardrum is less likely to rupture and transmits fewer vibrations to the delicate mechanisms of the middle and inner ear than a taut one. Thus we have to some degree built-in, automatic protection against the assaults of noise pollution—but not nearly enough, according to physicians who are convinced that more and more cases of deafness are caused by the incessant battering of the modern world against our eardrums. Human eardrums are not made to withstand the sound of jet planes taking off, for example.

The Nose and Tongue

The sense receptors on the tongue and within the nasal cavity work very closely together to give us our sense of taste. These five kinds of receptors—the olfactory cell in the nose and the four special cells or taste buds on the tongue for discriminating salty, sweet, sour, and bitter tastes—also have a functional similarity. All are chemical detectors, and all require moisture in order to function. In the nose, airborne substances must first be moistened by mucus (from the olfactory glands) before they can stimulate olfactory cells. In the mouth, the saliva does the wetting.

The general number and distribution of the four types of taste receptors are described earlier in this chapter under "The Digestive System and the Liver." These nerve endings, numbering in the hundreds of thousands, merge into two nerve bundles traveling away from the tongue to the

The term *labyrinth* is sometimes used to refer collectively to the cochlea, semicircular canals and associated structures of the inner ear. The space or cavity within the labyrinth is called the *vestibule,* which gives its name to the vestibular nerve.

How We Hear

Just as our eye has certain special equipment—its focusing apparatus—to prepare light for the retina, so our ear has special equipment to prepare vibrations for reception by the organ of Corti.

This equipment consists of structures that amplify the vibrations reaching the ear, or, more rarely, damping (decreasing) the vibrations caused by very loud or very close occurrences.

Sound waves are really vibrations in the air that reach the eardrum at the narrow end of the funnel-shaped auditory canal. These vibrations set the membrane of the eardrum vibrating ever so slightly. Behind the eardrum, the first ossicle encountered is the hammer, which is attached to the eardrum by a projection descriptively called the hammer-handle.

From the eardrum, vibrations travel up the handle and set the hammer vibrating. The hammer, in turn, sets the anvil vibrating; and the anvil, the stirrup. The stirrup then knocks like an impatient caller on the oval window of the inner ear, and the then vibrating oval window stirs the fluids within the cochlea. This chain of events can account for a tremendous amplification of vibrations—so that we are literally able to "hear a pin

Taste: The Nose and Tongue

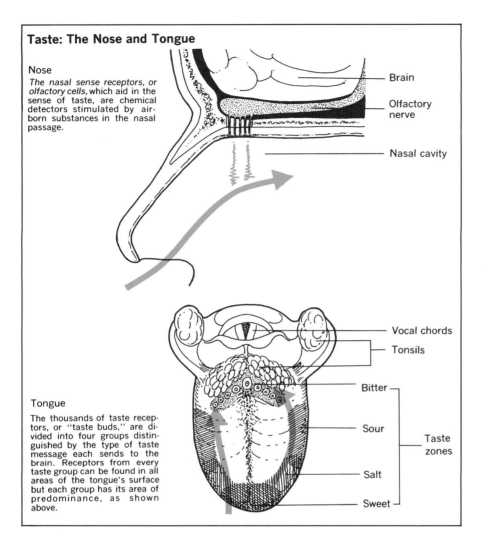

Nose

The nasal sense receptors, or olfactory cells, which aid in the sense of taste, are chemical detectors stimulated by airborn substances in the nasal passage.

Brain

Olfactory nerve

Nasal cavity

Vocal chords

Tonsils

Bitter

Sour

Salt

Sweet

Taste zones

Tongue

The thousands of taste receptors, or "taste buds," are divided into four groups distinguished by the type of taste message each sends to the brain. Receptors from every taste group can be found in all areas of the tongue's surface but each group has its area of predominance, as shown above.

brain's "taste center." The receptors toward the rear of the tongue collect into the *glossopharyngeal nerve;* those at the front and middle are directed along the *lingual nerve.*

Our smell receptors are clustered in an area about a half-inch wide on ceiling of the nasal cavity. This is called, appropriately enough, the smell patch. The nerve endings pass upward through the sievelike *ethmoid bone,* separating the nasal cavity from the brain, and connect to the olfactory bulb, which is the "nose end" of the *olfactory nerve.* At the other end of the olfactory nerve is the "nose brain" or *rhinencephalon*—a tiny part of the cerebrum in man, but quite large in dogs and other mammals whose sense of smell is keener than man's.

Although man's sense of smell is probably his least used sense, it still has a quite remarkable sensitivity. With it we can detect some chemicals in concentrations as diluted as one part in 30 billion—for example, the active ingredient in skunk spray. Also, man's ability to smell smoke and to detect gas leaks and other warning scents has prevented many a tragedy.

Skin

The sensations stimulated by the various types of sense receptors in the skin are described at the outset of this section. It is worth noting, however, at the end of our tour of the sense organs that the senses associated with the skin are really in a class by themselves. Perhaps the most telling indication of their unique place in the hierarchy of senses is the fact that practically our entire central nervous system is given over to handling the impulses transmitted by these receptors. See also Ch. 16, *Diseases of the Eye and Ear.*

The Urinogenital System and the Kidneys

In large part our good health depends on the quality of the body's internal environment. There is a kind of ecological principle at work within us—if one chain threatens to break, one system becomes polluted, one balance is tilted, then the whole environment is in imminent danger of collapsing. The major responsibility for keeping our internal environment clean and unclogged lies with our two kidneys. They are the filters and purifiers of body fluids: the body's pollution-control stations, its recycling plants, and its waste-disposal units.

The Kidneys

The kidneys are located just behind our abdominal cavity on either side of the spinal cord, their tops usually tucked just under the bottommost rib. Each of our kidneys is four to five inches long and weighs about half a pound. The right kidney is normally placed a bit below the left, to accommodate the bulky liver lying also on the right side above it. Neither kidney is fixed rigidly; both can shift position slightly. Lying outside the muscular sheath of the abdonimal cavity, the kidneys are more vulnerable than most internal organs to outside blows, but good protection against all but the severest jolts is afforded by surrounding fatty cushions, the big back muscles, and the bone and musculature associated with the spinal column.

As it has with the lungs, the liver, and most other vital organs, nature has supplied us with a large reserve capacity of kidney tissue—a life-giving overabundance in the event of kidney disease or injury. Indeed, normal function of only one-half of one kidney can sustain a person's life.

The kidney's task of purifying our internal environment—that is, our circulating blood—is really a double task. Each kidney must purify the blood that passes through it, sending back into circulation only "clean blood"; and it must dispose of the impurities it has taken from the blood. The latter is accomplished by the urine draining down a tube, or *ureter,* leading from each of the two kidneys

to one common urinary *bladder.* Urine is discharged from the bladder down another tube called the *urethra* to the external opening for urination.

How the Kidneys Process Body Fluids

Blood is brought to the kidney by a renal artery, is treated in the kidney's unique microscopic structures, and exists via the renal vein. (*Renal* means associated with the kidneys.) The sheer volume of blood processed by both our kidneys is prodigious: between 400 and 500 gallons are processed every day.

Internal Structure

Within each kidney are over a million microscopic units called *nephrons.* The nephron is the basic functional unit of the kidney—a little kidney in itself—and is really a superbly engi-

neered and coordinated arrangement of many smaller structures, all working together.

Blood arriving at the kidney from the renal artery is quickly channeled into finer and finer vessels, until finally it flows into a kind of cat's cradle or "ball of wool" structure called a *glomerulus* (composed of intertwining, microscopic vessels called glomerular capillaries). The entire structure of the nephron is built around the microscopic glomerulus (Latin, "tiny ball"). Surrounding the glomerulus, like a hand lightly cupping a ball of wool, is another structure called *Bowman's capsule.* Fluid and dissolved materials filter out of the blood from the glomerular capillaries through the membranes into Bowman's capsule.

Substances in Bowman's Capsule

The fluids and dissolved materials filtering into Bowman's capsule are by no means all wastes and impurities. In fact, some of the substances must soon be reclaimed. Among the waste substances captured by Bowman's capsule and destined for excretion in urine are various nitrogen salts and other waste products of cellular metabolism, as well as actual or potential poisons that have entered or accumulated in the bloodstream. Nonwaste substances include needed sugars and salts, and water.

Reclaiming Essential Substances

Before we leave the glomerulus altogether behind, it should be noted that like any capillary bed, this small ball of blood vessels has not only an inflow from the renal artery but also outflow vessels leading eventually back to the renal vein.

From the cupped lips of Bowman's capsule, fluid and dissolved substances from the blood trickle into a single tube called a kidney *tubule.* The

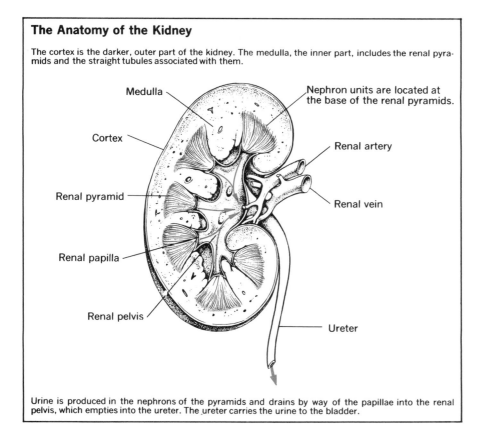

The Anatomy of the Kidney

The cortex is the darker, outer part of the kidney. The medulla, the inner part, includes the renal pyramids and the straight tubules associated with them.

Medulla

Cortex

Renal pyramid

Renal papilla

Renal pelvis

Nephron units are located at the base of the renal pyramids.

Renal artery

Renal vein

Ureter

Urine is produced in the nephrons of the pyramids and drains by way of the papillae into the renal pelvis, which empties into the ureter. The ureter carries the urine to the bladder.

The Nephron

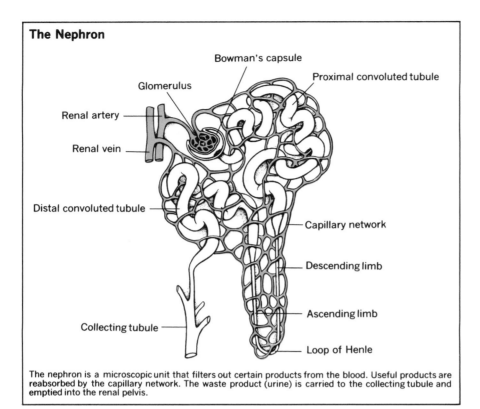

Bowman's capsule

Glomerulus

Proximal convoluted tubule

Renal artery

Renal vein

Distal convoluted tubule

Capillary network

Descending limb

Ascending limb

Collecting tubule

Loop of Henle

The nephron is a microscopic unit that filters out certain products from the blood. Useful products are reabsorbed by the capillary network. The waste product (urine) is carried to the collecting tubule and emptied into the renal pelvis.

outflow vessels from the glomerulus wind closely over and around the tubule, forming a capillary network around it. By this means the nonwaste substances are reclaimed and returned to refresh the blood moving away from the nephron.

The tubule itself makes many twists and turns—including one hairpin turn so stunning that it has its own medical name—*Henle's loop*. So much twisting and turning gives the tubule a great deal more surface area than a simple, straight tube would have within the same space, thus increasing the amount of water and dissolved substances that can be recaptured by the encircling capillaries.

If there were no recapturing system in the kidneys, death would probably result from dehydration. Even if that could be avoided, the loss of essential salts and other substances would prove fatal in a short time.

The arithmetic of the situation goes something like this: every day, an estimated 42 gallons of fluid filter out of the glomeruli and into the two kidneys' approximately two and a half million tubules. Dissolved in this 42 gallons—representing about three times the body's weight—are about two-and-a-half pounds of common salt, just one of the many substances in the fluid that our body needs in sufficient amounts. The loss of either water or common salt at a rapid rate would prove fatal in a matter of hours.

But so efficient is the tubule-capillary recapturing system that only an average of less than two quarts of fluid, containing just one-third ounce of salt, pass daily out of the kidneys into the ureter and are excreted as urine. In other words, over 99 percent of both the water and common salt removed from the blood at Bowman's capsules is returned to the blood.

The Kidneys and Blood Pressure

A surprising insight into the critical role played by our kidneys in almost every body function is provided by the relation of blood pressure to kidney function. The blood in the glomerular capillaries must be at higher pressure than the fluid around them, so that the fluid and its dissolved substances can push through the capillary membranes toward Bowman's capsule. If blood pressure in the body falls too low (severe *hypotension*) the formation of urine ceases.

On the other hand, if a portion of the kidney is suffering from anemia due to some disorder, kidney cells secrete *pressor hormones*, which serve to elevate the blood pressure. Thus high blood pressure (*hypertension*) may be a sign of kidney disorder.

The Urinary Tract

From the ends of the million or so tubules in each kidney, urine drains into larger and larger collecting basins (called *calyces,* singular *calyx*) which drain in turn into the kidney's master urine reservoir, the *kidney pelvis.* Then, drop by drop, urine slides down each ureter to the urinary bladder.

Urine is held in the bladder by the contraction of two muscle rings, or *sphincters,* one located just inside the bladder before it meets the urethra, and the other encircling the urethra itself. When about a half-pint has accumulated, nerves convey the urge to urinate to the brain, and the person voluntarily causes the sphincters to relax, emptying the bladder. (In exceptional circumstances, the elastic-walled bladder can hold two or three quarts of urine.) Up to the point where the bladder drains, the male and female urinary tracts are very similar, but after the bladder, any similarity stops.

Female Urethra

The female's urethra, normally about

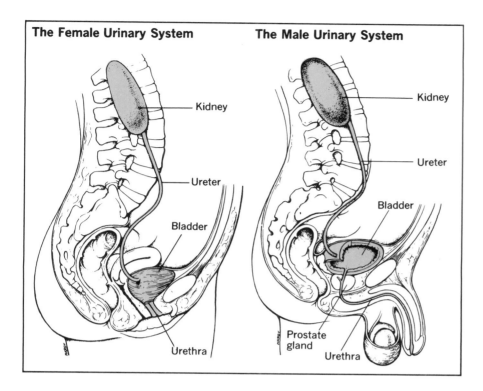

The Female Urinary System

- Kidney
- Ureter
- Bladder
- Urethra

The Male Urinary System

- Kidney
- Ureter
- Bladder
- Prostate gland
- Urethra

gynecologist and *obstetrician.*

However, all the distinctly male sex glands and organs are linked more or less directly into the eight- or nine-inch length of the male urethra.

The Genitals

The Female Reproductive System

As indicated above, the urinary and genital systems of women are dealt with by two different medical specialties. For this reason, the female genitals are discussed elsewhere. For a description and illustration of the female reproductive system, see Ch. 3, *The Teens.* For a description of infections of the female reproductive tract, see Ch. 25, *Women's Health.*

The Male Reproductive System

From its emergence below the bladder, the male urethra serves as a conduit for all the male sexual secretions.

Prostate Gland

Directly below the bladder outlet, the

one and a half inches long, is not much more than a short channel by which urine is eliminated from the bladder. Its very shortness often gives it an undesired significance, because it represents an easy upward invasion route for bacteria and other infection-causing microbes from the outside. Acute and painful inflammations of the urethra (*urethritis*) and bladder (*cystitis*) are thus common in women. These lower urinary tract infections, however, can usually be halted before spreading further up the urinary tract by the administration of any of several antimicrobial drugs. See Ch. 25, *Women's Health* for more information on these disorders.

Male Urethra

In contrast to the female, the male's urethra is involved with reproductive functions. So closely connected are the male's lower urinary tract and genital organs that his urethra (from bladder to the outside) is properly called the urinogenital (or genitouri-

nary) tract. This is the reason why the medical specialty known as *urology* deals with both the urinary and genital apparatus of men; but with only the urinary tract of women. The urologist's specialty does not extend to the female genital and childbearing organs, which are the concern of the

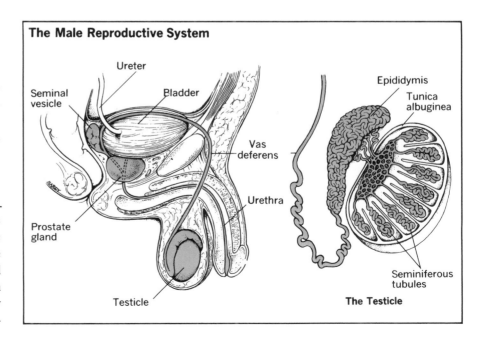

The Male Reproductive System

- Seminal vesicle
- Ureter
- Bladder
- Vas deferens
- Urethra
- Prostate gland
- Testicle
- Epididymis
- Tunica albuginea
- Seminiferous tubules

The Testicle

prostate gland completely enwraps the urethra. The prostate secretes substances into the urethra through ejaculatory ducts; these substances are essential in keeping alive the spermatozoa that arrive from their manufacturing sites in the *testicles* (or *testes*).

Testicles

The two testicles hang down within a wrinkled bag of skin called the *scrotum*. Although the vulnerable position of the testicles remains something of an evolutionary mystery, one clue is that the optimum production of spermatozoa takes place at a temperature some degrees lower than the normal internal body temperature.

Spermatozoa produced in the testicles travel upward toward the urethra through a seminal duct or tube called the *vas deferens* (one from each testicle). (These are the ducts, incidentally, that are tied and cut in the male sterilization procedure known as a vasectomy.) The sperm cells are then stored, until ejaculation, in little reservoirs called *seminal vesicles* which are situated on either side of the urethra in the area just above the prostate gland.

The portion of the male urethra from the bladder to where it emerges from the encircling prostate, having received the emission of both the prostate and the testicles, is called the prostatic or posterior urethra. The remainder, mainly consisting of the conduit running down the middle of the shaft of the penis, ending in the external opening called the *meatus,* is known as the anterior urethra. See also Ch. 17, *Diseases of the Urinogenital System.*

The Heart

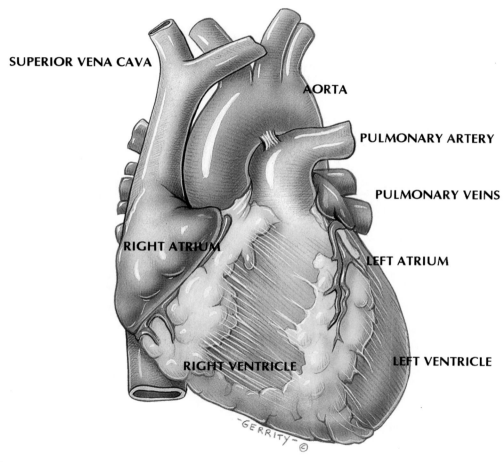

SUPERIOR VENA CAVA

AORTA

PULMONARY ARTERY

PULMONARY VEINS

RIGHT ATRIUM

LEFT ATRIUM

RIGHT VENTRICLE

LEFT VENTRICLE

The heart is a muscular pump that works tirelessly pushing the roughly six quarts of blood in the human body through its nearly 70,000 miles of arteries, veins, and capillaries. Blood from the upper body returns to the heart through the superior vena cava; blood from the lower body returns through the inferior vena cava. The vena cava leads into the right atrium, where blood passes through the tricuspid valve into the right ventricle. The blood is then pumped through the pulmonary valve into the pulmonary artery, where it travels to the lungs to pick up oxygen and get rid of carbon dioxide. The blood returns to the heart through the pulmonary veins, enters the left atrium, and passes through the mitral valve into the left ventricle. The blood is then pumped through the aortic valve into the aorta from whence it will travel to the rest of the body.

Coronary Artery Bypass Surgery

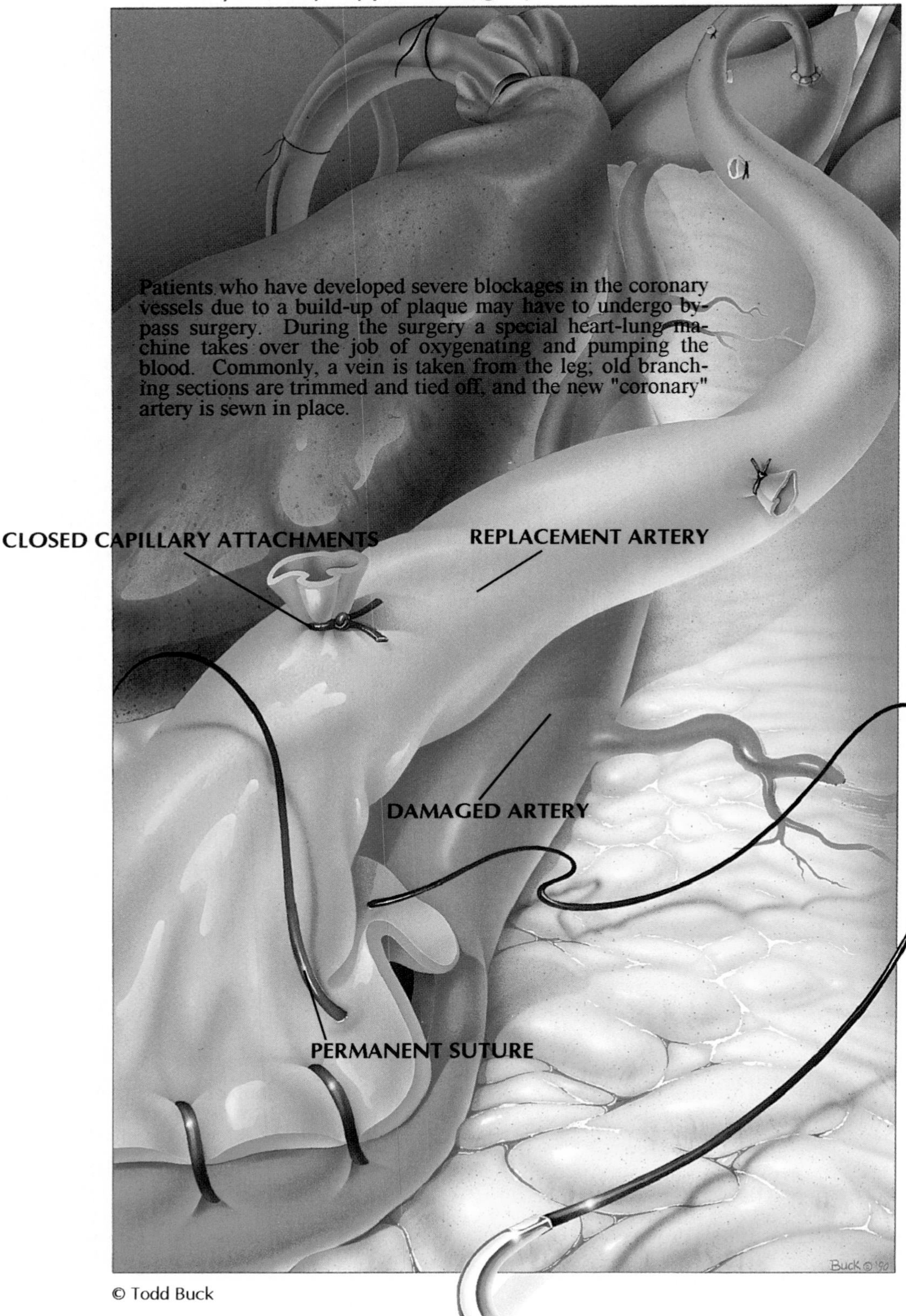

Patients who have developed severe blockages in the coronary vessels due to a build-up of plaque may have to undergo bypass surgery. During the surgery a special heart-lung machine takes over the job of oxygenating and pumping the blood. Commonly, a vein is taken from the leg; old branching sections are trimmed and tied off, and the new "coronary" artery is sewn in place.

CLOSED CAPILLARY ATTACHMENTS

REPLACEMENT ARTERY

DAMAGED ARTERY

PERMANENT SUTURE

Angioplasty

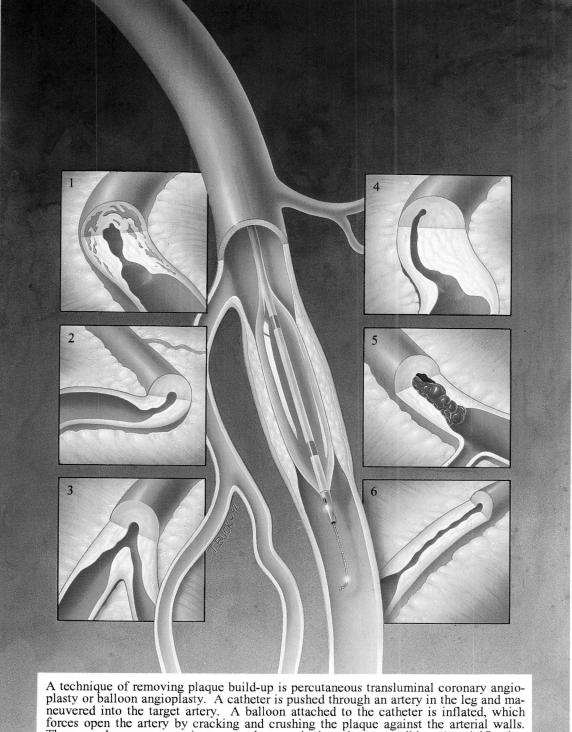

A technique of removing plaque build-up is percutaneous transluminal coronary angio-plasty or balloon angioplasty. A catheter is pushed through an artery in the leg and ma-neuvered into the target artery. A balloon attached to the catheter is inflated, which forces open the artery by cracking and crushing the plaque against the arterial walls. There are, however, some instances where angioplasty is not possible: 1) calcification of the plaque (the pressure of the balloon could cause the plaque to puncture the arterial walls); 2) an angled arterial segment (too hard to maneuver the catheter); 3) bifurcation of the vessel (pressure on one vessel could block the other); 4) excentricity (when build-up is unbalanced, the thinner side would receive too much pressure from the bal-loon, possibly damaging or rupturing the vessel); 5) a thrombus, or clot, in the vessel (the catheter could push the clot into the heart, triggering a heart attack); and 6) a long lesion (the balloon catheter is ineffective on a long length of vessel).

The Lungs

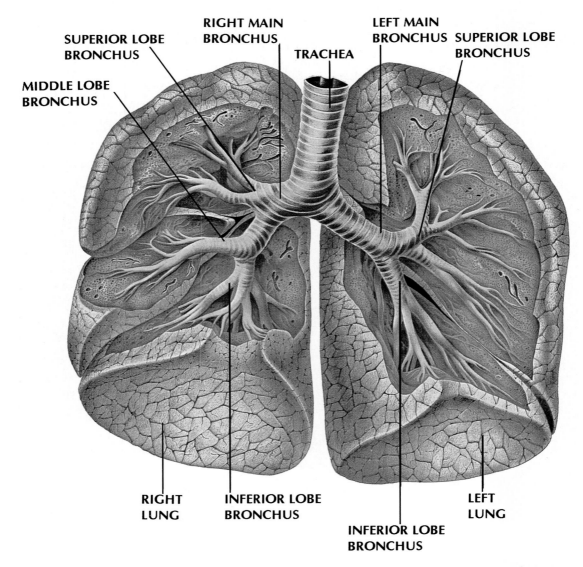

SUPERIOR LOBE BRONCHUS

RIGHT MAIN BRONCHUS

TRACHEA

LEFT MAIN BRONCHUS

SUPERIOR LOBE BRONCHUS

MIDDLE LOBE BRONCHUS

RIGHT LUNG

INFERIOR LOBE BRONCHUS

LEFT LUNG

INFERIOR LOBE BRONCHUS

Lung cancer kills more Americans than any other cancer. Only 10 to 20 percent of those who get lung cancer are still alive five years later. Smoking is recognized as the main cause of lung cancer in men and accounts for 90 percent of all lung cancer deaths. The lungs, when functioning normally, absorb oxygen from the air to pass to the blood and expel carbon dioxide, which is passed back into the air. The tar and nicotine from cigarettes damage the tissues that perform these functions.

The Renal System

The renal system is responsible for ridding the body of liquid waste. The kidneys filter and purify the blood (between 400 and 500 gallons a day), discharging the impurities through each ureter to the bladder, where the urine is held until it is passed out of the body through the urethra to the external opening for urination. Problems with the kidney's function can cause stones, fluid retention, and uremia. The kidneys are one of the most essential organs to human survival.

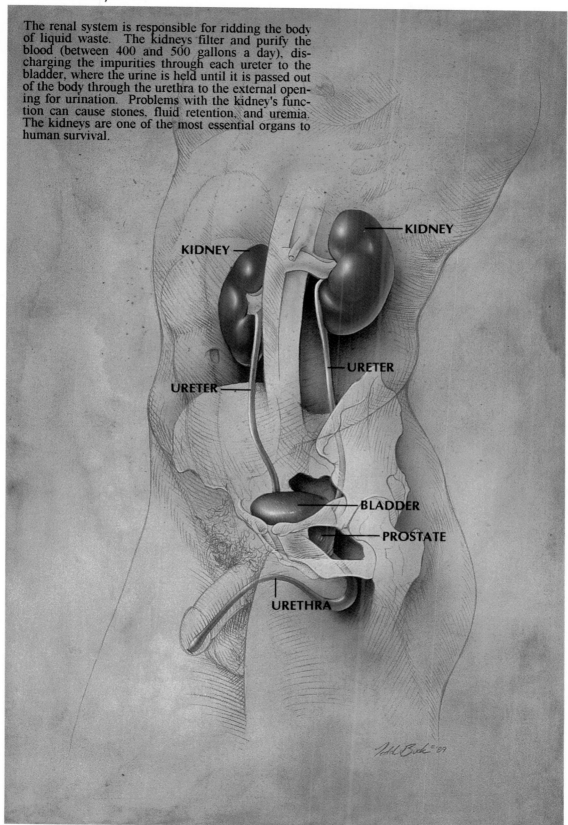

KIDNEY

KIDNEY

URETER

URETER

BLADDER

PROSTATE

URETHRA

The Prostate

The prostate gland surrounds the urethra at the base of the bladder in men. It secretes fluids necessary for healthy sperm. After about 50 years of age, the prostate in many men becomes enlarged and its secretions are reduced. The enlarged prostate may compress the urethra, restrict the flow of urine, and thus make urination difficult, which can lead to bladder and kidney damage.

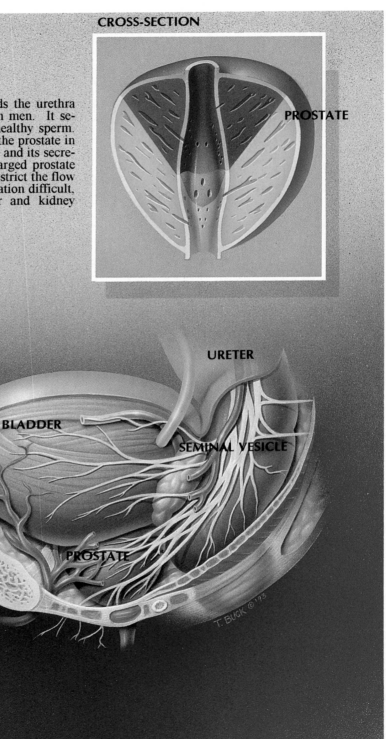

CROSS-SECTION

PROSTATE

URETER

BLADDER

SEMINAL VESICLE

PROSTATE

T. BUCK © '93

© Todd Buck

The Spine

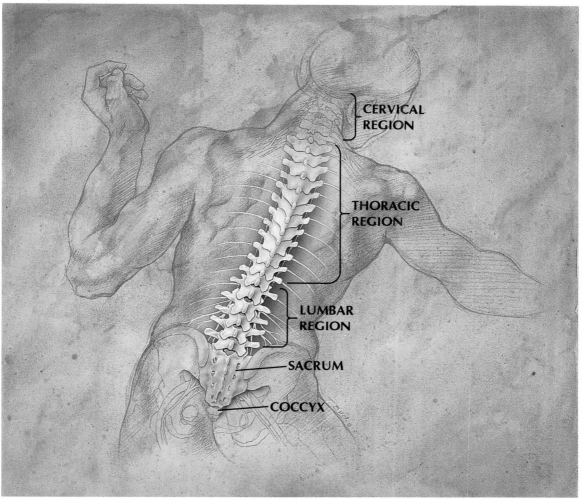

© Todd Buck

The spine is an impressive structure made up of 26 vertebrae held together by muscles, tendons, and ligaments. The spine not only supports our upper body and head, it also serves as a flexible, protective tubing for the spinal cord, the master nerve bundle of the body. From the top down, the first 7 vertebrae form the cervical region; the next 12 constitute the thoracic, or chest, region; the next 5 make up the lumbar, or lower, section of the back (hence, lumbago); the 25th vertebra is the sacrum, which in infants consists of five separate vertebrae that fuse to form the sacrum in adults; the 26th vertebra is the coccyx, which was originally 4 separate vertebrae in infancy. Damage to any of the vertebrae can cause back pain. Other common causes of back pain are pulled or strained muscles, tendons, and ligaments. Tension in the upper back muscles can cause headaches. Heavy lifting or poor posture can cause chronic lower back pain.

The Muscles

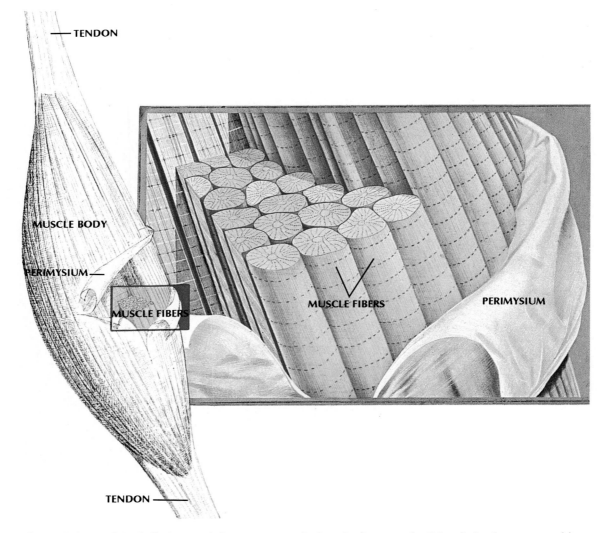

Some 600 muscles of all sizes and shapes are attached to the framework of the skeletal system, making up nearly half of a normal adult's weight. There are three types of muscles in the body: skeletal, smooth, and cardiac. The smooth and cardiac muscles are involuntary and control the body's vital functions. The skeletal muscles are the ones we consciously control when we want to move. They come in two kinds: fast twitch for bursts of energy and slow twitch for efficient oxygen use. Muscles are prone to tears, strains, bruises, and cramping.

2

The First Dozen Years

Birth, Infancy, and Maturation

Before the Baby Arrives

When a husband and wife decide to have a baby they should both undergo complete physical examinations. This will make it possible to detect and treat abnormalities like diabetes and anemia that might affect the future pregnancy. A pregnant woman should have periodic checkups so that her physician can observe both her progress and that of the growing fetus. Such observation will help to assure a pregnancy and delivery that are free from troublesome complications.

What the Newborn Baby Looks Like

At birth the baby's skin is wrinkled or scaly, and may be covered by a cheesy substance called *vernix caseosa*. During the first two weeks the skin will become quite dry to the touch. The skin of white newborns is red, and sometimes turns yellow during the first few days. Black newborns often are not as dark as they might be later. Their skin becomes just as yellow as that of white babies, but the change is more difficult to observe.

The newborn's head is large in proportion to the rest of its body. The genitals too may seem large, especially in girls. Newborn girls may have

swollen genitalia that is a result of *edema* (fluid in the tissues, causing puffiness), but the swelling is usually present for only a few days after birth.

The eyes, slate blue in color, can open and react to light, but are unable to focus. Noises produce a *startle response*, a complex involuntary reaction marked by a sudden, jerky, arm and leg movement. The newborn cries a great deal, sucks, and may sneeze.

The infant's stomach may look rather large and protuberant, and, of course, it has the stump of the umbilical cord dangling from it. The umbilical cord has been cut and tied near the navel, and will eventually fall off.

If you feel the front and back of the baby's head, you will notice one or two soft spots, called the *anterior* and *posterior fontanelles*. The posterior fontanelle usually closes at the baby's second month of life, and the anterior at 18 months or earlier.

You also may feel many different ridges in the baby's head. These are the borders of the different skull bones, which fuse as the baby gets older. They are present so that the skull can grow as the baby's brain and head continue to grow.

Soon after birth, you may detect a

swelling on the baby's head just under the scalp. This is called *caput succedaneum*. It is nothing to worry about, as it dissolves a day or two after birth. Occasionally, another swelling known as *cephalhematoma* may also be present. This, too, disappears, within a few weeks.

The baby's weight will, of course, vary. Most full-term babies weigh between six and eight pounds. Babies of diabetic mothers are often heavier, and may weigh up to twelve pounds.

Some Advice to New Mothers

Unless the new father and mother are really prepared to change some of the conditioned patterns of their relationship, both can be in for a very difficult time. The father suddenly finds himself taking second place in his wife's attentions and affection. The new mother is tired physically and mentally. In-laws and other relatives may infringe on the couple's privacy and interfere with their right to make their own decisions. The new mother may find it hard to reconcile her maternal instinct with her desires as a woman and wife.

All of these problems can be minimized if the mother follows a few commonsense guidelines:

- The new baby is a shared responsibility. Do not shut your husband out of the experience of parenthood. Let him learn to feed the baby, diaper her, hold her, get acquainted with her. Make your husband feel just as important to the baby as you are, and just as important to you as he was before the baby was born.

- Arrange for some kind of assistance in your home, and don't wait until the day you bring the baby home to do it. Plan ahead. You will be physically and emotionally tired after childbirth, no matter how marvelous you may feel when you leave the hospital. During the hospital stay the baby was cared for by a trained staff. At home the burden will fall mainly on you, unless you take steps to get help. If you cannot get your mother or another relative to stay with you, engage a housekeeper or some other trained person. The investment will pay off for you, the baby, and your husband.

- If it is at all possible, arrange to have a separate area for the baby. It is best for a baby not to be kept in the parents' room. Parents must have privacy. If you do not have a bedroom for the baby, section off some spot where you can put a crib and a dressing table to hold the supplies you will need when you feed, change, bathe, and dress her.

- Don't make the baby the focus of attention 24 hours a day. If she fidgets and fusses at times, try not to get nervous. Don't run to her at every whimper so long as you know she has been fed, is dry, and nothing is really wrong. Relax. The baby will be very sensitive to your emotional responses, particularly when you hold her. Through your physical contact you will develop a kind of communication with your baby which she will sense when you pick her up or feed her.

- As important as it is for you and your husband to avoid overhandling the baby, it is more important that family and friends be made to follow a "hands off" policy except at your discretion. A new baby should not be subjected to excessive stimulation. For example, you

---

Newborn Infant

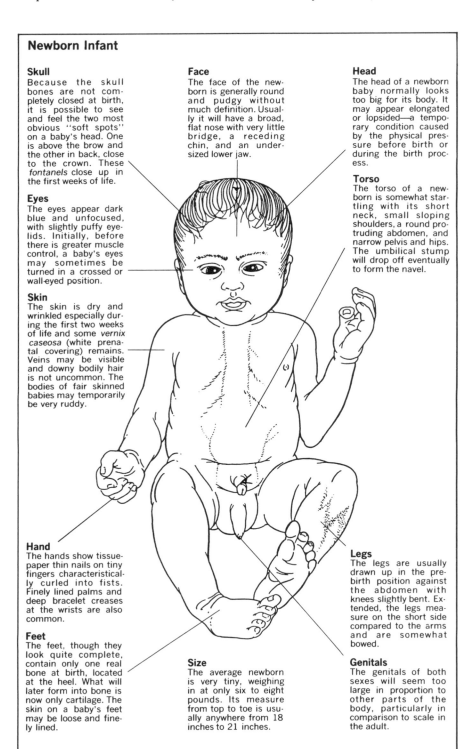

Skull
Because the skull bones are not completely closed at birth, it is possible to see and feel the two most obvious "soft spots" on a baby's head. One is above the brow and the other in back, close to the crown. These *fontanels* close up in the first weeks of life.

Eyes
The eyes appear dark blue and unfocused, with slightly puffy eyelids. Initially, before there is greater muscle control, a baby's eyes may sometimes be turned in a crossed or wall-eyed position.

Skin
The skin is dry and wrinkled especially during the first two weeks of life and some *vernix caseosa* (white prenatal covering) remains. Veins may be visible and downy bodily hair is not uncommon. The bodies of fair skinned babies may temporarily be very ruddy.

Hand
The hands show tissue-paper thin nails on tiny fingers characteristically curled into fists. Finely lined palms and deep bracelet creases at the wrists are also common.

Feet
The feet, though they look quite complete, contain only one real bone at birth, located at the heel. What will later form into bone is now only cartilage. The skin on a baby's feet may be loose and finely lined.

Face
The face of the newborn is generally round and pudgy without much definition. Usually it will have a broad, flat nose with very little bridge, a receding chin, and an undersized lower jaw.

Size
The average newborn is very tiny, weighing in at only six to eight pounds. Its measure from top to toe is usually anywhere from 18 inches to 21 inches.

Head
The head of a newborn baby normally looks too big for its body. It may appear elongated or lopsided—a temporary condition caused by the physical pressure before birth or during the birth process.

Torso
The torso of a newborn is somewhat startling with its short neck, small sloping shoulders, a round protruding abdomen, and narrow pelvis and hips. The umbilical stump will drop off eventually to form the navel.

Legs
The legs are usually drawn up in the pre-birth position against the abdomen with knees slightly bent. Extended, the legs measure on the short side compared to the arms and are somewhat bowed.

Genitals
The genitals of both sexes will seem too large in proportion to other parts of the body, particularly in comparison to scale in the adult.

may notice that if you pick her up and put her back in her crib, and then let someone else hold her a few minutes later, the baby may cry. If you slam a door, the baby's body reacts in the startle reflex, the involuntary reaction previously described. A baby needs a quiet, organized home, free from the kind of upsetting distraction that comes from being surrounded and fussed over by too many people. You and your husband must decide when you want the baby to have visitors and how those visitors are to behave. You must do this even if it causes hurt feelings among your friends and relatives. When the baby is a little older there will be time enough for friends and relatives to admire and play with her.

Feeding the Baby

One of the first questions a mother-to-be must ask herself is how she will feed her baby.

Breast-feeding is certainly the simplest method, and many women believe that a both mother and child get more emotional satisfaction from it than from bottle-feeding. It is also, obviously, less expensive.

Breast-Feeding

Almost any healthy woman who wants to breast-feed her baby can do so. All she needs is the desire and motivation. No special preparation is necessary except, perhaps, some stimulation of the breasts, as prescribed by her physician during pregnancy.

On the other hand, a variety of different factors might necessitate a change from breast to bottle-feeding. Although breast-feeding may be discontinued at any time, some mothers may feel a sense of failure or frustration at being unable to continue having

the intimate relationship that so many other mothers enjoy. No harm will come to the baby by being switched to a formula. Once started on a formula, however, it may be difficult to go back to breast-feeding on a regular basis. For a while, at least, the mother will have to stimulate her breasts artificially to increase their milk-producing capacity.

The First Few Days

When a mother first starts to breast-feed, she may be worried that she won't have sufficient milk for the baby. Her breasts are just beginning to fill up with a creamy, yellowish substance called *colostrum*. Transitional and then regular breast milk will not come in for three to five days or longer. Colostrum contains more protein and less fat than breast milk. Secretions of colostrum are small, but during this time the baby does not need very much fluid, and the colostrum will give her adequate nutrition.

Actually, it is important that the milk does not fill the breasts right away because engorgement would be so severe that the baby would not be able to suck well or strongly enough to empty them. During engorgement, the mother's breasts feel extremely tender and full. A good nursing brassiere will lift and support the breasts and alleviate the tender sensation during the one- or-two day period of the engorgement.

Some Advice to Nursing Mothers

If you do not have enough milk for the first few days, don't worry about it. Let the baby suck on your nipples for three, five, or even ten minutes. Don't keep her on your breasts for twenty or thirty minutes right from the beginning. Start with three minutes the first day, five minutes the

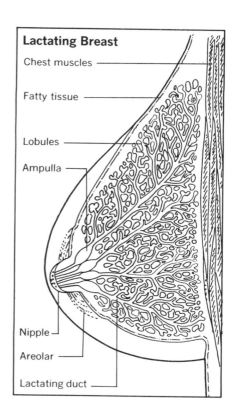

Lactating Breast
Chest muscles
Fatty tissue
Lobules
Ampulla
Nipple
Areolar
Lactating duct

second, and so on until you work up to fifteen or twenty minutes. In this way you will toughen your nipples so that your breasts will become accustomed to the baby's sucking. A bland cream may be used to massage the nipple area, particularly if the nipples become sore or cracked.

Be sure to use both breasts. By emptying the breasts, milk production is stimulated; thus an adequate milk supply is dependent upon using both breasts. To avoid any soreness or tenderness, use one breast longer than the other during each nursing period.

Let us assume, for example, that at the first feeding of the day you nurse the baby on the left breast for a long period, then on the right for a short period. During the next feeding the right breast will become the first one on which the baby nurses (for the long period), and the left will be nursed second (for the short period). After a few weeks you should be nursing the baby on the first breast for twenty minutes and on the other for ten minutes.

The Feeding Schedule

Depending on how often the baby wants to feed, you will be wise to adhere to a modified demand schedule. Don't watch the clock and feed the baby every four hours on the dot. You might feed at approximately every fourth hour, which means that you could start a second feeding early—at a three-hour interval—or late—at a five-hour interval. And, needless to say, never wake your baby up at night. She will awaken you.

Bottle-feeding

New parents have a choice between prepackaged formulas and the homemade variety. Either provides the same basic nutritional requirements.

The basic homemade formula for newborns consists of evaporated milk, water, and sugar or one of the sugar derivatives. Twice as much water as evaporated milk is used with one to two tablespoons of sweetening. A similar formula can be made with whole milk in somewhat different proportions. As the baby gets older, the formula will be changed from time to time by your physician.

If one formula does not agree with the baby, it will not help to put her on a similar formula; its ingredients are likely to be virtually the same. You must switch to a radically different formula, such as one containing no milk at all or no carbohydrates. It is up to your physician to advise you which modified formula to try.

As to how much formula should be given at each feeding, let the baby decide. If she is satisfied with two-and-a-half ounces, she is probably getting enough. If she wants up to four-and-a-half ounces, give it to her. The amount is not important as long as

your physician feels the baby is in good health.

A final thing to remember about feeding is this: whether you use breast or bottle, you must give your baby the love, warmth, and body contact that she needs. As you feed her, you are not only providing nutritional nourishment for her growing body but giving her emotional and mental food for her developing personality.

The First Six Months

It is extremely important that the baby have regular health supervision. Your baby's physician—whether pediatrician or general practitioner—will check the baby's height and weight on each visit, and make certain she is growing and gaining at a satisfactory rate. Often, the first sign of illness in a baby is a change in her height and weight pattern.

Although no two children develop at the same rate, it is possible to make certain generalizations about their development. See the charts in this chapter showing the growth rates for boys and girls.

By two months a baby often holds her head up when she lies on her stomach or when she is being held up. She recognizes large objects, and she knows her bottle or feeding position. She can probably smile.

Sometime during the second or third month, your physician will start a series of injections against diphtheria, whooping cough, and tetanus (called *DTP*), as well as oral immunizing agents against polio—the *Sabin vaccine*. See the chart in the "Alphabetic Guide to Child Care" under "Immunization" later in this chapter.

The Three-Month Mark

By three months most babies are eating some solids specially processed

for babies—fruits, cereals, vegetables, meats—in addition to having formula. They may, of course, still be entirely on breast milk. Your physician will also suggest the use of vitamin supplements, in the form of drops, which can be added to the baby's milk or solid food. All babies need vitamins A, C, and D. Occasionally, vitamin B is also prescribed. If fluorides are not present in your drinking water, they are often added to the baby's vitamins to retard tooth decay.

At Four Months

By four months the baby will look at moving objects. Do not be surprised if her eyes cross. This is a normal condition during early infancy, and may even persist for a year.

At about this time, the baby may also learn to turn over from front to back—an important milestone. Some babies may have developed bald or flat places on the back of the head from lying more or less in one position. At about this time the condition should begin to disappear.

The Second Six Months

At six months most babies smile when they are brought to the physician's office. At one year of age a visit to the physician is more likely to produce tears and screams. The friendly, sociable attitude of the six-month-old gives way to one in which strangers are shunned or mistrusted, and everyone other than mother may qualify as a stranger.

By the sixth month the baby may roll over when placed on her back. She may learn to crawl, sit, pull herself up, and even stand. By a year she may start to walk, although walking unaided does not often occur so soon.

At this stage the baby is full of life and activity. She won't lie still when you change her diaper, and often needs distraction. She cries if you put her down or leave her alone. Unless you are firm and resist running to her first whimper, you may set the stage for spoiling her as she gets older. Of course, if she continues to cry for any considerable length of time—not more than half an hour—make sure there is nothing wrong with her besides her displeasure at your not appearing like a genie because she screams or fusses.

Other Changes

Other changes occur at this age. Where before she had been a good sleeper, she may now not want to go to sleep or she may awaken at night. Let her know that you are nearby, but don't make a habit of playing with her in the middle of the night—not if you value your sleep.

If you should notice, as many parents do at about this time, that your baby seems to be left-handed, do not try to make her right-handed. Each of us inherits a preference for one hand or the other, and it is harmful to try to change it. In any case, you are not likely to know for sure which hand your child prefers until the second year of her life.

In this second six-month period, the baby will probably take some of her milk from a cup. Don't be surprised if she takes juices out of a cup but insists on taking milk from a bottle. If she tries to hold the bottle or cup herself, let her. Of course, it may be wise to keep a mop handy at first, but after few months her skills will improve. In any case, nonbreakable cups are recommended.

Diet and Teeth

The baby's diet is soon expanded to include pureed baby foods. You might even want to try the somewhat lumpier junior foods; as more of her teeth erupt, the baby will enjoy lumpier food more and more. Teething biscuits can be added to the diet, too. By the time she is one year old she will usually have six teeth (incisors), although, because no two children are alike, she may have none at all. By the end of the first year she will have lost some of her appetite, and her rapid weight gain will cease. This is entirely natural in a period when the outside world is taking more and more interest.

As she starts to move around she wants to investigate everything. Keep dangerous objects—detergents, poisons, and medicines, especially baby aspirin—out of her reach. Tell her "no" to emphasize the seriousness of certain prohibitions. She should understand what "no" means by the time she is one-year-old, and will also probably respond to other simple commands.

It is essential that your baby's health supervision be continued without interruption. During the second six months of life she will complete her protection against diphtheria, whooping cough, tetanus (DTP), and polio (Sabin), and be tested for exposure to tuberculosis (the tuberculin test).

Behavioral Development during Infancy

During a child's first year she needs a warm and loving emotional environment in the home. It is during this time that a child establishes what psychiatrists and psychologists call basic trust. That is, she learns to be a trusting individual who feels that her important needs—those of being cared for, fed, and comforted—will be met by other human beings, initially by her mother.

Emotional Needs

Such activities as holding and cuddling the infant, talking to her, and playing with her in an affectionate, relaxed way are important for her emotional growth. Experiments with animals have shown that if the infant animal does not get sufficient cuddling and physical contact from its mother during its early development, it is unable to perform adequately as an adult later in life. It has also been shown that infants growing up in an environment lacking warm, loving, close physical and emotional contact with a mother or a mother-substitute often fail to thrive and may even die.

Fondling and Sucking

During the first year, most of an infant's satisfactions and gratifications are through the skin's perception of being touched—through physical contact with her mother and other caring adults—and through the mouth, especially sucking. Infants have a great need to suck even when they are not hungry, and this sucking should be both allowed and encouraged.

Parents frequently worry that if they respond to a baby's crying by picking her up they will spoil her, and the baby will cry often in order to get attention. In general, it could be said that during its first year an infant cannot be spoiled. When an infant cries she usually does so because she is uncomfortable, hungry, sick, or needs some physical attention.

Social Responses

As she matures, one of a child's tasks is to begin to see herself as separate from the world around her. During early infancy, the infant does not see herself as an individual who is separate from her mother, from other adults, and from the rest of the world. But, gradually, some time within the first year of life, this feeling of separateness and individuality begins to emerge in the developing infant.

One of the important and gratifying events in the early months of a child's life is the smiling responses. For the first time the infant can respond in a social way to other human beings. It is often at this time that the infant's mother and father begin to think of her as a real person and an individual. Thus the smile could be considered one of the infant's first social communications.

Suspicion of Strangers

Somewhere around the age of eight months, an infant who has in the past without complaint allowed anyone to pick her up begins to distinguish her mother from other individuals. When picked up by another the infant usually cries, acts frightened, and, in general, looks unhappy. This response indicates that she can now tell her mother and other individuals apart—an important and normal step in an infant's development.

Fear of Separation

Some time later, usually around the age of one year, the infant begins to become fearful upon separation from her mother. When her mother walks out of the room or leaves the baby with a sitter, the child may respond with crying, fear, and anger. This again indicates that the infant can now tell her mother from strangers and does not like being separated from her. Although the response is normal and usually subsides within three to four months, parents should learn to leave the child in the hands of a competent sitter, and walk out without guilt or anger. The child must learn that separations are temporary and that parents do return.

The Second Year: The Toddler Stage

It is during the second year of a child's life that begins to develop independence and separateness from his mother. Beginning with his growing ability to walk, usually some time early in the second year (age 12 to 16 months), an infant starts to explore the world around him more actively. He experiments with greater and greater distances and increasing independence from his mother.

Toward the end of the second year, children frequently become quite independent, trying to do many things for themselves, and resenting their parents or other well-meaning adults doing things for them. Even if the child is not yet capable of performing the tasks he attempts, he should be encouraged in these early moves toward independence. It is also during the second year that speech begins to develop, with the child's first words usually being "ma ma," "da da," "milk," and the ever-present "no."

Developing Relationships with Mother and Father

It is in this phase of the child's life that he develops a real relationship with his mother. In most homes, mother is the loving, warm, secure comforter in his life, the giver of rewards and disciplinarian of his activities, the center of his life. During this period it is imperative that the child's father spend as much time with his son or daughter as possible, so that the child begins to recognize the difference between his relationship to his mother and father.

In some cases the father, because of the demands of business, may find it impossible to spend enough time with his family. This is an unfortunate fact, but one that can be dealt with positively, because it is the quality of the time a father spends with his child rather than the quantity that is most important.

Testing Himself and the World around Him

The toddler is insatiably curious. He wants to explore and investigate everything. Take him outdoors as much as possible. Let him meet children of his own age so that he can play and learn the beginnings of social contact.

Physically, the toddler tries to do many things apart from walking, running, and climbing—including quite a few things that he can't do. He is easily frustrated and may have a short attention span. (Girls are better than boys in this respect.) Don't be impatient with your toddler; don't punish him for his clumsiness. He has a great many experiences ahead of him, and many skills to learn and develop.

You can now expect a negative reaction to your control. Obviously, you must set limits on your child's behavior—on what is acceptable and what is not, while still giving him the freedom to express his emotions and energies in vigorous physical play. Make the rules easy to understand so that the child will not become confused about what is expected of him. And do not set up impossible standards.

The Third Year

The third year is extremely important. Children are usually toilet trained, show marked growth in their language abilities, and demonstrate a continuing and growing independence.

Negativism

From two to about three and perhaps beyond, a child is extremely negative.

When asked to do anything or when asked about anything, he often responds by saying, "No, no, no, no, no." This saying of the word "no" on the slightest provocation indicates a child's wish to become separate and independent from parents, to do what he wants to do when he wants to do it, and to be free from the control of others.

The child's desire for independence can be respected and encouraged by parents within limits, but this does not mean that a parent must give in to a child on every issue. A parent should try to determine what is really important and not make an issue over petty matters that can best be handled with relaxed good humor.

Language Development and Play

A rapid spurt in language development takes place at this time. A child may increase his vocabulary from about 50 words at the beginning of the third year to an almost countless vocabulary at the end of the third year. It is during this year, too, that children first show marked interest in imaginative play activities. Play, including making up stories, using toy trucks and cars, blocks, dolls, and toy furniture, is vital activity for children and should be encouraged by parents. It is through play that children express their feelings, often feelings that cannot be expressed in ordinary ways. The child also experiences what it feels like to be an adult by playing the role of physician, fire fighter, police officer, teacher, mother or father. In addition, during play children discharge tensions and learn to use their muscles and bodies.

Exploring the Body

From very early infancy, all children show a strong interest in their own and in other's bodies. During infancy this takes the form of playing with his own or his mother's body. A baby puts his fingers in his own mouth, in his mother's mouth, ears, eyes, and pats her on the tummy or on the breast. An infant also explores and touches his own body, including the genital region. This interest is normal and need not be discouraged.

Dental Development

The roots of all 20 primary teeth are complete at the child's third year of life. These teeth, which began erupting between 6 and 7 months of age, are called the *central incisors*. The primary teeth, the last of which usually fall out between the eleventh and thirteenth year, are smaller and whiter than the permanent teeth, of which there are 32. The first permanent tooth erupts between 7 and 8 years of age, while the last, the third molars, or *wisdom teeth*, erupt between the seventeenth and twenty-first year.

The Preschooler

This is the age when many children go to school for part of the day and begin learning how to get along with other children in play and in organized activities. They also begin to meet adults other than their parents.

First Separation from Mother

During the ages of three and four, the preschooler develops increasing interest in the world around him, in children his own age, and in himself. One of the key problems that the preschooler has to deal with is his impending separation from his mother when he becomes old enough to go to school. This can often be made less painful by arranging for the child to spend at first short and then increasingly longer periods of time away from his mother. By using baby-sitters both in the evening and during the day, by later having the child spend three or more half-days a week at a preschool, and lastly by enrolling him in kindergarten for either all day or half a day, five days a week, the mother can ease the child's adjustment to the world outside the home.

Although his first nearly full-time separation from mother is difficult for the child, it may be difficult for the mother as well. Mothers often feel that this initial separation from their child will eventually lead to their child's growing up and leaving home. Parents are often nostalgic and somewhat regretful about their children's first going off full time to school. The child's fearful anticipation of a strange situation can be eased by a mother's anticpating school with the child, talking with him about it and reassuring him regarding his fears of abandonment or separation.

Differences between Boys and Girls

A word might be mentioned here concerning differences between boys and girls. At the age of five most girls are ready to attend kindergarten; they can sit in their seats for long periods of time, pay attention to a teacher, and be interested in a task. Boys, because of their somewhat slower rate of maturity, are often less ready than girls for coping with a classroom situation at the age of five.

A child of five grows at a slower rate than in earlier years, but his body is nonetheless changing. The protruding abdomen and knock-knees of the toddler begin to disappear.

Television

Students of the medium suggest that television offers some worthwhile programs for the young child. At the same time, the experts warn that television watching can, over time, become addictive. A basically passive experience, it may also decrease the quality of family life and raise early obstacles to literacy and learning.

The parent's main task, insofar as television watching is concerned, is to find ways to use "the tube" to help the child develop. Parents can, for example, turn on programs that their child enjoys, that do not frighten or overexcite, and that the toddler can learn from. The television should not be used as an "electronic baby-sitter"; as much as possible, parents should watch when their child does. If a child is 18 months old or older the experts say parents should select the special programs they want their child to see. Television should not, finally, be used as a reward for being good. Such an approach can suggest the TV is more important than interesting games and other worthwhile activities.

Personal Hygiene

Good habits of cleanliness should be established. The child should know that hand-washing before meals is essential even when the hands look clean. He will learn this only if he sees parents do it. As he gets older he should select his own clean clothing and know that dirty clothing should be washed. A daily routine of washing or bathing should be set up, and the child should be encouraged to observe it.

School-Age Children: Parent–Child Relationships

Beginning around the age of four, boys show a decided preference for their mothers. A boy may, for example, tell his mother that when he grows up he would like to marry her

and kick father out of the house. At times he may even suggest that he would work to support her and that life would be much nicer if daddy were not around.

This interest in his mother is often expressed in what may be thought of as sexual ways. That is, the child of this age enjoys his mother's affection, including kissing, hugging, and close bodily contact. This wish to have mother all to himself and to have father out of the picture is called the *Oedipal complex* by psychiatrists and psychologists, after the ancient Greek tragedy, *Oedipus Rex*, in which Oedipus kills his father and marries a woman whom he later discovers to be his mother.

At about this same age, similar emotional developments take place in a girl. She will likely be somewhat seductive, coy, and coquettish with her father, and may talk about marrying father (or a man like father) and having mother out of the picture. This phase of emotional attachment between a girl and her father is called the *Electra complex* after the Greek play, *Electra*.

At these times, both the girl and the boy have a strong, although not always conscious, wish to displace the parent of the same sex and have the opposite-sexed parent all to themselves. Strong conflicts disturb children in this phase of development, for they also realize that they love and need the same-sexed parent to instruct them, to guide them, to provide for them, and to love them.

Identification

Both males and females eventually resolve these conflicts by abandoning their so-called sexual attachment to the opposite-sexed parent, forming a closer attachment to the same-sexed parent and trying to be like that parent. This is not a conscious decision,

but one that a child makes without realizing it. This process of *identification* with the parent of the same sex starts very early, perhaps as early as the second year, and continues through adolescence, but it is especially noticable from five to ten.

Much of the energy that had previously been utilized in loving the parent of the opposite sex is now spent in loving the parent of the same sex. The boy follows father around, wants to do whatever he does, and holds as his greatest ambition to be exactly like father when he grows up—even to marrying a woman like the one father did.

The girl during this same period spends the energy that was once expended in love for her father in an attempt to learn to be like mother and perhaps eventually to marry a man resembling in some way her father. This, however, does not mean that children do not continue to love the opposite-sexed parent; it means only that their primary attachment during these years is to the same-sexed parent. It is this process of identification with the same-sexed parent that facilitates the chief task of the school-age child from 5 or 6 to 11: the task of learning.

Six Years to Adolescence

The years from 6 to 11 have generally been regarded as quiet years as far as emotional development is concerned. Many of the tasks of earlier childhood have been completed, and the relatively stormy years of adolescence have not yet begun. A child's interests begin to turn more and more away from his family and to other children his own age, usually children of the same sex. At this stage, a child's interest in learning is broad and intense.

During this period children begin to be more and more individualistic. Some are solitary, others sociable; some are athletic, others not. One likes only other children, another prefers the company of adults. Some children have imaginary fears that disappear with age or when the fears are discussed with an adult who can explain how or why they originated.

Curiosity about Sex

The child's earlier curiosity about naked people may change to a concern about being clothed and being with people who are clothed. Questions about sex should be answered simply and truthfully.

Adolescence

Adolescence arrives anywhere from 9 to 14 years of age. A girl usually enters adolescence at 10, a boy at about 12. Adolescence lasts through the teens.

In female children, there is growth of the breasts and nipples; the pelvis matures, and the external genitalia develop. Axillary (underarm) and pubic hair appear. On the average, girls have their first menstrual period around age thirteen, but it can occur between 10 and 16 years of age. Be sure to explain menstruation to your daughter before the beginning of adolescence.

In male children, the penis and testes develop. Facial, axillary, and pubic hair appear. The voice begins to deepen.

In both boys and girls, there is a rapid growth in height and weight which is related to sexual development. In general the average height of the adolescent is double what is was at age two. See Ch. 3, *The Teens.*

Alphabetic Guide to Child Care

The following Guide is an alphabetically arranged list of articles dealing with many of the problems that confront parents. It includes articles on physical disorders and ailments of childhood; behavioral and emotional problems; and on situations that occur normally in the life of almost every child which may cause tension or distress for parents, child, or both. It is hoped that having information about such normal developmental tensions will help to minimize them.

A note on the cross-references: Where a particular subject is covered elsewhere within this Guide, the reference is printed in small capital letters. (For example: See also TONSILLITIS.) References to sections in other chapters are printed in italic type along with the chapter number. (For example: See "Tonsils and Adenoids" in Ch. 20, *Surgery.*)

Accidents

All children have accidents and injure themselves. Some do more frequently or more seriously than others. Parents should treat the ones that are minor and seek immediate medical attention for ones that are major. The parents' response to an injury can greatly determine the child's response to it. Calm, responsible behavior will keep the child calmer, even in a serious accident.

For minor injuries such as cuts and bruises, treatment can be completed at home. Cuts and scrapes should be washed thoroughly with warm (not hot) water and 3 percent hydrogen peroxide. A skin disinfectant can be applied, only if the cut is not deep. A

bandage should be applied during the day to keep dirt out. The cut should be left uncovered when possible, though, to allow it to dry and heal. Once the cut or scrape has scabbed over, a bandage need not be used, unless the scab is damaged or tears off.

Sprains, unless very minor, are difficult to treat at home. It is not likely that a parent can determine the damage to muscle tissue. Sprains can be more painful than breaks and can inflict severe damage to ligaments and tendons. X rays are usually required to determine the damage done to the limb.

Minor sprains that show slight swelling or discoloration of the skin can be treated by applying ice to the injured area as soon as possible after the accident. Keep the limb elevated for ten to twenty minutes with the ice pack on the injured joint. Have the child avoid using the limb for a while. Once movement can be made without serious pain, warm water soaks or baths will help reduce swelling. If pain persists for more than 24 hours, consult a physician.

Bruises are caused by bleeding under the surface of the skin with no cut to the surface of the skin. Black eyes are bruises under the eye tissue. Minor bruises can be treated with cold water or ice packs to the area hurt. (Eyes should receive only water packs, ice against the eye is not recommended.) As the bruise fades a purple or yellow tint to the skin will remain for a few days or so as the body removes the last of the dried blood from the bruised tissue. Bruises can take several days to fade and heal. If it takes longer, a doctor should be consulted.

Head injuries in children are also common. A sharp blow to the head, or a fall, can trigger vomiting in a child. This, in itself, is not a danger signal. Danger signals are:

- Both pupils in eyes not dilated equally.
- Eyes do not move together when following something.
- Child sleeps immediately, or is hard to waken during a nap. Any child should be awakened every three hours to check, for 24 hours after the accident.
- More than one episode of vomiting.
- Any sign of mental disorder— speech or movement difficulties, dazed focus or attention, or any type of non-response.
- Increasing headache.
- Blood or fluid from nose or ears. If any one of these symptoms appear, contact the local hospital emergency facilities immediately.

For more information, see Ch. 35, *Medical Emergencies,* and "The Emergency Room" in Ch. 20, *Surgery.*

Adenoidectomy

See "Tonsils and Adenoids" in Ch. 20, *Surgery.*

Adenoids, Swollen

The adenoids are clusters of lymph tissue located behind the soft palate where the nasal passages join the throat. Along with the tonsils and lymphoid tissues elsewhere in the body, the adenoids are involved in warding off infection. When they themselves become inflamed because of bacterial or viral invasion, they become swollen. Swelling may also occur because of allergy.

Swollen adenoids may block the air passages sufficiently to cause mouth breathing, which in turn will not only give the child an "adenoidal" look, but will lead to more frequent upper respiratory infection, as well as to eventual malformation of the lower jawbone. Chronic swelling may also block the eustachian tube, causing pain in

the ear and increasing the possibility of ear infection as well as of intermittent hearing loss. The child's physician can keep track of the severity of such symptoms during periodic checkups and can evaluate the need for surgery. See also TONSILLITIS. For a description of adenoidectomy, see "Tonsils and Adenoids" in Ch. 20, *Surgery.*

Adopted Children

No matter what their individual differences about child rearing, all specialists agree that an adopted child should be told that she was adopted. It doesn't matter that the adoptive parents have come to feel that the child is completely their own. Biologically, she isn't, and it is her human right to find this out not from a neighbor or schoolmate but from the people she trusts as her parents. The fact of her adoption should be talked about naturally in the child's presence even before she can understand what it means. If she is being raised in a loving atmosphere and feels secure in the acceptance of her adoptive parents, she isn't likely to be upset by the reality of her situation.

When the child becomes curious about the circumstances of her adoption, or if she wants to know about her "real" mother and father, she should be given no more—and no less—information than the adoption agency provided originally.

A widow or divorcee who remarries when her children are still very young may be faced with the possibility that her second husband wants to legally adopt the offspring of her first marriage. Far-reaching consequences are involved in such a decision, and it should not be undertaken lightly. The problem should be discussed with a lawyer who can present the facts in a detached way so that the decision will

cause the least anguish and fewest unpleasant consequences.

Aggressiveness

In the rough and tumble of play, some puppies are obviously more aggressive than others, and one of them is clearly determined to be top dog. The same is true of children, especially in any society where energy and enterprise are rewarded.

Aggressive tendencies are natural; the form they take is up to the civilizing efforts of the parents. It is they who have the responsibility of helping a child understand that bullying and bossiness are unacceptable. It seems that because of inheritance, body build, or temperament, some youngsters, whether male or female, are more clearly aggressive than others. It is especially for such children that healthy outlets must be provided for aggression—in the form of toys and playground activities when they are little, and in suitable physical and intellectual endeavors when they get older.

Guilt Feelings

Making a child feel guilty about the strength of his aggressive feelings or thwarting them constantly won't wipe out or destroy the feelings; they'll simply be turned inward, or take the form of nail-biting, or express themselves in some sneaky and antisocial way. Parents who are upset by children's play that simulates violence and who disapprove of toy guns should make their feelings clear without making the youngster feel like a monster because he enjoys them. Aggressiveness that expresses itself in violence and bloodshed—as it so often does in Westerns and in TV programs—should not be the day-in-day-out entertainment to which children are exposed no matter what the parental feelings are.

Boy/Girl Differences

As for a boy who doesn't seem aggressive enough to suit a parent's idea of what a boy should be, or a girl who seems too aggressive to conform to family notions about what "feminine" is all about: these stereotypes are being reexamined and discarded by many people because they are too confining and too rigid to permit the full development of a child's personality. It's no disgrace for a boy to cry, and it should be a source of pride to have a daughter who's determined to be the best math student in the fourth grade.

Allergies

See NUTRITION, and Ch. 24, *Allergies and Hypersensitivities.*

Anger

Anger is a feeling that everyone is familiar with. There are moments when even the most controlled and civilized adult experiences the kind of anger that might become blind rage. A child whose bike has been stolen has a right to her anger; a child whose baby brother has broken a valuable doll is justifiably angry. Some youngsters seem to be angry all the time because they feel they're always being pushed around by adults. (Many adults are always angry because they feel they're being pushed around by other adults.) Almost continuous anger seems especially common among some children of six, seven, and eight. Their theme song is "It isn't fair" and they get to be known as injustice-collectors, angry at their friends, siblings, teachers.

Means of Expressing Anger

When parents know that a child's anger comes from a healthy feeling of outrage or because of confusion, they should allow the anger to be expressed—in words or tears. But it does have to be made clear that smashing things in a fit of rage or having a tantrum is unacceptable. A child at the mercy of powerful feelings of rage can be frightened by them and should be helped to understand and control them. It's also a comfort to children to know that grown-ups get terribly angry from time to time, but that part of growing up consists in being able to handle one's feelings and in learning how to express them in the right way at the right time. Thus, a father who is in a rage with his boss will find ways of letting him know that he feels an injustice has been done rather than swallow his anger at work and let it out against his wife or children as soon as he comes home.

Animal Bites

See "Animal Bites" in Ch. 35, *Medical Emergencies.*

Anxiety

Children become chronically anxious when their parents constantly criticize them for failing to measure up to some unachievable standard of perfection. Likewise, parents become anxious about being parents when they criticize themselves for failing to measure up to some unachievable standard of perfection.

Anxiety is one of the most widespread and most debilitating stresses from which people of all ages suffer in the United States, chiefly because many Americans have been victimized by the notion that everybody can be everything. Thus, a parent will expect a little child to be good, bright, neat, polite, aggressive enough to complete adequately but not so aggressive that the other children don't like him, relaxed and cheerful at the same time that he's supposed to do all his chores and the homework and remember to be nice to his baby-sister. What child burdened with such expectations isn't going to feel anxious about fulfilling them so that he can gain his parents' love and approval?

Parents may waste emotional energy feeling anxious because they think they're inadequate mothers or fathers, perhaps because they lose their tempers from time to time or because they're often too tired to play with their toddler and stick him in the playpen just to keep him out of trouble. A child will also be made chronically anxious if he's always being threatened with punishment, or if he's made to feel that he's bad when he's trying to be good but doesn't know how. The way to keep anxiety at a minimum is to have achievable goals. Is the child healthy, moderately well-behaved, cheerful, and inspiring no complaints from his teachers? Are you as a parent helping him to be healthy, moderately well-behaved, cheerful, and cause no trouble at school? If pressure on the child is small, and he still seems anxious, counseling may be considered.

Asthma

Asthma, also known as *bronchial asthma,* is a respiratory disturbance in which breathing becomes difficult and labored and is accompanied by a wheezing sound. It is a chronic disorder in which the bronchial tubes suddenly contract or go into spasm, thus cutting off the passage of air from the windpipe to the lungs. Spasms are accompanied by secretion of mucus into the air passages and a swelling of the bronchial tubes, causing the intake and outflow of air to be further obstructed. The disorder may be triggered by a variety of factors; in children it is associated chiefly with allergy and emotional stress. In some cases, asthma may accompany a bacterial or viral infection of the nose or throat.

The Asthma Attack

It can be very frightening to witness a child's first asthma attack, because judging from the sounds and the effort involved in breathing, the child seems to be suffocating. Call the child's pediatrician promptly. Until the physician can be consulted for emergency treatment, parents should try to be calm and reassuring. Immediate symptoms can be alleviated by prescribed medicines given orally or by injection, or by placing the child in a moist environment, such as in the bathroom with the shower turned on (but not *in* the shower). Otherwise, the child should be kept in bed in a humidified room. The condition itself should be carefully assessed by the physician to decide whether desensitization to a particular food or pollen is necessary, whether a pet has to be given away, or whether the child's emotional needs are being neglected. Chronic asthma should not go untreated because frequent and acute attacks can affect general health. Medicines now available can sometimes prevent acute attacks if taken daily by inhalation when one is well.

Autism

See under MENTAL ILLNESS.

Baby-sitters

Whenever anyone other than a parent is responsible for the well-being of children, great care should be taken in selecting the individual. Baby-sitters should get along well with your children, feel comfortable dispensing reasonable disciplinary measures should the children misbehave, and be capable of taking charge in case an emergency situation develops.

Ground Rules

All aspects of the sitter's responsibilities and privileges should be covered in conversations before the first sitting. Parents should clearly explain their expectations of the sitter and details should be ironed out, including pay scale and whether or not the sitter is allowed to invite company over.

Clear and explicit instructions should always be left with the sitter about what to do and who to call in the event of an emergency, including important telephone numbers, such as where you can be reached.

Beds

Infants should not be left on a full size bed to nap or they could become wedged between the mattress and the solid object and suffocate. Crib mattresses are designed to fit tightly against the frame avoiding the risk of suffocation. To further protect an infant from suffocation, he should not be given a pillow while napping or sleeping. An infant who rolls over and is unable to lift his head may suffocate in the pillow.

Bedtime

From babyhood on, the routine of bedtime should be as relaxed as possible for both parent and child. Little babies love to be chanted to (even off-key) or talked to in a gentle tone of voice (even though they don't understand the words) or rocked a bit in their crib. Toddlers may want to hear the same story every night for months, or may cling to the bedtime bottle for quite a while after they've begun to use a cup in the daytime.

Keeping things peaceful at bedtime doesn't mean giving in to the child's pressures or whims, but involves keeping one's voice calm, pleasant, and firm. Adjustments in the bedtime hour should be made from time to time not because of a child's wheedling, but because you decide that the occasion calls for it. However, the youngster who keeps calling out after having been tucked in—for water, for a last hug or trip to the bathroom—isn't determined to make a nuisance of himself; he's just a little scared and wants to make absolutely sure that you're still there. If the family tradition calls for prayers at bedtime, keep the tone cheerful. No child can be expected to relish, "And if I die before I wake I pray the Lord my soul to take" as an accompaniment to sleep.

Bedwetting

Enuresis, the medical term for bedwetting, is the involuntary release of urine, usually during sleep at night. A child who wets his bed recurrently after he has learned to control urination during toilet-training has enuresis. Controlling urination through the night may not occur until after the age of three. About 15 percent of boys and 10 percent of girls are bedwetters at the age of 5; most outgrow it by the time they reach puberty.

Children who are bedwetters should be examined to rule out any physical abnormality in the urinary tract. Obstruction at the neck of the bladder where it joins the urethra or obstruction at the end of the urethra may cause uncontrollable dribbling of urine, but this usually occurs during the day as well as at night. Disease of the nerves controlling the bladder, sometimes hereditary, can cause loss of urine. It can also occur in children who are mentally retarded or mentally ill, or because of an acute or chronic illness. In the latter cases, the problem disappears when the child regains his health.

Emotional problems

If all physical abnormalities for bedwetting have been explored and eliminated as possible causes, the emotional problems of the child and his family should be examined. The condition often develops in conjunction with a stressful change in the child's environment. Typical examples are the birth of a sibling, the absence of a parent, or separation anxiety on the first day of school. An understanding attitude rather than a hostile or punitive one on the part of the parent is extremely important in helping a child with enuresis. The bedwetting may be his outlet for emotions he feels he cannot adequately express. Bringing the child's hidden feelings into the open and dealing with them sympathetically usually causes the problem to disappear.

Treatment

Limiting the intake of liquids before bedtime, encouraging the child to urinate before going to bed, or waking the child soon after he's gone to sleep and getting him to go to the bathroom may also help. Behavior modification techniques include the use of positive reinforcement and rewards for dry nights as well as devices with small alarms that awaken the child when he urinates in his sleep. If the condition persists, a doctor may prescribe medication, such as imipramine.

Behavior Problems

See AGGRESSIVENESS, ANGER, DELINQUENCY, DESTRUCTIVENESS, DISHONESTY, DISOBEDIENCE.

Birthmarks

See "Pigment Disorders and Birthmarks" in Ch. 21, *Skin and Hair*.

Biting

Some children learn that their strongest weapon when angry is their teeth. They may bite siblings, friends, and occasionally parents. Because of the enormous risk of infection from the bite, and because it can inflict extreme pain to the person bitten, biting should be strongly discouraged by any child.

Blindness

See HANDICAPPED CHILD.

Booster Shots

See IMMUNIZATION.

Boredom

Babies are usually too hungry or too sleepy—or too cranky—to be bored. Toddlers have so much to investigate around the house that boredom is not likely to be one of their problems. As a child gets older and complains about having nothing to do, you might get him involved in a household chore by saying, "Let's . . ." rather than "Why don't you" or "How would you like to." "Let's tidy the cans on the pantry shelf" or "Let's make some cookies" can make a three-year-old feel useful and interested.

Coping with Boredom Can be Productive

A child who is never allowed to be bored because his parents or older siblings feel that they have to entertain him or play with him is deprived of the possibility of calling on his own resources and learning how to amuse himself. The fact that an only child may have to live through stretches of boredom often contributes to his exploring his own abilities in a creative way. Sometimes just asking a child to "Tell *me* a story" can work wonders. Some parents solve the recurrent problem of boredom by organizing informal play groups of three or four children; others find a nursery school the best solution.

Convalescence

An older child who is recovering from an illness that has kept him out of school and isolated him from his friends may require some special project to work on in addition to catching up on his homework. A period of protracted convalescence is a good time to introduce a new hobby or craft such as model-making or clay sculpture that may solve the boredom problem for years to come.

Brain Damage

Brain damage refers to an organic defect of the brain—that is, tissue destruction—caused by an injury to the nervous system occurring before, during, or after birth. Such injury can be caused by toxic chemicals as well as by physical trauma. It can result in any of a variety of neurological disorders, such as cerebral palsy or other impairment of motor coordination, mental retardation, convulsive seizures, hyperkinesis, or perceptual difficulties.

Minimal Brain Damage

Minimal brain damage (or, more formally, *minimal brain dysfunction*) refers to a condition of some children who suffer from a motor or perceptual impairment that may affect their ability to learn or use language, interfere with memory, or make it difficult for them to control their attention. Some learning disabilities are attributed to minimal brain damage. See also DYSLEXIA.

Brothers and Sisters

Rivalry and jealousy and bickering are inevitable among brothers and sisters; companionship, a helping hand, and good times together are part of the picture too. Parents can keep resentments and quarrels at a minimum by not playing one child off against the other or by refraining from holding up one child as an example of virtue to another. In an atmosphere of equal recognition, brothers and sisters will love and respect each other most of the time and fight only occasionally. Special privileges granted on the basis of such distinctions as "Well, he's the oldest" or "She's the youngest" or exceptions made because "He's a boy" or "She's only a girl" can cause resentments that last a lifetime.

Burns

See "Burns" in Ch. 35, *Medical Emergencies.*

Camps

There seems to be no end to the diversity of camps available for summer enrollment. Most urban and suburban communities have day camps in which children may be accepted for certain minimum periods. They range from expensive groups that offer sightseeing trips, swimming instruction, and other special attractions to groups that cost very little and function more or less like day-care centers. "Sleep-away" camps run by organizations such as the Scouts and the 4-H Clubs are comparatively cheap and will register a child for a week rather than for a month or for the entire summer. Camps subsidized by community funds or private endowment are available for urban children from poor families.

Special Camps

The proliferation of special camps has been a blessing to the parents of handicapped children: those with diabetes, muscular dystrophy, learning disabilities, obesity, and other problems need no longer be deprived of a camping experience with their peers. In many cases, particularly for overweight youngsters, the summer experience can be a major health contribution.

In general, an effort should be made to choose a camp that suits the tastes and temperament of the child. A youngster who hates competitive sports is likely to have a miserable time in a camp that emphasizes team spirit. He may enjoy a place that offers lots of nature study, hiking, and animal care. A child eager to improve his swimming should go to a camp with better-than-average water sport facilities rather than one that concentrates on arts and crafts and offers only a nearby pond for all water activities. Information about camps that have official standing can be obtained by writing to The American Camping Association, 5000 State Rd., 67 N, Martinsdale, IN 46151.

Cancer

Rare as it may be and affecting only one child in about 7,000 each year, cancer still claims the lives of more children between the ages of one and fourteen than any other single disease. Among the cancers that more commonly affect children in their early years are the following: *acute lymphocytic leukemia,* in which white blood cells proliferate in the bone marrow in such great quantities that they disrupt normal blood production; *neuroblastoma,* which may occur in any part of the body but characteristically involves a tumorous growth in the sympathetic nerve tissues of the adrenal glands; *brain* or *spinal cord tumor; Hodgkin's disease,* or cancer of the lymph nodes; *Wilms' tumor,* a rare kidney cancer that accounts for about one-fifth of all childhood cancers; *retinoblastoma,* an eye tumor that is probably hereditary and is most frequently encountered in children under four; and *bone cancer* that may attack the long bones of the forearm and leg during the growing years. Many of these cancers can now be arrested, and some can be cured if symptoms are detected early enough. See Ch. 18, *Cancer,* for further information about cancer.

Early Symptoms

Early detection is best accomplished by calling to a physician's attention any of these symptoms that last for more than a few days: continued crying or pain for which there appears to be no explanation; intermittent nausea and vomiting; the development of lumps or swellings in or on any part of the child's body; stumbling or walking unsteadily; a loss of appetite and general lassitude; any marked change in bowel or bladder habits; any unexplained discharge of blood, whether in the stool or urine, or in heavy nosebleeds, or any marked slowness of bleeding to stop after an injury.

Celiac Disease

Celiac disease, officially known as *malabsorption syndrome*, is the designation for a group of congenital enzyme deficiencies in which certain nutriments are not properly absorbed from the intestinal tract. *Celiac* means having to do with the abdomen. Celiac disease is characterized by frothy, bulky, and foul-smelling stools containing undigested fats. Diarrhea may alternate with constipation, the child has severe stomach cramps, and the abdomen becomes conspicuously bloated. If the disease is untreated, anemia results, and the child's growth is impaired. Early symptoms should be brought to a physician's attention so that a correct diagnosis can be made based on laboratory investigation of the stools. Treatment consists of a special, gluten-free diet under a physician's continuing supervision. *Gluten* is a protein component of wheat and rye; special breads, cookies, etc., must therefore be used. If the diet is strictly adhered to, full recovery can be expected although it may take over a year.

Cerebral Palsy

Cerebral palsy is the general term for a group of abnormal conditions commonly associated with a brain disorder that causes the loss or impairment of muscle control. Approximately one child in about 7,000 suffers from some degree of this disability. Damage to the nervous system that results in cerebral palsy may have occurred before birth, during delivery, or in rare cases, as a consequence of accident, injury, or severe illness during infancy or childhood. Because symptoms vary widely, each individual case is assessed for proper treatment by a team of therapists under the supervision of a specialist, usually a pediatrician. One of the most important aspects of treatment involves parental understanding of the fact that it is essential that they help the child to help himself as much as possible. Guiding the youngster towards self-acceptance and independence requires the patience, persistence, and resourcefulness of the entire family, and may require a certain amount of group therapy and counseling. For a discussion of symptoms and treatment, see "Cerebral Palsy" in Ch. 8, *Diseases of the Muscles and Nervous System.*

Cheating

See DISHONESTY.

Checkups

Medical and dental checkups are essential to everyone's health, but they are especially important for the growing child. An infant should be examined by a physician every month for the first six months, and less frequently after that. The pediatrician usually recommends a schedule for immunization and future checkups. If possible, parents should try to maintain continuity with the same physician so that when an illness occurs, the child sees the physician as an old friend rather than a threatening stranger. Continuity also gives the physician a total picture of the child in sickness and in health and enables him to diagnose variations from the normal with more accuracy. Parents who cannot afford the services of a private physician can be assured of good infant and child care at a local child-health station or at the well-baby clinic of a nearby hospital. Between checkups, it's a good idea for parents to keep a running list of questions or problems they would like to discuss with the doctor at the next visit.

Chicken Pox

Chicken pox cannot be prevented at this time. It does not usually cause any severe complications in a child, but it can be serious in an adult. It is highly infectious and spreads rapidly.

Chicken pox is caused by a virus. Its incubation period is two to three weeks. Symptoms include those of the common cold, a fever, general malaise, and a rash.

The rash, which may be either mild or severe, is different from that produced by measles or by rubella. The measles rash is red and blotchy. Chicken pox has bunches of blisters close together. These blisters are filled with fluid, and there is a reddened area around each lesion. As new blisters appear, the older ones become encrusted. The rash may affect the mouth, nose, ears, vagina, penis, or scrotum. In an older child the symptoms may be more severe than in a younger one, and may be accompanied by headache and vomiting.

Treatment

The only way to treat chicken pox is symptomatically. The rash is very itchy, and an affected child must be prevented from scratching. Otherwise, he may develop a secondary infection and be left pitted and scarred.

Treatment involves the use of lotions, such as Calamine, applied locally to the pox to relieve the itching. If the child is old enough, it's a good idea to let him paint it on himself. Your physician may also prescribe medicine to be taken orally to help the child stop scratching the blisters. In a few days, the rash clears up, the lesions dry, and the crusts fall off.

Child Abuse and Neglect

Child abuse and neglect have been defined in various ways.

In 1962, Dr. C. Henry Kempe, chief pediatrician at the University of Colorado Medical Center, coined the term *battered child syndrome*. According to Dr. Kempe's definition, the victim of battering is "any child who [has] received *nonaccidental* injury or injuries as a result of acts or omissions on the part of his parents or guardians." Under the Child Abuse Prevention and Treatment Act (Public Law 93-247), passed by Congress in 1974 and amended in 1978, child abuse and neglect are defined as

> the physical or mental injury, sexual abuse or exploitation, negligent treatment, or maltreatment of a child under the age of 18 by a person who is responsible for the child's welfare under circumstances which indicate that the child's health or welfare is harmed or threatened thereby.

Abuse and neglect clearly take many forms. *Physical abuse* may involve punching, scalding, suffocating, headcracking, and stomping. *Sexual abuse* can mean intercourse, incest, rape, sodomy, or impairing of a minor's morals (see SEXUAL ABUSE). *Physical neglect* occurs when parents or parent surrogates fail to provide the essentials of a normal life. These include food, clothing, shelter, care, and supervision. Under *emotional abuse or neglect* authorities include parental failure to provide love and proper direction, parental rejection, and deprivation of mothering.

Incidence

Figures on the incidence of child abuse and neglect are difficult to confirm. Many such cases are never reported. At least one agency, the National Center on Child Abuse and Neglect, a federal agency, has concluded that more than one million children are maltreated each year. Another estimate indicates that some 3,000 children die annually in New York City alone as a result of physical abuse.

Most of the abuse victims are three years old or younger. Some authorities believe that the cases of neglect are far more numerous than those of actual abuse.

Control

Approaches to control of the problem of child abuse and neglect have been both legislative and social. Laws passed by all 50 states require physicians and other professionals to report suspected cases of child abuse. In increasing numbers the states also require reports from nurses, teachers, counselors, social workers, clergymen, law enforcement officers, attorneys, and coroners. Some states provide for penalties, including fines up to $1,000 or prison sentences of as much as one year, for persons mandated to report but failing to do so.

Control measures have focused in addition on the rehabilitation of abusive parents and protection of abused children. The National Center on Child Abuse and Neglect, established in 1974 as part of the Children's Bureau of the federal Office of Child Development, receives funding that makes possible protective services for the short-term care of endangered children outside the home. The Center also provides counseling for parents, foster-care payments, and other services.

On the principle that the abusive parent must be treated if child abuse and neglect are to be controlled, various organizations have instituted parent-oriented programs. Parents Anonymous sponsors therapy sessions in which abusive parents can meet to help themselves and each other. "Helplines" operating in many communities offer aid and counseling to parents who have abused a child but are afraid to contact a social service or other agency. A number of other agencies and groups provide emergency, counseling, outreach, and related services to parents or parent surrogates. Some helplines have workers available to visit homes in life-threatening situations.

Other groups and agencies take a multidisciplinary approach. Alliance, a division of Catholic Charities, brings together existing community agencies that work together in teams to treat child abuse and neglect cases. Hospital-based treatment programs may include a physician, nurse, social worker, and consulting psychiatrist. Lay therapists may visit homes under other programs, and "foster grandparents" over 65 years of age may be recruited to care for battered children who have been hospitalized.

Sources of Help

Persons seeking help or advice on abused and neglected children can look in their communities' yellow pages under the heading "Social Services Organizations." A number of organizations that offer assistance are listed in the SEXUAL ABUSE section. Others include:

- Parents Anonymous, 1733 South Sepulveda, Ste. 270, Los Angeles, CA 90045; 213/410-9732.

- American Association for Protecting Children (a division of the American Humane Association), 9725 E. Hampden Ave., Denver, CO 80231; 303/695-0811.

- Parents without Partners, 8807 Colesville Rd., Silver Springs, MD 20910; 301/588-9354.

- Parents United, P.O. Box 952, San Jose, CA 95108; 408/279-1957.

Cholesterol

Cholesterol poses two types of problems in children. The first is a lack of cholesterol in children whose parents have kept them from infancy on low cholesterol diets. Parents should keep in mind that the body requires some cholesterol to function correctly and that the protein derived from meat and eggs is almost essential to growing bodies. Children who are not fed meat, dairy products, or eggs need to have the protein, amino acids, and other nutrients replaced by either pills or a very well balanced diet. Certain vitamins cannot be found in a vegetarian diet, such as one type of vitamin B. Children on restrictive low-fat, low-cholesterol diets can suffer growth failure and malnutrition unless the diet is supervised by a doctor.

The second problem is an extremely elevated cholesterol level. Although general testing of children for high cholesterol is not recommended, one statistic that proved reliable in spotting 9 out of 10 children with raised levels was the amount of television watched. Children who watched two or more hours of television a day were more likely to have cholesterol levels exceeding 200 mg. More importantly, less than half of those children who had raised levels and watched two hours of television came from families who had a history of high cholesterol. This means that these children are not from high-risk families, but they still manage to increase their cholesterol because of their eating patterns and lack of exercise in their daily routine. The flag that points to the problem is excessive TV viewing. Snacking while watching TV, and not exercising, are the suspected culprits.

Circumcision

Circumcision is a surgical procedure in which the foreskin, or *prepuce*, that covers the cone-shaped tip of the male infant's penis is removed. The Book of Genesis speaks of circumcision as a religious rite. Once relatively common in the United States, the procedure has become more rare. The American Academy of Pediatrics has stated that "routine circumcision of the newborn infant lacks medical justification."

Usually performed a few days after birth, the procedure takes only a few minutes and can be done in various ways. A scalpel may be used, for example. Possible complications include excessive bleeding, infection, and urinary obstruction resulting from contraction of the skin at the base of the foreskin. But complications are infrequent.

The parents of the newborn male infant should decide whether to have their son circumcised or not. They may first consult their obstetrician or pediatrician. Most decisions are made on the basis of family, religious, or cultural traditions. Many family health insurance policies today provide no coverage for the procedure.

Cleft Palate and Cleft Lip

A *cleft palate* is a split in the roof of the mouth sometimes extending to the lip and into the nose. The split is caused by the failure of the two sides of the face to unite properly during prenatal development. The condition occurs in about 1 out of 1,000 births and is sometimes associated with a foot or spine deformity. It is in no way related to mental retardation.

An infant born with a cleft palate cannot suck properly unless a special device, called an *obturator*, is inserted into the split to close it against the flow of air. Where this is undesirable, feeding may be done with a spoon or a dropper.

Because the condition eventually causes speech distortion, it should be corrected at about 18 months of age, before the child begins to talk. The surgery consists of reconstructing the tissue. Sometimes, even at this early age, the child may need some corrective speech therapy following the operation.

If the split occurs only in the lip, commonly called a *harelip*, surgery may be recommended when the infant weighs about 15 pounds, usually at the age of 12 to 15 months. When the operation is performed this early, there is no danger of speech impairment, and the result is only a thin scar.

Clothing

Standards have been set up the U.S. government for infants' and children's sleepwear to be flame retardant or flame resistent. Even flame retardant material, though, will burn when fire is held against the cloth. The difference is that when the flame is removed, the retardant material ceases to burn. Nontreated material will continue to burn and fuel further flames.

Until recently this meant that sleepwear for small children had to be non-natural fibers. Synthetic material could be coated so that it would not continue to burn after the flame was removed. Cotton does continue to burn and increases the likelihood of serious injuries to a child in case of fire. However, recent improvements in chemical treatment of cotton has provided the clothing industry with flame retardant cotton. Check clothing labels to see if the cotton is treated. If it is not labeled as flame retardant or resistent, it should not be considered for sleepwear.

Labeling should be checked on all clothing to be used as sleepwear.

Many manufacturers produce clothing for infants that looks like sleepwear but is labeled daywear or playwear to avoid the need for flame retardant treatment of the cloth. If the clothing is not marked flame retardant, or is not specifically labeled as sleepwear, it should not be used to clothe a sleeping child.

Clubfoot

Clubfoot is a bone deformity characterized by an inturning or outturning of the foot. An orthopedist must put the clubfoot and part of the leg into a cast to correct the condition. If casting does not cure the abnormality, orthopedic surgery may be necessary.

Occasionally, a benign and easily correctable condition involving a child's legs may have been produced by the position the baby was in while still in the uterus.

The mother can help to correct the condition by daily passive exercises of the baby's feet. She does this by turning the feet correctly for a few minutes every day. To maintain the corrected position, the application of plaster is sometimes necessary. Such a procedure requires the attention of an orthopedic surgeon.

Colic

During the first three or four months, many babies have occasional attacks of *colic*, a general term applied to infantile digestive discomfort. After feeding, the baby may cry out in pain and draw up her arms and legs. Her abdomen may feel hard. Apart from making sure the baby is as comfortable as can be, there's not much that can be done for colic. You must try not to let the baby's crying make you a nervous wreck, for your nervousness will be communicated to the baby, which will only create a vicious circle of increasing tension. Usually

colic tapers off at about the third month. If the baby's colic attacks are very frequent or persistent, consult your pediatrician.

Color Blindness

Color blindness is a genetic inability to distinguish between certain colors, most commonly between red and green. This defect, which is characteristically male, is inherited through the mother. That is, a woman whose father was color blind can pass the trait to her son without herself suffering the defect. About 8 million people in the United States have the red/green form of color blindness which can neither be cured nor corrected. Many of them are scarcely aware of their deficiency. Parents who suspect that their child may have this minor disability can arrange for simple testing.

Common Cold

By recent count, there are about 150 different viruses that cause common cold symptoms, and because not a single one of them can be treated effectively by medicines, coping with a cold seems to be part of the human condition. Parents who are sniveling, sneezing, and coughing should ask the physician what precautions to take when handling the baby.

Young children with stuffy noses and breathing difficulties should be kept indoors, near a humidifier or steam kettle if the air is especially dry. Nose drops should not be given unless the physician says so. Older children may not want to miss school because of a cold. If they do go, they should be given lots of liquid when they get home and steered in the direction of an afternoon nap. Colds in and of themselves are unavoidable and not serious, but the proper pre-

cautions should be taken to prevent complications, such as an ear infection or a sore throat.

Competitiveness

See AGGRESSIVENESS.

Conscience

See GUILT AND CONSCIENCE.

Constipation

Parents who are anxious about the frequency of their own bowel movements or who are excessively refined in their attitudes towards defecation are pretty sure to transmit these feelings to their children unless they make some effort not to. Concerns of this kind are one sure way of constipating a child. Actually, if a child is eating a proper diet, getting enough exercise, and drinking a sufficiency of liquids, constipation is not likely to be a problem.

Frequency of Bowel Movements

Not everyone has a bowel movement every day. On the other hand, some people routinely have more than one movement a day. There is considerable variation among normal patterns of bowel movements. This should be borne in mind before parents conclude that their child is constipated. Children need to be assured that they are not necessarily abnormal if they deviate from the one-a-day pattern.

However, any abrupt change in the normal pattern of bowel movements should be noted, and if it persists contact a physician. Frequent small movements can be a sign of constipation.

A youngster on a light diet because of illness, or one who is dehydrated because of a fever, may suffer from mild constipation that will clear up when he recovers. If constipation becomes chronic, don't resort to enemas or laxatives on your own; discuss the problem with your physician who will want to check on other symptoms that might indicate an intestinal disorder.

Cradle Cap

This condition is marked by yellowish crusts on the baby's scalp. It is usually harmless, and can be taken care of by regular shampooing. Occasionally, a special soap as well as a very fine comb may be helpful.

Crib Death

See SUDDEN INFANT DEATH SYNDROME.

Crossed Eyes (Strabismus)

Do not be alarmed if your baby's eyes do not focus. Crossed eyes are a common condition that usually corrects itself somewhere between the ages of six and twelve months. If crossing of the eyes persists after one year, an ophthalmologist (eye specialist) should evaluate the baby's vision.

If a real problem does develop, one eye—or each eye alternately—may cross, turn outward, or focus below or above the other. Frequently the reason for "turning" is that there is a larger refractive error in one eye than in the other. Eyeglasses will often correct this condition.

Occasionally, eye muscle weakness is the cause of crossed eyes. This is most often true of premature children. The weakness of some muscles causes overaction of other muscles.

Eyeglasses will often prevent the need for eye surgery. Sometimes, however, surgery will be necessary to straighten the eyes. Either before or after surgery the eyes may need further attention in the form of eye drops, a patch to cover one eye, or glasses.

Croup

Croup, a most harassing and terrifying experience for new parents, is a spasm of the windpipe or trachea, especially involving the larynx. When such a spasm occurs, an affected child has great trouble in breathing and produces a cough that sounds like the bark of a dog. In some cases, the child can't breathe at all.

An attack of croup is an emergency. The younger the child, the more dangerous it is. You must get the baby's airway open. The best thing to do is to take the child into the bathroom, shut the door, and turn on the hot water of the shower full force, or of the bathtub and sink if you don't have a shower. The idea is to fill the room with hot steam in order to loosen the mucus plug in the baby's trachea, thus enabling him to cough up the mucus.

Get to your physician as soon as possible so that more effective treatment can begin. If the croup is viral in origin, antibiotics may not help; but when the infection is caused by bacteria, your physician will put the child on one of the antimicrobial agents. If your child is subject to croup, it is a good idea to invest in a hot or cold air vaporizer and use it whenever he has congestion resulting from a cold.

In a really severe emergency, when the windpipe closes completely, a *tracheostomy* must be performed so that the throat can be opened and an airway inserted. A tracheostomy should be performed in a hospital, but if for some reason it is performed elsewhere, the child should be hospitalized as quickly as possible.

Curiosity

If we weren't born curious, we'd never learn a thing. Even before a child can walk and talk, curiosity motivates a good part of her behavior: putting things into her mouth, poking at things, pointing at people, and as the natural urge to speak becomes stronger, holding things up or bringing them to mother or father in order to find out what they're called.

Respecting Curiosity

A parent who respects the child's curiosity will be attentive to it and satisfy it as part of the ongoing learning experience. It doesn't take any extra time when a toddler is sitting in your lap to say the words for the parts of your face (and hers) as she touches them, or the words for her articles of clothing as she tries to help put them on. Dealing with the "why" stage of curiosity is more complicated, especially because in many instances, the child is asking "Why?" for the sheer joy and sense of power of being able to do so.

Many parents who don't know anything about mechanics or astronomy have developed a sense of security by heading for the children's shelves at the local library and reading the simplest books on the subject that interest their preschool children so that they can answer some of their questions. Of course, no one can answer all the questions that a child might ask during an average day. Some should be answered by mother, some by father, and some will have to wait. There's no harm in telling a four-year-old child who wants to know why the wind makes a whistling sound that she'll find out about such things when she goes to school. That's a much better answer than "Don't ask so many questions." Questions should always be listened to even if the answers aren't readily available.

As the child reaches the age of eight and can do a certain amount of reading, it's a good idea to invest in a fairly simple encyclopedia. With such a source of information available, it's possible to respond to some questions with "Let's go find the answer together."

Each family must decide for itself where the line is to be drawn between legitimate curiosity and unacceptable snoopiness or nosiness as children get older and become interested in such matters as how rich the neighbors are, or "What were you and mommy fighting about when I was falling asleep last night?"

Cystic Fibrosis

Cystic fibrosis is an inherited disease in which the child cannot handle the normal secretions of the respiratory tract. There is a lack of ciliary action—the beating movement by the hairs of the cells lining the bronchial tubes of the lungs. Thick mucus collects at the base of the lungs, obstructing the smaller air passages and causing labored breathing and chronic cough.

Respiratory Complications

Bacteria multiply in the accumulated lung secretions, predisposing the patient to chronic bronchitis and other respiratory infections, such as pneumonia. Lung tissue changes can result eventually in severe, permanent damage to the lungs.

Digestive Complications

The abnormally thick, viscous mucus produced by the cystic fibrosis patient tends to obstruct the ducts or openings of the mucus-secreting glands. When such mucus obstructs the pancreas, it interferes with its ability to supply important digestive enzymes to the intestinal tract, thus leading to poor digestion and malabsorption of a number of important nutrients. A child with cystic fibrosis may therefore be poorly nourished in spite of an adequate diet.

Other Complications

Tissue changes in the lungs can restrict blood flow to the heart, leading to increased blood pressure and chronic heart strain. Loss of large amounts of salt through malfunctioning sweat glands can become a very serious problem for youngsters in hot weather, causing dehydration and heat exhaustion. Laboratory tests usually find an abnormally high concentration of salt in the sweat of cystic fibrosis patients. (Indeed, the skin of a cystic fibrosis patient is apt to taste salty.) Some tissues may show three times the normal concentration of sodium and twice the normal levels of potassium.

Treatment

There is no known cure for cystic fibrosis. Treatment includes the use of humidifiers and inhalation medication in the form of aerosols to loosen secretions. Another method used is *postural drainage*—lying facedown with the head lower than the feet to let gravity help loosen secretions. Antibiotics are used to control infections; special diets with reduced fat intake and added nutrients are prescribed to compensate for abnormal digestive function. Other medical techniques are utilized in individual cases to maintain normal heart and lung function.

Scientists have discovered a molecular defect in the gene that regulates the expulsion and absorption of chloride and sodium ions by lung cells. Using inactivated cold viruses, doctors have been able to transmit a normal gene to the cells of the trachea and bronchi. Because the new normal gene does not become a part of the cells the treatment is not permanent and must be repeated.

Once considered strictly a disease of early childhood, an increasing number of cases of cystic fibrosis have been detected in recent years among adolescents and adults. Symptoms of the disease, including respiratory difficulty with chronic coughing, may resemble those of an allergic reaction.

How the Disease Is Inherited

Cystic fibrosis is transmitted to a child only when both parents are carriers of the trait. When only one parent carries the trait, however, some of the children can become carriers. Through marriage with other carriers, they may then become the parents of a child afflicted with the disorder.

Information on new treatment techniques, the location of treatment centers, and genetic counseling may be obtained from the national headquarters of the Cystic Fibrosis Foundation, 6931 Arlington Rd., Ste. 200, Bethesda, MD 20814.

Daydreaming

See FANTASIES.

Deafness

Major advances have been made in recent years in educating and socializing incurably deaf children who are normal in all other ways. Starting with a proper assessment of the child's degree of deafness at the earliest possible time and the fitting of a hearing aid are two crucial considerations. The child's instruction in lipreading and the use of her own vocal equipment are professionally supervised, and the rest of the family is very much involved in the whole process. Nowadays an important advance in speech therapy is the use of a feedback system that make it possible for the youngster to be self-corrective. Parents seeking information about special schools and services, summer camps, and other facilities can write to the following agencies: Alexander Graham Bell Association for the Deaf, 3417 Volta Place, N.W., Washington, D.C. 20007; American Speech-Language-Hearing Association, 10801 Rockville Pike, Rockville, MD 20852. See also HEARING.

Death

Some children's first experience of death is the loss of a grandparent; others may have to confront the fact of death for the first time when a beloved pet dies. A child wants to know where people or animals go when they die. Parents should be as honest as possible in answering such questions and tell their offspring what they themselves truly believe. Those parents who believe that there is life after death should say so; those who do not should say that they do not. Whatever one's beliefs, there are better ways to phrase them than "Grandma is in heaven watching you" or "People who are naughty go to hell when they die."

Death of a Parent

A child who has to cope with the death of a parent may be so disoriented that his behavior will seem odd to the adults around him. He may pretend that the death never happened; others may protect themselves from the shock by burying their feelings and never talking about the dead parent. Still others may feel rage at hav-

ing been abandoned. Many youngsters are overwhelmed by guilt, feeling that in some magic way they caused the death because from time to time they secretly wished it. In cases where the bereft child cannot cope with the loss, it may be advisable to provide some help in the form of psychiatric therapy.

Delinquency

Juvenile delinquents are minors who are guilty of breaking the law or who are engaged in associations and activities considered harmful to children's morals, such as running errands for gamblers, acting as a lookout during a robbery, or sniffing glue for kicks. Swiping a candy bar or a comic book at the age of ten doesn't define a child as a hardened delinquent, but where such behavior becomes chronic, it's a sign that something is wrong that needs to be corrected. With the guidance of a therapist, it may turn out that the child alone is not entirely responsible for his delinquent tendencies. See also DESTRUCTIVENESS, DISHONESTY, DISOBEDIENCE.

Dental Care

The proper attitude toward dental care is best instilled not by lectures or warnings, but by example. Parents who themselves go regularly to the dentist for checkups, who take care of their teeth by keeping them clean with routine brushing and the use of dental floss, can do more for their child's dental health than those who depend on stern warnings to shape the attitudes of their children. Parents can hardly expect their offspring to be heroic about dental visits when they themselves scarcely ever go unless they have a toothache.

Start Early

Dental care can begin by having the toddler accompany the parent to the dentist so that his baby teeth can be inspected and he can be given a special toothbrush of his own with instructions about how to use it. In communities where the water supply is not fluoridated, the dentist may recommend an ongoing program of fluoride application to the teeth themselves. Some families find that a pediatric dentist who specializes in children's dentistry can deal with a frightened or anxious child more expertly than the family dentist. Other families use the services of the dental clinics that are part of the dental schools of large universities.

No matter who is in charge of the family's dental health, it is important that professional attention is given to the child's dental development at every stage: fillings for decay in the first teeth, routine cleanings and checkups, and preventive orthodontics where advisable. Another aspect of dental care involves keeping the consumption of sweets to a minimum, and making sure that the child's daily diet contains the proper nutrients for building healthy teeth. See also ORTHODONTICS. For full discussion, see Ch. 22, *Teeth and Gums*.

Destructiveness

"It was an accident!" is a common cry when a child destroys a valuable object because of carelessness. And it probably was an accident. Parents who don't want precious bric-a-brac or other delicate possessions broken had better put them out of the reach of curious and clumsy little fingers. Young children should not be punished because their toys always seem to be destroyed; better to give them playthings that are sturdy and comparatively indestructible.

The child who is destructive unwittingly should not be spoken to in the same way as one would speak to a boy who willfully breaks his sister's doll or a girl who spitefully tears her brother's model-making manual. Destructiveness born of anger ("I was so furious, I smashed a dish") may happen rarely, but when it does, it should be commented on as an unsuitable way of dealing with the problem that caused the anger in the first place. When destructiveness gets out of hand or involves group activities amounting to vandalism, parental action should be taken with the guidance of a professional counselor.

Developmental Disability

Any disability that interferes with a child's normal development is a *developmental disability*. The term has been used more specifically, however, to refer to mental retardation, cerebral palsy, epilepsy, and autism.

Diabetes

No one knows why some children develop diabetes. Diabetes is a noncontagious disease that results from the body's inability to produce enough insulin for the normal metabolism of sugar. The diabetic child is thus improperly nourished because the sugar that should be incorporated into the tissues is excreted in the urine. Finding sugar in the urine facilitates early diagnosis. Also, because this disorder causes a disturbance in the metabolism of fat, there is an increase of fat in the blood, detectable in a routine blood count. Juvenile onset diabetes can be more volatile that adult onset diabetes. Control is usually though injectable insulin.

Insulin treatment has undergone some improvements in the past few years. Human insulin is now readily available; beef-pork insulin was common in usage before. There is less likely to be an allergic reaction to human insulin produced through genetic reproduction. Also, doses can be adjusted to the individual though the mix of fast-acting and slow-acting preparations.

Early Signs

Parents who are themselves diabetic will be alert to any symptoms in their offspring. The disease occurs more frequently in children where there is a family history of diabetes. However, because the disorder may occur in children where there is no previous family history of diabetes, alertness to the following signs is advisable: an abnormally frequent need to urinate; an excessive desire for fluids; itching of the genitals; general listlessness; frequent boils and carbuncles; slow healing of cuts and bruises.

If a diagnosis of diabetes is made by the physician, the child may be hospitalized for a few days for a series of definitive tests, and all the members of the family will be educated in the best way to supervise the child's diet and daily routine so that serious complications can be avoided. Professional guidance is also available to ensure that the youngster's emotional adjustment is a healthy one. For a full discussion see Ch. 15, *Diabetes Mellitus*.

Diaper Rash

See RASHES.

Diapers

Some controversy has built up in the past few years over which is more ecologically sound—cloth diapers or paper diapers. Paper diapers in landfills take more than one hundred years to deteriorate. If the plastic lining is removed, it is believed that the paper will deteriorate only weeks faster than the diaper left intact. Effective recycling of paper diapers does not yet exist, and it may be years before the material can be sanitized to the point of recyclability.

Cloth diapers, on the other hand, require strong soaps and chemicals to clean. To insure the sterility and whiteness of the cloth, bleach and harsh detergents are used. These go into the water supply and affect the plant and animal life. The energy used for hot water to wash the diapers also adds to the environmental cost.

Many parents try to use paper diapers only while traveling or in places where having a soiled diaper to carry or clean would be extremely inconvenient. This infrequent use of paper diapers allows for the occasional convenience of the throwaway while reducing paper waste.

Some parents believe that cloth diapers cause more diaper rash; other parents believe that the sealed paper diaper causes more diaper rash. The biggest cause of diaper rash is excessive moisture against the baby's skin, which can be avoided by frequent diaper changes, for whatever diaper used. Excessive use of powders and creams can also increase the problem because of the pasty substance that forms when these encounter moisture.

Diarrhea

Diarrhea, or loose and watery bowel movements, is common in babies because they are more sensitive to certain intestinal germs than older children. They may also be reacting to a change in their formula or to the roughage in a newly introduced fruit or vegetable. In older children, diarrhea may occur not only as a symptom of bacterial or viral infection, or because of food poisoning, but also as an allergic response, or because of overexcitement or anxiety.

Diarrhea in an infant should always be brought to a doctor's attention if it continues for more than 24 hours. The same holds true for an older child, especially when there are also symptoms of cramps, fever, or aches and pains in the joints. Persistent diarrhea from any cause, because it can lead to serious dehydration especially in infants, requires prompt medical attention.

Diphtheria

Diphtheria is a severe and contagious bacterial infection, often fatal if untreated. Once one of the most threatening of all childhood diseases, there are now fewer than 1,000 cases a year in the United States because of widespread and effective immunization.

The first symptoms—fever, headache, nausea, and sore throat—may be confused with the onset of other disorders. However, there is a manifestation of diphtheria that is uniquely its own: patches of grayish yellow membrane form in the throat and grow together into one large membrane that interferes with swallowing and breathing. The diphtheria bacteria also produce a powerful toxin that can eventually cause irreversible damage to the heart and nerves. Diagnosis is usually verified by laboratory identification of the bacteria in a throat culture.

If diphtheria does occur, it is best treated in a hospital. The prompt prescription of antitoxin serum and antibiotics results in recovery in practically all cases. See IMMUNIZATION.

Disabled Child

Whether a handicap is hereditary or acquired, mental or physical, temporary or permanent, it is always a con-

dition that prevents a child from participating fully on an equal footing in the activities of her own age group. But how fully she can participate and her attitude toward her disability are usually a reflection of the attitudes of her parents, teachers, and the community. Of primary importance is an assessment at the earliest possible age of the extent to which the handicap can be decreased or corrected.

Exactly how deaf is the deaf child? Can surgery repair a rheumatic heart? Is a defect of vision operable? Is the child with cerebral palsy mentally retarded or is the seeming mental malfunction a reversible effect of the physical condition? Parents should investigate all the available services offered by voluntary organizations and community groups that might help them and their child. See Ch. 36, *Voluntary Health Agencies*.

One promising development in recent years is the attempt to integrate handicapped children, whenever possible, into the mainstream of education rather than segregate them in special classes. School systems in various parts of the United States are placing deaf, blind, physically disabled, and emotionally disturbed youngsters into classrooms with their nonhandicapped peers and providing them with essential supportive services at various times during the school day. The experience of dealing with nonhandicapped children will provide them with a more realistic preparation for their adult lives.

Discrimination

See PREJUDICE.

Dishonesty

Nobody is honest about everything all the time, and that goes for children as well as adults. It's unrealistic to ex-

pect a child never to lie about anything.

Little children like to make things up and can't be held strictly accountable for some of their tall stories when they're still at an age at which fact and fantasy are not clearly distinguished. A colorful exaggeration needn't call for an accusation of lying. It's better to respond with, "That's an interesting story," or "You're just imagining."

Lying and Punishment

As youngsters get older, they should feel secure enough to tell the truth about having been naughty, knowing that although they may be punished, they will get approval for having told the truth. Children shouldn't be so fearful of their parents that dishonesty is their only protection against a beating.

Cheating

Children who are pressured beyond their ability to perform are the ones likeliest to cheat; so are those for whom winning has been held up constantly as a transcendent value. A child who has been caught cheating at school is usually punished by the authorities. If the incident is discussed at home, the parents might reexamine their values before adding to the child's burdens. A youngster who cheats regularly at games will suffer the natural punishment of exclusion by his peers.

Stealing

Young children who embark on group enterprises of stealing "for fun"—whether it's taking candy from the corner market or shoplifting from a department store—needn't be viewed as case-hardened criminals unless the stealing becomes habitual.

A nine-year-old who swipes a candy bar once or twice and regrets it belongs in a different category from one who is hired as a lookout for older delinquents. Children usually have respect for other people's property when they have property of their own that they value and don't want anyone else to take.

Disobedience

Father gets a parking ticket because he forgot about alternate sides of the street on Wednesdays; mother has a whipped cream dessert in spite of her physician's orders not to. Are mother and father disobedient? When Junior comes home from the playground at five instead of obeying orders to come home at four, is his disobedience any worse than theirs? Genuine forgetfulness, negligence, or occasional breaking of a rule is only human. Willful chronic disobedience is another matter.

Some children with a strong urge toward independence may test out many parental rules by disobeying them on purpose. A child who has been ordered not to spend any time with another child because the families are feuding, may, by flouting the order, be telling his parents that he has a right to choose his own friends. Where disobedience affects a youngster's health or safety or morals, it's time for parental action, not necessarily in the form of punishment, but in taking stock of the situation to find out why the child won't obey.

Divorced Parents

See "Separation and Divorce" in Ch. 5, *The Middle Years.*

Dreams and Nightmares

Children go through periods of having "bad dreams" or nightmares that wake them up in the middle of the night in a state of terror and bewilderment. It won't do to say, "It's just a dream." To a young child who is just beginning to grasp the difference between what's real and what isn't, nightmare can be extremely threatening. If the child wants to describe the dream after she collects herself, she should be allowed to do so even at 3:00 A.M. She may amplify and exaggerate a little bit, but that's only to let you know that she's been very brave through it all. Parental patience is called for; with a certain amount of reassurance, the child can usually be led back to bed and to sleep.

Youngsters whose sleep is regularly interrupted by nightmares or who are in the grip of the same nightmare may be feeling anxious about a daytime activity or may be feeling guilty about some undiscovered naughtiness. A tactful chat can sometimes reveal what the trouble is so that it can be disposed of during waking hours.

Night Terrors

Some children may have occasional nightmares—often called *night terrors*—in which they scream or tremble in terror. They may sit up in bed while still asleep, or even walk around. Their terror is certainly real, but the parents should remember that the cause of it is purely imaginary. Accordingly, they have no reason to be alarmed; in spite of the child's appearance, she is not in any danger, and no drastic action is called for.

Simply comfort the child, who frequently will be disoriented and confused in a half-awake state, until she can go back to sleep. She will probably have no recollection of the episode the next morning.

If night terrors occur only occasionally, there is no cause for concern, although it might be a good idea to check on the television shows your child is watching before bedtime. If there is a great deal of tension in the household, that could be a contributing cause. If night terrors are persistent or frequent, however, a physician should be consulted. See also SLEEPWALKING.

Dyslexia

Dyslexia is a condition in which an otherwise average or intelligent child suffers from a complex of motor-perceptual disabilities that interfere with the orderly processing and acquisition of language. The disability that results in an inhibition of symbol recognition essential for learning how to read, write, and spell is thought to originate in some form of brain circuitry malfunction that may have been caused by injury or by genetic defect. Recent researchers have established some connection between dyslexia and a faulty pathway between the lower brain—the cerebellum—and the inner ear, causing the dyslexic child to suffer from a mild and permanent form of motion sickness that interferes with learning.

Symptoms

The symptoms of dyslexia vary considerably and may include: garbled or disordered development of speech during the early years; an inability to learn the relationship between sounds and symbols for purposes of reading aloud; an inability to learn how to spell or how to organize written expression; confusion about serial order, as in naming the days of the week or in number concepts; unusual difficulty in doing simple repetitive tasks.

If a parent suspects that a child is suffering from dyslexia, a diagnosis should be made on the basis of tests administered by trained professionals. The child's pediatrician or the school guidance counselor should be consulted about where such tests are best given and assessed. Should the child be diagnosed as dyslexic, an appropriate remedial program or an accredited special school can help surmount some of the learning difficulties.

Earache

Earache is one of the most common complaints of childhood.

As Secondary Infection

Earache is often attributable to bacterial infection of the middle ear and should be treated promptly by a physician. Because the eustachian tube that connects the back of the throat with the middle ear is shorter and wider in a child than in an adult, it affords easier entry to bacteria. Infections of the ear may thus occur as the result of a sore throat or a postnasal drip. Infectious mucus from the nose is often forced into the middle ear by way of the eustachian tube because young children are inclined to sniff it back rather than to blow it out. And when a child is mastering the technique of noseblowing, he should be told that neither one nor both of the nostrils should be pressed closed in the process. Rather, both nostrils should be blown out gently at the same time, and with the mouth open. If gentle blowing doesn't clear the nostrils, the nose should be wiped as necessary.

Recognizing Earache in an Infant

Earache in an infant may be combined with fever and the kind of crying associated with sharp pain. A toddler may indicate the source of discomfort by pulling at the earlobe. Until the pediatrician can prescribe proper medication, discomfort can be relieved by applying a heating pad to the involved ear and giving the child a non-aspirin pain reliever.

Other Causes

Earache may also accompany teething or tooth infection, or it may be the result of pressure caused by water that has been trapped in the ear after swimming or bathing. In small children, an earache may be a sign that the youngster has stuffed a bean or a tiny plastic object so far into his ear that it won't come out as easily as it went in. If you suspect such an occurrence, avoid poking and prodding in an attempt to remove the object. The child should be taken to a physician or to a hospital so that the object can be removed with the proper instruments and the ear examined and treated for possible injury.

Consequences of Neglect of Earache

An earache should always be brought to a physician's attention without delay because untreated middle ear infections can lead to irreversible hearing loss. The leading cause of mild hearing loss in toddlers is believed to be *serous otitis media*, or serous infection of the middle ear. This condition is specifically an inflammation of the middle ear with an accumulation of fluid behind the eardrum. When the condition is chronic or improperly treated during the first three years, it may impair hearing permanently and as a consequence lead to a failure to develop normal language skills. Occasionally the physician may have to make a small opening in the eardrum to drain the fluid, a procedure known as a *myringotomy*. Tubes may be inserted to drain the ear. The small tubes will eventually pop out themselves. Other treatments may include surgery on the eustachian to expand constricted areas and allow drainage through the auditory tube. The isthmus of the auditory tube is the narrowest point in the canal and may close during swelling or inflammation. See also HEARING.

Eczema

See under RASHES.

Education

See SCHOOL.

Epilepsy

Epilepsy in childhood most commonly takes the form of petit mal or psychomotor episodes.

Petit Mal Seizures

Petit mal episodes are characterized by brief lapses of consciousness, sometimes occurring many times a day. The child does not fall down but simply stops what he is doing and may appear to stare absently.

Psychomotor Seizures

Psychomotor episodes are characterized by the performance of some activity during a brief lapse of consciousness. The child may walk around in circles, or sit down and get up in a purposeless way. During this type of seizure the child may babble nonsensically or chant the same word over and over. Such an attack may last no more than a few minutes, and when the child recovers he is likely to have no memory of its occurrence.

In many instances, parents who expect a certain amount of bizarre behavior from their youngsters may not realize that a form of epilepsy is the cause. Should such incidents occur frequently, they should be called to the attention of the physician who may think it advisable to have the child examined by a neurologist.

A parent witnessing a *grand mal* or convulsive epileptic seizure for the first time may be unduly alarmed and take measures that may harm the child rather than help. For a description of emergency measures during a grand mal seizure, see Ch. 35, *Medical Emergencies.* For a full discussion of epilepsy, see Ch. 8, *Diseases of the Muscles and Nervous System.*

Exercise

Some children seem to sit around a great deal; others are on the move from morning until bedtime. A youngster might be listless or lethargic because there's something the matter that needs to be investigated by a physician. This type of sitting around is quite different from playing with dolls for hours at a time or looking at picture books instead of running around. A young child who really cannot sit still at all may have a problem that needs diagnosing by a physician, too. Practically all children are found between these extremes.

Exercise as a Developmental Need

Toddlers must be allowed to get the exercise necessary for the development of their bodies. They shouldn't be confined in a playpen for most of the day. Three- and four-year-olds who don't go to a nursery school and have no play equipment in their backyard (if they have a backyard), should be taken whenever possible to a local park or playground that has swings, slides, seesaws, jungle gyms, or other devices that are safely designed and installed. Most schools have some kind of supervised gym activity or a free time for yard play, and if they don't, they should. If this sched-

uled exercise is insufficient for a nine- or ten-year-old, inquiries can be made about athletic facilities at a local YMCA, settlement house, church, or fraternal organization.

Choice of Activities

As children get a little older, they should be permitted to choose the exercise that appeals to them unless there's a good reason for its being forbidden. A girl who wants to join a sandlot baseball team shouldn't be forced to go to a ballet class, and a boy inspired by the dancing he's seen on TV shouldn't be discouraged if the family can afford the lessons. Exercise needn't be synonymous with competition unless the youngster wants it to be. See also "Physical Fitness" in Ch. 3, *The Teens.*

Eyeglasses

Now that infants and youngsters have periodic eye checkups with their physicians, and regular tests are given to all students, more children are wearing glasses than in former years. In addition to *strabismus* (crossed eyes), the three major eye problems encountered in children are *myopia* (nearsightedness), *hyperopia* (farsightedness), and *astigmatism.*

Myopia

The *myopic* or nearsighted child cannot see distant objects well but can see close objects clearly. A very young child so afflicted may stumble and fall easily. An older child attending school may make errors in copying because she has difficulty in making out the words and figures written on the chalkboard. She may be called a behavior problem or may even be said to be mentally retarded. Most cases of myopia can be helped with glasses.

Hyperopia

The *hyperopic* (also called *hypermetropic*) or farsighted eye is shorter from front to rear than the normal eye, and if not corrected will often hinder close work like reading. When a farsighted child reads she often complains of blurring of the printed page, sleepiness, and headache. Farsightedness is often associated with crossed eyes and is usually correctable with glasses.

Astigmatism

In *astigmatism* or distorted vision, there is an uneven curvature of the cornea or lens surface of the eye. This condition causes some light rays to focus further back than others and produces a blurred, distorted image on the retina.

Either a farsighted or nearsighted eye can be *astigmatic;* the abnormality can usually be corrected by properly prescribed eyeglasses.

Fantasies

Every normal child has fantasies, some highly pleasurable, some fearful and frightening. Young children sometimes have a hard time sorting out what they imagine from what's real; this may be especially true when a nightmare interferes with sleep. Many children quite consciously say, "Let's pretend" or "Let's make believe" when they embark on a dress-up activity; others simply and straightforwardly act out their fantasies by playing games of violence with toy guns. An only child may create a fantasy companion with whom she has conversations; a child who is encouraged to draw may give shape to her fantasies in pictures that mean a lot to her but not much to anyone else.

Daydreaming

Some children infuriate their energetic parents by sitting around and daydreaming (with one sock on and one off) instead of doing their chores. Whatever form fantasies may take, they are an inevitable part of growing up and should be respected, unless they become the equivalent of a narcotic escape from reality rather than a means of enriching it. When a child's fantasy life appears to be turning into a substitute for his real one, the time has come to consult a psychiatric authority.

Fears and Phobias

Babies are fearful about being dropped, and they're frightened by a sudden loud noise. (You *can* make babies cry by saying, "Boo!" When they get older and catch on, they'll think it's fun to be scared.) Toddlers are taught to be afraid of a hot stove, and as children get a little older, they develop night fears that become bad dreams. Many parents transmit, deliberately or unknowingly, some of their fears to their children: fear of dogs, or thunder and lightning, or infection by germs.

Only a thin line separates sensible caution from anxiety. Where a threat of punishment is involved, an anxiety may develop that can last a lifetime. Parents should control the impulse to say such things as, "Don't eat that, it's going to make you sick" or "Don't climb so high, you're going to fall" or "Don't play in the mud; the germs will make you sick." Or, worse yet, "If you do that, the bogey man will get you" or "God will punish you."

Phobias

If fears are often legitimate and usually outgrown through reassuring ex-periences, phobias are deep-seated unconquerable fears. Many adults suffer from them; two of the most common are *claustrophobia*, the fear of being in an enclosed place, and *acrophobia*, the fear of heights. *Phobia* is a clinical term and shouldn't be used to describe a youngster's aversion to school at a particular time, or his apprehension about elevators and escalators. If parental reassurance can help a child overcome fears of this type, they need not be classed as phobias.

Fever

As every parent knows, babies can run very high fevers. In itself, a rectal temperature of 103° F or 104° F is not necessarily cause for alarm. (Normal rectal temperature is about ½° F to 1° F higher than the oral norm of 98.6° F.) Of course, you should take the immediate step of calling your pediatrician to find out what's causing the fever.

If a baby's fever goes over 104° F, the infant may experience convulsions. To avoid this possibility, he may be bathed with cool water or with equal parts of water and alcohol. (The alcohol is not necessary.) If convulsions do occur, protect the baby from injuring himself by seeing that his head and body don't strike anything hard. The convulsion, though frightening, is usually brief and ends of its own accord. Get in touch with your physician without delay.

Although the mechanism that results in fever is not precisely understood, the elevation in temperature is almost always a sign that the child's normal body processes are being disturbed. A child old enough to talk can let you know that his throat is sore or that he has an earache.

Possible Causes

Fever is often the sign of the onset of an infectious disease such as measles or influenza; it usually accompanies severe sunburn; it may be a warning that the infection of a local cut is spreading through the rest of the body. When it comes suddenly and rises quickly, along with cramps or diarrhea, it may indicate a gastrointestinal infection or food poisoning. No matter what a child's age, if temperature by mouth rises above 101° F, a physician should be informed of the fever and accompanying symptoms.

Treatment

Until a diagnosis is made and treatment prescribed, the feverish youngster should be put to bed and kept on a diet of light foods and lots of liquids. If the elevated temperature is combined with stiff neck, aching joints, or headache, nonaspirin medication can be given for relief according to dose instructions indicated.

Fluoridation

Although it has been unequivocally established that fluoridated drinking water is the best safeguard against tooth decay, many parts of the United States continue to resist this public health measure, thus placing a special burden on the parents of preschool children. Families in such communities are strongly urged to consult their dentist or the closest dental clinic connected with a university's college of dentistry for advice on the appropriate measures to be taken to protect their children's teeth. A consultation of this nature is advisable as soon as the baby shows signs of teething, because the fluoride treatments should begin as early as possible.

In many areas where the water supply remains unfluoridated, programs in the public schools supply youngsters with fluoride tablets every day. Although this method of applying the chemical is less effective than its availability in the drinking water, it is a step in the right direction. Concerned parents can make an effort to initiate such programs where none exists by contacting state public health officials.

Foot Care

Unless the child's pediatrician indicates the need for corrective or orthopedic shoes, parents need have little concern for pigeon toes or bowed legs or flat feet. If a shoe salesman suggests remedial footwear, his suggestions should be discussed with a physician before complying with them. A good general rule to follow about the fit of shoes is that they should be about three-quarters of an inch longer than the foot itself. For a child whose feet have a tendency to perspire heavily, sweat socks made of cotton or wool are to be preferred to those made of synthetics. Blisters that form on the instep, heel, or any other part of the foot because of ill-fitting footwear must be treated promptly to avoid serious infection.

Friends

Everyone needs friends. Some children need only one; others seem to enjoy having several. A three-year-old who is just beginning to learn about sharing may be more relaxed playing with just one other child; a ten-year-old may like the hurly-burly of a group of friends to get together with when school is out.

Parents Please Stay Out

Parents should try to steer clear of squabbles between children. One day, Nancy and Harriet are best friends, the next, bitter enemies, because of some real or imagined outrage. Left to their own devices, the children will probably patch things up. If parents get involved, the situation gets magnified out of all proportion. It's not unusual in such situations for the two sets of parents to stop speaking to each other and the two little girls to go back to being best friends again.

Keeping Bad Company

What's to be done about "unsuitable" friends? Some parents may think a particular child is unacceptable because she's too aggressive or too foul-mouthed. If your child seems fond of her nonetheless, voice your opinions, but don't forbid the youngster from coming to the house. Any attempt to break up the friendship is likely to be resisted until your child learns from experience that your judgment was the right one. Children who are discouraged from bringing their friends home because they make a mess or make too much noise are actually deprived of feeling at home in their own house.

Friendships between girls and boys may begin in nursery school and continue for years afterward. Although the tone of the friendship may change, the closeness can be very valuable if it doesn't exclude other relationships.

Frostbite

See Ch. 35, *Medical Emergencies.*

Guilt and Conscience

Children often feel as guilty about bad thoughts as they do about bad deeds. After being angry, a child may feel as badly about having had a fleeting wish to hurt his mother as he would have felt had he actually hurt her. A child should be helped to understand that his thoughts are his own, that his thoughts cannot harm anybody, and that he will not be punished for his thoughts. He should understand that it is only actions of certain kinds that cannot be allowed and that will result in a reprimand or punishment. In other words, a child should not be made to feel guilty for angry or aggressive thoughts toward other members of his family, but only for angry and aggressive acts.

A parent might say to a child, "I understand that you really disliked your brother when you hit him, in fact, even hated him and would have liked to hurt him. It's okay for you to be angry with him, but I am not going to let you hurt him." A clear distinction should be made between hostile feelings and hostile behavior.

Headaches

Children get headaches just as adults do. The difficulty in diagnosing and treating them comes from the different symptoms that children experience. It is believed that up to 10 percent of preadolescents suffer from migraine headaches.

Symptoms of headaches in children include aggression, agitation, vomiting, nausea, visual problems, insomnia, and profuse sweating. Causes are the same as they are in adults: tension, stress, eye strain, migraine, or emotional or physical problems. For a child experiencing frequent or severe headaches, a physician should be consulted to eliminate the possibility of an underlying physical disorder, such as near or farsightedness. Once the doctor has determined that no physical disorder exists, treatment of the psychological cause should be considered. Undue pressure from home or the school can create as much stress on a child as an adult experiences in the workplace.

Medication of children should be taken only under the supervision of a qualified doctor. Children respond to certain medications much differently than adults, and care must be taken in administering the types and quantities of drugs. Also treatment of any child with aspirin should be supervised because of the risk of Reye's Syndrome.

Diagnosis and treatment of children with headaches is difficult. Parents should continue to seek treatment for their children until they are satisfied that the problem has been addressed and is being remedied.

Health Records

It may seem somewhat troublesome to keep orderly health records for every member of the family, but the accumulated information can be extremely helpful if it can be supplied at a moment's notice to a physician or a hospital. Chronologically arranged facts can also provide the material eventually needed by summer camps and school applications and insurance policies.

A notebook containing essential data about past illnesses, accidents, allergies, surgery, and other facts can be extraordinarily helpful and time-saving in supplying a physician with a medical history that simplifies diagnosis and treatment. Such a notebook should have separate sections for immunizations and booster shots and their dates; annual weight and height progress; illnesses with dates and special notations; accidents with dates and any permanent consequences; hospitalization and reason;

individual problems relating to allergies, hearing, vision, speech, and the like. Visits to physician and dentist should be recorded, and the blood type entered in a conspicuous place. If possible, parents should also provide a summary at the back of the notebook of their own major illnesses, disabilities, and surgical history.

Hearing

Approximately half of all adult hearing problems are thought to have originated in childhood. About five out of every hundred children reveal some hearing disability when screening tests are given. Total deafness among children is uncommon, and where it does exist, its symptoms become manifest to parents and physicians alike during infancy.

Partial Hearing Loss

Partial hearing disability, on the other hand, is common, and is likely to be overlooked until it may be too late to correct its consequences.

A physician begins to suspect a hearing problem when the mother of a young baby tells him that the child does not react to her voice, to noises, or to other auditory stimuli. As the child gets older, he may not speak properly. Because he has never heard speech, he cannot imitate its sound and may fail to develop normal language skills. Sometimes these children, like visually handicapped children, are mistakenly called mentally retarded or are classified as suffering from hyperkinesis or brain dysfunction. Often the undetected hearing disability stemmed from a middle ear infection that was treated inadequately or not treated at all.

Language Problems

A hearing loss of 15 decibels is considered sufficiently large to produce language problems for a very young child, causing a major handicap in the acquisition of language skills. Specialists therefore recommend that parents ask that their physician test a baby's hearing, especially during and after an ear infection. If a compensatory hearing aid is necessary, the baby should be supplied with one immediately. Speech will not develop normally—that is, the language function of the brain will be impaired—unless the essential sounds of language can be perceived during the first two years of life.

Just as glasses or surgery can help eye problems, simple hearing aids, the surgical removal of excessive lymphoid tissue blocking the eustachian tube, or special instruction in lip reading can often help a hearing problem and open up a new world for the child afflicted with a hearing disability.

Heart Disease

See RHEUMATIC FEVER. See also "Congenital Heart Disease" in Ch. 10, *Heart Disease*.

Hernia

A *hernia* is a condition in which part of an organ protrudes through a weak spot or other abnormal opening in the wall of a body cavity. There are three types of hernias that may occur in children.

Umbilical Hernia

The most common is an *umbilical hernia*, in which there is a protrusion of some of the contents of the abdomen through an opening in the abdominal wall at the navel where the umbilical cord was attached. When the baby cries or strains, the protrusion becomes more obvious, and when the baby is at rest, the bulge recedes. An umbilical hernia usually disappears by the time a child reaches the second year. Because it represents no danger to any of the body functions, the condition need be no cause for concern. It is very common in non-Caucasian children.

Inguinal Hernia

The second most common type of hernia in childhood is known as an *indirect inguinal hernia*, occurring frequently in boys. At birth it may have the appearance of a marble located under the skin at the groin. In time, it may descend into the scrotum that encloses the testicles. This type of hernia is usually corrected by simple surgery that repairs the weakened musculature. The weak muscles are often present on both sides.

Hiatus Hernia

Another congenital hernia is known as a *hiatus hernia* (or *diaphragmatic hernia*) in which part of the stomach protrudes upward through the part of the esophagus that opens into the diaphragm. In some cases, this structural defect is self-healing. Surgical correction is advised only if the hernia interferes with respiration. See also Ch. 11, *Diseases of the Digestive System*.

Hospitalization

Most children at some time in their first 15 years of life require at least one hospitalization, ranging in time from a few days to many months. This can be a frightening experience and may leave permanent emotional scars on a child. Parents can do many things to make the experience less harmful.

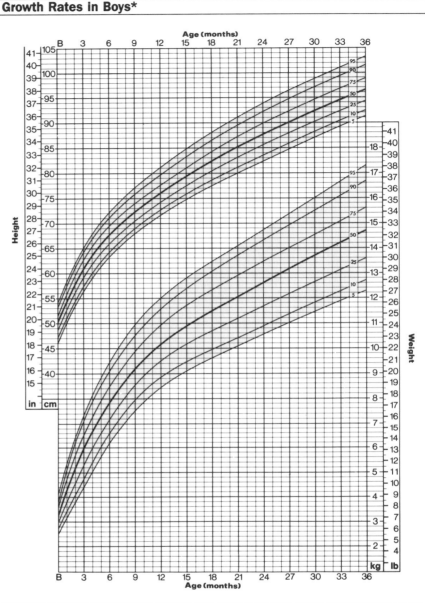

Growth Rates in Boys*

*Adapted from National Center for Health Statistics *NCHS Growth Charts*, 1976. Monthly Vital Statistics Report. Vol. 25, No. 3, Supp. (HRA) 76-1120. Health Resources Administration, Rockville, Maryland, June, 1976. Data from The Fels Research Institute, Yellow Springs, Ohio. © 1976 Ross Laboratories

These charts indicate the rate of growth of boys and girls from birth to 36 months in the United States. In each chart the upper gray area indicates the range of growth in height from the 5th to 95th percentile, and the lower gray area indicates a similar range in weight. (If a boy or girl is in the 95th percentile in height, 95% of all other boys and girls are not as tall as he or she. If someone is in the 50th percentile in weight, half of other children weigh more and half weigh less. If one is in the 25th percentile

Preparing the child for the hospital stay may be the most important task for the parent. There are many books available for different age groups on going to the hospital. Authorities generally agree that parents should:

● Try to answer all the questions the child asks. If you have no answer, try to find one.

● Be as honest as possible. The child will want to know why he or she

Growth Rates in Girls*

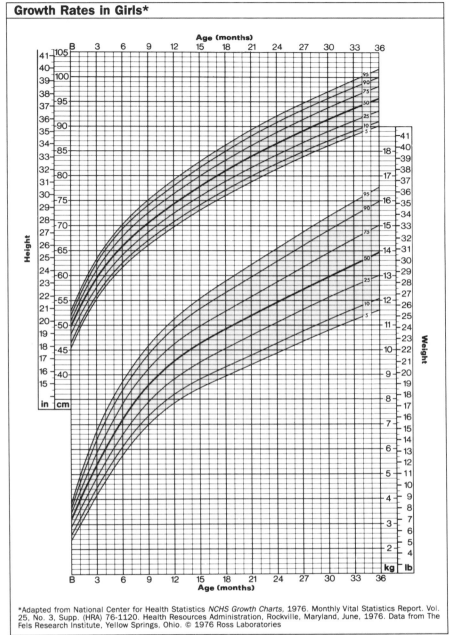

*Adapted from National Center for Health Statistics *NCHS Growth Charts,* 1976. Monthly Vital Statistics Report. Vol. 25, No. 3, Supp. (HRA) 76-1120. Health Resources Administration, Rockville, Maryland, June, 1976. Data from The Fels Research Institute, Yellow Springs, Ohio. © 1976 Ross Laboratories

of weight, 75% of other children weigh more and 25% weigh less. Thus, the percentile indicates how your child compares in height or weight with other children of the same sex and age in the United States.) Height, indicated at the left-hand side of each chart, is shown in inches and in centimeters. Weight, indicated at the right-hand side of each chart, is shown in kilograms and in pounds. The bottom and top lines of each chart indicate age in months.

has to go to the hospital, what will be done there, how long it will take, and whether it will hurt.

- Be reassuring. The child should know that he or she will receive

good care and that the hospital visit will be temporary.

- Explain what the hospital is and what it is like—with wheeled carts, people in uniform, and so on.

- Using sheets as gowns, role-play to make it clear that under the gowns will be helping people.

- Let the child know when they will be in the hospital and how long they will stay.

Most hospitals today try to work with parents to make the child feel at home and to allay the child's fears. Many hospitals offer rooms so that parents can "room in"—and stay near the young patient. A playroom may be available. Hospital staff members may hold parent-nurse sessions to introduce mothers and fathers to the hospital's schedule, locations of facilities, and other details. Parents of a child who has to be hospitalized can, by learning as much as possible and cooperating with the staff, help alleviate a child's natural fears of separation, of mutilation, and of the strange new situation.

Fear of Separation

Hospitalization for an operation or an illness affects different children at different stages of their development in different ways. Very young children may be particularly worried about separations from their mothers. Parents can help with this fear by assuring the child that separation will not be permanent.

If at all possible, the child's mother or another member of the family should stay with the child during much of the hospital stay. During an extended hospitalization, of course, this may become difficult or impossible. Barring accidents, children should always be forewarned of a hospitalization; if they are not, they may feel they were deceived by their parents and lose trust in them.

Fear of Mutilation

Children of about 4 to 10 or 11 may be more worried about possible damage or mutilation of their bodies than about separations from their families. They often have fears that parts of their bodies may be cut out or that in some way they may be permanently harmed. They may feel that when they come back from the hospital they will not be the same as they were when they went in. Matter-of-fact reassurance by the parents can be most helpful in alleviating these fears.

Fear of the Strange

Both younger children and older children aged 10, 11, or 12 may fear the new or strange, such as the anesthetic that goes with an operation. The child should be allowed to talk out fears. Simple explanations usually help. A child can, for example, understand that when you get sick taking medicine can sometimes make you better. At other times an operation, or surgery, is the only thing that will help. In the hospital, physicians or nurses may have to make tests to find out what is wrong. One such test is the X ray, which is simply a "picture" of a part of the child's body.

The parent can prepare the child for the operating room and for the operation. Everything in this special place, for example, must be kept perfectly clean, so nurses and physicians wear long-sleeved gowns. They also wash carefully before the operation begins. They wear sterile gloves so that they can touch patients without passing on germs. They also wear masks, shoe coverings, and caps. They may make a small opening in the patient's skin so that they can take out or get rid of whatever is making the child sick. The physicians and nurses use stitches, or sutures, to pull the skin edges together and allow healing to begin. Some stitches may

be under the skin; these simply melt, or dissolve, by themselves.

A dressing may be placed over the part of the child's body that was opened up. These pieces of soft cloth protect the skin opening and keep out germs. When the dressing comes off, a white scar may remain. The scar will not open up and it will not hurt. It will be a sign that the child was sick, got well, and came home.

Hostility

See ANGER.

Hyaline Membrane Disease

Hyaline membrane disease, now technically called the *respiratory distress syndrome*, is a disorder that affects approximately 50,000 newborn babies each year, and until recently was fatal for about half of them. The disorder occurs especially among premature infants, those born by caesarian section, and those with diabetic mothers. In premature infants, the immaturity of the lungs may result in a collapse of the air space within the lungs themselves when the first breath is exhaled. Each new breath then becomes a greater struggle, and with the spread of lung collapse, exhaustion and asphyxiation may occur.

A treatment known as *continuous positive airway pressure* is now being successfully used in many of the special hospital units equipped for newborns with disabilities. The therapy involves a pressure chamber that forces high-oxygen air into the lungs and keeps these air spaces open. The method has already prevented thousands of infant deaths. Newborns who need this assistance acquire the ability to breathe normally in about a week.

Hyperactivity

Hyperactivity or, more properly,

attention-deficit disorder, is a childhood syndrome describing children who are unable to concentrate and who are overactive and excitable often to the point of disrupting or disturbing nearly every social situation in which they participate. The disorder is more common in boys than in girls, and experts estimate that 3 to 6 percent of American children have some degree of it, although it has been properly diagnosed in only about half of those afflicted.

Hyperactivity is believed to be a neurological disorder (often inherited) involving the brain mechanisms that regulate attention and impulse control. It is usually treated with small daily doses of a stimulant, such as Ritalin or Dexedrine. Drug treatment combined with behavioral therapy and disciplinary tactics can be effective at calming the child down enough to gradually teach him appropriate behavior. For more information on hyperactivity/attention-deficit disorder write:

- ADDA Southern Region, Attention-Deficit Disorder Association, Nancy Eisenberg, 12345 Jones Road, Suite 287, Houston, TX 77070, (713) 955-3720

- CHADD, Children with Attention Deficit Disorders, 499 NW 70th Avenue, Suite 109, Plantation, FL 33317, (305) 587-3700

- NADDA, National Attention-Deficit Disorder Association, P. O. Box 972, Mentor, OH 44061, (800) 487-2282

Immunization

Recently developed vaccines against measles, mumps, and rubella (German measles) should eventually wipe out these diseases in the same way that smallpox has been eliminated practically everywhere in the world. Routine immunization follows a schedule of shots administered with minor variations by most pediatricians and child care clinics. Severe reactions are rare, but should they occur, they should be reported to the physician promptly.

Keeping Records

Records should be kept of the child's immunization history so that booster shots can be given at proper intervals. Because families move from one place to another, changing physicians as they relocate, it saves a great deal of time and trouble if immunization data is written down rather than committed to memory. See HEALTH RECORDS.

DTP Injections

DTP stands for diphtheria, tetanus, and pertussis (or whooping cough). DTP injections are usually given in the muscles of the mid-thigh or upper arm, at intervals of one month, sometimes longer. To prevent fever or other severe reactions, the two- to five-month-old baby should receive one grain of baby aspirin within a few hours after the injection. If she nevertheless develops fever or has other severe reactions, your physician may have to give lower doses, and therefore give more than three injections. Very rarely is a severe reaction reported with smaller doses of the vaccine. If there is such a reaction, no further injections of pertussis vaccine will be given.

Occasionally, redness or a lump appears at the site of the injection. This is a local reaction. It is harmless and will disappear within a few weeks. If it does not, consult your physician.

It is recommended that a booster or recall shot be given at one-and-a-half and at three years of age. Another recall injection of only TD (tetanus-diphtheria toxoid) is given at six years and at twelve years.

DTP Reactions

Adverse reactions to the DTP vaccine have been reported in a few cases. The reactions ranged from permanent neurological damage to such mild symptoms as persistent crying and unusual sleepiness. Crying may be high-pitched and may continue as long as three hours or more. Sleepiness may resemble a shocklike state. Some children may run temperatures of 105° F or higher. In cases of suspected adverse reactions to DTP or any other vaccine, a pediatrician or family physician should be called immediately.

Parents may want to discuss their children's medical histories with their family physicians or pediatricians before taking a child in for an inocculaton. The American Academy of Pediatrics suggests that children with personal histories of convulsions or allergic reactions to DTP or other vaccines should not be given the DTP vaccine. The same is true of children born prematurely.

Independence

Many parents feel that the most memorable moment in a child's progress towards independence comes when he takes his first steps alone. Upright and walking! Most children accomplish this by going independently from the secure arms of one adult to the waiting arms of another.

Recommended Schedule for Active Immunization of Normal Infants and Children		
Recommended Age	**Vaccine**[a]	**Comments**
2 months	DTP, OPV	Can be initiated earlier in areas of high incidence
4 months	DTP, OPV	2-month interval desired for OPV to avoid interference
6 months	DTP	OPV optional for areas where polio might be imported (e.g., some areas of southwestern United States)
12 months	TB test	May be given simultaneously with MMR at 15 months (see text)
15 months	Measles, Mumps, Rubella; DPT, OPV	MMR preferred
24 months	Hemophilus b polysaccharide vaccine	
24 months	Hemophilus b	Hemophilus b polysaccharide vaccine for Hemophilus influenza type b
4–6 years[b]	DTP, OPV	

[a] DTP—diphtheria and tetanus toxoids with pertussis vaccine. OPV—oral, attenuated poliovirus vaccine contains poliovirus types 1, 2, and 3. Tuberculin test—mantoux (intradermal PPD) preferred. Frequency of tests depends on local epidemiology. The Committee recommends annual or biennial testing unless local circumstances dictate less frequent or no testing (see tuberculosis for complete discussion. MMR—live measles, mumps, and rubella viruses in a combined vaccine (see text for discussion of single vaccines versus combination). Td—adult tetanus toxoid (full dose) and diphtheria toxoid (reduced dose) combination.

[b] Up to the seventh birthday.

As youngsters move toward greater independence, they will do so with confidence if they can start out from a secure foundation of rules and limits, and return to the security of acceptance and understanding should they come to grief.

The Toddler Stage

The toddler relishes the independence of being able to explore the house or the playground but he won't go very far before he returns to check in with the person in charge of him so that he can start out all over again. He voices his independence, too: "no" to naps; "no" to outings; "no" to a bath. This is the phase during which parents must be wary of asking "Would you like to" or "Do you want to" instead of just proceeding with the business at hand. Patience is required for the self-assertive fumblings and clumsy efforts at self-feeding and putting clothes on. Assistance should be subtle and tactful, not hurried and bossy: "Baby do, daddy help," is the general idea.

School Age

As the child moves into the larger arena of school and friendships, "I'm not a baby any more" may become a complaint if he wants more freedom than he's permitted to have. At this stage, he begins to learn that responsibility goes hand-in-hand with freedom and independence. Old enough to ride the bike farther and farther from home means taking on the responsibility of keeping it in good repair and obeying all the traffic rules.

Influenza

See "The Common Cold, Influenza, and Other Viral Infections" in Ch. 12, *Diseases of the Respiratory System*.

Insect Stings and Bites

When a child is bitten or stung by an insect, he often complains about the pain or the itching, but with the application of a lotion or salve to relieve discomfort and a bandage to prevent infection, the incident is soon forgotten. There are times, however, when a sting or a bite may require emergency treatment.

It has been estimated that about four children out of every 1,000 have serious allergic reactions to the sting of a hornet, wasp, bee, yellow jacket, or the fire ant. A child who has sustained multiple stings, or whose body, tongue, or face begins to swell because of a single sting should be taken to the hospital immediately. Tests can clearly distinguish between those children who are highly sensitive to stings and those who are not.

Preventive Measures

A physician should be consulted about the advisability of testing youngsters who are going off to camp for the first time or who are planning long hikes. Rather than curtail the activities of a child who turns out to have an acute sensitivity, it may make sense to plan a series of desensitization treatments against the particular venom. For children who are very allergic to insect stings, an emergency kit containing adrenaline is now available and should always be carried.

Mosquitoes

Every effort should be made to eradicate mosquitoes by eliminating their breeding places. A mosquito bite can be a serious threat to a child's health because these insects transmit several diseases. Where mosquitoes are a problem, infants and children should be protected against them by screens, netting, and the application of repellents.

Ticks

Families that travel and those that have pets should guard against the possibility of infection by disease-bearing ticks. A species of tick known as *Ixodes dammini* can transmit an illness called Lyme disease while another common tick may carry Rocky Mountain spotted fever.

Rashes may appear as symptoms of infection by either tick. The Lyme disease rash may be circular and hot to the touch. It may have a diameter as wide as 28 inches. Untreated in either children or adults, Lyme disease may trigger chills, fever, general feelings of malaise, fatigue, and attacks of arthritis that may last weeks or months to years. Heart and nerve abnormalities may appear. Penicillin is used to bring Lyme disease under control in pregnant women and children.

Less prevalent than Lyme disease, Rocky Mountain spotted fever usually produces a rash on the soles of the feet and the palms of the hands. Prompt medical attention is essential to prevent possible complications. See ROCKY MOUNTAIN SPOTTED FEVER and LYME DISEASE under RASHES.

Intelligence and IQ

Intelligence is a quality, not a quantity. It therefore cannot be measured as precisely as height or weight; nor can it be exemplified as definitely as mechanical skill or athletic ability or musical talent. Although child development authorities and educators may disagree about how to assess intelligence, they generally agree on the following premise: no matter what is inherited and what is instilled by experience, children function best in later life if their earliest years of nurture bring out and develop their inborn capacities.

Encouragement and Enrichment

Beginning with proper prenatal diet and care, a healthy baby is born, and from then on, her intellectual capacities are shaped by experience. Loving and attentive parents give her the self-confidence to explore and learn. She is encouraged to express herself in language. She is exposed to a variety of experiences that will stimulate her curiosity and interest: plants, drawing materials, pets, picture books, outings to the beach. Her efforts to use her intelligence by asking questions are respected and encouraged rather than minimized and ignored.

IQ Tests

Once a child gets to school her capabilities may or may not be measured by a standard IQ test. Such tests, which have been abandoned in some states, assess specific areas of intelligence and are graded according to a statistical norm. Newer techniques for measuring intelligence are designed to compensate for a cultural bias that some authorities believe exists in the standard tests.

Jealousy

See BROTHERS AND SISTERS, NEW BABY.

Kidney Diseases

For a discussion of kidney diseases, see Ch. 17, *Diseases of the Urinogenital System*, and Ch. 18, *Cancer*.

Learning

See CURIOSITY, INTELLIGENCE AND IQ, READING, SCHOOL.

Lead Poisoning

Lead poisoning in children is usually associated with the ingestion of paint and plaster flakes containing high levels of lead. This is a problem in city slums where old buildings are being leveled, or in cases where youngsters manage to gnaw on repainted cribs and other furniture originally covered with lead-base paint. In homes being renovated, the dust from removal of lead paint can cause an increase in lead levels in the blood.

Lead poisoning is a serious danger to the health of approximately half a million children in the United States. Irreversible brain damage and anemia can occur if the condition becomes chronic; convulsions and death may occur in an acute case. To lessen such hazards, legislation now requires new cars to use only lead-free gasoline.

Learning Disability

A child with a learning disability is one who, though otherwise normal, cannot acquire certain skills or assimilate certain kinds of knowledge at the same rate as most other children. Obviously, almost every child lags behind her peers at one time or another in certain subjects; but the difficulties of a learning disabled child are far more severe. A 16-year-old who suffers from a learning disability may, for example, be capable only of third- or fourth-grade math while functioning at her own grade level in other subjects. Some learning disabilities are attributed to minimal brain damage, but in most cases the cause is unknown. See also DYSLEXIA.

Leukemia

See CANCER.

Lying

See DISHONESTY.

Malnutrition

Poor nutrition or undernourishment can occur not only as a result of a faulty diet, but also because a child may have a metabolic defect that prevents her body from making proper use of a particular essential nutrient. Temporary malnutrition may also accompany a long illness in which the child's appetite wanes.

Although malnutrition is usually associated with poverty and child neglect, it can also occur because of ignorance, carelessness, or fanaticism. Children have been found to be malnourished by parents following a macrobiotic diet or a faddish type of vegetarianism. Using vitamins as a substitute for food can also cause certain types of undernourishment.

Older children, especially girls approaching puberty, may embark on starvation diets in an attempt to ward off inevitable body changes and end up seriously malnourished. The general signs of malnutrition are increasing physical weakness, vague and unfocused behavior, as well as the particular symptoms associated with anemia and vitamin deficiencies. See also Ch. 27, *Nutrition and Weight Control*.

Measles

Measles is by far the most dangerous of the common childhood diseases because of its possible complications, such as meningitis, encephalitis, and severe secondary staphylococcus infection. Fortunately, widespread protection is available in the live measles vaccine, which should be given to every child over one year of age.

Symptoms

Measles, a highly contagious disease caused by a virus, has an incubation period of one to two weeks. The most noticeable symptom is the rash that begins on the head and face within a few days after the onset of the disease, and gradually erupts all over the body, blending into big red patches. Other symptoms include fever up to 104° F or higher, a severe cough, sore throat, stuffy nose, inflammation of the *conjunctiva* (the mucous membrane on the inner part of the eyelid and extending over the front of the eyeball), sensitivity of the eyes to light, enlarged lymph nodes, and a generalized sick feeling.

Any child who has contracted measles should be seen by a physician and watched carefully for possible complications. Moreover, if he is of school age, the school should be promptly notified. This, of course, is true for any contagious disease.

Treatment

Measles can be treated only symptomatically. During the incubation period, an injection of gamma globulin will lessen the severity of the disease, or occasionally prevent it. If there are other children at home besides the affected one, they should also receive gamma globulin injections. Antibiotics are of no help unless there is a secondary bacterial infection.

It is now suspected that vaccinations given in the United States and Canada during the 1960s and 1970s were not triggering permanent immunity to measles. Anyone who has been vaccinated during that period should consult his or her physician about reimmunization. The number of

cases, including adult cases, of measles has risen dramatically. This is partly because of the need for revaccination in adults; it is also because many parents are not having their children immunized. Measles can be fatal and vaccination can protect against needless deaths from this preventable disease.

All parents should make certain that their children are vaccinated against this potentially serious disease. See IMMUNIZATION.

Medication

New parents can save themselves time and trouble by getting into the habit of writing down a physician's instructions about medication when the child requires it. Although dosages are usually clearly indicated on labels prepared by the pharmacist according to the prescription, the physician may add comments about how or when to change the dosage.

How to Give Medicines to Children

As for administering medication, a calm and assured approach and a minimum of fuss are more effective than wheedling and urging. A very young child may need to be distracted by cheerful conversation as the spoon goes into her mouth; an older child can be given some factual information about the medication and what it will do. No matter what the youngster's age, parents should never trick or fool her about what she's being given, nor should candied medicine be used under any circumstances. Setting up this type of confusion in a young mind can lead to an overdose of "candy" serious enough to require emergency hospitalization.

Overusing Medication

As a child gets older, she will become increasingly conscious of the medication her parents take. Families that are constantly swallowing one or another kind of pill—diet pills, sleeping pills, tranquilizers—might give some thought to their attitude towards drugs and how these attitudes are affecting their children. Generally, it's a good idea to refrain from medicating a child unless the pediatrician recommends it.

Old Medicines

Once the illness for which a particular medication has been prescribed is definitely over, the remains of the bottle or the leftover capsules should be flushed down the toilet. Old, outdated pills can be dangerous. For safety's sake, parents should review the contents of the medicine cabinet on a regular basis and get rid of any medications left over from a previous illness. Basic medications that are essential for occasional emergencies should be reviewed for continuing effectiveness. Some of these might have a limited shelf life and be completely ineffective should they be needed.

Meningitis

Meningitis is an inflammation of the *meninges*, the thin membranes that cover the spinal cord and the brain. The inflammation, which may be caused by a virus or by bacteria, is more common among children than adults, and may occur in epidemics. This is especially true if the infectious agent is meningococcal (*meningococcal meningitis*), because the meningococcal bacteria are also found in the throat and are transmitted by coughing, sneezing, and talking. This type occurs mostly in young adults. Another type of meningitis that commonly occurs among young children during the spring and summer is caused by such organisms as the mumps virus and the coxsackievirus.

Symptoms

Whatever the cause, the symptoms are generally the same: headache, fever, vomiting, and stiff neck. If untreated, the child may go into delirium and convulsions. Drowsiness and blurred vision may also occur, and if the disease develops in an infant, the pressure on the brain caused by the inflamed meninges will create a bulge on the soft spot (fontanelle) of the baby's head. No time should be lost in calling the physician about any of these symptoms.

Meningitis was almost always fatal before the availability of antibiotics, and although it is no longer the threat it once was, it must be treated promptly if irreversible consequences are to be avoided.

Mental Illness

Behind the search for the causes and treatment of mental illness in children is the current research in the relationship between that mysterious entity called the mind and that palpable physical organism called the brain. Parents of children diagnosed as mentally ill are themselves caught up in this distinction, often preferring to call their youngsters "emotionally disturbed." It is now estimated that about one-and-a-half million youngsters under 18 require some kind of treatment for mental illness, and this figure does not include the one million children diagnosed as hyperkinetic. The two most serious forms of childhood mental illness are autism and schizophrenia.

Autism

The term "early infantile autism" was coined in the 1940s to describe babies and young children who show unpredictable deviations in development. Some never learn to speak; others refuse to look anyone directly in the eye. Autistic children may have one or two extraordinary skills and be incapable of remembering their own names. In spite of a tendency on the part of a few specialists to ascribe autism to a rejecting mother's refusal to love the infant, most authorities now describe this mysterious disorder as an organic condition caused by neurological rather than by psychological abnormalities. The same conclusions are more or less being reached about schizophrenia.

Schizophrenia

In schizophrenia, a child is likely to exhibit any of the following symptoms: confused speech and thinking; lack of emotional responsiveness; withdrawal into fantasy; and, occasionally, hallucinations. There are indications that genetic inheritance plays some role in this disorder, and that environmental influences are also involved.

Studies suggest that symptoms originate in abnormalities of brain chemistry that may be corrected by the proper medication. Over the past twenty years, many special schools, both day schools and residential ones, have been established for training autistic and schizophrenic children. The most successful enlist the cooperation of parents as cotherapists. The National Society for Children and Adults with Autism was organized to initiate schools, offer counseling to parents, and foster research. The Society operates a National Information and Referral Service that can be addressed at 1234 Massachusetts Ave., NW,

Ste. 1017, Washington, DC 20005. See also HYPERKINESIS.

Mental Retardation

An estimated six million people in the United States are in some degree mentally retarded—almost three percent of the population. Mental retardation occurs among all nationalities, races, and religions, and among the children of those in the highest social and economic groups as well as the lowest.

What Is Mental Retardation?

Mental retardation is a developmental disability in which the individual's rate of development as a child is consistently slower than average. Learning cannot be acquired at the usual rate, and the child encounters difficulties in social adjustment.

Degrees of Mental Retardation

Mentally retarded children (and adults) are classified into four categories depending upon the degree of retardation.

Mildly retarded children—those with IQs roughly between 50 and 70—belong to by far the largest category; nearly 90 percent of all retarded people fall into this group. IQ scores by themselves can be misleading, but they are a convenient guide to probable learning and development patterns if understood properly—that is, simply as one of the criteria by which the degree of a child's disability can be estimated. The retardation of mildly retarded children is usually not apparent until they are of school age. With special educational help, such children can achieve satisfying progress in school and, as adults, will be capable with proper training of handling any of a wide variety of regular jobs. They may be indistinguishable from nonretarded people and can be expected to take their places in the life of their community.

Moderately retarded children—those with IQs somewhat below 50—belong to a group that comprises about 6 percent of all retarded people in the United States. The retardation of these children is usually apparent before they begin school, often during the child's first year, in the form of delayed developmental landmarks—for example, late sitting, late standing, late walking, and delayed talking. Many children with Down's syndrome (Mongolism) fall into this group. These children require a more sheltered environment than the mildly retarded, but can be trained as adults to do productive, satisfying work.

Severely and profoundly retarded children often have other handicaps, such as impaired motor coordination or defective vision or hearing. The great majority of these children can be taught to care for their basic needs, and many can do useful work under supervision.

Causes

There are numerous causes of mental retardation. Some cases are specifically caused by congenital factors (conditions existing at or before birth). Among these are the following: deprivation of oxygen to the brain of a baby during the birth process; the mother's contraction of rubella (German measles) during the first three months of pregnancy; complications resulting from Rh factor blood incompatibility between mother and baby; a grossly inadequate prenatal diet of the mother; syphilis; hydrocephalus (accumulation of spinal fluid in the brain); or any other pressure or injury to the brain of the fetus.

Some forms of retardation result from hereditary factors, the genetic makeup of the parents. Down's syndrome and phenylketonuria (PKU) fall in this category.

Mental retardation can also occur as a result of disease. Inflammation of the brain is a possible complication of measles—now wholly preventable by the administration of the measles vaccine. Other causes are brain injuries that result from a severe blow to the head, as from a fall. Some of these injuries are deliberately inflicted, usually by parents. (See CHILD ABUSE AND NEGLECT.) Among environmental hazards, lead and mercury poisoning are of particular importance. Lead-based paint chips have been eaten by unattended children. (See LEAD POISONING.)

If retardation is suspected by parents, medical advice should be sought immediately and a thorough evaluation of the child conducted. Some types of retardation can be greatly benefited by medical and educational treatment. It should be emphasized that all retarded children can learn and that many can be helped to the extent that they can become productive citizens. Parents would like further information about mental retardation or who are in need of counseling should write to the Association for Retarded Citizens, P.O. Box 6109, Arlington, TX 76005. See also DISABLED CHILD.

Money

Money may not be the root of all evil, but it certainly is the cause of a lot of family quarrels. To communicate to children the value of money and how to use it, spend it, save it, borrow it, lend it, and earn it, parents should try to clarify their own attitudes and settle their own differences.

Young children hear money talked about all the time: "We can't afford it," "That's a bargain," "That's a waste of money." What does it all mean to a preschooler?

The Weekly Allowance

The best way for a child to get first-hand experience in dealing with "I need" and "I want" in terms of cash on hand is to give her a weekly allowance. There isn't any point in doing this until she has mastered addition and subtraction. If the prospect of getting an allowance is motivation for improving her number skills at school, so much the better. The amount of the allowance should be calculated in terms of what it's supposed to cover. These details should be spelled out so that there's no confusion about who is responsible for paying for what. As the child gets older, the amount is adjusted for increasing needs—social occasions such as a ten-year-old might enjoy when she and her friends stop for an ice-cream cone on the way home from school.

Saving

If the family feels that a child should be required to save part of her allowance, a piggy bank and a brief talk about the virtues of saving are essential. Some children get so anxious about money that they turn into misers. When this occurs, it may be advisable to point out that the money is not meant to be hoarded but to be spent on needs and treats. Children who receive birthday or other special presents in the form of money from relatives can open a bank account and learn about interest accrual. Although the money is rightfully theirs, they might be encouraged to consult the family before they spend it all on a passing enthusiasm.

Mumps

Mumps, a mild disorder in most children, is caused by a virus and has an incubation period of from two to three weeks. The most familiar symptom is swollen glands involving the jaw. The glands usually affected are the *parotid glands*—large salivary glands below and slightly in front of the ear—although other glands may be affected, too. Other symptoms include fever and a general sick feeling. No rash is present. Mumps lasts about five days; then the swelling disappears.

In an adolescent boy, the disease sometimes causes an inflammation of the testes (called *orchitis*) and may be very painful. In addition, if it involves both testes, there is a possibility—fortunately only a very slight one—that sterility will result.

In older children mumps occasionally produces the complication called *mumps meningoencephalitis*. The signs of this more serious disease are headache, fever, and extreme debilitation. Finally, there may be an inflammation of the pancreas, which can cause severe abdominal pain and vomiting.

Because mumps is now preventable, every boy and girl should be given the mumps vaccine. Boys should be given the vaccine before puberty.

Muscular Dystrophy

See Ch. 8, *Diseases of the Muscles and Nervous System.*

Nausea and Vomiting

Nausea, the signal that vomiting may occur, is often described as feeling sick to the stomach. The feeling is experienced when irritated nerve endings in the stomach and elsewhere send messages to the vomiting reflex in the brain. When the nerve irritation is acute, vomiting occurs.

Physical Causes

Although nausea and vomiting are usually associated with a child's upset stomach or the sudden onset of a high fever and an acute infection, many youngsters feel nauseated and throw up because of motion sickness in a car or plane, or as the result of severe pain occasioned by a bad fall or other accident. A physician should always be consulted when nausea and vomiting are accompanied by fever, cramps, or diarrhea. For the child who feels sick in a moving vehicle, the physician can prescribe suitable medication. For a youngster who has swallowed a toxic substance, vomiting must often be induced. See Ch. 35, *Medical Emergencies*, for further information on poisoning.

Emotional Stress

Chronic nausea may result from emotional stress. A child who doesn't want to go to school because of some threatening situation, or who is always too anxious before a test because of pressures to do well, or who is fearful about some athletic challenge but ashamed to admit it—children under these pressures are likely to develop symptoms of nausea. However, instead of dismissing the recurrence of nausea and vomiting as typical of an oversensitive child, parents should try to find out the source of the problem and, if necessary, arrange some family therapy sessions with the child.

Nervous Habits

Nervous habits both express and release inner tension, and because growing up isn't an easy process, it's inevitable that most children have one or another way of dealing with their fears, anxieties, and emotional pressures. There's no point in parental scolding or ridicule or punishment, because any of these approaches simply adds yet another pressure to those that exist already. After all, most adults have nervous habits too—whether it's smoking, or picking at a cuticle, or tooth-grinding—and no amount of nagging is likely to put a stop to any of them.

Some nervous habits can be unhealthy, and some can be socially unacceptable but essentially harmless. All are unconscious, and most eventually disappear with age. Among the habits that may need looking into in order to decide that they have no basis in a physical disorder are squinting and throat-clearing. Hair-twirling and foot-shaking can be entirely ignored. Nail-biting may persist for years, or it may yield to vanity or the comments of friends.

Thumb-sucking, abandoned at two, may recur at three because of the arrival of a new baby or because of the stresses of going to nursery school. Many school-age children continue to suck their thumbs when they're going to sleep. There's no need to worry about this habit unless the dentist notices the beginning of an orthodontic problem, in which case, the dentist and not you should discuss it with the child. Nose-picking in public is almost always abandoned when a child enters school. If a big fuss has been made about it, he may continue the habit at home as a gesture of defiance—or because it really is unconscious. When done in private, it's completely harmless.

Masturbation bothers many parents more than it should. In and of itself, there's no harm in it, but as a chronic expression of anxiety, it might be dealt with tactfully and indirectly by trying to get to the source of the tension rather than by punishing or humiliating the child.

New Baby

It's a good idea for parents to talk about the anticipated arrival of a new baby with their child or children before the pregnancy is really obvious. Conversations can be casual, and questions should be answered simply and factually. If any basic changes are to be made—especially if a child is to be shifted to a bed so that the new arrival can have the crib—this transition should be accomplished before the infant appears. Adults should refrain from asking such questions as "Would you like a little brother or a little sister?" or "Isn't it wonderful that there's going to be a new baby in the family?" Preparations made in advance of going to the hospital should, if possible, consider whether the child would prefer to stay at home or with a relative during mother's absence. When the baby is brought home and well-wishers arrive with presents, it's comforting for the first-born to sit in mother's or daddy's lap while visitors coo over the infant in the crib. Thoughtful baby-present givers will always include a little present for the baby's older siblings, too. Parents should do their best to make baby's big brother or sister feel that the new baby is his or hers no less than mother's or father's. See also BROTHERS AND SISTERS.

Nightmares

See DREAMS AND NIGHTMARES.

Night Terrors

See DREAMS AND NIGHTMARES.

Nosebleeds

Children are likely to have nosebleeds more often than adults, and they are usually no cause for alarm. A blood vessel near the nostril may be injured by energetic noseblowing, the presence of a foreign object, or by an accidental blow or an intentional wallop.

Apply Pressure

A minor nosebleed is most effectively stopped by applying pressure over the bleeding area. A child old enough to follow instructions should be told to sit down, hold the head slightly forward, and compress the soft portion of the nose between thumb and forefinger, maintaining the pressure for about five minutes and breathing through the mouth. Application of an ice pack to the outside of the nose is usually helpful. Fingers should be withdrawn very slowly in order not to disturb the clot that should have formed.

Packing the Nostril

If this method doesn't stop the bleeding, a small twist of sterile cotton can be inserted gently into the nostril so that some of it protrudes. Light pressure should be applied once again for five minutes and the cotton allowed to remain in place for a while. Should the bleeding continue in spite of these measures, the child should be taken to a hospital emergency clinic.

Nutrition

Children's nutritional requirements are not the same as adults. Although that may seem like an obvious statement, the fact is many parents do not take it into account when planning meals.

Infants are incapable of digesting many products. Introduction of new food to an infant should be done one item at a time. If the baby has an allergic reaction, the parent then knows what it is in response to. If the baby has eaten two or three new items, it isn't possible to tell without another feeding which one the child is allergic to.

Children can outgrow some intolerances to food. A baby that could not properly digest citrus fruit may be able to handle it well a few months or years later. Some allergies, though, get worse with each exposure. Common food allergies and intolerances include nuts, berries, milk, eggs, and fish.

Children do not require the same quantity of food as an adult. Small children will eat less at a meal, but may need to eat more frequently during the day. Their stomach holds less so they get hungry more frequently.

Children also do not require the same quantity of minerals and vitamins as adults. Childrens' vitamins are available but should not be used to replace a healthy diet. Good eating habits in children establishes a pattern that they are likely to follow for the rest of their lives. Also, children should not become adapted to the idea of taking a pill every day.

Several studies show that children who are obese can diet effectively and that they are more likely to keep the weight off than adults are. Overweight children who diet for a period even as short as 10 weeks are less obese than overweight children who never diet at all. One study demonstrated that dieting in childhood does not completely prevent obesity but it does limit the amount of weight gain to less than half that gained by those who never dieted as children.

Weight is an extremely sensitive subject to children. Adolescents in particular are susceptible to negative self-images based on weight, and to criticism by others. Disorders related to eating are covered in *The Teens* under Anorexia and Bulimia.

Weight gain can commonly be traced to the amount of television a child watches. Obesity and television viewing are related through two habits. The first is that for every hour the child is plopped in front of a television is an hour the child is not playing and exercising. The other is that television watching is usually accompanied by snacking on high-fat, high-salt or sugar pre-processed food.

Orthodontics

Orthodontics is the branch of dentistry that specializes in the correction of *malocclusion* (an improper alignment of the upper and lower teeth at the point where they meet) or to irregularity of tooth positioning. Emphasis is now being placed on the prevention of malocclusion before it can occur. General practitioners of dentistry, *pedodontists* (specialists in children's dentistry), and orthodontists now believe that the need for expensive, time-consuming, and emotionally unsettling orthodontics can sometimes be avoided by beginning treatment as early as the age of four.

The positioning of the permanent teeth is the result not only of inheritance, but of other variables, such as lip-biting and thumb-sucking. Premature loss or partial disintegration of primary teeth also has a strong influence on whether the permanent teeth will be properly positioned.

Preventive Orthodontics

By the time the child is five, an X ray will show exactly how all the permanent teeth are situated in the gums. In some cases, it may be possible to guide these teeth as they erupt. If potential overcrowding and eventual crookedness are indicated, some baby teeth may be pulled to make room for the permanent ones. Normal positioning may also be accomplished by establishing a different balance of muscular forces.

Corrective Appliances

Corrective orthodontics uses many different types of appliances for the repositioning of permanent teeth, all of which operate on the same principle of applying pressure to the bone. Widening the arch of the upper jaw, for example, is accomplished by the use of a screw appliance fixed to the upper teeth so that the two halves of the hard palate are slightly separated along the middle suture, permitting new bone to fill in the space. Specialists point out that a bonus of this orthodontic correction is increased respiratory ease for youngsters who were formerly mouth-breathers.

Parents who have been advised by the family dentist that an orthodontic consultation is advisable for a child, and who are concerned about the eventual economic burden that prolonged treatment might represent, should get a second opinion from the clinical staff of a dental school associated with a university. See also DENTAL CARE.

Pacifiers

Some parents can't stand the sound of a baby's crying; others can't stand the sight of a baby sucking on a pacifier. Whatever the preference, what the baby needs during the early months is satisfaction for the sucking impulse. For most babies, this need seems to taper off at about six months; with those babies in whom the need remains strong, the thumb seems to be a convenient substitute for the pacifier. Whatever decision is arrived at between you and your physician, the important thing to keep in mind is that the pacifier is no substitute for holding and cuddling the baby when she wants comforting, and that sometimes a parent is more dependent on a pacifier than the baby is.

If pacifiers are used regularly, more than one should be available, and they should be inspected periodically to make sure that bits and pieces of rubber haven't been chewed so loose that they may be swallowed and lodge in the windpipe.

Pets

Rural children usually have their own pet animals even if the animals aren't allowed in the house. Suburban families are likely to own a dog that's a pet as well as a discouragement to prowlers. It's the city child who may have to wage a persistent campaign before his parents capitulate to the idea of a pet. Yet even the smallest apartment can accommodate a pet bird or a small fish tank; a cat and a litter box won't cause extra crowding. Of course, dogs offer the greatest companionship but also impose the greatest responsibility; they do have to be housebroken and walked in all weathers at least twice a day. If a child brings a stray animal home, the dog or cat must be checked by a vet before it becomes a household member. Once a youngster can read, the acquisition of a pet hamster or a guinea pig or a pair of gerbils will provide the incentive for trips to the library for books on care and feeding.

Choosing a Dog

When a dog is to be the choice, it's often cheaper and more satisfactory to select one from the litter of a healthy dog you know than to buy one in a pet shop or from a commercial kennel. The Anti-Cruelty and other animal shelters can provide pets at little or no charge to families. The breed chosen should be suitable in terms of size, temperament, and cost of feeding. Relative advantages and disadvantages should be checked out at the library by the child whose responsibility the pet will be.

For an only child, a pet animal is almost a must, not only for companionship, but so that there's a being in the house who's smaller and more helpless than she is. In families where allergies are a problem, the physician should be consulted about the type of pet that will cause the least discomfort to a vulnerable member of the household.

Pica

Pica is the technical term for an abnormal desire to eat substances that are not fit for food, such as clay, earth, plaster and the like. This tendency is not to be confused with the tendency of babies and toddlers to put unsuitable things into their mouth. Pica is habitual and compulsive, and may result in serious disabilities. Because the phenomenon is especially conspicuous among poor and neglected children, some authorities associate it with nutritional deficiency, others with unsatisfied emotional needs. Signs of pica should be brought to the attention of a physician or a social service agency that can provide guidance on how the child's circumstances should be altered even if the total environment cannot be changed. See also LEAD POISONING.

Pills

See MEDICATION.

Pinworms or Threadworms

See Ch. 11, *Diseases of the Digestive System*.

PKU

PKU stands for *phenylketonuria*, an inherited metabolic defect. Approximately one baby in 10,000 is born with this disease, in which the body is incapable of producing certain enzymes that are essential for the metabolic conversion of the amino acid phenylalanine. The disorder causes the amino acid and some of its by-products to accumulate in the bloodstream to a dangerous degree. If the condition goes undetected and untreated, irreversible brain damage and mental retardation are the result.

PKU babies are characteristically blond and blue-eyed, with sensitive skin and faulty muscle coordination. In many parts of the United States, state laws require that three days after birth, all babies be given the blood test that detects the presence of PKU so that treatment can begin at once if necessary. Supervised treatment usually continues for several years, and in some communities is available at special therapy centers. Parents or prospective parents who would like to find out whether any member of the family is a carrier of the recessive gene that transmits the PKU disorder can arrange for diagnostic testing and genetic counseling based on the results.

Play

See FANTASIES, TOYS, SAFETY.

Pneumonia

See "Pneumonia" in Ch. 12, *Diseases of the Respiratory System*.

Poison Ivy, Oak, and Sumac Rashes

Poison ivy and poison oak are two plants readily found across the United States. Poison sumac is found in marshes in the southern and eastern states. Children frequently come in contact with the plants while playing, hiking, or camping. The oils from the surface of the plant brush against the skin and usually, within hours, a itchy painful rash appears on the skin.

If contact with poisonous plants is suspected, the first thing one should do is wash the area of skin thoroughly with soap and water as soon after exposure as possible. Removing the poisonous oils can eliminate or reduce the inflammation. Care should be taken not to spread the oils from the infected skin to other skin. Particular care should be given to not touch or rub your eyes after contact with one of these plants. You should also be cautious of rubbing your eyes after scratching infected or exposed skin.

The rash is an itchy red group of small blisters. Cold water dressings can help reduce the itching. Use clean cotton cloth soaked in a solution of one teaspoon of salt per pint of water. Antihistamine medication can help reduce the itching and rash. If the rash persists, becomes infected, is severe, or covers a large part of the child's body, consult a physician immediately.

Poisons and Poisoning

Every year, hundreds of thousands of children swallow some poisonous substance—in too many cases with fatal results—because of parental carelessness, or because the child hasn't been given clear and unequivocal instructions about the difference between "candy" and medicine. Poisoning because of the ingestion of sugar-coated aspirin is a continuing problem; iron-containing multiple vitamins that seem to be a gourmet treat to some children also present a problem because iron in excess doses is a stomach irritant.

Safety Measures

Toddlers can do themselves damage because they're curious about everything, and their sense of taste isn't all that discriminating. Thus it's an absolute necessity to see that all household cleansers and strong chemicals are kept on high shelves rather than on the floor. Many bottles containing medicines come with safety caps that presumably cannot be opened by children—for instance, because pressure must be applied—but can be opened by adults. The experience of many parents, however, is that whereas their children can often open such caps, *they* frequently have a great deal of difficulty. Suffice it to say that the perfect childproof bottle cap has yet to be designed.

Because it's practically impossible for anyone except an expert to know what substances are poisonous to children in what amounts, or which seeds of which plants are harmful if swallowed, many authorities feel strongly that parents should immediately call the closest Poison Control Center for first-aid information rather than try to cope with antidotes or emetics on their own. The Centers are available by phone on a 24-hour-a-day basis. See Ch. 31, *Medical Emergencies*, to find the Poison Control Center nearest you. Make a note of the telephone number and make sure it's available to baby-sitters as well as to all responsible family members.

Poliomyelitis

Until the Salk vaccine was developed in the 1950s, there was no protection against polio (or, as it was then popularly called, *infantile paralysis*). The disease caused paralysis of the extremities and could cause death by paralyzing the muscles used in breathing.

The Salk vaccine utilizes doses of killed virus and is given by injection. Although it is still widely used in many parts of the world, in the United States the Sabin live virus vaccine, which is given orally, has virtually supplanted it. Repeated series of booster shots are unnecessary because the immunity persists for years.

It is advisable that a child receive three doses of the Sabin vaccine, six to eight weeks apart, starting at about the age of two months. One method employs *trivalent* vaccine, in which each dose contains three kinds of vaccine—to give protection against three strains of polio. Three separate doses are necessary, however, to insure full protection. The other method employs *monovalent* vaccines, in which each dose insures protection against a different type of polio.

Posture

"Stand up straight" is an order that many parents issue to their children with the regularity of drill sergeants. Actually, most youngsters tend to slump and have a potbellied look until they're about nine years old. This inelegant posture is not necessarily the sign of any disorder.

Youngsters who are regularly checked by a physician and given a good bill of health are not in any danger of developing a permanent curvature of the spine because they slouch. However, certain kinds of chronically poor posture may be an expression of some disorder that should be checked. Among these are flat feet, nearsightedness or astigmatism, or a hearing loss.

Emotional problems may also be expressed in a child's bearing. Anxiety can lead to carrying one shoulder higher than the other as if warding off a blow. Shyness or insecurity may cause a hangdog stance. For pubescent girls, embarrassment about burgeoning breasts may result in a round-shouldered slump. Some of these causes of poor posture should be discussed with a physician; others may be temporary and shouldn't be turned into major problems by incessant and unproductive nagging. A better corrective is participation in a dancing class or an exercise class. Sports such as ice-skating and bicycle-riding are good posture correctives, too.

Prejudice

The A student (female) who avoids studying mathematics because "girls aren't supposed to be good in math" and the black boy who goes out for the track team even though he'd rather be in the science club "because blacks are better at sports than at brainwork" have unconsciously accepted the prejudiced views of other people about them. What a waste for themselves and society!

Children who are raised in an atmosphere of contempt for and fear and mistrust of Catholics, Jews, Italians, blacks, women, men, are likely to spend the better part of their lives alternating between apprehension and arrogance. It's difficult to believe that adults can have a prejudice such as, "All Orientals are sneaky," which is supposed to describe millions of human beings, or "She's only a girl," which makes a judgment about one-half of the human race.

Being the Object of Discrimination

Parents who have themselves been discriminated against have to prepare their children for the reality of discrimination and how to cope with it. A child raised in an atmosphere of love and respect will have enough self-esteem to refuse to accept anyone else's false notions about him.

Privacy

Every child has a right to a certain amount of privacy even when he's very young. If, for instance, a parent or older child doesn't allow anyone into the bathroom when he's using it, a four- or five-year-old should be given the same option. When children share the same room, or even the same furniture, each one should have a drawer of his own and a shelf of his own for his things. Respecting his private property will lead him to respect other people's. A youngster does like the privacy of playing with his friends without having a parent hovering around all the time, and he certainly doesn't want anyone listening in on his phone conversations by the time he's nine or ten.

Parents have a right to privacy, too! Children should be led to understand—pleasantly but firmly— that some adult conversations are private and not meant for their ears. They should also be taught that when an older member of the family is behind a closed door, it's rude to barge in without knocking.

Puberty

See Ch. 3, *The Teens.*

Punishment

Severe physical punishment should be avoided. Ideally, punishment should be carried out because it has an instructional value for the child rather than because it helps a parent relieve his or her feelings of anger or frustration. Severe physical punishments— for example, the use of sticks, belts, or hard blows to the body—are extremely frightening and may even be permanently injurious to the child. They are also illegal actions, constituting child abuse. Frequently, this kind of discipline can evoke even further anger on the part of the child and lead to further misbehavior.

Duration

Punishments should not be long and drawn out, but should be as immediate as possible and last only a reasonable length of time. For example, withdrawal of television privileges for a month for a seven-year-old's misbehavior would be excessively long, because at the end of the month it would be difficult for her to remember what she had done that was wrong. Excessively long punishments are also difficult to enforce. If possible, a punishment should be related to the misbehavior for which the child is receiving the punishment.

Immediacy

Punishment "when father gets home" or a day later frequently has little meaning for the child and is unlikely to help her stop misbehaving. Rewards for good behavior should also be immediate; affection and approval for most children are often more powerful rewards than candy and money.

Rashes

Rashes of one kind or another are among the most common occurrences of childhood. Whether it's the discomfort of diaper rash soon after birth, the childhood markings of chicken pox, or a case of poison ivy, most skin eruptions aren't too serious and are usually of brief duration.

The First Six Months

Skin rashes are especially common during the first six months. They may result from overheating or overdressing, or to the use of detergents, powders, perfumes, and oils which cause *contact dermatitis.* In addition, certain foods may make the baby break out in facial rashes. Prolonged contact with wet diapers causes *diaper rash,* from the ammonia produced by urine.

Skin rashes can usually be prevented or controlled by:

- Control of temperature
- Proper clothing
- Avoidance of irritating perfumes, powders, and detergents in laundering baby clothes
- Avoidance, in certain circumstances, of milk or other foods, as suggested by your physician
- Avoidance of rubber pants over diapers
- Applications of ointments to rashy areas

If a disturbing skin condition persists or gets worse, your physician will check for special infections like impetigo or fungus, and, should they exist, recommend proper treatment. During the early years, most children develop the characteristic rashes of the contagious childhood diseases, and at these times, a physician's care is usually essential for the prevention of complications.

Eczema

Some children suffer from intermittent eczema that has a tendency to run in families. Eczema can be extremely uncomfortable, because the more it itches, the more it is scratched, and the more it's scratched, the more it itches. This cycle may be triggered by an allergy to a particular food or pollen; it may be a contact dermatitis caused by a particular fabric, or it might flare up because of emotional tension created by family arguments or anxiety about schoolwork. Eczema should be treated by the family physician who may be able to discover its source and prevent further attacks.

Other Allergic Rashes

Other rashes that are essentially allergic in origin are those resulting from contact with poison ivy, oak, or sumac. For information about these and other skin conditions, including hives, see "Disorders of the Skin," in Ch. 21, *Skin and Hair*.

The discomfort of many rashes can be eased by ointments or salves. Plain cornstarch is helpful for prickly heat. Rashes that are bacterial in origin, such as impetigo, or parasitic, have to be treated by a physician with antibiotic or fungicidal preparations.

Roseola

Among the more common rashes of early childhood is the one known as *roseola infantum*. It is believed to be caused by a virus. It begins with a high fever that subsides in a few days. There are no other specific signs of illness, and the end of the disorder—when the fever is usually gone—is signaled by the appearance of a body rash of red spots that disappear overnight. The one aspect of roseola that requires medical attention is the fever. Because high temperature can produce convulsions in infants and babies, efforts should be made to reduce it by sponging and nonaspirin medication. Antibiotics are not indicated unless there's some sign of a secondary infection.

Pityriasis Rosea

A long-lasting rash thought to be viral in origin is *pityriasis rosea*, easily identifiable because the onset of this infection is preceded by one large raised red scaly eruption known as the herald patch. The rash itself appears symmetrically and in clusters on the trunk, arms, and legs, and in some children on the hands and feet as well as the face. Unfortunately, this rash may last for more than a month. There is no treatment for it, and, although it leaves without a trace and almost never recurs, it can cause severe itching that should be eased with a salve or ointment. Soap is very irritating and should be avoided.

Rocky Mountain Spotted Fever

Among the diseases caused by organisms known as rickettsiae and transmitted to people by the animal ticks that are infected with them is *Rocky Mountain spotted fever*, also called *tick fever*. In addition to rising temperature, headache, nausea, and malaise, this disease produces a characteristic rash that starts on the ankles, lower legs, and wrists, and then spreads to the rest of the body. Children who wander about in the woods during the summer or whose pets run loose in tick-infested areas should be watched for the presence of a tick on the skin and the ensuing rash. Rocky Mountain spotted fever is a serious disease against which youngsters should be protected by wearing the proper clothing.

Lyme Disease

A rash may be the first visible symptom of Lyme disease, which had been reported in 34 American states by the late 1980s. Caused by a tick-carried bacterium, the disease can produce symptoms similar to those of arthritis, multiple sclerosis, and heart disease. The initial rash can extend over an area 28 inches across. Antibiotics including tetracycline and penicillin may be used in treatment. The risk of infection may be reduced by frequent inspections of skin areas and prompt removal of the pinhead-sized ticks. If not embedded, ticks can be brushed off; if embedded, they can be lifted out with a tweezers. The skin should be washed carefully with an antiseptic such as rubbing alcohol.

Reading

Children who see their parents reading or who've heard an older sibling say, "Don't interrupt me when I'm reading" are much more likely to want to learn how to read than those who have never seen an older person absorbed in a book or magazine.

Reading Difficulties

No matter how much the world changes, the child who can't read easily is handicapped. Where a true reading problem exists, parents should confer with the school about a practical solution. If a learning disability appears to be the explanation, tutoring or a special class may be essential. See DYSLEXIA.

Reading for Information

Many youngsters who don't see the point in reading for pleasure when there are so many other things they'd prefer to do may dash off to the library if they want information about horses or sailing ships or sewing. Families who would like their youngsters to read more than they do have the responsibility of providing a quiet corner, a decent reading light, and an occasional hour of uninterrupted leisure and privacy. Parents who object to their ten-year-old daughter's habit of "always having her nose in a book" instead of "getting some fresh air and exercise" should withhold their criticism unless the physician recommends a change in the child's activities.

Retardation

See MENTAL RETARDATION.

Reye's Syndrome

Reye's Syndrome is a childhood disease that affects the nervous system and the liver and can result in death. The symptoms normally occur after the child has suffered from the flu or a respiratory illness. The symptoms include vomiting, rash, and disorientation or confusion. If not immediately treated, seizures, respiratory arrest, and coma follow shortly. There is no cure but the dangerous manifestations of the disease can be treated to avoid complications, permanent damage, or death.

The syndrome is believed to be linked to treating the child with aspirin or aspirin-containing medication during the initial illness. Cases of Reye's Syndrome have decreased sharply since 1980, with the increase in public awareness of the link between the disease and the use of aspirin for children.

Given the risk of Reye's Syndrome, it is highly recommended that parents avoid aspirin for children during any illness with fever, flu, diarrhea, or respiratory symptoms. If symptoms persist or if aspirin was given just before the onset of symptoms, please notify a physician. Reye's Syndrome is diagnosed symptomatically.

Rheumatic Fever

Once called growing pains, rheumatic fever is actually a disease of the connective tissues, a secondary manifestation of a primary infection by streptococcus bacteria of the throat or tonsils. Its chief symptoms are pains and tenderness in the joints and sore throat.

Rheumatic fever may be mild enough to escape attention or it may be disabling for a period of months. The insidious aspect of the disease is that it may damage the child's heart in such a way that tissue is permanently scarred and function is impaired in the form of a heart murmur. Acuteness of symptoms varies. Any time from a week to a month after the occurrence of strep throat, the child may complain of feeling tired and achy. Fever usually accompanies the fatigue, and pains in the joints may precede swelling and the development of nodules under the skin in the areas of the wrists, elbows, knees, and vertebrae. The pediatrician can usually detect an abnormal heart finding. The sooner treatment begins, however, the less likely the risk of permanent heart damage.

Close supervision of the affected child may be essential over a long period. Antibiotics, aspirin, hormones (cortisone), and other medicines control the course of the disease and protect the child from its potentially disabling effects. See also "Rheumatic Fever and Rheumatic Heart Disease" in Ch. 10, *Heart Diseases*.

Roseola Infantum

See under RASHES.

Rubella (German Measles)

Rubella was once thought of as a benign disease. Then it was discovered that it could have serious consequences if it were contracted by a woman during the first three months of her pregnancy. The virus that causes rubella is transmitted from the infected woman to her unborn baby, and has been linked to birth defects of the heart, eye, ear, and liver, and to mental retardation.

In addition, a baby who has been exposed to the disease in utero may infect others even though he himself is not affected by it and shows no symptoms. (In fact, most babies are immune to rubella during their first year.) The rubella virus is highly contagious and spreads rapidly.

Rubella has been on the increase in recent years, largely due to the number of young adults who have never been vaccinated. Although it can be a mild illness, it can also cause severe birth defects if contracted by a pregnant woman. Because of the risk of miscarriage and birth defects, pregnant women are advised against getting the immunization during the course of their pregnancy. Anyone who suspects that they or their children were not vaccinated should seek immunization immediately.

The incubation period for rubella is two to three weeks. Symptoms include earache, swollen glands behind the ears, a low-grade fever, and a usually mild, blotchy rash that erupts over the body but lasts only a few days.

Runaways

In growing numbers children and youth ran away from home in the early and middle 1980s. The runaways left home for various reasons. Some were escaping physical or sexual abuse while many others had severe long-term psychological and other problems. A smaller percentage faced temporary or less severe home or school difficulties. Other reasons include "status criminal offense problems"—minor violations of the law that would not be violations at all if committed by an adult—and "poor communication" with parents. Truancy is an example of a status offense. Many children who leave home are not technically "runaways." Professionals call these children *throwaways* because they have in fact been thrown out of the parents' home.

Social service professionals believe many young persons leave home to escape from "dysfunctional families." In such families, parental separation or divorce, poverty, unemployment, and high mobility have, separately or in combination, made the home ineffective as a nurturing environment. The young person may become labeled as a "failure" or "troublemaker"; and a lack of warmth may characterize parent–child relations. In other cases delinquency among a youngster's friends may exert a powerful influence.

The runaways represent diverse age and economic groups. They come from a variety of racial backgrounds. A large proportion are in the 15 to 16 age group. But runaways range in age from 10 or younger to 18.

Parents faced with the fact that a child has run away have to make difficult choices. The child who stays away overnight or for two or more nights has usually not traveled more than 10 miles from home. He or she is usually staying with friends. Only about one in five ventures more than 50 miles from home. The parent or parents of a runaway, considering such facts and not wishing simply to wait, can:

- Look for the youngster themselves. Recommended by many social workers as a logical first step, such a search may involve calls to relatives or the child's friends, checks on favorite haunts, and "driving around" in areas that the young person knows and frequents.

- Report the runaway to police. A "first impulse" alternative, calling the police may not be in the child's best interest. For one thing, the police, especially in large cities, are swamped with such reports. Parental searches actually succeed in finding runaways more frequently than police do. As a second consideration, once reported to police the youngster may be drawn into the juvenile-justice system. In some states, that could result in incarceration with adult offenders or delinquent juveniles. Other states provide that a runaway cannot be held—or cannot be held more than a brief, specified period.

- Contact a local branch of the National Network of Runaway and Youth Services. A private, nonprofit organization with more than 500 community-based shelter programs, the Network serves runaway, homeless, and other "problem" young people. It offers shelter and hotline services 24 hours a day, seven days a week. While not a search operation, the Network also provides crisis and long-term individual and family counseling, outreach, advocacy, referrals for medical, legal, and mental health assistance, and followup services.

- Contact the National Communications System. Supported by the U.S. Department of Health and Human Services, the system operates a nationwide toll-free telephone hotline. Services provided center on referral and crisis intervention aid.

Some national or local services have been established primarily to help runaways obtain clothing, shelter, and food. These organizations also try to mediate between parents and children and to bring families together. Three such groups operate the Runaway Hotline (800/231-6946), the National Runaway Switchboard (800/621-4000), and the National Center for Missing and Exploited Children (800/843-5678).

What happens after a child returns home may determine whether he or she will run away again. Family counselors suggest that parents remain calm. No matter how stressful the runaway incident may have been, parents should try to accept their child as a person. Many runaways, counselors say, are "testing the waters," or experimenting, or seeking a sense of self and identity. If the family can discuss what has happened, the problems that caused the young person to run away may be resolved.

In difficult situations, counseling may be necessary. More and more parents are turning also to inpatient psychiatric services. Usually, these parents have tried other solutions before turning to psychiatry. Contributing to the trend toward hospitalization and professional treatment is the increasing availability of insurance to cover the expected costs.

Safety

See "Accident Prevention" in Ch. 36, *Voluntary Health Agencies.*

Scarlet Fever

Scarlet fever used to be a disease that everyone dreaded. It is highly contagious, and can result in severe after-effects like rheumatic fever, or the kidney disease known as nephritis.

It is now known that scarlet fever is simply a streptococcal infection—a strain of a specific organism that also causes a diffuse red rash. It can be dealt with quite simply by your physician, the usual treatment being a ten-day course of penicillin, which cures the streptococcal infection and prevents most complications.

Schizophrenia

See under MENTAL ILLNESS.

School

In the United States, an elementary school is a place where children are taught not only how to read, write, handle numbers, and correlate sets of facts, they are also taught how to get along with children different from themselves, how to express themselves creatively, and how to become responsible citizens of a democratic society. If the reality of education falls short of these goals, parents are supposed to exert influence on the proper authorities to see that they are in fact accomplished.

Nursery School

For a child, leaving the protection of the family if only for a half-day in a nearby nursery school is a big step forward. The step is likely to be taken with eagerness if parents present the school as a pleasurable place to be, and not as a dumping ground for a youngster who's in the way of a new baby or a working mother.

Elementary School

The elementary grades represent a major change in many different ways, but most importantly because new authority figures begin to displace parents as the source of all wisdom. Adults and older siblings can help a child make a happy and productive adjustment to school by talking about it with interest and respect. Wherever possible, one or another parent should be present at parent-teacher meetings and participate in the activities of the child's group, such as class trips, visiting days, and the like.

Homework

When youngsters come home with school assignments that they find baffling, parents should feel free to ask the teacher for clearer instructions. If the child is at fault through inattention or ignorance, it might be pointed out to her that whether or not she gets a good education depends on how hard she's ready to work and not how efficiently the teacher can spoon-feed her.

Private Schools

Some families feel that the local public school is not the best place for their children to learn during the lower grades. Alternative private schools, whether denominational, discriminatory, or for gifted children, may have advantages that are less apparent to the child than to the parents, especially if attendance isolates the youngster from her friends in the neighborhood.

Staying Home from School

It's not unusual for a child to avoid going to school once in a while by saying she's sick. She may actually need a rest from the routine every few months. This is quite different from truly getting sick at the thought of facing school. A child who is nauseated in the morning, or who throws up, or who has a stomachache at breakfast, is probably experiencing feelings of anger, resentment, or anxiety beyond her ability to cope with them. Whatever it is in the school situation that's worrying her, she should be given the opportunity to talk about what's going on and the reassurance that efforts will be made to help straighten things out.

For children with disabilities, special facilities are often provided within the structure of the local school so that they can spend at least part of their day with their own age group.

Sex Education

Children need and deserve to have access to correct information about sexual functioning. If there is a natural openness in a family about questions of all types, children first start asking questions about sex when they are three or four; it is then that parents can begin describing sexual functioning to their children.

Questions about Body Parts

The first questions about sex usually have to do with the functioning of body parts. For example, children want to know where urine comes from, what happens to food when they eat it, where feces come from, and where babies come from. Explanations should be given in a straightforward, unembarrassed manner. Children should not be overloaded with information that they do not understand, but parents should be willing to answer questions to the best of their ability.

With older children, particularly 11- and 12-year-olds, it is often helpful for sexual questions to be answered by the parent of the same sex. Reading a book on sexual development together with the child can be a good experience for both parent and child. Parents frequently wonder if sex education may not lead children to engage in experimentation. Most of the evidence on this question indicates that children are more likely to experiment sexually when they are ignorant than when their questions about sex are reasonably and accurately answered.

Sexual Abuse and Incest

Of all the forms of child abuse (see CHILD ABUSE), sexual abuse, including incest, is the most common. Estimates of the number of sexual assaults on children in the United States range as high as five million annually. As many as 80 percent of these assaults occur within families. In many cases the adults reside outside the family but are closely acquainted with their victims.

Child sexual abuse takes many forms. While tens of thousands of children and young people are sexually attacked or molested, thousands of others are filmed, photographed, or otherwise exploited for the private recreational purposes of abusers. An estimated 50,000 children disappear annually; most of them are never found. Experts say many of these lost children are forced into a kind of sex-slavery, becoming victims of the "kiddie porn" (child pornography) trade. Within the home, sexual abuse may include rape, inappropriate fondling, exhibitionism, sexual intercourse, sodomy, and other acts.

Who are the victims of child sexual abuse? They are both males and females; they range in age from a few months to 16 years or older. The mean age at which a child experiences sexual abuse is nine. The victims represent all socioeconomic groups, all races, all geographic regions.

Safety Tips for Parents

1. Know your children's friends.
2. Never leave your child unattended.
3. Be involved in your child's activities.
4. Listen when your child tells you he or she does not want to be with someone.
5. Pay attention when someone shows greater than normal interest in your child.
6. Have your child fingerprinted and know where to locate dental records.
7. Be sensitive to changes in your child's behavior or attitudes.
8. Take a photograph of your child each year (4 times each year if under age 2).
9. Be prepared to describe your children accurately—including clothing, visible identifying marks, or special characteristics.
10. Develop a set procedure should you and your child become separated while away from home.
11. Do not buy items that visibly display your child's name.
12. Be sure your child's school or day-care center will not release your child to anyone other than you or someone you officially designate.
13. Instruct the school to contact you immediately if your child is absent or if someone other than you arrives to pick up him or her without advance notice from you.

Protecting Your Children

Parents have the delicate task of maintaining a loving, touching family relationship while also teaching their child or children to recognize and reject "bad touches." Parents do not want to instill in their child fear, hysteria, or paranoia. But they should want their child to know how to escape or avoid abuse within or outside the home. Without dwelling on the details of what *could* happen, show what a bad touch involves—generally, a pinch, hard slap, or a touch in a body area normally covered by a bathing suit. One exception, of course, is a physician's examination. Parental approval makes such an examination acceptable.

Children can and should learn to say "no" to an adult, psychologists tell us. Having said "no," whether the would-be abuser is a friend, relative, or stranger, your child should leave the scene quickly. Then he or she should report the incident to a parent. "Be sure to emphasize that if someone asks them not to tell that they should immediately tell," advises one authority. Parents should make it clear that they will not be mad if they receive such a report.

Parents need to instruct children periodically in the ways to respond appropriately to abusers' approaches. But then they have to listen if the child wants to talk. Children have to be sure both of the parents' love and their willingness to pay attention.

Symptoms to Watch For

A child encountering molestation or sexual abuse of any kind is undergoing an emotionally stressful experience. But the young person may be too shy to reveal what has happened. If a parent suspects that a son or daughter has been molested, one authority suggests, asking directly if anything has happened.

What symptoms might cause suspicion? As published in "Child Protection Alert," a publication of the American Christian Voice Foundation, there are at least 25 symptoms that you should watch for:

1. Explicit (sometimes bizarre) sexual knowledge

2. Precocious sexually related experimentation or speech

3. Toilet training relapses

4. Smearing of feces or urine

5. Gagging and unexplained vomiting

6. Speech problems

7. Regressive behavior

8. Masturbation

9. Withdrawal from normal human contact

10. Stomach and head pains

11. Bedwetting

12. Suicidal depression and/or self-destructive tendencies

13. Excessive fear of selected individuals or locations

14. Loss of appetite

15. Unexplained bruises or injuries in genital areas

16. Blood spotting or unexplained substances on underwear

17. Abrupt or radical behavioral or attitude changes

18. Lack of self-esteem or self-worth

19. Ulcers, colitis, anorexia, or other stress related disorders

20. Alcohol or drug abuse

21. Frequent nightmares

22. Excessive passivity

23. Vaginal or urinary tract infections

24. Infections of the mouth, gums, or throat. (Be vigilant for venereal diseases of the anus or throat. Incidences are no longer uncommon in children.)

25. Unexplained gifts, extra money, or the presence of pornography in your child's possession

Sources of Help

Where does a parent seek help once it's certain that molestation or abuse has occurred? The recommended first stage is to notify the police or local rape crisis center, or (where incest is the crime) the state child protection agency. To avoid adding to your child's stress, parents should *not* confront the offender while the child is present. Make sure the young victim has a complete physical examination if only to reassure the boy or girl that no permanent physical damage has been done. Depending on need, you may also want to ensure that the child gets counseling. Resource centers that provide diverse kinds of aid include:

- CHILD HELP National Child Abuse hotline: 800/422-4453

- Child Find hotline: 800/A-WAY-OUT for mediation; 800/I-AM-LOST for abducted children children or people identifying missing or abducted children.

- National Center for Missing and Exploited Children: 800/843-5678 or 202/634-9821

- The Adam Walsh Child Resource Center: 305/475-4848

- National Crime Information Center (F.B.I.): 202/324-2311

- National Runaway Switchboard: 800/621-4000

Sibling Rivalry

See BROTHERS AND SISTERS, NEW BABY.

Sickle-cell Anemia

See Ch. 9, *Diseases of the Circulatory System.*

Sisters and Brothers

See BROTHERS AND SISTERS.

Sleep

See BEDTIME, DREAMS AND NIGHTMARES, SLEEPWALKING.

Sleepwalking

Sleepwalking may be distressing to the parent who witnesses it, but it usually does the child no harm. If the child seems to be about to do something dangerous, it's a good idea to wake her up with a few reassuring remarks and guide her back to bed. In most sleepwalking incidents, the child goes back to bed by herself and gets up the next day without the slightest recollection of her nighttime prowl. Parents shouldn't tease or scold or make the child feel peculiar about walking in her sleep. It can be ignored unless it continues over a long period, and then it might be mentioned to your physician.

Smallpox

Smallpox has been eradicated everywhere in the world. Vaccination against smallpox has therefore been discontinued in the United States.

Smoking

Young children who see older children in the family or at home smoking cigarettes are going to equate smoking with being grown up even if their parents don't smoke. A ten-year-old who sneaks off to experiment with a cigarette shouldn't be treated like a criminal, but he should be told that he is harming himself. Parents who smoke and wish they didn't should concentrate on their own efforts to stop and hope that their offspring get the message. In any event, it might help to emphasize how hard it is to stop smoking once one has acquired the habit.

Sore Throat

"It hurts when I swallow" is a common complaint of childhood. It may be connected with a cold or tonsillitis, but if there is tenderness at the sides of the neck and a rise in temperature, the physician should be called promptly so that tests can be made to see whether the child has strep throat. Often a throat culture is necessary. A streptococcus throat infection that is undiagnosed and untreated can have serious consequences. See also STREP THROAT, TONSILLITIS.

Speech Impediments

Among the more common speech defects are *lisping* (the substitution of *th* for *s* and *z* sounds); *lallation* (the inability to pronounce *l* or *r* correctly), and stuttering. Although many children do outgrow their speech disabilities, a considerable number do not.

Therapy

Corrective therapy should be undertaken without too much delay. There have been many advances in the techniques used by speech pathologists, including the audiovisual devices and feed-back systems that promote self-correction. A list of certified speech pathologists can be obtained from the American Speech-Language-Hearing Association, 10801 Rockville Pike, Rockville, MD 20852. See also STUTTERING.

Stealing

See DISHONESTY.

Stepchildren

See Ch. 5, *The Middle Years*. See also ADOPTED CHILDREN.

Stomachache

A wide variety of disorders begins with some kind of abdominal pain, but in most cases, a stomachache is temporary and unaccompanied by any other symptoms. Digestive upsets are frequent in infancy, becoming rarer as the baby approaches the fourth month. See COLIC.

After the baby's first year, a stomachache may signal the onset of a cold or some other infection. The physician should be called if any of the following conditions occurs:

- When the stomach pain is accompanied by fever, vomiting, or diarrhea

- If moderate pain lasts for a considerable time—several hours, for example

- If the pain is obviously acute—the child is doubled over

- If the location off the pain shifts from one place to another

Never give a child a laxative or an enema except on a physician's orders.

A youngster who complains regularly of stomachaches without any other symptoms, and who might also complain of headaches or constipation shouldn't be dismissed as a worrier. The problem should be discussed with your physician so that an investigation can be made of possible causes. In many cases, constipation is the source of stomach pain. When the constipation is cleared up, the stomach pains cease.

Stomach pain may also be of psychosomatic origin, in children as well as in adults. If the pain cannot be explained after a physical examination and tests have been made, parents should consider how they can lighten some of the stresses and tensions in the child's life.

Strabismus

See CROSSED EYES.

Strep Throat

Streptococcal infections, commonly called strep throat, are caused by bacteria that inflame and infect the tissues in the throat. Symptoms include sore throat, swollen glands, redness or blotchy white spots on the throat and tonsils. Severe throat pain may occur for three to four days of the two-week run of the illness. Strep infections should be treated immediately after diagnosis by a physician with antibiotics such as erythromycin or penicillin.

Strep throat poses several risks to the health of both the adult and child sufferer. If left untreated, strep bacteria may produce the toxin that triggers scarlet fever, which also requires treatment with penicillin.

Strep can also lead to rheumatic fever. Rheumatic fever can develop into rheumatic heart disease, leaving the child with a heart murmur. Also treated with penicillin, the disease leaves little damage if caught and treated early.

The last serious problem to arise from a strep infection is relatively new. There a new strep type produces the same symptoms as toxic shock syndrome. The rare form of streptococcus causes low blood pressure, rash, high fever, and rapid organ and blood destruction. It ends in death in 20 percent of the cases. It affects children and adults. Due to the rapid onset of serious and deadly symptoms, it is essential that medical treatment be sought immediately if you or your child suffers any one of the signs of this disease.

Stuttering

Stuttering, or stammering, is a speech dysfunction where the words are spoken with hesitation, repetition, prolongation, or stumbling on one or more syllable of a word. Parents should bear in mind, though, that many children stutter when they are learning to speak. At this stage it is not a permanent problem, and the child will usually outgrow it as ease with language increases.

For a child who continues to show hesitation in speech after the age of four or five, the parents should consider getting professional guidance of a physician, speech therapist, or counselor as recommended by the child's pediatrician. The speech problem may be related to cerebellar disease or a neuromuscular defect or a problem with the voice box. There is also some research being done on hearing problems with stutterers. Some patients respond well to speech therapy when the sound of their voice is played back on a delay through earphones. The slight delay allows them to speak without hesitation. Why this works is not fully understood.

Stuttering can also be related to emotional or psychological problems. Stress from early childhood speech impairment may create a psychological block to speaking. Other problems may enter into the reason for stuttering. It is not uncommon for there to be both emotional and physical reasons for stuttering.

For more information, please call the toll-free hotline for the National Center for Stuttering at 800/221-2483. They will provide information and guidance to parents.

Sudden Infant Death Syndrome

Sudden Infant Death Syndrome, sometimes referred to as SIDS and generally known as *crib death*, claims about 10,000 babies every year. It is the chief single cause of fatalities in infants, usually occurring between the ages of one month and six months. Although there are a number of plausible theories being investigated, its cause remains unknown. In some cases, autopsies indicate a hidden infection or an unsuspected abnormality, but in 80 percent of the deaths, no obvious explanation can be found. One cause appears to be an inherited heart irregularity, and another is respiratory distress, discussed under HYALINE MEMBRANE DISEASE. Improved hospital facilities for the care of premature babies who are considered to be at higher risk than those born at full term, as well as prenatal tests and ultrasonic alarm systems that monitor breathing are expected to reduce the number of SIDS victims.

Parents of infant SIDS victims often suffer intensely, apart from their natural grief, from feelings of guilt, as if they were somehow careless or negligent. They must be reassured that they could not possibly have foreseen the susceptibility of their child to this affliction and that there is therefore no way they could have averted its tragic result. They will have suffered enough without the wholly unwarranted feeling that they were somehow responsible.

Swallowed Objects

Babies in a crib or playpen can certainly be depended on to put anything within reach into their mouths, so it's a good idea to make sure that surfaces are cleared of anything that would cause a crisis if it were swallowed. Plastic toys and rattles should be inspected for loose parts. Pins, buttons, and small change should be kept in drawers. It's no serious matter if a child swallows a cherry stone or a plum pit or a small button, because these are not likely to cause problems in their passage through the digestive system. They will be disposed of in regular bowel movements.

Emergencies

Emergencies occur when the object is stuck in the windpipe or when it goes into the bronchial passage. If it is in the windpipe and isn't coughed up right away, use the first aid maneuver for "Obstruction in the Windpipe," Ch. 35, *Medical Emergencies* without delay. If is doesn't work the first time, do it again—and again. You must clear the windpipe. If all efforts fail, rush the child to a hospital.

Swearing

Sooner or later most children learn swear words, either from hearing their parents use them or from their peers. Young children may use curse words without knowing what they mean or without appreciating how offensive they may be.

Nowadays it is virtually impossible for children to avoid hearing words in everyday use that were strictly taboo when their parents were growing up. However jolting it may be to hear foul words issuing from their angelic-looking children, parents should be neither surprised nor unduly upset if this happens occasionally, especially if they themselves use curse words. They might well point out to the child, however, that many people object strongly to such language, and if they want to be treated courteously by adults, they had better watch their language.

Swimming

Every child should learn to swim, and the earlier the better. Families fortunate enough to have their own large pools can accomplish this in their own backyards; others may spend summers near a suitable body of water.

Although there's nothing like the ocean for water play, it's not a good place to try to teach a small child how to swim. There are too many extraneous hazards, such as undertow, waves, and unexpected depths. Many communities have outdoor public pools; most large cities have indoor and outdoor pools where professional instruction is available. Even when a child can swim moderately well, she should not be allowed to do so alone, and she shouldn't be allowed to go out in a boat by herself either. Rubber floats, rafts, and the like shouldn't be made available to youngsters until they can swim. A nonswimmer depending on such a device is in trouble if it should drift away from her in deep water.

Talking

The ability to speak is part of the human heritage. How soon and how clearly a child begins to do so depends on several factors. First and foremost is the ability to hear.

Hearing and Speech

Any illness or infection in infancy that has caused even a small hearing loss will interfere with the baby's perception of sounds. This in turn will prevent the normal development of those parts of the brain that govern the imitative aspect of speech.

A Stimulating Environment

How much attention and stimulation the baby gets from his environment and the people around him will have a great effect on how much he tries to say and the age at which he begins to say it. Being listened to and automatically corrected instead of being ignored or teased is the indispensable feedback process that enriches the learning of language. The clarity of the child's speech depends to a large extent on the examples before him; what his ears hear his brain will order

his vocal equipment to imitate. Parents who want a child to outgrow baby talk should avoid responding to the baby in kind. Normal adult speech should become the norm toward which the child is constantly striving. See also HEARING, SPEECH IMPEDIMENTS, SWEARING.

Tantrums

See ANGER.

Tay-Sachs Disease

Tay-Sachs disease is an inherited disorder of the nervous system. It causes degeneration of the nerves, starting after six months of age. Infant development through pregnancy and the first six months is normal, but the disease can be detected through genetic testing. The first symptoms to appear are subtle, becoming more obvious with motor deterioration. They include a slowing of development, loss of vision, and eventually convulsions. A cherry-red spot develops on the retina of the eye. The child will lose the motor coordination that he already had, and will deteriorate to the point where he will be unable to lift his head. The child will not normally survive past the age of four.

Tay-Sachs is found with higher prevalence among the following populations: Ashkenazi Jews, Eastern European Jews, and French Canadians. Testing is recommended to anyone from these populations, and testing is also recommended for all Jews to determine if one is a carrier of the disease.

Tay-Sachs is a form of cerebral sphingolipidosis. It is the infantile onset of the disorder. The others are Jansky-Bielschowsky disease (early juvenile), Spielmeyer-Vogt and Batten-Mayou disease (late juvenile), and Kufs' disease (adult onset).

Symptoms are similar and include blindness within two years of the onset of the disorder.

Teething

Babies of four to six months drool a great deal and put their fingers in their mouth. These habits, and the telltale small bumps you may detect on the baby's gums, are the signs of teething. But they don't necessarily mean that the first tooth is about to erupt. That may not happen until he is nearly one year old, although it usually happens earlier.

Teething may or may not be painful. If the baby does fret, medication is available to alleviate the pain. (A little anesthesia, such as Ambesol, rubbed on the gums is a home remedy that often helps.)

Tetanus

Tetanus (also called *lockjaw* because it causes spasms of the jaw) can occur at any age as the result of contamination of a simple wound. The causative organism is usually found in soil, street dust, or feces.

The disease is preventable by immunization. The triple vaccine DTP should be started at two to three months of age. See also IMMUNIZATION.

When a child suffers a puncture wound, dog bite, or other wound that may be contaminated, ask your physician to give the child a booster dose of tetanus toxoid if she has not had a shot within one year.

Tick Fever

See "Rocky Mountain Spotted Fever" under RASHES.

Toilet Training

During the toddler stage parents begin to teach their child how to control his bowel and urinary functions.

When to Start

A simple question parents always ask is, "How do I know when my child is ready to be toilet trained?"

Generally, children do not have muscular control over their bowel movements and urination until about the age of two, so attempting to toilet-train a child much before this is usually wasted effort. If it is accomplished, the result is usually a training of the parents rather than of the infant. Toilet training should usually take place some time between the age of two and three and one-half.

A child is emotionally ready when he understands what is meant by toilet training and is willing to perform toilet functions without expressing fear of them. This may occur at any age, but is perhaps most apt to start between the ages of 18 and 24 months. With a first child it is usually later than with a second or third child, because the first child has no siblings to emulate. But a first child should be trained, usually, by the time he is three. Training the child to stay dry through the long night hours may take even longer.

Resistance to Toilet Training

Early toilet training—training that is begun during a child's first year—may work, but as a child develops and asserts his personality and independence, he will resent any insistence on manipulating the control of his bodily functions. He may get even by refusing to empty his bowels when put on the potty. Worse yet, if another baby has entered the scene, the early-trained child may develop constipation, or may revert to wetting and having bowel movements in his training pants.

When you feel the child is ready for training, establish the fact that going to the bathroom is a normal part of daily life. If the child expresses fear, don't struggle with him. Don't fight about it. Take him right off the potty and let him know that you are not concerned or displeased. A genuine complication can arise if the child connects his fear of toilet functions with your displeasure at his failures.

Training can usually be facilitated by praise from the parents for putting the bowel movement and the urine in the proper place, rather than by punishment. Excessive punishment or the threat of it usually results in anger on the child's part and increasing stubbornness and resistances to toilet training. Praise immediately following the proper performance of the act is far more effective in encouraging compliance with the parents' goals.

Tonsillectomy

See "Tonsils and Adenoids" in Ch. 20, *Surgery*.

Tonsillitis

The tonsils are two masses of soft spongy tissue that are partly embedded in the mucous membrane of the back of the throat. Bacterial or viral infection of this tissue is known as tonsillitis. It used to be considered advisable to remove the tonsils if they became enlarged—which they normally do in the process of filtering out mild infections.

Nowadays, an occasional bout of tonsillitis isn't considered sufficient reason for surgical removal of the tonsils, especially because they're likely to be less prone to infection as the child gets older. However, even a mild case of tonsillitis should be called to a physician's attention. Acute symptoms such as swollen tonsils, sudden high fever, swollen neck glands, and severe pain when swallowing must be treated promptly since they might be an indication of a strep throat. The proper antibiotics are always effective in controlling this infection so that it doesn't turn into rheumatic fever or involve the kidneys. Tonsillitis caused by a virus usually responds to aspirin, bed rest, and a soft diet. See also ADENOIDS. For a description of tonsillectomy, see "Tonsils and Adenoids" in Ch. 20, *Surgery*.

Toy Safety

Toys come with a recommended age of use. It is important that parents heed the information. Some toys are unsuitable for certain ages, not only because of an inability to use it correctly, but because there may be pieces of the toy that are harmful. These are just a few examples of toys that can be safe at one age and not another; games may have small pieces can be swallowed by little children; electrical toys should only be handled by children old enough to understand the danger. Toys hanging in the crib should not be used by infants old enough to pull themselves up to a standing position because they may strangle on cords and strings of the toy. It should be noted that it is not always the case that only younger children should avoid older children's toys. Toys that are safe for younger children may tip, break, or pinch with the increased size and weight of an older child.

Not all toys come with recommendations or fulfill the safety standards set up by the U.S. government. Cheap imitations may not meet the rigid standards of the more established companies' toys. Several hundred toys are recalled each year, and more may have not yet been tested. It is important that a parent take responsibility for evaluating the safety of any toy to be given to a youngster.

For detailed and important information on age recommendations for toys

(*Which Toy for Which Child*) and for a listing of products recommended for their reliability and safety, please write to U.S. Consumer Product Safety Commission, Washington, DC 20207 or call 1-800-638-CPSC. *The ABC's of Toys and Play* is also a worthwhile publication on how to select toys for children. It is published by Toy Manufacturers of America, Inc., 200 Fifth Avenue, New York, NY 10010.

Tuberculosis

See Ch. 12, *Diseases of the Respiratory System.*

Twins and Triplets

Multiple births may be *identical*—that is, the result of the splitting of a single egg fertilized by a single sperm—or they may be *fraternal*, which means that they developed from different eggs fertilized by different sperm. Most multiple births are fraternal; except for their birthdays, most twins and triplets are no more alike than other brothers and sisters of the same family.

Although there is no ready explanation for the occurrence of multiple births, the tendency is thought to be genetically determined through the mother. Twins occur about once in every 86 births, triplets once in every 8,000. Multiple births can be anticipated by a physician at least a month before delivery. They usually arrive about two weeks early, and if they give any indications of prematurity, they receive special hospital attention.

Urinary Infections

Urinary infections of either viral or bacterial origin are more common among girls than boys, especially during the preschool years. Such an infection is sometimes the explanation for a fever unaccompanied by other symptoms. Any inflammation that creates a burning sensation during urination should be cultured and treated promptly because it can spread from the bladder to the kidneys and create a major problem.

Girls can be spared frequent infection if tactful suggestions are made at an early age about their toilet routines. Fecal matter is high in bacterial content, so little girls should learn to wipe their bottoms from front to back. This procedure reduces the possibility of contaminating the urethra after a bowel movement.

Vaporizer

A vaporizer is a device similar to a humidifier that moistens the air with steam and thus alleviates some of the discomfort of respiratory congestion. During the winter months when heated interiors are likely to be especially dry and when colds are more common, children and grown-ups can benefit from moist air that keeps the throat and nasal and bronchial passages from feeling like sandpaper. Medication shouldn't be added to a vaporizer except at the physician's recommendation. If the device is used near a child's bed throughout the night, it should be placed on a surface high enough to prevent bumping into it accidentally should the child wake up in the middle of the night to go to the bathroom.

Vomiting

See NAUSEA AND VOMITING.

Warts

See Ch. 21, *Skin and Hair.*

Water Beds

Because of the softness and the motion of a waterbed, infants up to *at least* twelve months of age should never be left unattended on a waterbed. Infants left even briefly on a waterbed have suffocated. The risks are that the infant will become trapped between the mattress and the frame or wall, or become wedged between a sleeping adult and the mattress, or sink face first into the mattress and be unable to push himself up. Several infant deaths originally attributed to SIDS are now considered suffocation due to a waterbed. At least 24 infants have died while left to nap on the parents' waterbed in the last decade.

Whooping Cough

Whooping cough (also called *pertussis*), like diphtheria a bacterial disease, occurs more frequently than diphtheria because immunity to it wears off, especially in the older child in whom the disease may appear as a severe bronchitis.

Whooping cough can be very serious in young babies because it can cause them to choke and be unable to catch their breath. If your child does contract whooping cough, call your physician immediately. He or she may give a specific drug against the organism that causes the disease as well as a specific antitoxin against the poison that the bacillus releases.

It is advisable to immunize children against whooping cough as early as possible. The effective triple vaccine known as DTP provides immunization not only against whooping cough, but against diphtheria and tetanus as well.

Worms and Parasites

See Ch. 11, *Diseases of the Digestive System.*

3

The Teens

Puberty and Growth

The bridge between childhood and adulthood is a period of growth and change called puberty. There seems to be no standard pattern for the physical changes of puberty. Two boys of the same age who have been nearly identical throughout childhood may appear to set off along entirely different paths of physical development as they enter the teenage years. One may quickly shoot up to a height of five feet eight inches within a couple of years while his companion lags for a while at preteen size, then begins growing into a six-footer. One may develop a heavy beard in his early high-school years while the other boy will have no use for a razor until he is in college. However, both boys are normal youngsters, and each will eventually attain all of the physical attributes of adulthood.

Similarly, one girl may begin menstruating in her 11th year while a classmate will not experience her first menstruation until she is 16. One girl may need a bra while still in grammar school but her friend will fret about a small bustline for many years. But both girls can look forward to normal womanhood. Each has an individual pattern of development, and if there

is any rule of thumb about puberty it is that each youngster has his or her own time schedule for the transformation into a mature man or woman.

Puberty: Changes in Girls

The physical changes that occur in the female body during puberty probably are more dramatic than those associated with a boy progressing into manhood. One definite milestone for the girl is her first *menstruation,* commonly regarded as the first sign of puberty. Actually, the first menstruation, known as the *menarche,* is only one of several signs of puberty, along with the slimming of the waist, gradual broadening of the hips, the development of breasts, the appearance of hair about the genitals and in the armpits, and a change in the rate of growth.

The Menarche

The age at which a girl first experiences menstruation generally varies over a period of ten years and depends upon the structural development of the youngster, her physical

condition, the environment, and hereditary factors. Menarche can occur as early as the age of 7, and most physicians would not be overly concerned if a girl did not begin to menstruate until she was approaching 17. The age range of 9 to 16 usually is considered normal. The median age for the start of menstruation is around 13½ years, which means that 50 percent of all females are younger than 13 years and 6 months when they reach the menarche, and half are on the older side of that age when they first menstruate. In general, the pubertal experiences of a girl follow a pattern like that of her mother and sisters; if the mother began menstruating at an early age, the chances are that her daughters will also.

If the girl has not reached the menarche by the age of 18, she should be examined by a *gynecologist,* a physician who specializes in problems related to the female reproductive system. A medical examination also should be arranged for any girl who experiences menstruation before she reaches the age of eight or nine years.

When menarche occurs on the early side of childhood, the condition

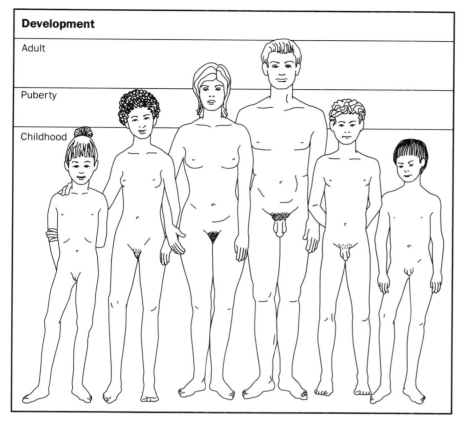

Development

Adult

Puberty

Childhood

tropical and arctic climates seem to be related to early menarche. The first menstrual periods also are likely to occur during the school year, September to June, rather than during the summer vacation.

The First Menstrual Cycles

The first menstrual cycles tend to be very irregular and have been known to be as short as 7 days and as long as 37 weeks. Even when regularity becomes established, the adolescent menstrual cycle usually is longer than the average for adult women. The typical menstrual cycle of a young girl may be about 33 days, compared to an average of 28 days for an adult woman. About three years elapse before the menstrual cycles become regular. In the meantime, irregular menstrual patterns can be considered as normal for girls during puberty.

The first menstrual cycles also are *anovulatory.* In other words, the young girl's ovaries have not matured sufficiently to produce an *ovum,* or egg cell, that can be fertilized by the sperm of a male. There are, of course, the exceptions that make newspaper headlines when a little girl gives birth to a baby. But anovulatory menstruation generally is the rule for the first few months after the menarche.

Delayed Puberty

Delayed puberty probably causes as much anguish as precocious puberty. The last girl in a group of childhood chums to develop breasts and experience the menarche may feel more self-conscious than the first girl in the class to menstruate. If the signs that usually precede menarche have not appeared by the age of 17 or 18, a medical examination should be considered, even though the girl may be a late-late-bloomer at the other end of

is sometimes called *precocious puberty.* The child may suddenly begin menstruating before her mother has told her what to expect, a situation that can prove embarrassing to both child and parents. It may first be detected by a teacher at school; occasionally, a young girl may be aware of bleeding from the vagina but because of fear or false modesty does not report the event to her mother or teacher. For this reason, parents should be alert for changes associated with early puberty and be prepared to explain the facts of life to their children. Also, in the case of precocious puberty, parents should arrange for medical consultation to be certain the bleeding actually is the result of first menstruation and not the effects of an injury or tumor.

Growth Spurt before Menarche

During the year or two preceding the menarche there is a growth spurt of

two or three inches. This is because of the hormone changes of puberty. The *hormones* are chemical messengers secreted by glands in various parts of the body and carried rapidly through the bloodstream to organs or other glands where they trigger reactions. The spurt in growth preceding menarche results from the secretion of a growth hormone that is produced by the pituitary gland, and androgen, a hormone secreted by the adrenal glands. They produce rapid growth of the bones and muscles during puberty. The girl who is first among her classmates to menstruate often is larger than those who are of the same age but have not yet reached the menarche.

From numerous research studies of the menarche, it has been learned that poor nutrition and psychological stress sometimes delay the onset of menstruation, that girls reared in cities tend to menstruate earlier, and that climate is a factor, although both the spectrum from the 7- or 8-year-old child who has menstruated.

The absence of menstruation after a girl is 18 can be the result of a wide variety of factors. The cause sometimes can be as simple as an *imperforate hymen,* a membrane that blocks the opening of the vagina. It can be the result of a congenital malformation of the reproductive organs, such as imperfect development of the ovaries. Accidents, exposure to carbon monoxide gas, or diseases like rheumatic fever or encephalitis in earlier years can result in brain damage that would inhibit the start of menstruation. The relationship between emotional upset and delayed menarche was vividly demonstrated during World War II when some girls who suffered psychological traumas also experienced very late signs of puberty.

Preparing Your Daughter for Menstruation

A mother's main responsibility is to convince her daughter at the beginning of puberty that menstruation is a perfectly normal body function. The mother should explain the proper use of sanitary napkins or tampons and encourage her daughter to keep records of her menstrual periods on a calendar.

The mother also should explain that menstruation usually is not a valid reason to stay in bed or avoid school or work. The girl should be advised that bathing and swimming should not be postponed because of menstruation. There are many old wives' tales about menstruation that are not true. But there may be some truth to stories that loss of menstrual blood can be weakening, particularly if the girl's diet does not replace the body stores of iron which may be lowered during menstrual flow. Iron is a key element of the red blood cell, and if iron-rich

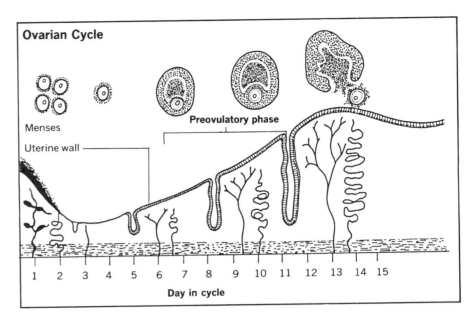

Ovarian Cycle

Menses

Uterine wall

Preovulatory phase

1 2 3 4 5 6 7 8 9 10 11 12 13 14 15

Day in cycle

foods are not included in the meals of women during their years of menstruation they can eventually suffer a form of iron-deficiency anemia.

Hormone Activity: Becoming a Woman

Although the sex hormones are the key to what makes girls grow into women and boys into men, both sexes appear to receive secretions of male and female sex hormones in approximately equal amounts for about the first ten years of life. But as puberty approaches, the adrenal glands of girls seem to increase production of a female sex hormone, *estrogen.* Meanwhile, a nerve center in the hypothalamus area of the brain stimulates the pituitary gland, the master gland of the body, to secrete another kind of hormone, *gonadotropin.* Gonadotropin in turn activates a *follicle-stimulating hormone* that causes a maturation of the ovaries, which are part of the original equipment girls are born with but which remain dormant until the start of puberty.

During the second decade of life, the hormone activity stimulates the development of body tissues that not only grow in size but give a girl more

womanly contours. However, the fully mature contours of a woman usually do not appear until after the ovaries are functioning and still another female sex hormone, *progesterone,* has been introduced in the system. The ovaries, uterus, Fallopian tubes, and vagina gradually mature as the menarche draws near.

Puberty: Changes in Boys

The appearance of male sexual characteristics during puberty is also influenced by hormonal changes. But the manifestation of male puberty is somewhat more subtle. The pituitary gland in a boy also secretes a gonadotropic hormone that stimulates maturation of *gonads.* In the male, the gonads are the *testicles,* the source of *sperm.* But whereas maturation of the ovaries in females leads to the menarche, there is no obvious sign in the boy that *spermatozoa* are being produced.

However, the secondary sexual characteristics, such as the growth of a beard and pubic hair, the spurt of growth of bones and muscles, the increase in size of the sex organs, and the deepening of the voice, are all in-

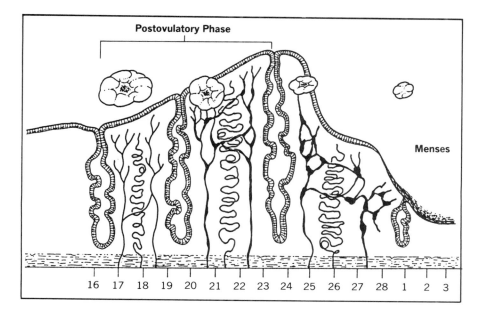

Postovulatory Phase

Menses

16 17 18 19 20 21 22 23 24 25 26 27 28 1 2 3

dications of puberty. The changes in a boy's characteristics during puberty are usually spread over a period of two years, beginning with an increase in the size of the penis and testicles and reaching completion with the production of spermatozoa in the testicles. During the two-year period there usually is a noticeable increase in the chest size of a boy, with the broad shoulders of manhood appearing during the peak of bone and muscle growth. Generally, the appearance of pubic and facial hair, as well as hair in the armpits, follows the growth of the shoulder and chest area and precedes the change in voice.

The Testicles

The testicles are contained in a walnut-size sac of skin called the *scrotum*. It is held outside the body by a design of nature in order to maintain a temperature for spermatozoa production that is less than internal body temperature. Muscle fibers in the scrotum hold the testicles closer to the body for warmth in cold weather and relax to allow the sperm-producing organ to be farther away from the body when surrounding temperatures are warm.

In some cases, one or both testicles do not descend from the abdomen during the male child's early years. The result is that the undescended testicle or testicles will not produce sperm. An *incompletely descended testicle* always lies somewhere along the normal path to the scrotum. An *ectopic* testicle has deviated from that path and lies somewhere near the inguinal canal, at the junction of the thigh and the lower part of the abdomen. In a third departure from normal

development, a *retractile testicle* has stopped short of the scrotum. It can be manipulated into the normal position or may descend to that position at puberty.

The danger of malignant change—of tumor development—usually warrants surgical removal of the incompletely descended and the ectopic testicle. A testicle trapped in the inguinal region may become inflamed because of the pressure of larger body parts in the area. In some cases, physicians are able to assist the descent into the scrotum through administration of hormones or by surgery. At some point during puberty, a medical examination should include a check on the condition of the testes.

Genital Size

Many boys are as sensitive about the size of their genitals as girls are about breast size. In the case of an empty scrotum because of undescended testicles, it is possible to have the scrotum injected with silicone plastic for cosmetic or psychological reasons so the sac appears less flaccid or larger. The size of the penis may become the

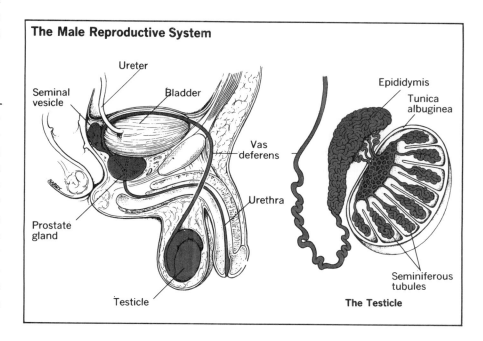

The Male Reproductive System

Ureter

Seminal vesicle

Bladder

Epididymis

Tunica albuginea

Vas deferens

Urethra

Prostate gland

Testicle

Seminiferous tubules

The Testicle

subject of discussion in the school shower room. If a boy appears sensitive about the subject, he should be assured that there is a wide variation in normal sizes and that like ears, noses, and other body parts the dimensions have little to do with function.

Nocturnal Emission

Another cause for concern by adolescent boys is the *nocturnal emission.* The nocturnal emission, sometimes called a *wet dream,* is the automatic expulsion of *semen* through the penis while the young man is asleep. The semen is secreted by the *prostate gland,* the *seminal vesicle,* and other glands that open into the *urethra.* The opalescent white fluid carries spermatozoa during intercourse and if the young male does not engage in sexual intercourse or does not masturbate, the semen simply accumulates until it overflows during a nocturnal emission. It is a harmless, normal occurrence.

Bone Growth

As the growth spurt subsides in the late teens, the *cartilage plates,* or *epiphyses,* in the long bones of the body close. Until the growth plates become filled in with calcium deposits, each long bone is in effect three bones—a central shaft separated from the ends by the cartilage growth plates. The growth plates are not completely replaced by bone until a female is about 20 and a male 23 years old. But the rate of growth begins to taper off as sexual maturity is achieved. After that, young women tend to retain fatty tissue and young men gain in muscle mass. It is a time to begin weight watching so that the hazards of obese adult life can be avoided. But the ravenous appetites developed

during the period of rapid body growth and intense physical activity can easily evolve into bad eating habits during the teen years.

Skin and Hair Problems

Hereditary influences may determine many of the physical and psychological traits that an individual first becomes aware of in the teen years. Because of the various crossovers of the 23 sets of *chromosomes* and the nearly infinite combinations of *genes,* it is not always easy to predict how a child is going to appear as a young adult. But some features, such as hair color and eye color, usually can be identified with one or both parents; other traits may seem to be those of uncles, aunts, or grandparents. Heredity and hormones frequently are involved in the distribution of hair on the body and the oiliness of the skin, both of which can cause concern to teenagers who are plagued by an overabundance or lack of these cosmetic traits. An example of hereditary influences on hair patterns can be seen in early baldness. A receding hairline is not a trait of the parents but rather an influence of the genetic makeup of a grandparent—the trait skips a generation.

Removal of Excess Hair

While not much can be done about baldness that is hereditary, there are ways of handling the problems of excess hair. If a woman has excess hair on her face, arms, and legs, it can be removed by shaving, with wax, by electrolysis, or depilatories. Shaving is the most direct but not always the most satisfactory method of hair removal because it is intended only as a temporary measure. An alternate shortcut is bleaching with diluted hydrogen peroxide; the hair is still there

but it is not as noticeable. Another method involves the use of hot wax spread on the skin and allowed to harden. When it is removed quickly, the hair is pulled away.

Depilatories are chemicals that destroy the hair at the skin line. Both hot wax and depilatories have longer-lasting effects than shaving, but they must be repeated at intervals of several weeks.

Depilatories, too, can produce unpleasant allergenic reactions. The only permanent method of removing excess hair is *electrolysis,* which is a time-consuming technique. Each hair root has to be burned out individually with an electric current. Electrolysis is recommended only for small areas and because of the time and expense involved would not be feasible for removing excess hair from regions other than the face.

Acne

There is some evidence that *acne* is partly hereditary. But it is such a common problem among teenagers— it has been estimated that up to 90 percent of all youngsters endure some degree of acne—that it must have been inherited from a mutual ancestor like Adam or Eve. In fact, one of the deterrents to effective control of the skin disorder is that acne is so common that it is neglected by many youngsters. Waiting to outgrow acne can be a serious mistake, because the pimples, blemishes, blackheads, and boils that make life miserable for so many teenagers can be eliminated or considerably reduced. They can also cause scarring. A physician should be consulted in cases of severe or especially persistent acne.

Overactive Oil Glands

Acne is not a serious threat to the life of a youngster, but it can be seriously disfiguring at a time of life when most young people are sensitive about their appearance. It can occur at any time from puberty into early adulthood, and it is caused by poor adjustment of the skin to secretions of sebaceous glands. The imbalance resulting from hormones in the bloodstream will correct itself eventually. But to prevent permanent scarring, a program of simple skin care must be followed faithfully.

Acne is caused by overly-active oil glands in the skin. When the oil glands become clogged, blackheads and pimples appear. The color of blackhead is not caused by dirt but rather by a chemical change in the secretions of the oil glands. To treat acne, a person should wash the skin to clear the plugged pores and oil glands. This is done by keeping the skin dry enough to peel away soiled layers and remove dirt from the pores. Most topical medications seek to keep the skin sufficiently dry to enhance peeling.

Skin Care

The face should be washed several times a day with warm water and mild soap. It should be dried thoroughly and gently with a clean towel. Careless handling of blemishes, such as squeezing blackheads, and picking at pimples and scabs can result in scarring. Teenagers also should avoid touching their faces. If the condition of the skin is worse than a few mild blemishes, a dermatologist will be able to prescribe topical medication, antibiotics, or hormones to treat the problem. Treatment often takes several months before there is noticeable improvement.

Other Precautions

Young women should not use cold creams or cosmetics unless they have been approved by a physician. Young

men who shave must be careful to avoid cutting pimples. A physician also should be consulted about how diet can help control acne. Although the skin disorder is not a dietary disease, there is some evidence that certain foods tend to aggravate it. However, there is a lack of agreement among physicians as to whether chocolate, carbonated beverages, nuts, sweets, and other specific snack items may be the culprits. And there always is the possibility that because each youngster develops along an individual path, a food item that causes one teenager's face to break out with blemishes will not affect a sibling or classmate in the same way.

Diet

It is no surprise that many American teenagers have poor eating habits. A survey by the Food and Nutrition Board of the National Research Council recently showed that 40 percent of boys between 13 and 19 years of age and 60 percent of the girls in the same age group subsisted on diets that were substandard. Generally, the young people surveyed had abandoned the healthy eating habits of their families. They habitually skipped breakfast and failed to make up the nutritional loss during other meals.

There are several reasons for this phenomenon. Perhaps the most prominent reason is that teens are anxious to break away from their home. They therefore rebel against any form of convention or parental advice. The popularity of fast food institutions and snack shops is a also great contributor to the problem. Such places have become frequent hangouts for teenagers after school and on weekend evenings. With social gatherings in these surroundings, teenagers begin to develop poor eating habits. Frequently, they fill themselves

up with non-nutritive foods and have no appetite later for balanced meals. At home, teenagers are great snack-eaters, and much snacking occurs while they are watching television. The combination of inactive television-watching and munching on junk foods leads to an unhealthy physical condition in teenagers.

Calories and Nutrition

A calorie is a unit of energy, and the human body requires a certain amount of energy each day in order to sustain life and continue normal physical activity. The amount of caloric intake varies according to the individual. Much of it depends on physical activity, size, and metabolic rate.

Calories in themselves are not bad. However, excessive intake of calories can lead to severe weight and health problems. Often the problem is not calories but the consumption of "empty calories" or non-nutritive foods. For instance, an unhealthy snack of a soda (100 calories) and French fries (roughly 450 calories) adds up to 550 "empty" calories. Conversely, a glass of skim milk (80 calories) and an apple (60 calories) is a healthy snack that adds up to only 140 calories.

To maintain the proper balance between foods consumed and energy used in work and play, a teenager must regulate his or her caloric intake. Much of the regulation occurs naturally. For example, when a person eats a lot, he or she is not hungry for a longer period of time than usual. Often, people crave foods that have been lacking in their diet. Thus, without conscious effort, most people are able to limit their consumption of foods to normal levels.

Nonetheless, it is important for teenagers to learn healthy eating habits and be aware of the potential of gaining weight. It is the awareness that is important for teenagers, not the strict regulation of body weight and caloric intake. Regularly checking one's weight on a scale is not a good idea. It will only foster unhealthy obsessions in teenagers who will worry about the loss or gain of a single pound. This can lead to skewed images of a teenager's physique and perhaps serious eating disorders. It is more important that a teenager monitor weight through the fit of his or her clothing.

Calcium and Phosphorus

Among the important minerals in teenage diets are calcium and phosphorus. Milk is the most easily available source of calcium and phosphorus, which are required for the development of strong bones during the period of life in which the body is still growing. Calcium also is required for the effective contraction of muscle tissues and is vital for normal heart function. The recommended daily intake of milk for teenagers is four eight-ounce glasses. It can be served as fluid whole milk, as skim milk, buttermilk, evaporated milk, or as nonfat dry milk. Cheese or ice cream can be substituted for part of the fluid milk allowance. One cup of ice cream is equivalent in calcium to one-half cup of milk. A one-inch cube of cheddar cheese is equal to two-thirds of a cup of milk, which also is equivalent in calcium to one cup, or eight ounces, of cottage cheese. Cream cheese can be substituted for milk in a two-to-one ratio; that is, two ounces of cream cheese are equal to one ounce of milk.

Iron

Iron is needed for the formation of *hemoglobin,* the substance that gives red blood cells their red coloration and is responsible for the transport of oxygen and carbon dioxide in the bloodstream. Hemoglobin has such an affinity for oxygen that without it humans would require 60 times as much blood to transport oxygen from the lungs to tissues throughout the body. Studies indicate that girls are five times as likely to need additional supplies of iron in their diets because of blood loss through menstruation. Recommended sources of iron are liver, heart, kidney, liver sausage, meat, shellfish, egg yolk, dark molasses, bread, beans and other legumes. If basic food lists seem drab and boring, the teenager might think of the iron sources in terms of a peanut butter sandwich or two hamburgers; either choice would provide the daily iron needs for a girl. Other minerals that are important to a teenager's diet include the following:

- Sulfur is needed by the body for hair, skin, nails, and cartilage, and is available by eating nearly any protein-rich foods.

- Iodine is needed for normal thyroid control of body metabolism and is supplied in the form of iodized table salt.

- Potassium is a tonic for the nervous system and the muscles and is available in adequate amounts in most kinds of meats, as well as bananas, orange juice, and milk.

- Magnesium collaborates chemically with calcium and phosphorus for normal muscle and nerve function, and is found in most forms of protein.

Note: Many of these nutrients are readily available in a normal diet. In most cases, it is not necessary to supplement a teenager's diet with these minerals. Children and teens should not rely on vitamin pills to make up for an unhealthy diet. It is better to eat nutritionally.

Weight Problems

Teens who are seriously overweight or who are contemplating radical weight reduction programs should be examined by a physician. Otherwise, unfair comparisons with other persons of the same age and height may lead to wrong conclusions about the need to gain or lose weight. The weight–height standards are based on averages, and there are many youngsters who are above or below the average but quite healthy and normal.

Another reason for a medical exam is to check the possibility of disease as the cause of the weight problem. The exam will also indicate whether the youngster has some other disorder that could be aggravated by a sudden weight loss.

Achieving optimum weight is only one step toward proper physical conditioning. A youngster who has been able to avoid physical activity by living in an elevator apartment, riding a bus to school, and watching TV after school hours instead of working or playing could be right on the button as far as weight for his age and height are concerned, but his muscular development and heart and lung capacity could be at the same time at a very low ebb.

Anorexia Nervosa

One of the most common eating disorders is anorexia nervosa, which occurs most often in teenage girls. It is a psychological disorder that in extreme cases results in death. The victims starve themselves in an exaggerated attempt to lose weight.

The most obvious trait is excessive and unnatural thinness. When anorexics become critically thin, they develop downy hair, called lanugo. Other symptoms include obsession with exercise and "healthy" eating habits, emphasis on self-control and discipline, high achievement in school, alternative periods of strict fasting and binging, and rituals surrounding food preparation and eating.

Anorexics may weigh themselves several times a day and avoid eating when they are hungry. Most, according to experts, are usually preoccupied with their appearance or bodily "image" as a result of personality or ego problems and social insecurities. Anorexics frequently suffer from amenorrhea–cessation or delay of menstruation. Amenorrhea can have serious physical consequences.

Treatment of anorexia nervosa involves psychiatric counseling and, sometimes, hospitalization to ensure weight gain.

Bulimia

When binges become "gorge and purge" sessions—stretches of overeating followed by self-induced vomiting—the condition is called bulimia. Purging can involve vomiting, using laxatives, or taking diuretics. Bulimia may exist in conjunction with anorexia nervosa or it may afflict people who are of normal size or are slightly overweight. Like anorexics, most bulimics are female, who perceive themselves as larger and fatter than they really are. Studies have shown that 11 percent of high school females and 10 percent of female college students suffer from anorexia nervosa and/or bulimia.

Much of the problem stems from a poor self-image, some social insecurities, and a lack of self-control. Treatment involves psychiatric counseling. Physical damages may include a ruptured esophagus, dental caries, and hypoglycemia. For more information, or guidance to resources in your community, please contact the National Association of Anorexia Nervosa and Associated Disorders, Box 7, Highland Park, IL 60035; 312/831–3438.

Physical Fitness

It is important for young people to understand the major benefits of daily exercise. Good physical conditioning is as important as weight control during the teen years. While not everybody can be an athletic champion, almost anyone can improve his or her heart, lungs, and muscles. All that is required is time, discipline, determination, and patience. Teenagers are advised to join school athletic teams or exercise independently after school. Walking to school rather than driving is another means of getting exercise.

Exercise Goals

One of the goals of physical conditioning for teenagers is to tone and develop muscles. Muscles that are exercised regularly will grow in size and strength. Those that are not will atrophy (shrink in size).

Exercise allows for an increase in the number of individual muscle fibers as well as an increase in the number of blood capillaries that supply the muscle tissue with nutritive substances. Consequently, the muscles become more efficient and more toned.

In addition to muscle development, physical conditioning should include optimum cardiopulmonary fitness. The increase in heart activity and oxygen consumption is the basis for aerobic workouts. Aerobic means, literally, "with oxygen." Aerobic training involves maintaining a steady rate of physical activity so that the heart, lungs, and muscles work together at a level that is more demanding than a body's state of rest. Jogging, running, and rapid walking are common examples of aerobic training.

Exercise Precautions

The individual goals should be kept within sensible limits to avoid injury or impaired health. Overexertion can cause dizziness, nausea, and hyperventilation. Teenagers should avoid excessive exercise during severely hot and humid weather. To avoid dehydration, drink plenty of water before and after exercising.

Choosing Proper Equipment

When exercising, it is essential that a teenager use proper athletic gear to avoid injuries. The knees are one of the most vulnerable body parts. As such, a teenager must be fitted with high-quality athletic shoes, which should be replaced as soon as they wear out. A podiatrist can provide insoles for proper foot balance for pavement or grass field. Protective gear, such as a mouth piece, shin guard, or riding helmet, is also important.

The Use of Steroids

In recent years, a substantial number of male teenagers have been abusing steroids in the hopes of developing bulky muscles. While this nonmedical use of anabolic steroids is illegal, its use is rampant.

There are considerable risks involved with taking steroids at such a young age. Adverse physical effects include stunted growth, acne, vomiting, and, for boys, enhanced breast development. In girls, side effects may be the development of permanent facial hair and deepened voices. For all users, there is a risk of long-term dependence or addiction to the drug. The psychological effects are equally serious. They include irritability, violent behavior, depression, mania, psychosis, and in some cases suicide.

Care of the teeth

During the teen years, careful supervision by the dentist and cooperation from the teenager are especially necessary. The poor eating habits of many teenagers are reflected in their cavity rate, which is usually higher during adolescence than in later life.

If a young person is conscientious about oral care, he can avoid not only a high cavity rate, but also bad breath and the unpleasant appearance of food particles left on the teeth. These problems are really caused by the same thing—*dental plaque.* For more information on this subject, see Ch. 22, *The Teeth and Gums.*

Need for Frequent Checkups

During the adolescent period, the dentist will often recommend more frequent checkups than in the past. Small cavities are treated before they become deeper and infect the pulp, the inner chamber of the tooth, containing nerves and blood vessels. Should the pulp become infected, the tooth must have special treatment, usually a root canal process, or be extracted.

The dentist also treats tooth decay, or *caries,* more popularly known as cavities, to prevent their spread. While they are not thought to be contagious, cavities begin as a break in the tooth surface, which later enlarges. Food debris can become lodged in the cavity, be attacked by bacteria, and cause a cavity on the next tooth. The only way to avoid such a problem is to have the affected tooth treated immediately.

Front teeth often decay for the first time during this period. They are restored with a silicate or plastic filling close in color to the tooth rather than silver or gold, which would be unattractive. Unfortunately, these materials are not permanent and will need to be replaced in time. As a result, neglect of diet and oral cleanliness by an adolescent may mean that

he may need many replacement fillings in the same cavity over his lifetime.

Orthodontic Treatment

The development and growth of teeth is completed during the adolescent period. When oral growth is improper, the adolescent needs treatment by an *orthodontist,* a dental specialist who treats abnormalities of the bite and alignment of teeth and jaws. Correction of such conditions as buck teeth, which mar a person's appearance, is a major reason for orthodontic treatment. But there are also major health reasons for orthodontic care. If teeth, for example, come together improperly, efficient chewing of food is impossible. The digestive system is strained because chunks of improperly chewed food pass through it. Orthodontic treatment will, therefore, result in lifelong better health and appearance. For more information, see Ch. 22, *The Teeth and Gums.*

Stimulants and Alcohol

Initial exposure to caffeine, tobacco, drugs, and alcohol usually occurs during adolescence. Teenagers should be fully educated regarding their physical effects and potential danger. They should learn how to use them, if at all, sensibly and in moderation, and to resist peer-group pressures.

Caffeine

Caffeine, which is naturally present in coffee and tea and is used in many carbonated beverages and medications, stimulates the central nervous system to overcome fatigue and drowsiness. It also affects a part of the nervous system that controls respiration so that more oxygen is

pumped through the lungs. In large amounts, caffeine can increase the pulse rate, but there are few long-range effects because the substance is broken down by the body tissues within a few hours and excreted. Because of the action of caffeine in stimulating an increased intake of oxygen, it sometimes is used to combat the effects of such nervous system depressants as alcohol.

Nicotine

Nicotine is one of nearly 200 substances in tobacco. It affects the human physiology by stimulating the adrenal glands to increase the flow of adrenaline. The blood vessels become constricted and the skin temperature drops, producing effects not unlike exposure to cold temperatures. When comparatively large amounts of nicotine are absorbed by the body, the pulse becomes rapid and the smoker has symptoms of dizziness, faintness, and sometimes nausea and diarrhea. The release of adrenaline, triggered by nicotine, will produce temporary relief from fatigue by increasing the flow of sugar in the blood. However, the effect is transient, and the feeling of fatigue will return again after the increased blood sugar has been expended.

Other Properties of Tobacco

The nicotine in tobacco can be absorbed simply by contact with the mucous membranes of the mouth; the tobacco does not have to be smoked to get the nicotine effects. Burning tobacco produces a myriad of substances found in the smoke of many plant materials when they are dried and burned. More than 50 different compounds are known to occur in concentrations of one microgram or more in each puff of tobacco smoke. Again, laboratory tests have demonstrated that the substances in burning tobacco do not have to be inhaled; most of the chemical compounds can be absorbed through the mucous membranes while a puff of smoke is held in the mouth for a few seconds. At least ten of the substances in tobacco smoke have been shown to produce cancer in animals. Other chemicals in tobacco tars are known as *cocarcinogens;* although they do not produce cancer themselves, they react with other substances to produce cancers.

Smoking and Disease

The relationship among tobacco smoking and cancer, heart disease, and emphysema-bronchitis is well established, even if some of the cause and effect links are missing. Large-scale studies of the death rates of smokers and nonsmokers have been carried on for more than 20 years. One group, consisting of nearly a quarter-million war veterans, yielded results indicating that smokers are from 10 to 16 times as likely to die of lung cancer as nonsmokers. (The higher ratio is for heavy smokers.) Similar results have been obtained from studies of smokers and nonsmokers with heart disease and lung ailments.

Buerger's Disease

One of the possible, although rare, effects of smoking is the aggravation of symptoms of a particularly insidious circulatory disorder known as *Buerger's disease*. As noted above, one of the effects of nicotine is a drop in skin temperatures. Smoking a single cigarette can cause the temperature of the fingers and toes to drop as much as 15 degrees Fahrenheit; the average is a little more than a 5-degree drop. The temperature change re-

sults from constriction of the blood vessels at the extremities. Blood clots may develop in the vessels that have been constricted, cutting off the flow of blood to the tissues of the area. When there is numbness or pain in the extremities, the condition should receive swift medical attention to prevent serious consequences.

Carbon Monoxide Accumulation

Another little publicized effect of smoking is the accumulation of carbon monoxide in the blood. Carbon monoxide is one of the lethal gases emitted in automobile exhaust. It is also produced by burning plant materials such as tobacco. It is a dangerous gas because of its strong affinity for the hemoglobin of red blood cells. Unlike oxygen and carbon dioxide, which become temporarily attached, then released, from the hemoglobin molecule, carbon monoxide becomes permanently locked into the red blood cell chemistry so that the cells are no longer effective for their normal function of transporting oxygen to the body tissues. With the oxygen-carrying capacity of part of the red blood cells wiped out, brain cells and other tissues suffer a mild oxygen starvation and the results are a form of intoxication.

A strong whiff of carbon monoxide can be fatal. Smokers, of course, do not get that much of the substance into their blood, but they do pick up enough carbon monoxide to render up to eight percent of their red blood cells ineffective. Experiments at Indiana University show that pack-a-day smokers have the same level of carbon monoxide in their blood as subjects who inhale an atmosphere of one-fourth of one percent carbon monoxide. That level of carbon monoxide increases the shortness of breath during exercise by approxi-

mately 15 percent, and, the study shows, about three weeks of abstinence from smoking are required to permit the oxygen-carrying capacity of the blood to return to normal. It is the carbon monoxide of burning plant materials that produces most of the "high" associated with the smoking of many substances.

Alcohol

Alcohol usually is not considered a potentially dangerous drug because it is easily available at cocktail lounges and liquor stores and is served generously at parties. Alcohol has been used by man for thousands of years, at times as a sedative and anesthetic, and when used in moderation has the effect of a mild tranquilizer and appetite stimulant. But when consumed in excess amounts, alcoholic beverages can produce both psychological and physical dependence. It can produce illusions of being a pick-me-up, but studies indicate that this is due to a letdown of inhibitions and the weakening of some functions of the central nervous system, particularly in the cerebral cortex.

Parents and teachers share an important responsibility to educate young people about the use and misuse of alcohol. Like marihuana, the effects of alcohol on human beings are not thoroughly understood. Some users develop a tissue tolerance for alcohol so that their body tissues require increasing amounts. When alcohol is withdrawn from such users, they develop tremors, convulsions, and even hallucinations. However, there are many varied reactions to the use of alcohol, and an individual may react differently to alcoholic drinks at different times. See Ch. 29, *Substance Abuse.*

Drugs

During the 1960s there was an alarming increase in drug use among teenagers—a problem that deservedly received nationwide attention. Education concerning the hazards and occasional tragedies accompanying drug use is imperative.

Marihuana

Marihuana affects the central nervous system, including the brain, after it enters the bloodstream. According to some researchers, the substance accumulates in the liver. Some of the effects of marihuana are not unlike those of tobacco. The rate of the heartbeat is increased, body temperature drops, and blood sugar levels are altered. The drug user also feels dehydrated, the appetite is stimulated, coordination of movements becomes difficult, there are feelings of drowsiness or unsteadiness, and the eyes may become reddish. Taken in higher strengths, marihuana can cause hallucinations or distortions of perception.

Varying Effects

Scientists are uncertain about the pathways of the drug in the central nervous system and its effects on other body systems. The drug's effects seem to vary widely, not only among individual users but also according to the social setting and the amount and strength of the marihuana used. The effects, which usually begin within 15 minutes after the smoke is inhaled and may continue for several hours, vary from depression to excitement and talkativeness. Some users claim to experience time distortions and errors in distance perception. But others sharing the same marihuana cigarette may experience no effects at all.

Although marihuana is not addictive, in that users do not develop a physical dependence upon the substance and withdrawal of the drug produces no ill effects, there are dangerous results from the use of marihuana. Marihuana users find it hard to make decisions that require clear thinking, some users develop psychotic reactions or an emotional disorder called "acute marihuana panic," and there is some evidence that the active ingredient is transmitted by expectant mothers to their unborn children.

Hallucinogens

Marihuana sometimes is described as a *hallucinogen* because of visual hallucinations, illusions, and delusions reported by users after they have inhaled the smoke from a large number of "joints" or "sticks" of the drug. But marihuana should not be confused with the true hallucinogenic drugs such as *mescaline* and *LSD* (lysergic acid diethylamide) which are known by doctors as *psychomimetic* drugs because they mimic psychoses.

LSD and Mescaline

LSD and mescaline have marked effects on perception and thought processes. Teenagers usually become involved with the use of LSD because they are curious about its effects; they may have heard about its purported "mind-bending" properties and expect to gain great personal insights from its use. Instead of great insight, however, the user finds anxiety, depression, confusion, and frightening hallucinations. The use of LSD is complicated by the reappearance of hallucinations after the individual has quit using the drug; the very possibility of repeated hallucinations causes a sense of terror.

Morphine and Heroin

Besides the hallucinogenic drugs, there are *opium* derivatives, *morphine* and *heroin*. Morphine is one of the most effective pain relievers known and is one of the most valuable drugs available to the physician. Morphine and heroin depress the body systems to produce drowsiness, sleep, and a reduction in physical activity. They are true narcotics, and their appeal is in their ability to produce a sense of euphoria by reducing the individual's sensitivity to both psychological and physical stimuli.

Addictive Properties

A great danger lies in the ability of the body tissues to develop a physical dependence on morphine and its derivative cousin, heroin. The degree to which heroin's "desirable" effects are felt depends in part on how the user takes it. *Sniffing* is the mildest form of abuse, followed by *skin-popping*—subcutaneous injection—and then by *mainlining*—injecting directly into a vein, which is the method used by almost all those dependent on heroin.

The body adjusts to the level of the first doses so that increasingly larger injections of the drug are required to produce the same feelings of euphoria. The ability of the body to adjust to the increasingly larger doses is called *tolerance*. And with tolerance goes *physical dependence,* which means that when heroin or morphine is withdrawn from the user he experiences a violent sickness marked by tremors, sweating and chills, vomiting and diarrhea, and sharp abdominal pains. Another shot of heroin or morphine temporarily ends the withdrawal symptoms. But the user, now dependent upon the drug, must continue regular doses or face another bout of the withdrawal sickness. Heroin has no value as a medicine and is available only through illicit channels at a high price. The heroin addict usually is unable to hold a job because of effects of the drug and often turns to crime in order to finance his daily supply of the narcotic.

Shortened Life Span

The health of a narcotics addict declines so that his life span is shortened by 15 to 20 years. He usually is in continual trouble with the law because of the severe penalties for illegal possession of narcotics. If he sells narcotics, as many heroin addicts are driven to do to get enough money to support their habit, the punishment is even more severe.

Amphetamines and Barbiturates

Other commonly abused drugs are *amphetamines,* also known as *uppers* or *pep pills,* and *barbiturates,* sometimes called *downers* or *goof balls.* Amphetamines are used by physicians to curb the appetite when weight reduction of patients is needed and to relieve mild cases of depression. However, some physicians doubt that amphetamines should be used as a weight-control medication because of the risks involved; other experts have questioned whether the drugs are actually effective for that purpose.

Amphetamines stimulate the heart rate, increase the blood pressure, cause rapid breathing, dilate the pupils of the eyes, and produce other effects such as dryness of the mouth, sweating, headache, and diarrhea. Ordinarily, amphetamines are swallowed as tablets, but a more extreme form of amphetamine abuse involves the injection of the drug, usually Methedrine, directly into the vein.

Dangers of Amphetamines

The danger in the use of amphetamines is that they induce a person to do things beyond his physical endurance, cause mental disorders that require hospitalization, and, in large doses, can result in death. Although they do not produce the kind of physical dependence observed in the use of narcotics, amphetamine withdrawal for a heavy user can result in a deep and suicidal depression.

Barbiturates

Barbiturates are sedatives used by physicians to treat high blood pressure, epilepsy, and insomnia, and to relax patients being prepared for surgery. They slow the heart rate and breathing, lower blood pressure, and mildly depress the action of nerves and muscles.

Dangers of Barbiturates

Barbiturates are highly dangerous when taken without medical advice. They distort perception and slow down reaction and response time, contributing to the chances of accidents. Barbiturates are a leading cause of accidental poison deaths because they make the mind foggy and the user forgets how many pills he has taken, thus leading to overdosage. They also cause physical dependence with withdrawal symptoms that range from cramps and nausea to convulsions and death. See also Ch. 29, *Substance Abuse.*

Adolescent Suicide

Suicides among teenage boys and girls increased greatly in number during the middle 1980s. Health experts termed the phenomenon an "epidemic of self-destruction." In some areas suicides or suicide attempts took place in clusters. Often, groups of close friends were involved. In some cases of cluster suicides or attempts, it appeared that a suicidal attitude was contagious.

Suicide became the second leading cause of death among adolescents. In the nearly 30 years beginning in the late 1950s, the suicide rate among teenagers tripled. Preadolescents also began to take their own lives more frequently: public health personnel reported suicides among children as young as three.

Risk Factors

As educators, social workers, psychiatrists, and others became involved in community efforts to prevent teenage suicides, a number of "risk factors"—signs of an intent to take one's life—were isolated. Changes in a teenager's behavior, whether in peer relationships, school activities, or academic performance, were said to be primary indicators. So were emotional shifts, particularly toward anger or irritability. Depression and withdrawal, experts said, might accompany the emotional changes. Sadness, changes in eating and sleeping habits, and preoccupation with death were other signs.

Young people considering suicide showed other symptoms. Many reported headaches, stomachaches, and other ailments. Some talked about taking their own lives. A young person who had lost a close friend through suicide was at unusual risk, according to studies. Family histories of suicide and parental depression were cited as indirectly contributing factors.

Parent Involvement

For parents concerned about the possibility of a child's or teen's suicide, such clues are only clues. The parent still has the task of trying to resolve the potential suicide. Authorities make the following suggestions.

Act at Once

Where a preadolescent or adolescent gives clear signals—usually risk factors appearing in combination—that suicide might be contemplated, parents should seek help immediately. Local suicide hotlines or suicide prevention centers should be contacted; counseling may have to be started.

School Help

Many schools cooperate in efforts to prevent suicides. The schools may sponsor group meetings at which students talk out their feelings about suicide, and such meetings may be appropriate as a first or second step. A representative of the community crisis or prevention center normally takes part in such meetings. Many schools have special counselors, psychologists, and others who can serve as direct lines to sources of help.

Out-of-School Contacts

Group meetings provide all teenage participants with the names and locations of out-of-school contact persons who may be able to help them in a crisis. Most crisis agencies operate 24 hours a day, seven days a week, providing aid during the "danger hours" between late afternoon and midnight. Parents may want also to contact clergy, trusted friends or relatives, or others.

Peer Support

Where possible, peer support should be mobilized in the effort to prevent a suicide. Many young people, especially the friends of a depressed or otherwise suicidal teenager, can help—and will do so rather than hear later that a suicide has taken place. But parents should, according to experts, remember that a youngster

with high status among his or her peers may influence those peers. Committing suicide, the high-status young person may convince others that "life isn't worth it." Surviving boy- or girlfriends are especially at risk.

Social and Sexual Maturation

The Prospect of Adulthood

As a youngster passes from childhood into adolescence, it is the psychological adjustments rather than the physical changes that are most likely to produce difficulties. The emotional problems, of course, are related to the hormonal activity of the developing body. However, the conflicts that frequently are upsetting to both the adolescent and other members of his family are the result of adjustments that must be made between the young person and the society in which he must live.

In our own culture, the teenager must continually adjust to a complex set of rules and regulations. He frequently may feel that he must accept the responsibilities of adulthood before he is entitled to the privileges of being treated as an adult. Childhood is only a step behind, but he has learned to suppress or ignore childhood relationships. He can easily forget the point of view of children and even resent the ability of his parents to recall the "cute" incidents of his earlier years. At the same time, he may be startled by the suggestion that within a few short years he and his teenage friends will face the selection of a career, marriage, establishment of a home, and a lifetime of responsibili-

ties he may feel ill-prepared to assume.

Future Outlook for Teenagers

While a teenager may feel competent enough to handle adult responsibilities and decisions, he or she may have misgivings about what the future holds. Fear and uncertainty of the unknown can cause anxiety in teenagers, though they may not express it. They are aware that the choices they make—what college or vocational school they select, what profession they choose, who they marry, where they decide to live—can affect their entire lives.

An abundance of educational opportunities and careers choices is available for any teenager. It is the parents' responsibility to expose teenagers to all of the options and to guide them toward attainable goals. Parents should recognize a teen's strengths and weakness and direct him or her to the most appropriate educational institution or profession. Career and college guidance counselors at high school are very helpful.

In the past few decades, the outlook for males and females have become nearly identical. There are virtually no educational or professional barriers that separate men and women. There are male nurses and female doctors, husbands who stay at home and wives who work.

The career options and lifestyles that teenagers may select are seemingly endless. Traditional social conventions are changing. Many marriages occur after both spouses have established careers, allowing for arrangements that were not possible for many parents of current teenagers. Given the professional opportunities for women, many families are dual-income, or, in some cases, the men choose to stay at home. Much of this depends on the economic needs of a particular family, but the options are there for nearly any kind of work situation and lifestyle. Such instances of role-reversal and dual-income families have provided a new and promising outlook for teenagers.

Advanced Education

The educational requirements for current jobs place an added strain on the pace of growing up. Many teenagers must have some vague professional goals in order to choose the proper means of attaining them. This primarily includes an appropriate education. All professions require a certain level of education and expertise. While much of the experience is learned on the job, many professions require college degrees and even graduate degrees. In many blue-collar professions, training is essential. It can be obtained through vocational schools, apprenticeships, or training programs.

Need for Independence

Adolescence is a time when a child slowly develops into an adult. With physical changes come psychological changes as well. As such, a teenager wants to be treated like an adult, not a child. These demands are often manifested in rebellious actions and disdainful remarks.

In a desire to act independently, a teenager may exhibit reclusive behavior in order to avoid contact with parents. He or she may be reluctant to divulge information. Sneaking out of the house is a common gesture. These are distinct attempts to dodge unsolicited advice from parents who are only too anxious to give it.

Parents should not be offended by these actions, rather they should allow their child to explore the world independently. Such an education will make them more confident and well-

adjusted as adults. Teenagers who are not allowed much freedom are often more difficult to control and can cause more damage out of spite.

Conflicts between Parent and Teenager

Some conflicts between the generations are avoidable. The parents may be protective and slow to cut the apron strings because they love their children and want to prevent them from becoming involved in unhappy situations. The teenager resents the overprotective actions of the parents, regarding them as evidence that they do not trust their own children.

A keystone in the training for adulthood is the concept that being an adult entails more than just privileges and the authority to make decisions; along with decision-making goes a responsibility to the family and society for the consequences of one's decisions and actions.

Few parents, of course, would refuse to bail out a teenage son or daughter in real trouble. And even when a youngster is rebellious enough to leave home, he should know that the door will always be open to him when he decides to return. Again, limiting the options available to a teenager can lead to a snowballing of bad decisions and resulting complications.

In many cases, the conflicts between parents and teenagers derive from the illusion that a younger child has more freedom of choice. A small child may actually seem to have a freer choice of friends he can bring into his home and the games he can play with them. But there are always limitations to a child's choices, and parents are more understanding of the bad choices by attributing mistakes to the fact that "he's only a child."

Older youngsters become involved

in situations in which the decisions are more important. A boy and girl at the age of five can "play house" together in an atmosphere of innocence. However, the same boy and girl could hardly suggest to their parents that they intended to play house at the age of 15. If the boy and girl, although next-door neighbors, are of different social or ethnic backgrounds, they may become aware of parental prejudices in addition to new rules of propriety as they grow into their teenage years.

Decisions of the teen years can involve the use of tobacco, alcohol, owning an automobile, handling of money, overnight trips with friends, association with friends who use drugs illegally, and relationships with members of the opposite sex. The consequences of all alternatives should be outlined for the adolescent.

Search for Identity

Part of the youngster's struggle for independence will involve what sometimes is described as a search for identity. A child accepts without much questioning that he is a member of a certain family and lives in a certain neighborhood. But as he grows older, he becomes aware of his status in the family as well as the status of his family in society. A seven-year-old could not care less about the background of his family or that of his second-grade friends. As he becomes a teenager he learns that such subjects may be matters of concern to parents and their circle of friends. He may imitate the attitudes of his family or disregard them, perhaps inviting criticism that he is rebellious.

More important to the youngster, however, is a growing concern about his position and role in life and where it may lead. He is still in the so-called formative years and is sensitive to countless influences in the world about him. Teenagers become concerned with approaching education and career decisions. It is natural for them to identify with older members in the family, teachers, and celebrities.

Need for Privacy

For the teenage girl, party invitations, dances, and diaries are important and an increasing amount of privacy is required. Even if she must share a room with a sister, there should be a part of the room that is her territory. She should have personal belongings that are not shared by a parent or sibling. If she has her own room, everything in the room probably will be regarded as her property. Even her mother should respect her privacy by knocking on the door and getting permission to enter her private world.

Although sometimes less sensitive about such matters, boys also are likely to insist on a certain amount of privacy as they grow older. They may share a room with a brother but they need trunks or other containers with locks in which they can keep personal possessions. Proof that such desire for privacy is not a passing fad for young men is found in their adult compulsion for private offices and a den or workshop area at home.

Contacts with Older Friends

Young teenagers, through part-time jobs as babysitters or errand boys, usually come in contact with young adults outside the family circle for the first time. The young adults may accept the teenagers as peers, which is flattering to the youngsters, who may in turn admire and imitate the young adults. If the teenager has been able to identify closely with his family's sense of propriety, the contacts can be a good social experience. But if the youngster has not been able to identify effectively with his parents and family members, he may be vulnerable to misguiding influences. Because of the urge for adult status, the teenager may find a premature outlet for testing his abilities to live the adult life in the company of young adults. He (or she) can absorb a lot of information—and misinformation—about sex, alcohol, drugs, and other subjects.

Teenagers certainly should not be cautioned against contacts with all young adults, but they should also have a reliable older person aside from their parents with whom they can discuss matters they would not discuss with a mother or father. The alternate adult might be a clergyman, the family physician, a teacher, or even a favorite aunt or uncle. Such an arrangement provides the youngster with a means of learning a bit more about life in an independent manner and from a different point of view than could be obtained within his own immediate family circle.

Relationships with the Opposite Sex

First teenage contacts with the opposite sex tend to be awkward and sometimes embarrassing despite the best efforts and intentions of parents. The meetings may be at school dances or movie dates, perhaps in the presence of a chaperon who is a teacher or parent.

Overcoming Insecurity

Some youngsters will feel more secure than others in social gatherings; those who feel insecure may not participate at all when such opportunities first arise. As the youngsters grow older, however, they find that more and more of their friends are dating or going to dances or parties to meet members of the opposite sex.

Some boys or girls who feel insecure may find that they are more gregarious or less ill-at-ease if they fortify themselves with a couple of drinks of an alcoholic beverage, or with drugs, before they join their friends. Youngsters who feel the need for stimulants or depressants in order to enjoy parties usually can be helped with psychological counseling to overcome their fears of inadequacy.

Young people should be assured that getting together at parties of mixed sexes is a natural thing to do. It has been going on for generations and although an individual youngster may feel ill-at-ease at his first few dances or parties, he probably will survive. As the boy or girl attends more parties the chances increase that he or she will meet a person of the opposite sex who is particularly attractive. If the feeling is mutual, the acquaintanceship may develop into more or less steady dating.

Going Steady

Steady dating, which leads to a formal engagement and marriage in many cases, should not be encouraged at an early age or before a young person has had an opportunity to date a number of prospective partners. At the same time, it should not be discouraged to the point of producing a rebellious reaction. As was pointed out earlier, some girls admit going steady with a boy for no other reason than to demonstrate their independence of judgment.

Controlling the Sexual Impulse

Teenagers who spend a lot of time together at parties, in their homes, or at recreational meetings such as beach outings are likely to be physically attracted to each other. It may begin with kissing, dancing, holding hands, or simply a natural urge to neck or pet. In more primitive societies, the couple might simply indulge in sexual intercourse without any concern for the possible consequences. But in our own society, young people are expected to control their natural urges.

Influence of the Mass Media

Complicating sincere efforts of a teenager to make the right decisions in relations with the opposite sex is the constant exposure of youngsters to movies, magazine articles, books, and other media suggesting that sexual relations between unmarried couples are not only acceptable but a common practice. Compared to the image of young love as displayed in movie promotion advertising, a teenage boy and girl may believe that a few ardent hugs and kisses in a secluded spot may be as innocent as making a plate of fudge together in the girl's kitchen.

Some girls, but not all, are as easily aroused as boys by close bodily contact with the opposite sex. Physical contact for most boys arouses sexual desire, partly because of the physiological makeup of the male.

The Sex Drive in Boys

Males are so constituted that during periods of abstinence from intercourse, their sperm builds up. During periods of sperm buildup, the male sex drive increases in strength. There are no standards or averages for the male sex drive; instead there is a wide variety of sexual appetites and abilities.

A girl who cuddles too closely to a boy may trigger a response she did not expect and may not want. Depending upon the boy and the status

of his sex drive at that time, he might accept the girl's approaches as a suggestion that she is willing to have intercourse or is at least interested in petting. If the girl is simply being friendly, the results can be embarrassing to one or both of the youngsters. If the boy is the type who likes to discuss the details of his dates with friends, the girl may discover a sudden and unwelcome change in attitude by other boys of the group.

Walking hand-in-hand, or with an arm around the waist, and kissing that is not too passionate, usually are acceptable ways for young teenagers to display affection. And there are activities such as hiking or bicycle riding that afford a boy and girl a chance to be together and apart from the rest of the world. There also are picnics, ball games, movies, and concerts that permit togetherness without setting the stage for hard-to-control sexual impulses.

Masturbation

Another manifestation of the natural sex drives of young persons is masturbation. Discouraged by the rules and standards of society from fulfilling sex urges in the same manner as married couples, teenagers discover they can find sexual satisfaction in masturbation. Despite the stories that warn of physical or mental decay for youngsters who masturbate, the practice is not harmful unless the parents make an issue of it.

If there are dangers in masturbation, they are likely to be the isolation and loneliness associated with the practice and the confusion and anxiety that can result if the young person feels guilty or is punished or criticized for masturbating. Masturbation is such a natural reaction that most youngsters discover it by themselves even if the subject is never discussed by friends or family members. But for

many young people, masturbation may violate religious or other beliefs or values. These youngsters may want to discuss the practice with a physician, understanding clergy, or some other trusted person.

Sex Education

Because boys and girls in their teens may be capable of producing children and are known to have strong sexual urges, they should be provided with authoritative information about human reproduction and birth control. It is up to the parents to make decisions regarding the proper sources of such information, how much information should be given, and at what age.

One of the reasons for the popularity of sex education in the schools is that teachers can get the parents off the hook by explaining the facts of life to youngsters. However, by forfeiting their prerogative to explain sex and human reproduction to their own children, parents must depend upon the teacher to make an acceptable presentation to the youngsters. The likely alternative is that youngsters will obtain a considerable amount of misinformation from friends and acquaintances at street-corner seminars or by experimentation.

In the days when the majority of the population lived on farms or near rural areas, children learned a few things about sex and reproduction simply by working with farm animals. They learned that cats produced kittens, dogs produced puppies, cows produced calves, and so on. This on-the-job type of sex education also provided farm youngsters with a smattering of genetics, because cross-breeding strains of animals frequently had economic consequences. It was not too difficult for the rural youngsters to relate their barnyard education to human experience.

Children enrolled in sex education

classes in the urban areas of America today receive similar information—dogs have puppies, cats have kittens, etc.—by watching movies and reading books. However, the lessons may be superficial or incomplete, depending upon the teacher and the prescribed curriculum. For example, the children in one eastern school were taught that the baby develops in the mother's abdomen, which led some youngsters to believe the baby lived in the mother's stomach until born. "Why isn't the baby digested by the stomach acid?" asked one confused girl. And when asked how the baby gets out when it's time to be born, the teacher told the students that such questions should be answered by their parents. The point here is that parents should establish some rapport with their children to be sure they are learning a practical set of facts about adult love, sex, and reproduction, including the possible emotional and physical consequences of premarital sexual intercourse.

Although parents may find it difficult or embarrassing to explain the facts of life to their own children, it is one of the most important contributions that can be made to a maturing youngster. At the present time, at least one out of six teenage girls in the United States will have an unwanted pregnancy. Obviously, thousands of parents and teachers are not providing adequate instruction in sex education subjects.

The Male Reproductive System

Any instruction in the facts of life should begin by use of the proper names for the body parts involved. In the male, the external sex organs are the *penis* and the *testicles,* or *testes.* The penis contains a tiny tube, the *urethra,* through which urine is eliminated. Much of the fleshy part of the

penis is composed of spongy tissue. When the penis is stimulated sexually, the spongy areas become filled with blood, which makes the penis larger and firm, a condition called an *erection.* The testicles contain male *sperm cells,* also called *spermatozoa.*

The sperm travel up tubules inside the abdomen to a storage organ, or reservoir, the *seminal vesicle.* The sperm storage area also contains a thick white fluid called *semen* that is secreted by glands that open into the urethra. One of the glands, the *prostate,* serves partly as a control valve to prevent urine from mixing with the semen, since both are discharged through the urethra. The semen, containing millions of sperm, empties periodically in a more or less automatic action, being squeezed out of the seminal vesicle by pulsating contractions. The contractions and ejection of semen are called *ejaculation.* During the sex act, or *intercourse,* with a female, the semen is ejaculated into the woman's vagina.

The Female Reproductive System

The *vagina* is the proper name for the tubular female sex organ. At the end of the vagina is an opening, called the *cervix,* which leads into the *uterus.* The uterus, or *womb,* is shaped somewhat like an upside-down pear. When a baby develops within the mother's abdomen, it grows inside the uterus. The uterus also is the source of the bloody discharge that occurs periodically during the fertile years of women. When the blood is discharged it is called *menstruation,* or the menstrual period. The menstrual blood passes out through the vagina, which stretches to become the *birth canal* when a baby is being born. The urethra of a female empties outside the vagina.

The Menstrual Cycle and Conception

Unlike the male reproductive organs, which produce perhaps millions of spermatozoa each day, the female reproductive system ordinarily releases only one germ cell, called an *ovum* or egg, at a time. An ovum is released at an average frequency of once every 28 days. It should always be remembered that the 28-day figure is only an average; the actual time may vary considerably for reasons that are only partly known. The cycles are more likely to be irregular for teenage girls than for mature women. An ovum is released from one of the two *ovaries,* or sex glands, comparable in function to the male testicles, located on either side of the uterus. The ovum, or egg, is transported from the ovary to the uterus through a *Fallopian tube.*

If the ovum encounters male sperm during its passage from the ovary to the uterus, there is a good chance that fertilization, or *conception,* will occur through a union of a spermatozoon and the egg. The fertilized ovum, called a *zygote,* soon divides into a cluster of human tissue cells that become the embryo of a baby. For further information about pregnancy, see under Ch. 4, *The Beginning of a Family.*

During the time that the egg is maturing in the ovary and passing into the uterus after its release, the membrane lining of the uterus becomes thicker because it accumulates blood and nutrients. If the ovum is fertilized, it finds a spot in the membrane where it becomes attached and develops rapidly into an embryo, gaining its nourishment from the blood and nutrient-enriched lining of the uterus. If the ovum is not fertilized, it passes through the uterus, and the blood-rich membrane sloughs off. The blood and some of the cells of the membrane become the discharged material of menstruation. The unfertilized ovum could pass through undetected because it is nearly microscopic.

After menstruation has begun, the female reproductive cycle starts over again. The lining of the uterus once more builds up its supply of blood and nutrients to support a fertilized ovum. Ordinarily, the next ovum will be released about 14 days after a menstrual period begins. If a female does not have intercourse, or avoids intercourse during the time the ovum is released, or in some other manner is able to prevent sperm from reaching an ovum, she will not become pregnant but will experience a menstrual period at intervals that average around 28 days.

When fertilization of an ovum occurs, menstruation ceases and no further egg cells are released until the outcome of the pregnancy has been determined. In other words, the cycles of ovulation and menstruation start anew after the baby is born or the pregnancy has been terminated.

Contraception

The first rule of birth control is that no method is guaranteed to be 100 percent effective. Sexual intercourse nearly always is accompanied by some risk of pregnancy, and the teenagers who try to beat the odds should be willing to take the responsibility for the results. Teenagers should be provided with the basic facts of birth control as soon as they are capable of producing children themselves. But the emphasis should be on the relative unreliability of the techniques which do not require a visit to a physician's office. Many birth controldevices and substances can bepurchased without a physician's prescription. But if young men and women were aware of their chances of effecting a pregnancy while using such methods, they probably would have second thoughts about taking the risk. See Ch. 4, *The Beginning of a Family,* for a full discussion of birth control methods.

Venereal Disease

Equally important in the education of teenagers is a knowledge of the hazards of venereal disease. A poster prepared for a New York campaign against venereal disease carried the words "If your son is old enough to shave, he's old enough to get syphilis." The American Social Health Association estimates that 300,000 teenagers each year become infected with one or more forms of venereal disease. Most insidious has been the recent increase in gonorrhea, partly because girls who carry the infection may show no symptoms. A girl may have a slight but seemingly unimportant vaginal discharge. She may not be aware that she has gonorrhea until she is contacted by health officials after her boyfriend has reported to a physician for treatment. For more information on venereal disease, see Ch. 17, *Diseases of the Urinogenital System.*

Two reasons for the rising incidence of gonorrhea after it was once thought to be virtually eliminated by antibiotics are that condoms, once used as a mechanical barrier by males, have become less popular since teenage girls have obtained the use of oral contraceptives, and that new strains of the bacteria are resistant to the antibiotics. Some boys delay treatment when they realize they are infected with VD; they believe it makes them appear "tough" to be able to go without medical treatment even when it endangers their health. Because of rebelliousness, youngsters may have a venereal disease and either refuse to tell their parents or boast about it, depending upon which approach they think will make them appear independent.

It is a bitter irony for many parents to realize that their children might carry the spirit of independence and privacy into areas that could endanger their health, for untreated syphilis can result in blindness, insanity, and heart disease. Such grave consequences can be avoided in most cases by establishing effective channels of communication between parents and teenagers, or between teenagers and another responsible adult.

The Generation Gap

Despite the attention devoted in recent years to the so-called generation gap, the gap is nothing new to the process of evolving from childhood to adulthood. Every generation has had its generation gap—a period in which the fledgling adult tests his ability to make his own way in the world. In previous eras youngsters were considered old enough to take on an adult role when they were big enough physically. A boy left home to become a farm hand or a factory apprentice. A girl would leave home to become a live-in maid with another family. Sometimes the generation gap was masked by great social upheavals such as a war or a wave of emigration. The fictional hero of many romantic stories was a young man who left home to make his own way in the world, discovering in the process a girl who wanted to be rescued from her environment. With a few jet-age variations the adolescent boys and girls of today experience the same emotional struggles as nature develops their minds and bodies toward becoming another generation of adults.

4

The Beginning of a Family

Family Planning

When and How to Plan

Planning a family basically means figuring out when you want children, how many you want, and how long you choose to wait between pregnancies. It is always recommended that you discuss these things before marriage. It is going to be a major sticking point in a relationship if you want four children and your partner's idea of family is a parakeet.

When to have a family is also important. If you are in your twenties or early thirties and wish to have children, you have several years for doing so. If you are in your late thirties or older, having children may be an immediate priority. This is true for both men and women. Although most men are physically capable of fathering children throughout their lives, they should be young enough to participate actively in the raising of the children. If you father a child when you are 51 years old, you will be 72 when the child graduates from college. This is something to consider when you make the decision to become a parent.

Any plan should leave room for flexibility. Priorities and situations may change during the course of a re-

lationship. Both partners should be aware of this possibility and be flexible to the shifting situations.

Almost no couple expects problems with fertility or conception when they plan a family. Yet approximately 10 percent of all couples have enough difficulty conceiving that they require fertility testing or treatment.

For those whom infertility is not an issue, planning pregnancies involves decisions about birth control and spacing of pregnancies.

Timing Between Pregnancies

The minimum time a couple should leave between pregnancies is set by the period of time the baby is breast-fed. Breastfeeding and pregnancy tax the mother's and the fetus's health. It is recommended that any mother who is breastfeeding a child, and is pregnant, wean the child.

For the recovery of the physical health of the mother, two years is the average recommended wait. This puts the children almost three years apart in age.

The length of time between children should take into consideration the age and health of the parents, the number of children the couple wants, and the difficulty they have in conceiving. For a couple that suffers through a miscarriage for every successful pregnancy, a long wait may not be recommended. It should also be noted here, though, that a good gynecologist/obstetrician will be able to recommend what is in the mother's best health interest in spacing of pregnancies. For any couple that experiences difficulties with pregnancies, a doctor's advice on their particular situation should be the primary source of information.

Once physical considerations are understood, it becomes a matter of personal priority for the parents. Some parents prefer to wait until one child is in school, or at least out of diapers, before having another child. Having two toddlers can be quite trying on a parent's energy and patience. For first-time parents, having children close in age may help in arranging the parents' schedule around the children. The problems of arranging for day care may only be extended a year or two if the children are close in age. For children five years apart, working parents have at least one child in day care for ten years. For more discussion on child care and day care, see the end of this chapter.

Conception

Once you decide that you would like to have a child, planning the pregnancy involves two basic schedules. The first is deciding when you want the child to arrive. This includes deciding when pregnancy would be convenient. The second is discovering when fertility occurs each month in the woman's cycle.

When to Get Pregnant

In deciding when the best time of the year to have a baby arrive, several things should be taken into account. If you plan on taking time off from work for the child, you should consider the work you do and when a break in the work load would prove easiest to pull away. If you are a teacher, summer months may provide an ideal time for birth. If you can schedule delivery in June, the baby will be almost three months old before you start back to school in the fall. For others, a sabbatical or independent project may be timed to coincide with periods at home.

Weather may also help you decide when you wish to get pregnant. Buying winter clothing for the last stage of pregnancy can be costly. Getting a winter coat, and sweaters, and longjohns to fit during the eighth and ninth month of pregnancy may require buying clothes you won't ever wear again. Getting summer dresses and cotton pants for the last trimester of the pregnancy may be cheaper. Some women, however, cannot bear the thought of being eight months pregnant in the August heat.

Holiday schedules are also important. Some children love having birthdays around Christmas and Hanukkah. Other children hate it, feeling that their birthdays are overlooked in the festivities of the season. Pre-holiday births may allow a family to see distant relatives without taking an added trip across the country. For parents who work, holiday births may allow them to spend vacation time with their newborn.

Each family works on a slightly different schedule than the next. Their needs and what works best for them have to be determined on an individual basis. Even within that family, schedules may shift between the birth of one child and the next. Planning can help ease the burden of time off and child care that may be essential to making a family work.

How to Get Pregnant

Once you have decided on starting or continuing a family, planning the pregnancy involves calculating the fertile period in the menstrual cycle. For some parents, this requires no effort at all. Some women get pregnant immediately after stopping birth control. For others, months of timing ovulation may be required for successful conception.

The best method to figure out an ovulation cycle is to work with your physician. There are some things you can do in advance to help, though. Write down the starting and ending date of your period, for several months. If anything significant happens during the month that may have changed the cycle, such as an illness, note it in your calendar.

Your physician can give your specific information on physical characteristics and signs of ovulation that you should watch for. Basal body temperature fluctuates just before ovulation. If you chart your temperature every day at the same time, usually first thing in the morning, you should notice a slight change in the body temperature approximately two weeks before your period. The rise in temperature of about .4 to .8 degrees Fahrenheit appears normally within 24 hours of ovulation. It should last a few days and then the temperature should return to a normal level.

Some women do not get a sharp increase in temperature. It may be more subtle, more gradual, or even may drop in temperature slightly. It is important that you chart more than a couple months to get a better general view of your own body's rhythm.

Checking the viscosity of mucous production can also give some signs of ovulation. Cervical mucous production becomes more transparent and more elastic as ovulation occurs. There are also physical characteristic changes that can be noted under a microscope.

By establishing and keeping a calendar for these changes, a woman should be able to, with the help of her obstetrician or gynecologist, determine when she is fertile. If, after several months of intercourse during periods of fertility, the couple still has not conceived, the physician will recommend testing for egg and sperm production.

The Menstrual Cycle

The menstrual cycle runs, on average, every 28 days. As many women have cycles longer than 28 days as have cycles shorter than 28 days. Some women's cycles are not always the same length. Cycles may vary each month, with no true regularity. Some may alter between two lengths. For example, a woman may have a cycle that is 28 days, followed by a cycle of 30 days. She may then repeat the pattern. For women who have extremely irregular cycles, birth control pills can help regulate their menstrual flow. When they stop taking the pill,

Male Ejaculation

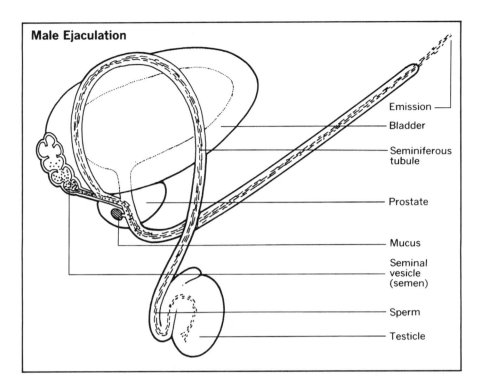

Emission

Bladder

Seminiferous tubule

Prostate

Mucus

Seminal vesicle (semen)

Sperm

Testicle

though, they may return to their previous irregularity.

Some women have lower abdominal pain midway through their cycle that accompanies ovulation. Called *mittelschmerz*, the pain can vary from a dull ache lasting hours to a sharp pain that only lasts minutes. The pain is believed to be caused by the release of the ovum from the ovary.

A new cycle is marked from the first day of menstruation. On the first day after menstruation stops, the body's hormonal levels are at their lowest for estrogen and progesterone. The uterine lining is at its thinnest. As the level of estrogen rises the blood-lined wall of the uterus builds. The wall prepares for the embedding of a fertilized egg. For the average cycle (28 days) the wall continues to build for two weeks.

While this is occurring, at least one egg is developing in an ovary. The ovary that develops the egg may alternate from left side to right. How this is controlled by the body's hormonal system is not yet understood. After approximately two weeks, the

body releases luteinizing hormone (LH), triggering the release of the ripe egg from the ovary.

The egg travels down the fallopian tube. This may take from one to five days. While the egg is in the fallopian tube, the body continues to prepare the uterine wall for implantation of a fertilized egg.

If intercourse takes place during this period of time, the egg and the sperm meet up in the fallopian tube. One sperm will penetrate the egg wall and the egg immediately produces a

barrier that prevents a second sperm from penetrating. The fertilized egg, called the blastula during that stage of development, continues to travel down the fallopian tube to the uterus.

If the egg implants on the tube wall, or lodges against something and cannot continue on to the uterus, it will continue growing in the fallopian tube. It will only take a matter of days for the embryo to outgrow the size of the tube. Spots of blood will be the first sign of an *ectopic pregnancy*, or a pregnancy that develops outside the uterus. The accompanying pain will continue to get worse until treatment is sought. After a few days of spotting and pain the fallopian tube will rupture, producing tremendous pain and blood flow. This is an extreme emergency and medical attention should be sought immediately.

If the embryo successfully makes the journey to the uterine lining, it will usually implant against the blood-filled wall. The embryo will develop a cord attachment to the wall, establishing the placental link between the mother and the embryo. Through this cord flows the blood that will keep the embryo alive and nourish its development.

Some eggs will not successfully lodge against the wall. They may pass undetected with the menstrual blood. They may also temporarily lodge

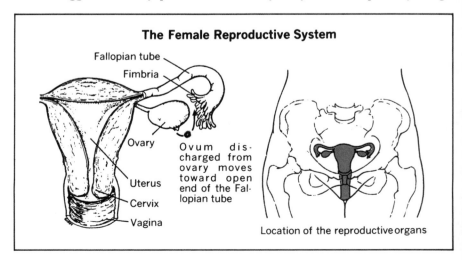

The Female Reproductive System

Fallopian tube

Fimbria

Ovary

Uterus

Cervix

Vagina

Ovum discharged from ovary moves toward open end of the Fallopian tube

Location of the reproductive organs

against the wall, delaying menstruation, but then be dispelled by the body. One in ten pregnancies is estimated to end in some form of miscarriage. See the section on Miscarriage, in this chapter, for more information.

If the embryo successfully attaches, it will usually continue to develop normally through to completion of pregnancy. The presence of the embryo triggers hormonal signals that shut off the menstrual cycle. This prevents further development of eggs in the ovaries, keeps the uterine lining intact, and seals the cervix to prevent infection and allow amniotic fluid to fill the uterus.

If the egg is unfertilized during its passage through the fallopian tube, it will either pass into the uterus and then wash out with the menstrual blood or will deteriorate before leaving the body.

Approximately a week past ovulation the ovary will trigger an increase in progesterone production. This, in turn, will cause the deterioration of the uterine wall's blood lining. The deterioration takes about four days before menstruation begins.

Menstruation is the passing of the blood from the uterine wall. The blood is shed, on average, two weeks after the day of ovulation. Menstruation lasts from three to seven days. The flow of blood will vary during the course of menstruation, with the heaviest flow occurring early on after onset.

Extremely heavy periods, called *menorrhagia,* may occasionally occur during one's lifetime. If it is a persistent problem, consult with your gynecologist. *Dysmenorrhea* is the technical term for periods with cramps. As anyone who has had cramps can testify, they can be quite painful. There are several medications that can be taken to ease or relieve the pain of cramping with menstruation. Most require a physician's prescription.

Some over-the-counter medications, such as ibuprofen, can also help. Cramps are the accompanying contractions of the uterus that force the lining to be shed. Many women stop having dysmenorrhea after the birth of their first child. Other women who previously had no problem suffer from cramps after childbirth. Birth control pills can also eliminate or reduce menstrual pain.

Birth Control

Spacing of pregnancies can be controlled by birth control. Several options are available to couples who wish to prevent pregnancy either permanently or temporarily. Temporary measures mean that, once the method of control is stopped, the woman can become pregnant. Permanent birth control is almost always surgically achieved and it involves cutting or removing part or all of the reproductive system. Once a permanent surgical procedure has been done, it is extremely difficult or impossible to reverse. For that reason, it is rarely performed on patients who have never had children.

In the discussion of different types of birth control, a failure rate is given. The failure rate is determined by the number of people who conscientiously use the birth control and still get pregnant. The rate is per year, not per use. So if one person in one hundred has a failure, that means that one woman in hundred gets pregnant during one year of use.

Oral Contraceptives

The birth control pill comes in various types. The main ingredient in all of them is synthetic estrogen. Synthetic estrogen has two common types: mestranol and estradiol. The quantity of estrogen in a pill can vary from .03 milligram to .1 milligram for the average dosage. The pill will also contain synthetic progestogen, of which there are several types. Commonly used progestogens are norgestrel, norethindrone, and ethynodiol diacetate. Levels of progestogen can vary from .15 milligram to 2 milligrams.

The two hormones work in combination to prevent ovulation. Pills with the hormones are taken every day for 21 days. Some pill packages come with seven extra pills containing inactive ingredients. The cycle is 28 days, so the schedule will either be 21 days on pills, 7 days off, or 21 days on hormone pills, and 7 days on placebos (pills with no effect). The reason doctors prescribe the 21/7 set of pills is that the patient is less likely to forget a pill if one is taken every day without exception.

After the 21st pill with hormones is taken, the level of estrogen drops as the placebo (or no pill) is used. After 24 to 48 hours, the menstrual cycle will begin. It will usually be lighter in flow and take fewer days than previous periods. The pill may also eliminate cramping.

The effectiveness rating of the pill is less than one pregnancy for 100 women (a year) for pill doses of .35 milligrams or higher of estrogen. For pill doses of less than .35 milligrams of estrogen, there is a very slightly higher pregnancy rate.

Some women experience side effects with oral contraceptive pills. Side effects may be minor, from headaches to weight gain, or they may be major, from blood clots to strokes. The increase in risk is directly affected by the patient's age and smoking habits. Women over the age of 35 or smokers increase the risk of heart attack, stroke, and blood clots considerably by taking the pill. The pill does not have any linkage to uterine cancer, cervical cancer, or breast cancer. If a woman already has breast cancer, taking the pill is not recommended because it may stimulate tumor growth, but it is not linked to beginning cancerous development.

Oral contraceptives can only be obtained through prescription by a licensed physician. The physician will determine the dosage the woman takes, and will usually start on the lightest effective dosage. Dosage is insufficient if the woman experiences bleeding during the 21 day cycle, heavy menstrual flow, or other unusual symptoms. Consult with your prescribing physician if you experience problems. Occasionally switching from one type of synthetic estrogen to another, without increasing dosage, can remedy a problem.

Once on the pill, women who decide to get pregnant should stop taking the pill. Restarting ovulation may take a few months so it may be a while before the woman becomes pregnant. *It is not dangerous* for a woman to become pregnant immediately after stopping oral contraceptives. It is not a major health concern if pill taking overlaps pregnancy slightly. It may cause some problems if pill-taking continues past the first trimester.

There is no medical reason for stopping the use of oral contraceptives if there are no side effects. It was once believed that a woman should cease pill taking for a period of months, either every year or every ten years. Neither has proved to be of medical benefit.

The Mini-Pill

The mini-pill is the nickname of the progestin-only oral contraceptive. For women who run higher health risks by taking estrogen, the progestin pill may be an alternative. The risk of pregnancy is at least 1 percent higher than for the combination pill, and missing a day increases the likelihood of unwanted pregnancy (a higher risk than missing a combination pill). The risk of ectopic pregnancy (the fetus develops outside the uterus, usually in the fallopian tube) is also greater. Ectopic pregnancy can be an extremely painful, serious complication with the risk of sterility to at least one fallopian tube. Any woman on the mini-pill who suffers from lower stomach pain should be tested immediately for a possible ectopic pregnancy.

IUDs

Intrauterine devices (IUDs) are small metal pieces inserted semi-permanently into the woman's uterus. Barring complications they remain in place for one to two years. One type sold in the United States is a form called the Copper T. It is made of copper and is t-shaped, measuring less than 1 inch in length. The other is a double s-shape. Two small threads descend from the tail of the device, through the cervix into the vagina. These threads are used to check position of the IUD and to withdraw the IUD after the prescribed period of time.

IUDs are recommended only for women who have already had one successful delivery, are active in a mutually monogamous relationship, and who do not plan on getting pregnant for a few years. The device is inserted at the doctor's office after verification that the woman is not pregnant, has no current pelvic infection or disease, and has never had an ectopic pregnancy.

Because of the problematic history of the IUD, most of the devices were taken off the market. The Dalkon Shield was associated with a number of serious problems and triggered numerous lawsuits against the company. Since then, research and testing of IUDs has improved. However, there are still serious potential complications from using an IUD, so a woman who gets one is required by the IUD manufacturer to sign a Patient Consent, after the side effects have been explained by her doctor. The side effects are too numerous to list here, but the major ones are septic or spontaneous abortion, perforation of the uterus or cervix, ectopic pregnancy, or fetal damage during pregnancy. Common minor complaints are cramping, heavy menstrual flow, anemia, or amenorrhea (no period).

Pregnancy rates for IUDs vary from less than 1 pregnancy for 100 women using the device, to 8 pregnancies per 100. Individual devices have varying rates and their effectiveness is also determined by the size of the woman's uterus. The larger the uterine cavity, the less likely she will conceive while using the IUD. Some women accidently expel the IUD; this occurs less frequently with the large size IUDs inserted into larger width uteruses.

Condoms

Condoms are rubber or natural material sheaths that fit over the glans and shaft of the penis. Natural material condoms are usually made from sheep intestinal tissue and will protect against unwanted pregnancy but may allow the AIDS virus to pass through. For this reason, rubber condoms are preferred for both protection against pregnancy and disease.

Several types of condoms are available to the general public. They are purchased without a prescription at a drug store, pharmacy, or other general merchandise shop. They come with or without lubrication on the rubber, and with or without a reservoir tip. The reservoir tip is intended to hold the semen after ejaculation.

Similar to the male-worn condom is the female-worn condom—a rubber sheath inserted into the vagina. The physical appearance of the female-condom is a tube, with a sealed ring at the top. The plastic ring, similar to a diaphragm ring, fits against the cervix at the top of the vagina. Attached to the diaphragm-like ring is the long, round sheath of rubber. The sheath covers the entire vaginal wall and the end of the sheath (another, larger ring) remains outside the body around the vaginal opening.

Condoms, even without the use of a spermicide, have a low failure rate. When used correctly, the rate is 2 pregnancies for every 100 users. In actuality, the pregnancy rate is closer to 10 percent, since the condom is frequently used incorrectly. One of the more common errors is placing the tip of the condom too close to the glans of the penis, leaving no room for the semen after ejaculation. Other reasons are tearing or mispositioning of the condom during intercourse, although this is extremely rare. Another, more common problem is the use of petroleum jelly for lubrication. Petroleum products deteriorate rubber material. Only water-based lubricants should be used. Also, the penis should be withdrawn while still erect, to insure that the condom remains in place throughout intercourse. Correct storage of the condom, away from heating sources, helps keep the condom in good condition.

Condoms, when used with spermicides, have an even lower failure rate, at less than 1 percent. Spermicide foams and creams kill any sperm that may pass beyond the condom barrier. Spermicides also help protect against venereal disease. Condoms, and condoms with spermicides, offer the best protection against contracting a venereal disease during intercourse.

Spermicides

Spermicides come in creams, foams, and jellies. They may be inserted into the vagina with a plastic applicator, or by suppository or tablet. The spermicide should surround the cervix. The specific requirements vary from type to type, but usually the spermicide must be applied within 30 minutes before intercourse. It must be reapplied for each episode of intercourse. The spermicide should remain in place for at least eight hours after intercourse.

Spermicides are most commonly used with diaphragms, condoms, or other barrier methods of birth control. On their own, spermicides have an estimated failure rate of 15 percent. The two most common ingredients in spermicides are nonoxynol and oxtoxynol. The percentage of the spermicide in the cream, jelly, or foam will vary from 1 percent to more than 12 percent. Some people may have allergic responses to the higher percentage spermicides, but the higher concentrations are more effective in preventing pregnancy.

Diaphragms and Other Barriers

Barrier methods of birth control work by placing a physical barrier, usually of rubber, over the cervical opening to the uterus. The barrier remains in place for at least several hours after intercourse to prevent sperm from entering into the uterus. Barriers are used in conjunction with spermicidal creams, foams, or jellies to enhance protection against sperm passage.

The single-most common form of barrier is the diaphragm. The diaphragm is prescribed by a physician after sizing a women for the dimensions of the diaphragm. If a woman loses or gains more than ten pounds, or becomes pregnant, she should be checked to see if the diaphragm size has to be changed.

The rim of the diaphragm is coated with a spermicidal agent and then is put in place before intercourse. Another application of spermicide is required for each episode of intercourse. The diaphragm should be removed 24 hours after the last episode of intercourse and should be washed thoroughly before reuse.

The failure rate for diaphragms when used with spermicides is 3 percent, when used correctly. The difficulty in using a diaphragm is that positioning of the diaphragm and correct size of the diaphragm are all essential to the success rate. The percentage of failure of different brands of diaphragms, combined with experience of the woman in using it and whether she has had children, can increase the failure rate to as high as 20 percent.

Cervical caps are smaller types of rubber barriers. They are currently unavailable in the United States, except for those women participating in the initial pre-FDA studies on their effectiveness. One of the reasons they are not currently marketed in the U.S. is because the failure rate can be extremely high on them, as high as 44 percent.

A contraceptive sponge is also available as a barrier method. The contraceptive sponge works something like a diaphragm, but is thrown out after use. The sponge is moistened before placement against the cervix, and it releases spermicides for 24 hours after intercourse. It must be removed after 24 hours. The failure rate is almost 18 per 100 users for women who have never had children. It becomes much higher with women who have had children, at 28 percent failure.

Natural Birth Control Methods

Natural birth control is called that when it requires no outside preven

cally; others are irreparable and the women will not be able to conceive naturally.

Hysterosalpingography

This is a long name for the X-ray technique that is used to check for defects and blockage in the fallopian tubes and uterus. (Hystero refers to the uterus, salpingo for the fallopian tube, and graphy for the X-ray technique.) A radiopaque dye is injected into the uterus and fallopian tubes. Then an X ray is made to check for unusual formations and blockages that may be obstructing the path of the egg to the uterus. Two X rays will be taken; one on the day of the dye insertion, and one 24 hours later.

Transcervical Balloon Tuboplasty (TBT)

One of the surgical techniques used to unblock damaged fallopian tubes is called transcervical balloon tuboplasty (TBT). A deflated balloon at the end of a flexible guiding tube is inserted into the fallopian tube and inflated. As angioplasty works on blocked arteries, the tuboplasty works by inflating in the area that is restricted, forcing the tube open. The inflation is done several times to force the scar tissue open and clear the passageway. The surgery is done through outpatient care, which means that it can be performed without a costly overnight stay at a hospital. It is shown to be effective for more than half of the women deemed treatable for fallopian tube blockage.

Treatment of Uterine Disorders

Several problems can arise from uterine dysfunction or disease. Tumors, polyps, and endometrial growth can prevent implantation of fertilized eggs in the uterine lining. There are several surgical procedures, mostly done in the doctor's office, that can correct the problems. *Dilation and curettage (D and C), endometrial biopsy,* and *endometrial curettage* are procedures that allow the physician to remove unusual growths from the cervix and uterine walls.

Hormonal Deficiencies

Hormones regulate the development and release of the ovum from the ovary and prepare the uterine wall for reception of the fertilized egg. Low levels of certain hormones can disrupt any one of the numerous stages of the menstrual cycle. Hormonal problems affect one third of all infertile women.

Anovulatory cycles are menstrual cycles in which no egg is released. *Amenorrhea* is when there is no menstruation, with or without ovulation. *Inadequate endometrium* is when the lining of the uterus is not sufficient for the fertilized egg to lodge on. All of these conditions can be treated with synthetic hormones. Many couples are able to conceive after hormonal treatment. The physician determines the hormone levels through a series of exams. Urine testing, mucous testing, and biopsies will give the different hormone levels for the various hormones required for successful fertilization.

Sperm Count and Formation

The single largest contributing factor to male infertility is sperm count or formation. Testing of sperm involves three studies: count, motility, and morphology.

Sperm Count

The number of sperm present in a single ejaculation should be at least 20 million in one milliliter. For a full determination of sperm count before a male is diagnosed as infertile, testing should be performed more than once. *Oligospermia* is the reduced count of sperm; *azoospermia* is the complete absence of sperm.

Several factors influence sperm production. Alcohol consumption, drug use, and restrictive clothing all reduce sperm count. Blocked ducts in the epididymis or in the vas deferens can also reduce the number of sperm present during ejaculation. Low hormone levels may reduce sperm count. Methods for reversing or correcting low sperm count problem can range from the simple—elimination of affecting factors such as alcohol—to the difficult—surgical reparation of the vas deferens to remove blockage.

Sperm Motility

Motility is the ability of the sperm to travel through the fluid present. A normal score for sperm motility is that two hours after ejaculation, 50 percent of the sperm are still actively swimming. If the sperm die unusually quickly, it is less likely that one will make the passage through the female cervix and uterus and meet up with the egg in the fallopian tube.

Sperm Morphology

The structure of the sperm (morphology) is a small oval body with a whip-like tail that is used to propel the sperm through the uterus. The tip of the sperm body has a cap with enzymes that deteriorate the protective coating on the ovum when the two press together. Sperm that is misshapen, or missing a tail or the enzyme cap, will not be able to successfully penetrate an ovum. In a morphology test, at least 60 percent of the sperm should be normally structured.

Motility and morphology problems present barriers to natural fertilization. With new techniques, *in-vitro fertilization* can take place, barring other complications with the sperm. Some men are able to successfully impregnate their spouses without surgical intervention, despite deficient sperm; others may require extensive intervention.

Immunological Problems

In some partners, the female will develop an immunological response to the male's semen. This means that her immune system attacks the sperm, responding the same way it would to an invasion by a virus. The immune system destroys the sperm before it can reach the ovum. Why this occurs is unknown, but the response fades if exposure to the sperm is eliminated. The treatment for immunological attacks is eliminating intercourse or using condoms for several months until the female's immune system shuts off the mechanism that responds to the sperm.

Alternative Forms of Conception

There have been a number of breakthroughs in conception for couples who experience difficulty in beginning a pregnancy. There are methods for overcoming problems in sperm production, egg production, fertilization, and immune compatibility. For couples wishing to have a biological child related to both parents, one parent, or neither parent but carried by the female, these are the current methods of fertilization.

IVF

In-vitro fertilization (IVF) is the method of conception where the egg is fertilized by the sperm in a glass dish. Several eggs are removed, surgically and non-surgically, from the female. The sperm are concentrated and added to the dish to fertilize the eggs. One or two days later, a couple fertilized eggs are reinserted into the female to impregnate her. More that one are usually implanted because not all will be viable. The remaining fertilized eggs can be frozen for future implantation into the biological parent. The eggs can be donated to parents who do not have the reproductive capability to produce eggs and semen or who have genetic disorders that they do not want to pass on. The success rate for impregnation is not high; about 11 to 15 percent.

GIFT

Gamete intrafallopian transfer (GIFT) is similar to IVF in the first stage. Eggs are removed from the female and placed in a dish with sperm. The difference between IVF and GIFT is that the eggs and sperm are then immediately reinserted into the female's fallopian tube before or while the eggs are being fertilized. This allows the process to resemble more closely the natural process of conception. Fertilization of the egg should take place in the fallopian tube where the eggs and sperm are deposited and then the gamete (fertilized egg) can travel the path to the uterus as it would naturally. The success rate of GIFT is around 17 percent. This rate is expected to improve as GIFT is practiced more frequently.

ZIFT

Zygote intrafallopian transfer follows the same procedure as GIFT except that the eggs and sperm are kept together for eighteen hours before reinsertion. Fertilized eggs are then reinserted into the fallopian tubes where they should make the journey to the uterine lining as they would in natural conception.

Artificial Insemination

Artificial insemination is the oldest of the methods used to circumvent infertility problems. The method involves nonsurgical insertion of sperm into the vagina or uterus. This can be done to provide more concentrated sperm count from the father, or provide sperm from a donor if the father is infertile. This is mainly successful on women who are not experiencing infertility problems themselves.

Surrogacy

For women who are unable to carry a fetus to term in a pregnancy, one of the alternatives is to have another women carry the fetus. Depending on the physical problems of the parents, the surrogate mother may carry a donor egg or the egg of the infertile mother. The egg may be fertilized by a donor or by the father. In some cases the surrogate provides the egg and undergoes one of the procedures above with the father's sperm. Surrogates have been relatives, friends, or hired women whom the couple does not know. The legal involvement is complicated for surrogacy and requires serious consideration before undertaking this arrangement.

Pregnancy

Once you have conceived, the baby has nine months of growth and change to prepare itself for the outside world. There are numerous physiological changes to the mother as the baby grows inside her, and many emotional changes and discoveries for both parents.

As soon as a women realizes she may be pregnant, she should schedule an appointment with a gynecologist/obstetrician. The doctor will perform a blood test that can confirm the mother's pregnancy status. Once a women finds that she is pregnant and decides to proceed with the pregnancy, her doctor will schedule her for monthly exams, through the 28th week of pregnancy. Then she may see her doctor every other week from the 30th week to the 36th. After the 36th week of pregnancy, she should be seen every week until delivery. Delivery should occur before the 42nd week.

First Trimester

The first three months of pregnancy take the embryo from a single free-floating cell to a formed two-inch recognizable fetus. The mother's breasts enlarge to prepare for the production of milk. The uterus increases in size to make room for the growing fetus and the surrounding liquid, called *the amnion.* The placenta forms to process the mother's blood and carry nutrients and water to the fetus. The umbilical cord is the connection between the mother and her child. Through this cord the nutrients travel to the baby and waste material travels back to be processed out by the mother's system.

Because of the direct link between the mother's blood and the baby's blood, the mother must be diligent about the foods and drugs she ingests. Many chemicals can pass through the placenta; some will do irreparable harm to the forming baby. Alcohol, caffeine, chemicals from cigarette smoke, and some medications will pass through the placenta and have been shown to harm the developing fetus. In large quantities, they can cause brain damage, deformity, or death. Any medication should be approved by the pregnant woman's obstetrician before use.

The first examination should be to confirm your pregnancy and run an initial screening for health problems and general health history. A complete physical will either be done then or at a following appointment.

At your first visit with your obstetrician, after you know you are pregnant, your doctor should give you information on what to expect.

During Pregnancy

A pregnant woman needs special foods to maintain her own health as well as to safeguard the health of her baby. She should have additional vitamin D, folic acid, and iron, usually recommended as dietary supplements. More important for most women is the provision of adequate protein in the diet to prevent toxemia of pregnancy or underweight babies. Between 70 and 85 grams of protein a day should be eaten during pregnancy, even if this results in a weight gain of as much as 25 pounds. Adequate nutrition is more important than restricting weight gain to 20 pounds or less.

Morning Sickness

During the second and third months of pregnancy, usually, morning sickness may plague the expectant mother. With the raised hormone levels, and the increased pressure on the internal organs from the growing uterus, the stomach can become easily upset. Morning sickness usually occurs during the first hours after awakening, and can start immediately upon rising.

Although the mechanism of morning sickness is not understood, it is believed that the combination of having gone all night without food and the pressure on the stomach from lying down create the nausea. Munching on crackers and dry toast before arising and continuing to snack through the day will help. Some women experience morning sickness throughout the day; others never experience it. Morning sickness can range from slight nausea to regular vomiting and increased inability to hold down food.

Frequent Urination

As the uterus grows it puts pressure on the surrounding organs. This pressure will shift during the pregnancy from the bladder to the intestines, then to the lungs, as the size of the uterus expands. During the first trimester the main pressure occurs on the bladder, creating the need for the pregnant woman to urinate more frequently. It may cause her to awaken at night to use the bathroom.

Fatigue

Many women experience fatigue during the first trimester of pregnancy. Some women will also continue to experience fatigue throughout the pregnancy. Others experience a respite from being tired during the second trimester. Some of the fatigue may come from restless sleep or interrupted sleep caused by changes in the mother's body. It also stems from the shift of energy to the developing fetus, taxing the mother's body. This new draw of energy requires an increased intake of food by the mother to compensate for the increased need. Despite the fact that the mother may not look pregnant, her nutritional needs increase immediately upon becoming pregnant.

Second Trimester

It is usually sometime during the fourth month that a woman starts "showing." This means that the stomach becomes slightly, but visibly, distended with the growth of the fetus. This may not be noticeable when the woman is fully clothed.

By the end of the second trimester, the pregnant woman will probably have felt the baby move. The baby will begin by rolling and moving about in the amnion surrounding it. It eventually fills the space to keep from moving extensively, but arm and leg jabs will become more apparent and more vigorous as the baby grows. The baby will double in size during the second trimester, getting to an average length of 13 inches by the end of the sixth month. All of the organs and all of the features are in place and developing.

Constipation

The pressure of the growing uterus will shift slowly from the bladder to the intestines. This will relieve the need to urinate as frequently as before, but there will be increased difficulty with bowel movements because of the added pressure. This will result in constipation for some pregnant women.

Varicose Veins

With increased body weight concentrated in the pelvic area, some women experience problems with varicose veins. Leg veins are under increased pressure and may bulge into visible bubbles on the surface of the skin. This may be caused by weakened venal (vein) walls, expanded blood volume, and decreased tension in the muscles. By using aids such as support panty hose and avoiding prolonged standing, the pregnant woman can alleviate some of the problems. Her physician can guide her to other methods of avoiding or exacerbating the problem.

Breathlessness

Breathlessness can start in the second trimester, triggered by hormonal changes that affect the capillaries in the lungs. It will continue into the last trimester because the uterus will push up on the diaphragm, the muscle that controls lung expansion.

Third Trimester

The baby continues to grow, adding fat cells and filling out. The eyes, ears, and mouth are all functioning. The lungs are beginning to expand and contract, taking in amniotic fluid in preparation for breathing air. During the eighth or early ninth month, the baby will rotate into a head down position to prepare for descent through the birth canal. By the ninth month the baby is too big in the womb to make large movements. The sensations the mother feels are the baby jabbing and poking with arms and legs.

Depending on the status of lung development and on the emergency care available, a baby born during the third trimester can survive. The lungs are ill-equipped to deal with the intake of oxygen, but new treatments are available to help the child survive.

Contractions

Some women experience mild uterine contractions throughout the second and third trimester of pregnancy; others only experience contractions toward the end of the third trimester. These contractions can be thirty seconds to several minutes in duration. They usually start at the top of the uterus and the woman experiences a tightening sensation that moves down the uterus to the pelvic floor. The contractions should not be extremely painful, and if they become uncomfortable, changing position or lying down may relieve them. The contractions, known as *Braxton Hicks contractions*, are preparing the uterine muscles for delivery. The contractions may be difficult to distinguish from true labor toward the end of the pregnancy. False alarms, where the expectant mother thinks labor has begun, are caused by this. Lying down should alleviate Braxton Hicks contractions, but not true labor.

Fatigue

As in the first trimester, fatigue can become a daily obstacle. The pregnant woman's body is carrying a large weight and large drain on her energy system. As the baby gets closer to delivery, the amount of energy required increases, increasing the likelihood that the mother will tire easier.

Awkwardness

Falling, tripping, dropping things, and general inability to get into and out of chairs and cars is a normal part of pregnancy. The shift in a woman's center of gravity can occur rapidly during the last trimester, giving her little time to adjust. Moving and stepping over things becomes more difficult as the woman's line of vision with her feet and the ground becomes blocked. Her added weight can make some movements more difficult. And the swelling that comes from general edema can make handling small objects more cumbersome. All of these problems disappear after delivery.

Edema

General swelling of the extremities, the hands and feet particularly, is a normal aspect of pregnancy. About 75 percent of pregnant women experience some swelling from retention of fluids. It is usually helpful to *increase* water intake to alleviate some of the swelling. Increased fluids help the body flush out excess liquids. Talk to your doctor if swelling becomes a problem. *Pre-eclampsia* and *toxemia* occur in a small percentage of women, where swelling is extreme and life threatening if not treated. Your doctor will monitor for pre-eclampsia by checking your blood pressure, weight gain, and degree of swelling.

Breathing Difficulties

As the size of the baby grows, the baby and the uterus will push on the diaphragm muscle that controls breathing. This added pressure keeps the woman from deep breathing and can be painful. Also the baby may temporarily lodge a foot against her ribs or diaphragm, causing sharp pains. During the last two weeks or so, the baby will drop into the pelvic girdle and the pressure will be relieved on the diaphragm. This is called *lightening*. (Note: Shortness of breath, rapid and shallow breathing and/or rapid pulse should be reported immediately to a doctor.)

Prenatal Diagnosis and Tests

During your pregnancy, you will undergo a few or many of the following examinations. Depending on your health and potential health risks, these tests may be performed more than once; some may be done each month. Other tests may be added. Each provides you and the physician with information about your health and the health of the developing baby. Prenatal care increases the chances of having a healthy baby tremendously. Less than 2 percent of the women who see their obstetrician regularly after the second month of pregnancy have an underweight baby.

Home Pregnancy Tests

Home pregnancy tests can now be purchased in almost any pharmacy or drugstore. The prices range from $5.00 to more than $20.00. All the tests work on the same principle— they test for the presence of the hormone Human Chorionic Gonadotropin (HCG), which is present at high levels during pregnancy. A chemical in the home testing kit will change colors when HCG is present. The tests are 99 percent accurate in labs, but probably around 95 percent accurate in home use, where circumstances are not as controlled. A false-negative test will register if the HCG levels are not high enough yet. A false-positive reading may occur if you have unusually high HCG readings or another chemical which mimics HCG in the test. If you have not had your period and you suspect that you may be pregnant, it is advisable to have a doctor's test regardless of the results of the home kit. You should seek medical advice as soon as possible.

Blood tests

Blood is tested during your first examination to determine if you are pregnant. Either during the same examination or at a follow-up examination, blood is tested for the following: anemia; infectious diseases, including sexually transmitted diseases and AIDS; immunities to childhood diseases, especially German measles; and diabetes. Sometime before delivery blood will be checked again for diabetes, sexually transmitted diseases, and hepatitis.

Rh Compatibility Test

Rh is the part of the blood type that labels the blood positive or negative. The only time this poses a problem is when the mother is Rh negative and the father is Rh positive and the offspring develops Rh positive blood. This used to pose serious threat to the pregnancy, but can now be treated adequately with drugs.

Urine tests

The physician will check your urine, probably at each visit, for sugar (diabetes), protein (toxemia), bacteria (infection), and perhaps drug use.

Pelvic Exams

Pelvic exams are done throughout pregnancy to check the position of the fetus and the status of the vaginal walls and the cervix. As you approach delivery, the cervix muscle will *efface* and *dilate*, meaning that the walls will thin and the cervical opening will increase. During your early visits to the doctor, a pap smear will be performed to check for infections and unusual growths on the cervix. Other smear tests will be done for diseases such as chlamydia. These tests may be repeated late in pregnancy.

Ultrasound

By using sound waves to reflect off the fetus in the uterus, the doctor is able to determine the size, position, and occasionally the sex of the forming baby. Ultrasound can be performed anytime after about the fifth week of pregnancy. Your physician will let you know what scheduling is used in his or her office. Some obstetricians perform ultrasound to get an accurate date on the pregnancy by the size of the fetus; others may wait to do one reading later to determine general position and health.

Ultrasonography is performed *transabdominally* (across the stomach) or *transvaginally* (through the vagina). If the ultrasound is done transabdominally, then the woman must drink plenty of fluids beforehand to fill the bladder. This allows the bladder to push the uterus up for better positioning as well as provide an obvious sighting for the bladder so it is not misidentified.

Amniocentesis

To determine the genetic makeup of the developing baby, a small portion of the amniotic fluid can be drawn out of the womb to pick up floating cells, which contain the baby's genetic information. This allows the doctor and the pregnant woman the opportunity to screen for different inheritable diseases. Amniocentesis is usually performed on higher risk patients during the fourth or fifth month of pregnancy. Armed with the information provided, the parents can choose to carry the baby to term, abort the fetus, or have intrauterine surgery performed to remedy problems with the fetus.

The fluid is drawn out by a syringe that is inserted into the woman's naval to the level of the uterus. Using ultrasound to avoid the placenta and the fetus, the needle draws up fluid.

This procedure runs about a one in one hundred risk of causing amniotic leaking, and a one in two hundred risk of infection. The risk of triggering spontaneous abortion is even lower.

Chorionic Villus Sampling (CVS)

A newer procedure than the amniocentesis, the CVS samples the tissue that forms between the interior uterine wall and the beginning placenta. The needle-like tube is inserted either through the vagina or the stomach and guided by ultrasound to the chorionic villus. This testing procedure is usually performed during the third month of pregnancy.

The benefits of the test are that it can be performed earlier in the pregnancy, and a determination to discontinue the pregnancy poses less risk to the woman when decided during the

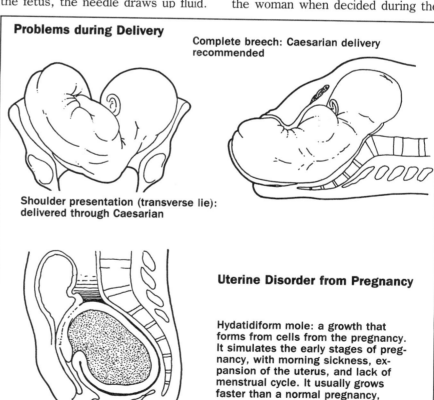

Problems during Delivery

Complete breech: Caesarian delivery recommended

Shoulder presentation (transverse lie): delivered through Caesarian

Uterine Disorder from Pregnancy

Hydatidiform mole: a growth that forms from cells from the pregnancy. It simulates the early stages of pregnancy, with morning sickness, expansion of the uterus, and lack of menstrual cycle. It usually grows faster than a normal pregnancy, though, and can be diagnosed through ultrasound and tissue examination.

first trimester. Amniocentesis can only be done after the start of the second trimester. The risk is that, because it is a newer procedure, the spontaneous abortion rate following CVS is higher than the rate for amniocentesis. As doctors become more practiced with the procedure it is believed the rate will even out.

Fetal Monitoring

External and internal monitoring of the fetus are done to check on the heart rate and stress of the fetus. External monitoring involves registering the heartbeat via ultrasound readings and, if needed, a pressure gauge to measure contractions.

Internal monitoring is done only during delivery and if some level of distress is suspected or likely in the fetus. The monitoring electrode is placed on the baby's scalp through the opening in the cervix. This can only be done after dilation has started. A catheter that measures pressure can also be inserted into the uterus to measure contraction pressure. Both of these units can be connected to the monitor reader by cord or by radio wave.

Monitoring is now a regular procedure during delivery. It allows the doctors to check on the health of the baby and provides an early warning if the baby is in distress. It should be set up so that it does not interfere at all with the birthing process.

Apgar Test Score

When the baby is born, you will probably be given an Apgar score that refers to the general health of the baby. The scores range from 0 to 10 and are based on five criteria: skin color and

Birth Sequence

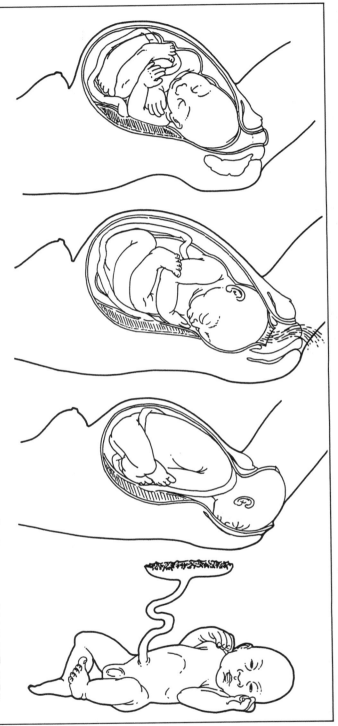

Dilated cervix
During the first stage of labor the cervix dilates to form a passageway into the vagina, the birth canal. Contractions of the uterus may occur at intervals of approximately 5 to 15 minutes, with brief periods of rest in between, which permit oxygen to flow to the fetus.

Ruptured amniotic sac
Ruptured amniotic sac ordinarily signals the onset of the second and generally shorter stage of labor. Contractions during this stage occur in more frequent succession and are more intense. The so-called *bag of waters*, which contains the amniotic fluid, is ordinarily discharged during a strong contraction but may even rupture before labor begins.

Delivery
As the fetus moves into the lower pelvic region the mother naturally experiences a conscious impulse to bear down and help its entry into the world. She may feel a few moments of increased pressure or pain as the infant's head gradually appears and is followed by the rest of its body.

Placental stage
Placental stage is the third stage of labor and is characterized by the expulsion from the womb of the placenta, or *afterbirth*, to which the baby is connected by the umbilical cord. This cord is not cut until all the placental blood has pulsed into the baby's body.

appearance, heart rate, respiratory effort, muscle tone, and reflex responses. Stillborns rate a zero with no pulse, blue skin, and no response system; extremely healthy babies can score a 10 with good coloration, good crying, and strong pulse and muscular activity.

Birthing

There are three basic stages to birthing: labor, delivery, and placental delivery. The average length of birthing is 14 hours for the first birth and 8 hours for births after that. This is only an average though. Some women will experience mild true contractions for 24 hours before significant dilation begins. Some women have labors that last an hour or less. Although it may seem ideal for women who have experienced extremely long labors to have a 20 minute birthing process, there are risks with short labors. The most likely thing with short labors is that you won't get to the hospital on time. Since no one knows when labor will begin or how long it will last, it is extremely important for every woman who is pregnant to have a good understanding of what happens during birthing and what to do as soon as labor begins.

Labor

Labor is marked with the beginning of regular contractions of the uterus. In some women this will be similar to the Braxton Hicks contractions they have been experiencing during the days preceding labor. For others the true labor contractions will be much harder and much more severe in pressure and duration.

Latent Phase

During the initiation of labor the contractions will be some distance in time apart—up to a half hour. Contractions may be regularly spaced or may come irregularly. Because of the possible differences in pressure and duration, some women do not recognize the early stages of labor.

Contractions should come more rapidly, eventually getting to a pace of every five minutes. The contractions are slowly opening the cervix (dilatation) and thinning the cervical muscle (effacement) to allow for the passage of the baby into the vaginal canal. The muscle will eventually thin and open to 10 centimeters during the last part of labor.

Call your doctor when you know labor has begun. Most doctors recommend that women wait out this period at home. Talk to your doctor about what activities are recommended and what should be avoided during this phase. Since the latent phase of labor can last up to one full day, resting is important.

Active Phase

The contractions come more rapidly, last longer, and are stronger in pressure. The contractions force the cervical muscle to dilatation of 7 centimeters. If the amniotic sac did not break during the latent phase, it will break now. The attending physician may choose to break the sac to help the baby's head to *crown*. Crowning occurs when the baby's head moves into the pelvic bone region and becomes visible through the vaginal canal. The act of crowning will normally break the amniotic sac if it has not already ruptured.

By the active phase you should be attended by your health care person. Contractions will reduce to every two or three minutes and may last one full minute. If the attending physician decides that the vaginal canal is not wide enough to accommodate the size of the baby's head, he or she may decide to perform an *episiotomy*. This procedure involves a small incision in the

tissue between the vagina and the anus or off to the side of the vagina. The majority of first births have this procedure; about half the women who have given birth before have an episiotomy again.

Transitional Phase

This can be the most difficult part of the birthing process because it comes at the end of the hard work of labor. The extremely strong contractions are still two to three minutes apart but are now lasting over a minute. The contractions have peaks in pressure that are much stronger than previous contractions. The cervix dilates to a full 10 centimeters, usually in less than an hour. This is the point where breathing exercises learned in birthing classes will come in handy. You may be too anxious, annoyed, or fatigued to consider them though. The coach is there to help with this. At the end of the transition the baby's head forces through the canal and the largest width of the head passes the cervical opening.

Delivery

At this point you can start to push. The point from the end of transition to the actual delivery of the baby should be less than one hour and in some women can take less than fifteen minutes. The baby will usually descend head first with the head facing the back of the mother's body. Other possible positions include the baby facing front, the baby descending feet or butt first (breech delivery) or an arm or leg descending first. All fetal positions except head first, face back, may require medical intervention.

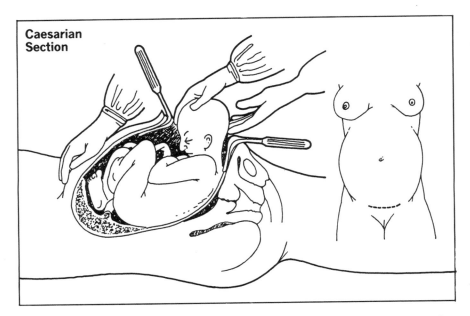

Caesarian Section

Placental Delivery

The last part of the birthing process is the delivery of the placenta. The delivery of the placenta usually follows the birth of the baby by less than one hour. It can occur within five minutes or it may take some time. Nursing the baby during this period helps because the stimulation of the nipples causes uterine contractions that help separate the placenta from the uterine wall, arrest bleeding, and shrink the size of the uterus. The placenta should be delivered in one solid piece.

It is during this time that any tears or surgical cuts will be repaired by the doctor. The episiotomy will be stitched.

Caesarian Sections

In some cases the mother is not able to deliver a baby through the vaginal canal. This can be due to several possible circumstances. If the baby is in one of several breech positions, such as arm or leg descended, the doctor may elect to perform a caesarian instead of attempting to shift the baby for vaginal delivery. If the baby's head is too large to pass through the pelvic girdle bones, or if the pelvic opening is too small to accommodate even a normal size infant, caesarian section will be performed. Also, if the mother does not dilate entirely or if the contractions are not adequate to push the baby into the birth canal, a caesarian will be performed.

In all these circumstances, caesarians are performed to avoid undue stress on the fetus and the mother during the birthing process. The uterus will only be able to provide life support to the infant for a few days after labor has begun. As the physical status of the placenta deteriorates, the loss of oxygen-rich blood will harm the fetus. The pressure from continued contractions will also eventually stress the fetus. Vaginal walls and the cervical muscle will swell from the extended pressure of contractions. It becomes essential to the health of both the mother and the child that labor not continue for too long.

A caesarian section begins with a local anesthesia to the mother that numbs the belly region. An incision is made after anesthesia that opens a small section of the stomach (usually right above the pubic hair). A second incision is made into the uterine wall.

If amniotic fluid remains in the uterus, it will be suctioned away with the same type of tube the dentist uses. The baby is then lifted from the uterus either by hand or by forceps. The umbilical cord is clipped. The placenta may be delivered through the surgical opening. Then both layers of the incision are stitched closed (frequently with metal or plastic clips).

Birthing Places

There are several alternatives for where you can have your baby delivered. Check with your community and your attending physician to see what is available and review what you are comfortable with.

Hospitals

Some hospitals offer a variety of options to the traditional sterile delivery rooms that were common for women over the past forty years. They may have private patient rooms where the mother can decide who attends the birth. All the equipment that will be needed is in the room. The baby may still sleep in the nursery, but will be brought to the mother for feeding.

Birthing Room

Birthing rooms are a step away from private patient rooms. The room is equipped for most emergencies, except caesarians. The father and others can be present throughout the delivery. The atmosphere in the room is designed to be homey and comfortable. For most of the labor the woman will remain on a traditional bed. The bed can then be broken down into a birthing bed for the final stage of labor and delivery. The baby will most probably remain in the room with the mother during her recovery.

Home Delivery

Not usually recommended for first-time pregnancies, the home delivery is just that—delivering the baby in your home. Your attending medical personnel will be there for assistance, but except in emergencies, the full labor and delivery will take place in the home. Screening for this is intensive, because there is little that can be done in emergencies except to take the woman to the hospital in an ambulance.

Birthing Assistants

Along with the choices one can make on where to give birth, one also has choices for who will assist.

Obstetricians

Traditional medical practitioners, obstetricians, are fully trained medical doctors who specialize in pregnancy and birth. They usually assist in deliveries in the hospital, either in delivery rooms or birthing rooms. There may be some in your community, though, who will perform home births.

Nurse Practitioners

Nurse practitioners have several years of medical training although there are procedures that a doctor can perform that a nurse practitioner cannot. The nurse practitioner specializing in birthing will be able to assist in all deliveries, with an attending physician for caesarian sections.

Although arrangements vary from clinic to clinic, there is usually one obstetrician on staff with several nurse practitioners. It is likely that you would only see the doctor once or twice during the course of your pregnancy. The nurse practitioner would be able to handle most of your concerns.

Midwives

Certified midwives may also hold nursing degrees, although this is not a requirement in all states. They will assist in all deliveries, but, like the nurse practitioner, cannot perform caesarian sections. They are trained for all aspects of pregnancy and delivery.

Complications of Pregnancy

Occasionally something goes wrong during pregnancy or childbirth. This may be some problem that can be treated either with medication or surgically. There are some problems, though, that cannot be remedied. In some cases, the mother may lose the fetus.

Miscarriage

When the body rejects the embryo or developing fetus for whatever reason, this is considered a miscarriage or *spontaneous abortion*. There are numerous reasons why a miscarriage may take place. A shift in hormone level, a defect in the embryo, or another factor that interferes with the normal development of the fetus.

Early Miscarriage

Occurring in the first trimester of pregnancy, early miscarriage may be as frequent as one in ten pregnancies. Many miscarriages go undetected because the woman may not realize she has conceived and the body sheds the developing egg before any signs of pregnancy occur. In most of these miscarriages, it is believed that the egg would not have survived to delivery because of physiological defects. Other reasons may include inadequate hormonal development of the uterine lining and a faulty immune reaction to the embryo.

Symptoms

Symptoms of early miscarriage include cramps from the uterine area, not unlike menstrual cramps. This is caused by the uterine contractions that force the lining to be shed. Heavy bleeding accompanies or follows the cramping when the lining is expelled. The bleeding may also be present without accompanying pain. Light bleeding that persists for a few days or more can also signal an impending spontaneous abortion. With any of these symptoms, the attending physician should be contacted immediately.

Upon examination the doctor will determine if the cervix has become dilated—a sign of miscarriage. The physician will guide you through treatment that follows a miscarriage, or will help to arrest the symptoms if a miscarriage has not yet taken place.

Late Miscarriage

Occurring during the second or early third trimester, late miscarriages are physically more difficult to endure. (Psychologically both early and late miscarriages can be difficult if the woman has prepared for the upcoming baby.) Late miscarriages can be caused by trauma, insufficient uterine or cervical capability, or exposure to chemical or drug substances that trigger a miscarriage.

Symptoms

Bleeding, a pink discharge, a brown discharge, or cramping may precede a late term miscarriage. Some women will experience uterine contractions and spotting without it signaling difficulty with the pregnancy. However, any changes in the mother's condition or any experience of the symptoms above should be discussed with the attending physician immediately.

The mother will be examined by the attending medical person to see if the cervix has begun to dilate. If a miscarriage has begun, several steps may be used to prevent it continuing. Continual bed rest, hospitalization, and surgery are just a few of the possible remedies, depending on the reasons for the threat of miscarriage. If the miscarriage does occur, the doctor will try to determine the reasons for it to prevent a reoccurrence in subsequent pregnancies.

Late miscarriages will follow the stages of labor in some women, once miscarriage has become inevitable. The woman will have to expel the fetus and the uterine lining, along with the placenta. A dilatation and curettage (D & C) may be required to clean the uterus after a miscarriage to ensure that no infection sets in. Once the doctor determines that the uterus is sound, and that the reason for miscarriage has been remedied (if possible) then a new pregnancy may begin.

Stillbirths

A baby delivered after about the 20th week of pregnancy will be diagnosed as a stillbirth instead of a miscarriage.

Symptoms

Following the pattern of the late miscarriage, stillbirths can be late miscarriages or they can be full deliveries. The fetus may have already died *in utero* or may die during the labor and delivery. Many of the reasons that apply to late miscarriage also apply here. Other reasons for stillbirths can include deterioration of the uterus, umbilical strangulation, infection of the amnion or uterine lining, or other physiological defects.

Abortions

Different than a spontaneous abortion, an *induced abortion* is when the doctor ends the pregnancy medically. This can occur for several reasons. The woman may elect to have the pregnancy terminated. This is legal through the first trimester in all states, and through the second trimester in some states. If the fetus threatens the life of the mother or has died *in utero*, the pregnancy can be terminated at any point.

There are several methods of inducing an abortion. All involve opening the cervical muscle to remove the fetus. This requires local anesthesia in a first trimester abortion, and can require general anesthesia after the first trimester. Performed in a doctor's office or in the hospital, the medical procedure is considered less risky than birthing. If performed by unqualified personnel or in unsanitary conditions, the risks increase greatly. When the tissue from the pregnancy remains after an abortion, infection can set in. It is therefore extremely important that competent medical personnel be sought to perform abortions.

During the first trimester a D & C can be used to remove the embryo. The uterus can also be aspirated by vacuum. This is a method that removes all the embryonic tissue at once. Second trimester abortions usually involve a chemical injected into the uterus that triggers the body to expel the fetus and induce labor. A pill, RU 486, has been introduced in Europe that triggers spontaneous abortion. It is still being tested for use in the United States.

Genetic Disorders

There are 4,300 genetic defects that can be passed on to offspring. Of those 4,300 there are about 600 that are common enough to be tested for in couples where the risk is considered high. It is estimated that three percent of all births are to children carrying a genetic defect. These can range from mild disorders such as night blindness to serious and life threatening disorders such as Tay-Sachs and sickle cell anemia. If one grandparent or immediate family member carries a known genetic disorder, the attending physician may recommend genetic testing and counseling. Even if abortion is not considered by the parents, genetic testing will allow the parents to prepare for any eventuality.

Child Care

Bringing the Baby Home

Once the child is born, the mother will spend a couple days to a couple weeks in the hospital, depending on her condition after delivery. Caesarian deliveries can keep a woman in the hospital for several days to assist in recovery from the surgery.

Preparation for the baby should be made before delivery, if at all possible. This includes preparing the baby's sleeping area, buying clothes, diapers, and other essentials for the baby. Some parents worry about how they would handle coming home to a nursery if the baby did not survive or was required to remain at the hospital for some time.

Many parents find that, if they did lose the child, disassembling the nursery helped in the mourning process. It may be more difficult for parents to come home to a house where there are no signs of the infant, than to return to a nursery where they have to confront their loss.

In most circumstances, though, the parents return home from the birthing process with baby in hand. It is more than likely that the new mother will be tired from the hard work of delivery. The father will also have been functioning with little sleep if he assisted in delivery and is helping with the feeding and care of the newborn. So having the nursery set up with essentials is one way of assuring that the new family is not adding to the increased demand in their time with this new member.

Essentials in the nursery should include: diapers (cloth, disposable, or both) t-shirts in more than one size, a washtub, a car seat, a crib with a mattress that fits snugly against the sides, blankets, a bunting suit and clothing appropriate to the season, soft terry towels and washcloths, flame resistant pajamas, and a chair for the parent to sit in during feedings. Other items to consider are: a baby monitor that lets you hear the baby when you are in another room, a nightlight, a little music box or recorder that plays lullabies, bottles for feeding, a bottle warmer, pacifiers, clips to hold the pacifier to the baby's clothes, a mobile that hangs over the crib, a stroller, a baby carrier (sling or backpack), a diaper bag, baby oil, powder, shampoo, hypoallergenic soap, and other assorted toiletries. Some of these you may receive as gifts; others you will no doubt want to supply yourselves.

It is important when purchasing items such as carriers, cribs, car seats, and other equipment where safety plays a major role, that you consult with consumer guides, professional recommendations, and that you contact the U.S. Consumer Product Safety Commission, Washington D.C. 20207, (800) 638-2772 to find out if any complaints are registered on the products you are considering. It is worth your baby's safety to take the time to research the things that your baby will spend so much time using. You cannot determine quality by price and, remember, the manufacturer isn't going to put warnings about defects on products they sell.

When buying clothes for the baby, keep in mind that many babies are born bigger than the newborn size of clothing. There is no guarantee for your baby's size, so you should be equipped with several sizes of clothing in case you come home with a big baby. You don't want a nine pound baby and a roomful of six-pound size t-shirts.

Post-Partum Depression

It is estimated that 50 percent of all women suffer from some form of the blues when returning home with their baby. This can be caused by several things. There is a let-down that comes from having an event that you have prepared months for be over. This can be accompanied by the fact that the pregnant woman is the center of attention until the baby comes. Then the baby is the center of attention.

The physical fatigue that comes with birthing, nursing, and caring for a child that has to be fed night and day can also lead to exhaustion and depression.

Some parents take several weeks to bond with their babies. The baby may feel like a stranger when the parent (not just the mother) holds him. The baby, for all practical purposes, *is* a stranger. You are just getting to know his wants, needs, and desires. Each baby is unique in the way he wants to be held, in what the different types of crying mean, and how he responds in general to life around him. Even experienced parents must get used to this new being and his new personality. This takes time. So the sensation that you are not madly in love with or attuned to the child is neither unusual nor incomprehensible. The feelings will develop as you become more comfortable with your baby.

The feelings of inadequacy that arise from all of these potential sources of depression may increase the depression. You may feel like an inadequate or deficient parent because you are not as good a parent as you expected. The ability to be a parent takes time and learning. You should allow adequate time to develop the skills that make you comfortable with your new baby.

If, after several weeks, you still have feelings of depression and inadequacy, talk to your doctor about counseling. It may be a passing problem or it may be tied to other aspects of your life. A good counselor should be able to help you sort everything out and get to the root of your insecurity with your baby. But, again, allow yourself a normal amount of time to adjust without brow-beating yourself about it.

Both fathers and mothers can suffer from post-partum depression. It is important that the new parents communicate with each other about their feelings and their needs. Chances are that the other parent will not only understand what you are feeling, but will be experiencing some of the same feelings as well.

Other methods of handling this period can include talking with other parents about the new stresses that accompany parenthood. Support groups, new parent groups, and other such gatherings may already exist in your community. If not, try to start one, provided it doesn't add a major burden on your time.

If you miss some aspect of your life before baby, such as going out, then make some effort to treat yourself to such an occasion. Talk with friends and keep from isolating yourself if you feel a need to share company. If, however, the problem is too much company and no private time, then feel free to establish visiting hours, as you would have in a hospital when someone else is watching out for your health and well-being.

Serious post-partum depression

Severe post-partum depression that requires immediate counseling has the same symptoms that require immediate counseling even without a baby. The symptoms include: suicidal thoughts, violent urges (particularly directed inward or toward the baby), chronic insomnia, extreme lethargy, loss of appetite, complete inability to function, and general sense of despair. Any of these symptoms should be discussed thoroughly with your physician and/or a counselor as soon as possible.

Diet for Nursing Mothers

A nursing mother has special dietary needs in addition to those satisfied by the normal adult diet. She should drink an extra quart of milk and eat two more servings of citrus fruit or tomatoes, one more serving of lean meat, fish, poultry, eggs, beans, or cheese, and one more serving of leafy green or yellow vegetables.

After the Birth: Physical Changes

The mother's body will take several weeks to get back to something resembling the pre-pregnancy state. Weight gain, uterine expansion, and breastfeeding all change the body and take some time to undo.

Weight gain

Depending on how much weight the mother has gained during the course of the pregnancy, it can take several weeks to several months to get back down to her pre-pregnancy size. If you have gained the recommended 20 to 25 pounds during pregnancy, it will take about two months to lose the ex-

tra weight if you don't diet. If you are breastfeeding, dieting should only be done under strict supervision of your doctor.

The uterus will remain distended for several weeks following delivery. Breastfeeding helps reduce the size of the uterus because a hormone (oxytocin) that increases uterine contractions is released during breastfeeding.

Extra water is maintained in the mother's body during the pregnancy, and this water takes some time to eliminate. The extra fluids will be eliminated from the mother through frequent urination and heavy sweating. It is important that the new mother continue to replenish her fluids despite this apparent flood of liquids leaving her body. Increased intake may help increase the speed with which the body eliminates the unneeded fluids.

The body will also pick up extra weight in the breasts if the mother continues to breastfeed. For mothers who are bottlefeeding, it will take several days for the breasts to reduce in size.

Exercising to help tone and shape the pelvic, stomach, and thigh muscles, is a good method of speeding your return to your usual size. Talk with your physician for post-partum exercises that will not tax your muscles but will help build back up and firm them.

Lochia

For several days following a delivery, whether vaginal or caesarian, the body will excrete through the vagina a discharge that will shift from dark brown to yellowish-white. This discharge is the product of the body shedding the last particles of blood and fluids from the uterus.

Warning signs that are not part of the normal discharge include: bright red blood after about the fourth day, heavy bleeding that requires pad changes of more than one an hour (at any time following delivery), foul smelling discharge, heavily clotted blood, or an absence of discharge during the first two weeks following delivery. Other symptoms to watch for include: lower abdominal pain after the second day and/or lower abdominal swelling. *All of these symptoms require immediate consultation of your doctor.*

Perineal pain

With or without an episiotomy, the perineal area is normally sore following vaginal deliveries. The head of the baby has pushed against the muscles and the muscles are likely to be bruised. Talk to your physician about methods of alleviating soreness if the pain moves beyond irritating. For mild pain try soaking baths, sitting on inner tubes or cushions, lying on your side instead of sitting up, and continuing with Kegel exercises to alleviate some of the discomfort.

Fever

Puerperal fever is a sign of infection following delivery. Although it is extremely uncommon now (it was once a major killer of post-partum women) any fever that lasts for more than a few hours, or which gets over 100 degrees, should be reported immediately to your doctor. It may be just a virus or from the changes taking place for breastfeeding, but your doctor should be notified of any fever during the first month you are home.

General fears and concerns

Most parents have some fears and concerns surrounding the birth of their baby and the general routine that is required once the baby is home. Other concerns are around the various changes and symptoms that both the mother and the baby go through following birth. Some may involve simple things like dry skin; some may be more disconcerting, like rashes and red patches. If you cannot find any answers in your stock of books on pregnancy and babies, or if you are really concerned, you should not hesitate to call your doctor. If he or she feels that you need guidance and are panicky, then request some good books to help you understand what to expect. In any case, no concerned and caring doctor will object to a new parent needing reassurance about the mother's and the baby's health. It is better to ask questions and find out that there is nothing to worry about than to not ask questions and leave a potentially serious problem ignored.

Child Care and Day Care

Once you have a child, you make a choice about how that child is to be cared for during the years before school. The majority of families in the United States can no longer afford to have one parent stay home to raise a child. This means that, for at least part of the week, the child will be cared for by someone other than a parent.

Most parents have caretakers either come to their home or they drop the child off at the caretaker's place. The child will be there three to eight hours a day. Some children are in child care for up to twelve hours, depending on the parents' schedule.

For children with only one primary caretaker, and this counts for more than one quarter of American children, time in day care is essentially the same amount of time as the average adult full-time employee. The quality of the care is as influential on the child's upbringing as the quality of the parental care received during non-work hours. Because of this, child care selection is extremely important to the safety and well-being of any child entrusted to someone else.

Child Care in the Home

Nannies, au pairs, child care workers, and babysitters, are the names for people who come to, or live in, the homes of the child for whom they care. The arrangements can range from one caretaker to one child, to one caretaker for two or three families' small children. The ability of the parents to pay for child care determines the type of care selected.

Few families can afford the salary and the living space required of the live-in nanny. For those who can, the nanny provides a registered, reliable, trained caretaker who will supervise the child for as many years as the parents deem necessary. Au pairs are much the same type of worker, except they usually do not have educational training for child care. They tend to be younger workers, less likely to stay for more than a year or two in the same position. Many au pairs are foreign students seeking a chance to live abroad for a while.

Child care workers and babysitters may come to take care of the child during assigned hours. They may live somewhere else and their work hours are scheduled for regular work patterns. They may work for one family, or a few families may pool together resources and use one caretaker for several children. One child care worker should care for no more than four or five children at a time, to provide the best safety and education for the children.

When hiring someone to come watch your children in your home, several things should be considered. The most important is to check the personal history of whomever is being considered. This now means going beyond personal recommendations. Check for police records, work papers, history of employment, and any other documentation that the person can provide to show stability, reliability, honesty, and integrity *while working with children*. In most situations, the caretaker will be unsupervised while working with your small children. Children's versions of events may not fully explain events you should know about, or may exaggerate problems with the caretaker that are not important. You have to have complete faith that this person is delivering the service you expect in a manner that meets with your full approval. If you have the opportunity to observe at least one full day of activity under the care of the worker, you should take it. This gives you a sample of how your child will spend important hours of his development. It also allows you to watch how a worker deals with the frustrations and problems that come up every day when dealing with youngsters.

Child Care Centers and Programs

Many states are now requiring registration of child care centers. Even for individuals who run informal-style child care in their own home, licensing may be required. The state will set up rules of how much space is needed per child, how many staff employees per child, what kind and variety of food is to be served, what activities are allowed, and what type of insurance is needed to cover for accidents while at the center. Check to see if your state has a licensing program,

and what the licensing requirements are. If your state does have such a program, you should only use licensed facilities for your child. If there is no mandatory licensing, find out if there is a voluntary licensing program for day care. You should check references thoroughly for programs that have no governmental inspection. Even with licensing, you want to ask the same types of questions that the licensor asks:

- How many staff per student?

- With whom is a sick staff member replaced?

- What food is provided for the children?

- What activities are provided for?

- What instruction and education is the child given?

- What are the age ranges of the children enrolled?

- How many children does the facility accommodate?

- How many children per classroom or room?

- Are any activities off the center grounds? Is permission obtained in advance to take the child off the grounds?

- What is the policy for sick children? Are they allowed in the classroom? If a child is brought to the center, obviously sick, what procedures are followed by the day care staff?

- If a child gets sick or injured while at day care, what procedures are followed?

- What is the policy of allowing children to leave with someone other than a parent? Is advance notice required? Is the parent the only acceptable guardian to be picking up a child? (Although it may seem initially that you would only want a

parent picking a child up, you may wish to carpool, or have a babysitter or a relative pick up a child. You want to make absolutely sure, though, that the child cannot leave with anyone who walks in and asks to take the child home.)

- What are their hours? What are their pickup times? If you are late, what do they do with the child?

- What is the discipline policy of the center? (This is of fundamental importance that the policies be explained in advance of enrollment.)

- Do they expel children? For what reasons?

Look around the facilities. Are they clean, well kept, and brightly lit? Are there appropriate ranges and types of toys for your child's age? Are there any safety violations or potentially dangerous aspects to the room's design (such as an open staircase without guardgates).

Attend the facilities while day care is in session. Observe the interaction of the children to see if they are well cared for, occupied in a manner you find suitable, and playing or interacting positively. Get references from parents whose children are the same age as yours and are currently using the day care program.

Once you have enrolled in the program, continue to monitor the classroom atmosphere. Occasionally drop by early before picking a child up to watch the activities. Continue to talk to other parents who have children in the same program. And, above all, continue to talk to and listen to your child about how he has spent his day.

Day care can be one of the most influential and rewarding experiences for a child. Your child will learn to interact with other adults, and perhaps other children, depending on the type of care you select. It will provide him or her with early educational experi- ence that will be the foundation of the entire learning experience. If it is a positive experience from the start, it is likely that your child will continue to enjoy learning throughout his or her lifetime.

5

The Middle Years

Maintaining good health over the years is far simpler, less expensive, and more comfortable than restoring health that has become poor. Because some diseases cannot be cured after they are contracted, it is only logical to try to prevent all possible health problems. The techniques of modern preventive medicine are available to Americans of every age.

All people are not beautiful or handsome, but nearly everyone can have the kind of attractiveness and vitality that comes from good health. The health of an individual depends upon the kind of body he inherits and the care he gives it. Good health can be thought of as a state of social, physical, and mental well-being, a goal virtually everybody can attain—if the responsibility for maintaining one's own health, with occasional help from the health experts, is accepted.

Keeping Fit

Physical Changes

Physically, middle age should be a pleasant plateau—a time to look back on a vigorous youth, enjoy an active present, and prepare for a ripe old age.

Middle age should not be measured by chronological age but by biological age, the condition of various parts of the body. You might say that the middle-aged body is like a car that has been driven a certain number of miles. It should be well broken in and running smoothly, but with plenty of reserve power for emergencies, and lots of mileage left.

Biological age should be measured by the state of the heart, arteries, and other essential organs, the length of life and comparative health of parents and grandparents, temperament and outlook on life, and outward appearance. The way you have fed or treated yourself is important. Eating the wrong kinds of food, being overweight, smoking too much, or worrying too much can add years to biological age.

However, no one should be surprised if he is not in quite the shape he was when he was 25 or 30 years old. At age 40 to 50 it is perfectly normal to have only 80 percent of the maximum breathing capacity, 85 percent of the resting cardiac output, 95 percent of the total body water, and 96 percent of the basal metabolic rate. These factors, however, should not slow anyone down very much.

There is one difference, though, that can be anticipated in middle age. Reaction time and decision-making processes may be a bit slower. This is because the nervous system is one of the most vulnerable to aging. The cells of the central nervous system begin to die early in life and are not replaced, while other organs are still growing and producing new cells. Specific response to input is delayed because it takes a greater length of time for an impulse to travel across the connections linking nerve fibers.

Thus, though you may function as usual under normal conditions, you may find it a little harder to respond to physical or emotional stress. However, if you have followed a sound health maintenance program, including good nutrition, enough mental and physical exercise and rest, and moderate living habits, you should respond to unusual physiological or emotional stress quite adequately.

The Importance of Checkups

Physical disabilities associated with

chronic disease increase sharply with age, starting with the middle years. While more than half (54 percent) of the 86 million persons who have one or more chronic conditions are under age 45, the prevalence of disability from illness is greatest in the 45 and older age group. Of those under 45 who have chronic conditions, only 14 percent are limited in activity as compared with almost 30 percent of the 45 to 64 age group. And only 1 percent of those under 45 with chronic illness are completely disabled, as compared with 4 percent in the 45 to 64 age group.

These figures suggest that it is wise to have an annual checkup so that any disease process or condition can be nipped in the bud. Further evidence of the value of medical checkups comes from the Aetna Life Insurance Company, which compared two groups of policyholders over a five-year period. Those who did not have checkups and health counseling had a death rate 44 percent higher than the group who did. Regular checkups will not only help prolong life, they will also help you to live it more comfortably.

Here are some other good reasons for having a physical checkup:

- If an organ has been attacked by serious disease in youth, it may deteriorate at an early adult age.

- Heredity may play an important role in determining the speed at which various organs age. If your parents and grandparents had arteriosclerosis, there is a chance you might develop this condition in your middle years.

- Your environment (smog, poor climate, etc.) might affect the rate at which your body ages, particularly the skin.

- Individual stresses and strains or abuses or overuse (of alcohol, for example) may create a health problem in middle age.

- The endocrine glands (pituitary, thyroid, parathyroids, adrenals, ovaries, testicles) play important roles in aging. Serious disease of one or more of these glands may lead to premature aging of an organ dependent upon its secretions.

- At middle age you are more likely to be beset by emotional strains at work or at home that could make you an early candidate for heart disease, arteriosclerosis, and other degenerative disorders.

- The earlier a chronic disease is detected, the better the chance that it can be arrested before permanent damage is done. This is especially true in the case of glaucoma, diabetes, heart disease, cancer of the lung or breast or other cancers—all of which could have their onset in middle age.

To help detect disease and other debilitating conditions, many physicians utilize automated medical screening, which combines medical history with selected physiological measurements and laboratory tests to give the physician a complete health profile of the patient. This profile should indicate the probability of any chronic condition, which the physician could then pinpoint with more thorough tests.

Also, annual checkups enable the physician to observe changes taking place over a period of time. For example, he is able to observe gradually changing blood chemistry levels or a progressive increase in eye pressure that could signal the onset of disease.

Don't Try To Be Your Own Physician

A panel of medical specialists from the University of California at Los Angeles recently found that many men of 40 years and older were dosing themselves with unnecessary pills and "conserving" their energy by increasing bed rest to the point that it actually became enervating.

These physicians point out that increasing dependence on pills can be harmful as well as expensive. Laxatives are a good example of a popular commercial medicine taken unnecessarily by large numbers of people. Perhaps only one person in 100,000 may have an actual motor disability of the bowels, and most constipation can be easily corrected through proper foods and exercise, without resorting to laxatives. Also, taking vitamin pills or avoiding all high-cholesterol foods is unnecessary—unless recommended by a physician.

But, most important, "conserving" energy through prolonged bed rest or avoiding exercise can be fatal. The panel members pointed out that before age 40, a person exercises to improve his performance, but that after age 40 he exercises to improve his chances of survival.

Physical Fitness and Exercise

In middle age most of us stop performing most forms of exercise other than those that we enjoy doing. In other words, we find it easier to bend an elbow than lift weights. This is unfortunate, because in middle age most of us need regular exercise to maintain both mental and physical fitness and to increase endurance, strength, and agility.

As noted earlier, in middle age there is some decrease in breathing capacity, cardiac output, and metabolic rate; yet exercise can improve these functions. The more often the normal heart and circulatory system are required to move blood to active regions of the body through exercise or movement, the more efficient they become. Protracted exercise also improves the work of the lungs by increasing their ability to expand more fully, take in more air, and utilize a greater proportion of the oxygen in the inhaled air.

While exercise alone cannot eliminate obesity, it can help prevent it by improving digestion and bowel movements and by burning up excess calories. Exercise can also make you feel, look, and think better. Some traditional formal exercises, however, like touching the toes while keeping your knees stiff, or doing deep knee bends, are potentially harmful in middle age; they put too much stress on weak parts of the back and legs.

Despite protests about not having enough time, everyone has time to exercise, particularly if it is worked into the daily routine—for example, walking instead of riding to the train, office, store, or bus stop. You might find you'll get there faster, especially in traffic-clogged metropolitan areas, and you'll save money as well. More important, those minutes of "stolen" exercise accrue over the years in the form of improved health.

Sports and Games

If you don't like formal exercise, you can get exercise informally—through a favorite sport, whether it be golf, tennis, swimming, jogging, skiing, cycling, or whatever. Many sports and games are stop-and-go activities that do not provide helpful, rhythmic exercise, but here's how you can make them more beneficial.

Golf

Instead of riding in a golf cart between shots, walk—in fact, stride vigorously, lifting your head and chest. And don't make golf a cut-throat competition or business pursuit. Relax and enjoy it—count your blessings rather than your bogeys.

Tennis

Like golf, tennis can be a cut-throat competitive sport or a pleasant pursuit. If it's played with muscles tied in knots from nervous tension, it will not provide any fun or healthful exercise. Also, players over 30 are well-advised to play more doubles than singles and to avoid exhausting themselves in the heat of competition.

Swimming

Along with fast walking and jogging, swimming is one of the best all-around exercises. When swimming, most of the muscles are exercised and lung capacity and cardiac output are improved. The exercise potential can be increased by doing pull-ups with the diving board or ladder and by bobbing up and down in the water.

Jogging

This popular sport can be combined with walking, done in a group or alone, either outdoors or indoors, and alternated with other exercises. Moreover, it doesn't require any special equipment and has been recognized by fitness experts as one of the best exercises for the heart and circulation. However, it is wise to get your physician's advice and approval before embarking on a jogging program.

Skiing

Skiing is healthful as well as fun. You can get in shape for skiing and improve your ability by jogging and by practicing some of the techniques needed in skiing—such as the rhythmic left-right-left-right twist of foot, knee, and leg in short turns. To do this exercise, stand up straight with your feet quite close together and flex your knees forward so that the weight goes onto the balls of the feet. Now, arms apart for balance, twist your feet and knees to the left without twisting your upper body. As you do this, try the modified half-bends of the traversing position that all ski schools teach. Then reverse the position to the right, and keep repeating.

Other Sports

Other worthwhile sports for healthful exercise include badminton, bicycling, canoeing, rowing, table tennis, skating, and squash. However, they should be sustained for at least 30 minutes at a time, ideally four times a week, and should be combined with supplemental exercises.

A Word of Warning

Everyone should beware of becoming a weekend athlete and punishing himself with an overdose of exercise or sports only on weekends. It makes as much sense as stuffing yourself on weekends and starving the rest of the week. It's far more sensible—and healthful—to engage in sports activities for an hour or so at a time on a daily basis.

Exercises

Participating in sports activities is not the only way to keep fit. Special exercises can help reduce tension and build muscles. For instance, one way to relax is to do rhythmic exercises, particularly for the trunk, that help to improve circulation. You can also try exercises that will relieve tense muscles and improve breathing. The exercises described below were developed by Dr. Josephine L. Rathbone of Columbia University.

Breathing to Relax

Lie on your back on the floor with knees bent and feet resting on the floor. Take a deep breath, letting both the abdominal wall and chest rise. Hold the air for a few seconds, then expel it through your mouth with a gasp. Repeat four or five times at regular intervals.

For Tense Arms

Standing erectly, swing both arms forward, then to the side, letting them drop during the swings so that your hands brush your thighs with each motion. Keep your shoulders low. Repeat a few times. Then, sit on the edge of a chair and clench one hand tightly. Swing your arm vigorously in large circles, keeping your hand clenched. Then repeat with other arm.

For Tense Legs

Sit on the edge of a table with lower legs hanging free. Then, alternately, swing them backward and forward. Try to keep your legs moving in rhythm.

For Stomach Tension

Kneel with your feet under your hips and swing your trunk down to one side and around, sweeping your arms in a wide circle, coming up again on the opposite side. Or stand with your hips supported against the wall, feet apart and a few inches from the wall. Bend your body forward, arms drooping, and let your body sway from side to side, with your arms and head loose.

Relaxing at Work or Home

Relieve tension while sitting by holding the spine erect, shoulders low. Turn your head so that the chin touches first one collarbone, then the other. Move slowly and rhythmically.

Yoga

You can also relax and become revitalized through various Yoga exercises. Courses are taught at many recreational centers. Some of the exercises require only a minimum of time, and can be done not only before and after the workday but in the office during the lunch hour.

Isometrics

Isometric exercises—pitting one muscle against another without moving—can also be practiced at odd moments. These exercises should, however, be done only by healthy persons, and not by anyone with a cardiac problem. To strengthen arm and shoulder muscles through isometrics, put the fist of one hand against the palm of the other and push without moving. Or push up with your arms from a chair or the edge of a table. Strengthen arm and neck muscles by grasping the back of the neck with laced fingers and pulling forward—again, without movement.

All of the above exercises and sports can put you on the road to physical fitness. Just remember, whatever form of exercise or sport you choose, make it fun and do not strain yourself unduly.

Rest and Sleep

Rest and sleep adequate for one's personal needs are another vital component of good health and good appearance. They also influence human relationships and mental alertness. Scientists believe that during sleep the body replaces tissue cells and eliminates waste products created by fatigue at a faster rate than when awake.

Sleep also rests the heart and blood system, because heart muscle contractions and blood pressure are slower then. Excessive fatigue from lack of sleep increases susceptibility to a number of ailments, including the common cold. If an individual gets an adequate amount of sleep (usually seven to eight hours for an adult), he will feel ready to meet the day's activities. If not, his memory may not be sharp, and he may be irritable because his nervous system has had inadequate rest.

A quiet, dark, ventilated room, a fairly firm mattress, and performance of a moderate amount of exercise during the day will aid sleep. When worry, frustration, or anxiety make it difficult to sleep, a conscious attempt to relax will help. Sedatives or sleeping pills should not be taken unless they are prescribed or recommended by a physician.

Personal Hygiene

Disease germs can enter the body only in a limited number of ways. One of the major ways is through the skin. The skin is a protective covering which, when broken, can admit harmful bacteria or viruses easily.

Simple precautions are very effective. The hands come into contact with disease germs more than any other part of the body. Therefore, they should be washed whenever they are dirty, prior to preparing food or eating, and after using the lavatory.

The rest of the body must also be kept clean, because adequate bodily cleanliness will remove substances that, by irritating the skin, make it more susceptible to infection. Bathing also improves the muscle tone of the skin. Hair should also be washed frequently enough to prevent accumulation of dust and dead skin cells.

Openings in the body are also paths by which disease germs can enter the body. The nose and ears should be carefully cleaned only with something soft, for instance, a cotton swab. Genital orifices should be kept clean by frequent bathing. Any unusual discharge from a body opening should be promptly reported to a physician. The problem can then be treated at its earliest stage—the easiest time to solve the problem.

Personal hygiene includes care of the nails. They should always be kept clean and fairly short. Hangnails can be avoided by gently pushing back the cuticle with a towel after washing the hands.

Care of the Feet

"My feet are killing me!" is a complaint heard more frequently in middle age, especially from women. The devil in this case usually takes the shape of fashionable shoes, where the foot is frequently squeezed into shapes and positions it was never designed to tolerate. Particularly unhealthy for the foot was the formerly fashionable spike heel and pointed toe.

Any heel two inches or higher will force the full weight of the body onto the smaller bones in the front of the foot and squeeze the toes into the forepart of the shoes. This hurts the arch, causes calluses on the sole of the foot, and can lead to various bone deformities.

The major solution to this problem is to buy good shoes that really fit. The shoes should be moderately broad across the instep, have a straight inner border, and a moderately low heel. To fit properly, shoes should extend one-half inch to three-fourths inch beyond the longest toe.

Avoid wearing shoes that have no support; also, avoid wearing high heels for long periods of time. Extremely high heels worn constantly force the foot forward and upset body balance. Changing heel height several times a day will rest the feet and give the muscles in the back of the legs a chance to return to their normal position. It's highly desirable to wear different shoes each day, or at least alternate two pairs. This gives the shoes a chance to dry out completely. Dust shoes with a mild powder when removed.

Shoes should not be bought in the morning. They should be tried on near the end of the day, when the feet have broadened from standing and walking, and tightness or rubbing can be more easily detected.

As to hosiery, socks and stockings should extend a half-inch beyond the longest toe. Stretch socks are fine in many cases, but plain wool or cotton socks help if your feet perspire a lot.

Foot Exercises

Exercise your feet by trying these simple steps recommended by leading podiatrists:

- Extend the toes and flex rapidly for a minute or two. Rotate the feet in circles at the ankles. Try picking up a marble or pencil with your toes; this will give them agility and strength.

- Stand on a book with your toes extended over the edge. Then curl your toes down as far as possible, grasping the cover.

- After an unusually active day, refresh the feet with an alcohol rub. Follow this with a foot massage, squeezing the feet between your hands. When you are tired, rest with your feet up. Try lying down for about a half-hour with your feet higher than your head, using pillows to prop up your legs.

- Walk barefoot on uneven sandy beaches and thick grass. This limbers up the feet and makes the toes work. Walking anywhere is one of the best exercises for the feet if you learn to walk properly and cultivate good posture. Keep toes pointed ahead, and lift rather than push the foot, letting it come down flat on the ground, placing little weight on the heel. Your toes will come alive, and your feet will become more active.

Foot Ailments

Doing foot exercises is particularly important in middle age, because the foot is especially vulnerable to the following problems.

Bunions

A bunion is a thickening and swelling of the big joint of the big toe, forcing it toward the other toes. There is also a protuberance on the inner side of the foot. Unless treated, this condition usually gets progressively worse. Surgery is not always necessary or successful. Often, special shoes to fit the deformed foot must be worn.

Stiff Toe

People suffering from this problem find that the big joint of the big toe becomes painful and stiff, possibly due to a major accident or repeated minor trauma. This condition usually corrects itself if the joint is protected for a few weeks, usually by a small steel plate within the sole of the shoe.

Hammer Toe

This clawlike deformity is usually

caused by cramping the toes with too small shoes. The pressure can be eased with padding and, in some cases, the deformity can be corrected by surgery.

Ingrown Toenail

Cutting the nail short and wearing shoes that are too tight are major causes of ingrown toenails; the edge of the nail of the toe—usually the big toe—is forced into the soft outer tissues. In some cases the tissues can be peeled back after soaking the foot in hot water, and the offending part of the nail can be removed. To prevent ingrown toenails, the nails should be kept carefully trimmed and cut straight across the nail rather than trimmed into curves at the corners. For severe or chronic cases of ingrown toenails it is best to seek professional treatment.

Morton's Toe

This is the common name for a form of *metatarsalgia,* a painful inflammation of a sheath of small nerves that pass between the toes near the ball of the foot. The ailment is most likely to occur in an area between the third and fourth toe, counting from the large toe, and usually is due to irritation produced by pressure that makes the toes rub against each other. In most instances, the pressure results from wearing improperly fitted shoes, shoes with pointed toes, or high heel shoes, which restrict normal flexing of the metatarsals (the bones at the base of the toes) while walking.

Temporary relief usually is possible through removal of the shoes and massaging of the toes, or by application of moist, warm heat to the afflicted area. In cases of very severe pain, a doctor may inject a local anesthetic into the foot. Additional relief sometimes can be obtained by wearing metatarsal arch supports in the shoes. However, continued irritation of the nerves can result in the growth of a tumor that may require surgical removal.

Care of the Teeth

An attractive smile is often the first thing that one notices about others. In addition to creating an attractive appearance, healthy teeth and gums are a basic requirement for good overall health. The dentist should be visited at whatever intervals he recommends, usually every six months.

Neglect of oral hygiene and the forgoing of dental checkups are commonplace in the middle years. An often-heard excuse is that the eventual loss of teeth is inevitable. Years ago, loss of teeth really was unavoidable. Today, however, thanks to modern dental practices, it is possible for nearly everyone to enjoy the benefits of natural teeth for a lifetime.

Problems of Aging

When the human body reaches middle age, a number conditions that are the result of advancing years begin to make themselves felt. These include wrinkling of the skin, baldness, varicose veins, and the body's decreased ability to deal with nicotine, caffeine, alcohol, and excess calories.

Skin

The skin usually starts to show its age in the mid to late 30s. At that time it starts to lose its elasticity and flexibility, and becomes somewhat thinner. Little lines—not yet wrinkles—start to show up, usually crow's feet around the eyes.

Wrinkling takes place at different times with different people, and sometimes in different areas of the skin. Heredity may play a part.

Treatment for Wrinkles

While wrinkles do not hurt, many people want to do something about them. Experienced physicians and dermatologists have a number of techniques for removing or minimizing wrinkles. One accepted method is *dermabrasion,* or planing of the skin. The physician sprays on a local anesthetic, then scrapes the skin with a motor-driven wire brush or some other abrasive tool. The treatment usually takes one session, and no hospital stay is required. There will be some swelling and scab formation, but this should clear up in a week to ten days.

Another method is called *cryotherapy,* in which the physician freezes the skin with carbon dioxide. This induces peeling, which improves the appearance of flat acne scars and shallow wrinkles.

The use of retinoic acid, or Retin-A™, for the treatment of wrinkles has become popular in recent years. Retinoic acid was originally used for the treatment of acne and has not yet been studied for long-term use for wrinkles. The effect is temporary on wrinkles and skin will return to original condition after discontinued use. Some side effects include heightened sensitivity to sunlight and skin irritation or rash.

Skin Texture Change

Besides wrinkling, the skin has a tendency in some people to become thinner, leathery, and darkened as they move towards the 40s and 50s. This effect can be minimized if the skin is toned up with cold cream and other emollients that provide the moisture and oil the skin needs. Also, overexposure to the sun—one of the prime agers of the skin—should be avoided.

In fact, most physicians feel that the sun is a lethal agent, and that exposing the face to too much sun is like putting it in a hot oven. Many say that the sun destroys some inherent good qualities of facial skin, and ruins any chance of improving the appearance through cosmetic surgery.

Cosmetic Surgery

Cosmetic surgery for both men and women is becoming increasingly popular and sophisticated. Cosmetic surgery procedures include *rhinoplasty* (nose); *facial plasty* or *rhytidoplasty* (face lift); *blepharoplasty* (upper eyelids and bags under the eyes); breast augmentation and reduction; as well as the dermabrasion and other methods mentioned earlier. See "Plastic and Cosmetic Surgery" in Ch. 20, *Surgery.*

Baldness

The problem of baldness has its roots in ancient history. Men were worried about baldness 4,000 years ago. But until recently, medical opinion agreed largely with the statement by Dr. Eugene Van Scott, head of the Dermatology Service of the National Cancer Institute: "Baldness is caused by three factors: Sex, age, and heredity. And we can't do a thing about any of these."

Other causes of male baldness include infections, systemic diseases, drugs that have a toxic effect, mechanical stress, friction, and radiation. Diet does not usually affect baldness, but chronic starvation or vitamin deficiencies can contribute to dryness, lack of luster, and hair loss. Also, ex-

cessive intake of vitamin A can cause hair loss.

In women, loss of hair is quite common toward the end of pregnancy, after delivery, and during menopause. A hysterectomy, crash dieting, severe emotional stress, high fever, a major illness such as thyroid disease or diabetes, certain allergies, and the use of systemic drugs such as steroids and amphetamines—all can produce hair loss.

There are two common types of baldness in men: male pattern baldness (*alopecia*) and patchy baldness (*alopecia areata*). The latter is more common in women.

Male Baldness

Male pattern baldness may begin as early as the early 20s or 30s. Hair

falls out from the crown until a fringe of hair remains at the sides and along the back of the head. At the onset, a bald spot may appear on the crown of the head; balding spots in other areas may merge to form the fringe pattern.

In patchy baldness, hair may fall out suddenly in patches. In this case, hair usually returns after going through three growth periods. The new hair may be thinner than the original hair. Although patchy baldness is self-limiting and often self-curing, therapy is indicated for some patients. The therapy may consist of injections of soluble steroid suspensions directly into the scalp. Regrowth may begin in three to four weeks, but remains localized at the sites of injections.

Hair transplants remain the most dependable way to grow new hair—especially in men with male pattern baldness. The process involves cut-

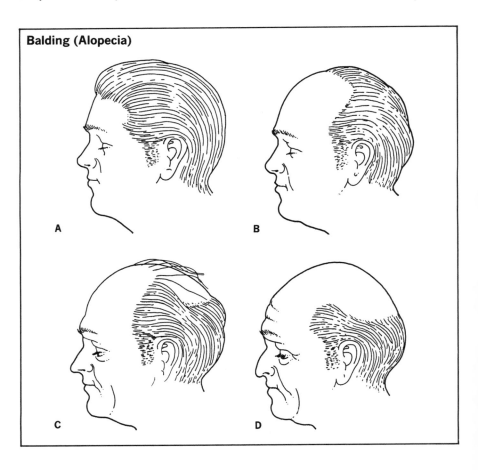

Balding (Alopecia)

A   B   C   D

ting out *punch grafts,* small patches or plugs of hair and follicle-bearing tissue, from the back or sides of the head. The grafts are immediately inserted into recipient incisions that are slightly smaller than the plugs. In a two- or three-hour session a physician can transplant 60 to 80 plugs of hair. Adequate coverage of a balding crown usually requires 200 to 400 plugs.

Female Baldness

The hair on the crown of a woman's head may thin out, but women seldom become bald as men do. Progesterone, administered in careful, dose-regulated treatments, has been used successfully by some dermatologists. The progesterone is applied to the scalp as a cream or ointment.

Drug Treatments

Other forms of therapy have come into experimental use for both men and women. Many of them involve the use of drugs. In one treatment carefully monitored doses of cortisone are injected into the scalp. In another, the drug psoralen may either be applied to the scalp directly or taken internally. A combination of drugs including 8-methoxypsoralen and inosiplex may be used in conjunction with ultraviolet irradiation.

Most acclaimed of all the new drug therapies is minoxidil, a derivative of the blood pressure-reducing drug Loniten. Physicians simply order Loniten reformulated as a topical solution. Thicker than water, the minoxidil has been used generally by prescription as a gel. Visible improvement is never guaranteed, and in most cases results can take from four months to a year.

Minoxidil must be prescribed by a physician and requires medical monitoring about every four months. It must be used indefinitely to maintain new hair growth. Early findings suggest that the drug works best on men who have not been bald for a long time. Some dermatologists believe that patients with minoxidil-generated growths of hair can gradually, over time, switch to low-dose, modified use patterns.

Excess Hair

For some middle-aged women, the problem is too much hair in the wrong place, instead of too little. Excess hair can grow on the face, chest, arms, and legs. In some instances, unwanted hair may be a sign of an endocrine disorder that can be detected by a physician. In other cases, it can be caused by chronic irritation, such as prolonged use of a cast, bandage, or hot-water bottle; it can also be due to excess exposure to the sun, iodine or mercury irritation, or localized rubbing.

Excess hair can be bleached, shaved, tweezed, waxed, or removed by chemical depilatories and electrolysis. Only electrolysis is permanent. See "Hair Removal" in Ch. 21, *Skin and Hair.*

Varicose Veins

Another complaint of middle-aged men and women is *varicose veins.* About half the women over 50 years of age have these enlarged veins with damaged valves in their thighs and calves.

Varicose veins can occur in various parts of the body. They are, however, most common in the legs.

Varicose veins are usually caused by years of downward pressure on the veins, causing the valves to break down. This often happens to people who must stand for many hours at a time. The large, bluish irregularities are plainly visible beneath the skin of

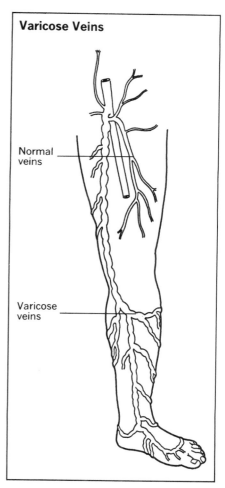

Varicose Veins

Normal veins

Varicose veins

the thighs and calves, and they cause a heavy dragging sensation in the legs and a general feeling of tiredness and lack of energy.

Treatment

In most instances, the best treatment involves surgery to tie off the main veins and remove all superficial veins that lend themselves to this procedure (called *stripping*). In other cases, varicose veins can be relieved by wearing elastic stockings or compression bandages.

Varicose veins that remain untreated can cause *varicose ulcers,* which usually form on the inner side of the leg above the ankle. Treatment calls for prolonged bed rest, warm applications, and surgical ligation and stripping of the varicose veins responsible for the ulcers. Thus, it is wise to consult a physician if varicose veins appear.

Menopause

The permanent end of a woman's menstrual cycle is called *menopause*. The duration of time it takes for the body to change over to a non-menstruating hormonal structure varies. It may be as short as a year; some women may experience menopausal signs and occasional periods for up to ten years.

The average age bracket for menopause is between 40 and 50 years of age. However, about 12 percent of women reach menopause between ages 36 and 40; 15 percent between 51 and 55; and 6 percent either earlier than 40 or later than 55. What this basically means is that menopause can normally occur anywhere between 36 and 56 years of age.

The *premenopausal period* is the period of time before frequently irregular menstruation or cessation of menstruation. The body begins to undergo changes that may go unnoticed. Ovulation may be irregular and skip menstrual cycles. The estrogen and progesterone levels may lower.

Signs that accompany the premenopausal period include increasing or lessening menstrual flow, skipped or shortened periods, and occasional irregularly timed menstruation.

The *perimenopausal period* is the onset of noticeable changes. The menstrual cycle may abruptly cease, or become unpredictable and irregular. Hormone levels of estrogen and progesterone continue to decline. Egg production becomes increasingly irregular or ceases entirely. Egg production may or may not correspond to menstrual flow. A woman can continue ovulating without having a pe-

riod, or may have periods without ovulation.

The most familiar signs of menopause occur during the perimenopausal period. These occurrences should be considered "signs" and not "symptoms" since they do not represent anything going wrong. They are not a sign of illness.

The one sign that everyone is aware of is the "hot flash." Referred to as flashes or flushes, this is a rapid increase in blood vessel dilation at the surface of the skin. The skin temperature can rise between four to eight degrees. The internal body temperature may drop with the increase of the surface temperature. A common hot flash pattern is a sudden feeling of extreme warmth, occasionally accompanied by heavy sweating, and chills following, as the internal body temperature cools. For some women, flashes occur daily; for others they may only occur once every several weeks. Some menopausal women never experience them. Many women experience flashes but are not disturbed by them.

Hot flashes at night, which produce heavy sweating and chills, are sometimes referred to as "night sweats." They may just be nighttime flashes. They can, though, lead to loss of sleep and thereby trigger fatigue, irritability, and insomnia. Problems with sleep should be discussed with your physician.

Dressing for fluctuations in body temperature may help reduce some undesirable side effects. Wear layers of clothing so when you are warm you can take off the top layer. The top layers are available, then, if you get cold later. It is commonly feared by some women that others can tell when one is experiencing a hot flash. This is rarely true; the usual physical response is a slight blush that goes unnoticed by others. Reassurance by friends can help relieve anxiety.

Other signs of menopause that may be problematic or startling when they occur include flooding. This is the sudden onset of a very heavy menstrual flow. It can occur without warning and normal amounts of menstrual protection may not be adequate. As with the hot flashes, this may never happen, or it may happen extremely infrequently, or it may be a recurrent problem. It is, however, usually only a problem in terms of hygiene and embarrassment. Flooding alone is not normally a symptom of an underlying problem. If there is no underlying disease, no surgery or treatment is required for this. If you are distressed by flooding and need reassurance, or *if it is accompanied by pain* please see a physician.

Vaginal changes that occur during menopause can include a thinning of the vaginal wall. This is normally associated with the reduction of estrogen production. The vagina will produce less lubrication and hold less moisture. The signs of this may include perceived dryness, itching, irritation from walking, and pain or discomfort during intercourse. Because the loss of lubrication may be the underlying cause, using douches and feminine hygiene sprays are not recommended. A water-based lubricant, such as K-Y Jelly™, is recommended for discomfort, particularly with intercourse. You should avoid oil-based lubricants, such as Vaseline™, as they are more difficult for the body to absorb and may create problems with infection.

Mood swings are also commonly cited as a sign of menopause. They may accompany the hormonal swings of the early stages of menopause or they may occur later. Many women do not have noticeable mood change at all.

The change of mood may be sudden or may be slow. Depression has been noted by some women, with its passing as the body adapts to the new hormonal levels. Knowing that it is caused by hormonal changes may help some women adjust to temporary shifts in mood. Debilitating or distressing changes should always be discussed with your doctor.

The *post-menopausal period* is the rest of one's life after menopause. The menstrual cycle has ceased entirely. The production of eggs has stopped. The body's production of estrogen and progesterone is very low. The body is back to a stable, predictable physical pattern.

Hysterectomies and Hormonal Supplements

When problems arise with the reproductive organs, or the body's response to the fluctuation in hormone production, there are a few methods of alleviating the problems.

Hysterectomy, the surgical removal of the uterus, and oophorectomy, the surgical removal of the ovaries, are medical procedures done to alleviate major medical problems or remove cancerous tissue. Cancer of the uterus, ovaries, or cervix are frequently treated with removal of the cancerous and surrounding tissue. Hemorrhaging that has not responded to hormonal or other surgical techniques (such as a dilation and curettage—D&C) may be corrected with a hysterectomy.

Other problems that can be alleviated surgically are noncancerous fibroid growths, endometriosis (the uterine tissue invades other tissues), and physical impairment or deterioration of the uterus or ovaries, as is the case with collapse of the uterus through the cervix.

There are several types of hysterectomies, differing in how much of the sexual reproduction system is removed.

A *subtotal hysterectomy* is the removal of the uterus, leaving the cervix, fallopian tubes, and the ovaries in place. A *total hysterectomy* is the removal of the cervix as well as the uterus. *Oophorectomy* and *ovariectomy* are both used to describe the surgical removal of one or both of the ovaries. *Ovariohysterectomy* is the removal of the ovaries, fallopian tubes, and uterus. The quantity of tissue removed will be determined by the patient and the doctor, based on the reasons for the operation. For removal of cancerous tissue, all organs may need to be removed. For sterilization, only a subtotal hysterectomy may be necessary.

Although hysterectomies are common, they are still considered major surgery and should be approached as such, by both the doctor and the patient. Recoveries can take six weeks or longer.

A physician may prescribe estrogen and progesterone supplemental pills to reduce or eliminate some of the adverse physical reactions to menopause. Hormonal treatment may reduce or eliminate hot flashes and vaginal wall thinning and drying. It can reduce heavy menstrual bleeding. However, hormone therapy increases a woman's risk for heart disease and strokes. It is also believed to increase the risk of breast cancer. The risks and benefits should be explained by and discussed with your physician before starting any treatment.

Male Sexuality and Aging

Most men are capable of having intercourse, and fathering children, throughout their lives. Aging can reduce some physical capacity in sexual performance, but the vast majority of men remain sexually capable through old age.

Physical problems that can be encountered, however, involve testicular failure and testicular cancer.

Testicular cancer is relatively rare, affecting less than 2 percent of the adult male population with cancer. Symptom include include a noticeable lump in the the testicle, swelling, and some alteration in the consistency of the affected testicle. The symptoms may also include dull aching from the lower abdomen, groin or scrotum. Men are now recommended to do monthly physical check for lumps, as women are recommended to do self-breast exams. The reason is that testicular cancer, when caught early, has a very high survival rate. If left unchecked until the yearly physical, the cancer has a chance to spread.

Testicular failure is when the body shuts off the functions of the testes. This may be caused by hormonal deficiency and can be cured through hormonal replacement therapy. Since hormonal therapy can lead to prostate problems, it is recommended that a physician closely monitor any medication for testicular failure.

Vasectomy

Vasectomy is the sterilization of the male by cutting the vas deferens, the tubes that transport the sperm. The surgery is normally performed in the doctor's office with local anesthesia. Incisions are made on each side of the scrotum or on the center of the scrotum. The tubes are then cut, and tied or cauterized on each end.

Vasovasotomy is the surgical procedure that attempts to reconnect the vas deferens after a vasectomy. This operation is done for men wishing to reverse the surgical sterilization. Success at this procedure can vary from 30 to 75 percent, depending on the type of initial sterilization procedures, and the skill of the surgeon in reconnection of the tubes.

Drugs, Chemicals, and Alcohol

Most substances consumed in excess cause temporary problems at the least, and permanent damage to your health at the worst. One of the problems with excess is that as you age, you are able to tolerate less. Most people recognize that, as they grow older, they are less able to handle the rigors of exercise and stress. It is not expected, though, that they will tolerate less the effects of cigarettes, alcohol, and chemicals such as caffeine.

There are two basic risks that come from indulgence of these substances. One is from long-term use; the other is from individual instances of overindulgence.

- With the continued use of a substance such as nicotine over a long period of time, the cumulative effects on the body begin to take a toll. The body removes the substance less rapidly from the system. The delicate tissues of the kidneys, liver, lungs, or other vital organs may become damaged or destroyed from processing what the body basically responds to as a poison. The risk is that you will become one of those to suffer the consequences of long-term use. Some of the damage may be reversed if the habit is broken. Other effects may be permanent, risking scarred tissue, destruction of the organ, and, eventually, death.

- Binging in drinking, or taking drugs, always runs the risk of an overdose—forcing major trauma to the body and, perhaps, resulting in death. Binging on cigarettes, food, and caffeine may not result in such an immediate and dramatic response, but the short-term damage can also be substantial to the body. As you age, your body will tolerate such abuses less and less well.

Nicotine

Nicotine is thought to get into the system through the membranes of the mouth and related areas. Thus, a person who holds an unlighted cigar in his mouth may absorb nicotine.

While a little nicotine is not harmful, most steady smokers absorb too much nicotine for their own good. Lung cancer kills over 142,000 persons a year. Lung cancer only had a 13% survival rate, for living five years after diagnosis and treatment. Also, cigarette smoking is believed to be a primary cause of *emphysema* (a disease that decreases efficiency of the lungs) which kills over 15,000 persons a year. Approximately 100,000 cigarette smokers die from heart attacks each year.

In their book *Vigor for Men Over 30,* the authors, Drs. Warren R. Guild, Stuart Cowan, and Samm Baker, suggest these tips on giving up smoking:

- *Try a program of enjoyable physical activity.* They suggest that if the urge to smoke becomes overpowering, the smoker should take a brisk walk, do a set of invigorating exercises at home or in the office, or engage in an enjoyable sport.

- *Don't use antismoking drugs or other nostrums without a physician's advice.* Such devices may do more harm than good. Your physician is the one who can advise you on the best way to cut down on smoking, and he can help you cope with any withdrawal symptoms such as nervousness, dizziness, or insomnia.

- *Don't try to cut down on too many things at the same time.* Concentrate on cutting down on your smoking, and relax about cutting down on diet and drinking, too. One reduction at a time is best.

- *You've got to quit completely.* Like the alcoholic, you've got to say, "This is my *last* cigarette"—and mean it.

- *Quit when there's a major break in your routine.* The recovery from an operation or illness is a good time to stop. After you have established the habit of *not* smoking, make that habit a part of your daily life.

- *Try something different to throw desire off the track.* Take a shower—you can't light a match under water. Also, you can't hold a cigarette if you're playing table tennis or practicing your golf swing.

Caffeine

Laboratory studies show that caffeine appears to work on the central nervous system: fatigue and drowsiness fade while mental activities quicken. But too much caffeine can produce headaches, irritability, and confusion.

Although tea leaves contain almost twice as much caffeine as an equal weight of coffee, smaller amounts of tea are used to make a cup of tea, thus lessening the per-cup intake rate. Cola and chocolate also contain caffeine. Although these drinks are not addictive, abstaining from them is no easy matter, as anyone who has tried to give up coffee drinking can attest.

Ordinarily, drinking a few cups of coffee or other caffeine beverage is not harmful—unless your physician tells you to cut down. But if you find that you need a caffeine beverage to keep going, you might be better off taking a rest instead.

Alcohol

Many physicians feel that a person's capacity to handle liquor diminishes after age 40, and that alcohol intake should be cut down after this age.

Also, some people seem to develop an allergic reaction to alcohol—an allergy that can be fatal. One physician described the extra dry martini as "the quick blow to the back of the neck."

Drinking too much and too fast can jar the whole system. It tends to make the drinker nervous and on edge instead of providing calming relief from tensions. The hard-pressed executive is especially vulnerable to the quick, fast drink he takes to provide instant relaxation when he is fatigued.

"The key to the real value of alcohol is intelligent drinking," says Dr. Harry J. Johnson, of the Life Extension Institute. Dr. Johnson says that he sometimes recommends a drink or two before dinner, which he says is the best time to indulge. However, Dr. Johnson suggests a tall, well-diluted highball taken in a peaceful, quiet setting.

How to Avoid Drinking

If you find that drinking is a problem at business luncheons, conventions, and cocktail parties, Dr. Warren R. Guild recommends the following commonsense ways to pass up drinks:

- Say "no thanks" if you do not like the taste or effect of alcohol. Order a juice or nonalcoholic beverage just to have something to sip. Actually, many more jobs and clients have been lost through drinking too much than by not drinking at all.

- Wait for others to order drinks. If someone else refuses a drink, you can decline too. Or, you could say, "I'm not having one but you go ahead." This usually sets the pace for drinking.

- Instead of a powerhouse martini, try vermouth on the rocks, beer, wine, or a well-diluted highball.

- Use dieting as a reason to cut down or out on drinking. You have a good excuse—a drink has 100 or more calories.

- Make arrangements with your favorite restaurant or bar to serve you "your usual." You could make this a nonalcoholic drink.

Remember that alcohol definitely decreases your ability to concentrate, absorb, or produce thoughts or ideas. After drinking you will not be as efficient at writing, drawing, handling objects, or driving. If the level of alcohol in your blood exceeds 0.05 percent—which, depending on weight, is approximately the equivalent of two ounces of hard liquor or two bottles of beer at one session—*you are not a safe driver.*

Treating a Hangover

What if you do drink too much and have a hangover? Is there anything you can do about it? Dr. Harold T. Hyman, formerly of the Columbia University College of Physicians and Surgeons, recommends calling a physician if the case is particularly bad. You should keep in mind that alcohol is toxic, and can be deadly in large quantities. It is not unheard of to have people die of alcohol poisoning, when they have ingested too much alcohol in one evening. Blacking out, passing out, and vomiting are all signs of severe overindulgence and should not be treated lightly.

Less acute sufferers should, on awakening after a binge, take warmed fluids (tea, consommé, clam broth). As soon as your stomach feels in shape, eat warm, soft foods at frequent intervals—poached egg, milk toast, pureed soup, mashed potatoes. Despite your craving for cold, carbonated fluids, avoid them; they may cause stomach cramps.

To prevent a hangover as you drink, Dr. Guild recommends taking *fructose.* Fructose, or *levulose,* is a crystalline sugar, the sweetest of the sugars. It increases the rate at which the body metabolizes and eliminates alcohol. It seems to work best when the alcohol is combined with something naturally high in fructose, as the tomato juice in a Bloody Mary, for example. Or just sip tomato juice between drinks.

Looking for quick panaceas in the medicine cabinet to cure a hangover or any other condition seems to become increasingly popular after age 40. Panaceas are all right up to a point, but indiscriminate self-treatment can do a great deal of harm, because it may mask a more serious illness or may prevent a condition from clearing up if left alone. In drinking, as in eating, the key is moderation.

Proper diet

Proper diet is an important contribution an individual can make to his good health, because foods build body tissues and provide energy for the body to work. Adequate diet planning is not difficult. The basic rules of good nutrition must be learned. See Ch. 27, *Nutrition and Weight Control,* for a full treatment of diet and nutrition. Applying these rules to a daily diet will take only a few minutes of planning when the menu is decided upon, and will reap enormous rewards in good health and appearance. The hardest part of planning a balanced diet is to avoid selecting food solely on the basis of taste or convenience and ignoring nutritional value.

Vitamins

Eating a proper, balanced diet will fulfill vitamin and other nutritional requirements. Therefore, there is no need for a healthy person who eats nutritious foods to take vitamin pills. Vitamins and other food supplements should be taken only on the advice of a physician or dentist. If a person decides he is deficient in some dietary element and purchases a patent medicine to treat the problem, he may only make it worse. It is rare to find someone deficient in only one element, and by trying to treat himself, he may delay seeking the advice of a physician.

Breakfast

Many Americans neglect breakfast, an important contribution to good diet. Studies prove that men, women, and children need an adequate breakfast. A good breakfast can provide a start in obtaining the day's vitamin and mineral requirements. It is also a help to dieters and those trying to maintain a stable weight, since those who have eaten a good breakfast are able to avoid mid-morning snacks such as sweet rolls, cakes, and the like, which are usually high in carbohydrates and calories.

Weight and Health

Overweight is one of the biggest deterrents to successful middle age, and is also one of the greatest threats to health and longevity. As one physician said, "Consider how few really obese persons you see over 60 years of age." Unfortunately, in middle age most of us maintain the eating habits of our youth while we cut down on our exercise. The result: added weight that acts as a deterrent to our physical well-being.

The overweight person is more likely to develop arthritis, diabetes, heart disease, high blood pressure, kidney trouble, and many other disabling or fatal disorders.

As reported in *Nation's Business,* "If you are overweight by 10 percent, your chances of surviving the next 20 years are 15 percent less than if you had ideal weight; if you are 20 percent overweight, your chances are 25 percent less; if you are 30 percent overweight, 45 percent less." In other words, the odds are against the overweight.

If you do not know what your ideal weight should be, a physician can tell you. To check yourself, try the "pinch" test. Take a pinch of skin on your upper arm just below the shoulder. If more than a half-inch separates your fingers, you are too fat. Try the same test on your stomach when you're standing erect. And, of course, your mirror can reveal the tell-tale signs of middle-age fat—the double chin, sagging belly, flabby arms and legs.

Good Eating Habits

Is there any magic way to reduce? The only sure way is to *eat less,* and to continue this practice all the time. It will not help if you go on a crash diet and then resume your normal eating habits. And while exercise will help control weight and burn up excess calories, probably the best exercise is to push yourself away from the table before you've overeaten.

Calories do count, and usually the caloric intake of a person in the 40- to 55-year age bracket should be about one-third less than that of a person between ages 25 and 40. Again, your physician or a good calorie-counter can help you determine what to eat and how much.

Here are some additional tips from nutritionists to help you lose weight:

- *Cut down on quantity.* Eat just enough to satisfy your appetite—not as much as you can. Even low-calorie foods will add weight if you eat enough of them.

- *Eat less more often.* Spread your food intake over several meals or snacks. Some hospitals have been experimenting with five meals a day, spreading the recommended total food intake over two full meals a day (brunch and dinner) and three snacks (continental breakfast, afternoon snack, and evening). They find that the stomach handles small amounts of food better, that metabolism keeps working at a good pace all day, and that blood sugar levels (your energy reserve) do not drop between meals.

- *Avoid high-calorie foods.* Cut out breads, rolls, jellies, jams, sauces, gravies, dressings, creams, and rich desserts. These are the villains that add calories and are not as rich in nutrients.

- *Look for natural flavors.* Cultivate an interest in the natural flavor of what you eat. Try vegetables without butter, coffee and tea without cream and sugar. You might want to substitute a squeeze of lemon on your vegetables or noncaloric sweeteners in your beverages.

- *Serve only just enough.* Keep portions small and put serving dishes with leftovers out of sight. Taking seconds is often just a habit. Cultivate the idea of just one serving, and you will find it satisfies the appetite. Another idea: serve meals on smaller plates. the portion will look big if only in relationship to the size of the plate.

In order to maintain a healthy body and a youthful appearance while dieting, you must make sure you eat the necessary proteins and nutrients.

This can be done by selecting foods from the four basic food groups. See Ch. 27, *Nutrition and Weight Control.*

As a panel of experts on middle age said in a recent interview: "Two factors are vital to successful middle age: physical activity and a variety of interests. Move around but don't rush around. Keep an open mind and a closed refrigerator. Remember that variety is more than the spice of life— it's the wellspring of life. The person who pursues a variety of activities will usually stay fit long after middle age."

Living Life to the Fullest

No wise man ever wished to be younger.   —JONATHAN SWIFT

Staying young is looked on by most of the rest of the world as a peculiarly American obsession. This obsession is certainly fostered and exploited by the advertising industry, but its causes have to be looked for elsewhere.

In many countries, it is the old who are venerated for their wisdom and authority. This point of view is likely to prevail in societies that stay the same or that enjoyed their greatest glories in the past.

America is another matter. Because of its history, it is literally a young country. It is also a nation built on the idea of progress and hope in the future. And to whom does the future belong if not to youth?

Keeping up with change is unfortunately identified by too many people with how they look rather than how they think or feel. To be young in heart and spirit has very little to do with wearing the latest style in clothes—no matter how unbecom-

ing—or learning the latest dances. Maintaining an open mind receptive to new ideas, keeping the capacity for pleasure in the details of daily living, refusing to be overwhelmed by essentially unimportant irritations can make the middle years more joyful for any family.

A Critical Time

Nowadays, the average American can expect to reach the age of 70. Thus, for most people, the middle years begin during the late 30s. Ideally, these are the years of personal fulfillment accompanied by a feeling of pride in accomplishment, a deeper knowledge of one's strengths and limitations, and a growing understanding and tolerance of other people's ideas and behavior.

Emotional Pressures

In many families, however, the pleasures of maturity often go hand in hand with increased pressures. It's no simple matter for the typical husband and wife in their 40s to maintain emotional health while handling worries about money, aging parents, anxiety about willful teenagers, tensions caused by marital friction, and feelings of depression about getting older. To some people, the problems of the middle years are so burdensome that instead of dealing with them realistically—by eliminating some, by compromising in the solution of others—they escape into excessive drinking or into sexual infidelity. It doesn't take much thought to realize that those escapes do nothing except introduce new problems.

Physical Symptoms of Emotional Problems

For others, deep-seated conflicts that come to a head during the middle

years may be expressed in chronic physical symptoms. Many physicians in the past intuitively understood the relationship between emotional and physical health, but it is only in recent years that medical science has proved that feelings of tension, anxiety, suppressed anger, and frustration are often the direct cause of ulcers, sexual impotence, high blood pressure, and heart attacks, not to mention sleeplessness and headaches.

Of course, there are no magic formulas that guarantee the achievement of emotional well-being at any time of life. Nor does any sensible person expect to find a perfect solution to any human problem. However, it is possible to come to grips with specific difficulties and deal with them in ways that can reduce stress and safeguard emotional health.

Sexuality during the Middle Years

In spite of the so-called sexual revolution and all its accompanying publicity, it is still very difficult for most people to sort out their attitudes towards sexual activity. It is a subject that continues to be clouded by feelings of guilt and anxiety, surrounded by taboos, and saddled with misinformation. For each individual, the subject is additionally complicated by personal concepts of love and morality.

Many people were shocked when the Kinsey reports on male and female sexual behavior appeared. More recently, militant efforts have been made in various communities to prevent the schools from including sex education in their courses of study. Yet marriage counselors, family physicians, ministers, and all other specialists in human relations can attest to the amount of human misery caused by ignorance about sex—all the way from the ignorance that results in a 15-year-old's unwanted pregnancy to the ignorance of a 50-year-old man about his wife's sexual needs.

Sexuality After Menopause

Sexual relations between partners can continue throughout the life of the marriage. There is no reason that a person cannot remain sexually active, barring medical complications, for one's entire life.

Sexual function will change with aging. It takes longer for a man to obtain an erection and it takes longer to achieve orgasm for both partners. Women may suffer from thinning and drying of the vaginal walls following menopause, but the difficulties that this may cause are easily remedied. Lubricants that are water-based (unlike petroleum jelly, which is oil-based) can be used to replace natural lubricants. If it takes longer to arouse one partner, then set aside a little more time for romance.

It may be easier for the couple to enjoy lovemaking in the morning, after a good night's rest, rather than the end of the evening when they both may be tired. Since it is likely that there will be no children in the house to interrupt, couples may find that there is a renewed interest in sex, because of a new-found freedom that comes with having grown children and having no fear of pregnancy.

There are circumstances, though, that may arrive that hinder or block sexual relations. These are discussed in brief here.

Problems with Sexual Activity

Occasional problems with sexual drive or capabilities are normal. Most people will experience some fluctuation during their lifetime. If a problem persists beyond a few weeks, or if any pain is associated with sexual intercourse, you should consult with

your doctor. Although the causes may be psychological, it is best that you do not draw this conclusion without speaking with a medical expert first. Some of the problems that may be experienced follow.

Impotence

Impotence is defined as a lack of adequate erection to complete intercourse. This can be experienced on a temporary basis because of fatigue, overindulgence in alcohol or drugs, stress, or other factors that physically affect the system. It can be experienced on a more long-term basis and still not be physiological in origin.

Some of the psychological causes for impotence include: resentment, hostility, and anger at one's spouse; stress and anxiety from any aspect of one's life; and fear of sexual inadequacy and impotence. This last point is important because the fear of impotence can bring on impotence. If one experience of impotence triggers fear, the cycle of fear and inability to perform can prolong recovery. It is important to remember that over half the cases of impotence are psychologically based and are cured once the cause is resolved.

Physiological reasons for impotence usually involve the blood flow and the nerve response to the penis. In diabetics, the combination of nerve loss and restricted blood flow can reduce sexual capacity. With some men, artery blockage restricts the flow of blood to the penis. Surgery may be able to remedy some causes of impotence. Your doctor can advise you on any specific problems you encounter.

New Treatments

Where other approaches fail, the impotent male can either undergo a test for erectability or try one of the new

treatments currently available. Conducted during sleep, the tests provide evidence indicating that impotence in any given case has physical or psychological causes. Physical causes may include such diseases as diabetes; some drugs or medication, including those used to treat high blood pressure; and alcohol abuse, hardening of the arteries, or testosterone or thyroid hormone deficiencies.

These tests have shown that physical causes underlie impotence in nearly half of all cases. As a result much research has been conducted into physical "cures." All of the tests operate on the accepted medical principle that "normal" men have approximately five erections during every sleep period. In what is called the *stamp test,* a strip of stamps is wrapped around the penis before the subject retires for the night. Fitted snugly around the shaft of the penis, the strip tears along one of the perforated edges if the subject experiences an erection while sleeping.

Two other tests are more reliable. In one, a *snap gauge band* made of elastic fabric and Velcro is wrapped around the penis; the band has three snaps designed to open at various stages of penile rigidity. A third test utilizes a *Nocturnal Penile Tumescence Monitor* to tell exactly when erections occur, with what rigidity, and for how long. Two circular elastic silicone bands are attached to the penis; sensor wires connect the bands to an apparatus like an electrocardiograph machine.

Of the prosthetic devices used to "cure" impotence, three can be implanted in the penis in operations that take one to three hours under local anesthetic. The simplest utilizes two semirigid rods that keep the penis permanently erect. A second implanted type, made of flexible, plastic-covered metal wire, also maintains the penis in a constantly erect state but can be bent into an erect or downward position. A third type works hydraulically to pump the penis into a naturally erect state. Two expandable metal tubes implanted in the penis function with an attached tiny pump in the scrotum and a water reservoir placed behind the muscles of the lower abdomen. Pressure on the pump causes the penis to erect; valves make possible penile relaxation.

Disinterest

Disinterest, which was referred to as frigidity in women, can be experienced by both women and men. It may be traced to hostility or resentment toward the partner, lack of adequate satisfaction during intercourse, other psychological impediments, or physical problems. Some medications can reduce libido; depression may also reduce the sex drive. Consult with your physician to

eliminate physical reasons, and follow up with therapy if no physical ailments are suspected.

Self-Image Problems

If you do not believe yourself to be physically appealing, it is likely that you will regard a partner with suspicion and hostility if he or she finds you physically appealing. You may be willing to perceive insult and ill-intent where none is meant if you do not believe yourself to be a desirable partner.

Self-image is one of the most important aspects of sexuality. The belief that one is too old, too fat, too thin, too wrinkly, too whatever can be a huge obstacle to a satisfying life. Self-image is estimated to be a problem for half of the male population and the majority of the female population. One cannot change the view others have of beauty, but one can improve a

self-image. This may require counseling, but is worth it in the long-run, since the ability to be happy rests with the ability to be happy with oneself.

Sexual Activity and Disability

Disabilities, whether the result of genetics, disease, accident, or aging, need not be a complete barrier to sexual satisfaction. Most disabilities allow some form of sexual gratification and with an understanding partner, this can be worked out. Counseling and training may be needed to develop the emotional support and understanding necessary to achieve a fulfilling relationship with your partner, but if both are willing participants in the learning process, this can be achieved. Talk with your physician or a therapist specializing in disabilities about your situation. If they cannot provide guidance, they should be able to direct you to someone who can.

Coping With Retirement

For more people, retirement makes up several years of their lives. As the average age of men and women extend into the seventies, the number of years one spends in retirement increases. These years can be spent with a fulfilling and exciting lifestyle, or they can pass slowly, with little to look forward to. It is important that people consider their retirement before they get to it. If they have not done so and find themselves at retirement age, it is important that they set goals and prioritize how they want the days to be spent.

Preparation for Retirement

The single biggest concern to most retirees is finance. With Social Security under constant scrutiny by the government, it is important that everyone consider what money they have coming in from sources other than the Social Security program.

Start planning for your retirement by figuring out *exactly* what money you will have coming in, and when, for your retirement. Questions you will need to investigate include:

- What are you and your spouse's pension benefits from work?
- How are these benefits affected by the death of the spouse, before and after retirement age?
- What are you scheduled to receive from Social Security?
- What are your savings and other benefits worth?
- What other sources of income will be available to you after retirement?

You should fill in the *Request for Earnings and Benefit Statement* form SSA-7004 every three years to insure that the government records of your earnings are accurate. They are only obliged to correct your records for the previous three years. This also keeps you informed of what you are entitled to for your income credits. The form is available through all Social Security offices.

You should also be aware that the age of retirement for Social Security is no longer strictly held at 65 years of age. For people born between 1954 and 1960, the age is 66. For those born in 1960 and after, the age is 67. There is a reduction of payments related to your age, if you retire early.

Once you have figured out what money you have coming in, you need to do a budget for what you will be spending after retirement. This is tricky since inflation and property-cost fluctuations can be hard to predict. However, it is better to guess than to just ignore this step.

You need to figure out basic expenses, and then extra expenses and perks. If you would love to sail around the world, don't just assume you can't do it. Calculate it into your retirement needs and see if you can save enough now with investments to allow for your dreams.

Basic expenses should include as a minimum:

- Property and income taxes
- House repairs, rent, and other living quarter expenses
- Medical insurance and expenses
- Food, clothing, and day-to-day purchases
- Expenses remaining for children (college, etc.)
- Emergency income for nursing homes, catastrophic illness or other incapacitating problems
- General entertainment and activity costs

Once these are down on paper, discuss what your goals and ambitions are for the years ahead. Budget in

those expenses. Some possibilities include, but certainly are not limited to:

- returning to school
- traveling
- pursuing a hobby
- moving to another climate
- starting another career or business

Assume that you will live to at least 95. This way you likely to have enough for the majority of your retirement. You are better off overpredicting, rather than underpredicting, your age at death.

Calculate your expenses for the total of the thirty years. You can set inflation at 5% or higher, or use a guide to retirement earnings. Then figure out what you will have as income when you retire. If you have enough saved, and enough pension to provide for all your needs, then you are set for retirement. If not, you need to calculate what you have still to save.

There are several guides available for a more exact method of predicting costs and savings. The American Association of Retired Persons (AARP) can guide you to sources. Their address is: 601 E Street, NW, Washington DC, 20049; phone (202) 434-2277.

When to Retire

Once you have figured out your financial needs and earnings for retirement, you can estimate how many years you have saved for, and how many years you still need to work to gain enough income to provide for retirement. If you can afford early retirement, and you have activities that would fulfill you, it should be considered as an option. If you find that you have to continue working beyond the time you had assumed for retirement, you may be able to manage with less hours or a job with less pressure without influencing your pension.

Beyond Retirement

Once you have the finances figured out for your retirement (or if you have retired), you need to figure out how you are going to spend your time. These years can be the most rewarding and exciting of your life. There are literally hundreds of ways for you to spend your time. If you are thoughtful about your retirement planning, you may find that you still don't have enough time in the day to do everything that you want.

Volunteer Work

Volunteer work can be one of the most rewarding ways to spend your time. Depending on your community, there will be a variety of places that are happy to train and utilize volunteers in different positions. Depending on your personal needs, volunteer positions can range from basic tasks—such as greeting visitors, assisting patients in reading, or escorting people—to jobs that resemble working positions, such as accounting, staff management, and teaching. You can select what you want to do with the level of effort you are interested in putting in. You can do more than one volunteer position to fill different needs. You may want to work one or two days with children, and then take on a more pressured, or less pressured, position elsewhere for another day of activity. You should research and ask around about the organizations that take volunteers. Most arts organizations, museums, zoos, hospitals, schools, day care centers, and nonprofit organizations rely on their volunteers for many jobs.

Community Activism

You may be interested in pursuing your volunteer work in another arena entirely. Political and social activism is based on volunteer support. That support is both financial- and assistance-based. You are in a position, once you retire, to take your expertise to an organization that fights for the positions you support and believe in. If no organization exists in the area you want to dedicate your time, then start one. Chances are good that if you are interested in something, others are out there who are also interested. This resolves two potential problems in retirement: activity and social contact. you will meet people with similar interests by participating in community organizations.

Home Management

Once you have retired, you will probably be spending a few more hours, at least, in your home. This is when the dripping faucet, the faded carpet, and the stained walls will become more annoying. Do not take on more repair work than you can do physically or afford financially. Plan repairs and redecorating to accommodate your time and your budget. Overhauling your home may be a goal, but it should be planned as such and not decided on one afternoon. The stress of remodeling and renovating should be taken into account with your physical health.

Leaving the Children and Children Leaving

One of the major turning points in many lives is when the children grow up and leave the house. Children will usually move out of their parents houses, for at least part of the year, between the ages of 18 and 21. The majority of children are permanently out of the house by the time they are 22.

For many families, this shift from being a full-time caregiver to a child to a parent of independent adults is a difficult one. Regardless of the continued contact through visits and calls, the separation of living space may be difficult for the parent to adjust to. It may also be difficult for the child to adjust to; transition to adulthood can be rocky.

Once the children are off on their own, the parent may find him- or herself with a sense of loss, lack of purpose, or anxiety. All of this may be attributed to the last child moving out, or it may be to a combination of events, such as a child leaving and a sixtieth birthday. If you or your spouse experience any prolonged or severe bouts of depression, it is important to consult with a therapist, even if you are sure you recognize the source of the depression. Recovering from the depression is what you should be working toward.

Many parents, however, find the empty home an enjoyable change. After adapting to the new patterns of living without children, they find that the respite from caring for others can be exhilarating. For some parents, this may be the first time in two decades where their days are completely their own to decide. It provides the opportunity to put oneself first. Although there may be some residual guilt about self-indulgence, it should pass quickly. This is the opportunity to nurture and care for yourself and your spouse as you have cared for your children. And, as any parent will attest, your children will continue to provide you with parenting concerns for the rest of your life.

The biggest consideration you should focus on during this transition is your emotional and mental state. As with any major life change, the period of transition will create stress, mood changes, and susceptibility to depression. If you experience any of the warning signs of depression (suicidal or violent thoughts, inertia, or chronic insomnia are some of the signs), please contact your physician or therapist.

Separation and Divorce

Marriage in this country is based on the highly personal concept of love rather than on such traditional foundations as a property merger between two families or an arrangement determined by the friendship of the young people's parents. It is often assumed, therefore, that if mutual love is the basis for embarking on a marriage, its absence is a valid reason for dissolving it, either by legal separation or divorce.

The idea of divorce is not particularly modern; in practically every time and place where a form of marriage has existed, so has some form of divorce, with reasons ranging from excessive wife-beating to failure to deliver a piece of land mentioned in the marriage contract.

The High Rate of Divorce

What is new is the high rate of divorce. Figures now indicate that in the United States as a whole, approximately one in every four marriages is terminated by legal arrangement. However, these figures by no means indicate that the family as an institution is on the way out, because a constantly increasing number of people who get divorced get married again.

There are many reasons for the growing rate of separation and divorce:

- Over the last 50 years, a continually increasing percentage of the population has been getting married.

- Although the trend toward earlier marriages has leveled off in recent years, a significant number of people still marry at earlier ages than was common in the past. (The number of divorces is highest among the poorly educated group who marry under the age of 21.)

- The legal requirements for separation and divorce are less rigid than formerly.

- With increasing independence and earning capacity, women are less frightened of the prospect of heading a family.

- The poorer groups in the population, in which desertion was a common practice, are more often obtaining divorces.

Contrary to popular belief, there are more divorces among the poor than among the rich, and more among the less well-educated than among the educated. Also, most divorces occur before the fifth year of marriage.

Telling the Truth to Children

Most people with children who are contemplating a breakup of their marriage generally make every effort to seek professional guidance that might help them iron out their differences. When these efforts fail and steps are taken to arrange for a separation or divorce, it is far healthier for parents to be honest with each other and with their children than to construct elaborate explanations based on lies.

A teenager who is given the real reason for a divorce is less likely to have something to brood about than

one who is told lies that he can see through. If the real reason for a divorce is that the parents have tried their best to get along with each other but find it impossible, the child who is in his teens or older can certainly understand this. If the marriage is coming to an end because the husband or wife wants to marry someone else, the explanation to the child should avoid assigning blame. When the rejected parent tries to enlist the child's sympathy by blackening the character of the parent who is supposedly the cause of the divorce, results are almost always unpleasant. Under no circumstances and no matter what his age should a child be called on to take the side of either parent or to act as a judge.

Nor should children be told any more about the circumstances of the breakup of a marriage than they really want to know. Young people have a healthy way of protecting themselves from information they would find hurtful, and if they ask few questions, they need be told only the facts they are prepared to cope with. Of course, as they grow older and live through their own problems, they will form their own view of what really happened between their parents.

After the Separation

Traditionally, in separation and divorce proceedings, the children have remained in the custody of the mother, with financial support arrangements and visiting rights spelled out for the father. Although an increasing number of fathers have been awarded custody of their children in recent years, it is still commonly the mother who must face the problems of single parenthood after divorce. Although teenage children may need some extra attention for a while, there is no need for a mother to make

a martyr of herself, nor should she feel guilty when she begins to consider remarrying.

The father should be completely reliable in his visiting arrangements, and if he has remarried, should try to establish good relationships between the offspring of his former marriage and his new family.

Losing a Spouse

As you and your spouse get older, you should begin to prepare for the fact that one of you will probably survive the other. This can be the most difficult challenge you face. Having a spouse or a child die can be the most strenuous and difficult parts of life. It can occur at any time during adulthood. Widows and widowers are not just people in their 70s and 80s. One can lose a spouse at 21 or 41 and experience the same sense of loss and confusion.

Depending on the preparations made before the spouse dies, the concerns of the surviving spouse may range from mourning and adjusting to single life to attempting to arrange financial support, dividing inheritance, and struggling to sort through all the legal and financial matters that may be left by the deceased.

Preparing a will is one of the things you can do in preparation for your own and your spouse's death. You cannot assume that everything will be easily handled if you die and your spouse is surviving. Wills provide some legal assistance to the surviving spouse to sort through finances during the difficult times that follow the spouse's death.

It is important for anyone, of any age, to maintain a strong support group of friends and family. Without this, any change in one's life will be confronted alone. With a strong group of supporters, almost any tragedy can be weathered. Meeting people and making friends can be a difficult thing to do. By joining clubs, support groups, and organizations, you are reaching out to people with similar backgrounds or interests. It is likely that you will be able to establish some contacts through such activities. You and your spouse may wish to pursue this together, or you may each seek out friends of your own interest. If you have relocated or do not, for whatever reason, have a circle of friends you can turn to, it is important to establish one. It makes the transition to widowhood easier if your support group is in place.

If you have already lost a spouse and have not prepared for it, you can still seek out a support group in your community. This may be found in churches and synagogues, community centers, and in local organizations. As explained before, it is important to watch for any warning signs of serious depression and seek professional counseling immediately if any are experienced.

Loss of a Parent

The loss of a parent may affect your family when you or your partner lose a parent, or when you lose a spouse and your children have lost a parent.

It is important to work through the mourning period. Some people respond to death by attempting to plow through the time, as if unscathed by the event. Others shut down entirely and refuse consolation or assistance in coping. Neither response may be in the best interest of the mourner.

Coping with death is a personal experience. Each individual will respond uniquely to a loss of a family member. And each individual may respond differently to different losses. Mourning one's parent will be different than mourning one's spouse. It is important for everyone to remember this when adjusting to a death in the family.

The mourning period can range from several days to several months. There is no correct period of time to spend in mourning. If you are not comfortable with the amount of time you are taking to get over the loss, then feel free to speak to someone about it. But there is no rule of thumb for how long you should spend mourning.

Any inability to function through day-to-day activities, such as eating, sleeping, bathing, grocery shopping, or other mundane events, should be taken as a sign of serious depression and not part of general mourning. You may not feel like socializing, but you should still have the energy to take good hygienic care of yourself. As always, any behavior that is threatening to life and health should be referred to professional counseling immediately. You should watch for such signs in yourself, your parents and your children after experiencing any family member's death.

6

The Later Years

Aging and What To Do About It

Growing older could mean growing healthier. In many ways you are as old as you think and feel. Consider these points:

- No disease results just from the passage of years.

- We age piecemeal—each organ separately rather than uniformly.

- In retirement you have less daily stress and strain, and you have more time to take care of yourself.

What, then, makes a person think and feel old?

The Aging Process

Physically, we mature at about 25 to 30, when the body reaches maximum size and strength. Then, body tissues and cells are constantly being rebuilt and renewed. Nutrition, rest, exercise, and stress influence the length of time that the body can maintain a balance between the wearing down and rebuilding of body tissues. When more cells die than can be reproduced, they are replaced by a fibrous, inert substance called *colagen*. The living process slows down to compensate, and we begin aging; strength and ability start to decline.

But this happens at various intervals. For instance, vision is sharpest at age 25; the eye loses its ability to make rapid adjustments in focus after age 40. Hearing is sharpest at about age 10, then diminishes as you grow older. Sensitivity to taste and smell lessens after age 60.

The decline in strength and muscle ability is long and gradual; there are even gratifying plateaus. At age 50, a man still has about four-fifths of the muscle strength he had when he was 25.

Although physical abilities may decline, mental abilities may actually improve during the middle years, and memory and the ability to learn can remain keen. Dr. Alfred Schwartz, dean of education at Drake University, was asked: "Can a 70-year-old man in reasonably good health learn as rapidly as a 17- year-old boy?" Dr. Schwartz answered:

Indeed he can—provided he's in the habit of learning. The fact that some older people today are not active intellectually is no reflection on their ability to learn. There is ample proof that learning ability does not automatically decline with age.

Regardless of what you may have heard, organic brain damage affects less than one percent of those over age 65.

But in thinking about physical change, remember that this is just one aspect of aging. Age is determined by emotional and intellectual maturity as well as by chronological years.

Can a person do anything to retard aging?

Most *gerontologists* feel that the reason more people don't live longer is that they are not willing to follow a regimen of diet, exercise, rest, recreation—coupled with the exclusion of various excesses. And while there isn't anything you can do to set back the clock, you can keep in good health by making sure to have regular physical examinations, sufficient exercise, adequate rest, nutritious food, and a positive mental attitude.

A Positive Mental Attitude

Mark Twain once said: "Whatever a

man's age he can reduce it several years by putting a bright-colored flower in his buttonhole." A lively, fresh outlook is essential for enjoyable living at any age. Most physicians believe there is a direct connection between one's state of mind and physical health. This is especially true when you are faced with the challenges of retirement. Plato said: "He who is of a calm and happy nature will hardly feel the pressure of age, but to him who is of an opposite disposition, youth and age are equally a burden."

Experts in the field of aging have found that most older people can relieve transitory depression by a deliberate shift of thought or by physical activity. If you look upon retirement as an opportunity to take better care of yourself and to pursue old and new interests, you'll go a long way toward better health.

The Annual Checkup

For peace of mind and to maintain and improve your health, make it a habit to see your physician at least once a year. To remind themselves, many people make an appointment on their birthday. An annual checkup is especially important in later years and should not be put off or neglected.

During a routine checkup, the physician pays special attention to enlarged lymph nodes of the neck, armpits, and groin, and the front of the neck. He also checks the condition of veins and arteries and looks at your knees and arches—which are of particular importance to older people.

He makes tests for arteriosclerosis, high blood pressure, diabetes, brain tumors, and other diseases. He can feel and tap your body to check your lungs, liver, and spleen, and he can take electrocardiographs to detect changes in your heart. Simple tests can note bladder and kidney conditions.

In addition, the physician usually asks about personal habits—smoking, drinking, eating. He also wants to know about any unusual symptoms you might have. Be completely frank with your physician, answer his questions as directly as possible, and give all information that might be helpful.

When explaining the nature of your ailment or symptom, tell him what part of the body is involved, what changes are associated with the symptoms, and whether symptoms occurred after a change of diet or medicine. Tell him about any previous experiences with this condition and what treatments you might have had.

It is extremely important to tell your physician about any pills you are taking—including aspirin, tranquilizers, and sleeping tablets. Even the most common drug can affect the potency of medication he might prescribe.

After he has taken your case history and after he has all the reports from your tests, the physician will want to talk with you, explain his findings, and perhaps make some recommendations. Take his advice; don't try to be your own physician.

If you have questions, don't be afraid to ask them. Have him explain the nature of your ailment, how long it may take for relief or cure, how the therapy or medication is expected to work, and the possible impact on your everyday activities.

Hopefully, by following his advice you'll stay healthy and well. However, if you are at home and feel ill, call your physician if:

- Your symptoms are so severe you can't endure them.

- Apparent minor symptoms persist without explainable cause.

- You are in doubt.

For more information, see "The Physical Examination" in Ch. 26, *Physicians and Diagnostic Procedures.*

Oral Health

It is especially important in later years to have regular dental checkups. After age 50, over half of the American people have some form of *periodontal disease*, and at age 65 nearly all persons have this disease.

Brushing teeth and gums regularly is a defense against periodontal disease. Use dental floss to remove all food particles and plaque from areas between the teeth, especially after each meal. See "Periodontal Disease" in Ch. 22, *The Teeth and Gums*, for more information on this subject.

Dentures

If you do lose some teeth, they should be replaced with bridges or partial or full dentures, because the cheeks and lips will otherwise sag and wrinkle and make you look older than you really are. Chewing ability and the clarity of speech are also impaired if missing teeth are not replaced. See "Dentures" in Ch. 22, *The Teeth and Gums.*

Diet and Health

Just what are your food requirements as you grow older? Basically you need the same essential nutrients that you have always needed, except that you face special problems. You need to:

- Select food more carefully to eat adequate proteins, vitamins, and minerals—while cutting down on calories.

- Get the most nutritious food for the least money and make the most of what you buy.

- Avoid bad eating habits—make mealtime a pleasure rather than a chore.

- Learn new techniques to stretch meals, use leftovers, and substitute lower-priced items with the same nutritional value for higher-priced foods. In other words, learn how to shop well.

Basic Requirements

How can you get the essential nutrients every day? A good rule is first to eat recommended servings from the Basic Four Food Groups (see below) established by the National Research Council. Then, eat other foods that you like, as long as they do not go over the recommended daily caloric intake. The average man in the 55-to-75-year age group should consume 2,200 calories a day; the average woman in the same age group, 1,600 calories a day. This is a drop of between 500 and 600 calories a day from what was needed at age 25. As you grow older, your physical activity decreases and your metabolism slows, causing body fats to build up at a much higher rate and making you more prone to hardening of the arteries and certain heart conditions.

Here are the Basic Four Food Groups:

Meat Group

Two or more servings from this group of foods are recommended daily. A serving is two to three ounces of cooked meat, fish, or poultry; two eggs; occasionally one cup of cooked dry beans or peas; one-half cup peanut butter; or one cup cottage cheese.

Dairy Foods

Dairy food requirements may be satisfied by two cups of milk or its equivalent in cheese, ice cream, etc. A one and one-third ounce slice of cheddar-type cheese or one scant pint of ice cream is equivalent to one cup of milk. Imitation ice cream or ice milk where vegetable fat has been substituted for butterfat has just as much protein.

Vegetables and Fruit

The daily vegetable and fruit requirement consists of four or more servings. A serving is one-half cup. Include one serving of citrus fruit each day and dark green or deep yellow vegetables every other day.

Bread and Cereal Group

Each day have four or more servings of whole grain, enriched, or restored products such as breads, cereals, rice, hominy grits, noodles, or macaroni. One serving is a slice of bread; one-half to three-fourths cup cooked cereal, pasta, or rice; one medium potato.

Use other foods such as sweets, baked goods, or desserts to complete meals and treat the sweet tooth. But remember to count calories. Nutritionists have found that skinny animals live longer than fat ones, and this seems to be true of people, too.

Beware of food fads and so-called health foods unless these are recommended by your physician. Also, do not buy vitamins and mineral tablets unless prescribed. When you obtain vitamins from food, your body uses the amount necessary to maintain proper health, appetite, and resistance to infection. Your body promptly eliminates excesses of vitamin C and the B complex, and stores an excess of vitamins A and D in your liver and other body organs. It may take up to seven years of practically complete deprivation for a previously healthy adult to show signs of a vitamin deficiency.

Some older people may go on low-fat diets because of fear of cholesterol caused by talk and advertisements for unsaturated fats. Get a physician's recommendation before curtailing your fat intake—too little fat and dairy products can be as harmful as too much.

Also, unless prescribed, do not take iron tonics or pills. Usually you'll get adequate iron intake if you eat meat, eggs, vegetables, and enriched cereals regularly. Adding more iron to a normal diet may even be harmful.

Eating Habits

If you find that mealtime is a chore rather than a pleasure, try these tips to enhance your meals:

- Try a two-meal-a-day schedule. Have a late breakfast and early dinner when you are really hungry. But be sure to get your Basic Four requirements in these two meals.

- Drink a glass of water as soon as you wake up to promote good digestion, weight control, and bowel movements.

- Try a walk or light exercise to stimulate appetite and to regulate body processes. Moderate exercise also will help regulate weight because it burns up calories.

- You might sip glass of wine before dinner. Recent research shows wine is very useful to older people in improving appetite and digestion. Port, a light sherry, and vermouth with a dash of soda are good appetite stimulators.

- Make meals interesting by including some food of distinctive flavor to contrast with a mild-flavored food; something crisp for contrast with softer foods, even if it is only a pickle or a lettuce leaf; some brightly colored food for eye appeal.

- Pep up your food with a judicious use of herbs and spices or flavor-enhancers like wine, bottled sauces, fruit juices, and peels.

- If some food causes you distress, eliminate it and substitute something else of equal nutritive value. Green salad may include too much roughage for the intestinal tract; ham or bacon may be supplying your body with too much salt, which increases water retention. Or you may be drinking too much coffee, tea, or soft drinks.

- Be realistic about your chewing ability. Food swallowed whole may be causing digestive problems. If your teeth are not as good as they were or if you are wearing dentures, try cubing, chopping, or grinding foods that are difficult to chew. Let your knife or meat grinder do part of the work.

- Try a different atmosphere or different setting for your meals. Use candlelight, music, and your best linen on occasion. Move outdoors when the weather is good; eat your lunch in the park and dinner on the patio.

- Occasionally invite a friend or relative to dine with you. It's surprising what stimulating conversation and an exchange of ideas can do to boost your mood and appetite.

- Try a new recipe or a new food. Thanks to modern transportation, foods are available in larger cities from many areas and other countries. Eat eggplant or okra, avocado or artichoke, gooseberry jam, or garbanzo beans in a salad. And why not have a papaya with lemon juice for breakfast?

Cooking Hints

Try these ideas for preparing food more easily; they are especially useful if you have only a single gas or electric burner:

- Combine your vegetables and meat—or some other protein food—in a single pot or pan. You can cook many hot, nourishing meals of this kind: Irish stew, braised liver or pot roast with vegetables, ham-and-vegetable chowder or fish chowder, a New England boiled dinner.

- Combine leftovers to make a one-dish meal. Leftover meat combines beautifully with vegetables, macaroni, or rice. Add a cheese or tomato sauce or a simple white sauce and heat in a baking dish. Chopped tomatoes or green onions or chives will give extra flavor and color to the dish.

- Round out one-dish meals with a crisp salad topped with cut strips of leftover cooked meat or poultry or another raw food, bread, a beverage, and perhaps a dessert.

- Mix leftover cooked vegetables with raw fresh ones, such as chopped celery, cucumber slices, tomatoes, green pepper, shredded cabbage, to make an interesting salad.

- Cream vegetables, meat, fish, or chicken. Or serve them with a tasty sauce. Use canned tomato or mushroom soup for a quick and easy sauce. If the dish is a bit skimpy, a hard-boiled egg may stretch it to serving size.

- Add a bit of relish, snappy cheese, or diced cucumber to a cooked dressing for meat or vegetable salad.

- If you cook a potato, an ear of corn, or some other vegetable in the bottom of a double boiler, you can use the top to warm rolls, heat leftover meat in gravy, or heat such foods as creamed eggs or fish.

The Value of Exercise

As you grow older, exercise can help you look, feel, and work better. Various organs and systems of the body, particularly the digestive process, are stimulated through activity, and, as a result, work more effectively.

You can improve your posture through exercise that tones supporting muscles. This not only improves appearance but can decrease the frequency of lower-back pain and disability.

Here are some other benefits of exercise: it can increase your ability to relax and tolerate fatigue; it improves muscle tone; reduces fat deposits; increases working capacity of the lungs; improves kidney and liver functions; increases volume of blood, hemoglobin, and red blood cells, leading to improved utilization of oxygen and iron.

Also, physically active people are less likely to experience a heart attack or other forms of cardiovascular disease than sedentary people. Moreover, an active person who does suffer a coronary attack will probably have a less severe form. The Public Health Service studied 5,000 adults in Framingham, Mass., for more than a decade. When any member of the group suffered a heart attack, his physical activity was reviewed. It was found that more inactive people suffered more fatal heart attacks than active members.

Walking for Exercise

Exercise need not be something you *must* do but rather something you *enjoy* doing. One of the most practical and enjoyable exercises is walking. Charles Dickens said:

Walk and be happy, walk and be healthy. The best of all ways to lengthen our days is to walk, steadily and with a purpose. The wandering man knows of certain ancients, far gone in years, who have staved off infirmities and dissolution by earnest walking—hale fellows close upon eighty and ninety, but brisk as boys.

The benefits of walking were revealed in a recent Health Insurance Plan study of 110,000 people in New York City. Those who had heart attacks were divided into two groups— walkers and nonwalkers. The first four weeks of illness were reviewed for both groups. At the end of the time 41 percent of the nonwalkers were dead, while only 23 percent of the walkers were. When all physical activity was considered, 57 percent of the inactive had died compared to only 16 percent of those who had some form of exercise.

Walking is as natural to the human body as breathing. It is a muscular symphony; all the foot, leg, and hip muscles and much of the back musculature are involved. The abdominal muscles tend to contract and support their share of the weight, and the diaphragm and rib muscles increase their action. There is automatic action of the arm and shoulder muscles; the shoulder and neck muscles get play as the head is held erect; the eye muscles are exercised as you look about you.

Other Types of Exercise

Swimming and bicycling exercise most of the muscles, and gardening is highly recommended. The fresh air is beneficial, the bending, squatting, and countless other movements exercise most parts of the body.

Surprisingly, most games do not provide good exercise. According to a physical fitness research laboratory at the University of Illinois, the trouble with most games is that the action is intermittent—starting and stopping—a burst of energy and then a wait. The bowler swings a ball for two and one-half seconds and gets about one minute of actual muscular work per game. Golf is a succession of pause, swing, walk—or, more often, a ride to the next pause, swing, and so on. Also, you spend a lot of time standing and waiting for the party ahead and for your partners. Tennis gives one more exercise but it too involves a great deal of starting and stopping, as does handball. No game has the essential, tension-releasing pattern of continuous, vigorous, rhythmic motion found in such activities as walking, running, or jogging.

For formal exercises, you could join a gym, but you might find your enthusiasm waning after a few weeks. You could also exercise at home; there are many excellent books on exercise that provide programs for you to follow at home on a daily basis.

But everyone's exercise capacity varies. It is best to discuss any new exercise program with your physician, especially if you have some illness or are out of practice. Then select an exercise which is pleasant for you and suitable to your condition.

It is most important always to warm up before any strenuous exercise. The U.S. Administration on Aging's booklet, *The Fitness Challenge in the Later Years*, states:

> The enthusiast who tackles a keep-fit program too fast and too strenuously soon gives up in discomfort, if not in injury. A warm-up period should be performed by starting lightly with a continuous rhythmical activity such as walking and gradually increasing the intensity until your pulse rate, breathing, and body temperature are elevated. It's also desirable to do some easy stretching, pulling, and rotating exercises during the warm-up period.

The booklet outlines an excellent program—*red* (easiest), *white* (next), and *blue* (the most sustained and difficult). Each program is "designed to give a balanced workout utilizing all major muscle groups."

A Word of Caution

You may be exercising too strenuously if the following happens:

- Your heart does not stop pounding within 10 minutes after the exercise.

- You cannot catch your breath 10 minutes after the exercise.

- You are shaky for more than 30 minutes afterwards.

- You can't sleep well afterwards.

- Your fatigue (not muscle soreness) continues into the next day.

Sensible, moderate exercise geared to your own physical capacity can help to give you a sense of all-around well-being. As Dr. Ernest Simonson, associate professor of physiological hygiene at the University of Minnesota Medical School, has said:

> Those who exercise regularly never fail to mention that it makes them feel better in every way. It's common logic if one feels better, his attitude towards others will be more congenial. When one is in a cordial, happy frame of mind, he will likely make wiser decisions, and his world in general will look better.

Weight Control

Importantly, both diet and exercise affect the individual's ability to control his weight (see Ch. 27, *Nutrition and Weight Control*; "Weight Problems" in Ch. 23, *Aches, Pains, Nuisances, Worries*; and Ch. 37, *Physical Fitness*). Healthy habits in both areas provide a complete answer for many older persons. For others, some additional effort is required.

The same diet rules that help the older person feel well and function adequately will make weight control simpler. But persons beyond middle age who have weight problems should make extra efforts to bring their weight down. Extra pounds of fat only make it harder for the vital organs to function; excess poundage also forces the heart to work harder. A variety of diets may be used to bring your weight back to where it should be. But the calorie-counter program may suffice for most persons.

Exercise provides the second key to weight control. Many physicians feel that older persons of both sexes should walk at least a mile daily. Other exercises acclaimed by physicians include golf, gardening, working on or around the house, and similar activities. Some other basic rules regarding exercise and diet should be noted:

- Avoid junk, or high carbohydrate, food where possible.

- Make certain you are eating foods that provide enough protein.

- Eat to assuage hunger, not to drive away boredom.

- Remember that appetite usually decreases with age, and act accordingly.

- Avoid vitamins unless they are prescribed by your physician, and use them accordingly.

- Try every day to eat foods in the four basic groups.

- Keep moving; walk daily—to the store, post office, church, around the block.

- If you exercise already, do it regularly; a little exercise daily is better than a lot on weekends.

- If you don't exercise but are thinking of starting a program of work-outs of some kind, start slowly and build up—following your physician's recommendations.

- If stress gives you problems, find ways to relax without eating or drinking; consider light exercises, yoga, meditation, breathing exercises, or some other method.

Skin Problems

As a person grows older, his skin begins to wrinkle; oil and sweat glands slow down, causing the skin to become dry. Also, the skin may lack the elasticity and tone of normal skin, and this might cause changes in facial contours.

However, the skin, like other parts of the body, tends to age according to various factors. Among prime agers of the skin are exposure to sunlight and weather; the sailor and chronic sunbather may have older-looking skin than their years. Also, hereditary and racial factors influence skin age.

Itching

The skin often itches as one grows older. Itching usually stems from external irritations or internal diseases. External irritations may be more severe in winter because of lack of humidity and because the skin oil does not spread properly. Too many baths or wearing wool garments could also cause itching. You can correct this by cutting down on bathing, maintaining correct temperature and humidity, and applying skin creams.

If itching does not clear up in about two weeks, the trouble may be due to any of a number of internal diseases, some of them serious. Thus, it is wise to see your physician if itching persists.

Skin Cancer

Skin cancer can be easily diagnosed and treated. The two most common types are *basal cell* and *squamous cell*.

The basal cell type begins with a small fleshy *nodule*, usually on the face. It may take several months to reach one-half to one inch in diameter. In about a year it begins to ulcerate and bleed. Then it forms a crust, which it sheds at intervals, leaving another ulcer. A physician can usually remove the ulcer by a local operation.

Smoking and exposure to the sun aid squamous cell cancer. Lesions or horny growths may appear on the lips, mouth, and genitalia, and they tend to spread and increase in size. Again, your physician can treat or operate effectively. See also Ch. 18, *Cancer*.

Vitiligo

Vitiligo is an autoimmune disease that causes loss of pigment in skin. No cure exists for vitiligo, which affects about 1 percent of the U.S. population, but treatments include drugs and exposure to ultraviolet A radiation. The condition, itself, is not physically painful, but it is emotionally damaging.

Senile Purpura

Sometimes the skin develops *senile purpura* as one grows older. The characteristic hemorrhages of this condition usually appear on the extremities, and the purple color gradually fades and leaves mottled areas of yellow-brown. Generally, the skin is thin, fragile, and transparent in appearance.

Stasis Dermatitis

Sometimes in association with such conditions as varicose veins, the skin

Worry

Worry increases tension and elevates blood pressure. Try to cultivate a philosophical approach to the daily ups and downs. See Ch. 10, *Heart Disease.*

Strokes

Strokes are not hopeless; even severely paralyzed patients may make remarkable progress. A *stroke* occurs when the blood supply to a part of the brain tissue is cut off and, as a result, the nerve cells in that part of the brain can't function. When this happens, the part of the body controlled by these nerve cells can't function either.

Whenever the blood supply is cut off from an area, small neighboring arteries get larger and take over part of the work of the damaged artery. In this way nerve cells that have been temporarily put out of order may recover, and that part of the body affected by the stroke may eventually improve or even return to normal.

Once a stroke has occurred, a sound rehabilitation program can help the patient resume as many normal activities as possible. This program can be worked out in cooperation with the physician, patient, family, and local organizations. See Ch. 9, *Diseases of the Circulatory System.*

Arthritis

There are two main types of arthritis: *rheumatoid arthritis* and *osteoarthritis.*

Rheumatoid arthritis—which can cause pain and swelling in joints, nerves, muscles, tendons, blood vessels, and connective tissue in the whole body—can strike at any age, but it occurs mainly in the 25-to-40-year age group. The exact cause of rheumatoid arthritis is unknown.

Osteoarthritis is a degenerative joint disease that affects almost everyone who lives long enough; it is a product of normal wear and tear on the joints over the years. Poor posture and obesity are contributing causes, as are heredity and trauma.

Osteoarthritis is usually mild, and it seldom cripples. Pain is generally moderate. Unlike rheumatoid arthritis, which is inflammatory, spreads from joint to joint, and affects the whole body, osteoarthritis confines its attack locally to individual joints. Rarely is inflammation a problem.

Osteoarthritis is likely to develop in any joint that has been required to take a lot of punishment or abuse: the knee or hip joints of someone who is overweight; joints injured in an accident; joints injured or overused in sports; joints subjected to unusual stresses and strains in work or play; joints with hidden defects that were present at birth.

There is no specific cure for arthritis, but the pain and swelling can be controlled. In other than acute cases, common aspirin has proved the safest and most popular medication.

Adequate rest for both the body and the affected joint is a fundamental treatment. Heat, controlled exercise, hydrotherapy, and massage are all effective if done under a physician's supervision. See "Arthritis and Other Joint Diseases" in Ch. 7, *Diseases of the Skeletal System.*

Cancer

Cancer strikes at any age, but it does strike more frequently in the later years. Many factors are believed to contribute to cancer; frictional and chemical irritations like cigarette smoking, irritation of the skin and mouth (such as poor dentures), exposure to the sun, X rays, or radioactive elements. Common sites are the lips, mouth, stomach, intestines, rectum, liver, pancreas, lungs, breast, kidney, bladder, skin, uterus, and prostate.

Early detection and prompt treatment are the best protection against cancer. If any of the following seven danger signals lasts longer than two weeks, be sure to get a checkup.

- Unusual bleeding or discharge
- A lump or thickening in the breast or elsewhere
- A sore that does not heal
- Change in bowel or bladder habits
- Hoarseness or cough
- Indigestion or difficulty in swallowing
- Change in wart or mole

Great strides have been made in treating cancer through surgery, radiotherapy, and chemotherapy. See Ch. 18, *Cancer.* For cancers affecting women only, see "Cancers of the Reproductive System" and "Cancer of the Breast" in Ch. 25, *Women's Health.*

The Eyes

The eye does age. After age 40, failing vision is usually caused by natural hardening of the lens, making it difficult to see close objects. However, failing vision may also be the first symptom of a serious bodily disorder, or of glaucoma or of a cataract, which requires a physician's immediate attention.

Both glaucoma and cataract can be treated effectively. About 90 percent of glaucoma cases can be checked with eye drops and about 95 percent of cataracts can be removed by a painless operation.

Other diseases that may develop in later years affect the blood vessels of the eye. A common condition is *senile macula degeneration* which causes a blind spot to appear when the victim looks directly at something. The exact cause of senile macula degeneration is not known. See under Ch. 16, *Diseases of the Eye and Ear.*

Diabetes

Most likely candidates for diabetes are overweight persons past 40, particularly those who have a hereditary history of diabetes, and especially older women.

The exact cause of diabetes is not known, but it is a functional disorder in which the body cannot handle certain foods—mainly sugars and starches. Symptoms include increased thirst, constant hunger, frequent urination, loss of weight, itching, easy tiring, changes in vision, and slow healing of cuts and scratches.

Treatment and control consist of planned diet, exercise, and, in many cases, insulin shots or oral medication. Well-controlled diabetics can lead active lives. See Ch. 15, *Diabetes Mellitus.*

Constipation

There is no truth in the notion that a daily bowel movement is necessary for good health. A movement every day or twice a day may be all right for one person; for another every three or four days may be enough.

The two most common causes of chronic constipation are physical inactivity and poor food and water habits. Ironically, constipation may be caused by swallowing a cathartic nightly to induce a bowel movement. The habit eventually leads to chronic constipation because normal bowel movement ceases and bowel evacuation depends on using a cathartic.

To maintain proper bowel movement, try the following:

- Drink eight to ten glasses of water a day. Take two glasses of water on an empty stomach as soon as you get up.

- Drink more fruit juices and eat more dried and fresh fruits.

- Get at least one-half hour of moderate exercise daily. Walking, for example, is excellent, particularly if you relax while you walk.

- Give yourself enough time for normal bowel movement and set up a regular time for evacuation.

- If you are constipated, consult your physician to make sure it is simple and functional. See under Ch. 23, *Aches, Pains, Nuisances, Worries.*

Back Problems

As we grow older, the back muscles—weakened by inactivity, poor posture, and almost unavoidable wear and tear—start to complain.

Other causes of back problems are muscle and joint strain, changes in the spine, psychological tension, and internal diseases. Here are some tips to help avoid backache:

- Learn to lift correctly. Use your leg muscles, which are stronger than back muscles, by placing your feet closer to the base of the object, bending your knees outward, and pushing up with your legs.

- Avoid subjecting your back to any sudden, erratic motion.

- Try to improve your posture when sitting and walking.

- Sleep on a firm bed; a bed board may be helpful.

- Get regular exercise of a type that stimulates all your muscles rather than just a few.

- If you sit for a long period, get up and stretch occasionally.

- Beware of excess weight. Extra weight on the abdomen pulls on the vertebrae at the small of the back, increasing the spine's normal curve and causing pain.

- Try never to become overfatigued or exhausted, either physically or mentally. Emotional pressure, from work or personal problems, causes muscle tension. See "Backaches" in Ch. 23, *Aches, Pains, Nuisances, Worries.*

Because the feet are farthest away from the heart's blood supply, they are often the first areas affected by circulatory diseases. Also, arthritis and diabetes might first show up in the feet.

Warning signs include continued cramping of the calf muscles, pain in the arch and toes, and unusually cold feet—especially if accompanied by a bluish skin. Brittle or thickened toenails or burning, tingling, and numbness may also signal a circulatory disease.

Foot ulcers may be one of the first signs of diabetes. Some *bunions*—swollen, tender, red joints—are caused by arthritis. Swelling around the feet and ankles suggests a possible kidney disorder.

If you have these symptoms, go to a *podiatrist* (a foot doctor) or to your own physician. They are trained to recognize these symptoms.

Most older people, however, suffer from minor aches and pains in the feet that are caused by poor foot care or abuse. See "The Vulnerable Extremeties" in Ch. 23, *Aches, Pains, Nuisances, Worries.*

Care of the Feet

To prevent these problems, treat yourself to daily foot care. Dry your feet thoroughly and gently after bathing and inspect the skin for abrasion, rough spots, or cracks. Dry carefully between the toes. If the skin is dry or scaly, lubricate it with lanolin or olive oil. Next, apply a medicated foot powder recommended by your podiatrist or physician over the entire foot, especially between the toes, as a preventive measure against athlete's foot.

When you cut your nails, do it with a strong light and be careful to cut straight across the nail to prevent ingrown toenails. Avoid the use of strong medications containing salicylate and strong antiseptics like iodine, carbolic acid, lysol, or bleach. Harsh chemicals that attack toughened skin can irritate normal tissue and cause infection. Avoid using hot water bottles, electric pads, or any form of extreme heat or cold. Diabetics should visit a podiatrist regularly.

The Prostate

Men over 50 may have an enlarged *prostate*. (This is not caused by sexual excesses or venereal disease.) The exact cause is not known, but it's estimated that some type of enlarged prostate is present in about 10 percent of 40-year-olds and 80 percent of 80-year-olds.

The prostate is a rubbery mass of glands and muscle tissue about the size and shape of a horse chestnut. It is wrapped around the urethra and base of the bladder at the point where they join. The prostate functions as part of a man's sexual apparatus, providing a fluid that transports and nourishes the spermatozoa.

Symptoms of an enlarged prostate include difficulty in urination. There might be an initial blocking of the urine, or the stream may lack force. You may feel that you can't empty the bladder, and you may have urgent needs to urinate. You may have pain or blood in the urine from straining.

If you have any of these symptoms, your physician can easily check for enlarged prostate by a simple rectal examination. If he discovers an enlargement, he can usually treat it in early stages with simple massage. But if it has progressed too far, he may have to operate.

An operation is usually performed through the urethra or by an incision in the lower abdomen. The choice depends upon the individual problems of the patient and the judgment of the surgeon. In either case, the patient usually recovers completely in a short time.

A rectal examination can also discover early stages of cancer of the prostate, which is not uncommon in men over 40. Some 20 percent of men over 60 have this condition, and it is most common in men over 70.

Unfortunately, this disease does not manifest itself early, so it is important that men over 40 have the diagnostic rectal examination. If the disease is detected early and treated—usually by surgery, hormonal therapy, and possibly radiation—the cure rate is very high. If found late, the cure rate is low.

When treatment is by surgery, the entire prostate and upper urethra may be removed. In some cases, the disease may be retarded or relieved by treatment with female hormones. (The male hormone is known to hasten prostate cancer.)

In both enlargement and cancer of the prostate, early detection is vital to a successful cure. That is why it is important to have a rectal examination. See also "Cancer of the Prostate" in Ch. 18, *Cancer*.

Alzheimer's Disease

Alzheimer's disease is a group of brain disorders marked by progressive deterioration and affects both memory and reasoning abilities. Victims of Alzheimer's, which is a form of dementia, or mental deterioration (see "Dementia" in Ch. 8, *Diseases of the Muscles and Nervous System*), undergo various behavioral changes. These include an inability to concentrate, anxiety, irritability, agitation, withdrawal, and petulance. Persons suffering from Alzheimer's may wander about and lose their way. They may have temper tantrums and engage in obsessional behavior, such as repeatedly washing dishes. Time and place disorientation may be accompanied by delusions and depression. In the later stages of the disease, sufferers often lose bladder and bowel control.

Diagnosing Alzheimer's in its early stages is difficult despite its numerous symptoms. Laboratory tests that could identify the disorder do not exist. Adding to the problems of diagnosis, various other disorders have similar symptoms. The best medical alternative, a complete physical examination, generally includes a review of any drugs or medications the patient has been taking as well as standard laboratory tests. The latter help to rule out other diseases or disorders that may be treatable. A clinical evaluation can include a CT (computed tomography) scan, an EEG (electroencephalogram), and assessment of evidence from family members and the patient regarding the latter's (or patient's) mental state.

Even when diagnosed with relative certainty, Alzheimer's disease cannot be cured. But some symptoms, including depression and delusions, can be treated, slowing the progress of the disorder. Where Parkinson's disease or heart problems accompany Alzheimer's, treatment can focus on alleviation of those conditions.

A small proportion of Alzheimer's cases have been linked to the possession of a flawed gene that causes cells to produce too much of a protein called beta amyloid. It is not known, however, whether excess beta amyloid protein is the cause, or the result, of brain cell devastation.

Scientists have also linked the possession of another gene, apolipoprotein E4, to an increased susceptibility to the most common form of Alzheimer's. It is not known whether the likelihood of a person with the E4 gene contracting Alzheimer's is affected by environmental factors. There is some evidence that persons on estrogen replacement therapy or anti-inflammatory drugs are less likely to develop the disease.

Meeting the Challenge of Leisure

Leisure Activities

In ten years of retirement, you will have the leisure time equivalent of working 40 hours a week for 21 years. You cannot fish this time away and you cannot rest it away. Whatever you do for long must have meaning—must satisfy some basic need and want. Certain needs remain constant throughout life:

- Security—good health, income, and a recognized role in society

- Recognition—as an individual with your own abilities and personality

- Belonging—as a member of a family, social group, and community

- Self-expression—by developing abilities and talents in new areas and at new levels

- Adventure—new experiences, new sights, and new knowledge

There are many activities that can satisfy these basic needs and wants to keep you mentally and physically in top shape.

Travel

Travel satisfies your need for adventure in many ways. If you travel off-season at bargain rates, you'll find that time truly is money. Most travel problems stem from rushing to meet a schedule. Making every minute count on a fast-paced European tour can be expensive and exhausting. For the same transatlantic fare, you can spend a full year in Europe at one-third the daily cost of a three-week vacation.

Wherever you travel, it isn't enough just to sightsee. Try to center your travel around an interest or a hobby. You can take art or music tours—tours that stress education, night life, culture, or special interests. You can travel on your own or with a group. But whatever you do, participate; don't just observe.

Doing things instead of just observing adds new dimensions to the pleasure of going places. For people who participate, travel means the adventure of enjoying exciting new places, people, and experiences. To help plan your trip, write to the government tourist offices of foreign countries (ask your library for addresses); to the National Park Service, Washington, DC; and to state or local chambers of commerce (no street addresses necessary).

Gardening

Gardening satisfies one's need for self-expression in many ways. Being outside in the fresh air and planting living things can bring satisfaction and peace of mind.

Gardening is a many-faceted hobby that offers many challenges. You can go into plant breeding, growing for resale, introducing new plants, collecting the rare and unusual, plant selecting, or simply cultivating what you find personally appealing and satisfying.

Your local library or bookstore has many books on the subject. There are local and national garden clubs that you can join to learn about your hobby and to meet other people who are interested in gardening. Write the Government Printing Office, Washington, DC 20401, for help and advice. In addition, state extension directors at state colleges and universities, county agricultural agents, and local plant nurseries can give expert advice and information.

Reading

Reading offers excitement, adventure, pursuit of knowledge, and an introduction to new people and places. Your local library is the best place to launch a reading program—and you may be surprised to find that it offers more than books. Most libraries have art and music departments, audiovisual services (films and microfilm copies), foreign language departments, periodical rooms (newspapers and magazines), writing classes, genealogy workshops, and special courses of general interest.

Hobbies

A hobby can be any physical or mental activity that gives you happiness, relaxation, and satisfaction. It should not be just a time killer—it should offer some tangible reward. Also, it should have continuity, not be too expensive, and not make undue demands on time and energy. Perhaps you would prefer a series of hobbies, some serious and some just for fun. They can be related to your work or completely unrelated. In any event, a hobby should be something you've always wanted to do.

Before selecting a hobby, consider these points:

- Do you like to do things alone? Consider arts, crafts, reading, sewing, fishing—activities that are not dependent on others, although you can enjoy them with others.

- Do you like groups? Seek hobbies that include other people—organizational, sport, game, or craft activities.

- Do you like to play to win? Try your luck in competitive or team games that stress winning.

- Do you have to be an expert? Too many of us are afraid to try new activities because we hate to fail or look clumsy. But be fair; judge your efforts in light of your past experience and present progress; do not compare yourself to someone who's been at it longer than you.

- Do you put a price tag on everything? Many people will not engage in an activity if it costs too much. Yet, many hobbies fail because they're tried on a shoestring without adequate equipment. Also, some people do not want to do anything unless it brings in money. If so, perhaps you should look for something that's an offshoot of the work or business you know best.

Creative Crafts

Creative crafts are difficult for most of us because we are conservative, afraid to make mistakes, sensitive because of buried and almost forgotten blunders. Yet creativity is essential to life. Without it we don't live fully; through creative skills we refurbish old interests and develop new ones.

Most of us are happiest with creative crafts that do not require intri-cate work or fine detail and that are not too demanding physically. Some crafts best suited to retirement years include weaving, rug making, sewing, ceramic work, knitting, plastic molding, woodwork, leathercraft, and lapidary.

You can learn these and other crafts and also market your products through senior centers, adult education classes, and senior craft centers.

Volunteer Work

Through community service and volunteer work, thousands are not only helping others but are serving themselves. Such activities keep time from hanging heavy, give purpose to retirement, and in some cases may lead to paying jobs and a second career.

Participating in community activities is not difficult. In some communities a call to the city clerk is enough to get started. In others, a letter to the mayor will bring faster results. In larger cities, call the Volunteer Bureau in your area; this is a United Fund agency that acts as a clearing house for volunteer jobs.

If you wish to have the type of volunteer job that leads to a second career, you might consider doing work for one of the government programs utilizing the skills of older people. All of these programs have been assembled under the umbrella of one organization called ACTION. For additional information about any of the following programs, write to ACTION, Washington, DC 20525.

- The Foster Grandparent Program hires low-income men and women over 60 to give love and attention to institutionalized and other needy children.

- The Peace Corps is seeking the skills of retirees. However, you must be skilled in some trade or profession, pass a tough physical examination, and complete a rigorous orientation and training program. For information, write to ACTION, Washington, DC 20525, and request a copy of *Older Volunteers in the Peace Corps*. It lists specific skills needed in the Peace Corps.

- Other programs within ACTION include the Retired Senior Volunteer Program, the Service Corps of Retired Executives, the Active Corps of Executives, and VISTA (Volunteer in Service to America). Many of the workers in these programs are paid.

There are other volunteer jobs that may not pay a salary, but do fill a basic need by allowing you to pass along your skills and ideals to younger people. You can do this through the Boy Scouts, Girl Scouts, Boys Clubs of America, YMCAs and YWCAs, hospitals, schools for the handicapped and mentally retarded, and many other organizations.

Continuing Social and Intellectual Activities

The one organ we can depend upon in old age is the brain. At 80, a person can learn at approximately the same speed he could when he was 12 years old. But like any organ, the brain must be kept active and alert by constant use.

One of the best ways to exercise the brain is through some process of continuing education. This does not have to mean going back to school or taking formal classes. Continuing education can take the form of participating in discussions in senior centers, "Y's," town meetings, or study courses. You can find out about educational opportunities and possibilities by contacting local, state, or national offices of education; state employment offices; the information service of your Community Council or Health and Welfare Federation; the Adult Education section of the U.S. Office of Education, Washington, DC 20202; the National Education Association, 1201 Sixteenth Street, NW, Washington, DC 20036; the State Commission on Aging (write to your state capital).

Your local library may have some suggestions (and perhaps offers some classes), and your local "Y" is probably offering some programs.

The federal government continues to be a prime source of educational literature. Each year the government prints about 50 million books, pamphlets, brochures, reports, and guidebooks on everything from astrology to zoology. For a free price list of specified subjects, write to the Superintendent of Documents, Government Printing Office, Washington, DC 20401.

Formal and informal learning situations can help you keep pace with change and the future. Continuing education prepares you to live contentedly with a free, independent spirit and mind—while providing you with the means for improved social integration, participation, and satisfaction.

Sexual Attitude and Activity in the Aged

We have come far since the Victorian era when talk about sex was taboo. Now science is taking a candid look at sex in the later years and is exploding old myths as well as exploring new truths. Such enlightenment can help reduce any remaining guilt in this area.

After Age 60

In one study to determine the pattern of sexual behavior after 60, researchers at Duke University quizzed 250 people aged 60 to 93 about their sexual activities. Of the 149 who were married, 81 reported they were still sexually active; even in the single group, 7 of the 101 questioned reported "some sexual activity."

Dr. Gustave Newman, who conducted the study, reported 10 percent of the couples over 60 as having sexual relations more than once a week, though couples over 75 unanimously reported less activity.

"No age is an automatic cut-off point for sex," claims the late Dr. Isadore Rubin in his study, *Sexual Life After Sixty*. "But," he continues,

sexuality cannot flourish in a climate where rejection of aging as a worthwhile stage of life leads inevitably to self-rejection by many older persons . . . the men and women who "act old" in their sexual activity before their bodies have really called a halt become sexually old long before their time.

Physiological and Psychological Changes and Sex

Postmenopausal women may experience painful intercourse due to a decrease in vaginal lubrication. This problem is easily remedied with the use of nonpetroleum-based vaginal creams or jellies.

Many women take a renewed interest in sex after menopause. Dr. William H. Masters and Mrs. Virginia E. Johnson in their study *Human Sexual Response* credit the tendency of many women to experience a second honeymoon in the early 50s to the fact that they no longer have to worry about pregnancy and usually have resolved most of the problems of raising a family.

On the other hand, they tell us:

Deprived of normal sexual outlets, women exhaust themselves physically in conscious or unconscious efforts to dissipate their accumulated and frequently unrecognized sexual tensions. Many demonstrate their basic insecurities by casting themselves unreservedly into their religion, the business world, volunteer social work, or overzealous mothering of their mature children or grandchildren.

While some women become more responsive as they grow older, Masters and Johnson point out, "There is no question that the human male's responsiveness wanes as he ages."

Men may experience less sexual urgency, delayed or partial erection, and less defined ejaculations because the body's secretion of the male hormone testosterone decreases with age and the conduction of nerve impulses is less rapid. Also, arteries in the penis are less able to maintain the blood pressure necessary for a full erection.

Another common concern for older men is impotence, that is, diminished or no sexual response. Nearly everyone experiences impotence from time to time, often from such routine problems as fatigue, stress, or illness. The incidence of impotence, however, definitely increases with age. (By age 65, 30 percent of men report chronic impotence; by age 75, 55 percent do.)

Impotence has been linked to such problems as diabetes, Parkinson's disease, liver or kidney disease, and lower back problems. Other causes are certain medications, excessive alcohol consumption, drug abuse, and smoking. Most cases of impotence, however, can be traced to psychological problems such as anxiety, depression, or marital problems. About 80 percent of these cases can still be overcome with psychotherapy.

Sexual dysfunction in women is often called *frigidity* and implies a *cold* woman who cannot become excited sexually. As with men, there are both organic and psychological causes which can often be treated.

Although sex for most healthy men and women over 60 may not be quite the same as it was for them in their 20s, that does not mean it cannot be good, or even better. A change in attitudes and expectations about sex may have surprising results. Couples may find new enjoyment in reducing the pace of lovemaking and exploring different ways of giving each other pleasure besides intercourse.

Health Concerns

For those not so healthy older men and women, especially most of those who have suffered heart attacks, there is no reason for them not to have sex. After a heart attack most are able to resume sexual activity within a few months, although patients with angina pectoris may be advised to proceed cautiously.

According to Dr. Philip Reichert, former executive secretary of the American College of Cardiology:

> We must get rid of the notion that every heart patient lives under an overhanging sword and that he faces the constant threat of sudden death. The congenial married couple, accustomed to each other and whose technique is habituated through many years of companionship, can achieve sexual satisfaction without too great an expenditure of body energy or too severe a strain upon the heart. . . .

Hypertension sufferers may sometimes indulge in a restricted form of sexual activity with medical supervision. And modern therapy and surgical methods can often prevent or delay impotence caused by prostate disease or diabetes.

Where any health problem is involved, it is best to analyze your sex needs and those of your partner; consult with your physician and partner as to how you can both attain satisfaction without harm to your health; see your physician regularly and report

accurately distress symptoms and the conditions causing them.

Recent research has dispelled other long-held ideas about sex, too—among them the myth that masturbation is childish and harmful to health. Moreover, Rubin points out: "All studies of older persons have shown that autoerotic activity, while not as common as in the younger years, is far more prevalent in later years than most of us have imagined."

Dr. Lester W. Dearborn, marriage consultant, in pointing out the role masturbation plays in the lives of the single or widowed, comments:

> It is to be hoped that those interested in the field of geriatrics will . . . encourage the aging to accept masturbation as a perfectly valid outlet when there is a need and other means of gratification are not available.

Cellular Therapy and Hormone Treatment

To keep older people vigorous and active, some researchers have experimented with *cellular therapy* as a means of retarding aging. Dr. Paul Niehans, a Swiss physician, introduced the idea of cellular therapy in the 1930s with his theory that organs begin to deteriorate in old age when the body fails to replace the cells that compose it. He prescribed a treatment whereby a person is injected with cells from healthy embryonic animal organs. (He used sheep, pigs, and calves.) He believed that the animal cells from a particular organ would migrate to the same organ in the aging body and reactivate it. Thus, kidney troubles could be cured with cells from an embryonic animal kidney. Although such notables as Sir Winston Churchill, Pope Pius XII, Somerset Maugham, and Dr. Konrad Adenauer submitted to it, cellular therapy is not widely accepted in the

United States today as an effective agent against aging.

More to the point, most researchers feel, are the current experiments with hormones. Hormones help women through the tension of menopause and are used to treat impotence and loss of sexual desire. However, some studies have linked estrogen hormone therapy statistically with uterine cancer. For this reason and because of side effects, hormones face many years of testing before they will be used extensively to retard aging.

Mental Outlook

Good health plus a romantic outlook promote sex appeal at any age. Showing affection, whether sexually or not, keep you sparkling and lively no matter what your age.

A good wholesome attitude toward life, a hearty sense of humor, a sympathetic interest in other people—all help make up the indefinable something that makes us appealing to the opposite sex. Cleanliness, neat suitable apparel, and good posture all add to the image we create of ourselves in other people's minds. So do the manners we reflect in the courtesies we show the people around us—the thoughtful little things we do for them, our reactions to the things they do for us.

If you're a woman over 65 who is looking for companionship, you'll probably find a good personality uplift will get you farther than a face or bust lift. If you're a man who is hoping to find feminine companionship, you will probably find a good spiritual overhaul more image-enhancing than dyeing your hair. Also, a good night's sleep is the best aphrodisiac.

The Right Housing

Selecting retirement housing is like

selecting a spouse; there are many possibilities, but few that are right.

Ideally, the right housing should take care of you rather than requiring you to take care of it. It should give you shelter, security, and privacy; allow you freedom; and keep you near friends, relatives, and a grocer who delivers.

To Move or Not to Move

What is the right housing for you—the one that you are in or some other place? The answer to this question depends upon the state of your pocketbook and the state of your health.

Advantages of Moving

Right now you might be in good health, but this could change. Would stairs become a problem? Could you keep up the house and garden? Would you want more adequate heat? Older people are more comfortable when the temperature is over 75° F. You might also need better lighting in several rooms.

If you are retired, you might find that you cannot keep up expenses on the old house. You might find that your larger, older house does not suit the reduced size of your family or your need for work or recreation. You could probably save money by living in a smaller place that requires less upkeep. You could also arrange to move nearer children and grandchildren, or into an area where you could find new opportunities for work and recreational activities.

Advantages of Staying Put

But by staying in your home you would remain in familiar surroundings and near old friends. You could maintain your comfortable routine and remain independent as long as possible. If you have unused space, you could move into the first floor and shut off the second floor to save on heat and maintenance. Or you could convert part of the house into apartments.

Where to Live?

Many older persons fulfill ambitions of long standing by moving to warmer climates after retirement. The question whether such a move should be undertaken should be considered with other questions relating to housing.

Moving to a different climate makes sense for many reasons. Many elderly persons feel threatened or restricted by cold winters and their usual accompaniments—snow, sleet, and high winds. Having more leisure time, older persons feel that warmer temperatures will make it possible to take part in more activities for more hours of the day than if they "stay put." Some persons move so that they can live closer to friends who have already moved—or to children or other relatives. Some move to play golf or tennis outdoors the year around.

An individual or couple considering a move to a warmer climate should look at a number of basic considerations. A key one relates to the cost of living in the new area or state. Living on incomes that may have been substantially reduced by retirement, older persons without special preferences may select that state that offers the cheapest living. Studies indicated in 1979 that the "10 best states to retire to" from a personal-financial point of view were, in order:

1. Utah, because of lower energy costs, growing job opportunities, moderate living costs. A drawback: Utah may have extremely cold winters.

2. Louisiana, because of cheap living costs—about 10 percent lower than other states—and low real estate taxes.

3. South Carolina, for the same reasons. A drawback: physician shortages in some communities.

4. Nevada, because of new housing, jobs, no state income or inheritance taxes, and average living costs.

5. Texas, with moderate housing costs away from major cities, and normal, if rising, living costs.

6. New Mexico, where energy costs are low, jobs are increasing in number, and cheap housing is plentiful.

7. Alabama, the cheapest and lowest as regards costs of living. Drawbacks: few new jobs, medical care lacking in some areas.

8. Arizona, because of good, relatively inexpensive housing, warm climate, good medical care. Drawbacks: rising living costs, high taxes.

9. Florida, with a warm climate, no income tax, good medical services. Drawbacks: living costs high in coastal areas; property taxes rising.

10. Georgia, because of mild climate, low living costs. Drawbacks: slow growth in jobs, locally poor medical services.

"Retirement to the sun" entails many other decisions. States like New Mexico offer a wide range of sites, from urban to desert, from high mountains to empty plains. Some of the states with favorable tax laws and cheap living costs have little to offer in the way of cultural attractions. Other states may lack recreational activities.

Psychological Trauma

Moving 100 or 1,000 or 2,000 miles to live in a warmer climate obviously involves some pain of separation and loss. The psychological trauma occasioned by a departure from old friends and familiar surroundings has caused major problems for some older persons. For that reason, the psychological challenge should be given deep consideration *before* any move is made.

How to alleviate the trauma of leaving the familiar for the unfamiliar? Some persons spend a year in the new locale, return home, and *then* make up their minds to move or not to move. Others, including those who cannot afford such trial living, at least visit the target region to "get a feel" for it and its way of life. Whatever your situation, the wisdom of considering at least five factors cannot be disputed:

- In the new home under the sun, will you be able to entertain family, including children and grandchildren, and in that way to minimize the pain of separation?

- Are friends or relatives already located in the new area—and can you live near them (not *with* them, if possible)?

- Will you be able to swing into enough new activities to eliminate any possibility that you might feel useless, wasted, or frustrated?

- Can you maintain your old, or a decent, standard of living once you have moved?

- Can you stand the first 9 to 12 months in the new home without climbing the walls? Studies have shown that those who can last out a year or more will very likely adjust and continue to enjoy life.

Requirements of Retirement Housing

Whatever you plan to do, your retire-ment housing should be located near or be easily accessible to shops and recreation centers by public transportation. To make living arrangements more pleasant, individual housing units should contain at least 400 square feet, and there should be two or more rooms.

The new dwelling unit should be equal to or better than the housing you have been used to in the past. It should be suitable for comfortable living in both health and sickness—easily adaptable to convalescent needs with either two bedrooms or a bedroom and sleeping alcove.

In addition, retirement housing should incorporate the following:

- All rooms on one floor, and that floor reached by few, if any, steps

- No thresholds or tripping hazards

- Nonslip surfaces in hallways, bedrooms, and kitchens

- Handrails by all steps and inclines

- Adequate illumination in halls, near steps, and in other potentially hazardous areas

- Fully automatic central heating

- Doors and halls wide enough to accommodate a wheelchair

Public Housing

If you decide to move and to rent instead of buying, consider public housing projects. These projects are available to single men and women 62 or older, as well as to families whose head is 62 or older or has a spouse at least 62. Local housing authorities build, purchase, or lease the units and set entrance requirements and maximum income limits. Rents are comparatively low.

The Housing and Urban Development Agency also makes loans for nonprofit (and profit) sponsors that will build housing for senior citizens with moderate or higher incomes.

Retirement Hotels and Communities

You might also consider retirement hotels, which are especially numerous in Florida, California, and Texas. These hotels are usually refurbished former resorts that provide room and board at a fixed monthly rent.

Retirement communities offer housing of various types, usually apartments, cooperatives, and individual units. It usually costs about $450 a month or more to cover mortgage payments, living, and maintenance expenses.

Would you like retirement community living? It's usually the life for people who like people and who enjoy being active. For those who don't, it can be a bit tiring. Some couples do not like the closeness and activity found in a retirement community and prefer living in a less social environment.

Lifetime Care Facilities

In contrast to the emphasis on independent living in retirement communities, many projects sponsored by church, union, and fraternal organizations stress lifetime care (room, board, and medical care for life), with fees based on actuarial tables of life expectancy at age of entry. Housing alone costs from $10,000 to $30,000, depending upon age and type of living accommodation, *plus* a monthly charge of around $250 per person to cover meals, medical care (exclusive of Medicare), maintenance, and other expenses. In many cases, lifetime care for a couple could cost around $90,000.

Cooperatives and Condominiums

In addition to lifetime care facilities,

many church, fraternal, and union groups offer other types of housing. In the case of church-sponsored housing, residence usually is not restricted to members of the sponsoring faith.

Some of these units are operated as *cooperatives;* others as *condominiums.* The major difference in the two is that condominium owners have titles to their units, while cooperative residents are stockholders in the cooperative association with occupancy rights to specific units. Condominium owners pay their own taxes; cooperative residents pay taxes in their monthly charges.

Mobile Homes

You might also want to consider a mobile home. A suitable one must be at least 10 feet wide and 50 feet long.

What is it like to live in a mobile-home park? Certainly, there is a closeness in these parks that you would not have in a normal neighborhood. Typically, the mobile home is placed on a lot 25 to 30 feet wide and 75 feet deep. This means that you could have 12 families within a radius of 100 feet.

Residents visit back and forth and hold frequent picnics, barbecues, and other social activities. This would not be the way of life for someone who did not enjoy group activities.

Be Realistic

To find out what type of housing is best for you, look around the area to see where you want to live. Each community is different, shaped by the people who live there. Talk to the residents and do some serious thinking before you move, not forgetting to carefully consider your financial position in regard to the new locale. Try to be realistic; don't expect to find the perfect climate for health and happiness. The nearest thing to it would be a place that encourages outdoor life, is neither too hot nor too cold, has a relative humidity of around 55 percent, and enough variety in weather, with frequent but moderate weather changes, to be interesting and not too monotonous.

If you have any doubts about the location as far as health is concerned, check with your physician.

When Faced with Ill Health

How can you help yourself or others when faced with a serious or terminal illness?

Alvin I. Goldfarb, M.D., former consultant on Services for the Aged, New York State Department of Mental Hygiene, notes the importance of self-esteem, self-confidence, sense of purpose, and well-being to a person who is seriously ill or dying. Supported by the idea, "I've led a good and full life," older people can face a serious or terminal illness with dignity. Sometimes this acceptance may be almost an unspoken and tacit understanding between the aging and society to help the separation process along.

When a person is terminally ill, the chances are that he is not in severe pain. With the increasing supply of pain-relieving drugs and the possibility of sedation, very few elderly patients suffer greatly with pain. While a fear of death probably exists in most people, when death is actually encountered the fear is seldom overwhelming, even though it may deeply affect others directly involved with the dying patient.

Most patients are at least aware of the possibility of dying soon; those with lingering conditions are particularly adept at self-diagnosis. But more often, they notice a change in social relationships with friends, family, and medical personnel.

Patient–physician relationships can be vital in helping the seriously ill patient retain peace of mind. It is the physician's responsibility to give compassion and recognize fear, even when it is hidden. Likewise, he should respond to a patient's hidden wish to discuss his illness. Of course, there is no set formula for communicating with seriously ill patients. Each individual needs a different approach, and most physicians are sensitive to this.

Many physicians report that death, except in unusual cases, is not accompanied by physical pain. Rather, there is often a sense of well-being and spiritual exaltation. Physicians think this feeling is caused by the anesthetic action of carbon dioxide on the central nervous system and by the effect of toxic substances. Ernest Hemingway wrote, "The pang of death, a famous doctor once told me, is often less than that of a toothache."

Stages of Death

According to physicians, people die in stages—rapidly or slowly, depending on circumstances. First comes *clinical death*, when respiration and heartbeat cease. The brain dies as it is deprived of oxygen and circulating blood, and *biological death* occurs.

Life can be restored in the moments between clinical death and brain death if circulation and respiration are continued through the use of medical devices that stimulate the heart and lungs.

After the brain ceases to function, cellular death begins. Life is not considered to be completely lost until the brain stops functioning. It is possible for surgeons to remove viable organs after biological death for transplant or other use.

Many clergymen and physicians insist that we need more honest communication about death, as such communication is probably the single most useful measure to avoid unnecessary suffering. Sound knowledge never made anyone afraid. And although death will probably always remain essentially a mystery, scientists will continue to search for a better understanding of its nature. By such means they may learn a great deal more about life.

The Autopsy

Family members adjusting to the death of a loved one may face the question of whether or not an autopsy should be performed. More and more, medical experts are underscoring the need for an autopsy as a means of confirming the cause of death. The postmortem examination may also "provide a reasonable context for accepting death," according to Daniel W. McKeel, director of autopsy pathology at Washington University School of Medicine. From a family and genetic point of view, the autopsy may reveal information about specific conditions or medical problems in the deceased that survivors can use to guide their own health practices and concerns.

Contrary to some reports, the autopsy need not delay funeral arrangements or disfigure the body so as to require a closed casket. Autopsies are generally mandatory in homicide, suicide, burn deaths, deaths resulting from on-the-job injuries, operating room deaths, and questionable or unwitnessed deaths.

7

Diseases of the Skeletal System

The bones and joints of the human body, although designed to withstand a great deal of stress, are subject to a variety of disorders that can affect people of all ages. Some skeletal deformities are the result of congenital defects, and can be treated by physical therapy or surgery with varying degrees of success. Arthritis and related joint diseases, caused by wear and tear over the years, probably affect more people than any other skeletal disorder.

Man's erect posture makes the spine especially vulnerable to problems of alignment, often causing considerable pain. Bone tissue can also be invaded by tumors and by infections of the bone marrow. Also, stress to bones and joints can cause fractures or dislocations, which require prompt medical treatment to prevent deformity or loss of mobility.

Congenital Defects

As the fetus develops in the womb, its bony skeleton first appears as soft cartilage, which hardens into bone before birth. The calcium content of the mother's diet aids the fetus in bone formation and in the development of the normal human skeleton. Thus the basic skeletal structure of an individual is formed before his birth. In some instances, the bones of the fetus develop abnormally, and such defects are usually noticeable soon after delivery.

The causes of skeletal birth defects are not always known. Some may result from hereditary factors; others have been traced to the mother's exposure to X rays, radiation, chemicals, drugs, or to disease during pregnancy. Among the more common birth defects are extra fingers, toes, or ribs, or missing fingers, hands, toes, feet, or limbs. Sections of the spine may be fused together, often without causing serious problems later in life, although some fused joints can hinder the motion of limbs. The sections of the skull may unite prematurely, retarding the growth of the brain.

Defects of the Skull, Face, and Jaw

Various malformations of the skull, face, and jaw can appear at birth or soon after. They include *macrocephaly* (enlarged head) and *microcephaly* (very small head). Microcephaly is caused by the premature fusion of the cranial sutures in early childhood. If brain growth increases very rapidly during the first six months of life in infants whose skulls have fused prematurely, the brain cannot expand sufficiently within the rigid skull, and mental retardation results. Surgery is used to widen the sutures to permit normal brain development.

Cleft lip and *cleft palate* are common facial deformities and are visible at birth. These are longitudinal openings in the upper lip and palate. They result from failure of the area to unite in the normal manner during embryonic stages of pregnancy. They should be corrected at an early age. If surgery is performed in infancy there is a good chance that the child will mature with little or no physical evidence of the affliction and with no psychological damage as a result of it. See "Cleft Palate and Cleft Lip" in Ch. 2, *The First Dozen Years*, for further information.

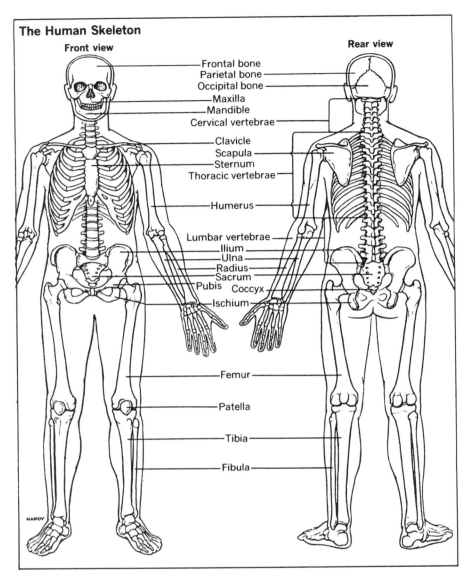

The Human Skeleton

Front view

- Frontal bone
- Parietal bone
- Occipital bone
- Maxilla
- Mandible
- Cervical vertebrae
- Clavicle
- Scapula
- Sternum
- Thoracic vertebrae
- Humerus
- Lumbar vertebrae
- Ilium
- Ulna
- Radius
- Sacrum
- Pubis
- Coccyx
- Ischium
- Femur
- Patella
- Tibia
- Fibula

Rear view

HARDY

Defects of the Rib Cage

Every normal human being has 12 pairs of ribs attached to the spine, but some people are born with extra ribs on one or both sides.

Although such extra ribs are usually harmless, one that projects into the neck can damage nerves and the artery located in that area. In adults extra neck ribs may cause shooting pains down the arms, general periodic numbness in the arms and hands, weak wrist pulse, and possible diminished blood supply to the forearm. Surgery may be required to remove the rib and thereby relieve the pres-

sure on the nerves or artery. Minor symptoms are treated by physiotherapy.

Congenital absence of one or more ribs is not uncommon. An individual may be born with some ribs fused together. Neither condition creates any serious threat to health.

Congenital Dislocation of the Hip

Dislocation of the hip is the most common congenital problem of the pelvic area. It is found more often in girls than in boys in a five to one ratio. Babies born from a breech presenta-

tion, buttocks first, are more likely to develop this abnormality than those delivered head first. The condition may be the result of inherited characteristics.

Clinical examination of infants, especially breech-born girls, may reveal early signs of congenital hip dislocation, with the affected hip appearing shorter than the normal side. If the condition is not diagnosed before the infant is ready to walk, the child may begin walking later than is normal. The child may develop a limp and an unsteady gait, with one leg shorter than the other.

Early diagnosis of this condition is important, followed by immediate reduction and immobilization by means of a plaster cast or by applying traction. Permanent deformity, dislocation, uneven pelvis, retarded walking, limping, and unsteady gait are possible complications if this condition remains untreated. Surgery is sometimes required.

Arthritis and Other Joint Diseases

Arthritis is probably the most common of all disabling diseases, at least in the temperate areas of the world. It has been estimated that 10 percent of the population suffers from one of the many forms of arthritis. In the United States alone, more than 13 million persons each year seek professional medical care for arthritis. Of this number, some three million must restrict their daily activities, and about 750,000 are so disabled by arthritis that they are unable to attend school, work, or even handle common household tasks.

Arthritis apparently is not associated with any stage of civilization; it has been diagnosed in the skeletons of prehistoric humans. There is even evidence that arthritic diseases afflict a variety of animals, including the dinosaurs that inhabited the earth more than 100 million years ago. Arthritis caused pain and suffering to such famous personages as Goethe, Henry VI, Charlemagne, and Alexander the Great.

Arthritis and *rheumatism* are terms sometimes used interchangeably by the layman to describe any abnormal condition of the joints, muscles, or related tissues. Many rheumatic or arthritic diseases have popular names, such as "housemaid's knee," "baseball finger," or "weaver's bottom." Physicians usually prefer to apply the term *arthritis* to disorders of the joints, especially joint disorders accompanied by inflammation. More than 75 different diseases of the joints have been identified; they are classified according to their specific signs, symptoms, and probable causes. The list includes bursitis, gout, and tendinitis in addition to the major disorders, rheumatoid arthritis and osteoarthritis.

Rheumatoid arthritis and osteoarthritis are examples of two types of arthritic ailment that are quite different diseases. Rheumatoid arthritis usually develops from unknown causes before the age of 45 and is marked by a nonspecific inflammation of the joints of the extremities; the inflammation is accompanied by changes in substances found in the blood. A victim of rheumatoid arthritis may develop limb deformities within a short period of time. Osteoarthritis, on the other hand, is most likely to produce symptoms after the age of 45. Here the cause is simply wear and tear on the cartilage cushions of the joints, mainly weight-bearing ones such as the hips and knees. Both kinds of joint disorders afflict millions of persons with painful and disabling symptoms.

Osteoarthritis

The most common form of arthritis is *osteoarthritis*, which is also known by the terms *hypertrophic arthritis* and *degenerative joint disease*. It can be said quite accurately that if you live long enough you will experience osteoarthritis. In fact, osteoarthritis is most common in areas of the world where people have the greatest longevity. The first signs of osteoarthritis may appear on X-ray pictures of persons in their 30s and 40s, even though they have not yet felt pain in the weight-bearing joints, the hips and knees, where discomfort usually appears first. Studies show that nearly everybody has at least the beginning signs or symptoms of osteoarthritis after they reach their 50s. It affects both men and women, although women may not experience symptoms until after they have reached the menopause.

Causes

A somewhat simplified explanation of the cause of osteoarthritis is this: the joints between the bones of a young person are cushioned and lubricated by cartilage pads and smooth lining membranes; normal wear and tear on

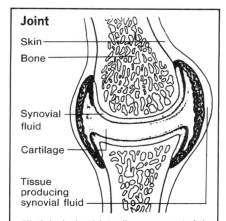

Joint
Skin
Bone

Synovial fluid

Cartilage

Tissue producing synovial fluid

All of the body's joints allow movement of the bones through this combination of ball and socket contours. Cartilage allows the bones to move without scraping or catching. Synovial fluid helps reduce friction in the movement.

the joints during a lifetime of activity gradually erodes the protective layers between the bones. In addition, the bones may develop small growths at the joints, a factor that aggravates the situation. There is evidence that heredity plays a role in the development of these bone growths, which are ten times more likely to occur in women than in men.

While hips and knees are among the most likely targets of osteoarthritis, the disease also can involve the hands, the shoulders, or back. Weight-bearing joints are commonly involved when the patient is overweight and spends a great deal of time standing or walking.

Symptoms

Except for the descriptions of aches and pains by victims of osteoarthritis and X-ray examination of the joints, a physician frequently has little information to go on in making a diagnosis of this disease. In some cases, there may be enlargement of the joint and some tenderness. But few cases are marked by the excessive warmth, for example, associated with rheumatoid arthritis. There are no laboratory tests that can distinguish the disorder from other rheumatic or arthritic diseases.

Osteoarthritis seldom causes the degree of discomfort experienced by patients afflicted by rheumatoid arthritis; the disease is not as disabling for most patients, and even the stiffness associated with osteoarthritis is milder, usually lasting only a few minutes when activity is attempted, while the stiffness of rheumatoid arthritis may continue for hours.

Arthritis of the Hip

Although most cases of osteoarthritis are not seriously disabling, arthritis of

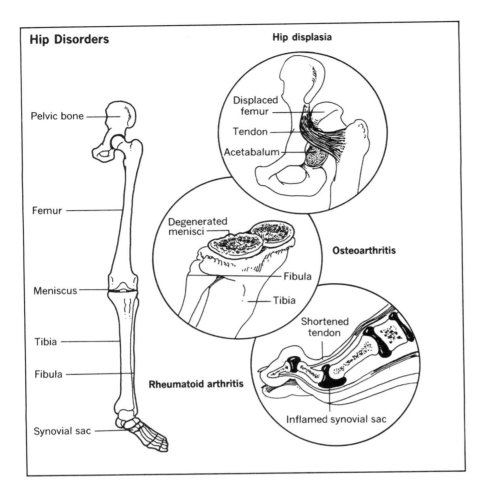

Hip Disorders

Pelvic bone

Femur

Meniscus

Tibia

Fibula

Synovial sac

Hip displasia

Displaced femur

Tendon

Acetabalum

Degenerated menisci

Fibula

Tibia

Osteoarthritis

Shortened tendon

Rheumatoid arthritis

Inflamed synovial sac

the hip is a prominent cause of disability in older persons. It produces pain in the hips, the inner thigh, the groin, and very often in the knee. Walking, climbing steps, sitting, and bending become very painful, because the joint is destroyed by degeneration of bone and cartilage. Stress and strain on the hip joint further aggravate the condition, which becomes worse with advancing age.

Surgery to replace the head of the femur or the entire hip joint with metal or plastic parts has brought relief from pain and restored mobility to some patients suffering from severe arthritis of the hip.

Small children sometimes suffer from transient arthritis of the hip, of unknown cause, manifested by pain, limitation of hip movement, and impeded walking. Because the condition usually disappears within six weeks, the only treatment is bed rest. Transient arthritis must not be mistaken for the more serious pyrogenic hip arthritis of children and adults, marked by high fever.

Spinal Arthritis

The aging process is the prinicipal cause of spinal arthritis. Other contributing factors are disk lesions and injury. Spinal arthritis causes pronounced bone degeneration and disability. The sufferer experiences severe back pain radiating to the thighs as a result of interference of the nerve roots from *osteophytes*, or spurs, formed in the joints. In mild cases, physical therapy may be the only treatment required.

Treatment of Osteoarthritis

For most patients, osteoarthritis is not likely to be crippling or disabling. The effects generally are not more serious than stiffness of the involved joints, with occasional discomfort and some pain. When weight-bearing joints are involved, the basic remedies are weight control and adequate rest for the areas affected. In some instances, the patient may have to learn new postural adjustments; symptoms often appear in another joint after the first has been affected because the patient tends to favor the joint that first caused pain and shifts weight or muscle stress to the second joint.

Physical therapy and corrective exercises are helpful. A physician may recommend the use of aspirin or another analgesic for the pain. Steroid drugs may be injected into an injured joint, but usually only for temporary relief. Surgery is sometimes recommended for removal of troublesome bone spurs or to correct a serious problem in a weight-bearing joint, where a metal cup or other device may be inserted as part of an artificial joint.

Rheumatoid Arthritis

Rheumatoid arthritis occurs at a much earlier age than osteoarthritis, appearing at any time from infancy to old age, but most commonly afflicting persons between the ages of 20 and 35. Women are three times as likely to be victims of rheumatoid arthritis as are men, although men seem to lose that advantage after the age of 50. All races seem to be equally vulnerable. Recent studies also suggest that two common beliefs about rheumatoid arthritis probably are untrue. The facts show that the disease is not hereditary and that it is not more prevalent in cold, damp climates.

Symptoms

Rheumatoid arthritis can begin as part of an acute illness, with high fever and intense inflammation of the joints, or it can develop insidiously with little or no discomfort except for fatigue, loss of appetite, weight loss, and perhaps a mild fever. Sometime later the victim becomes aware of aches and pains in the joints and muscles and seeks medical attention. Frequently, deformities develop before the patient realizes that rheumatoid arthritis may be the cause of swollen joints, pain, redness, or excessive warmth about the affected area.

The inflammation of a joint caused by rheumatoid arthritis may continue for weeks or it may last for a period of years. During inflammation, tendons become shortened and muscles lose their normal balance. The result is the deformity of joints commonly associated with rheumatoid arthritis, such as a swan-neck shape in the fingers. Muscular weakness develops and there is a loss of grip strength in the hands when that area is affected. Patients may be unable to make a tight fist.

A common symptom of rheumatoid arthritis is a stiffness that develops during periods of rest but gradually disappears when activity resumes. After a night's sleep, the stiffness may persist for a half hour or much longer. The stiffness may result, at least in part, from the muscular weakness that accompanies the disease.

Although the effects of rheumatoid arthritis are most commonly observed in the hands or feet of patients, other body joints such as the elbows, shoulders, knees, hips, ankles, spine, and even the jawbones may be involved. It is possible for all of a patient's joints to be involved, and the involvement often is symmetrical; that is, both hands will develop the symptoms at the same time and in the same pattern.

Probable Causes

The exact cause of rheumatoid arthritis is unknown, although a variety of factors have been associated with the onset of the disease. Emotional upsets, tuberculosis, venereal disease, psoriasis, and rheumatic fever are among conditions associated with the beginnings of the disease. Various viruses and other microorganisms have been isolated from the inflamed tissues of patients, but medical researchers have been unable to prove that any of the infectious agents is the cause. Efforts have also been made to transmit rheumatoid arthritis from a known victim to a normal volunteer by transfusions and injections of substances found in the victim's tissues, but without success in tracing the causative factor.

Treatment

The symptoms of rheumatoid arthritis intensify or abate spontaneously and unpredictably. Available methods of treatment do not cure the disease but relieve the symptoms so that the pain is reduced and some normal movement is facilitated. Proper nutrition, heat, rest, and exercise are also helpful. A number of drugs can reduce the inflammation of the joints, but they may have undesirable toxic side effects. Accordingly, before any drug therapy is embarked upon, the patient should seek the advice of a physician specializing in arthritic disorders.

Aspirin

The most common drug used to treat all kinds of arthritis is aspirin; it is also the most economical. Occasional side effects, such as irritation of ulcers or other gastrointestinal upsets, as well as buzzing in the ears, can result from aspirin use, especially in massive doses; such complications can some-

times be avoided by the use of specially coated aspirin tablets. The size of the dose usually is started at a minimum level and gradually increased until the physician finds a level that is most helpful to the patient but does not result in serious side effects.

Several other types of medication have been tried as alternatives to aspirin. One of the newer drugs, *indomethacin*, is about as effective as aspirin, but when taken in large doses it also seems to cause side effects, including nausea, heartburn, and headache.

Sulindac, a nonsteroidal antiinflammatory drug (NSAI), made its appearance on the U.S. market in the late 1970s. Under the trade name Clinoril, sulindac came into wide use in the treatment of a variety of arthritic disorders. These included osteoarthritis, rheumatoid arthritis, gouty arthritis, and painful shoulder.

Sulindac both relieves pain and reduces fever while attacking inflammations. In those respects it resembles other antiarthritis drugs such as fenoprofen (trade name: Nalfon), naproxen (trade name: Naprosyn), and tolmetin (trade name: Tolectin). Sulindac can be ingested on a twice-daily basis; but in use it was found to have adverse side effects, some of them serious. For example, some patients reported abdominal pains, nausea, and constipation. Diarrhea can also occur. Some side effects involved the central nervous system, and included dizziness, drowsiness, and headache.

Among other drugs used to treat arthritis, DMSO (dimethylsulfoxide) attracted widespread attention in the early 1980s. Research indicated that DMSO might have value as an antiarthritic agent. The Arthritis Foundation of the United States indicated, however, that DMSO might serve as "a short-term analgesic for pain due to limited conditions." A liquid that arthritis sufferers rubbed on their skin,

DMSO was reported to have such negative side effects as skin rashes and halitosis.

Many other drugs promising relief for victims of arthritis have made their appearance in recent years. For example, penicillamine (trade name: Cuprimine) was found to help patients with rheumatoid arthritis. Experiments with many other drugs—including aclofenac, flurbiprofen, and proquazone—are under way.

Steroids

The cortisone-type (steroid) drugs have proven effective in controlling severe cases of rheumatoid arthritis. They can be given orally or injected directly into the affected joints. However, these drugs generate a number of undesirable side effects, and withdrawal often results in a severe recurrence of the original symptoms. Thus, steroid drug therapy is a long-term process that can make the patient totally dependent on the medication. Some physicians are reluctant to inject steroid drugs into the joints because the effect is temporary and there is a danger of introducing infection by repeated use of the needle. In addition, some patients do not seem to respond to the steroid drugs and X-ray studies of the joints may show progressive destruction of the tissues despite the medications.

Rest

Bed rest is recommended for acute cases and up to 10 hours of sleep per day is advised for mild cases of rheumatoid arthritis. The patient also should take rest periods during the day whenever possible, reducing fatigue and stress on the affected joints. As in severe cases of osteoarthritis, the patient should try to adjust his daily work habits to avoid strain on weight-bearing joints.

Exercise

Patients tend to avoid moving arthritic joints because of pain and stiffness. Exercise of an arthritic joint, however, helps prevent the adjoining muscles from shrinking and weakening. A program of physiotherapy—including hot packs and exercise—can be extremely helpful.

The exercise program should carry the joints through their normal range of movement. Exercises should be performed every day but not carried to the point of fatigue. In addition to exercises intended to prevent limitation of normal joint movement, isometric-type exercises should be used to maintain or increase muscle power in other parts of the body that might otherwise be neglected because of limited activity by the patient.

Posture

The patient should be encouraged to maintain proper posture as much as possible, through correct positioning of the body when standing, sitting, or reclining in bed. A sheet of thick plywood may be used under a mattress to prevent it from sagging. Chairs should be firm with straight backs. Pillows should be avoided whenever possible.

Crutches, canes, leg braces, and other devices may be needed by the patient in advanced stages of rheumatoid arthritis. In some cases, orthopedic surgery is recommended to help reconstruct the limbs and joints as a part of rehabilitation.

Heat

Massages or vibrating equipment are not recommended as part of the therapy for rheumatoid arthritis patients. Heat in the form of hot baths, hot compresses, or heating pads, however, may be helpful. Paraffin baths are particularly helpful in treating hands or wrists.

Diet

While osteoarthritis patients are advised to lose as much weight as possible, rheumatoid arthritis patients tend to suffer from weight loss and nutritional deficiencies. Part of the cause may be a loss of appetite that is a characteristic of the disease and part may be the gastrointestinal problems that frequently accompany the disorder and that may be aggravated by the medications prescribed. Some physicians advise that rheumatoid arthritis patients include adequate amounts of protein and calcium in their diets as a preventive measure against a loss of bone tissue.

Juvenile Rheumatoid Arthritis

A form of arthritis quite similar to adult rheumatoid arthritis afflicts some children before the age of 16. Called *juvenile rheumatoid arthritis* or *Still's disease*, it includes a set of symptoms that nevertheless differentiate it from adult rheumatoid arthritis. In addition to the rheumatoid joint symptoms, the patient may have a high fever, rash, pleurisy, and enlargement of the spleen. The onset of the disease may appear in the form of an unexplained childhood rash and fever, with arthritic symptoms developing as much as several weeks later. A possible complication is an eye inflammation that can lead to blindness if untreated.

Treatment

Juvenile rheumatoid arthritis is treated with aspirin or steroid drugs, or both, along with other kinds of therapy used for the adult version of rheumatoid arthritis. Steroid therapy is often more effective against rheumatoid arthritis in children than in adults. There may be a complete remission of the disease or the patient may experience rheumatoid symptoms into adult life.

Ankylosing Spondylitis

A kind of arthritis that affects the spine, causing a fusion of the joints, is known as *ankylosing spondylitis*. About 90 percent of the patients are young adult males. There is some evidence that it may be a hereditary disease.

Like other forms of arthritis, ankylosing spondylitis is insidious in its start. The patient may complain of a backache, usually in the lumbar area of the back. Some victims of the disease have claimed they were without pain but felt muscle spasms and perhaps tenderness along the lower part of the spine. Then stiffness and loss of motion spread rapidly over the back.

Along with fusion of the spine, the ligament along the spine calcifies like a bone. X-ray photographs of the spinal column may show the backbone to resemble a length of bamboo. A complication is that the spine is bent and chest expansion is limited by the fusion so that normal breathing is impaired.

Treatment of the disease consists of physical therapy and exercises to prevent or limit deformity and the use of aspirin or other drugs to reduce pain.

Gout

Gout is an arthritic disease associated with an abnormality of body chemistry. There is an excessive accumulation of uric acid in the blood resulting from the chemical abnormality, and the uric acid, in the form of sharp urate crystals, may accumulate in the joints, where they cause an inflammation with symptoms like those of arthritis. A frequent target of the urate crystals is the great toe, which is why gout patients occasionally are pictured as sitting in a chair with one foot propped upon a pillow.

Primary Gout

There are two forms of gout, primary gout and secondary gout. Primary gout is presumed to be linked to a hereditary defect in metabolism and afflicts mostly men, although women may experience the disease after menopause. The painful inflammation may develop overnight following an injury or illness or after a change in eating habits. The patient may suddenly feel feverish and unable to move because of the tenderness of the affected joint, which becomes painfully swollen and red.

Although the great toe is a common site for the appearance of gout, it also may develop in the ankle, knee, wrist, hand, elbow, or another joint. Only one joint may be affected, or several joints might be involved at the same time or in sequence. The painful attack usually subsides within a week or so but it may return to the same joint or another joint after an absence of a few years. The inflammation subsides even if it is not treated, but untreated gout may eventually result in deformity or loss of use of the affected joint. During periods between attacks the patient may show no signs of the disease except for high blood serum levels of uric acid and the appearance of *tophi*, or *urate* (a salt or uric acid) deposits, visible in X-ray photographs of the joints.

Secondary Gout

Secondary gout is related to a failure of the kidneys to excrete uric acid products or a variety of diseases that are characterized by overproduction of certain types of body cells. Failure of the kidneys to filter out urates can, in turn, be caused by various drugs, including aspirin and diuretics. Gout symptoms can also be caused by efforts to lose weight rapidly through a starvation diet, because this speeds up the breakdown of stored body fats. Among diseases that may precipitate an attack of secondary gout are Hodgkin's disease, psoriasis, and some forms of leukemia.

Chronic Gouty Arthritis

A form of arthritis called *chronic gouty arthritis* is associated with patients who have abnormal levels of uric acid in their blood. While they may or may not be plagued by attacks of acute joint pain, the urate deposits apparently cause a certain amount of stiffness and soreness in various joints, especially during periods of stormy weather or falling barometric pressure. The tophi or urate crystals may spread to soft tissues of the body, such as bursae, the cartilage of the ear, and tendon sheaths. More than ten percent of gout patients eventually develop kidney stones formed from urate deposits in the kidney.

Treatment of Gout

Because gout was traditionally associated with certain meats that are rich in chemicals called *purines*, special diets were once a routine part of the treatment. In recent years, there has been less emphasis placed on maintaining a low-purine diet for gout patients. This change in therapy is mainly the result of the relatively good success in maintaining proper uric-acid levels in gout patients with medications. However, adequate fluid intake is still recommended to prevent development of urate kidney stones.

Infectious Arthritic Agents

There are at least 12 types of arthritis

and rheumatism that are associated with infections involving bacteria, viruses, fungi, or other organisms. One of these diseases is known as *pyrogenic arthritis*. The arthritis-causing organisms infect a joint and induce pain and fever and limitation of joint movement by muscle spasm and swelling. Treatment includes bed rest and antibiotics. If untreated, destruction of the joints is possible.

Gonococcal Arthritis

This disease is transmitted by the gonococcal bacteria associated with venereal disease. As in the venereal disease itself, the arthritic effects are more likely to be treated at an early stage in men than in women because men are more likely to develop obvious infections of the urethra and thus seek medication from a physician. In females, the initial infection is likely to go unrecognized and untreated by antibiotics. The infection, meanwhile, may spread to body joints and produce acute attacks of arthritis. The symptoms tend to appear first in the wrists and finger joints; there may also be skin lesions that occur temporarily in areas near the joints.

Tuberculous Arthritis

As the name suggests, this disease is associated with tuberculosis and can be serious, leading to the destruction of involved joints. The infection spreads to the joints from other areas of the body. The early symptoms include pain, tenderness, or muscle spasm. In children and young adults the infection tends to settle in the spinal joints. If there is an absence of pain, the disease may go unnoticed until changes in posture or gait are observed. If untreated, the disease may progress toward spinal deformity. When detected early in the course of the disease, treatment with anti-

tuberculosis drugs and physical therapy may control the disorder. In some cases, surgery may be required.

Rubella Arthritis

This form of arthritis derives from an infection involving the rubella virus. The arthritis symptoms may appear shortly after a rash appears, or they may be delayed until after the rash has faded. The onset of the arthritis effects may be accompanied by fever and a general feeling of illness; pain and swelling are most likely to occur in the small joints of the wrists, knees, or ankles. The physician usually advises aspirin for the pain while it lasts, usually about a week. Eventually all signs and symptoms may subside without joint destruction.

Bacteria That Cause Arthritis

A type of bacteria that causes spinal meningitis also may cause symptoms of arthritis. The pain usually is not severe and may be limited to a few body joints. Antibiotics are administered to control the infection, although this form of the disease does not respond as rapidly to the medication as some of the other versions of arthritis caused by infection.

Several other kinds of bacteria may invade the joints and precipitate or aggravate arthritic symptoms. They include the increasingly common strains of bacteria that have become resistant to control by antibiotics. Patients who are being treated with steroid drugs or those whose resistance to infection has been lowered by disease are among the most vulnerable victims.

Fungal Arthritis

While fungal infections are relatively rare causes of arthritis, there are at least four kinds of fungus that have been identified as the responsible or-

ganisms in joint inflammations. The fungus seems to be carried by the bloodstream to the area of the joint where it causes an inflammation in the tissues surrounding the bony structures. The infection usually can be treated with special antibiotic remedies that destroy fungal organisms, but surgery is occasionally necessary to ensure eradication of the source of the inflammation.

Psoriatic Arthropathy

Arthritis also may be associated with psoriasis (a chronic skin condition marked by bright red patches and scaling) in a disease known as *psoriatic arthropathy*. This variation of the disease is marked by a deep pitting of the nails along with a chronic arthritic condition. The disease may be mild or very destructive and the sacroiliac region of the spine may be involved. The uric acid levels associated with gout frequently are elevated in patients with psoriasis, so gout symptoms also can appear. Unfortunately, one of the medications commonly used in the treatment of rheumatoid arthritis and gout, chloroquine, cannot be used as therapy for psoriatic arthropathy symptoms because the drug aggravates the psoriasis. Otherwise, the treatment is quite similar to that used for rheumatoid arthritis—analgesics such as aspirin and steroid drugs. In severe cases, methotrexate may be administered to control both the joint and skin symptoms.

Other Arthritic Diseases

Two kinds of arthritis once associated with venereal diseases are no longer considered a hazard of intimate contact. One is syphilis-caused arthritis, which is a possible problem but actually quite rare because of improved control of syphilis. The second is *Rei-*

ing heart. Called the *cine CT*, the imaging procedure enables cardiologists to measure blood flow through grafted coronary arteries. Only by using a catheter could physicians take such measurements earlier. With the cine CT it is also possible to measure the weights of different parts of the heart with almost 100 percent accuracy and to detect minute holes in the hearts of children suffering from congenital heart defects. Surgeons use these pictures to become familiar with a defective heart before surgery.

More advanced than either the CT scanner or radiography, *nuclear magnetic resonance* (NMR) uses neither X radiation, as does the CT scanner, nor needle-injected contrast fluids. Instead, NMR uses magnetic forces 3,000 to 25,000 times as strong as the earth's magnetic field. Taking three-dimensional "pictures" of various parts of the body, NMR "sees" through bones. It can differentiate between the brain's gray and white matter. NMR can also show blood moving through an artery or the reaction of a malignant tumor to therapy.

Another type of contrast study is called a *myelogram*. A radiopaque liquid similar to that used in angiography is introduced through a spinal needle into the sac-enclosed space around the spinal cord. Any obstructive or compressive lesion of the spinal cord is thus seen on the radiograph and helps to confirm the diagnosis.

Each of these contrast studies helps the physician better understand the structures of the brain or spinal cord and may be essential for him to make a correct diagnosis.

Cerebral Palsy

The term *cerebral palsy* is not a diagnosis but a label for a problem in locomotion exhibited by some children. Definitions of cerebral palsy are

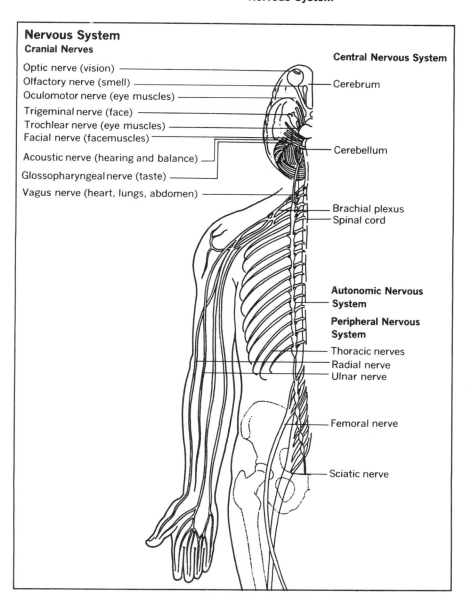

Nervous System
Cranial Nerves

Optic nerve (vision)
Olfactory nerve (smell)
Oculomotor nerve (eye muscles)
Trigeminal nerve (face)
Trochlear nerve (eye muscles)
Facial nerve (face muscles)
Acoustic nerve (hearing and balance)
Glossopharyngeal nerve (taste)
Vagus nerve (heart, lungs, abdomen)

Central Nervous System
Cerebrum
Cerebellum
Brachial plexus
Spinal cord

Autonomic Nervous System
Peripheral Nervous System
Thoracic nerves
Radial nerve
Ulnar nerve
Femoral nerve
Sciatic nerve

many and varied, but in general refer to nonprogressive abnormalities of the brain that have occurred early in life from many causes. The label implies that there is no active disease process but rather a static or nonprogressive lesion that may affect the growth and development of the child.

Symptoms

Included in the category of cerebral palsy are such problems as limpness (flaccidity), *spasticity* of one or all limbs, incoordination, or some other disorder of movement. In some pa-

tients, quick jerks affect different parts of the body at different times (*chorea*); in others, slow, writhing, incoordinated movements (*athetosis*) are most pronounced in the hands and arms. Incoordination of movement may also occur in muscles used for speaking and eating, so that speech becomes slurred, interrupted, or jerky; the patient may drool because incoordinated muscle action prevents efficient swallowing of saliva. This does little to improve the physical appearance of the child and, unfortunately, he may look mentally subnormal.

The fact that a patient has an abnormality that is responsible for difficulty in locomotion or speech does not mean that the child is mentally retarded. There is some likelihood that he will be mentally slow, but patients in this group of disease states range from slow to superior in intelligence, a fact that emphasizes that each child must be assessed individually.

A complete examination must be completed, and to determine the patient's functional status complete psychological testing should be performed by a skilled psychologist.

Treatment

Treatment for cerebral palsy is a continuing process involving a careful surveillance of the patient's physical and psychological status. A physical therapist, under the physician's guidance, will help to mobilize and maintain the function of the neuromuscular system. Occasionally, an orthopedic surgeon may surgically lengthen a tendon or in some way make a limb more functional. A speech therapist can provide additional speech training, and a vocational therapist can help the patient to find appropriate work. The key professional is the primary physician, usually the pediatrician, who with care and understanding guides the patient through the years.

Bell's Palsy

Bell's palsy is a paralysis of the facial nerve that was first described by Sir Charles Bell, a Scottish surgeon of the early nineteenth century. It may affect men and women at any age, though it occurs most commonly between the ages of 30 and 50. The onset of the facial paralysis may be abrupt: the patient may awaken one morning unable to move one side of his face. He can't wrinkle one side of his forehead or raise the eyebrow; the eye will not close on the affected side, and when attempting to smile, the face is pulled to the opposite side. Occasionally the patient may experience discomfort about the ear on the involved side. There is no difficulty in swallowing, but because the muscles about the corner of the mouth are weak, drooling is not uncommon, and food may accumulate in the gutter between gum and lip.

Bell's palsy may affect the branch of the facial nerve that supplies taste sensation to the anterior part of the tongue and the branch that supplies a small muscle in the middle ear (the *stapedius*) whose function it is to dampen loud sounds. Depending on the extent to which the facial nerve is affected, the patient may be unable to perceive taste on the side of the paralysis and may be unusually sensitive to sounds, a condition known as *hyperacusis*.

The most probable causes of Bell's palsy are inflammation of the facial nerve as it passes through a bony canal within the skull or inflammation of that bony canal with subsequent swelling and compression of the nerve. It is not uncommon that the patient has a history of exposure to a cold breeze, such as sleeping in a draft or riding in an open car. Any patient who has a facial weakness should be carefully evaluated by a physician, preferably a neurologist, to be quite certain that there is no other neurologic abnormality. When the diagnosis of Bell's palsy is certain, some therapeutic measures can be taken.

Treatment

There is no specific treatment for Bell's palsy, but many physicians recommend massage, application of heat, and exercise of the weak muscles, either passive (by external manipulation) or active (by use). These therapeutic measures do not specifically influence the course of the facial nerve paralysis, but they are thought to be useful in maintaining tone of the facial muscles and preventing permanent deformity. Occasionally a V-shaped adhesive tape splint can be applied to the affected side of the face, from the corner of the mouth to the temple. Some physicians treat the condition with steroids such as cortisone, which may hasten recovery if begun at the onset of the illness.

In treating Bell's palsy, it is important to remember that when the eyelid does not close normally, the conjunctiva and cornea are not fully lubricated, and corneal lesions may develop from excessive dryness or exposure to the air. For this reason, some ophthalmic lubrication may be recommended by the physician.

About 80 percent of the patients with Bell's palsy recover completely in a few days or weeks, and about 10 to 15 percent recover more slowly, over a period of three to six months. The remaining 5 to 10 percent will have some residual facial deformity.

Parkinson's Disease

Parkinson's disease is a potentially devastating neurological disease that results in a progressive loss of muscle control. Patients with *parkinsonism* are easily recognized because of the characteristic symptoms of gradually worsening tremors, rigidity, decreased ability to make voluntary movements and, in many cases, loss of cognitive functions. Scientifically described nearly a century and a half ago, the disease is associated with the death, or degeneration, of the brain cells that supply dopamine, a chemical that transmits signals between nerve cells. Such degeneration is normal in the human brain, but in patients suffering from Parkinson's disease the loss of dopamine-producing neurons occurs at an accelerated rate. The onset of parkinsonism may follow encephalitis, a brain injury, or exposure to toxic substances, but the symptoms usually occur in patients who are middle-aged or older and, in these instances, there is no known cause for the degeneration of the nerve cells.

Symptoms

The tremors or shaking usually involve the fingers and the wrist, but sometimes the arms, legs, or head are involved to the extent that the entire body shakes. Characteristically, the tremors occur when the patient is at rest. The tremors stop or are much less marked during a voluntary muscle movement. Tremors do not occur when the patient is asleep.

Early in the disease, the patient notices what appear to be the normal signs of aging—a little shakiness, stiffness, jerky motions, and difficulty with movements such as rising out of a low, deep chair. Very gradually the signs increase. The shaking begins to interfere with daily activities and other signs develop, including what most patients with parkinsonism perceive as the most distressing symptom, *bradykinesia,* the gradual loss of spontaneous movement. In advanced stages of the disease, such bradykinesia results in periods when the patient's body is completely unable to move itself. These "frozen" periods are known as *akinesia.* And, while the emotional balance of the parkinsonian patient is generally unaffected by the disease, he may lose the ability to control the facial and vocal muscles which allow him to convey a range of different emotions. Although the patient may continue to have natural emotional responses, he cannot indicate them in the normal manner, by smiling or frowning or by raising or

lowering his voice. Instead, his face appears expressionless, his voice flat. The patient frequently experiences periods of depression and tremendous frustration.

While most patients with Parkinson's disease continue to retain their cognitive abilities, in severe or advanced cases, the patient may suffer some degree of mental deterioration or dementia.

Treatment

Once it was determined nerve pathways in the brains of patients with parkinsonism were depleted of dopamine, modern treatment of the disease began to focus on providing the remaining healthy nerve cells with the means to make the crucial it. First introduced in the 1960s, levodopa, a natural brain chemical also used by the nerve cells to make dopamine, is the traditional treatment for sufferers of Parkinson's disease. Levodopa (or L-dopa), and levodopa-containing compounds, force the dying nerve cells in the brain to produce more dopamine. L-dopa also reduces all of the main symptoms of the disease. However, because the dopamine-producing cells continue to die, levodopa is usually rendered useless within ten years. For this reason, physicians sometimes delay treatment until a patient shows more severe symptoms. The drug, selegiline, also known as deprenyl, works to increase and extend the effects of Levodopa.

Side effects associated with L-dopa include nausea, involuntary movements, some mental changes, cardiac irregularities, and urinary retention. The undesirable side effects of nausea and confusion have been somewhat countered by the use of drugs like carbidopa, an *extracerebral decarboxylase inhibitor,* that prevent the levadopa from changing into dopamine

before it enters the brain. "End-of-dose" akinesia, the return of symptoms a few hours after taking medication, can be relieved in some cases by taking the patient off drug treatments entirely for several days. Patients are usually hospitalized during this "drug holiday" and some take part in speech and physical therapy programs.

Other drugs include those in the anticholinergic and dopamine agonist categories. Anticholinergic drugs are used to treat the early stages of the disease and include: trihexyphenidyl hydrochloride, benztropine mesylate, diphenhydramine hydrochloride, biperiden, and procyclidine hydrochloride. All of these drugs reduce tremors and rigidity to a modest degree, but none affects bradykinesia. Patients using the drugs may experience such side effects as gingivitis or inflammation of the gums, constipation, mild dizziness, nausea, nervousness, and slightly blurred vision. More serious side effects could include urinary retention, confusion, and psychosis. The two drugs in the dopamine agonist category, bromocriptine and pergolide, stimulate the brain's dopamine receptors, "convincing" the receptors they are dopamine. Bromocriptine and pergolide are used alone and in conjunction with levodopa.

While drug therapy remains the primary course of treatment, research has made advances in other areas, such as studies of possible environmental causes and factors and experimental surgeries involving the transplant of adrenal glands from the parkinsonian patient and the implantation of fetal tissue.

Epilepsy

Epilepsy is a common disorder of the human nervous system. In the United States, about five persons of every

1,000, or more than one million people, suffer from epilepsy.

Epilepsy affects all kinds of people, regardless of sex, intelligence, or standard of living.

Epilepsy has been one of the most misunderstood diseases throughout its long history. Because of the involvement of the brain, epilepsy has commonly been associated with psychiatric disorders. Epilepsy differs strikingly from psychiatric disorders in being manifested in relatively brief episodes that begin and end abruptly.

Causes and Precipitating Factors

A single epileptic seizure usually occurs spontaneously. In some cases, seizures are triggered by visual stimuli, such as a flickering image on a television screen, a sudden change from dark to very bright illumination, or vice versa. Other patients may react to auditory stimuli such as a loud noise, a monotonous sound, or even to certain musical notes. A seizure is accompanied by a discharge of nerve impulses, which can be detected by electroencephalography. The effect is something like that of a telephone switchboard in which a defect in the circuits accidentally causes wrong number calls. The forms that seizures take depend upon the location of the nervous system disturbances within the brain and the spread of the nerve impulses. Physicians have found that certain kinds of epilepsy cases can be traced to specific areas of the brain where the lesion has occurred.

Epilepsy can develop at any age, although nearly 85 percent of all cases appear before the age of 20 years. Hence, it is commonly seen as an affliction of children. There is no indication that epilepsy itself can be inherited, but some evidence exists that certain individuals inherit a greater tendency to develop the condition from precipitating causes than is true

for the general population. According to the Epilepsy Foundation, studies show that if neither parent has epilepsy, the chances are one in 100 that they will have an epileptic child, but the chances rise to one in 40 if one parent is epileptic.

About 70 percent of epilepsy cases are *idiopathic*—that is, they are not attributable to any known cause. In the remaining 30 percent, the recurrent seizures are *symptomatic*—they are symptoms of some definite brain lesion, either congenital or resulting from subsequent injury. Because it can reasonably be assumed that some of the idiopathic cases are a result of lesions that have not been identified, epilepsy is perhaps best regarded not as a specific disease but as a symptom of a brain abnormality due to any of various causes.

Aura Preceding a Seizure

Unusual sensory experiences have been reported to occur before a seizure by about half the victims of epilepsy. The sensation, which is called an *aura,* may appear in the form of an unpleasant odor, a tingling numbness, a sinking or gripping feeling, strangulation, palpitations, or a gastrointestinal sensation. Some patients say the sensation cannot be described. Others report feeling strange or confused for hours or even days before a seizure. Such an early warning is known as a *prodrome.*

The various types of epilepsy can be broadly grouped under four general categories: grand mal, petit mal, focal, and psychomotor. Only one feature is common to all types of epilepsy—the sudden, disorderly discharge of nerve impulses within the brain.

Grand Mal Seizure

The *grand mal* is a generalized convulsion during which the patient may

initially look strange or bewildered, suddenly groan or scream, lose consciousness and become stiff (*tonic phase*), hold the breath, fall to the ground unless supported, and then begin to jerk the arms and legs (*clonic phase*). There may be loss of bowel and bladder control. The tongue may be bitten by coming between clenched jaws. The duration of the entire seizure, both the tonic and clonic phases, is less than two minutes—frequently less than one minute—followed by postconvulsive confusion or deep sleep that may last for minutes or hours.

Variations in the Pattern

The sequence of events in grand mal seizures is not invariable. The tongue-biting and urinary and fecal incontinence do not occur as frequently in children as in adult patients. Children may also demonstrate a type of grand mal seizure in which the patient suddenly becomes limp and falls to the floor unconscious; there is no apparent tonic or clonic phase and the muscles do not become stiff. Other cases may manifest only the tonic phase, with unconsciousness and the muscles remaining in a stiffened, tonic state throughout the seizure. There also is a clonic type of seizure, which begins with rapid jerking movements that continue during the entire attack. In one very serious form of convulsive seizure known as *status epilepticus,* repeated grand mal seizures occur without the victim's becoming conscious between them.

Petit Mal Seizure

Petit mal seizures are characterized by momentary staring spells, as if the patient were suspended in the middle of his activity. He may have a blank stare or undergo rapid blinking, sometimes accompanied by small twitching movements in one part of

The Back

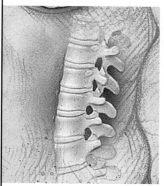

The back, especially the lower back, is a source of chronic pain for many individuals. Muscle strain because of overexertion, poor posture, or poor support because of weak stomach muscles are common causes of back pain that are best handled with rest and then proper exercise. A slipped disk (when one of the cushioning cartilaginous disks between each vertebra moves out of position) is more serious, although often brought on by the same causes as muscle strain. Changes in lifestyle, including exercise habits and stress reduction, are recommended over surgery.

Autoimmune Diseases

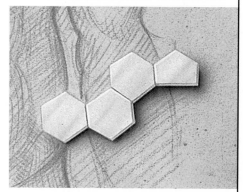

Autoimmune diseases are cases where the body's immune system attacks the body's own tissues and organs in the same way it attacks invading microbes; somehow the lymphocytes incorrectly identify the body's tissues as outside invaders. (Allergies are related disorders when the lymphocytes incorrectly identify harmless outside sources as harmful.) Autoimmune diseases include insulin dependent diabetes mellitus, systematic lupus erythematosus, rheumatoid arthritis, and dermatomyositis. Treatment involves first correcting any major deficiencies and then diminishing the activity of the immune system with drugs such as corticosteroids or immunosuppressant drugs.

The Breasts

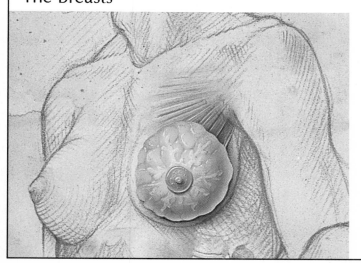

Breast cancer is the most common of cancers affecting women, killing more women than any other cancer except lung cancer. The cause of breast cancer is unknown. If caught early enough it can be treated effectively. Monthly self-examination of the breasts is important. Annual mammography for women over 40 is also recommended. Should a lump be found, and a biopsy determine that it is cancerous, it is not always necessary that the entire breast, lymph glands, and muscle be removed (radical mastectomy). (In fact many physicians consider this procedure obsolete.) In most cases a simple mastectomy (removal of the breast alone) or a lumpectomy (removal of the tumor only) followed by radiation, chemotherapy, or hormonal treatments is just as effective.

Caesarian sections are done in an increasingly high percentage of cases in the United States, often routinely if a woman has had one with the previous pregnancy. While there are very important instances when C-sections are absolutely necessary (the baby is in a difficult breech position, the baby's head is too large to pass through the pelvic girdle, the pelvic opening is too small to accommodate even a normal size infant), a C-section should never be done to accommodate the patient's (or her doctor's) schedule or as "defensive medicine" to avoid perceived threats of malpractice. Women who have had C-sections can have successful vaginal births (VBACs) and should be encouraged and supported to do so.

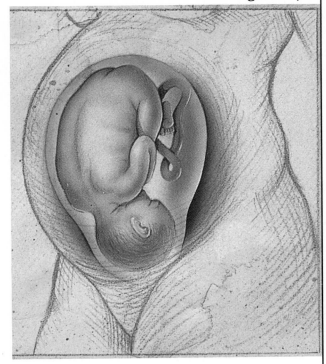

The Uterus, Ovaries, and Fallopian Tubes

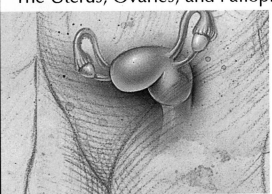

The female reproductive system is susceptible to cancers. It is also susceptible to endometriosis, a painful overgrowth of uterine tissues that eventually blocks the fallopian tubes, causing infertility. One common disorder of the uterus is the development of benign fibroid tumors. Although fibroid tumors can grow to large sizes, distorting the shape of the uterus and causing painful menstrual periods, full removal of the uterus (hysterectomy) is not always necessary. Laser surgery to remove the fibroids alone is an effective, and much less drastic, treatment.

The Prostate and Urethra

The prostate gland is a small cone-shaped object that surrounds the male urethra. It is normally about half an inch long and weighs less than an ounce. Ejaculatory ducts empty through the prostate into the urethra, and other ducts drain glandular secretions of the prostate into the urethra. Because of the intimate association of the prostate and the urinary tract, a disorder in one system can easily affect the other. Cancer of the prostate that threatens to metastasize may necessitate removal of the entire gland (prostatectomy).

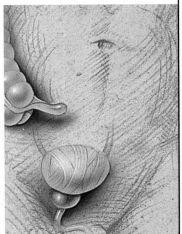

Common Medical Problems of the Human Body

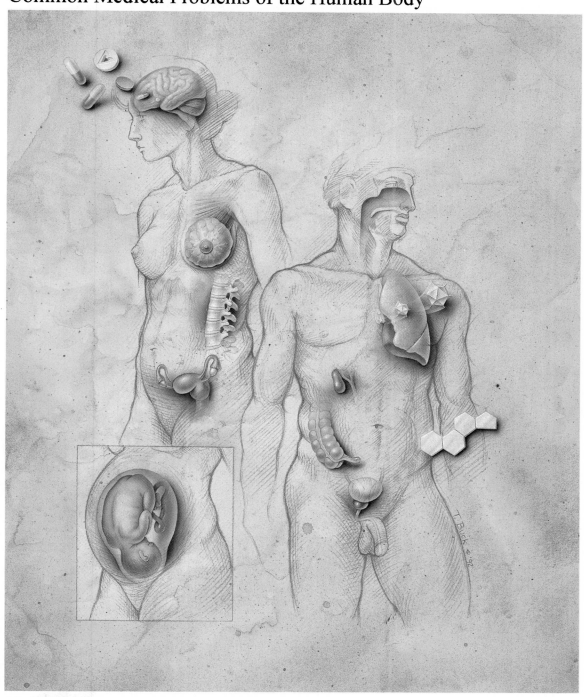

The Brain

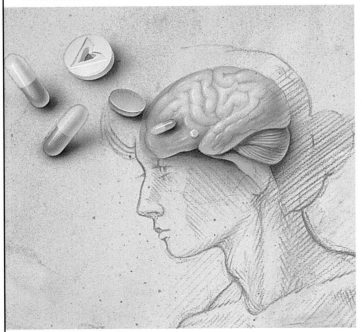

Drug addiction affects the brain in ways that are still not clearly understood. Physical dependence occurs when the body has developed a physical need for the drug. Psychological dependence occurs when the user feels he or she cannot manage without the drug. Drugs of potential abuse fall into six categories: stimulants, depressants, narcotics, hallucinogens, cannabinoids, and inhalants.

The Sinuses

The sinuses comprise eight hollow spaces within the skull that open into the nose. They act as resonating chambers for the voice; help filter particles from the air before they reach the lower airway; and lighten the weight of the skull of the vertebral bones of the neck. Sinusitis is the inflammation of the mucous membranes that line the sinuses. Severe headache, face pain, fever, swelling, a stuffed nose, and post-nasal drip are common symptoms. Sinusitis usually clears up within a few days, but some people suffer from chronic sinusitis. Smoking and allergies are only two of many causes. While there are many treatment possibilities, including a change in lifestyle or habits, surgery is a last resort that is seldom effective.

The Appendix

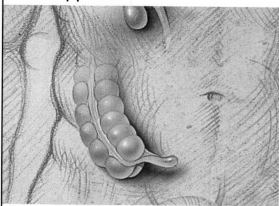

The appendix is a short, wormlike appendage at the junction of the small and large intestines. Inflammation of the appendix is one of the most common causes of abdominal surgery today, particularly among children. It is often removed routinely to prevent possible future problems if a patient is having abdominal surgery for some other reason. Severe pain in the area of the appendix should not be ignored. There may be one pain localized on the lower right side of the abdomen and another, more generalized colicky sort of pain sometimes associated with gas in the intestine. There may also be nausea, vomiting, loss of appetite, and fever. If appendicitis is left untreated the organ may rupture and its contents infect the tissues outside of the intestinal tract, a condition known as peritonitis.

The Gallbladder

The biliary tract is very often plagued by the presence of stones, either in the gallbladder or in one of the bile ducts. Gallstones are mostly a mixture of calcium carbonate, cholesterol, and bile salts. A sharp pain to the right of the stomach is usually the first warning sign of gallstones, especially if felt soon after a fatty meal. Changes in diet and certain drugs can manage many gallstone problems. However, removal of the gallbladder is necessary if it becomes severely damaged or obstructed. Laparoscopic cholecystectomy involves inserting an optical cutting device through tiny punctures in the naval and along the rib cage, allowing the surgeon to grab hold of, drain, and remove the gallbladder.

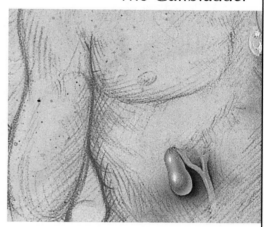

The Lungs

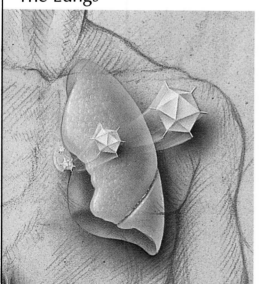

Two common respiratory infections are colds and the flu; they account for more time lost from work than any other single condition. Surveys indicate that about 25 percent of the population experience four or more infections a year, 50 percent experience two or three a year, and the remaining 25 percent have one or no infections a year. Several viruses have been implicated as the cause for the common cold but no one virus has been isolated. Several varieties of influenza virus have been identified; however, an annual inoculation is recommended for certain high risk groups such as the elderly, for whom the flu can be life threatening. There is no cure for the flu or the common cold, but fluids, analgesics, and bed rest help relieve the symptoms. Because these illnesses are viral in nature, antibiotics, which work against bacteria, are not effective treatment.

The Ear

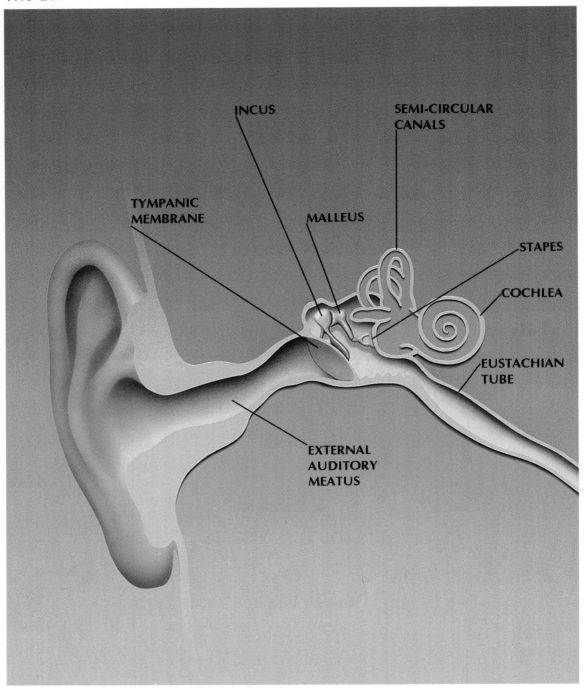

INCUS

SEMI-CIRCULAR CANALS

TYMPANIC MEMBRANE

MALLEUS

STAPES

COCHLEA

EUSTACHIAN TUBE

EXTERNAL AUDITORY MEATUS

© William Graham

Hearing is a complex process. The outer ear collects and guides sound waves to the large tympanic membrane. Vibrations of the tympanic membrane are passed on to three linked bones, the malleus, the incus, and the stapes, which magnify the waves and pass them to another smaller membrane, the oval window. The vibrations next pass through the fluid surrounding the cochlea (the organ of hearing) and then through fluid inside it, spreading along the membrane. Vibrations are picked up by tiny hairlike sense cells, which transmit their information to thousands of nerve fibers. The main nerve of hearing is the auditory nerve, which carries the nerve impulses to the hearing area of the cerebral cortex.

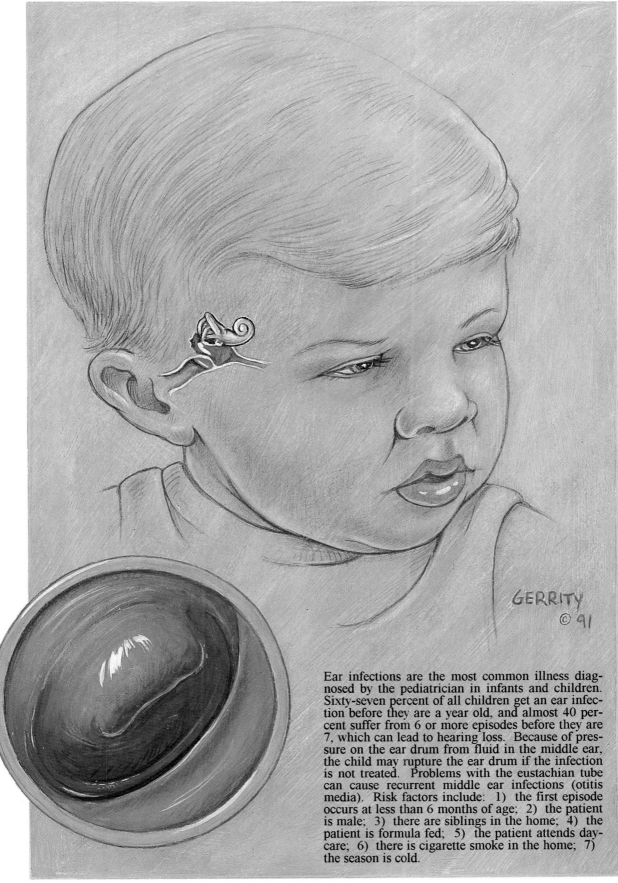

GERRITY
© 91

Ear infections are the most common illness diagnosed by the pediatrician in infants and children. Sixty-seven percent of all children get an ear infection before they are a year old, and almost 40 percent suffer from 6 or more episodes before they are 7, which can lead to hearing loss. Because of pressure on the ear drum from fluid in the middle ear, the child may rupture the ear drum if the infection is not treated. Problems with the eustachian tube can cause recurrent middle ear infections (otitis media). Risk factors include: 1) the first episode occurs at less than 6 months of age; 2) the patient is male; 3) there are siblings in the home; 4) the patient is formula fed; 5) the patient attends day-care; 6) there is cigarette smoke in the home; 7) the season is cold.

Carpal Tunnel Syndrome

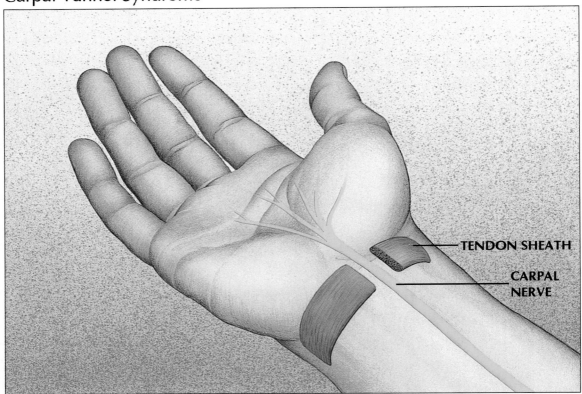

TENDON SHEATH

CARPAL NERVE

© William Graham

People who do heavily repetitive work with their hands, such as typists and meatpackers, may develop carpal tunnel syndrome. Overuse of certain tendons in the wrist may cause them to swell or thicken, and they may begin pressing on a nerve. The person may experience a tingling sensation, numbness of the fingers, aching, discomfort, and impaired hand function. While splinting and rest relieve most cases, surgery is sometimes necessary to correct severe problems. An incision is made from the palm to the wrist. A section of tissue is removed, relieving pressure on the nerve and restoring normal function and feeling.

the body or another—hands, legs, or facial muscles. He does not fall down. These spells, called *absence* or *lapse attacks,* usually begin in childhood before puberty. The attacks are typically very brief, lasting half a minute or less, and occur many times throughout the day. They may go unnoticed for weeks or months because the patient appears to be daydreaming.

Focal Seizure

Focal seizures proceed from neural discharges in one part of the brain, resulting in twitching movements in a corresponding part of the body. Usually, one side of the face, the thumb and fingers of one hand, or one entire side of the body is involved. The patient does not lose consciousness and may in fact remain aware of his surroundings and the circumstances during the entire focal convulsion. Focal convulsions in adults commonly indicate some focal abnormality, but this is less true in a child who may have a focal seizure without evidence of a related brain lesion.

With their knowledge of the nerve links between brain centers and body muscles, physicians are able to determine quite accurately the site of a brain lesion that is involved with a focal seizure.

Jacksonian Epilepsy

One type of focal seizure has a distinctive pattern and is sometimes called a *Jacksonian seizure,* and the condition itself *Jacksonian epilepsy.* The attack begins with rhythmic twitching of muscles in one hand or one foot or one side of the face. The spasmodic movement or twitching then spreads from the body area first affected to other muscles on the same side of the body. The course of the twitching may, for example, begin on the left side of the face, then spread to the neck, down the arm, then along the trunk to the foot. Or the onset of the attack may begin at the foot and gradually spread upward along the trunk to the facial muscles. There may be a tingling or burning sensation and perspiration, and the hair may stand up on the skin of the areas affected.

Psychomotor Seizures

Psychomotor seizures, or *temporal lobe seizures,* often take the form of movements that appear purposeful but are irrelevant to the situation. Instead of losing control of his thoughts and actions, the patient behaves as if he is in a trancelike state. He may smack his lips and make chewing motions. He may suddenly rise from a chair and walk about while removing his clothes. He may attempt to speak or speak incoherently, repeating certain words or phrases, or he may go through the motions of some mechanical procedure, like driving a car, for example.

The patient in a psychomotor seizure usually does not respond to questions or commands. If physically restrained during a psychomotor episode, the patient may appear belligerent and obstreperous, or he may resist with great energy and violence. Usually, the entire episode lasts only a few minutes. When the seizure ends, the patient is confused and unable to recall clearly what has happened.

The aura experienced by victims of psychomotor seizures may differ from that of other forms of the disorder. The psychomotor epileptic may have sensations of taste or smell, but more likely will experience a complex illusion or hallucination that may have the quality of a vivid dream. The hallucination may be based on actual experiences or things the patient has seen, or it may deal with objects or experiences that only seem familiar though they are in fact unfamiliar. This distortion of memory, in which a strange experience seems to be a part of one's past life, is known as *déjà vu,* which in French means literally "already seen."

Other visual associations involved in various forms of epilepsy include those in which the patient experiences sensations of color, moving lights, or darkness. Red is the most common color observed in visual seizures, although blue, yellow, and green also are reported. The darkness illusion may occur as a temporary blindness, lasting only a few minutes. Stars or moving lights may appear as if visible to only one eye, indicating that the source of the disturbance is a lesion in the brain area on the opposite side of the head. Visual illusions before an epileptic attack may have a distorted quality, or consist of objects arranged in an unnatural pattern or of an unnatural size.

Auditory illusions, on the other hand, are comparatively rare. Occasionally a patient will report hearing buzzing or roaring noises as part of a seizure, or human voices repeating certain recognizable words.

Treatment of the Epileptic Patient

Usually the physician does not see the patient during a seizure and must rely on the description of others to make a proper diagnosis. Because the patient has no clear recollection of what happens during any of the epileptic convulsions, it is wise to have someone who has seen an attack accompany him to a physician. First, the physician begins the detective work to find the cause of the seizure. He will examine the patient thoroughly, obtain blood tests, an electroencephalogram, and a lumbar puncture, if indicated. Even after all these studies, however, the physician often can find no specific cause that can be eradicated. Efforts are then made to control the symptoms.

The treatment of epilepsy consists primarily of medication for the prevention of seizures. It is usually highly effective. About half of all patients are completely controlled and another quarter have a significant reduction in the frequency and severity of attacks. The medication, usually in tablet or capsule form, must be taken regularly according to the instructions of the physician. It may be necessary to try several drugs over a period of time to determine which drug or combination of drugs best controls the seizures. Phenobarbital and diphenylhydantoin (Dilantin) may be prescribed for the control of grand mal seizures and focal epilepsy, and the physician may find that a combination of these drugs or others offers the best anticonvulsant control. Trimethadione frequently is administered to petit mal patients; primidone or phenobarbital may be prescribed for psychomotor attacks.

Surgery may be recommended when drugs fail to control the seizures. But this approach usually is used only as a last resort and is not always effective.

However, medicine and surgery are not the only treatments for epilepsy patients. Emotional factors are known to influence convulsive disorders. Lessening a patient's anger, anxiety, and fear can help to control the condition. An understanding family and friends are important, as are adequate rest, good nutrition, and proper exercise. The exercise program should not include vigorous contact sports, and some activities such as swimming should not be performed by the patient unless he is accompanied by another person who understands the condition and is capable of helping the epileptic during a seizure.

There is nothing permanent about epilepsy, although some patients may endure the symptoms for much of their lives. It is a disorder that changes appreciably and constantly in form and manifestations. Some experts claim that petit mal and psychomotor cases if untreated may progress to more serious cases of grand mal seizures. On the other hand, epilepsy that is given proper medical attention may eventually subside in frequency and severity of attacks. In many cases, seizures disappear or subside within a short time and treatment can be discontinued gradually.

While some effort has been made by medical scientists to determine if there is an "epileptic personality," evidence indicates there is no typical personality pattern involved. Whatever behavior patterns and emotional reactions are observed are the result of individual personality makeup rather than being directly related to epilepsy. Most epilepsy patients are capable of performing satisfactory work at various jobs; one study showed that only nine percent were partially dependent and four percent were incapable of holding a job. In some areas there may be restrictions on issuing driver's licenses to epileptics or other legal regulations that limit normal activities for epilepsy patients. As a result, some epileptics may conceal their condition or avoid medical treatment that might be reported to government agencies.

Because of ignorance and misinformation, some people regard epilepsy as frightening or mysterious, and patients may suffer unnecessarily and unjustly. In fact, behavioral abnormalities in patients with seizures are commonly the reflection of how they are viewed by others. The patient should be carefully observed by an understanding physician who watches not only for medical but for psychological problems.

When epilepsy has been diagnosed in a child, the parents must be instructed about the condition and the need for continuous careful medical supervision. If the child is old enough to understand, he also should learn more about the nature of the condition. Misbeliefs should be corrected. Both parents and child should understand that seizures are not likely to be fatal and that a brain lesion does not lead to mental deterioration. Parents and child should learn what actions should be taken in the event of a seizure, such as loosening clothing and taking steps to prevent injury. Natural concern should be balanced with an understanding that overprotection may itself become a handicap. The child should be encouraged to participate in social and physical activities at school and in the neighborhood as long as they do not strain his capabilities. Finally, parents should not feel guilty about the child's condition and think that some action of theirs contributed to the child's condition. See "Epileptic Seizures" in Ch. 31, *Medical Emergencies,* for a description of what to do when a seizure occurs.

Further information about epilepsy, including causes, effects, treatment, rehabilitation, and laws regulating employment and driver permits, can be obtained from the Epilepsy Foundation of America, 4351 Garden City Dr., Landover, MD 20785, and from the U.S. Department of Health, Education and Welfare, Public Health Service, National Institutes of Health, Bethesda, MD 20014.

Amyotrophic Lateral Sclerosis

Amyotrophic lateral sclerosis, ALS, is a degenerative neurological disease in which the nerve cells that control muscles die, resulting in loss of muscle movement and the wasting away of muscles from lack of use.

Symptoms

The first signs of ALS, commonly known as Lou Gehrig's Disease (named for the New York Yankees player who died of it at 38), are the inability to do simple tasks, such as turn a door knob or button a shirt. The condition starts on one side of the body, then moves to the other side. As muscles begin to degenerate, the person loses weight. Eventually, ALS sufferers lose control of their ability to speak, to move, to swallow, or sometimes even to breathe. Mentally, they remain alert, trapped in a withering body.

Treatment

Although there is no cure for ALS, scientists have discovered a defective gene believed to be the cause of the inherited form of the disease (about 10 percent of cases). The gene is responsible for producing an enzyme that destroys free radicals, by-products of normal metabolism that can destroy healthy cells if left unchecked. There is hope that antioxidant drugs, which act in a similar way to the enzyme, may offer relief.

Multiple Sclerosis

Multiple sclerosis is a disease in which the myelin sheath that insulates nerves is progressively destroyed through attacks by white blood cells of the immune system. The disease affects mainly the brain and spinal cord. It is termed *multiple* because there are distinct and separate areas of the nervous system involved, seemingly distributed in a random pattern.

Multiple sclerosis rarely appears before the age of 15 or after 55. A person aged 30 years is statistically at peak risk of developing the disease. The typical patient, statistically speaking, is a woman of 45 who was born and raised in a temperate climate. Women are more susceptible to the disease than men by a ratio of 1.7 to 1, and women are more likely than men to experience the onset of symptoms before the age of 30.

Symptoms and Diagnosis

There are no laboratory tests that are specific for multiple sclerosis, although there are certain tests that may suggest the presence of the disease. Diagnosing the disorder depends to a large extent upon tests that rule out other diseases with similar signs and symptoms. The first symptom may be a transitory blurring of vision or a disturbance in one or more of the limbs, such as numbness, a tingling sensation, clumsiness, or weakness. There may be a partial or total loss of vision in one eye for a period of several days, or the patient may experience double vision, dizziness or pain when moving the eye. In some cases, the patient may develop either a lack of sensation over an area of the face or, paradoxically, a severe twitching pain of the face muscles. In more advanced cases, because of involvement of the spinal cord, the patient may have symptoms of bladder or bowel dysfunction and male patients may experience impotence.

When brain tissues become invaded by multiple sclerosis, the patient may suffer loss of memory and show signs of personality changes, displaying euphoria, cheerfulness, irritability, or depression for no apparent reason.

Multiple sclerosis is marked by periods of remission and recurrence of symptoms. Complete recovery can occur. About 20 percent of the patients may have to spend time confined to bed or wheelchair. In severe cases, there can be complications such as infections of the urinary tract and respiratory system.

Treatment

There is no known cure for multiple sclerosis and, until recently, treatment techniques generally were aimed at relieving symptoms, shortening the periods of exacerbation, and preventing complications that could be crippling or life-threatening. Most patients experience recurrences of symptoms that last for limited periods of days or weeks, followed in cycles by periods of remission that may last for months or years, making it difficult to determine whether the therapy applied is actually effective or if the disease is merely following its natural fluctuating course.

Among the medications now used are anti-inflammatory drugs such as adrenocorticotrophin (ACTH), a hormone that seems to reduce the severity and duration of recurrences. Cortisone and prednisone, two steroid hormones, also can be used and have an advantage over ACTH in that they can be taken by mouth rather than by intramuscular injection. Not all patients react favorably to steroid drugs and serious side effects may be experienced.

Beta interferon, the first drug to be approved by the FDA for any form of multiple sclerosis, is believed to significantly reduce the number of acute episodes of the disease and lessen the severity of the episodes that occur. Brain scans reveal that nerve damage is reduced in patients taking beta interferon. While these findings are significant, studies will continue on whether beta interferon, also known as Betaseron, can slow or prevent the worsening of MS over time.

Physical therapy and antispasmodic medications may be employed for patients suffering weakness or paralysis of the limbs. Bed rest during periods of exacerbation is important; continued activity seems to worsen the severity and duration of symptoms during those periods. Muscle relaxants and tranquilizers may be prescribed in some serious cases and braces could be required for patients who lose some limb functions.

Causes

The cause of multiple sclerosis has not been established.

A theory that researchers consider promising suggests that a virus similar but not identical to HTLV-I (human T-cell leukemia virus-I) may cause multiple sclerosis. HTLV-I causes an unusual form of leukemia. Some T-cells, a type of white blood cell, have been found to contain genetic material from this virus. These T-cells were taken from the cerebrospinal fluid of MS victims, establishing a possible link between the cells and the virus.

Infections of the Nervous System

Like any other organ system, the brain and its associated structures may be host to infection. These infections are usually serious because of the significantly high death rate and incidence of residual defects. If the brain is involved in the inflammation, it is known as *encephalitis;* inflammation of the brain coverings, or *meninges,* is called *meningitis.*

Encephalitis

Encephalitis is usually caused by a virus and, because the symptoms are not specific, the diagnosis is usually made by special viral immunologic tests. Both sexes and all age groups can be afflicted. Most patients complain of fever, headache, nausea or vomiting, and a general feeling of mal-

aise. The mental state varies from one of mild irritability to lethargy or coma, and some patients may have convulsions. The physician may suspect encephalitis after completing the history and the physical examination, but the diagnosis is usually established by laboratory tests that include examination of the cerebrospinal fluid (CSF), the EEG, and viral studies of the blood, CSF, and stool. Because there is no specific treatment for viral encephalitis at the present time, particular attention is paid to general supportive care.

Meningitis

Meningitis can occur in either sex at any time of life. The patient often has a preceding mild respiratory infection and later complains of headache, nausea, and vomiting. Fever and neck stiffness are usually present early in the course of the disease, at which time the patient is commonly brought to the physician for examination. If there is any question of meningitis, a lumbar puncture is performed and the CSF examined. It is not possible to make a specific diagnosis of meningitis without examination of the cerebrospinal fluid.

Meningitis is usually caused by bacteria or a virus. It is important to learn what the infectious agent is in order to begin appropriate therapy. Bacterial infections can be treated by antibiotics, but there is no known specific treatment for viral (*aseptic*) meningitis. Meningitis is a life-threatening disease and, despite modern antibiotic therapy, the mortality rate varies from 10 to 20 percent.

Poliomyelitis

Poliomyelitis is an acute viral illness affecting males and females at any time of life, though most commonly before the age of ten. It is also called

polio, infantile paralysis, or *Heine-Medin disease.*

Polio is caused by a virus that probably moves from the gastrointestinal tract via nerve trunks to the central nervous system, where it may affect any part of the nervous system. The disease, however, most often involves the larger motor neurons (*anterior horn cells*) in the brain stem and spinal cord, with subsequent loss of nerve supply to the muscle. The neuron may be partially or completely damaged; clinical recovery is, therefore, dependent on whether those partially damaged nerves can regain normal function.

There are two categories of polio victims: asymptomatic and symptomatic. Those persons who have had no observed symptoms of the disease, but in whom antibodies to polio can be demonstrated, belong in the *asymptomatic* group. The *symptomatic* group, on the other hand, comprises patients who have the clinical disease, either with residual paralysis (paralytic polio) or without paralysis (nonparalytic polio).

Symptoms

The symptoms of poliomyelitis are similar to those of other acute infectious processes. The patient may complain of headache, fever, or *coryza* (head cold or runny nose), or he may have loose stools and malaise. One-fourth to one-third of patients improve for several days only to have a recurrence of fever with neck stiffness. Most patients, however, do not improve, but rather have a progression of their symptoms, marked by neck stiffness and aching muscles. They are often irritable and apprehensive, and some are rather lethargic.

Whether or not the patient will have muscle paralysis should be evident in the first few weeks. Some have muscle paralysis with the onset of symptoms; others become aware of loss of muscle function several weeks after the onset. About half of the patients first notice paralysis during the second to the fifth day of the disease. Patients experience a muscle spasm or stiffness, and may complain of muscle pain, particularly if the muscle is stretched.

The extent of the muscle paralysis is variable, ranging from mild localized weakness to inability to move most of the skeletal muscles. Proximal muscles (those close to the trunk, like the shoulder-arm or hip-thigh) are involved more often than distal muscles (of the extremeties), and the legs are affected more often than the arms. When the neurons of the lower brain stem and the spinal cord at the thoracic level and above are affected, the patient may have a paralysis of the muscles used in swallowing and breathing. This circumstance, obviously, is life-threatening, and particular attention must be paid to the patient's ability to handle saliva and to breathe. If independent, spontaneous respiration is not possible, patients must be given respiratory assistance with mechanical respirators.

Treatment

There is no specific treatment for acute poliomyelitis. The patient should be kept at complete bed rest and given general supportive care, assuring adequate nutrition and fluid intake. Muscle spasm has been treated with hot as well as cold compresses, and no one method has been universally beneficial. Careful positioning of the patient with the musculature supported in a position midway between relaxation and contraction is probably of benefit, and skilled physical therapy is of great importance.

Immunization

Since the early 1900s, attempts had been made to produce an effective vaccine against poliomyelitis, with success crowning the efforts of Dr. Jonas Salk in 1953. Today, vaccination is accomplished with either the Salk vaccine (killed virus), which is given intramuscularly, or the Sabin (live attenuated virus), given orally. There is little question that immunization with poliomyelitis vaccine has proven to be highly effective in eradicating the clinical disease within the community, and it is now a part of routine immunization for all children.

Dementia

Dementia is a term for mental deterioration, with particular regard to memory and thought processes. Such deterioration can be brought about in various ways: infection, brain injury, such toxic states as alcoholism, brain tumors, cerebral arteriosclerosis, and so forth.

The presenile dementias (*Alzheimer's disease*) represent a group of degenerative diseases of the brain in which mental deterioration first becomes apparent in middle age. Commonly, the first clue may be demonstrations of unusual unreasonableness and impairment of judgment. The patient can no longer grasp the content of a situation at hand and reacts inappropriately. Memory gradually fades and recent events are no longer remembered, but events that occurred early in life can be recalled. The patient may wander aimlessly or get lost in his own house. There is progressive deterioration of physical appearance and personal hygiene, and, finally, the command of language deteriorates. Unfortunately, there is a relentless progression of the process, and the patient becomes confined to bed and quite helpless.

Whether the mental deterioration seen in some aged patients, senile dementia, is a specific brain degeneration or is secondary to cerebral arteriosclerosis is not yet settled. It does appear, however, that senile dementia is probably secondary to a degenerative process similar to that of Alzheimer's disease but occurring late in life.

Whether or not dementia can be halted depends upon its cause. If, for example, the dementia is secondary to brain infection or exposure to toxic material, eradication of the infectious agent or removal of the toxin may be of distinct benefit in arresting the dementing process. Unfortunately, there is no specific treatment for the brain degenerative processes.

Muscle Diseases

When one hears the words "muscle disease," one may think of only muscular dystrophy and picture a small child confined to a wheelchair. But there are many diseases other than muscular dystrophy in which muscle is either primarily or secondarily involved, and many of these diseases do not have a particularly bad prognosis. Muscle diseases may make their presence known at any time, from early infancy to old age; no age group or sex is exempt.

Any disease of muscle is called a *myopathy*. The hallmark of muscle disease is weakness, or loss of muscle power. This may be recognized in the infant who seems unusually limp or *hypotonic*. Often the first clue to the presence of muscle weakness is a child's failure to achieve the developmental milestones within a normal range of time. He may be unusually clumsy or have difficulty in running, climbing stairs, or even walking. Occasionally a teacher is the first one to be aware that the child cannot keep up with classmates and reports this fact to the parents. The onset of the muscle weakness can be so insidious that it may go unnoticed or be misinterpreted as laziness until there is an obvious and striking loss of muscle power.

This is true in the adult as well who at first may feel tired or worn out and then realize that he cannot keep up his previous pace. Often his feet and legs are involved in the beginning. He may wear out the toes of his shoes and may then recognize that he must flex his ankles more to avoid tripping or dragging the toes. Or he finds that he must make a conscious effort to raise the legs in climbing stairs; he may even have to climb one step at a time. Getting out of bed in the morning may be a chore, and rising from a seated position in a low chair or from the floor may be difficult or impossible. Those with arm involvement may recognize that the hands are weak; if the shoulder muscles are involved, there is often difficulty in raising the arms over the head. The patient may take a long time in recognizing the loss of muscle power because the human body can so well compensate or use other muscles to perform the same motor tasks. If the weakness is present for a considerable length of time, there may be a wasting, or a loss of muscle bulk.

Diagnostic Evaluation of Muscle Disease

In evaluating patients with motor weakness, the physician must have a complete history of the present complaints, past history of the patient, and details of the family history. A general physical and neurological examination is required, with particular reference to the motor, or musculoskeletal system. In most cases, the physician will be able to make a clinical diagnosis of the disease process, but occasionally the examination does not reveal whether the nerve, the muscle, or both are involved. In order to clarify the diagnosis, some additional examinations may be required, mainly determination of serum enzymes (a good indicator of loss of muscle substance), a muscle biopsy, and an electromyogram.

Serum Enzymes

Enzymes are essential for the maintenance of normal body chemistry. Because the normal concentration in the blood serum of some enzymes specifically related to muscle chemistry is known, the determination of concentrations of these enzymes can provide additional evidence that muscle chemistry is either normal or abnormal.

Muscle Biopsy

The first step is the surgical removal of a small segment of muscle, which is then prepared for examination under the microscope. The examination enables the physician to see any abnormality in the muscle fibers, supporting tissue, small nerve twigs, and blood vessels. The muscle biopsy can be of great value in making a correct

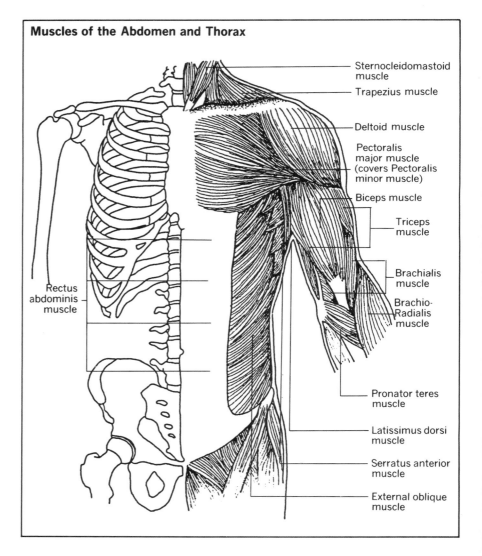

Muscles of the Abdomen and Thorax

Sternocleidomastoid muscle
Trapezius muscle
Deltoid muscle
Pectoralis major muscle (covers Pectoralis minor muscle)
Biceps muscle
Triceps muscle
Brachialis muscle
Brachio-Radialis muscle
Pronator teres muscle
Latissimus dorsi muscle
Serratus anterior muscle
External oblique muscle
Rectus abdominis muscle

diagnosis, but occasionally, even in good hands, there is not sufficient visible change from the normal state to identify the disease process.

Electromyograph (EMG)

This is a technique for studying electrical activity of muscle. Fine needles attached to electronic equipment are inserted into the muscle to measure the electrical activity, which is displayed on an *oscilloscope,* a device something like a television screen. It is not a particularly painful process when performed by a skilled physician, and the information gained may be important in establishing a diagnosis.

Muscular Dystrophy

Muscular dystrophy (MD) is defined as an inborn degenerative disease of the muscles. Several varieties of MD have been described and classified according to the muscles involved and the pattern of inheritance. There is no specific treatment for any form of MD, but the patient's life can be made more pleasant and probably prolonged if careful attention is paid to good nutrition, activity without overfatigue, and avoidance of infection. Physical therapists can be helpful in instructing the patient or the parents in an exercise program that relieves joint and muscle stiffness. Sound, prudent psychological support and guidance cannot be overemphasized.

Duchenne's Muscular Dystrophy

In 1886, Dr. Guillaume Duchenne described a muscle disease characterized by weakness and an increase in the size of the muscles and the supporting connective tissue of those muscles. He named the disease *pseudohypertrophic* (false enlargement) *muscular paralysis,* but it is now known as *Duchenne's muscular dystrophy.*

Duchenne's MD is observed almost entirely in males. It is inherited, however, like many other sex-linked anomalies, through the maternal side of the family. The mother can pass the clinical disease to her son; her daughters will not demonstrate the disease but are potential carriers to their sons. More than one-quarter of the cases of Duchenne's MD are sporadic, that is, without any known family history of the disease. There are rare cases of Duchenne's MD in females who have *ovarian dysgenesis,* a condition in which normal female chromosomal makeup is lacking.

The disease process in Duchenne's MD may be apparent during the first few years of life when the child has difficulty in walking or appears clumsy. The muscles of the pelvis and legs are usually affected first, but the shoulders and the arms soon become involved. About 90 percent of the patients have some enlargement of a muscle or group of muscles and appear to be rather muscular and strong; however, as the disease progresses, the muscular enlargement disappears. Most patients progressively deteriorate and at the age of about 10 to 15 are unable to walk. Once the child is confined to a wheel-

Muscles of the Back

Trapezius muscle
Infraspinatus muscle
Deltoid muscle
Rhomboid muscle
Teres major muscle
Triceps muscle
Latissimus dorsi muscle (covers spinal erector muscle)
External oblique muscle
Internal oblique muscle
Gluteus maximus muscle

chair or bed, there is a progressive deformity with muscle contracture, with death usually occurring toward the end of the second decade. A small percentage of patients appear to have a remission of the disease process and survive until the fourth or fifth decade. Despite herculean attempts to unravel the riddle of muscular dystrophy, the problem is yet unsolved.

A benign variety of MD, *Becker type,* begins at 5 to 25 years of age and progresses slowly. Most of the reported patients with Becker type are still able to walk 20 to 30 years after the onset of the disease.

Facio-Scapulo-Humeral Muscular Dystrophy

This type of muscular dystrophy affects males and females equally and is thought to be inherited as a dominant trait. The onset may be at any age from childhood to adult life, but is commonly first seen in adolescence. There is not false enlargement of the muscles. The muscles affected, as indicated by the name of the disease, are those of the face and shoulders, usually with abnormal winging of the *scapula* (either of the large, flat bones at the backs of the shoulders). There is also a characteristic appearance of lip prominence, as if the patient were pouting. Occasionally there is an involvement of the anterior leg muscles and weakness in raising the foot. The disease progresses more slowly than Duchenne's type, and some patients can remain active for a normal life span.

Limb-Girdle Muscular Dystrophy

This type of muscular dystrophy is less clearly delineated than the others. Males and females are equally affected and the onset is usually in the second or third decade, but the process may start later. It is probably in-

herited as a recessive trait, but many cases are sporadic. It may first affect the muscles of the pelvis or the shoulder, but in 10 to 15 years both pelvis and shoulder girdles are usually involved. The disease varies considerably from patient to patient; sometimes the disease process appears to be arrested after involvement of either the pelvis or the shoulder, and the course thereafter may be a benign one. Most, however, have significant difficulty in walking by middle age.

Other Varieties of Muscular Dystrophy

These include ocular, oculopharyngeal, and a distal form (involving the muscles of the hands or feet).

Ocular MD

This type involves the muscles that move the eye as well as the eyelids; occasionally, the small muscles of the face and the shoulder girdle are affected.

Oculopharyngeal MD

This type involves not only the muscles that move the eye and the eyelids but may also affect the throat muscles, so that patients have difficulty in swallowing food (*dysphagia*).

Distal MD

This type is rare in the United States but has been reported in Scandinavia. Both sexes can be affected. Usually after the fifth decade, the patient recognizes weakness of the small muscles of the hands and anterior leg muscles that assist in raising the toes. The disease is relatively benign and progresses slowly.

The Myotonias

This is a group of muscle diseases characterized by *myotonia,* a continu-

ation of muscle contraction after the patient has voluntarily tried to relax that contraction. It is best observed in the patient who holds an object firmly in his hand and then tries to release his grasp suddenly, only to realize that he cannot let go quickly. There are two major members of this group of diseases and several other less common variants.

Treatment

As in the case of muscular dystrophy, there is no specific treatment for myotonia. Some drugs, such as quinine, have limited value in decreasing the abnormally prolonged muscular contractions, but as yet no treatment has been completely effective.

Myotonia Congenita

This condition is usually present at birth, but is recognized later in the first or second decade of life when the child complains of stiffness or when clumsiness is noted. A child with this condition appears very muscular and has been called the "infant Hercules." The unusual muscular development persists throughout life, but the myotonia tends to improve with age.

Myotonic Dystrophy

The other major variety of myotonia, *myotonic dystrophy,* is a disease in which many organ systems in addition to muscle are involved. Both males and females are affected equally, and the onset may occur at any time from birth to the fifth decade. It is not unusual for a patient to recognize some clumsiness, but he may not be aware that he has a muscle disease. The myotonia may range from mild to severe. There is a striking similarity in the physical appearance of patients with myotonic dystrophy, the features of which include frontal baldness in the male, wasting and weakness of the temporal muscles (that control closing the jaws), muscles of the forearm, hands, and anterior leg muscles. Other physical abnormalities include cataracts in about 90 percent of the patients, small testicles, and abnormality of the heart muscle. Thickening and other bony abnormalities have been seen in the skull radiogram and, with time, many patients become demented.

Polymyositis

Polymyositis is a disorder of muscular and connective tissues affecting both sexes, males more commonly than females. It can occur at any age, although usually after the fourth decade. It is characterized by muscle weakness with associated muscle wasting; about half of the patients complain of muscle pain or tenderness. The disease may begin suddenly, but often follows an earlier mild, febrile illness. Changes in the skin are common, including a faint red-violet discoloration, particularly about the eyelids, and these changes are often associated with mild swelling. There may be a scaly rash. Some patients have ulcerations over the bony prominences. About one-quarter of the patients with polymyositis complain of joint stiffness and tenderness and an unusual phenomenon in which the nail beds become blue (*cyanotic*) after minor exposure to cold.

Treatment

The treatment involves the administration of cortisone preparations, which may be required for many years. General supportive care, including appropriate physical therapy, is recommended.

Myasthenia Gravis

Myasthenia gravis is characterized by muscle weakness and an abnormal muscle fatigability (pathologic fatigue); patients are abnormally weak after exercise or at the end of the day. The disease affects males and females at any period, from infancy to old age, but it is most common during the second to the fourth decades. There is no complete explanation for myasthenia gravis, but it is believed that there is some defect in the transmission of a nerve impulse to the muscle (*myoneural junction defect*). The disease may occur spontaneously, during pregnancy, or following an acute infection, and there appears to be a curious association with diseases in which there is an immunologic abnormality, such as tumors of the thymus gland, increased or decreased activity of the thyroid gland, and rheumatoid arthritis.

Usually there is an insidious onset of generalized weakness or weakness confined to small groups of muscles. Normal muscle power may be present early in the day, but as the hours pass the patient notices that one or both eyelids droop (*ptosis*) or he may see double images (*diplopia*). If he rests and closes his eyes for a short time, the ptosis and the diplopia clear up, only to return after further muscle activity. The weakness can also be seen in the trunk or the limbs, and some patients have involvement of the muscles used in speaking, chewing, or swallowing (*bulbar* muscles). Some are weak all the time and have an increase in that weakness the longer they use their muscles. The muscles used in breathing may be affected in patients with severe myasthenia, and these patients must be maintained on a respirator for varying periods of time.

Treatment

Myasthenia gravis is treated with drugs that assist in the transmission of the nerve impulse to the muscle. Medication is very effective, but the patient should be carefully observed by the physician to determine that the drug dose and the time of administration are adjusted so that the patient may have the benefit of maximal muscle power. Surgical removal of the thymus gland, *thymectomy,* may prove of benefit to some patients in lessening the symptoms of muscle weakness; however, not all patients have clinical improvement of the disease after thymectomy, and patients must be selected very carefully by the physician. Myasthenia gravis is another chronic disease in which long-term careful observation by the physician is most important in obtaining an optimal medical and psychological outcome.

9

Diseases of the Circulatory System

It's called the river of life, the five or six quarts of blood that stream through the 60,000 tortuous miles of arteries, veins, and capillaries.

Blood contains many elements with specific functions—red cells to transport oxygen from the lungs to body tissues, white cells to fight off disease, and tiny elements called *platelets* to help form clots and repair tears in the blood vessel wall. All float freely in an intricate complex of liquid proteins and metals known as *plasma*.

Because of the blood's extreme importance to life, any injury to it—or to the grand network of channels through which it flows—may have the most serious consequences. The troubles that beset the circulation may be grouped conveniently into two categories: diseases of the blood and diseases of the blood vessels.

Diseases of the Blood

Diseases of the blood include disorders that affect the blood elements directly (as in the case of *hemophilia*, where a deficiency in clotting proteins

is at fault) as well as abnormalities in the various organs involved in maintaining proper blood balance (i.e., spleen, liver and bone marrow). The various ills designated and described below are arranged according to the blood component most affected (i.e., clotting proteins, red blood cells, and white blood cells).

Hemorrhagic or Clotting-Deficiency Diseases

The blood has the ability to change from a fluid to a solid and back to a fluid again. The change to a solid is called *clotting*. There are mechanisms not only for sealing off breaks in the circulatory system when serious blood loss is threatened, but also for breaking down the seals, or clots, once the damage has been repaired and the danger of blood loss is eliminated. Both mechanisms are in continuous, dynamic equilibrium, a delicate balance between tissue repair and clot dissolution to keep us from bleeding or literally clogging to death.

Clotting involves a very complex chain of chemical events. The key is the conversion of an inactive blood protein, *fibrinogen*, into a threadlike

sealant known as *fibrin*. Stimulus for this conversion is an enzyme called *thrombin*, which normally also circulates in an inactive state as *prothrombin* (formed from vitamin K in the daily diet).

For a clot to form, however, inactive prothrombin must undergo a chemical transformation into thrombin, a step requiring still another chemical—*thromboplastin*. This agent comes into play only when a tissue or vessel has been injured so as to require clot protection. There are two ways for thromboplastin to enter the bloodstream to spark the chain of events. One involves the release by the injured tissue of a substance that reacts with plasma proteins to produce thromboplastin. The other requires the presence of blood platelets (small particles that travel in the blood) and several plasma proteins, including the so-called antihemophilic factor. Platelets tend to clump at the site of vessel injury, where they disintegrate and ultimately release thromboplastin, which, in the presence of blood calcium, triggers the prothrombin-thrombin conversion.

The clot-destroying sequence is very similar to that involved in clot formation, with the key enzyme, *fi-*

brinolysin, existing normally in an inactive state (*profibrinolysin*). There are also other agents (e.g., *heparin*) in the blood ready to retard or prevent the clotting sequence, so that it does not spread to other parts of the body.

Naturally, grave dangers arise should these complex mechanisms fail. For the moment, we shall concern ourselves with hemorrhagic disorders arising from a failure of the blood to clot properly. Disorders stemming from excessive clotting are discussed below under "Diseases of the Blood Vessels" because they are likely to happen as a consequence of preexisting problems in the vessel walls.

Hemophilia

Hemophilia is probably the best known (although relatively rare) of the hemorrhagic disorders, because of its prevalence among the royal families of Europe. In hemophilia the blood does not clot properly and bleeding persists. Those who have this condition are called *hemophiliacs* or bleeders. The disease is inherited, and is transmitted by the mother, but except in very rare cases only the male offspring are affected. Hemophilia stems from a lack of one of the plasma proteins associated with clotting, *antihemophilic factor* (*AHF*).

The presence of hemophilia is generally discovered during early childhood. It is readily recognized by the fact that even small wounds bleed profusely and can trigger an emergency. Laboratory tests for clotting speed are used to confirm the diagnosis. Further investigation may occasionally turn up the condition in other members of the family.

In advanced stages, hemophilia may lead to anemia as a result of excessive and continuous blood loss. Bleeding in the joints causes painful

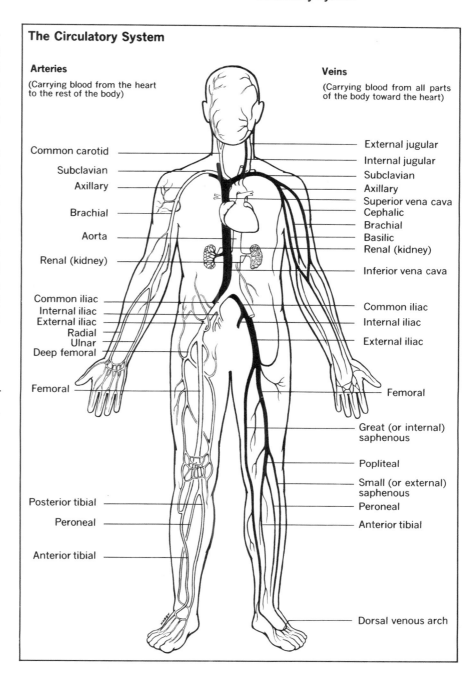

The Circulatory System

Arteries
(Carrying blood from the heart to the rest of the body)

- Common carotid
- Subclavian
- Axillary
- Brachial
- Aorta
- Renal (kidney)
- Common iliac
- Internal iliac
- External iliac
- Radial
- Ulnar
- Deep femoral
- Femoral
- Posterior tibial
- Peroneal
- Anterior tibial

Veins
(Carrying blood from all parts of the body toward the heart)

- External jugular
- Internal jugular
- Subclavian
- Axillary
- Superior vena cava
- Cephalic
- Brachial
- Basilic
- Renal (kidney)
- Inferior vena cava
- Common iliac
- Internal iliac
- External iliac
- Femoral
- Great (or internal) saphenous
- Popliteal
- Small (or external) saphenous
- Peroneal
- Anterior tibial
- Dorsal venous arch

swelling, which over a long period of time can lead to permanent deformity and hemophilic arthritis. Hemophiliacs must be under constant medical care in order to receive quick treatment in case of emergencies.

Treating bleeding episodes may involve the administration of AHF alone so as to speed up the clotting sequence. If too much blood is lost a complete transfusion may be necessary. Thanks to modern blood bank techniques, large quantities of whole blood can be made readily available. Bed rest and hospitalization may also be required. For bleeding in the joints, an ice pack is usually applied.

Proper dental hygiene is a must for all hemophiliacs. Every effort should be made to prevent tooth decay. Parents of children with the disease should inform the dentist so that all necessary precautions can be taken. Even the most common procedures, such as an extraction, can pose a serious hazard. Only absolutely essential surgery should be performed on hemophiliacs, with the assurance that large amounts of plasma are on hand.

Purpura

Purpura refers to spontaneous hemorrhaging over large areas of the skin and in mucous membranes. It results from a deficiency in blood platelets, elements essential to clotting. Purpura is usually triggered by other conditions: certain anemias, leukemia, sensitivity to drugs, or exposure to ionizing radiation. In newborns it may be linked to the prenatal transfer from the maternal circulation of substances that depress platelet levels. Symptoms of purpura include the presence of blood in the urine, bleeding from the mucous membranes of the mouth, nose, intestines, and uterus. Some forms of the disease cause arthritic changes in joints, abdominal pains, diarrhea and vomiting—and even gangrene of the skin, when certain infectious organisms become involved.

To treat purpura in newborns, physicians may exchange the infant's blood with platelet-packed blood. Sometimes drug therapy with *steroids* (i.e., cortisone) is prescribed. In adults with chronic purpura it may be necessary to remove the spleen, which plays an important role in eliminating worn-out blood components, including platelets, from the circulation. Most physicians prescribe large doses of steroids coupled with blood transfusions. Purpura associated with infection and gangrene also requires appropriate antibiotic therapy.

Red Cell Diseases

Half the blood is plasma; the other half is made up of many tiny blood cells. The biggest group in number is the red blood cells. These cells contain a complicated chemical called *hemoglobin,* which brings oxygen from the lungs to body cells and picks up waste carbon dioxide for expiration. Hemoglobin is rich in iron, which is what imparts the characteristic red color to blood.

Red blood cells are manufactured by bones all over the body—in the sternum, ribs, skull, arms, spine and pelvis. The actual factory is the red bone marrow, located at bone ends. As red cells mature and are ready to enter the bloodstream, they lose their nuclei to become what are called *red corpuscles* or *erythrocytes.* With no nucleus, a red corpuscle is relatively short-lived (120 days). Thus, the red cell supply must be constantly replenished by bone marrow. And a busy factory it is because 20 to 25 trillion red corpuscles normally travel in the circulation. The spleen is responsible for ridding the body of the aged corpuscles, but it is not an indiscriminate sanitizer; it salvages the hemoglobin for reuse by the body.

To measure levels of red cells, physicians make a blood count by taking a smidgen of blood from a patient's fingertip. The average number of red cells in healthy blood is about five million per cubic millimeter for men, and four and one-half million for women.

Anemia

Anemia exists when the red cell count stays persistently below four million. Abnormalities in the size, shape, or hemoglobin content of the erythrocytes may also account for anemic states. Any such irregularity interferes with the red cell's ability to carry its full share of oxygen to body tissues. It also tends to weaken the red cells so that they are more likely to be destroyed under the stresses of the circulation.

Anemia may result from:

- nutritional deficiencies that deprive the body of elements vital to the production of healthy cells

- diseases or injuries to organs associated with either blood cell formation (bone marrow) or blood cell destruction (spleen and liver)

- excessive loss of blood, the consequences of surgery, hemorrhage, or a bleeding ulcer and

- Heredity, as in the case of *sickle cell anemia* (where the red cells are misshapen)

Hemolytic Anemia

There are also several kinds of disorders known as *hemolytic anemias* that are linked to the direct destruction of red cells. Poisons such as snake venom, arsenic, and lead can cause hemolytic anemia. So can toxins produced by certain bacteria as well as by other organisms, such as the parasites that cause malaria, hookworm, and tapeworm. Destruction of red cells may also stem from allergic reactions to certain drugs or transfusions with incompatible blood.

The various anemias range from ailments mild enough to go undetected to disorders that prove inevitably fatal. Many are rare; following are the more common.

Pernicious Anemia

Pernicious anemia, or *Addison's anemia,* is associated with a lack of hydrochloric acid in the gastric juices, a defect which interferes with the body's ability to absorb vitamin B_{12} from the intestine. Because the vitamin acts as an essential stimulus to the production of mature red blood cells by the bone marrow, its lack leads to a reduced output. Moreover, the cells tend to be larger than normal, with only half the lifespan of the normal erythrocyte.

The symptoms are characteristic of most anemias: pale complexion, numbness or a feeling of "pins and needles" in the arms and legs, shortness of breath (from a lack of oxygen), loss of appetite, nausea, and diarrhea (often accompanied by significant weight loss). One specific feature is a sore mouth with a smooth, glazed tongue. Advanced stages of the disease may be marked by an unsteady gait and other nervous disorders, owing to degeneration of the spinal cord. Red cell count may drop to as low as 1,000,000. Several kinds of tests may be necessary to differentiate pernicious anemia from other blood diseases—a test for hydrochloric acid levels, for example.

Pernicious anemia, however, is no longer so pernicious, or deadly, as it once was—not since its cause was identified. Large, injected doses of vitamin B$_{12}$ usually restore normal blood cell production.

Sickle-Cell Anemia

Sickle-cell anemia, an inherited abnormality, occurs almost exclusively among black people. Widespread in tropical Africa and Asia, sickle-cell anemia is also found in this country, affecting perhaps 1 in 500 American blacks. The blood cells are sickle-shaped rather than round, a structural aberration arising from a defect in the manufacture of hemoglobin, the oxygen-carrying component. Such misshapen cells have a tendency to clog very small capillaries and cause the complications discussed below.

A differentiation should be made between sickle-cell anemia, the full-blown disease, and sickle-cell trait. Anemia occurs when the offspring inherits the sickle-cell gene from both

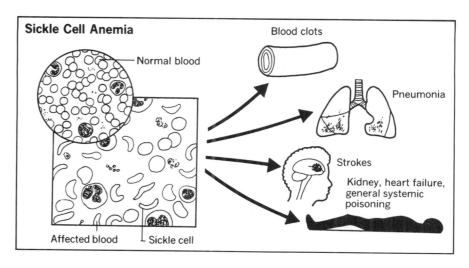

Sickle Cell Anemia — Normal blood — Affected blood — Sickle cell — Blood clots — Pneumonia — Strokes — Kidney, heart failure, general systemic poisoning

parents. For these people life stretches out in endless bouts of fatigue punctuated by a series of crises of excruciating pain lasting days or even weeks. In some cases there is permanent paralysis. The crises often require long-term hospitalization. The misshapen cells increase the patient's susceptibility to blood clots, pneumonia, kidney and heart failure, strokes, general systemic poisoning because of bacterial invasions, and, in the case of pregnant women, spontaneous abortion. Ninety percent of the patients die before age 40, with most dead by age 30. Half are dead by age 20, with a number also suffering from poor physical and mental development.

Those with only one gene for the disease have *sickle-cell trait*. They are not likely to have too much trouble except in circumstances where they are exposed to low oxygen levels (the result, say, of poor oxygenation in a high-altitude plane). Administration of anesthesia or too much physical activity may also bring on some feverish attacks. Those with the trait are also carriers of the disease because they can pass it on to the next generation. Two out of every 25 black Americans are said to be carrying the trait.

Iron-Deficiency Anemia

Iron-deficiency anemia is a common

complication of pregnancy, during which time the fetus may rob the maternal blood of much of its iron content. Iron is essential to the formation of hemoglobin. The deficiency can be further aggravated by digestive disturbances (e.g., a lack of hydrochloric acid) that may hinder the absorption of dietary iron from the intestines. Some women may not observe proper dietary habits, thereby aggravating the anemic state. Successful treatment involves increasing iron intake, with iron supplements and an emphasis on iron-rich foods, including eggs, cereals, green vegetables, and meat, especially liver.

Polycythemia

Polycythemia is the opposite of anemia; the blood has too many red corpuscles. The most common form of the disease is *polycythemia vera* (or *erythremia*). In addition to the rise in corpuscle count, there is a corresponding rise—as much as threefold—in blood volume to accommodate the high cell count, and increased blood viscosity. Symptoms include an enlarged spleen, bloodshot eyes, red mouth, and red mucous membranes—all resulting from excess red cells. Other common characteristics are weakness, fatigue, irritability, dizziness, swelling in the ankles, choking sensations, vise-like chest pains (angina pectoris), rapid heartbeat, and sometimes severe headaches. There is also an increased tendency toward both clotting and hemorrhaging.

The disease occurs primarily in the middle and late years and is twice as prevalent in males as in females. The cause is unknown, but polycythemia is characterized by stepped-up bone marrow production activity.

Radioactive phosphorus therapy is one method for controlling this hyperactivity. Low iron diets and several forms of drug therapy have been tried with varying degrees of effectiveness. A one-time panacea, bloodletting—to drain off excess blood— appears to be of considerable value. Many patients survive for years with the disease. Premature death is usually the result of vascular thrombosis (clotting), massive hemorrhage, or leukemia.

The Rh Factor

Rh disease might also be considered a form of anemia—in newborns. The disorder involves destruction of the red blood cells of an as-yet unborn or newborn infant. It is brought about by an incompatibility between the maternal blood and fetal blood of one specific factor—the so-called Rh factor. (Rh stands for rhesus monkey, the species in which it was first identified.) Most of us are Rh positive, which is to say that we have the Rh protein substance on the surface of our red cells. The Rh factor is, in fact, present in 83 percent of the white population and 93 percent of the black. Those lacking it are classified as Rh negative.

A potentially dangerous situation exists when an Rh negative mother is carrying an Rh positive baby in her uterus. Although the mother and unborn baby have separate circulatory systems, some leakage does occur.

When Rh positive cells from the fetus leak across the placenta into the mother's blood, her system recognizes them as foreign and makes antibodies against them. If these antibodies then slip across into the fetal circulation, damage is inevitable.

The first baby, however, is rarely affected because it takes time for the mother's body to become sensitized to the Rh positive cells. But should she become pregnant with another child, the now-sensitized mother's blood produces a large quantity of destructive antibodies that could result in stillbirth, death of the infant shortly after birth or, if the child survives, jaundice and anemia.

Modern medicine has reduced the fatality rate and considerably improved the prognosis. Severely affected newborns are being treated by complete blood transfusion—even while still in the womb—to draw off all the Rh positive cells. After birth and as it grows older, the child will once again produce Rh positive cells in its bone marrow—but by that time the danger from the mother's antibodies is past. Recently an Rh vaccine to prevent the problem from ever occurring was developed. After Rh negative women give birth to their first Rh positive baby, they are immunized with the anti-Rh serum to prevent them from manufacturing these dangerous antibodies.

White Blood Cell Diseases

For every 600 to 700 or more red corpuscles, there is one white blood cell, or *leukocyte*. White cells, unlike red corpuscles, have nuclei; they are also larger and rounder. About 70 percent of the white cell population have irregularly-shaped centers, and these are called *polymorphonuclear leukocytes* or *neutrophils*. The other 30 percent are made up of a variety

of cells with round nuclei called *lymphocytes*. A cubic millimeter of blood normally contains anywhere from 5,000 to 9,000 white cells (as compared with the four to five million red cells).

White cells defend against disease, which explains why their number increases in the bloodstream when the body is under infectious assault. There are some diseases of the blood and blood-forming organs themselves that can increase the white count. Disorders of the spleen, for example, can produce white cell abnormalities, because this organ is a major source of lymphocytes (cells responsible for making protective antibodies). Diseases of the bone marrow are likely to affect neutrophil production.

Leukemia

Leukemia, characterized by an abnormal increase in the number of white cells, is one of the most dangerous of blood disorders. The cancerlike disease results from a severe disturbance in the functioning of the bone marrow. Chronic leukemia, which strikes mainly in middle age, produces an enormous increase in neutrophils, which tend to rush into the bloodstream at every stage of their development, whether mature or not. Patients with the chronic disease may survive for several years, with appropriate treatment.

In acute leukemia, more common among children than adults, the marrow produces monster-sized, cancerous-looking white cells. These cells not only crowd out other blood components from the circulation, they also leave little space for the marrow to produce the other elements, especially the red cells and platelets. Acute leukemias run their fatal course in a matter of weeks or months—although there have been dramatic instances of sudden remission. The cause is unknown, but recent evidence strongly suggests that a virus may be responsible for at least some forms of the disease.

Modern treatment—radiation and drugs—is aimed at wiping out all of the malignant cells. A critical stage follows treatment, however. For with the disappearance of these abnormal cells and the temporary disruption of marrow function, the patient is left with his defenses against infection down. He also runs a great risk of hemorrhage. Therefore, he is usually kept in isolation to ward off infections. In addition he may be given white cell and platelet transfusions along with antibiotic therapy. Eventually—and hopefully—the marrow will revert to normal function, freed of leukemic cell production. For additional information on leukemia, see Ch. 18, *Cancer.*

Other White Cell Diseases

Agranulocytosis

Agranulocytosis is a disease brought on by the direct destruction of neutrophils (also called *granulocytes*). Taken over a long period of time, certain types of drugs may bring about large-scale destruction of the neutrophil supply. Symptoms include general debilitation, fatigue, sleeplessness, restlessness, headache, chills, high fever (often up to 105° F.), sore mouth and throat, along with psychologically aberrant behavior and mental confusion. White cell count may fall as low as 500 to 2,000. Sometimes agranulocytosis is confused with leukemia.

Treatment involves antibiotic therapy to ward off bacterial invasion, a likelihood that is increased owing to the lowered body resistance. In advanced cases, hospitalization and transfusions with fresh blood are necessary. Injections of fresh bone marrow may also be prescribed.

Leukopenia

Leukopenia is less severe than agranulocytosis. It too involves a reduction of circulating white cells to counts of less than 5,000. It is usually the result of allergic reactions to some chemical or drug.

Infectious Mononucleosis

Infectious mononucleosis, also known as *glandular fever* or *kissing disease,* is characterized by the presence in the bloodstream of a large number of lymphocytes, many of which are abnormally formed. The disease is mildly contagious—kissing is thought to be one popular source of transmission—and occurs chiefly among children and adolescents. The transmitting agent, however, has yet to be discovered, though some as yet unidentified organism is strongly suspected.

The disease is not always easy to diagnose. It can incubate anywhere from four days to four weeks, at which point the patient may experience fever, headache, sore throat, swollen lymph nodes, loss of appetite, and a general feeling of weakness.

The disease runs its course in a matter of a week or two, although complete recovery may take a while longer. Bed rest and conservative medical management is often enough for complete patient recovery. A few severe cases may require hospitalization because of occasional complications, such as rupture of the spleen, skin lesions, some minor liver malfunctions, and occasionally hemolytic anemia or purpura.

Diseases of the Blood Vessels

Diseases of the blood vessels are the result primarily of adverse changes in the vessel walls, such as hardening of the arteries, stroke, and varicose veins.

A healthy circulation depends to a large extent not only on the condition of the blood-forming organs but on the pipelines through which this life-sustaining fluid flows. The arteries, which carry blood away from the heart, and the veins, which bring it back, are subject to a wide range of maladies. They may become inflamed, as in the case of arteritis, phlebitis, and varicose veins; or they may become clogged—especially the arteries—as a result of atherosclerosis (hardening of the arteries) or blood clots (thrombosis and embolism), which can prevent the blood from reaching a vital organ.

The Inflammatory Disorders

Arteritis

Arteritis, or inflammation of the arterial wall, usually results from infections (e.g., syphilis) or allergic reactions in which the body's protective agents against invading organisms, the antibodies, attack the vessel walls themselves. In these instances, the prime source of inflammation must be treated before the arterial condition can heal.

Phlebitis

Phlebitis is an inflammation of the veins, a condition that may stem from an injury or may be associated with such conditions as varicose veins, malignancies, and infection. The extremities, especially the legs, are vulnerable to the disorder. The symptoms are stiffness and hot and painful swelling of the involved region. Phlebitis brings with it the tendency of blood to form blood clots (*thrombophlebitis*)

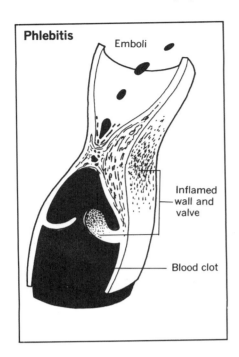

Phlebitis

Emboli

Inflamed wall and valve

Blood clot

at the site of inflammation. The danger is that one of these clots may break away and enter the bloodstream. Such a clot, on the move, called an *embolus,* may catch and become lodged in a smaller vessel serving a vital organ, causing a serious blockage in the blood supply.

Physicians are likely to prescribe various drugs for phlebitis—agents to deal with the suspected cause of the disorder as well as *anticoagulants* (anticlotting compounds) to ward off possible thromboembolic complications.

Varicose Veins

Varicose veins, which are veins that are enlarged and distorted, primarily affect the leg vessels, and are often troublesome to people who are on their feet for hours at a time. Varicose veins develop because either the walls or the valves of veins are weakened. Some people may be born with weakened veins or valves. In others, the damage may develop from injury or disease, such as phlebitis. More women than men seem to have this condition, but it is common among both sexes. In women, the enlarged

veins sometimes occur during pregnancy, but these may well diminish and disappear after delivery. Some elderly people are prone to this condition because the blood vessels lose their elasticity with aging, with the muscles that support the vein growing less sturdy.

In most instances, the surface veins lying just beneath the skin are involved. If there are no other complications, these cases are seldom serious, although they may be disturbing because of unsightliness. Physicians have remedies, including surgery, for making varicose veins less prominent.

When varicose veins become severe, it is usually because the vessels deeper in the leg are weak. Unchecked, this situation can lead to serious complications, including swelling (*edema*) around the ankles and lower legs. The skin in the lower leg may beome thin and fragile and easily irritated. Tiny hemorrhages may discolor the skin. In advanced stages, hard-to-treat leg ulcers and sores may erupt.

Most of the complicating problems can be averted with early care and treatment. Physicians generally prescribe elastic stockings even in the mildest of cases and sometimes elastic bandages to lend support to the veins. They may recommend some newer techniques for injecting certain solutions that close off the affected portion of the vein. On the other hand, surgery may be indicated, especially for the surface veins, in which the varicose section is either tied off or stripped, with the blood being rerouted to the deeper vein channels. See under "Vascular Surgery" in Ch. 20, *Surgery,* for more information about surgical treatment of varicose veins.

While long periods of standing may be hard on varicose veins, so are uninterrupted stretches of sitting, which

may cause blood to collect in the lower leg and further distend the veins. Patients are advised to get up and walk about every half hour or so during any extended period of sitting. A good idea, too, is to sit with the feet raised, whenever possible, to keep blood from collecting in the lower legs.

The Vessel-Clogging Disorders

Atherosclerosis

Atherosclerosis (hardening of the arteries) is the nation's most serious health problem, the underlying cause of a million or more deaths each year from heart attack and stroke. It is the process whereby fats carried in the

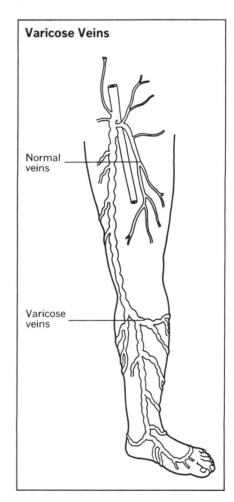

Varicose Veins

Normal veins

Varicose veins

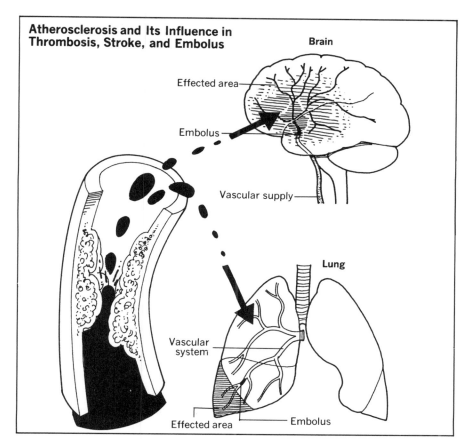

Atherosclerosis and Its Influence in Thrombosis, Stroke, and Embolus

Brain

Effected area

Embolus

Vascular supply

Lung

Vascular system

Effected area

Embolus

roughened wall surfaces, forming clots. If the clot blocks the coronary arteries, it may produce a heart attack—damage to that part of the heart deprived by vessel obstruction. For a detailed account of atherosclerosis and heart attack, see under Ch. 10 *Heart Disease.*

Stroke

Stroke, like heart attack, is a disorder usually resulting from blockage brought on by the atherosclerotic process in vessels supplying the brain. This sets the stage for a *thrombus,* or blood clot fixed within a vessel, which would not be likely to occur in arteries clear of these fatty deposits. A stroke may be a result of an interruption of blood flow through arteries in the brain or in the neck vessels leading to the brain.

Sometimes the shutoff of blood flow, or *embolism,* may be triggered by a wandering blood clot that has become wedged in cerebral vessels. This kind of clot, known as an *embolus,* is a thrombus that has broken free into the circulation.

A stroke may also stem from hemorrhaging, where a diseased artery in the brain bursts. A cerebral hemor-

bloodstream gradually pile up on the walls of arteries, like rust in a pipe. The vessels become brittle and roughened; the channel through which blood flows grows narrower. Eventually the organs and tissues supplied by the diseased arteries may be sufficiently deprived of their normal oxygen delivery so as to interfere with proper function. Such a cutback in the pipeline supply is called *ischemia.* This fat deposit poses its greatest hazard when it occurs in the vessels serving the heart, brain and, sometimes, the lower extremities.

A reduced supply of blood to the lower extremities may cause irreversible damage and ultimately lead to death of the leg tissues unless proper circulation is restored. Bacterial invasion may follow; the area may swell, blacken, and emit the distinctly offensive smell of the deadly infection. Such a condition is known as *gangrene,* a severe disorder that may

require amputation above the site of blockage if other measures, including antibiotic therapy, fail. Diabetics more commonly than others may develop atherosclerotic obstructions in leg arteries. Such persons must take care to avoid leg injuries, because even minimal damage in an already poorly served tissue area can bring on what is termed *diabetic gangrene.*

When the coronary arteries nourishing the heart are involved, even a moderate reduction in blood delivery to the heart muscle may be enough to cause angina pectoris, with its intense, suffocating chest pains.

Thrombosis

Thrombosis, a blood clot that forms within the vessels, is a great ever-present threat that accompanies atherosclerosis. The narrowed arteries seem to make it easier for normal blood substances to adhere to the

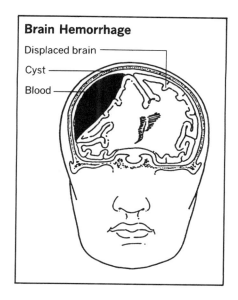

Brain Hemorrhage

Displaced brain

Cyst

Blood

rhage is most likely to occur when a patient has atherosclerosis in combination with hypertension (high blood pressure). (For a discussion of hypertension, see "Hypertensive Heart Disease" in Ch. 10, *Heart Disease.*) Hemorrhage is also a danger when an aneurysm forms in a blood vessel. An *aneurysm* is a blood-filled pouch that balloons out from a weak spot in the artery wall. Sometimes, too, pressure from a mass of tissue—a tumor, for example—can produce a stroke by squeezing a nearby brain vessel shut.

When the blood supply is cut off, injury to certain brain cells follows. Cells thus damaged cannot function; neither, then, can the parts of the body controlled by these nerve centers. The damage to the brain cells may produce paralysis of a leg or arm; it may interfere with the ability to speak or with a person's memory. The affected function and the extent of disability depend on which brain region has been struck, how widespread the damage is, how effectively the body can repair its supply system to this damaged area, and how rapidly other areas of brain tissue can take over the work of the out-of-commission nerve cells.

Symptoms

Frequently there are symptoms of impending stroke: headaches, numbness in the limbs, faintness, momentary lapses in memory, slurring of speech, or sudden clumsiness. The presence of these symptoms does not always mean a stroke is brewing; sometimes they are quite harmless. But should they be stroke warning signals, the physician can take some preventive action. He may recommend anticoagulant therapy as well as drugs to bring down elevated blood pressure. In some cases, he might decide to call for surgical replacement of diseased or weakened sections of arteries leading to the brain.

Treatment

Following a stroke, medical personnel may use *single photon emission computed tomography* (SPECT) to assess quickly the effects of a stroke. A refinement of nuclear scanning (See Chapter 26, Physicians and Diagnostic Procedures), SPECT shows the nature and extent of brain damage. The next critical step is intensive rehabilitation. Not everyone needs a rehabilitation regimen; some strokes have little effect. Some persons recover quickly from what appears to be a severe stroke. Others may suffer serious damage, and may take a long time to recover even partially. Treatment can usually help—especially those who are partially paralyzed and those with *aphasia,* the inability to speak properly because of damage to the brain's speech center.

Embolism

An embolus, or thrombus that has broken away into the bloodstream, is, as we have seen, sometimes the direct cause of a stroke. A heart attack may also cause a stroke. Bacterial action may soften a thrombus so that it separates into fragments and breaks free from its wall anchorage. Thrombi are not the only source of emboli; any free-floating mass in the bloodstream, be it an air bubble, clumps of fat, knots of cancer cells, or bacteria, can prove dangerous.

Usually, however, emboli originate as thrombi in the veins, especially the leg veins. Breaking free, the clump of clot material wanders into the bloodstream to be carried towards the right chamber of the heart and then onward into the lungs, unless dissolved before that. Once in the pulmonary arteries there is a growing threat that the moving mass will catch in one of the smaller branches of the lung circulation. This life-threatening blockage is called a *pulmonary embolism.*

This disorder takes at least 50,000 lives a year; most occur during or following prolonged periods of hospitalization and bed rest. The lack of activity slows the blood flow and increases the danger of thrombi—and ultimately emboli. Prevention requires getting the patient out of bed as soon and as often as possible to stimulate leg circulation. The non-ambulatory patient, meanwhile, is encouraged to move his legs by raising them, or changing positions so as to step up blood flow.

The detection of a large embolus—symptoms include shortness of breath and chest pains—may require emergency surgery for removal. In most instances, however, treatment means administering anticoagulants to prevent new clots from emerging while allowing the body to rid itself of the embolus.

10
Heart Disease

Heart disease is the commonly used, catch-all phrase for a number of disorders affecting both the heart and blood vessels. A more apt term is cardiovascular disease, which represents America's worst health scourge. More than 68 million Americans of all ages (about 27 percent of the total U.S. population) are afflicted with some kind of cardiovascular disease. When considered together heart and circulatory system diseases, including stroke, account for more than one-half of all deaths each year in the United States, a total of more than one million people. Cardiovascular disease comprises several symptoms and disorders: coronary artery disease (including atherosclerosis, angina pectoris, and heart attack), hypertensive heart disease, rheumatic heart disease, and congenital heart disease.

Coronary Artery Disease

To keep itself going, the heart relies on two pencil-thick main arteries. Branching from the aorta, these vessels deliver freshly oxygenated blood to the right and left sides of the heart. The left artery is usually somewhat larger and divides into two sizable

vessels, the circumflex and anterior branches. The latter is sometimes called the artery of sudden death, since a clot near its mouth is common and leads to a serious and often fatal heart attack. These arteries wind around the heart and send out still smaller branches into the heart mus-

cle to supply the needs of all cells. The network of vessels arches down over the heart like a crown—in Latin *corona*—hence the word *coronary*.

Coronary artery disease is the most frequent cause of death from cardiovascular disease. It is brought on by obstructions (plaque) that de-

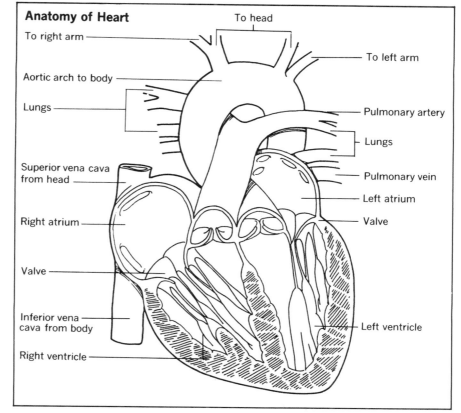

Anatomy of Heart

To right arm —
To head
To left arm
Aortic arch to body —
Lungs —
Pulmonary artery
Lungs
Superior vena cava from head —
Pulmonary vein
Left atrium
Right atrium —
Valve
Valve —
Inferior vena cava from body —
Left ventricle
Right ventricle —

velop in the coronary vessels nourishing the heart muscle, a condition termed *atherosclerosis*. These fatty blockages impair adequate delivery of oxygen-laden blood to the heart muscle cells. The result may be *angina pectoris*: short episodes of viselike chest pains that strike when the heart fails to get enough blood; or it may be a fullblown attack, where blood-starved heart tissue dies.

Heart attacks strike about 1.6 million annually, killing about 600,000. Overall, more than six million adults either definitely have or are suspected of having some degree of coronary disease; for this reason it has been labeled the "twentieth-century epidemic," or the "black plague of affluence."

Risk Factors of Coronary Artery Disease

1. Sedentary lifestyle
2. High cholesterol
3. High blood pressure
4. Obesity
5. Cigarette Smoking
6. Diabetes

Controlling the Risk Factors of Coronary Artery Disease

- Exercise regularly. Consult your physician for the best program for your age and physical condition.

- Eat less saturated fat and cholesterol. Substitute polyunsaturated vegetable fats or monounsaturated fats. Eat more poultry, fish, and complex carbohydrates.

- Undergo periodic tests of your total cholesterol level. A total cholesterol reading under 200 is desirable; a reading from 200 to 239 ranks as "borderline high" and indicates the need for dietary adjustments; levels above 240 are considered "abnormal" and indicate a need to consult a physician and possibly undergo drug therapy.

- Control high blood pressure. Those whose blood pressure is consistently 140/90 or higher are considered to have high blood pressure. There is some evidence that hypertension in women should be treated differently from that in men.

- Don't smoke. The heart attack death rate is 50 to 200 percent higher, depending on age and number of cigarettes consumed, among men who smoke as compared with nonsmokers. Giving up the habit can decrease the coronary risk to that of the nonsmokers within two years; the danger of smoking is reversible.

- Get down to your proper weight and stay there. Excess weight taxes the heart, making it work harder.

- An aspirin every other day has been shown to lessen the chance of having a heart attack for men at risk. Because aspirin decreases the clotting ability of the blood, it should not be taken by those with high blood pressure, a family history of stroke, bleeding disorders, ulcers, or impaired liver of kidney function. You should consult your physician before taking aspirin regularly.

Atherosclerosis

Coronary artery disease exists when flow of blood is impaired because of narrowed and obstructed coronary arteries. In virtually all cases, this blockade is the result of atherosclerosis, a form of *arteriosclerosis,* the thickening and hardening of the arteries. *Atherosclerosis,* from the Greek for porridge or mush, refers to the process by which fat carried in the bloodstream piles up on the inner wall of the arteries like rust in a pipe. As

more and more fatty substances, including cholesterol, accumulate, the once smooth wall gets thicker, rougher, and harder, and the blood passageway becomes narrower.

This fatty clogging goes on imperceptibly, a process that often begins early in life. To some extent, the body protects itself by developing, over a long period of time, alternative arterial connections, termed *collateral circulation,* through which the blood flow bypasses the diseased arteries. Eventually, however, blood flow may be obstructed sufficiently to cause the heart muscle cells to send out distress signals. The brief, episodic chest pains of angina pectoris announce that these cells are starving and suffering for lack of blood and oxygen. Flow may be so severely diminished or totally plugged up that a region of the heart muscle dies. The heart has been damaged; the person has had a heart attack.

The preventive measures for atherosclerosis are the same as those for a heart attack: exercise regularly, cut down on cholesterol and fat, don't smoke, control high blood pressure, and keep weight down. Avoiding these risk factors greatly decreases the chance of developing serious atherosclerosis.

Angina

Angina pectoris means chest pain (from the Latin *angere* meaning choke and *pectoralis* meaning chest). Angina occurs when the heart is called upon to pump more blood to meet the body's stepped-up needs. To do so means working harder and faster. If one or more of the heart's supply lines is narrowed by disease, the extra blood and oxygen required to fuel the pump cannot get through to a region of the heart muscle. Anginal pain

Angina Pectoralis

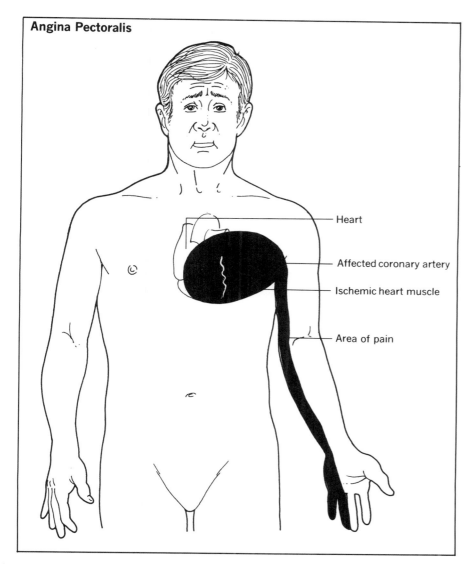

Heart

Affected coronary artery

Ischemic heart muscle

Area of pain

is a signal that muscle cells are being strained by an insufficiency of oxygen; they are, as it were, gasping for air.

The attacks usually are brief, lasting only a matter of minutes. Attacks stop when the person rests. Some people apparently can walk through an attack, as if the heart has gotten a second wind, and the pain subsides.

Symptoms

Angina attacks are likely to appear when sudden strenuous demands are placed on the heart. They may come from physical exertion—walking uphill, running, sexual activity, or the effort involved in eating and digesting

a heavy meal. Watching an exciting movie or sporting event can trigger it; so might cold weather. An attack can occur even when the individual is lying still or asleep—perhaps the result of tension or dreams. The most obvious characteristic of an angina attack is pain.

Usually the pain is distinctive and feels like a vest being drawn too tightly across the chest. Sometimes it eludes easy identification. As a rule, however, the discomfort is felt behind the breastbone, occasionally spreading to the arms, shoulders, neck, and jaw. Not all chest pain indicates angina; in most cases it may simply be gas in the stomach.

Treatment

It is important to note that angina is a symptom, not a disorder. In most cases it is the result of atherosclerosis, and thus the program recommended for reducing the risk of atherosclerosis also applies to angina. In addition, treatment may involve merely rearranging activity to avoid overly taxing physical labors or emotional situations likely to induce discomfort. A major medication used for angina is *nitroglycerin*. It dilates small coronary blood vessels, allowing more blood to get through. Nitroglycerine pellets are not swallowed but are placed under the tongue, where they are quickly absorbed by blood vessels there and sped to the heart; discomfort passes in minutes. Nitroglycerin is also available in a sprayable form. Often anginal attacks can be headed off by taking the tablets or spray before activities likely to bring on an attack. Some people experience temporary, mild headaches as a side effect of taking nitroglycerin.

Still other drugs have been found to relieve angina pains. One group, called the beta-blockers, slows down the heart's action and thus its need for oxygen. Widely used to treat high blood pressure as well as heart disease, the beta-blockers may cause shortness of breath. For that reason, physicians usually prescribe other medications for persons with asthma.

The first of the beta-blockers to come into use was *propranolol*. But at least five chemically related drugs may be prescribed: atenolol, timolol, metoprolol, nadolol, and pindalol. Physicians generally try to fit one of these drugs to the problems of the individual patient. There is some evidence that propranolol and nitroglycerin taken together may increase the effectiveness of therapy.

A second group of drugs for angina is known as the calcium slow channel blockers, or simply calcium channel blockers. These drugs prevent coronary spasms, one cause of angina chest pains, by blocking the flow of calcium ions to the heart and thus dilating the arteries and increasing blood flow to the heart. The heart's demand for oxygen is lessened, and blood pressure is lowered. Three chemically different calcium channel blockers in use are verapamil, nifedipine, and diltiazem.

Angina does not mean a heart attack is inevitable. Many angina patients never have one, whether the result of collateral circulation, treatment with medication, or lifestyle changes. Should attacks of angina begin to worsen in spite of these, however, angioplasty or coronary bypass surgery may be necessary.

Heart Attack

Heart attack is the common term for *myocardial infarction,* or death of heart muscle, which is also described as *coronary occlusion* (total closure of the coronary artery) or *coronary thrombosis* (formation of a blood clot, which closes the artery).

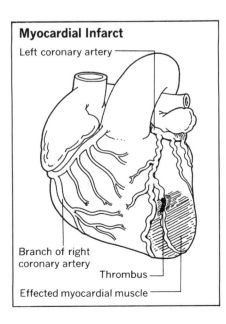

Myocardial Infarct

Left coronary artery

Branch of right coronary artery

Thrombus

Effected myocardial muscle

Although heart attacks can occur at any age, the frequency of heart attacks begins to build rapidly between the ages of 30 and 44 when roughly .05 percent of the total U.S. population experience heart attacks. Of this number only 2 percent are women. Between the ages of 45 and 64 the percentage increases to .2, with 24 percent of that number being women. After age 65 .33 percent of the population experience heart attack, 46 percent of which are women.

Symptoms

Sometimes heart attacks are so vague or indistinct that the victim may not know he has had one. Often a routine electrocardiogram turns up an abnormality indicative of an *infarct,* or injured area, thus the importance of periodic checkups. Special blood tests can also detect an elevation in the number of white blood cells or a rise in the enzyme content, resulting from leakage when heart muscle cells are injured.

Most heart attacks, however, do not sneak by. There are well-recognized symptoms. The most common are:

- A feeling of strangulation, crushing, or compressing

- A prolonged, oppressive pain or unusual discomfort in the center of the chest that may radiate to the left shoulder and down the left arm or up the neck into the jaw

- Abnormal perspiring

- Sudden, intense shortness of breath

- Nausea or vomiting (because of these symptoms, an attack is sometimes taken for indigestion; usually, coronary pains are more severe)

- Occasionally, fainting

Treatment

Knowing these warning signals and taking proper steps may make the difference between life and death. Call a physician or get to a hospital as soon as possible. Time is crucial. Most deaths occur in the initial hours after attack. About 40 percent, for example, die within one hour after onset of a major heart attack.

Often, death is not due to any widespread damage to the heart muscle, but rather to a disruption in the electric spark initiating heart muscle contraction—the same spark measured by the electrocardiogram. These out-of-kilter rhythms, including complete heart stoppage or cardiac arrest, are often reversible with prompt treatment.

For patients whose heart attack is the result of a blood clot (thrombus) the administration of thrombolytic drugs, which dissolve the clot and thus limit the extent of damage to the heart, increase the survival rate by 50 percent. Other drugs used to treat the heart include antiarrhythmics, which restore a regular beat to an irregularly beating heart, and vasopressors or inotropic agents that stimulate the heart and enhance heart function. Among the many cardiostimulants, or inotropic drugs, is a large group called partial beta 1 agonists that accelerate the rehabilitation process and increase exercise tolerance.

Of two other classes of therapeutic drugs, calcium and beta channel blockers are used to slow the heart rate, while angiotensin converting enzyme (ACE) inhibitors increase blood flow to the kidneys. The ACE inhibitors also block an enzyme that raises blood pressure. Among the diuretics are Dyazide and furosemide, marketed as Lasix. Both help to prevent fluid accumulation in the lungs.

Because most heart attacks are the result of reduced blood flow due to clots or buildup of deposits on arterial walls, following a heart attack the problem arteries must be identified. This is done in a procedure called *coronary arteriography* (cardiac catheterization), where blocked arteries are identified by X-ray "movies" taken of an injected opaque dye. Another technique, nuclear magnetic resonance (NMR), uses magnetic forces to scan the interior of the body for abnormalities. In heart disease diagnoses, NMR can identify specific problems in specific areas of the heart and its arteries.

Once clogged arteries are identified, they must be cleared. This is most commonly done by *percutaneous transluminal coronary angioplasty,* or balloon angioplasty. In balloon angioplasty, a catheter is pushed through an artery in the leg or shoulder and maneuvered into a coronary artery that has been narrowed by the build up of cholesterol, minerals, cell debris, and other material (plaque), which cuts off the flow of blood. A balloon attached to the catheter is then inflated, forcing open the affected artery by cracking and crushing the plaque against the arterial walls, compressing it but not removing it. The catheter and balloon are then removed. One problem with angioplasty is re-stenosis, or the return of narrowing deposits, which occurs within six months in 30 percent of coronary arteries. Devices that not only break down but remove plaque are thus being developed.

In cases where the blocked section of the artery is too long, difficult to reach, or located at a tortuous area or branch point of the artery, coronary artery bypass surgery must be performed.

Coronary Care Units

Special hospital centers called coronary care units (CCUs) have been created to provide for heart attack victims. Headed by a cardiologist and staffed by highly trained nurses, the CCU provides around-the-clock electronic devices that keep watch over each patient's vital functions, particularly the heart's electrical activity. The critical period is the first 72 hours, when up to 90 percent of heart attack patients experience some type of electrical disturbance or *arrhythmia* (irregular heartbeat).

Patient rooms in the CCU are designed to ensure privacy and a tranquil, cheerful environment. Rooms may be separated from one another by curtains or partial or full walls. Beds usually stand in a space adequate for movement of heavy equipment such as the portable X-ray apparatus.

Each patient is connected via electrodes attached to the skin to a heart monitor, which records the rhythm and rate of the heartbeat and the blood pressure, enabling nurses to check on a patient's condition without leaving the nurse's station. An alarm system on the monitor notifies the nurse when a major change is taking place in the patient's condition.

Other CCU equipment includes defibrillators for treatment of the condition called ventricular fibrillation (see section on arrhythmias), electroshock equipment, intravenous pacemakers, and a crash cart stocked with such items as the drugs needed for emergency cardiac care (ECC) and endotracheal tubes.

The advent of coronary care has produced striking results. Where in use, these units have reduced heart attack deaths among hospitalized patients up to 30 percent. If all heart victims surviving at least a few hours received such care, more than 50,000 lives could be saved annually.

Emergency Care

Most heart attack victims never reach the hospital. About one-third die before they receive medical care. Evidence suggests that many of these sudden deaths result from ventricular fibrillation or cardiac arrest — reversible disturbances when treated immediately.

These considerations led to the concept of mobile coronary care units — of bringing the advanced techniques of heart resuscitation to the victims. Originated in 1966 in Belfast, Northern Ireland, the practice of having a flying squad of specially equipped ambulances ready to race with on-the-spot aid to heart attack patients has been spreading to more U.S. communities, successfully reducing mortality.

An emergency technique called *cardiopulmonary resuscitation* (CPR), also known as *cardiac massage* or *closed-chest massage,* has also reduced out-of-hospital heart attack mortality figures. Used in conjunction with mouth-to-mouth breathing, cardiac massage is an emergency procedure for treating cardiac arrest. The lower part of the breastbone is compressed rhythmically to keep oxygenated blood flowing to the brain until appropriate medical treatment can be applied to restore normal heart action; often cardiac massage alone is enough to restart the heart. Training for the technique is widely available at hospitals or local branches of the Red Cross. Regular refresher courses are important, however, because improper use of the technique could fracture a rib or rupture a weakened heart muscle if too much pressure is applied.

Coronary Artery Bypass Surgery

Coronary artery bypass surgery involves removing a short length of vein from the leg and using it to reroute blood flow in the heart around severely blocked arteries. One to nine segments of these arteries may receive bypasses, although four to five is the most common.

Instead of a leg vein, it is often preferable to use either of the two (or both) internal mammary arteries for the bypass. (One common problem with using a leg vein is the tendency to develop blockages similar to those in the arteries it was intended to bypass; the mammary arteries are more resistant to the build up of atherosclerosis.

Although coronary artery bypass surgery relieves the debilitating angina or reduces the risk from severely blocked arteries by restoring adequate blood flow to the heart, it does not cure the underlying disease—atherosclerosis. Thus to reduce the risk of further complications or the need for another bypass operation, the patient must take care to follow the recommended dietary and lifestyle changes for reducing atherosclerosis.

Heart Surgery

Direct surgery on the heart is possible because of the development of the heart-lung machine, which takes over the job of oxygenating and pumping blood into circulation, thus giving surgeons time to work directly on a relatively bloodless heart.

Heart surgery is performed to correct congenital defects (see section on congenital heart disease), problems associated with coronary artery disease, hypertension, rheumatic fever, and congestive heart failure (see these sections), and injuries or diseases of the heart. Heart valves and arteries may be repaired or replaced, or the heart itself may be replaced.

The major valves of the heart—mitral, aortic, pulmonary, and tricuspid—may all become either obstructed (thus restricting the blood flow), a condition called *stenosis,*

or they may fail to close properly (causing backflow of blood), a condition called *regurgitation.*

Stenosis may be corrected by a valvotomy, which enlarges the constricted valve opening. Some cases of valve regurgitation can be repaired surgically, others require the replacement of the valve.

Heart transplant may be required when such diseases of the heart as *cardiomyopathy* (heart muscle disease), *myocarditis* (inflammation of the myocardium), and *pericarditis* (inflammation of the sac surrounding the heart) do not respond to lifestyle changes or medication.

Heart transplantation has been performed with increasing success for more than 20 years. The best candidates for transplantation are psychologically stable, otherwise healthy individuals under 60. About 80 percent of transplant patients survive for at least a year. Some have lived for more than a decade.

Two problems associated with heart transplantation are the acquisition and storing of donor hearts and overcoming the body's rejection response to transplants. The former means a long waiting list for potential transplant patients. Controlling the latter is becoming increasingly more successful with immunosuppressive drugs. For more information, see "Heart Surgery" in Ch. 20, *Surgery.* See also "Organ Transplants" in Ch. 20, *Surgery.*

Recuperation

Beyond the 72-hour crisis period, the patient will still require hospitalization for three to six weeks to give the heart time to heal. During the first two weeks or so, the patient is made to remain completely at rest. In this period, the dead muscle cells are being cleared away and gradually re-

placed by scar tissue. Until this happens, the damaged area represents a dangerous weak spot. By the end of the second week, the patient may be allowed to sit in a chair and then to walk about the room. Recently, some physicians have been experimenting with getting patients up and about earlier, sometimes within a few days after their attack. Although most patients are well enough to be discharged after three or four weeks, not everyone mends at the same rate, which is why physicians hesitate to predict exactly when the patient will be released or when he will be well enough to resume normal activity.

About 15 percent of in-hospital heart attack deaths come in the postacute phase owing to an *aneurysm,* or ballooning-out, of the area where the left ventricle is healing. This is most likely to develop before the scar has toughened enough to withstand blood pressures generated by the heart's contractions. The aneurysm may kill either by rupturing the artery or by so impairing pumping efficiency that the heart fails and the circulation deteriorates.

Most heart attack patients are able to return to their precoronary jobs eventually. Some, left with anginal pain, may have to make adjustments in their jobs and living habits. What kind of activity the patient can ultimately resume is an individual matter to be worked out by the patient with his physician. The prescription usually involves keeping weight down and avoiding undue emotional stress or physical exertion; moderate exercise along with plenty of rest is encouraged.

Before or after a heart attack victim returns to work and more normal life habits, physicians may want to know how he or she will react to stresses, medicines, and other factors and conditions. This is done by using "ambulatory electrocardiographic monitoring"—a portable EKG—which delivers electrocardiographic readings for 6 to 24 hours or longer while the patient goes about his normal activities. Electrodes are attached to the patient's chest over the heart. The electrodes connect with a tape recorder that makes electrocardiograms. Completely portable because of its weight—less than two pounds—the tape recorder/monitor is carried on a strap hung over the patient's shoulder or is attached to the wearer's belt.

The monitor's recordings are especially useful in diagnosing arrhythmias, which may occur at unpredictable times. Patients using the ambulatory monitor are generally asked to supplement the cardiographic record by keeping notes on their activities. These notes show the physician the activities in which the patient was engaged from hour to hour during the day. The notes may be matched up with the EKG to show what stresses accompanied particular activities. Some monitors have a special band on which the patient can record oral reports of his activities. The monitor's tape record and the patient's written or dictated notes help the physician give more specific instructions to the patient regarding his activities to facilitate recovery.

Arrhythmias

A disturbance in the rhythm of the heart is termed *arrhythmia* and can range from a mild "skipped beat" to a life-threatening failure to pump. The latter is called *ventricular fibrillation* and is usually associated with heart disease or occurs soon after a heart attack. The phenomenon of *cardiac arrest* (sudden death) is most often caused by ventricular fibrillation and is the leading cause of death in young and middle-aged men.

In ventricular fibrillation, the lower chambers of the heart contract in an uncoordinated and inefficient manner, causing blood-pumping to cease completely. The patient may experience palpitations, lightheadedness, chest discomfort, shortness of breath, or loss of consciousness. Treated within one minute, the patient has a 90 percent or better chance of surviving. A delay of three minutes means a survival rate of less than 10 percent because of extensive and irreversible brain and heart damage.

Treatment involves the use of an instrument called a *defibrillator.* Through plates applied to the chest, the device sends a massive jolt of electricity into the heart muscle to get the heart back on the right tempo.

More significantly, it is now also possible to head off ventricular fibrillation, so that the already compromised heart will not have to tolerate even brief episodes of the arrhythmia. Ventricular fibrillation is invariably heralded by an earlier, identifiable disturbance in the heartbeat. Most frequently, the warning signal is a skipped or premature ventricular beat. Picked up by the coronary care monitoring equipment, the signal alerts the unit staff to administer heart-calming medicaments that can ward off the danger. One such drug is *lidocaine,* a long-used dental anesthetic found to have the power to restore an irritated heart to electrical tranquility.

Less serious arrhythmias than ventricular fibrillation include *atrial flutter* (where the atria contract too often), *atrial fibrillation* (where they contract in an ineffective and uncoordinated manner), and *paroxysmal atrial tachycardia* (where the heart rate may race at between 140 and 240 beats per minute for minutes or even days).

Most all conditions of arrhythmia are associated with heart disease or heart attacks and can be controlled

with lifestyle changes and medications designed to pace the heart. Others are caused by a malfunctioning mitral valve of the heart or the sinus node (the area of the heart that sends electrical signals to the chambers, controlling the beat; i.e., the heart's pacemaker).

Hypertensive Heart Disease

Hypertension is the most common of the cardiovascular diseases, affecting about 22 million Americans, with more than half having some degree of heart involvement. A little more than 60,000 deaths are directly attributable to hypertension and hypertensive heart disease.

Hypertension, or elevated blood pressure, results from a persistent tightening of the body's very small arterial branches, the *arterioles.* This clenching increases the resistance to blood flow and sends the blood pressure up, just as screwing down the nozzle on a hose builds up pressure in the line. The heart must now work harder to force blood through. Over a period of time, the stepped-up pumping effort may cause the heart muscle to thicken and enlarge. Eventually, the overworked circulatory system may break down, with resultant failure of the heart or kidneys, or the onset of stroke. The constant hammering of blood under high pressure on the walls of the arteries causes them to thicken, making them less flexible (a condition called arteriosclerosis) and also accelerates the development of atherosclerosis and heart attacks.

How Blood Pressure is Measured

Blood pressure is measured in millimeters of mercury with an instrument called a *sphygmomanometer.* The device consists of an inflatable cuff attached to a mercury meter. The physician wraps the cuff around the arm and inflates it with air from a squeeze-bulb. This drives the mercury column up toward the top of the gauge while shutting off blood flow through the brachial artery in the arm. With a stethoscope placed just below the cuff, the physician releases the air and listens for the first thudding sounds that signal the return of blood flow as the blood pressure on the wall of the artery equals the air pressure in the cuff. He records this mercury meter reading. This number represents the *systolic* pressure, the force developed by the heart when it contracts.

By continuing to let air out, the physician reaches a point where he can no longer hear the pulsing sounds of flowing blood. He marks the gauge reading as the *diastolic* pressure, the pressure on the artery when the heart is relaxing between beats. Thus, two numbers are used to record blood pressure the systolic followed by the diastolic.

Recorded when the patient is relaxed, normal systolic pressure for most adults is between 100 and 140, and diastolic between 60 and 90. Many factors, such as age and sex, account for the wide variations in normal readings from individual to individual. Systolic blood pressure, for example, tends to increase with age.

Normally, blood pressure goes up during periods of excitement and physical labor. Hypertension is the diagnosis when repeated measurements show a persistent elevated pressure of 140 or higher for systolic and 90 or more for diastolic.

In addition to the sphygmomanometer reading in the examination for high blood pressure, the physician shines a bright light in the patient's eyes so that he can look at the blood vessels in the retina, the only blood vessels that are readily observable.

Any damage there resulting from hypertension is usually a good index of the severity of the disease and its effects elsewhere in the body.

An electrocardiogram and X ray may be in order to determine if and how much the heart has been damaged. The physician may also perform some tests of kidney function to ascertain whether hypertension, if detected, is of the essential or secondary kind, and if there has been damage to the kidneys as well.

Causes

More than 90 percent of all hypertension cases are classified as essential. This simply means that no single cause can be defined. Rather, pressure is up because of a number of factors—none of which has yet been firmly implicated—operating in some complex interplay.

One theory holds that hypertension arises from excessive activity of the sympathetic nervous system, which helps regulate blood vessel response. This notion could help explain why tense individuals are susceptible to hypertension. Emotional reactions to unpleasant events or other mental stresses prompt the cardiovascular system to react as it might to exercise, including widespread constriction of small blood vessels and increased heart rate.

The theory suggests that repeated episodes of stress may ultimately affect pressure-sensitive cells called *baroreceptors*. Situated in strategic places in the arterial system, these sensing centers are thought to be preset to help maintain normal blood pressure just as a thermostat works to keep a house at a preset temperature. Exposure to regularly recurrent elevated blood pressure episodes may bring about a resetting of the baroreceptors—or *barostats*—to a new, higher normal. Once reset, the

barostats operate to sustain hypertension.

Symptoms

Essential hypertension usually first occurs when a person is in his thirties. In the early stages, one may pass through a transitional or prehypertensive phase lasting a few years in which blood pressure rises above normal only occasionally, and then more and more often until finally it remains at these elevated levels.

Symptoms, if they exist at all, are likely to be something as nonspecific as headaches, dizziness, or nausea. As a result, without a physical examination to reveal its presence, a person may have the disease for years without being aware of it. That can be dangerous, because the longer hypertension is left untreated, the greater the likelihood that the heart will be affected.

About 10 percent of causes fall under the *secondary hypertension* classification because they arise as a consequence of another known disorder. Curing the underlying disorder also cures the hypertension. Usually it is brought on by an obstruction of normal blood flow to the kidney because of atherosclerotic deposits in one or both of its major supply lines, the renal arteries. Adrenal gland problems such as Cushing's Syndrome or a tumor of the adrenal gland can also cause hypertension. Many patients can be cured or substantially improved through surgery.

Treatment

Lifestyle changes are the most important thing an individual can do to reduce his blood pressure. These include reducing intake of salt, alcohol, and caffeine, controlling weight, and increasing physical exercise. Should these changes have no significant effect on the blood pressure after three to six months, a program of medication may be required. The outlook is good for almost all patients with essential hypertension, whether mild or severe, because of the large arsenal of antihypertensive drugs at the physician's disposal. Not all drugs will benefit all patients, but where one fails another or several in combination will almost invariably succeed. Even the usually lethal and hard-to-treat form of essential hypertension described as *malignant* is beginning to respond to new medications. *Malignant hypertension,* which may strike as many as 5 percent of hypertensive victims, does not refer to cancer, but rather describes the rapid, galloping way blood pressure rises.

Mild hypertension often may be readily treated with tranquilizers and mild sedatives, particularly if the patient is tense, or with one of a broad family of agents known as *diuretics.* These drugs flush the body of excess salt decreasing the amount of fluid in blood vessel walls and thus reducing the blood pressure.

Against more severe forms, there are a large number of drugs which work in a variety of ways to offset or curb the activity of the sympathetic nervous system so that it relaxes its hold on the constricted arterioles.

Rheumatic Fever and Rheumatic Heart Disease

Rheumatic heart disease is the possible sequel of rheumatic fever and claims the lives of 13,000 annually. It generally strikes children between the ages of 5 and 15. All told, 1.6 million persons are suffering from rheumatic heart disease, with about 100,000 new cases reported each year. Triggered by streptococcal attacks in childhood and adolescence, rheumatic fever may leave permanent

heart scars. The heart structures most often affected are the valves.

Causes

The cause of rheumatic fever is still not entirely understood. It is known that rheumatic fever is always preceded by an invasion of bacteria belonging to the group A beta hemolytic streptococcus family. Sooner or later, everybody has a strep infection, such as a strep throat. Most of us get over it without any complications. But in 1 out of every 100 children the strep infection produces rheumatic fever a few weeks later, even after the strep attack has long since subsided. The figure may rise to 3 per 100 during epidemics in closed communities, such as a children's camp.

The invasion of strep sparks the production of protective agents called antibodies. For some reason, in a kind of biological double cross, the antibodies attack not only the strep but also make war on the body's own tissues—the very tissues they are called upon to protect. Researchers are now suggesting the possible reason, although all the evidence is not yet in. According to a widely held theory, the strep germ possesses constituents (*antigens*) that are similar in structure to components of normal, healthy cartilage and connective tissues—found abundantly in joints, tendons and heart valves—in susceptible individuals. Failing to distinguish between them, the antibodies attack both. The result: rheumatic fever involving joint and valve inflammation and, perhaps, permanent scarring.

Symptoms

Rheumatic fever itself is not always easy to diagnose. The physician must detect at least two of the following major symptoms or one major and

two minor symptoms, derived by the American Heart Association.

Major:

- Swelling or tenderness in one or more joints (arthritis); usually, several joints are involved one after the other in migratory fashion

- Carditis or heart inflammation

- An unusual raised skin rash, which often disappears in 24 to 48 hours

- Chorea, or St. Vitus's dance, so-called because of the uncoordinated, jerky and involuntary motions of the arms, legs, or face, which result from rheumatic inflammation of brain tissue; (it may last six to eight weeks and even longer, but when symptoms disappear there is never any permanent damage and the brain and nervous system return to normal)

- Hard lumps, under the skin and over the inflamed joints, usually indicating severe heart inflammation

Minor:

- Joint aches without inflammation

- Fever

- Previous rheumatic fever or evidence of rheumatic heart disease

- Abnormal heartbeat on EKG

- Blood test indicating inflammation

Confirmation of rheumatic fever also requires other clinical and laboratory tests, to determine, for example, the presence of strep antibodies in the patient's blood. Rheumatic fever does not always involve the heart; even when it does, permanent damage is not inevitable. Nor does the severity of the attack have any relationship to the development of rheumatic heart disease.

The real danger arises when heart valve tissue becomes inflamed, affecting the valve's ability to close properly. When the acute attack has passed and the inflammation finally subsides, the valves begin to heal, with scar tissue forming.

Scar tissue may cause portions of the affected valve leaflets to fuse together. (*Leaflets* are the flaps of the heart valves.) This restricts leaflet motion, impeding the full swing action and thereby blood flow through the valve. This condition is called valvular *stenosis*. The leaflets may become shrunken or deformed by healing tissue, causing *regurgitation* or backspill because the valve fails to close completely.

Both stenosis and regurgitation are often present. Most susceptible are the *mitral valve,* which regulates flow from the upper to the lower left chambers of the heart, and the *aortic valve,* the gateway between the left ventricle and the general circulation. Rarely attacked are the two valves in the right chambers.

Treatment

During the acute stages of rheumatic fever, the patient is given heavy doses of antibiotics to rid the body of all strep traces, aspirin to control swelling and fever, and sometimes such hormones as ACTH and cortisone to reduce inflammation.

In the past, rheumatic fever spelled mandatory bed rest for months. Now the routine is to get the patient up and about as soon as the acute episode is over to avert the problem of psychological invalidism. The biggest restriction, especially for young people, is that no participation in competitive sports or other severely taxing exercises is allowed for two to three months while a close watch is kept on cardiac status.

The patient with valve damage can in many cases be treated medically, without the need for surgical intervention. He may, of course, have to desist from certain strenuous activities, but in all other ways he can lead a relatively normal life. Surgical relief or cure is available, however, for patients with severe damage or those who may, with age, develop progressive narrowing or leakage of the valves.

Surgery

Stenotic valves can be scraped clear of excess scar tissues, thereby returning the leaflets to more normal operation. In some cases individually scarred leaflets are replaced with synthetic substitutes. The correction of severe valvular regurgitation requires replacement of the entire valve with an artificial substitute, or, as some surgeons prefer, with a healthy valve taken from a human donor dying of other causes.

Prevention

The development of antibiotics has made rheumatic fever preventable. These drugs can knock out the strep before the germs get a chance to set off the inflammatory defense network sequences, but early detection is necessary. Among the symptoms of strep are a sore throat that comes on suddenly, with redness and swelling; rapidly acquired high fever; nausea and headaches. The only sure way to tell, however, is to have a throat swab taken by passing a sterile piece of cotton over the inflamed area. This culture is then exposed for 24 hours to a laboratory dish containing a substance that enhances strep growth. A positive identification calls for prompt treatment to kill the germs before the complications of rheumatic fever have a chance to set in.

Unfortunately, many strep infections may be mild enough to escape detection. The child may recover so quickly that the parents neglect to take the necessary precautions, but the insidious processes may still be going on in the apparently healthy child. This is a major reason why rheumatic fever is still with us, though in severe decline.

Heart Murmurs and Recurrences of Rheumatic Fever

The prime sign that rheumatic heart disease has developed is a heart murmur—although a heart murmur does not always mean heart disease. The murmur may be only temporary, ceasing once the rheumatic fever attack subsides and the stretched and swollen valves return to normal. To complicate matters more, many heart murmurs are harmless. Such functional murmurs may appear in 30 to 50 percent of normal children at one time or another.

As many as three in five patients with rheumatic fever may develop murmurs characteristic of scarred valves—sounds of blood flowing through ailing valves that fail to open and close normally.

Anyone who has had an attack of rheumatic fever has about a 50–50 chance of having one again unless safeguards are taken. As a result, all patients are placed on a daily or monthly regimen of antibiotics. The preventive dose, although smaller than that given to quell an in-progress infection, is enough to sabotage any attempts on the part of the strep germs to mount an attack.

There is some encouraging evidence that rheumatic fever patients who escape heart damage the first time around will do so again should a repeat attack occur. On the other hand, those with damaged valves will probably sustain more damage with subsequent strep-initiated attacks.

Endocarditis

One of the additional bonuses of antibiotic therapy is that it has all but eliminated an invariably fatal complication to which rheumatic patients were especially vulnerable—an infection of the heart's inner lining, or *endocardium*, called *subacute bacterial endocarditis*. The scar tissue provides an excellent nesting site for bacteria to grow.

The responsible germs are found in most everyone's mouth and usually invade the bloodstream after dental surgery. Fortunately, it is easy to prevent or cure because the germs offer little resistance to antibiotics. As a precaution, dentists are usually advised to give rheumatic fever patients larger doses of penicillin (or other antibiotics to those allergic to penicillin) before, during, and after dental work.

Congenital Heart Disease

Congenital heart disease includes that collection of heart and major blood vessel deformities that exist at birth in 8 out of every 1,000 live births, or 25,000 cases yearly. Nine thousand deaths annually are attributable to these inborn heart abnormalities.

There are some 35 recognized types of congenital heart malformations. Most—including all of the 15 most common types—can be either corrected or alleviated by surgery. The defects result from a failure of the infant's heart to mature normally during development in the womb.

The term *blue baby* refers to the infant born with a heart impairment that prevents blood from getting enough oxygen. Because

blood low in oxygen is dark bluish red, it imparts a blue tinge to the skin and lips.

The cause of inborn heart abnormalities is not known in most cases. Some defects can be traced to maternal virus infection, such as German measles (rubella), during the first three months of pregnancy when the fetus' heart is growing rapidly. Certain drugs, vitamin deficiencies or excessive exposure to radiation are among other environmental factors known to be associated with such defects.

Heart abnormalities may come singly or in combination. There may be, for example a hole in the walls separating the right and left heart chambers or a narrowing of a valve or blood vessel which obstructs blood flow, or a mixup in major blood vessel connections—or a combination of all of these.

Diagnosis

A skilled cardiologist often can make a reasonably complete diagnosis on the basis of a conventional physical examination including visual inspection of the infant's general condition, blood pressure reading, X ray, blood tests, and electrocardiogram. For more complex diagnosis, the physician may call for either *angiography* or *cardiac catheterization*. The former, a variation of coronary arteriography, allows direct X-ray visualization of the heart chambers and major blood vessels. In cardiac catheterization, a thin plastic tube or catheter is inserted into an arm or leg vein. While the physician watches with special X-ray equipment, the tube is advanced carefully through the vein until it reaches the heart chambers, there to provide information about the nature of the defect.

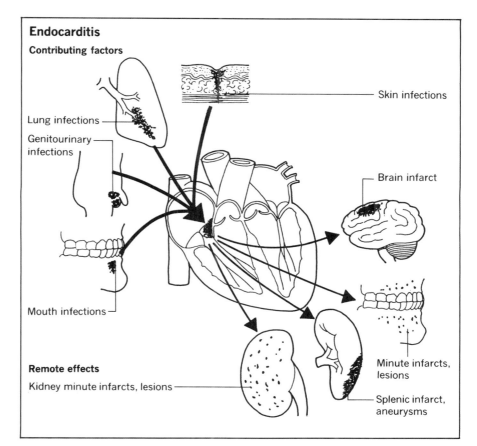

Endocarditis

Contributing factors

Skin infections

Lung infections

Genitourinary infections

Brain infarct

Mouth infections

Minute infarcts, lesions

Remote effects

Kidney minute infarcts, lesions

Splenic infarct, aneurysms

Advanced techniques known as computed tomography (CT), positron emission tomography (PET), and nuclear magnetic resonance (NMR) may also be used. Both the CT and PET scanners require injection of a contrast fluid so that a "picture" can be taken. The CT scanner takes X-ray images of "slices" of the patient's body with the aid of a computer. The PET scanner works on an electronic principle, with detectors located in a circle around the subject. Also computerized, NMR diagnoses by employing magnetic forces to "see" through bones, revealing such details as the differences between healthy and diseased tissues.

Treatment

From these tests, the cardiologist together with a surgeon can decide for or against surgery. Depending on the severity of the disease, some conditions may require an immediate operation, even on days-old infants. In other conditions, the specialists may instead recommend waiting until the infant is older and stronger before surgery is undertaken. In a number of instances, the defect may not require surgery at all.

Open-heart surgery in infants with inborn heart defects carries a higher risk than does the same surgery in older children. Risks must be taken often, however, because about one-third will die in the first month if untreated, and more than half within the first year.

Refinements in surgical techniques and postoperative care have given surgeons the confidence to operate on infants who are merely hours old with remarkable success. Specially adapted miniature heart-lung machines may also chill the blood to produce *hypothermia,* or body cooling. This slows metabolism and reduces tissue oxygen needs so that

the heart and brain can withstand short periods of interrupted blood flow.

A good deal has been learned, too, about the delicate medical management required by infants during the surgical recovery period. All of this accounts for the admirable record of salvage among infants who would have been given up for lost only a few years ago.

Congestive Heart Failure

Heart failure may be found in conjunction with any disease of the heart— coronary artery disease, hypertension, rheumatic heart disease, or congenital defects. It occurs when the heart's ability to pump blood has been weakened by disease. To say the heart has failed, however, does not mean it has stopped beating. The heart muscle continues to contract, but it lacks the strength to keep blood circulating normally throughout the body. Physicians sometimes refer to the condition as cardiac insufficiency or *dropsy,* although the latter term is seldom heard anymore.

When the heart fails to pump efficiently, the flow slows down, causing blood returning to the heart through the veins to back up. Some of the fluid in the blood is forced out through the thin walls of small blood vessels into surrounding tissues. Here the fluid piles up, or congests.

The result may be swelling, or *edema,* which can occur in many parts of the body but is most commonly seen in the legs and ankles. Fluids sometimes collect in the lungs, interfering with breathing and making the person short of breath. Heart failure also affects the ability of the kidneys to rid the body of sodium and water. Fluid retained in this way adds to the edema.

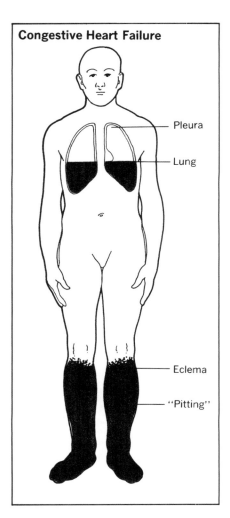

Congestive Heart Failure

Pleura

Lung

Edema

"Pitting"

Treatment

Treatment usually includes a combination of rest, drugs, diet, and restricted daily activity. *Digitalis,* in one of its many forms, is usually given to strengthen the action of the heart muscle. It also slows a rapid heartbeat, helps decrease heart enlargement, and promotes secretion of excess fluids. Care must be taken to find the right dose, because this will vary from person to person. When edema is present, diuretics are prescribed to speed up the elimination of excess salt and water. Many improved diuretics are available today. A sodium-restricted diet is generally necessary to reduce or prevent edema. Patients will also probably need bed rest for a while, with gradual return to slower-paced activity.

Most important, however, is the adequate treatment of the underlying disease that led to heart failure in the first place.

Heart Block

Sometimes the scars resulting from rheumatic fever, heart attack, or surgical repair of the heart may damage the electrical network in a way that blocks normal transmission of the signal between the upper and lower chambers. The disruption, called *atrioventricular block,* manifests in three degrees of intensity. First degree heart block is only detectable by an EKG and is merely a short delay in the normal transmission. Second degree heart block shows up as an irregular pulse—some of the beats are blocked. In third degree heart block, none of the beats reach the lower chambers; they begin beating on their own, but at a much slower rate, meaning that blood flow is seriously affected, especially to the brain. Blackouts and convulsions may ensue.

For first degree heart block and many forms of second degree, there are nervous system stimulants to keep the heart from lagging. For third degree heart block and some forms of second degree, however, drugs are not enough. An artificial electronic pacemaker, implanted in the body and connected to the heart by wires, has been successfully applied to many thousands of people throughout the world. This pacemaker fires electrical shocks into the ventricle wall to make it beat at the proper rate. Most devices are powered by tiny lithium batteries that last up to 10 years.

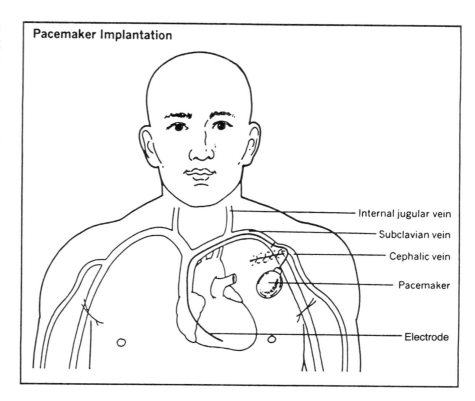

Pacemaker Implantation

Internal jugular vein

Subclavian vein

Cephalic vein

Pacemaker

Electrode

11

Diseases of the Digestive System

Digestive Functions and Organs

The function of the digestive system is to accept food and water through the mouth, to break down the food's chemical structure so that its nutrients can be absorbed into the body, a process called *digestion,* and to expel undigested particles. This process takes place as the food passes through the entire *alimentary tract.* This tract, also called the *gastrointestinal tract,* is a long, hollow passageway that begins at the mouth and continues on through the esophagus, the stomach, the small intestine, the large intestine, the rectum, and the anus. The salivary glands, the stomach glands, the liver, the gallbladder, and the pancreas release substances into the gastrointestinal tract that help the digestion of various food substances.

Digestion

Digestion begins in the mouth where food is shredded by chewing and mixed with saliva, which helps break down starch into sugars and lubricates the food so that it can be swallowed easily. The food then enters the *esophagus,* a muscular tube that for-cibly squeezes the food down toward the stomach, past the *cardiac sphincter,* a ring of muscle at the entrance of the stomach that opens to allow food into the stomach.

The stomach acts as a reservoir for food, churns the food, mixes it with gastric juices, and gradually releases the food into the small intestine. Some water, alcohol, and glucose are absorbed directly through the stomach into the bloodstream. Enzymes secreted by the stomach help break down proteins and fats into simpler substances. Hydrochloric acid secreted by the stomach kills bacteria and prepares some minerals for absorption in the small intestine. Some food may leave the stomach one minute after it enters, while other parts of a meal may remain in the stomach for as long as five hours.

The food passes from the stomach to the first section of the small intestine, the *duodenum,* where it is acted on by pancreatic enzymes that help break down fats, starches, proteins, and other substances. While the food is in the duodenum it is also digested by *bile,* which is produced by the liver and stored in the gallbladder. During a meal, the gallbladder discharges its bile into the duodenum. The bile promotes the absorption of fats and vitamins.

The semidigested food is squeezed down the entire length of the intestines by a wavelike motion of the intestinal muscles called *peristalsis.* Digestion is largely completed as the food passes through 20 feet of small intestine, which absorbs the digested food substances and water and passes them into the bloodstream. The food nutrients are distributed by the bloodstream throughout the body and used by the body cells.

Those parts of the food that are indigestible, such as the skins of fruits, pass into the large intestine, or *colon,* along with bacteria, bile, some minerals, various cells, and mucus. This combination of substances makes up the *feces,* which are stored in the colon until *defecation.* Some water and salts in the feces are absorbed through the walls of the colon into the bloodstream. This conserves the body's fluids and dries the feces. The formation of a semisolid fecal mass helps precipitate defecation.

The Oral Cavity

The Salivary Glands

The smell of food triggers the salivary glands to pour saliva into the mouth; that is what is meant by "mouth-watering" odors. During a meal, saliva is released into the mouth to soften the food as it is chewed.

Stones

Stones will sometimes form in the salivary glands or ducts, blocking the ducts and preventing the free flow of saliva into the mouth. After a meal, the swollen saliva-filled glands and ducts slowly empty. The swelling may sometimes be complicated by infection. Surgical removal of the stones is the usual treatment; sometimes the entire gland is removed.

Tumors

Tumors sometimes invade the salivary gland. An enlarged gland may press on the auditory canal and cause deafness, or it may result in stiffness of the jaw and mild facial palsy. The tumors can grow large enough to be felt by the fingers, and surgery is required to remove them.

Inflammation of the Parotid Glands

Inflammation of the upper (*parotid*) salivary glands may be caused by an infection in the oral cavity, by liver disease, or by malnutrition.

Mumps

One of the commonest inflammations of the salivary glands, called *mumps,* occurs especially in children. It is a highly contagious virus disease characterized by inflammation and swelling of one or both parotid salivary

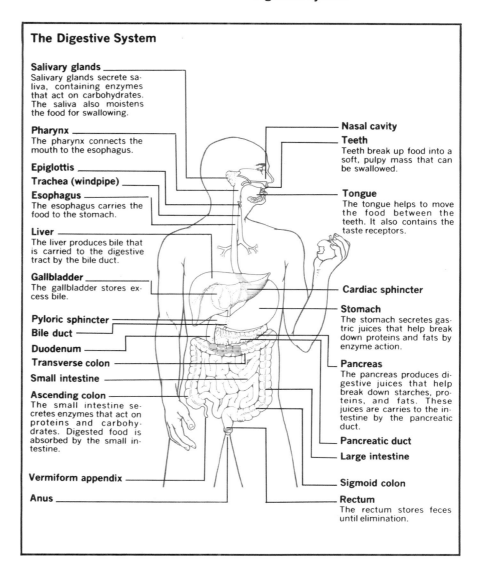

The Digestive System

Salivary glands
Salivary glands secrete saliva, containing enzymes that act on carbohydrates. The saliva also moistens the food for swallowing.

Pharynx
The pharynx connects the mouth to the esophagus.

Epiglottis

Trachea (windpipe)

Esophagus
The esophagus carries the food to the stomach.

Liver
The liver produces bile that is carried to the digestive tract by the bile duct.

Gallbladder
The gallbladder stores excess bile.

Pyloric sphincter

Bile duct

Duodenum

Transverse colon

Small intestine

Ascending colon
The small intestine secretes enzymes that act on proteins and carbohydrates. Digested food is absorbed by the small intestine.

Vermiform appendix

Anus

Nasal cavity

Teeth
Teeth break up food into a soft, pulpy mass that can be swallowed.

Tongue
The tongue helps to move the food between the teeth. It also contains the taste receptors.

Cardiac sphincter

Stomach
The stomach secretes gastric juices that help break down proteins and fats by enzyme action.

Pancreas
The pancreas produces digestive juices that help break down starches, proteins, and fats. These juices are carries to the intestine by the pancreatic duct.

Pancreatic duct

Large intestine

Sigmoid colon

Rectum
The rectum stores feces until elimination.

glands, and can have serious complications in adults. See "Alphabetic Guide to Child Care" in Ch. 2, *The First Dozen Years,* for a fuller discussion of mumps.

Bad Breath (Halitosis)

Poor oral hygiene is the principal cause of offensive mouth odor, or *halitosis.* It can result from oral tumors, abscesses from decaying teeth, and gum disease or infection. The foul smell is primarily a result of cell decay, and the odors are characteristic of the growth of some microorganisms.

When halitosis results from poor oral sanitation, the treatment is obvious—regular daily tooth brushing and the use of an antiseptic mouthwash. If the halitosis is because of disease of the oral cavity, alimentary tract, or respiratory system, the cure will depend on eradicating the primary cause.

Nonmalignant Lesions

The oral cavity is prone to invasion by several types of microorganisms that cause nonmalignant lesions. The most prominent follow.

Canker Sores

These are of unknown origin and

show up as single or multiple small sores near the molar teeth, inside the lips, or in the lining of the mouth. They can be painful but usually heal in a few days.

Fungus Infections

Thrush is the most common oral fungus infection and appears as white round patches inside the cheeks of infants, small children, and sometimes adults. The lesions may involve the entire mouth, tongue, and pharynx. In advanced stages the lesions turn yellow. Malnutrition, especially lack of adequate vitamin B, is the principal cause. Thrush is also one of the opportunistic infections commonly found in persons with AIDS. See also "AIDS" in Ch. 19, *Other Diseases of Major Importance.* Fungus growth may be aided by the use of antibiotic lozenges, which kill normal oral bacteria and permit fungi to flourish.

Tooth Decay and Vitamin Deficiencies

Lack of adequate vitamins in the daily diet is responsible for some types of lesions in the oral cavity. Insufficient vitamin A in children under five may be the cause of malformation in the crown, dentin, and enamel of the teeth. Lack of adequate vitamin C results in bleeding gums. Vitamin D insufficiency may lead to slow tooth development.

An inadequate and improper diet supports tooth decay, which in turn may be complicated by ulcers in the gums and abscesses in the roots of the decaying teeth. A diet with an adequate supply of the deficient vitamins will cause the symptoms to disappear. Infections, abscesses, cysts, or tumors in the mouth require the attention of a physician, dentist, or dental surgeon. See Ch. 22, *The Teeth and Gums.*

Chancres

These are primary syphilis lesions, which commonly develop at the lips and tongue. They appear as small, eroding red ulcers that exude yellow matter. They can invade the mouth, tonsils, and pharynx. Penicillin therapy is usually required.

The Esophagus

Varices

Varices (singular: *varix*) are enlarged and congested veins that appear in the esophagus because of increased blood pressure to the liver in patients with liver cirrhosis. This disease is most common in chronic alcoholics. Esophageal varices can be complicated by erosion of the mucous lining of the esophagus as a result of inflammation or vomiting. This causes hemorrhaging of the thin-walled veins, which can be fatal.

Bleeding esophageal varices may require hospitalization, immediate blood transfusions, and surgery.

Hiatus Hernia

The lower end of the esophagus or part of the stomach can sometimes protrude through the diaphragm. This *hiatus hernia,* sometimes referred to as a *diaphragmatic hernia,* can be a result of congenital malformation; in adults, the principal cause is weakness of the muscles around the opening of the esophagus leading into the stomach.

In individuals who are obese and who have large stomachs, the stomach contents may be forced back into the lower esophagus, causing this area to herniate. Other causes include stooping, bending, or kneeling, which increases pressure in the stomach. Pregnancy may increase abdominal pressure in the same manner as obesity.

Typical symptoms are vomiting when the stomach is full, heartburn with pain spreading to the ears, neck, and arms, swallowing difficulty with the food sometimes sticking in the esophagus, and a swollen abdomen. The vomiting may occur at night, with relief obtained by getting up and walking about for a few minutes. Belching will relieve the distension, and *antacids* (acid neutralizers) may be prescribed to counter gastric hyperacidity.

Conservative treatment involves

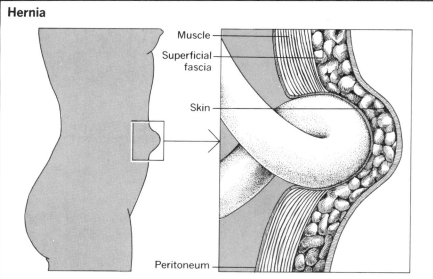

Hernia

Muscle
Superficial fascia
Skin
Peritoneum

Hernias result when a part of the intestine pushes through layers of muscle against the body's layers of skin.

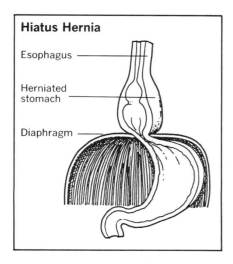

Hiatus Hernia

Esophagus

Herniated stomach

Diaphragm

eating small portions at frequent intervals. Dieting and a reduction in weight cause the symptoms to disappear. When the symptoms are due to pregnancy, they disappear after delivery. When medical management is not successful, surgical repair of the hernia is necessary. See also "Hernias" later in this chapter.

Achalasia

Achalasia is abnormal dilation of the lower esophagus caused by failure of the cardiac sphincter to relax and allow food to enter the stomach. Food collects in the esophagus and does not flow into the stomach. The patient feels as though the food is sticking in the middle of his chest wall. Small amounts of food may eventually pass into the stomach, and the mild pain or discomfort disappears.

If the condition persists, the pain may increase to become a continuous burning sensation at each meal, due to inflammation of the esophagus by accumulated food. If the patient lies down, some of this esophageal content will regurgitate and enter the pharynx. If the vomitus gets into the lungs, the end result may be *aspiration pneumonia*, a form of pneumonia caused by inhaling particles of foreign matter.

The disease is difficult to control,

and the condition tends to return, so that surgery is often used to create a permanent opening between the esophagus and stomach.

Swallowing Difficulty

Difficulty in swallowing is called *dysphagia*, which should not be confused with *dysphasia*, a speech impairment. Dysphagia may be caused by lesions in the mouth and tongue, acute inflammatory conditions in the oral cavity and pharynx (mumps, tonsillitis, laryngitis, pharyngitis), lesions, cancers, or foreign bodies in the esophagus. Strictures in the esophagus—from esophageal ulcers or from swallowing corrosive liquids—will also impair swallowing.

Stomach and Intestines

Indigestion (Dyspepsia)

There are times when the gastrointestinal tract fails to carry out its normal digestive function. The resulting indigestion, or *dyspepsia*, generates a variety of symptoms, such as heartburn, nausea, pain in the upper abdomen, gases in the stomach (*flatulence*), belching, and a feeling of fullness after eating.

Indigestion can be caused by ulcers of the stomach or duodenum and by excessive or too rapid eating or drinking. It may also be caused by emotional disturbance.

Constipation

Constipation is the difficult or infrequent evacuation of feces. The urge to defecate is normally triggered by the pressure of feces on the rectum and by the intake of food into the stomach. On the toilet, the anal sphincter is relaxed voluntarily, and the fecal material is expelled. The

need to defecate should be attended to as soon as possible. Habitual disregard of the desire to empty the bowels reduces intestinal motion and leads to constipation.

Daily or regular bowel movements are not necessary for good health. Normal bowel movements may occur at irregular intervals due to variations in diet, mental stress, and physical activity. For some individuals, normal defecation may take place as infrequently as once every four days.

Simple Constipation

In simple constipation, the patient may have to practice good bowel movement habits, which include a trip to the toilet once daily, preferably after breakfast. Adequate fluid intake and proper diet, including fresh fruits and green vegetables, can help restore regular bowel movement. Laxatives can provide temporary relief, but they inhibit normal bowel function and lead to dependence. When toilet-training young children, parents should encourage but never force them to have regular bowel movements, preferably after breakfast.

Chronic Constipation

Chronic constipation can cause feces to accumulate in the rectum and *sigmoid*, the terminal section of the colon. The colonic fluid is absorbed and a mass of hard fecal material remains. Such impacted feces often prevent further passage of bowel contents. The individual suffers from abdominal pain with distension and sometimes vomiting. A cleansing enema will relieve the fecal impaction and related symptoms.

In the overall treatment of constipation, the principal cause must be identified and corrected so that normal evacuation can return.

Intestinal Obstructions

Obstruction to the free flow of digestive products may exist either in the stomach or in the small and large intestines. The typical symptoms of intestinal obstruction are constipation, painful abdominal distension, and vomiting. Intestinal obstruction can be caused by the bowel's looping or twisting around itself, forming what is known as a *volvulus*. Malignant tumors can either block the intestine or press it closed.

In infants, especially boys, a common form of intestinal obstruction occurs when a segment of the intestine folds into the section below it. This condition is known as *intussusception,* and can significantly reduce the blood supply to the lower bowel segment. The cause may be traced to viral infection, injury to the abdomen, hard food, or a foreign body in the gastrointestinal tract.

The presence of intestinal obstructions is generally determined by consideration of the clinical symptoms, as well as X-ray examinations of the abdomen. Hospitalization is required, since intestinal obstruction has a high fatality rate if proper medical care is not administered. Surgery may be needed to remove the obstruction.

Diarrhea

Diarrhea is the frequent and repeated passage of liquid stools. It is usually accompanied by intestinal inflammation, and sometimes by the passing of mucus or blood.

The principal cause of diarrhea is infection in the intestinal tract by microorganisms. Chemical and food poisoning also brings on spasms of diarrhea. Long-standing episodes of diarrhea have been traced to inflammation of the intestinal mucosa, tumors, ulcers, allergies, vitamin deficiency, and in some cases emotional stress. Diarrhea, in conjunction with

other symptoms, can also indicate infection with human immunodeficiency virus (HIV), the suspected cause of AIDS. See "AIDS" in Ch. 19, *Other Diseases of Major Importance.*

Patients with diarrhea commonly suffer abdominal cramps, lose weight from chronic attacks, or have vomiting spells. A physician must always be consulted for proper diagnosis and treatment; this is especially important if the attacks continue for more than two or three days. Untreated diarrhea can lead to dehydration and malnutrition; it may be fatal, especially in infants.

Dysentery

Dysentery is caused by microorganisms that thrive in the intestines of infected individuals. Most common are *amoebic dysentery,* caused by amoebae, and *bacillary dysentery,* caused by bacteria. The symptoms are diarrhea with blood and pus in the stools, cramps, and fever. The infection is spread from person to person through infected excrement that contaminates food or water. The bacteria and amoebae responsible can also be spread by houseflies which feed on feces as well as on human foods. It is

a common tropical disease and can occur wherever human excrement is not disposed of in a sanitary manner.

Dysentery must be treated early to avoid erosion of the intestinal wall. In bacillary dysentery, bed rest and hospitalization are recommended, especially for infants and the aged. Antibiotic drugs may be administered.

In most cases the disease can be spread by healthy human carriers who must be treated to check further spread.

Typhoid

Enteric fever or *typhoid* is an acute, highly communicable disease caused by the organism *Salmonella typhosa.* It is sometimes regarded as a tropical disease because epidemic outbreaks are common in tropical areas where careless disposal of feces and urine contaminates food, milk, and water supplies. In any location, tropical or temperate, where unsanitary living predominates, there is always the possibility that the disease can occur. Flies can transmit the disease, as can shellfish that live in typhoid-infested waters.

The typhoid bacilli do their damage to the mucosa of the small intestines.

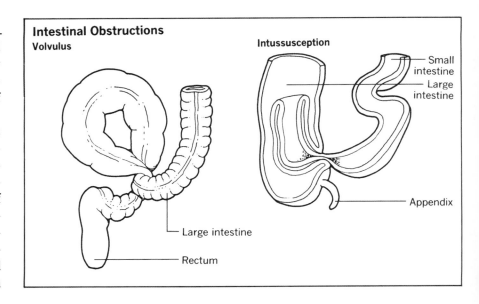

Intestinal Obstructions
Volvulus

Large intestine

Rectum

Intussusception

Small intestine
Large intestine

Appendix

They enter via the oral cavity and stomach and finally reach the lymph nodes and blood vessels in the small bowel.

Symptoms

Following an incubation period of about ten days, general bodily discomfort, fever, headache, nausea, and vomiting are experienced. Other clinical manifestations include abdominal pain with tenderness, greenish diarrhea (or constipation), bloody stools, and mental confusion. It is not unusual for red spots to appear on the body.

If untreated, typhoid victims die within 21 days of the onset of the disease. The cause of death may be perforation of the small bowel, abdominal hemorrhage, toxemia, or other complications such as intestinal inflammation and pneumonia.

Treatment and Prevention

A person can best recover from typhoid if he receives diligent medical and nursing care. He should be isolated in a hospital on complete bed rest. Diet should be restricted to highly nutritious liquids or preferably intravenous feeding. Destruction of the bacilli is achieved by antibiotic therapy, usually with Chloromycetin.

The best way to prevent the spread of typhoid is to disinfect all body refuse, clothing, and utensils of the person infected. Isolation techniques practiced in hospitals prevent local spread. Milk and milk products should always be pasteurized; drinking water should be chlorinated.

Human beings can carry the disease and infect others without themselves becoming ill; they are usually not aware that they are carriers. Within recent years, a vaccination effective for a year has been developed.

People traveling to areas where sanitation practices may be conducive to typhoid should receive this vaccination. In such areas, it is usually a good practice to boil drinking water as well.

Foreign Bodies in the Alimentary Tract

Anyone who accidentally swallows a foreign body should seek immediate medical aid, preferably in a hospital. Foreign bodies that enter the gastrointestinal tract may cause obstruction anywhere along the tract, including the esophagus. For emergency procedures, see "Obstruction of the Windpipe" in Ch. 31. *Medical Emergencies*.

Dental plates and large chunks of meat have been known to cause fatal choking. A foreign body in the esophagus may set off a reflex mechanism that causes the trachea to close. The windpipe may have to be opened by means of a *tracheostomy* (incision in the windpipe) to restore breathing. If the object swallowed is long and sharp-pointed, it may perforate the tract.

Foreign bodies in the esophagus are usually the most troublesome. Small fish bones may stick to the walls of the esophagus; large pieces of meat may block the tract. X-ray studies aid the physician in locating the swallowed object and in determining how best to deal with it.

Small objects like coins and paper clips may pass through the digestive tract without causing serious problems. Their progress may be checked by X rays of the abdomen. Examination of stools will indicate whether or not the entire object has been expelled. With larger objects, the problem of blockage must be considered. It is sometimes necessary for a surgeon to open the stomach in a hospital operating room and remove the foreign object.

Ulcers

A *peptic ulcer* is an eroded area of the mucous membrane of the digestive tract. The most common gastrointestinal ulcers are found in the lower end of the esophagus, stomach, or duodenum and are caused by the excessive secretion of gastric acid which erodes the lining membrane in these areas.

The cause of ulcers is obscure, but any factor that increases the gastric acidity may contribute to the condition. Mental stress or conflict, excessive food intake, alcohol, and caffeine all cause the stomach to increase its output of hydrochloric acid.

The disease is sometimes considered to be hereditary, especially among persons with type O blood. Symptoms usually appear in individuals of the 20-to-40 age group, with the highest incidence in persons over age 45. Peptic ulcers of the stomach (*gastric ulcers*) and duodenal ulcers occur more frequently in men than in women. Ulcers are common in patients with arthritis and chronic lung disease.

Symptoms

Early ulcer symptoms are gastric hyperacidity and burning abdominal pain that is relieved by eating, vomiting, or the use of antacids. The pain may occur as a dull ache, especially when one's stomach is empty, or it may be sharp and knifelike.

Other manifestations of a peptic ulcer are the following: nausea, associated with heartburn and regurgitation of gastric juice into the esophagus and mouth; excessive gas; poor appetite with undernourishment and weakness in older victims; and black stools resulting from a bleeding ulcer.

The immediate goal of ulcer therapy is to heal the ulcer; the long-term goal is to prevent its recurrence. An ulcer normally heals through the formation of scar tissue in the ulcer crater. The healing process, under proper medical care, may take several weeks. The disappearance of pain does not necessarily indicate that the ulcer has healed completely, or even partially. The pain and the ulcerative process may recur at regular intervals over periods of weeks or months.

Although treatment can result in complete healing and recovery, some victims of chronic peptic ulcers have a 20-to-30-year history of periodic recurrences. For such patients, ulcer therapy may have to be extended indefinitely to avoid serious complications. If a recurrent ulcer perforates the stomach or intestine, or if it bleeds excessively, it can be quickly fatal. Emergency surgery is always required when perforation and persistent bleeding occur.

Treatment

The basic principles of ulcer therapy are diet, rest, and the suppression of stomach acidity. A patient with an active gastric ulcer is generally hospitalized for three weeks to make certain that he receives the proper diet and to remove him from sources of emotional stress, such as business or family problems. During hospitalization the healing process is monitored by X-ray examination. If there is no evidence of healing within three to four weeks, surgery may be advisable. For patients with duodenal ulcers, a week or two of rest at home with proper diet may be sufficient.

Ulcer diets consist of low-residue bland foods taken in small amounts at frequent intervals, as often as once an hour when pain is severe. The preferred foods are milk, soft eggs, jellies, custards, creams, and cooked cereals. See "Minimal Residue Diet" in Ch. 27, *Nutrition and Weight Control.* Because ulcer diets often lack some essential nutrients, prolonged

dietary treatment may have to be augmented with daily vitamin capsules. Antispasmodic medication may be prescribed to reduce contractions of the stomach, decrease the stomach's production of acid, and slow down digestion. Antacids, such as the combination of aluminum hydroxide and magnesium trisilicate, may be required after meals and between feedings. Spicy foods, alcohol, coffee, cola and other caffeine-containing drinks, large meals, and smoking should be strictly avoided.

In addition to common antacids, some new drugs have been introduced to help treat ulcers and other digestive disorders. Tagamet in particular, a brand name for the drug cimetidine, has been found to be effective in treating duodenal ulcers. It has also been used to prevent ulcer-related stomach, esophagus, and duodenal problems. The drug acts primarily to reduce secretions of gastric acid. But side effects have been reported, some of them serious. These include mental confusion, fever, slowed pulse, and others. Metiamide, another drug used to control the production of gastric acids in the digestive system, has been found to attack the leukocytes or white cells of the blood. Other problems have been reported with metiamide.

If the ulcer does not respond to medical therapy, or if pain persists, surgery may be the preferred treatment. Such surgery is elective surgery, a matter of choice, as opposed to the emergency surgery required by large, bleeding, or perforated ulcers. After the removal of the acid-producing section of the stomach, some patients may develop weakness and nausea as their digestive system adjusts to the reduced size of their stomach. A proper diet of special foods and fluids, plus sedatives, can alleviate the condition. The chances for complete recovery are good. For

a full description of surgical treatment of peptic ulcers, see "Peptic Ulcers" in Ch. 20, *Surgery.*

Diverticula

A *diverticulum* is an abnormal pouch caused by herniation of the mucous membrane of the digestive tract. The pouch has a narrow neck and a bulging round end. Diverticula are found in the esophagus, stomach, duodenum, colon, and other parts of the digestive tract.

The presence of diverticula in any segment of the digestive tract is referred to as *diverticulosis.* When diverticula become inflamed the condition is known as *diverticulitis.* The latter is a common form of disease of the sigmoid colon and is found in persons past the age of 45.

In mild cases, there may be no symptoms. On the other hand, a diverticulum may sometimes rupture and produce the same symptoms as an acute attack of appendicitis—vomiting and pain with tenderness in the right lower portion of the abdomen. Other symptoms are intermittent constipation and diarrhea, and abdominal pain.

Diverticulosis is treated by bed rest, restriction of solid food and increase of fluid intake, and administration of antibiotics. Surgery is recommended when diverticulosis causes obstruction of the colon or creates an

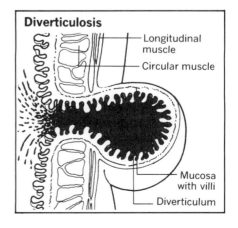

Diverticulosis

Longitudinal muscle

Circular muscle

Mucosa with villi

Diverticulum

opening between the colon and the bladder, or when one or more diverticula rupture and perforate the colon. The outlook for recovery following surgery is good.

Hemorrhoids (Piles)

Hemorrhoids, or *piles,* are round, purplish protuberances at the anus. They are the results of rectal veins that become dilated and rupture. Hemorrhoids are very common and are often caused by straining because of constipation, pregnancy, or diarrhea.

Hemorrhoids may appear on the external side of the anus or on the internal side; they may or may not be painful. Rectal bleeding and tenderness are common. It is important to emphasize, however, that not all rectal bleeding results from hemorrhoids. Small hemorrhoids are best left untreated; large painful ones may be surgically reduced or removed. *Prolapsed* piles—those that have slipped forward—are treated by gentle pressure to return the hemorrhoidal mass into the rectum. The rectal and anal opening must be lubricated to keep the area soft. Other conditions in the large bowel can simulate hemorrhoids and need to be adequately investigated.

Hernias

Hernias in the digestive tract occur

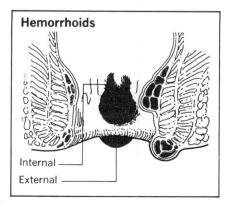

Hemorrhoids

Internal

External

when there is muscular weakness in surrounding body structures. Pressure from the gastrointestinal tract may cause a protrusion or *herniation* of the gut through the weakened wall. Such hernias exist in the diaphragmatic area (*hiatus hernias,* discussed above), in the anterior abdomen (*ventral hernias*), or in the region of the groin (*inguinal hernias*). Apart from hiatus hernias, inguinal hernias are by far the most common.

One of the causes of intestinal obstruction is a *strangulated hernia.* A loop of herniated bowel becomes

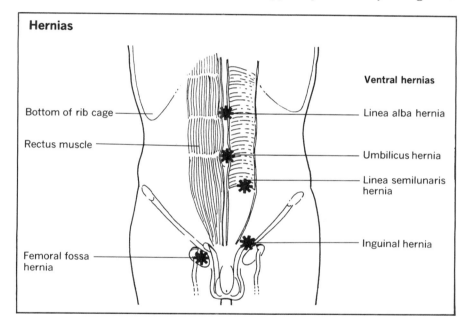

Hernias

Bottom of rib cage

Rectus muscle

Femoral fossa hernia

Ventral hernias

Linea alba hernia

Umbilicus hernia

Linea semilunaris hernia

Inguinal hernia

tightly constricted, blood supply is cut off, and the loop becomes gangrenous. Immediate surgery is required since life is threatened from further complications.

Except for hiatus hernias, diagnosis is usually made simple by the plainly visible herniated part. In men, an enlarged scrotum may be present in untreated inguinal hernias. The herniating bowel can be reduced, that is, manipulated back into position, and a truss worn to support the reduced hernia and provide temporary relief. In all hernias, however, surgical repair is the usual treatment.

Gastritis

Gastritis is inflammation of the mucosa of the stomach. The patient complains of *epigastric* pain—in the middle of the upper abdomen—with distension of the stomach, loss of appetite, nausea, and vomiting.

Attacks of acute gastritis can be traced to bacterial action, food poisoning, peptic ulcer, the presence of alcohol in the stomach, the ingestion of highly spiced foods, or overeating and drinking. Occasional gastritis, though painful, is not serious and may disappear spontaneously. The general treatment for gastritis is similar to the treatment of a gastric ulcer.

Enteritis

Enteritis, sometimes referred to as *regional enteritis,* is a chronic inflammatory condition of unknown origin that affects the small intestine. It is called regional because the disease most often involves the terminal ileum, even though any segment of the digestive tract can be involved. The diseased bowel becomes involved with multiple ulcer craters and ultimately stiffens because of fibrous healing of the ulcers.

Regional enteritis occurs most often in males from adolescence to middle age. The symptoms may exist for a long period before the disease is recognized. Intermittent bloody diarrhea, general weakness, and lassitude are the early manifestations. Later stages of the disease are marked by fever, increased bouts of diarrhea with resultant weight loss, and sharp lower abdominal pain on the right side. This last symptom sometimes causes the disease to be confused with appendicitis, because in both conditions there is nausea and vomiting. Occasionally in women there may be episodes of painful menstruation.

Treatment involves either surgical removal of the diseased bowel or conservative medical management and drug therapy. In acute attacks of enteritis, bed rest and intravenous fluids are two important aspects of treatment. Medical management in less severe occurrences includes a daily diet rich in proteins and vitamins, excluding harder foods such as fresh fruits and vegetables. Antibiotics are prescribed to combat bacterial invasion.

Colitis

Colitis is an inflammatory condition of the colon, of uncertain origin, and often chronic. It may result from a nervous predisposition which leads to bacterial or viral infection. The inflammation can cause spasms that damage the colon, or can lead to bleeding ulcers that may be fatal.

In milder forms, colitis first appears with diarrhea in which red bloody streaks can be observed. The symptoms may come and go for weeks before the effects become very significant. As the disease process advances, the diarrhea episodes become more frequent; more blood and mucus are present in the feces. These are combined with abdominal pain, nausea, and vomiting. Because of the loss of blood, the patient often becomes anemic and thin. If there are ulcer craters in the mucosa, the disease is called *ulcerative colitis*.

Hospitalization is necessary in order to provide proper treatment that will have a long-term effect. Surgery is sometimes necessary if an acute attack has been complicated by perforation of the intestines or if chronic colitis fails to respond to medical management.

Nonoperative treatment includes control of diarrhea and vomiting by drug therapy. Antibiotics are given to control infection and reduce fever, which always accompanies infection. A high protein and vitamin diet is necessary. But if the diarrhea and vomiting persist, intravenous feeding becomes a must. Blood transfusions may be required for individuals who have had severe rectal bleeding. Because there is no absolute cure, the disease may recur.

Appendicitis

The *vermiform appendix* is a narrow tubular attachment to the colon. It can become obstructed by the presence of undigested food such as small seeds from fruits or by hard bits of feces. This irritates the appendix and causes inflammation to set in. If it is obstructed, pressure builds within the appendix because of increasing secretions, a situation that can result in rupture of the appendix. A ruptured appendix can be rapidly fatal if *peritonitis,* inflammation of the peritoneal cavity, sets in.

In most cases the onset of appendicitis is heralded by an acute attack of pain in the center of the abdomen. The pain intensity increases, shifts to the right lower abdomen with nausea, vomiting, and fever as added symptoms. Some individuals, however, suffer from recurrent attacks of dull pain without other signs of gastrointestinal disease, and these may not be significant enough to warrant immediate hospitalization.

Diagnosis of appendicitis is usually dependent on the above symptoms, along with tenderness in the appendix area, increased pulse rate, and decreasing blood pressure. The last two are very significant if the appendix ruptures and peritonitis sets in. Whenever these symptoms are observed, the patient should be rushed to the nearest hospital.

Immediate surgical removal of the diseased appendix by means of a small incision is necessary in all nonperforated acute cases. This type of operation (*appendectomy*) is no longer considered major surgery. If the appendix ruptures and peritonitis is evident, emergency major surgery is necessary to drain the infection and remove the appendix. In the absence of postoperative complications, the patient recovers completely. One of the major problems of appendicitis is early diagnosis to prevent dangerous complications.

Intestinal Parasites

Not all the diseases of man are caused by microscopic organisms. Some are caused by parasitic worms, *helminths,* which invade the digestive tract, most often via food and water. In recent years government health agencies have largely eliminated the prime sources of worm infection: unwholesome meat or untreated sewage that finds its way into drinking water. Nevertheless, helminths still exist. Drugs used to expel worms are called *vermifuges* or *anthelmintics*.

The following are among the major intestinal parasites.

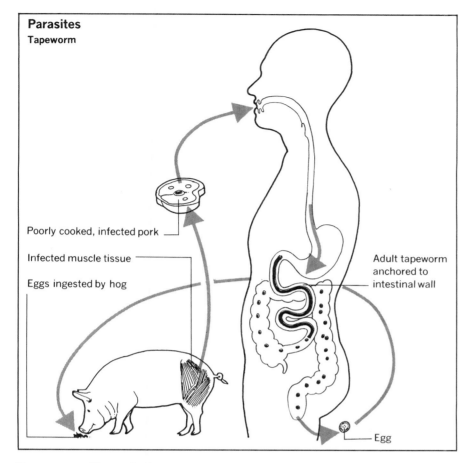

Parasites

Tapeworm

Poorly cooked, infected pork

Infected muscle tissue

Eggs ingested by hog

Adult tapeworm anchored to intestinal wall

Egg

Tapeworms (Cestodes)

These ribbon-shaped flatworms are found primarily in beef, fish, and pork that have not been thoroughly cooked. There are several species ranging from inch-long worms to tapeworms that grow to about 30 feet and live for as long as 16 years.

Tapeworms attach themselves to intestinal mucosa and periodically expel their eggs in excreta. If such feces are carelessly disposed of, the eggs can reach drinking water and be taken in by fish or ingested by grazing cattle. The eggs hatch in the animal's large bowel and find their way into the bloodstream by boring through the intestinal wall. Once in the blood they eventually adhere to muscles and live a dormant life in a capsule.

People who eat raw or partially cooked meat and fish that are infested with tapeworms become infected. The worms enter the bowel, where they feed, grow, and produce eggs. When the egg-filled segments are excreted, the cycle begins anew. Tapeworm infection is usually asymptomatic. It is discovered when egg-laden segments in feces are recognized as such.

Medication must be given on an empty stomach, followed later by a laxative. This will dislodge the worms and enable the body to purge itself of them. A weekly check of stools for segments of the worms may be necessary to confirm that the host is free of the parasites.

Hookworms

There are many species of these tiny, threadlike worms which are usually less than one centimeter long. They are found principally in tropical and subtropical areas of China, North Africa, Europe, Central America, and the West Indies, but they are by no means extinct in the United States.

The eggs are excreted in the feces of infected individuals, and if fecal materials are not well disposed of, the eggs may be found on the ground of unsanitary areas. In warm, moist conditions they hatch into larvae that penetrate the skin, especially the feet of people who walk around barefooted. The larvae can also be swallowed in impure water.

Hookworm-infected individuals, most often children, may experience an inflammatory itch in the area where the larvae entered. The host becomes anemic from blood loss, due to parasitic feeding of the worms, develops a cough, and experiences abdominal pain with diarrhea. Sometimes there is nausea or a distended abdomen. Diagnosis is confirmed by laboratory analysis of feces for the presence of eggs.

Successful treatment requires administration of anthelmintic drugs, preferably before breakfast, to destroy the worms. Weekly laboratory examination of the feces for evidence of hookworm eggs is a necessary precaution in ascertaining that the disease has been eradicated. Untreated hookworm infestation often leads to small bowel obstruction.

Trichinosis

This sometimes fatal disease is caused by a tiny worm, *Trichinella spiralis,* which is spread to man by eating improperly cooked pork containing the tiny worms in a capsulated form. After they are ingested the worms are set free to attach themselves to the mucosa of the small intestines. Here they mature in a few days and mate; the male dies and the female lays eggs that reach the muscles via the vascular system.

Trichinella organisms cause irritation of the intestinal mucosa. The infected individual suffers from abdominal pains with diarrhea, nausea, and vomiting. Later stages of the disease are marked by stiffness, pain, and swelling in the muscles, fever with sweating, respiratory distress, insomnia, and swelling of the face and eyelids. Death may result from complications such as pneumonia, heart damage, or respiratory failure. Despite government inspection of meats, all pork should be well-cooked before eating.

Threadworms (Nematodes)

These worms, also called pinworms, infect children more often than adults. Infection occurs by way of the mouth. The worms live in the bowel and sometimes journey through the anus, where they cause intense itching. The eggs are laid at the anal opening, and can be blown about in the air and spread in that manner. The entire family must be medically treated to kill the egg-laying females, and soothing ointment should be applied at the rectal area to relieve the itching. Good personal hygiene, especially hand washing after toilet use, is an essential part of the treatment.

Roundworms (Ascaris)

These intestinal parasites closely resemble earthworms. The eggs enter the digestive tract and hatch in the small bowel. The young parasites then penetrate the walls of the bowel, enter the bloodstream, and find their way to the liver, heart, and lungs.

Untreated roundworm infestation leads to intestinal obstruction or blockage of pancreatic and bile ducts caused by the masses of roundworms, which usually exist in the hundreds. Ingestion of vermifuge drugs is the required treatment.

Food Poisoning

Acute gastrointestinal illnesses may result from eating food that is itself poisonous, from ingesting chemical poisons, or from bacterial sources. The bacteria can either manufacture *toxins* (poisonous substances) or cause infection. Improperly canned fish, meats, and vegetables may encourage the growth of certain toxin-manufacturing organisms that resist the action of gastric juice when ingested. A person who eats such foods may contract a type of food poisoning known as *botulism*. The symptoms include indigestion and abdominal pain, nausea and vomiting, blurred vision, dryness in the mouth and throat, and poor muscular coordination.

If the toxins become fixed in the central nervous system, they may cause death. Emergency hospitalization is required, where antitoxins are administered intravenously and other measures are taken to combat the effects of botulism.

Salmonella food poisoning is caused by a species of bacteria of that name and is spread by eating contaminated meat, or by eating fish, egg, and milk products that have not been properly cooked or stored or have been inadequately refrigerated. The organisms are also transmitted by individuals who handle well-prepared food with dirty hands. Victims suffer from vomiting, diarrhea, abdominal pain, and fever. This type of food poisoning can be fatal in children and the aged, especially if the latter are ailing. Medical treatment with hospitalization, administration of broad-spectrum antibiotics, and intravenous fluids (to replace water loss due to vomiting) is required.

Some people develop allergic reactions to certain foods and break out in severe rashes after a meal containing any of these foods. Among such foods are fruits, eggs, and milk or milk products. Vomiting or diarrhea

may also occur. The best treatment is to avoid eating such foods and, when necessary, supplement the diet with manufactured protein and vitamins.

Liver Disease

Cirrhosis

Chronic disease of the liver with the destruction of liver cells is known as *cirrhosis*. A common cause is excessive intake of alcoholic beverages along with malnutrition. However, there are other predisposing factors, such as inflammation of the liver (*hepatitis*), syphilis, intestinal worms, jaundice or biliary tract inflammation, and disorders in blood circulation to the liver.

Victims of cirrhosis are usually anemic and have an elevated temperature, around 100° F. Alcoholics very often lose weight, suffer from indigestion, and have distended abdomens.

Accurate diagnosis of cirrhosis depends on complex laboratory tests of liver function, urine, and blood. If liver damage is not too far advanced, treatment of the complications and underlying causes can aid the liver cells in the process of regeneration. In long-standing chronic disease, liver damage may be irreversible. Alcoholics who forgo alcohol may be restored to health, depending on the extent of liver damage, with a proper diet rich in proteins and vitamins.

Successful treatment of liver cirrhosis may require long hospitalization with drug therapy and blood transfusions. During alcoholic withdrawal, the patient may require close medical observation and psychiatric help. If the patient's jaundice improves and his appetite returns, recovery in milder cirrhosis cases is possible.

Jaundice

In diseases of the liver and biliary tract, excessive bile pigment (*bilirubin*) is recirculated into the bloodstream. It enters the mucous membranes and skin, giving them the characteristic yellow pigmentation of the disease.

Gallstones or tumors that obstruct the free flow of bile are one cause of jaundice. Other causes include hepatitis, overproduction of bile pigments with resultant accumulation of bile within the liver, cirrhosis, and congenital closure of the bile ducts, the last a common cause of jaundice in infancy.

Apart from the typical yellow appearance of the skin, jaundice generates such symptoms as body itching, vomiting with bile (indicated by the green appearance and bitter taste), diarrhea with undigested fats present in the stools, and enlargement of the liver with pain and tenderness in the right upper abdomen.

Treatment of jaundice requires continued medical care with hospitalization. Surgery may be necessary to remove stones in the biliary tract or other obstructions. If there is bacterial infection, antibiotic therapy is necessary.

Hepatitis

Inflammation of the liver results in the disease known as *hepatitis*. The most common cause is an infectious process brought on by viruses, jaundice, or high fevers. Other causes of hepatitis include intestinal parasites, circulatory disturbances (such as congestive heart failure), hypersensitivity to drugs, damage to the liver or kidneys, or bacterial infection elsewhere in the body.

Serum hepatitis or *hepatitis B* is spread through blood contact with infected body fluids. The most common means of transmitting hepatitis B is sexual contact, but with an increased number of blood transfusions for complex surgery and rising intravenous drug use by addicts, the danger of transmitting hepatitis B by infected blood, needles or syringes has correspondingly increased. While hepatitis B and the HIV virus which causes AIDS are spread in the same manner, hepatitis B is one hundred times as contagious as HIV.

Infectious hepatitis or *hepatitis C* is the most common cause of viral hepatitis. This form of the virus primarily attacks children and young adults, especially those that congregate in large numbers. Epidemics of the C virus have broken out at schools, summer camps, music festivals and military installations. The virus is spread by food and water contaminated by feces from infected individuals; good sanitation thus becomes a vital preventative factor. Recent discoveries indicate the C virus remains in the blood long after all symptoms have disappeared, making those that are exposed to it chronic carriers of the virus.

Symptoms

The incubation period of infectious hepatitis lasts from one to six weeks —that of hepatitis B is longer— followed by fever with headache, loss of appetite (especially for fatty foods), and gastrointestinal distress (nausea, vomiting, diarrhea, or constipation). As the disease progresses, the liver becomes enlarged and the patient jaundiced. There may be some pain in the right upper abdomen.

Treatment

Untreated hepatitis causes severe liver damage, even liver failure accompanied by coma. Sometimes death occurs. Several assaults on the liver reduce its regeneration process and promote cirrhosis and cancer of the liver.

The original vaccine developed for hepatitis B was made from blood plasma, and thus constituted a potential risk of transmitting the AIDS virus. To eliminate this danger, new vaccines were genetically engineered from artificial genes. Three doses of the vaccine are needed to achieve a protection level of greater than 95 percent. The vaccine can also be administered soon after exposure to the virus with comparable protection levels. Infants should be vaccinated and those born to infected mothers can be protected by immune globulin administered at the time of the vaccine sequence. National guidelines recommending vaccination only for high risk groups, such as health care workers, infants of infected mothers and sexually active adults with more than one sex partner, are believed to be too conservative; ideally everyone should be vaccinated.

The immune system hormone, alpha interferon, is the only known treatment for hepatitis C, and only a low percentage respond to this treatment without suffering a relapse. It is not known yet whether or not the hormone treatment eradicates the virus.

In all cases, bed rest, preferably hospital isolation, is a necessary step in the initial treatment stages. Drug therapy with steroids may hasten the recovery process, which may take three to four weeks and usually leaves the patient very weak.

Gallbladder Disease

The biliary tract is very often plagued by the presence of stones, either in the gallbladder or in one of the bile ducts. Gallstones are mostly a mixture of calcium carbonate, cholesterol, and bile salts, and can occur either as one large stone, a few smaller ones, or several very small stones.

When fats from the daily diet enter

the small intestines, the concentrated bile from the gallbladder is poured into the duodenum via the bile ducts. Bile is necessary if fats are to be digested and absorbed. If stones are present in the biliary tract, the gallbladder will contract, but little or no bile will reach the fats in the small bowel.

A sharp pain to the right of the stomach is usually the first warning sign of gallstones, especially if the pain is felt soon after a meal of fatty foods—eggs, pork, mayonnaise, or fried foods. The presence of stones very often causes inflammation of the gallbladder and such symptoms as occasional diarrhea and nausea with vomiting and belching. The abdominal area near the gallbladder is usually very tender.

Untreated gallbladder disease leads to several possible complications. The obstructed bile pigments may be recirculated in the bloodstream, causing jaundice. Obstruction of the ducts causes increased pressure and may also result in perforation of the gallbladder or ducts. Acute inflammation of the biliary tract is always a possibility due to the irritation caused by the concentrated bile.

A gallbladder that is full of stones or badly diseased must be surgically removed for the patient's health to improve. In milder cases, other treatment and special diet can prevent attacks.

Treatment and Diagnosis of Gastrointestinal Disorders

Some medications used in treating gastrointestinal disorders, such as antacids and laxatives, can be purchased without prescription. Such medications should be taken only upon a physician's advice.

Treatment of gastrointestinal diseases may require low-residue diets—that is, a diet of foods that pass through the digestive tract very readily without a large amount of solid fecal residue. Included are low-fat meals, liquids, and finely crushed foods. Diagnostic tests may require overnight fasting, fat-free meals, or eating specific foods. Bland meals are vital in the treatment of peptic ulcers and should consist of unspiced soft foods and milk. Raw fruits and vegetables, salads, alcohol, and coffee do not belong in a bland diet. See under Ch. 27, *Nutrition and Weight Control,* for further information on special diets.

X-ray examinations play an important role in diagnosis of gastrointes-tinal disorders, such as ulcers, diverticula, foreign bodies, malignant lesions, obstruction, achalasia of the esophagus, and varices.

Plain film radiographs are used in initial studies in cases where intestinal obstruction or perforation is suspected. Metallic foreign bodies are easily demonstrated on plain X rays of the digestive tract.

GI Series

By filling the digestive tract with *barium sulfate,* a substance opaque to X rays, a radiologist can locate areas of abnormality. Barium sulfate can be mixed as a thin liquid or paste and be swallowed by the patient during studies of the esophagus, stomach, and small intestines. The type of radiological examination that utilizes such a barium meal is known as a *GI* (gastrointestinal) *series.* The large bowel is examined with the barium mixture administered through the rectum like a standard enema, known as a *barium enema.* This procedure makes it possible to visualize the inner walls of the colon. For further information on diagnostic procedures, see Ch. 26, *Physicians and Diagnostic Procedures.*

12

Diseases of the Respiratory System

The human body cannot survive for more than a very few minutes in an environment that lacks oxygen. Oxygen is required for the normal functioning of all living body cells. This vital gas reaches the body cells via the bloodstream; each red blood cell transports oxygen molecules to the body tissues. The oxygen comes from the atmosphere one breathes, and it enters the bloodstream through the very thin membrane walls of the lung tissue, a fresh supply of oxygen entering the bloodstream each time a person inhales. As the red blood cells circulating through the walls of the lung tissue pick up their fresh supply of oxygen, they release molecules of carbon dioxide given off by the body cells as a waste product of metabolism. When a person exhales, the lungs are squeezed somewhat like a bellows, and the carbon dioxide is expelled from the lungs.

The automatic action of breathing in and out is caused by the alternate contraction and relaxation of several muscle groups. The main muscle of breathing is the *diaphragm,* a layer of muscle fibers that separates the organs of the chest from the organs of the abdomen. Other muscles of res-

piration are located between the ribs, in the neck, and in the abdomen. As the diaphragm contracts to let the lungs expand, the other muscles increase the capacity of the *thorax,* or chest cavity, when one inhales. The muscles literally squeeze the lungs and chest when an individual exhales.

Any disease of the muscles and bones of the chest wall or of the passages leading from the nose to the lung tissue—containing the small air sacs where the gases are actually exchanged—will interfere to some extent with normal function. As with any organ of the body, there is a great reserve built into the lungs that assures that small to even moderate amounts of diseased tissue can exist without compromising their ability to sustain life. However, when disease of the lungs, air passages, thoracic (rib) cage, or any combination of these parts decreases the capacity of the reserve areas, then the oxygen supply to all the organs and tissues of the body becomes deficient, and they become incapable of performing their vital functions.

Diseases of the thoracic cage are relatively uncommon. Certain forms of arthritis cause fixation of the bony

cage and limit expansion when breathing. Various muscle and nervous system diseases weaken the muscles used to expand the chest for breathing.

Diseases of the *bronchi* or air passages tend to narrow those tubes and thereby limit the amount of air that can pass through to the tiny *alveoli,* or air sacs. Other conditions affect the alveoli themselves, and, if widespread enough, allow no place for the oxygen and carbon dioxide to be exchanged.

The most common forms of lung disease are infections caused by vi-

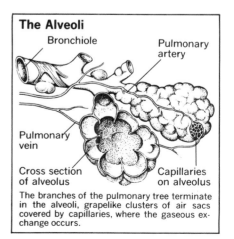

The Alveoli

Bronchiole

Pulmonary artery

Pulmonary vein

Cross section of alveolus

Capillaries on alveolus

The branches of the pulmonary tree terminate in the alveoli, grapelike clusters of air sacs covered by capillaries, where the gaseous exchange occurs.

Interaction between Heart and Lungs

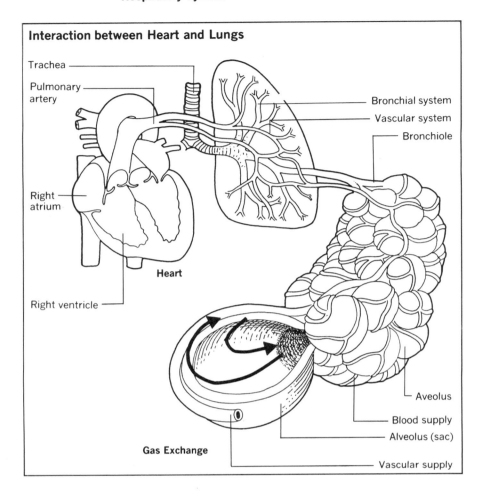

Trachea

Pulmonary artery

Bronchial system

Vascular system

Bronchiole

Right atrium

Heart

Right ventricle

Aveolus

Blood supply

Alveolus (sac)

Gas Exchange

Vascular supply

ruses, bacteria, or fungi. Infection is always a potential threat to the lung because this organ is in constant contact with the outside air and therefore constantly exposed to infectious agents. It is only through elaborate defenses that the body is able to maintain normal functions without interference by these agents.

The major defenses are simply mechanical and consist mainly of the hairs in the nose and a mucous blanket coating the inside of the bronchi. The very small hairs (called *cilia*) in the breathing passage act as a filtering system; mucous membranes of the bronchi help to intercept small particles as they are swept along by the action of the cilia. Whenever these structures are diseased, as in chronic bronchitis, there is a much greater likelihood of acquiring infection.

The Common Cold, Influenza, and Other Viral Infections

The Common Cold

The common cold is the most prevalent illness known to mankind. It accounts for more time lost from work than any other single condition. The infection rate varies from one individual to another.

Surveys indicate that about 25 percent of the population experience four or more infections a year, 50 percent experience two or three a year, and the remaining 25 percent have one or no infections in a year. There is also some variation from year to year for each person, explained often by the amount of exposure to young children, frequent extreme changes in

weather, fatigue, and other factors.

For years it has been felt that chilling plays a role in causing the common cold, and, although difficult to prove, there is almost certainly some truth to the idea. By some as yet unclear process, chilling probably causes certain changes in our respiratory passages that make them susceptible to viruses that otherwise would be harmless.

The common cold affects only the upper respiratory passages: the nose, sinuses, and throat. It sometimes is associated with fever. Several viruses have been implicated as the cause for the common cold. But in the study centers that investigate this illness, isolation of a cold virus is only achieved in about one half of the cases. These viruses are not known to produce any other significant illnesses. Most likely they inhabit the nose and throat, often without producing any illness at all.

Symptoms

The major part of the illness consists of about three days of nasal congestion, possibly a mild sore throat, some sneezing and irritation of the eyes (though not as severe as in hay fever), and a general feeling of ill health often associated with some muscle fatigue and aching. After three days the symptoms abate, but there is usually some degree of nasal congestion for another ten days.

Prevention is difficult, and there is no specific treatment. The natural defenses of the body usually are capable of resolving the infection. Attention should be paid to avoiding further chilling of the body, exhausting activity, and late hours that can further lower the defenses and lead to complications.

Complications

Ear infection may develop because of

blockage of the *Eustachian tube,* which leads from the back of the throat to the inner part of the ear. That complication is heralded by pain in the ear. Bronchitis and pneumonia may be recognized early by the development of cough and production of *sputum* (phlegm). *Sinusitis* develops when the sinus passages are obstructed so that the infected mucus cannot drain into the pharynx (as in postnasal drip). The pain develops near the sinus cavity involved. These complications can and should be treated with specific drugs, and, if they develop, a physician should be consulted.

Influenza

A number of other viruses cause respiratory illness similar to the common cold, but are much more severe in intensity and with frequently serious, and even fatal, complications. The best known member of the group is the *influenza* (flu) virus. It can cause mild symptoms that are indistinguishable from those of the common cold, but in the more easily recognizable form it is ushered in by fever, cough, and what physicians refer to as *malaise*—chills, muscle ache, and fatigue.

The symptoms of influenza appear quickly; they develop within hours and generally last in severe form from four to seven days. The disease gradually recedes over the following week. The severity of the local respiratory and generalized symptoms usually forces the influenza patient to stay in bed.

Not only is the individual case often severe, but an outbreak of influenza can easily spread to epidemic proportions in whole population groups, closing factories, schools, and hospitals in its wake. There have been 31 very severe *pandemics* (epidemics that sweep many countries) that have

occurred since 1510. The most devastating of these pandemics occurred in 1918; it led to the death of 20 million people around the world. Rarely is death directly attributable to the influenza virus itself, but rather to complicating bacterial pneumonia or to the failure of vital organs previously weakened by chronic disease.

Flu Shots

Inoculation is fairly effective in preventing influenza, but is not long-lasting and has to be renewed each year. Unfortunately, there are several different types of influenza virus, and a slightly different vaccine is needed to provide immunity to each type of infection. Each recent epidemic in the United States has been the result of a different strain, and although there have been several months' warning before the epidemics started, it has been difficult to mass-produce a vaccine in time to use it before the epidemic developed.

Treatment

Once acquired, there is no cure for influenza, but the body defenses are usually capable of destroying the virus if given the necessary time and if the defenses are not depressed by other illness. Fluids, aspirin, and bed rest help relieve the symptoms. Special attention should be paid to sudden worsening of fever after seeming recovery, or the onset of sputum production. In elderly people more intensive medical care is often necessary, including hospitalization for some.

Pneumonia

Pneumonia might be defined as any inflammation of the lung tissue itself, but the term is generally applied only to infections of an acute or rapidly de-

veloping nature caused by certain bacteria or viruses. The term is generally not used for tuberculous or fungal infections. The most common severe pneumonia is that caused by the *pneumococcus bacterium.*

Pneumonia develops from inhaling infected mucus into the lower respiratory passages. The pneumococcus is often present in the nasal or throat secretions of healthy people, and it tends to be present even more often in the same secretions of an individual with a cold. Under certain conditions these secretions may be *aspirated,* or inhaled, into the lung. There the bacteria rapidly multiply and spread within hours to infect a sizable area. As with the common cold, chilling and fatigue often play a role in making this sequence possible. Any chronic debilitating illness also makes one very susceptible to pneumonia.

Symptoms

Pneumonia develops very suddenly with the onset of high fever, shaking chills, chest pain, and a very definite feeling of total sickness or malaise. Within hours enough pus is produced within the lung for the patient to start coughing up thick yellow or greenish sputum that often may be tinged or streaked with blood. The patient has no problem in recognizing that he has suddenly become extremely ill.

Prior to penicillin the illness tended to last about seven days, at which time it would often suddenly resolve almost as quickly as it started, leaving a healthy but exhausted patient. But it also could frequently lead to death or to serious complications, such as abscess formation within the chest wall, meningitis, or abscess of the brain. Because penicillin is so very effective in curing this illness today, physicians rarely see those complications.

Treatment

The response of pneumococcal pneumonia to penicillin is at times one of the most dramatic therapeutic events in medicine. After only several hours of illness the patient presents himself to the hospital with a fever of 104° F, feeling so miserable that he does not want to eat, talk, or do anything but lie still in bed. Within four to six hours after being given penicillin he may have lost his fever and be sitting up in bed eating a meal. Not everyone responds this dramatically, but when someone does, it is striking.

Prevention

There is no guaranteed way to prevent pneumonia. The advice to avoid chilling temperatures, overexertion, and fatigue when one has a cold is directed principally toward avoiding pneumonia. Anybody exposed to the elements, especially when fatigued and wearing damp clothing, is particularly susceptible to pneumonia; this explains its frequent occurrence among army recruits and combat troops. The elderly and debilitated become more susceptible when exposed to extremes of temperature and dampness.

Pneumonia is not really a contagious illness except in very special circumstances, so that isolation of patients is not necessary. In fact, all of us carry the pneumococcus in our noses and throats, but we rarely have the constellation of circumstances that lead to infection. It is the added physical insults that allow pneumonia to take hold.

Other Kinds of Pneumonia

All bacteria are capable of causing pneumonia and they do so in the same manner, via the inhalation of infected upper airway secretions. Some diseases, such as alcoholism, tend to predispose to certain bacterial pneumonias. Usually these are not as dramatic as those caused by the pneumococcus, but they may be much more difficult to treat and thereby can often be more serious.

Far less severe are the pneumonias caused by certain viruses or a recently discovered organism that seems to be intermediate between a virus and a bacterium. The term *walking pneumonia* is often applied to this type, because the patient is often so little incapacitated that he is walking about and not in bed. These pneumonias apparently occur in the same way as the bacterial pneumonias, but the difference is that the infecting agent is not capable of producing such severe destruction. These pneumonias are usually associated with only mild temperature elevation, scant amount of sputum production, and fewer general body symptoms. They should be suspected when coughing dominates the symptoms of a cold, especially if it turns from a dry or nonproductive cough to one that produces sputum. Antibiotic therapy tends to hasten recovery and prevent the complication of bacterial pneumonia.

Pleurisy

No discussion of pneumonia is complete without mention of *pleurisy*. This term refers to any inflammation of the lining between the chest wall and the lung. Infection is only one of the causes, but probably the most common, of inflammation of the *pleura*. Pleurisy is almost always painful, the pain being felt on inhaling and exhaling but not when the breath is quietly held for a brief period. It is a symptom that always deserves the attention of a physician and investigation of its cause. The same type of pain on breathing can often be mimicked by a strain of the chest wall muscles, but the difference can usually be determined by a physician's examination. If not, a chest X ray will help to reveal the cause of the pain.

Tuberculosis

At the turn of the century *tuberculosis* was the leading cause of death in the world; now it is eighteenth. The change in status is due both to the discovery of antibiotics and to modern preventive measures. In this century most other infectious diseases have likewise decreased in incidence and severity for similar reasons. The general decline leaves tuberculosis still at the top of the list as the leading cause of death among infectious diseases. And tuberculosis remains a very serious health problem, accounting for 40,000 new illnesses every year in the United States. In contrast to a disease like influenza, physicians already have the tools with which to eliminate tuberculosis. But many factors, primarily social, make that a very distant possibility.

Tuberculosis is caused by one specific type of bacterium. Certain ethnic groups seem particularly susceptible to the disease, but the reasons are unclear. The American Indian and the Eskimo are two susceptible groups. However, there is no recognized hereditary factor. The disease is different from many commonly known infections in several ways. Unlike pneumonia, tuberculosis is a chronic and painless infection, measured more in months than in days. Because of this pattern, it not only takes a long time to develop serious disease, but it also takes a long time to effect a cure.

Another very important difference between tuberculosis and many other infections is its ability to infect individuals without causing symptoms of illness, but then to lie dormant as a potential threat to that person for the rest of his life. The early stages of the disease do not produce any symptoms. Consequently a patient develops large areas of diseased tissue before he begins to feel sick. Screening procedures, therefore, are very important in detecting early disease in patients who feel perfectly healthy. Another is the skin testing of schoolchildren, which is carried out routinely in many communities today.

How Tuberculosis Spreads

Tuberculosis is contracted by inhaling into the lungs bacteria that have been coughed into the air by a person with advanced disease. It is, therefore, contagious, but not as contagious as measles, mumps, or chicken pox. Unlike those illnesses, it usually requires fairly close and prolonged contact with a tuberculous patient before the infection is passed on. Once the bacteria are inhaled, the body defenses are usually capable of isolating them into small areas within the tissues, thereby preventing any significant destruction or disease. However, though defenses are able to isolate the bacteria, they are not able to destroy all of them. Some bacteria persist in a state in which they are unable to break out and destroy tissue, but they always maintain the potential to do so at a time when the body defenses are impaired.

In about 20 percent of individuals the body defenses are not initially capable of isolating the tubercle bacilli. These individuals, mostly children, develop progressive tuberculosis directly following their initial contact. Others are successful in preventing actual disease at the time of initial contact, but they join a large group with the potential for active disease at some time in the future. Most of the new cases of active tuberculosis come

from this second group; their defenses break down years after the initial contact and resultant infection.

Weight loss, malnutrition, alcoholism, diabetes, and certain other chronic illnesses are particularly likely to lead to deterioration of the defense mechanisms holding the tuberculosis organisms in check. Still other individuals develop active disease with no recognizable condition to account for the loss of defenses. In fact, the most likely age group to develop active disease as a result of breakdown of past infection is the 20- to 30-year-old group.

Once active disease has appeared it usually involves the chest, although it can develop anywhere in the body. There is gradual spread of inflammation within lung tissue until large areas are involved. Holes, or cavities, are formed as a result of tissue destruction. These contain large numbers of tuberculosis organisms and continue to enlarge as new tissue is destroyed at the edges. At any stage of this development organisms may find their way into the bloodstream and new foci of disease can spring up throughout the body. The sputum becomes loaded with organisms that are coughed into the air and go on to infect other individuals. The infected sputum from one area of the lung may gain access to other areas and cause development of diseased tissue there as well.

Treatment

Before the modern era of drug treatment all these events followed an inexorable course to death in 85 percent of people with active tuberculosis. Only a lucky few were able to survive as cured, usually because their disease was found at an early stage. That survival was often at the expense of years confined to a sanatorium. Because of its almost uniform

outcome and the required separation from family and home, tuberculosis was formerly looked upon with quite as much dread as cancer is today.

The sanatorium rest cure of tuberculosis was first developed in the mid-nineteenth century at a time when the cause of the disease was unknown. In 1882, Robert Koch first demonstrated the tuberculosis organism, thereby proving the disease was an infection. As the twentieth century progressed, general public health measures helped limit the number of new cases, and new surgical procedures were developed to treat the disease. These measures were effective enough to arrest tuberculosis in another 25 percent of cases, brightening somewhat the dismal outlook of the past century.

But the discovery of specific antibiotics in the 1940s made the real difference in tuberculosis. Because of drug treatment, surgery is rarely resorted to today, although it still may be helpful in certain patients. Now patients with tuberculosis can face a relatively bright future without having to be hospitalized for prolonged periods or enduring periods of endless disability.

Tuberculosis Control

People still contract tuberculosis, and people still die from it. Two of the principal causes of death are delayed therapy and interruptions in therapy, the latter leading to the development of tuberculosis organisms that are unaffected by drugs. Both of these causes are often under the control of the patient. The first can be avoided by seeing a physician whenever one develops a cough that lasts more than two weeks, especially when it is not associated with the typical symptoms of a cold at the outset. The other symptoms of developing tuberculosis are also seen in other illnesses, and should always lead one to recognize that he is sick and needs to consult his physician. These symptoms are weight loss, loss of appetite, fever, and night sweats. When tuberculosis is diagnosed, the patient must follow carefully the directions regarding medication, which is always continued for a long time after the patient has regained his feeling of well-being.

There are other ways, however, to attack tuberculosis, even before one becomes sick. Once a person has had contact with tuberculosis, even though he usually does not develop active disease, he produces antibodies against the bacteria. A person with such antibodies can be recognized by injecting under the skin specially prepared material from dead tuberculosis bacteria, which gives rise to a reaction within the skin after two days. This material is called *tuberculin* and the test is known as the *tuberculin test.*

There are now many mass screening programs of tuberculin testing for schoolchildren, hospital personnel, and industrial groups. Those with positive skin test reactions are screened further for the presence of active disease. If they are found to be active cases, they are treated during what is usually an early and not very severe stage of the disease. The other people with positive tuberculin tests, without any evidence of active disease, are candidates for *prophylactic* (preventive) *therapy.* This therapy employs *isoniazid* (*INH*), the most effective of many drugs for the treatment of tuberculosis and one that has virtually no side effects. Treatment for one year has been shown to reduce greatly the chance of future progress from the merely infected state to the state of active disease.

The goal of prophylactic therapy is chiefly to prevent the far more serious development of active disease. But in addition, by preventing disease before it develops, physicians can prevent the infection of others, since the typical patient with tuberculosis has already infected some of those living with him before he becomes ill and seeks medical attention. The surface has just been scratched in this regard, however, as there are estimated to be 25 million people in the United States who would demonstrate reactions to tuberculin tests. Many of these people have never been tested and are not aware of the potential threat within them.

In most foreign countries the tuberculosis problem is much more serious. An estimated 80 percent of the populations of the countries of Asia, Africa, and South America would show positive tuberculin skin tests, with the number of active cases and deaths being proportionately high.

Sarcoidosis

Sarcoidosis (or *Boeck's sarcoid*), a disease that affects black people more often than whites, has symptoms closely resembling those of tuberculosis and other diseases. The most obvious symptom is the formation of skin nodules, often of the face, but the nodules, called *granulomas* (small tumors composed chiefly of granulation tissue), commonly occur in many other places as well, especially in the lungs and lymph nodes. They can occur also in the liver, bones, eyes, and other tissues.

Although sarcoidosis occurs all over the world, it is more common in temperate regions, and in the United States occurs more frequently in the southeastern states than elsewhere. Men and women are about equally affected. The onset of the disease occurs usually in the third or fourth decade of life.

Diagnosis and Treatment

The disease is diagnosed by an examination of chest X rays, which will show the proliferation of nodules in the lungs. Surgical biopsy and microscopic examination of skin tissue or tissue from a lymph node is usually necessary to confirm the presence of the disease.

There is no specific treatment for sarcoidosis, and in spite of its similarities in some respects to tuberculosis, no connection between the two disorders has been established. Steroids are sometimes used to treat the skin lesions, but in many cases the skin nodules clear up eventually without any treatment. About half of the patients, however, do not recover completely, and the disease becomes chronic—though of varying severity. Ultimately the granulomas can change into fibrous scars that may pose serious threats to the patient, depending upon where the scarring occurs. Respiratory distress, heart failure, and glaucoma, for example, can result from tissue changes in the lungs, heart, and eyes, respectively.

Respiratory Diseases Caused by Fungi

Two fungal diseases affecting respiration are of great importance in particular regions of the United States. They are both caused by types of fungi capable of growing within mammalian tissue, thereby infecting and destroying it. Both cause chronic diseases very similar to tuberculosis and may lead to death, though that is a far less common outcome—even when untreated—than in tuberculosis.

The spores of the fungi are inhaled from the air, and the response of the body is similar to that in tuberculosis in that most people become merely infected (the spores being contained by body defenses) while a few develop progressive disease. The body also produces anitbodies, and consequently skin tests similar to the tuberculin test can identify infected individuals.

Histoplasmosis (named for a fungus called *histoplasma*) organisms are prevalent in the Midwest, generally in the areas of the Ohio, Mississippi, and Missouri rivers. Largely unknown prior to World War II, histoplasmosis has been studied extensively since. Local epidemics have brought it to public attention on several occasions. The fungus grows readily in soil containing large amounts of bird (chickens, pigeons, starlings) or bat excrement. One of the better ways to assure exposure is to clean out an old chicken coop. The concentration of organisms may reach such high levels in bat caves that entry by spelunkers may prove fatal. In contrast to tuberculosis, the amount of exposure seems to play a very important role in determining the extent of the disease. There also seem to be few cases of late breakdown (the rule in tuberculosis). Most people develop the active disease, if at all, at the time of their initial exposure.

Coccidioidomycosis (for *Coccidioides* fungus) also generates in the soil, in this case in California, the southwest United States, and Mexico. It grows best in hot, dry soil. The common names for this disease are *desert rheumatism* or *valley fever*. Infection and disease occur in a similar pattern to that of histoplasmosis. Skin testing of large population groups for both these fungi in the appropriate geographical areas indicates that the majority of exposed individuals quite adequately contain the initial infection and never develop any illness or active disease.

Because Americans travel into infected regions, these diseases are being seen more frequently in people who do not live where the fungi are found. Both conditions, fortunately, are often self-limited, even when active disease develops. For more se-

vere cases there is a drug, *amphotericin-B,* which is quite effective; however, because it is also quite toxic to the patient, it must be given in progressive doses starting with a small initial dose, to permit the body's tolerance to build up. It is hoped that less toxic agents will be found in the future that will be just as effective against the fungus.

Allergic Respiratory Diseases

Hay fever (*allergic rhinitis*) and *asthma* are two very common allergic diseases of the respiratory tract. The two have much in common as to age at onset, seasonal manifestations, and causation. Hay fever involves the *mucosa,* or lining, of the upper respiratory tract only, whereas asthma is confined to the bronchial tubes of the lower respiratory tract. Physicians usually distinguish two main types of asthma, allergic and infectious. The infectious type of asthma resembles bronchitis, with cough and much wheezing as well. The discussion here will be confined to the allergic form of asthma.

In hay fever and asthma the allergenic substance causing the reaction is usually airborne, though it can be a food. In most cases the offender is pollen from a plant. The pollen is inhaled into the nostrils and alights upon the lining of the respiratory passages. In the allergic individual, antibodies react with the proteins in the pollen and cause various substances to be released from the tissue and blood cells in the immediate area. These substances, in turn, produce vessel enlargement in the area and an outpouring of mucus, plus certain irritating symptoms that result in a stuffy or runny nose and itchy eyes. The same reactions occur in the bronchial lining in asthma, but the substances released there also cause constriction of the bronchial muscle and conse-

quent narrowing of the passages. This muscular effect and the narrowing caused by greatly increased amounts of mucus in the passages are both responsible for the wheezing in asthma.

Hay Fever

Hay fever is never a threat to life, but in severe cases it can upset one's life patterns immensely. For unknown reasons it is more common in childhood, where it is often seen in conjunction with eczema or asthma. The tendency to develop hay fever, eczema, and asthma is hereditary. The transmission of the hereditary factors is complex, so that within a family group any number of individuals or none at all may exhibit the trait.

Most people with hay fever have their only or greatest difficulty in the summer months because of the airborne pollens from trees, grasses, flowers, and molds that are prevalent then. The most notorious of all pollens is the ragweed pollen. This weed pollinates around August 15 and continues to fill the air until late September. In many cities an official pollen count is issued every day, and those with severe difficulty can avoid some trouble by staying outside as little as possible on high-count days. *Antihistamine* drugs are used to counteract the nasal engorgement in hay fever. These drugs counteract the effect of *histamine,* which is one of the major substances released by the allergic reaction.

Allergic Asthma

Allergic asthma is the result of the allergic reaction taking place in the bronchial mucosal lining rather than in the nasal lining. A person may suffer from both asthma and hay fever. The common inciting factors are pollens, hair from pets (especially cats), house dust, molds, and certain foods (especially shellfish). When foods are responsible, the reaction initially occurs within the bloodstream, but the major effect is felt within the lung, which is spoken of as the target organ.

Most allergic asthma is seen in children. For unclear reasons it usually disappears spontaneously at puberty. In those who continue to have difficulty after puberty, the role of infection as a cause for the asthma usually becomes more prominent. Allergic asthma attacks start abruptly and can usually be aborted rather easily with medication.

People with asthma are symptom-free much of the time. When exposed to high concentrations of pollen they begin wheezing and producing sputum. Wheezing refers to the high-pitched squeaking sound that is made by people exhaling through narrowed bronchi. Associated with the wheezing and sputum is a distinct sensation of shortness of breath that varies in severity according to the nature of the attack. Milder attacks of asthma often subside spontaneously, merely with relaxation. This is especially true when the wheezing is induced by nonspecific factors, such as a cloud of dust, cold air, or exercise. Asthmatic individuals have more sensitive air passages and they are more easily bothered by these nonspecific irritants.

Treatment

For more severe attacks of asthma there are several types of treatment.

There are oral medications that dilate the bronchi and offset the effects of the allergic reaction. (Antihistamines, however, exert no effect on asthma and may even worsen the condition.) Also available are injectable medications, such as adrenaline, and sprays that contain substances similar to adrenaline and that can be inhaled. Any or all of these methods may be employed by the physician. During times of high exposure it is often helpful to take one of the oral medications on a regular basis, thereby avoiding minor episodes of wheezing.

A recently discovered remedy for asthma is particularly useful to persons—primarily infants and small children, who cannot swallow tablets. The remedy comes in capsules containing tiny pellets of the drug theophylline. Once the capsule is twisted open, the pellets can be sprinkled on soft foods, including strained baby food, applesauce, pudding, or hot or cold cereal. The pellets give relief for about 12 hours, long enough to protect children during sleep.

The best therapy for asthma and hay fever is avoidance of the allergen responsible for attacks. Obviously, cats and certain foods can be avoided more readily than pollens and other airborne substances. The first requisite, however, is to identify the offender. The most important method of identification is the patient's medical history. Sometimes the problem is easy, as when the patient states that he only has trouble during the ragweed season. At other times a great

amount of detective work may be required. Skin testing is used to complement the history. The skin test merely involves the introduction under the skin (usually within a tiny scratch) of various materials suspected of being allergens. If the individual has antibodies to these substances he will form a hive at the site of introduction. That he reacts does not necessarily mean that his asthma is due to that test substance, because many people have reactions but no hay fever or asthma. The skin test results need to be interpreted in the light of the history of exposure.

If the substance so identified cannot be avoided, then hyposensitization may prove useful. This form of treatment is based on the useful fact that the human body varies its ability to react depending upon the degree and the frequency of exposure. In a hyposensitizing program small amounts of pollen or other extract are injected frequently. Gradually the dose of extract is increased. By this technique many allergic individuals become able to tolerate moderate exposure to their offending material with few or no symptoms. Hyposensitization does not succeed in everyone, but it is usually worth attempting if other approaches are unsuccessful. For more information see Ch. 21, *Allergies and Hypersensitivities.*

13

Lung Disease

Two present-day problems of major proportions are not diseases in themselves, but both are detrimental to health. These are smoking and air pollution. The former is a habit that, in some users, can produce as serious results as narcotics or alcohol addiction. Knowledge of air pollution has grown with the increased public awareness of our environment. It is quite clear that there are many serious consequences produced by the products with which we foul our air. Both tobacco and air pollution are controllable: one by individual will, the other by public effort.

Smoking

Eighty-five million Americans smoke, and the vast majority of these people smoke cigarettes. This discussion will therefore center on cigarettes. The number of new smokers is increasing, which offsets the number of quitters, thereby producing a new gain in smokers each year. There was a temporary absolute decline in 1964 when the first U.S. Surgeon General's report on smoking outlined the many hazards, but that trend quickly reversed itself. The tobacco industry spends $280 million per year to promote smoking. The U.S. Public Health Service and several volunteer agencies spend $8 million in a contrary campaign to discourage smoking.

Dangers of Smoking

Scientists know much about the ways in which smoking produces health dangers. As they burn, cigarettes release more than 4,000 different substances into the atmosphere. Carried in the cigarette smoke, these substances enter the smoker's lungs or simply dissipate in the air. Three of the substances, carbon monoxide, "tar," and nicotine, are the primary threats to health.

Smoking has "mainstream" effects on the smoker who inhales. But there are "sidestream" effects as well. For example, persons who habitually breathe the smoke from others' cigarettes may be inhaling higher concentrations of possibly harmful chemicals than the smokers themselves. These nonsmokers may experience such unpleasant symptoms as watery eyes and headaches. If they have lung or heart diseases, suffer from asthma or some allergies, or wear contact lenses, the nonsmokers may find that their symptoms are worsening.

Some of the direct effects of breathing tobacco smoke suggest its capacity for producing disease in the smoker. Smoking lowers skin temperature, often by several degrees, principally through the constricting effect of nicotine on blood vessels. Carbon monoxide levels rise in the blood when a person is smoking. Even a single cigarette may impair somewhat the smoker's ability to expel air from the lungs. Adverse changes in the activity of several important chemicals in the body can be demonstrated after smoking.

Smoking has been strongly implicated in bronchitis and emphysema, lung and other cancers, heart disease, and peripheral vascular disease. Cigarette smoking causes more "preventable" deaths in the United States than any other single factor. Of the five leading causes of American deaths, smoking is related to four. According to verified statistics, a smoker faces a 70 percent greater risk of dying prematurely than a nonsmoker of comparable age. Smoking-related diseases take six times as many American lives annually as automobile accidents.

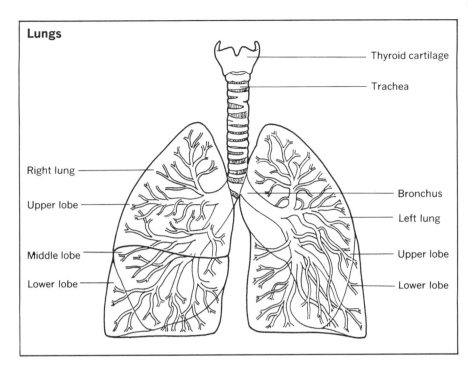

Lungs

- Thyroid cartilage
- Trachea
- Right lung
- Upper lobe
- Middle lobe
- Lower lobe
- Bronchus
- Left lung
- Upper lobe
- Lower lobe

A Cause of Cancer

Lung cancer takes more American lives annually than any other type of cancer. Some 80 percent of all lung cancer deaths, over 90,000 in a typical year, may be attributed to cigarette smoking. On average, 7 in 10 lung cancer patients die within a year of diagnosis.

The cigarette smoker's risks are not confined to lung cancer. Such serious and sometimes fatal diseases as cancers of the mouth, pharynx, larynx, and esophagus may also be smoking-related. Of all cancer deaths, 30 percent are related to smoking. Smoking leads to 10 times as many cancer deaths as all other reliably identified cancer causes combined.

Heart Disease

Heart disease caused by smoking cigarettes takes more American lives than does cancer. But smoking is implicated in about 30 percent of all deaths resulting from coronary heart disease, the most common cause of American deaths. In 1982, about 170,000 U.S. citizens died of heart disease resulting from smoking.

In the mid-1980s, statistics showed that one living American in every 10 would die prematurely as a result of smoking-related heart disease. The smoker who refused to give up smoking after a heart attack was inviting a second attack to a significant degree. But the person who quit smoking would after some 10 years face a heart-disease risk about equal to that of a nonsmoker.

Women and Smoking

Where women accounted for one lung cancer death in six in 1968, one-fourth of all such deaths occurred among women in 1979. Those figures suggest what later statistics have borne out: that lung cancer would soon replace breast cancer as the leading cause of cancer death among women.

Women were once thought to be less susceptible to smoking-related diseases than men. But later epidemiological studies have proved the opposite. When the earlier studies were conducted, women had simply not been smoking as long as men, or in such numbers. As the picture has changed, the statistics have changed. Like men, women smokers who experience other heart disease risk factors, including hypertension and high serum cholesterol levels, face a greatly increased risk of coronary heart disease.

The Dose-Response Relationship

The number of cigarettes an individual smokes is one of the determinants of eventual damage even though individual susceptibility is also important. Thus a definite dose-response relationship exists between smoking and disease. If a person smokes one pack a day for one year he has smoked one pack-year; if he smokes one pack a day for two years or two packs a day for one year, he has smoked two pack-years, and so on. Calculating by pack-years, it appears that 40 pack-years is a crucial time period above which the incidence of cancer of the lung, emphysema, and other serious consequences rises rapidly. Smoking three packs a day, it takes only about 13 years to reach this critical level.

Breaking the Smoking Habit

Obviously, the best way not to smoke is never to start. Unfortunately, young people are continuing to join the smoking ranks at a rapid rate. The teenager often is one of the hardest persons to convince of the hazards of smoking. He is healthy, suffers less from fatigue, headaches, breathlessness, and other immediate effects of smoking, and he often feels the need to smoke to keep up with his peers. Once he starts, it is not long before he becomes addicted. The addiction to cigarettes is very real. It is more psychological dependency than the physical addiction associated with narcotics, but there are definite physical addiction aspects to smoking that are mostly noted when one stops.

For most people it is quite a challenge to stop smoking. There are many avenues to travel and many sources now available to aid one on the way. They include smoking clinics that offer group support and medical guidance to those anxious to quit. The clinics vary in their format but basically depend on the support given the smoker by finding other individuals with the same problems and overcoming the problems as a group. The medical guidance helps people recognize and deal with withdrawal symptoms as well as helping them with weight control.

Withdrawal Symptoms

Withdrawal symptoms vary from person to person and include many symptoms other than just a craving for a cigarette. Many people who stop smoking become jittery and sleepless, start coughing more than usual, and often develop an increased appetite. This last withdrawal effect is especially disturbing to women, and the need to prevent weight gain is all too often used as a simple excuse to avoid stopping the cigarette habit or to start smoking again. The weight gained is usually not too great, and one generally stops gaining after a few weeks. Once the cigarette smoking problem is controlled, then efforts can be turned to weight reduction. Being overweight is also a threat to health, but ten extra pounds, even if maintained, do not represent nearly the threat that confirmed smoking does.

Despite all efforts, many individuals who would like to stop smoking fail in their attempts. The best advice

for them is to keep trying. Continued effort will at least tend to decrease the amount of smoking and often leads to eventual abstinence, even after years of trying. If a three-pack-per-day smoker can decrease to one pack a day or less, he has helped himself even though he is still doing some damage. For prospective quitters it is important to remember that cigarette smoking is an acquired habit, and that the learning process can be reversed. The problem most people have is too little knowledge of the dangers and too much willingness to believe that disease and disability cannot strike them, just the other fellow.

Air Pollution

While 85 million Americans pollute the air they breathe individually with cigarettes, all 210 million of us collectively pollute the atmosphere we all breathe. Some people are obviously more responsible than others, but air, water, and land pollution is a disease of society and can only be solved through a concerted effort by the whole society. Pollution has always been a problem to man. As we have become more urbanized the problem has grown. It has now reached what many consider to be crisis proportions in our large cities and even in some of our smaller ones.

We have had ample warning. In 1948 a killer smog engulfed Donora, Pennsylvania, killing 20 persons and producing serious illness in 6,000 more. In 1952 a lingering smog over London was blamed for 4,000 deaths in a few weeks. New York City has had several serious encounters with critical smog conditions that have accounted for many illnesses and deaths. The exteriors of many buildings in our cities are showing signs of vastly increased rates of decay due to the noxious substances in the air. It

is estimated that air pollution costs the United States $11 billion a year in damage, illness, and in other ways. Even if all this loss of life and property were not a result it would clearly be more pleasant to live in a clean atmosphere than in a foul one.

Emphysema and Bronchitis

Emphysema and chronic bronchitis are diseases that involve the whole lung. They can be of varying severity, and both are characterized by the gradual progression of breathlessness.

Because chronic bronchitis is almost invariably associated with pulmonary emphysema, the combined disorder frequently is called *obstructive-airway disease*. The disease involves damage to the lung tissue, with a loss of normal elasticity of the air sacs (*emphysema*), as well as damage to the *bronchi*, the main air passages to the lungs. In addition, chronic bronchitis is marked by a thickening of the walls of the bronchi with increased mucus production and difficulty in expelling these secretions. This results in coughing and sputum production.

The condition known as *acute bronchitis* is an acute process generally caused by a sudden infection, such as a cold, with an exaggeration of bronchitis symptoms. If a spasm of the bronchi occurs, accompanied by wheezing, the ailment is called infectious or nonallergic asthma.

Obstructive-airway disease is very insidious, and characteristically people do not, or will not, notice that they are sick until they suddenly are very sick. This is partly because of chronic denial of the morning cough and breathlessness, but also because we are fashioned in such a way as to have great reserve strength in our organs. As the disease progresses one starts using up his reserve for exertion. Be-

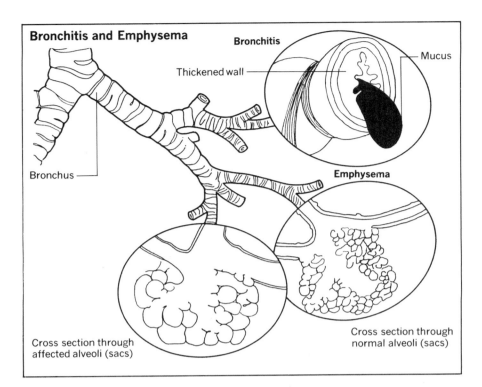

Bronchitis and Emphysema

Bronchitis

Thickened wall

Mucus

Bronchus

Emphysema

Cross section through affected alveoli (sacs)

Cross section through normal alveoli (sacs)

For more severe disease a program of breathing exercises and graded exertion may be beneficial. When these people develop heart trouble as a result of the strain on the heart, a treatment to strengthen the heart is rewarding. For those with the most advanced stage of the disease new methods of treatment have been devised in recent years. One of the most encouraging is the use of controlled oxygen administration, treatment that can sometimes allow a patient to return to an active working life from an otherwise helpless bed-and-chair existence. But it must be remembered that all these measures produce little effect if the patient continues to smoke.

Vaporizers, Nebulizers, IPPB

Mechanical methods have been developed to help control emphysema, bronchitis, acute and chronic asthma, and other respiratory disorders. These methods include the use of vaporizers, nebulizers, and intermittent positive pressure breathing (IPPB).

The vaporizer is a device that increases the moisture content of a home or room. In doing so, the vaporizer relieves the chronic condition that makes breathing difficult: the increased humidity loosens mucus and reduces nasal or bronchial congestion. One simple type of vaporizer or humidifier is the "croup kettle" or hot-steam type that releases steam into the air when heated on the stove or electrical unit. A more formal type of vaporizer is the electric humidifier that converts water into a spray. In dispersing the spray into the atmosphere, the vaporizer raises the humidity level without increasing the temperature.

The nebulizer also converts liquid into fine spray. But the nebulizer dispenses medications, such as isoproterenol hydrochloride, directly into

cause most people's life styles allow them to avoid exertion easily, the victim of this disease may have only rare chances to notice his breathlessness. Then, suddenly, within a period of a few months he becomes breathless with ordinary activity because he has used up and surpassed all his reserve. He goes to a physician thinking he has just become sick. Usually this event occurs when the patient is in his fifties or sixties and little can be done to correct the damage. The time for prevention was in the previous 30 years when elimination of smoking could have prevented much or all of the illness.

Chronic cough and breathlessness are the two earliest signs of chronic bronchitis and emphysema. A smoker's cough is not an insignificant symptom. It indicates that very definite irritation of the bronchi has developed and it should be respected early. Along with the cough there is often production of phlegm or sputum, especially in the morning, because of less effective emptying of the bronchial tree during the relatively

motionless period of sleep. Another early manifestation of disease is the tendency to develop chest infections along with what would otherwise be simple head colds. With these chest infections there is often a tightness or dull pain in the middle chest region, production of sputum and sometimes wheezing.

Treatment

Once emphysema or bronchitis are diagnosed there are many forms of therapy that can help. Stopping smoking is the most important measure, and will in itself often produce dramatic effects. The more bronchitis the patient has, the more noticeable the effect, as the bronchial irritation and mucous production decrease, cough lessens, and a greater sense of well-being ensues. The emphysema component does not change, as the damage to the air sacs is irreversible, but the progression may be greatly slowed. When chest infections develop they can be treated with antibiotics.

the throat through a mouthpiece and pressure-injector apparatus like an atomizer. Used in limited doses according to a physician's instructions, nebulization can relieve the labored or difficult breathing symptoms common to various respiratory diseases, among them asthma and bronchitis. The patient controls the dosage while using the nebulizer simply by employing finger pressure and obeying instructions.

In IPPB, a mask and ventilator are used to force air into the lungs and enable the patient to breathe more deeply. The ventilator supplies intermittent positive air pressure. The IPPB method of treatment has been used to help persons suffering from chronic pulmonary disease that makes breathing difficult. But IPPB may also be used with patients who cannot cough effectively; these patients include those who have recently undergone surgery. Newer IPPB units are highly portable; but they must be cleaned carefully with an antibacterial solution before use, and should always be used carefully to avoid producing breathing difficulties or aggravating heart problems.

Smoking and Obstructive Diseases

The problems encountered by patients with obstructive disease do not encompass merely that disease alone. Because of their smoking history these patients are also prone to develop lung cancer. All too often a person with a potentially curable form of lung cancer is unable to undergo surgery because his lungs will not tolerate the added strain of surgery. Patients with obstructive disease are also more prone to pneumonia and other infectious pulmonary conditions. When these develop in the already compromised lung, it may be impossible for the patient to maintain adequate oxygen supply to his vital

tissues. If oxygen insufficiency is severe and prolonged enough, the patient dies from pulmonary failure.

Despite the emphasis placed on smoking as the predominant factor for the development of obstructive disease, there are people with the disease who have never smoked. For many of these individuals there is no known cause for their disease. However, a group of younger people with obstructive disease has been found to be deficient in a particular enzyme. (Enzymes are agents that are necessary for certain chemical reactions.) Individuals with this deficiency develop a particularly severe form of emphysema, become symptomatic in their third or fourth decade, and die at a young age. They may not smoke, but if they do, the disease is much more severe. Just how the enzyme deficiency leads to emphysema is not clear, but a great amount of research is being conducted on this new link to try to learn more about the causes of emphysema.

The Pneumoconioses

Pneumoconiosis is a chronic reaction of the lung to any of several types of inhaled dust particles. The reaction varies somewhat but generally consists of initial inflammation about the inhaled particle followed by the development of scar tissue. The pneumoconioses develop predominantly from various occupational exposures to high concentrations of certain inorganic compounds that cannot be broken down by the cells of the body. The severity of the disease is proportional to the amount of dust retained in the lung.

Silica is the most notorious of these substances. People who work in mining, steel production, and any occupation involved with chipping stone, such as manufacturing monuments, are exposed to silica dust. Many of the practices associated with these occupations have been altered over the years because of the recognition of the hazard to workers. Other important pneumoconioses involve talc and asbestos particles, cotton fibers, and coal dust. Coal dust has gained wide attention in recent years with the heightened awareness of *black lung,* a condition seen in varying degrees in coal miners. The attention has resulted in a federal black lung disease law under which more than 135,000 miners have filed for compensation.

Although there are individual dif-

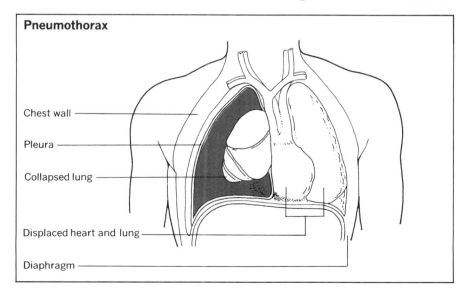

Pneumothorax

Chest wall

Pleura

Collapsed lung

Displaced heart and lung

Diaphragm

ferences in reaction to the varied forms of pneumoconiosis, the ultimate hazard is the loss of functioning lung tissue. When enough tissue becomes scarred, there is interference with oxygenation. Those people with pneumoconiosis who smoke are in great danger of compounding their problem by adding obstructive disease as well.

Prevention

Once the scarring has taken place there is no way to reverse the process. Therefore, the answer to the pneumoconioses is to prevent the exposure. Attention to occupational diseases in the United States has lagged about 30 years behind Europe, so that we are just now beginning to show concern about certain industrial practices condemned as hazardous in many European countries in the 1940s. New lung diseases caused by inhaled substances are discovered every year, and more will undoubtedly be found in the future. People in industries in which there is exposure to industrial dust should be aware of the potential danger and should be prepared to promote the maintenance of protective practices and the investigation of new ideas and devices. Where masks have been supplied, the workers should wear them, a practice too often neglected.

Pulmonary Embolism

Pulmonary embolism is a condition in which a part of a blood clot in a vein breaks away and travels through the heart and into the pulmonary circulatory system. Here the vessels leading from the heart branch like a tree, gradually becoming smaller until finally they form *capillaries*, the smallest blood vessels. Depending on its size, the clot will at some point reach

a vessel through which it cannot pass, and there will lodge itself. The clot disrupts the blood supply to the area supplied by that vessel. The larger the clot, the greater is the area of lung that loses its blood supply, and the more drastic the results to the patient.

This condition develops most commonly in association with inflammation of the veins of the legs (*thrombophlebitis*). People with varicose veins are particularly susceptible to thrombophlebitis. Because of constrictions produced by garters or rolled stockings, or just sitting with crossed legs for a long time, the sluggish blood flow already present is aggravated, and a clot may form in a vessel. Some people without varicose veins can also develop clots under the same conditions. The body often responds to the clot with the reaction of inflammation, which is painful. However, when there is no inflammatory response, there is no warning to tell that a clot has formed. In either situation there is always a chance that a piece may break off the main clot and travel to the lung. Of recent concern in this regard are studies that appear to link oral contraceptives with the incidence of clotting, thereby leading to pulmonary embolism. The number of women affected in this way by the use of oral contraceptives is small, but enough to be of concern.

The symptoms of pulmonary embolism are varied and may be minor or major. Most common are pleurisy—marked by chest pain during breathing—shortness of breath, and cough with the production of blood. Once the pulmonary embolism is diagnosed the treatment is simple in the less severe cases, which are the majority. But in cases of large clots and great areas of lung deprived of blood supply there may be catastrophic effects on the heart and general circulation.

Prevention

Certain preventive measures are worthwhile for all people. Stockings should not be rolled, because that produces a constricting band about the leg that impairs blood flow and predisposes to clot formation. Especially when taking long automobile or airplane rides one should be sure to stretch the legs periodically. Individuals with varicose veins or a history of thrombophlebitis should take these precautions more seriously. People who stand still for long periods during the day should wear elastic support stockings regularly and elevate their feet part of the day and at night.

When considering the use of oral contraceptives the physician must weigh the risks of developing clots from the drug against the psychological, social, and physical risks of pregnancy. The risk from oral contraceptives is lessened if the woman does not have high blood pressure. Any persistent pain in the leg, especially in the calf or behind the knee, deserves the attention of a physician. Anyone with varicose veins or anyone taking oral contraceptives should be especially attentive to these symptoms.

Pneumothorax

Another less common lung condition is spontaneous *pneumothorax* or collapse of a lung. This most commonly occurs in the second and third decade of life and presents itself with the sudden development of pain in the chest and breathlessness. The collapse occurs because of a sudden leak of air from the lung into the chest cavity.

The lung is ordinarily maintained in an expanded state by the rigid bony thorax, but if air leaks out into the space between the thorax and the lung, the lung collapses. This condition is rarely very serious but the patient needs to be observed to be sure that the air leak does not become greater with further lung collapse.

Treatment

Often a tube has to be placed in the chest, attached to a suction pump, and the air pumped out from the space where it has collected. When the air is removed the lung expands to fill the thoracic cage again. Some individuals tend to have several recurrences. Because the reason for the collapse is poorly understood, there is no satisfactory method of preventing these recurrences except by surgery. This is rarely required. In a person with a proven propensity for recurrence it is usually advisable to open the chest and produce scarring of the lung surface so that it becomes fixed to the thoracic cage. Although it is usually successful, even this procedure does not always solve this bothersome problem.

14

Diseases of the Endocrine Glands

Glands are organs that produce and secrete substances essential for normal body functioning. There are two main types of glands: the *endocrine* and the *exocrine*. The endocrines, or *ductless,* glands send their secretions directly into the bloodstream. These secretions, which are biochemically related to each other, are called *hormones*. The exocrines, such as the sebaceous or sweat glands, the mammary (or milk) glands, and the lachrymal (or tear) glands, have ducts that carry their secretions to specific locations for specific purposes.

The exocrine glands are individually discussed elsewhere in connection with the various parts of the body where they are found. This section is devoted to diseases of the ductless glands, which include:

- The *pituitary,* which controls growth and the activity of the adrenal, thyroid, and sex glands

- The *thyroid,* which controls the rate of the body's chemical activity or metabolism

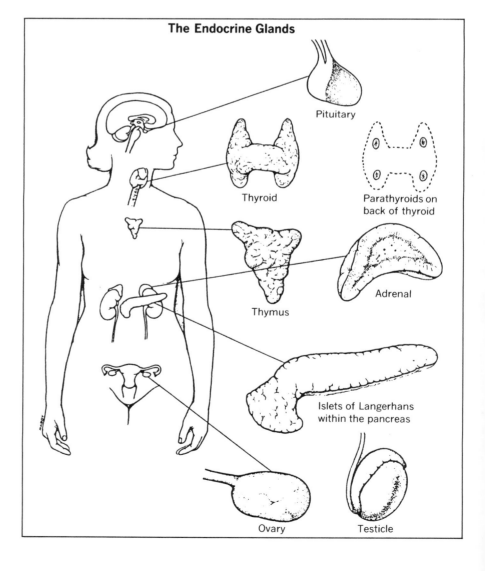

The Endocrine Glands

Pituitary

Thyroid

Parathyroids on back of thyroid

Thymus

Adrenal

Islets of Langerhans within the pancreas

Ovary

Testicle

- The *adrenals,* which affect metabolism and sex characteristics
- The *male gonads* or testicles and the *female gonads* or ovaries
- The *parathyroids,* which regulate bone metabolism

Unlike the exocrine glands, which can function independently of one another, the endocrines form an interrelated system. Thus a disorder in one of them is likely to affect the way the others behave. Glandular disorder can sometimes be anatomical, but it is usually functional. Functional disease can result in the production and release of too little or too much of a particular secretion.

When too much of a hormone is being secreted, the prefix *hyper-* is used for the condition, as in *hyperthyroidism.* When too little is being secreted, the prefix *hypo-* is used, as in the word *hypofunction,* to indicate that a gland operates below normal.

Abnormalities of the endocrine glands that cause changes in their functioning are responsible for a wide variety of illnesses. These illnesses are almost always accompanied by symptoms that can be recognized as distinctly abnormal. Prompt and accurate diagnosis can usually prevent the occurrence of irreversible damage. For many people with glandular disorders, treatment may have to be lifelong. They can feel well and function almost normally, but they must follow a program of regulated medication taken under a physician's supervision.

Anterior Pituitary Gland

The anterior pituitary gland, also called the *hypophysis,* is located in the center of the brain. It produces two types of secretions: a growth hor-

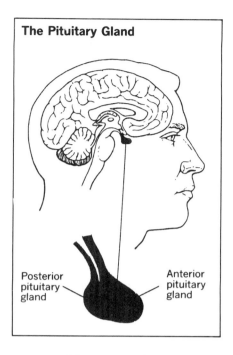

The Pituitary Gland

Posterior
pituitary
gland

Anterior
pituitary
gland

mone and hormones that stimulate certain other glands.

The anterior pituitary gland is subject to neurochemical stimulation by

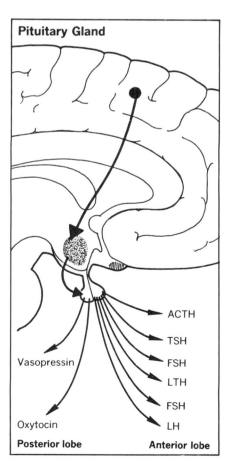

Pituitary Gland

Vasopressin

Oxytocin

Posterior lobe

ACTH

TSH

FSH

LTH

FSH

LH

Anterior lobe

the *hypothalamus,* a nearby part of the brain. This stimulation results in the production of the hormones that promote testicular and ovarian functioning, and does not occur normally until around 12 years of age in girls and 14 in boys. The beginning of this glandular activity is known as the onset of *puberty.*

Puberty is sometimes delayed for no apparent reason until age 16 or 17. Because the hypothalamus is affected by emotional factors, all of the endocrine glands governed by the anterior pituitary can also be affected by feelings. Psychological factors can therefore upset the relationships in the glandular system and produce the physical symptoms of endocrine disorders.

It is extremely rare for the anterior pituitary to produce too much or too little of its hormones, but sometimes hypofunction may follow pregnancy because of thrombosis or changes in the blood vessels.

A truly hypofunctioning anterior pituitary gland can cause many serious disturbances: extreme thinness, growth failure, sexual aberration, and intolerance for normal variations in temperature. When appropriate diagnostic tests determine the deficiency, the patient is given the missing hormones in pill form.

Absence of the growth hormone alone is unknown. Most cases of *dwarfism* result from other causes. However, excess production of the growth hormone alone does occur, but only rarely. If it begins before puberty when the long bones are still growing, the child with the disorder will grow into a well-proportioned giant. When it begins after puberty, the head, hands, feet, and most body organs except the brain slowly enlarge. This condition is called *acromegaly.* The cause of both disorders is usually a tumor, and radiation is the usual treatment.

The thyroid, adrenal cortex, testicles, ovaries, and pancreatic glands are target glands for the anterior pituitary's stimulating hormones, which are specific for the functioning of each of these glands. Therefore, a disorder of any of the target organs could be caused either by an excess or a deficiency of a stimulating hormone, creating a so-called *secondary disease.* There are various tests that can be given to differentiate primary from secondary disorders.

The Thyroid Gland

The thyroid gland is located in the front of the neck just above its base. Normal amounts of *thyroxin,* the hormone secreted by the thyroid, are necessary for the proper functioning of almost all bodily activities. When this hormone is deficient in infancy, growth and mental development are impaired and *cretinism* results.

Hypothyroidism

In adulthood, a deficiency of thyroxin hormone is caused primarily by a lack of sufficient iodine in the diet. In *hypothyroidism,* the disorder resulting from such a deficiency, the metabolic rate is slower than normal, the patient has no energy, his expression is dull, his skin is thick, and he has an intolerance to cold weather.

Treatment consists of increasing the amount of iodine in the diet if it is deficient or giving thyroid hormone medication. Normal metabolic functioning usually follows, especially if treatment is begun soon after the symptoms appear.

Hyperthyroidism

An excess amount of thyroid hormone secretion is called *hyperthyroidism* and may relate to emotional stress. It

causes physical fatigue but mental alertness, a staring quality in the eyes, tremor of the hands, weight loss with increased appetite, rapid pulse, sweating, and intolerance to hot weather.

Long-term treatment is aimed at decreasing hormone production with the use of a special medicine that inhibits it. In some cases, part of the gland may be removed by surgery; in others, radiation treatment with radioactive iodine is effective.

Hyperthyroidism may recur long after successful treatment. Both hypothyroidism and hyperthyroidism are common disorders, especially in women.

Other Thyroid Disorders

Enlargement of part or all of the thyroid gland occurs fairly often. It may be a simple enlargement of the gland itself caused by the lack of iodine, as in *goiter,* or it may be caused by a tumor or a nonspecific inflammation. Goiter is often treated with thyroxin, but it is easily prevented altogether by the regular use of iodized table and cooking salt. Treatment of other problems varies, but surgery is usually recommended for a tumor, especially if the surrounding organs are being obstructed.

The Adrenal Glands

The adrenals are paired glands located just above each kidney. Their outer part is called the *cortex.* The inner part is called the *medulla* and is not governed by the anterior pituitary. The cortex produces several hormones that affect the metabolism of salt, water, carbohydrate, fat, and protein, as well as secondary sex characteristics, skin pigmentation, and resistance to infection.

An insufficiency of these hormones

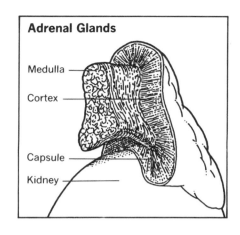

Adrenal Glands

Medulla
Cortex
Capsule
Kidney

can be caused by bacterial infection of the cortex, especially by *meningococcus;* by a hemorrhage into it; by an obstruction of blood flow into it; by its destruction because of tuberculosis; or by one of several unusual diseases.

In one type of sudden or acute underfunctioning of the cortex, the patient has a high fever, mental confusion, and circulatory collapse. Unless treated promptly, the disorder is likely to be fatal. When it persists after treatment, or when it develops gradually, it is called *Addison's disease* and is usually chronic. The patient suffers from weakness, loss of body hair, and increased skin pigmentation. Hormone-replacement treatment is essential, along with added salt for as long as hypofunction persists.

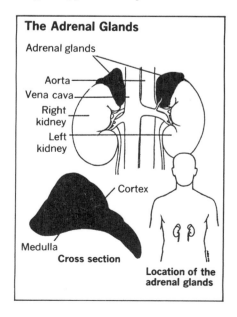

The Adrenal Glands

Adrenal glands
Aorta
Vena cava
Right kidney
Left kidney
Cortex
Medulla
Cross section
Location of the adrenal glands

The formation of an excess of certain cortical hormones (i.e., hormones produced in the adrenal cortex)—a disorder known as *Cushing's syndrome*—may be caused by a tumor of the anterior pituitary gland, which produces too much specific stimulating hormone, or by a tumor of one or both of the adrenal glands. It is a rare disease, more common in women, especially following pregnancy. Symptoms include weakness, loss of muscle tissue, the appearance of purple streaks in the skin, and an oval or "moon" face.

Treatment involves eliminating the overproducing tissue either by surgery or irradiation and then replacing any hormonal deficiencies with proper medication.

An excess of certain other cortical hormones because of an increase in cortical tissue or a tumor can result in the early onset of puberty in boys, or in an increase in the sexuality of females of any age. Surgical removal of the overproducing tissue is the only treatment.

The Adrenal Medulla

The medulla of the adrenal glands secretes two hormones: *epinephrine* (or *adrenaline*) and *norepinephrine*. Although they contribute to the proper functioning of the heart and blood vessels, neither one is absolutely indispensable. Disease caused by hypofunction of the medulla is unknown. Hyperfunction is a rare cause of sustained high blood pressure. Even more rarely, it causes episodic or paroxysmal high blood pressure accompanied by such symptoms as throbbing headache, profuse perspiration, and severe anxiety. The disorder is caused by a tumor effectively treated by surgical removal. Cancer of the adrenal medulla is extremely rare and virtually incurable.

Changes in hormone production can be caused by many intangible factors and are often temporary disorders. However, persistent or recurrent symptoms should be brought to a physician's attention. The accurate diagnosis of an endocrine disease depends on careful professional evaluation of specific laboratory tests, individual medical history, and thorough examination. No one should take hormones or medicines that affect hormone production without this type of evaluation, since their misuse can cause major problems.

Male Sex Glands

The male sex glands, or *gonads,* are the two testicles normally located in the *scrotum.* In addition to producing sperm, the testicles also manufacture the male hormone called *testosterone.* This hormone is responsible for the development and maintenance of secondary sex characteristics as well as for the male *libido,* or sexual impulse. Only one normal testicle is needed for full function.

Testicular Hypofunction

Hypofunction of one or both of the testicles can result from an abnormality in prenatal development, from infections such as mumps or tuberculosis, from injury, or from the increased temperature to which undescended testicles are exposed.

When hypofunction occurs before puberty, there is failure in the development of secondary sex characteristics. The sex organs do not enlarge; facial, pubic, and armpit hair fails to appear; and the normal voice change does not occur. Fertility and libido also fail to develop. A person with this combination of abnormalities is called a *eunuch.*

If the disorder is secondary to anterior pituitary disease, it is called *Froehlich's syndrome.* When it occurs after puberty, the body changes are less striking, but there may be a loss of fertility and libido. The primary disease is usually treated by surgery, and testosterone may be given. If the disorder is secondary to anterior pituitary disease, the gonad-stimulating hormone should be administered.

Testicular hypofunction is rare because it results only when both testicles are damaged in some way. Although mumps may involve the testicles, it is rarely the cause of sterility, even though this is greatly

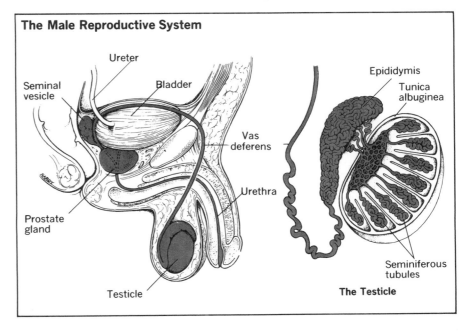

The Male Reproductive System

Ureter

Seminal vesicle

Bladder

Vas deferens

Urethra

Prostate gland

Testicle

Epididymis

Tunica albuginea

Seminiferous tubules

The Testicle

feared. Even so, everyone should be immunized against mumps in infancy.

It is advisable to wear an appropriate athletic supporter to protect the testicles when engaged in strenuous athletics or when there is a possibility that they might be injured. However, nothing that restricts scrotal movement should be worn regularly, since movement is essential for the maintenance of constant testicular temperature.

A sudden decrease in sexual drive or performance may be caused by disease, trauma, or emotional factors. In certain cases administering male hormones may relieve the condition. However, a decrease in sexual drive is one of the natural consequences of aging. It is not a disease and should not be treated with testosterone.

Testicular Hyperfunction

Testicular hyperfunction is extremely rare and is usually caused by a tumor. Before puberty, the condition results in the precocious development of secondary sex characteristics; after puberty, in the accentuation of these characteristics. Such a tumor must be removed surgically or destroyed by irradiation.

Cancer can develop in a testicle without causing any functional change. It is relatively uncommon. When it appears, it shows up first as a painless enlargement. The cancer cells then usually spread quickly to other organs and have a fatal result. Prompt treatment by surgery and irradiation can sometimes arrest the condition.

Because an undescended testicle may become cancerous, it should be repositioned into the scrotum by surgery or removed.

Female Sex Glands

The female gonads are the *ovaries,* situated on each side of and close to

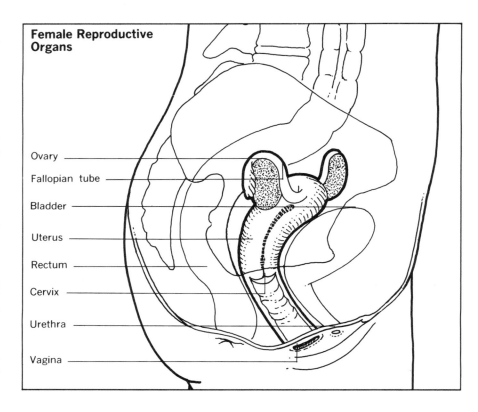

Female Reproductive Organs

Ovary
Fallopian tube
Bladder
Uterus
Rectum
Cervix
Urethra
Vagina

the uterus or womb. In addition to producing an *ovum* or egg each month, they manufacture the female hormones *estrogen* and *progesterone,* each making its special contribution to the menstrual cycle and to the many changes that go on during pregnancy. Estrogen regulates the secondary sex characteristics such as breast development and the appearance of pubic and axillary hair.

The periodicity of the menstrual cycle depends on a very complicated relationship between the ovaries and the anterior pituitary. Birth control pills, most of which contain estrogen and progesterone, interrupt this relationship in such a way that no ovum is produced and pregnancy therefore should not occur.

Changes in normal ovarian hormone function create problems similar to changes in normal testicular hormone function, except of course

for the female–male differences. In general, the diseases responsible for these changes are the same in males and females. However, changes in female hormone function are very often caused by emotional stress or by other unspecific circumstances.

Ovarian Hypofunction

Hypofunction of the ovaries may cause failure to menstruate at all or with reasonable regularity. A disruption of the menstrual cycle is an obvious indication to the woman past puberty that something is wrong. Less obvious is the reduction or complete loss of fertility that may accompany the disorder.

Both menstrual and infertility problems should be evaluated by a trained specialist, preferably a gynecologist, to find out their cause. If it should be hormonal deficiency, treatment may consist of replacement hormone therapy. In many cases, however, effective treatment consists of eliminating the emotional stress that has affected the stimulation relationship between the anterior pituitary and the ovaries, thereby inhibiting hormone production. Occasionally, hormone treatment for infertility causes several ova to be produced in the same month, increasing the possibility of a multiple pregnancy.

Menopause

All women eventually develop spontaneous ovarian hypofunction. This usually happens between the ages of 45 and 50 and is called the *climacteric* or *menopause*. When it happens before the age of 35, it is called premature menopause.

Normal menopause results from the gradual burning out of the ovaries so that estrogen is deficient or absent altogether. Most women experience very few changes or symptoms at this time other than the cessation of menstruation, usually preceded by progressive irregularity and reduction of flow.

A few women become excessively irritable, have hot flashes, perspire a great deal, gain weight, and develop facial hair. Such women, as well as those who have premature menopause, are likely to benefit greatly from estrogen replacement therapy for a few years. However, because recent statistical studies have implicated sustained use of estrogen therapy as increasing the risk of uterine cancer in postmenopausal women, the American Cancer Society has cautioned physicians to supervise such women closely. At the present time, most physicians feel that the treatment should be given temporarily and only when menopause symptoms are causing special discomfort.

Ovarian Hyperfunction

Hyperfunction of the ovaries after puberty is one cause of increased menstrual flow during or at the end of each cycle. This is called functional bleeding and is caused by excess estrogen. The disorder is treated with progesterone, which slows down estrogen production. In cases where this treatment fails, it is sometimes necessary to remove the uterus by an operation called a *hysterectomy*.

Some diseases of the ovaries, such as infections, cysts, and tumors, do not necessarily cause functional changes, but they may call attention to themselves by being painful, or a physician may discover them during a pelvic examination. Treatment may be medical, surgical, or by irradiation, depending on the nature of the disorder. See Ch. 25, *Women's Health,* for fuller treatment of ovarian and other disorders affecting women.

A rather common cause of short-lived ovarian pain is connected with *ovulation,* which occurs about 14 days before the next expected menstrual period. This discomfort is called *mittelschmerz,* which is German for "middle pain," and can be treated with aspirin or any other simple analgesic.

The Pancreas

The pancreas, a combined duct and endocrine gland, is to some extent regulated by the anterior pituitary. See Ch. 15, *Diabetes Mellitus,* for a discussion of the pancreas and diabetes.

Posterior Pituitary Gland

The posterior lobe of the pituitary gland, the parathyroid glands, and the adrenal medulla are not governed by the anterior pituitary gland. The posterior pituitary produces a secretion called *antidiuretic hormone* which acts on the kidneys to control the amount

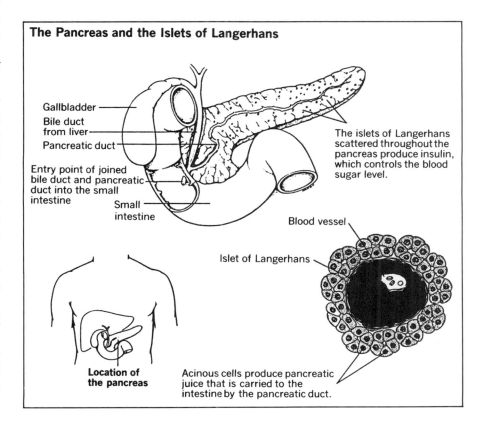

The Pancreas and the Islets of Langerhans

Gallbladder

Bile duct from liver

Pancreatic duct

Entry point of joined bile duct and pancreatic duct into the small intestine

Small intestine

Location of the pancreas

The islets of Langerhans scattered throughout the pancreas produce insulin, which controls the blood sugar level.

Blood vessel

Islet of Langerhans

Acinous cells produce pancreatic juice that is carried to the intestine by the pancreatic duct.

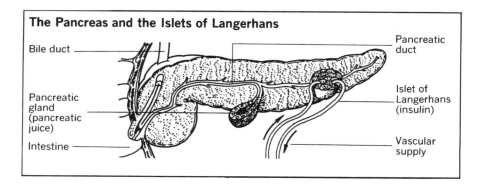

The Pancreas and the Islets of Langerhans

Bile duct

Pancreatic gland (pancreatic juice)

Intestine

Pancreatic duct

Islet of Langerhans (insulin)

Vascular supply

of urine produced. A deficiency of this hormone causes *diabetes insipidus,* which results in the production of an excessive amount of urine, sometimes as much as 25 quarts a day. (A normal amount is about one quart.) The natural consequence of this disorder is an unquenchable thirst. It is an extremely rare disease, the cause of which is often unknown, although it may result from a brain injury or tumor. Treatment involves curing the cause if it is known. If not, the patient is given an antidiuretic hormone.

The Parathyroid Glands

The parathyroid glands are located in or near the thyroid, usually two on each side. They are important in the regulation of blood calcium and phosphorus levels and therefore of bone metabolism. Hypofunction of these glands almost never occurs except when they have been removed surgically, usually inadvertently during a thyroid operation. In underfunctioning of the parathyroids, blood calcium levels fall and muscle spasm results. The patient is usually given calcium and replacement therapy with parathyroid hormone to correct the disorder.

Hyperfunction is rare and is slightly more common in women. A benign tumor, or *adenoma,* is the usual cause. The amount of calcium in the blood rises as calcium is removed from the bones, which then weaken and may break easily. The excess calcium is excreted in the urine and may coalesce into kidney stones, causing severe pain. Treatment for hyperfunction of the parathyroids consists of surgical removal of the affected glands.

15

Diabetes and Other Autoimmune Diseases

THE STRUCTURE OF THE IMMUNE SYSTEM

The immune system is what protects us from different types of disease. When an invading bacteria, virus, or other antigen enters the human body, a network of cells move in to attack and destroy the invading substance. This may happen without any side effects to the infected person, or the person may develop side effects from the battle between the immune system and the invader.

Blood cells known as macrophages roam through the body looking for foreign elements. When they find one, they digest it and produce something called peptides. These peptides serve as a marker that identifies the invading substance.

White blood cells (lymphocytes) then bind to the marker to "learn" the shape. The white blood cells seek out more of the substance to destroy it, while sending out a signal to the immune system to build up more forces. A result of this buildup is an increased white blood cell count, which is why doctors test blood to see if any infection is present. If you have an elevated white blood cell count, your im-

mune system has detected an invading infection.

One type of white blood cell, the b-lymphocyte, secretes antibody proteins. The proteins work to destroy the invading antigen. Another type, T-lymphocytes, are white blood cells that "read" the markers and alert the immune system to the presence of an infection. T cells can also destroy invading bodies. There are two types of t cells: the helper T and the killer T.

Antibodies are just what the word sounds like, they are cells designed against a foreign body: anti-body. After a specific antibody is built up in the blood, some cells always remain to identify the invader more rapidly the next time the infection strikes. With viral infections, once the body knows the shape, it will eliminate the virus before it can make the person sick. Measles and mumps are illnesses that you can only get once because the body learns to attack those cells after the first exposure. Colds, flus, and other common illnesses occur over and over because there are so many strains of them. You do not have the same type of cold virus twice. One single white cell can produce 10 million antibodies every hour. At that speed, a recognized virus doesn't

have a chance to survive in your system and make you sick.

This system of defense from infections, viruses, toxins, and other contaminants is extremely important to human survival. Without an immune system, you would not survive for very long. Babies born without functioning immune systems have to be kept in sterile rooms to protect them. The simplest infection can spread and kill a person if there is no counterattack from within the body.

AUTOIMMUNE DISEASES

Autoimmune diseases are created when the human body stops recognizing one internal part as its own. If fails to recognize the "self" cells and attacks them as if they were foreign bodies. In normal immune system development, white cells are run through a test before leaving the thymus gland. If they fail to distinguish between foreign cells and self cells, they are destroyed. It is this process which keeps the healthy body from releasing an immunological army that could destroy all cells it encounters. In autoimmune diseases, the immune system stops recognizing a very specific part of the body and proceeds to destroy it. Medical researchers are still investigating why this happens and possible preventive measures.

Types of Autoimmune Diseases

The recognized autoimmune diseases are:

- Addison's disease
- anemia (pernicious)
- Crohn's disease
- diabetes mellitus
- glomerulonephritis
- Goodpasture's syndrome
- Graves' disease
- Hashimoto's thyroiditis
- hemolytic anemia
- lupus erythematosus (systemic)
- multiple sclerosis
- myasthenia gravis
- pemphigus
- rheumatoid arthritis
- scleroderma
- Sjögren-Larsson syndrome
- thrombocytopenic purpura

The area attacked can vary. In diabetes mellitus, the T cells attack the pancreas, destroying the organ's ability to produce insulin. Without insulin, the body cannot break down sugar. If left unchecked, the sugar amounts will reach dangerous levels in the blood and eventually cause death.

In multiple sclerosis, the immune system attacks the long nerve fibers (white matter) of the nervous system. Lesions appear in the brain, and loss of nerve function results. The loss can be the ability to feel things with one's hands, the ability to control the legs while walking, muscle weakness, blurred vision, and assorted other functions.

Each of the autoimmune diseases attacks a different site, or attacks the same sites differently. It is estimated that 5 percent of the adult population in the Western Hemisphere suffer from an autoimmune disease.

Although there is a genetic link for autoimmune diseases, it is not solely through inheritance that someone gets the disease. People with two parents with the disease may not develop the disease, and others with no family history of autoimmune disease have been known to develop one. In identical twins, most autoimmune diseases occur less than 50 percent of the time in both twins.

Managing autoimmune diseases

Scientists are studying what turns the autoimmune disease on. The possibilities include the patient having a previous infection, unusual levels of stress, weight gain, or high hormonal levels. It could also be a combination of these factors.

An autoimmune disease does not progress smoothly. There are periods of rapid decline, and periods of remission where the disease is not as influential on the body. The care that the patient takes with following doctor's orders can help in alleviating some, but not all, of the symptoms.

The diseases vary as well from individual to individual. Some patients with diabetes mellitus will live relatively normal, healthy lives for decades with almost no side effects from the disease besides dependence on insulin. Other patients, even under strict diet and insulin monitoring, may suffer from many of the side effects such as neuropathy (death of the nerves in the arms and legs), blindness, and kidney failure. Why patients' reactions vary like this is not understood.

It is essential, though, that anyone with an autoimmune disease understand what behaviors and habits are harmful and avoid them. For a diabetic, controlling one's diet is essential. Although it requires constant monitoring, no diabetic can avoid the strict attention to dietary needs that diabetes requires. Ignoring the diet rules can kill a diabetic in days.

For people with lupus and psoriasis, stress increases the severity of the disease. Because the nerves release peptides that increase the body's immune response during periods of stress, the effect or the disease becomes worse during stressful times. Patients with stress-enhanced diseases may have to take meditation courses, change jobs, and practice daily relaxation exercises to lower their stress level.

Systemic lupus erythematosus is capable of attacking any human tissue. For reasons unknown to scientists, it is almost exclusively a disease that affects females. Only 10 percent of the sufferers are male. The disease attacks a variety of areas in the body, and the attacks differ from patient to patient. The most common areas, though, are the joints, kidneys, and the brain. It also undergoes periods of remission, but anxiety over having another attack can actually trigger another attack. Optimism about the disease's course by the patient can improve the patient's outlook.

Graves' disease also affects more women than men, but not as disproportionately as lupus. Graves' is one of several autoimmune diseases that affects the thyroid. It increases the hormone that regulates the metabolism, making weight gain a common side effect.

There are usually support and awareness groups for autoimmune disease sufferers. Check in your phone book for a local affiliation, and check with your physician. He or she can put you in contact with an organization that will assist you with information and encouragement. Since your mental attitude is very important in the treatment of the disease, it is in your best interest to take care of your spirits as well as your body.

Early detection

If you have a blood relative with an autoimmune disease, you should familiarize yourself and your family with the early symptoms of the disease. If there are tests that can be run (most of these diseases have simple blood tests), then you should discuss with your physician how often you should be tested for the disease. Ask about family testing and at what age your children should start getting tested.

With some of these diseases, science is developing some preventative treatments that may help keep a child from developing the disease. For example, diabetes specialists have several test groups in place to check different preventative measures. If one works it may become available to the general population.

Your strongest weapon is information. Know what to look for, what to expect, and be active in getting medical checks for the diseases for which you and your family are at risk. Avoid the things (like weight gain) that may increase your chances of getting an autoimmune disorder, and maintain general good health.

Diabetes mellitus (DM)

Diabetes has been known for several thousand years. Late in the nineteenth century, when diabetes was well recognized as an abnormality in carbohydrate metabolism (the ability to burn sugar), several scientists discovered that the experimental removal of certain cells, the islets of Langerhans, from the pancreas, produced diabetes in dogs. This observation led to the 1921 discovery and isolation of naturally produced insulin. Insulin is a hormone produced by the islets of Langerhans. Injection of insulin into the bodies of people with diabetes proved to be the first and, to this day, the most effective means of treating the disease.

Until injectable insulin was developed, death occurred within a year or two of the onset of the disease, and usually within weeks or months of development of the symptoms. With injectable insulin, the life expectancy rose dramatically.

An early pioneer in the treatment of diabetes with insulin was Dr. Elliott Joslin of Boston. Dr. Joslin realized that the diabetic patient needed to have a full understanding of his disease so that he could take care of himself. He knew that the diabetic, with the chronic abnormality of a delicate and dynamic metabolic process, could not be cared for successfully solely by knowledgeable physicians. The patient and his family had to be informed about the disease and be active in the day-to-day management of diabetes.

In many ways this marked the beginning of what has become patient-management of illness. It is important for every type of illness and injury, but it is essential to the welfare of patients with chronic illness.

Characteristics of Diabetes

The fundamental problem in diabetes is the body's inability to metabolize glucose (burn sugar), fully and continually. This is a vital process in creating body cell energy. Glucose is a chemical derivative of carbohydrates in food after they have been digested. Carbohydrates are mostly from plants. They may come in the form of starches (such as corn), sucrose (regular sugar), and fructose (fruit sugars). All natural sweeteners, including honey, are forms of sugar. Nonnatural sweeteners such as Equal, Sweet and Low, and others are not sugar and do not affect the body the same way.

Glucose is stored under normal conditions in the form of glycogen, an animal starch, in the liver and muscles for use later as energy fuel. It is reconverted to glucose and burned by the body when energy is needed.

Insulin

Insulin is necessary for both the storage and reconversion of glucose. The metabolic failure to burn sugar may occur because of an insufficiency of insulin, an inability of the body to respond to the normal triggers for producing insulin, or for a combination of those reasons. In any event, the failure to metabolize glucose results in an abnormal, and unhealthy, accumulation of sugar in the bloodstream.

This failure to break down sugar resembles starvation in its effect. A starved person eats no food, and the diabetic eats food but is unable to gain the benefits of the food because the body is unable to break the food down into a usable form. Eventually the body will start to digest fat, protein, and muscle cells from the body to maintain the energy level. This causes a rise in acid level in the blood which, when left untreated, will cause coma and death. Before insulin was discovered, this was why diabetics died.

For most of the 20th century, insulin was prepared commercially in the United States from beef or pork pancreas. There were difficulties from this because of allergic reactions in some patients. Patients who required insulin injections but were allergic to it also had to use steroids and other immune suppressing substances to keep the allergic reaction down. This made them more susceptible to other infections.

Researchers developed an insulin drug that is manufactured with an synthetic duplicate of human genes. Unlike animal insulins, Humulin, the first consumer health product made with DNA, can be produced in unlimited quantities. It has far fewer side effects and is less costly to produce. Research continues to refine and improve the quality of injectable insulin. The effort is to get insulin to match the body's natural insulin as closely as possible in both genetic structure and the speed with which it interacts with sugar.

Insulin is given by injection, usually subcutaneously (under the skin), because the stomach acids will destroy it, if it is swallowed. Insulin comes in several versions, classified by the speed with which it works. Fast-acting insulin usually follows meals. Slow-acting insulin is for evening, and periods between meals. A combination may be administered.

How insulin doses are determined

A diabetic's basic insulin dose initially has to be established by the physician, according to several factors. The severity of the disease, the general level of exercise, the general quantity of food eaten, and the general health of the patient all play a role in determining insulin needs. This is part of the reason for hospitalizing a patient after he or she is diagnosed with diabetes.

Once the dose has been established, the quantity of insulin has to be assessed before every injection. This is done through blood testing and an analysis of the expected activity level to follow the injection and the expected food consumption. The dia-

Injection of Insulin Dose

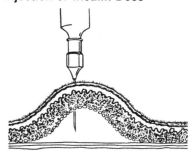

1. Wipe site of injection with cotton swab dipped in alcohol.
2. With one hand, pinch up skin at injection site. Place syringe perpendicularly to the skin and quickly insert needle for its entire length in order to insure injection of sufficient depth (*see illustration*).The more rapidly the needle is inserted, the less the pain will be. Stainless steel needles are preferred.
3. Inject insulin dose.

Sites of Insulin Injections

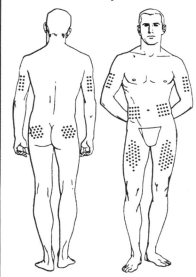

It is important to change the site of injection daily for best absorption of insulin.

betic undergoes training for all these evaluations during his or her hospital stay.

Blood testing

The methods of testing blood have become much more easy and accurate in the past 10 years. A simple pinprick to a finger for a small drop of blood is all that is needed to get an accurate blood reading. Electronic monitors are available that read the blood sample automatically. If a patient cannot

afford an electronic sampler, financial assistance may be available through the American Diabetics Association.

After a five-year study, it was determined that the most effective method of testing and determining insulin levels in diabetics was to test blood three to four times daily. At least once a week the diabetic should waken in the middle of the night to test blood levels. With this close monitoring of the blood sugar levels, peaks in sugar or insulin levels are less extreme, and the diabetic can avoid some of the deterioration that high sugar levels can cause.

Understanding Diabetes

There are two types of diabetes, insulin dependent and noninsulin dependent. Except for the symptoms, they are unrelated.

Noninsulin dependent diabetes

In noninsulin dependent diabetes, the patient's pancreas stops producing insulin, or produces insulin intermittently. Although the reasons for the pancreatic shutdown are unknown, the suspicion is there is undue stress on the pancreas. Triggers for noninsulin dependent diabetes are weight gain (including pregnancy), bad diet, lack of exercise, and general unfitness. Patients with noninsulin dependent diabetes can usually be treated by an oral tablet to boost insulin production and a change in diet and behavior. Patients with extreme stress on the pancreas may have to take injectable insulin. This disease is not assumed to be inherited, although the similar body build and lifestyle of parent and child will make the offspring of a noninsulin dependent diabetic more prone to developing the disease.

Pregnancy-induced diabetes, commonly called gestational diabetes, is usually the result of the stress on the body from carrying the developing fetus. In most women, the disease ends soon after the pregnancy. In some cases, though, the woman will develop insulin-dependent diabetes after the pregnancy. The first course of treatment in pregnant women is usually to control diet. If that is unsuccessful, or the pancreas production of insulin is too low, either pills or injections may be used.

Noninsulin dependent diabetes can occur at any age, but is most common in older adults.

Insulin dependent diabetes

Often referred to as juvenile onset diabetes, diabetes mellitus, and type I diabetes, all are the autoimmune form of diabetes. The disease can develop at any age; it is as common to develop in a 20-year-old as in a 40-year-old. There are no age restrictions for developing diabetes.

By the time a patient experiences symptoms, the area of insulin production in the pancreas has been nearly destroyed by the body's immune system. It is suspected that the initial immune attack on the pancreas can start as early as one year before any symptoms are experienced.

The warning signs of diabetes are excessive thirst, excessive urination, a sweet smell to the breath, and fatigue and lightheadedness. Other possible symptoms can include unexplained weight loss (sometimes rapid), extreme hunger, and disorientation. You can have one or more of these symptoms. But it is unlikely you will have all of them.

If at any point in your life you experience any one of the symptoms you should consult your doctor imme-

diately. There are very simple blood and urine tests to determine if you have excessive sugar levels.

If it is determined that your sugar level is high, it is probable that you will be hospitalized immediately. One reason for this is to get you into a controlled environment where your food intake, sugar levels, and urine can be monitored regularly and frequently for several days. The other and more important reason is that excessive sugar levels in the blood are damaging to the kidneys, eyes, and circulatory system, and can cause death in a matter of days if left untreated.

Once you are in the hospital, you will be trained in giving yourself insulin injections, monitoring your diet, and decreasing your sugar consumption. There is nothing complicated about the diet or the insulin amounts. The blood sugar monitoring devices are quick, accurate, and easy to use. The insulin injections are painless once you learn how to do them. The difficult part for most patients is changing their diet. This takes understanding, determination, and will power. But it is essential that the patient follow the diet guidelines.

Diabetic side effects

The most important side effects to familiarize yourself with are sugar reactions and shock, and insulin reactions and shock. They are caused by either excessive sugar or excessive insulin.

Sugar reaction and shock

Sugar shock is triggered when the insulin in the body is not sufficient to break down the sugar. The excess sugar begins travelling through the blood stream. Since the body is unable to digest the sugar without insulin present, the body must turn to an-

other source of energy. Ketone levels build when the body begins to break down fat cells for energy. The by-product of the ketones is an acid buildup in the blood.

The earliest stage of the problem is called diabetic ketosis; a slightly later stage is called diabetic acidosis.

The symptoms of this are the same as the onset of diabetes, because the same thing happened when the patient was first diagnosed—early diabetic ketosis or acidosis was setting in. The symptoms are: excessive urination, excessive thirst, disorientation, weight loss, dry and hot skin, and fatigue. Call your physician immediately if you experience any of these symptoms.

When the blood gets too acidic, the body goes into shock. If the patient is left untreated, he or she will go into a coma. This occurs several days after diabetic ketosis starts. The unconscious patient will have deep, labored breathing, and a fruity odor to his or her breath.

Sugar shock resembles an insulin reaction, although they can be distinguish from each other. If you find a diabetic in a coma and you do not know the cause, assume the cause is an insulin reaction and treat him initially with sugar. This will give immediate relief to an insulin reaction but will not significantly affect sugar shock.

Diabetic acidosis and sugar shock occur for many reasons. The patient does not take his insulin or oral drugs for several days. He may take too little insulin. He may overeat or underexercise for a number of days. Illness can change the patterns of exercise and diet; the patient may need to change doses of insulin. In any case, the patient should be brought to a hospital immediately, where he or she may be admitted for further observation.

Insulin reaction and shock

Insulin reactions are caused when the quantity of sugar is insufficient to burn up the insulin in the blood. When there is not enough sugar, the blood sugar level falls, and the brain is deprived of an essential source of energy. This was commonly known as hypoglycemia, although the term is not currently used in medicine.

Insulin shock can be brought on by excessive insulin injection, excessive exercise, or undereating. Stomach viruses that cause vomiting and diarrhea need to be especially monitored in diabetics because the illnesses change the amount of sugar being absorbed by the body. Less insulin is usually required than normal.

The first sign of an insulin reaction is usually mild hunger. Sweating, dizziness, palpitations, shallow breathing, trembling, mental confusion, strange behavior, and loss of consciousness follow rapidly. The symptoms will appear fairly quickly. There is much less time to treat insulin reactions and shock than there is to treat sugar shock. Insulin reactions should always be treated as an immediate medical emergency.

Diabetics who use insulin should always have sugar or quick dissolving candy on hand for treating insulin reactions. They must learn to recognize the early symptoms of increased insulin levels.

If you find a diabetic unconscious, give sugar to him or her immediately, then call an ambulance. Some shocks need to be treated with intravenous glucose. Notify the medical team immediately that the patient is a diabetic.

Medical bracelets

Because immediate treatment can be lifesaving with a diabetic, it is important that the diabetic have some identification on him or her *at all times* explaining that he or she suffers from diabetes. If the patient loses consciousness, this ID can save his or her life. Your physician or pharmacist can help you get an ID piece to wear.

Long-term side effects

Long-term side effects are caused by sugar crystals passing through small tubes of the circulatory system. If the sugar crystals are larger than the tubes, as is the case with capillaries, then the tubes are scratched, torn or destroyed by the sugar.

This damage can cause plaque to build up on the inside of the arteries, leading to atherosclerosis and heart disease. It can cause scarring and hemorrhaging in the kidneys, leading to kidney failure and kidney disease. It can cause hemorrhaging in the back of the eyes because of tears to the capillaries and reduction of blood flow to the hand and feet, because of tears in the capillaries that provide blood to the extremities.

This lack of blood flow makes healing take longer, and infections become more likely. With reduced blood flow, the body cannot battle the infection as well, so infections are likely to be worse. Blisters won't heal as well, and scratches and cuts, particularly on the feet, are likely sources of infections.

Since the blood flow to the extremities is reduced, the nerves are not as well nourished and may begin to die off in the hands and feet. This causes unusual sensations and pain as it happens and leads to numbness in the extremities.

With reduced feeling, the diabetic is less likely to notice the small injuries, making him or her even more prone to infections. Particular care must be paid to the condition of hands and feet, and daily visual checks should be made of hands and feet to make sure no injuries go undetected.

Catching injuries early helps immeasurably in preventing serious infection.

The diabetic is at risk of losing arms and legs because of the eventual decreased blood flow to the limbs. As nerve impulse is lost from these regions, the body is unable to recognize when an injury occurs. This becomes a problem for the diabetic because exercise is an important part of the daily health care for the disease. So, the diabetic must consider the types of exercise he or she will do with some care.

Early in the disease, these concerns are minimal, since there is still strong nerve response from the limbs. However, as the disease progresses, it may become important to reassess the types of athletics the patient is involved in. Diabetics should consider swimming over running, since there is less impact on the limbs in non-weight-bearing exercise.

Even with good management, there is some chance that the diabetic may lose eyesight, limbs, or kidney functions. Many years ago, these were considered end-stage complications of diabetes. This is no longer the case. Disease management has allowed diabetics to undergo amputations and still survive years after the surgery. With the improvement of prosthetic devices, the ability to lead normal lives is maintained. Laser surgery for retinal hemorrhaging in the eyes has improved the treatment of eye disease in diabetics. And improved dialysis allows patients regular treatment without the discomfort that was previously associated with dialysis.

Improvements in treatment and management occur regularly, with occasionally dramatic results. Research in autoimmune diseases, and particularly diabetes, is enhancing the understanding of and the treatment of the disease.

Long-term treatment

With diabetes and other autoimmune diseases, long-term treatment is a team effort. You, as the sufferer, have an equally important role in the management of your disease as the physician has. You are responsible for the day-to-day actions that increase or decrease the controllable elements that affect your disease. These controls are as essential to the course of the disease as any medical effort your doctor will provide.

So, if diet is an important element to disease management, then you should approach it with the same seriousness that you expect the doctor to approach your treatment. If you are to reduce stress in your life, then do it. Arguing about the importance, the feasibility, or the difficulty of making these changes helps no one, and only puts off the tasks you have to do.

The medical treatment of these diseases will change dramatically over the next several years. Autoimmune diseases are an area of intensive medical study, and the methods for treatment will improve as medical experts learn more about the disease. If you join a support group, are active in researching medical information about your disease, and develop a good relationship with your doctor, this should provide you with the resources to keep up-to-date on new treatments of autoimmune diseases. You are your strongest advocate. It is up to you to make sure you know everything there is to know about your treatment.

16

Diseases of the Eye and Ear

Most people never experience any impairment of the senses of smell, taste, and touch. But it is indeed lucky and unusual to reach old age without having some problems connected with sight or with hearing or both.

The Eyes

All sensations must be processed in the brain by a normally functioning central nervous system for their proper perception. In addition, each sensation is perceived through a specific sense organ. Thus, sight is dependent on at least one functioning eye.

The eye is an optical system that can be compared to a camera, because the human lens perceives and the retina receives an image in the same way that a camera and its film does. Defects in this optical system are called errors in refraction and are the most common type of sight problem.

Myopia

Nearsightedness or *myopia* is a refractive error that causes faraway objects to be seen as blurred and indistinct. The degree of nearsightedness can be measured by testing each eye with a Snellen Test Chart. Normal vision is called 20/20. This means that at 20 feet the eye sees an image clearly and accurately.

Eyesight of less-than-normal acuity is designated as 20/50 or 20/100 and so on. This means that what the deficient eye can see accurately at a distance of 20 feet or less, the normal eye can see accurately at 50 or 100 feet.

Myopia, the most common of all refractive errors, results from an elongation of the eyeball that prevents images from being focused on the retina. Myopia usually develops between the ages of 6 and 15. Prescription eyeglasses or contact lenses can correct the refractive error.

Other corrective measures involve physically altering the shape of the cornea. In radial keratotomy, the cornea is flattened through surgical cuts in order to change the way light is bent by the eye. This technique is rarely performed, as it severely weakens the cornea. A revolutionary alternative to radial keratotomy is laser surgery. A laser beam trims and sculpts the cornea in seconds.

Farsightedness and Astigmatism

The opposite of myopia is *hyperopia,* or farsightedness, which results from a shortening of the eyeball. The two conditions may be combined with *astigmatism,* in which vertical and horizontal images do not focus on the same point, mainly because of some abnormality of the front surface of the cornea. Properly fitted glasses can correct all of these deficiencies.

Presbyopia

A fourth refractive error combines with the other three to make up about 80 percent of all visual defects. It is known as *presbyopia,* or old-sight, and results from an inability of the lens to focus on near objects. Almost everyone is affected by presbyopia some time after the age of 40, because of the aging of the lens itself or the muscles which expand and contract it. Presbyopia can be easily corrected with glasses.

All these conditions represent variations in the sight of one or both eyes from what is considered the norm.

Eye

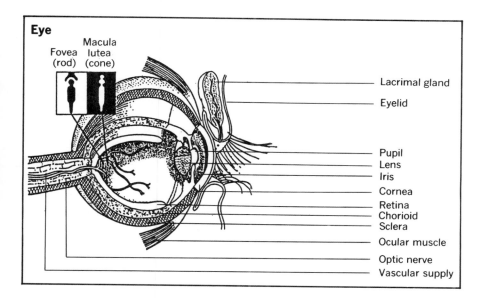

Fovea (rod)
Macula lutea (cone)

Lacrimal gland
Eyelid

Pupil
Lens
Iris
Cornea
Retina
Chorioid
Sclera
Ocular muscle
Optic nerve
Vascular supply

Because seating distance from a school blackboard, the size of print, and the distance at which signs must be read are all based on what is considered to be normal vision, eye defects are handicaps, some mild and some severe.

Many people can function normally without glasses if the defects are minor. But because uncorrected refractive errors can cause headaches and general fatigue as well as eye aches and eye fatigue, they should receive prompt medical attention.

Color Blindness

Color blindness is a visual defect that occurs in about eight percent of men but is extremely rare in women. It is hereditary, and usually involves an inability to differentiate clearly between red, green, and blue. It is a handicap for which there is no known cure at the present time.

Glaucoma

Glaucoma is a serious problem that affects about two percent of those people who are over 40. It is caused not only by the aging process, but also and more importantly by anatomical changes inside the eye that pre-

vent the normal drainage of fluid. The pressure inside the eye is therefore increased, and this pressure causes further anatomical change that can lead to blindness.

Glaucoma may begin with occasional eye pain or blurred vision, or it may be very insidious, cause no symptoms for years, and be discov-

ered only at an eye examination. Glaucoma is the number one cause of blindness, and an annual check for its onset by a specialist is particularly recommended for everyone over 40. The test is quick, easy, and painless, and should symptoms appear, early treatment, either medical or surgical or both, can reduce the likelihood of partial or complete loss of sight.

Cataracts

Another serious eye problem is the development of *cataracts*. These are areas in the lens that are no longer transparent. The so-called *senile cataract* is common among elderly people because of degenerative changes in the lens. The condition causes varying degrees of loss of vision which are readily noticed by the patient. If the vision is reduced a great deal, the entire lens can be removed surgically and appropriate glasses or contact lenses can be provided.

Focusing

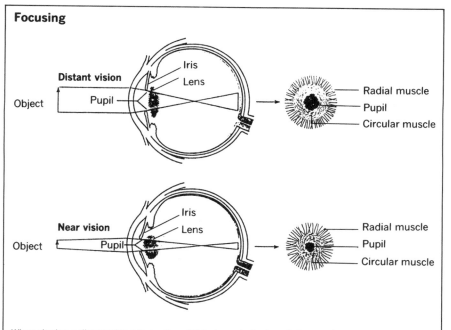

Distant vision

Object
Pupil
Iris
Lens

Radial muscle
Pupil
Circular muscle

Near vision

Object
Pupil
Iris
Lens

Radial muscle
Pupil
Circular muscle

When viewing a distant object (more than 20 feet away), the lens flattens and the pupil dilates, allowing more light to enter the eye. The pupil is dilated by the action of the outer radial muscles of the iris, which contract and thus stretch the previously contracted circular muscles. When viewing a near object, the lens becomes more oval and the pupil contracts as more light enters the eye. This prevents overstimulation of the retina. The pupil is reduced in size by the contraction of the inner circular muscles, which serve to stretch the previously contracted radial muscles.

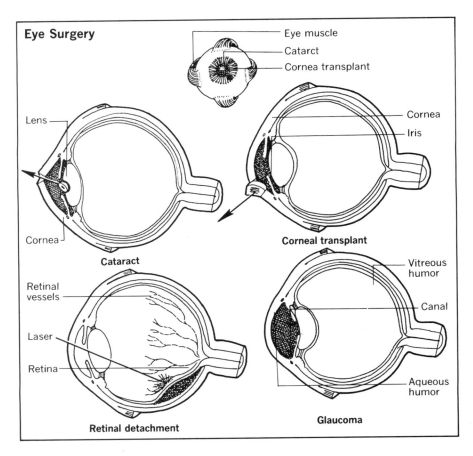

Eye Surgery

Eye muscle
Catarct
Cornea transplant

Lens

Cornea

Cataract

Cornea
Iris

Corneal transplant

Retinal vessels

Laser

Retina

Retinal detachment

Vitreous humor

Canal

Aqueous humor

Glaucoma

Detached Retina

Among the most serious eye disorders is the condition known as *separated* or *detached retina*. It occurs when fluid from inside the eye gets under the retina (the inner membrane at the back of the eye, on which the image is focused) and separates it from its bed, thus breaking the connections that are essential for normal vision. The most common cause of the detachment is the formation of a hole or tear in the retina. However, the condition may also develop following a blow to the head or to the eye, or because of a tumor, nephritis, or high blood pressure.

The symptoms of the onset of retinal separation are showers of drifting black spots and frequent flashes of light shaped like pinwheels that interfere with vision. These disturbances are usually followed by a dark shadow in the area of sight closest to the nose.

A retinal detachment is treated by surgical techniques in which the accumulated fluid is drained off and the hole in the tissue is sealed. About 60 percent of all cases are cured or considerably improved after surgery. The earlier the diagnosis, the more favorable is the outcome. Proper postoperative care usually involves several weeks of immobilization of the head so that the retinal tissue can heal without disturbance.

Trauma

Like any other part of the body, the eye can be injured by a major accident or *trauma*, although it is somewhat protected by the bones surrounding it. Trauma can cause most of the problems previously described. In addition, small objects can get into the eye easily, and particles of soot and other wind-borne dirt can cause great discomfort. The tearing that results

from the irritation usually floats foreign substances away, but occasionally they have to be removed by an instrument.

When a particle in the eye or under the eyelid is not easily dislodged and begins to cause redness, it should be removed by someone qualified to do so. The eye should never be poked at or into by untrained hands.

Leaving contact lenses in the eye for too long can cause discomfort that lasts for quite a while even after they have been taken out. Bacterial or viral infections of the outer surface of the eye such as *conjunctivitis* or *pinkeye*, or of the eyelids, are quite common and should be treated by a physician if they are extensive or chronic.

Contact Lenses

Contact lenses, which are fitted directly over the iris and pupil of the eye in contact with the cornea (the tissue covering the outer, visible surface of the eye), are preferred by some people for the correction of vision defects. In some cases of severe astigmatism or nearsightedness, or following cataract surgery, contact lenses can be more effective and comfortable than eyeglasses. But the chief reason for their popularity has been cosmetic. They are practically invisible.

Hard contact lenses adhere to the eye by suction; a partial vacuum is created between the inner surface of the lens and the outer surface of the eyeball.

Soft plastic contact lenses are *hydrophilic* (literally, water-loving) and adapt their shape to the shape of the moist cornea, to which they adhere. Thus they are relatively easily fitted, and patients seldom experience discomfort in adjusting to them. It is virtually impossible for dust particles to get under them. Many ophthalmologists, however, advise that the soft lens be sterilized daily.

The soft lens has proved valuable in the treatment of some eye disorders. But it often leads to problems among wearers. It may scratch or tear, for example, and generally it has

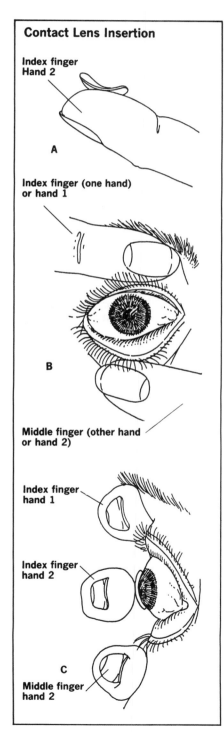

Contact Lens Insertion

Index finger
Hand 2

A

Index finger (one hand)
or hand 1

B

Middle finger (other hand
or hand 2)

Index finger
hand 1

Index finger
hand 2

C

Middle finger
hand 2

been limited to the correction of certain kinds of nearsightedness and farsightedness.

Extended wear lenses (EWLs) were introduced in the 1970s. Made of soft plastic like the older lenses, but thinner and more porous, they could be worn as long as 30 days. But wearing EWLs too long was found to cause such problems as scarring of the cornea; neurovascularization, the growth of tiny blood vessels that can cloud the vision and in extreme cases threaten the wearer's sight; the development of microcysts during sleep; and bacterial infections of the eye or eyelid, such as *Acanthamoeba keratitis.*

Disposable lenses and cosmetic contacts appeared in the late 1980s. Worn for a week and then discarded, disposable lenses reduce the danger of keratitis and other infections. But they cost about 50 percent more than the regular EWLs. Cosmetic contacts simply change the color of the eyes. Disposables should not be worn longer than prescribed, and cosmetic lenses should not be shared to prevent the spread of eye diseases and other infections. Clean the lenses according to instructions and seek medical help quickly if problems arise.

Diseases That Affect Vision

In addition to the various disorders involving only the eye, there are a number of generalized diseases that affect vision. Among these are arteriosclerosis, diabetes mellitus, and hypertension or high blood pressure, which often cause abnormalities in the blood vessels of various parts of the eye. These abnormalities can lead to tissue changes that cause the patient to see spots or to notice that his vision is defective.

Diseases of the brain, such as mul-

tiple sclerosis, tumors, and abscesses, although rare, can result in double vision or loss of lateral or central vision. Any sudden or gradual changes in vision should be brought to a physician's attention promptly, since early diagnosis and treatment is usually effective and can prevent serious deterioration.

The Ears

The ear, like the eye, is a complicated structure. Its major parts consist of the auditory canal, middle ear, and inner ear. Hearing results from the perception of sound waves whose loudness can be measured in decibels and whose highness or lowness of pitch can be measured by their frequency in cycles per second.

Sound waves usually travel through the auditory canal to the eardrum or *tympanic membrane,* vibrating it in such a way as to carry the vibrations to and along the three interlocking small bones in the middle ear to the inner ear. Here the vibrations are carried to the auditory nerve through a fluid-filled labyrinth called the communicating channel.

An abnormality at any of these points can produce a hearing deficiency. Normal hearing means the ability to hear the spoken voice in a relatively quiet room at a distance of about 18 feet. How well a person hears can be tested by an audiometer, which measures decibels and frequency of sound.

Wax Accumulation

A very common cause of hearing deficiency is the excessive accumulation of wax in the auditory canal, where it is continually being secreted. When the excess that blocks the passage of sound waves is removed—sometimes by professional instrumenta-

Ear

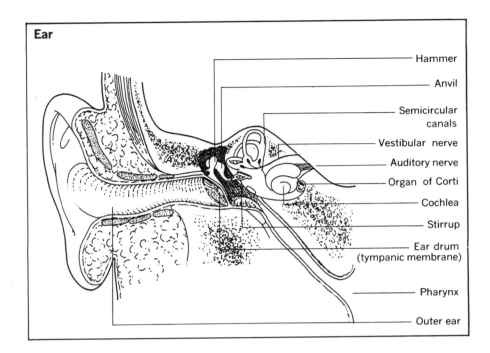

- Hammer
- Anvil
- Semicircular canals
- Vestibular nerve
- Auditory nerve
- Organ of Corti
- Cochlea
- Stirrup
- Ear drum (tympanic membrane)
- Pharynx
- Outer ear

tion—hearing returns to normal. Anyone whose hearing is temporarily impaired in this way should avoid the use of rigid or pointed objects for cleaning out the accumulated wax.

Infection

Infections or other diseases of the skin that lines the auditory canal can sometimes cause a kind of local swelling that blocks the canal and interferes with hearing. Although such a condition can be painful, proper treatment, usually with antibiotics, generally results in a complete cure.

A major cause of hearing deficiency acquired after birth is recurrent bacterial infection of the middle ear. The infecting organisms commonly get to the middle ear through the *Eustachian tube,* which connects the middle ear to the upper throat, or through the eardrum if it has been perforated by injury or by previous infection.

The infection can cause hearing loss, either because it becomes chronic or because the tissues become scarred. Such infections are usually painful, but ever since treatment with antibiotics has become pos-

sible, they rarely spread to the mastoid bone as they used to in the past.

Disorders Caused by Pressure

The Eustachian tube usually permits the air pressure on either side of the eardrum to equalize. When the pressure inside the drum is less than that outside—as occurs during descent in an airplane or elevator, or when riding through an underwater tunnel, or during skin diving—the eardrum is pushed inward. This causes a noticeable hearing loss or a stuffy feeling in the ear that subsides as soon as the pressure equalizes again. Yawning or swallowing usually speeds up the return to normal.

When the unequal pressure continues for several days because the Eustachian tube is blocked, fluid begins to collect in the middle ear. This is called *serous* (or *nonsuppurative*) *otitis media* and can cause permanent hearing damage.

Eustachian tube blockage is more commonly the result of swelling around its *nasopharyngeal* end because of a throat infection, a cold, or an allergy. Nose drops help to open

up the tube, but sometimes it may be necessary to drain the ear through the eardrum or treat the disorder with other surgical procedures.

Otosclerosis

A very common cause of hearing loss that affects about 1 in 200 adults— usually women—is *otosclerosis.* This disorder is the result of a sort of freezing of the bones in the middle ear caused by an overgrowth of tissue. The onset of the disorder usually occurs before age 30 among about 70 percent of the people who will be affected. Only one ear may be involved, but the condition does get progressively worse. Although heredity is an important factor, the specific cause of otosclerosis is unknown. In some cases, surgery can be helpful.

Injury

A blow to the head, or a loud noise close to the ear such as the sound of a gunshot or a jet engine, especially when repeated often, can cause temporary and sometimes permanent hearing defects. Anyone who expects to be exposed to damaging noise should wear protective earmuffs. Injury to the auditory nerve by chemicals or by medicines such as streptomycin can also cause loss of hearing.

Ringing in the Ears

Sometimes people complain of hearing noises unrelated to the reception of sound waves from an outside source. This phenomenon is called *tinnitus* and occurs in the form of a buzzing, ringing, or hissing sound.

It may be caused by some of the conditions described above and may be relieved by proper treatment. In many cases, however, the cause is unknown and the patient simply has to learn to live with the sounds and ignore them.

Impairment of Balance

The *labyrinths* of the inner ear are involved not only in hearing but also in controlling postural balance. When the labyrinths are diseased, the result can be a feeling of *vertigo* or true dizziness. This sensation of being unable to maintain balance is quite different from feeling lightheaded or giddy.

Vertigo can be an incapacitating disorder. Sometimes it is caused by diseases of the central nervous system such as epilepsy or brain hemorrhage, but more often by inflammation sometimes caused by infection of the labyrinth. It can be sudden and recurrent as in *Ménière's disease,* or somewhat gradual and nonrecurrent. It may or may not be accompanied by

vomiting or hearing loss. Treatment for the condition varies depending on the cause.

Deafness

Deafness at birth or in a very young baby is an especially difficult problem because hearing is necessary for the development of speech. Although the deafness itself may be impossible to correct, its early recognition and management can usually prevent muteness from developing.

Many communities now have special schools for deaf children, and new techniques and machines are constantly being devised for helping them to learn how to speak, even if imperfectly. Any doubt about an infant's ability to hear should therefore be brought to a physician's attention immediately.

Deafness at birth can be caused by a maternal infection such as rubella (German measles) during pregnancy. Because children are often the ones who spread this disease, youngsters should be immunized against it.

Hearing Aids

Hearing loss that cannot be treated medically or surgically can often be compensated for by an accurately fitted hearing aid. This device, which now comes in many sizes, shapes, and types, converts sound waves into electrical impulses, amplifies them, and reconverts them into sound waves. A hearing aid can be placed in the auditory canal for air conduction of sound waves, or it can be worn behind the ear for bone conduction. See under "Hearing Loss" in Ch. 6, *The Later Years,* for further information about hearing aids.

17

Diseases of the Urinogenital System

The parts of the urinogenital tract that produce and get rid of urine are the same for men and women: the kidneys, ureters, bladder, and urethra. To understand some of the problems that can arise from diseases of the urinary tract, it is necessary to know a few facts about the anatomy and function of these parts.

The two kidneys are located on either side of the spinal column in the back portion of the abdomen between the last rib and the third lumbar vertebra of the spine. They are shaped like the beans named after them but are considerably larger.

Their function is to filter and cleanse the blood of waste substances produced in the course of normal living and, together with some other organs, to maintain a proper balance of body fluids. The kidneys do this job by filtering the fluid portion of the blood as it passes through them, returning the necessary solids and water to the bloodstream, and removing waste products and excess water, called *urine*. These products then flow into the *ureters,* the ducts that connect the kidneys and bladder.

The *bladder* holds the urine until voiding occurs. The duct from the bladder to the urinary opening is called the *urethra*. In the male, it passes through the penis; in the female, in front of the anterior wall of the vagina.

Symptoms of Kidney Disorders

Normal kidney function can be disrupted by bacterial or viral infection, by tumors, by external injury, or by congenital defects. Some of the common symptoms that may result under these circumstances are:

- *Anuria:* inability to produce or void urine

- *Dysuria:* pain, often of a burning quality, during urination

- Frequency: abnormally frequent urination, often of unusually small amounts

- Hesitancy: difficulty in starting urination

- Urgency: a very strong urge to urinate, often strong enough to cause loss of urine

- *Oliguria:* reduced production of urine

- *Polyuria:* voiding larger than normal amounts of urine

- *Nocturia:* frequent voiding at night

- *Hematuria:* voiding blood in the urine

Because any of these symptoms may indicate a disease of the urinary tract, their appearance should be brought to the attention of a physician without delay.

Kidney Failure

Kidney failure can occur gradually—either from kidney disease or as a secondary condition resulting from another disease—or suddenly, as from an infection.

Acute Kidney Failure

The sudden loss of kidney function over a period of minutes to several days is known as acute kidney failure. It may be caused by impairment of blood supply to the kidneys, by severe infection, by nephritis (discussed below), by poisons, and by various other conditions that injure both kidneys.

Urogenital Systems

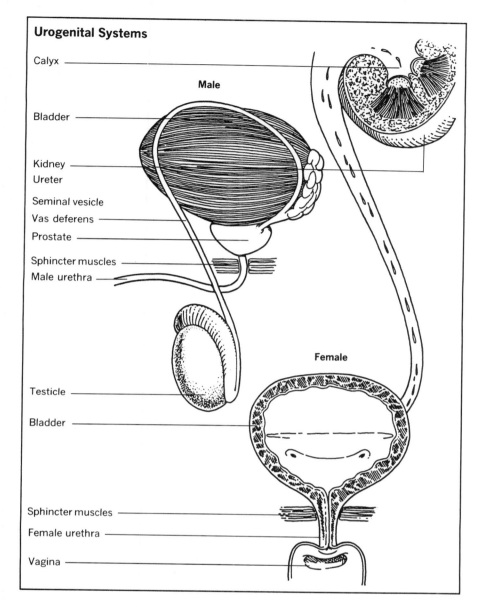

Calyx

Male

Bladder

Kidney

Ureter

Seminal vesicle

Vas deferens

Prostate

Sphincter muscles

Male urethra

Female

Testicle

Bladder

Sphincter muscles

Female urethra

Vagina

The body can function adequately throughout a normal lifespan with only one healthy kidney, but if both are impaired sufficiently over a short period of time, there will be symptoms of acute kidney failure: production of a decreased amount of urine (*oliguria*) sometimes with blood in it; fluid retention in body tissues, a condition known as *edema;* increasing fatigue and weakness; nausea and loss of appetite.

If damage to the kidneys has not been too severe, the patient begins to have a *diuresis,* or greater than normal urine output. When this hap-

pens—usually after one or two weeks of reduced urine output—he is kept on a restricted diet and reduced fluid intake after recovery until normal kidney function returns.

Causes

Heredity is rarely a factor in acute kidney failure, although people born with one kidney or with congenital defects of the urinary tract may lack the normal reserve capacity to prevent it. It is also unusual for external injury to result in a loss of function in both kidneys. However, severe internal

shock accompanied by a reduction of blood flow to the kidneys can cause acute kidney failure.

Prevention and Treatment

Acute kidney failure can occur at any age. Prevention hinges on the proper control of its many causes. About 50 percent of patients with this disease may succumb to it; in cases of severe kidney failure involving widespread destruction of tissue, mortality may be almost 100 percent.

When acute kidney failure occurs as a complication of another serious illness, its prevention and treatment are usually managed by physicians in a hospital. If the patient is not already under a physician's supervision when he has the characteristic symptoms, he should immediately be brought to a medical facility for diagnosis and treatment.

Chronic Kidney Failure and Uremia

Many progressive kidney diseases can eventually lead to a group of symptoms called *uremia.* Other diseases, such as severe high blood pressure, diabetes, and those leading to widespread damage of kidney tissue, can also cause uremia.

In this condition, as in acute kidney failure, waste products and excess fluid accumulate in the body and cause the symptoms of chronic kidney failure. Certain congenital defects in the urinogenital system such as *polycystic kidney disease,* in which cysts in the kidneys enlarge slowly and destroy normal kidney tissue, may lead to uremia. Hereditary diseases such as hereditary nephritis may cause chronic kidney failure, but this is uncommon. Injury is also rarely the cause of uremia.

Although kidney failure is more likely to occur in older people because of the decreased capacity of the body to respond to stress, uremia can occur in any age group if kidney damage is severe enough. The onset of uremia may be so gradual that it goes unnoticed until the patient is weak and seems chronically ill. Voiding unusually large amounts of urine and voiding during the night are early symptoms.

Sleepiness and increasing fatigue set in as the kidney failure progresses, and there is a loss of appetite accompanied sometimes by nausea and hiccups. As the disease gets more serious, increasing weakness, anemia, muscle twitching, and sometimes internal bleeding may occur. High blood pressure is another characteristic symptom. Because of fluid retention, there will often be marked signs of facial puffiness and swelling of the legs.

Kidney damage that leads to chronic kidney failure is irreversible and the outlook for the victim of uremia is poor. The technique of dialysis (discussed below) has, however, prolonged many lives and continues to be a life-saving procedure for many.

Dialysis

An effective method of treatment of kidney failure developed in the 1960s is based on an artificial kidney that cleanses the patient's blood if his own kidneys are not functioning properly. The procedure, known as *dialysis* (or *hemodialysis*), removes dangerous waste products and excess fluids from the patient's bloodstream. It is the accumulation of waste products and fluids that probably causes the symptoms of acute kidney failure and that can be fatal if not reversed in one way or another.

Dialysis for Chronic Kidney Failure

For patients suffering chronic kidney failure or uremia, dialysis is a life-preserving but unfortunately expensive

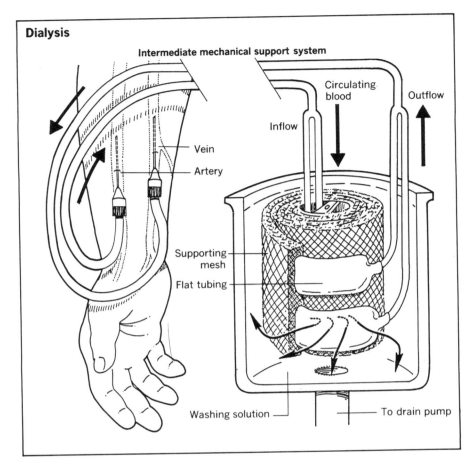

Dialysis

Intermediate mechanical support system

Circulating blood

Inflow

Outflow

Vein

Artery

Supporting mesh

Flat tubing

Washing solution

To drain pump

procedure. The patient must be dialyzed with the artificial kidney unit two or three times a week, usually for six to eight hours at a time. Although the technique does not cure uremia, it can keep the patient comfortable provided that his diet is carefully restricted and supervised.

Dialysis in the Home

One approach that promises to be helpful in reducing the excessive cost is the development of home dialysis programs prepared with the cooperation of hospitals having departments specializing in kidney disease. Home dialysis is not suitable for everyone; the patient must be mature and stable enough to be relied on to undertake the procedure on schedule and in the prescribed manner. The overall costs of home dialysis, however, are about one-third those of in-hospital dialysis.

Medicare Coverage

Medicare coverage is now available for a part of the costs for dialysis maintenance for those suffering from permanent kidney failure, even if they are under 65 years of age. Coverage includes training in self-dialysis and the cost of dialysis equipment and applies to dialysis done in the home as well as in hospitals or other approved facilities. For details of this coverage, see your local social security office or write for the free booklet, *Medicare Coverage for Kidney Dialysis and Kidney Transplant Services,* published by the Social Security Administration.

Kidney Transplant Surgery

Some people suffering from kidney disease may benefit greatly from the surgical transplant of a donor's kidney. The donor kidney may be taken from a live relative or from someone recently deceased. The organ is removed from the donor's abdomen, usually flushed with a salt solution, and then reattached to a large artery and vein in the recipient's abdomen and to his ureter.

The successfully transplanted kidney functions just as the patient's own did when he was healthy, removing wastes and excess fluids from his bloodstream and excreting the resulting urine through the bladder. The recipient of a kidney transplant must take special medication to prevent the rejection of the newly installed organ by his own body tissues. With proper medical care, recipients have lived for many years with their transplanted organs.

Medicare Coverage

Medicare coverage is now available for a part of the costs of kidney transplant surgery for those under 65 as well as those over 65. This coverage includes hospital charges for costs incurred by the donor. For details of this coverage, see your local social security office or write for the free booklet, *Medicare Coverage of Kidney Dialysis and Kidney Transplant Services,* published by the Social Security Administration.

Nephritis

Nephritis is a disorder characterized by inflammation of the *glomeruli* of the kidneys. The glomeruli are tiny coiled blood vessels through which the liquid portion of the blood is filtered as it enters the outer structure of the kidneys. There are about one million of these tiny blood vessels in each kidney. The fluid from the blood passes from them into many little ducts called *tubules.* Water and various substances are secreted into and absorbed from the liquid in the tubules. The final product of this passage of filtered fluid from the glomeruli through the tubules to the ureters and then to the bladder is urine. It contains the excess fluid and waste products produced by the body during normal functioning.

When the glomeruli become inflamed, the resulting disease is called *glomerulonephritis.* There are several forms of this disease. One type is thought to be caused by the body's allergic reaction to infection by certain streptococcal bacteria. Another type sometimes accompanies infection of the valves of the heart. The relationship between glomerulonephritis and strep infections is not fully understood at present, and the same may be said for nephritis, which is associated with allergic reaction to certain drugs and to heart valve infections.

Glomerulonephritis may occur ten days to two weeks after a severe strep throat infection. For this reason, any severe sore throat accompanied by a high fever should be seen and diagnosed by a physician. Prompt treatment with antibiotics may decrease the possibility of kidney involvement.

Nephritis Symptoms

The inflammation and swelling of the glomeruli cause a decrease in the amount of blood that the kidney is able to filter. As a result of the slowing down of this kidney function, the waste products of metabolism as well as excess fluid accumulate in the body instead of being eliminated at the normal rate.

In a typical case, a person will develop a severe sore throat with fever and a general feeling of sickness. These symptoms will disappear, but after one or two weeks, there will be a return of weakness and loss of appetite. The eyes and the face may become puffy, the legs may swell, and there may be shortness of breath—all because of the retention of excess fluid in the body. The amount of urine is small and the color is dark brown, somewhat like coffee. Abdominal pain, nausea, and vomiting may occur, always accompanied by fatigue. In most cases, the blood pressure increases, leading to headaches.

Although there is a hereditary type of nephritis, the more common types of the disease have other causes. When the disease is suspected, the physician examines a specimen of urine under a microscope and looks for red blood cells. These cells, which usually do not pass through the walls of the normal glomerulus in large numbers, do pass through the damaged walls of the inflamed blood vessels characteristic of nephritis. Evidence of decreased kidney function is also found by special blood tests.

Nephritis occurs in all age groups. Children under ten have an excellent chance of recovery, about 98 percent. In adults, from 20 to 50 percent of the cases may be fatal or may progress to chronic nephritis, which often leads to uremia and death.

Treatment

It is absolutely essential for anyone with a streptococcal infection, which may lead to acute glomerulonephritis, to receive prompt and proper treatment. Penicillin is considered the most effective antibiotic at present.

Once acute nephritis is present, the treatment consists of bed rest, some fluid restriction, and protein restriction if kidney failure occurs. If there is a total loss of kidney function, a specially restricted diet is prescribed. Complete lack of urine output—*anuria*— may last as long as ten days, but the patient can still make a full recovery if the treatment is right. Usually a gradual return of kidney function occurs over a period of several months.

Nephrosis

The *nephrotic syndrome*, commonly referred to as *nephrosis*, is a disease in which abnormal amounts of protein in the form of *albumin* are lost in the urine. Albumin consists of microscopic particles of protein present in the blood. These particles are important in maintaining the proper volume of fluids in the body, and they have other complicated functions as well. The loss of albumin in the urine affects the amount that remains in the blood, and it is this imbalance, together with other body changes, that results in the retention of excess fluid in the tissues, thus causing facial puffiness and swelling of the legs.

The disease is caused by damage to the glomeruli, but at the present time the exact nature of the damage is uncertain. It may be caused by an allergic reaction, by inflammation, or it may be a complication of diabetes. The nephrotic syndrome may also appear because of blood clots in the veins that drain the kidneys.

Although the disease is more common among children than among adults, it may affect a person of any age. The main symptom is painless swelling of the face, legs, and sometimes of the entire body. There is also loss of appetite, a tired, rundown feeling, and sometimes abdominal pain, vomiting, and diarrhea.

Recovery from nephrosis varies with age. More than 50 percent of child patients are completely free of kidney ailments after the first attack. Adults are more likely to develop some impairment of kidney function, or the disease may become chronic, with accompanying high blood pressure. In some people, protein loss may continue over the years, al-though the kidneys function in an apparently normal manner without any visible symptoms.

Treatment

Treatment of the nephrotic syndrome has been greatly helped by the use of the adrenal hormones known as *steroids*. The treatment is effective for about two-thirds of child patients and for about one-fourth to one-third of adults. Some patients may relapse after therapy is completed, sometimes years after such therapy has been discontinued. For this reason, steroids are sometimes continued after initial treatment but in reduced dosage, to avoid some of the unpleasant side effects such as acne and facial swelling.

Unlike the dietary treatment for uremia, a high protein diet is used with nephrotic patients so that the protein loss can be replaced. Salt intake is usually restricted because salt contributes to fluid retention and may cause high blood pressure or heart failure. If fluid retention doesn't respond to steroid treatment, other medicines called *diuretics*, which increase urinary output, are used.

Anyone with unusual swelling of the face, limbs, or abdomen should see a physician promptly. Even though the swelling is painless, it may be the first sign of the onset of a serious kidney problem.

Infection in the Urinary Tract

Infection in the urinary tract is a common disorder that can be serious if the kidneys themselves are involved.

Cystitis

Infection of the bladder is called *cystitis*. The symptoms include a burning sensation when urine is passed, the frequent need to urinate, occasionally blood in the urine, and sometimes difficulty in starting to urinate. Cystitis is rarely accompanied by high fever.

The problem may be recurrent and is more usual with women than men, probably because the female urethra is shorter and closer to the rectum, permitting bacteria to enter the bladder more easily. These bacteria multiply in the urine contained in the bladder, causing irritation to the bladder walls and producing the symptoms described above.

Cystitis should be treated promptly because the infection in the bladder can easily spread to the kidneys, with serious consequences. Treatment usually consists of antibiotics after urine analysis and culture have determined the type of bacteria causing the infection. Cystitis and other kidney infections are especially common during pregnancy because of the body changes that occur at this time. At no time is cystitis itself a serious disease, but it must be diagnosed and treated promptly to avoid complications.

Other Causes of Infection

Infection of the bladder and kidneys may occur because of poor hygiene in the area of the urethra, especially in women. It is also caused by some congenital defects in the urinary tract or by the insertion of instruments used to diagnose a urinary problem.

Sometimes bacteria in the bloodstream can settle in and infect the kidneys. Patients with diabetes seem to be more prone to urinary infections—indeed to infections generally—than other people. Any obstruction to the flow of urine in the urinary tract, such as a kidney stone, increases the possibility of infection in the area behind the obstruction. Damage to the nerves controlling the bladder is another condition that increases the chances of infection in that area.

Pyelonephritis

Infection in the kidneys is called *pyelonephritis*. Although it sometimes occurs without any symptoms, a first attack usually causes an aching pain in the lower back, probably due to the swelling of the kidneys, as well as nausea, vomiting, diarrhea, and sometimes severe pain in the front of the abdomen on one or both sides, depending on whether one or both kidneys are involved. Fever may be quite high, ranging from 103° F to 105° F, often accompanied by chills.

Although the symptoms of pyelonephritis may disappear in a few days without treatment, bacterial destruction of the kidney tissue may be going on. This silent type of infection may eventually disrupt normal kidney function and result in a chronic form of the disease, which in turn can lead to uremia. If the disease is not halted before this, it can be fatal.

Anyone with symptoms of acute pyelonephritis must have prompt medical attention. To diagnose the disease properly, the urine is analyzed and the number and type of bacteria in the urine are determined. The disease is brought under control by the right antibiotics and by administering large amounts of fluids to flush out the kidneys and urinary tract, thus decreasing the number of bacteria in the urine. In its chronic form the disease is much more difficult to cure because bacteria that are lodged deep in the kidney tissue do not seem to be susceptible to antibiotics and are therefore almost impossible to get rid of.

Kidney Stones

Another cause of infection in the bladder and kidneys is obstruction in the urinary tract by *kidney stones*. These stones, crystallizations of salts that form in the kidney tissue, may be quite small, but they can grow large enough to occupy a considerable part of one or both of the kidneys. The smaller ones often pass from the kidney through the ureters to the bladder, from which they are voided through the urethra. However, obstruction of the flow of urine behind a kidney stone anywhere in the urinary tract usually leads to infection in the urine. This type of infection may lead to attacks of acute pyelonephritis.

Removal of Stones

Kidney stones must be removed unless they cause no symptoms of infection. Removal may be accomplished by flushing out the urinary tract with large fluid intake, by surgical methods, or by lithotripsy, a method of dissolving the stones with electrical shock waves so that the fragments can be flushed out of the body. Any accompanying infection may be treated with antibiotics. A drug, *potassium citrate,* may also be used to keep kidney stones from forming. See "Urinary Stones" in Ch. 20, *Surgery.*

Why kidney stones form in some people and not in others is not clearly understood. Because of metabolic disorders, certain substances may build up in the body. The increased excretion of these substances in the urine as well as excessive amounts of calcium in the blood may encourage kidney stone formation. People who have gout are also likely to develop them.

Renal Colic

Sometimes the formation and passage of stones cause no symptoms. However, when symptoms do occur with the passage of a kidney stone, they can be uncomfortably severe. The pain that results from the passage of a stone through the ureter, referred

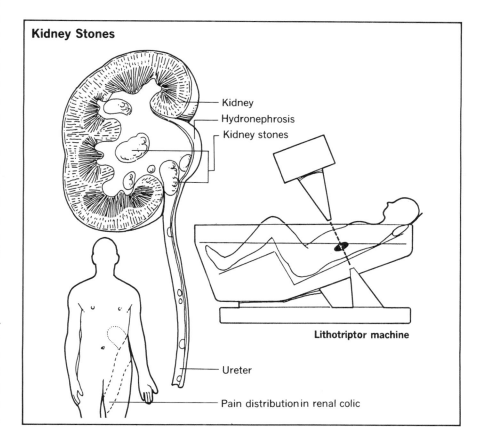

Kidney Stones

Kidney
Hydronephrosis
Kidney stones

Lithotriptor machine

Ureter

Pain distribution in renal colic

to as *renal colic,* is usually like an intense cramp. It begins in the side or back and moves toward the lower abdomen, the genital region, and the inner thigh on the affected side. The attack may last for a few minutes or for several hours. Sometimes bloody urine may be passed accompanied by a burning sensation.

Kidney stones are more likely to form in middle-aged and older people than in young ones. A history of stones is sometimes found in several generations of a family, since the metabolic disorders encouraging their formation have a hereditary basis.

Treatment for an acute attack of renal colic usually relieves the pain several hours after the patient has taken medication and fluids. If they are not promptly treated, kidney stones may lead to serious infection and eventual impairment of function.

Tumors of the Urinary Tract

Benign and malignant tumors of the kidney are not common problems. However, anyone with pain in the midback, blood in the urine, or a mass in the abdomen should have the symptoms diagnosed. If a malignant tumor is discovered early enough, it can be removed with the affected kidney, and normal function can be maintained by the healthy kidney that remains.

Malignant kidney tumors are most often found in children or adults over 40, and more often in men than in women. A tumor of any type can usually be diagnosed by X-ray studies. Where this technique is inadequate, an operation is necessary to search for the suspected growth. About one-fourth of all patients with a malignant kidney tumor live for more than ten years after surgery.

A malignant tumor of the bladder is a serious problem because it obstructs kidney drainage and may

cause death from uremia. The main symptom is the painless appearance of blood in the urine, although sometimes a burning sensation and a frequent need to urinate are also present. Treatment usually includes surgical removal of the bladder followed by radiation treatment of the affected area to destroy any malignant cells that remain after the operation.

Some malignant bladder tumors grow very slowly and do not invade the bladder wall extensively. Surgical treatment for this type, called *papillary tumors,* is likely to be more successful than for tumors of the more invasive kind.

The Prostate Gland

The *prostate gland,* which contributes to the production of semen, encircles the base of the male urethra where it joins the bladder. When it begins to enlarge, it compresses the urethra and causes difficulty in voiding. Urination may be difficult to start, and when the urine stream appears it may be thinner than normal.

Because urine may remain in the bladder, there is the possibility of local infection that may spread to the kid-

neys. If the kidneys become enlarged because of this type of obstruction, a condition of *hydronephrosis* is said to exist. This disease can cause impaired kidney function and lead to uremia.

Benign Prostatic Enlargement

Enlargement of the prostate gland occurs in about half the male population over 50, and the incidence increases with increasing age. The condition is called *benign prostatic enlargement* and must be treated surgically if sufficient obstruction is present. For temporary relief, a catheter can be inserted into the bladder through the urethra, allowing the urine to drain through the catheter and out of the body. If surgery is necessary, the entire prostate may be removed or only that part of it that surrounds the urethra.

Symptoms of benign prostatic enlargement are quite distinctive: increased difficulty in voiding; an urge to continue to urinate after voiding has been completed; burning and frequent urination, caused in part by infection from urine retained in the bladder.

The cause of benign prostatic en-

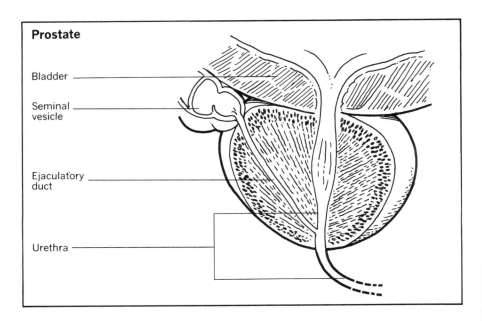

Prostate

Bladder

Seminal
vesicle

Ejaculatory
duct

Urethra

largement is thought to be a change during the aging process in the hormones that affect prostate tissue, but the exact nature of the change and its effect is not clear. It is likely that hormone-containing medicines will eventually be developed that will prevent or reverse prostate tissue growth.

Acute Prostatitis

Acute prostatitis occurs typically in young men. Symptoms include pain on urinating, sometimes a discharge of pus from the penis, pain in the lower back or abdomen indicating a tender and enlarged prostate, and fever. It is caused by a bacterial infection and usually responds promptly to antibiotics.

Cancer of the Prostate

Cancer of the prostate is a common type of malignancy in older men. It accounts for about 10 percent of male deaths from cancer in the United States. The disease may be present without any symptoms or interference with normal function and is therefore difficult to diagnose. A very high proportion of men over 80—probably more than 50 percent—has been found to have had cancer of the prostate at autopsy.

When symptoms are present, they are likely to be the same as those of benign prostatic enlargement. The disease can be diagnosed only by a biopsy examination of a tissue sample taken from the prostate during surgery. If malignancy is found, the gland is surgically removed when feasible to do so; the testes are removed too so that the level of male hormones in the body is lowered.

Male hormones increase the growth of malignant prostate tissue, but because female hormones slow it down, they may be administered after a diagnosis of prostate malignancy. If

the tumor has spread to bone tissue, radiation treatment of the affected areas may slow down cancerous growth and relieve pain.

Men over 40 should have a rectal examination once a year, since tumors of the prostate and benign prostatic enlargement can often be diagnosed early in this way.

Urinary Incontinence

Urinary incontinence, or the involuntary release of urine, is a highly treatable disorder of the urinogenital system. Controlled urination is a complex, synchronized process coordinated by the central nervous system involving the kidneys, the bladder, the urethra and the muscles of the pelvic floor and abdominal wall. Urine from the kidneys flows into the bladder, where it is stored until nerves in the spinal cord indicate that it is full. When this occurs, the muscles of the bladder contract in a reflex action and squeeze the urine into the urethra. In toilet training, the brain learns to control this reflex action by tightening the muscles of the pelvic wall and refusing release until an appropriate time. Disruption of nearly any part of this system can cause incontinence. Neurological problems affecting the central nervous system, infections of the genital or urinary systems, and anatomical abnormalities all can cause urinary incontinence in adults. Sometimes, though, no known cause can be discovered.

Contrary to popular myth, urinary incontinence is not the inevitable consequence of aging and is almost always treatable. A wide range of techniques including behavior modification, medication and surgery can improve or cure most cases.

Behavioral techniques, being the easiest and safest to administer, are usually tried first. These techniques involve bladder training and exercise

of the pelvic muscles and bladder sphincter. Done at home, exercises such as Kegel exercises require a certain amount of practice and commitment, as it often takes several months to strengthen the relevant muscles. Medications are also available which relax the bladder or contract the muscles of the sphincter and pelvic wall. These medications can have undesirable side effects. Finally, surgery can tighten the pelvic muscles or create a vaginal "hammock" or support for the urethra to prevent it from prematurely releasing urine. A doctor should be consulted for a complete diagnosis and individualized treatment program.

Sexually Transmitted Diseases

The name of Venus, the Roman goddess of love, is preserved in the term *venereal disease* because they are transmitted by sexual contact. But today the broader phrase *sexually transmitted disease* (STD) is more commonly used to refer to both venereal and other diseases that may be passed from one person to another during sexual activity. STDs include some diseases, among them *acquired immunodeficiency syndrome,* or AIDS (see "AIDS" in Ch. 19, *Other Diseases of Major Importance*), that had not been identified as separate disorders until the 1970s or 1980s.

Sexually transmitted diseases were spreading at epidemic rates by the middle 1980s. Because all are contagious by definition, and can often cause serious complications, the symptoms should be treated without delay. At least two of the STDs, AIDS and genital herpes, or herpes simplex type II, are incurable. Some drugs and medications can, however, ameliorate specific symptoms of both diseases.

Except for pelvic inflammatory disease (PID), a serious complication among women, STDs afflict both men and women. Of the 11 most common STDs, chlamydia is the most prevalent. Public health officials believe the disease has spread because it has no obvious symptoms and victims can live for years without realizing they have it.

AIDS

While neither a disease of the urinogenital system nor an STD, strictly speaking, acquired immunodeficiency syndrome (AIDS) ranks as one of the most feared diseases today. Because the disease may be transmitted by intravenous needles that are shared by drug abusers as well as through sexual contact and contaminated blood it cannot strictly be called an STD. The disease strips the body of its acquired immunity against infection and leaves its victims susceptible to a variety of opportunistic infections. These include a rare form of pneumonia and Karposi's sarcoma, a rare type of cancer. AIDS is uniformly fatal.

A virus called the *human immunodeficiency virus* (HIV) is thought to be the cause of AIDS. Researchers speculate, however, that more than one virus may be the causative agent in AIDS. Exposure to the disease does not mean inevitably that a person will contract AIDS. Perhaps no more than 10 to 20 percent of the individuals who have been exposed to HIV will develop full-blown cases of AIDS. Many will develop what has been termed ARC, AIDS-related complex, which is less often fatal and not considered by authorities to be AIDS per se.

Diagnosis

No simple means of diagnosing AIDS exists. Physicians can test for certain opportunistic infections. They also study symptoms as reported by individuals. Damage to white blood cells (specifically the T-cells), revealed by tests, may indicate the presence of the disease. The only test available now, commonly called the "AIDS test," can only test for the presence of antibodies. These antibodies are indicative of exposure to HIV and do not indicate the presence of the virus itself. Because the test was developed for blood donor screening its use by individuals concerned about possible exposure to HIV is not advocated by most health professionals. A positive test showing AIDS antibodies does not necessarily mean that the person will contract the disease, nor does a negative test mean the person has not become infected. The present blood screening test has a relatively high degree of unreliability and so should therefore not be relied upon as the sole indicator of exposure to AIDS.

The symptoms of AIDS range across a broad grouping of complaints that are common to various illnesses. Because these complaints are so common, diagnosis becomes even more difficult. The symptoms include night sweats, diarrhea, fatigue, weight loss of 10 or more pounds over a short period, swollen lymph nodes, fever, and loss of appetite. The symptoms may appear from six months to five years or more after infection.

Treatment

There is no treatment for AIDS as yet; therefore, physicians can only treat the specific symptoms that occur from the various opportunistic diseases that attack AIDS patients. Also, an antiserum has been found to keep the AIDS virus from invading human cells in laboratory tests. The antiserum, a blood substance, reacts with a thymus gland hormone called thymosin alpha 1. Researchers hope the antiserum will eventually lead to development of an AIDS vaccine. The development of such a vaccine, however, is thought to be some years away.

Chlamydia

Chlamydia is a bacterial infection that can cause sterility in men and women and has been called "the disease of the '80s." Most women with the disease have no obvious symptoms. For that reason, physicians suggest that sexually active women undergo tests for chlamydia at least once a year. The disease is spreading more rapidly than any other STD.

Persons at highest risk of contracting chlamydia are under 35 years of age. A bacterium, *Chlamydia trachomatis,* causes the disease, which is spread to adults during sexual contact and to babies of infected mothers during birth. Complications affect both sexes: both men and women may become infertile, and women may have pregnancy problems that could kill a fetus. In some cases the disease may be fatal for the mother. Babies infected during birth may develop infections of the eyes, ears, or lungs.

Diagnosis

A new diagnostic technique has led to hope that chlamydia can be brought under control. The technique, *antigen detection testing,* is a relatively simple and painless laboratory procedure.

Symptoms that indicate the possibility of chlamydia may or may not appear. Men may experience a discharge from the penis or a burning sensation while urinating. Women may have vaginal itching, bleeding between menstrual periods, and chronic abdominal pain. The symptoms may appear two to four weeks after infection.

Treatment

Even though chlamydia is spreading more rapidly than other STDs, it ranks among the lesser STD threats. Treatments involve drug therapies with tetracycline or doxycycline. Erythromycin has also been used successfully. The drugs usually take effect in about seven days. The partner of a person who is undergoing treatment for chlamydia should also be treated.

Gonorrhea

The second most common STD, *gonorrhea,* has afflicted mankind for centuries. Gonorrhea, caused by the bacteria gonococcus, lives in the mucous membranes of the body, including the vagina, rectum, throat, or hollow of the cheek. Cervical, penile, or rectal gonorrhea are contracted through intercourse; oral sex may lead to throat gonorrhea. Women may acquire gonorrhea in a single contact with an infected male; but men face only about a 20 to 40 percent risk of contracting the disease from a female.

Untreated, gonorrhea can lead to various complications. Women can suffer from pelvic inflammatory disease. In relatively unusual cases gonococci can enter the bloodstream and cause blood poisoning. The babies of infected mothers may be born blind. Gonococci settling in joints may cause arthritis. Very rarely the disease leads to *endocarditis,* an inflammation of the lining of the heart, or to *meningitis,* an inflammation that destroys the membrane surrounding the brain and spinal cord.

Except for PID, men experience most of the basic symptoms of untreated gonorrhea. Thus male problems can range from back pains to sterility.

Diagnosis

Anyone suspecting the presence of gonorrhea should arrange for a medical examination as quickly as possible. A test "just in case" may be advisable if, for example, a sex partner indicates that he or she has contracted the disease. Women are cautioned against douching before a visit to a physician or public health clinic; nor should self-treatment with antibiotics be attempted. In either case diagnosis may become more difficult.

Gonorrhea is more difficult to detect in women than in men. As many as four out of five women infected with cervical gonorrhea may not realize for days or weeks that they have the disease. When symptoms do appear, they include vaginal discharges and discomfort when urinating. These symptoms, appearing three to eleven days after exposure, may become steadily worse. Urinating may become extremely painful. With rectal gonorrhea, burning sensations, bleeding or mucous discharges may accompany defecation. Approximately nine of ten males know within a week to ten days that they have been infected. Male symptoms are, commonly, a puslike discharge from the penis and a burning sensation while urinating.

Treatment

Penicillin is the most effective treatment for gonorrhea. For persons allergic to penicillin, physicians usually prescribe tetracycline or erythromycin in oral doses. All three drugs are effective in most cases.

Researchers believe the possibility that they will find a vaccine for gonorrhea is strong. Experimental vaccines have been successfully tested on laboratory animals.

Genital Herpes

Genital herpes, or herpes simplex type II, is transmitted by physical—usually sexual—contact. The virus is one of the herpesviruses that also cause shingles, mononucleosis, or chicken pox. The disease is transmitted through skin-to-skin contact with herpes sores or the secretions of an infected person. The virus enters the body through the mucous membranes of the genitals, mouth, or anus.

The first attack of genital herpes usually occurs one to two weeks after exposure. Sores may appear; the afflicted person may have difficulty urinating or defecating. The symptoms usually disappear in ten days to three weeks, but for most herpes victims a recurrence can be expected within six months. Later attacks may be milder, but the disease is incurable and can be transmitted even when no symptoms are visible.

Stress and depression, authorities say, can trigger herpes attacks. Women suffering from the disease face increased risks of cervical cancer. They may also pass the virus to babies during delivery. So exposed, the babies may die within a few weeks; some newborns are deformed, blind, or mentally handicapped. Because of the danger that the herpesvirus poses to newborns, women with genital herpes should alert their obstetricians so that delivery can be by cesarian section. By avoiding vaginal mucous membranes, the infant will not be exposed to the virus.

Diagnosis

Physicians can usually diagnose herpes by visual examination while the characteristic sores are evident. A physician may also take a herpes culture from the base of the lesion.

Treatment

While no cure for genital herpes exists, the drug acyclovir has been found to reduce the severity of the flareups. Acyclovir is applied as a topical ointment, usually for initial outbreaks. In an oral form the drug alleviates subsequent attacks. The oral preparation has been reported to be effective in about seven cases out of ten.

Whether treated or not, later outbreaks of herpes are generally shorter and less severe than the first. Physicians agree that acyclovir effects improvement in the majority of cases, but some reserve judgment concerning the drug's long-term effects.

Trichomoniasis

A type of leukorrhea, *trichomoniasis* is caused by the *Trichomonas vaginalis,* an organism that causes an irritating itching condition in women. Men usually have no symptoms. The organism, a parasite, favors warm, moist areas, such as genital tissues; but some experts believe it can sometimes survive in damp cloths, douching syringes, towels, around toilet seats, on beaches, and around swimming pools. Thus the disease can, it is believed, be spread without sexual contact.

Complications can follow trichomoniasis. Women victims experience discomfort and pain. Chronic infection, according to some researchers, may make a woman more susceptible to cervical cancer. Constant irritation of the cervix is said to produce such susceptibility.

Diagnosis

The trichomoniasis leukorrhea consists of a yellow to green frothy discharge. The itching that accompanies the infection tends to begin or worsen immediately after a menstrual period. Some women report a burning sensation when they urinate. In diagnosis the physician uses a test similar to a Pap smear (see "Pap Smear" in Ch.

25, *Women's Health*), made with a specimen taken from the vagina. Under a microscope the trichomonas organisms are easy to identify because they are pear-shaped and have three to five whiplike tails.

Treatment

Several drugs are available for treating trichomoniasis. They include tablets taken orally and suppositories inserted in the vagina. Most commonly prescribed is metronidazole. Cures may be effected quickly. One dose of two grams (eight 250 mg tablets) may be adequate for both the victim and his or her partner. The oral medication may, however, be continued for weeks or months if the infection resists the drug.

Trichomoniasis victims have reported such side effects as nausea, depression, and hives. Because many persons are allergic to metronidazole, physicians may suggest the use of vaginal douches made up of vinegar and water, or of vaginal suppositories. The latter relieve trichomoniasis symptoms, but do not cure the disease.

Venereal Warts

Venereal warts, also called *genital warts,* may be painless but they can be serious and thus require medical attention. If left untreated, researchers say, venereal warts can increase the risk of penile cancer in men and cervical cancer in women. A pregnant woman with these growths may transmit the virus to her infant during delivery. Warts may then develop in the newborn's windpipe, causing later breathing problems.

The *human papilloma viruses* cause venereal warts, which may appear in a variety of places in the pubic area. The growths are usually small pink bumps, but they can grow to-

gether to resemble tiny cauliflowers. In most cases, the growths itch and produce a foul-smelling discharge.

Diagnosis

A physician can usually diagnose venereal warts from their external appearance. To make certain that the warts are not syphilis growths, however, the physician may take a biopsy. A tiny part of the wart is removed for study under a microscope. The papilloma virus can then be identified.

Women with external venereal warts may also have the growths on the cervix. A Pap test is required for detection of these internal warts.

Treatment

The drug podophyllin can be used in solution to remove venereal warts. The solution is painted on the growths, left for six hours, then washed off. The warts usually disappear within a few days. The treatment may have to be repeated several times. If any wart cells remain, the problem will most likely recur.

Podophyllin is not effective in all cases. Where it cannot achieve a cure, other methods, including surgery, may have to be attempted. Among these other methods, which are not always successful, are freezing and burning of the growths. Some studies have indicated that the hormone interferon can prevent recurrences of the disease. Interferon therapy may, however, produce such flulike side effects as fatigue and fever.

Syphilis

Historically, syphilis has ranked among mankind's chief health scourges. Modern medicine has brought it largely under control, but it can still be life-threatening.

Syphilis strikes men about three times as often as women. Approximately half of the male victims are homosexuals. A spiral-shaped bacterium called *Treponema pallidum* causes the disease. Transmittal takes place during sex with a person in the infectious stage in which open sores or rashes are typical symptoms. The *Treponema* bacteria fill the sores and in infecting another person invade the mucous membranes of the genitals, mouth, or rectum. The *spirochete,* or spiral bacterium, succumbs to heat, dryness, ordinary antiseptics, or even soap and water. But it can tolerate cold and survive freezing.

Stages

Unless it is treated early, syphilis progresses from a primary to secondary and sometimes tertiary stages. In the primary stage, the victim may have a painless chancre, or ulcer, that may be small, single, or multiple and that may look like any common skin ulcer. The reddish-brown ulcers generally appear between ten days and three months after exposure to the disease, with a typical incubation time of three weeks.

The secondary and latent stages of syphilis can lead to serious complications unless treatment is undertaken. A month to six weeks after the first ulcers appear, secondary lesions may develop, taking the form of a rash or almost any other kind of skin eruption. The lesions may appear on the trunk of the body, on the face, the arms and legs, or the palms of the hands and soles of the feet. The lesions may or may not itch, and they may not appear at all. The victim may, however, experience fevers and flu symptoms as well as hair loss. A latent stage of many years' duration follows untreated secondary syphilis. In this stage only a blood test can reveal the presence of the bacteria in the body.

If still untreated, late or tertiary-stage syphilis follows the secondary and latent stages in about one case in four. Tertiary syphilis involves the gradual destruction of the central nervous system, the heart, the bones, the liver, the stomach, or other organs. The bacteria can cause paralysis, convulsions, heart failure, insanity, and even death. Attacking the circulatory system, syphilis can cause an *aneurysm,* dilated section, of the aorta just above the heart. The blood flow to the heart is reduced; a ruptured aneurysm can produce a fatal hemorrhage. While gummas, rubbery syphilitic tumors inside organs, may respond to antibiotics in the late stage of syphilis, damage to the heart valves and arteries may be irreversible.

General Paresis

Permanent tissue damage to the brain and nerves can result from syphilitic invasion of the central nervous system; this the chronic, progressive form of syphilis known as *general paresis.* The damage occurs gradually, and early symptoms may include headaches, a tendency to forget things, or difficulty in concentrating. Mental effects may progress from memory loss to psychotic symptoms of delusions of grandeur.

Tabes Dorsalis

Late syphilis involving deterioration of the sheaths of spinal nerves (demyelination) and other destructive changes in the spinal cord is known as *tabes dorsalis.* The patient may become uncoordinated in movement. Tremors of the hands and fingers may be noticed, as well as tremors of the lips and tongue. Vision may be affected, and sensory effects can range from sharp sudden pains to a loss of feeling. The patient may lose control of bladder function or the ability to walk.

Congenital Syphilis

The latent syphilitic condition is not uncommon, and it is a period of great danger to the fetus if an infected woman, especially a recently infected woman, becomes pregnant at this time. The fetus can acquire syphilis through the placenta and be born with congenital syphilis. Or it can be stillborn or die shortly after birth. Some of the signs of syphilis in an infant born with the congenital form of the disease are similar to those of secondary syphilis. Others are very different, more closely resembling tertiary syphilis. Because of the hazards to the child, most physicians test the mother's blood for the presence of the spirochete during the first three months of pregnancy and during the last three months; syphilis acquired during pregnancy is especially likely to affect the fetus. Treatment of the mother has the added benefit of treating the fetus. Treatment begun before the eighteenth week of pregnancy will prevent syphilis from developing; treatment begun after the eighteenth week will cure the fetus of syphilis.

Diagnosis

Because the symptoms of syphilis may appear sporadically or not at all, and because they so closely resemble the symptoms of other diseases, diagnosis usually calls for a blood test. If a chancre has developed, the physician may take a scraping from the lesion and order a special microscopic examination.

Treatment

Long-lasting penicillin, given by intravenous injection, usually cures syphilis. But the disease can, as noted, cause irreversible damage if allowed to spread unchecked. For persons who are allergic to penicillin, physicians may prescribe tetracycline or erythromycin. Both are effective as treatments.

Pelvic Inflammatory Disease

Pelvic inflammatory disease (PID) is a serious complication of STDs. It affects women as a result of infection from a number of diseases including chlamydia and gonorrhea. To produce PID, a disease has to progress to the point where it leads to inflammation and abscesses of a victim's Fallopian tubes, ovaries, and pelvis.

One woman in about seven who contract PID becomes infertile. On the average, three of four women experiencing attacks of the disease will be unable to conceive.

Diagnosis and Treatment

Physicians can diagnose PID by conducting abdominal and pelvic examinations as well as various laboratory tests.

Antibiotics are prescribed in some cases. In more severe cases, surgery may be necessary. The surgery usually results in infertility.

Lymphogranuloma Venereum

This disease, also known as LGV and *lymphogranuloma inguinale*, is a venereal disease that produces a primary lesion like a small blister, which ruptures to form a small ulcer. It is caused by a virus that is spread by sexual intercourse, although sexual contact is not necessary for transmission of the disease. It can be acquired by contact with the fluid excreted by a lesion.

The primary lesion usually appears in the genital area within one to three weeks after contact with an infected person. It may appear only briefly or be so small as to go unnoticed. But the disease spreads to neighboring lymph nodes, where the next sign of the disorder appears 10 days to a month later. The swelling of the lymph nodes (forming *buboes*) is often the first symptom to be noted by the patient; the lymph nodes become matted together and hard, forming channels (or *fistulas*) through which pus drains to the surface of the skin. Enlargement of the lymph nodes may produce painful swelling of the external genitalia. The lymph-node involvement may spread to the anal region, leading to rectal constriction and painful bowel movements.

Diagnosis and Treatment

Because the lesions of lymphogranuloma venereum may resemble those of syphilis, chancroid, or certain nonvenereal diseases, physicians usually make a number of tests to determine whether or not the condition is, in fact, LGV. Therapy includes administration of antibiotics and sulfa drugs for a period of about a week to a month, depending on the severity of the infection.

Chancroid

Chancroid, or *soft chancre,* is a venereal disease transmitted by a bacterium that causes a tender, painful ulcer. The ulcer, which may erode deeply into the tissues, follows the formation of a primary pustule at the site of infection. The pustule appears within five days after contact with an infected person. While essentially a venereal disease, like other venereal diseases it is transmissible without sexual intercourse. Physicians, for

example, have been known to develop a soft chancre on a finger after examining an infected patient.

Diagnosis and Treatment

Physicians usually do tests to make sure that the lesion is not a syphilitic chancre. Although the disease can spread from the genital region to other parts of the body, the soft chancre generally is self-limiting. Therapy consists of administration of sulfa drugs or tetracycline.

Granuloma Inguinale

Granuloma inguinale, also called *granuloma venereum,* is not the same, in spite of the similarity in name, as lymphogranuloma venereum. The former is an insidious, chronic venereal disease that produces lesions on the skin or mucous membrane of the genital or anal regions. The first sign of the infection may be a painless papule or nodule that leaves an ulcer with a reddish granular base. If untreated, the lesions tend to spread to the lower abdomen and thighs. In time, the sores produce a sour, pungent odor.

Treatment

Antibiotics such as streptomycin and tetracycline are prescribed. Relapses may occur and cure may be slow, especially in cases of long standing.

External Venereal Maladies

The two conditions described below, one related to viruses and one a parasitic infestation, may generally be considered sources of discomfort and disfigurement rather than threats to general health. Both of these STDs are transmissible by other means besides sexual contact.

Molluscum Contagiosum

A viral disease transmitted during sexual intercourse is known by the medical term *molluscum contagiosum*. The disease can also be transmitted by ordinary person-to-person contact, as between members of a family or children in a classroom. The virus causes raised lesions containing a waxy white material. The lesions, which may be very small or as large as an inch in diameter, occur on the skin or mucous membranes, commonly in the anal or genital area but sometimes on the face or torso. The lesions may last for several months or several years, then disappear spontaneously, or they may be removed by medications or surgery.

Pubic Lice

Infestations of pubic lice constitute a unique kind of venereal disease. Pubic lice, known popularly as crabs, are a species somewhat larger than body and head lice but still almost invisible to the naked eye. These whitish, oval parasites usually remain in the hair of the anal and genital regions, but they may sometimes be found attached to the skin at the base of any body hair, including eyelashes and scalp. A very few pubic lice in the anal and genital areas can cause intense irritation and itching. The itching results in scratching which, in turn, produces abrasions of the skin. The lice may also produce patches of bluish spots on the skin of the inner thighs and lower abdomen. Another sign of their presence is the appearance of tiny brown specks deposited by the lice on the inside of undergarments.

Pubic lice are commonly spread by sexual contact, but they can be acquired from toilet seats, clothing, towels, bedclothes, combs, or any article of intimate use. Creams or ointments containing various parasiticides are available for disinfestation. They are applied every night for several nights, but overuse should be avoided because of the danger of injury to the tender tissues of the genital and anal region. Some physicians recommend soaking the infested part of the body several times daily in a mild solution of potassium permanganate. Lice on the eyebrows and eyelashes may have to be removed individually with a pair of tweezers. Treatment must be repeated after one week to kill the nits (eggs) that have hatched since the first treatment. Clothing and other contaminated materials must be cleaned to prevent reinfestation.

Complications of an infestation of pubic lice include intense itching (known medically as *pruritus*) and secondary infections from scratching. These may require special medical care and administration of antibiotics, corticosteroid creams, or other appropriate remedies.

18
Cancer

Cancer has always figured uniquely in the diseases of mankind. For centuries people spoke of it only in whispers, or not at all, as if the disease were not only dreadful but somehow shameful as well. Today, the picture is changing and rapidly. This decade may see the time— undreamt of only scant years ago— when half of those stricken by cancer will survive its ravages. And much of the mystery that cloaked the disease in an awful shroud has been dissipated, although the last veils remain to be stripped away.

Of course, cancer remains a formidable enemy. More than a million Americans are under medical care for cancer; an estimated 500,000 will die of it each year. Of all Americans now alive, one in three will be stricken. Cancer is the greatest cause of lost working years among women and ranks third after heart disease and accidents in denying men working years.

But in context, the picture is not as bleak as it might seem. At the beginning of the twentieth century, survival from cancer was relatively rare. At the end of the 1930s, the five-year survival rate (alive after five years) was one in five or fewer. Ten years

later it had shot up to one in four, and in the mid-fifties to one in three. This figure has remained relatively stable because the survival rate for some of the more widespread cancers has leveled off despite the best efforts of physicians to devise better forms of treatment. For such cancers, which include those of the breast, colon, and rectum, improvements will come through earlier detection and even prevention. Dr. Richard S. Doll, Professor of Medicine at Oxford University, has said that we could prevent 40 percent of men's cancer deaths and 10 percent of women's simply by applying what we already know. For example, according to the American Cancer Society, the risk of death from lung cancer is 15 to 20 times greater among men who smoke cigarettes than among men who have never smoked. The relative risk of lung cancer among women smokers is five times that of women who have never smoked.

Considerable progress is being made on many fronts in the war against cancer. It ranges from advances in early detection to breakthroughs in treatment. The past 25 years have seen a 50 percent dip in the death rate from cervical cancer,

mostly because of increasing acceptance of the Pap test, which can detect the disease at a very early stage. At the same time, children with acute lymphocytic leukemia, which used to be invariably fatal in weeks or months, have benefited from new therapies, with at least half now surviving three years, some more than five years, and a few on the verge of being pronounced cured. Similar advances in the treatment of a cancer of the lymph system called *Hodgkin's disease* have improved the five-year survival rate from 25 percent at the end of World War II to about 55 percent today.

What Is Cancer?

Cancer would surely be easier to detect and treat if it were a single entity with a single simple cause. But it is not. Experts agree that there are actually some 100 different diseases that can be called cancers. They have different causes, originate in different tissues, develop for different reasons and in different ways, and demand vastly different kinds of treatment. All have one fatal element in common,

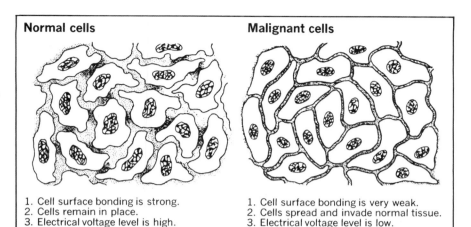

Normal cells
1. Cell surface bonding is strong.
2. Cells remain in place.
3. Electrical voltage level is high.
4. Cells divide at a low rate.

Malignant cells
1. Cell surface bonding is very weak.
2. Cells spread and invade normal tissue.
3. Electrical voltage level is low.
4. Cells divide at a rapid pace.

however; in every case, normal cells have gone wild and lost their growth and development controls.

Initial Stages

The cancer may start with just one or a few cells somewhere in the body that undergo a change and become malignant, or cancerous. The cells divide and reproduce themselves, and the cancer grows.

Most cancers arise on the surface of a tissue, such as the skin, the lining of the uterus, mouth, stomach, bowel, bladder, or bronchial tube in the lung, or inside a duct in the breast, prostate gland, or other site. Eventually, they grow from a microscopic clump to a visible mass, then begin to invade underlying tissues. As long as the cells remain in one mass, however, the cancer is localized.

Later Stages

At some later phase, in a process called *metastasis,* some of the cancer cells split off and are swept into the lymph channels or bloodstream to other parts of the body. They may be captured for a while in a nearby lymph node (a stage called *regional involvement*), but unless the disease is arrested, it will rapidly invade the rest of the body, with death the almost

certain result. Some cancers grow with a malevolent rapidity; some are dormant by comparison. Some respond to various therapies, such as radiation therapy; others do not. About half of the known types of cancer are incurable at any stage. Of the remaining half, it is obviously imperative to diagnose and treat them as early as possible.

How Cancers Are Classified

The cancers described above, arising in *epithelial* (covering or lining) tissue, are called *carcinomas* as a group. Another class of malignant tumors, similar in most basic respects, is the *sarcomas,* which originate in connective tissue, such as bones and muscles. A third group of cancers—*leukemia* and the *lymphomas*—includes diseases of the blood-forming organs and the lymphatic system, respectively, and does not produce tumors. They arise and spread in a basically different way.

What Causes Cancer?

In its battle with cancer, medical science devotes constant attention to a search for those factors in our environment that can produce cancer in human beings. They include a large number of chemical agents such as

those in tobacco smoke, and including asbestos fibers and other occupational chemical hazards; ionizing radiation such as that from X rays, nuclear bombs, and sunlight; injury or repeated irritation; metal or plastic implants; flaws in the body's immune reaction; genetic mistakes; parasites; and—many scientists believe—viruses.

It is this last factor that is generating perhaps the most interest among medical scientists today. It has been shown that viruses cause a variety of cancers in animals; yet they have never been proved responsible in human cancer, although they have been linked to at least six different ones. Recently, researchers discovered an enzyme in a virus believed to cause cancer and also in the tissues of leukemia patients. This enzyme may be the key to the mechanism by which a virus induces a malignant change in normal cells.

Scientists have also discovered that certain substances in the environment which by themselves may not stimulate the growth of a cancer can be dangerously activated to become carcinogenic by the presence of one or more other substances. Each of these potential cancer-causing agents is called a *cocarcinogen.* It is possible that some cocarcinogens are present in ordinary fruits and vegetables, in certain food additives, and in such other substances as the synthetic estrogen diethylstilbestrol (DES). For more information on DES, see Ch. 25, *Women's Health.*

Major Forms of Cancer

The following material includes discussions of the major forms of cancer with the exception of those cancers that affect women only. For additional information on many kinds of tumors for which surgery may be indicated, see also Ch. 20, *Surgery.*

Breast Cancer

See under *Women's Health,* Ch. 25.

Lung Cancer

Lung cancer kills more Americans than any other cancer. The average annual death toll for recent years is more than 90,000 men and more than 45,000 women. It represents 36 percent of all cancers in men, 20 percent of all cancers in women. There has been a dramatic increase in the incidence of lung cancer in women over the past 35 years to where it has surpassed breast cancer as the leading cause of cancer death among women. The five-year survival rate for this disease is between 10 and 20 percent.

Symptoms

Although some early lung cancers do not show up on an X-ray film, they are the ones that usually produce coughing as an early symptom. For this reason, any cough that lasts more than two or three weeks—even if it seems to accompany a cold or bronchitis—should be regarded as suspicious and investigated in that light. Blood in the sputum is another early warning sign that must be investigated immediately; so should wheezing when breathing. Later symptoms include shortness of breath, pain in the chest, fever, and night sweats.

Detection

If many lives could be saved by preventing lung cancer in the first place,

others could be saved by early detection. By the time most lung cancers are diagnosed, it is too late even for the most radical approach to cure—removal of the afflicted lung. Experts estimate that up to five times the present cure rate could be achieved if very early lung cancers could be spotted. They therefore recommend a routine chest X ray every six months for everyone over 45.

Causes

Lung cancer is one of the most preventable of all malignancies. Most cases, the majority of medical experts agree, are caused by smoking cigarettes. The U.S. Public Health Service has indicted smoking as "the main cause of lung cancer in men." Even when other agents are known to produce lung cancers—uranium ore dust or asbestos fibers, for example—cigarette smoking enormously boosts the risk among uranium miners and asbestos workers. Smoking accounts for 90 percent of all lung cancer deaths.

It is known that the lungs of some cigarette smokers show tissue changes before cancer appears, changes apparently caused by irritation of the lining of the *bronchi*—the large air tubes in the lung. Physicians believe these changes can be reversed before the onset of cancer if the source of irritation—smoking—is removed. This is why a heavy smoker who has been puffing away for many years but then stops smoking has a better chance of avoiding lung cancer than one who continues smoking.

Until recently, the evidence linking cigarette smoking and lung cancer was purely statistical, although overwhelming. No one had succeeded in producing lung cancer in laboratory animals by having them ingest smoke. However, lung cancer has been induced in dogs specially trained to in-

hale cigarette smoke, as reported by the American Cancer Society.

Cigarette smoking has also been implicated in other kinds of lung disease, including the often-fatal emphysema, and in cardiovascular diseases. To any sensible person, then, the options would seem clear: If you don't smoke, don't start. If you do smoke, stop. If you can't stop, cut down, and switch to a brand low in tars and nicotine—suspected but not proved to be the principal harmful agents in cigarette smoke.

Colon-Rectum Cancer

Cancer of the colon (large intestine) and rectum is the second leading cause of cancer death in the United States. Each year it claims an estimated 55,000 lives, and produces about 150,000 new cases—more than any other kind of cancer except skin cancer. It afflicts men and women about equally. The five-year survival rate from this form of cancer, usually after surgery, is 60 to 70 percent where the cancer was localized and 30 to 40 percent where there was regional involvement. However, authorities now believe that this rate could be upped substantially through early diagnosis and prompt treatment.

Symptoms

It is important, then, to be alert to the early symptoms of these cancers. Cancers of the colon often produce changes in bowel habits that persist longer than normal. The change may be constipation or diarrhea, or even both alternating. Cancers of the colon also often produce large quantities of gas, which cause abdominal discomfort ranging from a feeling of overfullness to pain, intermittent at first and then coming as regular cramps.

Both colon cancer and rectal cancer may also cause bleeding. Sometimes such bleeding is evidenced in the stool or on the tissue (the most frequent first sign of rectal cancer); but if the bleeding is slight and occurs high enough up the colon, it may not be visible at all. After a period of weeks, however, the persistent bleeding causes anemia in the patient.

All such symptoms should be investigated promptly. Unfortunately, many persons tend to ignore them. Chronic constipation, for example, or gas, is easy to dismiss for the nuisance that it usually is. Even rectal bleeding, which demands immediate medical consultation, is often ignored by hemorrhoid sufferers, who fail to realize that hemorrhoids and cancer, though unrelated, can and sometimes do exist in the same persons at the same time.

Detection

For these reasons, the key to successful and early diagnosis of colon and rectum cancer lies in making a *proctoscopy* part of the regular annual health checkup. In this procedure, performed in a physician's office, a lighted tube called a *proctoscope* is passed into the rectum. Through it, the physician can examine the walls visually for signs of tumor. If the physician thinks it advisable to check the sigmoid colon also, the procedure is called a *proctosigmoidoscopy,* and a similar instrument called a *sigmoidoscope* is used. The American Cancer Society now recommends that everyone over age 40 have a proctoscopy or proctosigmoidoscopy in routine annual checkups.

Therapy

The indicated treatment for colon-rectum cancer is surgical removal of the affected part of the bowel. Adjacent portions and related lymph nodes may also be removed, and if the surgeon sees that the cancer is widespread, he may have to perform extensive surgery. This may require that he create a *colostomy*—a temporary or permanent opening in the abdominal wall through which solid wastes may pass. Although this method of voiding the bowels is somewhat inconvenient at first, most colostomy patients adjust to it very easily and lead perfectly normal, active, and healthy lives. The wall of prudish silence that used to surround the disease and the colostomy is fortunately crumbling. An organization for colostomy patients called the United Ostomy Association keeps up with current information on diet, colostomy equipment, and other problems the members have in common.

Radiotherapy is sometimes used before the operation (occasionally to make surgery possible) and sometimes afterward to treat recurrence of the cancer. Various chemical agents have been found useful in treating colon-rectum cancer that has spread to the lymph nodes or more widely.

Skin Cancer

With as many as 500,000 new cases occurring annually, skin cancer is the largest single source of malignancy in the United States. An estimated 6,000 persons die of this disease each year. Since 1980, the number of cases of malignant melanoma, the most deadly form of skin cancer, has risen by more than 90 percent.

Experts believe that many cases of skin cancer could be prevented if more people avoided exposure to the sun. Radiation in sunlight not only burns and dries the skin; it also is thought to suppress the human immune system and thus contribute in-directly to skin problems. Long and continued exposure to the sun has been associated with cataracts as well as with skin aging and wrinkling.

Symptoms

Persons with skin problems should report promptly to their physicians any sores that refuse to heal, or changes in warts or moles. Pimples that itch and recur may also be symptoms of skin cancer.

Therapy

Most skin cancers remain localized. They can usually be removed by excisional surgery, with an electric needle, or by cryosurgery (freezing). X-ray irradiation and chemotherapy may also be used.

Causes

Most skin cancers appear after the age of 40. Scientists point to the ultraviolet radiation in sunlight as the primary cause, with ultraviolet-B (UV-B), the shorter wavelength band, as the more dangerous. But dermatologists recommend that ultraviolet-A (UV-A), used often in high-intensity sunlamps and tanning beds, be avoided as well. While UV-A is spread more evenly throughout the day, UV-B is largely concentrated around midday.

Fair-skinned individuals who burn readily, rather than tanning, are more vulnerable to radiation-caused cancer than darker-skinned persons. Geographic location is also important. Skin cancer occurs more frequently in the southern belt of states, particularly in the sunny Southwest.

Chemicals, too, can cause skin cancer. Before the relationship was discovered, skin cancer was an occupational hazard for many thousands of unprotected workers who dealt with arsenic and various derivatives of coal and petroleum.

Kinds

Of the three primary kinds of skin cancer, two are both common and relatively curable. These are basal-cell and squamous-cell *carcinoma.* Early detection almost ensures that a cure can be effected.

A *melanoma,* or so-called *black cancer,* is a malignant tumor that arises from a mole. The moles may begin as flat, soft, brown, and hairless protrusions, but they can change suddenly into darker, larger growths that itch and bleed. They can also metastasize, spreading cancer cells to other parts of the body through the bloodstream and the lymphatic system.

Unlike other types of skin cancer, melanomas may grow in skin areas not usually exposed to the sun, such as the feet, in the genital area, or under the belt or collar. Chronic irritation from tight clothing is one suspected cause. Melanomas rarely occur before middle age; nearly three-fourths of the victims are women.

Oral Cancer

Cancers of the mouth and lips strike an estimated 24,000 persons in the United States each year and kill a shocking 8,500. Shocking because anyone with the aid of a mirror and a good light can see into his mouth and therefore spot even very small cancers early in their development.

Symptoms

Any sore, lump, or lesion of the mouth or lips should be regarded as suspicious if it persists more than two weeks without healing, and a physi-

cian or dentist should then be consulted without delay. The five-year survival rate for localized mouth cancers—when they are usually no larger than the little fingernail—is 67 percent—about two out of three. But if regional involvement occurs, the rate falls to 30 percent—fewer than one out of three.

Detection

Just as the Pap test screens for cervical cancer by scraping up sloughed-off cells that are then examined under a microscope, so one day your dentist may routinely scrape mouth cells to detect oral cancer. When more than 40,000 patients were screened over a five-and-one-half-year period at the Western Tennessee Cancer Clinic, about 230 cases of oral cancer were diagnosed, of which 35 percent would have been missed otherwise.

Right now, a weekly or monthly personal inspection of your mouth is the best detective method available. The American Cancer Society has materials explaining the best way to conduct such an examination.

Therapy

Oral cancers are treated by surgical removal or by irradiation.

Causes

No one can pinpoint the causes of oral cancer definitely, but there are a number of leading suspects. They are smoking, in all its forms; exposure to wind and sun (for lip cancer); poor mouth hygiene; sharp or rough-edged teeth or improperly fitted, irritating dentures; dietary inadequacies, and constant consumption of alcohol or very hot foods and liquids.

Ovarian and Uterine Cancer

See under *Women's Health,* Ch. 25.

Stomach Cancer

Before World War II, cancer of the stomach was the most common type of cancer among men and women in the United States. The death rate from stomach cancer in the 1930s was about 30 per 100,000 population. In recent years, stomach cancer has declined in proportion to other forms of the disease, such as lung, breast, and uterine cancer. However, stomach cancer is still one of the more frequently diagnosed types of cancer and the death rate is relatively high, at nearly 10 per 100,000 population.

Today, men are twice as likely to be victims of stomach cancer as women. The disease is seldom found in persons under 40 years of age, but after that age the incidence increases steadily, reaching a peak before the age of 60. One of the disease's mysterious incidental factors is its peculiar geographical distribution, the highest rates of occurrence being in Japan, Chile, Iceland, northern Russia, and the Scandinavian countries.

Symptoms

Stomach cancer seems to develop slowly and insidiously, with initial symptoms that may be disregarded by the patient because they mimic ordinary gastric distress. The victim may experience a distaste for foods, particularly meats, and display a slow but progressive loss of weight. There may be sensations of fullness, bloating, or pain after meals. The same symptoms may be noted between meals and be aggravated by eating. The pain may vary from intermittent stomachaches to intense pain that seems to extend into the patient's back. The patient also experiences fatigue or weakness and anemia, and, as the cancerous condition progresses, may have periods of vomiting. The vomitus is dark, much like the color of coffee grounds, and there may be other signs of bleeding in the patient's stools.

Cancer's Seven Warning Signals*

1. Change in bowel or bladder habits
2. A sore that does not heal
3. Unusual bleeding or discharge
4. Thickening or lump in breast or elsewhere
5. Indigestion or difficulty in swallowing
6. Obvious change in wart or mole
7. Nagging cough or hoarseness

If you have a warning signal, see your doctor without delay.

*from the American Cancer Society

Detection

X rays of the stomach and examination of the stomach interior by gastroscopy usually locate and define the cancerous area; they may also reveal another cause of the symptoms, such as a peptic ulcer. During the physical examination, the physician may find a tissue mass and tenderness in the stomach area. The laboratory report usually will show signs of anemia from blood loss, the presence of blood in a stool sample, and the level of hydrochloric acid in the stomach; a lack of hydrochloric acid is found in more than half the stomach cancer patients. A biopsy study of the suspected tissue usually completes the diagnosis.

Therapy

Unfortunately, because of the insidious nature of stomach cancer, the disease becomes easier to diagnose as it progresses. By the time cancer has been confirmed, the most expedient form of treatment is surgery to remove the affected area of the stom-ach. If the cancer is small and has not spread by metastasis to lymph nodes in the region, the chances are relatively good that the patient will survive five years or more; the odds against surviving five years without surgery are, by comparison, about 50 to 1 at best. Chemotherapy treatments may be used in cases where surgery is not feasible, but the use of medicines instead of surgery for stomach cancer is not a routine procedure and generally is not recommended.

Occasionally, a stomach tumor is found to be noncancerous. The tumor may be a polyp, a *leiomyoma* (a growth consisting of smooth muscle tissue), or a *pseudotumor* (false tumor), such as an inflammatory fibroid growth. Such benign tumors produce symptoms ranging from gastric upset to internal bleeding and should be removed by surgery.

Causes

Many possible factors have been suggested as causes of stomach cancer. Dietary factors include hot food and beverages, as well as fish and smoked foods. Food additives have been implicated despite the fact that the incidence of stomach cancer has been declining during the period in which the use of additives has been increasing. Cured meats and cheeses, preserved with nitrites to retard spoilage, reportedly foster the development of carcinogenic chemical compounds in the digestive tract.

On the other hand, the widespread use of refrigeration has been offered as an explanation for the declining incidence of stomach cancer, since refrigeration reduces the need for chemical food preservatives.

Beyond the influence of diet, medical epidemiologists have found that genetic factors may play a role in the development of stomach cancer. Statistical analysis of large population studies of stomach cancer shows a tendency for the disease to occur in persons with blood type A, or with below-normal levels of hydrochloric acid in the stomach, or with inherited variations in the stomach lining. There also seems to be a good possibility that stomach cancers evolve from noncancerous changes in the stomach lining, as from polyps or peptic ulcers.

Bladder Cancer

As with stomach cancer, the incidence of cancer of the bladder rises progressively with age and occurs much more frequently in men than in women. Extensive occurrence of bladder cancer is commonly associated with industrial growth, but internationally its incidence ranges from a high rate in England to a low one in Japan; in the United States, the highest incidence of bladder cancer is in southern New Jersey. A study by the Roswell Park Memorial Institute, a cancer research center in Buffalo, New York, found that persons of Italian-American parentage were more likely to have bladder cancer than those of different parentage, and that women living in urban areas were more likely to develop the disease than their country cousins. American blacks have less bladder cancer than American whites.

Bladder cancer appears at an annual rate of about 40,000 new cases each year in the United States and causes more than 15,000 deaths annually.

Symptoms

A change in bladder habits is among the first signs of bladder cancer. The change might be the presence of pain while urinating, a noticeable difficulty in urinating, or a difference in the frequency of urination.

Another symptom of the disease is the appearance of blood in the urine. The degree of blood coloration is not necessarily related to the severity of the cancer; any sign of blood in the urine should be investigated. Nor should the absence of pain be allowed to minimize the seriousness of urinary bleeding as a symptom of a diseased bladder. Even without pain, the presence of blood can indicate a problem such as an obstruction to the urinary flow that can lead to uremia, a toxic condition caused by retention of urinary waste products in the system.

Detection

Cancer of the bladder is frequently diagnosed from common signs and symptoms, particularly the appearance of blood in the urine. A laboratory examination of the patient's urine may also reveal the presence of cancer cells that have been washed out of the bladder. The disease can be detected by a *pyelogram*—a kind of X-ray picture made by filling the urinary system with a fluid that makes tissue details appear in sharp contrast—and by examination of the membrane lining the bladder. The bladder lining may be examined by surgical biopsy or by *cystoscopy,* the viewing of the interior of the bladder by means of a device inserted in the urethra—or both.

Examination of the bladder lining is needed to determine the type of tumor that may be the cause of the symptoms. One type, called a *papillary tumor,* or *papilloma,* is relatively harmless and usually does not invade the wall of the bladder as does the more dangerous type, sometimes described as a solid lesion. The degree of invasion of the bladder tissues by the infiltrating mass determines the type of treatment recommended. However, any tumor found in the lining of the bladder must be removed, because the papillary type can progress into a solid lesion if not treated.

Therapy

The cure of a bladder tumor can be approached in several ways, the choice of treatments depending upon the size and type of growth, the location of the tumor, and so on. Chemotherapy, using drugs such as thiotepa, has been successful in treating papillary bladder tumors; the chemical is applied directly to the bladder lining. A kind of electric cautery known as *fulguration* also may be used to destroy the tissue growth; it may be employed by cystoscopy or as part of a surgical approach. Radiation therapy also may be used by implanting radium needles in the affected bladder tissue. Surgical excision of the cancerous area, with or without radiation, chemotherapy, or cautery, may be the procedure chosen. In advanced cases of bladder cancer, the bladder may be removed and its function performed by the construction of a substitute organ from other tissues or by the relocation of the upper ends of the ureters at other urine-collecting points.

Causes

Cancer of the bladder may be caused by irritation from bladder stones or by toxic chemicals excreted from the kidneys. A high incidence of bladder cancer has been found among persons who are heavy cigarette smokers; a possible explanation is that certain carcinogenic tobacco-burning by-products are absorbed into the blood and excreted through the kidneys. The evidence includes studies showing that when such patients quit smoking, the carcinogens no longer appear in their urine.

Occupational factors have been associated with cancer of the bladder since 1895, when it was discovered that persons who worked with aniline chemical dyes were among those most likely to develop the disease. The incidence of the disease among chemical workers was found to be 30 times greater than that of the general population. The aniline dye workers developed bladder cancer at an average age 15 years younger than among the general population. The effect of the chemical dyes was verified by the development of cancer in the bladders of laboratory animals exposed to the dyes. In recent years, it has been found that many other chemicals can cause bladder cancer.

Besides the influence of industrial environmental factors, bladder cancer is associated with *schistosomiasis,* a disease occurring in Africa, Asia, South America, and other regions. Schistosomiasis develops after bathing or wading in water infested by a blood fluke. The organisms penetrate the skin and migrate to the intestines or urinary bladder, producing an inflammation that eventually leads to cancer. See Ch. 19, *Other Diseases of Major Importance,* for a fuller description of the disease.

Cancer of the Prostate

Cancer of the prostate is one of the most common cancers among men and is second only to lung cancer as a lethal type of tumor for men. About 30,000 people die of prostate cancer each year. The incidence increases with advancing age from the fifth decade of life, when prostatic cancer cells are found in nearly 20 percent of all men examined, to those in their 70s, an age when 60 percent of the men have been found to have cancer cells in their prostate glands. Fortunately, only 15 percent of the men with evidence of latent carcinoma of the prostate ever develop clinical symptoms of cancer before death. But after the age of 75, there are almost as many deaths, due to prostatic cancer as to lung cancer.

Symptoms

Cancer of the prostate is a disease noted for its secondary symptoms. It usually is detected because a physician begins analyzing symptoms that could suggest other disorders. There may, for example, be blood in the urine, indicating a serious problem that could be located anywhere along the urinary tract. Because the prostate encircles the urethra, which is the outlet from the bladder, any prostatic problem can cause disturbances in the normal passage of urine, including increased frequency of urination or discomfort in urinating. However, these also could be the symptoms of ailments other than cancer of the prostate.

Detection

Diagnosis of prostatic cancer usually begins with an examination of the prostate through the wall of the rectum. This technique is a regular part of a physical examination for men over the age of 40. If during the examination of the prostate the physician feels a lump or hardened area, further tests are ordered. The presence of a lump in the prostate need not be evidence of cancer; about half of the lumps and nodules are caused by fibrosis, calcium deposits, or other noncancerous bodies. Transrectal ultrasound is a newer detection method used in conjunction with the traditional digital rectal examination.

Additional tests may include examination by a cystoscope, which is inserted through the urethra to provide a view of the tissues of the area, plus a laboratory examination of tissue samples and prostatic fluid samples. A microscopic study of the samples may reveal the presence of cancer cells. The examination of prostatic cells for signs of cancer is similar to the technique used in the Pap test for cancer of the cervix in women.

In the search for evidence of cancer of the prostate, diagnostic clues may be found in blood chemistry tests and by the examination of a urinary pyelogram that could indicate obstructions from the prostate walls. Additional information may be forthcoming from an evaluation of the patient's medical history; low back pain complaints, for example, may result from prostate disorders.

Therapy

Surgery is the usual treatment for cancer of the prostate when the tumor is confined to the prostate gland. The surgical removal of the prostate may be supplemented by the administration of estrogens, or hormone therapy. If the cancer has spread to other areas, a frequent complication of prostatic cancer, an additional form of therapy could be the administration of radioactive drugs or some other form of radiation. An additional measure may be *orchiectomy,* the surgical removal of the testicles, performed because of the close physiological relationship between the testicles and the prostate. Impotence is a major result of prostate cancer, and if female hormones are administered, water retention, painful breast enlargement, and cardiovascular complications can result. An alternative to orchiectomy or hormone therapy is the monthly injection of luteinizing hormone-

releasing hormone agonists, which disrupts the normal production of testosterone.

Causes

Cancer of the prostate seems to be associated with activity of the sex hormones in men. It has been reported that all patients with prostatic cancer previously had a normal history of sex-hormone activity. The cancer symptoms begin to appear at a period of life when male sex-hormone activity is waning. Laboratory studies of the urine of patients show a decrease in levels of male sex hormones after the age of 40. As in female breast cancer, which also is related to sex-hormone activity, there are certain tissues of the body that appear to be more sensitive to influences of hormones. Changes in hormonal activity lead to increasing numbers of cells in those tissues and abnormal tissue growth.

Cancer of the Kidney

Cancer of the kidneys is most likely to occur in young children or in adults over the age of 40. The most common form of kidney cancer in children is known as *Wilms' tumor.* In adults, kidney cancer is usually in the form of a growth called *Grawitz's tumor,* or *hypernephroma,* a malignant growth that occurs chiefly among men.

Wilms' Tumor

Wilms' tumor, also called *nephroblastoma,* accounts for perhaps 25 percent of all cancers in children. About 90 percent of the cases develop before the age of seven; it has been diagnosed in infants less than five months old.

Symptoms

The symptoms can include fever, abdominal pain, weight loss, lack of appetite, blood in the urine, and an abdominal mass that may grow quickly to enormous size. The growth may be accompanied by symptoms of hypertension.

Detection

Examination of the patient may show the tumor to be on either the left or the right kidney. In a small percentage of the cases both kidneys are affected. A biopsy usually is performed in order to verify the presence of cancer cells in the growth.

Therapy

Treatment is most effective when the disease is diagnosed before the age of two. Surgery, radiation, and chemotherapy may be employed. The choice of chemotherapeutic agents may be varied as follow-up examinations reveal side effects or tumor resistance to one of the previously administered medications.

The five-year survival rate for victims of Wilms' tumor is about 65 percent when surgery and other measures are employed at an early stage. If not controlled, the cancer cells from Wilms' tumor tend to spread by metastasis to the lungs, liver, and other organs.

Causes

Wilms' tumor is believed to be congenital in nature. Studies of the tumor cells indicate that it may develop from embryonic kidney tissue that fails to evolve as a normal part of that organ.

Grawitz's Tumor

In about half of the cases of Grawitz's tumor, the common adult kidney cancer, the disease manifests itself through a combination of three symptoms: abdominal mass, pain in the area of the kidneys, and blood in the urine. In the other half of the cases, the cancer has metastasized and is found in the brain, lung, liver, or bone.

Detection

The physician may get important information about the seriousness of the tumor through laboratory studies of blood and urine samples; these can indicate the presence of substances that appear in body fluids when cancer cells are active.

Information can also be obtained by angiogram studies. An angiogram is an X-ray picture of an organ that has been injected with a dye to make the blood vessels, which carry the dye, markedly visible. A kidney angiogram shows different dye patterns for a normal organ, a kidney with a cyst, or a kidney with a tumor. The diagnosis usually is confirmed by biopsy or surgical exploration.

Therapy

Surgery and radiation treatment are the usual forms of therapy for adult kidney tumors, and the chances of ten-year survival, even after removal of a cancerous kidney, are fairly good.

Causes

Causes of adult kidney tumors remain largely unknown, but they have been thought to be associated with other disorders, such as infections or the presence of kidney stones.

Cancer of the Pancreas

Pancreatic cancer affects men about twice as frequently as women and accounts for about five percent of the cancer deaths. It is most likely to develop after the age of 40, and persons who are diabetic seem to be particularly susceptible to the disease.

Symptoms

The pancreatic cancer patient complains of apparent digestive disorders, such as abdominal pain, nausea, loss of appetite, and perhaps constipation. The abdominal distress may improve or worsen after eating and the pain may increase when the patient lies on his back. He will suffer weight loss and there will be jaundice. Many victims of pancreatic cancer also complain of itching sensations. Abdominal pain is usually persistent.

Detection

Along with signs of jaundice and scratching, the examining physician will evaluate laboratory reports of urine, blood, and stool analyses. Glucose tolerance tests and bilirubin levels are helpful in defining the source of the disorder. Negative findings of X-ray studies of the gastrointestinal tract, kidney-bladder area, and gallbladder can suggest a pancreatic disorder; by their normal condition, the physician can conclude that the disease is elsewhere in the abdominal region.

Therapy

Surgery is the usual treatment recommended for cancer of the pancreas; the precise location of the tumor within the pancreas may determine the exact surgical procedure to be undertaken. Removal of the tumor surgically has a more hopeful outcome if it is located at the head of the pancreas; cancers in the body or tail of the pancreas usually are not detected until the disease has spread to other parts of the body. Radiation and chemotherapy are not as effective in the treatment of pancreatic cancer as in other organs.

Cancer of the Liver

Cancer of the liver is commonly found to be the result of metastasis from other parts of the body. Cancers that originate in the liver account for less than 2 percent of the cancers reported in the United States and occur more frequently in men than in women, most frequently after the age of 40. Cancer of the liver is usually fatal.

Symptoms

Weakness, weight loss, and pain in the upper abdomen or right side of the chest are among the symptoms of liver cancer. A fever apparently unrelated to any infection also may mark the onset of liver cancer.

Detection

An enlarged liver with masses of abnormal tissue may be detected by an examining physician. Laboratory tests usually reveal alterations in metabolism that are associated with changes in the liver cells caused by the cancer growth. A biopsy test of the abnormal liver tissue may confirm the presence of cancer. A more direct approach is to perform exploratory surgery for examination of the liver.

Therapy

If the tumor is located during exploratory surgery and the area can be ex-

cised, part of the liver is removed. Chemotherapy may also be used.

A nonsurgical therapy for liver cancer involves the use of so-called "radiolabeled antibodies." To these molecules of antibodies, the defensive compounds of the body, radioactive substances are attached. The antibodies then seek out the cancer cells, and the radioactivity helps them destroy the cancer. The procedure has been used experimentally on patients whose tumors were too large for surgical instruments.

Causes

While the exact cause of primary liver cancer is unknown, a large proportion of cases is associated with cirrhosis of the liver. In recent years, some types of liver cancer have been traced to exposure of industrial workers to chemicals known to be carcinogenic. The high incidence of primary liver cancer in Asia and Africa is related to *aflatoxins* (molds) in grains and legumes, such as peanuts.

Secondary cancers of the liver are the result of primary cancers in other body areas; the liver is vulnerable to metastasis from cancers in every organ except the brain because of the pattern of blood circulation that carries cancer cells through the body.

Cancer of the Brain

Cancers in the brain tissue frequently are the result of metastasis from other body organs. They travel through the bloodstream, primarily from cancers of the lung, kidney, gastrointestinal tract, and breast. They become implanted in both the cerebrum and cerebellum, and, although there is wide distribution of the cancer cells, they are clustered mainly near the surfaces of the brain tissues. Primary brain tumors are more com-

mon among children than among adults; in children, other cancer sites are not likely to have had time to develop to the stage of metastasis required for the transmission of malignant cells to the brain.

A cancer that seems to originate in the brain tissues is known as *glioblastoma multiforme,* a malignant growth that may strike at any age but is more likely to occur during middle age. The glioblastoma may develop in nearly any part of the brain structure, including the brain stem, and spread extensively into a large tumorous mass.

Symptoms

Symptoms of brain cancer may include headache, dizziness, nervousness, depression, mental confusion, vomiting, and paralysis. The symptoms sometimes are interpreted as those of a psychiatric disorder, and treatment of the organic disease may be postponed until too late.

Detection

Diagnosis may be difficult, and the physician must evaluate the symptoms in terms of other findings from laboratory tests, X rays, and other techniques. In some cases, cancer cells may be detected in samples of spinal fluid.

Therapy

Treatment of brain cancers usually requires surgery or radiation or both, depending upon the type of tumor, its location, and other factors. Whether or not the brain tumor is a true cancer is not as important as early treatment; any abnormal tissue growth in the brain causes destructive pressure against vital tissues.

Cancer of the Larynx

Cancer of the larynx is chiefly a disease of men, afflicting about eight times as many men as women, usually around the age of 60. It is not one of the major types of cancer, with about 9,000 new cases appearing each year in the United States; but more than 35 percent of these cases are fatal. About 70 percent involve tumors on the vocal cords and are classed as *intrinsic* cancers of the larynx. The remainder of the cases involve tissues originating outside the vocal cords and are designated as *extrinsic*.

Symptoms

One of the first symptoms of intrinsic cancer of the larynx is hoarseness. Later the patient loses his ability to speak and has difficulty breathing. The same series of symptoms occurs in cases of extrinsic cancer except that there is an initial period of pain or discomfort in the throat before hoarseness begins. *Adenopathy,* or swelling of the lymph nodes in the area, also may be an early symptom of extrinsic cancer of the larynx.

Detection

Diagnosis of cancer of the larynx is relatively simple because the throat's interior can be examined by a physician and tissue samples can be removed for biopsy study. Detection of extrinsic cancer may be complicated by the fact that it is more likely to metastasize than intrinsic forms.

Therapy

In early cases of intrinsic cancer, or for small lesions that appear in the middle of the vocal cords, radiation may be the therapy of choice.

Surgery may be required for more serious cases, with radiation treatments before or after surgery, or both. The surgery, called a *laryngectomy,* may involve partial or total removal of the larynx. If a partial laryngectomy is performed, an effort is made to save as much of the vocal cords as possible. The voice will be changed after surgery, but it will be functional. The respiratory tract will be preserved. When total laryngectomy is required, the entire larynx is removed and the neck is dissected to determine if cancer cells have migrated to the lymph nodes in the neck. A new trachea is constructed by plastic surgery to permit normal or nearly normal respiration.

Thyroid Cancer

Cancer of the thyroid gland is relatively uncommon, with fewer than three new cases per 100,000 population per year. The death rate is even less, about one thyroid-cancer death per year per 200,000 persons. One reason for the low death rate is that many of the cancers are detected during examination or surgery for goiter or other throat symptoms.

Symptoms

These include rapid growth of the thyroid gland, hoarseness, paralysis of nerves in the larynx, and enlarged lymph nodes in the neck and surrounding area. Diagnosis is aided by the rate at which suspected areas of cancer in the thyroid gland absorb radioactive iodine; the pattern of radioactive uptake helps pinpoint tissue abnormalities.

Therapy

Treatment may include surgery to remove the cancer and part of the surrounding tissue, plus removal of lymph nodes that may contain cancer cells that have metastasized from the thyroid tumor. In addition, other lymph nodes that are in the path of drainage from the thyroid gland may be removed. Surgery usually is more successful in young patients than in older persons. Radiation sometimes is used, either from an external source or by injection of large doses of radioactive chemicals.

Causes

Among causes of cancer of the thyroid gland is exposure of children and young adults to radiation therapy of the head and neck region; many such patients later develop thyroid cancer.

Hodgkin's Disease

Hodgkin's disease is one of the *lymphomas*—cancers of the lymphatic system. It occurs most commonly among young adults, although it can appear at any age. Men are more likely to be victims than are women.

Symptoms

One of the first symptoms of Hodgkin's disease is a painless enlargement of a lymph node, usually in the area of the neck. The enlarged lymph nodes usually are firm and rubbery at first. The patient may experience a severe and persistent itching for several weeks or months before the first enlarged lymph node appears.

Other symptoms may include shortness of breath, fever, weight loss, anemia, and some pressure or pain as the disease progresses and nerve tissue becomes involved. Gradually, the lymph nodes that originally were separate and movable become matted and fixed, and sometimes inflamed. Over a period of months to years, the disease spreads through other parts of the body.

Therapy

Hodgkin's disease is ordinarily confirmed by removal of an affected lymph node for biopsy study. If the disease is limited to one or two localized areas the usual therapy is radiation treatments. Surgical excision of the nodes may be employed in special cases, as when a mass of nodes threatens a vital organ. But intense radiation exposure is generally more effective than surgery. Radiation treatments when properly applied may have a cure rate of as high as 95 percent. In cases where the disease has spread over a large area of the body, the treatment of choice may be chemotherapy utilizing nitrogen mustard, steroid drugs, and other substances.

Causes

The cause of Hodgkin's disease is unknown. Because of the fever and other symptoms associated with the disorder, and because it appears to occur more frequently among members of the same family or community than in the population as a whole, it has been suggested that Hodgkin's disease is a viral disease that has a malignant effect on the human lymphatic system.

Leukemia

Because leukemia involves blood cells circulating through the body rather than a fixed mass of tissue, leukemia is sometimes not considered a true cancer. However, leukemia cells, when studied under the microscope and in cell cultures, behave like cancer cells found in tumors.

There are at least ten different kinds of blood cells that have been identified with various forms of the disease. In addition, there are both acute and chronic forms of leukemia, such as *acute granulocytic leukemia* and *chronic lymphocytic leukemia,* named after the particular kind of white blood cells that are most affected.

Leukemia affects the blood-forming tissues, such as the bone marrow, resulting in an overproduction of white blood cells. The disease is particularly lethal to children under the age of 15; more than 10 percent of the leukemia deaths each year are among children. The incidence by age group varies according to the specific type of leukemia, however; one variety of acute granulocytic leukemia can occur at any age, but chronic lymphocytic leukemia usually does not appear before the age of 40. Men are more likely than women to be the victims of one of the various forms of leukemia.

Symptoms

Common symptoms to all leukemias include fever, weight loss, fatigue, bone pain, anemia as expressed in paleness, and an enlarged spleen or masses under the skin caused by an accumulation of leukemic cells. There may be skin lesions and a tendency to bleed. Infections may become more common and less responsive to treatment because of a loss of the normal blood cells needed to resist disease.

Detection

Diagnosis of leukemia from early symptoms may be difficult because they resemble those of mononucleosis and other infections. Biopsies of bone marrow and careful blood studies usually identify the disease.

Therapy

Treatment usually is directed toward reducing the size of the spleen and the number of white cells in the blood, and increasing the level of blood hemoglobin to counteract the effects of anemia. Antibiotics may be included to help control infections when natural resistance to disease has been lowered. X-ray treatments, radioactive phosphorus, anticancer drugs, and steroid hormone medications are administered according to the needs of the individual patient and the type of leukemia being treated.

Acute leukemia may be fatal within a few weeks of the onset of symptoms. But chronic cases receiving proper treatment have been known to survive more than 25 years. Remission rates are improving, partly because of new drugs and methods of treatment. The new chemotherapeutic approaches include the following:

- For acute leukemia in children, *methotrexate* has been used with increasing success. One of the antimetabolites, the family of drugs that interfere with development of essential cell components, methotrexate reduces the production in the blood of folic acid. In that way the drug competes with the cancer cells for the vital enzyme folic reductase—and inhibits the cancer's growth.

- In adults, chronic and acute forms of leukemia may be treated with *chlorambucil* or *cyclophosphamide.* Both drugs are types of nitrogen mustard. Both may produce such side effects as suppression of bone marrow, loss of hair, nausea, dizziness, and vomiting.

- In cases of acute leukemia in childhood, the vinca alkaloid drugs have proved valuable. These drugs, such as *vincristine sulfate,* are extremely powerful. They attack active cancer cells more directly than they attack normal cells. They may lead to such side effects as headaches, convulsions, and loss of some muscular control.

Other drugs in the alkaloid and other drug families have been used to treat leukemia. The others include *cytosine arabinoside,* which works to prevent cell synthesis — including cancer-cell synthesis; 6-Mercotopurine, which inhibits some metabolic processes; and *busulfan* and similar drugs, which work against multiplication of the cancer cells. Antitumor antibiotics that prevent growth of cancer cells include daunoribicin, doxorubicin, and bleomycin.

Causes

There is no general theory about the cause of leukemia. Animals are known to be susceptible to a form of leukemia transmitted by virus, but there is no solid evidence that human leukemias are caused by viral infections. Survivors of nuclear explosions as well as persons exposed to large doses of X rays have developed leukemia at a higher-than-normal rate than other people. There is evidence that at least one type of acute leukemia may be a result of an inherited genetic defect.

Other Cancers

Lymphosarcoma

Another of the cancers that involve the lymphatic system is called *lymphosarcoma* — a malignant lymphoma that tends to metastasize in lymphatic tissue. The most common first symptom is a swelling of the lymph nodes, and the diagnosis and treatment are similar to those of Hodgkin's disease. Lymphosarcoma can occur at any time and in any part of the body where there is lymphatic tissue, including the gastrointestinal tract, the tonsils, the tongue, or the nasopharynx area.

Reticulum-Cell Sarcoma

The lymphomas also include *reticulum-cell sarcoma.* (A sarcoma is a malignant tumor in the connective tissue. Reticulum cells are a particular kind of connective tissue.) The disease is marked by the invasion of normal tissue by increased numbers of reticulum cells or fibers. As in the treatment of leukemia, it is important to know which of the various types of cancer has affected the lymphatic system, because each of the lymphomas responds to a different therapeutic routine.

Myeloma and Multiple Myeloma

Myelomas, once considered rare but now reported in increasing numbers, are cancerous growths that seem to originate in the bone marrow. The average age at onset is about 65. Men are twice as likely as women to be victims of myelomas.

The disease is marked by bone destruction, mainly in the pelvis, ribs, and spine. The bones break easily, sometimes causing collapse of the spinal column and pressure on the spinal cord. There also may be anemia, kidney damage, and changes in the blood chemistry. When the myelomas occur at numerous sites in the bone marrow throughout the body, the disease is known as *multiple myeloma.*

Treatment

Various methods of treating lymphomas have evolved despite serious difficulties. Lymphomas appear in many different forms, and can change form in the process of spreading to another part of the body. Different types may be found in a single lymph gland.

Despite these difficulties, many chemotherapeutic agents have been found useful in treatment of lymphomas. To an extent, the preferred drugs fall in the same categories as those used in treating leukemia. The principal drugs, thus, include:

- alkalyting agents, such as nitrogen mustard, cyclophosphamide, and chlorambucil;

- vinca alkaloids, among them vincristine and vinblastine;

- procarbazine, which works like the alkalyting agents;

- antibiotics, which work to reduce or eliminate tumors, including Adriamycin and actinomycin D; and

- the corticosteroids, combinations of agents including hormones, acids, and other body elements.

These and other drugs have been used in various combinations in the treatment of lymphomas. One of the more successful has been named for the four drugs that are included in the protocol, or treatment series. The four are nitrogen mustard, vincristine (Oncovin), Procarbazine, and Prednisone; the combination treatment is known as MOPP. The treatment is used at certain stages of lymphoma, and has encouraged medical specialists to consider lymphoma as potentially curable.

In addition to drug therapy, methods of treating lymphomas include irradiation therapy, or radiotherapy, and a combination of drugs and radiotherapy.

19

Other Diseases of Major Importance

This chapter discusses a number of diseases of major importance that are not dealt with elsewhere: acquired immune deficiency syndrome (AIDS), a disease characterized by a defect in the body's natural immune system; plague, of great historical importance but fortunately now uncommon in the United States; two infectious diseases—tularemia and Rocky Mountain Spotted Fever; and seven tropical diseases that afflict millions of people in the warmer regions of the world and that occasionally occur elsewhere—malaria and yellow fever, leishmaniasis, trypanosomiasis, filariasis, schistosomiasis, and leprosy.

AIDS

First reported widely in 1981, AIDS has become a priority of the U.S. Public Health Service. Researchers have isolated a virus, the *human immunodeficiency virus* (*HIV*), that they believe causes AIDS. This virus was initially called the *human T-cell leukemia virus III* (*HTLV-III*). Persons with AIDS (PWAs) are susceptible to a variety of unusual or rare illnesses called *opportunistic diseases*. These include *Pneumocystis carinii* pneu-

monia (PCP); Kaposi's sarcoma; thrush, or *Candida albicans*; dementia (AIDS dementia complex or ADC); herpes simplex; and meningitis.

Groups at highest risk of contracting AIDS include homo- and bisexual men and intravenous drug users in large cities; hemophiliacs; female prostitutes; heterosexuals with multiple partners in areas where AIDS is common; and recipients of multiple blood transfusions from areas where the disease was common between 1983 and 1985. Evidence suggests that the HIV virus may also be affecting more and more young people, particularly runaways. In "passive transmission," a mother can pass AIDS to her child before or during birth.

Increasingly, medical authorities view AIDS as a disease with which victims may live for years. But AIDS is incurable. No treatment has successfully restored the immune system of an AIDS patient to normal functioning. Making the task of researching AIDS more difficult, the virus can lie inactive in the human body for as long as 10 years without causing any symptoms. Where this occurs, a "carrier" of AIDS can infect others with the disease.

Symptoms

Once infection with AIDS occurs, the human body may take from six weeks to a year or more to produce antibodies. These appear in response to the virus's invasion of the blood stream. The symptoms that can follow may resemble those of flu or even the common cold. Symptoms may include swollen glands, or enlarged lymph nodes, in the neck, armpits, or groin; night sweats; fever; unexplained rapid weight loss; chronic, unexplained diarrhea; fatigue; loss of appetite, and bruising and bleeding that do not heal.

Prevention

To prevent the spread of AIDS, the U.S. Public Health Service has recommended that persons at risk of contracting the disease should:

- Not donate blood or plasma, sperm, body organs, or other tissues

- Limit sexual contacts and be assertive with sexual partners about engaging only in safe sexual practices

- Not engage in sexual acts in which

exchange of body fluids, including semen, takes place

- Refrain from sharing toothbrushes, razors, or other implements that could be contaminated with blood

- If a drug user, limit drug use, do not let others use needles you have used, and do not leave needles or other drug paraphernalia where others might find and use them

- If a woman who has had a positive antibody test (see below), or who is the sexual partner of a man with a positive antibody test, avoid or postpone pregnancy

The Public Health Service has reported that no evidence indicates that the AIDS virus can be transmitted through casual kissing or other casual social contacts. But persons who have had positive antibody tests should let their physicians and dentists know about the test results. The physician and dentist can then cooperate in preventing the spread of the virus if the patient has become infected. There has been no risk of contracting AIDS through blood donations or transfusions since the introduction of blood-screening procedures in 1985.

Treatment

Although there is no known cure, a blood test called the *ELISA* (enzyme-linked immunosorbent assay) test has been developed to detect the presence of antibodies to the AIDS virus in human blood. The test has helped to eliminate nearly all questionable blood and plasma from the nation's blood supply—not to diagnose individuals. Laboratories have also used the Western Blot test to verify positive results from ELISA. In 1989, the FDA approved marketing of the HIVAG-1 test, the first designed to help physicians detect the AIDS virus

and to monitor its development in the human body. Already in use, a rapid screening test, the Recombigen HIV-1 Latex Agglutination test, can detect AIDS virus antibodies in five minutes.

More than 50 pharmaceutical companies have begun to develop vaccines, antiviral drugs, and other diagnostic tests for AIDS patients. The drugs in use include zidovudine, or AZT, the only compound proven effective against AIDS; alpha interferon, used to treat AIDS-generated cancer; and aerosolized pentamidine, approved in 1989 for broadened use with patients afflicted at least once with Pneumocystis pneumonia. AZT offered hope to some 600,000 Americans infected with AIDS after it was discovered that the drug can delay the onset of active symptoms.

At least 25 potential anti-HIV compounds were in various stages of testing in the late 1980s. The drugs worked in different ways. Researchers believed some of the agents might be most effective when used in combination. For example, alpha interferon has been combined in tests with AZT to reduce AZT's toxic effects, including anemia and liver problems. Various experimental drugs are designed to prevent the AIDS virus from binding to body cells, from entering into cells, or from developing into "virus factories" once inside human cells. Still others are designed to combat groups of AIDS symptoms, known as AIDS-Related Complex (ARC). Among the test drugs were several natural human products that bolster the immune system or antiviral defenses, including Imreg-2, interleukin-2, and virus-fighting interferons.

The FDA has taken steps to reduce the time elapsing between testing of drugs for treating life-threatening diseases and introduction of those compounds into the marketplace. The goal is to make possible

decisions on the approvability of various drugs much sooner than would once have been possible. In line with this program, the FDA approved expanded studies of the drugs foscarnet and ganciclovir, both of them potential compounds for the prevention of AIDS-related blindness.

Plague

Bubonic plague, one of the many diseases transmitted to humans through direct or indirect contact with animals, usually is listed among the scourges of past centuries. At least three great epidemics of bubonic plague have been recorded, including the Black Death of the 14th century, when the disease claimed at least 50 million lives. The most recent worldwide epidemic of the plague occurred in the 1800s. While recent cases of the plague in North America have been relatively rare, the disease organism is still carried by rodents, including squirrels, rats, and rabbits; and cases of the plague still occur in the western United States. Increased activity in western areas by hunters, campers, and other outdoor enthusiasts has resulted in a higher incidence of the disease among humans in recent years. The disease also is fairly common in Asia, Africa, and South America.

Symptoms

The infection is transmitted from animals to man through the bite of a flea carrying the disease organism. Symptoms usually develop in several days but may take as long as two weeks after the flea bite. The victim experiences chills and fever, with the temperature rising above 102° F. He may experience headaches, a rapid heart beat, and difficulty walking. Vomiting and delirium also are among the symptoms of plague. There may be pain and tenderness of the lymph nodes, which become inflamed and swollen; the enlarged lymph nodes are known as *buboes,* a term that gives its name to the type of plague involved. The buboes occur most frequently in the legs and groin because these are the most frequent sites for flea bites.

The site of the flea bite may or may not be found after the symptoms develop. If present, it may be marked by a swollen, pus-filled area of the skin.

Diagnosis of plague can be confirmed by laboratory tests that might include examination of the bacteria taken in samples from buboes or other diseased areas of the body, inoculation of laboratory animals with suspected disease organisms, and studies of the white blood cells of the patient.

Complications can include pneumonia and hemorrhages, with bleeding from the nose or mouth or through the gastrointestinal or urinary tracts, and abscesses and ulcerations. The pneumonic form of plague can be transmitted from one person to another like colds or other infectious diseases; in other words, plague organisms are spread by being exhaled by one person and inhaled by another.

Treatment and Prevention

As in other infectious diseases, early treatment is most effective. Antibiotics are administered every day for a period of one to two weeks, and buboes are treated with hot, moist applications. The buboes may be drained if necessary after the patient has responded to antibiotic medications. Antibiotics have reduced the fatality rate from plague infections from a high of 90 percent to a maximum of about 10 percent. Vaccines are available but are of limited and temporary

value. Prevention requires eradication of rats and other possibly infected rodents (some 200 species are known to carry the disease), use of insecticides to control fleas, and avoidance of contact with wild animals in areas where plague is known to exist. Domestic animals also should be protected from contact with possibly infected wild animals.

Tularemia

An infectious disease known as *tularemia,* sometimes called *rabbit fever,* is transmitted from animals to humans who come in contact with the animal tissues. It also can be transmitted through the bites of ticks or flies or by drinking contaminated water. Like the plague-disease organism, tularemia can be transmitted by inhalation of infected particles from the lungs of a diseased person, although such occurrences are rare.

Symptoms

Within a couple of days to perhaps two weeks after exposure to the tularemia germ, the patient develops chills and a fever with temperatures rising to 103° F. or higher. Other symptoms include headache, nausea and vomiting, extreme weakness, and drenching sweats. Lymph nodes become enlarged and a pus-filled lesion develops at the site of the infection. Usually only one pustular papule develops on a finger or other skin area, marking the point of the insect bite or contact with infected animal tissues; but there may be several such sores in the membranes of the mouth if that is the point of infection. It is not uncommon for the eyes or lungs to become involved.

Laboratory tests, along with a record of contact with wild animals or game birds, eating improperly cooked

meats, being bitten by deer flies or ticks, or drinking water from ponds or streams, usually helps verify the cause of the symptoms as tularemia. In some cases the contact with the disease organism can be made through bites or scratches of infected dogs or cats, but most frequently the disease of humans originates through handling of the meat or fur of wild animals or by camping or hiking in areas where the disease is endemic.

Treatment

Treatment includes bed rest and administration of antibiotics. Adequate fluid intake is important and oxygen may be required. Aspirin usually is given also, to relieve headache and muscle aches. Hot compresses are applied to the enlarged lymph node areas; it may be necessary to drain the swollen, infected nodes. If the disease is complicated by pneumonic tularemia or infection of the eye, the patient usually is hospitalized. Success of the therapy depends upon early and adequate treatment. The disease is rarely fatal when properly treated with antibiotics, but it can be lethal if the symptoms are ignored. Anyone who develops the symptoms of tularemia after handling wild animals or being exposed to biting insects or contaminated water in rural or rugged country should seek immediate medical help.

Hunters, campers, hikers, and others venturing into the great outdoors should protect their bodies against invasion by ticks by wearing long-sleeved shirts and long trousers with cuffs securely fastened. Regular checks should be made of the scalp, groin, and armpits for ticks. Any ticks found should be detached quickly and the bite area cleansed with soap and water, followed by an alcohol cleansing. If the head of the tick breaks off, it can be removed by the same techniques used to remove a splinter from the skin. Raw water from ponds and streams should be boiled or disinfected with chemicals before using. Rubber gloves should be worn while dressing the meat of wild game or birds, and the meat should be thoroughly cooked. On the positive side, once the disease occurs, the recovered patient develops immunity to tularemia.

Rocky Mountain Spotted Fever

The name of an increasingly common tick-borne disease, *Rocky Mountain spotted fever,* is misleading, because humans are most likely to become infected in regions far from the Rocky Mountains. The disease, also known as *tick fever,* has become most prevalent in rural and suburban areas of the southern and eastern United States. It is caused by a rickettsial organism transmitted by a tick bite. Wild rodents are a reservoir of the infected ticks that carry the disease.

Symptoms

Rocky Mountain spotted fever may be relatively mild or dangerously severe. The symptoms of headache, chills, and fever may begin suddenly and persist for a period of two or three weeks. Fever temperatures may reach 104° F and may be accompanied by nausea and occasional vomiting. Headaches have been described in some cases as excruciating, with the pain most intense along the forehead. Muscles of the legs, back, and abdomen may ache and feel tender. The most serious cases seem to develop within a few days after a tick bite; milder cases usually are slower to develop. A rash usually develops a few days after the onset of other symptoms and is most likely to be concentrated on the forearm, ankles, feet, wrists, and hands. If untreated, Rocky Mountain spotted fever symptoms may abate in two weeks, but the infection can be fatal, particularly in persons over the age of 40.

Treatment

Treatment includes administration of antibiotics and, in some cases, steroid hormones. Careful nursing care and adequate intake of protein foods and liquids also are needed.

Preventive measures are similar to those recommended to guard against tularemia. Wear adequate protective clothing that forms a barrier against tick invasion of the skin surfaces, check the scalp and other hairy body areas regularly for ticks, and remove and destroy any ticks found. In addition, ground areas known to be inhabited by wood ticks should be sprayed with an effective insecticide safe for humans; insect repellents also should be applied to clothing and exposed skin surfaces when venturing into wooded or brushy areas. Ticks may become attached to dogs and other animals and care should be used in removing them from the pets, because the disease organism can enter the body through minor cuts and scratches on the skin. A vaccine is available for protection of persons who are likely to use possibly infested tick areas for work or recreation. Immunity usually is established by two inoculations, about a month apart, and booster shots as needed.

Tropical Diseases

Most people living in the temperate climates of North America and Europe are spared the ravages of some of the most lethal and debilitating diseases known to mankind. They include malaria, which probably has killed more people than any other disease in history, yellow fever, leishmaniasis, trypanosomiasis, filariasis, schistosomiasis, and leprosy.

While many persons probably have never heard of some of these diseases and at least a few doctors might have trouble in diagnosing the symptoms, they affect hundreds of millions of people each year and could pose a threat to persons living in any part of the world. They are generally classed as tropical diseases, but so-called tropical or exotic diseases have been prevented from spreading into temperate regions partly because of alert medical care and preventive measures by public health experts. Malaria, for example, has been found as far north as the Arctic Circle, as far south as the tip of South America, and at one time was a disease of epidemic proportions in such northern cities as Philadelphia and London. These diseases have altered the course of history, ending the life of Alexander the Great as he tried to conquer the world, nipping in the bud Napoleon's plans to retake Canada from the English, defeating French efforts to build the Panama Canal, and contributing to the black-slave trade between Africa and the Americas.

The major tropical diseases are caused by a variety of organisms, including viruses, protozoa, and worms. Some are transmitted by insect bites, some by contact with contaminated water, and others, like leprosy, are spread by means that remain a mystery despite centuries of medical experience with millions of cases of the disease. Space does not permit detailed discussion of all tropical diseases; only those regarded by medical authorities as among the most significant to world health are described in this chapter.

Malaria

Malaria, one of the most common diseases in the world, gets its name from an Italian word for "bad air" because of an ancient belief that a mysterious substance in the air was the cause of the ailment. It is now known that the disease is caused by any of at least four parasites carried by Anopheles mosquitoes. According to the World Health Organization (WHO), some 200 million persons are affected by the disease, including one-fourth of the adult population on the continent of Africa. WHO estimates that at least one million children die each year of malaria. The disease was relatively rare in the United States until the 1960s, when hundreds of cases began to appear among military personnel who apparently contracted the disease in southeast Asia but did not develop symptoms until they returned to the United States; the disease later occurred in soldiers who had never left the United States, apparently transmitted by domestic Anopheles mosquitoes that had become infested with the malaria parasites.

Symptoms

The symptoms of malaria differ somewhat among various patients because the four known kinds of plasmodia, or protozoa, that cause the infection do not produce the same specific effects. However, the general symptoms common to all forms of malaria are fever, chills, headache, muscle pains, and, in some cases, skin disorders such as cold sores, hives, or a rash. A malaria attack may begin with a severe chill that lasts from twenty minutes to an hour, followed by a fever lasting from three to eight hours with temperature rising to more than 104° F. The fever usually is accompanied by profuse sweating, and the afflicted person is left exhausted by the cycle of chills and fever. The attacks become more or less successively milder, less frequent, and more irregular, and finally cease, although there may be relapses.

One kind of malarial organism seems to cause attacks that occur every other day, while another type produces attacks that appear quite regularly on every third day; still another type of malaria plasmodium seems to cause a fever that is continuous. While the liver seems to be a favored target organ, other body systems can be involved, with related complications. If the organism reaches the brain, the patient may suffer convulsions, delirium, partial paralysis, or coma. If the organism invades the lungs, there may be coughing symptoms and blood-stained sputum. In some cases, there may be gastrointestinal symptoms with abdominal pain, vomiting, or diarrhea.

Medical examination of malaria patients frequently reveals signs of anemia, an enlarged spleen, liver abnormalities, and edema, or swelling because of fluid accumulation. Blood studies may show the malaria parasites in the blood, damaged red blood cells, and an abnormal white blood cell count. The four species of malaria organism are distinctive enough to be identified in laboratory tests.

Treatment

Treatment includes administration of antimalarial drugs such as quinine, chloroquine, or primaquine. Newer antimalarial drugs are sometimes used in combinations because of the development of drug-resistant strains of the organism in South America and Asia. There is no vaccine that protects against malaria.

Causes

The protozoa that cause malaria are carried by the Anopheles mosquito,

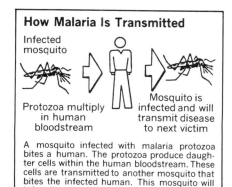

How Malaria Is Transmitted

Infected mosquito → Protozoa multiply in human bloodstream → Mosquito is infected and will transmit disease to next victim

A mosquito infected with malaria protozoa bites a human. The protozoa produce daughter cells within the human bloodstream. These cells are transmitted to another mosquito that bites the infected human. This mosquito will infect the next human it bites, thus perpetuating the malaria cycle.

but humans are the intermediate host. This means that both infected humans and infected mosquitoes are needed to continue the life cycle of the organism. The disease therefore can be controlled if Anopheles mosquito populations are eradicated and humans are not carrying the protozoa in their blood. When these organisms get into human blood, they invade the red blood cells and multiply until the blood cells rupture to release offspring called *daughter cells*. When the mosquito bites a human for a blood meal, the daughter cells enter the mosquito stomach, where they complete their life cycle and migrate to the mosquito's salivary gland to be injected into the next human, and so on. It takes from ten days to six weeks following a mosquito bite for the first malaria symptoms to develop, the time differences varying with the species of protozoa involved. The malaria mosquito in recent years has developed resistance to insecticides, and areas of infestation have spread in some countries where irrigation for farming has been expanded.

Yellow Fever

Yellow fever, which sometimes produces symptoms similar to those of malaria, also is transmitted by a mosquito. But yellow fever is a virus disease carried by the Aedes mosquito.

Yellow fever also can be harbored by other animals, while the malaria organism that affects humans is not transmitted between humans and lower animals. Like malaria, yellow fever has in past years spread deeply into North America with cases reported along the Gulf Coast, the Mississippi River Valley, and as far north as Boston. A vaccine is available for protection against yellow fever.

Leishmaniasis

Leishmaniasis is similar to malaria in that the disease organisms are protozoa transmitted to humans by an insect bite, but the insect in this case is the sandfly. There are several forms that leishmaniasis can take. The kind considered most lethal, with a mortality rate of up to 95 percent of untreated adults, is known as *kala-azar*, a term derived from the Hindi language meaning "black disease". Kala-azar also is known as *black fever, dumdum fever,* and *visceral leishmaniasis*. It occurs from China through Russia and India to North Africa, the Mediterranean countries of Europe, and in parts of Central and South America. Kala-azar has appeared in the United States in cases contracted overseas.

Symptoms

The symptoms may not appear for a period of from ten days to more than three months after the bite of a sandfly, although the disease organism may be found in blood tests before the first symptoms occur. Symptoms include a fever that reaches a peak twice a day for a period of perhaps several weeks, then recurs at irregular intervals while the patient experiences progressive weakness, loss of weight, loss of skin color, and a rapid heartbeat. In some cases, depending upon the type of infection, there may be gastrointestinal complaints and bleeding of the mucous membranes, particularly around the teeth. There also can be edema, an accumulation of fluid in the tissues that conceals the actual loss of body tissue. Physical examination shows an enlarged spleen and liver plus abnormal findings in blood and urine tests.

American Cutaneous Leishmaniasis

The American cutaneous form of leishmaniasis usually begins with one or more skin ulcers resulting from sandfly bites, with the skin of the ear the target site of the insect in many cases. The skin lesion may enlarge, with or without secondary infection by other disease organisms, and spread into the lymphatic system of the body. From the lymph system, the infecting protozoa may invade the mouth and nose, producing painful and mutilating skin ulcers and other destructive changes in the tissues. Bacterial infections and respiratory problems can lead to the death of the patient. In some areas of Central and South America, more than 10 percent of the population suffer from the disfiguring effects of leishmaniasis. Diagnosis usually is confirmed by medical tests that identify the leishmaniasis organism in the patient's tissues.

Old World Cutaneous Leishmaniasis

A milder form, sometimes known as Old World cutaneous leishmaniasis, occurs from India westward to the Mediterranean countries and North Africa. An ulcer appears at the site of a sandfly bite, usually several weeks after the bite, but it heals during a period of from three months to a year. A large pitted scar frequently remains to mark the site of the ulceration, but the invading organism does not spread deeply into the body tissues as in the severe types of leishmaniasis.

Treatment

Therapy for leishmaniasis cases includes administration of various medications containing antimony, along with antibiotics for the control of secondary infections. Bed rest, proper diet, and, in severe cases, blood transfusions also are advised.

Causes

The leishmaniasis organisms injected into the human body by the sandfly bite multiply through parasitic invasion of the tissue cells, particularly blood cells that usually resist infection. They may invade the lymph nodes, spleen, liver, and bone marrow, causing anemia and other symptoms. In populated areas, sandflies can be eradicated by insecticides. Unfortunately, rodents and other wild and domestic animals serve as a reservoir for the leishmaniasis protozoa and tend to perpetuate the disease in rural and jungle areas of warm climates.

Trypanosomiasis

Trypanosomiasis is a group of diseases caused by similar kinds of parasitic protozoa. The diseases, which include two kinds of African *sleeping sickness* and *Chagas' disease* of Central and South America, affect about 10 million people. The sleeping-sickness forms of trypanosomiasis are transmitted by species of the tsetse fly, while Chagas' disease is carried by insects known as *assassin bugs* or *kissing bugs*. Besides affecting humans, the trypanosomiasis organisms infect other animals, including cattle, horses, dogs, and donkeys, and have made an area of nearly four million square miles of Africa uninhabitable. According to the World Health Organization, the African land devastated by trypanosomiasis contains large fertile areas capable of supporting 125 million cattle, but domestic animals cannot survive the infestation of tsetse flies.

Sleeping Sickness

The two kinds of African sleeping sickness, Gambian and Rhodesian, are similar. Gambian, or mid-African, sleeping sickness is transmitted by a tsetse fly that lives near water; Rhodesian, or East African, sleeping sickness is carried by a woodland species of tsetse fly that uses antelopes as a reservoir of the infectious organism. The most likely victims of tsetse fly bites are young men, probably because they are more likely to be exposed to the insects.

Symptoms

The symptoms of trypanosomiasis infections from tsetse fly bites can vary considerably according to various factors, such as the general health of the victim. A small area of inflammation, called a *chancre*, appears at the site of the tsetse fly bite about two days after the incident; some patients complain of pain and irritation in the area around the bite for several weeks, but others have no symptoms. Then, for a period of perhaps several months, episodes of fever occur, with temperatures rising to 106° F. The bouts of fever may be accompanied by skin rashes, severe headaches, and heart palpitations. Loss of appetite and weight follow, with insomnia, an inability to concentrate, tremors, and difficulty in speaking and walking. There also may be signs of anemia and delayed reaction to a painful stim-

ulus. Eventually, the protozoa can invade the central nervous system, producing convulsions, coma, and death.

Sleeping sickness, which may progress gradually, gets its name from the appearance of the patient, who develops a vacant expression and drooping eyelids, along with blurred speech, general lethargy, and occasional periods of paralysis.

Gambian and Rhodesian Varieties

A major difference between the Gambian and Rhodesian forms of African sleeping sickness is that the Rhodesian variety, which has similar symptoms, is more acute and progresses more rapidly than the Gambian. The fevers are higher, weight losses greater, the disease more resistant to treatment, and the span of time from first symptoms to death much shorter. Even with intensive treatment, Rhodesian sleeping sickness patients have only a 50–50 chance of survival, while 90 to 95 percent of the Gambian sleeping sickness patients recover when properly treated for the disease.

Treatment

Several chemotherapeutic agents are available for treatment of Gambian and Rhodesian sleeping sickness; they include suramin, pentamidine, and tryparsamide given by injection. Good nutrition, good nursing care, and treatment of secondary infections are additional therapeutic measures.

Chagas' Disease

Chagas' disease, or American trypanosomiasis, is a primary cause of heart disease from Mexico through much of South America. The protozoan infection is rare in the United

States, but cases have been reported. The first symptoms may be edema of the face. The accumulation of fluid occuring in the area of the eyelids, conjunctivitis, hard reddish nodules on the skin, along with the fever and involvement of the heart, brain, and liver tissues. The assassin or kissing bugs by which the disease is spread tend to bite the face, especially around the lips or eyelids, accounting for the swelling of those facial areas. The bite may be painful, or if the victim is sleeping at the time, it may not be noticed at all.

Symptoms

The protozoa multiply rapidly at the site of the bug bite, frequently producing symptoms resembling those of leishmaniasis—intermittent fever, swollen spleen, and enlarged liver, after signs of an insect bite. After several days, the trypanosomiasis organisms spread from the site of infection into other tissues, especially the heart and brain, where they cause tissue destruction, inflammation, and often death.

Treatment

There is no specific treatment for Chagas' disease, and, except for experimental drugs, most therapeutic measures are intended to treat the symptoms.

Like the African sleeping sickness forms of trypanosomiasis, the American type can involve reservoirs of wild and domestic animals; the disease has been found in cats and dogs as well as in opossums and armadillos. Persons traveling in endemic areas should use preventive measures that are appropriate, such as insect sprays and repellents. Efforts to eradicate large areas of insects carrying the trypanosomiasis organisms have been futile; in some instances it has been found to be more effective to move villages away from the insects than to try to remove the insects from the villages.

Filariasis

The species of mosquitoes that transmit malaria and yellow fever, diseases caused by protozoa and viruses, also transmit *filariasis,* caused by a parasitic worm—a nematode or roundworm. Filariasis affects 300 million people living in tropical and subtropical areas of the world. The worm invades the subcutaneous tissues and lymph system of the human body, blocking the flow of lymph and producing symptoms of inflammation, edema, abscesses, and, in one form of the disease, blindness. Filariasis is not unknown to Americans; some 15,000 soldiers contracted the disease during World War II fighting in the Pacific Theater, and cases have been reported along the Carolina coast area. But most of the victims of filariasis live in a region extending from Africa through Asia to the islands of New Guinea and Borneo.

Symptoms

Symptoms of filariasis can develop insidiously during an incubation period that may last from three months to a year after infection. There can be brief attacks of a low-grade fever, with chills and sweating, headache, nausea, and muscle pain. The patient also may feel sensitive to bright lights. Signs and symptoms more specifically related to filariasis are the appearance of red, swollen skin areas with tender spots that indicate the spread of the threadlike worms through the lymphatic system. Most likely sites for the first signs of filariasis are the lymph vessels of the legs, with later involvement of the

groin and abdomen, producing the swollen lower frontal effect known as *elephantiasis.* Diagnosis of the disease is confirmed by finding the tiny worms in the lymph; the infecting organism also may be found in blood tests, but only at certain times. The worms of one form of the disease are only 35 to 90 millimeters long in the adult stage, and those of a second type of the disease are only half that size. Larvae, or embryos, of the worms may be only 200 microns (one-fifth of a millimeter) in size.

Treatment

An oral medication, diethylcarbamazine, is available to kill the larvae in the system; the drug has only limited value in destroying the adult worms. The drug is taken orally for three weeks, but courses may have to be repeated over a period of two years because relapses can occur. Other therapeutic measures include bed rest during periods of fever and inflammation, antibiotics to control secondary infections, and, occasionally, surgery to remove damaged tissues that may interfere with normal working activities following recovery.

Onchocerciasis

The type of filariasis that causes blindness is transmitted by a species of blackfly that introduces or picks up the worm larvae while biting. As in mosquito-transmitted filariasis, the worms work their way through the skin to the lymphatic system but tend to migrate to eye structures. Blackfly filariasis, also called *onchocerciasis,* occurs most frequently in Africa and from southern Mexico to northern South America. More than one million cases of onchocerciasis have been found in the upper basin of the Volta River of Africa, with thousands of patients already blinded by the infection.

Loiasis

A third variation of filariasis is called *loiasis.* It is carried from man to monkey or from monkey to man by a biting fly. The larvae develop into adult worms that migrate under the skin and sometimes through the eye. Migration of a worm through the skin causes swelling, irritation, and redness. The disease is treated with drugs to kill the larvae, as well as by antihistamines and, occasionally, surgery to remove the adult worms.

Control of filariasis requires eradication of the flies and mosquitoes that transmit the parasitic worms and perhaps the wild animals that can serve as reservoirs. As in the examples of other tropical diseases, it frequently is easier to separate the humans from the areas infested by the insects than to eradicate the insects.

Schistosomiasis

A worm of a different sort—the trematode, a flatworm of the class *Trematoda,* which includes the flukes—is responsible for *schistosomiasis.* This disease occurs in various forms in Africa, Asia, South America, and the Caribbean, including Puerto Rico. About 200 million people are infected with schistosomiasis, also called *bilharziasis.*

Life Cycle of the Fluke Parasite

The process of infection by one kind of fluke involves free-swimming larvae that penetrate the skin of a human who has entered waters containing the organism. The larvae follow the human bloodstream to the liver, where they develop into adult worms. The adult worms then move into the blood vessels of the host and lay eggs. Some of the eggs find their way into the intestine or urinary bladder and are excreted with the urine or feces of the host. If they find their way to fresh water, the eggs hatch and the released organisms find their way to the body of a snail. Inside the snail they multiply into thousands of new larvae over a period of one or two months, after which they return to the water and invade the skin of another human. In this manner the fluke worm continues its life cycle, infecting more humans who venture into the contaminated waters.

Symptoms

Skin rashes and itching, loss of appetite, abdominal discomfort, and diarrhea are among early symptoms of schistosomiasis infections. There also may be fever and generalized aches and pains. During a period of from one to two or more months after the initial infection, more severe symptoms may occur as a result of a growing number of adult worms and eggs in the body, which produce allergic reactions. Those symptoms may include diarrhea, abdominal pain, coughing spells, and high fever and chills. Medical examination may reveal a tender and enlarged liver plus signs of bleeding in the intestinal tract. Complications may result from obstruction by masses of worms and eggs or by rupturing of the walls of body organs during migration of the organisms. Diagnosis usually can be confirmed by examination of the victim's stools or of the lining of the rectum for the presence of eggs of the fluke worms.

Treatment

Therapy may consist of administration of antimony-based drugs, tartar emetic, measures to relieve the symptoms, and, when deemed necessary, surgery. In some cases, a medication may be administered to flush the eggs of the fluke worm

through a specific part of the circulatory system during a surgical procedure in which a filter is inserted in a vein to trap the eggs; thousands of fluke worms can be removed by this technique. Some of the medications used in treating schistosomiasis can have serious side effects and are used cautiously. However, the alternative may be prolonged emaciation of the victim, with a bloated abdomen and early death by cancer or other causes related to the infection. The female fluke worm has been known to continue depositing eggs during a life span of 30 years, causing frequent recurrence of acute symptoms.

Other Forms of Schistosomiasis

There are several other forms of schistosomiasis that cause variations in symptoms. One kind involves the liver and central nervous system, resulting in death of the victims within as little as two years after infection. Another form seems to involve the urinary bladder, causing frequent, painful, and blood-tinged urination with bacterial infection as a complication.

Swimmer's Itch

A mild form of schistosomiasis is known by the popular name *swimmer's itch*. It can occur anywhere from Asia to South America and as far north as Canada and western Europe, affecting bathers in both fresh water and sea water. As in the severe forms of schistosomiasis, snails are the intermediate hosts, and wild animals and birds provide a reservoir of the organism. The effects are treated as a skin allergy, and shallow local waters used for swimming are treated with chemicals to eradicate the snails. Careful drying and examination of the skin after swimming in possibly infected waters can control to some de-

gree the invasion of the skin by fluke larvae. A chemical skin cream that tends to repel fluke larvae also is available as a protective measure.

Leprosy

More than 10 million people are victims of *leprosy,* an infectious disorder also known as *Hansen's disease.* Although leprosy is more common in tropical regions, where up to 10 percent of some population groups may be affected, the disease also occurs in several northern countries, including the United States, where the disease is found in coastal states from California through Texas and Louisiana, and from Florida to New York. Ancient medical writings indicate that leprosy was known in China and India about 3,000 years ago but did not spread to the eastern Mediterranean until A.D. 500 or 600. Thus, the disease described in the Bible as leprosy probably was not the same disease known today by that name.

Symptoms

The manifestations of leprosy resemble those of several other diseases, including syphilis, sarcoidosis, and vitiligo, a skin disease marked by patches where pigmentation has been lost. The lesions of leprosy, which may begin as pale or reddish areas of from one-half inch to three or four inches in diameter, appear on body surfaces where the temperature is cooler than other body areas. These cooler surfaces include the skin, nose and throat, eyes, and testicles. The early cosmetic symptoms are followed gradually by a loss of feeling in the affected areas because of involvement of the nerve endings in those tissues. At first the patient may notice a loss of ability to distinguish hot and cold sensations in the diseased area.

Then there may be a loss of tactile sensation. Finally, there is a loss of pain sensation in the affected tissues.

A case of leprosy may progress into one of two major forms, *tuberculoid leprosy* or *lepromatous leprosy,* or a combination of the two forms. The advanced symptoms can include more severe nerve damage and muscular atrophy with foot drop and contracted hands, plus damage to body areas from burns and injuries that are not felt but that can become infected. Damage to nose tissues can lead to breathing difficulties and speech problems. Crippling and blinding are not uncommon in untreated causes of leprosy, and death may occur as a result of secondary infections.

Treatment

A number of different sulfone drugs have been found effective against the mycobacterium that apparently causes leprosy, but the drugs also produce such side effects as fever and anemia. When intolerance to sulfones occurs, other medications are offered, including thiourea, mercaptan, and streptomycin. Steroid hormones are used to help control adverse reactions.

Causes

The disease organism, *Mycobacterium leprae,* or *Hansen's bacillus,* is believed to enter the skin or the respiratory system of the victim, probably during childhood. It rarely infects adults except under unusual circumstances, as through skin tattooing. Some medical scientists believe the infection may be transmitted through an insect bite, since the disease organism has been found in insects. However, the true process of leprosy infection remains unknown, and efforts to cultivate the mycobacterium in laboratory tissue cultures have been futile, although the disease can be induced in the footpads of experimental animals. Doctors have not found it necessary to isolate patients with the disease except during the period when treatments begin. Regular and thorough skin examinations of persons who have been in contact with leprosy patients and early detection and treatment of the disease by specialists are the recommended means of control.

20

Surgery

Surgery Today

Computer and video screens surround the operating table, their displays projecting larger-than-life sections of a patient's internal organs. Monitors beep and blip in the foreground as a surgical assistant quickly hands the surgeon his tools—two slender fiber-optic tubes, one equipped with telescopic lens, video camera and light source, the other fitted with a laser. The surgeon makes two tiny incisions in the patient's abdomen, each smaller than a dime, and then inserts the instruments. The telescopic lens and camera help the surgeon locate the organ. Watching his movements on the video screen, he uses the laser to first carefully cut away a lesion and then seal the organ where the cut was made. Even as the piece of tissue is being sent to the laboratory for biopsy, the patient's incisions have been stitched and covered with Band-Aids.

This scene is reenacted every day in hospitals across the country. New developments in techniques, instruments and knowledge have revolutionized the field of surgery, moving it into what once was considered only the realm of science fiction. Doctors routinely make microscopic incisions with beams of light, freeze cancerous cells with liquid nitrogen, and use computer-operated cameras to view the interior landscape of the body. While the range of surgical procedures remains vast, the procedures, themselves, have changed. For example, a patient undergoing surgery to remove his gall bladder previously faced an operation that sliced through the major muscles of the abdomen to reach the organ and then kept him in the hospital for a week with restricted physical activity for up to six weeks following the procedure. Today, the same patient would most likely undergo a laparoscopic cholecystectomy, a procedure in which surgeons make four tiny incisions in the abdomen and then insert delicate instruments and cameras that they manipu-

late from outside. In less than an hour, the diseased gall bladder is extricated through one of the incisions. After an overnight stay in the hospital followed by a week of rest, the patient is back to his normal activities.

Just when operations, such as open heart surgery, were becoming more and more complex, as well as risky, technological innovations simplified the field. Less invasive surgical techniques, new antibiotics and anesthesia, improved imaging techniques, and advances in preoperative management all have contributed to making the surgical experience of the average patient safer and less painful and his recovery time much quicker.

Surgical Innovations

Researchers and surgeons have begun to view the best surgical techniques as those that manage to dispense with the typical symbols of their craft—the knife and scalpel. Advanced technology is changing the way a surgeon plans and executes an operation.

Videoscope Surgery & Imaging Techniques

One of the primary reasons why overall health care has improved in the last decade is the development of slender, fiber-optic tubes, or *scopes*, that can be inserted deep inside the body through nearly invisible incisions. Fitted with cameras, telescopic lenses, and lights and hooked up to video screens, scopes enable surgeons to see images of a patient's internal organs, usually with greater clarity than if they were looking directly at the organ. The appeal of videoscope surgery to both surgeons and patients is simple; while it enables doctors to pinpoint the location and type of the problem they're facing, it dramatically reduces surgical trauma for the patient. Conventional "open" surgery results in high levels of stress to the patient's body. Surgeons must cut through skin, muscles, fat and, depending on the surgery, bone. The use of videoscopes dramatically lowers the number of conventional operations, especially in the area of exploratory surgery, in which surgeons perform an operation to discover the nature of a patient's problem. Some doctors predict that the day will come when making any kind of incision will be viewed as a failure.

Various scopes are named for the area of the body in which they are generally used. *Laparoscopes* are used in the abdomen, *arthroscopes* are applied to the joints, *thoracoscopes or endoscopes* are used in the chest, and *angioscopes* are used inside the walls of blood vessels.

Improved imaging techniques such as *computerized tomography (CT)* and *magnetic resonance imaging (MRI)* have also moved the science of surgery forward. The CT scan provides surgeons with cross-section x-ray images of the inside of the body. All of the organs can be seen and evaluated. The MRI, on the other hand, creates three-dimensional images of the body's interior using a magnetic field and radio waves instead of X rays. Using these improved methods, surgeons can narrow the scope of the procedure considerably and meticulously plan every aspect of the operation.

Laser Surgery

First used in eye surgery in the 1960s, laser technology is coming to be regarded as a conventional surgical technique. Laser surgeons are the new breed of surgeons and precision separates their tools from the traditional knife and scalpel. Without even cutting skin, a surgeon can often completely eradicate a problem with absolute precision even in the most inaccessible areas of the body. Lasers cause little trauma, if any, to the patient, thus offering less invasive, even noninvasive, solutions.

An acronym for **L**ight **A**mplification by **S**timulated **E**mission of **R**adiation, the laser is a precisely controlled light beam that is narrowly focused and then aimed at a minute target. In each laser, various frequencies of light are converted into an intense beam of single wavelength, or color. The color determines how the beam will interact with particular kinds of tissue, and may be different for different kinds of surgery. Lasers may function continuously or in pulsed bursts. The type of laser determines the number of pulses per second, the duration of the pulses and whether the light will be used to cut through tissue, vaporize it, or seal it.

Various lasers take their names from the different substances that produce the beam.

The *carbon dioxide laser*, with a wavelength in the far infrared spectrum, penetrates tissue to a depth of only one millimeter. CO_2's ability to turn the body's water content into steam allows it to sear, cook, or cut tissue to a precisely controlled depth, sealing blood vessels and nerve endings in a bloodless procedure. The CO_2 laser has been used widely to treat some types of cancer, gynecological disorders, and brain tumors.

The *argon laser*, functioning in the blue-green frequencies, reacts with the color red and will penetrate the skin until it comes in contact with blood. Because it readily coagulates with blood in the operating area, the argon laser has been particularly useful in the fields of opthalmology, plastic surgery, and dermatology.

The *YAG laser*, with a wavelength in the near infrared spectrum, is used to cook or vaporize tissue that will then be removed from the body. The most invasive of all surgical laser devices, the YAG laser can penetrate 4 to 5 millimeters.

Dye lasers can be tuned to react to different wavelengths of light, simply by adding or diluting tint. The *free-electron laser*, also tunable, uses magnets to stimulate pulsed light from a stream of electrons.

The *excimer laser* breaks up intermolecular bonds and decomposes matter, allowing precise surgery through holes so small no stitches are necessary. When certain gases are stimulated and combined and then returned to a disassociated state, their electrons emit photons of light in ultraviolet wavelengths. For example, patients undergoing excimer laser surgery to repair corneal damage do not experience the thermal effects or shock waves of conventional lasers. Without even touching the cornea, the excimer vaporizes with cool UV light the molecular links that bond the tissue.

Microscopic Surgery

The development of microsurgery—the use of operating microscopes—allows surgeons access to parts of the body that would otherwise be too small to see. Many tumors, formerly considered inoperable, now can be removed through microsurgery. Often the use of microscopes is paired with another innovative technology, such as the use of lasers, because what the surgeon can't see with the naked eye, he also can't cut with a scalpel. Using the microscope to locate and isolate a tumor, the surgeon then destroys it with a laser beam. Microsurgery is often used on brain tumors with success.

Cryosurgery & Hypothermic Arrest

Precancerous skin conditions, such as acute keratosis, as well as skin cancers, are being treated with extreme cold in a procedure called cryosurgery. Liquid nitrogen, applied to the growth, freezes and kills the abnormal cells. Once it thaws, the dead tissue falls off or is easily removed. Anesthesia is not necessary in cryosurgery, but patients may experience pain after treatment. Scarring may also occur.

The human body's vulnerability to extreme temperature fluctuations and how it has reacted in past cases has provided surgeons and researchers with valuable information that they have been able to use to develop new surgical techniques. The notion that the human body can survive without circulation at very low temperatures arose from cases in which children who lost consciousness in extremely cold water were later revived after hours of submersion. Normally, the brain only lasts three to five minutes without oxygen. In a new, experimental procedure called *hypothermic arrest*, the body is cooled to approximately 40 degrees below normal, where it needs much less energy and the brain can actually survive for up to sixty minutes without oxygen. Hypothermic arrest has been used almost exclusively for brain surgery.

Surgery Classifications

Surgery is classified according to whether it is vital to life, necessary for continued health, or desirable for medical or personal reasons. Although there are many ways in which surgical procedures are classified, the following breakdown is one that is widely accepted among surgeons.

Emergency Surgery

Unpredictable events that result in the need for medical immediate attention are classified as emergency surgeries. An automobile accident, a fire, a violent crime, or even a sudden change in a chronic medical problem, like a perforated ulcer or a strangulated hernia, can create situations in which the life of the patient depends upon the time it takes to get the victim into the hands of a trained surgeon. Emergency surgery cases typically involve the treatment of gunshot and stab wounds, fractures of the skull and other major bones, severe eye injuries, or life-threatening situations, such as obstruction of the windpipe caused by choking on a piece of food.

Emergency surgery may be one of the most common routes for patients entering the operating room. Accident patients present tremendous challenges to surgeons, because emergency room patients frequently have multiple injuries involving several organ systems. Such victims are often unconscious or otherwise unable to communicate coherently about their injuries, and there may be little or no time to obtain medical histories or information about their blood types, allergies to medicines, etc.

When possible, vital information about the patient and the circumstances surrounding the injury or sudden need for surgery is obtained by medical personnel who question anybody who might provide one or more clues. Efforts to maintain life are begun even while blood samples are taken for laboratory analysis and X-ray photographs made of the chest, abdomen, and other body areas that may be involved. When life is in immediate peril, resuscitation, induction of anesthesia, and surgery might proceed simultaneously as soon as a diagnosis is made.

Urgent Surgery

Next in priority for the surgeon are cases in which an operation is vital but can be postponed for a few days. A person injured in an automobile accident but conscious and suffering a minor bone fracture may be classed as an urgent rather than emergency surgery case, and the delay would give surgeons and other medical personnel time to study X-rays carefully, evaluate blood tests and other diagnostic data, and otherwise plan corrective therapy while under less pressure. Kidney stones, an acute, inflamed gall bladder, or cancer of a vital organ are examples of urgent surgery.

Elective Surgery

Elective surgery is usually subdivided into three categories: required, selective, and optional.

Required Surgery

Physical ailments that are serious enough to need corrective surgery but that can be scheduled a matter of weeks or months in advance generally are designated as required surgery cases. Conditions such as a chronically inflamed gall bladder, cataracts, bone deformities, or diseased tonsils and adenoids would be examples of conditions that require surgery.

Selective Surgery

Selective surgery covers a broad range of conditions that are of no real threat to the immediate physical health of the patient but nevertheless should be corrected by surgery in order to improve his comfort and emotional health. Certain congenital defects such as cleft lip and cleft palate would be included in this classification, as well as removal of certain cysts and nonmalignant fatty or fibrous tumors.

Optional Surgery

Of the lowest priority are operations that are primarily of cosmetic benefit, such as removal of warts and other nonmalignant growths on the skin, blemishes of the skin, and certain cases of varicose veins. Optional surgery also includes various kinds of plastic surgery undertaken for cosmetic effect. Among popular types of plastic surgery are operations to reduce or enlarge the shape of female breasts, reshape the nose, correct protruding ears, remove bags under the eyes, decrease facial wrinkles.

Types of Surgery

Surgery is further divided according to the following groups of major operations.

Surgeries with the suffix *-ectomy* involve the partial or complete removal of an organ, the most common being the appendectomy.

Operations to restore, reconstruct or refigure body parts are denoted by the suffix *-plasty*; thus cosmetic surgery to reshape the nose is called rhinoplasty.

Surgeries with the suffix *-otomy* involve the perforation or incision of organs or tissue, as in radial keratotomy, laser surgery performed on the eye.

The Surgical Team

Most surgical operations are performed not by the surgeon alone, but by a surgical team. Depending upon the complexity of the surgical procedure involved, the surgeon may have one or more assistants working him. The assistants may be interns or hospital residents who participate in the operation as a part of the advanced training in surgical techniques, or they may be other surgeons who are specialists in a particular field. An abdominal surgeon or orthopedic surgeon, for example, may be assisted by a neurosurgeon if the operation is likely to require a special knowledge of the nervous system as it affects another organ system.

The Anesthetist

The anesthetist, who is also likely to be a physician, specializes in maintaining the proper degree of anesthesia in the patient, while also helping to maintain the body's life systems. In addition to making the patient unaware of pain during the operation—sometimes by making him unconscious, sometimes without affecting consciousness—the anesthetist must keep the muscles and nervous reflexes in a proper state for the type of surgery to be performed. Each of the various functions, muscle relaxation, for example, requires a different anesthetic drug. Their performance

must be perfectly coordinated to prevent complications during the operation. Obviously, the anesthetist must prepare a different combination of drugs for a child, an elderly person, a pregnant woman in labor, or a man with heart disease.

Other Members of the Surgical Team

As noted earlier, there are occasions when several surgeons are working more or less simultaneously on an accident victim with injuries to multiple organ systems. In such cases of emergency surgery, a general surgeon may supervise and coordinate the work of the other surgeons. The Chief Operating Room Nurse supervises and coordinates the activities of the scrub nurses who assist the surgeon in the actual operation, and the supply and circulating nurses who aid the rest of the surgical team by making available as needed the various towels, drapes, sponges, sutures, instruments, and other equipment.

One or more of the nurses wear gowns and gloves that have been sterilized so they can work directly with the surgeon and hand him equipment or supplies that he requests. Such a nurse is called a *scrub nurse* because he scrubs his hands and arms for ten minutes before the operation, just as the surgeon does. Other nurses in the operating room who do not wear sterilized gowns and gloves are not permitted to handle equipment directly but may be permitted to pick up sterilized materials with an instrument that has been sterilized. One or more orderlies, who are responsible for lifting the patient and keeping the operating room in tidy condition, complete a surgical team.

Preoperative Procedures

Preparation of a patient for surgery involves a variety of procedures determined by the urgency of the operation, the anatomical area involved, the nature of the disease or injury requiring surgery, the general condition of the patient, and other factors. Emergency surgery of an accident victim in critical condition obviously requires a greatly accelerated pace of preparing the patient for the operating room; medical personnel may cut away the clothing of the victim in order to save precious minutes. An operation on the intestine, on the other hand, may require a full week of preparation, including the five or so days needed to evaluate laboratory tests and sterilize the bowel with drugs. However, most preop procedures, as they are commonly called, generally follow a similar pattern designed to insure a safe and sound operation. Even in a case of emergency surgery, certain information must be compiled to help guide the surgeon and other hospital staff personnel in making the right decisions affecting proper care of the patient during and after the operation.

Medical History

The medical history should reveal the general health of the patient and any factors that might increase the risk of surgery. Perhaps one of his parents or another close relative suffered from heart disease or diabetes; such facts might suggest a predisposition of the patient to problems associated with those disorders. The data should also show whether the patient has a tendency to bleed easily and whether he has been following a special diet, such as a sodium-restricted diet.

It is important that the patient reveal to his own physician, the surgeon, and the anesthetist, the names of any drugs or other medications used. It also is vital that the medical personnel have a complete record of any patient experiences, including allergic reactions to certain drugs, that might help predict drug sensitivities that could complicate the surgery. The simple fact that a patient suffers from asthma or hay fever might indicate that he may be more sensitive than other individuals to drugs that might be administered.

Allergic Reactions

Some patients are allergic to penicillin or other antibiotics. Others may be sensitive to aspirin or serums. Still others could be allergic to iodine, Merthiolate, or even adhesive tape. All of these factors, if they are known and if they apply to the patient about to undergo surgery, should be brought to the attention of the medical staff.

Medications Currently Being Used

Among medications routinely used by the patient that should be brought to the attention of the surgeon and anesthetist are insulin for diabetes, digitalis drugs for heart diseases, and cortisone for arthritis. Depending upon various factors relating to the individual case, the patient may be directed to continue using the medication as usual, change the size of the dose before or after surgery, or discontinue the drug entirely for a while.

A patient who has been taking certain sedatives or drinking alcohol beverages regularly for a prolonged period before surgery may begin to experience withdrawl symptoms or he may have developed a tolerance for the anesthetic used, which means that he would require a larger than usual dose to get the desired effect. A patient who has been using epinephrine-type eye drops for glaucoma may be asked to increase the dosage before surgery as an adjustment to one of the drugs used in conjunction.

Diuretics, tranquilizers, and anticoagulant drugs are among other medications commonly used by patients that could affect the manner in which a surgical procedure is carried out. Patients should take a sample of the medication or the pharmacist's label from a container of the medication to the hospital so the medical staff can verify the type of drug used.

Psychological Evaluation

Of increasing importance in recent years has been a phychological evaluation of the patient. Individuals with a past history of mental disease or patients whose complaints may be based on psychoneurotic factors may react differently to surgery than persons who could be described as psychologically well balanced. The preoperative interviews also may seek to obtain information about the patient's abuse of drugs or alcohol.

Physical Examination

In addition to the medical history evaluation, the surgeon will need vital information about the physical condition of the patient. This requires a complete physical examination, including a chest X ray, an electrocardiogram of the heart activity, a neurological examination, and a check of the condition of the blood vessels in various areas of the body. Other body areas may be checked as warranted by complaints of the patient or by the type of surgery to be performed. An examination of the rectum and colon may be suggested, for example, if the medical history includes problems related to the digestive tract. Adult women patients usually receive a Pap test and possibly a pelvic examination. Samples of blood and urine are taken for laboratory analysis, including blood typing in the event a transfusion is needed. The laboratory tests for older patients frequently are more detailed and may include an examination of a stool sample. Any or all of these tests can be conducted days or hours in advance of the surgery.

Additional blood and urine samples may be taken immediately after admission to recheck the body chemistry, and a brief physical examination may be made to make sure the patient does not have any open wounds or infections that might complicate the chances of recovery or introduce a dangerous strain of bacteria into the sterile environment of the operating room.

Legal Authorization

Before the preoperative preparations are complete, chances are good that a member of the hospital staff will make sure that the patient has signed a legal permit authorizing the operation. The permit describes the operation, special diagnostic or therapeutic procedure to be performed and it may be signed by a close relative or legal guardian if for some reason the patient is unable to take responsibility for this action. For example, a parent will be asked to sign a permit authorizing an operation on his child.

Exceptions may be made in cases of emergency surgery where the patient is unable to sign a permit and a relative or a guardian cannot be located in time. But there are in-house procedures of consultation among staff members who accept the responsibility. Laws regarding permission to perform surgery may vary locally.

Preop Meals

A light but adequate evening meal is served if the surgery is scheduled for the following morning, but no solid food is permitted for 12 hours before surgery. No fluids are allowed during the eight hours before surgery. Children and patients with certain diseases, such as diabetes, may be given special orders regarding nutrients.

Preparation of the Skin Area

The area of the skin around the surgery site is carefully prepared beginning the evening before the operation. A member of the hospital staff may assist or direct the cleaning of the area with soap and warm water. The cleaned skin area is usually scrubbed again in the operating room as further protection against possible infection.

Shaving

Whether or not the skin area is to be shaved depends upon the amount of hair present. If there is no hair, the tiny nicks or cuts made by a razor would constitute an unnecessary hazard of infection. Where hair is present, however, shaving is essential in order to make available a very clean skin surface. Also, it is important that no hair or hair fragments be close enough to the surgical incision to fall beneath the skin; the bit of hair beneath the skin could cause a serious infection after surgery.

Anesthetics and How They Are Used

Anesthesia is a word derived from ancient Greek, meaning "without perception," or a loss of sensation. During a major or minor operation, as in having a tooth extracted by a dentist,

it is helpful to both the patient and the physician if there is a lack of sensation during the procedure. But eliminating pain isn't the only consideration in the choice of anesthetic and other drugs used in conjunction with it. The age of the patient, chronic ailments, the site of the operation, and the emotional status of the patient are among factors considered. If a patient has undergone surgery previously and had an adverse effect from a particular kind of anesthesia, this information would have an important influence on the choice of an alternative type of anesthetic.

For many types of surgery, the kind of anesthetic chosen may be the result of an agreement among the surgeon, the patient, and the anesthetist. Some patients, given a choice, would prefer to remain conscious during an appendectomy or hernia repair; others would rather not. The surgeon frequently recommends the use of a general anesthetic because the procedure may require more time than the patient can be comfortable with in an operating room situation. Therefore, patients should realize that when a surgeon recommends a general anesthetic for an operation in which a local or spinal anesthetic might be adequate, it is for their own welfare.

General Anesthetics

General anesthetics are those that produce "sleep," or unconsciousness, along with *analgesia,* or absence of pain. They also cause a kind of amnesia in that the patient remembers nothing that occurs during the period in which the anesthetic is effective. At the same time, general anesthetics produce a certain loss of muscle tone and reflex action. A general anesthetic, however, should not interfere significantly with such normal bodily functions as respiration and circulation, nor should it produce permanent damage to body tissues.

How They Work

General anesthetics cause the patient to fall into a kind of sleep state by depressing the central nervous system, an effect that is reversible and lasts only until the drug has been eliminated by the body tissues. The general anesthetic reaches the central nervous system rather quickly because it is introduced directly or indirectly into the bloodstream. The use of a gas to produce anesthesia is an indirect method of producing unconsciousness.

A gas-type anesthetic, such as nitrous oxide or cyclopropane, can be delivered under compression from tanks or cylinders, or it may be stored in the operating room as a liquid that is converted to a vapor, like ether or halothane. The compressed-gas anesthetics are administered with the help of an anesthetic machine. The liquid forms of gases may be dripped through a mask over the patient's face; or the liquid may be vaporized and directed to the patient by anesthetic equipment. Whether the source of the anesthetic is compressed gas or a volatile liquid, the purpose is the same: to get the anesthetic into the patient's lungs. There the gas enters the bloodstream through the walls of the blood vessels of the tiny sacs that make up the lungs.

Kinds of General Anesthetics

Nearly a dozen different kinds of gases are available as general anesthetics. Each has certain advantages and disadvantages and interacts differently with other drugs used by the patient. The effects of each on chronic diseases of the patient must be weighed. Some gases induce anesthesia more rapidly than others; some are tolerated better by patients. These are among the many factors that can determine which gas or mixture of gases might be selected by the anesthetist for a particular surgical procedure.

Intravenous Anesthetics

Not all general anesthetics come in the form of compressed gases or volatile liquids. Several commonly used general anesthetics are administered intravenously, by injection into the bloodstream. The group includes barbiturates, such as thiopental, and narcotics, such as morphine. Ketamine is a general anesthetic drug that can be injected into the muscles as well as into the bloodstream. The intravenous anesthetics may be used instead of the gaseous general anesthetics or in combination with them. Thiopental is often administered to a patient first, to bring on sleep quickly, after which an inhaled general anesthetic is applied. Like the gaseous general anesthetics, each of the injected general anesthetics has its own peculiarities and may have different effects on different individuals. The rate of recovery from thiopental anesthesia varies according to the ability of a patient's body tissue to eliminate the drug; narcotics can affect the patient's respiration; ketamine may produce hallucinations in some patients.

Regional Anesthetics

Regional anesthetics include *local anesthetics* and *spinal anesthetics*. They are more likely to be used than general anesthetics when the patient is ambulatory and the surgery involves removal of moles or cysts, plastic surgery, certain eye, ear, nose, and throat procedures, and certain operations such as hernia repair that gen-erally are uncomplicated. Regional anesthetics also may be recommended by the surgeon for operations to correct disorders in the arms or legs.

The surgical procedure may require that the patient remain conscious so he can follow instructions of the surgeon in manipulating muscles or bones to test the function of a body part being repaired. In such cases, a regional anesthetic would be preferred; a regional also would be advised for a patient with severe heart or lung disease that might be complicated by the effects of a general anesthetic. A restless child, on the other hand, might be given a general anesthetic for a relatively minor operation, because the youngster would not be likely to remain motionless for the duration of the operation.

Topical Anesthetics

Regional anesthetics generally are administered by infiltration of a drug into the tissues involved or into the nerve trunks leading into the area of incision. A simple kind of regional anesthesia is the topical application of a substance to a sensitive membrane of a body organ. For example, the eye drops applied by an ophthalmologist may anesthetize a patient's eyes to make it easier for him to examine them. Topical anesthetics are not very effective when applied to the skin, which forms a tough barrier against most invasive substances, but they can effectively anesthetize the inner surfaces of the mouth, nose, throat, and other inner body surfaces. The anesthetic might be administered by sprays, gargles, or by direct application. Topical anesthetics commonly are used to prepare the throat and upper lung passages for examination with medical instruments.

Local Anesthetics

Local anesthetics, which are similar to those used by the dentist, are usually injected via a hypodermic needle into the tissues surrounding the area to be operated on. The injection of an anesthetic into the tissue area sometimes is referred to as a *field block.* A variation of this technique is the *nerve* or *plexus block,* in which a hypodermic needle is used to inject the drug into the region of one or more key nerve trunks leading to the site of the incision. Local anesthetics are not recommended by most surgeons if there is an inflammation or infection of the tissues around the surgery site. The drugs used for local anesthetics can lower the patient's resistance to the infection while at the same time the inflammation may reduce the effectiveness of the drug as a pain-killer.

Intravenous Administration

Sometimes a regional anesthetic is administered intravenously by injecting it into a vein that runs through the site of the surgery. The drug is confined to the area, such as an arm or leg, by applying a tourniquet about the limb. Because of the possible dangers in suddenly releasing a potent anesthetic drug into the general bloodstream after the operation is ended, the tourniquet is intermittently tightened and released to slow the flow to a mere trickle. A sudden release also would quickly end the pain-killing effect in the area of the incision.

Spinal Anesthetics

Spinal anesthesia is similar to a nerve or plexus block method of eliminating pain sensation in a region of the body, except that the nerves receive the drug at the point where they leave the spinal cord. The drugs may be the same as those used as local anesthetics. They are injected either by hypodermic needle or by catheter into tissues surrounding the spinal cord. Although there are several variations of spinal anesthesia—each involving the precise layer of tissue or space around the spinal cord which is the immediate target area of the injection—for all practical purposes the objective is the same. They are all intended to produce a lack of sensation in the spinal nerves along with a loss of motor function so there will be no movement of the body area to be operated on during surgery.

The spinal anesthetic may affect not only the targeted nerve system but neighboring spinal nerves as well, generally all the spinal nerves below the point of drug injection. For its purposes, spinal anesthesia can be a highly effective alternative to a general anesthetic. However, side effects are not uncommon. Severe headache is one of the most frequent complaints of patients. Temporary adverse effects can occur after use of other regional anesthetics as well and may be owing in part to individual allergic reactions to the drug used.

Care after Surgery

The last thing you may remember as a patient, before receiving a general anesthetic, is being wheeled into the operating room and lifted by hospital orderlies onto the operating table. You may not see the surgeon, who could be scrubbing for the operation or reviewing the information compiled on your case. The anesthetist and a few nurses may be in the operating room. You are feeling relaxed and drowsy because of the preanesthetic medications. A tube may be attached to your arm to drip an intravenous solution into a vein. The anesthetist may administer a dose of a drug such as sodium pentothal, a not unpleasant medication that brings on a deep sleep within a matter of seconds.

The Recovery Room

You will probably remember nothing after that point until you gradually become aware of the strange sounds and sights of a recovery room. The recovery room may contain a number of patients who have undergone surgery at about the same time, especially in a large hospital. Each is reclining in bed equipped with high railings to prevent a groggy, confused patient just recovering from a general anesthetic from falling onto the floor.

Nurses move briskly about the room, checking the conditions of the various patients. As each patient gains some awareness of the situation, a nurse puts an oxygen mask over his face and explains the purpose: to help restore the tiny air sacs of the lungs to their normal condition. During administration of the anesthetic, the air sacs can become dry and partially collapsed. The humidified oxygen mixture helps restore moisture to the inner surfaces of the lungs; by breathing deeply of the oxygen, the patient expands the air sacs to their normal capacity. Before the use of oxygen masks in the recovery room and deep-breathing techniques for patients recovering from the effects of an anesthetic gas, there was a much greater danger of pneumonia developing as a postoperative complication.

Nurses assigned to the recovery room are given a report on each patient arriving from the operating room and instructions about such matters as the position of the patient in the bed. One patient may have to lie flat on his back, another on his side, a third in a sitting position, and still another with the head lower than the feet. If the patient has received a general anesthetic, the nurses may be instructed to turn him from one side to the other at regular intervals until he is able to turn himself.

The patient's blood pressure, pulse, and respiration are checked at regular intervals by the recovery room nurses, who also watch for any signs of bleeding or drainage from the area of incision. The surgeon is notified immediately of any signs of complications. Because the recovery room usually is located next to the operating room, the surgeon can quickly identify complications and attend the problem without delay. Most surgical patients will remain in the recovery room for a few hours at the most, and when they appear to be able to manage somewhat on their own they are returned to their beds in the regular nursing area of the hospital.

The Intensive Care Unit

Critically ill patients or those with heart, lung, kidney, or other serious disorders usually are assigned to an intensive care unit where each bed may be isolated from the others in a glass booth designed to provide privacy and quiet during the recovery period. Patients can still be clearly observed from the central nursing station.

Patients in an intensive care unit are given continuous care by nurses. Electronic equipment is used to monitor pulse, blood pressure, heartbeat, and, when needed, brain function and body temperature. Other devices are available for making bedside measurements of bodily function and to obtain laboratory data such as blood chemistry without moving the patient from his bed.

Pain

Most surgical patients will be concerned about how much pain they will feel after leaving the operating room. It is not unusual to expect greater pain than is actually experienced; the incision may cause no more discomfort than the problem that required surgical therapy. Obviously, a minor operation will result in less painful discomfort than a major operation. Generally, the pain or discomfort associated with a surgical incision may last for one or two days, then subside over a period of perhaps three or four days. After that an occasional twinge may be felt in the area of the incision when shifting the body puts extra stress on the muscles or other tissues involved in the operation. During the hospital stay, medications will be available to help relieve any serious pain resulting from the operation.

Signs of Recovery or Complication

While the patient may be concerned about pain following surgery, the physicians and nurses are more likely to direct their attention toward other signs and symptoms that will help them to gauge the rate of recovery, such as the patient's body temperature, skin coloring, urine output, and his ability to cough. The health professionals are well aware that surgery, and drugs or anesthetics administered in conjunction with surgery, can be disruptive to normal bodily activities. A major operation is more likely to cause changes in the patient's physiology than a minor operation.

Vital Signs

Nurses can be expected to make regular checks of temperature, pulse, and respiration because these common measures of the body functions (sometimes called *vital signs*) can provide early-warning signals of possible post operative complications. A patient may have a temperature of 100° F. even after a major operation, but because of increased metabolic activity of the body following surgery, a slightly elevated thermometer reading is considered normal. The pulse and respiration also may be slightly above the patient's rate before surgery, but the mild change again is caused by the normal stress reaction of the body. However, a temperature rising above 100° F. and/or a significantly faster pulse or respiration rate suggests that a complication may have developed.

If a nurse seems interested in the patient's ability to cough, it is because the cough reflex helps the patient get rid of mucus accumulation in his lungs, especially after the use of a general anesthetic. If coughing is difficult, a plastic tube may be inserted into the patient's throat to help clear the breathing passages. Normal breathing can also be restored by steam inhalation, aerosol sprays of water or special medications, or positive pressure breathing equipment that forces air into the lungs. Failure to expand the air passages of the lungs leads to serious respiratory complications.

Urine output is also checked. This is just one more way of watching the rate of recovery of a patient and alerting the staff to any signs of complications. If for some reason the patient is unable to pass urine, a *catheter,* or plastic tube, is inserted into the bladder to drain it. The volume of urine drained is collected and measured.

The Incision Area

Some blood may accumulate under the skin in the area of the incision or in nearby tissues, causing a discoloration of the skin. But this effect is seldom a serious matter, and the discoloration gradually vanishes. In some cases of excess blood accumulation, the surgeon may simply remove one or two sutures and drain away the blood. Any continued bleeding about the incision would, of course, be a complication.

A more common complication is infection of the incision area by bacteria that enter the wound. An infection may develop any time from one day to one week after an operation. However, most postoperative infections of incision wounds are easily controlled by antibiotics, drainage, or natural defenses against disease. The surgeon or other physicians will make regular inspections of the incision during the first few days after surgery to make sure it is healing properly.

Postoperative Nourishment

A light meal may be offered the patient a few hours after surgery. The patient may or may not feel like eating, especially if he still feels a bit nauseated from the effects of a general anesthetic. At this stage fluid intake is probably more important, especially if the patient has not been allowed to have even a sip of water since the previous evening. If the surgery was not performed on the stomach or intestinal tract, a small amount of water or tea may be permitted within a few hours after the operation. It is unlikely in any case that the patient will feel a great desire for fluid, because intravenous solutions may have been dripping slowly into a vein since he entered the operating room. Intravenous solutions can satisfy hunger as well as thirst because they may contain proteins, carbohydrates, and essential vitamins and minerals dissolved in a finely formulated broth. Perhaps unnoticed by the patient, the

amount of fluid intake will be routinely measured by members of the hospital staff.

Ambulation

Ambulation—getting the patient out of bed and moving about—is an important part of postoperative care. Experience has shown that recovery from surgery is more effective if the patient spends increasing amounts of time each day in simple physical activity. The degree of ambulation depends upon the magnitude of the surgery and the general physical health of the patient. But in a typical case of hernia surgery or an appendectomy, the patient may be asked, on the first or second day after the operation, to sit on the edge of his bed and dangle his legs for a while. On the second or third day, he may be allowed to walk about the room, and may in fact prefer to walk to the bathroom rather than use a bedpan or urinal. On the following day, he may walk up and down the halls with the help of a nurse or other hospital staff member.

Each patient is encouraged to handle the ambulation phase of recovery at his own pace, and there are few hard and fast rules. Of two persons entering the operating room on the same day for the same kind of elective surgery, one may feel like walking to the bathroom a few hours after surgery while the second may prefer to remain in bed and use a bedpan a week after surgery. The surgeon and attending physicians may encourage and in some cases even insist upon early ambulation, however, because it reduces the rate of complications.

Back at Home

Dressings used to cover the incision are changed regularly, as the incision is inspected once each day, more frequently if warranted. If the patient is

anxious to be discharged from the hospital as early as possible, the surgeon may give him instructions for changing his own dressings. The surgeon will also outline a plan for recovery procedures to be followed after he leaves the hospital. The plan will include a schedule of visits to the surgeon's office for removal of stitches that may remain and a final inspection of the incision. The surgeon will also offer his advice on how the patient should plan a return to normal activities, including a return to his job and resumption of sports or recreational programs.

Special Diets

Proper foods are as important as proper medicines in helping a patient recover from surgery. Despite the common complaints about hospital meals, the nutrients that are provided in certain special diets for surgical patients are as carefully prescribed and prepared as are some medications that are served in pill or capsule form.

Surgical nutrition has become increasingly important in recent years because of an awareness by physicians that an operation, minor or major, is not unlike an organic disease that creates physiological stresses and a nutritional imbalance in the patient's body. To help compensate for alterations in the patient's physiology as it recovers from the effects of surgery, special diets may be ordered.

Bland Soft Diet

A bland soft diet frequently is ordered for patients who are unable to handle a regular diet but whose condition is not serious enough to require a liquid diet. The foods are selected because they are low in cellulose and connective tissue; they are bland, smooth, and easily digested. The choice of food, nevertheless, represents as great a variety as one might be served in a restaurant or at home, except for an absence of spices and other substances that would be stimulating to the gastrointestinal tract. Included in the surgical soft diet might be lean meat, fish, poultry, eggs, milk, mild cheese, cooked tender or pureed fruits and vegetables, refined cereals and breads with butter or margarine, plus gelatin desserts, puddings, custards, and ice cream.

Liquid Diet

Liquid diets for surgical patients may be prepared with or without milk. They are usually ordered for patients with impaired function of the gastrointestinal tract. A liquid diet without milk may include a cereal gruel made with water, clear bouillon or broth, gelatin, strained fruit juce, and coffee or tea. Liquid diets with milk are similar but may also include creamed soups, sherbets, ice cream, cereal gruel made with milk instead of water, cocoa and beverages of milk or cream. Beverage options permitted are tomato juice and some carbonated beverages such as ginger ale.

Diets Following Particular Kinds of Surgery

Peptic Ulcers

A special diet for peptic ulcer patients may include a half-and-half mixture of milk and cream, plus mashed potatoes, eggs, toast and butter, pureed vegetables, cottage cheese, rice, plain puddings and gelatin desserts. But meat soups, tea, coffee, raw vegetables, and fried foods are prohibited.

Rectal Surgery

Following rectal surgery, and other procedures in which it is necessary to prevent bowel movements for a period of several days, a low residue diet is ordered. A low residue diet (or *minimal residue diet,* as it is also called) might offer eggs, poached or boiled, rice, soda crackers, cereals made with water, butter, bouillon or clear broths, carbonated beverages, tea, coffee, and certain meats, including oysters, sweetbreads, and tender bits of beef or veal. An alternative low residue diet is the bland soft diet with all milk-containing items eliminated.

Gallbladder Surgery

Gallbladder surgical patients may expect a modified fat diet that eliminates as much as possible fats and gas-producing food items. It includes foods that provide protein and carbohydrate sources of energy to replace fats and includes primarily fish, poultry, lean cuts of beef, cottage cheese, cereal products and bread, and certain fruits and vegetables. However, foods prohibited are mainly pork products and fatty cuts of other meats, cream, chocolate, melons, apples, fried foods of any kind, onions, cabbage, turnips, cucumbers, radishes, green peppers, and dried beans and peas.

Restricted Salt Intake

Chronic heart failure patients and those with liver ailments or edema are placed on a low-sodium diet before and after surgery. The low-sodium diet is fairly simple in that it is prepared mainly with foods from which sodium or salt either is naturally absent or has been removed. Many salt-free or low-sodium foods are available commercially from manufacturers that also supply special di-

etetic foods for persons suffering from diabetes.

Fractures or Burns

Special consideration is given the diets of patients who are recovering from accidents that result in fractures or burns. Because of complex body responses to such injuries, there may be an abnormal loss of nitrogen from the tissues and a breakdown of muscle tissue, which is a rich source of nitrogen, an important component of protein. As a result, adequate amounts of protein need to be provided to surgical patients with burn injuries and broken bones.

Potassium Loss

Normal body stores of potassium also may be diminished during and immediately after surgery, but potassium can be replaced in the tissues by including in the meals adequate amounts of meats, fish, poultry, bananas, raisins, figs, dates, and prunes, as well as dried peaches and dried apricots. Prune, tomato, orange, and pineapple juices also are a rich source of potassium for postoperative patients.

Replacement of Water Losses

While water is not always thought of as a food, it is an important part of the gastronomic intake of the surgical patient; adequate amounts of water need to be provided the person recovering from an operation. The postoperative patient usually requires larger than normal amounts of water even though he may not feel inclined to help himself to as much fluid intake as he would at home or on the job. In addition to normal water losses through perspiration, urine, and breathing, there may be additional water losses through vomiting. Water replacement may be provided through sufficient amounts of fruit juices and other beverages offered during meals and between meals.

Apprehensions about Surgery

Most people feel anxious when faced with the need for surgery. This is to be expected. After all, a certain amount of anxiety normally accompanies any prolonged or incapacitating illness or infirmity. When surgery is the recommended therapy, it's natural for the patient to feel some anxiety about the surgery even if he's optimistic about a favorable result.

Factors That Reduce the Risk of Modern Surgery

Much of the risk of surgery these days is eliminated through the careful preoperative screening examinations reviewed earlier. A patient with a chronic disease who might have been a surgical risk a generation ago may have one or more options not available in past years, such as regional anesthetics that allow surgeons alternatives to general anesthetics that would be less than satisfactory. Antibiotics and other backup medications are available to control possible complications after surgery. Recovery room techniques and intensive care units with electronic monitoring of vital life systems provide added insurance of safe recovery. And, of course, surgeons today have the added experience of many millions of successful operations involving a range of procedures such as kidney and heart transplants, open heart surgery, and replacement of important organ parts with plastic substitutes. These and other procedures, including the implanting of electronic heart

pacemakers, were beyond the dreams of surgeons of past years.

Surgery for the Older Patient

With the rapid increase in the proportion of older people in the population, the surgical patient is more likely to be an older person with problems associated with aging. An older man who underwent surgery to remove his prostate gland before World War II had a life expectancy of a few years after the operation. Today, such procedures in older men are considered routine cases with little or no effect on longevity. It is not unusual nowadays to find men and women in their 70s and 80s who have undergone five or six major operations since reaching the traditional retirement age and without any significant restrictions on their physical activities.

Part of the reason for the greatly improved outlook for surgery on older patients may be that older persons today are simply in better health because of the improved medical care available. Thus they are better surgical risks than their parents would have been at the same age. Advanced preoperative and postoperative care has also improved the outlook for the older patient. He may be admitted to the hospital a few days earlier than the younger patient for more intensive examinations, and he may remain a few days longer for postoperative care. Convalescence for the older patient may take longer, and in some instances the recovery may not be as complete as that of a younger person. But in general, modern surgical techniques are likely to offer a safe and effective therapy for people of advanced age with complaints that can be corrected by an operation.

In addition to the physical benefits, surgery may improve the mental capacity, personality, and sensitivity of older persons who had been de-

pressed about a disorder before surgery. The patient who complained that he is no longer the person he used to be physically may have assumed that his medical problem was simply a result of growing old and overlooked the possibility that the complaint was due to a disease that might respond to treatment.

Surgery for the Child

A child, on the other hand, may have his own reasons to be apprehensive about the trip to a hospital for surgery. Most children seem to worry that the operation will hurt or that other procedures, such as taking a blood sample for testing, will be painful.

Telling the Truth

Many surgeons recommend that the child be told as realistically as possible, in terms he can understand, what can be expected. The youngster should not be given a sugar-coated story about the operation which might give the impression that he is embarking upon a happy adventure. At the same time, the child should not be frightened by suggestions that he may be given drugs to make him unconscious while he is strapped to a table so that strangely masked and gowned strangers can cut him open with sharp knives.

Children are more likely to appreciate surgery if they are told that a friendly person will help them go to sleep; that the operation will hurt a little but the pain will go away after a while; and that the operation will make them feel better or help correct a problem so they can be more active like other children. A small child should always understand that he may have to remain overnight at the hospital without his parents, but that he will have other adults to take care of him and there probably will be other children at the hospital to keep him company.

Common Surgical Procedures

In this section some of the more common surgical procedures are described. The operations discussed are organized by the system or region of the body with which they are concerned. The following areas are covered in this order:

- Male Reproductive System (for surgical procedures involving the female reproductive system, see Ch. 25, *Women's Health*);

- Urinary Tract;

- Abdominal Region;

- Oral Cavity and Throat;

- Ear Surgery;

- Eye Surgery;

- Chest Region;

- Vascular Surgery;

- Orthopedic Surgery; and

- Neurosurgery.

Many of the conditions treated in this chapter from a surgical point of view are also treated elsewhere, in the chapter devoted to diseases of the appropriate body system or organ; the reader is invited to turn to those chapters for additional information. For example, although heart surgery is discussed in this chapter, heart disease is treated in greater detail in Ch. 10, *Heart Disease*.

Male Reproductive System

Surgical procedures of the prostate, testis, scrotum, and penis are considered in this section. Undescended testicles and vasectomy are also among the subjects discussed.

Prostate Surgery

The prostate gland is a small cone-shaped object that surrounds the male urethra, the tube that carries urine from the urinary bladder to the penis. It is normally about one-half inch long and weighs less than an ounce. Ejaculatory ducts empty through theprostate into the urethra, and other ducts drain glandular secretions of the prostate into the urethra. Because of the intimate association of the prostate gland and the urinary tract, a disorder in one system can easily affect the other. A urinary infection can spread to the prostate and an abnormality of the prostate can interfere with the normal excretion of urine.

Enlargement of the Prostate

A relatively common problem is the tendency of the prostate to grow larger in middle-aged men. The gradual enlargement continues from the 40s on, but the symptoms usually go unnoticed until the man is in his 60s. At that point in life, the prostate may have become so enlarged that it presses on the urethra and obstructs the flow of urine from the neighboring bladder. The older man may experience various difficulties in emptying his bladder. He may have to urinate more frequently, and suddenly find himself getting out of bed at night to go to the bathroom. He may not be able to develop a urine stream of the size and force he had in earlier years. He may have trouble getting the stream of urine started and it may end in a dribble.

In addition to the somewhat embarrassing inconveniences caused by prostate enlargement, the urinary bladder may not drain properly and can eventually lose its own muscle tone needed for emptying. Residual urine in the bladder can become a source of infection, and backflow into the ureters can gradually affect those tissues and the kidneys. It has been estimated that 20 percent of all older men may need treatment of some kind, including surgery, for correcting this problem of the prostate gland.

Factors Indicating the Need for Surgery

Factors that may decide in favor of surgical removal of the prostate include residual urine in the patient's bladder; blood in the urine, with evidence that the blood comes from the prostate; the severity of the inconveniences associated with irregular urination; and complications such as the presence or threat of failure of the wall of the urinary bladder, the formation of stones, and symptoms and signs of infection.

Surgical Methods

There are several methods of performing a *prostatectomy* (excision of all or part of the prostate) for relief of the symptoms of an enlarged prostate, a condition that may appear on the patient's medical records as *benign prostate hyperplasia*. All of the methods are relatively safe and in none of the techniques is the entire prostate removed. One method, called *transurethral resection*, requires insertion of an instrument into the urethra through the penis. The instrument, a *resectoscope*, uses a high-frequency electric current to cut away the tissue inside the gland. This technique avoids open surgery and

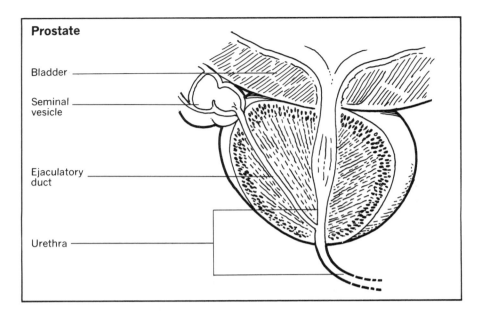

Prostate

Bladder

Seminal vesicle

Ejaculatory duct

Urethra

requires a postoperative hospital stay of only a few days.

Open Surgery

The other techniques involve *open surgery,* that is, surgery in which an incision is made in the pelvic or rectal area to make the prostate gland accessible so that its inner tissues can be removed. The differences in the various open surgery techniques depend upon such factors as where the incision should be made and the risks associated with the approaches. The incision is made either in the *perineum,* the region between the rectum and the testicles, or through the abdomen. Only a small percentage of patients experience complications or regrowth of the prostate tissues to produce a second enlargement problem. Impotence is usually not an aftereffect of the surgery, and libido is normal.

Infections of the Prostate

Infections of the prostate gland can involve obstruction of the urethra, but the problem usually can be resolved by the use of medications and tech-

niques other than surgery. An abscess, however, may require an incision to drain the prostate. Surgery also may be recommended for the treatment of stones, or calculi, that develop in the prostate and cause obstruction or contribute to infections.

Cancer of the Prostate

Cancer of the prostate also may occur in older men, causing obstruction or the urinary flow or contributing to infection of the urinary tract. If examination including biopsy studies confirms the presence of cancer, the surgeon may recommend radical prostatectomy. In this procedure an incision is made either through the lower abdomen or through the perineum to remove the entire prostate gland and surrounding tissues, such as the seminal vesicles. Hormonal therapy, chemotherapy, and radiation treatments also may be administered.

Tumors of the Testis

Tumors of the testis occur most frequently in men between the ages of 18 and 35. Such a tumor appears as a firm and enlarged testis and usually

without pain unless bleeding is involved as a symptom. Testicular tumors generally are malignant and spread rapidly to other parts of the body, including the lungs. The onset of the disorder can be so insidious that the patient may seek medical advice for a more obvious secondary problem, such as the apparent development of mammary glands on his chest, the result of disruption of his normal male hormonal balance.

Special laboratory tests and other examination techniques usually are required to determine which of several possible kinds of testicular tumors may be involved and the extent of the metastasis of the cancer cells to other body areas. If cancer of a testicle is confirmed, it is removed by an incision through the groin area, and neighboring lymph nodes also will be taken out. The surgical procedure usually is supplemented with chemotherapy and radiation. The prognosis, or chances for recovery, following surgical removal of a testicular tumor depends upon the particular kind of cancer involved and how far the disease had progressed before medical treatment was begun.

Tumors of the Scrotum and Penis

Tumors of the scrotum and penis are relatively uncommon but do occur. Cancer of the scrotum is usually associated with exposure to cancer-causing chemicals. Boys who worked as chimney sweeps a century ago tended to develop cancer of the scrotum from body contact with soot in coal-burning fireplaces. Cancer of the penis occurs usually in men who have not been circumcised. In either type of cancer, the treatment usually requires removal of the affected tissues. This can mean castration in the case of scrotal cancer or amputation of a part or all of the penis, depending upon the extent of the cancerous growth. Surgery that requires removal of a part of the reproductive system can have a devastating psychological effect on a man, but the alternative is likely to be early death from the spread of cancer.

Undescended Testicles

About 10 percent of cases of tumors of the testis occur in men with an undescended testicle. Because the chances of a tumor developing in an undescended testicle are as much as 50 times greater than the incidence for the normal male population, the existence of an undescended testicle can warrant corrective surgery.

Ordinarily, the testicles descend from their fetal location in the abdomen into the scrotum about two months before birth. But in one case in 200 male births, a child is found with a failure of one or, less commonly, both testicles to descend properly into the scrotum. In addition to the risk of cancer, undescended testicles are associated with lack of fertility and other problems, such as hernias.

Cryptorchidism

In male babies and young boys, an undescended testicle sometimes can be encouraged to enter the scrotum by manipulation or administration of hormones. Many surgeons recommend that the developmental problem of undescended testicles, or *cryptorchidism,* be corrected before a child enters school, although the surgical procedure for correcting the situation can be postponed until adolescence or adulthood. The operation for correcting an undescended testicle is called *orchidopexy* and involves an incision in the groin to release the testicle and its attached cord from fibrous tissue holding it in the abdomen. The testicle may be brought directly down into

the scrotum, where it may be anchored temporarily with a suture, or it may be brought down in stages in a series of operations to permit the growth and extension of blood supply to the testis. The original location of the undescended testicle determines which procedure is used.

Vasectomy

Vasectomy is a birth control technique that is intended to make a man permanently sterile. It does not involve the removal of any of the male reproductive system and does not result in a loss of potency or libido. A vasectomy is a relatively simple operation that can be performed in a physician's office in less than 30 minutes and requires only a local anesthetic. The operation is similar to but much less complicated than the procedure in which a woman may be sterilized by cutting or tying her Fallopian tubes. A vasectomy requires no hospitalization, and the man is able to return to work or other normal activities after a day or two.

How the Procedure Is Done

The vasectomy procedure requires a small incision, about one-half inch in length, on either side of the scrotum. The surgeon removes through the incision a short length of the *vas deferens,* the tube that carries spermatozoa from the testicles, and ties a piece of surgical thread at two points about an inch apart. Then a small piece of the vas deferens between the tied-off points is snipped out of the tube. The procedure is done on each side. With the ducts of the vas deferens cut and tied, sperm from the testicles can no longer move through their normal paths to the prostate, where they would become mixed with semen from the prostate and seminal vesicles and be ejaculated during sexual intercourse.

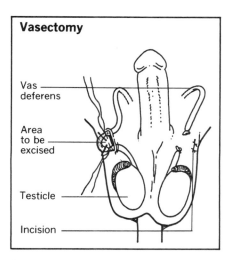

Vasectomy

Vas deferens

Area to be excised

Testicle

Incision

Sterility Is Usually Permanent

A vasectomy does not immediately render a man sterile. Sperm already stored in the seminal "pipeline" can still be active for a period of a month to six weeks, and a woman who has intercourse with a vasectomized man during that period can become pregnant. On the other hand, a man who undergoes a vasectomy should not expect that the severed ducts can be connected again should he want to become a father in the future. Sperm banks have been offered as a possible alternative for the man who might want to store some of his spermatozoa for future use, but there is little evidence that the sperm will remain fertile in a sperm bank for more than a year or 18 months. In rare cases, men who have undergone vasectomies have unintentionally become fertile again because of *canalization,* or creation of a new channel connecting the severed ends of the vas deferens; in one case the canalization occurred 8 years after the vasectomy was performed.

The vasectomy is regarded as an extremely safe operation, and complications are infrequent. Some swelling and discomfort are reported by a small percentage of men undergoing the operation. Steroid hormone drugs are sometimes administered to control these aftereffects.

Urinary Tract

Surgical procedures involving urinary stones and tumors of the bladder, ureter, urethra, and kidney are considered in this section. Also discussed are kidney cysts and conditions affecting the adrenal glands which might require surgery.

Urinary Stones

Most stones that occur in the urinary tract are formed in the kidneys, but kidney stones can travel to other areas, such as the ureters, and cause problems there. Various types of stones can develop in the kidneys from several different causes. A common cause is a metabolic disorder involving calcium, proteins, or uric acid. Other causes are infections or obstructions of the urinary tract, the use of certain drugs, such as diuretics, or vitamin deficiency.

Symptoms

Kidney stones seldom cause problems while they are forming, but movement of the stones irritates the urinary tract and can cause severe pain; the irritation of the tissues may cause bleeding that will ultimately show up in the urine. Other symptoms may indicate obstruction of the flow of urine, and infection. In some cases obstruction of a ureter can lead to failure of the kidney. X-ray techniques can usually verify the cause of the patient's symptoms and locate the urinary stone. Most stones cast a shadow on X-ray film, and by injecting special dyes into the urinary system, the degree of obstruction by a stone can be determined.

Ureter Stones

Most stones released by the kidney are small enough to pass through a ureter to the bladder and be excreted while urinating. But if a stone is large enough it can become lodged in a ureter, causing excruciating pain that may be felt both in the back and in the abdomen along the path of the ureter. Ureter stones often can be removed by manipulation, using catheter tubes that are inserted through the bladder. If the stuck stone cannot be manipulated from the ureter, an operation in a hospital is required. However, the surgical procedure is relatively simple and direct. An incision is made over the site of the stuck stone, and the ureter is exposed and opened just far enough to permit removal of the stone. The operation is safe and requires perhaps a week in the hospital.

Kidney Stones

If the urinary stone is lodged in the kidney, the surgical procedure also is a relatively safe one although more complicated and requiring a longer hospital stay. The surgeon must work through skin and muscle layers to reach the kidney, then cut into the kidney if necessary to remove the stone. If the obstruction has been serious enough to impair normal kidney function or if infection has damaged the kidney tissue, the surgeon may elect to remove the affected kidney. Fortunately, the human body can get along fairly well with one good functioning kidney, so a *nephrectomy,* as the procedure is called, may not be as drastic a maneuver as the patient might imagine. If, on the other hand, the affected kidney has not been seriously damaged, the stone or stones can be removed with instruments or by the surgeon's fingers and the incision in the kidney sewed up so that it can resume its normal functions.

More modern techniques for removing kidney stones include two that hold promise of eliminating nearly all surgical methods. One involves the use of the lithotriptor, a machine that shatters the stones with an electrical shock wave. The wave is focused on the stones with the aid of a reflector and two sophisticated X-ray machines that "aim" the target beam. No surgery is required, and the patient is usually back at work within a week. A second means of attacking kidney stones is a drug, *potassium citrate,* which keeps the stones from forming. The drug actually corrects the metabolic disorders that cause the formation of kidney stones.

Vesical Stones

Occasionally, urinary stones are found in the neck of the bladder or in the bladder itself. They are called *vesical stones* and, depending upon their size and other factors, may be removed by several techniques, including use of a cystoscope inserted through the urethra. In some cases the stone can be broken into smaller pieces for removal. If it appears unlikely that the stone can be removed directly or by crushing it, the surgeon can make an incision directly to the bladder in a manner similar to the approach used in removing a stone from the ureter.

Bladder Tumors

About three-fourths of the tumors of the bladder occur in men past the age of 45. Although the specific cause of bladder tumors is unknown, physicians suspect that a cancer-producing chemical is involved. Several studies have found an association between the disease and cigarette smoking or occupations that require contact with organic chemicals used in making dyes. Tumors that appear in the female bladder are less likely to be cancerous than those that occur in the male bladder.

Symptoms and Diagnosis

The first symptom of bladder tumor is blood in the urine. The tumor itself may cause no pain, but an early complication could be an infection producing inflammation and discomfort in the region of the bladder. If the tumor blocks the normal flow of urine, the patient may feel pain or discomfort in the area of the kidneys; this condition is most likely to happen if the tumor is located at the opening of a ureter leading from a kidney to the bladder. An early examination of the bladder may fail to locate a small tumor, although X rays might show the growth as a bit of shadow on the film, and obstruction of a ureter could be seen. Nonetheless, examination of the interior of the bladder by a cystoscope is necessary to confirm the presence of the tumor. A biopsy can be made by removing a few tissue cells from the area in a manner quite like the procedure for making a Pap-smear test for possible cancer of the cervix in a female patient.

Treatment

Most early and simple cases of bladder tumor can be corrected by a procedure called *saucerization* by an instrument that removes the abnormal tissue, leaving a shallow wound that normally will grow over with healthy tissue cells. But a tumor that invades deeply into the wall of the bladder requires more radical therapy, such as surgery to cut away the part of the bladder that is affected by the growth. Radiation also may be employed to control the spread of tumor cells, particularly if laboratory tests indicate that the type of tumor cells involved are sensitive to radiation.

Surgical Procedure

If it is necessary to cut away a part of the bladder, the surgeon simply shapes a new but smaller organ from the remaining tissues. If a total *cystectomy* is required to save the life of the patient, the entire bladder is removed, along with the prostate if the patient is a man. When the bladder is removed, a new path for the flow of urine is devised by the surgeons, usually to divert the urine into the lower end of the intestinal tract.

Tumors of the Ureter or Urethra

Tumors of the ureter, above the bladder, or of the urethra, below the bladder, may begin with symptoms resembling those of a bladder tumor, although X rays might show the growth as a bit of shadow on the normal flow of urine. Treatment also usually requires removal of the affected tissues with reconstructive surgery as needed to provide for a normal flow of urine from the kidneys.

Kidney Tumors

Wilms' Tumor

Tumors of the kidney generally occur either in children before the age of eight or in adults over the age of 25. The type of tumor that affects children usually is the Wilms' tumor, one of the most common kinds of cancer that can afflict a youngster. The tumor grows rapidly and may be painful even though there may be no obvious signs of urinary tract disorder in the child's urine. The tumor frequently becomes so large that it appears as an abdominal swelling. A Wilms' tumor usually occurs only on one side of the body, but in a small percentage of the cases the disorder can develop in both right and left kidneys. Kidney function may continue normally during growth of the tumor, but cancerous cells from the tumor may be carried by the bloodstream to other parts of the body, by metastasis, causing the problem to spread to the lungs and other vital organs.

Treatment usually requires surgical removal of the affected kidney and radiation therapy; the tumor cells responsible for the growth are sensitive to radiation. The younger the child and the earlier treatment is started, the better are the child's chances for recovery from a Wilms' tumor.

Adult Kidney Tumor

The adult type of kidney tumor, which is more likely to affect men than women, may also appear as an enlarged abdominal mass. But, unlike the Wilms' tumor, the adult kidney tumor presents as an early symptom blood in the urine. Bleeding from the kidney may be painless. X-ray studies may show an enlarged and sometimes distorted kidney. The patient may have symptoms indicating metastasis of the tumor cells to the lungs, bones, or other body systems. Adult kidney tumors are almost always malignant.

Treatment usually requires nephrectomy, or surgical removal of the diseased kidney. Radiation therapy may be provided in addition to the surgery, although the kind of tumor cells involved in the adult type of kidney tumor usually are resistant to radiation. Chemotherapy also may be offered. The chances for complete recovery from a kidney tumor depend upon several factors, such as the location of the tumor in the kidney and the extent of metastasis of the cancerous cells to other organ systems.

Kidney Cysts

A cyst is a small pouch enclosed by a membrane; technically, the urinary bladder and gall bladder are cysts. But the cysts of medical disorders are small pouches or sacs filled with a fluid or viscous substance; they may appear on the skin, in the lungs, or in other body systems, such as the kidneys.

Symptoms

Kidney cysts produce symptoms that resemble the symptoms of cancer of the kidney; in a few cases kidney cysts are associated with tumors that cause bleeding into the cysts. In addition to the troublesome symptoms of flank pain and blood in the urine, untreated cysts can grow until they damage normal kidney tissue and impair the function of the organ's functions. Simple or solitary kidney cysts usually do not occur before the age of 40.

Diagnosis

X-ray techniques are made to determine the exact nature of kidney cyst symptoms, but in some cases exploratory surgery is recommended to differentiate a cyst from a tumor. The cyst is excised, frequently by cutting away the exposed wall of the growth. The chances of the cyst reforming are very slight.

Polycystic Kidney Disease

A different kind of kidney cyst disease, consisting of many small cysts, may be found in younger persons, including small children. The symptoms again may be flank pain and blood in the urine; examination may show some enlargement of the kidney. This form of the disease, sometimes called *polycystic kidney disease,* can be complicated by uremia and hypertension as the patient grows older. Treatment usually is medical unless the cysts interfere with urine flow by obstructing the upper end of the ureter. If the outlook for recovery through conservative treatment is poor, the surgeon may consider a kidney transplant operation.

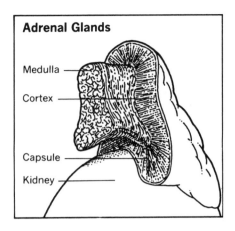

Adrenal Glands

Medulla

Cortex

Capsule

Kidney

Adrenal Glands

The adrenal glands are small hormone-producing organs that are located just above the kidneys. Although the combined weight of the two glands may be only one-fourth of an ounce, the adrenals affect a number of important body functions, including carbohydrate and protein metabolism and fluid balance. Surgery of the adrenal glands may be needed for the correction of various bodily disorders associated with oversecretion of the adrenal hormones; it may also be indicated to help control of cancer of the breast in women and cancer of the prostate in men.

Tumors of the Adrenal Glands

Tumors of the adrenal glands produce a disorder known as *primary hyperaldosteronism,* which is marked by symptoms of muscle weakness, hypertension, abnormally large outputs of urine, and excessive thirst. Another kind of tumor invasion of the adrenal glands can produce symptoms of hypertension with headaches, visual blurring, and severe sweating. Still another adrenal-related disorder, called *Cushing's syndrome,* tends to affect women under the age of 40. The symptoms may range from hypertension and obesity to acne, easy

bruising, and *amenorrhea* (cessation of menstruation). Adrenal tumors may also alter secondary sex characteristics of men and women; they may result in body hair and baldness in women and increased sex drive in men.

Despite the tiny size of the adrenal glands, they are complex organs, and the varied disorders caused by tumors of the glands may depend upon the precise kind of tumor cells involved and the precise area of the glands affected by the tumor, as well as the interactions of the adrenal hormones with hormones from other glands, such as the pituitary, or master gland of the body, located at the base of the brain.

Preoperative Tests

Before adrenal surgery for correction of a disorder is begun, the surgeon may ask for detailed laboratory tests and other diagnostic information. A radioactive scan to help locate and identify the kind of tumor more precisely may be ordered. Women patients who have been using oral contraceptives usually have to discontinue use of "the pill" for two months or more, because the medication can interfere with laboratory studies of hormones in the bloodstream.

Long-Range Effects

Physicians handling the case also must evaluate the long-range effects of an adrenal gland operation because normal metabolism is likely to be disrupted by removal of the glands, if that should be necessary. Hormone medications usually are needed in such cases to replace the hormones normally secreted. An *adrenalectomy* (removal of an adrenal gland) sometimes is explained as the substitution of a controllable disease for a life-threatening disease that cannot be controlled by medical therapy. If only one of the adrenal glands must be removed, however, the patient may be able to recover and resume a normal life without the need for hormone medications.

Surgical Procedure

The surgical approach to the adrenal glands is similar to that used in kidney operations. The incision may be made through the abdomen or through the flank. The surgery may be primarily exploratory, or the surgeon may excise a part of a gland, an entire gland, or both glands, depending upon the extent of the disease, or upon other factors, such as the need to control cancers in other parts of the body.

Abdominal Region

This section discusses the following procedures or conditions: appendicitis, peptic ulcers, hiatus hernia, adhesions, cancer of the stomach and of the intestines, gallbladder surgery, inguinal hernia, and hemorrhoids.

Appendicitis

Inflammation of the appendix is one of the most common causes of abdominal surgery today, particularly among children. But appendicitis was not recognized as a disease until 1886, leading some doctors to believe that this digestive tract infection may be related to a change in eating habits that occurred within the past century. The vermiform appendix, the site of the inflammation, is a short, wormlike (or *vermiform*) appendage at the junction of the small and large intestines. Its function in humans is unknown; plant-eating animals have an appendix, but carnivorous animals, like cats, do not. Humans live quite well without an appendix, so it seems reasonable to have a diseased appendix removed.

Symptoms

The appendix can cause trouble if it becomes obstructed by a foreign body, a tumor, an infection, or other cause of inflammation. Pain is a common symptom; there may be two kinds of pain at the same time: one, localized on the lower right side of the abdomen, near the site of the appendix; the other, more generalized and colicky, of the kind sometimes associated with gas in the intestine. Some patients experience diarrhea or a constant urge to defecate, an effect attributed to irritation of the bowel by the abnormal activity of the appendix. Frequently there is loss of appetite, nausea and vomiting, and a fever.

The symptoms of appendicitis may begin suddenly, but frequently take from 6 to 18 hours to develop into a pattern typical of the disease, so most cases permit ample time for a doctor to examine the patient and make a diagnosis before the problem becomes critical. During the period that any symptoms suggest a possibility of appendicitis, the patient should avoid the use of any laxatives.

Ruptured Appendix

A potentially serious complication of untreated appendicitis is rupture of the appendix, which can produce a slightly different set of symptoms because of the onset of *peritonitis,* a dangerous inflammation of tissues outside the intestinal tract. The contents of the ruptured appendix leak into the body cavity, spreading the bacterial infection and irritating the lining (peritoneum) of the abdominal cavity. Diarrhea and a fever of more than 101° F. are frequently associated with a perforated or ruptured appendix. The colicky pain may disappear suddenly, because the internal pressure ends with perforation of the wall of the appendix, but it is quickly replaced by the pain of peritonitis. The severe pain of peritonitis usually is made worse by any body movement, including the abdominal muscle movement required for coughing or sneezing.

Appendicitis with perforation is much more common in older persons, perhaps because the early symptoms of colicky pain that younger people notice are not felt by older people, so the disease is not detected until it has reached an advanced stage. Appendicitis also requires special attention in pregnant women, because the enlarged uterus crowds and repositions segments of the intestinal tract and the potential threat grows more serious during the last trimester of pregnancy.

Surgical Procedure

Laboratory tests usually are checked before surgery proceeds if there is no evidence of perforation. The usual symptoms of appendicitis can be produced by a number of other ailments, and the symptoms may diminish with bed rest, time, and medications. However, appendicitis must be considered in any case of acute abdominal complaints, and many surgeons and physicians follow the rule of "When in doubt, operate." Surgery for appendicitis is fairly simple and safe if the appendix has not perforated. An incision is made in the lower right side of the abdomen, the connection between the end of the large intestine and appendix tied off with surgical thread, and the appendix cut away from the stump. The actual operation, if uncomplicated by peritonitis or other factors, may require only a few minutes. A hospital stay of a few days is usually required during which the diet is readjusted from nothing by mouth at first, to a liquid diet, then a soft diet, etc. Normal work activities usually can be resumed within two or three weeks following surgery. Complications other than those related to peritonitis are rare. In untreated cases involving peritonitis, however, the risk is very high.

Peptic Ulcers

The cause of peptic ulcers is still unknown, although the disease affects about 10 percent of the population at some time in life. Men are four times as likely as women to develop ulcers; the incidence is highest in young and middle-aged men. Peptic ulcers may occur in the stomach, where they are called *gastric ulcers,* or in the duodenum, where they are called *duodenal ulcers.* Ninety percent of the ulcer cases that reach the physician's office for treatment are in the duodenum, a short length of the small intestine just beyond the stomach. Autopsy studies indicate that gastric ulcers may be as common as duodenal ulcers, but are frequently not detected during the life of the individual.

Causes

The development of ulcers is associated with the possible action of gastric acid on the lining of the stomach and duodenum in people who may have inherited a sensitivity to the substances. Ulcers are also related to the use of certain drugs and exposure to severe burns, injury, emotional stress, and disease.

Symptoms

A common symptom is a gnawing pain in the area of the stomach from 30 minutes to several hours after eating; the pain is relieved by food or antacid medications. The pain sometimes is likened to heartburn and may be described as radiating from the abdomen to the back. Some patients report the discomfort is more like a feeling of hunger or cramps; they may be awakened from sleep by the feeling that is relieved by a midnight snack of milk or other foods. Attacks of ulcers may be seasonal, occurring in certain patients only in the spring and autumn. In severe cases there may be bleeding without any sensation of abdominal pain; bleeding occurs from erosion of the lining of the stomach or duodenum and penetration of blood vessels in those membranes.

Complications other than bleeding can include perforation of the wall of the stomach or duodenum by continued erosion, or inflammatory swelling and scarring by an ulcer at a narrow part of the digestive tract, causing an obstruction. A duodenal ulcer can erode into the head of the pancreas, which secretes its digestive juices into the small intestine in that area. The pain may then become more or less continuous regardless of efforts to palliate it with food or antacids.

Symptoms vary only slightly between duodenal and gastric ulcers. Gastric ulcer pain usually begins earlier after a meal, attacks generally last longer, and symptoms, including vomiting and loss of appetite, may be more severe than in duodenal ulcer. But because of the similarities, physicians usually rely on laboratory tests and X-ray studies to determine the precise location in the digestive tract of the peptic ulcer.

Duodenal Ulcers

Duodenal ulcers nearly always occur within an inch of the pyloric valve separating the stomach from the small intestine. The pain or discomfort follows a cycle. The patient may experience no pain until after breakfast. The pain is relieved by the noon meal but returns in the afternoon and occurs again in the evening. Milk or other bland food or medications relieve the pain that may appear at various times in the cycle. The symptoms of duodenal ulcers also go through periods of remission and recurrence over months or years. Most duodenal ulcers are treated with diet, drugs, and measures that encourage rest and relaxation.

Surgical Procedures

Surgery for either duodenal or gastric ulcer is designed to reduce gastric acid secretion rather than simply to excise the ulcer from the normal digestive tract tissue. One surgical approach, called *subtotal gastrectomy,* involves cutting away a portion of the stomach in the area where it joins the duodenum. There are several variations of this technique, including one in which the remaining portion of the stomach is attached to the jejunum, a segment of the small intestine. The ulcerated portion of the duodenum may be removed during the reconstructive surgery of the digestive tract, or it may be left in the duodenal segment that is closed during the gastrectomy procedure. An interesting effect is that a duodenal ulcer usually heals, when left in place, after the gastric juices are routed into the intestine through the jejunum. The reconstructed stomach and stomach-to-intestine connection cause no serious problems in eating after the patient has recovered.

A second surgical approach, called a *vagotomy,* involves cutting a part of the vagus nerve trunk that controls the secretion of stomach acid. There are several variations of vagotomy, each technique affecting a different portion of the vagus nerve distribution to the stomach.

Gastric Ulcers

Stomach or gastric ulcers tend to develop in older persons more often than duodenal ulcers, and the problem seems to be less importantly related to the overproduction of gastric acid. The real hazard of stomach ulcers is that a significant percentage are found to be a kind of cancer and do not respond to the usual therapies for controlling peptic ulcer symptoms. If it is determined that a stomach ulcer is a malignant growth, a partial gastrectomy is performed in the same manner as an operation of the type for duodenal ulcers. The vagotomy approach is not used for treatment of a stomach ulcer unless the ulcer is excised at the same time.

Hiatus Hernia

The term *hiatus hernia* actually describes a diaphragmatic hernia or weakness in the diaphragm, the horizontal muscular wall separating the organs of the chest from the organs of the abdomen. A *hernia* is an abnormal protrusion of an organ or tissue through an opening. A *hiatus,* or opening, occurs naturally to permit the esophagus to carry food from the mouth to the stomach. Blood vessels and nerves also pass through the diaphragm. The diaphragm is an important group of muscles for contracting and expanding the lungs, forcing air in and out of the lung tissues.

Hiatus hernias are rare in children, but as people grow older, there may be a weakening of the diaphragm muscles and associated tissues. Aided by a tendency toward obesity and the use of girdles and other tight garments, a portion of the stomach may be pushed through the opening designed by nature for use of the esoph-

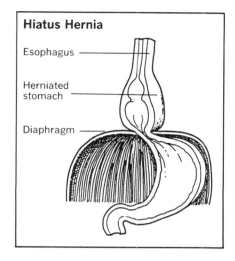

Hiatus Hernia

Esophagus

Herniated stomach

Diaphragm

agus. Aside from the discomfort of having a part of the stomach in the chest, there are potential dangers of incarceration of the stomach, with obstruction, strangulation, and hemorrhage with erosion of the stomach lining. In severe complications, the entire stomach along with intestines and other abdominal organs may be forced through the hiatus hernia into the chest area.

The most common kind of hiatus hernia is sometimes called *sliding hiatus hernia* from the tendency of the stomach to slide in and out of the thorax, or chest cavity, when the patient changes body positions or as a result of the pressure of a big meal in the gastrointestinal tract. Sometimes the herniated stomach does not move at all but remains fixed, with a significant portion of the stomach above the diaphragm. Hiatus hernia causes heartburn symptoms, including regurgitation of digested food and gastric acid from the stomach, when one is lying down or straining or stooping. The effect also may be noticeable in a woman during pregnancy.

Nonsurgical Treatment

Many cases of hiatal hernia can be treated without surgery through a change of eating habits and the use of

antacid medications. The patient may be advised to eat small amounts more frequently during the day with dietary emphasis on high-protein, low-fat foods. Some physicians recommend that patients use liquid antacid medications rather than antacid tablets or lozenges.

Surgical Treatment

When surgery is recommended to correct hiatus hernia, the repair may be performed either through the abdominal wall or through the chest. About three-fourths of the procedures are handled through abdominal incisions, because surgeons often find other abdominal problems that need to be corrected at the same time, such as peptic ulcers or gall bladder disease. The opening through the diaphragm is firmly closed with sutures to prevent upward movement of the stomach. The stomach and lower end of the esophagus may be anchored in place in the abdomen. The chances of recurrence are about one in ten, although some patients may continue to have a few of the symptoms of the disorder for a while after the hernia repair.

Adhesions

Adhesions may develop between various abdominal organs and the peritoneum, the membrane lining the abdominal cavity. The bowel may acquire adhesions that result in obstruction of the intestinal tract. Adhesions may form between the liver and the peritoneum or between the liver and the diaphragm. The symptoms may be pain or cramps in the area where tissues are literally stuck together; in more serious cases that involve bowel obstruction, symptoms may include constipation, vomiting, and distension of the abdomen. Adhesions do not show on X-ray film and can be difficult to diagnose unless the patient's medical history suggests a cause for the bands or filaments of tissues responsible for the adhesions.

Causes

The causes may be peritonitis, injury, infection, internal bleeding, or foreign objects. Adhesions occur after an operation, perhaps because of a bit of blood resulting from surgery or as a result of a speck of talc from the surgeon's glove or a fiber from a surgical drape which produces a foreign-body reaction, much like an allergic reaction, when it comes in contact with abdominal tissues. Disease organisms may enter the female abdominal cavity through the Fallopian tubes to produce adhesions, especially in the case of gonorrhea, which can escape early detection in women because of the lack of obvious symptoms.

Complications

Adhesions can cause complications, such as changing the position of the intestinal tract through twisting or otherwise distorting its path so that bowel movements are obstructed. If the involved portion of the intestine becomes so seriously damaged that it no longer functions properly, the surgeon may have to remove that section. Generally, when the surgeon is correcting the problem of adhesions, a relatively simple procedure of cutting away the tissue bands or filaments holding organs in abnormal ways, he inspects the organs to determine if they appear to be in good working order. That part of the operation may add 15 or 20 minutes to the time spent on an operating table, but it helps insure that the patient will not have to be returned soon for further surgery.

Cancer of the Stomach

There are several possible types of stomach tumors, but one kind, called *adenocarcinoma,* is one of the greatest killers of men over the age of 45. Although the incidence of stomach cancer in the United States has declined considerably since the end of World War II, the death rate from this problem in the United States alone is about 15,000 per year. In central and eastern Europe the incidence of stomach cancer is about four times, and in Japan seven times, that of the United States. Almost two-thirds of the stomach cancers develop near the pylorus, the opening from the stomach into the small intestine; only five percent involve the entire stomach area.

Symptoms

Symptoms include a feeling of heaviness rather than pain following a meal. The patient in many cases mysteriously loses his appetite for meat and begins to lose weight. There may be vague symptoms of an upset stomach, with some vomiting, especially if the tumor begins to obstruct the pylorus such that stomach contents cannot be emptied into the intestine. The vomitus usually is the color of coffee grounds, suggesting a loss of blood from the stomach lining because of the tumor, and the patient's stools also may be dark in coloration because of internal bleeding. The physician frequently can confirm his suspicions about the cause of the symptoms by laboratory analysis of a specimen of cells from the stomach, by X-ray studies of the stomach, or by an examination with a gastroscope that permits a direct view of the interior of the stomach. In some cases the physician will be able to feel an abnormal mass in the stomach by pal-

pating the stomach area of the abdomen with his hands.

Treatment

Treatment is by cutting away the tumor and surrounding tissues that may be involved, including parts of neighboring organs. The lymph nodes in the region of the stomach are also removed. The remaining part of the stomach is used to build a new digestive organ, as in a case of partial gastrectomy for correcting a peptic ulcer problem. However, before beginning reconstructive surgery, the physician usually orders biopsy tests of the remaining tissues to make sure the new stomach will not be made of tissues in which tumor cells have spread. If the edges of the remaining stomach wall are found to contain tumor cells, the surgeon simply extends the area to be removed. As in subtotal gastrectomy for peptic ulcers, the remaining portion of the stomach may be connected directly to the upper portion of the small intestine, at the duodenum or the jejunum.

Meals are provided in the form of intravenous feedings for the first few days following surgery. Sips of water may be permitted on the second or third day after the operation with the amounts gradually increased to one or two ounces of water per hour as the new digestive system adjusts to fluid intake. Then soft or bland foods can gradually be taken orally in a half-dozen small feedings each day. It may take three or four months for the new stomach to distend and adjust to normal eating habits of the patient.

Postoperative Effects

Some patients may experience a variety of symptoms ranging from nausea to cramps and diarrhea while recovering from stomach surgery. The symptoms form what is known as the *dumping syndrome,* which occurs within a half hour after a meal, presumably by rapid distension of the upper portion of the small intestine as fluid rushes, or is dumped, into that part of the digestive tract from the new stomach. The effects can be controlled by a change of diet to eliminate starches and sugars, by delaying the intake of fluids until after the meal, by medications, and by training the patient to lie in a recumbent or semirecumbent position to lessen discomfort following a meal. The symptoms occur in only a small proportion of stomach surgery patients, and they usually diminish gradually during the period of recovery.

Cancer of the Intestines

Small Intestine

Tumors of the small intestine are not common, but they also are not rare. It has been estimated that less than five percent of all tumors of the gastrointestinal tract occur in the small intestine. Of tumors that do develop in this portion of the gastrointestinal tract, about 90 percent are benign, or noncancerous, growths. The symptoms of small intestine tumors may include bleeding, obstruction, and perforation of the intestinal wall. However, most tumors of the small intestine produce no symptoms at all. When tumors are found in the small intestine they usually are found at the same time in other parts of the body, and usually in a patient over 40 years of age, although the more malignant growths can occur in younger persons. Treatment of a cancer of the small bowel is by removing the affected section and administration of radiation therapy for certain kinds of cancerous tumors.

Large Intestine

Tumors of the large intestine, unlike those of the small bowel, account for a large proportion of cancers of the human body and for most of the malignant growths of the entire gastrointestinal tract. More than 40,000 deaths each year in the United States are a result of cancers of the colon and rectum portions of the large bowel. And about three-fourths of all large-intestine tumors develop near the rectal portion of the bowel, where, ironically, they should be easily available for detection during physical examination.

Tumors of the large intestine can be found in persons of any age, but they occur most frequently in patients who are of middle age or older, reaching a peak of incidence around the age of 65. Men are more likely to develop cancer of the rectum, but women are more frequently affected by cancer of the colon. While cancer of the large intestine tends to occur among members of the same families at a rate that is two or three times the normal incidence, it is believed that family environment factors, such as life style and diet, are the causative influences, rather than hereditary factors. People who develop cancer of the large intestine usually eat foods that are low in cellulose and high in animal fats and refined carbohydrates.

Bowel cancers appear to grow in size at a very slow rate, doubling about once every 20 months, so a number of years may elapse between the start of a bowel tumor and the appearance of signs or symptoms of cancer.

Symptoms

The location of the growth can influence the types of symptoms experienced. Cancer in the right colon may be found as an abnormal mass during a physical examination by a physician after complaints of fatigue and weakness and signs of anemia. The tumor can develop to a rather large size without producing signs of blood in the stools. Cancer in the left colon, by contrast, may be found after complaints of alternate periods of constipation and frequent urge to defecate, pain in the abdomen, and stools marked by dark and bright red blood. When the cancer is in the rectum, the patient may find blood mixed with the bowel movements but experience no pain in the early stages. Other symptoms of cancer of the large intestine may mimic those of appendicitis, hemorrhoids, peptic ulcer, or gall bladder disease.

As noted above, most cancers of the large bowel are close enough to the end of the intestinal tract to be observed directly by palpation or the use of fiberoptic instruments, such as a sigmoidoscope or colonoscope, which can be inserted into the rectum or colon. Biopsy samples can be removed for study and X-ray pictures taken after administration of a barium enema, which coats the bowel membrane in such a way that abnormal surfaces are clearly visible.

Surgical Procedures

Surgical procedures for treatment of cancer of the large intestine vary somewhat according to the location of the growth, but the objective is the same: to remove the affected portion and reconstruct the bowel so that normal digestive functions can resume. Radiation therapy and chemotherapy may be used in the treatment of certain advanced cases. When surgical treatment is begun soon after the first symptoms are diagnosed, the chances of curing cancer of the large bowel are very good.

If there are complications, such as obstruction of the portion of the large intestine, the surgery may be conducted in a series of stages over a period of several weeks. The several stages involve a colostomy procedure in which an opening is made in the wall of the abdomen to permit a portion of the intestinal tract to be brought to the surface of the body. After the complicating problem is treated and resection of the cancerous segment is completed, the colostomy is closed by sewing the open end of the bowel to the remaining portion and closing the opening in the abdomen.

Preoperative Steps

Some special preoperative measures are ordered for patients awaiting surgery for treatment of bowel cancer. They consist primarily of several days of liquid diets, laxatives, and enemas to make the interior of the intestinal tract as clean as possible. Other measures will be directed toward correction of anemia and compensation for possible loss of blood resulting from the cancer's invasion of bowel tissues.

Gallbladder Surgery

Gallbladder disease is one of the most common medical disorders in the United States. It has been estimated that more than 15 million Americans are affected by the disease and about 6,000 deaths a year are associated with it. The incidence increases at middle age; 1 of every 5 women over the age of 50 and 1 of every 20 men can expect to be treated for gallbladder symptoms. Approximately 1,000 people in the United States enter operating rooms each day for removal of gallstones, a primary cause of the symptoms of the disorder.

Gallstones

Gallstones generally are formed from crystals of cholesterol that gradually increase in size in the gallbladder; some, however, are formed from other substances, such as bile salts and breakdown products of red blood cells. Because they are very small in size, the stones may produce no symptoms at first. But as they grow in size they become more threatening and eventually can block the normal flow of bile from one of the bile ducts emptying into the intestine. Bile contains substances needed by the body to digest fats in the diet.

Symptoms

A common symptom of *chronic chole-cystitis,* or gallstone disease, is a pain that appears suddenly in the upper abdomen and subsides slowly over a period of several minutes to several hours. The pain may occur after a meal or with no apparent relationship to meals. There can be tenderness in the upper right side of the body, with pain extending to the shoulder. The pain also can appear on the left side or near the center of the upper abdomen, producing misleading symptoms suggesting a heart attack. Nausea, heartburn, gas, indigestion, and intolerance to fatty foods are among other possible symptoms. The gallbladder attacks may occur frequently or there may be remissions (periods without symptoms) lasting for several months or years.

A careful and extensive physical examination, including X-ray studies of the gallbladder area, may be needed to confirm the presence of gallstones. Until recently, the most commonly used test was the oral cholecystogram (OCG), in which the patient swallowed an iodine-based "dye," or contrast agent. X rays taken about 12 hours after administration of the dye might or might not provide useful "pictures" of the gallstones. As a result, ultrasound has largely replaced X rays as a primary test for suspected gallstones.

Acute Cholecystitis

About three-fourths of the cases of acute cholecystitis are patients who have had previous attacks of gallstone disease. In the acute phase there is persistent pain and abdominal tenderness, along with nausea and vomiting in many cases and a mild fever. Complications may include perforation, or rupture, of the gallbladder, leading to peritonitis, or development of adhesions to neighboring organs such as the stomach or intestine.

Treatment

Surgical treatment of chronic or acute cholecystitis is basically an elective procedure that can be scheduled at a time convenient to the patient. But acute cases with complications may require emergency operations. The patient can usually be maintained, after surgery, on intravenous fluids and pain-killing medications.

In gallstone surgery, the abdomen is opened so that the surgeon can examine the gall bladder and the ducts leading from it for stones. The gallbladder may be freed of stones and a temporary drainage tube inserted, with an opening to the outside of the upper abdomen. But usually the surgeon removes the entire gallbladder in an operation called a *cholecystectomy.* The bile duct, which remains as a link between the liver and the small intestine, gradually replaces the gallbladder in function. Conventional cholecystectomies are rarely performed now. The less invasive laparoscopic cholecystectomy has almost completely replaced the conventional surgical removal of diseased gallbladders. In the innovative method, a laparoscope removes the entire gallbladder and any stones it contains. Using videoscope surgery, everything is neatly pulled through tiny incisions in the abdomen.

A number of alternatives to surgery have been developed. A gastroenterologist may use an endoscope on older patients or those in poor health. The endoscope, a tube inserted through the chest wall, enables the physician to view the gallbladder's duct area and to widen its opening so that small gallstones can slip through the small intestine. Using a small basket on the endoscope, the physician can sometimes catch and withdraw or crush the stones.

Other nonsurgical treatments include chemical preparations. Chenodeoxycholic acid, or chenodiol, has been given orally to dissolve smaller, floating cholesterol stones. But the drug has little effect against pigment stones or stones with a high calcium content, and can cause diarrhea as a side effect.

Among the most advanced techniques is *choledocholithotripsy,* a nonsurgical method using shock waves to destroy gallstones. Already in use as a method of shattering kidney stones, lithotripsy requires only a local anesthetic and the recovery period lasts only a few days. The physician uses a hollow tool—the lithotriptor—that is inserted through the patient's chest until it approaches the stones. With a foot switch, the physician then triggers a jolt of high-voltage, low-current electricity that shatters the stones.

In another advance, drugs have been utilized to dissolve gallstones. A drug called *methyl tertbutyl ether* (MTHE) has been found to break down gallstones as large as golf balls. Still partly experimental, the compound could replace most surgical operations for gallstones.

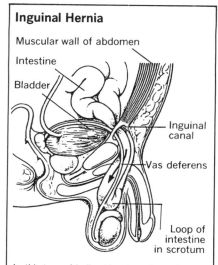

Inguinal Hernia

Muscular wall of abdomen

Intestine

Bladder

Inguinal canal

Vas deferens

Loop of intestine in scrotum

In this type of indirect hernia, a loop of small intestine has pushed through the weakened inguinal canal in the abdominal wall and descended into the scrotal sac.

Inguinal Hernia

An inguinal hernia (hernia of the groin) can develop in either men or women at almost any age from infancy to late adult years. But the incidence of inguinal hernia is much more common in males. An inguinal hernia is one in which the intestinal tract protrudes through the opening of one of the inguinal rings on either side of the groin. In males, the inguinal rings are temporary openings through which the testicles descend into the scrotum before birth; in females, the openings permit the passage of a ligament supporting the ovary.

Causes

Normally, the inguinal rings are closed after the birth of the child. However, they may fail to close completely or the muscles and connective tissues may become stretched or weakened in later years to permit a portion of the abdominal contents, usually part of the intestine, to protrude. A number of factors can contribute to the development of a hernia, including physical strain from exercise or lifting, straining over a

bowel movement, coughing spells, pregnancy, pressure of abdominal organs, or obesity.

Reducible and Irreducible Hernias

The hernia may be *reducible,* that is, the bulge in the abdominal wall may disappear when the body position is changed, as in lying down, only to reappear upon standing. An *irreducible* hernia does not allow the hernia sac contents to return to the abdominal cavity; an irreducible hernia also may be called *incarcerated,* a term aptly describing the hernia as being trapped. A serious complication is strangulation of the hernia contents, which usually involves obstruction of normal blood flow and resulting damage or destruction of the incarcerated intestines. A strangulated hernia may be life-threatening because of the possibility of gangrene in body tissues damaged by incarceration.

Surgical Procedure

Some hernias are called *direct,* some *indirect,* for purposes of medical records. These terms indicate to the surgeon specific layers of muscle and connective tissue that have been breached and are of no real significance to the patient, because the surgical repair procedures are essentially the same for either type. In the absence of complications, the operation is fairly simple and usually can be performed with either a general or a local anesthetic. An incision is made in the lower abdomen in the area of the hernia, the protruding organ is returned to its normal position, and the weakened or ruptured layers of muscle and connective tissue are repaired and reinforced to provide a strong internal wall that will hold the abdominal contents in place. In some cases the surgeon will use available tissues from

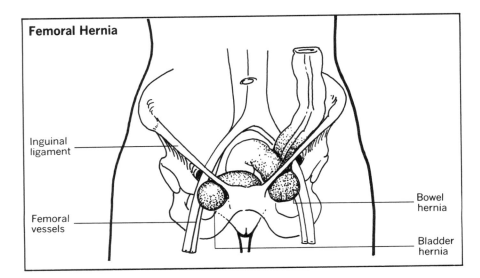

Femoral Hernia

Inguinal ligament

Femoral vessels

Bowel hernia

Bladder hernia

the patient's own body in building a new wall against future hernias. The surgeon also may use a variety of materials, including silk, catgut, stainless steel, tantalum mesh gauze, or mesh screens made of plastics, in building a new barrier.

Recovery

The hospital stay for hernia repair is relatively brief, usually from three days to a week; some healthy children undergo surgery early in the morning and return home in the evening of the same day. The patient usually is instructed to avoid exercise or exertion for a couple of weeks and can return to work in a month to six weeks, depending upon the work load expected. Hernias tend to recur in only a small percentage of cases among adults and very rarely in children.

Femoral Hernia

About five percent of all hernias of the groin area are femoral hernias, with the hernia bulge appearing along the thigh. Femoral hernias occur about four times as frequently among women and usually appear in middle age. While a femoral hernia is not necessarily limited to obese patients, it is more likely to be associated with being overweight, and the movement of a bowel segment or the urinary bladder into the hernia frequently is preceded by a fat pad—a mass of fatty tissue. Femoral hernias are more prone to incarceration and strangulation than inguinal hernias. The surgical treatment of femoral hernias is similar to that used in the repair of inguinal hernias, although the incision may be made through the thigh in a few cases.

Hemorrhoids

Hemorrhoid, a term derived from Greek words meaning "blood flowing," refers to a system of arteries and veins that serve the rectal area. The medical problem known as *hemorrhoids,* or *piles,* is a tortuous en-

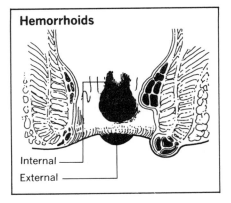

Hemorrhoids

Internal

External

largement of the hemorrhoidal veins, a problem similar to the varicose veins of the legs. Causes of the varicosities of the hemorrhoidal veins include the human peculiarity of standing and walking in an erect posture—animals that walk on all fours do not get hemorrhoids.

Women during pregnancies are particularly subject to hemorrhoidal problems because of the pressure on the veins of the lower body area. Other causes are constipation and straining at stool; diseases of the digestive tract resulting in anal infection; and cirrhosis of the liver, which obstructs blood flow and puts increased pressure on the hemorrhoidal veins.

Symptoms

Symptoms usually include bleeding, which may stain the patient's clothing; irritation and discomfort, including itching, in the anal region; and occasionally pain with inflammation. Because rectal bleeding also can be a sign of a number of other diseases, the physician usually makes a thorough examination to rule out other possible causes, such as cancer or ulcerative colitis.

Treatment

If the hemorrhoids do not warrant surgery, medical treatments may be prescribed. *Prolapsed hemorrhoids* (veins that protrude from the anus) can be reduced by gentle pressure. Bed rest, warm baths, and medications are also a part of medical treatments. A type of injection chemotherapy sometimes is used to control bleeding and eliminate the varicosed veins.

Surgery can be used to excise all the affected tissues, and the disorder also can be treated by cryosurgery in which the hemorrhoids are destroyed by a probe containing supercold liquid nitrogen or carbon dioxide. The patient usually is able to recover and return to work within one or two weeks after surgical removal of the hemorrhoidal tissues.

Oral Cavity and Throat

This section discusses oral cancers, tonsils and adenoids, and surgery of the thyroid. For a discussion of cosmetic surgery of the face area, see "Plastic and Cosmetic Surgery" later in this chapter.

Oral Cancers

There are many potential problems of the mouth, or oral cavity, besides an occasional toothache. Surgical treatment frequently is needed to correct a disorder or to prevent a life-threatening situation from developing. Cancers of the lips, tongue, hard and soft palate, and other areas of the mouth, for example, affect about 25,000 people in the United States each year. Elsewhere in the world, the incidence varies considerably according to sex and location; the rate in Hong Kong for men is three times the figure for women, and the incidence of oral cancer for women in Hong Kong is nearly 10 times as high as that of women in Japan. Environmental factors such as tobacco and contact with chemical and physical agents have been suggested as causes, although one form of oral cancer, known as *Burkitt's lymphoma,* is believed to be transmitted by a mosquito-borne virus.

Cancer of the Lip

Oral cancers tend to occur after the age of 45. Some types of oral cancer, particularly when the lips are af-

fected, are found most frequently in persons exposed to a great deal of sunlight. Farmers, sailors, and other outdoor workers develop such tumors around the age of 60, with the lesion appearing on the lower lip. Like other cancers, cancer of the lip may begin as a tiny growth, but, if untreated, can spread through neighboring tissues and eventually destroy part of the chin. Treatment may include both radiation therapy and surgical excision of the growth; if surgery is performed when the tumor is small, the scar is likewise small. Obviously, the larger the tumor is allowed to grow, the more difficult the treatment.

Cancer of the Cheek

Similarly, cancers that develop on the inner surface of the cheek usually can be excised and the wound closed with simple surgery if treatment is started early. If the cancer is allowed to grow before treatment, the surgery becomes more complicated with removal of tissues extending to the outer skin layers and repair of the wound with skin grafts. Radiation therapy also may be used to augment the surgical repair.

Cancer of the Mouth

Cancer of the floor of the mouth may be second only to lip cancer in rate of occurrence of oral cavity tumors; together they may account for half of the oral cavity cancers in the United States. A tumor of the floor of the mouth may involve the under surface of the tongue, the lower jawbone, and other tissues of the area. A small lesion detected early can be controlled in most cases by excision of the growth and radiation therapy.

Cancer of the Tongue

The tongue may be the site of cancerous growths beginning in the 30s of the patient's life, particularly if the individual is a heavy user of tobacco and alcohol and has been neglectful of proper oral hygiene, such as brushing the teeth regularly. If the growth is at the tip of the tongue rather than underneath or along the sides, the operation is easier and there is less chance that the normal function of the tongue will be impaired by removing the growth and surrounding tissue cells. Radiation therapy for cancer of the tongue sometimes involves the implantation of needles containing radium into the tongue. The procedure is done while the patient is under a general anesthetic. Tumors at the base of the tongue, as well as some growths on the floor of the mouth, sometimes are approached through an incision in the neck.

Other Surgery

Apart from cancers, surgery of the oral cavity may be needed to treat genetic defects, such as cleft lip and cleft palate, damage to tissues from injuries, and noncancerous tumors of the soft tissues, such as cysts.

Tonsils and Adenoids

Tonsils and adenoids are glands of lymphoid tissue lying along the walls near the top of the throat. The tonsils are located on the sides of the pharynx, or throat, near the base of the tongue. Unless an adult's tonsils are inflamed, they may not be easily visible to a physician or other person looking into the throat, but when inflamed and swollen they can be seen without difficulty. The adenoids are located higher in the pharynx and cannot be seen by looking into the back of the mouth without special instruments, because the palate, or roof of the mouth, blocks the view.

Tonsillitis

The function of the tonsils and adenoids apparently is that of trapping infectious organisms that enter the body through the nose and mouth. But sometimes the glands do such a good job of collecting infections that they lose their effectiveness, becoming enlarged and inflamed, a condition known as *tonsillitis*. The patient develops fever and sore throat and the breathing passages become obstructed. The infections can spread through the nearby Eustachian tubes to the ears, causing *otitis media* (inflammation of the middle ear), resulting in deafness. Disease organisms also can spread from the tonsils and adenoids to the kidneys, joints, heart, eyes, and other body areas. Many youngsters survive occasional bouts of tonsillitis, and the infections can be treated with antibiotics and medications to relieve pain and fever symptoms. But many surgeons recommend that the tonsils and adenoids be removed if tonsillitis occurs repeatedly.

Tonsillectomy

A *tonsillectomy* (removal of the tonsils) is not a complicated operation, but it usually is performed under a general anesthetic if the patient is a child. A local anesthetic may be used for an adult. The adenoids usually are removed at the same time; they consist of the same type of lymphoid tissue in the same general area, and adenoids develop similar problems from the same kinds of infectious agents. An overnight stay in the hospital may be required or it may be possible for the patient to have the tonsils and adenoids removed in the morning and be released from the hospital in the evening of the same day, after a few hours of postoperative rest under medical observation.

Preoperative and Postoperative Care

The patient may receive antibiotic medications two or three days prior to surgery and is instructed to avoid eating foods or drinking fluids for at least 12 hours before the operation. If the patient has a cold or other viral infection, the surgery may be delayed or postponed. Some surgeons also prefer to avoid tonsillectomy operations during the hay-fever season. If there is any evidence of bleeding after the patient is released, such as spitting blood, he is returned to the hospital and the surgeon is notified; the bleeding usually can be controlled without difficulty. The patient also returns for checkups a couple of weeks after the operation and again about six months later.

Adenoidectomy

In some cases, a surgeon may recommend an *adenoidectomy* (removal of the adenoids) without a tonsillectomy. This is particularly true when the patient suffers from recurrent ear infections and hearing loss. An adenoidectomy is a relatively simple operation performed under a local anesthetic when the patient is an adult or older teenager; a general anesthetic is preferred for younger patients.

The surgeon can reach the adenoid mass through the open mouth of the patient. The tissue grows on a palate ledge near the point where the nasal passage enters the back of the mouth cavity. Using a special instrument, the surgeon cuts away the adenoid tissue within a few minutes. A medicated pack is inserted into the post-nasal area to help control bleeding and the patient is moved to a recovery room. The only aftereffects in most cases are a soreness in the postnasal area for a few days and, occasionally, a temporary voice change that is marked by a nasal tone while the wound heals.

Thyroid Surgery

The thyroid gland lies along the trachea, or windpipe, at a point just below the Adam's apple. Secretions of the thyroid gland are vital for metabolic activities of the body, and the gland's functions are closely orchestrated with those of other endocrine glands of the body. When the thyroid is less active than normal, mental and physical functions are slow and the patient gains weight. When the gland is overly active, body functions operate at an abnormally fast pace, with symptoms of weight loss, irritability, heart palpitations, and bulging eyes. Occasionally, lumps develop on the thyroid, requiring medical or surgical treatment. A lump on the thyroid gland may be a nodular, or nontoxic, goiter. Or it could be a tumor. A nodular goiter poses several threats: it can make the thyroid gland become overactive, it can press on the windpipe and cause hoarseness, or it can develop into a cancer. Some growths of the thyroid gland can be treated effectively with medications, radiation, or a combination such as radio-

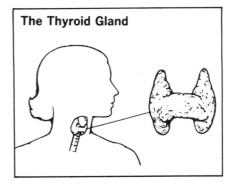

The Thyroid Gland

active iodine. However, when conservative forms of therapy no longer appear to control the condition, or when it is suspected that a thyroid growth may be a malignant cancer, surgical removal of the affected area is advised promptly.

Surgical Procedure

The operation itself is fairly simple. An incision is made through the skin folds of the neck, neck muscles beneath the skin are separated, and the affected portion of the gland is cut away. The neck and throat area may be sore and painful for a few days after the operation; within a few weeks the patient can resume normal activities. A thin scar remains at the line of incision, but it is usually partly concealed by skin folds of the neck.

Ear Surgery

Surgical treatment of the ear usually is directed toward restoring the function of normal hearing which may have been lost or impaired by disease or injury. The eardrum, or tympanic membrane, can be perforated or ruptured by direct injury, by the shock waves of an explosion, or by an infection of the middle ear. Infection or injury also can disrupt hearing function by damaging the ossicles, a chain of tiny bones that transmit sound waves from the eardrum to the inner ear. Disease, aging effects, and exposure to loud noises can cause hearing loss or impairment.

Surgery of the ear usually involves working with the middle ear, the compartment between the eardrum and the inner ear, which contains the nerve endings that carry impulses to the auditory centers of the brain. The middle ear contains three ossicles, known by their common names of *hammer, anvil,* and *stirrup*—terms that suggest their functions in translating movements of air molecules into the vibrations the brain understands as sounds.

Otitis Media

One common disease of the middle ear is otitis media, which can occur by infection from a number of different kinds of organisms. Otitis media also can develop from secretions or fluids such as milk being forced into the ear through the Eustachian tube, particularly in infants who are fed while they are in a reclining position. The symptoms of otitis media are pain in the ear, fever, and loss of hearing; a small child may indicate the symptoms by crying and tugging at the ear.

Surgical Procedure

Many cases of otitis media respond to medical treatment, such as the use of antibiotics, but for patients who suffer severe pain or who have middle ears filled with pus, a surgical procedure called *myringotomy* is performed. "Myringotomy" means simply perforating the eardrum. But the operation usually is peformed in a hospital, under a local anesthetic, and with great care to avoid disturbing the ossicles or other ear structures beyond the eardrum. The middle ear is drained and the eardrum either heals spontaneously or can be subsequently repaired with a graft from the patient's own tissues.

Surgery to Correct Hearing Loss

Occasionally surgery is required to correct a conductive hearing loss involving the structures of the middle ear. Such problems happen more frequently among older persons because of abnormal tissue growths that in effect "freeze" the ossicles, so that they no longer work with normal flexibility. Ossicular disorders also can occur in younger persons, including children, because of congenital defects, injury, or repeated infections, as of otitis media. The exact procedure for restoration of hearing depends upon the type of disorder. If one of the ossicles has slipped out of position or has become rigidly attached to another structure, like the tympanic membrane, the tiny bones can be repositioned or freed from the tissues that may have immobilized them. It is not unusual for the surgeon, working in a space about the size of a pea and viewing his progress through a microscope, to literally take the middle ear structures apart, rebuild the organ with bits of plastic or metal shaped like the ossicles, and reconstruct the eardrum with tissue grafts. This kind of surgery is called *microsurgery.*

Inner Ear Disturbances

Disorders of the inner ear usually are treated with medications. Surgery in that area is seldom performed unless there is a great risk to the life of the patient. Little can be done to restore hearing loss caused by nerve deafness except with hearing aids; these are designed to pick up sounds on the affected side of the head and route the sounds by electronic circuitry to an area where they can be picked up by remaining functional auditory nerves.

Eye Surgery

Among common types of eye surgery are procedures for correcting eye muscles, glaucoma, cataracts, cornea and retina disorders. Operations on the eye muscles are intended to correct crossed eyes or similar problems in which the two eyes fail to work together.

Crossed Eyes

The condition technically known as *strabismus,* in which one eye drifts so that its position is not parallel with the other, is caused by a congenitally weak muscle. Infants often appear to have crossed eyes, but in most cases the drifting corrects itself by the time the baby is six months old. If the condition persists beyond that time, a physician should be consulted. He may recommend the use of an eye patch over the stronger eye so that the weaker one will be exercised. If this does not achieve the desired result, he may prescribe special glasses and eye exercises as the child gets older, so that there is no impairment of vision.

Corrective Surgery

If corrective surgery proves necessary after these measures, it is usually done before the child enters school. The operation is a simple one involving the muscle and not the inside of the eye itself. Each eye has six *extraocular* muscles—muscles originating outside the eyeball—to move the eye up, down, left, right, etc.; the surgeon lengthens or shortens these muscles, as may be required, to coordinate the eye movements. The operation is safe and requires only a brief hospital stay.

Amblyopia

If the lack of eye coordination is not corrected, a kind of blindness called *amblyopia* can result in one of the eyes. This condition occurs particularly in young children who depend upon the vision of one good eye; the function of the other eye is allowed to deteriorate. It has been estimated that about two million Americans have lost a part of their vision in this manner. Crossed eyes should receive professional attention early enough to prevent a permanent visual handicap.

Cataract

Cataract is a condition in which there is a loss of transparency of the lenses of the eyes. Each lens is made up of layers of cells naturally formed to focus a visual image on the retina at the rear of the eyeball. As a result of aging, or because of an injury to the eye, the lens may develop cloudy or opaque areas, or *cataracts,* that result in a blurring of vision. About five percent of the population of the United States have cataracts. Some physicians claim that anyone who lives long enough can expect to have cataracts, although age is not the only determining factor.

Surgical Correction

The condition can be corrected rather easily by several different kinds of surgical procedures. Among these, a relatively simple, advanced technique involves a microsurgery procedure called *extracapsular extraction* followed by implantation of a new lens. Using this method, the surgeon first makes a tiny incision in the cornea. Reaching through that incision, the surgeon then makes a circle of tiny cuts in the lens. The lens and its cataract are then drawn through the opening in the cornea. The back part of the lens remains in place to support the implant lens.

Extracapsular extraction has begun to replace older techniques. These include dissolving the tissues holding the lens in place with a liquid enzyme, freezing the lens with a supercold probe, and grinding the lens tissue with a high-speed instrument. Extracapsular extraction requires only a local anesthetic injected into the facial muscles. Because the sutures are tiny, healing time can be as short as a few weeks.

Laser surgery has also been used effectively following cataract lens replacements. The neodymium yttrium-aluminum garnet (Nd:YAG) laser has helped to clear the capsular membrane that sometimes clouds the eye after such surgery.

The timing of cataract surgery presents the patient with a difficult decision. To help you make up your mind, the physician may use a potential acuity meter (PAM) to show what kind of vision you should have after a cataract is removed. The PAM projects a light beam that flashes a standard eye chart through tiny clear areas in the cataract. Because the beam hits your retina directly, you can read the chart without interference.

Lens implants normally effect greatly improved vision. But for optimum results most patients need to wear eyeglasses or contact lenses after the operation. Because implanted lenses cannot focus as your eye's natural lens does, you will probably need reading glasses. The artificial lenses may require some adjustments to compensate for visual illusions as to distances and shapes, but the blurring of progressive blindness will have been eliminated.

Sometimes after cataract operations, patients notice that the rear part of the lens left in to support the implant has begun to cloud. In such a case a surgeon may use a laser beam to punch a tiny hole in the clouded area. The hole lets light rays reach the retina unimpeded.

Cornea Transplant

The cornea of the eye is a clear window of several cells in thickness at the very front of the eye. While it is protected by the constant sweeping of the corneal surface by the eyelid and the washing of the surface by the tears, it is vulnerable to injury and infection, allergies, and metabolic disorders. The simple habit of rubbing the eyes can distort the shape of the cornea, changing the normal round shape to a cone shape. Eventually, a cornea may degenerate from wear and tear and become so clouded that the patient can no longer see clearly, if at all. It is possible, however—and has been since the 1930s—to replace a clouded cornea with an undamaged cornea from a deceased person. Corneas are contributed by donors and stored in eye banks.

Surgical Procedures

When only a portion of the cornea needs to be replaced, as is often the case, a disk encompassing the damaged cornea is carefully cut out and a piece of new cornea of precisely the same size and shape is sewn into the remaining tissue of the old cornea. The reconstructed cornea is treated with antibiotics and bandaged for several weeks. More than three-fourths of the cornea transplants are successful; the chances of success depend upon many factors, including the health of the remaining tissues of the original cornea.

Glaucoma

Glaucoma, a leading cause of blindness, is a disease caused by a failure of the fluid produced inside the eye to drain properly. The fluid, or *aqueous humor,* is produced in the anterior chamber of the eye, between the cornea and the lens. In a normal eye it drains through a duct at the base of the cornea at the same rate at which it is produced. But if the drainage system is obstructed, fluid buildup creates pressure backward through the eye. If untreated, such pressure can cause gradual blindness by crushing the nerves at the back of the eye.

Treatment

Some cases of glaucoma can be treated with medications that control the rates of fluid production and drainage. But when medications are no longer effective or when an acute attack occurs, with symptoms of severe eye pain sometimes accompanied by abdominal pain, nausea, and vomiting, surgery within a matter of hours is recommended. Several surgical procedures for the treatment of glaucoma are available; all are designed to release the fluid pressure in the eye. One common procedure involves cutting a small opening in the iris. Another technique is to insert a fine wire into the duct that normally drains the fluid and literally ream it open.

Other surgical and nonsurgical treatments for glaucoma have been developed. For example, laser surgery has proved effective for treating both open-angle and closed-angle glaucoma. In the former, the eye's internal drain system does not work properly, causing pressure to build up in the eye. In closed-angle glaucoma, fluid cannot pass properly from the front to the back of the eye, again producing dangerous pressure. The neodymium yttrium-aluminum garnet (Nd:YAG) laser is usually used in treatment to "drill" a tiny hole and destroy swollen blood vessels that block normal fluid drainage. Because marihuana has also been found to reduce pressure in the eye, manufacture of the chemical known as THC (delta-9-tetrahydrocannabinol), the key marihuana ingredient, was authorized by the Food and Drug Administration in 1985 and begun in 1986. THC has also been used to relieve the nausea accompanying cancer chemotherapy and to slow multiple sclerosis.

An estimated 10 million people in the world are afflicted by glaucoma, and the chances of developing increase with age. Women are twice as likely to develop the disease as men, and there is some evidence that the risk is hereditary. However, it also is easily preventable and controllable, since glaucoma usually develops slowly and can be detected during routine eye examinations in its early stages.

Retinal Detachment or Disease

Retinal detachment can occur from bleeding in the retinal area, an injury, a change in the shape of the eyeball, or other causes. The surgical treatment to correct the problem usually is related to the specific cause. For example, if fluid or blood has accumulated behind the retina, it is drained away. Alternatively, pressure may be directed within the eyeball to push the retina back into its proper position. For some cases, such as those associated with *diabetic retinopathy,* a kind of retinal bleeding in diabetes patients, a laser beam is used to seal the blood vessels responsible for the tiny hemorrhages in the eye.

Chest Region

This section deals with surgery of the lungs and heart. For a discussion of cosmetic surgery of the chest area, as of the breast, see "Plastic and Cosmetic Surgery" later in this chapter.

The Lungs

Before the era of modern drugs such as antibiotics, lung disorders were the leading cause of death in the United States. Lung diseases are still common enough. With every breath taken in, the lungs are vulnerable to damage from disease organisms, chemicals, and air pollutants, many of which did not exist 50 years ago when pneumonia and tuberculosis were among the greatest threats to human life. Because the lungs are not as sensitive to pain as some other organs, a respiratory disorder may develop insidiously with few or no symptoms. When pain is felt in the chest area, the source of the pain may be the chest wall, the esophagus, or the bronchial tubes that branch from the trachea into smaller units that distribute air through the lung tissues. Other symptoms of respiratory disease may be coughing, shortness of breath, or sputum that contains blood.

Tuberculosis

Any of the above signs or symptoms could be associated with tuberculosis, which also can cause loss of appetite, weight loss, lethargy, and heavy perspiration, especially during the night. Tuberculosis is still one of the most common causes of death in the world, and new cases are found in the United States each year at a rate of 18 per 100,000 population. In addition, an estimated 35 million Americans are tuberculin-positive, indicating they have been in contact with the infectious organism but have developed an immune response to it. For an explanation of how tuberculosis is spread and of tests devised to check its spread, see "Tuberculosis" in Ch. 12, *Diseases of the Respiratory System.*

Surgical Treatment of Tuberculosis

A dozen different drugs are available for medical treatment of tuberculosis and several types may be taken in combination by a patient. Intensive treatment may require a hospital stay of several months and use of the drugs for at least 18 months. However, because of the adverse side effects of drugs, resistance of the bacterium to the drugs, and other reasons, surgery may be required. If

one of the five lobes of lung tissue— the right lung has three lobes, the left lung two—has been severely damaged by tuberculosis, it may be removed by surgeons. In some instances, physicians may recommend that surgery be undertaken to allow one of the lungs to rest while it recovers from the infection. This is accomplished by crushing the phrenic nerve, under a local anesthetic, creating a partial paralysis of the diaphragm. Partial lung collapse also can be accomplished by removing parts of the ribs over the affected lung.

Lung Cancer

Cancer of the lung may appear with early symptoms of coughing, wheezing, or the appearance of blood in sputum; in about 10 percent of cases there is chest pain or shortness of breath. However, it is not unusual for the lung cancer patient to have no complaints of illness. Chest X rays during a routine physical examination may reveal the disease. In many cases, the cancer develops from metastases of cancers that have spread

from other body systems. Medical therapy for lung cancer patients, including the use of radiation, is primarily for the purpose of relieving pain or other symptoms. The only effective cure is surgical excision of the affected lung tissue along with the nearby lymph nodes. Surgical treatment is most effective in young adults when the tumor has not invaded neighboring tissues, although the five-year survival rate for lung cancer is still poor.

Heart Surgery

Heart surgery procedures that are routine in many hospitals today were unheard of a generation ago. Since World War II, techniques have been devised to permit attachment of a heart-lung machine to the human body so that the patient's blood can be circulated and refreshed with oxygen while the heart itself is stopped temporarily for surgery.

Heart Valve Repair

While the blood flow is shunted away from the heart, surgeons can replace

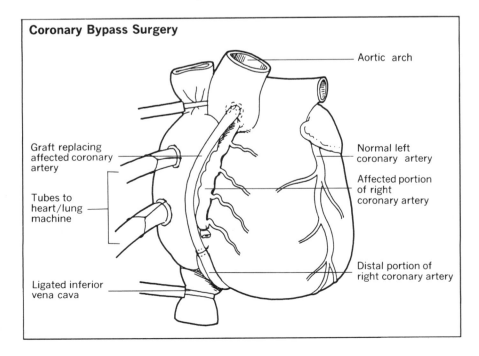

Coronary Bypass Surgery

- Aortic arch
- Graft replacing affected coronary artery
- Tubes to heart/lung machine
- Ligated inferior vena cava
- Normal left coronary artery
- Affected portion of right coronary artery
- Distal portion of right coronary artery

a diseased heart valve that may have become calcified with deposits that keep it from closing normally. An artificial valve made of metal and plastic may be used to replace the patient's diseased mitral valve that no longer effectively controls the flow of blood from the left atrium to the left ventricle of the heart. Artificial valves also can be installed between the right chambers of the heart. In some cases, a diseased valve leaf may be repaired with a graft of tissue from the patient's body.

Installation of artificial heart valves has had a remarkably good record of success; some surgeons recommend the procedure over other techniques for treatment of heart valve diseases and report the operation has been well tolerated by patients over 70. While some activites may be restricted, life expectancy is increased for most patients, and they are able to have comfortable and more normal lives after such operations.

Septal Defect

Another kind of heart surgery is used to correct a septal defect. The rightand left atria of the heart are separated by a septum, a wall of muscular tissue. A similar but much thicker septum separates the left and right ventricles. Occasionally, usually because of a birth defect, the septum does not close completely and blood flows from one side to the other through the opening in the heart wall. The problem is solved by putting the patient on a heart-lung machine while the heart is opened and the septum closed either by sewing the opening or by stitching into the septum a patch of plastic material.

Coarctation of the Aorta

An equally dramatic bit of heart surgery is used to correct a defect called

coarctation, or narrowing, of the aorta, the main artery leading from the heart. This short, pinched section interferes with normal blood flow. If untreated, the patient may die of a ruptured aorta or heart failure. Treatment requires an operation in which the narrowed section of the aorta is cut away and the two normal-sized ends sewed together. In some cases, a piece of plastic material is sewed into the reconstructed aorta to replace the coarctated section.

Aortal-Pulmonary Artery Shunt

A comparatively simple bit of heart surgery is employed to correct a defect that occurs in some newborn children. Before birth, when the lungs are not needed because fresh blood is supplied from the placenta via the umbilical cord, the aorta is connected by a shunt to the pulmonary artery. After birth the shunt closes in most cases so the pulmonary artery can carry the blood from the heart to the lungs for oxygenation. In some children this shunt fails to close. To correct the defect and prevent heart failure, the surgeon opens the child's chest, ties off the open shunt, and cuts the ligated connection.

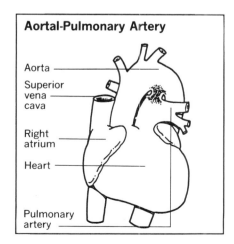

Aortal-Pulmonary Artery

Aorta

Superior vena cava

Right atrium

Heart

Pulmonary artery

Vascular Surgery

This section consists of discussions of aneurysms, varicose veins, phlebitis, and intermittent claudication.

Aneurysm

When a blood vessel develops a balloonlike malformation the defect is called an *aneurysm.* A common complication of the aneurysm is that it may rupture if not treated. A ruptured aneurysm of a large blood vessel, or of a small blood vessel in a critical area such as the brain, can be fatal or severely disabling.

Surgical Procedures

If the aneurysm develops at a vital site such as the aorta, heroic surgical measures may be required to correct the problem. Before the important artery can be clamped off, the patient may have to be attached to a heartlung machine and the body temperature lowered so as to reduce normal body functions to a minimum. After the aneurysm is removed, that section of the aorta may have to be replaced with a piece of plastic artery. Not all aneurysms require such complicated methods of repair; if the ballooning section of artery develops as a saclike appendage, it frequently can be tied off and removed while the relatively small opening between the blood vessel and the sac is sewed closed.

Surgical removal of an aneurysm is the only available treatment for the disorder. The surgery is much less complicated if the abnormal section of the blood vessel is replaced before it ruptures than after. When the patient has recovered from correction of the aneurysm, he can resume a rather active, normal life style.

Varicose Veins

Varicose veins can develop in many parts of the body. But they are most obvious and commonly a problem when they appear in the legs, especially in the *saphenous veins,* large veins that lie close to the surface of the skin.

Causes

The cause of varicose veins is a failure of tiny valves in the blood vessels to function properly, so that venous blood destined for the heart flows backward and forms pools that can make the veins distended, tortuous, and painful. Varicose veins are related to the erect posture of humans; the heart pumps blood through arteries to the extremities, but the return flow must fight the pull of gravity. Ordinarily, venous blood gets a boost up the legs by a pumping action of leg-muscle contractions. Valves in the legs are designed to let the blood move upward but are supposed to block any backward flow. People whose jobs require them to stand all day are among those likely to suffer from a breakdown of the normal functioning of the valves. Women who have had multiple pregnancies and obese individuals are also apt to develop varicose veins.

Ulceration

Varicose veins can cause ulcers in the lower leg near the ankle that bleed through the skin after an injury to the area.

Treatment

One kind of surgical treatment of the varicosed vein is *ligation,* which means "tying" or "binding". An incision is made in the leg, usually in the area of the groin. The diseased sa-phenous vein is severed from its connection with the larger, femoral vein and is tied off. The function of a ligated vein is taken over by other veins in the leg. An alternate kind of surgery for varicose veins, sometimes called *stripping,* requires either a series of small incisions along the path of the vein, from the groin to the ankle, or an internal stripping by use of a special, long, threadlike instrument. The diseased vein is then removed and any connections with other veins ligated.

Varicose vein surgery is used for treatment of the *superficial* veins—those that are close to the skin. The operation is simple and can be performed under a local anesthetic in many cases. When multiple varicose veins are on both legs, all of the problem veins can be stripped and ligated at the same time. A hospital stay of several days may be required, and dressings are needed on the treated legs for two or three weeks after the operation.

Phlebitis

A problem related to varicose veins is *phlebitis,* a disease that usually involves the larger, deep veins of the legs with inflammation, pain, and swelling. Phlebitis is much more serious than varicose veins because a large vein is involved and a clot usually forms, obstructing return blood flow of the limb. The danger is that the clot will break loose—that is, become an *embolus*—and travel to the lungs, where it can obstruct a vital blood vessel, with serious or even fatal results. The obstructing clot is called an *embolism.*

Causes and Treatment

Causes of phlebitis can be injury, infection, poor circulation, or simply sitting for long periods of time. Medical therapy may include wet dressings and medications, especially anticoagulant drugs to thin the blood and reduce the chances of clot formations. Supportive bandages, leg exercises, and elevation of the legs may also be recommended.

Surgical Procedure

Surgery is reserved usually for cases in which medical therapy fails to control the risk of emboli forming. The surgical procedure is directed toward treatment of the deep vein that is the source of the phlebitis symptoms. The surgeon may open the vein to remove the clot, or a device can be inserted in the vein to strain out any clots that may form in the vein and travel toward the lungs. In some cases the surgeon may block the upward flow of blood from the affected vein, allowing other veins in the leg to assume that function. However, if other veins already have been stripped or ligated in the treatment of varicose veins, it is unlikely that a surgeon would occlude or block the flow of blood in a deep leg vein.

Intermittent Claudication

Intermittent claudication is a disorder of blood circulation of the legs involving the arteries. It is primarily a disease of aging, with gradual, progressive narrowing of the lumen (interior space) of the arteries by atherosclerosis. Atherosclerosis of the arteries occurs in other parts of the body, including the arms. Intermittent claudication is marked by muscle fatigue and pain when the leg muscles are used, as in walking. The symptoms are relieved by rest. The condition can be relieved by drugs, particularly medications that help dilate the arteries, but in severe cases surgery to reconstruct the leg arteries is the solution.

Surgical Procedure

The surgeon may build a bypass artery by grafting a length of plastic tubing into the affected blood vessel and around the area blocked by atherosclerotic narrowing. Sometimes surgeons will use a piece of a vein from the patient's body to make a bypass artery; for example, a vein from the arm may be transformed into an artery for the leg. Another procedure involves simply removing the portion of the artery blocking the normal flow of blood.

Orthopedic Surgery

Orthopedics originally was the name given the subject of treating deformities in children; the original Greek term could be translated as "normal child." But the medical world now uses the word to describe treatment of the bones, muscles, joints, and associated tissues of the body's locomotion apparatus. Orthopedic surgery, therefore, might involve repair of a broken big toe, as well as treatment of a whiplash injury to the neck.

This section discusses disorders of the spine, including herniated (or "slipped") disk, fractures, and torn ligaments.

Slipped Disk

The spinal column of 33 stacked vertebrae is a common source of painful problems that require orthopedic treatment. In addition to helping support the weight of the body above the hips, the vertebrae are subjected to a variety of twists, turns, and strains during a typical day. Much of the nearly continuous shock exerted on the spinal column is absorbed by the gel-like disks between the vertebrae.

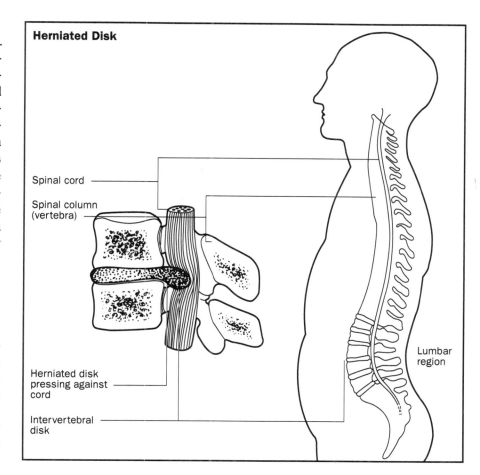

Herniated Disk

Spinal cord

Spinal column (vertebra)

Herniated disk pressing against cord

Intervertebral disk

Lumbar region

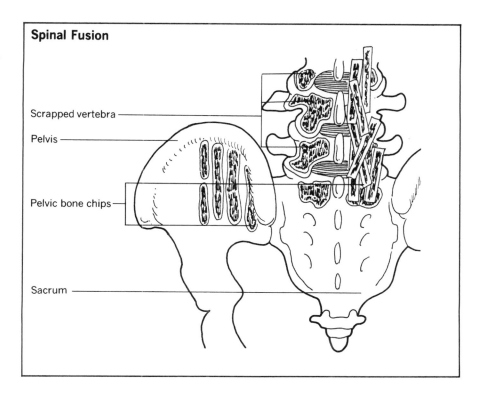

Spinal Fusion

Scrapped vertebra

Pelvis

Pelvic bone chips

Sacrum

Symptoms

Eventually, one of the disks may *herniate,* or slip out of place, causing pressure on a spinal nerve. The result can be severe pain that radiates along the pathway of the nerve as far as the lower leg. The pain may be accompanied by muscular weakness and loss of reflexes, even perhaps by a loss of feeling in part of the leg affected by a pinched or squeezed nerve. This condition, known popularly as a *slipped disk,* has symptoms of low back pain or leg pain that are similar to those of other disorders, such as intermittent claudication, arthritis, strained muscles, and prostatitis. Also, a herniated disk can occur near the top of the spinal column with symptoms of head and neck-area pains. But more than 90 percent of herniated disk cases involve the lumbar region of the spinal column, in the lower back.

Diagnosis

Physicians usually can confirm a herniated disk problem by a technique called *myelography,* in which a dye is injected into the spinal canal and X-ray pictures taken. Another procedure, called *electromyography,* can help determine which nerve root is involved.

Treatment

Conservative measures generally are used at first to reduce the pain and other symptoms. They include bed rest on a hard mattress, medications, and sometimes the use of traction and back braces. If conservative therapy fails to correct the problem and the diagnosis has been well established by a myelogram, surgery may be advised to remove the herniated disk.

Spinal Fusion

The surgeon may recommend a procedure called *spinal fusion,* in which the edges of several of the vertebrae are roughened and a piece of bone from the pelvis grafted onto the roughened edges. The bone graft will fuse with the vertebrae and in effect make the several vertebrae a single bone. However, the fused vertebrae will not interfere noticeably with body movements after the fusion is completed, which takes about six months. The operation requires a hospital stay of from one to two weeks and the patient must wear a body cast for the first few weeks and then use a back brace for a period of possibly several months. The patient usually can return to work and resume some normal activities within a couple of months after the operation. Strenuous activity, however, is usually restricted after an operation on the spinal column.

Other Spinal Disorders

Spondylolisthesis

Spinal fusion surgery also may be used to correct two other kinds of spinal disorders. One disorder is known as *spondylolisthesis,* a condition in which one of the vertebrae slips out of alignment. Spondylolisthesis usually occurs at the bottom of the group of lumbar vertebrae, where that section of the spinal column rests on the sacrum.

Scoliosis

The other disorder is *scoliosis,* or abnormal curvature of the spinal column. If the case of scoliosis is mild and causes no severe symptoms, it may be treated with conservative measures such as braces and special

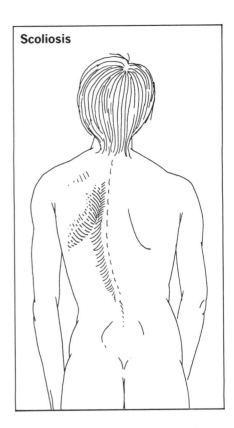

Scoliosis

exercises. Surgical treatment of scoliosis may involve not only spinal fusion but reinforcement of the spinal column with metal rods attached to the vertebrae to hold them in proper alignment.

Disorders of the cervical portion of the spinal column, in the area of the neck, may cause symptoms similar to those of a herniated disk in the lower back. But there is pain in the neck and shoulders and weakness in the arms. Surgical treatment also is similar, with removal of a herniated disk portion or fusion of cervical vertebrae when conservative therapy, with bed rest, neck braces, and medications, does not prove helpful.

Fractures

Many fractures of the spinal column also are treated by fusion operations, use of casts, braces, bed rest, or traction, in addition to therapy directed toward the specific problem. Spinal fractures frequently are compression fractures of vertebrae caused by falling in a sitting or standing position or mishaps in which a bony process of a vertebra is broken. Spinal fractures that result in permanent damage to the spinal cord, with resulting paralysis, are relatively uncommon.

Reduction of Fractures

Fractures of the long bones of the arms and legs are treated by a method called *reduction,* the technique of aligning the broken ends of the bones properly so the healing process will not result in a deformity. Reduction also requires that the muscles and surrounding tissues be aligned and held in place by immobilizing them as the break heals.

If the break is simple enough, the limb can be immobilized by putting a plaster cast around the part of the involved limb after the fractured ends of the bone and associated tissues have been realigned. In complicated cases with a number of bone fragments resulting from the fracture and surrounding tissues in some disarray, the patient usually is given a general anesthetic while the surgeon recognizes the shattered limb like a player assembling pieces of a jigsaw puzzle. If some of the needed pieces are missing, the surgeon may fill the gaps with bone from a bone bank, although bank materials usually are not as effective in the healing process as pieces of the patient's own bones.

Use of Internal Appliances

A common technique of modern fracture surgery is the application of wires, screws, pins, metal plates, and other devices to provide internal fixation of a broken long bone during the healing process. Nails and pins may be used to fasten the fractured neck of a femur, the long bone of the upper leg, to the shaft of that bone. A steel rod may be driven through the shaft of a long bone to align the broken sections. Screws may be used to hold together bone ends of a fracture in which the break runs diagonally across the shaft. Screws also may be employed to hold a metal plate or strip of bone from the patient's own body across the break. The screws, nails, and other devices generally are well tolerated by the body and may be left in the bones indefinitely if they do not cause adverse reactions after the healing process is completed.

Traction

Traction frequently is employed to hold a limb in alignment while a fracture is healing. A clamp sometimes is placed at one end of the fractured limb and a weight attached by wires over a pulley is connected to the clamp. Depending upon the kind of fracture and type of traction prescribed, a system of several weights and pulleys may be rigged around the bed of a patient to fix the bone and related tissues in correct positions.

Torn Cartilage

Joints of the body can be vulnerable to damage from sudden twisting and turning actions, particularly when the force of the individual's body weight is added to the pressure on the joint. The effect of such forces on the knee joint can result in tearing of the half-moon-shaped cartilages that cushion friction of the upper and lower leg bones where they are joined. Sports fans are particularly aware of the vulnerability of the knee joint because of the high incidence of knee injuries to athletes, especially in football and basketball. Obese individuals are also particularly liable to develop cartilage problems in the knee.

Symptoms

When a cartilage of the knee joint is torn, the patient may feel pain and weakness in the area of the injury. Swelling usually occurs, and in more than half the cases the knee cannot be straightened, because it has become "locked" by the cartilage. There may be a remission of symptoms, but surgery frequently is required sooner or later.

Surgical Procedure

The surgeon makes an incision in the area of the kneecap and cuts away the torn cartilage. Full recovery takes several weeks after the first few post-operative days, during which the patient remains in bed with the affected leg elevated. Special exercises are required to overcome muscle weakness in the leg and to help the patient learn to use the leg with part of the cartilage cushion missing.

Neurosurgery

Neurosurgery may be employed to treat a wide assortment of disorders involving the nervous system, from the brain to nerve endings in the fingers and toes. Neurosurgery may involve treatment of epilepsy, Parkinson's disease, and psychiatric disorders, as well as herniated disks of the spinal column and aneurysms that affect the nervous system. Causes of neurosurgical problems can be injury, tumors, infectious diseases, or congenital disorders.

This section includes discussions of trigeminal neuralgia, brain tumors, and head injuries.

Trigeminal Neuralgia

Trigeminal neuralgia is one of many types of pain that sometimes can be treated by surgery. The disorder, also known as *tic douloureux* or *facial neuralgia,* tends to develop in persons between 40 and 60 years of age, causing attacks of acute pain and muscular twitching in the area of the face containing branches of the trigeminal nerve. The painful attacks occur with no apparent reason but seem to be associated with certain stimuli, such as touch or temperature changes, at points around the face and mouth. During periods of attacks, the patient may avoid eating, shaving, or any other activity that might trigger a spasm of severe pain. But the pain attacks also may cease, with or without treatment, for three or four months, only to resume for weeks or months.

Treatment

Alcohol injections and medications may offer relief of symptoms, but when symptoms continue, surgery frequently is recommended. The operation consists of an incision to reach the root of the nerve and cut the divisions that appear to be involved with the painful symptoms. However, cutting the nerve can result in loss of feeling for the entire side of the face, including the cornea of the eye, so that the patient must wear special glasses to protect the cornea. An alternative procedure that is not always effective involves exposing the nerve root and rubbing it, a technique that seems to produce a temporary loss of sensation in the nerve fibers.

Brain Tumor

Brain tumors are popularly associated with neurosurgery skills. And while brain surgery requires great skill and knowledge of brain anatomy, which in itself is quite complicated, most brain tumor operations are conducted safely and successfully. Diagnosing,

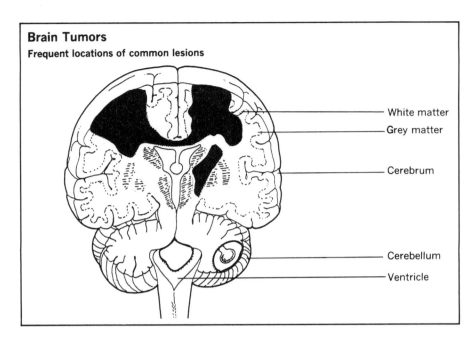

Brain Tumors
Frequent locations of common lesions

White matter
Grey matter
Cerebrum
Cerebellum
Ventricle

locating, and identifying a brain tumor are challenges faced by the physician before surgery begins. There are a dozen major types of brain tumors plus some minor types. The types of tumors tend to vary according to the age of the patient; the patient's age and the type of tumor may suggest where it develops.

Symptoms

Because brain tumors can cause organic mental changes in the patient, the symptoms of changed behavior can be mistaken for neurotic or psychotic disorders, with the result that a patient may spend valuable time receiving psychiatric treatment rather than surgical treatment; autopsies of a significant number of patients who die in mental hospitals reveal the presence of brain tumors. In addition to mental changes, the person suffering from a brain tumor may complain of headaches, experience convulsions, or display signs of neurological function loss, such as abnormal vision.

Diagnosis

The specific signs and symptoms,

along with X-ray studies, electroencephalograms, and other tests, help the physicians determine the site and extent of growth of a brain tumor. A recently developed technique called *CT scanning* (for *computed tomography*) aids the neurosurgeon by producing a series of X-ray pictures of the interior of the skull as if they were "slices" of the brain taken in thicknesses of about two-thirds of an inch. The detailed anatomical portrait of the patient's brain helps pinpoint the disorder and indicate whether it is a tumor or another kind of abnormality.

Surgical Procedure

The usual method of removing a brain tumor after it has been diagnosed and located is a procedure called a *craniotomy.* The entire head is shaved and cleaned to eliminate the possibility that a stray bit of hair might fall into the incision that is made in the scalp. After the scalp has been opened, a series of holes are drilled in a pattern outlining the working area for the surgeon; a wire saw is used to cut the skull between the drilled holes.

Removing the tumor is a delicate operation, not only because of the need to avoid damage to healthy brain tissue but because accidental severing of a blood vessel in the brain could produce a critical hemorrhage. The surgeon tries to remove the entire tumor, or as much of the tumor as appears possible without damaging vital brain tissues or blood vessels. All the various types of brain tumors are considered dangerous, whether malignant or benign, because within the rigid confines of the skull there is no opportunity for outward release of pressure. Therefore any growth may compress or destroy vital brain tissues if left untreated.

After the tumor is removed, the piece of skull removed at the start of the operation is replaced and the scalp flap is sewed in place. Radiation therapy may be administered for a month to six weeks after surgery to destroy any tumor tissue left behind or tumor cells that may have drifted into the spinal canal. Some tumors near the base of the brain may be treated effectively with radiation alone if the tumor cells are radiosensitive. Tumors of the pineal gland and the pituitary gland also may be treated with radiation.

Laser Surgery

In an alternative procedure, *laser neurosurgery,* a brain surgeon may use a laser beam to vaporize the tumor. The hair is removed from all or part of the skull; a section of the skull is removed with a power or hand saw after being marked out with tiny holes; and the surgeon then uses the laser to destroy the tumor. Typically, the surgeon may actually control two laser beams: a helium-neon type that guides the surgical work, and a carbon dioxide (CO_2) laser that does the vaporizing.

Because the "no-touch" CO_2 laser works slowly, an operation may require 10 or more hours. The laser beam can focus on and destroy one tumor cell at a time, targeting areas of tissue 1/50th the thickness of a human hair, or it can attack a number of cells in a group. The surgeon controls the electrical power that activates the beam with a foot pedal. In effect, the laser causes the tumor cells to heat up beyond the boiling point and then to explode into vapor. At the same time, the beam coagulates the tiny blood vessels that it passes through, preventing bleeding.

Head Injuries

Brain Hemorrhage

Head injuries, such as a blow to the head, can produce massive hemorrhages within the skull. As in the case of brain tumors, the expanding pool of blood within the skull gradually compresses the brain tissue and can result in death unless the problem is corrected. The damage of a brain hemorrhage can be insidious, with no immediate signs or symptoms of the problem until irreversible changes have occurred in the brain tissue. The patient may receive what may appear to be a minor head injury, for example, and not lose consciousness. Or he may be unconscious for a brief period, then recover and seem very alert. But gradually, over a period of hours or even days, neurological signs of disintegrating brain function appear.

Treatment

The treatment requires a procedure similar to that used for removing brain tumors. An opening is made in the skull to remove the blood or blood clot and relieve pressure upon the brain tissues. The chances for full recovery depend somewhat upon the

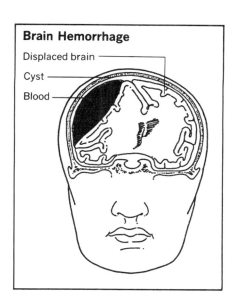

Brain Hemorrhage
Displaced brain
Cyst
Blood

extent of brain damage caused by the hemorrhage before treatment.

Skull Fracture

Surgical treatment for a skull fracture may combine techniques of various other methods for fractures and brain injuries. The scalp is shaved and cleaned carefully so the surgeon can determine the extent of the injury and its location with respect to vital tissues under the skull. With the help of X rays and signs of neurological damage, the surgeon frequently can tell how severe the fracture may be and whether there is bleeding beneath the skull.

Treatment

If the skull appears to be intact but there are signs of a brain hemorrhage, the skull is opened to remove the blood or blood clot and relieve pressure on the brain. If the skull fracture is compound and depressed, or with skull fragments in the brain tissue, efforts also must be made to elevate the depressed bone section so it does not press on vital brain areas and to remove bits of bone or

the ears. Those directly in front of the ears are visible only under very close scrutiny. Even after a face lift, however, the same wrinkles will eventually reappear, owing to the characteristic use of the individual's facial muscles.

Eyelids

The shape and size of the eyelids can be changed by an operation called a *blepharoplasty*. In this procedure, an incision is made in the fold of the upper eyelid, and excess skin and fat are removed. The technique can be used to correct congenital deformities, such as hanging upper eyelids that do not fully open. When a comparable incision is made below the lash line on the lower lid, the surgeon can remove the fat that causes bags under the eyes.

Ears

Surgery to correct protruding orover-large ears is called *otoplasty*. Though it can be performed on adults, it is usually performed on children before they enter school, to prevent the psychological problems that often result from teasing. In the procedure, an incision is made behind the ear, cartilage is cut, and the ear is repositioned closer to the skull. Otoplasty can also build up or replace an ear missing because of a birth defect or accident.

Scar Reduction

Unsightly scars that are the result of a birth defect or an injury can usually be reduced by plastic surgery to thin hairlines. The procedure is effective only if there has been no extensive damage to surrounding areas of underlying tissue, as sometimes occurs in severe burns. The operation in-

volves the removal of the old scar tissue, undermining the surrounding skin, and pulling it together with very fine stitches.

Uncommon Surgical Procedures

Organ Transplants

The notion of man's ability to rebuild human bodies from the parts of other humans or from artificial organs probably is as old as the dreams that men might someday fly like birds or travel to the moon. Some of the oldest documents, thousands of years old, tell of medical efforts to transplant organs, limbs, and other tissues to save lives or enable disabled persons to pursue normal activities. In recent decades, medical scientists have discovered how to overcome some of the obstacles to organ transplanting, just as other scientists have learned to fly higher and faster than birds and travel beyond the moon.

Tissue Compatibility

A major obstacle to organ transplants has been one of *histoincompatibility* (*histo* means "tissue"): the tissues of the person receiving the transplant tend to reject the tissues of the transplanted organs. The problem is quite similar to that of allergies or the body's reaction to foreign bodies, including infectious organisms. Each individual has a set of antigens that are peculiar to that person, because of genetic variations among different persons. The histoincompatible antigens are on the surfaces of the tissue cells. But in most cases the antigens on the cells of the transplanted organ

do not match those of the person receiving the transplant, so the recipient's body in effect refuses to accept the transplant.

The major exception to this rule is found in identical twins, who are born with the same sets of antigens. The organs of one twin can be transplanted to the body of the other twin with a minimum risk of rejection. Antigens on the tissue cells of brothers and sisters and of the parents will be similar, because of the biological relationship, but they will not be as compatible as those of identical twins. Even less compatible are antigens of people who are not related.

Types of Grafts

There is virtually no problem in transferring tissues from one area to another of the same patient. Skin grafts, bone grafts, and blood-vessel transplants are commonly made with a patient's own tissues, which have the same antigens, as in spinal fusions, repair of diseased leg arteries, and so on. Tissue transplants within an individual's body are called *autografts*. Transplants of tissues or organs from one human to another are called *homografts*. *Heterografts* are tissues from one species that are transplanted to another; they offer the greatest risk of histoincompatibility and are used mainly as a temporary measure, such as covering a severely burned area of a person with specially treated pieces of pigskin. The heterograft will be rejected, but it will provide some protection during the recovery period.

Much of the experience of surgeons in handling tissue transplants between humans came from early experiments in skin grafting. It was found that histoincompatibility in transplants of skin appeared to sensitize the recipient tissues in the same way that allergy sensitivity rises.

Thus, when a second skin graft from the same donor is attempted, the graft is rejected more rapidly than the first graft because of the buildup of antibodies from the first rejection. The same sort of rejection reaction can occur in transplants of kidneys, hearts, and other organs unless the problem of histoincompatibility is overcome.

Immunosuppressive Chemicals

In order to make the host body more receptive to an organ transplant, *immunosuppressive* chemicals are injected into the recipient's tissues to suppress their natural tendency to reject the foreign tissue. However, the technique of suppressing the immune response of the host tissues is not without hazards. By suppressing the natural rejection phenomenon, the transplant recipient is made vulnerable to other diseases. It has been found, for example, that persons who receive the immune response suppression chemicals as part of transplant surgery develop cancers at a rate that is 15 times that of the general population. Transplant patients also can become extremely vulnerable to infections, such as pneumonia.

Antigen Matching

The breakthrough in human organ transplantation was helped by the development of a system of matching antigens related to lymphocytes—a type of white blood cell—of the donor and recipient. At least a dozen lymphocyte antigens have been identified, and it is possible to match them by a process similar to matching blood factors of patients before making a blood transfusion. If all or most of the antigens of the donor tissue and the recipient match, the chances for a successful transplanting procedure are greatly enhanced.

Antigen matching is less important in some kinds of homografts, such as replacing the cornea of the eye. The cornea is a unique kind of tissue with no blood vessels, and therefore is unlikely to be invaded by antibodies of the recipient. Pieces of human bone also may be used in homografts with a minimum risk of rejection, although surgeons usually prefer to use bone from the patient's own body in repairing fractures and in other orthopedic procedures.

Types of Transplants

Cornea Transplant

Cornea transplants helped to pioneer the art of homografts. The first successful cornea transplants were made during the 1930s. In addition to the absence of rejection problems because of incompatible antigens, cornea transplants probably succeeded in the early days of homografts because only small pieces of the tissue were used.

Kidney Transplant

Kidney transplants began in the 1950s. Antigen typing was unknown at that time, but physicians had learned of the genetic factors of blood groups and found from experience that although kidney transplants from siblings and parents could eventually be rejected, the rejection phenomenon was delayed. The first truly successful kidney transplant operation was performed in Boston in 1954 between twin brothers; doctors had tested the tissue compatibility of the twins first by making a small skin transplant to see if it would be rejected. Knowledge acquired later of immunosuppressive drugs enabled surgeons to make kidney transplants between persons who were not twins.

More than 5,000 kidney transplant operations have been performed with an 82 percent survival rate of two years or more when the donor was related to the recipient. When a cadaver kidney was transplanted, the two-year survival rate was 65 percent. It has been estimated that as many as 10,000 kidney disease patients each year could benefit from a transplanted organ, but a lack of available kidneys in satisfactory condition restricts the number of transplants. An alternative for some kidney patients awaiting an organ transplant is hemodialysis, a process that performs as an artificial kidney.

Heart Transplant

The first successful human heart transplant was performed by Dr. Christiaan Barnard in Cape Town, South Africa, in 1968. The patient survived more than 18 months and led a relatively active life until the second heart failed because of a rejection reaction. Many heart transplant operations have been performed since 1968, with varying success, sometimes leading to complete recovery and sometimes to recovery for long periods of time. Heart transplants were found to be more difficult than some other organ transplants, such as of the kidney, because the heart must be taken from the donor at virtually the moment of death and immediately placed in the body of the recipient. Because of concern about determining the moment of death, the medical profession has offered guidelines for answering this complex ethical and legal question.

Success of a heart transplant operation may depend on the health of other organ systems in the patient's body; persons in need of heart transplants usually have medical problems involving the lungs and kidneys as a result of the diseased heart. And heart transplant patients frequently seem less able to tolerate the use of immunosuppressive drugs that must be administered after surgery. The introduction of cyclosporine as an immunosuppressant changed the picture substantially, however. Medical evidence indicated that cyclosporine would lead to a five-year survival rate among heart transplant patients of 50 percent or more. Because cyclosporine speeds rehabilitation after an operation, average hospital stays for patients receiving the immunosuppressant have been reduced from 72 to 42 days.

Conducted before cyclosporine came into common use, one study of a group of transplant patients showed that fewer than 40 percent survived beyond the first year. Several lived more than two years after the operation.

Bone-Marrow Transplant

Limited success has been reported in efforts to perform bone-marrow transplants. Bone-marrow transplants are performed to supply patients with active leukocytes to fight cancer and other diseases. The successful early cases have involved transplants between sisters and brothers who had been typed for tissue compatibility.

Other Kinds of Transplants

Surgeons also have experimented with varying success with human transplants of livers, lungs, and pancreas tissue. Lung transplant efforts have been hampered by infection, rejection, and hemorrhage. Because the lungs are exposed to pathogenic organisms in the environment they are especially vulnerable to infections when the host tissues have been treated with immunosuppressive chemicals. Liver transplants are diffi-

cult to perform because of a lack of satisfactory donor organs and the complex circuitry of arteries, veins, and bile duct that must be connected to the recipient before the liver can begin to function.

Most major organ transplants are considered only in terms of a "last ditch" effort to prolong the life of a patient who is critically ill. While homografts are not always a perfect success and may lengthen a patient's life by only a few years, remarkable strides in these surgical techniques have been made over a relatively short period of time. Surgeons who specialize in organ transplants state that even greater progress could be made if a greater supply of donor organs were available.

Reattachment of Severed Members

Because an individual's tissues present no histocompatibility problem with other parts of his own body, severed fingers and other members can be rejoined to the rest of the body if vital parts are not damaged beyond repair. Children sometimes suffer amputation of a part of a finger during play or in accidents at home. For example, a finger tip can be severed when caught in a closed door of an automobile. If the severed part of the finger is saved and the patient is given immediate medical care, the finger usually can be rejoined and sutured in place with a very good chance of survival of the graft.

Rejoining a Severed Limb

One of the most dramatic cases of a rejoined limb in American medical annals involved a 12-year-old whose right arm was severed at the shoulder when he was crushed between a train and a tunnel wall in 1962. Railroad

workers called an ambulance, and the boy, his severed arm still encased in his sleeve, was rushed to a hospital. The boy was given plasma by physicians who packed the severed arm in ice and flushed out the blood vessels of the arm with anticoagulant drugs and antibiotics. During three hours of surgery, the major veins and artery of the arm were carefully stitched to the vessels at the shoulder. For the next five hours, surgeons joined the bones, located the main nerve trunks and connected them to the nerve ends in the shoulder, and repaired the muscles. The boy was released from the hospital three weeks after the accident but returned for additional operations to connect various nerve fibers. That operation was a success, but similar attempts to rejoin severed arms of middle-aged men have failed despite heroic attempts by surgeons to restore the limbs as functioning parts of the body.

A Chinese factory worker suffered accidental amputation of his right hand when it was caught in a metal-punching machine, and was rushed to a hospital in Shanghai. Chinese medical reports of the case indicate that a procedure similar to the one used on the American boy was followed. Blood vessels were rejoined first to permit the flow of blood to tissues. This was followed by surgery to connect the tendons and main nerve trunks. The bones of the forearm, where the amputation occurred, were joined and held in place with metal plates and screws. Physicians reported that the graft was successful, and the patient, a 27-year-old man, was able to move his fingers again within three weeks after the accident.

Medical records indicate that major reattachments of severed limbs are still rare, although rejoined finger tips, ears, and other parts not involving main arteries, veins, or nerve trunks are not as uncommon.

21

Skin and Hair

Not many people have perfectly proportioned faces and bodies, but practically anyone, at any age, can present an attractive appearance if skin is healthy-looking and glowing and hair is clean and shining. Healthy skin and hair can be achieved through good health habits, cleanliness, and personal grooming. Expensive skin-and-hair products may boost self-confidence, but they are a poor substitute for proper diet, exercise, enough sleep, and soap and water or cleansing creams.

The condition of skin and hair reflects a person's physical and emotional health. Of course, general appearance is determined not only by what is going on inside the body but also by outward circumstances, such as extremes of temperature or the use of harsh soaps. Appearance can also be altered temporarily by cosmetics and permanently by surgery.

The Skin

The skin is one of the most important organs of the body. It serves as protection against infection by germs and shields delicate underlying tissue against injury. Approximately one-third of the bloodstream flows through the skin, and as the blood vessels contract or relax in response to heat and cold, the skin acts as a thermostat that helps control body temperature. The two million sweat glands in the skin also regulate body temperature through the evaporation of perspiration. The many delicate nerve endings in the skin make it a sense organ responsive not only to heat and cold but also to pleasure, pain, and pressure.

Certain cells in the skin produce a protective pigmentation that determines its color and guards against overexposure to the ultraviolet rays of the sun. By absorption and elimination, the skin helps regulate the body's chemical and fluid balance. One of the miracles of the skin is that it constantly renews itself.

Structure of the Skin

The skin is made up of two layers. The outer later, or *epidermis,* has a surface of horny, nonliving cells that form the body's protective envelope. These cells are constantly being shed and replaced by new ones, which are made in the lower or inner layer of the epidermis.

Underneath the epidermis is the *dermis,* the thicker part of the skin. It contains blood vessels, nerves, and connective tissue. The sweat glands are located in the dermis, and they collect fluid containing water, salt, and waste products from the blood. This fluid is sent through tiny canals that end in pores on the skin's surface.

The oil, or *sebaceous,* glands that secrete the oil that lubricates the surface of the skin and hair are also located in the dermis. They are most often associated with hair *follicles.* Hair follicles and oil glands are found over most of the body, with the exception of the palms of the hands and the soles of the feet.

The layer of fatty tissue below the dermis, called *subcutaneous* tissue, acts as an insulator against heat and cold and as a shock absorber against injury.

Skin Color

The basic skin color of each person is determined at birth, and is a part of his heritage that cannot be changed.

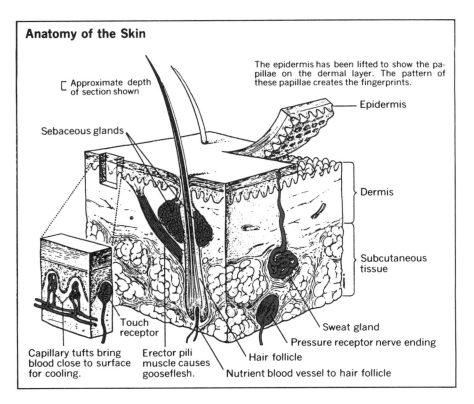

Anatomy of the Skin

Approximate depth of section shown

The epidermis has been lifted to show the papillae on the dermal layer. The pattern of these papillae creates the fingerprints.

Sebaceous glands

Epidermis

Dermis

Subcutaneous tissue

Touch receptor

Sweat gland

Pressure receptor nerve ending

Capillary tufts bring blood close to surface for cooling.

Erector pili muscle causes gooseflesh.

Hair follicle

Nutrient blood vessel to hair follicle

Melanin

There are four pigments in the normal skin that affect its color: melanin, oxygenated hemoglobin, reduced hemoglobin, and various carotenes. Of these, *melanin* is the most powerful. The cells that produce it are the same in all races, but there is wide variation in the amount produced, and wide variation in its color, which ranges from black to light tan. Every adult has about 60,000 melanin-producing cells in each square inch of skin.

Melanin cells also affect eye color. When the cells are deep in the eye, the color produced is blue or green. When they are close to the surface, the eye is brown. An *albino*, a person with no melanin, has eyes that appear pink, because the stronger pigment that ordinarily masks the blood vessels is lacking.

Hemoglobin

The pigment that gives blood its color, called *hemoglobin*, has the next greatest effect on skin color. When it is combined with oxygen, a bright red is the result, and this in turn produces the rosy complexion associated with good health in light-skinned people. When such people suffer from reduced hemoglobin because of anemia, they appear to be excessively pale. A concentration of reduced hemoglobin gives the skin a bluish appearance. Because hemoglobin has a weaker coloring effect than the melanin that determines basic skin color, these variations are more visible in lighter-skinned individuals.

Carotenes

The weakest pigments in the skin are the *carotenes*. These produce a yellowish tone that is increased by eating excessive amounts of carrots and oranges. In people with black or brown skin, excess carotene is usually masked by the melanin pigment.

Aging Skin

Skin appearance is affected by both internal and external factors. A baby's skin has a silken quality because it has not yet begun to show the effects of continued exposure to sun and wind. The skin problems associated with adolescence reflect the many glandular changes that occur during the transition to adulthood. As the years pass, the skin becomes the most obvious indicator of aging.

Heredity, general health, and exposure to the elements are some of the factors that contribute to aging skin. Because people with darker skin have built-in protection against the ravages of the sun, their skin usually has a younger appearance than that of lighter-skinned people of comparable age.

In general, the skin of an older person is characterized by wrinkles and shininess. It feels thinner when pinched because it has lost its elasticity and part of the underlying fat that gives firmness to a younger skin.

Constant exposure to sunlight is now thought to play a more important role in the visible aging of skin than the aging process itself. Such exposure also appears to be directly related to the greater frequency of skin cancer among farmers, sailors, and others who spend most of their working hours out of doors.

Care of the Skin

Healthy, normal skin should be washed regularly with mild soap and warm water to remove grease, perspiration, and accumulated dirt. For those with a limited water supply or inadequate bath and shower facilities, sponge baths are a good substitute if the sponge or washcloth is thoroughly rinsed as various parts of the body are washed. Many people feel that a shower is a much more efficient way of getting clean than a bath, since the bath water becomes the receptacle for the dirt washed from the body, instead of its being rinsed away.

No matter what method is used, all soap should be thoroughly rinsed off the skin after washing. Unless specifically prescribed by a physician, medicated or germicidal soaps should not be used, since they may be an irritant. Skin should be dried with a fluffy towel, and bath towels should never be shared. Hands should be washed several times a day, and fingernails kept clean.

Facial skin requires special care because of its constant exposure. The face should be cleaned in the morning and before bedtime. Some women may prefer to use a cleansing cream rather than soap and water. Everyone should avoid massaging soap into the skin, because this may cause drying.

Dry and Oily Skin

Both heredity and environment account for the wide variation in the amount of oil and perspiration secreted by the glands of different people. Also, the same person's skin may be oily in one part of the body and dry in another.

Dry Skin

This condition is the result of loss of water from the outer surface of the epidermis and its insufficient replacement from the tissues below. Some causes of the moisture loss are too frequent use of soap and detergents, and constant exposure to dry air. Anyone spending a great deal of time in air-conditioned surroundings in which the humidity has been greatly lowered is likely to suffer from dry skin.

To correct the condition, the use of soap and water should be kept to a minimum for those parts of the body where the skin is dry. Cleansing creams or lotions containing lanolin should be used on the face, hands, elbows, and wherever else necessary. If tub baths are taken, a bath oil can be used in the water or applied to the skin after drying. Baby oil is just as effective and much cheaper than glamorously packaged and overadvertised products. Baby oil or a protective lotion should also be used on any parts of the body exposed to direct sunlight for any extended length of time. Applying oil to the skin will not, however, prevent wrinkles.

Oily Skin

The amount of oil that comes to the surface of the skin through the sebaceous glands is the result not only of heredity but also of temperature and emotional state. In warm weather, when the skin perspires more freely, the oil spreads like a film on the surface moisture. Nonoily foundation lotions can be helpful in keeping the oil spread to a minimum, and so can frequent washing with soap and water. When washing is inconvenient during the day, cleansing pads packaged to fit in pocket or purse are a quick and efficient solution for both men and women.

Too much friction from complexion brushes, rough washcloths, or harsh soaps may irritate rather than improve an oily skin condition.

Deodorants and Antiperspirants

Sweat glands are present almost everywhere in the skin except for the lips and a few other areas. Most of them give off the extremely dilute salt water known as sweat, or perspiration. Their purpose is to cool the body by evaporation of water. Body odors are not produced by perspiration itself but by the bacterial activity that takes place in the perspiration. The activity is most intense in warm, moist parts of the body from which perspiration cannot evaporate quickly, such as the underarm area.

Deodorants

The basic means of keeping this type of bacterial growth under control is through personal cleanliness of both skin and clothing. Deodorant soaps containing antiseptic chemicals are now available. Though they do not kill bacteria, they do reduce the speed with which they multiply.

Underarm deodorants also help to eliminate the odor. They are not meant to stop the flow of perspiration but rather to slow down bacterial growth and mask body odors with their own scent. Such deodorants should be applied immediately after bathing. They are usually more effective if the underarm area is shaved, since the hair in this unexposed area collects perspiration and encourages bacterial growth.

Antiperspirants

Antiperspirants differ from deodorants in that they not only affect the rate of bacterial growth but also reduce the amount of perspiration that reaches the skin surface. Because the action of the chemical salts they contain is cumulative, they seem to be more effective with repeated use. Antiperspirants come under the category of drugs, and their contents must be printed on the container. Deodorants are considered cosmetics, and may or may not name their contents on the package.

No matter what the nature of the advertising claim, neither type of product completely stops the flow of perspiration, nor would it be desirable to do so. Effectiveness of the various brands differs from one person to another. Some may produce a mild allergic reaction; others might be too weak to do a good job. It is practical to experiment with a few different brands, using them under similar conditions, to find the type that works best for you.

Creams and Cosmetics

The bewildering number of creams and cosmetics on the market and the exaggerated claims of some of their advertising can be reduced to a few simple facts. Beauty preparations should be judged by the user on their merits rather than on their claims.

Cold Creams and Cleansing Creams

These two products are essentially the same. They are designed to remove accumulated skin secretions, dirt, and grime, and should be promptly removed from the skin with a soft towel or tissue.

Lubricating Creams and Lotions

Also called night creams, moisturizing creams, and conditioning creams, these products are supposed to prevent the loss of moisture from the skin and promote its smoothness. They are usually left on overnight or for an extended length of time. Anyone with dry skin will find it helpful to apply a moisturizer under foundation cream. This will help keep the skin from drying out even further, and protect it against the effects of air-conditioning.

Vanishing Creams and Foundation Creams

These products also serve the purpose of providing the skin with moisture, but are meant to be applied immediately before putting on makeup.

Rejuvenating Creams

There is no scientific proof that any of the "royal jelly," "secret formula," or "hormone" creams produce a marked improvement on aging skin. They cannot eliminate wrinkles, nor can they regenerate skin tissue.

Medicated Creams and Lotions

These products should not be used except on the advice of a physician, since they may cause or aggravate skin disorders of various kinds.

Lipsticks

Lipsticks contain lanolin, a mixture of oil and wax, a coloring dye, and pigment, as well as perfume. Any of these substances can cause an allergic reaction in individual cases, but such reactions are uncommon. Sometimes the reaction is caused by the staining dye, in which case a "nonpermanent" lipstick should be used.

Cosmetics and the Sensitive Skin

Anyone with a cosmetic problem resulting from sensitive skin should consult a *dermatologist,* a physician specializing in the skin and its diseases. Cosmetic companies will inform a physician of the ingredients in their products, and he or she can then recommend a brand that will agree with the patient's specific skin problems. The physician may also recommend a special nonallergenic preparation.

Eye Makeup

Eye-liner and mascara brushes and pencils—and lipsticks, for that matter—can carry infection and should never be borrowed or lent.

Hypoallergenic makeup, which is specially made for those who get allergic reactions to regular eye makeup, is available and should be used by anyone so affected.

Suntanning Creams and Lotions

Growing awareness that exposure to the sun may cause skin cancer (see "Skin Cancer" in Ch. 18, *Cancer*) has led to a demand for a variety of skin creams and lotions. The preparations protect the skin or speed the tanning process. Many of the "sunblocks" and "sunscreens" keep the ultraviolet radiation in sunlight from reaching the skin. They are adapted to six basic skin types, ranging from type 1, which burns easily and never tans, to types 5 and 6, which never burn and usually tan well.

Skin lotions and creams are rated according to a "sun protection factor" (SPF). Among the basic ratings are SPF 4, providing "moderate protection;" SPF 8, a "maximal" sunscreen; and SPF 15, with "ultra" protection. Other ratings range up to SPF 50. Some medical authorities question the need for sunscreens rated higher than 15 or 20. Food and Drug Administration ratings go only to SPF 15. Many newer sunscreens are greaseless, hypoallergenic, waterproof, or PABA-free. PABA, or para-aminobenzoic acid, is a sunscreen chemical that can irritate skin and stain clothing.

Sunscreen ratings indicate, in theory, how long the user can stay in the sun without burning. A lotion or cream with a rating of SPF 2 should allow users to remain exposed twice as long as they could with no protection at all. The Skin Cancer Foundation believes that persons who burn in the sun should uniformly wear an SPF 15 protective preparation.

Persons who want suntans have many products from which to choose. "Tanning accelerators" in lotion form speed up the tanning process. A pocket-sized "sun exposure meter" operated electronically alerts the user when overexposure may be taking place. The meter is programmed with the individual's skin type and SPF.

Tanning Pills

Case-studies have proven that tanning pills can cause serious medical problems, possibly resulting in death. Ailments include aplastic anemia (a decrease in the production of red blood cells), orange skin, headaches, weight loss, easy bruising, and increased fatigue. Treatment involves blood transfusion therapy. Physicians believe that the ingredient canthaxanthin is responsible for the disorders.

This drug is not approved as a prescription or an over-the-counter preparation by the Federal Drug Administration. Ultimately, this product serves no purpose, and it is best to avoid using it.

Hair

Hair originates in tiny sacs or follicles deep in the dermis layer of skin tissue. The part of the hair below the skin surface is the root; the part above is the shaft. Hair follicles are closely connected to the sebaceous glands, which secrete oil to the scalp and give hair its natural sheen. Hair grows from the root outward, pushing the shaft farther from the scalp.

Texture

Each individual hair is made up of non-living cells that contain a tough protein called *keratin*. Hair texture differs from one part of the body to

another. In some areas, it may be soft and downy; in others, tough and bristly. Hair texture also differs between the sexes, among individuals, and among the different races.

If an individual hair is oval in cross-section, it is curly along its length. If the cross-section is round, the hair is straight. Thick, wiry hair is usually triangular or kidney-shaped. The fineness or coarseness of hair texture is related to its natural color.

Curling

Anyone using a home permanent preparation should read and follow instructions with great care. If a new brand is tried, the instructions should be read all over again, since they may be quite different from the accustomed ones.

Electric curling irons are not safe, because they may cause pinpoint burns in the scalp that are hardly noticeable at the time but may lead to permanent small areas of baldness. The danger can be minimized, however, if instructions for use are followed exactly. It is especially important that the iron not be hot enough to singe the hair. Setting lotions used with rollers or clips have a tendency to dull the hair unless they are completely brushed out.

Straightening

The least harmful as well as the least effective way of straightening the hair temporarily is the use of pomades. They are usually considered unsatisfactory by women because they are too greasy, but are often used by men with short, unruly hair. Heat-pressing the hair with a metal comb is longer-lasting but can cause substantial damage by burning the scalp. The practice of ironing the hair should be discouraged, since it causes dryness and brittleness, with resultant breakage.

Chemical straighteners should be used with great care, since they may cause serious burns. Special efforts must be made to protect the eyes from contact with these products.

Hair Color

In the same way that melanin colors the skin, it also determines hair color. The less melanin, the lighter the hair. As each hair loses its melanin pigment, it gradually turns gray, then white. It is assumed that the age at which hair begins to gray is an inherited characteristic and therefore can't be postponed or prevented by eating special foods, by taking vitamins, or by the external application of creams. The only way to recolor gray hair is by the use of a chemical dye.

Dyes and Tints

Anyone wishing to make a radical change in hair color should consult a trained and reliable hairdresser. Trying to turn black hair bright red or dark red hair to blond with a home preparation can sometimes end up with unwanted purplish or greenish results. When tints or dyes are used at home to lighten or darken the hair color by one or two shades, instructions accompanying the product must be followed carefully. Anyone with a tendency to contract contact dermatitis should make a patch test on the skin to check on possible allergic reactions. Hair should be tinted or dyed no more often than once a month.

Dye Stripping

The only safe way to get rid of an unwanted dye color that has been used on the hair is to let it grow out. The technique known as stripping takes all color from the hair and reduces it to a dangerously weak mass. It is then redyed its natural color. Such a procedure should never be undertaken by anyone except a trained beautician, if at all.

Bleaching

Hydrogen peroxide is mixed with a hair lightener to prebleach hair before applying blond tints. Bleaching with peroxide alone can cause more damage to the hair than dyeing or tinting it with a reliable commercial preparation, because it causes dryness, brittleness, and breakage.

General Hair Care

Properly cared for hair usually looks clean, shiny, and alive. Unfortunately, too many people mask the natural good looks of their hair with unnecessary sprays and "beauty" preparations.

Washing the Hair

Hair should be washed about once a week—more often if it tends to be oily. The claims made by shampoo manufacturers need not always be taken too seriously, since most shampoos contain nothing more than soap or detergent and a perfuming agent. No shampoo can restore the natural oils to the hair at the same time that it washes it. A castile shampoo is good for dry hair, and one containing tincture of green soap is good for oily hair.

Thorough rinsing is essential to eliminate any soap deposit. If the local water is hard, a detergent shampoo can be rinsed off more easily than one containing soap.

Drying the Hair

Drying the hair in sunlight or under a heat-controlled dryer is more satisfactory than trying to rub it dry with a towel. Gentle brushing during drying reactivates the natural oils that give hair its shine. Brushing in general is excellent for the appearance of the hair. Be sure to wash both brush and comb as often as the hair is washed.

Hair pomades should be avoided or used sparingly, since they are sometimes so heavy that they clog the pores of the scalp. A little bit of olive oil or baby oil can be rubbed into dry hair after shampooing. This is also good for babies' hair.

There is no scientific evidence that creme rinses, protein rinses, or beer rinses accomplish anything for the hair other than making it somewhat more manageable if it is naturally fine and flyaway.

Dandruff

Simple dandruff is a condition in which the scalp begins to itch and flake a few days after the hair has been washed. There is no evidence that the problem is related to germ infection.

Oiliness and persistent dandruff may appear not only on the scalp but also on the sides of the nose or the chest. In such cases, a dermatologist should be consulted. Both light and serious cases often respond well to prescription medicines containing tars. These preparations control the dandruff, but there is no known cure for it.

Nits

Head lice sometimes infect adults as well as children. These tiny parasites usually live on the part of the scalp near the nape of the neck, and when they bite, they cause itching. They attach their eggs, which are called *nits,* to the shaft of the hair, and when they are plentiful, they can be seen by a trained eye as tiny, silvery-white ovals. This condition is highly contagious and can be passed from one head to another by way of combs, brushes, hats, head scarfs, and towels. A physician can be consulted for information on effective ways of eliminating nits—usually by the application of chemicals and the use of a fine-tooth comb.

Baldness

Under the normal circumstances of combing, brushing, and shampooing, a person loses anywhere from 25 to 100 hairs a day. Because new hairs start growing each day, the loss and replacement usually balance each other. When the loss rate is greater than the replacement rate, thinning and baldness are the result.

Alopecia

The medical name for baldness is *alopecia,* the most common form of which is *male pattern baldness.* Dr. Eugene Van Scott, Professor of Dermatology of Temple University's Health Sciences Center, sums up the opinion of medical authorities on the three factors responsible for this type of baldness: sex, age, and heredity. Unfortunately, these are three factors over which medical science has no control.

Other Causes of Baldness

Other forms of baldness may be the result of bacterial or fungal infections, allergic reactions to particular medicines, radiation, or continual friction. It has also been suggested that constant stress from hair curlers or tightly pulled ponytails can cause loss

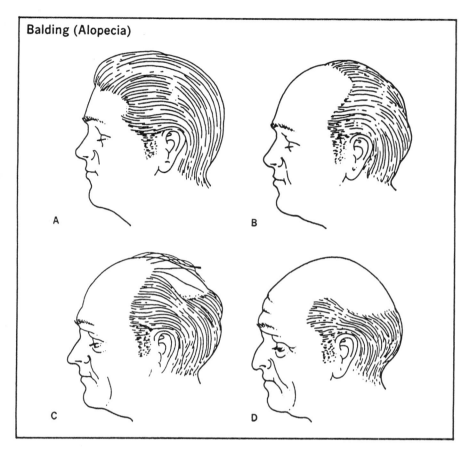

Balding (Alopecia)

A

B

C

D

of hair. These forms of baldness usually disappear when the cause is eliminated.

Although diet has very little to do with baldness, poor nutrition can result in hair that is dry, dull, and brittle enough to break easily. Any serious illness can lead to hair loss as well. It is thought that vitamin A taken in grossly excessive amounts can contribute to hair loss.

Women ordinarily lose some of their hair at the end of pregnancy, after delivery, and during the menopause, but regrowth can be expected in a few months.

It is now possible for anyone suffering from temporary baldness or from male pattern baldness to choose from a wide variety of attractively styled wigs and hairpieces.

A surgical procedure for treating male pattern baldness and baldness in women is called hair transplantation; it is discussed in Ch. 20, *Surgery.*

Hair Removal

Over the centuries and around the world, fashions in whiskers and beards come and go, but the average American male still subjects at least part of his face to daily shaving. Although feminine shaving practices are a more recent phenomenon, most American women now consider it part of good grooming to remove underarm and leg hair with a razor as often as twice a week. Shaving removes not only the dead skin cells that make up the protective layer of the body's surface but also some of the living skin underneath. Instead of being harmful, this appears to stimulate rather than damage new skin growth.

Male Shaving

The average beard grows about two-tenths of an inch a day. However, the density of male face hair varies a great deal depending on skin and hair color. In all races, the concentration is usually greatest on the chin and in the area between the nose and upper lip.

There is no proof that an electric razor is safer or better for all types of skin than a safety razor. Both types result in nicks and cuts of the living skin tissue, depending on the closeness of the shave.

Twice as many men prefer wet shaving to dry because the use of soap and hot water softens the hair stubble and makes it easier to remove. Shaving authorities point out that thorough soaking is one of the essentials of easy and safe shaving. Leaving the shaving lather on the face for at least two minutes will also soften whiskers a good deal.

The razor should be moistened with hot water throughout the process, and the chin and upper lip left for last so that the heavier hair concentration in these areas has the longest contact with moisture and lather.

Oily Skin

Men with oily skin should use an aerosol shaving preparation or a lather type applied with a brush. These are really soaps and are more effective in eliminating the oils that coat the face hair, thus making it easier to shave.

Dry Skin

A brushless cream is advisable for dry skin, since it lubricates the skin rather than further deprives it of oil.

Ingrown Hairs

One of the chief problems connected with shaving is that it often causes ingrown hairs, which can lead to pore-clogging and infection. Hair is more likely to turn back into the skin if it is shaved against the grain, or if the cutting edge of the blade is dull and rough rather than smooth. Men with coarse, wiry, curly, rather than fine, hair may find that whisker ends are more likely to become ingrown than men with fine hair. The problem is best handled by shaving with the grain, using a sharp blade, and avoiding too close a shave, particularly in the area around the neck.

Shaving and Skin Problems

For men with acne or a tendency to skin problems, the following advice is offered by Dr. Howard T. Behrman, Director of Dermatological Research, New York Medical College:

- Shave as seldom as possible, perhaps only once or twice a week, and always with the grain.

- If wet shaving is preferred, use a new blade each time, and shave as lightly as possible to avoid nicking pimples.

- Wash face carefully with plenty of hot water to make the beard easy to manage, and after shaving, rinse with hot water followed by cold.

- Use an antiseptic astringent face lotion.

- Instead of plucking out ingrown hairs, loosen them gently so that the ends do not grow back into the skin.

- Although some people with skin problems find an electric shaver less irritating, in most cases, a wet shave seems best.

Female Shaving

Millions of American women regularly shave underarm and leg hair, and most of them do so with a blade razor.

In recent years, various types of shavers have been designed with blade exposure more suited to women's needs than the standard type used by men. To make shaving easier and safer, the following procedures are recommended.

- Since wet hair is much easier to cut, the most effective time to shave is during or immediately following a bath or shower.

- Shaving cream or soap lather keeps the water from evaporating, and is preferred to dry shaving.

- Underarm shaving is easier with a contoured razor designed for this purpose. If a deodorant or antiperspirant causes stinging or irritation after shaving, allow a short time to elapse before applying it.

- Light bleeding from nicks or scrapes can be stopped by applying pressure to a sterile pad placed on the injured area.

Unwanted Hair

The technical word for excess or unwanted hair on the face, chest, arms, and legs is *hirsutism*. The condition varies greatly among different ethnic strains, and so does the attitude toward it. Women of southern European ancestry are generally hairier than those with Nordic or Anglo-Saxon ancestors. Caucasoid peoples are hairier than Negroid peoples. The sparsest amount of body hair is found among the Mongolian races and American Indians. Although heredity is the chief factor of hirsutism, hormones also influence hair growth. If there is a sudden appearance of coarse hair on the body of a young boy or girl or a woman with no such former tendency, a glandular disturbance should be suspected and investigated by a physician.

A normal amount of unwanted hair on the legs and under the arms is usually removed by shaving. When the problem involves the arms, face, chest, and abdomen, other methods of removal are available.

Temporary Methods of Hair Removal

Bleaching

Unwanted dark fuzz on the upper lip and arms can be lightened almost to invisibility with a commercially prepared bleach or with a homemade paste consisting of baking soda, hydrogen peroxide (bleaching strength), and a few drops of ammonia. Soap chips can be used instead of baking soda. The paste should be left on the skin for a few minutes and then washed off. It is harmless to the skin, and if applied repeatedly, the hair will tend to break off as a result of constant bleaching.

Chemical Depilatories

These products contain alkaline agents that cause the hair to detach easily at the skin surface. They can be used on and under the arms, and on the legs and chest. However, they should not be used on the face unless the label says it is safe to do so. Timing instructions should be followed carefully. If skin irritation results, this type of depilatory should be discontinued in favor of some other method.

Abrasives

Devices that remove hair from the skin surface by rubbing are cheap but time-consuming. However, if an abrasive such as pumice is used regularly, the offending hairs will be shorter with each application. A cream or lotion should be applied to the skin after using an abrasive.

Waxing

The technique of applying melted wax to the skin for removal of excess facial hair is best handled by an experienced cosmetician. The process involves pouring hot wax onto the skin and allowing it to cool. The hairs become embedded in the wax, and are plucked out from below the skin surface when the wax is stripped off. Because this method is painful and often causes irritation, it is not very popular, although the results are comparatively long-lasting.

Plucking

The use of tweezers for removing scattered hairs from the eyebrows, face, and chest is slightly painful but otherwise harmless. It is not a practical method for getting rid of dense hair growth, however, because it takes too much time.

Permanent Hair Removal by Electrolysis

The only permanent and safe method of removing unwanted hair is by *electrolysis*. This technique destroys each individual hair root by transmitting electric current through fine wire needles into the opening of the hair follicle. The hair thus loosened is then plucked out with a tweezer. The older type of electrolysis machine uses galvanic current. The newer type, sometimes called an *electrocoagulation machine,* uses modified high-frequency current. In either case, the efficiency and safety of the technique depends less on the machine than on the care and skill of the operator.

Because the process of treating each hair root is expensive, time-consuming, and uncomfortable, it is not recommended for areas of dense hair growth, such as the arms or legs. Before undertaking electrolysis either at a beauty salon or at home, it would be wise to consult a dermatologist about individual skin reaction.

Nails

Fingernails and toenails are an extension of the epidermis, or outer layer of the skin. They are made of elastic tissue formed from keratin, the substance that gives hair its strength and flexibility.

Some of the problems associated with fingernails are the result of too much manicuring. White spots, for example, are often caused by too much pressure at the base of the nail when trying to expose the "moon"—the white portion that contains tissue not yet as tough as the rest of the nail.

To ensure the health of toenails, feet should be bathed once a day and the nails cleaned with a brush dipped in soapy water. Shoes should fit properly so that the toenails are not subjected to pressure and distortion. To avoid ingrown toenails, trimming should be done straight across rather than by rounding or tapering the corners.

Splitting

Infection or injury of the tissue at the base of a fingernail may cause its surface to be rigid or split. Inflammation of the finger joints connected with arthritis will also cause nail deformity. For ordinary problems of splitting and peeling, the nails should be kept short enough so that they don't catch and tear easily. For practical purposes, the top of the nail should not be visible when the palm is held about six inches from the eye. As the nails grow stronger, they can be grown longer without splitting.

Brittleness

This condition seems to be caused by such external factors as the chemicals in polish removers, soaps, and detergents. It is also a natural consequence of aging. Commercial nail-hardening preparations that contain formaldehyde are not recommended, because they are known to cause discoloration, loosening, or even loss of nails in some cases.

Nail damage can be reduced by wearing rubber gloves while doing household chores. Hand cream mas-

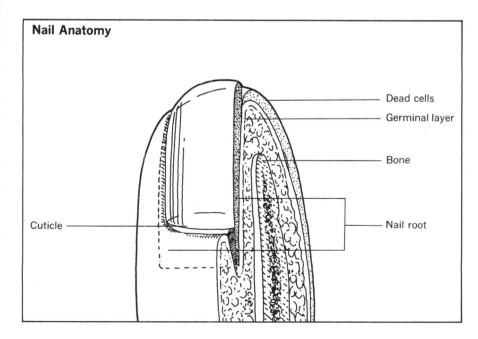

Nail Anatomy

Dead cells

Germinal layer

Bone

Nail root

Cuticle

saged into the skin around the nails will counteract dryness and lessen the possibility of hangnails. Although nail polish provides a shield against damage, it should not be worn all the time, particularly if the nail is polished right down to the base; this prevents live tissue from "breathing."

Disorders of the Skin

The skin is subject to a large number of disorders, most of which are not serious even though they may be temporarily uncomfortable. A disorder may be caused by one or another type of allergy; by excessive heat or cold; or by infection from fungi, bacteria, viruses, or parasites. Many skin ailments are caused or aggravated by emotional disturbances.

The symptoms and treatment of the more common disorders are discussed in the following pages. Any persistent change in skin condition should be brought to the attention of a physician.

Allergies and Itching

Itching and inflammation of the skin may be caused by an allergic reaction, by exposure to poisonous plants, or by a generalized infection.

Dermatitis

Dermatitis is the term used for an inflammation of the skin. The term for allergic reactions of the skin resulting from surface contact with outside agents is *contact dermatitis*. This condition is characterized by a rash and may be brought out by sensitivity to cosmetics, plants, cleaning materials, metal, wool, and so on. Other forms of dermatitis can be caused by excesses of heat or cold, by friction, or by sensitivity to various medicines. Dermatitis is usually accompanied by itching at the site of the rash.

Poison Ivy

This common plant, unknown in Europe but widespread everywhere in the United States except in California and Nevada, produces an allergic reaction on the skin accompanied by a painful rash and blisters. Some people are so sensitive to it that they are affected by contact not only with the plant itself but with animal fur or clothing that might have picked up the sap weeks before.

A mild attack of poison ivy produces a rash and small, watery blisters that get progressively larger. The affected area of the skin becomes crusty and dry, and after a few weeks, all symptoms vanish. If the exposed area is thoroughly washed with laundry soap immediately after contact, the poison may not penetrate the skin.

If the symptoms do develop, they can be relieved with Burow's solution—one part solution to fifteen parts of cool water—or with the application of calamine lotion. If the symptoms are severe, and especially if the area around the eyes is involved, a physician should be consulted. He may prescribe an application or an injection of cortisone.

The best way to avoid the unpleasantness of a poison ivy attack is to learn to recognize the plant and stay away from it. Children especially should be warned against putting the leaves and berries in their mouths.

Poison oak and poison sumac produce somewhat the same symptoms and should also be avoided. Under no circumstances should these plants be burned to eliminate them, because the inhaling of the contaminated smoke even from a distance can cause a serious case of poisoning. The application of special sprays, if the instructions are followed carefully, will get rid of the plants without affecting people or the neighborhood greenery.

Hives

These are large, irregularly shaped swellings on the skin that burn and itch. The cause is unknown, but allergic reactions to certain foods and medicine or to insect bites have been suggested as possible causes. The swellings of hives usually disappear within a day or so, but they can be very uncomfortable while they last. The itching and burning can often be relieved by applying cold water and a calamine solution. However, some people are sensitive to cold and develop wheals when subjected to intense cold. Commercial preparations containing surface anesthetics are seldom effective and may cause allergic reactions.

If the outbreak of hives can be traced to a specific food, such as shellfish or strawberries, the food should be eliminated from the diet. If a medicine such as penicillin or a sulfa drug is the cause, a physician should be told about the reaction.

Eczema

This condition is an allergic reaction that produces itching, swelling, blistering, oozing, and scaling of the skin. It is more common among children than among adults and may sometimes cover the entire body, although the rash is usually limited to the face, neck, and folds of the knees and elbows. Unlike contact dermatitis, it is likely to be caused by an allergy to a food or a pollen or dust. Advertised cures for eczema cannot control the cause and sometimes make the condition worse. A physician should be consulted if the symptoms are severe, particularly if the patient is an infant or very young child.

Itching

The technical name for the localized or general sensation on the skin that can be relieved by scratching is *pruritus*. Itching may be caused by many skin disorders, by infections, by serious diseases such as nephritis or leukemia, by medicines, or by psychological factors such as tension. A physician should always be consulted to find the cause of persistent itching, because it may be the symptom of a basic disorder. Repeated scratching may provide some relief, but it can also lead to infection.

Anal Pruritus

If itching in the anal area is so severe that only painful scratching will relieve it, the condition is probably *anal pruritus*. It is often accompanied by excessive rectal mucus that keeps the skin irritated and moist. This disorder is most commonly associated with hemorrhoids, but many other conditions, such as reactions to drugs, can cause it. Anxiety or tension can also contribute to it. Sitz baths with warm water are usually recommended. Every effort should be made to reduce scratching and to keep the anal skin clean and dry. Cortisone cream may be prescribed in persistent cases.

Skin Irritations and Weather

Extremes of weather produce local inflammations and other skin problems for many people.

Chapping

In cold weather, the sebaceous glands slow down the secretions that lubricate the skin, causing it to become dry. When dry skin is exposed to wintry weather, it becomes irritated and is likely to crack, particularly around the lips. Chapped skin is especially sensitive to harsh soaps. During such periods of exposure, the skin can be protected with a mild cream or lotion. A lubricating ointment should be used on the lips to prevent them from cracking. Children who lick their lips continually no matter what the weather can benefit from this extra protection. Chapped hands caused by daily use of strong soaps and detergents can be helped by the use of a lubricating cream and rubber gloves during housework.

Frostbite

Exposure to extreme cold for a prolonged period may cause freezing of the nose, fingers, toes, or ears, thus cutting off the circulation to the affected areas. Frostbitten areas are of a paler color than normal and are numb. They should not be rubbed with snow or exposed to intense heat. Areas should be thawed gradually, and a physician should be consulted for aftercare in extreme cases.

Chilblain

A localized inflammation of the skin called *chilblain* is common among people who are particularly sensitive to cold because of poor circulation. Chilblain may occur in the ears, hands, feet, and face, causing itching, swelling, and discoloration of the skin. Anyone prone to chilblain should dress protectively during the cold weather and use an electric pad or blanket at night. Affected parts should not be rubbed or massaged, nor should ice or extreme heat be applied directly, since these measures may cause additional damage. Persistent or extreme attacks of chilblain should be discussed with a physician.

Chafing

This condition is an inflammation of two opposing skin surfaces caused by the warmth, moisture, and friction of their rubbing together. Diabetics, overweight people, and those who perspire heavily are particularly prone to chafing. Chafing is accompanied by itching and burning, and sometimes infection can set in if the superficial skin is broken. Parts of the body subject to chafing are the inner surfaces of the thighs, the anal region, the area under the breasts, and the inner surfaces between fingers and toes.

To reduce the possibility of chafing, lightweight clothing should be worn and strenuous exercise avoided during hot weather. Vaseline or a vitamin A and D ointment may be applied to reduce friction. In general, the treatment is the same as that for diaper rash in infants. If the condition becomes acute, a physician can prescribe more effective remedies.

Prickly Heat

This skin rash is usually accompanied by itching and burning. It is caused by an obstruction of the sweat ducts such that perspiration does not reach the surface of the skin but backs up and causes pimples the size of a pinhead. If the obstruction is superficial, the pimples are white; if it is deeper, they are red. The condition can be brought on by other minor skin irritations, by continued exposure to moist heat, such as a compress, or by exercise in humid weather. Infants and people who are overweight are especially prone to prickly heat.

The discomfort can be eased by wearing lightweight, loose-fitting clothing, especially at night, and keeping room temperature low. Alcoholic beverages, which tend to dehydrate the body, should be avoided. Tepid baths and the application of cornstarch to the affected skin areas will usually relieve itching. If the rash remains for several days, a physician should be consulted to make sure it does not arise from some other cause.

Calluses and Corns

As a result of continued friction or pressure in a particular area, the skin forms a tough, hard, self-protecting layer known as a *callus*. Calluses are common on the soles of the feet, the palms of the hands, and, among guitarists and string players, on the tips of the fingers. A heavy callus that presses against a bone in the foot because of poorly fitted shoes can be very painful. The hard surface can be reduced somewhat by the use of pumice, or by gently paring it with a razor blade that has been washed in alcohol.

Corns are a form of callus that appear on or between the toes. They usually have a hard inner core that causes pain when pressed against underlying tissue by badly fitted shoes. A hard corn that appears on the surface of the little toe can be removed by soaking for about ten minutes and applying a few drops of ten percent salicylic acid in collodion. The surface should be covered with a corn pad to reduce pressure, and the corn lifted off when it is loose enough to be released from the skin. Anyone suffering from a circulatory disease and particularly from diabetes should avoid home treatment of foot disturbances. Those with a tendency to callus and corn formations should be especially careful about the proper fit of shoes and hose. A *chiropodist* or *podiatrist* is a trained specialist in foot care who can be visited on a regular basis to provide greater foot comfort.

Fungus Infections

Fungi are plantlike parasitic growths found in the air, in water, and in the soil. They comprise a large family that includes mushrooms, and are responsible for mildew and mold. Only a small number cause disease.

Ringworm

This condition is caused not by a worm but by a group of fungi that live on the body's dead skin cells in those areas that are warm and damp because of accumulated perspiration. One form of ringworm attacks the scalp, arms, and legs, especially of children, and is often spread by similarly affected pets. It appears as reddish patches that scale and blister and frequently feel sore and itchy. Ringworm is highly contagious and can be passed from person to person by contaminated objects such as combs and towels. It should therefore be treated promptly by a physician. Ringworm can best be prevented by strict attention to personal cleanliness.

Athlete's Foot

Another form of ringworm, *athlete's foot,* usually attacks the skin between the toes and under the toenails. If not treated promptly, it can cause an itching rash on other parts of the body. Athlete's foot causes the skin to itch, blister, and crack, and as a result, leaves it vulnerable to more serious infection from other organisms. The disorder can be treated at home by gently removing the damaged skin, and, after soaking the feet, thoroughly drying and dusting between the toes with a medicated foot powder. Some of the powder should be sprinkled into shoes. If the condition continues, a fungicidal ointment can be applied in the morning and at night. Persistent cases require the attention of a physician.

Scabies

An insectlike parasite causes the skin irritation called *scabies,* otherwise known as "the itch." The female itch mite burrows a hole in the skin, usually in the groin or between the fingers or toes, and stays hidden long enough to build a tunnel in which to deposit her eggs. The newly hatched mites then work their way to the skin surface and begin the cycle all over again. There is little discomfort in the early period of infestation, but in about a week, a rash appears, accompanied by extreme itching, which is usually most severe at night. Constant scratching during sleep can lead to skin lesions that invite bacterial infection.

Scabies is very contagious and can spread rapidly through a family or through a community, such as a summer camp or army barracks. It can also be communicated by sexual contact.

Treatment by a physician involves the identification of the characteristic tunnels from which sample mites can be removed for examination. Hot baths and thorough scrubbing will expose the burrows, and medical applications as directed by the physician usually clear up the condition in about a week.

Bacterial Infections

The skin is susceptible to infection from a variety of bacteria. Poor diet and careless hygiene can lower the body's resistance to these infectious agents.

Boils

These abscesses of the skin are caused by bacterial infection of a hair follicle or a sebaceous gland. The pus that accumulates in a boil is the result of the encounter between the bacteria and the white blood cells that fight them. Sometimes a boil subsides by itself and disappears. Sometimes the pressure of pus against the skin surface may bring the boil to a head; it will then break, drain, and heal if washed with an antiseptic and covered with a sterile pad. Warm-water compresses can be applied for ten minutes every hour to relieve the pain and to encourage the boil to break and drain. A fresh, dry pad should be applied after each period of soaking.

Anyone with a serious or chronic illness who develops a boil should consult a physician. Since the bacteria can enter the bloodstream and cause a general infection with fever, a physician should also be consulted for a boil on the nose, scalp, upper lip, or in the ear, groin, or armpit.

Carbuncles

This infection is a group of connected boils and is likely to be more painful and less responsive to home treatment. Carbuncles may occur as the result of poor skin care. They tend to occur in the back of the neck where the skin is thick, and the abscess tends to burrow into deeper tissues. A physician usually lances and drains a deep-seated carbuncle, or he may prescribe an antibiotic remedy.

Impetigo

This skin infection is caused by staphylococcal or streptococcal bacteria, and is characterized by blisters that break and form yellow crusted areas. It is spread from one person to another and from one part of the body to another by the discharge from the sores. Impetigo occurs most frequently on the scalp, face, and arms and legs. The infection often is picked up in barber shops, swimming pools, or from body contact with infected people or household pets.

Special care must be taken, especially with children, to control the spread of the infection by keeping the fingers away from infected parts. Bed linens should be changed daily, and disposable paper towels, as well as paper plates and cups, should be used during treatment. A physician should be consulted for proper medication and procedures to deal with the infection.

Barber's Itch

Sycosis, commonly called *barber's itch,* is a bacterial infection of the hair follicles of the beard, accompanied by inflammation, itching, and the formation of pus-filled pimples. People with stiff, curly hair are prone to this type of chronic infection, because their hair is more likely to curve back and reenter the skin. The infection should be treated promptly to prevent scarring and the destruction of the hair root. In some cases, physicians recommend antibiotics. If these are not effective, it may be necessary to drain the abscesses and remove the hairs from the inflamed follicles. During treatment, it is best to avoid shaving, if possible. If one must shave, the sterilization of all shaving equipment and the use of a brushless shaving cream are recommended.

Erysipelas

An acute streptococcal infection of the skin, *erysipelas* can be fatal, particularly to the very young or very old, if not treated promptly. One of its symptoms is the bright redness of the affected areas of the skin. These red patches enlarge and spread, making the skin tender and painful. Blisters may appear nearby. The patient usually has a headache, fever, chills, and nausea. Erysipelas responds well to promptly administered antibiotics, particularly penicillin. The patient is

usually advised to drink large amounts of fluid and to eat a nourishing, easily digested diet.

Viral Infections

The most common skin conditions caused by viruses are cold sores, shingles, and warts, discussed below.

Cold Sores

Also called fever blisters, *cold sores* are technically known as *herpes simplex.* They are small blisters that appear most frequently in the corners of the mouth, and sometimes around the eyes and on the genitals. The presumed cause is a virus that lies dormant in the skin until it is activated by infection or by excessive exposure to sun or wind. There is no specific cure for cold sores, but the irritation can be eased by applying drying or cooling agents such as camphor ice or cold-water compresses. Recurrent cold sores, especially in infants, should be called to a physician's attention.

Recent studies have shown that a variety of the herpes simplex virus called HSV-II (for herpes simplex virus-Type II) can be a serious danger to the fetus of a pregnant woman. For a discussion of this condition, see Ch. 25, *Women's Health.* The variety that causes cold sores is called Type I.

Shingles

The virus infection of a sensory nerve, accompanied by small, painful blisters that appear on the skin along the path of the nerve—usually on one side of the chest or abdomen—is called *shingles.* The medical name for the disorder, which is caused by the chicken pox virus, is *herpes zoster,* Latin for "girdle of blisters." When a cranial nerve is involved, the blisters appear on the face near the eye. The preliminary symptom is neuritis with severe pain and, sometimes, fever. The blisters may take from two to four weeks to dry up and disappear. Although there is no specific cure, the pain can be alleviated by aspirin. In severe cases, or if the area near the eye is involved, a physician should be seen.

Warts

These growths are caused by a virus infection of the epidermis. They never become cancerous, but can be painful when found on the soles of the feet. In this location, they are known as *plantar warts,* and they cause discomfort because constant pressure makes them grow inward. Plantar warts are most likely to be picked up by children because they are barefooted so much of the time, and by adults when their feet are moist and they are walking around in showers, near swimming pools, and in locker rooms. Warts can be spread by scratching, by shaving, and by brushing the hair. They are often transmitted from one member of the family to another. Because warts can spread to painful areas, such as the area around or under the fingernails, and because they may become disfiguring, it is best to consult a physician whenever they appear.

In many ways, warts behave rather mysteriously. About half of them go away without any treatment at all. Sometimes, when warts on one part of the body are being treated, those in another area will disappear. The folklore about "witching" and "charming" warts away has its foundation in fact, because apparently having faith in the cure, no matter how ridiculous it sounds, sometimes brings success. This form of suggestion therapy is especially successful with children.

There are several more conventional ways of treating warts. De-

pending on their size and the area involved, electric current, dry ice, or various chemicals may be employed. A physician should be consulted promptly when warts develop in the area of the beard or on the scalp, because they spread quickly in these parts of the body and thus become more difficult to eliminate.

Sebaceous Cysts

When a sebaceous gland duct is blocked, the oil that the gland secretes cannot get to the surface of the skin. Instead, it accumulates into a hard, round, movable mass contained in a sac. This mass is known as a *sebaceous cyst.* Such cysts may appear on the face, back, ears, or in the genital area. A sebaceous cyst that forms on the scalp is called a *wen,* and may become as large as a billiard ball. The skin in this area will become bald, because the cyst interferes with the blood supply to the hair roots.

Some sebaceous cysts just disappear without treatment. However, those that do not are a likely focus for secondary infection by bacteria, and they may become abscessed and inflamed. It is therefore advisable to have cysts examined by a physician for possible removal. If such a cyst is superficial, it can be punctured and drained. One that is deeper is usually removed by simple surgical procedure in the physician's office.

Acne

About 80 percent of all teenagers suffer from the skin disturbance called *acne.* It is also fairly common among women in their twenties. Acne is a condition in which the skin of the face, and often of the neck, shoulders, chest, and back, is covered to a greater or lesser extent with pimples, blackheads, whiteheads, and boils.

The typical onset of acne in adolescence is related to the increased activity of the glands, including the sebaceous glands. Most of the oil that they secrete gets to the surface of the skin through ducts that lead into the pores. When the surface pores are clogged with sebaceous gland secretions and keratin, or when so much extra oil is being secreted that it backs up into the ducts, the result is the formation of the skin blemishes characteristic of acne. Dirt or makeup does not cause acne.

The blackheads are dark not because they are dirty but because the fatty material in the clogged pore is oxidized and discolored by the air that reaches it. When this substance is infected by bacteria, it turns into a pimple. Under no circumstances should such pimples be picked at or squeezed, because the pressure can rupture the surrounding membrane and spread the infection further.

Although a mild case of acne usually clears up by itself, it is often helpful to get the advice of a physician so that it does not get any worse.

Cleanliness

Although surface dirt does not cause acne, it can contribute to its spread. Therefore, the affected areas should be cleansed with a medicated soap and hot water twice a day. Hair should be shampooed frequently and brushed away from the face. Boys who are shaving should soften the beard with soap and hot water. The blade should be sharp and should skim the skin as lightly as possible to avoid nicking pimples.

Creams and Cosmetics

Nonprescription medicated creams and lotions may be effective in reducing some blemishes, but if used too often, they make the skin dry. They should be applied according to the manufacturer's instructions and should be discontinued if they cause additional irritation. If makeup is used, it should have a nonoily base and be completely removed before going to bed.

Forbidden Foods

Although acne is not caused by any particular food, it can be made worse by a diet overloaded with candy, rich pastries, and fats. Chocolate and cola drinks must be eliminated entirely in some cases.

Professional Treatment

A serious case of acne, or even a mild one that is causing serious emotional problems, should receive the attention of a physician. He or she may prescribe antibiotics, usually considered the most effective treatment, or recommend sunlamp treatments. A physician can also be helpful in dealing with the psychological aspects of acne that are so disturbing to teenagers.

Psoriasis

Psoriasis is a noncontagious chronic condition in which the skin on various parts of the body is marked by bright red patches covered with silvery scales. The areas most often affected are the knees, elbows, scalp, and trunk, and less frequently, the areas under the arms and around the genitals.

The specific cause of psoriasis has not yet been discovered, but it is thought to be an inherited abnormality in which the formation of new skin cells is too rapid and disorderly. In its mild form, psoriasis responds well to a variety of long-term treatments.

When it is acute, the entire skin surface may be painfully red, and large sections of it may scale off. In such cases, prompt hospitalization and intensive care are recommended.

Conditions That Can Bring On an Outbreak

The onset or aggravation of psoriasis can be triggered by some of the following factors:

- bruises, burns, scratches, and overexposure to the sun

- sudden drops in temperature—a mild, stable climate is most beneficial

- sudden illness from another source, or unusual physical or emotional stress

- infections of the upper respiratory tract, especially bacterial throat infections and the medicines used to cure them

Treatment

Although there is no specific cure for psoriasis, these are some of the recommended treatments:

- controlled exposure to sunlight or an ultraviolet lamp

- creams or lotions of crude coal tar or tar distillates, used alone or in combination with ultraviolet light

- psoralen and ultraviolet light (PUVA), a combined systemic-external therapy in which a psoralen drug is taken orally before exposure to ultraviolet light

- systemic drugs, such as methotrexate, which can be taken orally

- steroid hormone medications applied to the skin surface under dressings

Pigment Disorders and Birthmarks

The mechanism that controls skin coloration is described above under "Skin Color." Abnormalities in the creation and distribution of melanin result in the following disorders, some of which are negligible.

Freckles

These are small spots of brown pigment that frequently occur when fair-skinned people are exposed to the sun or to ultraviolet light. For those whose skin gets red rather than tan during such exposure, freckles are a protective device. In most cases, they recede in cold weather. A heavy freckle formation that is permanent can be covered somewhat by cosmetic preparations. No attempt should be made to remove freckles with commercial creams or solutions unless supervised by a physician.

Liver Spots

Flat, smooth, irregularly placed markings on the skin, called *liver spots,* often appear among older people, and result from an increase in pigmentation. They have nothing to do with the liver and are completely harmless. Brownish markings of similar appearance sometimes show up during pregnancy or as a result of irritation or infection. They usually disappear when the underlying cause is eliminated.

Liver spots are permanent, and the principal cause is not aging but the accumulated years of exposure to sun and wind. They can be disguised and treated in the same way as freckles. A liver spot that becomes hard and thick should be called to a physician's attention.

Moles

Clusters of melanin cells, called *moles,* may appear singly or in groups at any place on the body. They range in color from light tan to dark brown; they may be raised and hairy or flat and smooth. Many moles are present at birth, and most make their appearance before the age of 20. They rarely turn into malignancies, and require medical attention only if they become painful, if they itch, or if they suddenly change in size, shape, or color.

There are several ways of removing moles if they are annoying or particularly unattractive. They can be destroyed by the application of an electric needle, by cauterizing, and by surgery. A mole that has been removed is not likely to reappear. The hairs sometimes found in moles can be clipped close to the surface of the skin, or they can be permanently removed. Hair removal often causes the mole to get smaller.

Vitiligo

The condition called *vitiligo* stems from a loss of pigment in sharply defined areas of the skin. There is no known cause for this abnormality of melanin distribution. It may affect any part of the body and may appear any time up to middle age. It is particularly conspicuous when it occurs among blacks, or when a lighter skinned person becomes tanned except around the paler patches. There is no cure for vitiligo, but cosmetic treatment with pastes and lotions can diminish the contrast between affected areas and the rest of the skin.

Birthmarks

About one-third of all infants are born with the type of birthmark called a *hemangioma,* also known as a vascular birthmark. These are caused by a clustering of small blood vessels near the surface of the skin. The mark, which is flat, irregularly shaped, and either pink, red, or purplish, is usually referred to as "port wine stain." There is no known way to remove it, but with cosmetic covering creams, it can usually be successfully masked.

The type of hemangioma that is raised and bright red—called a strawberry mark—spontaneously disappears with no treatment in most cases during early childhood. If a strawberry mark begins to grow rather than fade, or if it begins to ulcerate, a physician should be promptly consulted.

See Ch. 18, *Cancer,* for a discussion of skin cancer; see Ch. 3, *The Teens,* for a discussion of adolescent skin problems; see Ch. 23, *Aches, Pains, Nuisances, Worries,* for further discussion of minor skin problems.

22

The Teeth and Gums

Although a human baby is born without teeth, a complete set of 20 *deciduous,* or baby, teeth (also called *primary teeth*) already has formed within the gums of the offspring while it still is within the mother's womb. The buds of the permanent or secondary teeth are developing even before the first baby tooth appears at around the age of six months. The baby teeth obviously are formed from foods eaten by the mother. Generally, if the mother follows a good diet during pregnancy, no special food items are required to ensure an adequate set of deciduous teeth in the baby.

It takes about two years for the full set of deciduous teeth to appear in the baby's mouth. The first, usually a central incisor at the front of the lower jaw, may erupt any time between the ages of three and nine months. The last probably will be a second molar at the back of the upper jaw. As with walking, talking, and other characteristics of infants, there is no set timetable for the eruption of baby teeth. One child may get his first tooth at three months while another must wait until nine months, but both would be considered within a normal range of tooth development.

The permanent teeth are never far behind the deciduous set. The first permanent tooth usually appears around the age of six years, about four years after the last of the baby teeth has erupted. But the last of the permanent molars, the third molars or *wisdom teeth,* may not break through the gum line until the offspring is an adult.

Types of Teeth

The permanent teeth number 32. In advancing from deciduous to permanent teeth, the human gains six teeth in the lower jaw, or *mandible,* and six in the upper jaw, or *maxilla,* of the mouth. The primary set of teeth includes the following:

UPPER JAW	LOWER JAW
2 central incisors	2 central incisors
2 lateral incisors	2 lateral incisors
2 cuspids	2 cuspids
2 first molars	2 first molars
2 second molars	2 second molars

The permanent set of teeth has an equivalent combination of incisors, cuspids, and first and second molars. But it also includes:

2 first bicuspids	2 first bicuspids
2 second bicuspids	2 second bicuspids
2 third molars	2 third molars

An *incisor* is designed to cut off particles of food, which is then pushed by muscles of the tongue and cheeks to teeth farther back in the mouth for grinding. The front teeth, one on each side, upper and lower, are central incisors. Next to each central incisor is a lateral incisor.

A *cuspid* is so named because it has a spear-shaped crown, or *cusp.* It is designed for tearing as well as cutting. Cuspids sometimes are called *canine teeth* or *eyeteeth; canine teeth* owe their name to the use of these teeth by carnivorous animals, such as dogs, for tearing pieces of meat. There are four cuspids in the mouth, one on the outer side of each lateral incisor in the upper and lower jaws.

Bicuspids sometimes are identified

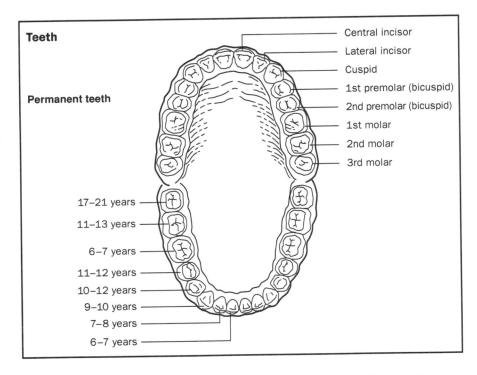

Teeth

Permanent teeth

- Central incisor
- Lateral incisor
- Cuspid
- 1st premolar (bicuspid)
- 2nd premolar (bicuspid)
- 1st molar
- 2nd molar
- 3rd molar

17–21 years
11–13 years
6–7 years
11–12 years
10–12 years
9–10 years
7–8 years
6–7 years

as *premolars.* The term "bicuspid" suggests two cusps, but a bicuspid may in fact have three cusps. The function of the bicuspids is to crush food passed back from the incisors and cuspids. The permanent set of teeth includes a total of eight bicuspids.

The *molars,* which also number eight and are the last teeth at the back of the mouth, are the largest and strongest teeth, with the job of grinding food. The third molars, or wisdom teeth, are smaller, weaker, and less functional than the first and second molars.

Structure of the Tooth

The variety of shapes of teeth make them specialized for the various functions in preparing food for digestion—biting, chewing, and grinding. All varieties, however, have the same basic structure.

Enamel

The outer covering of the part of the tooth that is exposed above the gum line is *enamel,* the hardest substance in the human body. Enamel is about 97 percent mineral and is as tough as some gemstones. It varies in thickness, with the greatest thickness on the surfaces that are likely to get the most wear and tear.

Enamel begins to form on the first tooth buds of an embryo at the age of about 15 weeks, depending upon substances in the food eaten by the mother for proper development. Once the tooth has formed and erupted through the gum line, there is nothing further that can be done by natural means to improve the condition of the enamel. The enamel has no blood supply, and any changes in the tooth surface will be the result of wearing, decay, or injury.

While the health and diet of the mother can affect the development of tooth enamel in the deciduous teeth, certain health factors in the early life of a child can result in defective enamel formation of teeth that have not yet erupted. Some infectious or metabolic disorders, for example, may result in enamel pitting.

Dentin

Beneath the enamel surface of a tooth is a layer of hard material—though not as hard as enamel—called *dentin,* which forms the bulk of a tooth. The dentin forms at the same time that enamel is laid down on the surface of a developing tooth, and the portion beneath the crown of the tooth probably is completed at the same time as the enamel. However, the dentin, which is composed of calcified material, is not as dense as the enamel; it is formed as myriad tubules that extend downward into the pulp at the center of the tooth. There is some evidence that dentin formation may continue slowly during the life of the tooth.

Cementum

The *cementum* is a bonelike substance that covers the root of the tooth. Though harder than regular bone, it is softer than dentin. It contains attachments for fibers of a periodontal ligament that holds the tooth in its socket. The periodontal ligament serves as a kind of hammock of fibers that surround and support the tooth at the cementum surface, radiating outward to the jawbone. This arrangement allows the tooth to move a little while still attached to the jaw. For example, when the teeth of the upper and lower jaws are brought together in chewing, the periodontal ligament allows the teeth to sink into their sockets. When the teeth of the two jaws are separated, the hammocklike ligament permits the teeth to float outward again.

Pulp

The cavity within the dentin contains the *pulp.* There is a wide pulp chamber under the crown of the tooth and a pulp canal that extends from the chamber down through the root or roots. Some teeth, such as the molars, may contain as many as three roots, and each of the roots contains a pulp canal.

The pulp of a tooth contains the blood vessels supplying the tooth and the lymphatic system. Although the blood supply arrangement is not the same for every tooth, a typical pattern includes a dental artery entering through each passageway, or *foramen,* leading into the root of a tooth. The artery branches into numerous capillaries within the root canal. A similar system of veins drains the blood from the tooth through each foramen. A lymphatic network and nerve system also enter the tooth through a foramen and spread through the pulp, as branches from a central distribution link within the jawbone. The nerve fibers have free endings in the tooth, making them sensitive to pain stimuli.

Supporting Structures

The soft, pink gum tissue that surrounds the tooth is called the *gingiva,* and the bone of the jaw that forms the tooth socket is known as *alveolar bone.* The gingiva, alveolar bone, and periodontal ligaments sometimes are grouped into a structural category identified as the *periodontium.* Thus, when a dentist speaks of periodontal

disease, he is referring to a disorder of these supporting tissues of the teeth. The ailment known as *gingivitis* is an inflammation of the gingiva, or gum tissue around the teeth.

Care of the Teeth and Gums

Years ago, loss of teeth really was unavoidable. Today, thanks to modern practices of preventive dentistry, it is possible for nearly everyone to enjoy the benefits of natural teeth for a lifetime. But natural teeth can be preserved only by daily oral-hygiene habits and regular dental checkups.

The Dental Examination

During the teen years, careful supervision by the dentist and cooperation from the teenager are especially necessary. The poor eating habits of many youngsters are reflected in high cavity rates, which may be greater during adolescence than in later life. Neglect of proper dental care also occurs in the middle years when an often used excuse is that eventual loss of teeth is inevitable. After the permanent teeth are established, the dentist should be visited every six months, or at whatever intervals he recommends for an individual patient who may need more or less care than the typical patient.

The dentist, like the family physician, usually maintains a general health history of each patient, in addition to a dental health history. He examines each tooth, the gums and other oral tissues, and the *occlusion,* or bite. A complete set of X-ray pictures may be taken on the first visit and again at intervals of perhaps five to seven years. During routine visits, the dentist may take only a couple of X-ray pictures of teeth on either side of the mouth; a complete set of X rays may result in a file of 18 or 20 pictures covering every tooth in the mouth.

X rays constitute a vital part of the dental examination. Without them the dentist cannot examine the surfaces between the teeth or the portion of the tooth beneath the gum, a part that represents about 60 percent of the total length of the tooth. The X rays will reveal the condition of the enamel, dentin, and pulp, as well as any impacted wisdom teeth and the alveolar bone, or tooth sockets. Caps, fillings, abscessed roots, and bone loss resulting from gum disease also are clearly visible on a set of X rays.

Other diagnostic tests may be made, such as a test of nerve response. Sometimes the dentist will make an impression of the teeth, an accurate and detailed reverse reproduction, in plaster of paris, plastic impression compound, or other material. Models made from these impressions are used to study the way the teeth meet. Such knowledge is often crucial in deciding the selection of treatment and materials.

After the examination, the dentist will present and explain any proposed treatment. After oral restoration is completed, he will ask the patient to return at regular intervals for a checkup and *prophylaxis,* which includes cleaning and polishing the teeth. Regular checkups and prophylaxis help prevent periodontal diseases affecting the gum tissue and un-

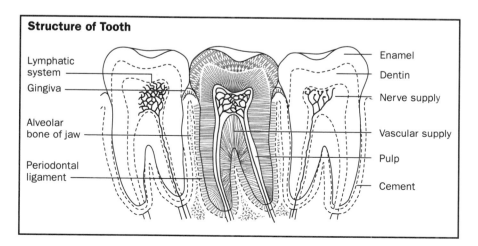

Structure of Tooth

Lymphatic system
Gingiva
Alveolar bone of jaw
Periodontal ligament

Enamel
Dentin
Nerve supply
Vascular supply
Pulp
Cement

derlying bone. Professional cleaning removes hard deposits that trap bacteria, especially at the gum line, and polishing removes stains and soft deposits.

Dental Care in Middle Age

Although periodontal (gum) disease and cavities—called *dental caries* by dentists—continue to threaten oral health, two other problems may assume prominence for people of middle age: replacing worn-out restorations, or fillings, and replacing missing teeth. No filling material will last forever. The whitish restorations in front teeth eventually wear away. Silver restorations tend to crack and chip with age because they contract and expand slightly when cold or hot food and drinks come in contact with them. Even gold restorations, the most permanent kind, are subject to decay around the edges, and the decay may spread underneath.

If a needed restoration is not made or a worn-out restoration is not replaced, a deep cavity may result. When the decay reaches the inner layer of the tooth—the dentin—temporary warning twinges of pain may occur. If the tooth still is not restored, the decay will spread into the pulp that fills the inner chamber of the tooth. A toothache can result from inflammation of the pulp, and although the pain may eventually subside, the pulp tissue dies and an abscess can form at the root of the tooth.

Dental Care during Pregnancy

It may be advisable for a pregnant woman to arrange for extra dental checkups. Many changes take place during pregnancy, among them increased hormone production. Some pregnant women develop gingivitis (inflammation of the gums) as an indirect consequence of hormonal changes. A checkup by the dentist during the first three months of pregnancy is needed to assess the oral effects of such changes, and to make sure all dental problems are examined and corrected. Pregnant women should take special care to brush and floss their teeth to minimize these problems.

Infection

To avoid the problem of toxic substances or poisons circulating in the mother's bloodstream, all sources of infection must be removed. Some of these sources can be in the mouth. An abscessed tooth, for example, may not be severe enough to signal its presence with pain, but because it is directly connected to the bloodstream it can send toxic substances and bacteria through the mother's body with possible harmful effects to the embryo.

It is during pregnancy that tooth buds for both the deciduous and permanent teeth begin to form in the unborn child. If the mother neglects her diet or general health care during this period, the effects may be seen in the teeth of her child.

Maintaining Good Oral Hygiene

Fluoridation

Among general rules to follow between dental checkups are using fluorides, maintaining a proper diet, and removing debris from the teeth by brushing and by the use of dental floss. Fluorides are particularly important for strengthening the enamel of teeth in persons under the age of 15. Many communities add fluorides to the water supply, but if the substance is not available in the drinking water, the dentist can advise the patient about other ways of adding fluoride to water or other fluids consumed each day. Studies show that children who drink fluoridated water from birth have up to 65 percent fewer cavities than those who do not drink fluoridated water. However, using excessive amounts of fluoride in the drinking water can result in mottled enamel.

Diet

Although a good diet for total health should provide all of the elements needed for dental health, several precautions on sugars and starches should be added. Hard or sticky sweets should be avoided. Such highly refined sweets as soft drinks, candies, cakes, cookies, pies, syrups, jams, jellies, and pastries should be limited, especially between meals. One's intake of starchy foods, such as bread, potatoes, and pastas, should also be controlled. Natural sugars contained in fresh fruits can provide sweet flavors with less risk of contributing to decay if the teeth are brushed regularly after eating such foods. Regular chewing gum may help remove food particles after eating, but it deposits sugar; if you chew gum, use sugarless gum.

Because decay is promoted each time sugars and other refined carbohydrates are eaten, between-meals snacks of sweets should be curtailed to lessen the chances of new or additional caries. Snack foods can be raw vegetables, such as carrots or celery, apples, cheese, peanuts, or other items that are not likely to introduce refined carbohydrates into the mouth between meals.

Brushing

Brushing the teeth is an essential of personal oral hygiene. Such brushing rids the mouth of most of the food

Brushing

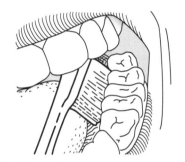

Begin by brushing the tops of the upper and lower molars, using a scrubbing motion without much pressure. A soft toothbrush with a straight handle is most recommended.

Next, keeping the brush parallel to the teeth, angle the bristles against the lower gums and brush back and forth with short strokes against both sides of every tooth. Use the same technique for the upper teeth.

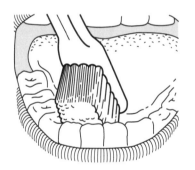

Apply the tip of the brush to the backs of upper and lower front teeth. Scrub in an up-and-down motion holding the brush handle directly out in front.

debris that encourages bacterial growth, which is most intense 20 minutes after eating. Therefore, the teeth should be cleaned as soon as possible after a meal.

There is no one kind of toothbrush that is best for every person. Most dentists, however, recommend a soft toothbrush with a straight handle and flat brushing surface that can clean the gums without irritating them. As for claims about whether toothbrushes should have bristles with square corners or rounded shapes, a dentist may point out that there are both curved and straight surfaces in the mouth, so what one design offers in advantages may be offset by equivalent disadvantages. There also are special brushes for reaching surfaces of crooked teeth or cleaning missing-tooth areas of the mouth.

Although several different methods may be used effectively, the following is the technique most often recommended. Brush the biting surfaces, or tops, of the back upper and lower teeth. The lines and grooves on these surfaces make them prone to decay. They should be brushed first, before moisture has softened the brush. The cheek and tongue surfaces of the lower teeth are brushed next. Hold the brush parallel to the teeth with the bristle edges angled against and touching the gums. Using short strokes, move the brush back and forth several times before proceeding to the next one or two teeth. Use the same technique on all the inner surfaces of your teeth as well. For the hard-to-brush inner surfaces of the front teeth, hold the handle of the brush out in front of the mouth and apply the tip in an up-and-down motion. For all brushing, a scrubbing motion—but without too much pressure—should be used.

Some people prefer electric toothbrushes, which require less effort to use than ordinary toothbrushes. These are available with two basic motions—up and down and back and forth. Your dentist may advise which kind best serves an individual's needs and proper use of equipment. Some dentists point out that back-and-forth brushing applied with too much pressure can have an abrasive effect on tooth enamel because it works against the grain of the mineral deposits. The American Dental Association also evaluates electric toothbrushes and issues reports on the safety and effectiveness of various types.

Removing Debris with Dental Floss

Brushing often does not clean debris from between the teeth. But plaque and food particles that stick between the teeth usually can be removed with dental floss. A generous length of floss, about 18 inches, is needed to do an effective job. The ends can be wrapped several times around the

Flossing

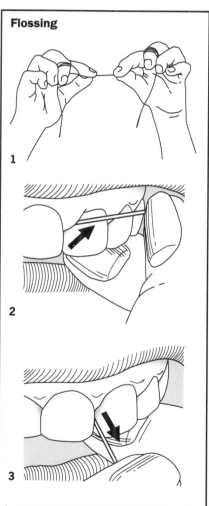

1. Wrap floss several times around middle fingers and pull center section taut between thumbs or index fingers.
2. Insert floss between teeth and gently slide back and forth against every tooth. Work floss into the space between tooth and gumline.
3. To remove, pull floss gently downward along the angle of the tooth. Snapping it in and out may cause gum irritation.

first joint of the middle finger of each hand. Using the thumbs or index fingers, the floss is inserted between the teeth with a gentle, sawing, back-and-forth motion. Then it is slid gently around part of a tooth in the space at the gum line and gently pulled out; snapping the floss in and out may irritate the gums. After brushing and flossing, the mouth should be rinsed with water. A mouthwash is unnecessary, but it may be used for the good taste it leaves in the mouth.

The dentist may recommend the use of an oral irrigating device as part of dental home care. These units produce a pulsating stream of water that flushes food debris from between teeth. They are particularly useful for patients wearing orthodontic braces or for those who have had recession of the gums, creating larger spaces between the teeth.

The person who wants to see the areas of plaque on his teeth can chew a *disclosing tablet,* available at most pharmacies, which leaves a harmless temporary stain on plaque surfaces. Some dentists recommend the use of disclosing tablets about once a week so that patients can check on the effectiveness of their tooth-cleaning techniques.

Tooth Decay

In addition to wear, tear, and injury, the major threat to the health of a tooth is bacteria. Bacteria can cause tooth decay, and the human mouth is a tremendous reservoir of bacteria because the mouth is warm, dark, moist, and usually contains tiny particles of food that help nourish the organisms. The bacteria found in the mouth are of two kinds, *aerobic* and *anaerobic.* Aerobic bacteria need ox-ygen to survive; anaerobic bacteria do not. Anaerobic bacteria can find their way through cracks and crevices into areas of the mouth or teeth where there is little or no oxygen and continue their *cariogenic,* or decay, activity.

Saliva

Saliva offers some protection against the decay germs, for reasons not well understood, but there are crevices and deep pockets around the teeth and gums where saliva does not penetrate. Paradoxically, saliva itself contains millions of different bacterial organisms. Dental scientists have calculated that one ounce of saliva may contain as many as 22 billion bacteria. Even a presumably healthy mouth may contain more than ten varieties of bacteria, plus protozoa and yeast cells. The yeast cells and at least three of the different kinds of bacteria are capable of producing acids that erode the tough enamel surface of a tooth.

Bacterial Acids and Plaque

The acids produced by decay bacteria actually are waste products of the organisms' digestive processes; bacteria, like other living creatures, eventually excrete waste products after a meal. As unpleasant as the thought may be, tooth decay can be the result of feeding a colony of germs in the mouth. Bacterial growth—hence the production of harmful acids—is encouraged by the consumption of too many foods composed of refined sugars. The sugars of candies, cakes, soft drinks, and the like are easier for the bacteria to eat and digest than those of fruits, vegetables, and other less thoroughly processed foods. Even a tiny bit of food remaining in the mouth after a meal may be enough to support many millions of bacteria for 24 hours or more.

An additional contributing factor to tooth decay is *plaque* formation. Plaque is a sticky, transparent substance that forms a film over the surface of the teeth. Plaque forms every day, which is the reason that the teeth must be brushed every day. Plaque frequently begins with deposits of soft food debris along the gum line after a meal; it consists mainly of bacteria and its products. When mixed with mucus, molds, tissue cells from the membranes lining the mouth, and mineral salts, it takes the form of a white, cheesy substance called *materia alba.* If not removed regularly by brushing and the use of dental floss, this substance becomes a thick, sticky mass that has been compared to epoxy cement. Then it becomes a rough-surfaced hard substance with the texture of stone, otherwise known as *dental calculus,* or *tartar.*

Other Causes of Decay

Bacterial acid is not the only way in which the tooth enamel may be damaged to permit the entry of decay bacteria. Certain high-acid foods and improper dental care can erode the molecules of enamel. Temperature extremes also can produce cracks and other damage to the enamel; some dental scientists have suggested that repeated exposure to rapid temperature fluctuations of 50° F., as in eating alternately hot and cold foods or beverages, can cause the enamel to develop cracks.

Complications of Tooth Decay

Once decay activity breaks through the hard enamel surface, the bacteria can attack the dentin. Because the dentin is about 30 percent organic material, compared to 5 percent in the enamel layer, the decay process can advance more rapidly there. If the tooth decay is not stopped at the dentin layer, the disease organisms can enter the pulp chamber, where they will multiply quickly, producing an acute inflammation and, if unchecked, spread through the blood vessels to other parts of the body. Osteomyelitis, an infection of the membrane covering the skeletal bones, and endocarditis, an extremely dangerous heart ailment, are among diseases in other parts of the body that can begin with untreated tooth decay.

Periodontal disease, described below, is another possible complication of tooth decay.

Treatment of Tooth Decay

The portion of a tooth invaded by decay is called a *cavity;* it may be compared to an ulcer that develops because of disease in soft tissues. In treating the decay process, the dentist tries to prevent further destruction of the tooth tissue. The dentist also tries to restore as much as possible the original shape and function of the diseased tooth. The procedure used depends on many factors, including the surfaces affected (enamel, dentin, etc.) and the tooth face and angle involved, as well as whether the cavity is on a smooth area or in a pit or fissure of the tooth surface.

The decayed portions of the tooth are removed with various kinds of carbide burrs and other drill tips, as well as with hand instruments. The dentist may also use a caries removal system that reduces or eliminates drilling. In this system two solutions are combined in one liquid and squirted in a pulsating stream onto the decayed area. The stream does not harm gums or healthy teeth; rather, it softens the caries so that it can easily be scraped away. Used, generally, in conjunction with rotary or hand instruments, the "squirt" sys-

Tooth Restoration

The portion of the tooth affected by decay is known as a *cavity*. After removal of this diseased area (2), using drill, hand instrument, or other method, the dentist fills the cleaned cavity with a base or liner material (3). Finally, the tooth is filled with a restorative substance such as an amalgam, inlay, or ceramic material.

tem may make anesthesia unnecessary.

In other cases an anesthetic may be injected for the comfort of the patient. The dentist usually asks whether the patient prefers to have an anesthetic before work commences. In the cleaning process, an effort is made to remove all traces of diseased enamel or dentin, but no more of the tooth material than is necessary.

The cleaned cavity is generally filled in a layering procedure. The layers of liners and bases used before insertion of the filling are determined by the depth of the cavity and other factors. If pulp is exposed, special materials may be applied to help the pulp recover from the irritation of the procedure and to form a firm base for the amalgam, inlay, or other restorative substance that becomes the filling.

In the 1980s, new ceramic materials came into use for fillings. Many dentists believed that ceramics could provide more natural-looking restorations. With ceramics, also, teeth would be less sensitive to changes of temperature—a problem with some more traditional materials.

Tooth Extraction

When it becomes necessary to re-

move a diseased, damaged, or malpositioned tooth, the procedure is handled as a form of minor surgery, usually with administration of a local anesthetic to the nerves supplying the tooth area. However, there is no standard routine for extraction of a tooth, because of the numerous individual variations associated with each case. The dentist usually has a medical history of the patient available, showing such information as allergies to drugs, and medications used by the patient that might react with those employed in oral surgery. Because the mouth contains many millions of bacteria, all possible precautions are taken to prevent entry of the germs into the tooth socket.

The condition of the patient is checked during and immediately after tooth extraction, in the event that some complication develops. The patient is provided with analgesic (pain-killing) and other needed medications, along with instructions regarding control of any postoperative pain or bleeding. The dentist also may offer special diet information with suggested meals for the recovery period, which usually is quite brief.

Dry Socket

Severe pain may develop several days after a tooth has been extracted if a blood clot that forms in the socket becomes dislodged. The condition, commonly called *dry socket,* can involve infection of the alveolar bone that normally surrounds the roots of the tooth; loss of the clot can expose the bone tissue to the environment and organisms that produce *osteitis,* or inflammation of the bone tissue. Dry socket may be treated by irrigating the socket with warm salt water and packing it with strips of medicated gauze. The patient also is given analgesics, sedatives, and other medications as needed to control the pain and infection.

General anesthetics are sometimes necessary for complicated oral surgery. In such cases, there are available dental offices or clinics that are as well equipped and staffed as hospital operating rooms.

Endodontic Therapy

Tooth extraction because of caries is less common today than in previous years, although an estimated 25 million Americans have had all of their teeth removed. Modern preventive dentistry techniques of *endodontics* now make it possible to save many teeth that would have been extracted in past decades after the spread of decay into the pulp canal. The procedures include *root canal therapy, pulp capping,* and *pulpotomy.*

Root Canal Therapy

Once the tooth has fully developed in the jaw, the nerve is not needed, so if the pulp is infected the nerve as well as the pulp can be removed. Only minor effects are noticeable in the tooth structure after the pulp is removed, and the dentist compensates for these in filling the tooth after root canal therapy.

Briefly, the procedure of root canal

Root Canal Therapy

(1) The first step of root canal, or removal of the nerve of a tooth, begins with examining the infected pulp to determine its vitality. (2) The depth of the root is measured by X ray and, after administering local anesthetic, the dentist extracts the pulp with drill or hand instrument marked to indicate when the end of the root has been reached. (3) When the entire pulp and nerve have been removed the canal is sterilized to prevent infection. (4) After filling the tooth with silver or a tough plastic substance known as *gutta-percha,* or sometimes a combination of both, the dentist then caps the tooth.

---

work begins by examination and testing of the pulp viability. The pulp may be tested by heat, cold, or an electrical device called a *vitalometer,* which measure the degree of sensation the patient feels in a tooth. If the pulp is dead, the patient will feel no sensation, even at the highest output of current.

After the degree of vitality in the pulp has been determined, a local anesthetic is injected and the dentist begins removing the pulp, using rotary drills and hand instruments. By means of X-ray pictures, the dentist measures the length of the root, which may be about one and a half times the length of the crown. Stops or other markers are placed on the root excavation tools to show the dentist when the instrument has reached the end of the root. The canal is then sterilized and filled with gutta-percha—a tough plastic substance—silver, or a combination of the two, and a cap is added.

Pulp Capping

Pulp capping consists of building a cap over the exposed pulp with layers of calcium hydroxide paste, which is covered by zinc oxide and topped with a firm cement.

Pulpotomy

A pulpotomy procedure involves removal of the pulp in the pulp chamber within the crown of the tooth, while leaving the root canal pulp in place. The amputated pulp ends are treated and a pulp-capping procedure is used to restore the crown of the tooth.

Periodontal Disease

It is important in the middle years of life and later to continue good oral-hygiene habits and the practice of having regular dental checkups. Studies have found that after the age of 50 more than half the people in America have periodontal disease. At the age of 65, nearly everybody has this disease.

The Course of the Disease

The combination of bacterial action described above and the roughness of the resulting calculus injures the surrounding gum tissue and makes it susceptible to infection and recession. The irritation causes swelling, inflammation, and bleeding into the crevices between the teeth and gums, which is one of the early signs of impaired tissue health.

The inflammation of the gums, known as *gingivitis,* can spread to the roots of the teeth if not treated. The gums separate from the teeth, forming pockets that fill up with more food particles and colonies of bacteria. As the disease progresses, the bone support for the teeth is weakened and the affected teeth begin to loosen and drift from their normal position. Finally, unless the disease is treated in time, the teeth may be lost.

Periodontal disease is sometimes called *pyorrhea,* a Greek word meaning a discharge of pus. But "pyorrhea" is a somewhat misleading term, because it identifies only one manifestation of the disease, an abscess that usually forms along the side of an affected tooth. In some cases, a membrane forms around the abscess, creating a pus-filled cyst in the tooth socket.

Other Signs and Complications

Another manifestation of periodontal disease is periodontal atrophy, or recession of the gingiva, or gum tissue, and the underlying bone away from the outer layer of the tooth that joins it to its socket. Recession tends to expose the dentin below the gum line, which is not protected by a layer of enamel. The exposed dentin may be hypersensitive to hot or cold foods or beverages, air, and sweet or sour food flavors.

Inflammation of the gingival tissue in periodontal disease may be increased in intensity by toxic chemicals from tobacco smoke, bacterial infections, vitamin deficiencies, and defective dental restorations. The normal pink color of the gingival tissue may be altered by periodontal disease to a bright red or a darker coloration ranging to bluish purple.

The inflamed gingival tissue may lead to a complication called *periodontitis* in which the bone under the gum tissue is gradually destroyed, widening the crevice between the tooth and surrounding tissues. Pregnant women seem particularly vulnerable to periodontitis and gingivitis if they have been experiencing periodontal disorders, because the temporary hormonal imbalance of the pregnancy tends to exaggerate the effects of this condition.

One kind of gingivitis that involves projections of gum tissue between the teeth is sometimes referred to as *trench mouth,* because it was not an uncommon form of periodontal disease affecting soldiers during World War I. The infection is associated with poor oral hygiene, along with nutritional deficiencies and general depressed condition of health.

Causes

At one time it was assumed that periodontal diseases were associated with the life styles of persons living in more technologically advanced societies, where soft, rich foods are eaten regularly, providing materials toward the formation of plaque and support of bacteria in the plaque. But recent investigations show that people living in the less developed nations, who are relatively free of tooth decay, eventually develop periodontal disease. However, this does not alter the fact that the accumulation of plaque and harmful bacteria are the chief causes of periodontal disease, as well as of tooth decay.

Although periodontal disease generally becomes troublesome in middle age, there is some evidence that early symptoms of gingival disorders occur during childhood or adolescence. Also, because more people live longer today, periodontal disease has become more common than in the past.

Bruxism

Bruxism—the nervous habit, often unconsciously done, of clenching and grinding the teeth—can contribute to the development of periodontal disease. Bruxism frequently occurs during sleep.

Malocclusion

Another contributing cause to periodontal disease is repeated shock or undue pressure on a tooth because of

---

Periodontal Disease

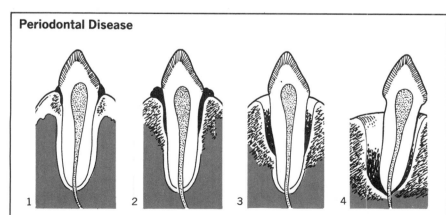

(1) If allowed to build up at the gumline, deposits of plaque and calculus result in damage to the gum tissues (periodontal disease). (2) As gums become increasingly irritated and inflamed, they may bleed easily and begin to recede from the tooth itself. (3) Untreated, the inflammation spreads to the roots of the teeth. Bacteria and particles of food lodge in the pockets between tooth and gums, aggravating the condition. (4) A tooth held by the diseased gum loses most of its bony support structure, causing it to loosen and move out of position. Eventually, such teeth may need to be extracted.

malocclusion, or an improper bite. This effect accelerates damage to the tooth and gum structure during such simple activities as biting and chewing.

Treatment

Periodontal treatment may include a variety of techniques ranging from plaque removal to oral surgery to form new contours on the alveolar bone surrounding the tooth. If treatment is not begun until periodontal disease is well advanced, it may be difficult to fit replacement teeth, or *dentures,* as substitutes for lost teeth. Dentures fit over the ridges of the jaws, and if the top edge of the ridge has been destroyed by periodontal disease, the procedure for holding the denture firmly in place will be complicated.

Dental Implants & Dentures

If it becomes necessary to have some teeth removed, they should be replaced as soon as possible with dental implants, a bridge, or partial or full dentures.

Why Missing Teeth Must Be Replaced

Most patients show some concern over the replacement of natural teeth with dentures, associating the loss of teeth with old age in the same way that others resist wearing eyeglasses or using a hearing aid. Millions of persons of all ages have improved their eating, speaking, and physical appearance by obtaining attractive and well-fitted dental implants or dentures. Also, each tooth functions to hold the teeth opposite and on either side in place. Missing teeth would mean shifting teeth and a host of other problems. For example, food particles could lodge in the spaces created by the shifting teeth, followed by the formation of plaque and the development of periodontal disease, resulting in the loss of additional teeth.

Dental Implants

Dental implants, or *osseointegration,* are an effective alternative to ordinary dentures because they serve as substitutes for natural tooth roots that rely on the jawbone for support. Implants are capable of supporting dentures or replacing individual teeth or bridges.

Although physicians have been experimenting with dental implants for centuries, researchers only recently developed the most advanced version of the implant using titanium, whose primary advantage is that bone tissue actually fuses to it.

An implant consists of a small post that protrudes from the gum tissue and is anchored either in the jaw bone (endosseous) or fitted directly over the jaw bone (subperiosteal). Prosthetic teeth are attached to the posts. These prosthetic teeth can be perma-

nent or removable; cleaning and care depends upon the type.

While they tend to cost more than dentures, dental implants are more secure, easier to maintain, and less likely to irritate the gums or harm adjacent natural teeth.

Because it is a surgical procedure that can take up to three visits over a period of several months, most implant surgeries occur in two stages. First, the general dentist or oral surgeon implants the metal "roots" and then, in a second surgery, attaches the metal posts with the prosthetic teeth. Consult with your dentist to determine if this procedure is compatible with your dental problems.

Fitting of Dentures

Modern techniques and materials of construction and the skill of modern dentists should assure well-fitting, natural looking dentures. The dentist selects the tooth shade and shape that are best for an individual's face size, contours, and coloring. No one, however, has perfectly arranged, perfectly white natural teeth. Tooth coloring depends upon genetic factors and changes as one grows older.

Bridges and Partial Dentures

Several different types of dental appliances may be constructed to fill empty spaces. Some, such as dental bridges, may be cemented to the remaining natural teeth. Others, such as complete sets of dentures, are removable.

A bridge may be made entirely of gold, a combination of gold and porcelain, or combinations of gold and porcelain and other materials. If there is a sound natural tooth on either side of

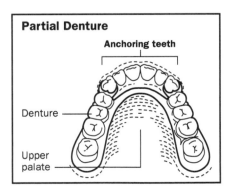

Partial Denture

Anchoring teeth

Denture

Upper palate

the space, a *pontic*, or suitable substitute for the missing tooth, may be fused to the metal bridge. The crown retainer on either side of the pontic may then be cemented to crowns of the neighboring natural teeth.

If there are no natural teeth near the space created by an extracted tooth, a partial denture may be constructed to replace the missing teeth. This appliance usually fastens by a clasp onto the last tooth on each side of the space. A bar on the inside of the front teeth provides stability for the partial denture. A "Maryland bridge," a fixed partial denture, eliminates the need for crowns to anchor false teeth.

A removable partial denture should be taken out and cleaned with special brushes whenever the natural teeth are brushed. Your dentist should check bridges and partial dentures periodically to make sure they have not become loosened. A loose clasp of a partial denture can rock the teeth to which the device is attached, causing damage and possible loss.

New materials have brought bonding into more common use as an alternative to crowning and for cosmetically restoring chipped, malformed, stained, or widely spaced teeth. In the bonding process the dentist applies first liquid plastic and then thin layers of tooth-colored plastics known as composite resins. The layers are sculpted and polished.

Complete Dentures

Before a full set of removable dentures is constructed, the dentist determines whether there are any abnormalities in the gum ridges, such as cysts or tooth root tips that may have to be removed. If the gums are in poor condition, treatments may be needed to improve the surfaces of the ridges on which the dentures will be fitted. The dentist may also have to reconstruct the bone underlying the gums—the alveolar ridge. Human bone "harvested" from another part of the patient's body were used in such reconstruction for decades, but have been replaced by ceramic materials such as arehydroxylapatite and beta tricalcium phosphate.

The dentist now makes an impression of the patient's mouth. Tooth and shade choices are discussed. Several other appointments may be arranged before the new dentures are delivered to the patient, either for "try-ins" of dentures as they are being constructed and for adjustments after completion of the set.

Although dentures do not change with age, the mouth does. Therefore, it is necessary for the denture-wearer to have occasional check-ups during which the dentist examines oral tissues for irritation, determines how the dentures fit with respect to possible changing conditions of the mouth, and if a replacement should be recommended. The dentist also seeks to correct any irritations of the oral tissues of the mouth and polishes the dentures, making them smooth and easier to clean between check-ups.

Care of Dentures

Dentures should be cleaned daily with a denture brush and toothpaste; once a week they should be soaked for seven or eight hours in a denture cleaner. To avoid breaking them during the brushing process, fill a wash basin with water and place it under the dentures while they are being cleaned; if they are dropped, the dentures will be cushioned by the water. A harsh abrasive that could scratch the denture surface should not be used. Scratches allow stains to penetrate the surface of the dentures, creating permanent discoloration.

The use of adhesives and powders is only a temporary solution to ill-fitting dentures. In time, the dentist may rebuild the gum side of the denture to conform with the shape of the patient's gum ridge. The patient should never try to make his own changes in the fit of dentures. Rebuilding the gum side of the dentures, or relining, as it is called, usually begins with a soft temporary material if the patient's gums are in poor condition, and requires several appointments over a period of two or three weeks while the gum tissues are being restored to good health.

Orthodontics

*O*rthodontics is a term derived from the Greek words for straight, or normal, teeth. Straight teeth are easier to keep clean and they make chewing food more efficient. There also is a cosmetic benefit in being able to display a smile with a set of straight teeth, although many dentists consider the cosmetic aspect of orthodontics as secondary to achieving proper occlusion, or bite.

Causes of Improper Bite

Orthodontic problems can be caused by hereditary factors, by an infectious or other kind of disease, by the premature loss of primary teeth, by the medications used in treatment, or by individual factors such as injury or loss of permanent teeth. A person may have congenitally missing teeth resulting in spaces that permit drifting

Improper Bite

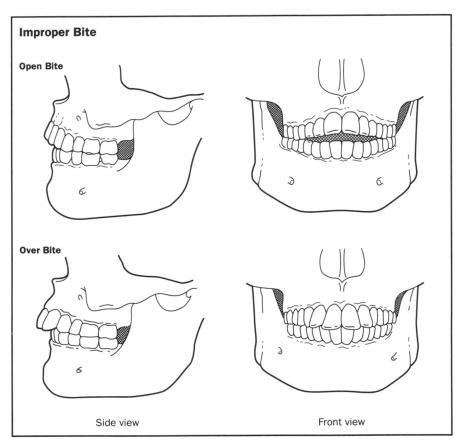

Open Bite

Over Bite

Side view   Front view

In the normal or ideal occlusion positions of the teeth, the first and second permanent upper molars fit just slightly behind the same molars of the lower jaw; all of the teeth of the upper jaw are in contact with their counterparts of the lower jaw. In this pattern of occlusion, all of the biting surfaces are aligned for optimum use of their intended functions of cutting, tearing, or grinding.

There are numerous variations of malocclusion, but generally, in simple deformities, the teeth of the upper jaw are in contact with lower jaw teeth once removed from normal positions. Other variations include an *open bite,* in which the upper and lower incisors do not contact each other, or *closed bite,* in which there is an abnormal degree of overlapping (*overbite*) of the front teeth.

Diagnosis is made with the help of X-ray pictures, photographs of the face and mouth, medical histories, and plaster models of the patient's teeth and jaws. The plaster models are particularly important because the dentist can use them to make experimental reconstructions without touching an actual tooth of a patient. For example, the dentist can remove one or more teeth from the plaster model and reorganize neighboring teeth in the jawbones to get an accurate representation of the effects of extracting teeth or forcing teeth into different developmental situations.

Orthodontic Appliances

Once a plan of orthodontic treatment has been determined by the dentist, he may choose from a dozen or more types of bands, braces, or other orthodontic appliances, some removable and some nonremovable, for shaping the teeth and jaws of the patient. A typical orthodontic appliance may include small curved strips or loops of metal cemented to the surfaces of the

of neighboring teeth or collapse of the dental arch. Or he may develop extra (supernumerary) teeth resulting from an inherited factor. The supernumerary teeth may develop during the early years of life while the deciduous teeth are in use. A supernumerary tooth may force permanent teeth into unnatural positions.

Nutritional disorders can also affect the development of jaws and teeth, while certain medications can cause abnormal growth of gingival, or gum, tissues, resulting in increased spaces between the teeth.

Teeth that erupt too early or too late, primary teeth that are too late in falling out when permanent teeth have developed, and habits such as grinding of the teeth, thumb-sucking, or pushing the tongue against the teeth are among other factors that can result in *malocclusion,* or improper bite, and the need for orthodontic treatment.

Diagnosis of Orthodontic Problems

Each child should visit a dentist before the eruption of his permanent teeth for an examination that may determine the need for orthodontic treatment. Because there are many genetic and other influences that help shape the facial contours and occlusion of each individual, there are no standard orthodontic procedures that apply to any or all children. The dentist may recommend what treatment, if any, would be needed to produce normal occlusion and when it should begin; some dentists advise only that necessary procedures for correcting malocclusion be started before the permanent set of teeth (excluding wisdom teeth) has become established, or around the age of 12 or 13. However, there are few age limits for orthodontic care, and an increasing number of adults are receiving treatment today for malocclusion problems that were neglected during childhood.

Orthodontic Appliance

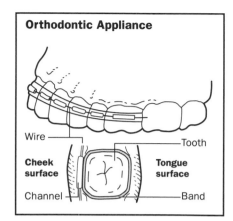

teeth as anchors for arch wires that pass around the dental arch. Springs and specially designed rubber bands, called elastics, are sometimes used to bring about alignment of the two jaws, or to align teeth within a dental arch.

In addition to the appliances that are attached to and between the upper and lower dental arches, the dentist may prescribe the use of an elastic tape device with a strap that fits around the back of the patient's neck and is attached also to the arch wire inside the mouth, thus providing a force from outside the mouth to bring teeth into alignment.

Orthodontic appliances are custom-designed and built for the individual patient. This requires several rather long sessions or one all-day session in the dental chair while the appliance is being organized and properly anchored. Thereafter, the patient must return at regular intervals spaced a few weeks to a month apart so the dentist can make adjustments in the appliance, determine if any of the bands have pulled away from tooth surfaces, and prevent plaque from building up in places that the braces may make impervious to brushing.

The patient, meanwhile, must follow a diet that prohibits sticky foods or items that may damage the appliance or any of its parts. A conscientious program of oral hygiene, including regular cleaning by the dentist or hygienist, also is necessary because, as indicated above, it is more difficult to do a thorough job of cleaning the teeth when orthodontic appliances are in the mouth.

Orthodontics for Adults

Although orthodontic treatment originally was applied only to children, the technique has been requested with increasing frequency for the correction of a variety of facial and dental disorders. Receding chins, buck teeth, sunken cheeks, sunken mouths, and other abnormalities have been treated successfully in adults beyond the age of 40. Orthodontists have observed that adult patients usually are more patient and cooperative during the long periods of treatment than youngsters.

The upper age limit for orthodontic work has not really been established, but doctors at the National Institute of Dental Research believe it is possible to treat adult patients with protrusion of the upper jaw and related disfigurements until the age of 70. This is possible because the upper jaw does not completely unite with the frontal bone of the skull, according to the experts, until after the age of 70 in most people.

Orthodontic treatments can be relatively expensive and involve many visits to a dentist's office over a long period of time. Any parent of a prospective patient or a responsible older patient seeking orthodontic work for himself should have a frank discussion with the dentist regarding the time and money to be invested in the corrective procedures before making an agreement to begin the work. In nearly every case some arrangement can be made for covering the costs of dental work that is vital to the health and welfare of a patient.

23

Aches, Pains, Nuisances, Worries

And Other Things You Can Live With But Could Get Along Very Well Without

None of the variety of discomforts discussed in this chapter is a laughing matter. The best thing about most of them is that they will pass, given your commonsense attention, or will disappear if you follow your physician's advice. This includes taking the medications prescribed by your physician exactly as directed. In a few cases, such as allergies or gout, long-term drug therapy may be necessary on a self-supervised basis, once treatment has been established by a physician. Of course, when symptoms of any kind persist or get worse, you should waste no time in seeking a professional diagnosis.

There may be somebody, somewhere, who has never felt rotten a day in his life. But most of us are not so fortunate. Among the most common nuisance ailments are:

- upper respiratory infections
- allergies
- occasional headaches
- backaches
- weight problems
- weather discomforts
- disturbances of normal sleep patterns
- aching feet
- indigestion

The unpleasant feeling associated with any of these common disorders can almost always be banished with a modicum of care and thought. For example, allergic reactions to particular foods can be curtailed by identifying the offending food and avoiding it. Self-diagnosis and self-discipline can often enable one to cope with weight problems. A backache may be cured by attention to posture, or adjusting your office chair. A sensible approach to clothing and exposure can often do away with weather discomforts.

For many minor disorders and discomforts, particularly those caused by stress, massage may be the answer. Massage is a process that is at least 3,000 years old and has been used to help relieve tension, increase muscle tone, improve blood and oxygen circulation, and aid major body functions. Massage has also helped alleviate aches and pains resulting from exercise, improve posture, and increase joint flexibility. Among the disorders for which massage should not be used are osteoporosis, varicose veins, inflamed joints, herniated discs, tumors, and some cardiovascular problems.

Massage invariably involves kneading, manipulation, and methodical pressure on various body parts. The process should never be painful. The three kinds of massage in most common use are Swedish, a pleasant, muscle-kneading procedure; Shiatsu, or "acupressure," which depends on finger and hand pressure on so-called energy meridians in the body; and reflexology, a system that calls for pressure on various points of the foot.

When symptoms do not respond to

self-help—as when sporadic difficulty in sleeping burgeons into a string of near-sleepless nights, or when abdominal pain you interpret as indigestion is intense or frequent in spite of avoiding rich or heavy foods, it's time to see a physician.

The Common Cold and Upper Respiratory Infections

Common cold is the label attached to a group of symptoms that can be caused by one or more of some 20 different viruses. Colds are considered highly contagious, but some physicians think that people don't entirely catch others' colds—in a sense they catch their own. While the viruses that carry the infection are airborne and practically omnipresent, somebody in good health is usually less susceptible to a cold than someone who is run down. Both environmental factors (such as air pollution) and emotional ones (such as anxiety or depression) seem to increase susceptibility.

Symptoms

Symptoms differ from person to person and from cold to cold with the same person. Generally, a cold starts with sneezes, a running nose, teary eyes, and a stuffed head. Sometimes the nasal membranes become so swollen that a person can breathe only through the mouth; sometimes the senses of smell and taste simply disappear. The throat may be sore; a postnasal drip may cause a constant cough when the person is lying down at night.

When these symptoms are acute and are accompanied by fever and aching joints, the illness is usually referred to as influenza or "the flu." There are many different viruses that cause influenza, and new ones are always turning up. Unfortunately, there is as yet no medicine that can cure either a cold or a flu attack, although many people do get relief from symptoms by taking various cold remedies. Antibiotics are sometimes prescribed by doctors to prevent more serious bacterial diseases, such as pneumonia, from developing, but antibiotics are not effective against the cold viruses.

Treatment

Some people can get away with treating a cold with contempt and an occasional aspirin, and go about their business. Others are laid low for a few days. If you are the type who is really hit hard by a cold, it isn't coddling yourself to stay home for a couple of days. In any event, a simple cold usually runs its course, lasting anywhere from a few days to two weeks.

Discomfort can be minimized and recovery speeded by a few simple steps: extra rest and sleep, drinking more liquids than usual, and taking one or two aspirin tablets every four hours. Antihistamine preparations or nose drops should be avoided unless specifically prescribed by a physician.

A painful sore throat accompanied by fever, earache, a dry, hacking cough, or pains in the chest are symptoms that should be brought to the attention of a physician.

Prevention

Although taking massive doses of vitamin C at the first sign of a cold is said by some authorities to prevent the infection from developing, there is not yet general agreement on the effectiveness of this treatment.

Actually, there are several commonsense ways of reducing the risk of infection, particularly for those people who are especially susceptible to catching a cold. For most people, getting a proper amount of sleep, eating sensibly, avoiding exposure to sudden chill, trying to stay out of crowds, and trying to keep emotional tensions under control can increase resistance to colds and other minor respiratory infections.

Inoculation against particular types of viruses is recommended by many physicians in special cases: for pregnant women, for the elderly, and for those people who have certain chronic heart and lung diseases. Flu shots are effective against a particular virus or viruses for a limited period.

Allergies

Discomforts of various kinds are considered allergies when they are brought on by substances or conditions that ordinarily are harmless. Not too long ago, perturbed allergy sufferers would say things like:

"I can't use that soap because it gives me hives."

"Smelling roses makes me sneeze."

"Eating almonds gives me diarrhea."

Nowadays, such complaints are commonly recognized as indications of allergies.

Symptoms

Allergic symptoms can range from itching eyes, running nose, coughing, difficulty in breathing, welts on the skin, nausea, cramps, and even going into a state of shock, depending upon the severity of the allergic individual's response. Almost any part or system of the body may be affected, and almost anything can pose an allergic threat to somebody.

Allergens

Substances that trigger an allergic reaction are called *allergens.* The system of an allergic individual reacts to such substances as if they were germs, producing *antibodies* whose job it is to neutralize the allergens. But the body's defense mechanism overreacts: in the process of fighting off the effects of the allergens, various chemicals, particularly *histamines,* are dumped indiscriminately into the bloodstream. It is the overabundance of these "good" chemicals that causes the discomforts associated with allergies.

Allergens are usually placed in the following categories:

- Those that affect the respiratory tract, or *inhalants,* such as pollens, dust, smoke, perfumes, and various airborne, malodorous chemicals. These bring on sneezing, coughing, and breathing impairment.

- Food substances that affect the digestive system, typically eggs, seafood, nuts, berries, chocolate, and pork. These may cause not only nausea and diarrhea but also hives and other skin rashes.

- Medicines and drugs, such as penicillin, or a particular serum used in inoculations.

- Agents that act on the skin and mucous membranes, such as insecticides, poison oak, and poison ivy, particular chemical dyes, cosmetics, soaps, metals, leathers, and furs.

- Environmental agents, such as sunlight or excessive cold.

- Microbes, such as particular bacteria, viruses, and parasites.

Treatment

In general, approaches to treatment for allergies fall into three categories: removing or avoiding as many allergens from the environment as possible; using creams, inhalers, pills, and other medications to control the symptoms; and undergoing immunotherapy (allergy shots) to reduce the allergic response. The type of treatment selected often depends on test findings that indicate what is causing the allergic reaction; the tests may produce such identification quickly or they may have to be continued for weeks or months before the allergen is finally tracked down.

As soon as the source of the allergen is identified, the obvious course is to avoid it, if possible. Avoidance may not, however, be possible. Few persons can avoid breathing pollen in the spring and fall. Giving up a house pet may be almost as difficult, but may be necessary as a health or comfort measure.

New medications that control the symptoms of allergies have been marketed in recent years. Newer antihistamines, for example, relieve allergic reactions but do not cause the drowsiness associated with earlier medications. Other medicines that have been used to treat allergies include adrenaline, ephedrine, and cortisone. Aerosol drugs may be used to attack specific symptoms. Some, for example, may be inhaled to treat the linings of the nose and throat.

In addition to histamines, other body chemicals are released during an allergy "attack." Researchers have found that these chemicals include leukotrienes. Consequently, antileukotrienes have tested as medications.

Direct or specific immunotherapy constitutes the third approach to treatment of allergy. The shots are effective in reducing allergic responses. A person with a substance allergy receives increasing amounts of the substance over a period of years. For example, a person who is allergic to insect stings receives injections of the particular insect's venom.

A life-threatening allergic reaction calls for emergency treatment, usually with adrenalin. Physicians suggest that persons with very intense food allergies or who are allergic to insect stings should carry special kits that include an adrenalin-filled syringe. The allergy victims administer the medication to themselves in case of *anaphylaxis* — an acute, life-threatening response (see "Allergic Shock" in Ch. 31, *Medical Emergencies*).

Persons subject to severe, disabling allergy attacks by a known allergen should also carry a card describing both the allergen and the allergic reactions. Detailed information on the latest developments in allergy treatment is available from the Asthma and Allergy Foundation of America, 1302 18th St., NW, Suite 800, Washington, DC 20036. See also Ch. 24, *Allergies and Hypersensitivities*.

Headaches

The common headache is probably as ancient as primitive man. The headache, a pain or ache across the forehead or within the head, may be severe or mild in character, and can last anywhere from under half an hour to three or four days. It may be accompanied by dizziness, nausea, nasal stuffiness, or difficulty in seeing or hearing. It is not a disease or illness but a symptom.

Causes

Headaches in today's modern world can arise from any of a number of underlying causes. These include excessive drinking or smoking, lack of sleep, hunger, drug abuse, and eyestrain. Eyestrain commonly results from overuse of the eyes, particularly under glaring light, or from failure to correct defective vision.

Treatments for headaches are as varied as the causes of headaches. Diagnosis may take some time, but if you suffer from severe or chronic headaches, it is important to consult your doctor. Headaches may point to an underlying problem, such as high blood pressure.

Headaches that are non-debilitating may be treated with analgesics such as aspirin or ibuprofen. Debilitating headaches such as tension, migraine, or cluster headaches can be treated with prescription drugs if your doctor advises it.

Chronic headaches should be diagnosed so the sufferer does not have to always depend on medication to treat the problem. Long-term solutions may include meditation, relaxation exercises, and exercise to reduce tension and stress. Dietary changes such as eliminating chocolate, caffeine, cheese, alcohol, sugar, or other products may also help.

Migraine

Migraine, also called *sick headache,* is a particularly severe, intense kind of headache. An attack may last several days and necessitate bed rest. Dizziness, sensitivity to light, and chills may accompany a migraine headache.

The exact cause of migraine is unknown, but researchers suspect a hereditary link, since the majority of migraine patients have one or more close relatives with migraine.

Migraine headaches can occur from changes in body hormone balances, sudden body temperature changes, bright light or noise, shifts in barometric pressure, and alcohol and drug use. It may also be caused by a combination of these triggers.

For chronic migraine sufferers, keeping a daily journal of food consumed, activities done, emotional status, and (for women) menstrual cy-

cles, may help provide an indication of why migraines occur.

Migraines can be avoided by eliminating any apparent triggers. The fluctuation in estrogen is believed to be a major cause of migraines. Some foods only bring on headaches during certain times of the menstrual cycle. Hormone replacement therapy, some types of birth control pills, and menopause may increase incidence of migraines, although menopause may also end migraines in women who had them for years.

Tension Headaches

Tension headaches are characterized by a painful pressure in the head. Such headaches can be caused by stress, depression, or poor posture and should be treated with analgesics such as aspirin and ibuprofen, a massage or a cold shower. Tension headaches can occur at any time; you can even wake up with one. The best long-term treatment is learning to reduce or manage the stress in your life.

Cluster Headaches

Cluster headaches cause pain around a specific area of the head, and eye tearing, nasal stuffiness, and a burning sensation on the side of the head affected. The headaches usually last only a few hours but are usually described as excruciating. These headaches usually occur after a person has fallen asleep and typically affect men and heavy smokers. Since the pain is resistant to over-the-counter medicine, cluster headaches can be treated with corticosteroids, such as prednisone, or inhaling 100 percent oxygen.

Backaches

"Oh, my aching back" is probably the most common complaint among peo-

ple past the age of 40. Most of the time, the discomfort—wherever it occurs, up or down the backbone—can be traced to some simple cause. However, there are continuous backaches that have their origin in some internal disorder that needs the attention of a physician. Among the more serious causes are kidney or pancreas disease, spinal arthritis, and peptic ulcer.

Some Common Causes

Generally a backache is the result of strain on the muscles, nerves, or ligaments of the spine. It can occur because of poor posture, carelessness in lifting or carrying heavy packages, sitting in one position for a long time in the wrong kind of chair, or sleeping on a mattress that is too soft. Backache often accompanies menstruation, and is common in the later stages of pregnancy. Emotional tension can also bring on back pain.

Prevention

In general, maintaining good posture during the waking hours and sleeping on a hard mattress at night—if necessary, inserting a bed board between the mattress and bedsprings—are the first line of defense against backaches. Anyone habitually carrying heavy loads of books or groceries, or even an overloaded attach;aae case, should make a habit of shifting the weight from arm to arm so that the spine doesn't always get pulled in one direction. Workers who are sedentary for most of the day at a desk or factory table should be sure that the chair they sit in provides firm support for back muscles and is the right height for the working surface.

Treatment

Most cases of simple backache respond to rest, aspirin, and the application of heat, applied by a hot water bottle or heating pad. In cases where the pain persists or becomes more acute, a physician should be consulted. He may find that the trouble is caused by the malfunctioning of an internal organ, or by pressure on the sciatic nerve (*sciatica*). With X rays he may also locate a slipped disk or other abnormality in the alignment of the vertebrae of the spine. See "Back Pain and Its Causes" in Ch. 7, *Diseases of the Skeletal System.*

Weight Problems

A few people can maintain the weight that is right for their body build without ever having to think about it. However, most experts believe that just about half the people in the United States may be risking shorter lives because they are too heavy. By one estimate, approximately one out of five American men and one out of four American women are 10 percent or more overweight, a group that may be called the borderline obese.

There is no longer any reasonable doubt that, if you are overweight, you have statistically a greater chance of high blood pressure, diabetes, and *atherosclerosis* (lumpy deposits in the arteries). And because atherosclerotic heart disease alone accounts for 20 percent of deaths among adults in the United States, it is understandable why physicians consider weight truly a national problem.

Causes

In practically all cases, weighing too much is the result of eating too much and exercising too little. In many cases, the food eaten is of the wrong kind and leisure time is used for riding around in a car rather than walking, or for watching television rather than playing tennis.

Many people like to think that they weigh too much only because they happen to like good food; but the real explanations may be considerably more complicated. In some cases, overeating has been found to have emotional sources: feelings of inadequacy; the need to compensate for a lack of affection or approval, or an unconscious desire to ward off the attention of the opposite sex. Psychological weight problems of this kind can be helped by consulting a psychiatrist or psychologist.

Treatment

There are many overweight people who merely need the support and encouragement that come from participating in a group effort, and for them, joining one of the various weight-control organizations can be extremely beneficial in taking off extra pounds and keeping them off.

Permanent results are rarely achieved by crash diets, faddish food combinations, or reducing pills. Not only are such solutions usually temporary; they may actually be harmful. See "Weight" in Ch. 27, *Nutrition and Weight Control,* for further information about weight problems.

Weather Discomforts

Using good sense about clothing, exercise, and proper diet is probably our best protection against the discomforts caused by extremes of temperature. Sometimes circumstances make this exercise of good sense impossible, with unpleasant but rarely serious results, if treatment is promptly administered. Following are some of the more common disorders resulting from prolonged exposure to excessive heat or cold, and what you can do to alleviate them.

Heat Cramps

In a very hot environment, a person may drink great quantities of water while "sweating buckets" of salty perspiration. Thus, the body's water is replaced, but its salt is not. This salt-water imbalance results in a feeling of faintness and dizziness accompanied by acute stomach cramps and muscle pains in the legs. When the symptoms are comparatively mild, they can be relieved by taking coated salt tablets in five-to-ten-grain doses with a full glass of tepid or cool—not iced—water. Salt tablets along with plenty of fluids should be taken regularly as a preventive measure by people who sweat a great deal during hot weather.

Sunburn

If you have not yet been exposed to much sun, as at the beginning of summer, limit your exposure at first to a period of 15 to 20 minutes, and avoid the sun at the hours around midday even if the sky is overcast. Remember, too, that the reflection of the sun's rays from water and beach sand intensifies their effect. Some suntan lotions give effective protection against burning, and some creams even prevent tanning; but remember to cover all areas of exposed skin and to reapply the lotion when it's been washed away after a swim.

Treatment

A sunburn is treated like any other burn, depending upon its severity. See "Burns" in Ch. 31, *Medical Emergencies.* If there is blistering, take care to avoid infection. Extensive blistering requires a physician's attention.

Heat Exhaustion

This condition is different from heatstroke or sunstroke, discussed below. Heat exhaustion sets in when large quantities of blood accumulate in the skin as the body's way of increasing its cooling mechanism during exposure to high temperatures. This in turn lowers the amount of blood circulating through the heart and decreases the blood supply to the brain. If severe enough, fainting may result. Other symptoms of heat exhaustion include unusual pallor and profuse cold perspiration. The pulse may be weak, and breathing shallow.

Treatment

A person suspected of having heat exhaustion should be placed in a reclining position, his clothing loosened or removed, and his body cooled with moist cloths applied to his forehead and wrists. If he doesn't recover promptly from a fainting spell, smelling salts can be held under his nose to revive him. As soon as he is conscious, he can be given salt tablets and a cool sugary drink—either tea or coffee—to act as a stimulant. Don't give the patient any alcoholic beverages.

Sunstroke or Heatstroke

Sunstroke is much more of an emergency than heat exhaustion and requires immediate attention. The characteristic symptom is extremely high body temperature brought on by cessation of perspiration. If hot, dry, flushed skin turns ashen gray, a physician must be called immediately. Too much physical activity during periods of high temperature and high humidity is a direct contributing cause.

Treatment

See "Heatstroke" in Ch. 31, *Medical Emergencies,* for a description of the

emergency treatment recommended for this condition.

Chapped Skin

One of the most widespread discomforts of cold weather is *chapped skin.* In low temperatures, the skin's sebaceous glands produce fewer oils that lubricate and protect the skin, causing it to become dry. Continued exposure results in reddening and cracking. In this condition, the skin is especially sensitive to strong soaps.

Treatment

During cold, dry weather, less soap should be used when washing, a bath oil should be used when bathing, and a mild lotion or creme should be applied to protect the skin from the damaging effects of wind and cold. A night cream or lotion containing lanolin is also helpful, and the use of cleansing cream or oil instead of soap can reduce additional discomfort when cleansing chapped areas. The use of a colorless lip pomade is especially recommended for children when they play out of doors in cold, dry weather for any length of time.

Chilblain

A *chilblain* is a local inflammation of the skin brought on by exposure to cold. The condition commonly affects people overly sensitive to cold because of poor circulation. When the hands, feet, face, and ears are affected, the skin in these areas itches and burns, and may swell and turn reddish blue.

Treatment

The best way to avoid chilblains is to wear appropriate clothing during cold weather, especially warm socks,

gloves, and ear coverings. The use of bed socks and a heating pad at night is also advisable. Once indoors, cold, wet feet should be dried promptly, gently, and thoroughly. Rubbing or massaging should be avoided, because these can cause further irritation. People who suffer from repeated attacks of chilblains should consult a physician for diagnosis of circulatory problems.

Frostbite

Frostbite is a considerably more serious condition than chilblains, because it means that a part or parts of the body have actually been frozen. The fingers or toes, the nose, and the ears are most vulnerable. If frostbitten, these areas turn numb and pale and feel cold when touched. The dangerous thing about frostbite is that pain may not be a warning. If the condition is not treated promptly, the temperature inside the tissues keeps going down and eventually cuts off blood circulation to the overexposed parts of the body. In such extreme cases, there is a possible danger of gangrene.

Treatment

In mild cases, prompt treatment can slowly restore blood circulation. The frozen parts should be rewarmed *slowly* by covering them with warm clothing or by soaking them in lukewarm water. Nothing hot should be applied—neither hot water nor a heating pad. Nor should the patient be placed too close to a fireplace or radiator. Because the affected tissues can be easily bruised, they should not be massaged or rubbed. If you are in doubt about restoring circulation, a physician should be called promptly or the patient taken to a hospital for emergency treatment.

Sleep and the Lack of It

Until rather recently, it was assumed that sleep was the time when the body rested and recovered from the activities of wakefulness. Although there is still a great deal to learn about why we sleep and what happens when we are sleeping, medical researchers have now identified several different phases of sleep, all of them necessary over the long run, but some more crucial than others.

How much sleep a person needs varies a great deal from individual to individual; and the same individual may need more or less at different times. Children need long periods of unbroken sleep; the elderly seem to get along on very little. No matter what a person's age, too little sleep over too long a time leads to irritability, exhaustion, and giddiness.

Insomnia

Almost everybody has gone through periods when it is difficult or impossible to fall asleep. Excitement before bedtime, temporary worries about a pressing problem, spending a night in an unfamiliar place, changing to a different bed, illness, physical discomfort because of extremes of temperature—any of these circumstances can interfere with normal sleep patterns.

But this is quite different from *chronic insomnia,* when a person consistently has trouble falling asleep for no apparent reason. If despite all your commonsense approaches insomnia persists, a physician should be consulted about the advisability of taking a tranquilizer or a sleeping pill. Barbiturates should not be taken unless prescribed by a physician.

The Vulnerable Extremities

Aches and pains in the legs and feet occur for a wide variety of reasons, some trivial and easily corrected, others serious enough to require medical attention. Those that originate in such conditions as arthritis and rheumatism can often be alleviated by aspirin or some of the newer prescription medications.

Gout

Gout, which is usually a metabolic disorder, is a condition that especially affects the joint of the big toe, and sometimes the ankle joint, causing the area to become swollen, hot, and acutely painful. Although the specific cause of gout is not yet clearly understood, the symptoms can be alleviated by special medication prescribed by a physician. An attack of gout can be triggered by a wide variety of causes: wearing the wrong shoes, eating a diet too rich in fats, getting a bad chill, surgery in some other part of the body, or chronic emotional anxiety, as well as the use of certain medicines, such as diuretics ("water-pills"). See also "Gout" in Ch. 7, *Diseases of the Skeletal System.*

Fallen Arches

Fallen arches can cause considerable discomfort because the body's weight is carried on the ligaments of the inside of the foot rather than on the sole. When the abnormality is corrected by orthopedic shoes with built-in arches for proper support, the pressure on the ligaments is relieved. A physician rather than a shoe salesman should be consulted for a reliable diagnosis. In some cases, the physician may also recommend special exercises to strengthen the arch.

Flat Feet

Flat feet can usually be revealed by a simple test—making a footprint on level earth or hard-packed sand. If the print is solid rather than indented by a curve along the big-toe side of the foot, the foot is flat. Aching ligaments in the area of the instep are often a result, but can be relieved by proper arch supports inside the shoes. Corrective arch supports are particularly important for young children, for anyone who is overweight, and for anyone who has to stand a great deal of the time.

Blisters

Although blisters are sometimes a sign of allergy, fungus infection, or sunburn, they most commonly appear on the feet because of the friction of a shoe or of hosiery that does not fit properly. A *water blister* is a collection of lymph that forms inside the upper level of the skin; a *blood blister* goes down deeper and contains some blood released from broken capillaries. A normal amount of walking in shoes and hosiery that fit comfortably—neither too loose nor too tight—rarely results in blisters. When blisters do appear, it is best to protect them from further friction by the use of a sterile bandage strip.

Treatment

A blister that causes acute pain when one is walking can be treated as follows: after cleaning the area with soap and water, pat it dry and swab it with rubbing alcohol. Sterilize the tip of a needle in a flame, let it cool a little, and then puncture the edge of the blister, absorbing the liquid with a sterile gauze. The loose skin can be removed with manicure scissors that have been sterilized by boiling for ten minutes. The surface of raw skin should then be covered with an adhesive bandage. This procedure is best done before bedtime so that healing can begin before shoes are worn again.

If redness appears around the area of any blister and inflammation appears to be spreading, a physician should be consulted promptly.

Bunions

A *bunion* is a deformation in the part of the foot that is joined by the big toe. The swelling and pain at the joint is caused by inflammation of the *bursa* (a fluid-filled sac) that lubricates the joint. Although bunions often develop because of wearing shoes that don't fit correctly, they most frequently accompany flat feet. Pain that is not too severe can be relieved by the application of heat; the condition may eventually be cured by doing foot exercises recommended by a physician, who will also help in the choice of correct footwear. A bunion that causes acute pain and difficulty in walking can be treated by a simple surgical procedure.

Calluses

A *callus* is an area of the skin that has become hard and thick as a result of constant friction or pressure against it. Pain results when the callus is pressed against a nerve by poorly fitting shoes. A painful callus can be partially removed by rubbing it—very cautiously—with a sandpaper file or a pumice stone sold for that purpose. The offending shoes should then be discarded for correctly fitted ones. Foot care by a podiatrist is recommended for anyone with recurring calluses and corns (see below), and especially for those people who have diabetes or any disorder of the arteries.

Corns

A *corn* is a form of callus that occurs on or between the toes. When the thickening occurs on the outside of the toe, it is called a *hard corn;* when it is located between the toes, it is called a *soft corn.* The pain in the affected area is caused by pressure of the hard inside core of the corn against the tissue beneath it. The most effective treatment for corns is to wear shoes that are the right size and fit. Corns can be removed by a podiatrist, but unless footwear fits properly, they are likely to return.

Treatment

To remove a corn at home, the toes should be soaked in warm water for about ten minutes and dried. The corn can be rubbed away with an emery file, or it can be treated with a few drops of 10 percent salicylic acid in collodion, available from any druggist. Care should be exercised in applying the solution so that it doesn't reach surrounding tissue, because it is highly irritating to normal skin. The area can then be covered with a corn pad to relieve pressure. This treatment may have to be repeated several times before the corn becomes soft enough to lift out. Diabetics or those suffering from any circulatory disorder should never treat their own corns.

Bursitis

Bursitis is a pain and swelling in a joint caused when the bursa, a sac-like cushion between the bones and tendons, becomes worn or torn from constant use.

Forms of bursitis include: housemaid's knee, characterized by a swollen kneecap that has become inflamed by injury or constant pressure; bunions, where the joint of the big toe is swollen and inflamed by poorly fitting shoes; and weaver's bottom, where the bursa around the pelvic girdle become damaged from long periods of sitting on hard surfaces.

Bursitis can be treated by resting the inflamed joint, applying heat, taking an anti-inflammatory drug, such as aspirin or ibuprofen, or getting a corticosteroid injection or antibiotic therapy. For chronic bursitis, surgery may be required, and physical therapy to repair the joint may follow treatment.

Tendinitis

Tendinitis is inflammation of a tendon, and tenosynovitis is inflammation of the tendon sheath from injury. These problems tend to occur together. The tendon becomes injured by excessive or unusual use, such as a weekend athlete might experience, or from extreme strain on the tendon by overexertion in lifting, carrying, or moving something heavy. The tendon may also be injured by repetitive movement. The areas most susceptible to tendon injuries are the shoulder, hips, hamstrings, ankles, and heels.

Tendinitis can be treated with aspirin or ibuprofen, corticosteroid injections, elevating the injured limb and applying ice, and using a sling. Tendinitis can be avoided by doing warm-up exercises before engaging in an athletic activity, and by not overexerting.

If the pain is persistent or causes you to avoid using the limb, you should seek professional medical advice. Because rest and then gradually increased exercise of the injured area is required, your doctor will have to help you develop a plan for recovery.

Carpal tunnel syndrome

Carpal tunnel syndrome is caused when a median nerve, which provides feeling in the wrist, thumb and fingers, is compressed and becomes swollen and inflamed. The result is a painful stiffness of the hand, wrist, or fingers. The pain also can reach an arm or shoulder.

The debilitating condition is caused by repetitive motion caused by overusing the wrist. It typically affects people who type, such as secretaries and reporters, and is common among carpenters, meat cutters, gymnasts, knitters, racquetball players, and supermarket checkers. Water retention and weight gain in pregnant women often causes them to develop carpal tunnel syndrome which disappears after the baby is born.

Treatments include halting the activity that caused the syndrome, performing the activity differently, and using a split to keep the wrist from bending while it heals. Anti-inflammatory drugs are also used. In severe cases, a carpal tunnel sufferer may be injected with corticosteroid drugs or undergo surgery to cut the bandlike ligament that is pressing on the median nerve.

Unnecessary delays in treating carpal tunnel may cause loss of function, although the condition need not reach such a stage.

The Exposed Integument

Common skin and scalp annoyances such as rashes, itches, dandruff, excessive perspiration, and infections of various kinds (such as athlete's foot and ringworm), as well as acne, wrinkles, and baldness, are discussed in Ch. 21, *Skin and Hair*.

Splinters

If lodged superficially in the hand, a splinter will usually work its own way out, but a splinter of no matter what size in the sole of the foot must be removed promptly to avoid its becoming further embedded by pressure and causing infection. The simplest method of removal is to pass a needle through a flame; let the needle cool; then, after the skin surface has been washed with soap and water or swabbed with alcohol, press the point of the needle against the skin, scraping slightly until the tail of the splinter is visible and loosened. It can then be pulled out with tweezers that have been sterilized in boiling water or alcohol.

Hangnails

Hangnails are pieces of partly living skin torn from the base or side of the fingernail, thus opening a portion of the underskin to infection. A hangnail can cause considerable discomfort. It should not be pulled or bitten off; but the major part of it can be cut away with manicuring scissors. The painful and exposed area should then be washed with soap and water and covered with a sterile adhesive bandage. Hangnails are likely to occur when the skin is dry. They can therefore be prevented by the regular use of a hand cream or lotion containing lanolin.

"Normal" Disorders of the Blood and Circulation

Almost everybody is bothered occasionally by minor disturbances of the circulatory system. Most of the time these disturbances are temporary, and in many cases where they are chronic they may be so mild as not to interfere with good health. Among the more common disturbances of this type are the following.

Anemia

Anemia is a condition in which there is a decrease in the number of red blood cells or in the hemoglobin content of the red blood cells. *Hemoglobin* is the compound that carries oxygen to the body tissues from the lungs. Anemia in itself is not a disease but rather a symptom of some other disorder, such as a deficiency of iron in the diet; excessive loss of blood resulting from an injury or heavy menstrual flow; infection by industrial poisons; or kidney or bone marrow disease. A person may also develop anemia as a result of hypersensitivity (allergy) to various medicines.

In the simple form of anemia, caused by a deficiency of iron in the diet, the symptoms are rarely severe. There may be feelings of fatigue, a loss of energy, and a general lack of vitality. Deficiency anemia is especially common among children and pregnant women, and can be corrected by adding foods high in iron to the diet, such as liver, lean meat, leafy green vegetables, whole wheat bread, and dried peas and beans.

If the symptoms persist, a physician should be consulted for diagnosis and treatment. For more information on anemia, see "Diseases of the Blood" in Ch. 9, *Diseases of the Circulatory System.*

Varicose Veins

Varicose veins are veins that have become ropy and swollen, and are therefore visible in the leg, sometimes bulging on the surface of the skin. They are the result of a sluggish blood flow (poor circulation), often combined with weakened walls of the veins themselves. The condition is common in pregnancy and occurs frequently among people who find it necessary to sit or stand in the same position for extended periods of time. A tendency to develop varicose veins may be inherited.

Even before the veins begin to be visible, there may be such warning symptoms as leg cramps, feelings of fatigue, or a general achiness. Unless the symptoms are treated promptly, the condition may worsen, and if the blood flow becomes increasingly impeded, ulcers may develop on the lower area of the leg.

Treatment

Mild cases of varicose veins can be kept under control, or even corrected, by giving some help to circulation, as follows:

- Several times during the day, lie flat on your back for a few minutes, with the legs slightly raised.

- Soak the legs in warm water.

- Exercise regularly.

- Wear lightly reinforced stockings or elastic stockings to support veins in the legs.

If varicose veins have become severe, a physician should be consulted. He or she may advise injection treatment or surgery. See also "The Inflammatory Disorders" in Ch. 9, *Diseases of the Circulatory System.*

Chronic Hypertension

Hypertension, commonly known as *high blood pressure,* is a condition that may be a warning of some other disease. In many cases, it is not in itself a serious problem and has no one underlying specific cause: this is called *functional, essential,* or *chronic hypertension.* The symptoms of breathing difficulty, headache, weakness, or dizziness that accompany high blood pressure can often be controlled by medicines that bring the pressure down, by sedatives or tranquilizers, and in cases where overweight is a contributing factor, by a change in diet, or by a combination of these.

More serious types of high blood pressure can be the result of kidney disease, glandular disturbances, or diseases of the circulatory system. Acute symptoms include chronic dizziness or blurred vision. Any symptoms of high blood pressure call for professional advice and treatment. See "Hypertensive Heart Disease" in Ch. 10, *Heart Disease.*

Tachycardia

Tachycardia is the medical name for a condition that most of us have felt at one time or another—abnormally rapid heartbeat, or a feeling that the heart is fluttering, or pounding too quickly. The condition can be brought on by strong feelings of fear, excitement, or anxiety, or by overtaxing the heart with sudden exertion or too much exercise. It may also be a sign

of heart disease, but in such cases, it is usually accompanied by other symptoms.

The most typical form of occasional rapid heartbeat is called *paroxysmal tachycardia,* during which the beat suddenly becomes twice or three times as fast as it is normally, and then just as suddenly returns to its usual tempo. When the paroxysms are frequent enough to be disturbing and can be traced to no specific source, they can be prevented by medicines prescribed by a physician.

Nosebleed

Nosebleeds are usually the result of a ruptured blood vessel. They are especially common among children, and among adults with high blood pressure. If the nosebleed doesn't taper off by itself, the following measures should be taken: the patient should be seated—but not lying down—clothing loosened, and a cold compress placed on the back of the neck and the nose. The soft portion of the nostril may be pressed gently against the bony cartilage of the nose for at least six minutes, or rolled wads of absorbent cotton may be placed inside each nostril, with part of the cotton sticking out to make its removal easier. The inserted cotton should be left in place for several hours and then gently withdrawn.

Fainting

Fainting is a sudden loss of consciousness, usually caused by an insufficient supply of blood and oxygen to the brain. Among the most common causes of fainting are fear, acute hunger, the sight of blood, and prolonged standing in a room with too little fresh air. Fainting should not be confused with a loss of consciousness resulting from excessive alcohol intake or insulin shock. A person about to faint

usually feels dizzy, turns pale, and feels weak in the knees.

Treatment

If possible, the person should be made to lie down, or to sit with his head between his knees for several minutes. Should he lose consciousness, place him so that his legs are slightly higher than his head, loosen his clothing, and see that he gets plenty of fresh air. If smelling salts or aromatic spirits of ammonia are available, they can be held under his nose. With these procedures, he should revive in a few minutes. If he doesn't, a physician should be called.

Troubles Along the Digestive Tract

From childhood on, most people are occasionally bothered by minor and temporary disturbances connected with digestion. Most of the disturbances listed below can be treated successfully with common sense and, if need be, a change in habits.

The Mouth

The digestive processes begin in the mouth, where the saliva begins chemically to break down some foods into simpler components, and the teeth and the tongue start the mechanical breakdown. Disorders of the teeth such as a malocclusion or poorly fitted dentures that interfere with proper chewing, should promptly be brought to the attention of a dentist.

Inflammation of the Gums

Also known as *gingivitis,* inflammation of the gums is caused by the bacteria that breed in food trapped in the spaces between the gums and the teeth. The gums become increasingly swollen, may bleed easily, and be sore enough to interfere with proper chewing. The condition can be prevented by cleaning the teeth thoroughly and frequently, which includes the use of dental floss or the rubber tip on the toothbrush to remove any food particles lodged in the teeth after eating. Because gingivitis can develop into the more serious condition of *pyorrhea,* persistent gum bleeding or soreness should receive prompt professional treatment. See Ch. 22, *The Teeth and Gums.*

Canker Sores

Canker sores are small ulcers inside the lips, mouth, and cheeks. Their specific cause is unknown, but they seem to accompany or follow a virus infection, vitamin deficiency, or emotional stress. They may be additionally irritated by citrus fruit, chocolate, or nuts. A canker sore usually clears up in about a week without special treatment. A bland mouth rinse will relieve pain and, in some cases, speed the healing process.

Coated Tongue

Although a coated tongue is commonly supposed to be a sure sign of illness, this is not the case. The condition may occur because of a temporary lack of saliva.

Glossitis

Glossitis, an inflammation of the tongue causing the tongue's surface to become bright red or, in some cases, glazed in appearance, may be a symptom of an infection elsewhere in the body. It may also be a symptom of anemia or a nutritional deficiency, or it may be an adverse reaction to certain forms of medication. If the in-

flammation persists and is accompanied by acute soreness, it should be called to a physician's attention.

Halitosis or Bad Breath

Contrary to the millions of commercial messages on television and in print, bad breath cannot be cured by any mouthwash, lozenge, spray, or antiseptic gargle now on the market. These products can do no more than mask the odor until the basic cause is diagnosed and cured. Among the many conditions that may result in bad breath (leaving out such fleeting causes as garlic and onions) are the following: an infection of the throat, nose, or mouth; a stomach or kidney disorder; pyorrhea; respiratory infection; tooth decay; improper mouth hygiene; and excessive drinking and smoking. Anyone who has been made self-conscious about the problem of bad breath should ask his physician or dentist whether his breath is truly offensive and if it is, what to do about it.

Gastritis

Gastritis, one of the most common disorders of the digestive system, is an inflammation of the lining of the stomach that may occur in acute, chronic, or toxic form. Among the causes of *acute gastritis* are various bacterial or viral infections; overeating, especially heavy or rich foods; excessive drinking of alcoholic beverages; or food poisoning. An attack of acute gastritis may be severely painful, but the discomfort usually subsides with proper treatment. The first symptom is typically sharp stomach cramps, followed by a bloated feeling, loss of appetite, headache, and nausea. When vomiting occurs, it rids the stomach of the substance causing the attack but usually leaves

the patient temporarily weak. If painful cramps persist and are accompanied by fever, a physician should be consulted about the possibility of medication for bacterial infection. For a few days after an attack of acute gastritis, the patient should stay on a bland diet of easily digested foods, taken in small quantities.

Toxic Gastritis

Toxic gastritis is usually the result of swallowing a poisonous substance, causing vomiting and possible collapse. It is an emergency condition requiring prompt first aid treatment and the attention of a physician. See "Poisoning" in Ch. 31, *Medical Emergencies.*

Chronic Gastritis

Chronic gastritis is a recurrent or persisting inflammation of the stomach lining over a lengthy period. The condition has the symptoms associated with indigestion, especially pain after eating. It can be caused by excessive drinking of alcoholic beverages, constant tension or anxiety, or deficiencies in the diet. The most effective treatment for chronic gastritis is a bland diet from which caffeine and alcohol have been eliminated. Heavy meals should be avoided in favor of eating small amounts at frequent intervals. A tranquilizer or a mild sedative prescribed by a physician may reduce the tensions that contribute to the condition. If the discomfort continues, a physician should be consulted about the possibility of ulcers. See Ch. 11, *Diseases of the Digestive System.*

Gastroenteritis

Gastroenteritis is an inflammation of the lining of both the stomach and the intestines. Like gastritis, it can occur in acute or toxic forms as a result of food poisoning, excessive alcohol intake, viral or bacterial infections, or food allergies. Vomiting, diarrhea, and fever may be more pronounced and of longer duration. As long as nausea and vomiting persist, no food or fluid should be taken; when these symptoms cease, a bland, mainly fluid diet consisting of strained broth, thin cereals, boiled eggs, and tea is best. If fever continues and diarrhea doesn't taper off, a physician should be called.

Diarrhea

Diarrhea is a condition in which bowel movements are abnormally frequent and liquid. It may be accompanied by cramps, vomiting, thirst, and a feeling of tenderness in the abdominal region. Diarrhea is always a symptom of some irritant in the intestinal tract; among possible causes are allergy, infection by virus or bacteria, accidentally swallowed poisonous substances, or excessive alcohol. Brief attacks are sometimes caused by emotions, such as overexcitement or anxiety.

Diarrhea that lasts for more than two days should be diagnosed by a physician to rule out a more serious infection, a glandular disturbance, or a tumor. Mild attacks can be treated at home by giving the patient a light, bland diet, plenty of fluids, and the prescribed dosage of a kaolin-pectin compound available at any drugstore.

Constipation

Many people have the mistaken notion that if they don't have a bowel movement every day, they must be constipated. This is not necessarily so. From a physician's viewpoint, constipation is determined not by an arbitrary schedule of when the bowel should be evacuated but by the indi-

vidual's discomfort and other unpleasant symptoms. In too many instances, overconcern and anxiety about bowel movements may be the chief cause of constipation.

The watery waste that results from the digestion of food in the stomach and small intestine passes into the large intestine, or colon, where water is absorbed from the waste. If the waste stays in the large intestine for too long a time, so much water is removed that it becomes too solid and compressed to evacuate easily. The efficient removal of waste material from the large intestine depends on wavelike muscular contractions. When these waves are too weak to do their job properly, as often happens in the elderly or the excessively sedentary, a physician may recommend a mild laxative or mineral oil.

Treatment

Constipation is rarely the result of an organic disorder. In most cases, it is caused by poor health habits; when these are corrected, the disorder corrects itself. Often, faulty diet is a major factor. Make sure that meals contain plenty of roughage in the form of whole-grain cereals, fruit, and leafy green vegetables. Figs, prunes, and dates should be included from time to time. Plenty of liquid intake is important, whether in the form of juices, soups, or large quantities of water. Scheduling a certain amount of exercise each day strengthens the abdominal muscles and stimulates muscle activity in the large intestine. Confronting the sources of worries and anxieties, if necessary with a trained therapist, may also be helpful.

An enema or a laxative should be considered only once in a while rather than as regular treatment. The colon should be given a chance to function properly without relying on artificial stimulation. If constipation resists

these commonsense approaches, the problem should be talked over with a physician.

Hemorrhoids

Hemorrhoids, commonly called *piles,* are swollen veins in the mucous membrane inside or just outside the rectum. When the enlargement is slight, the only discomfort may be an itching sensation in the area. Acute cases are accompanied by pain and bleeding. Hemorrhoids are a very common complaint and occur in people of all ages. They are usually the result of straining to eliminate hard, dry stools. The extra pressure causes a fold of the membranous rectal lining to slip down, thus pinching the veins and irritating them.

Because hemorrhoids may be a symptom of a disorder other than constipation, they should be treated by a physician. If neglected, they may bleed frequently and profusely enough to cause anemia. Should a blood clot develop in an irritated vein, surgery may be necessary.

Treatment

Advertised cures should be avoided because they are not only ineffective but can cause additional irritation. Laxatives and cathartics, which may temporarily solve the problem of constipation, are likely to aggravate hemorrhoids.

If pain or bleeding becomes acute, a physician should be consulted promptly. Treatment can be begun at home. Sitting for several minutes in a hot bath in the morning and again in the evening (more frequently if necessary) will provide temporary relief. Preventing constipation is of the utmost importance.

Anal Fissure

This is a condition in which a crack or

split or ulcerated place develops in the area of the two anal sphincters, or muscle rings, that control the release of feces. Such breaks in the skin are generally caused by something sharp in the stool, or by the passage of an unusually hard and large stool. Although discomfort often accompanies a bowel movement when there is a fissure, the acute pain typically comes afterward. Healing is difficult because the injured tissue is constantly open to irritation. If the condition persists, it usually has to be treated by a minor surgical procedure. Intense itching in this area is called *anal pruritis*.

Minor Ailments in the Air Pipes

In addition to all the respiratory discomforts that go along with the common cold, there are various other ailments that affect breathing and normal voice production.

Bronchitis

Usually referred to as a chest cold, *bronchitis* is an inflammation of the bronchial tubes that connect the windpipe and the lungs. If bronchitis progresses down into the lungs, it can develop into pneumonia. Old people and children are especially susceptible to acute bronchitis. The symptoms include pain in the chest, a feeling of fatigue, and a nagging cough. If the infection is bacterial, it will respond to antibiotics. If it is viral, there are no specific medicines. The attack usually lasts for about ten days, although recovery may be speeded up with bed rest and large fluid intake.

Chronic Bronchitis

Chronic bronchitis is a condition that may recur each winter, or may be present throughout the year in the form of a constant cough. The condition is aggravated by smoking and by irritants such as airborne dust and smog. The swollen tissues and abnormally heavy discharge of mucus interfere with the flow of air from the lungs and cause shortness of breath. Medicines are available that lessen the bronchial phlegm and make breathing easier. People with chronic bronchitis often sleep better if they use more than one pillow and have a vaporizer going at night.

Coughing

Coughing is usually a reflex reaction to an obstruction or irritation in the trachea (windpipe), pharynx (back of mouth and throat), or bronchial tubes. It can also be the symptom of a disease or a nervous habit. For a simple cough brought on by smoking too much or breathing bad air, medicines can be taken that act as sedatives to inhibit the reflex reaction. Inhaling steam can loosen the congestion (a combination of swollen membranes and thickened mucus) that causes some types of coughs, and hot drinks such as tea or lemonade help to soothe and relax the irritated area. Constant coughing, especially when accompanied by chest pains, should be brought to a physician's attention. For a discussion of whooping cough and croup, see the respective articles under the "Alphabetic Guide to Child Care" in Ch. 2, *The First Dozen Years*.

Laryngitis

Laryngitis is an inflammation of the mucous membrane of the larynx (voice box) that interferes with breathing and causes the voice to become hoarse or disappear altogether. This condition may accompany a sore throat, measles, or whooping cough, or it may result from an allergy. Pro-

longed overuse of the voice, a common occupational hazard of singers and teachers, is also a cause. The best treatment for laryngitis is to go to bed, keep the room cool, and put moisture into the air from a vaporizer, humidifier, or boiling kettle. Don't attempt to talk, even in a whisper. Keep a writing pad within arm's reach and use it to spare your voice. Drinking warm liquids may help to relieve some of the discomfort. If you must go out, keep the throat warmly protected.

Chronic laryngitis may result from too many acute laryngitis attacks, which can cause the mucous membrane to become so thick and tough that the voice remains permanently hoarse. The sudden onset of hoarseness that lasts for more than two weeks calls for a physician's diagnosis.

Hiccups

Hiccups (also spelled *hiccoughs*) are contractions of the diaphragm, the great muscle responsible for forcing air in and out of our lungs. They may be brought on by an irritation of the diaphragm itself, of the respiratory or digestive system, or by eating or drinking too rapidly. Common remedies for hiccups include sipping water slowly, holding the breath, and putting something cold on the back of the neck. Breathing into a paper bag is usually effective because after a few breaths, the high carbon dioxide content in the bag will serve to make the diaphragm contractions more regular, rather than spasmodic. If none of these measures helps, it may be necessary to have a physician prescribe a sedative or tranquilizer.

The Sensitive Eyes and Ears

Air pollution affects not only the lungs but the eyes as well. In addition to all the other hazards to which the eyes are exposed, airborne smoke, chemicals, and dust cause the eyes to burn, itch, and shed tears. Other common eye troubles are discussed below.

Sty

This pimplelike inflammation of the eyelid is caused by infection, which may be linked to the blocking of an eyelash root or an oil gland, or to general poor health. A sty can be treated at home by applying clean compresses of hot water to the area for about 15 minutes at a time every two hours. This procedure should cause the sty to open, drain, and heal. If sties are recurrent, a health checkup may be indicated.

Pinkeye

Pinkeye, an acute form of *conjunctivitis,* is an inflammation of the membrane that lines the eyelid and covers the eyeball, causing the eyes to become red and the lids to swell and stick together while one is sleeping. The condition may result from bacterial or viral infection—in which case it is extremely contagious—or from allergy or chemical irritation. A physician should be consulted.

Conjunctivitis can be treated by washing the eyes with warm water, drying them with a disposable tissue to prevent the spread of infection, and applying a medicated yellow oxide of mercury ophthalmic ointment (as recommended by your physician) on the inner edges of the lids. This should be done upon rising in the morning and upon retiring at night. The eyes should then be closed until the ointment has spread. Apply compresses of hot water three or four times a day for five-minute periods.

Eyestrain

Eyestrain—with symptoms of fatigue, tearing, redness, and a scratchy feeling in the eyelids—can be caused by a need for corrective glasses, by a disorder of the eye, or by overuse of the eyes. One of the most common causes of eyestrain, however, is improper lighting. Anyone engaged in close work, such as sewing or miniature model building, and at all times when reading, should have light come from behind and from the side so that no shadow falls on the book or object being scrutinized. The light should be strong enough for comfort—not dazzling. Efforts should be made to avoid a shiny or highly polished work surface that produces a glare. To avoid eyestrain when watching television, be sure the picture is in sharp focus; the viewer should sit at least six feet from the screen; and see that the room is not in total darkness.

Ear Infections

Ear infections related to colds, sore throats, or tonsillitis can now be kept from spreading and entering the mastoid bone by the use of sulfa drugs and antibiotics. Any acute earache should therefore be called to a physician's attention promptly. Aspirin can be taken for temporary relief from pain; holding a heating pad or a hotwater bottle to the affected side of the face may also be helpful until proper medication can be prescribed.

Earwax

An excessive accumulation of earwax can cause pain and interfere with hearing. A small wad of cotton should be used to gently clean the ear canal, and sharp objects such as hairpins and matchsticks should never be used.

Hardened earwax can be softened by a few drops of hydrogen peroxide.

Sometimes a doctor may have to flush out earwax that is deeply imbedded.

Ear Blockage

A stopped-up feeling in the ear can be caused by a cold, and also by the change in air pressure experienced when a plane makes a rapid descent. The obstruction of the eustachian tube can usually be opened by swallowing hard or yawning.

Ringing in the Ear

The general word for a large variety of noises in the ear is *tinnitus.* Tinnitus can be ringing, buzzing, or other low level continual sounds. Everyone experiences some form of ear ringing on occasion, such as after listening to loud music or noise. However, chronic noise is symptomatic of other problems. Tinnitus can be caused by tension in the jaw muscle from stress, grinding of the teeth, or structural problems with the jaw. It can also be caused by high blood pressure, infections, or as a reaction to chemicals, such as nicotine. If you experience continual or chronic ringing, you should discuss it with your physician.

Tinnitus is treated by avoiding excessive noise, masking irritating ear noises with music or amplified sounds from a hearing aid or cleaning ear wax out of ears. A doctor's opinion should also be sought to determine if the ringing is caused by an inner ear infection. Avoiding caffeine, nicotine and alcohol also helps.

The Path from the Kidneys

Cystitis

Cystitis is the general term for inflammation of the bladder caused by various types of infection. It is more common in women than in men. Infecting microbes may come from outside the body by way of the urethra, or from some other infected organ, such as the kidney. When the bladder becomes inflamed, frequent and painful urination results.

Cystitis may also occur as a consequence of other disorders, such as enlargement of the prostate gland, a structural defect of the male urethra, or stones or a tumor in the bladder. Although there is no completely reliable way to prevent cystitis, some types of infection can be prevented by cleansing the genital region regularly so that the entrance of the urethra is protected against bacterial invasion. Cystitis is usually cured by medicines prescribed by a physician. For a detailed discussion of cystitis and related conditions affecting women, see "Disorders of the Urinary System" in Ch. 25, *Women's Health.*

Prostatitis

Prostatitis is an inflammation of the prostate gland (present in males only), caused by an infection of the urinary tract or some other part of the body. It may occur as a result of venereal infection. The symptoms of painful and excessive urination generally respond favorably to antibiotics. *Acute prostatitis* is less common: the patient is likely to have a high fever, as well as a discharge of pus from the penis. These symptoms should be brought to a physician's attention without delay.

Excessive Urination

A need to empty the bladder with excessive frequency can be merely a nuisance caused by overexcitement or tension, or it can be the sign of a disorder of the urinogenital system. A physician should be consulted if the problem persists.

The All-Important Feet

The *podiatrist* is the specialist who treats foot problems. Causes of foot ailments range from lack of cleanliness to ill-fitting shoes and overindulgence in athletic activities (see "Care of the Feet" in Ch. 5, *The Middle Years,* "The Vulnerable Extremities" in Ch. 23, *Aches, Pains, Nuisances, Worries*).

An ache, pain, or other disorder of the foot can be particularly annoying because it usually hampers mobility. A severe problem can keep a person bedridden, sometimes in the hospital, for substantial periods of time. As humans, we move about on our feet. They deserve the best of care from us, as their owners, and from the podiatrist in case a serious problem arises.

Podiatry, the science of foot care, has become more and more important as Americans have taken to athletics and exercises of various kinds. Most of these activities require the use of the feet. Increasing numbers of persons in the adult years are also taking up walking, jogging, or running as diversions or exercises.

Podiatrists believe that some persons "walk old"—they give the appearance, by the way they walk, of greater age than their chronological years. Others "walk young," or walk normally. Those who walk old may be inviting foot problems, and a fact of podiatric science is that every foot problem has its reflection in another part, or other parts, of the body.

By contrast, good foot and body posture often suggests that the owner of the feet enjoys good health in other parts of the body. Foot care may in effect help other body parts to function better. Because many problems with parts of the body remote from the feet make good foot posture and normal walking difficult or impossible, individuals with diverse problems, such as back pains, sometimes go to

a podiatrist for treatment. The back pain may disappear when the feet have been brought into good working order.

Diabetes and the Feet

"Care" for the feet of diabetics means prevention. The diabetic tries to keep his feet so healthy that he avoids major problems. He knows that diabetes affects blood circulation, and that the leg and foot are extremely vulnerable to circulatory problems. Where blood cannot reach a limb or member, gangrene becomes a possibility.

Foot Care

What kind of care serves the diabetic best? Effective care means that the diabetic takes steps quickly to treat such problems as abrasions or ulcers that refuse to heal. Other conditions that warn of possible future problems are dry skin, numbness, and dry or brittle nails. Ulcers that appear in the skin of the foot and that appear to have roots in deeper layers of tissue serve as danger signals. Such ulcers may appear on the site of an injury, cut, or scratch. A physician will usually prescribe medication, dietary adjustments, or other measures.

Ulcers may result from neglect of a corn or callus. But such neglect itself indicates the risks that diabetics incur: they may neglect to have a foot problem such as a corn treated because their disease has, over time, reduced the sensitivity of their feet. They may lose much of their ability to feel pain, heat or cold, or stress in the foot. Because of such problems, diabetics generally follow certain rules of foot care, including the following:

- Give the feet a daily examination for cuts, bruises, or other abnormalities

- Use only prescribed medications in caring for the feet—and avoid over-the-counter preparations

- Visit a podiatrist regularly, as often as once a month, and avoid medical "treatment" of one's own feet or even cutting one's own toenails

- Wash the feet daily in warm, not hot, water and dry them carefully, including the area between the toes

- Use a gentle lubricant on the feet after washing and drying—and never go barefoot

- Avoid the use of items of clothing that may interfere with circulation, including wraparound garters and support hosiery

- Avoid "holey" socks, darned socks, or anything else that may irritate the soles of the feet and

- Avoid constrictive boots or shoes

Jogging and Running

The podiatrist usually tries to learn about a patient's work, his hobbies and sports, and other facts before undertaking treatment. In particular, the podiatrist asks whether the patient runs or jogs or takes part in other strenuous exercises. With such background information, he or she can suggest appropriate treatment.

A podiatrist will advise runners or joggers on the kind of footwear that would be best—especially if problems have been encountered or may be expected. Shoe inserts may be custom-designed if needed. The podiatrist may also advise runners and joggers to run on softer surfaces rather than cement. Jogging or running "in place," without forward movement, is to be avoided if possible; even when jogging inside the home or apartment, the jogger should move from room to room.

Podiatrists point out that even the more serious knee and ankle problems incurred in running and jogging can be treated. "Jogger's ankle," pain resulting from too much jogging and the attendant strain, can be controlled if the jogger will use moderation. Beginning joggers in particular should start slowly and gradually increase their level of participation. Runners'

knee problems may be cured in many cases by treatment that enables the feet to carry the weight of the body properly. In part, the treatment requires practice in throwing the body weight onto the balls of the feet, not on the inner sides of the feet. The remainder of the body, including the knees, can be kept in proper alignment with the feet if the weight falls where it should.

Podiatrists also advise runners, joggers, and others taking part in sports to make certain *all* their clothing and equipment are appropriate. That applies especially in skiing, ice-skating, and other sports requiring extensive foot use. Proper equipment helps runners and joggers avoid colds and similar respiratory problems.

With proper equipment, including good shoes, and a moderate approach, runners and joggers can avoid many other potentially troublesome physical difficulties that could require podiatric care. These others include fallen arches; corns, calluses, and bunions; and "aging feet" that grow weaker from lack of proper foot attention.

24

Allergies and Hypersensitivities

Allergy is a broad term used to describe an unusual reaction of the body's tissues to a substance that has no noticeable effect on other persons. About 17 out of every 100 persons in America are allergic, or hypersensitive, to one or more substances that are known to precipitate an unusual reaction. Such substances, known as *allergens,* include a variety of irritants, among them mold spores, pollens, animal dander, insect venoms, and house dust. Some individuals are allergic to substances in soap, which produce a skin irritation. Others react to the smell of a rose by sneezing. Still others react with an outbreak of hives, diarrhea, or other symptoms to allergens in foods.

How Allergens Affect the Body

Allergic symptoms can range from itching eyes, running nose, coughing, difficulty in breathing, and welts on the skin to nausea, cramps, and even going into a state of shock, depending upon the severity of the particular individual's sensitivity and response. Almost any part or system of the body can be affected, and almost anything can pose an allergic threat to somebody.

The Role of Antibodies

The system of an allergic individual reacts to such substances in the way it would react to an invading disease organism: by producing *antibodies* whose job it is to neutralize the allergen. In the process of fighting off the effects of the allergen, the body's defense mechanism may overreact by dumping a chemical mediator, *histamine,* indiscriminately into the individual's bloodstream. It is the overabundance of this protective chemical that causes the discomforts associated with allergies.

At the same time, the antibodies can sensitize the individual to the allergen. Then, with each new exposure to the allergen, more antibodies are produced. Eventually the symptoms of allergy are produced whenever the allergen is encountered. Most allergic reactions, including hay fever, asthma, gastrointestinal upsets, and skin rashes, are of the type just described; their effect is more or less immediate. A second type, known as the delayed type, seems to function without the production of antibodies; contact dermatitis is an example of the delayed type.

Eosinophils

Some individuals seem to be sensitive to only one known allergen, but others are sensitive to a variety of substances. Persons who suffer acute allergic reactions have abnormally high levels of a type of white blood cell called *eosinophil.* The eosinophil contains an enzyme that may have some control over the allergic reaction, and varying degrees of the enzyme's efficiency appear to account for individual differences in the severity of allergic reactions.

Allergic Symptoms in Children

Many of the common allergies appear during the early years of life. It has been estimated that nearly 80 percent of the major allergic problems begin to appear between the ages of 4 and 9. Allergic youngsters may have nasal speech habits, breathe through the mouth, have coughing and wheezing spells, or rub their eyes, nose, and ears because of itching. A not uncommon sign of allergic reaction in a child may be dark circles under the eyes caused by swelling of the mucous membranes to such an extent that blood does not drain properly from the veins under the lower eyelids. Nose twitching and mouth wrinkling also are signs that a youngster has allergic symptoms.

Common Allergens

The allergens responsible for so many unpleasant and uncomfortable symptoms take a variety of forms too numerous and sometimes too obscure for any book to enumerate. Discussed below are some of the more common types of allergens.

Foods

Foods are among the most common causes of allergic reactions. While nearly any food substance is a potential allergen to certain sensitive individuals, those most frequently implicated are cow's milk, orange juice, and eggs, all considered essential in a child's diet. However, substitute foods are almost always available. Many natural foods contain vitamin C, or ascorbic acid, found in orange juice. Ascorbic acid also is available in vitamin tablets. All of the essential amino acids and other nutrients in cow's milk and eggs also can be obtained from other food sources, although perhaps not as conveniently packaged for immediate use. Other common food offenders are chocolate, pork, seafoods, nuts, and berries. An individual may be allergic to the gluten in wheat, rye, and oats, and products made from those grains.

Inhaled Allergens

Allergens also may affect the respiratory tract, bringing on sneezing,

coughing, and breathing impairment. The substances involved can be pollens, dust, smoke, perfumes, and various airborne chemicals.

Mold Spores

A person also can become allergic to a certain mold by inhaling the spores, or reproductive particles, of fungus. In the nose, the mold spores trigger a reaction in cells of the tissues beneath the mucous membranes that line the nasal passages. This in turn leads to the symptoms of allergy. Because they are small, mold spores can evade the natural protective mechanisms of the nose and upper respiratory tract to reach the lungs and bring on an allergic reaction in that site. Usually, this leads to the buildup of mucus, wheezing, and difficulty in breathing associated with asthma.

Less frequently, inhaling mold spores can result in skin lesions similar to those of eczema or chronic hives. In all but the very warmest areas of the United States, molds are seasonal allergens, occurring from spring into late fall. But unlike pollens, molds do not disappear with the killing frosts of autumn. Actually, frost may help increase the activity of molds, which thrive on dying vegetation produced by cold temperatures.

Dust and Animal Hair

House dust and animal hair (especially cat and dog hair) are also responsible for respiratory allergies in many people. Asthma attacks are often triggered by contact with these substances. Symptoms of dust allergy are usually most severe in the spring and fall, and tend to subside in the summer.

Man-Made Allergens

An example of respiratory allergy

caused by man-made allergens is the complaint known as "meat wrappers' asthma," which results from fumes of the price-label adhesive on the polyvinyl chloride film used to package foods. The fumes are produced when the price label is cut on a hot wire. When the fumes are inhaled, the result is burning eyes, sore throat, wheezing and shortness of breath, upset stomach, and other complaints. Studies show that exposure to the fumes from the heat-activated label adhesive for as little as five minutes could produce airway obstruction in food packagers.

Another source of respiratory allergy is the photochemical smog produced by motor vehicle exhaust in large city areas. The smog is composed of hydrocarbons, oxides of nitrogen, and other chemicals activated by the energy of sunlight. When inhaled in the amounts present along the nation's expressways, the smog has been found to impair the normal function of membranes in the lungs.

Drugs

Medicines and drugs, such as penicillin, or serums used in inoculations, can cause allergic reactions. Estimates of the incidence of allergy among those receiving penicillin range from one to ten percent. The National Institutes of Health has calculated that just three common drugs—penicillin, sulfonamides, and aspirin—account for as much as 90 percent of all allergic drug reactions. The allergic reactions include asthmatic symptoms, skin rash, shock, and other symptoms similar to tissue reactions to other allergens. Medical scientists theorize that chemicals in certain drugs probably combine with protein molecules in the patient's body to form a new substance that is the true allergen. However, it also has been noted that some persons show allergic reactions to placebo drugs, which may contain sugar or inert substances rather than real drugs.

Insect Venom

Insect stings cause serious allergic reactions in about four of every 1,000 persons stung by bees, fire ants, yellow jackets, wasps, or hornets. A single sting to a sensitive person may lead to a serious drop in blood pressure, shock, and possibly death. There are more than 50 reported fatalities a year, and experts suspect that other deaths occur as a result of insect stings but are listed as heart attacks, stroke, or convulsions.

Sensitivity tests of persons who might be acutely allergic to insect stings have been difficult to develop, because allergic individuals reacted in the same way as nonallergic persons to skin tests performed with extracts from insect bodies. More recently, physicians have found that using pure insect venom produces a reaction that determines whether a person is allergic to the sting. Medical scientists also have isolated the major allergen in an insect venom for use in diagnosing and treating patients who are particularly sensitive to stings.

Skin Allergies

Allergies affecting the skin take many forms, the most common being eczema, urticaria (hives), angioedema (swelling of the subcutaneous tissues), and contact dermatitis. Among the most common causes are foods, cosmetics, fabrics, rubber, metals, plants and flowers, plastics, insecticides, furs and leather, jewelry, and many industrial chemicals. Studies of patients who seem to be especially sensitive to skin allergies show that they have higher than average amounts of a body protein called *immunoglobulin E* in their systems.

Contact dermatitis usually is distinguished by skin swelling, hives, or blisters. The area affected is usually the skin that comes in direct contact with the allergen, so a watch band allergy response will appear as a band around the wrist where the watchband touches the skin. Long-term exposure will cause dry, cracked, darkened patches on the skin.

Poisonous Plants

Poison ivy, poison oak, and poison sumac contain an extremely irritating oily resin that sensitizes the body; repeated contact seems to increase the severity of the allergic reactions. About 50 percent of the population who come in contact with the resin will experience a severe form of dermatitis, and up to 10 percent will be temporarily disabled by the effects. Exposure to the resin may come from direct contact with the plant, from contact with other objects or animals that have touched the plant, or from inhaling smoke from the burning plant.

Cosmetics and Jewelry

A wide variety of cosmetics and jewelry can cause allergic reactions through skin contact. Even jewelry that is presumably pure gold can contain a certain amount of nickel that will produce a mild reaction that causes a skin discoloration, sometimes aided by chemical activity resulting from perspiration in the area of jewelry contact. Among cosmetics that may be involved in allergic reactions are certain permanent-wave lotions, eyelash dyes, face powders, permanent hair dyes, hair-spray lacquers, and skin-tanning agents. Of course, not all persons are equally sensitive to the ingredients known to be allergens, and in most cases a similar product

with different ingredients can be substituted for the cosmetic causing allergic reactions. For more information on skin allergies, see "Disorders of the Skin" in Ch. 21, *Skin and Hair.*

Environmental Allergies

Environmental agents such as sunlight, excessive cold, and pressure are known to produce allergic reactions in certain individuals. Cold allergy, for example, can result in hives and may even lead to a drop in blood pressure, fainting, severe shock, and sometimes death. Research into the causes of cold allergy has shown that cold urticaria, or hives, results from a histamine released from body tissues as they begin to warm up after a cold stimulus. Extremely high histamine levels coincide with episodes of very low blood pressure, the cause of fainting.

Although reaction of the body tissues to the invasion of microbes, such as bacteria, viruses, and other microorganisms, generally is not thought of as an allergic situation, the manner in which the body musters its defenses against the foreign materials is essentially the same as the way the antibodies are mobilized to neutralize other allergens. Thus, there is a similarity be tween infectious diseases and allergies.

Temporary Allergies

Occasionally, a change in the body's hormonal balance may trigger a hypersensitivity to a substance that previously had no effect on the individual. Pregnant women are especially susceptible to these temporary allergies, which almost always disappear after childbirth. Some women during pregnancy, on the other hand, experience complete relief from allergies that have plagued them since childhood.

People who suffer from seasonal allergies, such as hay fever, often have heightened allergic reactions to dust, animal dander, and even certain foods, such as chocolate and pineapple, during the season when ragweed pollen or other airborne allergens are plentiful.

Diagnosis of Allergies

Some allergic reactions are outgrown; some don't develop until adulthood; some become increasingly severe over the years because each repeated exposure makes the body more sensitive to the allergen. In many instances, the irritating substance is easily identified, after which it can be avoided. In other cases, it may take a long series of tests before the offending allergen is tracked down.

Medical History

If a person suspects he may have an allergy, the first thing he should do is consult a physician to see if the help of an allergy specialist should be sought. The physician or allergist will first take a complete medical history and check the patient's general health. Not infrequently the source of an allergy can be found by general questioning about the patient's life style. For example, the reaction may occur only on or immediately after the patient eats seafood. Or a patient may have an apparently chronic allergy but be unaware that it may be related to daily meals that include milk and eggs. A patient who keeps several cats or sleeps every night with a dog in the bedroom may not realize that an asthmatic condition actually is an allergic reaction to dander from the fur of a pet animal.

The history taken by the physician will include questions about other known allergies, allergies suffered by other members of the family, variations in symptoms according to the weather, time of day, and season of the year. The symptoms may be related to a change in working conditions or the fact that the symptoms, if perhaps a result of house dust, diminish during periods of outdoor exercise. A person sensitive to cold may unwittingly exacerbate the symptoms with cold drinks, while another person who is sensitive to heat may not realize that symptoms can be triggered by hot drinks but relieved by cold drinks, and so on.

Skin Testing

If the patient is referred to an allergy specialist, the allergist will continue the detective story by conducting skin tests.

Scratch Test

Based on information in the medical history of the patient and the allergist's knowledge of molds, pollens, and other airborne allergens in the geographical area, "the allergist" will conduct what is called a *scratch test.*

A diluted amount of a suspected allergen is applied to a small scratch on the patient's arm or back. If the results of the scratch test are inconclusive, a more sensitive test may be tried.

Intracutaneous Test

In the *intracutaneous* test, a solution of the suspected allergen is injected into the underlayer of skin called the *dermis.* The intracutaneous test also may be used to verify the results of a positive scratch test. With either test, a positive reaction usually consists of a raised reddish welt, or *wheal.* The welt should develop within 15 or 20 minutes if that particular allergen is the cause of the symptoms.

Culture Plates

If the allergen has been identified, or if the allergist still suspects a substance in the environment of the patient despite negative or inconclusive tests, the patient may be given a set of culture plates to place around his home and office or work area. If the allergen has been identified, the culture plates can help the physician and patient learn where his exposure to the substance takes place. If the allergen is not known, the cultures may pick up samples of less common allergens that the specialist can test.

Mucosal Test

Another kind of approach sometimes is used by allergists when skin tests fail to show positive results despite good evidence that a particular allergen is the cause of symptoms. It is called the *mucosal test.* The allergist using the mucosal test applies a diluted solution of the suspected allergen directly to the mucous membranes of the patient, usually on the inner surface of a nostril or by aerosol spray into the bronchial passages. In some cases, the allergic reaction occurs immediately and medication is administered quickly to counter the effects. Because of the possibility of a severe reaction in a hypersensitive patient, the mucosal test is not employed if other techniques seem to be effective.

Relief from Allergies

Other Tests

Allergists have other ways to test for allergies. They can, for example, use the *prick test,* a kind of skin test in which a physician or nurse pricks the skin as many as 30 or 40 times. On each pricked spot a drop of a watery solution is dropped; the solution contains a small amount of one allergen. A red welt appears on the spot within 15 to 30 minutes if the patient is allergic. Using another approach, an *elimination diet,* an allergist may specify a diet that omits certain foods for stated periods. Improvement in the patient's condition while avoiding certain foods usually indicates that the individual has an allergy to that food.

A variation of the prick test involves injection of small amounts of food in solution under the skin or application of the solution under the tongue. If the injection or drops provoke reactions, an allergy is indicated.

Avoidance

For a patient sensitive to a particular type of allergen, such as molds, complete avoidance of the substance can be difficult, but some steps can be taken to avoid undue exposure. For example, the mold allergy sufferer should avoid areas of his home, business, or recreational areas that are likely spots for mold spores to be produced. These would include areas of deep shade or heavy vegetation, basements, refrigerator drip trays, garbage pails, air conditioners, bathrooms, humidifiers, dead leaves or wood logs, barns or silos, breweries, dairies, any place where food is stored, and old foam, rubber pillows and mattresses.

Medication

To supplement avoidance measures, the allergist may prescribe medications that will significantly reduce or relieve the irritating symptoms of the allergic reaction. Antihistamines, corticosteroids, and a drug called cromolyn sodium are among medications that may be prescribed, depending upon the nature and severity of the patient's reactions to the allergen.

Immunotherapy

If avoidance measures and medications do not control the symptoms effectively, the allergist may suggest *immunotherapy.* Immunotherapy consists of injections of a diluted amount of the allergen, a technique similar to that used in the skin tests. A small amount of a very weak extract is injected once or twice a week at first. The strength of the extract is gradually increased, and the injections are given less frequently as relief from the symptoms is realized. The injections are continued until the patient has experienced complete relief of the symptoms for a period of two or three years. However, some people may have to continue the injections for longer time spans. Even though the treatments may relieve the symptoms, they may not cure the allergy.

Identification Cards

Any person subject to severe disabling allergy attacks by a known allergen should carry a card describing both the allergic reaction and the allergen. Detailed information can be obtained from the Asthma and Allergy Foundation of America, 1302 18th St., NW, Washington, DC 20036. See also "Allergic Respiratory Diseases" in Ch. 12, *Diseases of the Respiratory System,* and "Asthma Attack" in Ch. 31, *Medical Emergencies.*

25

Women's Health

The special health matters that are related to a woman's reproductive system belong to the branch of medicine known as *gynecology. Obstetrics* is a closely related specialty associated with pregnancy and childbirth. The distinction is something of a technicality for most patients, since obstetricians usually are quite capable of handling gynecological cases and vice versa. The practice of obstetrics and gynecology is commonly combined in a medical service identified by the contraction *Ob-Gyn.* However, there are medical matters that are specifically concerned with female reproductive organs and related tissues but have little to do with obstetrics. For a discussion of obstetrics, see "Infertility, Pregnancy, and Childbirth" in Ch. 4, *The Beginning of a Family.*

The Gynecological Examination

What should a woman expect on her first visit to a gynecologist? First, the gynecologist will interview her, asking about her family, her medical history, and any fears or apprehensions she may have about her personal health. The woman's answers and comments are written into her medical records for future reference. The information can contain important clues that may help in diagnosing any present or future disorders.

A sample of urine and a sample of blood are usually obtained for laboratory tests. During the ensuing physical examination, the woman lies on a special examination table with her feet in metal stirrups and her knees apart. A nurse will be present to assist the doctor. While she is in the *lithotomy position,* the woman's abdomen will be palpated for lumps or other abnormalities. The breasts also will be palpated for possible lumps. Then an external inspection of the vulva and surrounding areas is made by the physician, followed by internal inspection, in which a speculum is used to spread apart the sides of the vagina so that the cervix is exposed. A digital examination (using the fingers) is made of the walls of the vagina and rectum and the neighboring tissue areas, in a search for possible growths or other abnormal conditions. And a sample of cells and secretions from the cervix is taken for a Pap-smear test.

In addition to the examination of the breasts and reproductive system, the gynecologist usually conducts a general physical examination, recording information about height, weight, blood pressure, heart and lung condition, and so on. The routine physical examination, like the medical history, provides additional clues that, when added to the results of the examination of the breasts and reproductive system, will give a complete picture of the patient's gynecological health.

Following the examination, the gynecologist discusses his appraisal of the woman's condition and answers questions. He will discuss whatever treatment she needs. Medications can be explained at this time, including reasons why certain drugs can or should not be taken. If any surgery or further testing is recommended, those aspects of the health picture also should be discussed in some detail.

Results of some laboratory tests and the Pap smear are not usually available for several days. But the physician or nurse will contact the patient when the results are available and advise if she should return in the near future for follow-up testing. The American Cancer Society and the American College of Physicians and Gynecologists agree (1) that all

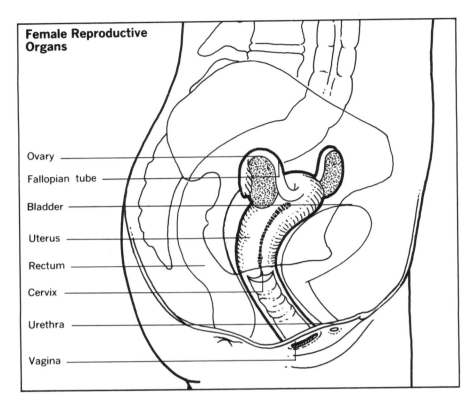

Female Reproductive Organs

Ovary

Fallopian tube

Bladder

Uterus

Rectum

Cervix

Urethra

Vagina

women should have their first Pap smear when they become sexually active or at age 18, whichever occurs first; (2) that every woman should have a yearly Pap smear for the following two years; and (3) that later tests should be administered at the physician's discretion if the first three Pap smears are negative. The woman also should discuss arrangements for future checkups or Pap smear tests rather than wait until signs or symptoms of a serious disorder warrant an immediate visit.

Menstrual Disorders

Among the health concerns of women that specifically belong to gynecology are menstrual disorders. Normally, the first menstrual period (menarche) occurs about age 12 or 13, or sometimes earlier or later. Periods are generally irregular for the first year or two, and then they tend to recur at intervals of 24 to 32 days. Each period begins about two weeks after ovulation, or the release of an egg cell (ovum) from the ovary—unless, of course, the ovum happens to be fertilized in the interval and pregnancy interrupts the whole process.

The menstrual flow, which lasts from three to seven days, is composed mainly of serum, mucus, and dead cells shed from the lining (endometrium) of the uterus. The loss of blood is minimal, usually from two to four ounces. The volume of flow, as well as the time schedule, tends to be fairly regular for most women. When one's menstrual pattern varies noticeably from the expected pattern, and in the absence of pregnancy, it may be a sign of a physical or emotional disorder.

Amenorrhea

Failure to menstruate is called *amenorrhea*. Amenorrhea is a natural effect of pregnancy and of nursing a baby. In an older woman, it may be a sign of menopause. But if a nonpregnant or nonnursing woman after menarche and before menopause (say between the ages of 17 or 18 and 52) fails to menstruate for two or more periods, she should bring it to the attention of a doctor—unless, of course, she has undergone a hysterectomy or other surgical or medical treatment that eliminates menstruation.

Primary Amenorrhea

When menarche has not occurred by the age of 16 or 17, the absence of menstruation is called *primary amenorrhea*. In such a case, a physical examination may show that an imperforate hymen or a closed cervix is obstructing the flow of menses, or a congenital defect may be interfering with menstruation. In almost all cases, menarche can be started with a bit of minor surgery, by treatment of any existing systemic disease, or by the injection of sex hormones; or it will start spontaneously later.

Secondary Amenorrhea

When menstrual periods cease after menarche, the condition is known as *secondary,* or *acquired, amenorrhea.* Secondary amenorrhea may involve missing a single menstrual period or many periods in consecutive months. Among possible causes of interrupted menstruation are certain medications, drugs of abuse, emotional stress, normal fluctuations in ovarian activity in the first few years after menarche, and a number of organic diseases. Medicines that can disrupt normal menstrual activity include tranquilizers and other psychotropic (mind-affecting) drugs that apparently influence hormonal activity in the brain centers, amphetamines, and oral contraceptives. When a particular medication is found to be the cause of amenorrhea, the medical treatment may be judged to be more important than maintaining normal menstrual cycles. When the use of oral contraceptives is followed by amenorrhea for six or more months, normal menstrual activity may resume eventually, but it can often be started sooner by a prescribed medication. Among drugs of abuse known to cause amenorrhea are alcohol and opium-based drugs.

Just as the mind-altering effects of psychotropic drugs involve the hypothalamus and pituitary glands in the brain, which control the hormones that regulate menstrual functions, emotional stress seems to have a parallel influence on the incidence of amenorrhea. *Anorexia nervosa,* a disorder associated with emaciation resulting from an emotional disturbance, also can result in an interruption of menstruation.

Other factors contributing to secondary amenorrhea are measles, mumps, and other infections; cysts and tumors of the ovaries; changes in the tissues lining the vagina or uterus; premature aging of the ovaries; diabetes; obesity; anemia; leukemia; and Hodgkin's disease. In many cases, normal or near-normal menstrual function can be restored by medical treatment, such as administration of hormones, or by surgery, or both. In one type of amenorrhea, marked by adhesion of the walls of the uterus, curettage (scraping of the uterus) is followed by insertion of an intrauterine contraceptive device (IUD) to help hold the uterine walls apart.

Menorrhagia

Almost the opposite of amenorrhea is *menorrhagia,* an excessive menstrual flow. The causes of menorrhagia are as varied as those associated with amenorrhea. They include influenza and other infectious diseases, emotional stress, polyps of the cervical or uterine tissues, hypertension, congestive heart failure, leukemia, and blood coagulation disorders. Menorrhagia may occur during the early stages of a young woman's reproductive life soon after reaching puberty, and medical treatment may be necessary to control the excessive loss of blood. In some cases, dilation and curettage is recommended in addition to the administration of hormones and other medications, such as iron tablets to correct anemia resulting from the loss of red blood cells.

Dilation and Curettage

Dilation and curettage, generally referred to as *D and C,* is a procedure in which the cervix is dilated and the cavity of the uterus is cleaned out by a scooplike instrument, a curette. The same procedure is sometimes used to abort an embryo or to remove a tumor or a polyp.

Although it takes only a few minutes to perform a D and C, the procedure is done in a hospital while the patient is anesthetized. There is no afterpain, only a dull discomfort in the lower pelvic region similar to menstrual awareness.

A physical examination is usually made to determine if there are tumors anywhere in the reproductive organs. Except where tumors are found to be a causative factor, most women will resume normal menstrual cycles after treatment of menorrhagia with medications and D and C. For women beyond the age of 40, the physician may recommend a hysterectomy to prevent recurrence of excessive menstrual blood loss.

Polymenorrhea and Metrorrhagia

These medical terms refer to two other ways in which menstrual periods may depart from typical patterns. *Polymenorrhea* is abnormally frequent menstruation, so that menstrual periods occur at intervals of less than 21 days. This short interval may be the natural established pattern for some women. If it is not, the cause may be physical or emotional stress. *Metrorrhagia* is marked by menstrual bleeding that occurs erratically at unpredictable times. It may be the result of a cyst in the lining of the uterus, a tumor in the reproductive tract, polyps, or some hormonal imbalance, including a disorder of the thyroid gland.

Dysmenorrhea

Abdominal or pelvic pain occurring just before or along with the onset of menstruation is known as *dysmenorrhea.* The symptoms include severe colicky abdominal cramps, backache, headache, and, in some cases, nausea and vomiting. As with amenorrhea, there are two general types of dysmenorrhea, primary and secondary.

Primary Dysmenorrhea

This type includes all cases in which no organic disorder is associated with the symptoms, which are presumed to be a result of uterine contractions and emotional factors. More than 75 percent of all cases are of this type. Primary dysmenorrhea generally begins before age 25, but it may appear at any time from menarche to menopause. It frequently ends with the birth of the first child.

Since primary dysmenorrhea by definition occurs in the absence of organic disease, the diagnosis can be made only after a careful medical history is compiled and a special study of the reproductive organs is made to ensure that no disorder has been overlooked. In some cases, oral contraceptives may be prescribed because of the effect such drugs have in suppressing ovulation; the contraceptives prevent the natural production of the hormone progesterone, which is responsible for certain tissue changes associated with the discomfort of dysmenorrhea. Analgesic drugs to relieve pain and medications that help to relax muscles may be prescribed. Medication is often less beneficial, however, than emotional support—including the easing of any stress at home, school, or work, and reassurance about the worries sometimes associated with menstruation.

Secondary Dysmenorrhea

This condition comprises all menstrual pain that is a result of or associated with an organic disease of the reproductive organs, such as endometriosis, to cite just one example. Secondary dysmenorrhea can occur at any age.

Premenstrual Syndrome

Premenstrual syndrome (PMS) has emerged in recent years as a major challenge to the medical profession. PMS clinics have begun to offer specialized counseling, physical examinations, and treatment for women unable to cope with the disorder. Treatment regimens or therapies range from aspirin to large doses of sex hormones, diet programs, and exercise.

A group of related symptoms, PMS involves both psychological and physical changes. Among the psychological are lethargy, tension, irritability, depression, and feelings of aggression. The physical signs may include headache, bloating, asthma,

and more exotic problems, such as recurrent herpes or hives. In all, more than 300 different symptoms have been attributed to PMS.

The symptoms, gynecologists warn, should become "disturbing" before they are labeled PMS. Restlessness, minor cramps, and other premenstrual problems may indicate that menstruation is about to start but do not necessarily point to PMS. Such minor problems are called *menstrual molimina*. Cramping and other painful conditions occurring during menstruation are referred to as *dysmenorrhea* (see above).

Of the many treatments for PMS, none has proved uniformly effective. This is because the cause or causes of PMS are not totally understood. Most commonly, physicians believe the disorder represents some basic imbalance in the major female hormones, estrogen and progesterone. Thus one treatment calls for administration of "natural" progesterone to correct the supposed imbalance.

Another common treatment suggested for PMS is vitamin B_6, although the treatment remains partly experimental. Some researchers and physicians, however, have reported

disturbing neurological side-effects.

Other theories and treatments exist. Some physicians who have studied PMS and its symptoms believe *prolactin,* a pituitary hormone that stimulates milk secretion, and PMS are associated. A diet and nutrition theory has evolved out of findings that some women report improvement after going on a hypoglycemic diet.

Treated over a substantial period, PMS victims often find that diagnostic tests combined with diet and exercise regimens and vitamin therapy bring good results. If such initial attempts fail, the physician may prescribe medications. In all cases of PMS, according to researchers, psychological support for the sufferer may be important to treatment effectiveness.

Minor Menstrual Problems

Blood Clots

There is not usually any cause for alarm if blood clots are expelled during menstruation. Ordinarily, the menstrual flow is completely liquefied, but a few clots tend to appear

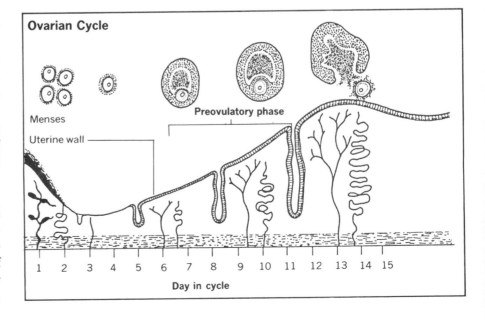

when the flow is profuse. However, if many clots appear and the flow seems excessive, medical advice is recommended, since these conditions may be a sign of fibroid tumors in the uterus.

Oral Contraceptives

Women on combination birth-control pills can expect to see a changed menstrual pattern. The flow becomes slighter than before and very regular. For a discussion of oral contraceptives, see "Family Planning" in Ch. 4, *The Beginning of a Family.*

Odor

The menstrual flow of a healthy woman generally has a mild odor that develops when it is exposed to the air or to the vulva. Some women are concerned about this odor, although it usually is not offensive. When it is, it tends to be associated with inadequate bathing. Detergents are added to some commercial tampons and pad products, and special deodorants have been developed to mask the odor. However, such materials produce allergic reactions in some women, and they can have the unfortunate effect of masking an odor that may be the sign of an abnormal condition.

Onset of Menopause

Menstrual irregularities almost always precede the natural cessation of menstrual function. For a full discussion of menopause, see Ch. 5, *The Middle Years.*

Postmenopausal Bleeding

Bleeding that occurs after the final cessation of menstrual activity should be seen as an urgent signal to seek medical advice. The bleeding may be painless or painful and may range from occasional spotting that is brownish or bright red to rather profuse bleeding that continues for several days or more. The various signs and symptoms should be noted carefully because they can help suggest to a physician the possible cause of bleeding. Bleeding after the menopause is often a sign of cancer of the cervix or the lining of the uterus, but there is a wide variety of other pos-

sible causes, including polyps, ulcers, hypertensive heart disease, an ovarian tumor, or infection. In many cases, the problem can be treated by dilation and curettage or withdrawal of any hormone medications, such as estrogens prescribed for menopausal symptoms, or both. In these cases, if D and C and treatment and discontinuance of hormone therapy fail, the physician may advise a hysterectomy.

Infections of the Reproductive Tract

Vaginal and other reproductive tract infections are among the most common gynecological problems, and among the most stubborn to treat successfully.

Leukorrhea

A whitish, somewhat viscid discharge from the vagina, which is known medically as *leukorrhea,* may be quite normal, especially if it is not continual but occurs only intermittently—prior to menstruation, for example, or associated with sexual excitation. It may also be increased when oral contraceptives are used.

Constant leukorrhea, on the other hand, often is a symptom of an abnormality. Leukorrhea resulting from disease can occur at any age. It is generally associated with an infection of the lower reproductive tract. The discharge may occur without any discomfort, but in some cases there is itching, irritation, and *dyspareunia*—or painful intercourse.

Laboratory tests of vaginal secretions may be needed to help identify the precise cause of the discharge. Leukorrhea can result from vaginal ulcers; a tumor of the vagina, uterus, or

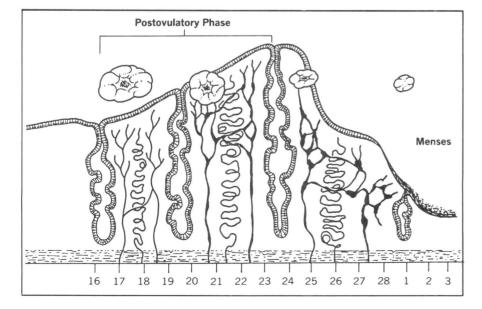

Postovulatory Phase

Menses

16 17 18 19 20 21 22 23 24 25 26 27 28 1 2 3

fallopian tubes; gonorrhea; or infection by any of various disease organisms of the vulva, vagina, cervix, uterus, or tubes. It may also result from an abnormality of menstrual function, or even emotional stress.

Treatment, of course, depends on the cause. If the discharge is because of an infection, care must be taken to avoid being reinfected or transmitting the disease organism through sexual contact or possibly contaminated underclothing, etc.

Moniliasis

Moniliasis, also known as *candidiasis,* is an infection by a yeastlike fungus that invades mucous membrane and sometimes skin in various parts of the body. Inside the mouth, the organism causes thrush, most commonly in babies. When the organism invades the vaginal area, it causes a scant white discharge of a thick consistency resembling that of cottage cheese. There is itching, burning, and swelling of the labial and vulvar areas. The symptoms tend to worsen just before the menstrual period. The occurrence of the disease is thought by some researchers to be fostered by oral contraceptives. Antibiotic therapy, may increase the moniliasis organism, because it destroys many of the benign organisms that regularly share the same environment.

Moniliasis is treated with suppositories, creams, and other medications. The woman's partner should be treated at the same time to prevent a cycle of reinfection because the fungus will otherwise spread to the genital tissues of the man.

Trichomoniasis

A type of leukorrhea that consists of a copious yellow to green frothy and

fetid discharge is caused by infection by the *Trichomonas* organism. The organism causes an irritating itching condition that tends to set in or worsen just after a menstrual period. The condition is diagnosed by a test similar to a Pap smear, made with a specimen taken from the vagina. Trichomonas organisms, if present, are easy to identify under a microscope; they are pear-shaped protozoa with three to five whiplike tails.

The organism favors warm, moist areas, such as genital tissues, but it can also survive in damp towels and washcloths, around toilet seats, and on beaches and the perimeters of swimming pools. Thus it can spread from one member of a family to other members and from one woman to other women. *Trichomoniasis* is not technically a venereal disease, but it can be transmitted by sexual contact. When one partner is infected with trichomoniasis, both must be treated at the same time and a condom must be worn during intercourse.

Several drugs are available for treating trichomoniasis, including tablets taken orally and suppositories inserted in the vagina. The tablets are taken for ten days, then an examination is made to determine if any *Trichomonas* organisms are still present. Medication may be continued for several months if the infection resists the drug—studies show that the organism appears to survive in about 10 percent of treated cases.

Herpes Simplex Virus Type 2

Herpes is acquired by contact with the mucous membranes of an infected person. The mucous membrane of the mouth and lips, the genitals, or the rectum may be affected. The causative agent is known as *herpes simplex virus Type II,* or *HSV-II.* It is similar to but not the same as the vi-

rus that causes fever blisters, or cold sores, which is Type *I* (HSV-I). The virus is associated with some spontaneous abortions. If the mother has blisters at the time of delivery, the virus can be transmitted to the baby as he or she passes through the vagina. The central nervous system, including the brain, may be damaged by the virus if the baby becomes infected. To avoid exposure to the virus, a caesarian delivery is recommended.

Symptoms

Patients with their first HSV-II infection usually complain of intense itching, painful blisterlike eruptions, and ulcerated patches with a discharge. Other symptoms may include genital pain and vaginal bleeding. Fever, swelling, difficult urination, and a general feeling of ill health and lack of appetite may accompany the infection.

Symptoms may subside after a few weeks, but recurrences are common, though they are less painful and of shorter duration. There is no known cure for the viral infection.

Treatment

No drug has been found to attack the viruses while they are "hibernating" in cells at the base of the spine. But one antiviral drug, *acyclovir,* has been found to reduce recurrent outbreaks and to block flareups for up to several months. Taken orally in pill form, acyclovir is ingested daily. Some patients can stop treatment and have no further flare-ups. Researchers have discovered that the capsules kill or neutralize the herpes viruses only when they are active. Because of evidence that the virus may be related to the subsequent development of cervical cancer, women sufferers should have Pap-smear tests at intervals of six months instead of the usual twelve.

Pelvic Inflammatory Disease

Pelvic inflammatory disease, or PID, is on the increase in the female population. Commonly caused by bacteria from other diseases such as chlamydia or gonorrhea, PID may go for years without detection. Frequently symptomless, PID infects and destroys the interior of the reproductive system. It attacks the fallopian tubes and uterine lining, leaving permanent scarring. The increase in the number of ectopic pregnancies (fallopian tube pregnancies) is believed to stem from the increase in women who have scarring from PID. The increase in sterility in the population is also linked directly to PID scarring.

One is seven women in the United States has been infected with PID. Treatment for both partners involves antibiotics to kill the bacteria, and treatment of any original disease that may have caused it. Douching should be avoided if PID is suspected. Symptoms include abdominal tenderness or pain, vaginal discharge, or dull ache or twitching in the uterine cavity.

Blood tests and cultures for chlamydia or other diseases should be done. Two-thirds of PID cases are from sexual transmission. If left untreated, PID can cause sterility, miscarriage, ectopic pregnancy, blood infection, and eventually death.

Disorders of the Urinary System

Both men and women are subject to disorders of the urinary system, but there are a few disorders that affect women chiefly or women only, for reasons related to anatomical structure. See also Ch. 17, *Diseases of the Urinogenital System.*

Inflammation of the Bladder

Any inflammation of the bladder is known medically as *cystitis.* Factors such as urinary tract stones, injury, and obstructions to the normal flow of urine can aggravate or cause cystitis in either sex. Cystitis resulting from infectious organisms, however, is much more common in women than in men. This is understandable in view of the relative shortness of the female urethra—the tube through which urine is discharged from the bladder and through which infectious organisms can reach the bladder from the outside. In addition, the anus and the vagina, both of which may frequently be sources of infection, are situated relatively close to the external opening of the female urethra.

In women generally, the symptoms of cystitis may include a burning sensation around the edges of the vulva. There is usually a frequent urge to urinate and difficulty or pain (*dysuria*) associated with urination. Urinary retention and dehydration, which are generally under the control of the individual, can contribute to the spread of infection once it begins. The lining of the urinary bladder is relatively resistant to infection by most microorganisms as long as the normal flow of liquids through the urinary tract is maintained. In cases that do not yield quickly to copious fluid intake, there are medications that may be prescribed to cure the infection. Where urinary frequency or difficulty is accompanied by the appearance of blood in the urine, a physician should be consulted immediately.

Honeymoon Cystitis

One type of cystitis tends to occur mostly in young women during the first few weeks of frequent sexual activity, to which it is attributed. Sexual activity may result in swelling of the urethra and the neck of the bladder, making urination difficult. The inflammation of these tissues can in turn make them more susceptible to infection. A treatment recommended specifically for honeymoon cystitis is to drink large quantities of water or other fluids and to empty the bladder before and after engaging in sexual intercourse. Adequate lubrication, such as petroleum jelly, is also important. Medical care should be sought if the condition persists.

Urethral Disorders

The urethra is perforce involved in the inflammation of cystitis because it is the route by which infectious organisms reach the bladder. In addition, there are disorders that are essentially confined to the urethra.

Urethral Caruncle

Urethral caruncle is a rather uncommon urinary tract disorder that tends to be confined to women after the menopause. A *caruncle* (not to be confused with *carbuncle*) is a small, red, fleshy outgrowth. It may be visible near the opening of the urethra. A caruncle growing from the cells of the urethra may be a sign of a bacterial infection, a tumor, or any of several other possible conditions. Symptoms may include vaginal bleeding, pain, tenderness, painful sexual intercourse (dyspareunia), a whitish, viscid discharge, and difficulty in urinating. A physician should be consulted when such symptoms are present. A tissue biopsy and Pap smear may be taken to diagnose the condition. Caruncles are easily treated and of no long-term consequence.

Urethral Diverticulum

Another disorder of the urethra is a *urethral diverticulum,* or outpocket-

The Female Urinary System

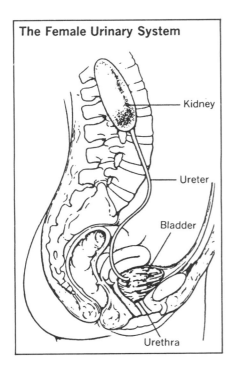

Kidney

Ureter

Bladder

Urethra

ing of the urethra. The problem can be caused by a developmental malformation, an injury, inflammation, a cyst, a urinary stone, or a venereal disease. Stones are a common cause, and in some patients there may be more than one diverticulum. The symptoms may include discomfort and urinary difficulty, as well as dyspareunia. The disorder can be diagnosed with the help of X-ray photographs of the region of the urethra and bladder after they have been filled with a radiopaque substance that flows into any diverticula that may be present.

Treatment of a urethral diverticulum includes antibiotics to stop infection, medications to relieve pain and discomfort, and douches. In some cases, surgery is needed to eliminate the diverticula.

Structural Anomalies

Various kinds of injury may be sustained by the female reproductive system and other abdominal organs, chiefly as a result of childbearing. The structural damage can generally be repaired by surgical measures.

Fistula

An abnormal opening between two organs or from an organ to the outside of the body is known as a *fistula*. Fistulas may involve the urinary and reproductive systems of a woman. Damage to the organs during pregnancy or surgery, for example, can result in a fistula between the urethra and the vagina, causing urinary incontinence. A similar kind of fistula can develop between the rectum and the vagina as a result of injury, complications of pregnancy, or surgery. Disorders of this sort must be repaired surgically.

Prolapsed Uterus

The uterus normally rests on the floor of the pelvis, held in position by numerous ligaments. Damage to the ligaments and other supporting tissues causes the uterus to descend, or *prolapse*, into the vagina. There are various degrees of prolapse, ranging from a slight intrusion of the uterus

into the vagina to a severe condition in which the cervix of the uterus protrudes out of the vaginal orifice. Prolapse of the uterus resembles a hernia but is not a true hernia, because the opening through which the uterus protrudes is a normal one.

Backache and a feeling of heaviness in the pelvic region may accompany the condition. Many women complain of a "dragging" sensation. An assortment of complications may involve neighboring organ systems; bleeding and ulceration of the uterus are not uncommon. Coughing and straining can aggravate the symptoms.

Like the various types of hernia, a prolapsed uterus does not improve without treatment but tends instead to worsen gradually. The only permanent treatment is surgical repair. In mild cases, a woman may get relief from symptoms through exercises intended to strengthen the muscles of the pelvic region. Supporting devices, such as an inflatable, doughnut-shaped pessary, are available as temporary methods of correcting a prolapse. Preventive exercises may be recommended for childbearing women who want to avoid weakened muscles and ligaments leading to prolapse.

Prolapsed Uterus

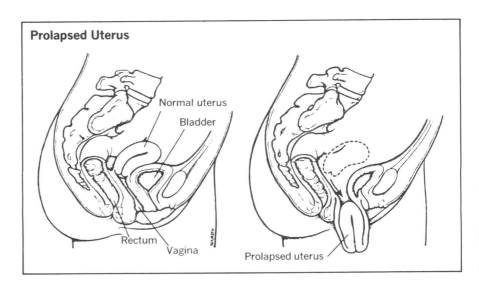

Normal uterus

Bladder

Rectum

Vagina

Prolapsed uterus

Tipped Uterus

The uterus may be out of its normal position without being prolapsed. A malpositioned uterus may be "tipped" forward, backward, or otherwise be out of alignment with neighboring organs. A malpositioned uterus may cause no symptoms, or it may be associated with dysmenorrhea or infertility. If a malpositioned uterus causes pain, bleeding, or other problems, the condition can be corrected surgically, or a pessary support may relieve the symptoms. Displacement of the uterus occasionally is the result of a separate pelvic disease that requires treatment.

Hernias of the Vaginal Wall

The wall of the vagina may be ruptured in childbirth, especially in a multiple delivery or birth of a larger-than-average baby. The kind of hernia depends on the exact site of the rupture and what organ happens to lie against the vaginal wall at that point. The condition may be further complicated by a prolapsed uterus. Careful examination of the patient and X-ray pictures may be necessary to determine whether just one or several of the urinary, reproductive, and gastrointestinal organs in the pelvic cavity are involved.

Cystocele

Cystocele is a hernia involving the bladder and the vagina. Structurally, part of the bladder protrudes through the wall of the vagina. The symptoms, in addition to a feeling of pressure deep in the vagina, may be urinary difficulties, such as incontinence, a frequent urge to urinate, and inability to completely empty the bladder. Residual urine in the bladder may contribute to infection and inflammation of the bladder. Treatment includes

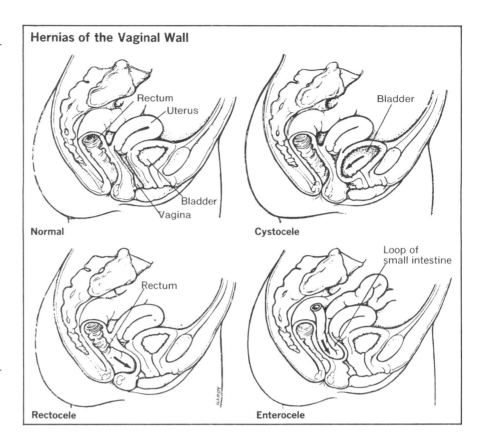

Hernias of the Vaginal Wall

Rectum / Uterus / Bladder / Vagina — **Normal**

Bladder — **Cystocele**

Rectum — **Rectocele**

Loop of small intestine — **Enterocele**

surgery to correct the condition, pessaries if needed to support the structures, and medications to control infection.

Rectocele

A hernia involving the tissues separating the vagina and the rectum, behind the vagina, is called a *rectocele*. The symptoms are a feeling of fullness in the vagina and difficulty in defecating. Enemas or laxatives may be needed to relieve constipation because straining, or even coughing, can aggravate the condition. Surgery is the only permanently effective treatment. Special diets, laxatives, and rectal suppositories may be prescribed pending surgery.

Enterocele

A herniation of the small intestine into the vagina is called an *enterocele*.

Some of the symptoms are similar to those of other hernias involving the vaginal wall, and in addition, a patient with an enterocele may experience abdominal cramps shortly after eating. An enterocele can be dangerous, as well as uncomfortable, because a segment of the small bowel can become trapped and obstructed, requiring emergency surgery.

Varicose Veins

Varicose veins of the vulva, vagina, and neighboring areas are another possible effect of pregnancy, although the legs are more often affected. Obesity, reduced physical activity during pregnancy, and circulatory changes associated with pregnancy can contribute to the development of varicose veins. The symptoms generally are limited to discomfort, although there can be bleeding, particularly at the time of childbirth.

Varicose veins that occur in the vulva and vagina during pregnancy and cause discomfort can be treated surgically during the early months of pregnancy. Some drugs and supportive therapy can be used to help relieve symptoms. But many physicians recommend that surgical stripping of veins be delayed until after the pregnancy has been terminated. A complication of untreated varicose veins can be development of blood clots in the abnormal blood vessels. For a discussion of varicose veins of the legs during pregnancy, see "Leg Cramps and Varicose Veins" in Ch. 4, *The Beginning of a Family*.

Benign Neoplasms

The word *neoplasm* refers to any abnormal proliferation of tissue that serves no useful function. There are numerous kinds of neoplasms but just two main groups—cancerous, or *malignant;* or noncancerous, or *benign.* In ordinary speech the word *benign* suggests some positive benefit, but a benign neoplasm, though noncancerous, may in fact be harmful to health or at least worrisome. Benign neoplasms that are of particular concern to women are discussed below.

Cysts

A *cyst* is a sac containing a gaseous, fluid, or semisolid material. (Certain normal anatomical structures, like the urinary bladder, are technically known as cysts—hence the term *cystitis* for inflammation of the bladder.) Abnormal, or neoplastic, cysts can develop at several sites within the urinary and reproductive systems.

Vaginal Cysts

A cyst may develop in a gland at the opening of the vagina as a result of infection with a venereal or other disease. Such a cyst can block the flow of secretions from the gland and produce swelling and pain. Dyspareunia, or painful intercourse, is sometimes a symptom. A vaginal-gland cyst usually is treated with antibiotics and hot packs. In some cases, it may be necessary for a physician to make an incision to drain the cyst.

Ovarian Cysts

Cysts in the ovaries may be caused by a malfunction of physiological process or by a pathological condition. Some pathological cysts are malignant. The cysts in the ovaries generally are filled with fluid that may range in color from pale and clear to reddish brown, depending upon the source of the fluid. Some cysts are too small to be seen with the naked eye, whereas others may be four or five inches in diameter when symptoms begin to cause discomfort. There are several different kinds of ovarian cysts.

Follicular Cyst

A *follicular,* or *retention,* cyst is a physiological cyst and is one of the most common types. It develops in an old follicle in which an ovum for some reason has failed to break out of its capsule during the ovulation process. Ordinarily, the contents of such a follicle are resorbed, but sometimes a cyst develops. It rarely grows larger than about two inches in diameter. It may rupture but usually disappears after a few months. The symptoms may include pain with some uterine bleeding and dyspareunia. Treatment consists of warm douches, analgesics, and hormone therapy designed to restore normal ovarian activity. If the

symptoms persist or the cyst continues to increase in size, or if serious complications occur, the physician may recommend exploratory surgery.

Occasionally such cysts, whether or not they rupture, produce symptoms that mimic those of appendicitis, with severe abdominal pain. The abdomen may become so tender that a physician cannot palpate the organs in order to distinguish between an ovarian cyst and appendicitis, particularly if the right ovary is involved. The symptoms occur at the time that ovulation would be expected. If the physician cannot be certain that the cause of the abdominal pain is indeed a cyst, for which surgery is not needed, he may recommend surgery anyway— just to be on the safe side.

Multiple follicular cysts, involving the ovaries on both sides (*bilateral polycystic ovaries*) can result in a syndrome (or group of symptoms) that includes infertility, obesity, and abnormal growth of body hair. All of these effects are related to a disruption of normal sex-hormone activity; they generally occur in young women, from teenagers to those in their 20s. The therapy includes both medical and surgical efforts to restore normal menstrual function, a diet to control obesity, and the use of various depilatory techniques to remove unwanted body hair.

Corpus Luteum Cyst

This kind of cyst may develop in the ovary following ovulation or during the early part of a pregnancy. The corpus luteum is a small, temporary gland that forms in the empty follicle after the ovum has been released from the ovary. Its function is to produce the hormone progesterone, which is important in preparing the endometrium, the lining of the uterus, to receive a fertilized ovum. The corpus luteum, however, also can be overproductive of a brownish fluid that fills the former follicular space, causing it to swell to a diameter of two or three inches. The cyst causes symptoms of pain and tenderness and may also result in a disruption of normal menstrual cycles in a woman who is not pregnant.

Most corpus luteum cysts gradually decrease in size without special treatment, except to relieve the symptoms. There may, however, be complications, such as torsion, or painful twisting of the ovary, or a rupture of the cyst. A ruptured corpus luteum cyst can result in hemorrhage and peritonitis, requiring immediate surgery.

Chocolate Cyst

So called because of their brownish-red color, chocolate cysts consist of misplaced endometrial tissue growing on the ovary instead of in its normal position lining the uterus. Chocolate cysts are among the largest of the ovarian cysts, ranging up to five or six inches in diameter. They cause symptoms associated with a variety of disorders of the reproductive system, including infertility, dyspareunia, and dysmenorrhea. Surgery usually is a favored method of therapy, the precise procedure depending upon the amount of ovarian tissue involved. A small chocolate cyst can be cauterized, but a large cyst may require removal of a portion of the ovary. See also "Cancer of the Ovary" later in this chapter.

Cysts of the Breast

Cysts may form in the milk glands or the ducts leading from the glands. They are caused by imbalances in ovarian hormones and they tend to develop in mature women approaching the menopause. The cysts tend to fluctuate in size, often enlarging just before or during menstruation, and there may be a discharge from the nipple. Pain and tenderness are usually present, although painless cysts are sometimes discovered only when a woman examines her breasts for possible lumps. Cysts may be almost microscopic in size or as large as an inch or more in diameter. It is not uncommon for more than one cyst to occur at the same time in one breast or both.

A medical examination is recommended when any kind of lump can be felt in the breast tissue. This is particularly important for women who have passed menopause. The physician frequently can determine whether a lump is a result of a cyst or cancer by the patient's history and by physical examination, especially when repeated at intervals of several weeks. Mammography and biopsy study of a small bit of tissue are used to confirm the diagnosis.

Women who are troubled by breast cysts may be helped by wearing a good brassiere at all times, even during sleep, to protect tender areas. The only medications available are those that relieve pain and discomfort—symptoms that usually subside when the menopause is reached.

Other Noncancerous Masses

A benign lump in the breast can be caused by either a fat deposit or an abscess. A fatty mass frequently forms if an injury to the breast damages adipose tissue. Because of a similarity of the symptoms to those of breast cancer, a biopsy is usually required to distinguish the lesion from a cancer. The involved tissue may in any case be removed surgically.

An abscess of the breast as a result of an infection, although a rare problem, may produce a lump that requires treatment with antibiotic medications or by an incision to drain the pus. Breast infections leading to abscesses are most likely to occur in nursing mothers but can also develop in women who are not lactating. When an infection develops in a breast being used to nurse a baby, nursing has to be discontinued temporarily while the infection is treated. See also "Cancer of the Breast" later in this chapter.

Polyps

A *polyp* is a strange-looking growth, even for an abnormal growth of tissue. It has been described as having the appearance of a tennis racket or a small mushroom. Polyps are found in many parts of the body, from the nose to the rectum. Usually they are harmless. But a polyp can result in discomfort or bleeding and require surgical excision. A polyp on the breast, for example, can become irritated by rubbing against the fabric of a brassiere. Although polyps generally are not cancerous, it is standard procedure to have the polyp tissue, like any excised tissue, tested in the laboratory. If malignant cells accompany a polyp, they are usually found at the base of the growth, which means that some of the tissue around the polyp must be excised along with the growth itself. Once a polyp is removed it does not grow again, although other polyps can occur in the same region.

Cervical Polyp

Polyps in the cervix are not uncommon, occurring most frequently in the years between menarche and menopause. A cervical polyp may be associated with vaginal bleeding or leukorrhea; the bleeding may occur after douching or sexual intercourse. In some cases, the bleeding is severe. Cervical polyps can usually be located visually by an examining physician and removed by minor surgery.

Endometrial Polyp

Endometrial polyps, which develop in the lining of the uterus, usually occur in women who are over 40, although they can develop at any age after menarche. They are frequently the cause of nonmenstrual bleeding. They tend to be much larger than polyps that grow in other organs of the body: an endometrial polyp may be rooted high in the uterus with a stem reaching all the way to the cervix. Such a polyp is usually located and removed during a D- and C- procedure. As in the case of a cervical polyp, the growth and a bit of surrounding tissue are studied for traces of cancer cells.

Benign Tumors

Tumors are rather firm growths that may be either benign or malignant. In practice, any tumor is regarded with suspicion unless malignancy is ruled out by actual laboratory tests. Even a benign tumor represents a tissue abnormality, and if untreated can produce symptoms that interfere with normal health and activity.

Fibromas

Among the more common of the benign tumors is the *fibroma,* commonly known as a *fibroid tumor,* composed of fibrous connective tissue. About one of every 20 ovarian tumors is a fibroma, and a similar growth in the uterus is the most common type of tumor found in that organ. Fibromas also occur in the vulva.

Ovarian Fibroma

Ovarian fibromas are usually small, but there are instances in which they have grown to weigh as much as five pounds. A large fibroma can be very painful and produce symptoms such as a feeling of heaviness in the pelvic area, nausea, and vomiting. The growth may crowd other organs of the body, causing enlargement of the abdomen and cardiac and respiratory symptoms. The only treatment is surgical removal of the tumor, after which there is usually a quick and full recovery.

Uterine Fibroma

Fibroid tumors of the uterus can also grow to a very large size, some weighing many pounds. Like ovarian fibromas, they can press against neighboring organs such as the intestine or the urinary bladder, producing constipation or urinary difficulty. More commonly, there is pain and vaginal bleeding, along with pelvic pressure and enlargement of the abdomen. It is possible in some cases for a fibroid tumor to grow slowly in the uterus for several years without causing serious discomfort to the patient. If the tumor obstructs or distorts the reproductive tract, it may be a cause of infertility.

Treatment of fibroid tumors varies according to their size, the age of the patient and her expectations about having children, and other factors. If the tumor is small and does not appear to be growing at a rapid rate, the physician may recommend that surgery be postponed as long as the tumor poses no threat to health. For an older woman, or for a woman who does not want to bear children, a hysterectomy may be advised, especially if symptoms are troublesome. If the patient is a young woman who wants to have children, the physician is likely to advise a *myomectomy,* a surgical excision of the tumor, since a fibroid tumor of the uterus can cause serious complications during pregnancy and labor. It can result in abortion or premature labor, malpresentation of the fetus, difficult labor, and severe loss of blood during childbirth. While fibroid tumors of the uterus are not malignant, special tests are made of the endometrial tissue as part of any myomectomy or hysterectomy to rule out the possibility that cancer cells may be involved in the disorder.

Endometriosis

Endometriosis is the medical term for a condition in which endometrial tissue, the special kind of tissue that lines the uterus, grows in various areas of the pelvic cavity outside the uterus. Endometrial cells may invade such unlikely places as the ovaries (the most common site), the bladder, appendix, Fallopian tubes, intestinal tract, or the supporting structure of the uterus. The external endometrial tissue may appear as small blisters of endometrial cells, as solid nodules, or as cysts, usually of the ovary, which may be four inches or more in diameter, like the chocolate cysts of the ovaries. Such a mass of sometimes tumorlike endometrial cells is called an *endometrioma.*

The misplaced endometrial tissue causes problems because it goes through menstrual cycles just as the endometrium does within the cavity of the uterus. The endometrial tissue proliferates after ovulation and may cause almost constant pain, wherever it is located, for a few days before the start of menstruation. The symptoms subside after the menstrual flow begins. The effects may include dyspareunia, rectal bleeding, backache, and generalized pain in the pelvic region as sensitive tissues throughout the pelvic cavity are irritated by monthly cycles of swelling and bleeding.

Because infertility is associated with endometriosis, which can become progressively worse, young women who want to bear children are sometimes encouraged to begin efforts to become pregnant as early as possible if they show signs or symptoms of the disorder. Treatment includes hormone medication and surgery to remove the lesions of endometriosis or the organ involved. For patients with extensive spread of endometrial tissue outside the uterus, the physician may recommend removal of one or both ovaries. Destruction of the ovaries surgically or by radiation therapy may be employed to eliminate the menstrual cycle activity that aggravates the symptoms of endometriosis. These procedures cause sterility and premature menopause, but some women prefer this to the discomfort of endometriosis. The hormone therapy inhibits the ovulation phase of the menstrual cycle. Without ovulation, the endometrial tissue does not proliferate. For this reason, pregnancy often eliminates or eases the symptoms of endometriosis during parturition and for a period of time thereafter.

Dyspareunia

Dyspareunia, or painful intercourse, is often associated with endometriosis and is attributed to irritation of nerve fibers in the area of the cervix from the pressure of sexual activity. There are many other possible causes of painful intercourse, some functional and some organic in nature. In addition to endometriosis, the problem may be owing to a vaginal contracture, a disorder involving the muscles of the pelvic region, inflammation of the vagina or urethra, prolapsed or malpositioned uterus, *cervicitis* (inflammation of the cervix), or a disorder of the bladder or rectum. A cause of dyspareunia in older women may be a degeneration of the tissues lining the vagina, which become thin and dry. Temporary therapy for dyspareunia may include water-soluble lubricants, anesthetic ointments, steroid hormones, analgesics, and sedatives.

In appropriate cases, surgery is effective in correcting an organic cause of painful sexual intercourse. Functional or psychogenic (of psychological origin) causes of dyspareunia usually require psychological counseling for the patient and her sexual partner.

Backache

Still another effect of endometriosis that can suggest other disorders is backache. When endometrial tissue invades the pelvic region, there may be a fairly constant pain in the back near the tailbone or the rectum. Usually the backache subsides only after the cause has been eliminated. Temporary measures include those advised for other kinds of backache: sleeping on a firm mattress, preferably reinforced with a sheet of plywood between springs and mattress; application of dry heat or warm baths; sedatives to relieve tension, and analgesics to relieve the pain.

A backache that radiates down the back and into a leg, following the path of a sciatic nerve, can be the result of a disorder of the ovaries or uterus. An ovarian cyst or infection of the Fallopian tubes can produce a backache that seems to be centered in the lumbosacral area of the spinal column. Such backaches, sometimes called gynecologic backaches, tend to occur most frequently during a woman's childbearing years and more often affect women who have had several children than women who have not been pregnant. Tumors also can produce backache symptoms. X-ray pictures, myelograms, and laboratory studies may be required in order to rule out the possibilities that the back pain may be caused by a tumor, a herniated or "slipped" disk, or a deformity of the spinal column that might have been aggravated by one or more pregnancies. Most backaches, however, relate to poor posture or mus-

cle tension. Anxiety or other kinds of emotional stress can aggravate the symptoms. See also "Backaches" in Ch. 23, *Aches, Pains, Nuisances, Worries,* and "Back Pain and Its Causes" in Ch. 25, *Women's Health.*

Cancers of the Reproductive System

Cancer of the Cervix

The cervix of the uterus is the ninth most common site of cancers affecting women. As compared with all cancers of the reproductive organs of women, it rates third, after uterine cancer and ovarian cancer. It has been estimated that about 13,000 cases of cervical cancer are found among American women each year, and approximately 4,500 deaths every year are a result of this disease.

The number of cases of preinvasive cervical cancer is down because of the increased number of women who undergo regular gynecological examination. When cancer is diagnosed early, the survival rate increases tremendously for the patient.

The actual causes of cervical cancer are still unknown. Current medical thinking suggests that there is no causal relationship between cervical cancer and the use of oral contraceptives.

Preinvasive Stage

The earliest signs of cervical cancer tend to appear between the ages of 25 and 45. At this early, *preinvasive* stage, the cancer is described as *in* situ—confined to its original site. If the cancer is not treated at this stage, the disease spreads and becomes a typical invasive cancer within five to ten years. Signs of bleeding and ulceration usually do not appear until this has occurred. However, because of the relatively slow growth of cervical cancer in the early stage, the disease usually can be detected by a Pap smear test before it becomes invasive.

Invasive Cancer

Cancer that has spread beyond the cervix is far more difficult to treat. Surgery, radiation or chemotherapy, and regular examinations to catch any recurrence of cancer will probably be necessary. It is unusual for anyone to develop invasive cancer without knowing it, if she has undergone regular, routine pelvic exams.

Diagnostic Methods

Pap Smear Test

The *Pap smear* test (named for Dr. George Papanicolaou, who developed the technique in 1928) is a quick and simple method of detecting cancerous cells in secretions and scrapings from mucous membrane. It requires the collection of small samples of cells from the surface of the cervix and from the cervical canal. Such samples are obtained by inserting a plastic spatula or a brush-tipped tube into the vagina, into which a speculum has been placed previously. The device is scraped gently over the area of the cervix. The physician may collect also a sample of vaginal secretions, which may contain possibly cancerous cells not only from the cervix but from the ovaries and uterus as well. (This is the only way a Pap smear test can be done if a woman has had a complete hysterectomy and has no cervix.) All cell samples are placed (smeared) on microscope slides and treated with a chemical preservative. The slides are sent to a laboratory for study and a report is made to the examining physician, usually within a few days, on the findings.

Results from the Pap smear are reported as: normal, inadequate sampling, showing infection, or showing cell abnormalities. Except for the normal results, Paps will be done again to ensure accuracy. No one should wait more than six months for a follow-up reading on an infectious diagnosis and treatment. For all others, follow-up should be immediate. Cell abnormalities are divided into at least three categories: low-grade lesions (noncancerous), high-grade lesions (noncancerous), and cancer.

Other Diagnostic Tests

When a report of positive findings is returned by the laboratory, the physician immediately arranges for further studies. These involve examination of the cervix visually by a special microscopic technique known as *colposcopy,* and the removal of small tissue samples. These studies are usually done in a physician's office. In some cases a biopsy is necessary. The biopsy sample is taken when possible from the same location on the cervix as the Pap smear that resulted in positive findings. The Loop Electrosurgical Excision Procedure (LEEP) is a method of combining the biopsy and the excision of the diseased tissue. An electrified loop removes the abnormal tissue from the cervix. The small circle that is removed can then be examined for signs of cancer. The electrical charge of the loop cauterizes the cut to prevent infection and bleeding. Treatment ordinarily is not started until all of the studies have verified that there is cancer in the tissues of the cervix; other disorders, such as cervicitis, venereal infection, and polyps, can mimic symptoms of cervical cancer.

Therapy

The kind of treatment recommended for a case of cervical cancer generally depends upon several factors, such as the stage of cancer development and the age and general health of the patient. For a young woman who wishes to have children despite cancer *in situ,* which is limited to the cervix, surgeons may excise a portion of the cervix and continue watching for further developments with frequent Pap smears and other tests. The treatment of choice for cervical cancer in the early stage, however, is surgical removal of the body of the uterus, as well as of the cervix—a procedure called a *total hysterectomy.* This is the usual treatment for women over the age of 40 or for those who do not wish to have children. Sometimes more extensive surgery is necessary.

Radiation treatment may be advised for women who are not considered to be good surgical risks because of other health problems. Radiation may be recommended along with surgery for women with advanced cervical cancer in order to help destroy cancer cells that may have spread by metastasis to other tissues.

The five-year cure rate for cervical cancer is about 99 percent when treatment is started in the early, pre-invasive stage. The chances of a cure drop sharply in later stages, but the five-year cure rate is still as high as 65 percent if treatment is started when the cancer has just begun to spread to the vagina or other nearby tissues.

Cancer of the Body of the Uterus

Cancer of the body of the uterus, or *endometrial cancer,* is more common than cancer of the cervix. Uterine cancer is the most common type of cancer of the reproductive organs. Cervical cancer primarily affects women before middle age; uterine cancer occurs more frequently among women beyond the menopause, with its highest rate occurring among women between the ages of 50 and 70. Survival rate for cancer of the uterus is high, with 82 percent living 5 years after diagnosis. Risk factors for uterine cancer include obesity, diabetes, and ovarian cysts. Other potential risks are for women who have taken estrogen-only pills for menopausal symptoms and women who have taken tamoxifen for breast cancer.

Diagnostic Methods

Early symptoms usually include bleeding between menstrual periods or after menopause, and occasionally a watery or blood-stained vaginal discharge. Most patients experience no pain in the early stages, although pain is a symptom in advanced uterine cancer or when the disease is complicated by an infection. Unfortunately, there is no simple test, like the Pap smear for cervical cancer, that provides a good diagnostic clue to the presence of endometrial cancer. The Pap smear does occasionally pick up cells sloughed off by the endometrium, and laboratory tests can tell if they might be malignant. The best chance for early diagnosis is for a woman to report to her gynecologist or physician any signs of abnormal bleeding between periods, or postmenopausal bleeding. Unusual bleeding should be followed up by the doctor with examination of the uterine lining.

A physician who is suspicious of symptoms of endometrial cancer must depend upon direct methods to confirm or rule out the disease. The usual method is a dilatation and curettage (D and C), during which a small sample of uterine lining will be removed for biopsy, or a sample may be withdrawn by suction (aspirated) from the uterine cavity. The cervix is dilated (opened) and the uterine lining scraped with a curette. Aspiration can be done in the physician's office with local anesthesia of the cervix or with no anesthesia. There is little or no discomfort following aspiration.

Therapy

If the diagnostic D and C is done when the abnormal bleeding associated with uterine cancer first begins, the chances of a cure are very good. The first step, if the general health of the patient permits surgery, is complete removal of the uterus, ovaries, and fallopian tubes—a procedure called a *radical hysterectomy.* Radiation may also be administered to control the spread of cancer cells.

A hysterectomy should not affect a woman's normal sexual activity. Sexual relations usually can be resumed about six to eight weeks after the operation, or when the incision has healed. If the incision is made through the pubic region or vagina, there should be little or no visible scar. See "Family Planning," in Chapter 4.

Estrogen and Cancer

There is a higher incidence of cancer of the uterus among women who have tumors of the ovary that produce estrogen, as well as among women whose menopause begins later than the usual age (and hence who have produced estrogen naturally for a longer-than-usual period). Because of the statistical associations between uterine cancer and estrogen-producing tumors, as well as other factors, the American Cancer Society has cautioned that physicians should exert "close supervision of women on estrogen, with an awareness that sustained use [of estrogens] may stimulate dormant factors in the body and lead to development of endometrial cancer." For women who are prescribed estrogen for menopause, it is recommended that the estrogen be given in combination with a synthetic progestin. Unopposed estrogen increases the growth of cancerous tumors already present, and is suspected of increasing the risk of new cancer growths.

Among the conditions for which estrogen has been prescribed for women of middle age and beyond are uncomfortable effects of menopause, such as itching and irritation caused by dryness of the vagina, and what is commonly referred to as "hot flashes." See *The Middle Years,* Ch. 5, "Menopause" for more information.

Diethylstilbestrol

An estrogenlike synthetic compound has definitely been implicated in the development of a type of cancer, *adenocarcinoma,* which primarily affects epithelial tissue. The synthetic hormone known chemically as *diethylstilbestrol* (DES) or stilbestrol was taken for the most part in the late 1940s and through the 1960s by pregnant women for the treatment of such complications as bleeding and threatened miscarriage. Around 1971, physicians became aware that some of the daughters whose mothers had taken DES during their pregnancy had developed an unusual cell formation in vaginal tissue, vaginal and cervical cancers, and some anatomical abnormalities. Cancers have been discovered in daughters as young as seven years of age. An unknown but substantial number of women in the

United States alone received DES while pregnant, but approximately 1 in 1000 have been found to be afflicted with cervical or vaginal cancers. The National Cancer Institute has urged that all mothers and daughters who may have been exposed to DES during the mother's pregnancy arrange to be examined by a physician for possible effects of the drug.

The use of DES for pregnant women has been discontinued, although the compound is still available for treating certain cases of breast cancer and menopausal symptoms in nonpregnant women.

Cancer of the Ovary

Ovarian cancer is the fifth most common type of cancer in women, with an average of 21,000 new cases each year. It is second to uterine cancer in the number of cases of cancer of the reproductive system. It has, however, a much lower survival rate. Because of the difficulty in diagnosing ovarian cancer, the cancer is more likely than other forms to go unchecked until it has spread to other areas of the body. Less than 2 in 5 women will survive five years after diagnosis. There are several different kinds of malignant tumors of the ovary; some originate in the ovaries and others are caused by cells that have metastasized from a cancer at some other site, such as the uterus.

There are no age limits for cancer of the ovary, although most cases are detected in women between 50 and 70. A physician at a routine pelvic examination may notice a lump or other abnormal growth in the abdominal region. The symptoms reported by patients usually include abdominal discomfort or digestive problems, possibly because ovarian cancers often grow large enough to press on neighboring organs and cause urinary

difficulties, constipation, or other digestive disorders. A clue is given in some cases by endometrial bleeding as a result of abnormal hormone production by the affected ovary. However, the more common kinds of ovarian cancers do not produce hormones. Occasionally, cancer cells from an ovarian tumor will be found in a Pap smear sample. But there are no direct, simple tests for cancer of the ovary.

Treatment for ovarian cancer varies with the individual case. As with cancer at other sites, surgery is generally necessary. The extent of the surgery depends upon the type of lesion and other factors. In an advanced case of an older woman, total hysterectomy along with removal of the ovaries and fallopian tubes would be the treatment of choice. But if the patient is a young woman and the cancer is not extensive, the surgeon may excise the affected ovary and leave the remainder of the reproductive system intact. Radiation and chemotherapy are commonly applied in addition to surgery. The most important risk factor is having relatives who have had ovarian cancer. If a mother, grandmother, or sibling have been diagnosed with ovarian cancer, then the woman is recommended to undergo regular blood tests to check for malignancy. Let your doctor know if you have a family history of ovarian cancer.

Cancer of the Breast

Cancer of the breast is one of the oldest and best-known types of cancer. It is described in an ancient Egyptian papyrus of 5,000 years ago. The hormonal factors involved in the physiology of breast cancer have been

studied by physicians for more than 100 years. But it remains the most common of cancers affecting woman. It kills more women than any other kind of cancer, except lung cancer. About 150,000 women in the United States develop breast cancer each year, and 35 percent die of the disease. Nearly everyone knows a friend or relative who has been stricken by breast cancer. Yet the cause of breast cancer is still unknown.

Women whose female relatives have had breast cancer are more likely to be victims than women from families in which breast cancer is not present. The disease appears to be linked statistically also to women who do not have children before their 30s or who do not have any children; to mothers who do not nurse their babies; to women who reach the menopause later than normal; and to women who began menstruation earlier in life than normal. There is increasing evidence also that ovarian activity may play an important role in the development of breast cancer. Women with ovarian tumors and women who use supplementary estrogen have been shown by some studies to be at increased risk, while the process of having many children and nursing them, which suppresses estrogen hormone activity, is associated with a decreased risk of developing breast cancer. However, 55 percent of the diagnosed cases are for women who have no known risk factors.

Cancer of the breast may occur as early as the teens, but this is rare. It is generally not found before the age of 30, and the incidence peaks around the time of menopause. Then there is a second period after the age of about 65 when the incidence of breast cancer rises again.

Breast cancer usually begins in the ducts of the milk glands; the first noticeable sign is a lump in the breast.

The lump may appear anywhere in the breast, but the most common site is the upper, outer quadrant. Most lumps are not usually cancerous, but a biopsy (described below) must be performed to check the tissue involved.

In a typical case of breast cancer, a small tumor half an inch in diameter, large enough to be detected during careful self-examination, can grow to a cancer two inches in diameter in six months to a year. The lump generally causes no pain; pain is rarely associated with early breast cancer. If the tumor is allowed to grow unchecked, it may cause pulling of the skin from within. This effect may appear as a flattening of the breast or a dimpling of the skin, or a sinking, tilting, or flattening of the nipple. Less frequently, the tumor begins in a duct near the nipple, causing irritation of the skin of the nipple and a moist discharge. In such cases a scab eventually forms at that site. In time, cancer cells spread to the nearby lymph nodes and the danger becomes very serious of metastasis to any part of the body.

Detection of Breast Cancer

Fortunately, breast cancer can be treated effectively if it is detected early enough. Some 95 percent of breast cancers are discovered by the patient herself when she notices a lump. In all too many cases the discovery is made by chance and the lump may be quite large. The cure rate for breast cancer could be greatly improved if all women made a routine of monthly self-examination and then consulted a physician immediately if they found the least indication of a thickening or lump. Most such lumps are benign, but it is most important that the ones that are malignant be identified without delay.

The American Cancer Society and the National Cancer Institute recommend that every woman follow a prescribed method of self-examination just after the menstrual period, continuing every month after the menopause. The procedure consists of carefully looking at and feeling the breasts, and takes only a few minutes. A detailed description of the proper procedure is available in pamphlet form from the Superintendent of Documents, U.S. Government Printing Office, Washington, D.C. 20402. Ask for Public Health Service Publication No. 1730. A film entitled *Breast Self-Examination,* produced by the American Cancer Society and the National Cancer Institute, is also available.

If a tumor can be detected as even a small lump, it must have been developing for some time. There is a truism about breast cancer to the effect that a cancer that is undetectable is curable—leaving unspoken the implication that a cancer that is detectable may not be curable. In recent years, methods of early detection have been refined to the point that tumors once undetectable can now be detected before any lump becomes palpable.

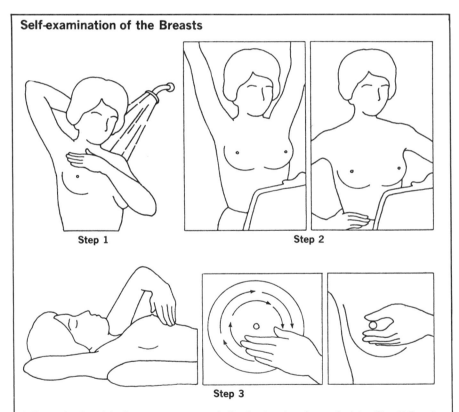

Self-examination of the Breasts

Step 1

Step 2

Step 3

Self-examination of the breasts as recommended by the American Cancer Society. *(Step 1)* Examine breasts during a shower or bath; hands glide easier over wet skin. With fingers flat, move the left hand gently over every part of the right breast, then the right hand over the left breast. Check for any lump, hard knot, or thickening. *(Step 2)* Before a mirror, inspect the breasts with arms at the sides, then with arms raised. Look for any changes in the contour of each breast, a swelling, dimple of skin, or changes in the nipple. Then rest palms on hips and press down firmly to flex the chest muscles. Left and right breasts will not match exactly—few women's breasts do. But regular inspection will show what is normal for you. *(Step 3)* While lying down with a pillow or folded towel under the right shoulder and with the right hand behind the head, examine the right breast with the left hand. With fingers flat, press gently in small circular motions around an imaginary clock face. Begin at 12 o'clock, then move to 1 o'clock, and so on around back to 12. A ridge of firm tissue in the lower curve of each breast is normal. Next, move in an inch toward the nipple and keep circling to examine every part of the breast, including the nipple. This requires at least three more circles. Then repeat the procedure slowly on the left breast with the pillow under the left shoulder and left hand behind the head. Notice how the breast structure feels. Finally, squeeze the nipple of each breast gently between thumb and index finger. Any discharge, clear or bloody, should be reported to a physician immediately.

Thermography

One early warning detection technique involves the use of *thermography,* which is based on the fact that tumor cells produce slightly more heat than normal tissue. Hence a device that is sufficiently heat sensitive can detect and pinpoint the location of an incipient tumor. A harmless tumor, too, would have a higher-than-normal temperature. Further tests would be needed to determine the true cause of the "hot" tissue-reading.

Mammography

Mammography is an X-ray technique developed specifically for examination of breast tissue. A tumor shows up on a mammogram as an opaque spot because of mineral concentrations associated with the growth. However, like thermography, mammography cannot determine whether a tumor is benign or malignant or if the opaque spot on the film is because of some other mineral-rich tissue rather than a tumor. The examining physician uses mammography only as one among other diagnostic tools.

Guidelines from medical groups such as the American Medical Association and the American Cancer Society are as follows:

- Physical breast exams by doctors once a year, and monthly self-exams for all age groups from puberty to 40 onward.
- No known risk factors, ages 40-49, physical breast exam by doctor every year, mammogram every one to two years.
- Risk factors ranked medium to high, ages 40-49, physical breast exams and mammograms once a year or more frequently with the advice of a physician.
- Age 50, with or without risk factors, mammogram and physical breast exam every year.

Some gynecologists recommend a mammogram at the age of 35 so that there is an opportunity for comparison when mammograms are done after the age of 40. Consult with your physician about his or her personal recommendations. Some insurance companies will pay for yearly mammograms; others pay for biannual mammogram exams. Some states require insurance companies by law to pay for at least one exam. Check with your insurance company about their policy. Medicare covers mammograms for women over the age of 65.

Xeroradiography

Xeroradiography is a method that, like mammography, uses X rays, but it entails only about half the exposure to radiation. The pictures are developed by xerography, the process made familiar by Xerox copying machines. The picture consists of dots in varying shades of blue. The process produces a sharp picture, making interpretation simpler and more accurate than is possible with X-ray photographs. When performed by experienced medical technicians, xeroradiography can detect from 85 to 95 percent of all breast cancer, including those too small to be located by palpation. The xeroradiography examination and the physician's examination of the breast usually take only about 20 minutes.

Other Methods

Other diagnostic tools have come into use. *Ultrasound* and *diaphanography,* for example, have reportedly proved their value, especially when combined with other techniques, including mammography. Ultrasound depends on sound waves that vibrate at frequencies beyond the range of human hearing; transmitted into the breast, ultrasound can distinguish between lumps that are cystic and fluid-filled—and therefore benign—and those that

are solid. Other tests, however, may be needed to differentiate between benign solid and malignant solid lumps. In diaphanography, or transillumination, a technician or physician shines an ordinary white light through the breast in the dark. An overhead camera takes pictures with infrared film. Diaphanography can determine whether breast lumps are fibrous, benign, or malignant.

Fine needle aspiration has also proved useful in diagnosing breast cancer. The surgeon uses a needle to draw out a sample approximately 0.5 cm in size. Microscopic examination of the sample follows.

Biopsy

When a physician believes there is good evidence of a cancer in a breast as a result of thermography, xeroradiography, mammography, palpation of lumps, and other factors, the next step is a biopsy study. An entire nodule of breast tissue is removed for microscopic examination of the tissue cells. It is sent to the pathology department, which usually reports within 90 minutes whether the tissue is noncancerous or malignant.

If the lesion is not cancerous—and between 60 and 80 percent of biopsies of breast lumps are not—the patient is taken back to the recovery room and, as soon as possible, reassured that the tumor was benign. The incision made for the biopsy leaves an almost indiscernible scar. In some cases, a hollow needle may be used to withdraw tissue, leaving no scar. This is called a *needle biopsy.*

The Two-Step Procedure

Because of the psychological and physical problems associated with breast cancer, the test and operation can take place in two separate stages.

In many cases, it may be necessary to perform both operations on the same day.

Presurgical Staging involves administration of various tests that are carried out before a mastectomy. The tests show whether the cancer has already spread, or metastasized, to parts of the body other than the breast and local lymph node regions. Staging is widely regarded as a necessary procedure in all cases of breast cancer. A mastectomy has the single purpose of preventing the spread of cancer; the patient has to know, for her own peace of mind, whether it has already spread.

A two-step procedure involves other choices. Where the biopsy is to be carried out separately, the patient may ask to have it done under local anesthesia, as an outpatient. That possibility can be explored with the surgeon. If a general anesthetic appears preferable, the patient may have to spend a night in the hospital. But the *diagnostic biopsy*—involving surgical removal of the entire tumor—and mastectomy can still be performed separately. After a biopsy specimen is removed, the specimen may be subjected to an estrogen-receptor assay. The assay tells the surgeon whether or not the cancer depends on the female hormone estrogen for its growth. That information provides a clue to possible future treatment.

For many women, the one- to two-day wait for the results of a biopsy is worth the time involved, especially because it may be possible to perform the biopsy under local anesthesia on an outpatient basis.

Following the biopsy, the patient receives the pathologist's report on whether the finding is positive or negative. If positive, precise information will usually be given on the type of cancer and where it is located in the breast. Then the patient may want to obtain a second opinion on the permanent-section pathology report and slides. The second opinion is also given by a pathologist. It helps in making decisions on surgery.

Mastectomy

If the lesion is malignant, the surgeon proceeds with the mastectomy. Depending upon the seriousness of the case and the procedure recommended by the surgeon and the pathologist, the operation may remove just the breast tissue, leaving the skin and nipple for reconstructive surgery; remove the skin tissue as well; or remove breast tissue and tissue from around the breast area. The type of surgery is determined by the type and size of the cancerous growth, the risk of further growth, and other factors. The physician and the patient should discuss the reasons for each type of surgery before deciding which to perform. In the United States until recently, radical mastectomy was the usual procedure for breast cancer treatment. Today, at least five different types of mastectomy may be performed. The five:

- *Simple mastectomy*: The breast tissue is removed, but the surrounding muscles and lymph nodes remain.

- *Radical mastectomy*: The breast, lymph nodes, and surrounding muscle are removed.

- *Modified radical mastectomy*: The underlying muscle stays intact while the breast, lymph nodes, and surrounding tissue are removed.

- *Subcutaneous mastectomy*: The breast is removed but not the nipple and skin. This procedure usually is done to allow the most natural looking reconstructive surgery.

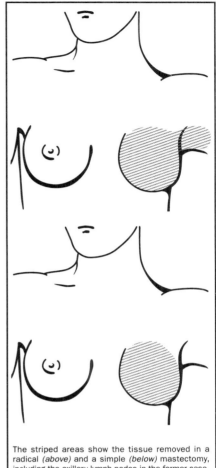

The striped areas show the tissue removed in a radical *(above)* and a simple *(below)* mastectomy, including the axillary lymph nodes in the former case.

- *Lumpectomy or segmental mastectomy*: Only the cancer and surrounding tissue are removed. No reconstructive surgery is usually necessary.

Survival rates depend as much on timely use of pre- and postoperative radiotherapy and postoperative chemotherapy as on the type of operation. But the kind of operation may determine whether the patient will be able to function normally in a relatively short period of time.

Some surgeries allow reconstruction of the breast either during or after a mastectomy, using artificial material to create a breast to match the natural one.

Breast implants

Breast implants for reconstruction are the same types used for cosmetic breast enlargement. There are two basic types: silicone-gel and saline filled. The saline sacs duplicate the natural breast's shape. The sac is inserted under the skin and then filled slightly larger than the final size. After the skin has adjusted to the enlarged sac, some of the liquid is drained to give the breast a natural sag, in most cases closely matching the remaining breast.

Although silicone-gel implants have been widely discouraged for cosmetic use since 1992, they are still considered an important rehabilitation option for women with breast cancer or women with premalignant conditions requiring mastectomies, according to the American Cancer Society. The silicone implant is carefully inserted under the skin tissue and the body forms a scar tissue seal around the sac.

Reactions to silicone-gel implants may include side effects such as hardening of scar tissue around the implant, ruptured silicone sacs, and obscured diagnostic X rays. The link between silicone and diseases of the immune system is still under study. In addition, implants also may block the results of mammographic X rays. However, studies show that implants do not increase the risk of breast cancer or cancer in other parts of the body.

According to the United States Food and Drug Administration, women should only consider removing implants if they are experiencing difficulties. Women should have periodic exams to check for ruptures. Those who want implants for cosmetic purposes should know the importance of detecting early cancer through mammography and the chance of having results obscured by implants.

Postoperative Therapies

The type of surgery recommended in any given case of breast cancer has significance for postoperative therapy. Breast surgery may be extensive where the cancer has spread to the lymph nodes or to other parts of the body; the use of chemotherapy and radiation therapy may be aggressive.

Options include:

- surgery only;

- surgery with radiation; chemotherapy; or hormone therapy

- surgery with a combination of these treatments; or

- radiation or chemotherapy without surgery.

The choices of alternative therapies should be made with an eye to still other factors.

Radiation

A lumpectomy, or segmental mastectomy, is usually followed by radiation therapy. Radiation treatments are typically given five days a week for five weeks. A "booster" treatment may follow completion of the initial series of treatments. Side effects from radiation therapy include fatigue; reddened, moist, or dry skin at the site of the radiation; decreased or heightened sensitivity; enlarged pores; and sometimes changes in breast size.

Chemotherapy

Adjuvant (auxilliary) chemotherapy, which follows surgery, is the usual treatment where breast cancer has spread to the lymph nodes and the patient has not entered menopause. Postmenopausal women may be given tamoxifen, an antiestrogen drug, or may undergo chemotherapy. Except for some high-risk patients, adjuvant chemotherapy is not recommended for women with noncancerous nodes.

Hormone Therapy

Less toxic than chemotherapy, hormone treatments are normally given to those women whose cancer has not spread to the underarm nodes and whose tumors were hormone-dependent. This is especially the case if a patient is postmenopausal. For these women tamoxifen would also be a standard treatment if the cancers had spread to the lymph nodes.

The Rape Victim

The woman who has been raped faces special problems. Authorities agree that long-term health threats can be minimized if the victim takes certain precautions. Complications arising from sexual assault include contracting sexually transmitted disease (STD) or other diseases; becoming pregnant; and experiencing the aftereffects of contusions and abrasions. In addition to these, and much harder to gauge, is the emotional trauma that the rape victim suffers, perhaps for the rest of her life.

Experts suggest that women try to protect themselves against rape and follow certain procedures in the event that a rape occurs.

Precautions

Because rapists generally attack without warning, the woman who feels that she is at risk can sometimes do little more than exercise vigilance in protecting herself. There are precautions, however, that women may take. Self-defense or martial-arts courses may be the answer for some. Although weapons may impart a sense of security, authorities are divided on the issue of their value. Additionally, the weapons themselves may be illegal in some cities or states. Noisemakers, including whistles and siren devices, may or may not be either available or effective, depending upon the circumstances.

Among the possible nonviolent methods of self-protection are the following:

- If you are being followed by a man who is more than 20 or so feet away, you can scream or use a noisemaker.
- Where possible, if followed, you should go into a store and tell the proprietor or clerk that you want to use a telephone.
- Again where possible, bring third parties into the situation—a chance pedestrian, perhaps another woman, or a passing group.
- Remain out of doors if your choice lies between entering a hallway or lobby or staying outside.
- Never go home if you know there is no one home. Instead ring all the door bells on apartment doors or go to a neighbor you know will be home.
- If you find it necessary to walk alone at night, walk in the street—again if possible and safe.
- Take a taxicab home if you have to travel late at night, and ask the driver to wait until you get indoors.
- Even when entering your own building, check the entrance and both sides before going inside.
- If you live alone, pretend you don't.

If a Rape Occurs

The rape victim may face a long period in which recovery and normal living seem impossible. The ability to enjoy life, sex, love, and work may appear to be elusive, even nonexistent. Six months or a year may pass without bringing relief from bad dreams, feelings of guilt, insomnia, and many other physical and psychological aftereffects. But authorities say that what a victim does after experiencing rape may make the transition to normal living easier while also protecting her against recurring health problems.

The Sympathetic Ear

Preferably before, but certainly after reporting to the police, the victim should confide in another person—whether husband, lover, close woman friend, counselor, pastor, hotline volunteer, or someone else trustworthy. The person confided in should go to the police station with the victim—if not the first time, then on any later occasions. The person confided in should be able to provide support, to make sure the victim's rights are protected, and to listen sympathetically to the victim's story.

Going to the Hospital

The rape victim should go as soon as possible to a hospital and undergo the pelvic and other examinations that physicians administer in such cases. If the woman goes to the hospital immediately, she should not wash herself or change clothes. A shower can remove valuable medical evidence. The pelvic examination is designed to find evidence of abrasions or internal damage, and for collection of any semen left by the rapist. Physicians will also examine for any of the rapist's hair, blood, skin, or semen. Any such evidence may be important in court later.

The hospital visit has other pur-

poses. A physician can also administer preventive injections for sexually transmitted diseases and, if desired, an antipregnancy medication. The latter medication must be taken within three days if it is to be effective.

Importantly, the hospital visit may or may not bring the rape case automatically to the attention of the police. That would be true in some areas but not in all. Ultimately, the victim has to report the crime.

Reporting to the Police

Failure to report a rape immediately or after a few days probably means the rapist will not be apprehended. Even so, as many as nine out of ten rapes go unreported simply because most victims cannot face the added trauma of being questioned in detail and, possibly, rude treatment. The woman who does report to the police should, however, do so as soon as possible; each passing day increases the possibility that the police will want to know the reasons for the delay. But reporting late, experts stress, is better than not reporting at all. Reporting a rape does not mean that the victim has to press charges later.

Rape Crisis Centers

Rape crisis centers operate in most communities of any size. The staffs of these centers include many rape victims who have decided to devote time to helping other victims. To find help or advice, or an experienced person to accompany you to the police station with, you can:
- Check the front of your telephone directory for the number of a rape hotline.
- Call Women Against Rape (WAR) if the group has an office in your area. WAR should be listed in the telephone book under "Women."
- Failing the other alternatives, the local YWCA or women's center should have a rape crisis number.

26

Physicians and Diagnostic Procedures

Many people dislike going to the doctor; many fear going to the hospital. And many are overwhelmed by the enormity of the health care industry; much of its costs and procedures seem incomprehensible to us and out of control. Too often, these people put off seeing a doctor until they develop a debilitating problem. Yet many people overlook the one very important way they can alleviate some of their anxiety over their own medical care: choosing a doctor. Having a doctor you trust and with whom you can communicate well not only makes it more likely that you will make appointments for regular checkups, tests, and immunizations, but you will feel comfortable reporting any symptoms that may be the first signs of serious illness, many of which, when diagnosed early, can be treated successfully.

Your Primary Care Physician

Your primary care physician is your regular doctor, the person you see for checkups, and the first person you call when signs of illness appear.

More than likely, he or she will be a *general practitioner,* a *family practitioner,* or an *internist* (see below). In selecting a primary care physician you should try to get a few recommendations from other patients, doctors, nurses, or hospital workers. Don't hesitate to make an appointment for an informational interview to meet the doctor in person and ask any questions about his or her methods, background, and philosophy that may be important to you.

Another important thing to check is the doctor's training—how much and from where. Check the American Medical Association's *The Directory of Medical Specialists* and other such directories in the library to find out whether the doctor has graduated from a fully accredited medical school and where he or she received further training.

In addition, remember that good communication is often the key to good health care. Make sure your doctor understands your questions and concerns and make sure you understand your doctor's answers and instructions. Don't hesitate to ask why you're being given a particular

medication, or what is the purpose of any tests that are recommended. There are alternatives to some medications, and many tests are very expensive and not always necessary. If you are ever uncomfortable with what your doctor has ordered, seek a second opinion; your doctor should be happy to recommend someone. If not, find out why.

General Practitioner

All doctors must complete four years of schooling at an approved medical school, receive one year of postgraduate training in a supervised clinical setting, and pass a state board examination to become licensed to practice medicine. At this point in his or her training a doctor qualifies as a *general practitioner.* Like the stereotypical old-time country doctor, they treat just about everything from warts to measles, set broken bones, deliver babies, and dispense antibiotics and painkillers.

Family Practitioner

The general practitioner has largely been replaced by the *family practi-*

tioner. Family practitioners must complete a three-year residency that covers certain aspects of internal medicine, pediatrics, obstetrics, and orthopedics, and then pass an exam. They treat the same things that general practitioners treat.

Internist

Like the family practitioner, the *internist* must complete a three-year residency and then pass an exam. Generally, they choose to specialize further in such problems as heart disease, cancer, or diabetes.

Osteopath

A doctor of osteopathy (D.O.) or *osteopath* has similar qualifications as a doctor of medicine. Osteopathy was founded by Andrew Taylor Still (1828-1917) on the principle that the body possesses a natural ability both to defend itself against disease and to heal itself as long as it is intact physically and physiologically and has adequate nutrition and favorable environmental conditions. Osteopaths place great emphasis on the importance of normal body mechanics and use of the hands for detecting and correcting problems.

Medical Specialties

There are 23 major specialties that are recognized by the American Medical Association.

Allergy and Immunology: *Allergists* and *immunologists* diagnose and treat allergies and specialize in the reactions of tissues of the immune system to stimulation by antibodies.

Anesthesiology: An *anesthesiologist* decides which types of pain killers will be used, administers it during surgery, and monitors its effects after surgery.

Colon and Rectal Surgery: A *proctologist* is concerned with disorders of the rectum and anus. A *gastroenterologist* studies problems of the digestive tract, including the lower part of the large intestine.

Dermatology: A *dermatologist* diagnoses and treats diseases of the skin, hair, and nails.

Emergency Medicine: An *emergency medicine specialist* practices emergency medicine in a trauma center.

Family Practice: The role of the *family practitioner* is discussed above.

Internal Medicine: The role of the *internist* is discussed above. An internist may specialize in any of the following:

cardiology, the study of diseases of the heart; *endocrinology,* the study of diseases of the glands; *gastroenterology,* the study of disorders of the digestive tract; *hematology,* the study of blood and blood-forming tissues; *infectious diseases; medical oncology,* the study of tumors; *nephrology,* the study of the anatomy, physiology, and pathology of the kidneys; *pulmonary diseases,* the study of disorders of the lungs and respiratory system; and *rheumatology,* the study of connecting and supporting tissues.

Neurological Surgery: The *neurological surgeon* deals with the diagnosis, treatment, and surgical management of disorders and diseases of the brain, spinal cord, and nervous systems.

Nuclear Medicine: The *nuclear medicine specialist* is concerned with the use of radioactive material in the diagnosis and treatment of disease.

Obstetrics and Gynecology: An *obstetrician* specializes in the treatment of pregnant women and delivers babies. A *gynecologist* specializes in the treatment of women and their particular diseases, especially the reproductive system. Often, physicians specialize in both areas.

Ophthalmology: An *ophthalmologist* specializes in the medical and surgical treatment of the eye. They also treat eye diseases.

Orthopedic Surgery: An *orthopedist* diagnoses, treats, and surgically corrects disorders and injuries associated with the bones, joints, muscles, cartilage, and ligaments.

Otorhinolaryngology: An *otorhinolaryngologist* treats and performs surgery on the ears, nose, and throat.

Pathology: A *pathologist* investigates the course and causes of diseases.

Pediatrics: A *pediatrician* specializes in all medical aspects of child care. Subspecialties of pediatrics include: *pediatric cardiology, pediatric endocrinology, pediatric hematology/ oncology, neonatal/perinatal medicine,* and *nephrology.*

Physical Medicine and Rehabilitation: A *physiatrist* deals with the full or partial restoration of use and function to body parts that have been injured or diseased, or have been defective at birth.

Plastic Surgery: A *plastic surgeon* performs operations designed to restore features to their former appearance following a disfiguring accident or correct features that the owner feels are unsightly.

Psychiatry and Neurology: A *psychiatrist* treats behavior disorders, often with psychotherapy, but also with drugs. A *neurologist* diagnoses and treats disorders of the brain and nervous system as well as of the muscles.

Radiology: A *radiologist* uses X rays in the diagnoses and treatment of diseases.

Surgery: A *general surgeon* specializes in the diagnosis and surgical treatment of a wide range of diseases, although most surgeons choose to specialize further.

Urology: A *urologist* diagnoses and treats disorders of the urinary-tract organs, and in men, problems of the reproductive system.

The Physical Examination

One of the first questions many people have about the physical exam is "How often should I have one?" Visits for infants from birth to 18 months are typically scheduled at 2, 4, 6, 15, and 18 months. Visits for children from 2 to 18 are typically scheduled once a year. Visits for individuals aged 19 to 65 are recommended every 1 to 3 years, for most people beginning on the low side (every 3 years) and progressing to every year as one approaches age 65. After age 65 annual visits are recommended.

A typical physical examination will include a careful health appraisal by an examining physician, including a detailed health history of the patient and study of the patient's body appearance and functions. Because no two persons are alike and the differences among patients are likely to increase with advancing years, the examining physician's interest in a set of signs and symptoms may vary with different patients as he or she pieces evidence together to come up with a complete evaluation of a particular patient.

The patient's *medical history* is important because the physician needs to know any medical problems the patient may have had in the past, including any operations or pregnancies, any medications the patient is allergic to or currently taking, and any incidence of family illnesses that may make the patient more susceptible to such things as heart disease, cancer, and so on.

The physician may begin the exam with a simple, obvious question like, "Why are you here?" or "What seems to be the matter?" Even if you feel fine and are just in for a routine physical, don't underestimate the importance of even the slightest *symptoms* you may be experiencing; things like aches, pains, headaches, a bloated feeling, gas, bad breath, and so on may not sound very important in an of themselves, and in fact are often only temporary annoyances, but any symptom experienced regularly over a period of time should be reported.

The physician will also want to know something about your lifestyle—whether or not you smoke, drink, exercise regularly, and so on.

After the medical history has been recorded or updated, the physician may begin a general inspection of the patient's body, beginning with the head and neck and working down to the feet. The physician looks for possible deformities, scars or wounds, including insect bites, or pulsations or throbbing areas. Bruises, areas of skin peeling or flaking, areas of heavy skin pigmentation or loss of pigmentation, hair distribution, perspiration or goose bumps, firmness or slackness of the skin, warts, calluses, and other features are noted.

The physician usually checks the exterior of the body by a method known as *palpation,* which means feeling with the fingers and hands. Rough vibrations from a disorder in the respiratory system, the trembling sensation of blood encountering an obstruction, or the grating feeling of a bone deformity can be detected during palpation. In addition to palpation, the physician may apply *percussion,* or tapping, of certain body areas. Tapping the chest, for example, gives the physician some information about the condition of the lungs. A related technique, *auscultation,* involves listening to sounds within the body through a stethoscope. During percussion, the physician listens for changes in sounds that range from resonance over hollow spaces to dullness over solid or muscular areas. Lack of resonance over a normally resonant area of the lung might indicate fluid, pneumonia, or perhaps an abnormal mass. Percussion may also give the first sign of enlargement of organs, such as the liver, heart, or spleen. During auscultation, the physician listens for normal or abnormal breathing sounds. He can usually detect specific aberrations in lung function by noises made as the air rushes in and out of the lungs through the bronchi. In auscultation of the heart, the physician listens for extra heartbeats, rubbing sounds, the rumbling noises of a heart murmur, or the sounds of normally functioning heart valves opening and closing.

The physician may also use the stethoscope to listen to sounds beyond the chest area. He or she may listen to the sounds of blood flowing through vessels of the neck, bowel sounds through the wall of the abdomen, and the subtle noises made by joints, muscles, and tendons as various limbs are moved.

Weight and height are checked as part of any routine examination. These factors are especially important in a health examination for children to determine the rate of growth, even though youngsters of the same age can vary considerable in height and weight and still be within the so-called normal range. Sudden changes in the rate of growth or abnormal growth may be signs that special attention should be given to possible problems. Adults also can vary greatly in weight and height, but special concern may be indicated by the physician if the individual is exceptionally tall, short, fat, or skinny. Posture also provides clues to the true condition of a patient; a person who has a slouch or holds one shoulder higher than the other may have an abnormal spinal curvature. The physician may watch the patient's manner of walking because a person's gait can suggest

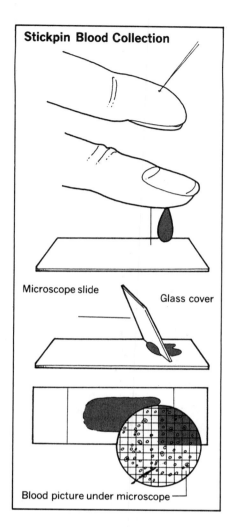

Stickpin Blood Collection

Microscope slide

Glass cover

Blood picture under microscope

muscle, bone, or nervous-system disorders.

Common Screening Tests

A variety of tests may be given in a routine physical exam, depending on the patient's age, family history, current state of health, the length of time between the last visit, and so on. Some of the following tests will be done each time the patient visits the doctor and some are necessary only when specific complaints or concerns are raised or when an individual reaches a certain age or risk category. Some tests have remained the same for years, and some change or are replaced with newer tests. Your doctor should explain any new test to you.

Blood Pressure and Pulse Rate

The patient's blood pressure and pulse rate are checked on every office visit, no matter what the reason is for the visit. Blood pressure is measured with a *sphygmomanometer* and a stethoscope. The sphygmomanometer has attached to it an inflatable cuff, which is wrapped around the upper arm; a rubber bulb is used to inflate the cuff and increase pressure in it so that it can control the blood flow in the arm. The physician locates the pulse with the stethoscope and increases the cuff pressure until the pulse (heartbeat) can no longer be heard. Then the physician slowly deflates the cuff and lets the reading on the gauge fall gradually until he hears the first beat of the heart. The reading on the gauge at that point is recorded as the *systolic pressure* (the first number). The physician continues to relax the pressure in the cuff and watches for the reading at the point where the thumping of the heart disappears again. That number is recorded as the *diastolic pressure* (the second number).

The pulse is checked for rate and quality, which means the force of the pulse beat and the tension between beats. The pulse rate for small children may be well over 100 beats per minute and still be considered normal. But in an adult who is relaxed and resting, any pulse rate over 100 suggests that something is wrong. An adult pulse rate of less than 60 in a nonathlete might also indicate an abnormal condition.

Eyes, Mouth, Nose, and Ears

Inspection of the eyes is usually done with the aid of an *ophthalmoscope,* by means of which the physician can visualize the retina on the back inner surface of each eye, and its associated arteries, veins, and nerve fibers. Dis-

tended retinal veins may be a sign of a variety of disorders, including diabetes or heart disease; signs of hardening of the arteries also may be observed in the eyes before other indications are found elsewhere. The condition of retinal blood vessels may also signal the development of hypertension.

A device called an *otoscope* is inserted in the outer ear to examine the external auditory canal and eardrum. The condition of the tongue, teeth, and gums can reveal much about health habits of the individual.

Cholesterol Measurement

The blood cholesterol level is an important risk factor for coronary artery disease. For most people a blood cholesterol level above 200 mg/dl should be cause for concern, indicating a need for further tests and perhaps a change in life-style. It's a good idea to have your blood cholesterol checked at age 25 and then once every 3 to 5 years thereafter.

Blood Tests

Complete Blood Count

A CBC requires a sample of less than two teaspoons of blood. Four common measurements are taken from it: *Hemoglobin concentration* indicates the level of this substance that transports oxygen to all the cells in the body. A low *red blood cell count* may indicate anemia, as well as be a potential early warning sign for leukemia, kidney malfunction, internal bleeding, or sickle cell anemia. A too high red blood cell count could be an early clue to congenital heart disease, respiratory disease, or polycythemia vera. The *hematocrit* measures the ratio of red blood cells to the plasma in the blood. Like the hemoglobin concentration and the red blood cell count, the hematocrit can indicate anemia, and all three tests are generally given in order to help diagnose the specific type and cause of anemia. A high *white blood cell count* can indicate the presence of an infection, stress, a major injury, or even leukemia. A low count can be a sign of poor diet, certain infections, or another type of leukemia. If taken in the presence of a fever, the white blood cell count can help distinguish between a bacterial and a viral infection.

Blood Glucose

The glucose test determines the amount of sugar in the blood. Individuals who experience symptoms of diabetes mellitus (such as excessive thirst or urination), hypoglycemia (lightheadedness or fainting), or who are pregnant will most likely be given a blood glucose test. A very high level of blood sugar can indicate diabetes, while a very low level can indicate hypoglycemia. In either case or in border-line cases an *oral glucose tolerance test* is given. This test requires that the individual fast for 12 to 14 hours before the test. The patient is then given a concentrated sugar solution to drink, and blood is drawn at regular intervals over the next several hours. This test now replaces the urine test for sugar.

Blood Urea Nitrogen (BUN) and Blood Creatinine

Blood urea and creatinine are products of protein metabolism. A high level of either in the blood means that the kidneys are not filtering them properly from the blood, and thus may indicate kidney damage.

Blood Electrolytes

The four blood electrolytes are sodium, potassium, chloride, and bicarbonate, and they play important roles in the blood pH, the cells' water balance, kidney function, and so on. Most often this test is given to patients who are taking diuretics, those with liver, kidney, or heart disease, or those who may be experiencing dehydration or excessive vomiting or diarrhea.

Urinalysis

The urinalysis is a simple and important test that can indicate much about a person's overall health and identify potential problems, such as kidney disease, diabetes, and urinary tract infections. For a routine urinalysis a sample can be taken at any time of day, although the physician may specify the first morning's urine, or may give special instructions about food and water intake before taking the urine sample.

In the lab the technician will test the urine for its *specific gravity,* which can indicate whether the kidneys can effectively conserve body fluid; its *pH,* which is an indication of how well the kidneys are able to excrete acids from the body; its *protein content,* which in pregnant women can indicate toxemia of pregnancy an in others is a clue to the condition of the kidneys and the prostate; its *glucose content,* which could suggest diabetes; and its *bilirubin content,* which indicates a potential problem in the liver or bile ducts. The technician will also examine the urine under a microscope, looking for such things as pus cells, bacteria, or too many red blood cells, all of which could indicate potential problems.

Routine blood work and a urinalysis are both simple, common tests that can catch many potential problems early. When these tests do indicate abnormalities, other, more specific—and often more expensive—tests are required for confirmation before treatment can begin. Given the fact that any test can give a false result,

whether through human error or through individual variations, the question of whether or not healthy feeling individuals should even have these tests is a much-debated point in the medical community and one best discussed with one's primary care physician.

Electrocardiogram

An *electrocardiogram* is a kind of picture of the heart created by attaching electrodes to the chest, arms, and legs. The wires from the electrodes pick up electrical impulses produced by the heart. The wires are connected to the machine, which translates the impulses into the picture, traced by a pen on a moving sheet of paper. The test is simple, safe, and takes five to ten minutes to perform.

Since a normally beating heart produces a similar pattern of waves in everybody, abnormal waves can indicate a number of potential problems, such as irregular heart rhythms, damage to the heart muscle, enlargement of the heart's chambers, mineral imbalances in the blood, and whether the patient has had, or is having, a heart attack. The EKG is not foolproof, however, and can produce false results. It is perhaps overused as a screen for coronary artery disease. A "baseline" EKG is recommended at age 35 (when the patient is presumably in a good state of health) to give a pattern with which to compare all future EKGs.

Mammogram

A *mammogram* is an X ray of the breast done to detect breast cancer. It is estimated that yearly mammograms for women over 50 could lead to a one-third reduction in the number of deaths from breast cancer.

To be the most effective, the mammogram must be done on a machine

Electrocardiogram

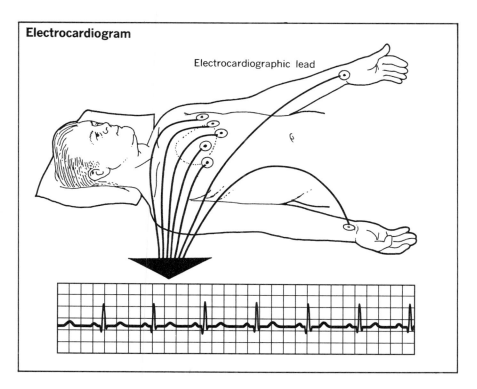

Electrocardiographic lead

designed especially for this purpose. The patient must remove all clothing from the waist up and either stands or sits with the breast placed on a small shelf that extends out from the machine. The patient is then pushed forward so that the edge of the shelf presses into the chest just below the breast. The compression device is brought down onto the breast, and pressure is applied for about a minute. This is the most uncomfortable part of the test, as much pressure is necessary in order to get the most detailed picture possible. Many women find that eliminating caffeine and foods that tend to cause water retention two weeks prior to the exam makes the breasts less sensitive.

The American Cancer Society recommends a baseline mammogram for women aged 35 to 40. Between the ages of 40 and 49 a mammogram is recommended every 1 to 2 years, and after age 50 an annual mammogram is essential. Regular breast exams before the age of 40 have not been proven to be of value.

Pap Smear

The *pap smear* tests for cervical cancer by the microscopic examination of cells from the vaginal walls and cervix. About 2 percent of all women over 40 develop cervical cancer, but 95 percent of these can be cured if the cancer is caught early.

The procedure can be done any time except during the menstrual period. The patient undresses from the waist down and lies down on her back with her legs spread apart and her feet in special stirrups. The gynecologist inserts a lubricated *speculum* into the vagina and opens it to expose the cervix and its os (mouth). The doctor then inserts a small applicator through the speculum and rubs it gently against the cervix and sometimes the os. The applicator is removed and rubbed onto a glass slide (the smear). The speculum is then removed.

The first pap smear should be done when a woman turns 18 or becomes sexually active (whichever occurs

first), and should be followed by pap smears for 2 consecutive years. Providing these tests are negative and there are no risk factors present, tests can be done less frequently at the discretion of one's doctor, although an annual pap smear for women between 25 and 60 is common.

Occult Blood Test

Colon cancer is the second most common form of cancer in the United States. An early warning sign of colon cancer is blood in the stool. It is called *occult,* or hidden, blood because it cannot be detected by sight. It is recommended that everyone over age 50 be tested for occult blood annually.

Home tests are available for occult blood, but because of the seriousness of the results it is often wise to at least discuss the results with a physician or have the physician do the test. Before collecting stool samples the patient must avoid eating red meat, turnips, horseradish, and high doses of vitamin C and consume more fruits, vegetables, and fibrous foods beginning three days before the first test and until the last sample is taken. A sample from three consecutive stools is necessary. Two tests are available and it is best to discuss with your physician which one to use. The *Guaiac test* uses a chemical that turns bluish in the presence of blood. Usually reliable, the test nevertheless fails for a number of reasons to detect colon cancer in about one third of patients who have it. The *HemoQuant* is another test that is better able to detect occult blood even after bacteria have altered it.

Sigmoidoscopy

Another, more expensive procedure for detecting colon cancer is *sigmoi-*

doscopy, the use of a sigmoidoscope to examine the lower segment of the large intestine. To ensure a clean lower bowel, the patient must eat a soft diet the day before the test, a liquid dinner and an enema. A light breakfast is permitted, and another enema will be given an hour before the test. The patient removes clothing from the waist down and lies on the left side with the knees drawn up to the chest. A thin, lubricated tube (there are two kinds, flexible and rigid; the flexible one is easier to tolerate and is a better optical tool) is inserted into the rectum and slowly advanced along the large intestine. The tube contains optical filaments and small instruments that allow the doctor to view the interior of the intestine and take samples if necessary. Air may be forced through the tube to expand the intestine, which can cause a feeling of discomfort. The procedure takes from 15 to 30 minutes. The American Cancer Society recommends a baseline sigmoidoscopy for everyone at age 50 (or 40 if there is a family history of colon cancer) and once every three years after that.

Sexually Transmitted Diseases

The prevalence of sexually transmitted diseases (STDs), such as syphilis, gonorrhea, chlamydia, genital herpes, and AIDS makes regular tests for these diseases in sexually active people who are not involved in monogamous relationships vitally important. Tests are typically blood tests or swab tests and should be done every year or two.

Tuberculosis

Tuberculosis is normally tested for with a simple *skin test*. Either the forearm is pricked with a small device with four prongs or a subcutaneous injection is used. In either case, the patient is asked to observe the area after 48 to 72 hours for signs of redness, raised bumps, or swelling. Individuals who regularly come into close contact with many people, such as those in education or health care, are advised to be tested often.

Stress Test

Stress tests are often given to older people who are about to begin an exercise program. The test is similar to the resting EKG, only instead of just lying still while hooked up to the machine, the patient exercises on a treadmill or stationary bicycle. Because the size of the opening in the vessels of the heart can decrease more than 60 percent before anything abnormal is apparent, the stress test allows the doctor to get a picture of the heart with an increased workload in order to see if it's getting a good supply of oxygen. If it's not, this could indicate a build-up of plaque on the arteries, or coronary artery disease. A routine stress test is often recommended at age 45, and as early as 35 if you have at least one risk factor for coronary artery disease.

Chest X ray

The *chest X ray* was once a routine part of the physical exam. Its expense, potential danger, and limited results in the absence of symptoms has made it less popular. (An individual X ray in and of itself is not harmful, but because exposure to radiation is cumulative throughout your life, a series of X rays over a lifetime can result in increased risk of cancer.)

If you are advised to have a chest X ray, you will be asked to remove all clothing from the waist up and to wear a gown. Depending on the particular area to be X rayed, you will either sit, stand, or lie down. The X-ray beam is centered on the target area, activated, and the film between you and the beam is exposed. Generally two or three exposures are taken for each target area.

Immunizations

Nearly everyone knows the importance of having their children immunized, but many people may not realize that it is important for adults to have regular immunizations as well. When a patient is immunized, he or she receives a shot of modified microbes (bacteria or viruses) or toxins. Although not strong enough to actually give the patient the disease, the dose of microbes does stimulate the patient's own immune system to build up antibodies against the disease, thus making him or her immune to future exposures. Vaccines do wear off, however, and it is best to keep a record of all immunizations and receive scheduled booster shots.

Diphtheria

Diphtheria is spread by airborne bacteria that release toxins that can attack the heart and other internal organs. Adults should receive a booster shot every ten years.

Tetanus

Tetanus is spread by bacteria that enter the body through a contaminated wound. Adults should receive a booster shot (often combined with the diphtheria shot) every ten years. If you sustain a contaminated wound, your doctor may recommend a tetanus booster is you have not had one in 5 years.

Influenza

The risk of death from the *flu* increases with age, and people over 65 are strongly advised to receive annual

The Human Skeleton

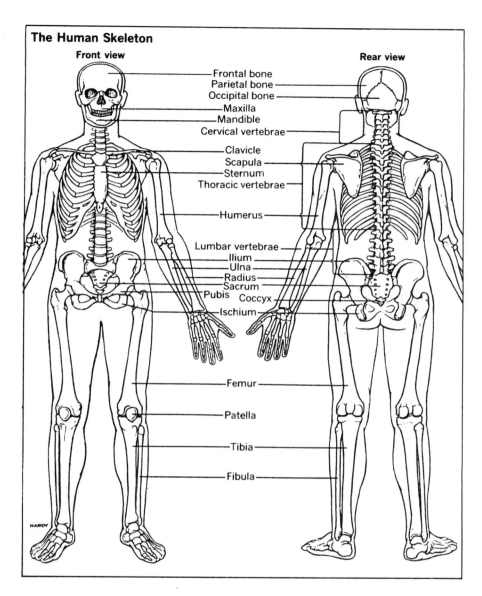

Front view

Rear view

- Frontal bone
- Parietal bone
- Occipital bone
- Maxilla
- Mandible
- Cervical vertebrae
- Clavicle
- Scapula
- Sternum
- Thoracic vertebrae
- Humerus
- Lumbar vertebrae
- Ilium
- Ulna
- Radius
- Sacrum
- Pubis
- Coccyx
- Ischium
- Femur
- Patella
- Tibia
- Fibula

HARDY

diagnosis, 2) they are immune, as demonstrated by a blood test, 3) they have a record of receiving live vaccine no earlier than their first birthday.

Hepatitis B

Like the HIV virus that causes AIDS, hepatitis B is spread through blood contact with virus-infected body fluids and the most common form of transmission is sexual contact. However, hepatitis B is 100 times as contagious as the HIV virus and the leading cause of cirrhosis and cancer of the liver. Because half of those infected with hepatitis B never develop symptoms but become unwitting chronic carriers of it, vaccination is strongly recommended, especially for those with a high risk of infection, such as health care workers, sexually active persons with multiple partners, intravenous drug users, hemodialysis patients, newborns with infected mothers, and residents and staff of institutions for the mentally retarded.

Children

The standard immunizations for children are 1) combined vaccines for diphtheria, pertussis, and tetanus (DTP); 2) a triple oral polio virus vaccine or TOPV; 3) vaccines for measles, mumps, and rubella (MMR); 4) HIB, hemophilus b for influenza. The Centers for Disease Control recommends the following schedule:

- 2 months: DPT, TOPV, HIB
- 4 months: DPT, TOPV, HIB
- 6 months: DPT and HIB
- 15 months: MMR (also at 12 mos)
- 18 months: DPT and TOPV
- 4 to 6 years: DPT, MMR, and TOPV
- 14 to 16 years: tetanus and diphtheria booster (Td)

flu shots in the fall. In 1976 about 500 cases of a rare paralytic condition called Guillain-Barre syndrome were associated with a swine flu vaccine. No influenza vaccines since have been associated with the development of Guillain-Barre.

Pneumococcal Pneumonia

Again, those at risk of death from influenza should also be immunized against *pneumonia*. Like the flu shot, the pneumonia shot is about 70 percent effective, so although being immunized against them is no guarantee against coming down with either

one, any common form of flu or pneumonia the patient might get will at least be non-life threatening.

Measles and Mumps

Many people born after 1957 have both not had and not been immunized against *measles* and *mumps* and thus are particularly susceptible. In addition, those vaccinated between 1963 and 1967 may have gotten a short-lasting killed-virus vaccine and should be revaccinated. Anyone born between 1957 and 1967 should be revaccinated unless 1) they had a case of measles confirmed by a physician's

Other Tests You May Encounter

If a definite diagnosis cannot be made on the basis of the medical history, preliminary physical exam, and routine diagnostic tests, more specialized tests may be required. What follows is a description, grouped by body system, of some of the other diagnostic tests.

The Skeletal System

The skeletal system includes the bones and cartilage, and the specialist is the orthopedic surgeon. Problems with the nervous system and joints often overlap skeletal problems and may necessitate tests by a neurologist or rheumatologist.

X rays are the most important diagnostic tool for special investigations of the bones. They can reveal a hairline fracture of a major bone, a bony deposit, or abnormal alignment.

Synovial aspiration, or a *synovial fluid exam,* involves the withdrawal of a tiny amount of synovial fluid with a needle inserted into a joint. The laboratory analysis of the fluid can help diagnose such problems as gout and some forms of arthritis.

Magnetic resonance imaging, or *MRI,* is a way of creating an image of a body part by taking advantage of the way protons behave in a magnetic field when exposed to a radiofrequency pulse: the way they line up and the form of the radiowave that they emit produces the image. The patient lies down on a table, and a surface coil (it comes in a variety of forms, depending on the body part to be examined) is applied. The surface coil is the device that emits the radiofrequency pulse. The patient's heartbeat and respiration are monitored, usually by a small band placed around a finger. Next the table moves the patient so that the area to be exam-

ined is inside the magnet. The magnet is in the form of a tunnel and may make some people feel claustrophobic. At this point the noise level increases and may be uncomfortable. Several images are taken, with the table moving slightly between each. MRI is safer than X rays because there is no exposure to radiation; however, pregnant women and people with implanted stimulatory devices, such as pacemakers, should not have MRI.

Nuclear imaging involves the injection, swallowing, instillation, or inhalation of a *radioactive isotope* (a marker, or tracer) into the body that goes where the problem is. The isotope is then located by a special camera, and an image is produced. Two uses of this technique for skeletal exams are the bone scan and the bone density test. These tests are more sensitive than X rays and can often identify a problem months before it shows up on the X ray. They are used when the X ray comes back normal, but symptoms persist.

In the *bone scan* the patient receives an injection of a bone-seeking nuclide in a vein. Scanning begins two to four hours later. Either the entire body or just the part concerned is imaged. Injuries, infections, and tumors can all be located with this technique.

The *bone density test* is used to diagnose osteoporosis, the decrease in both density that is the major cause of fractures in the elderly. The patient lies on a table while two L-shaped devices (an emitter above the table and a detector below the table) pass over him. The emitter emits energy and the detector detects it. Because the energy has to go through your body before it is detected by the detector, the amount that your body absorbs is an indication of your bone density. This procedure is called *absorptiometry.*

Ultrasonography is most often em-

ployed in skeletal exams to determine whether a "lump" or "bump" is solid or fluid-filled. Ultrasonography follows the same principle behind radar and sonar: Sound waves emitted by a transducer are directed at a particular part of the body, bounce back, and are translated into an image. Tissues, bones, water, air, and so on all vary consistently in the way they reflect the sound wave, thus making possible the interpretation of the reflected image.

Arthroscopy is a way of seeing inside the body by using an optical instrument equipped with lenses and lights (an arthroscope) which is inserted in a small opening. Anesthesia is generally required, and the area most often studied by this method is the knee. If a problem is found during the exam the doctor may opt to go ahead and take care of it then, a procedure for which the patient's prior permission is required.

The Muscles and Joints

The human body has more than 600 muscles of all sizes and shapes that, attached to the skeletal system, enable us to move as they contract. The joints are the spaces between two coupled bones that allow the bones to move in more than one direction. Muscles and joints are the domain of the rheumatologist.

The synovial fluid exam, X rays, MRI, nuclear imaging, and ultrasonography described under the skeletal system are used to examine the muscles and joints as well. When there is a problem with muscle control, inability to relax a muscle, or weakness in commonly used muscles, another test that may be ordered is the *electromyogram.* This test measures a muscle's electrical potential, which should be zero if the muscle is relaxed. An electrode is attached to the skin over the target muscle and another electrode, in the form of a small needle, is inserted in the muscle. Lead wires from the two electrodes are attached to a monitor, and measurements of the muscle's electrical activity are made while the patient contracts and relaxes it. This test helps determine whether the problem is with the muscle itself or with the nerves controlling it (in which case an electroneurogram is in order).

Joints are prone to stiffness and damage from swelling of the surrounding bursa and tendons. X rays and MRIs will detect damage to the bursa and tendous.

Skin

The dermatologist specializes in treating skin disorders. Many problems specific to the skin can be diagnosed by physical exam and questioning of the patient.

Skin tests are commonly done on allergy sufferers to determine what they are allergic to. In a *prick test* the forearm is cleansed and a drop of up to 35 different solutions is placed in rows on the arm. The doctor then takes a small needlelike object and pricks the center of each drop. After 15 minutes any of the solutions to which the patient is allergic will produce a slight swelling much like a mosquito bite. A *scratch test* is similar except a small scratch is made on the arm and then the drop is applied. In the *intradermal test* the solution is injected. A *patch test* is done when the patient has a rash, probably caused by something that touches the skin. Patches of possible allergens are placed on the back, and the patient returns in two days for a reading.

Sores that refuse to heal, change in the shape, color, and texture of warts or moles, and pimples that itch and recur are all considered symptoms of skin cancer and should be checked by your doctor. Because of the small size of most of these skin eruptions, they are commonly removed entirely and then a biopsy is performed on the tissue. They can be cut out (excised), removed with an electric needle, or frozen (cryosurgery).

The Nervous System

The brain, spinal cord, and network of nerves make up the nervous system. The neurosurgeon and the neurologist are the specialists.

In a *spinal tap,* or *spinal fluid exam,* the doctor inserts a needle into the lower back and removes a small amount of spinal fluid, which is then examined in the lab. The test usually causes severe headaches; it is used to diagnose infections, brain hemorrhages, tumors, polio, meningitis, and other conditions. *Myelography* is a similar study, much more painful, in which a small amount of spinal fluid is removed, dye injected in its place, and X rays are taken while the patient lies on a table. Slipped disks, some types of arthritis, and different types of tumors are commonly diagnosed this way, although the use of MRI

Nervous System
Cranial Nerves

Optic nerve (vision)
Olfactory nerve (smell)
Oculomotor nerve (eye muscles)
Trigeminal nerve (face)
Trochlear nerve (eye muscles)
Facial nerve (facemuscles)
Acoustic nerve (hearing and balance)
Glossopharyngeal nerve (taste)
Vagus nerve (heart, lungs, abdomen)

Central Nervous System

Cerebrum
Cerebellum
Brachial plexus
Spinal cord

Autonomic Nervous System
Peripheral Nervous System

Thoracic nerves
Radial nerve
Ulnar nerve
Femoral nerve
Sciatic nerve

(see skeletal system) and computerized axial tomography (CT) are also used and are often done first.

The CT exam is a noninvasive procedure that takes a series of X-ray pictures of "slices" of the targeted body part. The patient removes all removables from the area being studied and lies on a table (called a gantry) which is then moved into the machine. Several exposures are taken, with the table moving slightly between each. For some studies it is necessary to inject a special "dye," which could cause mild discomfort. Some people experience a claustrophobic reaction while inside the machine. CT is about 100 times more sensitive than conventional X rays and is good for detecting calcium deposits, tumors, cysts, and abscesses. Because of its sensitivity to tissue density, it can sometimes distinguish benign from malignant tumors.

The *brain scan* continues to be an diagnostic important tool. Areas of the brain can be "mapped," patterns are being discovered that allow diagnosis of such things as Alzheimer's disease, and the diagnosis of stroke can be validated days sooner than with CT.

The brain scan involves the injection in the arm of a radioactive isotope and the scanning of the brain by either a single photon emission computed tomography camera (SPECT) or a positron emission tomography camera (PET). The SPECT scanner uses gamma rays to create images, and the camera rotates around the stationary patient (thus there is no sensation of claustrophobia as with CT). The PET scanner uses positrons (a type of subatomic particle found in the nucleus of an atom) to create images. The PET scanner looks like a wall with a hole in the middle of it. The patient lies on a table, and the table is positioned so that the patient's head is in the opening of the wall. The scan is

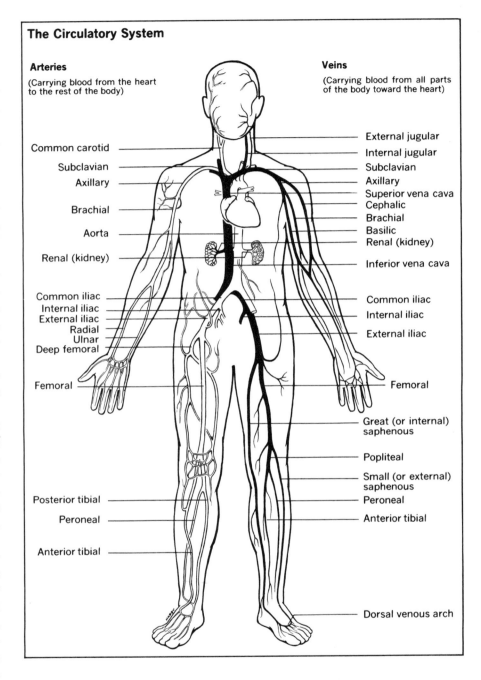

The Circulatory System

Arteries
(Carrying blood from the heart to the rest of the body)

Common carotid
Subclavian
Axillary
Brachial
Aorta
Renal (kidney)
Common iliac
Internal iliac
External iliac
Radial
Ulnar
Deep femoral
Femoral
Posterior tibial
Peroneal
Anterior tibial

Veins
(Carrying blood from all parts of the body toward the heart)

External jugular
Internal jugular
Subclavian
Axillary
Superior vena cava
Cephalic
Brachial
Basilic
Renal (kidney)
Inferior vena cava
Common iliac
Internal iliac
External iliac
Femoral
Great (or internal) saphenous
Popliteal
Small (or external) saphenous
Peroneal
Anterior tibial
Dorsal venous arch

able to read through different depths, so problems deeply buried in tissue can be detected without surgery.

When the blood supply to the brain is limited by the blocking of the carotid arteries (in the neck) a condition known as transient ischemic attack (TIA), momentary loss of brain function, can occur and can eventually lead to a stroke. Thus examining the carotid arteries is important if the pa-

tient possess symptoms or significant risk factors. This can be done by X ray and also by ultrasound. In the ultrasound test two techniques are generally used. The first creates images (called duplex) and the second measures the rate and quality of blood flow (called Doppler). Both involve the gentle movement of the transducer slowly over each side of the neck. The Doppler phase, however,

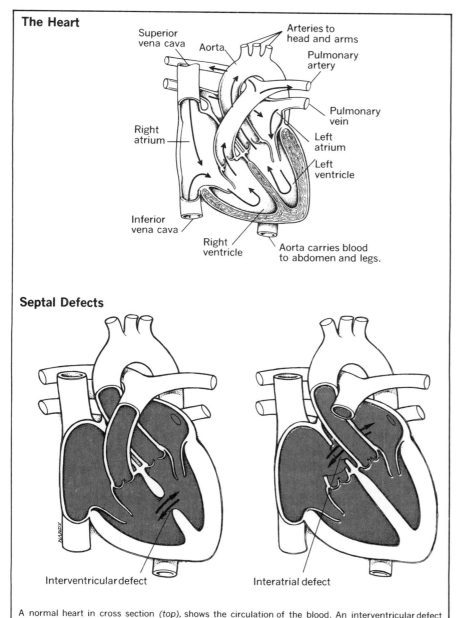

The Heart

Superior
vena cava

Aorta

Arteries to
head and arms

Pulmonary
artery

Pulmonary
vein

Right
atrium

Left
atrium

Left
ventricle

Inferior
vena cava

Right
ventricle

Aorta carries blood
to abdomen and legs.

Septal Defects

Interventricular defect

Interatrial defect

A normal heart in cross section *(top)*, shows the circulation of the blood. An interventricular defect *(bottom left)* allows blood to pass directly between the left and right ventricles. An interatrial defect *(bottom right)*, with the aorta seen in cross section over the left atrium, allows blood to pass freely between the two atria. Any septal defect interferes with the effectiveness of the pumping action of the heart.

When epilepsy is suspected, following certain head injuries, or when the patient is experiencing confusional states, sleep problems, and even impotence, an *electroencephalograph* (EEG) may be ordered. The patient sits in a chair while a technologist attaches 16 to 22 electrodes to his head. EKG leads are also placed on the chest. The patient then lies down and may even fall asleep. The technologist may instruct the patient to open and close his eyes while a strobe light flashes. The test takes about two hours.

The electromyogram was discussed under the section on muscles. If the muscle is not the problem, the nerves connected to it may be and a *nerve conduction study*, or *electroneurogram*, is ordered. This test measures the speed of the electrical impulse across a nerve and the speed of the muscle's response. Electrodes are affixed to the skin over the target muscle. The target nerve is then given a mild electric shock. The electrode over the muscle both measures the time between the shock and the response (the muscle will twitch) and the intensity of the response. The corresponding nonaffected muscles are also tested for comparison. There is no hazard, and the shock feels like a mild sting or burn.

The Circulatory System

The cardiologist specializes in diseases of the heart and circulatory system. Coronary artery disease is the most common form of heart disease and involves the blocking of the arteries to the heart. There can also be problems with the heart muscle itself, problems with the heart valves, or congenital problems resulting from birth defects.

The electrocardiogram and the stress test have already been discussed. Nuclear imaging, ultrasound,

is very noisy. The procedure takes about 30 minutes.

Patients who have experienced TIA, stroke, or vertigo often routinely undergo *ocular plethysmography* (OPG) to detect narrowing of the ophthalmic artery. The patient is seated in a chair with a headrest, blood pressure is taken in each arm, and EKG leads are placed on the

chest. The chair is semireclined and anesthetic drops are placed in each eye. The technologist then places tiny plastic cups into the corner of each eye. The cups are attached to wire leads connected to the machine. The patient is instructed to keep the eyes wide open. The machine then produces a slight suction on each eye and measures its pressure.

and X rays are also used to detect coronary artery disease. In order to detect exactly how bad the arteries are and determine the necessary correctional procedure, an *angiograph,* or *arteriograph,* is done.

The angiograph begins with the insertion of a special needle in a major artery (usually in the groin area, but other sites are the armpit, the hollow of the elbow, and the neck). A sudden spurt of blood indicates correct positioning. A wire is then inserted through the needle, which stops the bleeding. The wire is advanced to the target area, and the needle is removed. A catheter is then slid over the wire and advanced to the target area. The wire is then withdrawn. The next step is the injection of a special dye to the target area. To prevent its being diluted it must be injected at high velocity and in large quantity. For most people the injection is extremely uncomfortable, with some reporting severe pain, a feeling of heat, headache, chest pain, or dizziness. The next step involves the rapid imaging of the target area, either by a series of X-ray pictures or by X-ray movies (both noisy). Often different views are needed of the targeted area, which means that the catheter must be repositioned and the dye reinjected. Once the pictures are finished the catheter is slowly removed and pressure is applied, either by the doctor himself or by a mechanical device, to the hole to seal the artery. The pressure involved is intense and lasts for 10 to 15 minutes. Because it is necessary for the patient to be conscious during the procedure, the entire process may cause extreme anxiety, which in turn increases the risk of heart attack. The patient is normally given a sedative to relax him. An overnight stay in the hospital following the procedure is routine. *Venography* is a similar study of the veins.

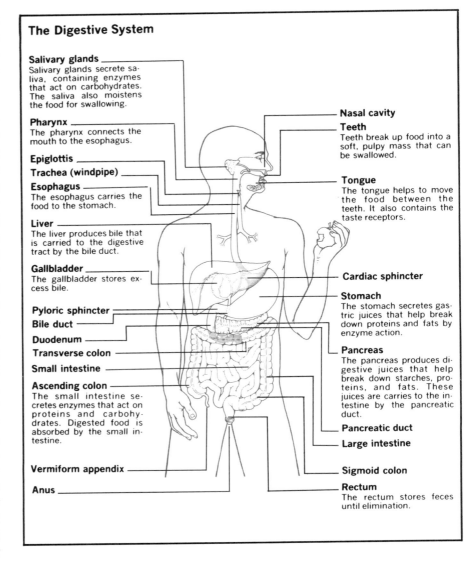

The Digestive System

Salivary glands
Salivary glands secrete saliva, containing enzymes that act on carbohydrates. The saliva also moistens the food for swallowing.

Pharynx
The pharynx connects the mouth to the esophagus.

Epiglottis

Trachea (windpipe)

Esophagus
The esophagus carries the food to the stomach.

Liver
The liver produces bile that is carried to the digestive tract by the bile duct.

Gallbladder
The gallbladder stores excess bile.

Pyloric sphincter

Bile duct

Duodenum

Transverse colon

Small intestine

Ascending colon
The small intestine secretes enzymes that act on proteins and carbohydrates. Digested food is absorbed by the small intestine.

Vermiform appendix

Anus

Nasal cavity

Teeth
Teeth break up food into a soft, pulpy mass that can be swallowed.

Tongue
The tongue helps to move the food between the teeth. It also contains the taste receptors.

Cardiac sphincter

Stomach
The stomach secretes gastric juices that help break down proteins and fats by enzyme action.

Pancreas
The pancreas produces digestive juices that help break down starches, proteins, and fats. These juices are carries to the intestine by the pancreatic duct.

Pancreatic duct

Large intestine

Sigmoid colon

Rectum
The rectum stores feces until elimination.

Not all people who experience sudden and severe chest pain are having a heart attack. A technique called *infarct detection* can confirm the diagnosis. Normally performed within the first 12 to 24 hours after the onset of the pain, the test involves the injection of an isotope (thallium-201) into a vein. The patient is then positioned under a gamma camera and an image is created of the heart that will make evident any occluded (blocked) vessels. A similar nuclear imaging process (under less duress) is used to obtain information about the heart's *wall motion* (how well the muscle relaxes and contracts) and *ejection fraction* (how much blood leaves a chamber of the heart when it contracts). Both tests give valuable information about the heart's health.

While X rays provide more detail, nuclear imaging can also be used to check *circulatory integrity,* or how open the veins and arteries are. Again, an isotope is injected into a vein near the target area and images are produced via a gamma camera.

Examination of the ejection fraction, valve function, and excessive pericardial fluid (the pericardial membrane surrounds the heart) can also be done with ultrasound. In a process similar to that described earlier for the carotid arteries, *echocardiography* produces an image of the working heart.

The Digestive System, the Liver, and the Pancreas

The gastroenterologist specializes in disorders of the digestive tract—the esophagus, stomach, duodenum, and intestine. The proctologist treats disorders of the large intestine, rectum, and anus.

As in many other systems, X rays are the traditional diagnostic tool for gastrointestinal problems. Nuclear imaging, however, may be used for some specific complaints. For example, if you're having trouble with heartburn an *esophageal reflux* test may be done to determine whether or not you have a hiatus hernia. The patient eats nothing the night before the exam. A small balloon is placed over the stomach, held in place by a special inflatable belt. The patient then stands in front of a gamma camera and drinks a glass of orange juice to which an isotope has been added. Pictures are taken as the fluid moves to the stomach. The patient then lies down on a table, and the cuff is inflated, causing the balloon to apply pressure to the stomach. Pictures are taken to see if this pressure causes the liquid in the stomach to back up into the esophagus. If it does, a hiatus hernia is the diagnosis.

An *endoscopy,* like the sigmoidoscopy and the arthroscopy, is a way of seeing inside the body, this time inside the gastrointestinal tract to the duodenum. X rays are usually done first, and the endoscopy is done if they are not definitive or if a tissue sample is needed for biopsy. The patient eats nothing the night before the exam. After undressing and putting on a gown, the patient lies down and drinks a bad-tasting liquid, the local anesthetic. The patient may opt for

no other medication, thus remaining completely conscious, or having an injection that makes him drowsy, but conscious, or having a general anesthetic, which puts him to sleep altogether. The second of the three is recommended. The first is the most painful; the third has a higher risk factor and requires hospitalization afterward.

The patient lies on his left side with the mouth open. The gastroscope is then put in the mouth and advanced down toward the stomach. The physician pauses at the places he needs to look at. Photographs are commonly taken, and samples of tissue or gastric juice may also be taken. The exam takes about 2 to 3 hours.

An *upper GI* may be in order if your doctor suspects an ulcer or tumor. No food is allowed for 8 hours before the test. An injection of glucagon (which may cause nausea or dizziness) is normally given to slow down the movements of the stomach. Next, the patient swallows a small cupful of granular material, which produces gas and causes the stomach to distend. Finally, the patient is given a glass of barium and stands with his back to the X-ray table. A fluoroscopic screen is positioned in front of the patient, and the radiologist instructs him to take small swallows of the barium. A series of pictures are taken, with the patient changing position several times. If the entire small intestine is being studied, the patient is next taken to a waiting area and returns every 15 to 30 minutes for more pictures. A stomach—duodenum study takes about a half hour. The longer study takes from 1 to 3 hours.

A *lower GI,* often called simply a *barium enema,* is much more involved. It is used when there is a suspicion of diverticulitis, bowel obstruction, colon polyps, colitis, and so on. -A strict diet is prescribed, along with laxatives, for several days before the

test. Two enemas are given on the morning of the study. For this exam the patient lies down on the X-ray table. The doctor inserts a lubricated, gloved finger into the patient's rectum to make sure there are no obstructions and then inserts the enema tip. The tip has a built-in balloon that can be inflated if the patient feels he cannot retain the enema. Like the upper GI, an injection of glucagon is often given to counteract the feeling of "fullness" felt by most people. The fluoroscope is then positioned, and the technologist begins the enema: a solution of barium is pumped into the rectum until it fills the large intestine. Air may then pumped into the rectum for greater contrast. Both the enema and the air can cause a feeling of fullness and discomfort. The patient retains the enema and the air until all the pictures are taken.

The gall bladder, an organ in the upper right abdomen responsible for storing the bile necessary for fat digestion, is a frequent site of infection and may also develop calculi or stones. Examination of the gall bladder can be done with X rays, ultrasound, or nuclear imaging. Most routine gall bladder studies are done with ultrasound. An 8-hour fast is required before the test. The patient is given a gown to wear, may be asked to drink a white liquid, and then lies down on the couch. The doctor applies a special lubricant to the abdominal area and moves the transducer over it. The patient can watch the results on a monitor.

If stones develop in the gall bladder and block the flow of bile, infection results, and the condition is called acute cholecystitis. Nuclear imaging is considered the most specific diagnostic tool for this condition. The patient fasts for 4 hours before the exam. An isotope is injected and the patient lies down under a gamma camera. Pictures are taken every 5 to 10 minutes for a half hour and then every 15 minutes for one and a half hours.

The liver makes the bile necessary for fat digestion, and the pancreas makes the enzymes necessary for fat digestion. Neither the entire liver nor the entire pancreas can be seen with X rays. X rays of the blood supply and ductal structures, however, enable the skilled specialist to make accurate assumptions about the condition of either. CT imaging can give a full picture of both organs and is much easier on the patient than X rays. Ultrasound is also useful.

If the results of lab tests suggest liver disease or if the organ is enlarged, a special *needle biopsy* may be done. The patient is normally asked to avoid eating the night before the test. Medication by mouth or injection may be given. The gastroenterologist feels the lower edge of the liver, selects a spot, and injects a small amount of local anesthetic under the skin. Next a larger needle with a syringe is inserted. There will be pressure and even a dull pain. The plunger of the syringe is pulled back, and liver cells are sucked inside. The needle is then removed and pressure is applied to the puncture site.

The Respiratory System

The respiratory system includes the pharynx, trachea, bronchi, and the lungs.

The routine chest X ray (described earlier) is commonly the first test done when symptoms indicate a possible problem in the respiratory system. When the bronchi must be seen in more detail, a *bronchogram* may be done. This requires the disabling of the "coughing reflex" by spraying a local or topical anesthetic in the patient's mouth and back of the throat. Then a thin metal tube shaped like a candy cane (a cannula) will be placed in the mouth with the curved end over

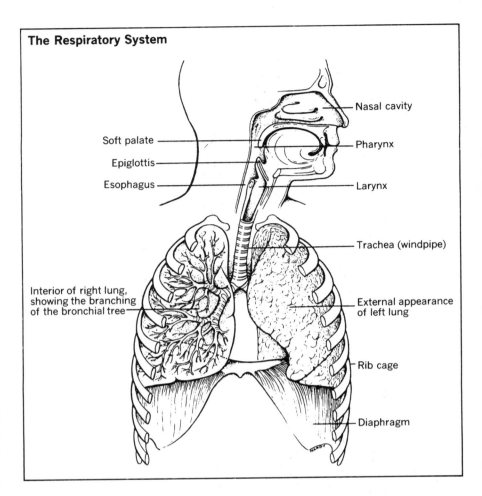

The Respiratory System

Soft palate — Epiglottis — Esophagus — Nasal cavity — Pharynx — Larynx — Trachea (windpipe) — Interior of right lung, showing the branching of the bronchial tree — External appearance of left lung — Rib cage — Diaphragm

the back of the tongue. Anesthetic is injected into the cannula, which then runs down the back of the throat, down into the bronchi. A rubber tube (catheter) is passed through the patient's nose, down the back of the throat, through the voice box, the trachea, and then into the bronchi of one or both lungs. A special dye is then instilled into the catheter, which runs down and fills the tubes. The dye highlights the bronchi, making them easier to see on the X ray displaying blockage and tight areas.

A *bronchoscopy* may be in order if X rays or CT reveal potential problems and the physician needs a closer look or a tissue sample. The process is similar to the bronchogram except a bronchoscope is inserted for viewing and the taking of tissue samples.

A group of tests called *pulmonary function tests* help the physician determine if certain symptoms may be due to either restrictive or obstructive lung disease. The test measures how much air can be forcibly exhaled after inhaling as deeply as possible, how much air remains in the lungs after a forcible exhalation, how much air is expired with each normal breath, and how well the lungs stretch with each breath in and how well they collapse with each breath out. The patient is put in a pressurized plexiglass cabin called a body box, which looks like a large phone booth. The patient's nose is closed off with a nose clip and a special mouthpiece is inserted in the mouth. The patient is positioned in front of a special apparatus that will measure and record the results. Once comfortable, the patient performs a series of breathing maneuvers on the instructions of the technologist. The tests take 15 to 45 minutes and may involve some straining as the maneuvers can get quite demanding.

The Endocrine System

There are 7 endocrine glands that make up the endocrine system: pituitary, thyroid, parathyroids, adrenals, pancreas, ovaries (women), and testicles (men). The glands secrete hormones that produce a specific effect or regulate a certain action of other body organs. Laboratory tests of blood and urine are important diagnostic tools for the glands, and all can be visualized with X rays, CT, nuclear imaging, and ultrasound if lab tests indicate a potential problem. Some

tests may necessitate the injection of a special dye to highlight the target area.

The Kidneys and the Urinary System

Laboratory tests of the urine are the most obvious way of beginning a diagnosis of kidney or urinary system problems. A resting EKG may also be done as well as nuclear imaging, ultrasound, and X rays. If a kidney biopsy is needed, the patient is normally given an anesthetic to make him drowsy and then lies face down on a table. The procedure is similar to that of the liver biopsy. First the anesthetic is injected, then the aspirating needle is inserted. This generally hurts a great deal but takes only a minute or so. An overnight stay is re-

quired for observation. A mild backache will last about a week.

An intravenous urography is a common test for urinary tract problems. Colon cleansing (strict diet, laxative, enemas) is often done before the test. A large amount of dye is injected into the patient's arm (or may drip in gradually from a diluted bottle of fluid). X ray exposures are taken at timed intervals. A compression cuff (like a large blood pressure cuff) may be put around the abdomen to apply pressure just below each kidney, and more pictures are taken until the radiologist is satisfied that enough information has been obtained. The patient voids his bladder, another picture is taken, and the test is over.

Ears, Nose, and Throat

The otorhinolaryngologist specializes in treating problems of the ears, nose, and throat. Difficulty hearing, faulty balance or vertigo, pain, and ringing in the ears (tinnitus) are common ear complaints. Congestion, discharge from the nose, postnasal drip, itching and sneezing, headaches over the eyes and top of the head, pain over the upper teeth and unexplained fever are complaints associated with the nose and sinuses. Problems with the voice, sore throat, or difficulty swallowing are common throat complaints.

An *audiogram* evaluates and measures the ears' ability to hear. The patient is seated in a booth, instructions about communicating with the technician are given, and earphones are placed over the ears. A series of different tones in varying degrees of loudness are played through the earphones and the patient indicates by hand signs which or both ears heard the sound.

A *tympanogram* is a way of recording the movement of the ear drum. A rubber plug is inserted in one ear and

A Guide to Some Home Medical Tests

Kind	Function	How It Works	Time Required
Blood glucose monitoring	Measures the level of glucose (a kind of sugar) in blood	Wash your hands thoroughly. Prick a finger or earlobe to obtain a drop of blood, then follow instructions.	1 to 2 minutes
Ovulation monitoring	Measures the quantity of luteinizing hormone (LH) in urine	A chemically treated strip is dipped in urine specimen and compared with a color guide.	20 minutes to 1 hour
Pregnancy	Detects human chorionic gonadotropin, produced by a developing placenta, in urine	Chemicals are mixed with a urine specimen in a small test tube. A ring formation or color change indicates pregnancy.	20 minutes to 2 hours
Urinary tract infections	Detects nitrite in urine	Chemically treated test strip is dipped in urine specimen on three consecutive mornings.	30 to 40 seconds
Occult fecal blood	Detects hidden blood in stools	A color change, appearing when stool specimen is brought into contact with peroxide and guaiac, indicates hidden blood.	30 seconds to 16 minutes
Gonorrhea	Detects the bacteria causing gonorrhea in the specimen of pus from the penis	Specimen, collected on a slide, is allowed to air-dry. Then follow directions.	Several days
Blood pressure	Measures the pressure of blood on the walls of the arteries	The center of a cuff is placed on the pulse point of the upper arm. With or without a microphone, the user listens for artery sounds.	2 to 5 minutes
Impotence	Detects, measures the rigidity of erections during sleep	Soft fabric band or stamps are placed around the penis before the subject goes to bed at night. The strips break at different degrees of pressure.	Overnight
Vision	Screens for visual acuity problems	Using three different tests, you read special eye charts.	2 to 3 minutes

Focusing

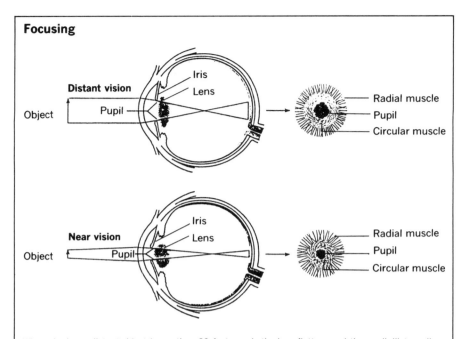

When viewing a distant object (more than 20 feet away), the lens flattens and the pupil dilates, allowing more light to enter the eye. The pupil is dilated by the action of the outer radial muscles of the iris, which contract and thus stretch the previously contracted circular muscles. When viewing a near object, the lens becomes more oval and the pupil contracts as more light enters the eye. This prevents overstimulation of the retina. The pupil is reduced in size by the contraction of the inner circular muscles, which serve to stretch the previously contracted radial muscles.

mild pressure is applied which is similar to the pressure experienced when flying in a plane. The tympanogram reveals if the eardrum is thickened due to infection, perforated, or if there is an obstruction in the middle ear.

Patients who experience dizziness may have an *electronystagmogram,* which measures and records the abnormal movements of the eye that can indicate a problem with the balance mechanism (vestibular system). Contacts or glasses are removed and the technician tapes a small metal disk under each eye and on the bridge of the nose. These sensors are attached by lead wires to a graph machine. Small lights are flashed on the wall, which the patient is asked to look at. The patient then lies down, closes his eyes, and turns onto each side. Water is then put in the ears. The procedure often produces dizziness or nausea that persists for several hours.

Smears and cultures are the common lab tests for nose and throat complaints. X ray examinations may also be done. In some cases a biopsy may be necessary. For the nose, a needle aspiration is the common method, either through the nose or upper gum of the mouth. A local anesthetic is given first. An excisional biopsy may be necessary, in which case a small piece of tissue is removed. For the throat an excisional biopsy is commonly done, normally under general anesthesia, and an overnight stay in the hospital may be required. A laryngoscope is used to obtain the sample. The throat will be sore for several days afterwards.

The Eyes

The ophthalmologist specializes in eye disorders. The common eye exam involves several tests: visual acuity, refraction, color defectiveness, determination, muscle integrity, pupillary reflex response, slit-lamp exam, intraocular pressure determination, and retinal exam. The *visual acuity* test is the familiar wall chart. The patient covers each eye in turn and tries to read as many letters as he can see. In the *refraction* test a special device with various lenses is positioned in front of the patient. Different lenses are tried while the patient again tries to read the letters on the wall chart, telling the doctor which is better.

Color blindness is usually tested for with a series of cards covered with an array of colored dots which form a number. Those with no color defect will be able to read the number. The doctor performs the *muscle integrity exam* simply by asking the patient to look in different directions and observing that the patient is able to. The *pupillary reflex response* is tested when the doctor directs the patient to look straight ahead while he shines a small light at each eye and watches what happens to the size of the pupil.

The slit-lamp examination is done in two parts and involves a special instrument called a biomicroscope. The patient's eyes may be stained with a special dye (a fine strip of paper is quickly touched to the side of each eye) and the chin and forehead are positioned on their respective rests. The ophthalmologist sits in front and looks into the eyes, viewing the sclera, iris, conjunctiva, cornea, and the lens. Next drops are put into the eyes to dilate the pupils, which takes about 20 to 30 minutes. With the pupils dilated, the doctor can then see the retina.

Glaucoma is a condition of increased pressure within the eyes that, if discovered too late, can cause blindness. The *intraocular pressure determination,* or *tonometry,* is the test for this problem. First, a drop of local anesthetic is put into each eye. Then the ophthalmologist uses a *tonometer,* a penlike tube with a small retractable tip, to touch the front of each eye. It is recommended that this painless procedure be done for those 40 and over every 2 to 3 years, or annually if there is a family history of glaucoma.

The final test in the general eye exam is the *retinal exam*. The room is darkened, and the doctor uses an ophthalmoscope to look through the pupil into the back of the eye.

Diagnostic Tests and the Patient's Rights

As medical costs continue to rise, questions about the necessity of various diagnostic tests will continue to be raised. For the healthy individual, it makes little sense to undergo more than the few routine screening tests necessary for his particular age group; there is always the chance of an error that may lead to additional tests at even greater expense, not to mention the emotional trauma that a false positive could cause.

For the patient experiencing particular symptoms, or those in high risk categories, the number and kind of diagnostic tests are a concern. *Batteries,* or sets, of tests are a particular cause for concern. The batteries can be complex, and the physician may not take the time to explain each one in detail so that the patient thoroughly understands what they mean in terms of discomfort, risk, and cost. The value of a particular test must also be weighed against its results. Expensive CT and MRI tests are the "study of choice" for many problems, but for others, the less expensive X ray might do just as well or better. When approaching diagnostic tests, then, the patient should make sure that he is as informed as possible about what is necessary. As already mentioned, having a physician with whom you can converse easily and understand is an important factor in the quality of the medical care you receive.

27

Nutrition and Weight Control

Just as it was for our earliest ancestors, food is an integral part of our daily lives. Not only is food essential for survival, but oftentimes the way in which we structure our lives—our work habits, our recreational activities—revolves around how, when, and where we get food and eat it.

Ironically, however, because most of us live a much faster-paced lifestyle than we did even twenty years ago, we spend less time choosing, preparing, and eating food. We grab breakfast on the run (if we eat it at all), hurry through lunch, and rarely take time to plan and prepare a leisurely, well-balanced dinner. Often everyone in the family is on a different schedule, with the result that all too often we rely on prepackaged microwave dinners or take out fast food. Consequently, many of us are not eating properly, spending money on expensive vitamins to make up for poor nutrition, starving ourselves to lose weight, or gaining extra pounds by filling up on empty calories.

Practicing good eating habits may take a little more time and planning than we think we can afford, but its benefits will pay off in the long run in a healthier, happier way of life.

Basic Nutritional Requirements

The process by which food is converted into useful energy is called *metabolism*. It begins with chemical processes in the gastrointestinal tract which change plant and animal food into less complex components so that they can be absorbed to fulfill their various functions in the body—growth, repair, and fuel. Different foods have different energy values, measured in calories. An ideal diet for the average healthy individual provides the highest nutritional benefits from the fewest number of calories. Information on the protein, fat, and carbohydrate content in specific foods, as well as the number of calories, may be obtained by consulting the tables "Nutrients in Common Foods." The Metric Equivalents table converts spoon and cup measures into metric measures.

Protein

Of the several essential components of food, *protein* is in many ways the most important. This is so not only because it is one of the three principal sources of energy, but also because

much of the body's structure is made up of proteins. For example, the typical 160-pound man is composed of about 100 pounds of water, 29 pounds of protein, 25 pounds of fat, 5 pounds of minerals, 1 pound of carbohydrate, and less than an ounce of vitamins. Because the muscles, heart, brain, lungs, and gastrointestinal organs are made up largely of protein, and since the protein in these organs is in constant need of replacement, its importance is obvious.

The recommended dietary allowance for protein is 0.8 g/Kg of body weight per day for persons aged 15 and up and 1 g/Kg of body weight for children under 15. (To convert your weight from pounds to kilograms, divide by 2.2. Thus a woman weighing 130 pounds weighs about 59 kilograms and needs about 47 grams of protein a day. A man weighing 175 pounds needs about 64 grams of protein a day.) Most Americans, however, eat about twice the amount they need, and while more may sound better, too much is too much. Your body uses what it needs. Some excess protein is excreted as urine; the rest is converted to fat.

Chemically, proteins are varying mixtures of amino acids that contain various elements, including nitrogen. There are 22 different amino acids that are essential for the body's protein needs. Nine of these must be provided in the diet and are thus called *essential* amino acids; the rest can be synthesized by the body itself.

Meat, fish, poultry, eggs, and milk or milk products are the primary protein foods and contain all of the necessary amino acids; they are therefore called *complete* proteins. Grains and vegetables are partly made up of protein, but more often than not, they do not provide the whole range of amino acids required for proper nourishment. When properly combined, however, vegetable proteins, too, can be complete. For example, mixing rice and dried beans provides the same quality of protein as a steak (with a lot less fat).

One gram of protein provides four calories of energy.

Carbohydrates

Carbohydrates are another essential energy source. Called *starches* or *sugars,* they are present in large quantities in grains, fruits, and nuts. As *complex carbohydrates,* or *polysaccharides,* they are found in the foods named and particularly in breads, breakfast cereals, flours, pastas, barley legumes, rice, and starchy vegetables. *Simple carbohydrates,* or mono- or disaccharides, are found in such foods as table sugars, candy, pastries, and soft drinks.

Complex carbohydrates are primary sources of calories, nutrients, and fiber—for such purposes as muscle contraction, weight reduction, and control of sodium and cholesterol. Simple carbohydrates, on the other hand, are pure sources of calories and contain little nutritional value. It is for this reason that they are often termed "empty" calories. Lack of adequate carbohydrates means the body will begin to convert body fat or protein into sugar.

Although there is no absolute dietary requirement for carbohydrates, it is generally recommended that more than half the energy requirement beyond infancy be provided by complex carbohydrates. One gram of carbohydrate provides four calories of energy. Thus the average man consuming about 2,900 calories per day should consume about 360 grams of carbohydrate. The average woman consuming about 2,200 calories per day should consume about 275 grams of carbohydrate.

Fats

Fats are a chemically complex food component composed of *glycerol* (a sweet, oily alcohol) and fatty acids. Fats exist in several forms and come from a variety of sources. One way to think of them is to group them as visible fats, such as butter, salad oil, or the fat seen in meat, and as invisible fats, which are mingled, blended, or absorbed into food, either naturally, as in nuts, meat, or fish, or during cooking. Another way is to think of them as solid at room temperature (fats), or as liquid at room temperature (oils).

Saturated and Unsaturated

Fats are also classified as *saturated* or *unsaturated.* This is a chemical distinction based on the differences in molecular structure of different kinds of fat. If the carbon atoms in a fat molecule are surrounded or boxed in by hydrogen atoms, they are said to be saturated. This type of fat tends to be solid at room temperature, and high consumption of it increases the cholesterol content of the blood, which can lead to heart disease. *Unsaturated* fats, such as those found in fish and vegetable oils, contain the least number of hydrogen atoms and do not add to the blood cholesterol content. They are either *monounsaturated* or *polyunsaturated.* In general, fats in foods of plant origin are more unsaturated than in those of animal origin (except for coconut and palm oils, which are highly saturated). It is recommended that you consume no more than 30 percent of your daily calories from fats; 10 percent of each of the three types, or, for our average man, about 32 grams total; for our average woman, about 24 grams total.

Fats play several essential roles in the metabolic process. First of all, they provide more than twice the number of calories on a comparative weight basis than do proteins and carbohydrates (one gram of fat contains nine calories). They also can be stored in the body in large quantities (in adipose tissue) and used as a later energy source. They serve as carriers of the fat-soluble vitamins A, D, E, and K, and—of no little importance—they add to the tastiness of food.

Vitamins

Vitamins, which are present in minute quantities in foods in their natural state, are essential for normal metabolism and for the development and maintenance of tissue structure and function. In addition to the fat-soluble vitamins noted above, there are a number of B vitamins, as well as vitamin C, also called *ascorbic acid.* If any particular vitamin is missing from the diet over a sufficiently long time, a specific disease will result.

Vitamin A

Vitamin A is essential for vision, growth, cell growth and development, reproduction, a strong immune

Average Daily Calorie Consumption

Men	Calories
Sedentary	2,500
Moderately active	3,000
Active	3,500
Very active	4,250

Women	Calories
Sedentary	2,100
Moderately active	2,500
Active	3,000
Very active	3,750

Guidelines for average daily calorie consumption by men and women. With increasing use of labor-saving devices, most Americans fall into the sedentary category.

Calorie Consumption for Some Activities

Type of Activity	Calories Per Hour
Sedentary: reading, sewing, typing, etc.	30–100
Light: cooking, slow walking, dressing, etc.	100–170
Moderate: sweeping, light gardening, making beds, etc.	170–250
Vigorous: fast walking, hanging out clothes, golfing, etc.	250–350
Strenuous: swimming, bicycling, dancing, etc.	350 and more

Low Calorie Diet

Sample Menus

	800 calories		1,200 calories		1,600 calories	
	Weight grams	Household measure	Weight grams	Household measure	Weight grams	Household measure
Breakfast						
Orange, sliced	125	1 medium	125	1 medium	125	1 medium
Soft cooked egg	50	One	50	One	50	One
Toast	25	1 slice	25	1 slice	25	1 slice
Butter	5	1 teaspoon	5	1 teaspoon	5	1 teaspoon
Coffee or tea	—	As desired	—	As desired	—	As desired
Milk	240	1 cup skim	240	1 cup skim	240	1 cup whole
Luncheon						
Clear broth	—	As desired	—	As desired	—	As desired
Salad (cottage cheese, tomato, plain lettuce leaf)	90	½ cup	90	½ cup	90	½ cup
Egg			50	One	50	One
Green peas					100	½ cup
Baked apple, unsweetened	80	1 small	80	1 small	80	1 small
Bread			25	1 slice	25	1 slice
Butter			5	1 teaspoon	5	1 teaspoon
Milk	240	1 cup skim	240	1 cup skim	240	1 cup whole
Coffee or tea	—	As desired	—	As desired	—	As desired
Dinner						
Roast beef, lean	60	2 ounces	90	3 ounces	120	4 ounces
Carrots, plain	100	½ cup	100	½ cup	100	½ cup
Tossed vegetable salad with vinegar	50	¾ cup	50	¾ cup	50	¾ cup
Pineapple, unsweetened	80	½ cup	80	½ cup	80	½ cup
Bread			25	1 slice	25	1 slice
Butter			5	1 teaspoon	10	2 teaspoons
Coffee or tea	—	As desired	—	As desired	—	As desired
Nourishment						
Peach					100	1 medium

These diets contain approximately 800, 1,200, and 1,600 calories. The 800 calorie diet, even with variations in selections of food, will not meet the recommended daily allowances in iron and thiamine. The approximate composition is as follows:

	800 calories	1,200 calories	1,600 calories
Protein	60 gm.	75 gm.	85 gm.
Fat	30 gm.	50 gm.	80 gm.
Carbohydrate	75 gm.	110 gm.	130 gm.

From the *Clinical Center Diet Manual*, revised edition, prepared by the Nutrition Department. The Clinical Center, National Institutes of Health, Public Health Service, U.S. Department of Health, Education, and Welfare (Public Health Service Publication No. 989), pp. 67–68.

system, and healthy hair, skin, and mucous membranes.

Vitamin A is fat soluble and is therefore stored by the body (in the liver). It comes in two forms: retinol, found only in animal foods (chiefly liver), and beta-carotene, found in fruits and vegetables (chiefly deep green or orange ones like spinach and sweet potatoes). Retinol is instantly available for bodily use, while beta-carotene must be converted by the body into retinol before it can be used. (Because the body will not convert excess beta-carotene into retinol, there is no danger of overdosing on this form of vitamin A. Retinol, however, can be extremely toxic at high levels.)

Symptoms of vitamin A deficiency include dry rough skin, slow growth, night blindness, thickening of bone, and increased susceptibility to infection. Vitamin A deficiency is rare in the United States.

Formerly measured in International Units (IU), vitamin A content is now expressed retinol equivalents (RE). One RE equals 10 IU of beta-carotene and 3.33 IU of retinol. The Recommended Daily Allowance (RDA) for vitamin A for adult males is 1000 RE and for adult women, 800 RE.

Vitamin D

Vitamin D is essential for proper metabolism of calcium, which is primarily responsible for the healthy growth of bones and teeth.

Vitamin D is fat soluble and therefore excessive intake can be toxic. It is consumed chiefly as an addition to milk and is also manufactured by the body by a reaction of sunlight on sterols present in the skin.

The major deficiency disease of vitamin D in children is rickets (deformation of the skeleton) and in adults excessive bone loss and fractures.

The RDA for adults over 24 is 5 micrograms.

Vitamin E (tocopherol)

Vitamin E is essential for healthy nerve function and reproduction.

Vitamin E is found principally in plant oils, particularly wheat germ oil and nuts. It is fat soluble, but there is little danger of toxicity because absorption by the body is relatively inefficient.

Vitamin E is measured in tocopherol equivalents (TE). The RDA for adult males is 10 TE and for adult women 8 TE. Deficiencies in a normal diet are rare.

Vitamin K

Vitamin K is essential for proper clotting of the blood.

Vitamin K is fat soluble and is found primarily in green leafy vegetables. Another form of the compound is synthesized by intestinal bacteria. Like vitamin E, there is little danger from ingesting too much vitamin K, and most diets provide an adequate supply.

The RDA for adult males over age 24 is 80 micrograms and for adult women 65 micrograms.

Vitamin C (ascorbic acid)

Vitamin C is essential for healthy skin, bones, teeth, and muscles, for producing and maintaining collagen, and for fighting infection.

Vitamin C is water soluble and therefore must be ingested every day. It is widely available in a variety of colorful fruits and vegetables, such as peppers, broccoli, cabbage, oranges, strawberries, and tomatoes. Unfortunately, vitamin C is also the most unstable of all vitamins and minerals: it is easily destroyed by heat and oxygen, and thus care should be taken in cooking and storing of fruits and vegetables.

The classic vitamin C deficiency disease is scurvy, typified by the wasting away of muscles, wounds and bruises that don't heal, and bleeding, deteriorating gums. Milder forms of vitamin C deficiency produce milder versions of these symptoms. Vitamin C deficiency has also been linked to such health problems as the common cold, anemia, atherosclerosis, asthma, cancer of the stomach and esophagus, infertility in males, rheumatoid arthritis, and cataracts.

Vitamin C is measured in milligrams (mg). The RDA for adults is 60 mg. Megadoses of vitamin C are often recommended to fight colds or as a general preventive measure against disease, although the body only uses as much as it needs; the rest is excreted in the urine. Toxicity is rarely a problem.

Thiamin (vitamin B$_1$)

Thiamin is essential for the proper metabolism of carbohydrates and for a healthy nervous system.

Thiamin is water soluble and is found primarily in cereals, wheat germ, port, and nuts. It is strongly susceptible to destruction during cooking. Deficiency is not common among the general population, but studies have shown heavy drinkers, pregnant women, and the elderly to be more deficient. Severe thiamin deficiency results in beriberi, a disease that weakens the body, disables the mind, and permanently damages the heart. Symptoms of deficiency include loss of appetite, nausea, vomiting, constipation, depression, fatigue, poor eye-hand coordination, irritability, headaches, and anxiety.

Thiamin is measured in milligrams. The RDA for adult males is 1.5 mg and for adult women 1.1 mg. Danger of toxicity is rare as excess thiamin is excreted in urine.

Riboflavin (vitamin B$_2$)

Riboflavin is essential for growth and repair of tissues and aids in DNA synthesis. It helps metabolize proteins, fats, and carbohydrates.

Most Americans get plenty of this water-soluble vitamin, which is readily found in liver, eggs, and milk products. Studies have found that children in low-income families, however, are less likely to get enough riboflavin. Signs of deficiency include a purplish-colored tongue; cracks at the corners of the mouth; sores and burning of the lips, mouth, and tongue; itchy inflamed eyelids; flaky skin around the nose, ears, eyebrows, or hairline; and light sensitivity of eyes. Deficiency in riboflavin often means deficiency in other B vitamins as well. Cataracts, birth defects, and anemia have been linked to riboflavin deficiency.

Unlike vitamin C and thiamin, riboflavin is not easily destroyed by cooking, although adding baking soda to vegetables when cooking creates an alkaline solution that destroys it. Risk of toxicity is very low, and excess riboflavin is excreted in the urine.

Riboflavin is measured in milligrams. The RDA for adult males is 1.7 mg and for adult women 1.3 mg.

Niacin (vitamin B$_3$)

Niacin is essential for the release of energy from carbohydrates, fats, and proteins and for the formation of DNA.

Most Americans get plenty of niacin from their diets; only heavy drinkers are at risk of deficiency. Severe deficiencies of niacin result in pellagra, a disease virtually wiped out in the United States since the 1930s with the advent of fortified flour and cereals with the vitamin.

Niacin is widely available in a variety of plant and animal foods, including fish, liver, turkey, cereals, and peanuts. The body is also able to convert the amino acid tryptophan into niacin, and thus proteins high in tryptophan also provide plenty of niacin.

Niacin in measure in milligrams (60 mg of tryptophan equal 1 mg of niacin). The RDA for adult males is 19 mg. and for women 15 mg.

Vitamin B_6

Vitamin B_6 is essential for fat and carbohydrate metabolism and for the formation and breakdown of amino acids. It also helps regulate blood glucose levels and is needed to synthesize hemoglobin.

Vitamin B_6 occurs in three forms: pyridoxine, pyridoxal, and pyridoxamine, which are converted by the body into pyridoxal phosphate and pyridoxamine phosphate. It is most readily found in nuts, kidney, liver, eggs, pork, poultry, dried fruits, and fish.

Although few Americans get the full RDA of vitamin B_6, there is no evidence of corresponding overt deficiency symptoms. The following health problems, however, have been linked to B_6 deficiency: asthma, carpal tunnel syndrome, cancer (melanoma, breast, and bladder), diabetes, coronary heart disease, premenstrual syndrome, sickle-cell anemia, and aging and dementia.

In moderate doses B_6 is not toxic. Although excessive amounts of this water-soluble vitamin are to a great extent flushed out of the body in the urine, high doses have produced neurological disturbances such as numbness in the hands, feet, and mouth.

Vitamin B_6 is measured in milli-

Recommended Dietary Allowances for Fat-Soluble Vitamins

	Age	Vit. A (mcg RE)	Vit. D (mcg)	Vit. E (mgTE)	Vit.K (mcg)
Infants	0 to .5	375	7.5	3	5
	.5 to 1	"	10	4	10
Children	1 to 3	400	"	6	15
	4 to 6	500	"	7	20
	7 to 10	700	"	"	30
Males	11 to 14	1,000	"	10	45
	15 to 18	"	"	"	65
	19 to 24	"	"	"	70
	25 to 50	"	5	"	80
	51 +	"	"	"	"
Females	11 to 14	800	10	8	45
	15 to 18	"	"	"	55
	19 to 24	"	"	"	60
	25 to 50	"	5	"	65
	51 +	"	"	"	"
Pregnant Nursing			10	10	"
	1st 6 months	1,300	"	12	"
	2nd 6 months	1,200	"	11	"

grams. The RDA for adult men is 2 mg and for women 1.6 mg.

Vitamin B_{12}

Vitamin B_{12} is important for normal growth, healthy nerve tissue, and normal blood formation.

Most Americans get plenty of B_{12}. It is found chiefly in animal foods: meat, fish, eggs, and milk products. Only strict vegetarians (vegans), who eat none of these foods are in danger of deficiency. Problems for everyone arise with age, however; the stomach may become less able to absorb B_{12} and deficiency may result. Pernicious anemia is the classic B_{12} deficiency disease and may take years to appear. Other health problems that may be linked to B_{12} deficiency include infertility, nervous system disorders, and walking difficulties.

Cooking results in few losses of B_{12}, and toxicity is not a danger. The RDA for B_{12} for adults is 2 micrograms.

Folacin (folic acid, or folate)

Folacin is essential for cell growth and division.

Women, especially pregnant women, and alcoholics are most likely to be folacin deficient. Signs of deficiency include anemia, weakness, pallor, headaches, forgetfulness, sleeplessness, and irritability. Vitamin B_{12} deficiency can aggravate folacin deficiency because B_{12} is essential to release folacin from bodily storage. Other health problems that may be associated with folacin deficiency include depression, dementia, neuropsychological disorders, toxemia of pregnancy, infections, and fetal damage.

Folacin is widely distributed in fruits and vegetables, but it is easily destroyed during cooking and storage. The RDA for folacin for adult men is 200 micrograms and for women, 180 micrograms.

Biotin

Biotin is essential for overall growth and well-being. It is important in the metabolism of fats and in the utilization of carbon dioxide.

The best sources of biotin are liver, egg yolks, soy flour, cereals, and

		Vit. C	Thiamin	Riboflav.	Niacin	Vit. B6	Folate	Vit. B12
	Age	(mg)	(mg)	(mg)	(mg)	(mg)	(mcg)	(mcg)
Infants	0 to .5	30	0.3	0.4	5	0.3	25	0.3
	.5 to 1	35	0.4	0.5	6	0.6	35	0.5
Children	1 to 3	40	0.7	0.8	9	1	50	0.7
	4 to 6	45	0.9	1.1	12	1.1	75	1
	7 to 10	"	1	1.2	13	1.4	100	1.4
Males	11 to 14	50	1.3	1.5	17	1.7	150	2
	15 to 18	60	1.5	1.8	20	2	200	"
	19 to 24	"	"	1.7	19	"	"	"
	25 to 50	"	"	"	"	"	"	"
	51 +	"	1.2	1.4	15	"	150	"
Females	11 to 14	50	1.1	1.3	"	1.4	180	"
	15 to 18	60	"	"	"	1.5	"	"
	19 to 24	"	"	"	"	1.6	"	"
	25 to 50	"	1.1	"	"	"	"	"
51 +		"	1	1.2	13	"	"	"
Pregnant		70	1.5	1.6	17	2.2	400	2.2
Nursing	1st 6 months	95	1.6	1.8	20	2.1	280	2.6
	2nd 6 months	90	"	1.7	20	"	260	"

Recommended Dietary Allowances for Water-Soluble Vitamins

yeast. It is also produced by intestinal bacteria, although it is not known whether this form is readily absorbed by the body. Deficiencies are most often produced by the ingestion of large amount of raw egg white, which contains a biotin-binding protein called avidin that prevents the absorption of biotin. Symptoms of deficiency include nausea, vomiting, swelling of the tongue, pallor, depression, hair loss, and dry scaly dermatitis.

The RDA for adults is a wide range: from 30 to 100 micrograms. Toxicity from a normal diet is not a concern.

Pantothenic acid

Pantothenic acid is essential for general growth and well-being. It is an important component in a number of metabolic reactions such as the release of energy from carbohydrates, fats, and proteins and the synthesis of sterols and steroid hormones.

Pantothenic acid is widely distributed among foods, chiefly animal tissues, cereals, and legumes. Evidence of dietary deficiency of pantothenic acid has not been clinically recognized in humans, and there is no specific disease associated with pantothenic acid deficiency.

Pantothenic acid is measured in milligrams. There is no RDA, but daily consumption by adults of between 4 and 7 mg is considered safe. Toxicity from a normal diet is not a concern.

Minerals

Minerals are another component of basic nutritional needs. All living things extract them from the soil, which is their ultimate source. Like vitamins, they are needed for normal metabolism and must be present in the diet in sufficient amounts for the maintenance of good health. The essential minerals are calcium, phosphorus, magnesium, iodine, iron, zinc, selenium, molybdenum, copper, manganese, fluoride, and chromium.

Calcium

Calcium is essential for bone growth, development, and retention as well as for proper nerve conduction, muscle contraction, blood clotting, and membrane permeability.

Dairy products are the primary sources of calcium, but the mineral is also found in green leafy vegetables and soft bones, such as those of sardines and salmon. Maximum calcium ingestion is extremely important during the years from birth to age 25, when the body reaches its peak bone mass. Deficiencies are most common in women and have been linked to the development of osteoporosis in the later years.

The RDA for calcium for children between the ages of 11 and 24 is 1,200 mg. For adults over 24 the RDA is 800 mg. Ingestion of very large amounts of calcium may inhibit the absorption of iron, zinc, and other essential minerals.

Phosphorus

Phosphorus is a structural component of all cells. It is a part of DNA, and is therefore essential in the growth, maintenance, and repair of all body tissues. It is also critical for energy transfer and production.

Phosphorus is present in nearly all foods, principally cereals and proteins. Deficiency is a serious concern only for premature infants fed exclusively human milk.

The RDA for phosphorus is the same as that for calcium. Toxicity from a normal diet is not a concern.

Magnesium

Like phosphorus, magnesium is a structural component in soft tissue cells and is therefore important in the growth, maintenance, and repair of these tissues. It is also important in energy production, lipid and protein synthesis, the formation of urea, muscle relaxation, and in the prevention of tooth decay.

The best sources of magnesium are nuts, legumes, unmilled grains, and green vegetables. Deficiencies from a normal diet are rare and are related instead to various diseases such as those of the gastrointestinal tract, kidney dysfunction, and malnutrition and alcoholism. Symptoms of deficiency include weakness, confusion, personality changes, muscle tremor, nausea, lack of coordination, and gastrointestinal disorders.

The RDA for adult men is 350 mg and for adult women 280 mg.

Iodine

Iodine is an essential component of thyroid hormone, which is important in cellular reactions, metabolism, and growth and development.

Iodized salt and water are the most common sources, and most animal foods contain adequate supplies depending on the soil quality and the amount of iodine added to animal feeds. Iodine is also added in the processing of bread dough. Deficiencies in the United States is not common. The classic deficiency disease in adults is goiter. Iodine deficient fetuses are at a risk of developing cretinism.

The RDA for iodine for adults is 150 micrograms.

Iron

As an essential component of hemoglobin, iron is necessary for the proper transfer of oxygen to cells. It is also important for energy production and collagen synthesis.

Many Americans don't get enough iron. Women and very young children get the least, followed by the elderly. Iron deficiency leads to anemia: muscles become weak, fatigue, listlessness, and a tendency to tire easily set in. Even mild iron deficiency, however, can affect a person's intellectual capabilities, especially children's. Symptoms of deficiency in children include irritability, hyperactivity, learning problems, shortened attention span, poor motivation, and poor intellectual performance.

There are two types of iron, heme and nonheme. Heme comes from animal foods and is much more readily absorbed than nonheme iron, which comes from vegetables. When eaten together, however, the rate of absorption for nonheme iron increases significantly. Also, iron eaten with just a little vitamin C dramatically increases its absorption. Tannins (in tea and red wine) block iron absorption. Iron-rich foods include liver and other organ meats, beef, dried fruits, legumes, dark green leafy vegetables, prune juice, and whole grain cereals.

The RDA for adult males is 10 mg and for adult women 15 mg. There is little danger of toxicity from a normal diet, although some people have an inherited defect in regulating iron absorption and can easily get too much.

Zinc

Zinc is essential for cell multiplication, tissue regeneration, sexual maturity, and proper growth. It is also important as a cofactor in more than 20 enzymatic reactions and serves as a binder in many others.

Severe zinc deficiency is not a problem in the United States, but the effects of mild deficiency—common especially in children, women, and the elderly—on overall health are feared to be widespread. Signs of deficiency include loss of appetite, stunted growth in children, skin changes, small sex glands in boys, delayed sexual maturation, impotence, loss of taste sensitivity, white spots on fingernails, delayed wound-healing, dull hair color.

Animal foods are good sources of zinc as are oysters, milk, egg yolks, and whole grains. Toxicity is rare. The RDA for adults is 12 mg.

Selenium

Selenium functions in a similar way to vitamin E, as an antioxidant helping to protect cells from destruction by toxic agents. Its consumption has also been associated with lower incidences of cancer and heart disease.

Good sources of selenium include whole grains, seafood, liver, kidney, meat, seeds, and nuts. Deficiency may be a problem in areas with selenium-poor soils. Selenium is toxic at higher than trace amounts. The RDA for adult males is 70 micrograms and for adult women 55 micrograms.

Molybdenum

Molybdenum is essential in the function of certain enzyme systems and is also necessary in iron metabolism.

Sources of molybdenum include meats, whole grains, legumes, leafy vegetables, and organ meats. The molybdenum content of vegetables varies widely depending on the content of the soil in which they were grown. Deficiency is not known in humans. Ingesting more than trace amounts is not recommended. The

RDA for adults is between 75 and 250 micrograms.

Copper

Copper is important as a cofactor in several enzyme systems and as a catalyst in the synthesis of hemoglobin. It also aids in collagen formation and is involved in the synthesis of phospholipids, which maintain health nerve fibers.

Copper deficiency is believed to be more common than once thought, and it has been linked to heart disease, central nervous system disorders, anemia, and bone disorders. Good sources of copper include shellfish, liver, nuts and seeds, meats, and green leafy vegetables. Copper supplements are not recommended because they can interfere with other minerals, and copper is toxic at more than trace amounts. The RDA for copper is 1.5 to 3 mg.

Manganese

Manganese has a variety of functions, some that other minerals can perform in its place. It is known to play a role in such things as collagen formation, urea formation, synthesis of fatty acids and cholesterol, digestion of proteins, normal bone formation and development, and protein synthesis.

Manganese deficiency has not been observed in humans. Sources of manganese include liver, kidney, spinach, whole grain cereals and breads, dried peas and beans, and nuts. Excessive intake of manganese can interfere with iron absorption. More than trace amounts of manganese are not recommended. The RDA is 2 to 5 mg.

Fluoride

Fluoride is essential for the development of healthy teeth and bones and the prevention of tooth decay.

Fluoride deficiency shows up in increased incidences of tooth decay. Fluoridated water is a most common source of fluoride for many people. For those without access to such water fluoride tablets or toothpaste are helpful. Fish, tea, milk, and eggs are also sources of fluoride. The RDA for adults is between 1.5 and 4 mg.

Chromium

Chromium is important for maintaining normal glucose metabolism. It also acts as a cofactor for insulin.

Chromium deficiency can show up in the form of glucose intolerance in malnourished children and in some diabetics. Sources of chromium include whole grains, brewer's yeast, meats, and cheeses. Hard water also contains chromium. Chromium intake should not exceed trace amounts. The RDA for adults is between 50 and 200 micrograms.

Fiber

Fiber in the diet is important for proper elimination. It provides bulk, and its use has been linked to the prevention of many health problems: constipation, appendicitis, colon cancer, diverticular disease, spastic colon, hiatal hernia, varicose veins, hemorrhoids, coronary heart disease, high blood pressure, gallstones, diabetes, obesity, ulcerative colitis, and Crohn's disease.

Fiber is found almost exclusively in plant foods and comes in basically two types: water soluble or water insoluble. Soluble fiber is found primarily in fruits and vegetables and in oat bran in the form of gums and pectin and affects the way the body metabolizes sugars and fats. Insoluble fiber is primarily associated with whole grains, the traditional 'bran,' such as wheat bran and rice bran, and is the fiber we think of when we think of laxatives. Generally, the less processed the food, the higher it is in either kind of fiber.

Fiber in high doses can affect the absorption of other vitamins and minerals as well as cause flatulence, bloating, nausea, diarrhea, and impaction or rupture of the bowl. Daily consumption of 35 to 40 grams of fiber is recommended for optimum health and safety.

Water

Water is not really a food in the fuel sense, but it is in many ways a crucial component of nutrition: the body's need for water is second only to its need for oxygen. It makes up from 55 to 65 percent of the body's weight, and is constantly being eliminated in the form of urine, perspiration, and expired breath. It must therefore be replaced regularly, for while a person can live for weeks without food, he can live for only a few days without water.

Normally, the best guide to how much water a person needs is his sense of thirst. The regulating mechanism of excretion sees to it that an excessive intake of water will be eliminated as urine. The usual water requirement is on the order of two quarts a day in addition to whatever amount is contained in the solids which make up the daily diet.

Basic Daily Diets

Everyone should have at least the

minimal amount of basic nutrients for resting or basal metabolism. The specific needs of each individual are determined by whether he is still growing, and by how much energy is required for his normal activities. All those who are still growing—and growth continues up to about 25 years of age—have relatively high food needs.

For Infants

That food needs of an infant are especially acute should surprise no one. The newborn baby normally triples his birth weight during his first year and is very active in terms of calorie expenditure.

For his first six months, breast milk or formula, or a combination of both, fills his nutritional needs. The amount of milk he should get each day is about two and a half ounces per pound of his body weight. This provides 50 calories per pound, and in the early months is usually given in six feedings a day at four-hour intervals.

If his weight gain is adequate and he appears healthy, and if his stomach is not distended by swallowed air, his appetite is normally a satisfactory guide to how much he needs. The formula-fed baby should get a supplement of 35 milligrams of ascorbic acid each day and 400 international units of vitamin D if the latter has not been added to the milk during its processing.

Solid Foods

Between two and six months of age, the baby should begin to eat solid foods such as cooked cereals, strained fruits and vegetables, egg yolk, and homogenized meat. With the introduction of these foods, it is not really necessary to calculate the baby's caloric intake. Satisfaction of appetite, proper weight gain, and a healthy appearance serve as the guides to a proper diet.

By one year of age, a baby should be getting three regular meals a day, and as his teeth appear, his food no longer needs to be strained. By 18 to 24 months, he should no longer need baby foods. For more information, see Ch. 2, *The First Dozen Years*.

The Years of Growth

A proper diet is crucial during the years from 2 to 18, since this is a period of tremendous growth.

Children should also learn about balanced diets, decent manners at the table, and develop a sense of timing about when to eat and when not to eat.

Creating a Pleasant Mealtime Atmosphere

- Children should never be bribed with candy, money, or the promise of special surprises as a way of getting them to eat properly.

- They should not be given the idea that dessert is a reward for finishing the earlier part of the meal.

- Relatively small portions should be served and completely finished before anything else is offered.

- Between-meal snacks should be discouraged if they cut down on the appetite at mealtime.

- From time to time, the child should be allowed to choose the foods that he will eat at a meal.

Parents should keep in mind that the atmosphere in which a child eats and the attitudes instilled in him toward food can be altogether as basic as the nourishment for his body.

Teenage Diet

From the start of a child's growth spurt, which begins at age 10 or 11 for girls and between 13 and 15 for boys, and for several years thereafter, adolescent appetites are likely to be unbelievably large and somewhat outlandish. Parents should try to exercise some control over the youngster who is putting on too much weight as well as over the one who is attracted by a bizarre starvation diet.

Adult Nutrition

The average American adult experiences slow, but steady, weight gain; for some, this develops into an obesity problem. Doctors no longer dismiss the average adult's weight gain as normal or acceptable, but view it as a hazard that could jeopardize the individual's health. A sensible diet is recommended.

For Older People

People over 60 tend to have changes in their digestive system that are related to less efficient and slower absorption. Incomplete chewing of food because of carelessness or impaired teeth can intensify this problem. Avoiding haste at mealtimes ought to be the rule.

In cases where a dental disorder makes proper chewing impossible, food should be chopped or pureed.

Recommended Dietary Allowances for Minerals

	Age	Calcium (mg)	Phospho. (mg)	Magnesium (mg)	Iron (mg)	Zinc (mg)	Iodine (mcg)	Selenium (mcg)
Infants	0 to .5	400	300	40	6	5	40	10
	.5 to 1	600	500	60	10	"	50	15
Children	1 to 3	800	800	80	"	10	70	20
	4 to 6	"	"	120	"	"	90	"
	7 to 10	"	"	170	"	"	120	30
Males	11 to 14	1,200	1,200	270	12	15	150	40
	15 to 18	"	"	400	"	"	"	50
	19 to 24	"	"	350	10	"	"	70
	25 to 50	800	800	"	"	"	"	"
	51 +	"	"	"	"	"	"	"
Females	11 to 14	1,200	1,200	280	15	12	"	45
	15 to 18	"	"	300	"	"	"	50
	19 to 24	"	"	280	"	"	"	55
	25 to 50	800	800	"	"	"	"	"
	51 +	"	"	"	10	"	"	"
Pregnant		1,200	1,200	320	30	15	175	65
Nursing	1st 6 months	"	"	355	15	19	200	75
	2nd 6 months	"	"	340	"	16	200	"

Food for older people should be cooked simply, preferably baked, boiled, or broiled rather than fried, and menus excessively rich in fats should be avoided. A daily multivitamin capsule is strongly recommended for those over 60.

Eating for Life

The U.S. Department of Agriculture and the U.S. Department of Health and Human Services recommend seven basic guidelines to avoid excess weight and maintain optimum health:

- Eat a variety of foods

- Maintain a desirable weight

- Avoid too much fat, saturated fat, and cholesterol

- Eat foods with adequate starch and fiber

- Avoid too much sugar

- Avoid too much sodium

- If you drink alcoholic beverages, do so in moderation

The guidelines are designed for healthy adult Americans, but are considered especially appropriate for people who may already have some of the risk factors for chronic diseases, including a family history of obesity, premature heart disease, diabetes, high blood pressure, or high blood cholesterol levels.

The U.S.D.A. and the U.S.D.H.H.S. also recommend the "Choose More Often" approach to healthful eating.

Choose More Often:

Low-fat meat, poultry, fish
Lean cuts of meat trimmed of fat (round tip roast, pork tenderloin, loin of lamb chop), poultry without skin, and fish, cooked without breading or added fat.

Low-fat or Non-fat diary products
1 percent or skim milk, buttermilk; nonfat or low-fat yogurt; lower fat cheeses (part-skim ricotta, fresh parmesan or feta); nonfat or low-fat yogurt, sherbet.

Dry beans and peas
All beans, peas, and lentils—the dry forms are higher in protein.

Whole grain products
Reduced-fat breads, bagels, and English muffins made from whole wheat, rye, bran, and corn flour or meal; whole-grain or bran cereals; whole wheat pasta; brown rice; bulgur.

Fats and oils high in unsaturates
Unsaturated vegetable oils, such as canola oil, corn oil, cottonseed oil, olive oil, soybean oil, and margarine; reduced- fat and calorie mayonnaise and salad dressings.

Some tips for following the "Choose More Often" approach when grocery shopping, food preparation, and eating out.

When Grocery Shopping

Focus on variety. Using the above guidelines, choose a wide selection of low-fat foods rich in fiber. Although the goal is to reduce fat to 30 percent or less, when choosing foods that do contain fat, try to choose ones that contain primarily unsaturated fats.

Read food labels. Many nutritional labels on packaged foods show the amounts of unsaturated and saturated fat, cholesterol, fiber, vitamins and minerals. Avoid those that contain animal lowest proportion of saturated fat, coconut or palm kernel oils. Choose products with the lowest proportion of saturated fat. The label also lists ingredients in order of amount from most to least by weight. Choose items that have a low-fat, high-fiber ingredient listed first.

Beware of sodium. Many processed, canned, and frozen foods are high in sodium. Cured or processed meats, cheeses, soups and condiments (soy sauce, mustard, tartar sauce) are high in sodium. Check labels for salt, onion or garlic salt, and any ingredient with sodium in its name. Compare products and choose the ones with lower levels.

When Preparing Food

Use small amounts of fat and fatty foods when planning meals.
When you do use fat, use it sparingly and allow the full flavor of the foods to dominate, instead of a single element like cheese or butter. Try to use only ½ teaspoon of fat per serving. Gradually introduce nonfat or low-fat alternatives into your diet.

Use less saturated fat. While reducing your total fat intake, substitute unsaturated fat and oils for saturated. Instead of butter, try vegetable oil, margarine or a low-fat cooking spray. To substitute, use equal portions, or less.

Use low-fat alternatives. Substitute 1 percent, skim, or reconstituted nonfat dry milk for whole milk. Use buttermilk, nonfat or low-fat yogurt, or evaporated skim milk in place of cream and sour cream. Try reduced-fat mayonnaise, sour cream and salad dressings.

Choose lean meat. Trim all visible fat from meat and poultry, including poultry skin. Canned, reduced fat and sodium stocks are now available for making soup.

Use low-fat cooking methods. Bake, steam, broil, microwave, or boil foods rather than frying. Avoid gravies and try vegetable-based instead of cream-based sauces.

Increase fiber. Substitute whole-grain flour for white flour. Have gen-erous servings. Whenever possible, eat the edible fiber-rich skin as well as the rest of the vegetable or fruit.

Use herbs, spices, and other flavorings. For a different way to add flavor to meals, try lemon juice, basil, chives, curry powder, onion, cracked pepper, and garlic in place of fats and sodium. Try low-fat recipes and adjust old ones to reduce fat and sodium.

When Eating Out

Choose the restaurant carefully. Are low-fat, high-fiber items on the menu, like pasta? How are meat, chicken, and fish dishes cooked—broiled, baked, or fried? Avoid fast food places.

Try ethnic cuisines. Italian and Asian restaurants often feature low-fat dishes—though you must be selective and alert to portion size. Try a small serving of pasta or fish in a tomato sauce at an Italian restaurant. Many Chinese, Japanese, and Thai dishes include a plenty of steamed vegetables and a high proportion of vegetables to meat. Steamed rice, steamed noodle dishes and vegetarian dishes are good choices, too. Ask for food without soy sauce or salt.

Make sure you get what you want. Be in control when you eat out. Ask how dishes are cooked. Don't hesitate to request that one food be substituted for another. Order a green salad or baked potato in place of french fries or order fruit or sherbet instead of ice cream. Request sauces and salad dressings on the side and use only a small amount. Ask that butter and rolls not be sent to the table. If you're not very hungry, order two low-fat appetizers rather than an entire meal, split a menu item with a friend, get a doggie-bag to take half of your meal home, or order a half-size portion. When you finish, let the waiter clear dishes to avoid post-meal nibbling.

Be reasonable. If you don't eat out very often, one meal won't ruin your health. If you feel like ordering a rich meal or having dessert, simply cut back on the extras; avoid the bread and butter, don't order an appetizer, have one glass of wine instead of two.

Malnutrition

The classic diseases of nutritional deficiency, or malnutrition, such as scurvy and pellagra, are now rare, at least in the United States. The chief reason for their disappearance is the application of scientific knowledge gained in this century of the importance of vitamins and minerals in the diet. Thus most bread is fortified with vitamins and minerals, and in addition, commercial food processing has made it possible for balanced diets of an appealing variety to be eaten all year round.

Many people do not get an adequate diet, either through ignorance or because they simply cannot afford it. A number of food programs have been created to assist them, but unfortunately, the programs don't reach everyone who needs help.

Causes of Malnutrition

Some people, either because of ignorance or food faddism, do not eat a balanced diet even though they can afford to. There are also large numbers of people with nutritional deficiency diseases who can be described as abnormal, at least in regard to eating. Some are alcoholics; others live alone and are so depressed that they lack sufficient drive to feed themselves properly. Combination of any of these factors increase the likelihood of poor nutrition and often lead to health-damaging consequences.

Disease

People can also develop nutritional deficiencies because they have some disease that interferes with food absorption, storage, and utilization, or that causes an increased excretion, usually in the urine, of substances needed for nutrition. These are generally chronic diseases of the gastrointestinal tract including the liver, or of the kidneys or the endocrine glands.

Medications

Nutritional deficiencies can also result from loss of appetite caused by medications, especially when a number of different medications are taken simultaneously. This adverse affect on the appetite is a strong reason for not taking medicines unless told to do so by a physician for a specific purpose.

Most people are not aware of inadequacies in their diet until there are some dramatic consequences. Nor is it easy to recognize the presence of a disorder that might be causing malnutrition. A physician should be consulted promptly when there is a persistent weight loss, especially when the diet is normal. He should also be informed of any changes in the skin, mucous membranes of the mouth or tongue, or nervous system function, because such symptoms can be a warning of dietary deficiency.

The family or friends of a person with a nutritional deficiency can often

Nutrients in Common Foods

Food	Food energy Calories	Protein Grams	Fat Grams	Carbohydrate Grams
Milk and Milk Products				
Milk; 1 cup:				
Fluid, whole	165	9	10	12
Fluid, nonfat (skim)	90	9	trace	13
Buttermilk, cultured (from skim milk)	90	9	trace	13
Evaporated (undiluted)	345	18	20	24
Dry, nonfat (regular)	435	43	1	63
Yogurt (from partially skimmed milk); 1 cup	120	8	4	13
Cheese; 1 ounce:				
Cheddar or American	115	7	9	1
Cottage:				
From skim milk	25	5	trace	1
Creamed	30	4	1	1
Cream cheese	105	2	11	1
Swiss	105	7	8	1
Desserts (largely milk):				
Custard, baked; 1 cup, 8 fluid ounces	305	14	15	29
Ice cream, plain, factory packed:				
1 slice or individual brick, ⅛ quart	130	3	7	14
1 container, 8 fluid ounces	255	6	14	28
Ice milk; 1 cup, 8 fluid ounces	200	6	7	29
Eggs				
Egg, raw, large:				
1 whole	80	6	6	trace
1 white	15	4	trace	trace
1 yolk	60	3	5	trace
Egg, cooked; 1 large:				
Boiled	80	6	6	trace
Scrambled (with milk and fat)	110	7	8	1
Meat, Poultry, Fish, Shellfish				
Bacon, broiled or fried, drained, 2 medium thick slices	85	4	8	trace
Beef, cooked without bone:				
Braised, simmered, or pot-roasted; 3 ounce portion:				
Entire portion, lean and fat	365	19	31	0
Lean only, approx. 2 ounces	140	17	4	0
Hamburger patties, made with				
Regular ground beef; 3-ounce patty	235	21	17	0
Lean ground round; 3-ounce patty	185	23	10	0
Roast; 3-ounce slice from cut having relatively small amount of fat:				
Entire portion, lean and fat	255	22	18	0
Lean only, approx. 2.3 ounces	115	19	4	0
Steak, broiled; 3-ounce portion:				
Entire portion, lean and fat	375	19	32	0
Lean only, approx. 1.8 ounces	105	17	4	0
Beef, canned: corned beef hash: 3 ounces	155	8	10	9
Beef and vegetable stew: 1 cup	220	16	11	15
Chicken, without bone: broiled; 3 ounces	115	20	3	0
Lamb, cooked:				
Chops; 1 thick chop, with bone, 4.8 ounces:				
Lean and fat, approx. 3.4 ounces	340	21	28	0
Lean only, 2.3 ounces	120	18	5	0

Nutrients in Common Foods *(continued)*

Food	Food energy Calories	Protein Grams	Fat Grams	Carbohydrate Grams
Roast, without bone:				
Leg; 3-ounce slice:				
Entire slice, lean and fat	265	20	20	0
Lean only, approx. 2.3 ounces	120	19	5	0
Shoulder; 3-ounce portion, without bone:				
Entire portion, lean and fat	300	18	25	0
Lean only, approx. 2.2 ounces	125	16	6	0
Liver, beef, fried; 2 ounces	120	13	4	6
Pork, cured, cooked:				
Ham, smoked; 3-ounce portion, without bone	245	18	19	0
Luncheon meat:				
Boiled ham; 2 ounces	130	11	10	0
Canned, spiced; 2 ounces	165	8	14	1
Pork, fresh, cooked:				
Chops; 1 chop, with bone, 3.5 ounces:				
Lean and fat, approx. 2.4 ounces	295	15	25	0
Lean only, approx. 1.6 ounces	120	14	7	0
Roast; 3-ounce slice, without bone:				
Entire slice, lean and fat	340	19	29	0
Lean only, approx. 2.2 ounces	160	19	9	0
Sausage:				
Bologna; 8 slices (4.1 by 0.1 inches each), 8 ounces	690	27	62	2
Frankfurter; 1 cooked, 1.8 ounces	155	6	14	1
Tongue, beef, boiled; 3 ounces	205	18	14	trace
Veal, cutlet, broiled; 3-ounce portion, without bone	185	23	9	0
Fish and shellfish:				
Bluefish, baked or broiled; 3 ounces	135	22	4	0
Clams: raw, meat only; 3 ounces	70	11	1	3
Crabmeat, canned or cooked; 3 ounces	90	14	2	1
Fishsticks, breaded, cooked, frozen; 10 sticks (3.8 by 1.0 by 0.5 inches each), 8 ounces	400	38	20	15
Haddock, fried; 3 ounces	135	16	5	6
Mackerel: broiled; 3 ounces	200	19	13	0
Oysters, raw, meat only; 1 cup (13–19 medium-size oysters, selects)	160	20	4	8
Oyster stew: 1 cup (6–8 oysters)	200	11	12	11
Salmon, canned (pink); 3 ounces	120	17	5	0
Sardines, canned in oil, drained solids; 3 ounces	180	22	9	1
Shrimp, canned, meat only; 3 ounces	110	23	1	—
Tuna, canned in oil, drained solids; 3 ounces	170	25	7	0
Mature Beans and Peas, Nuts				
Beans, dry seed:				
Common varieties, as Great Northern, navy, and others, canned; 1 cup:				
Red	230	15	1	42
White, with tomato or molasses:				
With pork	330	16	7	54
Without pork	315	16	1	60

detect his condition because they become aware of changes in his eating patterns. They can also note early signs of a deficiency of some of the B vitamins, such as cracks in the mucous membranes at the corners of the mouth, or some slowing of intellectual function.

Correction of Nutritional Deficiencies

Nutritional deficiencies are among the most easily preventable causes of disease. It is important to realize that even mild deficiencies can cause irreparable damage, particularly protein deprivation in young children, which can result in some degree of mental retardation. Periodic medical checkups for everyone in the family are the best way to make sure that such deficiencies are corrected before they snowball into a chronic disease. In most cases, all that is required is a change of eating habits.

Weight

Probably the most important dietary problem in the United States today is obesity. It is certainly the problem most talked about and written about, not only in terms of good looks, but more important, in terms of good health.

All studies indicate that people who are obese have a higher rate of disease and a shorter life expectancy than those of average weight. From a medical point of view, people who are too fat may actually suffer from a form of malnutrition, even though they look overnourished.

Being too fat and being overweight are not necessarily the same. Heavy bones and muscles can make a person overweight in terms of the charts, but only an excess amount of fat tissue can make someone obese. However, height and weight tables are generally used to determine obesity.

Table 1 lists standard desirable weights for people of various heights, calculated with indoor clothing and shoes on. Frame sizes are estimated in a general way. This table applies to anyone over the age of 25, indicating that weight gain for the rest of the life span is unnecessary for biological normalcy.

Table 2 gives average weights of American men and women, according to height and age. These measurements are made without clothing or shoes. Note that the weights are considerably higher than the corresponding ones of Table 1. There is a modest weight gain until the middle years and then a gradual loss.

To determine whether a person is obese according to the tables, the percent that he is overweight has to be calculated. An individual is usually considered obese in the clinical sense if he weighs 20 percent more than the standard tables indicate for his size and age.

The Pinch Test

Another method of determining obesity is to use the "pinch" test. In most adults under 50 years of age, about half of the body fat is located directly under the skin. There are various parts of the body, such as the side of the lower torso, the back of the upper arm, or directly under the shoulder blade, where the thumb and forefinger can pinch a fold of skin and fat away from the underlying bone structure.

If the fold between the fingers—which is, of course, double thickness when it is pinched—is thicker than one inch in any of these areas, the likelihood is that the person is obese.

Nutrients in Common Foods (continued)

Food	Food energy	Protein	Fat	Carbohydrate
	Calories	Grams	Grams	Grams
Beans, dry seed:				
Lima, cooked; 1 cup	260	16	1	48
Cowpeas or black-eyed peas, dry, cooked; 1 cup	190	13	1	34
Peanuts, roasted, shelled; 1 cup	840	39	71	28
Peanut butter; 1 tablespoon	90	4	8	3
Peas, split, dry, cooked; 1 cup	290	20	1	52
Vegetables				
Asparagus:				
Cooked; 1 cup	35	4	trace	6
Canned; 6 medium-size spears	20	2	trace	3
Beans:				
Lima, immature, cooked; 1 cup	150	8	1	29
Snap, green:				
Cooked; 1 cup	25	2	trace	6
Canned; solids and liquid; 1 cup	45	2	trace	10
Beets, cooked, diced; 1 cup	70	2	trace	16
Broccoli, cooked, flower stalks; 1 cup	45	5	trace	8
Brussels sprouts, cooked; 1 cup ...	60	6	1	12
Cabbage; 1 cup:				
Raw, coleslaw	100	2	7	9
Cooked	40	2	trace	9
Carrots:				
Raw: 1 carrot (5½ by 1 inch) or 25 thin strips	20	1	trace	5
Cooked, diced; 1 cup	45	1	1	9
Canned, strained or chopped; 1 ounce	5	trace	0	2
Cauliflower, cooked, flower buds; 1 cup	30	3	trace	6
Celery, raw: large stalk, 8 inches long	5	1	trace	1
Collards, cooked; 1 cup	75	7	1	14
Corn, sweet:				
Cooked; 1 ear 5 inches long	65	2	1	16
Canned, solids and liquid; 1 cup	170	5	1	41
Cucumbers, raw, pared; 6 slices (⅛-inch thick, center section)	5	trace	trace	1
Lettuce, head, raw:				
2 large or 4 small leaves	5	1	trace	1
1 compact head (4¾-inch diameter)	70	5	1	13
Mushrooms, canned, solids and liquid; 1 cup	30	3	trace	9
Okra, cooked; 8 pods (3 inches long, ⅝-inch diameter)	30	2	trace	6
Onions: mature raw; 1 onion (2½-inch diameter)	50	2	trace	11
Peas, green; 1 cup:				
Cooked	110	8	1	19
Canned, solids and liquid	170	8	1	32
Peppers, sweet:				
Green, raw; 1 medium	15	1	trace	3
Red, raw; 1 medium	20	1	trace	4
Potatoes:				
Baked or boiled; 1 medium, 2½-inch diameter (weight raw, about 5 ounces):				
Baked in jacket	90	3	trace	21
Boiled; peeled before boiling ...	90	3	trace	21
Chips; 10 medium (2-inch diameter)	110	1	7	10
French fried:				
Frozen, ready to be heated for serving; 10 pieces (2 by ½ by ½ inch)	95	2	4	15

Nutrients in Common Foods *(continued)*

Food	Food energy	Protein	Fat	Carbohydrate
	Calories	Grams	Grams	Grams
Ready-to-eat, deep fat for entire process; 10 pieces (2 by ½ by ½ inch)	155	2	7	20
Mashed; 1 cup:				
Milk added	145	4	1	30
Milk and butter added	230	4	12	28
Radishes, raw; 4 small	10	trace	trace	2
Spinach:				
Cooked; 1 cup	45	6	1	6
Canned, creamed, strained; 1 ounce	10	1	trace	2
Squash:				
Cooked, 1 cup:				
Summer, diced	35	1	trace	8
Winter, baked, mashed	95	4	1	23
Canned, strained or chopped; 1 ounce	10	trace	trace	2
Sweet potatoes:				
Baked or boiled; 1 medium, 5 by 2 inches (weight raw, about 6 ounces):				
Baked in jacket	155	2	1	36
Boiled in jacket	170	2	1	39
Candied; 1 small, 3½ by 2 inches	295	2	6	60
Canned, vacuum or solid pack; 1 cup	235	4	trace	54
Tomatoes:				
Raw; 1 medium (2 by 2½ inches), about ⅓ pound	30	2	trace	6
Canned or cooked; 1 cup	45	2	trace	9
Tomato juice, canned; 1 cup	50	2	trace	10
Tomato catsup; 1 tablespoon	15	trace	trace	4
Turnips, cooked, diced; 1 cup	40	1	trace	9
Turnip greens, cooked; 1 cup	45	4	1	8
Fruits				
Apples, raw; 1 medium (2½ inch diameter), about ⅓ pound	70	trace	trace	18
Apple juice, fresh or canned; 1 cup	125	trace	0	34
Apple sauce, canned:				
Sweetened; 1 cup	185	trace	trace	50
Unsweetened; 1 cup	100	trace	trace	26
Apricots, raw; 3 apricots (about ¼ pound)	55	1	trace	14
Apricots, canned in heavy syrup; 1 cup	200	1	trace	54
Apricots, dried: uncooked; 1 cup (40 halves, small)	390	8	1	100
Avocados, raw, California varieties: ½ of a 10-ounce avocado (3½ by 3¼ inches)	185	2	18	6
Avocados, raw, Florida varieties: ½ of a 13-ounce avocado (4 by 3 inches)	160	2	14	11
Bananas, raw; 1 medium (6 by 1½ inches), about ⅓ pound	85	1	trace	23
Blueberries, raw; 1 cup	85	1	1	21
Cantaloupes, raw, ½ melon (5-inch diameter)	40	1	trace	9
Cherries, sour, sweet, and hybrid, raw; 1cup	65	1	1	15
Cranberry sauce, sweetened; 1 cup	550	trace	1	142
Dates, "fresh" and dried, pitted and cut; 1 cup	505	4	1	134
Figs:				
Raw; 3 small (1½-inch diameter), about ¼ pound	90	2	trace	22
Dried; 1 large (2 by 1 inch)	60	1	trace	15

The Problem of Overweight

The percentage of overweight people in this country has been increasing steadily, chiefly because people eat more and use less physical energy than they used to. Americans do very little walking because of the availability of cars; they do very little manual labor because of the increasing use of machines. They may eat good wholesome meals, but they have the time for nibbling at all hours, especially when sitting in front of the television screen.

These patterns usually begin in childhood. Youngsters rarely walk to school any more; they get there by bus or car. They often have extra money for snacks and soft drinks, and frequently parents encourage them to overeat without realizing that such habits do them more harm than good.

Most overweight children remain overweight as adults. They also have greater difficulty losing fat, and if they do lose it, tend to regain it more easily than overweight adults who were thin as children. Many adults become overweight between the ages of 20 and 30. Thus, by age 30, about 12 percent of American men and women are 20 percent or more overweight, and by age 60, about 30 percent of the male population and 50 percent of the female are at least 20 percent overweight. As indicated above, the phenomenon of weight gain while aging does not represent biological normalcy.

Why People Put On Weight

Why does weight gain happen? Excess weight is the result of the imbalance between caloric intake as food and caloric expenditure as energy, either in maintaining the basic metabolic processes necessary to sustain life or in performing physical activity. Calories not spent in either of these ways become converted to fat and accumulate in the body as fat, or *adipose* tissue.

A *calorie* is the unit of measurement that describes the amount of energy potentially available in a given food. It is also used to describe the amount of energy the body must use up to perform a given function.

Counting Calories

If an adult gets the average 3,000 calories a day in his food from the age of 20 to 70, he will have consumed about 55 million calories. About 60 percent of these calories will have been used for his basic metabolic processes. The rest—22 million calories—might have resulted in a gain of about 6,000 pounds of fat, since each group of 3,500 extra calories could have produced one pound of fat.

In some ways, it's a miracle that people don't become more obese than they do. The reason, of course, is that most or all of these extra calories are normally used to provide energy for physical activity. Elsewhere in this chapter are some examples of calorie expenditure during various activities.

A reasonably good way for an adult to figure his daily caloric needs for moderate activities is to multiply his desirable weight (as noted in Table 1) by 18 for men and 16 for women. If the typical day includes vigorous or strenuous activities, extra calories will, of course, be required.

Parental Influences and Hereditary Factors

Although there are exceptions, almost all obese people consume more calories than they expend. The reasons for this imbalance are complex. One has to do with parental weight. If the weight of both parents is normal, there is only a 10 percent likelihood that the children will be obese. If one

Nutrients in Common Foods *(continued)*

Food	Food energy	Protein	Fat	Carbohydrate
	Calories	Grams	Grams	Grams
Fruit cocktail, canned in heavy syrup, solids and liquid; 1 cup	175	1	trace	47
Grapefruit:				
Raw; ½ medium (4¼-inch diameter, No. 64's)	50	1	trace	14
Canned in syrup; 1 cup	165	1	trace	44
Grapefruit juice:				
Raw; 1 cup	85	1	trace	23
Canned:				
Unsweetened; 1 cup	95	1	trace	24
Sweetened; 1 cup	120	1	trace	32
Frozen concentrate, unsweetened:				
Undiluted; 1 can (6 fluid ounces)	280	4	1	72
Diluted, ready-to-serve; 1 cup	95	1	trace	24
Frozen concentrate, sweetened:				
Undiluted; 1 can (6 fluid ounces)	320	3	1	85
Diluted, ready-to-serve; 1 cup	105	1	trace	28
Grapes, raw; 1 cup:				
American type (slip skin)	70	1	1	16
European type (adherent skin) ...	100	1	trace	26
Grape juice, bottled; 1 cup	165	1	1	42
Lemonade concentrate, frozen, sweetened:				
Undiluted; 1 can (6 fluid ounces)	305	1	trace	113
Diluted, ready-to-serve; 1 cup ...	75	trace	trace	28
Oranges, raw; 1 large orange (3-inch diameter)	70	1	trace	18
Orange juice:				
Raw; 1 cup:				
California (Valencias)	105	2	trace	26
Florida varieties:				
Early and midseason	90	1	trace	23
Late season (Valencias)	105	1	trace	26
Canned, unsweetened; 1 cup	110	2	trace	28
Frozen concentrate:				
Undiluted; 1 can (6 fluid ounces)	305	5	trace	80
Diluted, ready-to-serve; 1 cup	105	2	trace	27
Peaches:				
Raw:				
1 medium (2½-inch diameter), about ¼ pound	35	1	trace	10
1 cup, sliced	65	1	trace	16
Canned (yellow-fleshed) in heavy syrup; 1 cup	185	1	trace	49
Dried: uncooked; 1 cup	420	5	1	109
Pears:				
Raw; 1 pear (3 by 2½-inch diameter)	100	1	1	25
Canned in heavy syrup; 1 cup ...	175	1	trace	47
Pineapple juice; canned; 1 cup	120	1	trace	32
Plums:				
Raw; 1 plum (2-inch diameter), about 2 ounces	30	trace	trace	7
Canned (Italian prunes), in syrup; 1 cup	185	1	trace	50
Prunes, dried:				
Uncooked; 4 medium prunes	70	1	trace	19
Cooked, unsweetened; 1 cup (17–18 prunes and ⅓ cup liquid)	295	3	1	78
Prune juice, canned; 1 cup	170	1	trace	45
Raisins, dried; 1 cup	460	4	trace	124
Raspberries, red:				
Raw; 1 cup	70	1	trace	17

Nutrients in Common Foods *(continued)*

Food	Food energy	Protein	Fat	Carbohydrate
	Calories	Grams	Grams	Grams
Frozen; 10-ounce carton	280	2	1	70
Strawberries:				
Raw; 1 cup	55	1	1	12
Frozen; 10-ounce carton	300	2	1	75
Tangerines; 1 medium (2½-inch diameter), about ¼ pound	40	1	trace	10
Watermelon: 1 wedge (4 by 8 inches), about 2 pounds (weighed with rind)	120	2	1	29
Grain Products				
Biscuits, baking powder, enriched flour; 1 biscuit (2½-inch diameter)	130	3	4	20
Bran flakes (40 percent bran) with added thiamine; 1 ounce	85	3	1	22
Breads:				
Cracked wheat:				
1 pound (20 slices)	1,190	39	10	236
1 slice (½ inch thick)	60	2	1	12
Italian; 1 pound	1,250	41	4	256
Rye:				
American (light):				
1 pound (20 slices)	1,100	41	5	236
1 slice (½ inch thick)	55	2	trace	12
Pumpernickel; 1 pound	1,115	41	5	241
White:				
1–2 percent nonfat dry milk:				
1 pound (20 slices)	1,225	39	15	229
1 slice (½ inch thick)	60	2	1	12
3–4 percent nonfat dry milk:				
1 pound (20 slices)	1,225	39	15	229
1 slice (½ inch thick)	60	2	1	12
5–6 percent nonfat dry milk:				
1 pound (20 slices)	1,245	41	17	228
1 slice (½ inch thick)	65	2	1	12
Whole wheat, graham, or entire wheat:				
1 pound (20 slices)	1,105	48	14	216
1 slice (½ inch thick)	55	2	1	11
Cakes:				
Angel food: 2-inch sector (1/12 of cake, 8-inch diameter)	160	4	trace	36
Butter cakes:				
Plain cake and cupcakes without icing:				
1 square (3 by 3 by 2 inches)	315	4	12	48
1 cupcake (2¾-inch diameter)	120	2	5	18
Plain cake with icing:				
2-inch sector of iced layer cake (1/16 of cake, 10-inch diameter)	320	5	6	62
Rich cake:				
2-inch sector layer cake, iced (1/16 of cake, 10-inch diameter)	490	6	19	76
Fruit cake, dark; 1 piece (2 by 1½ by ¼ inches)	60	1	2	9
Sponge; 2-inch sector (1/12 of cake, 8-inch diameter)	115	3	2	22
Cookies, plain and assorted; 1 cookie (3-inch diameter)	110	2	3	19
Cornbread or muffins made with enriched, degermed cornmeal; 1 muffin 2¾-inch diameter)	105	3	2	18
Cornflakes: 1 ounce	110	2	trace	24
Corn grits, degermed, cooked: 1 cup	120	3	trace	27

parent is obese, there is a 50 percent probability that the children will be too, and if both are, the probability of obese offspring is 80 percent.

No one knows for certain why this is so. It is probably a combination of diet habits acquired in youth, conditioning during early years to react to emotional stress by eating, the absence of appropriate exercise patterns, and genetic inheritance.

Some obese people seem to have an impairment in the regulatory mechanism of the area of the central nervous system that governs food intake. Simply put, they do not know when to stop eating. Others, particularly girls, may eat less than their nonobese counterparts, but they are considerably less active. Some researchers think that obese people have an inherent muscle rhythm deficiency. A few people appear to have an abnormality in the metabolic process which results in the accumulation of fat even when the balance between calories taken in and expended is negative and should lead to weight loss.

Obesity and Health

There are many reasons why obesity is a health hazard. The annual death rate for obese people between the ages of 20 and 64 is half again as high as that for people whose weight is close to normal. This statistical difference is due primarily to the increased likelihood that the obese person will suffer from diabetes mellitus and from diseases of the digestive and circulatory systems, especially of the heart.

One possible reason for the increased possibility of heart disease is that there are about two-thirds of a mile of blood vessels in each pound of adipose tissue. Thus 20 or more pounds of excess weight are likely to impose a great additional work load on the heart.

Obese people are also poorer surgical risks than the nonobese, and it is often more difficult to diagnose and therefore to treat their illnesses correctly.

Permanent loss of excess weight makes the formerly obese person come closer to matching the life expectancy of the nonobese. However, losing and regaining weight as a repeated pattern is even more hazardous in terms of health than consistent obesity.

Psychological Consequences of Obesity

In ways that are both obvious and subtle, obesity often has damaging psychological consequences. This is particularly true for obese children, who tend to feel isolated and rejected by their peers. They may consider themselves victims of prejudice and blame their obesity for everything that goes wrong in their lives. In many cases, the destructive relationship between obesity and self-pity keeps perpetuating itself.

Obese adults are likely to experience the same feelings, but to a somewhat lesser degree. For some, obesity is an escape which consciously or unconsciously helps them to avoid situations in which they feel uncomfortable—those that involve active competition or relationships with the opposite sex.

Avoiding Excess Weight

Clearly, obesity is a condition that most people would like to avoid. Not putting on extra pounds does seem to be easier, in theory at least, than taking them off. One possible explanation for this is that additional adipose tissue consists of a proliferation of fat cells. Shrinking these cells is one thing, eliminating them is another. Our present lack of fundamental knowledge about the regulatory and

Nutrients in Common Foods (continued)

Food	Food energy	Protein	Fat	Carbohydrate
	Calories	Grams	Grams	Grams
Crackers:				
Graham; 4 small or 2 medium ...	55	1	1	10
Saltines; 2 crackers (2-inch square)	35	1	1	6
Soda, plain: 2 crackers (2½-inch square)	45	1	1	8
Doughnuts, cake type; 1 doughnut	135	2	7	17
Farina, cooked; 1 cup	105	3	trace	22
Macaroni, cooked; 1 cup:				
Cooked 8–10 minutets (undergoes additional cooking as ingredient of a food mixture)	190	6	1	39
Cooked until tender	155	5	1	32
Noodles (egg noodles), cooked; 1 cup	200	7	2	37
Oat cereal (mixture, mainly oat flour), ready-to-eat; 1 ounce	115	4	2	21
Oatmeal or rolled oats, regular or quick cooking, cooked; 1 cup	150	5	3	26
Pancakes, baked; 1 cake (4-inch diameter):				
Wheat (home recipe)	60	2	2	7
Buckwheat (with buckwheat pancake mix)	45	2	2	6
Pies; 3½-inch sector (⅛ of 9-inch diameter pie):				
Apple	300	3	13	45
Cherry	310	3	13	45
Custard	250	7	13	27
Lemon meringue	270	4	11	40
Mince	320	3	14	49
Pumpkin	240	5	13	28
Pretzels; 5 small sticks	20	trace	trace	4
Rice, cooked; 1 cup:				
Converted	205	4	trace	45
White	200	4	trace	44
Rice, puffed or flakes; 1 ounce	110	2	trace	25
Rolls:				
Plain, pan (16 ounces per dozen); 1 roll	115	3	2	20
Hard, round (22 ounces per dozen); 1 roll	160	5	2	31
Sweet, pan (18 ounces per dozen); 1 roll	135	4	4	21
Spaghetti, cooked until tender; 1 cup	155	5	1	32
Waffles, baked, with enriched flour: 1 waffle (4½ by 5½ by ½ inches)	215	7	8	28
Wheat, puffed: 1 ounce	100	4	trace	22
Wheat, rolled, cooked; 1 cup	175	5	1	40
Wheat flakes; 1 ounce	100	3	trace	23
Wheat flours:				
Whole wheat; 1 cup, sifted	400	16	2	85
All purpose or family flour: 1 cup, sifted	400	12	1	84
Wheat germ; 1 cup, stirred	245	17	7	34
Fats, Oils, Related Products				
Butter; 1 tablespoon	100	trace	11	trace
Fats, cooking:				
Vegetable fats:				
1 cup	1,770	0	200	0
1 tablespoon	110	0	12	0
Lard:				
1 cup	1,985	0	220	0
1 tablespoon	125	0	14	0
Margarine; 1 tablespoon	100	trace	11	trace
Oils, salad or cooking; 1 tablespoon	125	0	14	0

Nutrients in Common Foods (continued)

Food	Food energy	Protein	Fat	Carbohydrate
	Calories	Grams	Grams	Grams
Salad dressings; 1 tablespoon:				
Blue cheese	90	1	10	1
Commercial, plain (mayonnaise type)	60	trace	6	2
French	60	trace	6	2
Mayonnaise	110	trace	12	trace
Thousand Island	75	trace	8	1
Sugars, Sweets				
Candy; 1 ounce:				
Caramels	120	1	3	22
Chocolate, sweetened, milk	145	2	9	16
Fudge, plain	115	trace	3	23
Hard	110	0	0	28
Marshmallow	90	1	0	23
Jams, marmalades, preserves; 1 tablespoon	55	trace	trace	14
Jellies; 1 tablespoon	50	0	0	13
Sugar; 1 tablespoon	50	0	0	12
Syrup, table blends; 1 tablespoon	55	0	0	15
Miscellaneous				
Beverages, carbonated, cola types; 1 cup	105	–	–	28
Bouillon cubes; 1 cube	2	trace	trace	0
Chocolate, unsweetened; 1 ounce	145	2	15	8
Gelatin dessert, plain, ready-to-serve; 1 cup	155	4	0	36
Sherbet, factory packed; 1 cup (8-fluid-ounce container)	235	3	trace	58
Soups, canned, prepared with equal amount of water; 1 cup:				
Bean with pork	168	8	6	22
Beef noodle	140	8	5	14
Bouillon, broth, and consomme	30	5	0	3
Chicken consomme	44	7	trace	4
Clam chowder, Manhattan style	80	2	3	12
Tomato	90	2	3	16
Vegetable beef	80	5	2	10
Vinegar; 1 tablespoon	2	0	–	1

Adapted from *Nutritive Value of American Foods* by Catherine F. Adams, Agriculture Handbook No. 456, U.S. Department of Agriculture, issued November 1975. The cup measure used in the following table refers to the standard 8-ounce measuring cup of 8 fluid ounces or one-half liquid pint. When a measure is indicated by ounce, it is understood to be by weight—1/16 of a pound avoirdupois—unless a fluid ounce is indicated. All weights and measures in the table are in U.S. System units.

metabolic mechanisms relating to obesity limits the technique of preventing overweight to recommending a balance between caloric intake and expenditure.

The real responsibility for preventing the onset of obesity in childhood rests with parents. It is important for the parents to set a good example and to instill early on all of the fundamentals of good nutrition and healthy eating habits; these are of the utmost importance in this connection. Caloric expenditure in the form of regular exercise is equally important.

Exercising by Habit

This does not necessarily mean that exercise should be encouraged for its own sake. What it does mean is making a habit of choosing an active way of approaching a situation rather than a lazy way: walking upstairs rather than taking the elevator; walking to school rather than riding; walking while playing golf rather than riding in a cart; running to get the ball that has rolled away rather than ambling toward it. These choices should be made consistently and not just occa-

sionally if obesity is to be avoided. Those people who naturally enjoy the more active way of doing things are lucky. Those who don't should make an effort to develop new patterns, especially if obesity is a family problem.

Anyone with the type of physical handicap that makes a normal amount of exercise impossible should be especially careful about caloric intake.

Weight Reduction

The treatment of obesity is a complicated problem. In the first place, there is the question of who wants or needs to be treated and how much weight should be lost. Except in unusual situations, anyone who wants to lose weight should be encouraged to do so. Possible exceptions are teenagers who are not overweight but who want to be as thin as they can possibly be—the boy who is involved in an athletic event such as wrestling, or the girl who has decided she wants to look like a fashion model.

Crash dieting is usually unwise if the goal is to lose too much weight too rapidly and should be undertaken only after consulting a doctor about its advisability. As for adolescents who have become slightly overweight during puberty, they may be ill-advised to try to take off the extra pounds that probably relate to a temporary growth pattern.

Losing Weight Must Be Self-Motivated

Unless there are compelling medical reasons for not doing so, anyone weighing 20 percent or more over the normal limit for his age and body build should be helped to slim down. It is extremely important, however, for the motivation to come from the person himself rather than from outside pressure.

Unless an overweight person really wants to reduce, he will not succeed in doing so, certainly not permanently, even though he appears to be trying. He must have convinced himself—intellectually and emotionally—that the goal of weight loss is truly worth the effort.

It is very difficult not only for his friends and family but for the person himself to be absolutely sure about the depth of his motivation. A physician treating an overweight patient has to assume that the desire to reduce is genuine and will try to reinforce it whenever he can. However, if a patient has made a number of attempts to lose weight over a period of years and has either been unable to reduce to any significant degree, or has become overweight again after reducing, it is probably safe to assume that the emotional desire is absent, or that there are emotional conflicts that stand in the way.

It is very possible that such a person could be harmed psychologically by losing weight, since he might need to be overweight for some deep-seated reason. This can be true for both children and adults. Occasionally it is possible for a psychiatrist or psychologist to help the patient remove a psychological block against losing weight, after which weight reduction can occur if the caloric balance is straightened out.

Effective Planning for Weight Loss

The ultimate key to successful weight reduction is proper eating combined with proper physical activity. This balance is extremely difficult for many people to achieve because it involves a marked change in attitudes and behavior patterns that are generally solidly established and of long duration. Furthermore, once the changes are made, they will have to endure for a

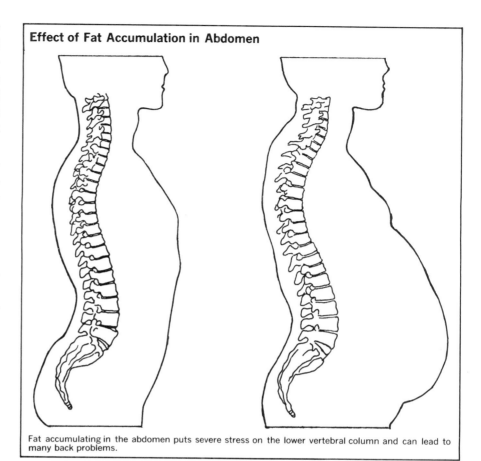

Effect of Fat Accumulation in Abdomen

Fat accumulating in the abdomen puts severe stress on the lower vertebral column and can lead to many back problems.

lifetime if the weight that has been lost is not to be regained.

It is therefore important that the reducing diet should be somewhat similar to the person's usual eating pattern in terms of style and quality. Intake of fat and calories should be reduced and that of fiber increased, and probably the word "dieting" should not be used to describe the process, since most people don't find the idea of permanent dieting congenial.

Similarly, the increased physical activity that must accompany the new eating style should be of a type that the person enjoys. It is virtually impossible for an overeating person to reduce merely by restricting his caloric intake, or merely by increasing his caloric expenditure. The two must go together.

Cutting Down Step by Step

The first thing to determine when planning to lose weight is the number of pounds that have to go. A realistic goal to set is the loss of about one pound a week. This may seem too slow, but remember that at this rate, fifty pounds can be lost in a year.

Getting Started

Start by weighing yourself on arising, and then for two weeks try to eat in your customary manner, but keep a careful record of everything that you eat, the time it is eaten, and the number of calories it contains. During this period, continue to do your usual amount of physical activity.

When the two weeks are over, weigh yourself again at the same time of day as before. If you haven't gained

Daily Food Guide				
	Child	**Preteen and Teen**	**Adult**	**Aging Adult**
Milk or milk products (*cups*)	2–3	3–4 or more	2 or more	2 or more
Meat, fish, poultry, and eggs (*servings*)	1–2	3 or more	2 or more	2 or more
Green and yellow vegetables (*servings*)	1–2	2	2	at least 1
Citrus fruits and tomatoes (*servings*)	1	1–2	1	1–2
Potatoes, other fruits, vegetables (*servings*)	1	1	1	0–1
Bread, flour, and cereal (*servings*)	3–4	4 or more	3–4	2–3
Butter or margarine (*tablespoons*)	2	2–4	2–3	1–2

1. The need for the nutrients in 1 or 2 cups of milk daily can be satisfied by cheeses or ice cream. (1 cup of milk is approximately equivalent to 1½ cups of cottage cheese or 2–3 large scoops of ice cream.)
2. It is important to drink enough fluid. The equivalent of 3–5 cups daily is recommended.
3. The recommended daily serving of meat, fish, and poultry (3 oz.) may be alternated with eggs or cheese, dried peas, beans, or lentils.
4. Iron-rich foods should be selected as frequently as possible by teenage and adult females to help meet their high requirement for this mineral (liver, heart, lean meats, shellfish, egg yolks, legumes, green leafy vegetables, and whole grain and enriched cereal products).

From *Your Age and Your Diet* (1971), reprinted with permission from the American Medical Association.

any weight, you are in a basal caloric state. Then check over your food list to see what might be eliminated each day without causing discomfort.

Try to think in terms of eliminating fats and simple carbohydrates first, because it is essential that you continue to get sufficient vitamins and minerals which are largely found in proteins and complex carbohydrates. The foods described in the "Daily Food Guide" chart should all continue to be included in your daily food consumption. If you are in the habit of having an occasional drink, remember that there are calories in alcohol but no nutrients, and that most alcoholic beverages stimulate the appetite.

Planning Meals

When you replan your meals, keep in mind that the items you cut down on must add up to between 300 and 400 calories a day if you are going to lose one pound a week.

Your total daily food intake should be divided among at least three meals a day, more if you wish. If you need to eat more food or to eat more often,

try snacking on low calorie foods such as cabbage, carrots, celery, cucumber, and cauliflower. All of these can be eaten raw between meals.

There is definitely something to be said in favor of having breakfast every morning, or at least most mornings. This may be psychologically difficult, but try to do it, because it will be easier to control your urge to eat too much later in the day.

Increasing Exercise

At the same time that you begin to cut down on your food intake, start to increase your daily exercise in whatever way you find congenial so that the number of calories expended in increased exercise plus the number of calories eliminated from your diet comes to 500 or more. This is your daily caloric loss compared with your so-called basal caloric state.

Achieving Your Goal

You may wish to double your daily caloric loss so that you lose two pounds a week. Do not try to lose any more

than that unless you are under close medical supervision.

If you gained weight during your two-week experimental period, you will have to increase your daily caloric loss by 500 for every pound gained per week. Thus, if you gained one pound during the two weeks, you will have to step up your daily caloric loss to 750 to lose a pound a week.

You'll have to keep plugging away to achieve your goal. It will be trying and difficult in many ways. You may get moody and discouraged and be tempted to quit. Don't. You'll probably go on periodic food binges. All this is natural and understandable, so try not to brood about it. Just do the best you can each day. Don't worry about yesterday, and let tomorrow take care of itself.

In many ways it can help, and in some cases it's essential, to have the support and encouragement of family and friends, particularly of those with whom you share meals. You may find it helpful to join a group that has been formed to help its members lose weight and maintain their weight loss. This is a good psychological support.

Maintaining Your Weight Loss

Once you have achieved your desired weight, you can test yourself to see what happens if you increase your caloric intake. Clearly, anyone who can lose weight in the manner described can't stay in a state of negative caloric imbalance indefinitely. But you will have to be careful, or you'll become overweight again. It's a challenge, but people who stick to a disciplined program can be rewarded by success.

Special Problems

If you do not succeed in losing weight in spite of carrying out the program described above, you may need professional help because of some special problem. A qualified physician may try some special diets, or he may even suggest putting you into a hospital so that he can see to it that you have no caloric food at all for as long as three weeks.

Perhaps the situation is complicated by a metabolic abnormality that can be corrected or helped by medication. Although such conditions are rare, they are not unheard of.

Obesity is almost never caused by a "glandular" problem—which usually means an underactive thyroid. Do not take thyroid pills to reduce unless your thyroid has been found to be underactive on the basis of a specific laboratory test.

The indiscriminate use of pills to reduce, even when prescribed, is never helpful in the long run, although it may appear to be at first. The unsupervised use of amphetamines, for example, can be extremely dangerous. See Ch. 29, *Substance Abuse*, for further information about the dangers of amphetamine abuse.

Because so many people are eager to reduce, and because losing weight isn't easy, there are many unethical professionals who specialize in the problem. Avoid them. All they are likely to do for you is take your money and make your situation no better—and often worse—than it was to begin with.

Underweight

Weighing too little is a problem that is considerably less common than weighing too much. In fact, in many cases, it isn't accurate to call it a problem at all, at least not a medical one.

There are some times, however, when underweight may indicate the presence of a disease, especially when a person rather suddenly begins and continues to lose weight, even though there has been no change in his eating habits. This is a situation

---

Sodium Restricted Diets
Diets Moderately Restricted in Sodium

If only a moderate sodium restriction is necessary, a normal diet *without added salt* may be ordered. Such an order is interpreted to mean that the patient will be offered the regular salted food on the general selective menu with the following exceptions:

1. No salt will be served on the tray.
2. Soups that are salted will be omitted.
3. Cured meats (ham, bacon, sausage, corned beef) and all salted cheeses will be omitted.
4. Catsup, chili sauce, mustard, and other salted sauces will be omitted.
5. Salt-free gravies, sauces, and salad dressings will be substituted for the regular salted items.
6. Salted crackers, potato chips, nuts, pickles, olives, popcorn, and pretzels will be omitted.

This diet contains approximately 3 grams of sodium or 7.5 grams of sodium chloride, depending on the type and quantity of the food chosen.

---

that calls for prompt medical evaluation. Fortunately, such a person may already be under a physician's care at the time the weight loss is first noticed.

More often, however, underweight is a chronic condition that is of concern to the person who feels his looks would improve if he could only add some extra pounds. This is especially true in the case of adolescent girls and young women.

What To Do About Weighing Too Little

Chronic underweight is rarely a reflection of underlying disease. It is rather an expression of individual heredity or eating patterns, or a combination of both. Treatment for the condition is the opposite of the treatment for overweight. The achievement of a positive caloric balance comes first; more calories have to be consumed each day than are expended. An underweight person should record his food history over a two-week period in the manner described for an overweight one. Once this has been done, various adjustments can be made.

First of all, he should see that he eats at least three meals a day and that they are eaten in a leisurely way and in a relaxed frame of mind. All of the basic foods should be represented in the daily food intake, with special emphasis on protein and complex carbohydrates. The daily caloric intake should then be gradually increased at each meal and snacks added, so long as the snacks don't reduce the appetite at mealtimes.

Carbohydrate foods are the best ones to emphasize in adding calories. Since the extra food intake may cause a certain amount of discomfort, encouragement and support from family and friends can be extremely helpful. Just as there may be psychological blocks against losing weight, there may well be a complicated underlying resistance to adding it.

Anyone trying to gain weight should remain or become reasonably active physically. Adding a pound or two a month for an adult—and a little more than that for a growing youngster—is an achievable goal until the desired weight is reached. When this happens, there will probably have to be some adjustments in eating and exercise patterns so that a state of caloric balance is achieved.

How Food Relates to Disease

Just as proper food is essential in the prevention of some diseases, it is helpful in the treatment of others. It also plays an important role in protecting and fortifying the general health of a patient while a specific illness is being treated.

The components of therapeutic diets are usually prescribed by the physician in charge, but some general principles will be presented here. Remember that diets designed to treat a given disease must supply the patient's basic nutritional requirements.

Ulcers

Special diet is a major treatment consideration in the case of peptic ulcer, whether located in the stomach (gastric) or in the small intestine (duodenal). A major aim of such a diet is the neutralizing of the acidity of gastric juices by the frequent intake of high protein foods such as milk and eggs. Foods which irritate an ulcer chemically, such as excessive sweets, spices, or salt, or mechanically, such as foods with sharp seeds or tough skins, and foods that are too hot or too cold, should be avoided. It is also advisable to eliminate gravies, coffee, strong tea, carbonated beverages, and alcohol, since all of these stimulate gastric secretion. Such a diet is called a *bland* diet. A soft diet is recommended for some forms of gastrointestinal distress and for those people who have difficulty chewing. It is often combined with the bland diet recommended for peptic ulcer patients to reduce the likelihood of irritation. See Ch. 11, *Diseases of the Digestive System,* for further information about ulcers.

Diabetes

As the section on diabetes mellitus indicates (see Ch. 15), the major objectives of the special diet are weight control, control of the abnormal carbohydrate metabolism, and as far as possible, psychological adjustment by the patient to his individual circumstances. To some extent, he must calculate his diet mathematically. First, his daily caloric needs have to be determined in terms of his activities:

If he is overweight or underweight, the total calories per pound of body weight will have to be adjusted downward or upward by about five calories per pound.

After his total daily caloric needs have been figured out, he can calculate the number of grams of carbohydrate, protein, and fat he should have each day: 58 percent of the calories should come from carbohydrates, 12 percent from protein, and 30 percent from fat. One-fifth of the total should be obtained at breakfast and the rest split between lunch and dinner. Snacks that are taken during the day should be subtracted equally from lunch and dinner.

It is important that meals and planned snacks be eaten regularly and that no food servings be added or omitted. Growing children from 1 to 20 years of age who have diabetes will require considerably more daily calories. A rough estimate is 1,000 calories for a one-year-old child and 100 additional calories for each year of age.

Salt-Free Diets

There are a number of chronic diseases which are treated in part by restricting the amount of sodium in the diet. These diseases, which are associated with fluid retention in the body, include congestive heart failure, certain types of kidney and liver diseases, and hypertension or high blood pressure.

The restriction of sodium intake helps to reduce or avoid the problem of fluid retention. The normal daily diet contains about seven or more grams of sodium, most of it in the form of sodium chloride or table salt. This amount is either inherent in the food or added during processing, cooking, or at mealtime. Half the weight of salt is sodium.

For people whose physical condition requires only a small restriction of the normal sodium intake, simply not salting food at the table is a sufficient reduction. They may decide to use a salt substitute, but before doing so should discuss the question with their physician.

A greater sodium restriction, for example, to no more than 5 grams a day, requires the avoidance of such high salt content foods as ham, bacon, crackers, catsup, and potato chips, as well as almost entirely eliminating salt in the preparation and serving of meals. Severe restriction—1 gram or less a day—involves special food selection and cooking procedures, as well as the use of distilled water if the local water has more than 20 milligrams of sodium per quart. In restricting sodium to this extent, it is important to make sure that protein and vitamins are not reduced below the minimum daily requirements. See "Sodium Restricted Diets."

Other Diseases Requiring Special Diets

There are several other disorders in which diet is an important consideration: all chronic gastrointestinal disorders, such as gallbladder stones, ulcerative colitis, enteritis, and diverticulitis; a variety of hereditary disorders such as phenylketonuria and galactosemia; atherosclerosis, especially when it is associated with elevated blood levels of cholesterol or triglycerides or both; liver disease such as cirrhosis; many of the endocrine diseases; kidney stones; and sometimes certain neurological diseases such as epilepsy. Diet also plays a special role in convalescence from most illnesses and in post-surgical care. A modified fat diet and low fat diet are recommended for some diseases of the liver and gallbladder. A minimal residue diet is recommended for some digestive troubles and before and after gastrointestinal surgery.

Diet and Individual Differences

Most discussions about food and eating tend to suggest that all normal people have identical gastrointestinal and metabolic systems. This is simply not true. There are many individual differences that explain why one man's meat is another man's poison. A person's intolerance for a given food may be caused by a disorder, such as an allergy or an ulcer, and it is possible that many of these intolerances will ultimately be related to enzyme deficiencies or some other biochemical factor.

More subtle are the negative physical reactions to particular foods as a result of psychological conditioning. In most such cases, the choice is between avoiding the food that causes the discomfort or eating it and suffering the consequences. Of course, compulsive overeating can also cause or contribute to discomfort. Practically no one can eat unlimited quantities of anything without having gastrointestinal discomfort or *dyspepsia.*

The establishment of so-called daily minimum food requirements suggests that every day's intake should be carefully balanced. Although this is beneficial, it is by no means necessary. Freedom from such regimentation can certainly be enjoyed during a holiday, or a trip to another country, or on a prolonged visit to relatives with casual food habits.

Sometimes a change in diet is dictated by a cold or an upset stomach or diarrhea. Liquids containing carbohydrates, such as tea with sugar and light soups, should be emphasized in treating a cold, while at the same time solid food intake should be somewhat reduced. In the case of an upset stomach or diarrhea, the discomfort may be eased by not eating or drinking anything at all for a whole day. This form of treatment may be helpful for an adult, but since children with diarrhea can become dehydrated in a day or so, professional advice is indicated when cutting down liquid intake.

Diet and Disease Prevention

More and more, medical specialists agree that diet can be helpful in preventing various diseases. Consensus has become general that a diet low in cholesterol and saturated fats can help prevent cardiovascular disease caused by atherosclerosis. Among the foods that reduce total cholesterol levels are rice bran and oat bran. Other sources of the soluble fiber that decreases blood cholesterol include peas, lentils, barley, and pectin fruits like apples, oranges, pears, and prunes. Also recommended are skinless poultry and fish, lean meat, and low-fat dairy products.

Food-Borne Diseases

There are several ways in which food can be the *cause* of disease, most commonly when it becomes contaminated with a sufficient amount of harmful bacteria, bacterial toxin, viruses, or other poisonous substances. The gastrointestinal diseases typically accompanied by nausea, vomiting, diarrhea, or stomach cramps that are produced in this way are not, strictly speaking, caused by the foods themselves, and are therefore called food-borne diseases.

Most food-borne illnesses are caused by a toxin in food contaminated by staphylococcal or salmonella bacteria. In general, milk, milk products, raw shellfish, and meats are the foods most apt to be contaminated. This is most likely to happen when such foods are left standing at room temperature for too long between the time they are prepared and the time they are eaten. However, food can also become contaminated at many different points in time and at various stages of processing. Standards enforced by federal and local government agencies provide protection for the consumer for foods bought for the home as well as for use in restaurants, although whether the protection is adequate is a matter of dispute.

Food Storage

Food is best protected from contamination when it is stored below 40 degrees Fahrenheit or heated to 145 degrees or more. Cold slows bacterial growth; cooking kills it. Bacteria present in food can double in number every 15 minutes at room temperature.

All food stored in the refrigerator should be covered except ripe fruits and vegetables. Leftover foods cannot be kept indefinitely, nor can frozen foods be stored beyond a certain length of time. Specific information about these time periods for individual items is available from the Agricultural Extension Service in each state.

Commercially processed foods sold in the United States are under government control and generally are safe. However, any food can spoil or become contaminated at any point in time, and the consumer should not buy or serve food whose container (package or can) has been broken, cracked, or appears unusual.

Food Additives

From time to time, concern is expressed about one or another food additive as a hazard to health. Most of these additives are put into foods during processing in order to increase their nutritional value, or to improve their chemical or physical characteristics, such as taste and color. Perhaps as many as 2,000 different substances are used in this way in the United States. Some are natural products such as vanilla, others are chemicals derived from other foods, and a few, like artificial sweeteners, are synthetic. Other additives are referred to as indirect, since they are residues in the food from some stage of growing, processing, or packaging. Although additives are controlled and approved by agencies such as the federal Food and Drug Administration, they continue to be a cause of concern to many people.

Pesticides

The pesticides and fertilizers used in growing fruits and vegetables and the additives given to livestock may pose additional health hazards to humans. The National Academy of Sciences, for example, in 1988 estimated the national risk of cancer from pesticide use alone at as many as 20,000 cases a year.

Although it is not known how much is too much, it only makes sense to try and eliminate as much of the risk as possible. This is fairly easy to do. First of all, eat a wide variety of foods to help minimize your exposure to any one pesticide. Eat what's in season and what's grown locally or domestically. (The right season and less transportation mean less chemicals to ripen and preserve food; food and animals from abroad are subject to different health standards that are hard to regulate and check.) Wash all meat and produce carefully; many toxins are easily removed with soap and water. Peel any fruit or vegetable with a wax coating. (Although it is generally

advisable to retain as much of the skin of produce as possible for higher vitamin content, wax coatings hold in toxic residues.) Trim produce.

You may also want to go further in reducing your chances of consumption of added toxins by buying organically grown and raised produce and meat. These foods are not widely available in all areas of the country, and they often cost quite a bit more than foods raised with chemicals, but many people not only feel safer eating these foods, but find them tastier as well. Home gardening without the use of chemical fertilizers and pesticides is another healthful option. Be sure to wash and trim carefully all organic or home-grown vegetables, however, to guard against ingestion of naturally occurring toxins such as fungus.

Psychological Aspects of Food and Meals

Food and meals play an important role in emotional well-being and interpersonal relationships as well as in physical health and appearance.

During Infancy

The infant whose needs are attended to by a loving family develops a general sense of trust and security. The major contribution to his emotional contentment is probably made at mealtimes, and perhaps in a special way if he is breast-fed.

For most infants, food comes to be identified with love, pleasure, protection, and the satisfaction of basic needs. If there is an atmosphere of tension accompanying his feeding times, his digestion can be impaired in such a way as to cause vomiting, fretting, or signs of colic. If the tension and the baby's reaction to it—and inevitably the mother's increasing tension as a consequence—become a

chronic condition, the result may be a failure to gain weight normally, and in extreme cases, some degree of mental retardation. Throughout life, good nutrition depends not only on eating properly balanced meals that satisfy the body's physiological requirements, but also on a reasonable degree of contentment and relaxation while eating.

Everybody develops individual emotional reactions and attitudes about food and its role as a result of conditioning during the years of infancy and childhood. These attitudes relate not only to food itself and to mealtimes in general, but also to other aspects of eating, including the muscle activities of sucking, chewing, and swallowing.

If food symbolized contentment during the early years, it probably will have the same role later on. If it was associated with conflict, then it may be associated throughout life with strife and neurotic eating patterns.

During Childhood

For the preschool child, mealtimes should provide the occasion for the development of interpersonal relationships, because they are a daily opportunity for both verbal and nonverbal self-expression. The child who eats with enthusiasm and obvious enjoyment is conveying one message; the one who dawdles, picks at food, and challenges his mother with every mouthful is conveying quite a different one.

Meals can become either positive or negative experiences depending in large part on how the adults in the family set the stage. Communication can be encouraged by relaxed conversation and a reasonably leisurely schedule. It can be discouraged by watching television or reading while eating, by not eating together, or by eating and running.

Reasonably firm attitudes about eating a variety of foods in proper quantities at proper times and avoiding excessive catering to individual whims can also help in the development of wholesome eating patterns.

Those who select and prepare the food can transmit special messages of love and affection by serving favorite dishes, by setting the table attractively, and by creating an atmosphere of grace and good humor. Or they can show displeasure and generate hostility by complaining about all the work involved in feeding everyone, or by constant criticism of table manners, or by bringing up touchy subjects likely to cause arguments at the table.

Diet Fads

There are many fads and fallacies about losing weight. Everyone wants an easy solution; cosmetic and food product manufacturers know this and develop products that play to this desire. Thus we have pills that are supposed to burn fat while we sleep; machines that are supposed to give us a "workout" while we're lying down by electrically stimulating our muscles; plastic suits that we wear while exercising that are supposed to produce dramatic weight loss; and special creams and body scrubbers that are supposed to take away unsightly cellulite.

The truth is that a pill will not burn calories for you, a machine will not do your exercise for you, a plastic suit will only make you lose water, not fat, and the idea that there is a special kind of fat called cellulite is a myth.

Cellulite, in fact, is fat, plain and simple; there are no special varieties. Much of the body's fat is stored directly beneath the skin where there is also a sheath of connective tissue, which tends to compartmentalize the fat cells. The more fat the more this

FOODS TO AVOID	FOODS TO EAT
High saturated fat percentages	Low or no saturated fat
Avocado 15-20%	Apples 0%
Biscuits 23%	Apricots 0%
Bread stuffing 25%	Cherries 0%
Sweet rolls 27 + %	Cranberry sauce 0%
Fried chicken 27%	Fruit 0%
Bran muffins 30%	Fruit juices 0%
Veal 30-50%	Herbs 0%
Chicken livers 33%	Peaches 0%
Ham 33%	Plums 0%
Lunch meats 35 + %	Rice, plain 0%
Duck 35%	Split peas 0%
Pancakes 35%	Vegetables, raw or steamed 0%
Pork 35%	Squid 1%
Beef brisket 40%	Cornmeal 10%
Ground beef 40%	Popcorn, plain 12%
Hotdogs 40%	Sweet and sour sauce 12%
Lamb 40-50%	Teriyaki sauce 14%
Rib roast 42%	Spaghetti, no egg 15%
Gravy 50 + %	Halibut 17%
Custard 50%	Chestnuts 19%
Cheese 50-80%	Salmon 19%
Cream 60%	Carp 20%
Ice cream 60 + %	Perch 20%
Beef heart 80%	Abalone 21%
Coconut 88%	Clams 21%
Cream substitute 90 + %	Trout 22%
Sour cream 91%	Octopus 27%

NOTE: The same percentage number may appear in both columns; the determining factor is then the grams of fat in each item. The left column has more grams of fat, even if the percentage is the same for an item in the right column.

tissue is stretched and the more the fat bulges around and through it, producing cellulite's characteristic dimpled effect. Women tend to have thinner skin and less flexible connective tissue, making them more "prone" to cellulite than men. There is no point in spending money on special creams or brushes; you cannot scrub away excess fat. You have to reduce your intake and burn it through exercise.

Similarly, most diet programs that consist of pills, powders, or foolish eating habits are ineffective and usually harmful. Many of them are addictive and those who benefit from the diet programs often gain back the weight lost once they return to their "normal" eating habits.

One controversial drug that appears frequently in pills is phenylpropanolamine hydrochloride (PPA). Producers of PPA claim that it acts as an appetite suppressant, though its effectiveness is questionable.

Taken in large doses, its effects resemble those of amphetamines. It can produce such side effects as anxiety, sleeplessness, headaches, irregular heart rhythm, and even lead to strokes or seizures.

Another diet drug, benzocaine, is present in chewing gum and candy. It deadens taste receptors, which supposedly suppresses one's appetite. It does not, however, stop the habit of munching, which is a great cause of weight gain.

Guar gum is another diet substance that gives the dieter a sense of fullness. It is a vegetable gum that swells when it absorbs moisture. When taken improperly, it can swell in the throat and cause an obstruction, resulting in suffocation. At least 1 death and 50 injuries have been reported as a result of ingesting guar gum diet products.

Anybody interested in losing a substantial amount of weight should consult with his or her physician. The physician will know of a nutritionist who can provide a healthy program for weight reduction. If a person chooses to try one of the over-the-counter diet programs, read the directions carefully.

Weight loss involves a complete change in one's lifestyle. The solution includes eating balanced meals, reducing the intake of fat, increasing proportionately the consumption of carbohydrates, and exercising three or four times a week. It is a slow process that does not offer the quick yet temporary loss offered by over-the-counter diet programs. Rather, it is a permanent commitment to a healthy way of life. Only then, can a person maintain an optimal weight.

28

Mental and Emotional Disorders

The ability to adapt is central to being emotionally fit, healthy, and mature. An emotionally fit person is one who can adapt to changing circumstances with constructive reactions and who can enjoy living, loving others, and working productively. In everyone's life there are bound to be experiences that are anxious or deeply disturbing, such as the sadness of losing a loved one or the disappointment of failure. The emotionally fit person is stable enough not to be overwhelmed by the anxiety, grief, or guilt that such experiences frequently produce. His sense of his own worth is not lost easily by a setback in life; rather, he can learn from his own mistakes.

Communication and Tolerance

Even the most unpleasant experiences can add to one's understanding of life. Emerging from a crisis with new wisdom can give a sense of pride and mastery. The emotionally fit person can listen attentively to the opinions of others, yet if his decision differs from that being urged by friends and relatives, he will abide by it and can stand alone if necessary, without

guilt and anger at those who disagree.

Communicating well with others is an important part of emotional fitness. Sharing experiences, both good and bad, is one of the joys of living. Although the capacity to enjoy is often increased by such sharing, independence is also essential, for one person's pleasure may leave others indifferent. It is just as important to appreciate and respect the individuality of others as it is to value our own individual preferences, as long as these are reasonable and do not give pain to others.

Ways of Expressing Disagreement

Communication should be kept open at all times. Anger toward those who disagree may be an immediate response, but it should not lead to cutting off communication, as it so frequently does, particularly between husbands and wives, parents and children.

Emotional maturity enables us to disagree with what another says, feels, or does, yet make the distinction between that person and how we feel about his thoughts and actions. To tell someone, "I don't like what you are doing," is more likely to keep

the lines of communication open than telling him "I don't like you." This is particularly important between parents and children.

It is unfortunately common for parents to launch personal attacks when children do something that displeases them. The child, or any person to whom this is done, then feels unworthy or rejected, which often makes him angry and defiant. Revenge becomes uppermost, and communication is lost; each party feels misunderstood and lonely, perhaps even wounded, and is not likely to want to reopen communication. The joy in a human relationship is gone, and one's pleasure in living is by that much diminished.

Function of Guilt

The same principles used in dealing with others can be applied to ourselves. Everyone makes mistakes, has angry or even murderous thoughts that can produce excessive guilt. Sometimes there is a realistic reason for feeling guilty, which should be a spur to take corrective action. Differentiate clearly between thoughts, feelings, and actions. Only actions need cause guilt. In the privacy of one's own mind, anything may be thought as long as it is not acted out; an emotionally fit person can accept this difference.

Role of the Subconscious

Emotional disorders are similar to other medical diseases and can be treated by physicians or other professionals just as any other disease can be treated. Fortunately, this truth is widely accepted today, but as recently as 200 years ago it was believed that the emotionally ill were evil, possessed by the devil. Their illness was punished rather than treated. The strange and sometimes bizarre actions of the mentally ill were feared and misunderstood.

Freud and Psychoanalysis

Although we have penetrated many of the mysteries of the mind, much remains to be discovered. Significant steps toward understanding mental functioning came about through the work of Sigmund Freud. Building upon the work of others before him and making his own detailed observations, Freud demonstrated that there is a subconscious part of the mind which functions without our awareness.

He taught that mental illness resulting from subconscious memories could be cured by *psychoanalysis,* which brings the memories out into consciousness. He believed that dreams are a major key to the subconscious mind and that thoughts, dreams, fantasies, and abnormal fears follow the rules of cause and effect and are not random. This is called *psychic determinism,* meaning that emotional disorders can be understood by exploring the subconscious. *Psychiatrists* help the patient understand how his mind works and why it

works that way—often the first step toward a cure.

Does psychic determinism rule out will power as a function of the mind? No, because the subconscious is only one part of the mind. Although it has an important influence, there are other forces influencing behavior and thought: the *id,* or instinctive force, the *superego,* or conscience, and the *ego,* or decision-maker. The more we know about how our minds work, what underlies our wishes and thoughts, the more control we can exercise in choosing how to behave in order to achieve our goals.

Role of Sexuality

Freud discovered that young children and even babies are aware of the sensations, pleasurable and painful, that can be experienced from all parts of the body. The sexual organs have a rich supply of nerves; the baby receives pleasure when these organs are touched, for example, during a bath or a diaper change. The child learns that when he touches these organs he obtains a pleasant feeling; therefore he repeatedly touches and rubs them (*infantile masturbation*).

This concept, that the child derives pleasure from his body and sex organs, is called *infantile sexuality.* It does not mean that the baby has adult sexual ideas or wishes. These do not develop until puberty. It does mean that parents have the responsibility to see to it that children learn early that sex is associated with tenderness and love between man and woman. Even young children are aware of what their parents do and how they treat each other.

Types of Mental Illness

Although there is considerable disagreement about the classification of mental disorders, a convenient sys-

tem used by many doctors divides mental illnesses into two general categories, organic and functional.

Some types of mental illness show little or no evidence of changes in brain tissue: these are called *functional* disorders. Another group of mental illnesses does involve some definable impairment of brain tissue resulting from disease, injury, the introduction of poisonous substances, malfunction of the body's metabolic processes, nutritional problems, or inherited defects. These are *organic* disorders. Organic brain damage may be *congenital*—that is, existing at or prior to birth—or *acquired.* Examples of congenital defects are *hydrocephalus,* an accumulation of fluid within the skull of a newborn infant that destroys brain tissue; *phenylketonuria* (PKU), a type of mental retardation associated with an inability of the child's body to metabolize a protein substance; and *Down's syndrome* (also called *Mongolism*), a form of retardation that occurs more frequently in children of older mothers and which is marked by certain physical features such as eyes that resemble those of Oriental people. Some examples of acquired defects are cerebrovascular accidents such as stroke; injuries to the brain, as from a fall or from the introduction of poisonous substances such as lead, arsenic, or mercury; and arteriosclerosis, resulting in senile psychosis in aged people.

This chapter will deal only with functional illness. Organic disorders are treated in the chapters on diseases of particular systems of the body and often in other sections as well. If you are in doubt about where to find information about a particular disorder, consult the index.

Who Is Mentally Ill?

Most people occasionally experience spells of anxiety, blue moods, or temper tantrums, but unless the psychological suffering they endure or inflict upon others begins to interfere with their job or marriage, they seldom seek professional guidance. There is no exacting scientific standard for determining when an eccentric pattern of behavior becomes a mental illness. Norms vary from culture to culture and within each culture, and, as every student of history and every parent knows, norms also change from generation to generation.

Just how can a determination be made as to who is mentally ill? No temperature reading, no acute pain, no abnormal growth can be looked for as evidence of a serious problem. Yet there are warning signs, and among the common ones are these:

- Anxiety that is severe, prolonged, and unrelated to any identifiable reason or cause

- Depression, especially when it is followed by withdrawal from loved ones, from friends, or from the usual occupations or hobbies that ordinarily afford one pleasure

- Loss of confidence in oneself

- Undue pessimism

- A feeling of constant helplessness

- Uncalled for or unexplainable mood changes—for example, an abrupt switch from happiness to unhappiness when nothing has happened to warrant it

- Rudeness or aggression that is without apparent cause or which is occasioned by some trivial incident

- An unreasonable demand for perfectionism, not only in oneself but in one's loved ones, friends, business associates, and even from things or situations

- Habitual underachievement, especially if one is adequately equipped to do the work one is called upon to perform

- The inability to accept responsibility, often manifested by a recurrent loss of employment

- Phobias

- Unreasonable feelings of persecution

- Self-destructive acts

- Sexual deviation

- A sudden and dramatic change in sleeping habits

- Physical ailments and complaints for which there are no organic causes

If one or more of these warning signs occur frequently or in severe form, a mental illness may be present, and professional help should be sought to evaluate the underlying problem.

Types of Functional Mental Illness

Functional mental disorders may be broken down into four general categories: neuroses; psychophysiological (or psychosomatic) disorders; personality or character disorders; and psychoses.

Neurosis

A *neurosis* (or *psychoneurosis*) is characterized primarily by emotional rather than physical symptoms—although physical symptoms may be present. The neuroses are usually categorized according to the type of reaction that the patient exhibits in his attempt to resolve the underlying emotional conflict. All of them involve anxiety as a prominent symptom.

Anxiety Reaction

The *anxiety reaction* is probably the most widespread of all the neurotic response patterns. Although, as noted above, all the neuroses share anxiety as a symptom, the most common and outstanding characteristic of the anxiety reaction is a feeling of dread or apprehension that is not related to any apparent cause. The anxiety is caused by conflicts of which the patient himself is unaware but which may be stimulated by thoughts or events in his present life. For example, the junior executive who is constantly apprehensive that his employer will ridicule his work and dismiss his ideas may be expressing an anxiety reaction to a childhood fear that equated ridicule with abandonment or mutilation.

While anxiety reaction symptoms are primarily mental or emotional—the patient feels inadequate or ineffectual, or behaves irrationally—anxiety is always accompanied by physiological changes such as sweating and heart palpitations. Fatigue and feelings of panic are also common symptoms.

Conversion Reaction

The *conversion reaction* (or *conversion hysteria*) describes a type of neurotic behavior in which the patient, instead of coming to grips with his underlying psychic conflict, manages to convert it into physical symptoms involving functions over which he ordinarily exerts complete control. Sometimes the physical symptoms are unimportant, but often they are markedly dramatic. For example, the soldier who becomes deaf to the sound of explosions even though there is no organic defect that would account for a loss of hearing has effectively obliterated a sensation that evokes associations too painful to acknowledge.

Obsessive-Compulsive Reaction

A person beset by persistent, unwanted ideas or feelings (*obsessions*), who is impelled to carry out certain acts (*compulsions*) ritualistically, no matter how irrational they are, is reacting to a psychic conflict in an *obsessive-compulsive* manner. The obsession may involve a feeling of violence or sexuality directed toward a member of his own family. Usually the feeling will never lead to any overt action of the type imagined, but the idea is nevertheless persistent and painful.

Obsessive-compulsive patients are typically exceptionally meticulous and conscientious, often intelligent and gifted in their work. But they expend an enormous amount of energy and time in observing compulsive acts. For example, they may take a dozen or more showers every day because they are obsessed with the idea that they are dirty or carrying a contagious disease. By performing an apparently harmless compulsive act, the patient is temporarily relieved of the obsession.

Depressive Reaction

Most people have blue moods from time to time in their lives. A person suffering from the *depressive reaction*, however, has persistent feelings of worthlessness and pessimism unrelated to events that might depress a normal person. An inability to cope with problem situations is gradually magnified into an inability to cope with anything at all. Attempts to mask the crisis by putting on a "front"—feigning cheerfulness and optimism—give way to episodes of total hopelessness. Suicide is often considered and sometimes attempted. Threats of suicide from a depressed person should always be regarded seriously.

Common physical symptoms are fa-tigue, loss of appetite, and insomnia. Treatments for depression include psychotherapy—short-term counseling or long-term analytical therapy—and non-addictive antidepressant medication, among them, Prozac, or fluoxetine.

Phobic Reaction

A *phobic reaction* is the result of an individual's attempt to deal with an anxiety-producing conflict, not by facing up to the actual source of that conflict but by avoiding something else. The substitute—whether it be an animal, closed places, or whatever—is responded to with the intense anxiety that is really felt for the true source of anxiety. This process is known as *displacement,* and the irrational fears or dreads are known as *phobias.*

Thus, a person who had been regularly punished as a child by having been forcibly confined in a closet might be unable to deal with the anxiety of the experience consciously. The anxiety might be displaced and emerge later in life in the form of terror of crowded or confined places—*claustrophobia.*

Phobias can involve almost anything one encounters in life—including things that go on in one's body and one's mind. Some of the most common phobias have to do with disease—*bacteriophobia,* for example, the fear of germs.

Scores of phobias exist, ranging alphabetically from *acrophobia,* the fear of heights, to *xenophobia,* the fear of strangers. Other well-known examples are *ailurophobia,* the fear of cats; *cynophobia,* the fear of dogs; *algophobia,* the fear of pain; *agoraphobia,* the fear of open spaces; *erythrophobia,* the fear of blushing; *mysophobia,* the fear of dirt and contamination; *nyctophobia,* the fear of the dark; and *lyssophobia,* the fear of rabies.

Dissociative Reaction

The *dissociative reaction* involves a basic disruption of the patient's personality. The dissociative reaction permits a person to escape from a part of his personality associated with intolerable anxiety. The escape is made in various ways: by forgetfulness or absent-mindedness, dream states (including sleepwalking), amnesia, and—most seriously—the adoption of multiple personalities, in which the patient behaves like one person at certain times and like an altogether different person at other times.

Psychophysiological Disorders

It has been estimated that one-half or more of the patients of a general practitioner either do not have any organic illness or do not have any organic disease that could account for the severity or extent of the symptoms described. These patients are obviously not inventing their symptoms. The symptoms—whether they be itching, constipation, asthma, or heart palpitations—are real enough. But in many cases they are either wholly or partly of psychological origin—*psychogenic* is the medical term.

The psychological and physiological aspects of humans are so closely interwoven that the problem of *psychophysiological* (or *psychosomatic*) disorders must be considered with attention to both aspects. Consider how many physiological changes in normal people can be induced by psychological states: sweating, blushing, gooseflesh, sexual arousal, weeping, the feeling of "a lump in the throat," etc. It should hardly be surprising, then, that when someone has a physical illness there are profound concomitant psychological factors that can materially affect the physiological disease.

In many cases, however, as noted above, there is no detectable organic disease. Anxiety and other disturbing emotions such as rage are sometimes dealt with by the individual by constructing a pattern of defense that involves physiological reactions. Confronted with an emotional conflict that cannot be handled consciously, the individual may channel his feelings inward and deal with it by the formation of troublesome physical symptoms. It must be stressed that this strategy is not consciously engineered by the patient and that the symptoms are genuinely experienced.

Psychophysiological disorders affect many parts of the body, but certain organs and tissues seem more vulnerable than others. The digestive tract, for example, is frequently beset by disorders that are psychophysiological, including diarrhea, constipation, regional enteritis (inflammation of the intestine), ulcerative colitis (ulcers and inflammation of the colon), and peptic ulcers. Hypertension is frequently associated with psychogenic causes. Muscle cramps, recurrent stiff necks, arthritis, backaches, and tension headaches are other common complaints. Many skin conditions such as hives and eczema can be triggered by or are aggravated by psychological factors.

The symptoms of a psychophysiological illness appear to have no logical relation to the conflict that is responsible for them, nor do they relieve the underlying anxiety.

Personality or Character Disorders

Another group of mental illnesses is the *personality* or *character disorders,* so called because they appear to stem from a kind of defect in or arrested development of the personality. Unlike neurotic patients, individuals with personality disorders do not especially suffer from anxiety, nor is their behavior markedly eccentric. But when observed over a period of time, the personality problem becomes evident.

Personality disorders fall into various categories including:

- The *passive-dependent* individual needs excessive emotional support and reassurance from an authority figure.

- The *schizoid* individual is withdrawn from and indifferent to other people.

- The *paranoid* individual is exquisitely sensitive to praise or criticism and often suspicious of expressed or implied attitudes toward him, and often is subject to feelings of persecution.

- The *cyclothymic* (or *cycloid*) individual is subject to sharply defined moods of elation or depression, seemingly without relation to external circumstances.

- The *sociopathic* individual is characteristically lacking in a sense of personal responsibility or of morality. Formerly called the *psychopathic* personality, the sociopath may be disposed to aggressive, hostile, sometimes violent behavior and frequently engages in self-destructive behavior such as alcoholism or addiction to drugs. Sociopathic behavior also includes sexual deviation.

Psychosis

The chief distinction between *psychosis* and neurosis is that a psychosis represents a more complete disintegration of personality and a loss of contact with the outside world. The psychotic is therefore unable to form relationships with people. Most people who suffer from nonpsychotic mental disorders are seldom, if ever, hospitalized, and then usually for very brief periods. But many psychotics are so crippled by their illness that they are hospitalized repeatedly or for protracted periods of time.

Schizophrenic Reaction

Schizophrenia, the most common and destructive of the psychotic reactions, is characterized by withdrawal from external reality, inability to think clearly, disturbances in affective reaction (capacity to feel and express emotion), and a retreat into a fantasy life—all of these resulting in a progressive deterioration of the patient's ordinary behavioral patterns.

Simple Schizophrenia

The patient with *simple schizophrenia* experiences a gradual loss of concern and contact with other people, and a lessening of the motivation needed to perform the routine activities of everyday life. There may be some personality deterioration, but the presence of hallucinations and delusions is rare.

Hebephrenic Schizophrenia

This form of schizophrenia is marked by delusions, hallucinations, and regressed behavior. Hebephrenics babble and giggle, and often react in inappropriately childish ways. Their silly manner can make them seem happier than other schizophrenics, but this disorder often results in severe personality disintegration—more severe, in fact, than in other types of schizophrenia.

Catatonic Schizophrenia

In *catatonic schizophrenia* there are dramatic disturbances of the motor functions. Patients may remain in a fixed position for hours, days, or even weeks. During this time their muscles may be rigid, their limbs held in awkward positions. They may have to be fed, and their urinary and bowel functions may be abnormal. This stuporous state may be varied by an occasional period of frenzied but purposeless excitement.

Paranoid Schizophrenia

The *paranoid schizophrenic* is preoccupied with variable delusions of persecution or grandeur. Men working with pneumatic drills on the street, for example, are really sending out supersonic beams designed to destroy his brain cells; the water supply is being poisoned by visitors from other planets; any mechanical malfunction, as of a telephone or an elevator, is part of a deliberate plot of harassment or intimidation.

Paranoid schizophrenia is often marked by the presence of hallucinations, by disturbances in mental processes, and by behavioral deterioration. The disorder is regarded as particularly serious—hard to deal with and likely to become permanent.

Paranoid Reaction

The patient with this disorder suffers from delusions, usually of persecution, sometimes of grandeur. In this respect, *paranoia* is very similar to paranoid schizophrenia. However, in paranoid schizophrenia the delusions are often variable, and usually there is a breakdown of the patient's behavioral patterns.

A case of true paranoia, by contrast, is characterized by an invariable delusion around which the patient constructs and adheres to a highly systematized pattern of behavior. When the delusion is of such a nature that its persistence does not engender a conflict between the patient and his surrounding social structure, the patient may never be suspected of mental illness, perhaps merely of eccentricity. If, however, the delusion does provoke conflict, the patient may react with destructive hostility, and hospitalization or some other kind of professional treatment will be necessary.

Manic-Depressive Reaction

This disorder, also called an *affective reaction,* is characterized by two phases—*mania* and *depression*.

The manic phase may be mild and bring elation and a general stepping up of all kinds of activity. The patient tends to talk endlessly and in an associative rather than a logical way. If the disorder is more severe, he may act or dress bizarrely; he may be a whirlwind of activity and become so excited and agitated that he foregoes food and sleep and ends in a state of total collapse.

In a mild depressive phase, the individual feels dull and melancholy, his confidence begins to drain away, and he becomes easily fatigued by daily routines. When the depressive phase is more severe, the patient starts to retreat from reality, gradually entering into a state of withdrawal that is very much like a stupor. At this point he hardly moves or speaks. He may be unable to sleep. Eventually he begins to question his value as a human being and is crushed by feelings of guilt. He may refuse to eat. Symptoms may progress to the point where an attempt at suicide is a real possibility.

Although the manic-depressive psychosis may alternate from one of its phases to the other, one or the other phase is usually dominant for a prolonged period of time. Depression is more often dominant than mania. Manic-depressive patients often recover spontaneously for periods of time, but relapses are fairly common. For treatment, see "Chemotherapy."

Depressive Reaction

The *depressive reaction* is a disorder connected with aging and its attendant changes in sexual functioning; it usually occurs at the time of the menopause in women, in the middle or late 40s, and somewhat later in men. Formerly called *involutional melancholia,* it is characterized, as that name suggests, by a sense of hopeless melancholy and despair.

Patients begin to feel that life has passed them by. They experience real physical symptoms such as loss of vigor, and develop various hypochondriacal complaints. Their interests become narrower, and they begin to retreat from the world.

As the melancholy deepens, there are periods of senseless weeping, bouts of intense anxiety, feelings of worthlessness, and growing concern—coupled with delusions—about dying and death. The depth of the depression is overwhelming, and the danger of suicide greater than in any other psychosis.

Treatment of Emotional Problems and Mental Disorders

When should help be sought for an emotional problem? Sometimes individuals themselves realize that they need help and seek it without urging. They may have symptoms such as anxiety, depression, or troublesome thoughts that they cannot put out of their mind. But many others who need help do not know it or do not want to know that they need it. They usually have symptoms that disturb others rather than themselves, such as irritability, impulsive behavior, or excessive use of drugs or alcohol that interferes with their family relationships and work responsibilities.

Other people in need of psychological guidance are those who have a physical disease that is based on psychological factors. They react to stress internally rather than externally. Instead of displaying anger, they feel it inside. We are all familiar with headaches or heartburn caused by tension; more serious diseases clearly associated with emotional factors are asthma, certain skin disorders, ulcerative colitis, essential hypertension, hyperthyroidism, and peptic ulcer. Other physical symptoms that may be related to psychological factors are some types of paralysis, blindness, and loss of memory.

In all these situations the patient's enjoyment of life is curtailed. He has no feeling of control over what he does and little or no tolerance for himself and others. Such an existence is completely unnecessary today, with the many agencies and specialists, capable of effectively treating these problems.

Mental Health Professionals

Who can help those with emotional problems? Confusion about the different professions in the mental health field is understandable. To add to the muddle, self-appointed counselors without professional training and experience have set themselves up in this field, so it is necessary to know whom to consult to obtain the best help possible.

Psychiatrists

Psychiatrists are medical doctors; that is, they have graduated from a medical school, served internships and afterwards residencies specializing in emotional disorders. They are specialists in the same way that a surgeon or an eye doctor is a specialist. Most are members of the American Psychiatric Association. They are experienced in treating medical illnesses, having done so for many years before being certified as specialists in emotional disorders. Generally they can be relied upon to adhere to the ethical and professional standards of the medical field.

The American Psychiatric Association, 1400 K St., N.W., Washington, D.C. 20005, can supply the names of members. The American Board of Psychiatry and Neurology, One American Plaza, Suite 800, Evanston, Illinois 60201, examines and certifies psychiatrists who pass its tests, so that the term "board certified" means that the psychiatrist has passed its tests. If a family physician is consulted about an emotional problem, he will often refer the patient to a psychiatrist, just as he would to any other specialist.

Psychologists

Psychologists have gone to college, majored in psychology, and most often have advanced degrees, for example, a doctorate in psychology. They are not medical doctors and may get a degree in psychology without ever working with a human being, e.g., by working in animal behavior, experimental psychology, or other fields. They may or may not have clinical training, but many acquire this training and experience with human beings. There is no guarantee that a psychologist has this background, however, without looking into the qualifications of each individual.

Psychotherapists

Psychotherapy is the general term for any treatment that tries to effect a cure by psychological rather than physical means. A psychotherapist may be a psychiatrist, or he may be a psychologist, or may have no training at all. Anyone can set up an office and call himself a psychotherapist, psychoanalyst, marriage counselor, family therapist, or anything else he desires. It is up to the patient to check on the training and background of a therapist. Any reputable therapist should be pleased to tell patients his credentials and qualifications for helping them. A psychoanalyst, for example, may be a psychiatrist with several years of additional training in psychoanalysis, or may be someone whose qualifications consist of a few college psychology courses.

Social Workers

Social workers are another group of trained persons who may also counsel those with emotional problems. They may work either with individuals, families, or groups after meeting the educational requirements for the profession, which include a bachelor's degree and two years of professional training leading to a master's degree in social work.

Professionals should be associated with recognized groups of their peers, or perhaps with a medical center or hospital. Generally a person with emotional problems should consult a psychiatrist first, who will then either treat the problem or be in a good position to advise what is necessary and who can best be available for treatment.

Types of Therapy

Functional mental illnesses are treated by a variety of tools, among them psychotherapy and chemotherapy (treatment with drugs).

Psychotherapy

As noted above, psychotherapy applies to various forms of treatment that employ psychological methods designed to help patients understand themselves. With this knowledge, or insight, the patient learns how to handle his life—with all its relationships and conflicts—in a happier and more socially responsible manner.

The best known form of psychotherapy is psychoanalysis, developed by Freud but modified by many others, which seeks to lift to the level of awareness the patient's repressed subconscious feelings. The information about subconscious conflicts is explored and interpreted to explain the causes of the patient's emotional upsets.

The technique employs a series of steps beginning with *free association,* in which the patient is encouraged to discuss anything that comes to mind, including things that the patient might be reluctant to discuss with anyone else but the analyst. Other steps include dream analysis and *transference,* which is the redirection to the analyst of repressed childhood emotions.

Group therapy is a form of therapeutic treatment in which a group of approximately six to ten patients, usually under the guidance of a therapist, participate in discussions of their mental and emotional problems. The therapist may establish the direction of the discussion or may remain mostly silent, allowing the patients' interaction to bring about the special cathartic benefits of this technique.

Family therapy is much like group therapy, with an individual family functioning as a group. It is felt that the family members may be better able to discuss the problems of relating to each other within the context of a group than they would be on an individual basis with a therapist.

Psychodrama is a therapeutic technique in which a patient or a group of patients act out situations centered about their personal conflicts. The psychodrama is "performed" in the presence of a therapist and, sometimes, other people.

Children are sometimes enrolled in programs of *play therapy* in which dolls, doll houses, and other appropriate toys are made available so that they can express their frustrations, hostilities, and other feelings through play. This activity, carried on under the observation of a therapist, is considered a form of catharsis in that it often prevents the repression of hostile emotions. In the case of a maladjusted child, it can also act as a helpful diagnostic tool—revealing the source of the child's emotional problem.

Chemotherapy

The relationship between body chemistry and mental illness has been studied for over half a century. The result of this study is the therapeutic technique known as *chemotherapy,* the treatment of disease with drugs or chemicals.

Present-Day Uses of Chemical Agents

The control of mental illness has taken a giant step forward with the development of *tranquilizers* and *antidepressants.* Tranquilizers counteract anxiety, tension, andoverexcitement; they are used to calm patients whose behavior is dangerously confused or disturbed. Antidepressants help to stimulate the physiological activity of depressed patients, thereby tending to relieve the sluggishness that attends depression.

Persons suffering from depression and patients with obsessive-compulsive behavior have been prescribed fluoxetine, commonly known as Prozac. Fluoxetine acts by inhibiting the central nervous system's uptake of serotonin, a neurotransmittor.

The treatment of the manic-depressive psychosis has been facilitated with the use of salts derived from lithium, a metal. Lithium salts seem to control the disease without producing the undesirable emotional and intellectual effects that resulted from the previous treatment with tranquilizers and antidepressants. The medication has been found to be particularly effective in treating patients with frequent manic episodes; it is also said to be effective as a preventive measure against future manifestations of mania or depression. Lithium may have adverse side effects and must be administered carefully.

Chemotherapy does not usually cure mental illness. It does, however, improve the patient's mental state, thereby enabling him to cope more effectively with the problems of everyday life.

Electroshock Treatment

Electroshock is a form of therapy in which a carefully regulated electric current is passed through a patient's head, thereby producing convulsions and unconsciousness.

Electroshock is primarily a treatment for the manic-depressive psychosis; to a lesser extent the therapy is used on schizophrenic patients. It often shortens depressed periods, and sometimes the patient seems totally free of the symptoms of his disorder. Unfortunately, the remission may be temporary; electroshock does not prevent further attacks. Also, transitory memory impairment often occurs.

Because of the recent advances in the techniques of chemotherapy, electroshock is used much less frequently than it was in the past.

Facilities Available for the Mentally Ill

The last decade has seen a number of hopeful changes in the facilities for treatment of mental disorders in the United States. The great majority of severely ill mental patients used to be cared for in county or state mental hospitals, many of which were crowded and able to offer custodial care but very little in the way of therapeutic programs. The picture has changed, however, and the extent and quality of care in these hospitals is expanding and improving.

Patients with mental illnesses are also being treated in greater numbers at general hospitals. As a matter of fact, more patients who need hospitalization for such illnesses are being admitted to general hospitals than to public mental hospitals.

Treatment for the mentally or emotionally disturbed is also provided in other facilities, including private mental hospitals, mental health clinics, and various social agencies.

Among the new facilities for treating mental illness is one which permits many patients who would formerly have been hospitalized, perhaps for the rest of their lives, to be served by community mental health centers. These centers offer both inpatient and outpatient care. The services they provide go beyond diagnosis and treatment to include rehabilitation, thus making it possible for more and more of today's mental patients to live at home, function in a job situation, and be a part of their own community.

Results of Treatment

What can be expected from treatment? Does a person who has been through treatment emerge bland, uncaring about others, with absolutely no problems, and without guilt for his misdeeds? Absolutely not. What treatment can do, said Freud, is to change neurotic misery into common unhappiness. There will always be things in life that are disappointing or otherwise upsetting. No treatment can eliminate such problems. After successful treatment, however, one should be better able to handle these stresses with flexible and constructive responses and to see his own difficulties in relation to the problems of others.

To feel emotionally fit is to have a capacity for enjoying life, working well, and loving others. Fear, shame, and guilt about undergoing needed treatment should not prevent anyone from reaching that potential.

29

Substance Abuse

Drug-Related Deaths up 59%." "Driving-and-Drinking Accident Claims 5 Lives." "Teen Drug Abuse—The News Is Bad."

The headlines tell a story with a moral, or lesson. The lesson is that the United States has a major health and social problem. Once called by a number of names, including *alcoholism, drug addiction,* and *drug abuse,* the problem today goes by the designation *substance abuse.* In this usage, the phrase applies to all forms of addiction or abuse, whether the substance is alcohol or such vegetation-derived drugs as marijuana, cocaine, and heroin.

In a broad sense, substances include any material aside from food that can be imbibed, injected, or taken into the body in any way and that changes or affects the body or mind. This definition covers aspirin, many medications, tobacco, and a broad range of other substances. But *substance abuse* refers to unhealthy or excessive use of any material, alcohol, or addictive drugs at an individual's discretion and not according to a physician's prescription.

The dimensions of the substance-abuse problem are almost incalculable. Americans in 1986 spent an esti-

mated $110 billion on addictive drugs alone. At least 40 percent of all Americans between the ages of 18 and 25 had experimented with one or more illegal substances. As one authority wrote,

Not only the poor, the uneducated, the deprived, or the shadow types are being destroyed. We're dealing with the privileged, the successful, the professional.

Alcohol Abuse

Alcohol abuse is not unique to the United States or to the twentieth century. Alcoholic beverages, and their use or abuse, have an ancient history. Long before humans began to keep records of any kind, these beverages were valued as food, medicine, and ceremonial drinks. When people today have a beer with dinner, or toast newlyweds with champagne, or share wine at a religious ritual or festival, they are continuing traditions that have deep roots in the past.

The consumption of alcoholic beverages has always been a fact of life.

So has, in a sense, alcohol abuse. The immigrants who came to the United States brought their ethnic ceremonies and drinking habits with them. The frontiersmen who moved continually west found liquor to be a source of release and comfort. Inevitably, alcohol use and abuse occurred.

Most drinkers have been, and are, able to control what they are doing and are none the worse for the habit. However, of the estimated 100 million drinkers in the United States, about 10 million have some kind of problem with alcohol: they are *alcohol abusers.* The 10 million alcoholics cost the economy some $60 billion annually. Drunken drivers are implicated in about half of the nearly 50,000 traffic deaths occurring yearly.

Scientists have come to believe that habitual alcohol abuse is a disease and should be treated as such. In 1956, the American Medical Association officially termed alcoholism an illness and a medical responsibility.

Kinds of Alcohol

The alcohol in beverages is chemically known as *ethyl alcohol.* It is often called *grain alcohol.* It is produced by the natural process of *fermentation:* When certain foods such as honey, fruits, grains, or their juices remain in a warm place, airborne yeast organisms begin to change the sugars and starches in these foods into alcohol. Ethyl alcohol is in itself a food in the sense that its caloric content produces energy in the body, but it contains practically no essential nutriments.

Methyl alcohol, also called *wood alcohol,* because it is obtained by the dry distillation of maple, birch, and beech, is useful as a fuel and solvent. It is poisonous if taken internally and can cause blindness and death. Other members of the same family of chemicals, such as *isopropyl alcohol,* are also used as rubbing alcohols—as cooling agents and skin disinfectants—and are also poisonous if taken internally.

Present-Day Drinking Trends

On a per capita basis, Americans drink twice as much wine and beer as they did a century ago, and half as much distilled spirits. Where the drinking takes place has also changed. There is less hard drinking in saloons and more social drinking at home and in clubs. The acceptance of drinking in mixed company has made it more a part of social situations than it used to be.

Here are some facts about the current consumption of alcoholic beverages in the United States:

● Drinking is more common among men than among women, but the gap is closing.

● It is more common among people who are under 40.

● It is more common among the well-to-do than among the poor.

● Beyond the age of 45, the number of drinkers steadily declines.

Teenagers and Alcohol

One fact emerges clearly and consistently from all the surveys of teenage drinking in all parts of the country: the drinking behavior of parents is more related to what children do about drinking than any other factor. It is more influential than children's friends, their neighborhoods, their religion, their social or economic status, or their local laws.

Statistics on teenage (and adult) drinking vary from one ethnic group or one part of the country to another. But overall, the statistics show that about two-thirds of all Americans 18 and older consume alcoholic beverages. Some three-quarters of all students in the tenth to twelfth grade range also drink.

In general, drinking is an activity that is associated with growing up. For boys, it represents manhood; for girls, sophistication.

Kinds of Alcoholic Beverages

The way any alcoholic drink affects the body depends chiefly on how much alcohol it contains. The portion of alcohol can range from less than 1/20th of the total volume, in the case of beer, to more than one-half in the case of rum. As a general rule, distilled drinks have a higher alcohol content than fermented ones.

The five basic types of beverages are beers, table wines, dessert or cocktail wines, cordials and liqueurs, and distilled spirits such as brandy and whisky. The labels of beers and wines usually indicate the percentage of alcohol by volume. The labels of distilled spirits indicate *proof.*

Proof

The proof number is twice the percentage of alcohol by volume. Thus a rye whisky that is 90-proof contains 45 percent alcohol, 80-proof bourbon is 40 percent alcohol, and so on. The word *proof* used in this way comes from an old English test to determine the strength of distilled spirits. If gunpowder soaked with whisky would still ignite when lighted, that fact was "proof" that the whisky contained the right amount of alcohol. The amount, approximately 57 percent, is still the standard in Canada and Great Britain.

How Alcohol Affects the Body

The overall effects of alcohol on the body and on behavior vary a great deal depending on many factors. One factor should be noted at once: if the blood reaching the brain contains a certain percentage of alcohol, there are marked changes in reaction. As the percentage increases, the functioning of the brain and central nervous system is increasingly affected. As the alcohol is gradually metabolized and eliminated, the process reverses itself.

If at any given time the blood contains a concentration of about 3/100 of one percent (0.03 percent), no effects are observable. This amount will make its way into the bloodstream after you have had a highball or cocktail made with one and one-half ounces of whisky, or two small glasses of table wine, or two bottles of beer. It takes about two hours for this amount of alcohol to leave the body completely.

Twice that number of drinks produces twice the concentration of alcohol in the bloodstream (0.06 percent) with an accompanying feeling of warmth and relaxation.

If the concentration of alcohol in the bloodstream reaches 0.1 percent—when one part of every thousand parts of blood is pure alcohol—the person is legally drunk in most states.

The motor areas of the brain are affected; there is a noticeable lack of coordination in standing or walking. If the percentage goes up to 0.15 percent, the physical signs of intoxication are obvious, and they are accompanied by an impairment of mental faculties as well.

A concentration of as much as 0.4 percent can cause a coma. At the level of 0.5 to 0.7 percent there may be paralysis of the brain centers that control the activities of the lungs and heart, a condition that can be fatal.

Alcohol affects the brain and nervous system in this way because it is a depressant and an anesthetic.

How Alcohol Moves through the Body

Although it is negligible as nourishment, alcohol is an energy-producing food like sugar. Unlike most foods, however, it is quickly absorbed into the bloodstream through the stomach and small intestine without first having to undergo complicated digestive processes. It is then carried to the liver, where most of it is converted into heat and energy. From the liver, the remainder is carried by the bloodstream to the heart and pumped to the lungs. Some is expelled in the breath and some is eventually eliminated in sweat and urine. From the lungs, the alcohol is circulated to the brain.

People who use good judgment when drinking rarely, if ever, get drunk. The safe and pleasurable use of alcoholic beverages depends on the drinker's weight and his or her physical condition and emotional state. Other factors include the following:

1. *The Concentration of Alcohol in the Beverage* The higher the alcohol content in terms of total volume, the faster it is absorbed. Three ounces of straight whisky—two shot glasses— contain the same amount of alcohol as 48 ounces (or four cans) of beer.

2. *Sipping or Gulping* Two shots of straight whisky can be downed in seconds or, more normally, in a few minutes. The same amount diluted in two highballs can be sipped through an entire evening. In the latter case, the body has a chance to get rid of much of the alcohol.

3. *Additional Components of the Drink* The carbohydrates in beer and wine slow down the absorption of alcohol in the blood. Vodka mixed with orange juice travels much more slowly than a vodka martini.

4. *Food in the Stomach* The alcohol concentration in two cocktails consumed at the peak of the hunger before dinner can have a nasty effect. Several glasses of wine with a meal or a brandy sipped after dinner get to the bloodstream much more slowly and at a lower concentration. The sensible drinker doesn't drink on an empty stomach.

The Hangover

The feeling of discomfort that sometimes sets in the morning after excessive drinking is known as a hangover. It is caused by the disruptive effect of too much alcohol on the central nervous system. The symptoms of nausea, headache, dry mouth, diarrhea, fatigue, dizziness, heartburn, and a feeling of apprehension are usually most acute several hours after drinking and not while there is still any appreciable amount of alcohol in the system.

Although many people believe that "mixing" drinks, such as switching from whisky drinks to wine, is the main cause of hangovers, a hangover can just as easily be induced by too much of one type of drink or by pure alcohol. Nor is it always the result of drinking too much because emotional stress or allergy may well be contributing factors.

Some aspects of a hangover may be caused by substances called *congeners*. These are the natural products of fermentation found in small amounts in all alcoholic beverages, among them tannic acid and fusel oil. Some congeners have toxic properties that produce nausea by irritating certain nerve centers.

In spite of accumulated lore about hangover remedies, there is no certain cure for the symptoms. Neither raw eggs, oysters, alkalizers, sugar, black coffee, nor another drink has any therapeutic value. A throbbing head and aching joints can sometimes be relieved by aspirin and bed rest. Stomach irritation can be eased by bland foods such as skim milk, cooked cereal, or a poached egg. Persons seeking relief may also try analgesics such as aspirin or acetaminophen for the headache, antacids if the problem is upset stomach, or over-the-counter medications for the diarrhea.

Alcohol and General Health

As a result of new studies of the effect of alcohol on the body, many myths have been laid to rest. In general, it is known that in moderate quantities, alcohol causes the following reactions: the heartbeat quickens slightly, appetite increases, and gastric juices are stimulated. In other words, a drink makes people "feel good." But drinking does have harmful effects when consumed in large quantities.

Tissue Impairment

Habitual drinking of straight whisky can irritate the membranes that line the mouth and throat. The hoarse voice of some heavy drinkers is the result of a thickening of vocal cord tissue. As for the effect on the stomach, alcohol doesn't cause ulcers, but it does aggravate them.

There is no evidence to support the belief that port wine or any other alcoholic beverage taken in moderation will cause gout. Studies have shown that as many as 60 percent of all patients with this disease had never drunk any wine at all.

Brain Damage

Alcohol abuse continued over many years has been found to contribute to cognitive defects. These may, in turn, indicate brain impairment. Researchers do not know what the defects represent—whether greater susceptibility to the problems of aging or an actual, alcohol-caused "premature aging" effect. Whatever the case, long-term chronic alcohol abuse leads to more rapid aging of the brain. Neuropsychologically, the alcoholic's brain resembles that of an older nonalcoholic.

Long-term abuse can have many other effects. These include withdrawal symptoms beginning 12 to 48 hours after a person stops drinking, sometimes followed by *delirium tremens* (DTs), which brings hallucinations and can be fatal; the Werner-Korsakoff syndrome, a type of beriberi characterized by a lack of the B vitamins; alcoholic peripheral neuropathy, involving damage to the nerve tissue outside the brain and spinal cord; and liver damage, including alcoholic hepatitis and cirrhosis. In the latter the liver becomes hard and yellowed.

Alcohol and Immunity to Infection

Moderate drinkers who maintain proper health habits are no more likely to catch viral or bacterial diseases than nondrinkers. But heavy drinkers, who often suffer from malnutrition, have conspicuously lower resistance to infection. Even well-nourished heavy drinkers have a generally lower immunity to infection than normal. When the blood-alcohol level is 0.15 percent or higher, the alcohol appears to weaken the disease-fighting white blood cells.

Alcohol and Stroke

Studies have shown that heavy drinkers face nearly three times the teetotaler's risk of hemorrhagic stroke. Light drinkers face twice the risk. About one stroke in four occurring in the United States is hemorrhagic, but these strokes are more likely to be fatal than those caused by blood clots.

Alcohol and Life Expectancy

It is difficult to isolate drinking in itself as a factor in longevity. One study reported the shortest life span for heavy drinkers, a somewhat longer one for those who don't drink at all, and the longest for moderate drinkers. But other factors, such as general health and heredity, play important roles.

Alcohol and Sex Activity

Alcohol in sufficient quantity depresses the part of the brain that controls inhibitions. This liberating effect has led some people to believe that alcohol is an aphrodisiac, in men. This is a conclusion that is far from the truth. At the same time that alcohol increases the sexual appetite, it reduces the ability to perform.

Alcohol as an Irritant

Many otherwise healthy people cannot tolerate alcoholic beverages of any kind, or of a particular kind, without getting sick. In some cases, the negative reaction may be psychological in origin—connected with a disastrous experience with drunkenness in the early years or with an early hatred for a drinker in the family. Some people can drink one type of beverage but not another because of a particular congener, or because of an allergy to a specific grain or fruit. People suffering from such diseases as peptic ulcers, kidney and liver infections, and epilepsy should never drink any alcoholic beverages unless allowed to do so by a physician.

Uses and Hazards

At practically all times and in many parts of the world today, alcoholic beverages of various kinds have been and are still used for medicinal purposes. This should not be taken to mean that Aunt Sally is right about the curative powers of her elderberry wine, or that grandpa knows best when he says brandy is the best cure for hiccups. Today an American physician may recommend a particular alcoholic beverage as a tranquilizer, a sleep-inducer, or an appetite stimulant.

Use of Alcohol with Other Drugs

Alcoholic beverages should be avoided by anyone taking barbiturates or other sedatives. See "Drug Use and Abuse" later in this chapter for a discussion of barbiturates.

Alcohol and Driving

For many people, coordination, alertness, and general driving skills are impaired at blood-alcohol levels below the legal limit (0.1 percent). There are some people who become dangerous drivers after only one drink. Attempts are constantly being made, but so far with less than perfect success, to educate the public about the very real dangers of drunken driving.

Possible Causes of Alcohol Abuse

A popular myth holds that alcohol causes alcohol abuse. It doesn't—any more than sugar causes diabetes. Various theories have been evolved to explain what does cause alcohol abuse.

Physiological Causes

Although several physiological factors seem to be involved in the progression of alcohol abuse, no single one can be pinpointed as the cause of the disease. Among the theories that have come under investigation are the following: abnormal sugar metabolism, disorders of the endocrine glands, and dietary deficiencies.

Psychological Causes

Recent studies have pointed to a possible relationship between personality and alcohol abuse. Researchers indicate that one definable segment of the alcoholic population has the character disorder known as *antisocial personality*. Once called a *sociopath,* the person with an antisocial personality is usually charming in a social sense, manipulative, impulsive and rebellious, and egocentric. An estimated 25 percent of the alcoholic population falls in this category; in the general population the prevalence of antisocial personalities is about 3 percent.

Sociological Factors

Practically all studies of alcohol abuse in the United States indicate that ethnic groups vary dramatically in their rates of problem drinkers. A great deal of attention has therefore been focused on *learned attitudes* toward alcoholic beverages and how they are used or abused. Generally, in the low-incidence groups attitudes toward drinking are clearly defined and understood by all the members of the group. Drunkenness is consistently frowned upon. In the high-incidence groups, researchers have found extensive conflict over alcohol. The basic rules aren't clearly defined, and there are no clear-cut standards for acceptable and unacceptable drinking behavior.

Genetic Factors

Research into the genetics of alcohol abuse has led to a theory of "familial abuse." The theory holds that the person with a close relative who is alcoholic is at far greater risk of succumbing to the disease than are others without such connections. Familial abuse or "familial alcoholism" characterizes as many as three in four of all abusers. Therapy has thus begun to focus on the families of alcohol abusers—particularly young sons—as the ones most susceptible to the disease.

Recognizing the Danger Signals of Problem Drinking

The chronic alcohol abuser shows physical symptoms that a physician can recognize. Among them are hand tremors, deterioration of eye functions, reduced bladder control, liver disorders, anemia, memory lapses, and others. But there are many other symptoms that family members and friends can observe, among them these:

- Alcohol use as a way of handling problems or escaping from them
- Increased use of alcohol with repeated occasions of unintended intoxication

- Sneaking drinks or gulping them rapidly in quick succession
- Irritation, hostility, and lying when the subject of alcohol abuse is mentioned
- A noticeable deterioration in appearance, health, and social behavior
- Persistent drinking in spite of such symptoms as headaches, loss of appetite, sleeplessness, and stomach trouble

Treatment

Methods of treating alcohol abuse fall generally into three categories. Choice of any one form of treatment depends on the particular needs of a client, including the degree of dependency. The three categories include the hospital, the intermediate, and the outpatient settings. Other approaches to treatment may be geared to individual or group needs.

The family physician can in most cases provide guidance on what kind of treatment would most benefit a particular patient. The alcohol abuser may be referred first to a toxicologist for an interview and recommendations on treatment. A review of the patient's history is a typical first step in treatment. Family involvement during therapy may be critically important. More than 4,200 centers offer treatment programs; of these, many are nonprofit clinics while others are units owned by for-profit health care chains. Many centers and clinics specialize in team approaches to therapy.

The Hospital Setting

Whether undertaken voluntarily or involuntarily (for example, by court order) the treatment formats offered in a hospital can be individualized.

Where some patients adjust best to inpatient care, others prefer partial hospitalization. In the latter case the patient is allowed to go home or to work at appropriate times, otherwise living in the hospital. In a hospital detoxification program, one designed to end physical addiction, the patient has a variable period, usually two weeks to a month, during which he or she undergoes a programmed regimen of activities. These may range from exercise classes to medications to bed rest and regulated diets.

The Intermediate Setting

The intermediate settings usually include at least halfway houses, quarterway houses, and residential care sites. The first of these offer not only living quarters but also job counseling, psychotherapy, and other services. In quarterway houses, the patient receives more attention in the form of counseling and psychotherapy. Residential care centers usually offer little beyond living quarters.

The Outpatient Setting

Again in the outpatient setting the patient has a range of treatment choices. Among them typically are individual counseling sessions held by a paraprofessional; individual therapy sessions with a professional who may have an advanced degree in social work, psychology, medicine, or a related specialty; and group therapy sessions supervised by either a paraprofessional or a professional.

Chemical Treatments

Some treatment programs utilize medications to help patients to "shake the habit." Tranquilizers may be used to reduce tensions and prepare the patient for a follow-up stage. In a program of *aversion therapy* a substance called emetine may be prescribed. Taken before an alcoholic drink, emetine causes nausea. The treatment should be undertaken only under medical supervision.

Where to Find Help

Volunteer organizations of various kinds offer the alcohol abuser and his or her family a wide range of services and programs. The best known is Alcoholics Anonymous (AA), which is supported by contributions from members. AA utilizes a group-support approach to treatment. Most larger communities have AA chapters as well as Al-Anon and Alateen units for family members, relatives, and friends of abusers. Alateen works with young people between 12 and 20 years of age. Counseling and referrals may be obtained from a local Alcoholic Treatment Center.

Information may also be obtained from the following national headquarters of organizations established to help alcohol abusers:

Alcoholics Anonymous World
   Services
P.O. Box 459
Grand Central Station
New York, NY 10163

National Association for Children of
   Alcoholics
31582 Coast Highway, Suite 201
South Laguna, CA 92677
(714/499-3889)

Al-Anon Family Group Headquarters
P.O. Box 862
Midtown Station
New York, NY 10018
(212/302-7240)

National Council on Alcoholism and
   Drug Dependence
12 W. 21 Street
New York, NY 10010
(212/206-6770)

Drug Abuse

Like alcohol abuse, drug abuse can wreck lives and break up families. But to many experts the problem of drug abuse is far more serious than alcohol abuse. The trade in addictive, harmful drugs is not only unlawful; it has grown year by year, to the point where many believe it is out of control. The U.S. government spent some $1.6 billion on efforts to combat illegal drug importation in 1986, calling on units of the military forces to join the campaign. Even so, heroin imports increased by about 10 percent and cocaine imports by about 4 percent.

The forms that drug abuse takes, and the numbers of drugs, are numerous and increasing. Many authorities believe we should examine our whole American society for the "pill-happy" context in which drug abuse occurs. Dr. Joel Fort, former consultant on drug abuse to the World Health Organization, called America

> "a drug-prone nation. . . . The average 'straight' adult consumes three to five mind-altering drugs a day, beginning with the stimulant caffeine in coffee, tea, and Coca Cola, going on to include alcohol and nicotine, often a tranquilizer, not uncommonly a sleeping pill at night and sometimes an amphetamine the next morning."

The social effects of drug abuse rank among the most alarming of all the symptoms of what has been called the drug crisis. By estimate, drugs are involved in one-third to one-half of all crimes committed in the United States in a typical year. In a single recent year, medical treatments for drug abusers cost the nation more than $2 billion. The costs of abuse to families, communities, and to abusers themselves cannot be calculated.

Making the problem of control of drug abuse unbelievably complex is the fact that literally thousands of drugs and drug combinations have basic roles in medical treatments. Legal and illicit uses may, because of the close connections, become confused. Physicians' instructions regarding use of such legal drugs as sleeping pills may be ignored or neglected. Legitimately prescribed drugs may, in some cases, unintentionally lead to abuse or dependency.

Other facts make it difficult to control drug abuse. More and more, for example, abusers are turning to multiple substance abuse. Cocaine "sniffers" may take alcohol in one form or another to soften the uncomfortable and even painful effects of cocaine withdrawal. Physicians report that "polydrug" abuse leads to progressive worsening of such medical symptoms as stomach ailments and liver problems.

Designer drugs add another complicating factor. Made in clandestine chemical laboratories, these drugs are imitations or analogs of such other drugs as cocaine, heroin, amphetamines, and many other basic substances. The new drugs are legal until declared illegal by the federal government's Drug Enforcement Administration because a chemist has altered their chemical compositions enough to take them out of the banned or controlled drug categories. Far more powerful than the basic drugs they imitate, the designer forms have been implicated in more than 200 deaths. Researchers indicate that there is no limit to the numbers of designer drugs that can be produced.

A designer drug called *new heroin* (*Ecstasy*) was, on analysis, found to contain the industrial chemical MPTP, a suspected causative element in cases of Parkinson's disease. A number of new-heroin abusers also had classic Parkinson's symptoms: rigidity, tremors in the arms, legs, and even the head, and slow or difficult movement. Thus new research has focused on MPTP as a possible clue to the degenerative brain processes that lead to Parkinson's.

Over-the-Counter Drugs

Americans consume over-the-counter (OTC) drugs in enormous quantities. Purchasable without a physician's prescription, these drugs have limited but real potential for abuse. They range from headache remedies to cold nostrums and from acne ointments to vitamins. In general, good practice is to use OTC drugs as seldom as possible, for short-term, minor illnesses. Medicines of proven effectiveness should be used exclusively: taking an aspirin for a headache is a good example. The U.S. Public Health Service offers these guidelines:

- Self-prescribed drugs should never be used continuously for long periods of time. . . . A physician is required for abdominal pain that is severe or recurs periodically; pains anywhere, if severe, disabling, persistent, or recurring; headache, if unusually severe or prolonged more than one day; a prolonged cold with fever or cough; earache; unexplained loss of weight; unexplained and unusual symptoms; *malaise* lasting more than a week or two. . . .

The Food and Drug Administration (FDA), a branch of the U.S. Public Health Service, is responsible for establishing the safety and usefulness of all drugs marketed in the United States, both OTC and prescription. You can be assured that OTC drugs are safe provided you take them in strict accordance with the label instructions. These indicate the appropriate dosages, among other things, and carry warnings against prolonged or improper use, such as "discontinue if pain persists," or "do not take if abdominal pain is present." This labeling information is regulated by the FDA.

Drug Classifications

In addition to alcohol, the drugs of potential abuse fall into six categories: stimulants, depressants, and narcotic preparations, all of which can have legitimate medical uses; hallucinogens; cannabinoids such as marijuana; and inhalants (or volatile inhalants) such as aerosol sprays, glues, and fuels. See the accompanying table:

Major Drug Classifications	
Type	**Examples**
Stimulants	Amphetamines Cocaine derivatives
Depressants	Valium Seconal
Narcotics (opioids)	Morphine Codeine
Hallucinogens	LSD Mescaline Psilocybin
Marijuana (cannabinoids)	Marijuana Hashish
Inhalants	Gasoline Amyl nitrate

Drug abuse can lead to at least three kinds of addiction or dependency. *Physical addiction* results in unpleasant withdrawal symptoms, including, nausea, headache, or cold sweats when the abuser does not take the drug. Sudden withdrawal from some physically addictive drugs can cause heart failure. *Psychological addiction,* more subtle, is a stage at which the abuser believes he or she cannot cope without the drug. In *functional addiction,* the abuser grows dependent on such drugs as decongestant nasal sprays to remain free of an annoying physical condition.

Definitions of Dependence and Addiction

Dependence and addiction is used to describe the compulsive and uncontrollable use of a substance. The use continues despite negative effects on health, lifestyle, work, or other aspects of one's life. Lack of the substance leads to craving, physical or psychological discomfort, and, at times, an overwhelming desire to obtain more of the substance to alleviate the negative sensations experienced from withdrawal.

Psychological dependence or addiction occurs when the user feels he or she cannot manage without the drug. This can occur for several reasons, with several types of drugs. The condition can be mild or can be extraordinarily severe.

Psychological addiction to painkillers—and this can include ibuprofen (Motrin), aspirin, and acetaminophen (Tylenol)—occurs when the user feels that pain may be too great without regular medication. As pain occurs without use, it fulfills the user's expectations. The pain may be real or may be psychosomatic (triggered by psychological expectations of pain), but it reassures the user that the drug is needed and does good. The problem is that with many types of drug, the effectiveness decreases as use increases.

Psychological addiction can accompany physical addiction, and it is usually difficult to distinguish where psychological needs leave off and physical needs begin. Many addictions are a combination of psychological and physical.

Physical dependence or addiction occurs when the body has developed a physical need for the drug. Physical dependence is usually recognized when the user stops taking the drug. Withdrawal symptoms occur when the body is denied the chemicals to which it has become habituated. Withdrawal symptoms can include dizziness, anxiety, restless sleep, dull ache, acute pain, heart tremors, seizures and convulsions, and heart attack. Sudden withdrawal from some physically addictive drugs can kill the user. Many of the street drugs, such as cocaine and heroin, and many of the prescription drugs, such as Xanax and codeine, can produce severe symptoms if withdrawal is sudden from quantities that were abusive.

Tolerance is the term used for the effect that occurs when the quantity of drug is progressively increased to achieve the desired result. For some chemicals, the body becomes habituated to one quantity and the dosage must be increased to maintain the same level of relief or pleasure experienced from the drug. Increased tolerance for some drugs is what frequently leads to levels that are physically addictive.

Three Classes of Prescription Drugs

Among the drugs that may be prescribed for you are some that have a tremendous potential for abuse. They include *stimulants,* such as amphetamines; *depressants,* such as sleeping pills; and *narcotic* painkillers, including morphine and codeine. When abused (that is, when taken in any way other than according to a physician's strict instructions) these drugs constitute a substantial part of America's burgeoning national drug problem.

Stimulant Drugs

The legitimate use of stimulant drugs and their great capacity for abuse stem from the same property: their ability to speed up the processes of the central nervous system. Physicians may prescribe amphetamines primarily to curb the appetites of patients who are dieting or to counteract mild depression. More rarely, they use stimulant drugs to treat *narcolepsy,* a disease in which the patient is subject to irresistible bouts of sleep, and to counteract the drowsiness caused by sedatives. Amphetamines and an amphetamine-like drug (Ritalin) may be used to treat some hyperactive children who are extremely excitable and easily distracted. For reasons that are imperfectly understood, the drug calms these children instead of stimulating them.

Amphetamines

The major forms of the amphetamines are: amphetamine (Benzedrine), the more powerful dextroamphetamine (Dexedrine), and methamphetamine (Methedrine, Desoxyn). The street name for these drugs is "speed."

The consumption of amphetamines is reportedly far greater than the prescription books indicate. Some 10 billion tablets are produced in the United States annually, enough for 50 doses for every man, woman, and child. Of this amount, probably half is diverted into illicit channels. Underground laboratories manufacture even more.

Abusers of amphetamines include students cramming for exams, housewives trying to get through the day without collapsing from exhaustion, and the businessman who has tossed and turned all night in a strange hotel bedroom and needs to be alert for a conference the next morning.

Used judiciously, amphetamines can improve performance, both mental and physical, over moderate periods of time. In effect, they delay the deterioration in performance that fatigue normally produces. Required to carry out routine duties under difficult circumstances and for extended periods, some astronauts have used amphetamines under long-range medical supervision.

Amphetamines give some persons feelings of self-confidence, well-being, alertness, and an increased ability to concentrate and perform. Others may experience an increase in tension ranging from the uncomfortable to an agonizing pitch of anxiety. High doses may produce dry mouth, sweating, palpitations, and raised blood pressure. Because amphetamines only defer the effects of fatigue, the letdown can be dangerous, especially for such users as long-distance truck drivers. In addition, the feelings of self-confidence about improved performance may be highly deceptive. Some college students who have crammed for exams while on speed have turned in blank examination books, or written a whole essay on one dense line.

Amphetamine abusers quickly develop a tolerance to the drug. They may have continually to increase dosages, and may undergo different kinds of drug experiences. Psychological dependence can build rapidly.

Amphetaminelike Stimulants

Several drugs that are chemically unrelated to the amphetamines produce very similar effects on the body. They are, also, equally amenable to abuse. Among them are methylphenidate (Ritalin) and phenmetrazine (Preludin). The latter has been commonly used as a diet pill.

Cocaine

Ranked as powerful stimulants to the central nervous system, cocaine and its derivatives have become the trendy drugs of the late 20th century. An alkaloid found in the leaves of the coca bush, *Erythroxylon coca,* cocaine in its crystalline form is a white powder that looks like moth flakes. Cocaine can be sniffed, smoked, or taken intravenously. Abusers of cocaine may or may not develop a tolerance for the drug. But some evidence indicates that the same dose repeated frequently will not produce similar effects over a period of time.

Very little street-purchased cocaine is pure. Usually, the drug is mixed, or cut, with other drugs or with substances that resemble it, such as talcum powder or sugar.

Physical dependence on cocaine is rare. Psychological dependence is much more common. When physical dependence occurs, the withdrawal symptoms may include hunger, irritability, extreme fatigue, depression, and restless sleep. With psychological dependence, abusers come to need the feeling of euphoria induced by cocaine. When a dose wears off, the abuser may go into a period of deep depression.

The use of cocaine as a legal anesthetic need not lead to addiction. It has been used particularly in surgical operations on the mouth, eyes, and throat because it can constrict blood vessels and because it is rapidly absorbed by the mucous membranes.

Cocaine's effects as a stimulant last only a short time. Generally, the effects depend on the size of the dose. A small dose may produce sensations of euphoria and illusions of increased strength and sensory awareness. A large dose may magnify these effects. The abuser may engage in irrational behavior, and may experience such physical side effects as sweating, di-

lation of the pupils, and rapid heartbeat.

In extreme cases abusers may have hallucinations and feelings of paranoia and depression. They may imagine that insects are crawling over their skins (formication) and may have chest pains. Injections by needle may produce skin abscesses. Both heavy and light users may develop runny noses, eczema around the nostrils, and deterioration of the nasal cartilage. The latter occurs because cocaine is usually "snorted" into the nostrils through a straw or a roll of paper, or from a spoon.

Death results, occasionally, from overdoses of cocaine, with respiratory arrest as a prime cause. The abuser may also have high fever, heart rhythm disturbances, or convulsions.

Crack Cocaine

By a simple process dealers in cocaine can convert cocaine in white powder form, cocaine hydrochloride, into cocaine alkaloid, called *freebase.* The process involves mixing powdered cocaine with baking soda and water to form a paste. Once the concoction hardens, it looks like lumpy, off-white granulated sugar. Unlike powdered cocaine, the drug in this form, called *crack* or *rock,* can be smoked, eliminating the need for needles.

However made, crack is a purified cocaine base that is usually smoked in a special pipe with wire screens, or sprinkled on a tobacco or marijuana cigarette. The drug produces a high that may start in eight seconds and last two minutes. By contrast, snorted cocaine takes effect after about five minutes.

Crack produces a very intense euphoria along with other physical symptoms. Because the drug in this form is far more potent than powdered cocaine, the heartbeat speeds up and the abuser's blood pressure may rise. Heart-lung problems may follow, and seizures can occur. Death may ensue. Because of the variations in the strength and purity of crack, and because of the variability of a body's response, death can occur on the first use or the thousandth. Abuse of crack may lead to physical addiction in weeks, with the victim needing continually larger doses to achieve a high.

Depressant Drugs

Making up a second class of medically useful drugs that are also widely abused, the depressants act as sedatives on the central nervous system (CNS). They may also act as hypnotic, or sleep-inducing, agents.

The depressants include mainly the barbiturates, which are both sedative and hypnotic, and the tranquilizers, which can calm without producing sleep. Though they are available as main or secondary constituents of more than 80 brand name preparations, the barbiturates are readily abused.

Tranquilizers act selectively on the brain and the central nervous system. Divided into major and minor tranquilizers, these drugs are similar to barbiturates in many ways, including their sedative or calming effect. The major tranquilizers, called *neuroleptics* because they are useful in the treatment of mental disorders, are *haloperidol* and *chlorpromazine*. These drugs lead to virtually no addiction or dependence even in long-term therapy.

The minor tranquilizers, among them *meprobamate* (Miltown), *chlordiazepoxide* (Librium), and *diazepam* (Valium), are, by contrast, highly addictive. Abusers take such drugs to achieve euphoric states as well as to offset the effects of alcohol, amphetamines, and other drugs.

Barbiturates

Barbiturates have many legitimate uses. For example, they may be prescribed to overcome insomnia, reduce high blood pressure, alleviate anxiety, treat mental disorders, and sedate patients both before and after surgery. Barbiturates may help to bring epileptic and other convulsions under control.

Barbiturates are metabolized, or broken down chemically, by the liver. They are then eliminated by the kidneys at different speeds depending on their types: slow- or long-acting, intermediate and short-acting, or ultra-short-acting. The first of these, primarily phenobarbital and barbital, take effect on the brain in one to two hours and last for six to 24 hours. The intermediate and short-acting barbiturates, including secobarbital and pentobarbital, take effect in 20 to 45 minutes and last five to six hours. The best known of the ultra-short-acting drugs, sodium pentothal or thiopental, can produce unconsciousness in a few minutes. Used mostly in hospitals as an anesthetic, pentothal is also injected by dentists to produce instant unconsciousness.

Abuse

Barbiturate abusers usually select the ultra-short-acting form of the drug because of the rapid action. Abusers as a group generally fall into four categories, with some overlap.

The "silent abuser" takes sleeping pills at first to get some sleep, probably with a physician's prescription. Progressively, the drug helps the abuser to deal with tension and anxiety. Indulging at home, he or she finds the barbiturates producing an alcohol-like high, with slurred speech, confusion, poor judgment and coordination, and sometimes wild emotional swings. Eventually the abuser is obtaining the drug through illicit channels. Some may end up spending most of their time in bed.

A second group, taking barbiturates for stimulation, has already developed a high tolerance that makes drug stimulation possible. Some other abusers find that the drug releases inhibitions.

Made up mostly of young people who are experimenting with various drugs, a third group uses barbiturates to "come down" from an amphetamine high. Members of this group may find themselves in a vicious cycle of stimulation and sedation. To obtain both effects at once, some abusers take the barbiturate-amphetamine combination in the same swallow—a so-called "set-up."

A fourth group, abusers of heroin and other narcotics, uses barbiturates as a substitute when drugs of choice are not available. They may also combine barbiturates with heroin to prolong its effect. In one hospital surveyed, 23 percent of the narcotics users said they were also dependent on barbiturates.

Effects and Dangers

Barbiturate abuse is generally considered to be far more dangerous than narcotic abuse. Every year brings some 3,000 deaths from barbiturate overdose, accidental or intentional. For such reasons many physicians believe barbiturates are the most dangerous of all drugs. Chronic abuse can lead to psychological dependence and increased tolerance, followed often by physical dependence of a particularly anguishing kind.

Abrupt withdrawal from barbiturates can be much more dangerous than withdrawal from heroin. Within a day the abuser withdrawing from barbiturates may experience headaches, muscle twitches, anxiety, weakness, nausea, and blood pressure drops. If the abuser stands up suddenly he or she may faint. Delirium and convulsions may come later. The latter can be fatal. Thus the withdrawal must always be undertaken under medical supervision. Even with supervision, a withdrawal from barbiturates may take two months.

Abuse of barbiturates presents other dangers. Unintentional overdosing frequently occurs when a person takes a regular dose to get to sleep and then remains awake or awakens soon afterward; tired and confused, the person may take another or repeated doses. Death may result. Mixing barbiturates and alcohol can produce the same outcome.

Other Barbiturate-Type Drugs

Some depressants are chemically unrelated to the barbiturates but have similar effects. These include *glutethimide, ethchlorvynol* (Placidyl), and *methyprylon* (Noludar). These too lead to tolerance when abused and sometimes to psychological and physical dependence.

Tranquilizers

The minor tranquilizers are manufactured as capsules and tablets in many sizes, shapes, and colors. They may also be purchased in liquid form for injection. Used legitimately to treat emotional tension and as muscle re-

Varieties of abused drugs

Name	Form	Drug
amphetamine methamphetamine	capsule, pill, liquid, powder, tablet, lozenge; swallowed	stimulant
barbiturate	sleeping pills, capsules, tablets; swallowed; injected	depressant, sedative
cocaine	white powder; sniffed, smoked, injected	stimulant, local anesthetic
hashish	resin; smoked	relaxant, euphoriant, hallucinogen (in large or strong doses)
heroin	powder; injected, or sniffed	narcotic
inhalants (for example, gasoline, paint, glue, aerosols, amyl nitrite)	aerosols, volatile substances, solvents; sniffed	
LSD (d-lysergic acid diethylamide)	tablet, capsule, liquid; swallowed	hallucinogen (psychedelic)
marijuana, marihuana	dried leaves; smoked	relaxant, euphoriant, hallucinogen (in large or strong doses)
mescaline	tablet, capsule; swallowed	hallucinogen
PCP	powder; smoked, swallowed	anesthetic (used only with animals)

laxants, these tranquilizers have high abuse potential because they produce both psychological and physical dependence. Tolerance develops with prolonged abuse.

Miltown, Librium, and Valium produce effects similar to those of barbiturates. But the minor tranquilizers act more slowly and have longer duration. Once considered completely harmless, these drugs came into such vogue that in the 1970s the federal government intervened. Both Valium and Librium as well as some other drugs were placed under federal control. From 1975 on anyone requiring a prescription for these drugs was limited to five prescription refills within a six-month period following the initial prescription. If more of the medication was required after that, a new prescription had to be written.

Withdrawal from the minor tranquilizers can be as dangerous and painful as withdrawal from barbiturates. Combining the tranquilizing drugs with others, including alcohol, is a highly dangerous form of abuse. Each drug reinforces the effects of the other. The result may be greater

than the combined effects of the different drugs.

Narcotics (Opiates)

Narcotics are drugs that relieve pain and induce sleep by depressing the central nervous system. Under U.S. law, narcotics are addictive drugs that produce rapid and severe physical and psychological dependence; that category includes opium and such opium derivatives as heroin, morphine, and codeine. The narcotics, or *opioids*, also include the so-called synthetic opiates, among them *meperidine* and *methadone.*

Opium

The seedpods of the opium poppy, *Papaver somniferum,* produce a gummy resin that has narcotic effects when eaten or smoked. Opium has been used in many lands and many cultures since prehistoric times. It was used medicinally in ancient Egypt. But not until recently did its addictive properties become known.

Of the more than two dozen active compounds, or *alkaloids,* that can be isolated from opium, the two most important are morphine and codeine.

Morphine

Morphine, named after Morpheus, the Roman god of dreams, is the chemical substance in opium that gives it sedative and analgesic properties. Isolated initially in the early 1800s, morphine was later synthesized in pure form. On the illicit drug market it appears usually as a white powder.

Morphine can relieve almost any kind of pain, particularly dull, continuous pain. It may also relieve the fear and anxiety that go with such suffering. In addition to drowsiness, euphoria, and impairment of mental and physical performance, morphine may have adverse effects including nausea, vomiting, and sweating. Intravenous injections of the drug may produce an orgasmic high sensation beginning in the upper abdomen and spreading throughout the body. Taken in overdose, morphine can lead to respiratory depression that is sometimes severe enough to cause coma and death. Morphine is highly addictive and is used only short-term in hospitals because longer exposure easily leads to problems. Naloxone (Narcan) may be administered intravenously as an antidote for morphine overdose.

Codeine

Taking its name from the Greek word *kodeia,* meaning poppyhead, codeine is a mild pain-reliever that can be produced from gum opium or through conversion from morphine. The effects of codeine peak in 30 to 60 minutes; they disappear in three to four hours. Codeine is milder than either morphine or heroin in analgesic effect, and is an ingredient in some popular nonprescription cough syrups. All forms can induce addiction problems with regular use.

Heroin

Originally thought to be nonaddictive, heroin was for a time used as a cure for opium and morphine addiction. It was then found to be more addictive than either of those drugs. It was prohibited in the United States in 1924 and became a staple on the drug black market. Heroin is several times as powerful as morphine.

All of the opiates, including heroin, produce feelings of well-being or euphoria. They also lead to dulled senses and to reduction or elimination of normal fears, tensions, and anxiety. The drug also produces sleepiness and lethargy; *nodding* is one of the characteristic symptoms of abuse. Possible side effects include nausea, flushing, constipation, slowed respiration rates, retention of urine, and, eventually, malnutrition resulting from loss of appetite. When first injecting heroin, nausea and vomiting can occur almost immediately.

The heroin abuser rapidly develops tolerance to the drug. Continually larger doses are then required to produce the same degree of euphoria. Used chronically, heroin leads to both psychological and physical dependence. The former is far more important, and is more difficult to break.

Caught in a cycle involving desperate efforts to obtain enough money, often by criminal means, and getting high, the heroin abuser is not necessarily driven by the search for escape. He or she may want, equally, to avoid withdrawal symptoms. For the chronic abuser these symptoms can
be difficult and painful, and may include anxiety, sweating, muscle aches, vomiting, and diarrhea.

Heroin sold on the streets is cut with quinine, milk sugar, or baking soda. It may be cut several times before reaching the abuser. A bag may contain only 1 to 5 percent heroin. If the addict unknowingly buys a dose containing 30 percent or more pure heroin, the higher concentration can spell grave illness or death.

Because heroin can be taken in different ways, the drug's narcotic effects are variable. Sniffing is the mildest form of abuse, followed by skin-popping or subcutaneous injection anywhere on the body, and mainlining, injection directly into a vein, usually the large vein inside the elbow. Abscesses at the preferred site of injection are common, and the vein may become inflamed.

Heroin use does not necessarily lead to dependence. Many persons have experimented with the drug without becoming addicted. Others "joy-pop"—use the drug on weekends, usually for recreational purposes or "kicks."

Little agreement exists regarding treatments for heroin abuse. A promising yet controversial method is the substitution of controlled doses of *methadone* for heroin. Methadone is a synthetic opiate that does not produce the euphoria of heroin. The substitution can help the abuser to lead a normal life, but he or she may still be addicted—to methadone.

Other forms of treatment utilize group psychotherapy, often in live-in communities modeled after the West Coast's *Synanon.* Some experts believe that only multiple-approach treatment formats, combining chemical treatment, psychiatry, user communities, and rehabilitation, can be effective. But the five-year cure rate for heroin abusers is low—only about one-third of that for alcoholics.

Synthetic Opiates

Prescription pain-relievers such as Demerol, Dilaudid, Pantopon, and other synthetic opiates can become addicting if used indiscriminately. They occasionally appear on the illicit drug market. With the increased availability of methadone in treatment clinics, methadone itself is used illicitly, often in combination with alcohol or other drugs, and especially when heroin is in short supply.

The Hallucinogens: LSD and Others

LSD (lysergic acid diethylamide) is one of a class of drugs legally classed as *hallucinogens*—agents that cause the user to experience hallucinations, illusions, and distorted perceptions. Others include *mescaline, psilocybin* and *psilocin, PCP, DMT* (dimethyltryptamine), and *DOM* or *STP*.

A colorless, tasteless, odorless compound, LSD is a semisynthetic acid of immense potency. A single effective dose requires, on the average, only 100 millionths of a gram. A quantity of LSD equivalent to two aspirin tablets would furnish 6,500 such doses. When sold on the street, LSD is generally mixed with colored substances. It may be manufactured in capsule, tablet, or liquid form.

History of LSD

With names such as *California sunshine, acid, purple haze,* and others, LSD reached a peak of popularity in the 1960s. Today it cannot be made legally except for use in certain supervised experiments. Physicians may use it to treat alcoholism and some mental disease, but without uniformly convincing results. It may be sold illegally in sugar cubes, candy, cookies, on the surfaces of beads, even in the mucilage of stamps and envelopes. One dose may produce a 4- to 18-hour *trip,* a hallucinogenic experience.

In the 1960s this trip made LSD the drug of choice for many substance abusers. Among those who claimed that LSD and other psychedelic drugs were consciousness-expanding were well-known public figures. The drugs, in brief, were supposed to enhance the user's appreciation of everything in the environment, to increase creativity, open the gates of awareness to mind-bending mystical or religious experiences, and perhaps to bring about profound changes, hopefully for the better, in the user's personality.

While some users reported such results, various studies suggested that the improvements were illusory. Members of some groups nonetheless felt that it was "in" to be an *acidhead,* an LSD user. One authority estimates that less than 1 percent of the total population have experimented with LSD. Partly because knowledge of dangers in LSD use has become common, the drug has passed the peak of its popularity even though it can still be obtained illegally.

Addictive Aspects

Abuse of LSD is difficult; the drug produces such a spectacular high that daily ingestion is virtually out of the question. Thus LSD use does not lead to physical dependence. But the heavy user can develop a tolerance for the drug very quickly. The tolerance disappears after a few days of abstinence.

Effects

Taking LSD, the individual is usually prepared for minor physical discomforts: a rise in temperature, pulse, and blood pressure; the sensation of hair standing on end; and some nausea, dizziness, and headache. The trip begins about an hour after the drug is first taken. Vision is affected the most profoundly. Colors become more intense and more beautiful; those in a painting may seem to merge and stream. Flat objects become three-dimensional.

The LSD user's reactions are closely related to his or her expectations. Thus one trip may be mind-expanding, filled with brilliant sights and sensations as well as euphoric feelings of oneness with the universe. Another trip may bring anxiety, panic, fear, and depression verging on despair. The latter experience can be terrifying; some bad trips have ended in psychiatric wards, with the tripper suffering from a severe mental disorder, a *psychosis.* An individual's body image may be distorted; in the LSD-induced vision he or she may have no head, for example. Such psychotic episodes, or breaks, may clear up within a day or two. Others can last for months or years.

Some trips have ended in tragedy. Convinced that they could fly or float through the air, some trippers have walked through high windows to their deaths. Others have walked in front of trains or cars.

In effect, no one can predict what psychological changes LSD use will produce. One reason is that no one really knows how LSD works inside the body to affect the mind. What is known is that the drug moves quickly to the brain and throughout the body, acting on both the central and autonomic nervous systems. But all traces of the drug disappear from the brain in some 20 minutes. The effects, as noted, last many more hours.

As with all drugs, LSD should not be ingested by persons who have psychotic tendencies or who are unstable. A disquieting side effect, usually occurring after chronic or heavy use, appears in the flashback, a reexperiencing of the effects of the drug weeks or months after a trip. One theory holds that flashbacks are induced by stress or fatigue, or by resort to other drugs, but the theory remains a theory.

Studies have reported some statistical findings. One research project found that the children of LSD users are 18 times more likely to have birth defects than the children of nonusers. Some research also suggests that the drug may have toxic effects on some cells of the human body. An unproved, and possibly unprovable, theory indicates that there may be a link between LSD use and breaks in chromosomes that could conceivably lead to leukemia or to birth defects in users' children.

Other Hallucinogens

Many other substances, both natural and synthetic, are used as hallucinogens. Most of them produce effects similar to those of LSD, but are far less potent.

Mescaline

Mescaline is the active ingredient of *peyote,* a Mexican cactus that has been used by American Indians for centuries to achieve mystical states in religious ceremonies. Users consume cactus "buttons" either ground up or whole. Mescaline itself may be obtained as a powder or a liquid. It can also be synthesized in a laboratory.

Psilocybin and Psilocin

Psilocybin and psilocin are the active hallucinogenic ingredients in the Aztec mushroom *Psilocybe mexicana.* The mushroom grows in southern Mexico and has been eaten raw by the natives since about 1500 B.C. Both derivatives can be made in the laboratory.

PCP (Phencyclidine Hydrochloride)

First developed in 1959 as an anesthetic, PCP in its pure form is a white crystalline powder that is readily soluble in water or alcohol. It appears on the drug black market as tablets, capsules, and colored powders. Abusers snort, smoke, or eat PCP. They can also inject the drug, but do not usually do so. PCP appears as an adulterant in many drug mixtures—in mescaline, psilocybin, or LSD, for example. PCP reportedly has as many or more undesirable effects as positive ones, among them forgetfulness, loss of behavior control, feelings of depersonalization, paranoid episodes, hallucinations, and suicidal impulses.

DMT (Dimethyltryptamine)

Called the "businessman's high" because its effects may last only 40 to 50 minutes, DMT is similar in structure to psilocin. DMT can be smoked or injected; in either case the effect is a powerful wave of exhilaration. An ingredient of various plants native to South America, DMT has long been used by Indian tribes in the form of intoxicating drinks or snuff, often very dangerous. In the United States, DMT is synthesized from tryptamine in the laboratory.

DOM or STP

DOM or STP is a synthetic compound originally developed by the Dow Chemical Company for possible use in the treatment of mental disorders. The drug was never released. Manufactured illicitly, it was allegedly given the name STP for Serenity, Tranquility, Peace. The drug is powerful, it produces vivid hallucinations, and it seems to last as long as LSD. It is also extremely poisonous, and can bring on fever, blurred vision, difficulty in swallowing, and occasionally death from convulsions. In some cases abusers suffer from manic psychoses lasting for days.

Marijuana (Cannabinoids)

Marijuana, or *marihuana,* is a Mexican-Spanish word originally used to refer to a poor grade of tobacco. Later it came to mean a smoking preparation made from the Indian hemp plant (*Cannabis sativa*). A tall, weedy plant related to the fig tree and the hop, cannabis grows freely in many parts of the world and in a variety of grades depending on climate and method of cultivation. The different grades produce drugs of varying strengths. Some 300 million people around the world obtain drug preparations of one kind or another from cannabis.

Drugs are obtained almost exclusively from the female hemp plants. The male plants produce the fiber for hemp. When the female plants are ripe, late in the summer, their top leaves and especially the clusters of flowers at their tops develop a minty, sticky, golden-yellow resin, which eventually blackens. This resin contains the highest concentrations of THC (tetrahydrocannabinol), the group of substances containing the active principles of the drug. The pure resin of carefully cultivated plants is the most potent form of cannabis. It is available in cakes, called *charas* in India, and as a brown powder called hashish in the Middle East.

An estimated 15,000 tons of marijuana are illegally smuggled into the United States annually. But cannabis cultivation has become a major underground business inside the United

States. Most illegal shipments of the drug come from Colombia, Jamaica, and Mexico.

Abuse Potential

Marijuana has puzzling aspects. Scientists have not succeeded in establishing exactly what substances in the cannabis plant produce drug effects, or how. THC is, of course, believed to be the most important active element, but chemists believe it is not the only one.

Beyond that, marijuana seems to be in a special class as a drug. It is classed as a hallucinogen, but is less potent than the true hallucinogens. It is not a narcotic, and it resembles both stimulants and depressants in some of its effects. Its use does not lead to physical dependence, nor does the user or abuser develop tolerance. Some users, in fact, find that with regular use they need less marijuana to achieve the desired high.

Users do acquire a slight to moderate psychological dependence—less, in some experts' opinions, than do regular users of alcohol or tobacco. Thus much of the theorizing about marijuana is conjecture despite the fact that millions of persons use it regularly or occasionally.

Effects

Experimenters and newcomers to marijuana smoking may experience little at the beginning. A sense of panic may accompany early exposure to the drug. More serious reactions have been reported, however, including *toxic-psychosis* (psychosis caused by a toxic agent) with accompanying confusion and disorientation. But such reports are rare. Experimenters using large doses of marijuana, hashish, or THC have induced what they termed hallucinations and psychotic reactions.

The experienced smoker may feel halfway between elation and sleepiness. He or she may have some altered perceptions of sound or color, for example, and a greatly sloweddown sense of time. It is usually possible to control the extent of the high by stopping when a given point is reached. The smoker often experiences mild headache or nausea.

Medical Evidence

Research and medical use of marijuana have led to some relatively tentative findings. Some evidence indicates, for example, that the drug may produce genetic damage. More definitely, marijuana has been found to be effective for reducing the pressure of fluids in the eyes of patients suffering from glaucoma. In a 1976 case, the Food and Drug Administration (FDA) approved the use of marijuana for such treatment.

In 1985 the FDA licensed a small drug firm to manufacture THC for use in combating the nausea associated with cancer chemotherapy. Other studies indicated that the drug may also be useful in the treatment of such other diseases as multiple sclerosis.

The debate over full legalization of marijuana promises to continue. Few argue that all penalties for major suppliers should be dropped, at least as long as marijuana remains illegal. But many persons see a contradiction in sending a young person to prison for smoking a marijuana cigarette while his or her parents can drink three martinis every evening.

Inhalants

The inhalants as a class include solvents used in cleaning compounds, aerosol sprays, fuels, and glues. Abusers of these substances sniff or inhale the fumes for recreational and mind-altering purposes. But the substances, primarily chemical compounds, were never meant for human consumption. With some exceptions, they are available commercially and thus have appeal for persons who cannot afford or cannot obtain the more conventional drugs.

Strictly speaking, tobacco, cocaine, and marijuana could be considered inhalants. But the term more commonly refers to three categories of products: solvents, aerosols, and anesthetics. Among the solvents are commercial items such as gasoline, transmission fluid, paint thinner, and airplane cement. The aerosol products include shoeshine compounds, insecticides, spray paints, and hair spray. The type of inhalant used appears to vary according to geographic location, the ethnic backgrounds of abusers, and availability.

Anesthetics comprise a special group of inhalants. Some of them, including nitrous oxide, ether, and chloroform, were used recreationally before medical applications were found for them. Because they are not widely available, they are not abused as much as solvents and aerosols.

Abuse Patterns

Young teenagers are primary inhalant abusers. But some groups or classes of adults, such as prisoners in institutions, also use inhalants. Reasons for abuse vary; among teenagers they range from hostility and lack of affection to peer pressure. Adults, say authorities, are attracted by the ready availability of many inhalants. Alcoholics may resort to inhalants while trying to forestall the symptoms of withdrawal from alcohol.

Effects

Among the active chemicals in many inhalants are toluene, naphtha, carbon tetrachloride, acetone, and others. The fumes from these chemicals enter the bloodstream quickly. They are then distributed to the brain and liver. Entering the central nervous system, the fumes depress such body functions as respiration and heartbeat.

Classed as depressants, inhalants are sometimes referred to as "deliriants." The reason is that they can produce illusions, hallucinations, and mental disturbances. These effects usually result in cases of overdose; in moderate doses, the abuser feels sedated, has changed perceptions and impaired judgment, and may experience fright or even panic. Depending on the dosage, the abuser may also feel intoxicated, and may have lowered inhibitions along with feelings of restlessness, uncoordination, confusion, and disorientation.

Prolonged abuse can lead to nausea, muscular weakness, fatigue, and weight loss. Other effects of such abuse can be extensive damage to the kidneys, bone marrow, liver, and brain. Inhalants have been implicated in some forms of cancer. A high can last from a few minutes to an hour or more. Repeated dosing can produce physical and psychological dependence; but inhalants are not considered as dangerously addictive as other depressants.

In the 1960s the many deaths resulting from glue-sniffing made inhalant abuse a matter of nationwide concern. Studies reported later that about two-thirds of these deaths came about because the abusers, usually children, put plastic bags over their heads to intensify the effect and suffocated.

More recently, deaths have occurred from children experimenting with all types of aerosol sprays and fumes and dying either from toxic poisoning or suffocating in their own vomit after they pass out.

Where to Find Help

Substance abuse has many disturbing aspects aside from the physical, psychological, and social damage that it can cause. With addictive medicines, the progression from a *therapeutic* dose—the amount prescribed by a physician—to a *toxic* dose may seem, to some persons, natural and even inevitable. Ingestion or injection of a *lethal* dose may follow as an unintended consequence.

Other factors are causes for concern. The proliferation of illicit street drugs, the rapidity with which dependence or addiction can develop, and the costs and complexity of treatment or detoxification programs all add to the dangers inherent in abuse as a spreading phenomenon. Researchers are discovering weapons that may help in some cases to make treatment more effective: *naloxone* (Narcan), for example, can be given intravenously to reduce the toxic effects of narcotics. But too often a drug has done irreversible harm in a human system before help arrives.

American society has begun to mobilize resources to aid those who need information, assistance, or counsel, for themselves or others, in cases of substance abuse. A National Partnership to Prevent Drug and Alcohol Abuse has established a network of community groups to inform teenagers about narcotics and their potentially disastrous effects. Among helplines and hotlines is one operated by Fair Oaks Hospital in Summit, New Jersey, with the toll-free number 800-COCAINE. Counselors serving with 800-COCAINE are linked to a network of treatment centers and hospitals throughout the country. The addresses and telephone numbers of four national groups, including Fair Oaks Hospital and its program, are:

National Federation of Parents for Drug-Free Youth
1423 N. Jefferson
Springfield, MO 65802
417/836-3709

American Counsel for Drug Education
204 Monroe, Suite 110
Rockville, MD 20850
301/294-0600

National Parent Resource Institute for Drug Education (PRIDE)
50 Hurt Plaza, Suite 210
Atlanta, GA 30303
404/577-4500

Fair Oaks Hospital
19 Prospect Street
Summit, NJ 07901
800/COCAINE

30

The Environment and Health

How pure is the soil in which our food grows? How clean is the air we breathe or the water we drink? How healthy are the animals that provide substantial portions of our diets?

The Environmental Protection Agency (EPA) monitors, among other things, the level of pollutants in drinking water, the disposal of toxic wastes, the threat of radiation from nuclear power plants and the seepage of poisonous chemicals.

Harmful ingredients in the environment may be the result of pollution, accidental or intentional. Some enter the environment as a result of deliberate planning. Asbestos, for example, a mineral fiber that will not burn, was used widely to insulate and fireproof buildings. The EPA banned the use of asbestos in construction in the 1970s, after researchers proved the fiber caused diseases and several forms of cancer.

Major health hazards fall in four categories: Air, water and noise pollution and food contamination. Other hazards include toxic wastes, nuclear radiation, and work-place dangers.

Air Pollution

Air pollutants can damage health in a number of ways. Even where little scientific proof links these pollutants to specific maladies, much statistical or circumstantial evidence suggests that air pollution can lead to various forms of respiratory disease. Some cases of air pollution outside the workplace and exclusive of nuclear radiation hazards have been documented.

Inversions

An inversion is a freak weather condition in which a mass of warm air rests like a lid on top of cooler air. The warm air traps the lower air and prevents the pollutants in it from being ventilated. The results can be deadly, as in 1948 in Donora, Pennsylvania. Situated in a valley, at the center of an industrial complex, the town found its air becoming more and more polluted over a six-day period, as daytime visibility dwindled to a few yards. Residents eventually had difficulty breathing; more than half of the valley's 14,000 inhabitants were coughing and gasping for breath. Thousands were hospitalized and twenty-two persons died. Physicians used adrenalin to keep older people alive.

Sulfur Dioxide

Sulfur dioxide enters the air from many sources. In the main, however, it is spewed into the atmosphere when heavy fuel oil and coal are burned to provide heat, generate electricity, and provide industrial power. Large cities are especially vulnerable because of their concentrations of heavy industry.

Sulfur dioxide apparently irritates the lungs and leads to a reduction of the lungs' oxygen-handling capacity. Persons who are particularly susceptible to carbon and sulfur dioxide-filled smogs are those suffering from bronchial asthma, chronic bronchitis, and emphysema. The respiratory systems of such persons are already defective. In emphysema, for example, the elasticity of the air sacs in the lungs has progressively broken down, usually after prolonged infection or repeated bronchial irritation. Cigarette smoking can produce such irritation; the sulfur dioxide only worsens the situation.

Lead

Substantial evidence indicates that lead in the air can cause neurological harm and impair body chemistry and bone growth. Most of the airborne lead comes from auto and smelter emissions. These are inhaled directly or they may "soak" food crops. Children are most immediately affected because they have fewer natural defenses against toxic absorption than adults. But adults too may feel the effects of such absorption. They may, for example, feel tired, cramped, or confused.

Because their bodies absorb and metabolize substances rapidly, children may have rates of lead absorption four times as high as those of adults. Workers in some industries, including the ceramic, glass, and lead industries, are also at risk. One study showed that 44 percent of the lead workers in two U.S. smelters suffered from clinical poisoning.

Specific effects of lead poisoning range across a broad spectrum. The formation of red blood cells may be inhibited even by low-level exposure to lead in the air. At higher levels, lead may cause anemia. In children, bone cell growth may be stunted; in pregnant women, lead may prevent the normal development of the fetal skeleton. But lead affects the brain primarily, in some cases interfering with motor skills, auditory development, memory, and the nervous system. Children with higher levels of lead absorption have been found to have serious learning disabilities. Fortunately, lead levels may fluctuate, and the lead in blood and soft tissue may pass out of the human system four to six weeks after exposure ends. But lead remains in bone for periods lasting as long as three decades.

Other Fuel Contaminants

Auto exhausts are major sources of other air pollutants besides lead. Exhaust emissions, for example, may include nitrogen oxides, carbon monoxide, hydrocarbons, and soot. The latter is made up of visible particles of carbon suspended in the air.

Nitrogen oxides irritate the eyes and the respiratory tract. When nitrogen oxide and hydrocarbons mix in sunlight, they form other noxious substances in the typical photochemical smog that has a yellowish cast. The new ingredients include *ozone,* a poisonous form of oxygen, and peroxyacetyl nitrate (PAN), which is intensely irritating to the eyes. Los Angeles was the first city to experience these smogs; they now occur in many other cities as well.

Worst of all, auto exhaust hydrocarbons include varieties that are possible *carcinogens,* causes of cancer in susceptible individuals.

Acid Rain

While so-called *acid rain* has not been found to harm humans directly, scientists say it has begun to damage the natural food chain in certain regions. As industrial smokestacks emit pollutants, including sulfur and nitrogen oxides, these rise into the upper atmosphere. Mixed with water vapor and other substances, the airborne chemicals are changed by sunlight, becoming tiny acid droplets. The droplets fall to earth as rain or snow, raising the acid content of freshwater lakes and damaging trees and other plants. Under conditions of extreme acidity, fish populations have disappeared; where the food web is disrupted, aquatic animals, algae, and bacteria may dwindle in number. The effects of acid rain on crops and trees are less apparent but are thought to be harmful.

To some extent, acid rain is a geographic phenomenon in North America. Factories in the midwestern industrial belt throw off most of the pollutants, which are then carried east and north. Southeastern Canada and the northeastern and eastern regions of the United States are the areas primarily affected.

Indoor Air Pollution

Reports of illness associated with office and other nonresidential buildings have given rise to what has been termed the "sick building syndrome." The causes of this syndrome, or complex of symptoms, have not been completely and precisely explained. Among the possible explanations are the following:

- Building ventilation has been reduced to conserve energy, with the result that ventilation is simply inadequate

- Indoor air has become contaminated by emissions from the building fabric and associated systems, furnishings, office equipment, or maintenance materials

- Entrainment or cross contamination has taken place, with contaminants generated in a different part of the building or in a separate building drawn in by an air-handling system

- Bioeffluents, or volatile human substances, spread throughout a building, polluting the air with pyruvic acid, lactic acid, acetaldehyde, butyric acid, carbon dioxide, and other body effluents

- Combustion byproducts from smoking tobacco have produced substances, smoke included, that contaminate indoor air

- Microorganisms or airborne particles from molds, dust mites, and other sources cause such illnesses as Legionnaires Disease

A common tendency has been to identify a public building's heating, ventilating, and air conditioning (HVAC) system as the cause of indoor air pollution. But that conclusion may be premature and overly nonspecific. The symptoms described by persons affected by the sick building syndrome should be studied closely. At least four separate illnesses have been isolated according to their symptoms and causes. Hypersensitivity Pneumonitis and Humidifier Fever usually produce such symptoms as coughing, wheezing, chest tightness, muscular aches, chills, headache, fever, and fatigue. While these conditions are rarely fatal, Legionnaires Disease, produced by the bacterium *Legionella pneumonophilae,* is notable because of its 15 to 20 percent mortality rate. Both Legionnaires Disease and the relatively less serious Pontiac Fever are identified by their pneumonialike symptoms.

Carbon Monoxide

Carbon monoxide poisoning is one of the most common dangers of modern living. A colorless, odorless and tasteless gas produced whenever organic, or carbon-containing, substances burn, carbon monoxide can be lethal in poorly-ventilated spaces. The gas rapidly combines with hemoglobin to replace oxygen in the blood. The heart and the brain are most vulnerable, since they rely heavily on oxygen to function properly, and symptoms generally mimic those associated with impaired heart or brain functions: shortness of breath, nausea, headache, fatigue, weakness, dizziness, irritability, and reduced ability to concentrate. During winter is when most deaths attributed to carbon-monoxide poisoning occur, primarily due to clogged furnace exhaust systems and doors and win-

dows too tightly sealed against the cold. Other common sources are tobacco smoke, motor vehicle exhaust, house fires, wood-burning stoves and fireplaces, factory machines with gas-powered engines, charcoal-burning barbecues, kerosene heaters and water heaters that run on gas or oil. Improvements in ventilation systems and public warnings to consumers have lowered the number of carbon monoxide deaths in recent years. In addition, most hardware stores sell carbon monoxide detection devices that sound an alarm when unsafe levels of carbon monoxide are reached. Many cities now require all homeowners and landlords to install them.

Involuntary or Passive Smoking

While it has long been established that cigarettes are harmful to smokers, only in the last two decades has research begun to establish the risks of cigarette smoke to nonsmokers, those who passively inhale "secondhand" smoke. In 1986, the Surgeon General's Report examined the smoke inhaled directly by smokers and the smoke passively inhaled by nearby nonsmokers, concluding that the chemical composition of both types of smoke was similar enough to warrant further study and to issue a preliminary warning about the potential dangers. Since then, a heated debate has raged. While some research has linked passive smoking to an increased risk of diseases, including lung cancer, other research indicates a negligible effect. Despite the frequent contradictions in data, public opinion has sided with nonsmokers who fear potential harm from environmental tobacco smoke. Fewer and fewer public places even allow smoking and many cities, including New York, have legislatively declared

nearly all public spaces smoke-free environments.

The only exception to the debate on the risks of passive smoking are very young children exposed to passive smoke. Studies have proven that pregnant women who smoke not only increase their risk of miscarriage and stillbirth, but also risk delivering infants with low birthweight who, as a result, are highly susceptible to health and development problems. Infants and toddlers of smoking parents have an increased incidence of bronchitis and pneumonia and are much more likely to be hospitalized for respiratory infections than children of nonsmoking parents.

Household Chemicals

Depending on its location, structural characteristics, and other factors, the typical home may have as many as 350 or more organic chemical pollutants in its interior air. Household chemical products like spray paints, insecticides, and furniture polish disperse tiny (and toxic) droplets into the air, adding the propellant to the chemicals in the basic product. Among the hazard-producing chemicals, some solvents in particular are known or suspected carcinogens. One of the worst is methylene chloride, found in paint sprays and paint strippers and in some hair sprays and insecticides. Product labels may identify methylene chloride as a "chlorinated solution" or as "aromatic hydrocarbons."

Radon

After cigarette smoking, say scientists, the second leading cause of lung cancer may be radon gas. Considered by many to be the most dangerous of all indoor air pollutants, radon, a naturally occurring radioactive gas, diffuses out of the ground into houses that happen to be built above subsurface sources.

Invading homes, according to theU.S. Environmental Protection Agency, radon causes between 5,000and 20,000 lung cancer deaths annually. The gas breaks down into unstable elements called "radon daughters"; these become attached to particles of dust or other matter floating in the air. If breathed in, the radon daughters lodge in the linings of the lungs. Radioactive decay takes place almost at once, with the daughters emitting alpha particles that damage the adjacent lung cells, sometimes causing cancer.

Private homes can be tested for radon and, if hazardous levels are found, can be equipped with ventilation or other equipment to remove the health threat. A charcoal-based detector is available. Finally, many firms can conduct home radon checks for a fee.

Water Pollution

To an increasing extent, water pollution has prevented or limited use of many once-valuable sources of water. This progressive deterioration of the nation's water supply has resulted from years of abuse in which natural lakes and waterways were inundated with quantities of raw sewage, waste products of industrial plants and slaughterhouses, petroleum residues, poisonous herbicides and insecticides, and so on. But the pollutants generally fall into two categories: materials that change with time and contact with water, and materials that remain unchanged in form. Organic materials in sewage and such industrial wastes as pulp and paper effluents belong in the first group; inorganic salts like sodium sulfate and such inert inorganic materials as pesticides represent the second.

Communities generate thousands of tons of municipal sewage daily. Industries, the greatest users of water, utilize more than half of all the water consumed in the United States for raw material, heating and cooling processes, and transporting, sorting, and washing operations. Agriculture, the second largest user, requires millions of gallons of water for irrigation and drainage; for spraying orchards and crops, often with insecticides, fungicides, or herbicides; for removal of animal and other organic wastes; and for manufacturing operations such as meat packing and canning.

Chemical Contamination

The continuing proliferation of chemicals, many of them toxic, suggests the dimensions of the problems relating to water pollution. One estimate by the EPA's Office of Toxic Substances indicated that more than 70,000 chemicals are manufactured or processed commercially in the United States. About 1,000 new chemical compounds are added annually. Literally hundreds of these compounds find their ways into the nation's water supply, some in potentially dangerous concentrations.

How directly and to what degree chemical contaminants contribute to America's health bill cannot be gauged with accuracy. But the roles of these contaminants as carcinogens is widely accepted. Federal health officials have estimated that environmental carcinogens, including those in water, account for 55 to 60 percent of all U.S. cancer cases annually. Some estimates run much higher.

Heavy Metals

A study by the U.S. Geological Survey reported that small amounts of seven toxic metals were present in many of the nation's lakes and streams, with dangerous concentrations occurring occasionally. The metals are mercury, arsenic, cadmium, chromium, cobalt, lead, and zinc. Aside from being generally poisonous, some of these metals are implicated in specific health problems. Cadmium, as one example, has been linked to hypertension caused by kidney malfunction. Some other substances represent special situations.

Mercury

Because mercury is heavier than water, experts thought for years that it could be dumped into lakes, the oceans, and waterways. In theory, the mercury would lie harmlessly on the bottom. In reality, bacteria can convert some of the metallic part of the element into water-soluble form. The new compound enters the food chain and ends up in fish. When dangerous levels of this form of mercury were found in some waters and in food fish, warnings were issued regarding canned tuna and swordfish. The government later announced that 97 percent of the tuna on the market was safe to eat. But lakes and rivers across the country were closed to commercial and sport fishing.

An extremely toxic substance, mercury can, even in small concentrations, produce blindness, paralysis, and brain damage. The U.S. Food and Drug Administration has established the safe limit of mercury in food at half a part per million—about the equivalent of a thimbleful in an Olympic-sized swimming pool.

PCBs

Among the chief water pollutants today are the *polycholorinated biphenyls* (PCBs), highly toxic chemicals used industrially in carbonless copying paper and as an additive in lubricants, paints, printing inks, coatings, waxes, and many other products. PCBs, which are *biodegradable* (capable of decomposing) only over a period of years, have been found in unusually large quantities in waterways downstream from manufacturing plants. The EPA banned the direct discharge of PCBs into any U.S. waterway in 1977 after tests showed that fish in some rivers, like the Hudson, had levels of PCBs far higher than the permissible levels.

No one knows what the long-term effects of ingesting small quantities of PCBs will be. But the chemical is a suspected carcinogen. PCB's have also caused severe skin and eye irritations and have been implicated in reproductive disorders, kidney damage, and liver ailments. Researchers believe that the millions of pounds of PCBs in the nation's water or in landfills will take many years to dissipate.

Sludge

Sewage treatment plants around the country also face the major health challenge of disposing of the sludge, or solid matter, that is removed from sewage in the treatment process. Sludge contains not only human wastes but the residues of petroleum products, detergents, toxic heavy metals such as cadmium, lead, and zinc, and many other contaminants. Disposal methods range from dumping on land to burning and to composting for use as fertilizer. But environmental experts maintain that the use of sludge as fertilizer constitutes a health hazard; and major food processors will not accept food grown with sludge as fertilizer. In refusing such food, the companies are following guidelines set by the National Food Processors Association, which has expressed concern for farm workers'

health and for the health of the consumer.

The sludge comes from an estimated 6.8 billion gallons of sewage flushed daily into America's sewers. The sewage itself contains microorganisms that can endanger health. You may be risking gastrointestinal upsets if you swim at a beach that is posted with a sign proclaiming "polluted water." Scientists warn that the fish caught in sewage-polluted coastal waters and harbors may not only be cancerous, they may also be carcinogenic. A number of states including Michigan and New York have restricted or banned sales of tainted fish such as naturally grown carp, catfish, and striped bass.

Oil Spills

With the increasing reliance on supertankers to carry industrial and heating oil from abroad, the danger of major water-polluting oil spills in coastal areas has grown substantially. Several of these huge ships have gone aground and broken apart under heavy pounding by sea waves. Their cargoes have spilled into the oceans, where currents usually carry them many miles before they float ashore or sink to the ocean floor. The oil reaching land fouls beaches and kills water birds. Similar accidents on inland waterways have polluted rivers and lakes, killing fish and spoiling recreational areas.

Noise Pollution

"Pollution" refers generally to the various forms of physical pollution by liquids, gases, or solids. Few persons realize that we are all threatened by a pollutant so common that it tends to be overlooked: noise.

Noise assails us nearly everywhere. It fills homes with loud music or the dog's barking or the grinding of the washing machine and the workplace with the chatter of drill presses and the roar of huge engines. Neither city dwellers nor country people can live noise-free today; none of us can escape car and truck horns, motorcycles that belch sound, and the noisy throb of machinery.

Effects of Sound on the Eardrum

Noise is not just annoying; it is potentially dangerous, both physically and mentally. It has been described as "a slow agent of death." A form of energy, sound or noise is caused by anything that vibrates, that moves back and forth. Our ears receive the effects of this vibrating motion from a distance, great or small, via sound waves. These waves are successive series of regions of compressed air and partial vacuums, or areas of high and low air pressure. Sound can also travel through liquids and solids. We *hear* sound because our eardrums are moved back and forth by the changes in air pressure. The eardrum, or *tympanic membrane*, may perceive a sound that moves it only one billionth of a centimeter—the threshold of hearing. If the intensity of sound pressure becomes too great, we experience pain, and the eardrum or the delicate structures inside the ear may be damaged.

The intensity of sounds is often measured in units called *decibels,* or *db.* These units are logarithmic, that is, 10 db is ten times as powerful as 1 db, 20 db is 100 times as powerful, 30 db is 1,000 times as powerful, and so on. On this scale, 0 db is at the threshold of hearing; rustling leaves, 20 db; a quiet office, about 50 db; conversation, 60 db; heavy traffic, 90 db; a pneumatic jackhammer six feet

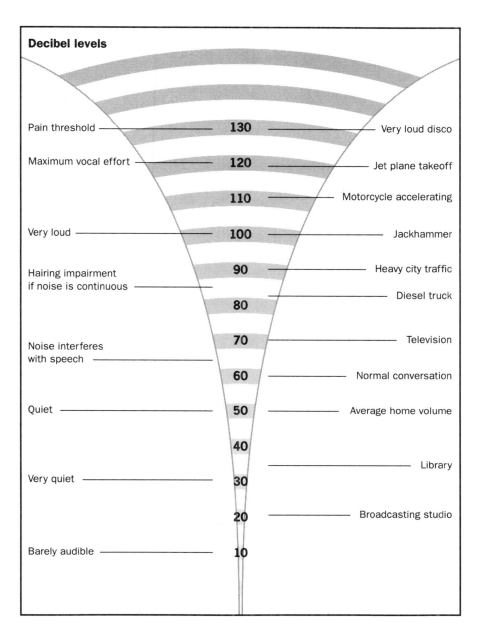

Decibel levels

Pain threshold	**130**	Very loud disco
Maximum vocal effort	**120**	Jet plane takeoff
	110	Motorcycle accelerating
Very loud	**100**	Jackhammer
	90	Heavy city traffic
Hairing impairment if noise is continuous	**80**	Diesel truck
Noise interferes with speech	**70**	Television
	60	Normal conversation
Quiet	**50**	Average home volume
	40	
Very quiet	**30**	Library
	20	Broadcasting studio
Barely audible	**10**	

away, 100 db; a jet aircraft 500 feet overhead, 115 db; a Saturn rocket's takeoff, 180 db.

For most people, the pain threshold is about 120 db; deafening ear damage can result at 150 db. But damage of various kinds can come from much lower exposures. Temporary hearing impairment can result from sounds over the 85 db now found in modern kitchens with all appliances going. If the ears do not get a chance to recover, the impairment will become permanent.

Damage to the Inner Ear

Although very loud noise can damage the eardrum, most physiological damage from noise occurs in the snail-shaped, liquid-filled *cochlea,* or inner ear. Sound transmitted to the cochlea produces waves in the liquid, which in turn move delicate and minute structures called hair cells or *cilia* in that part of the cochlea known as the organ of Corti. The motion of the cilia is transformed into electrical impulses that conduct the sensation of sound to the brain.

The cilia can easily be fatigued by noise, causing a temporary loss of hearing, or a shift in the threshold of hearing. If they are not given a chance to recuperate, they will be permanently damaged, and irreversible hearing loss will result. There are some 23,000 cilia in the average cochlea; different sets of cilia respond to different frequency bands. The cilia responding to sound frequencies of 4,000 to 6,000 cps (cycles per second) are especially vulnerable to damage. The region of 85 to 95 db is generally regarded as the beginning of dangerous sound intensities. In general, the louder the noise, the longer it lasts, the higher it is, and the purer in frequency, the more dangerous it is. Thus, jet engines and powerful sirens are particularly hazardous.

Noise and Stress

The EPA has estimated that some 20 million Americans live or work at noise levels that could cause hearing losses; about 18 million have experienced at least some hearing loss because of noise exposure. But sound, or noise, can lead to physical and psychological problems ranging from irritability to migraine headaches. Linked with many such problems is stress, which has been found to cause high blood pressure, insomnia, ulcers, digestive disorders, alcoholism, anxiety, and many other ills.

Excessive noise has been implicated in such problems as adrenaline flow, elevated heart rates, and blood pressure. All are associated with heart disease. Noise can also affect children in special ways. For example, researchers believe it can retard language development and impair reading ability. Pregnant women exposed to excessive noise may show symptoms of stress and may pass on the harmful effects to their unborn babies. Studies in several countries have shown that the newborns of women living near airport runways experience a higher than normal incidence of birth defects.

Noise-related stress has a definite effect on mental well-being. No one knows exactly how, but noise can produce irritability, tension, and nervous strain. More seriously, British medical authorities have reported a significantly higher incidence of mental illness among people exposed constantly to aircraft noise.

Workplace Noise

Workplace noise presents special problems. Persons working in such industries as construction, mining, steel, lumber, and textiles are almost universally exposed to loud noises. Certain operations in other industries expose workers to high decibel levels. Overexposure takes place when employees work eight hours a day at sites with noise levels exceeding 90 decibels. Such standards, established by the government's Occupational Safety and Health Administration (OSHA), provide also that overexposure occurs where workers are subjected to higher decibel levels for shorter periods.

Workplace noise can lead to problems similar to those produced by-overexposure elsewhere. But many workers have little choice as regards the places where they work. For their parts, companies may have limited options insofar as noise control or abatement is concerned. Changing the gears of a machine or building an enclosure around it may not always be feasible.

Some professional musicians find it difficult or impossible to avoid excessive noise on the job. Rock music artists, for example, spend hours at a stretch in enclosed places that magnify sound that is already greatly amplified. Such persons may be at serious risk of incurring hearing losses.

Food Hazards

Contaminants found in water often make their way into food products in the cooking and packaging processes, so that many of the comments on water pollution apply here. Some dilute water pollutants become highly concentrated as they pass up the food chain and end in fish or other foods for man. Mercury was cited earlier as one example. Contamination of food with harmful microorganisms is an everpresent concern wherever standards of cleanliness and sanitation are low.

Additives

Food entails a whole new set of problems because of the thousands of new ingredients that have been added to it, directly and indirectly, in recent years. These substances include many that have been deemed necessary because of the revolution in food technology: the rise of packaged convenience foods of all kinds. Labels on today's convenience foods list preservatives, nutrients, flavors, colors, and processing agents. The trouble with food additives is that we have had little time to learn about their long-term effects on the body. The Food and Drug Administration does set standards in this area; but in the opinion of many experts, these safeguards are inadequate.

What do the additives do and what are they? What kinds of health hazards do they present? The principal kinds are explained below.

Nutrients

Some additives are simply vitamins and minerals that increase the nutritional value of food. Iodine is added to salt as a goiter preventative; vitamins A and D go into fortified milk. The vitamin and mineral additives are generally beneficial.

Preservatives

Preservatives do what the name implies: they protect against spoilage from molds, yeasts, or bacteria, or prevent oxidation. In the first category are such substances as salt, sugar, vinegar, and—among the controversial additives—sodium nitrate, sodium nitrite, and the sulfiting agents. Where some of these substances guard against illnesses like salmonella and *Clostridium botulinum,* or botulism, a deadly form of food poisoning, the controversial types may cause serious illnesses and even cancers. For example, nitrates and nitrites can combine with the amines in protein to become nitrosamines, powerful carcinogens.

The antioxidants include lecithin from soybeans, ascorbic acid (vitamin C), and *butylated hydroxytoluene* (BHT) and *butylated hydroxyanisole* (BHA). The latter two have been studied because they appear to protect against stomach cancer and liver damage.

Flavors

Of the more than 1,500 different flavors used in food, some are natural and some synthetic. Among the natural flavors are cinnamon, vanilla, and citrus oils. The synthetics, some of which, like vanillin, have exactly the same chemical compositions as their originals, include monosodium glutamate (MSG), hydrolyzed vegetable protein, and maltol. MSG in particular has become controversial because it can cause "Chinese restaurant syndrome," with temporary headaches, dizziness, and other unpleasant symptoms.

Colors

As a group, the color additives are the most controversial. But they range from beta carotene, a yellow coloring that is used in carrots and sweet potatoes and is beneficial, to a number of coal tar dyes. The FDA has banned as unsafe more than a dozen of the latter in recent years. Others are readily available and are widely used in cereals, baked goods, ice cream, and beverages.

Processing Agents

Many useful processing agents, including yeast and baking soda, are standard kitchen items. They help to control stability, moisture, texture, and other food qualities and characteristics.

Chemical Residues

Some toxic substances found in food appear in the natural environment. An example: the trace amounts of arsenic in cow's milk. Other poisons are introduced into the environment by humans. These, including fungicides, herbicides, and pesticides, have aroused deep concern among environmentalists and a growing number of private physicians.

American farmers use more than 350 approved agricultural chemicals, including about one billion pounds of insecticides annually. Because of such heavy use, about 52 percent of the average American's diet contains one or more kinds of chemical residues. Measured often in parts-per-billion, these can collect in human bodies. Permanent damage can result, according to researchers. Among the compounds are not only weed- and bug-killers like parathion but also growth-enhancers like daminozide.

Researchers warn of other problems with contaminated food. The use of antibiotics in livestock feed, for example, promotes the development of bacteria that resist antibiotics. As one result, humans who eat beef or pork that is improperly cooked may acquire infections that resist penicillin or tetracycline.

Irradiated Foods

Consumer groups have urged further study and cautious use of irradiation as a means of preserving many foods. At least 30 countries have approved radiation exposure to retard spoilage and aging; but concerns remain. They focus particularly on the nutritional losses thay may occur if foods are exposed to more than one kind of preservative, on the effects of radiation exposure on workers handling irradiated foods, and on environmental hazards that could emerge in the transport, storage, and handling of radioactive food-processing wastes.

The possible long-term effects of irradiation have led to other concerns. Radiation kills the salmonella microorganism, but may not affect more virulent and dangerous bacteria such as those responsible for botulism and may, over time, strengthen those other organisms. Irradiation might even produce dangerous mutations of some bacteria. Researchers point out further that meat can become contaminated after irradiation, indicating that other preservatives might have to be used.

Other Hazards

Toxic Wastes

Various estimates place the number of toxic-waste disposal sites in the United States at 14,000 to 20,000. Poisonous substances left over from industrial processes are buried or simply dumped at these sites, many of which present serious health hazards. Primarily, according to scientists, the open dumps, landfills, bulk storage containers, and surface impoundments at the thousands of sites spill toxic chemicals into the surrounding soil and through it into groundwater systems. Noxious fumes and even flames burst from some sites at unpredictable moments. The wastes include a huge variety of substances, among them chlorinated solvents, aromatic hydrocarbons, pesticides, trace metals, and PCBs.

The locations of many waste disposal sites remain unknown, often, until a health or environmental problem is detected. Thus the health threats posed by waste dumps may lie dormant for years and may surface only after a container has rusted through or seepage has brought poisonous slush into contact with drinking-water sources.

Waste chemicals can enter the body through skin contact and inhalation as well as ingestion. But the latter is the most common method. Where dosage is substantial, ingestion usually leads to toxic effects on the liver and kidneys. Other parts of the body may be affected as well. Skin contact may produce lesions while inhalation can have direct respiratory effects.

Improved methods of disposing of toxic wastes have combined with public awareness and governmental action to build hopes of reduced waste problems in the future. In the meantime, as environmentalists contend, the thousands of existing toxic-waste sites pose continuing health hazards.

Nuclear Radiation

Among the most dangerous of all pollutants is nuclear or "ionizing" radiation. Made up of particles of energy, this radiation can attack the atoms that form the body's cells, causing both short- and long-term damage. Human tissues like skin, bone-marrow, and intestinal cells, all of which reproduce rapidly, feel the impact of radiation most intensely. But different isotopes in ionizing radiation concentrate in different body tissues, sometimes causing cancer or genetic mutations many years after exposure. Of the most common radioactive elements in radiation from a nuclear power plant, barium resembles calcium and therefore concentrates in the bones while iodine 131 concentrates in the thyroid.

Completely invisible, radiation reaches the earth from various natural and manmade sources. Some comes from the sun and outer space; larger amounts are given off by radioactive materials, including waste from nuclear power plants, the fallout from nuclear weapons explosions, and various electronic devices. The numbers of such devices are increasing steadily; among them are lasers, X-ray machines, TV sets, and microwave ovens.

The damage done to the human body as a result of exposure to radiation varies with the intensity of the "dose" and the isotopes involved. A dose of radiation above 1,000 rem, a unit of measurement, is always fatal. Smaller doses, with exposure over an extended period of time, may also be fatal. Victims can protect themselves to a limited degree if given time. For example, they can guard against thyroid cancer by taking potassium iodide. Ingested in pill form, the medication loads the thyroid gland with iodine, thus "blocking" the iodine 131 isotope and preventing its concentration in the thyroid.

In a simple operation physicians can transplant marrow into persons exposed to the barium isotope, and thus reduce the possibility of bone-marrow syndrome. This illness cripples the body's immune system. But donor marrow must match that of the victim, and the relatives of a victim are those most likely to supply marrow that is a genetic match. If the relatives have also been exposed to radiation, no donors may qualify.

Workplace Dangers

Air and noise pollution are, as noted, common in certain industries. The materials and machines used in manufacturing processes are the usual causes of such pollution. Many controls have been mandated by the federal Occupational Safety and Health Administration, but researchers have reported that some industries are experiencing increased health hazards, largely because of the materials they use.

High-tech microelectronics plants are especially threatened. According to scientists, many such plants use toxic chemicals that have been linked to reproductive disorders in both men and women. Among the high-tech hazards usually cited are glycol ethers, widely used as a solvent by manufacturers of printed circuit boards; arsenic, an element in the manufacture of some semiconductor chips; and lead, used in soldering and other operations. Some semiconductor plants are also employing radio-frequency radiation in potentially dangerous amounts to etch and clean silicon wafers.

Musculoskeletal Disorders

Carpal tunnel syndrome and other neurological and musculoskeletal disorders frequently occur in the workplace and are usually the result of a repetitive motion or series of movements which strain or damage nerves and muscles. Poor posture, uncomfortable or poorly-designed chairs and equipment, and lengthy periods of the same repetitive motion exposes the nerves and muscles of the body, often the hands and arms, to agonizing pain. In most cases, behavior modification, exercises, surgeries, and specially-designed furniture or equipment can completely eradicate pain and incidence of these disorders. A physician should be consulted for individualized diagnosis and treatment.

31

Health Insurance

Health insurance has two basic purposes. It provides for reimbursement to families or individuals for health care costs. It may also guarantee replacement income when a person is unable to work because of sickness or injury. Reimbursement insurance can cover virtually all types of expenses connected with hospital care, medical treatment, and related services. Disability insurance usually calls for periodic payments to make up for lost income.

From another perspective, health insurance offers protection to both groups and individuals. The groups may be company work forces that have *group insurance* as a benefit. Individuals can buy insurance from as many as 1,000 commercial insurance companies offering a huge variety of plans.

Some insurers are general insurance companies. Others are hospital and medical service plans such as Blue Cross and Blue Shield, group medical prepayment plans such as health maintenance organizations (HMOs), and others.

What Health Insurance Is and Does

"Health insurance" means a number of things. It may be called "accident and health insurance" or "disability insurance." Various types of policies have other names. The different descriptions indicate that the policies vary as regards the types of expenses covered. While some policies cover hospital expenses only, others may cover virtually all kinds of medical expenses.

Two Types of Coverage

In general, private health insurance coverage is one of two kinds: *group* and *individual*. Employers, unions, and other kinds of organizations typically provide group insurance as an employee or membership benefit. An individual can buy individual insurance whether or not he or she is covered under a group policy. But a good group policy usually covers all the major health problems or contingencies that a person could face under normal circumstances.

Group insurance has a number of specific advantages over individual coverage, among them the following:

- Because a number of people can be included under a single contract, with consequent savings to the insurer in sales, administrative, and claims costs, the insurer can charge less per individual covered.

- In most cases the company, union, or organization holding the group contract pays part or all of the individual premiums.

- With group insurance the health of the individual insured person is usually not a major factor in determining eligibility. The insurance company is more interested in the average age and overall health status of the group. The health of individuals may become a selection factor, however, where small groups, 10 or fewer persons, are involved.

- Unless an individual leaves a job or gives up a membership, his or her group coverage cannot be canceled. Termination of the group plan itself would, of course, terminate coverage.

Despite such advantages, individual and family policies fulfill at least two fundamental needs. First, they provide coverage for persons who are not members of an insured group. Such policies may also cover those who cannot, for whatever reason, obtain group coverage. Second, the individual or family policy can provide supplementary coverage where a group plan does not meet all basic health insurance needs.

Group and individual plans differ in basic ways. Where a group policy establishes the level of benefits for all group members, the individual policy can more easily be tailored to specific requirements.` With the individual policy, too, each person or family is enrolled separately. The cost of individual insurance is usually substantially higher because the insurer considers the age, health status of the insured, and other factors when setting premium rates.

Principles of Health Insurance

Private or commercial health insurance programs function according to some key principles. Primarily, these programs are based on the theory that a relatively small, regular payment, the premium, can protect the insured against what might be a sizable loss.

A companion principle holds that the insured must pay the expenses of operating an insurance system. These expenses include the costs of maintaining offices, investigating claims, and otherwise administering the system as well as paying benefits.

Two other principles underlie the operation of most health insurance programs:

• The *large-loss principle,* which holds that the insured should try to obtain protection only against those costs or losses that he or she could not bear financially. Under this principle the contract may exclude from reimbursement some specific kinds of costs. Most such policies contain a "deductible" clause specifying that the insured must pay a certain amount of initial costs.

Major medical insurance plans probably exemplify best the large-loss, or large-risk, principle. These policies nearly always provide for a deductible. The higher the deductible, as a rule, the lower the premium.

• The *first-dollar principle,* under which the policy pays the full cost of all covered hospital and medical expenses. Policies of this kind have no deductible clauses.

Advocates of first-dollar policies stress the need for preventive health care. The policy in theory encourages the insured to see a physician and obtain treatment before a health problem becomes worse or even unmanageable.

Kinds of Insurance Plans

Voluntary or private health insurance plans offer protection against a broad range of hospital and medical expenses. Some policies offer protection against a single illness such as cancer while others insure individuals, families, or groups against nearly all medical contingencies. Some of the many kinds of coverage are as follows:

Hospital

Blue Cross plans and most other commercial plans provide room benefits at a specified rate per day. Usually, they also cover miscellaneous hospital services, including drugs, operating room, and laboratory services up to a given cost level. Some commercial plans and most Blue Cross plans cover all costs in a semiprivate, or shared, room.

Surgical

Typically, health insurance policies cover the costs of surgery according to a schedule that establishes specified amounts for listed procedures. The insurance contract sets a payment of so many dollars for an appendectomy or a tonsillectomy, for example, with that payment going toward coverage of the surgeon's bill. In the case of Blue Shield, certain surgeons perform surgical operations for low-income subscribers for no additional charge.

Regular Medical

This is a form of insurance that provides coverage of physicians' fees in cases that do not involve surgery. The medical care may be provided in the home, in a hospital, or in a physician's office. A regular medical policy may also cover diagnostic X-ray and other laboratory expenses.

Major Medical

As noted, major medical policies usually provide for deductibles. After an insured has reached a specified hospital-medical expense level, the insurer will also pay, for example, 80 percent of all remaining expenses to a set maximum. The maximum may be $1 million or more. Some policies offer unlimited coverage. In some cases the policy sets a maximum, perhaps $5,000, $10,000, or $25,000, for a given illness in a one- or three-year period. Where an insurance company and the insured pay percentages of all costs beyond a deductible, the policy is said to be a form of "coinsurance."

Comprehensive or Comprehensive Major Medical

This kind of health policy combines hospital, major medical, and surgical coverage in one contract. Generally, little or no deductible applies to hospital and surgical charges. But the major medical coverage ordinarily comes with a deductible.

Dental

Basic or comprehensive protection, covering the costs of hospital care, surgery, and physicians' services, may also include dental insurance. A basic plan may establish a set of allowances for each procedure to an annual maximum of, for example, $500 or $1,000. A comprehensive policy would cover, typically, 80 percent of all dental expenses above a specified minimum.

Special Perils

While frowned upon by many insurance experts, "special perils" plans continue to appear. They cover such specific health hazards as cancer, polio, and vision problems.

Auto and Travel

Many insurance companies offer auto and travel policies that cover insured persons in the event of injury or death in an accident. Such policies may provide protection against almost any travel accident in various kinds of vehicles.

Income

Insurance against loss of income gives the insured person a flow of cash if, because of illness or disability, he or she cannot work. A commercial policy that limits coverage to accidental disability usually costs much less than broader coverage, or it provides for greater benefits. Accidental disability payments, usually monthly, may continue for life. Payments for disability resulting from illness are commonly limited to 6, 12, or more months depending on the terms of the contract.

Many policies provide only for *hospital income insurance.* Such insurance pays a stipulated cash payment for every day of hospitalization. Insurance companies offer these policies to individuals only, not to groups.

Basic Protection

Of the various kinds of comprehensive health insurance, the so-called "basic protection" plan ranks among the most common. Basic protection offers coverage for the costs of hospital care and services and physicians' services.

Most basic protection policies specify that hospital room and board benefits will be paid in one of two ways. One kind of policy provides for reimbursement for actual room and board charges up to a set daily maximum. Another kind offers a service type of benefit equaling the hospital's established semiprivate room and board rates. If the insured occupies a private room, he or she pays the additional room charge.

Surgical-Expense Insurance

Basic policies that provide hospital expense coverage generally offer surgical-expense benefits as well. That means coverage may extend to operations and postoperative, inpatient physicians' visits. The policy then becomes a "hospital-and-surgical-expense" or "hospital-surgical" plan.

Surgical-expense insurance normally pays benefits whether illness or accident makes the surgery necessary. Coverage may include benefits for anesthetics. A schedule of surgical procedures and specified maximum benefits for each may be part of such a policy. Physicians' fees may be covered to a "reasonable and customary" level for the particular city or region. In this case the policy would not contain a surgical schedule.

Physician's-Expense Insurance

The counterpart of the surgical-expense policy is the physician's-expense plan. This policy offers benefits to help cover the costs of nonsurgical physicians' services in a hospital, home, or office. The terms of the policy usually provide for maximum payments for specified services. The latter may include diagnostic X-ray and other laboratory expenses.

Policy Provisions

Purchasing health insurance calls for close attention to the provisions of any given policy. Little standardization exists among the hundreds of types of policies, a factor that makes the buyer's task a difficult one. In four areas in particular the buyer should scrutinize closely the "fine print" in an individual, but not a group, policy.

Provisions Relating to Other Policies

Many policies include clauses that limit or prohibit payments where the policyholder has other insurance covering the same loss or expense. In this way insurers protect themselves against overpayments for specific losses. A typical clause of this kind reduces benefits payments to the policy's prorated share of the insured person's actual expenses.

Preexisting Conditions

Most individual health insurance policies exclude preexisting conditions. That means they do not cover at all, or do not cover for a stated period, physical or health problems that existed before the policy became effective. The waiting period that must elapse before coverage for a preexisting condition begins may be 30, 60, or more days.

Cancellation and Renewal

All health policies contain cancellation and renewal provisions. One type, the most favorable to the policyholder, specifies that the insurer cannot cancel or refuse to renew the policy before the insured turns 65. The same clause may state that the premium cannot be increased. Because it provides guaranteed coverage, this kind of policy is usually the most expensive.

Many policies contain a widely used modification of the no-cancel, guaranteed renewal clause. This alternative provides that the company must continue the coverage until the insured reaches 65, but that the premium can be increased for entire groups of insured persons. In a third variation, some policies permit the insurer to cancel or refuse to renew the coverage at any time by giving written notice to the policyholder. This kind of policy is the least advantageous to the insured.

"Good-Health" Discounts

Increasingly, the disability, hospital, or medical policy provides for discounts for persons in good health. For example, the policy may specify that the applicant be a nonsmoker who exercises three to five times a week and does not have a high-risk job or hobby. Race-car driving would fall in the latter category.

Discounts of 5 to 15 percent have been available to nonsmokers since the 1960s. New discount arrangements broaden the range of qualifying factors and increase the discount levels. The new trend takes as a model the life insurance plan that may offer discounts of up to 50 percent if the applicant observes basic rules of health and safety. These include, in addition to those named, adhering to a nutritious diet, using seat belts while riding in a car, and avoiding excess salt in diet.

Meeting Special Needs

Some health insurance policies are designed to meet special needs. One common kind of coverage protects persons who are above-average risks: persons with poor health histories, existing problems or illnesses, or chronic disorders of one kind or another. Other types of policies serve other purposes.

Existing Health Problems

Because persons with existing health problems are not average risks, insurance for them may be costly. But an approach to insurance may be made in at least three ways.

1. A policy may exclude entirely the usual benefits for the specified existing condition. The insurance may then provide protection for all or many other conditions. Standard rates or premiums may be charged.

2. Charging a standard rate, the insurer may amend the policy to provide for a longer waiting period before coverage begins. In such a case standard benefits may be available.

3. The policy may call for a higher than normal premium to compensate for the greater degree of risk. Regular benefits might be available.

Some special health coverages have become relatively common. For example, dental-expense insurance helps pay for normal dental care as well as accidental damage. Insurance companies, prepayment plans, and some state dental associations make such coverage available, usually providing for a deductible and for coinsurance.

Special coverage may, finally, be provided for eye care. Many group policies have such coverage.

Insuring the Unemployed and Divorced

Most Americans have health insurance as a job-related benefit. Coverage terminates, however, if an individual quits his or her job, is laid off, or loses the job for whatever reason.

An employee who is leaving a job should find out how long, if at all, coverage will continue after employment terminates. A normal period would be 30 days. In that period the employee is usually allowed to convert the coverage from group to individual. The conversion option means the employee can remain insured by the same company while retaining, usually, reduced benefits. The premium payments generally increase, sometimes dramatically. Where a group policy permits conversion, the insured has the right to convert regardless of existing health problems. No medical examination is required.

Many group policies provide for conversion from group to individual coverage where a divorced person was dependent for protection on the former spouse's group plan. The person needing health coverage has to apply within the specified period, but cannot be rejected for health reasons.

By the middle 1980s, some 25 states had laws requiring "group continuance." By the terms of these laws a divorced spouse or unemployed person could remain in the group and receive the same benefits as before. The insured had only to assume the group cost formerly contributed by the employer for each insured individual. The effect of the group continuance laws was to make it possible for divorced or unemployed persons to retain group coverage for about half of what an individual policy would cost. With some exceptions, state laws limited group continuance periods to a year or less.

"Medigap" Insurance

An estimated 95 percent of all Americans over 65 are protected by Medicare. But the government program covers only a portion of all possible physician and hospital expenses— less than 50 percent. To help bridge the gap between Medicare and the 100 percent coverage that most persons need and want, private insurance companies have developed "medigap" policies.

What do the medigap policies cover? Their terms vary. Most help insured persons to expand existing Medicare coverages. But few offer even partial protection against hospital and medical costs that Medicare does not cover, or does not cover fully. These areas include: routine physical checkups; most prescription drugs; hearing tests and hearing aids; eye examinations and eyeglasses; most dental care, including dentures; private nursing care; and custodial home nursing care.

Because neither Medicare nor medigap insurance covers these areas thoroughly, many elderly persons remain vulnerable. But some medigap policies, including those offered by Blue Cross/Blue Shield and some associations for the elderly, provide for good hospital and physician coverage.

Congress set minimum standards for medigap insurance in 1980. But the Better Business Bureau has warned that the older person in need of additional insurance should shop carefully. Some groups, the BBB states, offer insurance as a means of building membership rolls. The BBB also advises as follows:

- Older buyers should make sure they have the Medicare medical insurance (Part B) as well as the hospital coverage (Part A).

- Insurance buyers should check the reputation of any potential private insurer with the state insurance department and the local Better Business Bureau. Insurance companies are also rated according to their financial health in *Best's Insurance Reports: Life and Health Insurance,* available in most libraries.

- The practice of switching from one insurance company to another because of premium levels can be hazardous: rates charged by any company can increase.

- As a rule, premiums should not be paid for years in advance. Your needs may change.

Five Innovative Plans

Pressures to cut the costs of medical care have given rise to basic changes in the methods of delivering such care in the United States. No longer do most persons simply call their family physicians and, if the physician so advises, go to a specific hospital. More and more, insurance plans and programs offer both choices and restrictions. Five innovative programs in particular have gained in popularity.

Health Maintenance Organizations (HMOs)

Operating clinic-style facilities, HMOs require that their subscribers pay a set monthly premium. In return the HMO provides full medical care. But members have to select their physicians from a list provided by the HMO. If hospitalization is necessary, the subscriber goes to a hospital selected by the organization.

Charging premiums that may be 10 to 20 percent lower than those for equivalent insurance coverage, HMOs provide incentives to avoid unnecessary expenses or treatments. HMOs, for example, encourage subscribers to make use of preventive care to stay healthy. Thus most HMOs offer eye and hearing checkups, as well as podiatry and dental services, at little or no cost beyond a monthly fee.

Many subscribers point to the convenience of HMOs as their major attraction. Subscribers not only have the convenience of full medical and hospital services at one facility; they pay no deductibles and have no claim forms to fill out.

HMOs have won federal support. New rules published in 1985 encouraged Medicare recipients to drop out of the government's medical insurance program and to join HMOs. The usual HMO restrictions on choices of physicians and hospitals would apply; applicants would join a central hospital facility, with its own physicians and specialties, and would be directed to specific physicians approved for HMO patients. Those who make the change have to retain the Medicare Part B coverage.

Former Medicare beneficiaries have various ways to report grievances. They can, for example, write to the U.S. Department of Health and Human Services Office of Health Maintenance Organizations, Compliance Division, Room 9-11, Parklawn Building, 5600 Fishers Lane, Rockville, MD 20857.

Preferred Provider Organizations (PPOs)

In the PPO, subscribers receive care at a discount if they go to physicians and hospitals recommended by the insurer. Generally, the insurance company underwriting the PPO allows employees in insured groups to go to a nonparticipating physician. But in such a case the costs of care rise considerably, sometimes to twice those charged by the listed physicians.

Under the PPO arrangement, physicians, hospitals, and insurers work together to keep down overall costs. A PPO hospital provides care for insured persons at reduced rates. In exchange, the hospital enjoys increased utilization of its facilities.

Managed Care

Unlike the HMO and the PPO, a managed care program gives members the freedom to pick the physicians and hospitals they prefer. But severe cost-containment rules apply. The restrictions may include the following:

- Preadmission reviews of hospital stays by panels of physicians and nurses. A panel would have to agree in all cases, except for maternity care and emergencies, that hospitalization and the proposed care are necessary.

- Reviews during hospitalization to ensure that continued inpatient care is necessary.

- Mandatory second opinions before some operations to make certain a particular procedure is necessary.

- As in some newer group plans,

surgery is performed on an outpatient basis where possible.

Companies adopting managed care plans may offer HMO and PPO plans as well. An eligible employee in such a firm then has a choice of program.

Hospital Chains

Competition among health care providers has led to still another approach to both cost control and hospital utilization. Some for-profit hospital chains have bought insurance companies to obtain insurance licenses, then provided health insurance programs that required the insured to use the chain's facilities.

A variation on the HMO and PPO systems, the hospital chain approach makes possible insurance costs that are 10 to 15 percent lower than those of traditional plans. Chain officials contend that the lower charges are justified by more efficient hospital operation.

Insurance experts note characteristics of the hospital chains' programs that appear to justify caution on the part of the potential buyer. For example, the policies sold by the chains usually impose limits on lifetime benefits. Unlike the plans of such nonprofit groups as Blue Cross/Blue Shield, the chains' policies provide for the termination of certain benefits at specified ages.

Nursing Home Care

Increasingly, major insurance companies have begun to devise policies that would cover the costs of nursing home care for the elderly. Such spe-

cialized plans face a double difficulty. First, the insurance company needs to make a profit off the program of coverage. Second, nursing home costs ranging generally from $15,000 to $50,000 and more per year raise the possibility of enormous claims that could continue for years.

Long-term care insurance marks a start toward a solution. Major insurers have begun to market policies that differ on such points as home health care benefits and the right to renew. But because no actuarial figures are available to show, for example, how many younger policyholders would be needed to offset older beneficiaries, the companies have worked through organizations such as the American Association of Retired Persons (AARP). The memberships of such groups are usually numerous enough to reduce the risks of major claims.

If given a choice, the person shopping for a long-term care policy should ask at least these questions:

- Does the policy put a ceiling on benefits, and at what point?

- Exactly what does the policy cover? No such policies provide coverage for *all* the ills of aging.

- To be eligible for benefits, must the patient be hospitalized before he or she enters a long-term care facility?

- Must a patient's diagnosis cite an organic disease before eligibility can begin?

- Are "mental health" problems, possibly including Alzheimer's disease and senility, excluded from coverage?

32

Home Care of the Sick

Patients suffering from serious illnesses or from certain communicable diseases should be hospitalized. Home care facilities do not normally include the expensive and delicate medical equipment required for the complete care of these diseases.

If, however, the physician in charge of a case decides that his patient does not need hospitalization and that adequate home nursing care can be provided, the well-being of the patient can be greatly enhanced by his being cared for in the comfortable and familiar surroundings of his own home.

When the decision to treat a patient at home is made, it must be understood that the physician's orders regarding rest, exercise, diet, and medications have to be rigorously adhered to. Nursing responsibilities assigned to the patient and whoever else is tending to the patient's recovery should be carried out as conscientiously as they would be if the patient's care were entrusted to a team of medical professionals in a hospital environment.

The physician in charge of a case should, of course, be notified of any significant changes in the condition of the patient. The physician should be contacted if, for example, the patient complains of severe pain, pain of long duration, or pain that apparently is not directly related to an injury or surgical procedure. The location and characteristics of the pain should be noted, and the physician will want to know whether the pain is affected by changing the position of the patient or if it seems to be related to the intake of food or fluids.

In addition to being informed of such potentially dangerous developments, the physician should get daily or frequent reports on the patient's progress. The easiest and best way to see that this is done is to keep a written record of the following functions, symptoms, and conditions of the patient:

- Morning and evening body temperature, pulse rate, and respiration rate
- Bowel movements—frequency, consistency of stools, presence of blood
- Urination—amount, frequency, presence of burning sensation, color
- Vomiting or nausea

- The amount and kind of solid foods and liquids taken by the patient
- Hours of sleep
- Medications given (should be administered only on the instructions of the physician)
- Patient's general appearance (includes any unusual swelling, skin rash, or skin discoloration)
- General mental and psychological condition of the patient, such as signs of irritability or despondency

Checking the Pulse and Respiration

The pulse and respiration are usually checked in the morning and again in the evening; the physician may recommend other times as well.

Pulse

The home nurse should learn how to measure the pulse rate in beats per minute. A watch with a second hand or a nearby electric clock will help count the passage of time while the pulse beat is counted. The pulse can be felt on the inner side of the wrist, above the thumb; the pulse also can be checked at the temple, the throat, or at the ankle if for some reason the wrist is not conveniently accessible.

The patient should be resting quietly when the pulse is counted; if the patient has been physically active the pulse count probably will be higher than normal, suggesting a possible disorder when none actually exists. Temperature extremes, emotional upsets, and the digesting of a meal also can produce misleading pulse rates.

What is a normal pulse rate? The answer is hard to define in standard or average terms. For an adult male, a pulse rate of about 72 per minute is considered normal. The pulse of an adult woman might range around 80 per minute and still be normal. For children, a normal pulse might be one that is regularly well above 100 per minute. Also, a normal pulse may vary by a few beats per minute in either direction from the average for the individual. The home nurse with a bit of practice can determine whether a patient's pulse is significantly fast or slow, strong or weak, and report any important changes to the physician.

Respiration

The patient's respiration can be checked while his pulse is taken. By observing the rising and falling of the patient's chest, a close estimate of the rate of respiration can be made. An average for adults would be close to 16 per minute, with a variation of a few inhalations and exhalations in either direction. The rate of respiration, like the pulse rate, is higher in children.

Sometimes the respiration rate can be noted without making it obvious to the patient that there is concern about the information; many persons alter their natural breathing rate uncon-

sciously if they know that function is being watched.

Body Temperature

A fever thermometer, available at any drugstore, is specially shaped to help the home nurse read any tiny change in the patient's temperature, such changes being measured in tenths of a degree. Instead of being round in cross-section like an ordinary thermometer, a fever thermometer is flat on one side and ridge-shaped on the other. The inner surface of the flat side is coated with a reflective material and the ridge-shaped side actually is a magnifying lens. Thus, to read a fever thermometer quickly and properly, one looks at the lens (ridged) side.

How To Take the Temperature

The usual ways of taking temperature are by mouth (oral) or by the rectum (rectal), and fever thermometers are specialized for these uses. The rectal thermometer has a more rounded bulb to protect the sensitive tissues in the anus. Normal body temperature taken orally is 98.6° F. or 37° C. for most people, but slight variations do occur in the normal range. When the temperature is taken rectally, a normal reading is about 1° F. higher—99.6° F. or about 37.5° C.—because rectal veins in the area elevate the temperature slightly.

Before a patient's temperature is taken, the thermometer should be carefully cleaned with soap and water, then wiped dry, or sterilized in alcohol or similar disinfectant. The thermometer should then be grasped firmly at the shaft and shaken briskly, bulb end downward to force the mercury down to a level of 95° F. or lower—or 35° C. or lower if the thermometer is calibrated according to the Celsius temperature scale. See the chart *Body*

Body Temperature in Degrees		
Fahrenheit		**Celsius**
105.5		40.8
105		40.6
104.5		40.3
104		40
103.5		39.7
103		39.4
102.5		39.2
102		38.9
101.5		38.6
101		38.3
100.5		38.1
100		37.8
99.5		37.5
99		37.2
98.6	Normal	37.0
97.8	Range	36.6

Temperature in Degrees for comparative values of the Fahrenheit and Celsius scales.

If the temperature is taken orally, the thermometer should be moistened in clean fresh water and placed well under the tongue on one side. If the temperature is taken rectally, the thermometer should be dipped first in petroleum jelly and then inserted about one inch into the opening of the rectum. If an oral thermometer is used in the rectum, special care should be taken to make sure that the lubrication is adequate and that it is inserted gently to avoid irritating rectal tissues. Whichever method is used, the thermometer should be left in place for at least three minutes in order to get an accurate reading.

If circumstances preclude an oral or rectal temperature check, the patient's temperature may be taken under the arm; a normal reading in that area is about 97.6° F. or 36.5° C.

Above-Normal Temperature

If the patient's temperature hovers around one degree above his normal reading, the home nurse should note the fact and watch for other signs of a fever that would indicate the presence of an infection or some other bodily disorder. A mild fever immediately after surgery or during the course of an infectious disease may not be cause for alarm. Also, the normal body temperature of a mature woman may vary with hormonal changes during her menstrual cycle. But when oral temperatures rise above 100° F. the change should be regarded as a warning signal. A rise of as much as three degrees above normal, Fahrenheit, for a period of several hours or more, could be critical, and a physician should be notified immediately.

Sleep

Another item to be checked each day for the at-home medical records is the patient's sleeping habits. While there is no standard number of hours of sleep per day preferred for healthy individuals, a regular pattern of sleep is very important during recovery from disease or injury, and an obvious change from such a pattern can suggest tension, discomfort, or other problems. Typical daily sleep periods for most adults range from 7 to 9 hours, while children and infants may sleep as much as 12 to 20 hours per day and be considered normal; sleep in the form of naps should be included in total amounts per day.

Making the Patient Comfortable

A good deal of the patient's time at home will be devoted to sleep or rest, most or all of it in bed. The bed should give firm support to the body; if the mattress does not offer such support, place a thick sheet of plywood between the springs and mattress. Pillows can be placed under the head and shoulders of the patient to raise those parts of the body from time to time. When the patient is lying on his back,

a small pillow can be slipped under the knees to provide support and comfort. A small pillow can also be placed under the small of the back if necessary. Additional pillows may be placed as needed between the ankles or under one foot or both feet.

If the pressure of bed clothing on the feet causes discomfort, a bridge made from a grocery carton or similar box can be placed over the feet but beneath the blankets. To help maintain muscle tone and circulation in the feet and legs, a firm barrier can be placed as needed at the foot of the bed so the patient can stretch his legs and push against the barrier while lying on his back.

Changing Position

Helping the patient change position in bed is an important home-nursing technique. Unless a definite effort is made to help the patient change positions at regular intervals, the sick person may tend to curl up into a sort of fetal position, with the hips and knees flexed and the spine curved. While this position may be preferred by the patient in order to increase body warmth or to relieve pain, the practice of staying in one position for longer periods of time can lead to loss of muscle tone and even deformities.

Moving or positioning the patient in bed should, of course, be done according to directions outlined by the doctor for the specific medical problem involved. Body movements should not aggravate any injury or other disorder by placing undue strain or stress on a body part or organ system that is in the healing stage. At the same time, the patient should be stimulated and encouraged to change positions frequently and to use as much of his own strength as possible.

If the patient is likely to need a very long period of bed rest, and the family can afford the modest expense,

it may be wise to purchase or rent a hospital-type bed. The basic hospital bed is higher from the floor than ordinary beds, making the tasks of changing bed linens, taking temperatures, etc., easier for the home nurse. More sophisticated hospital beds have manual or electrical controls to raise the head and foot of the bed.

Helping the Patient Sit Up

The patient can be helped to a sitting position in bed by placing one arm, palm upward, under the patient's shoulder while the patient extends an arm around the nurse's back or shoulders. The nurse also may slip both hands, palms facing upward, under the patient's pillow, raising it along with the patient's head and shoulders. The same procedures can be used to help move a patient from one side of the bed to the other if the patient is unable to move himself.

When the patient has been raised to a sitting position, he should try to brace his arms behind him on the bed surface with elbows straightened. If the patient feels dizzy or faint as a result of the effort, he can be lowered to the back rest position again by simply reversing the procedure.

When the patient is able to support himself in a sitting position, he should be encouraged to dangle his legs over the side of the bed, and—when his strength permits—to move to a chair beside the bed and rest for a while in a seated position.

Bathing the Patient

A patient who is unable to leave the bed will require special help in bathing. When bath time comes, the nurse will need a large basin of warm water, soap, a washcloth, and several towels, large and small. A cotton blanket also should be used to replace the regular blanket during bathing, and pillows should be removed from the bed unless they are necessary at the time.

One large towel should be placed under the patient's head and another should be placed on top of the bath blanket, with part of the towel folded under the bath blanket. This preliminary procedure should help protect the bed area from moisture that may be spilled during the bathing procedure.

The bath should begin at the area of the eyes, using only clear water and brushing outward from the eyes. Soapy water can be applied to the rest of the face, as needed, with rinsing afterward. After the face, bathing and rinsing are continued over the chest and abdomen, the arms and hands, the legs and feet, and the back of the body from the neck downward to the buttocks. The external genitalia are washed last.

During the washing procedure, the nurse uses firm strokes to aid circulation and checks for signs of pressure areas or bed sores. Skin lotions or body powders may be applied, and a back rub given, after washing. The teeth may be brushed and the patient may want to use a mouthwash. After the personal hygiene routine is completed, a fresh pair of pajamas can be put on. If bed linen needs to be changed, the bathing period provides a good opportunity for that chore.

Changing the Bed Linen

Changing the bed linen while the patient is in bed can be a challenge for any home nurse. However, there are a few shortcuts that make the task much easier. First, remove all pillows, or all but one, as well as the top spread if one is used. Loosen the rest of the bedding materials on all sides and begin removing the sheets from

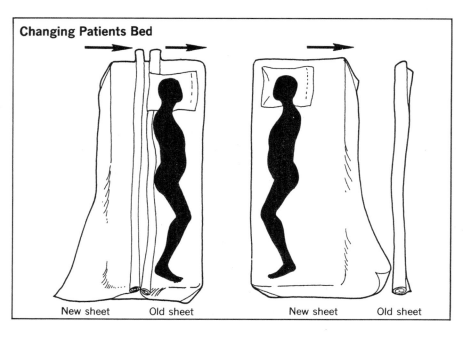

Changing Patients Bed

New sheet   Old sheet   New sheet   Old sheet

the head of the bed, top sheet first. By letting the patient hold the top edge of the blanket, or by tucking the top edges under his shoulder, the blanket can remain in place while the top sheet is pulled down, under the blanket, to the foot of the bed. If the top sheet is to be used as the next bottom sheet, it can be folded and placed on the side with the top spread.

Next, the patient must be moved to one side of the bed and the bottom sheet gathered in a flat roll close to the patient. Then the clean bottom sheet is unfolded on the mattress cover and the edges, top, and bottom, tucked under the mattress. The rest of the clean sheet is spread over the empty side of the bed and pushed in a flat roll under the soiled sheet next to the patient's back.

The next step is to roll the patient from one side of the bed onto the clean sheet that has been spread on the other side. The soiled bottom sheets can be pulled out easily and the new bottom sheet spread and tucked in on the other side.

The new top sheet can be pulled up under the blanket, which has been used to cover the patient throughout

the change of bed linens. Finally, the top spread and pillows can be replaced, after the pillow cases have been changed. A special effort should be made, meanwhile, to keep the mattress cover and bottom sheet of the patient's bed as flat and smooth as possible and to allow room for the feet to move while the sheets are firmly tucked in at the foot of the bed.

The home nurse should handle the soiled linens carefully if the patient is being treated for an infectious disease; they should never be held close to the face.

Bowel Movements and Urination

If the patient is expected to remain bedridden for a long period of time, the home nurse should acquire a bedpan and perhaps a urinal from a drugstore. A sheet of oilcloth, rubber, or plastic material should also be provided to protect the bed during bowel movements and urination.

If the patient is unable to sit up on a bedpan because of weakness, his body can be propped up with pillows. If he is capable of getting out of bed but is unable to walk to the bathroom, a commode can be placed near the bed and the patient can be helped from the bed to the commode and back. Another alternative is to use a wheelchair or any chair with casters to move the patient between the bedroom and bathroom.

Administering an Enema

Occasionally, a physician may recommend an enema to help the patient empty his bowels or to stimulate the peristaltic action associated with normal functioning of the intestinal tract.

Since enemas are seldom an emergency aspect of home nursing, there usually is time to purchase disposable enema units from a drugstore. The disposable enema contains about four or five ounces of prepared solution packaged in a plastic bag with a lubricated nozzle for injecting the fluid into the patient's rectum. The entire package can be thrown away after it has been used, thus eliminating the need to clean and store equipment. The alternative is to use a traditional enema bag filled with plain warm water or a prescribed formulation.

An enema is best administered while the patient is lying on his side with his knees drawn up toward his chest. When using the disposable enema unit, the home nurse simply squeezes the solution through the lubricated nozzle that has been inserted into the rectum. When using an enema bag, the home nurse should lubricate the nozzle before insertion. After insertion of the nozzle, the enema bag should be held or suspended above the patient so that, upon the opening of the valve that controls the flow of the enema, the liquid will flow easily into the patient's rectum.

Feeding the Patient

It may be necessary at times for the home nurse to feed a patient unable to feed himself. An effort should be made to serve meals to the patient in an attractive and, when possible, colorful manner. The bedding should be protected with towels or plastic sheeting and the patient made as comfortable as possible with his head raised.

Liquids should be offered in a spoon filled about two-thirds full with any drops on the bottom of the spoon carefully wiped off. The spoon should be held so that the area between the tip and the side touch the patient's lower lip. Then the spoon is tilted toward the tip so the liquid will run into the patient's mouth. The process takes time, and much patience is required of the nurse. The patient may be slow to swallow and in no hurry to finish the meal.

If the patient can take liquids through a glass tube or plastic straw, the home nurse should see to it that the end of the tube inserted in the container of liquid is always below the surface of the fluid so that the patient will swallow as little air as possible.

A patient who can drink liquids from a spoon or tube may be able to drink from a cup. In making the step from tube or spoon to cup, the home nurse can help the patient by holding the cup by its handle and letting the patient guide the cup to his lips with his own hands.

The nurse should always make sure the patient is fully alert before trying to put food or liquid into his mouth; a semiconscious person may not be able to swallow. The nurse also should test the temperature of the food; cold foods should be served cold and warm foods should be served warm. But foods should never be too hot or too cold for the patient. Finally, the dishes, tubes, or other devices used to feed the patient should be carefully cleaned before storing them.

Ice Bags and Hot-Water Bottles

Ice bags and hot-water bottles frequently are used in home nursing to relieve pain and discomfort. The temperature of the water in a hot-water bottle or bag should be tested before it is placed near a patient's body. The maximum temperature of the water should be about 130° F., and preferably a few degrees cooler. The hot-water container should never be placed directly against the skin of a patient; it must be covered with soft material, such as a towel, to protect the patient against burns. A patient who is receiving pain-killing medications could suffer serious tissue damage from a hot-water bottle without feeling severe pain.

When ice is the preferred method of relieving pain, it can be applied in a rubber or plastic bag sealed to prevent leakage and covered with a soft cloth. Cold applications to very young and old persons should be handled cautiously and with medical consultation, particularly if ice packs are to be applied to large body areas for long periods of time; individuals at both age extremes can lack the normal physiological mechanisms for coping with the effects of cold temperatures.

Steam Inhalators

If the at-home patient suffers from a respiratory ailment that is relieved by steam inhalation, there are several devices to provide the relief he needs. One is the commercial electric inhalator that boils water to which a few drops of a volatile medication are added to provide a pleasantly moist and warm breathing environment. If a commercial inhalator is not available, a similar apparatus can be made by fashioning a cone from a sheet of newspaper and placing the wide end of the cone over the top and spout of a teapot containing freshly boiled water. The narrow end of the cone will direct the hot water vapor toward the face of the patient. If a medication is to be added, it can be applied to a ball of cotton placed in the cone; the steam or water vapor will pick up the medication as it passes through the cone.

If medicated vapor is intended for a small child or infant, the end of the cone can be directed into a canopy or tent made of blankets placed over a crib or the head of a bed. This arrangement should produce an effective respiratory environment for the child while keeping his body safely separated from the hot teakettle.

Still another method of providing steam inhalation for a patient requires only an old-fashioned washstand pitcher and bowl plus a grocery bag. An opening is cut in one corner of the bottom of the bag which is placed upside down over the pitcher filled with hot steaming water and, if needed, a medication. The patient simply breathes the hot moist air seeping through an opening in the bag. The pitcher of steaming water is placed in a bowl or basin as a safety precaution.

Sickroom Devices

With a bit of imagination, many sickroom devices can be contrived from items already around the house. A criblike bed railing can be arranged, for example, by lining up a series of ordinary kitchen chairs beside a bed; if necessary, they can be tied together to prevent a patient from falling out of bed. The bed itself can be raised to the level of a hospital bed by placing the bed legs on blocks built from scrap lumber. Cardboard boxes can be shaped with scissors and tape into bed rests, foot supports, bed tables, or other helpful bedside aids.

Plastic bags from the kitchen can be used to collect tissues and other materials that must be removed regularly from the sickroom. Smaller plastic bags may be attached to the side of the bed to hold comb, hairbrush, and other personal items.

Keeping Health Records

The family that keeps good records of past injuries and illnesses, as well as immunization information and notes on reactions to medications, has a head start in organizing the home care of a member who suddenly requires nursing. The file of family health records should include information about temperatures and pulse rates taken during periods of good health; such data can serve as benchmark readings for evaluating periods of illness. Also, if each member of the family can practice taking temperatures and counting pulse and respiration rates during periods of good health, the family will be better able to handle home nursing routines when the need arises.

Home Care Equipment Checklist

Following is a convenient checklist of basic supplies needed for home care of the sick:

1. Disinfectants for soaking clothing and utensils used by the sick. Not all disinfectants are equally effective for every purpose. For clothing and food utensils, corrosive or poisonous disinfectants are to be avoided. Antiseptics do not kill bacteria; they only retard their growth. Among the common disinfectants that can be used in the home are:

- Alcohol, 75 percent by weight, used for disinfecting instruments and cleaning the skin
- Lysol, for decontaminating clothing and utensils
- Soap with an antibacterial agent for scrubbing the hands

- Carbolic acid (phenol) for disinfecting instruments and utensils (it is corrosive, poisonous, and very effective if used in 5 percent solution)
- Cresol in 2.5 percent solution for disinfecting sputum and feces (less poisonous than phenol and can be obtained as an alkali solution in soap)
- Boric acid, a weak antiseptic eyewash
- Detergent creams, used to reduce skin bacteria

2. Disposable rubber gloves, to be used when handling patients with open wounds or contagious diseases, as well as for cleaning feces.

3. Paper napkins and tissues for cleaning nasal and oral discharges.

4. Rectal and oral thermometers. The former is used primarily for infants, while the latter is used for adults and older children. Thermometers should always be thoroughly disinfected after use by soaking in isopropyl alcohol, and they should be washed prior to reuse.

5. Eating and drinking utensils to be used only by the patient. Disposable utensils are preferable.

6. Urinal, bedpan, and sputum cup for patients who cannot go to the toilet. After use, they should be thoroughly disinfected with cresol and washed with liquid soap containing an antibacterial agent.

7. Personal toilet requisites: face cloths and towels, toilet soap, washbasin, toothbrush and toothpaste, comb, hairbrush, razor, and a water pitcher (if running water is not accessible to the patient).

8. Measuring glass graduated in teaspoon and tablespoon levels for liquid medication.

9. Plastic waste-disposal bags that can be closed and tied.

33

Health Care Delivery

A Changing Service

Unending change has characterized American health care in recent decades. The general practitioner in private practice, once the institutionalized symbol of medical care in the United States, has largely given way to specialists of many kinds. Where the general practitioner once sent a handwritten bill for services to the family home, he or she may now send a computerized invoice to an insurance company or a government agency. The "house call" has virtually disappeared.

Technology has taken over. Hospitals and other health care institutions may pay sums in seven figures for equipment that can save lives but that also demands to be used. A "technological imperative" requires that the new approach or instrument or drug at least be tried—experimented with, proven useful or useless, and made available to those who need it. In diagnosis and therapy in particular, physicians and other professionals are continually seeking the new and better.

Some seven million people work in the American health care system. Half a million of those are physicians. The facilities in which the system's personnel work range from rural clinics to high-technology urban medical centers. On balance, the consumer dealing with this system has many choices. Understanding those choices may make the difference between a beneficial experience and a frustrating search for help.

Health care reaches the American public at three broadly defined levels. The three are primary, secondary, and tertiary care.

Primary Care

Essentially, *primary care* refers to "first contact" care as provided in physicians' offices or hospitals. Such care may also be provided in emergency rooms and outpatient clinics. The individual can obtain primary care without referral by a physician, but referrals from this level of care are generally necessary to ensure that the patient will receive treatment at the next higher level. Among the types of services provided at the primary care level are health maintenance for infants and children, screening for infectious and communicable diseases, and treatment for minor injuries.

Secondary Care

At the *secondary care* level the patient usually comes under the care of a specialist, often in a community hospital or other, similar setting. Secondary level specialties include such well-known areas of medicine as obstetrics and gynecology, dermatology, otolaryngology, and cardiology. While physicians often refer their patients for secondary level care, many persons "refer themselves."

Tertiary Care

At the tertiary care level, the patient receives highly specialized, high-technology care and treatment. Complex programs and unusual procedures, among them open heart surgery, heart or kidney transplantation, and neurological surgery, are provided by physicians with extensive training and the advantages of sophisticated equipment for diagnosis and treatment. Often, care at this level is obtainable only if the patient enters a hospital with specialized facilities. Of the various tertiary care institutions, three key ones are hospitals specializing in a certain disease or a group of diseases, hospitals associated with medical schools, and large regional referral centers. Many such institutions would be expected to have diagnostic equipment for such procedures as cardiac catheterization, nuclear magnetic resonance testing, and CT scanning.

Importantly, the three levels of care overlap. The distinctions among them are not always clearly drawn or defined. For the patient, the most important factor may be the need for referrals at some levels and not at others.

Health Care Delivery Formats

The average American visits a physician five times a year. That statistic appears in a U.S. Public Health Service survey that also defines a visit as an encounter with a physician or other health professional under a physician's direction or supervision. The "encounter" can take place in the physician's office, in the patient's home, by telephone, or in some other ambulatory care setting. The physician initiates about half of the encounters, usually as part of follow-up care.

Office and Clinic Care

In the main, the patient sees his or her physician in an office or at a site reserved for group practice; in a hospital outpatient department; in an ambulatory surgical center; or in a freestanding surgical center.

Office-Based Practice

Most physicians practice on their own; even so, the solo practice is declining as a way of medical life. The solo practitioner survives in isolated or rural areas, but hardly at all elsewhere. For the physician, solo practice is both simpler because of the independence and freedom it

guarantees and more complex because the service responsibility may continue 24 hours a day, seven days a week. For the patient, the main advantage of solo practice is both the closer relationship that can develop and less fragmented care.

Partnerships

Very common today is the partnership, an agreement between two or more physicians under which the participants share office space, staff, and equipment. The physicians retain their independence in the sense that they have their own practices, but they usually share patient responsibilities under given circumstances. A physician who has to be out of contact with the office may, for example, give a patient another partner's number so as to have continuous backup. Spreading the care responsibilities and reducing the workload, each physician may also have more time for each patient.

The patient may find major advantages in the partnership. He or she can become acquainted with the physician's partner and in this way obtain personalized care at all times. Backup support may be especially important in obstetrics, where deliveries may occur without warning, and in cardiology, where emergencies are equally unscheduled.

Groups

Where three or more physicians associate in an arrangement that is normally less formal than a partnership, it is termed a *group*. The physicians belonging to the group may practice in a single specialty or in diverse fields of medicine. An example of the latter would be a group of three doctors offering internist, obstetrics-gynecological, and pediatric services. In other

ways the group shares the advantages and disadvantages of the typical partnership. Like the partnership, the group has one particular advantage, however: other physicians are available for consultation and education. The group format may also make possible relatively sophisticated laboratory and other facilities.

Health Maintenance Organizations

The health maintenance organization (HMO) ranks as a special kind of group practice, one that involves a fixed monthly or annual fee system rather than a fee-for-service arrangement. The fixed fee ensures that the HMO member will receive, at no additional charge, all necessary health services, including hospitalization and the care of specialists. Preventive medicine at no extra cost to the member is a feature of the HMO that has ensured reduced usage of hospital facilities.

Preferred Provider Organizations

Like the HMO, the preferred provider organization (PPO) is at least partly a response to rising health-care costs. Forming a PPO, a group of physicians contracts individually with an insurance company or employer to provide health services for fees that are usually lower than those prevailing in the community or area. The PPO does charge on a fee-for-service basis, but employees making use of the organization's medical services save money because they avoid the copayments of conventional insurance plans and the standard deductibles. Physicians belonging to the PPO have a stable pool of employed members whose health problems may be extremely diverse. For the employer or insurance company, a particular advantage is the ability to bargain for lower fees.

Three Alternative Systems

Obviously, office and clinic care takes many forms. Three alternatives that provide relatively minor, low-level services are the hospital outpatient department, the ambulatory surgical center, and the freestanding emergency center. Each plays a particular role in the health care delivery network.

Hospital Outpatient Departments

Outpatient departments once offered free services as a means of training medical students and residents or because physicians volunteered their services for such departments. Today, outpatient departments charge for their services while delivering health care that varies broadly as regards quality. One hospital in three has an outpatient department or a clinic for ambulatory care while nine of ten community hospitals offer outpatient care in their emergency departments.

Ambulatory Surgical Centers

Sometimes called surgicenters, the ambulatory surgical center may be attached to a hospital or be completely independent. In either case, the surgicenter may be an effective alternative in the traditional situation where a patient needs an abortion, a dilatation and curettage (D & C), hernia repair, or tissue biopsy. Because they perform lower-risk procedures, ambulatory surgical centers can keep costs down. Local anesthesia is the norm, and usually the patient goes home on the day of the operation.

Freestanding Emergency Centers

Sometimes called *urgicenters,* freestanding emergency centers resemble hospital emergency departments.

But private, for-profit groups usually run them. Open from 12 to 24 hours daily, they operate on a drop-in basis, meeting a definite need where a hospital emergency room is far away or when all physicians' offices have shut down for the day. Typically, emergency centers treat sprains and bruises, cuts that require stiches, and upper respiratory infections. Charges for such services usually range from visits to physicians' offices on the low side to hospital emergency rooms on the high side.

Community Health Care Facilities

Providing more evidence of the complexity of the United States' health care delivery complex, community health facilities fill a void in health services at a very basic level. At least five different modes of providing health care need to be considered as community facilities.

School and College Health Programs

Once concerned primarily with the control of communicable diseases and screenings for dental, vision, and hearing problems, school and college health programs have taken on new functions. At the elementary and high-school levels, they may help with health and sex education programs, keep vaccination records, and consult with parents. Colleges and universities generally provide infirmary services, meaning inpatient care for acute illness. At larger schools, programs may deal with contraception and pregnancy problems, substance abuse, and neuroses.

Industrial Health Programs

Treatment of work-related injuries and minor illnesses remains a key

function of industrial health programs. The programs also continue to give minor physical exams and to provide general medical and dental care. But they have expanded their services in recognition of the value of preventive medicine. Newer or more modern programs offer comprehensive work-site education and screening programs, alcohol abuse counseling, stop-smoking clinics, and aerobic fitness classes.

Health Screening

Provided by local health departments and voluntary health agencies (see Chapter 36), health screening varies from community to community as regards both availability and reliability. Depending on community funding, a local health department may or may not provide tests that screen for infectious or parasitic diseases, including sexually transmitted diseases (see Chapter 17), and chronic disorders such as high blood pressure, sickle cell anemia, or diabetes. Many health departments make referrals to follow-up medical care.

Neighborhood and Primary Health-Care Centers

Neighborhood and primary health-care centers were established first in the 1960s to provide ambulatory care in underserved communities, both rural and urban. Staffed often by U.S. Public Health Service medical personnel or by nurse practitioners, the centers either limited their services according to income requirements or served specific communities. Because of cuts in federal spending, experts note, many such centers have been or are being phased out.

Women, Infant, and Child Care

Also federally funded, the women, infant, and child care program emphasizes provision of well-baby care, nutritious food, and nutrition education for pregnant women, infants, and children under three. Estimates indicate that the program saves three dollars for every dollar spent. But federal budget cuts have begun seriously to scale back the program.

Disease Prevention and Control

County or city health departments usually establish disease prevention and control programs to help control the spread of communicable diseases. Methods used include immunization, screening, and follow-up. Typical concerns include immunization for childhood diseases like diphtheria, measles, and polio; tuberculosis and sexually transmitted diseases; and influenza immunization for older persons.

Hospitals

Viewed a century ago as a deathhouse, the hospital has a new image in the 1980s. With an entirely revised role built on its ability to provide comforts and even amenities, the hospital has added a "hotel" function to its fundamental "healing" function. But the hotel role does not affect the hospital's main medical purpose: to provide, within budgetary and other limits, sophisticated, technologically upto-date care. The hospital has become the place to go for diagnostic and therapeutic care that a physician's office cannot provide.

A basic method of classifying hospitals is by length of the patient's stay. Viewed this way, hospitals fall into two groups, long-term or extendedcare institutions and short-term hospitals. The former will be discussed later; the second group includes community, teaching, and public hospitals.

Community Hospitals

Most Americans receive medical care in community hospitals. Usually quite small, with 50 to 500 beds, this kind of hospital generally provides good to excellent secondary-level care. Traditionally, community hospitals were nonprofit corporations that depended heavily on community support. Today, the community hospital is increasingly likely to be proprietary. That means it is run for profit by investor-owned groups or corporations.

The costs of medical care at a proprietary community hospital may not be significantly different from those charged by a voluntary or nonprofit hospital.

Teaching Hospitals

Ranging in size from a few hundred to a few thousand beds, teaching hospitals universally offer training for undergraduate medical students, postgraduate students, or fellows. Also, nearly all have ties to major medical schools. A state government may own a teaching hospital that is used by state medical schools; others are owned by the associated university or by a nonprofit corporation. Teaching hospitals provide care at all three levels.

Public Hospitals

Public hospitals include not only county hospitals but others supported by public funds, among them public health service hospitals, Veterans Administration (VA) hospitals, and municipal short-term-stay hospitals. Many such institutions that are owned by federal, state, or city governments are teaching hospitals, and many also have associated rehabilitation units and nursing homes.

The Elderly: Home Care

Surprisingly, most elderly persons live at home and receive care from relatives and others who may visit the home to help out. Younger family members may need home care because of illness or injury, but typically the disabled or ill older person is the one receiving such care. A number of community resources are available to make home care—or self-care for those living alone—easier. These resources include home health workers, such services as Meals-on-Wheels, and various day-care programs.

Invaluable aids for those responsible for home care for an aging relative are unskilled companions and temporary help. With this kind of assistance, the elderly person may be able to enjoy continuity of care and independence while maintaining ties with family, home, and community.

Home Health Services

Some 2,500 home health agencies operate under the general direction of physicians to provide two kinds of services: skilled and supportive. Of the many types of home health service providers, the best known are private, either profit-making or nonprofit; public health agencies such as neighborhood health centers; hospital-based services; and local or county health department or community and church programs. The nationwide Visiting Nurses Association is perhaps the most familiar.

Different communities and areas enjoy different levels and types of home health services. But most such agencies provide care to anyone who requests it. Fees vary, and may be paid by the individual or the family accepting the care. In other cases the government or individual insurance plans may reimburse the family, partially or totally, for the fees charged.

Hospital social workers or discharge-planners, the Area Agency on Aging, the local office of the Social Security Administration, day-care centers, and churches and synagogues normally provide information on home health services.

Voluntary Health Agencies

Many voluntary health agencies provide aid and support to the disabled or sick elderly person (see Chapter 36). Such groups and organizations as the American Cancer Society and the Easter Seal Society may even offer "friendly visitor" services in specific communities. Most of the groups see education of the public as functional to their roles. Thus they may provide films, lecturers, books and pamphlets, and other materials of interest to groups and organizations of many kinds. Many such agencies have specialized equipment for those who need it as well as listings of community resources.

Drugstores and Medical Supply Houses

Two other basic sources of specialized equipment and sickroom supplies, the medically oriented drugstore and the medical supply house, play important roles. In many cases the family discharging home care responsibilities can obtain wheelchairs, walkers, portable oxygen equipment, and hospital beds from one source or the other. Often, the supplier will rent or sell the specialized equipment; the choice may be the family's to make.

Community Facilities for the Aged

An entire new category of health care facilities has come into being in recent years in response to the needs of the elderly. These community facilities are designed specifically for those elderly persons living at home who are not housebound.

Adult Day Care

A broad variety of community-based centers schedule adult day-care programs for the elderly. To some extent the programs provide an alternative to institutionalization. In each case the programs are tailored to meet specific needs. Each type has a basic therapeutic objective.

Day Hospitals

Generally located at an extended-care facility or hospital, the day hospital provides medical care and supervision for persons recovering from acute illnesses. A physician's referral is normally required; fees closely parallel those charged for other hospital services. The day hospital that treats primarily patients discharged from an institution is sometimes called an aftercare clinic.

Medical Day Care

Where chronically ill or disabled persons do not require frequent or intensive medical intervention, the medical day care service may be the solution. Located usually in a long-term care institution or freestanding center, such a care service may include nursing and other supports. A physician's referral is required, and rehabilitation and maintenance are primary therapeutic goals. Reimbursement is by third-party (insurance company) payments on a sliding scale. Medicaid pays for medical day care in some states.

Mental Health Day Care

Offering a supervised environment along with mental health services to adults with organic or functional mental illness, the mental health day care service is usually located in a psychiatric institution or freestanding center. Referral by a psychiatrist is required. Three basic therapeutic goals are supervision, assistance with coping skills, and safety for the patient. Reimbursement is by third-party payment.

Social Adult Day Care

Title XX of the Social Security Act provides for funding of many social adult day care facilities, all of which are geared to the needs of adults who have difficulty functioning independently. Both families and health facilities can make referrals, but examination by a physician is normally required before admission. Third-party reimbursement is the norm. Program objectives and services vary widely, and are usually formulated by the funding source and the sponsoring organization. Program participants may attend part-days or full days five days a week; the facility may provide a midday meal and transportation within a specified area.

Nutrition Services

Nutrition ranks as a critical need for both homebound and more independent elderly persons. Meals-on-Wheels, a community service offered under voluntary auspices but funded partly by public funds, caters to the homebound. For a reasonable charge the service provides at least one hot meal daily for persons 60 and older. For the elderly attending senior centers, the Area Agency on Aging provides both adequate nutrition and a chance to socialize. Agency personnel can keep in touch with clients' physical and social situations, giving the program an important outreach and prevention dimension.

Extended-Care, Long-Term Care, Nursing Homes

Closely related, the extended-care facility, long-term care facility, and nursing home nonetheless meet different needs. A relatively recent innovation, the extended-care facility provides a service that falls between that given in an acute-care hospital and that provided in a skilled nursing facility or nursing home.

Extended-Care Facility

Despite its name, the extended-care facility provides short-term inpatient care. This type of facility is designed mainly to aid patients who have been hospitalized but no longer need the full complement of hospital services. Such patients still require professional nursing and medical supervision. Typically attached to a hospital, the extended-care facility may also serve those who are not acutely ill but who require skilled care.

Because most extended-care facilities are physically attached to hospitals, patients often simply move from one hospital wing to another. Some nursing homes also meet the standards set for qualification as extended-care facilities by the Joint Commission on the Accreditation of Hospitals (JCAH). For the most part, extended-care facilities charge much less than the typical hospital.

Long-Term Care Facilities

Patients with chronic conditions that cannot be treated effectively in a general hospital generally qualify for care in a long-term care facility. Such conditions range from tuberculosis to mental retardation. The facilities also include chronic disease hospitals, rehabilitation hospitals, and psychiatric hospitals for both children and adults.

Nursing Homes

Also falling in the category of long-term care facilities, nursing homes comprise a special group of facilities of different kinds. They offer services ranging from sheltered living arrangements to around-the-clock nursing care. All nursing homes rank as residential facilities.

The approximately 18,000 nursing homes in the United States have between 1.3 and 1.5 million beds. Three-quarters of these nursing homes are proprietary, or for-profit, institutions that house about two-thirds of all the beds. Nonprofit organizations operate 15 percent of all the nation's nursing homes and make available about 20 percent of the beds. The government operates the remaining homes.

Nursing homes accommodate persons of all ages. A few younger residents have serious congenital illnesses or disorders, or have been recently discharged from a hospital. Others are recovering from recent surgery. But most patients are the chronically ill elderly. Typically, a nursing home resident is a woman in her 80s, single or widowed. Afflicted with three or more serious chronic illnesses, she has very likely exhausted all her assets except her monthly Social Security payments.

Residential-Care Facilities

Standing at the lowest level of nursing home care, the residential-care facility is usually appropriate for the person who can no longer live alone and manage household chores. This "typical" resident does not need extensive medical attention but does require sheltered living, prepared meals, and some medical monitoring. The latter may include supervision of medications and tracking of signs and symptoms.

Intermediate-Care Facilities

The intermediate-care facility supplements typical RCF services with regular, but not round-the-clock, nursing care for residents who are unable to survive on their own. The intermediate-care facility may also make provision for social and recreational activities. Programs of physical therapy and rehabilitation, occupational therapy, speech therapy, and social work services may also be offered.

Skilled Nursing Facilities

With staffs of registered nurses, licensed practical nurses, and nurses' aides, skilled nursing facilities can provide 24-hour care. They are, thus, appropriate for persons in need of intensive nursing care and rehabilitation. Like intermediate-care facilities, skilled nursing facilities are state-certified for the most part, a factor that makes them eligible for public funds as payment for services. Lack of certification may mean that an ICF or SNF has serious deficiencies.

Hospices

Described sometimes as more a philosophy than a type of physical facility, the hospice is a form of care for the terminally ill. The family and the patient merit equal consideration in the typical hospice; the purpose is to minimize the twin fears associated with dying, fear of isolation and fear of pain. Typical palliative care involves the careful control of pain and the management of other symptoms of terminal disease or illness.

A growing number of communities have hospice facilities. But no pattern appears in the types of institutions— or sections of institutions—devoted to the care of the terminally ill. A hospice may be a wing in a hospital or simply a group of hospital beds that can be made available as needed. A hospice may also be a separate building or institution. While families provide much of the care as long as patients are at home, a team including a physician, nurses, counselors, home health aides and others may be continually on call. The team provides continuity between home and hospice when patients must be institutionalized. At all times, the individual patient's comfort is a prime consideration.

Patients enter hospice programs at their own requests. A physician's referral, indicating that the prognosis is no more than six months, may also be required.

34

Voluntary Health Agencies

Major Agencies

The establishment of more than 100 voluntary health agencies since the beginning of this century has been a major factor in the growth of health services to the American public. These agencies, whose activities are made possible by donations of time and money from the public, occasionally augmented by government grants for special projects, have the following objectives: spreading information about various diseases to the professional and lay public; sponsoring research; promoting legislation; and operating referral services on the community level to patients in need of diagnosis, treatment, and financial aid.

Some of these agencies, such as the American Diabetes Association or the Arthritis Foundation, focus on a particular disease; others deal with problems arising from related disorders, such as the National Association for Mental Health and the American Heart Association. Still others, such as Planned Parenthood and the American Social Health Association, have programs vital not only to individuals, but to society as a whole.

To coordinate the activities of these many groups, to promote better health facilities, and to establish standards for the organization and conduct of these agencies, the National Health Council was founded in 1920. Its membership includes government, professional, and community associations, as well as the 21 voluntary health agencies described below, which command a total budget of almost $1.5 billion and involve the services of almost 12 million volunteers.

All of these organizations function on the national, state, and community level. Information and literature may be obtained through local chapters or by writing to the national office of the organization. Volunteers may offer their services in a variety of ways: as office workers, fund raisers, speakers, and community coordinators.

On the following pages, voluntary health agencies are discussed under the subjects with which they are concerned; the subjects are arranged alphabetically. Following these agencies is a brief discussion of other voluntary health agencies. Because of limitations of space, however, many worthwhile organizations have had to be omitted.

Accident Prevention

The National Safety Council, 444 North Michigan Avenue, Chicago, Illinois 60611, was founded in 1913 to improve factory safety but soon broadened its activities to preventing every type of accident. The Council is now composed of groups and individuals from every part of the population: business, industry, government, education, religion, labor, and law. Its main efforts are devoted to building strong support for official safety programs at the national, state, and community levels in specific areas, such as traffic, labor, and home.

The Council believes that practically all accidents can be prevented with the application of the right safeguards. These safeguards include public education and awareness of danger, enforcement of safety laws and regulations, and improved design standards for machines, farm equipment, and motor vehicles.

It maintains the world's largest library of accident prevention materials, distributes a wide variety of safety literature, and issues awards for outstanding safety achievements. It also serves as a national and international clearing house of information about the causes of accidents and how they can be prevented.

In addition to campaigning for increased safety legislation on the national and state level, the Council's current programs include a defensive driving course, which provides effective adult driver training on a mass scale; a safety training institute; environmental and occupational health and "Right-to-Know" educational materials; and several approaches to the alcohol and driving problem.

Its publication, *Family Safety and Health,* has record circulation of more than two million readers, and its manual called *Fundamentals of Industrial Hygiene* provides more than 1,000 pages of material essential to the safety of factory workers.

The Council in recent years has expanded its safety promotion work to include both on- and off-the-job safety for workers and their families, as well as 24-hour-a-day safety for all persons in all activities.

Alcoholism

The National Council on Alcoholism and Drug Dependence, 12 W. 21st Street, New York, New York 10010, is the only national voluntary health agency founded to combat alcoholism as a disease by an extensive program on the professional and community level. The Council is completely independent of Alcoholics Anonymous, although the two organizations cooperate fully.

In nearly 200 cities where the Council has affiliates, alcoholism information centers have been established that provide referral services for alcoholics and drug addicts and their families as well as educational materials for all segments of the community, including physicians and nurses, the clergy, the courts, social workers, and welfare agencies. Local affiliates also help to develop labor-management programs that provide help for employees who suffer from the disease.

The Council also sponsors research, professional training, and legislative action. Its publications department distributes a variety of fact sheets, pamphlets, posters, and videos. For a listing of publications or information on the Council's programs, write the national headquarters or contact the nearest local affiliate.

Arthritis

The Arthritis Foundation, 1314 Spring Street N.W., Atlanta, Georgia 30309, was established to help arthritis sufferers and their physicians through programs of research, patient services, public health information, and education on the professional and popular level. Its long-term goal is to find the cause, prevention, and cure for the nation's number one crippling disease.

The Foundation operates local chapters throughout the United States whose chief concern is the patient who has or might have arthritis. These chapters are centers for information about the disease itself and also serve as referral centers for treatment facilities. In addition, they distribute literature and sponsor forums on the latest developments in research and patient care.

Some chapters support arthritis clinics and home care programs; most conduct patient self-help programs such as discussion groups and exercise classes. Parent groups are often maintained for parents of children with arthritis.

Two special groups work within the Foundation: the Arthritis Health Professions Association which devotes itself to continuing education for health professionals caring for arthritis patients and the American Juvenile Arthritis Organization for those with a special interest in arthritis in children.

A major part of the Foundation's work at the national level is providing funds for fellowships to young physicians and scientists so that they may continue their work in arthritis research and in funding through annual grants research at major institutions throughout the United States.

Cancer

The American Cancer Society, 1599 Clifton Rd. N.E., Atlanta, Georgia 30329, was established in 1913 by a small group of physicians and volunteer workers to inform the public about the possibility of saving lives through the early diagnosis and treatment of cancer. The Society now has 57 regional groups, one in each state plus one in the District of Columbia and six other metropolitan areas, devoted to the control and eradication of cancer. In addition to the physicians, research scientists, and other professional workers engaged in the Society's activities, more than two million volunteers are connected with its many programs.

The American Cancer Society conducts widespread campaigns to educate the public in the importance of annual medical checkups so that cancerous symptoms can be detected while they are still curable. Such checkups should include an examination of the rectum and colon and, for women, examination of the breasts and a Pap test for the detection of uterine cancer.

In another of its campaigns, the Society emphasizes the link between cigarette smoking and lung cancer. It also sponsors an extensive program to persuade teenagers not to start smoking. During its annual April Crusade against Cancer, the Society distributes approximately 40 million copies of a leaflet containing lifesaving information on early detection of cancer.

On the professional level, the major objective of the Society is to make every physician's office a cancer-detection center. To achieve this goal, it publishes a variety of literature, offers refresher courses, sponsors seminars, and cooperates closely with local and state medical societies and health departments on the diagnosis and treatment of cancer. It also arranges national and international conferences for the exchange of information on the newest cancer-fighting techniques, and finances a million-dollar-a-year clinical fellowship program for young physicians.

Among its special services to patients are sponsorship of the International Association of Laryngectomies, for people who have lost their voices to cancer; and Reach to Recovery, a program for women who have had treatment for breast cancer and who need support and guidance to return to normal living. On the community level, the American Cancer Society operates a counseling service for cancer patients and their families, referring them to the proper medical facilities and social agencies for treatment and care. Through its "loan closets," it provides sickroom necessities, hospital beds, medical dressings, and so on.

Some local divisions offer home care programs through the services of the Visiting Nurse Association or a similar agency. Although the Society does not operate medical facilities, treat patients, or pay physicians' fees, some of the chapters support cancer detection programs and professionally supervised rehabilitation services.

Cerebral Palsy

The United Cerebral Palsy Associations, 7 Penn Plaza, Suite 804, New York, New York 10001, founded in 1948 by a small group of concerned parents, now has 203 affiliates across the country where those who have the condition may obtain treatment referral, therapy, and education. The Associations also play an important role in vocational training, job placement programs, housing, and recreational services.

The Research and Educational Foundation of this organization supports studies investigating possible causes of cerebral palsy. The Foundation also gives grants to universities and medical schools for research into the causes and prevention of cerebral palsy and new methods of therapy, for training medical and other professional personnel in the management of this condition.

Cystic Fibrosis

The Cystic Fibrosis Foundation, 6931 Arlington Road, No. 200, Bethesda, Maryland 20814, was organized in 1955 by a group of concerned parents whose children were born with this lung disease. The Foundation now concerns itself with all serious lung ailments of children regardless of their medical names, and it engages in a broad program of research, medical education, public information, and the sponsorship of diagnostic and treatment centers.

The Foundation's 58 local chapters offer advice and information to parents of children with severe lung disease, and have direct connections with the more than 120 Cystic Fibrosis Centers throughout the country. They refer patients to sources of financial aid, make arrangements for the purchase of drugs at a discount, and lend home treatment equipment to families who cannot afford to buy it.

The national organization makes grants for research activities, conducts professional conferences, and publishes literature for physicians and the general public on various aspects of childhood lung diseases.

Diabetes

The American Diabetes Association, National Service Center, P.O. Box 25757, 1660 Duke Street, Alexandria, Virginia 22314, was established as a professional society in 1940. In recent years it has enlarged its scope so that it currently has 800 affiliated local chapters throughout the country that promote the creation of better understanding of diabetes among patients and their families; the exchange of knowledge among physicians and other scientists; the spreading of accurate information to the general public about early recognition and supervision of the disease; and the sponsorship of basic research.

Since 1948, the American Diabetes Association has conducted an annual Diabetes Detection Drive supported by widespread publicity in all news media. During this drive, approximately three million testing kits are provided to state and county medical societies to facilitate the early detection and prompt treatment of the disorder. This annual activity hopes to find the estimated 1,600,000 people who are unaware that they have diabetes.

Among the Association's publications of special interest to diabetics and their families are the *Diabetes Forecast,* a national magazine that presents news items on research and treatment; *Meal Planning with Exchange Lists,* prepared with the cooperation of the American Dietetic Association and the U.S. Public Health Services; and *A Cookbook for Diabetics,* which contains attractive recipes for meals that can be served to diabetics.

Other activities of the Association include encouraging the employment of diabetics and providing special groups such as teachers, police, and social agencies with information on the condition. It also established a classification of the disease according to its severity. Guidelines on emergency medical care and the scientific journal *Diabetes* are available to physicians.

Drug Abuse

The American Social Health Association, which was organized originally to combat the spread of venereal disease, expanded its program in 1960 to include drug abuse education. For information about its activities in this field, see below under "Sexually Transmitted Diseases."

Eye Diseases

The National Society to Prevent Blindness, 79 Madison Avenue, New York, New York 10016, was founded in 1908 to reduce the number of cases of infants born with impaired sight. In subsequent years, it merged with the American Association for the Conservation of Vision and the Ophthalmological Foundation. The Society is now concerned with investigating all causes of blindness and supports measures and community services that will eliminate them. It also distributes information on the proper care and use of the eyes.

The organization's first and most significant victory was the adoption of laws by almost all states requiring that silver nitrate solution be routinely dropped into the eyes of all newborn babies to counteract the possibility of congenital blindness. This resulted in a dramatic drop in the number of children suffering from eye impairment dating from birth.

For almost half a century, the Society has actively campaigned to reduce the number of people suffering from glaucoma, one of the leading causes of blindness in the United States. It has also conducted a national program to educate the elderly in the ease, safety, and advantages of surgery for cataracts, the leading cause of blindness among the aged.

Since 1926, the Society has been conducting preschool vision screening programs administered by teams that travel from big cities to isolated rural communities. Current activities also include research into the cause, treatment, and prevention of eye diseases leading to blindness; assembling data and publishing reports; cooperating with community agencies to improve eye health; promoting conditions in schools and industry to safeguard vision; and advocating eye examinations in early childhood so that disorders can be properly and promptly corrected.

Family Planning

Planned Parenthood Federation of America, 810 Seventh Avenue, New York, New York 10019, is the nation's oldest and largest voluntary family planning organization. Tracing its origins to 1916, when Margaret Sanger founded the first U.S. birth control clinic in Brooklyn, New York, Planned Parenthood maintains that every individual has the fundamental right to choose when or whether to have a child.

Planned Parenthood has five key goals:

- To increase the availability and accessibility of high-quality and affordable reproductive health care services and information, especially for underserved groups

- To reduce adolescent pregnancy and unwanted births to teens

- To meet the challenge of changes in health care delivery systems and maintain high-quality, efficiently run, and creative Planned Parenthood programs

- To further Planned Parenthood's role in the provision of education of human sexuality, reproduction, and population, and on the bioethical and legal implications of reproductive technology

- To increase access to safe and effective methods of voluntary fertility regulation for individuals in developing countries

Each year, more than three million individuals in 49 states and the District of Columbia obtain medical, educational, and counseling services through more than 900 clinics operated by Planned Parenthood's 171 affiliates. The organization is active in more than 100 developing countries throughout the world. In addition, Planned Parenthood conducts clinical research, provides professional training of health and education personnel, and serves as a resource to health agencies, government agencies at the state and federal levels, legislators and other policy makers, and the media.

Heart Disease

The American Heart Association, 7320 Greenville Avenue, Dallas, Texas 75231, was founded in 1924 as a professional organization of cardiologists. It was reorganized in 1948 as a national voluntary health agency to promote a program of education, research, and community service in the interests of reducing premature death and disability caused by diseases of the heart and blood vessels. The complex of heart disorders, including atherosclerosis, stroke, high blood pressure, kidney diseases, rheumatic fever, and congenital heart disturbances, is by far the leading cause of death in the United States.

Since its first Annual Heart Fund Campaign in 1949, the Association has contributed more than $150 million to research and has been a major factor in the reduction of cardiovascular mortality statistics. It has spent more than $2 million since 1959 studying human heart transplantation procedures, and has contributed to the development of an artificial heart, plastic heart valves, and synthetic arteries.

Public and professional education programs designed to reduce the risk of heart attack through avoidance of cigarette smoking, obesity, and foods high in cholesterol are conducted on a nationwide and community level by the Association's affiliates throughout the country. The local chapters are also engaged in service programs for rheumatic fever prevention, stroke rehabilitation, school health, cardiopulmonary resuscitation, and industrial health. In addition, they conduct information and referral services for patients and their families.

The American Heart Association publishes many technical and professional journals as well as material designed for the general public.

Hemophilia

The National Hemophilia Foundation, 110 Green Street, Room 406, New York, New York 10012, was established in 1948 to serve the needs of hemophiliacs and their families by ensuring the availability of treatment and rehabilitation facilities. It is estimated that there are as many as 100,000 males suffering from what is

popularly known as "bleeder's disease," an inherited condition passed from mothers to sons.

The long-term goal of the Foundation is to develop a national program of research and clinical study that will provide new information about early diagnosis and effective treatment of the disorder as well as trained professional personnel to administer patient care.

The development in recent years of blood-clotting concentrates is the most important advance to date in the treatment of the disease. This development, supported in part by the Foundation's 48 chapters, makes it possible for patients to have elective surgery and dental work, and to eliminate much of the pain, crippling, and hospitalization of those suffering from hemophilia.

The need for blood supplies from which to extract the clotting factor caused the Foundation to embark on an extensive campaign for blood donations. For this purpose, it has been working closely since 1968 with the American Red Cross and the American Association of Blood Banks. It also maintains close ties with various laboratories and research groups in the development of more powerful concentrates that can be manufactured and sold at the lowest possible cost.

The organization's activities include a national network of facilities with blood banks, clinics, and treatment centers as well as referral services. It has also established a Behavioral Science Department to explore the nonmedical aspects of hemophiliacs' problems, such as education, vocational guidance, and psychological needs.

Kidney Disease

The National Kidney Foundation, 30 E. 33rd Street, Suite 1100, New

York, New York 10016, formerly the National Kidney Disease Foundation, was founded in 1950 by a group of parents whose children had a disease with no cure—nephrosis. The ultimate goal was the total eradication of all diseases of the kidney and urinary tract. Today, although there remains no cure for nephrosis, the disease is almost totally treatable. In the past two decades the National Kidney Foundation and its 49 affiliates nationwide have supported more than $20 million in research to find the answers to kidney and urinary tract related diseases.

The National Kidney Foundation and its affiliates sponsor a wide variety of programs in treatment, service, education, and prevention that are designed to aid the patient in the community. Examples of some affiliate programs include: information and referral programs for patients and their families, drug banks, support groups, summer camp programs for children on dialysis and transplantations, transportation services, counseling and screening, and direct financial assistance to needy patients.

The National Kidney Foundation seeks continually to increase the number of organs available for transplantation through its nationwide Organ Donor Program. To date, more than 50 million donor cards have been distributed by the Foundation and its affiliates. Distribution of public and professional educational materials continues to heighten public awareness of organ donation and the "Gift of Life" it can provide to thousands of people waiting for a kidney transplant.

Mental Health

The National Mental Health Association, 1021 Prince Street, Alexandria, Virginia 22314-2971, was founded in 1909 to work toward the improved care and treatment of people with mental illnesses, the promotion of mental health, and the prevention of mental disorders. The original National Committee for Mental Hygiene merged with the National Mental Health Foundation and the Psychiatric Foundation in 1950 to create the organization as it now stands.

The association implements its service programs through its 650 affiliates (local chapters and larger state divisions) across the country. These mental health associations tailor their efforts to the needs of their communities.

The National Mental Health Association is composed of one million volunteers and supporters who have a keen interest in mental health. They include family members whose loved ones have been affected by mental illnesses, current or former consumers, mental health professionals, and lay citizens.

Recent and ongoing activities include:

• Coordinated a national coalition to address the needs of people with mental illnesses who are homeless.

• Serves as a prime source of referral and educational information on mental illnesses and mental health issues through the NMHA Mental Health Information Center.

• Assists local and state MHA affiliates in serving communities through patient and family support groups, housing programs, suicide-prevention hotlines, and school mental health education programs.

• Helped extend the civil rights protection of the 8th and 14th Amendments to the U.S. Constitution to the mentally disabled by representing persons with severe mental illnesses before the Supreme Court.

• Specified a "state-of-the-art" program to prevent severe mental and emotional disabilities in a landmark 1986 report by its National Commission on the Prevention of Mental-Emotional Disabilities.

• Serves as the public-interest policy voice for mental health issues in the Congress and state legislatures.

Multiple Sclerosis

The National Multiple Sclerosis Society, 205 East 42nd Street, New York, New York 10017, was founded in 1946 with the primary goal of supporting research on this chronic neurological disease whose cause and cure are unknown. Some 250,000 Americans are estimated to have multiple sclerosis (MS).

Research aimed at finding the cause and methods of arresting MS is being conducted worldwide. From the beginning the Society has made every effort to increase professional and public awareness of the symptoms of MS and the best ways of treating them. This is done through a network of 143 chapters and branches and some 470,000 active members. The chapters, which are either affiliated with or support MS clinics around the country, provide home and hospital visits, recreational programs, referrals for medical care, job counseling, and other services. The chapters also arrange educational programs for physicians and social workers as well as for patients and their families. The society sponsors public education awards in magazine, radio, and television writing and conducts Project Rembrandt, a biennial competition for artists with MS.

The national office distributes publications for physicians and the interested public, including guides for the development of patient services and a quarterly magazine, *Inside MS*.

Films, slide presentations, videocassettes and audiocassettes are available for purchase or loan.

Physical Disabilities

The National Easter Seal Society, 70 East Lake Street, Chicago, Illinois 60601, has grown from its pioneering origins in 1919 to a national organization that serves more than one million disabled people of all ages. Among its network of facilities are comprehensive rehabilitation centers, treatment and diagnostic centers, and vocational training workshops, residential camps, special education programs, and transportation services in many different parts of the country.

Because many disabled children and adults in rural areas and small communities are unaware of the services available to them, the Society gives top priority to publicizing its information, referral, and follow-up activities. In recent years, it has also established mobile treatment units in hospitals and nursing homes in rural areas.

Other innovative activities include screening and testing programs to detect hearing loss in newborns and learning disabilities in preschool children, and providing treatment and referral for those who are disabled by respiratory diseases.

The Society collaborates with federal and professional agencies in all programs designed to eliminate architectural barriers to the disabled, and was instrumental in the enactment of legislation making it mandatory that all buildings constructed with government funds be fully and easily accessible to the disabled. It also initiates and supports significant studies in rehabilitation procedures as well as scientific research in bone transplant techniques.

Extensive literature is distributed to professionals, the public, parents, and employers. It also assembles special educational packets for parents of the disabled.

Sexually Transmitted Diseases

The American Social Health Association, P.O. Box 13827, Research Triangle Park, North Carolina 27709, was organized in 1912 to promote the control of venereal disease and to combat prostitution. In the mid-1980s the Association faced new challenges in the field of sexually transmitted diseases (STDs) while also developing new strategies to augment and complement existing AIDS information programs, promote attention to chlamydia, the most widespread STD in the United States, exert influence in Congress for additional federal funding for STD prevention and control programs, and place STD information in the hands of high-school students.

The Association is in close touch with government agencies such as the Public Health Service, the National Institutes of Health, and the various branches of the armed forces. Through these channels, it promotes its program for STD education in the schools and for research toward the discovery of an immunizing vaccine against syphilis and gonorrhea.

It is the major national voluntary repository for information and consultation on STDs, and maintains the world's most comprehensive collection of source workshops, residential camps, special education programs, and materials on STDs. It constantly helps communities in diagnosing their problems and produces a number of publications for teachers, guidance counselors, and youth workers.

The Association stresses the importance of introducing family life ed-

ucation into the curriculum of elementary and secondary schools and of establishing training programs on this subject in teachers' colleges. These efforts have resulted in the inclusion of family life education in an increasing number of school systems throughout the United States.

Tuberculosis and Respiratory Diseases

The American Lung Association, 1740 Broadway, New York, New York 10019, is the direct descendant of the first voluntary health organization to be formed in the United States. In 1904, when the National Association for the Study and Prevention of Tuberculosis was organized, this disease was the country's leading cause of death. Since 1973, with the sharp increase in the problems relating to smoking and air pollution, the association has been known by its present name, which was adopted to reflect the broader scope of its activities.

It now concerns itself not only with the elimination of tuberculosis but with chronic and disabling conditions, such as emphysema, and with acute diseases of the respiratory system, such as influenza. Through its affiliates and nationwide state organizations, it is actively engaged in campaigns against smoking and air pollution.

The early endeavor of the association to have tuberculosis included among the reportable diseases was accomplished state by state, and since the 1920s all states have required that every case in the country be brought to the attention of local health officials.

Public awareness of better care and the development of effective drugs have dramatically reduced the num-

ber of TB patients, but the association continues to concern itself with the fact that provisional data indicate that there are still about 22,000 new cases each year.

Through its local affiliates, the American Lung Association initiates special campaigns to combat smoking and air pollution, using radio and television announcements, car stickers, posters, and pamphlets, as well as films and exhibits. Educational materials on respiratory diseases are regularly distributed by the national office to local associations for physicians, patients, and the general public. Funds raised by the annual Christmas Seal drive also support research and medical education fellowships.

Other Voluntary Health Agencies

In addition to those voluntary health agencies that are members of the National Health Council, many other organizations function on a national scale and offer specialized services as well as literature and guidance to professionals, patients, parents, and concerned families. The following is a partial list.

Alcoholics Anonymous World Services, P.O. Box 459, Grand Central Station,New York, New York 10163, is a fellowship of men and women who share their experiences and give each other support in overcoming the problem of alcoholism. Chapters exist throughout the country and offer referral services, literature, and information about special hospital programs.

Al-Anon Family Group Headquarters, Inc., P.O. Box 862 Midtown Station, New York, New York 10016, is not affiliated with Alcoholics Anonymous, but cooperates closely with it. Al-Anon, which includes Alateen for younger members, is a primary community resource and self-help fellowship for the families and friends of alcoholics. Members share their experiences, strength, and hope at regularly held meetings, and learn to cope with the effects of being close to an alcoholic. Headquarters registers, services, and provides literature to 33,000 groups worldwide, of which 19,000 are in the United States.

Asthma and Allergy Foundation of America, 1835 K Street, N.W., Suite P-900, Washington, D.C. 20006, was established to help solve all health problems related to allergic diseases by sponsoring research and treatment facilities. It also grants scholarships to medical students specializing in the study of allergy.

Alzheimer's Association, 70 E. Lake Street, Suite 600, Chicago, Illinois 60601, was founded in 1980 to heighten public awareness of this degenerative brain disorder, provide support for patients and their families, aid research efforts, advocate for legislation that responds to the needs of Alzheimer's disease patients and their family members, and commemorate National Alzheimer's Disease Awareness Month each November. The network includes more than 200 chapters and affiliates across the country representing over 1,000 Family Support Groups. To obtain the most up-to-date information on Alzheimer's disease legislation and research, and for referral to local chapters, call the Association's toll-free information and referral number, 800-621-0379 (in Illinois only, 800-572-6037) or write to the Association.

The *American Foundation for AIDS Research* (AmFAR), 5900 Wilshire Blvd., 2nd Floor, East Satellite, Los Angeles, California 90036, was created in the fall of 1985 as a result of the unification of two not-for-profit public foundations: the AIDS Medical Foundation (AMF), incorpo-

rated in the State of New York in April 1983; and the National AIDS Research Foundation (NARF), incorporated in the State of California in August 1985. AmFar is an independent, national organization whose directors, committee members, and staff are professionals in the field of AIDS.

The Foundation has two main missions. First, it supports and facilitates laboratory and clinical research projects selected on the basis of scientific merit and relevance to achieve an understanding of the pathogenesis of AIDS, its prevention through the use of a vaccine, and its treatment. Second, the Foundation works to develop data and to serve as a source of accurate and up-to-date information about an epidemic that has profound psychosocial repercussions in our society.

American Foundation for the Blind, 15 West 16th Street, New York, New York 10011, is a national nonprofit organization working with local and national services to improve the quality of life for all blind and visually impaired persons. It stocks many different consumer products and publications and has recorded and produced millions of talking book records for the Library of Congress.

Through its staff of national consultants and its regional offices, the Foundation maintains a direct liaison with state, regional, and local agencies.

The *Association for Voluntary Surgical Contraception,* 122 East 42nd Street, New York, New York 10168, was founded in 1943 to promote the right of each individual to choose sterilization as a method of birth control. A nonprofit membership organization, the AVSC has increasingly collaborated with governmental and private sector providers to ensure effective access to sterilization facilities. The Association also sponsors training,

education, and program support for sterilization and family planning counselors and others; prepares annual estimates of male and female voluntary sterilizations in the United States; issues a quarterly newsletter, the *AVSC News,* and other publications, and initiates and monitors research into medical, legal, psychological, ethical, and public health aspects of voluntary sterilization.

The C.D.C. National AIDS Hotline, (800) 342-2437 is operated by the Federal Centers for Disease Control and provides confidential and anonymous information and referrals to local health organizations, counselors, and support groups. *The C.D.C. National AIDS Clearinghouse,* P.O. Box 6003, Rockville, MD 20849, provides free educational materials on HIV and AIDS.

The Epilepsy Foundation of America, 4351 Garden City Drive, Landover, Maryland 20785, is the result of a merger in 1967 of two similar organizations. At present, the Foundation has 85 local affiliates that provide information, referral services, and counseling. It conducts a research grant program for medical and psychosocial investigation and distributes a wide variety of literature on request to physicians, teachers, employers, and the interested public on such subjects as anticonvulsant drugs, insurance, driving laws, and emergency treatment. The national office also maintains an extensive research library.

The Leukemia Society of America, 733 Third Avenue, New York, New York 10017, was organized in 1949 and now has 57 chapters. It supports research in the causes, control, and eventual eradication of the disease that, though commonly thought of as a disorder of the blood, is in fact a disorder of the bone marrow, lymph nodes, and spleen, which manufacture blood. The society has a continuing program of education through special publications directed to physicians, nurses, and the public. Through its local affiliates, it conducts patient-aid services that provide counseling, transportation, and—to those who need financial assistance—drugs, blood transfusions, and laboratory facilities.

The Muscular Dystrophy Association, Inc., 810 Seventh Avenue, New York, New York 10019, has as a primary goal the scientific conquest of muscular dystrophy and related neuromuscular diseases. The Association supports scientific investigators worldwide. In addition, through its 170 chapter affiliates nationwide, MDA provides a comprehensive patient and community services program to individuals diagnosed with any one of 40 neuromuscular disorders. The Association maintains a network of some 240 MDA clinics coast to coast to provide diagnostic services and therapeutic and rehabilitative follow-up care as well as genetic, vocational, and social service counseling to patients and their families. MDA also sponsors a summer camping program for youngsters aged 6 to 21 as well as adult outings, with activities geared to the special needs of those with neuromuscular diseases.

RESOLVE, (HelpLine: (617) 623-0744) is a national non-profit consumer organization serving the unique needs of the infertile population and allied professionals with support, education and advocacy. RESOLVE, 1310 Broadway, Somerville, MA 02144-1731. Membership services include national newsletter, telephone helpline, physician referral service.

The Association for Retarded Citizens of the United States, P.O. Box 6109, Arlington, Texas 76006, established in 1950, is the nation's largest voluntary organization specifically devoted to promoting the welfare of children and adults with mental retardation. It is estimated that there are six million such persons in the United States. Through its 1,500 affiliates the association conducts and supports research, sponsors employment programs, advocates for progressive public policy, and works for better community services. Counseling and referral services, as well as extensive literature for professionals and concerned families, are available on request.

The March of Dimes Birth Defects Foundation, 1275 Mamaroneck Avenue, White Plains, New York 10605, was founded in 1938 to combat infantile paralysis (polio). In the 30 years since the conquest of polio, through the development of the Salk and Sabin polio vaccines, the March of Dimes has dedicated itself to the prevention of birth defects, the nation's number one child health problem. It does this through programs of birth defects research and medical service and education that provide new knowledge and understanding of birth defects and their prevention. More than a quarter-million babies are born with one or more of the 3,000 known birth defects each year. The Foundation also has established the Salk Institute in La Jolla, California, directed by Dr. Jonas Salk, for the purpose of carrying on basic research in life processes to discover what causes birth defects and other diseases.

Special Health Services and Agencies

Many factors have contributed to the growth of the American system of health services. Specialists in various medical specialties have tried to meet needs for new types of health care.

Medical care has become so effective that individual life expectancy has increased enormously; as one result, the number of Americans aged 65 and older tripled in the three-quarters of a century between 1900 and 1975. As the population of the United States has grown older, in percentage terms, the problems of the aged have received more attention. New methods and devices have been developed for the care and assistance of the ill or disabled of any age.

Special health services and agencies help to fill such needs. Many older persons have utilized the services of trained individuals who make survival possible—sometimes at home—or slow down the rate of deterioration. Other institutions and agencies perform simple maintenance tasks for the aged or the seriously ill or handicapped, or help with rehabilitation. Social service agencies and groups with health roles, for example, provide adult day care, homemaker assistance, and home health services that may include the following:

- Part-time or occasional nursing care, often under the supervision of a registered nurse

- Physical, occupational, or speech therapy

- Medical social services that help the patient and his or her family to adjust to the social and emotional conditions accompanying illness or disability of any kind

- Assistance from a home health aide, including help with such tasks as bathing and going to the bathroom, taking medications, exercising, and getting into and out of bed

- Under some circumstances, medical attention from interns or residents in training

35

Medical Emergencies

Anyone attempting to deal with a medical emergency will do so with considerably more confidence if he has a clear notion of the order of importance of various problems. Over and above all technical knowledge about such things as tourniquets or cardiac massage is the ability of the rescuer to keep a cool head so that he can make the right decisions and delegate tasks to others who wish to be helpful.

Cessation of Breathing

The medical emergency that requires prompt attention before any others is cessation of breathing. No matter what other injuries are involved, artificial respiration must be administered immediately to anyone suffering from respiratory arrest.

To determine whether a person is breathing naturally, place your cheek as near as possible to the victim's mouth and nose. While you are feeling and listening for evidence of respiration, watch the victim's chest and upper abdomen to see if they rise and fall. If respiratory arrest is indicated, begin artificial respiration immediately.

Time is critical; a human body has only about a four-minute reserve supply of oxygen in its tissues, although some persons have been revived after being submerged in water for ten minutes or more. Do not waste time moving the victim to a more comfortable location unless his position is life threatening.

If more than one person is available, the second person should summon a physician. A second rescuer can also assist in preparing the victim for artificial respiration by helping to loosen clothing around the neck, chest, and waist, and by inspecting the mouth for false teeth, chewing gum, or other objects that could block the flow of air. The victim's tongue must be pulled forward before artificial respiration begins.

Normal breathing should start after not more than 15 minutes of artificial respiration. If it doesn't, you should continue the procedure for at least two hours, alternating, if possible, with other persons to maintain maximum efficiency. Medical experts have defined normal breathing as eight or more breaths per minute; if breathing resumes but slackens to a rate of fewer than eight breaths per minute, or if breathing stops suddenly for more than 30 seconds, continue artificial respiration.

Mouth-to-Mouth and Mouth-to-Nose Artificial Respiration

Following is a description of the techniques used to provide mouth-to-mouth or mouth-to-nose artificial respiration. These are the preferred methods of artificial respiration because they move a greater volume of air into a victim's lungs than any alternative method.

After quickly clearing the victim's mouth and throat of obstacles, tilt the victim's head back as far as possible, with the chin up and neck stretched to ensure an open passage of air to the lungs. If mouth-to-mouth breathing is employed, pull the lower jaw of the victim open with one hand, inserting your thumb between the victim's teeth, and pinch the nostrils with the other to prevent air leakage through the nose. If using the mouth-to-nose technique, hold one hand over the mouth to seal it against air leakage.

Next, open your own mouth and

Cardiopulmonary Resuscitation (CPR)

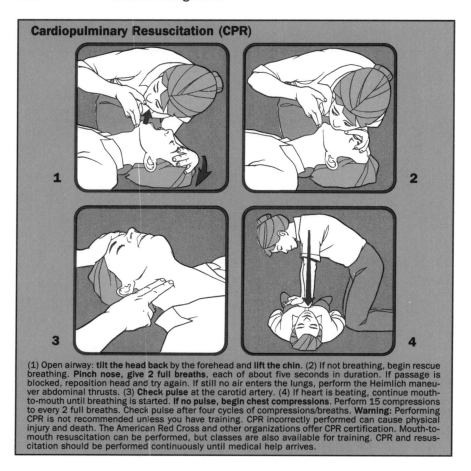

(1) Open airway: **tilt the head back** by the forehead and **lift the chin.** (2) If not breathing, begin rescue breathing. **Pinch nose, give 2 full breaths,** each of about five seconds in duration. If passage is blocked, reposition head and try again. If still no air enters the lungs, perform the Heimlich maneuver abdominal thrusts. (3) **Check pulse** at the carotid artery. (4) If heart is beating, continue mouth-to-mouth until breathing is started. **If no pulse, begin chest compressions.** Perform 15 compressions to every 2 full breaths. Check pulse after four cycles of compressions/breaths. **Warning:** Performing CPR is not recommended unless you have training. CPR incorrectly performed can cause physical injury and death. The American Red Cross and other organizations offer CPR certification. Mouth-to-mouth resuscitation can be performed, but classes are also available for training. CPR and resuscitation should be performed continuously until medical help arrives.

take a deep breath. Then blow forcefully into the victim's mouth (or nose) until you can see the chest rise. Quickly remove your mouth and listen for normal exhalation sounds from the victim. If you hear gurgling sounds, try to move the jaw higher because the throat may not be stretched open properly. Continue blowing forcefully into the victim's mouth (or nose) at a rate of once every three or four seconds. (For infants, do not blow forcefully; blow only small puffs of air from your cheeks.)

If the victim's stomach becomes distended, it may be a sign that air is being blown into the stomach; press firmly with one hand on the upper abdomen to push the air out of the stomach.

If you are hesitant about direct physical contact of the lips, make a ring with the index finger and thumb of the hand being used to hold the victim's chin in position. Place the

ring of fingers firmly about the victim's mouth; the outside of the thumb may at the same time be positioned to seal the nose against air leakage. Then blow the air into the victim's mouth through the finger-thumb ring. Direct lip-to-lip contact can also be avoided by placing a piece of gauze or other clean porous cloth over the victim's mouth.

Severe Bleeding

If the victim is not suffering from respiration failure or if breathing has been restored, severe bleeding is the second most serious emergency to attend to. Such bleeding occurs when either an artery or a vein has been severed. Arterial blood is bright red and spurts rather than flows from the body, sometimes in very large amounts. It is also more difficult to control than blood from a vein, which

can be recognized by its dark red color and steady flow.

Emergency Treatment

The quickest and most effective way to stop bleeding is by direct pressure on the wound. If heavy layers of sterile gauze are not available, use a clean handkerchief, or a clean piece of material torn from a shirt, slip, or sheet to cover the wound. Then place the fingers or the palm of the hand directly over the bleeding area. The pressure must be *firm and constant* and should be interrupted only when the blood has soaked through the dressing. *Do not remove the soaked dressing.* Cover it as quickly as possible with additional new layers. When the blood stops seeping through to the surface of the dressing, secure it with strips of cloth until the victim can receive medical attention. This procedure is almost always successful in stopping blood flow from a vein.

If direct pressure doesn't stop ar-

Pressure Points

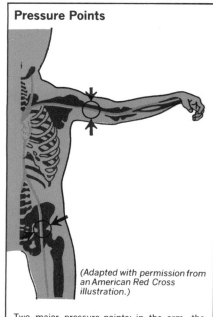

(Adapted with permission from an American Red Cross illustration.)

Two major pressure points: in the arm, the brachial artery; in the leg, the femoral artery. Continue to apply direct pressure and elevate the wounded part while utilizing pressure points to stop blood flow.

Pressure Points

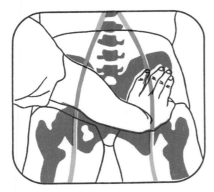

(Top) Use the femoral artery for control of severe bleeding from an open leg wound. Place the victim flat on his back, and put the heel of your hand directly over the pressure point. Apply pressure by forcing the artery against the pelvic bone. *(Bottom)* Use the brachial artery for control of severe bleeding from an open arm wound. Apply pressure by forcing the artery against the arm bone. Continue to apply direct pressure over the wound, and keep the wounded part elevated.

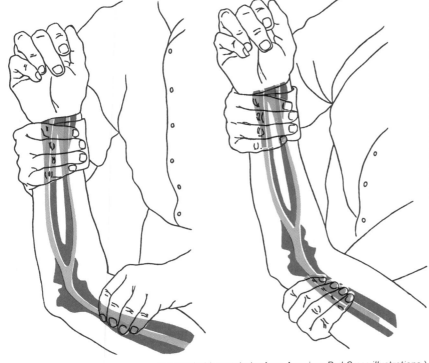

(Adapted with permission from American Red Cross illustrations.)

terial bleeding, two alternatives are possible: pressure by finger or hand on the pressure point nearest the wound, or the application of a tourniquet. No matter what the source of the bleeding, if the wound is on an arm or leg, elevation of the limb as high as is comfortable will reduce the blood flow.

Tourniquets

A tourniquet improperly applied can be an extremely dangerous device, and should only be considered for a hemorrhage that can't be controlled in any other way.

It must be remembered that arterial blood flows away from the heart and that venous blood flows toward the heart. Therefore, while a tourniquet placed on a limb between the site of a wound and the heart may slow or stop arterial bleeding, it may actually increase venous bleeding. By ob-

structing blood flow in the veins beyond the wound site, the venous blood flowing toward the heart will have to exit from the wound. Thus, the proper application of a tourniquet depends upon an understanding and differentiation of arterial from venous bleeding. Arterial bleeding can be recognized by the pumping action of the blood and by the bright red color of the blood.

Once a tourniquet is applied, it should not be left in place for an excessive period of time, since the tissues in the limb beyond the site of the wound need to be supplied with blood.

Shock

In any acute medical emergency, the possibility of the onset of shock must always be taken into account, especially following the fracture of a large bone, extensive burns, or serious wounds. If untreated, or if treated too late, shock can be fatal.

Shock is an emergency condition in which the circulation of the blood is so disrupted that all bodily functions are affected. It occurs when blood pressure is so low that insufficient blood supply reaches the vital tissues.

Types of Circulatory Shock and Their Causes

● *Low-volume shock* is a condition brought about by so great a loss of blood or blood plasma that the remaining blood is insufficient to fill the whole circulatory system. The blood loss may occur outside the body, as in a hemorrhage caused by injury to an artery or vein, or the loss may be internal because of the blood loss at the site of a major fracture, burn, or bleeding ulcer. Professional treatment involves replacement of blood loss by transfusion.

Arterial Bleeding

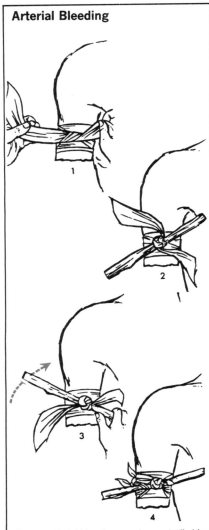

Severe arterial bleeding can be controlled by the correct application of a tourniquet. (1) A long strip of gauze or other material is wrapped twice around the arm or leg above the wound and tied in a half‑knot. (2) A stick, called a windlass, is placed over the knot, and the knot is completed. (3) The wind‑lass is turned to tighten the knot and finally, (4) the windlass is secured with the tails of the tourniquet. Improper use of a tourniquet can be very dangerous.

- *Neurogenic shock,* manifested by *fainting,* occurs when the regulating capacity of the nervous system is impaired by severe pain, profound fright, or overwhelming stimulus. This type of shock is usually relieved by having the victim lie down with his head lower than the rest of his body.
- *Allergic shock,* also called *anaphylactic shock,* occurs when the func-

tioning of the blood vessels is disturbed by a person's sensitivity to the injection of a particular foreign substance, as in the case of an insect sting or certain medicines.

- *Septic shock* is brought on by infection from certain bacteria that release a poison which affects the proper functioning of the blood vessels.
- *Cardiac shock* can be caused by any circumstance that affects the pumping action of the heart.

Symptoms

Shock caused by blood loss makes the victim feel restless, thirsty, and cold. He may perspire a great deal, and although his pulse is fast, it is also very weak. His breathing becomes labored and his lips turn blue.

Emergency Treatment

A physician should be called immediately if the onset of shock is suspected. Until medical help is obtained, the following procedures can alleviate some of the symptoms:

1. With a minimum amount of disturbance, arrange the victim so that he is lying on his back with his head somewhat lower than his feet. (**Exception:** If the victim's breathing is difficult, or if he has suffered a head injury or a stroke, keep his body flat but place a pillow or similar cushioning material under his head.) Loosen any clothing that may cause constriction, such as a belt, tie, waistband, shoes. Cover him warmly against possible chill, but see that he isn't too hot.

2. If his breathing is weak and shallow, begin mouth-to-mouth respiration.

3. If he is hemorrhaging, try to control bleeding.

4. When appropriate help and transportation facilities are available, quickly move the victim to the nearest hospital or health facility in order to begin resuscitative measures.

5. *Do not* try to force any food or stimulant into the victim's mouth.

Cardiac Arrest

Cardiac arrest is a condition in which the heart has stopped beating altogether or is beating so weakly or so irregularly that it cannot maintain proper blood circulation.

Common causes of cardiac arrest are heart attack, electric shock, hemorrhage, suffocation, and other forms of respiratory arrest. Symptoms of cardiac arrest are unconsciousness, the absence of respiration and pulse, and the lack of a heartbeat or a heartbeat that is very weak or irregular.

Cardiac Massage

If the victim of a medical emergency manifests signs of cardiac arrest, he should be given cardiac massage at the same time that another rescuer is administering mouth-to-mouth resuscitation. Both procedures can be carried on in the moving vehicle taking him to the hospital.

It is assumed that he is lying down with his mouth clear and his air passage unobstructed. The massage is given in the following way:

1. The heel of one hand with the heel of the other crossed over it should be placed on the bottom third of the breastbone and pressed firmly down with a force of about 80 pounds so that the breastbone moves about two inches toward the spine. Pressure should not be applied directly on the ribs by the fingers.

2. The hands are then relaxed to allow the chest to expand.

3. If one person is doing both the cardiac massage and the mouth-to-mouth respiration, he should stop the massage after every 15 chest compressions and administer two very quick lung inflations to the victim.

4. The rescuer should try to make the rate of cardiac massage simulate restoration of the pulse rate. This is not always easily accomplished, but compression should reach 60 times per minute.

The techniques for administering cardiac massage to children are the same as those used for adults, except that much less pressure should be applied to a child's chest, and, in the case of babies or young children, the pressure should be exerted with the tips of the fingers rather than with the heel of the hand.

Caution

Cardiac massage can be damaging if applied improperly. Courses in emergency medical care offered by the American Red Cross and other groups are well worth taking. In an emergency in which cardiac massage is called for, an untrained person should seek the immediate aid of someone trained in the technique before attempting it himself.

Obstruction in the Windpipe

Many people die each year from choking on food; children incur an additional hazard in swallowing foreign objects. Most of these victims could be saved through quick action by nearly any other person, and without special equipment.

Food choking usually occurs because a bite of food becomes lodged at the back of the throat or at the

opening of the trachea, or windpipe. The victim cannot breathe or speak. He may become pale or turn blue before collapsing. Death can occur within four or five minutes. But the lungs of an average person may contain at least one quart of air, inhaled before the start of choking, and that air can be used to unblock the windpipe and save the victim's life.

Finger Probe

If the object can be seen, a quick attempt can be made to remove it by probing with a finger. Use a hooking motion to dislodge the object. Under no circumstances should this method be pursued if it appears that the object is being pushed farther downward rather than being released and brought up.

Back Blows

Give the victim four quick, hard blows with the fist on his back between the shoulder blades. The blows should be given in rapid succession. If the victim is a child, he can be held over the knee while being struck; an adult should lie face down on a bed or table, with the upper half of his body suspended in the direction of the floor so that he can receive the same type of blows. A very small child or infant should be held upside down by the torso or legs and struck much more lightly than an adult.

The Heimlich Maneuver

If the back blows fail to dislodge the obstruction, the Heimlich maneuver should be given without delay. (Back blows may loosen the object even if they fail to dislodge it completely; that is why they are given first.) The lifesaving technique known as the *Heimlich maneuver* (named for Dr. Henry J. Heimlich) works simply by

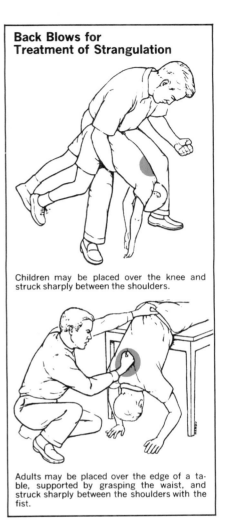

Back Blows for Treatment of Strangulation

Children may be placed over the knee and struck sharply between the shoulders.

Adults may be placed over the edge of a table, supported by grasping the waist, and struck sharply between the shoulders with the fist.

squeezing the volume of air trapped in the victim's lungs. The piece of food literally pops out of the throat as if it were ejected from a squeezed balloon.

To perform the Heimlich maneuver, the rescuer stands behind the victim and grasps his hands firmly over the victim's abdomen, just below the victim's rib cage. The rescuer makes a fist with one hand and places his other hand over the clenched fist. Then, the rescuer forces his fist sharply inward and upward against the victim's diaphragm. This action compresses the lungs within the rib cage. If the food does not pop out on the first try, the maneuver should be repeated until the air passage is unblocked.

The Heimlich Maneuver

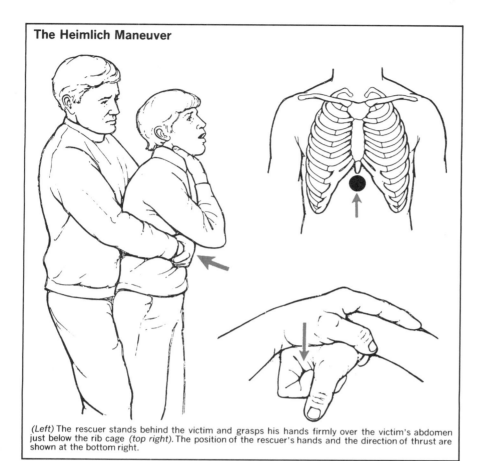

(Left) The rescuer stands behind the victim and grasps his hands firmly over the victim's abdomen just below the rib cage *(top right)*. The position of the rescuer's hands and the direction of thrust are shown at the bottom right.

When the victim is unable to stand, he should be rolled over on his back on the floor. The rescuer then kneels astride the victim and performs a variation of the Heimlich maneuver by placing the heel of one open hand, rather than a clenched fist, just below the victim's rib cage. The second hand is placed over the first. Then the rescuer presses upward (toward the victim's head) quickly to compress the lungs, repeating several times if necessary.

The Heimlich maneuver has been used successfully by persons who were alone when they choked on food; some pressed their own fist into their abdomen, others forced the edge of a chair or sink against their abdomen.

Poisoning

In all cases of poisoning, it is imper-ative to get professional assistance as soon as possible.

Listed below are telephone numbers for Poison Control Centers throughout the United States. These health service organizations are accessible 24 hours a day to provide information on how best to counteract the effects of toxic substances.

In the event of known or suspected poisoning, call the center nearest you immediately. Give the staff member to whom you speak as much information as possible: the name or nature of the poison ingested, if you know; if not, the symptoms manifested by the victim.

If for any reason it is impossible to telephone or get to a Poison Control Center (or a doctor or hospital), follow these two general rules:

1. If a strong acid or alkali or a petroleum product has been ingested, dilute the poison by administering large quantities of milk or water. Do not induce vomiting.

2. For methanol or related products such as window cleaners, antifreeze, paint removers, and shoe polish, induce vomiting—preferably with syrup of ipecac.

Calling for Help

Every household should have a card close by the telephone—if possible attached to an adjacent wall—that contains the numbers of various emergency services. In most communities, it is possible to simply dial the operator and ask for the police or fire department. In many large cities, there is a special three-digit number that can be dialed for reaching the police directly.

An ambulance can be summoned either by asking for a police ambulance, by calling the nearest hospital, or by having on hand the telephone numbers of whatever private ambulance services are locally available. Such services are listed in the classified pages of the telephone directory.

Practically all hospitals have emergency rooms for the prompt treatment of accident cases. If the victim is in good enough physical condition, he can be placed in a prone position in a family station wagon for removal to a hospital. However, under no circumstances should a person who has sustained major injuries or who has collapsed be made to sit upright in a car. First aid must be administered to him on the spot until a suitable conveyance arrives.

Every family should find out the telephone number of the nearest Poison Control Center (see section in this chapter) and note it on the emergency number card.

The Emergency-Free Home

Every year, hundreds of thousands of Americans go to hospital emergency rooms to obtain treatment for injuries or illnesses incurred in their homes. But many of these emergency health problems could have been prevented. In too many cases, no one took action to eliminate home hazards simply because they were easy to overlook or were not readily detectable.

Millions more Americans suffer less serious home injuries and do not go to hospitals.

With a little forethought, many of these home accidents can be prevented. This chapter provides basic guidelines for home safety.

First Aid Needs

The first step toward home safety is preparedness. This means ensuring that basic first aid equipment and medications are in the home, readily available.

Both materials and medicines should be chosen with care. Key considerations are the ages of those who live in the home, special requirements of particular family members, the seasons of the year, and other factors that may suggest a need for certain products or preparations.

First aid supplies should be kept in a medicine cabinet or in a larger storage place out of reach of children. Basic first aid items include:

- Fragrance-free soap (to clean hands and wounds)
- Pain-relief tablets
- Children's acetaminophen elixir
- Betadine (painless, disinfecting wound cleanser)
- Bacitracin, or other multiple antibiotic ointment (for minor cuts)
- 5% hydrocortisone ointment (for local pain, itching)
- Ipecac syrup and activated charcoal for poison antidotes (always call poison control center first)
- Isopropyl alcohol and antiseptic towelettes
- Ammonia inhalant
- Calamine lotion
- Flashlight
- Old credit card (to scrape bee stings)
- Scissors
- Cotton-tip applicators and cotton balls
- Stretch fabric bandage (for sprains)
- assorted bandages
- latex gloves (for handling wounds)
- sterile gauze pads (for compresses)
- waterproof adhesive tape
- ice pack
- tweezers (for removing splinters)
- oral and rectal thermometers
- heating pad

Medicines and Medications

Don't overstock medications and, if possible, consult a physician or emergency hotline before attempting any emergency measures. Many medications only serve to delay proper medical attention. For example, syrup of ipecac, a preparation that induces vomiting in emergency situations, is a basic necessity in a household with children. However, if ipecac is used after the ingestion of certain liquids, the results can be very damaging and even fatal.

Leftover antibiotics should never be used a second time without consulting a physician. Because of their cost, many people are reluctant to dispose of leftover antibiotics, but severe allergic reactions could result or make it difficult for a physician to diagnose an illness if symptoms have been masked.

Antibiotics prescribed in series should be taken until the series is completed. Finally, no such medications should be passed on to friends or relatives for their use. Borrowed medications could harm, rather than help, the recipient.

What drugs or medications should be in your medicine cabinet? Some basic items are:

- Cold and allergy medications, including an antihistamine, a decongestant, a cough suppressant, an expectorant
- An antacid for indigestion
- An anti-odor foot cream or powder
- An anti-diarrheal medicine
- A laxative
- Eyedrops
- Aspirin or an aspirin-free pain reliever
- Other items as required for chronic conditions.

Here are some additional safety rules regarding medicine cabinets:

- If possible, locate the medicine cabinet in a cool, dry, dark place, out of the reach of children.
- Check the contents periodically and throw away out-of-date or spoiled items (including aspirin that smells like vinegar).
- Remove the cotton from any medicine cabinet containers that may

use cotton stoppers (because the cotton can absorb a medication's active ingredients).

- If even one pill in a bottle has deteriorated or spoiled, throw out the entire batch.

- Keep liquids in their amber containers to protect the contents from light.

- To discard medications, flush them down the toilet, then remove the labels on the containers to prevent others from refilling the prescriptions.

- Keep emergency phone numbers (physician, pharmacist, fire, police, and so on; see the list of emergency phone numbers on the inside front cover of this volume) on the medicine cabinet or near it. When in doubt about which medication to use, call a doctor or pharmacist.

Reducing the Risk of Medicine Poisoning

Following certain safety rules can help ensure against the possibility of medicine poisoning. The rules are most important in homes where there are very young children or very old family members.

Medicines or preparations that are potentially harmful should be kept in a locked cabinet. If there are a number of such preparations in the home, they should probably be kept in a separate, locking storage place. If this is not possible, they should at least be stored out of the reach of young children.

Other safety rules are simply common sense. For example, one should never transfer a medicine into an unlabeled container. Old medicine containers should be thrown away. Special care should be taken with the dosages of both liquid and solid drugs. Sleeping tablets, tranquilizers, and

even aspirin can, if taken in overdose, seriously harm the body.

If children resist taking their medicine, parents should never encourage them by pretending that the medicine is candy. Nor should parents rely too heavily on anti-tamper packaging. The shrink-wraps, push-and-turn bottle caps, foil inner seals, and other anti-tamper devices are valuable but not foolproof.

In any case of medicine poisoning, do not wait to seek help. Stay calm, call your physician or the nearest hospital or poison control center, and get instructions on correct procedures. If you take a poisoned family member to a hospital or elsewhere for help, you should bring with you the container(s) from which pills or liquid were taken. Do not administer salt and water to induce vomiting; the mixture is potentially fatal.

Dangers of Alternative Medicines and Quack Remedies

Americans spend billions of dollars each year on "alternative" medicinal supplies and equipment. In too many cases the quack remedies not only do not help, they may do serious harm.

Examples of items that flood the marketplace but should not be found in your home are numerous. Among the many unproved procedures and preparations are hair analysis and cytotoxic tests for food allergies; oral chelation therapy, with vitamin and mineral capsules or tables for cardiovascular disease; and various "metabolic" programs, "non-toxic holistic medicines," radical dietary changes and regimens, and programs calling for massive doses of vitamins.

Still others include detoxification and drastic "cleansing" enemas, herbal mixtures to be applied to a sore or inflamed area, immune boosters that once were sold as cancer cures and now are promoted as treatments

for AIDS, and laetrile, an unproven cancer treatment.

The following guidelines can help protect your family from such noneffective medications:

- Beware of testimonials in ads or on labels that purportedly come from satisfied users.

- Do not believe any promises of "money-back guarantees." They are rarely dependable.

- Be wary of advertising that claims a product is effective against numerous ailments.

- Be wary of promises of a "cure" or of "complete relief" from pain.

- Discount any "FDA-tested" or "FDA-recommended" testimonials. Federal law states that the Food and Drug Administration cannot be mentioned as giving marketing approvals.

- Beware of mentions of "natural" ingredients. The definition of natural is elusive, and the word is often abused.

- Think twice before buying *anything* that is advertised with such terms as these: "amazing," "vanish," "discovery," "breakthrough," "painless," "exclusive," or "instant."

- Finally, warns the FDA, "If the product sounds too good to be true, it probably is."

Emergency-Proofing Your Home

The modern home is a marvel of devices and appliances, such as space heaters, washers, dryers, refrigerators, gas and electric furnaces, and many others. To a great extent, the hazards of large or small appliances are associated with fire. But householders should also take precautions against the dangers of electrocution, falls caused by poorly placed electrical cords, and other accident-producers.

Household items that are most likely to be hazardous are heating-cooling equipment, cooking equipment, heat tapes and humidifiers, and small electrical appliances.

Heating-Cooling Equipment

In the first category are furnaces, air conditioners, space heaters, and similar equipment. The primary safety rule with heating equipment is to make sure it is operating properly and efficiently. For furnaces of any kind, an annual checkup—usually in the summer or fall—is advisable. Many homeowners have maintenance policies that include such checkups.

All *space heaters* come with instructions for installation and operation. These instructions should be followed closely. Space heaters should be located so that they have plenty of room around them. They should be placed at a safe distance from all papers, clothing, draperies, furniture, and children. Manufacturers' labels usually indicate what the proper clearance is for a particular model.

As with furnaces, space heaters should be kept in good working condition. Missing controls should be replaced; so should missing or defective guards or screens.

Electric space heaters should have tip-over shutoff switches that turn off the current if the unit is knocked over. These heaters should also have guards around their coils. The guard can be a wire grille or other protective "fence" that keep fingers or fabrics away from the heating element.

If an extension cord is used with the space heater, the cord should have a power rating at least as high as the heater's rating. The cord should be in a safe place and out of the reach of children.

An important rule: Do not use a portable electric heater in a bathroom, near a sink, or close to water. This presents the risk of electrocution.

Gas space heaters may be vented or unvented. Both kinds need special care and attention.

If a gas space heater is vented, it should be vented correctly. That is, the vent pipe should be properly sized and free of cracks, leaks, and blockages, with tight joints and crack-free heat exchanger (to prevent leakage of carbon monoxide). If in doubt about the venting, call a servicer or your gas supplier.

When using an unvented gas space heater, you should always have a door or window slightly open in the room where the heater is located.

With either kind of gas heater, light the match *first* before you turn on the gas for the pilot light. This prevents flareups due to accumulated gas.

Woodburning, kerosene, or oil space heaters not only need to be installed properly; it would also be wise to have them inspected by a local fire safety official. Then you should use only the fuel, and in some cases the *grade* of fuel, for which the heater was designed.

The chimney of the heater or stove should be cleaned regularly, once every couple of months at least. In the case of a woodburning heater, it is best to use only paper or wood for kindling. *Never* use gasoline or another flammable or combustible fluid to start a woodburning stoves.

Cooking Equipment

The U.S. Consumer Product Safety Commission (CPSC) reports that more than 100,000 fires each year are associated with cooking equipment, especially stoves. These fires cause an estimated $300 million in property losses.

Some basic safety precautions can prevent most of these fires. For example, householders can avoid storing flammable or combustible items above the stove, including potholders, plastic utensils, or towels. Children's favorite foods, including cookies or candy, should never be kept above the range or in its immediate vicinity.

Clothing can be a trap for the unwary. Loose-fitting sleeves should not be worn while cooking. Also, you should never leave a stove unattended, especially when a burner is turned to a high setting.

Heat Tapes and Humidifiers

Heat tapes and ultrasonic humidifiers can pose home safety and health hazards. Heat tapes, used to keep exposed water pipes from freezing, present fire hazards. Ultrasonic humidifiers filled with tap water may discharge dangerous mineral particles into the air.

Electric heat tapes, or pipe heating cables, plug into wall or floor outlets. Once plugged in, they emit heat through their molded plastic insulation. Used in crawl spaces and in the substructures of homes and mobile homes, many tapes remain plugged in year-round. A thermostat in the power supply cord turns the tape on when the temperature falls below a certain level.

Improper installation of heat tapes has become a major cause of home fires in recent years. In many cases, lack of attention to the instructions that come with the product has resulted in faulty installation. Some homeowners lap the tape over itself when winding the tape around the pipe. Others ignore manufacturers' warnings that specific lengths of tape be used to protect pipes of given diameters and lengths.

If your home has heat tapes already installed you should (1) inspect all tapes, or have a licensed electrician inspect them, for proper installation or deteriorated installation; (2) check older tapes for cracks in the plastic insulation or bare wires, and replace worn tapes at once; (3) make certain, if you have plastic pipes, that the tapes you are using are recommended specifically for your kind of plastic piping; and (4) inspect all tapes to make sure none is wrapped over the thermal insulation on a pipe or near flammable objects.

Ultrasonic humidifiers using tap water have been found to spread such impurities as lead, aluminum, asbestos, or dissolved organic gases into the air. All these substances can be health hazards. To avoid such problems, use bottled, demineralized water or install demineralizing filters on your tap-water supply.

Other humidifiers pose no such mineral particle threat.

Home Electrical Safety

Have you conducted an audit of the connections, cords, gadgets (aside from major appliances), and other electrical equipment in your home? If not, such an audit is virtually a must.

You can start checking all lighting, including bulbs and sockets, all cords and extension cords, and all TV or audio equipment. Bulbs with wattages too high for the size of a fixture may overheat and cause a fire, so you should replace oversized bulbs with others of appropriate wattages. If the correct wattage is not indicated, use a bulb no larger than 60 watts.

Make sure all electrical cords are placed out of traffic areas so that people will not trip or fall over them. Stepping on cords can damage them, too, and produce fire hazards. Also check to make sure that cords do not have furniture resting on them. Cords should not be frayed, should not be wrapped around themselves or any

object, and should *never* be attached to walls with nails or staples.

Extension cords should be equipped with safety covers and should never carry more than their proper loads. Cords and electrical devices will normally have electrical ratings.

Wall outlets and switches should be checked to make sure they are working properly and fixed if they are not. You can test them by touching: an unusually warm outlet or switch may indicate an unsafe wiring condition. Plugs should fit into outlets snugly, and all outlets should have face plates so that no wiring is exposed.

Kitchen countertop appliances should be placed so that they remain dry. If they give off heat, as does a toaster, they should have some space to "breathe." Countertop appliances should be unplugged when not in use.

Cords for countertop appliances are critically important. These should never be placed so that they can come into contact with hot surfaces; especially cords around toasters, ovens, and ranges. The same rule holds with water or wet surfaces.

Because ground fault circuit interrupters (GFCIs) can prevent many electrocutions, the Consumer Product Safety Commission recommends that all countertop outlets be equipped with them. They should also be used in bathrooms and other areas where there is a risk of electrical shock. Test your GFCIs regularly in accordance with the manufacturers' instructions.

Most current building codes require that bathrooms be equipped with GFCIs. Older homes may not have them.

Other electrical appliances and equipment require safety care. These items can include hair dryers, curling irons, and electric blankets. A universal rule is that such devices be unplugged when not in use. Plugged in

and allowed to fall into water, they can cause an electrocution. They should also be in good operating condition, with no damaged wiring or other parts.

Do not use portable electric heaters in the bathroom or other rooms where they may come into contact with water. Keep *any* use of electrical devices or appliances in such rooms to a minimum.

Electric blankets also have to be used with care. They should be in good condition and have no charred spots on either the upper or the lower blanket surface. Before using them, look for cracks or breaks in wiring, connectors, and plugs.

To prevent overheating, do not cover electric blankets with other blankets, comforters, or other bedding. They should also be used flat, not folded back, and should not be tucked in except in accordance with the manufacturers' instructions.

Basement, garage, and workshop power tools and outlets constitute another extremely important area of safety concern. Power tools should have three-pronged plugs to indicate that they are double insulated. These plugs reduce the risk of electric shock.

Check your fuse box or circuit breaker. A fuse of the wrong size can present a fire hazard. If you do not know what sizes are correct, an electrician can tell you. Your circuit breakers should be "exercised" periodically if they are to remain in good working order. This procedure is simple:

1. Turn off your freezer, refrigerator, and air conditioner.

2. Flip each circuit breaker off and on three times.

3. Turn the appliances back on.

Repeat this routine at least once a year. Also check the GFCIs on your basement, garage, or workshop equipment to make sure they are working properly.

Receptacles located outdoors represent a final stage in your electrical audit. These receptacles or outlets should have waterproof covers that keep water out and prevent malfunctions. The covers should be *closed* when not in use. If your home has no GFCIs on outside receptacles, have them installed.

As regards electric lawn movers and other electric garden tools and appliances, the basic rules of safety apply. But remember: extension cords used outside should be specifically designed for such use, or you may be risking a fire or a serious shock.

Home Fire Prevention and Protection

Many home fires have nothing to do with gadgets or appliances. Both the simplest and the most complex of our daily amenities can be fire hazards. Extremely flammable liquids provide power for our cars. Fabrics and upholstered furniture can ignite and burn. Some of us carry fire sources, matches or cigarette lighters, in our pockets.

In the sections that follow, effort will be made to call attention to the most important of these hazards.

Matches, Lighters, and Cigarettes

Some prohibitions that help to immunize your home against accidental fires are matters of common sense. Others have more technical origins.

Some 140 young children die each year in fires that they or their friends or siblings started. Children start thousands more home fires while playing with matches or lighters. Thus a basic rule is that children should not have access to either matches or cigarette lighters. Both

should be kept out of sight and reach.

Adults should never use either matches or lighters as toys or sources of amusement. Cigarette butts should not be left burning in ashtrays that children can reach.

Ashtray and cigarette discipline is always appropriate. Lighted butts should not be thrown into the trash. A lighted butt can start a major fire. Ashtrays should not be placed on the arms of chairs, where they can be knocked off. As a precaution, check the furniture where smokers have been sitting to make sure that no lighted cigarettes have fallen unnoticed behind or between cushions or under furniture.

In a recent year, 46,700 mattress and bedding fires took some 700 lives. Thus, "No smoking in bed" represents a cardinal rule of home safety.

Furniture Precautions

Because many home fires start on pieces of furniture, you should take special care when selecting the items you need. In particular, you should look for furniture designed to reduce the likelihood of furniture fires that may be started by cigarettes.

This task has become simpler in recent years. Manufacturers are making upholstered furniture far more fire resistant than they have in the past. All furniture that meets the standards of the Upholstered Furniture Action Council (UFAC) carries a gold-colored tag with red letters that states, "Important Consumer Safety Information from UFAC."

Other precautions help reduce the risks of injury or death from furniture fires. For example, look for upholstery fabrics made primarily from such thermoplastic fibers as nylon, polyester, acrylic, and olefin. These resist ignition by burning cigarettes better than do rayon or cotton, both cellulose fabrics.

Flammable Liquids

The federal Hazardous Substances Act establishes three labeling categories for liquid products:

1. *Extremely flammable liquids* include gasoline, the white gas commonly used in camping stoves, contact adhesives, and wood stains that produce ignitable vapors at room temperature. Once ignited, the vapors act as wicks to carry the fire to the container of the liquid.

2. *Flammable liquids* produce ignitable vapors at higher temperatures. This group includes paint thinners, some paints, and automotive products such as brake fluids.

3. *Combustible liquids* can be ignited but are less likely to catch fire than the other kinds. This category includes furniture polishes, oil-based paints, fuel oil, diesel oil, and kerosene.

Remember: some products do not carry *flammable* labels because they will not catch fire in liquid form as they come from the container (such as paint strippers). Once they are applied, however, they become quite flammable because their flame-suppressant chemicals evaporate.

Use solvent-based products with adequate moving air ventilation, and ventilate the work area. These precautions will keep fumes from building up and igniting. They will also protect you from the toxic effects of invisible and sometimes explosive vapors.

Wise Use of Flammable Liquids

At one time or another, nearly everyone has to use flammable liquids. Here are some fundamental rules for wise use:

● Never use such liquids near flames or a source of sparks, including pilot lights.

- Use gasoline only as a fuel, not as a cleaning fluid.

- Always shut off power mowers, chain saws, or other gas-powered equipment before refueling them. Refuel outdoors and wait for hot parts to cool before adding fuel.

- Use only liquids identified as *charcoal starters* to get charcoal fires going. Never pour on additional fluid after starting the fire.

Proper Storage

Gasoline and other extremely flammable liquids should be stored outside your house or apartment, but they should *not* be stored in the trunk of your car. Children should not be able to reach your safe-storage place. For added insurance, lock up all flammable liquids.

Never keep gasoline in glass bottles, plastic jugs, or other makeshift containers. If possible, invest in a gasoline container with such safety features as a pressure release valve or a flame arrester.

Flammable Fabrics

There are four basic safety principles regarding the flammability of fabrics:

1. All fibers used in ordinary clothing can burn. But some catch fire and burn less readily than others. The more-fire-resistant fabrics are fire-resistant cotton, wool, rayon, polyester, and modacrylic. Fabrics that burn most readily are acetate, untreated cotton and rayon, and linen.

2. The way in which a fabric is made determines the way it burns. As a rule, heavy, tightly constructed fabrics ignite with difficulty and burn more slowly than fabrics that are light, open, or fuzzy. Once ignited, however, the heavier fabrics burn longer than the lightweights and can cause very serious injuries.

3. "Flame resistant" does not mean "noncombustible." The phrase only indicates that a fabric is designed to resist ignition and burning. Fabrics are incapable of providing you with protection if you reach into a fireplace, a wood-burning stove, or an oven. To maintain a fabric's flame-resistant qualities, follow the manufacturer's instructions regarding care and cleaning.

4. A garment's style has much to do with safety. The safest clothes are those that fit closely, have large neck openings and quick release closures, and are wrap-style.

Remember the three rules for extinguishing a clothing fire:

1. Don't run.

2. Do try to remove the burning article of clothing.

3. If that fails, drop to the floor or ground and roll back and forth.

Smoke Detectors

There are two basic rules regarding smoke detectors. First, every home should have at least one smoke detector, approved by a recognized national testing laboratory. Second, at least one smoke detector should be placed on each floor of your home.

Both types of detectors, ionization and photoelectric detectors, if well designed and engineered, are effective. The particular layout of your home may determine whether you need plug-in or battery-powered devices. Both have advantages and disadvantages.

The battery-powered smoke detector can run out of power, usually after about a year. It then gives a warning sound, at which time you need to install new batteries.

The plug-in detector operates like a permanently burning lamp. However, it cannot operate if fire or some other interference breaks the electrical circuit that powers the detector. Other tips:

- Place detectors high up, on a ceiling or wall, close to where people sleep. Otherwise the alarm may not be heard.

- Never place a smoke detector in the kitchen or very near it. Airborne kitchen grease and cooking fumes can easily activate the device, touching off a false alarm.

- Even if a battery-powered detector does not give a signal that its batteries are running down, change the batteries at least once a year.

- With a photoelectric detector, the light source should be replaced as soon as it burns out.

- Test photoelectric detectors regularly with real smoke—from a just-extinguished candle, for example. Test ionization detectors using a *lighted* candle. Test detectors every two to four weeks.

Fire Extinguishers

Fire extinguishers complement your smoke alarms and should be part of your home "immunization" program. The extinguishers should be kept in areas where fires are most likely to occur: the kitchen, home workshop, or rooms where flammable materials are kept, where people may be smoking, or where there are hazard-producing activities or materials.

Fire extinguishers are rated according to size. A five-pound extinguisher rated ABC (meaning it can be used to fight fires of any kind) is considered minimal for home protection. Many homeowners, however, buy two-and-one-half-pound extinguishers specifically to fight small kitchen fires.

The best protection against home fires may be a common garden hose.

Using extensions, it can be made long enough to reach every room in the house. You can also attach nozzles that make it possible to sprinkle, spray, or direct a solid stream. Keep the hose in one place so that it is always ready to use.

An Escape Plan

Fire causes most home emergencies, but other conditions can be just as disastrous. An accident outside the home may force immediate evacuation; so may natural disasters such as storms or floods.

An escape plan should be part of your program for immunizing your home against emergencies. The plan can save lives by preventing panic.

For Fires

In cases of fire, you need to have two exits from each part of the house. You may want to consider installing rope or chain safety ladders outside windows that are too high above the ground for safe jumping. If you live in an apartment, you should obtain escape instructions from your building management or landlord or your local fire department.

Through informal fire drills, you can help to ensure that each member of your household understands the escape plan. You should include small children in all rehearsals, and repeat them periodically. Everyone should know where they are to meet to be sure everyone got out safely.

Young children should understand clearly that they have to evacuate when everyone else does. They *must* escape; they cannot hide under a bed or in a closet.

Three rules are critically important:

1. *Stay low.* Since most smoke rises, you need to keep low, crawling on hands and knees when necessary, to pass safely through a smoke-filled hallway or room.

2. *Feel doors before you open them.* If you find that the door panels, the knob, or the molding surrounding the door are hot to the touch, it may mean that the fire is just outside. Move toward another exit.

3. *Use wet cloths.* To avoid excessive smoke inhalation, a major cause of fire-related deaths, you can wet pillow cases, towels, or other fabrics and hold them over your face while you make your way to an exit.

For Natural Disasters

In case of natural disasters, you need to obtain accurate, current information as well as warnings, advice, or instructions from agencies. Disregarding such instructions or advice can endanger you and your family.

Your home should be equipped with a battery-powered portable radio. The radio could mean the difference between disaster and survival if your power is interrupted. You should have spare, sealed-in-the-package batteries for the radio. To prolong their lives, you can keep them in a refrigerator freezer.

Other avenues of communication in an emergency are available in most communities in the United States. These include amateur radio, citizens' band (CB) radio, community disaster warnings, special signals and communications methods, and (of course) the telephone.

Amateur radio or "ham" operators have proven to be unusually helpful in emergencies. To locate such an operator in your community, you can inquire among your neighbors or write, enclosing a self-addressed, stamped envelope, to the Amateur Radio Relay League, 225 Main St., Newington, CT 06111.

Poisonous or Harmful Substances

Each year, more than 100,000 children under the age of five become victims of accidental ingestion of poisonous or harmful substances. These include medicines and such flammable liquids as gasoline, but they also include a vast range of liquids, solids, and gases that find their ways into the home.

Substances that require special precautions range from carbon monoxide to spoiled food, cleaning fluids, detergents, and pesticides. Some general guidelines are as follows:

● Bring such substances into your home only if necessary, and then in the smallest possible quantity.

● Keep all products in their original containers, never in containers customarily used for food or drinks.

● If a product comes in a child-resistant container, never transfer it to a container that has no such protection.

● Carefully separate foods from potentially harmful products.

● After using a product that comes in a child-resistant container, resecure the cap or other closure.

● Make sure that all products that entail any risk or hazard are properly labeled, and turn on lights before using such products.

● Store potentially hazardous products in a separate area from other household products, preferably in a locked cabinet.

Because not all the harmful substances that enter your home have warnings on their containers, you should make it your business to learn whether hazards exist.

Contamination from Pets

The case of a one-year-old boy in Columbus, Ohio alerted the U.S. government to some of the hazards that can enter your home with pets.

Four days after his mother gave him a baby turtle, the child became ill with fever, abdominal pain, and bloody diarrhea. The following day, his brother showed similar symptoms. Analysis of stool cultures showed that the children had been infected with salmonella, a disease-causing organism carried by the turtle.

The children recovered. Subsequently, however, the U.S. Food and Drug Administration (FDA) banned the sale and public distribution of small turtles with shells less than four inches long. Included in the ban are turtle eggs. Aside from salmonella, turtles can introduce into your home other bacteria that can cause fever, diarrhea, and various gastrointestinal problems. Infection can lead to additional complications and even death.

Almost any kind of pet can introduce disease-causing organisms into the home. "Some pet store owners may . . . be ignorant of the potential diseases and illnesses that can be caused not only by turtles, but by other reptiles, birds, and mammals sold as pets," according to an FDA official.

Among household pets, dogs are susceptible to infection by a variety of worms and other parasites. Worms present a particularly insidious problem because the host pets can become seriously sick unless owners take curative steps. Also, many varieties of worms can infect dogs, and the symptoms can be extremely diverse and complex.

Generally, humans cannot be infected by dog-borne illnesses. But

hookworm is an exception. As the FDA notes, "Although canine hookworms can't mature in people, the larvae can migrate through the skin and subcutaneous tissue, causing serious skin lesions."

Lead Poisoning

Many ceramic-ware products sold in the United States are coated with glazes that are applied and fused onto a shaped piece of clay. Cadmium may be used to enhance the vividness of the colors.

Both cadmium and lead are toxic metals. Both can, under given conditions, leach into foods stored in some glazed ceramic containers.

Since 1971, the FDA has limited the amounts of lead that can leach or soak out of ceramic ware into foods. But cases of lead poisoning and various studies have renewed concerns about lead from all sources and from many different consumer products. These products include the 60 percent of all ceramic foodware imported into the United States from foreign countries.

Lead can, however, invade the home environment in other ways or from other sources. Some paints manufactured before 1978 contained lead (see Lead Poisoning, pp. 163–4). That paint still covers the walls, floors, and furniture of many older apartments and homes. In some communities, water reaches homes by way of old lead service pipes and water system mains.

You can reduce the risks to a safe minimum and avoid the stomach disorders and other problems, including brain damage in severe cases, that lead can produce.

Ceramic-ware Lead Poisoning

The following precautions can help prevent lead poisoning from ceramic ware:

1. *Avoid storing foods in ceramic ware.* Much preferred and far safer are glass or plastic containers. The high acid content of many foods increases the amounts of lead that the food can absorb.

2. *Be especially wary of products imported from or bought in foreign countries.* Manufacturers in those countries do not necessarily adhere to high safety standards. You may be wise either to avoid purchasing dinnerware made in other countries or to use such products for other purposes, such as decoration.

3. *Avoid using antiques or collectibles to hold food and vegetables.* They may be family heirlooms, or they may have been bought at garage or rummage sales, antique shops, or flea markets, but ceramic ware of uncertain origin may be dangerous.

4. *Beware of ceramic items made by amateurs or hobbyists.* Hobbyists can obtain safe glazes today, but you may not be able to tell whether the maker actually used such a glaze.

You have another choice if you want to use ceramic items to store foods or liquids: you can have your ceramic ware tested by a qualified commercial laboratory. Check your local health department or the telephone book for laboratories in your area.

Paint Lead Poisoning

Parents of young children should learn to recognize the symptoms of such poisoning and to consult as quickly as possible with a doctor, local hospital or clinic, or public health department. Delay can, in serious cases, lead to mental retardation, paralysis, and even death.

A difficulty in recognizing paint lead poisoning is that the symptoms are similar to those of many other childhood ailments. A child with lead poisoning may complain of stomachaches or may vomit. Headaches, a loss of appetite, crankiness, and excessive tiredness may be other symptoms. The child may lose interest in normal play.

A second problem is that a child can be poisoned by chewing on or eating dirt, dust, newspapers, some pottery, some furniture, or many other nonfood substances containing lead. But hospital or clinic blood tests for lead poisoning take only minutes. If a high concentration of lead is found in the blood, treatment may be necessary. Follow the directions and guidance of your doctor or local health department.

Depending on your child's age, you may be able to explain that he or she should eat nothing but food. Babysitters should be instructed about lead poisoning hazards and should keep children in their care from eating paint, newspapers, or other nonfood substances.

To remove the threat of paint lead poisoning, keep your home in good shape, free of water leaks from faulty plumbing, defective roofs, or exterior holes that could admit rain or dampness. Repaint the interior surfaces of your home every four to five years. Here are some further precautions:

1. Replaster any plaster walls that may be cracking or peeling.

2. Using a broom or stiff brush, remove all the pieces of loose paint from the walls.

3. Sweep up and put into a paper bag all the pieces of paint and plaster and place them in a trash can. *Do not burn them.*

4. While removing lead-based paint by scraping or sanding, keep children and pregnant women away (preferably outside the home) and take precautions to protect yourself. The dust you raise may be harmful.

The Allergen-Free Environment

Some 35 million Americans suffer from allergies. They may have hay fever, asthma, food intolerances or sensitivities, or adverse skin reactions to the stings of hornets, bees, or wasps. While medical scientists do not completely understand the causes and workings of allergies, great progress is being made in this area.

One result of allergy research is that most people with allergies are able to lead normal lives in spite of diverse symptoms and reactions. For hay fever sufferers, doctors can prescribe drugs to relieve irritating nasal inflammation, or allergic rhinitis. Cromolyn sodium may be prescribed to relieve the symptoms of asthma; the sodium can be inhaled through a spinhaler, nebulizer machine, or metered dose inhaler.

For most allergy victims, the best defense is to avoid the substances or circumstances that bring on attacks or symptoms. If there are allergy sufferers in your family, you may want to establish a home environment that is as allergen-free as possible. Furry pets are a major cause of allergic reactions. Carpeting, unless laid on a cement floor, serves as the perfect incubator for dust mites. Books can also harbor mites. Both feather and foam rubber pillows can be hazards. The best protection is cleanliness.

Radon, A Special Case

Radon is a colorless, odorless, radioactive gas that is almost impossible to detect without instruments. It seeps through the crevices or spaces in the soil or rock on which a home is built. It can enter your home through cracks, drains, and the tiny holes or pores in walls.

Persons exposed to radon face serious health risks, specifically lung cancer. Also, continued exposure to radon increases the risk of illness.

Many persons never realize that the gas is invading their homes.

Detection of radon requires special equipment but moderate cost. Two commercially available radon detectors are the charcoal canister and the alpha track detector. The former calls for a test period of three to seven days, and the latter requires two to four weeks. Trained personnel can provide other methods of detection. Reports on measurements of radon gas are made in terms of picocuries per liter (pCi/l).

Readings of above 1.0 WL (working level) or above 200 pCi/l, require immediate follow-up measurements.

Doing it yourself to close off the radon entry points in your basement begins with caulking. Using urethane or silicone caulk, seal up the gap (if any) between the basement floor and all walls; fill cracks in the mortar joints between concrete blocks; and lay a thick bead of caulk around the perimeter of sump openings. Treated plywood or a metal sheet can then be used to cover the sump, with more caulk used as a sealant.

Use ready-mix concrete to seal any large openings around pipes, pipe-chase openings, and spaces along the top rows of concrete-block walls. Inject insulation into the top rows of concrete-block walls before sealing them. Foam backing can be applied before the concrete sealing is applied to pipe-chase openings.

Ventilation supplements your efforts to close all gaps and holes in your basement's floors and walls. Without creating uncomfortable drafts, you can ventilate under your basement slab *if:* (1) you have a continuous slab with no large, unsealed openings to the earth beneath, and (2) there is a sufficiently porous bed under the slab to permit ventilating air to circulate through it. Given both conditions, you can create your own subslab vent system with pipes and a fan; the air intake and exhaust pipes should be located in opposite corners of the basement.

Other methods of ventilating your basement include forced-air systems using fans to maintain a balanced air exchange rate; heat-recovery ventilators that replace radon-tainted air with outside air; and use of a product called Enka-drain, which traps radon in a nylon mesh airspace that is then vented through an exhaust pipe.

Because it is a gas, radon always moves from a higher pressure area (the ground) to a lower-pressure one (your house). That means you have a final alternative to ventilation: pressurize your basement and home by providing outside air supplies for wood stoves, fireplaces, gas dryers, and furnaces.

Safety for the Old and the Young

Some precautions can help prevent home accidents. Older persons need special consideration because they may not be as mobile or as observant as they once were. Young children tend to actively and continuously explore what they see as their world.

Safety for Children

Some steps that will make home life safer for children are obvious. Toy boxes or chests should not have lids that can crush small fingers, for example. Windows should have safety locks so that children cannot open them more than two or three inches.

The bars of a child's bed should not be more than two-and-one-half inches apart. Baby carriages should not tip over easily, and should have safety harnesses.

Other precautions: High chairs should not have sharp edges or points, open tubes that might trap small limbs, or mechanisms that could

pinch. Night clothes *must* be flame-resistant, and all clothes should be free of cords or other ties. Clothing for toddlers should allow free movement and growth.

Examine your child's room. Beds or cots should be solid and smooth, with no sharp projections and no horizontal bars that could make it easy for your child to climb out. If you are using a baby bed, it should have a dropside mechanism that is childproof. Avoid plastic sheets in favor of absorbent cotton, and the sheets should be fitted or tightly tucked in.

Children's furniture should be soft, low, and free of sharp edges. The furniture should be positioned so that young children cannot climb onto shelves or window sills.

Toys should be selected carefully and maintained in a safe condition. The Consumer Product Safety Commission notes that all toys that come into your home should be adapted to your child's age, interests, and skill level. They should have quality design and construction. Instructions of use should be read carefully and followed. Labels can guide you to some extent. Plastic wrappings, if any, should be discarded immediately.

Check periodically for breakage or wear and tear that makes toys unsafe. Check, too, for surfaces with splinters. Repaint toys only with lead-free paint, and look for and remove rust or weak parts on outdoor toys in particular. Here are some important safety measures regarding toys:

- Teach your child to put his toys away when they are not in use. It's safer.

- Make sure all toys conform to laws that ban small, swallowable parts.

- Prohibit toy caps, some noise-making guns, and other toys that can produce loud noises that might damage hearing. (The law requires labels on boxes or caps that ex-

plode with a sound above a certain level: "WARNING: Do not fire closer than one foot to the ear. Do not use indoors.")

- Avoid leaving long strings or cords, on toys or off, in cribs or where young children can get at them.

- Keep out of your home dangerous projectiles such as guided missiles, dart guns, flying toys, and lawn darts. If you have very young children, exercise caution with balloons and other toys that may be best suited for older children.

- Monitor any electric toys so that they cannot shock or burn. Electric toys have to meet specific requirements for maximum surface temperatures, electrical construction, and appropriate warning labels. Electric toys with heating elements are not recommended for children under eight years old.

- Make sure infants' toys, such as rattles and teethers, are large enough that they cannot be swallowed.

A house check is in order if you have children. Is all furniture safe? Are stairs fitted with a handrail? Are there safety gates at the top and bottom? Are the stairs well lighted and free of ill-fitting carpets? In the bathroom, are all bath toys safe? Are they plastic? (They should be.) Have hand grips and rubber mats been properly placed, and are they also safe? Do you have non-slip flooring?

In the kitchen, in addition to the safety tips already noted, you will want to make sure that heavy items are out of the reach of little children; that only safe-to-play-with items are kept in children's-level cupboards; that doors have locks or bolts, where necessary; and that you use table mats instead of cloths if you eat at the kitchen table.

In the garage, do-it-yourself materials and tools should be kept in locked toolboxes, on safe, high shelves, or hanging out of reach. Discarded refrigerators or freezers should either be padlocked or have their doors removed.

Safety for the Elderly

Make your home safe for older family members or visitors before someone falls and incurs the most common of all injuries for older people: a broken hip. In addition to the safety measures that make your home safe for children, you can take further steps to protect older people in your home:

- Provide night lights in rooms that may need them, and make sure bathrooms and other rooms have light switches near entry doors.

- If possible, eliminate extension cords.

- Install light switches at the top and bottom of stairways.

- Provide toilet facilities on the same floor as an older person's bedroom.

- If necessary, install a higher toilet seat.

- Install handrails or grab bars for the toilet, bathtub, and stairway, and apply non-slip appliqués to tub bottoms and shower floors.

- Remove casters from furniture, or keep castered furniture against a wall.

- Where possible, give floors and carpets non-slip surfacing.

- Make the top and bottom stair step a different color than the others.

- Tape or tack down the edges of area rugs, runners, and mats that have a tendency to roll up or curl, or simply get rid of them.

- To prevent scalds, keep tempera-

tures in your water heater below 120° F.

Examine your home through the eyes of an older person. Would you have access to a telephone if you were to fall? Can you install at least one telephone that could be reached if you were unable to stand? In the kitchen, are towels or dishcloths hanging close to the toaster or the stove? Do you have good, even lighting over the stove, sink, and countertop? Do you need additional lighting under a cabinet or over a countertop where you slice or cut foods?

Because hundreds of elderly persons are treated annually for injuries resulting from falls from boxes or chairs, a step-stool can be an extremely practical item of furniture. But the stool itself should be safe. It should have tight screws and braces, and it should have a handrail to hold while standing on the top step. If the stool has broken parts, it should be discarded.

Before stepping up, the stool should be fully opened and stable.

Clothing

Clothing can present a number of safety hazards for older people. The CPSC has estimated that 70 percent of all persons who die from clothing fires are over 65 years of age.

Some of those fires have started when older persons reached over hot or burning stove or range surfaces. It is safest not to wear clothes that have loose, flowing sleeves, or at least to tie or pin the sleeves snugly to your arm and wrist. Loose sleeves present another hazard: they can catch on pot or pan handles, overturning hot water or food and causing scalds. Awareness of how clothing can contribute to home safety also extends to the selection of nightwear.

Any program for making the home safe for older persons should include

most of the other steps noted in this chapter, including those referring to electrical safety and flammable fabrics.

The Food Department

Threats to your health can enter your home in a grocery bag. They can develop in your home in the forms of mold or bacteria on food. Poor food handling practices, inside and outside the home, contribute to these health hazards. The greatest threats are a lack of sanitation, insufficient cooking, and improper storage (see also "Food Hazards," pp. 967–970).

Bacteria cause about 95 percent of all cases of food poisoning. People can ingest illness-producing bacteria in contaminated foods; the bacteria then multiply and spread infections in the digestive tract or the bloodstream. Such digestive problems occur most often in warm weather, when food may be taken to picnics or on cookout without proper refrigeration.

Contamination may also take place if parasitic animals such as the roundworm, found sometimes in pork, enter the body. The roundworm produces a disease called trichinosis.

There are four main kinds of bacteria that can contaminate foods and cause diseases: salmonella; "staph," or *staphylococcus aureus;* botulism; and *clostridium perfringens,* which causes diarrhea. However, you can avoid contamination if you take precautions. The four kinds of bacteria can produce symptoms as mild as an upset stomach or as severe as death, as in the case of botulism.

Food-Borne Poisons and Allergens

When shopping, you usually have to take on faith the food manufacturer's and the grocer's claims that their food is safe. But you can certainly be selective. You may want to avoid foods that touch off negative or allergic reactions. If certain foods have given you gastrointestinal or other problems in the past, it would be wise to avoid those foods when shopping.

You may have allergies—for example, to sulfites, the additives in many foods that can cause serious or even fatal reactions. Today, the labels on food packaging provide an abundance of dietary information to aid consumers in making choices.

Buying intelligently and carefully constitutes your first line of defense against food-borne illness and disease. Here are some guidelines for the conscientious shopper:

- Watch for possible spoilage in everything you buy, and *never* purchase food in a torn package or a dented or bulging can.

- Exercise your right to doubt: check display cases to make sure frozen foods are stored above the frost lines or load lines. Never buy frozen food that has softened.

- Always pick up meat, poultry, and dairy products last when making your grocery rounds.

- Never leave a sackful of groceries in the car on a hot day. Make the grocery store your last stop on the way home, and make sure perishable groceries are wrapped in an insulated bag for the trip home.

- Once home, put everything away quickly in the appropriate storage place, whether refrigerator, freezer, or storage cupboard.

Different foods require different storage methods. The labels on many packaged or canned foods provide instructions for storage procedures.

Food preparation under the wrong conditions creates many of the problems that Americans face when they sit down to eat. The wrong conditions range from unclean hands, hair, fingernails, and clothing to failure to wash one's hands thoroughly after us-

ing the toilet. You should wash your hands thoroughly after smoking or blowing your nose. You should also wash your hands after handling raw meat, poultry, or eggs and before working with other foods. Other precautions: Do not use your hands to mix foods; use clean utensils instead. Avoid using the same spoon more than once to taste food while preparing it. Never eat any food directly from the jar or can; this could contaminate the can's contents. Scrub potatoes and other raw foods before cooking them. Carefully clean all utensils, work surfaces, dishes, and kitchen equipment before using them. And drink only pasteurized milk.

It is best to serve foods soon after they are cooked; otherwise, refrigerate them. You can refrigerate hot or warm foods if you are sure they will not raise the refrigerator temperature above 45° F.

The temperatures at which you keep foods affect directly your home's level of food safety. Hot foods should be kept above 140 degrees for safety while cold foods should be stored at 40 degrees or lower. The danger zone in which foods can develop bacteria, sometimes in the space of two or three hours, lies between 60° and 125°. Keeping food warm for several hours in an oven can be hazardous if the oven's temperature is between 60° and 125°.

Some foods require special attention. Eggs, for example, should be used only if they are fresh, clean, uncracked, and odor-free. You may make exceptions if the eggs are unspoiled and if they are to be used in recipes that call for thorough cooking. When serving a dish that has eggs as a major ingredient, cool the dish quickly after it is cooked, preferably in cold water, if it is not to be served hot. Then refrigerate it.

Meat, poultry, and fish are also sensitive. If frozen, they should be

thawed in the refrigerator. If you need to thaw these products more quickly, you can place them, sealed in watertight wrappers, in cold water. To cook frozen items of these types, allow about one-and-one-half times the ordinary cooking times for thawed products of the same weight and shape.

Meats, poultry, or fish should be stuffed just before they are cooked, not a day or two ahead of time. The stuffing should reach a temperature of at least 165° F. during cooking. Use reliable timetables or follow package directions when cooking these products, and take extra care with ground meat. Because it is handled several times in packaging, ground meat should be cooked thoroughly and never eaten raw. Some *hams* need to be cooked, and should be if you have any doubt.

Fish, meat, and poultry should be cooked entirely in a single process, not cooked partially one day and then finished on another. Poultry should always be cooked thoroughly. If you store poultry products before the day on which you plan to cook them, you should store the giblets and the rest of the bird separately in the refrigerator. Use the hot dogs and cold meat within a few days after purchasing, and never more than a week later.

Freezer practices should be grounded in common sense. A fundamental rule is that freezing does not kill the bacteria in food; it only keeps existing bacteria from multiplying. Thawing enables those bacteria to begin to proliferate again.

Do not refreeze food that has been frozen and thawed. To protect frozen foods, wrap or package each item carefully to keep air away from the product. Different items can be kept safely in a freezing compartment for different periods of time, depending on the product. Label each item with the date it went into the freezer and the type of food.

Emergency Transport

In the majority of situations, the transfer of an injured person should be handled only by experienced rescue personnel. If you yourself must move a victim to a physician's office or hospital emergency room, here are a few important rules to remember:

1. Give all necessary first aid before attempting to move the victim. Do everything to reduce pain and to make the patient comfortable.

2. If you improvise a stretcher, be sure it is strong enough to carry the victim and that you have enough people to carry it. Shutters, doors, boards, and even ladders may be used as stretchers. Just be sure that the stretcher is padded underneath to protect the victim and that a blanket or coat is available to cover him and protect him from exposure.

3. Bring the stretcher to the victim, not the victim to the stretcher. Slide him onto the stretcher by grasping his clothing or lift him—if enough bearers are available—as shown in the illustration.

4. Secure the victim to the stretcher so he won't fall off. You may want to tie his feet together to minimize his movements.

5. Unless specific injuries prevent it, the victim should be lying on his back while he is being moved. However, a person who is having difficulty breathing because of a chest injury might be more comfortable if his head and shoulders are raised slightly. A person with a severe injury to the back of his head should be kept lying on his side. In any case, place the patient in a comfortable position that will protect him from further injury.

6. Try to transport the patient feet first.

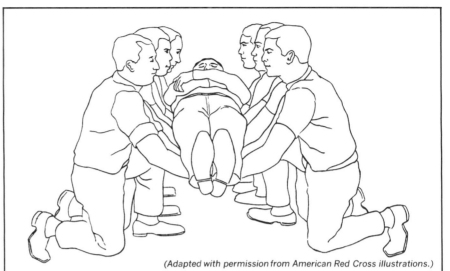

(Adapted with permission from American Red Cross illustrations.)

How to lift an injured or unconscious person to place him on a stretcher. Three bearers on each side of the victim kneel on the knee closer to the victim's feet. The bearers work their hands and forearms gently under the victim to about the midline of the back. On signal, they lift together as shown; on a following signal, they stand as a unit, if that is necessary. In lowering the victim to a stretcher or other litter, the procedure is reversed.

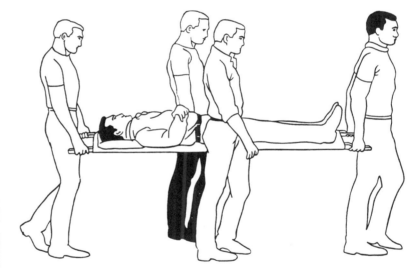

The proper way to carry a victim on a stretcher. One bearer is at the head, one at the foot, and one at either side of the stretcher. The victim should be carried feet first.

7. Unless absolutely necessary, don't try to put a stretcher into a passenger car. It's almost impossible to get the stretcher or injured person into a passenger car without further injuring him. If there is no ambulance, a station wagon or truck makes a good substitute.

8. When you turn the patient over to a doctor or take him to an emergency room of a hospital, give a complete account of the situation to the person taking charge. Tell the doctor what you've done for the patient and what you suspect might cause further problems.

Alphabetic Guide to Medical Emergencies

Abdominal Wound

Abdominal wounds can result from gunshots during hunting or working with firearms, from falling on a knife or sharp object at home or work, or from a variety of other mishaps ranging from automobile accidents to a mugging attack. Such a wound can be a major emergency requiring surgery and other professional care. Call a physician or arrange for quick transportation to a hospital as quickly as possible.

Emergency Treatment

If there is severe bleeding, try to control it with pressure. Keep the victim lying on his back with the knees bent; place a pillow, coat, or a similar soft object under the knees to help hold them in the bent position. If abdominal organs are exposed, do not touch them for any reason. Cover the wound with a sterile dressing. Keep the dressing moistened with sterile water or the cleanest water available. Boiled water can be used to moisten the dressing, but be sure it has cooled before applying.

If the victim is to be moved to a hospital or physician's office, be sure the dressing over the wound is large enough and is held in place with a bandage. In addition to pain, you can expect the victim to experience nausea and vomiting, muscle spasms, and severe shock. Make the victim as comfortable as possible under the circumstances; if he complains of thirst, moisten his mouth with a few drops of water, but do not permit him to swallow the liquid.

Abrasions

Emergency Treatment

Wash the area in which the skin is scraped or rubbed off with soap and water, using clean gauze or cotton. Allow the abrasion to air-dry, and then cover it with a loose sterile dressing held in place with a bandage. If a sterile dressing is not available, use a clean handerchief.

Change the dressing after the first 24 hours, using household hydrogen peroxide to ease its removal if it sticks to the abrasion because of clotted blood. If the skinned area appears to be accompanied by swelling, or is painful or tender to the touch, consult a physician.

Acid Burns

Among acids likely to be encountered at work and around the home are sulphuric, nitric, and hydrochloric acids. Wet-cell batteries, such as automobile batteries, contain acid powerful enough to cause chemical destruction of body tissues, and some metal cleaners contain powerful acids.

Emergency Treatment

Wash off the acid immediately, using large amounts of clean, fresh, cool water. Strip off or cut off any clothing that may have absorbed any of the acid. If possible, put the victim in a shower bath; if a shower is not available, flood the affected skin areas with as much water as possible. However, do not apply water forcefully since this could aggravate damage already done to skin or other tissues.

After as much of the acid as possible has been eliminated by flooding with water, apply a mild solution of sodium bicarbonate or another mild alkali such as lime water. Caution should be exercised, however, in neutralizing an acid burn because the chemical reaction between an acid and an alkali can produce intense heat that would aggravate the injury; also, not all acids are effectively neutralized by alkalis—carbolic acid burns, for example, should be neutralized with alcohol.

Wash the affected areas once more with fresh water, then dry gently with sterile gauze; be careful not to break the skin or to open blisters. Extensive acid burns will cause extreme pain and shock; have the victim lie down with the head and chest a little lower than the rest of the body. As soon as possible, summon a physician or rush the victim to the emergency room of a hospital.

Aerosol Sprays

Although aerosol sprays generally are regarded as safe when handled according to directions, they can be directed accidentally toward the face with resulting contamination of the eyes or inhalation of the fumes. The pressurized containers may also contain products or propellants that are highly flammable, producing burns when used near an open flame. When stored near heat, in direct sunlight, or in a closed auto, the containers may explode violently.

Emergency Treatment

If eyes are contaminated by spray particles, flush the eye surfaces with water to remove any particles of the powder mist. Then carefully examine eye surfaces to determine if chemicals appear to be imbedded in the surface of the cornea. If aerosol spray is inhaled, move the patient to a well-ventilated area; keep him lying down, warm, and quiet. If breathing fails, administer artificial respiration. Victims of exploding containers or burning contents of aerosol containers should be given appropriate emergency treatment for bleeding, burns, and shock.

The redness and irritation of eye injuries should subside within a short time. If they do not, or if particles of spray seem to be imbedded in the surface of the eyes, take the victim to an ophthalmologist. A physician should also be summoned if a victim fails to recover quickly from the effects of inhaling an aerosol spray, particularly if the victim suffers from asthma or a similar lung disorder or from an abnormal heart condition.

Alkali Burns

Alkalis are used in the manufacture of soap and cleaners and in certain household cleaning products. They combine with fats to form soaps and may produce a painful injury when in contact with body surfaces.

Emergency Treatment

Flood the burned area with copious amounts of clean, cool, fresh water. Put the victim under a shower if possible, or otherwise pour running water over the area for as long as is necessary to dilute and weaken the corrosive chemical. Do not apply the water with such force that skin or other tissues are damaged. Remove clothing contaminated by the chemical.

Neutralize the remaining alkali with diluted vinegar, lemon juice, or a similar mild acid. Then wash the affected areas again with fresh water. Dry carefully with sterile gauze, being careful not to open blisters or otherwise cause skin breaks that could result in infection. Summon professional medical care as soon as possible. Meanwhile, treat the victim for shock.

Angina Pectoris

Angina pectoris is a condition that causes acute chest pain because of interference with the supply of oxygen to the heart. Although the pain is sometimes confused with ulcer or acute indigestion symptoms, it has a distinct characteristic of its own, producing a feeling of heaviness, strangling, tightness, or suffocation. Angina is a symptom rather than a disease, and may be a chronic condition with those over 50. It is usually treated by placing a nitroglycerine tablet under the tongue.

An attack of acute angina can be brought on by emotional stress, overeating, strenuous exercise, or by any activity that makes excessive demands on heart function.

Emergency Treatment

An attack usually subsides in about ten minutes, during which the patient appears to be gasping for breath. He should be kept in a semireclining position rather than made to lie flat, and should be moved carefully only in order to place pillows under his head and chest so that he can breathe more easily. A physician should be called promptly after the onset of an attack.

Animal Bites/Rabies

Wild animals, particularly bats, serve as a natural reservoir of rabies, a disease that is almost always fatal unless promptly and properly treated. But the virus may be present in the saliva of any warm-blooded animal. Domestic animals should be immunized against rabies by vaccines injected by a veterinarian.

Rabies is transmitted to humans by an animal bite or through a cut or scratch already in the skin. The infected saliva may enter through any opening, including the membranes lining the nose or mouth. After an incubation period of about ten days, a person infected by a rabid animal experiences pain at the site of infection, extreme sensitivity of the skin to temperature changes, and painful spasms of the larynx that make it almost impossible to drink. Saliva thickens and the patient becomes restless and easily excitable. By the time symptoms develop, death may be imminent. Obviously, professional medical attention should begin promptly after having been exposed to the possibility of infection.

Emergency Treatment

The area around the wound should be washed thoroughly and repeatedly with soap and water, using a sterile gauze dressing to wipe fluid away from—not toward—the wound. Another sterile dressing is used to dry the wound and a third to cover it while the patient is taken to a hospital or physician's office. A tetanus injection is also indicated, and police and health authorities should be promptly notified of the biting incident.

If at all possible the biting animal should be indentified—if a wild animal, captured alive—and held for observation for a period of 10 to 15 days. If it can be determined during that period that the animal is not rabid, further treatment may not be required. If the animal is rabid, however, or if it cannot be located and impounded, the patient may have to undergo a series of daily rabies vaccine injections lasting from 14 days for a case of mild exposure to 21 days for severe exposure (a bite near the head, for example), plus several booster shots. Because of the sensitivity of some individuals to the rabies vaccines used, the treatment itself can be quite dangerous.

Recent research, however, has established that a new vaccine called HDCV (human diploid cell vaccine), which requires only six or fewer injections, is immunologically effective and is not usually accompanied by any side effects. The new vaccine has been used successfully on people of all ages who had been bitten by animals known to be rabid.

Appendicitis

The common signal for approaching appendicitis is a period of several days of indigestion and constipation, culminating in pain and tenderness on the lower right side of the abdomen. Besides these symptoms, appendicitis may be accompanied by nausea and a slight fever. Call a physician immediately and describe the symptoms in detail; delay may result in a ruptured appendix.

Emergency Treatment

While awaiting medical care, the victim may find some relief from the pain and discomfort by having an ice bag placed over the abdomen. Do not apply heat and give nothing by mouth. A laxative should not be offered.

Asphyxiation

See GAS POISONING.

Asthma Attack

Emergency Treatment

Make the patient comfortable and offer reassurance. If he has been ex-amined by a physician and properly diagnosed, the patient probably has an inhalant device or other forms of medication on his person or nearby.

The coughing and wheezing spell may have been triggered by the presence of an allergenic substance such as animal hair, feathers, or kapok in pillows or cushions. Such items should be removed from the presence of the patient. In addition, placing the patient in a room with high humidity, such as a bathroom with the shower turned on, may be helpful.

Asthma attacks are rarely fatal in young people, but elderly persons should be watched carefully because of possible heart strain. In a severe attack, professional medical care including oxygen equipment may be required.

Back Injuries

In the event of any serious back injury, call a physician or arrange for immediate professional transfer of the victim to a hospital.

Emergency Treatment

Until determined otherwise by a physician, treat the injured person as a victim of a fractured spine. If he complains that he cannot move his head, feet, or toes, the chances are that the back is fractured. But even if he can move his feet or legs, it does not necessarily mean that he can be moved safely, since the back can be fractured without immediate injury to the spinal cord.

If the victim shows symptoms of shock, do not attempt to lower his head or move his body into the usual position for shock control. If it is absolutely essential to move the victim because of immediate danger to his life, make a rigid stretcher from a wide piece of solid lumber such as a door and cover the stretcher with a blanket for padding. Then carefully slide or pull the victim onto the stretcher, using his clothing to hold him. Tie the body onto the stretcher with strips of cloth.

Back Pain

See SCIATICA.

Black Eye

Although a black eye is frequently regarded as a minor medical problem, it can result in serious visual problems, including cataract or glaucoma.

Emergency Treatment

Inspect the area about the eye for possible damage to the eye itself, such as hemorrhage, rupture of the eyeball, or dislocated lens. Check also for cuts around the eye that may require professional medical care. Then treat the bruised area by putting the victim to bed, covering the eye with a bandage, and applying an ice bag to the area.

If vision appears to be distorted or lacerations need stitching and antibiotic treatment, take the victim to a physician's office. A physician should also be consulted about continued pain and swelling about the eye.

Black Widow Spider Bites

Emergency Treatment

Make the victim lie still. If the bite is on the arm or leg, position the victim so that the bite is lower than the level of the heart. Apply a rubber band or similar tourniquet between the bite and the heart to retard venom flow toward the heart. The bite usually is marked by two puncture points. Apply ice packs to the bite. Summon a physician or carry the patient to the nearest hospital.

Loosen the tourniquet or constriction band for a few seconds every 15 minutes while awaiting help; you should be able to feel a pulse beyond the tourniquet if it is not too tight. Do not let the victim move about. Do not permit him to drink alcoholic beverages. He probably will feel weakness, tremor, and severe pain, but reassure him that he will recover. Medications, usually available only to a physician, should be administered promptly.

Bleeding, Internal

Internal bleeding is always a very serious condition; it requires immediate professional medical attention.

In cases of internal bleeding, blood is sometimes brought to the outside of the body by coughing from the lungs, by vomiting from the stomach, by trickling from the ear or nose, or by passing in the urine or bowel movement.

Often, however, internal bleeding is concealed, and the only symptom may be the swelling that appears around the site of broken bones. A person can lose three or four pints of blood inside the body without a trace of blood appearing outside the body.

Some Symptoms of Internal Bleeding

The victim will appear ill and pale. His skin will be colder than normal, especially the hands and feet; often the skin looks clammy because of sweating. The pulse usually will be rapid (over 90 beats a minute) and feeble.

Emergency Treatment

Serious internal bleeding is beyond the scope of first aid. If necessary treat the victim for respiratory and cardiac arrest and for shock while waiting for medical aid.

Bleeding, Minor

Bleeding from minor cuts, scrapes, and bruises usually stops by itself, but even small injuries of this kind should receive attention to prevent infection.

Emergency Treatment

The injured area should be washed thoroughly with soap and water, or if possible, held under running water. The surface should then be covered with a sterile bandage.

The type of wound known as a puncture wound may bleed very little, but is potentially extremely dangerous because of the possibility of tetanus infection. Anyone who steps on a rusty nail or thumbtack or has a similar accident involving a pointed object that penetrates deep under the skin surface should consult a physician about the need for antitetanus inoculation or a booster shot.

Blisters

Emergency Treatment

If the blister is on a hand or foot or other easily accessible part of the body, wash the area around the blister thoroughly with soap and water. After carefully drying the skin around the blister, apply an antiseptic to the same area. Then sterilize the point and a substantial part of a needle by heating it in an open flame. When the needle has been thoroughly sterilized, use the point to puncture the blister along the margin of the blister. Carefully squeeze the fluid from the blister by pressing it with a sterile gauze dressing; the dressing should soak up most of the fluid. Next, place a fresh

sterile dressing over the blister and fasten it in place with a bandage. If a blister forms in a tender area or in a place that is not easily accessible, such as under the arm, do not open it yourself; consult your physician.

The danger from any break in the skin is that germs or dirt can slip through the natural barrier to produce an infection or inflammation. Continue to apply an antiseptic each day to the puncture area until it has healed. If it appears that an infection has developed or healing is unusually slow, consult a doctor. Persons with diabetes or circulatory problems may have to be more cautious about healing of skin breaks than other individuals.

Blood Blisters

Blood blisters, sometimes called hematomas, usually are caused by a sharp blow to the body surface such as hitting a finger with a hammer while pounding nails.

Emergency Treatment

Wash the area of the blood blister thoroughly with soap and water. Do not open it. If it is a small blood blister, cover it with a protective bandage; in many cases, the tiny pool of blood under the skin will be absorbed by the surrounding tissues if there is no further pressure at that point.

If the blood blister fails to heal quickly or becomes infected, consult a physician. Because the pool of blood has resulted from damage to a blood vessel, a blood blister usually is more vulnerable to infection or inflammation than an ordinary blister.

Boils

Boils frequently are an early sign of diabetes or another illness and should be watched carefully if they occur often. In general, they result from germs or dirt being rubbed into the skin by tight-fitting clothing, scratching, or through tiny cuts made during shaving.

Emergency Treatment

If the boil is above the lip, do not squeeze it or apply any pressure. The infection in that area of the face may drain into the brain because of the pattern of blood circulation on the face. Let a physician treat any boil on the face. If the boil is on the surface of another part of the body, apply moist hot packs, but do not squeeze or press on the boil because that action can force the infection into the circulatory system. A wet compress can be made by soaking a wash cloth or towel in warm water.

If the boil erupts, carefully wipe away the pus with a sterile dressing, and then cover it with another sterile dressing. If the boil is large or slow to erupt, or if it is slow to heal, consult a physician.

Bone Bruises

Emergency Treatment

Make sure the bone is not broken. If the injury is limited to the thin layer of tissue surrounding the bone, and the function of the limb is normal though painful, apply a compression dressing and an ice pack. Limit use of the injured limb for the next day or two.

As the pain and swelling recede, cover the injured area with a foam-rubber pad held in place with an elastic bandage. Because the part of the limb that is likely to receive a bone bruise lacks a layer of muscle and fat, it will be particularly sensitive to any pressure until recovery is complete.

Botulism

The bacteria that produce the lethal toxin of botulism are commonly present on unwashed farm vegetables and thrive in containers that are improperly sealed against the damaging effects of air. Home-canned vegetables, particularly string beans, are a likely source of botulism, but the toxin can be found in fruits, meats, and other foods. It can also appear in food that has been properly prepared but allowed to cool before being served. Examples are cold soups and marinated vegetables.

Emergency Treatment

As soon as acute symptoms—nausea, diarrhea, and abdominal distress—appear, try to induce vomiting. Vomiting usually can be started by touching the back of the victim's throat with a finger or the handle of a spoon, which should be smooth and blunt, or by offering him a glass of water in which two tablespoons of salt have been dissolved. Call a physician; describe all of the symptoms, which also may include, after several hours, double vision, muscular weakness, and difficulty in swallowing and breathing. Save samples of the food suspected of contamination for analysis.

Prompt hospitalization and injection of antitoxin are needed to save most cases of botulism poisoning. Additional emergency measures may include artificial respiration if regular breathing fails because of paralysis of respiratory muscles. Continue artificial respiration until professional medical care is provided. If other individuals have eaten the contaminated food, they should receive treatment for botulism even if they show no symptoms of the toxin's effects, since symptoms may be delayed by several days.

Brown House (or Recluse) Spider Bites

Emergency Treatment

Apply an ice bag or cold pack to the wound area. Aspirin and antihistamines may be offered to help relieve any pain or feeling of irritation. Keep the victim lying down and quiet. Call a physician as quickly as possible and describe the situation; the physician will advise what further action should be taken at this point.

The effects of a brown spider bite frequently last much longer than the pain of the bite, which may be comparatively mild for an insect bite or sting. But the poison from the bite can gradually destroy the surrounding tissues, leaving at first an ulcer and eventually a disfiguring scar. A physician's treatment is needed to control the loss of tissue; he probably will prescribe drugs and recommend continued use of cold compresses. The victim, meanwhile, will feel numbness and muscular weakness, requiring a prolonged period of bed rest in addition to the medical treatments.

Bruises/Contusions

Emergency Treatment

Bruises or contusions result usually from a blow to the body that is powerful enough to damage muscles, tendons, blood vessels, or other tissues without causing a break in the skin.

Because the bruised area will be tender, protect it from further injury. If possible, immobilize the injured body part with a sling, bandage, or other device that makes the victim feel more comfortable; pillows, folded blankets, or similar soft materials can be used to elevate an arm or leg. Apply an ice bag or cold water dressing to the injured area.

A simple bruise usually will heal without extensive treatment. The swelling and discoloration result from blood oozing from damaged tissues. Severe bruising can, however, be quite serious and requires medical attention. Keep the victim quiet and watch for symptoms of shock. Give aspirin for pain.

Bullet Wounds

Bullet wounds, whether accidental or purposely inflicted, can range from those that are superficial and external to those that involve internal bleeding and extensive tissue damage.

Emergency Treatment

A surface bullet wound accompanied by bleeding should be covered promptly with sterile gauze to prevent further infection. The flow of blood should be controlled as described under "Severe Bleeding" in this chapter. *Don't* try to clean the wound with soap or water.

If the wound is internal, keep the patient lying down and wrap him with coats or blankets placed over and under his body. If respiration has ceased or is impaired, give mouth-to-mouth respiration and treat him for shock. Get medical aid promptly.

Burns, Thermal

Burns are generally described according to the depth or area of skin damage involved. First-degree burns are the most superficial. They are marked by reddening of the skin and swelling, increased warmth, tenderness, and pain. Second-degree burns, deeper than first-degree, are in effect open wounds, characterized by blisters and severe pain in addition to redness. Third-degree burns are

deep enough to involve damage to muscles and bones. The skin is charred and there may be no pain because nerve endings have been destroyed. However, the area of the burn generally is more important than the degree of burn; a first- or second-degree burn covering a large area of the body is more likely to be fatal than a small third-degree burn.

Emergency Treatment

You will want to get professional medical help for treatment of a severe burn, but there are a number of things you can do until such help is obtained. If burns are minor, apply ice or ice water until pain subsides. Then wash the area with soap and water. Cover with a sterile dressing. Give the victim one or two aspirin tablets to help relieve discomfort. A sterile gauze pad soaked in a solution of two tablespoons of baking soda (sodium bicarbonate) per quart of lukewarm water may be applied.

For more extensive or severe burns, there are three first-aid objectives: (1) relieve pain, (2) prevent shock, (3) prevent infection. To relieve pain, exclude air by applying a thick dressing of four to six layers plus additional coverings of clean, tightly woven material; for extensive burns, use clean sheets or towels. Clothing should be cut away—never pulled—from burned areas; where fabric is stuck to the wound, leave it for a physician to remove later. Do not apply any ointment, grease, powder, salve, or other medication; the physician simply will have to remove such material before he can begin professional treatment of the burns.

To prevent shock, make sure the victim's head is lower than his feet. Be sure that the victim is covered sufficiently to keep him warm, but not enough to make him overheated; exposure to cold can make the effects

of shock more severe. Provide the victim with plenty of nonalcoholic liquids such as sweetened water, tea, or fruit juices, so long as he is conscious and able to swallow.

To prevent infection, do not permit absorbent cotton or adhesive tape to touch the wound caused by a burn. Do not apply iodine or any other antiseptic to the burn. Do not open any blisters. Do not permit any unsterile matter to contact the burn area. If possible, prevent other persons from coughing, sneezing, or even breathing toward the wound resulting from a burn. Serious infections frequently develop in burn victims from contamination by microorganisms of the mouth and nose.

Long-Term Treatment

A highly effective method of treating serious burns involves, first, removal of samples of uninjured skin from victims' bodies. Laboratory workers then "grind up" the healthy skin samples and separate them into groups of cells. Placed in flasks and bathed in a growth-stimulating solution, the cells grow rapidly; while the colonies are small, they double in size every 17 hours. New skin appears. The procedure can be repeated until enough has been grown to cover the burned areas.

Because the "test-tube skin" is developed from samples of a victim's own skin, the body does not reject it. It can be grafted onto a burned area in patches until the entire burn is covered. The new skin has no hair follicles or sweat glands, and is thinner than normal skin. But it offers hope to some 10 to 15 percent of those persons who are hospitalized with burn injuries.

See also CHEMICAL BURNS OF THE EYE.

Carbuncles

Carbuncles are quite similar to boils

except that they usually develop around multiple hair follicles and commonly appear on the neck or face. Personal hygiene is one factor involved in the development of carbuncles; persons apparently susceptible to the pustular inflammations must exercise special care in cleansing areas in which carbuncles occur, particularly if they suffer from diabetes or circulatory ailments.

Emergency Treatment

Apply moist hot packs to the boil-like swelling. Change the moist hot packs frequently, or place a hot-water bottle on the moist dressing to maintain the moist heat application. Do not handle the carbuncle beyond whatever contact is necessary to apply or maintain the moist heat. The carbuncle should eventually rupture or reach a point where it can be opened with a sterile sharp instrument. After the carbuncle has ruptured and drained, and the fluid from the growth has been carefully cleaned away, apply a sterile dressing.

Frequently, carbuncles must be opened and drained by a physician.

Cat Scratch Fever

Although the scratch or bite of a house cat or alley cat may appear at first to be only a mild injury, the wound can become the site of entry for a disease virus transmitted by apparently healthy cats. The inflammation, accompanied by fever, generally affects the lymph nodes and produces some aches and pains as well as fatigue. Although the disease is seldom fatal, an untreated case can spread to brain tissues and lead to other complications.

Emergency Treatment

Wash the scratch thoroughly with water and either soap or a mild detergent. Apply a mild antiseptic such as hydrogen peroxide. Cover with a sterile dressing.

Watch the area of the scratch carefully for the next week or two. If redness or swelling develop, even after the scratch appears healed, consult your physician. The inflammation of the scratch area may be accompanied by mild fever and symptoms similar to those of influenza; in small children, the symptoms may be quite serious. Bed rest and antibiotics usually are prescribed.

Charley Horse

A charley horse occurs because a small number of muscle fibers have been torn or ruptured by overstraining the muscle, or by the force of a blow to the muscle.

Emergency Treatment

Rest the injured muscle and apply an ice pack if there is swelling. A compression dressing can be applied to support the muscle. Avoid movement that stretches the muscle, and restrict other movements that make the victim uncomfortable. If pain and swelling persist, call a physician.

During the recovery period, which may not begin for a day or two, apply local heat with a hot water bottle or an electric heating pad, being careful not to burn the victim. A return to active use of the muscle can begin gradually as pain permits.

Chemical Burns of the Eye

Emergency Treatment

Flush the victim's eye immediately with large quantities of fresh, clean water; a drinking fountain can be used

to provide a steady stream of water. If a drinking fountain is not available, lay the victim on the floor or ground with his head turned slightly to one side and pour water into the eye from a cup or glass. Always direct the stream of water so that it enters the eye surface at the inside corner and flows across the eye to the outside corner. If the victim is unable, because of intense pain, to open his eyes, it may be necessary to hold the lids apart while water pours across the eye. Continue flushing the eye for at least 15 minutes. (An alternate method is to immerse the victim's face in a pan or basin or bucket of water while he opens and closes his eyes repeatedly; continue the process for at least 15 minutes.)

When the chemical has been flushed from the victim's eye, the eye should be covered with a small, thick compress held in place with a bandage that covers both eyes, if possible; the bandage can be tied around the victim's head. **Note:** Apply nothing but water to the eye; do not attempt to neutralize a chemical burn of the eye and do not apply oil, ointment, salve, or other medications. Rush the victim to a physician as soon as possible, preferably to an ophthalmologist.

Chemicals on Skin

Many household and industrial chemicals, such as ammonia, lye, iodine, creosote, and a wide range of insecticides can cause serious injury if accidentally spilled on the skin.

Emergency Treatment

Wash the body surface that has been affected by the chemical with large amounts of water. Do not try to neutralize the chemical with another substance; the reaction may aggravate the injury. If blisters appear, apply a sterile dressing. If the chemical is a refrigerant, such as Freon, or carbon dioxide under pressure, treat for frostbite.

If the chemical has splashed into the eyes or produces serious injury to the affected body surface, call a physician. The victim should be watched closely for possible poisoning effects if the chemical is a pesticide, since such substances may be absorbed through the skin to produce internal toxic reactions. If there is any question about the toxicity of a chemical, ask your doctor or call the nearest poison control center.

Chigger Bites

Emergency Treatment

Apply ice water or rub ice over the area afflicted by bites of the tiny red insects. Bathing the area with alcohol, ammonia water or a solution of baking soda also will provide some relief from the itching.

Wash thoroughly with soap, using a scrub brush to prevent further infestation by the chiggers in other areas of the body. Rub alcohol over the surrounding areas and apply sulfur ointment as protection against mites that may not have attached themselves to the skin. Continue applications of ice water or alcohol to skin areas invaded by the insects. Clothing that was worn should be laundered immediately.

Chilblains

Emergency Treatment

Move the victim to a moderately warm place and remove wet or tight clothing. Soak the affected body area in warm—but not hot—water for about ten minutes. Then carefully blot the skin dry, but do not rub the skin. Replace the clothing with garments that are warm, soft, and dry.

Give the victim a stimulant such as tea or coffee, or an alcoholic beverage, and put him to bed with only light blankets; avoid the pressure of heavy blankets or heavy, tight garments on the sensitive skin areas. The victim should move the affected body areas gently to help restore normal circulation. If complications develop, such as marked discoloration of the skin, pain, or blistering and splitting of the skin, call a physician.

Cold Sores/Fever Blisters

Emergency Treatment

Apply a soothing ointment or a medication such as camphor ice. Avoid squeezing or otherwise handling the blisters; moisture can aggravate the sores and hinder their healing. Repeated appearances of cold sores or fever blisters, which are caused by the herpes simplex virus, may require treatment by a physician.

Concussion

See HEAD INJURIES.

Contusions

See BRUISES.

Convulsions

Emergency Treatment

Protect the victim from injury by moving him to a safe place; loosen any constricting clothing such as a tie or belt; put a pillow or coat under his head; if his mouth is open, place a folded cloth between his teeth to keep him from biting his tongue. Do not force anything into his mouth. Keep the patient warm but do not disturb him; do not try to restrain his convulsive movements.

Send for a physician as quickly as possible. Watch the patient's breathing and begin artificial respiration if breathing stops for more than one minute. Be sure that breathing actually has stopped; the patient may be sleeping or unconscious after an attack but breathing normally.

Convulsions in a small child may signal the onset of an infectious disease and may be accompanied by a high fever. The same general precautions should be taken to prevent self-injury on the part of the child. If placed in a bed, the child should be protected against falling onto the floor. Place him on his side—not on his back or stomach—if he vomits. Cold compresses or ice packs on the back of the neck and the head may help relieve symptoms. Immediate professional medical care is vital because brain damage can result if treatment is delayed.

See also EPILEPTIC SEIZURES.

Cramps

See MUSCLE CRAMPS.

Croup

Croup is a breathing disorder usually caused by a virus infection and less often by bacteria or allergy. It is a common condition during childhood, and in some cases, may require brief hospitalization for proper treatment.

The onset of a croup attack is likely to occur during the night with a sudden hoarse or barking cough accompanied by difficulty in breathing. The coughing is usually followed by choking spasms that sound as though the child is strangling. There may also be a mild fever. A physician should be called immediately when these symptoms appear.

Emergency Treatment

The most effective treatment for croup is cool moist air. Cool water vaporizers are available as well as warm steam vaporizers. Another alternative is to take the child into the bathroom, close the door and windows, and let the hot water run from the shower and sink taps until the room is filled with steam.

It is also possible to improvise a croup tent by boiling water in a kettle on a portable hot plate and arranging a blanket over the back of a chair so that it encloses the child and an adult as well as the steaming kettle. A child should never be left alone even for an instant in such a makeshift arrangement.

If the symptoms do not subside in about 20 minutes with any of the above procedures, or if there is mounting fever, and if the physician is not on his way, the child should be rushed to the closest hospital. Cold moist night air, rather than being a danger, may actually make the symptoms subside temporarily.

Diabetic Coma and Insulin Shock

Diabetics should always carry an identification tag or card to alert others of their condition in the event of a diabetic coma—which is due to a lack of insulin. They also should advise friends or family members of their diabetic condition and the proper emergency measures that can be taken in the event of an onset of diabetic coma. A bottle of rapid-acting insulin should be kept on hand for such an emergency.

Emergency Treatment

If the victim is being treated for diabetes, he probably will have nearby a supply of insulin and a hypodermic apparatus for injecting it. Find the insulin, hypodermic syringe, and needle; clean a spot on the upper arm or thigh, and inject about 50 units of insulin. Call a physician without delay, and describe the patient's symptoms and your treatment. The patient usually will respond without ill effects, but may be quite thirsty. Give him plenty of fluids, as needed.

If the victim does not respond to the insulin, or if you cannot find the insulin and hypodermic syringe, rush the victim to the nearest physician's office.

Insulin shock—which is due to a reaction to too much insulin and not enough sugar in the blood—can be treated in an emergency by offering a sugar-rich fluid such as a cola beverage or orange juice. Diabetics frequently carry a lump of sugar or candy that can be placed in their mouth in case of an insulin shock reaction. It should be tucked between the teeth and cheek so the victim will not choke on it.

If you find a diabetic in a coma and do not know the cause, assume the cause is an insulin reaction and treat him with sugar. This will give immediate relief to an insulin reaction but will not affect diabetic coma.

Diarrhea

Emergency Treatment

Give the victim an antidiarrheal agent; all drugstores carry medications composed of kaolin and pectin that are useful for this purpose. Certain bismuth compounds also are recommended for diarrhea control.

Put the victim in bed for a period of at least 12 hours and withhold food and drink for that length of time. Do not let the victim become dehydrated; if he is thirsty, let him suck on pieces of ice. If the diarrhea appears to be subsiding, let him sip a mild beverage like tea or ginger ale; cola syrup is also recommended.

Later on the patient can try eating bland foods such as dry toast, crackers, gelatin desserts, or jellied consomme. Avoid feeding rich, fatty, or spicy foods. If the diarrhea fails to subside or is complicated by colic or vomiting, call a physician.

Dizziness/Vertigo

Emotional upsets, allergies, and improper eating and drinking habits—too much food, too little food, or foods that are too rich—can precipitate symptoms of dizziness. The cause also can be a physical disorder such as abnormal functioning of the inner ear or a circulatory problem. Smoking tobacco, certain drugs such as quinine, and fumes of some chemicals also can produce dizziness.

Emergency Treatment

Have the victim lie down with the eyes closed. In many cases, a period of simple bed rest will alleviate the symptoms. Keep the victim quiet and comfortable. If the feeling of dizziness continues, becomes worse, or is accompanied by nausea and vomiting, call a physician.

Severe or persistent dizziness or vertigo requires a longer period of bed rest and the use of medicines prescribed by a physician. While recovering, the victim should avoid sudden changes in body position or turning the head rapidly. In some types of vertigo, surgery is required to cure the disorder.

Drowning

Victims of drowning seldom die because of water in the lungs or stomach. They die because of lack of air.

Emergency Treatment

If the victim's breathing has been impaired, start artificial respiration immediately. If there is evidence of cardiac arrest, administer cardiac massage. When the victim is able to breathe for himself, treat him for shock and get medical help.

Drug Overdose (Barbiturates)

Barbiturates are used in a number of drugs prescribed as sedatives, although many are also available through illegal channels. Because the drugs can affect the judgment of the user, he may not remember having taken a dose and so may take additional pills, thus producing overdose effects.

Emergency Treatment

If the drug was taken orally, try to induce vomiting in the victim. Have him drink a glass of water containing two tablespoons of salt. Or touch the back of his throat gently with a finger or a smooth blunt object like the handle of a spoon. Then give the victim plenty of warm water to drink. It is important to rid the stomach of as much of the drug as possible and to dilute the substance remaining in the gastrointestinal tract.

As soon as possible, call a physician or get the victim to the nearest hospital or physician's office. If breathing fails, administer artificial respiration.

Drug Overdose (Stimulants)

Although most of the powerful stimulant drugs, or pep pills, are available only through a physician's prescription, the same medications are available through illicit sources. When taken without direction of a supervising physician, the stimulants can produce a variety of adverse side effects, and when used frequently over a period of time can result in physical and psychological problems that require hospital treatment.

Emergency Treatment

Give the victim a solution of one tablespoon of activated charcoal mixed with a small amount of water, or give him a glass of milk, to dilute the effects of the medication in the stomach. Then induce vomiting by pressing gently on the back of the throat with a finger or the smooth blunt edge of a spoon handle. Vomiting also may be induced with a solution made of one teaspoonful of mustard in a half glass of water. Do not give syrup of ipecac to a victim who has been taking stimulants.

As soon as possible call a physician or get the victim to the nearest hospital or physician's office. If breathing fails, administer artificial respiration.

Earaches

An earache may be associated with a wide variety of ailments ranging from the common cold or influenza to impacted molars or tonsillitis. An earache also may be involved in certain infectious diseases such as measles or scarlet fever. Because of the relationship of ear structures to other parts of the head and throat, an infection involving the symptoms of earache can easily spread to the brain tissues or the spongy mastoid bone behind the ear. Call a physician and describe all of the symptoms, including temperature, any discharge, pain, ringing in the ear, or deafness. Delay in reporting an earache to a doctor can result in complications that require hospital treatment.

Emergency Treatment

This may incude a few drops of warm olive oil or sweet oil held in the ear by a small wad of cotton. Aspirin can be given to help relieve any pain. Professional medical treatment may include the use of antibiotics.

Ear, Foreign Body in

Emergency Treatment

Do not insert a hairpin, stick, or other object in the ear in an effort to remove a foreign object; you are likely to force the object farther into the ear canal. Instead, have the victim tilt his head to one side, with the ear containing the foreign object facing upward. While pulling gently on the lobe of the ear to straighten the canal, pour a little warmed olive oil or mineral oil into the ear. Then have the victim tilt that ear downward so the oil will run out quickly; it should dislodge the foreign object.

Wipe the ear canal gently with a cotton-tipped matchstick, or a similar device that will not irritate the lining of the ear canal, after the foreign body has been removed. If the emergency treatment is not successful, call a physician.

Electric Shocks

An electric shock from the usual 110-volt current in most homes can be a serious emergency, especially if the person's skin or clothing is wet. Under these circumstances, the shock may paralyze the part of the brain that controls breathing and stop the heart completely or disorder its pumping action.

Emergency Treatment

It is of the utmost importance to break the electrical contact *immediately* by unplugging the wire of the appliance involved or by shutting off the house current switch. **Do not touch the victim of the shock while he is still acting as an electrical conductor.**

If the shock has come from a faulty wire out of doors and the source of the electrical current can't be reached easily, make a lasso of dry rope on a long sturdy dry stick. Catch the victim's hand or foot in the loop and drag him away from the wire. Another way to break the contact is to cut the wire with a dry axe.

If the victim of the shock is unconscious, or if his pulse is very weak, administer mouth-to-mouth respiration and cardiac massage until he can get to a hospital.

Epileptic Seizures

Epilepsy is a disorder of the nervous system that produces convulsive seizures. In a major seizure or *grand mal,* the epileptic usually falls to the ground. Indeed, falling is in most cases one of the principal dangers of the disease. Then the epileptic's body begins to twitch or jerk spasmodically. His breathing may be labored, and saliva may appear on his lips. His face may become pale or bluish. Although the scene can be frightening, it is not truly a medical emergency; the afflicted person is in no danger of losing his life.

Emergency Treatment

Make the person suffering the seizure as comfortable as possible. If he is on a hard surface, put something soft under his head, and move any hard or dangerous objects away from him. **Make no attempt to restrain his movements, and do not force anything into his mouth.** Just leave him alone until the attack is over, as it should be in a few minutes. If his mouth is already open, you might put something soft, such as a folded handerchief, between his side teeth. This will help to prevent him from biting his tongue or lips. If possible, turn the person's head so if he vomits, the matter will be expelled, and he won't hurt himself. If he seems to go into another seizure after coming out of the first, or if the seizure lasts more than ten minutes, call a physician. If his lower jaw sags and begins to obstruct his breathing, support of the lower jaw may be helpful in improving his breathing. After a seizure has stopped, turn the person's head to the side so he can breathe normally.

When the seizure is over, the patient should be allowed to rest quietly. Some people sleep heavily after a seizure. Others awake at once but are disoriented or confused for a while. If it is the first seizure the person is aware of having had, advise him to see his physician promptly.

Eye, Foreign Body in

Emergency Treatment

Do not rub the eye or touch it with unwashed hands. The foreign body usually becomes lodged on the inner surface of the upper eyelid. Pull the upper eyelid down over the lower lid to help work the object loose. Tears or clean water can help wash out the dirt or other object. If the bit of irritating material can be seen on the surface of the eyeball, try very carefully to flick it out with the tip of a clean, moistened handkerchief or a piece of moistened cotton. Never touch the surface of the eye with dry materials. Sometimes a foreign body can be removed by carefully rolling the upper lid over a pencil or wooden matchstick to expose the object.

After the foreign object has been removed, the eye should be washed with clean water or with a solution made from one teaspoon of salt dissolved in a pint of water. This will help remove any remaining particles of the foreign body as well as any traces of irritating chemicals that might have been a part of it. Iron particles, for example, may leave traces of rust on the eye's surface unless washed away.

If the object cannot be located and removed without difficulty, a small patch of gauze or a folded handkerchief should be taped over the eye and the victim taken to a physician's office—preferably the office of an ophthalmologist. A physician also should be consulted if a feeling of irritation in the eye continues after the foreign body has been removed.

Fever

Emergency Treatment

If the fever is mild, around 100°F. by mouth, have the victim rest in bed and provide him with a light diet. Watch closely for other symptoms, such as a rash, and any further increase in body temperature. Aspirin usually can be given.

If the temperature rises to 101°F. or higher, is accompanied by pain, headache, delirium, confused behavior, coughing, vomiting, or other indications of a severe illness, call a physician. Describe all of the symptoms in detail, including the appearance of any rash and when it began.

Fever blisters

See COLD SORES.

Finger Dislocation

Emergency Treatment

Call a physician and arrange for inspection and treatment of the injury. If a physician is not immediately available, the finger dislocation may be reduced (put back in proper alignment) by grasping it firmly and carefully pulling it into normal position. Pull very slowly and avoid rough handling that might complicate the injury by damaging a tendon. If the dislocation cannot be reduced after the first try, go through the procedure once more. But do not try it more than twice.

Whether or not you are successful in reducing the finger dislocation, the finger should be immobilized after your efforts until a physician can examine it. A clean flat wooden stick can be strapped along the palm side of the finger with adhesive tape or strips of bandage to hold it in place.

Fingernail Injuries/Hangnails

Emergency Treatment

Wash the injured nail area thoroughly with warm water and soap. Trim off any torn bits of nail. Cover with a small adhesive dressing or bandage.

Apply petroleum jelly or cold cream to the injured nail area twice a day, morning and night, until it is healed. If redness or irritation develops in the adjoining skin area, indicating an infection, consult a physician.

Fish Poisoning

Emergency Treatment

Induce vomiting in the victim to remove the bits of poisonous fish from the stomach. Vomiting usually can be started by pressing on the back of the throat with a finger or a spoon handle that is blunt and smooth, or by having the victim drink a solution of two tablespoons of salt in a glass of water.

Call a physician as soon as possible. Describe the type of fish eaten and the symptoms, which may include nausea, diarrhea, abdominal pain, muscular weakness, and a numbness or tingling sensation that begins about the face and spreads to the extremities.

If breathing fails, administer mouth-to-mouth artificial respiration; a substance commonly found in poisonous fish causes respiratory failure. Also, be prepared to provide emergency treatment for convulsions.

Food Poisoning

Emergency Treatment

If the victim is not already vomiting, try to induce it to clear the stomach. Vomiting can be started in most cases by pressing gently on the back of the throat with a finger or a blunt smooth spoon handle, or by having the patient drink a glass of water containing two tablespoons of salt. If the victim has vomited, put him to bed.

Call a physician and describe the food ingested and the symptoms that developed. If symptoms are severe, professional medical treatment with antibiotics and medications for cramps may be required. Special medications also may be needed for diarrhea caused by bacterial food poisoning.

Fractures

Any break in a bone is called a fracture. The break is called an *open* or *compound fracture* if one or both ends of the broken bone pierce the skin. A *closed* or *simple fracture* is one in which the broken bone doesn't come through the skin.

It is sometimes difficult to distinguish a strained muscle or a sprained ligament from a broken bone, since sprains and strains can be extremely painful even though they are less serious than breaks. However, when there is any doubt, the injury should be treated as though it were a simple fracture.

Emergency Treatment

Don't try to help the injured person move around or get up unless he has slowly tested out the injured part of his body and is sure that nothing has been broken. If he is in extreme pain, or if the injured part has begun to swell, or if by running the finger lightly along the affected bone a break can be felt, *do not* move him. Under no circumstances should he be crowded into a car if his legs, hip, ribs, or back are involved in the accident. Call for an ambulance immediately, and until it arrives, treat the person for shock.

Splinting

In a situation where it is imperative to move someone who may have a fracture, the first step is to apply a splint so that the broken bone ends are immobilized.

Splints can be improvised from anything rigid enough and of the right length to support the fractured part of the body: a metal rod, board, long cardboard tube, tightly rolled newspaper or blanket. If the object being used has to be padded for softness, use a small blanket or any other soft material, such as a jacket.

The splint should be long enough so that it can be tied with a bandage, torn sheet, or neckties beyond the joint above and below the fracture as well as at the site of the break. If a leg is involved, it should be elevated with pillows or any other firm support after the splint has been applied. If the victim has to wait a considerable length of time before receiving professional attention, the splint bandaging should be checked from time to time to make sure it isn't too tight.

In the case of an open or compound fracture, additional steps must be taken. Remove that part of the victim's clothing that is covering the wound. Do not wash or probe into the wound, but control bleeding by applying pressure over the wound through a sterile or clean dressing.

Frostbite

Emergency Treatment

Begin rapid rewarming of the affected tissues as soon as possible. If possible, immerse the victim in a warm bath, but avoid scalding. (The temperature should be between 102°F. and 105°F.) Warm wet towels also will help if changed frequently and applied gently. Do not massage, rub, or even touch the frostbitten flesh. If warm water or a warming fire is not available, place the patient in a sleeping bag or cover him with coats and blankets. Hot liquids can be offered if available to help raise the body temperature.

For any true frostbite case, prompt medical attention is important. The depth and degree of the frozen tissue cannot be determined without a careful examination by a physician.

Gallbladder Attacks

Although gallstones can affect a wide variety of individuals, the most common victims are overweight persons who enjoy rich foods. The actual attack of spasms caused by gallstones passing through the duct leading from the gallbladder to the digestive tract usually is preceded by periods of stomach distress including belching.

X rays usually will reveal the presence of gallstones when the early warning signs are noted, and measures can be taken to reduce the threat of a gallbladder attack.

Emergency Treatment

Call a physician and describe in detail the symptoms, which may include colic high in the abdomen and pain extending to the right shoulder; the pain may be accompanied by nausea, vomiting, and sweating. Hot water bottles may be applied to the abdomen to help relieve distress while waiting for professional medical care. If the physician permits, the victim may be allowed to sip certain fluids such as fruit juices, but do not offer him solid food.

Gas Poisoning

Before attempting to revive someone overcome by toxic gas poisoning, the most important thing to do is to remove him to the fresh air. If this isn't feasible, all windows and doors should be opened to let in as much fresh air as possible.

Any interior with a dangerous concentration of carbon monoxide or other toxic gases is apt to be highly explosive. Therefore, gas and electricity should be shut off as quickly as possible. **Under no circumstances should any matches be lighted in an interior where there are noxious fumes.**

The rescuer needn't waste time covering his face with a handkerchief or other cloth. He should hold his breath instead, or take only a few quick, shallow breaths while bringing the victim to the out-of-doors or to an open window.

Emergency Treatment

Administer artificial respiration if the

victim is suffering respiratory arrest. Arrange for medical help as soon as possible, requesting that oxygen be brought to the scene.

Head Injuries

Accidents involving the head can result in concussion, skull fracture, or brain injury. Symptoms of head injury include loss of consciousness, discharge of a watery or blood-tinged fluid from the ears, nose, or mouth, and a difference in size of the pupils of the eyes. Head injuries must be thought of as serious; they demand immediate medical assistance.

Emergency Treatment

Place the victim in a supine position, and, if there is no evidence of injury to his neck, arrange for a slight elevation of his head *and* shoulders. Make certain that he has a clear airway and administer artificial respiration if necessary. If vomitus, blood, or other fluids appear to flow from the victim's mouth, turn his head gently to one side. Control bleeding and treat for shock. Do not administer stimulants or fluids of any kind.

Heart Attack

A heart attack is caused by interference with the blood supply to the heart muscle. When the attack is brought on because of a blood clot in the coronary artery, it is known as *coronary occlusion* or *coronary thrombosis.*

The most dramatic symptom of a serious heart attack is a crushing chest pain that usually travels down the left arm into the hand or into the neck and back. The pain may bring on dizziness, cold sweat, complete collapse, and loss of consciousness. The face has an ashen pallor, and there may be vomiting.

Emergency Treatment

The victim **must not be moved** unless he has fallen in a dangerous place. If no physician is immediately available, an ambulance should be called at once. No attempt should be made to get the victim of a heart attack into an automobile.

Until help arrives, give the victim every reassurance that he will get prompt treatment, and keep him as calm and quiet as possible. Don't give him any medicine or stimulants. If oxygen is available, start administering it to the victim immediately, either by mask or nasal catheter, depending on which is available.

If the victim is suffering from respiratory arrest, begin artificial respiration. If he is suffering from cardiac arrest, begin cardiac massage.

Heat Exhaustion

Heat exhaustion occurs when the body is exposed to high temperatures and large amounts of blood accumulate in the skin as a way of cooling it. As a result, there is a marked decrease in the amount of blood that circulates through the heart and to the brain. The victim becomes markedly pale and is covered with cold perspiration. Breathing is increasingly shallow and the pulse weakens. In acute cases, fainting occurs. Medical aid should be summoned for anyone suffering from heat exhaustion.

Emergency Treatment

Place the victim in a reclining position with his feet raised about ten inches above his body. Loosen or remove his clothing, and apply cold, wet cloths to his wrists and forehead. If he has fainted and doesn't recover promptly, smelling salts or spirits of ammonia should be placed under his nose. When the victim is conscious, give him sips of salt water (approximately one teaspoon of salt per glass of water), the total intake to be about two glasses in an hour's time. If the victim vomits, discontinue the salt solution.

Heatstroke/Sunstroke

Heatstroke is characterized by an acutely high body temperature caused by the cessation of perspiration. The victim's skin becomes hot, dry, and flushed, and he may suffer collapse. Should the skin turn ashen gray, a physician must be called immediately. Prompt hospital treatment is recommended for anyone showing signs of sunstroke who has previously had any kind of heart damage.

Emergency Treatment

The following measures are designed to reduce the victim's body temperature as quickly as possible and prevent damage to the internal organs:

Place him in a tub of very cold water, or, if this is not possible, spray or sponge his body repeatedly with cold water or rubbing alcohol. Take his temperature by mouth, and when it has dropped to about 100°F., remove him to a bed and wrap him in cold, wet sheets. If possible, expose him to an electric fan or an air conditioner.

Hiccups

Emergency Treatment

Have the victim slowly drink a large glass of water. If cold water is not effective, have him drink warm water containing a teaspoonful of baking soda. Milk also can be employed. For babies and small children, offer sips of warm water. Do not offer carbonated beverages.

Another helpful measure is breathing into a large paper bag a number of times to raise the carbon dioxide level in the lungs. Rest and relaxation are recommended; have the victim lie down to read or watch television.

If the hiccups fail to go away, and continued spastic contractions of the diaphragm interfere with eating and sleeping, call a physician.

Insect Stings

Honeybees, wasps, hornets, and yellow jackets are the most common stinging insects and most likely to attack on a hot summer day. Strongly scented perfumes or cosmetics and brightly colored, rough-finished clothing attract bees and should be avoided by persons working or playing in garden areas. It should also be noted that many commercial repellents do not protect against stinging insects.

Emergency Treatment

If one is stung, the insect's stinger should be scraped gently but quickly from the skin; don't squeeze it. Apply Epsom salt solution to the sting area. Antihistamines are often helpful in reducing the patient's discomfort. If a severe reaction develops, call a physician.

There are a few people who are critically allergic to the sting of wasps, bees, yellow jackets, or fire ants. This sensitivity causes the vocal cord tissue to swell to the point where breathing may become impossible. A single sting to a sensitive person may result in a dangerous drop in blood pressure, thus producing shock. Anyone with such a severe allergy who is stung should be rushed to a hospital immediately.

A person who becomes aware of having this type of allergy should consult with a physician about the kind of medicine to carry for use in a crisis.

Insulin Shock

See DIABETIC COMA AND INSULIN SHOCK.

Jaw Dislocation

The jaw can be dislocated during a physical attack or fight; from a blow on the jaw during sports activities; or from overextension of the joint during yawning, laughing, or attempting to eat a large mouthful of food. The jaw becomes literally locked open so the victim cannot explain his predicament.

Emergency Treatment

Reducing a dislocated jaw will require that you insert your thumbs between the teeth of the victim. The jaw can be expected to snap into place quickly, and there is a danger that the teeth will clamp down on the thumbs when this happens, so the thumbs should be adequately padded with handkerchiefs or bandages. Once the thumbs are protected, insert them in the mouth and over the lower molars, as far back on the lower jaw as possible. While pressing down with the thumbs, lift the chin with the fingers outside the mouth. As the jaw begins to slip into normal position when it is pushed downward and backward with the chin lifted upward, quickly remove the thumbs from between the jaws.

Once the jaw is back in normal position, the mouth should remain closed for several hours while the ligaments recover from their displaced condition. If necessary, put a cravat bandage over the head to hold the mouth closed. If difficulty is experienced in reducing a jaw dislocation, the victim should be taken to a hospital where an anesthetic can be applied. A dislocated jaw can be extremely painful.

Jellyfish Stings

Emergency Treatment

Wash the area of the sting thoroughly with alcohol or fresh water. Be sure that any pieces of jellyfish tentacles have been removed from the skin. Aspirin or antihistamines can be administered to relieve pain and itching, but curtail the use of antihistamines if the victim has consumed alcoholic beverages. The leg or arm that received the sting can be soaked in hot water if the pain continues. Otherwise, apply calamine lotion.

If the victim appears to suffer a severe reaction from the sting, summon a doctor. The victim may experience shock, muscle cramps, convulsions, or loss of consciousness. Artificial respiration may be required while awaiting arrival of a doctor. The physician can administer drugs to relieve muscle cramps and provide sedatives or analgesics.

Kidney Stones

Emergency Treatment

Call a physician if the victim experiences the agonizing cramps or colic associated with kidney stones. Discuss the symptoms in detail with the doctor to make sure the pain is caused by kidney stones rather than appendicitis.

Comforting heat may be applied to the back and the abdomen of the side affected by the spasms. Paregoric can be administered, if available, while waiting for medical care; about two teaspoonsful of paregoric in a half glass of water may help relieve symptoms.

Knee Injuries

Emergency Treatment

If the injury appears to be severe, including possible fracture of the kneecap, immobilize the knee. To immobilize the knee, place the injured leg on a board that is about four inches wide and three to four feet in length. Place padding between the board and the knee and between the board and the back of the ankle. Then use four strips of bandage to fasten the leg to the padded board—one at the ankle, one at the thigh, and one each above and below the knee.

Summon a physician or move the patient to a physician's office. Keep the knee protected against cold or exposure to the elements, but otherwise do not apply a bandage or any type of pressure to the knee itself; any rapid swelling would be aggravated by unnecessary pressure in that area. Be prepared to treat the patient for shock.

Laryngitis

Laryngitis is associated with colds and influenza and may be accompanied by a fever. The ailment can be aggravated by smoking, and it is possible that the vocal cords can be damaged if the victim tries to force the use of his voice while the larynx is swollen by the infection.

Emergency Treatment

Have the victim inhale the warm moist air of a steam kettle or vaporizer. A vaporizer can be improvised in an emergency by pouring boiling water into a bowl and forming a "tent" over the steaming bowl with a large towel or sheet, or by placing a large paper bag over the bowl and cutting an opening at the closed end of the bag so the face can be exposed to the steam. The hot water can contain a bit of camphor or menthol, if available, to make the warm moist air more soothing to the throat, but this is not necessary.

Continue the use of the vaporizer for several days, as needed. The victim should not use the vocal cords any more than absolutely necessary. If the infection does not subside within the first few days, a physician should be consulted.

Leeches

Emergency Treatment

Do not try to pull leeches off the skin. They will usually drop away from the skin if a heated object such as a lighted cigarette is held close to them. Leeches also are likely to let go if iodine is applied to their bodies. The wound caused by a leech should be washed carefully with soap and water and an antiseptic applied.

Lightning Shock

Emergency Treatment

If the victim is not breathing, apply artificial respiration. If a second person is available to help, have him summon a physician while artificial respiration is administered. Continue artificial respiration until breathing resumes or the physician arrives.

When the victim is breathing regularly, treat him for shock. Keep him lying down with his feet higher than his head, his clothing loosened around the neck, and his body covered with a blanket or coat for warmth. If the victim shows signs of vomiting, turn his head to one side so he will not swallow the vomitus.

If the victim is breathing regularly and does not show signs of shock, he may be given a few sips of a stimulating beverage such as coffee, tea, or brandy.

Motion Sickness

Emergency Treatment

Have the victim lie down in a position that is most comfortable to him. The head should be fixed so that any view of motion is avoided. Reading or other use of the eyes should be prohibited. Food or fluids should be restricted to very small amounts. If traveling by car, stop at a rest area; in an airplane or ship, place the victim in an area where motion is least noticeable.

Drugs, such as Dramamine, are helpful for control of the symptoms of motion sickness; they are most effective when started about 90 minutes before travel begins and repeated at regular intervals thereafter.

Muscle Cramps

Emergency Treatment

Gently massage the affected muscle, sometimes stretching it to help relieve the painful contraction. Then relax the muscle by using a hot water bottle or an electric heating pad, or by soaking the affected area in a warm bath.

A repetition of cramps may require medical attention.

Nosebleeds

Emergency Treatment

Have the victim sit erect but with the head tilted slightly forward to prevent blood from running down the throat.

Apply pressure by pinching the nostrils; if bleeding is from just one nostril, use pressure on that side. A small wedge of absorbent cotton or gauze can be inserted into the bleeding nostril. Make sure that the cotton or gauze extends out of the nostril to aid in its removal when the bleeding has stopped. Encourage the victim to breathe through the mouth while the nose is bleeding. After five minutes, release pressure on the nose to see if the bleeding has stopped. If the bleeding continues, repeat pressure on the nostril for an additional five minutes. Cold compresses applied to the nose can help stop the bleeding.

If bleeding continues after the second five-minute period of pressure treatment, get the victim to a physician's office or a hospital emergency room.

Poison Ivy/Poison Oak/Poison Sumac

Emergency Treatment

The poison of these three plants is the same and the treatment is identical. Bathe the skin area exposed to poison ivy, poison oak, or poison sumac with soap and water or with alcohol within 15 minutes after contact. If exposure is not discovered until a rash appears, apply cool wet dressings. Dressings can be made of old bed sheets or soft linens soaked in a solution of one teaspoon of salt per pint of water. Dressings should be applied four times a day for periods of 15 to 60 minutes each time; during these periods, dressings can be removed and reapplied every few minutes. The itching that often accompanies the rash can be relieved by taking antihistamine tablets.

Creams or lotions may be prescribed by a physician or supplied by a pharmacist. Do not use such folk remedies as ammonia or turpentine; do not use skin lotions not approved by a physician or druggist. Haphazard application of medications on poison ivy blisters and rashes can result in complications including skin irritation, infection, or pigmented lesions of the skin.

Rabies

See ANIMAL BITES.

Rape

Rape has been defined as any unlawful sexual intercourse or sexual contact by force or threat. Most commonly, men commit rape against women; but homosexual rape involving men only may occur, for example, in a prison.

Of the million or more Americans who are raped each year, one in five is under the age of 12. Boys are the victims of sexual assault as often as girls. In seven to ten percent of all reported adult cases, men are the victims.

Emergency Response

The victim of rape may not always be able to help him- or herself. Because violence may accompany the rape, the victim may find it impossible to seek help at once. But where possible, the recommended course of action is to go to a hospital for physical examination. Reporting to a hospital in itself may reduce the feelings of shock, depression, anxiety, and revulsion that generally follow a sexual assault. The physical examination that takes place at the hospital may produce evidence that could be important in a court trial if the rapist is later apprehended. Victims are also advised to report the rape to the police as soon as possible.

For additional information on ways to avoid rape and what to do if it occurs, see "The Rape Victim" in Ch. 25, *Women's Health.*

Sciatica/Lower Back Pain

Although lower back pain is frequently triggered by fatigue, anxiety, or by strained muscles or tendons, it may be a symptom of a slipped or ruptured disk between the vertebrae or of a similar disorder requiring extensive medical attention.

Emergency Treatment

Reduce the pressure on the lower back by having the victim lie down on a hard flat surface; if a bed is used there should be a board or sheet of plywood between the springs and mattress. Pillows should be placed under the knees instead of under the head, to help keep the back flat. Give aspirin to relieve the pain, and apply heat to the back. Call a physician if the symptoms do not subside overnight.

Scorpion Stings

Emergency Treatment

Apply ice to the region of the sting, except in the case of an arm or leg, in which event the limb may be immersed in ice water. Continue the ice or ice-water treatment for at least one hour. Try to keep the area of the sting at a position lower than the heart. No tourniquet is required. Should the breathing of a scorpion sting victim become depressed, administer artificial respiration. If symptoms fail to subside within a couple of hours, notify a physician, or transfer the victim to a doctor's office or hospital.

For children under six, call a physician in the event of any scorpion sting. Children stung by scorpions may become convulsive, and this condition can result in fatal exhaustion unless it receives prompt medical treatment.

Snakebites

Of the many varieties of snakes found in the United States, only four kinds are poisonous: copperheads, rattlesnakes, moccasins, and coral snakes. The first three belong to the category of pit vipers and are known as *hemotoxic* because their poison enters the bloodstream. The coral snake, which is comparatively rare, is related to the cobra and is the most dangerous of all because its venom is *neurotoxic.* This means that the poison transmitted by its bite goes directly to the nervous system and the brain.

How to Differentiate among Snakebites

Snakes of the pit viper family have a fang on each side of the head. These fangs leave characteristic puncture wounds on the skin in addition to two rows of tiny bites or scratches left by the teeth. A bite from a nonpoisonous snake leaves six rows—four upper and two lower—of very small bite marks or scratches and no puncture wounds.

The marks left by the bite of a coral snake do not leave any puncture wounds either, but this snake bites with a chewing motion, hanging on to the victim rather than attacking quickly. The coral snake is very easy to recognize because of its distinctive markings: wide horizontal bands of red and black separated by narrow bands of yellow.

Symptoms

A bite from any of the pit vipers produces immediate and severe pain and darkening of the skin, followed by weakness, blurred vision, quickened pulse, nausea, and vomiting. The bite of a coral snake produces somewhat the same symptoms, although there is less local pain and considerable drowsiness leading to unconsciousness.

If a physician or a hospital is a short distance away, the patient should receive professional help *immediately*. He should be transported lying down, either on an improvised stretcher or carried by his companions—with the wounded part lower than his heart. He should be advised to move as little as possible.

Emergency Treatment

If several hours must elapse before a physician or a hospital can be reached, the following procedures should be applied promptly:

1. Keep the victim lying down and as still as possible.

2. Tie a constricting band *above* the wound between it and the heart and tight enough to slow but not stop blood circulation. A handkerchief, necktie, sock, or piece of torn shirt will serve.

3. If a snakebite kit is available, use the knife it contains; otherwise, sterilize a knife or razor blade in a flame. Carefully make small cuts in the skin where the swelling has developed. Make the cuts along the length of the limb, not across or at right angles to it. The incisions should be shallow because of the danger of severing nerves, blood vessels, or muscles.

4. Use the suction cups in the snakebite kit, if available, to draw out as much of the venom as possible. If suction cups are not available, the venom can be removed by sucking it out with the mouth. Although snake venom is not a stomach poison, it should not be swallowed but should be rinsed from the mouth.

5. This procedure should be continued for from 30 to 60 minutes or until the swelling subsides and the other symptoms decrease.

6. You may apply cold compresses to the bite area while waiting for professional assistance.

7. Treat the victim for shock.

8. Give artificial respiration if necessary.

Splinters

Emergency Treatment

Clean the area about the splinter with soap and water or an antiseptic. Next, sterilize a needle by holding it over an open flame. After it cools, insert the needle above the splinter so it will tear a line in the skin, making the splinter lie loose in the wound. Then, gently lift the splinter out, using a pair of tweezers or the point of the needle. If tweezers are used, they should be sterilized first.

Wash the wound area again with soap and water, or apply an antiseptic. It is best to cover the wound with an adhesive bandage. If redness or irritation develops around the splinter wound, consult a physician.

Sprains

A sprain occurs when a joint is wrenched or twisted in such a way that the ligaments holding it in position are ruptured, possibly damaging the surrounding blood vessels, tendons, nerves, and muscles. This type of injury is more serious than a strain and is usually accompanied by pain, sometimes severe, soreness, swelling, and discoloration of the affected area. Most sprains occur as a result of falls, athletic accidents, or improper handling of heavy weights.

Emergency Treatment

This consists of prompt rest, the application of cold compresses to relieve swelling and any internal bleeding in the joint, and elevation of the affected area. Aspirin is recommended to reduce discomfort. If the swelling and soreness increase after such treatment, a physician should be consulted to make sure that the injury is not a fracture or a bone dislocation.

Sting Ray

Emergency Treatment

If an arm or leg is the target of a sting ray, wash the area thoroughly with salt water. Quickly remove any pieces of the stinger imbedded in the skin or flesh; poison can still be discharged into the victim from the sting-ray sheath. After initial cleansing of an arm or leg sting, soak the wound with hot water for up to an hour. Apply antiseptic or a sterile dressing after the soak.

Consult a physician after a sting-ray attack. The physician will make a thorough examination of the wound to determine whether stitches or antibiotics are required. Fever, vomiting, or muscular twitching also may result from an apparently simple leg or arm wound by a sting ray.

If the sting occurs in the chest or abdomen, the victim should be rushed to a hospital as soon as possible because such a wound can produce convulsions or loss of consciousness.

Strains

When a muscle is stretched because of misuse or overuse, the interior bundles of tissue may tear, or the tendon that connects it to the bone may be stretched. This condition is known as strain. It occurs most commonly to the muscles of the lower back when heavy weights are improperly lifted, or in the area of the calf or ankle as the result of a sudden, violent twist or undue pressure.

Emergency Treatment

Bed rest, the application of heat, and gentle massage are recommended for back strain. If the strain is in the leg, elevate it to help reduce pain and swelling, and apply cold compresses or an ice bag to the area. Aspirin may be taken to reduce discomfort.

In severe cases of strained back muscles, a physician may have to be consulted for strapping. For a strained ankle, a flexible elastic bandage can be helpful in providing the necessary support until the injured muscle heals.

Stroke

Stroke, or apoplexy, is caused by a disruption of normal blood flow to the brain, either by rupture of a blood vessel within the brain or by blockage of an artery supplying the brain. The condition is enhanced by hardening of the arteries and high blood pressure, and is most likely to occur in older persons. A stroke usually occurs with little or no warning and the onset may be marked by a variety of manifestations ranging from headache, slurred speech, or blurred vision, to sudden collapse and unconsciousness.

Emergency Treatment

Try to place the victim in a semireclining position, or, if he is lying down, be sure there is a pillow under his head. Avoid conditions that might increase the flow of blood toward the head. Summon a physician immediately. Loosen any clothing that may be tight. If the patient wears dentures, remove them.

Before professional medical assistance is available, the victim may vomit or go into shock or convulsions. If he vomits, try to prevent a back-flow of vomitus into the breathing passages. If shock occurs, do not place the victim in the shock position but do keep him warm and comfortable. If convulsions develop, place a handkerchief or similar soft object between the jaws to prevent tongue biting.

Sty on Eyelid

Sties usually develop around hair follicles because of a bacterial infection. They are most likely to develop in association with poor health and lowered resistance to infection.

Emergency Treatment

Apply warm, moist packs or compresses to the sty for periods of 15 to 20 minutes at intervals of three or four hours. Moist heat generally is more penetrating than dry heat.

The sty should eventually rupture and the pus should then be washed carefully away from the eye area. If the sty does not rupture or is very painful, consult a physician. Do not squeeze or otherwise handle the sty except to apply the warm moist compresses.

Sunburn

Emergency Treatment

Apply cold wet compresses to help relieve the pain. Compresses can be soaked in whole milk, salt water, or a solution of cornstarch mixed with water. The victim also may get some relief by soaking in a bathtub filled with plain water. Soothing lotions, such as baby oil or a bland cold cream, can be applied after carefully drying the skin. Don't rub the burn area while drying. Avoid the use of "shake" lotions, like calamine, which may aggravate the burn by a drying action. The victim should, of course, avoid further exposure to sunlight.

If pain is excessive, or extensive blistering is present, consult a physi-cian. Avoid application of over-the-counter topical anesthetics that may cause allergic skin reactions.

A severe or extensive sunburn is comparable to a second-degree thermal burn and may be accompanied by symptoms of shock; if such symptoms are present the victim should be treated for shock. See also BURNS, THERMAL.

Sunstroke

See HEATSTROKE.

Tick Bites

The most common tick-borne illness is Lyme disease which is carried by a bacterium that infects mice, ticks, deer and humans. It is distinguished by a red bull's eye rash, fatigue, chills headaches and fever within three to 30 days after infection and has been fatal in some rare cases. Lyme disease can be treated with antibiotics which should be administered in the condition's early stages.

Emergency Treatment

Do not try to scrape or rub the insect off the skin with your fingers; scraping, rubbing, or pulling may break off only part of the insect body, leaving the head firmly attached to the skin. Rubbing also can smear disease organisms from the tick into the bite. To make the tick drop away from the skin, cover it with a heavy oil, such as salad, mineral, or lubricating oil. Oil usually will block the insect's breathing pores, suffocating it. If oil is not readily available, carefully place a heated object against the tick's body; a lighted cigarette or a match that has been ignited and snuffed out can serve as a hot object.

Carefully inspect the bite area to be sure that all parts of the tick have been removed. Use a pair of tweezers to remove any tick parts found. Then carefully wash the bite and surrounding area with soap and water and apply an antiseptic. Also, wash your hands and any equipment that may have come in contact with the tick. Consult a physician if symptoms of tick fever or tularemia, such as unexplained muscular weakness, occur following a bite.

Toothaches

Emergency Treatment

Give an adult one or two aspirin tablets; a young child should be given no more than one-half of an adult tablet. The aspirin should be swallowed with plenty of water. Do not let it dissolve in the mouth or be held near the aching tooth. Aspirin becomes effective as a painkiller only after it has gone through the digestive tract and into the bloodstream; if aspirin is held in the mouth, it may irritate the gums.

Oil of cloves can be applied to the aching tooth. Dip a small wad of cotton into the oil of cloves, then gently pack the oil-soaked cotton into the tooth cavity with a pair of tweezers. Do not let the tweezers touch the tooth.

If the jaw is swollen, apply an ice bag for periods of 15 minutes at a time, at intermittent intervals. Never apply heat to a swollen jaw when treating a toothache. Arrange to see your dentist as soon as possible.

Tooth, Broken

Emergency Treatment

Apply a few drops of oil of cloves to the injured tooth to help relieve pain. If oil of cloves is not available, give an adult one to two regular aspirin tablets. One-half of a regular tablet can be given to a young child.

Make an emergency filling from a wad of cotton containing a few drops of oil of cloves. An emergency filling also can be made from powdered chalk; it is important to protect the cavity from infection while providing pain relief.

If the tooth has been knocked out of the socket, retrieve the tooth, because it can be restored in some cases. Do not wash the tooth; ordinary washing can damage dental tissues. A dentist will take care of cleaning it properly. Wrap the tooth in a damp clean handkerchief or tissue or place the tooth in a container of slightly salty warm water for the trip to the dentist.

Unconsciousness

Unconsciousness is the condition that has the appearance of sleep, but is usually the result of injury, shock, or serious physical disturbance. A brief loss of consciousness followed by spontaneous recovery is called *fainting*. A prolonged episode of unconsciousness is a *coma*.

Emergency Treatment

Call a physician at once. If none is available, get the victim to the nearest hospital. If the loss of consciousness is accompanied by loss of breathing, begin mouth-to-mouth respiration. If the victim is suffering cardiac arrest, administer cardiac massage. Don't try to revive the victim with any kind of stimulant unless told to do so by a physician.

Vertigo

See DIZZINESS.

36

Commonly Prescribed Generic Drugs

Name	Action	Prescribed for	
Trade Names (CD) = combined drug)			
Acetaminophen	Believed to reduce concentration of chemicals involved in production of pain, fever, and inflammation (analgesic; antipyretic)	Relief of mild to moderate pain; reduction of fever	
Anacin-3 Bancap (CD) Capital (CD) Codalan (CD) Co-Gesic (CD) Comtrex (CD) Congesprin (CD) for children	Co-Tylenol (CD) Darvocet-N (CD) Datril Dolacet (CD) Dorcol (CD) for children Dristan (CD) Esgic (CD)	Excedrin (CD) Hycomine (CD) Hyco-Pap (CD) Lorcet (CD) Midrin (CD) Pacaps (CD) Percocet (CD) Percogesic (CD)	Penaphen (CD) Protid (CD) Repan (CD) Sinarest (CD) Sine-Aid (CD) Sinutab (CD) Talacen (CD) Tylenol Tylenol Infant Drops Tylenol Junior Strength Tylox (CD) Unisom (CD) Vicodin (CD) Wygesic (CD)
Alprazolam	Believed to depress the central nervous system, slowing nervous response, and relieving nervousness and tension	Relief of anxiety attacks and insomnia; reduction of symptoms of chronic anxiety	
Xanax			
Amitriptyline	Believed to restore to normal levels the constituents of brain tissue that transmit nerve impulses (antidepressant)	Relief of emotional depression; gradual improvement of mood	
Elavil Endep Etrafon (CD)	Limbitral (CD) Triavil (CD)		
Ampicillin	Interferes with ability of susceptible bacteria to produce new protective cell walls as they grow and multiply (antibiotic)	Elimination of infections responsive to action of this drug	
Omnipen Polycillin	Principen Unasyn		

Name	Action	Prescribed for
Trade Names (CD = combined drug)		
Antacids (Aluminum Hydroxide) (Calcium Carbonate) (Sodium Bicarbonate)	Neutralizes stomach acid; reduces action of digestive enzyme pepsin (relief from gastric hyperacidity)	Relief of heartburn, sour stomach, acid indigestion, and discomfort associated with peptic ulcer, gastritis, esophagitis, hiatal hernia

Absorbable: Sodium bicarbonate:	Alka-Seltzer Brioschi Bromo-Seltzer	Less absorbable: Aluminum hydroxide:	Amphojel Calcium carbonate:	Alka-2 Amitone

Aspirin (Acetylsalicylic Acid)	Dilates blood vessels in skin, thus hastening loss of body heat (antipyretic); reduces tissue concentration of inflammation and pain (analgesic; antirheumatic)	Reduction of fever; relief of mild to moderate pain and inflammation; prevention of blood clots, as in phlebitis, heart attack, stroke

Bayer
Easprin
Empirin
St. Joseph's Children's Aspirin
Alka-Seltzer (CD)
Anacin (CD)
	Ascriptin (CD)
	Axotal (CD)
	Buff-A Comp (CD)
	Bufferin (CD)
	Congespirin (CD)
	   for children
	Darvon (CD)
		Ecotrin
		Equagesic (CD)
		Excedrin (CD)
		4-Way Cold Tablets (CD)
		Fiorinal (CD)
		Midol (CD)
			Norgesic (CD)
			Percodan (CD)
			Robaxisal (CD)
			Soma Compound
			   (CD)
			Supac (CD)
			Synalgos-DC (CD)
				Talwin (CD)
				Zorprin

Atropine (Belladonna, Hyoscyamine)	Prevents stimulation of muscular contractions and glandular secretions in organ involved (antispasmodic [anticholinergic])	Relief of discomfort associated with excessive activity and spasm of digestive tract; irritation and spasm of lower urinary tract; painful menstruation

Antrocol (CD) Arco-Lase Plus (CD)	Donnagel-PG (CD) Donnatal (CD)	Donnatal Donnazyme (CD) Lomotil (CD)	Ru-Tuss (CD) SK-Diphenoxylate (CD)	Urised (CD)

Bendroflumethiazide	Increases elimination of salt and water (diuretic); relaxes walls of smaller arteries, allowing them to expand; combined effect lowers blood pressure (antihypertensive)	Elimination of excessive fluid retention (edema); reduction of high blood pressure

Naturetin	Corzide (CD)	Rauzide (CD)

Beta-Adrenergic Blocking Agents	Decreases physical responses at beta-adrenergic receptors, slowing heart rate, dilating the vascular and bronchial systems (antihypertensive); believed to reduce cardiac output and nervous system responses in some forms of the medication	Treatment of high blood pressure; medication to reduce the incidence of another attack in heart attack patients; prevention of migraine headaches in chronic sufferers of migraines

Blocadren Corgard	Lopressor Normodyne	Sectral Tenormin	Visken

Brompheniramine	Blocks action of histamine after release from sensitized tissue cells, thus reducing intensity of allergic response (antihistamine)	Relief of symptoms of hay fever (allergic rhinitis) and of allergic reactions of skin (itching, swelling, hives, rash)

Dimetane Bromfed (CD) Dimetapp (CD)	Poly-histine-DX (CD)

Butabarbital	Believed to block transmission of nerve impulses (hypnotic; sedative)	Low dosage: relief of moderate anxiety or tension (sedative effect); higher dosage: at bedtime to induce sleep (hypnotic effect)
Butisol Pyridium Plus (CD)		

Butalbital	Affects the actions of the central nervous system, relieving anxiety (anxiolytic), and relaxing muscles (barbiturate sedative)	Relief of headaches related to tension or stress, psychic tension; relaxation of muscle strain and contraction in the head, neck, and shoulders

Esgic (CD) Fioricet (CD) Fiorinal (CD)	Medigesic (CD) Phrenilin (CD) Repan (CD)	Sedapap (CD)

Name	Action	Prescribed for
Trade Names (CD = combined drug)		
Caffeine	Constricts blood vessel walls; increases energy level of chemical systems responsible for nerve tissue activity (cardiac, respiratory, psychic stimulant)	Prevention and early relief of vascular headaches such as migraine; relief of drowsiness and mental fatigue
No-Doz Anacin (CD) Cafergot (CD)	Esgic (CD) Fiorinal (CD) Excedrin Extra Maximum Strength Strength (CD) Midol (CD)	Pacaps (CD) Wigraine (CD) Vivarin
Carisoprodol	Believed to block transmission of nerve impulses and/or to produce a sedative effect (muscle relaxant)	Relief of discomfort caused by spasms of voluntary muscles
Soma (CD) Soma Compound (CD)		
Chloral Hydrate	Believed to affect wake-sleep centers of brain (hypnotic)	Low dosage: relief of mild to moderate anxiety or tension (sedative effect); higher dosage: at bedtime to relieve insomnia (hypnotic effect)
SK-Chloral Hydrate		
Chloramphenicol	Prevents growth and multiplication of susceptible bacteria by interfering with formation of their essential proteins (antibiotic)	Elimination of infections responsive to action of this drug
Chloromycetin Ophthochlor Ophthocort		
Chlordiazep-oxide	Believed to reduce activity of some parts of limbic system (tranquilizer)	Relief of mild to moderate anxiety and tension without significant sedation
Libritabs Librium Librax (CD)	Limbitrol (CD) Menrium (CD)	
Chlorpheniramine	Blocks action of histamine after release from sensitized tissue cells, thus reducing intensity of allergic response (antihistamine)	Relief of symptoms of hay fever (allergic rhinitis) and of allergic reactions of skin (itching, swelling, hives, rash)

Chlor-Trimeton
Teldrin
Comtrex (CD)
Contac
Dristan (CD)
	PediaCare (CD)
	   for children
	Tylenol Cold Med-
	   ication (CD)	

Chlorpromazine	Believed to inhibit action of dopamine, thus correcting an imbalance of nerve impulse transmission thought to be responsible for certain mental disorders (antiemetic; tranquilizer)	Relief of severe anxiety, agitation, and psychotic behavior
Thorazine		
Chlorzoxazone	Inhibits nerve responses that trigger muscle contractions	Pain relief of muscle tension and injuries to the muscles and joints; relaxation of muscular tension for use in combination with physical therapy
Paraflex	Parafon (CD) Remular	
Codeine	Believed to affect tissue sites that react specifically with opium and its derivatives (antitussive; narcotic analgesic)	Relief of moderate pain; control of coughing

Acetaco (CD)
Actifed with Co-
   deine (CD)
Ambenyl (CD)
Calcidrine Syrup
   (CD)
Codalan (CD)
Codimal PH (CD)
	Dimetane-DC
	   (CD)
	Empirin with Co-
	   deine (CD)
	Fiorinal with Co-
	   deine (CD)
	IoTuss (CD)
	Naldecon-CX (CD)
		Novahistine DK
		   (CD)
		Nucofed (CD)
		Pediacof (CD)
		Phenaphen with
		   Codeine (CD)
		Phenergan with
		   Codeine (CD)
			Promethazine
			   (CD)
			Robitussin A-C
			   (CD)
			Soma Compound
			   (CD)
			Triaminic with Co-
			   deine (CD) Tussar (CD)
			Tylenol with Co-
			   deine (CD)

Name	Action	Prescribed for
Trade Names (CD = combined drug)		
Desiprimine	Blocks the movement of certain stimulant chemicals in and out of nerve endings, has a sedative effect and acts as an anticholinergic drug, counteracting the effects of the hormone, acetylcholine. Also believed to reestablish chemical balance in the brains of people suffering depression.	Depression, cocaine withdrawal, panic disorder, and bulimia nervosa.
Norpramin	Pertofrane	
Dexamethasone	Believed to inhibit several tissue mechanisms that induce inflammation (adrenocortical steriod [anti-inflammatory])	Symptomatic relief of inflammation (swelling, redness, heat, pain)
Decadron Dalalone	Hexadrol Neodecadron	
Dextroamphet-amine (d-Amphetamine)	Increases release of nerve impulse transmitter (central stimulant); this may also improve concentration and attention span of hyperactive child (primary calming action unknown); alters chemical control of nerve impulse transmission in appetite control center of brain (appetite suppressant [anorexiant])	Reduction or prevention of sleep epilepsy (narcolepsy); reduction of symptoms of abnormal hyperactivity (as in minimal brain dysfunction); suppression of appetite in management of weight reduction
Dexedrine	Biphetamine (CD)	
Diazepam	Believed to reduce activity of some parts of limbic system (tranquilizer)	Relief of mild to moderate anxiety and tension without significant sedation
Valium		
Dicyclomine	Believed to produce a local anesthetic action that blocks reflex activity responsible for spasm (antispasmodic)	Relief of discomfort from muscle spasm of the gastrointestinal tract
Bentyl		
Digitoxin	Increases availability of calcium within the heart muscle, thus improving conversion of chemical energy to mechanical energy; slows pacemaker and delays transmission of electrical impulses (digitalis preparations [cardiotonic])	Improvement of heart muscle contraction force (as in congestive heart failure); correction of certain heart rhythm disorders
Crystodigin		
Digoxin	Same as above	Same as above
Lanoxicaps	Lanoxin	
Diphenhy-dramine	Blocks action of histamine after release from sensitized tissue cells, thus reducing intensity of allergic response (antihistamine)	Relief of symptoms of hay fever (allergic rhinitis) and of allergic reactions of skin (itching, swelling, hives, rash)

Ambenyl (CD)
Benadryl
Benadryl DM (CD)
Bromanyl (CD)
Dytuss (CD)
	Tylenol Cold Night
	  Time (CD)
	Unisom Dual Re-
	  lief (CD)	

Doxylamine	Same as above	Same as above
Unisom	Cremacoat 4 (CD) Nyquil (CD)	
Ephedrine	Blocks release of certain chemicals from sensitized tissue cells undergoing allergic reaction; relaxes bronchial muscles; shrinks tissue mass (decongestion) by contracting arteriole walls in lining of respiratory passages (adrenergic [bronchodilator])	Prevention and symptomatic relief of bronchial asthma; relief of congestion of respiratory passages
Primatene Mist Bronkolixir (CD) Bronkotabs (CD)	Medicone-Derma Mudrane (CD) HC (CD) Nyquil (CD) Marax (CD) Primatene (CD)	Quadrinal (CD) Tedral (CD) Quelidrine (CD) Rynatuss (CD)

Name	Action	Prescribed for
Trade Names (CD = combined drug)		
Ergotamine	Constricts blood vessel walls, thus relieving excessive dilation that causes pain of vascular headaches (migraine analgesic [vasoconstrictor])	Prevention and early relief of vascular headaches such as migraines or histamine headaches
Ergomar Ergostat	Medihaler Ergotamine Bellergal (CD) Cafergot (CD)	Wigraine (CD)
Erythromycin	Prevents growth and multiplication of susceptible bacteria by interfering with formation of their essential proteins (antibiotic)	Elimination of infections responsive to action of this drug
A/T/S E.E.S. E-Mycin ERYC	EryDerm Erythrocin Erymax Ilosone EryPed Ilotycin Ery-Tab P.C.E.	Staticin/T-Stat Wyamycin S SK-Erythromycin Pediazole (CD)
Estrogens (Estrogenic Substances) Conjugated Estrogens, Esterified Estrogens (Estrone and Equilin) Estradiol Mestranol	Prepares uterus for pregnancy or induces menstruation by cyclic increase and decrease in tissue stimulation; when taken regularly, blood and tissue levels increase to resemble those during pregnancy, thus preventing pituitary gland from producing hormones that induce ovulation; reduces frequency and intensity of menopausal symptoms (female sex hormone)	Regulation of menstrual cycle; oral birth control; prevention of pregnancy; relief of symptoms of menopause
Estratab Premarin Estratest (CD)	Mediatric (CD) Brevicon (CD) Menrium (CD) Demulen (CD) PMB (CD) Enovid (CD)	Modicon (CD) Ortho-Novum (CD) Norethin (CD) Norinyl (CD)
Fluoxetine	Believed to inhibit nerve uptake of serotonin to reduce depression (antidepressant, sedative)	Relief from acute depression or major depressive episodes
Prozac		
Griseofulvin	Believed to prevent growth and multiplication of susceptible fungus strains by interfering with their metabolic activities (antibiotic; antifungal)	Elimination of fungus infections responsive to actions of this drug
Fulvicin-U/F	Fulvicin P/G Grifulvin V	Grisactin Gris-PEG
Guaifenesin	Loosens phlegm and mucous from the bronchial passages by reducing viscosity and adhesiveness (expectorant)	Relief of painful coughs due to colds and influenzas; usually taken in conjunction with a decongestant
Codiclear (CD) Codimal (CD)	Dilaudid (CD) Guaifed (CD) Donatussin (CD) Mudrane (CD)	Naldecon (CD) Quibron (CD) Robitussin (CD) Triaminic (CD)
Hydralazine	Lowers pressure of blood in vessels by causing direct relaxation and expansion of vessel walls—mechanism unknown (antihypertensive)	Reduction of high blood pressure

Apresoline
Apresazide (CD)
	Apresoline-Esidrex Ser-Ap-Es (CD)
	   (CD)
		Serpasil-
		   Apresoline (CD)

Hydrochlorothiazide	Increases elimination of salt and water (diuretic); relaxes walls of smaller arteries, allowing them to expand; combined effect lowers blood pressure (antihypertensive)	Elimination of excessive fluid retention (edema); reduction of high blood pressure
Esidrix HydroDIURIL Oretic Aldactazide (CD)	Aldoril (CD) (CD) Apresazide (CD) Dyazide (CD) Apresoline-Esidrix Esimil (CD)	Hydropres (CD) Moduretic (CD) Inderide (CD) SK-Hydro- Maxzide (CD) chlorothiazide Timolide (CD)
Hydrocodone	Believed to affect opiate receptors in the nervous system, reducing pain and relaxing muscles (narcotic analgesic)	Relief of moderate to severe pain; severe cough and cold symptoms
Anexsia (CD) Azdone (CD) Bancap (CD) Codiclear (CD)	Codimal (CD) Entuss (CD) Co-Gesic (CD) Hyco-Pap (CD) Donatussin (CD) Hydrocet (CD) DuoCet (CD) Lorcet (CD)	Lortab (CD) Ru-Tuss with Hy- drocodone (CD) Triaminic (CD)

Name	Action	Prescribed for
Trade Names (CD = combined drug)		
Hydrocortisone (Cortisol)	Believed to inhibit several tissue mechanisms that induce inflammation (adrenocortical steroid [anti-inflammatory])	Symptomatic relief of inflammation (swelling, redness, heat, pain)
Aeroseb-HC Carmol HC Cortef Eldecort F-E-P Hydrocortone Hytone	Penecort Cortisporin (CD) Synacort Derma-Sone (CD) Vanoxide-HC Di-Hydrotic (CD) Vioform- Hill Cortac (CD) Hydrocortisone Hysone (CD) VōSoL HC Iodo-Cortifair (CD) Corticaine (CD) Oticol (CD)	Otocort (CD) Proctocort Proctocream (CD) Proctofoam (CD)
Hydroxyzine	Believed to reduce excessive activity in areas of brain that influence emotional health (antihistamine; tranquilizer)	Relief of anxiety, tension, apprehension, and agitation
Atarax Vistaril	Marax (CD) SK-Hydroxyzine	
Ibuprofen	Believed to inhibit prostaglandin sythetase production, acting as an anti-inflammatory agent; reduces fever (antipyretic), reduces inflammation and pain (antirheumatic, analgesic)	Relief of inflammation and pain from rheumatoid arthritis, osteoarthritis, and primary dysmenorrhea
Advil Children's Advil	IBU-TAB Motrin Medipren Nuprin	PediaProfen for Rufen children SK-Ibuprofen
Imipramine	Blocks the movement of certain stimulant chemicals in and out of nerve endings, has a sedative effect and acts as an anticholinergic drug, counteracting the effects of the hormone, acetylcholine. Also believed to reestablish chemical balance in the brains of people suffering depression.	Depression, panic disorder, childhood bed-wetting (older than age 6), chronic pain (from migraines, tension headaches, diabetic disease, tic douloureux, cancer, herpes lesions, arthritis, and other sources), and bulimia.
Janimine	Tofranil Tofranil-PM	
Insulin (Human, beef, pork)	Facilitates passage of sugar through cell wall to interior of cell (hypoglycemic)	Control of diabetes
Humulin Iletin Insulatard NPH	Lente Insulin NPH Insulin Mixtard Regular Insulin Novolin Semilente Insulin	Ultrlente Insulin Velosulin
Isoniazid	Believed to interfere with several metabolic activities of susceptible tuberculosis organisms (antibacterial; tuberculostatic)	Prevention and treatment of tuberculosis
INH	Laniazid Rifamate (CD)	
Isopropamide	Prevents stimulation of muscular contraction and glandular secretion in organ involved (antispasmodic [anticholinergic])	Relief of discomfort from excessive activity and spasm of digestive tract
Darbid		
Isoproterenol/ Isoprenaline	Dilates bronchial tubes by stimulating sympathetic nerve terminals (Isoproterenol: adrenergic [bronchodilator]; Isoprenaline: sympathomimetic)	Management of acute bronchial asthma, bronchitis, and emphysema
Isuprel Medihaler-Iso Norisodrine	Duo-Medihaler Isuprel Hydrochloride (CD) (CD)	
Isosorbide Dinitrate	Acts directly on muscle cells to produce relaxation which permits expansion of blood vessels, thus increasing supply of blood and oxygen to heart (coronary vasodilator)	Management of pain associated with angina pectoris (coronary insufficiency)
Dilatrate	Iso-Bid Isordil	Sorbitrate

Name	Action	Prescribed for
Trade Names (CD = combined drug)		
Labetalol Hydro-chloride	Selectively blocks both alpha- and beta-adrenergic impulses, contributing to lowered blood pressure. Unlike other beta-blocking drugs, it rarely affects heart rate.	High blood pressure
Normodyne	Trandate	
Levodopa	Believed to be converted to dopamine in brain tissue, thus correcting a dopamine deficiency and restoring more normal balance of chemicals responsible for transmission of nerve impulses (anti-Parkinsonism)	Management of Parkinson's disease
Larodopa Sinemet		
Liothyronine (T-3)	Increases rate of cellular metabolism and makes more energy available for biochemical activity (thyroid hormone)	Correction of thyroid hormone deficiency (hypothyroidism)
Cytomel Euthroid (CD) Thyrolar (CD)		
Lithium	Believed to correct chemical imbalance in certain nerve impulse transmitters that influence emotional behavior (anti-depressant)	Improvement of mood and behavior in chronic manic-depression
Eskalith Cibalith-S	Lithane Lithobid	
Meclizine	Blocks transmission of excessive nerve impulses to vomiting center (anti-emetic)	Management of nausea, vomiting, and dizziness associated with motion sickness
Antivert Bonine Meclizine HCl		
Meperidine/ Pethidine	Believed to increase chemicals that transmit nerve impulses (narcotic analgesic)	Relief of moderate to severe pain
Demerol Mepergan (CD)		
Meprobamate	Not known (tranquilizer)	Relief of mild to moderate anxiety and tension (sedative effect); relief of insomnia resulting from anxiety and tension (hypnotic effect)
Equanil Miltown	Deprol (CD) Meprospan Equagesic (CD) PMB (CD)	
Methadone	Believed to increase chemicals that transmit nerve impulses (narcotic analgesic)	Treatment of heroin addiction; sometimes for relief of moderate to severe pain
Dolophine Methadone Hydro-chloride		
Methyclothiazide	Increases elimination of salt and water (diuretic); relaxes walls of smaller arteries, allowing them to expand; combined effect lowers blood pressure (antihypertensive)	Elimination of excess fluid retention (edema); reduction of high blood pressure
Aquatensen	Enduron Diutensen (CD)	Enduronyl (CD)
Methylphenidate	Believed to increase release of nerve impulse transmitter, which may also improve concentration and attention span of hyperactive child (primary action unknown) (central stimulant)	Management of fatigue and depression; reduction of symptoms of abnormal hyperactivity (as in minimal brain dysfunction)
Ritalin		

Name	Action	Prescribed for
Trade Names (CD = combined drug)		
Metoprolol	Interferes with the action of a specific part of the nervous system, rather than affecting the entire system.	High blood pressure, angina pectoris, abnormal heart rhythms, preventing second heart attack, migraine headaches, tremors, aggressive behavior, antipsychotic drug side effects, improving cognitive performance, congestive heart failure (in a small number of individuals), and bleeding from the esophagus.
Lopressor	Toprol XL	
Nicotinic Acid/ Niacin	Corrects a deficiency of nicotinic acid in tissues; dilation of blood vessels is believed limited to skin—increased blood flow within head has not been demonstrated; reduces initial production of cholesterol and prevents conversion of fatty tissue to cholesterol and triglycerides (vitamin B-complex component; cholesterol reducer)	Management of pellagra; treatment of vertigo, ringing in ears, premenstrual headache; reduction of blood levels of cholesterol and triglycerides
Niacor Nicobid Nicolar	Nicotinex Elixir Slo-Niacin	
Nitrofurantoin	Believed to prevent growth and multiplication of susceptible bacteria by interfering with function of their essential enzyme systems (antibacterial)	Elimination of infections responsive to action of this drug
Furacin	Macrodantin	
Nitroglycerin	Acts directly on muscle cells to produce relaxation which permits expansion of blood vessels, thus increasing supply of blood and oxygen to heart (coronary vasodilator)	Management of pain associated with angina pectoris (coronary insufficiency)
Nitro-Bid Nitrodisc Nitro-Dur	Nitroglyn Nitrostat Nitrol Transderm-Nitro Nitrong Tridil	
Nystatin	Prevents gorwth and multiplication of susceptible fungus strains by attacking their walls and causing leakage of internal components (antibiotic; antifungal)	Elimination of fungus infections responsive to action of this drug
Mycostatin Nilstat Nystex	Mycolog (CD) Myco-Triacet (CD) Mytrex (CD)	
Oral Contraceptives	Suppresses the two pituitary gland hormones that produce ovulation (oral contraceptives)	Prevention of pregnancy
Ovcon Brevicon Demulen Enovid-E	Loestrin Nordette LO/Ovral Norinyl Micronor Norlestrin Medicon Ortho-Novum	Ovral Triphasil Ovrette Ovulen Tri-Norinyl
Oxycodone	Believed to affect tissue sites that react specifically with opium and its derivatives (narcotic analgesic)	Relief of moderate pain; control of coughing
Percocet (CD) Percodan (CD) SK-Oxycodone with Acetaminophen (CD)	SK-Oxycodone Roxicet (CD) with Aspirin Roxicodone (CD) Roxiprin (CD) Tylox (CD)	
Oxytetracycline	Prevents growth and multiplication of susceptible bacteria by interfering with their formation of essential proteins (antibiotic)	Elimination of infections responsive to action of this drug
Terra-Cortril (CD)	Terramycin Urobiotic (CD)	

Name	Action	Prescribed for
Trade Names (CD = combined drug)		
Papaverine	Causes direct relaxation and expansion of blood vessel walls, thus increasing volume of blood which increases oxygen and nutrients (smooth muscle relaxant; vasodilator)	Relief of symptoms associated with impaired circulation in extremities and within brain
SK-Papaverine Pavabid		
Paregoric (Camphorated Tincture of Opium)	Believed to affect tissue sites that react specifically with opium and its derivatives to relieve pain; its active ingredient, morphine, acts as a local anesthetic and blocks release of chemical that transmits nerve impulses to muscle walls of intestine (antiperistaltic)	Relief of mild to moderate pain; relief of intestinal cramping and diarrhea
Donnagel-PG (CD) Parepectolin (CD)		
Penbutolol	Interferes with the action of a specific part of the nervous system, rather than affecting the entire system.	High blood pressure
Levatol		
Penicillin G	Interferes with ability of susceptible bacteria to produce new protective cell walls as they grow and multiply (antibiotic)	Elimination of infections responsive to action of this drug
Bicillin C-R Pentids Pfizerpen	SK-Pencillin G Wycillin	
Penicillin V	Same as above	Same as above
Betapen-VK Pen-Vee K Ledercillin	SK-Pencillin VK Veetids	
Pentobarbital	Believed to block transmission of nerve impulses (hypnotic; sedative)	Low dosage: relief of mild to moderate anxiety or tension (sedative effect); higher dosage: at bedtime to induce sleep (hypnotic effect)
Cafergot PB (CD) Nembutal		
Phenazopyridine	Acts as local anesthetic on lining of lower urinary tract (urinary-analgesic)	Relief of pain and discomfort associated with acute irritation of lower urinary tract as in cystitis, urethritis, and prostatitis
Azo Gantanol (CD) Azo-Standard	Pyridium Thiosulfil-A (CD) Urobiotic (CD)	
Pheniramine	Blocks action of histamine after release from sensitized tissue cells, thus reducing intensity of allergic response (antihistamine)	Relief of symptoms of hay fever (allergic rhinitis) and of allergic reactions of skin (itching, swelling, hives, and rash)
Triaminic Citra Forte (CD) Dristan (CD) Fiogesic (CD)	Poly-Histine-D (CD) Ru-Tuss with Hydrocodone (CD) Robitussin AC (CD) S-T Forte (CD) Triaminicin (CD)	Tussagesic (CD) Tussirex (CD)
Phenobarbital/ Phenobarbitone	Believed to block transmission of nerve impulses (anticonvulsant; hypnotic; sedative)	Low dosage: relief of mild to moderate anxiety or tension (sedative effect); higher dosage: at bedtime to induce sleep (hypnotic effect); continuous dosage: prevention of epileptic seizures (anticonvulsant effect)
SK-Phenobarbital Solfoton Antrocol (CD)	Bellergal-S (CD) Mudrane (CD) Bronkolixir (CD) Mudrane GG (CD) Bronkotabs (CD) Phazyme (CD)	Primatene (CD) Quadrinal (CD) T-E-P (CD)

Name	Action	Prescribed for
Trade Names (CD = combined drug)		
Phentermine	Believed to alter chemical control of nerve impulse transmitter in appetite center of brain (appetite suppressant [anorexiant])	Suppression of appetite in management of weight reduction
Adipex-P	Fastin	Ionamin
Phenylbutazone	Believed to suppress formation of chemical involved in production of inflammation (analgesic; anti-inflammatory; antipyretic)	Symptomatic relief of inflammation, swelling, pain, and tenderness associated with arthritis, tendinitis, bursitis, superficial phlebitis
Butazolidin		
Phenylephrine	Shrinks tissue mass (decongestion) by contracting arteriole walls in lining of nasal passages, sinuses, and throat, thus decreasing volume of blood (decongestant [sympathomimetic])	Relief of congestion of nose, sinuses, and throat associated with allergy

Codimal (CD)
Comhist (CD)
Cogespirin (CD)
  for children
Coryban-D Cough
  Syrup (CD)
Dallergy (CD)
Dimetapp (CD)
Donatussin (CD)
Dristan, Advanced
  Formula (CD)

Dura-Tap/PD (CD)
Dura-Vent/PD
  (CD)
Entex (CD)
Extendryl (CD)
4-Way Nasal
  Spray (CD)
Histor-D (CD)
Hycomine (CD)
Korigesic (CD)
Naldecon (CD)

Neo-Synephrine
  (CD)
P-V-Tussin (CD)
Pediacof (CD)
Phenergan VC
  (CD)
Protid (CD)
Quelidrine (CD)
Ru-Tuss (CD)
Rynatan (CD)
Rynatuss (CD)

Sinarest (CD)
S-T Decongest
  (CD)
S-T Forte (CD)
Tamine S.R. (CD)
Tussar DM (CD)
Tussirex (CD)

Name	Action	Prescribed for
Phenylpropano-lamine	Same as above	Same as above

Help
Propagest
Rhindecon
Alka-Seltzer Plus
  (CD)
Allerest (CD)
Appedrine, Maxi-
  mum Strength
  (CD)
Bayer Children's
  Cold Tablets
  (CD)
Bayer Cough Sy-
  rup for Children
  (CD)
Codimal Expecto-
  rant (CD)
Comtrex (CD)

Conex (CD)
Congesprin (CD)
  for children
Contac (CD)
Control (CD)
Coryban-D (CD)
CoTylenol Chil-
  dren's Liquid
  (CD)
Cremacoat 3 (CD)
Dehist (CD)
Dexatrim (CD)
Dieutrim (CD)
Dimetane (CD)
Dimetapp (CD)
Dura-Tapp/PD
  (CD)
Dura-Vent (CD)

Dura-Vent/A (CD)
Entex (CD)
4-Way (CD)
Fiogesic (CD)
Heat & Chest
  (CD)
Histalet (CD)
Hycomine (CD)
Naldecon (CD)
Nolamine (CD)
Ornacol (CD)
Ornade (CD)
Poly-Histine (CD)
Prolamine, Extra
  Strength (CD)
Quadrahist (CD)
Resaid (CD)
Rescaps (CD)

Rhinolar (CD)
Ru-Tuss (CD)
S-T Decongest
  (CD)
S-T Forte (CD)
Sinubid (CD)
Sinulin (CD)
Sinutab (CD)
Tamine S.R. (CD)
Tavist-D (CD)
Triaminic (CD)
Triaminicin (CD)
Triaminicol (CD)
Tuss-Ade (CD)
Tuss-Ornade (CD)

Name	Action	Prescribed for
Phenytoin (formerly Diphenylhydantoin)	Believed to promote loss of sodium from nerve fibers, thus lowering their excitability and inhibiting spread of electrical impulse along nerve pathways (anticonvulsant)	Prevention of epileptic seizures
Dilantin		
Pilocarpine	Lowers internal eye pressure (antiglaucoma [miotic])	Management of glaucoma
Almocarpine	Isopto Carpine Pilocar	
Potassium	Maintains and replenishes potassium content of cells (potassium preparations)	Management of potassium deficiency
Kaon Kay Ciel	K-Lor Kaochlor	Klorvess Pima Syrup
Prednisolone	Believed to inhibit several mechanisms that induce inflammation (adrenocortical steroid [anti-inflammatory])	Symptomatic relief of inflammation (swelling, redness, heat, and pain)
Delta-Cortef Hydeltra-T.B.A.	Metimyd Metreton	Predate

Name	Action	Prescribed for
Trade Names (CD = combined drug)		
Prednisone	Same as above	Same as above
Deltasone Liquid Pred	SK-Prednisone Sterapred	
Probenecid	Reduces level of uric acid in blood and tissues; prolongs presence of penicillin in blood (antigout [uricosuric])	Management of gout
Benemid SK-Probenecid ColBENEMID (CD) Col-Probenecid (CD) Polycillin-PRB (CD)		
Promethazine	Blocks action of histamine after release from sensitized tissue cells, thus reducing intensity of allergic response (antihistamine); blocks transmission of excessive nerve impulses to vomiting center (antiemetic); action producing sedation and sleep is unknown (sedative)	Relief of symptoms of hay fever (allergic rhinitis) and of allergic reactions of skin (itching, swelling, hives, rash); prevention and management of nausea, vomiting, and dizziness associated with motion sickness; production of mild sedation and light sleep
Phenergan	Mepergan (CD)	
Propantheline	Prevents stimulation of muscular contraction and glandular secretion within organ involved (antispasmodic [anticholinergic])	Relief of discomfort associated with excessive activity and spasm of digestive tract
Pro-Banthine	SK-Propantheline	
Propoxyphene	Increases chemicals that transmit nerve impulses, somehow contributing to the analgesic effect (analgesic)	Relief of mild to moderate pain
Darvon Darvocet-N (CD) Darvon Compound (CD) Dolene (CD)	SK-65 APAP (CD) SK-65 Compound (CD) Wygesic (CD)	
Propranolol	Affects the entire beta-adrenergic portion of the nervous system.	High blood pressure, angina pectoris, abnormal heart rhythms, preventing second heart attack, preventing migraine headaches, tremors, aggressive behavior, antipsychotic drug side effects, acute panic, stage fright and other anxieties, and schizophrenia and is used to treat bleeding from the stomach or esophagus and symptoms of hyperactive thyroid.
Inderal Inderal LA		
Pseudoephedrine (Isoephedrine)	Shrinks tissue mass (decongestion) by contracting arteriole walls in lining of nasal passages, sinuses, and throat, thus decreasing volume of blood (decongestant [sympathomimetic])	Relief of congestion of nose, throat, and sinuses associated with allergy
Sudafed Actifed (CD) Ambenyl-D (CD) Anafed (CD) Anamine (CD) Brexin (CD) Bromfed (CD) Chlor-Trimeton (CD) Chlorafed (CD)	Codimal-L.A. (CD) Gunifed (CD) Congess (CD) Histalet (CD) CoTylenol Cold Isoclor (CD) Medication (CD) Kronofed-A (CD) Deconamine (CD) Novafed (CD) Dimacol (CD) Novahistine (CD) Dorcol (CD) Nucofed (CD) Extra-Strength Phenergan (CD) Sine-Aid (CD) Poly-Histine-DX Fedahist (CD) (CD)	Respaire-SR (CD) Robitussin-DAC (CD) Sine-Aid (CD) Triafed (CD) Tussend Expectorant (CD) Zephrex (CD)

Name	Action	Prescribed for
Trade Names (CD = combined drug)		
Pyrilamine/ Mepyramine	Blocks action of histamine after release from sensitized tissue cells, thus reducing intensity of allergic response (antihistamine)	Relief of symptoms of hay fever (allergic rhinitis) and of allergic reactions of skin (itching, swelling, hives, and rash)
Albatussin (CD) Kronohist (CD) Ru-Tuss (CD) Citra Forte (CD) Mydol PMS (CD) Triaminic (CD) Codimal (CD) P-V-Tussin (CD) Triaminicin (CD) 4-Way Nasal Poly-Histine-D Triaminicol (CD) Spray (CD) (CD) Fiogesic (CD) Primatene-M (CD)		
Quinidine	Slows pacemaker and delays transmission of electrical impulses (cardiac depressant)	Correction of certain heart rhythm disorders
Cardioquin Quinidex Duraquin SK-Quinidine Quinaglute		
Reserpine	Relaxes blood vessel walls by reducing availability of norepinephrine (antihypertensive; tranquilizer)	Reduction of high blood pressure
Sandril Demi-Regroton Diutensen-R (CD) Regrotin (CD) Serpasil (CD) Hydromox R (CD) Salutensin (CD) SK-Resperine Diupres (CD) Hydropres (CD) Ser-Ap-Es (CD)		
Rifampin	Prevents growth and multiplication of susceptible tuberculosis organisms by interfering with enzyme systems involved in formation of essential proteins (antibiotic; tuberculostatic)	Treatment of tuberculosis
Rifadin Rifamate Rimactane		
Secobarbital	Believed to block transmission of nerve impulses (hypnotic; sedative)	Low dosage: relief of mild to moderate anxiety or tension (sedative effect); higher dosage: at bedtime to induce sleep (hypnotic effect)
Seconal		
Sulfamethox- azole	Prevents growth and multiplication of susceptible bacteria by interfering with their formation of folic acid (antibacterial)	Elimination of infections responsive to action of this drug
Gantanol Azo Gantanol (CD) Bactrim (CD) Septra (CD)		
Sulfisoxazole	Same as above	Same as above
Gantrisin SK-Soxazole Azo Gantrisin (CD) Pediazole (CD) for children		
Tetracycline	Prevents growth and multiplication of susceptible bacteria by interfering with their formation of essential proteins (antibiotic)	Elimination of infections responsive to action of this drug
Achromycin V Robitet SK-Tetracycline Topicycline Sumycin (CD)		

Name	Action	Prescribed for
Trade Names (CD = combined drug)		
Theophylline (Aminophylline, Oxtriphylline)	Reverses constriction by increasing activity of chemical system within muscle cell that causes relaxation of bronchial tube (bronchodilator)	Symptomatic relief of bronchial asthma
Accurbron Bronkodyl Constant-T Elixicon LABID Respbid Somophyllin	Sustaire Synophylate Theobid Theoclear Theo-Dur Theolair Theon Theo-Organidin Theophyl Aerolate (CD) Amesec (CD) Aquaphyllin (CD) Brondecon (CD)	Bronkolixir (CD) Quibron (CD) Bronkotabs (CD) Slo-bid (CD) Elixophyllin (CD) Slo-Phyllin (CD) Marax (CD) T.E.H (CD) Primatene (CD) T-E-P (CD) Quadrinal (CD) Tedral (CD) Theozine (CD)
Thyroid Liothyronine Thyroglobulin Levothyroxine	Makes more energy available for biochemical activity and increases rate of cellular metabolism by altering poocesses of cellular chemicals that store energy (thyroid hormones)	Correction of thyroid hormone deficiency (hypothyroidism)
Armour Thyroid Cytomel Euthroid Levothroid	Proloid S-P-T Synthroid Thyrolar Choloxin L-Thyroxine Thyrolar (CD)	
Tolbutamide	Stimulates secretion of insulin by pancreas (hypoglycemic)	Correction of insulin deficiency in adult diabetes
Orinase		
Triazolam	Works directly on the brain by making it easier to go to sleep while also decreasing the number of times a patient wakes during the night.	Short-term treatment of insomnia or sleeplessness, difficulty falling asleep, frequent nighttime awakening, and waking too early in the morning.
Halcion		
Trimethoprim	Prevents growth and multiplication of susceptible organisms by interfering with formation of proteins (antibacterial)	Elimination of infections responsive to action of this drug
Proloprim Trimpex Bactrim (CD)	Cotrim (CD) Septra (CD) Sulfatrim (CD)	
Triprolidine	Blocks action of histamine after release from sensitized tissue cells, thus reducing intensity of allergic response (antihistamine)	Relief of symptoms of hay fever (allergic rhinitis) and of allergic reacitons of skin (itching, swelling, hives, and rash)
Actidil Actifed (CD) Actifed-C (CD) Triafed (CD) Trifed (CD)		
Vitamin C (Ascorbic Acid)	Believed to be essential to enzyme activity involved in formation of collagen; increases absorption of iron from intestine and helps formation of hemoglobin and red blood cells in bone marrow; inhibits growth of certain bacteria in urinary tract; enhances effects of some antibiotics (vitamin)	Prevention and treatment of scurvy; treatment of some types of anemia; maintenance of acid urine
Cetane Cevalin Cevi-Bid Cevi-Fer (CD) Mediatric (CD)		

Index